PISA 2012 Results: What Makes Schools Successful?

RESOURCES, POLICIES AND PRACTICES
(VOLUME IV)

WITHDRAWAL

OECD
BETTER POLICIES FOR BETTER LIVES

This work is published on the responsibility of the Secretary-General of the OECD. The opinions expressed and arguments employed herein do not necessarily reflect the official views of the Organisation or of the governments of its member countries.

This document and any map included herein are without prejudice to the status of or sovereignty over any territory, to the delimitation of international frontiers and boundaries and to the name of any territory, city or area.

Please cite this publication as:

OECD (2013), *PISA 2012 Results: What Makes Schools Successful? Resources, Policies and Practices (Volume IV)*, PISA, OECD Publishing.
http://dx.doi.org/10.1787/9789264201156-en

ISBN 978-92-64-20114-9 (print)
ISBN 978-92-64-20115-6 (PDF)

Note by Turkey: The information in this document with reference to "Cyprus" relates to the southern part of the Island. There is no single authority representing both Turkish and Greek Cypriot people on the Island. Turkey recognises the Turkish Republic of Northern Cyprus (TRNC). Until a lasting and equitable solution is found within the context of the United Nations, Turkey shall preserve its position concerning the "Cyprus issue".

Note by all the European Union Member States of the OECD and the European Union: The Republic of Cyprus is recognised by all members of the United Nations with the exception of Turkey. The information in this document relates to the area under the effective control of the Government of the Republic of Cyprus.

The statistical data for Israel are supplied by and under the responsibility of the relevant Israeli authorities. The use of such data by the OECD is without prejudice to the status of the Golan Heights, East Jerusalem and Israeli settlements in the West Bank under the terms of international law.

Photo credits:
© Flying Colours Ltd/Getty Images
© Jacobs Stock Photography/Kzenon
© khoa vu/Flickr/Getty Images
© Mel Curtis/Corbis
© Shutterstock/Kzenon
© Simon Jarratt/Corbis

Corrigenda to OECD publications may be found on line at: *www.oecd.org/publishing/corrigenda*.

Foreword

Equipping citizens with the skills necessary to achieve their full potential, participate in an increasingly interconnected global economy, and ultimately convert better jobs into better lives is a central preoccupation of policy makers around the world. Results from the OECD's recent Survey of Adult Skills show that highly skilled adults are twice as likely to be employed and almost three times more likely to earn an above-median salary than poorly skilled adults. In other words, poor skills severely limit people's access to better-paying and more rewarding jobs. Highly skilled people are also more likely to volunteer, see themselves as actors rather than as objects of political processes, and are more likely to trust others. Fairness, integrity and inclusiveness in public policy thus all hinge on the skills of citizens.

The ongoing economic crisis has only increased the urgency of investing in the acquisition and development of citizens' skills – both through the education system and in the workplace. At a time when public budgets are tight and there is little room for further monetary and fiscal stimulus, investing in structural reforms to boost productivity, such as education and skills development, is key to future growth. Indeed, investment in these areas is essential to support the recovery, as well as to address long-standing issues such as youth unemployment and gender inequality.

In this context, more and more countries are looking beyond their own borders for evidence of the most successful and efficient policies and practices. Indeed, in a global economy, success is no longer measured against national standards alone, but against the best-performing and most rapidly improving education systems. Over the past decade, the OECD Programme for International Student Assessment, PISA, has become the world's premier yardstick for evaluating the quality, equity and efficiency of school systems. But the evidence base that PISA has produced goes well beyond statistical benchmarking. By identifying the characteristics of high-performing education systems PISA allows governments and educators to identify effective policies that they can then adapt to their local contexts.

The results from the PISA 2012 assessment, which was conducted at a time when many of the 65 participating countries and economies were grappling with the effects of the crisis, reveal wide differences in education outcomes, both within and across countries. Using the data collected in previous PISA rounds, we have been able to track the evolution of student performance over time and across subjects. Of the 64 countries and economies with comparable data, 40 improved their average performance in at least one subject. Top performers such as Shanghai in China or Singapore were able to further extend their lead, while countries like Brazil, Mexico, Tunisia and Turkey achieved major improvements from previously low levels of performance.

Some education systems have demonstrated that it is possible to secure strong and equitable learning outcomes at the same time as achieving rapid improvements. Of the 13 countries and economies that significantly improved their mathematics performance between 2003 and 2012, three also show improvements in equity in education during the same period, and another nine improved their performance while maintaining an already high level of equity – proving that countries do not have to sacrifice high performance to achieve equity in education opportunities.

Nonetheless, PISA 2012 results show wide differences between countries in mathematics performance. The equivalent of almost six years of schooling, 245 score points, separates the highest and lowest average performances

of the countries that took part in the PISA 2012 mathematics assessment. The difference in mathematics performances within countries is even greater, with over 300 points – the equivalent of more than seven years of schooling – often separating the highest- and the lowest-achieving students in a country. Clearly, all countries and economies have excellent students, but few have enabled all students to excel.

The report also reveals worrying gender differences in students' attitudes towards mathematics: even when girls perform as well as boys in mathematics, they report less perseverance, less motivation to learn mathematics, less belief in their own mathematics skills, and higher levels of anxiety about mathematics. While the average girl underperforms in mathematics compared with the average boy, the gender gap in favour of boys is even wider among the highest-achieving students. These findings have serious implications not only for higher education, where young women are already under-represented in the science, technology, engineering and mathematics fields of study, but also later on, when these young women enter the labour market. This confirms the findings of the OECD Gender Strategy, which identifies some of the factors that create – and widen – the gender gap in education, labour and entrepreneurship. Supporting girls' positive attitudes towards and investment in learning mathematics will go a long way towards narrowing this gap.

PISA 2012 also finds that the highest-performing school systems are those that allocate educational resources more equitably among advantaged and disadvantaged schools and that grant more autonomy over curricula and assessments to individual schools. A belief that all students can achieve at a high level and a willingness to engage all stakeholders in education – including students, through such channels as seeking student feedback on teaching practices – are hallmarks of successful school systems.

PISA is not only an accurate indicator of students' abilities to participate fully in society after compulsory school, but also a powerful tool that countries and economies can use to fine-tune their education policies. There is no single combination of policies and practices that will work for everyone, everywhere. Every country has room for improvement, even the top performers. That's why the OECD produces this triennial report on the state of education across the globe: to share evidence of the best policies and practices and to offer our timely and targeted support to help countries provide the best education possible for all of their students. With high levels of youth unemployment, rising inequality, a significant gender gap, and an urgent need to boost growth in many countries, we have no time to lose. The OECD stands ready to support policy makers in this challenging and crucial endeavour.

Angel Gurría
OECD Secretary-General

Acknowledgements

This report is the product of a collaborative effort between the countries participating in PISA, the experts and institutions working within the framework of the PISA Consortium, and the OECD Secretariat. The report was drafted by Andreas Schleicher, Francesco Avvisati, Francesca Borgonovi, Miyako Ikeda, Hiromichi Katayama, Flore-Anne Messy, Chiara Monticone, Guillermo Montt, Sophie Vayssettes and Pablo Zoido of the OECD Directorate for Education and Skills and the Directorate for Financial Affairs, with statistical support from Simone Bloem and Giannina Rech and editorial oversight by Marilyn Achiron. Additional analytical and editorial support was provided by Adele Atkinson, Jonas Bertling, Marika Boiron, Célia Braga-Schich, Tracey Burns, Michael Davidson, Cassandra Davis, Elizabeth Del Bourgo, John A. Dossey, Joachim Funke, Samuel Greiff, Tue Halgreen, Ben Jensen, Eckhard Klieme, André Laboul, Henry Levin, Juliette Mendelovits, Tadakazu Miki, Christian Monseur, Simon Normandeau, Mathilde Overduin, Elodie Pools, Dara Ramalingam, William H. Schmidt (whose work was supported by the Thomas J. Alexander fellowship programme), Kaye Stacey, Lazar Stankov, Ross Turner, Elisabeth Villoutreix and Allan Wigfield. The system-level data collection was conducted by the OECD NESLI (INES Network for the Collection and Adjudication of System-Level Descriptive Information on Educational Structures, Policies and Practices) team: Bonifacio Agapin, Estelle Herbaut and Jean Yip. Volume II also draws on the analytic work undertaken by Jaap Scheerens and Douglas Willms in the context of PISA 2000. Administrative support was provided by Claire Chetcuti, Juliet Evans, Jennah Huxley and Diana Tramontano.

The OECD contracted the Australian Council for Educational Research (ACER) to manage the development of the mathematics, problem solving and financial literacy frameworks for PISA 2012. Achieve was also contracted by the OECD to develop the mathematics framework with ACER. The expert group that guided the preparation of the mathematics assessment framework and instruments was chaired by Kaye Stacey; Joachim Funke chaired the expert group that guided the preparation of the problem-solving assessment framework and instruments; and Annamaria Lusardi led the expert group that guided the preparation of the financial literacy assessment framework and instruments. The PISA assessment instruments and the data underlying the report were prepared by the PISA Consortium, under the direction of Raymond Adams at ACER.

The development of the report was steered by the PISA Governing Board, which is chaired by Lorna Bertrand (United Kingdom), with Benő Csapó (Hungary), Daniel McGrath (United States) and Ryo Watanabe (Japan) as vice chairs. Annex C of the volumes lists the members of the various PISA bodies, as well as the individual experts and consultants who have contributed to this report and to PISA in general.

Table of Contents

BOXES

FIGURES

This book has...

StatLinkS

**A service that delivers Excel® files
from the printed page!**

Look for the *StatLinks* at the bottom left-hand corner of the tables or graphs in this book.
To download the matching Excel® spreadsheet, just type the link into your Internet browser,
starting with the ***http://dx.doi.org*** prefix.
If you're reading the PDF e-book edition, and your PC is connected to the Internet, simply
click on the link. You'll find *StatLinks* appearing in more OECD books.

Executive Summary

The organisation of learning environments is related to education outcomes. As in other organisations, decisions taken at one level in a school system are affected by decisions taken at other levels. For example, what happens in the classroom is influenced by decisions taken at the school level; and decisions taken at the school level are affected by the decisions – particularly those concerning resources, policies and practices – taken by district, regional and/or national education administrations.

Stratification in school systems, which is the result of policies like grade repetition and selecting students at a young age for different programmes or "tracks", is negatively related to equity; and students in highly stratified systems tend to be less motivated than those in less-stratified systems.

In systems where students are more likely to repeat a grade, the impact of students' socio-economic status on their academic performance is stronger than in systems where this type of stratification is not practiced. In 35 of 61 countries and economies examined, when comparing two students with similar mathematics performance, the student who is more socio-economically disadvantaged is more likely to have repeated a grade. Across OECD countries, an average of 12% of students reported that they had repeated a grade at least once. Among the 13 countries and economies that had grade repetition rates of more than 20% in 2003, these rates dropped by an average of 3.5 percentage points by 2012, and fell sharply in France, Luxembourg, Macao-China, Mexico and Tunisia.

How resources are allocated in education is just as important as the amount of resources available to be allocated.

PISA results show that beyond a certain level of expenditure per student, excellence in education requires more than money. Among countries and economies whose per capita GDP is more than USD 20 000, including most OECD countries, systems that pay teachers more (i.e. higher teachers' salaries relative to national income per capita) tend to perform better in mathematics.

High-performing countries and economies tend to allocate resources more equitably across socio-economically advantaged and disadvantaged schools.

That said, PISA results show that in many school systems, resources are not allocated equitably: On average across OECD countries, while disadvantaged schools tend to have smaller classes, they tend to be more likely to suffer from teacher shortages, and shortages or inadequacy of educational materials and physical infrastructures than advantaged schools.

Most countries and economies with comparable data between 2003 and 2012 have moved towards better-staffed and better-equipped schools.

Of the 36 countries and economies with comparable data for this period, 21 saw a reduction in student-teacher ratios; 20 of 38 countries and economies with comparable data saw a reduction in teacher shortages; and more school principals in 2012 than in 2003 reported that schools are in good physical condition.

Students in 2012 were more likely than their counterparts in 2003 to have attended at least one year of pre-primary education.

While more 15-old students reported to have enrolled in pre-primary education during the period, many of the students who reported that they had not attended pre-primary school are disadvantaged – the students who could benefit most from pre-primary education.

If offered a choice of schools for their child, parents are more likely to consider such criteria as "a safe school environment" and "a school's good reputation" more important than "high academic achievement of students in the school".

The criteria parents use to choose a school for their child not only vary across school systems, but also within systems. In all countries and economies with data from parents, socio-economically disadvantaged parents are more likely than advantaged parents to report that they considered "low expenses" and "financial aid" to be very important criteria in choosing a school.

In 37 participating countries and economies, students who attend private schools (either government-dependent or government-independent schools) are more socio-economically advantaged than those who attend public schools.

The difference in the average socio-economic status of students in private schools compared with those in public schools is particularly large in Brazil, Costa Rica, Mexico, Peru, Poland and Uruguay. Only in Chinese Taipei is the average socio-economic status of students who attend public schools more advantaged than that of those who attend private schools.

Schools in high-performing systems tend to have more responsibility for curricula and assessments.

Schools with more autonomy tend to perform better than schools with less autonomy when they are part of school systems with more accountability arrangements and greater teacher-principal collaboration in school management.

Between 2003 and 2012 there was a clear trend towards schools using student assessments to compare the school's performance with district or national performance and with that of other schools.

On average across OECD countries, in 2003, 46% of students attended schools whose principal reported that the school uses student assessment data to compare itself against national or district performance; by 2012, 62% of students attended such schools. Similarly, the percentage of students who attended schools that use assessment data to compare themselves to other schools increased from 40% to 52% during the period. The use of student-assessment data to compare against national or regional benchmarks or with other schools increased most notably in Brazil, Denmark, Ireland, Luxembourg and Portugal, and declined only in Finland between 2003 and 2012.

Systems with larger proportions of students who arrive late for school and skip classes tend to show lower overall performance.

Schools with more student truancy and more disciplinary problems are also those with more socio-economically disadvantaged student populations. But even when comparing schools of similar socio-economic status, students in schools with more disciplinary problems tend to perform worse than their peers in schools with a better disciplinary climate.

According to students' reports, teacher-student relations improved between 2003 and 2012 in all but one country, Tunisia, where they remained stable.

The share of students who "agree" or "strongly agree" that they get along with most teachers increased by 12 percentage points on average across OECD countries during the period and increased by more than ten percentage points in 22 countries and economies.

Between 2003 and 2012, disciplinary climate also improved on average across OECD countries and across 27 individual countries and economies.

Disciplinary climate improved the most in the Czech Republic, Hong Kong-China, Iceland, Japan, Luxembourg and Norway, but deteriorated in Germany and Tunisia during the period. PISA results also show that in 45 countries and economies, schools whose student population is predominantly socio-economically disadvantaged tend to have a more negative disciplinary climate.

Reader's Guide

Data underlying the figures

The data referred to in this volume are presented in Annex B and, in greater detail, including some additional tables, on the PISA website (*www.pisa.oecd.org*).

Four symbols are used to denote missing data:

a   The category does not apply in the country concerned. Data are therefore missing.

c   There are too few observations or no observation to provide reliable estimates (i.e. there are fewer than 30 students or fewer than 5 schools with valid data).

m   Data are not available. These data were not submitted by the country or were collected but subsequently removed from the publication for technical reasons.

w   Data have been withdrawn or have not been collected at the request of the country concerned.

Country coverage

This publication features data on 65 countries and economies, including all 34 OECD countries and 31 partner countries and economies (see map in the section *What is PISA?*).

The statistical data for Israel are supplied by and under the responsibility of the relevant Israeli authorities. The use of such data by the OECD is without prejudice to the status of the Golan Heights, East Jerusalem and Israeli settlements in the West Bank under the terms of international law.

Two notes were added to the statistical data related to Cyprus:

1. Note by Turkey: The information in this document with reference to "Cyprus" relates to the southern part of the Island. There is no single authority representing both Turkish and Greek Cypriot people on the Island. Turkey recognises the Turkish Republic of Northern Cyprus (TRNC). Until a lasting and equitable solution is found within the context of the United Nations, Turkey shall preserve its position concerning the "Cyprus issue".

2. Note by all the European Union Member States of the OECD and the European Union: The Republic of Cyprus is recognised by all members of the United Nations with the exception of Turkey. The information in this document relates to the area under the effective control of the Government of the Republic of Cyprus.

Calculating international averages

An OECD average corresponding to the arithmetic mean of the respective country estimates was calculated for most indicators presented in this report. The OECD average is used to compare performance across school systems. In the case of some countries, data may not be available for specific indicators, or specific categories may not apply. Readers should, therefore, keep in mind that the term "OECD average" refers to the OECD countries included in the respective comparisons.

Rounding figures

Because of rounding, some figures in tables may not exactly add up to the totals. Totals, differences and averages are always calculated on the basis of exact numbers and are rounded only after calculation.

All standard errors in this publication have been rounded to one or two decimal places. Where the value 0.0 or 0.00 is shown, this does not imply that the standard error is zero, but that it is smaller than 0.05 or 0.005, respectively.

Reporting student data

The report uses "15-year-olds" as shorthand for the PISA target population. PISA covers students who are aged between 15 years 3 months and 16 years 2 months at the time of assessment and who are enrolled in school and have completed at least 6 years of formal schooling, regardless of the type of institution in which they are enrolled and of whether they are in full-time or part-time education, of whether they attend academic or vocational programmes, and of whether they attend public or private schools or foreign schools within the country.

Reporting school data

The principals of the schools in which students were assessed provided information on their schools' characteristics by completing a school questionnaire. Where responses from school principals are presented in this publication, they are weighted so that they are proportionate to the number of 15-year-olds enrolled in the school.

Focusing on statistically significant differences

This volume discusses only statistically significant differences or changes. These are denoted in darker colours in figures and in bold font in tables. See Annex A3 for further information.

Abbreviations used in this report

ESCS	PISA index of economic, social and cultural status	PPP	Purchasing power parity
GDP	Gross domestic product	S.D.	Standard deviation
ISCED	International Standard Classification of Education	S.E.	Standard error
ISCO	International Standard Classification of Occupations	STEM	Science, Technology, Engineering and Mathematics

Further documentation

For further information on the PISA assessment instruments and the methods used in PISA, see the *PISA 2012 Technical Report* (OECD, forthcoming). The reader should note that there are gaps in the numbering of tables because some tables appear on line only and are not included in this publication. To consult the set of web-only data tables, visit the PISA website (*www.pisa.oecd.org*).

This report uses the OECD StatLinks service. Below each table and chart is a url leading to a corresponding Excel™ workbook containing the underlying data. These urls are stable and will remain unchanged over time. In addition, readers of the e-books will be able to click directly on these links and the workbook will open in a separate window, if their internet browser is open and running.

What is PISA?

"What is important for citizens to know and be able to do?" That is the question that underlies the triennial survey of 15-year-old students around the world known as the Programme for International Student Assessment (PISA). PISA assesses the extent to which students near the end of compulsory education have acquired key knowledge and skills that are essential for full participation in modern societies. The assessment, which focuses on reading, mathematics, science and problem solving, does not just ascertain whether students can reproduce knowledge; it also examines how well students can extrapolate from what they have learned and apply that knowledge in unfamiliar settings, both in and outside of school. This approach reflects the fact that modern economies reward individuals not for what they know, but for what they can do with what they know.

PISA is an ongoing programme that offers insights for education policy and practice, and that helps monitor trends in students' acquisition of knowledge and skills across countries and economies and in different demographic subgroups within each country. PISA results reveal what is possible in education by showing what students in the highest-performing and most rapidly improving school systems can do. The findings allow policy makers around the world to gauge the knowledge and skills of students in their own countries in comparison with those in other countries, set policy targets against measurable goals achieved by other school systems, and learn from policies and practices applied elsewhere. While PISA cannot identify cause-and-effect relationships between policies/practices and student outcomes, it can show educators, policy makers and the interested public how education systems are similar and different – and what that means for students.

A test the whole world can take

PISA is now used as an assessment tool in many regions around the world. It was implemented in 43 countries and economies in the first assessment (32 in 2000 and 11 in 2002), 41 in the second assessment (2003), 57 in the third assessment (2006) and 75 in the fourth assessment (65 in 2009 and 10 in 2010). So far, 65 countries and economies have participated in PISA 2012.

In addition to OECD member countries, the survey has been or is being conducted in:

East, South and Southeast Asia: Himachal Pradesh-India, Hong Kong-China, Indonesia, Macao-China, Malaysia, Shanghai-China, Singapore, Chinese Taipei, Tamil Nadu-India, Thailand and Viet Nam.

Central, Mediterranean and Eastern Europe, and Central Asia: Albania, Azerbaijan, Bulgaria, Croatia, Georgia, Kazakhstan, Kyrgyzstan, Latvia, Liechtenstein, Lithuania, the former Yugoslav Republic of Macedonia, Malta, Moldova, Montenegro, Romania, the Russian Federation and Serbia.

The Middle East: Jordan, Qatar and the United Arab Emirates.

Central and South America: Argentina, Brazil, Colombia, Costa Rica, Netherlands-Antilles, Panama, Peru, Trinidad and Tobago, Uruguay and Miranda-Venezuela.

Africa: Mauritius and Tunisia.

Decisions about the scope and nature of the PISA assessments and the background information to be collected are made by participating countries based on recommendations from leading experts. Considerable efforts and resources are devoted to achieving cultural and linguistic breadth and balance in assessment materials. Since the design and translation of the test, as well as sampling and data collection, are subject to strict quality controls, PISA findings are considered to be highly valid and reliable.

...

Map of PISA countries and economies

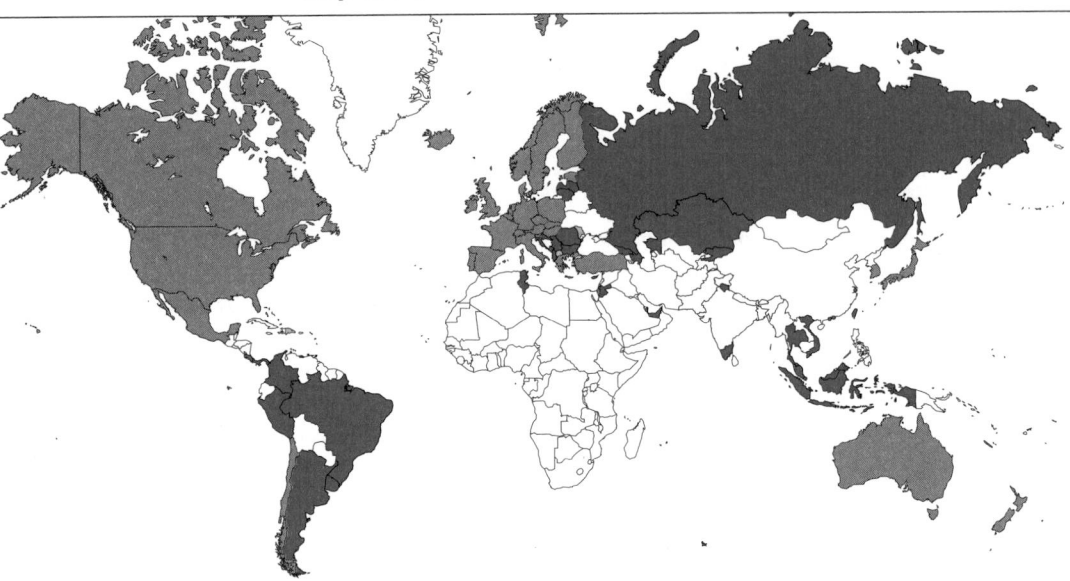

■ OECD countries

Australia	Japan
Austria	Korea
Belgium	Luxembourg
Canada	Mexico
Chile	Netherlands
Czech Republic	New Zealand
Denmark	Norway
Estonia	Poland
Finland	Portugal
France	Slovak Republic
Germany	Slovenia
Greece	Spain
Hungary	Sweden
Iceland	Switzerland
Ireland	Turkey
Israel	United Kingdom
Italy	United States

■ Partner countries and economies in PISA 2012

Albania	Montenegro
Argentina	Peru
Brazil	Qatar
Bulgaria	Romania
Colombia	Russian Federation
Costa Rica	Serbia
Croatia	Shanghai-China
Cyprus[1,2]	Singapore
Hong Kong-China	Chinese Taipei
Indonesia	Thailand
Jordan	Tunisia
Kazakhstan	United Arab Emirates
Latvia	Uruguay
Liechtenstein	Viet Nam
Lithuania	
Macao-China	
Malaysia	

■ Partner countries and economies in previous cycles

Azerbaijan
Georgia
Himachal Pradesh-India
Kyrgyzstan
Former Yugoslav Republic of Macedonia
Malta
Mauritius
Miranda-Venezuela
Moldova
Panama
Tamil Nadu-India
Trinidad and Tobago

1. Note by Turkey: The information in this document with reference to "Cyprus" relates to the southern part of the Island. There is no single authority representing both Turkish and Greek Cypriot people on the Island. Turkey recognises the Turkish Republic of Northern Cyprus (TRNC). Until a lasting and equitable solution is found within the context of the United Nations, Turkey shall preserve its position concerning the "Cyprus issue".

2. Note by all the European Union Member States of the OECD and the European Union: The Republic of Cyprus is recognised by all members of the United Nations with the exception of Turkey. The information in this document relates to the area under the effective control of the Government of the Republic of Cyprus.

PISA's unique features include its:

- policy orientation, which links data on student learning outcomes with data on students' backgrounds and attitudes towards learning and on key factors that shape their learning, in and outside of school, in order to highlight differences in performance and identify the characteristics of students, schools and school systems that perform well;

- innovative concept of "literacy", which refers to students' capacity to apply knowledge and skills in key subjects, and to analyse, reason and communicate effectively as they identify, interpret and solve problems in a variety of situations;

- relevance to lifelong learning, as PISA asks students to report on their motivation to learn, their beliefs about themselves, and their learning strategies;

- regularity, which enables countries and economies to monitor their progress in meeting key learning objectives; and

- breadth of coverage, which, in PISA 2012, encompasses the 34 OECD member countries and 31 partner countries and economies.

Key features of PISA 2012

The content

- The PISA 2012 survey focused on mathematics, with reading, science and problem solving as minor areas of assessment. For the first time, PISA 2012 also included an assessment of the financial literacy of young people, which was optional for countries and economies.

- PISA assesses not only whether students can reproduce knowledge, but also whether they can extrapolate from what they have learned and apply their knowledge in new situations. It emphasises the mastery of processes, the understanding of concepts, and the ability to function in various types of situations.

The students

- Around 510 000 students completed the assessment in 2012, representing about 28 million 15-year-olds in the schools of the 65 participating countries and economies.

The assessment

- Paper-based tests were used, with assessments lasting a total of two hours for each student. In a range of countries and economies, an additional 40 minutes were devoted to the computer-based assessment of mathematics, reading and problem solving.

- Test items were a mixture of multiple-choice items and questions requiring students to construct their own responses. The items were organised in groups based on a passage setting out a real-life situation. A total of about 390 minutes of test items were covered, with different students taking different combinations of test items.

- Students answered a background questionnaire, which took 30 minutes to complete, that sought information about themselves, their homes and their school and learning experiences. School principals were given a questionnaire, to complete in 30 minutes, that covered the school system and the learning environment. In some countries and economies, optional questionnaires were distributed to parents, who were asked to provide information on their perceptions of and involvement in their child's school, their support for learning in the home, and their child's career expectations, particularly in mathematics. Countries and economies could choose two other optional questionnaires for students: one asked students about their familiarity with and use of information and communication technologies, and the second sought information about their education to date, including any interruptions in their schooling and whether and how they are preparing for a future career.

WHO ARE THE PISA STUDENTS?

Differences between countries in the nature and extent of pre-primary education and care, in the age of entry into formal schooling, in the structure of the school system, and in the prevalence of grade repetition mean that school grade levels are often not good indicators of where students are in their cognitive development. To better compare student performance internationally, PISA targets a specific age of students. PISA students are aged between 15 years 3 months and 16 years 2 months at the time of the assessment, and have completed at least 6 years of formal schooling. They can be enrolled in any type of institution, participate in full-time or part-time education, in academic or vocational programmes, and attend public or private schools or foreign schools within the country or economy. (For an operational definition of this target population, see Annex A2.) Using this age across countries and over time allows PISA to compare consistently the knowledge and skills of individuals born in the same year who are still in school at age 15, despite the diversity of their education histories in and outside of school.

The population of participating students is defined by strict technical standards, as are the students who are excluded from participating (see Annex A2). The overall exclusion rate within a country was required to be below 5% to ensure that, under reasonable assumptions, any distortions in national mean scores would remain within plus or minus 5 score points, i.e. typically within the order of magnitude of 2 standard errors of sampling. Exclusion could take place either through the schools that participated or the students who participated within schools (see Annex A2, Tables A2.1 and A2.2).

There are several reasons why a school or a student could be excluded from PISA. Schools might be excluded because they are situated in remote regions and are inaccessible, because they are very small, or because of organisational or operational factors that precluded participation. Students might be excluded because of intellectual disability or limited proficiency in the language of the assessment.

In 28 out of the 65 countries and economies participating in PISA 2012, the percentage of school-level exclusions amounted to less than 1%; it was less than 5% in all countries. When the exclusion of students who met the internationally established exclusion criteria is also taken into account, the exclusion rates increase slightly. However, the overall exclusion rate remains below 2% in 30 participating countries and economies, below 5% in 57 participating countries and economies, and below 7% in all countries except Luxembourg (8.4%). In 11 out of the 34 OECD countries, the percentage of school-level exclusions amounted to less than 1% and was less than 3% in 30 OECD countries. When student exclusions within schools were also taken into account, there were 11 OECD countries below 2% and 26 OECD countries below 5%.

(For more detailed information about the restrictions on the level of exclusions in PISA 2012, see Annex A2.)

WHAT KINDS OF RESULTS DOES THE TEST PROVIDE?

The PISA assessment provides three main types of outcomes:

- basic indicators that provide a baseline profile of students' knowledge and skills;
- indicators that show how skills relate to important demographic, social, economic and educational variables; and
- indicators on trends that show changes in student performance and in the relationships between student-level and school-level variables and outcomes.

Although indicators can highlight important issues, they do not provide direct answers to policy questions. To respond to this, PISA also developed a policy-oriented analysis plan that uses the indicators as a basis for policy discussion.

WHERE CAN YOU FIND THE RESULTS?

This is the fourth of six volumes that present the results from PISA 2012. It begins by examining the relationships between education outcomes and various school and system characteristics, including the use of vertical and horizontal stratification, resource allocation, how the school system is organised and governed, and the learning environment in the school and classroom. Chapter 2 discusses the ways in which students are selected and grouped into certain education levels, grade levels, schools, programmes and different classes within schools based on their performance; Chapter 3 examines the allocation of human, material and financial resources throughout school systems and the amount of time dedicated to instruction and learning; Chapter 4 explores the inter-relationships among school autonomy, school competition, public and private management of schools, school leadership, parental involvement, and assessment and accountability arrangements; and Chapter 5 discusses student- and teacher-related aspects of the learning environment, including student truancy, teacher-student relations, the disciplinary climate and teacher morale. Whenever comparable data are available, trends between 2003 and 2012 are highlighted. Case studies, examining the policy reforms adopted by countries that have improved in PISA, are presented throughout. The concluding chapter discusses the policy implications of the PISA results.

The other five volumes cover the following issues:

Volume I, *What Students Know and Can Do: Student Performance in Mathematics, Reading and Science,* summarises the performance of students in PISA 2012. It describes how performance is defined, measured and reported, and then provides results from the assessment, showing what students are able to do in mathematics. After a summary of mathematics performance, it examines the ways in which this performance varies on subscales representing different aspects of mathematics literacy. Given that any comparison of the outcomes of education systems needs to take into consideration countries' social and economic circumstances, and the resources they devote to education, the volume also presents the results within countries' economic and social contexts. In addition, the volume examines the relationship between the frequency and intensity of students' exposure to subject content in school, what is known as "opportunity to learn", and student performance. The volume concludes with a description of student results in reading and science. Trends in student performance in mathematics between 2003 and 2012, in reading between 2000 and 2012, and in science between 2006 and 2012 are examined when comparable data are available. Throughout the volume, case studies examine in greater detail the policy reforms adopted by countries that have improved in PISA.

Volume II, *Excellence through Equity: Giving Every Student the Chance to Succeed,* defines and measures equity in education and analyses how equity in education has evolved across countries and economies between PISA 2003 and 2012. The volume examines the relationship between student performance and socio-economic status, and describes how other individual student characteristics, such as immigrant background and family structure, and school characteristics, such as school location, are associated with socio-economic status and performance. The volume also

reveals differences in how equitably countries allocate resources and opportunities to learn to schools with different socio-economic profiles. Case studies, examining the policy reforms adopted by countries that have improved in PISA, are highlighted throughout the volume.

Volume III, *Ready to Learn: Students' Engagement, Drive and Self-Beliefs,* explores students' engagement with and at school, their drive and motivation to succeed, and the beliefs they hold about themselves as mathematics learners. The volume identifies the students who are at particular risk of having low levels of engagement in, and holding negative dispositions towards, school in general and mathematics in particular, and how engagement, drive, motivation and self-beliefs are related to mathematics performance. The volume identifies the roles schools can play in shaping the well-being of students and the role parents can play in promoting their children's engagement with and dispositions towards learning. Changes in students' engagement, drive, motivation and self-beliefs between 2003 and 2012, and how those dispositions have changed during the period among particular subgroups of students, notably socio-economically advantaged and disadvantaged students, boys and girls, and students at different levels of mathematics proficiency, are examined when comparable data are available. Throughout the volume, case studies examine in greater detail the policy reforms adopted by countries that have improved in PISA.

Volume V, *Skills for Life: Student Performance in Problem Solving,* presents student performance in the PISA 2012 assessment of problem solving, which measures students' capacity to respond to non-routine situations in order to achieve their potential as constructive and reflective citizens. It provides the rationale for assessing problem-solving skills and describes performance within and across countries and economies. In addition, the volume highlights the relative strengths and weaknesses of each school system and examines how they are related to individual student characteristics, such as gender, immigrant background and socio-economic status. The volume also explores the role of education in fostering problem-solving skills.

Volume VI, *Students and Money: Financial Literacy Skills for the 21st Century,* examines 15-year-old students' performance in financial literacy in the 18 countries and economies that participated in this optional assessment. It also discusses the relationship of financial literacy to students' and their families' background and to students' mathematics and reading skills. The volume also explores students' access to money and their experience with financial matters. In addition, it provides an overview of the current status of financial education in schools and highlights relevant case studies.

The frameworks for assessing mathematics, reading and science in 2012 are described in *PISA 2012 Assessment and Analytical Framework: Mathematics, Reading, Science, Problem Solving and Financial Literacy* (OECD, 2013). They are also summarised in this volume.

Technical annexes at the end of this report describe how questionnaire indices were constructed and discuss sampling issues, quality-assurance procedures, the reliability of coding, and the process followed for developing the assessment instruments. Many of the issues covered in the technical annexes are elaborated in greater detail in the *PISA 2012 Technical Report* (OECD, forthcoming).

All data tables referred to in the analysis are included at the end of the respective volume in Annex B1, and a set of additional data tables is available on line (*www.pisa.oecd.org*). A Reader's Guide is also provided in each volume to aid in interpreting the tables and figures that accompany the report. Data from regions within the participating countries are included in Annex B2.

References

OECD (forthcoming), *PISA 2012 Technical Report*, PISA, OECD Publishing.

OECD (2013), *PISA 2012 Assessment and Analytical Framework: Mathematics, Reading, Science, Problem Solving and Financial Literacy*, PISA, OECD Publishing.
http://dx.doi.org/10.1787/9789264190511-en

1

How Resources, Policies and Practices are Related to Education Outcomes

This chapter examines the relationships between education outcomes and various school and system characteristics, including the use of vertical and horizontal stratification, resource allocation, how the school system is organised and governed, and the learning environment in the school and classroom. Trends in these relationships up to 2012 are also discussed.

This volume focuses on how the organisation of learning environments relates to education outcomes in countries and economies that participated in PISA 2012. As in other organisations, decisions taken at one level in a school system are affected by the context and by decisions taken at other levels (see the *PISA 2012 Assessment and Analytical Framework* [OECD, 2013a]). For example, what happens in the classroom is influenced by the context and decisions made at the school level; and decisions made at the school level are affected by the context and decisions made at higher levels in school administrations (i.e. districts or national ministries) (Gamoran, Secada and Marrett, 2000). Thus, when analysing the organisational arrangement of school systems it is important to consider the organisation of learning environments at the school and school system levels together.

Data collected through the PISA 2012 student, parent and school questionnaires are used to describe how schools are organised. Some student-level data are aggregated at the school level to approximate school features, and some school-level data are aggregated at the system level to approximate system characteristics. School-level data from PISA are complemented by OECD system-level data.[1]

This volume also analyses how the organisation of schools and its relationships with education outcomes have changed over time. Comparisons are made between PISA 2012 and PISA 2003, the last time mathematics was assessed in depth. To account for the extent to which the observed relationships are influenced by the level of economic development of countries and economies, the comparison of school systems discussed in this chapter also considers national income per capita (per capita GDP).

The first chapter examines the relationships between education outcomes and various school and system characteristics. Chapters 2, 3, 4 and 5 then describe these school and system characteristics in detail: Chapter 2 describes how and when students are distributed across different grade levels, programmes and schools; Chapter 3 focuses on resources invested in education at the system level and examines how resources are allocated across schools within systems; Chapter 4 describes school-governance issues, including school autonomy, school choice, and assessment and accountability arrangements; and Chapter 5 focuses on learning environments at school, examining how these are related to other aspects of school organisation discussed in Chapters 2 through 4.

■ Figure IV.1.1 ■
Structure of Volume IV

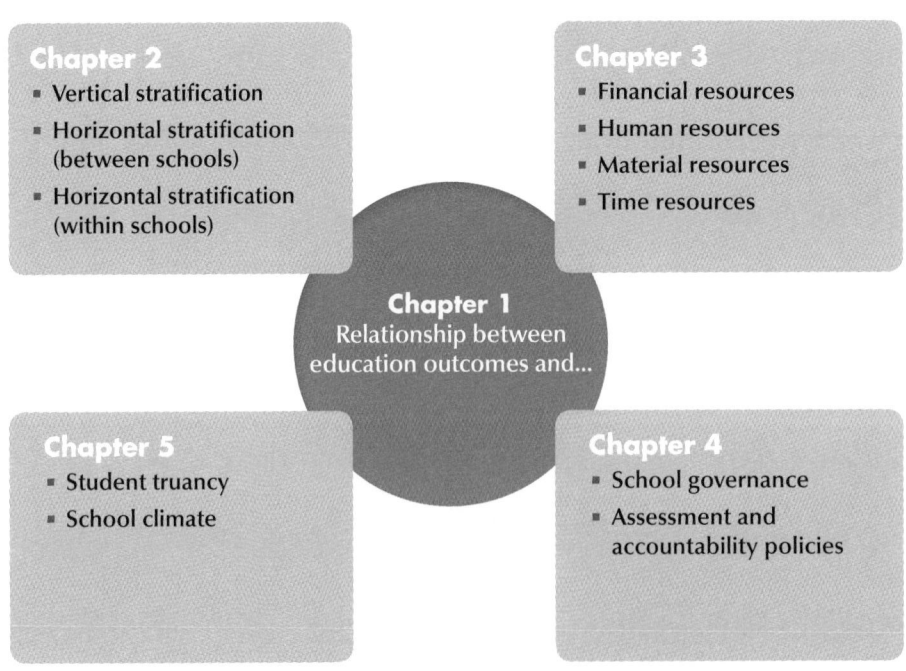

What the data tell us

- Stratification in school systems, the result of policies like grade repetition and early selection, is negatively related to equity.

- Among countries and economies whose per capita GDP is more than USD 20 000, including most OECD countries, systems that pay teachers more (i.e. higher teachers' salaries relative to national income) tend to perform better in mathematics.

- High-performing countries and economies tend to allocate resources more equitably across socio-economically advantaged and disadvantaged schools.

- School autonomy has a positive relationship with student performance when accountability measures are in place and/or when school principals and teachers collaborate in school management.

- Systems with larger proportions of students who arrive late for school and skip classes tend to show lower overall performance in mathematics.

PERFORMANCE DIFFERENCES AMONG SCHOOL SYSTEMS, SCHOOLS AND STUDENTS

As discussed in Volume I, academic performance among 15-year-old students varies widely, and that variation is related both to individual student characteristics and to the characteristics of schools and school systems in which those students are enrolled.

In the PISA 2012 assessment of mathematics, about half of the variation in student performance is observed between schools and school systems. Figure IV.1.2 shows that among OECD countries, 10% of the variation in mathematics performance observed among students is attributable to differences in performance among school systems, 36% is attributable to differences in performance among schools within a country, and 54% is attributable to differences in performance among students in a school. Among all countries and economies that participated in PISA 2012, 23% of the performance variation among students is observed at the system level, 31% is observed at the school level, and 46% is observed at the student level.

■ Figure IV.1.2 ■
Variation in mathematics performance between systems, schools and students

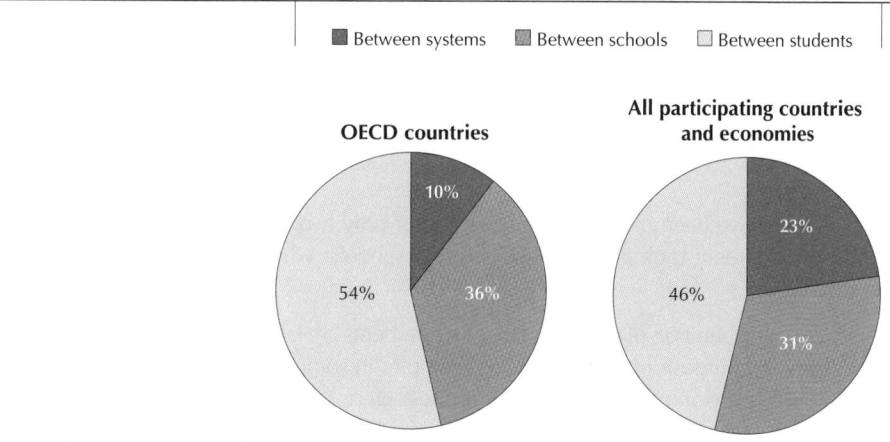

■ Between systems   ■ Between schools   ☐ Between students

OECD countries

All participating countries and economies

Source: OECD, PISA 2012 Database.

This chapter relates features of school organisation and the learning environment to the performance of students within countries and economies and analyses how countries and economies differ in the relationships among these features, overall performance in mathematics, and the level of equity in school systems. The cross-national analyses provide an overview of how system-level attributes and major organisational arrangements relate to student performance and equity in school systems. As always, such relationships require further study in order to determine causality (Box IV.1.1).

Box IV.1.1. **Interpreting the data from students, parents and schools**

PISA 2012 asked students and school principals (and, in some countries, parents) to answer questions about the learning environment and organisation of schools, and the social and economic contexts in which learning takes place. Information based on reports from school principals or parents has been weighted so that it reflects the number of 15-year-olds enrolled in each school. These are self-reports rather than external observations and may be influenced by cultural differences in how individuals respond. For example, students' perceptions of classroom situations may reflect the actual classroom situation imperfectly, or students may choose to respond in a way that does not accurately reflect their genuine thoughts because certain responses may be more socially desirable/acceptable than others.

Several of the indices presented in this volume summarise the responses of students, parents or school principals to a series of related questions. The questions were selected from larger constructs on the basis of theoretical considerations and previous research. Structural equation modelling was used to confirm the theoretically expected dimensions of the indices and validate their comparability across countries. For this purpose, a model was estimated separately for each country or economy and collectively for all OECD countries. For detailed information on the construction of these indices, see Annex A1.

In addition to the general limitation of self-reported data, there are other limitations, particularly those concerning the information collected from principals, that should be taken into account when interpreting the data:

- An average of 346 principals was surveyed in each OECD country, but in 7 countries and economies, fewer than 150 principals were surveyed. In all of these countries and economies, the weighted school participation rate after all replacements is 95% or higher. In 6 of these 7 countries and economies, this was because fewer than 150 schools were attended by 15-year-old students.

- Although principals can provide information about their schools, generalising from a single source of information for each school and then matching that information with students' reports is not straightforward. Students' opinions and performance in each subject depend on many factors, including all the education that they have acquired in previous years and their experiences outside the school setting.

- Principals' perceptions may not be the most appropriate sources of some information related to teachers, such as teachers' morale and commitment.

- The learning environment examined by PISA may only partially reflect the learning environment that shaped students' experiences in education earlier in their school careers, particularly in school systems where students progress through different types of educational institutions at the pre-primary, primary, lower secondary and upper secondary levels. To the extent that students' current learning environment differs from that of their earlier school years, the contextual data collected by PISA are an imperfect proxy for students' cumulative learning environments, and the effects of those environments on learning outcomes is likely to be underestimated.

- In most cases, 15-year-old students have been in their current school for only two to three years. This means that much of their academic development took place earlier, in other schools, which may have little or no connection with the present school.

- In some countries and economies, the definition of the school in which students are taught is not straightforward because schools vary in the level and purpose of education. For example, in some countries and economies, sub-units within schools (e.g. study programmes, shifts and campuses) were sampled instead of schools as administrative units.

Despite these caveats, information from the school questionnaire provides unique insights into the ways in which national and sub-national authorities seek to realise their education objectives.

In using results from non-experimental data on school performance, such as the PISA Database, it is also important to bear in mind the distinction between school effects and the effects of schooling, particularly when interpreting

...

the modest association between factors such as school resources, policies and institutional characteristics and student performance. The effect of schooling is the influence on performance of not being schooled compared with being schooled. As a set of well-controlled studies has shown, this can have a significant impact not only on knowledge but also on fundamental cognitive skills (e.g. Ceci, 1991; Blair et al., 2005). School effects are education researchers' shorthand for the effect on academic performance of attending one school or another, usually schools that differ in resources or policies and institutional characteristics. Where schools and school systems do not vary in fundamental ways, the school effect can be modest. Nevertheless, modest school effects should not be confused with a lack of an effect by schooling.

The analyses that relate the performance and equity levels of school systems to education policies and practices are carried out through a correlation analysis. A correlation is a simple statistic that measures the degree to which two variables are associated with each other, but does not prove causality between the two. Since the relationships are in general examined only after accounting for countries' per capita income, omitted variables could be related to these variables and their relationship in a significant way.

Given the nested nature of the PISA sample (students nested in schools that, in turn, are nested in countries), other statistical techniques, such as Hierarchical Linear Models or Structural Equation Modeling may seem more appropriate. Yet, even these sophisticated statistical techniques cannot adequately take into account the nature of the PISA sample for the system-level analyses because participating countries and economies are not randomly selected. The system-level correlations presented here are consistent with results from earlier PISA analyses, which used more sophisticated statistical techniques. Given that the limitations of a correlation analysis using PISA data are not completely overcome by using more sophisticated statistical tools, the simplest method was used. The robustness and sensitivity of the findings are checked against other specifications. Cautionary notes are provided to help the reader correctly interpret the results presented in this volume.

In contrast, the within-system analyses are based on multilevel regression models appropriate for the random sampling of schools and the random sampling of students within these schools.

Comparisons of results between resources, policies and practices and mathematics performance across time (trends analyses) should also be interpreted with caution. Changes in the strength of the relationship between policies and practices and mathematics performance cannot be considered causal because they can occur for two reasons. First, a particular set of resources, policies and practices might have been chosen by higher-performing students or higher-performing schools while lower-performing students/schools did not choose that set of resources, policies and practices. Under this interpretation, the relationship between mathematics performance and resources, policies and practices becomes stronger because higher-performing students and schools choose them. Second, a particular set of resources, policies and practices may have promoted student learning more in 2012 than in 2003. PISA trends data indicates where changes have taken place, but although they cannot provide precise explanations of the nature of the change, trends data shed light on the ways in which a school system is evolving. However, further analysis is needed to unveil the underlying processes (Box IV.1.3 provides more details on interpreting trends analysis results).

MEASURING THE SUCCESS OF SCHOOL SYSTEMS

"Successful" school systems are defined here as those that perform above the OECD average in mathematics (494 points) and in which students' socio-economic status has a weaker-than-average impact on mathematics performance (on average across OECD countries, 14.6% of the variation in mathematics scores is accounted for by the socio-economic status of students). As shown in Volume II, Australia, Canada, Estonia, Finland, Hong Kong-China, Japan, Korea, Liechtenstein and Macao-China perform at higher levels than the OECD average and also show a weaker relationship between socio-economic status and performance (Figure IV.1.3).

The following sections analyse some of the features shared by these successful school systems that relate to their allocation of resources, policies and practices. The analysis is also extended to the school level within countries, before and after accounting for the socio-economic status of students and schools (Box IV.1.2).

■ Figure IV.1.3 ■
Student performance and equity

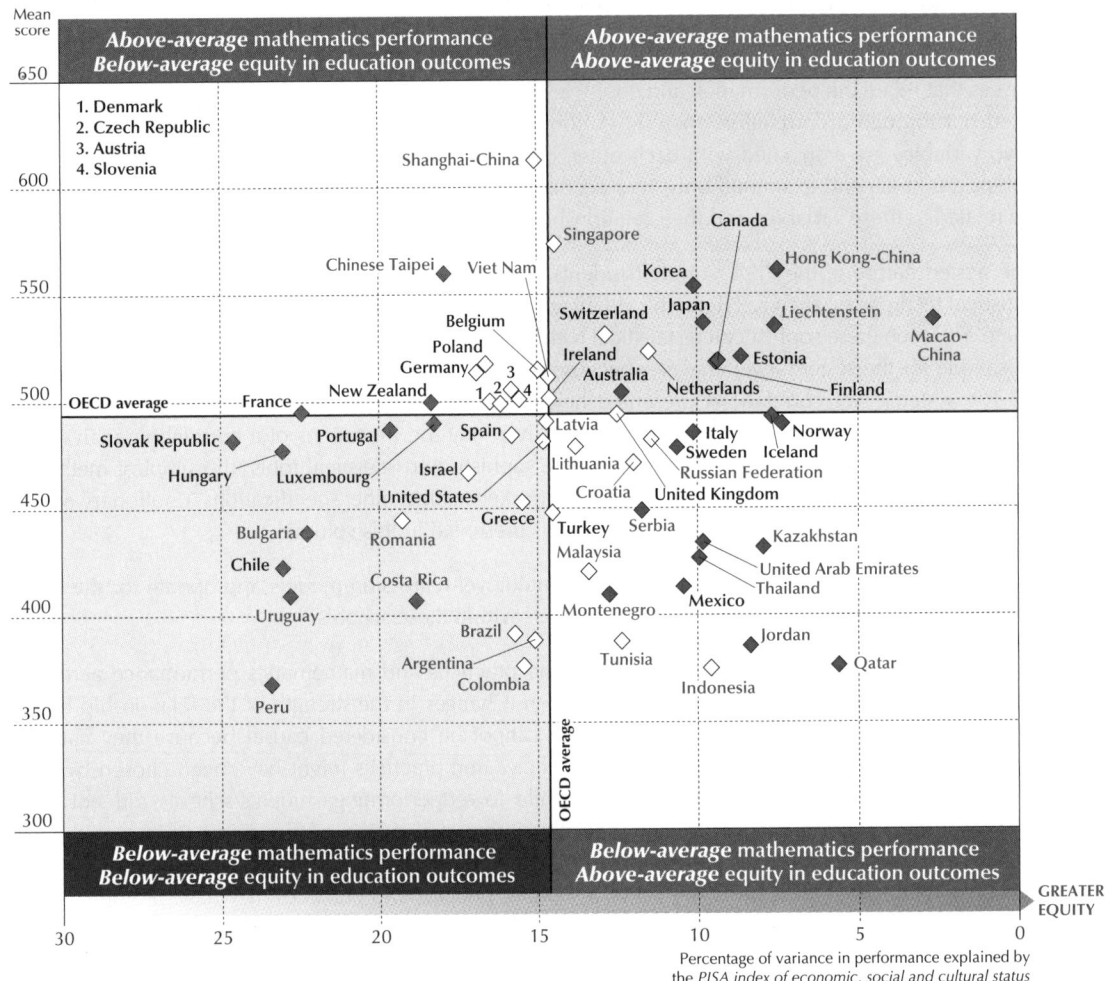

◆ Strength of the relationship between performance and socio-economic status is **above** the OECD average

◇ Strength of the relationship between performance and socio-economic status is not statistically significantly different from the OECD average

◆ Strength of the relationship between performance and socio-economic status is **below** the OECD average

Source: OECD, PISA 2012 Database, Table II.2.1.

StatLink http://dx.doi.org/10.1787/888932957403

Box IV.1.2. **How PISA examines resources, policies, practices and education outcomes**

When examining the relationship between education outcomes and resources, policies and practices, this volume takes into account the socio-economic differences among students, schools and school systems. The advantage of doing this lies in comparing similar entities, namely school systems and schools with similar socio-economic profiles. At the same time, there is a risk that such adjusted comparisons underestimate the strength of the relationship between student performance and resources, policies and practices, since most of the differences in performance are often attributable to both policies and socio-economic status. For example, it may be that in better-performing schools, parents have high expectations for the school and exert pressure on the school to fulfil those expectations. After accounting for socio-economic factors, an existing relationship between parents' expectations of the school and student performance may no longer be apparent as an independent relationship because these

...

schools often have an advantaged student population. Even though the relationship between parental expectations and student performance may exist, it is no longer observed, simply because it has been statistically accounted for by the socio-economic differences with which it overlaps.

Conversely, analyses that do not take socio-economic status into account can overstate the relationship between student performance and resources, policies and practices, as the level of resources and the kinds of policies adopted may also relate to the socio-economic profile of students, schools and countries and economies. At the same time, analyses without adjustments may paint a more realistic picture of the schools that parents choose for their children. They may also provide more information for other stakeholders who are interested in the overall performance of students, schools and systems, including any effects that may be related to the socio-economic profile of schools and systems. For example, parents may be primarily interested in a school's absolute performance standards, even if a school's higher achievement record stems partially from the fact that the school has a larger proportion of advantaged students.

The analyses in this volume present relationships both before and after accounting for socio-economic differences, and focus on differences among school systems and among schools within school systems. Unless otherwise noted, comparisons of student performance refer to the performance of students on the mathematics scale.

Relationships between the organisational characteristics of a school system and the school system's performance in PISA, as well as the impact of socio-economic status on performance, are established through a correlational analysis. The analysis is conducted both before and after accounting for the school systems' per capita income (i.e. per capita GDP). The analyses are undertaken first for OECD countries and then for all countries and economies that participated in PISA (Tables IV.1.1, IV.1.2, IV.1.3, IV.1.4 and IV.1.5).[2]

Within school systems, these relationships are established through multilevel regression analysis. In each of the following sections, a set of interrelated resources, policies and practices are considered jointly to establish their relationship with student performance. For the reasons explained above, two approaches are used: an unadjusted approach that examines the relationships as they present themselves to students, families and teachers in the schools, irrespective of the socio-economic context; and a "like-with-like" approach that examines the relationships after accounting for the socio-economic status and demographic background of students and schools.

HOW LEARNING OUTCOMES ARE RELATED TO THE WAYS IN WHICH SCHOOL SYSTEMS SELECT AND GROUP STUDENTS

Volume II highlights the challenges school systems face in addressing the needs of diverse student populations. To meet these challenges, some countries and economies have adopted non-selective and comprehensive school systems that seek to provide all students with similar opportunities, leaving it to each teacher and school to cater to the full range of student abilities, interests and backgrounds. Other countries and economies respond to diversity by grouping students, whether between schools or between classes within schools, with the aim of serving students according to their academic potential and/or interests in specific programmes. Teaching in these schools or classes is adapted to students with different needs; class size and teacher assignments are determined accordingly. Often, the assumption underlying these stratification policies is that students' talents will develop best when students reinforce each other's interest in learning, and create an environment that is more conducive to effective teaching.

The analysis presented in this chapter covers not only curricular differentiation (i.e. tracking or streaming) and school selectivity, but also other forms of horizontal and vertical stratification. Vertical stratification refers to the ways in which students progress through school as they become older. Even though the student population is differentiated into grade levels in practically all schools that participate in PISA, in some countries, all 15-year-old students attend the same grade level, while in other systems they are dispersed throughout various grade levels as a result of policies governing the age of entrance into the school system and/or grade repetition.

Horizontal stratification refers to differences in instruction within a grade or education level. Horizontal stratification, which can be adopted by the school system or by individual schools, groups students according to their interests and/or performance. School systems make decisions on offering specific programmes (vocational or academic, for example),

setting the age at which students are admitted into these programmes, and determining the extent to which students' academic records are used to select students for their schools. Individual schools make decisions about whether to transfer students out of the school because of poor performance, behavioural problems or special needs, and whether to group students in classes according to ability. Chapter 2 complements this analysis with a detailed description of how different school systems implement these policies and practices and how various forms of stratification are interrelated.

Policies that regulate the selection and sorting of students into schools and classrooms can be related to performance in various ways. On the one hand, creating homogeneous student populations may allow teachers to direct classroom instruction to the specific needs of each group, maximising the learning potential of each group. On the other hand, selecting and sorting students may segregate students according to socio-economic status and result in differences in opportunities to learn. Grouping higher-achieving students together limits the opportunity for under-achieving students to benefit by learning from their higher-achieving peers. In addition, if student sorting is related to teacher sorting, such that high-achieving students are matched to the most talented teachers, under-achieving students may be relegated to lower-quality instruction. Student selection and sorting may also create stereotypes and stigmas that could eventually affect student engagement and learning.

Vertical stratification

PISA shows that the degree of school systems' vertical stratification tends to be negatively related to the equity aspect of education outcomes. In systems where 15-year-old students are found in different grade levels, the impact of students' socio-economic status on their academic performance is stronger than in systems with less vertical stratification. Across OECD countries, 32% of the variation in the impact of students' socio-economic status on their mathematics performance can be explained by differences in the degree of vertical stratification within the system, after accounting for per capita GDP (Table IV.1.1).[3] In contrast, the relationship between vertical stratification and average performance differs between OECD countries on the one hand and across all participating countries and economies on the other. School systems where 15-year-old students attend a wider range of grade levels tend to have lower overall performance in mathematics, across all participating countries and economies, even after accounting for per capita GDP,[4] while no clear relationship is observed across OECD countries, where the dispersion of 15-year-olds across grades is generally less pronounced. To some extent, this is the expected result of a deliberate effort by some countries and economies to make education more inclusive by accommodating students who started school at relatively late ages or who are at greater risk of dropping out.

How is grade repetition related to student performance? The literature suggests that the effect of grade repetition varies, depending on when during their school careers students are retained (Schwerdt and West, 2012). Although some research suggests that grade repetition does not benefit learning (Hauser, 2004; Alexander, Entwisle and Dauber, 2003; Jacob and Lefgren, 2009; Manacorda, 2012), and there is a general understanding that grade repetition is costly for a system (West, 2012; OECD, 2011a), grade repetition is still used in many countries (Goos et al., 2013). Sometimes the prospect of grade repetition, itself, is seen as a source of motivation towards better engagement with school, and is accompanied by other interventions to help a student succeed.

PISA examines the issue of grade repetition not at the individual student level but at the system level in order to avoid selection bias (Heckman and Li, 2003).[5] Grade repetition tends to be negatively related to equity, and this is especially obvious when the relationship is examined across OECD countries, as shown in Figure IV.1.4. Across OECD countries, 20% of the variation in the impact of students' socio-economic status on their mathematics performance can be explained by differences in the proportion of students who repeated a grade, even after accounting for per capita GDP. Across OECD countries, grade repetition is unrelated to the system's overall performance; but across all PISA participating countries and economies, systems in which more students have repeated a grade tend to be those that have lower overall performance in mathematics (Table IV.1.1).[6]

Requiring that students repeat grades implies some cost, not only the expense of providing an additional year of education (i.e. direct costs), but also the cost to society in delaying that student's entry into the labour market by at least one year (i.e. opportunity costs) (OECD, 2011a). Among the countries that practice grade repetition and that have relevant data available, in Estonia, Iceland, Ireland and Israel, the direct and opportunity costs of using grade repetition for one age group can be as low as 0.5% or less of the annual national expenditure on primary- and secondary-school education – or between USD 9 300 and USD 35 100 per repeater (Figure IV.1.5 and Table IV.1.6). In Belgium and the Netherlands, the cost is equivalent to 10% or more of the annual national expenditure on primary- and secondary-school education – or as high as USD 48 900 per repeater or more. These estimates are based on the assumption that students who repeat grades attain lower secondary education, at most. If they were to attain higher levels of education, the costs would be even greater.[7]

■ Figure IV.1.4 ■

Grade repetition and equity

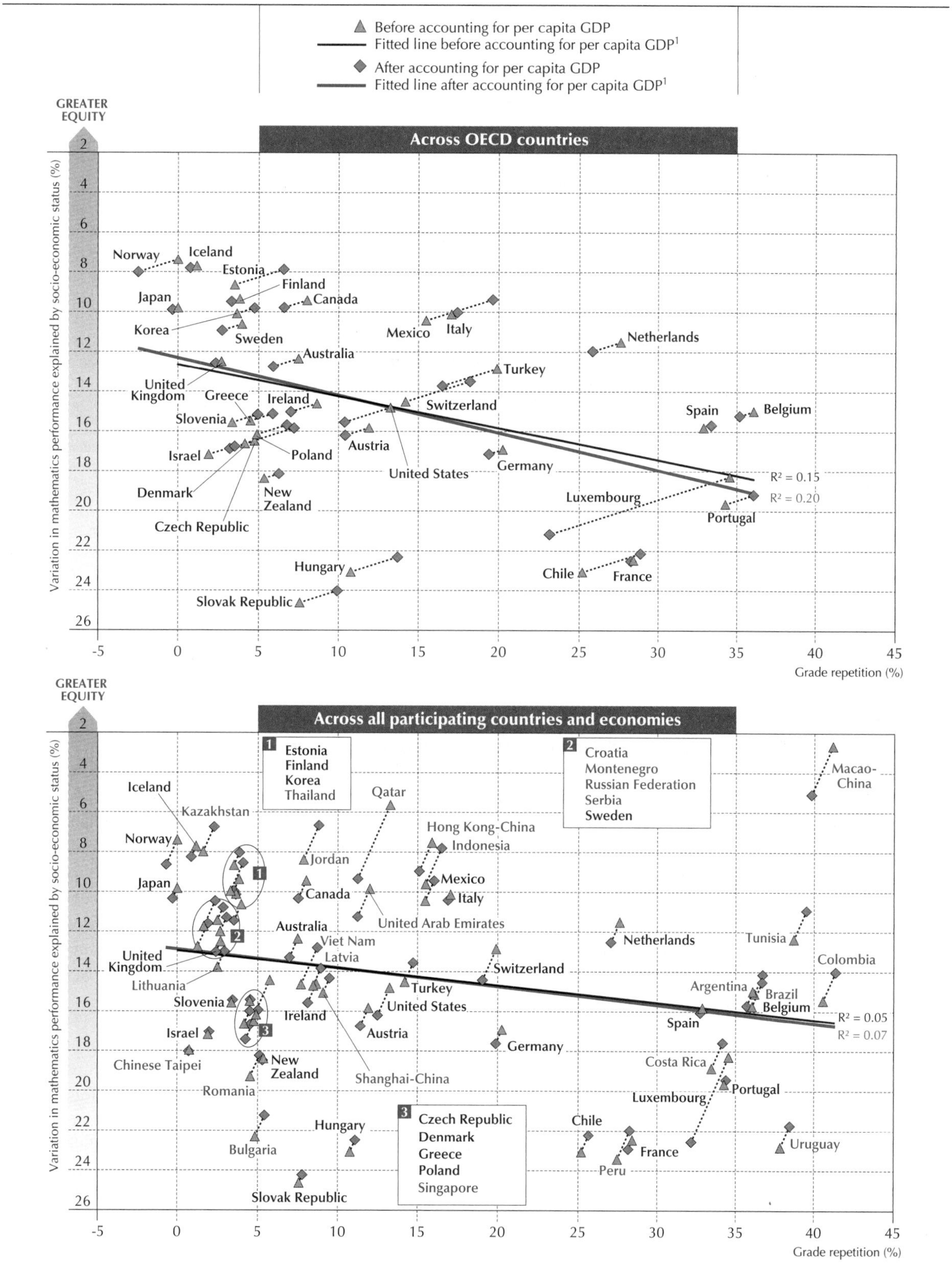

▲ Before accounting for per capita GDP
— Fitted line before accounting for per capita GDP[1]
◆ After accounting for per capita GDP
— Fitted line after accounting for per capita GDP[1]

Across OECD countries

GREATER EQUITY

Variation in mathematics performance explained by socio-economic status (%)

$R^2 = 0.15$
$R^2 = 0.20$

Grade repetition (%)

Across all participating countries and economies

GREATER EQUITY

Variation in mathematics performance explained by socio-economic status (%)

1 Estonia
Finland
Korea
Thailand

2 Croatia
Montenegro
Russian Federation
Serbia
Sweden

3 Czech Republic
Denmark
Greece
Poland
Singapore

$R^2 = 0.05$
$R^2 = 0.07$

Grade repetition (%)

Note: Grade repetition refers to the percentage of students who have repeated a grade at least once in primary or secondary school.
1. A significant relationship (p < 0.10) is shown by the solid line.
Source: OECD, PISA 2012 Database, Table IV.1.1.
StatLink ⟐⟐⟐ http://dx.doi.org/10.1787/888932957403

■ Figure IV.1.5 ■

Cost of grade repetition

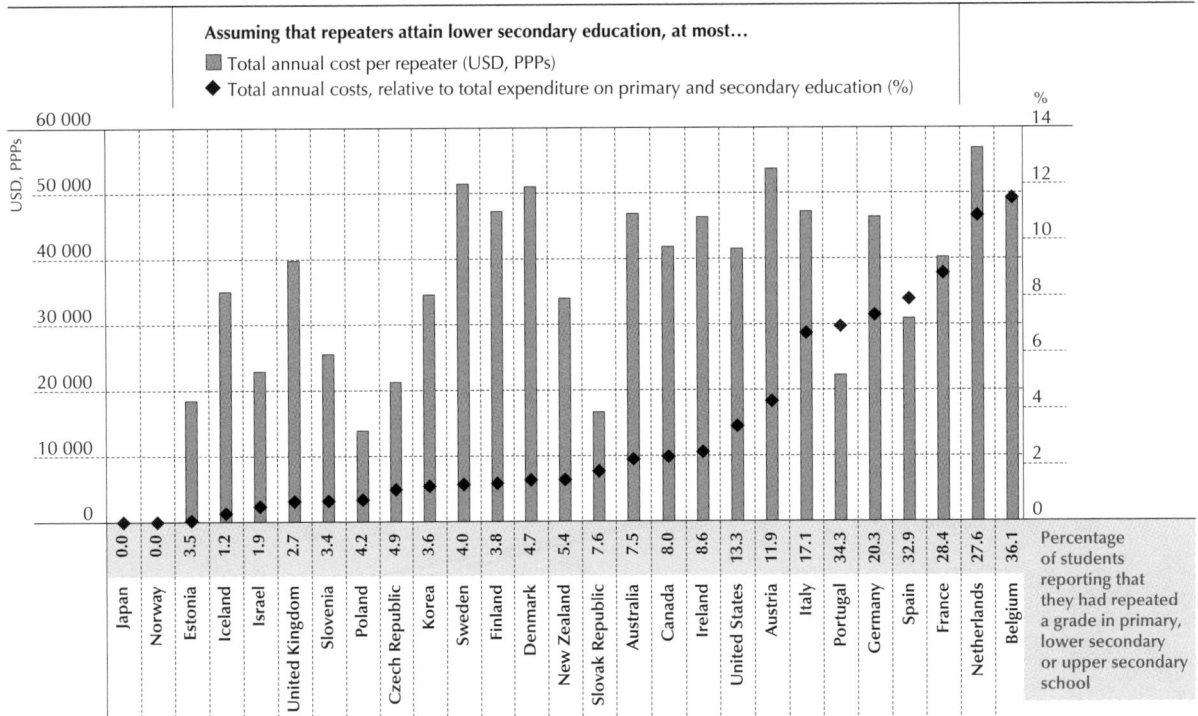

Note: Only countries and economies with available data are shown.
Countries and economies are ranked in ascending order of the total annual cost, relative to total expenditure on primary and secondary education.
Source: OECD, PISA 2012 Database, Tables IV.1.6 and IV.2.2.
StatLink ᴍᴤ￫ http://dx.doi.org/10.1787/888932957403

Horizontal stratification

In general, horizontal stratification is unrelated to a system's average performance. The exception is that systems that group students, within schools, for all classes based on their ability tend to have lower performance across all participating countries and economies, after accounting for per capita GDP (partial correlation coefficient=-0.25). However, between-school horizontal stratification is negatively related to equity in education opportunities. The impact of the socio-economic status of students and/or schools on performance is stronger in school systems that sort students into different tracks, where students are grouped into different tracks at an early age, where more students attend vocational programmes, where more students attend academically selective schools, or where more students attend schools that transfer low-performing students or students with behaviour problems to another school. Across OECD countries, 39% of the variation in the impact of socio-economic status of students and schools on students' mathematics performance can be explained by differences in the ages at which students are selected into different programmes, even after accounting for per capita GDP (Table IV.1.1).

The reason why the age at which stratification begins is closely associated with the impact of socio-economic status on performance may be because the frequency and the nature of student selections/transitions differ between early- and late-stratified systems. In systems that stratify students early, students might be selected more than once before the age of 15. When students are older, more information on individual students is available, and decisions on selecting and sorting students into certain tracks are thus better informed. In addition, students are more dependent upon their parents and their parents' resources when they are younger. In systems that stratify students early, parents with more advantaged socio-economic status may be in a better position to promote their children's chances than disadvantaged parents. In systems where these decisions are taken at a later age, students play a larger role in deciding their own education pathways, and teachers and parents have enough information to make more objective judgements.

As expected, schools that select students for admittance based on students' academic performance tend to show better school average performance, even after accounting for the socio-economic status and demographic background of students and schools and various other school characteristics, on average across OECD countries (Table IV.1.12c).

■ Figure IV.1.6 ■

School admissions policies and mathematics performance

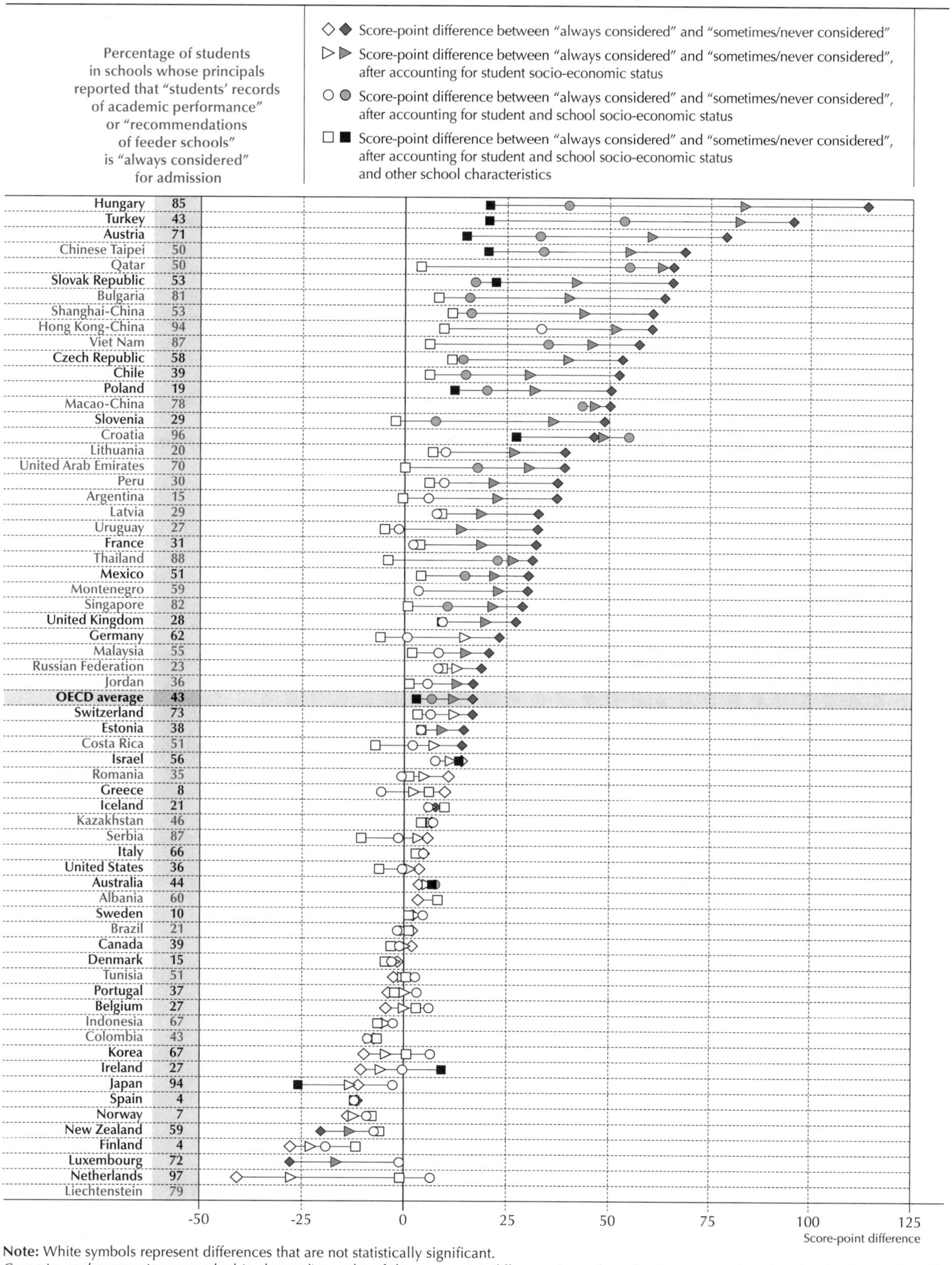

◇ ◆ Score-point difference between "always considered" and "sometimes/never considered"

▷ ▶ Score-point difference between "always considered" and "sometimes/never considered", after accounting for student socio-economic status

○ ● Score-point difference between "always considered" and "sometimes/never considered", after accounting for student and school socio-economic status

□ ■ Score-point difference between "always considered" and "sometimes/never considered", after accounting for student and school socio-economic status and other school characteristics

Percentage of students in schools whose principals reported that "students' records of academic performance" or "recommendations of feeder schools" is "always considered" for admission

Country	%
Hungary	85
Turkey	43
Austria	71
Chinese Taipei	50
Qatar	50
Slovak Republic	53
Bulgaria	81
Shanghai-China	53
Hong Kong-China	94
Viet Nam	87
Czech Republic	58
Chile	39
Poland	19
Macao-China	78
Slovenia	29
Croatia	96
Lithuania	20
United Arab Emirates	70
Peru	30
Argentina	15
Latvia	29
Uruguay	27
France	31
Thailand	88
Mexico	51
Montenegro	59
Singapore	82
United Kingdom	28
Germany	62
Malaysia	55
Russian Federation	23
Jordan	36
OECD average	43
Switzerland	73
Estonia	38
Costa Rica	51
Israel	56
Romania	35
Greece	8
Iceland	21
Kazakhstan	46
Serbia	87
Italy	66
United States	36
Australia	44
Albania	60
Sweden	10
Brazil	21
Canada	39
Denmark	15
Tunisia	51
Portugal	37
Belgium	27
Indonesia	67
Colombia	43
Korea	67
Ireland	27
Japan	94
Spain	4
Norway	7
New Zealand	59
Finland	4
Luxembourg	72
Netherlands	97
Liechtenstein	79

-50   -25   0   25   50   75   100   125

Score-point difference

Note: White symbols represent differences that are not statistically significant.

Countries and economies are ranked in descending order of the score-point difference in mathematics between students in schools whose principals reported that "students' records of academic performance" or "recommendations of feeder schools" are "always considered" for admission and students in schools where these two factors are "sometimes" or "never considered" for admission.

Source: OECD, PISA 2012 Database, Tables IV.1.12c, IV.1.31 and IV.2.7.

StatLink ᵐᔕᔖ http://dx.doi.org/10.1787/888932957403

However, a school system's performance overall is not better if it has a greater proportion of academically selective schools. In fact, in systems with more academically selective schools, the impact of the socio-economic status of students and schools on student performance is stronger (Table IV.1.1).

Trends in the relationship between mathematics performance and stratification

With the exception of Brazil and Turkey, in all countries and economies, students who entered primary school at age 5 or younger, or at age 6, 7 or 8 or older improved their performance between PISA 2003 and PISA 2012 to a similar degree. By contrast, in Brazil and Turkey, performance among students who had started primary school at age 8 or older improved to a greater degree between 2003 and 2012 than that of students who had started school at younger ages (Table IV.1.21). In Brazil, and as shown in Table IV.2.17 (see Chapter 2), more students in 2012 than in 2003 had started school at age 8 or older. Combining these two results suggests that students who would have started school at age 7 in 2003 but did so at age 8 in 2012 were more likely to perform better than students who entered school at age 8 in 2003. It may also be the case that in Turkey students who started school later were more likely to come from socio-economically disadvantaged backgrounds and, as discussed in Volumes I and II, the greatest improvements in performance over the period were observed among low-achieving and disadvantaged students, who are more likely to be those who entered school at a later age in 2012 compared with their counterparts in 2003.

■ Figure IV.1.7 ■

Change between PISA 2003 and PISA 2012 in the relationship between grade repetition and mathematics performance

Score-point difference in mathematics performance between students who had repeated a grade and those who hadn't

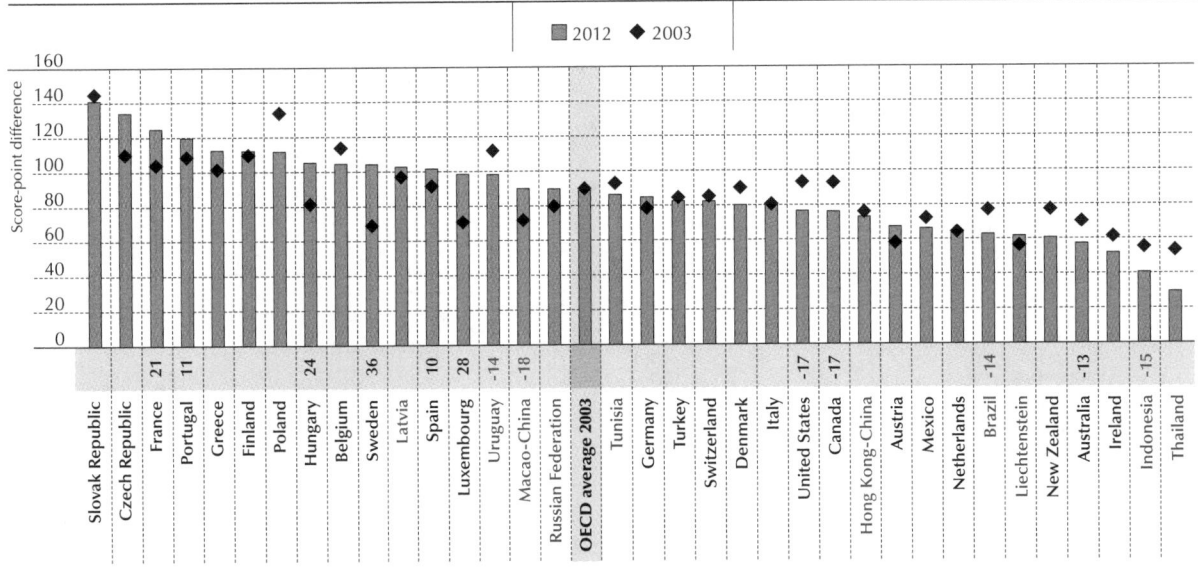

Notes: The change in the score-point difference in mathematics performance between 2003 and 2012 (2012 - 2003) is shown above the country/economy name. Only statistically significant differences are shown.
OECD average 2003 compares only OECD countries with comparable mathematics scores since 2003.
Only countries and economies with comparable data from PISA 2003 and PISA 2012 are shown.
Countries and economies are ranked in descending order of the score-point difference in mathematics performance between students who reported in 2012 that they had repeated a grade and those who hadn't.
Source: OECD, PISA 2012 Database, Table IV.1.22.
StatLink ⬛ᴎ⬛ http://dx.doi.org/10.1787/888932957403

In PISA 2012, more than 20% of students in 16 countries and economies reported that they had repeated a grade; 11 of these countries and economies have comparable data for PISA 2003. On average across these 11 countries and economies (Macao-China, Tunisia, Uruguay, Brazil, Belgium, Luxembourg, Portugal, Spain, France, the Netherlands and Germany), in 2003, the difference in mathematics performance between students who had repeated a grade and those who hadn't was 90 score points; by 2012, that difference had increased slightly, to 94 score points. This performance advantage among those who had not repeated a grade increased in Macao-China, Luxembourg, Portugal, Spain and France (and also in Sweden and Hungary, two countries with lower grade repetition rates). In this group of

countries and economies, either the penalty in performance for repeating a grade became larger during the period, or low-achieving students were more likely to have been required to repeat a grade. The performance advantage of non-repeaters decreased in Brazil and Uruguay, where either the adverse effects on performance of repeating a grade weakened during the period, or these school systems held back more students with relatively higher scores in mathematics in 2012 than they did in 2003. Among countries that rely less on grade repetition, the performance advantage increased in Sweden and Hungary and narrowed by more than 10 points in Canada, the United States, Indonesia and Australia (Figure IV.1.7; see also Table IV.2.18 in Chapter 2 for repetition rates).

Trends at different levels of the school system (grade levels or lower/upper secondary, for example) shed light on the extent to which students are more – or less – prepared to enter the next level. Declining trends among 15-year-old students in the 9th grade, for example, may signal an increasing challenge for 10th-grade teachers, as the students they teach now are not as well prepared for 10th-grade coursework as students were a decade ago. Similarly, declining trends in performance among upper secondary students indicate that it is becoming more difficult for school systems to ensure that their students are ready to make the transition into tertiary education or the labour market. On average across OECD countries[8] and in most other countries and economies, the overall trends in mathematics performance discussed in Volume I are seen in both lower and upper secondary education. In 2012, lower secondary students in Turkey, Brazil, the Russian Federation, Portugal, Mexico, Poland, Thailand, Belgium, Indonesia, Tunisia, Germany and Latvia scored higher in mathematics than did their counterparts in 2003, signalling that lower secondary 15-year-old students were better prepared to enter upper secondary education in 2012 than in 2003. In Portugal, the Russian Federation, Turkey, Italy, Korea and Mexico, 15-year-olds in upper secondary students in 2012 were better prepared to make the transition into tertiary education or the labour market than their counterparts were in 2003 (Table IV.1.23).

Box IV.1.3. Trends in the relationship between resources, policies and practices and mathematics performance

Educational resources, policies and practices interact in different ways with students' mathematics performance. The relationship between education policies and practices and students' mathematics performance varies across school systems; it may also vary across time with certain resources, policies or practices becoming more strongly related to mathematics over time. The sections on trends discuss how certain resources, policies and practices have become more strongly – or weakly – related to students' mathematics performance. They compare the strength of the relationship observed in PISA 2003 to that observed in PISA 2012, taking advantage of the fact that many of the resources, policies and practices measured in PISA 2012 were also measured in PISA 2003. These factors include vertical and horizontal stratification practices, learning time and assessment practices. The trends sections in the following chapters describe the ways in which countries and economies have changed their stratification practices (Chapter 2), their level of resources (Chapter 3), their autonomy and assessment/accountability policies (Chapter 4), and their learning environments (Chapter 5).[9]

Changes in the relationship between resources, policies and practices described in this section should be interpreted with caution as they may arise for a variety of reasons. One possible interpretation of the fact that a particular policy or practice has become more strongly related to students' mathematics performance is that it has promoted student learning better in 2012 than in 2003. Alternative explanations are also possible, such as the fact that better-performing students (or schools) may have chosen to adopt this policy during the period, or that lower-performing students (or schools) chose not to. Changes in the relationship between resources, policies and practices and mathematics performance between PISA 2003 and PISA 2012 cannot be considered causal. They shed light on ways in which a school system is evolving and need further analysis to reveal the processes and nature of the change. Moreover, because PISA can only show whether the policy or practice has become more – or less – strongly related to students' mathematics performance among the particular students, schools and school systems that adopted it, it is not possible to know whether the observed changes can be generalised to include other school systems, schools and students (see endnote 10 for further details on interpreting trends results).

Nonetheless, these changes over time show where certain policies may have become more closely related to student learning. They also highlight where certain challenges to excellence in performance remain or have become more apparent, as in the case of those policies and practices that continue to be related to lower performance or that have become even more strongly associated with poorer mathematics performance.

On average across OECD countries, there was no change in the performance advantage among students in higher grades. In Luxembourg, however, the difference became more pronounced by PISA 2012: in 2003, students in the modal grade outperformed those in the grades below (by an average of 30 score points) and scored lower than those in the grades above (by an average of 80 points); by 2012 these differences had widened significantly to 46 and 89 points, respectively. By contrast, in Belgium, Ireland, Thailand and Australia, these performance differences across grade levels were smaller in 2012 than in 2003 (Table IV.1.23).

On average across OECD countries, the advantage in mathematics performance increased for students in schools that do not use ability grouping compared with students in schools where ability grouping is practiced in some or all classes. Students in schools where no ability grouping is practiced scored eight points higher in mathematics in 2012 compared to their counterparts in 2003, while students in schools where ability grouping is practiced in some or all classes scored lower in PISA 2012 than their counterparts in PISA 2003 did. This could mean that schools that do not group students by ability became more effective than schools that use ability grouping. Alternatively, it could mean that schools that do not group students by ability are increasingly those that select higher-performing students and so appear to have higher average performance than schools that do practice ability grouping. The advantage of schools that do not use ability grouping narrowed in Uruguay and Brazil, where, by 2012, it was no longer statistically significant, and in Luxembourg. The performance advantage among students in schools that do not use ability grouping was observed in PISA 2012, but not in PISA 2003, in Macao-China and Iceland, while the performance disadvantage observed among students who attend schools that do not group students by ability disappeared by 2012 in Turkey and Belgium (Table IV.1.24).[11]

HOW LEARNING OUTCOMES ARE RELATED TO SYSTEMS' RESOURCE ALLOCATION

Adequate resources are crucial for providing students with high-quality opportunities to learn. At the same time, those resources translate into better learning outcomes only if they are used efficiently. As Chapter 3 shows, school systems in the countries and economies that participated in PISA vary in the amount of resources – including financial, human and material resources and students' learning time – that they invest in education. Research is inconclusive on the subject, but usually shows a weak relationship between the quantity of educational resources and student performance, since more of the variation in performance can be explained by the quality of resources and how these resources are used, particularly among the industrialised countries (Fuller, 1987; Greenwald, Hedges and Laine, 1996; Buchmann and Hannum, 2001; Rivkin, Hanushek and Kain, 2005; Murillo and Román, 2011; Hægeland, Raaum and Salvanes, 2012; Nicoletti and Rabe, 2012).

Financial resources

A first glance at PISA results gives the impression that high-income countries and economies – and those that are able to and spend more on education – have better student performance. High-income countries and economies (defined here as those with a per capita GDP above USD 20 000) have more resources to spend on education: high-income countries and economies cumulatively spend, on average, USD 89 702 on each student from age 6 to 15, while countries that are not considered to be in that group spend, on average, USD 25 286 (Tables IV.3.1 and IV.3.2 discussed in Chapter 3). Moreover, high-income countries and economies have an average mathematics performance almost 70 score points higher than that of countries whose per capita GDP is below the USD 20 000 threshold.

Yet the relationship among a country's/economy's income per capita, its level of expenditure on education per student, and its PISA score is far more complex (Baker, Goesling and LeTendre 2002; OECD, 2012). While among countries and economies whose cumulative expenditure per student is below USD 50 000 (the level of spending in the Czech Republic, the Slovak Republic and Hungary), higher expenditure on education is predictive of higher PISA mathematics scores; however, this is not the case among high-income countries and economies, which include most OECD countries. It seems that for this latter group of countries and economies, factors other than wealth are better predictors of student performance.

Among the former group of countries and economies, systems with a cumulative expenditure of USD 10 000 higher than other systems score an average of 27 points higher in the PISA mathematics assessment. For example, Jordan, with a cumulative expenditure per student of USD 7 125, has an average PISA mathematics score of 386 points – 35 points lower than Malaysia, which has a cumulative expenditure per student that is roughly USD 10 000 higher than that of Jordan.

However, among those countries and economies whose cumulative expenditure per student is more than USD 50 000, the relationship between spending per student and performance is no longer apparent, even after accounting for differences in purchasing power. Thus, among these countries and economies, it is common to find some with substantially different levels of spending per student yet similar mathematics performance. For example, the United States and the Slovak Republic score at 481 points in mathematics, but the United States' cumulative expenditure per student is more than double that of the Slovak Republic. Also, countries and economies with similar levels of expenditure can perform very differently.

■ Figure IV.1.8 ■

Spending per student from the age of 6 to 15 and mathematics performance in PISA 2012

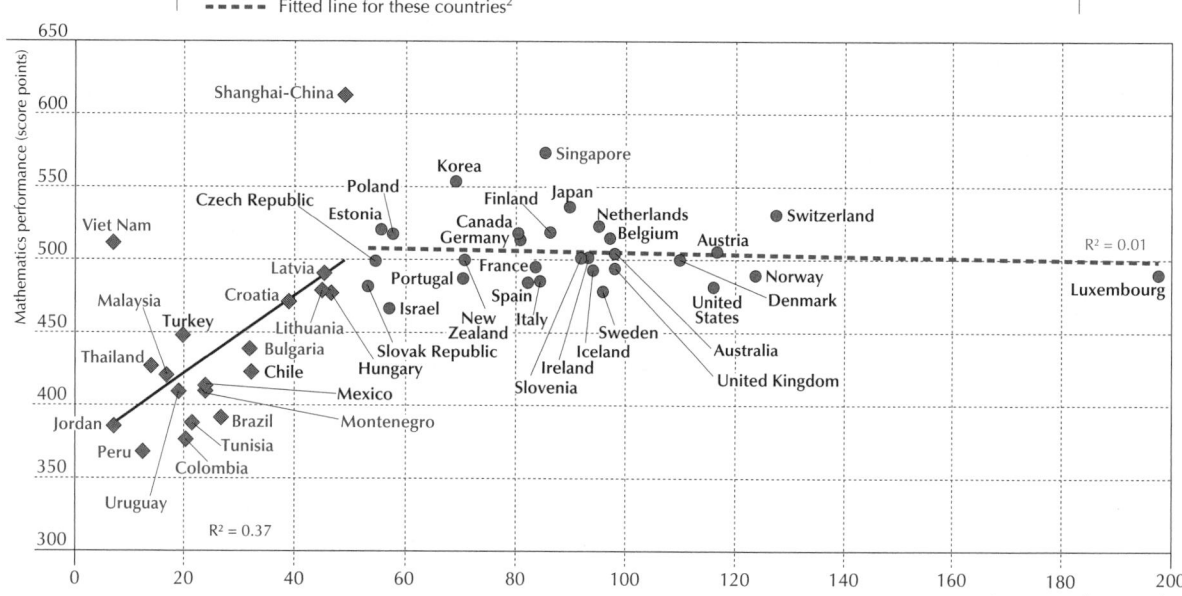

Note: Only countries and economies with available data are shown.
1. A significant relationship (p < 0.10) is shown by the solid line.
2. A non-significant relationship (p > 0.10) is shown by the dotted line.
Source: OECD, PISA 2012 Database, Tables I.2.3a and IV.3.1.
StatLink ⌐🔢 http://dx.doi.org/10.1787/888932957403

■ Figure IV.1.9 ■

Change between 2003 and 2012 in average spending per student from the age of 6 to 15 and change in mathematics performance

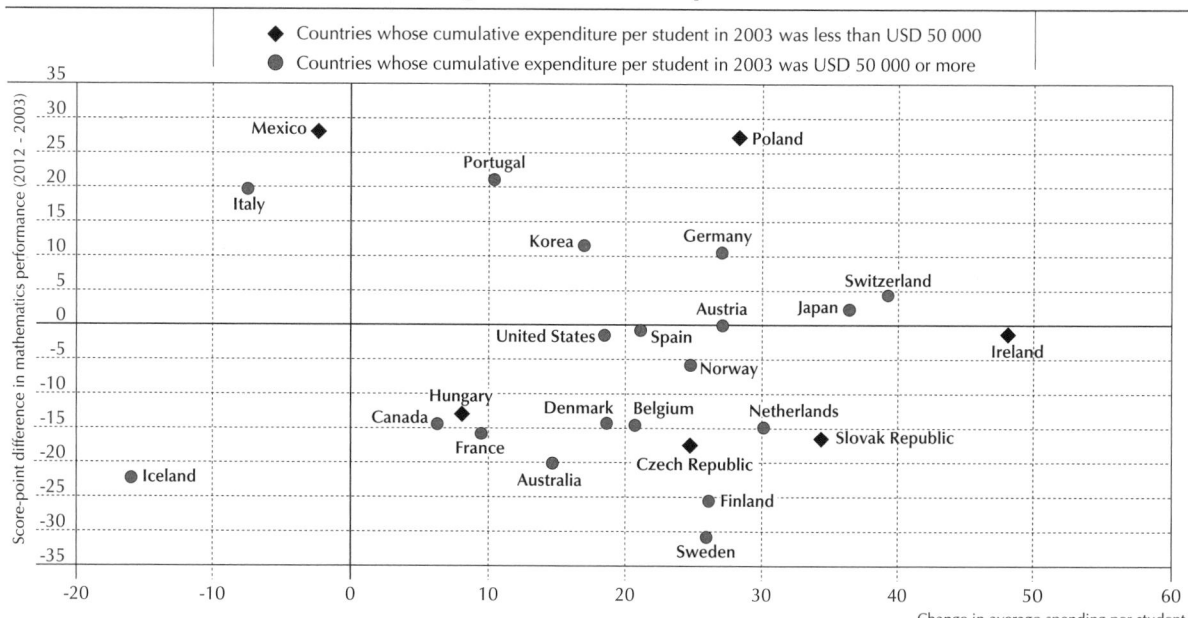

Note: Only countries with comparable data from PISA 2003 and PISA 2012 are shown.
Source: OECD, PISA 2012 Database, Tables I.2.3b and IV.3.1.
StatLink ⌐🔢 http://dx.doi.org/10.1787/888932957403

For example, Italy and Singapore both have a cumulative expenditure per student of roughly USD 85 000, but while Italy scored 485 points in mathematics in PISA 2012, Singapore scored 573 points (Figure IV.1.8).

Trend data between PISA 2003 and PISA 2012 shed light on how changes in spending per student relate to changes in performance.[12] As shown in Figure IV.1.9, the PISA data show no relationship between increases in expenditure and changes in performance, not even for the countries where cumulative expenditure per student was less than USD 50 000 in 2003. Mexico, for example, is among the countries and economies with the greatest improvement in average mathematics performance between 2003 and 2012, but its levels of expenditure remained relatively stable between 2001 and 2011. Similar improvements in average mathematics performance were observed in Poland, where per-student cumulative expenditure nearly doubled during the period (Figure IV.1.9). Caution is required when interpreting the change in per-student expenditure: if the spending is related to capital investment or other purposes that did not change the instructional environment of the 15-year-olds assessed by PISA, then it would not be expected that the returns to these investments accrue to the students whose performance is measured by PISA. Also, in some countries, an increase in per-student expenditure might be a consequence of a decreasing student population rather than a real increase in investment in education.

Whatever the reason for the lack of a relationship between spending per student and learning outcomes, at least in the countries and economies with larger education budgets, excellence in education requires more than money. How resources are allocated is just as important as the amount of resources available to be allocated. One finding from PISA is that high-performing systems tend to prioritise higher salaries for teachers, especially in high-income countries (Figure IV.1.10).

■ Figure IV.1.10 ■

Teachers' salaries and mathematics performance

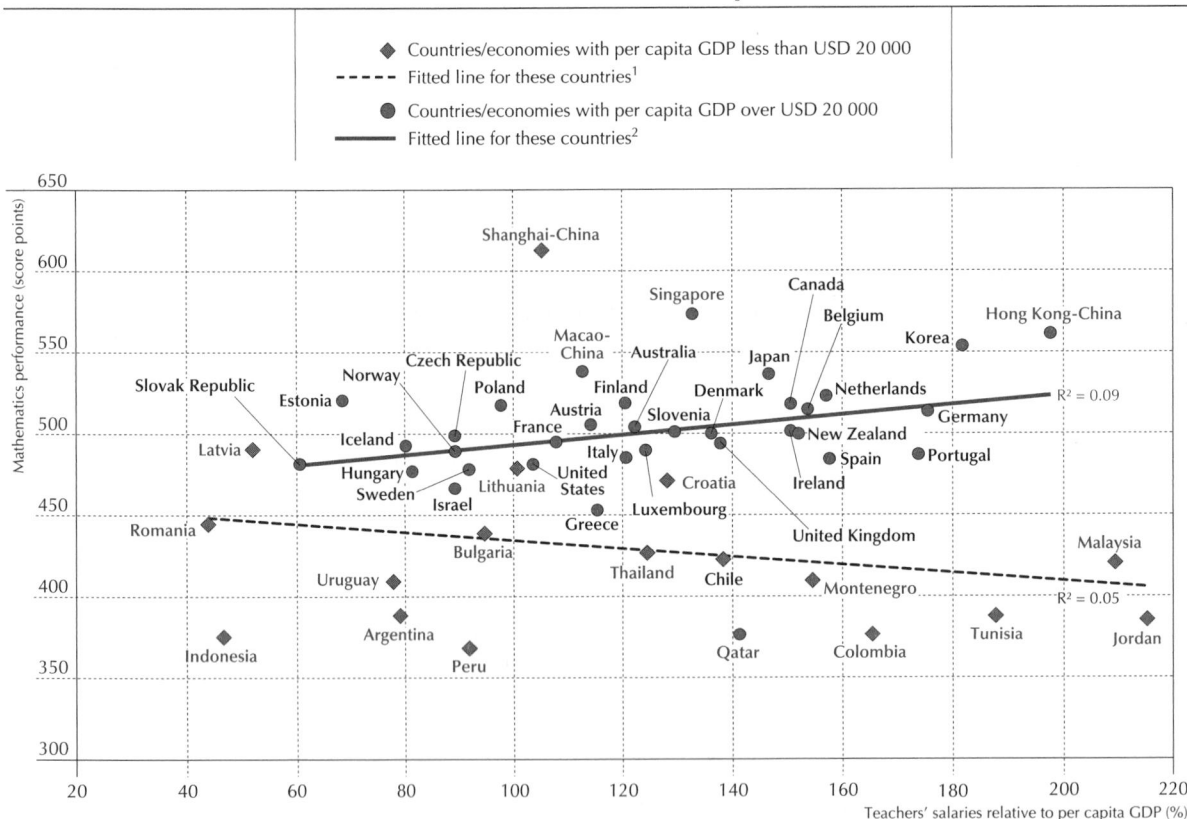

Notes: Teachers' salaries relative to per capita GDP refers to the weighted average of upper and lower secondary school teachers. The average is computed by weighting teachers' salaries for upper and lower secondary school according to the respective 15-year-old students' enrolment (for countries and economies with available information on both the upper and lower secondary levels).

Only countries and economies with available data are shown.

1. A non-significant relationship (p > 0.10) is shown by the dotted line.

2. A significant relationship (p < 0.10) is shown by the solid line.

Source: OECD, PISA 2012 Database, Tables I.2.3a and IV.3.3.

StatLink ᵃᵢˢ᛫ http://dx.doi.org/10.1787/888932957403

Among countries and economies whose per capita GDP is more than USD 20 000, including most OECD countries, systems that pay teachers more (i.e. higher teachers' salaries relative to national income per capita) tend to perform better in mathematics. The correlation between these two factors across 33 high-income countries and economies is 0.30, and the correlation is 0.40 across 32 high-income countries and economies excluding Qatar.[13] In contrast, across countries and economies and economies whose per capita GDP is under USD 20 000, a system's overall academic performance is unrelated to its teachers' salaries, possibly signalling that a host of resources (material infrastructure, instructional materials, transportation, etc.) also need to be improved until they reach a certain threshold, after which improvements in material resources no longer benefit student performance, but improvements in human resources (through higher teachers' salaries, for example) do.[14]

Human resources

As with spending per student, the mere volume of human resources tends to be unrelated to the academic performance or equity of school systems, after accounting for the level of national income.[15] Of course, a school system that lacks quality teachers, infrastructure and textbooks will almost certainly perform at lower levels than other systems. In fact, at the school level, teacher shortage appears to be related to poorer performance in most countries. In 33 countries and economies, schools where a higher share of principals reported that teacher shortages hinder learning tend to show lower performance (see Table IV.3.10, in Chapter 3). However, the degree of teacher shortage is related to the amount of other resources allocated to schools and to schools' socio-economic intake. But even after accounting for the socio-economic status and demographic background of students and schools and various other school characteristics, in the Czech Republic, Slovenia and Switzerland schools whose principals reported that teacher shortages hinder learning tend to show lower average performance (Table IV.1.12c). On average across OECD countries, almost half of the performance differences between schools are accounted for jointly by school resources and students' and schools' socio-economic status and demographic profile (Table IV.1.8a).[16] This suggests that much of the impact of socio-economic status on performance is mediated by the resources invested in schools.

Material resources

The educational resources available in a school tend to be related to the system's overall performance, while the adequacy of the physical infrastructure appears to be unrelated. After accounting for per capita GDP, 33% of the variation in mathematics performance across OECD countries can be explained by differences in principals' responses to questions about the adequacy of science laboratory equipment, instructional materials (e.g. textbooks), computers for instruction, Internet connectivity, computer software for instruction, and library materials (Table IV.1.2).

How resources are allocated to disadvantaged and advantaged schools is also related to systems' levels of performance. In higher performing systems, principals in socio-economically advantaged and disadvantaged schools reported similar levels of quality of physical infrastructure and schools' educational resources, both across OECD countries and across all countries and economies participated in PISA 2012 (Table IV.1.3). As shown in Figure IV.1.11, even after accounting for per capita GDP, 30% of the variation in mathematics performance across OECD countries can be explained by the level of similarities in principals' report on school s' educational resources between socio-economically advantaged and disadvantaged schools.

At the school level, in 32 countries and economies, principals' perceptions about the adequacy of the educational resources in their school are positively related to the school's average performance (Table IV.3.16, which is discussed in Chapter 3). However, schools with more adequate educational resources are also those that have other characteristics closely related to higher performance. But, even after accounting for the socio-economic status and demographic profile of students and schools and various other school characteristics, in Qatar, Romania and Costa Rica schools with more adequate resources tend to perform better (Table IV.1.12c). This suggests that much of the impact of socio-economic status on performance is mediated by the resources invested in schools (Table IV.1.8a).

Time resources

The average learning time in regular mathematics lessons is positively related to student performance at the school level. Even after accounting for the socio-economic status and demographic profile of students and schools and various other school characteristics, in 15 countries and economies, schools with longer learning time in mathematics classes tend to perform better in mathematics (Table IV.1.12c). However, at the system level, across all OECD countries and all countries and economies that participated in PISA 2012 there is no clear pattern between a system's overall mathematics performance and whether students in that system spend more time in regular mathematics classes or not (Table IV.1.2).[17] Since learning outcomes are the product of both the quantity and the quality of instruction time, this suggests that cross-system differences in the quality of instruction time blur the relationship between the quantity of instruction time and student performance.

■ Figure IV.1.11 ■

Systems' allocation of educational resources and mathematics performance

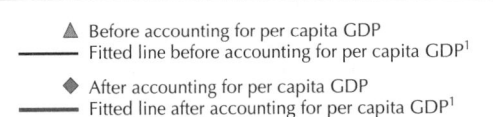

▲ Before accounting for per capita GDP
── Fitted line before accounting for per capita GDP[1]

◆ After accounting for per capita GDP
── Fitted line after accounting for per capita GDP[1]

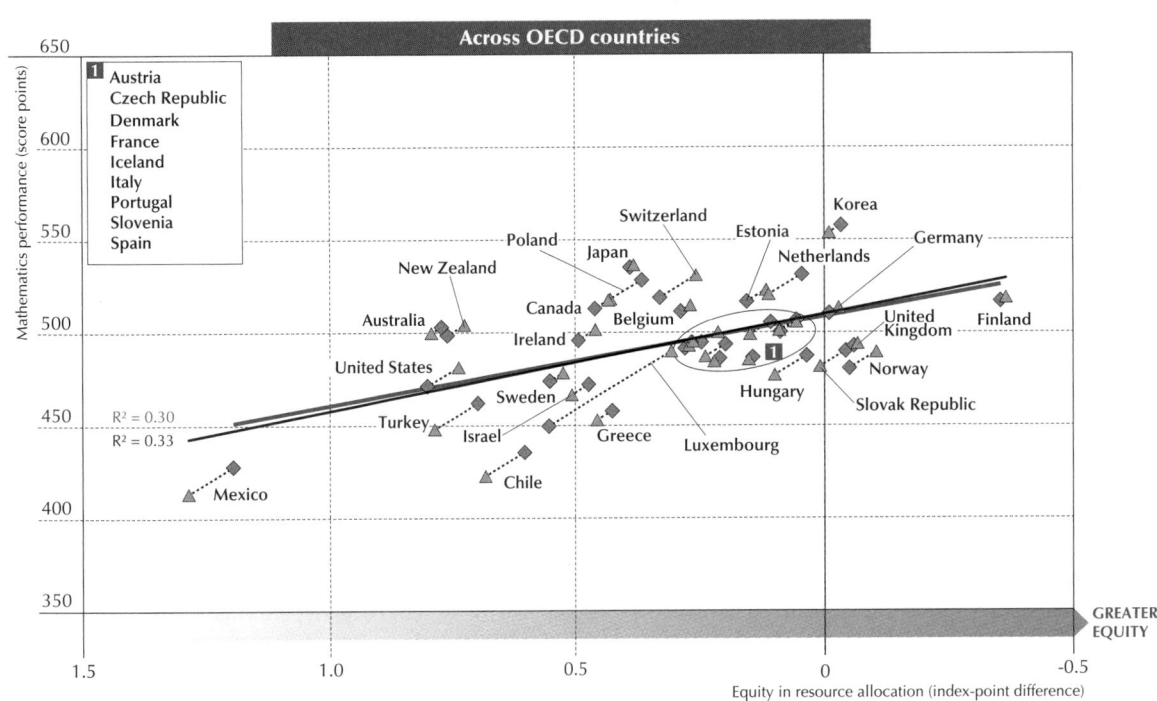

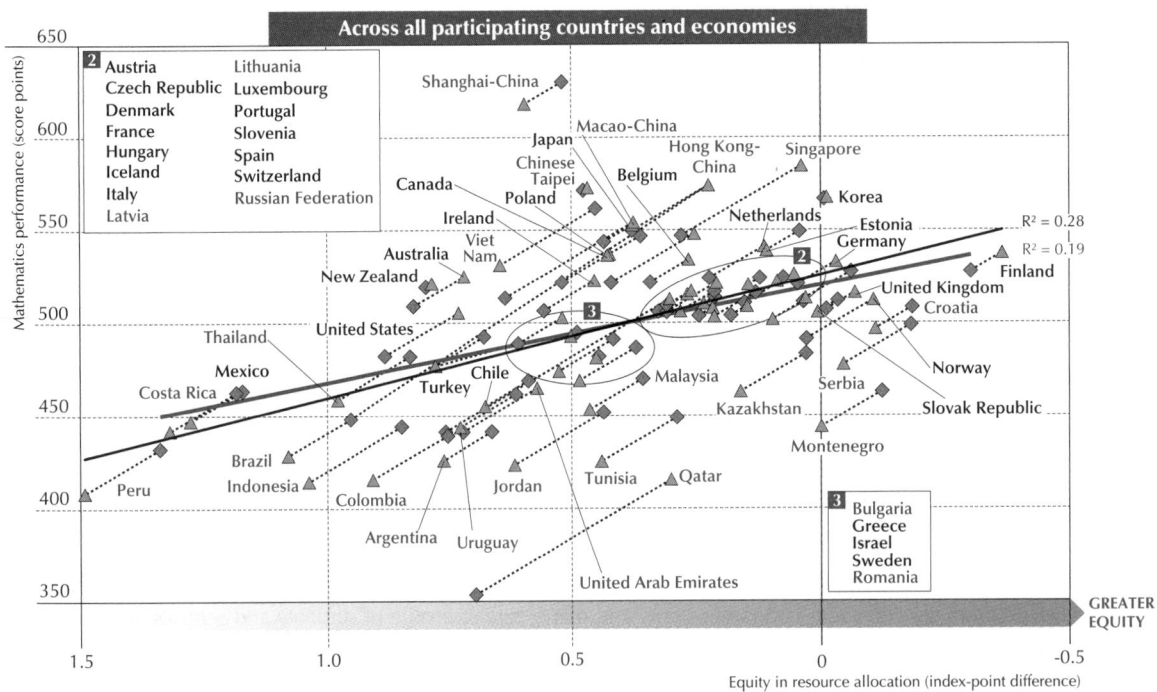

Note: Equity in resource allocation refers to the difference in the *index of quality of schools' educational resources* between socio-economically advantaged and disadvantaged school.

1. A significant relationship (p < 0.10) is shown by the solid line.

Source: OECD, PISA 2012 Database, Table IV.1.3.

StatLink ⌜⌐ᔭᴾ http://dx.doi.org/10.1787/888932957403

Some schools offer supplementary mathematics lessons in addition to those provided during regular school hours. Schools often decide to offer these after-school lessons because their students need more time to learn mathematics. Not surprisingly then, the schools that offer after-school mathematics lessons are often those with lower average performance in mathematics (Tables IV.1.8b, IV.1.8c, IV.1.12b and IV.1.12c). However, at the system level and across all OECD countries and also across all participating countries and economies, the proportion of students in schools with after-school mathematic lessons tends to be unrelated to the system's overall performance level (Table IV.1.2).

Schools whose students spend more hours on homework or other study set by teachers tend, on average, to perform better, even after accounting for the socio-economic status and demographic background of students and schools and various other school characteristics (Tables IV.1.8b, IV.1.8c, IV.1.12b and IV.1.12c). This is not an obvious finding, since one could expect that lower-performing students spend more time doing homework. However, there may be other factors, such as higher-performing schools requiring more homework from their students. At the system level, the average number of hours that students spend on homework or other study set by their teachers tends to be unrelated to systems' overall performance level (Table IV.1.2).

In summary, at the school level, there is some relationship between the time students spend learning in and after school and their performance, but no clear pattern of this relationship is observed at the system level. This might be because of differences across systems in how the time is spent and how much students learn within a given amount of time. In addition, the nature and purpose of after-school lessons are not always the same. In some schools and school systems, after-school lessons are provided mainly to support struggling students, while in others they are mainly for enrichment.

Across all countries and economies, school systems where schools tend to offer more creative extracurricular activities (i.e. band, orchestra or choir; school plays or musicals; and art clubs or art activities) tend to show better overall performance in mathematics, even after accounting for per capita GDP; but this relationship is not observed across OECD countries (Table IV.1.2). In 47 countries and economies, schools that offer more creative extracurricular activities tend to perform better in mathematics (see Table IV.3.31, discussed in Chapter 3). However, the extent to which schools offer these activities is also related to schools' socio-economic profile and other characteristics. But, even after accounting for the socio-economic status and demographic profile of students and schools and various other school characteristics, in Qatar, Viet Nam, Israel, the United Arab Emirates, Jordan, Estonia and Uruguay schools that offer more of these activities tend to perform better in mathematics (Table IV.1.12c) (Box IV.1.4 offers more details on the policies and programmes implemented recently by Israel[18]).

As shown in Volume II, students who attended pre-primary education tend to perform better at the age of 15 than those who did not attend pre-primary education. This relationship is also apparent at the school level. In 17 countries and economies, schools with more students who had attended pre-primary education for more than one year tend to show better average performance (Table IV.1.12c). At the system level, across all PISA participating countries and economies, there is also a relationship between the proportion of students who had attended pre-primary education for more than one year and systems' overall performance in mathematics. Some 32% of the variation in mathematics performance across all countries and economies can be explained by the difference in the percentage of students who attended pre-primary education for more than one year, after accounting for per capita GDP (Table IV.1.2). However, across OECD countries, there is no clear relationship.

Trends in the relationship between mathematics performance and educational resources

As discussed in Chapter 3, all but 11 countries reduced their student-teacher ratios between 2003 and 2012 (Table IV.3.35). The relationship between the student-teacher ratio and the mathematics performance of schools was weak in 2003 and remained so in 2012. In Tunisia, the negative relationship between student-teacher ratios and performance observed in 2003 – whereby students who attend schools with smaller student-teacher ratios perform better – weakened by 2012. Conversely, the positive relationship between student-teacher ratios and students' mathematics performance – whereby students in schools with more favourable student-teacher ratios actually score lower - strengthened in Italy during the period and remained positive and moderately strong in Liechtenstein, Belgium, the Netherlands and Hong Kong-China. In all other countries and economies, the relationship between the student-teacher ratio and student performance in mathematics was weak in both 2003 and 2012 (Figure IV.1.12).

■ Figure IV.1.12 ■

Change between 2003 and 2012 in the relationship between students' mathematics performance and student-teacher ratios in their schools

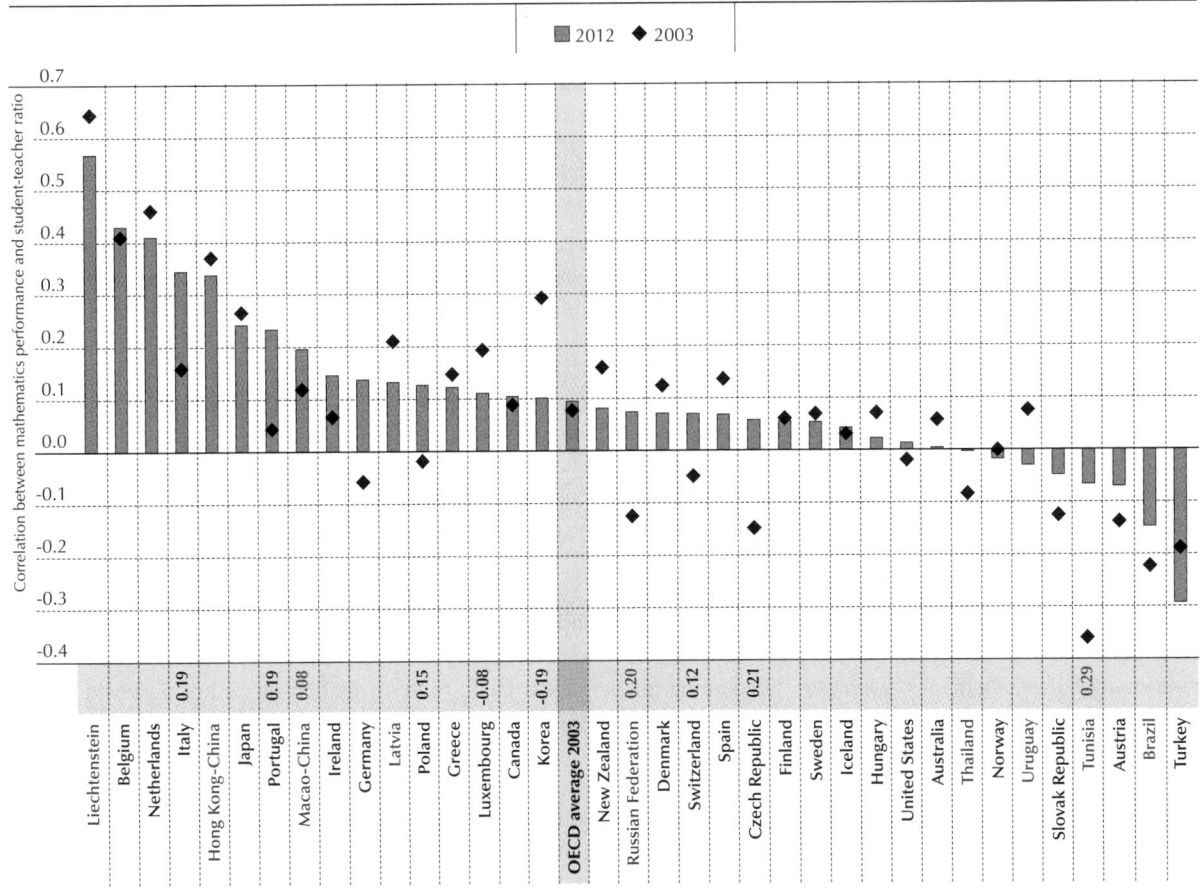

Notes: The change in the correlation between mathematics performance and schools' student-teacher ratios between 2003 and 2012 (2012 - 2003) is shown above the country/economy name. Only statistically significant differences are shown.

OECD average 2003 compares only OECD countries with comparable mathematics scores and student-teacher ratios since 2003.

Only countries and economies with comparable data from PISA 2003 and PISA 2012 are shown.

Countries and economies are ranked in descending order of the correlation between students' mathematics performance and the student-teacher ratio in their schools in 2012.

Source: OECD, PISA 2012 Database, Table IV.1.25.

StatLink ⛐🔢 http://dx.doi.org/10.1787/888932957403

Between 2003 and 2012, there was an increase in the amount of time students spend in mathematics classes (see Table IV.3.46 in Chapter 3); yet the relationship between learning time and mathematics performance was weak in both PISA 2003 and PISA 2012: in both PISA assessments, students exposed to more mathematics instruction did not perform better than students exposed to less mathematics instruction. This could be because, in some countries and economies, low-performing students tend to spend more time in mathematics classes to catch up with their peers; in others, higher-performing students may spend more time in mathematics lessons because they enjoy the subject more. In both cases, students may benefit from more time spent in the classroom, but the average relationship is negligible. The relationship was weak and positive in PISA 2003 and became stronger in PISA 2012 in Thailand, Japan and Turkey, meaning that students in these countries who spent more time in mathematics classes performed even better in mathematics in 2012 than their peers did in 2003. This relationship was also positive, but weakened during the period, in Greece and Belgium (Table IV.1.26).

One notable trend concerning educational resources was the widening of the performance gap between students who had attended pre-primary school and those who had not. In 2003, the average advantage in mathematics performance among students who had attended pre-primary education compared to those 15-year-olds who had not was 40 points; by 2012 the difference had grown to 51 score points. Students who had not attended pre-primary education are at an

increasing disadvantage compared to their peers who had, and this disadvantage widened by more than 25 points in the Slovak Republic, the Czech Republic, Iceland, Italy, Finland, Spain, Greece, Thailand and Luxembourg. Participation in pre-primary education increased significantly in all of these countries and economies, and by more than five percentage points in Finland, Luxembourg and Portugal (see Table IV.3.50 in Chapter 3), signalling not only that enrolments grew, but that the relationship between attendance and later performance strengthened. In these countries and economies, where the relationship between attendance in pre-primary school and students' mathematics performance grew stronger, attendance in pre-primary school may have improved students' readiness for school or determined students' paths through education to a greater degree in 2012 than it did in 2003.

However, this trend can also signal that, despite an expansion in enrolments in pre-primary programmes, the group of students who do not attend pre-primary schools are increasingly from socio-economically and academically disadvantaged backgrounds. In fact, from 2003 to 2012 there was an increase in the socio-economic disparity between students who had attended pre-primary education and those who had not. This means that the students who could benefit the most from these programmes, those from disadvantaged backgrounds, are those less likely to participate in them. This growing socio-economic divide between students who had attended pre-primary education and those who hadn't is wide in the Slovak Republic and is also observed in Greece, Luxembourg, Poland, Finland, the Russian Federation and Latvia; it narrowed, however, in Macao-China, Germany, Korea, Uruguay and Portugal during the period (Figures IV.1.13 and IV.1.14).

■ Figure IV.1.13 ■

Change between 2003 and 2012 in the relationship between students' mathematics performance and their attendance in pre-primary school

Score-point difference in mathematics performance between students who reported that they had attended pre-primary education (ISCED 0) for more than one year and those who hadn't

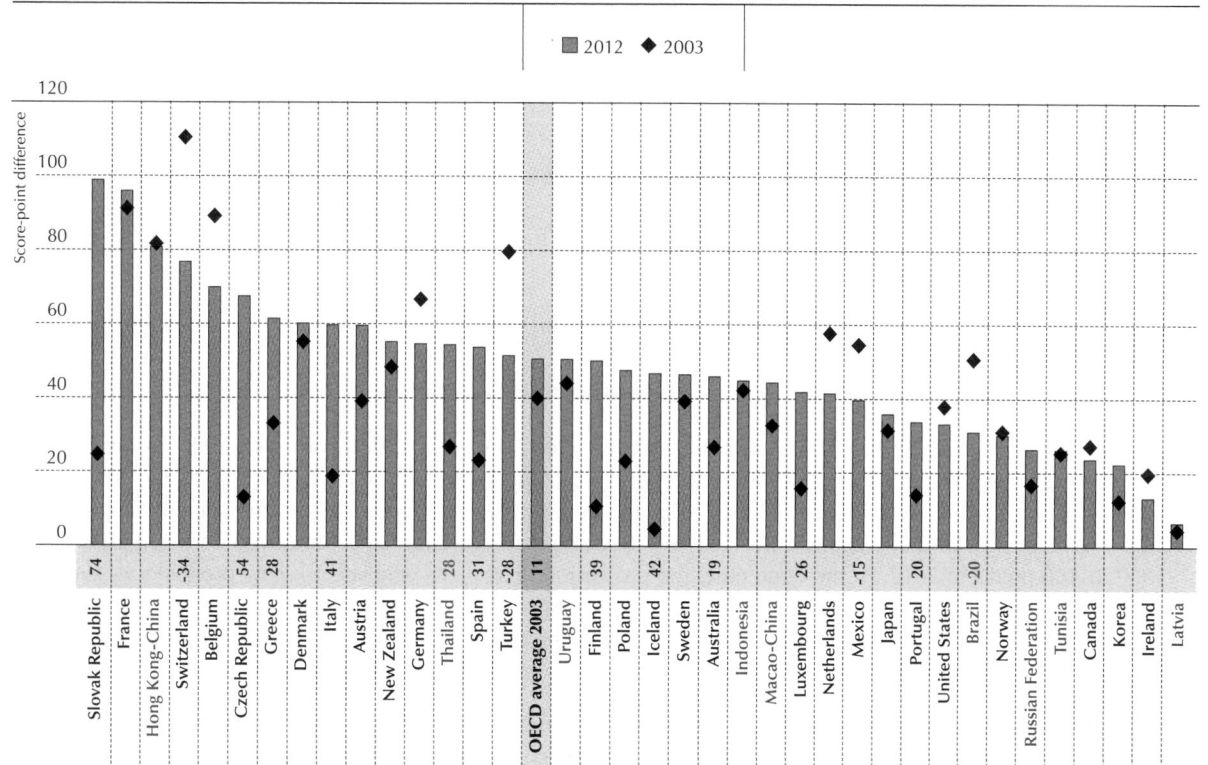

Notes: The change in the score-point difference in mathematics performance between 2003 and 2012 (2012 - 2003) is shown above the country/economy name. Only statistically significant differences are shown.
OECD average 2003 compares only OECD countries with comparable mathematics scores since 2003.
Only countries and economies with comparable data from PISA 2003 and PISA 2012 are shown.
Countries and economies are ranked in descending order of the score-point difference in mathematics performance between students who reported in 2012 that they had attended pre-primary education (ISCED 0) for more than one year and those who hadn't.
Source: OECD, PISA 2012 Database, Table IV.1.27.
StatLink ᵐˢᵖ http://dx.doi.org/10.1787/888932957403

■ Figure IV.1.14 ■

Change between 2003 and 2012 in the relationship between students' socio-economic status and their attendance at pre-primary school

Index-point difference in the PISA index of economic, social and cultural status *between students who reported that they had attended pre-primary education (ISCED 0) for more than one year and those who hadn't*

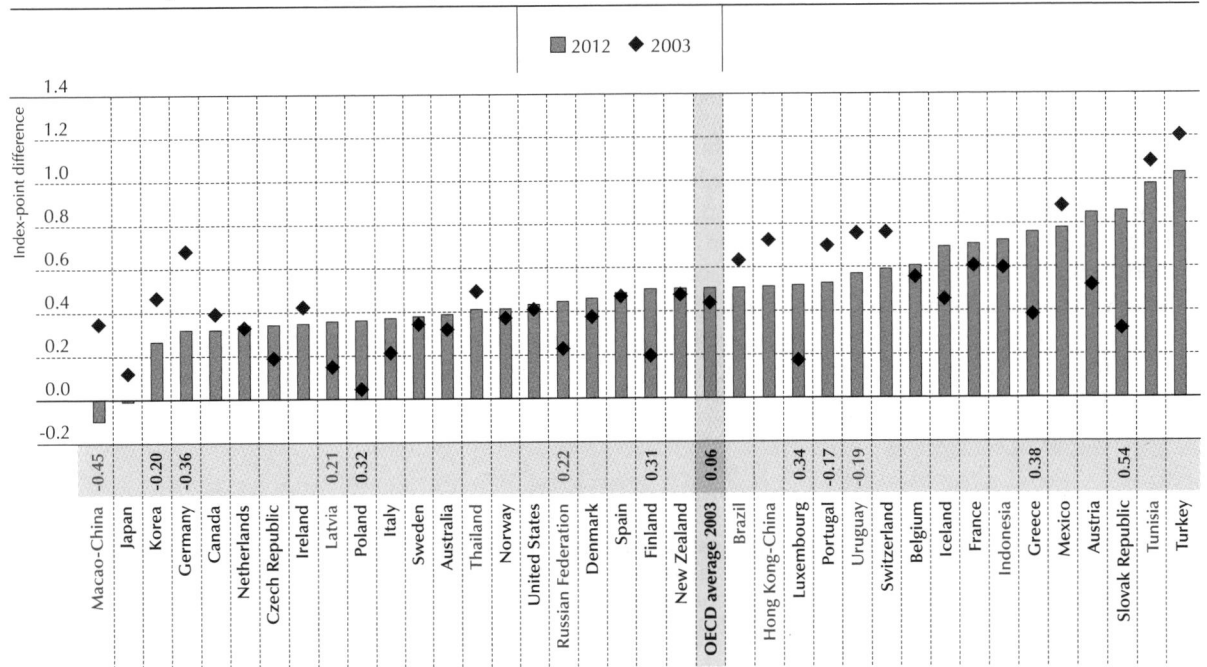

Notes: The change in the index-point difference in the *PISA index of economic, social and cultural status* performance between 2003 and 2012 (2012 - 2003) is shown above the country/economy name. Only statistically significant differences are shown.

OECD average 2003 compares only OECD countries with comparable values on the *PISA index of economic, social and cultural status* since 2003. Only countries and economies with comparable data from PISA 2003 and PISA 2012 are shown.

Countries and economies are ranked in ascending order of the index-point difference in the PISA index of economic, social and cultural status *between students who reported in 2012 that they had attended pre-primary education (ISCED 0) for more than one year and those who hadn't.*

Source: OECD, PISA 2012 Database, Table IV.1.27.

StatLink ᘔᔐᕯ http://dx.doi.org/10.1787/888932957403

Box IV.1.4. **Improving in PISA: Israel**

Israel's performance in PISA has improved in all subject matters. Since PISA 2006, for example, it has improved by an average of 4.2 points per year in mathematics and 2.8 points per year in science; since 2000, the country's score in reading has improved by an average of 3.7 points per year. Average performance in mathematics improved from 442 points in PISA 2006 to 466 points in PISA 2012 and reading performance improved from 452 points in 2000 to 486 points in 2012. At the same time, the proportion of students who score below proficiency Level 2 shrank considerably and the proportion of those who score at or above proficiency Level 5 increased. In 2006, for example, 42% of students did not attain proficiency Level 2 in mathematics; by 2012, that proportion had decreased to 34%. The share of top performers in mathematics grew from 6% to 9% over the same period.

Israel's school system is arranged along six different education streams, reflecting the cultural diversity of the country. Three of these streams cater to the Hebrew-speaking community (secular schools, religious schools and ultra-orthodox schools), and three cater to the Arab-speaking community (schools for the Arab, Druze and Bedouin minorities). For most streams (all but the ultra-orthodox), the Ministry of Education has high capacity to influence and monitor the type and quality of teaching and learning through resource allocation, regulations and guidelines. Only ultra-orthodox schools, which are only partially funded by the state, often do not follow the programmes and policies established by the Ministry.

...

The *Meitzav* and the *Bagrut* are two external evaluations that characterise Israel's education system. The *Meitzav* assessments are conducted in the second year of primary school (Grade 2), the fifth year of primary school (Grade 5), and the second year of lower-secondary school (Grade 8). The *Meitzav* assessment is used for system-level evaluation and assesses a quarter of Israel's schools each year in Hebrew or Arabic skills in Grade 2, depending on the language spoken by the child; and also in mathematics, English and science and technology in the Grade 5 and Grade 8 assessments. The *Bagrut* is the upper secondary exit-level examination, which is also used for university-level admissions, thus having direct consequences for students and a strong influence on what students learn and how they are taught. Students who graduate but do not pass the *Bagrut* are awarded a certificate of completion of upper-secondary education; those who pass obtain a diploma that allows students to apply to university.

Israel's school system has expanded dramatically in the past 20 years. As a result of a 40% increase in the 5-24 year-old population between 1990 and 2010, and a change in the composition of the student population (much of the increase in the number of primary and secondary school students has been in the Arab-speaking and ultra-orthodox streams), the Israeli school system has been in constant change.

Reforms prompted by assessment results

Education policy discussions flourished after participation in international assessments revealed Israel's relatively poor performance and inequitable school system. In PISA 2000, which Israel implemented in 2002 as part of PISA+, for example, Israel performed well below the OECD average in reading, mathematics and science. These policy discussions led to the formation of the *Dovrat Committee* in 2003 whose aim was to propose reforms and policies to the government to improve both the performance and equity of the school system. Although only some of the recommendations, delivered in 2004, were ultimately implemented, many of the current policies and reforms follow the committee's strategic recommendations. The recommendations included providing universal pre-school from age three, improving the links between pre-primary and primary schools by either organising pre-schools into clusters or adding pre-school classes to primary schools, lengthening the school day for all students, and re-defining the role of school principals by giving them more responsibilities and higher pay. Following the *Dovrat Committee*'s recommendations, in 2005, the National Authority for Measurement and Evaluation (RAMA) was established to conduct periodic evaluations of the education system and schools, contributing to the process of results-based management at all levels.

Current education policy follows the framework outlined by *New Horizons*, a programme launched in 2007 that advances reform for pre-primary, primary and lower secondary schools on several fronts and follows an agreement between education authorities and the primary and lower-secondary teachers' union. Initially, it was implemented on a voluntary basis, in schools were a majority of teachers agreed, then became compulsory in the 2009-10 school year. School principals' careers were distinguished from that of teachers. Following the reforms on principals' careers originally laid out by the *Dovrat Committee,* principals must now have earned a special tertiary-level degree and have been granted more responsibility and autonomy in evaluating teachers. Each school is given a monthly in-service training opportunity; the principal and managerial staff decide how to make the best use of it. Teachers' working hours were increased from 30 to 36 hours per week. In parallel, government policies expanded the duration of compulsory education to Grade 12 and set a maximum class size of 32 students which has been partially implemented, mainly among socio-economically disadvantaged schools. In addition, extra funding was given to primary schools to teach reading, writing and mathematics at the first two years in small groups of 20 students.

Changes in teachers' pay and working conditions, school support and assessments

In addition, teachers' pay scales were increased and flattened (salaries for junior teachers were doubled, while those for veteran teachers increased by 25%) and promotion was made contingent on triennial evaluations and fulfilling the requirement of 60 hours of in-service training per year. These changes to teachers' working conditions sought to improve teacher morale and reduce retention and recruitment problems that stem from the growing student population, the caps on class size, and the expansion of compulsory schooling.

New Horizons also mandates that the increased number of working hours for teachers be focused on small-group teaching for under-performing students. Small-group teaching programmes were piloted in the early 2000s together with cash-reward programmes (although cash-reward programmes for students proved more cost-effective, they did not have broad public support). Other programmes to promote equity focus on the Arab-speaking minorities,

...

particularly the Bedouin minority. The most recent of these five-year programmes began in 2008 and supports extra hours of study, provides rent assistance for teachers, improves the quality of educational facilities, offers support teams to assist low-performing schools, and strengthens Arabic-language skills. To advance towards greater equity, other policies introduced a socio-economic component in the allocation of resources in primary schools and lower secondary; but only 5% of the school budget is devoted to this compensatory mechanism.

More recently, *Courage to Change* policies outlines the framework for reform in upper secondary schools. In conjunction with *New Horizons, Courage to Change* allows schools that offer lower and upper secondary education to take part in the reforms. *Courage to Change* was signed in 2012 and the policies are set to be implemented gradually so that full implementation is expected by 2015.

Other programmes have sought to attract university-level graduates into the teaching profession in general and to science areas in particular. In *Academics for Teaching*, participants undergo an intensive teacher-training programme (no tuition fees and a monthly allowance), and teach full time with a commitment to teach for three years. They receive a normal teachers' salary in addition to a supplement, and after the three years they can enrol, for free, in a master's degree in return for an additional two years' commitment. Other programmes to attract individuals to the teaching profession are *Outstanding Achievers for Education* (to attract students with good performance at the tertiary level), *Teach First* (to promote teaching as an interim career move following graduation from university), *Educational Pioneer* (to encourage those already working with youth in other contexts to become teachers), and the *Atidim* programme (to encourage English and science teachers to work in remote and disadvantaged areas).

In 2007, the schedule of the *Meitzav* assessment was converted to a new biennial-rotating, so that individual schools are assessed every two years and on a particular subject every four years with system-level results available annually based on a quarter of the country's schools. In the years where a particular subject is not assessed in a particular school, individual schools implement, internally, a version of the *Meitzav* which come with supporting pedagogical material. The internal *Meitzav* is graded internally by the teachers and results are not reported to an external entity. Changes to the *Bagrut* examination have shifted the weight given to questions that can be answered by rote learning so that more space is given to projects that require students' individual inquiry, sending a strong signal to secondary schools about the competencies that students should have acquired by the end of compulsory education.

Note: The statistical data for Israel are supplied by and under the responsibility of the relevant Israeli authorities. The use of such data by the OECD is without prejudice to the status of the Golan Heights, East Jerusalem and Israeli settlements in the West Bank under the terms of international law.

Sources:

Beller, M. (2013), *Assessment in the Service of Learning: Theory and Practice*, RAMA, Ramat Gan.

OECD (2010), "Israeli Education Policy: How to Move Ahead in Reform", *Economics Department Working Paper,* No. 781, OECD Publishing.

OECD (2011b), *OECD Economic Survey: Israel*, OECD Publishing.

Wolff, L. and E. Breit (2012), "Education in Israel", *Institute for Israeli Studies Research Paper,* No. 8, University of Maryland.

HOW LEARNING OUTCOMES ARE RELATED TO THE GOVERNANCE OF EDUCATION SYSTEMS

School autonomy

Since the early 1980s, school reforms have focused on giving schools greater autonomy over a wide range of institutional operations in an effort to raise performance levels (Whitty, 1997; Carnoy, 2000; Clark, 2009; Machin and Vernoit, 2011). More decision-making responsibility and accountability has devolved to school principals, and, in some cases, management responsibilities have devolved to teachers or department heads. Schools have become increasingly responsible for curricular and instructional decisions as well as for managing financial and material resources and personnel. These reforms are adopted on the premise that schools themselves are more knowledgeable about their own needs and the most effective ways to allocate resources and design the curriculum so that they can better meet the needs of their students.

■ Figure IV.1.15 ■

School autonomy over curriculum and assessment and mathematics performance

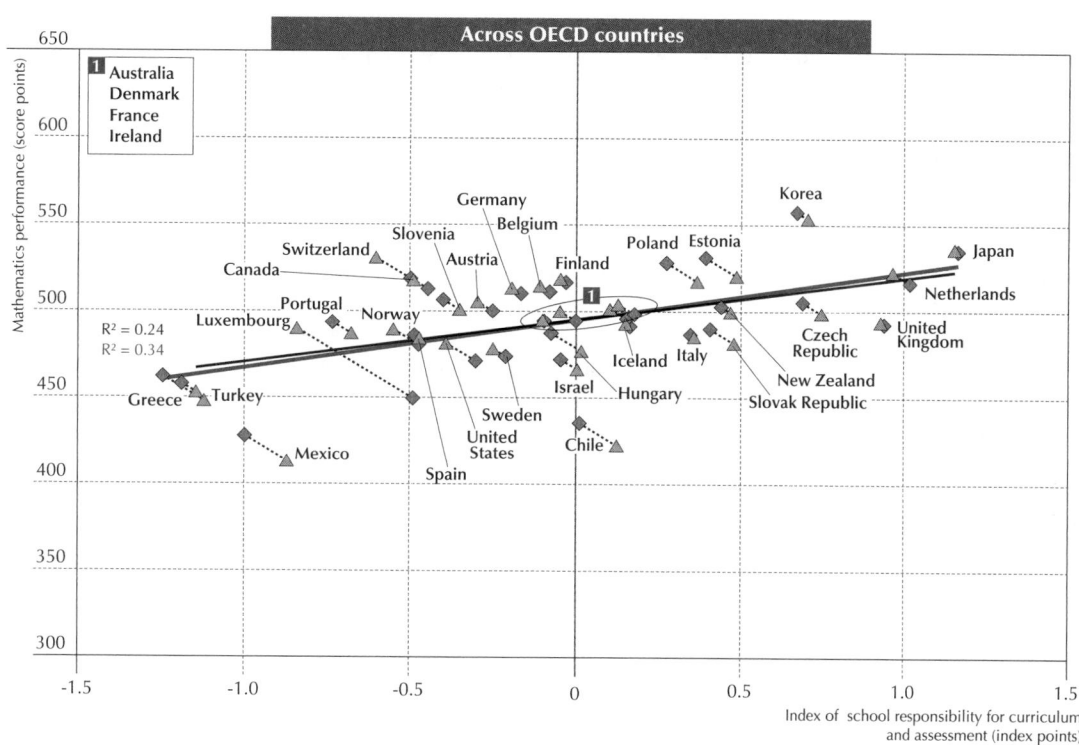

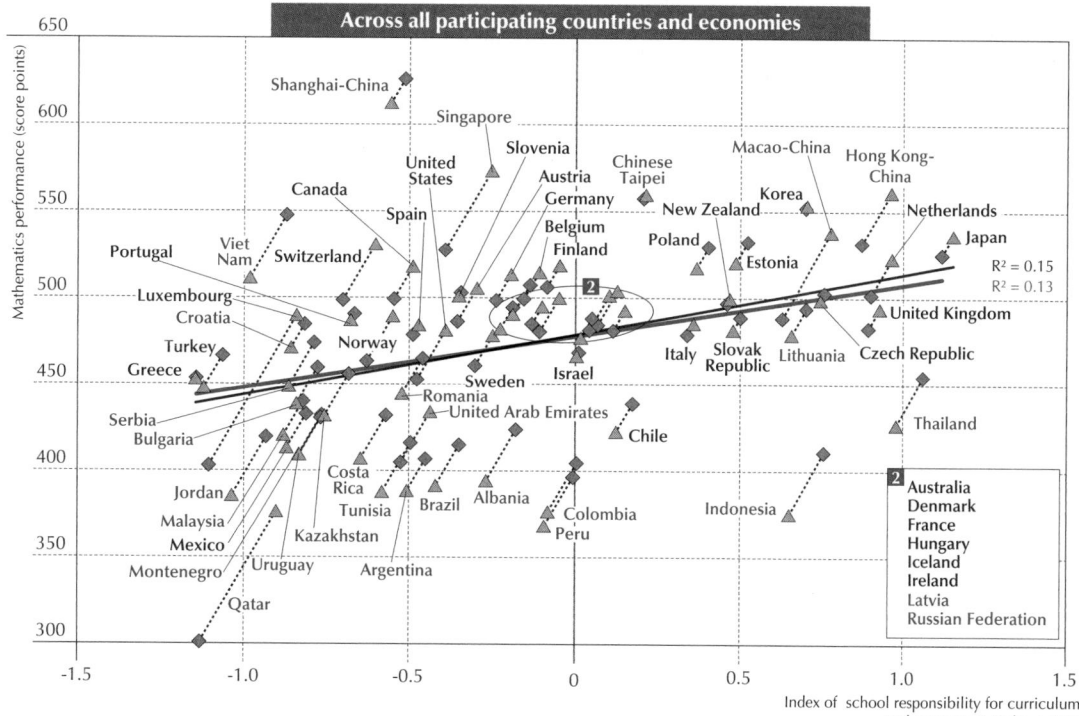

1. A significant relationship (p < 0.10) is shown by the solid line.
Source: OECD, PISA 2012 Database, Table IV.1.4.

StatLink ᕵᔍᕵ http://dx.doi.org/10.1787/888932957403

PISA shows that school systems that grant more autonomy to schools to define and elaborate their curricula and assessments tend to perform better than systems that don't grant such autonomy, even after accounting for countries' national income (Figure IV.1.15). School systems that provide schools with greater discretion in deciding student-assessment policies, the courses offered, the content of those courses and the textbooks used are also school systems that perform at higher levels in mathematics. In contrast, greater responsibility in managing resources appears to be unrelated to a school system's overall performance (Table IV.1.4).

The positive relationship between schools' autonomy in defining and elaborating curricula and assessment policies and student performance that is observed at the level of the school system can play out differently within countries and economies. In 17 countries and economies, schools that have more autonomy in this area tend to perform better, while the opposite is observed in seven countries and economies (Table IV.4.3, discussed in Chapter 4). The degree of school autonomy is also related to the socio-economic status and demographic background of students and schools and various other school characteristics, such as whether the school is public or private. But even after accounting for all of these aspects, a positive relationship is observed in Costa Rica, Thailand, Latvia and Finland (Table IV.1.12c).

Within systems too, there is a relationship between school autonomy and learning outcomes, but this relationship interacts with the accountability arrangements of school systems. For example, information on the results of external examinations and assessments often provide a basis on which schools and parents can make informed and appropriate decisions for students (Fuchs and Woessmann, 2007). Data from PISA 2012 show that in systems where a greater share of schools post achievement data publicly, considered here as one form of accountability, there is a positive relationship between school autonomy in resource allocation and student performance. The first panel in Figure IV.1.16 shows that, in the participating countries and economies where schools do not post achievement data publicly, after students' and schools' socio-economic status and demographic profile are taken into account, a student who attends a school with greater autonomy in defining and elaborating curricula and assessment policies tends to perform seven points lower in mathematics than a student who attends a school with less autonomy in these areas.

■ Figure IV.1.16 ■

School autonomy and mathematics performance, by system-level accountability features

Predicted score-point difference in mathematics performance between students in schools with more autonomy and those in schools with less autonomy (more - less)

──────── School autonomy for resource allocation (across OECD countries)

▪▪▪▪▪▪▪ School autonomy for curriculum and assessment (across OECD countries)

─────── School autonomy for resource allocation (across all participating countries and economies)

- - - - - School autonomy for curriculum and assessment (across all participating countries and economies)

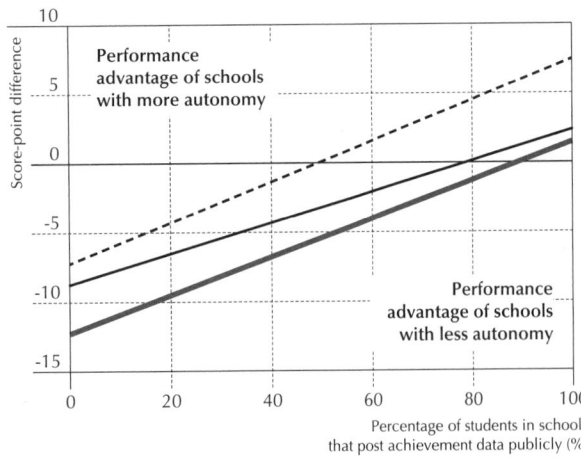

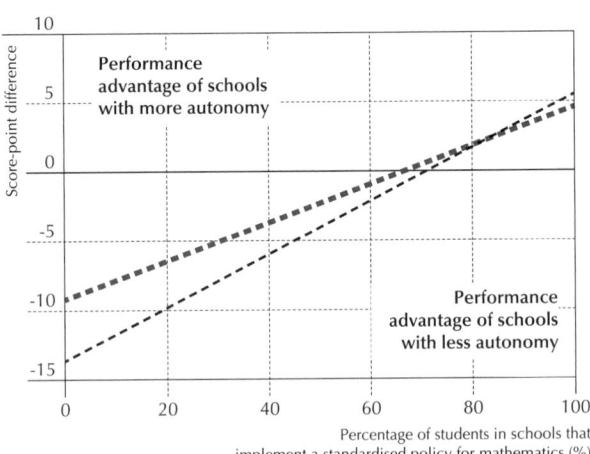

Notes: Schools with more autonomy are those with 1.0 point on the autonomy index and schools with less autonomy are those with -1.0 point on the autonomy index.

These predicted relationships are based on a net model after accounting for socio-economic status of students and schools, demographic backgrounds and school type.

Source: OECD, PISA 2012 Database, Tables IV.1.13 and IV.1.14.

StatLink ᴀᴤᴵᴤ᠊ http://dx.doi.org/10.1787/888932957403

In contrast, in a school system where all schools post achievement data publicly, a student who attends a school with greater autonomy scores seven points higher in mathematics than a student who attends a school with less autonomy. A similar interaction between school autonomy in resource allocation and a system's accountability arrangements, particularly those of posting achievement data publicly, is observed; however the performance advantage for schools with greater autonomy in this regard is relatively small (Table IV.1.13).

Similar interactions between school autonomy and system-level accountability are observed when system accountability takes the form of a standardised policy for mathematics, such as a school curriculum with shared instructional materials accompanied by staff development and training. The right panel of Figure IV.1.16 shows that the relationship between school autonomy in defining and elaborating curricula and assessment policies and school average performance in mathematics is influenced by the extent to which systems have a standardised policy for mathematics. In OECD countries where no school implements a standardised policy for mathematics, a student who attends a school with greater autonomy in curricula and assessments tends to score nine points lower in mathematics than a student who attends a school with less autonomy. In contrast, in a school system where all students are in schools that implement such a standardised policy, a student who attends a school with greater autonomy scores five points higher in mathematics than a student who attends a school with less autonomy (Table IV.1.14).

The relationship between school autonomy and performance also appears to be affected by whether there is a culture of collaboration between teachers and principals in managing a school. Figure IV.1.17 shows that, in school systems where principals reported less teacher participation in school management (i.e. 1.5 index points lower than the OECD average), even after students' and schools' socio-economic status and demographic profile are taken into account, a student who attends a school with greater autonomy in allocating resources tends to score 17 points lower in mathematics than a student who attends a school with less autonomy. In contrast, in a school system where principals reported more teacher participation in school management (i.e. 1.5 index points higher than the OECD average), a student who attends a school with greater autonomy scores 9 points higher in mathematics than a student who attends a school with less autonomy (Table IV.1.15).

■ Figure IV.1.17 ■

School autonomy and mathematics performance, by system-level teacher participation in school management

Predicted score-point difference in mathematics performance between students in schools with more autonomy and those in schools with less autonomy (more - less)

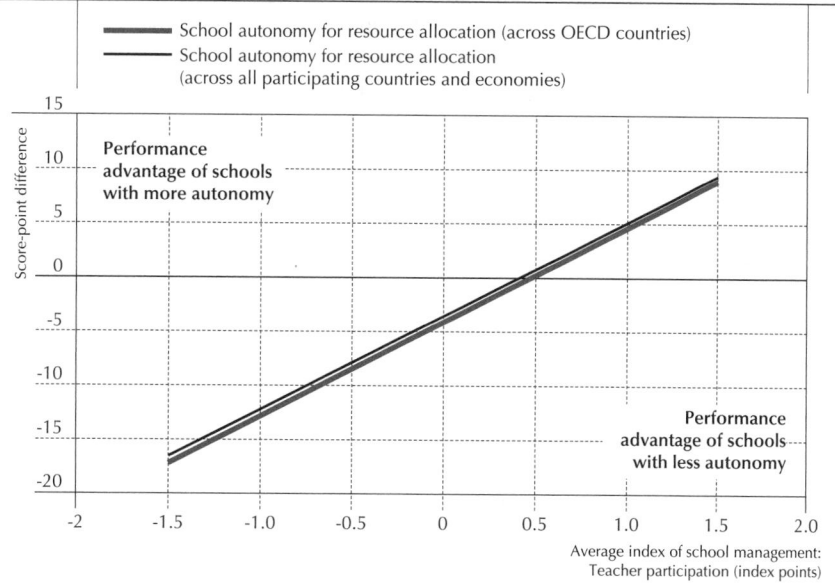

Notes: Schools with more autonomy are those with 1.0 point on the autonomy index and schools with less autonomy are those with -1.0 point on the autonomy index.

These predicted relationships are based on a net model after accounting for socio-economic status of students and schools, demographic backgrounds and school type.

Source: OECD, PISA 2012 Database, Table IV.1.15.

StatLink ㎳ http://dx.doi.org/10.1787/888932957403

School competition

Since the early 1980s, reforms in many countries have also granted parents and students greater choice in the school the students will attend. Students and their families are granted the freedom to seek and attend the school that best serves students' education needs; that, in turn, introduces a level of competition among schools to attract students. Assuming that students and parents have all the required information about schools and choose schools based on academic criteria, the competition creates incentives for institutions to organise programmes and teaching in ways that better meet diverse student requirements and interests, reducing the costs of failure and mismatches.

Yet some of the assumptions underlying such reforms have been called into question (Schneider, Teske and Marshall, 2002; Hess and Loveless, 2005; Berends and Zottola, 2009). It is unclear, for example, whether parents have the necessary information to choose the best schools for their children. It is also unclear whether parents always give sufficient priority to high achievement, at the school level, when making these choices (see Chapter 4). School choice may also lead to the unintended racial/ethnic or socio-economic segregation of schools (Gewirtz, Ball and Rowe, 1995; Whitty, 1998; Karsten, 1999; Viteritti, 1999; Schneider and Buckley, 2002; Plank and Sykes, 2003; Hsieh, 2006; Heyneman, 2009; Bunar, 2010a; Bunar, 2010b; Söderström and Uusitalo, 2010). Recently, in some school systems greater responsibility for assigning students to schools is given to the education authority (see Box IV.4.2 as an example in Belgium [French community]).

The degree of competition among schools is one way to measure school choice. Competition among schools is intended to provide incentives for schools to innovate and create more effective learning environments. System-level correlations in PISA do not show a relationship between the degree of competition and student performance (Table IV.1.4). At the school level, in 28 countries and economies, schools that compete for student enrolment with other schools tend to show better performance, before accounting for schools' socio-economic intake. In seven countries and economies, schools whose socio-economic intake is more advantaged are also more likely to compete with other schools for students (Table IV.1.16). Only in the Czech Republic and Estonia do schools that compete with other schools for students in the same area tend to perform better, on average, than schools that do not compete, after accounting for the socio-economic status and demographic background of students and schools and various other school characteristics (Table IV.1.12c).

On the other hand, the results indicate a weak and negative relationship between the degree of competition and equity. Among OECD countries, systems with more competition among schools tend to show a stronger impact of students' socio-economic status on their performance in mathematics. Caution is advised when interpreting this result, as the observed relationship could be affected by a few outliers.[19] But, this finding is consistent with research showing that school choice – and, by extension, school competition – is related to greater levels of segregation in the school system, which may have adverse consequences for equity in learning opportunities and outcomes.

Public and private stakeholders

The evidence on the impact of public and private funding and management on student performance is mixed. Cross-country studies conducted by Woessmann (2006) based on the PISA 2000 assessment, and by Woessmann, et al. (2009) and West and Woessmann (2010), based on the PISA 2003 assessment, concluded that countries that combine private management and public funding tend to produce better overall academic performance. Studies in Chile (Lara, Mizala and Repetto, 2009), the Czech Republic (Filer and Münich, 2003), Sweden (Sandström and Bergström, 2005), the United Kingdom (Green et al., 2011) and the United States (Couch, Shugart and Williams, 1993; Peterson et al., 2003) show that larger proportions of private school enrolments are related to better performance, based on cross-sectional or longitudinal data or the data before and after structural changes. But the debate on performance is far from conclusive, as other studies report little, negative or insignificant effects, and the results often depend on methodological choices. For example, other studies based on state-level data from the United States concluded that higher private school enrolment is not significantly related to performance (Wrinkle et al., 1999; Sander, 1999; Geller, Sjoquist and Walker, 2006). A few studies show small negative effects (Smith and Meier, 1995), negative effects for low-income districts (Maranto, Milliman and Scott, 2000), or that the relationship depends on the education outcome that is measured (Greene and Kang, 2004).

Across OECD countries and all countries and economies that participated in PISA 2012, the percentage of students enrolled in private schools is not related to a system's overall performance (Table IV.1.4).

■ Figure IV.1.18 ■
School competition and mathematics performance

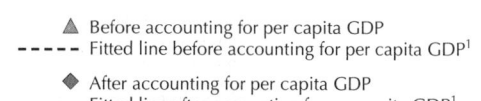

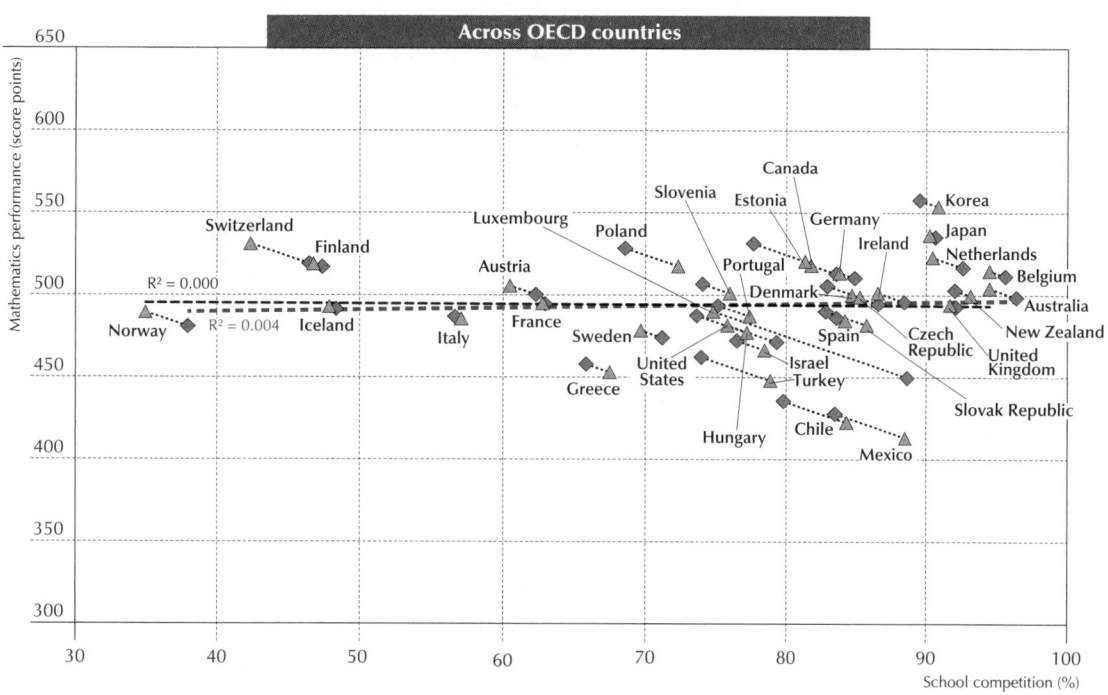

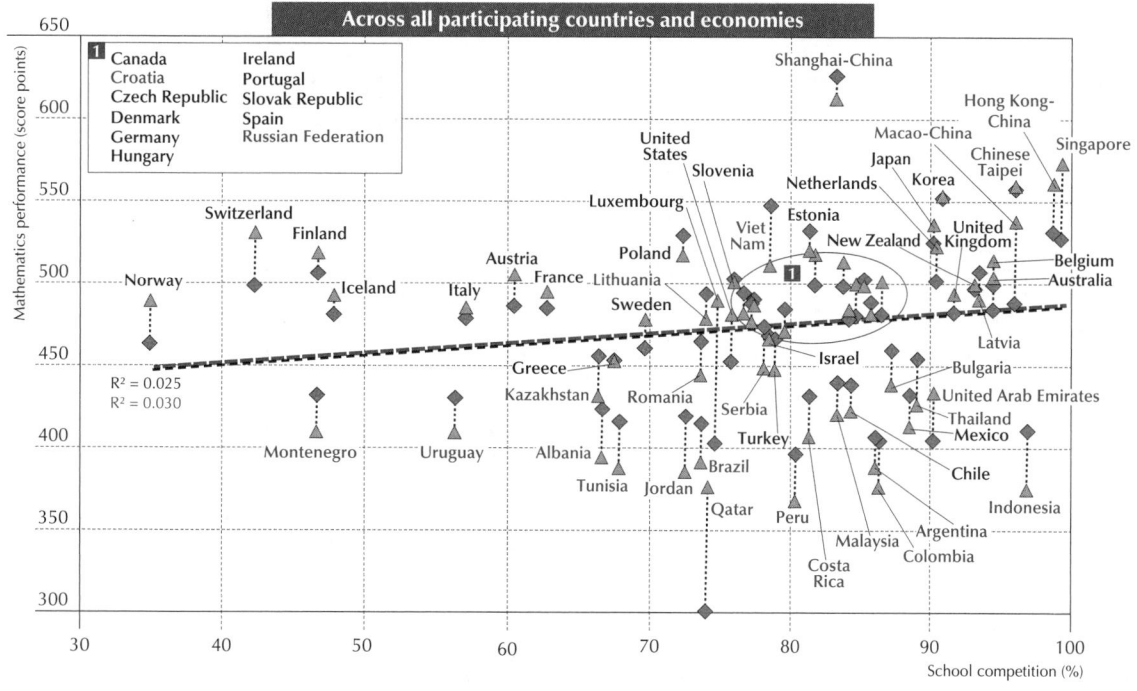

Note: School competition refers to the percentage of students in schools whose principal reported that one or more schools compete for students in the same area.

1. A non-significant relationship (p > 0.10) is shown by the dotted line.

Source: OECD, PISA 2012 Database, Table IV.1.4.

StatLink ᘯᏕᏁᎵ http://dx.doi.org/10.1787/888932957403

■ Figure IV.1.19 ■
School type and mathematics performance

Score-point difference in mathematics performance between public and private schools (government-dependent and government-independent schools combined)

◇ ◆ Observed performance difference

▷ ▶ Performance difference after accounting for the *PISA index of economic, social and cultural status* **of students**

○ ● Performance difference after accounting for the *PISA index of economic, social and cultural status* **of students and schools**

	Percentage of students attending:		
	Government or public schools[1]	Government-dependent private schools[2]	Government-independent private schools[3]
Chinese Taipei	68	5	28
Hong Kong-China	7	92	1
Thailand	83	12	5
Viet Nam	93	0	7
Luxembourg	85	13	2
Switzerland	94	1	5
Indonesia	59	17	24
Italy	95	2	3
Kazakhstan	97	1	2
Japan	70	0	30
Czech Republic	92	7	1
Netherlands	34	66	0
Estonia	98	2	1
Albania	92	0	8
Ireland	44	54	2
United States	95	0	5
Hungary	84	16	0
Sweden	86	14	0
Korea	53	31	16
United Kingdom	56	36	8
Finland	97	3	0
Denmark	77	19	4
OECD average	**82**	**14**	**4**
France	83	17	0
Shanghai-China	91	0	9
Australia	61	26	13
Spain	68	24	7
Slovak Republic	91	9	0
Mexico	91	0	9
Germany	95	5	0
Austria	91	8	1
Colombia	86	4	10
Chile	37	48	14
Canada	92	4	3
Poland	97	2	1
Jordan	83	1	16
Argentina	68	26	7
United Arab Emirates	55	1	45
Portugal	90	6	4
Peru	85	0	15
Costa Rica	87	4	10
Brazil	87	1	13
New Zealand	95	0	5
Malaysia	97	0	3
Slovenia	98	2	0
Uruguay	83	0	17
Qatar	62	1	37

Performance advantage of private schools   **Performance advantage of public schools**

-125   -100   -75   -50   -25   0   25   50   75   100
Score-point difference

Note: White symbols represent differences that are not statistically significant.
1. Schools that are directly controlled or managed by: a public education authority or agency; or a government agency directly or a governing body, most of whose members are either appointed by a public authority or elected by public franchise.
2. Schools that receive 50% or more of their core funding (i.e. funding that supports the basic educational services of the institution) from government agencies.
3. Schools that receive less than 50% of their core funding (i.e. funding that supports the basic educational services of the institution) from government agencies.
Countries and economies are ranked in descending order of the score-point difference in mathematics performance between public and private schools (government-dependent and government-independent schools combined).
Source: OECD, PISA 2012 Database, Table IV.4.7.
StatLink ⟨≋⟩ http://dx.doi.org/10.1787/888932957403

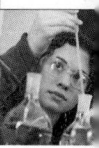

At the school level, when average performance is compared simply between public and private schools, without accounting for background aspects, private schools tend to show better performance than public schools in 28 countries and economies (Figure IV.1.19 and Table IV.4.7 in Chapter 4). The score-point difference ranges from 12 points in Ireland to 108 points – or the equivalent of nearly three years of schooling – in Qatar. By contrast, in Chinese Taipei, Hong Kong-China, Thailand and Luxembourg, the average score among public schools is higher than that among private schools by 13 to 60 points. The proportion of students in private schools is unrelated to the magnitude of the difference in performance between students who attend private and public schools.[20] Students who attend private schools tend to be more socio-economically advantaged than students who attend public schools. Thus, after accounting for the socio-economic status of students and schools, private schools outperform public schools in only 13 countries and economies, and public schools outperform private schools in eight countries and economies (Table IV.4.7). In addition, after accounting for the demographic background of students and schools and various other school characteristics, private schools outperform public schools in 10 countries and economies, while public schools show better average performance than private schools in five countries and economies (Table IV.1.12c).

Assessment and accountability

Tests that have direct and high-stakes consequences for students can serve as powerful incentives for students to put greater effort into learning. For teachers, student-based standardised assessments provide a way to compare the performance of their students to performance achieved elsewhere in the school systems and can also be used to customise pedagogy accordingly. At the school level, achievement data can be used to determine how resources and additional support are allocated and/or may trigger intervention by higher authorities. Achievement data can also be used to inform policies to create more efficient learning environments and to prompt schools, teachers and the students themselves to work towards centrally established education outcomes.

Critics of the use of standardised tests based on students' test performance rather than on improvements in test scores argue that standardised tests may reinforce the advantages of schools that serve students from socio-economically advantaged backgrounds (Ladd and Walsh, 2002; Downey, Von Hippel and Hughes, 2008). In addition, teachers may respond strategically to accountability measures by sorting out or retaining disadvantaged students (Jacob, 2005; Jennings, 2005). Standardised tests might have the adverse effect of limiting school goals to passing or proficiency on particular tests and focusing instruction on those students who are close to average proficiency and ignoring those who are far below or above the average (Neal and Schanzenback, 2010).

In order to avoid the negative impact of "teaching to the test," evaluations are expanding and becoming more diverse in most OECD countries. Countries do not solely focus on student assessments; they also evaluate schools and appraise teachers and school leaders. All school staff and students need to be engaged in a broader range of evaluation exercises, targeting both schools and teachers; student feedback is an important contribution to be used for formative purposes (OECD, 2013b).

PISA shows that the degree to which systems seek feedback from students regarding lessons, teachers or resources tends to be related to systems' level of equity. PISA 2012 asked school principals to report whether written feedback from students regarding lessons, teachers or resources is sought for quality-assurance and improvement of the school. Systems where more students attend schools with such practices tend to show less impact of student socio-economic status on performance. This is observed across OECD countries and across all participating countries and economies. As shown in Figure IV.1.20, across OECD countries, some 10% of the variation in the impact of students' socio-economic status on their mathematics performance can be accounted for by differences in the degree to which systems use this approach, after accounting for per capita GDP (Table IV.1.4). Systems seeking written feedback from students also tend to perform better across OECD countries.[21]

At the school level, on average across OECD countries, schools seeking written feedback from students tend to perform better, even after accounting for the socio-economic status of students and schools (Table IV.1.18). However, this relationship also varies by country/economy. After accounting for the socio-economic status of students and schools, in Switzerland, Belgium, Mexico, Portugal, Colombia and Macao-China, schools with higher average performance tend to use this approach, while in Qatar, New Zealand, Shanghai-China and Montenegro, schools with lower average performance tend to do so (Table IV.1.18). After accounting for the socio-economic status and demographic background of students and schools and various other school characteristics, in Viet Nam and Colombia schools with better average performance tend to use this practice, while in Qatar, New Zealand, Croatia and Chile, the opposite is observed (Table IV.1.12c).

■ Figure IV.1.20 ■

Written feedback from students and equity

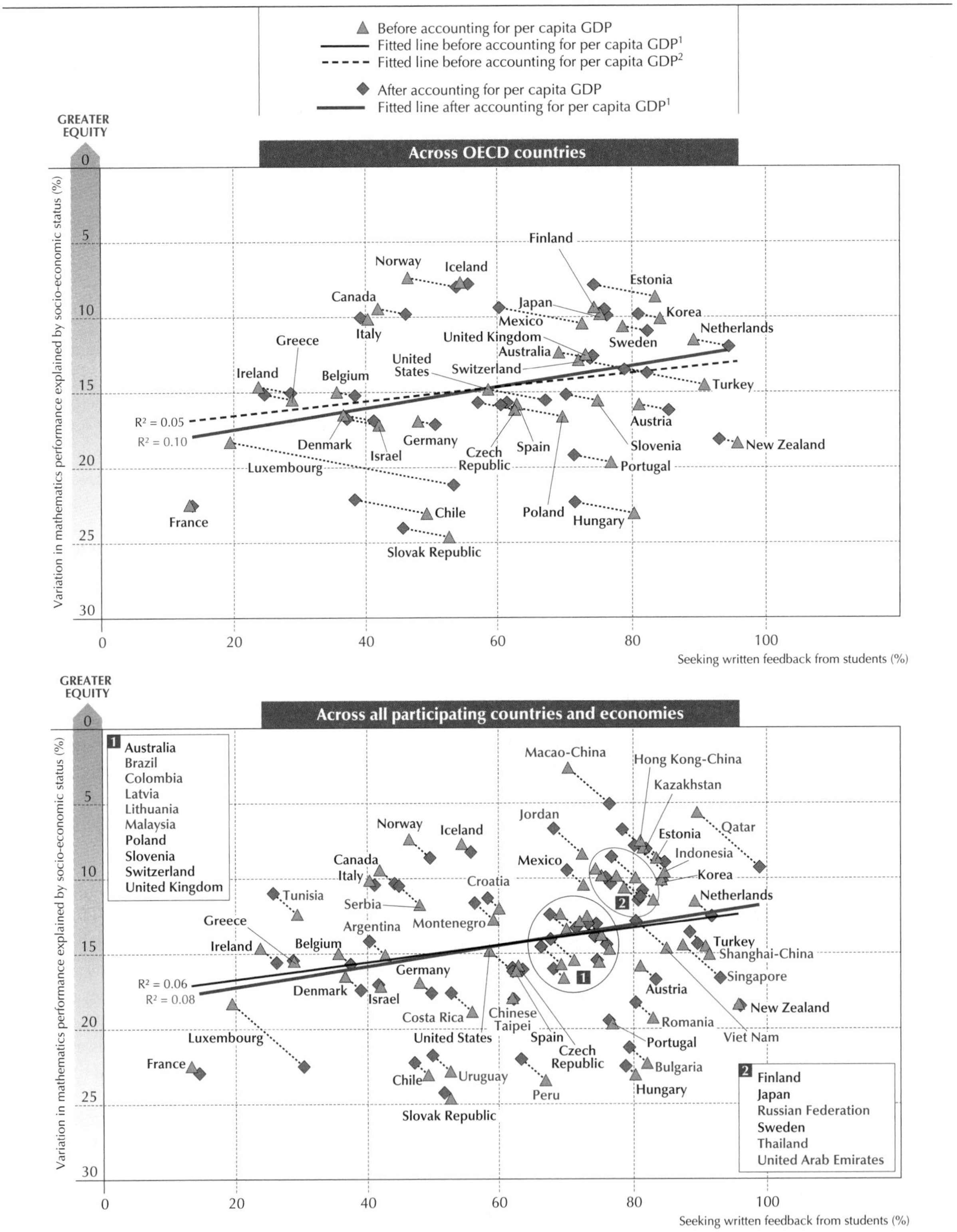

▲ Before accounting for per capita GDP
—— Fitted line before accounting for per capita GDP[1]
----- Fitted line before accounting for per capita GDP[2]

◆ After accounting for per capita GDP
—— Fitted line after accounting for per capita GDP[1]

Across OECD countries

GREATER EQUITY

Variation in mathematics performance explained by socio-economic status (%)

Seeking written feedback from students (%)

Across all participating countries and economies

GREATER EQUITY

1
Australia
Brazil
Colombia
Latvia
Lithuania
Malaysia
Poland
Slovenia
Switzerland
United Kingdom

2
Finland
Japan
Russian Federation
Sweden
Thailand
United Arab Emirates

Variation in mathematics performance explained by socio-economic status (%)

Seeking written feedback from students (%)

Note: Seeking written feedback from students refers to the percentage of students in school whose principal reported that written feedback from students regarding lessons, teachers or resources is sought for quality assurance and improvement of schools.
1. A significant relationship (p < 0.10) is shown by the solid line.
2. A non-significant relationship (p > 0.10) is shown by the dotted line.
Source: OECD, PISA 2012 Database, Table IV.1.4.
StatLink ⟨msl⟩ http://dx.doi.org/10.1787/888932957403

Systems with poorer overall performance tend to be those where more students are in schools whose principals reported that achievement data are tracked over time by an administrative authority. This observation holds across OECD countries and across all participating countries and economies (Table IV.1.4). This relationship is also observed at the school level in Qatar, Korea, Albania and Shanghai-China (Table IV.1.12c). In these countries and economies, schools with lower average performance tend to be those where an administrative authority tracks their achievement data over time. This negative relationship may reflect the fact that low-performing schools or systems use this practice in order to monitor school performance and hold lower-performing schools accountable. Indeed, systems where this practice is more common tend to have greater equity in education opportunities. Systems where more principals reported their achievement data are tracked over time by an administrative authority tend to show a weaker impact of the socio-economic status of students and schools on student performance in mathematics (Table IV.1.4).[22]

Across all countries and economies that participated in PISA 2012, but not across OECD countries, the extent to which schools provide an opportunity for teacher mentoring is related to equity. In the systems where more schools provide teacher mentoring, students' socio-economic status has less impact on their performance, both before and after accounting for per capita GDP (Table IV.1.4).

The analysis above has shown that system-level policies through which schools post results publicly interact with school autonomy in ways that yield better student performance. When looking at these policies in isolation at the school level, schools that post achievement data publicly perform higher in 21 countries and economies (Tables IV.1.17). But, after accounting for the socio-economic status and demographic profile of students and schools, no relationship is observed in most countries and economies (Table IV.1.12c).

Trends in the relationship between mathematics performance and school governance

Chapter 3 highlights how, in some countries and economies, the relative enrolment in public schools has increased while in others it has declined, but on average across OECD countries, the share of students attending public and private schools remained stable between 2003 and 2012. In PISA 2003, students in private schools outperformed students in public schools by 19 points in mathematics, but this difference was not observed when comparing students with similar socio-economic status. In fact, after comparing students of similar socio-economic status who attend schools with a similar socio-economic profile, students in public schools outperformed their peers in private schools by 14 points in mathematics (Table IV.4.19).

Between PISA 2003 and PISA 2012 all these differences shifted in favour of students in private schools. The overall difference in performance between public and private school students across OECD countries widened by nine points (up to 28 points in favour of students in private schools); after accounting for students of similar socio-economic status, the difference, which was not significant in 2003, was 11 points in favour of private-school students in 2012. However, after accounting for students of similar socio-economic status who attend schools with similar socio-economic profiles, the public-school advantage remained, but narrowed to nine score points.[23]

During the same period, the performance gap between private and public schools narrowed in Brazil, Ireland, Mexico and Thailand, either before or after accounting for students' socio-economic status. In Ireland, the difference in mathematics performance between students in public and private schools narrowed by 18 points, and by 2012 was one of the smallest among OECD countries, although it remains statistically significant. This trend is largely explained by the change in the socio-economic status of the students attending both types of schools. In Thailand, there was no performance gap between the two types of schools in 2003; but in 2012, public schools outperformed private schools by more than 30 score points – and this difference holds even when comparing students and schools of similar socio-economic status. In Mexico and Brazil, the performance of students in public schools also improved relative to that of students with similar socio-economic status who attend private schools. The socio-economic status of students in public schools has increased in Korea and Ireland. In 2003, students in public schools came from lower socio-economic backgrounds than students in private schools, on average. But by 2012, students in public and private schools had similar socio-economic status. In Ireland, the proportion of students from relatively advantaged socio-economic backgrounds who attended public schools grew so significantly over the period that by 2012 the socio-economic disadvantage associated with public schools was among the lowest in Ireland among all OECD countries (Figure IV.1.21 and Table IV.4.19).

■ Figure IV.1.21 ■

Change between 2003 and 2012 in the relationship between students' mathematics performance and their attendance in private or public schools, after accounting for socio-economic status

Score-point difference in mathematics performance between students in public and private schools, after accounting for students' PISA index of economic, social and cultural status

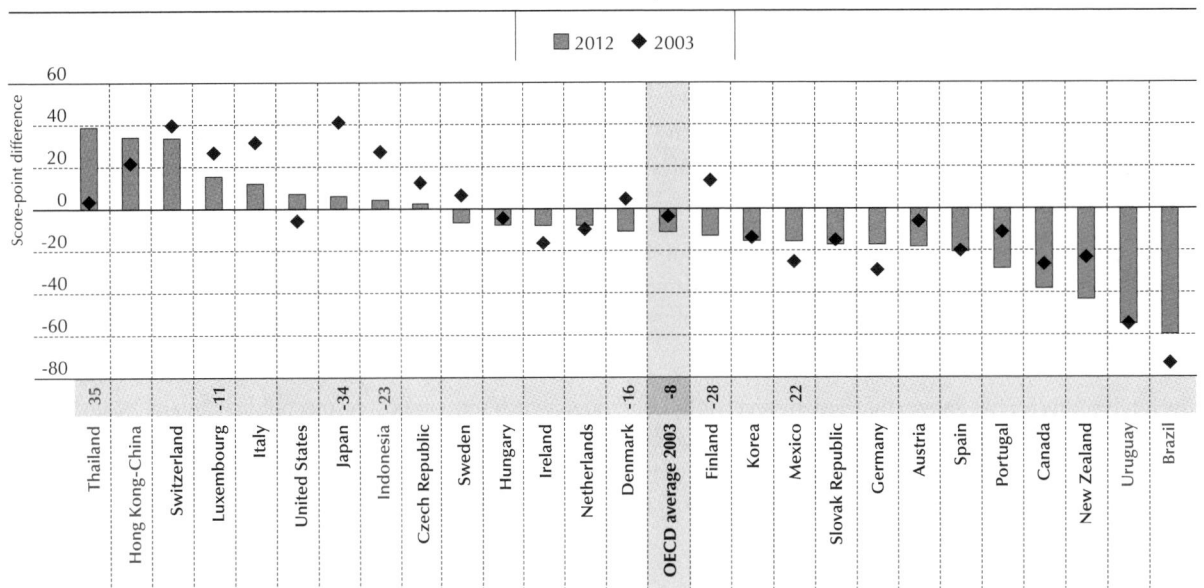

Notes: The change in the score-point difference in mathematics performance between 2003 and 2012 (2012 - 2003) is shown above the country/economy name. Only statistically significant differences are shown.

OECD average 2003 compares only OECD countries with comparable mathematics scores and attendance in private and public schools since 2003. Only countries and economies with comparable data from PISA 2003 and PISA 2012 are shown.

Countries and economies are ranked in descending order of the score-point difference in mathematics performance between public and private schools, after accounting for students' PISA index of economic, social and cultural status in 2012.

Source: OECD, PISA 2012 Database, Table IV.4.19.

StatLink ⟲ http://dx.doi.org/10.1787/888932957403

HOW LEARNING OUTCOMES ARE RELATED TO SYSTEMS' LEARNING ENVIRONMENTS

The results from earlier PISA assessments showed that students who are in a school climate characterised by high expectations, classrooms conducive to learning, and good teacher-student relations tend to perform better than those who are not. Building on these findings, this chapter examines disciplinary climate, teacher-student relations, teacher-related factors affecting school climate, student-related factors affecting school climate, students' sense of belonging, teacher morale, and the level of student truancy, including arriving late for school, skipping school and dropping out.

Research studying effective schools suggests a strong relationship between the quality of the learning environment and both student performance and the level of equity in the school system. Students learn more in schools that provide an orderly environment, where students feel supported by teachers, and that enjoy clearly articulated leadership by the principal, for example (Scheerens and Bosker 1997). Research also has shown that most of the variation in learning environments is found between classes or courses rather than between schools. As these differences at the classroom levels are included in within-school variation in the analyses based on PISA data, caution is advised when interpreting results.

Studies of effective schools find that a school culture that prioritises high academic achievement is positively related to student achievement. In such an environment, characterised by amiable and supportive teacher-student relationships that extends beyond the boundaries of the classroom, the values held by both teachers and students are clear. In these schools, academic activities and student performance are considered central to the success of the school (Scheerens and Bosker, 1997; Sammons, 1999; Taylor, Pressley and Pearson, 2002).

Student truancy

Student truancy tends to be negatively related to systems' overall performance. Among OECD countries, after accounting for per capita GDP, systems with higher percentages of students who arrive late for school tend to have lower scores in mathematics, and systems with higher percentages of students who skip school also tend to score lower in mathematics.

■ Figure IV.1.22 ■
Students skipping school and mathematics performance

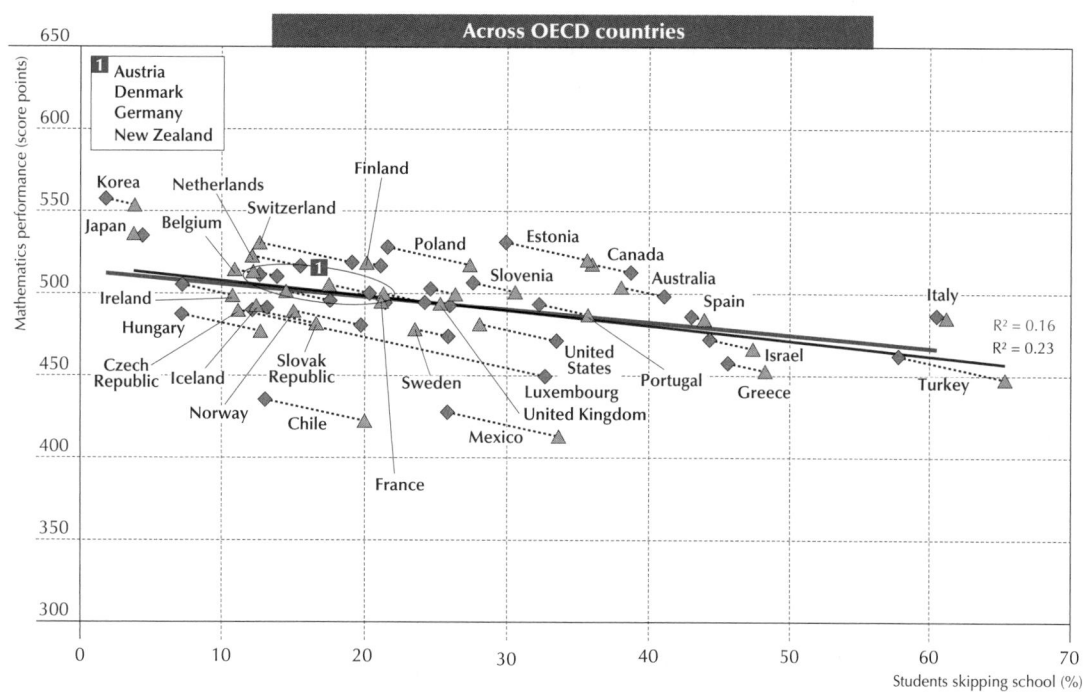

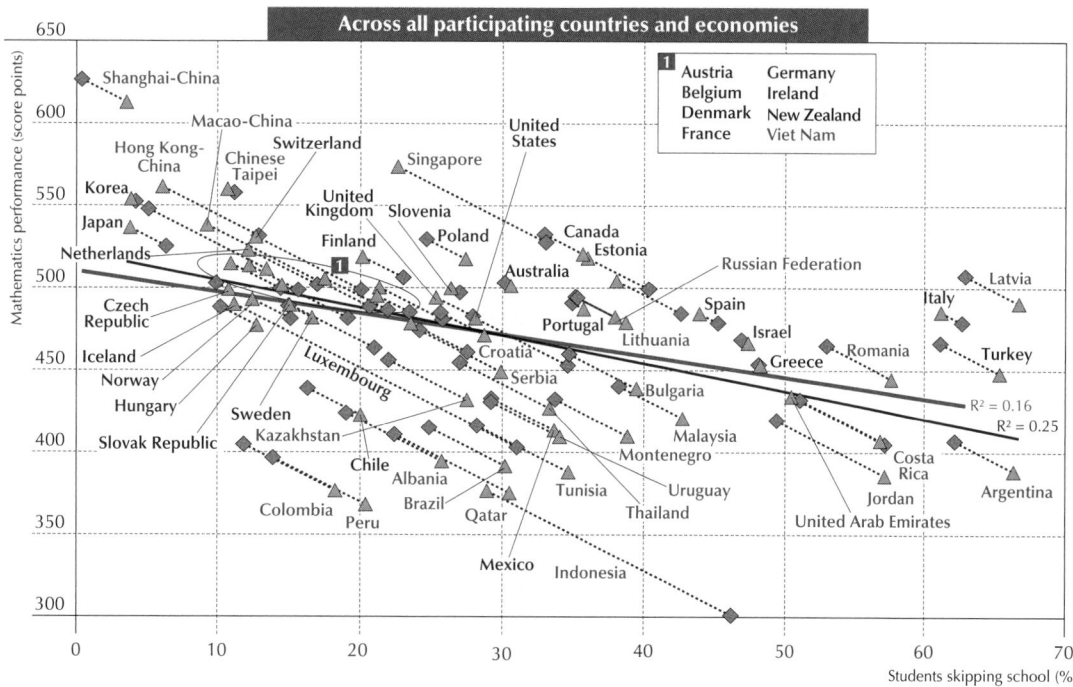

Note: Students skipping school refers to the percentage of students who had skipped a class or a day of school at least once in the two weeks prior to the PISA test.

1. A significant relationship (p < 0.10) is shown by the solid line.

Source: OECD, PISA 2012 Database, Table IV.1.5.

StatLink ⟨ms⟩ http://dx.doi.org/10.1787/888932957403

Among all countries and economies, after accounting for per capita GDP, systems with larger proportions of students who arrive late for school and skip classes tend to show lower overall performance (Table IV.1.5). As shown in Figure IV.1.22, after accounting for per capita GDP, 16% of the variation in mathematics performance across OECD countries can be explained by differences in the proportion of students who skip school. A similar result is observed among all countries and economies that participated in PISA 2012.

This negative relationship is also observed at the school level. In 29 countries and economies, schools with more students who arrive late for school tend to show lower average performance as do schools with more students who skip school. In Korea, Japan, Chinese Taipei, the Netherlands, Croatia, Slovenia, Viet Nam and New Zealand, a 10 percentage-point increase of such students corresponds to a decrease in average school performance of between 10 and 34 points, after accounting for the socio-economic status and demographic background of students and schools and various other school characteristics (Table IV.1.12c). In Korea and Japan, a 10 percentage-point increase in such students corresponds to a drop in average school performance of 25 points and 22 points, respectively. In these countries, an below-OECD-average proportion of students attends schools where over 10% of students skipped a day or a class at least once in the two weeks prior to the PISA test, (9% in Korea and 7% in Japan, while the OECD average proportion is 73%) (see Table IV.5.4, which is discussed in Chapter 5).

School climate

Disciplinary climate is also consistently related to higher average performance at the school level. In 48 participating countries and economies, schools with better average performance tend to have a more positive disciplinary climate, even after accounting for the socio-economic status and demographic background of students and schools and various other school characteristics (Table IV.1.12c). In-depth analysis of schools' disciplinary climates and other school features in Chapter 5 shows that, in almost all countries and economies, a school's average disciplinary climate is related to the average socio-economic status of its student population, but it is also related to other school features as well. On average across OECD countries, school size, school location, school type, and the incidence of teacher shortage are related to a school's disciplinary climate, even after accounting for all other school features (see Table IV.5.13 in Chapter 5).

Trends in the relationship between mathematics performance and the learning environment

Among OECD countries, the performance disadvantage among students who reported that they arrived late for school at least once in the two weeks prior to the PISA assessment was significantly larger in 2012 than it was in 2003. In 2003 students who had arrived late for school scored an average of 23 points lower than students who had not arrived late; by 2012, this difference had grown to 27 points. This disadvantage grew significantly, and by more than 10 score points, in the Czech Republic, Luxembourg, Norway, New Zealand, Portugal, Korea, the Slovak Republic, Canada and Ireland. In these countries and economies either the performance disadvantage associated with arriving late for school grew, or students who had arrived late for school were increasingly those who were low achievers. To the extent it is the latter association, the performance disadvantage related to arriving late for school grew because low-achieving students were more likely to have arrived late. If it's the case that low-achieving students are becoming more likely to arrive late, then it's precisely the group of students that would benefit the most from enhanced engagement with school that is arriving late and showing signs of disengagement with school. In Belgium, Turkey, Uruguay and Latvia, the performance difference between students who had arrived late for school and those who had not shrank (Table IV.1.28).

The proportion of students in a school who reported arriving late for school gives some indication of the learning environment. In both PISA 2003 and PISA 2012, students in schools with a larger concentration of students who reported to have arrived late performed worse than students in schools with a smaller proportion of students who reported so. But between 2003 and 2012 the performance disadvantage worsened among students who attended schools with a larger concentration of students who reported to have arrived late. In 2003 and on average across OECD countries, students in schools where more than one in four of their peers reported to have arrived late scored 18 points lower on the PISA mathematics assessment than students in schools where fewer than one in four of their peers so reported; by 2012, this performance difference grew significantly to 26 points. This could mean that, in 2012, a large concentration of students who had arrived late for school disrupted student learning to a greater extent than in 2003, or that schools with a higher concentration of students who had arrived late were enrolling more lower-achieving students. Whatever the reason, lower-achieving schools were more likely in 2012 than in 2003 to have learning climates that were not as conducive to learning (Table IV.1.29).

HOW THE FEATURES OF SCHOOLS AND SCHOOL SYSTEMS ARE INTERRELATED

Many of the aspects related to the organisation of school systems are closely interrelated. Figure IV.1.23 shows the relationship between school organisation and aspects of the learning environment. The aspects included in this figures are those that show a significant relationship,[24] either with performance or equity (i.e. the strength of the relationship between student socio-economic status and performance in mathematics), both across OECD countries and across all countries and economies that participated in PISA 2012.

Across OECD countries, two inter-related aspects of vertical stratification (the variation in grade levels in which 15-year-old students are enrolled, and the percentage of students who repeated one or more grades) are negatively related to school autonomy in curricula and assessments. This means that comprehensive systems that have to manage heterogeneous student populations within schools grant greater autonomy to schools to determine course content and assessment policies (Figure IV.1.23 and Table IV.1.19).

School systems that grant more discretion to schools to determine curricula and assessment policies tend to be those with fewer students who skip school. This relationship is observed both across OECD countries and across all countries and economies that participated in PISA 2012 (Figure IV.1.23 and Tables IV.1.19 and IV.1.20).

In summary, when all the indicators listed in Figure IV.1.23 and per capita GDP are related to a school system's overall performance, around 60% of the variation in performance across OECD countries is accounted for. Across all PISA-participating countries and economies, these system characteristics together with national income account for around 75% of the variation across school systems.

At the school level, after considering the socio-economic and demographic profile of students and schools as well as school organisation and the learning environment, across OECD countries, an average of 87% of the between-school variation in mathematics performance can be explained by the aspects measured by PISA (Figure IV.1.24 and Table IV.1.12a). Almost a quarter of the performance variation between schools is solely accounted for by aspects of school organisation and the learning environment measured by PISA, independent of the effect of the socio-economic status and demographic profile of students and schools. As school organisation and the learning environment are related to the socio-economic status and demographic profile of students and schools, about half of the between-school variation in performance is explained by these factors combined.

Box IV.1.5. How to interpret the figures

Figure IV.1.24 shows the extent to which variation in student performance is related to a particular school characteristic. The values that underlie the figures are extracted from Table IV.1.12a. The total length of the bar represents between-school variation in student performance for each country. The longer the bar, the greater the differences in student performance among schools.

Figure IV.1.24 considers the extent to which between-school variation can be explained by differences in schools' policies, practices, resources and the learning environment, either independently of students' and schools' socio-economic status and demographic profile (light blue) or jointly with those factors (dark blue). This means that the total length of the two sections (light blue and dark blue combined) present the overall variation attributable to schools' policies, practices, resources and the learning environment.

The variation jointly accounted for by both schools' policies, practices, resources and the learning environment, and students' and schools' socio-economic status and demographic profile (dark blue) indicates the extent to which school policies, practices, resources and the learning environment are inequitably distributed according to students' and schools' socio-economic status and demographic profiles.

The figure also shows the amount of variation attributable to socio-economic status and demographic background independent of schools' policies, practices, resources and the learning environment (light grey), and the amount of variation that is not attributable either to socio-economic and demographic background or to schools' policies, practices, resources and the learning environment (dark grey).

The variation in performance is presented as a percentage of the average variation in student performance across OECD countries, so that performance differences can be compared across all participating countries and economies. The OECD average variation in student performance is set to 100%.

■ Figure IV.1.23 ■

Relationship between selected policy, practice and resource indicators

Correlation coefficients between two relevant measures

Correlation coefficients range from -1.00 (i.e. a perfect negative linear association) to +1.00 (i.e. a perfect positive linear association). When a correlation coefficient is 0, there is no linear relationship between the two measures.

Upper triangle is across OECD countries
Lower triangle is across all participating countries and economies

		Math. perf.	Inequity	Std. dev. grade levels	% repeated one or more grades	No. years age of selection–age 15	Teachers' salaries rel. per capita GDP[1]	Avg. index quality educ. resources	% attended pre-primary >1 year	Diff. index quality educ. resources adv/disadv schools[2]	Avg. index school resp. curriculum/assess.	% use achievement data tracked	% seek written feedback	% arrived late	% skipped lessons/day
	Mathematics performance			-0.31x	-0.25	0.10	0.31	**0.58**	0.30x	**-0.55**	**0.58**	-0.31	0.34	**-0.44**	**-0.40**
	Inequity			**0.56**	**0.45**	0.32x	-0.02	0.04	-0.04	0.04	-0.11	0.04	-0.31	0.01	-0.12
Vertical stratification	Standard deviation of grade levels in which 15-year-olds are enrolled	**-0.36**	**0.26**		**0.71**	**0.45**	0.18	-0.08	-0.20	0.17	-0.31	0.02	-0.16	0.01	0.12
	Percentage of students who repeated one or more grades	**-0.34**	**0.25**	**0.80**		0.25	**0.42**	0.10	0.06	0.07	-0.31	-0.02	-0.24	-0.01	0.01
Horizontal stratification (between schools)	Number of years between age of selection and age 15	0.12	**0.42**	0.19	0.16		-0.05	0.01	0.17	-0.28	-0.02	-0.29	0.16	**-0.48**	-0.24
Financial resources	Teachers' salaries relative to per capita GDP[1]	-0.05	-0.21	-0.04	0.16	-0.12		**0.37**	-0.18	0.03	0.00	-0.13	0.06	-0.08	-0.09
Material resources	Average index of quality of schools' educational resources	**0.51**	0.15	-0.28x	-0.20	0.16	0.05		0.12	-0.20	0.28	-0.20	0.10	**-0.36**	-0.23
Time resources	Percentage of students reporting that they had attended pre-primary education for more than one year	**0.57**	0.23x	-0.25x	-0.08	0.23	-0.24x	**0.46**		**-0.44**	0.34	-0.35	-0.09	**-0.50**	**-0.46**
Inequity in the allocation of material resources	Difference in the index of quality of schools' educational resources between socio-economically advantaged and disadvantaged schools[2]	**-0.44**	0.12	**0.44**	**0.35**	**-0.28**	-0.06	**-0.42**	**-0.32**		-0.31	**0.39**	0.03	**0.34**	**0.37**
School autonomy	Average index of school responsibility for curriculum and assessment	**0.37**	-0.11	-0.08	-0.11	-0.03	-0.14	0.21	**0.39**	-0.14		-0.20	0.26	-0.36x	**-0.41**
Assessment and accountability policies	Percentage of students in schools that use achievement data to have their progress tracked by administrative authorities	**-0.32**	-0.07	0.00	-0.06	-0.22	0.11	-0.22	**-0.39**	0.25	**-0.28**		0.22	**0.55**	0.28
	Percentage of students in schools that seek written feedback from students for quality assurance and improvement	0.20	**-0.29**	-0.06	-0.25x	0.01	-0.08	0.17	-0.03	0.06	0.17	0.21		0.02	0.02
Student truancy	Percentage of students who arrived late for school in the two weeks prior to the PISA test	**-0.43**	0.22x	0.08	0.12	-0.20	-0.18	**-0.36**	**-0.34**	0.28	**-0.33**	**0.37**	-0.18		**0.60**
	Percentage of students who skipped some lessons or a day of school in the two weeks prior to the PISA test	**-0.41**	-0.08	0.01	0.00	-0.18	-0.12	**-0.25**	**-0.39**	0.25	**-0.40**	**0.32**	-0.06	**0.65**	

Notes: Values that are statistically significant at the 10% level (p<0.10) are indicated in italics and at the 5% level (p<0.05) are in bold. X indicates that the Pearson's correlation coefficient is significant at least at the 10% level but Spearman's rank correlation coefficient is not significant at the 10% level. Inequity refers to variation in mathematics performance explained by the *PISA index of economic, social and cultural status of students*. Correlations with mathematics performance and inequity are partial correlation coefficients after accounting for per capita GDP.

1. Weighted average of upper and lower secondary school teachers. The average is computed by weighting teachers' salaries for upper and lower secondary school according to the respective 15-year-old students' enrolment (for countries and economies with available information on both the upper and lower secondary levels).
2. See Box IV.3.1 for the definition of socio-economically advantaged and disadvantaged schools.
Source: OECD, PISA 2012 Database, Tables IV.1.1, IV.1.2, IV.1.3, IV.1.4, IV.1.5, IV.1.19 and IV.1.20.
StatLink ⟡ http://dx.doi.org/10.1787/888932957403

■ Figure IV.1.24 ■

How school characteristics are related to mathematics performance

Expressed as a percentage of the average variation in mathematics performance in OECD countries
(100% is the average total variation in mathematics performance across OECD countries)

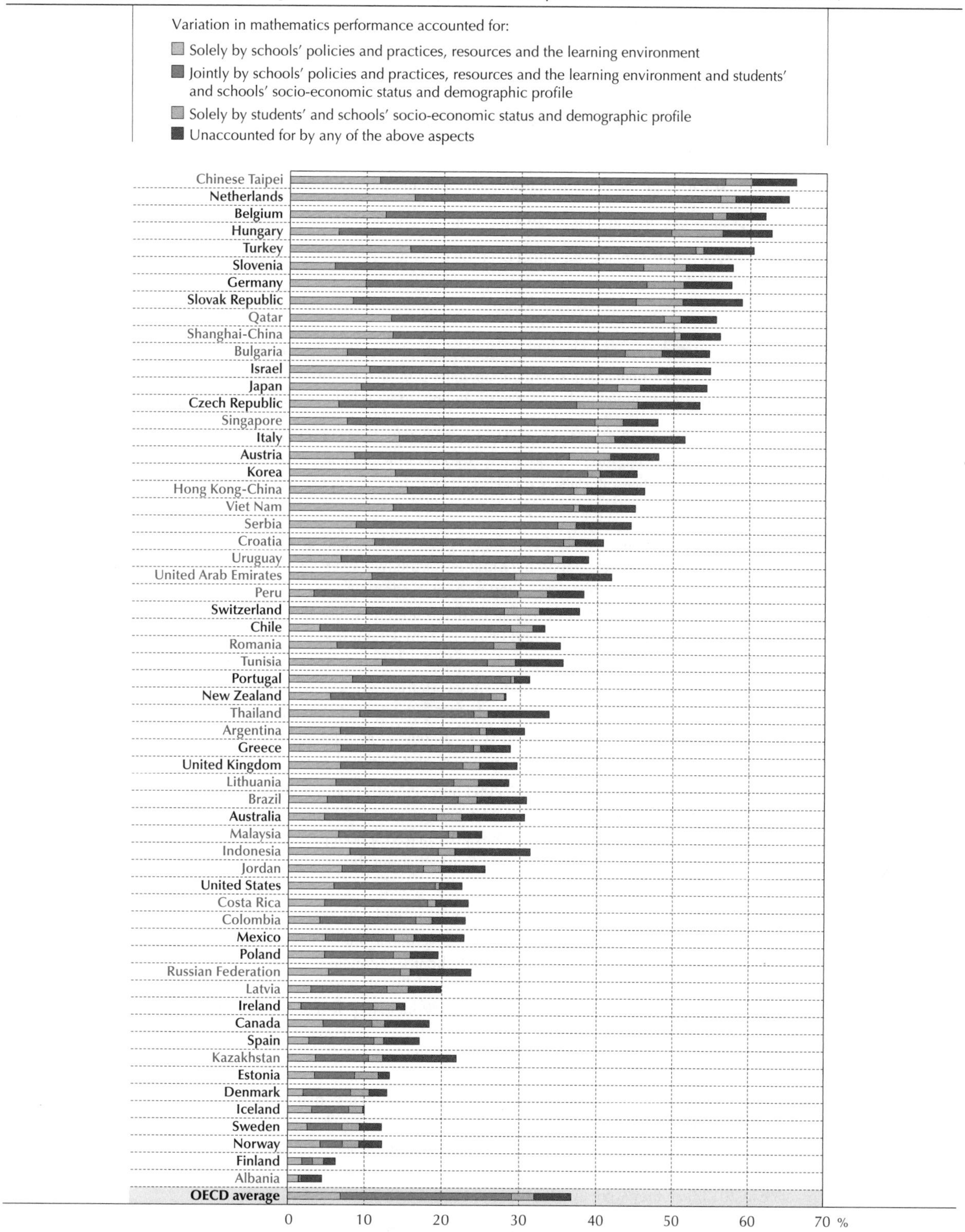

Variation in mathematics performance accounted for:

▢ Solely by schools' policies and practices, resources and the learning environment

■ Jointly by schools' policies and practices, resources and the learning environment and students'
and schools' socio-economic status and demographic profile

▢ Solely by students' and schools' socio-economic status and demographic profile

■ Unaccounted for by any of the above aspects

Chinese Taipei
Netherlands
Belgium
Hungary
Turkey
Slovenia
Germany
Slovak Republic
Qatar
Shanghai-China
Bulgaria
Israel
Japan
Czech Republic
Singapore
Italy
Austria
Korea
Hong Kong-China
Viet Nam
Serbia
Croatia
Uruguay
United Arab Emirates
Peru
Switzerland
Chile
Romania
Tunisia
Portugal
New Zealand
Thailand
Argentina
Greece
United Kingdom
Lithuania
Brazil
Australia
Malaysia
Indonesia
Jordan
United States
Costa Rica
Colombia
Mexico
Poland
Russian Federation
Latvia
Ireland
Canada
Spain
Kazakhstan
Estonia
Denmark
Iceland
Sweden
Norway
Finland
Albania
OECD average

0   10   20   30   40   50   60   70 %

Countries and economies are ranked in descending order of the between-school variation accounted for by schools' policies, resources and the
learning environment and students' and schools' socio-economic status and demographic profile, whether solely or jointly.
Source: OECD, PISA 2012 Database, Table IV.1.12a.
StatLink ⟐⟐⟐ http://dx.doi.org/10.1787/888932957403

Notes

1. These data are extracted from *Education at a Glance 2013: OECD Indicators* (OECD, 2013c) for the countries that participate in the regular annual OECD data collection that is administered through the INES Network. For other countries and economies, a special system-level data collection was conducted in collaboration with PISA Governing Board members and National Project Managers.

2. While Pearson's correlation coefficients are presented in Tables IV.1.1, IV.1.2, IV.1.3, IV.1.4 and IV.1.5, Spearman's rank correlation coefficients are also examined in order to confirm the robustness of the results. When outliers drive the results, Pearson's correlation coefficients are stronger than Spearman's correlation coefficients. Thus, the cases where Pearson's correlation coefficient is significant at least at the 10% level but Spearman's rank correlation coefficient is not significant at the 10% level are flagged in the tables. The same procedure is applied to partial correlation coefficients.

3. The percentage is obtained by squaring the partial correlation coefficient and then multiplying it by 100.

4. Partial correlation coefficients are -0.36 among all participating countries and economies (significant at the 5% level).

5. Selection bias in this case refers to how to separate the effect of grade repetition from differences in achievement due to the selection of students who must repeat grades.

6. The partial correlation coefficient is -0.34.

7. These estimates do not address either the potential benefits of grade repetition or the costs if school systems do not allow for grade repetition. For example, students who had repeated a grade might be better prepared for the labour market than if they had not done so. And schools might have to spend more to offer remedial classes to struggling students if those students are not permitted to repeat a year.

8. Throughout this section, and the entire volume, trends in the OECD average refer to the group of OECD countries that have comparable data from PISA 2003 and PISA 2012. In general, this excludes Chile, Estonia, Israel and Slovenia, which did not take part in PISA 2003. For school-level resources, policies and practices, this also excludes France, which did not distribute the school questionnaire to school principals in PISA 2003.

9. Trends analyses on student performance are available only for the 39 countries and economies that participated in PISA 2012, distributed the PISA 2003 questionnaire, and have comparable samples for the two assessments. PISA 2003 did not include questions on school competition, teacher appraisal, school transfers, skipping school, dropping out of school, attending after-school lessons, parental pressure or parental involvement. It is thus not possible to determine trends for these. Similarly, some questions relating to the same policy or practiced changed between PISA 2003 and PISA 2012, making it impossible to track trends related to them. Such is the case for school admission policies, teaching staff qualifications, and school's responsibility for resource allocation and curricula.

With respect to school admission policies, in 2003, question SC10 asked, for each admission criteria, "How much consideration is given to the following factors when students are admitted to your school?" offering the following response options "Prerequiste", "High priority", "Considered" or "Not considered". In 2012, question SC32 asked, "How often are the following factors considered when students are admitted to your school?" and offered "Never", "Sometimes" and "Always" as response options.

With respect to teaching staff qualifications, although both PISA 2003 and PISA 2012 questionnaires asked school principals about the total number of teachers in the school and the number of those who hold an ISCED 5A (university-equivalent) degree and those who have a teaching certificate, the questions are not comparable. PISA 2012 asked school principals, in broad terms, about the number of teachers in the school who hold an ISCED 5A degree; PISA 2003 asked about the number of teachers in the school who hold an ISCED 5A degree in pedagogy.

Finally, with respect to schools' responsibility for resource allocation and curricula, in the PISA 2003 questionnaire, school principals were asked, "In your school, who has the main responsibility for <each governance attribute>" and were offered the following response options: "Not a main responsibility of the school", "School's governing board", "Principal", "Department Head" or "Teachers". In the PISA 2012 questionnaire, school principals were asked, "Regarding your school, who has a considerable responsibility for <each governance attribute>" and were offered the following response options: "Principal", "Teachers", "School governing board", "Regional or local education authority", "National education authority". In both PISA 2003 and PISA 2012, school principals could select as many response options as appropriate.

10. Caution is required when interpreting how the relationship between students' mathematics performance and educational resources, policies and practices has evolved over time. Two reasons explain why this change can occur. First, the resource, policy or practice could have become more strongly related to mathematics performance because it promotes mathematics performance more in 2012 than it did in 2003. Second, higher-performing students and schools may have been more likely to implement this particular resource, policy or practice in 2012 than they were in 2003.

The use of student-assessment data for judging teacher effectiveness provides an example:

In PISA 2003, and on average across OECD countries that have comparable data from PISA 2003 and PISA 2012, students in schools where observations by external personnel were used to monitor teacher practice outperformed students in schools where observations by external personnel were not used to monitor teacher practice. In PISA 2012, however, students in schools that use such observations to monitor teacher practice underperformed compared with students in schools that did not use observations by external personnel for this purpose. This relationship holds, on average, across OECD countries, but is observed in only six OECD countries. One possible explanation for this reversal is that, on average across OECD countries, monitoring teachers by external personnel became less effective as a tool to promote learning. This explanation implies that the underlying process of using external observations to monitor teacher practice became less effective during the period. If, indeed, there was such a change, the specifics of this change remain unknown. PISA data cannot distinguish whether the reduced effectiveness of external monitoring – assuming that this explains the observed change – results from a change in the way the external monitors conducted their observations, the way school principals and teachers reacted to these observations, or the way students reacted to the teachers' and principals' reactions to the external observations. In addition, it is not possible to conclude from PISA trends analyses whether this hypothetical reduction in the effectiveness of external observations also applies to schools and school systems that had not yet chosen to use this type of observation, since instruction and learning may benefit from external observations of teacher practices.

Another explanation for this trend posits that the efficacy of external observations remained unchanged over the period, but that the types of schools that chose to use them have changed. Under this argument, better-performing schools tended to use external monitoring in 2003, but were less likely to do so by 2012. It could be the case that schools that used external observations in 2012 were those that were aware of their lower performance levels compared to schools in 2003. This alternative explanation suggests that schools used external observations *because* they showed poorer performance, as opposed to performing poorly because they used external observations. That causation between students' performance and the use of external observations could go either way underscores the importance of applying caution in interpreting these results.

11. It is difficult to explain these trends without further analyses of how students are selected into schools and the heterogeneity of these student populations. PISA was unable to undertake these analyses because variables on schools' admission criteria are not comparable between PISA 2003 and PISA 2012 (see note 3).

12. Comparisons of expenditure data from 2003 and 2012 are limited to a subset of 24 countries. Analyses for 2012 consider 48 countries and economies with information on cumulative expenditure on education for students aged 6 to 15. Of the countries and economies analysed in 2012, 16 did not participate in PISA 2003 and 7 do not have information on cumulative expenditure in 2003. Seven of the countries and economies not included in the trends analysis had cumulative expenditure per student above USD 50 000 and 17 had cumulative expenditures under USD 50 000 in 2012.

13. Across OECD countries, the correlation is 0.32.

14. The correlation is -0.22 across 17 countries and economies whose per capita GDP is less than USD 20 000.

15. Statistically significant coefficients in Table IV.1.2 are mainly the result of outliers. For example, the correlation between the student-teacher ratio and performance is -0.48 across OECD countries, but it is 0.09 after excluding two countries with extreme student-teacher ratios (31 in Mexico and 22 in Chile, while the average ranges from 8 to 18 in other OECD countries).

16. 46% = 17% / (8%+3%+17%+9%).

17. Across OECD countries, the correlation between mathematics performance and average learning time in regular mathematics lessons is -0.30 (significant at the 10% level), but this is mainly because of outliers.

18. Chapters 2, 3 and 4 of this volume and other volumes of this series highlight other country's improvements in PISA and outline their recent policy trajectories (e.g. Poland in Chapter 2, Tunisia in Chapter 3 and Colombia in Chapter 4 of this volume, Brazil, Turkey, Korea and Estonia in Volume I, Mexico and Germany in Volume II, and Japan and Portugal in Volume III).

19. Across OECD countries, the correlation between the degree of competition and equity is 0.33 (significant at the 10% level), while it is 0.23 after excluding Norway, where there is less school competition than in other countries (i.e. the degree of school competition is 35% in Norway, while it varies from 42% to 94% in other OECD countries).

20. Across all participating countries and economies with available data, the correlation between the percentage of students in private schools and the difference in mathematics performance between public and private schools is 0.14.

21. After accounting for per capita GDP, the correlation is 0.34 across OECD countries and 0.20 across all participating countries and economies.

22. Across OECD countries, the correlation is -0.33 after accounting for per capita GDP and it is -0.31 across all participating countries and economies.

23. The set of countries used to calculate trends in OECD averages includes only those OECD countries that have comparable data in PISA 2003 and PISA 2012 for the variable being examined.

24. Significant at the 10% level (p < 0.10).

References

Alexander, K., D. Entwisle and **S. Dauber** (2003), *On the Success of Failure: A Reassessment of the Effects of Retention in the Early Grades,* Cambridge University Press, Cambridge.

Baker, D., B. Goesling, and **G. LeTendre** (2002), "Socioeconomic Status, School Quality, and National Economic Development: A Cross-National Analysis of the 'Heyneman-Loxley Effect' on Mathematics and Science Achievement", *Comparative Education Review*, Vol. 46, No. 3, pp. 291-312.

Beller, M. (2013), *Assessment in the Service of Learning: Theory and Practice*, RAMA, Ramat Gan.

Berends, M. and **G. Zottola** (2009), "International Perspectives on School Choice", in M. Berends et al. (eds.), *Handbook of School Choice,* Routledge, London.

Blair, C., et al. (2005), "Rising Mean IQ: Cognitive Demand of Mathematics Education for Young Children, Population Exposure to Formal Schooling, and the Neurobiology of the Prefrontal Cortex", *Intelligence*, Vol. 33, pp. 93-106.

Buchmann, C. and **E. Hannum** (2001), "Education and Stratification in Developing Countries: A Review of Theories and Research", *Annual Review of Sociology,* Vol. 27, pp. 77-102.

Bunar, N. (2010a), "The Controlled School Market and Urban Schools in Sweden", *Journal of School Choice,* Vol. 4, pp. 47-73.

Bunar, N. (2010b), "Choosing for Quality or Inequality", *Journal of Education Policy,* Vol. 25, pp. 1-18.

Carnoy, M. (2000), "Globalization and Educational Reform", in N. Stromquist and K. Monkman (eds.), *Globalization and Education: Integration and Contestation across Cultures*, Rowman and Littlefield Publishers, Oxford.

Ceci, S. (1991), "How Much Does Schooling Influence General Intelligence and Its Cognitive Components? A Reassessment of the Evidence", *Developmental Psychology*, Vol. 27, No. 5, pp. 703-722.

Clark, D. (2009), "The performance and competitive effects of school autonomy", *Journal of Political Economy*, Vol. 117, No. 4, pp. 745-783.

Couch, J., W. Shugart and **A. Williams** (1993), "Private school enrolment and public school performance", *Public Choice*, Vol. 76, pp. 301-312.

Downey, D., P. Von Hippel and **M. Hughes** (2008), "Are 'Failing' Schools Really Failing? Using Seasonal Comparison to Evaluate School Effectiveness", *Sociology of Education*, Vol. 81, No. 3, pp. 242-270.

Filer, R.K. and **D. Munich** (2003), "Public Support for Private Schools in Post-Communist Europe: Czech and Hungarian Experiences" in D.N. Plank and G. Sykes (eds.), *Choosing Choice: School Choice in International Perspective*, Teachers College Press, New York.

Fuchs, T. and **L. Woessmann** (2007), "What Accounts for International Differences in Student Performance? A Re-Examination Using PISA Data", *Empirical Economics,* Vol. 32, No. 2-3, pp. 433-464.

Fuller, B. (1987), "What Factors Raise Achievement in the Third World?", *Review of Educational Research,* Vol. 57, No. 3, pp. 255-292.

Gamoran, A., W. Secada and **C. Marrett** (2000), "The Organizational Context of Teaching and Learning: Changing Theoretical Perspectives", in M. Hallinan (ed.), *Handbook of the Sociology of Education*, Springer, New York.

Geller, C.R., D.L. Sjoquist and **M.B. Walker** (2006), "The Effect of Private School Competition on Public School Performance in Georgia", *Public Finance Review,* Vol. 34, No. 1, pp. 4-32.

Gewirtz, S., S. Ball and **R. Bowe** (1995), *Markets, Choice and Equity in Education,* Open University Press, Buckingham.

Goos, M., et al. (2013), "How Can Cross-Country Differences in the Practice of Grade Retention Be Explained? A Closer Look at National Educational Policy Factors", *Comparative Education Review,* Vol. 57, No. 1, pp. 54-84.

Green, F., et al. (2011), "The Changing Economic Advantage from Private Schools", *Economica,* Vol. 79, No. 316, pp. 658-678.

Greene, K.V. and **B.G. Kang** (2004), "The Effect of Public and Private Competition on High School Outputs in New York State", *Economics of Education Review,* No. 23, pp. 497-506.

Greenwald, R., L. Hedges and **R. Laine** (1996), "The Effect of School Resources on Student Achievement", *Review of Educational Research,* Vol. 66, No. 3, pp. 361-396.

Hægeland, T., O. Raaum and **K.G. Salvanes** (2012), "Pennies from Heaven? Using Exogenous Tax Variation to Identify Effects of School Resources on Pupil Achievement", *Economics of Education Review*, Vol. 31, No. 5, pp.601-614.

Hauser, R. (2004), "Progress in Schooling", in K. Neckerman (ed.), *Social Inequality,* Russell Sage Foundation, New York.

Heckman, J.J. and **X. Li** (2003), "Selection Bias, Comparative Advantage and Heterogeneous Return to Education: Evidence from China in 2000", IZA Discussion Paper Series, No. 829.

Hess, F. and T. Loveless (2005), "How School Choice Affects Student Achievement", in J. Bettsand and T. Loveless (eds.), *Getting Choice Right: Ensuring Equity and Efficiency in Education Policy*, Brookings Institution Press, Washington, D.C.

Heynemann, S. (2009), "International Perspectives on School Choice", in M. Berends et al. (eds.), *Handbook of School Choice*, Routledge, London.

Hsieh, H. and M. Urquiola (2006), "The Effects of Generalized School Choice on Achievement and Stratification: Evidence from Chile's Voucher Program", *Journal of Public Economics*, Vol. 90, No. 8-9, pp. 1477-1503.

Jacob, B. (2005), "Accountability, Incentives and Behavior: The Impact of High-Stakes Testing in Chicago Public Schools", *Journal of Public Economics,* Vol. 89, No. 5-6, pp. 761-796.

Jacob, B.A. and L. Lefgren (2009), "The Effect of Grade Retention on High School Completion", *American Economic Journal: Applied Economics*, Vol. 1, No. 3, pp. 33-58.

Jennings, J. (2005), "Below the Bubble: 'Educational Triage' and the Texas Accountability System", *American Educational Research Journal,* Vol. 42, No. 2, pp. 231-268.

Karsten, S. (1999), "Neoliberal Education Reform in the Netherlands", *Comparative Education,* Vol. 35, No. 3, pp. 303-317.

Ladd, H. and R. Walsh (2002), "Implementing Value-Added Measures of School Effectiveness: Getting the Incentives Right", *Economics of Education Review,* Vol. 21, No. 1, pp. 1-17.

Lara, B., A. Mizala and A. Repetto (2009), "The Effectiveness of Private Voucher Education: Evidence from Structural School Switches", Working Paper No. 263, CEA, Universidad de Chile.

Machin, S. and J. Vernoit (2011), *Changing School Autonomy: Academy Schools and their Introduction to England's Education*, Paper No. CEE DP 123, Centre for the Economics of Education, London.

Manacorda, M. (2012), "The Cost of Grade Retention", *Review of Economics and Statistics,* Vol. 94, No. 2, pp. 596-606.

Maranto, R., S. Milliman and S. Scott (2000), "Does Private School Competition Harm Public Schools? Revisiting Smith and Meier's 'The Case Against School Choice'", *Political Research Quarterly*, Vol. 53, No. 1, pp. 177-192.

Murillo, F.J. and M. Román (2011), "School Infrastructure and Resources Do Matter: Analysis of the Incidence of School Resources on the Performance of Latin American Students", *School Effectiveness and School Improvement*, Vol. 22, No. 1, pp. 29-50.

Neal, D. and D. W. Schanzenback (2010), "Left Behind by Design: Proficiency Counts and Test-Based Accountability", *The Review of Economics and Statistics*, Vol. 92, No. 2, pp. 263-283.

Nicoletti, C. and B. Rabe (2012), *The Effect of School Resources on Test Scores in England,* working paper no. 2012-13, Institute for Social and Economic Research, Essex.

OECD (2013a), *PISA 2012 Assessment and Analytical Framework: Mathematics, Reading, Science, Problem Solving and Financial Literacy*, PISA, OECD Publishing.
http://dx.doi.org/10.1787/9789264190511-en

OECD (2013b), *Synergies for Better Learning: An International Perspective on Evaluation and Assessment*, OECD Publishing.
http://dx.doi.org/10.1787/9789264190658-en

OECD (2013c), *Education at a Glance 2013: OECD Indicators,* OECD Publishing.
http://dx.doi.org/10.1787/eag-2013-en

OECD (2012), "Does Money Buy Strong Performance in PISA?", *PISA in Focus*, No. 13, PISA, OECD Publishing.
http://dx.doi.org/10.1787/5k9fhmfzc4xx-en

OECD (2011a), "When Students Repeat Grades or Are Transferred Out of School: What Does it Mean for Education Systems?", *PISA in Focus*, No. 6, PISA, OECD Publishing.
http://dx.doi.org/10.1787/5k9h362n5z45-en

OECD (2011b), *OECD Economic Survey: Israel*, OECD Publishing.
http://dx.doi.org/10.1787/eco_surveys-isr-2011-en

OECD (2010), "Israeli Education Policy: How to Move Ahead in Reform", *Economics Department Working Paper,* No. 781, OECD Publishing.
http://dx.doi.org/10.1787/5kmd3khjfjf0-en

Peterson, P., et al. (2003), "School Vouchers: Results from Randomized Experiments", in C. Hoxby (ed.), *The Economics of School Choice*, University of Chicago Press, Chicago, pp. 107-144.

Plank, D. and G. Sykes (eds.) (2003), *Choosing Choice: School Choice in International Perspective,* Teachers College Press, New York.

Rivkin, S., E. Hanushek and **J. Kain** (2005), "Teachers, Schools and Academic Achievement", *Econometrica,* Vol. 73, No. 2, pp. 417-458.

Sammons, P. (1999), *School Effectiveness: Coming of Age in the Twenty-First Century*, Swets and Zeitlinger, Lisse.

Sander W. (1999), "Private Schools and Public School Achievement", *Journal of Human Resources,* Vol. 34, No. 4, pp. 697-709.

Sandström, M. and **F. Bergström** (2005), "School Vouchers in Practice: Competition will Not Hurt You", *Journal of Public Economics,* Vol. 89, No. 2-3, pp. 351-380.

Scheerens, J. and **R. Bosker** (1997), *The Foundations of Educational Effectiveness*, Pergamon Press, Oxford.

Schneider, M. and **J. Buckley** (2002), "What Do Parents Want From Schools? Evidence from the Internet", *Educational Evaluation and Policy Analysis*, Vol. 24, No. 2, pp. 133-144.

Schneider, M., P. Teske and **M. Marshall** (2002), *Choosing Schools: Consumer Choice and the Quality of American Schools*, Princeton University Press, Princeton, New Jersey.

Schwerdt, G. and **M. West** (2012), *Effects of Early Grade Retention on Student Outcomes over Time: Regression Discontinuity Evidence from Florida*, Program on Education Policy and Governance Working Paper Series, PEPG 12-09.

Smith, K. and **K. Meier** (1995), "Public Choice in Education: Markets and the Demand for Quality Education", *Political Research Quarterly*, Vol. 48, pp. 461-478.

Söderström, M. and **R. Uusitalo** (2010), "School Choice and Segregation: Evidence from an Admission Reform", *The Scandinavian Journal of Economics*, Vol. 112, No. 1, pp. 55-76.

Taylor, B., M. Pressley and **P. Pearson** (2002), "Research-Supported Characteristics of Teachers and Schools that Promote Reading Achievement", in B. Taylor and P. Pearson (eds.), *Teaching Reading: Effective Schools, Accomplished Teachers,* CIERA, Mahwah, New Jersey.

Viteritti, J. (1999), *Choosing Equality,* Brookings Institution Press, Washington, D.C.

West, M.R. (2012), *Is Retaining Students in the Early Grades Self-Defeating?*, CCF Brief No. 4, Center on Children and Families at Brookings.

West, M.R. and **L. Woessmann** (2010), "Every Catholic Child in a Catholic School: Historical Resistance to State Schooling, Contemporary School Competition, and Student Achievement across Countries", *Economic Journal*, Vol. 120, No. 546, pp. 229-255.

Whitty, G. (1997), "Creating Quasi-Markets in Education: A Review of Recent Research on Parental Choice and School Autonomy in Three Countries", *Review of Research in Education*, Vol. 22, pp. 3-47.

Whitty, G., S. Power and **D. Halpin** (1998), *Devolution and Choice in Education,* Open University Press, Buckingham.

Woessmann, L. (2006), "Public-Private Partnerships and Schooling Outcomes Across Countries", *CESifo Working Paper Series*, No. 1662, Center for Economic Studies, Institute for Economic Research, Munich.

Woessmann, L., et al. (2009), *School Accountability, Autonomy, and Choice around the World*, Edward Elgar, Cheltenham.

Wolff, L. and **E, Breit** (2012), "Education in Israel", *Institute for Israeli Studies Research Paper*, No. 8, University of Maryland.

Wrinkle, R., et al. (1999), "Public School Quality, Private Schools, and Race", *American Journal of Political Science*, Vol. 43, No. 4, pp. 1248-1253.

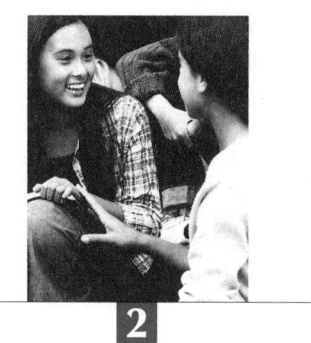

2

Selecting and Grouping Students

This chapter discusses the ways in which students are selected and grouped into certain education levels, grade levels, schools, programmes and different classes within schools based on their performance. It offers an analysis of whether students in school systems with similar degrees of stratification share similar dispositions for learning mathematics, and examines how stratification practices and policies have changed since 2003.

This chapter focuses on how 15-year-old students are selected and grouped into education levels, grade levels, different schools, programmes, and different groups within schools. The reason for this focus is that, as shown in Chapter 1, in highly stratified systems, education is less equitable.

This chapter first describes various ways of grouping and selecting students, hereafter referred to as vertical and horizontal stratification (Figure IV.2.1). Then comparisons are made across countries to examine which features related to social and academic inclusion are shared among school systems with similar degrees of stratification. This is followed by a section analysing whether students in school systems with similar degrees of stratification share similar dispositions for learning mathematics. The chapter concludes with a look at how systems' selection and grouping of students have changed since PISA 2003.

■ Figure IV.2.1 ■
Selecting and grouping students as covered in PISA 2012

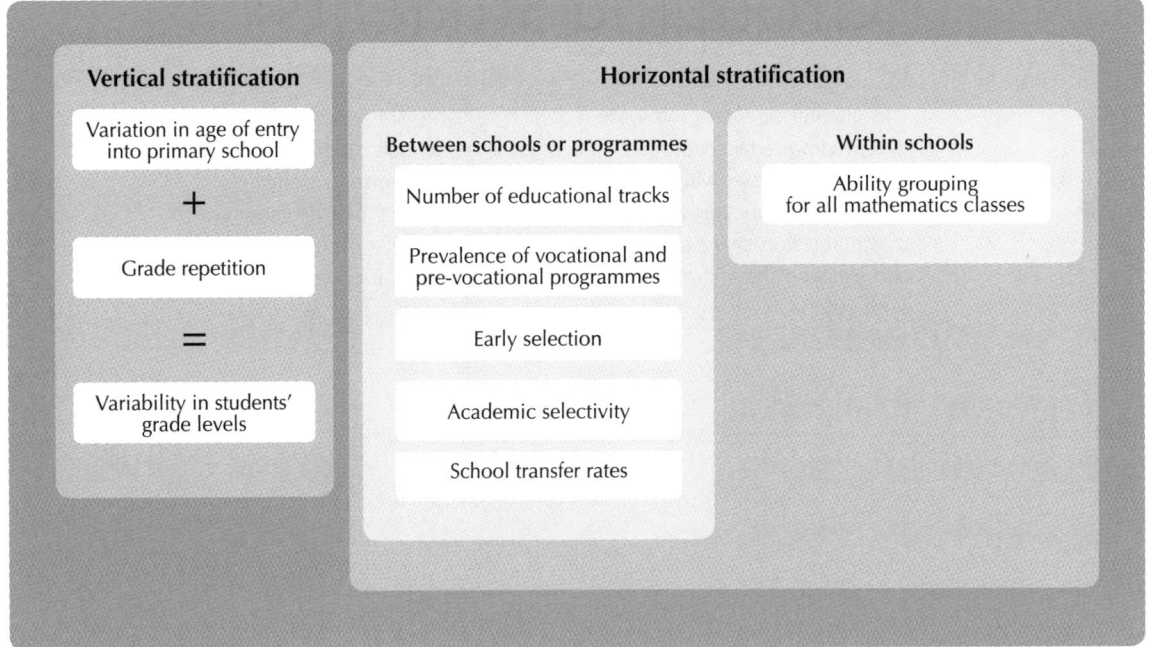

What the data tell us

- Across OECD countries, an average of 12% of students reported that they had repeated a grade at least once. In Japan, Malaysia and Norway, no 15-year-old student had repeated a grade, while in Colombia and Macao-China over 40% of students had repeated a grade at least once. Among the 13 countries and economies with grade repetition rates of more than 20% in 2003, these rates dropped by an average of 3.5 percentage points by 2012, and fell sharply in France, Luxembourg, Macao-China, Mexico and Tunisia.

- When comparing two students with similar mathematics performance, the student who is more socio-economically disadvantaged than the other is more likely to have repeated a grade.

- Students in comprehensive school systems – those that do not separate students into different schools according to their performance, such as the systems in Australia, Canada, Iceland, New Zealand, the United Kingdom and the United States – tend to regard learning mathematics as important for their later life, regardless of the system's overall performance.

HOW STUDENTS PROGRESS THROUGH THE SCHOOL SYSTEM

One-room schools, where all students, regardless of age, shared the same classroom and were taught by the same teacher, were commonplace in many countries in the early 19th century. As student populations grew in size and diversity, schooling was increasingly differentiated "vertically": younger students would concentrate on basic studies, and as they progressed, they would enter more complex and differentiated study programmes. This vertical stratification resulted in the creation of different grades and education levels (Sorensen, 1970; Tyack, 1974). This section describes two of the main factors that have an impact on 15-year-old students' grade level: the age of entry into the school system and grade repetition. It then examines how school systems differ in the way 15-year-old students are distributed across grade and education levels.

Students' ages at entry into the school system

Most school systems establish an age of entry into formal schooling. However practical this may be, children do not necessarily develop cognitively or emotionally at the same rate, and certain parents may believe that their children could benefit from starting schooling earlier, or waiting an extra year before they start schooling, a practice known as academic redshirting (Graue and DiPerna, 2000).

In PISA 2012, students were asked at what age they entered primary school, in order to assess the degree of heterogeneity in the student population that schools and teachers have to manage. In general, most students will be within one year of each other when they enter school in education systems that enforce a specific starting age. In countries where parents have more freedom to choose the age at which their children enter school, children may be two or more years above or below the modal age of entry. Thus, the proportion of students who entered school outside this modal two-year window indicates, approximately, the diversity of students' ages at entry into the school system.

Across OECD countries, an average of 51% of students reported that they started primary school at the age of six and 27% reported that they started at the age of seven. Some 20% of students started primary school at the age of five or earlier, while 2% started at the age of eight or older.[1] In 41 participating countries and economies, 90% or more of students started primary school within the national modal two-year window. In Japan and Poland, all students reported that they had started primary school within that window. By contrast, students in Brazil, Qatar, Canada, the United Arab Emirates, Peru and Colombia started primary school when they were younger or older. In Brazil, 67% of students started primary school at the age of six or seven, while 20% started at the age of eight or older and 13% started at the age of five or younger. At least one in two students in Ireland reported that they had started primary school at the age of four, but school is compulsory only at age six (Figure IV.2.2 and Table IV.2.1).

Grade repetition

Grade repetition is also a form of vertical stratification as it seeks to adapt curricula to student performance, thus creating more homogeneous classes. However, Chapter 1 explains that grade repetition is negatively related to equity in education: systems where more students repeat a grade tend to show a stronger impact of students' socio-economic status on their performance.

PISA asked 15-year-old students whether they had repeated a grade in primary, lower secondary or upper secondary school. Across OECD countries, an average of 12% of students reported that they had repeated a grade at least once: 7% of students had repeated a grade in primary school, 6% of students had repeated a lower secondary grade, and 2% of students had repeated an upper secondary grade. In Japan, Malaysia and Norway, no 15-year-old student reported to have repeated a grade, while in 24 countries and economies, over 0% but 5% of students or fewer reported that they had repeated a grade. In contrast, between 20% and 29% of students in France, the Netherlands, Peru, Chile and Germany had repeated a grade at least once; between 30% and 39% of students in Tunisia, Uruguay, Argentina, Belgium, Brazil, Luxembourg, Portugal, Costa Rica and Spain had repeated a grade at least once; and in Macao-China and Colombia over 40% of students had repeated a grade at least once (Figure IV.2.2 and Table IV.2.2).

Among these systems with high rates of grade repetition, over 20% of students in Portugal, Macao-China, Colombia, Uruguay, Luxembourg, the Netherlands, Brazil and Belgium had repeated a grade at least once in primary school. Over 20% of students in Tunisia, Macao-China, Colombia, Spain, Uruguay, Argentina and Costa Rica had repeated a lower secondary grade at least once; and over 10% of students in Turkey, Chile and Italy had repeated an upper secondary grade at least once (Table IV.2.2). Caution is required in comparing these results across systems, since the number of years in primary, lower secondary and upper secondary education differs according to the structure of the school systems.

■ Figure IV.2.2 ■

How students are grouped in a school system (vertical stratification)

		Age of entry into primary school		Repeaters	15-year-olds in different grades and education levels			
	Average age of entry into primary school	Percentage of students who started primary school at: (Age 5 or younger / Age 6 / Age 7 or older)		Percentage of students who reported that they had repeated a grade at least once in primary, lower secondary or upper secondary school	Percentage of students in: (Grade below the modal grade / The modal grade / Grade above the modal grade)	Lower secondary education (%)	Upper secondary education (%)	Variation in student grade level — S.D.
OECD								
Australia	5.2			7.5		81	19	0.55
Austria	6.2			11.9		6	94	0.61
Belgium	5.9			36.1		10	90	0.67
Canada	5.2			8.0		14	86	0.42
Chile	6.0			25.2		5	95	0.71
Czech Republic	6.4			4.9		56	44	0.59
Denmark	6.6			4.7		100	0	0.41
Estonia	6.9			3.5		98	2	0.47
Finland	6.7			3.8		100	0	0.39
France	5.9			28.4		30	70	0.57
Germany	6.2			20.3		98	2	0.67
Greece	6.3			4.5		5	95	0.33
Hungary	6.7			10.8		12	88	0.63
Iceland	5.8			1.2		100	0	0.00
Ireland	4.5			8.6		62	38	0.75
Israel	6.2			1.9		13	87	0.41
Italy	5.9			17.1		2	98	0.51
Japan	6.0			0.0		0	100	0.00
Korea	6.6			3.6		6	94	0.24
Luxembourg	6.2			34.5		60	40	0.67
Mexico	6.1			15.5		37	63	0.68
Netherlands	6.1			27.6		70	30	0.57
New Zealand	5.1			5.4		6	94	0.35
Norway	5.8			0.0		100	0	0.08
Poland	7.0			4.2		100	0	0.25
Portugal	5.9			34.3		45	55	0.75
Slovak Republic	6.3			7.6		45	55	0.69
Slovenia	6.2			3.4		5	95	0.32
Spain	5.8			32.9		100	0	0.67
Sweden	6.8			4.0		98	2	0.25
Switzerland	6.5			19.9		77	23	0.63
Turkey	6.9			14.2		3	97	0.61
United Kingdom	5.0			2.7		0	100	0.22
United States	5.9			13.3		12	88	0.55
OECD average	6.1			12.4		46	54	0.48
Partners								
Albania	6.4			3.2		42	58	0.55
Argentina	5.9			36.2		37	63	0.86
Brazil	7.2			36.1		20	80	0.95
Bulgaria	6.9			4.8		5	95	0.36
Colombia	6.0			40.6		39	61	1.11
Costa Rica	6.6			33.5		61	39	0.91
Croatia	6.7			2.7		0	100	0.40
Hong Kong-China	6.1			15.9		33	67	0.68
Indonesia	6.3			15.5		48	52	0.80
Jordan	6.0			7.9		100	0	0.32
Kazakhstan	6.5			1.6		72	28	0.55
Latvia	6.8			8.5		96	4	0.49
Liechtenstein	6.6			18.9		88	12	0.69
Lithuania	6.6			2.5		100	0	0.44
Macao-China	6.2			41.2		55	45	0.90
Malaysia	7.0			0.0		4	96	0.20
Montenegro	6.6			1.3		0	100	0.40
Peru	6.1			27.5		30	70	0.97
Qatar	5.8			13.3		18	82	0.72
Romania	6.8			4.5		100	0	0.37
Russian Federation	6.7			2.5		82	18	0.53
Serbia	6.9			1.6		2	98	0.19
Shanghai-China	6.7			9.1		44	56	0.65
Singapore	6.7			5.7		2	98	0.42
Chinese Taipei	6.8			0.8		36	64	0.48
Thailand	6.2			3.3		21	79	0.47
Tunisia	5.9			38.7		37	63	0.95
United Arab Emirates	6.0			12.0		15	85	0.75
Uruguay	5.9			37.9		41	59	0.95
Viet Nam	6.2			7.7		10	90	0.45

% 0   20   40   60   80   100   0   20   40   60   80   100 %

Source: OECD, PISA 2012 Database, Tables IV.2.1, IV.2.2 and IV.2.4.
StatLink ᴹˢᴾ http://dx.doi.org/10.1787/888932957308

PISA 2012 shows that in 35 out of 61 countries and economies examined, disadvantaged students are more likely to have repeated a grade than advantaged students, even after accounting for student performance in mathematics (Table IV.2.3). This means that when comparing two students with similar mathematics performance, the student who is more socio-economically disadvantaged than the other is more likely to have repeated a grade. As shown in Figure IV.2.3, on average across OECD countries, if a student scoring 300 points in mathematics is socio-economically advantaged, the likelihood that he or she had repeated a grade is 35 out of 100, while the likelihood of repeating a grade is 45 out of 100 if this student is socio-economically disadvantaged. In general, the higher a student's score, the less likely it is that the student had repeated a grade. But disadvantaged students are still at higher risk of repeating a grade than their advantaged counterparts. For example, if a student who scores 400 points is advantaged, the likelihood that he or she had repeated a grade is 14 out of 100, while the likelihood is 19 out of 100 if this student is disadvantaged.

This finding is consistent with the results of other studies showing that the incidence of grade repetition is highest among students from socio-economically disadvantaged backgrounds (Gomes-Neto and Hanushek, 1994). A study based on PISA 2009 data found that, in about half of the countries examined, students' socio-economic status is related to the likelihood of repeating a grade, even after accounting for student academic performance (Monseur and Lafontaine, 2012). In fact, data from PISA 2009 revealed that, among OECD countries, 53% of the variation in the likelihood of a student repeating a primary grade is observed at the student level, 28% at the school level, and 19% at the system level (Goos et al., 2013).

■ Figure IV.2.3 ■

Probability of students having repeated a grade, by students' socio-economic status (OECD average)

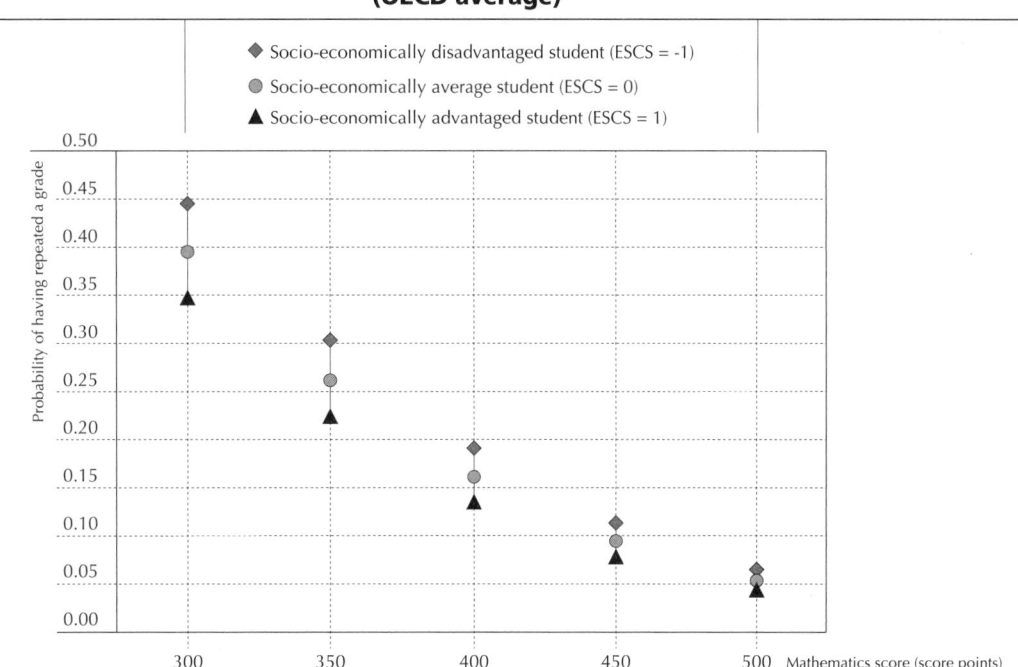

Notes: ESCS is the *PISA index of economic, social and cultural status.*
Students having repeated a grade refers to students who have repeated a grade in primary, lower secondary or upper secondary school.
Source: OECD, PISA 2012 Database, Table IV.2.3.
StatLink ⌗⌐ http://dx.doi.org/10.1787/888932957308

Students' grade and education levels

As a consequence of the variations in the age of starting primary school and/or in grade repetition, students in the same age group can be found in different grade and education levels. This is particularly important for PISA as participation is based on students' age.

As shown in Figure IV.2.2, 15-year-old students tend to be enrolled at similar grade levels in Iceland, Japan, Norway, Serbia, Malaysia, the United Kingdom, Korea and Sweden, while there are relatively greater variations in the grade levels

in which 15-year-olds in Colombia, Peru, Uruguay and Tunisia are enrolled. The modal grade for 15-year-old students depends on the school system: in PISA-participating countries it is usually grade 9, 10 or 11. Depending on the timing of the start of the academic year and the PISA data collection, in some systems, about an half of all 15-year-old students are in one grade and another half are in another grade either just above or just below. Across OECD countries, 74% of students are at the modal grade, 9% are in grades above the modal grade, and 17% are in grades below the modal grade. All 15-year-old students in Japan and Iceland, and over 95% of them in Norway, Serbia, Malaysia and the United Kingdom, are at the modal grade, while fewer than one in two students is in the modal grade in Costa Rica, Colombia, Brazil, Macao-China, Peru, Indonesia and the Netherlands (Table IV.2.4).

As 15-year-olds are enrolled in various grades, some of them are in lower secondary education while others are in upper secondary education. Across OECD countries, 46% of 15-year-old students are in lower secondary education and 54% are in upper secondary education. Over 99% of 15-year-old students in Iceland, Jordan, Romania, Lithuania, Spain, Finland, Norway, Denmark and Poland are in lower secondary education, while over 99% of 15-year-old students in Croatia, Japan, the United Kingdom and Montenegro are in upper secondary education (Figure IV.2.2 and Table IV.2.4).

HOW EDUCATION SYSTEMS ORGANISE SCHOOL PROGRAMMES

Students with different socio-economic status, different levels of achievement and different interests are found in every grade. School systems address this diversity in different ways. Some seek to adapt curricula so that students with different interests and academic preparation are exposed to a curriculum and pedagogy that is better suited to them. This type of stratification, referred to as "horizontal" stratification in this report, is the product of decisions made at the system level, such as offering the choice of general/academic and vocational programmes or basing entry into the school on academic achievement (Dupriez et al., 2008), or by decisions made at the school level, such as transferring students to other schools. Some schools group students based on their ability across classes. School-level policies are less relevant in systems with other types of grouping/sorting of students at the system level, as these education systems have already differentiated students to a large degree. The rationale behind using these differentiating mechanisms is to homogenise the student population so that its educational needs can be met more effectively. But there is some concern that tracking replicates existing social and economic inequities, as socio-economically disadvantaged students tend to be disproportionately grouped into lower tracks (Oakes, 2005). By contrast, other school systems seek to address the diversity in student populations by individualising education experiences within an established cohort of students over a longer period of time, and delay any type of stratification until the later years of secondary education or in higher education.

The number of study programmes and age of selection

In comprehensive school systems, all 15-year-old students follow the same programme, while in differentiated school systems, students are streamed into different programmes. Some of these programmes may be primarily academic, others offer primarily vocational components, and yet others may offer combinations of academic and vocational programmes (Kerckhoff, 2000; LeTendre et al., 2003). Differentiated systems must also decide at which age students will be sorted into these different programmes. Chapter 1 presents evidence that in countries and economies that sort students into different education programmes at an early age, the impact of students' socio-economic status on their performance is stronger than in systems that select and group students later. Education reforms in Poland shifted the age of selection to increase the amount of time students spend in comprehensive schools with evidence suggesting it has helped improve student performance in mathematics, reading and science (OECD, 2011a). Box IV.2.1 provides more details on Poland's trajectory in PISA and their recent education reforms.

On average across OECD countries, school systems begin selecting students for different programmes at the age of 14. However, this varies greatly across countries. Among OECD countries, the first age of selection varies from age 10 in Austria and Germany, to age 16 in Australia, Canada, Chile, Denmark, Finland, Iceland, New Zealand, Norway, Poland, Spain, Sweden, the United Kingdom and the United States. Among partner countries and economies, the first age of selection varies from around age 11 in Uruguay and 12 in Singapore, to age 16 in Jordan, Latvia, Lithuania and Peru (Figure IV.2.4 and Table IV.2.5).

The number of school types or distinct education programmes available to 15-year-old students also varies across countries. Among OECD countries, it varies from one distinct programme in Australia, Canada, Chile, Denmark, Estonia, Finland, Iceland, New Zealand, Norway, Poland, Spain, Sweden, the United Kingdom and the United States, to five or more programmes in the Czech Republic, the Netherlands and the Slovak Republic. Among partner countries and economies with available data, it ranges from one programme in Indonesia and Jordan and two programmes in Brazil, Colombia,

Hong Kong-China, Macao-China, Romania and Thailand, to five or more programmes in Montenegro, Uruguay, Croatia, Malaysia, Shanghai-China, the United Arab Emirates, Latvia and Lithuania (Figure IV.2.4 and Table IV.2.5).

In PISA, students were asked to report on the kind of programme in which they were enrolled. Then their responses were categorised according to programme orientation. As shown in Figure IV.2.4, across OECD countries, an average of 82% of 15-year-old students are enrolled in a programme with a general curriculum, 14% are enrolled in a programme with a pre-vocational or vocational curriculum, and 4% are in modular programmes that combine any or all of these characteristics. In Brazil, Denmark, Finland, Hong Kong-China, Iceland, Jordan, Liechtenstein, New Zealand, Norway, Peru, Qatar, Romania, Singapore, Tunisia and the United States, all 15-year-old students are in a general programme. In Serbia, Croatia, Austria, Montenegro and Slovenia, more than one in two students are enrolled in a vocational or pre-vocational programme. In Canada, all 15-year-olds, and in the Slovak Republic one out of four students, are enrolled in a modular programme (Table IV.2.6).

Admission and placement policies establish frameworks for selecting students for academic programmes and for streaming students according to career goals, educational needs and academic performance. In countries with large differences in student performance between programmes and schools or where socio-economic segregation is firmly entrenched because of residential segregation, admission and grouping policies have high stakes for parents and students. The most effective schools may be those more successful in attracting motivated students and in retaining good teachers; conversely, a "brain drain" of students and staff can undermine schools. Once admitted to school, students become members of a community of peers and adults and, as shown in Volume II, the socio-economic context of the school in which students are enrolled tends to be much more strongly related to student performance than students' individual socio-economic status.

In some school systems, the school catchment area determines admission into school. The school catchment area is used as a criterion because of: administrative responsibilities to ensure adequate capacity for students in those areas and plan for future needs; formal institutional areas, such as official communities or neighbourhoods that require separate education administration for legal, historical, or economic purposes; and deliberate isolation of populations due to racial, ethnic or socio-economic differences with other populations. According to principals' reports, on average across OECD countries, 41% of students are in schools where residence in a particular area is always considered as part of the criteria for admission. In Poland, the United States, Greece, Canada and Finland, more than two in three students are enrolled in such schools. By contrast, fewer than 10% of students in Belgium, Serbia, Slovenia, Macao-China, Peru, Croatia, Montenegro, Singapore, Mexico, Japan and Romania are enrolled in schools that always consider residence in a particular area for admission (Table IV.2.7). Among these countries and economies, over 94% of 15-year-old students are at upper secondary education in Croatia, Japan, Montenegro, Serbia, Singapore Slovenia and Greece, while 100% of 15-year-old students are at lower secondary education in Romania (Table IV.2.4).

Some school systems are highly selective and base admission on students' academic performance. Across OECD countries, 43% of students are in academically selective schools whose principals reported that at least "students' records of academic performance" or "recommendations of feeder schools" is always considered for admission. In the Netherlands, Croatia, Hong Kong-China, Japan, Thailand, Serbia, Viet Nam, Hungary, Singapore and Bulgaria, over 80% of students are in academically selective schools, while in Finland, Spain, Norway, Greece, Sweden, Denmark, Argentina, Poland and Lithuania, fewer than 20% of students are enrolled in such schools (Figure IV.2.4 and Table IV.2.7).

As expected, systems in which schools tend to select their students based on residence in a particular area are generally less academically selective. However, in Switzerland and Liechtenstein, schools are selective according to both catchment area and students' academic performance and/or recommendations of feeder schools (Figure IV.2.5).

The criteria used for admitting students to schools differ between lower and upper secondary education in some school systems where lower and upper secondary education are not provided in the same school. Across OECD countries, an average of 49% of 15-year-old students in lower secondary education attend schools that use residence in a particular area as one of the criteria for admitting students, while 32% of 15-year-old students at the upper secondary level attend such schools. In contrast, academic selectivity is more prevalent at the upper secondary than the lower secondary level. Across OECD countries on average, 32% of lower secondary students attend schools whose principals reported that at least either "students' records of academic performance" or "recommendations of feeder schools" is always considered for admission, while 56% of upper secondary students attend such schools. The difference in academic selectivity between 15-year-old students at the lower and upper secondary levels is notable in Hungary, the Czech Republic, the Slovak Republic, Sweden, Bulgaria, Shanghai-China, Korea and Austria, where the difference is over 40 percentage points (Table IV.2.8).

■ Figure IV.2.4 [Part 1/2] ■

How students are grouped across and within schools (horizontal stratification)

	Number of education programmes available for students at age 15	Early selection (first age of selection in the education system)	Percentage of students who are enrolled in a programme whose curriculum is: ■ General ▢ Pre-vocational or vocational ■ Modular	Percentage of students in schools whose principals reported that "students' records of academic performance" or "recommendations of feeder schools" are considered for admission — At least one of these two factors is "always" considered
Australia	1	16		44
Austria	4	10		71
Belgium	4	12		27
Canada	1	16		39
Chile	1	16		39
Czech Republic	6	11		58
Denmark	1	16		15
Estonia	1	15		38
Finland	1	16		4
France	3	15		31
Germany	4	10		62
Greece	2	15		8
Hungary	3	11		85
Iceland	1	16		21
Ireland	4	15		27
Israel	2	15		56
Italy	4	14		66
Japan	2	15		94
Korea	3	14		67
Luxembourg	4	13		72
Mexico	3	15		51
Netherlands	7	12		97
New Zealand	1	16		59
Norway	1	16		7
Poland	1	16		19
Portugal	3	15		37
Slovak Republic	5	11		53
Slovenia	3	14		29
Spain	1	16		4
Sweden	1	16		10
Switzerland	4	12		73
Turkey	3	11		43
United Kingdom	1	16		28
United States	1	16		36
OECD average	3	14		43
Albania	3	15		60
Argentina	3	15		15
Brazil	2	15		21
Bulgaria	3	13		81
Colombia	2	15		43
Costa Rica	m	m		51
Croatia	5	14		96
Hong Kong-China	2	15		94
Indonesia	1	15		67
Jordan	1	16		36
Kazakhstan	m	m		46
Latvia	5	16		29
Liechtenstein	3	15		79
Lithuania	5	16		20
Macao-China	2	15		78
Malaysia	5	15		55
Montenegro	6	15		59
Peru	3	16		30
Qatar	4	15		50
Romania	2	14		35
Russian Federation	3	16		23
Serbia	m	m		87
Shanghai-China	5	15		53
Singapore	4	12		82
Chinese Taipei	3	15		50
Thailand	2	15		88
Tunisia	m	m		51
United Arab Emirates	5	15		70
Uruguay	6	11		27
Viet Nam	4	15		87

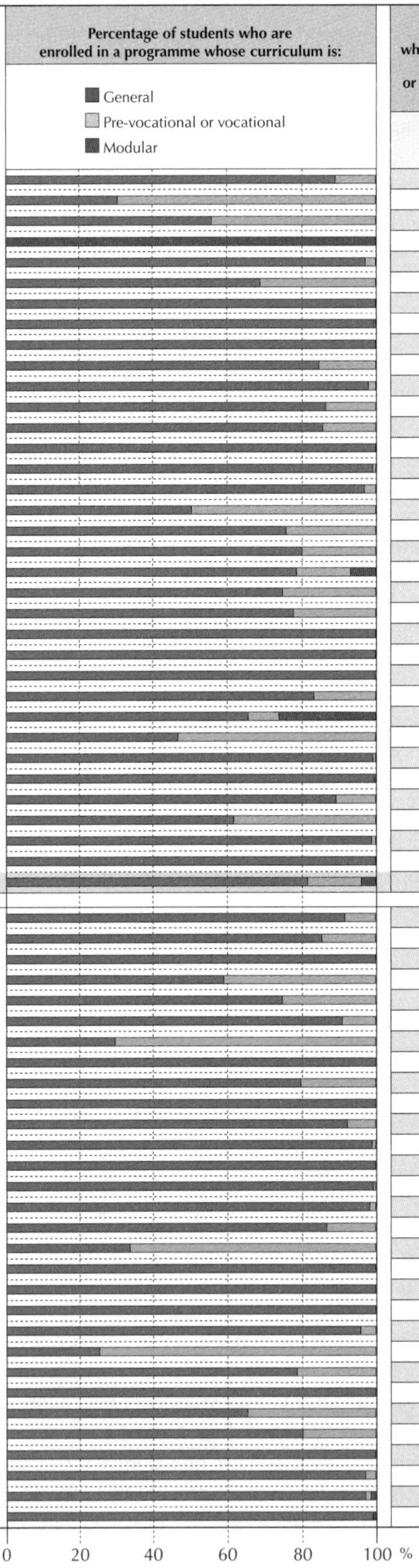

0   20   40   60   80   100 %

Source: OECD, PISA 2012 Database, Tables IV.2.5, IV.2.6, IV.2.7, IV.2.9 and IV.2.11.
StatLink ⬛ http://dx.doi.org/10.1787/888932957308

 WHAT MAKES SCHOOLS SUCCESSFUL? RESOURCES, POLICIES AND PRACTICES – VOLUME IV

■ Figure IV.2.4 [Part 2/2] ■

How students are grouped across and within schools (horizontal stratification)

Percentage of students in schools whose principal reported that "mathematics classes study similar content, but at different levels of difficulty" and/or "different classes study different content or sets of mathematics topics that have different levels of difficulty"

■ No ability grouping for any class
□ One form of grouping for some classes
■ One form of grouping for all classes

	Percentage of students in schools whose principal reported that a student in the national modal grade for 15-year-olds would "very likely" be transferred to another school because of "low academic achievement", "behavioural problems" or "special learning needs"
OECD	
Australia	3
Austria	65
Belgium	28
Canada	5
Chile	23
Czech Republic	10
Denmark	2
Estonia	4
Finland	0
France	17
Germany	6
Greece	25
Hungary	15
Iceland	1
Ireland	2
Israel	20
Italy	17
Japan	6
Korea	26
Luxembourg	19
Mexico	20
Netherlands	10
New Zealand	4
Norway	1
Poland	4
Portugal	4
Slovak Republic	24
Slovenia	22
Spain	3
Sweden	3
Switzerland	10
Turkey	27
United Kingdom	3
United States	4
OECD average	13
Partners	
Albania	10
Argentina	11
Brazil	15
Bulgaria	31
Colombia	15
Costa Rica	23
Croatia	17
Hong Kong-China	9
Indonesia	35
Jordan	43
Kazakhstan	9
Latvia	11
Liechtenstein	46
Lithuania	3
Macao-China	36
Malaysia	26
Montenegro	10
Peru	19
Qatar	11
Romania	22
Russian Federation	5
Serbia	20
Shanghai-China	7
Singapore	2
Chinese Taipei	28
Thailand	14
Tunisia	24
United Arab Emirates	16
Uruguay	4
Viet Nam	20

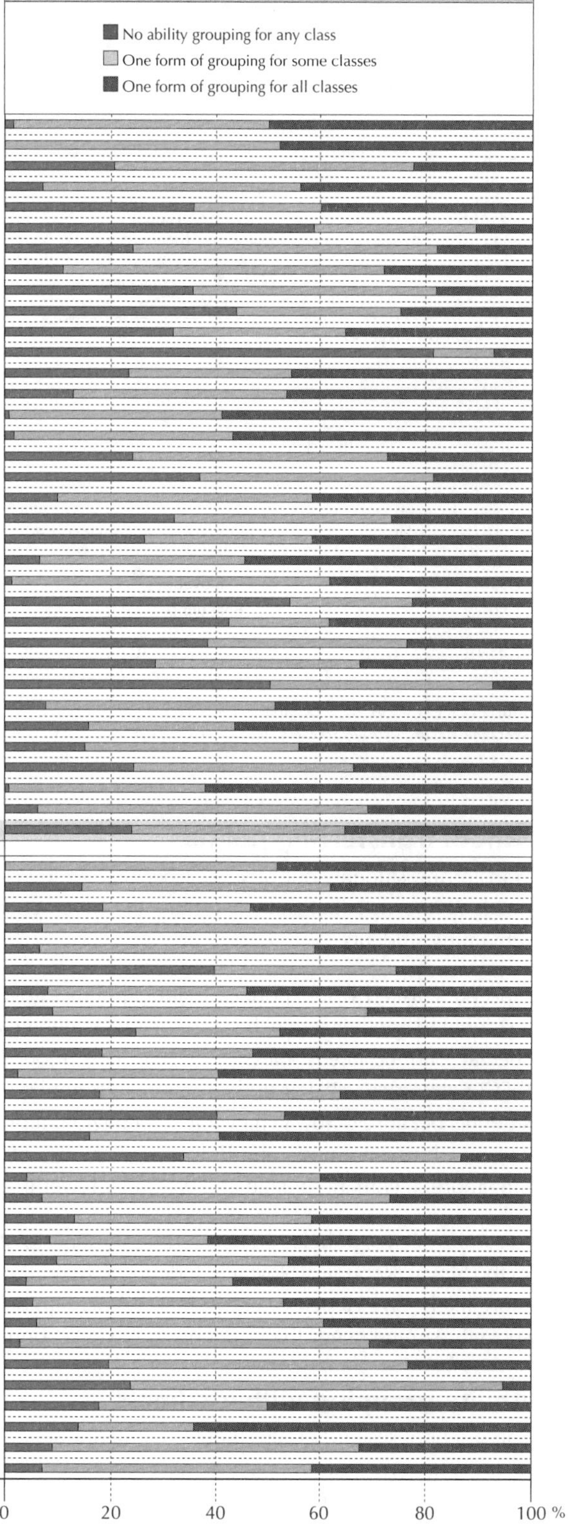

Source: OECD, PISA 2012 Database, Tables IV.2.5, IV.2.6, IV.2.7, IV.2.9 and IV.2.11.
StatLink ▩▩ http://dx.doi.org/10.1787/888932957308

■ Figure IV.2.5 ■
School admissions policies

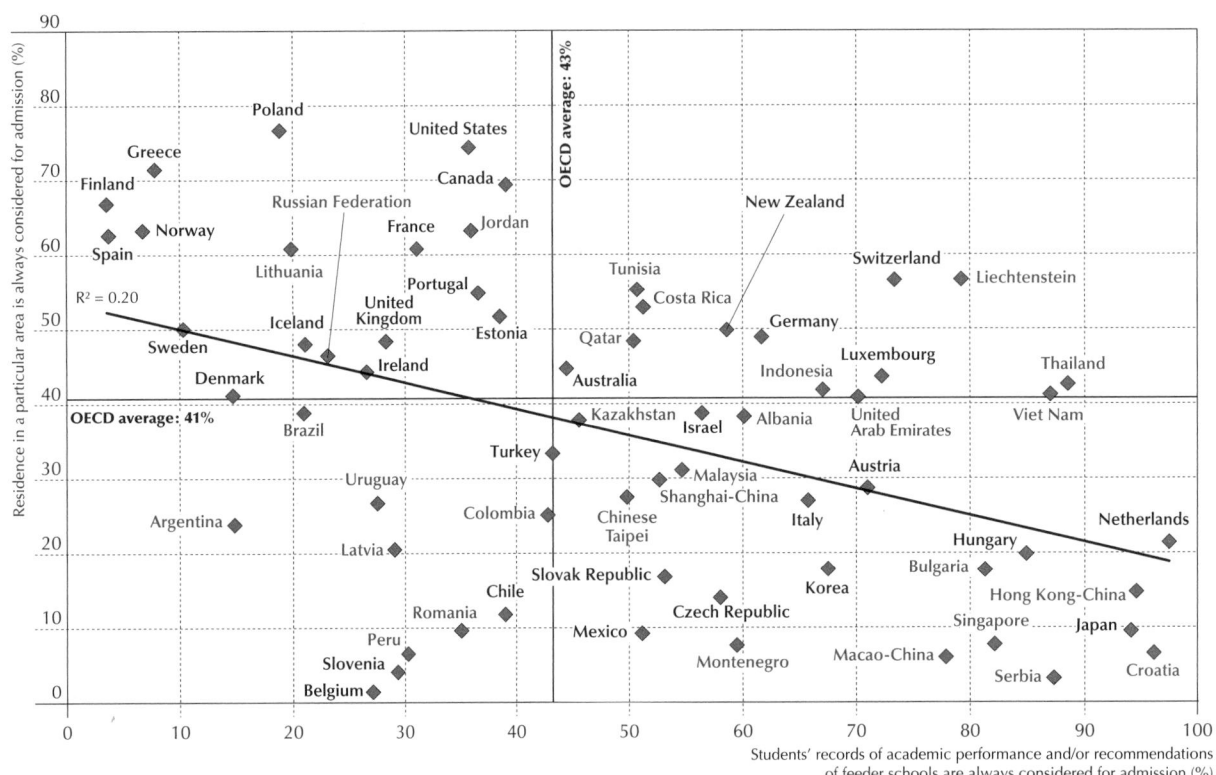

Source: OECD, PISA 2012 Database, Table IV.2.7.
StatLink ⌐ᵢₛ⌐ http://dx.doi.org/10.1787/888932957308

School transferring policies

Transferring students out of school because of low academic achievement, behavioural problems or special learning needs is one way that schools reduce the heterogeneity in the learning environment and facilitate instruction for the remaining students.

PISA 2012 asked school principals about policies governing student transfers, namely about the likelihood of transferring a student to another school because of low academic achievement, high academic achievement, behavioural problems, special learning needs, parents' or guardians' request, or other reasons. As shown in Figure IV.2.4, on average across OECD countries, 13% of students attend a school whose principal reported that the school would "very likely" transfer students because of low achievement, behavioural problems or special learning needs. In Austria, Liechtenstein, Jordan, Macao-China, Indonesia and Bulgaria, over 30% of students attend such schools, while in Finland, Norway, Iceland, Singapore, Denmark, Ireland and Australia, fewer than 3% of students attend such schools (Table IV.2.9).

In some systems, policies on transferring students to other schools differ between lower and upper secondary education. In the Slovak Republic, Slovenia, Indonesia, Israel, Hungary, Italy and Korea, students in upper secondary education are more likely – by 10 percentage points or more – to be transferred because of low achievement, behavioural problems or special learning needs than students in lower secondary education (Table IV.2.10).

Ability grouping within schools

Some school systems group students within the schools they attend. The rationale behind this practice is much the same as for other types of grouping or selecting of students, namely to better meet the students' needs by creating a more homogeneous learning environment and facilitating instruction. Because individual schools are nested within a broader organisation, the uses of ability grouping within schools is partly determined by the homogeneity/heterogeneity that results from other forms of stratification, such as school-admittance policies, grade retention or transfer policies.

Students can be grouped by ability across or within classes. Across OECD countries, 67% of students attend schools whose principal reported that students in mathematics classes study similar content, but at different levels of difficulty at least in some classes, and 54% of students attend schools whose principal reported that mathematics classes vary in content and level of difficulty at least in some classes. In sum, three out of four students are in schools whose principals reported that the school uses one of these forms of between-class ability grouping in at least some mathematics classes. Over 95% of students in Albania, the United Kingdom, Ireland, New Zealand, Australia, Israel, Kazakhstan, Singapore, the Russian Federation and Malaysia attend schools where students are grouped by ability across classes, while fewer than 50% of students in Greece, Austria, the Czech Republic, Norway and Slovenia attend such schools (Table IV.2.11).

Students are sometimes grouped according to ability within classes. Across OECD countries, 49% of students attend schools whose principal reported that students are grouped by ability within their mathematics classes at least in some classes, while 79% of students attend schools whose teachers use pedagogy suitable for students with diverse abilities at least in some classes. In Israel, the United Kingdom, New Zealand, Ireland, Australia, Singapore, the Russian Federation and Iceland, over 80% of students are in schools whose principals reported that students are grouped by ability within their mathematics classes. In these countries, students are also grouped across classes based on ability: 87% to 99% of students in these countries are in schools where principals reported having ability grouping across classes, at least in some classes. By contrast, in Greece, Montenegro, Uruguay, Turkey, Tunisia, Poland and Brazil, within-class ability grouping is not so common: in these countries, fewer than 20% of students are in schools whose principal reported having within-class ability grouping in mathematics classes, while no consistent pattern in between-class ability grouping is observed in these countries. In Uruguay and Montenegro, around 92% of students are in schools with between-class ability grouping; in Tunisia and Brazil around 82% of students are in such schools; in Turkey, 76% are in such schools; in Poland, 58% of students are; and in Greece, 19% of students are in such schools (Table IV.2.11).

Box IV.2.1. **Improving in PISA: Poland**

Poland has been building on progress made between PISA 2000 and PISA 2009 and continued to improve its mathematics, reading and science performance in 2012. Since 2003, mathematics performance has improved at an annual rate of 2.6 points, moving from a below-OECD-average score of 490 in 2003 to an above-OECD-average score of 518 in 2012. The country has reduced the percentage of low-performing students from 22% to 14% and increased that of high performers from 10% to 17% in a period of nine years. Improvement in mathematics is observed throughout the performance distribution, as both low-achieving and high-achieving students have improved at a similar rate. This improvement in average performance, coupled with an improvement among both high- and low-achieving students as well as top and low performers is also observed in reading (mean reading performance improved by an average of 2.8 points per year since 2000) and science (mean science performance improved by an average of 4.6 points per year since 2006). Because improvements in mathematics performance have touched all students alike, there has been no change in the relationship between students' socio-economic status and their mathematics performance. However, the overall improvement has meant that disadvantaged students have greater chances of being resilient and beating the odds against them: in 2003, 5.3% of students were considered resilient; by 2012, 7.7% of students were.

Education policy in Poland has been marked by two recent waves of reform: the structural reform of 1999 and the curricular and examination reform of 2009. In 1998, the Ministry of Education presented the outline of a reform agenda to raise the level of education by increasing the number of people with secondary and higher-education qualifications, ensure equal education opportunities, and support improvements in the quality of education. The reform was also part of a broader set of changes, including reform of the national administration that reduced the number of administrative regions from 49 to 16, health care reform and pension-system reform.

The education reform envisaged changes in the structure of the education system; giving more responsibility for education to local authorities; reorganising the school network; modifying administration and supervision methods; changing the curriculum; introducing a new central examination system with independent student assessments; reorganising school finances through local government subsidies; and offering new teacher incentives, such as alternative promotion paths and a revised remuneration system.

...

The structural changes resulted in a new type of school: the lower secondary "gymnasium", which offered the same general education programme to all students and became a symbol of the reform. The belief was that the lower secondary gymnasia would allow Poland to raise the level of education, particularly in rural areas. The previous structure, comprising eight years of primary school followed by four or five years of secondary school or a three-year basic vocational school, was replaced by a system described as 6+3+3. This meant that education at primary school was reduced from eight to six years. After completing primary school, a pupil would then continue his or her education in a comprehensive, three-year lower secondary school. Thus, the period of general education, based on a common core curriculum and equal standards for all students, was extended by one year. Only after completing three years of lower secondary education would the student move on to a three- or four-year upper secondary school that provided access to higher education or to a three-year basic vocational school. Coincidentally, students' experience in schools has shifted towards common exposure to content and content difficulty. In 2003, 19% of 15-year-old lower-secondary students who took part in PISA attended schools whose principal reported that students were not placed in different groups for mathematics classes (either through groups within a particular class or between different classes in the same school). In 2012, 42% of 15-year-old lower-secondary students attended schools whose principal reported so, further highlighting the increasing degree to which Polish students are incorporating a comprehensive approach to mathematics instruction, in particular, and teaching, in general.

A core curriculum and new assessments

In parallel, the concept of a core curriculum was adopted. This gave schools extensive autonomy to create their own curricula within a pre-determined general framework, balancing the three goals of education: imparting knowledge, developing skills and shaping attitudes. The curricular reform was designed not only to change the content of school-based education and to encourage innovative teaching methods, but also to change the teaching philosophy and culture of schools. Instead of passively following the instructions of the education authorities, teachers were expected to develop their own teaching styles, which would be tailored to the needs of their students.

Introducing a curricular reform that encouraged autonomy required implementing a system for collecting information and monitoring the education system at the same time. Under this new system, each stage of education ends with a standardised national assessment (in primary education) and examination (in lower and upper secondary education). These assessments and examinations provide students, parents and teachers with feedback; policy makers at the national, regional and local levels can also use the results of the assessment to monitor the performance of the school system. The results from the lower secondary examination are used, together with students' marks, for admission to upper secondary schools. The final upper secondary exam also serves as an entrance exam for universities. The national assessment at the end of primary school and lower secondary examinations were first administered in 2002. The *Matura* exam was first administered as an external national examination in 2005. All of these examinations are organised, set and marked by the central examination board and regional examination boards, the new institutions that had been set up as part of the reform.

Introducing the national assessment and examination system not only provided an opportunity to monitor learning outcomes, it also changed incentives for students and teachers. It sent a clear signal to students that their success depended directly on their externally evaluated outcomes, and made it possible to assess teachers and schools on a comparable scale across the whole country. It also provided local governments with information on the outcomes of schools that were now under their organisational and financial responsibility.

After the reform, local governments became an even more important part of the Polish school system. School funds were transferred to local governments using a per-pupil formula. Those funds now constitute a large share of their budgets. The reform also introduced a new system of teacher professional development and teacher appraisal. Initially, many teachers upgraded their levels of education and professional skills to meet those new requirements.

Studies suggest that the 1999 structural reforms helped reduce the differences in performance between schools and helped improve the performance of the lowest-achieving students. For example, the between-school variation in reading performance decreased substantially between 2000 and 2009. Additional analyses suggest that the reform improved outcomes for students who would have ended up in basic vocational schools under the old system, but were given a chance to acquire more general skills in newly created lower secondary schools (OECD, 2011a). Undoubtedly, Polish students in 2012 perform at higher levels in PISA than students did in 2003; they are, however, less likely to feel they belong at school, to hold positive attitudes towards school or to show intrinsic or instrumental motivation to learn mathematics.

...

Building on earlier reforms

Poland's reforms have also been flexible, adjusting to the needs of a more diverse student population and increased demand to participate in secondary and tertiary education. In this context, in 2009 the Ministry of National Education expanded the reforms initiated in the late 1990s by modifying the national core curriculum for general education and school vocational-training programmes. The new curriculum shifted the focus from the narrow, subject-related requirements to more general, transversal skills and competencies. The new curriculum would focus on experiments, scientific inquiry, problem solving, reasoning and collaboration. National standardised assessments and examinations were adjusted accordingly. The modified lower secondary examination, implemented for the first time in 2012, is the culmination of a three-year information campaign that communicated this new curricular focus to promote changes in teaching practice. The new regulations provided for further extension of schools' and teachers' autonomy. The new framework curriculum requires schools to develop their own sets of programmes instead of using the programmes (and textbooks) from the list accepted by the Ministry. School heads were given flexibility in managing, within a three-year cycle, the instruction time defined for subjects in the curriculum framework. They only have to ensure that the outcomes defined in the national curriculum are attained.

The Ministry granted more autonomy to schools and teachers, while maintaining a system of accountability via standardised assessments and examinations. The system of quality assurance, evaluation and accountability were modified as well. In 2009, the Ministry of Education defined three complementary functions of school supervision: evaluation, control and support. External evaluation is conducted by inspectors and is based on a school self-evaluation process as well as on evidence gathered from documents and the opinions of teachers, students, parents and other stakeholders (local employers, community and administration). Value-added models are used to a greater extent, and schools can use a web-based platform to compare improvements in student performance with other schools and against regional or national benchmarks. A value-added model approach promotes equal opportunities as the analysis focuses on student and school progress and not on the achievement level, so even schools with the lowest-performing students can demonstrate the quality of their teaching.

PISA offers an opportunity to follow the trajectory of the reform by measuring the performance of the age groups that were affected by the reform in different ways. The first group, those assessed in 2000, was not affected by the reform. The group of 15-year-olds assessed in 2003 had started primary school in the former system, but attended the new lower secondary gymnasia. Those students all had the same curricula and were not divided into different school types. The students covered by PISA 2006 had been part of the reformed education system for most of their school career, while those assessed in 2009 and 2012 had been part of that system for their entire school career. In addition, students assessed in 2012 also benefitted from the curricular reform of 2009.

Source:
OECD (2011a), "The Impact of the 1999 Education Reform in Poland", *OECD Education Working Papers*, No. 49, OECD Publishing.

SOCIAL AND ACADEMIC INCLUSION AND VERTICAL AND HORIZONTAL STRATIFICATION

As discussed above, school systems have developed different ways to manage the diversity of the student population. Analysis of PISA data can show how – and whether – these various forms of vertical and horizontal stratification are negatively associated with equity, as discussed in Chapter 1, and how these are associated each other and with the socio-economic profiles of systems. Caution is advised, however, when interpreting these results. The results do not imply any causality between the indicators, but merely show that there are some commonalities or differences. In addition, variables that are omitted in this analysis might affect the observed relationships.

As expected, systems where 15-year-old students are distributed across a wider range of grades tend to have higher rates of grade repetition (across OECD countries, the correlation coefficient is 0.71). These more vertically differentiated systems also tend to be highly differentiated horizontally, which means that they tend to have more programmes available to 15-year-old students, (r=0.50) and they select and sort students in the students' early years at school (r=0.45) (Figure IV.2.6 and Table IV.2.12).

The indicators measuring horizontal stratification between schools are inter-correlated. Systems with more education programmes available to 15-year-old students tend to select and sort students at the earlier stage of their education (r=0.73 across OECD countries), also tend to have more students in vocational or pre-vocational programmes (r=0.54) and have more students in academically selective schools (r=0.60). Systems where students are selected and sorted early tend to have more students in vocational or pre-vocational programmes (r=0.50) and have more students in academically selective schools (r=0.53). These four indicators are also related to another indicator measuring horizontal stratification between schools. Across OECD countries, systems with more education programmes tend to have a greater incidence of school transfers (r=0.41). Systems in which more students are enrolled in vocational programmes tend to have a greater incidence of school transfers (r=0.75) as do systems in which students are selected and sorted early tend (r=0.53) and systems with more academically selective schools (r=0.32) (Figure IV.2.6 and Table IV.2.12).

There is no consistent pattern in the relationship between vertical stratification and ability grouping mathematics classes within schools. By contrast, indicators of between-school horizontal stratification are related to ability grouping within schools. For example, systems with more students in vocational or pre-vocational programmes tend to have less ability grouping within schools (r=-0.48 across OECD countries).

■ Figure IV.2.6 ■
System-level correlation between indicators of stratification

Correlation coefficients between two relevant indicators

Correlation coefficients range from -1.00 (i.e. a perfect negative linear association) to +1.00 (i.e. a perfect positive linear association). When a correlation coefficient is 0, there is no linear relationship between two indicators.

Legend: ☐ Across OECD countries ☐ Across all participating countries and economies

| | | | Vertical stratification | Horizontal stratification — Between schools | | | | | Within schools |
		Math. perf.	Inequity	Variability in students' grade levels	Number of educational tracks	Prevalence of vocational and pre-vocational programmes	Early selection	Academic selectivity	School transfer rates	Ability grouping for all mathematics classes
Mathematics performance				*-0.31*	0.10	0.04	0.10	0.20	-0.17	-0.07
Mathematics performance — Inequity				**0.56**	0.26	0.00	*0.32*	0.15	0.29	-0.10
Vertical stratification — Variability in students' grade levels		**-0.36**	0.26		**0.50**	0.20	**0.45**	0.21	*0.29*	0.04
Horizontal stratification — Between schools — Number of educational tracks		0.04	0.20	**0.26**		**0.54**	**0.73**	**0.60**	**0.41**	-0.13
Horizontal stratification — Between schools — Prevalence of vocational and pre-vocational programmes		0.09	-0.01	-0.12	**0.39**		**0.50**	**0.38**	**0.75**	**-0.48**
Horizontal stratification — Between schools — Early selection		0.12	**0.42**	0.16	**0.49**	0.28		**0.53**	**0.53**	-0.17
Horizontal stratification — Between schools — Academic selectivity		0.15	-0.09	0.05	**0.38**	0.37	0.28		*0.32*	0.08
Horizontal stratification — Between schools — School transfer rates		-0.19	0.05	0.16	0.09	0.37	0.20	**0.30**		-0.32
Within schools — Ability grouping for all mathematics classes		**-0.25**	-0.17	0.08	0.02	**-0.30**	*-0.22*	-0.02	-0.17	

Notes: Correlation coefficients that are statistically significant at the 5% level (p < 0.05) are indicated in bold and those at the 10% level (p < 0.10) are in italics.

Inequity refers to variation in mathematics performance explained by the *PISA index of economic, social and cultural status of students*. Correlations with mathematics performance and inequity are partial correlation coefficients after accounting for per capita GDP.

Ability grouping for all mathematics classes is the system-level percentage of students in schools whose principal reports that students are grouped by ability in all classes.

Source: OECD, PISA 2012 Database, Tables IV.1.1 and IV.2.12.

StatLink ᔐᔐ http://dx.doi.org/10.1787/888932957308

As Figure IV.2.6 shows, some of these stratification methods are interrelated. In order to determine the extent to which the various methods of stratification are associated with the social and academic profiles of school systems, PISA developed three indices: an *index of vertical stratification*; an *index of between-school horizontal stratification;*[2] and an *index of ability grouping within schools*. The *index of vertical stratification* is based on the degree of variation in 15-year-old students' grade levels in the system, which also reflects the different starting ages for schooling and the prevalence of grade repetition. The *index of between-school horizontal stratification* is based on five interrelated indicators of horizontal stratification between schools. The *index of ability grouping within schools* is based on the prevalence of within-school ability grouping across the school system (Table IV.2.16). All of these indices are standardised.[3]

Countries and economies in the top right quadrant in Figure IV.2.7 are those that have higher levels of vertical and horizontal (between-school) stratification than the OECD average. Countries and economies in the bottom left quadrant in Figure IV.2.7 are those that have lower levels of vertical and horizontal (between school) stratification than the OECD average.

■ Figure IV.2.7 ■

Vertical and horizontal stratification

▲ Level of within-school stratification **above** the OECD average

◆ Level of within-school stratification **below** the OECD average

Source: OECD, PISA 2012 Database, Table IV.2.16.
StatLink ᴍˢᴾ http://dx.doi.org/10.1787/888932957308

Each of the three stratification indices is then compared with various socio-economic and academic profiles of the school systems. The socio-economic profile includes the variation in students' socio-economic status within the system, and the level of social inclusion in the system, which indicates how much of the variation in students' socio-economic status is attributable to differences within schools. The academic profile includes the variation in students' mathematics performance within a system, and the level of academic inclusion in the system, which indicates how much of the variation in students' performance in mathematics is attributable to differences within schools.

As shown in Figure IV.2.8, the degree of stratification is associated with different aspects of the socio-economic and academic profile of the system. Systems with a greater degree of vertical stratification also tend to have students from more diverse socio-economic status (r=0.59 for OECD countries and r=0.57 for all countries and economies) and tend to have lower levels of social inclusion (r=-0.43 for OECD countries and r=-0.43 for all participating countries and economies) (Table IV.2.13).

Across OECD countries, systems that use more between-school horizontal stratification tend to have lower levels of socio-economic inclusion (r=-0.36), greater variation in student mathematics performance (r=0.34), and lower levels of academic inclusion (r=-0.83). The picture is similar when including partner countries and economies (r=-0.71). In contrast, the degree of within-school horizontal stratification in a system does not seem to be consistently associated with the system's socio-economic and academic profile (Figure IV.2.8 and Table IV.2.13).

■ Figure IV.2.8 ■

System-level correlation between indices of stratification and student characteristics

		Index of vertical stratification	Index of horizontal stratification (between schools)	Index of horizontal stratification (within schools)
OECD countries	Variation in student socio-economic status (standard deviation of ESCS)	**0.59**	0.11	-0.02
	Socio-economic inclusion index (1-rho)	**-0.43**	**-0.36**	0.03
	Variation in mathematics performance (standard deviation)	-0.03	*0.34*	0.06
	Academic inclusion index (1-rho)	-0.23	**-0.83**	0.19
All participating countries and economies	Variation in student socio-economic status (standard deviation of ESCS)	**0.57**	0.06	-0.05
	Socio-economic inclusion index (1-rho)	**-0.43**	-0.20	0.05
	Variation in mathematics performance (standard deviation)	*-0.21*	*0.21*	-0.14
	Academic inclusion index (1-rho)	*-0.24*	**-0.71**	0.10

Notes: Correlation coefficients that are statistically significant at the 5% level (p < 0.05) are indicated in bold and those at the 10% level (p < 0.10) are in italic.
ESCS refers to the *PISA index of economic, social and cultural status*.
Source: OECD, PISA 2012 Database, Table IV.2.13.
StatLink http://dx.doi.org/10.1787/888932957308

HOW SYSTEMS' GROUPING AND SELECTING OF STUDENTS IS RELATED TO STUDENTS' INSTRUMENTAL MOTIVATION

A student's aspiration can be defined as the "ability to identify and set goals for the future, while being inspired in the present to work toward those goals" (Quaglia and Cobb, 1996). Existing research on the impact of stratification on students' educational aspirations mainly focuses on the goal-setting aspects of aspiration. These studies used students' reports on the level of education they expected to attain at the end of their formal schooling as a measure of educational aspiration. They showed that in highly differentiated systems, the impact of a students' socio-economic status on his or her educational goals is stronger than in less differentiated systems (Buchmann and Dalton, 2002; Buchmann and Park, 2009; Monseur and Lafontaine, 2012). In highly differentiated systems, socio-economically disadvantaged students tend to be grouped into less academically orientated tracks or schools, and this has an impact on their educational aspirations, possibly because of the stigma associated with expectations of lower performance among students enrolled in these tracks and schools, or because less – and often poorer quality – resources are allocated to these schools.

In PISA 2012, students were asked about the extent to which they are motivated to work towards their goals. This is measured by students' instrumental motivation for mathematics. Both an *index of instrumental motivation for mathematics* and an *adjusted index of instrumental motivation for mathematics* are used in the analysis. Box IV.2.2 provides a description of these indices.

Box IV.2.2. **PISA index of instrumental motivation**

An *index of instrumental motivation for mathematics* is based on students' responses ("strongly agree", "agree", "disagree" or "strongly disagree") to the following four statements:

- Making an effort in mathematics is worth it because it will help me in the work that I want to do later on.
- Learning mathematics is worthwhile for me because it will improve my career prospects.
- Mathematics is an important subject for me because I need it for what I want to study later on.
- I will learn many things in mathematics that will help me get a job.

This index is scaled so that OECD countries have an average of 0 and a standard deviation of 1. Higher values on the index indicate greater student motivation. In order to allow for international comparisons, students' responses to these questions are also adjusted based on their responses to an anchoring vignette (see Annex A6).

Students tend to report their self-beliefs, motivation and attitudes within the context of what they expect to achieve. For example, if some schools expect their students to attain minimum performance standards and they are given fairly easy mathematics tasks, students would tend to report that they think they are good at mathematics. But if students want to be admitted into a very competitive university, they would tend to report that they are not good at mathematics unless they have shown excellent performance in very difficult mathematics classes. Without having information on the goals that students set for themselves, and the expectations that schools, teachers, parents and the students themselves have, it is difficult to compare differences in motivation between subgroups of students. Therefore, this section focuses solely on systems' overall level of students' motivation.

As shown in Figure IV.2.9, a negative relationship is observed between the levels of students' motivation and the degree to which systems sort and group students into different schools and/or programmes. In the systems that separate students into different schools or programmes more, students tend to report less instrumental motivation for mathematics than students in systems with less horizontal stratification between schools (Table IV.2.14). This relationship is observed for both non-adjusted and adjusted indices, across both OECD and partner countries and economies. This relationship is observed even after accounting for systems' overall performance levels (Table IV.2.15). In the highly stratified systems, the variation in students' motivation is not necessarily greater (see correlations for the standard deviation for the index in Table IV.2.14). Both unmotivated and motivated students reported less motivation than those in less stratified systems (see correlations for the 10th and 90th percentiles of the index in Table IV.2.14).

■ Figure IV.2.9 ■
Students' motivation and horizontal stratification

[Scatter plot: Adjusted index of instrumental motivation for mathematics (mean index) on the y-axis (ranging from -0.8 to 0.6) versus Index of horizontal differentiation between schools (mean index) on the x-axis (ranging from -1.2 to 2.4). Countries plotted include United States, United Kingdom, Australia, New Zealand, Colombia, Albania, Shanghai-China, Iceland, Peru, Singapore, Canada, Kazakhstan, Mexico, Costa Rica, Denmark, Ireland, Portugal, Viet Nam, United Arab Emirates, Sweden, Brazil, Israel, Uruguay, Norway, Chile, Tunisia, Finland, Estonia, Latvia, Malaysia, Liechtenstein, Lithuania, Thailand, Russian Federation, Jordan, Macao-China, Germany, Spain, Argentina, Greece, Switzerland, Czech Republic, Netherlands, Indonesia, Hungary, Croatia, Serbia, Japan, Qatar, Korea, Italy, Bulgaria, Austria, Poland, Chinese Taipei, Belgium, Turkey, France, Luxembourg, Hong Kong-China, Montenegro, Slovenia, Slovak Republic, Romania. Trend line with R² = 0.24.]

Source: OECD, PISA 2012 Database, Table IV.2.16.
StatLink ⊠⊡ http://dx.doi.org/10.1787/888932957308

When individual aspects of horizontal stratification between schools are examined:

- 15-year-old students in systems that offer a larger number of distinct education programmes tend to report less instrumental motivation than students in systems with fewer programmes or tracks (Table IV.2.14).

- Students in systems with larger proportions of students in vocational or pre-vocational programmes tend to report less instrumental motivation than students in systems with smaller proportions of students in non-academic programmes.

- Students in systems that group or select students early tend to report less instrumental motivation than students in systems that select students at a later age.

- Students in systems where a large proportion of students attends academically selective schools tend to report less instrumental motivation than students in systems where a smaller proportion of students attends selective schools.

- Students in systems where a large proportion of students attends schools that transfer problematic students to another school tend to report less instrumental motivation than students in systems that use school transfers less.

TRENDS IN STRATIFICATION SINCE PISA 2003

Since 39 of the 65 countries and economies that participated in PISA 2012 had also taken part in PISA 2003, it is possible to see how stratification practices evolved during the period. Overall, countries and economies that have high rates of grade repetition (i.e. where more than 20% of students have repeated a grade) have tended to reduce the rate of grade repetition. Trends in horizontal stratification show that, among OECD countries, a similar share of students attends schools where students are grouped by ability in at least some classes.[4]

The PISA 2003 and PISA 2012 questionnaires share many common questions, allowing for trends to be identified. However, some forms of stratification were not included in the PISA 2003 questionnaire, including transferring policies and students' programme orientation, so it is impossible to identify trends in these areas. Although questions relating to the use of academic criteria in selecting students into schools were asked in both questionnaires, the question and response options changed, rendering comparisons unreliable.

Grade repetition

Grade repetition is a policy through which school systems try to meet students' educational needs. By repeating a grade, slower students are given a second chance to master their coursework. Grade repetition also serves a motivational purpose because it is sometimes also used as a way to penalise students who do not perform well or do not put forth the necessary effort in school. With the prospect of repeating a grade – and thus not moving forward with their peers – students at risk may decide to put more effort into their studies to avoid retention. In practice, however, grade repetition has not been shown to benefit student learning (Allen et al., 2010; Alexander et al., 2003). Moreover, grade repetition may have adverse system-level effects as retained students are more likely to drop out, stay longer in the school system, or spend less time in the labour force (Rumberger, 2011; OECD, 2011b). As a result, some countries that had used grade repetition extensively have rejected that policy in favour of early support for struggling students.

The percentage of students who had repeated a grade in primary, lower secondary or upper secondary school fell significantly (by 0.5 percentage points) between 2003 and 2012 among the OECD countries that have comparable data. Yet not all school systems rely on grade repetition as a mode of stratification (Dupriez et al., 2008). Among the 13 countries and economies that had grade repetition rates of more than 20% in 2003, these rates dropped by an average of 3.5 percentage points during the period, and fell sharply in Tunisia, Mexico, France, Macao-China and Luxembourg. In 2012 in Tunisia, Mexico and France, the percentage of 15-year-olds who reported that they had repeated a grade in primary, lower secondary or upper secondary school was at least ten percentage points lower than it was in 2003. Grade repetition rates increased in Belgium and Spain during the same period. Among countries with lower overall repetition rates (those with repetition rates below 20% in 2003), an important increase in the grade repetition rate was observed in the Slovak Republic (moving from a grade repetition rate of 2.5% in 2003 to 7.6% in 2012) while an important reduction in the repetition rate was observed in Ireland (moving from a grade repetition rate of 14% in 2003 to 9% in 2012) (Figure IV.2.10 and Table IV.2.18).

Schools in the Russian Federation, Hungary, Australia, Greece and Mexico seem to have moved away from grade repetition. In these five countries and economies, the percentage of students attending schools that have no grade repetition increased by at least ten percentage points between 2003 and 2012. This increase could also signal that schools in these countries and economies have begun to differentiate themselves into those with high and low rates of grade repetition. However, this does not seem to be the case, as the percentage of students who attend schools with a large proportion of students who had repeated a grade has also shrunk (Table IV.2.19).

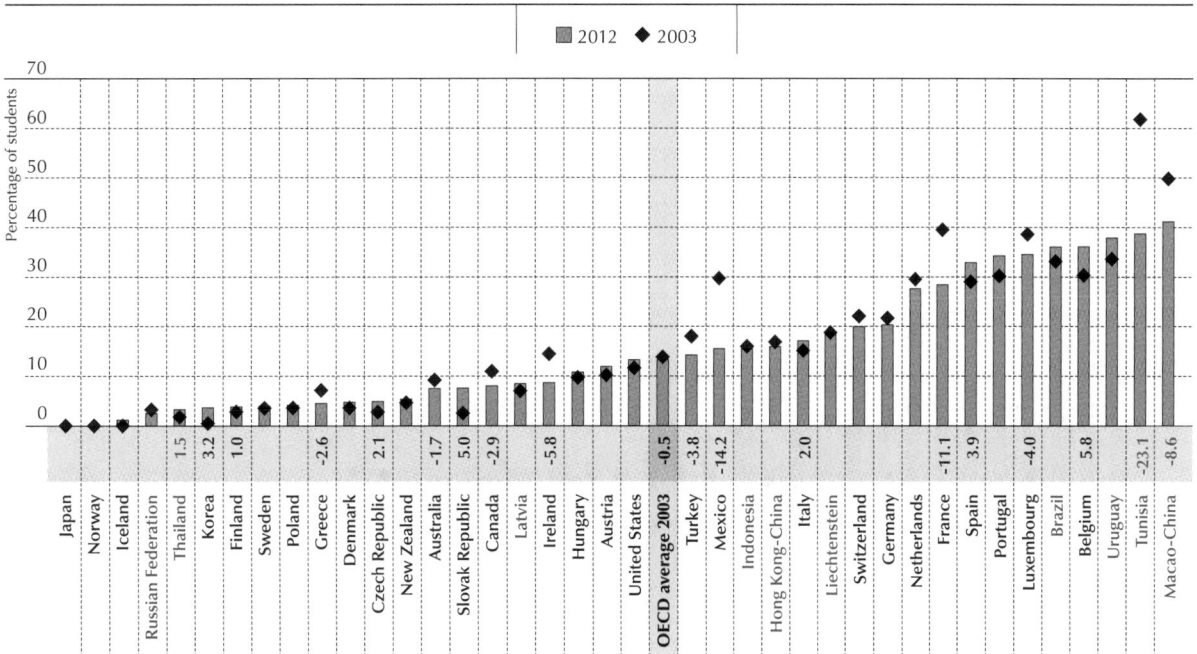

■ Figure IV.2.10 ■

Change between 2003 and 2012 in grade repetition rates

Percentage of students who repeated a grade in primary, lower secondary or upper secondary school

Notes: Only countries and economies with comparable data from PISA 2003 and PISA 2012 are shown.

The percentage-point difference in the share of students who repeated a grade in 2012 and 2003 (2012 - 2003) is shown above the country/economy name. Only statistically significant differences are shown.

OECD average 2003 compares only OECD countries with comparable grade repetition measures since 2003.

Countries and economies are ranked in ascending order of the percentage of students who reported having repeated a grade in primary, lower or upper secondary school in 2012.

Source: OECD, PISA 2012 Database, Table IV.2.18.

StatLink http://dx.doi.org/10.1787/888932957308

Ability grouping within schools

One form of horizontal stratification is ability grouping within the school. In organising mathematics instruction, for example, schools can differentiate their students according to their performance to create more homogeneous learning environments; other schools may opt to gather all students – irrespective of their academic performance – in the same classes to ensure that all students are granted the same opportunities to learn and thus have the same opportunities to succeed. Between 2003 and 2012, the share of students in schools where ability grouping is or is not practiced did not change, on average across countries with comparable data (Figure IV.2.11 and Table IV.2.21).

Although on average across OECD countries the share of students attending schools where no ability grouping is used for any class remained relatively stable, eight countries and economies saw an increase of more than ten percentage points in the share of students attending schools where ability grouping is used. In Tunisia and Germany, for example, the share of 15-year-old students attending schools that do not group by ability decreased by more than 20 percentage points; in Denmark, Japan, Hungary, Korea and Uruguay this share was reduced by more than 15 percentage points. Among these countries, different school systems shifted towards different forms of ability grouping. In Germany, for example, more students attended schools that group by ability in some classes or that group by ability in all classes in 2012 than in 2003. This could be the result of broader changes in Germany's school system. As described in Box II.3.2, the practice of between-school ability grouping that characterised German school system in the past has been replaced with a more comprehensive approach to schooling in which students with a greater diversity academic abilities are admitted to the same school. In order to adapt to these changes, some schools may choose to group students by ability in some or all classes. By contrast, in Denmark ability grouping in some classes has become more common, while the shares of students attending schools where ability grouping is not used in any class or is used in all classes has decreased. In Korea, ability grouping in all classes has become more common than both ability grouping in some classes and in no classes (Figure IV.2.11 and Table IV.2.21).

■ Figure IV.2.11 ■

Change between 2003 and 2012 in ability grouping

Percentage of students attending schools with no ability grouping for any mathematics class

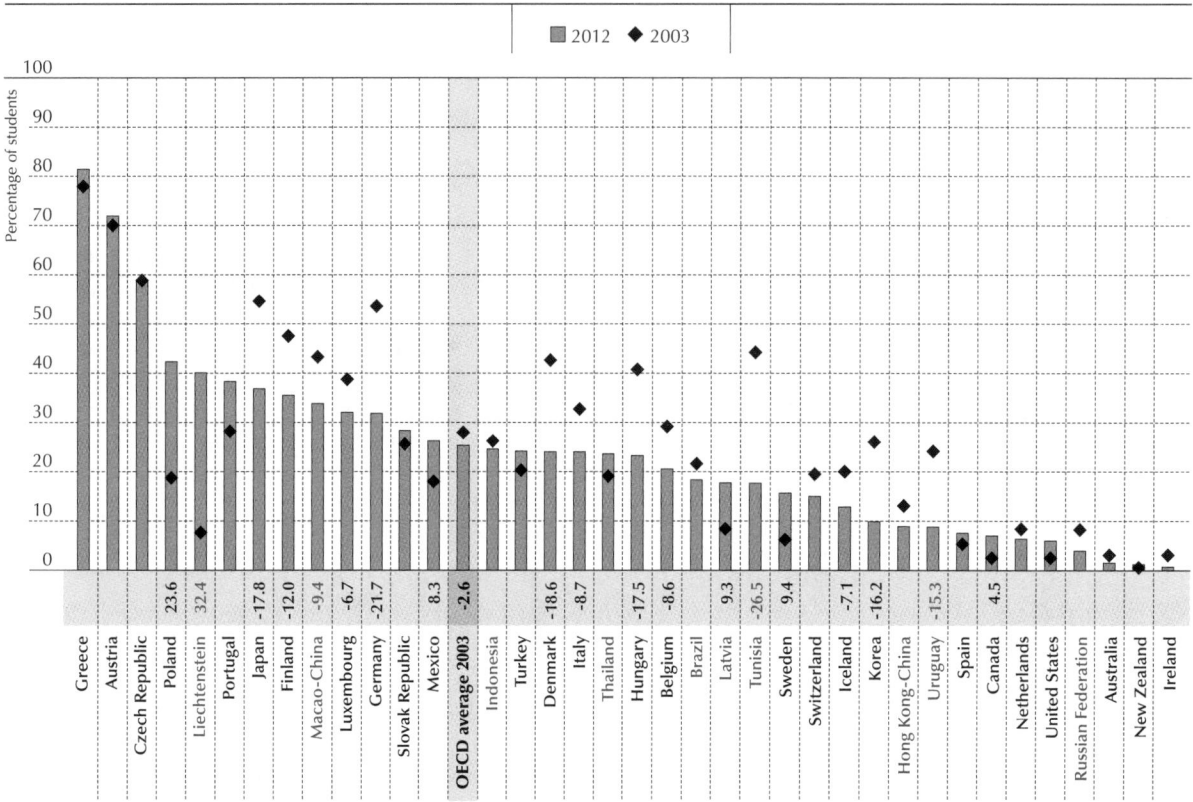

■ 2012 ◆ 2003

Country	value
Poland	23.6
Liechtenstein	32.4
Japan	-17.8
Finland	-12.0
Macao-China	-9.4
Luxembourg	-6.7
Germany	-21.7
Mexico	8.3
OECD average 2003	-2.6
Denmark	-18.6
Italy	-8.7
Hungary	-17.5
Belgium	-8.6
Latvia	9.3
Tunisia	-26.5
Sweden	9.4
Iceland	-7.1
Korea	-16.2
Uruguay	-15.3
Canada	4.5

Notes: Only countries and economies with comparable data from PISA 2003 and PISA 2012 are shown.
The percentage-point difference in the share of students in schools with no ability grouping in 2012 and 2003 (2012 - 2003) is shown above the country/economy name. Only statistically significant differences are shown.
OECD average 2003 compares only OECD countries with comparable ability grouping measures since 2003.
Countries and economies are ranked in descending order of the percentage of students who were in schools where no ability grouping in mathematics was used in 2012.
Source: OECD, PISA 2012 Database, Table IV.2.21.
StatLink ⟶ http://dx.doi.org/10.1787/888932957308

In seven countries and economies, a comprehensive approach to mathematics instruction within schools has become more common. In Poland, for example, ability grouping in some or all classes also became less common: the share of students in schools where no ability grouping is used for any class increased by 24 percentage points between 2003 and 2012. In Mexico there was a 29 percentage-point drop in the share of students in schools where ability grouping is practiced in some classes. These schools seem to have shifted either towards a comprehensive approach to mathematics (8 percentage-point increase) or to ability grouping in all classes (20 percentage-point increase) (Figure IV.2.11 and Table IV.2.21).

Notes

1. In some East Asian countries and economies (including Shanghai-China and Chinese Taipei where over 10% of students reported that they had started primary school at the age of eight or older), it is common to count age by starting at one when a child is born and adding an additional year for each subsequent lunar year.

2. This includes grouping students into different programmes.

3. Each of three variables contained in the *index of vertical stratification* is first standardised to have the OECD average as zero and the standard deviation across OECD countries as one. Then, these standardised variables are averaged to obtain the indicator. Similarly, each of five variables contained in the *index of between-school horizontal stratification* is standardised and then averaged. The *index of ability grouping within schools* is based on only one variable (i.e. the prevalence of within-school ability grouping across the school system), which is standardised to have the OECD average as zero and the standard deviation across OECD countries as one.

4. The PISA 2003 and PISA 2012 questionnaires share many common questions, allowing for trends to be identified. However, some forms of stratification were not included in the PISA 2003 questionnaire, including transferring policies and students' programme orientation, so it is impossible to identify trends in these areas. Although questions relating to the use of academic criteria in selecting students in schools were asked in both questionnaires, the question and response options changed, rendering comparisons unreliable. In 2003, question SC10 asked, for each admission criteria, "How much consideration is given to the following factors when students are admitted to your school?" offering the following response options "Prerequiste", "High Priority", "Considered" or "Not Considered". In 2012, question SC32 asked, "How often are the following factors considered when students are admitted to your school?" and offered "Never", "Sometimes" and "Always" as response options.

References

Alexander, K., D. Entwisle and **S. Dauber** (2003), *On the Success of Failure: A Reassessment of the Effects of Retention in the Early Grades,* Cambridge University Press, Cambridge.

Allen, C. S., et al. (2010), "Quality of Research Design Moderates Effects of Grade Retention on Achievement: A Meta-Analytic, Multi-Level Analysis", *Education Evaluation and Policy Analysis,* Vol. 31, No. 4, pp. 480-499.

Buchmann, C. and **B. Dalton** (2002), "Interpersonal Influences and Educational Aspirations in 12 Countries: The Importance of Institutional Context", *Sociology of Education*, pp. 99-122.

Buchmann, C. and **H. Park** (2009), "Stratification and the Formation of Expectations in Highly Differentiated Educational Systems", *Research in Social Stratification and Mobility*, Vol. 27, No. 4, pp. 245-267.

Dupriez, V., X. Dumay and **A. Vause** (2008), "How Do School Systems Manage Pupils' Heterogeneity?", *Comparative Education Review*, Vol. 52, No. 2, pp. 245-273.

Gomes-Neto, J. B. and **E. A. Hanushek** (1994), "Causes and Consequences of Grade Repetition: Evidence from Brazil", *Economic Development and Cultural Change*, Vol. 43, No. 1, pp. 117-148.

Goos, M., et al. (2013), "How Can Cross-Country Differences in the Practice of Grade Retention Be Explained? A Closer Look at National Educational Policy Factors", *Comparative Education Review*, Vol. 57, No. 1, pp. 54-84.

Graue, E. and **J. DiPerna** (2000), "Redshirting and Early Retention: Who Gets the 'Gift of Time' and What are Its Outcomes?", *American Educational Research Journal,* Vol. 37, No. 2, pp. 509-534.

Kerckhoff, A. (2000), "Transitions from School to Work in Comparative Perspective", in M. Hallinan (ed.), *Handbook of the Sociology of Education*, Springer, New York.

LeTendre, G., B. Hofer and **H. Shimizu** (2003), "What is Tracking? Cultural Expectation in the United States, Germany, and Japan", *American Educational Research Journal,* Vol. 40, No. 1, pp. 43-89.

Monseur, C. and **D. Lafontaine** (2012), "Structure des systèmes éducatifs et équité : un éclairage international", in M. Crahay (ed.), *Pour une école juste et efficace*, De Boeck, Brussels.

Oakes, J. (2005), *Keeping Track: Schools Structure Inequality Second Edition*, Yale University Press, New Haven and London.

OECD (2011a), "The Impact of the 1999 Education Reform in Poland", *OECD Education Working Papers*, No. 49, OECD Publishing. *http://dx.doi.org/10.1787/10.1787/5kmbjgkm1m9x-en*

OECD (2011b), "When Students Repeat Grades or Are Transferred Out of School: What Does it Mean for Education Systems?", *PISA in Focus*, No. 6, OECD Publishing. *http://dx.doi.org/10.1787/10.1787/5k9h362n5z45-en*

Quaglia, R. J. and **C. D. Cobb** (1996), "Toward a Theory of Student Aspirations", *Journal of Research in Rural Education,* Vol. 12, No.3, pp. 127-132.

Rumberger, R. (2011), *Why Students Drop Out of School and What Can Be Done About It*, Harvard University Press, Cambridge, Massachusetts.

Sorensen, A. (1970), "Organizational Differentiation of Students and Educational Opportunity", *Sociology of Education,* Vol. 43, No. 3, pp. 355-376.

Tyack, D. (1974), *The One Best System: A History of American Urban Education*, Harvard University Press, Cambridge, Massachusetts.

3

Resources Invested
in Education

This chapter examines the allocation of human, material and financial resources throughout school systems and the amount of time dedicated to instruction and learning. Resource allocation is also discussed as it relates to school location, the socio-economic profile of schools, programme orientation, education level, and whether a school is public or private. The chapter also analyses changes since 2003 in the level of resources devoted to education and how those resources are allocated.

This chapter examines the allocation of resources to school systems. Human, material and financial resources are examined in this chapter as well as the amount of time dedicated to instruction and learning as shown in Figure IV.3.1.

Although research on school effects has generally shown a modest relationship between educational resources and student learning (Fuller, 1987; Greenwald, Hedges and Laine, 1996; Buchmann and Hannum, 2001; Rivkin, Hanushek and Kain, 2005; Murillo and Román, 2011; Hægeland, Raaum and Salvanes, 2012; Nicoletti and Rabe, 2012), a basic set of resources is crucial for providing students with the opportunity to learn. This chapter focuses not only on the average level of resources available in each school system, but also on how school resources are allocated across schools within systems. Given that some research shows that allocating additional financial resources to disadvantaged schools reduces the achievement gap between disadvantaged and other schools (Lamb, Teese and Helme, 2005; Henry, Fortner and Thompson, 2010), resource allocation has implications for equity in a school system and, as such, is an important consideration for policy makers.

■ Figure IV.3.1 ■
Resources invested in education as covered in PISA 2012

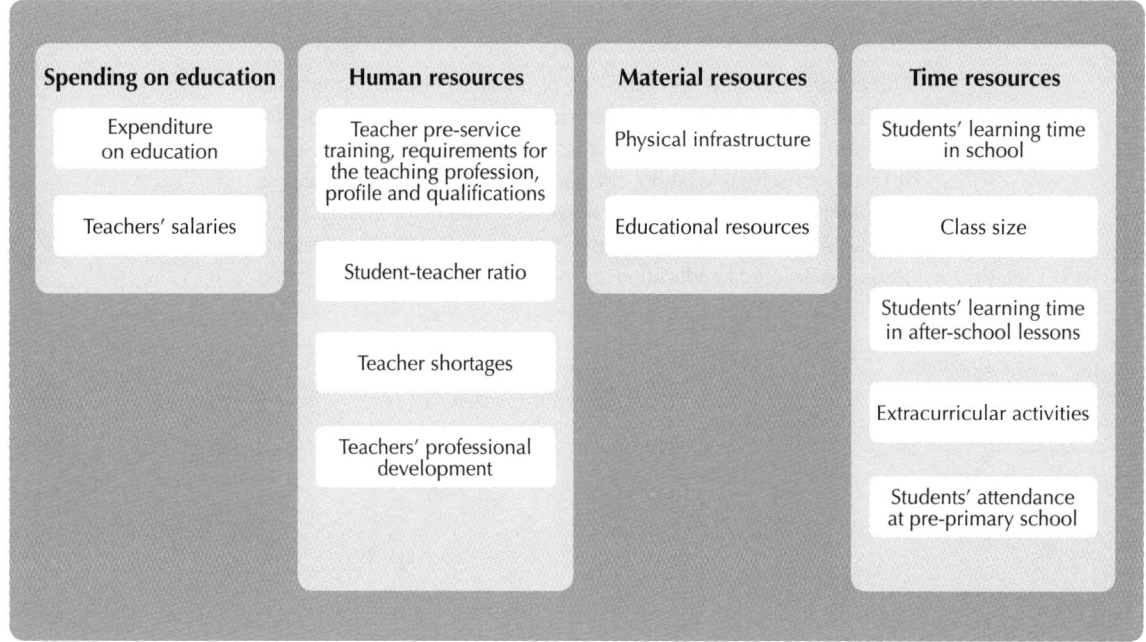

What the data tell us

- In Luxembourg, Jordan, Thailand, Turkey and Shanghai-China, more than three in ten students are in schools whose principals reported that a lack of qualified mathematics teachers hinders to some extent or a lot the schools' capacity to provide instruction (the OECD average is fewer than two in ten students attend such schools).

- On average across OECD countries, students who are in socio-economically disadvantaged schools tend to be in classes with four students fewer than students in advantaged schools; but disadvantaged schools tend to be more likely to suffer from teacher shortages, and shortages or inadequacy of educational materials and physical infrastructures than advantaged schools.

- Trends between 2003 and 2012 reveal a reduction in the student-teacher ratio, an increase in classroom instruction time dedicated to mathematics, and a reduction in the time students spend doing mathematics homework. These changes are seen across different types of schools and among both advantaged and disadvantaged students.

- Fifteen-year-old students in 2012 were more likely than 15-year-olds in 2003 to have attended at least one year of pre-primary education, but many of the students who did not attend were disadvantaged – the students who could benefit from pre-primary education the most.

In this chapter, resource allocation across schools is examined by comparing human, material and time resources allocated to schools according to various school features, such as school location, the socio-economic profile of schools, programme orientation, education level, and school type (see also Box IV.3.1). The chapter also analyses how the overall resource level and resource allocation across schools have changed since PISA 2003.

Chapter 1 shows that most of the relationship between school resources and performance is also related to schools' socio-economic intake. In other words, the quality and quantity of school resources can play an important role in mediating the impact of students' socio-economic status on performance.

FINANCIAL RESOURCES

Expenditure on education

Chapter 1 shows that improvements in performance require policies and practices that address more than spending on education, particularly among high-income countries and economies. High-performing systems tend to prioritise higher salaries for teachers.

Policy makers must constantly balance expenditure on education with expenditure for many other public services. Yet despite the competing demands for resources, expenditure on education has increased over the past few years. Between 2001 and 2010, expenditure per primary, secondary and post-secondary non-tertiary student[1] has increased 40%, on average across OECD countries with data available for both 2001 and 2010 (Table IV.3.1).

Financial resources can be allocated to salaries paid to teachers, administrators and support staff; maintenance or construction costs of buildings and infrastructure; and operational costs, such as transportation and meals for students.

Total expenditure by educational institutions per student from the age of 6 to 15[2] exceeds USD 100 000 (PPP-corrected dollars) in Luxembourg, Switzerland, Norway, Austria, the Unites States and Denmark. In Luxembourg, cumulative expenditure per students exceeds USD 190 000. In contrast, in Turkey, Mexico and the partner countries Viet Nam, Jordan, Peru, Thailand, Malaysia, Uruguay, Colombia, Tunisia and Montenegro, cumulative expenditure per student over this age period is less than USD 25 000 (Table IV.3.1). As expected, spending on education and per capita GDP are highly correlated (r=0.95 across OECD countries and r=0.94 across all participating countries and economies in PISA 2012). School systems with greater total expenditure on education tend to be those with higher levels of per capita GDP (Tables IV.3.1 and IV.3.2).

Teachers' salaries

Teachers' salaries represent the largest single cost in expenditure on education (OECD, 2013). School systems differ not only in how much they pay teachers but in the structure of their pay scales. Lower secondary teachers' salaries[3] in OECD countries are 124% of per capita GDP, corrected for differences in purchasing power parities. Relative to their country's national income, lower secondary teachers in Korea, Mexico, Germany, Portugal, Spain, the Netherlands, Ireland, New Zealand, Canada and the partner countries Jordan, Malaysia, Tunisia, Colombia and Montenegro earn the most. In these countries, annual earnings for lower secondary teachers are between 150% and 215% of per capita GDP. By contrast, annual earnings for lower secondary teachers are 70% or less of per capita GDP in the Slovak Republic, Estonia, Hungary and the partner countries Romania, Indonesia and Latvia. Upper secondary teachers' salaries in OECD countries are 129% of per capita GDP. In Germany, Turkey, Korea, Portugal, Spain and the partner countries and economies Hong Kong-China, Jordan, Malaysia, Tunisia and Colombia, upper secondary teachers' salaries are between 160% and 223% of per capita GDP. By contrast, in the Slovak Republic, Estonia and the partner countries Romania, Indonesia and Latvia, they are between 44% and 68% of per capita GDP (Table IV.3.3).

In all school systems, teachers' salaries rise during the course of a career, although the rate of change differs greatly. In Korea and the partner countries and economies Shanghai-China, Malaysia, Jordan, Singapore and Romania, salaries at the top of the scale are 2.5 times higher than starting salaries[4] and it takes between 20 and 40 years to reach the top salary. In Shanghai-China, this ratio is particularly high: the salary at the top of the scale is 4.5 times greater than the starting salary for lower secondary teachers, and it is 5.6 times greater for upper secondary teachers. By contrast, in Denmark, Iceland, Norway, Slovenia, Sweden, Finland, Germany, the Slovak Republic, the Czech Republic, Spain and the partner countries Peru, Montenegro and Croatia, teachers' salaries at the top of the scale is at most 1.4 times higher than starting salaries (Table IV.3.3).

■ Figure IV.3.2 ■

Expenditure on education and teachers' salaries

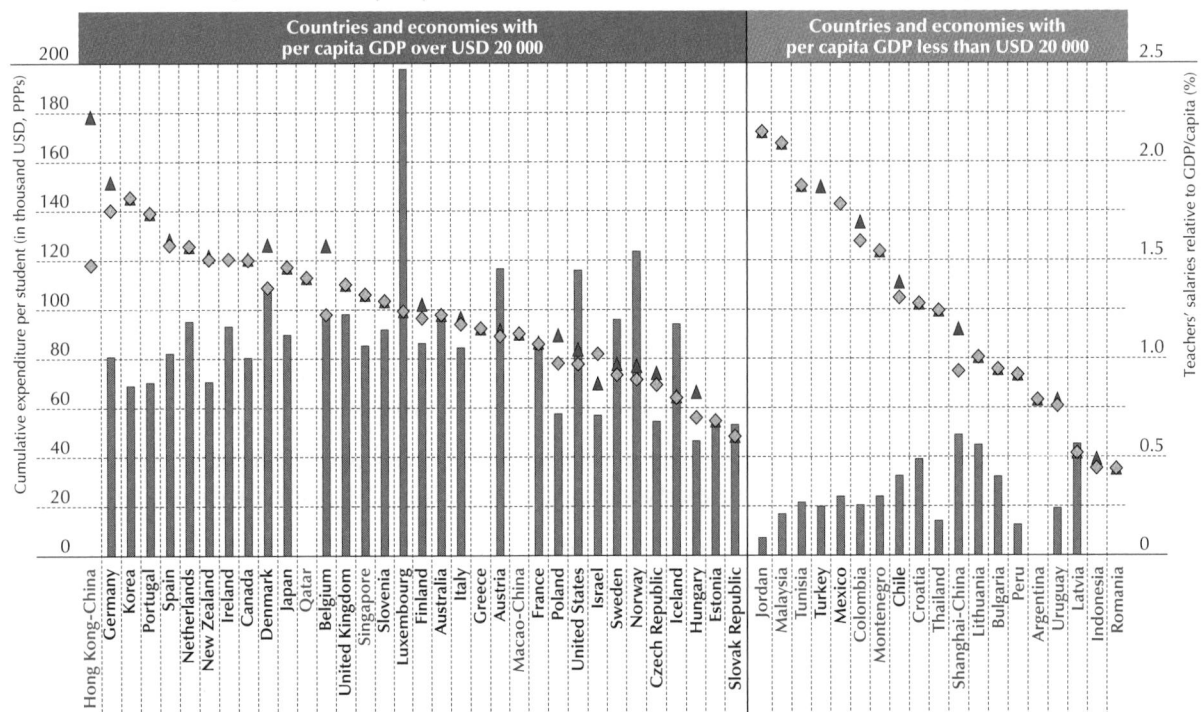

■ Cumulative expenditure by educational institutions per student aged 6 to 15

◆ Lower secondary teachers' salaries (after 15 years of experience/minimum training) relative to per capita GDP

▲ Upper secondary teachers' salaries (after 15 years of experience/minimum training) relative to per capita GDP

Notes: Teachers' salaries in Belgium are the average teachers' salaries of the French and Flemish communities of Belgium. Teachers' salaries in the United Kingdom are the average teachers' salaries in England and Scotland.

Countries and economies are ranked in descending order of teachers' salaries (average of lower and upper secondary teachers' salaries).

Source: OECD, PISA 2012 Database, Tables IV.3.1, IV.3.2 and IV.3.3.

StatLink ᵐˢᵖ http://dx.doi.org/10.1787/888932957327

Higher salaries can help school systems to attract the best candidates to the teaching profession, and they signal that teachers are regarded and treated as professionals. But paying teachers well is only part of the equation: school systems must also nurture and retain the best of their teachers. The next section examines these aspects more in detail.

HUMAN RESOURCES

According to results described in Chapter 1, schools that suffer from greater levels of teacher shortage tend to have lower scores in PISA.

Teachers are an essential resource for learning: the quality of a school system cannot exceed the quality of its teachers. Teachers interact with students daily and help students acquire the knowledge that they are expected to have by the time they leave school. Thus, attracting, developing and retaining effective teachers is a priority for public policy, although the policies related to teachers differ widely across countries (OECD, 2005). The type and quality of the training they receive, as well as the requirements to enter and progress through the teaching profession, have significant consequences on the quality of the teaching force.

Pre-service teacher training

Competitive examinations are required to enter pre-service teacher training (for public primary and secondary education) in Australia, Finland, Germany, Greece, Hungary, Ireland, Israel, Korea, Mexico and Turkey and the partner countries and economies Bulgaria, Colombia, Croatia, Indonesia, Lithuania, Macao-China, Romania, Shanghai-China, Chinese Taipei, the United Arab Emirates and Viet Nam (Table IV.3.4). In Austria, competitive examinations are required only

for teacher training in primary education. Pre-service teacher training is longest in Germany, where teacher pre-service training for primary teachers lasts 5.5 years, between 5.5 and 6.5 years for lower secondary teachers, and 6.5 years for upper secondary teachers. For teaching at primary levels, pre-service training is the shortest (three years) in Austria, Belgium, Spain and Switzerland; for teaching at lower secondary levels it is the shortest (three years) in Belgium; and for teaching at the upper secondary level, pre-service training is the shortest in England (UK) and Israel (3.5 years). A teaching practicum is required as part of pre-service training for primary teachers in all OECD countries except Chile and England (UK), and in all partner countries and economies except Brazil, Jordan and Tunisia. Teaching practicums are also required for lower secondary education in all OECD and partner countries and economies, except Brazil, Chile, England (UK), Jordan, Macao-China and Romania. Teaching practicums are also required for upper secondary education in all OECD and partner countries and economies except Austria, Chile, Denmark, England (UK) and Mexico among OECD countries, and partner countries and economies Brazil, Jordan, Macao-China and Romania.

Countries and economies can be categorised into four groups according to whether their public-school teacher pre-service training system requires a competitive examination and by the average duration of the training programme as shown in Figure IV.3.3.[5] Two groups require no entrance examination. One of these groups has a comparatively short pre-service training programme, and the other group has a comparatively long programme. The two additional groups require a competitive entrance examination, one with a short pre-service training programme and another with a comparatively long programme.

■ Figure IV.3.3 ■

Profiles of teacher pre-service training across countries and economies

	No examination to enter pre-service training	Competitive examination to enter pre-service training
Relatively short duration of pre-service training programme (less than 4.3 years)	Belgium (Fl.) Belgium (Fr.) England (UK) Hong Kong-China Iceland Japan Latvia Liechtenstein Montenegro New Zealand Poland Qatar Singapore Sweden United States Uruguay	Australia Bulgaria Croatia Greece Israel Lithuania Macao-China Romania Shanghai-China Chinese Taipei Viet Nam
Relatively long duration of pre-service training programme (more than 4.3 years)	Canada Czech Republic Denmark Estonia France Italy Luxembourg Malaysia Netherlands Norway Peru Portugal Scotland (UK) Slovak Republic Spain Switzerland	Austria Colombia Finland Germany Hungary Indonesia Ireland Korea Mexico Turkey
Countries and economies with no information on duration and/or examination	Albania Argentina Brazil Chile Costa Rica Jordan Kazakhstan	Russian Federation Serbia Slovenia Thailand Tunisia United Arab Emirates

Source: OECD, PISA 2012 Database, Table IV.3.4.

Requirements to enter the teaching profession

A competitive examination is required to enter the teaching profession for primary and secondary school in France, Germany, Greece, Israel, Italy, Japan, Korea, Luxembourg, Mexico, Spain, Turkey, the United States and the partner countries and economies Brazil, Colombia, Macao-China, Peru, Qatar, Romania, Shanghai-China, Chinese Taipei, Thailand, the United Arab Emirates and Viet Nam.

A credential or license, in addition to the education diploma, is required to start teaching or to become a fully qualified lower or upper secondary teacher in Australia, Canada, Denmark, England (UK), Germany, Iceland, Ireland, Israel, Italy, Japan, Korea, Mexico, New Zealand, Scotland (UK), Switzerland, the United States and the partner countries and economies Bulgaria, Croatia, Hong Kong-China, Indonesia, Malaysia, Montenegro, Shanghai-China, Chinese-Taipei, Thailand, the United Arab Emirates and Viet Nam.

A teaching practicum is required for lower or upper secondary teachers to obtain a credential/licence or is required after being recruited, during an induction/probation period, in Austria, Canada, Denmark, England (UK), Germany, Greece, Hungary, Ireland, Israel, Japan, Korea, Luxembourg, New Zealand, Scotland (UK), Spain, Turkey, the United States and the partner countries and economies Colombia, Croatia, Malaysia, Montenegro, Qatar, Romania, Shanghai-China, Chinese Taipei, the United Arab Emirates and Viet Nam.

Just over half of the participating countries and economies (18 OECD and 11 partner countries and economies) have a register for lower or upper secondary teachers. A register for teachers is an administrative record that contains a detailed profile of teachers, including such information as their qualifications, experience and career path. Continuing education is compulsory for remaining employed in the teaching profession at the lower and upper secondary levels in Belgium (French community), England (UK), Estonia, Finland, Hungary, Iceland, Israel, Japan, Luxembourg, the Netherlands, Scotland (UK), the United States and the partner countries and economies Croatia, Liechtenstein, Montenegro, Romania, Shanghai-China, Thailand, the United Arab Emirates and Viet Nam (Table IV.3.5).

Teacher profile and qualifications

How are these policies and requirements exercised at school? PISA 2012 asked school principals to report the composition and qualifications of teachers in their schools. Across OECD countries, the average 15-year-old student is in a school whose principal reported that 87% of teachers are fully certified. In 47 participating countries and economies, school principals reported that 80% of teachers or more are fully certified, while in Colombia and Chile, principals reported that fewer than 20% of teachers are fully certified. In addition, the average 15-year-old student in OECD countries attends a school whose principal reported that 85% of teachers have a university-level qualification (i.e. university or similar qualification). In 48 participating countries and economies, principals reported that more than 80% of teachers have such a qualification, while in Serbia, Uruguay and Argentina, principals reported that fewer than 20% of teachers have attained that qualification (Figure IV.3.4 and Table IV.3.6).

Box IV.3.1. **Socio-economically disadvantaged and advantaged schools**

Socio-economically disadvantaged and advantaged schools are identified within individual school systems by comparing the average socio-economic status of the students in the system and the average socio-economic status of the students in each school (Monseur and Crahay, 2008). Student socio-economic status is measured by the *PISA index of economic, social and cultural status* (ESCS).

Within each school system, schools are categorised into three groups:

- socio-economically advantaged schools: schools where the average socio-economic status of 15-year-old students is more advantaged than the average socio-economic status of students in the system as a whole;

- socio-economically average schools: schools where the average socio-economic status of 15-year-old students is not statistically different from the average socio-economic status of students in the system as a whole; or

- socio-economically disadvantaged schools: schools where the average socio-economic status of 15-year-old students is more disadvantaged than the average socio-economic status of students in the system as a whole.

The difference between a school average and the system average is statistically tested considering the confidence interval for school and system averages. Table IV.3.7 presents the percentage of students allocated to the three groups in PISA 2012. Table II.4.2 in Volume II presents average socio-economic, demographic and academic characteristics of schools in these three groups.

■ Figure IV.3.4 ■
Teachers' profiles and qualifications

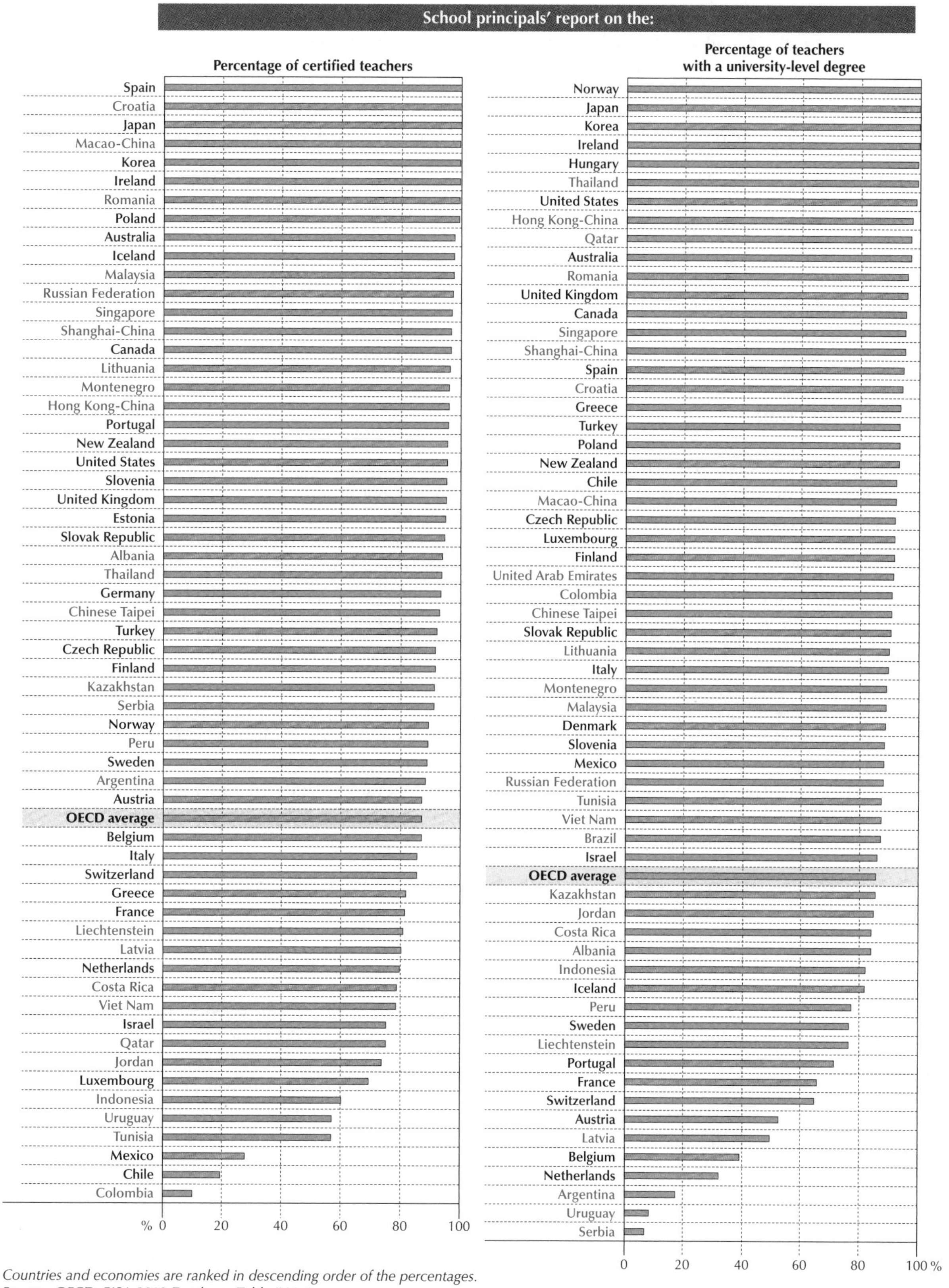

School principals' report on the:

Percentage of certified teachers

Spain	
Croatia	
Japan	
Macao-China	
Korea	
Ireland	
Romania	
Poland	
Australia	
Iceland	
Malaysia	
Russian Federation	
Singapore	
Shanghai-China	
Canada	
Lithuania	
Montenegro	
Hong Kong-China	
Portugal	
New Zealand	
United States	
Slovenia	
United Kingdom	
Estonia	
Slovak Republic	
Albania	
Thailand	
Germany	
Chinese Taipei	
Turkey	
Czech Republic	
Finland	
Kazakhstan	
Serbia	
Norway	
Peru	
Sweden	
Argentina	
Austria	
OECD average	
Belgium	
Italy	
Switzerland	
Greece	
France	
Liechtenstein	
Latvia	
Netherlands	
Costa Rica	
Viet Nam	
Israel	
Qatar	
Jordan	
Luxembourg	
Indonesia	
Uruguay	
Tunisia	
Mexico	
Chile	
Colombia	

% 0   20   40   60   80   100

Percentage of teachers with a university-level degree

Norway	
Japan	
Korea	
Ireland	
Hungary	
Thailand	
United States	
Hong Kong-China	
Qatar	
Australia	
Romania	
United Kingdom	
Canada	
Singapore	
Shanghai-China	
Spain	
Croatia	
Greece	
Turkey	
Poland	
New Zealand	
Chile	
Macao-China	
Czech Republic	
Luxembourg	
Finland	
United Arab Emirates	
Colombia	
Chinese Taipei	
Slovak Republic	
Lithuania	
Italy	
Montenegro	
Malaysia	
Denmark	
Slovenia	
Mexico	
Russian Federation	
Tunisia	
Viet Nam	
Brazil	
Israel	
OECD average	
Kazakhstan	
Jordan	
Costa Rica	
Albania	
Indonesia	
Iceland	
Peru	
Sweden	
Liechtenstein	
Portugal	
France	
Switzerland	
Austria	
Latvia	
Belgium	
Netherlands	
Argentina	
Uruguay	
Serbia	

0   20   40   60   80   100 %

Countries and economies are ranked in descending order of the percentages.
Source: OECD, PISA 2012 Database, Table IV.3.6.
StatLink ᵃˢᵖ http://dx.doi.org/10.1787/888932957327

Student-teacher ratio

PISA 2012 asked school principals to report the total number of teachers and students in their schools.[6] The student-teacher ratio is not equivalent to class size. For example, schools with large special education programmes tend to have many teachers, but the size of regular classes is not reduced by the school's high teacher-student ratio. Also, the amount of preparation time per day allotted to teachers may vary across schools and across school systems. More teachers are needed where more preparation time is given and class size remains constant.

Across OECD countries, the average student attends a school where the student-teacher ratio is 13 students to one teacher. Student-teacher ratios range from over 25 students per teacher in Mexico, Brazil and Colombia, to fewer than 10 students per teacher in Liechtenstein, Portugal, Luxembourg, Greece, Belgium, Poland, Latvia and Kazakhstan (Table IV.3.8).

Student-teacher ratios do not vary much within countries and economies, but in some countries there is a difference of around three or more students per teacher between socio-economically advantaged and disadvantaged schools. In Brazil, Turkey, Shanghai-China, Romania, Uruguay and Macao-China, disadvantaged schools tend to have more students per teacher than advantaged schools, while in Belgium, the Netherlands, Italy, Qatar, Estonia, the Russian Federation, Mexico, Peru and Japan advantaged schools have at least three more students per teacher than disadvantaged schools (Table IV.3.9).

Teacher shortages

In order to assess how school principals perceive the adequacy of the supply of teachers in their schools, they are asked to report on the extent to which they think instruction in their school is hindered by a lack of qualified teachers and staff in key areas. This information was combined to create a composite *index of teacher shortage*, such that the index has an average of 0 and a standard deviation of 1 for OECD countries. Higher values on the index indicate principals' perception that there are more problems with instruction because of teacher shortages. Caution is required in interpreting these results: school principals across countries and economies, and even within countries and economies, may have different expectations and benchmarks to determine whether there is a lack of qualified teachers. Nonetheless, these reports provide valuable information that can be used to assess whether schools or school systems are providing their students with adequate human resources.

According to school principals, teacher shortages hindered instruction the most in Luxembourg, Jordan, Thailand, Turkey and Shanghai-China. In these countries and economies, between 31% and 69% of students are in schools whose principals reported that a lack of qualified mathematics teachers hindered to some extent or a lot the schools' capacity to provide instruction (the OECD average is 17%). By contrast, in Poland, Bulgaria, Portugal, Serbia and Spain relatively few principals reported that teacher shortages hindered instruction. In these countries, only around 1% to 4% of students are in schools whose principals reported that a lack of qualified mathematics teachers hindered instruction to some extent or a lot (Figure IV.3.5 and Table IV.3.10).

Teacher shortages vary within countries, as measured by the standard deviation of the *index of teacher shortage*. Variation is comparatively large in Jordan, the United Arab Emirates, Colombia, Kazakhstan, Macao-China and Shanghai-China, while it is comparatively small in Poland, Bulgaria, Lithuania, Slovenia and Serbia (Figure IV.3.5 and Table IV.3.10). In 30 countries and economies, principals in socio-economically disadvantaged schools reported more teacher shortage than those in advantaged schools. Particularly wide gaps between advantaged and disadvantaged schools in teacher shortage are observed in Chinese Taipei, Australia, New Zealand, Brazil, Sweden, the Slovak Republic, Shanghai-China, Uruguay, Indonesia, Mexico, Turkey, Serbia, the Czech Republic, Chile, the United States, Ireland, Viet Nam and Peru, where the difference is greater than 0.5 index points (i.e. a half of the standard deviation of this index). In 14 countries and economies, principals of public schools tended to report more teacher shortage than those of private schools. In all of these countries and economies except the United Arab Emirates and Italy, principals of disadvantaged schools reported more teacher shortage than those of advantaged schools (Table IV.3.11).

On average across OECD countries, principals of schools located in rural areas reported more teacher shortage than principals of schools in towns, and they, in turn, reported more teacher shortage than principals of schools in cities. This is observed in Iceland, Mexico and Qatar. However, in the Slovak Republic, the Czech Republic, Hungary, Chile and Romania, principals of schools located in towns and cities reported similar levels of teacher shortage, while principals of schools located in rural areas reported more teacher shortage than principals of schools in towns. In contrast, principals of schools located in rural areas and in towns reported similar levels of teacher shortage,

◼ Figure IV.3.5 ◼
Impact of teacher shortage on instruction, school principals' views

A	Lack of qualified mathematics teachers
B	Lack of qualified science teachers
C	Lack of qualified language-of-instruction teachers
D	Lack of qualified teachers of other subjects

	Percentage of students in schools whose principals reported that the following phenomena hindered student learning "to some extent" or "a lot"				Index of teacher shortage ▬ Range between top and bottom quarters ◆ Average index	Variability in the index	Difference between private and public schools (priv.-pub.)	Difference between advantaged and disadvantaged schools (adv.-disadv.)
	A	B	C	D		S.D.	Index difference	Index difference
Luxembourg	69	71	18	40		0.92	1.41*	-0.44*
Jordan	46	50	44	46		1.48	0.57	-0.49
Thailand	45	47	44	57		1.10	0.29	-0.15
Turkey	31	42	28	36		1.03	c	-0.65*
Shanghai-China	36	37	32	41		1.24	-0.12	-0.70*
Israel	36	39	34	39		1.11	c	0.14
Colombia	32	34	30	48		1.40	0.38	-0.05
Peru	29	31	26	44		1.06	0.99*	-0.51*
Chile	43	42	27	33		1.19	0.48*	-0.59*
Netherlands	45	32	23	37		0.88	0.00	-0.05
Mexico	28	23	25	33		1.03	0.70*	-0.65*
Germany	18	38	7	39		0.87	0.41	-0.33
Viet Nam	30	33	31	31		1.18	1.12*	-0.53*
Russian Federation	27	24	22	39		1.13	c	-0.25
Uruguay	34	26	13	37		1.02	0.82*	-0.70*
Norway	19	13	20	26		0.87	c	-0.25
Kazakhstan	32	31	20	35		1.29	-0.27	0.11
Indonesia	13	16	13	23		0.93	-0.25	-0.68*
Belgium	25	21	9	42		0.96	0.08	-0.48*
Italy	16	14	15	25		0.92	0.55*	0.06
Malaysia	7	8	26	34		0.76	-0.64	0.08
Australia	32	25	12	23		1.04	0.50*	-0.80*
Brazil	18	22	13	38		1.04	0.76*	-0.79*
Iceland	23	28	9	19		0.83	c	-0.49*
United Arab Emirates	21	23	23	25		1.40	0.80*	-0.30
Singapore	6	6	24	25		0.84	c	-0.04
New Zealand	22	15	7	24		0.93	0.52	-0.80*
Korea	12	14	13	17		1.03	-0.07	0.24
Switzerland	14	23	4	26		0.89	0.20	-0.20
Liechtenstein	0	0	7	33		0.73	c	c
Estonia	17	18	6	16		0.78	0.37	0.19
Macao-China	28	24	15	27		1.25	c	-0.13*
Costa Rica	7	13	8	25		0.84	0.29	-0.05
OECD average	17	17	9	21		0.85	0.25*	-0.32*
Sweden	14	20	4	22		0.85	0.01	-0.76*
Argentina	10	14	12	24		1.01	0.22	-0.04
Tunisia	10	12	9	28		0.93	c	-0.12
Austria	14	16	14	21		0.99	0.26	-0.27
Qatar	17	21	10	14		1.10	0.85*	-0.12*
Ireland	14	6	5	30		0.84	-0.05	-0.54*
Chinese Taipei	12	16	11	22		1.17	-0.19	-1.16*
France	8	5	7	21		0.85	-0.27	-0.10
Denmark	3	7	2	15		0.71	0.28*	-0.39*
United Kingdom	16	14	8	11		0.88	0.23	-0.43*
Hong Kong-China	11	4	6	14		0.89	-0.14	-0.47*
Albania	8	13	5	18		0.94	0.21	m
Japan	8	9	3	12		0.89	0.07	-0.26
Canada	13	7	4	16		0.85	0.07	-0.29*
Slovak Republic	5	5	2	25		0.71	0.06	-0.70*
Latvia	3	6	5	4		0.76	c	0.09
Greece	5	9	7	9		0.94	c	-0.20
United States	9	9	2	11		0.91	-0.18	-0.58*
Czech Republic	5	4	1	10		0.70	0.41*	-0.60*
Croatia	12	10	1	9		0.77	c	-0.29
Finland	4	4	1	12		0.67	-0.10	-0.11
Montenegro	14	9	0	2		0.72	c	-0.28*
Romania	1	8	4	5		0.72	c	-0.21
Hungary	3	7	1	5		0.66	-0.21	-0.40*
Lithuania	1	3	1	2		0.59	c	-0.12
Slovenia	1	0	0	2		0.59	-0.30*	0.07*
Spain	2	2	1	7		0.64	0.09	-0.17*
Serbia	4	4	1	3		0.60	c	-0.62*
Portugal	1	1	1	2		0.65	0.12	-0.05
Bulgaria	1	1	0	8		0.48	c	-0.07
Poland	0	1	0	0		0.25	0.04	-0.02

-1.5   -1.0   -0.5   0   0.5   1.0   1.5   2.0   2.5   3.0   3.5   Index points

Notes: Higher values on the *index of teacher shortage* indicate greater incidence of teacher shortage. Differences that are significant at the 5% level (p < 0.05) are marked with *.
Countries and economies are ranked in descending order of the average index.
Source: OECD, PISA 2012 Database, Tables IV.3.10 and IV.3.11.
StatLink ᓬ꧁╗═╝ http://dx.doi.org/10.1787/888932957327

■ Figure IV.3.6 ■
Continuing education necessary to remain employed as a teacher
Mean percentage of mathematics teachers who have attended a programme of professional development with a focus on mathematics during the previous three months

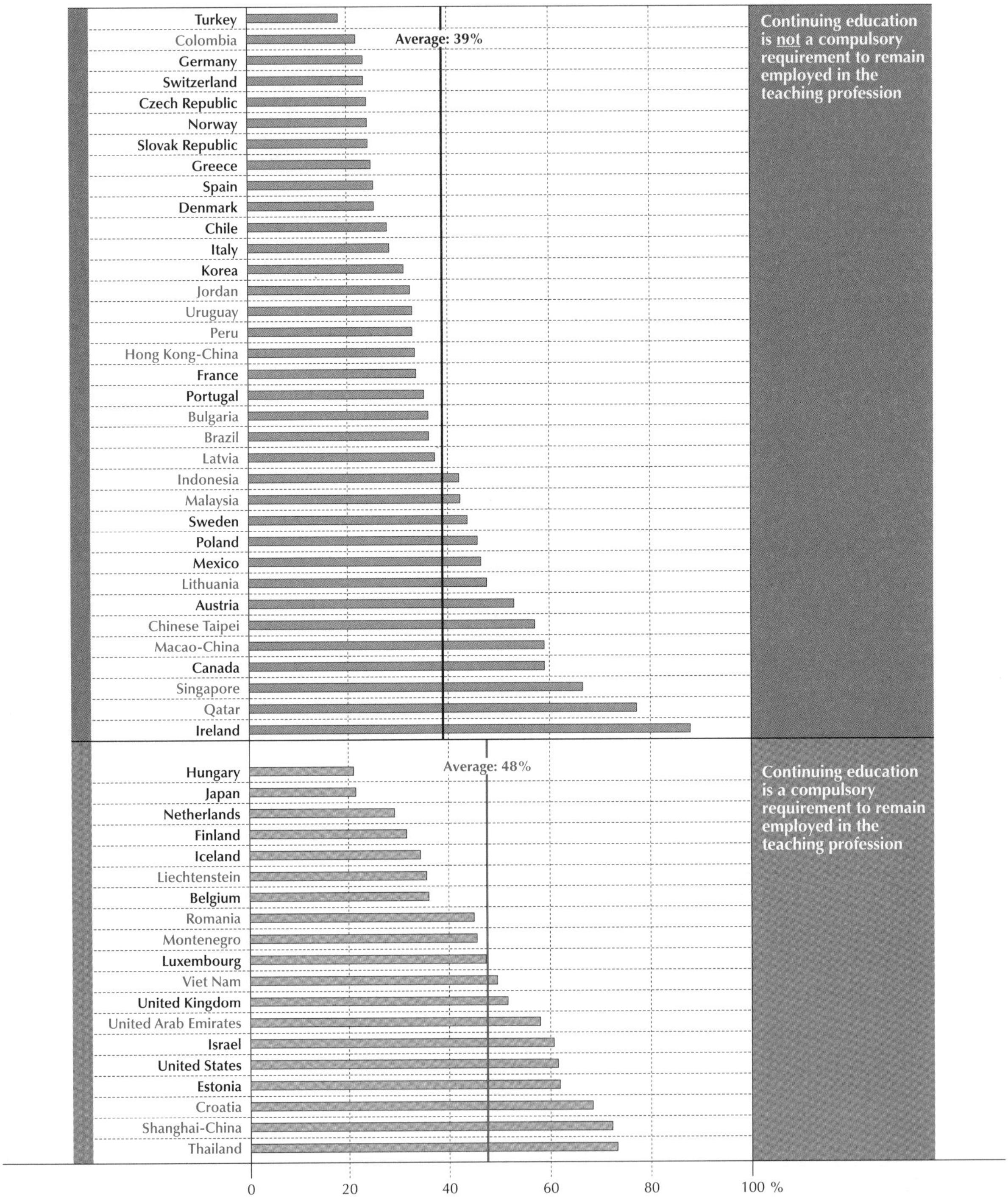

Continuing education is <u>not</u> a compulsory requirement to remain employed in the teaching profession

Average: 39%

Turkey
Colombia
Germany
Switzerland
Czech Republic
Norway
Slovak Republic
Greece
Spain
Denmark
Chile
Italy
Korea
Jordan
Uruguay
Peru
Hong Kong-China
France
Portugal
Bulgaria
Brazil
Latvia
Indonesia
Malaysia
Sweden
Poland
Mexico
Lithuania
Austria
Chinese Taipei
Macao-China
Canada
Singapore
Qatar
Ireland

Continuing education is a compulsory requirement to remain employed in the teaching profession

Average: 48%

Hungary
Japan
Netherlands
Finland
Iceland
Liechtenstein
Belgium
Romania
Montenegro
Luxembourg
Viet Nam
United Kingdom
United Arab Emirates
Israel
United States
Estonia
Croatia
Shanghai-China
Thailand

0   20   40   60   80   100 %

Notes: In Iceland, the majority of 15-year-olds are at the lower secondary level, therefore the information at the lower secondary in Table IV.3.5 is used. Belgium is grouped as "continuing education is compulsory requirement" even though it is not a compulsory requirement in the Flemish community of Belgium.
Countries and economies are ranked in ascending order of the percentages.
Source: OECD, PISA 2012 Database, Tables IV.3.5 and IV.3.12.
StatLink ⌐═╗ http://dx.doi.org/10.1787/888932957327

while in Colombia, Australia, Indonesia, Uruguay, Viet Nam, New Zealand, Montenegro, Chinese Taipei, the United Arab Emirates, Peru, Brazil, Norway, Ireland, Finland and Canada, principals of schools located in cities reported less teacher shortage than principals of schools in towns. In 34 countries and economies, the level of teacher shortage reported by principals does not vary by where school is located (Table IV.3.11).

Teachers' professional development

How is the requirement that teachers pursue continuing education implemented? Across OECD countries, the average 15-year-old student attends a school whose principal reported that 39% of those who teach mathematics in his or her school have attended a programme of professional development, with a focus on mathematics, during the previous three months. This proportion varies greatly across countries: in Ireland, Qatar, Thailand, Shanghai-China, Croatia, Singapore, Estonia, the United States, New Zealand and Israel, at least 60% of teachers attended such a programme, while in Turkey, Hungary, Japan, Colombia, Germany, Switzerland, the Czech Republic, Norway, the Slovak Republic and Greece, 25% of teachers or fewer did so (Figure IV.3.6 and Table IV.3.12). As expected, in those countries where it is compulsory for teachers to participate in continuing education, teachers are more likely to have attended professional development programmes (48% on average) than teachers in those countries/economies where it is not compulsory (39% on average) (as shown in Figure IV.3.6). The timing of the PISA data collection largely affects principals' responses on this proportion since they were asked to report teachers' attendance in professional development programmes during the three months prior to the assessment. For example, if most teachers in a country or economy participate in professional development programmes during summer holidays and the PISA data collection was conducted before the summer break in this country, the reported proportion would be underestimated.

In 18 countries and economies, more mathematics teachers in socio-economically advantaged schools than in disadvantaged schools attended a programme of professional development. The gap is especially wide in Luxembourg, Austria, Turkey, Serbia, Chinese Taipei and Shanghai-China, where the difference between advantaged and disadvantaged schools in the percentage of teachers who attended such a programme during the previous three months is 25 percentage points or more (Table IV.3.13).

On average across OECD countries, mathematics teachers in public schools are more likely (40%) than those in private schools (37%) to attend a programme of professional development. This is the case in Qatar, the United Arab Emirates, Canada, Thailand, France, Switzerland, Germany and Finland, where the difference ranges from 8 to 40 percentage points. In contrast, in Shanghai-China and Luxembourg, mathematics teachers in private schools are more likely than those in public schools to attend such a programme (Table IV.3.13).

Across OECD countries, there is no difference between schools located in towns and those located in cities, on average, in the likelihood of mathematics teachers attending a programme of professional development. But mathematics teachers in schools in rural areas are less likely to attend such a programme than those in schools located in towns. This is observed in Slovenia, Iceland, Denmark, Hungary, the Slovak Republic, Norway and Mexico. However, in 45 countries and economies, there is no difference among schools located in rural areas, towns and cities in the likelihood of mathematics teachers attending a professional development programme (Table IV.3.13).

MATERIAL RESOURCES

The educational resources available in a school tend to be related to the system's overall performance as well as schools' average level of performance, according to the results examined in Chapter 1. Furthermore, it is shown that high performing systems tend to allocate resource more equitably between socio-economically advantaged and disadvantaged schools.

While an adequate physical infrastructure and supply of educational resources does not guarantee good learning outcomes, the absence of such resources could negatively affect learning. What matters for student achievement and other education outcomes is not necessarily the availability of resources, but the quality of those resources and how effectively they are used (Gamoran, Secada and Marrett, 2000).

The PISA 2012 School Questionnaire asked school principals to report on not only the availability of school resources, on how the availability or non-availability of certain school resources affect teaching and learning in their schools.

■ Figure IV.3.7 ■

School principals' views on adequacy of physical infrastructure

A Shortage or inadequacy of school buildings and grounds
B Shortage or inadequacy of heating/cooling and lighting systems
C Shortage or inadequacy of instructional space (e.g. classrooms)

	Percentage of students in schools whose principals reported that the following phenomena hindered student learning "not at all" or "very little"			Index of quality of physical infrastructure — Range between top and bottom quarters ◆ Average index	Variability in the index S.D.	Difference between private and public schools (priv.-pub.) Index difference	Difference between advantaged and disadvantaged schools (adv.-disadv.) Index difference
	A	B	C				
Poland	79	89	91		0.82	0.06	-0.25
Qatar	66	93	74		0.98	0.36*	0.23*
United States	83	94	79		0.80	-0.09	0.47*
Czech Republic	86	88	87		0.78	0.04	-0.12
Singapore	78	92	84		0.80	c	0.25*
Latvia	87	84	91		0.77	c	-0.40*
Iceland	72	94	81		0.83	c	0.18*
Canada	75	87	79		0.86	-0.14	0.05
Switzerland	77	88	75		0.87	-0.28	0.03
Sweden	73	77	79		1.01	-0.36	0.60*
Hungary	74	89	79		0.84	-0.04	-0.10
France	68	82	73		0.93	0.04	-0.18
Bulgaria	68	81	80		0.91	c	-0.39*
Romania	78	84	83		0.71	c	0.18
Australia	70	79	73		0.95	-0.61*	0.51*
Russian Federation	62	75	80		0.95	c	-0.16
United Arab Emirates	67	76	71		1.18	-0.77*	0.69*
Liechtenstein	48	93	48		0.79	c	c
Estonia	70	83	67		0.99	-1.04*	-0.30
Malaysia	66	87	68		1.04	-0.26	-0.16
Chinese Taipei	65	83	65		1.04	-0.27	0.34
Slovenia	70	78	77		0.93	-0.42*	-0.20*
United Kingdom	60	80	70		1.07	-0.17	-0.45*
New Zealand	65	87	66		0.97	-1.12*	-0.23
Spain	68	74	70		1.03	-0.79*	0.57*
Lithuania	64	72	79		0.91	c	-0.50*
Hong Kong-China	53	95	65		0.85	0.36	0.29
Germany	69	83	60		0.94	-0.33	-0.14
OECD average	65	77	67		0.96	-0.37*	0.13*
Ireland	58	86	61		1.14	0.01	-0.11
Montenegro	56	78	73		0.82	c	0.25*
Macao-China	48	85	67		1.00	c	0.65*
Chile	74	60	76		1.10	-0.93*	0.92*
Japan	66	67	66		0.94	-0.56*	0.39*
Slovak Republic	56	73	68		1.00	0.29	-0.12
Belgium	57	76	59		0.96	0.12	0.13
Austria	61	74	52		1.07	-0.03	-0.07
Denmark	63	76	69		0.86	-0.27	-0.04
Korea	64	83	53		0.94	-0.08	-0.18
Shanghai-China	45	82	58		1.13	0.11	0.29
Greece	53	79	65		1.09	c	0.53*
Kazakhstan	53	67	52		1.17	-0.79	0.07
Turkey	53	84	61		0.97	c	0.78*
Portugal	58	49	68		0.91	-0.83*	0.73*
Netherlands	65	56	56		0.97	0.18	0.11
Norway	59	58	57		0.99	c	0.05
Finland	59	61	58		0.99	-0.66*	-0.38
Italy	58	61	60		1.04	-0.90*	0.04
Serbia	41	79	52		0.94	c	0.10
Brazil	54	49	67		1.16	-1.36*	1.30*
Argentina	56	50	59		1.25	-1.04*	1.25*
Mexico	61	54	60		1.06	-1.13*	0.82*
Viet Nam	50	46	69		1.01	-0.63	0.47*
Uruguay	52	52	57		1.24	-1.17*	1.32*
Albania	46	46	67		1.00	-1.59*	m
Peru	44	57	58		1.15	-1.01*	0.94*
Luxembourg	35	86	43		0.88	-0.25*	0.20*
Indonesia	68	32	71		0.85	-0.32*	0.66*
Israel	40	68	44		1.06	c	0.06
Jordan	48	43	60		1.18	-0.77*	0.54
Croatia	34	72	49		0.89	c	-0.24
Costa Rica	52	47	47		1.15	-1.54*	1.12*
Colombia	37	52	49		1.13	-1.16*	0.58*
Thailand	36	45	41		1.13	-0.93*	0.42*
Tunisia	30	12	33		0.93	c	0.18

-3.0 -2.5 -2.0 -1.5 -1.0 0.5 0 0.5 1.0 1.5 Index points

Notes: Higher values on the *index of quality of physical infrastructure* indicate better physical infrastructure. Differences that are significant at the 5% level (p < 0.05) are marked with *.

Countries and economies are ranked in descending order of the average index.

Source: OECD, PISA 2012 Database, Tables IV.3.14 and IV.3.15.

StatLink ᎘᎘ http://dx.doi.org/10.1787/888932957327

Physical infrastructure and educational resources

School principals were asked to report on whether their schools' capacity to provide instruction was hindered ("not at all", "very little", "to some extent", or "a lot") by a shortage or inadequacy of physical infrastructure, such as school buildings and grounds; heating/cooling and lighting systems; and instructional space, such as classrooms. The responses were combined to create an *index of quality of physical infrastructure* that has a mean of zero and a standard deviation of one in OECD countries. Positive values reflect principals' perceptions that the shortage of physical infrastructure hinders learning to a lesser extent than the OECD average, and negative values indicate that school principals believe the shortage hinders learning to a greater extent.

On average across OECD countries, 65% to 77% of students are in schools whose principals reported that shortages or inadequacy of school buildings and grounds, heating/cooling and lighting systems, or instructional spaces do not hinder at all or hinder very little their school's capacity to provide instruction. In Latvia, the Czech Republic, the United States, Poland, Romania, Singapore, Switzerland and Canada, 75% or more of students are in schools whose principals reported that shortages or inadequacy of school buildings and grounds do not hinder learning at all or hinder learning very little, while in Tunisia, Croatia, Luxembourg, Thailand and Colombia, fewer than 40% of students are in such school. The variation, between schools, in the quality of physical infrastructure and its effect on instruction reported by principals is notable in Argentina, Uruguay, Jordan, the United Arab Emirates, Kazakhstan and Brazil, while it is small in Romania, Latvia, the Czech Republic and Liechtenstein (Figure IV.3.7 and Table IV.3.14).

In 27 countries and economies, principals of disadvantaged schools tended to report more shortages or inadequacy of physical infrastructure than did principals of advantaged schools. This difference is of one index point or more on the *index of quality of physical infrastructure* (i.e. over one standard deviation of the index) in Uruguay, Brazil, Argentina and Costa Rica. In contrast, in Lithuania, the United Kingdom, Latvia, Bulgaria and Slovenia, principals of advantaged schools tended to report more shortages or inadequacy of physical infrastructure than did principals of disadvantaged schools. In 24 countries and economies, principals of public schools tended to report more shortages or inadequacy of physical infrastructure than did principals of private schools. The difference in reporting is over one index point (i.e. over one standard deviation of the index) in Albania, Costa Rica, Brazil, Uruguay, Colombia, Mexico, New Zealand, Argentina, Estonia and Peru. On average across OECD countries, principals in schools located in rural areas tended to report more shortages or inadequacy of physical infrastructure than principals of schools located in towns. However, in 33 countries and economies, the level of shortages or inadequacy of physical infrastructure reported by principals does not vary by where school is located (Figure IV.3.7 and Table IV.3.15).

School principals also reported their perceptions about educational resources in their school. They were asked to report whether their school's capacity to provide instruction was hindered by a shortage or inadequacy of: science laboratory equipment, instructional materials (e.g. textbooks), computers for instruction, Internet connectivity, computer software for instruction, and library materials. The responses were combined to create an *index of quality of schools' educational resources* that has a mean of zero and a standard deviation of one in OECD countries. Positive values reflect principals' perceptions that a shortage of educational resources hinders learning to a lesser extent than the OECD average, and negative values indicate that school principals believe the shortage hinders learning to a greater extent.

An average of around 80% of students across OECD countries attends schools whose principals reported that the school's capacity to provide instruction was not hindered at all or hindered very little by a shortage or inadequacy of instructional materials or a lack or inadequacy of Internet connectivity. Some 74% of students are in schools whose principals reported that instruction was not hindered at all or hindered very little by a shortage or inadequacy of library materials. Between 66% and 69% of students are in schools whose principals reported that instruction was not hindered at all or was hindered very little by shortages or inadequacy of science laboratory equipment, computer software for instruction or computers for instruction. Principals in Singapore, Qatar and Liechtenstein reported that instruction is not hindered by a shortage of educational resources, while in Colombia, Tunisia, Peru and Costa Rica, principals reported that instruction is hindered to some extent by a shortage of educational resources (Figure IV.3.8 and Table IV.3.16).

In 35 countries and economies, principals of disadvantaged schools reported more shortage or inadequacy of educational resources than did principals of advantaged schools. This difference amounts to more than one index point (i.e. more than one standard deviation) in Peru, Costa Rica, Mexico, Brazil and Indonesia. In contrast, in Finland, principals of disadvantaged schools reported less shortage or inadequacy of educational resources than did those of advantaged schools.

■ Figure IV.3.8 ■

School principals' views on adequacy of educational resources

A	Shortage or inadequacy of science laboratory equipment
B	Shortage or inadequacy of instructional materials (e.g. textbooks)
C	Shortage or inadequacy of computers for instruction
D	Lack or inadequacy of Internet connectivity
E	Shortage or inadequacy of computer software for instruction
F	Shortage or inadequacy of library materials

Index of quality of schools' educational resources

━━━ Range between top and bottom quarters

◆ Average index

	Percentage of students in schools whose principals reported that the following phenomena hindered student learning "not at all" or "very little"						Variability in the index	Difference between private and public schools (priv.-pub.)	Difference between advantaged and disadvantaged schools (adv.-disadv.)
	A	B	C	D	E	F	S.D.	Index difference	Index difference
Singapore	97	98	93	95	94	97	0.87	c	0.04*
Qatar	79	96	83	89	81	84	0.98	0.46*	0.30*
Liechtenstein	99	99	100	100	100	62	0.51	c	c
Australia	86	91	89	82	86	89	0.97	-0.59*	0.73*
Chinese Taipei	72	88	88	86	82	80	1.20	-0.12	0.47
Switzerland	81	89	76	81	85	89	0.93	0.25	0.26
United Kingdom	82	89	76	81	83	84	1.06	-0.39*	-0.07
Hong Kong-China	96	87	79	92	77	83	0.93	0.06	0.23
Japan	79	96	79	79	75	79	1.02	-0.42*	0.38
Slovenia	87	78	89	96	82	88	0.84	-0.76*	0.09*
France	88	87	69	77	79	89	0.98	0.17	0.26
United States	79	85	67	85	77	82	1.07	-0.59	0.74*
United Arab Emirates	75	83	72	71	71	73	1.21	-0.73*	0.58*
Poland	71	88	74	93	73	87	0.90	0.00	0.43*
Macao-China	78	82	87	75	79	79	1.02	c	0.38*
Belgium	83	90	71	78	80	79	0.98	-0.18	0.27
Canada	83	84	64	77	73	86	0.97	-0.38*	0.43*
Austria	62	85	73	82	72	88	1.16	0.16	0.06
Romania	74	71	74	94	82	83	0.82	c	0.53*
New Zealand	89	92	56	62	69	91	0.98	-1.33*	0.79*
Netherlands	82	91	54	71	67	84	0.95	0.06	0.12
Hungary	59	88	82	80	76	83	0.84	-0.21	0.10
Portugal	72	91	76	81	65	84	0.91	-0.70*	0.24
Lithuania	69	88	81	94	68	84	0.69	c	0.22
Shanghai-China	61	78	72	71	62	72	1.24	0.12	0.60*
Uruguay	82	76	71	71	57	72	1.03	-0.82*	0.73*
Ireland	75	87	70	77	61	55	0.97	0.23	0.46
Germany	71	89	68	70	69	82	0.89	0.04	-0.03
Korea	68	84	82	93	75	67	0.92	0.00	-0.01
OECD average	69	80	66	79	68	74	0.92	-0.39*	0.31*
Sweden	81	84	50	76	74	80	0.83	-0.27	0.52*
Czech Republic	66	72	81	93	72	68	0.80	0.02	0.15
Italy	63	88	75	83	66	73	0.89	-0.27	0.15
Luxembourg	76	77	59	93	92	70	0.78	-0.64*	0.31*
Latvia	74	78	70	91	77	77	0.73	c	0.03
Spain	69	91	61	70	58	73	0.86	-0.22*	0.22*
Bulgaria	53	75	63	90	67	69	0.88	c	0.49*
Denmark	80	77	58	66	64	81	0.78	-0.56*	0.21
Estonia	53	60	63	96	68	64	0.74	-0.19	0.11
Norway	64	81	63	68	58	62	0.82	c	-0.10
Finland	74	81	57	76	51	66	0.82	-0.35*	-0.36*
Malaysia	82	93	42	49	54	73	0.90	-0.92	0.47*
Iceland	44	75	42	85	59	67	0.85	c	0.27*
Greece	71	70	45	79	53	46	0.96	c	0.45*
Israel	53	70	51	65	57	63	1.10	c	0.51*
Chile	47	72	72	72	43	68	1.00	-0.67*	0.68*
Turkey	43	72	59	77	60	64	0.92	c	0.79*
Albania	32	82	47	59	52	55	0.83	-0.97*	m
Jordan	60	74	42	43	52	75	1.02	-0.92*	0.62*
Russian Federation	37	70	44	60	46	60	0.91	c	0.28
Viet Nam	32	73	54	64	52	55	0.99	-0.74*	0.65*
Montenegro	38	60	55	74	35	69	0.65	c	0.00
Croatia	43	65	50	74	36	59	0.66	c	-0.11
Brazil	36	86	47	52	40	58	1.05	-1.38*	1.09*
Argentina	45	62	49	46	49	69	1.07	-0.26	0.77*
Slovak Republic	43	20	64	79	50	46	0.69	-0.44*	0.01
Serbia	37	51	54	68	56	55	0.86	c	-0.04
Thailand	32	63	47	53	45	40	1.07	-0.71*	0.99*
Kazakhstan	32	53	40	45	38	52	0.96	-1.05*	0.16
Indonesia	40	62	42	52	46	53	1.12	-0.14	1.05*
Mexico	39	60	39	46	43	45	1.14	-1.30*	1.29*
Costa Rica	22	43	43	51	41	36	1.24	-1.76*	1.33*
Peru	28	42	40	43	33	29	1.24	-1.30*	1.50*
Tunisia	21	41	17	22	35	16	0.93	c	0.44*
Colombia	26	33	31	30	25	30	1.17	-1.63*	0.91*

-4.0   -3.0   -2.0   -1.0   0   1.0   2.0   3.0 Index points

Notes: Higher values on the *index of quality of schools' educational resources* indicate better quality of schools' educational resources. Differences that are significant at the 5% level (p < 0.05) are marked with *.

Countries and economies are ranked in descending order of the average index.

Source: OECD, PISA 2012 Database, Tables IV.3.16 and IV.3.17.

StatLink ⟶ http://dx.doi.org/10.1787/888932957327

In 26 countries and economies, principals of public schools reported more shortage or inadequacy of educational resources than did principals of private schools. In 36 countries and economies, the level of shortage or inadequacy of educational resources reported by school principals did not vary according to where the schools are located. On average across OECD countries, principals of schools located in cities reported less shortage or inadequacy of educational resources than did principals of schools located in towns; this is observed in 14 countries and economies. In contrast, in Austria, Belgium, Germany, Iceland and Qatar, principals of schools located in cities reported more shortages or in adequacy of educational resources did those of schools located in towns. In Argentina, Mexico, Chile, Thailand, Peru, Albania, Malaysia and Qatar, principals of schools located in rural areas reported more shortages or inadequacy than did principals of schools in towns (Figure IV.3.8 and Table IV.3.17).

■ Figure IV.3.9 ■
Equity in allocation of educational resources

BETTER EQUITY
IN RESOURCE
ALLOCATION

Equity in allocation of schools' educational resources
(Index-point difference)

-0.5 | Mean index is **below** the OECD average | Mean index is **above** the OECD average

Finland ◆   Germany
Korea
Croatia   Norway   United
Serbia ◆ Montenegro   Kingdom
0.0
Slovak Republic ◆   Latvia ◆ Austria
Estonia Italy   6 ◆ Slovenia   Singapore ◆
Kazakhstan ◆ Czech Republic   4 5
Denmark ◆   3 2 1 Hong Kong-China
Russian Federation ◆ Iceland Spain   Switzerland
                                          Qatar   R² = 0.01
Tunisia ◆   Japan
               Greece   Malaysia   Canada ◆   Macao-China
0.5   Israel ◆   Poland ◆ Chinese Taipei
                 Jordan Luxembourg   Romania
                   ◆ Chile   Ireland ◆ United Arab Emirates
                              Shanghai-China
          Argentina ◆ Turkey
Colombia ◆   United States Australia
                    Bulgaria
               Thailand   Uruguay New Zealand
1.0   Viet Nam Sweden
          Indonesia ◆
                   Brazil
     R² = 0.33

Costa Rica ◆   Mexico

1.5
          Peru   1. France
                                                 2. Belgium
                                                 3. Portugal
                                                 4. Lithuania
                                                 5. Netherlands
2.0   6. Hungary

OECD average: 0.05

MORE
RESOURCES

-1.5   -1.0   -0.5   0   0.5   1.0   1.5

Average level of schools' educational resources
(Mean index)

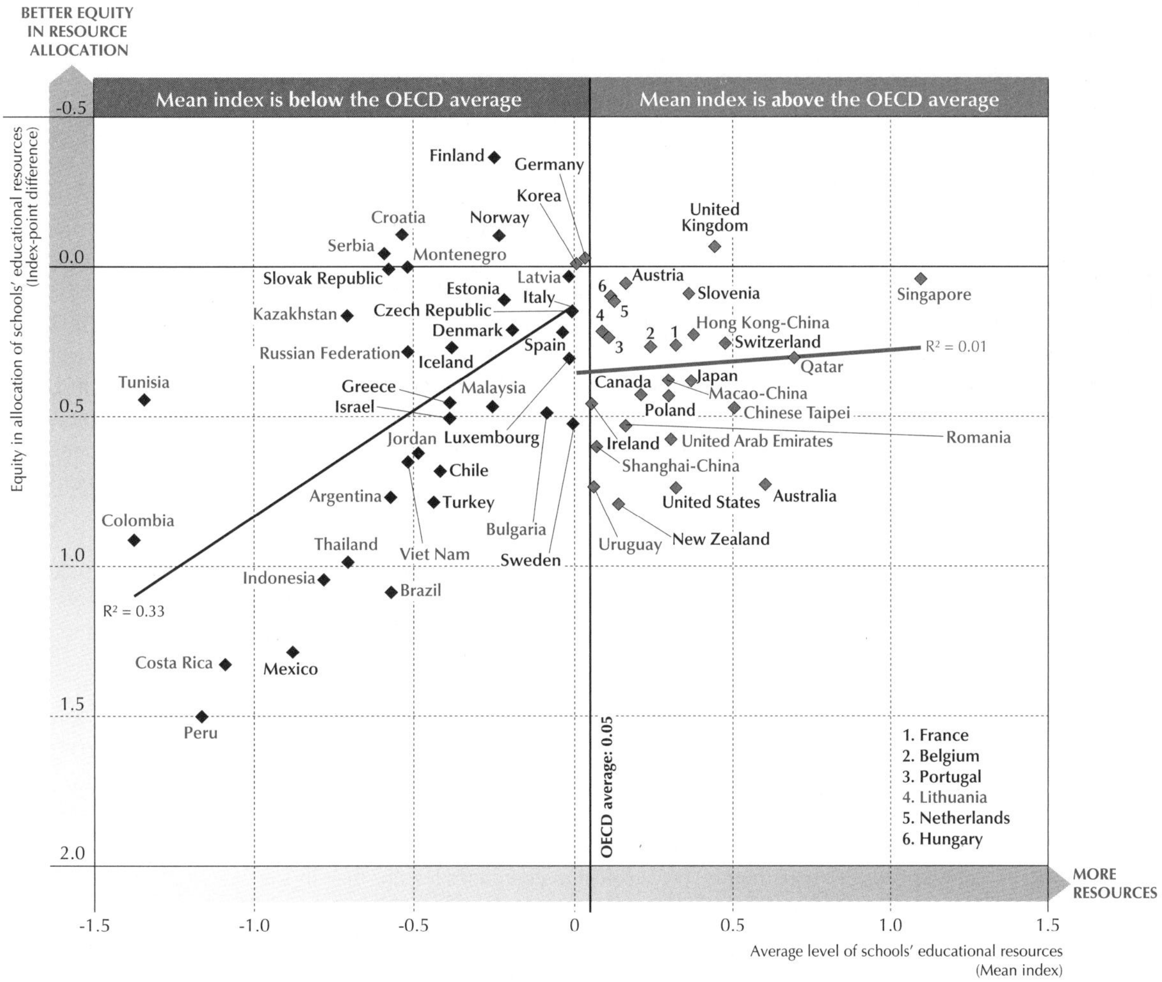

Notes: The vertical axis refers to the difference in the *index of quality of schools' educational resources* between socio-economically advantaged and disadvantaged schools (adv. - disadv.).
The horizontal axis refers to the mean *index of quality of schools' educational resources*.
Source: OECD, PISA 2012 Database, Tables IV.3.16 and IV.3.17.
StatLink ⌨ http://dx.doi.org/10.1787/888932957327

As shown in Figure IV.3.9, among the countries and economies where the average educational resource is below the OECD average, the overall level of educational resources is related to the level of equity in resource allocation between socio-economically advantaged and disadvantaged schools. The lower the overall level of schools' educational resources, the greater the gap in educational resources between advantaged and disadvantaged schools. Scarce resources tend to be more concentrated in advantaged schools, and disadvantaged schools tend to suffer from inadequacy

or shortage of resources; and the overall level of schools' educational resources is also related to systems' average performance (correlation coefficient is 0.70). By contrast, among countries and economies where the overall level of educational resources is above the OECD average, equity in resource allocation is not necessary linked to the overall level of resources; and the overall level of educational resources is not related to systems' average performance, either (correlation coefficient is 0.12).

School principals were asked to report in detail the number of computers available to students, at school, for educational purposes, and the number of these computers that are connected to the Internet. In Australia, Austria, New Zealand, Macao-China and the United Kingdom, at least one computer per student is available while in Turkey, Indonesia, Montenegro, Malaysia and Brazil five or more students share one computer. In a majority of countries and economies, over 95% of these computers are connected to the Internet; but in Indonesia, Kazakhstan, Tunisia and Peru, more than one in three of these computers are not connected to the Internet (Table IV.3.18).

Across OECD countries, about one in three students attends a school whose principal reported that less than 10% of work in class requires Internet access; more than one in two students are in schools where between 10% and 50% of work in class requires Internet access; and the remaining students (10%) attend schools where more than 50% of work in class requires Internet access (Table IV.3.19).

Box IV.3.2. **Improving in PISA: Tunisia**

Tunisia's performance in all three PISA subjects has improved over the past decade: in mathematics, by 3 score points per year; in reading, by 3.8 score points per year; and in science, by 2.2 score points per year. In 2003, the country's mean score in mathematics was 359 points; in 2012, it had improved to 388 points. This improvement reflects a considerable reduction in the proportion of students who scored below Level 2 in mathematics. In 2003, almost four out of five students (78%) failed to attain this baseline level of proficiency in mathematics; by 2012, this share had shrunk to around two out of three students (68%). Improvements in mathematics and reading scores are observed among both low- and high-achieving students, while improvements in science scores are seen only among low-achieving students.

Despite these improvements in the learning environment, 15-year-old students in 2012 had more negative dispositions towards school and mathematics than their counterparts in 2003 did; and the share of students who reported that they arrived late for school in the two weeks prior to the PISA test grew from 38% in 2003 to 52% in 2012.

Improvements in performance coincided with improvements in some aspect of the learning environment in Tunisia's schools. Students and principals reported fewer student- and teacher-related factors that hinder learning in 2012 than they did in 2003. In addition, the student-teacher ratio decreased from 19.4 in 2003 to 12.1 in 2012, and students attend schools whose principal is less likely to report that a shortage of teachers, educational material or physical infrastructure hinders student learning. Students are also more exposed to mathematics in school, as the average student in 2012 now spends 26 more minutes per week in mathematics lessons than the average student in 2003 did. Students in 2003 reported spending almost five hours per week on mathematics homework, while students in 2012 reported spending around three-and-a-half hours per week. In 2003, 62% of students reported that they had repeated a grade; by 2012, 38% of students so reported; as a result, 15-year old-students at the time of the PISA test in 2012 were more likely to be in upper secondary education than 15-year-olds in PISA 2003. Students in 2012 were also less likely than their counterparts in 2003 to be in schools that group students by ability.

In the 2000s, several policies were adopted with the aim of promoting student learning. The "School of Tomorrow" (*École de demain*) established the framework for these policies with planned implementation between 2002 and 2007. While the changes received wide support from teachers and parents, they have yet to be fully adopted because of the political uncertainty in Tunisia. Those policies that have been implemented focus on changing the curriculum and changing the way teachers teach. They also foster a culture of evaluation of schools and the school system, one of the reasons why Tunisia began participating in PISA in 2003 and continued to do so in every subsequent assessment.

...

In line with the PISA results outlined above, mandated teaching time for mathematics at the primary and top-level lower secondary schools was increased from four to five hours per week. The curriculum was further modified to introduce the teaching of physics and information technologies. Teachers were encouraged to modify their teaching methods to emphasise learning through student-directed problem solving and to make better use of information and communication technologies (ICT) in the teaching of Arabic, French, mathematics and sciences. To help teachers adopt of these new methods, national teaching manuals were revised and now include CDs with the relevant software for ICT-supported teaching.

In addition, Tunisia increased its budget for education, spending three times more per student at the secondary level and more than double at the primary level in 2011 than it did in 2001. These additional financial resources are devoted to providing information and communication technologies to schools, reducing class size, raising teachers' salaries, and improving the physical working conditions for teachers.

Sources :

Mhirsi, C. (2012), *Le Système Éducatif Tunisien à travers les Évaluations Internationales*, Colloque sur la Méthodologie de la Réforme du Système Éducatif (29-31 mars, 2012), Ministère de L'Éducation, Tunis.

Ministère de l'Éducation (2002), *La Nouvelle Réforme du Système Éducatif Tunisien : Programme pour la mise en œuvre du projet "École de demain"*, Ministère de l'Éducation, Tunis.

TIME RESOURCES

According to the results discussed in Chapter 1, at the school level, there is some relationship between the time students spend learning in and after school and their performance, but no clear pattern of this relationship is observed across countries and economies. Across all countries and economies that participated in PISA 2012, high-performing systems offer more creative extracurricular activities, and more students attend pre-primary education, and for a longer period of time, in these systems.

Ever since the seminal study by John B. Carroll (1963) on the extent of learning as a function of the instructional time a student receives relative to the time the student needs, educators and policy makers have attempted to understand how students' hours in school should be organised to maximise learning (Bloom, 1968). The literature suggests that optimising academic learning time is one of the key factors in improving academic achievement (Carroll, 1989; Hawley and Rosenholtz, 1984; Sheerens and Bosker, 1997; Marzano, 2003). The extent of students' exposure to content is the core of the concept of "opportunity to learn" (Schmidt and Maier, 2009), which is discussed in detail in Volume I.

While learning takes place in a variety of formal and informal settings, research indicates that structured lesson time at school is an important pre-requisite for students to develop the competencies that are assessed in the PISA 2012 framework (Scheerens and Bosker, 1997; Seidel and Shavelson, 2007; OECD, 2013a). Determining how learning time is associated with performance is difficult, given that many factors can influence the productivity of learning time. Yet research finds that the more time students spend learning, on average, the higher their grades (Fisher et al., 1980; Clark and Linn, 2003; Smith, 2002; Lavy, 2010).

What is less straightforward is how after-school lessons and individual study can promote academic achievement or be better organised to develop students' skills. While schools are structured learning environments with less variability than after-school programmes (Entwisle, Alexander and Olson 1997), both the quantity and quality of learning opportunities in informal settings are likely to vary more. Indirect evidence of this comes from studies examining the possible causes of the differences related to socio-economic status in the cognitive skills of young children entering school (Hart and Risley, 1995; Natriello, McDill and Pallas, 1990; Huttenlocher et al., 1991; Jencks and Phillips, 1998; Levin and Belfield, 2002). In these studies, differences in informal learning opportunities can be attributed to: more restricted vocabulary used by adults in the social networks of children coming from disadvantaged backgrounds; lower participation rates in pre-school education among children from disadvantaged backgrounds; the lack of educational resources available to parents with little education; and the fact that the achievement gap between social groups tends to grow during school breaks, reflecting differences in what children are exposed to while they are outside of school and formal learning environments.

Intended learning time in school

School systems make decisions about the overall amount of time devoted to instruction and what material students should be taught and at what age. Total intended instruction time is an estimate of the number of hours during which students are taught both compulsory and non-compulsory parts of the curriculum, as per public regulations. On average across OECD countries, students are expected to receive an average of around 7 700 hours of school (primary and secondary) by the time they are 14. Most of this instruction time is compulsory (OECD, 2013b). This total intended instruction time for students up to 14 years old ranges from over 9 400 hours in Australia, Greece and Chile and the partner country Colombia, to less than 6 000 hours in Estonia, Finland, Poland and Sweden and the partner countries and economies Argentina, Lithuania, Latvia, Croatia, the Russian Federation, Hong Kong-China, Bulgaria, Montenegro, Tunisia and Albania (Table IV.3.20).

Some systems allocate more learning time for older students than younger students, while other systems do the opposite. In the Czech Republic, Mexico, Hungary, Korea and the partner countries and economies the Russian Federation, Indonesia, Bulgaria, Chinese Taipei, Lithuania, Croatia, Macao-China and Latvia, the average number of hours per year of total intended instruction time for students between 12 and 14 years is more than that for students up to 9 years old (between 1.4 and 1.9 times more). By contrast, in Greece, Luxembourg, Turkey and the partner country Uruguay, the average number of hours per year of total intended instruction time for students aged between 12 and 14 is less than that for students up to 9 years old (between 0.67 and 0.98 times less) (Table IV.3.20).

Students' learning time in regular school lessons

PISA 2012 asked students to report the average number of minutes per class period and the number of class periods per week for mathematics, language of instruction and science.[7] Across OECD countries, students reported spending 3 hours and 38 minutes per week in mathematics lessons, 3 hours and 35 minutes per week in language-of-instruction classes, and 3 hours and 20 minutes per week in science lessons (Figure IV.3.10 and Table IV.3.21).

Student learning time in regular lessons varies greatly across school systems. Students in Chile spend around 6 hours and 40 minutes and students in Canada and the United Arab Emirates spend around 5 hours and 15 minutes in regular mathematics lessons per week. By contrast, students in Bulgaria, Montenegro, Croatia and Hungary spend less than 2 hours and 30 minutes in regular mathematics lessons per week. Meanwhile, students in Chile spend 6 hours and 14 minutes per week and students in Canada, Denmark and Tunisia spend between 5 hours and 6 minutes and 5 hours and 16 minutes per week in language-of-instruction classes. By contrast, students in Kazakhstan spend 1 hour and 49 minutes per week and students in the Russian Federation, Uruguay, Thailand, Bulgaria, Austria and Serbia spend between 2 hours and 15 minutes and 2 hours 25 minutes per week in language-of-instruction classes. Students in the United Arab Emirates and Canada spend 5 hours and 6 minutes; students in Lithuania spend 5 hours and 21 minutes per week in science lessons. By contrast, students in Montenegro spend 1 hour and 45 minutes, students in Italy spend 2 hours and 16 minutes, and students in Iceland spend 2 hours and 21 minutes per week in science lessons (Figure IV.3.10 and Table IV.3.21).

Students in school systems that provide an above-average amount of learning time in mathematics classes also tend to spend an above-average learning time in language of instruction lessons (r=0.85 across OECD countries and r=0.82 across all participating countries and economies). Students in systems that provide above-average learning time in regular mathematics lessons tend to spend more time in regular science lessons (r=0.59 across OECD countries and r=0.51 across all participating countries and economies). However, in some systems, such as those in Bulgaria and Lithuania, students spend less-than-average time in regular mathematics lessons, while they spend more-than-average time in regular science lessons.

Even within individual school systems, the amount of learning time in regular lessons, as reported by 15-year-old students, can vary. In most school systems, there is greater variation in learning time in regular science lessons than in regular mathematics or reading lessons. In Greece, Slovenia, Poland, Estonia, Ireland, Lithuania, Hungary, Finland and Serbia, the amount of learning time that students spend in regular mathematics lessons does not vary much, while in Chile, Peru, the United Arab Emirates, Argentina, Tunisia, Indonesia, Colombia and the United States, there are notable differences (Table IV.3.21).

On average across OECD countries, students who are in socio-economically disadvantaged schools tend to spend fewer minutes in regular mathematics lessons than students in advantaged schools. This is true in many countries and economies, especially in Japan, Chinese Taipei and Argentina, where students in advantaged schools spend an average of over 76 minutes more per week in regular mathematics lessons than students in disadvantaged schools. However, the opposite is observed in the United Arab Emirates, Germany, Switzerland, Austria, the United Kingdom and Qatar, where students in disadvantaged schools spend an average of between 5 to 35 minutes more per week in regular mathematics lessons than students in advantaged schools (Table IV.3.22).

■ Figure IV.3.10 ■

Student learning time in school and after school

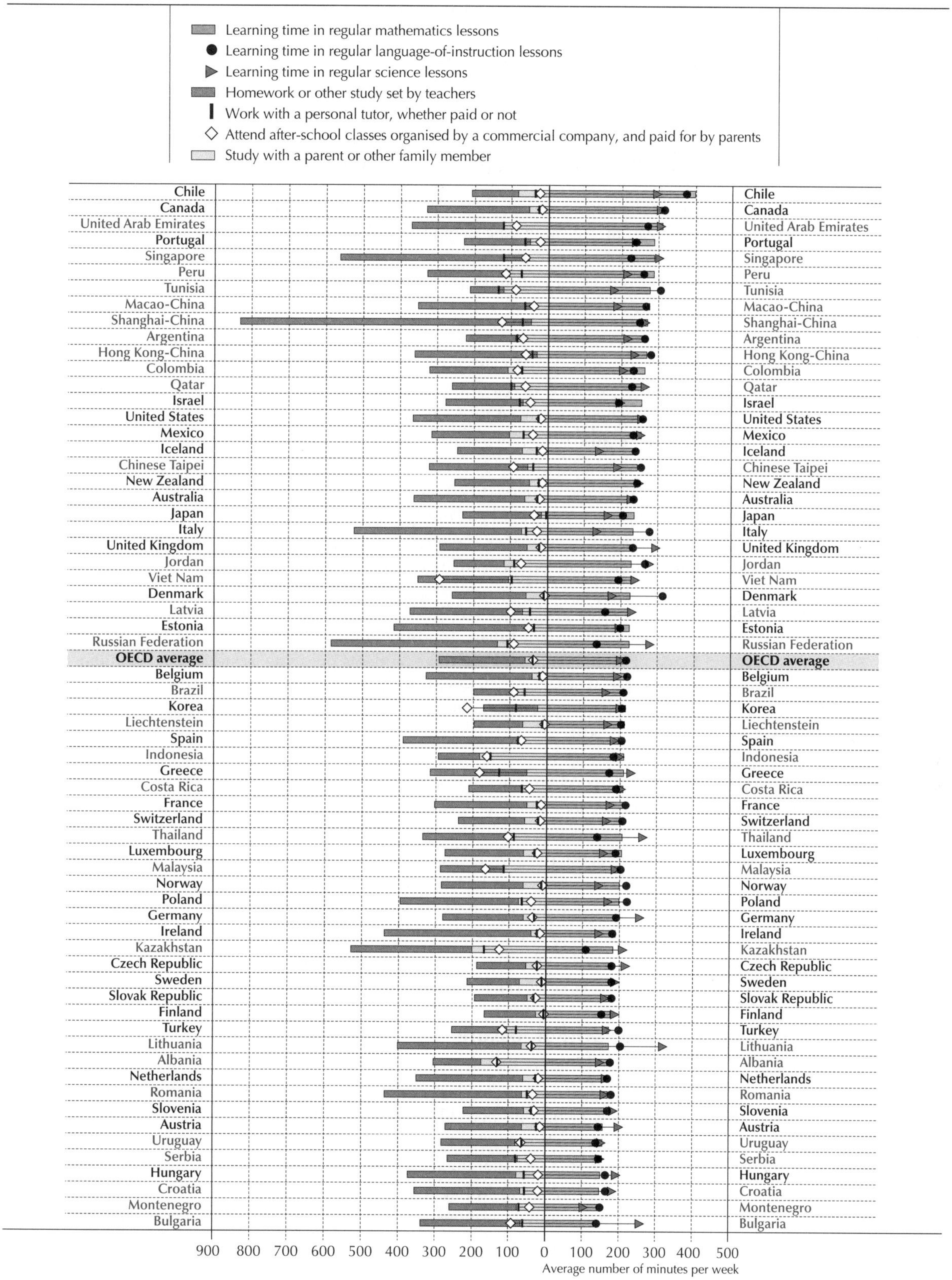

- ▨ Learning time in regular mathematics lessons
- ● Learning time in regular language-of-instruction lessons
- ▶ Learning time in regular science lessons
- ▨ Homework or other study set by teachers
- ❙ Work with a personal tutor, whether paid or not
- ◇ Attend after-school classes organised by a commercial company, and paid for by parents
- ▨ Study with a parent or other family member

Chile
Canada
United Arab Emirates
Portugal
Singapore
Peru
Tunisia
Macao-China
Shanghai-China
Argentina
Hong Kong-China
Colombia
Qatar
Israel
United States
Mexico
Iceland
Chinese Taipei
New Zealand
Australia
Japan
Italy
United Kingdom
Jordan
Viet Nam
Denmark
Latvia
Estonia
Russian Federation
OECD average
Belgium
Brazil
Korea
Liechtenstein
Spain
Indonesia
Greece
Costa Rica
France
Switzerland
Thailand
Luxembourg
Malaysia
Norway
Poland
Germany
Ireland
Kazakhstan
Czech Republic
Sweden
Slovak Republic
Finland
Turkey
Lithuania
Albania
Netherlands
Romania
Slovenia
Austria
Uruguay
Serbia
Hungary
Croatia
Montenegro
Bulgaria

900 800 700 600 500 400 300 200 100 0 100 200 300 400 500
Average number of minutes per week

Countries and economies are ranked in descending order of average time spent per week in regular mathematics lessons.
Source: OECD, PISA 2012 Database, Tables IV.3.21 and IV.3.27.
StatLink ᵐˢˡ http://dx.doi.org/10.1787/888932957327

These differences in learning time between disadvantaged and advantaged schools are also related to other school features, such as differences in learning time between lower or upper secondary levels, public or private schools, or academic or vocational schools, depending on the structure of individual school systems. As shown in Chapter 2, socio-economically disadvantaged students are, in general, more likely to repeat a grade, so they have a greater chance of being enrolled at the lower secondary level in some systems. Whether students in lower secondary school spend more time learning mathematics than those at the upper secondary level depends on the education system. For example, in Argentina students at the upper secondary level spend 40 minutes more per week in regular mathematics class than students in lower secondary school, while in Switzerland students at the lower secondary level spend 59 minutes more per week in regular mathematics class than students in upper secondary school (Table IV.3.22)

Because the PISA sample is age-based, students are drawn from various grade levels and from both lower and upper secondary levels. It is important to keep this in mind when comparing the amount of time students invest in reading, mathematics and science lessons, because these lessons may be compulsory at one level (and hence in one school system, depending on the education level 15-year-old students attend) and not in the other (see also Box IV.1.1).

Class size

Class size can affect learning in various ways. Large classes may limit the time and attention teachers can devote to individual students, rather than to the whole class; and they may also be more prone to disturbances from noisy and disruptive students. As a result, teachers may have to adopt different pedagogical styles to compensate, which may, in turn, affect learning. While some research shows that smaller classes can improve non-cognitive skills (Dee and West, 2011), research on class size has generally found a weak relationship between small classes and better performance (Ehrenberg et al., 2001; Piketty and Valdenaire, 2006). Class size seems to be more important in the earlier years of schooling than it is for 15-year-olds (Finn, 1998; Chetty et al., 2011; Dynarski, Hyman and Schanzenbach, 2011). Moreover, the effects of class size on student performance seem to be culture-specific: comparatively large classes are found in many Asian countries where average student performance is high.

Students were asked to report the average number of students who attend their language-of-instruction class. On average across OECD countries, there are 24 students in a language-of-instruction class. In Viet Nam, Chinese Taipei, Japan, Thailand, Shanghai-China and Macao-China, there are 35 or more students per class, while in Liechtenstein, Finland, Latvia, Belgium, Switzerland, Iceland, Kazakhstan and Denmark there are fewer than 20 students. Class size varies greatly in Mexico, Jordan and Thailand, while in Greece, Finland, Denmark, Romania, Poland, Luxembourg, Italy, Croatia and Portugal language-of-instruction classes for 15-year-olds are roughly the same size (Table IV.3.23).

Classes in advantaged schools tend to be larger than those in disadvantaged schools by four students, on average across OECD countries. This is true in 51 countries and economies, while in Singapore, Qatar and the United Arab Emirates, classes in advantaged schools tend to be smaller than those in disadvantaged schools. There is no difference in class size between public and private schools, on average across OECD countries; and upper secondary students tend to be in larger classes than lower secondary students, on average across OECD countries. This is true in 29 countries and economies, while the opposite is observed in Germany, Turkey, Singapore, Australia, Kazakhstan, Israel, the Russian Federation, Qatar and Ireland. On average across OECD countries, the size of classes in schools located in rural areas tend to be smaller than those in schools located in towns or cities, and there is no difference in class size between classes in schools located in towns and those in schools located in cities (Table IV.3.24).

Students' learning time in after-school lessons

Students were asked to report the number of hours they typically spend per week attending after-school lessons in mathematics, language of instruction and science. These are lessons that may be given at their school, at their home or somewhere else. Across OECD countries, students are more likely to attend after-school lessons in mathematics than in language of instruction or science. Around 73% of students reported that they do not attend after-school lessons in the language of instruction or science; more students attend after-school mathematics lessons, while 62% of students reported that they did not attend such lessons, another 30% of students reported that they attend after-school mathematics lessons, but for less than four hours per week, and 8% of students attend such lessons for four or more hours per week (Table IV.3.25).

Students' attendance in after-school lessons varies greatly across countries. In Viet Nam, Tunisia, Malaysia, Peru, Shanghai-China, Kazakhstan, the Russian Federation and Japan, around 70% or more of students attend after-school lessons in mathematics. In Viet Nam, Tunisia and Peru, between 28% and 36% of students attend these lessons for four hours or more per week.

■ Figure IV.3.11 ■
Attendance in after-school lessons

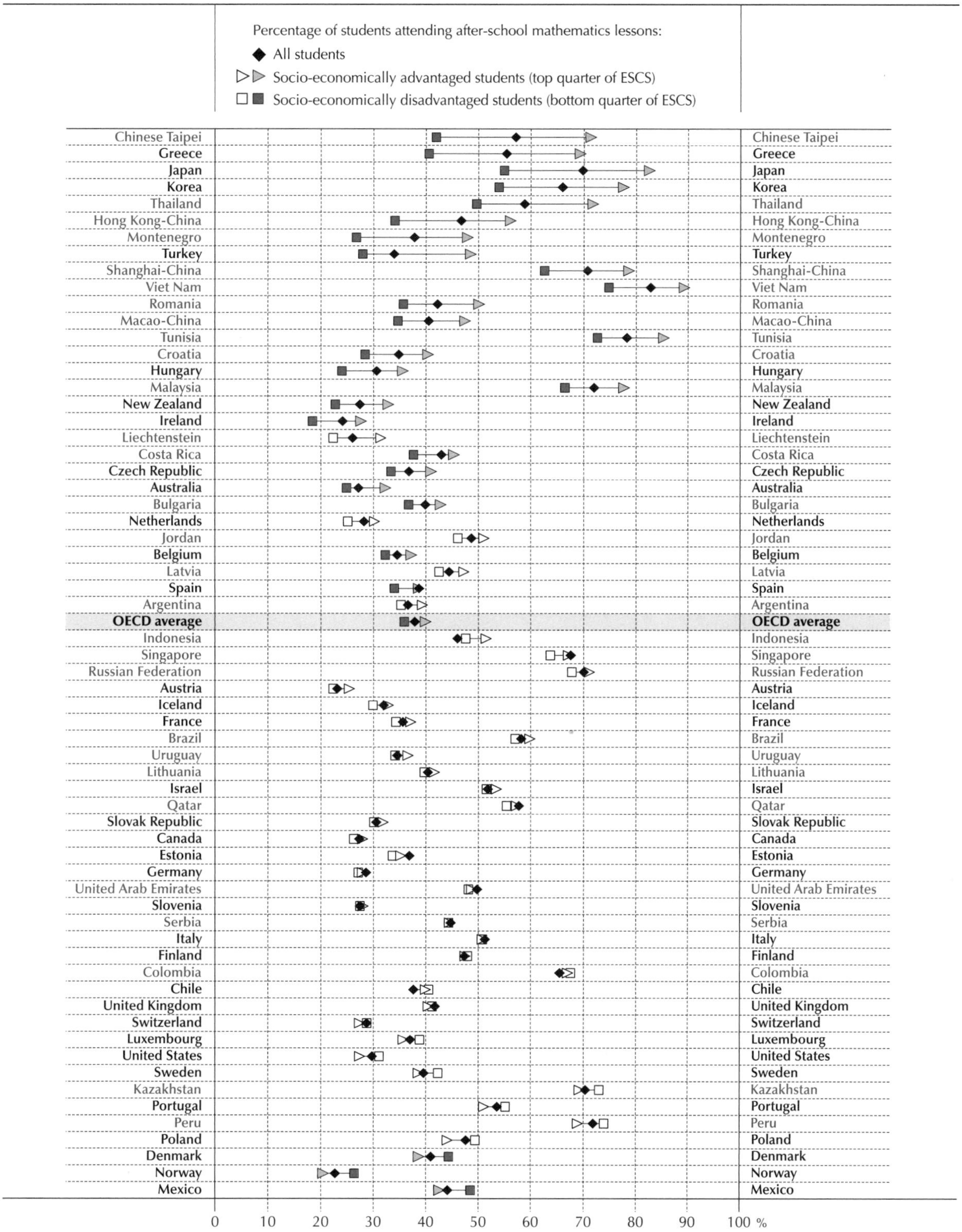

Percentage of students attending after-school mathematics lessons:
◆ All students
▷▷ Socio-economically advantaged students (top quarter of ESCS)
□■ Socio-economically disadvantaged students (bottom quarter of ESCS)

	Chinese Taipei
	Greece
	Japan
	Korea
	Thailand
	Hong Kong-China
	Montenegro
	Turkey
	Shanghai-China
	Viet Nam
	Romania
	Macao-China
	Tunisia
	Croatia
	Hungary
	Malaysia
	New Zealand
	Ireland
	Liechtenstein
	Costa Rica
	Czech Republic
	Australia
	Bulgaria
	Netherlands
	Jordan
	Belgium
	Latvia
	Spain
	Argentina
	OECD average
	Indonesia
	Singapore
	Russian Federation
	Austria
	Iceland
	France
	Brazil
	Uruguay
	Lithuania
	Israel
	Qatar
	Slovak Republic
	Canada
	Estonia
	Germany
	United Arab Emirates
	Slovenia
	Serbia
	Italy
	Finland
	Colombia
	Chile
	United Kingdom
	Switzerland
	Luxembourg
	United States
	Sweden
	Kazakhstan
	Portugal
	Peru
	Poland
	Denmark
	Norway
	Mexico

0   10   20   30   40   50   60   70   80   90   100 %

Notes: White symbols represent differences that are not statistically significant.
ESCS refers to the *PISA index of economic, social and cultural status.*
Countries and economies are ranked in descending order of the difference in the percentages between students who are in the bottom quarter of ESCS and those who are in the top quarter (top - bottom).
Source: OECD, PISA 2012 Database, Tables IV.3.25 and IV.3.26.
StatLink ⎙ http://dx.doi.org/10.1787/888932957327

By contrast, in Norway, Austria, Ireland, Liechtenstein, Australia, Canada, New Zealand, Slovenia, the Netherlands, Germany, Switzerland and the United States, 70% or more of students do not attend after-school lessons in mathematics. In these countries, between 2% and 7% of students attend these lessons for four hours or more per week (Figure IV.3.11 and Table IV.3.25). The nature and purpose of after-school lessons vary. In some schools and school systems, after-school lessons are provided mainly to support struggling students, while in others they are mainly for enrichment.

On average across OECD countries, socio-economically advantaged students are more likely to attend after-school lessons in mathematics (40%) than disadvantaged students (36%). This is true in 25 countries and economies; in Chinese Taipei, Greece and Japan, the difference is between 27 and 30 percentage points. By contrast, in Mexico, Norway and Denmark, the opposite is observed: the proportion of disadvantaged students who attend after-school lessons in mathematics is larger than that of advantaged students by 5 percentage points or more. Across OECD countries, lower secondary students are more likely to attend after-school lessons in mathematics than upper secondary students, on average; and students who attend schools in a city are more likely to attend these lessons than students in schools located in other areas (Figure IV.3.11 and Table IV.3.26).

Students were also asked to report the average time they spend each week on various types of after-school study activities, all school subjects combined. Across OECD countries, students reported that they spend 4.9 hours per week on homework or other study set by their teacher. Of this time, 1.3 hours are spent with another person overseeing the study and providing help if necessary, either at school or elsewhere. Students also reported that they spend 39 minutes per week working with a personal tutor, and 37 minutes per week attending after-school classes organised by a commercial company and paid for by their parents (Figure IV.3.10 and Table IV.3.27).

Students in Shanghai-China, the Russian Federation, Singapore, Kazakhstan, Italy, Ireland and Romania reported that they spend at least seven hours per week on homework or other study set by their teachers. In Shanghai-China, students spend almost 14 hours per week. By contrast, in Finland, Korea, the Czech Republic, the Slovak Republic, Liechtenstein, Brazil, Chile, Costa Rica, Tunisia, Sweden, Argentina, Slovenia, Portugal and Japan, students spend less than four hours per week on this. Students in Kazakhstan, Indonesia, Tunisia, Albania, Greece, the United Arab Emirates and Singapore reported that they spend two hours per week or more working with a personal tutor. Students in Viet Nam, Korea, Greece, Malaysia, Indonesia, Albania, Kazakhstan and Shanghai-China reported that they spend more than two hours per week attending after-school classes organised by a commercial company and paid for by their parents.

Hours that students spend doing homework or other study set by teachers vary between schools. On average across OECD countries, students who attend socio-economically advantaged schools tend to spend two hours per week longer on this than students who attend disadvantaged schools. This is true in 59 countries and economies. Across OECD countries, students in private schools spend more time doing homework or other study set by teachers than students in public schools, on average; upper secondary students spend more time on this than lower secondary students; students in schools located in cities spend more time than students in schools located in towns; and students in schools in cities or towns spend more time on this than students in schools located in rural areas (Table IV.3.28).

Some schools organise extra mathematics lessons at school. School principals reported on whether their school offers mathematics lessons in addition to the mathematics lessons offered during the usual school hours. Across OECD countries, two out of three students attend schools whose principals reported that such additional mathematics lessons are offered. In the Russian Federation, Hong Kong-China, Luxembourg, Viet Nam, Serbia, Macao-China, the United Kingdom, Kazakhstan, Korea, Malaysia, Singapore and Thailand, over 90% of students are in schools that offer these kinds of additional mathematics lessons, while fewer than half of students in Greece, Norway, Colombia, Denmark, Spain, Peru, Turkey, Costa Rica, Austria and Shanghai-China attend such schools (Table IV.3.29).

The additional mathematics lessons that are offered in some schools are usually for both enrichment and remedial purposes. Across OECD countries, 54% of students are in schools whose principals reported that the school offers enrichment and remedial mathematics lessons. Another 32% of students are in schools that offer remedial mathematics lessons only. Some 6% of students are in schools that offer enrichment mathematics lessons only. The remaining 7% of students are in schools that offer additional mathematics lessons based on the prior achievement level of the students. In most participating countries and economies, offering both enrichment and remedial mathematics lessons appears to be most common. However, in Luxembourg, Austria, the Netherlands, Spain, Chile, Belgium and Denmark, offering remedial mathematics lessons only is more common than offering both remedial and enrichment lessons. In these countries, there is at least an 18 percentage-point difference in the proportion of students in schools that offer remedial lessons only and those in schools that offer both remedial and enrichment lessons (Table IV.3.29).

■ Figure IV.3.12 ■
Extracurricular activities

Creative extracurricular activities at school

Percentage of students in schools whose principals reported
that the following activities are offered at school

- **A** Band, orchestra or choir
- **B** School play or school musical
- **C** Art club or art activities

Extracurricular mathematics activities at school

Percentage of students in schools whose principals reported that
the following activities are offered at school

- **D** Mathematics club
- **E** Mathematics competitions
- **F** Club with a focus on computers/information and communication technology
- **G** Either enrichment or remedial mathematics after-school lessons
- **H** Both enrichment and remedial mathematics after-school lessons

	A	B	C	Index of creative extracurricular activities at school
Macao-China	87	96	94	
Hong Kong-China	93	86	98	
United Kingdom	96	90	92	
Canada	88	91	89	
United States	92	86	88	
New Zealand	99	84	85	
Poland	81	88	87	
Singapore	98	70	86	
Lithuania	92	59	88	
Latvia	76	67	91	
Luxembourg	74	79	79	
Costa Rica	83	76	76	
Shanghai-China	74	67	87	
Thailand	68	72	87	
Germany	83	64	79	
Japan	85	42	95	
Slovenia	74	75	74	
Australia	91	68	64	
Estonia	83	58	75	
Chinese Taipei	74	50	89	
Korea	73	43	93	
Liechtenstein	79	60	72	
Kazakhstan	63	51	89	
Serbia	70	81	51	
France	42	72	83	
Switzerland	71	60	68	
Chile	69	48	80	
Montenegro	38	87	63	
Iceland	54	74	68	
Netherlands	58	63	65	
Hungary	69	51	65	
Qatar	28	78	80	
Albania	45	62	79	
Mexico	56	56	72	
Malaysia	42	42	94	
Peru	55	59	61	
Russian Federation	66	40	65	
Turkey	52	67	51	
Romania	51	56	63	
Colombia	52	54	68	
Indonesia	51	54	61	
Israel	60	52	56	
Bulgaria	49	52	62	
Finland	80	43	37	
Ireland	67	39	57	
Croatia	45	62	48	
United Arab Emirates	21	64	68	
Viet Nam	18	85	47	
Uruguay	70	52	27	
Sweden	68	46	30	
Tunisia	33	55	62	
Greece	57	45	43	
Italy	30	72	37	
Portugal	30	54	52	
Slovak Republic	31	48	57	
Jordan	25	54	55	
Brazil	23	58	46	
Belgium	31	52	40	
Czech Republic	41	24	52	
Denmark	46	39	30	
Austria	52	35	28	
Argentina	27	33	46	
Spain	29	45	22	
Norway	29	32	8	
OECD average	63	59	62	

	D	E	F	G	H	Index of extracurricular mathematics activities at school
Hong Kong-China	90	91	97	18	75	
Poland	94	100	78	8	77	
Malaysia	97	80	86	11	78	
Korea	76	76	85	19	77	
United Kingdom	73	94	77	21	62	
Thailand	80	53	91	13	77	
Macao-China	62	88	76	24	69	
Russian Federation	66	97	51	18	78	
Slovenia	64	99	59	37	57	
Kazakhstan	64	98	64	36	61	
Qatar	72	91	72	23	57	
Slovak Republic	85	91	93	22	40	
Singapore	21	87	95	12	75	
Hungary	51	79	57	18	66	
Albania	67	91	48	30	59	
Portugal	45	98	12	12	77	
New Zealand	25	97	53	19	57	
Chinese Taipei	42	59	68	21	67	
United Arab Emirates	58	86	65	24	42	
Montenegro	40	55	69	43	48	
Viet Nam	26	82	17	16	79	
Romania	44	68	49	63	34	
Lithuania	20	93	34	11	65	
Shanghai-China	68	67	70	22	27	
Latvia	35	92	29	16	52	
Croatia	20	71	40	22	63	
Serbia	18	75	46	40	45	
Estonia	30	92	42	30	42	
Tunisia	52	56	59	39	36	
United States	56	68	55	27	31	
Canada	42	77	54	34	31	
Australia	27	95	30	22	45	
Indonesia	37	68	46	33	40	
Bulgaria	36	80	58	25	32	
Luxembourg	20	79	34	72	23	
Italy	6	67	21	24	60	
Mexico	34	82	31	31	32	
Israel	10	48	47	36	47	
Czech Republic	33	85	38	21	22	
Germany	21	58	60	29	27	
Finland	8	88	12	33	37	
Argentina	41	42	51	32	23	
Brazil	8	92	17	12	41	
France	11	73	24	24	35	
Peru	30	81	31	28	19	
Jordan	33	38	44	36	28	
Japan	7	12	56	20	54	
Chile	13	42	49	51	24	
Costa Rica	32	61	22	25	23	
Iceland	7	67	23	23	31	
Ireland	19	61	26	26	22	
Turkey	19	23	57	18	30	
Uruguay	6	26	24	44	38	
Colombia	29	61	24	13	21	
Sweden	10	58	3	39	26	
Belgium	1	70	9	37	21	
Greece	9	75	17	15	15	
Switzerland	5	28	18	38	23	
Spain	8	66	13	27	11	
Liechtenstein	3	34	29	32	20	
Netherlands	3	47	5	34	14	
Austria	2	33	20	37	12	
Norway	6	32	19	26	8	
Denmark	7	11	9	27	13	
OECD average	27	67	38	28	37	

Index points 0   1   2   3   Index points 0   1   2   3   4   5

Countries and economies are ranked in descending order of the average index.
Source: OECD, PISA 2012 Database, Tables IV.3.31 and IV.3.32.
StatLink ᐧᐧᐧ http://dx.doi.org/10.1787/888932957327

Extracurricular activities

Instruction doesn't just occur inside classroom walls; extracurricular activities, such as sports activities and teams, debate clubs, academic clubs, bands, orchestras or choirs, can improve students' cognitive and non-cognitive skills. Skills such as persistence, independence, following instructions, working well within groups, dealing with authority figures, and fitting in with peers are needed for students to succeed in school – and beyond (Farkas, 2003; Carneiro and Heckman, 2005; Covay and Carbonaro, 2009, Howie et al., 2010).

School principals were asked to report whether their school offers various extracurricular activities to students in the modal grade for 15-year-olds. Across OECD countries, 90% of students are in schools that support a sports team or sporting activities; 73% are in schools that offer volunteering or service activities; 67% are in schools that offer mathematics competitions; 63% are in schools that support a band, orchestra or choir; 62% are in schools that offer an art club or art activities; 59% are in schools that produce a school play or musical; 56% are in schools that support a school yearbook, newspaper or magazine; 38% are in schools that support a club with a focus on computers and information and communications technologies (ICT); 30% are in schools that support a chess club; and 27% are in schools that support a mathematics club (Table IV.3.30).

Some of the principals' responses to these questions were combined to create two indices. One is an *index of creative extracurricular activities at school*, which is the sum of principals' responses on whether schools offer: band, orchestra or choir; school play or school musical; and art club or art activities. The other index is an *index of extracurricular mathematics activities at school*, which is the sum of principals' responses on whether schools offer: mathematics club; mathematics competitions; club with a focus on computers and ICT; and one more separate question regarding the availability of additional mathematics lessons (for remedial only, for enhancement only, or for both remedial and enhancement), which was described in the previous section. The *index of creative extracurricular activities at school* ranges from 0 to 3, as this is the sum of availability of three activities, and the *index of extracurricular mathematics activities at school* ranges from 0 to 5, as this is the sum of five activities (see Annex A1).

As shown in Figure IV.3.12, in Macao-China, Hong Kong-China and the United Kingdom, schools tend to offer more creative extracurricular activities (in these countries and economies, the index score ranges from 2.75 to 2.78), while schools in Norway, Spain, Argentina, Austria, Denmark and the Czech Republic do not offer many creative extracurricular activities (in these countries and economies, the index score ranges from 0.68 to 1.16). In 20 countries and economies, schools offer three or more out of five extracurricular mathematics activities, on average, while schools in Hong Kong-China, Poland, Malaysia and Korea offer four or more of these activities, on average. By contrast, schools in Denmark, Norway, Austria, the Netherlands, Liechtenstein, Spain, Switzerland and Greece offer fewer than one-and-a-half of these activities. School systems in which schools offer more creative extracurricular activities also tend to offer more extracurricular mathematics activities (r = 0.58 across OECD countries and r = 0.52 across all participating countries and economies).

Students' attendance at pre-primary school

Whether and for how long students are enrolled in pre-primary education is another important aspect of time resources invested in education. Many of the inequalities that exist within school systems are already present when students first enter formal schooling and persist as students progress through schooling (Entwisle, Alexander and Olson 1997; Downey, Von Hippel and Broh 2004; Mistry et al., 2010). Because research shows that inequalities tend to grow when students are not attending school such as during long school breaks (Entwisle, Alexander and Olson, 1997; Alexander, Entwisle and Olson, 2001; Downey, Von Hippel and Broh, 2004), earlier entry into the school system may reduce inequalities in education – as long as participation in pre-primary schooling is universal and the learning opportunities across pre-primary schools are of high quality and relatively homogeneous. Earlier entry into pre-primary school prepares students better for entry into – and success in – formal schooling (Hart and Risley, 1995; Heckman, 2000; Chetty et al., 2011).

Across OECD countries, 93% of students reported that they had attended pre-primary education. In 52 participating countries and economies, over 80% of students reported that they had attended pre-primary education. However, in Indonesia, Tunisia and Montenegro, between 32% and 46% of students reported that they had not attended pre-primary education, as did 70% of students in Turkey and 65% of students in Kazakhstan. In general, most students had attended pre-primary education for more than one year: across OECD countries, 74% of students reported that they had attended pre-primary education for more than one year. In 24 participating countries and economies, over 80% of students reported that they had attended pre-primary education for more than one year (Table IV.3.33).

An average of 67% of students in socio-economically disadvantaged schools had attended pre-primary education for more than one year, while 81% of students in advantaged schools had done so. This is true in almost all participating countries and economies. The difference is around 44 percentage points in Poland and Lithuania and between 39 and 30 percentage points in Croatia, Kazakhstan, Argentina, Finland and Malaysia. On average across OECD countries, students in private schools (79%) are more likely than students in public schools (73%) to have attended pre-primary education for more than one year; 15-year-old upper secondary students (73%) are more likely than lower secondary students (68%) to have attended pre-primary school; and students in schools located in towns or cities are more likely to attend pre-primary school than students in schools located in rural areas (Table IV.3.34).

Box IV.3.3 describes how indices like the *index of quality of schools' educational resources* are compared across PISA assessments.

Box IV.3.3. **Comparing PISA scale indices between 2003 and 2012**

PISA scale indices, like the *PISA index of economic, social and cultural status*, the *index of teacher shortage*, the *index of quality of physical infrastructure*, the *index of quality of educational resources,* the *index of disciplinary climate,* the *index of teacher-student relations,* the *index of teacher morale,* the *index of student-related factors affecting school climate* and the *index of teacher-related factors affecting school climate*, are based on information gathered from the student questionnaire. In PISA 2012, each index is scaled so that a value of 0 indicates the OECD average and a value of 1 indicates the average standard deviation across OECD countries (see Annex A1 for details on how each index is constructed). Similarly, in PISA 2003, each index was scaled so that a value of 0 indicated the OECD average and a value of 1 indicated the average standard deviation across OECD countries. To compare the evolution of these indices over time, the PISA 2012 scale was used and all index values for PISA 2003 were rescaled accordingly. As a result, the values of the indices for 2003 presented in this report differ from those produced in *Learning for Tomorrow's World: First Results from PISA 2003* (OECD, 2004).

TRENDS IN RESOURCES INVESTED IN EDUCATION SINCE PISA 2003

Overall, most countries and economies with comparable data between 2003 and 2012 have moved towards better-staffed and better-equipped schools. Trends between 2003 and 2012 also reveal an increase in classroom instruction time dedicated to mathematics and a reduction in the time students spend doing mathematics homework. Fifteen-year-old students in 2012 were also more likely than 15-year-olds in 2003 to have attended at least one year of pre-primary education.[8]

Between 2001 and 2010, financial investment in education increased significantly. On average across OECD countries with comparable data from PISA 2003 and PISA 2012,[9] national cumulative expenditure per student from the age of 6 to the age of 15 increased by 40% in real terms. Increases in cumulative expenditure per student are notable in the Slovak Republic, where investments nearly tripled during the period, and in Ireland and Poland, where they doubled. Moreover, in most countries and economies, growth in investment in education for students up to the age of 15 outpaced GDP growth, signalling that countries have privileged spending on education. Only in Iceland, Mexico and Italy did real cumulative expenditure decrease during the period (Tables IV.3.1 and IV.3.2).

On average across OECD countries with comparable data from PISA 2003 and PISA 2012, there has been a reduction in student-teacher ratios. In 2003, the average 15-year-old student attended a school with student-teacher ratio of 13.4 students per teacher; by 2012 this ratio had dropped to 12.6 students per teacher. Of the 36 countries and economies with comparable data for this period, 21 saw a reduction in student-teacher ratios, particularly Macao-China, Tunisia and Brazil, where the average student in 2012 attended a school where there were at least five fewer students per teacher than there were in 2003 (Tunisia's improvement in PISA and recent education policies and programmes is outlined in Box IV.3.2). By contrast, Hungary, the Netherlands, Denmark and Liechtenstein are the only countries with comparable data that saw an increase in student-teacher ratios during this period (Figure IV.3.13 and Table IV.3.35). The overall reduction in student-teacher ratios observed across OECD countries with comparable data applies to advantaged and disadvantaged students, advantaged and disadvantaged schools, private and public schools, lower and upper secondary students, and schools located in rural, town or urban areas (Table IV.3.36).

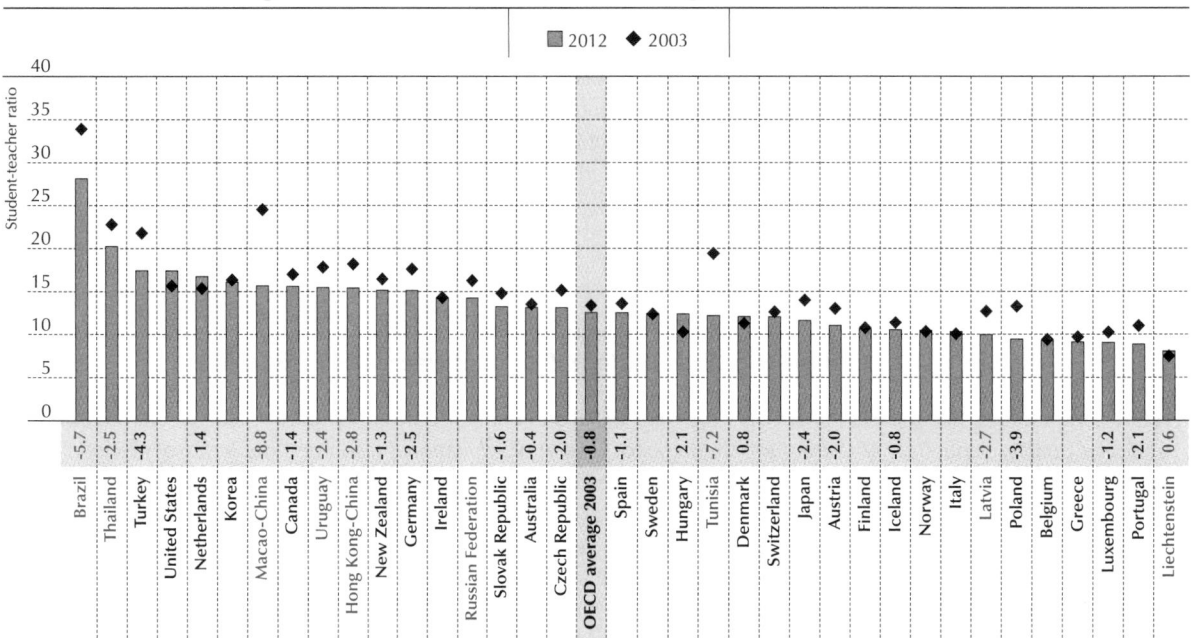

■ Figure IV.3.13 ■
Change between 2003 and 2012 in average student-teacher ratios

☐ 2012 ◆ 2003

Notes: Only countries and economies with comparable data from PISA 2003 and PISA 2012 are shown.
The change in student-teacher ratios (2012 - 2003) is shown above the country/economy name. Only statistically significant differences are shown.
OECD average 2003 compares only OECD countries with comparable results in 2012 and 2003.
Countries and economies are ranked in descending order of the student-teacher ratio in PISA 2012.
Source: OECD, PISA 2012 Database, Table IV.3.35.
StatLink ⬛ᴵˢᴸ http://dx.doi.org/10.1787/888932957327

School principals' reports also signal trends towards better-staffed schools. Students in 2012 were less likely than students in 2003 to attend schools whose principal reported that a lack of qualified teachers hinders learning. On average across OECD countries, students in 2012 were around five percentage points less likely than students in 2003 to attend schools whose principal reported that a lack of qualified mathematics teachers hinders instruction. In 2003, more than one in two students in Turkey, Luxembourg, Uruguay and Indonesia, attended schools whose principal signalled that a lack of qualified mathematics teachers hindered learning; in 2012 this was the case only for students in Luxembourg, among all countries and economies with comparable data from PISA 2003 and PISA 2012. Reductions in teacher shortages were observed in 20 of the 38 countries and economies with comparable data for the period. The largest reductions in teacher shortages were observed in Turkey and Indonesia, where students in 2012 were at least 35 percentage points less likely than students in 2003 to attend schools whose principals reported that a lack of qualified mathematics, science or language-of-assessment teachers hindered instruction to some extent or a lot. However, increases in teacher shortages are observed in eight countries and economies (Table IV.3.37). In Korea, for example, students in 2012 were ten percentage points more likely than students in 2003 to attend schools whose principal reported that a lack of qualified mathematics teachers hindered instruction to some extent or a lot. The fact that instruction was less hindered by a lack of qualified teachers in 2012 than in 2003, on average among OECD countries, was also observed across advantaged and disadvantaged schools, public and private schools, lower and upper secondary school programmes, and in schools located in rural, town or urban areas, on average (Table IV.3.39).

More school principals in 2012 than in 2003 reported that schools are in good physical condition. On average across the OECD countries with comparable data from PISA 2003 and PISA 2012, students are significantly less likely to attend schools whose principal reported that the inadequacy or shortage of school buildings, heating or cooling systems or instructional space hindered the capacity to provide instruction by six, four and five percentage points, respectively. Deterioration in the quality of overall material conditions, as measured by the *index of quality of physical infrastructure* were observed in 22 of the 38 countries with comparable data, particularly in Turkey. In Tunisia, Thailand and Korea more school principals in 2012 than in 2003 reported that the quality of the physical infrastructure – particularly a lack of sufficient instructional space – hindered learning (Table IV.3.40). The average positive trend among OECD countries

with comparable data, that instruction is less hindered by a lack of adequate physical infrastructure, is observed in both advantaged and disadvantaged schools, public and private schools, lower and upper secondary school programmes, and schools located in rural, town or urban areas, on average (Table IV.3.42).

Students in 2012 are also less likely than their counterparts were in 2003 to attend schools whose principal reported that the school's capacity to provide instruction is hindered by a lack of instructional materials. In 29 of the 38 countries and economies with comparable data, there is an increase in the *index of quality of schools' educational resources*, with the largest improvements observed in Turkey, Poland, Uruguay and the Russian Federation. In Turkey, for example, students are more than 40 percentage points less likely to attend schools whose principal reported that a lack of instructional materials (e.g. textbooks) or computer software for instruction hinders the school's capacity to provide instruction. By contrast, the *index of quality of schools' educational resources* fell – signalling a greater likelihood that students attend schools where a lack of material resources hinders the school's capacity to provide instruction – in Tunisia, Korea and Iceland (Figure IV.3.14 and Table IV.3.43). The overall trend among OECD countries, that a lack of educational resources hinders the school's capacity to provide instruction to a lower extent in 2012 than in 2003, was observed across all school types (advantaged and disadvantaged students, advantaged and disadvantaged schools, private and public schools, lower and upper secondary programmes, and urban and rural schools) (Table IV.3.45).

■ Figure IV.3.14 ■

Change between 2003 and 2012 in the index of quality of schools' educational resources (e.g. textbooks)

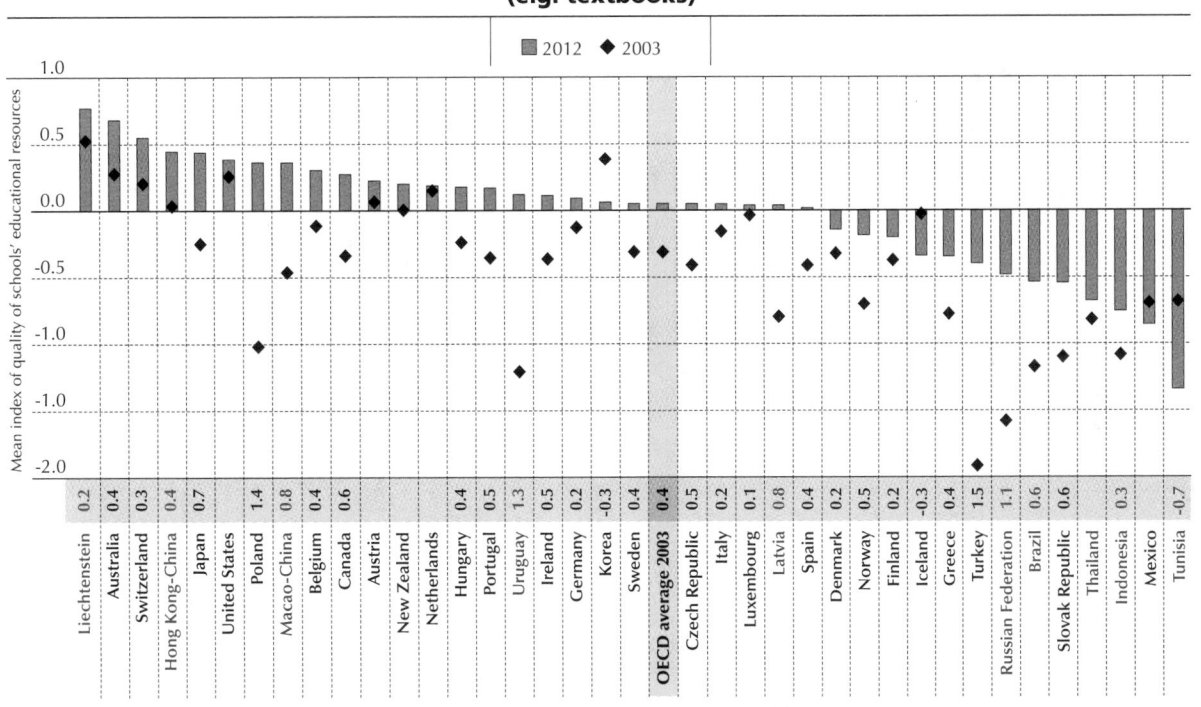

Notes: Only countries and economies with comparable data from PISA 2003 and PISA 2012 are shown.
The change in the *index of quality of schools' educational resources* (2012 - 2003) is shown above the country/economy name. Only statistically significant differences are shown.
For comparability over time, PISA 2003 values on the *index of quality of schools' educational resources* have been rescaled to the PISA 2012 scale of the index. PISA 2003 results reported in this figure may thus differ from those presented in *Learning for Tomorrow's World: First Results from PISA 2003* (OECD, 2004a) (see Annex A5 for more details).
OECD average 2003 compares only OECD countries with comparable results in 2012 and 2003.
Countries and economies are ranked in descending order of the mean index of quality of schools' educational resources *in PISA 2012.*
Source: OECD, PISA 2012 Database, Table IV.3.43.
StatLink ⓘ http://dx.doi.org/10.1787/888932957327

Across OECD countries, students spent an average of 13 minutes per week more in mathematics classes in 2012 than they did in 2003. Average time spent in regular school lessons in mathematics per week increased by more than an hour-and-a-half in Portugal and Canada, and by more than 30 minutes in Spain, Norway and the United States. As a result of these changes, mathematics instruction for 15-year-olds in Portugal increased from an average of 3 hours and 15 minutes

per week to 4 hours and 48 minutes per week. In Canada, average mathematic instruction time increased from 3 hours and 43 minutes to around 5 hours and 14 minutes. Increases in exposure to mathematics between 2003 and 2012 by more than 15 minutes per week when comparing are observed in an additional 14 countries and economies. In contrast, average learning time in mathematics shrank in ten countries and economies. Only in Korea – which had the fifth longest amount of learning time in 2003 – did the total learning time in mathematics fall by more than 30 minutes. Average weekly instruction time in mathematics also decreased in Turkey, Uruguay, Indonesia, Thailand and the Slovak Republic by at least 15 minutes per week. Countries and economies that saw an increase in weekly mathematics instruction time are not necessarily those that had shorter instruction time in 2003 (the correlation between instruction time in 2003 and change in instruction time between 2003 and 2012 is weak at -0.14) (Figure IV.3.15 and Table IV.3.46). The overall trend among OECD countries, that students spend more time in mathematics classes, is observed across all school types (advantaged and disadvantaged, private and public, lower and upper secondary programmes, and urban and rural schools) (Tables IV.3.47[1] and IV.3.47[2]).

■ Figure IV.3.15 ■

Change between 2003 and 2012 in the average time spent in mathematics lessons in school

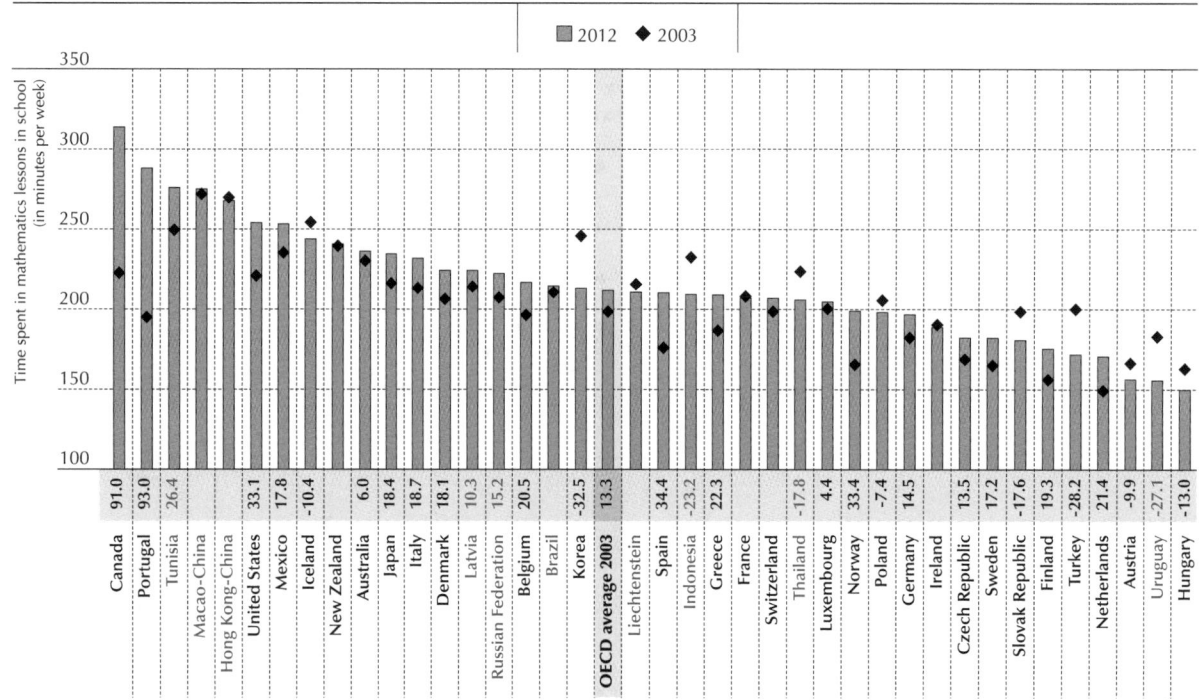

Notes: Only countries and economies with comparable data from PISA 2003 and PISA 2012 are shown.
The change in learning time (2012 - 2003) is shown above the country/economy name. Only statistically significant differences are shown.
OECD average 2003 compares only OECD countries with comparable results in 2012 and 2003.
Countries and economies are ranked in descending order of the average minutes students spent in mathematics lessons in school per week in PISA 2012.
Source: OECD, PISA 2012 Database, Table IV.3.46.
StatLink http://dx.doi.org/10.1787/888932957327

Trends also show that students spend less time on homework in 2012 that their counterparts in 2003 did. In 2003 and across OECD countries that had comparable data from 2003 and 2012, 15-year-old students reported spending 5.9 hours per week on homework or other study set by teachers. By 2012, this time had shrunk by one hour a week, to 4.9 hours. Average time spent on homework decreased in 31 of the 38 countries and economies with comparable data. It shrank by more than five hours per week in the Slovak Republic and by more than three hours per week in Hungary, Latvia and Greece. These reductions tend to be greatest among those countries and economies that recorded the most number of hours spent on homework in 2003 (correlation between average time spent in homework in 2003 and change to 2012 of -0.68). In 2003 in the Russian Federation, Italy and Hungary, the average student reported spending more than ten hours per week on homework; by 2012, the number of hours spent doing homework dropped by around two hours per week in Italy and by around three hours per week in the Russian Federation and Hungary. An exception to this trend

is Finland, where the average student in 2003 spent a relatively short time doing homework (3.7 hours per week) and in 2012, the average student spent almost one hour less on homework. As a result of these changes, the difference in time spent on homework between those countries where students do more homework and those where students do less has narrowed over time (Figure IV.3.16 and Table IV.3.48). The general trend among OECD countries, that students spend less time doing homework in 2012 than they did in 2003, was observed among both advantaged and disadvantaged students and across all school types (advantaged and disadvantaged, private and public, lower and upper secondary programmes, and urban and rural schools) (Table IV.3.49).

■ Figure IV.3.16 ■
Change between 2003 and 2012 in the average time spent doing homework

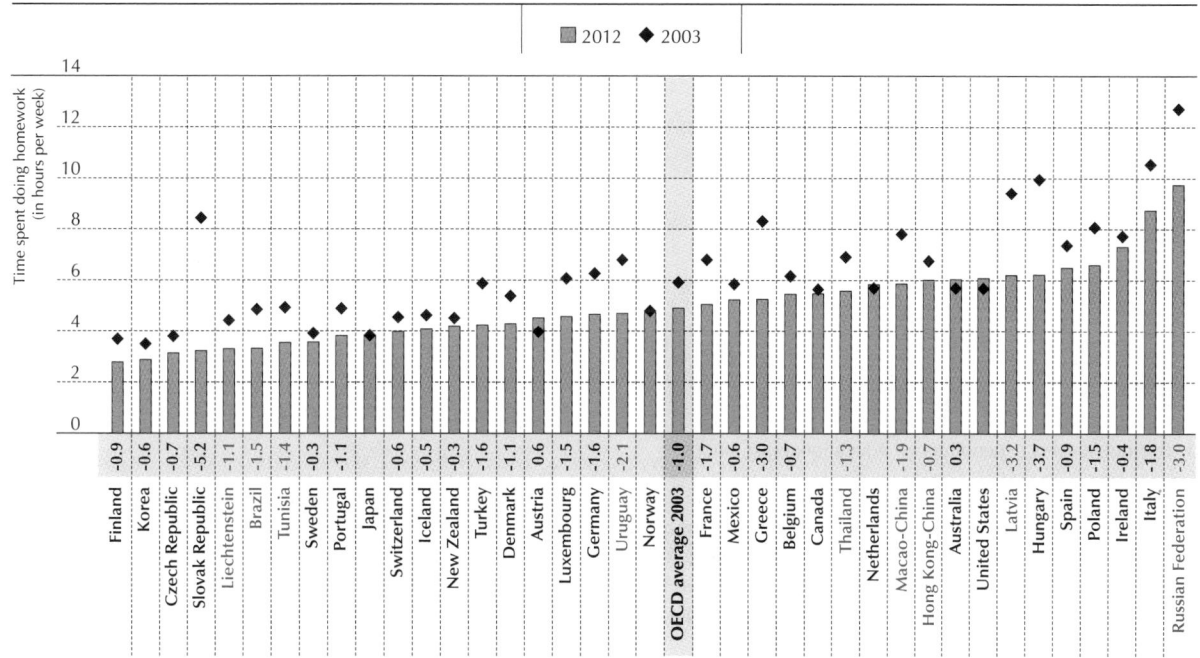

Notes: Only countries and economies with comparable data from PISA 2003 and PISA 2012 are shown.
The change in time spent doing homework (2012 - 2003) is shown above the country/economy name. Only statistically significant differences are shown.
OECD average 2003 compares only OECD countries with comparable results in 2012 and 2003.
Countries and economies are ranked in ascending order of the average time students spent doing homework in PISA 2012.
Source: OECD, PISA 2012 Database, Table IV.3.48.
StatLink 🔒🖘 http://dx.doi.org/10.1787/888932957327

Fifteen-year-old students' mathematics (and reading) achievement is related to their school readiness when they entered primary school (Duncan et al., 2008). Depending on the quality of the programme, pre-primary school can promote school readiness, particularly if these programmes last more than one year. In PISA 2003, and on average across the OECD countries that have comparable data between PISA 2003 and PISA 2012, 69% of 15-year-olds reported that they had attended a pre-primary school for more than one year; in 2012, 75% of students reported so. The United States saw an increase of more than 60 percentage points in the share of students who had attended pre-primary school for more than one year: while the great majority of 15-year-old students in 2003 had attended pre-primary school for one year or less, around three out of four 15-year-old students in 2012 had done so for more than one year. Increases in the share of students who had attended pre-primary school for more than one year are notable in Latvia, where the share of students who had attended pre-primary school for more than one year increased by almost 20 percentage points, with a similar reduction in the share of students who had not attended pre-primary school (Table IV.3.50).

Similarly, in 2012, 15-year-old students in Thailand, Denmark, Sweden and Ireland were at least ten percentage points more likely than their counterparts in 2003 to have attended pre-primary school for at least a year. By contrast, attendance in pre-primary school for more than one year declined significantly in the Russian Federation, Finland, Tunisia, Korea and France during the period. In the Russian Federation, attendance in pre-primary school for any period of time dropped by more than five percentage points, while in Tunisia, the four percentage-point drop is offset by a nine percentage-point reduction in the share of 15-year-olds who had not attended pre-primary education (Table IV.3.50).

The general trend observed among OECD countries, that a larger proportion of 15-year-old students had spent at least a year in pre-primary school, was observed among both advantaged and disadvantaged students, as well as in disadvantaged and advantaged schools, public and private schools, lower and upper secondary programmes, and urban and rural schools. The growth in this enrolment is significantly stronger among advantaged students than disadvantaged students, and among students attending advantaged schools than those attending disadvantaged schools. This signals that those students who could benefit the most from attending pre-primary education (i.e. those from disadvantaged backgrounds) are those who have benefited the least from the greater enrolment in pre-primary education (Table IV.3.51).

Notes

1. This only covers expenditure on educational institutions.

2. These resources are allocated throughout a student's educational career, and countries spend different amounts per student. Caution is required in interpreting this indicator, as school systems are organised in many different ways across countries. For example, some school systems include special education in school budgets while others don't. Some school systems sponsor extensive recreational, athletic, and extra-curricular activities that are not related to the kind of academic instruction. In addition, some countries require schools to pay the pensions and health insurance of school staff, while others include these costs in the national budget for all citizens.

3. This refers to the scheduled annual salary of a full-time classroom teacher with the minimum training necessary to be fully qualified, plus 15 years of experience.

4. Starting salaries refer to the average scheduled gross salary per year for a full-time teacher with the minimum training necessary to be fully qualified at the beginning of the teaching career. Maximum salaries refer to the maximum annual salary (top of the salary scale) for a full-time classroom teacher with the maximum qualifications recognised for compensation.

5. These groups are created using a cluster analysis with the Ward method (which groups countries and economies to minimise the variance within each cluster) using data available in Table IV.3.4. Variables that entered the analyses are: whether competitive examinations are required to enter pre-service teacher training (coded as 1 for "Yes" and 0 for "No" and taken as the average of the requirement in the primary, lower secondary and upper secondary levels); the duration of teacher-training programmes in years (as an average of the duration of training leading to teaching in the primary, lower secondary and upper secondary levels; when more than one duration is available for a particular level, the average is also taken); and the requirement of a practicum as part of pre-service training (coded as 1 for "Yes" and 0 for "No" and taken as the average of the requirement in the primary, lower secondary and upper secondary levels). Information for the duration of teacher-training programmes is unavailable for Brazil, Chile and the United Arab Emirates, so these countries are excluded from the cluster analysis.

6. Annex A1 provides detailed information on how student-teacher ratio is computed.

7. Based on these two sets of questions, the minutes per week that students spend learning mathematics, language of instruction and science in regular lessons are computed.

8. Although questions included in the PISA 2003 questionnaires allow for trend comparisons in resources invested in education, not all questions are common to both questionnaires. In particular, there were no comparable questions on teachers' continuing education programmes, teacher qualifications, class size, extracurricular activities or after-school learning.

9. Data for PISA 2003 come from *Education at a Glance 2004: OECD Indicators* (OECD, 2004b) and refer to the year 2001. Data for PISA 2012 come from *Education at a Glance 2012: OECD Indicators* (OECD, 2012) and refer to the year 2010. Results for the year 2001 have been adjusted by inflation to ensure comparability with 2010.

References

Alexander, K. L., D.R. Entwisle and **L.S. Olson** (2001), "Schools, Achievement, and Inequality: A Seasonal Perspective", *Educational Evaluation and Policy Analysis*, Vol. 23, No. 2, pp. 171-191.

Bloom, B. (1968), "Learning for Mastery", *UCLA-CSEIP Evaluation Comment*, Vol. 1, No. 2.

Buchmann, C. and **E. Hannum** (2001), "Education and Stratification in Developing Countries: A Review of Theories and Research", *Annual Review of Sociology*, Vol. 27, pp. 77-102.

Carneiro, P. and **J. Heckman** (2005), "Human Capital Policy", in J. Heckman and A. Krueger (eds.), *Inequality in America: What Role for Human Capital Policies?*, MIT Press, Cambridge, Massachusetts.

Carroll, J.B. (1989), "The Carroll Model: A 25-Year Retrospective and Prospective View", *Educational Researcher*, Vol. 18, No. 1, pp. 26-31.

Carroll, J.B. (1963), "A Model of School Learning", *Teachers College Record*, Vol. 64, pp. 723-733.

Chetty, R., et al. (2011), "How Does Your Kindergarten Classroom Affect Your Earnings? Evidence from Project STAR", *The Quarterly Journal of Economics*, Vol. 126, No. 4, pp. 1593-1660.

Clark, D. and **M.C. Linn** (2003), "Designing for Knowledge Integration: The Impact of Instructional Time", *Journal of the Learning Sciences*, Vol. 12, No. 4, pp. 451-493.

Covay, E. and **W. Carbonaro** (2009), "After the Bell: Participation in Extracurricular Activities, Classroom Behavior, and Academic Achievement", *Sociology of Education*, Vol. 83, No. 1, pp. 20-45.

Dee, T. S. and **M.R. West** (2011), "The Non-Cognitive Returns to Class Size", *Educational Evaluation and Policy Analysis*, Vol. 33, No. 1, pp. 23-46.

Downey, D., P. Von Hippel and **B. Broh** (2004), "Are Schools the Great Equalizer? Cognitive Inequality over the Summer Months and the School Year", *American Sociological Review*, Vol. 69, No. 5, pp. 613-635.

Duncan, G., et al. (2008), "School Readiness and Later Achievement", *Developmental Psychology*, Vol. 43, No. 6, pp. 1428-1446.

Dynarski, S., J.M. Hyman and **D.W. Schanzenbach** (2011), *Experimental evidence on the effect of childhood investments on postsecondary attainment and degree completion*, Working Paper No. 17533, National Bureau of Economic Research.

Ehrenberg, R., et al. (2001), "Class Size and Student Achievement", *Psychological Science in the Public Interest*, Vol. 2, No. 1, pp. 1-30.

Entwisle, D., K. Alexander and **L. Olson** (1997), *Children, Schools and Inequality*, Westview Press, Boulder, Colorado.

Farkas, G. (2003), "Cognitive Skills and Non-cognitive Traits and Behaviors in Stratification Process", *Annual Review of Sociology*, Vol. 29, pp. 541-562.

Finn, J. (1998), "Class Size and Students at Risk: What is Known? What is Next?", US Department of Education, Office of Educational Research and Improvement, National Institute on the Education of At-Risk Students, Washington, D.C.

Fisher, C.W., et al. (1980), "Teaching Behaviors, Academic Learning Time and Student Achievement: An Overview," in D. Denham and A. Lieberman (eds.), *Time to Learn*, National Institutes of Education, California, pp. 7-32.

Fuller, B. (1987), "What Factors Raise Achievement in the Third World?", *Review of Educational Research*, Vol. 57, No. 3, pp. 255-292.

Gamoran, A., W. Secada and **C. Marrett** (2000), "The Organizational Context of Teaching and Learning: Changing Theoretical Perspectives", in M. Hallinan (ed.), *Handbook of the Sociology of Education*, Springer, New York.

Greenwald, R., L. Hedges and **R. Laine** (1996), "The Effect of School Resources on Student Achievement", *Review of Educational Research*, Vol. 66, No. 3, pp. 361-396.

Hægeland, T., O. Raaum and **K.G. Salvanes** (2012), "Pennies from Heaven? Using Exogenous Tax Variation to Identify Effects of School Resources on Pupil Achievement", *Economics of Education Review*, Vol. 31, No. 5, pp.601-614.

Hart, B. and **T. Risley** (1995), *Meaningful Differences in the Everyday Experiences of Young American Children*, Paul H. Brookes Publishing, Baltimore, Maryland.

Hawley, W.D. and **S.J. Rosenholtz** (1984), "Effective Teaching", *Peabody Journal of Education*, Vol. 61, No. 4, pp. 15-52.

Heckman, J. (2000), "Policies to Foster Human Capital", *Research in Economics*, Vol. 54, No. 1, pp. 3-56.

Henry, G. T., C.K. Fortner and **C.L. Thompson** (2010), "Targeted Funding for Educationally Disadvantaged Students A Regression Discontinuity Estimate of the Impact on High School Student Achievement", *Educational Evaluation and Policy Analysis*, Vol. 32, No. 2, pp. 183-204.

Howie, L.D., et al. (2010). "Participation in activities outside of school hours in relation to problem behavior and social skills in middle childhood", *Journal of School Health*, Vol 80. No. 3, pp. 119-125.

Huttenlocher, J., et al. (1991), "Early Vocabulary Growth: Relation to Language Input and Gender", *Developmental Psychology*, Vol. 27, No. 2, pp. 236-248.

Jencks, C. and **M. Phillips** (1998), *The Black-White Test Score Gap*, Brookings Institution Press, Washington, D.C.

Lamb, S., R. Teese and **S. Helme** (2005), *Equity Programs for Government Schools in New South Wales: A Review*, Centre for Post-compulsory Education and Lifelong Learning, University of Melbourne, Melbourne.

Lavy, V. (2010), *Do Differences in School's Instruction Time Explain International Achievement Gaps in Math, Science, and Reading? Evidence from Developed and Developing Countries*, working paper no. 16227, National Bureau of Economic Research, Cambridge, Massachusetts.

Levin, H. M., and **C. R. Belfield** (2002), "Families as Contractual Partners in Education", *UCLA Law Review*, Vol. 49, No. 6, pp. 1799-1824.

Marzano, R.J. (2003), *What Works in Schools: Translating Research into Action*, Association for Supervision and Curriculum Development, Alexandria, Virginia.

Mhirsi, C. (2012), *Le Système Éducatif Tunisien à travers les Évaluations Internationales*, Colloque sur la Méthodologie de la Réforme du Système Éducatif (29-31 mars, 2012), Ministère de L'Éducation, Tunis.

Ministère de l'Éducation (2002), La Nouvelle Réforme du Système Éducatif Tunisien : Programme pour la mise en œuvre du projet "École de demain", Ministère de l'Éducation, Tunis.

Mistry, R.S., et al. (2010), "Family and Social Risk, and Parental Investments during the Early Childhood Years as Predictors of Low-Income Children's School Readiness Outcomes", *Early Childhood Research Quarterly*, Vol. 25, No. 4, pp. 432-449.

Monseur, C. and **M. Crahay** (2008), "Composition académique et sociale des établissements, efficacité et inégalités scolaires : une comparaison internationale. Analyse secondaire des données PISA 2006", *Revue française de pédagogie*, Vol. 164, pp. 55-65.

Murillo, F.J. and **M. Román** (2011), "School Infrastructure and Resources do Matter: Analysis of the Incidence of School Resources on the Performance of Latin American Students", *School Effectiveness and School Improvement*, Vol. 22, No. 1, pp. 29-50.

Natriello, G., E.L. McDill and **A.M. Pallas** (1990), *Schooling Disadvantaged Children: Racing Against Catastrophe*, Teachers College Press, New York.

Nicoletti, C. and **B. Rabe** (2012), *The Effect of School Resources on Test Scores in England*, working paper no. 2012-13, Institute for Social and Economic Research, Essex.

OECD (2013a), *PISA 2012 Assessment and Analytical Framework: Mathematics, Reading, Science, Problem Solving and Financial Literacy*, PISA, OECD Publishing.
http://dx.doi.org/10.1787/9789264190511-en

OECD (2013b), *Education at a Glance 2013: OECD Indicators*, OECD Publishing.
http://dx.doi.org/10.1787/eag-2013-en

OECD (2012), *Education at at Glance 2012: OECD Indicators*, OECD Publishing.
http://dx.doi.org/10.1787/eag-2012-en

OECD (2005), *Teachers Matter: Attracting, Developing and Retaining Effective Teachers*, OECD Publishing.
http://dx.doi.org/10.1787/9789264018044-en

OECD (2004a), *Learning for Tomorrow's World: First results from PISA 2003*, PISA, OECD Publishing.
http://dx.doi.org/10.1787/9789264006416-en

OECD (2004b), *Education at a Glance 2004: OECD Indicators*, OECD Publishing.
http://dx.doi.org/10.1787/eag-2004-en

Piketty, T. and **M. Valdenaire** (2006), *L'Impact de la taille des classes sur la réussite scolaire dans les écoles, collèges et lycées français : Estimations à partir du panel primaire 1997 et du panel secondaire 1995*, ministère de l'Éducation nationale, de l'Enseignement supérieur et de la Recherche, Direction de l'évaluation et de la prospective, Paris.

Rivkin, S., E. Hanushek and **J. Kain** (2005), "Teachers, Schools and Academic Achievement", *Econometrica,* Vol. 73, No. 2, pp. 417-458.

Scheerens, J. and **R. Bosker** (1997), *The Foundations of Educational Effectiveness*, Pergamon Press, Oxford.

Schmidt, W. and **A. Maier** (2009), "Opportunity to Learn", in G. Sykes, B. Schneider and D. Plank (eds.), *Handbook of Education Policy Research*, pp. 541-559, Routledge, New York.

Seidel, T. and **R.J. Shavelson** (2007), "Teaching effectiveness research in the past decade: The role of theory and research design in disentangling meta-analysis research", *Review of Educational Research*, Vol. 77, pp. 454-499.

Smith, B. (2002), "Quantity Matters: Annual Instructional Time in an Urban School System," *Educational Administration Quarterly*, Vol. 36, No. 5, pp. 652-682.

4

School Governance, Assessments and Accountability

This chapter explores the inter-relationships among school autonomy, school competition, public and private management of schools, school leadership, parental involvement, and assessment and accountability arrangements. The chapter also discusses trends since 2003 in school governance, assessments and accountability.

This chapter examines the balance between autonomy, accountability and collaboration among schools, teachers and parents by describing school autonomy, school competition, public and private involvement in schools, school leadership, parental involvement, and assessment and accountability arrangements.

Chapter 1 shows that the relationship between school governance and education outcomes is complex. At the school level, the relationships vary greatly, depending on the system. At the system level, school systems with high overall performance tend to grant more autonomy to schools in designing curricula and assessments and seek feedback from students for quality-assurance and improvement. In systems with more competition among schools, the impact of students' socio-economic status on their performance is stronger, while that impact is weaker in systems where more schools seek feedback from students and use teacher mentoring as part of quality-assurance and improvement activities.

■ Figure IV.4.1 ■
Governance, assessment and accountability as covered in PISA 2012

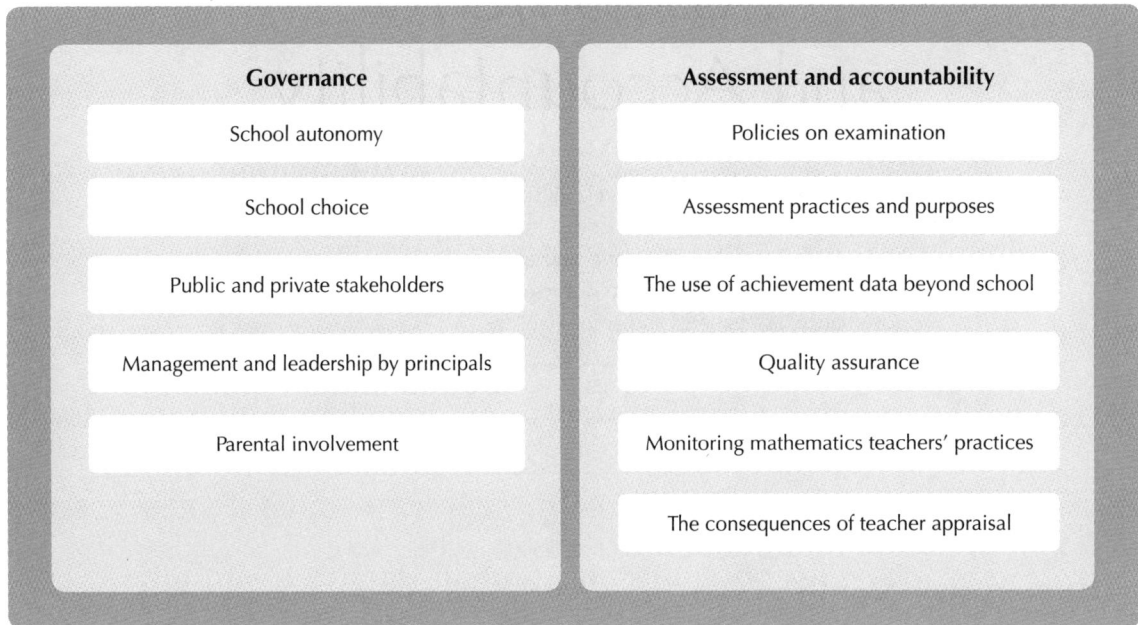

Governance	Assessment and accountability
School autonomy	Policies on examination
School choice	Assessment practices and purposes
Public and private stakeholders	The use of achievement data beyond school
Management and leadership by principals	Quality assurance
Parental involvement	Monitoring mathematics teachers' practices
	The consequences of teacher appraisal

What the data tell us

- In most countries, few individual schools have a major influence on teachers' salaries; however school principals and/or teachers have more responsibility for decisions related to selecting and hiring teachers, and determining course content.

- School systems in which more schools seek written feedback from students about lessons, teachers or resources tend to be more equitable.

- Between 2003 and 2012, students in most (27 out of 38) countries and economies became more likely to be in schools that use student assessments to compare the school's performance to that of other schools. During the same period, students in most countries and economies also became more likely to attend schools that use student assessment data to monitor teacher practice.

- If offered a choice of schools for their child, parents are more likely to consider such criteria as "a safe school environment" and "a school's good reputation" more important than "high academic achievement of students in the school".

GOVERNANCE OF SCHOOL SYSTEMS

School autonomy

Chapter 1 shows that systems where schools have more autonomy over curricula and assessments tend to perform better overall. Relationships between school autonomy and performance within countries are more complex, and the relationships vary according to the extent of accountability arrangements that systems have.

Among the many decisions that school systems and schools have to make, those concerning the curriculum and the way resources are allocated and managed have a direct impact on teaching and learning. Since the early 1980s, many school systems have granted individual schools increasing authority to make autonomous decisions on curricula and resource allocation on the premise that individual schools are good judges of their students' learning needs and of the most effective use of resources. The rationale was to raise performance levels by encouraging responsiveness to student and school needs at the local level (Whitty, 1997; Carnoy, 2000; Clark; 2009; Machin and Vernoit, 2011). This has involved increasing the decision-making responsibility and accountability of principals and, in some cases, the management responsibilities of teachers or department heads. Yet school systems differ in the degree of autonomy granted to schools and in the domains for which autonomy is awarded to schools.

PISA 2012 asked school principals to report whether the teachers, the principal, the school's governing board, the regional or local education authorities or the national education authority had considerable responsibility for allocating resources to schools (appointing and dismissing teachers; determining teachers' starting salaries and salary raises; and formulating school budgets and allocating them within the school) and responsibility for the curriculum and instructional assessment within the school (establishing student-assessment policies; choosing textbooks; and determining which courses are offered and the content of those courses). This information was combined to create two composite indices: an *index of school responsibility for resource allocation*, and an *index of school responsibility for curriculum and assessment*, such that both indices have an average of zero and a standard deviation of one for OECD countries. Higher values indicate more autonomy for school principals and teachers.[1]

In most countries and economies, few individual schools have a major influence on teachers' salaries. On average across OECD countries, around 70% or more of students are in schools whose principals reported that only national and/or regional education authorities have considerable responsibility for establishing teachers' starting salaries and determining teachers' salary increases (Figure IV.4.2). In contrast, school principals and/or teachers have more responsibility for decisions related to selecting and hiring teachers, dismissing teachers, formulating the school budget, and deciding on budget allocations within the school. School autonomy, as measured by the *index of school responsibility for resource allocation*, is greatest in Macao-China, the Netherlands, the Czech Republic, and the United Kingdom, as reported by school principals in these countries. In contrast, responsibility for resource allocation is least among schools in Turkey, Greece, Albania, Italy, Germany, Romania, Austria, France and Jordan (Table IV.4.1).

Schools within a country or an economy show varying degrees of autonomy in allocating resources. School principals in Turkey, Germany, Greece, Ireland, Romania and Belgium reported similar levels of autonomy in allocating resources, while in Peru, the Czech Republic, Chile, Indonesia, the United Arab Emirates, Macao-China, the Slovak Republic and the United Kingdom, some schools are permitted to allocate resources while for other schools these decisions are made by national or regional education authorities (Table IV.4.1). As expected, in virtually all participating countries and economies, private schools tend to have more autonomy in allocating resources than public schools. In 18 countries and economies, upper secondary schools tend to have more autonomy in allocating resources than lower secondary schools, while in Liechtenstein, Switzerland and Macao-China the reverse is true (Table IV.4.2).

In general, school systems that give responsibility for resource allocation to individual schools also tend to grant schools responsibility for curricular decisions, although this is not the case in some systems, such as Japan and Bulgaria.[2] Relatively higher levels of school autonomy in setting curricula and assessment practices are observed in Japan, Thailand, the Netherlands, Hong Kong-China and the United Kingdom, as measured by the *index of school responsibility for curriculum and assessment*. By contrast, Greece, Turkey, Jordan, Viet Nam, Qatar, Malaysia, Mexico, Serbia, Croatia, Luxembourg, Bulgaria, Montenegro and Uruguay are among those countries that grant the least responsibility to schools in making decisions about curricula and assessments (Figure IV.4.3 and Table IV.4.3).

Not all schools within the same system have the same level of discretion over their curricula and assessments. For example, in the United Arab Emirates, Peru, Tunisia and the Slovak Republic, some schools can formulate their own curricula and assessments while other schools must abide by decisions taken by the school governing board or national/regional authorities. The opposite is true in Serbia, Greece, Turkey, Bulgaria, Luxembourg and Croatia, where

all schools have similar levels of autonomy in designing their curricula (Table IV.4.3). In some countries and economies, there is a difference in the degree of school autonomy in deciding curricula and assessments between upper and lower secondary schools, but the pattern is not consistent: upper secondary schools tend to have more autonomy in this area than lower secondary schools in 12 countries and economies, while the reverse is observed in five other countries. In 26 countries and economies, private schools tend to have higher degrees of autonomy in making decisions about curricula and assessments, but in Estonia, the Slovak Republic and Slovenia, the reverse is observed (Table IV.4.2).

Box IV.4.1. **School autonomy and collaboration among schools**

Greater school autonomy does not lead to less collaboration among schools and school leaders; on the contrary: collaboration can complement school autonomy to promote greater empowerment of schools, and horizontal networks can also support more innovation by schools.

Sometimes school leaders in schools that have been granted greater autonomy have not yet been trained in all the areas for which they are now responsible (Pont, Nusche and Moorman, 2008). When school leaders lack sufficient expertise, the simplest types of co-operation, such as sharing managerial and administrative resources, can help reduce the school leaders' administrative workload and minimise inefficiencies. More important, more advanced types of collaboration, including collective learning, can help to develop leadership capacity (Pont, Nusche and Moorman, 2008). Networks of schools help to overcome the isolation of individual schools and educators by providing opportunities for organised professional exchange, development and enrichment (Sliwka, 2003).

In England (United Kingdom), for example, the government has been supporting a variety of approaches to enhance co-operation among schools and school leaders since the early 2000s. Funding for school-innovation projects often required schools to partner together and apply as school clusters, rather than as individual schools. More recently, when schools were invited to assume greater autonomy by applying for "academy" status, the government also encouraged strong academies to work with weaker schools to raise standards. Several academies have joined a "chain", which acts as a common trust for all of them. School-led partnerships among independent academies have also developed, such as the "Challenge Partners" network, which uses peer inspection as a way of fostering continuous improvement.

In Scotland (United Kingdom), "Heads Together" is a nationwide online community used by school leaders to share experiences, policies and ideas. It was launched after a successful pilot phase in 2003, and has since become part of the national intranet for schools, "Glow".

In Shanghai (China), policies support collaboration between better- and lower-performing schools with the aim of transferring leadership capacity from the former to the latter. One aspect is called empowered administration, a school-custody programme in which the government asks higher-performing public schools to administer weaker schools. Under this scheme, the high-performing school appoints its experienced leader, such as the deputy principal, to be the principal of the weaker school and sends a team of experienced teachers to lead in teaching. In this way, the ethos, management style and teaching methods of the good schools are transferred to the poorer-performing school. In addition, a consortium of schools is established, where strong and weak schools, old and new, public and private, are grouped into a consortium or cluster, with one strong school at the core (OECD, 2011).

Authentic and fruitful collaboration among autonomous actors, however, cannot simply be decreed. A general lesson that emerges from the OECD project on "Improving School Leadership" (Pont, Nusche and Moorman, 2008) is that if collaboration activities are perceived as being imposed from above rather than being pursued out of real commitment, their effectiveness will be limited.

Sources:

OECD (2011), *Strong Performers and Successful Reformers in Education: Lessons from PISA for the United States,* OECD Publishing. *http://dx.doi.org/10.1787/9789264096660-en*

Pont, B., D. Nusche and H. Moorman (2003), *Improving School Leadership: Volume 1, Policy and Practice,* OECD Publishing. *http://dx.doi.org/10.1787/9789264044715-en*

Sliwka, A. (2003), "Networking for Educational Innovation: A Comparative Analysis", OECD Networks of Innovation: Towards New Models for Managing Schools and Systems, OECD Publishing.

■ Figure IV.4.2 ■
School autonomy over resource allocation

Percentage of students in schools whose principals reported that only "principals and/or teachers", only "regional and/or national education authority", or both "principals and/or teachers" and "regional and/or national education authority", or "school governing board" has/have a considerable responsibility for the following tasks:

- **A** Selecting teachers for hire
- **B** Firing teachers
- **C** Establishing teachers' starting salaries
- **D** Determining teachers' salaries increases
- **E** Formulating the school budget
- **F** Deciding on budget allocations within the school

- **1** Only "principals and/or teachers"
- **2** Both "principals and/or teachers" and "regional and/or national education authority", or "school governing board"
- **3** Only "regional and/or national education authority"

Index of school responsibility for resource allocation
— Range between top and bottom quarters
◆ Average index

	A 1	A 2	A 3	B 1	B 2	B 3	C 1	C 2	C 3	D 1	D 2	D 3	E 1	E 2	E 3	F 1	F 2	F 3	Variability in the index S.D.
Macao-China	61	37	2	48	49	4	24	72	4	15	81	4	32	68	0	32	68	0	1.2
Netherlands	92	8	0	54	46	0	35	53	12	43	40	17	55	45	0	73	27	0	1.2
Czech Republic	95	5	0	94	6	0	74	18	8	72	22	6	56	36	9	78	21	1	1.4
United Kingdom	52	48	0	23	71	7	31	49	20	19	67	15	12	79	9	49	51	0	1.2
Bulgaria	92	7	1	90	9	1	55	26	18	65	30	5	25	41	33	60	38	2	1.1
Slovak Republic	95	5	0	92	8	0	45	13	42	48	19	33	50	27	23	63	31	6	1.2
Lithuania	82	18	0	84	16	0	38	39	22	33	45	21	15	64	21	30	57	13	1.2
Thailand	32	54	13	39	48	12	22	33	44	54	39	7	32	59	9	45	53	2	1.2
Sweden	90	10	0	44	35	22	40	24	36	52	40	8	45	44	11	86	13	1	1.2
Latvia	92	8	0	88	12	0	29	27	44	33	33	34	34	61	5	31	66	4	1.1
Chile	38	42	20	29	40	31	17	42	41	17	43	40	20	56	24	25	61	14	1.3
Hungary	68	32	0	73	27	0	32	16	52	28	23	49	34	43	23	30	65	5	1.1
Hong Kong-China	52	48	1	14	83	3	7	41	52	4	32	64	35	65	1	39	61	0	1.0
United Arab Emirates	31	29	40	27	35	38	20	37	43	16	43	42	23	51	25	24	50	26	1.2
Indonesia	20	31	48	16	35	48	15	34	51	17	37	46	44	50	6	46	46	8	1.3
Denmark	51	49	0	63	32	5	15	15	70	12	19	69	40	52	8	22	77	1	0.9
Peru	26	28	46	23	20	57	23	4	74	21	5	74	41	40	19	41	45	14	1.4
Estonia	84	16	0	90	10	0	11	14	74	14	30	55	34	54	11	61	35	4	0.8
New Zealand	75	25	0	28	71	0	10	9	82	15	24	61	23	77	0	46	54	0	0.7
United States	59	39	2	37	57	6	3	51	46	2	54	44	6	71	24	30	61	9	0.9
Chinese Taipei	66	24	10	54	36	10	10	14	76	16	14	71	29	34	37	53	35	12	1.0
Australia	63	20	17	39	17	43	8	12	80	9	14	77	38	47	15	62	37	1	1.0
Russian Federation	94	6	0	91	9	0	23	27	50	11	43	46	9	36	55	23	62	15	0.8
Iceland	96	3	1	92	7	1	8	15	77	8	11	81	50	37	13	61	31	8	0.6
OECD average	49	27	24	36	30	34	11	15	73	12	19	69	24	48	28	45	49	6	0.7
Liechtenstein	6	87	6	6	80	13	6	28	65	6	46	47	6	57	37	89	0	11	0.9
Slovenia	93	7	0	63	32	5	7	15	78	10	28	62	13	62	25	26	71	3	0.7
Switzerland	44	54	2	31	58	11	8	15	77	8	23	69	10	63	28	49	46	5	0.6
Norway	82	14	4	55	20	25	5	7	88	2	11	87	54	28	18	75	24	1	0.4
Luxembourg	11	59	30	13	54	33	1	20	79	1	20	79	13	69	18	17	83	0	0.8
Tunisia	32	12	57	31	9	61	28	7	66	28	6	67	33	23	43	40	35	25	0.8
Israel	70	26	3	55	33	13	4	9	86	8	12	80	17	29	54	59	28	13	0.6
Japan	14	19	67	8	25	67	2	29	70	3	32	65	18	28	54	65	27	7	0.8
Finland	41	45	14	23	36	41	7	8	85	7	15	78	31	39	30	87	12	1	0.6
Shanghai-China	34	56	10	19	61	20	2	22	76	5	26	69	15	46	39	26	69	5	0.7
Belgium	57	32	10	32	54	14	0	4	96	0	3	96	18	61	21	32	59	9	0.3
Mexico	26	20	54	16	18	65	6	13	80	6	13	81	31	32	37	44	36	19	0.8
Brazil	18	12	70	17	11	72	11	6	83	11	6	84	15	22	63	14	35	51	1.0
Kazakhstan	81	17	2	76	23	1	19	12	69	4	11	86	8	15	77	11	22	67	0.6
Montenegro	91	9	0	86	7	7	2	0	98	18	1	82	4	41	54	18	66	16	0.5
Croatia	22	77	1	24	73	2	1	1	98	1	2	97	8	68	25	11	80	10	0.3
Poland	80	18	2	76	21	3	7	12	81	5	14	81	4	44	52	25	47	28	0.4
Canada	48	38	14	11	33	56	2	16	82	2	17	82	21	42	37	65	29	6	0.6
Costa Rica	14	7	79	12	7	81	6	9	85	5	8	86	18	63	19	20	78	3	0.9
Colombia	19	3	78	16	5	79	13	2	85	3	8	88	25	40	36	27	68	4	0.9
Singapore	8	36	55	8	37	54	1	8	90	2	29	69	22	59	19	40	57	3	0.7
Qatar	34	50	16	30	50	20	5	46	50	5	44	51	10	56	34	26	53	21	0.4
Serbia	28	69	2	33	64	4	3	4	92	7	12	82	1	35	64	12	78	11	0.3
Spain	22	12	66	19	16	65	2	3	94	3	5	92	30	55	15	30	68	2	0.6
Ireland	19	68	13	1	76	23	0	4	96	0	5	95	11	66	24	36	51	12	0.2
Viet Nam	15	26	60	9	24	67	6	9	84	21	16	63	25	19	56	33	18	49	0.7
Korea	38	13	49	27	14	59	7	3	91	4	3	93	15	33	52	41	50	9	0.6
Uruguay	8	17	76	4	20	76	1	20	79	1	19	81	5	30	65	18	37	44	0.7
Portugal	21	55	24	14	16	69	1	8	91	1	8	91	23	59	18	33	64	3	0.5
Malaysia	7	13	79	4	14	83	1	6	94	3	14	83	60	24	16	57	22	21	0.5
Jordan	5	8	86	6	10	85	3	8	89	3	10	87	29	48	23	29	51	20	0.6
France	9	22	70	2	15	84	0	3	97	0	6	94	14	66	20	14	85	1	0.3
Austria	19	36	46	6	24	70	1	6	93	2	6	93	4	26	70	62	34	4	0.4
Romania	9	58	33	7	51	42	5	29	66	8	24	68	7	45	48	7	55	38	0.3
Germany	20	44	36	3	21	76	0	2	98	2	15	84	0	15	85	32	65	3	0.1
Italy	7	8	86	9	10	81	3	4	93	3	4	93	5	18	77	17	77	6	0.6
Albania	6	7	87	5	13	83	5	4	91	7	8	85	6	62	31	9	81	10	0.5
Greece	1	5	94	1	5	94	0	5	95	0	4	96	11	68	21	22	62	15	0.2
Turkey	1	6	93	1	5	94	0	2	98	0	2	98	6	73	21	7	79	14	0.1
Argentina	m	m	m	13	34	52	1	13	86	1	10	89	10	35	55	18	46	36	m

-1.5 -1.0 -0.5 0 0.5 1.0 1.5 2.0 2.5 3.0 Index points

Countries and economies are ranked in descending order of the average index.
Source: OECD, PISA 2012 Database, Table IV.4.1.
StatLink ᵐˢ⁹ http://dx.doi.org/10.1787/888932957346

■ Figure IV.4.3 ■

School autonomy over curricula and assessments

Percentage of students in schools whose principals reported that only "principals and/or teachers", only "regional and/or national education authority", or both "principals and/or teachers" and "regional and/or national education authority", or "school governing board" has/have a considerable responsibility for the following tasks:

- **A** Establishing student assessment policies
- **B** Choosing which textbooks are used
- **C** Determining course content
- **D** Deciding which courses are offered

- **1** Only "principals and/or teachers"
- **2** Both "principals and/or teachers" and "regional and/or national education authority", or "school governing board"
- **3** Only "regional and/or national education authority"

	A 1	A 2	A 3	B 1	B 2	B 3	C 1	C 2	C 3	D 1	D 2	D 3	Index of school responsibility for curriculum and assessment	Variability in the index S.D.
Japan	98	2	0	89	7	4	89	7	4	90	6	4		0.7
Thailand	42	54	4	47	53	0	76	24	1	63	37	0		0.7
Netherlands	95	5	0	93	7	0	91	7	2	75	25	0		0.8
Hong Kong-China	87	13	0	84	16	0	76	24	0	63	37	0		0.8
United Kingdom	62	38	0	100	0	0	83	14	3	70	30	0		0.8
Macao-China	66	34	0	81	19	0	66	33	2	36	61	2		0.9
Czech Republic	58	42	0	90	10	0	74	26	0	78	22	0		1.0
Korea	69	29	2	50	50	0	76	20	3	60	36	5		0.9
Lithuania	34	65	1	54	46	0	54	36	10	48	51	1		0.9
Indonesia	82	16	2	80	16	4	73	16	11	62	22	16		1.0
Estonia	39	61	1	70	30	0	35	62	2	48	52	0		0.9
Slovak Republic	76	22	2	68	27	5	61	35	3	56	42	3		1.0
New Zealand	58	38	4	96	4	0	71	28	1	71	29	0		0.9
Poland	57	43	0	82	18	0	83	17	0	36	33	31		0.8
Italy	79	21	0	90	10	0	60	27	12	29	55	15		0.9
Chinese Taipei	27	65	9	67	33	0	54	43	3	30	63	7		0.9
Iceland	63	36	0	77	23	0	51	37	11	39	52	9		1.0
Australia	56	40	3	81	18	0	36	48	16	63	36	2		0.9
Chile	46	51	3	57	36	7	37	35	27	31	60	9		1.0
Ireland	47	51	2	82	18	0	32	40	28	24	75	1		0.8
Hungary	35	64	1	57	43	0	26	59	14	10	65	25		0.9
Israel	57	42	1	45	50	5	47	49	4	30	64	5		0.9
OECD average	47	41	13	65	27	8	40	36	24	36	46	18		0.8
Finland	50	40	10	89	11	0	34	42	24	49	41	10		0.9
Denmark	38	51	11	57	43	0	45	47	8	20	70	10		0.9
Colombia	18	73	9	65	29	6	43	34	23	40	38	22		0.9
Peru	59	32	9	47	16	36	53	28	19	35	26	39		1.0
France	35	50	15	75	25	0	45	38	17	45	37	18		0.9
Belgium	56	40	4	83	15	2	30	45	25	25	62	13		0.8
Latvia	44	52	5	61	38	1	22	40	38	33	54	14		0.8
Germany	40	58	2	40	58	2	21	51	28	52	45	3		0.8
Russian Federation	17	73	10	45	52	3	19	64	17	30	61	10		0.8
Sweden	43	53	3	94	6	0	33	48	20	24	42	33		0.8
Singapore	17	83	0	26	72	2	20	66	15	20	75	5		0.8
Albania	46	22	32	81	15	4	35	30	34	33	35	32		0.9
Austria	38	38	23	60	40	0	35	39	26	10	72	18		0.8
Liechtenstein	54	46	0	16	78	6	6	74	20	9	78	13		0.9
Slovenia	41	55	4	55	44	1	25	63	12	20	73	8		0.7
United States	16	68	16	25	60	15	15	58	26	30	62	8		0.9
Brazil	20	58	22	73	25	2	30	35	35	13	33	54		0.8
United Arab Emirates	35	33	32	28	26	45	26	24	50	25	27	48		1.0
Spain	39	37	24	80	19	1	26	31	43	23	34	42		0.7
Canada	25	58	17	44	43	13	19	39	42	46	51	3		0.7
Argentina	59	33	8	81	18	1	24	36	41	6	24	69		0.7
Romania	22	55	24	38	42	20	26	43	31	16	57	26		0.7
Norway	35	35	29	85	14	1	23	43	34	15	35	51		0.7
Shanghai-China	25	69	6	21	40	39	20	48	32	18	53	29		0.8
Tunisia	27	28	45	29	9	63	28	15	58	29	10	62		1.0
Switzerland	47	42	11	37	38	25	17	46	37	11	61	28		0.6
Costa Rica	41	20	39	69	14	17	20	11	69	13	12	75		0.8
Portugal	18	63	19	79	21	0	6	28	66	10	72	18		0.5
Kazakhstan	34	49	17	16	33	52	7	39	55	16	65	19		0.6
Uruguay	13	45	43	25	41	34	8	33	59	5	42	53		0.6
Montenegro	65	2	33	20	2	78	24	2	75	23	9	68		0.6
Luxembourg	6	49	44	17	69	14	5	65	30	11	71	18		0.4
Bulgaria	18	56	26	45	55	1	8	32	60	2	58	40		0.4
Croatia	17	45	38	49	45	7	10	45	45	4	23	73		0.4
Serbia	51	42	7	34	54	12	5	34	61	0	15	85		0.2
Mexico	33	32	35	51	18	31	12	12	75	4	11	85		0.5
Malaysia	25	23	52	18	9	73	7	9	84	45	28	28		0.6
Qatar	5	48	47	17	46	36	10	44	45	14	40	45		0.5
Viet Nam	12	23	65	20	18	61	8	15	77	18	17	65		0.5
Jordan	14	27	58	6	6	87	4	7	89	6	13	81		0.6
Turkey	2	11	87	4	38	58	4	7	89	4	44	52		0.3
Greece	29	10	61	5	6	89	2	3	95	4	3	93		0.3

Index of school responsibility for curriculum and assessment
- ▬▬▬ Range between top and bottom quarters
- ◆ Average index

-1.5 -1.0 -0.5 0 0.5 1.0 1.5 2.0 2.5 3.0 Index points

Countries and economies are ranked in descending order of the average index.
Source: OECD, PISA 2012 Database, Table IV.4.3.
StatLink ᴍᴸᴾ http://dx.doi.org/10.1787/888932957346

Some caution is advised when interpreting the degree of responsibility schools have in allocating resources, formulating curricula and using student assessments. Decision-making arrangements vary widely across countries, so the questions posed to school principals were general; thus, responses may depend on how school principals interpreted the questions. For example, when school principals were asked who has considerable responsibility for formulating the school budget, some school principals might have related this question to the regular budget of the school, while others may not have had any involvement in the regular budget and may therefore have related the question to supplementary budgets, i.e. contributions from parents or the community.

School choice

Chapter 1 shows that schools systems emphasising greater competition for students among schools and greater school choice, do not necessarily perform better than systems with less competition among schools. This result reflects the fact that school competition is a multi-faceted concept, as described, in detail, below.

Students in some school systems are assigned to attend their neighbourhood school (see Chapter 2 for more details). However, in recent decades, reforms in many countries have tended to give greater choice to parents and students, to enable them to choose the schools that meet their children's educational needs or preferences (Heyneman, 2009). On the premise that students and parents have adequate information and choose schools based on academic criteria or programme quality, the competition for schools creates incentives for institutions to organise programmes and teaching in ways that better meet diverse student requirements and interests, thus reducing the cost of failure and mismatches. In some school systems this competition has financial stakes for schools such that schools not only compete for enrolment, but also for funding. Direct public funding of independently managed institutions, based on student enrolments or student credit-hours, is one model for this. Giving money to students and their families (through, for example, scholarships or vouchers) to spend on public or private educational institutions of their choice is another method. But some studies have questioned the validity of the underlying assumptions about parental and student choice (Schneider et al., 2002; Hess and Loveless, 2005; Berends and Zottola, 2009; Jensen et al., 2013); and, in some cases, adopting school-choice practices has led to greater socio-economic and academic segregation among schools.[3] In some school systems, more responsibility for regulating enrolment has been given to the education authority (Box IV.4.2).

Box IV.4.2. **Improving equity in Belgium's (French community) enrolment system**

The French community of Belgium, which offers parents and students a high degree of school choice, recently adopted a scheme to regulate enrolments in the first year of secondary education.[a] This was done to ensure that all families have equal access to the lower secondary school of their choice, to prevent dropout, and to maintain a good social, cultural and academic mix of students in every school.

Through the scheme, parents are given a pre-printed form on which they indicate their preferred school and any other choice of schools, in order of preference. Parents are also asked to report on the proximity of their home to the primary school their child attended, the proximity of their home to their preferred secondary school, the proximity of the preferred secondary school to the primary school the child attended, and other schools located in the municipality of their child's primary school. Parents are also asked whether the child aims to continue immersion learning begun in primary school and whether there is a partnership between the primary and preferred secondary schools. Each child is then given a ranking based on a composite index of these criteria.

If the number of applications received by the preferred lower secondary school does not exceed the number of places available, all enrolment applications are accepted. In all other cases, the school ranks the applications on the basis of objective, weighted geographical and educational criteria, and awards 80% of the places in accordance with the ranking, while ensuring that the remaining places are awarded to pupils from disadvantaged primary schools.

An Inter-Network Enrolment Commission manages the cases of those students who could not be enrolled in their first-choice school. These students are allocated places in the schools where there are still some available or are allocated one of the reserved places in the schools that are already 80% "full".

After this process is completed, enrolments may be resumed on a first-come, first-served basis. For more information, see the Eurypedia section on Belgium (French community)'s organisation of general lower secondary education.

---

a. For further information on this selection scheme, visit *http://www.inscription.cfwb.be/*

On average across OECD countries, 41% of students are in schools where residence in a particular area is always considered for admission, while 59% are in schools where residence in a particular area is never or sometimes considered for admission to school. In fact, in 27 countries and economies, 70% or more students are in schools where residence in a particular area is never or sometimes considered for admission to school. Over 90% of students in Belgium, Serbia, Slovenia, Macao-China, Peru, Croatia, Montenegro, Singapore, Mexico, Japan and Romania attend such schools. By contrast, in Poland, the United States, Greece and Canada, 30% of students or fewer attend such schools (Table IV.4.6).

Naturally, school systems in which more schools use admissions criteria other than the school catchment area tend to have more competition among schools. On average across OECD countries, 24% of students are in schools whose principals reported that there are no other schools in the areas that compete for students; 16% are in schools that compete with one other school; and 61% are in schools that compete with two or more other schools. Fewer than 50% of students in Norway, Liechtenstein, Switzerland, Montenegro, Finland and Iceland are in schools that compete with at least one other school for students, while over 90% of students in Singapore, Hong Kong-China, Indonesia, Macao-China, Chinese Taipei, Belgium, Australia, Latvia, New Zealand, the United Kingdom, Korea, the Netherlands, the United Arab Emirates and Japan attend such schools (Table IV.4.4).

School competition is more common at the upper secondary level of education, where there is generally greater differentiation of education programmes than at lower levels of education. For example, in Viet Nam, 38% of lower secondary students attend schools that compete with at least one other school, while 83% of upper secondary students attend such schools – a 45 percentage-point difference. In Bulgaria, Sweden, the Slovak Republic, Greece and the Czech Republic, the difference between the two groups is between 21 and 39 percentage points. In contrast, in a few school systems, there is more competition at the lower secondary than at the upper secondary level. For example, in Austria, 80% of lower secondary students attend schools that compete for students with at least one other school, while 59% of upper secondary students attend such schools (Table IV.4.5).

However, as Figure IV.4.4 shows, even when admission to schools is not based on catchment area, individual schools are not always competing with other schools for enrolment. Some schools use residential area as the criterion for selecting students, but there may be several schools within the area, such that schools still have to compete for enrolment with other schools. In contrast, not all schools that do not use the school catchment area as a criterion for admission compete with other schools for enrolment: there may, for example, be no other school in the area. Even if there are other schools in the same area, if these schools have different levels of academic achievement, different instructional or religious philosophies, or offer different programmes, school principals may not perceive that there are schools in the same area competing for enrolment. In Finland, Japan, Canada, Belgium, Qatar, Mexico and Singapore, schools that always consider residence in a particular area for admission to school are more likely to compete with other schools for enrolment than schools that never or sometimes use residence as a criterion for admission (the percentage-point difference in the prevalence of school competition between the two groups is between 0.7 and 16.4). In contrast, in Luxembourg, Peru, Montenegro, Shanghai-China, Ireland, Iceland and the United Kingdom, schools that never or sometimes consider residence in a particular area for admission to school are more likely to compete with other schools for enrolment than schools that always consider residence as a criterion for admission. The difference in the prevalence of school competition between the two groups is between 7.8 and 28.6 percentage points (Table IV.4.6).

Principals' perceptions of school competition are not necessarily the same as those of the parents of students in their schools. In 11 countries and economies, PISA asked parents of students who participated in PISA 2012 to report whether there are one or more other schools in the same area that compete with the school their child attends.[4] As expected, in all of these countries and economies, parents in schools whose principals reported that the school competes with other schools for students were more likely to report that there is at least one other school competing with the school their child attends, than parents in schools whose principals reported that the school does not compete with any other school. However, even among parents whose children attend schools that compete with one or more other schools, according to principals, the parents of between 20% and 45% of these students reported that no other school competes for enrolment with their child's school. There are various reasons for this discrepancy. For example, these parents might not have enough information about other schools in the area. Even if they are aware that there are other schools in the vicinity, those schools may already be full, parents might think that those schools are too far, the schools' level of academic achievement does not meet the parents' standards, or school fees are too high, so that parents do not consider these schools as competitors with their children's school (Table IV.4.9).

■ Figure IV.4.4 ■

School competition and school policy on catchment area

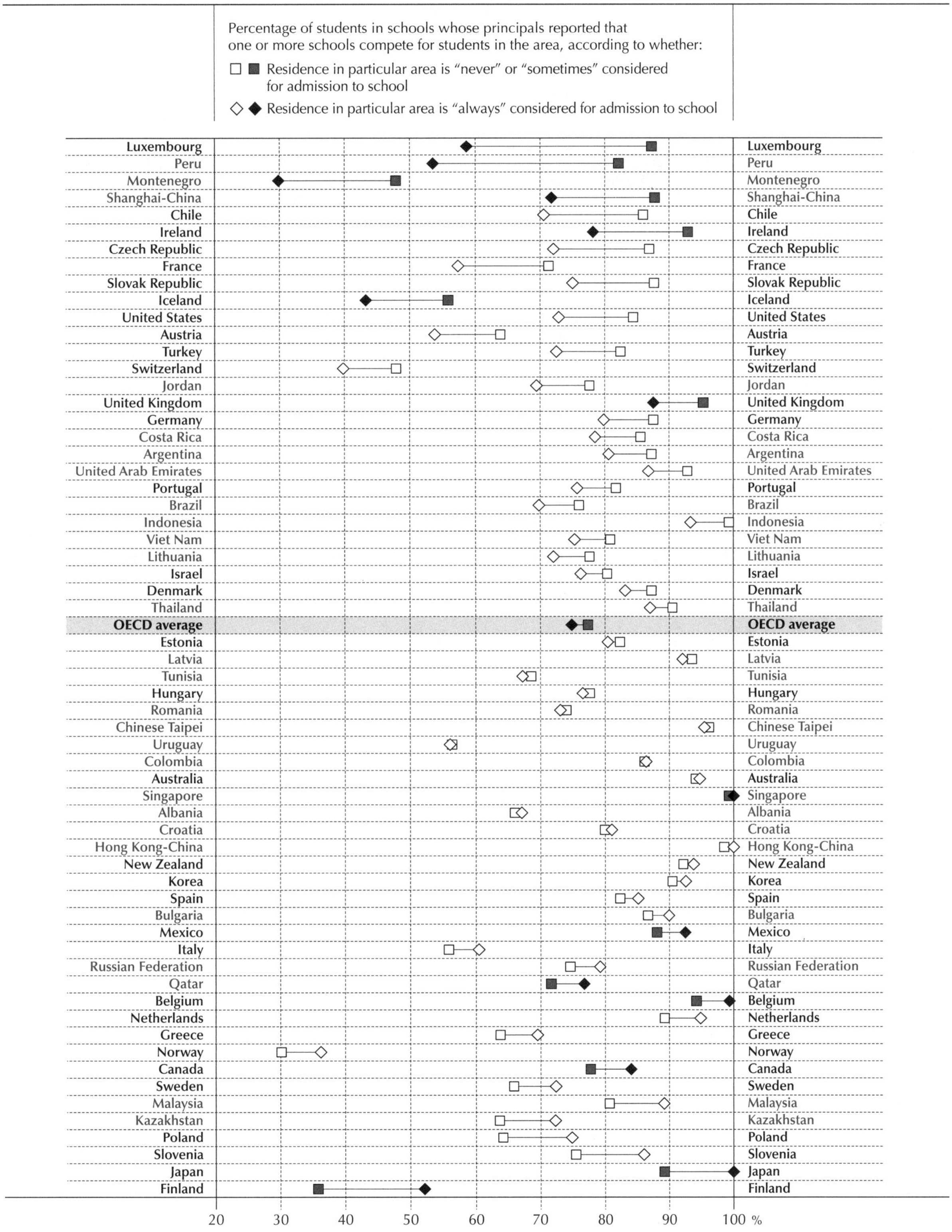
Percentage of students in schools whose principals reported that one or more schools compete for students in the area, according to whether:
□ ■ Residence in particular area is "never" or "sometimes" considered for admission to school
◇ ◆ Residence in particular area is "always" considered for admission to school
Luxembourg
Peru
Montenegro
Shanghai-China
Chile
Ireland
Czech Republic
France
Slovak Republic
Iceland
United States
Austria
Turkey
Switzerland
Jordan
United Kingdom
Germany
Costa Rica
Argentina
United Arab Emirates
Portugal
Brazil
Indonesia
Viet Nam
Lithuania
Israel
Denmark
Thailand
OECD average
Estonia
Latvia
Tunisia
Hungary
Romania
Chinese Taipei
Uruguay
Colombia
Australia
Singapore
Albania
Croatia
Hong Kong-China
New Zealand
Korea
Spain
Bulgaria
Mexico
Italy
Russian Federation
Qatar
Belgium
Netherlands
Greece
Norway
Canada
Sweden
Malaysia
Kazakhstan
Poland
Slovenia
Japan
Finland
20
30
40
50
60
70
80
90
100 %

Note: White symbols represent differences that are not statistically significant.
Countries and economies are ranked in descending order of the difference in the percentage of students in schools whose principal reported that one or more schools compete for students in the area between schools where residence in a particular area is "never" or "sometimes" considered, and schools where residence in a particular area is "always" considered for admission to school (never/sometimes - always).
Source: OECD, PISA 2012 Database, Table IV.4.6.
StatLink http://dx.doi.org/10.1787/888932957346

■ Figure IV.4.5 [Part 1/2] ■

**Parents' reports on criteria used to choose schools for their child,
by students' socio-economic status**

Percentage of parents who reported that the following criteria are very important in choosing a school for their child

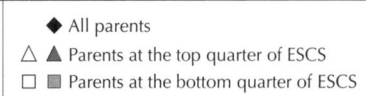

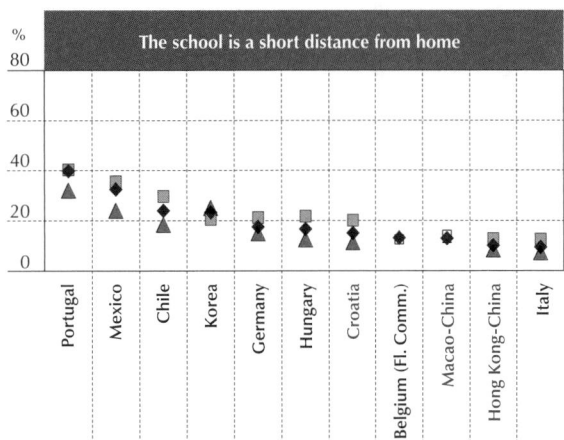

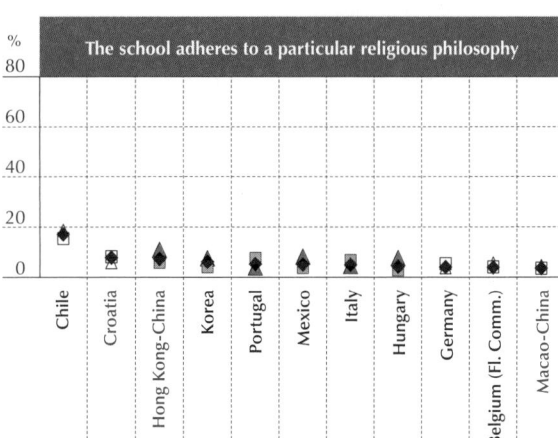

Notes: White symbols represent differences between top quarter and bottom quarter of ESCS (top - bottom) that are not statistically significant.
ESCS refers to the *PISA index of economic, social and cultural status*.
Countries and economies are ranked in descending order of the percentage of parents (all parents) who reported that each criterion is very important.
Source: OECD, PISA 2012 Database, Tables IV.4.10 and IV.4.11.

StatLink ᘉᓎ http://dx.doi.org/10.1787/888932957346

■ Figure IV.4.5 [Part 2/2] ■

Parents' reports on criteria used to choose schools for their child, by students' socio-economic status

Percentage of parents who reported that the following criteria are very important in choosing a school for their child

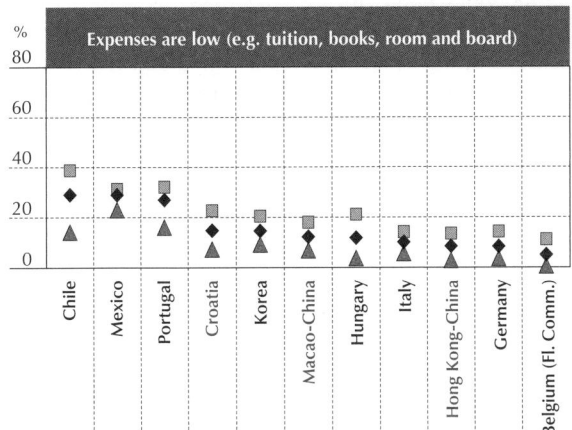

◆ All parents
△ ▲ Parents at the top quarter of ESCS
□ ■ Parents at the bottom quarter of ESCS

Notes: White symbols represent differences between top quarter and bottom quarter of ESCS (top - bottom) that are not statistically significant.
ESCS refers to the *PISA index of economic, social and cultural status*.
Countries and economies are ranked in descending order of the percentage of parents (all parents) who reported that each criterion is very important.
Source: OECD, PISA 2012 Database, Tables IV.4.10 and IV.4.11.
StatLink ᴹˢᴾ http://dx.doi.org/10.1787/888932957346

These results show that school competition is a multi-faceted concept, affected by such factors as local school markets, school performance, affordability, capacity and enrolment patterns. Often, a single indicator does not adequately capture the extent of school competition and the degree to which parents choose schools with better performance through school competition. To understand differences in how parents choose schools for their children, parents in the 11 countries that distributed the parent questionnaire were asked a series of questions regarding school choice. As shown in Figure IV.4.5, in nine of these countries and economies, over 50% of parents reported that a safe school environment is a very important criterion when choosing a school for their child. In four countries and economies, over 50% of parents reported that a school's good reputation is a very important criterion for choosing a school for their child. It is noteworthy that parents do not rate "high academic achievement of students in the school" as important as these two criteria. In Korea, 50% of parents reported high academic achievement of students as a very important criterion for choosing a school for their child, while in Belgium (Flemish community), Hungary, Italy, Germany, Hong Kong-China, Croatia and Macao-China, between 15% and 31% of parents reported so (Figure IV.4.5 and Table IV.4.10).

The criteria parents use to choose a school for their child not only vary across countries and economies, but also within countries and economies. In all countries and economies with data from parents, socio-economically disadvantaged parents are more likely than advantaged parents to report that they considered "low expenses" and "financial aid" to be very important criteria in choosing a school. As show in Figure IV.4.5, in Chile, 39% of disadvantaged parents reported that "low expenses" is a very important criterion in choosing a school, while 14% of advantaged parents reported so. In Portugal, 31% of disadvantaged parents reported that "financial aid" is a very important criterion in choosing a school, while 10% of advantaged parents reported so. In contrast, advantaged parents are more likely than disadvantaged parents to cite academic achievement as a "very important" consideration when choosing a school for their children. The greatest difference is observed in Korea, with a 21 percentage-point difference between disadvantaged parents (39%) who reported that they consider academic achievement to be very important in choosing a school, and advantaged parents (60%) who reported so. In Mexico, Portugal, Hungary, Belgium (Flemish community), Croatia, Chile, Hong Kong-China, Macao-China and Italy, the difference between the two groups is between 3 and 20 percentage points. The opposite is observed only in Germany, where 31% of disadvantaged parents reported that they consider academic achievement to be a very important criterion in choosing a school, while 21% of advantaged parents reported so (Figure IV.4.5 and Table IV.4.11).

These differences suggest that socio-economically disadvantaged parents believe that they have more limited choices of schools for their children because of financial constraints. If children from disadvantaged status cannot attend high-performing schools for this reason, then even school systems that offer parents more school choice for their children will be less effective in improving the performance of all students.

Public and private involvement

Schooling mainly takes places in public institutions, defined by PISA as schools managed directly or indirectly by a public education authority, government agency, or governing board appointed by government or elected by public franchise. Nevertheless, with an increasing variety of education opportunities, programmes and providers, governments are forging new partnerships to mobilise resources for education and to design new policies that allow the different stakeholders to participate more fully and to share costs and benefits more equitably. Private education is not only a way of mobilising resources from a wider range of funding sources; it is sometimes also regarded as a way of making education more cost-effective. Publicly financed schools are not necessarily also publicly managed. Instead, governments can transfer funds to public and private educational institutions according to various allocation mechanisms.

On average across OECD countries, 82% of 15-year-old students attend public schools, while 14% of students attend government-dependent private schools, which are managed directly or indirectly by a non-government organisation and receive 50% or more of their core funding (i.e. funding that supports the institution's basic educational services) from government agencies. Some 4% of students attend government-independent private schools, which are managed directly or indirectly by a non-government organisation and receive less than 50% of their core funding from government agencies. In Turkey, Israel, Montenegro, Serbia, Iceland, Tunisia, Romania, the Russian Federation, Bulgaria, Lithuania, Norway and Croatia, over 98% of students attend public schools. By contrast, in Macao-China, Hong Kong-China, the Netherlands, Chile and Ireland, fewer than one in two 15-year-old students attends public schools. In Hong Kong-China and Macao-China, over 80% of 15-year-old students attend government-dependent private schools (Table IV.4.7).

In 37 participating countries and economies, students who attend private schools (either government-dependent or government-independent schools) are more socio-economically advantaged than those who attend public schools. The difference between public and private schools in the average socio-economic status of their students is particularly large

in Uruguay, Costa Rica, Mexico, Brazil, Peru and Poland. Only in Chinese Taipei is the average socio-economic status of students who attend public schools more advantaged than that of those who attend private schools. Some 32% of students in Chinese Taipei attend private schools (Table IV.4.7).

Management and leadership by principals

Chapter 1 shows that the relationship between school autonomy and performance in mathematics varies according to the degree to which principals collaborate with teachers throughout the system. In systems where teachers and principals collaborate more frequently in managing schools, autonomy is positively related to performance in mathematics.

School principals can shape teachers' professional development, define the school's educational goals, ensure that instructional practice is directed towards achieving these goals, suggest modifications to improve teaching practices, and help solve problems that may arise within the classroom or among teachers. Principals are not only administrators, they can also become instructional leaders who motivate teachers to improve the quality of their practice and provide a framework for effective teacher collaboration (Blumberg and Greenfield, 1980; Bossert et al., 1981; Blase and Blase, 1998; Hallinger and Heck, 1998; and Wiseman, 2004). An international comparative study shows that effective principals are likely to display both administrate and instructional leadership (OECD, 2009).

PISA 2012 asked school principals to report how frequently various actions and behaviours related to managing their school, including teacher participation in school management, occurred in the previous academic year (Figure IV.4.6 and Table IV.4.8).

- On average across OECD countries, 72% of students are in schools whose principals reported that the school gives staff opportunities to make decisions concerning the school at least once a month (54% are in schools that give these opportunities from once a month to once a week; and 18% are in schools that give these opportunities more than once a week). Over 80% of students in Canada, Sweden, the United States, Finland, Portugal, Iceland, Australia, Jordan, Brazil, Norway, New Zealand, Colombia (Box IV.4.3), Chile, Denmark, Turkey, Germany and Thailand attend schools that give staff these opportunities at least once a month; while in Shanghai-China, Macao-China, Liechtenstein, Poland, France, Romania and Luxembourg, fewer than 50% of students attend such schools.

- Across OECD countries, an average of 70% of students are in schools whose principal reported that teachers are involved at least once a month in building a culture of continuous improvement in the school (47% of students are in schools where this occurs once a month to once a week; and 23% are in schools where this occurs more than once a week). Over 80% of students in Liechtenstein, the United States, Chile, Turkey, Australia, the United Arab Emirates, the United Kingdom, Malaysia, Uruguay, Germany, Singapore, Slovenia, Brazil, Indonesia, Thailand, Canada, Denmark, Sweden, Latvia, Jordan, Portugal and New Zealand attend schools where teachers are involved in this activity at least once a month; while in Luxembourg, France, Macao-China, Shanghai-China, Japan and Romania, fewer than 50% of students attend such schools.

- On average across OECD countries, 29% of students are in schools whose principal reported that teachers are asked to review management practices at least once a month (24% are in schools where teachers do so once a month to once a week; and 6% are in schools where teachers do so more than once a week). Over 50% of students in Turkey, Thailand, Malaysia, Jordan, Albania, Indonesia, Bulgaria, Uruguay, Brazil, Kazakhstan, the United States, the United Arab Emirates, Korea, Australia, Montenegro and the United Kingdom attend schools where teachers participate in this activity at least once a month; while in Luxembourg, France, Hungary, Switzerland and Shanghai-China, around 10% of students or fewer attend such schools.

Principals' responses to these questions are combined to develop a composite index, the *index of school management: teacher participation* (Figure IV.4.6 and Table IV.4.12). This index has an average of zero and a standard deviation of one for OECD countries. Higher values indicate greater teacher participation. In Turkey, Brazil, Jordan and Malaysia, principals reported that teachers are involved in managing school a greater extent, while principals in Shanghai-China, France and Romania reported that teachers are involved in this activity to a lesser extent (Figure IV.4.6 and Table IV.4.12).

Principals were also asked about their own management style. Responses to these questions are combined to develop three composite indices: an *index on framing and communicating the school's goals and curricular development*; an *index on instructional leadership*; and an *index on promoting instructional improvements and professional development*. Each of these indices has an average of zero and a standard deviation of one for OECD countries. Higher values indicate greater principals' leadership in each area (see Tables IV.4.13, IV.4.14 and IV.4.15, available on line).

■ Figure IV.4.6 ■
Principals' views on teacher participation in school management

Percentage of students in schools whose principals reported that he/she engaged in the following actions "more than once a week", "once a month to once a week", "3-4 times during the year" or "never or 1-2 times during the year"

A Provide staff with opportunities to make decisions concerning the school
B Engage teachers to help build a culture of continuous improvement in the school
C Ask teachers to participate in reviewing management practices

1 Never or 1-2 times during the year
2 3-4 times during the year
3 Once a month to once a week
4 More than once a week

Index of school management: Teacher participation

▬ Range between top and bottom quarters
◆ Average index

	A 1	A 2	A 3	A 4	B 1	B 2	B 3	B 4	C 1	C 2	C 3	C 4	Variability in the index (S.D.)
Turkey	2	14	41	44	3	9	42	46	6	19	45	29	1.0
Brazil	3	12	38	47	6	12	37	46	23	19	39	19	1.1
Jordan	6	8	49	37	8	11	42	39	23	9	43	26	1.2
Malaysia	5	25	46	24	2	14	50	34	10	20	46	24	1.0
Thailand	5	12	50	33	5	13	46	36	14	12	54	20	1.0
United States	4	9	59	29	2	5	54	40	26	19	44	12	1.0
Australia	2	12	62	24	2	11	49	38	22	26	42	10	0.9
Uruguay	7	13	52	28	7	10	53	30	26	16	45	14	1.1
Montenegro	11	31	27	32	5	19	26	50	20	28	35	16	1.1
Colombia	6	10	47	38	7	14	38	41	34	20	33	14	1.1
Kazakhstan	5	23	50	22	5	15	49	30	13	30	45	12	0.9
United Kingdom	3	23	53	21	2	14	42	43	22	27	40	10	0.9
Portugal	6	7	57	30	3	17	39	41	27	28	33	12	1.0
Chile	2	13	53	31	2	9	57	32	41	17	35	7	0.9
United Arab Emirates	7	21	52	19	6	9	50	35	29	18	37	16	1.0
Indonesia	11	20	49	19	6	12	50	33	16	23	48	12	1.0
Italy	5	31	43	22	3	20	38	38	21	33	34	13	1.0
Canada	2	8	67	23	5	13	46	36	35	21	39	5	0.9
Bulgaria	7	18	59	16	4	21	53	22	7	34	50	9	0.8
Albania	9	29	48	14	11	21	40	29	10	24	43	23	1.0
New Zealand	2	13	67	18	5	15	58	22	30	26	38	5	0.9
Qatar	14	17	45	24	6	19	42	33	32	30	28	11	1.1
Singapore	3	19	60	18	2	14	58	25	33	33	28	6	0.8
Argentina	11	22	36	31	4	18	32	46	46	22	19	14	1.1
Slovenia	7	22	53	18	4	13	57	26	40	25	30	5	0.9
Latvia	6	25	50	19	4	16	54	26	44	28	24	5	0.9
Ireland	3	26	49	22	7	25	38	30	38	30	22	11	1.1
Croatia	6	19	59	15	4	19	43	34	43	26	24	7	0.9
Greece	4	21	57	18	2	20	48	29	51	19	24	6	1.0
Sweden	2	10	71	17	3	16	56	26	64	17	16	2	0.7
Korea	9	17	62	12	14	21	59	6	29	20	43	9	1.0
Finland	4	9	70	17	7	19	54	21	63	18	16	4	0.9
Germany	1	15	53	31	2	14	52	32	79	10	10	1	0.7
Spain	4	22	55	19	4	31	43	21	39	37	19	6	0.9
Denmark	3	12	72	13	4	15	58	23	62	19	17	2	0.8
Serbia	3	31	45	21	5	26	40	29	53	25	17	5	0.9
OECD average	6	23	54	18	8	22	47	23	49	22	24	6	0.9
Norway	4	11	68	17	8	18	59	15	65	21	12	2	0.8
Russian Federation	3	36	53	9	13	20	53	15	17	39	42	2	0.8
Iceland	1	13	68	18	6	19	63	13	68	17	14	1	0.7
Chinese Taipei	11	25	51	12	13	26	48	13	25	29	39	6	1.0
Costa Rica	14	20	48	18	12	20	44	24	35	22	31	12	1.2
Estonia	4	35	44	17	4	22	51	23	71	12	13	4	0.8
Mexico	18	28	34	20	8	27	42	23	42	23	28	7	1.1
Hong Kong-China	7	33	51	8	11	34	43	12	16	43	40	1	0.8
Liechtenstein	0	56	43	1	0	0	96	4	74	12	12	2	0.6
Slovak Republic	9	28	55	8	3	25	55	17	35	33	30	2	0.8
Lithuania	6	29	50	15	12	26	39	23	61	25	10	4	0.9
Tunisia	14	35	26	26	16	34	26	25	31	35	24	10	1.2
Netherlands	5	36	45	14	6	22	57	15	57	24	18	1	0.8
Israel	8	25	52	15	11	24	46	19	60	21	16	4	1.0
Czech Republic	9	37	39	16	8	27	46	18	52	27	17	3	1.0
Viet Nam	19	16	60	5	14	20	56	10	40	23	34	4	0.9
Austria	8	27	46	19	11	24	50	15	75	11	13	1	0.9
Peru	14	34	34	18	19	25	33	23	47	29	20	4	1.1
Poland	13	43	33	11	15	33	40	12	36	42	20	2	0.8
Belgium	6	30	50	14	14	31	36	19	70	16	12	2	1.0
Japan	20	13	60	7	24	35	36	5	35	19	44	2	1.0
Hungary	5	30	60	5	20	24	44	12	82	11	6	0	0.7
Macao-China	24	46	24	7	15	46	35	4	28	48	18	6	0.8
Luxembourg	5	47	37	12	22	43	21	14	65	30	2	3	0.9
Switzerland	11	35	49	6	13	34	41	12	82	11	7	0	0.8
Romania	40	14	29	17	43	10	20	27	47	19	23	12	1.7
France	9	47	37	8	17	47	26	10	74	20	4	3	1.0
Shanghai-China	48	38	13	2	17	42	32	9	47	42	8	3	0.8

-2.5 -1.5 -0.5   0.5   1.5   2.5 Index points
-3.0 -2.0 -1.0   0   1.0   2.0

Countries and economies are ranked in descending order of the average index.
Source: OECD, PISA 2012 Database, Tables IV.4.8 and IV.4.12.
StatLink ᴹˢ■ http://dx.doi.org/10.1787/888932957346

Principals in Brazil, Kazakhstan, Qatar, Malaysia, the United Kingdom, the United States and the United Arab Emirates reported that they are more frequently involved in framing and communicating the school's goals and in curricular development than other countries and economies, while principals in Japan, Switzerland, Liechtenstein, Romania, Tunisia and Poland reported that they are involved in these less (Table IV.4.13). Principals in Qatar, the United States, Jordan, Brazil, Malaysia, Turkey, Australia and the United Kingdom tended to report they practice greater instructional leadership, while principals in Japan, Liechtenstein, France, Tunisia and Switzerland reported to practice this less than principals in other countries and economies (Table IV.4.14). In some countries, such as Brazil, Montenegro, Jordan, Turkey and Albania, principals also promote instructional improvements and professional development, while principals in Romania, Liechtenstein, the Netherlands and Japan reported that they are less active in this regard than principals in other countries and economies (Table IV.4.15).

In general, schools whose principals reported that they show leadership in framing and communicating the school's goals and curricular development also tend to be those whose principals reported showing leadership in instruction. The correlation between the *index of school management: framing and communicating the school's goals and curricular development* and the *index of school management: instructional leadership* is 0.67 on average across OECD countries, ranging from around 0.51 to 0.54 in Uruguay, Shanghai-China, Switzerland, Albania and Poland, to around 0.80 or more in Romania, Thailand, Costa Rica and Korea. Schools whose principals reported that they show leadership in instruction also tend to welcome teachers' participation in school management. On average across OECD countries, the *index of school management: instructional leadership* and the *index of school management: teacher participation* is 0.60, ranging from 0.37 in Luxembourg to over 0.80 in Romania, Montenegro, Liechtenstein and Thailand (Table IV.4.16).

These relationships at the school level are also mirrored at the system level. School systems in which principals are more frequently engaged in framing and communicating the school's goals and curricular development tend to be systems in which principals reported that they provide instructional leadership (correlation coefficient is 0.84 across OECD countries, and 0.87 across all participating countries and economies). In addition, systems with higher level of principals' instructional leadership tend to have more teachers participating in managing school (correlation coefficient is 0.78 across OECD countries, and 0.74 across all participating countries and economies) (Tables IV.4.12, IV.4.13 and IV.4.14).

Parental involvement

Parents are often expected to be partners with teachers and principals in order to better meet the learning objectives of their children (Gunnarsson et al., 2009; Zhao and Akiba, 2009). This partnership can take the form of: parents discussing educational matters with their children; parents supervising their children's progress through education; parents communicating with the school; and parents actively participating in school activities. While the first two forms of parental involvement involve interactions between parents and their children, the latter two involve interactions between parents and the school (Ho and Willms, 1996).

PISA 2012 asked principals to define the proportion of students' parents who participated in various school-related activities. Parents' discussing their child's progress on the initiative of one of their child's teachers seems to be one of the most common forms of parental involvement in school. As shown in Figure IV.4.7, across OECD countries, the average student attends schools whose principal reported that 47% of parents discussed their child's progress on the initiative of one of their child's teachers; 38% of parents discussed their child's behaviour on the initiative of one of their child's teachers; 27% of parents discussed their child's progress with a teacher on their own initiative; 23% of parents discussed their child's behaviour with a teacher on their own initiative; 11% of parents participated in local school government; 10% of parents assisted in fundraising for the school; 8% of parents volunteered in extracurricular activities, such as a book club, school play, sporting event or field trip; 5% of parents assisted a teacher in the school; 4% of parents volunteered in physical activities at school, such as building maintenance, carpentry, gardening or yard work; 2% of parents volunteered in the school library or media centre; 2% of parents appeared as a guest speaker; and 1% of parents volunteered in the school canteen. In Norway, Sweden, Macao-China, Denmark and Japan, the average student attends a school whose principal reported that around 70% of parents or more discussed their child's progress at the initiative of one of their child's teachers. By contrast, the average student in Tunisia, the Slovak Republic, Hungary, Croatia, Uruguay, Ireland and Austria attends a school whose principal reported that fewer than 30% of parents did so (Figure IV.4.7 and Table IV.4.17).

■ Figure IV.4.7 ■

Parental involvement

Based on school principals' reports

	Discussed their child's behaviour with a teacher on their own initiative	Discussed their child's behaviour on the initiative of one of their child's teachers	Discussed their child's progress with a teacher on their own initiative	Discussed their child's progress on the initiative of one of their child's teachers	Volunteered in physical activities, e.g. building maintenance, carpentry, gardening or yard work	Volunteered in extracurricular activities, e.g. book club, school play, sports, field trip	Volunteered in the school library or media centre	Assisted a teacher in the school	Appeared as a guest speaker	Participated in local school government, e.g. parent council or school-management committee	Assisted in fundraising for the school	Volunteered in the school canteen
	%	%	%	%	%	%	%	%	%	%	%	%
OECD												
Australia	19	30	26	41	5	7	2	5	2	5	14	4
Austria	17	22	26	29	2	5	1	4	1	6	8	1
Belgium	20	28	24	35	1	2	0	1	1	3	2	0
Canada	24	36	32	41	3	9	1	4	2	5	9	1
Chile	29	58	29	59	9	14	5	15	6	34	30	2
Czech Republic	18	31	24	40	1	2	0	0	0	5	5	a
Denmark	17	41	20	74	5	17	0	6	2	8	2	1
Estonia	17	27	22	40	5	16	1	10	6	9	3	0
Finland	26	45	28	55	1	4	0	0	1	4	10	1
France	26	40	25	41	1	3	1	1	2	9	3	0
Germany	22	30	27	35	4	7	1	6	2	5	4	0
Greece	33	33	51	39	5	7	2	a	3	20	14	1
Hungary	17	20	22	23	7	12	1	9	1	5	12	0
Iceland	16	41	19	57	2	8	0	2	2	4	13	4
Ireland	11	24	15	28	1	4	1	2	2	6	13	1
Israel	24	41	28	49	5	8	1	5	6	11	3	0
Italy	43	46	48	47	1	9	2	a	2	36	11	a
Japan	10	63	11	70	7	7	0	1	0	9	4	a
Korea	25	45	30	47	2	7	4	6	3	13	3	0
Luxembourg	26	44	32	48	1	4	1	1	2	6	6	0
Mexico	28	45	29	48	18	17	6	13	6	34	25	5
Netherlands	17	31	27	43	1	3	2	1	1	3	0	1
New Zealand	18	26	23	42	4	10	1	5	1	3	14	1
Norway	13	52	17	87	6	12	0	1	1	7	10	0
Poland	28	53	32	59	5	20	4	12	3	17	16	a
Portugal	35	47	38	53	1	4	0	1	2	7	4	0
Slovak Republic	26	32	19	23	4	10	1	1	1	17	13	0
Slovenia	30	36	38	34	2	4	2	4	2	15	26	0
Spain	35	52	40	62	2	6	1	5	2	14	9	0
Sweden	15	36	27	80	3	8	0	1	2	7	5	1
Switzerland	18	42	20	47	1	4	1	4	1	3	2	0
Turkey	32	41	30	36	10	13	8	12	7	22	11	2
United Kingdom	15	29	19	53	1	4	0	2	2	2	10	0
United States	24	33	32	41	7	14	3	6	3	11	23	1
OECD average	23	38	27	47	4	8	2	5	2	11	10	1
Partners												
Albania	42	58	45	58	10	19	9	14	18	48	19	5
Argentina	22	43	20	44	9	11	6	10	5	18	18	6
Brazil	24	41	25	42	2	6	2	3	3	21	5	1
Bulgaria	30	48	30	44	8	10	2	24	3	13	10	0
Colombia	37	59	39	58	13	16	10	14	12	51	28	6
Costa Rica	26	40	31	40	7	10	3	8	5	21	22	3
Croatia	31	27	32	27	2	7	1	a	2	18	11	a
Hong Kong-China	38	66	39	66	2	7	2	3	1	9	12	0
Indonesia	31	49	32	43	21	21	12	18	11	53	23	6
Jordan	29	33	28	30	12	14	8	11	13	31	5	5
Kazakhstan	57	56	61	65	41	52	33	46	34	51	15	11
Latvia	26	35	33	42	9	22	1	2	2	11	9	1
Liechtenstein	11	42	11	57	1	2	0	5	0	3	0	3
Lithuania	32	38	36	44	7	14	2	11	4	10	16	0
Macao-China	31	80	34	76	1	8	1	4	3	13	25	0
Malaysia	17	25	16	31	7	7	3	8	4	19	32	3
Montenegro	49	43	39	38	3	7	2	3	1	22	2	a
Peru	33	41	33	44	16	16	5	18	5	48	30	3
Qatar	40	47	43	52	10	22	17	18	20	28	16	4
Romania	39	46	40	49	16	22	13	12	11	35	31	2
Russian Federation	28	39	39	49	31	32	5	26	18	27	27	8
Serbia	39	50	36	45	2	4	0	1	2	23	20	0
Shanghai-China	49	58	46	55	8	13	6	12	8	12	13	3
Singapore	20	49	24	66	2	5	1	3	1	4	14	0
Chinese Taipei	39	41	34	38	6	10	4	5	3	13	9	1
Thailand	38	53	40	56	13	18	9	9	12	18	51	7
Tunisia	19	33	15	18	2	4	1	2	1	7	3	0
United Arab Emirates	35	38	39	42	12	21	15	15	15	25	9	4
Uruguay	10	23	18	27	3	5	3	3	2	10	8	0
Viet Nam	45	49	49	52	13	14	12	41	18	24	61	2

Source: OECD, PISA 2012 Database, Table IV.4.17.
StatLink ᵃˢᵐˢ http://dx.doi.org/10.1787/888932957346

Principals were also asked to report whether they receive: constant pressure from many parents who expect their school to set very high academic standards and to achieve them; pressure from a minority of parents to achieve higher academic standards; or whether such pressure from parents is largely absent. On average across OECD countries, 21% of students are in schools whose principals reported that they are pressured by many parents; 46% are in schools that are pressured by a minority of parents; and 33% are in schools that are not pressured by parents. In Singapore, Ireland, New Zealand, Sweden, the United Kingdom, Qatar, Viet Nam, Thailand, the United States, the United Arab Emirates and Australia, at least one out of three students are in schools whose principals reported that they are pressured by many parents; in Singapore, 60% of students attend such schools. By contrast, fewer than 10% of students in Macao-China, Hong Kong-China, Finland, Latvia, Croatia, Germany, Uruguay, Turkey, Lithuania, Serbia, Austria, Spain, Argentina, Korea, Belgium, Kazakhstan, and Switzerland are in schools that are pressured by many parents to meet high academic standards (Table IV.4.18).

All of parents' involvement in school activities – such as volunteering in physical activities, in extracurricular activities, and in the school library or media centre, assisting a teacher in the school, appearing as a guest speaker, or assisting in fundraising for the school – are highly correlated with each other, both across OECD countries and across all participating countries and economies. This means that when parents are highly involved in one of these school activities they also tend to be highly involved in other school activities. However, across OECD countries, the level of parents' involvement in school activities seems not to be related to the degree of their involvement in discussing their child's behaviour and/or progress with a teacher (Figure IV.4.8).

■ Figure IV.4.8 ■
Relationship among various aspects of parental involvement

Correlation coefficients between two relevant indicators

Correlation coefficients range from -1.00 (i.e. a perfect negative linear association) to +1.00 (i.e. a perfect positive linear association). When a correlation coefficient is 0, there is no linear relationship between two indicators.

Legend: ▢ Across OECD countries ▨ Across all participating countries and economies

Percentage of students whose parents...	Discussed their child's behaviour with a teacher on their own initiative	Discussed their child's behaviour on the initiative of one of their child's teachers	Discussed their child's progress with a teacher on their own initiative	Discussed their child's progress on the initiative of one of their child's teachers	Volunteered in physical activities, e.g. building maintenance, carpentry, gardening or yard work	Volunteered in extracurricular activities, e.g. book club, school play, sports, field trip	Volunteered in the school library or media centre	Assisted a teacher in the school	Appeared as a guest speaker	Participated in local school government, e.g. parent council or school management committee	Assisted in fundraising for the school	Volunteered in the school canteen
Discussed their child's behaviour with a teacher on their own initiative		**0.34**	**0.86**	-0.14	0.06	0.08	**0.48**	**0.35**	**0.39**	**0.68**	*0.30*	0.02
Discussed their child's behaviour on the initiative of one of their child's teachers	**0.51**		0.14	**0.68**	0.24	0.23	0.28	0.16	0.19	**0.44**	0.12	0.15
Discussed their child's progress with a teacher on their own initiative	**0.90**	**0.39**		-0.11	-0.05	-0.03	*0.30*	0.23	0.26	**0.50**	0.25	-0.01
Discussed their child's progress on the initiative of one of their child's teachers	0.10	**0.73**	0.15		0.10	0.24	-0.14	-0.11	-0.05	0.01	-0.11	0.10
Volunteered in physical activities, e.g. building maintenance, carpentry, gardening or yard work	**0.45**	*0.23*	**0.46**	0.13		**0.73**	**0.69**	**0.73**	**0.63**	**0.57**	**0.53**	**0.59**
Volunteered in extracurricular activities, e.g. book club, school play, sports, field trip	**0.49**	**0.26**	**0.51**	*0.22*	**0.91**		**0.49**	**0.75**	**0.54**	**0.48**	**0.41**	*0.36*
Volunteered in the school library or media centre	**0.61**	**0.30**	**0.58**	0.12	**0.81**	**0.82**		**0.77**	**0.74**	**0.73**	**0.49**	**0.45**
Assisted a teacher in the school	**0.57**	**0.26**	**0.60**	0.10	**0.83**	**0.78**	**0.80**		**0.76**	**0.74**	**0.53**	**0.40**
Appeared as a guest speaker	**0.59**	**0.30**	**0.61**	0.16	**0.84**	**0.84**	**0.92**	**0.85**		**0.61**	**0.38**	*0.35*
Participated in local school government, e.g. parent council or school management committee	**0.63**	**0.38**	**0.56**	0.06	**0.71**	**0.64**	**0.70**	**0.66**	**0.70**		**0.58**	**0.40**
Assisted in fundraising for the school	**0.40**	**0.28**	**0.41**	0.09	**0.45**	**0.35**	**0.39**	**0.54**	**0.45**	**0.48**		**0.46**
Volunteered in the school canteen	**0.41**	*0.25*	**0.38**	0.14	**0.81**	**0.73**	**0.73**	**0.63**	**0.78**	**0.66**	**0.41**	

Note: Correlation coefficients that are statistically significant at the 5% level ($p < 0.05$) are indicated in bold and those at the 10% level ($p < 0.10$) are in italic.
Source: OECD, PISA 2012 Database, Table IV.4.17.
StatLink ⧉ http://dx.doi.org/10.1787/888932957346

TRENDS IN GOVERNANCE OF SCHOOL SYSTEMS SINCE PISA 2003

In 2003, on average across OECD countries, 83% of students attended government or public schools, 14% attended government-depended private schools and 4% attended government-independent private schools.[5] These percentages have remained stable since then. In both PISA 2003 and PISA 2012 students enrolled in government or public schools had, on average, a lower socio-economic status than students attending private schools (by an order of around 0.4 points in the *PISA index of economic social and cultural status*). However, some countries and economies have seen an increase in enrolment in public schools (Figure IV.4.9), while in others there has been a shift towards private schools (Table IV.4.19). In Indonesia, Mexico, Spain and Finland, a larger proportion of 15-year-old students attended public schools in 2012 than did in 2003. In Indonesia there was a 21 percentage-point reduction in the share of students attending government-independent private schools, with a consequent 13 percentage-point increase in enrolment in government-dependent private schools and an 8 percentage-point increase in public school enrolments. In Mexico, Spain and Finland there was a four percentage-point increase in the share of students attending public schools. In Sweden, the share of students enrolled in public schools fell by ten percentage points, with a consequent greater share of students attending government-dependent private schools. A similar shift in enrolment towards government-dependent schools – an increase of six percentage points – was observed in Thailand, and, to a lesser degree, in Poland (Figure IV.4.9 and Table IV.4.19).

■ Figure IV.4.9 ■
Change between 2003 and 2012 in public school enrolments
Percentage of students enrolled in public schools

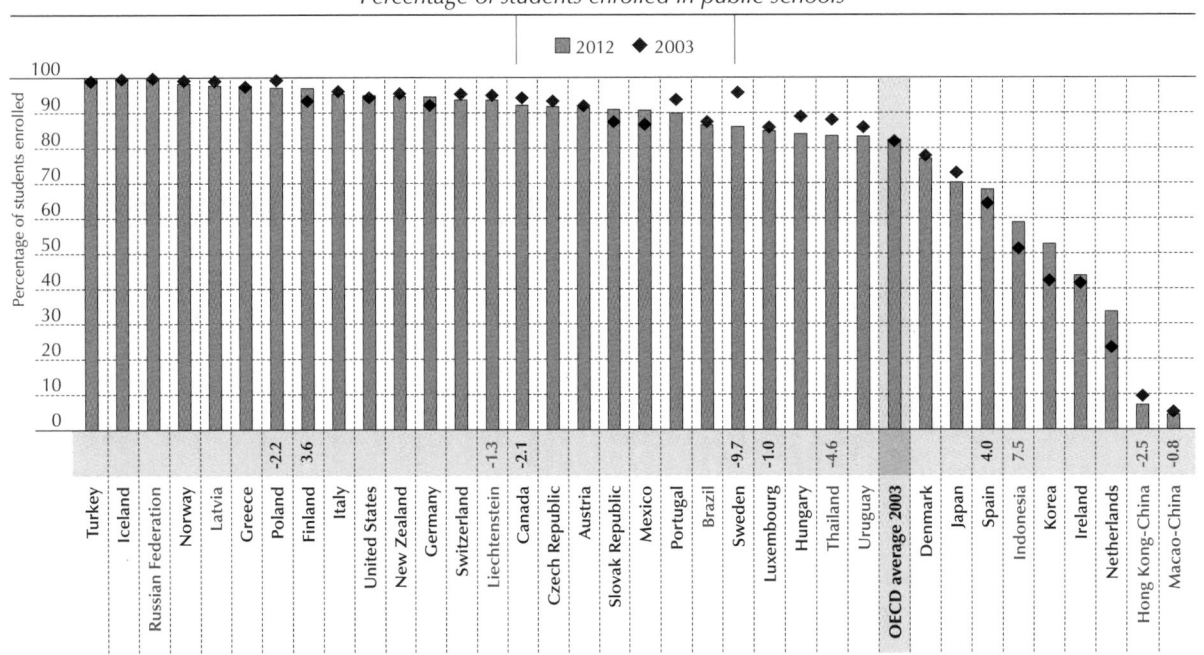

Notes: Only countries and economies with comparable data from PISA 2003 and PISA 2012 are shown.
The percentage-point difference in the share of students attending public schools (2012 - 2003) is shown above the country/economy name. Only statistically significant differences are shown.
OECD average 2003 compares only OECD countries with comparable data since 2003.
Countries and economies are ranked in descending order of the share of students in public schools in 2012.
Source: OECD, PISA 2012 Database, Table IV.4.19.
StatLink 🔗 http://dx.doi.org/10.1787/888932957346

In PISA 2003, students enrolled in public schools came from more socio-economically disadvantaged backgrounds than students enrolled in private schools, on average across OECD countries.[6] That year, only in Luxembourg were students from more advantaged backgrounds more likely to attend public schools. This general trend continued in most countries and economies through 2012. The disparity between the socio-economic status of students who attend public schools and those who attend private schools became wider in Mexico, Austria and Uruguay between 2003 and 2012. It became apparent in Denmark, while in 2003 there was no difference between the average socio-economic status of the two groups of students. In Luxembourg in 2012, students in public schools had the same average socio-economic status as those in private schools, in contrast to what was observed in 2003 (Table IV.4.19).

Only in Korea were public schools able to attract more advantaged students in 2012 than they did in 2003. While in 2003 the average student in public schools came from a substantially lower socio-economic background than students in private schools (a difference of 0.4 points in the *PISA index of social, economic and cultural status*), by 2012 there was no difference in the socio-economic status of the average student in public and private schools. It seems that between 2003 and 2012 public or government schools became better equipped to attract more advantaged students into their classrooms (Table IV.4.19). In addition, in Ireland and Brazil the socio-economic difference in students attending public and private schools narrowed between 2003 and 2012.[7]

Box IV.4.3. **Improving in PISA: Colombia**

With a population of 47 million, Colombia is Latin America's third most populated country after Brazil and Mexico. It began participating in PISA in 2006 and has shown an average annual improvement in reading performance of 3.0 points per year (from 385 points in 2006 to 403 points in 2012). Improvement in reading was led by the country's lowest-achieving students: those in the 10th percentile of reading performance increased their scores by more than 50 points, from 243 to 295 points, in six years. Similarly, science performance among low-achieving students has increased while that of high-achieving students has remained stable. These large improvements follow those observed in the years prior to Colombia's first participation in PISA, as Colombia was the most rapid improver in the Trends in International Mathematics and Science Study (TIMSS) between 1995 and 2007 (World Bank, 2010). These improvements are remarkable given the fact that, during the same period, Colombia has also increased its enrolment rates. Between 2002 and 2010, enrolment among 15- and 16-year-olds grew from 57% to 75%, there was a 40% reduction in the share of students aged 5 to 14 who were not in education, and 98.5% of primary school pupils progressed into secondary school (up from 89.6% in 2000).

Since the mid-1990s, Colombia has been engaged in improving both access to and the quality of schooling. Cash-transfer programmes, such as *Familias en Acción*, public campaigns (*Ni Uno Menos)* and direct investment (*Programa de Ampliación de la Cobertura y Mejoramiento de la Calidad de la Educación Secundaria, PACES*) increased student enrolments and reduced dropout rates, while targeted programmes, such as *Hogares Comunitarios de Bienestar Familiar* and *Grado Cero*, promoted enrolment in early childhood programmes which, in turn, reduced the incidence of grade repetition. The *Escuela Nueva* and similar programmes have improved student achievement in rural areas by allowing students to progress through a flexible curriculum and engaging students through active pedagogy, democratic decision-making, and community engagement (World Bank, 2010).

More recently, the *Todos a Aprender* programme, which began in 2012, adopts a comprehensive view towards school change, offering support to low-performing schools on several fronts. It first makes sure students can go to and stay in school by offering transportation and meals to disadvantaged students. It offers new pedagogical material for teachers, training for teachers to develop their classroom management and pedagogical skills with the assistance of tutors, and support in developing school-improvement plans.

The early 2000s also mark the beginning of *Revolución Educativa*, a major education-improvement programme that modified how education policy objectives are set, the way resources are allocated, how education is monitored, how the central government supports schools and local authorities (*Secretarías*), and teachers' career trajectories. The programme scaled-up the policies and practices adopted in the local government of Bogotá since 1995, particularly between 1998 and 2003 (MEN, 2010).

The *Revolución Educativa* established quinquennial (*Plan Sectorial*) and decennial (*Plan Decenal*) education-development plans, articulating policy objectives and areas of development. These plans, developed centrally by the Ministry of Education in consultation with stakeholders and adapted locally by the *Secretarías*, provided a framework for the development of individual policies and programmes. They shifted the objective of education to student-centred instruction, focusing on competencies and clearly defining the quality benchmarks that ought to be achieved as students progress through school. The plan also called for an integrated information system to promote the development and follow-up of school-improvement plans (MEN, 2010).

...

A major shift in school financing also occurred in the early 2000s. Between 2002 and 2010, total funding for education increased by 48.4%, 60% of which was an increase in public expenditure. More important, the structure of school financing shifted, such that, as of the 2000s, central government funding is allocated to *Secretarías* and then to schools based on enrolments, accounting for the accessibility of each school. A per-pupil financing system required an up-to-date online information system with which all students could be identified and followed through the school system, but no such system existed in Colombia. Information systems were developed to follow students as they are promoted and transition to other levels, as they transfer to other schools, drop out or graduate (*Sistema Integrado de Matrícula*), track schools, their staff and performance results (*Sistema Nacional de Información de Educación Básica*), track human resources to co-ordinate pay and human-resource management (*Sistema Integrado de Recursos Humanos*), track financial resources to help *Secretarías* manage their schools and budget (*Sistema de Gestión Financiera*), and support school-improvement plans and follow the management of schools. These information systems were created to be compatible with national and local social and welfare information systems (MEN, 2010).

The devolution of school management to local education authorities required support from the central government to ensure that each authority was able to assume their responsibilities. *Secretarías* were thus assisted in evaluating their processes and were provided the infrastructure necessary for adequate education and information management. In many authorities, plans were developed to ensure a stable workforce to give continuity to each management area. Large investments, with co-operation from the Inter-Amercian Development Bank, were made to train workers and promote a work culture of efficiency and countinuous improvement. The Ministry of Education was also restructured (MEN, 2010).

The monitoring of students and schools for management and school-improvement purposes is central to these reforms. Quality benchmarks and the competencies to be acquired by students at different levels of education were defined, and the annual national exam for entry into tertiary education (ICFES) and the triennial national assessments (SABER) were integrated in a common framework in accordance with these standards. Colombia also participates regularly in international assessments. All of these assessments and examinations are now co-ordinated by an independent institution, the *Instituto Colombiano de Evaluación de la Educación* (MEN, 2010).

The Ministry of Education provides guidelines so that every school develops an improvement plan and each *Secretaría* offers support for schools to achieve these objectives. Improvement plans focus on leadership, instructional management, financial and administrative management, and the relationship with the community. The Ministry worked closely with the *Secretarías* to ensure that each local authority had the capacity to support their individual schools, and encouraged collaboration with non-profit foundations, universities and foreign governments to support local authorities and individual schools in their improvement plans. Annual forums are held where good practices at the school, local authority and international levels are shared (MEN, 2010).

These reforms also changed the way teachers are selected into and progress through the profession. As of 2002, all new teachers are required to hold university-level degrees, and are recruited through an open and competitive selection process that includes an assessment of course content and pedagogy, a psychological evaluation, a personal interview and consideration of prior experience. The results of these processes are also used to determine in which schools to place teachers. By 2010, 22% of working teachers had been selected through this process. Career advancement shifted from a tenure-based system to one based on competencies, identified through a new teacher-evaluation system. Teacher salaries were raised to be aligned with those of other social science professionals. Salary increases were concentrated at the beginning of a teacher's career, to encourage continual improvement and promote retention. In parallel, teacher pre-service training programmes were accredited and a pilot programme to improve them began in 2009 (MEN, 2010).

Sources:

Ministerio de Educación Nacional (MEN) (2010), *Revolución Educativa 2002-2010, Acciones y Lecciones*, Ministerio de Educación Nacional, República de Colombia, Bogotá.

World Bank (2010), *Quality of Education in Colombia, Achievements and Challenges Ahead: Analysis of the Results of TIMSS 1995 – 2007*, World Bank, Washington, D.C.

ASSESSMENT AND ACCOUNTABILITY

Chapter 1 shows that equity in a school system is positively related to the degree to which systems seek feedback from students regarding lessons, teachers or resources, and to the degree to which teachers are mentored. Chapter 1 also shows that accountability arrangements, such as posting achievement data publicly and implementing standardised policies for mathematics, play an important role in relation to school autonomy and performance.

The shift in public and government concern away from mere control over the resources and content of education towards a focus on outcomes has, in many countries, led to the establishment of standards of quality for educational institutions. In most OECD countries, evaluation and assessment systems not only focus on students, but also on teachers and school leaders; and the use of performance data to improve teaching and learning has expanded in recent years (OECD, 2013a). The approaches to standard-setting that countries pursue range from defining broad education goals to formulating precise performance expectations in well-defined subject areas. PISA 2012 collected data on the nature of accountability systems and the ways in which the resulting information was used and made available to various stakeholders and the general public.

Assessments and examinations

Countries and economies implement different policies to evaluate their students' performance. System-wide evaluations can generally be classified as those that do not have direct consequences for students (assessments) and those that do (examinations). Assessments can be used to take stock of students' performance in order to make decisions on future instruction or to summarise performance for information purposes. Although assessments can be used to, for example, decide on allocation of resources to low-performing schools or tailor instruction to low-performing students, assessment results do not have direct tangible consequences for students. Results from examinations, by contrast, can be used to determine students' progression to higher levels of education (e.g. the transition from lower to upper secondary school), selection into different curricular programmes (e.g. into vocational or academic programmes), or selection into university programmes. Assessments and examinations provide students with benchmarks, and, in the case of examinations, with incentives to work hard in school in order to pass the examinations.

All PISA-participating countries and economies have an assessment or examination system in place.[8] Nineteen schools systems in OECD countries implement national assessments in all programmes in lower secondary schools and eight do so in upper secondary schools. Of these, in Belgium (Flemish community), Chile, Hungary, Korea, Mexico, Sweden and the United States national assessments are conducted in both lower and upper secondary schools (Tables IV.4.20 and IV.4.21). Twelve systems in OECD countries administer examinations in lower secondary schools and 21 systems in OECD countries conduct examinations in upper secondary schools. In some of these systems, however, not all students take these examinations, as they are only for students in general programmes (e.g. in lower secondary schools in Estonia, Germany and Portugal, and in upper secondary schools in Finland, Germany, the Netherlands and Portugal) or for students in pre-vocational or vocational programmes (e.g. in upper secondary schools in Spain) (Tables IV.4.22 and IV.4.23). Other examinations are used in Belgium (French Community), Japan, Norway, Switzerland and the United States (Table IV.4.24 and Table IV.4.25). Examinations not conducted by secondary schools are required for access to tertiary education programmes in all OECD countries for at least some fields of study, except in Iceland, the Netherlands and Portugal, where no examination is required. These tertiary-level entrance examinations are required for access to all fields of study in Chile, Greece, Japan, Korea, Mexico, Sweden and Turkey. In Chile, Italy, Japan and Turkey they are the only way to gain access to tertiary education programmes. In 13 OECD countries these tertiary entrance examinations are used to determine access to selective institutions (Table IV.4.26).

Countries and economies can be grouped into four categories of assessment-and-examination systems as shown in Figure IV.4.10. A first group of countries and economies tends to have assessments at the lower secondary level and national examinations at the upper secondary level, with few tertiary fields of study requiring a special examination for admission. A second group of countries and economies tends to have national examinations at both the upper and secondary levels. A third group of countries and economies tends to rely on not only national examinations, but also other types of examinations or on other types of examinations only. The fourth group of countries and economies tends to have no examinations at the lower or upper secondary level, but a large number of tertiary fields of study require examinations.[9]

Twelve school systems in OECD countries conduct national examinations in lower secondary school and 21 do so in upper secondary school; all partner countries and economies conduct them in upper secondary school. At the lower secondary level, these examinations are, in all cases, used to certify students' graduation or grade completion.

■ Figure IV.4.10 ■

Profiles of assessments and examinations across countries and economies

Assessment in lower secondary, national exams in upper secondary, few fields requiring tertiary exams	Only national exams in lower and upper secondary	National or other non-national examinations in lower or upper secondary	No national or other examinations, most fields requiring tertiary exams
Australia	Albania	Belgium (Fr. Comm.)	Austria
Croatia	Bulgaria	Liechtenstein	Belgium (Fl. Comm.)
Czech Republic	Denmark	Montenegro	Brazil
England (UK)	Estonia	Norway	Chile
Finland	France	Qatar	Colombia
Hong Kong-China	Germany	United Arab Emirates	Greece
Hungary	Indonesia	United States	Iceland
Israel	Ireland		Japan
Luxembourg	Italy		Korea
Scotland (UK)	Jordan		Macao-China
Singapore	Latvia		Mexico
Slovak Republic	Lithuania		Peru
Tunisia	Malaysia		Spain
	Netherlands		Sweden
	Poland		Turkey
	Portugal		Uruguay
	Romania		
	Russian Federation		
	Shanghai-China		
	Chinese Taipei		
	Thailand		
	Viet Nam		

Source: OECD, PISA 2012 Database, Tables IV.4.20, IV.4.21, IV.4.22, IV.4.23, IV.4.24, IV.4.25 and IV.4.26.

In Norway and Poland these examinations are used to determine access to selective upper secondary schools; and in Scotland, Norway and Ireland they are used to select students into certain programmes, courses or tracks in upper secondary school. In all OECD countries, the results from these examinations are shared directly with students, with an external audience in addition to education authorities, with school administrators (except in Italy), and directly with parents (except in Germany). Upper secondary examinations are also used in all OECD countries (except in general programmes in Poland) to certify completion or graduation and to determine students' access to tertiary education (except examinations in the United States and in pre-vocational and vocational programmes in Hungary and Spain). In 15 OECD countries these upper secondary examinations are also used to determine student selection for fields of study at the tertiary level (Tables IV.4.22 and IV.4.23)

Assessment practices and purposes

Principals were asked to report on how student assessments are used. Among the possibilities offered, assessments are most commonly used in OECD countries to inform parents about their child's progress: 98% of students, on average, are in schools whose principal reported that student assessments are used in this way. Some 81% of students are in schools whose principals reported that student assessments are used to monitor the school's progress from year to year; 80% are in schools that use student assessments to identify aspects of instruction or the curriculum that could be improved; 77% are in schools that use them to make decisions about whether students are held back or promoted; 63% are in schools that use them to compare the school to district or national performance; and about one in two students attends a school that uses student assessments to compare the school with other schools, to group students for instructional purposes, or to make judgements about teachers' effectiveness (Figure IV.4.11 and Table IV.4.30).

Systems in which more schools use student assessments for one purpose also tend to be systems where more schools use them for other purposes as well. The strongest relationship among the different uses of student assessment among the OECD countries is found between the proportion of students who attend schools whose principals reported that they use student assessments to compare the school to district or national performance and to compare the school to other schools (correlation coefficient is 0.85) (Figure IV.4.12). The only exception is "to make decisions about students' retention or promotion", which seems not to be related to any other assessment purposes; sometimes it has a negative relationship with other uses of student assessments. For example, across OECD countries, those where more schools use student assessments to make decisions about whether students are retained or promoted than in other countries tend to be less likely than other countries to use the assessments to compare the school's performance to district or national performance (Figure IV.4.12).

■ Figure IV.4.11 ■
Use of assessment practices

	Percentage of students in schools whose principal reported that assessments of students in the national modal grade for 15-year-olds are used for the following purposes:							
	To inform parents about their child's progress	To make decisions about students' retention or promotion	To group students for instructional purposes	To compare the school to district or national performance	To monitor the school's progress from year to year	To make judgements about teachers' effectiveness	To identify aspects of instruction or the curriculum that could be improved	To compare the school with other schools
	%	%	%	%	%	%	%	%
Australia	100	63	84	56	88	50	91	44
Austria	96	94	31	28	63	39	70	30
Belgium	97	96	17	23	60	35	73	18
Canada	100	95	74	82	92	30	87	62
Chile	100	89	44	54	94	61	92	39
Czech Republic	93	79	33	58	86	63	86	63
Denmark	99	10	52	55	57	27	85	56
Estonia	99	82	21	65	78	65	83	59
Finland	99	93	17	46	60	16	61	21
France	97	96	43	62	73	23	50	41
Germany	96	96	39	43	57	24	61	28
Greece	100	98	8	17	56	14	49	22
Hungary	94	69	47	78	93	58	77	71
Iceland	100	15	42	77	89	39	93	73
Ireland	100	62	81	77	86	47	68	35
Israel	100	82	97	66	95	82	92	54
Italy	99	87	53	65	82	30	92	37
Japan	99	90	45	17	52	76	79	15
Korea	95	56	86	70	90	85	96	67
Luxembourg	95	94	41	74	72	22	74	40
Mexico	99	91	73	77	92	77	88	71
Netherlands	99	98	61	70	89	68	78	64
New Zealand	100	77	94	93	100	68	99	87
Norway	98	1	48	68	84	30	74	52
Poland	99	98	55	58	96	79	95	59
Portugal	100	98	40	85	96	50	93	63
Slovak Republic	100	93	38	64	71	69	83	69
Slovenia	98	93	26	59	91	38	72	47
Spain	99	95	47	44	88	50	94	37
Sweden	94	43	25	90	96	44	84	85
Switzerland	94	86	40	41	48	36	51	27
Turkey	97	55	44	75	93	71	68	85
United Kingdom	99	69	96	96	100	88	96	90
United States	99	57	74	94	95	60	94	86
OECD average	98	77	51	63	81	50	80	53
Albania	99	77	74	77	91	87	87	78
Argentina	91	87	24	22	74	51	94	7
Brazil	97	91	47	83	97	80	89	56
Bulgaria	99	65	39	86	95	93	72	85
Colombia	99	93	44	68	94	60	95	64
Costa Rica	98	91	37	65	86	71	85	50
Croatia	100	88	52	66	95	56	85	62
Hong Kong-China	98	98	86	44	96	80	99	30
Indonesia	97	93	80	69	98	96	97	87
Jordan	97	92	81	70	85	72	89	55
Kazakhstan	100	95	65	92	100	100	99	91
Latvia	100	97	38	92	100	93	100	85
Liechtenstein	100	72	49	68	67	20	69	59
Lithuania	99	85	53	61	94	74	82	60
Macao-China	99	95	65	32	87	75	96	21
Malaysia	99	53	87	81	98	92	97	67
Montenegro	97	81	39	79	96	92	89	65
Peru	98	88	45	41	85	78	93	38
Qatar	97	88	86	83	96	87	97	81
Romania	77	70	57	68	72	75	76	69
Russian Federation	99	94	57	93	100	99	99	98
Serbia	98	84	36	34	96	57	86	57
Shanghai-China	98	51	55	50	87	86	96	57
Singapore	100	88	96	96	99	88	98	88
Chinese Taipei	96	45	35	37	78	48	94	42
Thailand	99	86	79	85	97	91	96	76
Tunisia	80	95	52	71	89	67	56	69
United Arab Emirates	100	91	87	77	96	94	97	72
Uruguay	95	92	25	16	87	31	86	12
Viet Nam	99	95	74	89	98	99	91	88

Source: OECD, PISA 2012 Database, Table IV.4.30.
StatLink 🔗 http://dx.doi.org/10.1787/888932957346

Using student assessments to make decisions about whether students are held back or promoted is prevalent in Greece, Portugal, Hong Kong-China, the Netherlands, Poland, Latvia, France, Belgium, Germany, Viet Nam, Tunisia, Kazakhstan and Canada (around 95% or more), while in Norway, Denmark, Iceland, Sweden and Chinese Taipei, fewer than one in two students attends a school that uses student assessment for that purpose (Table IV.4.30).

■ Figure IV.4.12 ■
Relationship among various aspects of assessment practices and purposes

Correlation coefficients between two relevant indicators
Correlation coefficients range from -1.00 (i.e. a perfect negative linear association) to +1.00 (i.e. a perfect positive linear association). When a correlation coefficient is 0, there is no linear relationship between two indicators.

	Percentage of students in schools whose principal reported that assessments of students in the national modal grade for 15-year-olds are used for the following purposes:								Index of assessment practices (sum of "yes" responses to these eight purposes)
	To inform parents about their child's progress	To make decisions about students' retention or promotion	To group students for instructional purposes	To compare the school to district or national performance	To monitor the school's progress from year to year	To make judgements about teachers' effectiveness	To identify aspects of instruction or the curriculum that could be improved	To compare the school with other schools	
To inform parents about their child's progress		0.03	*0.30*	0.08	0.20	0.12	*0.33*	0.02	0.28
To make decisions about students' retention or promotion	0.02		-0.19	**-0.34**	-0.17	0.03	-0.21	**-0.40**	-0.07
To group students for instructional purposes	0.16	-0.08		**0.55**	**0.55**	**0.55**	**0.56**	**0.45**	**0.69**
To compare the school to district or national performance	0.10	-0.18	**0.53**		**0.79**	*0.33*	**0.51**	**0.85**	**0.79**
To monitor the school's progress from year to year	0.18	-0.01	**0.53**	**0.67**		**0.53**	**0.69**	**0.75**	**0.91**
To make judgements about teachers' effectiveness	0.04	0.13	**0.55**	**0.47**	**0.65**		**0.62**	**0.54**	**0.64**
To identify aspects of instruction or the curriculum that could be improved	**0.29**	-0.07	**0.52**	**0.36**	**0.68**	**0.63**		**0.58**	**0.78**
To compare the school with other schools	0.05	*-0.21*	**0.48**	**0.88**	**0.68**	**0.61**	**0.42**		**0.72**
Index of assessment practices (sum of "yes" responses to these eight purposes)	**0.32**	0.11	**0.62**	**0.72**	**0.85**	**0.70**	**0.69**	**0.69**	

Across OECD countries
Across all participating countries and economies

(Left axis label: Percentage of students in schools whose principal reported that assessments of students in the national modal grade for 15-year-olds are used for the following purposes:)

Note: Correlation coefficients that are statistically significant at the 5% level (p < 0.05) are indicated in bold and at the 10% level (p < 0.10) are in italic.
Source: OECD, PISA 2012 Database, Table IV.4.30.
StatLink ᴍ᠍ᴘ http://dx.doi.org/10.1787/888932957346

A summary *index of assessment practices* is created by summing up how many times principals responded "yes" to the eight suggested uses of student assessments mentioned above. In theory, this index ranges from 0 to 8, but in fact the data show that it varies from 0 to 6, as no principal reported using assessments in seven or eight ways. This index mainly reflects principals' responses to all individual questions asked regarding the uses of assessments except "to make decisions about students' retention or promotion" (Figure IV.4.12). Across OECD countries, 33% of students are in schools whose principals reported that they use student assessments for six of the eight purposes; 26% are in schools that use student assessments for five of the eight purposes; 20% are in schools that use assessments for four of the eight purposes; and 21% are in schools that use student assessments for at most three of the eight purposes. In the Russian Federation, student assessments seems to be used for many purposes in most schools, as over 90% of students attend schools that use student assessments for six of the eight purposes. By contrast, in Greece, Switzerland, Finland, Denmark and Belgium, student assessments are not used for many of these purposes: more than 40% of students in these countries attend schools that use student assessments for at most three of the eight purposes (Table IV.4.30).

■ Figure IV.4.13 ■

Use of achievement data for accountability purposes

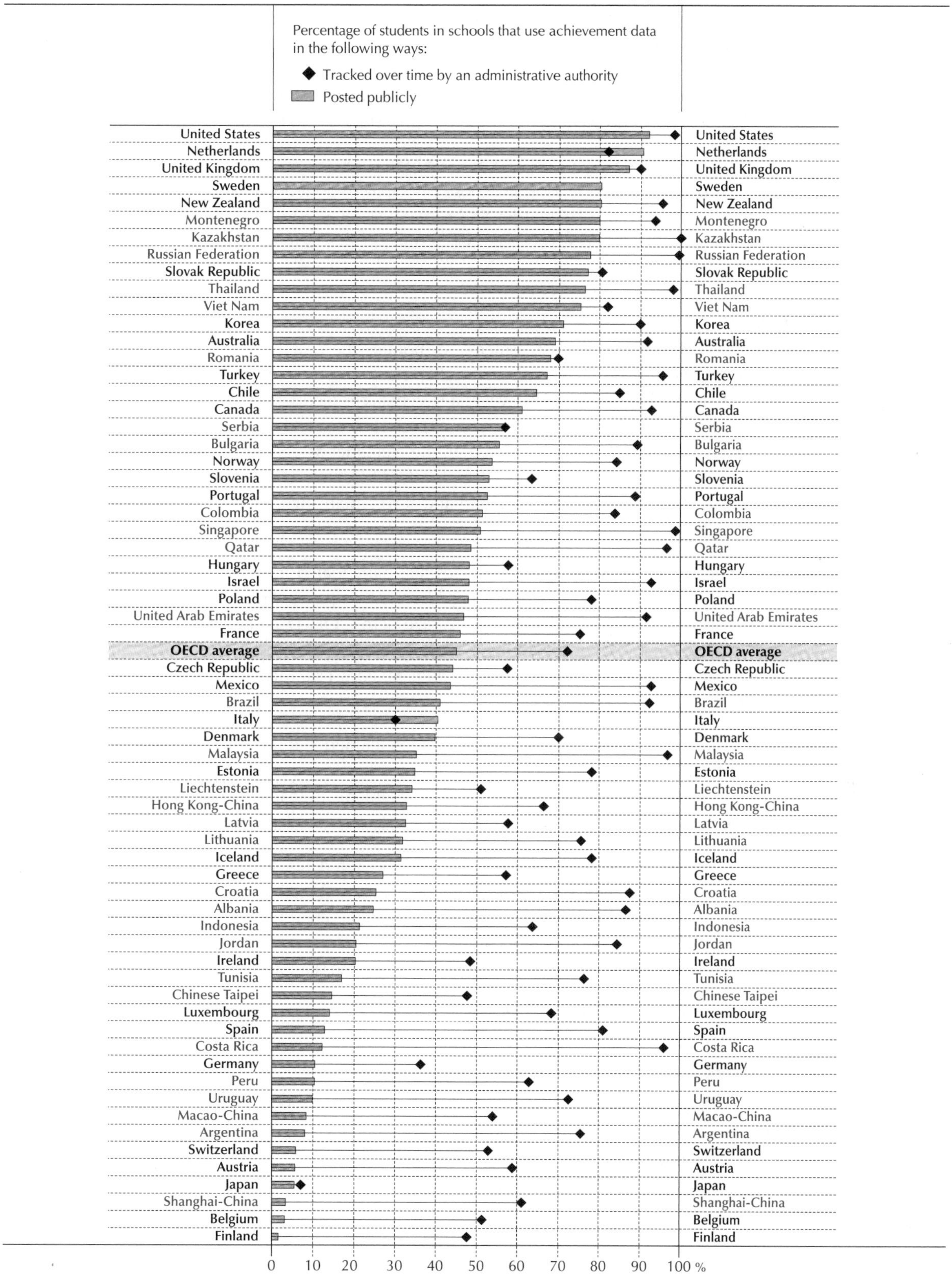

Percentage of students in schools that use achievement data in the following ways:

◆ Tracked over time by an administrative authority

▭ Posted publicly

United States
Netherlands
United Kingdom
Sweden
New Zealand
Montenegro
Kazakhstan
Russian Federation
Slovak Republic
Thailand
Viet Nam
Korea
Australia
Romania
Turkey
Chile
Canada
Serbia
Bulgaria
Norway
Slovenia
Portugal
Colombia
Singapore
Qatar
Hungary
Israel
Poland
United Arab Emirates
France
OECD average
Czech Republic
Mexico
Brazil
Italy
Denmark
Malaysia
Estonia
Liechtenstein
Hong Kong-China
Latvia
Lithuania
Iceland
Greece
Croatia
Albania
Indonesia
Jordan
Ireland
Tunisia
Chinese Taipei
Luxembourg
Spain
Costa Rica
Germany
Peru
Uruguay
Macao-China
Argentina
Switzerland
Austria
Japan
Shanghai-China
Belgium
Finland

0 10 20 30 40 50 60 70 80 90 100 %

Countries and economies are ranked in descending order of the percentage of students in schools where achievement data are posted publicly.
Source: OECD, PISA 2012 Database, Table IV.4.31.
StatLink ⫍⫎⫏⫐⫑ http://dx.doi.org/10.1787/888932957346

The use of achievement data beyond school

Achievement data are used for accountability purposes involving some stakeholders beyond school, teachers, partners and students. School principals were asked to report on whether achievement data are posted publicly, or tracked over time by an administrative authority. On average across OECD countries, 45% of students are in schools whose principals reported that achievement data are posted publicly. In the United States, the Netherlands, the United Kingdom, Sweden and New Zealand over 80% of students attend such schools, while in Finland, Belgium, Shanghai-China, Japan, Austria, Switzerland, Argentina, Macao-China and Uruguay, fewer than 10% of students do (Figure IV.4.13 and Table IV.4.31).

Tracking achievement data over time seems to be a more common practice than posting such data publicly. On average across OECD countries, 72% of students are in schools whose principals reported that achievement data are tracked over time by an administrative authority. In 31 countries and economies, over 80% of students attend schools whose principals reported this, while only in Japan do fewer than 10% of students (7%) attend such schools (Figure IV.4.13 and Table IV.4.31).

Quality assurance

Schools also use measures other than student assessments to monitor the quality of the education they provide. PISA 2012 asked school principals to report on whether their schools use various measures related to quality assurance and improvement. Chapter 1 shows that the degree to which a system seeks feedback from students regarding lessons, teachers or resources tends to be related to the system's overall performance; and also tends to be related to equity. In New Zealand, Liechtenstein, Shanghai-China, Turkey, Qatar, the Netherlands and Singapore, over 85% of students attend schools whose principals reported that the school seeks written feedback from students. In contrast, in France, Luxembourg, Ireland, Greece, Tunisia, Belgium and Denmark, fewer than 40% of students attend such schools (Figure IV.4.14 and Table IV.4.32).

Chapter 1 also shows that, across all countries and economies that participated in PISA 2012, systems where more schools use teacher mentoring for quality-assurance and improvement purposes tend to show a weaker impact of students' socio-economic status on their performance. On average across OECD countries, 72% of students attend schools whose principals reported that teacher mentoring is used for these purposes. In 37 countries and economies, over 80% of students attend such schools; in France, Iceland, Chile, Spain, Costa Rica, Germany and Argentina, fewer than 50% of students do (Figure IV.4.14 and Table IV.4.32).

A recent OECD review of evaluation and assessment in education concluded that it is important to engage all school staff and students in school self-evaluations, and to use student feedback about teachers for formative purposes (OECD, 2013a). While student feedback can help identify certain problems in teachers' practices, it cannot replace relevant professional feedback, advice and support by teaching experts since students are not pedagogical experts.

On average across OECD countries, 59% of students attend schools where students' written feedback is combined with other forms of evaluation (i.e. internal and/or external evaluations), while only 2% of students attend schools where students' written feedback is sought but neither internal nor external evaluations are used. Some 15% of students in Greece and 9% of students in Norway attend schools where students' written feedback is sought but neither internal nor external evaluations are used. Around 6% of students in Uruguay and Austria attend such schools (Figure IV.4.15 and Table IV.4.33).

As shown in Figure IV.4.14, school principals were also asked about other measures used related to the quality of teachers and schools. On average across OECD countries:

- 87% of students are in schools whose principals reported that internal evaluations or self-evaluations are used;
- 86% are in schools that have written specifications of the school's curriculum and education goals;
- 85% are in schools that systematically record data, including teacher and student attendance and graduation rates, test results and professional development of teachers;
- 74% are in schools that have written specifications of student-performance standards;
- 63% are in schools that use external evaluations;
- 62% are in schools that implement a standardised policy for teaching mathematics, such as a school curriculum with shared instructional materials accompanied by staff development and training; and
- 43% are in schools that regularly consult with one or more experts over a period of at least six months, with the aim of improving the school.

■ Figure IV.4.14 ■

Quality assurance and school improvement

Percentage of students in schools whose principal reported that their schools have the following for quality assurance and improvement:

	Written specification of the school's curriculum and educational goals	Written specification of student-performance standards	Systematic recording of data, including teacher and student attendance and graduation rates, test results and professional development of teachers	Internal evaluation/self-evaluation	External evaluation	Written feedback from students (e.g. regarding lessons, teachers or resources)	Teacher mentoring	Regular consultation with one or more experts over a period of at least six months with the aim of improving the school	Implementation of a standardised policy for mathematics (i.e. school curriculum with shared instructional materials accompanied by staff development and training)
	%	%	%	%	%	%	%	%	%
Australia	96	90	98	94	70	69	92	72	77
Austria	76	56	75	86	20	81	88	55	61
Belgium	82	48	77	79	69	36	72	40	42
Canada	95	85	90	81	62	42	86	69	80
Chile	83	76	87	90	55	49	21	40	50
Czech Republic	99	77	85	98	63	63	96	27	90
Denmark	66	38	80	88	58	37	52	50	24
Estonia	93	88	95	99	77	83	80	39	88
Finland	94	75	74	96	51	74	55	10	63
France	72	25	75	61	52	13	17	21	44
Germany	86	71	77	74	60	48	33	19	55
Greece	57	38	68	33	6	29	87	77	70
Hungary	96	91	80	97	57	80	71	17	69
Iceland	65	84	95	99	79	54	19	46	47
Ireland	75	48	89	83	82	24	64	53	81
Israel	96	78	96	82	60	42	94	54	87
Italy	98	84	52	76	34	40	78	23	56
Japan	98	49	54	96	77	75	88	5	38
Korea	99	95	94	97	79	84	88	59	65
Luxembourg	64	45	71	75	40	19	65	42	60
Mexico	93	83	94	94	75	73	54	52	68
Netherlands	91	86	99	91	81	89	98	47	47
New Zealand	99	88	98	100	89	96	97	63	81
Norway	97	73	84	61	53	46	70	33	29
Poland	68	83	99	97	79	70	87	39	82
Portugal	93	74	96	98	86	77	78	29	75
Slovak Republic	86	80	93	95	38	53	88	54	61
Slovenia	94	95	86	92	32	75	67	41	67
Spain	96	79	92	82	79	63	26	27	38
Sweden	70	95	95	90	65	79	68	32	29
Switzerland	70	43	63	84	63	72	71	27	54
Turkey	89	94	96	99	79	91	86	60	74
United Kingdom	97	93	100	100	91	73	96	80	74
United States	98	95	98	93	86	59	98	73	88
OECD average	86	74	85	87	63	61	72	43	62
Albania	96	97	97	95	68	69	92	68	91
Argentina	91	66	79	83	36	43	48	43	40
Brazil	94	74	83	96	82	69	93	50	72
Bulgaria	93	79	98	98	95	82	69	70	53
Colombia	96	95	88	98	82	71	67	55	50
Costa Rica	87	80	87	85	48	56	28	48	51
Croatia	93	68	95	92	81	60	98	58	79
Hong Kong-China	98	91	100	100	91	81	91	45	86
Indonesia	99	92	100	91	85	85	100	74	82
Jordan	91	92	93	90	71	72	68	57	76
Kazakhstan	97	99	100	99	95	81	97	87	92
Latvia	96	88	100	100	84	76	72	23	52
Liechtenstein	81	59	37	94	83	94	82	68	57
Lithuania	73	79	98	95	57	75	53	40	30
Macao-China	90	93	99	88	64	70	91	44	57
Malaysia	97	100	99	99	83	70	89	82	93
Montenegro	95	81	97	100	93	59	98	74	90
Peru	89	67	67	87	42	67	97	42	44
Qatar	100	98	100	99	87	90	100	90	98
Romania	88	87	89	88	84	83	85	66	74
Russian Federation	93	89	98	98	96	83	96	54	86
Serbia	82	55	97	96	53	48	98	58	41
Shanghai-China	100	86	97	100	88	91	98	93	94
Singapore	99	98	99	100	93	87	100	63	92
Chinese Taipei	94	88	92	84	75	62	73	32	57
Thailand	98	94	98	100	99	80	98	89	86
Tunisia	50	33	71	91	49	29	80	21	61
United Arab Emirates	95	96	99	98	94	77	92	73	82
Uruguay	75	59	96	85	45	53	74	27	29
Viet Nam	98	92	98	96	49	85	99	45	93

Source: OECD, PISA 2012 Database, Table IV.4.32.
StatLink ᴍˢᴾ http://dx.doi.org/10.1787/888932957346

■ Figure IV.4.15 ■

Internal or external evaluations and feedback from students

Percentage of students in schools whose principal reported that their schools seek written feedback from students (e.g. regarding lessons, teachers or resources)

Percentage of students in schools whose principal reported that there are:

- ■ Internal and/or external evaluations, and written feedback from students is sought
- ☐ Internal and/or external evaluations, but no written feedback from students is sought
- ■ Neither internal nor external evaluations, and no written feedback from students is sought
- ■ Neither internal nor external evaluations, but written feedback from students is sought

Country	Percentage
New Zealand	96
Liechtenstein	94
Shanghai-China	91
Turkey	91
Qatar	90
Netherlands	89
Singapore	87
Indonesia	85
Estonia	83
Russian Federation	83
Korea	84
Viet Nam	85
Bulgaria	82
Kazakhstan	81
Hong Kong-China	81
Thailand	80
Romania	83
Hungary	80
United Arab Emirates	77
Latvia	76
Portugal	77
Japan	75
Sweden	79
Austria	81
Lithuania	75
Finland	74
United Kingdom	73
Slovenia	75
Mexico	73
Colombia	71
Jordan	72
Switzerland	72
Poland	70
Malaysia	70
Albania	69
Brazil	69
Macao-China	70
Australia	69
Peru	67
Czech Republic	63
Spain	63
Chinese Taipei	62
Montenegro	59
OECD average	61
Croatia	60
United States	59
Costa Rica	56
Iceland	54
Slovak Republic	53
Serbia	48
Chile	49
Germany	48
Uruguay	53
Israel	42
Canada	42
Argentina	43
Norway	46
Italy	40
Denmark	37
Belgium	36
Tunisia	29
Ireland	24
Luxembourg	19
Greece	29
France	13

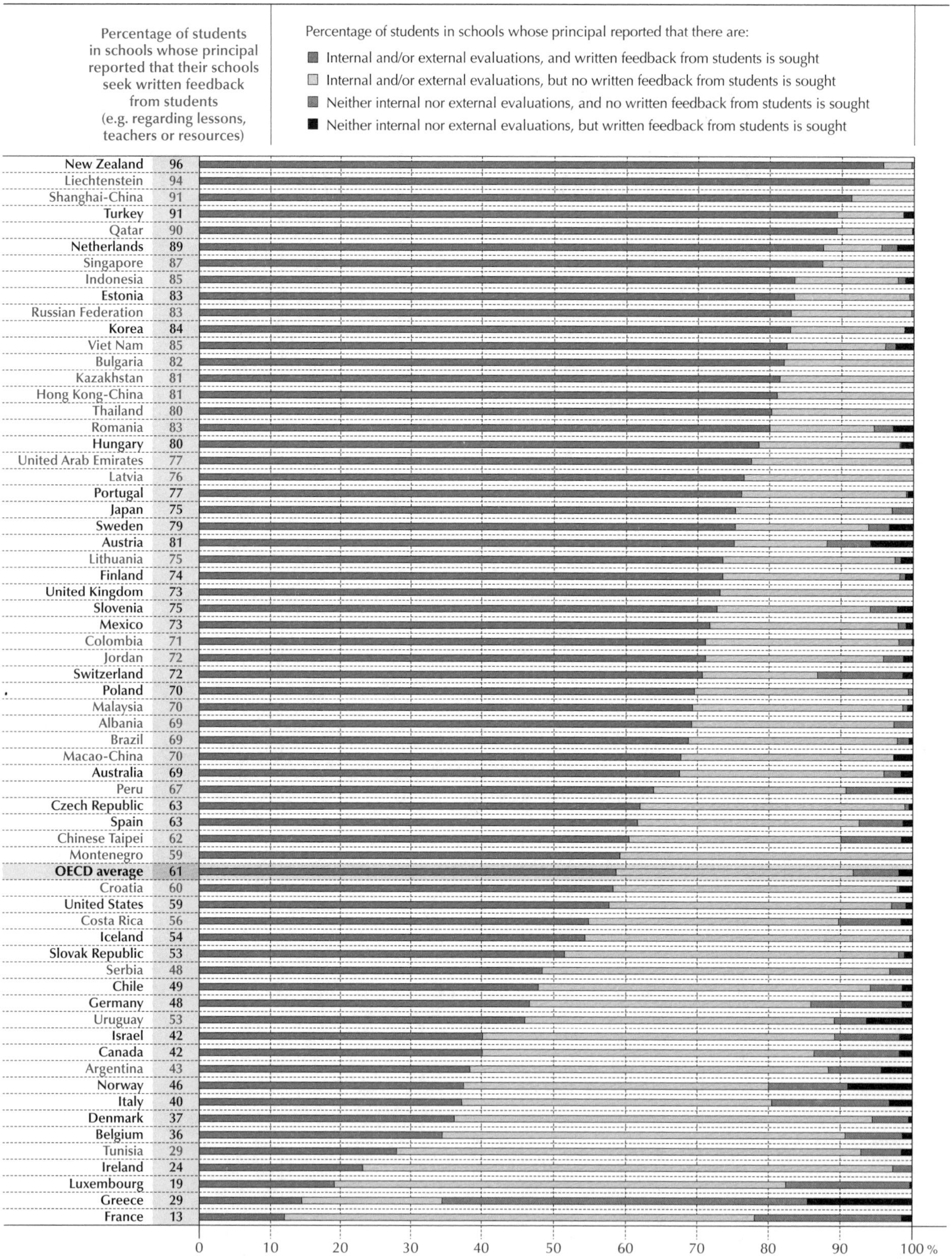

Countries and economies are ranked in descending order of the percentage of students in schools whose principal reported that the school has internal and/or external evaluations and seeks written feedback from students.

Source: OECD, PISA 2012 Database, Tables IV.4.32 and IV.4.33.

StatLink ᧗᧗ http://dx.doi.org/10.1787/888932957346

Chapter 1 shows that, in the systems where a standardised policy for mathematics is implemented more widely, school autonomy is positively related to performance. In Qatar, Shanghai-China, Viet Nam, Malaysia, Kazakhstan, Singapore, Albania and the Czech Republic, over 90% of students attend schools where a standardised policy for mathematics is implemented. In contrast, in Denmark, Norway, Uruguay, Sweden, Lithuania, Japan and Spain, fewer than 40% of students attend such schools (Figure IV.4.14 and Table IV.4.32).

A standardised policy for mathematics and school autonomy in establishing the curriculum and assessments are not mutually exclusive. At the system level, there is no relationship between the proportion of students in schools that use a standardised policy for mathematics and the *index of school responsibility for curriculum and assessments* (i.e. the correlation coefficient between the two is 0.04 across OECD countries) (Tables IV.4.3 and IV.4.32).

Monitoring mathematics teachers' practices

To examine in greater detail how the practice of mathematics teachers is monitored to ensure quality of teaching, PISA 2012 asked school principals to report on whether the following methods have been used to monitor the practice of mathematics teachers in their schools: test or assessments of student achievement; teacher peer review of lessons plans, assessment instruments, and lessons; principal or senior staff observations of lessons; and observation of classes by inspectors or other persons external to the school. On average across OECD countries, 78% of students are in schools whose principals reported that tests or assessments of student achievement have been used to monitor the practice of mathematics teachers; 69% are in schools where the principal or senior staff observe lessons; 60% are in schools that use teacher peer reviews of lesson plans, assessment instruments, and lessons; and 27% are in schools where classes are observed by inspectors or other persons external to the school (Figure IV.4.16 and Table IV.4.34).

In general, those countries that use one of these methods also use other methods. For example, across OECD countries, the percentage of students who attend schools that use teacher peer review and those who attend schools that use principal or senior staff observations of lessons are highly correlated (correlation coefficient is 0.59). The only exception is "observation of classes by inspectors or other persons external to the school". Among OECD countries, the proportion of students in schools using this method seems to be unrelated to the proportion of students in schools using other methods.

In Albania, Indonesia, Jordan, Kazakhstan, Malaysia, Qatar, the Russian Federation, Shanghai-China, Thailand and the United Kingdom, over 90% of students are in schools whose principals reported that the school uses tests or assessments of student achievement, teacher peer review, and principal or senior staff observations of lessons, while in Greece, Finland, France and Ireland, the use of these three methods is much less prevalent than the OECD average. By contrast, in Jordan, Shanghai-China, Tunisia, Liechtenstein, Viet Nam, the United Arab Emirates, Qatar and Kazakhstan, more than 80% of students attend a school where classes are observed by inspectors or other persons external to the school, while in Italy, Finland, Portugal, Slovenia, Luxembourg, Estonia and Chinese Taipei fewer than 10% of students do (Figure IV.4.16 and Table IV.4.34).

The consequences of teacher appraisals

Teacher appraisals can have many consequences, both positive and negative. On average across OECD countries, 81% of students attend schools whose principals reported that appraisals of and/or feedback to teachers lead directly to a role in school-development initiatives (e.g. curriculum-development group, development of school objectives); 79% are in schools where these lead directly to public recognition from the principal; 73% are in schools where these lead directly to opportunities for professional-development activities; 68% are in schools where these lead directly to changes in work responsibilities that make the job more attractive; 53% are in schools where these lead directly to a change in the likelihood of career advancement; 30% are in schools where these lead directly to a financial bonus or another kind of monetary reward; and 27% are in schools where these lead directly to a change in salary (Figure IV.4.17 and Table IV.4.35).

Across countries, the proportions of students in schools whose principals reported that teacher appraisals have one of these seven consequences are highly correlated. This means that countries with more students in schools where teacher appraisals have one of the abovementioned seven consequences also tend to have more students in schools where teacher appraisal has other consequences as well. For example, among OECD countries, in those countries where "a role in school-development initiatives" is frequently seen as a consequence of teacher appraisal, "a change in the likelihood of career advancement" is also a common consequence of teacher appraisal (correlation coefficient is 0.66).

■ Figure IV.4.16 ■
Monitoring mathematics teachers' practice

	Percentage of students in schools whose principal reported that the following methods have been used to monitor the practice of mathematics teachers at their schools:			
	Tests or assessments of student achievement	Teacher peer review of lesson plans, assessment instruments, and lessons	Principal or senior staff observations of lessons	Observation of classes by inspectors or other persons external to the school
	%	%	%	%
Australia	79	77	70	11
Austria	91	79	74	29
Belgium	66	76	65	48
Canada	73	60	82	21
Chile	77	80	91	25
Czech Republic	92	67	98	33
Denmark	75	41	64	17
Estonia	71	49	90	8
Finland	40	19	31	2
France	61	42	12	73
Germany	72	45	67	22
Greece	60	26	8	21
Hungary	74	75	97	13
Iceland	84	12	46	25
Ireland	65	34	13	48
Israel	96	51	75	34
Italy	74	87	17	1
Japan	69	54	81	26
Korea	84	99	96	68
Luxembourg	81	63	48	6
Mexico	93	76	77	41
Netherlands	83	54	87	42
New Zealand	84	92	97	32
Norway	72	54	48	11
Poland	100	64	94	16
Portugal	98	71	60	4
Slovak Republic	75	84	98	27
Slovenia	72	62	94	5
Spain	78	22	10	15
Sweden	68	59	80	27
Switzerland	61	63	83	29
Turkey	92	52	94	22
United Kingdom	95	93	97	68
United States	89	66	100	42
OECD average	78	60	69	27
Albania	98	92	99	62
Argentina	82	74	85	22
Brazil	88	75	50	23
Bulgaria	91	29	97	49
Colombia	84	60	43	11
Costa Rica	83	81	87	45
Croatia	72	62	93	34
Hong Kong-China	95	85	97	39
Indonesia	91	91	95	77
Jordan	94	93	98	97
Kazakhstan	99	99	100	82
Latvia	83	89	100	41
Liechtenstein	82	70	49	87
Lithuania	96	75	98	38
Macao-China	90	88	96	48
Malaysia	99	91	99	70
Montenegro	81	72	99	56
Peru	71	80	84	54
Qatar	97	98	100	82
Romania	68	69	73	58
Russian Federation	99	96	100	44
Serbia	50	59	95	34
Shanghai-China	92	91	97	90
Singapore	96	86	100	23
Chinese Taipei	82	61	61	8
Thailand	98	93	95	45
Tunisia	75	40	50	87
United Arab Emirates	96	85	100	84
Uruguay	58	63	88	66
Viet Nam	98	83	97	85

Source: OECD, PISA 2012 Database, Table IV.4.34.
StatLink ᐸᒥᔊᐵ http://dx.doi.org/10.1787/888932957346

■ Figure IV.4.17 ■

Consequences of teacher appraisals

		Percentage of students in schools whose principal reported that appraisals of and/or feedback to teachers lead directly to the following:					
		A change in salary	A financial bonus or another kind of monetary reward	Opportunities for professional-development activities	A change in the likelihood of career advancement	Public recognition from the principal	Changes in work responsibilities that make the job more attractive	A role in school-development initiatives (e.g. curriculum-development group, development of school objectives)
		%	%	%	%	%	%	%
OECD	Australia	13	6	86	68	83	63	87
	Austria	3	8	36	30	75	44	73
	Belgium	0	1	68	23	66	51	64
	Canada	3	3	79	44	73	44	84
	Chile	38	40	76	67	87	83	81
	Czech Republic	72	86	84	59	93	62	86
	Denmark	4	7	67	15	78	56	62
	Estonia	38	70	79	58	93	70	90
	Finland	19	23	71	27	76	68	81
	France	42	20	63	64	79	59	73
	Germany	7	8	56	44	53	49	68
	Greece	24	24	52	42	73	53	60
	Hungary	22	82	67	74	98	86	93
	Iceland	19	18	83	29	76	82	69
	Ireland	1	1	53	28	71	41	78
	Israel	23	26	81	79	95	90	84
	Italy	16	38	67	34	63	81	83
	Japan	27	34	67	53	65	87	92
	Korea	47	69	90	63	95	78	83
	Luxembourg	2	2	49	19	80	60	82
	Mexico	42	51	73	78	86	80	78
	Netherlands	22	27	91	70	92	74	86
	New Zealand	20	7	98	82	82	79	89
	Norway	9	3	84	51	79	77	85
	Poland	34	83	75	57	92	61	87
	Portugal	21	11	46	42	58	63	73
	Slovak Republic	49	83	85	72	95	81	94
	Slovenia	43	53	86	85	96	91	94
	Spain	9	9	46	23	67	55	63
	Sweden	87	19	93	61	89	82	94
	Switzerland	12	17	57	21	43	39	58
	Turkey	56	61	86	83	84	90	92
	United Kingdom	66	16	98	87	88	81	97
	United States	11	15	88	57	80	60	90
	OECD average	**27**	**30**	**73**	**53**	**79**	**68**	**81**
Partners	Albania	39	22	75	66	72	81	89
	Argentina	10	6	62	67	63	63	78
	Brazil	36	43	65	57	79	83	77
	Bulgaria	29	85	90	85	94	81	92
	Colombia	39	21	73	74	80	74	82
	Costa Rica	33	17	72	73	74	66	80
	Croatia	15	27	88	91	98	81	91
	Hong Kong-China	30	16	61	98	92	94	99
	Indonesia	85	80	97	97	92	97	99
	Jordan	59	60	81	79	96	95	90
	Kazakhstan	62	67	95	83	97	90	96
	Latvia	44	35	87	64	94	79	91
	Liechtenstein	6	6	88	26	27	60	95
	Lithuania	45	48	88	63	96	64	94
	Macao-China	62	69	80	89	91	92	95
	Malaysia	75	85	93	93	95	95	96
	Montenegro	18	22	85	70	94	85	91
	Peru	49	41	73	69	88	91	88
	Qatar	54	66	95	89	89	93	94
	Romania	30	33	66	72	76	73	73
	Russian Federation	94	90	92	92	96	83	95
	Serbia	13	24	65	45	84	70	70
	Shanghai-China	41	92	94	97	97	95	97
	Singapore	61	94	93	96	90	94	96
	Chinese Taipei	28	39	83	52	56	73	90
	Thailand	88	74	86	86	95	93	95
	Tunisia	72	66	90	87	90	88	74
	United Arab Emirates	58	50	93	89	96	94	97
	Uruguay	27	24	68	56	70	74	70
	Viet Nam	72	92	98	95	99	99	92

Note: The percentage refers to the percentage of students in schools whose principal reported that appraisals of and/or feedback to teachers lead directly to at least a small change.
Source: OECD, PISA 2012 Database, Table IV.4.35.
StatLink ᘌᴤᴾᴸ http://dx.doi.org/10.1787/888932957346

Box IV.4.4. **Teachers' perceptions of the consequences of appraisals: results from the first TALIS survey**[10]

The consequences for teachers of teacher appraisals and feedback vary significantly across systems and, within systems, by individual teachers. Overall, data from the first OECD Teaching and Learning International Survey (TALIS) (2007-08) show that in most participating countries, direct consequences for teachers' career and compensation are small or non-existent. However, teachers overwhelmingly report positive impact on their job satisfaction, and report that they find the feedback they received helpful for improving their work.[11] While teachers' perceptions of the impact of assessments may depend on whether the appraisal was positive or negative, and on which aspects of their work were reviewed, TALIS is able to provide a system-level measure of teachers' perceptions about the consequences of appraisal and feedback by surveying a large, representative sample of teachers.

Direct impact of appraisal and feedback on career and compensation

For most teachers surveyed in TALIS, the appraisal and feedback they received had little direct impact on their career or compensation. On average across participating countries, only 9% of teachers reported a moderate or large impact on their salary, and fewer than 11% reported an impact on a bonus or other monetary reward. Around 16% of teachers reported a (moderate or large) change in the likelihood of career advancement as a result of the appraisal or feedback received. Higher percentages are found in Central and East European countries, in Mexico, and in the partner countries Brazil and Malaysia.

This indicates that in most countries, career paths and teacher compensation are only indirectly linked, if at all, to teacher appraisal and feedback. This finding is consistent with the results of an OECD review of policy frameworks for teacher appraisal. Of the 28 systems reviewed, 22 had a regulatory framework for teacher appraisal. Only in Chile, Korea and Mexico are teacher appraisals linked to a reward scheme; and only in the Czech Republic, Estonia, Israel, Korea and Poland are teacher appraisals used to determine promotions. Most often, teacher appraisals are used in the context of a probationary period (13 countries) or of regular school-based appraisals (17 countries) (OECD, 2013b, p.16).

Impact of appraisal and feedback on public recognition and job satisfaction

For teachers who receive appraisals and/or feedback, a far more common outcome is some form of public recognition, either from the school principal or from teachers' colleagues. An average of more than one in three teachers (36%) reported a moderate or large change in the recognition they received; in Bulgaria, Lithuania, Malaysia and Poland, more than one in two teachers so reported. Some 30% of teachers, on average, reported that as a result of the appraisal and feedback they were given a role in school-development initiatives.

On average across countries, 51% of teachers reported a positive change in job satisfaction following the appraisal and/or feedback they received. In Malaysia and Mexico, more than one in three teachers reported "a large increase" in job satisfaction; in Brazil, Iceland and Poland, more than one in five teachers so reported. In most countries, very few teachers reported less job satisfaction after an appraisal/feedback, with larger proportions of discontent (more than 10%) found only in Korea and Turkey. TALIS thus shows that the effect of appraisal and feedback on teacher morale is largely positive.

Impact of appraisal and feedback on teaching and teachers' work

For 58% of teachers, the appraisal and feedback received also contained suggestions for improving certain aspects of teachers' work. Whether it contained specific suggestions or not, more than three out of four teachers agreed that the feedback and/or appraisal they received was helpful for improving their work as teachers. While only 53% of teachers in Korea reported so, more than 90% of teachers in Bulgaria and Malaysia did.

Teachers were also asked which teaching practices they changed as a result of the feedback and/or appraisal they received. In general, more than one in three teachers changed their instructional practices and/or their classroom-management practices as a result of feedback on their work as teachers. In many countries, more teachers reported

...

a moderate or large impact on their classroom-management practices, or on their handling of student discipline and behaviour problems, than on their instructional practices. In contrast, in Austria, Estonia, Italy, Korea, Lithuania, Malaysia and the Slovak Republic, more teachers reported changes in their instructional practices than in their classroom-management practices.

Sources:

OECD (2013b), *Teachers for the 21st Century: Using Evaluation to Improve Teaching*, OECD Publishing. *http://dx.doi.org/10.1787/9789264193864-en*

OECD (2009), *Creating Effective Teaching and Learning Environments: First Results from TALIS*, OECD Publishing. *http://dx.doi.org/10.1787/9789264072992-en*

TRENDS IN ASSESSMENT AND ACCOUNTABILITY POLICIES SINCE PISA 2003

Between PISA 2003 and 2012 there has been a clear trend towards using student assessments to compare the school's performance to district or national performance and to compare the schools' performance to that of other schools. For example, and on average across OECD countries, in 2003, 46% of students attended schools whose principal reported that the school uses student assessment data to compare itself against national or district performance; by 2012, 62% of students attended such schools (Figure IV.4.18 and Table IV.4.36).[12] Similarly, the percentage of students who attended schools that use assessment data to compare themselves to other schools increased from 40% to 52% during the period. Student assessment data are also increasingly used to make judgements about teachers' effectiveness (an increase of nine percentage points, on average across OECD countries) and to identify aspects of instruction or the curriculum that could be improved (an increase of six percentage points). In fact, assessment data are increasingly being used to monitor a school's progress from year to year (in 25 countries and economies), to compare the school with other schools (in 25 countries and economies), to compare the school's performance with national or district performance (in 23 countries and economies), and to make judgements about teachers' effectiveness (in 19 countries and economies) (Table IV.4.36).[13]

The use of student-assessment data for various purposes has increased most notably in Ireland and Denmark between 2003 and 2012. In Ireland, for example, students in 2012 were 60 percentage points more likely than their counterparts in 2003 to attend schools where student assessment data were used to compare the school with national or district performance (Figure IV.4.18); 37 percentage points more likely to be in schools where the data were used to monitor the school's progress from year to year; and more than 25 percentage points more likely to be in schools that used student assessments to judge teachers' effectiveness, to identify aspects of instruction or the curriculum that could be improved or to compare the school with other schools. In Denmark, students were at least 20 percentage points more likely in 2012 than in 2003 to attend schools where student-assessment data are used to group students for instructional purposes, inform parents about students' progress, compare the school's performance against national or district performance, monitor school progress, compare the school with other schools, identify aspects of the curriculum that could be improved, and make judgements about teachers' effectiveness (Table IV.4.36).

By contrast, the use of student assessments has declined in Finland and Hungary. In both of these countries, students in 2012 were less likely than their counterparts in 2003 to attend schools where assessments were used to make judgements about teachers' effectiveness. In Finland, students were less likely in 2012 than in 2003 to attend schools where assessment data are used to compare the school to other schools or to national or district performance. In Hungary, students were also less likely to attend schools where their assessment is used to make retention or promotion decisions or to identify aspects of the curriculum that could be improved, although assessment data are more likely to be used to group students for instructional purposes. Students in the Slovak Republic were less likely in 2012 than in 2003 to attend schools where assessment is used to group students for instruction purposes or to monitor school progress, but assessment data are being used more to compare the school with other schools. In Poland students in 2012 were also less likely than their counterparts in 2003 to attend schools where assessment data are used to compare school performance against national or regional benchmarks, but more likely to attend schools that use assessment data to group students for instructional purposes (Table IV.4.36).

■ Figure IV.4.18 ■

Change between 2003 and 2012 in using student assessment data to compare school performance

Percentage of students in schools where school performance is compared against regional or national benchmarks

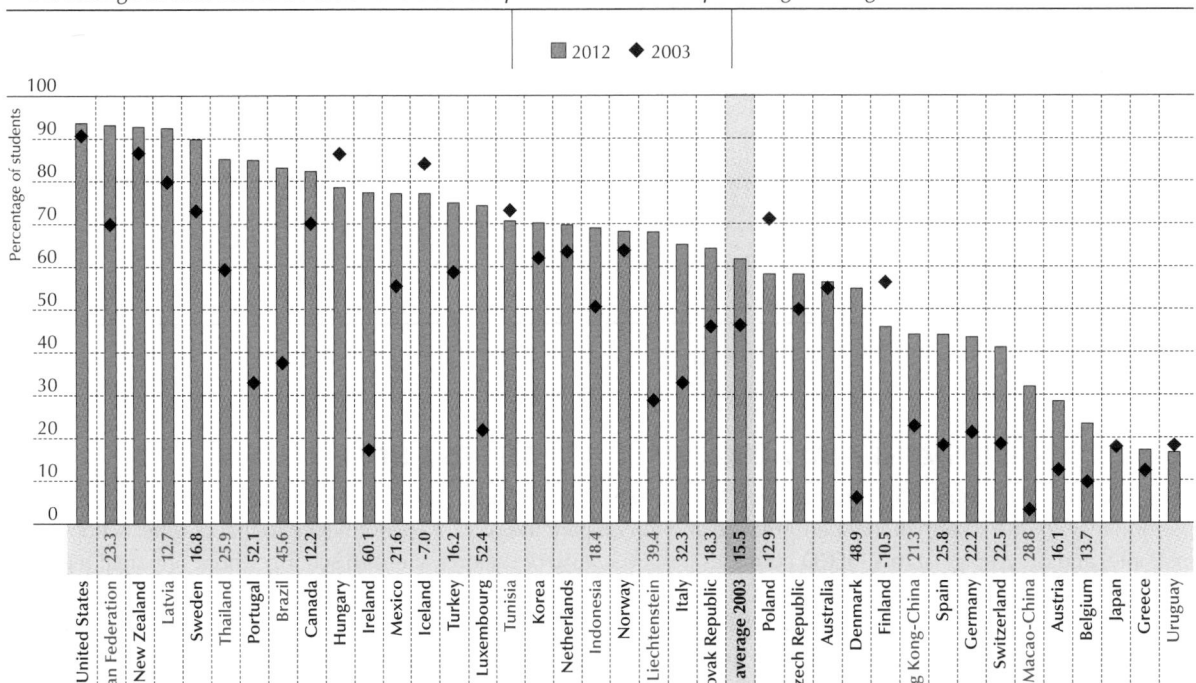

Notes: Only countries and economies with comparable data from PISA 2003 and PISA 2012 are shown.

The percentage-point difference in the share of students attending schools where student assessment data are used to compare the school against regional or national benchmarks in 2012 and 2003 (2012 - 2003) is shown above the country/economy name. Only statistically significant differences are shown.

OECD average 2003 compares only OECD countries with comparable data since 2003.

Countries and economies are ranked in descending order of the percentage of students in school where the principal reported using assessment data to compare the school against regional or national benchmarks in 2012.

Source: OECD, PISA 2012 Database, Table IV.4.36.

StatLink ⏢ http://dx.doi.org/10.1787/888932957346

As discussed above, teachers' practices can be monitored in several ways: through student achievement tests, peer reviews of lesson plans, class observations by the principal or senior staff or by external inspectors. With the exception of external observations, all of these types of teacher-monitoring practices have become more common since 2003. On average across OECD countries with comparable data from 2003 to 2012, students in 2012 were 20 percentage points more likely than their counterparts in 2003 to attend schools where the use of tests or assessments of student achievement are used to monitor teacher practice, and around eight percentage points more likely to attend schools that use peer reviews of lesson plans or principal or senior staff observations of lessons to the same end (Figure IV.4.19 and Table IV.4.37).

Using student assessments to monitor teachers' practices has become prevalent in PISA-participating countries and economies. In 2003, among all countries and economies with comparable data, 17 were those where fewer than 60% of students attended schools where student assessments were used to monitor teacher practices. By 2012, in only three countries with comparable data from 2003 – Greece, Uruguay and Finland – did fewer than 60% of students attend such schools; and in Finland, fewer than 40% of students attended such schools. In addition, 23 countries and economies saw an increase of more than 10 percentage points in the proportion of students who attend schools that use student assessments to monitor teachers' practices; and among the 14 countries and economies showing less of an increase or no increase, six showed more than 90% of students in such schools in 2003. Only two countries bucked this trend: Latvia, where the share of students in these types of schools decreased by 12 percentage points (from 95% in 2003 to 83% in 2012) and Finland, where fewer than 40% of students attend such schools (Figure IV.4.19 and Table IV.4.37).

■ Figure IV.4.19 ■

Change between 2003 and 2012 in using student assessment data to monitor teachers

*Percentage of students in schools whose principals report that student assessment is used
to monitor mathematics teachers' practice*

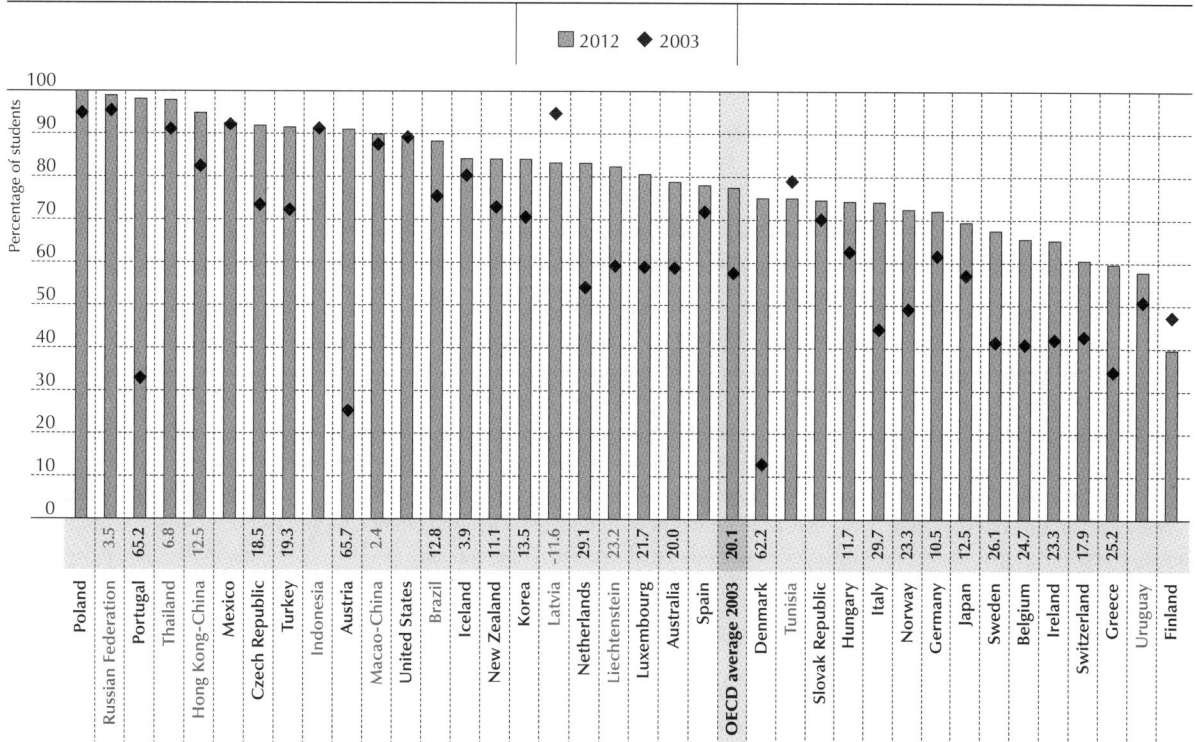

Notes: Only countries and economies with comparable data from PISA 2003 and PISA 2012 are shown.

The percentage-point difference in the share of students attending schools where student assessment data are used for teacher monitoring purposes in 2012 and 2003 (2012 - 2003) are shown above the country/economy name. Only statistically significant differences are shown.

OECD average 2003 compares only OECD countries with comparable data since 2003.

Countries and economies are ranked in descending order of the percentage of students in school where the principal reported to use assessment data for teacher monitoring purposes in 2012.

Source: OECD, PISA 2012 Database, Table IV.4.37.

StatLink ⌨ http://dx.doi.org/10.1787/888932957346

In 15 countries and economies with comparable data, it was at least ten percentage points more common in 2012 than in 2003 for students to attend schools where teachers were monitored through peer reviews of lesson plans, assessment instruments and lessons. These increases are notable in Sweden and Luxembourg, where the share of students attending such schools increased by more than 30 percentage points during the period. Only in Turkey, Tunisia, Spain and Finland did this proportion shrink by more than ten percentage points. In Turkey the percentage of students who attend schools where teachers are monitored through observations by external experts also decreased; but this drop was concurrent with an increase in the proportion of students in schools where teachers are monitored through student assessments. Tunisia also saw a decrease in the percentage of students in schools where teachers are monitored through observations by the principal or other senior staff (Table IV.4.37).

Notes

1. The ratio of the number of items for which "principals" and/or "teachers" have responsibility to the number of items for which "regional or local education authority" and/or "national education authority" have responsibility was computed. "School governing board " was not considered in the calculation.

2. System-level correlation between the *index of school responsibility for resource allocation* and the *index of school responsibility for curriculum and assessment* is 0.56 across OECD countries and 0.60 across all participating countries and economies. In Japan, the value on the *index of school responsibility for resource allocation* is relatively low compared with other countries, while the value on the *index of school responsibility for curriculum and assessment* is relatively high. In Bulgaria, the value on the *index of school responsibility for resource allocation* is relatively high, while the value on the *index of school responsibility for curriculum and assessment* is relatively low.

3. See Gewirtz, Ball and Bowe, 1995; Whitty, Power and Halpin, 1998; Karsten, 1999; Viteritti, 1999; Plank and Sykes, 2003; Hsieh and Urquiola, 2006; Heyneman, 2009; Bunar, 2010a; Bunar, 2010b; Söderström and Uusitalo, 2010; and Schneider and Buckley, 2002.

4. The parent questionnaire was distributed in Belgium (Flemish community), Chile, Croatia, Germany, Hong Kong-China, Hungary, Italy, Korea, Macao-China, Mexico and Portugal. Table III.6.14 (available on line) shows that in most countries and economies that distributed the parental questionnaire, participation was high, and the parents of virtually all students who participated in PISA responded to the questionnaire. Response rates were as high as 90% or more in Chile, Croatia, Hong Kong-China, Hungary, Italy, Korea, Macao-China and Mexico. The response rate in Portugal was 83%, while it was comparatively low in Germany (57%) and the Flemish community of Belgium (48%). Response rates for individual items vary as some parents responded to several questions but not to others. However, the extent of non-response to items in the parental questionnaire is similar to that of non-response to items in the student background questionnaire. Table III.6.14 illustrates how, in Belgium (Flemish community) and Germany, where response rates are low, and in Portugal, students whose parents responded to the parental questionnaire tend to score higher in PISA and have a more socio-economically advantaged status.

5. This average corresponds to the OECD average of countries that have comparable data in both PISA 2003 and PISA 2012.

6. This was also true in 19 countries and economies that participated in PISA 2003 and PISA 2012.

7. The PISA 2003 questionnaires did not include questions about principals' perspectives on school choice, leadership or parental involvement. Although PISA 2003 asked school principals about school autonomy as PISA 2012 did, the wording of these questions changed substantially, making it impossible to analyse trends in school autonomy. In the PISA 2003 questionnaire, school principals were asked "In your school, who has the main responsibility for <each governance attribute>" and offered the following response options: "Not a main responsibility of the school", "School's governing board", "Principal", "Department Head" or "Teachers". In the PISA 2012 questionnaire, school principals were asked "Regarding your school, who has a considerable responsibility for <each governance attribute>" and offered the following response options: "Principal", "Teachers", "School governing board", "Regional or local education authority", "National education authority". In both PISA 2003 and PISA 2012, school principals could select as many response options as appropriate.

8. Information is available for all OECD countries except Canada, New Zealand and Slovenia. Information is available for all participating partner countries and economies except Argentina, Costa Rica, Kazakhstan and Serbia. Turkey and Switzerland do not have information on the existence of assessments so they are excluded from the analysis.

9. These groups are created using a cluster analysis with the Ward method, which groups countries and economies to minimise the variance within each cluster, using data available in Tables IV.4.20 to IV.4.26. Variables that entered the analyses are: the existence of national assessments in lower secondary and upper secondary schools, the percentage of students taking national examinations in lower and upper secondary general programmes, the percentage of students taking other examinations in lower and upper secondary general programmes, and the percentage of tertiary fields of study requiring a non-secondary school examination for access. For those countries and economies where the percentage of students taking the examinations is unavailable, if examinations are compulsory, a percentage of 100 is used (Viet Nam), and if not compulsory, a percentage of 50 is used (Australia, upper secondary education). When the percentage of students taking other examinations is missing, a percentage value of 0 is used if no information on other examinations is provided (Australia, Korea, Romania, Slovenia, Tunisia, Turkey and Viet Nam); if these examinations do exist, then a value of 50 is used (Japan). When the number of fields of study requiring a tertiary examination is missing, a value of 0 is used (Tunisia).

10. The following countries and economies participated in the first TALIS survey, TALIS 2008: Australia, Austria, Belgium (Flemish community), Denmark, Estonia, Hungary, Iceland, Ireland, Italy, Korea, Mexico, Norway, Poland, Portugal, the Slovak Republic, Slovenia, Spain, Turkey, and the partner countries Brazil, Bulgaria, Lithuania, Malaysia and Malta. For the second TALIS survey, TALIS 2013, the following countries and economies are participating: Australia, Belgium (Flemish community), Canada (Alberta), Chile, the Czech Republic, Denmark, Estonia, Finland, France, Iceland, Israel, Italy, Japan, Korea, Mexico, the Netherlands, Norway, Poland, Portugal, the Slovak Republic, Spain, Sweden, the United Kingdom (England), the United States, and the partner countries Brazil, Bulgaria, Croatia, Latvia, Malaysia, Romania, Serbia, Singapore and the United Arab Emirates.

11. There is a possibility that certain negative consequences, such as teachers who were discouraged and left the profession or who were discharged from a particular school, is under-reported, because these teachers did not remain in the same school.

12. This average trend corresponds to the OECD average of countries that have comparable data in both PISA 2003 and PISA 2012. When rounded, the percentages of 84.65, 11.49 and 3.85 adds up to 101.

13. PISA 2012 also asked school principals about quality assurance and teacher appraisals. Because PISA 2003 did not include these questions, it is not possible to determine trends over time for these two aspects of assessment and accountability.

References

Berends, M. and **G. Zottola** (2009), "International Perspectives on School Choice", in M. Berends, et al. (eds.), *Handbook of School Choice*, Routledge, London.

Blase, J. and **J. Blase** (1998), *Handbook of Instructional Leadership: How Really Good Principals Promote Teaching and Learning*, Corwin Press, Thousand Oaks, California.

Blumberg, A. and **W. Greenfield** (1980), *The Effective Principal: Perspectives on School Leadership*, Allyn and Bacon, Boston, Massachusetts.

Bossert, S., D.C. Dwyer, B. Rowan and **G.V. Lee** (1981), *The Instructional Management Role of the Principal: A Preliminary Review and Conceptualization*, Far West Laboratory for Education Research, San Francisco, California.

Bunar, N. (2010a), "The Controlled School Market and Urban Schools in Sweden", *Journal of School Choice*, Vol. 4, pp. 47-73.

Bunar, N. (2010b), "Choosing for Quality or Inequality", *Journal of Education Policy*, Vol. 25, pp. 1-18.

Carnoy, M. (2000), "Globalization and Educational Reform", in N. Stromquist and K. Monkman (eds.), *Globalization and Education: Integration and Contestation across Cultures*, Rowman and Littlefield Publishers, Oxford.

Clark, D. (2009), "The Performance and Competitive Effects of School Autonomy", *Journal of Political Economy*, Vol. 117, No. 4, pp. 745-83.

Gewirtz, S., S. Ball and **R. Bowe** (1995), *Markets, Choice and Equity in Education*, Open University Press, Buckingham.

Gunnarsson, V., et al. (2009), "Does Local School Control Raise Student Outcomes? Evidence on the Roles of School Autonomy and Parental Participation", *Economic Development and Cultural Change*, Vol. 58, No. 1, pp. 25-52.

Hallinger, P. and **R. Heck** (1998), "Exploring the Principal's Contribution to School Effectiveness: 1980-1995", *School Effectiveness and School Improvement*, Vol. 9, pp. 157-91.

Hess, F. and **T. Loveless** (2005), "How School Choice Affects Student Achievement", in J. Betts and T. Loveless (eds.), *Getting Choice Right: Ensuring Equity and Efficiency in Education Policy*, Brookings Institution Press, Washington, D.C.

Heynemann, S. (2009), "International Perspectives on School Choice", in M. Berends *et al.* (eds.), *Handbook of School Choice*, Routledge, London.

Ho, E. and **D. Willms** (1996), "Effects of Parental Involvement on Eighth Grade Achievement", *Sociology of Education*, Vol. 69, No. 2, pp. 126-41.

Hsieh, H. and **M. Urquiola** (2006), "The Effects of Generalized School Choice on Achievement and Stratification: Evidence from Chile's Voucher Program", *Journal of Public Economics*, Vol. 90, No. 8-9, pp. 1477-1503.

Jensen, B., B. Weidmann and **J. Farmer** (2013), *The Myth of Markets in School Education*, Grattan Institute, Melbourne.

Karsten, S. (1999), "Neoliberal Education Reform in the Netherlands", *Comparative Education*, Vol. 35, No. 3, pp. 303-17.

Machin, S. and **J. Vernoit** (2011), *Changing School Autonomy: Academy Schools and their Introduction to England's Education*, Centre for the Economics of Education, London School of Economics, London.

Ministerio de Educación Nacional (MEN) (2010), *Revolución Educativa 2002-2010, Acciones y Lecciones*, Ministerio de Educación Nacional, República de Colombia, Bogotá.

OECD (2013a), *Synergies for Better Learning: An International Perspective on Evaluation and Assessment*, OECD Publishing. *http://dx.doi.org/10.1787/9789264190658-en*

OECD (2013b), *Teachers for the 21st Century: Using Evaluation to Improve Teaching*, OECD Publishing. *http://dx.doi.org/10.1787/9789264193864-en*

OECD (2011), *Strong Performers and Successful Reformers in Education: Lessons from PISA for the United States*, OECD Publishing. *http://dx.doi.org/10.1787/9789264096660-en*

OECD (2009), *Creating Effective Teaching and Learning Environments: First Results from TALIS*, OECD Publishing. *http://dx.doi.org/10.1787/9789264072992-en*

Plank, D. and **G. Sykes (eds.)** (2003), *Choosing Choice: School Choice in International Perspective,* Teachers College Press, New York.

Pont, B., D. Nusche and **H. Moorman** (2003), *Improving School Leadership: Volume 1, Policy and Practice*, OECD Publishing. *http://dx.doi.org/10.1787/9789264044715-en*

Schneider, M. and **J. Buckley** (2002), "What Do Parents Want From Schools? Evidence from the Internet", *Educational Evaluation and Policy Analysis*, Vol. 24, No. 2, pp. 133-44.

Schneider, M., P. Teske and **M. Marschall** (2002), *Choosing Schools: Consumer Choice and the Quality of American Schools*, Princeton University Press, Princeton, New Jersey.

Sliwka, A. (2003), "Networking for Educational Innovation: A Comparative Analysis", *OECD Networks of Innovation: Towards New Models for Managing Schools and Systems*, OECD Publishing.

Söderström, M. and **R. Uusitalo** (2010), "School Choice and Segregation: Evidence from an Admission Reform", *The Scandinavian Journal of Economics*, Vol. 112, No. 1, pp. 55-76.

Viteritti, J. (1999), *Choosing Equality,* Brookings Institution Press, Washington, D.C.

Whitty, G. (1997), "Creating Quasi-Markets in Education: A Review of Recent Research on Parental Choice and School Autonomy in Three Countries", *Review of Research in Education,* Vol. 22, pp. 3-47.

Whitty, G., S. Power and **D. Halpin** (1998), *Devolution and Choice in Education,* Open University Press, Birmingham and Philadelphia.

Wiseman, A.W. (2004), "Management of Semi-Public Organizations in Complex Environments", *Public Administration and Management*, Vol. 9, No. 2, pp. 166-81.

World Bank (2010), *Quality of Education in Colombia, Achievements and Challenges Ahead: Analysis of the Results of TIMSS 1995-2007,* World Bank, Washington, D.C.

Zhao, H. and **M. Akiba** (2009), "School Expectations for Parental Involvement and Student Mathematics Achievement: A Comparative Study of Middle Schools in the US and South Korea", *Compare*, Vol. 39, No. 3, pp. 411-28.

How the Quality of the Learning Environment is Shaped

This chapter discusses student- and teacher-related aspects of the learning environment, including student truancy, teacher-student relations, the disciplinary climate and teacher morale. It also examines trends in school climate and student truancy since 2003.

This chapter describes the learning environment and examines how it is related to other aspects of school organisation discussed in Chapters 2 through 4. The aspects of learning environments related to the issues of student truancy and school climate that are discussed in this chapter are summarised in Figure IV.5.1. Student truancy not only hurts the individual student, but when it is pervasive, it hurts the entire class. School climate such as the good quality of relationships and the general orderly atmosphere are important characteristics of effective schools. Chapter 1 shows that student truancy tends to be negatively related to both systems' and schools' overall performance; and a favourable disciplinary climate is consistently related to higher average performance at the school level. In general, learning environments improved between 2003 and 2012: more students reported positive teacher-student relations and positive disciplinary climates, and principals were more likely to report that teacher- and student-related factors rarely hindered learning.

■ Figure IV.5.1 ■
The learning environment as covered in PISA 2012

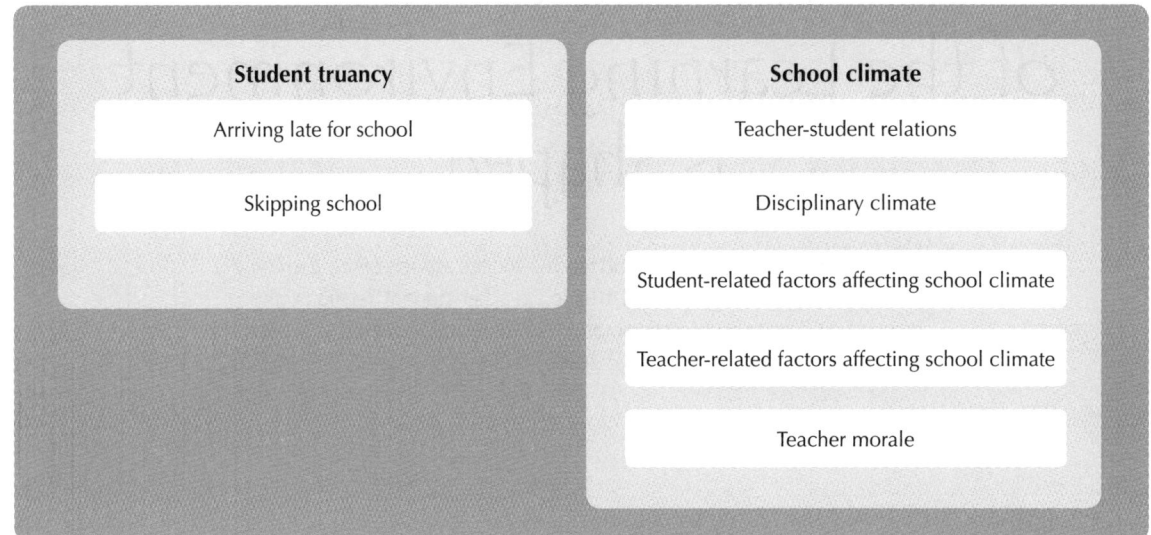

Student truancy	School climate
Arriving late for school	Teacher-student relations
Skipping school	Disciplinary climate
	Student-related factors affecting school climate
	Teacher-related factors affecting school climate
	Teacher morale

What the data tell us

- In virtually all school systems, schools with more negative disciplinary climates tend to have a higher incidence of students arriving late for school or skipping a day of school or a class.

- On average among OECD countries, schools with a more negative disciplinary climate tend to have a largely disadvantaged student population, have greater socio-economic diversity among students, and suffer from more teacher shortages.

- Consistent with trends showing that the overall learning environment improved between 2003 and 2012, students in 2012 were slightly less likely than students in 2003 to report that they had arrived late for school. According to students' reports, teacher-student relations have also improved during the period in all but one country, Tunisia, where they remained stable.

STUDENT TRUANCY

Student truancy (e.g. arriving late for school, unauthorised non-attendance) not only has serious adverse consequences on the lives of individual young people, but it can also cut into school learning time and distract from learning (Robins and Ratcliff, 1978; Gamoran and Nystrand 1992; Lamdin, 1996; Caldas, 1993; Hallfors et al., 2002; Roby, 2004; Fantuzzo, Grim and Hazan 2005; Henry, 2007; Sheldon, 2007; Saab and Klinger, 2010). If students who arrive late or skip classes fall far behind in their classwork and require extra assistance, the flow of instruction is disrupted and all students in the class may suffer.

Arriving late for school

PISA 2012 asked students to report the number of times they arrived late for school during the two weeks prior to the assessment. Across OECD countries, 65% of students reported that they had not arrived late for school during that period, 25% reported that they had arrived late once or twice, and 10% reported that they had arrived late three or more times. In Uruguay, Bulgaria, Costa Rica, Latvia, Sweden, Portugal, Israel, Chile, Peru and Tunisia, 50% to 60% of students had arrived late at least once in the prior two weeks. By contrast, around 15% to 19% of students in Hong Kong-China, Viet Nam, Shanghai-China and Liechtenstein had arrived late at least once, and 9% of students in Japan had arrived late at least once (Table IV.5.1).

Are students who arrive late for school concentrated in certain schools, or can they be found in any school? In order to answer this question, students' reports on arriving late for school were aggregated at the school level to calculate the proportion of students who had arrived late for school at least once in the two weeks prior to the PISA test (Figure IV.5.2). As shown in Figure IV.5.2, across OECD countries, 8% of students are in schools where one in ten students or fewer had arrived late for school during that period, 24% of students are in schools where between one in ten students and one in four students had arrived late for school at least once, 47% of students are in schools where between one and two in four students had arrived late for school, and 21% are in schools where more than two in four students had arrived late for school at least once in the previous two weeks. In Uruguay, Bulgaria, Costa Rica, Latvia, Sweden, Portugal, Israel, Peru, Tunisia, Chile and Greece, 50% to 80% of students are in schools where more than half of students had arrived late for school at least once in the previous two weeks. By contrast, in Shanghai-China, Hong Kong-China, Japan, Liechtenstein, Singapore, Viet Nam, Chinese Taipei, Luxembourg and Germany, fewer than 5% of students attend such schools. In Japan, 65% of students are in schools where one in ten students or fewer had arrived late for school during that period (Table IV.5.2).

In all school systems, the proportion of 15-year-old students who arrived late for school varies across schools. However, in some systems, these students seem to be concentrated in certain schools, while in other systems these students are distributed more equitably among all schools. For example, around 39% of students had arrived late for school at least once in the two weeks prior to the PISA test in Denmark and Montenegro (Figure IV.5.2 and Table IV.5.1). But these students are more concentrated in certain schools in Denmark than in Montenegro. In Montenegro, 83% of students are in schools where from one to two in four students had arrived late, while in Denmark, 52% of students are in such schools. Thus, in Montenegro, students will have similar experiences with late-arriving peers no matter which school they attend, while in Denmark, students' experiences with late-arriving peers will vary greatly, depending on the school they attend (Table IV.5.2).

Skipping school

Students were asked to report the number of times they skipped a whole day of school and the number of times they skipped some classes during the two weeks before the assessment. Across OECD countries, 85% of students reported that they had not skipped a day of school, 12% had skipped a day of school once or twice, and 3% had skipped a day of school three times or more during those two weeks. Similarly, across OECD countries, 82% of students had not skipped classes, 14% skipped classes once or twice, and 4% had skipped classes three times or more during that period (Table IV.5.3).

In Argentina and Turkey, more than 50% of students had skipped a day of school in the two weeks prior to the PISA test, while in Shanghai-China, Japan, Korea, Liechtenstein, Iceland, the Netherlands, Hong Kong-China, Ireland, Chinese Taipei, Colombia, Macao-China and Switzerland, fewer than 5% of students had done so. In general, those countries with high proportions of students who had skipped a day of school also tend to have high proportions of students who skip classes, while those countries and economies with small proportions of students who had skipped a day of school also tend to have small proportions of students who had skipped classes. An exception is Latvia, where about one in five students reported that he or she had skipped a day of school at least once during the period, while about two out of three students reported to have skipped classes at least once (Table IV.5.3).

Are students who skip a day of school concentrated in certain schools? Across OECD countries, an average of 27% of students are in schools where one in ten students or fewer reported that they had skipped a day or a class in the two weeks prior to the PISA test; 31% are in schools where between one in ten students and one in four students reported to have done so at least once; 30% are in schools where between a quarter and half of students reported to have done so; and 13% are in schools where more than half of students reported to have done so. In Argentina, Latvia, Turkey, Italy, Jordan, Romania, Costa Rica and the United Arab Emirates, over 50% of students attend schools where more than half of students reported that they had skipped a day of school or a class at least once in the two weeks prior to the assessment (Table IV.5.4).

■ Figure IV.5.2 ■
Students arriving late for school

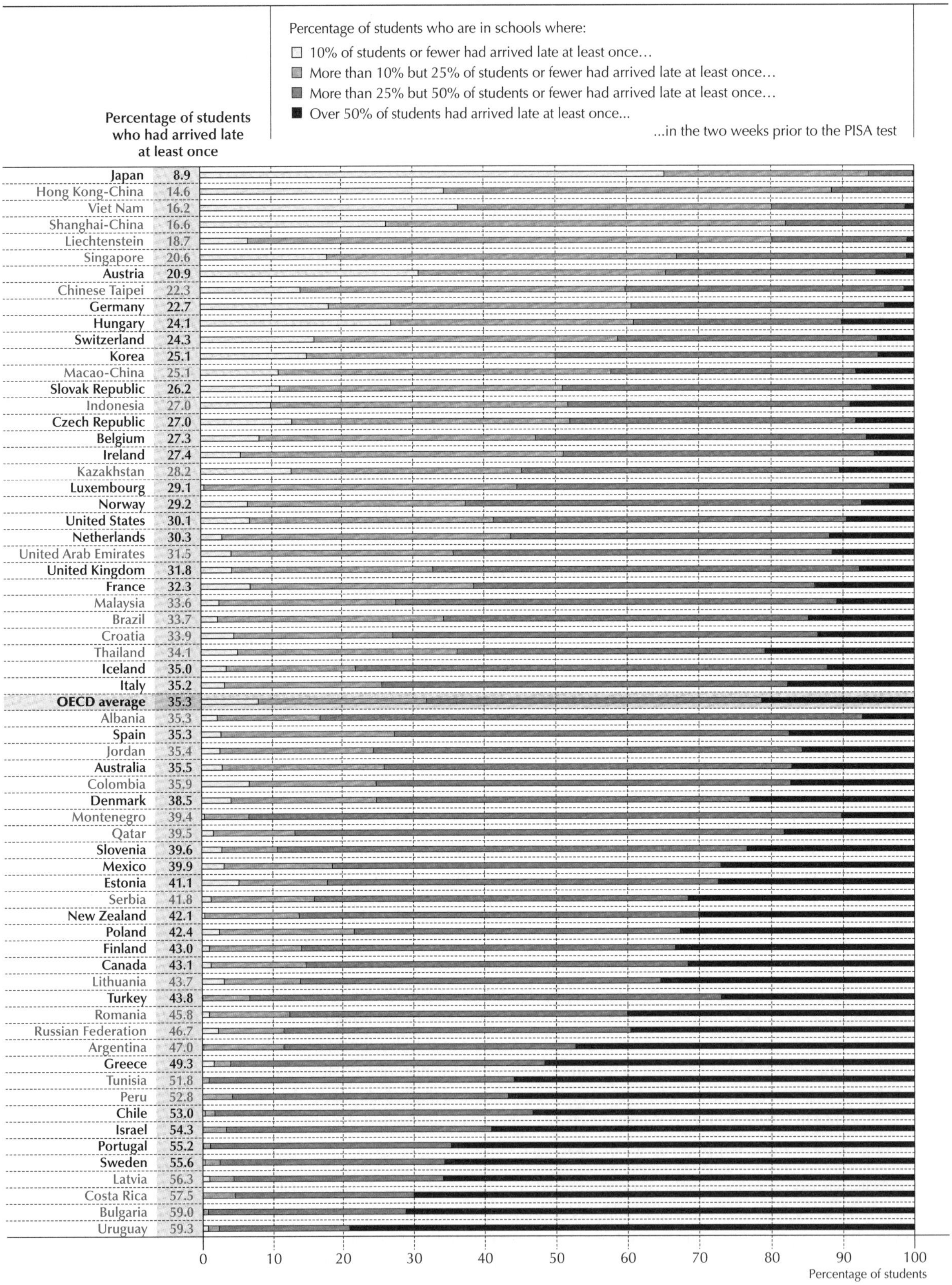

Percentage of students who are in schools where:

☐ 10% of students or fewer had arrived late at least once…
▨ More than 10% but 25% of students or fewer had arrived late at least once…
▨ More than 25% but 50% of students or fewer had arrived late at least once…
■ Over 50% of students had arrived late at least once…

…in the two weeks prior to the PISA test

	Percentage of students who had arrived late at least once
Japan	8.9
Hong Kong-China	14.6
Viet Nam	16.2
Shanghai-China	16.6
Liechtenstein	18.7
Singapore	20.6
Austria	20.9
Chinese Taipei	22.3
Germany	22.7
Hungary	24.1
Switzerland	24.3
Korea	25.1
Macao-China	25.1
Slovak Republic	26.2
Indonesia	27.0
Czech Republic	27.0
Belgium	27.3
Ireland	27.4
Kazakhstan	28.2
Luxembourg	29.1
Norway	29.2
United States	30.1
Netherlands	30.3
United Arab Emirates	31.5
United Kingdom	31.8
France	32.3
Malaysia	33.6
Brazil	33.7
Croatia	33.9
Thailand	34.1
Iceland	35.0
Italy	35.2
OECD average	35.3
Albania	35.3
Spain	35.3
Jordan	35.4
Australia	35.5
Colombia	35.9
Denmark	38.5
Montenegro	39.4
Qatar	39.5
Slovenia	39.6
Mexico	39.9
Estonia	41.1
Serbia	41.8
New Zealand	42.1
Poland	42.4
Finland	43.0
Canada	43.1
Lithuania	43.7
Turkey	43.8
Romania	45.8
Russian Federation	46.7
Argentina	47.0
Greece	49.3
Tunisia	51.8
Peru	52.8
Chile	53.0
Israel	54.3
Portugal	55.2
Sweden	55.6
Latvia	56.3
Costa Rica	57.5
Bulgaria	59.0
Uruguay	59.3

Percentage of students (x-axis: 0 10 20 30 40 50 60 70 80 90 100)

Countries and economies are ranked in ascending order of the percentage of students who had arrived late at least once in the two weeks prior to the assessment.
Source: OECD, PISA 2012 Database, Tables IV.5.1 and IV.5.2.
StatLink http://dx.doi.org/10.1787/888932957365

WHAT MAKES SCHOOLS SUCCESSFUL? RESOURCES, POLICIES AND PRACTICES – VOLUME IV

SCHOOL CLIMATE

Research into what makes schools effective finds that learning requires an orderly and co-operative environment both in and outside the classroom (Jennings and Greenberg, 2009). In effective schools, academic activities and student performance are valued by both students and teachers (Scheerens and Bosker, 1997; Sammons, 1999; Taylor, Pressley and Pearson, 2002). The school climate encompasses not only norms and values but also the quality of teacher-student relations and the general atmosphere (OECD, 2013). How does the climate in a classroom – e.g. the degree of discipline among students, the quality of the relationship between students and their teachers, the values promoted and shared between teacher and student and among the students themselves – vary, and how does it affect teaching and learning? Research has found that students, particularly disadvantaged students, learn more and have fewer disciplinary problems when they feel that their teachers take them seriously (Gamoran, 1993) and when they have strong and affective bonds with their teachers (Crosnoe, Johnson and Elder, 2004). Through these positive relationships, social capital is transmitted, communal learning environments are created, and adherence to norms conducive to learning are both promoted and strengthened (Birch and Ladd, 1998).

Teacher-student relations

Students were asked to indicate whether and to what extent they agree with several statements regarding their relationships with teachers at school, including whether they get along with their teachers, whether teachers are interested in their personal well-being, whether teachers take the student seriously, whether teachers are a source of support if the student needs extra help, and whether teachers treat the student fairly. These responses were combined to create a composite *index of teacher-student relations* such that the index has an average of zero and a standard deviation of one for OECD countries. Higher values indicate that students have a more positive perception of teacher-student relations. When comparing estimates across school systems, it is important to keep in mind that several factors beyond students' experiences in school may determine the patterns of these responses.

On average across OECD countries, at least three out of four students agreed or strongly agreed with four of these statements, as presented in Figure IV.5.3:

- 82% of students agreed or strongly agreed that students get along well with most teachers. While in Kazakhstan, Indonesia, Shanghai-China, Singapore, Hong Kong-China, Albania, Macao-China, Costa Rica, Portugal, Mexico, Thailand and Malaysia, over 90% of students responded so, fewer than 75% of students in Viet Nam, Qatar, Poland, Greece and Italy responded so.

- 82% of students agreed or strongly agreed that they would receive extra help from their teachers if they need it. In Viet Nam, Kazakhstan, Shanghai-China, Indonesia, Singapore, Canada, Portugal, Hong Kong-China, the United Kingdom, Thailand and Albania, over 90% of students responded so, while in Austria, Germany, Italy, Luxembourg, Croatia, Israel, Tunisia, Greece and Slovenia, fewer than 75% of students responded so.

- 81% of students agreed or strongly agreed that most of their teachers treat them fairly. Over 90% of students in Colombia, Albania, Kazakhstan and Shanghai-China responded so, while in Poland, France, Tunisia, Turkey, Greece and Macao-China, fewer than 75% of students responded so.

- 77% of students agreed or strongly agreed that most teachers are interested in students' well being. Over 90% of students in Kazakhstan, Indonesia, Latvia, Singapore, Portugal, Shanghai-China, Albania, Colombia and Costa Rica responded so, while in Poland, Slovenia, Japan, Tunisia, the Russian Federation and Luxembourg, at least one in three students did not respond so.

- 74% of students agreed or strongly agreed that most of their teachers really listen to what they have to say. Over 85% of students in Kazakhstan, Albania, Thailand, Peru, Portugal and Jordan responded so, while at least one in three students in Austria, Chinese Taipei, Poland, Macao-China and Germany did not respond so.

Although most students across OECD countries reported positive relationships between students and teachers, these relationships vary, as measured by the standard deviation of the *index of teacher-student relations*, which combines the abovementioned questions. Variation within countries (measured through the standard deviation at the student level) is smallest in the Netherlands, Indonesia, Viet Nam, Latvia, Estonia and Korea. In contrast, in Qatar, Israel, Jordan, Tunisia and Montenegro, teacher-student relations vary more (Table IV.5.5).

■ Figure IV.5.3 ■
Students' views of teacher-student relations

- **A** Students get along well with most teachers
- **B** Most teachers are interested in students' well-being
- **C** Most of my teachers really listen to what I have to say
- **D** If I need extra help, I will receive it from my teachers
- **E** Most of my teachers treat me fairly

Index of teacher-student relations based on students' reports
— Range between top and bottom quarters
◆ Average index

	Percentage of students who "agreed" or "strongly agreed" with the following statements					Variability in the index S.D.	Percentage of the index variation between schools %
	A	B	C	D	E		
OECD							
Australia	84	87	80	90	87	1.13	6.2
Austria	81	70	62	64	80	0.92	7.0
Belgium	80	77	74	85	79	0.78	9.1
Canada	86	86	81	92	90	0.95	5.7
Chile	83	85	77	83	76	0.95	6.1
Czech Republic	81	72	68	87	79	1.06	2.5
Denmark	89	85	80	85	87	0.96	4.8
Estonia	82	80	72	85	80	0.90	5.6
Finland	80	73	74	89	83	0.96	2.5
France	78	71	72	82	69	0.92	4.8
Germany	76	67	67	66	76	1.05	8.9
Greece	74	76	70	74	73	1.02	7.1
Hungary	83	73	83	77	77	0.95	10.3
Iceland	84	85	82	87	84	0.93	3.7
Ireland	82	84	73	84	87	1.09	3.5
Israel	79	78	75	74	81	1.00	4.1
Italy	75	71	70	71	71	1.04	6.8
Japan	80	59	73	81	79	1.08	3.8
Korea	90	72	69	89	80	1.02	7.8
Luxembourg	86	66	70	73	78	1.02	11.4
Mexico	91	90	84	85	89	1.09	10.3
Netherlands	84	78	74	83	85	1.01	6.8
New Zealand	84	85	78	89	88	1.00	7.4
Norway	82	75	67	81	77	1.03	6.7
Poland	74	54	62	76	66	0.94	1.7
Portugal	91	92	85	92	84	1.01	3.4
Slovak Republic	77	78	74	75	77	1.10	2.5
Slovenia	82	59	70	75	78	1.13	5.9
Spain	78	79	74	76	81	1.06	3.9
Sweden	85	82	77	83	83	1.03	0.5
Switzerland	82	78	76	84	83	1.11	1.6
Turkey	88	75	84	77	72	1.03	6.5
United Kingdom	85	86	76	91	86	0.89	6.1
United States	83	86	78	90	90	0.97	7.8
OECD average	82	77	74	82	81	0.98	6.9
Partners							
Albania	92	91	89	90	93	1.00	8.3
Argentina	82	79	79	78	84	0.87	10.2
Brazil	84	82	76	86	85	0.93	7.4
Bulgaria	82	80	81	87	80	1.13	5.1
Colombia	87	90	83	85	94	0.91	5.4
Costa Rica	91	90	82	80	89	1.02	6.9
Croatia	78	78	69	74	77	0.89	6.5
Hong Kong-China	92	79	71	91	83	1.05	6.6
Indonesia	95	94	78	93	88	0.92	8.2
Jordan	86	74	85	84	80	1.06	3.6
Kazakhstan	96	95	89	94	92	0.98	3.8
Latvia	84	92	75	90	85	0.91	9.3
Liechtenstein	82	74	71	79	84	0.89	6.0
Lithuania	89	83	82	87	87	1.05	6.6
Macao-China	91	82	66	87	75	1.08	3.2
Malaysia	90	89	67	89	83	1.03	8.6
Montenegro	86	81	77	77	81	1.11	7.0
Peru	90	90	86	85	86	1.06	8.3
Qatar	72	80	74	81	76	0.96	4.2
Romania	87	88	83	81	84	0.89	8.1
Russian Federation	88	66	80	86	83	1.03	4.7
Serbia	83	79	72	82	87	1.01	7.0
Shanghai-China	93	91	81	93	90	0.98	6.9
Singapore	92	92	83	93	89	0.96	7.4
Chinese Taipei	89	84	62	81	81	0.96	4.9
Thailand	90	89	87	90	87	1.02	4.4
Tunisia	78	64	72	74	72	1.06	8.7
United Arab Emirates	89	86	78	88	81	0.91	5.4
Uruguay	87	84	80	83	75	0.97	7.2
Viet Nam	70	77	74	95	82	1.00	6.8

-2.0 -1.5 -1.0 -0.5 0 0.5 1.0 1.5 2.0 2.5 Index points

Note: Higher values on the index indicate better teacher-student relations.
Source: OECD, PISA 2012 Database, Table IV.5.5.
StatLink ᵃˢᵖ http://dx.doi.org/10.1787/888932957365

Students' reports on their relationship with teachers vary both between and within schools. On average across OECD countries, most of the variation in the *index of teacher-student relations* is seen within schools (i.e. 93% of variation is seen within schools, while 7% is observed between schools). In other words, students who attend the same school vary in the extent to which they reported good relations with their teachers. In Montenegro, Hong Kong-China, Albania, Chinese Taipei and Luxembourg, around 2.5% or less of variation in the *index of teacher-student relations* is observed between schools; in contrast, in Germany, Australia, Liechtenstein and Indonesia, 10% or more of the variation is seen between schools (Figure IV.5.5 and Table IV.5.5).

Disciplinary climate

PISA 2012 asked students to describe the frequency with which interruptions occur in mathematics lessons. This included how often – "never", "in some", "in most" or "in all" mathematics lessons – students don't listen to what the teacher says; there is noise and disorder; the teacher has to wait a long time for students to quieten down; students cannot work well; and students don't start working for a long time after the lesson begins. These responses were combined to create a composite *index of disciplinary climate* such that the index has an average of zero and a standard deviation of one for OECD countries. Higher values indicate that students perceive a better disciplinary climate in the classroom.

Most students in OECD countries enjoy orderly classrooms during their mathematics lessons. As presented in Figure IV.5.4, on average across OECD countries:

- 78% of students reported that they never or only in some mathematics lessons cannot work well. In Viet Nam, Kazakhstan, Shanghai-China, Singapore and Korea, over 85% of students responded so, while in Tunisia, Qatar, Jordan, Argentina and Greece, 33% of students or more responded that this happens in most or every lesson.

- 73% of students reported that they never or only in some lessons don't start working for a long time after the lessons begins. Over 85% of students in Japan, Viet Nam, Kazakhstan, Shanghai-China and the Russian Federation gave this response, while over 40% of students in Tunisia, Jordan, Argentina, Brazil, the Netherlands, France and Qatar reported that this happens in most or every lesson.

- 72% of students reported that their teacher never or only in some lessons has to wait a long time for students to quiet down. Over 85% of students in Japan, Shanghai-China, Viet Nam, Kazakhstan, Hong Kong-China and Macao-China reported so, while over 40% of students in Argentina, Qatar, Chile and Tunisia reported that this happens in most or every lesson.

- 68% of students reported that students never, or only in some lessons, do not listen to what the teacher says. Over 80% of students in Viet Nam, Japan, Shanghai-China, Thailand, Indonesia, Kazakhstan, Albania and Korea reported so, while over 40% of students in Argentina, Serbia, Bulgaria, Croatia, Qatar, Montenegro, New Zealand, Finland, Brazil, Greece and France reported that this happens in most or every lesson.

- 68% of students reported there is never, or only in some lessons, noise and disorder. Over 80% of students in Kazakhstan, Japan, Viet Nam, Shanghai-China, Albania, Macao-China, the Russian Federation and Hong Kong-China reported so, while over 40% of students in Argentina, Finland, France, Tunisia, New Zealand, Qatar, Australia, Chile and Brazil reported that this happens in most or every lesson.

Disciplinary climate often varies widely within countries and economies, as measured by the standard deviation of the *index of disciplinary climate*, which combines the abovementioned questions. Variations within countries and economies (i.e. the standard deviation at the student level) are the smallest in Viet Nam, Thailand, Peru, Macao-China, Malaysia and Colombia. By contrast, in Qatar and Ireland there is more variation in disciplinary climate within the country (Table IV.5.6).

Variations in the *index of disciplinary climate* can occur between and within schools. On average across OECD countries, 86% of the variation in the *index of disciplinary climate* is seen within schools, while 14% is observed between schools. Higher levels of between-school variation mean lower levels of within-school variation. In other words, students who attend the same school share similar perceptions about the disciplinary climate in their classes. In the Czech Republic, Latvia, Iceland, and Liechtenstein, 20% or more of the variation in this index is observed between schools. In contrast, in Mexico, Montenegro, Luxembourg and Albania, less than 5% of the variation is seen between schools (Figure IV.5.4 and Table IV.5.6).

■ Figure IV.5.4 ■

Students' views of how conducive classrooms are to learning

A Students don't listen to what the teacher says
B There is noise and disorder
C The teacher has to wait a long time for students to quiet down
D Students cannot work well
E Students don't start working for a long time after the lesson begins

		Percentage of students who reported that the following phenomena occur "never or hardly ever" or "in some lessons"					Index of disciplinary climate based on students' reports	Variability in the index S.D.	Percentage of the index variation between schools %
		A	B	C	D	E			
OECD	Australia	62	57	68	78	73		1.03	9.6
	Austria	73	75	72	78	74		1.08	17.7
	Belgium	72	67	71	81	71		1.04	10.9
	Canada	71	66	75	82	72		0.97	12.1
	Chile	65	58	59	76	65		0.90	10.0
	Czech Republic	64	70	73	80	77		1.09	23.1
	Denmark	70	67	77	82	75		0.89	14.4
	Estonia	70	77	80	80	83		0.96	15.7
	Finland	57	51	64	78	65		0.86	8.5
	France	60	52	61	70	58		1.05	13.8
	Germany	64	71	68	73	71		1.02	9.0
	Greece	59	61	68	66	67		0.90	12.2
	Hungary	64	72	73	78	80		1.02	12.3
	Iceland	75	66	75	83	77		0.91	22.2
	Ireland	64	69	75	81	78		1.10	15.5
	Israel	77	76	76	78	80		1.07	9.8
	Italy	67	64	69	73	73		0.99	14.4
	Japan	91	90	93	84	90		0.90	17.2
	Korea	81	70	83	85	81		0.87	15.6
	Luxembourg	64	68	70	73	67		1.09	3.9
	Mexico	71	73	79	79	74		0.91	1.8
	Netherlands	71	63	66	80	56		0.92	14.2
	New Zealand	57	55	65	75	69		1.00	14.1
	Norway	72	71	76	79	71		0.87	7.8
	Poland	63	74	75	78	78		1.05	19.5
	Portugal	68	68	73	78	74		0.97	16.6
	Slovak Republic	61	71	68	74	69		0.93	15.9
	Slovenia	62	72	72	79	75		1.04	14.7
	Spain	66	68	67	77	70		1.03	14.5
	Sweden	66	62	66	75	68		0.89	11.8
	Switzerland	72	69	75	79	72		0.98	6.3
	Turkey	76	75	72	68	71		0.91	10.9
	United Kingdom	70	68	74	84	81		1.07	11.5
	United States	67	70	76	82	78		1.00	8.4
	OECD average	68	68	72	78	73		0.98	14.0
Partners	Albania	82	86	83	82	82		0.96	5.0
	Argentina	51	49	55	66	55		0.88	7.7
	Brazil	58	58	62	68	56		0.94	16.0
	Bulgaria	54	68	71	70	74		0.91	17.1
	Colombia	72	72	77	82	71		0.85	10.3
	Costa Rica	69	73	78	80	73		0.88	12.1
	Croatia	55	67	69	72	72		1.02	15.8
	Hong Kong-China	80	81	86	85	83		0.97	6.4
	Indonesia	83	74	75	84	84		0.88	13.9
	Jordan	63	62	62	62	50		1.07	15.4
	Kazakhstan	83	90	88	90	90		0.99	11.1
	Latvia	64	73	76	78	83		0.95	22.4
	Liechtenstein	75	75	79	80	80		1.01	20.0
	Lithuania	71	77	80	81	81		1.06	15.5
	Macao-China	76	85	85	84	79		0.79	18.1
	Malaysia	68	62	67	71	71		0.83	12.2
	Montenegro	56	73	75	72	73		1.01	3.6
	Peru	73	76	81	80	74		0.78	9.1
	Qatar	55	57	57	62	59		1.12	10.8
	Romania	67	74	75	73	72		1.00	10.3
	Russian Federation	73	82	81	83	86		1.02	17.9
	Serbia	52	69	69	70	70		1.02	15.4
	Shanghai-China	85	87	91	89	89		0.95	14.4
	Singapore	76	72	77	85	83		1.00	11.1
	Chinese Taipei	65	72	75	75	78		0.98	10.0
	Thailand	85	74	78	85	85		0.77	6.2
	Tunisia	64	53	60	59	50		0.87	18.0
	United Arab Emirates	67	68	68	73	70		1.04	11.0
	Uruguay	66	62	60	76	72		0.98	11.4
	Viet Nam	93	89	90	90	90		0.70	18.6

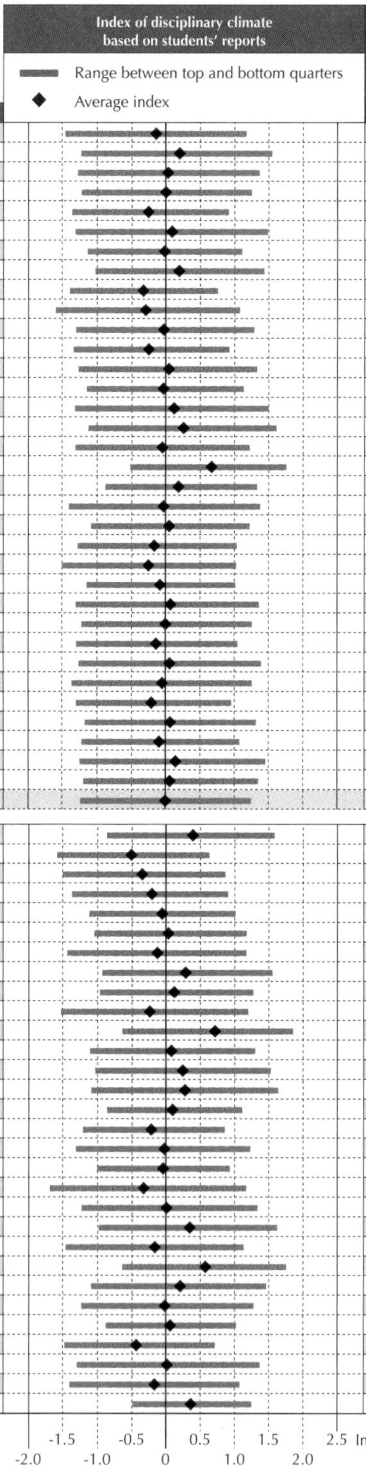

Range between top and bottom quarters
◆ Average index

-2.0 -1.5 -1.0 -0.5 0 0.5 1.0 1.5 2.0 2.5 Index points

Note: Higher values on the index indicate a better disciplinary climate.
Source: OECD, PISA 2012 Database, Table IV.5.6.
StatLink ᵐˢᴾ http://dx.doi.org/10.1787/888932957365

Student- and teacher-related factors affecting school climate

To examine the degree to which student behaviour influences learning, school principals were also asked to report the extent to which they think that learning in their schools is hindered by such factors as: student truancy, students skipping classes, students arriving late for school, students not attending compulsory school events or excursions, students lacking respect for teachers, disruption of classes by students, students using alcohol or illegal drugs, and students intimidating or bullying other students. The responses were combined to create an *index of student-related factors affecting school climate* that has a mean of zero and a standard deviation of one in OECD countries. Positive values reflect principals' perceptions that students' behaviour hinders learning to a lesser extent, and negative values indicate that school principals believe that students' behaviour hinders learning to a greater extent, compared to the OECD average.

In general, student truancy and disruption of classes are reported as more of a hindrance to learning than students' use of alcohol or illegal drugs, or students intimidating other students, not participating in compulsory events, or showing a lack of respect for teachers (Figure IV.5.5). On average across OECD countries:

- 94% of students attend schools whose principals reported that learning is not at all or very little hindered by students' use of alcohol or illegal drugs. Over 95% of students are in such schools in 29 participating countries and economies, while in Kazakhstan and Shanghai-China at least one in four students attends schools whose principals reported that learning is hindered by students' use of alcohol or illegal drugs to some extent or a lot.

- 89% of students are in schools whose principals reported that learning is not at all or very little hindered by students intimidating or bullying other students. Some 95% of students or more in Montenegro, Indonesia, Albania, the Slovak Republic, Latvia, the United Kingdom, Romania, Spain, Japan, Singapore, Lithuania and Iceland attend such schools, while over 20% of students in Kazakhstan, Shanghai-China, Finland, Colombia, the Netherlands, Brazil, Korea and Tunisia attend schools where learning hindered by students intimidating or bullying other students to some extent or a lot.

- 87% of students are in schools whose principals reported that learning is not at all or very little hindered by students not attending compulsory school events, such as sports days or excursions. Over 95% of students in Iceland, the United Kingdom, Lithuania, Albania, Macao-China, Portugal and Singapore attend such schools. In contrast, at least one in four students in Tunisia, Kazakhstan, Australia, Costa Rica, Malaysia and Slovenia attends schools whose principals reported that learning is hindered by students not attending compulsory school events to some extent or a lot.

- 81% of students are in schools whose principals reported that learning is not at all or very little hindered by students lacking respect for teachers. Over 90% of students in Viet Nam, Indonesia, Peru, Albania, Romania, Lithuania, Thailand, Singapore and the United Kingdom attend such schools. In contrast, at least one in three students in Kazakhstan, Croatia, Brazil, Korea, Jordan, Tunisia and the Russian Federation attends schools whose principals reported that learning is hindered by students' lack of respect for teachers to some extent or a lot.

- 69% of students are in schools whose principals reported that learning is not at all or very little hindered by students skipping classes. Over 90% of students in Indonesia, Singapore, the United Kingdom, Hong Kong-China, Macao-China, Liechtenstein, Iceland, Albania and Japan attend such schools. In contrast, at least one in two students in Croatia, the Slovak Republic, the Russian Federation, Serbia, Slovenia, Costa Rica, Kazakhstan, Canada, Turkey and Tunisia attends schools whose principals reported that learning is hindered by this behaviour to some extent or a lot.

- 69% of students attend schools whose principals reported that learning is not at all or very little hindered by students arriving late for school. Over 90% of students in Indonesia, Liechtenstein and Albania attend such schools. In contrast, at least one in two students in Tunisia, Costa Rica, Colombia, Canada, Serbia, Chile, Finland and Uruguay attends schools whose principals reported that learning is hindered by this behaviour to some extent or a lot.

- 68% of students are in schools whose principals reported that learning is not at all or very little hindered by student truancy. Over 90% of students in Liechtenstein, Iceland, Indonesia, the United Kingdom, Hong Kong-China, Qatar, Singapore and Chinese Taipei attend such schools. In contrast, more than two out of three students in Serbia, Tunisia, Colombia and Montenegro attend schools where learning is hindered by student truancy to some extent or lot.

- 68% of students attend schools whose principals reported that learning is not at all or very little hindered by students' disruption of classes. Over 90% of students in Japan, Romania, Indonesia, Albania, Viet Nam and Lithuania attend such schools. In contrast, more than one in two students in Liechtenstein, Brazil, Finland and Portugal attend schools where learning is hindered by this behaviour to some extent or a lot.

■ Figure IV.5.5 ■

School principals' views of how student behaviour affects learning

A	Student truancy
B	Students skipping classes
C	Students arriving late for school
D	Students not attending compulsory school events (e.g. sports day) or excursions
E	Students lacking respect for teachers
F	Disruption of classes by students
G	Student use of alcohol or illegal drugs
H	Students intimidating or bullying other students

	Percentage of students in schools whose principals reported that the following phenomena hindered learning "not at all" or "very little"								Index of student-related factors affecting school climate	Variability in the index S.D.
	A	B	C	D	E	F	G	H		
OECD										
Australia	68	75	66	70	77	68	96	81		1.02
Austria	56	59	60	86	78	63	94	83		0.95
Belgium	70	80	68	79	82	69	94	85		1.04
Canada	39	43	47	82	89	81	80	85		0.85
Chile	83	79	49	81	81	66	88	87		1.24
Czech Republic	84	60	90	85	84	66	98	95		0.96
Denmark	67	79	74	92	81	66	97	95		0.91
Estonia	64	63	70	86	86	66	99	83		0.88
Finland	52	65	49	88	68	41	98	70		0.65
France	62	72	73	90	86	73	88	95		1.01
Germany	80	83	69	88	82	58	98	85		0.69
Greece	69	78	73	89	82	59	92	89		1.05
Hungary	79	78	67	84	83	72	93	94		1.04
Iceland	93	92	84	99	87	64	96	95		0.86
Ireland	53	85	75	79	81	77	89	86		0.91
Israel	53	58	63	84	81	64	92	93		1.04
Italy	65	63	61	92	84	66	97	94		0.94
Japan	90	90	63	88	82	95	98	96		0.94
Korea	72	85	74	87	62	69	93	80		1.13
Luxembourg	73	88	72	92	84	60	99	89		0.67
Mexico	62	67	67	87	90	87	91	87		0.95
Netherlands	75	71	61	89	78	63	89	76		0.70
New Zealand	58	67	69	86	88	77	93	88		0.91
Norway	80	70	75	88	72	50	100	91		0.74
Poland	72	60	74	89	84	70	99	93		0.84
Portugal	67	59	71	95	69	46	92	91		1.07
Slovak Republic	65	28	69	80	68	54	99	98		0.85
Slovenia	46	34	65	75	90	74	94	95		0.80
Spain	80	75	84	88	76	62	96	96		0.96
Sweden	71	60	70	87	78	66	95	90		0.81
Switzerland	82	83	80	91	84	60	91	92		0.76
Turkey	37	46	57	88	79	72	94	91		1.01
United Kingdom	92	94	85	96	90	90	99	97		0.91
United States	60	69	66	95	85	84	83	88		0.94
OECD average	68	69	69	87	81	68	94	89		0.91
Partners										
Albania	80	90	91	96	95	94	98	98		0.93
Argentina	47	65	64	89	81	72	93	88		1.16
Brazil	48	52	57	82	58	40	82	77		1.17
Bulgaria	65	58	73	88	78	65	89	83		1.24
Colombia	33	57	45	82	77	54	81	72		1.03
Costa Rica	35	35	40	70	83	60	75	85		0.98
Croatia	37	25	60	91	58	51	90	87		0.96
Hong Kong-China	91	94	76	91	86	87	99	94		0.88
Indonesia	92	97	94	89	97	94	99	99		0.71
Jordan	45	63	62	80	64	59	90	80		1.38
Kazakhstan	34	38	50	67	52	58	58	57		1.66
Latvia	51	59	59	88	79	69	96	98		0.89
Liechtenstein	93	93	93	93	87	38	93	95		0.63
Lithuania	78	89	89	96	91	90	100	95		0.80
Macao-China	84	93	83	95	79	76	89	83		1.41
Malaysia	57	68	75	72	85	73	96	92		1.11
Montenegro	33	56	78	91	86	89	98	100		0.81
Peru	71	77	65	85	96	89	96	92		0.95
Qatar	91	75	72	82	82	83	96	95		1.15
Romania	76	75	86	92	94	95	98	96		0.93
Russian Federation	38	30	56	78	65	76	80	80		1.44
Serbia	15	33	48	80	74	69	96	92		0.81
Shanghai-China	67	66	73	88	68	61	71	68		1.82
Singapore	91	95	88	95	91	88	100	95		0.97
Chinese Taipei	90	89	79	91	80	76	91	88		1.35
Thailand	61	70	61	86	91	87	93	93		0.84
Tunisia	21	47	36	63	64	53	94	80		0.90
United Arab Emirates	82	82	74	76	80	79	90	89		1.31
Uruguay	54	64	49	83	81	64	94	81		1.26
Viet Nam	62	77	71	86	98	91	99	95		0.69

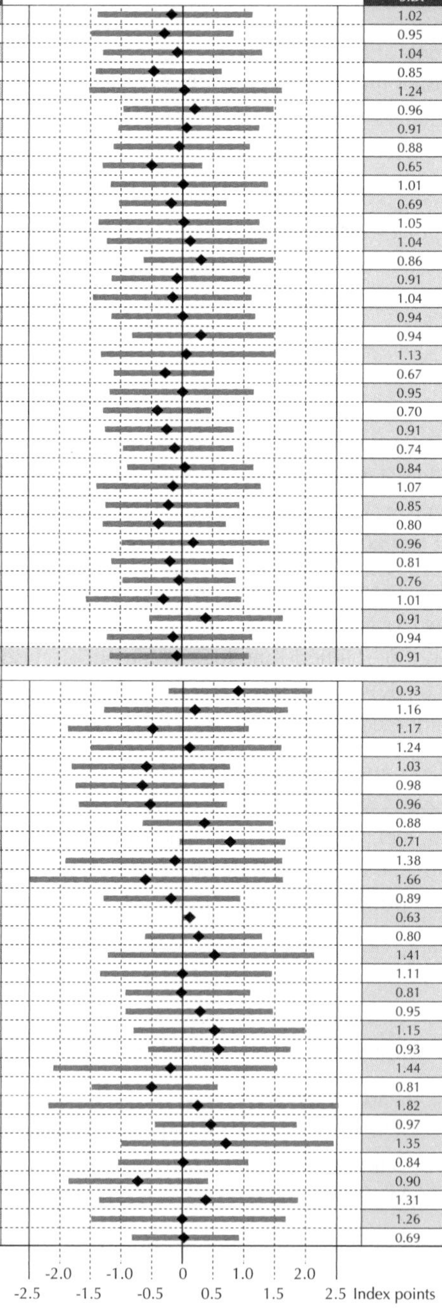

Index of student-related factors affecting school climate: ▬ Range between top and bottom quarters ◆ Average index

Scale: -2.5 -2.0 -1.5 -1.0 -0.5 0 0.5 1.0 1.5 2.0 2.5 Index points

Note: Higher values on the index indicate a better school climate.
Source: OECD, PISA 2012 Database, Table IV.5.8.
StatLink ⧉ http://dx.doi.org/10.1787/888932957365

As shown in Figure IV.5.6, in the countries and economies where more students reported truancy, more principals reported that student truancy hinders learning at school. For example, over 50% of students in Tunisia, Costa Rica, Chile and Uruguay reported that they had arrived late for school at least once in the two weeks prior to the PISA test – a larger proportion than in most other countries and economies. In these countries, 50% of students or more attend schools whose principals reported that students arriving late hinder learning. However, there is variation here as well. In Sweden, Portugal and Bulgaria, where over 50% of students reported that they had arrived late for school, only around 30% of students are in schools whose principals reported that students' late arrival hinders learning (Table IV.5.9).

Principals' reports on the extent to which students' behaviour hinders learning often vary widely within countries and economies, as measured by the standard deviation of the *index of student-related factors affecting school climate*. Variations within countries and economies are smallest in Liechtenstein, Finland, Luxembourg, Germany, Viet Nam, the Netherlands, Indonesia and Norway. By contrast, in Shanghai-China and Kazakhstan there is more variation in disciplinary climate within the country/economy (Figure IV.5.5 and Table IV.5.8).

School principals were also asked to report the extent to which they believe that learning in their schools is hindered by such factors as: students not being encouraged to achieve their full potential; poor teacher-student relations; teachers having to teach students of heterogeneous ability levels within the same class; teachers having to teach students of diverse ethnic backgrounds within the same class; teachers' low expectations of students; teachers not meeting individual students' needs; teacher absenteeism; school staff resisting change; teachers being too strict with students; teacher being late for classes; and teachers not being well-prepared for classes. The responses were combined to create an *index of teacher-related factors affecting school climate* that has a mean of zero and a standard deviation of one in OECD countries. Positive values reflect principals' perceptions that these teacher-related issues hinder learning to a lesser extent, and negative values indicate that school principals believe that these teacher-related issues hinder learning to a greater extent, compared to the OECD average.

In general, principals perceive that teachers being late for class, poor teacher-student relations, teachers not being prepared for class, and teachers being too strict with students do not hinder learning at their schools. On average across OECD countries over 90% of students attend schools whose principals reported that learning is not at all or very little hindered by one of these four behaviours (Figure IV.5.7):

- Virtually all students in Liechtenstein, Lithuania, the Czech Republic, Canada, the Slovak Republic, the United Kingdom, Hungary and the United States attend schools whose principals reported that learning is not at all or very little hindered by teachers being late for class, while fewer than 70% of students in Kazakhstan, Tunisia, Shanghai-China and Uruguay attend such schools.

- Virtually all students in Montenegro, the United Kingdom, Indonesia, Lithuania, Poland and Iceland attend schools whose principals reported that learning is not at all or very little hindered by poor teacher-student relations, while around 80% of students or fewer in Kazakhstan, Shanghai-China, Italy, Tunisia, Jordan, Israel and the Russian Federation attend such schools.

- Virtually all students in Hungary, Liechtenstein, the Czech Republic and Luxembourg attend schools whose principals reported that learning is not at all or very little hindered by teachers not being well-prepared for classes, while 70% of students or fewer in Kazakhstan, Shanghai-China, the Russian Federation and Jordan attend such schools.

- Nearly all students in Lithuania, Denmark, Norway, the United Kingdom and Portugal attend schools whose principals reported that learning is not at all or very little hindered by teachers being too strict with students, while two out of three students, at most, in Kazakhstan, Colombia and Thailand attend such schools.

On average across OECD countries, between 81% and 87% of students attend schools whose principals reported that learning is not at all or very little hindered by teacher absenteeism, teachers' low expectations of students, or teachers having to teach students of diverse ethnic backgrounds within the same class:

- Nearly all students in Hungary, Lithuania, Korea and Portugal attend schools whose principals reported that learning is not at all or very little hindered by teacher absenteeism, while fewer than one in two students in Uruguay, Tunisia and Argentina attends such schools.

- Around 96% or more of students in Liechtenstein, Finland, Hungary, Switzerland, Poland and Luxembourg are in schools whose principals reported that learning is not at all or very little hindered by teachers' low expectations of students, while two out of three students, at most, in Kazakhstan, Tunisia, Brazil, Uruguay, Shanghai-China, Jordan and Chile attend such schools.

■ Figure IV.5.6 ■
Student truancy reported by students and principals

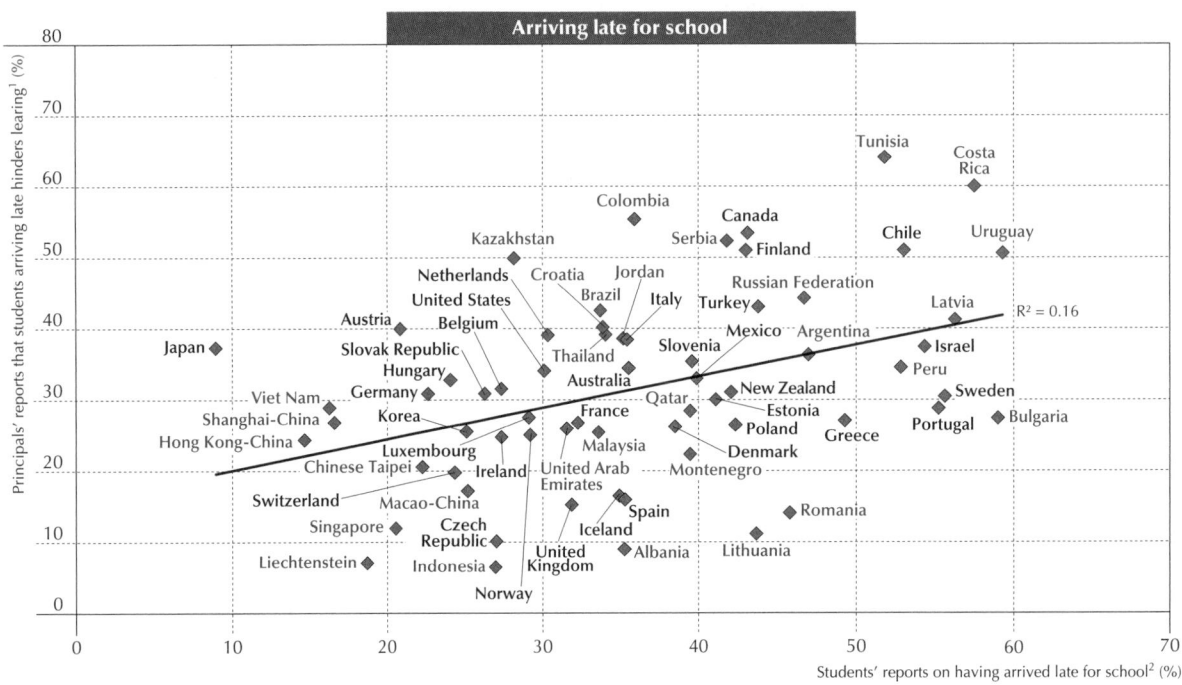

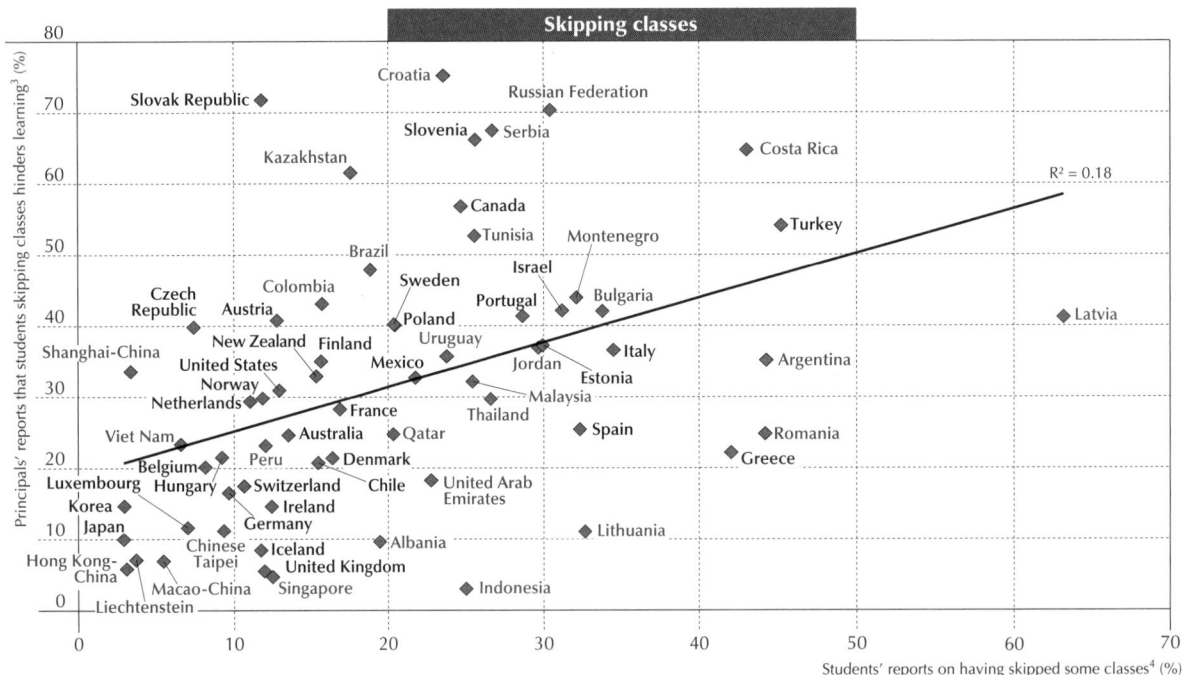

1. The vertical axis in the top figure refers to the percentage of students in schools whose principals reported that students arriving late for school hinders student learning "to some extent" or "a lot".

2. The horizontal axis in the top figure refers to the percentage of students who reported having arrived late for school at least once in the two weeks prior to the PISA test.

3. The vertical axis in the bottom figure refers to the percentage of students in schools whose principals reported that students skipping classes hinders student learning "to some extent" or "a lot".

4. The horizontal axis in the bottom figure refers to the percentage of students who reported having skipped some classes at least once in the two weeks prior to the PISA test.

Source: OECD, PISA 2012 Database, Tables IV.5.1, IV.5.3 and IV.5.9.

StatLink ⟐sL http://dx.doi.org/10.1787/888932957365

- Around 96% of students or more in Poland, Lithuania, Korea and Japan attend schools whose principals reported that learning is not at all or very little hindered by teachers having to teach students of diverse ethnic backgrounds within the same class. By comparison, two out of three students, at most, in Luxembourg, Liechtenstein, Switzerland, Greece, Austria and Malaysia attend such schools.

On average across OECD countries, between 74% and 79% of students attend schools whose principals reported that learning is not at all or very little hindered by students not being encouraged to achieve their full potential, teachers not meeting individual students' needs, or school staff resisting change:

- Around 93% or more of students in Liechtenstein, Lithuania, Malaysia, the United Kingdom, Finland, Poland and Thailand attend schools where learning is not at all or very little hindered by students not being encouraged to achieve their full potential. By comparison, fewer than one in two students in the Netherlands, Tunisia, Uruguay, the Russian Federation and Argentina attends such schools.

- Around 90% of students or more in Indonesia, the Czech Republic, Romania, Liechtenstein, Lithuania, the Slovak Republic, Albania and Poland are in schools where learning is not at all or very little hindered by teachers not meeting individual students' needs, while in the Netherlands, Shanghai-China and Turkey, one in two students, at most, attends such schools.

- Over 90% of students in Indonesia, Lithuania, Hungary, Viet Nam, the Czech Republic, Romania, Albania and Latvia are in schools where learning is not at all or very little hindered by school staff resisting change. By contrast, fewer than 60% of students in Italy, Colombia, Shanghai-China, the Netherlands, Argentina, Chile and France attend such schools.

Of all the indicators considered, teachers having to teach students of heterogeneous ability levels within the same class hinders learning most, according to principals. Across OECD countries on average, 45% of students attend schools whose principals reported that learning is not at all or very little hindered by this factor. More than two out of three students in the United Kingdom, Romania, New Zealand, Mexico, the United States and Ireland attend such schools, while one in four students, at most, in Hong Kong-China, Colombia, Poland, Viet Nam and Uruguay attend such schools.

Principals' reports on the extent to which teachers' behaviour hinders learning often vary widely within countries, as measured by the standard deviation of the *index of teacher-related factors affecting school climate*. Variations within countries and economies is smallest in the Netherlands, Liechtenstein, Germany, Viet Nam, and Luxembourg and largest in Kazakhstan and Shanghai-China (Figure IV.5.7 and Table IV.5.7).

Teacher morale

To examine the level of teacher morale in school, school principals were asked to report whether and to what extent they agree with the following statements: the morale of teachers in this school is high; teachers work with enthusiasm; teachers take pride in the school; and teachers value academic achievement. The responses were combined to create an *index of teacher morale* that has a mean of zero and a standard deviation of one in OECD countries. Positive values indicate principals' perceptions that teacher morale is higher and negative values indicate principals' perceptions that teacher morale is lower than the OECD average.

In general, school principals reported that teachers in their schools value academic achievement, take pride in their schools, work with enthusiasm and have high morale (Figure IV.5.8). On average across OECD countries:

- 97% of students attend schools whose principals agree or strongly agree that teachers value academic achievement. Over 90% of students in all participating countries and economies except Japan attend such schools. In Japan, 76% of students attend such schools.

- 95% of students attend schools whose principals agree or strongly agree that teachers take pride in their school. At least 90% of students in 58 participating countries and economies attend such schools, while between 82% and 89% of students in Tunisia, Greece, Turkey, Macao-China and Hong Kong-China attend such schools.

- 94% of students attend schools whose principals agree or strongly agree that teachers work with enthusiasm. At least 90% of students in 49 participating countries and economies attend such schools, while fewer than 80% of students in Tunisia, Brazil and Italy attend such schools.

- 91% of students attend schools whose principals agree or strongly agree that the morale of teachers in their schools is high. At least 90% of students in 48 participating countries and economies attend such schools, while 80% of students, at most, in Italy, Tunisia, Brazil, Spain, Portugal, Hong Kong-China, Korea and France attend such schools.

■ Figure IV.5.7 ■
School principals' views of how teacher behaviour affects learning

A	Students not being encouraged to achieve their full potential
B	Poor teacher-student relations
C	Teachers having to teach students of heterogeneous ability levels within the same class
D	Teachers having to teach students of diverse ethnic backgrounds (i.e. language, culture) within the same class
E	Teachers' low expectations of students
F	Teachers not meeting individual students' needs
G	Teacher absenteeism
H	Staff resisting change
I	Teachers being too strict with students
J	Teachers being late for classes
K	Teachers not being well prepared for classes

Index of teacher-related factors affecting school climate

— Range between top and bottom quarters

◆ Average index

	Percentage of students in schools whose principals reported that the following phenomena hindered learning "not at all" or "very little"											Variability in the index S.D.
	A	B	C	D	E	F	G	H	I	J	K	
OECD												
Australia	85	91	66	83	81	65	87	64	94	94	90	0.99
Austria	86	94	33	65	85	81	80	73	88	85	93	0.88
Belgium	82	97	42	76	92	84	75	66	86	91	87	0.83
Canada	90	95	62	80	94	78	91	66	92	99	96	0.97
Chile	54	88	29	89	66	68	75	57	86	79	73	1.02
Czech Republic	82	96	40	95	93	96	91	93	91	99	99	0.81
Denmark	86	97	61	88	91	86	85	84	99	95	97	0.94
Estonia	72	97	44	89	94	80	92	80	89	96	98	0.89
Finland	93	95	30	81	97	80	83	78	96	95	96	0.78
France	78	92	26	82	92	66	91	58	77	98	89	0.88
Germany	87	98	41	79	92	85	70	75	93	92	96	0.71
Greece	74	85	31	65	70	80	88	77	87	87	86	1.19
Hungary	71	93	38	88	96	86	99	95	92	99	100	0.89
Iceland	86	99	49	77	91	75	85	69	97	93	89	0.92
Ireland	87	98	67	85	86	82	88	81	89	90	90	0.99
Israel	75	79	45	83	79	73	74	79	86	83	82	1.02
Italy	72	74	64	84	79	76	89	47	80	94	87	0.95
Japan	72	90	28	96	80	74	97	69	81	93	87	0.81
Korea	80	86	39	98	75	74	99	86	84	96	90	1.14
Luxembourg	79	92	40	34	96	83	94	80	91	95	99	0.73
Mexico	61	94	69	92	74	75	83	65	77	80	85	0.99
Netherlands	35	93	41	85	75	29	60	54	89	84	82	0.53
New Zealand	91	96	72	81	86	67	93	73	97	97	94	0.79
Norway	75	90	30	76	82	56	70	74	99	87	94	0.80
Poland	93	99	22	99	96	90	93	89	97	98	97	0.86
Portugal	76	97	32	91	83	88	98	82	98	97	94	0.95
Slovak Republic	79	98	38	85	88	92	92	84	76	99	96	0.76
Slovenia	84	95	31	74	86	83	87	78	90	95	95	0.92
Spain	71	94	34	71	78	76	95	68	85	91	93	0.94
Sweden	79	93	55	70	81	74	79	79	97	97	92	1.02
Switzerland	89	98	44	56	96	87	95	75	94	98	98	0.77
Turkey	68	82	39	95	68	46	89	76	93	93	78	1.12
United Kingdom	93	100	86	95	95	81	84	85	99	99	96	1.05
United States	89	94	68	76	83	76	91	72	95	99	93	1.16
OECD average	79	93	45	81	85	76	87	74	90	93	92	0.91
Partners												
Albania	87	93	57	90	79	91	94	92	86	97	94	1.06
Argentina	48	91	51	94	72	73	41	55	83	77	82	0.93
Brazil	63	81	59	90	61	59	66	64	83	75	72	1.27
Bulgaria	72	83	62	89	79	79	84	88	91	87	79	1.33
Colombia	51	85	20	79	72	67	78	49	66	80	83	1.13
Costa Rica	55	96	39	91	79	67	72	62	87	80	86	0.91
Croatia	76	88	28	85	73	76	92	72	80	88	81	0.87
Hong Kong-China	63	95	18	95	70	55	89	82	94	96	93	0.86
Indonesia	58	99	48	72	94	97	97	98	96	96	97	0.99
Jordan	72	77	45	71	64	70	57	65	75	75	70	1.28
Kazakhstan	55	58	38	80	54	61	57	67	60	58	47	1.61
Latvia	83	93	25	87	86	87	95	91	91	98	94	0.89
Liechtenstein	100	93	57	48	100	93	88	74	93	100	100	0.66
Lithuania	97	99	44	98	93	92	99	95	99	100	96	0.76
Macao-China	62	83	54	93	78	57	84	82	84	87	78	1.31
Malaysia	93	95	45	66	87	87	87	89	86	89	90	0.98
Montenegro	71	100	50	91	78	86	94	84	96	92	97	0.79
Peru	53	92	65	87	81	69	84	65	73	80	77	1.08
Qatar	92	90	50	73	84	85	89	86	92	93	93	1.33
Romania	91	91	79	92	91	94	94	93	92	95	96	0.99
Russian Federation	45	80	44	92	68	64	74	65	76	76	66	1.27
Serbia	64	92	61	92	71	88	93	75	88	85	80	0.98
Shanghai-China	51	66	35	78	63	43	65	50	74	69	55	1.52
Singapore	90	93	52	73	88	77	96	86	94	96	94	1.09
Chinese Taipei	78	85	46	81	79	69	91	79	84	92	85	1.28
Thailand	93	97	26	81	87	86	89	89	66	85	86	0.83
Tunisia	41	76	42	94	59	66	36	61	71	65	88	0.81
United Arab Emirates	79	84	61	76	80	73	80	76	82	87	83	1.38
Uruguay	45	86	25	93	63	63	35	66	89	70	70	1.01
Viet Nam	79	96	22	89	79	80	96	95	77	96	89	0.72

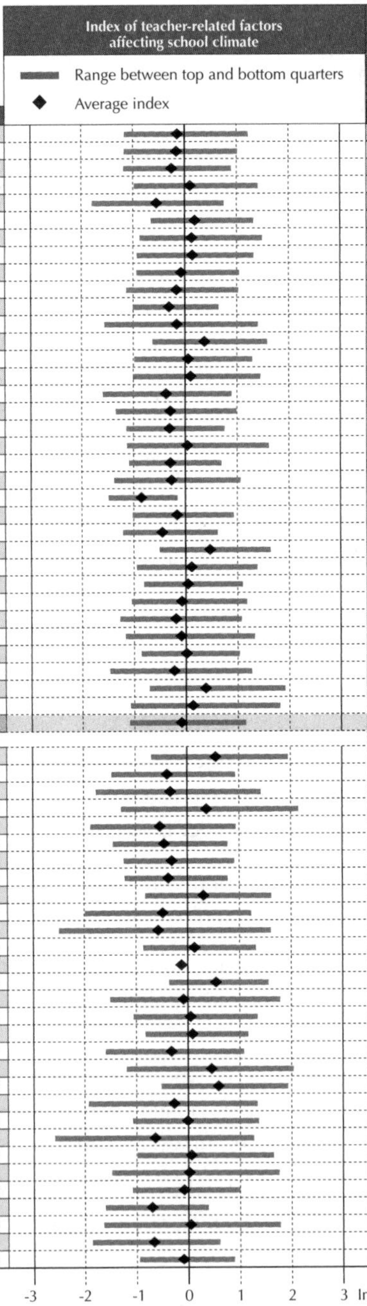

-3 -2 -1 0 1 2 3 Index points

Note: Higher values on the index indicate better school climate.
Source: OECD, PISA 2012 Database, Table IV.5.7.
StatLink ᵐˢᵖ http://dx.doi.org/10.1787/888932957365

■ Figure IV.5.8 ■
Schools' principals views of teacher morale

A	The morale of teachers in this school is high
B	Teachers work with enthusiasm
C	Teachers take pride in this school
D	Teachers value academic achievement

	Percentage of students in schools whose principals reported to "strongly agree" or "agree" with the following statements				Index of teacher morale — Range between top and bottom quarters, ◆ Average index	Variability in the index
	A	B	C	D		S.D.
OECD						
Australia	93	98	98	99		0.90
Austria	100	100	98	99		0.81
Belgium	89	95	95	95		0.90
Canada	90	96	99	100		0.95
Chile	86	91	93	93		0.98
Czech Republic	100	92	98	100		0.78
Denmark	99	99	96	99		0.92
Estonia	98	96	95	100		0.87
Finland	99	97	94	100		0.83
France	80	87	94	92		0.98
Germany	97	99	93	96		0.92
Greece	84	84	85	92		1.09
Hungary	97	88	95	99		0.90
Iceland	98	95	98	99		0.91
Ireland	94	96	99	100		0.96
Israel	95	91	96	97		0.95
Italy	73	80	92	97		0.92
Japan	97	98	90	76		0.94
Korea	79	97	91	93		1.06
Luxembourg	97	100	96	100		0.76
Mexico	95	94	94	95		1.01
Netherlands	97	100	96	95		0.85
New Zealand	94	100	99	100		0.91
Norway	99	98	96	100		0.91
Poland	86	97	99	99		0.90
Portugal	76	89	96	100		0.98
Slovak Republic	98	85	96	98		0.84
Slovenia	90	94	94	99		0.89
Spain	76	85	94	94		0.98
Sweden	97	97	94	100		0.87
Switzerland	96	98	99	97		0.89
Turkey	88	89	87	98		1.06
United Kingdom	91	98	98	100		0.92
United States	81	95	98	100		0.99
OECD average	91	94	95	97		0.92
Partners						
Albania	100	99	100	98		0.78
Argentina	94	92	97	98		0.89
Brazil	76	78	93	94		1.07
Bulgaria	100	94	97	93		0.88
Colombia	96	96	96	98		0.94
Costa Rica	96	93	95	93		1.02
Croatia	93	89	96	95		0.92
Hong Kong-China	78	98	89	100		0.89
Indonesia	100	98	99	100		0.91
Jordan	89	85	93	95		1.08
Kazakhstan	98	97	99	98		0.89
Latvia	100	98	100	99		0.78
Liechtenstein	100	100	100	100		0.70
Lithuania	99	95	97	98		0.83
Macao-China	93	93	89	91		0.83
Malaysia	97	97	97	100		0.95
Montenegro	100	97	97	97		0.94
Peru	94	94	91	96		0.99
Qatar	97	100	100	98		0.87
Romania	94	90	96	97		0.87
Russian Federation	98	92	97	98		0.87
Serbia	92	86	94	94		0.87
Shanghai-China	96	95	99	95		0.95
Singapore	94	98	95	99		0.95
Chinese Taipei	95	98	94	98		0.97
Thailand	90	94	97	96		1.01
Tunisia	74	68	82	92		1.16
United Arab Emirates	96	96	97	100		0.99
Uruguay	91	88	92	93		0.96
Viet Nam	91	98	95	97		0.85

-2.5 -2.0 -1.5 -1.0 -0.5 0 0.5 1.0 1.5 2.0 Index points

Note: Higher values on the index indicate higher teacher morale.
Source: OECD, PISA 2012 Database, Table IV.5.10.
StatLink ᵃˢᵖ http://dx.doi.org/10.1787/888932957365

Principals' reports on the extent to which teachers' behaviour hinders learning often vary widely within countries and economies, as measured by the standard deviation of the *index of teacher morale*. Variations within countries and economies are smallest in Liechtenstein, Luxembourg, Latvia, the Czech Republic, and Albania and largest in Tunisia (Figure IV.5.8 and Table IV.5.10).

INTER-RELATIONSHIPS AMONG LEARNING-ENVIRONMENT INDICATORS AT THE SCHOOL LEVEL

The seven indicators described above are, to a greater or lesser degree, inter-related at the school level. Schools with larger proportions of students who had arrived late for school at least once in the two weeks prior to the assessment also tend to have larger proportions of students who had skipped a class or a day of school at least once during that period. On average across OECD countries, the correlation coefficient is 0.44, and in 49 countries and economies, the correlation is 0.30 or higher. The relationship is particularly strong in Kazakhstan, Luxembourg, Macao-China, Poland, Romania, Bulgaria, Belgium, Austria, Serbia and Croatia, where the correlation coefficient is 0.60 or higher (Table IV.5.11).

In virtually all school systems, schools with more negative disciplinary climates tend to have a higher incidence of student truancy (arriving late for school or skipping a day or a class). This relationship is especially strong in Croatia, Korea, Chinese Taipei, Kazakhstan, Hungary, Thailand, Slovenia, the Slovak Republic, Bulgaria and New Zealand, where the correlation between the proportion of students who had skipped a day or a class at least once in the previous two weeks and the school's average *index of disciplinary climate* is between -0.55 and -0.42. In these countries and economies, there is also a strong relationship between the percentage of students who had arrived late for school at least once in the two weeks prior to the PISA test and that index (correlation is between -0.50 and -0.28) (Figure IV.5.9).

The relationship between student truancy and teacher-student relations seems more complex. In 28 countries and economies, schools with more negative teacher-student relations tend to be those with larger proportions of students who skipped a day or a class. By contrast, in Liechtenstein, Uruguay, Macao-China, Bulgaria, Peru, Italy and Luxembourg, there is a weak but positive relationship between these two factors. Similarly, in 27 countries and economies, schools with more negative teacher-student relations also tend to be those where more students arrived late for school; but in Malaysia, Italy, Luxembourg, Montenegro and Macao-China, a weak and opposite relationship is observed (Figure IV.5.9).

Schools whose principals reported that teachers' behaviour negatively affects learning to a great extent also tend to be those whose principals reported that their teachers' morale is low. On average across OECD countries, the correlation coefficient between the *index of teacher-related factors affecting school climate* and the *index of teacher morale* is 0.44. This relationship is particularly strong in Liechtenstein, Uruguay, Chile, the Slovak Republic, Hong Kong-China, Denmark, Mexico, Sweden, Argentina, Brazil, Thailand, Serbia, Costa Rica, the United States and Luxembourg, where the correlation coefficient is 0.50 or higher (Table IV.5.11).

In 45 countries and economies, schools with a student population that is predominantly socio-economically disadvantaged tend to have a more negative disciplinary climate. The correlation coefficient between the average student socio-economic status in a school and the school average *index of disciplinary climate* is over 0.40 in Chinese Taipei, Slovenia, Hungary, Croatia, Japan, Singapore, the United States, New Zealand and Shanghai-China. However, the opposite is observed in Tunisia, Indonesia and Viet Nam (Table IV.5.12). By contrast, the relationship between the average student socio-economic status in a school and the school average *index of teacher-student relations* varies, depending on the countries and economies. In 14 countries and economies, schools where students reported more positive relations with teachers are those with more advantaged student populations, while in 30 countries and economies, schools where students reported more positive relations with teachers are those with more disadvantaged student populations (Table IV.5.12).

On average across OECD countries as shown in Figure IV.5.10, school size, school location, school type, and the incidence of teacher shortage are related to a school's disciplinary climate, even after accounting for school features, such as the average socio-economic status of a school's student population, school size, school location, whether the school is public or private, and educational resources. Across OECD countries, schools with more advantaged student populations tend to have a more positive disciplinary climate; schools whose classes are larger or smaller than the national average tend to have a more positive disciplinary climate; schools located in cities tend to have a more negative disciplinary climate than schools located in towns; private schools tend to have a more positive disciplinary climate than public schools; schools whose principals reported more teacher shortage tend to have a more negative disciplinary climate; and schools with more socio-economically heterogeneous student populations tend to have a more negative disciplinary climate. On average across OECD countries, some 18% of the variation in school disciplinary climate is accounted for by these schools features (Table IV.5.13).

■ Figure IV.5.9 ■
Relationship between student truancy and school climate

	Correlation between:			
	Percentage of students who had arrived late for school at least once in the two weeks prior to the PISA test (at the school level) and...		Percentage of students who had skipped a day or a class at least once in the two weeks prior to the PISA test (at the school level) and...	
	School average index of teacher-student relations	School average index of disciplinary climate	School average index of teacher-student relations	School average index of disciplinary climate
Croatia	-0.17	-0.35	-0.03	-0.55
Korea	-0.32	-0.48	-0.31	-0.51
Chinese Taipei	-0.19	-0.33	-0.22	-0.49
Kazakhstan	-0.46	-0.47	-0.38	-0.49
Hungary	-0.09	-0.42	-0.05	-0.48
Thailand	-0.03	-0.50	-0.03	-0.46
Slovenia	-0.23	-0.35	-0.19	-0.45
Slovak Republic	-0.08	-0.37	0.00	-0.44
Bulgaria	0.11	-0.35	0.16	-0.42
New Zealand	-0.02	-0.28	-0.11	-0.42
France	0.00	-0.33	-0.05	-0.39
Uruguay	-0.06	-0.24	0.18	-0.37
United Arab Emirates	-0.04	-0.24	-0.09	-0.37
Lithuania	-0.23	-0.29	-0.34	-0.37
United States	-0.25	-0.34	-0.34	-0.36
Japan	-0.15	-0.36	-0.13	-0.35
Macao-China	0.05	-0.49	0.18	-0.35
Argentina	-0.02	-0.16	-0.03	-0.32
Belgium	0.08	-0.24	0.09	-0.31
Poland	-0.33	-0.33	-0.25	-0.30
Serbia	-0.01	-0.28	0.09	-0.30
Shanghai-China	-0.21	-0.44	-0.19	-0.29
Tunisia	-0.13	-0.17	0.02	-0.28
Greece	-0.29	-0.21	-0.20	-0.28
Switzerland	-0.30	-0.26	-0.37	-0.28
Russian Federation	-0.29	-0.35	-0.17	-0.28
Norway	-0.03	-0.14	-0.24	-0.28
Romania	0.09	-0.14	0.04	-0.27
Jordan	0.02	-0.29	-0.07	-0.27
Costa Rica	-0.16	-0.24	-0.06	-0.27
Sweden	-0.13	-0.12	-0.13	-0.26
Montenegro	0.06	-0.43	-0.08	-0.25
Iceland	-0.05	-0.12	-0.23	-0.25
Luxembourg	0.10	-0.20	0.08	-0.25
Portugal	-0.37	-0.20	-0.34	-0.24
Mexico	-0.22	-0.13	-0.17	-0.22
Colombia	-0.15	-0.26	-0.09	-0.22
Ireland	0.07	-0.32	-0.06	-0.22
Peru	0.04	-0.09	0.12	-0.22
Indonesia	0.05	-0.12	-0.08	-0.22
Germany	-0.06	-0.20	-0.03	-0.22
Chile	-0.07	-0.29	-0.22	-0.21
Singapore	-0.19	-0.40	-0.12	-0.20
Australia	-0.09	-0.15	-0.22	-0.20
Albania	-0.04	-0.22	-0.14	-0.20
Malaysia	0.26	-0.19	-0.12	-0.20
Denmark	-0.06	-0.25	-0.06	-0.19
Italy	0.14	-0.21	0.12	-0.18
Estonia	-0.04	-0.06	-0.21	-0.17
United Kingdom	-0.11	-0.07	0.01	-0.16
Brazil	-0.03	-0.05	-0.04	-0.15
Austria	-0.23	-0.27	-0.30	-0.14
Hong Kong-China	-0.04	-0.17	0.02	-0.13
Finland	-0.13	-0.29	-0.20	-0.13
Canada	-0.23	-0.13	-0.17	-0.12
Czech Republic	-0.25	-0.26	-0.16	-0.11
Viet Nam	0.02	-0.19	0.09	-0.10
Latvia	-0.09	-0.34	-0.02	-0.09
Netherlands	-0.15	-0.29	-0.21	-0.09
Israel	-0.05	0.01	-0.08	-0.08
Spain	-0.19	-0.13	0.01	-0.08
Turkey	0.10	-0.29	0.11	-0.01
Qatar	-0.25	-0.29	-0.12	-0.01
Liechtenstein	0.23	-0.52	0.28	0.11
OECD average	-0.12	-0.24	-0.14	-0.25

Note: Statistically significant correlations at the 5% level (p < 0.05) are shaded.
Countries and economies are ranked in ascending order of the correlation between students who had skipped a day or a class and school disciplinary climate.
Source: OECD, PISA 2012 Database, Table IV.5.11.
StatLink ᴍ🔢🔗 http://dx.doi.org/10.1787/888932957365

■ Figure IV.5.10 ■

Relationship between disciplinary climate and various school features

	School average PISA index of economic, social and cultural status (ESCS) (1 unit increase)	School size (per 100 students)	School size (per 100 students) (squared)	School in a small town or village (15 000 or fewer people)	School in a city (100 000 or more people)	Private school	School is pressured by parents to meet high academic standards	Index of quality of physical infrastructure (1 unit increase)	Index of quality of schools' educational resources (1 unit increase)	Index of teacher shortage (1 unit increase)	Socio-economic heterogeneity of school intake (standard deviation of ESCS within the school)	Academic heterogeneity of school intake (standard deviation of mathematics performance within the school)
OECD												
Australia	0.25					0.13				-0.04		
Austria	0.29	0.04										
Belgium	0.24					0.20						
Canada		-0.04	0.002									
Chile	0.10											
Czech Republic	0.46											
Denmark	0.31					0.31						0.00
Estonia									0.09	-0.07		
Finland	0.21				-0.08	0.28						
France	0.41											
Germany	0.18											
Greece	0.23											
Hungary	0.39		-0.002				0.28					
Iceland		0.02	-0.005	0.11	0.12		0.25	0.04	-0.03	-0.04	-0.28	
Ireland	0.30					0.16						
Israel												
Italy	0.31				-0.10			0.09				
Japan	0.66					-0.24		0.11	0.07			-0.01
Korea	0.37	-0.10	0.004	-0.47		0.16		0.12				-0.01
Luxembourg	-0.05		0.000	0.09		0.13	-0.12	-0.07	0.09	0.02	-0.83	0.01
Mexico		0.01			-0.10						-0.16	
Netherlands					-0.19						-0.08	
New Zealand	0.35											
Norway										0.10	-0.49	
Poland		-0.12	0.013									
Portugal					-0.16	0.31				0.08		
Slovak Republic	0.40											
Slovenia	0.54					0.10		-0.05	0.03		0.05	0.00
Spain	0.11					0.18		-0.07	0.09			
Sweden	0.27											
Switzerland					-0.16						-0.35	
Turkey	0.19										0.32	
United Kingdom												
United States	0.28											
OECD average	0.21	-0.02	0.001		-0.04	0.07				-0.02	-0.12	
Partners												
Argentina		-0.06	0.003				0.14					
Brazil						0.20	0.08					
Bulgaria		0.08	-0.004		-0.17					-0.11	-0.39	
Colombia												
Costa Rica						0.50						
Croatia	0.66	0.13	-0.008		-0.29							
Hong Kong-China											-0.55	-0.01
Indonesia											-0.31	
Jordan	-0.23					0.32				-0.07	-0.59	
Kazakhstan	0.38											
Latvia			0.007									
Lithuania	0.36											
Macao-China	0.21	0.03	-0.001				-0.10	0.00	-0.05	-0.04	-1.20	-0.01
Malaysia	0.15										0.11	-0.01
Montenegro	0.25	-0.06	0.003	0.02	-0.23		0.14	-0.02	0.04	-0.04	1.11	-0.01
Peru												
Qatar	0.05	0.00	0.000	-0.05	-0.13	0.45	0.20	-0.03	-0.02	-0.03	-0.28	
Romania	0.47				-0.16					0.08		
Russian Federation	0.30	-0.06	0.003	0.25								
Serbia	0.32										0.75	
Shanghai-China	0.39											
Singapore	0.34	0.03	-0.001				0.12	0.01	0.06	-0.02	-0.25	0.00
Chinese Taipei	0.46	-0.01										
Thailand				0.14								
Tunisia												
United Arab Emirates	0.15					0.20						
Uruguay	0.15										0.44	0.00
Viet Nam			0.001									

Notes: This figure shows only statistically significant regression coefficients at the 5% level (p < 0.05). Negative statistically significant correlations are shaded in grey; positive statistically significant correlations are shaded in blue.
These results are based on a model of regression of the school average disciplinary climate on all variables in this figure.
Source: OECD, PISA 2012 Database, Table IV.5.13.

StatLink ᴍˢᴾ http://dx.doi.org/10.1787/888932957365

Across countries and economies, the extent to which the variation in school disciplinary climate is accounted for by these school features differs. In Macao-China, Montenegro, Qatar, Japan, Chinese Taipei, Korea and Luxembourg, 35% or more of the variation is explained by these school features, while less than 8% of the variation is explained in Mexico, Estonia, Peru, Brazil, Finland and Poland (Table IV.5.13). In addition, depending on the country and economy, school disciplinary climate is related to a different set of school features, as shown in Figure IV.5.10.

STUDENT AND SCHOOL FEATURES RELATED TO THE LIKELIHOOD OF STUDENTS ARRIVING LATE FOR SCHOOL

PISA 2012 results show that, in all participating countries and economies, those students who had arrived late for school at least once in the two weeks prior to the assessment were also more likely to have skipped a class or day of school at least once during the same period. On average across OECD countries, 14 out of 100 students who had not arrived late for school in the previous two weeks would have skipped a class or day of school during the same period, while 38 out of 100 students who had arrived late for school in the previous two weeks would have also skipped a class or day of school during the same period (Table IV.5.14). Since students who arrive late for school are more likely to skip a class or a day, this section focuses on "arriving late for school" and examines which students are more likely to arrive late for school and the profile of the schools that these students are more likely to attend.

As shown in Figure IV.5.11a, boys are more likely than girls to have reported that they had arrived late at least once in the two weeks prior to the PISA test. In Japan, Thailand, Lithuania, Chinese Taipei, Shanghai-China, Poland, Viet Nam and Iceland, boys are between 25% and 40% more likely than girls to have arrived late for school. Students with an immigrant background are more likely than students without an immigrant background to have reported that they had arrived late at least once in the two weeks prior to the PISA test. As shown in Figure IV.5.11b, in Austria, Brazil, Belgium, Germany, France and Spain, students with an immigrant background are between 53% and 93% more likely than students wihout an immigrant background to have arrived late for school. In Finland, Switzerland, the Netherlands, Malaysia, Luxembourg, Lithuania, Denmark and Estonia, students with an immigrant background are over 30% more likely than students wihout an immigrant background to have arrived late for school (Table IV.5.15).

In another analysis, the various socio-economic and demographic background characteristics of students and schools (i.e. socio-economic status of students, gender, immigrant and language background, socio-economic profile of the school, school size and school location), as well as the type of school and the learning environment in the school are examined all together. On average across OECD countries, disadvantaged students, boys, and students with an immigrant background are more likely to have arrived late for school. Also, students in schools of average size (for the country or economy concerned), in schools located in cities, in schools with more negative disciplinary climates, and in schools with more negative teacher-student relations are more likely to have arrived late for school, while students in schools located in rural areas are less likely to have arrived late (Table IV.5.16).

Across countries and economies, the relationships between these student and school features and the likelihood of students arriving late vary; but, in most countries and economies, students' gender and average school disciplinary climate are consistently related to a higher likelihood of students' arriving late. In 32 countries and economies, boys are more likely to arrive late, and in 39 countries and economies students in schools with more negative disciplinary climates are more likely to arrive late for school, even after accounting for all these other student and school features (Table IV.5.16).

TRENDS IN SCHOOL CLIMATE AND STUDENT TRUANCY SINCE PISA 2003

Overall comparisons between PISA 2003 and PISA 2012 data suggest that, with the exception of a few countries and economies, student reports of teacher-student relations have improved. Comparisons also show that the disciplinary climate has improved in most of these countries and economies, and that students in 2012 are less likely to attend schools whose principal reported that student- and teacher-related factors negatively affect the learning climate.

According to students' reports, teacher-student relations improved between 2003 and 2012 in all but one country, Tunisia, where they remained stable. On average across OECD countries, the share of students who agreed or strongly agreed that they get along with most teachers increased by 12 percentage points during the period and increased by more than ten percentage points in 22 countries and economies.[1] For example, on average across OECD countries, seven in ten students reported getting along well with most teachers in 2003, while more than eight in ten did so in 2012.

■ Figure IV.5.11a ■

Students arriving late for school, by gender

Increased likelihood that boys reported having arrived late at least once in the two weeks prior to the PISA test

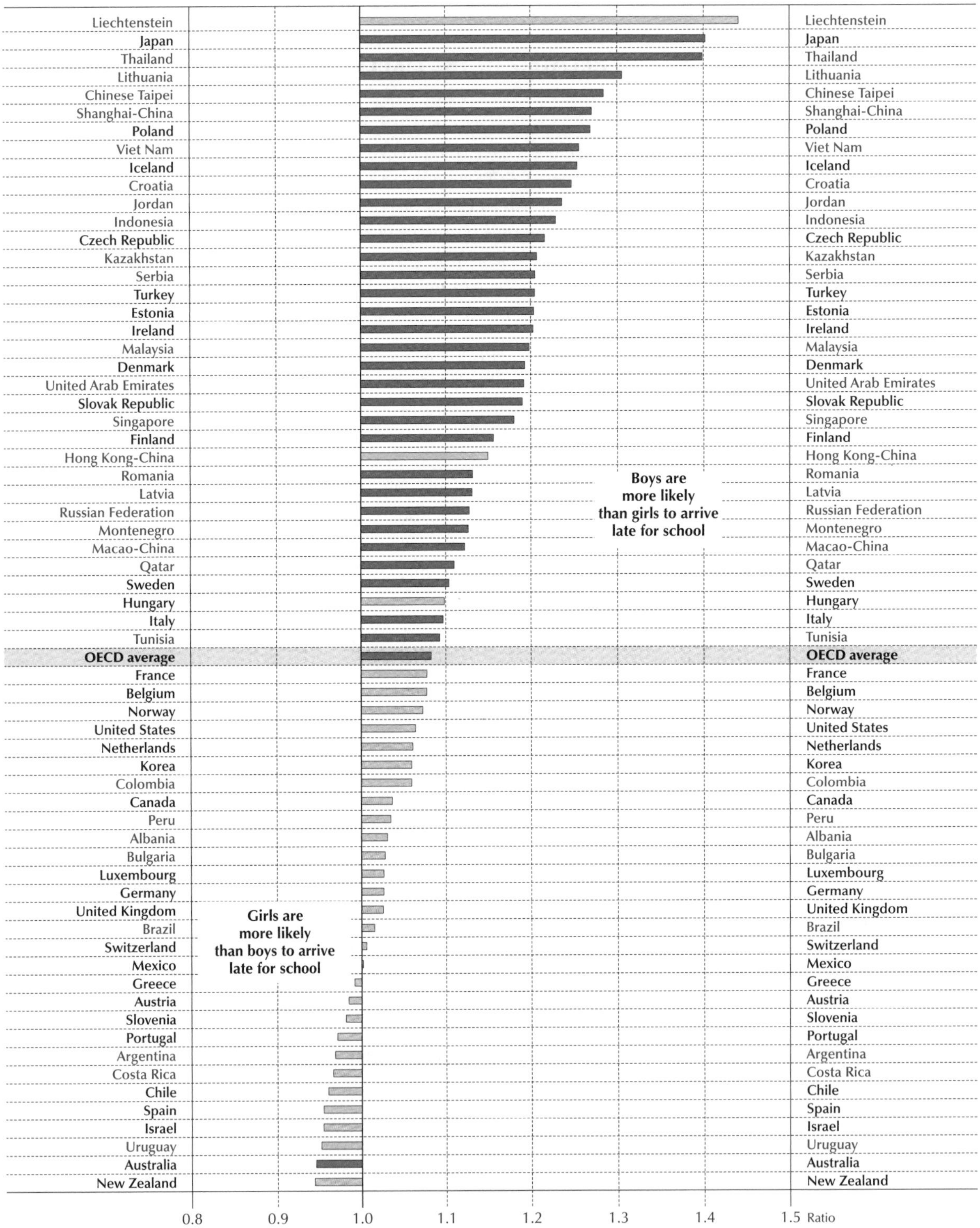

Liechtenstein	
Japan	
Thailand	
Lithuania	
Chinese Taipei	
Shanghai-China	
Poland	
Viet Nam	
Iceland	
Croatia	
Jordan	
Indonesia	
Czech Republic	
Kazakhstan	
Serbia	
Turkey	
Estonia	
Ireland	
Malaysia	
Denmark	
United Arab Emirates	
Slovak Republic	
Singapore	
Finland	
Hong Kong-China	
Romania	**Boys are more likely than girls to arrive late for school**
Latvia	
Russian Federation	
Montenegro	
Macao-China	
Qatar	
Sweden	
Hungary	
Italy	
Tunisia	
OECD average	
France	
Belgium	
Norway	
United States	
Netherlands	
Korea	
Colombia	
Canada	
Peru	
Albania	
Bulgaria	
Luxembourg	
Germany	
United Kingdom	**Girls are more likely than boys to arrive late for school**
Brazil	
Switzerland	
Mexico	
Greece	
Austria	
Slovenia	
Portugal	
Argentina	
Costa Rica	
Chile	
Spain	
Israel	
Uruguay	
Australia	
New Zealand	

0.8 0.9 1.0 1.1 1.2 1.3 1.4 1.5 Ratio

Note: Statistically significant differences between boys and girls are marked in a darker tone.
Countries and economies are ranked in descending order of the increased likelihood of boys to arrive late with respect to girls.
Source: OECD, PISA 2012 Database, Table IV.5.15.
StatLink ᎆᏚᎲ http://dx.doi.org/10.1787/888932957365

■ Figure IV.5.11b ■

Students arriving late for school, by students with and without immigrant backgrounds

Increased likelihood that students with an immigrant background reported having arrived late
at least once in the two weeks prior to the PISA test

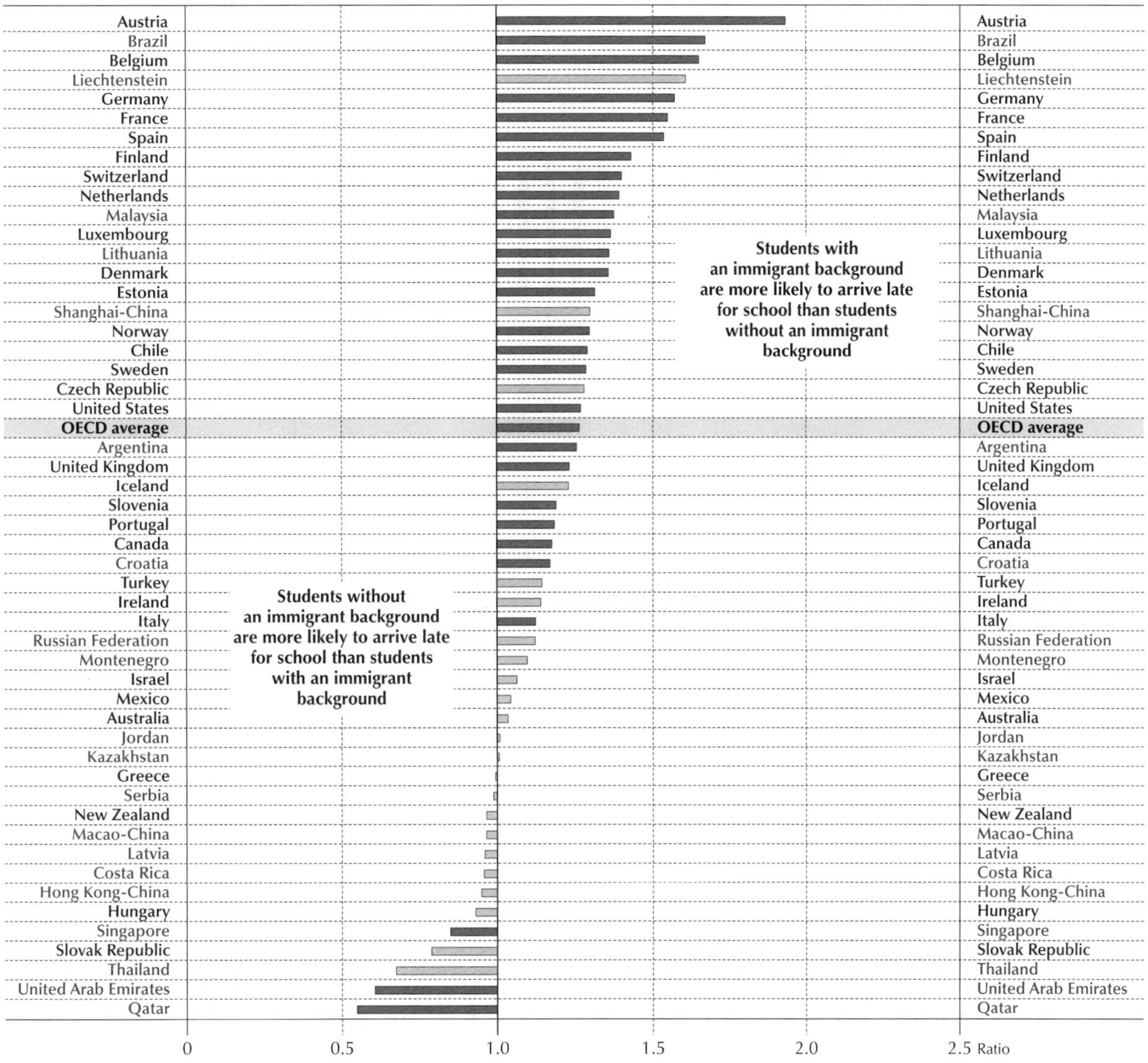

Austria		Austria
Brazil		Brazil
Belgium		Belgium
Liechtenstein		Liechtenstein
Germany		Germany
France		France
Spain		Spain
Finland		Finland
Switzerland		Switzerland
Netherlands		Netherlands
Malaysia		Malaysia
Luxembourg		Luxembourg
Lithuania	Students with an immigrant background are more likely to arrive late for school than students without an immigrant background	Lithuania
Denmark		Denmark
Estonia		Estonia
Shanghai-China		Shanghai-China
Norway		Norway
Chile		Chile
Sweden		Sweden
Czech Republic		Czech Republic
United States		United States
OECD average		**OECD average**
Argentina		Argentina
United Kingdom		United Kingdom
Iceland		Iceland
Slovenia		Slovenia
Portugal		Portugal
Canada		Canada
Croatia		Croatia
Turkey		Turkey
Ireland	Students without an immigrant background are more likely to arrive late for school than students with an immigrant background	Ireland
Italy		Italy
Russian Federation		Russian Federation
Montenegro		Montenegro
Israel		Israel
Mexico		Mexico
Australia		Australia
Jordan		Jordan
Kazakhstan		Kazakhstan
Greece		Greece
Serbia		Serbia
New Zealand		New Zealand
Macao-China		Macao-China
Latvia		Latvia
Costa Rica		Costa Rica
Hong Kong-China		Hong Kong-China
Hungary		Hungary
Singapore		Singapore
Slovak Republic		Slovak Republic
Thailand		Thailand
United Arab Emirates		United Arab Emirates
Qatar		Qatar

0   0.5   1.0   1.5   2.0   2.5 Ratio

Note: Statistically significant differences between students with and without an immigrant background are marked in a darker tone.
Countries and economies are ranked in descending order of the increased likelihood of students with an immigrant background to arrive late with respect to students without an immigrant background.
Source: OECD, PISA 2012 Database, Table IV.5.15.
StatLink ᵐˢᵖ http://dx.doi.org/10.1787/888932957365

Similar increases signalling better teacher-student relations were observed among students who reported that teachers are interested in their well-being, that teachers listen to what they have to say, that teachers will provide extra help if needed, and that teachers treat students fairly. Improvements in teacher-student relations are notable in Luxembourg, Iceland, Japan and the Russian Federation, where the likelihood of students responding favourably to all these questions increased and the *index of teacher-student relations* improved by at least 0.5 index points (Figure IV.5.12 and Table IV.5.17).

Disciplinary climate also shows signs of improvement on average across OECD countries and across 27 individual countries and economies. For example, on average across OECD countries, in 2003, 32% of students reported that the teacher had to wait a long time for students to quiet down in every class or most classes; by 2012, this percentage had dropped to 28%.

■ Figure IV.5.12 ■

Change between PISA 2003 and PISA 2012 in teacher-student relations

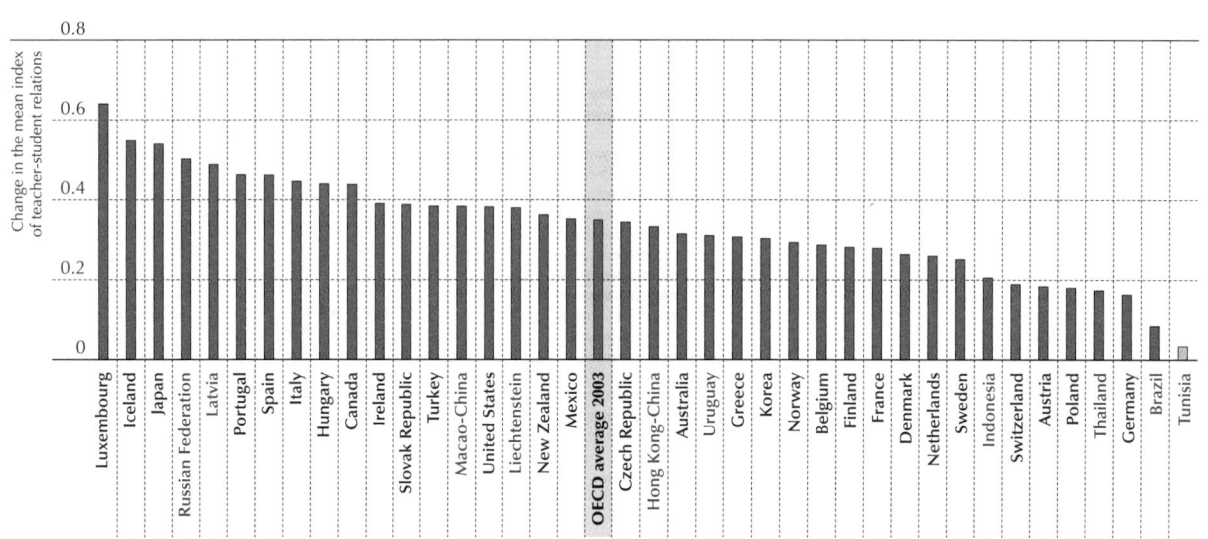

Notes: Statistically significant changes between PISA 2003 and PISA 2012 are marked in a darker tone.
Higher values on the index indicate better teacher-student relations.
Only countries and economies with comparable data from PISA 2003 and PISA 2012 are shown.
OECD average 2003 compares only OECD countries with comparable indices of teacher-student relations since 2003.
Countries are ranked in descending order of the change in index of teacher-student relations (2012 - 2003).
Source: OECD, PISA 2012 Database, Table IV.5.17.
StatLink ᵃᵢˢ⫶ http://dx.doi.org/10.1787/888932957365

■ Figure IV.5.13 ■

Change between PISA 2003 and PISA 2012 in disciplinary climate

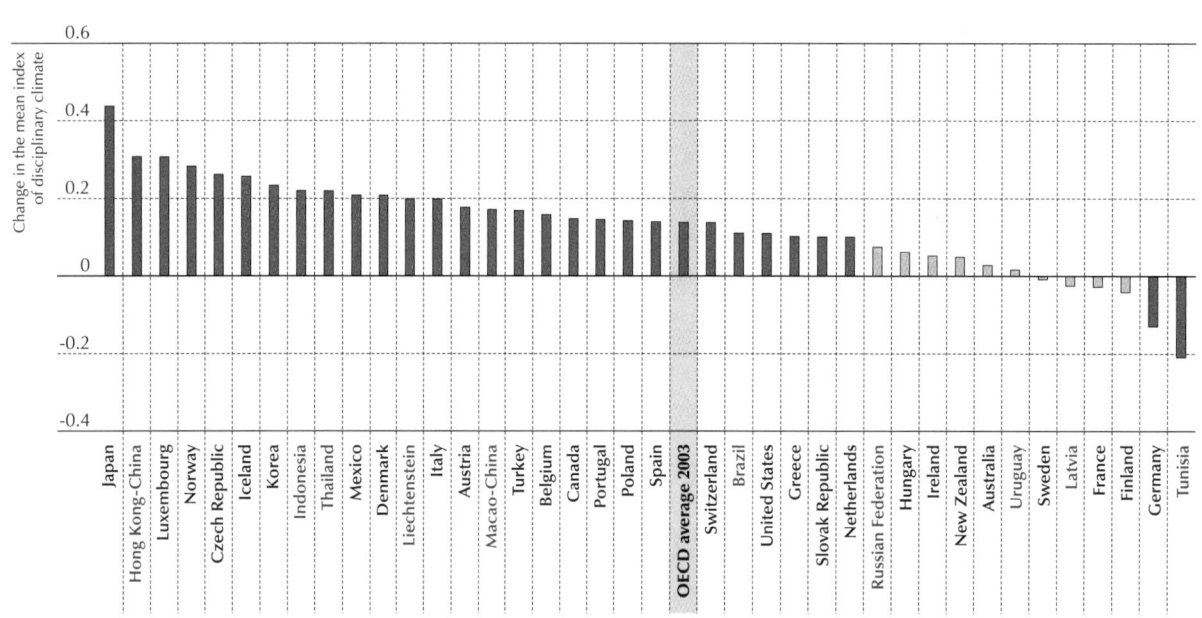

Notes: Statistically significant changes between PISA 2003 and PISA 2012 are marked in a darker tone.
Higher values on the index indicate better disciplinary climate.
Only countries and economies with comparable data from PISA 2003 and PISA 2012 are shown.
OECD average 2003 compares only OECD countries with comparable indices of disciplinary climate since 2003.
Countries and economies are ranked in descending order of the change in the index of disciplinary climate (2012 - 2003).
Source: OECD, PISA 2012 Database, Table IV.5.18.
StatLink ᵃᵢˢ⫶ http://dx.doi.org/10.1787/888932957365

As a result, the *index of disciplinary climate* improved by 0.14 index points. Disciplinary climate improved the most in Japan, Hong Kong-China, Luxembourg, Norway, the Czech Republic and Iceland: in these countries and economies, the increase in the *index of disciplinary climate* between 2003 and 2012 was significant and greater than 0.25 index points. In Japan, for example, students in 2012 were 10 percentage points more likely than students in 2003 to report that never or only in some lessons do students not listen to what the teacher says. In Luxembourg, students in 2012 were over 10 percentage points more likely than their counterparts in 2003 to report that never, or only in some lessons, is there is noise and disorder, that the teacher has to wait a long time for students to quiet down, or that students cannot work well. By contrast, students' reports on disciplinary climate declined in Tunisia and Germany during the period. In Germany, students in 2012 were significantly more likely to report that students do not listen to what the teacher says in every or in most mathematics lessons (36% so reported) than their peers were in 2003 (22% reported so) (Figure IV.5.13 and Table IV.5.18). See Box IV.3.3 for a description on how indices like the *index of disciplinary climate* are compared across PISA assessments.

Students in 2012 were less likely than students in 2003 to attend schools whose principal reported that teacher-related factors negatively affect learning. On average across OECD countries with comparable data, for example, students are 11 percentage points more likely to attend a school whose principal reported that teachers not meeting individual students' needs hinders learning very little or not at all. Similarly, students in 2012 were less likely to attend schools whose principal reported that teachers' low expectations of students, poor teacher-student relations or teacher absenteeism hinders learning. The decrease in the degree to which teacher-related factors negatively affect student learning is most apparent in Indonesia, Macao-China, Tunisia, Turkey and Portugal, where the *index of teacher-related factors affecting school climate* increased the most, by more than 0.75 points, between 2003 and 2012. By contrast, in Belgium and the Slovak Republic teacher-related factors hindered learning more in 2012 than in 2003 as the *index of teacher-related factors affecting school climate* fell during the period (Table IV.5.19).

Similarly, students in 2012 were also less likely to attend schools whose principal reported that there are more student-related factors that hinder learning. On average across OECD countries with comparable data, students in 2012 were eight percentage points more likely than their peers in 2003 to attend schools whose principal reported that the disruption of classes by students hinders learning very little or not at all. The decrease in reports that student-related factors hinder learning is most pronounced in Indonesia, Macao-China, the Russian Federation and Liechtenstein, where the *index of student-related factors affecting school climate* increased by more than 0.75 points. By contrast, student-related factors that affect the learning climate seem to have declined, as scores on the *index of student-related factors affecting school climate* fell significantly – indicating worse learning environments – in Korea, Uruguay, Belgium, the Slovak Republic and Finland (Table IV.5.20).

Consistent with the above-mentioned general trend towards more favourable learning environments, on average across OECD countries, students in 2012 were slightly less likely to report that they had arrived late for school than students were in 2003. In 15 countries and economies, fewer students in 2012 than in 2003 reported that they had arrived late in the two weeks prior to the PISA test. Improvements in punctuality are most marked in the Netherlands and Iceland, where the percentage of students who reported that they had not arrived late increased by 14 and 11 percentage points, respectively. The incidence of tardiness increased, however, in nine countries and economies, particularly in Turkey and Tunisia, where the percentage of students who reported that they had arrived late at least once in the two weeks prior to the test increased by more than 10 percentage points over the period. In Turkey, for example, 27% of students in 2003 reported that they had arrived late at least once in the previous two weeks, while in 2012, 44% of students reported so (Table IV.5.22).

In both Tunisia and Turkey, as well as in Latvia, Sweden, Uruguay, Poland and the Russian Federation, the share of students attending schools where the majority of students reported that they had arrived late increased by more than 10 percentage points between 2003 and 2012, thus showing an increase in the concentration of late-arriving students in particular schools (Table IV.5.23).

Note

1. This average trend corresponds to OECD countries with comparable data in PISA 2003 and PISA 2012. Other global averages reported in this section also correspond to the average across OECD countries with comparable data in PISA 2003 and PISA 2012. Although both PISA 2003 and PISA 2012 included questions referring to the learning climate, not all indicators have comparable data. In 2003, for example, questionnaires did not include questions on student truancy, skipping school. Thus, it is not possible to observe trends for these indicators.

References

Birch, S. and **G. Ladd** (1998), "Children's Interpersonal Behaviors and the Teacher-Child Relationship", *Developmental Psychology,* Vol. 34, No. 5, pp. 934-46.

Caldas, S.J. (1993), "Reexamination of Input and Process Factor Effects on Public School Achievement", *The Journal of Educational Research*, Vol. 86, No. 4, pp. 206-14.

Crosnoe, R., M. Johnson and **G. Elder** (2004), "Intergenerational Bonding in School: The Behavioral and Contextual Correlates of Student-Teacher Relationships", *Sociology of Education*, Vol. 77, No. 1, pp. 60-81.

Fantuzzo, J., S. Grim and **H. Hazan** (2005), "Project Start: An Evaluation of a Community-Wide School-Based Intervention to Reduce Truancy", *Psychology in the Schools*, Vol. 42, No. 6, pp. 657-67.

Gamoran, A. (1993), "Alternative Uses of Ability Grouping in Secondary Schools: Can We Bring High-Quality Instruction to Low-Ability Classes?", *American Journal of Education,* Vol. 102, No. 1, pp. 1-12.

Gamoran, A. and **M. Nystrand** (1992), "Taking Students Seriously", in F. Newman (ed.), *Student Engagement and Achievement in American Secondary Schools*, Teachers College Press, New York.

Hallfors, D., et al. (2002), "Truancy, Grade Point Average, and Sexual Activity: A Meta-Analysis of Risk Indicators for Youth Substance Use", *Journal of School Health*, Vol. 72, No. 5, pp. 205-11.

Henry, K.L. (2007), "Who's Skipping School: Characteristics of Truants in 8th and 10th Grade", *Journal of School Health*, Vol. 77, No. 1, pp. 29-35.

Jennings, P.A. and **M.T. Greenberg** (2009), "The Prosocial Classroom: Teacher Social and Emotional Competence in Relation to Student and Classroom Outcomes", *Review of Educational Research*, Vol. 79, No. 1, pp. 491-525.

Lamdin, D.J. (1996), "Evidence of Student Attendance as an Independent Variable in Education Production Functions", *The Journal of Educational Research*, Vol. 89, No. 3, pp. 155-62.

OECD (2013), *PISA 2012 Assessment and Analytical Framework: Mathematics, Reading, Science, Problem Solving and Financial Literacy*, PISA, OECD Publishing.
http://dx.doi.org/10.1787/9789264190511-en

OECD (2004), *Learning for Tomorrow's World: First Results from PISA 2003*, PISA, OECD Publishing.
http://dx.doi.org/10.1787/9789264006416-en

Robins, L. and **K. Ratliff** (1978), *Long Range Outcomes Associated with School Truancy*, Public Health Service, Washington, D.C.

Roby, D.E. (2004), "Research On School Attendance And Student Achievement: A Study Of Ohio Schools", *Educational Research Quarterly*, Vol. 28, No. 1, pp. 3-16.

Saab, H. and **D. Klinger** (2010), "School Differences in Adolescent Health and Wellbeing: Findings from the Canadian Health Behaviour in School-aged Children Study", *Social science and Medicine*, Vol. 70, No. 6, pp. 850-58.

Sammons, P. (1999), *School Effectiveness: Coming of Age in the Twenty-First Century*, Swets and Zeitlinger, Lisse.

Scheerens, J. and **R. Bosker** (1997), *The Foundations of Educational Effectiveness*, Pergamon Press, Oxford.

Sheldon, S.B. (2007), "Improving Student Attendance with School, Family, and Community Partnerships", *The Journal of Educational Research*, Vol. 100, No. 5, pp. 267-75.

Taylor, B., M. Pressley and **P. Pearson** (2002), "Research-Supported Characteristics of Teachers and Schools that Promote Reading Achievement", in B. Taylor and P. Pearson (eds.), *Teaching Reading: Effective Schools, Accomplished Teachers,* CIERA, Mahwah, New Jersey.

6

Policy Implications of School Management and Practices

In the wake of the recent global economic crisis, countries need to structure and manage school systems efficiently to maximise limited resources. This chapter considers how policies related to the governance of school systems and the learning environment in individual schools are associated with performance in PISA and equity at the country/economy and school levels.

The impact of the recent economic crisis on education budgets has only just begun to be observed; but it is evident that, in the context of the crisis, countries need to structure and manage school systems efficiently to maximise limited resources. However, as this volume shows, when it comes to education, money isn't everything. Performance in mathematics, reading and science is less related to a country's/economy's income or expenditure on education per student than to how those educational resources are allocated, and to the policies, practices and learning environments that determine the conditions in which students can work to achieve their full potential.

PISA conducts extensive, rigorous and internationally comparable assessments to measure the knowledge and skills of 15-year-old students. The purpose of the assessments is to inform policy makers and educators on the degree to which their students are prepared for life. Because PISA reports on the achievements of many countries and economies against a common set of benchmarks, it stimulates discussion within participating countries and economies about their education policies, with citizens recognising that their country's/economy's performance in education must be better-than-average if their children want better jobs and better lives. PISA informs this discussion by collecting reliable data on students' ability to apply high levels of knowledge and highly complex thinking to real-world problems. The PISA survey also gathers a wide range of background data about the students.

This volume makes the link between these two bodies of data, with the aim of associating patterns of students performance with a wide variety of background data, such as how much teachers are paid, the degree to which decisions are devolved from higher authorities to the school faculty, the nature of the assessments that students must take, how educational resources are allocated across schools, and whether the school climate is conducive to learning, to cite a few. In this way, while the causal nature of such relationships cannot be established, an extensive network of correlations can be drawn between certain dimensions of student performance and a large range of factors that could conceivably affect student performance. The intent of this volume is not to specify a formula for success; this volume does not contain policy prescriptions. Rather, the objective is to provide a resource for decision making. Education is highly value-laden. School systems tend to reflect the values and preferences of parents, students, administrators, politicians and/or many others. Yet such values and preferences evolve over time and education systems must change to accommodate them. Decision makers in domain of education can benefit from benchmarking research, learning about the range of factors that is related to success, taking inspiration from the success of others, and then adapting policies and practices to the local context while adding unique elements that make their own school system one of a kind.

ENSURE THAT THE LEARNING ENVIRONMENT IS CONDUCIVE TO LEARNING FOR ALL...

PISA shows that students tend to perform better in schools that provide an environment conducive to learning; it also shows that socio-economically disadvantaged students are less likely to be in orderly classrooms than advantaged students. However, even after accounting for the socio-economic status of schools and students, schools with less incidence of student truancy or better disciplinary climate tend to perform better.

In other words, students perform better in schools with a better school climate, partly because such schools tend to have more students from advantaged backgrounds who generally perform well, partly because this favourable socio-economic characteristic of students reinforces a climate conducive to learning, and partly for reasons unrelated to socio-economic factors. To the extent that improved disciplinary climate can be considered a pre-condition for improved student performance, these inter-relationships highlight how important it is to attract the most talented teachers into the most challenging classrooms, and to ensure that children from all socio-economic backgrounds are learning in a positive disciplinary climate.

Assessments and information systems, already in place in most countries ad economies, can be used to identify individual schools that need special assistance. Poland (Box IV.2.1), Mexico (Box II.2.4) and Colombia (Box IV.4.3), for example, have improved the information infrastructure of their education systems so that they can better identify and support struggling schools.

...AND OFFER SUPPORT TO ATTRACT AND RETAIN QUALIFIED TEACHERS.

It is encouraging, though, that learning environments have generally improved between 2003 and 2012, even if there are still schools with poor learning environments in all countries and economies. What kinds of interventions are most effective for these schools? PISA results show that, when comparing two schools, public or private, of the same size, in the same kind of location, and whose students share similar socio-economic status, disciplinary climate tends to be better in the school that does not suffer from a shortage of qualified teachers. Teacher shortage and disciplinary climate are inter-related. The nature of that relationship cannot be discerned from these data; for example, teachers may avoid

schools with more disciplinary problems, or a shortage of qualified teachers can adversely affect disciplinary climate. Whatever the case, public policy needs to break this vicious cycle. The fact that these inter-relationships are far weaker in some countries and economies than in others shows that this can be done.

The quality of a school cannot exceed the quality of its teachers and principals. Governments, like corporations, should know what is required to build an effective workforce: a pool of talented people from which to recruit new employees; a fair and rigorous recruitment process; initial and continuing training; adequate compensation; rewards for the best performers, support for those who need improvement, and ways of encouraging those who cannot or do not improve to leave the profession.

In building an effective teaching force, the true test always comes when these commitments are weighed against others. How do countries and economies pay teachers compared to the way they pay others with the same level of education? How are education credentials compared with other qualifications when people are being considered for jobs? Would most adults want their child to be a teacher? Does the media – and the public in general – show interest in schools and schooling? When it comes down to it, which matters more: a community's standing in the sports leagues or its standing in the student academic achievement league tables? Are parents more likely to encourage their children to study longer and harder? In effect, the answers to these questions show the extent to which a society values education.

Interestingly, countries that have improved their performance in PISA, like Estonia (Box I.5.1), Poland (Box IV.2.1), Brazil (Box I.2.4), Colombia (Box IV.4.3), Japan (Box III.3.1) and Israel (Box IV.1.4) for example, have established policies to improve the quality of their teaching staff by either adding to the requirements to earn a teaching license, providing incentives for high-achieving students to enter the profession, increasing salaries to make the profession more attractive and to retain more teachers, or by offering incentives for teachers to engage in in-service teacher-training programmes. While paying teachers well is only part of the equation, higher salaries can help school systems to attract the best candidates to the teaching profession. PISA results show that high-performing countries tend to pay more to teachers relative to their per capita GDP.

School systems also need to ensure that teachers are allocated to schools and students where they can make the most difference. Systems could re-examine teacher hiring/allocation systems to ensure that difficult schools get enough qualified teachers, develop incentive systems to attract qualified teachers in these difficult schools, and ensure that teachers in difficult schools participate in in-service training (results show that these teachers are less likely to participate in professional training).

SUPPORT SOCIO-ECONOMICALLY DISADVANTAGED SCHOOLS...

The analyses in this volume show that schools with more socio-economically disadvantaged students tend to have lower-quality resources than schools with more advantaged students. Fairness in resource allocation is not only important for equity in education, but it is also related to the performance of the education system as a whole. The results show that school systems with high student performance in mathematics tend to allocate resources more equitably between advantaged and disadvantaged schools. In these systems, there are smaller differences between higher-performing and lower-performing schools in principals' reports on teacher shortage, the adequacy of educational resources and physical infrastructure, and smaller differences in average mathematics learning time between schools with more advantaged and those with more disadvantaged students.

For example, Estonia, Finland, Germany, Korea and Slovenia all show higher-than-OECD average performance in mathematics. In these countries, principals in disadvantaged schools tended to report that their schools had adequate educational resources as much as, if not more than, principals in advantaged schools reported.

...BY USING APPROPRIATE APPROACHES, DEPENDING ON THE OVERALL LEVEL OF RESOURCES...

As might be expected, in systems where the overall level of educational resources is below the OECD average, there tends to be a greater gap in educational resources between advantaged and disadvantaged schools. Scarce resources tend to be more concentrated in advantaged schools, and disadvantaged schools tend to suffer from inadequacy or shortage of resources. The overall level of resources is also clearly linked to overall performance.

In contrast, among systems where the overall level of educational resources is above the OECD average, neither student performance nor equity in resource allocation is linked to the overall level of resources. In these cases, the challenge is to allocate resources efficiently and equitably.

...AND SUPPORT DISADVANTAGED STUDENTS AS WELL.

PISA shows that, in nearly all participating countries and economies, students who had attended pre-primary school tend to perform better at the age of 15 than students who had not attended, even after accounting for students' socio-economic status. PISA also shows how enrolment in pre-primary education changed over time. Fifteen-year-old students in 2012 were more likely than 15-year-olds in 2003 to have attended at least one year of pre-primary education. But the rate of increase in pre-primary enrolment is higher among advantaged students than disadvantaged students, which means that the socio-economic gap between students who had attended pre-primary education and those who had not has widened over time. Policies that ensure that disadvantaged students and families have access to high-quality pre-primary education and care can help reverse that trend. It is important to provide information and guidance for parents to increase enrolment in pre-primary education for all children, regardless of their socio-economic status. Governments should ensure that quality pre-primary education is available locally, especially when disadvantaged families are concentrated in certain geographic areas. Governments should also develop fair and efficient mechanisms for subsidising pre-primary education to ease the financial burden on families.

Israel (Box IV.1.4), Germany (Box II.3.2), Mexico (Box II.2.4), Turkey (Box I.2.5) and Brazil (Box I.2.4) have recently implemented targeted policies to improve the performance of low-achieving schools or students, or have distributed more resources to those regions and schools that need them most. Considering the importance of equity in resource allocation, the OECD has launched a new project[1] on this issue and more detailed information on how some high-performing countries allocate resources will be available as of 2015.

BALANCE PROFESSIONAL AUTONOMY WITH A COLLABORATIVE CULTURE AMONG SCHOOL STAFF.

In recent years, many school systems have been redefining school leadership roles to drive improvements in learning outcomes and to manage greater school autonomy and accountability. This comes at a time when increased decentralisation in many countries is being coupled with more school autonomy, more accountability for school and student results, better use of education theory and pedagogical processes, and broader responsibility for supporting schools' local communities, other schools and other public services. This marks a shift from Tayloristic management paradigms towards the kinds of paradigms that are more suited to managing professionals or "knowledge workers". In the former, one typically sees bureaucratic "command-and-control" systems that leave little discretion to the workers and supervisors on the factory floor or service-delivery level of the organisation. In the latter, the people responsible for actually making the product or delivering the services have much more control over the way resources are used, people are deployed, the work is organised and how the work gets done.

PISA results show that in higher-performing systems, schools have more autonomy, with incentives and the capacity to improve. In the school systems of Hong Kong-China, Japan, the Netherlands and Korea, for example, schools have more responsibility for establishing student disciplinary policies, student assessment policies, approving students for admission to the school, and choosing which textbooks are used and which courses are offered.

A stand-alone policy to grant schools greater autonomy, however, will not, in itself, result in better outcomes. Schools with more autonomy tend to perform better than schools with less autonomy when the school system, as a whole, uses such accountability arrangements as setting clear objectives of what students are expected to learn and sharing information about outcomes, and/or when principals and teachers work together to manage schools. Some countries, like Colombia (Box IV.4.3), Poland (Box IV.2.1) and Korea (Box I.4.1) have given schools and local authorities more autonomy and have recognised that autonomy works only in the context of collaboration and accountability. Others, like Portugal (Box III.4.1), have reshaped the organisation of schools to facilitate collaboration and economies of scale among individual schools by creating school clusters. These countries' approaches to autonomy suggest that it is the combination of various conditions, rather than a single policy in isolation, that is related to better outcomes.

RECOGNISE THAT THE QUALITY OF EDUCATION DOES NOT AUTOMATICALLY RESPOND TO MARKET MECHANISMS.

In contrast, some features, most notably the prevalence of private schools and competition for students, have no discernible relationship with student performance, at least at the system level. Socio-economically advantaged students, who tend to achieve higher scores, are also more likely to attend private schools and schools that compete for enrolment. Thus, after socio-economic status is accounted for, private schools do not perform better than public schools; and schools that compete with other schools for students do not perform better than schools that don't compete.

Although individual parents may derive an advantage for their child from the privileged socio-economic context – and attendant resources – of private schools, school systems as a whole do not seem to benefit from a greater prevalence of private schools or a higher degree of competition among schools.

In fact, school competition is a multi-faceted concept. Principals' perceptions of school competition is not necessary the same as that of the parents of students in their schools. More worryingly, in the countries and economies that administered the PISA parent questionnaire, disadvantaged parents are significantly more likely than advantaged parents to report that they considered "low expenses" and "financial aid" to be very important factors to consider when choosing a school. While parents from all backgrounds cite academic achievement as an important consideration when choosing a school for their children, advantaged parents are, on average, nine percentage points more likely than disadvantaged parents to cite this criterion as "very important". These differences suggest that disadvantaged parents may believe that their choice of schools for their child is limited, due to the cost of some schools. If children from disadvantaged backgrounds cannot attend high-performing schools because of financial constraints, then school systems that offer parents more choice of schools for their children will necessarily be less effective in improving the performance of all students.

PROVIDE OPPORTUNITIES FOR ALL STUDENTS...

PISA 2012 results, like those of earlier PISA assessments, show that, in general, school systems that cater to different students' needs by separating students into different institutions, grade levels and classes, known as stratification, have not succeeded in producing superior overall results, and in some cases they have lower-than-average and more inequitable performance. For example, cross-country/economy analysis shows that in the systems where more students repeat a grade, the impact of students' socio-economic status on their performance is stronger. Students in schools where no ability grouping is practiced also scored eight points higher in mathematics in 2012 compared to their counterparts in 2003, while students in schools where ability grouping is practiced in some or all classes had lower scores in PISA 2012 than their counterparts in PISA 2003.

In highly stratified systems, there may be more incentives for schools to select the best students, and fewer incentives to support difficult students if there is an option of transferring them to other schools. In contrast, in comprehensive systems, schools must find ways of working with students from across the performance spectrum. These different incentive systems may help explain the greater level of equity achieved in systems that use stratification less. School systems that continue to differentiate among students in these ways need to create appropriate incentives to ensure that some students are not "discarded" by the system.

Reflecting these results, Poland (Box IV.2.1), for example, reformed its school system by delaying the age of selection into different programmes; and schools in Germany (Box II.3.2) are also moving towards reducing the levels of stratification across education programmes.

...AND MOTIVATE STUDENTS.

The PISA 2012 results also show that students in more comprehensive systems reported that making an effort in mathematics and learning mathematics is important for their future career. This does not necessarily mean that if stratification policies were changed, students in stratified systems would have better instrumental motivation to learn, since PISA does not measure cause and effect. However, policy makers in highly stratified systems need to consider not only the equity aspect of education outcomes but also non-cognitive outcomes, such as students' attitudes towards learning.

ENGAGE STUDENTS IN SCHOOL EVALUATION AND TEACHER APPRAISAL TO IMPROVE TEACHING AND LEARNING.

Compared with PISA 2003, more schools are using student assessments to compare the school's performance to that of other schools or use student assessment data to monitor teacher practice. The scope of evaluations and assessments is not only limited to student assessments, but most schools use various forms of evaluations, such as self-evaluations, external school evaluation and teacher appraisals. PISA shows that, on average across OECD countries, 92% of students are in schools that use at least a self-evaluation or external evaluation to assure and improve school quality, and 60% of students are in schools that seek written feedback from students regarding lessons, teachers or resources in addition to using self-evaluations and/or external evaluations of the school. PISA results also show that in systems that attain a high level of equity, more schools tend to seek written feedback from students regarding lessons, teachers or resources.

The OECD review on evaluation and assessment in education (OECD, 2013) emphasises the importance of engaging all staff and students in school self-evaluations and using student feedback to teachers for formative purpose. Some countries engage students in school evaluations by establishing student councils or conducting student surveys in schools. In order to use the feedback from students effectively, school staff may need assistance in interpreting the evaluative information and translating it into action. Trust among school staff and students, and strong commitment from the school community, is key to making this practice work.

APPLY A COHESIVE, SYSTEMATIC AND CONTINUOUS APPROACH TO IMPROVE SCHOOL SYSTEMS.

Since education policies and practices, resources invested in education, the learning environment, socio-economic status, the demographic profile of schools and education outcomes are all interrelated, a cohesive and systematic approach is needed. In addition, since school systems change over time, intentionally or not, in response to external factors, efforts to improve school systems should be continuous. Korea (Box I.4.1), Turkey (Box I.2.5), Colombia (Box IV.4.3), Estonia (Box I.5.1) and Japan (Box III.3.1), among others, have established strategic development plans. These frameworks anticipate challenges (e.g. demographic changes) and provide guidance for coherent policies and programmes to be implemented at different levels of education. In most cases, they are flexible enough to allow for revisions and to be adapted to local contexts. What PISA findings tell policy makers, in the end, is that while there are several features that are shared among high-performing systems, among systems with greater equity or among high-performing schools, no one policy or practice spells success.

Note

1. The name of the project is OECD review of policies to improve the effectiveness of resource use in schools (school resources review).

References

OECD (2013), *Synergies for Better Learning: An International Perspective on Evaluation and Assessment,* OECD Reviews of Evaluation and Assessment in Education, OECD Publishing.
http://dx.doi.org/10.1787/9789264190658-en

Annex A

PISA 2012 TECHNICAL BACKGROUND

All figures and tables in Annex A are available on line

Notes regarding Cyprus

Note by Turkey: The information in this document with reference to "Cyprus" relates to the southern part of the Island. There is no single authority representing both Turkish and Greek Cypriot people on the Island. Turkey recognises the Turkish Republic of Northern Cyprus (TRNC). Until a lasting and equitable solution is found within the context of the United Nations, Turkey shall preserve its position concerning the "Cyprus issue".

Note by all the European Union Member States of the OECD and the European Union: The Republic of Cyprus is recognised by all members of the United Nations with the exception of Turkey. The information in this document relates to the area under the effective control of the Government of the Republic of Cyprus.

A note regarding Israel

The statistical data for Israel are supplied by and under the responsibility of the relevant Israeli authorities. The use of such data by the OECD is without prejudice to the status of the Golan Heights, East Jerusalem and Israeli settlements in the West Bank under the terms of international law.

ANNEX A1

CONSTRUCTION OF MATHEMATICS SCALES AND INDICES FROM THE STUDENT, SCHOOL AND PARENT CONTEXT QUESTIONNAIRES

How the PISA 2012 mathematics assessments were designed, analysed and scaled

The development of the PISA 2012 mathematics tasks was co-ordinated by an international consortium of educational research institutions contracted by the OECD, under the guidance of a group of mathematics experts from participating countries. Participating countries contributed stimulus material and questions, which were reviewed, tried out and refined iteratively over the three years leading up to the administration of the assessment in 2012. The development process involved provisions for several rounds of commentary from participating countries and economies, as well as small-scale piloting and a formal field trial in which samples of 15-year-olds (about 1 000 students) from participating countries and economies took part. The mathematics expert group recommended the final selection of tasks, which included material submitted by participating countries and economies. The selection was made with regard to both their technical quality, assessed on the basis of their performance in the field trial, and their cultural appropriateness and interest level for 15-year-olds, as judged by the participating countries. Another essential criterion for selecting the set of material as a whole was its fit to the framework described in Volume 1, in order to maintain the balance across various categories of context, content and process. Finally, it was carefully ensured that the set of questions covered a range of difficulty, allowing good measurement and description of the mathematics literacy of all 15-year-old students, from the least proficient to the highly able.

More than 110 print mathematics questions were used in PISA 2012, but each student in the sample only saw a fraction of the total pool because different sets of questions were given to different students. The mathematics questions selected for inclusion in PISA 2012 were organised into half-hour clusters. These, along with clusters of reading and science questions, were assembled into booklets containing four clusters each. Each participating student was then given a two-hour assessment. As mathematics was the focus of the PISA 2012 assessment, every booklet included at least one cluster of mathematics material. The clusters were rotated so that each cluster appeared in each of the four possible positions in the booklets, and each pair of clusters appeared in at least one of the 13 booklets that were used.

This design, similar to those used in previous PISA assessments, makes it possible to construct a single scale of mathematics proficiency, in which each question is associated with a particular point on the scale that indicates its difficulty, whereby each student's performance is associated with a particular point on the same scale that indicates his or her estimated proficiency. A description of the modelling technique used to construct this scale can be found in the *PISA 2012 Technical Report* (OECD, forthcoming).

The relative difficulty of tasks in a test is estimated by considering the proportion of test takers who answer each question correctly. The relative proficiency of students taking a particular test can be estimated by considering the proportion of test questions they answer correctly. A single continuous scale shows the relationship between the difficulty of questions and the proficiency of students. By constructing a scale that shows the difficulty of each question, it is possible to locate the level of mathematics literacy that the question represents. By showing the proficiency of each student on the same scale, it is possible to describe the level of mathematics literacy that the student possesses.

The location of student proficiency on this scale is set in relation to the particular group of questions used in the assessment. However, just as the sample of students taking PISA in 2012 is drawn to represent all the 15-year-olds in the participating countries and economies, so the individual questions used in the assessment are designed to represent the definition of mathematics literacy adequately. Estimates of student proficiency reflect the kinds of tasks they would be expected to perform successfully. This means that students are likely to be able to complete questions successfully at or below the difficulty level associated with their own position on the scale (but they may not always do so). Conversely, they are unlikely to be able to successfully complete questions above the difficulty level associated with their position on the scale (but they may sometimes do so).

The further a student's proficiency is located above a given question, the more likely he or she is to successfully complete the question (and other questions of similar difficulty); the further the student's proficiency is located below a given question, the lower the probability that the student will be able to successfully complete the question, and other questions of similar difficulty.

How mathematics proficiency levels are defined in PISA 2012

PISA 2012 provides an overall mathematics literacy scale, drawing on all the questions in the mathematics assessment, as well as scales for three process and four content categories. The metric for the overall mathematics scale is based on a mean for OECD countries set at 500 in PISA 2003, with a standard deviation of 100. To help interpret what students' scores mean in substantive terms, the scale is divided into levels, based on a set of statistical principles, and then descriptions are generated, based on the tasks that are located within each level, to describe the kinds of skills and knowledge needed to successfully complete those tasks.

For PISA 2012, the range of difficulty of tasks allows for the description of six levels of mathematics proficiency: Level 1 is the lowest described level, then Level 2, Level 3 and so on up to Level 6.

Students with a proficiency within the range of Level 1 are likely to be able to successfully complete Level 1 tasks (and others like them), but are unlikely to be able to complete tasks at higher levels. Level 6 reflects tasks that present the greatest challenge in terms

of mathematics skills and knowledge. Students with scores in this range are likely to be able to complete mathematics tasks located at that level successfully, as well as all the other mathematics tasks in PISA.

PISA applies a standard methodology for constructing proficiency scales. Based on a student's performance on the tasks in the test, his or her score is generated and located in a specific part of the scale, thus allowing the score to be associated with a defined proficiency level. The level at which the student's score is located is the highest level for which he or she would be expected to answer correctly most of a random selection of questions within the same level. Thus, for example, in an assessment composed of tasks spread uniformly across Level 3, students with a score located within Level 3 would be expected to complete at least 50% of the tasks successfully. Because a level covers a range of difficulty and proficiency, success rates across the band vary. Students near the bottom of the level would be likely to succeed on just over 50% of the tasks spread uniformly across the level, while students at the top of the level would be likely to succeed on well over 70% of the same tasks.

Figure I.2.21 in Volume I provides details of the nature of mathematics skills, knowledge and understanding required at each level of the mathematics scale.

Context questionnaire indices

This section explains the indices derived from the student and school context questionnaires used in PISA 2012.

Several PISA measures reflect indices that summarise responses from students, their parents or school representatives (typically principals) to a series of related questions. The questions were selected from a larger pool of questions on the basis of theoretical considerations and previous research. The *PISA 2012 Assessment and Analytical Framework* (OECD, 2013) provides an in-depth description of this conceptual framework. Structural equation modelling was used to confirm the theoretically expected behaviour of the indices and to validate their comparability across countries and economies. For this purpose, a model was estimated separately for each country and collectively for all OECD countries. For a detailed description of other PISA indices and details on the methods, see *PISA 2012 Technical Report* (OECD, forthcoming).

There are two types of indices: simple indices and scale indices.

Simple indices are the variables that are constructed through the arithmetic transformation or recoding of one or more items, in exactly the same way across assessments. Here, item responses are used to calculate meaningful variables, such as the recoding of the four-digit ISCO-08 codes into "Highest parents' socio-economic index (HISEI)" or, teacher-student ratio based on information from the school questionnaire.

Scale indices are the variables constructed through the scaling of multiple items. Unless otherwise indicated, the index was scaled using a weighted likelihood estimate (WLE) (Warm, 1989), using a one-parameter item response model (a partial credit model was used in the case of items with more than two categories). For details on how each scale index was constructed see the *PISA 2012 Technical Report* (OECD, forthcoming). In general, the scaling was done in three stages:

- The item parameters were estimated from equal-sized subsamples of students from all participating countries and economies.

- The estimates were computed for all students and all schools by anchoring the item parameters obtained in the preceding step.

- The indices were then standardised so that the mean of the index value for the OECD student population was zero and the standard deviation was one (countries being given equal weight in the standardisation process).

Sequential codes were assigned to the different response categories of the questions in the sequence in which the latter appeared in the student, school or parent questionnaires. Where indicated in this section, these codes were inverted for the purpose of constructing indices or scales. Negative values for an index do not necessarily imply that students responded negatively to the underlying questions. A negative value merely indicates that the respondents answered less positively than all respondents did on average across OECD countries. Likewise, a positive value on an index indicates that the respondents answered more favourably, or more positively, than respondents did, on average, across OECD countries. Terms enclosed in brackets < > in the following descriptions were replaced in the national versions of the student, school and parent questionnaires by the appropriate national equivalent. For example, the term <qualification at ISCED level 5A> was translated in the United States into "Bachelor's degree, post-graduate certificate program, Master's degree program or first professional degree program". Similarly the term <classes in the language of assessment> in Luxembourg was translated into "German classes" or "French classes" depending on whether students received the German or French version of the assessment instruments.

In addition to simple and scaled indices described in this annex, there are a number of variables from the questionnaires that correspond to single items not used to construct indices. These non-recoded variables have prefix of "ST" for the questionnaire items in the student questionnaire, "SC" for the items in the school questionnaire, and "PA" for the items in the parent questionnaire. All the context questionnaires as well as the PISA international database, including all variables, are available through *www.pisa.oecd.org*.

Scaling of questionnaire indices for trend analyses

In PISA, to gather information about students' and schools' characteristics, both students and schools complete a background questionnaire. In PISA 2003 and PISA 2012 several questions were kept untouched, enabling the comparison of responses to these

questions over time. In this report, only questions that maintained an exact wording are used for trends analyses. Questions with subtle word changes or questions with major word changes were not compared across time because it is impossible to discern whether observed changes in the response are due to changes in the construct they are measuring or to changes in the way the construct is being measured.

Also, in PISA, as described in this Annex, questionnaire items are used to construct indices. Whenever the questions used in the construction of indices remains intact in PISA 2003 and PISA 2012, the corresponding indices are compared. Two types of indices are used in PISA: simple indices and scale indices.

Simple indices recode a set of responses to questionnaire items. For trends analyses, the values observed in PISA 2003 are compared directly to PISA 2012, just as simple responses to questionnaire items are. This is the case of indices like student-teacher ratio and ability grouping in mathematics.

Scale indices, on the other hand, imply WLE estimates which require rescaling in order to be comparable across PISA cycles. Scale indices, like the *PISA index of economic, social and cultural status*, the *index of sense of belonging*, the *index of attitudes towards school*, the *index of intrinsic motivation to learn mathematics*, the *index of instrumental motivation to learn mathematics*, the *index of mathematics self-efficacy*, the *index of mathematics self-concept*, the *index of anxiety towards mathematics*, the *index of teacher shortage*, the *index of quality of physical infrastructure*, the *index of quality of educational resources*, the *index of disciplinary climate*, the *index of teacher-student relations*, the *index of teacher morale*, the *index of student-related factors affecting school climate* and the *index of teacher-related factors affecting school climate*, were scaled, in PISA 2012 to have an OECD average of 0 and a standard deviation of 1, on average, across OECD countries. These same scales were scaled, in PISA 2003, to have an OECD average of 0 and a standard deviation of 1. Because they are on different scales, values reported in *Learning for Tomorrow's World: First Results from PISA 2003* (OECD, 2004) cannot be compared with those reported in this volume. To make these scale indices comparable, values for 2003 have been rescaled to the 2012 scale, using the PISA 2012 parameter estimates.

These re-scaled indices are available at *www.pisa.oecd.org*. They can be merged to the corresponding PISA 2003 dataset using the country names, school and student-level identifiers. The rescaled *PISA index of economic, social and cultural status* is also available to be merged with the PISA 2000, PISA 2006 and PISA 2009 dataset.

Student-level simple indices

Age

The variable AGE is calculated as the difference between the middle month and the year in which students were assessed and their month and year of birth, expressed in years and months.

Study programme

In PISA 2012, study programmes available to 15-year-old students in each country were collected both through the student tracking form and the student questionnaire (ST02). All study programmes were classified using ISCED (OECD, 1999). In the PISA international database, all national programmes are indicated in a variable (PROGN) where the first six digits refer to the national centre code and the last two digits to the national study programme code.

The following internationally comparable indices were derived from the data on study programmes:

- Programme level (ISCEDL) indicates whether students are (1) primary education level (ISCED 1); (2) lower-secondary education level; or (3) upper secondary education level.

- Programme designation (ISCEDD) indicates the designation of the study programme: (1) "A" (general programmes designed to give access to the next programme level); (2) "B" (programmes designed to give access to vocational studies at the next programme level); (3) "C" (programmes designed to give direct access to the labour market); or (4) "M" (modular programmes that combine any or all of these characteristics).

- Programme orientation (ISCEDO) indicates whether the programme's curricular content is (1) general; (2) pre-vocational; (3) vocational; or (4) modular programmes that combine any or all of these characteristics.

Occupational status of parents

Occupational data for both a student's father and a student's mother were obtained by asking open-ended questions in the student questionnaire (ST12, ST16). The responses were coded to four-digit ISCO codes (ILO, 1990) and then mapped to the SEI index of Ganzeboom et al. (1992). Higher scores of SEI indicate higher levels of occupational status. The following three indices are obtained:

- Mother's occupational status (OCOD1).

- Father's occupational status (OCOD2).

- The highest occupational level of parents (HISEI) corresponds to the higher SEI score of either parent or to the only available parent's SEI score.

[Part 1/1]

Table A1.1 **Levels of parental education converted into years of schooling**

	Completed ISCED level 1 (primary education)	Completed ISCED level 2 (lower secondary education)	Completed ISCED levels 3B or 3C (upper secondary education providing direct access to the labour market or to ISCED 5B programmes)	Completed ISCED level 3A (upper secondary education providing access to ISCED 5A and 5B programmes) and/or ISCED level 4 (non-tertiary post-secondary)	Completed ISCED level 5A (university level tertiary education) or ISCED level 6 (advanced research programmes)	Completed ISCED level 5B (non-university tertiary education)
OECD						
Australia	6.0	10.0	11.0	12.0	15.0	14.0
Austria	4.0	9.0	12.0	12.5	17.0	15.0
Belgium[1]	6.0	9.0	12.0	12.0	17.0	15.0
Canada	6.0	9.0	12.0	12.0	17.0	15.0
Chile	6.0	8.0	12.0	12.0	17.0	16.0
Czech Republic	5.0	9.0	11.0	13.0	16.0	16.0
Denmark	7.0	10.0	13.0	13.0	18.0	16.0
Estonia	6.0	9.0	12.0	12.0	16.0	15.0
Finland	6.0	9.0	12.0	12.0	16.5	14.5
France	5.0	9.0	12.0	12.0	15.0	14.0
Germany	4.0	10.0	13.0	13.0	18.0	15.0
Greece	6.0	9.0	11.5	12.0	17.0	15.0
Hungary	4.0	8.0	10.5	12.0	16.5	13.5
Iceland	7.0	10.0	13.0	14.0	18.0	16.0
Ireland	6.0	9.0	12.0	12.0	16.0	14.0
Israel	6.0	9.0	12.0	12.0	15.0	15.0
Italy	5.0	8.0	12.0	13.0	17.0	16.0
Japan	6.0	9.0	12.0	12.0	16.0	14.0
Korea	6.0	9.0	12.0	12.0	16.0	14.0
Luxembourg	6.0	9.0	12.0	13.0	17.0	16.0
Mexico	6.0	9.0	12.0	12.0	16.0	14.0
Netherlands	6.0	10.0	13.0	12.0	16.0	15.0
New Zealand	5.5	10.0	11.0	12.0	15.0	14.0
Norway	6.0	9.0	12.0	12.0	16.0	14.0
Poland	a	8.0	11.0	12.0	16.0	15.0
Portugal	6.0	9.0	12.0	12.0	17.0	15.0
Slovak Republic[2]	4.0	9.0	12.0	13.0	18.0	16.0
Slovenia	4.0	8.0	11.0	12.0	16.0	15.0
Spain	5.0	8.0	10.0	12.0	16.5	13.0
Sweden	6.0	9.0	11.5	12.0	16.0	14.0
Switzerland	6.0	9.0	12.5	12.5	17.5	14.5
Turkey	5.0	8.0	11.0	11.0	15.0	13.0
United Kingdom (exclud. Scotland)	6.0	9.0	12.0	13.0	16.0	15.0
United Kingdom (Scotland)	7.0	9.0	11.0	13.0	17.0	15.0
United States	6.0	9.0	a	12.0	16.0	14.0
Partners						
Albania	6.0	9.0	12.0	12.0	16.0	16.0
Argentina	6.0	10.0	12.0	12.0	17.0	14.5
Azerbaijan	4.0	9.0	11.0	11.0	17.0	14.0
Brazil	4.0	8.0	11.0	11.0	16.0	14.5
Bulgaria	4.0	8.0	10.0	12.0	17.5	15.0
Colombia	5.0	9.0	11.0	11.0	15.5	14.0
Costa Rica	6.0	9.0	11.0	12.0	14.0	16.0
Croatia	4.0	8.0	11.0	12.0	17.0	15.0
Hong Kong-China	6.0	9.0	11.0	13.0	16.0	14.0
Indonesia	6.0	9.0	12.0	12.0	15.0	14.0
Jordan	6.0	10.0	12.0	12.0	16.0	14.5
Kazakhstan	4.0	9.0	11.5	12.5	15.0	14.0
Latvia	4.0	8.0	11.0	11.0	16.0	14.0
Liechtenstein	5.0	9.0	11.0	13.0	17.0	14.0
Lithuania	3.0	8.0	11.0	11.0	16.0	15.0
Macao-China	6.0	9.0	11.0	12.0	16.0	15.0
Malaysia	6.0	9.0	11.0	13.0	15.0	16.0
Montenegro	4.0	8.0	11.0	12.0	16.0	15.0
Peru	6.0	9.0	11.0	11.0	17.0	14.0
Qatar	6.0	9.0	12.0	12.0	16.0	15.0
Romania	4.0	8.0	11.5	12.5	16.0	14.0
Russian Federation	4.0	9.0	11.5	12.0	15.0	a
Serbia	4.0	8.0	11.0	12.0	17.0	14.5
Shanghai-China	6.0	9.0	12.0	12.0	16.0	15.0
Singapore	6.0	8.0	10.0	11.0	16.0	13.0
Chinese Taipei	6.0	9.0	12.0	12.0	16.0	14.0
Thailand	6.0	9.0	12.0	12.0	16.0	14.0
Tunisia	6.0	9.0	12.0	13.0	17.0	16.0
United Arab Emirates	5.0	9.0	12.0	12.0	16.0	15.0
Uruguay	6.0	9.0	12.0	12.0	17.0	15.0
Viet Nam	5.0	9.0	12.0	12.0	17.0	a

1. In Belgium the distinction between universities and other tertiary schools doesn't match the distinction between ISCED 5A and ISCED 5B.

2. In the Slovak Republic, university education (ISCED 5A) usually lasts five years and doctoral studies (ISCED 6) lasts three more years. Therefore, university graduates will have completed 18 years of study and graduates of doctoral programmes will have completed 21 years of study.

Source: OECD, PISA 2012 Database.

StatLink http://dx.doi.org/10.1787/888932937073

Some of the analyses distinguish between four different categories of occupations by the major groups identified by the ISCO coding of the highest parental occupation: Elementary (ISCO 9), semi-skilled blue-collar (ISCO 6, 7 and 8), semi-skilled white-collar (ISCO 4 and 5), skilled (ISCO 1, 2 and 3). This classification follows the same methodology used in other OECD publications such as *Education at a Glance* (2013b) and the *OECD Skills Outlook* (2013c).[1]

Educational level of parents

The educational level of parents is classified using ISCED (OECD, 1999) based on students' responses in the student questionnaire (ST13, ST14, ST17 and ST18).

As in PISA 2000, 2003, 2006 and 2009, indices were constructed by selecting the highest level for each parent and then assigning them to the following categories: (0) None, (1) ISCED 1 (primary education), (2) ISCED 2 (lower secondary), (3) ISCED Level 3B or 3C (vocational/pre-vocational upper secondary), (4) ISCED 3A (upper secondary) and/or ISCED 4 (non-tertiary post-secondary), (5) ISCED 5B (vocational tertiary), (6) ISCED 5A, 6 (theoretically oriented tertiary and post-graduate). The following three indices with these categories are developed:

- Mother's educational level (MISCED).
- Father's educational level (FISCED).
- Highest educational level of parents (HISCED) corresponds to the higher ISCED level of either parent.

Highest educational level of parents was also converted into the number of years of schooling (PARED). For the conversion of level of education into years of schooling, see Table A1.1.

Immigration and language background

Information on the country of birth of students and their parents is collected in a similar manner as in PISA 2000, PISA 2003, PISA 2006 and PISA 2009 by using nationally specific ISO coded variables. The ISO codes of the country of birth for students and their parents are available in the PISA international database (COBN_S, COBN_M, and COBN_F).

The index on immigrant background (IMMIG) has the following categories: (1) non-immigrant students (those students born in the country of assessment, or those with at least one parent born in that country; students who were born abroad with at least one parent born in the country of assessment are also classified as non-immigrant students), (2) second-generation students (those born in the country of assessment but whose parents were born in another country) and (3) first-generation students (those born outside the country of assessment and whose parents were also born in another country). Students with missing responses for either the student or for both parents, or for all three questions have been given missing values for this variable.

Students indicate the language they usually speak at home. The data are captured in nationally-specific language codes, which were recoded into variable LANGN with the following two values: (1) language at home is the same as the language of assessment, and (2) language at home is a different language than the language of assessment.

Relative grade

Data on the student's grade are obtained both from the student questionnaire (ST01) and from the student tracking form. As with all variables that are on both the tracking form and the questionnaire, inconsistencies between the two sources are reviewed and resolved during data-cleaning. In order to capture between-country variation, the relative grade index (GRADE) indicates whether students are at the modal grade in a country (value of 0), or whether they are below or above the modal grade level (+ x grades, - x grades).

The relationship between the grade and student performance was estimated through a multilevel model accounting for the following background variables: *i)* the *PISA index of economic, social and cultural status*; *ii)* the *PISA index of economic, social and cultural status* squared; *iii)* the school mean of the *PISA index of economic, social and cultural status*; *iv)* an indicator as to whether students were foreign-born first-generation students; *v)* the percentage of first-generation students in the school; and *vi)* students' gender.

Table A1.2 presents the results of the multilevel model. Column 1 in Table A1.2 estimates the score-point difference that is associated with one grade level (or school year). This difference can be estimated for the 32 OECD countries in which a sizeable number of 15-year-olds in the PISA samples were enrolled in at least two different grades. Since 15-year-olds cannot be assumed to be distributed at random across the grade levels, adjustments had to be made for the above-mentioned contextual factors that may relate to the assignment of students to the different grade levels. These adjustments are documented in columns 2 to 7 of the table. While it is possible to estimate the typical performance difference among students in two adjacent grades net of the effects of selection and contextual factors, this difference cannot automatically be equated with the progress that students have made over the last school year but should be interpreted as a lower boundary of the progress achieved. This is not only because different students were assessed but also because the content of the PISA assessment was not expressly designed to match what students had learned in the preceding school year but more broadly to assess the cumulative outcome of learning in school up to age 15. For example, if the curriculum of the grades in which 15-year-olds are enrolled mainly includes material other than that assessed by PISA (which, in turn, may have been included in earlier school years) then the observed performance difference will underestimate student progress.

[Part 1/1]

Table A1.2 **A multilevel model to estimate grade effects in mathematics accounting for some background variables**

Multilevel model to estimate grade effects in mathematics performance[1], accounting for:

	grade		PISA index of economic, social and cultural status		PISA index of economic, social and cultural status squared		school mean of the PISA index of economic, social and cultural status		first-generation students		percentage of first-generation students at the school level		student is a female		intercept	
	Coeff	S.E.	Coeff	S.E.	Coeff	S.E.	Coeff	S.E.	Coeff	S.E.	Coeff	S.E.	Coeff	S.E.	Coeff	S.E.
Australia	**35**	(2.3)	**20**	(1.4)	1	(1.1)	**68**	(7.1)	6	(3.9)	0	(0.2)	**-12**	(2.9)	**481**	(4.1)
Austria	**36**	(2.7)	**11**	(1.8)	-2	(1.6)	**62**	(8.2)	-9	(6.5)	0	(0.3)	**-28**	(3.3)	**526**	(5.8)
Belgium	**43**	(2.4)	**4**	(1.4)	1	(0.9)	**83**	(14.6)	-3	(4.7)	0	(0.6)	**-15**	(2.0)	**528**	(8.0)
Canada	**44**	(2.5)	**19**	(1.5)	3	(1.1)	**29**	(6.8)	6	(3.7)	0	(0.1)	**-13**	(1.9)	**506**	(4.0)
Chile	**33**	(1.8)	**9**	(1.5)	1	(0.7)	**37**	(3.6)	-2	(10.2)	-1	(1.1)	**-29**	(2.1)	**469**	(4.7)
Czech Republic	**47**	(3.5)	**13**	(2.0)	-3	(2.0)	**111**	(9.3)	1	(9.1)	-2	(0.9)	**-24**	(2.9)	**502**	(4.2)
Denmark	**34**	(3.9)	**26**	(2.2)	2	(1.6)	**44**	(8.0)	**-34**	(5.3)	0	(0.5)	**-18**	(2.2)	**483**	(5.4)
Estonia	**41**	(2.7)	**16**	(2.0)	2	(2.3)	**25**	(6.7)	-20	(17.0)	**-4**	(0.6)	**-7**	(2.5)	**530**	(3.3)
Finland	**52**	(4.4)	**22**	(2.1)	**6**	(1.9)	**38**	(13.2)	**-38**	(8.7)	-1	(0.8)	1	(3.1)	**501**	(7.7)
France	**49**	(4.8)	**16**	(2.3)	2	(1.7)	**60**	(9.5)	-6	(5.8)	0	(0.4)	**-18**	(2.7)	**509**	(6.3)
Germany	**41**	(2.1)	**5**	(1.5)	1	(1.4)	**108**	(8.3)	**-20**	(7.9)	**-2**	(0.7)	**-28**	(2.6)	**487**	(5.6)
Greece	**41**	(6.3)	**17**	(1.7)	1	(1.2)	**29**	(6.8)	8	(6.3)	0	(0.2)	**-15**	(2.6)	**458**	(4.5)
Hungary	**32**	(3.0)	**7**	(1.8)	3	(1.2)	**64**	(8.6)	42	(23.9)	**-1**	(0.5)	**-27**	(2.5)	**494**	(5.6)
Iceland	c	c	**19**	(3.2)	3	(1.9)	24	(9.4)	**-31**	(11.0)	-1	(0.5)	7	(3.5)	**454**	(8.4)
Ireland	**18**	(1.8)	**24**	(1.7)	1	(1.8)	**60**	(6.1)	**10**	(4.8)	0	(0.3)	**-15**	(3.0)	**491**	(4.4)
Israel	**35**	(4.2)	**21**	(2.6)	3	(1.5)	**91**	(14.8)	-12	(7.7)	1	(0.8)	**-11**	(4.2)	**446**	(9.7)
Italy	**35**	(1.9)	**3**	(0.9)	-1	(0.7)	**54**	(5.5)	**-13**	(3.4)	0	(0.1)	**-23**	(1.7)	**495**	(3.1)
Japan	c	c	3	(2.1)	1	(2.2)	**156**	(13.3)	c	c	c	c	**-14**	(3.2)	**548**	(5.5)
Korea	**40**	(14.6)	**25**	(4.7)	5	(3.0)	**75**	(20.8)	c	c	c	c	-10	(5.8)	**555**	(6.2)
Luxembourg	**50**	(2.3)	**12**	(1.8)	0	(0.8)	**55**	(5.4)	-7	(4.3)	0	(0.1)	**-23**	(2.7)	**481**	(4.7)
Mexico	**26**	(1.8)	**8**	(1.1)	**2**	(0.4)	**17**	(2.0)	**-44**	(6.0)	**-1**	(0.5)	**-14**	(1.5)	**451**	(3.1)
Netherlands	**35**	(2.6)	**6**	(1.6)	0	(1.1)	**108**	(22.6)	-14	(9.4)	-1	(1.1)	**-19**	(2.1)	**480**	(8.1)
New Zealand	**35**	(5.6)	**31**	(2.5)	-1	(1.8)	**60**	(8.4)	-1	(4.4)	0	(0.4)	**-10**	(3.2)	**502**	(9.6)
Norway	36	(17.8)	**24**	(2.5)	-2	(1.7)	29	(29.3)	**-21**	(7.8)	-1	(0.8)	3	(4.0)	**474**	(18.0)
Poland	**80**	(7.0)	**26**	(2.1)	-2	(1.8)	**37**	(6.9)	c	c	c	c	-5	(3.7)	**539**	(4.5)
Portugal	**51**	(2.9)	**17**	(1.5)	2	(0.9)	**27**	(4.0)	10	(7.1)	0	(0.5)	**-17**	(2.2)	**540**	(4.3)
Slovak Republic	**42**	(3.8)	**21**	(2.2)	-1	(1.4)	**39**	(7.5)	c	c	c	c	**-20**	(3.0)	**530**	(4.4)
Slovenia	**24**	(6.2)	1	(1.7)	4	(1.5)	**72**	(12.9)	**-34**	(6.7)	0	(0.8)	**-25**	(2.9)	**484**	(5.2)
Spain	**64**	(1.5)	**14**	(0.9)	**2**	(0.7)	**21**	(3.0)	**-16**	(3.0)	0	(0.2)	**-24**	(1.5)	**531**	(2.4)
Sweden	**67**	(6.7)	**27**	(2.1)	2	(1.4)	**29**	(7.8)	**-21**	(8.0)	0	(0.2)	3	(3.0)	**461**	(4.6)
Switzerland	**52**	(3.0)	**20**	(1.8)	-2	(1.2)	**20**	(7.9)	**-29**	(4.5)	-1	(0.3)	**-20**	(2.4)	**528**	(4.3)
Turkey	**29**	(2.9)	1	(2.4)	-1	(1.0)	**47**	(9.1)	c	c	c	c	**-22**	(2.7)	**553**	(17.0)
United Kingdom	**23**	(5.4)	**20**	(2.3)	3	(1.8)	**88**	(8.2)	4	(6.2)	0	(0.3)	**-9**	(3.2)	**465**	(4.9)
United States	**41**	(3.3)	**21**	(1.8)	**7**	(1.5)	**51**	(9.4)	9	(8.0)	1	(0.4)	**-12**	(3.5)	**457**	(6.5)
OECD average	**41**	(1.0)	**16**	(0.4)	**1**	(0.3)	**56**	(1.9)	**-10**	(1.6)	**0**	(0.1)	**-15**	(0.5)	**498**	(1.2)
Albania	6	(3.9)	m	m	m	m	m	m	c	c	c	c	0	(4.1)	**395**	(4.0)
Argentina	**31**	(1.7)	**9**	(1.7)	**2**	(0.9)	**38**	(7.1)	1	(12.1)	-2	(1.0)	**-18**	(2.3)	**446**	(5.3)
Brazil	**31**	(1.2)	**5**	(2.1)	0	(0.7)	**26**	(4.3)	**-49**	(19.1)	0	(1.4)	**-25**	(1.8)	**432**	(7.3)
Bulgaria	**30**	(4.2)	**12**	(1.6)	1	(1.1)	25	(12.6)	c	c	c	c	**-10**	(2.6)	**429**	(8.0)
Colombia	**25**	(1.3)	7	(2.4)	1	(0.7)	**26**	(4.1)	c	c	c	c	**-30**	(2.0)	**444**	(5.7)
Costa Rica	**26**	(1.3)	**8**	(1.6)	1	(0.6)	**25**	(4.2)	-7	(8.0)	0	(0.8)	**-29**	(2.3)	**447**	(7.5)
Croatia	**21**	(2.8)	**9**	(1.9)	-1	(1.3)	**71**	(13.7)	-10	(7.6)	-1	(0.9)	**-24**	(2.9)	**504**	(8.1)
Cyprus*	**39**	(6.0)	**18**	(1.8)	2	(1.1)	**61**	(8.7)	-5	(5.5)	0	(0.2)	**-14**	(2.4)	**439**	(5.3)
Hong Kong-China	**36**	(2.2)	4	(2.6)	1	(1.2)	**48**	(14.5)	**26**	(4.3)	0	(1.0)	**-22**	(3.3)	**613**	(18.1)
Indonesia	**17**	(2.7)	6	(2.3)	1	(0.6)	**27**	(5.6)	c	c	c	c	**-6**	(1.9)	**438**	(10.9)
Jordan	**37**	(5.3)	**12**	(2.1)	**2**	(0.8)	22	(14.9)	6	(6.6)	**2**	(1.0)	9	(11.7)	**393**	(11.4)
Kazakhstan	**16**	(2.5)	**14**	(2.4)	0	(1.5)	**36**	(10.3)	-5	(5.0)	0	(0.3)	-4	(2.2)	**459**	(5.2)
Latvia	**53**	(4.0)	**18**	(1.9)	2	(1.8)	**25**	(5.9)	c	c	c	c	-7	(3.0)	**510**	(3.8)
Liechtenstein	**40**	(8.9)	8	(4.1)	-5	(2.7)	**107**	(25.4)	-10	(9.3)	**-2**	(1.0)	**-27**	(5.2)	**543**	(20.9)
Lithuania	**32**	(3.4)	**17**	(1.8)	-2	(1.5)	**47**	(6.9)	c	c	c	c	-7	(2.6)	**483**	(4.1)
Macao-China	**50**	(1.7)	7	(2.9)	2	(1.4)	8	(12.2)	**24**	(3.0)	-1	(0.5)	**-26**	(2.3)	**544**	(14.2)
Malaysia	**79**	(7.0)	**15**	(2.3)	**2**	(0.9)	**53**	(7.2)	c	c	c	c	2	(2.1)	**466**	(6.5)
Montenegro	**9**	(3.1)	**13**	(1.9)	1	(1.0)	**76**	(15.6)	**16**	(7.0)	-2	(1.1)	**-11**	(3.2)	**437**	(8.6)
Peru	**25**	(1.3)	**8**	(2.1)	1	(0.6)	**36**	(3.8)	c	c	c	c	**-28**	(2.5)	**434**	(6.4)
Qatar	**28**	(2.2)	**6**	(1.4)	1	(0.7)	**26**	(7.9)	**32**	(3.3)	1	(0.1)	2	(4.1)	**310**	(5.4)
Romania	-5	(5.6)	**20**	(2.3)	**5**	(1.0)	**51**	(9.6)	c	c	c	c	-7	(2.8)	**475**	(7.4)
Russian Federation	**34**	(2.5)	**22**	(2.2)	-1	(1.5)	21	(9.6)	**-16**	(6.4)	-1	(0.5)	-2	(2.6)	**487**	(4.7)
Serbia	**33**	(10.4)	**8**	(2.1)	-1	(1.7)	**81**	(11.8)	-11	(11.5)	0	(0.9)	**-26**	(3.9)	**480**	(8.0)
Shanghai-China	**43**	(5.5)	6	(2.4)	-3	(1.4)	**52**	(6.5)	-27	(16.1)	-1	(1.0)	**-14**	(2.6)	**674**	(7.6)
Singapore	**44**	(3.3)	**21**	(2.2)	0	(1.2)	**81**	(12.6)	**29**	(4.8)	**-1**	(0.3)	-1	(2.7)	**608**	(9.4)
Chinese Taipei	**47**	(13.2)	**21**	(3.8)	-6	(2.1)	**114**	(9.6)	c	c	c	c	3	(4.1)	**638**	(9.6)
Thailand	**16**	(3.9)	**13**	(3.0)	3	(1.1)	-22	(10.8)	c	c	c	c	2	(3.5)	**418**	(17.5)
Tunisia	**36**	(1.7)	**7**	(2.0)	2	(0.7)	12	(7.0)	c	c	c	c	**-26**	(1.7)	**429**	(11.5)
United Arab Emirates	**33**	(1.5)	**9**	(1.3)	3	(0.8)	**23**	(7.4)	**31**	(2.1)	1	(0.1)	-2	(4.7)	**387**	(4.1)
Uruguay	**39**	(2.1)	**15**	(2.0)	3	(0.9)	**35**	(4.3)	c	c	c	c	**-19**	(2.3)	**480**	(4.7)
Viet Nam	**36**	(4.8)	**12**	(4.1)	3	(1.1)	26	(15.1)	c	c	c	c	**-22**	(4.4)	**550**	(32.4)

Note: Values that are statistically significant are indicated in bold (see Annex A3).
1. Multilevel regression model (student and school levels): Mathematics performance is regressed on the variables of school policies and practices presented in this table.
* See notes at the beginning of this Annex.
StatLink ⟲ http://dx.doi.org/10.1787/888932937073

Learning time

Learning time in test language (LMINS) was computed by multiplying students' responses on the number of minutes on average in the test language class by number of test language class periods per week (ST69 and ST70). Comparable indices were computed for mathematics (MMINS) and science (SMINS).

Student-level scale indices

Instrumental motivation to learn mathematics

The *index of instrumental motivation to learn mathematics* (INSTMOT) was constructed using student responses over the extent they strongly agreed, agreed, disagreed or strongly disagreed to a series of statements in question (ST29) when asked to think about their views on mathematics: Making an effort in mathematics is worth because it will help me in the work that I want to do later on; Learning mathematics is worthwhile for me because it will improve my career <prospects, chances>; Mathematics is an important subject for me because I need it for what I want to study later on; I will learn many things in mathematics that will help me get a job. See Annex A6 for the description of adjusted indices.

For trends analyses, the PISA 2003 values of the index of instrumental motivation to learn mathematics were rescaled to be comparable to those in PISA 2012. As a result, values for the index of instrumental motivation to learn mathematics for PISA 2003 reported in this volume may differ from those reported in *Learning for Tomorrow's World: First Results from PISA 2003* (OECD, 2004).

Disciplinary climate

The *index of disciplinary climate* (DISCLIMA) was derived from students' reports on how often the followings happened in their lessons of the language of instruction (ST81): *i)* students don't listen to what the teacher says; *ii)* there is noise and disorder; *iii)* the teacher has to wait a long time for the students to <quieten down>; *iv)* students cannot work well; and *v)* students don't start working for a long time after the lesson begins. In this index higher values indicate a better disciplinary climate.

For trends analyses, the PISA 2003 values of the index of disciplinary climate were rescaled to be comparable to those in PISA 2012. As a result, values for the index of disciplinary climate for PISA 2003 reported in this volume may differ from those reported in *Learning for Tomorrow's World: First Results from PISA 2003* (OECD, 2004).

Teacher-student relations

The *index of teacher-student relations* (STUDREL) was derived from students' level of agreement with the following statements. The question asked (ST86) stated "Thinking about the teachers at your school: to what extent do you agree with the following statements": *i)* Students get along well with most of my teachers; *ii)* Most teachers are interested in students' well-being; *iii)* Most of my teachers really listen to what I have to say; *iv)* if I need extra help, I will receive it from my teachers; and *v)* Most of my teachers treat me fairly. Higher values on this index indicate positive teacher-student relations.

For trends analyses, the PISA 2003 values of the index of student-teacher relations were rescaled to be comparable to those in PISA 2012. As a result, values for the index of student-teacher relations for PISA 2003 reported in this volume may differ from those reported in *Learning for Tomorrow's World: First Results from PISA 2003* (OECD, 2004).

Economic, social and cultural status

The *PISA index of economic, social and cultural status* (ESCS) was derived from the following three indices: *highest occupational status of parents* (HISEI), *highest educational level of parents* in years of education according to ISCED (PARED), and *home possessions* (HOMEPOS). The *index of home possessions* (HOMEPOS) comprises all items on the indices of WEALTH, CULTPOSS and HEDRES, as well as books in the home recoded into a four-level categorical variable (0-10 books, 11-25 or 26-100 books, 101-200 or 201-500 books, more than 500 books).

The *PISA index of economic, social and cultural status* (ESCS) was derived from a principal component analysis of standardised variables (each variable has an OECD mean of zero and a standard deviation of one), taking the factor scores for the first principal component as measures of the PISA *index of economic, social and cultural status*.

Principal component analysis was also performed for each participating country or economy to determine to what extent the components of the index operate in similar ways across countries or economy. The analysis revealed that patterns of factor loading were very similar across countries, with all three components contributing to a similar extent to the index (for details on reliability and factor loadings, see the *PISA 2012 Technical Report* (OECD, forthcoming).

The imputation of components for students with missing data on one component was done on the basis of a regression on the other two variables, with an additional random error component. The final values on the *PISA index of economic, social and cultural status* (ESCS) for 2012 have an OECD mean of 0 and a standard deviation of one.

ESCS was computed for all students in the five cycles, and ESCS indices for trends analyses were obtained by applying the parameters used to derive standardised values in 2012 to the ESCS components for previous cycles. These values will therefore not be directly comparable to ESCS values in the databases for previous cycles, though the differences are not large for the 2006 and 2009 cycles. ESCS values in earlier cycles were computed using different algorithms, so for 2000 and 2003 the differences are larger.

Changes to the computation of socio-economic status for PISA 2012

While the computation of socio-economic status followed what had been done in previous cycles, PISA 2012 undertook an important upgrade with respect to the coding of parental occupation. Prior to PISA 2012, the 1988 International Standard Classification of Occupations (ISCO-88) was used for the coding of parental occupation. By 2012, however, ISCO-88 was almost 25 years old and it was no longer tenable to maintain its use as an occupational coding scheme.[2] It was therefore decided to use its replacement, ISCO-08, for occupational coding in PISA 2012.

The change from ISCO-88 to ISCO-08 required an update of the International Socio-Economic Index (ISEI) of occupation codes. PISA 2012 therefore used a modified quantification scheme for ISCO-08 (referred to as ISEI-08), as developed by Harry Ganzeboom (2010). ISEI-08 was constructed using a database of 198 500 men and women with valid education, occupation and (personal) incomes derived from the combined 2002-07 datasets of the International Social Survey Programme (ISSP) (Ganzeboom, 2010). The methodology used for this purpose was similar to the one employed in the construction of ISEI for ISCO-68 and ISCO-88 described in different publications (Ganzeboom, de Graff and Treiman, 1992; Ganzeboom and Treiman,1996; Ganzeboom and Treiman, 2003).[3]

The main differences with regard to the previous ISEI construction are the following:

- A new database was used which is more recent, larger and cross-nationally more diverse than the one used earlier.
- The new ISEI was constructed using data for women and men, while previously only men were used to estimate the scale. The data on income were corrected for hours worked to adjust the different prevalence of part-time work between men and women in many countries.

A range of validation activities accompanied the transition from ISCO-88/ISEI-88 to ISCO-08/ISEI-08, including a comparison of *i)* the distributions of ISEI-88 with ISEI-08 in terms of range, mean and standard deviations for both mothers' and fathers' occupations and *ii)* correlations between the two ISEI indicators and performance, again separately undertaken for mothers' and fathers' occupations.

For this cycle, in order to obtain trends for all cycles from 2000 to 2012, the computation of the indices WEALTH, HEDRES, CULTPOSS and HOMEPOS was based on data from all cycles from 2000 to 2012. HOMEPOS is of particular importance as it is used in the computation of ESCS. These were then standardised on 2012 so that the OECD mean is 0 and the standard deviation is 1. This means that the indices calculated on the previous cycle will be on the 2012 scale and thus not directly comparable to the indices in the database for the previously released cycles. To estimate item parameters for scaling, a calibration sample from all cycles was used, consisting of 500 students from all countries in the previous cycles, and 750 from 2012, as any particular student questionnaire item only occurs in two-thirds of the questionnaires in 2012.

The items used in the computation of the indices has changed to some extent from cycle to cycle, though cycles they have remained much the same from 2006 to 2012. The earlier cycles were are in general missing a few items that are present in the later cycles, but it was felt leaving out items only present in the later cycles would give too much weight to the earlier cycles. So a superset of all items (except country specific items) in the five cycles was used, and international item parameters were derived from this set.

The second step was to estimate WLEs for the indices, anchoring parameters on the international item set while estimating the country specific item parameters. This is the same procedure used in previous cycles.

Family wealth

The *index of family wealth* (WEALTH) is based on students' responses on whether they had the following at home: a room of their own, a link to the Internet, a dishwasher (treated as a country-specific item), a DVD player, and three other country-specific items (some items in ST26); and their responses on the number of cellular phones, televisions, computers, cars and the number of rooms with a bath or shower (ST27).

Home educational resources

The *index of home educational resources* (HEDRES) is based on the items measuring the existence of educational resources at home including a desk and a quiet place to study, a computer that students can use for schoolwork, educational software, books to help with students' school work, technical reference books and a dictionary (some items in ST26).

Cultural possessions

The *index of cultural possessions* (CULTPOSS) is based on students' responses to whether they had the following at home: classic literature, books of poetry and works of art (some items in ST26).

The rotated design of the student questionnaire

A major innovation in PISA 2012 is the rotated design of the student questionnaire. One of the main reasons for a rotated design, which had previously been implemented for the cognitive assessment, was to extend the content coverage of the student questionnaire. Table A1.3 provides an overview of the rotation design and content of questionnaire forms for the main survey.

Table A1.3 **Student questionnaire rotation design**

Form A	Common Question Set (all forms)	Question Set 1 – Mathematics Attitudes/ Problem Solving	Question Set 3 – Opportunity to Learn/ Learning Strategies
Form B	Common Question Set (all forms)	Question Set 2 – School Climate/Attitudes towards School/Anxiety	Question Set 1 – Mathematics Attitudes/ Problem Solving
Form C	Common Question Set (all forms)	Question Set 3 – Opportunity to Learn/ Learning Strategies	Question Set 2 – School Climate/Attitudes towards School/Anxiety

Note: For details regarding the questions in each question set, please refer to the *PISA 2012 Technical Report* (OECD, forthcoming).

The *PISA 2012 Technical Report* (OECD, forthcoming) provides all details regarding the rotated design of the student questionnaire in PISA 2012, including its implications in terms of *i)* proficiency estimates, *ii)* international reports and trends, *iii)* further analyses, *iv)* structure and documentation of the international database, and *v)* logistics. The rotated design has negligible implications for proficiency estimates and correlations of proficiency estimates with context constructs. The international database (available at *www.pisa.oecd.org*) includes all background variables for each student. The variables based on the questions that students answered reflect their responses; those that are based on questions that were not administered show a distinctive missing code. Rotation allows the estimation of a full co-variance matrix which means that all variables can be correlated with all other variables. It does not affect conclusions in terms of whether or not an effect would be considered significant in multilevel models.

School-level simple indices

School and class size

The *index of school size* (SCHSIZE) was derived by summing up the number of girls and boys at a school (SC07).

Student-teacher ratio

The *student-teacher ratio* (STRATIO) was obtained by dividing the school size by the total number of teachers (SC09). The number of part-time teachers was weighted by 0.5 and the number of full-time teachers was weighted by 1.0 in the computation of this index.

The *student-mathematics teacher ratio* (SMRATIO) was obtained by dividing the school size by the total number of mathematics teachers (SC10Q11 and SC10Q12). The number of part-time mathematics teachers was weighted by 0.5 and the number of full time mathematics teachers was weighted by 1.0 in the computation of this index.

School type

Schools are classified as either public or private, according to whether a private entity or a public agency has the ultimate power to make decisions concerning its affairs (SC01). This information is combined with SC02 which provides information on the percentage of total funding which comes from government sources to create the *index of school type* (SCHLTYPE). This index has three categories: (1) government-independent private schools controlled by a non-government organisation or with a governing board not selected by a government agency that receive less than 50% of their core funding from government agencies, (2) government-dependent private schools controlled by a non-government organisation or with a governing board not selected by a government agency that receive more than 50% of their core funding from government agencies, and (3) public schools controlled and managed by a public education authority or agency.

Availability of computers

The *index of computer availability* (RATCMP15) was derived from dividing the number of computers available for educational purposes available to students in the modal grade for 15-year-olds (SC11Q02) by the number of students in the modal grade for 15-year-olds (SC11Q01). The wording of the questions asking about computer availability changed between 2006 and 2009. Comparisons involving availability of computers are possible for 2012 data with 2009 data, but not with 2006 or earlier.

The *index of computers connected to the Internet* (COMPWEB) was derived from dividing the number of computers for educational purposes available to students in the modal grade for 15-year-olds that are connected to the web (SC11Q03) by the number of computers for educational purposes available to students in the modal grade for 15-year-olds (SC11Q02).

Quantity of teaching staff at school

The *proportion of fully certified teachers* (PROPCERT) was computed by dividing the number of fully certified teachers (SC09Q21 plus 0.5*SC09Q22) by the total number of teachers (SC09Q11 plus 0.5*SC09Q12). The proportion of teachers who have an ISCED 5A qualification (PROPQUAL) was calculated by dividing the number of these kind of teachers (SC09Q31 plus 0.5*SC09Q32) by the total number of teachers (SC09Q11 plus 0.5*SC09Q12). The proportion of mathematics teachers (PROPMATH) was computed by dividing the number of mathematics teachers (SC10Q11 plus 0.5*SC10Q12) by the total number of teachers (SC09Q11 plus 0.5*SC09Q12). The proportion of mathematics teachers who have an ISCED 5A qualification (PROPMA5A) was computed by dividing the number of mathematics teachers who have an ISCED 5A qualification (SC10Q21 plus 0.5*SC10Q22) by the number of mathematics teachers (SC10Q11 plus 0.5*SC10Q12).

Although both PISA 2003 and PISA 2012 asked school principals about the school's teaching staff, the wording of the questions on the proportion of teachers with an ISCED 5A qualification changed, rendering comparisons impossible.

Academic selectivity

The index of academic selectivity (SCHSEL) was derived from school principals' responses on how frequently consideration was given to the following two factors when students were admitted to the school, based on a scale with response categories "never", "sometimes" and "always" (SC32Q02 and SC32Q03): students' record of academic performance (including placement tests); and recommendation of feeder schools. This index has the following three categories: (1) schools where these two factors are "never" considered for admission, (2) schools considering at least one of these two factors "sometimes" but neither factor "always", and (3) schools where at least one of these two factors is "always" considered for admission.

Although both PISA 2003 and PISA 2012 asked school principals about the school's criteria for admitting students, the wording of the questions changed, rendering comparisons impossible.

Ability grouping

The *index of ability grouping in mathematics classes* (ABGMATH) was derived from the two items of school principals' reports on whether their school organises mathematics instruction differently for student with different abilities "for all classes", "for some classes", or "not for any classes" (SC15Q01 for mathematics classes study similar content but at different levels and SC15Q02 for different classes study different content or sets of mathematics topics that have different levels of difficulty). This index has the following three categories: (1) no mathematic classes study different levels of difficulty or different content (i.e. "not for any classes" for both SC15Q01 and SC15Q02); (2) some mathematics classes study different levels of difficulty or different content (i.e. "for some classes" for either SC15Q01 or SC15Q02); (3) all mathematics classes study different levels of difficulty or different content (i.e. "for all classes" for either SC15Q01 or SC15Q02).

Extracurricular activities offered by school

The *index of mathematics extracurricular activities at school* (MACTIV) was derived from school principals' reports on whether their schools offered the following activities to students in the national modal grade for 15-year-olds in the academic year of the PISA assessment (SC16 and SC21 for the last one): *i)* mathematics club, *ii)* mathematics competition, *iii)* club with a focus on computers/Information, Communication Technology, and *iv)* additional mathematics lessons. This index was developed by summing up the number of activities that a school offers. For "additional mathematics lessons" (SC21), it is counted as one when school principals responded "enrichment mathematics only", "remedial mathematics only" or "without differentiation depending on the prior achievement level of the students"; and it is counted as two when school principals responded "both enrichment and remedial mathematics".

The *index of creative extracurricular activities at school* (CREACTIV) was derived from school principals' reports on whether their schools offered the following activities to students in the national modal grade for 15-year-olds in the academic year of the PISA assessment (SC16): *i)* band, orchestra or choir, *ii)* school play or school musical, and *iii)* art club or art activities. This index was developed by adding up the number of activities that a school offers.

Use of assessment

School principals were asked to report whether students' assessments are used for the following purposes (SC18): *i)* to inform parents about their child's progress; *ii)* to make decisions about students' retention or promotion; *iii)* to group students for instructional purposes; *iv)* to compare the school to district or national performance; *v)* to monitor the school's progress from year to year; *vi)* to make judgements about teachers' effectiveness; *vii)* to identify aspects of instruction or the curriculum that could be improved; and *viii)* to compare the school with other schools. The *index of use of assessment* (ASSESS) was derived from these eight items by adding up the number of "yes" in principals' responses to these questions.

School responsibility for resource allocation

School principals were asked to report whether "principals", "teachers", "school governing board", "regional or local education authority" or "national education authority" have a considerable responsibility for the following tasks (SC33): *i)* selecting teachers for hire; *ii)* firing teachers; *iii)* establishing teachers' starting salaries; *iv)* determining teachers' salary increases; *v)* formulating the school budget; and *vi)* deciding on budget allocations within the school. *The index of school responsibility for resource allocation* (RESPRES) was derived from these six items. The ratio of the number of responsibilities that "principals" and/or "teachers" have for these six items to the number of responsibilities that "regional or local education authority" and/or "national education authority" have for these six items was computed. Positive values on this index indicate relatively more responsibility for schools than local, regional or national education authority. This index has an OECD mean of 0 and a standard deviation of 1.

Although both PISA 2003 and PISA 2012 asked school principals about the school's responsibility for resource allocation, the wording of the questions changed, rendering comparisons impossible.

School responsibility for curriculum and assessment

School principals were asked to report whether "principals", "teachers", "school governing board", "regional or local education authority", or "national education authority" have a considerable responsibility for the following tasks (SC33): *i)* establishing student assessment policies; *ii)* choosing which textbooks are used; *iii)* determining course content; and *iv)* deciding which courses are offered.

The *index of the school responsibility for curriculum and assessment* (RESPCUR) was derived from these four items. The ratio of the number of responsibilities that "principals" and/or "teachers" have for these four items to the number of responsibilities that "regional or local education authority" and/or "national education authority" have for these four items was computed. Positive values on this index indicate relatively more responsibility for schools than local, regional or national education authority. This index has an OECD mean of 0 and a standard deviation of 1.

Although both PISA 2003 and PISA 2012 asked school principals about the school's responsibility for admission and instruction policies, the wording of the questions changed, rendering comparisons impossible.

School-level scale indices

School principals' leadership

The *index of school management: framing and communicating the school's goals and curricular development* (LEADCOM) was derived from school principals' responses about the frequency with which they were involved in the following school affairs in the previous school year (SC34): *i)* use student performance results to develop the school's educational goals; *ii)* make sure that the professional development activities of teachers are in accordance with the teaching goals of the school; *iii)* ensure that teachers work according to the school's educational goals; and *iv)* discuss the school's academic goals with teachers at faculty meetings. The *index of school management: instructional leadership* (LEADINST) was derived from school principals' responses about the frequency with which they were involved in the following school affairs in the previous school year (SC34): *i)* promote teaching practices based on recent educational research, *ii)* praise teachers whose students are actively participating in learning, and *iii)* draw teachers' attention to the importance of pupils' development of critical can social capacities. The index of school management: promoting instructional improvements and professional development (LEADPD) was derived from school principals' responses about the frequency with which they were involved in the following school affairs in the previous school year (SC34): *i)* take the initiative to discuss matters, when a teacher has problems in his/her classroom; *ii)* pay attention to disruptive behaviour in classrooms; and *iii)* solve a problem together with a teacher, when the teacher brings up a classroom problem. The *index of school management: teacher participation* (LEADTCH) was derived from school principals' responses about the frequency with which they were involved in the following school affairs in the previous school year (SC34): *i)* provide staff with opportunities to participate in school decision-making; *ii)* engage teachers to help build a school culture of continuous improvement; and *iii)* ask teachers to participate in reviewing management practices. Higher values on these indices indicate greater involvement of school principals in school affairs.

Teacher shortage

The *index of teacher shortage* (TCSHORT) was derived from four items measuring school principals' perceptions of potential factors hindering instruction at their school (SC14). These factors are a lack of: *i)* qualified science teachers; *ii)* qualified mathematics teachers; *iii)* qualified <test language> teachers; and *iv)* qualified teachers of other subjects. Higher values on this index indicate school principals' reports of higher teacher shortage at a school.

For trends analyses, the PISA 2003 values of the index of teacher shortage were rescaled to be comparable to those in PISA 2012. As a result, values for the index of teacher shortage for PISA 2003 reported in this volume may differ from those reported in *Learning for Tomorrow's World: First Results from PISA 2003* (OECD, 2004).

Quality of school's educational resources

The *index of quality of school educational resources* (SCMATEDU) was derived from six items measuring school principals' perceptions of potential factors hindering instruction at their school (SC14). These factors are: *i)* shortage or inadequacy of science laboratory equipment; *ii)* shortage or inadequacy of instructional materials; *iii)* shortage or inadequacy of computers for instruction; *iv)* lack or inadequacy of Internet connectivity; *v)* shortage or inadequacy of computer software for instruction; and *vi)* shortage or inadequacy of library materials. As all items were inverted for scaling, higher values on this index indicate better quality of educational resources.

For trends analyses, the PISA 2003 values of the index of quality of educational resources were rescaled to be comparable to those in PISA 2012. As a result, values for the index of quality educational resources for PISA 2003 reported in this volume may differ from those reported in *Learning for Tomorrow's World: First Results from PISA 2003* (OECD, 2004). One of the questions included to compute the index of quality of educational resources in PISA 2012 ("lack or inadequacy of internet connection") was not included in the PISA 2003 questionnaire. Estimation of the PISA 2003 index treats this question as missing and, under the assumption that the relationship between the items remains unchanged with the inclusion of the new questions, the PISA 2003 and PISA 2012 values on the index of quality of educational resources are comparable after the rescaling.

Quality of schools' physical infrastructure

The *index of quality of physicals' infrastructure* (SCMATBUI) was derived from three items measuring school principals' perceptions of potential factors hindering instruction at their school (SC14). These factors are: *i)* shortage or inadequacy of school buildings and grounds; *ii)* shortage or inadequacy of heating/cooling and lighting systems; and *iii)* shortage or inadequacy of instructional space (e.g. classrooms). As all items were inverted for scaling, higher values on this index indicate better quality of physical infrastructure.

For trends analyses, the PISA 2003 values of the index of quality of physical infrastructure were rescaled to be comparable to those in PISA 2012. As a result, values for the index of quality of physical infrastructure for PISA 2003 reported in this volume may differ from those reported in *Learning for Tomorrow's World: First Results from PISA 2003* (OECD, 2004).

Teacher behaviour

The *index on teacher-related factors affecting school climate* (TEACCLIM) was derived from school principals' reports on the extent to which the learning of students was hindered by the following factors in their schools (SC22): *i)* students not being encouraged to achieve their full potential; *ii)* poor student-teacher relations; *iii)* teachers having to teach students of heterogeneous ability levels within the same class; *iv)* teachers having to teach students of diverse ethnic backgrounds (i.e. language, culture) within the same class; *v)* teachers' low expectations of students; *vi)* teachers not meeting individual students' needs; *vii)* teacher absenteeism; *viii)* staff resisting change; *ix)* teachers being too strict with students; *x)* teachers being late for classes; and *xi)* teachers not being well prepared for classes. As all items were inverted for scaling, higher values on this index indicate a positive teacher behaviour.

For trends analyses, the PISA 2003 values of the index of teacher-related factors affecting school climate were rescaled to be comparable to those in PISA 2012. As a result, values for the index of teacher-related factors affecting school climate for PISA 2003 reported in this volume may differ from those reported in *Learning for Tomorrow's World: First Results from PISA 2003* (OECD, 2004). Four of the questions included to compute the index of teacher-related factors affecting school climate in PISA 2012 ("teachers having to teach students of heterogeneous ability levels within the same class," "teachers having to teach students of diverse ethnic backgrounds (i.e. language, culture) within the same class," "teachers being late for classes," and "teachers not being well prepared for classes") were not included in the PISA 2003 questionnaire. Estimation of the PISA 2003 index treats these indices as missing and, under the assumption that the relationship between the items remains unchanged with the inclusion of the new questions, the PISA 2003 and PISA 2012 values on the index of teacher-related factors affecting school climate are comparable after the rescaling.

Student behaviour

The *index of student-related factors affecting school climate* (STUDCLIM) was derived from school principals' reports on the extent to which the learning of students was hindered by the following factors in their schools (SC22): *i)* student truancy; *ii)* students skipping classes; *iii)* students arriving late for school; *iv)* students not attending compulsory school events (e.g. sports day) or excursions, *v)* students lacking respect for teachers; *vi)* disruption of classes by students; *vii)* student use of alcohol or illegal drugs; and *viii)* students intimidating or bullying other students. As all items were inverted for scaling, higher values on this index indicate a positive student behaviour.

For trends analyses, the PISA 2003 values of the index of student-related factors affecting school climate were rescaled to be comparable to those in PISA 2012. As a result, values for the index of student-related factors affecting school climate for PISA 2003 reported in this volume may differ from those reported in *Learning for Tomorrow's World: First Results from PISA 2003* (OECD, 2004). Two of the questions included to compute the index of student-related factors affecting school climate in PISA 2012 ("students arriving late for school," and "students not attending compulsory school events (e.g. sports day) or excursions") were not included in the PISA 2003 questionnaire. Estimation of the PISA 2003 index treats these questions as missing and, under the assumption that the relationship between the items remains unchanged with the inclusion of the new questions, the PISA 2003 and PISA 2012 values on the index of student-related factors affecting school climate are comparable after the rescaling.

Teacher morale

The *index of teacher morale* (TCMORALE) was derived from school principals' reports on the extent to which they agree with the following statements considering teachers in their schools (SC26): *i)* the morale of teachers in this school is high; *ii)* teachers work with enthusiasm; *iii)* teachers take pride in this school; and *iv)* teachers value academic achievement. As all items were inverted for scaling, higher values on this index indicate more positive teacher morale.

For trends analyses, the PISA 2003 values of the index of teacher morale were rescaled to be comparable to those in PISA 2012. As a result, values for the index teacher morale for PISA 2003 reported in this volume may differ from those reported in *Learning for Tomorrow's World: First Results from PISA 2003* (OECD, 2004).

Notes

1. Note that for ISCO coding 0 "Arm forces", the following recoding was followed: "Officers" were coded as "Managers" (ISCO 1), and "Other armed forces occupations" (drivers, gunners, seaman, generic armed forces) as "Plant and Machine operators" (ISCO 8). In addition, all answers starting with "97" (housewives, students, and "vague occupations") were coded into missing.

2. The update from ISCO-88 to ISCO-08 mainly involved *i)* more adequate categories for IT-related occupations, *ii)* distinction of military ranks and *iii)* a revision of the categories classifying different managers

3. Information on ISCO08 and ISEI08 is included from *http://www.ilo.org/public/english/bureau/stat/isco/index.htm* and *http://home.fsw.vu.nl/hbg.ganzeboom/isco08*

References

Ganzeboom, H.B.G. (2010), "A new international socio-economic index [ISEI] of occupational status for the International Standard Classification of Occupation 2008 [ISCO-08] constructed with data from the ISSP 2002-2007; with an analysis of quality of occupational measurement in ISSP ", paper presented at Annual Conference of International Social Survey Programme, Lisbon, 1 May 2010.

Ganzeboom, H.B.G. and **D.J. Treiman** (2003), "Three Internationally Standardised Measures for Comparative Research on Occupational Status ", in Jürgen H.P. Hoffmeyer-Zlotnik and Christof Wolf (eds.), *Advances in Cross-National Comparison: A European Working Book for Demographic and Socio-Economic Variables*, Kluwer Academic Press, New York.

Ganzeboom, H.B.G. and **D.J. Treiman** (1996), "Internationally Comparable Measures of Occupational Status for the 1988 International Standard Classification of Occupations", *Social Science Research*, Vol. 25, pp. 201-39.

Ganzeboom, H.B.G., P. de Graaf and **D.J. Treiman** (1992), "A Standard International Socio-Economic Index of Occupational Status", *Social Science Research*, Vol. 21, Issue 1, pp. 1-56.

Ganzeboom, H.B.G., R. Luijkx and **D.J. Treiman** (1989), "InterGenerational Class Mobility in Comparative Perspective", *Research in Social Stratification and Mobility*, Vol. 8, pp. 3-79.

ILO (1990), *ISCO-88: International Standard Classification of Occupations,* International Labour Office, Geneva.

OECD (forthcoming), *PISA 2012 Technical Report*, OECD Publishing.

OECD (2013a), *PISA 2012 Assessment and Analytical Framework: Mathematics, Reading, Science, Problem Solving and Financial Literacy*, PISA, OECD Publishing.
http://dx.doi.org/10.1787/9789264190511-en

OECD (2013b), *Education at a Glance 2013: OECD Indicators*, OECD Publishing.
http://dx.doi.org/10.1787/eag-2013-en

OECD (2013c), *OECD Skills Outlook 2013: First Results from the Survey of Adult Skills*, OECD Publishing.
http://dx.doi.org/10.1787/9789264204256-en

OECD (2004), *Learning for Tomorrow's World: First Results from PISA 2003*, PISA, OECD Publishing.
http://dx.doi.org/10.1787/9789264006416-en

OECD (1999), *Classifying Educational Programmes: Manual for ISCED-97 Implemention in OECD Countries*, OECD Publishing.
www.oecd.org/education/skills-beyond-school/1962350.pdf

Warm, T.A. (1989), "Weighted likelihood estimation of ability in item response theory", Psychometrika, Volume 54, Issue 3, pp. 427-450.
http://dx.doi.org/10.1007/BF02294627

ANNEX A2

THE PISA TARGET POPULATION, THE PISA SAMPLES AND THE DEFINITION OF SCHOOLS

Definition of the PISA target population

PISA 2012 provides an assessment of the cumulative yield of education and learning at a point at which most young adults are still enrolled in initial education.

A major challenge for an international survey is to ensure that international comparability of national target populations is guaranteed in such a venture.

Differences between countries in the nature and extent of pre-primary education and care, the age of entry into formal schooling and the institutional structure of education systems do not allow the definition of internationally comparable grade levels of schooling. Consequently, international comparisons of education performance typically define their populations with reference to a target age group. Some previous international assessments have defined their target population on the basis of the grade level that provides maximum coverage of a particular age cohort. A disadvantage of this approach is that slight variations in the age distribution of students across grade levels often lead to the selection of different target grades in different countries, or between education systems within countries, raising serious questions about the comparability of results across, and at times within, countries. In addition, because not all students of the desired age are usually represented in grade-based samples, there may be a more serious potential bias in the results if the unrepresented students are typically enrolled in the next higher grade in some countries and the next lower grade in others. This would exclude students with potentially higher levels of performance in the former countries and students with potentially lower levels of performance in the latter.

In order to address this problem, PISA uses an age-based definition for its target population, i.e. a definition that is not tied to the institutional structures of national education systems. PISA assesses students who were aged between 15 years and 3 (complete) months and 16 years and 2 (complete) months at the beginning of the assessment period, plus or minus a 1 month allowable variation, and who were enrolled in an educational institution with Grade 7 or higher, regardless of the grade levels or type of institution in which they were enrolled, and regardless of whether they were in full-time or part-time education. Educational institutions are generally referred to as schools in this publication, although some educational institutions (in particular, some types of vocational education establishments) may not be termed schools in certain countries. As expected from this definition, the average age of students across OECD countries was 15 years and 9 months. The range in country means was 2 months and 5 days (0.18 years), from the minimum country mean of 15 years and 8 months to the maximum country mean of 15 years and 10 months.

Given this definition of population, PISA makes statements about the knowledge and skills of a group of individuals who were born within a comparable reference period, but who may have undergone different educational experiences both in and outside of schools. In PISA, these knowledge and skills are referred to as the yield of education at an age that is common across countries. Depending on countries' policies on school entry, selection and promotion, these students may be distributed over a narrower or a wider range of grades across different education systems, tracks or streams. It is important to consider these differences when comparing PISA results across countries, as observed differences between students at age 15 may no longer appear as students' educational experiences converge later on.

If a country's scale scores in reading, scientific or mathematical literacy are significantly higher than those in another country, it cannot automatically be inferred that the schools or particular parts of the education system in the first country are more effective than those in the second. However, one can legitimately conclude that the cumulative impact of learning experiences in the first country, starting in early childhood and up to the age of 15, and embracing experiences both in school, home and beyond, have resulted in higher outcomes in the literacy domains that PISA measures.

The PISA target population did not include residents attending schools in a foreign country. It does, however, include foreign nationals attending schools in the country of assessment.

To accommodate countries that desired grade-based results for the purpose of national analyses, PISA 2012 provided a sampling option to supplement age-based sampling with grade-based sampling.

Population coverage

All countries attempted to maximise the coverage of 15-year-olds enrolled in education in their national samples, including students enrolled in special educational institutions. As a result, PISA 2012 reached standards of population coverage that are unprecedented in international surveys of this kind.

The sampling standards used in PISA permitted countries to exclude up to a total of 5% of the relevant population either by excluding schools or by excluding students within schools. All but eight countries, Luxembourg (8.40%), Canada (6.38%), Denmark (6.18%), Norway (6.11%), Estonia (5.80%), Sweden (5.44%), the United Kingdom (5.43%) and the United States (5.35%), achieved this standard, and in 30 countries and economies, the overall exclusion rate was less than 2%. When language exclusions were accounted for (i.e. removed from the overall exclusion rate), Norway, Sweden, the United Kingdom and the United States no longer had an exclusion rate greater than 5%. For details, see *www.pisa.oecd.org*.

Exclusions within the above limits include:

- At the school level: *i)* schools that were geographically inaccessible or where the administration of the PISA assessment was not considered feasible; and *ii)* schools that provided teaching only for students in the categories defined under "within-school exclusions", such as schools for the blind. The percentage of 15-year-olds enrolled in such schools had to be less than 2.5% of the nationally desired target population [0.5% maximum for *i)* and 2% maximum for *ii)*]. The magnitude, nature and justification of school-level exclusions are documented in the *PISA 2012 Technical Report* (OECD, forthcoming).

- At the student level: *i)* students with an intellectual disability; *ii)* students with a functional disability; *iii)* students with limited assessment language proficiency; *iv)* other – a category defined by the national centres and approved by the international centre; and *v)* students taught in a language of instruction for the main domain for which no materials were available. Students could not be excluded solely because of low proficiency or common discipline problems. The percentage of 15-year-olds excluded within schools had to be less than 2.5% of the nationally desired target population.

Table A2.1 describes the target population of the countries participating in PISA 2012. Further information on the target population and the implementation of PISA sampling standards can be found in the *PISA 2012 Technical Report* (OECD, forthcoming).

- *Column 1* shows the *total number of 15-year-olds* according to the most recent available information, which in most countries meant the year 2011 as the year before the assessment.

- *Column 2* shows the number of 15-year-olds enrolled in schools in Grade 7 or above (as defined above), which is referred to as the *eligible population*.

- *Column 3* shows the *national desired target population*. Countries were allowed to exclude up to 0.5% of students a priori from the eligible population, essentially for practical reasons. The following a priori exclusions exceed this limit but were agreed with the PISA Consortium: Belgium excluded 0.23% of its population for a particular type of student educated while working; Canada excluded 1.14% of its population from Territories and Aboriginal reserves; Chile excluded 0.04% of its students who live in Easter Island, Juan Fernandez Archipelago and Antarctica; Indonesia excluded 1.55% of its students from two provinces because of operational reasons; Ireland excluded 0.05% of its students in three island schools off the west coast; Latvia excluded 0.08% of its students in distance learning schools; and Serbia excluded 2.11% of its students taught in Serbian in Kosovo.

- *Column 4* shows the *number of students enrolled in schools that were excluded from the national desired target population* either from the sampling frame or later in the field during data collection.

- *Column 5* shows the *size of the national desired target population after subtracting the students enrolled in excluded schools*. This is obtained by subtracting Column 4 from Column 3.

- *Column 6* shows the *percentage of students enrolled in excluded schools*. This is obtained by dividing Column 4 by Column 3 and multiplying by 100.

- *Column 7* shows the *number of students participating in PISA 2012*. Note that in some cases this number does not account for 15-year-olds assessed as part of additional national options.

- *Column 8* shows the *weighted number of participating students*, i.e. the number of students in the nationally defined target population that the PISA sample represents.

- Each country attempted to maximise the coverage of the PISA target population within the sampled schools. In the case of each sampled school, all eligible students, namely those 15 years of age, regardless of grade, were first listed. Sampled students who were to be excluded had still to be included in the sampling documentation, and a list drawn up stating the reason for their exclusion. *Column 9* indicates the *total number of excluded students*, which is further described and classified into specific categories in Table A2.2.

- *Column 10* indicates the *weighted number of excluded students*, i.e. the overall number of students in the nationally defined target population represented by the number of students excluded from the sample, which is also described and classified by exclusion categories in Table A2.2. Excluded students were excluded based on five categories: *i)* students with an intellectual disability – the student has a mental or emotional disability and is cognitively delayed such that he/she cannot perform in the PISA testing situation; *ii)* students with a functional disability – the student has a moderate to severe permanent physical disability such that he/she cannot perform in the PISA testing situation; *iii)* students with a limited assessment language proficiency – the student is unable to read or speak any of the languages of the assessment in the country and would be unable to overcome the language barrier in the testing situation (typically a student who has received less than one year of instruction in the languages of the assessment may be excluded); *iv)* other – a category defined by the national centres and approved by the international centre; and *v)* students taught in a language of instruction for the main domain for which no materials were available.

- *Column 11* shows the *percentage of students excluded within schools*. This is calculated as the weighted number of excluded students (Column 10), divided by the weighted number of excluded and participating students (Column 8 plus Column 10), then multiplied by 100.

- *Column 12* shows the *overall exclusion rate*, which represents the weighted percentage of the national desired target population excluded from PISA either through school-level exclusions or through the exclusion of students within schools. It is calculated as the school-level exclusion rate (Column 6 divided by 100) plus within-school exclusion rate (Column 11 divided by 100) multiplied by 1 minus the school-level exclusion rate (Column 6 divided by 100). This result is then multiplied by 100.

[Part 1/2]

Table A2.1 **PISA target populations and samples**

		Population and sample information						
		Total population of 15-year-olds	Total enrolled population of 15-year-olds at Grade 7 or above	Total in national desired target population	Total school-level exclusions	Total in national desired target population after all school exclusions and before within-school exclusions	School-level exclusion rate (%)	Number of participating students	Weighted number of participating students
		(1)	(2)	(3)	(4)	(5)	(6)	(7)	(8)
OECD	Australia	291 967	288 159	288 159	5 702	282 457	1.98	17 774	250 779
	Austria	93 537	89 073	89 073	106	88 967	0.12	4 756	82 242
	Belgium	123 469	121 493	121 209	1 324	119 885	1.09	9 690	117 912
	Canada	417 873	409 453	404 767	2 936	401 831	0.73	21 548	348 070
	Chile	274 803	252 733	252 625	2 687	249 938	1.06	6 857	229 199
	Czech Republic	96 946	93 214	93 214	1 577	91 637	1.69	6 535	82 101
	Denmark	72 310	70 854	70 854	1 965	68 889	2.77	7 481	65 642
	Estonia	12 649	12 438	12 438	442	11 996	3.55	5 867	11 634
	Finland	62 523	62 195	62 195	523	61 672	0.84	8 829	60 047
	France	792 983	755 447	755 447	27 403	728 044	3.63	5 682	701 399
	Germany	798 136	798 136	798 136	10 914	787 222	1.37	5 001	756 907
	Greece	110 521	105 096	105 096	1 364	103 732	1.30	5 125	96 640
	Hungary	111 761	108 816	108 816	1 725	107 091	1.59	4 810	91 179
	Iceland	4 505	4 491	4 491	10	4 481	0.22	3 508	4 169
	Ireland	59 296	57 979	57 952	0	57 952	0.00	5 016	54 010
	Israel	118 953	113 278	113 278	2 784	110 494	2.46	6 061	107 745
	Italy	605 490	566 973	566 973	8 498	558 475	1.50	38 142	521 288
	Japan	1 241 786	1 214 756	1 214 756	26 099	1 188 657	2.15	6 351	1 128 179
	Korea	687 104	672 101	672 101	3 053	669 048	0.45	5 033	603 632
	Luxembourg	6 187	6 082	6 082	151	5 931	2.48	5 260	5 523
	Mexico	2 114 745	1 472 875	1 472 875	7 307	1 465 568	0.50	33 806	1 326 025
	Netherlands	194 000	193 190	193 190	7 546	185 644	3.91	4 460	196 262
	New Zealand	60 940	59 118	59 118	579	58 539	0.98	5 248	53 414
	Norway	64 917	64 777	64 777	750	64 027	1.16	4 686	59 432
	Poland	425 597	410 700	410 700	6 900	403 800	1.68	5 662	379 275
	Portugal	108 728	127 537	127 537	0	127 537	0.00	5 722	96 034
	Slovak Republic	59 723	59 367	59 367	1 480	57 887	2.49	5 737	54 486
	Slovenia	19 471	18 935	18 935	115	18 820	0.61	7 229	18 303
	Spain	423 444	404 374	404 374	2 031	402 343	0.50	25 335	374 266
	Sweden	102 087	102 027	102 027	1 705	100 322	1.67	4 739	94 988
	Switzerland	87 200	85 239	85 239	2 479	82 760	2.91	11 234	79 679
	Turkey	1 266 638	965 736	965 736	10 387	955 349	1.08	4 848	866 681
	United Kingdom	738 066	745 581	745 581	19 820	725 761	2.66	12 659	688 236
	United States	3 985 714	4 074 457	4 074 457	41 142	4 033 315	1.01	6 111	3 536 153
Partners	Albania	76 910	50 157	50 157	56	50 101	0.11	4 743	42 466
	Argentina	684 879	637 603	637 603	3 995	633 608	0.63	5 908	545 942
	Brazil	3 574 928	2 786 064	2 786 064	34 932	2 751 132	1.25	20 091	2 470 804
	Bulgaria	70 188	59 684	59 684	1 437	58 247	2.41	5 282	54 255
	Colombia	889 729	620 422	620 422	4	620 418	0.00	11 173	560 805
	Costa Rica	81 489	64 326	64 326	0	64 326	0.00	4 602	40 384
	Croatia	48 155	46 550	46 550	417	46 133	0.90	6 153	45 502
	Cyprus*	9 956	9 956	9 955	128	9 827	1.29	5 078	9 650
	Hong Kong-China	84 200	77 864	77 864	813	77 051	1.04	4 670	70 636
	Indonesia	4 174 217	3 599 844	3 544 028	8 039	3 535 989	0.23	5 622	2 645 155
	Jordan	129 492	125 333	125 333	141	125 192	0.11	7 038	111 098
	Kazakhstan	258 716	247 048	247 048	7 374	239 674	2.98	5 808	208 411
	Latvia	18 789	18 389	18 375	655	17 720	3.56	5 276	16 054
	Liechtenstein	417	383	383	1	382	0.26	293	314
	Lithuania	38 524	35 567	35 567	526	35 041	1.48	4 618	33 042
	Macao-China	6 600	5 416	5 416	6	5 410	0.11	5 335	5 366
	Malaysia	544 302	457 999	457 999	225	457 774	0.05	5 197	432 080
	Montenegro	8 600	8 600	8 600	18	8 582	0.21	4 744	7 714
	Peru	584 294	508 969	508 969	263	508 706	0.05	6 035	419 945
	Qatar	11 667	11 532	11 532	202	11 330	1.75	10 966	11 003
	Romania	146 243	146 243	146 243	5 091	141 152	3.48	5 074	140 915
	Russian Federation	1 272 632	1 268 814	1 268 814	17 800	1 251 014	1.40	6 418	1 172 539
	Serbia	80 089	75 870	74 272	1 987	72 285	2.67	4 684	67 934
	Shanghai-China	108 056	90 796	90 796	1 252	89 544	1.38	6 374	85 127
	Singapore	53 637	52 163	52 163	293	51 870	0.56	5 546	51 088
	Chinese Taipei	328 356	328 336	328 336	1 747	326 589	0.53	6 046	292 542
	Thailand	982 080	784 897	784 897	9 123	775 774	1.16	6 606	703 012
	Tunisia	132 313	132 313	132 313	169	132 144	0.13	4 407	120 784
	United Arab Emirates	48 824	48 446	48 446	971	47 475	2.00	11 500	40 612
	Uruguay	54 638	46 442	46 442	14	46 428	0.03	5 315	39 771
	Viet Nam	1 717 996	1 091 462	1 091 462	7 729	1 083 733	0.71	4 959	956 517

Notes: For a full explanation of the details in this table please refer to the *PISA 2012 Technical Report* (OECD, forthcoming). The figure for total national population of 15-year-olds enrolled in Column 2 may occasionally be larger than the total number of 15-year-olds in Column 1 due to differing data sources.
Information for the adjudicated regions is available on line.
* See notes at the beginning of this Annex.
StatLink http://dx.doi.org/10.1787/888932937092

[Part 2/2]
Table A2.1   **PISA target populations and samples**

	Population and sample information				Coverage indices		
	Number of excluded students	Weighted number of excluded students	Within-school exclusion rate (%)	Overall exclusion rate (%)	Coverage index 1: Coverage of national desired population	Coverage index 2: Coverage of national enrolled population	Coverage index 3: Coverage of 15-year-old population
	(9)	(10)	(11)	(12)	(13)	(14)	(15)
Australia	505	5 282	2.06	3.96	0.960	0.960	0.859
Austria	46	1 011	1.21	1.33	0.987	0.987	0.879
Belgium	39	367	0.31	1.39	0.986	0.984	0.955
Canada	1 796	21 013	5.69	6.37	0.936	0.926	0.833
Chile	18	548	0.24	1.29	0.987	0.987	0.834
Czech Republic	15	118	0.14	1.80	0.982	0.982	0.847
Denmark	368	2 381	3.50	6.10	0.938	0.938	0.908
Estonia	143	277	2.33	5.67	0.942	0.942	0.920
Finland	225	653	1.08	1.90	0.981	0.981	0.960
France	52	5 828	0.82	4.29	0.956	0.956	0.885
Germany	8	1 302	0.17	1.52	0.985	0.985	0.948
Greece	136	2 304	2.33	3.58	0.964	0.964	0.874
Hungary	27	928	1.01	2.55	0.974	0.974	0.816
Iceland	155	156	3.60	3.81	0.962	0.962	0.925
Ireland	271	2 524	4.47	4.47	0.955	0.955	0.911
Israel	114	1 884	1.72	4.07	0.959	0.959	0.906
Italy	741	9 855	1.86	3.30	0.967	0.967	0.861
Japan	0	0	0.00	2.10	0.979	0.979	0.909
Korea	17	2 238	0.37	0.82	0.992	0.992	0.879
Luxembourg	357	357	6.07	8.34	0.872	0.916	0.893
Mexico	58	3 247	0.24	0.74	0.993	0.993	0.627
Netherlands	27	1 056	0.54	4.27	0.956	0.956	1.012
New Zealand	255	2 030	3.66	4.60	0.954	0.954	0.876
Norway	278	3 133	5.01	6.09	0.939	0.939	0.916
Poland	212	11 566	2.96	4.56	0.954	0.954	0.891
Portugal	124	1 560	1.60	1.60	0.984	0.984	0.883
Slovak Republic	29	246	0.45	2.87	0.971	0.971	0.912
Slovenia	84	181	0.98	1.57	0.984	0.984	0.940
Spain	959	14 931	3.84	4.32	0.957	0.957	0.884
Sweden	201	3 789	3.84	5.42	0.946	0.946	0.930
Switzerland	256	1 093	1.35	4.14	0.958	0.958	0.914
Turkey	21	3 684	0.42	1.48	0.985	0.985	0.684
United Kingdom	486	20 173	2.85	5.36	0.946	0.946	0.932
United States	319	162 194	4.39	5.34	0.946	0.946	0.887
Albania	1	10	0.02	0.13	0.999	0.999	0.552
Argentina	12	641	0.12	0.74	0.993	0.993	0.797
Brazil	44	4 900	0.20	1.43	0.986	0.986	0.691
Bulgaria	6	80	0.15	2.49	0.974	0.974	0.773
Colombia	23	789	0.14	0.14	0.999	0.999	0.630
Costa Rica	2	12	0.03	0.03	1.000	1.000	0.496
Croatia	91	627	1.36	2.23	0.978	0.978	0.945
Cyprus*	157	200	2.03	3.27	0.967	0.967	0.969
Hong Kong-China	38	518	0.73	1.75	0.982	0.982	0.839
Indonesia	2	860	0.03	0.26	0.997	0.982	0.634
Jordan	19	304	0.27	0.38	0.996	0.996	0.858
Kazakhstan	25	951	0.45	3.34	0.966	0.966	0.806
Latvia	14	76	0.47	3.89	0.960	0.959	0.854
Liechtenstein	13	13	3.97	4.22	0.958	0.958	0.753
Lithuania	130	867	2.56	3.98	0.960	0.960	0.858
Macao-China	3	3	0.06	0.17	0.998	0.998	0.813
Malaysia	7	554	0.13	0.18	0.998	0.998	0.794
Montenegro	4	8	0.10	0.31	0.997	0.997	0.897
Peru	8	549	0.13	0.18	0.998	0.998	0.719
Qatar	85	85	0.77	2.47	0.975	0.975	0.943
Romania	0	0	0.00	3.36	0.965	0.965	0.964
Russian Federation	69	11 940	1.01	2.38	0.976	0.976	0.921
Serbia	10	136	0.20	2.80	0.971	0.951	0.848
Shanghai-China	8	107	0.13	1.48	0.985	0.985	0.788
Singapore	33	315	0.61	1.17	0.988	0.988	0.952
Chinese Taipei	44	2 029	0.69	1.21	0.988	0.988	0.891
Thailand	12	1 144	0.16	1.31	0.987	0.987	0.716
Tunisia	5	130	0.11	0.24	0.998	0.998	0.913
United Arab Emirates	11	37	0.09	2.05	0.979	0.979	0.832
Uruguay	15	99	0.25	0.28	0.997	0.997	0.728
Viet Nam	1	198	0.02	0.72	0.993	0.993	0.557

Notes: For a full explanation of the details in this table please refer to the *PISA 2012 Technical Report* (OECD, forthcoming). The figure for total national population of 15-year-olds enrolled in Column 2 may occasionally be larger than the total number of 15-year-olds in Column 1 due to differing data sources.
Information for the adjudicated regions is available on line.
* See notes at the beginning of this Annex.
StatLink http://dx.doi.org/10.1787/888932937092

[Part 1/1]

Table A2.2 **Exclusions**

	Student exclusions (unweighted)						Student exclusions (weighted)					
	Number of excluded students with functional disability (Code 1)	Number of excluded students with intellectual disability (Code 2)	Number of excluded students because of language (Code 3)	Number of excluded students for other reasons (Code 4)	Number of excluded students because of no materials available in the language of instruction (Code 5)	Total number of excluded students	Weighted number of excluded students with functional disability (Code 1)	Weighted number of excluded students with intellectual disability (Code 2)	Weighted number of excluded students because of language (Code 3)	Weighted number of excluded students for other reasons (Code 4)	Number of excluded students because of no materials available in the language of instruction (Code 5)	Total weighted number of excluded students
	(1)	(2)	(3)	(4)	(5)	(6)	(7)	(8)	(9)	(10)	(11)	(12)
OECD												
Australia	39	395	71	0	0	505	471	3 925	886	0	0	5 282
Austria	11	24	11	0	0	46	332	438	241	0	0	1 011
Belgium	5	22	12	0	0	39	24	154	189	0	0	367
Canada	82	1 593	121	0	0	1 796	981	18 682	1 350	0	0	21 013
Chile	3	15	0	0	0	18	74	474	0	0	0	548
Czech Republic	1	8	6	0	0	15	1	84	34	0	0	118
Denmark	10	204	112	42	0	368	44	1 469	559	310	0	2 381
Estonia	7	134	2	0	0	143	14	260	3	0	0	277
Finland	5	80	101	15	24	225	43	363	166	47	35	653
France	52	0	0	0	0	52	5 828	0	0	0	0	5 828
Germany	0	4	4	0	0	8	0	705	597	0	0	1 302
Greece	3	18	4	111	0	136	49	348	91	1 816	0	2 304
Hungary	1	15	2	9	0	27	36	568	27	296	0	928
Iceland	5	105	27	18	0	155	5	105	27	18	0	156
Ireland	13	159	33	66	0	271	121	1 521	283	599	0	2 524
Israel	9	91	14	0	0	114	133	1 492	260	0	0	1 884
Italy	64	566	111	0	0	741	596	7 899	1 361	0	0	9 855
Japan	0	0	0	0	0	0	0	0	0	0	0	0
Luxembourg	6	261	90	0	0	357	6	261	90	0	0	357
Mexico	21	36	1	0	0	58	812	2 390	45	0	0	3 247
Netherlands	5	21	1	0	0	27	188	819	50	0	0	1 056
New Zealand	27	118	99	0	11	255	235	926	813	0	57	2 030
Norway	11	192	75	0	0	278	120	2 180	832	0	0	3 133
Poland	23	89	6	88	6	212	1 470	5 187	177	4 644	89	11 566
Portugal	69	48	7	0	0	124	860	605	94	0	0	1 560
Korea	2	15	0	0	0	17	223	2 015	0	0	0	2 238
Slovak Republic	2	14	0	13	0	29	22	135	0	89	0	246
Slovenia	13	27	44	0	0	84	23	76	81	0	0	181
Spain	56	679	224	0	0	959	618	11 330	2 984	0	0	14 931
Sweden	120	0	81	0	0	201	2 218	0	1 571	0	0	3 789
Switzerland	7	99	150	0	0	256	41	346	706	0	0	1 093
Turkey	5	14	2	0	0	21	757	2 556	371	0	0	3 684
United Kingdom	40	405	41	0	0	486	1 468	15 514	3 191	0	0	20 173
United States	37	219	63	0	0	319	18 399	113 965	29 830	0	0	162 194
Partners												
Albania	0	0	1	0	0	1	0	0	10	0	0	10
Argentina	1	11	0	0	0	12	84	557	0	0	0	641
Brazil	17	27	0	0	0	44	1 792	3 108	0	0	0	4 900
Bulgaria	6	0	0	0	0	6	80	0	0	0	0	80
Colombia	12	10	1	0	0	23	397	378	14	0	0	789
Costa Rica	0	2	0	0	0	2	0	12	0	0	0	12
Croatia	10	78	3	0	0	91	69	539	19	0	0	627
Cyprus*	8	54	60	35	0	157	9	64	72	55	0	200
Hong Kong-China	4	33	1	0	0	38	57	446	15	0	0	518
Indonesia	1	0	1	0	0	2	426	0	434	0	0	860
Jordan	8	6	5	0	0	19	109	72	122	0	0	304
Kazakhstan	9	16	0	0	0	25	317	634	0	0	0	951
Latvia	3	7	4	0	0	14	8	45	24	0	0	76
Liechtenstein	1	7	5	0	0	13	1	7	5	0	0	13
Lithuania	10	120	0	0	0	130	66	801	0	0	0	867
Macao-China	0	1	2	0	0	3	0	1	2	0	0	3
Malaysia	3	4	0	0	0	7	274	279	0	0	0	554
Montenegro	3	1	0	0	0	4	7	1	0	0	0	8
Peru	3	5	0	0	0	8	269	280	0	0	0	549
Qatar	23	43	19	0	0	85	23	43	19	0	0	85
Romania	0	0	0	0	0	0	0	0	0	0	0	0
Russian Federation	25	40	4	0	0	69	4 345	6 934	660	0	0	11 940
Serbia	4	4	2	0	0	10	53	55	28	0	0	136
Shanghai-China	1	6	1	0	0	8	14	80	14	0	0	107
Singapore	5	17	11	0	0	33	50	157	109	0	0	315
Chinese Taipei	6	36	2	0	0	44	296	1 664	70	0	0	2 029
Thailand	2	10	0	0	0	12	13	1 131	0	0	0	1 144
Tunisia	4	1	0	0	0	5	104	26	0	0	0	130
United Arab Emirates	3	7	1	0	0	11	26	9	2	0	0	37
Uruguay	9	6	0	0	0	15	66	33	0	0	0	99
Viet Nam	0	1	0	0	0	1	0	198	0	0	0	198

Exclusion codes:
Code 1 Functional disability – student has a moderate to severe permanent physical disability.
Code 2 Intellectual disability – student has a mental or emotional disability and has either been tested as cognitively delayed or is considered in the professional opinion of qualified staff to be cognitively delayed.
Code 3 Limited assessment language proficiency – student is not a native speaker of any of the languages of the assessment in the country and has been resident in the country for less than one year.
Code 4 Other reasons defined by the national centres and approved by the international centre.
Code 5 No materials available in the language of instruction.
Note: For a full explanation of the details in this table please refer to the *PISA 2012 Technical Report* (OECD, forthcoming).
Information for the adjudicated regions is available on line.
* See notes at the beginning of this Annex.
StatLink ᴍꜱᴾ http://dx.doi.org/10.1787/888932937092

- *Column 13* presents an *index of the extent to which the national desired target population is covered by the PISA sample*. Canada, Denmark, Estonia, Luxembourg, Norway, Sweden, the United Kingdom and the United States were the only countries where the coverage is below 95%.

- *Column 14* presents an *index of the extent to which 15-year-olds enrolled in schools are covered by the PISA sample*. The index measures the overall proportion of the national enrolled population that is covered by the non-excluded portion of the student sample. The index takes into account both school-level and student-level exclusions. Values close to 100 indicate that the PISA sample represents the entire education system as defined for PISA 2012. The index is the weighted number of participating students (Column 8) divided by the weighted number of participating and excluded students (Column 8 plus Column 10), times the nationally defined target population (Column 5) divided by the eligible population (Column 2).

- *Column 15* presents an *index of the coverage of the 15-year-old population*. This index is the weighted number of participating students (Column 8) divided by the total population of 15-year-old students (Column 1).

This high level of coverage contributes to the comparability of the assessment results. For example, even assuming that the excluded students would have systematically scored worse than those who participated, and that this relationship is moderately strong, an exclusion rate in the order of 5% would likely lead to an overestimation of national mean scores of less than 5 score points (on a scale with an international mean of 500 score points and a standard deviation of 100 score points). This assessment is based on the following calculations: if the correlation between the propensity of exclusions and student performance is 0.3, resulting mean scores would likely be overestimated by 1 score point if the exclusion rate is 1%, by 3 score points if the exclusion rate is 5%, and by 6 score points if the exclusion rate is 10%. If the correlation between the propensity of exclusions and student performance is 0.5, resulting mean scores would be overestimated by 1 score point if the exclusion rate is 1%, by 5 score points if the exclusion rate is 5%, and by 10 score points if the exclusion rate is 10%. For this calculation, a model was employed that assumes a bivariate normal distribution for performance and the propensity to participate. For details, see the *PISA 2012 Technical Report* (OECD, forthcoming).

Sampling procedures and response rates

The accuracy of any survey results depends on the quality of the information on which national samples are based as well as on the sampling procedures. Quality standards, procedures, instruments and verification mechanisms were developed for PISA that ensured that national samples yielded comparable data and that the results could be compared with confidence.

Most PISA samples were designed as two-stage stratified samples (where countries applied different sampling designs, these are documented in the *PISA 2012 Technical Report* [OECD, forthcoming]). The first stage consisted of sampling individual schools in which 15-year-old students could be enrolled. Schools were sampled systematically with probabilities proportional to size, the measure of size being a function of the estimated number of eligible (15-year-old) students enrolled. A minimum of 150 schools were selected in each country (where this number existed), although the requirements for national analyses often required a somewhat larger sample. As the schools were sampled, replacement schools were simultaneously identified, in case a sampled school chose not to participate in PISA 2012.

In the case of Iceland, Liechtenstein, Luxembourg, Macao-China and Qatar, all schools and all eligible students within schools were included in the sample.

Experts from the PISA Consortium performed the sample selection process for most participating countries and monitored it closely in those countries that selected their own samples. The second stage of the selection process sampled students within sampled schools. Once schools were selected, a list of each sampled school's 15-year-old students was prepared. From this list, 35 students were then selected with equal probability (all 15-year-old students were selected if fewer than 35 were enrolled). The number of students to be sampled per school could deviate from 35, but could not be less than 20.

Data-quality standards in PISA required minimum participation rates for schools as well as for students. These standards were established to minimise the potential for response biases. In the case of countries meeting these standards, it was likely that any bias resulting from non-response would be negligible, i.e. typically smaller than the sampling error.

A minimum response rate of 85% was required for the schools initially selected. Where the initial response rate of schools was between 65% and 85%, however, an acceptable school response rate could still be achieved through the use of replacement schools. This procedure brought with it a risk of increased response bias. Participating countries were, therefore, encouraged to persuade as many of the schools in the original sample as possible to participate. Schools with a student participation rate between 25% and 50% were not regarded as participating schools, but data from these schools were included in the database and contributed to the various estimations. Data from schools with a student participation rate of less than 25% were excluded from the database.

PISA 2012 also required a minimum participation rate of 80% of students within participating schools. This minimum participation rate had to be met at the national level, not necessarily by each participating school. Follow-up sessions were required in schools in which too few students had participated in the original assessment sessions. Student participation rates were calculated over all original schools, and also over all schools, whether original sample or replacement schools, and from the participation of students in both the original assessment and any follow-up sessions. A student who participated in the original or follow-up cognitive sessions was regarded as a participant. Those who attended only the questionnaire session were included in the international database and contributed to the statistics presented in this publication if they provided at least a description of their father's or mother's occupation.

[Part 1/2]
Table A2.3 **Response rates**

		Initial sample – before school replacement				Final sample – after school replacement		
		Weighted school participation rate before replacement (%)	Weighted number of responding schools (weighted also by enrolment)	Weighted number of schools sampled (responding and non-responding) (weighted also by enrolment)	Number of responding schools (unweighted)	Number of responding and non-responding schools (unweighted)	Weighted school participation rate after replacement (%)	Weighted number of responding schools (weighted also by enrolment)	Weighted number of schools sampled (responding and non-responding) (weighted also by enrolment)
		(1)	(2)	(3)	(4)	(5)	(6)	(7)	(8)
OECD	Australia	98	268 631	274 432	757	790	98	268 631	274 432
	Austria	100	88 967	88 967	191	191	100	88 967	88 967
	Belgium	84	100 482	119 019	246	294	97	115 004	119 006
	Canada	91	362 178	396 757	828	907	93	368 600	396 757
	Chile	92	220 009	239 429	200	224	99	236 576	239 370
	Czech Republic	98	87 238	88 884	292	297	100	88 447	88 797
	Denmark	87	61 749	71 015	311	366	96	67 709	70 892
	Estonia	100	12 046	12 046	206	206	100	12 046	12 046
	Finland	99	59 740	60 323	310	313	99	59 912	60 323
	France	97	703 458	728 401	223	231	97	703 458	728 401
	Germany	98	735 944	753 179	227	233	98	737 778	753 179
	Greece	93	95 107	102 087	176	192	99	100 892	102 053
	Hungary	98	99 317	101 751	198	208	99	101 187	101 751
	Iceland	99	4 395	4 424	133	140	99	4 395	4 424
	Ireland	99	56 962	57 711	182	185	99	57 316	57 711
	Israel	91	99 543	109 326	166	186	94	103 075	109 895
	Italy	89	478 317	536 921	1 104	1 232	97	522 686	536 821
	Japan	86	1 015 198	1 175 794	173	200	96	1 123 211	1 175 794
	Korea	100	661 575	662 510	156	157	100	661 575	662 510
	Luxembourg	100	5 931	5 931	42	42	100	5 931	5 931
	Mexico	92	1 323 816	1 442 242	1 431	1 562	95	1 374 615	1 442 234
	Netherlands	75	139 709	185 468	148	199	89	165 635	185 320
	New Zealand	81	47 441	58 676	156	197	89	52 360	58 616
	Norway	85	54 201	63 653	177	208	95	60 270	63 642
	Poland	85	343 344	402 116	159	188	98	393 872	402 116
	Portugal	95	122 238	128 129	186	195	96	122 713	128 050
	Slovak Republic	87	50 182	57 353	202	236	99	57 599	58 201
	Slovenia	98	18 329	18 680	335	353	98	18 329	18 680
	Spain	100	402 604	403 999	902	904	100	402 604	403 999
	Sweden	99	98 645	99 726	207	211	100	99 536	99 767
	Switzerland	94	78 825	83 450	397	422	98	82 032	83 424
	Turkey	97	921 643	945 357	165	170	100	944 807	945 357
	United Kingdom	80	564 438	705 011	477	550	89	624 499	699 839
	United States	67	2 647 253	3 945 575	139	207	77	3 040 661	3 938 077
Partners	Albania	100	49 632	49 632	204	204	100	49 632	49 632
	Argentina	95	578 723	606 069	218	229	96	580 989	606 069
	Brazil	93	2 545 863	2 745 045	803	886	95	2 622 293	2 747 688
	Bulgaria	99	57 101	57 574	186	188	100	57 464	57 574
	Colombia	87	530 553	612 605	323	363	97	596 557	612 261
	Costa Rica	99	64 235	64 920	191	193	99	64 235	64 920
	Croatia	99	45 037	45 636	161	164	100	45 608	45 636
	Cyprus*	97	9 485	9 821	117	131	97	9 485	9 821
	Hong Kong-China	79	60 277	76 589	123	156	94	72 064	76 567
	Indonesia	95	2 799 943	2 950 696	199	210	98	2 892 365	2 951 028
	Jordan	100	119 147	119 147	233	233	100	119 147	119 147
	Kazakhstan	100	239 767	239 767	218	218	100	239 767	239 767
	Latvia	88	15 371	17 488	186	213	100	17 428	17 448
	Liechtenstein	100	382	382	12	12	100	382	382
	Lithuania	98	33 989	34 614	211	216	100	34 604	34 604
	Macao-China	100	5 410	5 410	45	45	100	5 410	5 410
	Malaysia	100	455 543	455 543	164	164	100	455 543	455 543
	Montenegro	100	8 540	8 540	51	51	100	8 540	8 540
	Peru	98	503 915	514 574	238	243	99	507 602	514 574
	Qatar	100	11 333	11 340	157	164	100	11 333	11 340
	Romania	100	139 597	139 597	178	178	100	139 597	139 597
	Russian Federation	100	1 243 564	1 243 564	227	227	100	1 243 564	1 243 564
	Serbia	90	65 537	72 819	143	160	95	69 433	72 752
	Shanghai-China	100	89 832	89 832	155	155	100	89 832	89 832
	Singapore	98	50 415	51 687	170	176	98	50 945	51 896
	Chinese Taipei	100	324 667	324 667	163	163	100	324 667	324 667
	Thailand	98	757 516	772 654	235	240	100	772 452	772 654
	Tunisia	99	129 229	130 141	152	153	99	129 229	130 141
	United Arab Emirates	99	46 469	46 748	453	460	99	46 469	46 748
	Uruguay	99	45 736	46 009	179	180	100	46 009	46 009
	Viet Nam	100	1 068 462	1 068 462	162	162	100	1 068 462	1 068 462

Information for the adjudicated regions is available on line.
* See notes at the beginning of this Annex.
StatLink ᠊᠊᠊ http://dx.doi.org/10.1787/888932937092

[Part 2/2]

Table A2.3 **Response rates**

		Final sample – after school replacement			Final sample – students within schools after school replacement			
		Number of responding schools (unweighted)	Number of responding and non-responding schools (unweighted)	Weighted student participation rate after replacement (%)	Number of students assessed (weighted)	Number of students sampled (assessed and absent) (weighted)	Number of students assessed (unweighted)	Number of students sampled (assessed and absent) (unweighted)
		(9)	(10)	(11)	(12)	(13)	(14)	(15)
OECD	Australia	757	790	87	213 495	246 012	17 491	20 799
	Austria	191	191	92	75 393	82 242	4 756	5 318
	Belgium	282	294	91	103 914	114 360	9 649	10 595
	Canada	840	907	81	261 928	324 328	20 994	25 835
	Chile	221	224	95	214 558	226 689	6 857	7 246
	Czech Republic	295	297	90	73 536	81 642	6 528	7 222
	Denmark	339	366	89	56 096	62 988	7 463	8 496
	Estonia	206	206	93	10 807	11 634	5 867	6 316
	Finland	311	313	91	54 126	59 653	8 829	9 789
	France	223	231	89	605 371	676 730	5 641	6 308
	Germany	228	233	93	692 226	742 416	4 990	5 355
	Greece	188	192	97	92 444	95 580	5 125	5 301
	Hungary	204	208	93	84 032	90 652	4 810	5 184
	Iceland	133	140	85	3 503	4 135	3 503	4 135
	Ireland	183	185	84	45 115	53 644	5 016	5 977
	Israel	172	186	90	91 181	101 288	6 061	6 727
	Italy	1 186	1 232	93	473 104	510 005	38 084	41 003
	Japan	191	200	96	1 034 803	1 076 786	6 351	6 609
	Korea	156	157	99	595 461	603 004	5 033	5 101
	Luxembourg	42	42	95	5 260	5 523	5 260	5 523
	Mexico	1 468	1 562	94	1 193 866	1 271 639	33 786	35 972
	Netherlands	177	199	85	148 432	174 697	4 434	5 215
	New Zealand	177	197	85	40 397	47 703	5 248	6 206
	Norway	197	208	91	51 155	56 286	4 686	5 156
	Poland	182	188	88	325 389	371 434	5 629	6 452
	Portugal	187	195	87	80 719	92 395	5 608	6 426
	Slovak Republic	231	236	94	50 544	53 912	5 737	6 106
	Slovenia	335	353	90	16 146	17 849	7 211	7 921
	Spain	902	904	90	334 382	372 042	26 443	29 027
	Sweden	209	211	92	87 359	94 784	4 739	5 141
	Switzerland	410	422	92	72 116	78 424	11 218	12 138
	Turkey	169	170	98	850 830	866 269	4 847	4 939
	United Kingdom	505	550	86	528 231	613 736	12 638	14 649
	United States	161	207	89	2 429 718	2 734 268	6 094	6 848
Partners	Albania	204	204	92	39 275	42 466	4 743	5 102
	Argentina	219	229	88	457 294	519 733	5 804	6 680
	Brazil	837	886	90	2 133 035	2 368 438	19 877	22 326
	Bulgaria	187	188	96	51 819	54 145	5 280	5 508
	Colombia	352	363	93	507 178	544 862	11 164	12 045
	Costa Rica	191	193	89	35 525	39 930	4 582	5 187
	Croatia	163	164	92	41 912	45 473	6 153	6 675
	Cyprus*	117	131	93	8 719	9 344	5 078	5 458
	Hong Kong-China	147	156	93	62 059	66 665	4 659	5 004
	Indonesia	206	210	95	2 478 961	2 605 254	5 579	5 885
	Jordan	233	233	95	105 493	111 098	7 038	7 402
	Kazakhstan	218	218	99	206 053	208 411	5 808	5 874
	Latvia	211	213	91	14 579	16 039	5 276	5 785
	Liechtenstein	12	12	93	293	314	293	314
	Lithuania	216	216	92	30 429	33 042	4 618	5 018
	Macao-China	45	45	99	5 335	5 366	5 335	5 366
	Malaysia	164	164	94	405 983	432 080	5 197	5 529
	Montenegro	51	51	94	7 233	7 714	4 799	5 117
	Peru	240	243	96	398 193	414 728	6 035	6 291
	Qatar	157	164	100	10 966	10 996	10 966	10 996
	Romania	178	178	98	137 860	140 915	5 074	5 188
	Russian Federation	227	227	97	1 141 317	1 172 539	6 418	6 602
	Serbia	152	160	93	60 366	64 658	4 681	5 017
	Shanghai-China	155	155	98	83 821	85 127	6 374	6 467
	Singapore	172	176	94	47 465	50 330	5 546	5 887
	Chinese Taipei	163	163	96	281 799	292 542	6 046	6 279
	Thailand	239	240	99	695 088	702 818	6 606	6 681
	Tunisia	152	153	90	108 342	119 917	4 391	4 857
	United Arab Emirates	453	460	95	38 228	40 384	11 460	12 148
	Uruguay	180	180	90	35 800	39 771	5 315	5 904
	Viet Nam	162	162	100	955 222	956 517	4 959	4 966

Information for the adjudicated regions is available on line.
* See notes at the beginning of this Annex.
StatLink 🔗 http://dx.doi.org/10.1787/888932937092

Table A2.3 shows the response rates for students and schools, before and after replacement.

- **Column 1** shows the *weighted participation rate of schools before replacement*. This is obtained by dividing Column 2 by Column 3, multiply by 100.

- **Column 2** shows the *weighted number of responding schools before school replacement* (weighted by student enrolment).

- **Column 3** shows the *weighted number of sampled schools before school replacement* (including both responding and non-responding schools, weighted by student enrolment).

- **Column 4** shows the *unweighted number of responding schools before school replacement*.

- **Column 5** shows the *unweighted number of responding and non-responding schools before school replacement*.

- **Column 6** shows the *weighted participation rate of schools after replacement*. This is obtained by dividing Column 7 by Column 8, multiply by 100.

- **Column 7** shows the *weighted number of responding schools after school replacement (weighted by student enrolment)*.

- **Column 8** shows the *weighted number of schools sampled after school replacement* (including both responding and non-responding schools, weighted by student enrolment).

- **Column 9** shows the *unweighted number of responding schools after school replacement*.

- **Column 10** shows the *unweighted number of responding and non-responding schools after school replacement*.

- **Column 11** shows the *weighted student participation rate after replacement*. This is obtained by dividing Column 12 by Column 13, multiply by 100.

- **Column 12** shows the *weighted number of students assessed*.

- **Column 13** shows the *weighted number of students sampled* (including both students who were assessed and students who were absent on the day of the assessment).

- **Column 14** shows the *unweighted number of students assessed*. Note that any students in schools with student-response rates less than 50% were not included in these rates (both weighted and unweighted).

- **Column 15** shows the *unweighted number of students sampled* (including both students that were assessed and students who were absent on the day of the assessment). Note that any students in schools where fewer than half of the eligible students were assessed were not included in these rates (neither weighted nor unweighted).

Definition of schools

In some countries, sub-units within schools were sampled instead of schools and this may affect the estimation of the between-school variance components. In Austria, the Czech Republic, Germany, Hungary, Japan, Romania and Slovenia, schools with more than one study programme were split into the units delivering these programmes. In the Netherlands, for schools with both lower and upper secondary programmes, schools were split into units delivering each programme level. In the Flemish community of Belgium, in the case of multi-campus schools, implantations (campuses) were sampled, whereas in the French Community, in the case of multi-campus schools, the larger administrative units were sampled. In Australia, for schools with more than one campus, the individual campuses were listed for sampling. In Argentina, Croatia and Dubai (United Arab Emirates), schools that had more than one campus had the locations listed for sampling. In Spain, the schools in the Basque region with multi-linguistic models were split into linguistic models for sampling.

Grade levels

Students assessed in PISA 2012 are at various grade levels. The percentage of students at each grade level is presented by country and economy in Table A2.4a and by gender within each country and economy in Table A2.4b.

[Part 1/1]

Table A2.4a **Percentage of students at each grade level**

		7th grade		8th grade		9th grade		10th grade		11th grade		12th grade and above	
		%	S.E.	%	S.E.	%	S.E.	%	S.E.	%	S.E.	%	S.E.
OECD	Australia	0.0	(0.0)	0.1	(0.0)	10.8	(0.5)	70.0	(0.6)	19.1	(0.4)	0.0	(0.0)
	Austria	0.3	(0.1)	5.4	(0.7)	43.3	(0.9)	51.0	(1.0)	0.1	(0.0)	0.0	c
	Belgium	0.9	(0.1)	6.4	(0.5)	30.9	(0.6)	60.8	(0.6)	1.0	(0.1)	0.0	c
	Canada	0.1	(0.0)	1.1	(0.1)	13.2	(0.6)	84.6	(0.6)	1.0	(0.1)	0.1	(0.0)
	Chile	1.4	(0.3)	4.1	(0.6)	21.7	(0.8)	66.1	(1.2)	6.7	(0.3)	0.0	c
	Czech Republic	0.4	(0.1)	4.5	(0.4)	51.1	(1.2)	44.1	(1.3)	0.0	c	0.0	c
	Denmark	0.1	(0.0)	18.2	(0.8)	80.6	(0.8)	1.0	(0.2)	0.0	c	0.0	c
	Estonia	0.6	(0.2)	22.1	(0.7)	75.4	(0.7)	1.9	(0.3)	0.0	c	0.0	c
	Finland	0.7	(0.2)	14.2	(0.4)	85.0	(0.4)	0.0	c	0.1	(0.1)	0.0	c
	France	0.0	(0.0)	1.9	(0.3)	27.9	(0.7)	66.6	(0.7)	3.5	(0.3)	0.1	(0.1)
	Germany	0.6	(0.1)	10.0	(0.6)	51.9	(0.8)	36.7	(0.9)	0.8	(0.4)	0.0	c
	Greece	0.3	(0.1)	1.2	(0.3)	4.0	(0.7)	94.5	(1.0)	0.0	c	0.0	c
	Hungary	2.8	(0.5)	8.7	(0.9)	67.8	(0.9)	20.6	(0.6)	0.0	c	0.0	c
	Iceland	0.0	c	0.0	c	0.0	c	100.0	c	0.0	c	0.0	c
	Ireland	0.0	(0.0)	1.9	(0.2)	60.5	(0.8)	24.3	(1.2)	13.3	(1.0)	0.0	c
	Israel	0.0	(0.0)	0.3	(0.1)	17.1	(0.9)	81.7	(0.9)	0.8	(0.3)	0.0	c
	Italy	0.4	(0.1)	1.7	(0.2)	16.8	(0.6)	78.5	(0.7)	2.6	(0.2)	0.0	(0.0)
	Japan	0.0	c	0.0	c	0.0	c	100.0	c	0.0	c	0.0	c
	Korea	0.0	c	0.0	c	5.9	(0.8)	93.8	(0.8)	0.2	(0.1)	0.0	c
	Luxembourg	0.7	(0.1)	10.2	(0.2)	50.7	(0.1)	38.0	(0.1)	0.5	(0.1)	0.0	c
	Mexico	1.1	(0.1)	5.2	(0.3)	30.8	(1.0)	60.8	(1.1)	2.1	(0.3)	0.1	(0.0)
	Netherlands	0.0	c	3.6	(0.4)	46.7	(1.0)	49.2	(1.1)	0.5	(0.1)	0.0	c
	New Zealand	0.0	c	0.0	c	0.1	(0.1)	6.2	(0.4)	88.3	(0.5)	5.4	(0.4)
	Norway	0.0	c	0.0	c	0.4	(0.1)	99.4	(0.1)	0.2	(0.0)	0.0	c
	Poland	0.5	(0.1)	4.1	(0.4)	94.9	(0.4)	0.5	(0.2)	0.0	c	0.0	c
	Portugal	2.4	(0.3)	8.2	(0.7)	28.6	(1.6)	60.5	(2.1)	0.3	(0.1)	0.0	c
	Slovak Republic	1.7	(0.3)	4.5	(0.5)	39.5	(1.5)	52.7	(1.4)	1.6	(0.5)	0.0	c
	Slovenia	0.0	c	0.3	(0.2)	5.1	(0.8)	90.7	(0.8)	3.9	(0.2)	0.0	c
	Spain	0.1	(0.0)	9.8	(0.5)	24.1	(0.4)	66.0	(0.6)	0.0	(0.0)	0.0	c
	Sweden	0.0	(0.0)	3.7	(0.3)	94.0	(0.6)	2.2	(0.5)	0.0	c	0.0	c
	Switzerland	0.6	(0.1)	12.9	(0.8)	60.6	(1.0)	25.6	(1.0)	0.2	(0.1)	0.0	c
	Turkey	0.5	(0.2)	2.2	(0.3)	27.6	(1.2)	65.5	(1.2)	4.0	(0.3)	0.3	(0.1)
	United Kingdom	0.0	c	0.0	c	0.0	(0.0)	1.3	(0.3)	95.0	(0.3)	3.6	(0.1)
	United States	0.0	c	0.3	(0.1)	11.7	(1.1)	71.2	(1.1)	16.6	(0.8)	0.2	(0.1)
	OECD average	0.5	(0.0)	4.9	(0.1)	34.7	(0.1)	51.9	(0.2)	7.7	(0.1)	0.3	(0.0)
Partners	Albania	0.1	(0.1)	2.2	(0.3)	39.4	(2.4)	58.0	(2.5)	0.3	(0.1)	0.0	c
	Argentina	2.0	(0.5)	12.0	(1.2)	22.6	(1.4)	59.4	(2.1)	2.8	(0.6)	1.1	(0.7)
	Brazil	0.0	c	6.9	(0.5)	13.5	(0.7)	34.9	(1.0)	42.0	(1.0)	2.6	(0.2)
	Bulgaria	0.9	(0.2)	4.6	(0.5)	89.5	(0.7)	4.9	(0.4)	0.0	(0.0)	0.0	c
	Colombia	5.5	(0.6)	12.1	(0.7)	21.5	(0.8)	40.2	(0.9)	20.7	(1.0)	0.0	c
	Costa Rica	7.4	(0.9)	13.7	(0.9)	39.6	(1.3)	39.1	(1.8)	0.2	(0.1)	0.0	c
	Croatia	0.0	c	0.0	c	79.8	(0.4)	20.2	(0.4)	0.0	c	0.0	c
	Cyprus*	0.0	(0.0)	0.5	(0.1)	4.5	(0.1)	94.3	(0.1)	0.7	(0.0)	0.0	(0.0)
	Hong Kong-China	1.1	(0.1)	6.5	(0.4)	25.9	(0.7)	65.0	(0.9)	1.5	(1.4)	0.0	c
	Indonesia	1.9	(0.4)	8.3	(0.8)	37.7	(2.6)	47.7	(3.0)	3.9	(0.6)	0.6	(0.6)
	Jordan	0.1	(0.0)	1.1	(0.1)	6.0	(0.4)	92.9	(0.4)	0.0	c	0.0	c
	Kazakhstan	0.2	(0.1)	4.9	(0.5)	67.2	(1.9)	27.4	(2.0)	0.2	(0.1)	0.1	(0.1)
	Latvia	2.1	(0.4)	14.8	(0.7)	80.0	(0.8)	3.0	(0.4)	0.0	(0.0)	0.0	c
	Liechtenstein	4.9	(0.7)	14.2	(1.5)	66.3	(1.3)	14.6	(0.2)	0.0	c	0.0	c
	Lithuania	0.2	(0.1)	6.2	(0.6)	81.2	(0.7)	12.4	(0.7)	0.0	(0.0)	0.0	c
	Macao-China	5.4	(0.1)	16.4	(0.2)	33.2	(0.2)	44.6	(0.1)	0.4	(0.1)	0.0	(0.0)
	Malaysia	0.0	c	0.1	(0.0)	4.0	(0.5)	96.0	(0.5)	0.0	(0.0)	0.0	c
	Montenegro	0.0	c	0.1	(0.0)	79.5	(0.7)	20.4	(0.1)	0.0	c	0.0	c
	Peru	2.7	(0.4)	7.8	(0.5)	18.1	(0.7)	47.7	(0.9)	23.7	(0.8)	0.0	c
	Qatar	0.9	(0.0)	3.1	(0.1)	13.8	(0.1)	64.8	(0.1)	17.1	(0.1)	0.3	(0.0)
	Romania	0.2	(0.1)	7.4	(0.5)	87.2	(0.6)	5.1	(0.4)	0.0	c	0.0	c
	Russian Federation	0.6	(0.1)	8.1	(0.5)	73.8	(1.6)	17.4	(1.8)	0.1	(0.1)	0.0	c
	Serbia	0.1	(0.1)	1.5	(0.7)	96.7	(0.7)	1.7	(0.2)	0.0	c	0.0	c
	Shanghai-China	1.1	(0.2)	4.5	(0.6)	39.6	(1.5)	54.2	(1.3)	0.6	(0.1)	0.1	(0.1)
	Singapore	0.4	(0.1)	2.0	(0.2)	8.0	(0.3)	89.6	(0.3)	0.1	(0.1)	0.0	c
	Chinese Taipei	0.0	c	0.2	(0.1)	36.2	(0.7)	63.6	(0.7)	0.0	c	0.0	c
	Thailand	0.1	(0.0)	0.3	(0.1)	20.7	(1.0)	76.0	(1.1)	2.9	(0.5)	0.0	c
	Tunisia	5.0	(0.6)	11.8	(1.3)	20.6	(1.4)	56.7	(2.7)	5.9	(0.5)	0.0	c
	United Arab Emirates	0.9	(0.2)	2.8	(0.2)	11.3	(0.8)	61.9	(1.0)	22.2	(0.7)	0.9	(0.2)
	Uruguay	6.9	(0.8)	12.2	(0.6)	22.4	(1.0)	57.3	(1.5)	1.3	(0.2)	0.0	c
	Viet Nam	0.4	(0.2)	2.7	(0.7)	8.3	(1.7)	88.6	(2.3)	0.0	c	0.0	c

Information for the adjudicated regions is available on line.
* See notes at the beginning of this Annex.
StatLink http://dx.doi.org/10.1787/888932937092

[Part 1/2]

Table A2.4b **Percentage of students at each grade level, by gender**

	Boys											
	7th grade		8th grade		9th grade		10th grade		11th grade		12th grade and above	
	%	S.E.	%	S.E.	%	S.E.	%	S.E.	%	S.E.	%	S.E.
OECD												
Australia	0.0	c	0.1	(0.0)	13.1	(0.9)	69.2	(0.9)	17.5	(0.6)	0.0	(0.0)
Austria	0.3	(0.1)	6.0	(0.9)	44.8	(1.4)	48.9	(1.5)	0.0	c	0.0	c
Belgium	1.0	(0.1)	7.1	(0.6)	33.8	(0.9)	57.1	(1.0)	1.0	(0.2)	0.0	(0.0)
Canada	0.1	(0.1)	1.3	(0.2)	14.8	(0.8)	82.7	(0.8)	0.9	(0.1)	0.1	(0.1)
Chile	1.4	(0.4)	5.0	(0.9)	24.2	(1.0)	63.1	(1.6)	6.4	(0.4)	0.0	c
Czech Republic	0.7	(0.2)	5.5	(0.6)	54.9	(2.0)	39.0	(2.1)	0.0	c	0.0	c
Denmark	0.1	(0.0)	23.4	(1.0)	75.7	(1.0)	0.8	(0.3)	0.0	c	0.0	c
Estonia	0.8	(0.3)	25.7	(1.0)	71.7	(1.1)	1.7	(0.4)	0.0	c	0.0	c
Finland	0.9	(0.4)	16.2	(0.6)	82.8	(0.7)	0.0	c	0.1	(0.1)	0.0	c
France	0.1	(0.1)	2.3	(0.4)	30.8	(0.9)	63.5	(1.0)	3.2	(0.5)	0.1	(0.1)
Germany	0.9	(0.2)	11.6	(0.7)	53.6	(1.1)	33.2	(1.2)	0.7	(0.3)	0.0	c
Greece	0.4	(0.2)	1.8	(0.6)	4.8	(1.0)	93.0	(1.4)	0.0	c	0.0	c
Hungary	3.9	(0.6)	12.1	(1.5)	67.1	(1.3)	17.0	(0.8)	0.0	c	0.0	c
Iceland	0.0	c	0.0	c	0.0	c	100.0	c	0.0	c	0.0	c
Ireland	0.0	c	2.4	(0.3)	63.6	(1.0)	21.1	(1.4)	13.0	(1.3)	0.0	c
Israel	0.1	(0.1)	0.3	(0.1)	18.9	(1.3)	79.6	(1.3)	1.2	(0.5)	0.0	c
Italy	0.5	(0.2)	2.1	(0.3)	19.3	(0.7)	75.8	(0.7)	2.3	(0.2)	0.0	c
Japan	0.0	c	0.0	c	0.0	c	100.0	c	0.0	c	0.0	c
Korea	0.0	c	0.0	c	6.4	(1.2)	93.4	(1.2)	0.2	(0.1)	0.0	c
Luxembourg	0.7	(0.1)	10.7	(0.2)	51.1	(0.2)	37.0	(0.2)	0.6	(0.1)	0.0	c
Mexico	1.3	(0.2)	6.3	(0.3)	33.0	(1.1)	57.2	(1.2)	2.1	(0.5)	0.0	(0.0)
Netherlands	0.0	c	4.4	(0.6)	49.5	(1.1)	45.7	(1.2)	0.4	(0.1)	0.0	c
New Zealand	0.0	c	0.0	c	0.2	(0.1)	7.0	(0.5)	88.0	(0.7)	4.8	(0.5)
Norway	0.0	c	0.0	c	0.6	(0.1)	99.1	(0.1)	0.3	(0.0)	0.0	c
Poland	0.9	(0.2)	5.7	(0.6)	93.0	(0.6)	0.4	(0.2)	0.0	c	0.0	c
Portugal	2.6	(0.5)	9.9	(0.9)	30.1	(1.7)	57.0	(2.2)	0.4	(0.2)	0.0	c
Slovak Republic	1.5	(0.3)	5.4	(0.8)	40.1	(2.0)	51.5	(2.1)	1.5	(0.5)	0.0	c
Slovenia	0.0	c	0.4	(0.3)	6.3	(1.0)	90.2	(1.0)	3.1	(0.4)	0.0	c
Spain	0.1	(0.1)	11.8	(0.6)	25.8	(0.6)	62.2	(0.7)	0.1	(0.1)	0.0	c
Sweden	0.1	(0.1)	4.6	(0.5)	93.7	(0.8)	1.7	(0.6)	0.0	c	0.0	c
Switzerland	0.5	(0.1)	13.9	(0.9)	60.6	(1.7)	24.7	(2.0)	0.2	(0.1)	0.0	c
Turkey	0.3	(0.1)	2.6	(0.5)	33.2	(1.5)	60.3	(1.5)	3.2	(0.4)	0.3	(0.1)
United Kingdom	0.0	c	0.0	c	0.0	(0.0)	1.7	(0.4)	94.7	(0.4)	3.7	(0.2)
United States	0.0	c	0.4	(0.2)	14.6	(1.1)	69.8	(1.1)	14.9	(0.9)	0.3	(0.2)
OECD average	0.6	(0.1)	5.9	(0.1)	35.6	(0.2)	50.1	(0.2)	7.5	(0.1)	0.3	(0.1)
Partners												
Albania	0.1	(0.1)	2.9	(0.4)	42.9	(2.7)	53.8	(2.8)	0.2	(0.1)	0.0	c
Argentina	2.8	(0.8)	15.0	(1.7)	25.8	(1.9)	52.6	(2.6)	3.0	(0.9)	0.8	(0.5)
Brazil	0.0	c	9.0	(0.7)	15.8	(0.8)	36.1	(1.1)	37.2	(1.0)	1.9	(0.2)
Bulgaria	1.3	(0.3)	5.8	(0.7)	88.2	(1.0)	4.6	(0.4)	0.0	c	0.0	c
Colombia	7.4	(0.8)	13.5	(1.0)	22.1	(1.0)	38.8	(1.4)	18.2	(1.2)	0.0	c
Costa Rica	9.3	(1.3)	16.4	(1.2)	38.5	(1.5)	35.7	(2.0)	0.0	(0.0)	0.0	c
Croatia	0.0	c	0.0	c	82.0	(0.6)	18.0	(0.6)	0.0	c	0.0	c
Cyprus*	0.0	(0.0)	0.5	(0.1)	4.7	(0.1)	94.0	(0.2)	0.7	(0.1)	0.0	c
Hong Kong-China	1.2	(0.2)	6.9	(0.5)	27.5	(0.7)	63.0	(1.0)	1.4	(1.3)	0.0	c
Indonesia	2.3	(0.4)	10.0	(1.1)	38.5	(3.0)	45.5	(3.7)	3.1	(0.6)	0.6	(0.6)
Jordan	0.1	(0.1)	0.8	(0.2)	5.7	(0.6)	93.4	(0.6)	0.0	c	0.0	c
Kazakhstan	0.3	(0.1)	5.5	(0.6)	68.4	(2.4)	25.4	(2.6)	0.2	(0.1)	0.2	(0.2)
Latvia	3.6	(0.8)	18.0	(0.9)	76.4	(1.3)	2.0	(0.3)	0.0	(0.0)	0.0	c
Liechtenstein	4.5	(1.2)	16.5	(2.1)	69.4	(2.2)	9.6	(0.6)	0.0	c	0.0	c
Lithuania	0.2	(0.1)	7.3	(0.6)	82.2	(0.9)	10.4	(0.8)	0.0	(0.0)	0.0	c
Macao-China	7.1	(0.2)	19.3	(0.2)	33.3	(0.2)	40.0	(0.2)	0.2	(0.1)	0.0	(0.0)
Malaysia	0.0	c	0.1	(0.1)	5.1	(0.7)	94.7	(0.7)	0.0	c	0.0	c
Montenegro	0.0	c	0.1	(0.1)	82.0	(0.3)	17.9	(0.3)	0.0	c	0.0	c
Peru	3.1	(0.5)	9.1	(0.8)	19.5	(0.7)	46.2	(1.0)	22.1	(0.9)	0.0	c
Qatar	1.2	(0.1)	3.6	(0.1)	14.0	(0.1)	64.6	(0.2)	16.1	(0.2)	0.4	(0.0)
Romania	0.3	(0.2)	6.5	(0.6)	88.7	(0.7)	4.5	(0.4)	0.0	c	0.0	c
Russian Federation	0.7	(0.2)	8.9	(0.7)	73.7	(1.5)	16.7	(1.8)	0.1	(0.1)	0.0	c
Serbia	0.1	(0.1)	1.9	(0.9)	96.7	(1.0)	1.4	(0.2)	0.0	c	0.0	c
Shanghai-China	1.3	(0.3)	5.3	(0.8)	41.6	(1.6)	51.2	(1.4)	0.6	(0.1)	0.0	(0.0)
Singapore	0.4	(0.1)	2.0	(0.3)	8.3	(0.4)	89.3	(0.5)	0.0	(0.0)	0.0	c
Chinese Taipei	0.0	c	0.2	(0.2)	37.4	(1.5)	62.4	(1.5)	0.0	c	0.0	c
Thailand	0.1	(0.1)	0.4	(0.2)	22.9	(1.3)	74.1	(1.5)	2.5	(0.5)	0.0	c
Tunisia	6.3	(0.8)	14.6	(1.6)	21.9	(1.6)	52.3	(3.0)	4.9	(0.5)	0.0	c
United Arab Emirates	1.3	(0.3)	3.1	(0.3)	12.9	(0.9)	60.3	(1.2)	21.8	(1.0)	0.6	(0.1)
Uruguay	9.4	(1.3)	13.1	(0.8)	24.0	(1.1)	52.4	(1.9)	1.2	(0.2)	0.0	c
Viet Nam	0.7	(0.3)	3.5	(0.8)	10.5	(2.2)	85.3	(2.8)	0.0	c	0.0	c

Information for the adjudicated regions is available on line.
* See notes at the beginning of this Annex.
StatLink ᴹˢᴸ http://dx.doi.org/10.1787/888932937092

[Part 2/2]

Table A2.4b **Percentage of students at each grade level, by gender**

		Girls											
		7th grade		8th grade		9th grade		10th grade		11th grade		12th grade and above	
		%	S.E.	%	S.E.	%	S.E.	%	S.E.	%	S.E.	%	S.E.
OECD	Australia	0.0	(0.0)	0.2	(0.1)	8.3	(0.3)	70.8	(0.6)	20.7	(0.6)	0.0	(0.0)
	Austria	0.3	(0.1)	4.7	(0.7)	41.8	(1.3)	53.1	(1.4)	0.1	(0.1)	0.0	c
	Belgium	0.9	(0.1)	5.7	(0.5)	28.0	(0.7)	64.4	(0.8)	1.0	(0.2)	0.0	c
	Canada	0.1	(0.0)	0.9	(0.1)	11.5	(0.5)	86.4	(0.5)	1.2	(0.1)	0.0	(0.0)
	Chile	1.3	(0.3)	3.3	(0.6)	19.3	(1.0)	69.0	(1.2)	7.1	(0.4)	0.0	c
	Czech Republic	0.1	(0.1)	3.5	(0.5)	47.1	(2.0)	49.4	(2.1)	0.0	c	0.0	c
	Denmark	0.1	(0.0)	13.0	(0.9)	85.6	(0.9)	1.3	(0.3)	0.0	c	0.0	c
	Estonia	0.3	(0.1)	18.6	(0.8)	79.0	(0.9)	2.2	(0.4)	0.0	c	0.0	c
	Finland	0.5	(0.1)	12.0	(0.4)	87.3	(0.4)	0.0	c	0.2	(0.1)	0.0	c
	France	0.0	c	1.6	(0.3)	25.1	(1.1)	69.4	(1.1)	3.8	(0.4)	0.1	(0.1)
	Germany	0.3	(0.1)	8.2	(0.6)	50.2	(1.0)	40.4	(1.1)	0.8	(0.4)	0.0	c
	Greece	0.3	(0.1)	0.5	(0.1)	3.1	(0.7)	96.1	(0.8)	0.0	c	0.0	c
	Hungary	1.8	(0.7)	5.7	(0.8)	68.4	(1.1)	24.1	(0.8)	0.0	c	0.0	c
	Iceland	0.0	c	0.0	c	0.0	c	100.0	c	0.0	c	0.0	c
	Ireland	0.1	(0.1)	1.4	(0.2)	57.3	(1.0)	27.6	(1.4)	13.7	(1.2)	0.0	c
	Israel	0.0	(0.0)	0.2	(0.1)	15.5	(1.0)	83.8	(1.0)	0.4	(0.1)	0.0	c
	Italy	0.3	(0.1)	1.2	(0.2)	14.0	(0.6)	81.5	(0.8)	3.0	(0.3)	0.0	(0.0)
	Japan	0.0	c	0.0	c	0.0	c	100.0	c	0.0	c	0.0	c
	Korea	0.0	c	0.0	c	5.4	(1.1)	94.4	(1.1)	0.2	(0.1)	0.0	c
	Luxembourg	0.7	(0.1)	9.7	(0.2)	50.2	(0.2)	39.0	(0.2)	0.4	(0.1)	0.0	c
	Mexico	0.8	(0.1)	4.1	(0.3)	28.7	(1.0)	64.2	(1.1)	2.1	(0.3)	0.1	(0.1)
	Netherlands	0.0	c	2.7	(0.4)	43.8	(1.1)	53.0	(1.1)	0.5	(0.2)	0.0	c
	New Zealand	0.0	c	0.0	c	0.1	(0.1)	5.3	(0.4)	88.6	(0.6)	5.9	(0.6)
	Norway	0.0	c	0.0	c	0.2	(0.1)	99.8	(0.1)	0.0	c	0.0	c
	Poland	0.2	(0.1)	2.6	(0.3)	96.7	(0.4)	0.6	(0.2)	0.0	c	0.0	c
	Portugal	2.2	(0.3)	6.6	(0.7)	27.2	(1.6)	63.8	(2.2)	0.2	(0.1)	0.0	c
	Slovak Republic	1.9	(0.5)	3.5	(0.5)	38.8	(1.9)	54.0	(1.9)	1.8	(0.5)	0.0	c
	Slovenia	0.0	c	0.2	(0.2)	3.8	(0.9)	91.2	(1.0)	4.7	(0.5)	0.0	c
	Spain	0.1	(0.0)	7.8	(0.5)	22.3	(0.7)	69.9	(0.8)	0.0	(0.0)	0.0	c
	Sweden	0.0	c	2.8	(0.3)	94.4	(0.6)	2.8	(0.6)	0.0	c	0.0	c
	Switzerland	0.6	(0.2)	11.9	(1.0)	60.7	(1.7)	26.6	(1.8)	0.2	(0.1)	0.0	c
	Turkey	0.7	(0.3)	1.7	(0.3)	21.9	(1.2)	70.8	(1.1)	4.8	(0.4)	0.2	(0.1)
	United Kingdom	0.0	c	0.0	c	0.0	(0.0)	1.0	(0.3)	95.4	(0.3)	3.6	(0.2)
	United States	0.0	c	0.1	(0.1)	8.8	(1.2)	72.7	(1.3)	18.3	(0.9)	0.2	(0.1)
	OECD average	0.4	(0.0)	3.9	(0.1)	33.7	(0.2)	53.8	(0.2)	7.9	(0.1)	0.3	(0.1)
Partners	Albania	0.1	(0.1)	1.4	(0.4)	35.7	(2.6)	62.5	(2.6)	0.3	(0.1)	0.0	c
	Argentina	1.2	(0.3)	9.1	(0.9)	19.7	(1.3)	65.8	(1.9)	2.7	(0.4)	1.4	(0.8)
	Brazil	0.0	c	5.0	(0.4)	11.5	(0.7)	33.8	(1.0)	46.4	(1.1)	3.3	(0.2)
	Bulgaria	0.5	(0.2)	3.3	(0.5)	90.9	(0.7)	5.2	(0.5)	0.0	(0.0)	0.0	c
	Colombia	3.9	(0.6)	10.8	(0.7)	21.0	(0.9)	41.4	(1.1)	22.9	(1.1)	0.0	c
	Costa Rica	5.7	(0.8)	11.3	(0.8)	40.5	(1.3)	42.1	(1.7)	0.4	(0.2)	0.0	c
	Croatia	0.0	c	0.0	c	77.5	(0.6)	22.5	(0.6)	0.0	c	0.0	c
	Cyprus*	0.0	c	0.5	(0.1)	4.2	(0.2)	94.6	(0.2)	0.7	(0.1)	0.0	(0.0)
	Hong Kong-China	0.9	(0.2)	6.0	(0.6)	24.2	(0.8)	67.3	(1.0)	1.6	(1.5)	0.0	c
	Indonesia	1.5	(0.4)	6.4	(0.8)	36.8	(2.9)	50.0	(3.0)	4.7	(0.8)	0.5	(0.5)
	Jordan	0.0	(0.0)	1.3	(0.2)	6.3	(0.5)	92.4	(0.6)	0.0	c	0.0	c
	Kazakhstan	0.1	(0.1)	4.4	(0.5)	65.9	(1.9)	29.3	(2.1)	0.2	(0.1)	0.0	c
	Latvia	0.6	(0.2)	11.6	(0.6)	83.7	(1.1)	4.1	(0.7)	0.0	c	0.0	c
	Liechtenstein	5.3	(1.3)	11.5	(1.9)	62.8	(1.9)	20.4	(0.8)	0.0	c	0.0	c
	Lithuania	0.1	(0.1)	5.2	(0.6)	80.2	(0.9)	14.4	(0.8)	0.0	(0.0)	0.0	c
	Macao-China	3.5	(0.1)	13.3	(0.2)	33.1	(0.3)	49.5	(0.3)	0.7	(0.2)	0.0	c
	Malaysia	0.0	c	0.0	c	2.9	(0.4)	97.1	(0.4)	0.0	(0.1)	0.0	c
	Montenegro	0.0	c	0.0	c	77.1	(0.3)	22.9	(0.3)	0.0	c	0.0	c
	Peru	2.3	(0.5)	6.6	(0.6)	16.8	(1.0)	49.1	(1.2)	25.3	(1.0)	0.0	c
	Qatar	0.5	(0.1)	2.7	(0.1)	13.6	(0.1)	64.9	(0.2)	18.2	(0.1)	0.2	(0.0)
	Romania	0.1	(0.1)	8.3	(0.6)	85.9	(0.9)	5.7	(0.6)	0.0	c	0.0	c
	Russian Federation	0.6	(0.2)	7.3	(0.5)	73.9	(2.0)	18.1	(2.0)	0.1	(0.1)	0.0	c
	Serbia	0.1	(0.1)	1.0	(0.6)	96.8	(0.7)	2.0	(0.3)	0.0	c	0.0	c
	Shanghai-China	0.8	(0.2)	3.8	(0.5)	37.6	(1.8)	57.0	(1.8)	0.6	(0.1)	0.1	(0.1)
	Singapore	0.4	(0.1)	2.1	(0.2)	7.6	(0.4)	89.8	(0.4)	0.2	(0.1)	0.0	c
	Chinese Taipei	0.0	c	0.1	(0.1)	35.0	(1.5)	64.9	(1.4)	0.0	c	0.0	c
	Thailand	0.0	(0.0)	0.2	(0.1)	19.0	(1.2)	77.5	(1.2)	3.3	(0.5)	0.0	c
	Tunisia	3.9	(0.5)	9.3	(1.1)	19.4	(1.5)	60.6	(2.5)	6.7	(0.6)	0.0	c
	United Arab Emirates	0.6	(0.1)	2.6	(0.4)	9.7	(1.1)	63.4	(1.7)	22.6	(1.3)	1.2	(0.3)
	Uruguay	4.6	(0.6)	11.4	(0.8)	21.0	(1.1)	61.7	(1.5)	1.4	(0.2)	0.0	c
	Viet Nam	0.1	(0.1)	2.1	(0.6)	6.4	(1.5)	91.4	(1.9)	0.0	c	0.0	c

Information for the adjudicated regions is available on line.
* See notes at the beginning of this Annex.
StatLink ⏷ http://dx.doi.org/10.1787/888932937092

ANNEX A3

TECHNICAL NOTES ON ANALYSES IN THIS VOLUME

Methods and definitions

Relative risk or increased likelihood

The relative risk is a measure of the association between an antecedent factor and an outcome factor. The relative risk is simply the ratio of two risks, i.e. the risk of observing the outcome when the antecedent is present and the risk of observing the outcome when the antecedent is not present. Figure A3.1 presents the notation that is used in the following.

■ Figure A3.1 ■

Labels used in a two-way table

p_{11}	p_{12}	$p_{1.}$
p_{21}	p_{22}	$p_{2.}$
$p_{.1}$	$p_{.2}$	$p_{..}$

$p_{..}$ is equal to $\frac{n_{..}}{n_{..}}$, with $n_{..}$ the total number of students and $p_{..}$ is therefore equal to 1, $p_{i.}$, $p_{.j}$ respectively represent the marginal probabilities for each row and for each column. The marginal probabilities are equal to the marginal frequencies divided by the total number of students. Finally, the p_{ij} represents the probabilities for each cell and are equal to the number of observations in a particular cell divided by the total number of observations.

In PISA, the rows represent the antecedent factor, with the first row for "having the antecedent" and the second row for "not having the antecedent". The columns represent the outcome: the first column for "having the outcome" and the second column for "not having the outcome". The relative risk is then equal to:

$$RR = \frac{(p_{11}/p_{1.})}{(p_{21}/p_{2.})}$$

Attributable risk or population relevance

The attributable risk, also referred to as population relevance in the text and tables of this volume, is interpreted as follows: if the risk factor could be eliminated, then the rate of occurrence of the outcome characteristic in the population would be reduced by this coefficient. The attributable risk is equal to (see Figure A3.1 for the notation that is used in the following formula):

$$AR = \frac{(p_{11}\,p_{22}) - (p_{12}\,p_{21})}{(p_{.1}\,p_{2.})}$$

The coefficients are multiplied by 100 to express the result as a percentage.

Statistics based on multilevel models

Statistics based on multi level models include variance components (between- and within-school variance), the index of inclusion derived from these components, and regression coefficients where this has been indicated. Multilevel models are generally specified as two-level regression models (the student and school levels), with normally distributed residuals, and estimated with maximum likelihood estimation. Where the dependent variable is mathematics performance, the estimation uses five plausible values for each student's performance on the mathematics scale. Models were estimated using Mplus® software.

In multilevel models, weights are used at both the student and school levels. The purpose of these weights is to account for differences in the probabilities of students being selected in the sample. Since PISA applies a two-stage sampling procedure, these differences are due to factors at both the school and the student levels. For the multilevel models, student final weights (W_FSTUWT) were used. Within-school-weights correspond to student final weights, rescaled to sum up within each school to the school sample size. Between-school weights correspond to the sum of student final weights (W_FSTUWT) within each school. The definition of between-school weights has changed with respect to PISA 2009.

The index of inclusion is defined and estimated as:

$$100 * \frac{\sigma_w^2}{\sigma_w^2 + \sigma_b^2}$$

where σ_w^2 and σ_b^2, respectively, represent the within- and between-variance estimates.

The results in multilevel models, and the between-school variance estimate in particular, depend on how schools are defined and organised within countries and by the units that were chosen for sampling purposes. For example, in some countries, some of the schools in the PISA sample were defined as administrative units (even if they spanned several geographically separate institutions, as in Italy); in others they were defined as those parts of larger educational institutions that serve 15-year-olds; in still others they were defined as physical school buildings; and in others they were defined from a management perspective (e.g. entities having a principal). The *PISA 2012 Technical Report* (OECD, forthcoming) and Annex A2 provide an overview of how schools were defined. In Slovenia, the primary sampling unit is defined as a group of students who follow the same study programme within a school (an educational track within a school). So in this particular case the between-school variance is actually the within-school, between-track variation. The use of stratification variables in the selection of schools may also affect the estimate of the between-school variance, particularly if stratification variables are associated with between-school differences.

Because of the manner in which students were sampled, the within-school variation includes variation between classes as well as between students.

Multiple imputation replaces each missing value with a set of plausible values that represent the uncertainty about the right value to impute. The multiple imputed data sets are then analysed by using standard procedures for complete data and by combining results from these analyses. Five imputed values are computed for each missing value. Different methods can be used according to the pattern of missing values. For arbitrary missing data patterns, the MCMC (Monte Carlo Markov Chain) approach can be used.

This approach is used with the SAS procedure MI for the multilevel analyses in this volume. Multiple imputation is conducted separately for each model and each country, except for the model with all variables (Tables IV.1.12a, IV.1.12b and IV.1.12c) in which the data were constructed from imputed data for the individual models, such as the model for learning environment, model for selecting and grouping students, etc. Where continuous values are generated for missing discrete variables, these are rounded to the nearest discrete value of the variable. Each of the five plausible value of mathematics performance is analysed by Mplus® software using one of the five imputed data sets, which were combined taking account of the between imputation variance.

Standard errors and significance tests

The statistics in this report represent estimates of national performance based on samples of students, rather than values that could be calculated if every student in every country had answered every question. Consequently, it is important to measure the degree of uncertainty of the estimates. In PISA, each estimate has an associated degree of uncertainty, which is expressed through a standard error. The use of confidence intervals provides a way to make inferences about the population means and proportions in a manner that reflects the uncertainty associated with the sample estimates. From an observed sample statistic and assuming a normal distribution, it can be inferred that the corresponding population result would lie within the confidence interval in 95 out of 100 replications of the measurement on different samples drawn from the same population.

In many cases, readers are primarily interested in whether a given value in a particular country is different from a second value in the same or another country, e.g. whether girls in a country perform better than boys in the same country. In the tables and charts used in this report, differences are labelled as statistically significant when a difference of that size, smaller or larger, would be observed less than 5% of the time, if there were actually no difference in corresponding population values. Similarly, the risk of reporting a correlation as significant if there is, in fact, no correlation between two measures, is contained at 5%.

Throughout the report, significance tests were undertaken to assess the statistical significance of the comparisons made.

Gender differences and differences between subgroup means

Gender differences in student performance or other indices were tested for statistical significance. Positive differences indicate higher scores for boys while negative differences indicate higher scores for girls. Generally, differences marked in bold in the tables in this volume are statistically significant at the 95% confidence level.

Similarly, differences between other groups of students (e.g. native students and students with an immigrant background) were tested for statistical significance. The definitions of the subgroups can in general be found in the tables and the text accompanying the analysis. All differences marked in bold in the tables presented in Annex B of this report are statistically significant at the 95% level.

Differences between subgroup means, after accounting for other variables

For many tables, subgroup comparisons were performed both on the observed difference ("before accounting for other variables") and after accounting for other variables, such as the *PISA index of economic, social and cultural status of students* (ESCS). The adjusted differences were estimated using linear regression and tested for significance at the 95% confidence level. Significant differences are marked in bold.

Performance differences between the top and bottom quartiles of PISA indices and scales

Differences in average performance between the top and bottom quarters of the PISA indices and scales were tested for statistical significance. Figures marked in bold indicate that performance between the top and bottom quarters of students on the respective index is statistically significantly different at the 95% confidence level.

Differences between subgroups of schools

In this Volume, schools are compared across several aspects, such as resource allocation or performance. For this purpose, schools are grouped in categories by socio-economic status of students and schools, public-private status, lower and upper secondary education and school location. The differences between subgroups of schools are tested for statistical significance in the following way:

- *Socio-economic status of students*: Students in the top quarter of ESCS are compared to students in the bottom quarter of ESCS. If the difference is statistically significant at the 95% confidence levels, both figures are marked in bold. The second and third quarters do not enter the comparison.

- *Socio-economic status of schools*: advantaged schools are compared to disadvantaged schools. If the difference is statistically significant at the 95% confidence levels, both figures are marked in bold. Average schools do not enter the comparison.

- *Public and private schools:* Government-dependent and government-independent private schools are jointly considered as private schools. Figures in bold in data tables presented in Annex B of this report indicate statistically significant differences, at the 95% confidence level, between public and private schools.

- *Education levels*: Students at the upper secondary education are compared to students at the lower secondary education. If the difference is statistically significant at the 95% confidence levels, both figures are marked in bold.

- *School location*: For the purpose of significance tests, "schools located in a small town" and "schools located in a town" are jointly considered to form a single group. Figures for "schools located in a city or large city" are marked in bold in data tables presented in Annex B of this report if the difference with this middle category ("schools located in a small town" and "schools located in a town") is significant at the 95% confidence levels. In turn, figures for "schools located in a village, hamlet, or rural area" are marked in bold if the difference with this middle category is significant. Differences between the extreme categories were not tested for significance.

Change in the performance per unit of the index

For many tables, the difference in student performance per unit of the index shown was calculated. Figures in bold indicate that the differences are statistically significantly different from zero at the 95% confidence level.

Relative risk or increased likelihood

Figures in bold in the data tables presented in Annex B of this report indicate that the relative risk is statistically significantly different from 1 at the 95% confidence level. To compute statistical significance around the value of 1 (the null hypothesis), the relative-risk statistic is assumed to follow a log-normal distribution, rather than a normal distribution, under the null hypothesis.

Attributable risk or population relevance

Figures in bold in the data tables presented in Annex B of this report indicate that the attributable risk is statistically significantly different from 0 at the 95% confidence level.

Standard errors in statistics estimated from multilevel models

For statistics based on multilevel models (such as the estimates of variance components and regression coefficients from two-level regression models) the standard errors are not estimated with the usual replication method which accounts for stratification and sampling rates from finite populations. Instead, standard errors are "model-based": their computation assumes that schools, and students within schools, are sampled at random (with sampling probabilities reflected in school and student weights) from a theoretical, infinite population of schools and students which complies with the model's parametric assumptions.

The standard error for the estimated index of inclusion is calculated by deriving an approximate distribution for it from the (model-based) standard errors for the variance components, using the delta-method.

Standard errors in trend analyses of performance: Link error

Standard errors for performance trend estimates had to be adjusted because the equating procedure that allows scores in different PISA assessments to be compared introduces a form of random error that is related to performance changes on the link items. These more conservative standard errors (larger than standard errors that were estimated before the introduction of the link error) reflect not only the measurement precision and sampling variation as for the usual PISA results, but also the link error (see Annex A5 for a technical discussion of the link error).

Link items represent only a subset of all items used to derive PISA scores. If different items were chosen to equate PISA scores over time, the comparison of performance for a group of students across time could vary. As a result, standard errors for the estimates of the change over time in mathematics, reading or science performance of a particular group (e.g. a country or economy, a region, boys, girls, students with an immigrant background, students without an immigrant background, socio-economically advantaged students, students in public schools, etc.) include the link error in addition to the sampling and imputation error commonly added to estimates in performance for a particular year. Because the equating procedure adds uncertainty to the position in the distribution (a change in the intercept) but does not result in any change in the variance of a distribution, standard errors for location-invariant estimates do not

include the link error. Location-invariant estimates include, for example, estimates for variances, regression coefficients for student- or school-level covariates, and correlation coefficients.

Figures in bold in the data tables for trends in performance presented in Annex B of this report indicate that the the change in performance for that particular group is statistically significantly different from 0 at the 95% confidence level. The standard errors used to calculate the statistical significance of the reported trend include the link error.

ANNEX A4
QUALITY ASSURANCE

Quality assurance procedures were implemented in all parts of PISA 2012, as was done for all previous PISA surveys.

The consistent quality and linguistic equivalence of the PISA 2012 assessment instruments were facilitated by providing countries with equivalent source versions of the assessment instruments in English and French and requiring countries (other than those assessing students in English and French) to prepare and consolidate two independent translations using both source versions. Precise translation and adaptation guidelines were supplied, also including instructions for selecting and training the translators. For each country, the translation and format of the assessment instruments (including test materials, marking guides, questionnaires and manuals) were verified by expert translators appointed by the PISA Consortium before they were used in the PISA 2012 Field Trial and Main Study. These translators' mother tongue was the language of instruction in the country concerned and they were knowledgeable about education systems. For further information on the PISA translation procedures, see the *PISA 2012 Technical Report* (OECD, forthcoming).

The survey was implemented through standardised procedures. The PISA Consortium provided comprehensive manuals that explained the implementation of the survey, including precise instructions for the work of School Co-ordinators and scripts for Test Administrators to use during the assessment sessions. Proposed adaptations to survey procedures, or proposed modifications to the assessment session script, were submitted to the PISA Consortium for approval prior to verification. The PISA Consortium then verified the national translation and adaptation of these manuals.

To establish the credibility of PISA as valid and unbiased and to encourage uniformity in administering the assessment sessions, Test Administrators in participating countries were selected using the following criteria: it was required that the Test Administrator not be the reading, mathematics or science instructor of any students in the sessions he or she would administer for PISA; it was recommended that the Test Administrator not be a member of the staff of any school where he or she would administer for PISA; and it was considered preferable that the Test Administrator not be a member of the staff of any school in the PISA sample. Participating countries organised an in-person training session for Test Administrators.

Participating countries and economies were required to ensure that: Test Administrators worked with the School Co-ordinator to prepare the assessment session, including updating student tracking forms and identifying excluded students; no extra time was given for the cognitive items (while it was permissible to give extra time for the student questionnaire); no instrument was administered before the two one-hour parts of the cognitive session; Test Administrators recorded the student participation status on the student tracking forms and filled in a Session Report Form; no cognitive instrument was permitted to be photocopied; no cognitive instrument could be viewed by school staff before the assessment session; and Test Administrators returned the material to the national centre immediately after the assessment sessions.

National Project Managers were encouraged to organise a follow-up session when more than 15% of the PISA sample was not able to attend the original assessment session.

National Quality Monitors from the PISA Consortium visited all national centres to review data-collection procedures. Finally, School Quality Monitors from the PISA Consortium visited a sample of seven schools during the assessment. For further information on the field operations, see the *PISA 2012 Technical Report* (OECD, forthcoming).

Marking procedures were designed to ensure consistent and accurate application of the marking guides outlined in the PISA Operations Manuals. National Project Managers were required to submit proposed modifications to these procedures to the Consortium for approval. Reliability studies to analyse the consistency of marking were implemented.

Software specially designed for PISA facilitated data entry, detected common errors during data entry, and facilitated the process of data cleaning. Training sessions familiarised National Project Managers with these procedures.

For a description of the quality assurance procedures applied in PISA and in the results, see the *PISA 2012 Technical Report* (OECD, forthcoming).

The results of adjudication showed that the PISA Technical Standards were fully met in all countries and economies that participated in PISA 2012, with the exception of Albania. Albania submitted parental occupation data that was incomplete and appeared inaccurate, since there was over-use of a narrow range of occupations. It was not possible to resolve these issues during the course of data cleaning, and as a result neither parental occupation data nor any indices which depend on this data are included in the international dataset. Results for Albania are omitted from any analyses which depend on these indices.

ANNEX A5

TECHNICAL DETAILS OF TRENDS ANALYSES

Comparing mathematics, reading and science performance across PISA cycles

The PISA 2003, 2006, 2009 and 2012 assessments use the same mathematics performance scale, which means that score points on this scale are directly comparable over time. The same is true for the reading performance scale used since PISA 2000 and the science performance scale used since PISA 2006. The comparability of scores across time is possible because of the use of link items that are common across assessments and can be used in the equating procedure to align performance scales. The items that are common across assessments are a subset of the total items that make up the assessment because PISA progressively renews its pool of items. As a result, out of a total of 110 items in the PISA 2012 mathematics assessment, 84 are linked to 2003 items, 48 to 2006 items and 35 to 2009 items. The number of PISA 2012 items linked to the PISA 2003 assessment is larger than the number linked to the PISA 2006 or the PISA 2009 assessments because mathematics was a major domain in PISA 2003 and PISA 2012. In PISA 2006 and PISA 2009, mathematics was a minor domain and all the mathematics items included in these assessments were link items. The *PISA 2012 Technical Report* (OECD, forthcoming) provides the technical details on equating the PISA 2012 mathematics scale for trends purposes.

Link error

Standard errors for performance trend estimates had to be adjusted because the equating procedure that allows scores in different PISA assessments to be compared introduces a form of random error that is related to performance changes on the link items. These more conservative standard errors (larger than standard errors that were estimated before the introduction of the link error) reflect not only the measurement precision and sampling variation as for the usual PISA results, but also the link error provided in Table A5.1.

Link items represent only a subset of all items used to derive PISA scores. If different items were chosen to equate PISA scores over time, the comparison of performance for a group of students across time could vary. As a result, standard errors for the estimates of the change over time in mathematics, reading or science performance of a particular group (e.g. a country or economy, a region, boys, girls, students with an immigrant background, students without an immigrant background, socio-economically advantaged students, students in public schools, etc.) include the link error in addition to the sampling and imputation error commonly added to estimates in performance for a particular year. Because the equating procedure adds uncertainty to the position in the distribution (a change in the intercept) but does not result in any change in the variance of a distribution, standard errors for location-invariant estimates do not include the link error. Location-invariant estimates include, for example, estimates for variances, regression coefficients for student- or school-level covariates, and correlation coefficients.

Link error for scores between two PISA assessments

The following equations describe how link errors between two PISA assessments are calculated. Suppose we have L score points in K units. Use i to index items in a unit and j to index units so that $\hat{\mu}_{ij}^{y}$ is the estimated difficulty of item i in unit j for year y, and let for example to compare PISA 2006 and PISA 2003:

$$c_{ij} = \hat{\mu}_{ij}^{2006} - \hat{\mu}_{ij}^{2003}$$

The size (total number of score points) of unit j is m_j so that:

$$\sum_{j=1}^{K} m_j = L$$

and

$$\bar{m} = \frac{1}{K} \sum_{j=1}^{K} m_j$$

Further let:

$$c_{.j} = \frac{1}{m_j} \sum_{j=1}^{m_j} c_{ij}$$

and

$$\bar{c} = \frac{1}{N} \sum_{j=1}^{K} \sum_{i=1}^{m_j} c_{ij}$$

then the link error, taking clustering into account, is as follows:

$$error_{2006,2003} = \sqrt{\frac{\sum_{j=1}^{K} m_j^2 (c_{.j} - \bar{c})^2}{K(K-1)\bar{m}^2}}$$

This approach for estimating the link errors was used in PISA 2006, PISA 2009 and PISA 2012. The link errors for comparisons of PISA 2012 results with previous assessments are shown in Table A5.1.

[Part 1/1]

Table A5.1 **Link error for comparisons of performance between PISA 2012 and previous assessments**

Comparison	Mathematics	Reading	Science
PISA 2000 to PISA 2012		5.923	
PISA 2003 to PISA 2012	1.931	5.604	
PISA 2006 to PISA 2012	2.084	5.580	3.512
PISA 2009 to PISA 2012	2.294	2.602	2.006

Note: Comparisons between PISA 2012 scores and previous assessments can only be made to when the subject first became a major domain. As a result, comparisons in mathematics performance between PISA 2012 and PISA 2000 are not possible, nor are comparisons in science performance between PISA 2012 and PISA 2000 or PISA 2003.
StatLink ᴍsᴘ http://dx.doi.org/10.1787/888932960500

Comparisons of performance: Difference between two assessments

To evaluate the evolution of performance, analyses report the change in performance between two cycles. Comparisons between two assessments (e.g. a country's/economy's change in performance between PISA 2003 and PISA 2012 or the change in performance of a subgroup) are calculated as:

$$\Delta_{2012-t} = PISA_{2012} - PISA_t$$

where $\Delta_{2012\text{-}t}$ is the difference in performance between PISA 2012 and a previous PISA assessment, where t can take any of the following values: 2000, 2003, 2006 or 2009. $PISA_{2012}$ is the mathematics, reading or science score observed in PISA 2012, and $PISA_t$ is the mathematics, reading or science score observed in a previous assessment (2000, 2003, 2006 or 2009). The standard error of the change in performance $\sigma(\Delta_{2012\text{-}t})$ is:

$$\sigma(\Delta_{2012-t}) = \sqrt{\sigma_{2012}^2 + \sigma_t^2 + error_{2012,t}^2}$$

where σ_{2012} is the standard error observed for $PISA_{2012}$, σ_t is the standard error observed for $PISA_t$ and $error_{2012,t}$ is the link error for comparisons of mathematics, reading or science performance between the PISA 2012 assessment and a previous (t) assessment. The value for $error_{2012,t}$ is shown in Table A5.1.

Comparing items and non-performance scales across PISA cycles

To gather information about students' and schools' characteristics, PISA asks both students and schools to complete a background questionnaire. In PISA 2003 and PISA 2012 several questions were left untouched, allowing for a comparison of responses to these questions over time. In this report, only questions that retained the same wording were used for trends analyses. Questions with subtle word changes or questions with major word changes were not compared across time because it is impossible to discern whether observed changes in the response are due to changes in the construct they are measuring or to changes in the way the construct is being measured.

Also, as described in Annex A1, questionnaire items in PISA are used to construct indices. Whenever the questions used in the construction of indices remains intact in PISA 2003 and PISA 2012, the corresponding indices are compared. Two types of indices are used in PISA: simple indices and scale indices.

Simple indices recode a set of responses to questionnaire items. For trends analyses, the values observed in PISA 2003 are compared directly to PISA 2012, just as simple responses to questionnaire items are. This is the case of indices like student-teacher ratio and ability grouping in mathematics.

Scale indices, on the other hand, imply WLE estimates which require rescaling in order to be comparable across PISA cycles. Scale indices, like the *PISA index of economic, social and cultural status*, the *index of sense of belonging*, the *index of attitudes towards school*, the *index of intrinsic motivation to learn mathematics*, the *index of instrumental motivation to learn mathematics*, the *index of mathematics self-efficacy*, the *index of mathematics self-concept*, the *index of anxiety towards mathematics*, the *index of teacher shortage*, the *index of quality of physical infrastructure*, the *index of quality of educational resources*, the *index of disciplinary climate*, the *index of student-teacher relations*, the *index of teacher morale*, the *index of student-related factors affecting school climate*, and the *index of teacher-related factors affecting school climate*, were scaled in PISA 2012 to have an OECD mean of 0 and a standard deviation of 1. In PISA 2003 these same scales were scaled to have an OECD average of 0 and a standard deviation of 1. Because they are on different scales, values reported in *Learning for Tomorrow's World: First Results from PISA 2003* (OECD, 2004) cannot be compared with those reported in this volume. To make these scale indices comparable, values for 2003 have been rescaled to the 2012 scale, using the PISA 2012 parameter estimates.

To evaluate change in these items and scales, analyses report the change in the estimate between two assessments, usually PISA 2003 and PISA 2012. Comparisons between two assessments (e.g. a country's/economy's change index of anxiety towards mathematics between PISA 2003 and PISA 2012 or the change in this index for a subgroup) is calculated as:

$$\Delta_{2012,t} = PISA_{2012} - PISA_t$$

where $\Delta_{2012,t}$ is the difference in the index between PISA 2012 and a previous assessment, $PISA_{2012}$ is the index value observed in PISA 2012, and $PISA_t$ is the index value observed in a previous assessment (2000, 2003, 2006 or 2009). The standard error of the change in performance $\sigma(\Delta_{2012-t})$ is:

$$\sigma(\Delta_{2012-t}) = \sqrt{\sigma_{2012}^2 + \sigma_t^2}$$

where σ_{2012} is the standard error observed for $PISA_{2012}$ and σ_t is the standard error observed for $PISA_t$. These comparisons are based on an identical set of items; there is no uncertainty related to the choice of items for equating purposes, so no link error is needed.

Although only scale indices that use the same items in PISA 2003 and PISA 2012 are valid for trend comparisons, this does not imply that PISA 2012 indices that include exactly the same items as 2003 as well as new questionnaire items cannot be compared with PISA 2003 indices that included a smaller pool of items. In such cases, for example the *index of sense of belonging,* trend analyses were conducted by treating as missing in PISA 2003 items that were asked in the context of PISA 2012 but not in the PISA 2003 student questionnaire. This means that while the full set of information was used to scale the sense of belonging index in 2012, the PISA 2003 sense of belonging index was scaled under the assumption that if the 2012 items that were missing in 2003 had been asked in 2003, the overall index and index variation would have remained the same as those that were observed on common 2003 items. This is a tenable assumption inasmuch as in both PISA 2003 and PISA 2012 the questionnaire items used to construct the scale hold as an underlying factor in the construction of the scale.

OECD average

Throughout this report, the OECD average is used as a benchmark. It is calculated as the average across OECD countries, weighting each country equally. Some OECD countries did not participate in certain assessments, other OECD countries do not have comparable results for some assessments, others did not include certain questions in their questionnaires or changed them substantially from assessment to assessment. For this reason in trends tables and figures, the OECD average is reported as assessment-specific, that is, it includes only those countries for which there is comparable information in that particular assessment. This way, the 2003 OECD average includes only those OECD countries that have comparable information from the 2003 assessment, even if the results it refers to the PISA 2012 assessment and more countries have comparable information. This restriction allows for valid comparisons of the OECD average over time.

References

OECD (forthcoming), *PISA 2012 Technical Report, PISA,* OECD Publishing.

OECD (2004), *Learning for Tomorrow's World: First Results from PISA 2003*, PISA, OECD Publishing.
http://dx.doi.org/10.1787/9789264006416-en

ANNEX A6
ANCHORING VIGNETTES IN THE PISA 2012 STUDENT QUESTIONNAIRE

Annex A6 is available on line only.

It can be found at: *www.pisa.oecd.org*

Annex B

PISA 2012 DATA

All tables in Annex B are available on line

Annex B1: Results for countries and economies
http://dx.doi.org/10.1787/888932957384
http://dx.doi.org/10.1787/888932957422
http://dx.doi.org/10.1787/888932957441
http://dx.doi.org/10.1787/888932957460
http://dx.doi.org/10.1787/888932957479
http://dx.doi.org/10.1787/888932957498
http://dx.doi.org/10.1787/888932957517

Annex B2: Results for regions within countries
http://dx.doi.org/10.1787/888932957536

Annex B3: List of tables available on line

The reader should note that there are gaps
in the numbering of tables because some tables
appear on line only and are not included in this publication.

ANNEX B1
RESULTS FOR COUNTRIES AND ECONOMIES

[Part 1/1]

Relationship between education outcomes and selecting and grouping students

Table IV.1.1 *System-level correlations*

OECD countries

		Mathematics performance				Variation in mathematics performance explained by the PISA index of economic, social and cultural status of students				Variation in mathematics performance explained by the PISA index of economic, social and cultural status of students and schools			
		Before accounting for GDP/capita		After accounting for GDP/capita		Before accounting for GDP/capita		After accounting for GDP/capita		Before accounting for GDP/capita		After accounting for GDP/capita	
		Corr.	p-value	Partial corr.	p-value	Corr.	p-value	Partial corr.	p-value	Corr.	p-value	Partial corr.	p-value
Vertical stratification	Standard deviation of grade levels that 15-year-old students attend	*-0.29*	(0.09)[1]	*-0.31*	(0.08)[1]	**0.56**	(0.00)	**0.56**	(0.00)	**0.37**	(0.03)	**0.38**	(0.03)
	Standard deviation of age of entry into primary school	-0.21	(0.24)	*-0.32*	(0.07)	0.06	(0.72)	0.11	(0.55)	-0.17	(0.34)	-0.14	(0.44)
	Percentage of students who repeated one or more grades	-0.14	(0.43)	-0.25	(0.16)	**0.39**	(0.02)	**0.45**	(0.01)	*0.33*	(0.06)	**0.38**	(0.03)
Horizontal stratification (between schools)	Number of school types or distinct education programmes available for 15-year-olds	0.13	(0.47)	0.10	(0.58)	0.23	(0.18)	0.26	(0.15)	**0.62**	(0.00)	**0.65**	(0.00)
	Percentage of students enrolled in a programme with a pre-vocational or vocational curriculum	0.00	(0.98)	0.04	(0.84)	0.02	(0.93)	0.00	(0.99)	**0.50**	(0.00)	**0.50**	(0.00)
	Number of years between age of selection and age 15	0.11	(0.55)	0.10	(0.57)	*0.31*	(0.07)[1]	*0.32*	(0.07)[1]	**0.61**	(0.00)	**0.63**	(0.00)
	Percentage of students in selective schools	0.22	(0.21)	0.20	(0.28)	0.13	(0.46)	0.15	(0.41)	**0.54**	(0.00)	**0.56**	(0.00)
	Percentage of students in schools that transfer students to other schools due to low achievement, behavioural problems or special learning needs	-0.20	(0.26)	-0.17	(0.33)	*0.30*	(0.09)	0.29	(0.10)	**0.48**	(0.00)	**0.47**	(0.01)
Horizontal stratification (within schools)	Percentage of students in schools that group students by ability for all mathematics classes	-0.06	(0.73)	-0.07	(0.71)	-0.10	(0.59)	-0.10	(0.59)	-0.23	(0.18)	-0.24	(0.19)

All participating countries and economies

		Mathematics performance				Variation in mathematics performance explained by the PISA index of economic, social and cultural status of students				Variation in mathematics performance explained by the PISA index of economic, social and cultural status of students and schools			
		Before accounting for GDP/capita		After accounting for GDP/capita		Before accounting for GDP/capita		After accounting for GDP/capita		Before accounting for GDP/capita		After accounting for GDP/capita	
		Corr.	p-value	Partial corr.	p-value	Corr.	p-value	Partial corr.	p-value	Corr.	p-value	Partial corr.	p-value
Vertical stratification	Standard deviation of grade levels that 15-year-old students attend	**-0.34**	(0.01)	**-0.36**	(0.00)	**0.25**	(0.05)	**0.26**	(0.04)	0.16	(0.22)	0.14	(0.26)
	Standard deviation of age of entry into primary school	*-0.22*	(0.07)[1]	**-0.32**	(0.01)	0.02	(0.85)	0.08	(0.54)	-0.05	(0.68)	-0.05	(0.67)
	Percentage of students who repeated one or more grades	**-0.26**	(0.04)[1]	**-0.34**	(0.01)	*0.22*	(0.09)	**0.25**	(0.05)	0.16	(0.21)	0.17	(0.18)
Horizontal stratification (between schools)	Number of school types or distinct education programmes available for 15-year-olds	0.04	(0.76)	0.04	(0.74)	0.19	(0.15)	0.20	(0.13)	**0.48**	(0.00)	**0.49**	(0.00)
	Percentage of students enrolled in a programme with a pre-vocational or vocational curriculum	-0.01	(0.94)	0.09	(0.49)	0.05	(0.71)	-0.01	(0.92)	**0.43**	(0.00)	**0.42**	(0.00)
	Number of years between age of selection and age 15	0.15	(0.24)	0.12	(0.35)	**0.37**	(0.00)	**0.42**	(0.00)	**0.56**	(0.00)	**0.61**	(0.00)
	Percentage of students in selective schools	0.18	(0.15)	0.15	(0.25)	-0.13	(0.30)	-0.09	(0.48)	**0.28**	(0.03)	**0.29**	(0.02)
	Percentage of students in schools that transfer students to other schools due to low achievement, behavioural problems or special learning needs	-0.19	(0.13)	-0.19	(0.14)	0.04	(0.76)	0.05	(0.70)	**0.26**	(0.04)	*0.23*	(0.08)
Horizontal stratification (within schools)	Percentage of students in schools that group students by ability for all mathematics classes	**-0.26**	(0.04)	**-0.25**	(0.04)	-0.15	(0.22)	-0.17	(0.18)	-0.20	(0.11)	*-0.23*	(0.07)

Note: Values that are statistically significant at the 10% level (p < 0.10) are indicated in italics and those at the 5% level (p < 0.05) are in bold.
1. While Pearson's correlation coefficients are presented in this table, Spearman's rank correlation coefficients are also computed in order to examine the robustness of the results. When Pearson's correlation coefficient is significant at least at the 10% level but Spearman's rank correlation coefficient is not significant at the 10% level, a superscript 1 appears in the cell.

StatLink ⌨ http://dx.doi.org/10.1787/888932957384

[Part 1/1]
Relationship between education outcomes and resources invested in education

Table IV.1.2   *System-level correlations*

OECD countries

		Mathematics performance				Variation in mathematics performance explained by the PISA index of economic, social and cultural status of students				Variation in mathematics performance explained by the PISA index of economic, social and cultural status of students and schools			
		Before accounting for GDP/capita		After accounting for GDP/capita		Before accounting for GDP/capita		After accounting for GDP/capita		Before accounting for GDP/capita		After accounting for GDP/capita	
		Corr.	p-value	Partial corr.	p-value	Corr.	p-value	Partial corr.	p-value	Corr.	p-value	Partial corr.	p-value
Financial resources	Cumulative expenditure by educational institutions per student aged 6 to 15	**0.41**	(0.02)	*0.32*	(0.08)[1]	-0.19	(0.30)	-0.13	(0.49)	-0.18	(0.31)	-0.12	(0.51)
	Teachers' salaries relative to GDP/capita[2]	*0.32*	(0.08)	*0.31*	(0.10)	-0.05	(0.77)	-0.02	(0.91)	0.08	(0.66)	0.11	(0.57)
Human resources	Percentage of teachers with university-level qualifications	-0.20	(0.28)	-0.15	(0.41)	-0.04	(0.84)	-0.07	(0.70)	-0.26	(0.16)	-0.30	(0.10)
	Average index of teacher shortage	-0.27	(0.13)	**-0.41**	(0.02)[1]	-0.14	(0.42)	-0.10	(0.57)	0.08	(0.66)	0.13	(0.48)
	Student-teacher ratio	**-0.48**	(0.00)[1]	**-0.42**	(0.02)[1]	-0.03	(0.88)	-0.08	(0.64)	-0.01	(0.94)	-0.07	(0.71)
	Percentage of mathematics teachers at the school who have attended a programme of professional development with a focus on mathematics during the previous three months	0.06	(0.75)	0.01	(0.97)	-0.11	(0.52)	-0.09	(0.61)	-0.28	(0.10)	-0.27	(0.13)
Material resources	Average index of quality of physical infrastructure	0.26	(0.13)	*0.31*	(0.08)[1]	0.02	(0.93)	0.00	(0.99)	-0.12	(0.51)	-0.13	(0.46)
	Average index of quality of schools' educational resources	**0.63**	(0.00)	**0.58**	(0.00)	-0.02	(0.92)	0.04	(0.81)	0.13	(0.46)	0.20	(0.26)
Time resources	Average learning time in regular mathematics lessons	*-0.32*	(0.07)[1]	*-0.30*	(0.09)[1]	0.05	(0.80)	0.03	(0.89)	-0.25	(0.15)	-0.28	(0.12)
	Percentage of students in schools offering after-school lessons in mathematics	0.15	(0.39)	0.17	(0.35)	0.20	(0.25)	0.20	(0.25)	0.22	(0.20)	0.22	(0.21)
	Average number of hours per week spent on homework or other study set by teachers, all school subjects combined	-0.03	(0.85)	-0.04	(0.80)	-0.13	(0.48)	-0.12	(0.49)	-0.12	(0.50)	-0.12	(0.51)
	Average index of creative extracurricular activities at school	0.20	(0.26)	0.18	(0.32)	-0.02	(0.91)	0.00	(0.98)	0.02	(0.91)	0.03	(0.85)
	Average index of extracurricular mathematics activities at school	0.13	(0.45)	0.27	(0.14)	0.23	(0.19)	0.19	(0.29)	0.16	(0.38)	0.12	(0.51)
	Percentage of students reporting that they had attended pre-primary education for more than one year	**0.36**	(0.04)[1]	*0.30*	(0.09)[1]	-0.07	(0.68)	-0.04	(0.84)	0.17	(0.34)	0.21	(0.23)

All participating countries and economies

		Mathematics performance				Variation in mathematics performance explained by the PISA index of economic, social and cultural status of students				Variation in mathematics performance explained by the PISA index of economic, social and cultural status of students and schools			
		Before accounting for GDP/capita		After accounting for GDP/capita		Before accounting for GDP/capita		After accounting for GDP/capita		Before accounting for GDP/capita		After accounting for GDP/capita	
		Corr.	p-value	Partial corr.	p-value	Corr.	p-value	Partial corr.	p-value	Corr.	p-value	Partial corr.	p-value
Financial resources	Cumulative expenditure by educational institutions per student aged 6 to 15	**0.55**	(0.00)	0.09	(0.52)	-0.15	(0.31)	-0.10	(0.48)	-0.13	(0.38)	-0.10	(0.50)
	Teachers' salaries relative to GDP/capita[2]	0.02	(0.91)	-0.05	(0.74)	*-0.24*	(0.09)[1]	-0.21	(0.14)	-0.08	(0.60)	-0.05	(0.73)
Human resources	Percentage of teachers with university-level qualifications	0.14	(0.28)	0.08	(0.52)	-0.16	(0.22)	-0.13	(0.32)	**-0.26**	(0.04)[1]	*-0.23*	(0.08)[1]
	Average index of teacher shortage	-0.14	(0.25)	-0.17	(0.18)	-0.13	(0.30)	-0.13	(0.30)	-0.06	(0.63)	-0.06	(0.62)
	Student-teacher ratio	**-0.37**	(0.00)	**-0.26**	(0.04)[1]	0.09	(0.50)	-0.03	(0.83)	0.00	(1.00)	-0.06	(0.66)
	Percentage of mathematics teachers at the school who have attended a programme of professional development with a focus on mathematics during the previous three months	0.10	(0.44)	0.02	(0.89)	-0.20	(0.11)	-0.17	(0.18)	*-0.23*	(0.07)	-0.20	(0.12)
Material resources	Average index of quality of physical infrastructure	**0.45**	(0.00)	**0.31**	(0.01)[1]	-0.01	(0.96)	0.13	(0.32)	-0.05	(0.67)	0.02	(0.86)
	Average index of quality of schools' educational resources	**0.66**	(0.00)	**0.51**	(0.00)	-0.10	(0.44)	0.15	(0.24)	0.04	(0.74)	*0.22*	(0.08)
Time resources	Average learning time in regular mathematics lessons	0.02	(0.85)	-0.07	(0.60)	-0.10	(0.46)	-0.06	(0.65)	**-0.27**	(0.03)	*-0.25*	(0.05)
	Percentage of students in schools offering after-school lessons in mathematics	0.10	(0.45)	0.13	(0.33)	-0.12	(0.35)	-0.14	(0.27)	-0.04	(0.78)	-0.03	(0.83)
	Average number of hours per week spent on homework or other study set by teachers, all school subjects combined	**0.31**	(0.01)[1]	**0.38**	(0.00)[1]	-0.07	(0.56)	-0.11	(0.41)	-0.12	(0.36)	-0.11	(0.38)
	Average index of creative extracurricular activities at school	**0.33**	(0.01)	**0.26**	(0.04)	-0.14	(0.26)	-0.08	(0.51)	-0.09	(0.48)	-0.05	(0.68)
	Average index of extracurricular mathematics activities at school	0.08	(0.51)	0.14	(0.26)	-0.12	(0.35)	-0.16	(0.20)	-0.11	(0.38)	-0.11	(0.39)
	Percentage of students reporting that they had attended pre-primary education for more than one year	**0.64**	(0.00)	**0.57**	(0.00)	0.09	(0.46)	*0.23*	(0.07)[1]	0.19	(0.12)	**0.28**	(0.03)

Note: Values that are statistically significant at the 10% level (p < 0.10) are indicated in italics and those at the 5% level (p < 0.05) are in bold.
1. While Pearson's correlation coefficients are presented in this table, Spearman's rank correlation coefficients are also computed in order to examine the robustness of the results. When Pearson's correlation coefficient is significant at least at the 10% level but Spearman's rank correlation coefficient is not significant at the 10% level, a superscript 1 appears in the cell.
2. Weighted average of upper and lower secondary school teachers. The average is computed by weighting teachers' salaries for upper and lower secondary school according to the respective 15-year-old students' enrolment (for countries and economies with valid information on both the upper and lower secondary levels).
StatLink http://dx.doi.org/10.1787/888932957384

[Part 1/1]
Relationship between education outcomes and allocation of resources
Table IV.1.3 *System-level correlations*

OECD countries

		Mathematics performance				Variation in mathematics performance explained by the PISA index of economic, social and cultural status of students				Variation in mathematics performance explained by the PISA index of economic, social and cultural status of students and schools			
		Before accounting for GDP/capita		After accounting for GDP/capita		Before accounting for GDP/capita		After accounting for GDP/capita		Before accounting for GDP/capita		After accounting for GDP/capita	
		Corr.	p-value	Partial corr.	p-value	Corr.	p-value	Partial corr.	p-value	Corr.	p-value	Partial corr.	p-value
Difference between socio-economically advantaged and disadvantaged schools[1] in:	Average index of teacher shortage	**0.41**	(0.02)	**0.47**	(0.01)	-0.20	(0.27)	-0.21	(0.23)	0.02	(0.90)	0.01	(0.96)
	Average index of quality of physical infrastructure	**-0.63**	(0.00)	**-0.63**	(0.00)	0.04	(0.83)	0.02	(0.91)	-0.06	(0.73)	-0.08	(0.66)
	Average index of quality of schools' educational resources	**-0.57**	(0.00)	**-0.55**	(0.00)	0.07	(0.71)	0.04	(0.83)	-0.09	(0.63)	-0.12	(0.51)
	Average learning time in regular mathematics lessons	0.16	(0.36)	0.24	(0.18)	-0.07	(0.70)	-0.10	(0.58)	0.26	(0.14)	0.24	(0.18)
	Average number of hours per week spent on homework or other study set by teachers, all school subjects combined	0.06	(0.75)	0.03	(0.87)	-0.06	(0.73)	-0.05	(0.79)	0.21	(0.23)	0.23	(0.20)
	Percentage of students reporting that they had attended pre-primary education for more than one year	-0.04	(0.81)	0.03	(0.88)	0.15	(0.40)	0.12	(0.50)	-0.23	(0.19)	-0.27	(0.13)

All participating countries and economies

		Mathematics performance				Variation in mathematics performance explained by the PISA index of economic, social and cultural status of students				Variation in mathematics performance explained by the PISA index of economic, social and cultural status of students and schools			
		Before accounting for GDP/capita		After accounting for GDP/capita		Before accounting for GDP/capita		After accounting for GDP/capita		Before accounting for GDP/capita		After accounting for GDP/capita	
		Corr.	p-value	Partial corr.	p-value	Corr.	p-value	Partial corr.	p-value	Corr.	p-value	Partial corr.	p-value
Difference between socio-economically advantaged and disadvantaged schools[1] in:	Average index of teacher shortage	-0.02	(0.88)	-0.04	(0.78)	-0.20	(0.12)	-0.20	(0.13)	-0.13	(0.29)	-0.13	(0.31)
	Average index of quality of physical infrastructure	**-0.46**	(0.00)	**-0.44**	(0.00)	0.08	(0.52)	0.04	(0.75)	0.00	(0.98)	-0.04	(0.78)
	Average index of quality of schools' educational resources	**-0.53**	(0.00)	**-0.44**	(0.00)	0.20	(0.12)	0.12	(0.36)	0.00	(0.99)	-0.07	(0.56)
	Average learning time in regular mathematics lessons	-0.05	(0.68)	0.12	(0.35)	0.02	(0.85)	-0.07	(0.57)	*0.21*	(0.09)	0.16	(0.21)
	Average number of hours per week spent on homework or other study set by teachers, all school subjects combined	**0.39**	(0.00)	**0.44**	(0.00)	0.11	(0.40)	0.11	(0.39)	*0.25*	(0.05)	**0.25**	(0.05)
	Percentage of students reporting that they had attended pre-primary education for more than one year	**-0.36**	(0.00)	-0.19	(0.14)	0.11	(0.39)	-0.02	(0.90)	-0.09	(0.49)	-0.21	(0.10)

Note: Values that are statistically significant at the 10% level (p < 0.10) are indicated in italics and those at the 5% level (p < 0.05) are in bold.
1. See Box IV.3.1 for the definition of socio-economically advantaged and disadvantaged schools.
StatLink ⌑ http://dx.doi.org/10.1787/888932957384

[Part 1/1]
Relationship between education outcomes and school governance, assessment and accountability policies
Table IV.1.4   *System-level correlations*

OECD countries

			Mathematics performance				Variation in mathematics performance explained by the PISA index of economic, social and cultural status of students				Variation in mathematics performance explained by the PISA index of economic, social and cultural status of students and schools			
			Before accounting for GDP/capita		After accounting for GDP/capita		Before accounting for GDP/capita		After accounting for GDP/capita		Before accounting for GDP/capita		After accounting for GDP/capita	
			Corr.	p-value	Partial corr.	p-value	Corr.	p-value	Partial corr.	p-value	Corr.	p-value	Partial corr.	p-value
School governance	School autonomy	Average index of school responsibility for curriculum and assessment	**0.49**	(0.00)	**0.58**	(0.00)	-0.08	(0.63)	-0.11	(0.54)	0.14	(0.44)	0.12	(0.52)
		Average index of school responsibility for resource allocation	-0.01	(0.95)	0.00	(1.00)	0.12	(0.50)	0.12	(0.52)	0.14	(0.44)	0.13	(0.46)
	School competition	Percentage of students in schools that compete with other schools in the same area	-0.02	(0.93)	0.07	(0.71)	0.26	(0.13)	0.24	(0.18)	*0.33*	(0.06)[1]	*0.31*	(0.08)[1]
		Percentage of students in private schools	0.14	(0.44)	0.11	(0.53)	0.06	(0.72)	0.08	(0.65)	0.18	(0.32)	0.19	(0.28)
Assessment and accountability policies	Percentage of students in schools that use achievement data to:	Post achievement data publicly	-0.21	(0.23)	-0.15	(0.42)	0.09	(0.61)	0.06	(0.76)	0.01	(0.96)	-0.03	(0.88)
		Have their progress tracked by administrative authorities	**-0.34**	(0.05)	*-0.31*	(0.08)	0.06	(0.73)	0.04	(0.83)	*-0.30*	(0.09)	*-0.33*	(0.06)
	Percentage of students in schools that:	Seek written feed-back from students for quality assurance and improvement	0.16	(0.36)	*0.34*	(0.05)	-0.22	(0.20)	*-0.31*	(0.07)	-0.05	(0.80)	-0.11	(0.53)
		Mentor teachers for quality assurance and improvement	0.24	(0.17)	0.26	(0.14)	-0.15	(0.40)	-0.15	(0.40)	0.03	(0.88)	0.02	(0.89)

All participating countries and economies

			Mathematics performance				Variation in mathematics performance explained by the PISA index of economic, social and cultural status of students				Variation in mathematics performance explained by the PISA index of economic, social and cultural status of students and schools			
			Before accounting for GDP/capita		After accounting for GDP/capita		Before accounting for GDP/capita		After accounting for GDP/capita		Before accounting for GDP/capita		After accounting for GDP/capita	
			Corr.	p-value	Partial corr.	p-value	Corr.	p-value	Partial corr.	p-value	Corr.	p-value	Partial corr.	p-value
School governance	School autonomy	Average index of school responsibility for curriculum and assessment	**0.38**	(0.00)	**0.37**	(0.00)	-0.13	(0.29)	-0.11	(0.38)	-0.04	(0.77)	-0.01	(0.93)
		Average index of school responsibility for resource allocation	0.14	(0.26)	0.10	(0.44)	-0.05	(0.67)	-0.03	(0.81)	-0.04	(0.73)	-0.02	(0.85)
	School competition	Percentage of students in schools that compete with other schools in the same area	0.12	(0.36)	0.19	(0.14)	0.11	(0.39)	0.06	(0.65)	0.10	(0.43)	0.12	(0.34)
		Percentage of students in private schools	0.17	(0.19)	0.01	(0.93)	*-0.22*	(0.09)[1]	-0.15	(0.23)	-0.10	(0.43)	-0.03	(0.82)
Assessment and accountability policies	Percentage of students in schools that use achievement data to:	Post achievement data publicly	-0.03	(0.83)	0.02	(0.90)	0.00	(0.98)	-0.04	(0.79)	-0.04	(0.77)	-0.05	(0.67)
		Have their progress tracked by administrative authorities	**-0.36**	(0.00)	**-0.32**	(0.01)	0.00	(0.98)	-0.07	(0.61)	**-0.28**	(0.02)	**-0.31**	(0.01)
	Percentage of students in schools that:	Seek written feed-back from students for quality assurance and improvement	0.13	(0.32)	0.20	(0.11)	**-0.26**	(0.04)	**-0.29**	(0.02)	-0.13	(0.29)	-0.18	(0.15)
		Mentor teachers for quality assurance and improvement	0.03	(0.79)	0.05	(0.72)	**-0.26**	(0.04)	**-0.27**	(0.04)	-0.07	(0.59)	-0.07	(0.57)

Note: Values that are statistically significant at the 10% level (p < 0.10) are indicated in italics and those at the 5% level (p < 0.05) are in bold.
1. While Pearson's correlation coefficients are presented in this table, Spearman's rank correlation coefficients are also computed in order to examine the robustness of the results. When Pearson's correlation coefficient is significant at least at the 10% level but Spearman's rank correlation coefficient is not significant at the 10% level, a superscript 1 appears in the cell.
StatLink ⫶ http://dx.doi.org/10.1787/888932957384

[Part 1/1]
Relationship between education outcomes and the learning environment
Table IV.1.5 *System-level correlations*

		OECD countries											
		Mathematics performance				Variation in mathematics performance explained by the PISA index of economic, social and cultural status of students				Variation in mathematics performance explained by the PISA index of economic, social and cultural status of students and schools			
		Before accounting for GDP/capita		After accounting for GDP/capita		Before accounting for GDP/capita		After accounting for GDP/capita		Before accounting for GDP/capita		After accounting for GDP/capita	
		Corr.	p-value	Partial corr.	p-value	Corr.	p-value	Partial corr.	p-value	Corr.	p-value	Partial corr.	p-value
Student truancy	Percentage of students who arrived late for school in the two weeks prior to the PISA test	**-0.51**	(0.00)	**-0.44**	(0.01)	0.07	(0.71)	0.01	(0.93)	*-0.30*	(0.08)	**-0.38**	(0.03)
	Percentage of students who skipped some lessons or a day of school in the two weeks prior to the PISA test	**-0.48**	(0.00)	**-0.40**	(0.02)	-0.05	(0.77)	-0.12	(0.52)	-0.15	(0.41)	-0.22	(0.23)

		All participating countries and economies											
		Mathematics performance				Variation in mathematics performance explained by the PISA index of economic, social and cultural status of students				Variation in mathematics performance explained by the PISA index of economic, social and cultural status of students and schools			
		Before accounting for GDP/capita		After accounting for GDP/capita		Before accounting for GDP/capita		After accounting for GDP/capita		Before accounting for GDP/capita		After accounting for GDP/capita	
		Corr.	p-value	Partial corr.	p-value	Corr.	p-value	Partial corr.	p-value	Corr.	p-value	Partial corr.	p-value
Student truancy	Percentage of students who arrived late for school in the two weeks prior to the PISA test	**-0.53**	(0.00)	**-0.43**	(0.00)	**0.31**	(0.01)	*0.22*	(0.09)[1]	-0.04	(0.74)	-0.11	(0.41)
	Percentage of students who skipped some lessons or a day of school in the two weeks prior to the PISA test	**-0.52**	(0.00)	**-0.41**	(0.00)	0.06	(0.65)	-0.08	(0.56)	-0.11	(0.40)	-0.19	(0.15)

Note: Values that are statistically significant at the 10% level (p < 0.10) are indicated in italics and those at the 5% level (p < 0.05) are in bold.
1. While Pearson's correlation coefficients are presented in this table, Spearman's rank correlation coefficients are also computed in order to examine the robustness of the results. When Pearson's correlation coefficient is significant at least at the 10% level but Spearman's rank correlation coefficient is not significant at the 10% level, a superscript 1 appears in the cell.
StatLink http://dx.doi.org/10.1787/888932957384

[Part 1/1]

Table IV.1.6 **Cost of grade repetition**

	Direct costs		Opportunity costs		Total costs (direct + opportunity costs)		
Number of 15-year-old students who have repeated a grade at least once in primary, lower secondary or upper secondary schools	Costs to systems to provide one additional year of education to repeaters		Assuming that repeaters attain at most ISCED 2 (i.e. using annual labour costs for ISCED 0/1/2 for 25-64 year-olds and unemployment rate for "below upper secondary")		Total annual costs	Total annual costs per repeater	Total annual costs, relative to total expenditure on primary and secondary education
			Number of 15-year-old students who enter the labour market at least one year later because of grade repetition (after adjusting unemployment rates)	Costs to systems by delaying students' entrance to the labour market by one additional year			
(students)	(USD, PPPs)		(students)	(USD, PPPs)	(USD, PPPs)	(USD, PPPs)	(%)
(1)	(2)		(3)	(4)	(5)	(6)	(7)
Australia	18 775	184 044 685	17 671	696 050 444	880 095 129	46 875	2.2
Austria	9 800	114 267 363	9 105	412 259 639	526 527 002	53 729	4.3
Belgium	42 564	413 403 011	37 431	1668 728 052	2082 131 063	48 918	11.5
Canada	27 893	224 253 077	24 624	942 393 439	1166 646 516	41 825	2.3
Chile[1]	57 746	186 232 081	55 203	m	186 232 081	3 225	1.8
Czech Republic	4 028	21 957 517	3 159	63 733 751	85 691 268	21 277	1.1
Denmark	3 116	34 198 882	2 838	124 706 884	158 905 766	50 994	1.5
Estonia	408	2 264 828	300	5 279 391	7 544 219	18 494	0.0
Finland	2 296	19 797 661	2 036	88 688 074	108 485 735	47 253	1.4
France	198 899	1662 432 344	173 300	6337531130	7999 963 475	40 221	8.8
Germany	153 407	1239 464 945	132 076	5871 727 799	7111 192 744	46 355	7.3
Greece	4 347	m	3 603	76 183 724	m	m	m
Hungary	9 819	45 755 284	7 550	112 804 733	158 560 017	16 148	m
Iceland	48	454 094	45	1 241 518	1 695 611	35 095	0.3
Ireland	4 667	43 459 946	3 654	172 792 186	216 252 132	46 334	2.5
Israel	2 059	11 741 465	1 909	35 467 449	47 208 914	22 923	0.5
Italy	88 929	750 706 413	80 586	3444 472 862	4195 179 275	47 174	6.7
Japan	0	0	0	0	0	0	0.0
Korea	21 997	151 857 955	21 413	609 568 404	761 426 358	34 616	1.3
Luxembourg[1]	1 907	37 683 413	1 791	m	37 683 413	19 760	2.5
Mexico[1]	205 280	490 879 781	197 080	m	490 879 781	2 391	0.7
Netherlands	54 202	515 310 514	51 254	2567 429 123	3082 739 637	56 875	10.9
New Zealand	2 869	20 270 349	2 682	77 367 987	97 638 336	34 031	1.5
Norway	0	0	0	0	0	0	0.0
Poland	15 758	90 836 603	13 096	128 301 062	219 137 665	13 906	0.8
Portugal	32 903	231 538 476	28 524	500 500 355	732 038 831	22 248	6.9
Slovak Republic	4 133	21 969 954	2 508	46 979 269	68 949 223	16 683	1.8
Slovenia	619	5 679 364	540	10 123 653	15 803 017	25 539	0.7
Spain	122 893	1009 912 235	90 434	2790 294 903	3800 207 139	30 923	7.9
Sweden	3 762	36 050 977	3 357	157 440 781	193 491 758	51 434	1.3
Switzerland[1]	15 844	201 726 074	14 643	m	201 726 074	12 732	1.3
Turkey[1]	123 017	243 831 343	112 629	m	243 831 343	1 982	0.8
United Kingdom	18 481	181 154 077	16 447	554 619 508	735 773 585	39 813	0.7
United States	469 032	5438 963 060	393 187	14037 167 584	19476 130 643	41 524	3.4
Brazil[2]	812 712	2175 263 001	775 658	4588 252 909	6763 515 910	8 322	m

1. In Chile, Luxembourg, Mexico, Switzerland and Turkey, the total costs are underestimated as the annual labour costs are not available in *Education at a Glance 2012: OECD Indicators*, Table A10.2 and the opportunity costs cannot be computed.
2. In Brazil, gross annual full time earnings are used, as annual labour costs are not available in *Education at a Glance 2012: OECD Indicators*, Table A10.2.
Source: OECD, PISA 2012 Database, Tables IV.2.2 and IV.3.1, *Education at a Glance 2012: OECD Indicators* (Tables A10.2 and X2.1), *Education at a Glance 2013: OECD Indicators* (Tables A5.4a and X2.2) and OECD.stat.
StatLink ᵃᵃˢᵖ http://dx.doi.org/10.1787/888932957384

[Part 1/2]
Variation in mathematics performance and variation explained by school characteristics combined

Table IV.1.12a *Within- and between-school variations*

		Variance		Remaining variance						Variance decomposition expressed as a percentage of the average variance in student performance in mathematics across OECD countries		
		Empty (or fully unconditional) model[1]		Model with demographic and socio-economic background[2]		Model with school-level variables[3]		Model with demographic and socio-economic background and with school-level variables[4]		Total variance in student performance	Total variance within schools as a percentage of total variance	Total variance between schools as a percentage of total variance
		Within-school	Between-school	Within-school	Between-school	Within-school	Between-school	Within-school	Between-school	%	%	%
OECD	Australia	6 720	2 602	6 389	1 092	6 720	966	6 381	692	110	79	31
	Austria	4 346	4 080	3 958	1 260	4 349	1 003	3 957	539	99	51	48
	Belgium	5 173	5 276	5 032	1 510	5 176	602	5 035	449	123	61	62
	Canada	6 342	1 563	5 978	882	6 341	631	5 971	491	93	75	18
	Chile	3 669	2 817	3 471	475	3 670	376	3 470	132	76	43	33
	Czech Republic	4 285	4 544	4 082	1 243	4 284	1 388	4 083	698	104	50	53
	Denmark	5 582	1 100	4 915	371	5 582	402	4 912	197	79	66	13
	Estonia	5 412	1 129	5 216	424	5 416	386	5 213	125	77	64	13
	Finland	6 533	530	5 977	289	6 533	250	5 973	129	83	77	6
	France	w	w	w	w	w	w	w	w	w	w	w
	Germany	4 333	4 890	4 063	1 371	4 337	950	4 063	529	109	51	58
	Greece	5 173	2 441	4 835	907	5 177	406	4 837	330	90	61	29
	Hungary	3 296	5 346	3 115	1 099	3 297	1 129	3 113	558	102	39	63
	Iceland	7 610	834	7 250	269	7 645	156	7 295	1	99	90	10
	Ireland	5 815	1 297	5 390	241	5 815	351	5 387	94	84	68	15
	Israel	6 320	4 659	5 950	1 471	6 321	974	5 949	585	129	74	55
	Italy	4 130	4 381	3 946	2 009	4 131	1 009	3 949	794	100	49	52
	Japan	4 094	4 620	4 027	1 538	4 094	1 003	4 027	746	103	48	54
	Korea	5 864	3 840	5 754	1 586	5 864	555	5 754	414	114	69	45
	Luxembourg	6 516	4 525	5 937	231	c	c	c	c	c	c	c
	Mexico	3 578	1 940	3 468	960	3 579	767	3 469	549	65	42	23
	Netherlands	2 858	5 534	2 712	1 984	2 860	772	2 713	607	99	34	65
	New Zealand	7 658	2 387	6 924	476	7 676	163	6 921	16	118	90	28
	Norway	7 063	1 045	6 630	616	7 065	437	6 624	253	95	83	12
	Poland	6 433	1 659	5 798	713	6 433	492	5 798	308	95	76	20
	Portugal	6 212	2 653	5 651	873	6 219	209	5 642	169	104	73	31
	Slovak Republic	5 020	5 008	4 619	1 359	5 025	1 185	4 629	658	118	59	59
	Slovenia	3 453	4 904	3 288	1 018	3 465	1 001	3 291	520	98	41	58
	Spain	6 263	1 454	5 577	627	6 262	499	5 575	393	91	74	17
	Sweden	7 266	1 042	6 661	462	7 267	438	6 665	244	98	86	12
	Switzerland	5 771	3 196	5 088	1 292	5 775	827	5 092	439	106	68	38
	Turkey	3 173	5 140	3 043	1 893	3 174	648	3 044	563	98	37	60
	United Kingdom	6 421	2 517	6 118	988	6 423	596	6 114	415	105	76	30
	United States	6 164	1 916	5 705	753	6 164	291	5 704	249	95	73	23
	OECD average	5 375	3 124	5 011	991	5 343	653	4 984	405	100	63	37
Partners	Albania	7 958	380	7 952	350	7 957	249	7 951	229	98	94	4
	Argentina	3 253	2 597	3 123	996	3 256	498	3 126	426	69	38	31
	Brazil	3 457	2 623	3 293	976	3 456	753	3 290	549	72	41	31
	Bulgaria	4 160	4 647	4 033	1 174	4 162	945	4 031	536	104	49	55
	Colombia	3 618	1 953	3 374	713	3 620	541	3 374	364	66	43	23
	Costa Rica	2 700	1 984	2 466	758	2 704	443	2 469	354	55	32	23
	Croatia	4 360	3 466	4 162	1 269	4 361	449	4 162	323	92	51	41
	Cyprus*	5 814	2 791	5 497	943	5 823	138	5 507	68	101	68	33
	Hong Kong-China	5 330	3 924	5 183	1 954	5 330	797	5 184	650	109	63	46
	Indonesia	2 457	2 665	2 398	1 511	2 457	1 008	2 399	829	60	29	31
	Jordan	3 852	2 166	3 745	1 070	3 853	672	3 737	475	71	45	25
	Kazakhstan	3 234	1 861	3 135	1 118	3 236	966	3 136	810	60	38	22
	Latvia	4 908	1 691	4 631	615	4 907	593	4 622	360	78	58	20
	Lithuania	5 463	2 424	5 197	855	5 466	602	5 198	334	93	64	29
	Macao-China	6 181	4 442	6 050	1 208	c	c	c	c	c	c	c
	Malaysia	4 449	2 129	4 282	818	4 449	362	4 282	264	77	52	25
	Montenegro	4 324	2 485	4 176	357	c	c	c	c	c	c	c
	Peru	3 865	3 244	3 625	677	3 869	726	3 624	402	84	45	38
	Qatar	5 487	4 722	5 243	1 516	5 490	587	5 248	391	120	65	56
	Romania	3 591	2 986	3 395	1 014	3 593	735	3 397	484	77	42	35
	Russian Federation	5 502	2 018	5 222	1 116	5 510	773	5 223	667	88	65	24
	Serbia	4 431	3 776	4 243	1 364	4 433	823	4 241	623	97	52	44
	Shanghai-China	5 401	4 767	5 201	1 579	5 403	506	5 202	439	120	64	56
	Singapore	7 033	4 070	6 696	1 029	7 033	704	6 691	389	131	83	48
	Chinese Taipei	7 710	5 613	7 287	1 492	7 711	799	7 288	497	157	91	66
	Thailand	3 941	2 866	3 843	1 459	3 951	828	3 850	674	80	46	34
	Tunisia	3 104	3 017	2 907	1 557	3 104	835	2 906	526	72	37	36
	United Arab Emirates	4 453	3 559	4 279	1 525	4 453	1 076	4 277	610	94	52	42
	Uruguay	4 546	3 297	4 282	867	4 550	396	4 284	292	92	53	39
	Viet Nam	3 509	3 823	3 308	1 787	3 511	697	3 310	638	86	41	45

1. Multilevel regression model consists of the student and school levels.
2. Multilevel regression model: Mathematics performance is regressed on the variables of demographic and socio-economic background shown in Table IV.1.12c.
3. Multilevel regression model: Mathematics performance is regressed on the school-level variables shown in Table IV.1.12b.
4. Multilevel regression model: Mathematics performance is regressed on the variables of demographic and socio-economic background and on the school-level variables shown in Table IV.1.12c.
* See notes at the beginning of this Annex.
StatLink http://dx.doi.org/10.1787/888932957384

[Part 2/2]
Variation in mathematics performance and variation explained by school characteristics combined
Table IV.1.12a *Within- and between-school variations*

| | Within-school variance expressed as a percentage of the average of within-school variance in student performance in mathematics across OECD countries | | | | Between-school variance expressed as a percentage of the average of between-school variance in student performance in mathematics across OECD countries | | | |
	Solely accounted for by students' and schools' socio-economic and demographic background	Solely accounted for by schools' characteristics	Jointly accounted for by students' and schools' socio-economic and demographic background and schools' characteristics	Remaining within-school variance	Solely accounted for by students' and schools' socio-economic and demographic background	Solely accounted for by schools' characteristics	Jointly accounted for by students' and schools' socio-economic and demographic background and schools' characteristics	Remaining between-school variance
	%	%	%	%	%	%	%	%
Australia	4.0	0.1	0.0	75.1	3.2	4.7	14.6	8.1
Austria	4.6	0.0	0.0	46.6	5.5	8.5	27.7	6.3
Belgium	1.7	0.0	0.0	59.2	1.8	12.5	42.5	5.3
Canada	4.4	0.1	0.0	70.3	1.7	4.6	6.4	5.8
Chile	2.3	0.0	0.0	40.8	2.9	4.0	24.7	1.6
Czech Republic	2.4	0.0	0.0	48.0	8.1	6.4	30.7	8.2
Denmark	7.9	0.0	0.0	57.8	2.4	2.0	6.2	2.3
Estonia	2.4	0.0	0.0	61.3	3.1	3.5	5.2	1.5
Finland	6.6	0.0	0.0	70.3	1.4	1.9	1.4	1.5
France	w	w	w	w	w	w	w	w
Germany	3.2	0.0	0.0	47.8	5.0	9.9	36.5	6.2
Greece	4.0	0.0	0.0	56.9	0.9	6.8	17.1	3.9
Hungary	2.2	0.0	0.0	36.6	6.7	6.4	43.3	6.6
Iceland	4.1	0.0	0.1	85.8	1.8	3.2	4.8	0.0
Ireland	5.0	0.0	0.0	63.4	3.0	1.7	9.4	1.1
Israel	4.4	0.0	0.0	70.0	4.6	10.4	32.9	6.9
Italy	2.1	0.0	0.0	46.5	2.5	14.3	25.4	9.3
Japan	0.8	0.0	0.0	47.4	3.0	9.3	33.3	8.8
Korea	1.3	0.0	0.0	67.7	1.7	13.8	24.9	4.9
Luxembourg	c	c	c	c	c	c	c	c
Mexico	1.3	0.0	0.0	40.8	2.6	4.8	9.0	6.5
Netherlands	1.7	0.0	0.0	31.9	1.9	16.2	39.8	7.1
New Zealand	8.9	0.0	0.0	81.4	1.7	5.4	20.7	0.2
Norway	5.2	0.1	0.0	78.0	2.2	4.3	2.9	3.0
Poland	7.5	0.0	0.0	68.2	2.2	4.8	9.0	3.6
Portugal	6.8	0.1	0.0	66.4	0.5	8.3	20.5	2.0
Slovak Republic	4.7	0.0	0.0	54.5	6.2	8.2	36.7	7.7
Slovenia	2.0	0.0	0.0	38.7	5.7	5.9	40.1	6.1
Spain	8.1	0.0	0.0	65.6	1.3	2.8	8.5	4.6
Sweden	7.1	0.0	0.0	78.4	2.3	2.6	4.5	2.9
Switzerland	8.0	0.0	0.0	59.9	4.6	10.0	17.8	5.2
Turkey	1.5	0.0	0.0	35.8	1.0	15.7	37.2	6.6
United Kingdom	3.6	0.1	0.0	71.9	2.1	6.7	15.9	4.9
United States	5.4	0.0	0.0	67.1	0.5	5.9	13.2	2.9
OECD average	4.2	0.3	0.0	58.6	2.9	6.9	22.2	4.8
Albania	0.1	0.0	0.0	93.6	0.2	1.4	0.1	2.7
Argentina	1.5	0.0	0.0	36.8	0.8	6.7	18.0	5.0
Brazil	2.0	0.0	0.0	38.7	2.4	5.0	17.0	6.5
Bulgaria	1.5	0.0	0.0	47.4	4.8	7.5	36.1	6.3
Colombia	2.9	0.0	0.0	39.7	2.1	4.1	12.5	4.3
Costa Rica	2.8	0.0	0.0	29.0	1.0	4.7	13.4	4.2
Croatia	2.3	0.0	0.0	49.0	1.5	11.1	24.4	3.8
Cyprus*	3.7	0.0	0.0	64.8	0.8	10.3	20.9	0.8
Hong Kong-China	1.7	0.0	0.0	61.0	1.7	15.3	21.5	7.6
Indonesia	0.7	0.0	0.0	28.2	2.1	8.0	11.5	9.8
Jordan	1.4	0.1	0.0	44.0	2.3	7.0	10.6	5.6
Kazakhstan	1.2	0.0	0.0	36.9	1.8	3.6	6.9	9.5
Latvia	3.4	0.1	0.0	54.4	2.7	3.0	9.9	4.2
Lithuania	3.2	0.0	0.0	61.2	3.2	6.1	15.3	3.9
Macao-China	c	c	c	c	c	c	c	c
Malaysia	2.0	0.0	0.0	50.4	1.1	6.5	14.3	3.1
Montenegro	c	c	c	c	c	c	c	c
Peru	2.9	0.0	0.0	42.7	3.8	3.2	26.4	4.7
Qatar	2.8	0.0	0.0	61.8	2.3	13.2	35.4	4.6
Romania	2.3	0.0	0.0	40.0	3.0	6.2	20.3	5.7
Russian Federation	3.4	0.0	0.0	61.5	1.2	5.3	9.4	7.9
Serbia	2.3	0.0	0.0	49.9	2.4	8.7	26.0	7.3
Shanghai-China	2.4	0.0	0.0	61.2	0.8	13.4	36.7	5.2
Singapore	4.0	0.1	0.0	78.7	3.7	7.5	32.1	4.6
Chinese Taipei	5.0	0.0	0.0	85.8	3.6	11.7	44.9	5.8
Thailand	1.2	0.0	0.0	45.3	1.8	9.2	14.7	7.9
Tunisia	2.3	0.0	0.0	34.2	3.6	12.1	13.5	6.2
United Arab Emirates	2.1	0.0	0.0	50.3	5.5	10.8	18.4	7.2
Uruguay	3.1	0.0	0.0	50.4	1.2	6.8	27.4	3.4
Viet Nam	2.4	0.0	0.0	38.9	0.7	13.5	23.3	7.5

1. Multilevel regression model consists of the student and school levels.
2. Multilevel regression model: Mathematics performance is regressed on the variables of demographic and socio-economic background shown in Table IV.1.12c.
3. Multilevel regression model: Mathematics performance is regressed on the school-level variables shown in Table IV.1.12b.
4. Multilevel regression model: Mathematics performance is regressed on the variables of demographic and socio-economic background and on the school-level variables shown in Table IV.1.12c.
* See notes at the beginning of this Annex.
StatLink ⌦ http://dx.doi.org/10.1787/888932957384

[Part 1/4]
Relationship between mathematics performance and the school's learning environment, resources, policies and practices

Table IV.1.12b

		Schools' policies on selecting and grouping students[1]								Resources invested in education at the school level[1]							
		Percentage of students who repeated one or more grades		School with ability grouping for all mathematics classes		School with high academic selectivity for school admittance		School is very likely to transfer students with low achievement, behavioural problems or special learning needs		Proportion of teachers with ISCED 5A (10% increase)		Percentage of mathematics teachers in the school who have attended a programme of professional development with a focus on mathematics during the previous three months		Student-teacher ratio		Index of teacher shortage (higher values indicate more shortages)	
		Change in score	S.E.	Change in score	S.E.	Change in score	S.E.	Change in score	S.E.	Change in score	S.E.	Change in score	S.E.	Change in score	S.E.	Change in score	S.E.
OECD	Australia	-0.6	(0.2)	-15.3	(17.1)	4.2	(3.0)	5.3	(7.8)	-0.6	(0.8)	-0.1	(0.0)	3.7	(0.8)	2.2	(1.7)
	Austria	-1.6	(0.4)	c	c	36.0	(8.9)	-1.5	(7.7)	4.4	(1.3)	0.1	(0.1)	0.0	(0.5)	-0.6	(3.3)
	Belgium	-2.0	(0.2)	4.1	(4.4)	2.0	(4.4)	1.7	(4.4)	0.4	(1.6)	0.0	(0.1)	0.8	(1.2)	-3.9	(2.3)
	Canada	-1.6	(0.2)	10.4	(7.1)	-5.5	(3.2)	-3.7	(8.0)	1.9	(0.6)	-0.1	(0.0)	2.0	(0.4)	2.7	(1.8)
	Chile	-0.9	(0.2)	0.1	(4.2)	5.5	(4.2)	-4.5	(4.1)	1.3	(1.0)	0.1	(0.1)	0.2	(0.3)	1.2	(1.8)
	Czech Republic	-1.5	(0.5)	-6.4	(6.1)	30.1	(7.8)	-5.4	(10.4)	9.2	(3.4)	-0.1	(0.1)	-1.1	(0.8)	-26.5	(5.1)
	Denmark	-2.3	(0.4)	-4.2	(4.6)	-3.2	(5.0)	-12.2	(9.9)	0.2	(0.7)	0.0	(0.1)	1.9	(0.7)	-2.6	(3.3)
	Estonia	-1.9	(0.5)	-5.4	(6.2)	9.3	(4.6)	-19.3	(13.4)	c	c	0.0	(0.1)	1.9	(1.0)	-0.1	(3.1)
	Finland	-1.5	(0.4)	-3.7	(3.3)	-17.3	(9.3)	-14.2	(17.2)	0.8	(1.2)	0.1	(0.0)	0.6	(1.0)	-1.9	(2.6)
	France	-1.7	(0.1)	0.2	(4.5)	6.0	(5.4)	-10.2	(6.0)	-1.4	(1.2)	0.0	(0.1)	0.8	(1.1)	0.5	(2.8)
	Germany	-2.6	(0.3)	-11.1	(6.1)	2.9	(5.5)	-2.9	(10.7)	c	c	-0.2	(0.1)	-0.4	(0.6)	-4.2	(3.3)
	Greece	-1.1	(0.5)	-7.0	(5.6)	10.7	(10.1)	1.1	(4.5)	-6.3	(2.0)	0.0	(0.1)	1.1	(0.9)	3.7	(3.0)
	Hungary	-1.2	(0.2)	-5.3	(8.4)	22.0	(10.9)	-19.2	(8.6)	8.0	(6.3)	0.1	(0.1)	-0.5	(0.7)	0.5	(5.0)
	Iceland	3.2	(1.9)	-5.1	(8.2)	13.8	(7.2)	-26.4	(25.4)	1.5	(1.1)	0.1	(0.1)	1.4	(0.8)	-5.8	(3.5)
	Ireland	-1.3	(0.4)	7.1	(13.0)	8.1	(5.4)	5.7	(12.1)	-17.4	(10.3)	-0.1	(0.1)	2.1	(1.0)	-7.9	(2.5)
	Israel	-1.5	(0.7)	36.3	(16.0)	18.5	(6.5)	-15.2	(7.7)	7.1	(1.7)	0.2	(0.1)	2.2	(1.4)	4.1	(3.3)
	Italy	-1.6	(0.4)	-9.8	(3.5)	3.8	(3.2)	1.0	(4.1)	-1.6	(1.2)	0.1	(0.1)	1.9	(0.6)	-1.7	(1.8)
	Japan	c	c	-19.2	(5.8)	-28.6	(11.1)	-13.5	(11.6)	38.1	(64.2)	0.0	(0.1)	1.0	(0.8)	2.0	(3.1)
	Korea	-0.5	(0.6)	-14.2	(9.6)	3.5	(6.4)	-5.4	(6.3)	6.1	(9.9)	0.2	(0.1)	0.0	(0.8)	-3.1	(3.2)
	Luxembourg	c	c	c	c	c	c	c	c	c	c	c	c	c	c	c	c
	Mexico	-0.6	(0.1)	-1.9	(2.4)	6.8	(2.5)	-2.7	(2.8)	0.9	(0.6)	0.0	(0.0)	0.0	(0.0)	0.8	(1.4)
	Netherlands	-2.4	(0.3)	-13.8	(8.7)	-10.3	(15.1)	9.6	(8.6)	5.7	(1.9)	0.1	(0.1)	1.4	(0.8)	0.4	(3.6)
	New Zealand	-0.3	(0.5)	-42.0	(14.5)	-9.6	(4.1)	3.1	(8.0)	-0.9	(1.8)	-0.1	(0.1)	0.0	(0.9)	-3.1	(2.2)
	Norway	c	c	2.4	(4.7)	-11.2	(8.5)	-59.1	(11.9)	c	c	0.1	(0.1)	-1.4	(1.4)	-3.0	(2.7)
	Poland	-2.9	(1.1)	-1.0	(4.7)	27.9	(7.6)	14.6	(9.1)	-0.3	(1.0)	0.1	(0.1)	3.4	(1.3)	0.9	(9.8)
	Portugal	-1.7	(0.1)	-4.1	(4.1)	-4.7	(3.8)	3.6	(12.6)	0.4	(0.4)	0.1	(0.1)	0.8	(0.8)	-0.9	(3.3)
	Slovak Republic	-0.7	(0.3)	-6.8	(6.3)	41.8	(8.3)	0.3	(7.4)	0.0	(3.0)	0.0	(0.1)	-0.9	(1.0)	-18.1	(4.6)
	Slovenia	-1.0	(1.7)	-1.1	(5.1)	8.4	(6.9)	1.5	(5.4)	4.6	(1.6)	-0.1	(0.1)	0.2	(0.6)	-3.2	(4.5)
	Spain	-1.3	(0.2)	-9.9	(6.6)	-9.0	(6.1)	10.3	(6.9)	-0.4	(1.0)	0.1	(0.1)	0.3	(0.5)	-3.4	(2.2)
	Sweden	-1.2	(0.5)	-5.1	(5.9)	1.1	(9.1)	13.4	(12.0)	0.5	(0.6)	0.0	(0.1)	1.9	(0.8)	-6.7	(2.6)
	Switzerland	-2.1	(0.2)	-27.1	(7.8)	10.5	(4.5)	1.7	(8.7)	1.7	(0.6)	0.1	(0.1)	0.1	(0.6)	-3.4	(2.6)
	Turkey	-1.2	(0.5)	-16.7	(6.9)	18.5	(5.3)	-6.3	(5.7)	-0.8	(1.3)	0.0	(0.1)	0.1	(0.4)	-1.3	(3.1)
	United Kingdom	-2.5	(0.6)	17.9	(12.1)	8.7	(5.0)	-19.2	(8.3)	-1.5	(0.9)	0.0	(0.1)	1.7	(1.1)	-4.5	(2.5)
	United States	-1.6	(0.2)	16.1	(10.1)	-7.6	(4.2)	-9.1	(13.3)	0.0	(5.7)	0.0	(0.1)	0.0	(0.1)	-1.3	(2.5)
	OECD average	**-1.3**	**(0.1)**	**-4.4**	**(1.4)**	**5.8**	**(1.2)**	**-5.4**	**(1.8)**	**2.1**	**(2.2)**	**0.0**	**(0.0)**	**0.8**	**(0.2)**	**-2.7**	**(0.6)**
Partners	Albania	0.7	(1.0)	c	c	6.5	(5.3)	1.9	(5.9)	0.1	(1.4)	0.0	(0.1)	c	c	-0.3	(2.5)
	Argentina	-0.8	(0.1)	8.0	(6.5)	4.5	(5.7)	2.0	(7.3)	1.1	(1.2)	0.2	(0.1)	0.0	(0.2)	-1.4	(2.9)
	Brazil	-1.2	(0.1)	-7.9	(4.9)	0.8	(4.2)	6.9	(4.9)	-0.5	(0.9)	0.0	(0.0)	-0.2	(0.1)	-0.9	(2.0)
	Bulgaria	-0.7	(0.5)	-28.6	(11.7)	11.3	(7.7)	4.2	(5.4)	c	c	0.1	(0.1)	0.0	(0.1)	8.6	(6.8)
	Colombia	-0.9	(0.2)	-2.0	(9.5)	-9.4	(4.4)	3.3	(6.0)	1.4	(1.1)	0.1	(0.1)	-0.3	(0.3)	3.1	(1.7)
	Costa Rica	-1.4	(0.2)	-3.5	(4.3)	-8.2	(4.6)	3.9	(4.9)	-0.4	(1.2)	0.0	(0.1)	0.2	(0.1)	2.5	(2.5)
	Croatia	-0.6	(0.9)	3.3	(9.0)	14.6	(8.0)	2.4	(6.8)	0.9	(3.3)	0.0	(0.1)	-0.2	(1.0)	0.7	(3.5)
	Cyprus*	-2.1	(0.4)	-10.8	(4.6)	-20.3	(5.6)	-7.6	(6.8)	-3.7	(1.5)	0.0	(0.1)	11.6	(1.7)	0.0	(2.0)
	Hong Kong-China	-1.8	(0.5)	-10.9	(8.0)	18.7	(11.3)	-18.8	(9.1)	-7.4	(3.0)	0.0	(0.1)	3.9	(1.5)	3.8	(4.7)
	Indonesia	-0.5	(0.2)	-5.5	(7.4)	-8.0	(6.5)	-2.5	(6.2)	-2.6	(1.9)	0.1	(0.1)	-0.5	(0.4)	-4.1	(3.8)
	Jordan	-2.3	(0.5)	-5.0	(6.6)	7.0	(5.1)	5.0	(5.1)	0.7	(1.1)	0.1	(0.1)	0.4	(0.5)	2.3	(2.0)
	Kazakhstan	-0.4	(1.0)	-4.8	(17.6)	3.5	(5.8)	-16.3	(7.0)	0.0	(0.9)	0.0	(0.1)	0.4	(0.8)	2.5	(2.9)
	Latvia	-1.1	(0.4)	-4.0	(5.7)	18.4	(5.9)	-0.4	(7.3)	0.4	(0.8)	-0.1	(0.1)	0.8	(1.0)	-3.3	(3.5)
	Lithuania	-2.2	(0.5)	1.0	(7.0)	8.6	(6.3)	-27.4	(12.7)	1.0	(1.2)	0.0	(0.1)	0.1	(0.4)	5.1	(4.1)
	Macao-China	c	c	c	c	c	c	c	c	c	c	c	c	c	c	c	c
	Malaysia	c	c	-1.2	(8.5)	4.5	(4.2)	-4.4	(4.8)	0.9	(0.9)	0.1	(0.1)	-0.3	(0.7)	4.6	(3.3)
	Montenegro	c	c	c	c	c	c	c	c	c	c	c	c	c	c	c	c
	Peru	-1.2	(0.2)	-16.2	(8.4)	4.5	(6.2)	4.1	(5.6)	-2.1	(1.4)	0.0	(0.1)	-0.1	(0.4)	0.2	(3.1)
	Qatar	-1.4	(0.3)	15.7	(10.4)	9.6	(7.5)	-20.1	(9.2)	10.1	(3.5)	0.1	(0.1)	-0.9	(0.2)	-3.0	(4.2)
	Romania	-0.6	(0.4)	-17.9	(9.4)	3.2	(5.2)	-9.1	(6.6)	-4.9	(3.3)	-0.1	(0.1)	0.6	(0.4)	-11.9	(4.4)
	Russian Federation	-0.9	(0.8)	-3.7	(10.9)	11.5	(5.9)	2.2	(11.2)	4.5	(2.0)	-0.1	(0.1)	-0.7	(0.8)	1.3	(2.8)
	Serbia	-4.4	(1.9)	-14.4	(15.8)	-5.4	(10.2)	-5.4	(7.7)	2.7	(1.5)	0.1	(0.1)	0.0	(0.8)	-9.8	(5.6)
	Shanghai-China	-1.4	(0.4)	-6.8	(10.8)	14.8	(6.0)	-8.2	(9.7)	-2.4	(3.3)	-0.1	(0.1)	0.6	(0.7)	-5.9	(2.4)
	Singapore	-1.0	(0.9)	-16.9	(16.6)	2.1	(5.6)	13.7	(25.1)	16.3	(7.1)	0.0	(0.1)	0.0	(0.6)	2.6	(3.7)
	Chinese Taipei	-9.0	(2.3)	1.5	(7.3)	17.8	(7.2)	-7.6	(6.7)	-0.5	(1.4)	-0.4	(0.1)	0.9	(0.8)	-4.8	(3.7)
	Thailand	0.1	(0.8)	-8.4	(6.6)	-1.4	(8.3)	-5.5	(6.5)	29.5	(13.2)	0.0	(0.1)	-0.5	(0.4)	7.0	(3.2)
	Tunisia	-1.3	(0.2)	-6.2	(8.6)	-0.6	(6.4)	3.7	(7.6)	2.0	(1.6)	0.0	(0.1)	0.2	(0.2)	-2.9	(3.2)
	United Arab Emirates	-0.9	(0.2)	18.6	(7.5)	0.0	(4.6)	-1.7	(5.4)	3.7	(1.6)	0.0	(0.1)	0.6	(0.5)	2.3	(2.0)
	Uruguay	-1.2	(0.2)	-4.8	(7.7)	-1.0	(5.6)	-23.9	(9.5)	3.3	(2.1)	-0.1	(0.1)	-0.5	(0.3)	2.9	(2.7)
	Viet Nam	-1.0	(0.4)	12.7	(12.9)	10.9	(8.1)	8.9	(7.1)	1.4	(1.0)	0.0	(0.1)	-1.8	(0.6)	1.1	(2.6)

Note: Values that are statistically significant are indicated in bold (see Annex A3).
1. Multilevel regression model (student and school levels): Mathematics performance is regressed on all the variables presented in this table.
* See notes at the beginning of this Annex.
StatLink http://dx.doi.org/10.1787/888932957384

[Part 2/4]

Table IV.1.12b **Relationship between mathematics performance and the school's learning environment, resources, policies and practices**

| | Resources invested in education at the school level[1] | | | | | | | | | | | | | | | |
| | Index of quality of schools' educational resources (higher values indicate better resources) | | Index of quality of physical infrastructure (higher values indicate better resources) | | School average of students' learning time per week in regular school mathematics lessons (minutes) | | Percentage of students who attended pre-primary education for more than one year (10% increase) | | School average of students' hours per week spent on homework or other study set by teachers, all school subjects combined (hours) | | School offering mathematics lessons in addition to those offered during regular school hours (1=yes, 0=no) | | Index of creative extracurricular activities at school | | Index of extracurricular mathematics activities at school | |
	Change in score	S.E.	Change in score	S.E.	Change in score	S.E.	Change in score	S.E.	Change in score	S.E.	Change in score	S.E.	Change in score	S.E.	Change in score	S.E.
OECD																
Australia	**4.4**	(2.2)	-4.0	(2.2)	0.1	(0.1)	**5.4**	(0.8)	**4.1**	(0.9)	3.0	(4.5)	**4.6**	(1.9)	-0.6	(2.1)
Austria	5.9	(3.4)	-2.4	(3.2)	0.2	(0.1)	-0.2	(2.5)	**8.4**	(3.1)	14.7	(8.1)	3.1	(3.9)	2.1	(3.6)
Belgium	-1.3	(2.3)	-0.7	(2.2)	0.5	(0.1)	**3.2**	(1.6)	3.5	(2.9)	3.7	(5.1)	-3.0	(2.2)	-1.8	(2.8)
Canada	-0.1	(1.9)	-0.1	(2.0)	0.0	(0.0)	1.1	(0.9)	**2.8**	(1.0)	2.7	(3.7)	-0.5	(2.5)	2.0	(1.3)
Chile	-0.5	(2.1)	3.5	(2.3)	-0.1	(0.0)	**7.7**	(1.7)	-0.8	(1.6)	-5.5	(5.4)	3.1	(2.2)	**4.1**	(1.7)
Czech Republic	1.9	(4.1)	**-12.8**	(4.3)	0.3	(0.1)	-0.2	(2.5)	3.0	(2.6)	11.8	(9.9)	**10.8**	(3.6)	-5.4	(3.7)
Denmark	1.3	(3.0)	-2.2	(2.1)	0.0	(0.1)	-1.8	(1.8)	**8.2**	(1.8)	6.2	(4.8)	-3.3	(2.1)	-3.8	(3.2)
Estonia	-2.4	(2.9)	**-4.6**	(2.3)	0.2	(0.2)	-1.9	(1.3)	**5.4**	(2.3)	2.5	(6.6)	4.8	(2.5)	-3.9	(2.0)
Finland	0.3	(1.8)	-2.0	(1.7)	-0.1	(0.1)	2.5	(2.3)	**3.5**	(1.1)	0.4	(4.8)	-1.2	(1.7)	-0.2	(1.9)
France	-1.1	(3.0)	-4.0	(2.2)	0.3	(0.1)	1.5	(1.5)	5.9	(3.5)	**-14.6**	(6.8)	-4.5	(2.9)	**8.8**	(2.7)
Germany	-4.6	(4.0)	3.3	(3.0)	-0.2	(0.2)	**5.7**	(2.1)	**16.4**	(2.9)	0.6	(6.9)	-0.5	(3.6)	**7.5**	(2.6)
Greece	-4.8	(3.0)	5.3	(2.9)	**2.4**	(0.5)	**6.3**	(1.4)	**3.8**	(1.6)	6.4	(8.4)	-0.5	(2.0)	4.3	(3.3)
Hungary	7.2	(4.6)	-4.7	(4.9)	0.2	(0.2)	**8.0**	(1.8)	0.7	(5.2)	-1.5	(10.1)	**6.4**	(2.9)	-1.1	(2.8)
Iceland	1.2	(4.7)	-5.0	(4.4)	-0.2	(0.2)	-2.5	(1.7)	6.8	(5.2)	10.7	(7.2)	**9.5**	(3.9)	-4.2	(3.0)
Ireland	1.4	(2.6)	-2.7	(2.0)	0.2	(0.2)	**5.1**	(1.1)	3.3	(1.8)	-10.5	(5.5)	1.7	(2.6)	3.5	(2.3)
Israel	**8.9**	(3.9)	-7.1	(3.7)	0.6	(0.1)	**-6.8**	(2.5)	**15.2**	(2.6)	**-30.9**	(10.8)	**9.9**	(3.3)	2.4	(3.0)
Italy	0.2	(1.8)	3.9	(1.6)	0.5	(0.1)	3.1	(0.7)	8.3	(1.7)	-6.6	(6.0)	4.2	(1.6)	3.6	(1.9)
Japan	-0.3	(3.3)	-4.9	(4.1)	0.6	(0.1)	5.8	(2.4)	26.5	(7.0)	-16.8	(8.8)	1.7	(3.9)	7.7	(3.8)
Korea	4.3	(5.0)	-4.3	(4.3)	0.3	(0.1)	9.1	(1.2)	4.1	(2.2)	-1.7	(10.1)	0.5	(3.7)	1.2	(3.9)
Luxembourg	c	c	c	c	c	c	c	c	c	c	c	c	c	c	c	c
Mexico	3.4	(1.5)	1.4	(1.4)	0.1	(0.0)	4.0	(0.8)	3.8	(0.8)	5.0	(3.3)	1.7	(1.2)	0.2	(1.0)
Netherlands	-3.8	(4.1)	3.0	(4.2)	0.0	(0.1)	7.9	(1.6)	5.7	(5.5)	0.4	(6.6)	-0.8	(3.0)	2.6	(4.0)
New Zealand	3.6	(3.3)	-5.6	(2.8)	0.0	(0.1)	4.2	(1.3)	7.0	(2.0)	9.1	(8.1)	8.1	(4.6)	1.9	(2.7)
Norway	**-8.8**	(3.9)	1.8	(3.2)	0.1	(0.1)	3.9	(2.0)	6.6	(2.4)	-0.5	(5.3)	-1.0	(3.1)	3.5	(3.1)
Poland	-1.3	(3.0)	-6.3	(3.7)	0.4	(0.2)	2.9	(1.5)	8.3	(1.2)	-5.1	(8.5)	2.7	(3.4)	-3.4	(3.4)
Portugal	2.3	(2.4)	-2.9	(2.4)	0.1	(0.1)	6.2	(1.7)	5.0	(1.4)	-0.7	(6.9)	-3.8	(2.4)	3.7	(2.5)
Slovak Republic	-1.1	(5.8)	-4.5	(3.4)	0.3	(0.1)	-0.6	(1.8)	5.7	(2.2)	-4.2	(9.5)	0.4	(3.1)	1.7	(3.7)
Slovenia	-3.3	(4.1)	-2.3	(3.4)	**1.8**	(0.2)	**-4.8**	(1.7)	6.2	(1.9)	4.8	(6.2)	1.3	(3.2)	1.2	(2.9)
Spain	0.0	(1.7)	-1.2	(1.8)	0.0	(0.1)	2.4	(0.9)	2.9	(1.3)	0.7	(3.8)	-0.5	(1.7)	0.9	(1.7)
Sweden	-1.6	(3.3)	1.3	(2.6)	0.1	(0.1)	2.4	(1.9)	2.5	(1.9)	-9.2	(6.1)	3.2	(2.5)	7.1	(2.8)
Switzerland	1.5	(3.5)	0.5	(3.8)	-0.2	(0.1)	0.1	(2.1)	-1.1	(1.0)	**-18.2**	(5.7)	5.3	(2.5)	10.9	(2.8)
Turkey	4.8	(4.2)	**-14.7**	(3.5)	**1.0**	(0.1)	2.1	(1.8)	**12.0**	(4.1)	**-15.3**	(7.3)	-3.2	(2.6)	9.0	(2.9)
United Kingdom	1.9	(2.4)	-3.5	(2.6)	**-0.2**	(0.1)	**6.2**	(1.2)	**7.0**	(1.6)	**-21.2**	(8.9)	1.4	(3.6)	-3.2	(2.0)
United States	-2.2	(3.4)	2.0	(4.1)	0.1	(0.1)	1.8	(1.4)	5.9	(2.0)	-3.4	(5.4)	6.1	(4.9)	4.9	(1.9)
OECD average	0.5	(0.6)	**-2.3**	(0.5)	**0.3**	(0.0)	**2.7**	(0.3)	**6.3**	(0.5)	**-2.5**	(1.2)	**2.1**	(0.5)	**2.0**	(0.5)
Partners																
Albania	5.6	(2.9)	-0.5	(3.0)	0.2	(0.2)	-0.6	(1.5)	2.6	(1.7)	4.4	(6.4)	**6.3**	(3.0)	-4.1	(2.0)
Argentina	1.6	(2.3)	-1.2	(2.2)	**0.3**	(0.1)	1.0	(1.3)	3.0	(1.5)	-8.1	(6.3)	2.6	(1.9)	0.7	(2.0)
Brazil	**4.1**	(1.9)	-0.5	(1.8)	-0.2	(0.1)	1.3	(1.3)	**4.0**	(1.0)	4.4	(5.3)	2.7	(2.3)	1.0	(2.8)
Bulgaria	0.6	(4.6)	-4.3	(3.6)	0.0	(0.1)	**8.7**	(1.7)	3.3	(2.3)	-0.2	(8.9)	-2.2	(3.3)	0.3	(3.3)
Colombia	3.5	(2.5)	-0.9	(2.3)	0.1	(0.1)	**4.3**	(1.4)	**4.0**	(1.6)	-1.9	(5.5)	-1.1	(2.4)	2.5	(2.1)
Costa Rica	7.5	(2.4)	0.0	(2.4)	0.0	(0.1)	**4.5**	(1.6)	2.5	(1.7)	-0.8	(5.6)	1.1	(2.8)	-2.9	(2.1)
Croatia	-2.1	(3.8)	**10.4**	(3.5)	**0.9**	(0.2)	2.9	(1.9)	**6.8**	(1.5)	-15.0	(8.3)	1.4	(2.3)	2.8	(2.6)
Cyprus*	8.7	(4.5)	1.8	(3.7)	**1.2**	(0.4)	**12.5**	(2.5)	3.5	(2.1)	7.8	(7.9)	**-14.1**	(4.7)	**-7.4**	(3.5)
Hong Kong-China	-6.2	(4.4)	**14.4**	(4.8)	-0.2	(0.2)	**11.2**	(2.2)	**27.9**	(5.5)	-9.2	(17.4)	-3.9	(6.6)	4.3	(4.5)
Indonesia	**7.1**	(3.6)	-3.0	(4.4)	0.1	(0.1)	**4.7**	(2.2)	**4.8**	(1.6)	-12.5	(7.1)	**8.1**	(3.4)	3.4	(2.8)
Jordan	3.0	(4.0)	-2.5	(2.8)	0.0	(0.3)	-0.5	(1.6)	**6.8**	(1.9)	-5.8	(6.2)	**5.2**	(2.6)	1.6	(1.6)
Kazakhstan	-0.3	(3.8)	2.5	(4.1)	**0.4**	(0.1)	0.7	(1.7)	3.0	(1.8)	-5.9	(11.9)	-4.8	(3.4)	-3.1	(3.0)
Latvia	1.3	(3.8)	5.5	(3.3)	**0.5**	(0.2)	**2.7**	(1.2)	2.3	(1.9)	5.0	(8.2)	3.9	(3.9)	0.6	(2.8)
Lithuania	4.4	(3.5)	**-5.7**	(2.9)	**0.7**	(0.2)	2.8	(1.4)	**6.4**	(1.2)	-3.5	(6.8)	1.8	(3.5)	1.7	(2.6)
Macao-China	c	c	c	c	c	c	c	c	c	c	c	c	c	c	c	c
Malaysia	2.7	(3.1)	-1.6	(2.6)	0.3	(0.1)	**5.4**	(1.5)	**4.7**	(1.4)	-13.7	(9.0)	0.9	(2.7)	-1.9	(2.5)
Montenegro	c	c	c	c	c	c	c	c	c	c	c	c	c	c	c	c
Peru	**9.6**	(2.9)	-4.6	(2.6)	0.0	(0.1)	2.4	(1.2)	2.8	(1.4)	1.7	(6.2)	**5.8**	(2.7)	-0.7	(2.3)
Qatar	**14.6**	(4.1)	**-14.4**	(4.3)	-0.3	(0.2)	**-15.8**	(4.8)	5.1	(3.5)	**33.4**	(10.4)	**20.1**	(4.6)	**-9.4**	(3.2)
Romania	**11.3**	(4.2)	**-10.0**	(4.9)	0.2	(0.2)	**8.9**	(1.6)	5.0	(3.0)	3.2	(6.7)	1.7	(3.1)	-1.2	(2.8)
Russian Federation	3.3	(4.1)	**-5.6**	(3.2)	**0.3**	(0.1)	1.1	(1.1)	**4.3**	(1.4)	-18.1	(14.0)	3.6	(2.7)	2.4	(2.9)
Serbia	-7.0	(4.2)	2.7	(3.7)	**0.6**	(0.2)	**6.7**	(2.4)	**11.1**	(2.0)	8.0	(11.8)	2.2	(3.8)	**8.1**	(2.9)
Shanghai-China	-1.8	(2.7)	-3.6	(3.0)	**-0.3**	(0.1)	**11.3**	(1.5)	-1.9	(3.3)	-2.1	(6.9)	2.3	(3.0)	3.6	(2.5)
Singapore	-4.2	(3.4)	0.9	(4.0)	**0.4**	(0.1)	**7.3**	(1.8)	**12.7**	(4.2)	-11.7	(10.0)	5.3	(4.4)	5.3	(3.3)
Chinese Taipei	1.0	(4.4)	**-10.3**	(4.5)	0.3	(0.1)	**14.6**	(1.8)	0.4	(4.5)	-3.1	(9.5)	1.6	(3.6)	6.3	(3.3)
Thailand	**7.7**	(3.4)	-0.7	(3.0)	0.0	(0.1)	**11.0**	(1.7)	0.1	(3.2)	9.2	(11.3)	-3.7	(4.2)	-0.2	(3.9)
Tunisia	0.1	(3.6)	-1.8	(3.8)	0.2	(0.1)	-0.4	(2.2)	5.3	(2.5)	6.8	(8.7)	**8.8**	(3.3)	-3.9	(2.3)
United Arab Emirates	**6.3**	(2.6)	-4.1	(2.2)	0.0	(0.0)	1.0	(1.2)	**6.9**	(1.3)	-0.2	(5.3)	**7.0**	(2.8)	-1.6	(2.1)
Uruguay	-1.6	(2.1)	**5.3**	(1.9)	0.1	(0.1)	2.1	(1.7)	**5.7**	(1.4)	5.4	(6.9)	3.5	(2.2)	3.7	(2.3)
Viet Nam	-2.2	(4.3)	1.6	(3.8)	0.0	(0.1)	**8.9**	(1.4)	2.5	(1.9)	-6.2	(14.6)	**11.6**	(3.3)	**-7.0**	(3.3)

Note: Values that are statistically significant are indicated in bold (see Annex A3).
1. Multilevel regression model (student and school levels): Mathematics performance is regressed on all the variables presented in this table.
* See notes at the beginning of this Annex.
StatLink http://dx.doi.org/10.1787/888932957384

[Part 3/4]

Table IV.1.12b Relationship between mathematics performance and the school's learning environment, resources, policies and practices

		School governance[1]																			
		Index of school responsibility for resource allocation (higher values indicate more autonomy)		Index of school responsibility for curriculum and assessment (higher values indicate more autonomy)		School competes with other schools for students in the same area		Private school		Index of school management: Instructional leadership		Index of school management: Teacher participation		Index of school management: Promoting instructional improvements and professional development		Index of school management: Framing and communicating the school's goals and curricular development		Use the same textbook in all mathematics classes for 15-year-olds (in the modal grade)		Mathematics teachers in the school follow a standardised curriculum that specifies content to be taught every month (at least)	
		Change in score	S.E.	Change in score	S.E.	Change in score	S.E.	Change in score	S.E.	Change in score	S.E.	Change in score	S.E.	Change in score	S.E.	Change in score	S.E.	Change in score	S.E.	Change in score	S.E.
OECD	Australia	1.3	(1.8)	-3.4	(1.8)	-13.8	(9.1)	**-12.3**	(5.6)	-2.0	(3.2)	3.1	(2.6)	-3.9	(2.1)	-3.1	(2.5)	3.4	(3.5)	3.1	(5.2)
	Austria	6.7	(5.6)	-7.1	(3.6)	-4.6	(6.5)	-19.4	(22.2)	-0.7	(5.3)	1.6	(5.0)	-1.1	(3.6)	-2.5	(5.2)	-14.0	(8.4)	-0.1	(7.1)
	Belgium	15.6	(10.4)	4.1	(2.3)	1.2	(6.9)	w	w	5.3	(3.1)	-3.6	(2.6)	-3.2	(2.6)	1.0	(2.5)	-1.1	(4.0)	-1.8	(4.9)
	Canada	**7.3**	(3.0)	1.1	(2.7)	2.3	(3.7)	-4.7	(8.7)	**-5.4**	(2.3)	-2.8	(2.4)	0.8	(2.0)	2.9	(2.0)	**7.0**	(3.2)	**-9.6**	(4.2)
	Chile	**8.6**	(1.6)	-1.8	(2.1)	2.1	(6.6)	**-37.5**	(7.2)	4.4	(3.4)	1.5	(3.0)	**-6.0**	(2.9)	-1.2	(3.0)	-1.7	(12.2)	-10.0	(6.4)
	Czech Republic	-3.7	(2.7)	5.0	(3.8)	**31.8**	(9.2)	-9.4	(15.2)	5.9	(4.0)	**8.7**	(3.2)	-6.7	(3.6)	**-12.7**	(6.4)	6.0	(8.8)	**-39.8**	(18.1)
	Denmark	-0.5	(2.4)	1.5	(2.2)	7.6	(5.9)	-12.0	(12.1)	-1.8	(2.9)	-4.3	(3.2)	2.4	(2.4)	4.4	(2.5)	**-10.3**	(5.2)	1.0	(4.0)
	Estonia	-1.1	(3.3)	-2.0	(2.2)	**11.9**	(4.3)	**-70.0**	(21.0)	7.0	(4.1)	1.6	(2.8)	-4.0	(3.5)	-5.2	(2.8)	**-17.8**	(7.6)	-6.0	(8.0)
	Finland	4.1	(3.0)	**4.9**	(1.8)	0.0	(3.7)	c	c	-2.3	(2.6)	-3.6	(2.1)	-1.7	(2.7)	1.9	(2.4)	-6.8	(5.6)	-0.7	(3.6)
	France	**-23.5**	(8.4)	3.1	(2.4)	6.1	(4.9)	c	c	-2.4	(2.8)	5.4	(3.2)	-4.3	(3.6)	-2.4	(3.5)	**21.3**	(9.0)	4.0	(4.6)
	Germany	**-44.5**	(19.7)	-4.8	(3.3)	8.9	(8.3)	**-87.5**	(19.8)	4.2	(5.8)	-4.0	(4.3)	**-12.8**	(4.4)	**14.4**	(3.8)	9.6	(7.6)	-11.4	(6.1)
	Greece	-20.8	(21.8)	**-18.7**	(9.3)	8.3	(5.7)	**-55.1**	(21.9)	6.7	(4.0)	-5.5	(3.0)	-1.0	(3.3)	-2.4	(2.9)	5.5	(17.0)	6.5	(6.9)
	Hungary	-1.4	(2.7)	-4.3	(3.6)	14.0	(7.6)	c	c	**13.9**	(5.6)	**-14.5**	(4.9)	-7.5	(4.9)	-1.6	(6.4)	-1.4	(9.2)	**-31.9**	(9.1)
	Iceland	5.1	(4.2)	1.2	(3.3)	4.4	(6.2)	c	c	4.8	(6.4)	-5.1	(6.0)	-0.1	(4.2)	-0.5	(6.0)	**24.8**	(7.6)	7.7	(7.6)
	Ireland	4.2	(9.6)	1.2	(2.7)	-4.4	(6.0)	**-53.4**	(13.8)	-3.0	(2.8)	2.8	(2.9)	-1.6	(3.1)	2.5	(3.0)	0.3	(4.8)	14.5	(9.2)
	Israel	-9.6	(7.1)	**7.9**	(3.7)	6.4	(7.0)	c	c	0.6	(5.7)	-2.4	(4.0)	-1.0	(5.1)	-0.7	(5.2)	**-23.3**	(7.4)	17.5	(11.6)
	Italy	**6.0**	(2.6)	-0.7	(1.6)	2.2	(3.2)	-2.3	(11.1)	1.3	(3.0)	-0.2	(2.2)	0.2	(2.1)	**-5.8**	(2.2)	-1.3	(3.2)	-4.2	(3.0)
	Japan	11.7	(6.3)	3.7	(4.2)	-13.7	(9.8)	**33.8**	(11.0)	4.6	(4.5)	0.6	(3.3)	0.2	(3.8)	-1.1	(5.2)	0.9	(7.4)	12.4	(8.8)
	Korea	-2.3	(4.9)	1.5	(2.7)	2.7	(10.2)	**-20.4**	(7.5)	-2.3	(5.9)	-2.1	(3.6)	2.8	(5.8)	-2.1	(4.8)	-9.4	(7.5)	-1.2	(7.3)
	Luxembourg	c	c	c	c	c	c	c	c	c	c	c	c	c	c	c	c	c	c	c	c
	Mexico	**4.7**	(2.3)	3.5	(2.2)	1.1	(3.9)	-5.1	(7.5)	-2.6	(2.0)	-2.1	(1.4)	1.8	(1.5)	2.0	(1.9)	-2.3	(2.7)	-3.8	(8.1)
	Netherlands	-0.5	(2.4)	-3.1	(4.1)	11.3	(7.4)	c	c	**16.3**	(4.9)	0.3	(4.8)	-4.8	(3.5)	**-8.2**	(4.0)	-1.4	(5.6)	6.7	(12.6)
	New Zealand	-2.4	(3.9)	-0.2	(2.5)	-7.1	(7.9)	**-22.7**	(11.3)	-6.3	(5.2)	-5.2	(3.6)	**9.1**	(3.8)	2.5	(4.3)	4.3	(6.3)	-3.7	(6.9)
	Norway	2.5	(4.7)	-0.6	(3.8)	1.3	(4.9)	c	c	2.0	(5.1)	-0.3	(3.8)	0.5	(4.3)	-0.3	(3.7)	4.1	(6.5)	-4.2	(7.1)
	Poland	-3.6	(5.9)	-0.3	(3.1)	3.3	(5.2)	-34.8	(19.5)	1.7	(3.4)	1.1	(4.5)	0.3	(3.5)	0.8	(4.7)	-1.1	(10.5)	**31.2**	(8.4)
	Portugal	4.0	(4.9)	**-12.8**	(4.5)	2.6	(4.9)	-22.7	(12.3)	-5.0	(3.0)	5.7	(3.0)	0.1	(3.1)	-1.9	(3.2)	15.9	(9.6)	-7.5	(9.0)
	Slovak Republic	-0.5	(2.8)	1.8	(3.7)	-0.7	(8.8)	**-71.5**	(24.2)	11.0	(5.7)	-4.1	(4.7)	**-13.2**	(5.2)	1.5	(5.6)	**-24.7**	(8.1)	7.2	(13.5)
	Slovenia	-0.8	(5.6)	0.1	(4.4)	9.6	(6.0)	c	c	**-15.2**	(4.9)	6.0	(4.8)	6.8	(4.4)	-0.9	(4.9)	0.0	(6.3)	-16.8	(14.1)
	Spain	**8.4**	(2.7)	-2.6	(2.2)	5.5	(4.1)	-5.5	(5.2)	-3.3	(1.9)	-0.9	(2.1)	-1.9	(1.7)	2.4	(2.4)	-0.3	(3.0)	5.8	(6.8)
	Sweden	1.6	(2.1)	-3.0	(2.8)	0.3	(5.5)	c	c	-3.3	(3.9)	1.3	(4.2)	-5.0	(3.0)	-0.8	(4.0)	-2.5	(5.4)	-2.7	(4.5)
	Switzerland	-6.5	(4.5)	-2.5	(5.0)	-5.5	(4.9)	16.1	(13.1)	4.8	(3.1)	-0.3	(2.8)	-3.2	(3.2)	-3.8	(2.8)	**-14.8**	(5.4)	-9.8	(5.7)
	Turkey	-52.2	(34.1)	-12.8	(8.8)	8.0	(6.4)	c	c	5.2	(3.9)	-2.1	(3.7)	**-8.1**	(3.3)	-1.6	(4.6)	-5.2	(35.8)	10.2	(9.1)
	United Kingdom	1.1	(1.9)	0.4	(2.5)	-14.2	(8.1)	-21.0	(11.4)	-0.1	(4.0)	1.3	(3.3)	**-6.6**	(2.6)	-3.2	(2.9)	-2.1	(4.9)	15.0	(8.1)
	United States	-4.5	(2.5)	-3.4	(2.9)	-9.8	(5.4)	**25.3**	(8.9)	2.2	(3.8)	1.6	(3.7)	1.6	(3.8)	**-10.5**	(3.9)	0.7	(4.6)	2.7	(11.3)
	OECD average	-2.6	(1.6)	**-1.3**	(0.7)	**2.4**	(1.1)	**-23.0**	(3.0)	1.4	(0.7)	-0.6	(0.6)	**-2.2**	(0.6)	-1.1	(0.7)	-1.1	(1.7)	-0.6	(1.5)
Partners	Albania	4.1	(5.0)	-0.6	(2.5)	7.2	(5.2)	0.5	(11.1)	-0.6	(4.4)	1.5	(2.9)	-3.4	(2.7)	0.5	(4.5)	13.3	(13.1)	-5.1	(13.2)
	Argentina	c	c	-1.5	(3.6)	8.5	(5.3)	-11.1	(9.1)	3.4	(3.1)	-0.5	(2.1)	-0.3	(2.3)	-4.4	(3.1)	4.2	(4.5)	-6.1	(4.7)
	Brazil	3.2	(5.3)	-0.7	(2.7)	6.3	(3.3)	**-36.6**	(17.2)	**-5.7**	(2.8)	4.0	(2.5)	0.8	(2.4)	**6.9**	(2.5)	**14.0**	(5.6)	-8.3	(6.3)
	Bulgaria	**5.6**	(2.6)	4.5	(7.2)	-2.8	(9.4)	-43.1	(33.3)	-2.9	(5.8)	0.4	(4.7)	**-8.6**	(4.0)	0.4	(5.5)	-8.3	(12.7)	**-30.2**	(14.6)
	Colombia	-1.5	(2.7)	2.7	(2.3)	-3.2	(5.6)	**-43.3**	(9.2)	**-10.3**	(3.2)	**7.7**	(2.3)	-2.5	(2.4)	-0.3	(2.5)	**-10.7**	(5.0)	**20.3**	(8.2)
	Costa Rica	-2.4	(5.4)	**11.7**	(4.1)	1.8	(5.5)	-6.5	(14.7)	5.4	(3.8)	**-6.9**	(2.8)	5.0	(3.2)	-4.5	(3.6)	0.2	(4.3)	-12.9	(7.8)
	Croatia	-8.6	(10.5)	-7.4	(4.9)	-0.7	(5.4)	-3.4	(33.1)	1.3	(4.1)	-0.2	(3.2)	-1.3	(3.0)	-3.0	(3.7)	**15.4**	(4.7)	-11.1	(7.2)
	Cyprus*	**-16.7**	(7.0)	**31.7**	(6.0)	1.4	(5.5)	-11.4	(15.1)	7.7	(4.6)	-5.7	(3.6)	**13.0**	(5.0)	**-16.5**	(4.7)	1.4	(15.6)	3.8	(8.9)
	Hong Kong-China	1.9	(4.6)	-3.9	(3.8)	-15.3	(29.1)	**49.7**	(21.2)	**-13.6**	(6.0)	3.9	(5.5)	1.7	(6.7)	3.5	(5.4)	9.1	(11.8)	10.7	(11.6)
	Indonesia	2.2	(2.7)	-3.1	(3.2)	-9.5	(22.7)	-12.6	(8.1)	6.7	(6.8)	-0.1	(5.1)	-1.6	(5.1)	-1.8	(6.0)	-5.0	(8.3)	-1.0	(11.3)
	Jordan	4.4	(7.4)	1.1	(6.6)	-0.1	(5.8)	**-25.7**	(9.3)	**-9.9**	(4.3)	-3.7	(2.8)	0.8	(3.2)	3.1	(3.2)	-17.8	(18.8)	**-18.8**	(7.3)
	Kazakhstan	3.0	(5.6)	-8.3	(5.4)	-6.7	(6.8)	-0.8	(15.4)	**13.9**	(4.9)	1.4	(3.6)	-2.6	(2.8)	**-10.5**	(5.0)	10.5	(8.5)	-0.2	(5.4)
	Latvia	0.7	(2.4)	1.8	(3.3)	**-20.0**	(8.6)	-4.9	(15.6)	2.4	(3.8)	6.8	(4.0)	-3.4	(2.8)	-5.3	(3.6)	-0.8	(15.6)	6.5	(9.4)
	Lithuania	-1.0	(2.1)	**-5.9**	(2.7)	-8.1	(5.5)	29.6	(19.5)	-4.2	(4.2)	-0.3	(3.1)	-5.3	(3.4)	2.2	(4.4)	-8.3	(7.7)	-4.5	(6.2)
	Macao-China	c	c	c	c	c	c	c	c	c	c	c	c	c	c	c	c	c	c	c	c
	Malaysia	1.4	(11.5)	-4.9	(3.7)	-2.1	(5.1)	-24.4	(36.6)	-3.5	(3.7)	**-9.5**	(3.1)	2.2	(3.6)	**5.6**	(2.9)	-5.0	(15.8)	6.8	(6.8)
	Montenegro	c	c	c	c	c	c	c	c	c	c	c	c	c	c	c	c	c	c	c	c
	Peru	4.2	(3.5)	-0.2	(2.7)	**16.0**	(6.6)	-20.1	(10.6)	-2.4	(3.4)	0.9	(3.6)	3.2	(3.2)	1.7	(3.7)	4.0	(6.3)	-5.9	(7.7)
	Qatar	3.2	(9.2)	**12.6**	(6.2)	**15.8**	(6.6)	**-57.5**	(22.6)	-10.0	(6.2)	0.4	(4.9)	2.2	(3.9)	-0.2	(4.8)	12.7	(9.8)	8.7	(16.1)
	Romania	6.1	(8.2)	-0.7	(3.8)	3.5	(5.6)	**-58.3**	(20.0)	0.7	(3.6)	1.4	(3.8)	-4.8	(3.1)	3.9	(3.3)	-3.3	(5.5)	**14.4**	(5.9)
	Russian Federation	3.4	(3.5)	**-6.4**	(3.0)	-0.5	(7.4)	-4.6	(21.3)	-3.4	(5.1)	2.8	(4.0)	-4.4	(3.6)	5.1	(5.1)	-11.7	(6.9)	-13.5	(9.8)
	Serbia	16.7	(12.7)	2.6	(15.0)	1.4	(9.3)	16.3	(47.2)	-2.1	(4.7)	1.5	(5.3)	1.8	(4.2)	-3.4	(5.1)	8.0	(6.1)	11.6	(8.6)
	Shanghai-China	5.3	(4.0)	-4.3	(3.8)	-0.5	(6.7)	-10.0	(12.1)	-4.7	(4.6)	1.6	(3.7)	-0.9	(4.0)	-1.2	(4.3)	-7.8	(11.4)	-2.5	(12.4)
	Singapore	9.2	(6.4)	-0.3	(3.5)	**-44.7**	(16.3)	41.6	(22.9)	-10.4	(6.1)	-1.3	(4.8)	6.1	(4.5)	0.0	(4.8)	5.3	(5.6)	-22.1	(21.5)
	Chinese Taipei	-3.8	(3.9)	2.1	(2.9)	2.4	(12.8)	11.0	(11.0)	13.2	(7.0)	2.6	(5.0)	**-13.5**	(5.6)	-4.0	(4.0)	1.4	(8.1)	0.2	(7.5)
	Thailand	1.2	(2.0)	5.4	(3.5)	2.5	(8.7)	-10.6	(15.0)	9.2	(4.8)	-2.0	(4.0)	1.9	(3.9)	-8.6	(4.6)	-3.6	(11.5)	-10.1	(6.4)
	Tunisia	-2.8	(5.1)	3.2	(4.2)	-0.6	(7.0)	-40.9	(40.8)	-3.0	(3.0)	-1.7	(3.2)	-0.9	(3.6)	1.0	(3.6)	0.7	(7.5)	0.7	(6.2)
	United Arab Emirates	**6.8**	(2.7)	4.1	(2.8)	2.9	(7.0)	-4.2	(7.8)	3.4	(4.4)	-5.7	(3.0)	-2.4	(2.4)	1.6	(3.7)	**-18.7**	(8.1)	11.5	(10.8)
	Uruguay	-6.5	(7.2)	0.4	(5.0)	7.0	(4.1)	**-36.8**	(13.9)	-0.6	(2.9)	-3.3	(2.6)	0.6	(2.3)	-1.0	(2.4)	0.0	(4.0)	0.2	(8.6)
	Viet Nam	-2.7	(4.0)	6.8	(5.9)	-1.8	(6.7)	**28.4**	(11.3)	-4.0	(4.4)	-0.6	(4.1)	-0.5	(4.0)	9.2	(6.3)	-1.1	(6.7)	**-32.8**	(14.4)

Note: Values that are statistically significant are indicated in bold (see Annex A3).
1. Multilevel regression model (student and school levels): Mathematics performance is regressed on all the variables presented in this table.
* See notes at the beginning of this Annex.
StatLink http://dx.doi.org/10.1787/888932957384

[Part 4/4]

Table IV.1.12b Relationship between mathematics performance and the school's learning environment, resources, policies and practices

	Assessment and accountability policies[1]										Learning environment and school climate at the school level[1]															
	Index of assessment practices		Schools that post achievement data publicly		Schools in which an administrative authority tracks data over time		Schools that seek written feedback from students (e.g. regarding lessons, teachers or resources)		Schools that have teacher mentoring		School average index of teacher-student relations (higher values indicate better climate)		School average index of disciplinary climate (higher values indicate better climate)		Index of teacher-related factors affecting school climate (higher values indicate positive teacher behaviour)		Index of student-related factors affecting school climate (higher values indicate positive student behaviour)		Index of teacher morale (higher values indicate better teacher morale)		Percentage of students who did not arrive late for school in the two weeks prior to the PISA test (10% increase)		Percentage of students who did not skip a whole school day in the two weeks prior to the PISA test (10% increase)	
	Change in score	S.E.	Change in score	S.E.	Change in score	S.E.	Change in score	S.E.	Change in score	S.E.	Change in score	S.E.	Change in score	S.E.	Change in score	S.E.	Change in score	S.E.	Change in score	S.E.	Change in score	S.E.	Change in score	S.E.	Change in score	S.E.
OECD																										
Australia	-0.8	(1.4)	6.2	(3.4)	4.6	(5.1)	-1.8	(3.5)	-1.0	(5.8)	**15.3**	(7.7)	**33.0**	(6.6)	1.2	(2.2)	**5.8**	(2.4)	-3.4	(2.0)	1.8	(1.1)	**5.0**	(1.1)
Austria	-0.9	(2.7)	20.9	(11.9)	2.4	(6.8)	6.7	(8.6)	4.3	(8.9)	**26.5**	(12.4)	**63.2**	(11.0)	-4.5	(4.4)	6.8	(3.7)	-6.8	(4.3)	0.8	(2.6)	2.7	(4.9)
Belgium	-0.9	(1.7)	14.5	(15.6)	3.5	(4.0)	7.0	(4.2)	7.4	(5.9)	-7.6	(9.9)	**31.6**	(8.2)	2.4	(2.9)	**5.2**	(2.5)	-1.4	(2.6)	**4.6**	(1.8)	**11.2**	(3.4)
Canada	**-4.0**	(1.5)	5.6	(3.1)	2.3	(5.1)	**6.9**	(3.0)	-8.6	(4.7)	-9.2	(7.7)	**27.2**	(7.4)	-3.2	(2.4)	**11.4**	(2.2)	**4.4**	(1.8)	**4.8**	(1.1)	**6.5**	(1.4)
Chile	**5.0**	(2.0)	3.2	(4.1)	-0.5	(5.4)	-6.9	(4.1)	2.6	(5.1)	**-20.6**	(8.1)	13.8	(7.5)	5.1	(3.1)	-2.3	(2.8)	3.4	(2.1)	**5.4**	(1.3)	**8.6**	(3.0)
Czech Republic	-0.3	(2.5)	**15.1**	(6.2)	-1.5	(6.6)	-7.0	(6.2)	10.8	(10.6)	**-35.6**	(13.0)	**35.8**	(8.4)	-5.0	(5.3)	**14.4**	(4.7)	-4.9	(4.4)	**4.3**	(2.2)	**12.1**	(3.6)
Denmark	**3.5**	(1.8)	-3.5	(4.0)	-1.9	(5.4)	-7.3	(3.8)	1.4	(3.8)	**19.2**	(9.6)	**32.4**	(7.9)	0.4	(3.0)	4.1	(3.2)	-0.6	(2.6)	-1.1	(1.1)	**6.5**	(2.5)
Estonia	-0.1	(1.9)	3.2	(4.2)	-4.5	(6.6)	-2.7	(5.4)	**13.9**	(5.7)	-1.3	(10.7)	**20.0**	(7.8)	**7.6**	(3.1)	-0.6	(2.8)	4.8	(2.6)	**3.5**	(1.4)	**6.4**	(2.4)
Finland	0.4	(1.3)	13.4	(10.6)	-3.4	(3.2)	0.4	(3.5)	1.9	(3.3)	5.7	(7.7)	1.1	(9.0)	-2.9	(2.1)	**6.4**	(2.9)	1.1	(2.0)	**4.8**	(1.3)	1.5	(2.4)
France	1.5	(2.0)	**10.7**	(4.7)	-2.7	(5.5)	7.8	(7.0)	-2.9	(5.7)	-17.9	(10.9)	**36.0**	(8.2)	-4.3	(3.9)	**7.3**	(3.3)	3.7	(2.6)	**5.8**	(1.6)	4.9	(3.0)
Germany	-3.8	(2.1)	2.0	(9.5)	-0.8	(6.3)	2.1	(5.7)	2.5	(5.4)	**-50.2**	(10.4)	**17.9**	(8.6)	2.3	(4.2)	5.6	(4.9)	-3.1	(3.3)	-2.4	(2.6)	6.2	(5.0)
Greece	2.4	(1.6)	-5.7	(5.3)	2.8	(4.0)	-6.6	(5.7)	**-13.1**	(6.6)	-9.6	(8.5)	**29.5**	(11.1)	1.2	(2.5)	-1.9	(3.3)	-0.9	(2.1)	-3.0	(1.9)	**5.0**	(2.2)
Hungary	4.2	(3.5)	2.1	(5.9)	-0.6	(6.5)	**18.4**	(7.9)	-8.0	(7.0)	-25.5	(13.7)	**37.3**	(9.8)	-4.0	(5.1)	1.4	(3.6)	6.3	(4.0)	**6.5**	(1.9)	6.3	(3.2)
Iceland	**9.5**	(4.0)	5.0	(7.1)	-13.0	(9.0)	**12.6**	(5.5)	5.9	(7.8)	**32.0**	(10.1)	17.9	(12.3)	-8.6	(4.7)	2.4	(5.3)	0.2	(3.8)	**6.5**	(2.1)	13.9	(10.6)
Ireland	**-5.5**	(2.5)	**15.6**	(6.4)	-1.2	(4.4)	0.7	(4.7)	4.9	(4.8)	**-25.2**	(11.8)	**26.5**	(8.6)	**-5.9**	(2.7)	**12.6**	(3.2)	-3.6	(2.9)	**5.0**	(1.9)	2.3	(6.0)
Israel	-3.8	(5.2)	**24.8**	(7.8)	-23.9	(12.8)	-10.0	(6.7)	-15.2	(12.4)	**-39.5**	(12.5)	**48.6**	(11.7)	-6.7	(6.5)	0.7	(5.2)	5.2	(4.2)	2.7	(2.3)	**12.7**	(3.7)
Italy	2.7	(1.5)	1.4	(3.1)	-3.3	(3.2)	3.9	(2.9)	-4.9	(3.3)	**-48.3**	(6.1)	**25.3**	(5.9)	-3.4	(2.3)	**7.7**	(2.2)	-0.2	(1.8)	**10.1**	(1.2)	**10.6**	(1.0)
Japan	0.1	(2.4)	4.5	(10.0)	-5.4	(11.1)	-9.3	(7.2)	**-20.9**	(9.9)	**36.3**	(13.0)	**37.0**	(13.4)	-3.1	(4.2)	-2.2	(4.4)	5.3	(3.6)	2.1	(4.5)	**33.5**	(9.1)
Korea	**7.7**	(3.1)	11.3	(6.1)	**-25.1**	(9.7)	-10.0	(8.7)	8.9	(9.4)	**44.8**	(15.3)	**30.7**	(12.5)	-3.2	(3.3)	1.3	(3.7)	1.3	(3.2)	**4.5**	(2.2)	**24.2**	(9.7)
Luxembourg	c	c	c	c	c	c	c	c	c	c	c	c	c	c	c	c	c	c	c	c	c	c	c	c
Mexico	1.5	(1.4)	-2.7	(2.5)	5.7	(4.9)	3.3	(3.0)	3.0	(2.4)	**-18.8**	(5.0)	**24.4**	(4.9)	-0.4	(1.9)	1.1	(1.7)	0.1	(1.3)	0.4	(0.9)	**4.0**	(1.0)
Netherlands	**-5.7**	(2.8)	6.0	(8.5)	-10.8	(6.9)	-1.6	(12.5)	12.2	(17.3)	17.2	(15.4)	**24.8**	(12.1)	**-12.5**	(5.6)	4.6	(5.0)	-5.2	(3.7)	**7.7**	(2.0)	**13.7**	(6.9)
New Zealand	-10.5	(6.1)	1.3	(5.4)	**19.3**	(7.1)	**-36.5**	(18.4)	5.0	(13.4)	**-31.7**	(9.7)	**48.7**	(8.6)	-3.1	(3.9)	**6.3**	(3.0)	**9.4**	(2.5)	**3.9**	(1.8)	**16.4**	(2.7)
Norway	**-4.3**	(1.7)	**10.2**	(4.5)	-5.9	(6.7)	7.7	(4.6)	-4.8	(5.1)	9.6	(11.6)	**40.4**	(10.0)	**9.5**	(4.1)	0.8	(4.0)	3.1	(3.2)	0.0	(1.7)	**8.7**	(4.2)
Poland	-2.0	(3.7)	3.3	(4.5)	1.6	(5.0)	-6.0	(5.2)	0.6	(8.7)	-6.3	(10.7)	**20.4**	(7.4)	4.0	(4.6)	2.0	(4.3)	-1.0	(3.4)	-0.7	(1.5)	**7.2**	(2.9)
Portugal	-1.3	(3.1)	2.2	(4.0)	-7.9	(6.9)	0.2	(4.4)	4.9	(4.7)	0.8	(10.3)	14.9	(10.7)	1.3	(2.8)	1.5	(2.0)	1.7	(2.4)	-0.2	(1.4)	2.9	(2.6)
Slovak Republic	-0.4	(2.8)	-2.9	(7.0)	-5.8	(7.1)	-6.9	(6.7)	**-23.3**	(8.1)	**-50.1**	(13.6)	**58.9**	(11.2)	1.0	(6.4)	-6.1	(6.1)	4.9	(4.3)	**6.2**	(2.4)	**10.6**	(3.5)
Slovenia	-3.4	(2.5)	-0.6	(5.4)	0.1	(7.0)	-4.3	(6.7)	-6.4	(5.1)	-20.0	(15.5)	**39.4**	(7.3)	6.4	(3.5)	0.9	(4.8)	-2.7	(3.0)	-0.7	(2.1)	**16.9**	(2.2)
Spain	-1.8	(1.8)	-1.1	(3.6)	4.9	(3.6)	6.0	(3.3)	-3.5	(3.9)	-5.3	(6.8)	**12.5**	(5.5)	-2.8	(2.5)	**7.3**	(2.2)	1.6	(1.8)	1.3	(1.1)	**8.1**	(1.2)
Sweden	0.1	(2.5)	0.2	(6.5)	w	w	0.7	(6.3)	-3.7	(4.9)	12.4	(10.0)	**33.3**	(10.6)	-5.1	(3.2)	6.0	(3.7)	2.1	(3.2)	**4.1**	(1.7)	6.6	(4.4)
Switzerland	-0.9	(1.8)	-10.3	(10.4)	2.6	(5.0)	-3.5	(5.8)	2.4	(5.0)	**21.3**	(10.7)	**33.3**	(11.3)	-0.2	(3.3)	3.0	(3.7)	-2.8	(3.1)	**-5.2**	(2.0)	**12.7**	(4.4)
Turkey	3.7	(2.9)	5.7	(5.5)	10.2	(16.5)	6.7	(7.5)	-7.3	(7.2)	**-61.4**	(11.4)	**94.3**	(12.3)	**-8.2**	(3.7)	3.7	(4.1)	**7.9**	(3.0)	1.7	(2.6)	-4.5	(2.3)
United Kingdom	**10.1**	(4.2)	-2.8	(7.8)	**-22.0**	(8.7)	-4.9	(5.2)	6.1	(6.7)	7.8	(10.6)	**41.4**	(7.4)	5.3	(2.8)	-4.7	(3.4)	2.7	(2.7)	**6.8**	(1.6)	**7.3**	(2.4)
United States	-4.1	(2.6)	7.6	(7.8)	**-41.2**	(20.4)	1.7	(4.8)	**47.9**	(19.2)	**31.9**	(10.6)	18.6	(13.0)	0.9	(2.6)	4.8	(3.9)	-0.3	(2.7)	**6.6**	(1.6)	-0.2	(2.4)
OECD average	-0.1	(0.5)	**5.0**	(1.2)	**-4.3**	(1.4)	-1.0	(1.2)	0.7	(1.4)	**-6.2**	(1.9)	**32.4**	(1.7)	-1.2	(0.7)	**3.6**	(0.7)	1.0	(0.5)	**3.0**	(0.3)	**8.8**	(0.8)
Partners																										
Albania	-0.6	(2.6)	-0.4	(6.4)	**-15.6**	(6.0)	-5.6	(6.1)	-5.5	(9.2)	-9.6	(11.3)	-13.8	(11.8)	0.5	(2.9)	-2.2	(3.1)	0.4	(3.3)	0.9	(2.2)	-0.1	(2.9)
Argentina	0.5	(1.8)	2.9	(6.7)	-7.7	(4.5)	0.4	(4.2)	-1.4	(3.9)	**-51.0**	(8.9)	**21.7**	(9.5)	1.7	(3.0)	3.1	(2.3)	4.2	(3.4)	**6.0**	(1.3)	**4.3**	(1.6)
Brazil	-0.6	(1.8)	-4.6	(3.7)	-5.3	(5.3)	-1.9	(3.2)	2.3	(5.7)	**-14.9**	(6.8)	**27.5**	(6.6)	-2.5	(2.2)	3.7	(1.9)	0.6	(1.8)	2.0	(1.1)	0.4	(1.2)
Bulgaria	2.9	(4.7)	**19.3**	(6.0)	-3.1	(9.7)	7.5	(7.4)	-2.5	(6.1)	**-56.4**	(10.9)	23.0	(12.6)	-3.6	(3.0)	5.6	(3.7)	**9.2**	(4.0)	2.9	(2.1)	**7.7**	(2.5)
Colombia	3.2	(2.7)	4.2	(4.1)	-3.3	(5.3)	**12.4**	(4.7)	-5.7	(4.8)	**-44.2**	(9.5)	13.2	(9.3)	-1.9	(2.2)	**7.2**	(2.8)	1.3	(2.6)	1.3	(1.3)	2.0	(3.2)
Costa Rica	-0.9	(2.0)	4.5	(6.0)	5.5	(11.1)	-5.6	(3.9)	2.1	(4.8)	-8.5	(11.2)	12.7	(10.0)	-2.5	(3.9)	3.2	(2.9)	**6.1**	(2.4)	-0.1	(1.2)	2.8	(2.1)
Croatia	**-5.1**	(2.3)	1.0	(4.5)	0.3	(6.9)	-7.5	(4.3)	-8.3	(20.9)	-4.6	(11.8)	**24.8**	(9.5)	-2.0	(3.5)	1.2	(3.3)	2.0	(2.9)	**6.9**	(2.1)	**12.1**	(2.9)
Cyprus*	**7.8**	(1.6)	1.3	(9.5)	**15.1**	(6.8)	0.0	(5.1)	4.9	(9.9)	17.4	(14.6)	**69.9**	(14.6)	7.4	(5.6)	-8.7	(4.6)	-2.6	(3.0)	-4.0	(2.6)	**12.1**	(2.4)
Hong Kong-China	-1.6	(4.4)	-3.8	(7.6)	-3.5	(6.2)	2.6	(7.7)	-9.4	(9.6)	-7.0	(22.8)	0.6	(14.5)	6.1	(5.3)	-3.2	(4.6)	**10.1**	(4.8)	-0.3	(4.3)	12.7	(9.1)
Indonesia	-9.6	(5.2)	0.3	(8.0)	-3.4	(6.6)	11.3	(10.7)	c	c	5.6	(14.8)	-8.9	(14.0)	-1.0	(3.6)	-1.5	(4.4)	1.4	(3.2)	**6.2**	(1.9)	5.4	(3.3)
Jordan	-0.7	(2.9)	-8.3	(6.2)	-1.0	(6.2)	5.3	(5.6)	-4.2	(4.6)	-4.6	(10.1)	**46.1**	(9.0)	-0.5	(2.9)	-0.8	(2.5)	**8.0**	(2.8)	-2.2	(1.7)	3.0	(2.1)
Kazakhstan	-7.7	(10.0)	1.8	(7.9)	c	c	-5.9	(9.6)	-0.6	(21.2)	-12.0	(14.6)	**43.8**	(12.9)	-3.4	(2.8)	4.0	(3.0)	-3.3	(2.8)	-1.4	(2.8)	3.0	(3.0)
Latvia	8.8	(8.3)	2.8	(5.4)	-2.3	(6.2)	6.1	(6.1)	3.6	(5.1)	**-29.9**	(8.6)	2.9	(8.2)	-0.7	(3.1)	4.3	(3.3)	2.0	(3.5)	2.6	(1.5)	**8.7**	(2.1)
Lithuania	**5.6**	(2.4)	-2.7	(5.0)	-0.9	(6.3)	**-12.5**	(5.9)	-0.8	(4.4)	10.4	(9.2)	**28.4**	(7.3)	6.4	(4.2)	-3.9	(4.4)	0.7	(3.2)	**4.0**	(1.5)	**6.9**	(2.3)
Macao-China	c	c	c	c	c	c	c	c	c	c	c	c	c	c	c	c	c	c	c	c	c	c	c	c
Malaysia	-5.3	(3.5)	-8.6	(5.8)	19.3	(15.0)	**11.1**	(4.1)	0.8	(5.9)	-8.0	(11.5)	**52.9**	(13.8)	**7.0**	(2.5)	0.5	(2.8)	-0.9	(2.4)	**6.5**	(1.9)	0.9	(1.7)
Montenegro	c	c	c	c	c	c	c	c	c	c	c	c	c	c	c	c	c	c	c	c	c	c	c	c
Peru	3.5	(2.3)	-1.4	(8.7)	-3.4	(5.1)	-10.3	(5.9)	7.7	(12.6)	-8.7	(10.5)	13.8	(12.7)	-1.6	(2.9)	-0.1	(3.3)	1.4	(3.2)	**4.2**	(1.4)	**8.2**	(2.6)
Qatar	**-8.0**	(3.9)	3.6	(6.3)	**-63.9**	(14.2)	**-29.0**	(14.1)	c	c	4.9	(16.2)	**64.9**	(18.6)	1.0	(3.1)	-1.4	(2.9)	1.1	(3.7)	**10.4**	(3.3)	-3.7	(3.4)
Romania	2.0	(2.4)	2.2	(5.7)	-8.0	(6.3)	-9.4	(7.0)	-2.5	(7.7)	**-35.1**	(13.0)	**54.5**	(9.2)	0.8	(3.2)	-1.0	(3.2)	1.5	(2.9)	-1.7	(2.3)	3.4	(2.7)
Russian Federation	5.0	(3.5)	2.0	(5.6)	**37.2**	(15.5)	6.4	(5.8)	0.5	(10.0)	**-25.7**	(12.8)	**25.3**	(9.3)	-1.0	(3.1)	**6.5**	(2.9)	5.4	(3.0)	1.8	(1.9)	**5.6**	(2.5)
Serbia	1.0	(3.4)	1.0	(6.9)	**-15.3**	(7.1)	**14.0**	(6.2)	8.6	(16.3)	**-38.2**	(15.1)	**41.2**	(12.3)	2.6	(4.1)	0.3	(5.8)	**-7.3**	(3.7)	**6.9**	(2.1)	6.3	(4.7)
Shanghai-China	3.9	(3.1)	-4.0	(12.4)	**-13.5**	(6.4)	-11.7	(9.0)	14.9	(14.9)	23.2	(14.7)	**39.0**	(13.6)	-0.3	(2.9)	2.2	(2.3)	-2.1	(2.7)	2.7	(2.8)	-8.5	(20.4)
Singapore	**-39.0**	(15.3)	**16.0**	(6.0)	18.5	(25.0)	**26.4**	(11.7)	-4.2	(25.0)	30.9	(19.5)	**37.6**	(12.6)	0.3	(4.4)	10.2	(5.3)	5.3	(2.8)	5.9	(3.7)	-1.7	(3.3)
Chinese Taipei	**-8.8**	(2.4)	15.2	(8.8)	6.6	(6.8)	-10.3	(6.6)	5.9	(7.3)	11.2	(21.1)	9.3	(16.8)	3.3	(3.0)	1.2	(3.1)	1.9	(3.9)	-0.3	(3.0)	**22.0**	(6.8)
Thailand	1.7	(4.3)	7.2	(6.4)	**46.5**	(14.1)	8.9	(6.2)	-21.3	(13.5)	-30.9	(18.1)	9.5	(18.1)	6.5	(4.2)	6.2	(4.1)	-1.6	(3.0)	1.9	(1.8)	**7.9**	(2.6)
Tunisia	-2.7	(2.5)	1.4	(8.8)	-1.5	(6.8)	1.3	(6.7)	-10.6	(8.1)	**-54.5**	(18.2)	**38.2**	(16.2)	4.2	(4.9)	-6.3	(4.6)	0.7	(2.8)	3.2	(2.7)	**8.7**	(2.3)
United Arab Emirates	1.0	(4.1)	-1.9	(5.0)	-6.9	(7.0)	-6.2	(5.5)	11.0	(7.9)	-11.0	(10.0)	**27.8**	(7.9)	2.8	(2.7)	0.1	(2.9)	1.8	(2.7)	**7.6**	(1.6)	**4.0**	(1.7)
Uruguay	3.3	(1.9)	4.2	(7.0)	-0.7	(5.0)	-1.4	(4.3)	4.3	(4.9)	**-30.4**	(12.7)	**25.2**	(9.7)	1.0	(3.3)	-0.4	(2.3)	1.0	(2.9)	0.7	(1.9)	2.0	(2.3)
Viet Nam	0.9	(5.1)	0.8	(7.1)	-9.7	(7.6)	**14.3**	(6.4)	-16.1	(20.4)	**-45.6**	(15.2)	34.4	(19.0)	-4.9	(4.5)	9.7	(5.6)	2.0	(4.5)	1.4	(3.5)	**14.2**	(4.9)

Note: Values that are statistically significant are indicated in bold (see Annex A3).
1. Multilevel regression model (student and school levels): Mathematics performance is regressed on all the variables presented in this table.
* See notes at the beginning of this Annex.

StatLink http://dx.doi.org/10.1787/888932957384

[Part 1/5]

Relationship among mathematics performance, the school's learning environment, resources, policies and practices, and student and school characteristics

Table IV.1.12c

	Schools' policies on selecting and grouping students[1]								Resources invested in education at the school level[1]							
	Percentage of students who repeated one or more grades		School with ability grouping for all mathematics classes		School with high academic selectivity for school admittance		School is very likely to transfer students with low achievement, behavioural problems or special learning needs		Proportion of teachers with ISCED 5A (10% increase)		Percentage of mathematics teachers in the school who have attended a programme of professional development with a focus on mathematics during the previous three months		Student-teacher ratio		Index of teacher shortage (higher values indicate more shortages)	
	Change in score	S.E.	Change in score	S.E.	Change in score	S.E.	Change in score	S.E.	Change in score	S.E.	Change in score	S.E.	Change in score	S.E.	Change in score	S.E.
OECD																
Australia	**-0.6**	(0.2)	-2.8	(15.6)	**6.9**	(2.7)	**12.2**	(7.1)	-0.7	(0.6)	0.0	(0.0)	**2.1**	(0.8)	1.5	(1.6)
Austria	**-0.9**	(0.3)	c	c	**15.0**	(7.2)	-2.2	(6.0)	**3.3**	(1.2)	0.0	(0.1)	**-1.3**	(0.5)	-2.1	(2.7)
Belgium	**-1.5**	(0.2)	5.8	(3.9)	3.0	(3.9)	1.5	(4.0)	0.7	(1.5)	0.1	(0.0)	0.6	(1.1)	-4.0	(2.1)
Canada	**-1.0**	(0.2)	10.0	(6.0)	-3.2	(2.9)	-5.0	(6.9)	**1.8**	(0.6)	-0.1	(0.0)	0.6	(0.4)	2.2	(1.7)
Chile	**-0.7**	(0.2)	-0.3	(3.0)	6.1	(3.2)	-0.8	(3.1)	0.4	(0.7)	0.1	(0.0)	0.0	(0.3)	-0.3	(1.4)
Czech Republic	0.1	(0.5)	-5.4	(5.3)	11.5	(6.0)	2.1	(7.3)	3.3	(2.7)	0.0	(0.1)	-0.4	(0.8)	**-18.9**	(4.3)
Denmark	**-1.5**	(0.3)	-1.5	(3.6)	-4.6	(3.8)	2.0	(11.2)	0.5	(0.7)	-0.1	(0.1)	-0.1	(0.7)	-0.9	(2.9)
Estonia	**-1.3**	(0.5)	-9.8	(5.4)	4.2	(3.3)	**-17.8**	(10.5)	c	c	0.0	(0.0)	0.4	(0.8)	-3.6	(2.3)
Finland	**-1.1**	(0.4)	-4.3	(2.9)	**-11.7**	(8.2)	**-12.9**	(11.0)	0.6	(0.9)	0.1	(0.1)	-1.6	(1.0)	-0.2	(2.4)
France	**-1.2**	(0.1)	3.5	(3.9)			-8.0	(5.7)	**-1.3**	(0.5)	0.0	(0.1)	-1.1	(1.0)	-1.6	(2.3)
Germany	**-1.2**	(0.3)	-5.1	(4.5)	-5.9	(4.7)	-3.4	(8.3)	c	c	-0.1	(0.1)	-0.9	(0.5)	**-5.0**	(2.8)
Greece	-0.9	(0.5)	**-10.4**	(5.0)	6.1	(8.8)	4.8	(4.5)	-3.0	(2.1)	0.1	(0.1)	0.1	(1.2)	1.3	(3.2)
Hungary	**-0.7**	(0.2)	-2.2	(6.3)	**20.6**	(10.3)	**-16.7**	(6.2)	-2.0	(6.1)	0.0	(0.1)	-0.3	(0.6)	4.9	(3.7)
Iceland	1.0	(1.6)	8.7	(6.9)	9.9	(5.3)	-1.5	(20.5)	0.8	(0.9)	0.1	(0.1)	0.0	(1.8)	0.1	(2.9)
Ireland	**-0.6**	(0.3)	10.6	(9.3)	**9.2**	(3.8)	11.6	(10.3)	-0.7	(11.4)	-0.1	(0.1)	1.1	(0.7)	-2.7	(2.0)
Israel	0.0	(0.8)	**24.3**	(10.0)	**13.3**	(6.4)	**-13.8**	(6.7)	2.1	(1.4)	0.1	(0.1)	-0.1	(1.4)	-0.3	(2.6)
Italy	**-1.0**	(0.4)	**-7.6**	(3.1)	2.9	(2.8)	0.4	(3.4)	**-2.0**	(1.0)	**0.1**	(0.1)	**1.5**	(0.5)	-0.5	(1.5)
Japan	c	c	**-15.0**	(5.4)	**-25.9**	(10.9)	-6.2	(10.7)	13.5	(60.6)	-0.1	(0.1)	-0.1	(1.3)	2.8	(2.8)
Korea	-0.5	(0.5)	-10.8	(8.8)	0.7	(5.6)	-6.4	(5.8)	5.0	(9.9)	0.1	(0.1)	-0.6	(0.7)	-2.5	(2.9)
Luxembourg	c	c	c	c	c	c	c	c	c	c	c	c	c	c	c	c
Mexico	**-0.5**	(0.1)	-0.6	(2.1)	4.0	(2.2)	-3.0	(2.4)	0.4	(0.5)	0.0	(0.0)	0.0	(0.0)	0.8	(1.2)
Netherlands	**-1.8**	(0.3)	**-18.5**	(7.9)	-0.9	(13.3)	0.9	(8.3)	2.7	(1.7)	0.1	(0.1)	0.4	(1.1)	0.6	(3.3)
New Zealand	-0.4	(0.5)	**-40.4**	(16.3)	-5.9	(4.7)	5.5	(7.2)	-1.1	(1.7)	-0.1	(0.1)	0.4	(0.8)	-2.8	(1.8)
Norway	c	c	2.6	(3.9)	-7.8	(7.8)	**-50.3**	(11.8)	c	c	0.1	(0.1)	**-2.9**	(1.2)	-1.6	(2.3)
Poland	-1.0	(0.9)	-4.4	(4.3)	**12.2**	(5.9)	**15.2**	(10.1)	0.2	(0.9)	0.1	(0.1)	**2.9**	(1.0)	7.9	(9.0)
Portugal	**-1.4**	(0.2)	-1.2	(4.1)	-2.3	(3.9)	-5.2	(9.9)	0.4	(0.4)	0.1	(0.1)	0.3	(0.9)	-1.8	(2.9)
Slovak Republic	0.2	(0.3)	-5.9	(5.6)	**22.1**	(8.4)	-0.1	(6.2)	-0.7	(2.2)	0.0	(0.1)	-1.2	(0.9)	-6.1	(3.7)
Slovenia	-1.0	(1.3)	-4.7	(4.1)	-2.2	(5.3)	2.2	(4.7)	**3.3**	(1.2)	0.0	(0.0)	-0.7	(0.9)	**-8.6**	(3.5)
Spain	**-0.9**	(0.3)	-4.6	(5.8)	**-12.1**	(6.4)	3.2	(6.3)	-0.2	(0.8)	0.1	(0.1)	0.2	(0.1)	-1.3	(2.0)
Sweden	-0.6	(0.4)	-5.8	(4.6)	1.1	(8.0)	2.8	(9.0)	-0.3	(0.5)	0.1	(0.1)	-0.1	(0.8)	-3.6	(2.5)
Switzerland	**-1.4**	(0.2)	-10.5	(6.0)	3.2	(3.7)	4.5	(6.6)	**1.2**	(0.4)	**0.1**	(0.1)	0.0	(0.6)	**-6.1**	(2.2)
Turkey	-0.8	(0.5)	**-19.2**	(6.5)	**20.5**	(5.2)	-9.3	(5.3)	-1.0	(1.3)	0.0	(0.1)	0.1	(0.4)	-0.6	(2.8)
United Kingdom	**-2.2**	(0.6)	**25.3**	(11.0)	**9.1**	(4.5)	**-16.6**	(5.7)	-1.3	(0.7)	-0.1	(0.0)	1.0	(1.1)	-3.2	(2.4)
United States	**-1.4**	(0.3)	11.9	(11.3)	-6.1	(3.9)	-0.8	(12.8)	1.6	(4.4)	0.0	(0.1)	0.1	(0.1)	-2.7	(2.3)
OECD average	**-0.9**	(0.1)	**-2.8**	(1.3)	**2.9**	(1.1)	**-3.4**	(1.5)	0.9	(2.1)	**0.0**	(0.0)	0.1	(0.2)	**-1.8**	(0.5)
Partners																
Albania	0.7	(0.9)	c	c	8.2	(5.3)	0.0	(5.8)	-0.1	(1.4)	0.0	(0.1)	c	c	-0.6	(2.5)
Argentina	**-0.8**	(0.2)	4.2	(5.8)	-0.5	(5.3)	2.8	(7.0)	0.7	(1.2)	**0.1**	(0.1)	0.1	(0.2)	-1.5	(2.8)
Brazil	**-0.9**	(0.1)	-6.3	(4.0)	1.2	(3.6)	4.9	(3.8)	-0.2	(0.8)	0.0	(0.0)	**-0.2**	(0.1)	-0.2	(1.7)
Bulgaria	-0.7	(0.5)	**-30.4**	(11.4)	8.3	(6.2)	-0.7	(4.5)	c	c	0.2	(0.1)	0.1	(0.1)	8.1	(4.9)
Colombia	-0.7	(0.2)	-1.3	(8.1)	-6.6	(3.8)	4.4	(5.5)	0.4	(0.8)	0.0	(0.1)	-0.4	(0.2)	2.4	(1.5)
Costa Rica	**-1.0**	(0.2)	-1.2	(3.9)	-7.1	(4.0)	3.4	(4.3)	-0.8	(1.1)	0.0	(0.1)	**0.4**	(0.1)	1.4	(2.4)
Croatia	-0.9	(0.7)	1.1	(9.2)	**27.2**	(9.3)	2.9	(6.2)	1.6	(2.9)	0.0	(0.1)	-1.0	(1.0)	0.2	(3.2)
Cyprus*	**-1.9**	(0.2)	**-10.7**	(4.8)	-5.3	(7.1)	0.1	(5.2)	-2.3	(1.4)	0.1	(0.1)	**14.7**	(2.3)	-0.5	(2.1)
Hong Kong-China	**-1.7**	(0.5)	-10.2	(7.1)	9.5	(10.3)	**-11.8**	(7.9)	-2.6	(3.1)	-0.1	(0.1)	**6.5**	(1.6)	2.4	(4.2)
Indonesia	-0.2	(0.2)	-5.9	(7.0)	-6.4	(6.0)	**-8.5**	(5.7)	-1.7	(1.6)	0.1	(0.1)	**-1.3**	(0.5)	-0.6	(3.5)
Jordan	**-1.5**	(0.4)	-4.0	(5.7)	1.2	(4.9)	3.6	(4.3)	1.1	(1.0)	0.0	(0.1)	0.1	(0.6)	1.0	(1.8)
Kazakhstan	-0.4	(0.5)	5.7	(14.1)	4.2	(5.8)	**-17.4**	(5.9)	-0.9	(0.9)	-0.1	(0.1)	**2.0**	(0.9)	3.1	(2.6)
Latvia	-0.3	(0.4)	2.7	(5.6)	9.1	(4.8)	2.6	(6.0)	-0.4	(0.6)	0.0	(0.0)	0.7	(1.4)	-3.1	(2.8)
Lithuania	**-1.2**	(0.5)	6.5	(5.7)	6.9	(5.2)	**-21.3**	(12.1)	0.3	(1.0)	0.1	(0.0)	-0.1	(0.2)	6.6	(3.6)
Macao-China	c	c	c	c	c	c	c	c	c	c	c	c	c	c	c	c
Malaysia	c	c	-3.1	(8.5)	1.9	(4.0)	-2.5	(4.5)	0.5	(0.9)	**0.1**	(0.0)	-0.7	(0.7)	3.5	(3.0)
Montenegro	c	c	c	c	c	c	c	c	c	c	c	c	c	c	c	c
Peru	-0.4	(0.2)	-7.4	(6.0)	6.1	(5.0)	3.9	(4.9)	**-2.1**	(1.1)	0.1	(0.1)	0.0	(0.3)	1.0	(2.5)
Qatar	-0.8	(0.3)	11.8	(11.2)	3.9	(5.9)	**-14.5**	(9.0)	**10.6**	(4.0)	0.2	(0.1)	**-0.7**	(0.2)	-4.6	(4.3)
Romania	-0.1	(0.4)	-16.4	(8.8)	1.2	(4.6)	-3.9	(6.1)	**-7.5**	(3.3)	-0.1	(0.0)	**1.0**	(0.4)	-7.4	(4.1)
Russian Federation	-0.7	(0.9)	2.0	(10.4)	9.4	(5.8)	-5.3	(9.2)	3.4	(2.1)	-0.1	(0.1)	-1.6	(1.0)	1.4	(2.8)
Serbia	**-2.9**	(1.5)	-12.6	(13.7)	-10.5	(9.5)	-3.7	(7.5)	1.2	(1.3)	0.0	(0.1)	-0.7	(1.0)	-6.1	(5.4)
Shanghai-China	**-1.2**	(0.4)	-0.4	(11.1)	11.6	(6.1)	-9.4	(9.2)	-2.0	(3.3)	-0.1	(0.1)	1.0	(0.7)	-4.1	(2.3)
Singapore	0.0	(0.8)	-9.9	(13.7)	0.8	(5.3)	**19.9**	(14.5)	**13.0**	(5.7)	0.1	(0.1)	-1.3	(0.6)	-0.5	(3.0)
Chinese Taipei	**-7.0**	(2.1)	8.0	(6.5)	**20.3**	(5.8)	-0.8	(5.9)	-0.2	(1.1)	**-0.3**	(0.1)	-0.8	(0.7)	-2.5	(3.3)
Thailand	0.3	(0.8)	-9.1	(6.2)	-4.0	(7.2)	-7.1	(5.7)	**22.7**	(11.6)	0.1	(0.1)	-0.8	(0.4)	7.3	(3.2)
Tunisia	**-1.1**	(0.2)	-7.9	(6.4)	0.5	(5.7)	1.2	(5.8)	2.8	(1.6)	0.0	(0.1)	-0.1	(0.1)	-3.8	(2.9)
United Arab Emirates	-0.5	(0.2)	16.5	(5.5)	0.1	(4.0)	-5.4	(4.5)	**3.9**	(1.2)	0.0	(0.0)	-0.1	(0.4)	1.8	(1.5)
Uruguay	**-0.8**	(0.2)	1.2	(7.1)	-4.8	(5.4)	-12.8	(11.5)	2.4	(2.1)	0.0	(0.0)	**-0.7**	(0.3)	2.2	(2.7)
Viet Nam	**-1.0**	(0.4)	7.2	(11.7)	6.1	(8.4)	5.0	(6.7)	1.7	(1.0)	0.0	(0.1)	**-1.7**	(0.8)	1.4	(2.8)

Note: Values that are statistically significant are indicated in bold (see Annex A3).
1. Multilevel regression model (student and school levels): Mathematics performance is regressed on all the variables presented in this table.
* See notes at the beginning of this Annex.
StatLink http://dx.doi.org/10.1787/888932957384

[Part 2/5]

Relationship among mathematics performance, the school's learning environment, resources, policies and practices, and student and school characteristics

Table IV.1.12c

| | Resources invested in education at the school level[1] | | | | | | | | | | | | | | | |
| | Index of quality of schools' educational resources (higher values indicate better resources) | | Index of quality of physical infrastructure (higher values indicate better resources) | | School average of students' learning time per week in regular school mathematics lessons (minutes) | | Percentage of students who attended pre-primary education for more than one year (10% increase) | | School average of students' hours per week spent on homework or other study set by teachers, all school subjects combined (hours) | | School offering mathematics lessons in addition to those offered during regular school hours (1=yes, 0=no) | | Index of creative extracurricular activities at school | | Index of extracurricular mathematics activities at school | |
	Change in score	S.E.	Change in score	S.E.	Change in score	S.E.	Change in score	S.E.	Change in score	S.E.	Change in score	S.E.	Change in score	S.E.	Change in score	S.E.
OECD																
Australia	3.1	(2.0)	-3.7	(2.0)	0.1	(0.1)	**3.6**	(0.8)	0.4	(0.8)	7.0	(4.0)	1.4	(1.6)	-2.7	(1.8)
Austria	4.3	(2.9)	-1.8	(2.4)	0.0	(0.1)	1.5	(2.0)	1.1	(2.9)	7.3	(6.5)	3.2	(3.3)	2.0	(3.1)
Belgium	-0.4	(2.1)	-0.3	(2.1)	0.4	(0.1)	2.9	(1.6)	2.0	(2.8)	1.4	(4.4)	-2.3	(1.9)	1.6	(2.6)
Canada	-1.8	(1.7)	1.1	(2.0)	**-0.1**	(0.0)	0.5	(0.9)	1.5	(0.9)	3.4	(3.4)	-2.6	(2.4)	0.8	(1.3)
Chile	-2.6	(1.6)	-0.2	(1.4)	-0.1	(0.0)	**3.1**	(1.4)	-2.2	(1.2)	-2.5	(3.8)	-0.4	(1.7)	2.3	(1.4)
Czech Republic	0.3	(3.5)	-5.0	(4.0)	0.1	(0.1)	-1.8	(1.0)	3.5	(2.1)	6.9	(7.8)	-0.2	(2.7)	-1.0	(2.8)
Denmark	0.7	(2.4)	1.0	(1.9)	0.0	(0.1)	-1.1	(1.5)	1.7	(1.6)	1.7	(3.9)	**-3.6**	(1.8)	-1.6	(2.5)
Estonia	-1.6	(2.5)	-2.0	(1.7)	0.2	(0.2)	-1.7	(1.0)	0.8	(2.1)	-6.2	(5.3)	**4.1**	(2.1)	-1.4	(1.8)
Finland	-1.6	(1.6)	-0.7	(1.5)	-0.2	(0.1)	-1.3	(2.1)	1.0	(1.3)	-1.4	(4.3)	-0.9	(1.6)	0.8	(1.7)
France	-1.5	(2.6)	-2.7	(2.4)	0.3	(0.1)	-0.7	(1.5)	**6.0**	(3.0)	-11.2	(5.9)	-3.7	(2.5)	**7.7**	(2.4)
Germany	1.6	(3.3)	-0.6	(2.8)	0.0	(0.1)	2.8	(2.2)	**12.0**	(2.7)	7.9	(6.4)	2.9	(3.3)	3.0	(2.3)
Greece	-4.4	(2.9)	2.7	(2.9)	**1.6**	(0.5)	**4.4**	(1.5)	3.0	(1.6)	-2.1	(9.1)	0.1	(1.8)	4.2	(3.4)
Hungary	5.0	(3.1)	-0.6	(3.4)	0.1	(0.1)	2.7	(1.7)	0.3	(4.9)	-0.8	(8.1)	1.1	(2.7)	-0.5	(2.1)
Iceland	-0.4	(3.8)	-5.5	(4.1)	-0.1	(0.2)	-4.1	(1.7)	1.9	(5.5)	7.5	(5.7)	5.4	(3.4)	-2.6	(1.9)
Ireland	1.5	(1.9)	-2.0	(1.4)	0.0	(0.2)	**2.8**	(1.0)	-1.3	(1.5)	1.1	(4.6)	2.5	(2.0)	-0.2	(1.7)
Israel	-1.1	(3.4)	0.4	(3.2)	0.2	(0.1)	-1.9	(1.9)	**9.2**	(2.0)	-9.2	(9.5)	**5.8**	(2.7)	-0.8	(2.8)
Italy	-0.8	(1.6)	2.6	(1.4)	0.4	(0.1)	0.5	(0.7)	**8.3**	(1.5)	-2.4	(5.0)	2.6	(1.5)	1.7	(1.7)
Japan	-1.6	(3.0)	-1.6	(3.4)	0.2	(0.1)	1.6	(1.9)	**13.4**	(6.6)	**-17.7**	(8.0)	3.0	(3.6)	**8.0**	(3.1)
Korea	3.8	(4.3)	-2.9	(3.9)	**0.3**	(0.1)	**5.6**	(1.4)	3.3	(2.0)	-3.0	(9.2)	2.9	(3.5)	0.1	(3.4)
Luxembourg	c	c	c	c	c	c	c	c	c	c	c	c	c	c	c	c
Mexico	0.0	(1.3)	1.2	(1.4)	0.1	(0.0)	**1.5**	(0.7)	1.3	(0.7)	2.7	(3.0)	-0.7	(1.1)	0.3	(0.9)
Netherlands	-1.1	(3.6)	0.0	(3.9)	0.0	(0.2)	**7.7**	(1.5)	-1.0	(4.9)	0.3	(6.1)	-5.6	(3.2)	2.2	(3.6)
New Zealand	1.6	(2.6)	-2.9	(2.6)	0.0	(0.1)	**4.0**	(1.5)	**3.6**	(1.7)	10.9	(7.7)	5.1	(4.0)	2.1	(2.2)
Norway	-5.4	(3.4)	0.2	(2.7)	0.2	(0.1)	2.3	(1.8)	0.3	(2.1)	-2.7	(5.0)	-2.0	(2.5)	2.3	(2.7)
Poland	-2.6	(2.6)	-3.0	(2.8)	0.1	(0.2)	1.6	(1.4)	2.1	(1.4)	6.0	(8.0)	1.8	(3.8)	-5.2	(3.1)
Portugal	4.0	(2.3)	-3.3	(2.2)	0.0	(0.0)	2.9	(1.9)	**3.2**	(1.3)	1.7	(6.0)	**-5.4**	(2.1)	3.8	(2.3)
Slovak Republic	-4.3	(4.5)	3.3	(3.0)	0.2	(0.1)	-0.3	(1.4)	0.3	(2.3)	-9.7	(7.9)	0.3	(2.4)	3.5	(3.1)
Slovenia	-0.2	(3.1)	-4.6	(2.7)	0.4	(0.2)	**-3.5**	(1.3)	1.5	(1.4)	-0.6	(5.4)	4.1	(2.5)	2.1	(2.2)
Spain	1.0	(1.6)	-0.5	(1.6)	-0.1	(0.1)	0.5	(0.9)	1.4	(1.2)	0.0	(3.1)	-1.3	(1.4)	1.4	(1.5)
Sweden	-5.1	(3.0)	2.5	(2.6)	-0.1	(0.1)	-1.5	(1.6)	-0.3	(1.6)	-3.8	(5.4)	2.0	(2.1)	4.4	(2.4)
Switzerland	-2.3	(2.4)	3.0	(2.9)	0.0	(0.1)	-1.6	(1.5)	-1.2	(0.8)	**-11.9**	(4.6)	-1.1	(2.0)	**8.4**	(2.4)
Turkey	1.8	(4.0)	**-13.4**	(3.2)	**0.9**	(0.1)	2.5	(1.6)	6.1	(4.5)	-8.3	(7.1)	-1.4	(2.7)	**7.0**	(2.8)
United Kingdom	1.2	(2.3)	-2.0	(2.8)	-0.1	(0.1)	**4.3**	(1.2)	**5.4**	(1.4)	**-17.7**	(7.0)	0.3	(3.1)	-3.1	(1.9)
United States	-2.9	(3.1)	3.7	(4.1)	0.1	(0.1)	-0.3	(1.4)	1.1	(2.4)	0.1	(5.0)	6.6	(4.7)	2.9	(2.0)
OECD average	-0.4	(0.5)	**-1.1**	(0.5)	**0.2**	(0.0)	**1.2**	(0.3)	**2.7**	(0.5)	-1.4	(1.1)	0.7	(0.5)	**1.6**	(0.4)
Partners																
Albania	3.6	(3.2)	-0.5	(2.9)	0.2	(0.2)	-1.1	(1.5)	2.1	(1.7)	5.3	(6.4)	5.3	(3.1)	-3.0	(2.0)
Argentina	0.1	(2.4)	-1.9	(2.3)	**0.2**	(0.1)	0.6	(1.3)	1.3	(1.5)	-3.6	(5.9)	1.8	(1.9)	-0.1	(1.9)
Brazil	3.0	(1.6)	-1.2	(1.6)	**-0.2**	(0.1)	-0.8	(1.2)	1.8	(1.0)	-3.0	(4.6)	0.9	(2.1)	2.5	(2.3)
Bulgaria	-2.3	(3.8)	-1.2	(2.8)	0.0	(0.1)	**3.1**	(1.5)	-2.3	(2.2)	-6.0	(7.3)	-3.1	(2.6)	1.6	(2.6)
Colombia	3.0	(2.3)	-0.3	(1.9)	0.1	(0.1)	2.0	(1.1)	-0.3	(1.7)	-0.7	(4.3)	1.0	(2.1)	1.4	(1.7)
Costa Rica	**5.3**	(2.2)	0.2	(2.2)	-0.2	(0.1)	2.3	(1.5)	0.5	(1.5)	-0.9	(5.1)	1.3	(2.6)	-2.4	(1.9)
Croatia	-0.9	(3.5)	**6.0**	(2.8)	**0.5**	(0.1)	1.8	(1.7)	1.0	(1.8)	**-20.5**	(7.7)	0.5	(2.1)	2.8	(2.4)
Cyprus*	**9.0**	(3.5)	-6.8	(3.8)	-0.5	(0.5)	**10.5**	(2.4)	-0.8	(2.3)	**16.5**	(6.2)	-0.1	(5.2)	**-6.6**	(3.0)
Hong Kong-China	-4.7	(4.1)	9.2	(4.9)	-0.3	(0.2)	**7.6**	(2.2)	**19.8**	(5.3)	-8.0	(15.9)	-5.5	(6.2)	3.1	(4.5)
Indonesia	3.7	(3.2)	-4.1	(3.8)	0.1	(0.1)	1.6	(2.1)	**3.5**	(1.4)	**-13.9**	(6.7)	6.4	(3.4)	3.5	(2.5)
Jordan	2.3	(3.1)	**-4.9**	(2.3)	-0.2	(0.2)	**-3.2**	(1.4)	1.0	(2.0)	-8.1	(5.1)	**5.2**	(2.5)	0.5	(1.5)
Kazakhstan	-1.7	(3.4)	3.2	(3.8)	**0.3**	(0.1)	-0.6	(1.7)	0.1	(1.5)	-11.9	(11.9)	-2.3	(2.9)	-0.5	(2.8)
Latvia	-1.6	(3.1)	4.9	(2.8)	0.2	(0.1)	0.1	(1.1)	0.6	(1.7)	4.9	(8.0)	4.6	(3.2)	-0.8	(2.8)
Lithuania	2.3	(3.2)	-0.4	(2.6)	**0.5**	(0.2)	1.8	(1.2)	0.4	(1.4)	-6.9	(6.2)	-2.8	(3.0)	0.9	(2.2)
Macao-China	c	c	c	c	c	c	c	c	c	c	c	c	c	c	c	c
Malaysia	0.1	(2.7)	1.0	(2.3)	**0.2**	(0.1)	**4.5**	(1.6)	1.9	(1.4)	-9.1	(8.6)	-0.9	(2.7)	-1.5	(2.4)
Montenegro	c	c	c	c	c	c	c	c	c	c	c	c	c	c	c	c
Peru	2.3	(2.5)	-3.3	(2.0)	0.2	(0.1)	-1.7	(1.1)	-1.7	(1.2)	-0.2	(5.2)	2.6	(2.2)	-0.3	(1.9)
Qatar	**10.5**	(3.0)	**-17.7**	(3.0)	-0.5	(0.3)	**-11.7**	(4.1)	2.1	(3.4)	**29.2**	(9.2)	**15.7**	(4.2)	**-6.8**	(2.9)
Romania	**7.4**	(3.6)	**-8.7**	(4.3)	0.1	(0.1)	**6.0**	(1.5)	1.4	(2.7)	4.2	(5.6)	-2.0	(3.0)	0.4	(2.4)
Russian Federation	1.8	(4.0)	-3.5	(3.0)	0.2	(0.1)	0.1	(1.1)	1.5	(1.5)	-21.0	(12.8)	2.4	(2.6)	3.8	(2.8)
Serbia	-6.3	(4.1)	4.8	(3.5)	0.2	(0.2)	4.9	(2.6)	**5.5**	(1.7)	5.6	(11.1)	0.6	(3.4)	**7.8**	(2.7)
Shanghai-China	-2.5	(2.7)	-1.6	(3.0)	**-0.3**	(0.1)	**8.3**	(1.6)	**-7.4**	(2.3)	-3.6	(6.4)	0.0	(3.0)	4.7	(2.4)
Singapore	0.4	(3.2)	-5.4	(3.7)	**0.3**	(0.1)	-0.5	(1.7)	**15.6**	(5.1)	-15.5	(8.2)	2.4	(4.0)	-1.3	(3.0)
Chinese Taipei	2.2	(3.4)	**-8.4**	(3.6)	**0.4**	(0.1)	4.2	(2.2)	3.4	(3.5)	-11.1	(9.2)	2.6	(2.9)	2.9	(2.9)
Thailand	3.1	(3.2)	1.7	(2.9)	0.0	(0.1)	**7.1**	(1.3)	-1.4	(3.0)	10.2	(10.6)	-2.5	(4.0)	-0.6	(3.6)
Tunisia	-4.2	(3.4)	-4.4	(3.1)	0.1	(0.1)	-3.6	(1.7)	-1.7	(2.3)	-1.0	(7.4)	4.0	(3.4)	-0.6	(2.1)
United Arab Emirates	2.3	(2.1)	-1.9	(1.8)	**-0.1**	(0.0)	1.3	(0.9)	**4.2**	(1.1)	**-10.9**	(4.4)	**5.3**	(2.3)	1.8	(1.7)
Uruguay	-2.1	(2.0)	**5.0**	(1.8)	0.1	(0.1)	2.1	(1.7)	**3.1**	(1.4)	4.6	(6.5)	**4.1**	(2.1)	2.8	(2.1)
Viet Nam	-2.9	(4.3)	2.2	(3.7)	0.0	(0.1)	**6.4**	(1.7)	2.6	(1.8)	-8.3	(14.3)	**7.8**	(3.5)	-6.0	(3.2)

Note: Values that are statistically significant are indicated in bold (see Annex A3).
1. Multilevel regression model (student and school levels): Mathematics performance is regressed on all the variables presented in this table.
* See notes at the beginning of this Annex.
StatLink http://dx.doi.org/10.1787/888932957384

[Part 3/5]

Table IV.1.12c **Relationship among mathematics performance, the school's learning environment, resources, policies and practices, and student and school characteristics**

	School governance[1]																			
	Index of school responsibility for resource allocation (higher values indicate more autonomy)		Index of school responsibility for curriculum and assessment (higher values indicate more autonomy)		School competes with other schools for students in the same area		Private school		Index of school management: Instructional leadership		Index of school management: Teacher participation		Index of school management: Promoting instructional improvements and professional development		Index of school management: Framing and communicating the school's goals and curricular development		Use the same textbook in all mathematics classes for 15-year-olds (in the modal grade)		Mathematics teachers in the school follow a standardised curriculum that specifies content to be taught every month (at least)	
	Change in score	S.E.	Change in score	S.E.	Change in score	S.E.	Change in score	S.E.	Change in score	S.E.	Change in score	S.E.	Change in score	S.E.	Change in score	S.E.	Change in score	S.E.	Change in score	S.E.
OECD																				
Australia	-2.1	(1.7)	-3.0	(1.7)	-12.2	(8.2)	0.8	(5.1)	-1.7	(3.0)	**4.5**	(2.3)	**-3.8**	(1.9)	-3.3	(2.1)	1.7	(3.0)	5.9	(5.0)
Austria	-3.8	(4.5)	-4.4	(2.9)	-4.7	(5.2)	6.8	(16.4)	2.4	(4.0)	2.8	(4.2)	-2.7	(3.1)	-3.4	(3.9)	-4.7	(7.4)	-1.6	(5.5)
Belgium	13.5	(9.8)	2.1	(2.2)	4.8	(7.6)	w	w	2.7	(2.6)	-2.0	(2.3)	-1.8	(2.3)	0.7	(2.2)	-1.5	(3.6)	-2.2	(4.4)
Canada	**7.2**	(2.9)	2.4	(2.4)	1.1	(3.6)	10.7	(8.8)	-3.9	(2.1)	-1.8	(2.1)	-0.1	(1.9)	3.3	(1.7)	0.7	(3.0)	**-8.1**	(4.0)
Chile	**4.4**	(1.3)	-0.5	(1.4)	2.0	(4.9)	-10.6	(6.0)	-0.3	(2.9)	3.2	(2.0)	**-5.0**	(2.2)	0.2	(2.1)	-4.8	(6.8)	-7.4	(5.1)
Czech Republic	-3.8	(2.0)	2.8	(3.0)	**21.6**	(7.9)	-2.2	(20.8)	1.6	(3.3)	2.4	(2.6)	-5.0	(3.0)	-5.1	(5.1)	-5.3	(8.2)	**-39.8**	(15.3)
Denmark	-1.7	(1.7)	0.8	(1.8)	8.6	(5.5)	-12.5	(8.7)	-0.6	(2.6)	-0.6	(2.4)	3.1	(1.9)	2.5	(2.1)	-3.2	(4.2)	1.2	(3.3)
Estonia	-2.6	(2.2)	-2.7	(1.7)	**9.2**	(4.4)	-29.6	(16.1)	0.8	(3.1)	-0.4	(2.6)	1.7	(2.8)	-0.9	(2.3)	**-11.9**	(5.9)	0.5	(5.8)
Finland	2.9	(2.2)	**4.7**	(1.6)	1.1	(2.9)	c	c	**-4.8**	(2.0)	-2.3	(1.8)	-0.7	(2.3)	2.9	(2.0)	-7.2	(4.9)	-1.2	(3.1)
France	**-20.2**	(7.3)	1.1	(2.4)	0.0	(4.4)	c	c	-1.9	(2.5)	4.0	(3.1)	-1.8	(3.2)	-1.9	(3.4)	**22.7**	(7.4)	4.4	(4.0)
Germany	**-66.5**	(15.6)	-2.0	(2.7)	-0.2	(6.0)	-24.5	(19.0)	2.6	(4.6)	-1.4	(3.8)	-5.9	(4.0)	**11.2**	(3.1)	2.2	(5.9)	-2.5	(5.0)
Greece	-11.9	(19.5)	-1.9	(9.4)	4.8	(5.9)	-11.3	(23.9)	5.8	(3.5)	-4.8	(3.1)	-0.6	(3.0)	-3.5	(2.8)	4.2	(17.4)	7.0	(5.8)
Hungary	-1.4	(2.1)	-3.6	(2.7)	7.0	(5.6)	c	c	6.1	(5.1)	-6.1	(4.3)	-2.2	(4.0)	1.0	(5.4)	-5.7	(7.1)	-11.9	(6.6)
Iceland	-2.4	(4.4)	2.6	(3.0)	-4.6	(5.9)	c	c	3.5	(5.0)	-5.2	(5.8)	0.1	(3.9)	-0.3	(4.6)	**16.3**	(5.0)	-4.3	(7.0)
Ireland	-2.9	(7.4)	1.1	(1.9)	-5.6	(4.4)	**-20.5**	(10.0)	-2.4	(2.3)	0.0	(2.3)	-1.6	(2.1)	3.3	(2.0)	-3.0	(3.6)	5.6	(5.6)
Israel	-7.6	(6.8)	4.7	(2.8)	9.3	(5.3)	c	c	0.7	(4.4)	-2.8	(3.2)	-1.4	(3.8)	0.5	(4.2)	**-18.1**	(6.5)	12.2	(9.4)
Italy	1.5	(2.2)	-0.3	(1.4)	1.1	(2.8)	**20.4**	(8.6)	-0.4	(2.8)	0.2	(2.0)	2.3	(1.8)	**-4.7**	(2.0)	-1.0	(2.8)	-2.3	(2.7)
Japan	8.0	(6.5)	4.3	(3.4)	-13.2	(7.9)	**46.9**	(10.1)	3.2	(4.1)	-5.1	(3.4)	1.3	(3.5)	1.5	(4.5)	-4.0	(6.6)	**17.6**	(8.0)
Korea	-0.9	(4.1)	0.7	(2.3)	2.8	(7.9)	-12.8	(6.7)	-7.2	(5.2)	-0.8	(3.2)	5.5	(5.2)	-1.8	(4.2)	-9.0	(6.7)	0.1	(6.8)
Luxembourg	c	c	c	c	c	c	c	c	c	c	c	c	c	c	c	c	c	c	c	c
Mexico	3.1	(1.9)	1.8	(2.3)	-3.6	(3.3)	**17.1**	(6.5)	-1.6	(1.7)	-0.4	(1.2)	0.4	(1.3)	1.5	(1.6)	-2.9	(2.4)	-1.2	(6.2)
Netherlands	0.6	(2.4)	-3.6	(3.6)	12.1	(9.2)	c	c	**12.3**	(4.1)	4.5	(4.3)	-2.6	(3.0)	**-9.5**	(3.5)	-2.0	(5.1)	4.4	(11.5)
New Zealand	-5.2	(3.1)	-1.7	(2.4)	**-13.7**	(6.3)	-12.5	(11.6)	-1.3	(3.6)	-6.0	(3.4)	6.2	(3.3)	-0.6	(3.7)	9.2	(5.0)	-2.0	(5.4)
Norway	3.4	(4.3)	-0.7	(3.6)	1.7	(4.7)	c	c	-2.5	(3.8)	5.0	(3.3)	3.9	(3.7)	-2.6	(3.3)	2.4	(5.7)	-5.4	(6.5)
Poland	-2.5	(5.3)	1.5	(2.8)	0.9	(5.4)	-0.1	(18.1)	2.4	(3.3)	-0.3	(3.6)	-1.7	(2.9)	-0.2	(3.8)	15.2	(10.2)	**18.6**	(7.1)
Portugal	1.1	(4.4)	**-11.7**	(3.9)	0.1	(5.5)	-1.0	(12.2)	-2.5	(2.7)	3.0	(2.9)	-2.9	(2.9)	1.5	(3.2)	14.9	(9.2)	-5.0	(8.7)
Slovak Republic	-2.2	(2.0)	0.7	(2.5)	-9.0	(7.2)	-7.0	(21.0)	7.8	(4.1)	1.1	(4.1)	**-14.8**	(4.4)	-5.3	(4.5)	-6.2	(6.0)	-4.7	(8.4)
Slovenia	-0.6	(3.4)	2.4	(2.8)	3.7	(4.8)	c	c	**-8.4**	(3.7)	**7.1**	(3.3)	1.4	(3.1)	-3.2	(3.2)	7.0	(4.6)	-13.3	(12.9)
Spain	**5.8**	(2.3)	-1.5	(2.2)	2.5	(4.2)	4.0	(4.7)	-2.3	(1.7)	0.7	(1.9)	-0.7	(1.5)	1.3	(2.3)	1.4	(2.7)	1.9	(5.1)
Sweden	1.3	(1.7)	-0.9	(2.4)	-5.9	(5.7)	c	c	-2.3	(3.4)	2.0	(3.6)	-2.7	(2.7)	-3.2	(3.6)	1.5	(4.8)	0.8	(4.1)
Switzerland	-1.5	(3.8)	0.1	(3.2)	-7.0	(4.0)	**75.8**	(11.3)	1.6	(2.4)	0.3	(2.7)	0.3	(2.6)	-3.4	(2.4)	**-15.1**	(4.4)	-5.1	(4.1)
Turkey	-46.5	(32.6)	-8.4	(8.0)	1.9	(6.5)	c	c	4.4	(3.9)	0.4	(3.6)	**-10.0**	(3.4)	-2.2	(4.8)	-8.8	(32.1)	7.7	(8.3)
United Kingdom	-0.4	(1.6)	0.0	(2.4)	-8.9	(7.5)	-1.6	(10.0)	4.2	(3.7)	-0.1	(3.0)	**-5.9**	(2.4)	-1.0	(2.5)	-5.3	(4.7)	**13.3**	(6.1)
United States	-3.6	(2.5)	-3.9	(2.8)	-10.5	(5.9)	**28.8**	(9.5)	0.6	(4.2)	3.7	(3.5)	0.0	(3.7)	**-9.0**	(3.9)	2.6	(4.6)	6.8	(9.2)
OECD average	**-4.2**	(1.4)	-0.5	(0.6)	-0.1	(1.0)	1.3	(2.7)	0.6	(0.6)	0.1	(0.6)	**-1.4**	(0.5)	-1.0	(0.6)	-0.5	(1.5)	-0.3	(1.2)
Partners																				
Albania	4.9	(4.9)	-0.4	(2.4)	4.3	(5.1)	3.2	(10.8)	-1.0	(4.2)	2.7	(2.9)	-4.3	(2.7)	1.0	(4.6)	8.9	(12.7)	-9.8	(14.5)
Argentina	c	c	-1.9	(3.6)	5.3	(6.4)	-5.6	(9.0)	2.9	(2.9)	-0.6	(2.0)	-1.4	(2.2)	-3.0	(2.8)	3.6	(4.2)	-4.1	(4.5)
Brazil	0.4	(3.9)	-0.2	(1.9)	0.3	(3.2)	-17.3	(12.0)	**-5.2**	(2.1)	3.5	(1.9)	0.5	(2.2)	**5.3**	(2.1)	3.9	(5.6)	-7.1	(5.9)
Bulgaria	**5.5**	(2.0)	-4.2	(6.7)	-6.5	(7.0)	26.6	(25.5)	-2.5	(4.3)	-1.1	(3.9)	-5.1	(3.2)	-1.3	(4.4)	-5.3	(10.8)	-6.1	(12.6)
Colombia	-1.3	(2.4)	2.8	(2.0)	-3.6	(5.9)	**-24.8**	(8.1)	**-7.3**	(2.9)	**6.7**	(2.0)	-1.3	(1.9)	-1.6	(2.3)	**-11.0**	(4.5)	**20.8**	(7.1)
Costa Rica	-4.1	(6.2)	**9.9**	(3.8)	2.4	(4.8)	16.0	(17.0)	4.7	(3.5)	**-6.2**	(2.6)	4.3	(3.0)	-3.3	(3.6)	-1.7	(3.8)	2.3	(7.9)
Croatia	-7.2	(9.1)	**-10.5**	(4.9)	-3.2	(4.6)	14.8	(28.8)	-0.7	(3.9)	3.1	(3.2)	-4.2	(2.7)	-1.3	(3.5)	**9.5**	(4.5)	-7.8	(6.7)
Cyprus*	**-13.8**	(4.7)	**20.2**	(6.3)	2.9	(4.9)	-5.9	(12.6)	5.6	(4.5)	-1.4	(3.2)	**8.1**	(4.1)	**-11.0**	(4.8)	-10.8	(12.8)	9.5	(8.8)
Hong Kong-China	-1.9	(4.6)	-0.8	(3.6)	23.2	(27.9)	41.4	(23.1)	-9.3	(5.7)	3.8	(5.1)	-0.2	(6.1)	0.4	(5.5)	3.1	(12.7)	2.6	(10.7)
Indonesia	**4.9**	(2.4)	-3.1	(2.7)	-9.3	(25.3)	**-17.6**	(8.1)	2.3	(6.4)	-0.7	(4.5)	3.0	(5.3)	-1.3	(6.2)	-6.7	(6.9)	1.6	(10.6)
Jordan	1.4	(6.3)	0.0	(5.1)	-2.0	(5.0)	-12.1	(8.5)	**-8.1**	(3.6)	**-6.0**	(2.4)	2.6	(3.0)	3.4	(2.7)	-16.9	(15.0)	-7.8	(8.7)
Kazakhstan	-0.1	(4.9)	-3.6	(5.0)	-6.9	(6.5)	18.5	(15.9)	**10.8**	(4.9)	2.8	(3.3)	-0.2	(2.6)	**-10.8**	(5.0)	3.4	(8.3)	4.1	(5.4)
Latvia	-0.1	(2.0)	**6.2**	(2.8)	**-24.4**	(6.3)	**40.5**	(14.3)	5.5	(3.3)	2.1	(3.5)	0.0	(2.6)	**-7.2**	(3.2)	-4.0	(20.2)	5.4	(9.4)
Lithuania	1.0	(1.7)	**-5.4**	(2.3)	**-13.2**	(5.2)	**85.4**	(18.3)	-2.9	(3.6)	-1.2	(2.6)	-4.6	(2.9)	3.5	(3.6)	-7.3	(6.1)	-1.7	(5.5)
Macao-China	c	c	c	c	c	c	c	c	c	c	c	c	c	c	c	c	c	c	c	c
Malaysia	2.4	(10.6)	-4.5	(3.7)	-4.1	(5.0)	-12.6	(33.7)	-5.1	(3.3)	**-6.1**	(2.9)	0.5	(3.2)	4.6	(2.7)	-4.1	(13.4)	10.0	(7.3)
Montenegro	c	c	c	c	c	c	c	c	c	c	c	c	c	c	c	c	c	c	c	c
Peru	2.1	(2.8)	2.0	(2.1)	4.1	(4.7)	-2.5	(9.0)	-3.2	(2.5)	5.0	(2.8)	-1.4	(2.5)	-2.2	(3.0)	7.9	(4.8)	1.0	(6.4)
Qatar	13.4	(9.1)	2.5	(6.1)	8.1	(6.8)	**-38.6**	(17.0)	-9.5	(5.2)	5.9	(4.3)	2.5	(3.8)	-1.7	(4.7)	15.4	(8.8)	-6.8	(15.3)
Romania	8.1	(6.6)	-0.8	(3.3)	-8.6	(4.8)	-19.9	(18.9)	0.4	(3.1)	1.8	(3.2)	-4.6	(2.7)	1.9	(3.0)	-5.4	(4.8)	**11.0**	(4.8)
Russian Federation	0.8	(3.1)	-5.2	(2.9)	-0.7	(7.2)	13.4	(23.3)	-1.9	(4.9)	1.2	(3.8)	-3.7	(3.6)	5.2	(4.9)	-9.9	(5.8)	-15.1	(8.7)
Serbia	15.2	(12.2)	6.1	(14.8)	9.1	(9.4)	75.9	(43.0)	-1.7	(4.4)	-2.8	(4.4)	3.3	(4.0)	-1.2	(5.0)	0.5	(6.0)	5.3	(7.2)
Shanghai-China	2.1	(3.9)	-4.5	(3.7)	1.6	(6.2)	-2.6	(11.6)	-5.3	(4.4)	2.6	(3.7)	0.2	(3.6)	-1.8	(4.1)	-0.3	(10.9)	-5.4	(11.0)
Singapore	-3.2	(4.9)	0.7	(2.7)	12.2	(16.4)	31.4	(20.7)	-6.8	(5.2)	-3.7	(3.8)	0.3	(3.7)	3.0	(3.9)	2.3	(4.8)	-7.9	(19.5)
Chinese Taipei	-3.8	(3.2)	1.3	(2.7)	-8.2	(11.0)	**24.2**	(9.4)	5.2	(6.0)	3.2	(4.6)	-9.4	(5.5)	-1.1	(3.5)	-3.9	(6.8)	-1.1	(6.0)
Thailand	0.8	(1.8)	**8.3**	(3.1)	2.3	(7.5)	-1.3	(13.9)	**9.7**	(4.7)	-1.4	(3.6)	3.2	(3.4)	**-10.7**	(4.3)	-2.8	(10.2)	-5.1	(5.9)
Tunisia	-2.6	(4.1)	2.9	(3.3)	-3.2	(6.1)	6.5	(24.7)	-2.9	(2.7)	-2.8	(2.8)	1.3	(2.8)	1.7	(2.9)	-3.7	(7.0)	-0.3	(5.3)
United Arab Emirates	3.4	(2.2)	1.8	(2.3)	-7.8	(5.4)	**24.6**	(6.5)	2.4	(3.5)	**-5.3**	(1.9)	-1.6	(1.9)	0.9	(2.7)	-10.8	(6.8)	10.1	(10.9)
Uruguay	-3.3	(5.9)	0.5	(4.4)	6.5	(3.9)	-3.1	(14.3)	-3.4	(2.4)	-0.7	(2.6)	1.2	(2.2)	-0.4	(2.3)	2.9	(3.8)	-1.6	(6.3)
Viet Nam	-1.3	(4.1)	0.8	(6.2)	-2.8	(6.4)	**32.9**	(12.0)	-2.6	(4.4)	-1.3	(4.2)	-0.1	(3.9)	9.1	(6.2)	1.4	(6.2)	**-27.2**	(13.7)

Note: Values that are statistically significant are indicated in bold (see Annex A3).

1. Multilevel regression model (student and school levels): Mathematics performance is regressed on all the variables presented in this table.

* See notes at the beginning of this Annex.

StatLink http://dx.doi.org/10.1787/888932957384

[Part 4/5]

Table IV.1.12c **Relationship among mathematics performance, the school's learning environment, resources, policies and practices, and student and school characteristics**

		Assessment and accountability policies[1]										Learning environment and school climate at the school level[1]											
		Index of assessment practices		Schools that post achievement data publicly		Schools in which an administrative authority tracks data over time		Schools that seek written feedback from students (e.g. regarding lessons, teachers or resources)		Schools that have teacher mentoring		School average index of teacher-student relations (higher values indicate better climate)		School average index of disciplinary climate (higher values indicate better climate)		Index of teacher-related factors affecting school climate (higher values indicate positive teacher behaviour)		Index of student-related factors affecting school climate (higher values indicate positive student behaviour)		Index of teacher morale (higher values indicate better teacher morale)		Percentage of students who did not arrive late for school in the two weeks prior to the PISA test (10% increase)		Percentage of students who did not skip a whole school day in the two weeks prior to the PISA test (10% increase)	
		Change in score	S.E.	Change in score	S.E.	Change in score	S.E.	Change in score	S.E.	Change in score	S.E.	Change in score	S.E.	Change in score	S.E.	Change in score	S.E.	Change in score	S.E.	Change in score	S.E.	Change in score	S.E.	Change in score	S.E.
OECD	Australia	-1.0	(1.2)	2.8	(3.1)	5.3	(4.4)	-2.4	(3.2)	-5.0	(4.9)	8.8	(7.5)	**26.9**	(5.9)	-0.5	(2.1)	2.8	(2.4)	-3.2	(1.8)	1.9	(1.0)	**3.6**	(1.0)
	Austria	-1.9	(2.1)	4.5	(9.7)	3.4	(5.8)	8.0	(6.6)	3.9	(7.3)	**36.2**	(10.9)	**36.0**	(9.0)	-2.4	(3.4)	3.7	(2.8)	**-9.7**	(3.6)	1.6	(2.0)	0.4	(3.5)
	Belgium	-1.1	(1.5)	11.0	(15.6)	3.1	(3.5)	5.9	(3.8)	6.4	(5.5)	-6.6	(9.0)	**28.2**	(7.5)	2.9	(2.7)	2.1	(2.2)	-2.7	(2.4)	**4.6**	(1.7)	**9.5**	(3.1)
	Canada	-2.5	(1.6)	**5.9**	(2.7)	-0.8	(4.6)	3.7	(2.9)	**-8.3**	(4.2)	-10.6	(6.7)	**23.2**	(6.7)	-3.2	(2.0)	**8.9**	(2.0)	**3.7**	(1.7)	**4.3**	(1.0)	**4.8**	(1.2)
	Chile	1.9	(1.4)	-3.0	(2.8)	-0.6	(3.7)	**-7.3**	(3.1)	5.1	(3.8)	-1.7	(6.9)	**13.2**	(5.4)	**5.3**	(2.3)	-1.3	(1.8)	1.1	(1.8)	**4.8**	(1.1)	**4.8**	(2.3)
	Czech Republic	1.2	(1.7)	0.8	(4.7)	0.8	(5.2)	-3.6	(5.4)	0.9	(10.3)	-5.6	(11.3)	**29.3**	(6.7)	-3.9	(4.2)	4.6	(3.7)	-5.4	(3.2)	2.1	(1.7)	**7.5**	(3.4)
	Denmark	**3.7**	(1.4)	-2.7	(3.2)	-2.1	(4.1)	-3.0	(3.3)	-2.0	(3.3)	5.6	(8.3)	**24.3**	(7.2)	0.4	(2.7)	0.8	(2.7)	-2.1	(2.1)	0.7	(1.0)	3.9	(2.2)
	Estonia	-0.3	(1.5)	-0.1	(3.6)	-3.0	(5.1)	-0.1	(4.1)	**8.8**	(4.2)	-1.0	(8.9)	**16.7**	(5.8)	3.8	(2.4)	0.0	(2.3)	2.6	(2.1)	**2.8**	(1.1)	**6.1**	(2.0)
	Finland	0.2	(1.1)	11.9	(13.4)	-3.6	(2.7)	0.4	(2.8)	1.1	(3.0)	3.1	(6.8)	-1.5	(6.9)	-2.4	(1.8)	**6.2**	(2.6)	-0.4	(1.8)	**4.3**	(1.2)	0.6	(2.0)
	France	**3.5**	(1.7)	8.0	(4.2)	-4.6	(4.6)	2.6	(6.4)	-6.2	(4.9)	-7.5	(9.9)	**19.9**	(7.1)	-6.0	(3.4)	**6.2**	(3.0)	1.6	(2.2)	**6.0**	(1.4)	2.2	(2.7)
	Germany	-0.9	(1.9)	-0.8	(7.5)	6.1	(4.6)	1.4	(4.8)	3.3	(4.0)	**-33.2**	(9.1)	**13.9**	(6.7)	0.7	(3.4)	4.1	(3.9)	**-5.5**	(2.7)	1.4	(1.8)	-0.1	(4.5)
	Greece	2.7	(1.5)	-6.4	(5.0)	2.2	(3.7)	-7.9	(5.6)	-8.7	(5.8)	0.9	(9.3)	**20.8**	(10.3)	0.0	(2.4)	-0.4	(3.1)	-1.5	(2.1)	-1.4	(2.1)	**5.3**	(2.0)
	Hungary	2.8	(2.9)	2.7	(4.7)	-5.1	(5.2)	10.4	(5.8)	-3.7	(5.7)	-10.6	(9.6)	**29.7**	(8.4)	-0.6	(3.7)	-1.9	(3.3)	3.7	(3.0)	**6.1**	(1.7)	-1.3	(2.8)
	Iceland	5.0	(3.5)	1.4	(5.9)	-4.7	(7.8)	4.4	(4.7)	1.3	(6.5)	6.7	(9.9)	**25.8**	(11.1)	-6.2	(4.7)	0.5	(5.1)	-1.7	(3.2)	**5.6**	(2.1)	2.0	(9.5)
	Ireland	**-3.7**	(1.7)	7.9	(4.7)	0.7	(3.3)	3.0	(3.4)	2.5	(3.2)	-2.8	(8.4)	**16.0**	(6.8)	-3.1	(2.2)	**5.9**	(2.5)	-2.8	(2.3)	**4.0**	(1.4)	0.8	(4.6)
	Israel	0.5	(4.5)	8.2	(6.4)	-15.3	(11.9)	1.5	(5.6)	-6.2	(9.6)	**-30.0**	(11.4)	**48.3**	(12.0)	-2.3	(5.1)	-0.8	(4.2)	3.1	(3.2)	-0.1	(2.2)	**7.6**	(2.9)
	Italy	**2.7**	(1.3)	0.8	(2.7)	-1.2	(2.9)	3.5	(2.5)	-2.9	(2.9)	**-31.0**	(5.8)	**24.6**	(5.1)	-2.5	(1.9)	**6.6**	(1.9)	-0.8	(1.6)	**9.7**	(1.0)	**8.9**	(0.9)
	Japan	2.5	(2.3)	4.2	(9.0)	5.6	(10.4)	-7.3	(6.2)	-11.9	(8.0)	24.0	(12.4)	**28.5**	(12.5)	-4.1	(3.8)	-0.9	(3.6)	2.3	(3.2)	5.2	(3.9)	**21.8**	(8.1)
	Korea	5.6	(3.2)	7.7	(5.8)	**-18.5**	(9.4)	-11.3	(7.9)	9.2	(8.8)	**29.4**	(13.8)	**35.7**	(12.3)	-2.8	(2.8)	3.3	(3.4)	0.4	(3.0)	**4.9**	(1.9)	**25.4**	(9.3)
	Luxembourg	c	c	c	c	c	c	c	c	c	c	c	c	c	c	c	c	c	c	c	c	c	c	c	c
	Mexico	0.2	(1.3)	**-4.5**	(2.2)	3.6	(4.4)	3.9	(2.7)	0.4	(2.1)	-6.6	(4.8)	**23.5**	(4.0)	0.1	(1.7)	1.2	(1.5)	0.2	(1.2)	1.4	(0.7)	**5.7**	(0.9)
	Netherlands	-2.5	(3.0)	1.7	(8.3)	-10.3	(5.7)	-9.1	(10.3)	15.7	(17.7)	17.4	(15.5)	16.9	(12.1)	-7.7	(5.7)	2.9	(4.6)	-1.5	(3.2)	**7.2**	(1.9)	**14.1**	(6.6)
	New Zealand	-9.1	(5.5)	5.6	(5.3)	11.3	(6.0)	**-30.1**	(13.4)	-5.9	(13.9)	**-19.6**	(9.4)	**30.7**	(7.7)	-3.4	(2.9)	1.8	(2.7)	**6.3**	(2.0)	3.0	(1.7)	**10.9**	(2.3)
	Norway	**-3.0**	(1.4)	6.9	(3.9)	-6.2	(6.0)	5.5	(4.0)	1.9	(4.3)	7.4	(10.4)	**47.0**	(8.8)	**10.6**	(3.8)	-2.4	(3.5)	-1.5	(2.8)	1.0	(1.5)	7.6	(3.9)
	Poland	-3.6	(3.3)	1.7	(4.3)	3.4	(4.3)	1.7	(4.9)	-7.6	(7.7)	-4.8	(9.4)	**20.6**	(7.1)	2.4	(4.0)	-0.1	(3.5)	-0.3	(2.8)	**2.8**	(1.4)	**5.5**	(2.2)
	Portugal	-0.7	(3.0)	4.9	(3.5)	-9.9	(6.6)	3.1	(4.4)	5.9	(4.5)	-0.6	(9.6)	**27.6**	(10.7)	0.1	(2.7)	1.4	(1.9)	0.1	(2.2)	-0.3	(1.3)	3.7	(2.5)
	Slovak Republic	-3.7	(2.0)	-3.8	(5.4)	0.9	(4.8)	-5.1	(5.2)	**-25.4**	(7.8)	-0.8	(12.6)	**46.0**	(9.6)	3.4	(4.5)	-5.3	(4.5)	2.5	(3.4)	**6.5**	(2.1)	3.9	(3.1)
	Slovenia	-2.5	(1.8)	0.2	(4.2)	-3.8	(4.8)	-4.9	(4.3)	-3.4	(4.0)	-1.1	(10.2)	**21.8**	(6.5)	2.3	(2.7)	0.6	(3.5)	-1.0	(2.4)	0.7	(1.7)	**11.8**	(1.8)
	Spain	-0.5	(1.6)	-5.4	(3.3)	4.2	(3.5)	3.9	(3.1)	-4.4	(3.3)	5.6	(6.4)	8.6	(5.0)	-2.7	(2.1)	**4.3**	(2.0)	-0.5	(1.6)	0.8	(1.0)	**6.3**	(1.1)
	Sweden	0.0	(2.5)	2.3	(5.2)	w	w	-0.7	(5.0)	-0.8	(4.0)	10.0	(8.5)	18.3	(9.8)	-4.0	(2.8)	2.5	(3.4)	0.9	(2.8)	**4.9**	(1.5)	3.5	(3.5)
	Switzerland	1.4	(1.4)	2.4	(9.3)	-0.1	(3.9)	-1.4	(4.7)	3.5	(4.0)	**18.0**	(7.6)	**29.5**	(8.9)	2.1	(3.0)	1.1	(3.1)	-2.5	(2.5)	-1.2	(1.7)	**7.7**	(3.7)
	Turkey	2.8	(2.9)	4.1	(5.2)	10.4	(15.2)	2.8	(7.2)	-10.8	(7.4)	**-44.9**	(11.5)	**93.4**	(12.5)	-6.2	(3.5)	4.4	(3.7)	**6.1**	(2.9)	2.1	(2.5)	-3.7	(2.2)
	United Kingdom	-2.4	(4.2)	2.5	(7.0)	-13.8	(8.0)	-0.5	(4.5)	-1.6	(6.2)	5.8	(9.1)	**35.6**	(6.4)	3.7	(2.5)	-5.7	(3.1)	2.0	(2.5)	**6.2**	(1.6)	3.4	(2.1)
	United States	**-6.2**	(2.9)	1.5	(10.0)	-6.3	(21.0)	-1.1	(4.4)	**58.4**	(22.5)	**26.4**	(10.9)	19.8	(12.3)	-1.0	(2.8)	3.2	(3.8)	0.5	(2.6)	**5.2**	(1.6)	-2.2	(2.6)
	OECD average	-0.3	(0.4)	**2.6**	(1.1)	-2.1	(1.3)	-0.9	(1.0)	0.4	(1.4)	-0.4	(1.7)	**27.2**	(1.5)	-0.8	(0.6)	**1.8**	(0.6)	-0.2	(0.4)	**3.3**	(0.3)	**5.8**	(0.7)
Partners	Albania	-4.1	(2.8)	1.7	(6.5)	**-17.5**	(5.7)	-11.0	(6.3)	-9.0	(8.9)	-9.6	(10.9)	-11.3	(11.8)	0.1	(2.8)	-1.9	(3.1)	1.4	(3.2)	0.5	(2.2)	-0.2	(2.9)
	Argentina	0.1	(1.8)	3.5	(6.3)	-6.0	(4.4)	2.2	(4.0)	0.6	(3.7)	**-34.7**	(10.1)	**19.7**	(9.4)	0.3	(2.8)	1.6	(2.3)	4.4	(3.1)	**4.9**	(1.3)	**4.4**	(1.5)
	Brazil	0.6	(1.7)	-1.7	(3.3)	-1.3	(4.7)	-1.2	(3.0)	6.8	(4.8)	-5.3	(6.3)	**32.6**	(6.0)	0.4	(1.9)	0.3	(1.7)	-0.1	(1.6)	**2.4**	(0.9)	0.7	(1.1)
	Bulgaria	0.7	(4.5)	**15.3**	(5.2)	2.4	(8.0)	7.4	(7.3)	2.1	(5.1)	-9.9	(9.4)	**30.3**	(11.4)	**-4.8**	(2.3)	**6.0**	(2.7)	5.1	(3.2)	**4.1**	(1.8)	**5.2**	(1.9)
	Colombia	3.3	(3.2)	1.5	(3.4)	-3.2	(4.5)	**12.9**	(3.8)	-6.1	(4.2)	**-27.1**	(8.8)	**16.9**	(7.7)	-2.3	(2.0)	**6.0**	(2.5)	-0.4	(2.2)	1.0	(1.0)	3.3	(2.6)
	Costa Rica	-0.5	(1.8)	6.4	(5.5)	2.9	(12.8)	-3.0	(3.7)	-1.5	(4.4)	-6.1	(10.5)	**26.5**	(10.1)	-0.4	(3.3)	1.1	(2.6)	**4.8**	(2.2)	-0.3	(1.1)	2.7	(1.8)
	Croatia	-1.6	(2.3)	1.9	(3.9)	-0.1	(6.5)	**-8.9**	(3.7)	-5.8	(24.7)	12.3	(12.0)	12.1	(8.9)	-2.4	(3.0)	0.9	(3.0)	-0.4	(2.5)	**8.8**	(2.1)	**12.8**	(2.7)
	Cyprus*	**4.7**	(1.7)	4.9	(9.2)	12.7	(6.6)	-1.1	(4.4)	4.3	(9.0)	23.9	(15.7)	**67.0**	(13.1)	1.5	(5.7)	-2.3	(5.1)	**-5.7**	(2.4)	-3.9	(2.2)	**11.9**	(2.3)
	Hong Kong-China	1.2	(4.4)	-3.6	(7.2)	1.7	(6.1)	-2.1	(7.3)	-2.8	(8.8)	-11.3	(21.0)	8.4	(13.6)	6.5	(4.5)	-1.2	(4.0)	6.0	(4.1)	-0.6	(4.4)	13.6	(8.2)
	Indonesia	-7.3	(4.7)	-5.2	(7.1)	1.6	(6.0)	11.8	(9.7)	c	c	-4.6	(13.9)	6.3	(12.8)	0.9	(3.2)	0.1	(4.2)	-1.3	(3.1)	**6.7**	(1.9)	2.2	(3.3)
	Jordan	3.3	(2.7)	-10.6	(5.7)	4.1	(5.2)	4.1	(4.8)	-0.4	(4.0)	-3.1	(9.2)	**50.2**	(9.9)	-2.2	(2.5)	1.7	(2.3)	**6.7**	(2.5)	0.7	(1.8)	3.4	(1.9)
	Kazakhstan	0.7	(19.3)	4.6	(11.4)	c	c	-5.4	(11.4)	-5.3	(17.1)	-11.4	(13.8)	**28.7**	(12.9)	-4.2	(2.8)	4.4	(2.8)	-2.6	(2.9)	-0.6	(2.6)	0.9	(2.9)
	Latvia	-6.7	(10.7)	4.0	(4.7)	2.1	(6.7)	6.3	(5.2)	2.2	(4.9)	1.8	(8.5)	4.1	(7.7)	0.5	(2.7)	1.6	(2.8)	1.1	(3.0)	**4.3**	(1.4)	**5.3**	(1.7)
	Lithuania	**4.0**	(2.0)	1.3	(4.5)	-3.1	(5.1)	-7.4	(4.9)	-3.9	(3.7)	7.7	(8.2)	**28.0**	(6.4)	3.7	(3.7)	-4.7	(3.5)	1.6	(2.7)	**4.8**	(1.3)	3.0	(1.9)
	Macao-China	c	c	c	c	c	c	c	c	c	c	c	c	c	c	c	c	c	c	c	c	c	c	c	c
	Malaysia	**-8.6**	(3.8)	-9.5	(5.7)	12.8	(17.3)	5.4	(4.2)	1.1	(5.3)	-10.5	(11.6)	**53.8**	(12.9)	**6.9**	(2.3)	-3.6	(2.5)	-1.7	(2.1)	**6.1**	(1.7)	1.4	(1.5)
	Montenegro	c	c	c	c	c	c	c	c	c	c	c	c	c	c	c	c	c	c	c	c	c	c	c	c
	Peru	2.3	(1.5)	-8.2	(6.9)	-0.8	(4.1)	1.5	(4.9)	-11.6	(13.1)	-8.7	(8.4)	**21.8**	(10.3)	1.4	(2.4)	-2.2	(2.9)	1.3	(3.0)	**3.0**	(1.1)	**9.1**	(2.2)
	Qatar	**-13.1**	(3.9)	-3.8	(5.3)	**-47.9**	(15.2)	**-33.6**	(11.4)	c	c	12.5	(16.1)	**55.5**	(15.0)	-0.2	(3.2)	-2.1	(3.2)	3.0	(3.2)	**9.3**	(3.1)	-1.4	(3.5)
	Romania	-0.4	(2.3)	5.6	(4.8)	-2.9	(5.6)	-6.3	(5.7)	1.1	(6.3)	-10.8	(12.1)	**31.2**	(9.1)	-0.7	(2.8)	0.1	(2.6)	2.3	(2.6)	2.8	(1.8)	0.9	(2.2)
	Russian Federation	5.9	(8.4)	0.3	(5.3)	32.4	(20.1)	2.6	(5.5)	-3.6	(10.2)	-21.6	(13.7)	18.5	(9.5)	0.7	(3.1)	4.0	(2.8)	2.7	(3.0)	2.9	(1.8)	5.0	(2.6)
	Serbia	2.3	(3.2)	1.2	(6.3)	-9.0	(6.2)	6.6	(5.9)	16.0	(13.1)	-13.0	(17.1)	**25.8**	(12.0)	2.0	(3.6)	1.2	(5.2)	-3.1	(3.7)	**9.0**	(2.1)	5.4	(4.2)
	Shanghai-China	2.9	(3.0)	2.0	(12.0)	**-12.8**	(5.9)	-11.7	(8.3)	26.1	(18.4)	-0.3	(14.2)	**48.5**	(12.6)	0.1	(2.8)	1.2	(2.2)	-1.8	(2.3)	3.9	(2.5)	4.1	(16.8)
	Singapore	-10.2	(13.3)	1.8	(4.8)	8.0	(24.7)	5.8	(10.6)	-8.4	(20.4)	15.3	(15.2)	**26.1**	(10.9)	1.6	(3.9)	4.5	(4.4)	**5.2**	(2.4)	3.5	(2.9)	0.0	(3.1)
	Chinese Taipei	-3.9	(2.1)	8.4	(6.5)	6.4	(6.0)	-1.0	(5.7)	2.4	(5.6)	19.0	(16.4)	7.6	(14.2)	5.1	(2.8)	-1.8	(2.9)	2.0	(3.3)	1.7	(2.4)	**15.1**	(5.9)
	Thailand	3.6	(4.0)	6.5	(6.1)	**38.0**	(13.8)	5.6	(5.5)	-12.9	(13.2)	-13.8	(16.9)	15.8	(17.9)	6.7	(4.2)	7.1	(4.0)	-3.6	(3.1)	2.0	(1.6)	**7.3**	(2.4)
	Tunisia	-3.2	(2.3)	4.2	(8.8)	-0.6	(5.6)	5.8	(6.3)	-4.0	(6.3)	**-30.1**	(15.1)	**67.4**	(14.1)	1.3	(3.9)	-4.1	(3.8)	0.8	(2.4)	2.2	(2.3)	**8.7**	(2.1)
	United Arab Emirates	**10.2**	(4.1)	**-8.5**	(3.8)	-3.1	(6.1)	-7.4	(4.7)	-1.3	(7.4)	1.2	(7.8)	**24.4**	(6.9)	0.7	(2.0)	3.0	(2.3)	2.3	(2.1)	**8.7**	(1.3)	2.1	(1.5)
	Uruguay	3.4	(1.8)	1.5	(6.9)	3.4	(4.6)	-0.6	(3.9)	-3.2	(4.5)	-16.8	(10.5)	**28.0**	(9.3)	-1.1	(3.2)	0.8	(2.2)	1.0	(2.6)	0.7	(1.8)	2.1	(2.1)
	Viet Nam	5.3	(7.6)	4.9	(7.3)	-9.7	(9.1)	**14.7**	(7.0)	-0.1	(20.2)	**-45.6**	(16.3)	**68.8**	(18.2)	-3.7	(4.7)	6.1	(5.3)	3.1	(4.1)	-0.7	(3.5)	**11.6**	(4.8)

Note: Values that are statistically significant are indicated in bold (see Annex A3).
1. Multilevel regression model (student and school levels): Mathematics performance is regressed on all the variables presented in this table.
* See notes at the beginning of this Annex.

StatLink http://dx.doi.org/10.1787/888932957384

[Part 5/5]

Table IV.1.12c Relationship among mathematics performance, the school's learning environment, resources, policies and practices, and student and school characteristics

		Student socio-economic and demographic background[1]										School socio-economic and demographic background[1]									
		Student is a female		Student without an immigrant background		Student's language at home is the same as the language of assessment		PISA index of economic, social and cultural status of student (1 unit increase)		PISA index of economic, social and cultural status of student (squared)		School average PISA index of economic, social and cultural status (1 unit increase)		School size (per 100 students)		School size (per 100 students) (squared)		School in a small town or village (15 000 or fewer people)		School in city (100 000 or more people)	
		Change in score	S.E.	Change in score	S.E.	Change in score	S.E.	Change in score	S.E.	Change in score	S.E.	Change in score	S.E.	Change in score	S.E.	Change in score	S.E.	Change in score	S.E.	Change in score	S.E.
OECD	Australia	**-13.3**	(1.9)	**-5.1**	(1.9)	**-9.4**	(3.4)	**25.1**	(1.2)	0.7	(1.0)	**38.1**	(5.6)	0.7	(1.1)	0.0	(0.0)	9.2	(4.8)	2.6	(3.5)
	Austria	**-26.6**	(2.7)	**13.9**	(3.6)	**30.0**	(4.4)	**9.0**	(1.7)	0.0	(1.3)	**29.1**	(9.0)	**8.3**	(1.4)	**-0.2**	(0.1)	**17.9**	(6.9)	5.7	(7.1)
	Belgium	**-15.6**	(1.9)	**14.2**	(2.3)	2.6	(2.5)	**8.9**	(1.4)	**2.4**	(0.9)	**22.9**	(7.1)	-0.8	(2.3)	0.0	(0.1)	1.6	(4.1)	-1.1	(4.9)
	Canada	**-11.3**	(1.7)	**8.0**	(2.2)	**-14.2**	(3.2)	**21.6**	(1.3)	**2.6**	(0.9)	**18.2**	(5.1)	1.7	(1.0)	0.0	(0.0)	4.0	(4.5)	-4.1	(3.8)
	Chile	**-27.1**	(2.0)	2.5	(4.6)	9.6	(9.9)	**8.6**	(1.4)	0.1	(0.7)	**25.1**	(3.5)	**3.4**	(0.6)	**-0.1**	(0.0)	5.4	(4.7)	**-8.5**	(3.7)
	Czech Republic	**-22.4**	(2.7)	0.6	(3.6)	**19.9**	(9.1)	**13.5**	(1.8)	-2.8	(1.7)	**89.1**	(8.6)	-0.3	(4.4)	0.2	(0.3)	12.9	(6.9)	4.9	(6.1)
	Denmark	**-14.6**	(2.3)	**21.1**	(2.9)	8.2	(4.3)	**27.0**	(1.9)	**3.2**	(1.3)	**24.8**	(5.0)	1.5	(1.2)	0.0	(0.0)	6.9	(4.0)	8.0	(4.4)
	Estonia	**-5.5**	(2.4)	2.4	(3.5)	**12.3**	(5.5)	**18.2**	(1.8)	3.1	(1.9)	**42.2**	(7.8)	-2.3	(2.4)	0.1	(0.1)	1.8	(4.8)	2.4	(5.0)
	Finland	0.0	(2.4)	**16.0**	(4.3)	**34.1**	(4.9)	**26.0**	(1.6)	**4.4**	(1.4)	**22.8**	(6.9)	-1.0	(3.7)	0.3	(0.3)	**8.1**	(3.7)	4.1	(3.6)
	France	**-20.5**	(2.3)	**14.4**	(2.4)	**13.2**	(4.6)	**19.9**	(1.9)	**4.3**	(1.4)	**11.9**	(5.1)	-1.7	(1.8)	0.1	(0.1)	c	c	**35.2**	(8.3)
	Germany	**-25.6**	(1.9)	**10.6**	(3.0)	**11.7**	(4.7)	**8.8**	(1.5)	1.0	(1.2)	**66.5**	(6.7)	1.2	(2.1)	0.0	(0.1)	**-12.0**	(5.5)	-7.5	(5.6)
	Greece	**-20.8**	(2.2)	-0.4	(2.8)	7.8	(7.1)	**17.4**	(1.5)	1.7	(1.1)	**14.2**	(6.6)	5.2	(3.8)	-0.3	(0.3)	7.6	(6.8)	4.4	(4.9)
	Hungary	**-27.5**	(2.2)	1.9	(4.2)	-5.7	(10.9)	**5.1**	(1.4)	0.9	(1.1)	**61.2**	(7.7)	**3.1**	(1.3)	**-0.1**	(0.0)	-13.0	(6.8)	-6.6	(5.6)
	Iceland	7.2	(4.1)	2.9	(4.6)	13.0	(15.5)	**18.9**	(3.4)	3.2	(2.0)	**40.0**	(10.4)	-6.8	(8.1)	0.6	(0.9)	-5.9	(6.2)	2.4	(6.5)
	Ireland	**-18.3**	(2.7)	-4.4	(2.8)	-0.7	(6.0)	**25.1**	(1.7)	1.9	(1.5)	**33.5**	(6.4)	1.5	(1.9)	-0.1	(0.1)	2.6	(4.4)	3.6	(4.8)
	Israel	**-18.2**	(3.0)	**-9.0**	(3.2)	7.0	(5.2)	**24.2**	(2.1)	**3.6**	(1.2)	**45.6**	(7.7)	2.6	(2.2)	-0.1	(0.1)	-7.5	(6.7)	-6.5	(5.8)
	Italy	**-25.8**	(1.4)	**11.5**	(1.6)	**3.9**	(1.9)	**5.3**	(0.7)	-0.1	(0.5)	**36.0**	(4.1)	1.5	(1.1)	-0.1	(0.1)	-2.7	(4.0)	1.2	(3.0)
	Japan	**-16.3**	(2.2)	2.5	(4.8)	**51.3**	(20.2)	**4.0**	(1.7)	1.0	(1.6)	**89.0**	(15.1)	3.0	(2.8)	-0.1	(0.1)	4.0	(17.2)	-0.1	(5.7)
	Korea	**-12.9**	(3.4)	7.0	(11.6)	90.3	(46.9)	**15.0**	(2.0)	**4.1**	(1.7)	21.1	(12.8)	-1.6	(3.1)	0.1	(0.1)	-12.9	(14.2)	-16.1	(9.7)
	Luxembourg	c	c	c	c	c	c	c	c	c	c	c	c	c	c	c	c	c	c	c	c
	Mexico	**-17.4**	(1.0)	**13.2**	(2.2)	**11.7**	(3.8)	**5.8**	(0.9)	**0.8**	(0.3)	**21.0**	(2.3)	**0.7**	(0.3)	0.0	(0.0)	2.2	(3.3)	2.7	(2.9)
	Netherlands	**-17.3**	(1.8)	**12.2**	(3.2)	**12.5**	(5.2)	**6.4**	(1.7)	**2.2**	(1.0)	**50.0**	(12.4)	2.9	(2.1)	-0.1	(0.1)	15.3	(8.0)	-4.0	(6.4)
	New Zealand	**-16.5**	(2.9)	**-8.2**	(2.9)	**22.6**	(5.9)	**35.1**	(2.3)	1.4	(2.3)	13.6	(7.4)	-1.2	(1.5)	0.1	(0.0)	-3.1	(4.9)	**-15.4**	(5.6)
	Norway	-1.0	(2.9)	**19.4**	(3.8)	11.1	(6.2)	**24.9**	(2.2)	-1.0	(1.5)	**39.4**	(9.6)	5.2	(5.9)	-0.5	(0.7)	-7.5	(4.6)	-8.3	(6.2)
	Poland	-4.5	(2.9)	1.8	(10.1)	10.8	(13.7)	**31.2**	(1.8)	**-4.7**	(1.7)	**28.3**	(11.2)	2.9	(4.3)	-0.2	(0.4)	3.2	(7.5)	10.0	(6.8)
	Portugal	**-13.4**	(2.3)	**7.7**	(3.1)	-6.9	(8.5)	**23.4**	(1.5)	0.1	(1.0)	4.2	(5.2)	-0.6	(1.7)	0.0	(0.1)	1.1	(4.3)	-5.3	(5.1)
	Slovak Republic	**-26.0**	(3.0)	6.8	(6.6)	**19.0**	(6.1)	**19.2**	(2.1)	-1.1	(1.3)	**47.4**	(9.5)	-1.7	(3.4)	**0.5**	(0.3)	-10.1	(7.6)	6.4	(7.0)
	Slovenia	**-25.9**	(2.9)	**14.7**	(3.1)	7.6	(6.1)	0.3	(1.4)	0.8	(1.3)	**88.0**	(7.2)	1.0	(2.8)	0.2	(0.2)	10.1	(6.9)	-5.3	(5.1)
	Spain	**-15.7**	(1.8)	**21.4**	(2.3)	**7.1**	(2.5)	**25.6**	(1.0)	0.2	(0.8)	5.0	(4.1)	-0.7	(0.8)	0.0	(0.0)	4.2	(3.6)	6.0	(3.4)
	Sweden	1.8	(2.8)	**24.2**	(3.3)	**13.8**	(5.9)	**25.0**	(1.9)	**2.9**	(1.4)	**19.5**	(8.3)	1.0	(2.1)	0.2	(0.1)	**-12.4**	(5.2)	5.3	(5.7)
	Switzerland	**-18.0**	(1.9)	**26.9**	(2.1)	**11.4**	(3.1)	**20.8**	(1.5)	-1.0	(1.2)	**50.5**	(6.7)	1.7	(1.2)	0.0	(0.0)	-4.9	(4.1)	4.3	(7.7)
	Turkey	**-22.2**	(1.9)	3.4	(5.9)	1.6	(4.4)	2.7	(1.8)	-1.1	(0.7)	**17.6**	(8.1)	**3.5**	(1.7)	**-0.1**	(0.1)	7.0	(9.8)	-0.5	(5.5)
	United Kingdom	**-13.4**	(2.6)	2.5	(3.4)	-1.3	(5.7)	**21.5**	(1.9)	**4.1**	(1.6)	**27.4**	(7.0)	0.6	(2.3)	0.0	(0.1)	-0.7	(4.6)	-5.9	(5.0)
	United States	**-8.1**	(2.5)	**-10.7**	(3.9)	5.6	(4.9)	**23.8**	(1.7)	**5.6**	(1.1)	7.8	(6.6)	-1.1	(1.0)	0.0	(0.0)	-7.9	(7.6)	2.7	(5.1)
	OECD average	**-15.5**	(0.4)	**7.4**	(0.8)	**12.5**	(1.9)	**17.2**	(0.3)	**1.3**	(0.2)	**34.9**	(1.4)	**1.0**	(0.5)	0.0	(0.0)	0.8	(1.2)	0.5	(1.0)
Partners	Albania	-1.2	(3.1)	2.5	(12.1)	9.4	(12.7)	c	c	c	c	c	c	c	c	c	c	-10.0	(6.5)	6.9	(7.1)
	Argentina	**-15.5**	(2.3)	**8.5**	(3.0)	6.5	(8.5)	**10.7**	(1.3)	**1.8**	(0.7)	10.8	(5.8)	-1.2	(1.5)	0.0	(0.1)	-7.6	(6.2)	-0.2	(5.0)
	Brazil	**-20.0**	(1.5)	**16.0**	(4.8)	6.8	(8.2)	**8.4**	(1.5)	0.3	(0.5)	**29.2**	(4.1)	**1.1**	(0.5)	0.0	(0.0)	**9.3**	(4.5)	**-10.7**	(3.3)
	Bulgaria	**-14.5**	(2.1)	0.9	(6.0)	**9.2**	(4.4)	**10.8**	(1.3)	0.1	(0.7)	**38.1**	(7.3)	-1.0	(2.6)	0.1	(0.2)	-3.6	(6.3)	9.0	(6.5)
	Colombia	**-24.3**	(2.1)	7.6	(5.8)	**24.7**	(12.1)	**13.2**	(2.4)	1.3	(0.7)	**18.8**	(5.1)	0.9	(0.5)	0.0	(0.0)	**15.5**	(6.9)	-1.7	(5.8)
	Costa Rica	**-23.0**	(1.8)	3.3	(2.9)	-9.6	(10.8)	**11.9**	(1.5)	**1.4**	(0.6)	**17.5**	(4.6)	-1.3	(0.9)	0.0	(0.0)	0.3	(4.3)	-0.8	(6.4)
	Croatia	**-24.6**	(2.5)	2.6	(2.4)	9.4	(8.5)	**9.4**	(1.6)	-1.5	(1.1)	**44.7**	(11.8)	0.2	(5.0)	0.1	(0.3)	-6.1	(6.0)	7.6	(5.3)
	Cyprus*	**-15.8**	(2.6)	5.3	(3.1)	2.4	(6.0)	**19.7**	(1.9)	1.1	(1.3)	20.6	(12.4)	**-23.3**	(5.0)	**1.4**	(0.4)	8.5	(9.0)	13.6	(9.7)
	Hong Kong-China	**-22.1**	(2.9)	**-6.8**	(3.2)	**24.5**	(5.5)	**6.4**	(2.3)	1.1	(1.1)	**25.6**	(8.2)	-7.2	(5.4)	0.3	(0.2)	c	c	c	c
	Indonesia	**-5.8**	(1.8)	8.1	(8.8)	**-12.5**	(2.3)	**8.8**	(2.5)	0.7	(0.6)	**15.5**	(6.8)	**5.3**	(2.6)	-0.1	(0.1)	8.1	(7.9)	7.3	(9.5)
	Jordan	-1.0	(7.5)	**-10.8**	(2.5)	8.2	(5.1)	**11.5**	(1.6)	0.5	(0.7)	**33.4**	(8.8)	-3.0	(1.9)	0.1	(0.1)	8.3	(6.8)	**10.9**	(5.0)
	Kazakhstan	-2.0	(1.8)	-3.5	(2.2)	2.9	(4.6)	**14.8**	(2.1)	-0.2	(1.4)	**33.8**	(9.8)	**-3.7**	(1.2)	**0.1**	(0.0)	18.8	(14.7)	13.2	(9.1)
	Latvia	-2.4	(2.9)	**6.2**	(3.0)	5.8	(5.6)	**21.0**	(1.7)	-1.8	(1.4)	**37.4**	(7.0)	-3.7	(3.4)	0.3	(0.2)	2.9	(7.9)	4.4	(8.4)
	Lithuania	**-9.7**	(2.4)	3.8	(4.0)	**20.4**	(8.3)	**17.8**	(1.6)	-1.7	(1.5)	**44.6**	(7.2)	2.2	(2.9)	-0.1	(0.2)	-4.7	(6.2)	-6.8	(6.4)
	Macao-China	c	c	c	c	c	c	c	c	c	c	c	c	c	c	c	c	c	c	c	c
	Malaysia	3.9	(2.1)	-3.2	(4.4)	-0.8	(3.6)	**19.6**	(2.2)	**2.8**	(0.8)	**14.3**	(5.9)	-0.6	(1.3)	0.0	(0.0)	2.7	(5.4)	0.6	(6.3)
	Montenegro	c	c	c	c	c	c	c	c	c	c	c	c	c	c	c	c	c	c	c	c
	Peru	**-26.6**	(2.0)	**20.2**	(6.5)	**16.2**	(5.2)	**10.4**	(1.7)	0.7	(0.5)	**31.6**	(5.6)	**3.1**	(1.1)	**-0.1**	(0.0)	0.2	(7.1)	0.5	(5.7)
	Qatar	8.0	(8.9)	**-34.2**	(2.4)	**13.1**	(4.4)	**10.7**	(2.4)	0.0	(0.9)	**30.0**	(10.2)	**3.4**	(1.3)	**0.0**	(0.0)	**23.7**	(9.8)	17.1	(9.6)
	Romania	**-12.6**	(2.4)	4.8	(7.2)	8.5	(9.5)	**18.2**	(1.9)	**2.3**	(0.9)	**27.4**	(7.4)	-0.5	(1.8)	0.0	(0.1)	-8.2	(7.1)	6.7	(6.0)
	Russian Federation	-1.7	(2.6)	3.7	(2.5)	**14.7**	(5.2)	**24.8**	(2.3)	-2.7	(1.7)	15.6	(9.2)	1.8	(2.5)	-0.1	(0.1)	2.4	(15.7)	-2.9	(16.9)
	Serbia	**-24.3**	(2.5)	**-6.8**	(2.6)	-7.8	(6.4)	**7.5**	(1.4)	-0.6	(1.2)	**57.1**	(11.1)	-1.1	(2.4)	0.1	(0.1)	-3.7	(9.4)	-2.3	(7.5)
	Shanghai-China	**-14.1**	(2.4)	**23.3**	(9.7)	**60.9**	(9.9)	**5.0**	(1.9)	**-4.2**	(1.3)	**29.8**	(9.2)	-1.1	(0.7)	0.0	(0.0)	c	c	c	c
	Singapore	1.1	(2.6)	**-13.0**	(2.7)	**8.8**	(2.8)	**17.9**	(2.2)	-1.6	(1.3)	**36.4**	(9.3)	**7.9**	(2.4)	-0.1	(0.1)	c	c	c	c
	Chinese Taipei	**-7.0**	(2.6)	7.8	(5.9)	**15.4**	(3.8)	**22.5**	(2.1)	**-2.8**	(1.4)	**43.9**	(11.4)	**1.7**	(0.6)	**0.0**	(0.0)	-4.3	(8.7)	8.8	(6.0)
	Thailand	-0.9	(2.0)	-11.9	(9.3)	**-12.5**	(3.1)	**16.6**	(1.9)	**3.2**	(0.7)	6.7	(6.2)	**1.9**	(0.9)	0.0	(0.0)	**13.0**	(5.7)	**11.9**	(5.6)
	Tunisia	**-23.4**	(1.9)	3.0	(5.6)	3.0	(9.9)	**12.5**	(1.8)	**2.7**	(0.6)	**30.8**	(5.8)	0.8	(3.0)	-0.1	(0.2)	-9.9	(6.8)	0.7	(7.1)
	United Arab Emirates	**-18.9**	(4.1)	**-25.6**	(2.2)	**6.1**	(2.5)	**13.6**	(1.4)	1.3	(0.8)	**40.6**	(6.2)	**1.8**	(0.5)	**0.0**	(0.0)	4.8	(5.2)	4.3	(6.2)
	Uruguay	**-18.0**	(2.1)	3.3	(4.2)	-12.1	(7.6)	**16.6**	(1.7)	**1.7**	(0.8)	**17.8**	(6.9)	**2.0**	(1.0)	0.0	(0.0)	8.3	(6.3)	6.2	(5.4)
	Viet Nam	**-24.2**	(2.1)	14.0	(10.2)	11.9	(7.1)	**9.9**	(2.5)	1.2	(0.7)	9.8	(8.9)	**4.8**	(1.8)	**-0.1**	(0.0)	8.3	(15.0)	16.0	(15.4)

Note: Values that are statistically significant are indicated in bold (see Annex A3).

1. Multilevel regression model (student and school levels): Mathematics performance is regressed on all the variables presented in this table.

* See notes at the beginning of this Annex.

StatLink http://dx.doi.org/10.1787/888932957384

[Part 1/1]

Table IV.1.13 School autonomy and performance, by system's extent of posting achievement data publicly

	OECD countries (OLS regression estimates)				All countries and economies that participated in PISA 2012 (OLS regression estimates)			
	Gross model		Net model		Gross model		Net model	
	Coef.	S.E.	Coef.	S.E.	Coef.	S.E.	Coef.	S.E.
School autonomy for resource allocation	2.54	(1.99)	**-6.13**	(1.81)	**7.04**	(1.47)	**-4.37**	(0.98)
× Percentage of students in schools that post achievement data publicly (additional 10%)	*0.61*	*(0.34)*	**0.69**	(0.28)	0.01	(0.25)	**0.56**	(0.18)
School autonomy for curriculum and assessment	0.56	(1.65)	-0.16	(1.13)	*-2.39*	(1.27)	**-3.61**	(0.79)
× Percentage of students in schools that post achievement data publicly (additional 10%)	-0.13	(0.33)	-0.04	(0.22)	0.45	(0.30)	**0.73**	(0.18)
Private school			0.46	(1.74)			0.03	(1.31)
PISA index of economic, social and cultural status of student (ESCS)			**18.20**	(0.31)			**18.78**	(0.29)
PISA index of economic, social and cultural status of student (ESCS squared)			**3.12**	(0.22)			**4.25**	(0.16)
Student is a female			**-13.60**	(0.56)			**-11.05**	(0.40)
Student's language at home is the same as the language of assessment			**6.96**	(1.29)			**5.61**	(0.97)
Student without an immigrant background			**10.62**	(1.00)			0.84	(0.89)
School average PISA index of economic, social and cultural status			**65.19**	(1.05)			**60.06**	(0.88)
School in a city (100 000 or more people)			**-5.81**	(1.14)			**-4.16**	(0.84)
School in a small town or village (15 000 or less people)			**5.38**	(1.26)			**6.66**	(0.95)
School size (100 students)			**2.60**	(0.23)			**1.78**	(0.16)
School size (100 students, squared)			**-0.05**	(0.01)			**-0.02**	(0.00)
N	256 739		256 739		420 028		420 028	

Notes: Estimates significant at the 5% level (p < 0.05) are in bold and those significant at the 10% level (p < 0.10) are in italics. Both net and gross models include country fixed effects, estimate no intercept, are run with using BRR weights to account for the sampling design. Each country contribute to the analysis with equal weights.
StatLink http://dx.doi.org/10.1787/888932957384

[Part 1/1]

Table IV.1.14 School autonomy and performance, by system's extent of implementing a standardised policy

	OECD countries (OLS regression estimates)				All countries and economies that participated in PISA 2012 (OLS regression estimates)			
	Gross model		Net model		Gross model		Net model	
	Coef.	S.E.	Coef.	S.E.	Coef.	S.E.	Coef.	S.E.
School autonomy for resource allocation	**13.88**	(2.69)	-0.25	(2.08)	**8.93**	(2.08)	**-4.21**	(1.55)
× Percentage of students in schools that implement a standardised policy for mathematics (additional 10%)	**-1.27**	(0.43)	-0.31	(0.30)	-0.28	(0.32)	0.40	(0.24)
School autonomy for curriculum and assessment	-2.86	(3.13)	**-4.61**	(1.99)	**-6.11**	(2.58)	**-6.82**	(1.67)
× Percentage of students in schools that implement a standardised policy for mathematics (additional 10%)	0.47	(0.49)	**0.69**	(0.30)	**0.86**	(0.40)	**0.96**	(0.27)
Private school			-0.14	(1.72)			-0.65	(1.33)
PISA index of economic, social and cultural status of student (ESCS)			**18.20**	(0.31)			**18.76**	(0.29)
PISA index of economic, social and cultural status of student (ESCS squared)			**3.13**	(0.22)			**4.25**	(0.16)
Student is a female			**-13.61**	(0.56)			**-11.05**	(0.40)
Student's language at home is the same as the language of assessment			**6.96**	(1.29)			**6.06**	(0.99)
Student without an immigrant background			**10.61**	(1.00)			0.84	(0.89)
School average PISA index of economic, social and cultural status			**65.24**	(1.05)			**60.10**	(0.88)
School in a city (100 000 or more people)			**-5.85**	(1.15)			**-4.26**	(0.84)
School in a small town or village (15 000 or less people)			**5.46**	(1.26)			**6.68**	(0.95)
School size (100 students)			**2.61**	(0.22)			**1.76**	(0.16)
School size (100 students, squared)			**-0.05**	(0.01)			**-0.02**	(0.00)
N	256 739		256 739		420 028		420 028	

Notes: Estimates significant at the 5% level (p < 0.05) are in bold and those significant at the 10% level (p < 0.10) are in italics. Both net and gross models include country fixed effects, estimate no intercept, are run with using BRR weights to account for the sampling design. Each country contribute to the analysis with equal weights.
StatLink http://dx.doi.org/10.1787/888932957384

[Part 1/1]

Table IV.1.15 School autonomy and performance, by system's extent of teachers participating in school management

	OECD countries (OLS regression estimates)				All countries and economies that participated in PISA 2012 (OLS regression estimates)			
	Gross model		Net model		Gross model		Net model	
	Coef.	S.E.	Coef.	S.E.	Coef.	S.E.	Coef.	S.E.
School autonomy for resource allocation	**6.17**	(0.86)	**-2.06**	(0.78)	**5.77**	(0.74)	**-1.78**	(0.57)
× Index of school management: teacher participation (1 unit increase)	**20.60**	(2.43)	**4.36**	(1.86)	**14.76**	(2.04)	**4.32**	(1.14)
School autonomy for curriculum and assessment	-0.39	(0.84)	-0.42	(0.57)	-0.87	(0.83)	-0.64	(0.49)
× Index of school management: teacher participation (1 unit increase)	-5.05	(3.43)	-0.63	(2.44)	**8.46**	(2.60)	**6.69**	(1.51)
Private school			-0.22	(1.73)			-1.55	(1.36)
PISA index of economic, social and cultural status of student (ESCS)			**18.20**	(0.31)			**18.74**	(0.29)
PISA index of economic, social and cultural status of student (ESCS squared)			**3.13**	(0.22)			**4.23**	(0.16)
Student is a female			**-13.58**	(0.56)			**-11.01**	(0.40)
Student's language at home is the same as the language of assessment			**7.01**	(1.30)			**6.25**	(0.99)
Student without an immigrant background			**10.59**	(1.00)			0.79	(0.89)
School average PISA index of economic, social and cultural status			**65.03**	(1.05)			**59.62**	(0.88)
School in a city (100 000 or more people)			**-5.84**	(1.14)			**-4.15**	(0.83)
School in a small town or village (15 000 or less people)			**5.38**	(1.26)			**6.64**	(0.95)
School size (100 students)			**2.61**	(0.23)			**1.79**	(0.16)
School size (100 students, squared)			**-0.05**	(0.01)			**-0.02**	(0.00)
N	256 739		256 739		420 028		420 028	

Notes: Estimates significant at the 5% level (p < 0.05) are in bold and those significant at the 10% level (p < 0.10) are in italics. Both net and gross models include country fixed effects, estimate no intercept, are run with using BRR weights to account for the sampling design. Each country contribute to the analysis with equal weights.
StatLink http://dx.doi.org/10.1787/888932957384

[Part 1/1]
Mathematics performance and school choice
Table IV.1.16 *Results based on school principals' reports*

	Mathematics performance, by school principals' reports on the number of schools competing for students in the same area												
	Two or more other schools		One other school		No other schools		Performance difference (one or more - none)		Performance difference (one or more - none) after accounting for student ESCS		Performance difference (one or more - none) after accounting for student and school ESCS	
	Mean score	S.E.	Mean score	S.E.	Mean score	S.E.	Score dif.	S.E.	Score dif.	S.E.	Score dif.	S.E.
Australia	506	(1.7)	474	(5.8)	509	(13.8)	-5	(14.2)	-11	(12.3)	-17	(10.4)
Austria	518	(5.5)	499	(8.9)	496	(6.3)	16	(8.7)	9	(7.3)	-1	(6.8)
Belgium	517	(3.1)	512	(13.7)	492	(20.3)	24	(21.6)	22	(17.0)	19	(13.2)
Canada	522	(2.4)	517	(5.4)	507	(4.0)	**14**	(4.8)	8	(4.3)	1	(4.1)
Chile	430	(3.9)	410	(6.8)	404	(10.9)	22	(11.5)	7	(9.0)	-3	(8.2)
Czech Republic	510	(4.4)	481	(10.1)	459	(11.3)	**47**	(12.2)	**37**	(10.6)	**21**	(10.2)
Denmark	504	(2.8)	493	(4.8)	492	(8.9)	9	(9.6)	7	(6.8)	7	(6.1)
Estonia	526	(2.8)	512	(5.1)	512	(3.9)	**11**	(4.6)	7	(4.4)	4	(4.6)
Finland	523	(3.0)	513	(3.6)	518	(3.3)	1	(4.2)	-3	(3.6)	**-8**	(3.0)
France	511	(6.4)	497	(11.5)	477	(6.6)	**29**	(10.1)	**16**	(8.2)	-3	(7.2)
Germany	529	(4.8)	503	(9.0)	474	(13.6)	**48**	(14.9)	**40**	(12.4)	13	(8.0)
Greece	467	(3.9)	466	(7.5)	425	(5.3)	**41**	(6.4)	**25**	(5.3)	5	(4.9)
Hungary	486	(6.7)	466	(9.9)	468	(9.8)	12	(12.3)	9	(8.9)	6	(7.8)
Iceland	492	(2.6)	507	(4.1)	489	(2.2)	**8**	(2.9)	1	(3.1)	-5	(3.1)
Ireland	501	(3.0)	510	(7.8)	506	(4.7)	-4	(5.5)	-4	(4.2)	-6	(4.3)
Israel	476	(6.1)	452	(11.4)	448	(11.4)	22	(13.2)	**21**	(9.5)	**22**	(7.0)
Italy	507	(4.5)	495	(6.0)	466	(3.6)	**36**	(5.4)	**29**	(4.5)	**15**	(3.4)
Japan	540	(4.3)	517	(19.2)	514	(17.3)	24	(18.8)	13	(14.7)	-13	(8.0)
Korea	560	(4.7)	533	(12.6)	547	(19.2)	7	(18.5)	2	(14.2)	-10	(9.9)
Luxembourg	486	(1.1)	543	(3.2)	474	(2.0)	**21**	(2.2)	**9**	(2.5)	**-8**	(2.3)
Mexico	420	(1.7)	400	(2.9)	395	(4.5)	**21**	(5.1)	**9**	(4.2)	-1	(3.7)
Netherlands	523	(6.0)	493	(14.4)	533	(20.2)	-15	(21.8)	-15	(19.3)	-16	(14.5)
New Zealand	499	(3.4)	535	(17.5)	496	(13.7)	5	(14.2)	-5	(9.9)	-12	(9.0)
Norway	503	(6.9)	488	(6.2)	487	(3.8)	9	(6.5)	5	(5.4)	1	(4.6)
Poland	524	(5.0)	518	(10.5)	504	(4.9)	**18**	(6.9)	6	(6.1)	-3	(6.6)
Portugal	499	(5.1)	478	(8.5)	466	(8.5)	**27**	(9.3)	13	(7.2)	3	(7.4)
Slovak Republic	493	(4.2)	446	(15.3)	448	(11.2)	**39**	(12.2)	13	(9.6)	-12	(9.6)
Slovenia	519	(1.8)	477	(3.3)	478	(2.2)	**33**	(2.8)	**25**	(2.8)	**8**	(3.3)
Spain	492	(2.3)	465	(4.8)	472	(4.3)	**15**	(5.0)	3	(4.2)	-5	(4.4)
Sweden	484	(3.4)	467	(6.8)	473	(4.3)	7	(4.8)	3	(4.1)	-2	(4.1)
Switzerland	530	(7.3)	552	(8.5)	528	(5.4)	11	(8.7)	4	(7.3)	-7	(6.0)
Turkey	460	(6.1)	410	(8.6)	425	(9.4)	**29**	(10.6)	16	(9.7)	-9	(9.2)
United Kingdom	495	(4.1)	493	(8.0)	502	(9.5)	-7	(10.1)	-7	(7.4)	-7	(7.1)
United States	484	(4.6)	462	(18.7)	482	(6.2)	0	(7.8)	-2	(6.8)	-4	(6.6)
OECD average	501	(0.8)	488	(1.7)	481	(1.7)	**17**	(1.9)	**9**	(1.5)	-1	(1.3)
Albania	399	(2.7)	393	(4.8)	387	(3.6)	**10**	(4.1)	c	c	c	c
Argentina	397	(3.8)	367	(10.7)	353	(7.3)	**40**	(8.2)	**21**	(7.9)	-6	(8.3)
Brazil	404	(3.6)	381	(4.6)	375	(2.7)	**22**	(4.0)	**8**	(3.3)	**-10**	(3.6)
Bulgaria	446	(5.3)	413	(9.0)	417	(17.7)	24	(19.3)	8	(13.6)	-6	(10.8)
Colombia	379	(4.0)	368	(11.2)	373	(8.1)	4	(9.2)	-4	(6.7)	-11	(6.2)
Costa Rica	412	(4.1)	397	(9.6)	398	(5.8)	11	(7.4)	5	(5.4)	-1	(4.5)
Croatia	477	(5.2)	485	(12.3)	445	(6.3)	**33**	(8.2)	**25**	(7.3)	11	(7.4)
Cyprus*	460	(1.8)	434	(3.1)	423	(1.9)	**29**	(2.6)	**15**	(2.6)	**-7**	(2.8)
Hong Kong-China	559	(3.4)	588	(29.3)	c	c	c	c	c	c	c	c
Indonesia	379	(4.5)	360	(6.4)	335	(26.2)	41	(26.5)	28	(28.9)	13	(31.9)
Jordan	397	(4.0)	365	(5.7)	380	(9.4)	8	(10.7)	3	(9.6)	-3	(8.4)
Kazakhstan	438	(4.6)	424	(9.1)	427	(5.8)	7	(7.8)	-2	(7.1)	**-18**	(6.9)
Latvia	491	(2.9)	491	(8.0)	484	(11.0)	8	(11.3)	-8	(7.3)	**-21**	(6.4)
Liechtenstein	c	c	c	c	562	(6.1)	**-68**	(9.2)	**-67**	(9.8)	**-55**	(9.9)
Lithuania	491	(4.1)	464	(6.1)	467	(5.2)	**16**	(6.1)	6	(4.8)	-7	(4.8)
Macao-China	534	(1.0)	549	(3.5)	c	c	c	c	c	c	c	c
Malaysia	426	(4.4)	413	(8.4)	410	(8.0)	12	(9.3)	5	(7.6)	-4	(7.2)
Montenegro	399	(2.4)	438	(2.7)	403	(1.3)	**14**	(2.4)	**11**	(2.4)	2	(2.4)
Peru	382	(4.3)	366	(10.4)	320	(7.1)	**59**	(8.1)	**30**	(6.2)	3	(6.3)
Qatar	392	(1.0)	342	(2.1)	359	(1.3)	**21**	(1.6)	**19**	(1.7)	**11**	(1.6)
Romania	449	(5.6)	434	(10.5)	443	(6.9)	2	(9.3)	-5	(6.3)	**-12**	(5.5)
Russian Federation	491	(3.8)	474	(5.9)	468	(7.8)	**19**	(7.7)	6	(6.8)	-5	(6.7)
Serbia	450	(5.1)	440	(12.9)	447	(10.4)	1	(12.3)	2	(10.8)	6	(9.6)
Shanghai-China	619	(4.5)	608	(10.4)	587	(14.9)	31	(16.4)	21	(13.5)	7	(12.9)
Singapore	569	(1.4)	646	(4.3)	c	c	c	c	c	c	c	c
Chinese Taipei	566	(3.8)	523	(9.8)	549	(46.1)	11	(46.8)	-4	(35.5)	-25	(18.3)
Thailand	425	(3.5)	440	(13.2)	421	(14.5)	7	(15.2)	0	(13.4)	-5	(12.4)
Tunisia	394	(6.7)	388	(7.2)	381	(7.9)	10	(9.7)	6	(8.2)	2	(7.6)
United Arab Emirates	437	(3.0)	427	(7.1)	424	(10.1)	12	(10.4)	3	(7.7)	-9	(4.9)
Uruguay	428	(5.7)	402	(9.3)	394	(5.2)	**27**	(7.9)	**12**	(5.8)	0	(5.1)
Viet Nam	515	(6.4)	532	(8.9)	475	(11.1)	**47**	(13.3)	**34**	(11.1)	**21**	(9.5)

Notes: Values that are statistically significant are indicated in bold (see Annex A3).
ESCS refers to the *PISA index of economic, social and cultural status* of students.
* See notes at the beginning of this Annex.
StatLink http://dx.doi.org/10.1787/888932957384

[Part 1/1]
Mathematics performance and use of achievement data for accountability purposes

Table IV.1.17 *Results based on school principals' reports*

Mathematics performance, by whether the school principal reported that achievement data of students in the national modal grade for 15-year-olds are used in the following ways:

	Posted publicly										Tracked over time by an administrative authority									
	No		Yes		Performance difference (yes - no)		Performance difference (yes - no) after accounting for student ESCS		Performance difference (yes - no) after accounting for student ESCS and school average ESCS		No		Yes		Performance difference (yes - no)		Performance difference (yes - no) after accounting for student ESCS		Performance difference (yes - no) after accounting for student ESCS and school average ESCS	
	Mean score	S.E.	Mean score	S.E.	Score dif.	S.E.	Score dif.	S.E.	Score dif.	S.E.	Mean score	S.E.	Mean score	S.E.	Score dif.	S.E.	Score dif.	S.E.	Score dif.	S.E.
OECD																				
Australia	492	(3.0)	510	(2.4)	17	(4.2)	10	(3.2)	2	(2.9)	494	(7.3)	505	(1.6)	12	(7.3)	9	(5.4)	6	(4.8)
Austria	505	(3.1)	528	(24.0)	24	(25.3)	22	(21.4)	20	(21.2)	498	(6.9)	511	(5.1)	13	(10.6)	10	(8.4)	5	(7.1)
Belgium	515	(2.3)	522	(30.5)	7	(31.3)	5	(24.9)	0	(20.4)	502	(4.6)	529	(4.3)	**27**	(7.8)	**22**	(5.8)	**14**	(4.7)
Canada	517	(2.5)	519	(2.7)	2	(3.8)	2	(3.4)	2	(3.4)	529	(5.3)	517	(2.0)	**-12**	(5.8)	-9	(4.8)	-6	(5.0)
Chile	418	(5.8)	425	(4.0)	7	(7.7)	4	(5.5)	2	(5.0)	403	(9.5)	426	(3.4)	**23**	(10.6)	9	(7.7)	0	(7.4)
Czech Republic	487	(4.8)	513	(5.4)	27	(7.5)	**17**	(6.1)	-2	(5.5)	496	(5.3)	502	(4.5)	6	(7.0)	4	(6.0)	-1	(6.1)
Denmark	503	(3.1)	498	(5.1)	-5	(4.9)	-3	(4.3)	-1	(4.2)	506	(4.7)	498	(3.0)	-8	(5.6)	-4	(4.0)	-1	(3.8)
Estonia	520	(2.8)	522	(3.6)	3	(4.9)	-1	(4.4)	-4	(4.3)	525	(5.6)	519	(2.3)	-6	(6.2)	-5	(5.4)	-3	(5.1)
Finland	518	(2.0)	530	(10.4)	12	(10.7)	12	(11.4)	12	(12.4)	520	(2.8)	517	(2.8)	-3	(4.1)	-5	(3.7)	-7	(3.6)
France	482	(5.7)	514	(5.5)	32	(9.9)	**22**	(7.5)	11	(6.3)	513	(9.1)	490	(4.4)	-22	(12.1)	-12	(8.6)	2	(6.2)
Germany	515	(4.0)	512	(14.7)	-2	(16.4)	-8	(12.2)	-7	(8.1)	511	(5.5)	520	(6.1)	8	(9.6)	10	(7.4)	**12**	(5.3)
Greece	451	(3.0)	456	(6.0)	5	(7.0)	1	(5.6)	-4	(5.4)	451	(5.3)	454	(4.6)	4	(8.5)	4	(6.4)	4	(5.4)
Hungary	460	(5.9)	497	(6.6)	37	(10.6)	**25**	(7.4)	10	(5.3)	467	(7.7)	486	(5.8)	19	(11.8)	11	(8.6)	1	(6.6)
Iceland	492	(2.0)	496	(3.0)	4	(3.4)	2	(3.4)	-1	(3.4)	502	(3.4)	491	(2.0)	**-11**	(3.8)	**-11**	(3.7)	**-11**	(3.7)
Ireland	499	(2.8)	514	(7.0)	15	(7.8)	9	(5.7)	3	(4.9)	508	(3.4)	496	(4.6)	**-12**	(6.3)	-7	(4.4)	-2	(3.4)
Israel	445	(7.5)	490	(6.3)	45	(11.0)	**31**	(9.0)	12	(8.1)	474	(16.4)	465	(4.6)	-9	(16.0)	-11	(13.8)	-14	(14.7)
Italy	478	(3.1)	501	(4.4)	23	(5.8)	**17**	(5.1)	7	(4.4)	487	(3.1)	487	(5.4)	0	(7.0)	-1	(5.9)	-3	(4.7)
Japan	535	(3.9)	553	(18.6)	18	(19.7)	15	(15.1)	0	(11.6)	538	(4.0)	511	(20.1)	-28	(21.4)	-17	(17.6)	9	(12.8)
Korea	542	(11.5)	558	(5.2)	16	(13.3)	14	(11.4)	11	(9.1)	580	(21.4)	551	(4.5)	-30	(22.3)	-25	(17.5)	-15	(12.5)
Luxembourg	483	(1.3)	532	(2.2)	50	(2.6)	**31**	(2.9)	5	(2.9)	495	(1.9)	487	(1.2)	**-8**	(2.1)	-4	(2.3)	3	(2.1)
Mexico	413	(2.0)	413	(2.3)	0	(3.3)	1	(2.7)	2	(2.5)	400	(5.8)	414	(1.4)	**15**	(6.1)	7	(4.8)	1	(4.6)
Netherlands	508	(21.9)	521	(4.9)	12	(23.8)	7	(19.4)	-5	(13.6)	523	(11.6)	519	(5.5)	-5	(14.3)	-7	(12.2)	-9	(9.2)
New Zealand	500	(9.4)	502	(3.4)	2	(11.3)	4	(7.1)	6	(5.1)	517	(14.7)	501	(2.8)	**-17**	(15.8)	**-17**	(6.8)	-17	(11.4)
Norway	483	(4.1)	497	(3.8)	14	(5.8)	9	(4.8)	4	(4.5)	491	(8.3)	490	(2.7)	-1	(8.5)	-4	(8.0)	-8	(7.7)
Poland	509	(3.7)	527	(6.8)	18	(7.8)	**14**	(6.0)	**11**	(5.3)	513	(6.0)	519	(4.4)	6	(7.5)	8	(5.8)	9	(5.3)
Portugal	481	(6.7)	492	(5.0)	11	(8.8)	**11**	(5.7)	**12**	(5.2)	502	(12.7)	485	(4.1)	-18	(13.8)	-7	(10.1)	0	(10.0)
Slovak Republic	476	(10.1)	483	(4.4)	8	(12.3)	1	(8.0)	-5	(5.5)	489	(13.5)	480	(4.8)	-9	(16.4)	-5	(10.5)	-3	(6.8)
Slovenia	512	(2.4)	495	(1.9)	-17	(3.4)	**-11**	(3.2)	1	(2.7)	507	(2.9)	501	(1.5)	-6	(3.5)	-4	(3.3)	0	(2.9)
Spain	484	(2.1)	486	(6.3)	2	(6.8)	-1	(4.7)	-3	(4.3)	486	(4.3)	484	(2.2)	-2	(4.9)	2	(4.0)	4	(4.1)
Sweden	478	(6.3)	479	(2.5)	1	(6.9)	-1	(5.7)	-2	(5.5)	w	w	w	w	w	w	w	w	w	w
Switzerland	530	(3.5)	571	(12.2)	42	(13.3)	**43**	(11.9)	**46**	(13.4)	518	(5.6)	544	(5.6)	**26**	(8.9)	**24**	(7.7)	**21**	(6.7)
Turkey	423	(6.0)	461	(6.2)	38	(8.4)	**27**	(7.2)	6	(7.7)	431	(21.2)	449	(5.0)	18	(22.0)	14	(18.9)	5	(18.4)
United Kingdom	492	(11.1)	496	(3.8)	4	(11.5)	0	(8.8)	-5	(7.0)	524	(19.3)	492	(4.0)	-32	(20.5)	-22	(14.6)	-8	(8.8)
United States	475	(13.5)	483	(4.0)	9	(14.5)	14	(12.4)	19	(12.0)	524	(12.4)	481	(3.8)	**-43**	(13.1)	-17	(11.8)	4	(11.4)
OECD average	489	(1.2)	503	(1.6)	14	(2.1)	10	(1.7)	5	(1.5)	498	(1.7)	494	(0.9)	-4	(2.0)	-2	(1.6)	-1	(1.4)
Partners																				
Albania	394	(2.4)	395	(3.9)	1	(4.6)	c	c	c	c	407	(5.0)	392	(2.2)	**-14**	(5.4)	c	c	c	c
Argentina	388	(3.9)	386	(10.4)	-2	(11.4)	-1	(8.7)	1	(7.5)	399	(7.6)	385	(4.1)	-14	(8.9)	-8	(7.0)	-1	(5.6)
Brazil	394	(3.6)	390	(3.5)	-4	(5.7)	-2	(4.2)	-1	(3.4)	399	(8.9)	391	(2.4)	-8	(9.9)	-7	(6.9)	-7	(5.7)
Bulgaria	407	(5.9)	465	(5.9)	59	(8.8)	**41**	(6.9)	23	(6.1)	426	(20.4)	440	(4.0)	14	(20.8)	13	(14.1)	11	(10.2)
Colombia	371	(4.7)	382	(4.4)	12	(7.0)	9	(5.1)	7	(4.4)	382	(6.2)	376	(3.1)	-6	(7.0)	-4	(5.8)	-2	(6.3)
Costa Rica	406	(3.3)	420	(7.1)	14	(7.7)	9	(6.0)	5	(6.5)	425	(26.5)	406	(2.9)	-18	(26.4)	-15	(19.8)	-11	(17.2)
Croatia	473	(5.1)	465	(8.5)	-8	(11.5)	-6	(9.1)	-3	(6.6)	476	(14.8)	470	(3.7)	-5	(15.8)	-6	(13.2)	-8	(10.4)
Cyprus*	433	(1.3)	469	(2.8)	36	(3.2)	**18**	(3.2)	-10	(3.4)	426	(2.3)	442	(1.3)	**16**	(2.7)	**14**	(2.7)	**12**	(2.7)
Hong Kong-China	552	(5.2)	580	(8.5)	28	(11.7)	**28**	(10.1)	26	(9.1)	564	(9.1)	560	(5.2)	-4	(12.6)	0	(10.5)	5	(9.8)
Indonesia	372	(4.9)	388	(9.4)	17	(10.1)	10	(9.5)	2	(8.4)	369	(8.5)	379	(5.0)	10	(10.3)	10	(8.6)	9	(7.3)
Jordan	388	(3.3)	377	(11.8)	-11	(13.0)	-11	(11.6)	-14	(9.8)	372	(8.5)	388	(3.4)	16	(9.0)	13	(8.2)	9	(8.8)
Kazakhstan	428	(6.8)	433	(3.5)	4	(8.0)	1	(7.5)	-2	(7.4)	c	c	432	(3.0)	c	c	c	c	c	c
Latvia	486	(3.6)	499	(4.6)	13	(6.0)	**10**	(4.9)	8	(4.6)	490	(5.3)	490	(3.0)	0	(6.2)	-2	(5.1)	-4	(4.7)
Liechtenstein	491	(4.6)	c	c	c	c	c	c	c	c	484	(5.3)	c	c	c	c	c	c	c	c
Lithuania	477	(3.3)	483	(4.3)	6	(5.5)	7	(4.2)	**9**	(3.8)	478	(7.0)	479	(3.1)	1	(8.2)	0	(6.3)	-1	(5.3)
Macao-China	536	(1.1)	564	(3.8)	28	(4.1)	**26**	(4.0)	23	(4.0)	537	(1.4)	537	(1.3)	0	(1.8)	1	(1.7)	1	(1.7)
Malaysia	418	(4.4)	426	(5.2)	9	(7.2)	7	(5.3)	5	(4.5)	404	(9.1)	421	(3.4)	17	(10.4)	6	(6.0)	-6	(10.1)
Montenegro	393	(2.0)	414	(1.3)	21	(2.6)	**18**	(2.8)	9	(2.7)	c	c	410	(1.1)	c	c	c	c	c	c
Peru	369	(3.8)	366	(12.8)	-3	(13.1)	-6	(8.7)	-8	(7.2)	360	(5.7)	373	(5.3)	12	(8.3)	6	(5.1)	1	(4.1)
Qatar	367	(1.1)	386	(1.0)	19	(1.3)	**18**	(1.5)	15	(1.4)	442	(4.6)	374	(0.8)	**-68**	(4.7)	**-63**	(4.5)	**-54**	(4.4)
Romania	438	(7.4)	448	(4.5)	10	(8.9)	9	(6.7)	9	(5.8)	444	(8.9)	443	(4.5)	1	(10.3)	1	(8.0)	1	(7.0)
Russian Federation	471	(5.8)	485	(3.8)	14	(7.4)	6	(5.7)	0	(5.2)	c	c	482	(3.0)	c	c	c	c	c	c
Serbia	444	(6.1)	452	(6.7)	8	(10.3)	6	(8.4)	1	(6.0)	455	(7.3)	443	(5.9)	-12	(10.7)	-9	(8.9)	-3	(6.5)
Shanghai-China	613	(3.3)	600	(26.2)	-13	(26.4)	-12	(22.9)	-11	(20.2)	607	(8.4)	616	(6.2)	10	(12.9)	5	(9.9)	-1	(7.2)
Singapore	560	(1.6)	588	(2.5)	28	(2.5)	**20**	(2.5)	7	(3.4)	c	c	575	(1.3)	c	c	c	c	c	c
Chinese Taipei	559	(4.2)	564	(16.6)	5	(18.9)	2	(12.7)	-1	(9.1)	562	(6.1)	557	(6.7)	-5	(10.9)	0	(8.2)	7	(6.5)
Thailand	411	(7.6)	432	(4.2)	21	(9.2)	**17**	(7.8)	14	(7.3)	394	(20.7)	427	(3.5)	33	(21.1)	**37**	(18.4)	**40**	(18.4)
Tunisia	389	(4.6)	379	(8.8)	-10	(10.0)	-7	(9.0)	-3	(9.6)	400	(8.6)	384	(4.8)	-16	(10.4)	-13	(8.6)	-8	(7.2)
United Arab Emirates	433	(3.7)	437	(3.4)	4	(5.2)	4	(4.9)	5	(5.0)	445	(10.2)	434	(2.8)	-11	(11.3)	-9	(10.1)	-6	(9.3)
Uruguay	409	(3.2)	411	(9.8)	2	(11.1)	6	(9.5)	9	(8.9)	418	(8.6)	406	(3.2)	-12	(10.1)	-5	(6.7)	0	(5.6)
Viet Nam	487	(9.6)	519	(5.0)	33	(10.7)	**28**	(9.3)	24	(9.0)	501	(8.2)	512	(6.0)	11	(10.4)	8	(8.5)	6	(9.3)

Notes: Values that are statistically significant are indicated in bold (see Annex A3).
ESCS refers to the *PISA index of economic, social and cultural status* of students.
* See notes at the beginning of this Annex.
StatLink http://dx.doi.org/10.1787/888932957384

[Part 1/5]
Mathematics performance and quality assurance and school improvement
Table IV.1.18   *Results based on school principals' reports*

	Mathematics performance, by whether the school principal reported that the school has the following measures aimed at quality assurance and improvement:									
	Written specification of the school's curriculum and educational goals					Written specification of student performance standards				
	No	Yes	Performance difference (yes - no)	Performance difference (yes - no) after accounting for student ESCS	Performance difference (yes - no) after accounting for student ESCS and school average ESCS	No	Yes	Performance difference (yes - no)	Performance difference (yes - no) after accounting for student ESCS	Performance difference (yes - no) after accounting for student ESCS and school average ESCS
	Mean score / S.E.	Mean score / S.E.	Score dif. / S.E.	Score dif. / S.E.	Score dif. / S.E.	Mean score / S.E.	Mean score / S.E.	Score dif. / S.E.	Score dif. / S.E.	Score dif. / S.E.
OECD Australia	499 (9.0)	504 (1.7)	5 (9.0)	-1 (7.8)	-6 (7.9)	500 (6.7)	505 (1.8)	4 (7.1)	-3 (5.6)	-9 (5.1)
Austria	510 (8.4)	506 (3.8)	-4 (10.4)	-3 (8.2)	-2 (7.9)	517 (5.5)	499 (5.0)	**-18** (8.7)	-10 (7.4)	1 (7.2)
Belgium	501 (12.1)	517 (3.0)	17 (14.0)	10 (10.5)	-2 (5.8)	505 (5.5)	525 (5.6)	**20** (10.2)	15 (7.7)	3 (5.4)
Canada	515 (8.5)	519 (2.0)	4 (9.1)	-6 (5.9)	**-14** (5.1)	515 (5.4)	519 (2.2)	4 (6.3)	-1 (5.3)	-5 (4.8)
Chile	412 (8.6)	425 (3.5)	13 (9.8)	6 (7.0)	1 (6.5)	418 (7.3)	424 (4.1)	6 (9.3)	3 (6.4)	1 (5.3)
Czech Republic	491 (12.1)	499 (3.6)	8 (12.9)	8 (11.0)	9 (14.4)	517 (7.9)	494 (4.1)	**-23** (9.2)	**-18** (7.3)	-8 (6.0)
Denmark	491 (3.8)	504 (3.3)	**13** (5.1)	**11** (3.3)	**9** (3.0)	502 (3.9)	497 (3.7)	-4 (5.7)	-2 (3.8)	-1 (3.2)
Estonia	526 (7.0)	520 (2.1)	-6 (7.3)	-8 (6.6)	-10 (6.7)	530 (6.2)	519 (2.2)	-11 (6.6)	-10 (6.7)	-9 (7.1)
Finland	520 (4.7)	518 (2.1)	-1 (5.1)	-3 (3.9)	-5 (4.0)	518 (3.0)	519 (2.5)	1 (3.9)	-2 (3.6)	-5 (4.0)
France	508 (9.0)	491 (4.3)	-17 (11.6)	-12 (8.6)	-8 (6.7)	509 (4.2)	460 (10.0)	**-49** (12.3)	**-33** (9.2)	-10 (6.3)
Germany	522 (15.8)	512 (4.0)	-10 (17.5)	2 (14.5)	18 (10.5)	525 (8.8)	509 (4.9)	-16 (11.7)	-8 (9.2)	2 (6.7)
Greece	458 (4.7)	448 (4.3)	-10 (7.3)	-10 (5.4)	-8 (4.6)	454 (3.8)	450 (6.4)	-4 (8.7)	-4 (6.6)	-3 (5.5)
Hungary	453 (44.7)	479 (3.6)	26 (46.1)	22 (36.4)	20 (27.1)	438 (15.3)	482 (3.8)	**44** (16.1)	**30** (10.0)	**14** (6.0)
Iceland	487 (2.7)	497 (2.2)	**10** (3.3)	2 (3.5)	**-7** (3.6)	492 (3.2)	494 (1.9)	2 (3.3)	**-6** (3.3)	**-13** (3.4)
Ireland	499 (6.1)	504 (3.1)	5 (7.6)	-1 (5.6)	-6 (4.2)	501 (3.9)	506 (3.6)	5 (5.8)	3 (4.4)	-1 (3.7)
Israel	500 (14.1)	465 (4.9)	**-35** (15.2)	-16 (9.3)	6 (9.7)	477 (8.5)	463 (5.7)	-14 (10.6)	-9 (8.3)	3 (7.3)
Italy	485 (18.8)	487 (2.3)	3 (18.9)	4 (15.3)	8 (11.5)	493 (5.5)	486 (2.7)	-6 (6.8)	-9 (6.1)	**-14** (5.8)
Japan	c c	537 (3.7)	c c	c c	c c	531 (5.0)	542 (7.7)	10 (10.8)	8 (8.9)	3 (5.8)
Korea	c c	555 (4.5)	c c	c c	c c	564 (14.8)	553 (4.8)	-11 (15.8)	-2 (14.5)	15 (15.1)
Luxembourg	484 (1.9)	498 (1.4)	**14** (2.1)	**5** (2.2)	**-10** (2.2)	482 (1.6)	504 (1.5)	**21** (2.0)	**10** (2.3)	**-5** (2.2)
Mexico	387 (4.5)	415 (1.4)	**28** (4.7)	**18** (4.2)	**10** (4.3)	409 (4.2)	414 (1.6)	5 (4.7)	2 (3.8)	0 (3.5)
Netherlands	503 (23.2)	521 (4.4)	19 (23.8)	18 (20.1)	12 (11.9)	535 (13.1)	517 (5.6)	-19 (15.2)	-14 (14.0)	-5 (9.5)
New Zealand	c c	501 (2.5)	c c	c c	c c	510 (12.6)	501 (2.7)	-9 (13.6)	-5 (8.4)	1 (6.6)
Norway	508 (21.6)	490 (2.6)	-18 (20.8)	-23 (19.4)	-29 (18.7)	484 (6.1)	493 (2.9)	8 (6.5)	4 (5.3)	2 (4.6)
Poland	515 (5.4)	520 (4.8)	4 (7.1)	1 (5.3)	-2 (5.0)	509 (6.9)	520 (4.1)	10 (7.8)	6 (6.3)	2 (6.4)
Portugal	488 (14.6)	486 (4.2)	-2 (15.8)	-6 (13.1)	-10 (12.5)	498 (5.9)	482 (5.1)	-16 (8.6)	**-13** (6.3)	-11 (6.6)
Slovak Republic	480 (16.5)	482 (4.3)	3 (18.8)	1 (12.8)	0 (8.8)	473 (10.5)	483 (4.5)	9 (12.7)	4 (8.6)	-1 (7.0)
Slovenia	513 (9.5)	503 (1.4)	-10 (10.0)	-8 (7.1)	-2 (7.6)	517 (5.3)	503 (1.4)	**-15** (5.5)	**-14** (5.3)	-12 (6.7)
Spain	488 (9.1)	484 (2.0)	-4 (9.4)	-5 (7.5)	-5 (7.3)	483 (4.7)	485 (2.0)	1 (4.9)	-1 (4.2)	-2 (4.1)
Sweden	472 (4.4)	481 (3.2)	9 (6.0)	5 (5.0)	3 (4.8)	476 (9.7)	478 (2.5)	3 (10.4)	4 (7.4)	6 (6.7)
Switzerland	517 (5.0)	540 (5.4)	23 (8.7)	**19** (7.1)	12 (5.9)	533 (4.4)	533 (6.0)	0 (8.0)	4 (6.9)	9 (6.0)
Turkey	445 (20.3)	449 (4.6)	4 (20.2)	3 (17.3)	-1 (13.3)	484 (31.6)	446 (4.2)	-38 (30.5)	-33 (26.5)	-23 (20.9)
United Kingdom	505 (20.1)	494 (3.8)	-10 (20.5)	-4 (13.7)	1 (11.7)	517 (8.2)	492 (4.2)	**-25** (10.0)	**-15** (6.4)	-5 (7.2)
United States	485 (29.5)	482 (3.5)	-3 (28.7)	5 (20.9)	11 (16.1)	484 (14.7)	482 (3.7)	-2 (15.0)	-8 (7.6)	**-13** (6.5)
OECD average	489 (2.7)	495 (0.6)	3 (2.8)	1 (2.2)	0 (1.8)	497 (1.6)	493 (0.8)	**-4** (1.9)	**-4** (1.5)	**-3** (1.2)
Partners Albania	398 (7.0)	394 (2.1)	-5 (7.5)	c c	c c	404 (13.0)	394 (2.1)	-10 (13.4)	c c	c c
Argentina	390 (12.9)	389 (3.9)	0 (14.3)	5 (10.2)	10 (7.0)	395 (6.3)	387 (4.1)	-9 (7.6)	-9 (5.7)	-10 (5.6)
Brazil	407 (19.6)	390 (2.1)	-17 (20.1)	-12 (15.2)	-5 (10.6)	387 (4.3)	393 (3.1)	6 (6.0)	1 (4.4)	-4 (3.8)
Bulgaria	428 (14.7)	441 (4.4)	13 (16.1)	0 (11.8)	-12 (9.5)	430 (13.4)	442 (4.6)	12 (15.2)	10 (10.8)	8 (7.2)
Colombia	368 (18.3)	377 (3.0)	8 (18.7)	11 (14.8)	14 (13.2)	365 (17.0)	377 (3.0)	12 (17.5)	9 (15.4)	7 (14.9)
Costa Rica	405 (7.4)	408 (3.4)	2 (8.0)	-1 (6.9)	-4 (6.8)	393 (5.2)	410 (3.5)	**17** (6.1)	**11** (5.0)	5 (5.3)
Croatia	483 (22.6)	471 (4.0)	-12 (24.1)	-11 (19.0)	-6 (12.6)	475 (9.8)	470 (4.7)	-5 (12.3)	-2 (9.8)	3 (7.4)
Cyprus*	c c	439 (1.1)	c c	c c	c c	430 (2.4)	441 (1.3)	**11** (2.8)	**6** (2.7)	-3 (2.7)
Hong Kong-China	c c	561 (3.3)	c c	c c	c c	551 (15.0)	562 (3.7)	12 (16.5)	6 (14.6)	-3 (12.4)
Indonesia	c c	376 (4.1)	c c	c c	c c	345 (12.9)	378 (4.4)	**33** (14.0)	**28** (11.3)	**22** (9.4)
Jordan	381 (13.1)	387 (3.2)	6 (13.5)	4 (12.7)	0 (12.8)	362 (9.0)	388 (3.3)	**25** (9.6)	**19** (8.8)	10 (9.9)
Kazakhstan	403 (12.5)	433 (3.1)	**29** (13.2)	**21** (10.3)	11 (8.5)	c c	432 (3.0)	c c	c c	c c
Latvia	467 (14.7)	490 (2.8)	22 (14.6)	17 (11.8)	15 (11.0)	471 (8.7)	490 (2.9)	**20** (9.3)	12 (6.8)	7 (5.4)
Liechtenstein	c c	557 (4.1)	c c	c c	c c	c c	490 (4.7)	c c	c c	c c
Lithuania	466 (7.7)	484 (3.3)	18 (9.1)	12 (7.1)	4 (5.6)	474 (7.0)	480 (3.4)	6 (8.4)	6 (6.7)	6 (5.8)
Macao-China	502 (3.2)	542 (1.0)	40 (3.4)	38 (3.6)	34 (3.5)	459 (4.1)	544 (1.0)	**85** (4.3)	**82** (4.3)	77 (4.3)
Malaysia	c c	420 (3.2)	c c	c c	c c	c c	421 (3.2)	c c	c c	c c
Montenegro	392 (3.4)	411 (1.1)	19 (3.7)	12 (3.7)	-6 (3.8)	419 (2.1)	408 (1.3)	**-11** (2.6)	**-7** (2.5)	3 (2.6)
Peru	341 (8.9)	371 (4.1)	30 (10.0)	**18** (6.7)	9 (5.8)	358 (5.4)	373 (5.0)	14 (7.5)	**10** (4.9)	7 (4.0)
Qatar	c c	375 (0.8)	c c	c c	c c	c c	375 (0.8)	c c	c c	c c
Romania	436 (12.6)	446 (3.9)	10 (13.3)	11 (9.4)	12 (7.7)	445 (13.0)	444 (4.1)	-1 (14.2)	-2 (11.2)	-3 (9.2)
Russian Federation	462 (12.1)	484 (2.9)	21 (11.9)	11 (11.7)	3 (11.7)	493 (10.1)	481 (3.3)	-12 (11.1)	-7 (9.3)	-3 (8.2)
Serbia	465 (13.2)	447 (5.0)	-18 (15.3)	-13 (13.0)	-5 (10.4)	444 (5.6)	455 (6.7)	11 (9.7)	7 (7.9)	-5 (6.1)
Shanghai-China	c c	613 (3.3)	c c	c c	c c	583 (12.8)	617 (3.5)	**34** (13.5)	18 (9.4)	-6 (7.7)
Singapore	c c	575 (1.3)	c c	c c	c c	c c	575 (1.2)	c c	c c	c c
Chinese Taipei	561 (18.8)	559 (3.9)	-3 (19.9)	0 (13.4)	5 (9.0)	568 (14.5)	558 (4.5)	-11 (16.9)	-5 (13.5)	3 (11.4)
Thailand	391 (6.0)	428 (3.6)	36 (7.1)	**26** (5.8)	**16** (7.4)	397 (15.6)	429 (3.6)	**32** (15.9)	23 (13.4)	15 (11.9)
Tunisia	392 (5.9)	385 (6.4)	-7 (9.2)	-3 (8.0)	1 (7.3)	385 (5.4)	397 (8.8)	12 (11.1)	10 (9.3)	8 (8.2)
United Arab Emirates	397 (11.0)	436 (2.1)	39 (11.1)	**29** (9.9)	**16** (10.0)	465 (11.5)	434 (2.3)	**-31** (12.0)	-24 (12.8)	-13 (14.8)
Uruguay	409 (8.3)	410 (4.2)	1 (11.0)	-3 (7.1)	-5 (5.9)	410 (5.6)	408 (5.6)	-2 (9.9)	3 (6.2)	7 (4.7)
Viet Nam	c c	511 (4.9)	c c	c c	c c	487 (19.1)	513 (4.9)	26 (19.5)	20 (16.6)	15 (14.9)

Notes: Values that are statistically significant are indicated in bold (see Annex A3).
ESCS refers to the *PISA index of economic, social and cultural status* of students.
* See notes at the beginning of this Annex.
StatLink ⬛⬛ http://dx.doi.org/10.1787/888932957384

[Part 2/5]
Mathematics performance and quality assurance and school improvement

Table IV.1.18 *Results based on school principals' reports*

Mathematics performance, by whether the school principal reported that the school has the following measures aimed at quality assurance and improvement:

	Systematic recording of data, including teacher and student attendance and graduation rates, test results and professional development of teachers										Internal evaluation/self-evaluation									
	No		Yes		Performance difference (yes - no)		Performance difference (yes - no) after accounting for student ESCS		Performance difference (yes - no) after accounting for student ESCS and school average ESCS		No		Yes		Performance difference (yes - no)		Performance difference (yes - no) after accounting for student ESCS		Performance difference (yes - no) after accounting for student ESCS and school average ESCS	
	Mean score	S.E.	Mean score	S.E.	Score dif.	S.E.	Score dif.	S.E.	Score dif.	S.E.	Mean score	S.E.	Mean score	S.E.	Score dif.	S.E.	Score dif.	S.E.	Score dif.	S.E.
OECD																				
Australia	492	(15.2)	504	(1.7)	13	(15.3)	5	(11.2)	-2	(8.2)	519	(7.9)	503	(1.7)	-16	(8.4)	-12	(7.5)	-10	(7.6)
Austria	507	(9.9)	507	(4.0)	1	(12.3)	0	(9.8)	-1	(8.3)	524	(13.1)	504	(3.8)	-20	(15.2)	-14	(11.4)	-6	(10.0)
Belgium	482	(7.2)	525	(3.2)	**43**	(8.9)	**32**	(6.8)	**16**	(5.6)	492	(9.0)	522	(3.5)	**30**	(11.4)	**21**	(8.5)	8	(5.3)
Canada	520	(7.9)	518	(2.2)	-2	(8.7)	-4	(7.1)	-6	(6.3)	520	(4.5)	518	(2.4)	-2	(5.6)	-6	(5.0)	**-10**	(4.8)
Chile	423	(9.9)	423	(3.3)	-1	(10.6)	6	(7.1)	9	(6.7)	404	(10.2)	425	(3.2)	**21**	(10.5)	13	(7.2)	7	(7.0)
Czech Republic	480	(13.9)	503	(3.5)	24	(14.6)	17	(11.8)	7	(8.5)	555	(19.5)	499	(3.7)	**-56**	(20.6)	**-45**	(12.2)	**-26**	(9.3)
Denmark	501	(8.6)	500	(2.6)	-1	(9.1)	-2	(6.0)	-3	(5.0)	502	(7.5)	500	(2.8)	-2	(8.1)	4	(5.4)	8	(4.6)
Estonia	533	(15.0)	520	(2.1)	-14	(15.5)	-12	(13.1)	-9	(11.1)	c	c	520	(2.0)	c	c	c	c	c	c
Finland	522	(2.7)	517	(2.5)	-5	(3.6)	-4	(3.2)	-3	(3.2)	511	(10.8)	519	(2.0)	8	(11.1)	10	(9.5)	11	(8.7)
France	518	(9.8)	488	(4.2)	**-30**	(12.1)	**-20**	(8.7)	-8	(6.8)	502	(7.0)	492	(5.8)	-10	(11.2)	-8	(7.8)	-6	(5.6)
Germany	521	(11.0)	512	(4.3)	-9	(13.1)	-5	(9.9)	4	(6.9)	498	(8.9)	520	(4.7)	22	(11.7)	14	(9.9)	6	(8.4)
Greece	448	(5.1)	455	(3.6)	6	(7.0)	3	(5.3)	-1	(4.8)	454	(3.7)	450	(7.0)	-3	(9.4)	-2	(6.7)	-1	(5.6)
Hungary	466	(15.7)	480	(4.0)	15	(17.8)	9	(12.8)	2	(9.1)	509	(23.8)	476	(3.6)	-32	(24.5)	-16	(17.1)	2	(16.0)
Iceland	461	(6.8)	496	(1.9)	**35**	(7.3)	**24**	(7.4)	14	(7.6)	c	c	494	(1.8)	c	c	c	c	c	c
Ireland	508	(10.3)	501	(2.7)	-6	(11.0)	-4	(7.8)	-3	(5.6)	506	(7.0)	501	(3.0)	-5	(8.0)	-3	(5.8)	0	(5.2)
Israel	485	(21.0)	465	(5.0)	-20	(22.2)	-14	(17.0)	-9	(13.0)	462	(13.9)	467	(5.0)	5	(15.0)	1	(12.4)	1	(10.0)
Italy	488	(3.6)	488	(3.6)	0	(5.6)	0	(4.7)	0	(4.1)	488	(5.7)	487	(2.6)	-1	(6.5)	0	(5.6)	2	(4.9)
Japan	530	(6.0)	542	(5.3)	12	(8.7)	9	(7.4)	7	(6.2)	488	(15.2)	538	(3.6)	**50**	(16.3)	**44**	(13.3)	29	(14.7)
Korea	546	(13.9)	554	(4.9)	8	(15.2)	6	(12.4)	1	(8.9)	c	c	553	(4.8)	c	c	c	c	c	c
Luxembourg	463	(1.8)	503	(1.4)	**40**	(2.1)	**21**	(2.3)	**-7**	(2.3)	500	(2.2)	490	(1.4)	**-10**	(2.3)	**-10**	(2.5)	**-12**	(2.3)
Mexico	407	(6.3)	414	(1.4)	7	(6.5)	7	(5.1)	6	(4.6)	407	(5.8)	414	(1.5)	6	(6.1)	5	(5.3)	4	(4.9)
Netherlands	c	c	521	(4.3)	c	c	c	c	c	c	526	(20.5)	519	(4.8)	-7	(21.9)	-3	(18.8)	7	(14.1)
New Zealand	465	(33.3)	503	(2.6)	37	(34.0)	24	(20.4)	18	(12.1)	c	c	502	(2.5)	c	c	c	c	c	c
Norway	492	(6.7)	490	(3.1)	-2	(7.5)	-1	(6.2)	0	(5.7)	484	(4.7)	494	(3.6)	10	(6.0)	6	(5.4)	3	(5.0)
Poland	c	c	517	(3.6)	c	c	c	c	c	c	518	(16.3)	517	(3.7)	-1	(16.6)	-1	(14.6)	-1	(15.0)
Portugal	524	(16.3)	485	(4.0)	**-39**	(17.2)	**-20**	(7.7)	-8	(7.0)	c	c	487	(3.8)	c	c	c	c	c	c
Slovak Republic	479	(18.7)	481	(3.7)	2	(19.9)	0	(14.1)	-2	(10.0)	428	(21.6)	484	(3.6)	**56**	(22.5)	**38**	(15.6)	22	(11.3)
Slovenia	504	(3.5)	503	(1.5)	-1	(3.9)	-2	(3.8)	-1	(3.3)	521	(8.9)	502	(1.4)	**-20**	(9.2)	**-15**	(6.8)	-7	(5.1)
Spain	491	(4.9)	484	(2.0)	-7	(5.2)	**-10**	(4.7)	**-12**	(5.2)	486	(3.3)	484	(2.1)	-2	(3.7)	-2	(3.7)	-2	(4.3)
Sweden	474	(9.8)	479	(2.4)	5	(10.1)	10	(8.2)	14	(7.4)	463	(9.0)	480	(2.5)	17	(9.9)	8	(6.6)	1	(6.3)
Switzerland	521	(5.8)	540	(5.6)	**19**	(9.4)	**17**	(7.8)	**14**	(6.5)	525	(9.4)	534	(3.7)	9	(10.4)	11	(8.5)	14	(7.6)
Turkey	456	(52.0)	448	(4.3)	-8	(51.2)	-2	(45.1)	11	(36.8)	c	c	449	(4.9)	c	c	c	c	c	c
United Kingdom	469	(16.9)	495	(3.6)	26	(17.1)	17	(15.1)	3	(13.3)	c	c	495	(3.6)	c	c	c	c	c	c
United States	c	c	482	(3.6)	c	c	c	c	c	c	472	(17.7)	483	(3.8)	11	(18.5)	3	(14.8)	-2	(12.7)
OECD average	489	(2.8)	495	(0.6)	5	(2.9)	3	(2.3)	2	(1.8)	491	(2.3)	495	(0.6)	2	(2.5)	2	(1.9)	2	(1.7)
Partners																				
Albania	389	(9.6)	394	(2.2)	5	(10.2)	c	c	c	c	397	(12.5)	394	(2.0)	-3	(12.7)	c	c	c	c
Argentina	385	(8.4)	391	(4.3)	5	(10.2)	3	(8.1)	-1	(7.5)	380	(7.6)	391	(3.9)	11	(9.7)	7	(7.1)	0	(7.9)
Brazil	382	(5.1)	393	(2.9)	11	(6.7)	6	(4.8)	1	(3.7)	374	(6.1)	392	(2.3)	**18**	(6.5)	8	(5.3)	-3	(5.4)
Bulgaria	c	c	440	(4.1)	c	c	c	c	c	c	c	c	439	(3.9)	c	c	c	c	c	c
Colombia	378	(10.1)	377	(3.3)	-1	(11.2)	1	(9.2)	3	(8.7)	309	(13.7)	378	(2.9)	**70**	(14.0)	**58**	(7.2)	**48**	(11.9)
Costa Rica	396	(5.4)	409	(3.3)	**12**	(5.8)	6	(4.8)	1	(6.1)	413	(10.4)	406	(3.2)	-7	(11.1)	-10	(8.9)	-12	(7.8)
Croatia	458	(20.5)	472	(3.8)	13	(21.6)	10	(18.2)	2	(13.0)	470	(19.2)	471	(4.0)	1	(20.6)	7	(17.2)	18	(11.8)
Cyprus*	424	(4.7)	440	(1.2)	**16**	(4.9)	**13**	(4.6)	8	(4.5)	434	(2.3)	440	(1.2)	**6**	(2.6)	2	(2.5)	-4	(2.5)
Hong Kong-China	c	c	561	(3.2)	c	c	c	c	c	c	c	c	561	(3.2)	c	c	c	c	c	c
Indonesia	c	c	375	(4.1)	c	c	c	c	c	c	371	(8.9)	376	(4.5)	5	(10.5)	0	(8.9)	-6	(8.1)
Jordan	389	(10.6)	385	(3.1)	-4	(10.6)	-3	(9.4)	-2	(8.7)	362	(7.4)	388	(3.4)	**26**	(8.4)	**25**	(8.3)	**22**	(9.5)
Kazakhstan	c	c	432	(3.0)	c	c	c	c	c	c	c	c	432	(3.1)	c	c	c	c	c	c
Latvia	c	c	490	(2.8)	c	c	c	c	c	c	c	c	488	(2.7)	c	c	c	c	c	c
Liechtenstein	557	(5.2)	497	(5.8)	**-60**	(7.8)	**-57**	(8.5)	**-50**	(8.5)	c	c	532	(3.9)	c	c	c	c	c	c
Lithuania	c	c	479	(2.7)	c	c	c	c	c	c	484	(17.6)	479	(2.9)	-6	(18.6)	-6	(15.6)	-7	(13.6)
Macao-China	c	c	539	(1.0)	c	c	c	c	c	c	511	(2.9)	542	(1.0)	**31**	(3.0)	**28**	(3.1)	**22**	(3.1)
Malaysia	c	c	420	(3.2)	c	c	c	c	c	c	c	c	420	(3.2)	c	c	c	c	c	c
Montenegro	c	c	409	(1.1)	c	c	c	c	c	c	c	c	410	(1.1)	c	c	c	c	c	c
Peru	363	(5.1)	370	(5.6)	7	(8.4)	4	(5.1)	2	(3.9)	363	(7.2)	368	(4.2)	5	(8.8)	3	(5.9)	2	(5.3)
Qatar	c	c	375	(0.8)	c	c	c	c	c	c	c	c	375	(0.8)	c	c	c	c	c	c
Romania	425	(11.4)	447	(3.9)	22	(12.2)	17	(9.5)	14	(8.8)	458	(13.3)	443	(4.0)	-16	(14.2)	-10	(11.1)	-6	(9.2)
Russian Federation	457	(29.1)	483	(3.1)	26	(29.5)	17	(23.3)	9	(20.2)	426	(15.8)	483	(3.1)	**57**	(16.5)	**39**	(16.3)	25	(18.1)
Serbia	480	(23.0)	450	(4.2)	-30	(23.8)	-28	(19.2)	-28	(19.3)	417	(15.1)	450	(4.0)	**33**	(15.5)	22	(13.8)	-4	(12.5)
Shanghai-China	c	c	614	(3.2)	c	c	c	c	c	c	c	c	613	(3.3)	c	c	c	c	c	c
Singapore	c	c	574	(1.3)	c	c	c	c	c	c	c	c	574	(1.3)	c	c	c	c	c	c
Chinese Taipei	555	(14.2)	559	(3.8)	4	(15.1)	13	(10.3)	27	(11.8)	544	(10.4)	562	(4.7)	18	(13.0)	9	(10.4)	-4	(9.9)
Thailand	c	c	428	(3.4)	c	c	c	c	c	c	c	c	427	(3.4)	c	c	c	c	c	c
Tunisia	372	(5.1)	395	(5.0)	**23**	(9.7)	**21**	(7.8)	**17**	(6.9)	392	(17.4)	388	(4.2)	-4	(18.1)	-2	(15.7)	2	(14.5)
United Arab Emirates	454	(19.8)	435	(2.5)	-19	(20.5)	-4	(15.9)	17	(18.5)	410	(16.1)	435	(2.5)	25	(16.4)	21	(13.3)	19	(11.9)
Uruguay	436	(19.6)	408	(3.0)	-28	(20.5)	-18	(11.9)	-10	(12.3)	404	(7.9)	411	(3.6)	7	(10.0)	6	(7.2)	5	(6.1)
Viet Nam	c	c	512	(4.8)	c	c	c	c	c	c	c	c	510	(4.8)	c	c	c	c	c	c

Notes: Values that are statistically significant are indicated in bold (see Annex A3).
ESCS refers to the *PISA index of economic, social and cultural status* of students.
* See notes at the beginning of this Annex.
StatLink ⧉ http://dx.doi.org/10.1787/888932957384

[Part 3/5]
Mathematics performance and quality assurance and school improvement

Table IV.1.18   *Results based on school principals' reports*

Mathematics performance, by whether the school principal reported that the school has the following measures aimed at quality assurance and improvement:

	External evaluation										Seek written feedback from students (e.g. regarding lessons, teachers or resources)									
	No		Yes		Performance difference (yes - no)		Performance difference (yes - no) after accounting for student ESCS		Performance difference (yes - no) after accounting for student ESCS and school average ESCS		No		Yes		Performance difference (yes - no)		Performance difference (yes - no) after accounting for student ESCS		Performance difference (yes - no) after accounting for student ESCS and school average ESCS	
	Mean score	S.E.	Mean score	S.E.	Score dif.	S.E.	Score dif.	S.E.	Score dif.	S.E.	Mean score	S.E.	Mean score	S.E.	Score dif.	S.E.	Score dif.	S.E.	Score dif.	S.E.
OECD																				
Australia	509	(3.5)	502	(2.3)	-7	(4.8)	-6	(4.2)	-5	(4.1)	500	(3.5)	506	(2.1)	6	(4.5)	1	(3.9)	-4	(3.9)
Austria	506	(4.2)	510	(9.5)	4	(12.3)	3	(10.4)	2	(9.3)	499	(12.4)	509	(4.0)	9	(14.8)	11	(11.3)	15	(8.7)
Belgium	503	(7.2)	521	(3.7)	18	(9.9)	9	(7.9)	-6	(5.9)	511	(3.1)	524	(6.3)	13	(8.2)	13	(6.4)	14	(5.8)
Canada	520	(3.0)	517	(3.0)	-3	(4.8)	-4	(4.1)	-6	(3.8)	514	(2.3)	525	(3.1)	10	(3.8)	6	(3.3)	2	(3.3)
Chile	412	(4.4)	432	(5.2)	20	(7.6)	13	(4.9)	8	(4.3)	418	(5.6)	428	(4.4)	10	(8.1)	5	(5.6)	2	(5.1)
Czech Republic	496	(6.8)	501	(5.1)	5	(9.6)	4	(7.6)	1	(6.0)	494	(7.9)	502	(5.5)	8	(11.3)	7	(9.2)	4	(7.1)
Denmark	505	(5.1)	497	(3.2)	-8	(6.5)	-4	(4.2)	0	(3.7)	500	(3.3)	499	(4.0)	-1	(5.1)	-1	(3.6)	-1	(3.5)
Estonia	524	(4.6)	519	(2.3)	-5	(5.2)	-3	(4.8)	-1	(4.8)	517	(4.6)	522	(2.4)	4	(5.4)	3	(5.3)	1	(5.6)
Finland	519	(2.5)	518	(3.1)	-1	(4.0)	-3	(3.6)	-3	(3.5)	517	(4.1)	519	(2.4)	2	(4.9)	2	(4.3)	2	(4.1)
France	499	(7.0)	493	(5.8)	-5	(11.2)	-5	(8.0)	-1	(6.2)	497	(3.5)	494	(16.0)	-3	(17.7)	-1	(13.9)	0	(10.8)
Germany	497	(6.7)	523	(5.3)	26	(10.3)	18	(7.9)	15	(5.8)	510	(6.2)	516	(6.7)	6	(11.0)	4	(8.7)	4	(5.7)
Greece	453	(2.9)	455	(24.4)	2	(25.6)	-2	(18.7)	-7	(14.5)	453	(3.2)	452	(6.9)	-1	(8.4)	-4	(6.5)	-9	(5.9)
Hungary	476	(8.5)	479	(5.8)	2	(8.5)	1	(8.9)	-2	(6.1)	464	(12.7)	481	(4.2)	17	(14.6)	13	(8.6)	8	(7.3)
Iceland	488	(3.3)	495	(1.8)	7	(3.2)	6	(3.2)	3	(3.2)	492	(2.5)	495	(2.2)	3	(3.1)	3	(3.1)	3	(3.1)
Ireland	513	(5.4)	500	(3.2)	-12	(7.0)	-8	(5.1)	-2	(4.7)	501	(3.2)	507	(6.1)	6	(7.5)	4	(5.0)	2	(3.7)
Israel	473	(8.5)	462	(5.5)	-11	(10.0)	-12	(7.7)	-12	(6.6)	464	(6.1)	468	(7.6)	4	(9.9)	5	(7.4)	9	(6.0)
Italy	486	(2.8)	491	(5.6)	5	(6.8)	5	(6.0)	5	(5.3)	486	(3.2)	490	(4.7)	4	(6.5)	4	(5.4)	4	(4.5)
Japan	537	(10.5)	536	(3.9)	-1	(11.6)	4	(9.5)	18	(8.0)	529	(9.6)	539	(3.7)	10	(10.5)	7	(9.1)	6	(7.8)
Korea	541	(9.1)	557	(5.6)	17	(11.2)	17	(8.9)	17	(6.5)	533	(12.7)	558	(5.2)	25	(14.3)	17	(12.7)	3	(10.9)
Luxembourg	479	(1.6)	511	(1.8)	32	(2.1)	21	(2.3)	6	(2.3)	491	(1.4)	496	(2.2)	5	(2.4)	2	(2.6)	-5	(2.4)
Mexico	412	(3.0)	414	(1.7)	2	(3.6)	1	(3.1)	0	(3.0)	398	(3.0)	419	(1.6)	21	(3.5)	17	(3.1)	14	(3.1)
Netherlands	509	(16.7)	522	(5.2)	13	(19.0)	13	(17.3)	11	(14.0)	463	(18.2)	526	(4.4)	63	(18.8)	50	(17.3)	6	(13.0)
New Zealand	512	(10.3)	501	(2.8)	-11	(11.2)	-3	(7.4)	6	(6.5)	536	(18.1)	501	(2.6)	-35	(18.8)	-33	(14.5)	-31	(12.5)
Norway	492	(4.0)	489	(4.3)	-3	(6.1)	-4	(5.3)	-5	(4.9)	486	(4.6)	496	(3.8)	10	(6.5)	7	(5.6)	4	(4.8)
Poland	516	(6.4)	518	(4.4)	2	(7.7)	1	(5.5)	0	(4.9)	515	(6.4)	518	(4.4)	3	(7.6)	4	(5.8)	4	(5.1)
Portugal	466	(9.9)	490	(3.9)	24	(10.0)	23	(7.1)	23	(6.8)	486	(9.0)	487	(4.9)	1	(11.1)	8	(6.7)	13	(6.2)
Slovak Republic	487	(5.6)	471	(7.3)	-16	(10.8)	-8	(7.3)	-1	(6.0)	474	(7.3)	489	(6.6)	15	(11.9)	6	(7.6)	-1	(5.2)
Slovenia	512	(1.8)	484	(2.2)	-28	(2.9)	-22	(2.9)	-7	(2.9)	503	(3.4)	503	(1.6)	0	(4.0)	-2	(3.5)	-5	(3.4)
Spain	480	(4.6)	486	(2.3)	6	(5.4)	1	(4.1)	-1	(3.8)	479	(3.9)	487	(2.3)	8	(4.7)	6	(3.7)	5	(3.6)
Sweden	468	(4.5)	483	(3.0)	15	(5.7)	11	(4.9)	7	(5.0)	472	(5.9)	480	(2.8)	9	(7.0)	4	(5.4)	2	(4.5)
Switzerland	535	(4.9)	531	(4.4)	-4	(6.8)	-3	(6.0)	-2	(5.9)	524	(6.7)	536	(4.1)	11	(8.1)	14	(6.7)	16	(5.9)
Turkey	459	(14.5)	446	(5.9)	-14	(16.9)	-9	(15.0)	-2	(12.7)	431	(16.3)	451	(5.1)	20	(17.1)	14	(15.1)	3	(13.4)
United Kingdom	536	(12.5)	490	(3.9)	-46	(13.5)	-31	(10.9)	-14	(9.1)	490	(10.6)	497	(3.7)	7	(11.7)	3	(7.6)	0	(5.5)
United States	498	(11.1)	480	(3.9)	-18	(12.0)	-11	(9.2)	-6	(7.6)	477	(5.5)	486	(5.3)	9	(8.0)	6	(6.2)	2	(5.4)
OECD average	495	(1.3)	495	(1.0)	0	(1.8)	0	(1.4)	1	(1.2)	489	(1.4)	497	(0.9)	8	(1.8)	6	(1.4)	3	(1.2)
Partners																				
Albania	390	(4.4)	395	(2.6)	5	(5.4)	c	c	c	c	396	(4.0)	393	(2.5)	-3	(5.0)	c	c	c	c
Argentina	394	(4.3)	382	(5.3)	-12	(6.7)	-10	(5.5)	-7	(5.7)	393	(4.6)	385	(5.6)	-9	(7.6)	-2	(5.7)	6	(4.6)
Brazil	387	(6.3)	392	(2.5)	5	(7.2)	6	(5.1)	8	(5.4)	383	(4.1)	395	(2.8)	12	(5.2)	8	(4.6)	3	(4.5)
Bulgaria	388	(20.2)	441	(4.1)	54	(21.1)	37	(15.1)	20	(12.4)	448	(12.0)	438	(4.8)	-10	(13.6)	-2	(10.2)	6	(7.9)
Colombia	369	(8.6)	379	(3.4)	10	(9.8)	8	(7.8)	6	(7.0)	360	(5.3)	384	(3.4)	24	(6.7)	17	(5.3)	11	(4.9)
Costa Rica	412	(4.7)	402	(4.8)	-9	(7.1)	-3	(5.4)	2	(4.9)	408	(5.3)	406	(4.1)	-1	(7.2)	-2	(5.2)	-2	(4.8)
Croatia	450	(9.7)	476	(4.4)	26	(11.7)	23	(9.8)	17	(8.7)	468	(7.2)	474	(5.8)	6	(10.8)	1	(8.9)	-7	(6.6)
Cyprus*	463	(2.6)	431	(1.2)	-32	(3.0)	-21	(2.9)	-4	(2.9)	444	(1.6)	433	(1.8)	-11	(2.5)	-12	(2.5)	-13	(2.5)
Hong Kong-China	564	(15.6)	561	(3.7)	-3	(17.1)	-3	(14.3)	-5	(11.6)	546	(9.6)	565	(4.6)	18	(12.3)	16	(10.7)	9	(10.1)
Indonesia	368	(7.5)	376	(4.7)	8	(8.8)	8	(8.0)	8	(8.0)	367	(7.8)	377	(4.6)	10	(9.3)	11	(7.8)	13	(7.0)
Jordan	375	(5.3)	390	(4.0)	14	(6.8)	11	(5.6)	7	(5.1)	388	(4.0)	385	(3.8)	-2	(5.2)	-4	(4.5)	-6	(4.4)
Kazakhstan	424	(13.4)	432	(3.0)	8	(13.4)	11	(11.5)	13	(9.7)	432	(7.5)	432	(3.4)	0	(8.4)	-2	(7.2)	-5	(6.7)
Latvia	488	(5.3)	489	(3.3)	1	(6.2)	0	(5.1)	-1	(5.6)	472	(6.9)	494	(3.2)	23	(7.9)	16	(6.4)	10	(5.7)
Liechtenstein	c	c	539	(4.4)	c	c	c	c	c	c	c	c	536	(4.2)	c	c	c	c	c	c
Lithuania	476	(4.8)	483	(4.1)	7	(7.0)	5	(5.6)	2	(4.8)	488	(6.3)	486	(3.3)	-11	(7.6)	-9	(6.0)	-7	(5.8)
Macao-China	528	(1.6)	544	(1.2)	16	(2.0)	12	(1.9)	8	(1.9)	525	(2.0)	544	(1.1)	19	(2.3)	16	(2.2)	11	(2.2)
Malaysia	412	(5.0)	422	(3.9)	10	(7.0)	5	(5.2)	-2	(4.9)	413	(6.7)	424	(3.6)	10	(7.7)	4	(6.3)	-2	(5.9)
Montenegro	c	c	411	(1.1)	c	c	c	c	c	c	433	(1.7)	394	(1.3)	-39	(2.2)	-31	(2.3)	-11	(2.4)
Peru	370	(4.3)	364	(7.1)	-6	(8.4)	-3	(5.5)	0	(4.3)	370	(7.0)	367	(4.7)	-3	(8.8)	-3	(5.3)	-3	(4.5)
Qatar	406	(2.1)	370	(0.8)	-36	(2.3)	-28	(2.4)	-14	(2.4)	427	(2.3)	369	(0.8)	-58	(2.4)	-52	(2.3)	-41	(2.3)
Romania	437	(11.6)	446	(4.1)	9	(12.5)	7	(9.0)	5	(7.3)	444	(9.7)	445	(4.3)	1	(11.0)	3	(7.9)	3	(6.3)
Russian Federation	461	(20.0)	483	(3.1)	22	(20.7)	11	(16.0)	3	(13.7)	469	(7.6)	485	(3.6)	16	(8.7)	8	(7.3)	2	(7.3)
Serbia	446	(6.8)	451	(6.7)	5	(10.9)	2	(9.1)	-5	(6.9)	444	(6.1)	458	(8.0)	13	(11.8)	9	(9.7)	-2	(6.7)
Shanghai-China	611	(10.4)	613	(3.8)	2	(11.8)	-1	(9.4)	-6	(6.9)	599	(20.2)	614	(3.3)	15	(20.9)	-1	(15.2)	-23	(8.8)
Singapore	552	(4.9)	576	(1.3)	23	(5.1)	18	(5.5)	8	(5.4)	548	(3.6)	578	(1.4)	30	(3.9)	21	(3.8)	6	(3.7)
Chinese Taipei	546	(11.7)	563	(4.6)	17	(13.9)	16	(10.3)	14	(7.3)	574	(6.2)	549	(5.7)	-25	(9.8)	-16	(7.2)	-1	(6.6)
Thailand	408	(10.7)	427	(3.5)	19	(11.7)	22	(18.3)	25	(25.7)	421	(7.9)	428	(3.9)	7	(9.0)	7	(7.3)	7	(6.5)
Tunisia	383	(6.0)	395	(6.9)	12	(9.8)	11	(8.3)	9	(7.4)	386	(5.2)	390	(8.1)	4	(10.1)	4	(8.5)	5	(7.9)
United Arab Emirates	425	(11.1)	436	(2.6)	10	(11.8)	5	(10.6)	-3	(11.3)	451	(6.2)	431	(2.9)	-20	(7.2)	-16	(6.6)	-12	(6.4)
Uruguay	413	(4.3)	404	(6.8)	-9	(9.7)	-6	(6.2)	-4	(4.7)	411	(4.9)	409	(5.0)	-2	(8.3)	-3	(5.7)	-3	(5.2)
Viet Nam	513	(7.5)	508	(6.8)	-5	(10.6)	-3	(8.4)	-1	(7.1)	495	(12.4)	514	(5.2)	19	(13.4)	15	(11.0)	11	(9.5)

Notes: Values that are statistically significant are indicated in bold (see Annex A3).
ESCS refers to the *PISA index of economic, social and cultural status* of students.
* See notes at the beginning of this Annex.
StatLink ᐧᐧᐧᐧᐧ http://dx.doi.org/10.1787/888932957384

[Part 4/5]

Mathematics performance and quality assurance and school improvement

Table IV.1.18   *Results based on school principals' reports*

Mathematics performance, by whether the school principal reported that the school has the following measures aimed at quality assurance and improvement:

	Teacher mentoring										Regular consultation with one or more experts over a period of at least six months with the aim of improving the school									
	No		Yes		Performance difference (yes - no)		Performance difference (yes - no) after accounting for student ESCS		Performance difference (yes - no) after accounting for student ESCS and school average ESCS		No		Yes		Performance difference (yes - no)		Performance difference (yes - no) after accounting for student ESCS		Performance difference (yes - no) after accounting for student ESCS and school average ESCS	
	Mean score	S.E.	Mean score	S.E.	Score dif.	S.E.	Score dif.	S.E.	Score dif.	S.E.	Mean score	S.E.	Mean score	S.E.	Score dif.	S.E.	Score dif.	S.E.	Score dif.	S.E.
OECD																				
Australia	505	(7.8)	504	(1.8)	-1	(8.5)	-3	(6.9)	-7	(5.9)	510	(3.7)	502	(2.0)	-7	(4.3)	-5	(3.6)	-4	(3.4)
Austria	505	(16.1)	508	(3.5)	3	(17.8)	4	(13.9)	5	(12.2)	510	(6.4)	505	(5.4)	-5	(10.2)	-8	(7.7)	**-13**	(6.2)
Belgium	491	(6.9)	527	(3.0)	**36**	(8.6)	**30**	(6.5)	**21**	(5.6)	513	(4.7)	518	(6.8)	4	(10.7)	7	(7.8)	10	(5.1)
Canada	526	(4.8)	517	(2.3)	-9	(5.7)	**-10**	(4.7)	**-11**	(4.3)	525	(3.3)	516	(2.6)	**-10**	(4.5)	**-12**	(3.8)	**-13**	(3.4)
Chile	419	(3.5)	436	(8.0)	18	(9.2)	12	(6.3)	9	(5.7)	419	(3.8)	427	(6.5)	8	(8.1)	6	(5.4)	5	(4.9)
Czech Republic	528	(7.9)	497	(3.6)	**-30**	(8.4)	**-32**	(8.7)	**-35**	(16.5)	506	(5.1)	484	(8.4)	-22	(11.6)	**-22**	(8.8)	**-21**	(6.3)
Denmark	498	(3.7)	501	(3.6)	3	(5.2)	0	(3.6)	-2	(3.4)	497	(4.0)	503	(3.6)	6	(5.5)	5	(3.7)	4	(3.4)
Estonia	503	(4.7)	525	(2.3)	**21**	(5.3)	**14**	(5.1)	8	(5.4)	522	(2.9)	517	(3.6)	-4	(4.8)	-6	(4.3)	-7	(4.2)
Finland	519	(2.7)	518	(2.5)	-1	(3.4)	-1	(2.9)	-2	(3.0)	519	(2.2)	516	(5.0)	-4	(5.5)	-3	(4.8)	-3	(4.9)
France	495	(4.0)	496	(13.5)	1	(15.6)	-6	(11.8)	-12	(9.7)	498	(4.0)	488	(12.6)	-10	(15.0)	-11	(11.1)	-13	(8.3)
Germany	514	(5.5)	511	(8.4)	-4	(12.0)	-4	(9.3)	-2	(6.7)	512	(4.3)	522	(11.0)	10	(13.1)	14	(9.3)	**17**	(5.4)
Greece	463	(11.6)	451	(2.9)	-13	(12.8)	-8	(9.6)	-4	(8.2)	466	(8.0)	449	(3.5)	-18	(10.1)	-13	(7.0)	-9	(5.5)
Hungary	465	(9.4)	482	(4.7)	17	(12.1)	12	(8.1)	7	(6.6)	478	(4.4)	476	(13.1)	-1	(15.4)	-3	(10.3)	-7	(6.9)
Iceland	492	(1.8)	501	(3.4)	**9**	(4.1)	**9**	(4.3)	8	(4.3)	491	(2.3)	494	(2.5)	2	(3.2)	4	(3.2)	5	(3.3)
Ireland	499	(4.4)	505	(3.4)	6	(5.9)	3	(4.2)	-1	(3.6)	507	(4.3)	497	(5.0)	-11	(7.6)	-8	(5.3)	-5	(3.7)
Israel	457	(33.3)	467	(4.7)	9	(33.8)	3	(29.5)	-7	(24.3)	479	(8.9)	460	(7.3)	-19	(12.6)	-11	(10.0)	-3	(8.1)
Italy	489	(5.7)	487	(2.7)	-2	(6.6)	-1	(5.5)	1	(4.3)	490	(2.8)	481	(5.3)	-9	(6.6)	-8	(5.5)	-7	(4.5)
Japan	553	(14.5)	534	(3.9)	-19	(15.6)	-12	(13.5)	3	(10.5)	537	(3.9)	522	(13.0)	-15	(14.2)	-14	(14.2)	-10	(15.0)
Korea	539	(15.1)	556	(5.1)	17	(16.6)	16	(13.2)	16	(9.6)	557	(6.6)	555	(6.9)	-2	(10.2)	3	(8.6)	**14**	(6.9)
Luxembourg	478	(2.0)	498	(1.3)	**19**	(2.1)	**15**	(2.2)	**8**	(2.1)	494	(1.6)	489	(1.7)	**-5**	(2.1)	**-5**	(2.1)	**-6**	(2.1)
Mexico	415	(2.5)	412	(2.5)	-3	(4.1)	-5	(3.2)	**-7**	(2.7)	411	(2.1)	415	(2.2)	4	(3.4)	-1	(3.0)	-5	(2.9)
Netherlands	428	(26.8)	522	(4.4)	**94**	(27.6)	**84**	(24.8)	**53**	(21.7)	526	(7.1)	512	(8.4)	-14	(12.7)	-12	(11.3)	-6	(9.4)
New Zealand	483	(24.0)	502	(2.5)	19	(24.5)	10	(14.7)	7	(13.2)	508	(5.4)	498	(3.0)	-9	(6.6)	-5	(4.8)	-2	(4.6)
Norway	484	(5.1)	493	(3.4)	9	(6.2)	7	(5.1)	7	(4.6)	493	(4.2)	487	(4.0)	-5	(6.2)	-5	(5.4)	-6	(5.3)
Poland	524	(12.1)	516	(3.5)	-8	(11.9)	-15	(8.9)	**-19**	(7.9)	512	(4.0)	526	(6.3)	**14**	(7.1)	10	(5.4)	7	(5.0)
Portugal	473	(9.4)	490	(4.0)	17	(10.2)	12	(7.0)	9	(6.6)	484	(4.8)	492	(8.1)	7	(10.0)	2	(5.9)	-1	(5.0)
Slovak Republic	515	(17.2)	476	(4.2)	**-39**	(19.5)	**-30**	(11.7)	**-21**	(8.8)	478	(7.0)	484	(6.5)	6	(11.6)	3	(8.5)	0	(6.6)
Slovenia	486	(2.1)	512	(1.8)	**26**	(2.9)	**19**	(3.0)	6	(2.9)	508	(2.0)	499	(2.5)	**-9**	(3.6)	-6	(3.2)	0	(3.0)
Spain	481	(2.4)	492	(4.3)	**12**	(5.4)	4	(3.9)	0	(3.8)	481	(2.6)	492	(3.7)	**11**	(4.9)	4	(3.4)	0	(3.2)
Sweden	482	(3.9)	476	(3.0)	-6	(5.0)	-1	(4.1)	2	(4.0)	478	(3.0)	479	(5.5)	1	(7.0)	0	(5.1)	0	(4.6)
Switzerland	516	(6.9)	540	(4.4)	**23**	(8.7)	**23**	(7.0)	**21**	(5.9)	535	(3.3)	526	(7.9)	-9	(8.3)	-8	(7.6)	-7	(7.6)
Turkey	429	(12.4)	451	(4.7)	21	(11.8)	12	(10.2)	-6	(9.6)	443	(8.9)	451	(6.5)	8	(11.8)	2	(10.2)	-11	(9.0)
United Kingdom	501	(10.2)	495	(3.8)	-6	(11.5)	-6	(7.7)	-8	(5.0)	524	(8.2)	487	(4.1)	**-38**	(8.9)	**-26**	(7.0)	-12	(6.3)
United States	c	c	483	(3.6)	c	c	c	c	c	c	500	(7.0)	477	(4.5)	**-23**	(8.6)	**-18**	(6.9)	**-15**	(6.0)
OECD average	490	(2.0)	497	(0.8)	**7**	(2.3)	**5**	(1.8)	1	(1.6)	497	(0.9)	493	(1.1)	**-5**	(1.6)	**-4**	(1.2)	**-4**	(1.0)
Partners																				
Albania	398	(5.9)	394	(2.2)	-5	(6.3)	c	c	c	c	388	(3.3)	397	(2.6)	**9**	(4.4)	c	c	c	c
Argentina	385	(5.2)	394	(4.3)	10	(7.0)	7	(5.3)	5	(4.8)	392	(4.4)	387	(5.7)	-6	(7.6)	-4	(5.7)	-3	(5.3)
Brazil	391	(10.9)	391	(2.3)	0	(11.2)	3	(7.3)	6	(4.2)	390	(3.5)	393	(3.6)	3	(5.6)	0	(4.1)	-4	(3.3)
Bulgaria	435	(8.8)	441	(5.5)	6	(11.6)	6	(8.0)	6	(5.7)	430	(8.5)	445	(5.8)	15	(11.8)	11	(8.3)	7	(6.3)
Colombia	372	(5.4)	379	(3.8)	7	(7.0)	4	(5.6)	1	(5.3)	371	(4.9)	382	(4.5)	10	(7.4)	3	(5.8)	-2	(5.2)
Costa Rica	407	(3.8)	409	(7.8)	3	(9.3)	1	(6.5)	0	(5.2)	414	(5.0)	399	(4.4)	**-15**	(7.4)	-7	(5.4)	0	(4.7)
Croatia	c	c	471	(3.6)	c	c	c	c	c	c	470	(8.1)	473	(5.1)	2	(11.0)	1	(9.1)	-1	(6.9)
Cyprus*	416	(4.9)	440	(1.2)	**24**	(5.2)	**13**	(5.1)	-2	(4.9)	454	(1.8)	428	(1.4)	**-26**	(2.3)	**-16**	(2.3)	-2	(2.2)
Hong Kong-China	567	(15.8)	561	(3.7)	-6	(17.4)	-7	(14.2)	-7	(11.7)	561	(5.2)	564	(6.6)	3	(10.1)	3	(8.6)	4	(8.1)
Indonesia	c	c	375	(4.1)	c	c	c	c	c	c	369	(6.2)	377	(5.2)	8	(8.2)	3	(7.2)	-2	(7.1)
Jordan	374	(6.8)	391	(3.9)	17	(8.3)	14	(7.3)	10	(6.8)	381	(5.2)	389	(4.6)	9	(7.5)	6	(6.5)	1	(5.9)
Kazakhstan	424	(22.4)	432	(3.1)	9	(22.8)	7	(20.3)	5	(17.6)	441	(9.7)	430	(3.1)	-11	(10.2)	-7	(8.7)	-3	(7.5)
Latvia	477	(5.4)	493	(3.5)	**16**	(6.8)	8	(5.6)	1	(5.5)	489	(3.7)	487	(5.0)	-2	(6.8)	-3	(5.3)	-3	(4.9)
Liechtenstein	c	c	537	(4.6)	c	c	c	c	c	c	500	(6.5)	552	(5.3)	**52**	(8.6)	**46**	(9.1)	8	(10.0)
Lithuania	478	(5.2)	480	(3.9)	2	(7.4)	-1	(6.0)	-6	(5.1)	480	(3.3)	478	(4.7)	-2	(6.0)	-4	(4.9)	-7	(4.6)
Macao-China	c	c	541	(1.0)	c	c	c	c	c	c	534	(1.4)	543	(1.3)	9	(1.9)	3	(2.0)	-5	(2.1)
Malaysia	410	(9.9)	422	(3.4)	11	(10.7)	7	(8.1)	2	(6.8)	414	(8.2)	423	(3.4)	9	(8.9)	5	(8.1)	2	(9.1)
Montenegro	c	c	410	(1.0)	c	c	c	c	c	c	430	(1.9)	402	(1.3)	**-28**	(2.3)	**-20**	(2.5)	1	(2.4)
Peru	c	c	369	(3.8)	c	c	c	c	c	c	370	(4.8)	366	(6.5)	-4	(8.5)	-2	(5.4)	0	(4.2)
Qatar	c	c	375	(0.8)	c	c	c	c	c	c	396	(2.5)	373	(0.8)	**-23**	(2.8)	**-15**	(2.8)	4	(2.8)
Romania	444	(14.1)	445	(4.1)	1	(15.3)	1	(11.1)	2	(8.9)	444	(6.9)	445	(5.0)	0	(9.1)	2	(7.0)	3	(6.3)
Russian Federation	476	(9.7)	482	(3.1)	7	(10.1)	-5	(9.9)	-14	(10.5)	475	(3.9)	489	(4.5)	14	(5.8)	10	(5.1)	7	(5.5)
Serbia	437	(42.1)	450	(4.0)	12	(42.9)	10	(35.9)	12	(22.3)	450	(6.4)	450	(6.4)	0	(10.1)	1	(8.3)	1	(6.7)
Shanghai-China	c	c	614	(3.4)	c	c	c	c	c	c	582	(22.5)	615	(3.5)	33	(23.3)	23	(19.2)	7	(15.4)
Singapore	c	c	574	(1.3)	c	c	c	c	c	c	561	(2.1)	578	(1.7)	**17**	(2.8)	**9**	(2.7)	-4	(2.7)
Chinese Taipei	570	(10.4)	553	(5.4)	-17	(13.5)	-14	(9.8)	-10	(6.4)	559	(5.5)	553	(10.1)	-6	(13.2)	-8	(10.2)	-11	(7.6)
Thailand	c	c	428	(3.6)	c	c	c	c	c	c	431	(15.6)	426	(3.4)	-4	(16.1)	-3	(13.4)	-2	(11.9)
Tunisia	400	(13.7)	386	(4.3)	-14	(14.7)	-8	(11.6)	0	(8.8)	389	(4.3)	380	(12.3)	-9	(13.4)	-7	(10.6)	-4	(8.3)
United Arab Emirates	411	(7.9)	437	(2.7)	**26**	(8.7)	**21**	(7.9)	14	(8.6)	419	(3.9)	441	(3.1)	**22**	(5.2)	**14**	(4.3)	0	(3.9)
Uruguay	427	(7.4)	405	(3.3)	**-23**	(8.6)	**-12**	(6.1)	-4	(5.5)	409	(3.6)	411	(9.7)	2	(11.7)	-2	(7.2)	-5	(5.4)
Viet Nam	c	c	510	(4.7)	c	c	c	c	c	c	509	(7.7)	514	(6.6)	5	(10.6)	6	(8.8)	7	(8.4)

Notes: Values that are statistically significant are indicated in bold (see Annex A3).

ESCS refers to the *PISA index of economic, social and cultural status* of students.

* See notes at the beginning of this Annex.

StatLink ᴍᴷᴸ http://dx.doi.org/10.1787/888932957384

[Part 5/5]
Mathematics performance and quality assurance and school improvement
Table IV.1.18   *Results based on school principals' reports*

	Mathematics performance, by whether the school principal reported that the school has the following measures aimed at quality assurance and improvement:									
	Implementation of a standardised policy for mathematics (i.e. school curriculum with shared instructional materials accompanied by staff development and training)									
	No		Yes		Performance difference (yes - no)		Performance difference (yes - no) after accounting for student ESCS		Performance difference (yes - no) after accounting for student ESCS and school average ESCS	
	Mean score	S.E.	Mean score	S.E.	Score dif.	S.E.	Score dif.	S.E.	Score dif.	S.E.
OECD										
Australia	501	(4.3)	506	(2.2)	5	(5.2)	1	(4.3)	-4	(4.0)
Austria	485	(6.8)	522	(5.0)	**37**	(10.3)	**26**	(8.9)	12	(8.2)
Belgium	510	(4.2)	521	(6.7)	11	(9.9)	7	(7.6)	0	(5.9)
Canada	519	(4.7)	518	(2.3)	-1	(5.8)	-3	(4.6)	-5	(4.1)
Chile	414	(5.1)	431	(4.8)	17	(7.7)	13	(5.2)	**10**	(4.5)
Czech Republic	488	(16.2)	500	(3.8)	12	(17.2)	11	(12.9)	9	(8.8)
Denmark	499	(3.3)	505	(4.3)	6	(5.6)	-1	(3.7)	**-7**	(3.5)
Estonia	533	(7.2)	519	(2.2)	**-14**	(7.3)	**-13**	(6.7)	-12	(6.7)
Finland	516	(4.0)	521	(2.1)	5	(4.5)	3	(3.9)	0	(3.7)
France	495	(6.3)	499	(6.8)	4	(11.6)	2	(8.2)	-1	(5.8)
Germany	496	(7.3)	530	(5.6)	**34**	(10.8)	**27**	(8.9)	**19**	(6.5)
Greece	444	(5.9)	456	(3.7)	12	(7.8)	7	(5.9)	0	(5.2)
Hungary	460	(10.7)	485	(5.2)	25	(14.1)	18	(10.2)	11	(7.2)
Iceland	491	(2.5)	494	(2.3)	3	(3.3)	2	(3.6)	-1	(3.6)
Ireland	506	(7.5)	501	(3.0)	-5	(8.1)	-4	(6.1)	-4	(4.7)
Israel	470	(15.2)	469	(5.1)	-2	(15.8)	-11	(12.1)	-16	(8.8)
Italy	477	(4.0)	495	(3.2)	**18**	(5.7)	**14**	(5.0)	6	(4.5)
Japan	527	(5.0)	552	(8.6)	**26**	(11.6)	**19**	(9.5)	3	(6.2)
Korea	556	(9.2)	555	(6.1)	-1	(11.8)	1	(9.6)	4	(7.0)
Luxembourg	490	(2.1)	494	(1.4)	3	(2.2)	2	(2.1)	-1	(2.1)
Mexico	407	(2.4)	416	(1.9)	**9**	(3.4)	**7**	(3.0)	5	(2.9)
Netherlands	529	(7.1)	513	(9.0)	-16	(13.5)	-14	(11.8)	-6	(10.1)
New Zealand	481	(8.0)	507	(3.1)	**26**	(9.4)	**19**	(6.5)	**14**	(5.3)
Norway	491	(3.7)	492	(5.3)	1	(6.7)	-3	(5.7)	-9	(4.9)
Poland	510	(7.1)	519	(4.0)	9	(7.5)	5	(6.0)	2	(6.2)
Portugal	485	(8.3)	487	(4.6)	2	(9.9)	-1	(6.8)	-3	(6.3)
Slovak Republic	475	(9.1)	485	(5.8)	9	(13.1)	4	(9.0)	-1	(6.4)
Slovenia	500	(2.5)	507	(1.6)	**7**	(3.0)	5	(3.0)	2	(3.0)
Spain	484	(3.0)	485	(2.8)	2	(4.5)	0	(3.3)	-1	(3.0)
Sweden	477	(2.8)	481	(4.7)	3	(5.7)	2	(4.7)	1	(4.5)
Switzerland	541	(5.1)	525	(4.5)	**-16**	(6.8)	-8	(5.8)	2	(5.5)
Turkey	437	(9.0)	452	(5.3)	15	(10.1)	11	(9.1)	4	(8.9)
United Kingdom	513	(8.0)	489	(5.2)	**-24**	(11.1)	**-21**	(8.6)	**-18**	(6.7)
United States	498	(12.7)	480	(4.1)	-18	(14.3)	-15	(12.2)	-12	(11.1)
OECD average	491	(1.3)	497	(0.8)	**6**	(1.6)	**3**	(1.3)	0	(1.1)
Partners										
Albania	390	(6.4)	395	(2.2)	5	(6.8)	c	c	c	c
Argentina	393	(4.7)	387	(5.0)	-6	(6.9)	-4	(5.2)	-1	(4.7)
Brazil	387	(4.5)	393	(3.0)	6	(6.1)	3	(4.1)	-2	(3.2)
Bulgaria	422	(7.3)	455	(5.7)	**33**	(10.2)	**22**	(7.6)	12	(6.6)
Colombia	367	(5.3)	387	(4.3)	**21**	(7.5)	**13**	(5.9)	6	(5.3)
Costa Rica	406	(4.7)	408	(4.8)	2	(7.2)	1	(5.1)	0	(4.4)
Croatia	459	(8.6)	475	(4.4)	15	(10.4)	11	(8.9)	3	(7.5)
Cyprus*	450	(4.1)	438	(1.1)	**-12**	(4.2)	**-12**	(4.7)	**-10**	(4.4)
Hong Kong-China	568	(13.3)	561	(4.0)	-7	(15.3)	-7	(13.7)	-8	(13.8)
Indonesia	362	(5.5)	377	(4.6)	15	(7.0)	9	(6.5)	2	(6.9)
Jordan	381	(7.5)	387	(4.0)	7	(9.3)	3	(8.0)	-1	(7.2)
Kazakhstan	427	(9.9)	432	(3.3)	5	(10.7)	1	(8.7)	-3	(8.2)
Latvia	488	(3.8)	489	(4.4)	2	(6.0)	1	(4.6)	0	(4.2)
Liechtenstein	c	c	496	(4.8)	c	c	c	c	c	c
Lithuania	478	(3.6)	481	(5.9)	4	(7.6)	-2	(6.4)	-10	(5.6)
Macao-China	538	(1.6)	538	(1.3)	0	(2.1)	-2	(2.0)	**-6**	(2.1)
Malaysia	431	(9.6)	421	(3.4)	-10	(10.5)	-4	(9.5)	4	(11.6)
Montenegro	380	(2.6)	413	(1.1)	**33**	(2.9)	**26**	(2.7)	**8**	(2.8)
Peru	360	(4.1)	378	(7.4)	**18**	(8.8)	8	(5.3)	1	(3.7)
Qatar	415	(5.6)	375	(0.8)	**-40**	(5.6)	**-32**	(5.6)	**-19**	(5.5)
Romania	446	(10.3)	444	(4.6)	-2	(12.3)	0	(9.1)	1	(7.5)
Russian Federation	471	(6.5)	484	(3.4)	13	(7.2)	6	(6.0)	1	(6.0)
Serbia	450	(5.6)	452	(8.3)	2	(11.4)	-1	(9.2)	-9	(6.3)
Shanghai-China	581	(18.7)	615	(3.4)	33	(19.0)	22	(13.8)	5	(12.1)
Singapore	570	(4.9)	572	(1.4)	3	(5.2)	0	(7.1)	-4	(12.0)
Chinese Taipei	557	(6.7)	558	(6.3)	1	(10.5)	-2	(8.3)	-6	(7.0)
Thailand	398	(7.9)	431	(4.0)	**34**	(9.6)	**26**	(8.4)	**20**	(8.6)
Tunisia	379	(5.5)	394	(5.9)	15	(8.7)	12	(7.4)	7	(6.8)
United Arab Emirates	432	(6.4)	436	(3.0)	4	(7.8)	1	(7.0)	-4	(6.7)
Uruguay	405	(3.8)	423	(8.3)	19	(10.6)	12	(7.3)	7	(6.1)
Viet Nam	505	(20.9)	512	(5.1)	6	(22.2)	1	(15.5)	-3	(11.0)

Notes: Values that are statistically significant are indicated in bold (see Annex A3).
ESCS refers to the *PISA index of economic, social and cultural status* of students.
* See notes at the beginning of this Annex.
StatLink ᴍᴧ∫ᴸ http://dx.doi.org/10.1787/888932957384

[Part 1/1]
Change between 2003 and 2012 in mathematics performance and age at which students start primary school

Table IV.1.21   *Results based on students' self-reports*

	PISA 2003				PISA 2012				Change between 2003 and 2012 (PISA 2012 - PISA 2003)			
	Mathematics performance, by the age at which students started primary school				Mathematics performance, by the age at which students started primary school				Mathematics performance, by the age at which students started primary school			
	5 years old or younger	6 years old	7 years old	8 years old or older	5 years old or younger	6 years old	7 years old	8 years old or older	5 years old or younger	6 years old	7 years old	8 years old or older
	Mean score (S.E.)	Mean score (S.E.)	Mean score (S.E.)	Mean score (S.E.)	Mean score (S.E.)	Mean score (S.E.)	Mean score (S.E.)	Mean score (S.E.)	Score dif. (S.E.)	Score dif. (S.E.)	Score dif. (S.E.)	Score dif. (S.E.)
OECD												
Australia	532 (2.1)	517 (3.3)	494 (10.1)	473 (16.2)	513 (2.0)	502 (2.3)	486 (5.4)	c c	**-19** (3.4)	**-15** (4.5)	-7 (11.6)	c c
Austria	549 (8.4)	521 (3.2)	474 (4.7)	429 (16.0)	542 (8.1)	518 (2.7)	467 (3.7)	394 (16.6)	-8 (11.8)	-3 (4.6)	-7 (6.3)	-35 (23.2)
Belgium	556 (3.8)	546 (2.8)	508 (5.6)	425 (18.8)	537 (3.0)	521 (2.3)	482 (6.4)	470 (18.2)	**-20** (5.2)	**-24** (4.1)	**-25** (8.8)	45 (26.2)
Canada	537 (1.6)	548 (2.7)	526 (6.8)	471 (18.1)	523 (1.8)	530 (2.6)	515 (5.5)	451 (9.3)	**-14** (3.1)	**-18** (4.2)	-11 (8.9)	-20 (20.4)
Czech Republic	562 (18.3)	541 (3.1)	494 (4.7)	450 (15.2)	551 (15.9)	517 (3.1)	475 (3.8)	392 (11.9)	-11 (24.3)	**-24** (4.8)	**-19** (6.3)	**-58** (19.4)
Denmark	533 (9.4)	523 (3.5)	516 (3.1)	488 (7.8)	497 (7.3)	505 (2.9)	506 (2.4)	471 (5.3)	**-36** (12.1)	**-18** (5.0)	**-10** (4.3)	-17 (9.6)
Finland	c c	553 (3.0)	544 (2.0)	457 (12.9)	520 (25.8)	530 (2.9)	519 (2.1)	421 (7.9)	c c	**-23** (4.6)	**-25** (3.5)	**-36** (15.2)
France	524 (4.3)	516 (2.7)	495 (6.6)	c c	517 (5.1)	499 (2.8)	469 (6.3)	434 (11.2)	-6 (6.9)	**-17** (4.4)	**-26** (9.3)	c c
Germany	559 (13.3)	529 (3.3)	488 (4.0)	398 (11.4)	565 (7.9)	530 (3.1)	486 (4.1)	391 (13.9)	6 (15.6)	1 (5.0)	-3 (6.0)	-7 (18.0)
Greece	c c	455 (4.1)	429 (3.5)	c c	461 (8.0)	464 (2.7)	431 (4.3)	406 (10.5)	c c	9 (5.2)	2 (5.9)	c c
Hungary	c c	515 (4.2)	483 (2.7)	418 (7.5)	c c	499 (4.1)	471 (3.7)	429 (8.4)	c c	**-16** (6.2)	**-12** (5.0)	11 (11.4)
Iceland	517 (3.3)	516 (1.8)	503 (13.4)	c c	502 (3.3)	495 (2.0)	458 (8.4)	c c	**-15** (5.0)	**-21** (3.3)	**-45** (16.0)	c c
Ireland	507 (2.4)	486 (7.4)	c c	c c	505 (2.1)	485 (7.5)	c c	c c	-1 (3.8)	-1 (10.7)	c c	c c
Italy	480 (4.7)	468 (3.0)	418 (11.2)	c c	508 (3.1)	486 (1.9)	447 (4.8)	432 (12.2)	27 (6.0)	19 (4.0)	28 (12.3)	c c
Japan	m m	m m	m m	m m	c c	538 (3.6)	c c	c c	m m	m m	m m	m m
Korea	535 (17.6)	545 (3.3)	514 (6.8)	c c	573 (20.0)	579 (5.3)	543 (4.9)	490 (8.2)	38 (26.7)	34 (6.5)	29 (8.6)	c c
Luxembourg	493 (4.6)	508 (1.7)	473 (3.4)	453 (12.1)	518 (6.0)	504 (1.6)	461 (2.3)	437 (7.1)	25 (7.8)	-4 (3.0)	**-11** (4.5)	-17 (14.1)
Mexico	414 (4.1)	392 (4.2)	365 (5.3)	323 (17.3)	430 (2.6)	418 (1.3)	395 (2.5)	357 (5.2)	17 (5.2)	25 (4.8)	30 (6.1)	34 (18.2)
Netherlands	551 (4.9)	551 (3.5)	527 (5.2)	495 (14.5)	536 (6.3)	531 (3.3)	503 (5.3)	465 (12.5)	-15 (8.2)	**-20** (5.2)	**-24** (7.7)	-30 (19.2)
New Zealand	527 (2.3)	514 (8.0)	527 (12.1)	c c	504 (2.4)	490 (6.5)	485 (11.5)	433 (19.5)	**-23** (3.8)	**-24** (10.5)	**-42** (16.8)	c c
Norway	485 (7.1)	493 (3.3)	504 (2.6)	c c	500 (3.5)	490 (3.1)	462 (6.8)	407 (16.2)	15 (8.1)	-2 (4.5)	**-42** (7.5)	c c
Poland	c c	489 (7.0)	495 (2.4)	453 (7.3)	c c	c c	517 (3.4)	c c	c c	c c	22 (4.6)	c c
Portugal	483 (4.0)	473 (3.4)	443 (6.1)	c c	503 (4.8)	495 (3.7)	453 (7.0)	449 (12.3)	20 (6.5)	22 (5.4)	10 (9.5)	c c
Slovak Republic	517 (11.8)	510 (3.4)	477 (4.3)	430 (18.2)	503 (12.7)	496 (4.1)	460 (4.5)	385 (17.1)	-14 (17.4)	**-15** (5.7)	**-17** (6.5)	-45 (25.1)
Spain	497 (4.1)	487 (2.4)	459 (7.4)	c c	489 (2.5)	489 (2.1)	429 (6.8)	c c	-8 (5.2)	2 (3.7)	**-30** (10.2)	c c
Sweden	536 (9.7)	510 (4.5)	517 (2.7)	437 (14.0)	472 (13.4)	484 (3.6)	484 (2.4)	423 (8.9)	**-65** (16.7)	**-27** (6.1)	**-32** (4.1)	-14 (16.7)
Switzerland	546 (6.2)	548 (5.6)	524 (3.2)	474 (8.9)	535 (4.2)	551 (3.7)	524 (3.6)	455 (5.9)	-10 (7.7)	2 (7.0)	0 (5.2)	-19 (10.8)
Turkey	c c	440 (11.2)	425 (7.7)	370 (8.8)	425 (15.5)	453 (6.0)	453 (5.1)	416 (5.9)	c c	13 (12.8)	27 (9.5)	**46** (10.7)
United States	492 (2.8)	488 (3.7)	478 (7.1)	416 (13.3)	483 (4.0)	491 (4.2)	469 (4.0)	420 (11.1)	-10 (5.3)	3 (5.9)	-9 (8.4)	4 (17.4)
OECD average 2003	519 (1.7)	506 (0.9)	485 (1.2)	437 (3.2)	508 (1.9)	503 (0.7)	476 (1.0)	427 (2.5)	**-5** (2.4)	**-5** (1.2)	**-9** (1.6)	**-10** (4.5)
Partners												
Brazil	354 (7.9)	383 (6.4)	364 (4.9)	303 (7.5)	385 (3.1)	409 (3.5)	399 (2.1)	371 (2.6)	**31** (8.7)	**26** (7.5)	**35** (5.7)	**68** (8.2)
Hong Kong-China	560 (6.4)	564 (4.3)	526 (4.9)	477 (11.3)	566 (5.4)	570 (3.3)	552 (5.1)	487 (10.1)	6 (8.6)	6 (5.8)	**26** (7.3)	10 (15.2)
Indonesia	374 (6.1)	371 (5.1)	351 (3.5)	327 (8.7)	394 (7.4)	382 (4.8)	367 (3.9)	336 (7.0)	**20** (9.8)	11 (7.2)	**16** (5.6)	10 (11.4)
Latvia	514 (15.2)	494 (4.6)	483 (3.6)	438 (6.9)	450 (14.6)	507 (3.9)	491 (2.7)	424 (8.8)	**-64** (21.2)	13 (6.3)	8 (4.9)	-14 (11.4)
Liechtenstein	c c	558 (7.6)	528 (6.4)	c c	c c	542 (7.8)	535 (7.5)	c c	c c	-15 (11.0)	6 (10.0)	c c
Macao-China	537 (8.4)	538 (4.3)	528 (7.0)	486 (15.8)	546 (3.7)	551 (1.6)	530 (2.9)	498 (7.2)	9 (9.4)	**13** (5.0)	2 (7.8)	13 (17.5)
Russian Federation	c c	478 (5.2)	469 (4.5)	424 (6.5)	515 (21.3)	496 (3.5)	477 (3.3)	424 (10.4)	c c	**18** (6.6)	8 (5.9)	0 (12.4)
Thailand	495 (22.7)	431 (4.4)	413 (3.1)	386 (14.4)	439 (8.9)	429 (3.7)	420 (6.9)	c c	**-56** (24.5)	-2 (6.1)	7 (7.8)	c c
Tunisia	389 (5.5)	361 (2.6)	331 (6.4)	c c	403 (5.3)	389 (4.0)	366 (6.9)	c c	14 (7.9)	**28** (5.1)	**35** (9.7)	c c
Uruguay	433 (4.4)	426 (3.2)	391 (7.8)	347 (20.9)	427 (4.4)	414 (3.0)	385 (8.5)	c c	-6 (6.5)	**-12** (4.8)	-5 (11.7)	c c

Notes: Values that are statistically significant are indicated in bold (see Annex A3).
Only countries and economies with comparable data from PISA 2003 and PISA 2012 are shown.
StatLink http://dx.doi.org/10.1787/888932957384

[Part 1/3]
Change between 2003 and 2012 in mathematics performance and grade repetition
Table IV.1.22   *Results based on students' self-reports*

	PISA 2003																							
	Mathematics performance, by whether students repeated a grade in:																							
	Primary school						Lower secondary school						Upper secondary school						Primary, lower secondary and upper secondary school					
	Never		Once or more		Difference between never and once or more (never - once or more)		Never		Once or more		Difference between never and once or more (never - once or more)		Never		Once or more		Difference between never and once or more (never - once or more)		Never		Once or more		Difference between never and once or more (never - once or more)	
	Mean score	S.E.	Mean score	S.E.	Score dif.	S.E.	Mean score	S.E.	Mean score	S.E.	Score dif.	S.E.	Mean score	S.E.	Mean score	S.E.	Score dif.	S.E.	Mean score	S.E.	Mean score	S.E.	Score dif.	S.E.
Australia	532	(2.1)	461	(6.7)	**70**	(6.2)	533	(2.1)	460	(8.8)	**73**	(9.3)	563	(3.0)	c	c	c	c	532	(2.1)	462	(5.9)	**70**	(5.5)
Austria	516	(3.0)	410	(11.8)	**106**	(12.1)	515	(3.1)	457	(11.2)	**58**	(11.4)	519	(3.2)	502	(6.3)	**17**	(7.4)	516	(3.1)	458	(8.7)	**58**	(9.0)
Belgium	564	(2.1)	419	(3.5)	**145**	(3.8)	556	(2.3)	473	(6.4)	**83**	(6.4)	560	(2.3)	502	(4.5)	**58**	(4.7)	569	(2.0)	455	(3.8)	**114**	(4.0)
Canada	544	(1.6)	441	(3.9)	**103**	(4.1)	545	(1.6)	459	(4.2)	**86**	(4.2)	551	(1.7)	464	(8.7)	**87**	(8.7)	547	(1.6)	454	(3.2)	**93**	(3.4)
Czech Republic	526	(3.1)	418	(11.9)	**108**	(11.8)	528	(3.1)	412	(15.8)	**116**	(15.0)	c	c	c	c	c	c	526	(3.0)	416	(10.0)	**110**	(9.4)
Denmark	520	(2.7)	427	(10.1)	**93**	(10.0)	521	(2.7)	446	(24.1)	**75**	(24.4)	585	(18.6)	c	c	c	c	520	(2.7)	430	(10.2)	**90**	(10.1)
Finland	548	(1.8)	432	(8.0)	**116**	(7.9)	547	(1.8)	c	c	c	c	c	c	c	c	c	c	548	(1.8)	438	(6.9)	**110**	(6.8)
France	539	(2.3)	417	(4.4)	**122**	(4.7)	545	(2.7)	462	(4.1)	**83**	(4.8)	c	c	c	c	c	c	553	(2.7)	449	(3.9)	**104**	(4.6)
Germany	527	(3.2)	407	(6.9)	**120**	(7.5)	526	(3.5)	474	(4.4)	**52**	(5.0)	c	c	c	c	c	c	528	(3.4)	450	(4.7)	**79**	(4.9)
Greece	452	(3.8)	351	(14.9)	**101**	(14.1)	454	(3.8)	347	(7.8)	**108**	(8.6)	460	(4.0)	386	(13.5)	**74**	(13.2)	453	(3.8)	352	(6.8)	**101**	(7.4)
Hungary	498	(2.9)	388	(8.3)	**111**	(9.2)	498	(2.9)	406	(8.3)	**92**	(8.3)	503	(3.0)	462	(7.6)	**41**	(7.4)	499	(3.0)	417	(5.4)	**81**	(5.9)
Iceland	516	(1.4)	c	c	c	c	516	(1.5)	c	c	c	c	c	c	c	c	c	c	516	(1.4)	c	c	c	c
Ireland	513	(2.4)	453	(4.6)	**60**	(4.4)	513	(2.4)	426	(16.9)	**87**	(16.9)	532	(3.8)	c	c	c	c	513	(2.4)	452	(4.5)	**61**	(4.4)
Italy	476	(2.8)	322	(25.6)	**153**	(25.8)	477	(2.8)	381	(9.3)	**97**	(8.9)	478	(2.8)	416	(4.8)	**62**	(4.3)	478	(2.8)	397	(5.9)	**81**	(5.5)
Japan	c	c	c	c	c	c	c	c	c	c	c	c	c	c	c	c	c	c	c	c	c	c	c	c
Korea	543	(3.2)	c	c	c	c	544	(3.2)	c	c	c	c	544	(3.3)	c	c	c	c	543	(3.2)	c	c	c	c
Luxembourg	516	(1.3)	411	(3.4)	**105**	(3.8)	517	(1.4)	473	(2.5)	**45**	(3.0)	556	(2.3)	c	c	c	c	522	(1.4)	451	(1.8)	**71**	(2.5)
Mexico	408	(3.3)	325	(4.3)	**83**	(4.2)	409	(3.2)	363	(6.2)	**46**	(5.8)	429	(1.9)	399	(10.3)	**30**	(10.2)	408	(3.4)	336	(4.2)	**72**	(4.1)
Netherlands	561	(2.7)	483	(4.4)	**78**	(4.9)	555	(2.7)	528	(6.5)	**27**	(5.8)	c	c	c	c	c	c	562	(2.8)	498	(4.3)	**64**	(4.2)
New Zealand	530	(2.1)	463	(8.4)	**67**	(8.8)	531	(2.1)	434	(16.6)	**96**	(16.2)	534	(2.2)	c	c	c	c	529	(2.2)	452	(8.0)	**77**	(8.2)
Norway	c	c	c	c	c	c	c	c	c	c	c	c	c	c	c	c	c	c	c	c	c	c	c	c
Poland	495	(2.2)	347	(10.1)	**149**	(9.6)	495	(2.2)	373	(11.5)	**123**	(11.1)	c	c	c	c	c	c	496	(2.2)	362	(8.8)	**134**	(8.5)
Portugal	497	(2.3)	377	(3.1)	**120**	(3.4)	497	(2.4)	397	(3.7)	**100**	(4.1)	508	(2.2)	c	c	c	c	500	(2.3)	391	(3.0)	**109**	(3.3)
Slovak Republic	503	(3.1)	352	(15.0)	**151**	(15.3)	504	(3.1)	355	(11.1)	**149**	(11.5)	c	c	c	c	c	c	503	(3.1)	358	(10.9)	**145**	(11.1)
Spain	493	(2.3)	375	(5.2)	**118**	(5.6)	506	(2.6)	425	(2.7)	**81**	(3.2)	c	c	c	c	c	c	512	(2.5)	421	(2.8)	**92**	(3.2)
Sweden	513	(2.4)	440	(11.7)	**73**	(11.6)	514	(2.3)	456	(21.6)	**58**	(21.7)	566	(15.3)	c	c	c	c	513	(2.4)	444	(11.8)	**69**	(11.7)
Switzerland	546	(3.2)	437	(3.6)	**109**	(4.7)	543	(3.5)	501	(5.1)	**42**	(4.8)	582	(12.4)	c	c	c	c	546	(3.4)	461	(3.2)	**85**	(3.9)
Turkey	439	(7.1)	323	(6.4)	**115**	(9.1)	444	(7.2)	341	(10.8)	**103**	(12.4)	450	(7.4)	378	(4.2)	**72**	(7.6)	439	(7.2)	355	(5.0)	**85**	(8.0)
United States	495	(2.7)	403	(5.4)	**92**	(5.1)	494	(2.7)	390	(6.8)	**104**	(7.0)	502	(2.8)	c	c	c	c	496	(2.7)	403	(4.1)	**93**	(4.0)
OECD average 2003	511	(0.6)	403	(1.9)	**107**	(1.9)	512	(0.6)	427	(2.3)	**83**	(2.3)	523	(1.7)	439	(2.9)	**55**	(3.0)	514	(0.6)	422	(1.3)	**90**	(1.3)
Brazil	385	(5.4)	292	(5.4)	**93**	(6.9)	389	(5.1)	317	(4.6)	**72**	(6.0)	410	(5.2)	395	(13.1)	**15**	(14.3)	384	(5.2)	307	(4.2)	**77**	(5.4)
Hong Kong-China	563	(4.4)	483	(5.2)	**80**	(5.2)	561	(4.3)	492	(10.7)	**69**	(9.5)	577	(4.4)	c	c	c	c	564	(4.4)	488	(5.3)	**76**	(4.4)
Indonesia	370	(4.1)	314	(4.4)	**57**	(5.5)	376	(4.3)	324	(13.1)	**51**	(12.6)	404	(8.3)	c	c	c	c	370	(4.1)	315	(4.4)	**55**	(5.4)
Latvia	491	(3.8)	390	(6.5)	**101**	(7.5)	491	(3.8)	404	(13.9)	**87**	(14.0)	533	(7.6)	c	c	c	c	491	(3.8)	394	(6.1)	**97**	(7.0)
Liechtenstein	546	(5.2)	c	c	c	c	542	(5.1)	514	(12.1)	**27**	(13.6)	c	c	c	c	c	c	546	(5.3)	490	(10.0)	**56**	(11.9)
Macao-China	556	(3.7)	483	(5.6)	**72**	(7.1)	557	(3.8)	492	(5.3)	**65**	(6.4)	583	(7.2)	c	c	c	c	563	(3.8)	491	(3.8)	**72**	(5.4)
Russian Federation	472	(4.2)	383	(10.7)	**89**	(11.3)	474	(4.2)	400	(13.3)	**74**	(13.7)	c	c	c	c	c	c	472	(4.3)	392	(8.6)	**80**	(9.2)
Thailand	418	(3.0)	c	c	c	c	419	(3.0)	378	(14.1)	**41**	(14.1)	443	(4.3)	c	c	c	c	419	(3.0)	366	(13.4)	**53**	(13.8)
Tunisia	412	(4.4)	315	(1.9)	**98**	(4.6)	403	(4.1)	328	(3.1)	**74**	(4.8)	426	(4.8)	c	c	c	c	417	(4.7)	324	(2.1)	**93**	(5.0)
Uruguay	452	(3.1)	329	(3.4)	**123**	(4.8)	454	(2.9)	354	(2.9)	**100**	(3.8)	467	(3.0)	434	(12.4)	**32**	(13.3)	460	(2.9)	348	(2.4)	**112**	(3.6)

OECD (Australia through United States); *Partners* (Brazil through Uruguay)

Notes: Values that are statistically significant are indicated in bold (see Annex A3).
Only countries and economies with comparable data from PISA 2003 and PISA 2012 are shown.
StatLink ⟐⟐ http://dx.doi.org/10.1787/888932957384

[Part 2/3]
Change between 2003 and 2012 in mathematics performance and grade repetition

Table IV.1.22   *Results based on students' self-reports*

		PISA 2012											
		Mathematics performance, by whether students repeated a grade in:											
		Primary school			Lower secondary school			Upper secondary school			Primary, lower secondary and upper secondary school		
		Never	Once or more	Difference between never and once or more (never - once or more)	Never	Once or more	Difference between never and once or more (never - once or more)	Never	Once or more	Difference between never and once or more (never - once or more)	Never	Once or more	Difference between never and once or more (never - once or more)
		Mean score / S.E.	Mean score / S.E.	Score dif. / S.E.	Mean score / S.E.	Mean score / S.E.	Score dif. / S.E.	Mean score / S.E.	Mean score / S.E.	Score dif. / S.E.	Mean score / S.E.	Mean score / S.E.	Score dif. / S.E.
OECD	Australia	510 (1.7)	454 (3.5)	**56** (3.8)	510 (1.7)	439 (8.5)	**71** (8.3)	511 (1.7)	c c	c c	510 (1.7)	453 (3.5)	**57** (5.5)
	Austria	512 (2.7)	416 (8.7)	**96** (9.0)	511 (2.6)	455 (7.5)	**56** (7.7)	514 (2.8)	470 (7.2)	**44** (7.5)	514 (2.8)	447 (5.4)	**67** (9.0)
	Belgium	544 (2.0)	428 (3.7)	**115** (3.9)	539 (2.1)	439 (3.5)	**101** (3.8)	536 (2.2)	488 (4.0)	**48** (4.0)	554 (2.0)	449 (2.9)	**105** (4.0)
	Canada	525 (1.9)	441 (4.8)	**84** (4.8)	525 (1.9)	452 (3.9)	**73** (4.3)	524 (1.9)	447 (10.8)	**77** (10.8)	526 (1.9)	450 (3.6)	**76** (3.4)
	Czech Republic	504 (2.8)	353 (12.6)	**150** (12.3)	506 (2.6)	382 (8.0)	**124** (7.5)	c c	c c	c c	506 (2.7)	372 (7.2)	**134** (9.4)
	Denmark	505 (2.1)	423 (6.8)	**82** (6.7)	504 (2.1)	429 (12.2)	**75** (12.1)	504 (2.1)	c c	c c	505 (2.1)	425 (6.3)	**80** (10.1)
	Finland	524 (1.8)	413 (6.4)	**111** (6.5)	522 (1.9)	412 (13.5)	**110** (13.3)	c c	c c	c c	524 (1.8)	412 (6.3)	**112** (6.8)
	France	524 (2.8)	386 (4.3)	**138** (4.6)	521 (2.7)	425 (4.5)	**95** (4.9)	519 (2.6)	435 (14.5)	84 (14.6)	532 (3.0)	407 (3.6)	**125** (4.6)
	Germany	534 (2.9)	416 (5.4)	**118** (5.8)	533 (3.0)	474 (4.7)	**59** (5.3)	c c	c c	c c	535 (3.0)	450 (4.3)	**85** (4.9)
	Greece	458 (2.5)	338 (11.4)	**120** (11.8)	459 (2.4)	345 (7.1)	**114** (7.6)	c c	c c	c c	458 (2.4)	346 (6.3)	**112** (7.4)
	Hungary	487 (3.4)	358 (9.3)	**128** (10.2)	486 (3.3)	388 (10.5)	**98** (11.2)	489 (3.5)	411 (6.5)	**78** (7.2)	489 (3.4)	384 (8.0)	**105** (5.9)
	Iceland	495 (1.7)	c c	c c	495 (1.7)	c c	c c	c c	c c	c c	495 (1.7)	430 (15.9)	65 c
	Ireland	506 (2.2)	456 (4.6)	**51** (4.3)	506 (2.2)	435 (15.1)	**71** (14.9)	508 (2.3)	c c	c c	506 (2.2)	455 (4.8)	**52** (4.4)
	Italy	496 (2.0)	392 (7.9)	**104** (7.8)	498 (2.0)	395 (3.4)	**103** (3.9)	498 (2.0)	437 (2.9)	**61** (3.0)	500 (2.0)	420 (2.3)	**80** (5.5)
	Japan	c c	c c	c c	c c	c c	c c	c c	c c	c c	c c	c c	c c
	Korea	555 (4.5)	530 (9.3)	25 (7.9)	556 (4.5)	530 (10.0)	25 (8.7)	556 (4.7)	532 (11.2)	25 (10.3)	555 (4.5)	526 (9.9)	29 c
	Luxembourg	517 (1.2)	405 (2.5)	**112** (2.7)	511 (1.3)	444 (2.4)	**67** (2.7)	506 (1.3)	409 (10.9)	**97** (11.2)	525 (1.3)	426 (1.8)	**98** (2.5)
	Mexico	424 (1.3)	351 (2.1)	**73** (2.4)	422 (1.3)	374 (4.4)	**48** (4.6)	429 (1.5)	378 (5.7)	**50** (5.7)	424 (1.4)	358 (2.0)	**66** (4.1)
	Netherlands	541 (3.2)	459 (5.1)	**82** (5.3)	529 (3.5)	518 (6.9)	12 (6.9)	531 (3.5)	487 (22.8)	44 (22.4)	542 (3.3)	477 (5.0)	**65** (4.2)
	New Zealand	504 (2.3)	445 (7.4)	**59** (7.6)	505 (2.3)	408 (12.8)	**97** (12.7)	505 (2.4)	404 (18.9)	101 (19.3)	505 (2.3)	444 (6.4)	**61** (8.2)
	Norway	c c	c c	c c	c c	c c	c c	c c	c c	c c	c c	c c	c c
	Poland	522 (3.6)	390 (9.5)	**132** (10.1)	523 (3.5)	417 (6.8)	**106** (7.4)	c c	c c	c c	522 (3.6)	411 (6.4)	**112** (8.5)
	Portugal	526 (2.7)	396 (3.2)	**130** (3.5)	525 (2.9)	421 (3.6)	**103** (4.0)	533 (2.9)	c c	c c	530 (2.7)	411 (3.1)	**120** (3.3)
	Slovak Republic	493 (3.4)	345 (7.6)	**147** (8.4)	496 (3.3)	360 (9.2)	**136** (9.7)	500 (3.6)	c c	c c	493 (3.4)	352 (6.5)	**141** (11.1)
	Spain	506 (1.7)	392 (2.3)	**114** (2.0)	514 (1.7)	419 (2.0)	**95** (1.9)	c c	c c	c c	519 (1.7)	417 (1.8)	**102** (3.2)
	Sweden	484 (2.1)	386 (6.4)	**98** (6.6)	484 (2.1)	377 (11.8)	**107** (12.0)	486 (2.3)	c c	c c	485 (2.1)	380 (5.6)	**104** (11.7)
	Switzerland	547 (3.0)	440 (3.3)	**107** (4.3)	542 (3.1)	500 (4.3)	**42** (5.1)	543 (3.3)	496 (15.1)	47 (15.6)	548 (3.1)	466 (2.8)	**82** (3.9)
	Turkey	459 (5.0)	348 (7.5)	**112** (9.3)	c c	c c	c c	464 (5.3)	383 (2.9)	**81** (5.9)	460 (5.2)	378 (2.8)	**82** (8.0)
	United States	493 (3.4)	419 (5.1)	**74** (5.2)	491 (3.5)	431 (7.3)	**59** (7.1)	491 (3.5)	444 (9.7)	47 (9.6)	494 (3.3)	417 (5.1)	**77** (4.0)
	OECD average 2003	507 (0.5)	407 (1.3)	**101** (1.4)	508 (0.5)	427 (1.6)	**82** (1.7)	507 (0.7)	444 (3.1)	**63** (3.2)	509 (0.5)	421 (1.1)	**89** (1.3)
Partners	Brazil	412 (2.3)	334 (2.2)	**78** (2.9)	411 (2.3)	358 (2.0)	**54** (3.1)	411 (2.3)	379 (2.9)	**32** (3.2)	415 (2.4)	353 (1.6)	**63** (5.4)
	Hong Kong-China	571 (3.2)	496 (5.6)	**75** (5.2)	569 (3.2)	503 (7.8)	**67** (8.0)	567 (3.3)	c c	c c	574 (3.2)	501 (5.2)	**73** (4.4)
	Indonesia	382 (4.2)	341 (5.3)	**41** (5.4)	384 (4.1)	359 (5.6)	25 (4.8)	392 (5.8)	374 (12.4)	18 (9.8)	382 (4.1)	341 (5.3)	**41** (5.4)
	Latvia	500 (2.8)	386 (7.3)	**114** (7.9)	500 (2.7)	414 (8.8)	**86** (8.9)	503 (3.2)	c c	c c	500 (2.8)	397 (6.4)	**103** (7.0)
	Liechtenstein	544 (4.2)	461 (17.0)	83 (17.9)	545 (4.3)	c c	c c	548 (4.9)	c c	c c	546 (4.4)	485 (11.3)	62 (11.9)
	Macao-China	565 (1.3)	468 (2.4)	**98** (2.8)	567 (1.3)	490 (2.1)	**77** (2.6)	557 (1.2)	c c	c c	576 (1.4)	486 (1.6)	**90** (5.4)
	Russian Federation	485 (2.9)	387 (12.9)	**98** (12.6)	486 (2.9)	408 (14.4)	**78** (14.6)	c c	c c	c c	485 (3.0)	395 (10.7)	**90** (9.2)
	Thailand	428 (3.4)	398 (13.4)	30 (12.3)	428 (3.4)	392 (11.4)	**37** (11.5)	431 (3.7)	c c	c c	428 (3.4)	398 (8.8)	30 (13.8)
	Tunisia	411 (3.9)	317 (3.7)	**94** (5.1)	416 (4.1)	339 (3.1)	**77** (5.1)	414 (4.2)	377 (8.3)	37 (8.4)	422 (4.2)	336 (2.9)	**86** (5.0)
	Uruguay	441 (2.7)	330 (3.3)	**111** (3.8)	443 (2.8)	357 (3.0)	**86** (3.5)	443 (2.6)	338 (12.6)	**106** (12.5)	447 (2.8)	349 (2.7)	**98** (3.6)

Notes: Values that are statistically significant are indicated in bold (see Annex A3).
Only countries and economies with comparable data from PISA 2003 and PISA 2012 are shown.
StatLink ⬛ꭆ⬛ http://dx.doi.org/10.1787/888932957384

[Part 3/3]
Change between 2003 and 2012 in mathematics performance and grade repetition

Table IV.1.22 — *Results based on students' self-reports*

Change between 2003 and 2012 (PISA 2012 - PISA 2003)

Mathematics performance, by whether students repeated a grade in:

	Primary school						Lower secondary school						Upper secondary school						Primary, lower secondary and upper secondary school					
	Never		Once or more		Difference between never and once or more (never - once or more)		Never		Once or more		Difference between never and once or more (never - once or more)		Never		Once or more		Difference between never and once or more (never - once or more)		Never		Once or more		Difference between never and once or more (never - once or more)	
	Score dif.	S.E.	Score dif.	S.E.	Score dif.	S.E.	Score dif.	S.E.	Score dif.	S.E.	Score dif.	S.E.	Score dif.	S.E.	Score dif.	S.E.	Score dif.	S.E.	Score dif.	S.E.	Score dif.	S.E.	Score dif.	S.E.
OECD																								
Australia	**-22**	(3.3)	-8	(7.8)	-14	(7.1)	**-23**	(3.3)	-21	(12.4)	-2	(12.5)	**-52**	(4.0)	c	c	c	c	**-22**	(3.3)	-9	(7.1)	**-13**	(6.7)
Austria	-4	(4.5)	6	(14.8)	-10	(15.2)	-4	(4.5)	-2	(13.6)	-2	(15.1)	-6	(4.7)	**-33**	(9.7)	**27**	(10.2)	-2	(4.6)	-11	(10.4)	9	(11.1)
Belgium	**-20**	(3.5)	10	(5.4)	**-30**	(5.2)	**-17**	(3.6)	**-34**	(7.6)	**18**	(7.6)	**-24**	(3.7)	**-14**	(6.3)	-10	(6.4)	**-15**	(3.4)	-6	(5.1)	-9	(5.5)
Canada	**-20**	(3.1)	-1	(6.4)	**-19**	(6.5)	**-20**	(3.1)	-7	(6.1)	**-13**	(5.3)	**-27**	(3.2)	-17	(14.0)	-10	(12.7)	**-20**	(3.1)	-3	(5.2)	**-17**	(5.1)
Czech Republic	**-22**	(4.5)	**-65**	(17.4)	**42**	(19.3)	**-21**	(4.4)	-29	(17.8)	8	(17.8)	c	c	c	c	c	c	**-21**	(4.5)	**-45**	(12.5)	24	(12.6)
Denmark	**-15**	(3.9)	-4	(12.4)	-11	(10.8)	**-17**	(3.9)	-17	(27.1)	1	(28.1)	**-81**	(18.8)	c	c	c	c	**-15**	(3.9)	-5	(12.1)	-10	(10.7)
Finland	**-24**	(3.2)	-19	(10.5)	-4	(9.5)	**-25**	(3.3)	c	c	c	c	c	c	c	c	c	c	**-24**	(3.2)	**-26**	(9.6)	3	(8.2)
France	**-15**	(4.1)	**-31**	(6.4)	**16**	(6.2)	**-25**	(4.3)	**-37**	(6.4)	12	(6.6)	c	c	c	c	c	c	**-22**	(4.5)	**-42**	(5.7)	**21**	(5.9)
Germany	7	(4.7)	9	(8.9)	-2	(10.0)	7	(5.0)	0	(6.8)	7	(7.9)	c	c	c	c	c	c	7	(4.9)	1	(6.6)	6	(7.6)
Greece	5	(5.0)	-13	(18.8)	18	(17.2)	4	(4.9)	-2	(10.7)	6	(11.5)	c	c	c	c	c	c	5	(4.9)	-6	(9.5)	11	(10.4)
Hungary	**-12**	(4.9)	**-29**	(12.6)	18	(14.3)	**-12**	(4.8)	-18	(13.6)	6	(13.7)	**-14**	(5.0)	**-51**	(10.2)	**37**	(9.9)	-10	(4.9)	**-33**	(9.8)	**24**	(11.1)
Iceland	**-21**	(2.9)	c	c	c	c	**-22**	(3.0)	c	c	c	c	c	c	c	c	c	c	**-21**	(3.0)	c	c	c	c
Ireland	-7	(3.7)	3	(6.8)	-10	(6.1)	-7	(3.8)	9	(22.7)	-16	(22.4)	**-24**	(4.9)	c	c	c	c	-7	(3.8)	3	(6.9)	-10	(6.2)
Italy	**20**	(4.0)	69	(26.8)	-50	(26.2)	**21**	(3.9)	15	(10.1)	6	(9.9)	**20**	(3.9)	**22**	(5.9)	-2	(5.6)	**21**	(4.0)	**22**	(6.6)	-1	(6.1)
Japan	c	c	c	c	c	c	c	c	c	c	c	c	c	c	c	c	c	c	c	c	c	c	c	c
Korea	**12**	(5.9)	c	c	c	c	**12**	(5.9)	c	c	c	c	**13**	(6.0)	c	c	c	c	**12**	(5.9)	c	c	c	c
Luxembourg	0	(2.6)	-6	(4.7)	6	(4.3)	**-7**	(2.8)	**-29**	(3.9)	**23**	(3.8)	**-50**	(3.3)	c	c	c	c	3	(2.7)	**-25**	(3.2)	**28**	(2.9)
Mexico	**16**	(4.1)	**26**	(5.1)	**-10**	(4.5)	**13**	(4.0)	11	(7.9)	2	(7.3)	0	(3.1)	-21	(12.0)	20	(11.8)	**16**	(4.1)	**22**	(5.0)	-6	(4.4)
Netherlands	**-20**	(4.6)	**-24**	(7.0)	4	(6.7)	**-26**	(4.9)	-10	(9.7)	-16	(8.9)	c	c	c	c	c	c	**-20**	(4.7)	**-20**	(6.9)	0	(6.0)
New Zealand	**-25**	(3.7)	-17	(11.4)	-8	(11.7)	**-25**	(3.7)	-27	(21.1)	1	(19.4)	**-29**	(3.8)	c	c	c	c	**-25**	(3.7)	-8	(10.5)	-17	(10.2)
Norway	c	c	c	c	c	c	c	c	c	c	c	c	c	c	c	c	c	c	c	c	c	c	c	c
Poland	**26**	(4.6)	**44**	(14.0)	-17	(14.9)	**28**	(4.6)	**44**	(13.5)	-17	(13.5)	c	c	c	c	c	c	**26**	(4.6)	**49**	(11.1)	-22	(11.6)
Portugal	**29**	(4.0)	**19**	(4.9)	10	(5.2)	**28**	(4.2)	**25**	(5.5)	3	(5.4)	**25**	(4.1)	c	c	c	c	**30**	(4.0)	**19**	(4.7)	**11**	(4.6)
Slovak Republic	**-10**	(5.0)	-7	(16.9)	-3	(17.3)	-8	(4.9)	5	(14.6)	-13	(15.1)	c	c	c	c	c	c	-9	(5.0)	-6	(12.8)	-4	(13.4)
Spain	**13**	(3.6)	**17**	(6.0)	-4	(6.2)	**8**	(3.6)	-6	(3.9)	**14**	(3.5)	c	c	c	c	c	c	7	(3.6)	-3	(3.8)	**10**	(3.3)
Sweden	**-29**	(3.7)	**-54**	(13.4)	25	(13.9)	**-29**	(3.7)	**-79**	(24.7)	**50**	(24.1)	**-80**	(15.6)	c	c	c	c	**-28**	(3.7)	**-64**	(13.2)	**35**	(13.6)
Switzerland	1	(4.8)	3	(5.3)	-2	(6.8)	-1	(5.1)	-1	(7.0)	0	(8.0)	**-39**	(13.0)	c	c	c	c	2	(5.0)	5	(4.7)	-3	(6.1)
Turkey	**21**	(8.9)	**25**	(10.0)	-4	(11.9)	c	c	c	c	c	c	14	(9.3)	5	(5.5)	9	(9.2)	**21**	(9.1)	**23**	(6.0)	-2	(9.5)
United States	-2	(4.7)	**15**	(7.7)	**-17**	(7.4)	-3	(4.8)	**41**	(10.2)	**-44**	(10.5)	**-10**	(4.9)	c	c	c	c	-2	(4.7)	**15**	(6.8)	**-17**	(6.9)
OECD average 2003	**-4**	(0.9)	-1	(2.4)	-3	(2.4)	**-7**	(0.8)	-7	(2.9)	1	(2.9)	**-21**	(1.9)	**-16**	(3.6)	**10**	(3.7)	**-4**	(0.9)	**-6**	(1.7)	2	(1.7)
Partners																								
Brazil	**27**	(6.2)	**42**	(6.2)	**-15**	(7.5)	**22**	(5.9)	**40**	(5.4)	**-18**	(7.1)	1	(6.0)	-17	(13.6)	18	(15.1)	**32**	(6.0)	**46**	(4.9)	**-14**	(6.2)
Hong Kong-China	8	(5.8)	13	(7.9)	-5	(7.2)	8	(5.7)	11	(13.4)	-3	(11.6)	-10	(5.8)	c	c	c	c	11	(5.8)	14	(7.7)	-3	(6.4)
Indonesia	12	(6.2)	**27**	(7.1)	-15	(7.2)	8	(6.3)	**35**	(14.4)	-26	(13.9)	-11	(10.4)	c	c	c	c	12	(6.1)	**26**	(7.1)	-15	(6.9)
Latvia	9	(5.1)	-4	(10.0)	13	(9.9)	9	(5.0)	10	(16.6)	-1	(15.4)	**-30**	(8.4)	c	c	c	c	9	(5.1)	3	(9.1)	6	(8.8)
Liechtenstein	-2	(7.0)	c	c	c	c	3	(7.0)	c	c	c	c	c	c	c	c	c	c	0	(7.1)	-5	(15.2)	5	(18.4)
Macao-China	10	(4.4)	-16	(6.4)	25	(7.5)	10	(4.5)	-3	(6.0)	13	(7.1)	**-27**	(7.5)	c	c	c	c	13	(4.5)	-5	(4.5)	18	(5.7)
Russian Federation	13	(5.5)	4	(16.8)	9	(17.6)	12	(5.4)	8	(19.7)	4	(22.7)	c	c	c	c	c	c	13	(5.6)	3	(13.8)	10	(14.3)
Thailand	10	(4.9)	c	c	c	c	9	(4.9)	13	(18.2)	-4	(18.6)	**-13**	(6.0)	c	c	c	c	9	(4.9)	33	(16.2)	-24	(16.7)
Tunisia	-1	(6.2)	2	(4.6)	-3	(7.2)	**13**	(6.1)	**10**	(4.8)	3	(6.6)	-12	(6.6)	c	c	c	c	5	(6.6)	**12**	(4.1)	-7	(7.0)
Uruguay	**-11**	(4.5)	0	(5.1)	-12	(6.1)	**-11**	(4.5)	3	(4.6)	**-14**	(5.1)	**-24**	(4.4)	**-97**	(17.8)	**73**	(18.4)	**-13**	(4.5)	1	(4.1)	**-14**	(4.9)

Notes: Values that are statistically significant are indicated in bold (see Annex A3).
Only countries and economies with comparable data from PISA 2003 and PISA 2012 are shown.
StatLink ᐃᔑᖦ http://dx.doi.org/10.1787/888932957384

[Part 1/3]
Change between 2003 and 2012 in mathematics performance and students' grade level

Table IV.1.23   *Results based on students' self-reports*

		PISA 2003														
		Mathematics performance, by students in:										Mathematics performance, by students enrolled in:				
		Grades below the modal grade		The modal grade		Grades above the modal grade		Performance difference (modal - below modal)		Performance difference (above modal - modal)		Lower secondary education (ISCED 2)		Upper secondary education (ISCED 3)		Performance difference (ISCED 3 - ISCED 2)	
		Mean score	S.E.	Mean score	S.E.	Mean score	S.E.	Score dif.	S.E.	Score dif.	S.E.	Mean score	S.E.	Mean score	S.E.	Score dif.	S.E.
OECD	Australia	464	(4.4)	522	(2.5)	560	(2.9)	58	(4.5)	38	(3.2)	516	(2.4)	560	(2.9)	44	(3.2)
	Austria	491	(3.8)	520	(4.3)	c	c	29	(4.9)	c	c	399	(9.2)	512	(3.0)	113	(9.4)
	Belgium	446	(3.8)	571	(2.1)	640	(10.8)	125	(4.3)	69	(10.8)	374	(6.9)	537	(2.3)	162	(7.0)
	Canada	480	(3.5)	546	(1.7)	581	(8.1)	66	(3.8)	35	(8.3)	480	(3.5)	546	(1.7)	67	(3.8)
	Czech Republic	496	(5.3)	535	(3.8)	c	c	39	(6.2)	c	c	495	(5.3)	537	(3.8)	42	(6.3)
	Denmark	451	(6.0)	519	(2.9)	561	(12.3)	68	(6.2)	42	(12.6)	513	(2.7)	583	(17.7)	70	(17.8)
	Finland	497	(4.6)	551	(1.9)	c	c	54	(4.6)	c	c	544	(1.9)	c	c	c	c
	France	446	(4.2)	553	(2.7)	612	(8.8)	107	(4.8)	59	(8.1)	446	(4.2)	555	(2.8)	109	(4.9)
	Germany	413	(4.7)	505	(3.1)	567	(3.6)	92	(4.6)	62	(3.6)	503	(3.3)	498	(9.8)	-5	(9.7)
	Greece	371	(7.3)	450	(4.3)	465	(5.2)	78	(8.3)	15	(5.0)	371	(7.3)	452	(4.0)	81	(8.1)
	Hungary	392	(7.2)	485	(3.2)	521	(3.6)	94	(7.7)	36	(3.0)	392	(7.2)	496	(3.0)	104	(7.6)
	Iceland	c	c	515	(1.4)	c	c	c	c	c	c	515	(1.4)	c	c	c	c
	Ireland	407	(9.5)	492	(3.0)	528	(3.9)	85	(9.9)	36	(4.5)	489	(3.0)	528	(3.9)	39	(4.6)
	Italy	398	(5.6)	478	(2.9)	486	(8.6)	79	(5.2)	8	(8.3)	321	(29.6)	468	(3.0)	147	(29.6)
	Japan	c	c	534	(4.0)	c	c	c	c	c	c	c	c	534	(4.0)	c	c
	Korea	532	(12.3)	542	(3.3)	c	c	10	(13.0)	c	c	532	(12.3)	542	(3.3)	10	(13.0)
	Luxembourg	444	(3.1)	474	(1.5)	554	(2.3)	30	(3.7)	80	(2.9)	468	(1.3)	554	(2.3)	87	(2.8)
	Mexico	355	(6.3)	421	(2.1)	460	(8.5)	66	(6.3)	39	(8.7)	357	(6.1)	422	(2.1)	66	(6.1)
	Netherlands	500	(4.0)	575	(2.9)	c	c	74	(4.1)	c	c	506	(3.7)	631	(2.9)	124	(4.6)
	New Zealand	455	(6.2)	526	(2.3)	582	(8.0)	71	(6.3)	56	(7.8)	455	(6.2)	528	(2.3)	73	(6.3)
	Norway	c	c	495	(2.4)	c	c	c	c	c	c	495	(2.4)	c	c	c	c
	Poland	366	(9.3)	495	(2.2)	c	c	128	(8.8)	c	c	490	(2.5)	c	c	c	c
	Portugal	393	(3.2)	504	(2.1)	c	c	111	(3.8)	c	c	393	(3.2)	505	(2.1)	112	(3.7)
	Slovak Republic	483	(5.3)	507	(4.6)	643	(11.5)	23	(7.2)	136	(12.3)	475	(5.5)	511	(4.5)	37	(7.4)
	Spain	420	(2.8)	513	(2.4)	c	c	93	(3.2)	c	c	485	(2.4)	c	c	c	c
	Sweden	406	(8.6)	509	(2.2)	563	(17.2)	103	(8.5)	54	(17.2)	506	(2.3)	566	(16.1)	59	(16.1)
	Switzerland	448	(4.2)	535	(3.4)	571	(11.8)	87	(4.5)	35	(10.9)	517	(3.3)	576	(15.0)	60	(14.2)
	Turkey	354	(11.9)	428	(8.9)	433	(6.3)	74	(12.3)	5	(8.0)	312	(13.9)	430	(6.8)	118	(15.2)
	United States	451	(4.0)	497	(3.0)	507	(7.2)	46	(3.8)	10	(7.5)	451	(4.0)	498	(2.8)	47	(3.8)
	OECD average 2003	437	(1.2)	510	(0.6)	546	(2.0)	73	(1.3)	45	(2.1)	457	(1.5)	524	(1.4)	77	(2.3)
Partners	Brazil	293	(4.0)	383	(4.3)	424	(6.5)	91	(5.7)	41	(4.9)	293	(4.0)	396	(4.6)	103	(6.1)
	Hong Kong-China	516	(4.9)	575	(4.6)	c	c	60	(3.7)	c	c	516	(4.9)	575	(4.6)	60	(3.7)
	Indonesia	313	(4.7)	348	(3.7)	396	(7.8)	35	(4.5)	48	(8.4)	340	(3.6)	396	(7.8)	56	(8.3)
	Latvia	426	(4.1)	491	(3.5)	537	(7.7)	65	(4.1)	45	(6.4)	479	(3.4)	537	(7.7)	58	(6.5)
	Liechtenstein	465	(8.5)	546	(4.6)	c	c	81	(9.3)	c	c	529	(4.2)	c	c	c	c
	Macao-China	473	(4.7)	546	(4.9)	583	(6.6)	73	(7.0)	37	(8.5)	509	(3.3)	583	(6.6)	75	(7.6)
	Russian Federation	443	(3.7)	480	(5.7)	527	(13.9)	37	(5.5)	48	(14.1)	443	(3.8)	480	(5.7)	38	(5.5)
	Thailand	394	(3.9)	434	(3.6)	523	(15.8)	40	(4.4)	89	(16.3)	394	(3.9)	436	(3.6)	42	(4.4)
	Tunisia	321	(2.3)	420	(4.3)	443	(9.8)	99	(4.7)	23	(8.0)	321	(2.3)	422	(4.5)	101	(4.9)
	Uruguay	345	(3.1)	458	(3.0)	489	(5.4)	113	(4.3)	31	(5.6)	345	(3.1)	461	(2.9)	116	(4.2)

Notes: Values that are statistically significant are indicated in bold (see Annex A3).
Only countries and economies with comparable data from PISA 2003 and PISA 2012 are shown.
StatLink http://dx.doi.org/10.1787/888932957384

[Part 2/3]
Change between 2003 and 2012 in mathematics performance and students' grade level
Table IV.1.23   *Results based on students' self-reports*

									PISA 2012									
	Mathematics performance, by students in:										Mathematics performance, by students enrolled in:							
	Grades below the modal grade		The modal grade		Grades above the modal grade		Performance difference (modal - below modal)		Performance difference (above modal - modal)		Lower secondary education (ISCED 2)		Upper secondary education (ISCED 3)		Performance difference (ISCED 3 - ISCED 2)	
	Mean score	S.E.	Mean score	S.E.	Mean score	S.E.	Score dif.	S.E.	Score dif.	S.E.	Mean score	S.E.	Mean score	S.E.	Score dif.	S.E.
Australia	467	(5.2)	503	(1.9)	528	(2.7)	**36**	(5.3)	**25**	(3.0)	499	(1.8)	529	(2.7)	**30**	(3.2)
Austria	482	(3.2)	528	(3.1)	c	c	**46**	(3.9)	c	c	405	(9.8)	512	(2.6)	**106**	(9.4)
Belgium	450	(2.8)	560	(2.0)	587	(11.3)	**110**	(3.1)	**27**	(11.5)	392	(5.0)	529	(1.9)	**137**	(7.0)
Canada	481	(2.9)	524	(2.0)	578	(8.2)	**43**	(3.3)	**55**	(8.3)	481	(2.9)	524	(2.0)	**44**	(3.8)
Czech Republic	368	(7.5)	491	(3.7)	523	(3.7)	**123**	(7.2)	**31**	(5.1)	480	(4.1)	523	(3.7)	**44**	(6.3)
Denmark	461	(3.7)	509	(2.2)	535	(17.0)	**48**	(3.7)	27	(17.1)	500	(2.3)	534	(41.9)	34	(17.8)
Finland	463	(4.9)	528	(1.7)	c	c	**65**	(4.6)	c	c	518	(1.9)	c	c	c	c
France	402	(3.7)	531	(2.7)	592	(13.2)	**129**	(4.3)	**61**	(11.8)	402	(3.7)	534	(3.0)	**132**	(4.9)
Germany	416	(4.2)	499	(3.3)	561	(3.5)	**83**	(4.8)	**62**	(3.8)	513	(2.9)	523	(16.3)	9	(9.7)
Greece	358	(7.1)	458	(2.6)	c	c	**101**	(7.6)	c	c	358	(7.1)	458	(2.6)	**101**	(8.1)
Hungary	389	(8.5)	480	(3.6)	517	(4.1)	**91**	(9.5)	**37**	(3.3)	389	(8.5)	489	(3.5)	**99**	(7.6)
Iceland	c	c	493	(1.7)	c	c	c	c	c	c	493	(1.7)	c	c	c	c
Ireland	445	(10.6)	495	(2.3)	515	(3.2)	**50**	(10.3)	**20**	(2.9)	493	(2.4)	515	(3.2)	**22**	(4.6)
Italy	425	(2.8)	499	(2.1)	522	(6.3)	**74**	(3.2)	**23**	(6.2)	362	(7.5)	488	(2.0)	**126**	(29.6)
Japan	c	c	536	(3.6)	c	c	c	c	c	c	c	c	536	(3.6)	c	c
Korea	520	(11.2)	556	(4.8)	c	c	**36**	(12.2)	c	c	520	(11.2)	556	(4.8)	**36**	(13.0)
Luxembourg	415	(2.4)	460	(1.3)	550	(1.6)	**46**	(2.5)	**89**	(1.8)	450	(1.3)	549	(1.6)	**99**	(2.8)
Mexico	385	(2.6)	429	(1.8)	455	(6.9)	**44**	(3.5)	**26**	(7.2)	385	(2.6)	430	(1.8)	**45**	(6.1)
Netherlands	436	(8.4)	495	(4.1)	556	(3.5)	**59**	(9.5)	**62**	(3.9)	488	(3.4)	605	(3.3)	**116**	(4.6)
New Zealand	455	(7.1)	501	(2.3)	536	(9.4)	**46**	(7.2)	**36**	(9.5)	455	(7.1)	503	(2.3)	**48**	(6.3)
Norway	c	c	490	(2.8)	c	c	c	c	c	c	489	(2.7)	c	c	c	c
Poland	411	(5.7)	522	(3.4)	c	c	**111**	(6.2)	c	c	517	(3.4)	c	c	c	c
Portugal	441	(3.8)	536	(2.9)	c	c	**94**	(4.6)	c	c	427	(3.7)	536	(2.9)	**109**	(3.7)
Slovak Republic	456	(4.8)	501	(5.4)	597	(14.1)	**45**	(7.3)	**96**	(13.7)	455	(4.8)	504	(5.2)	**49**	(7.4)
Spain	417	(2.1)	519	(1.8)	c	c	**101**	(2.1)	c	c	484	(1.9)	c	c	c	c
Sweden	372	(5.7)	480	(2.2)	564	(13.8)	**109**	(6.1)	**84**	(14.1)	476	(2.2)	564	(14.0)	**88**	(16.1)
Switzerland	444	(3.9)	530	(2.6)	578	(6.1)	**86**	(4.3)	**47**	(6.5)	515	(2.8)	584	(5.9)	**69**	(14.2)
Turkey	396	(4.6)	471	(5.4)	468	(7.4)	**75**	(5.8)	-3	(6.6)	368	(10.9)	450	(4.9)	**82**	(15.2)
United States	406	(5.6)	487	(3.5)	509	(5.0)	**81**	(5.9)	**22**	(4.1)	406	(5.6)	492	(3.4)	**86**	(3.8)
OECD average 2003	429	(1.1)	504	(0.6)	541	(2.0)	**74**	(1.2)	**44**	(2.0)	454	(1.0)	519	(2.1)	**74**	(2.3)
Brazil	363	(1.8)	425	(2.8)	439	(5.5)	**62**	(2.8)	**14**	(5.2)	333	(2.2)	406	(2.3)	**73**	(6.1)
Hong Kong-China	526	(3.5)	578	(2.9)	c	c	**51**	(3.2)	c	c	526	(3.5)	579	(3.2)	**52**	(3.7)
Indonesia	354	(3.9)	395	(6.4)	394	(6.7)	**41**	(7.6)	-1	(7.2)	354	(3.9)	395	(6.1)	**41**	(8.3)
Latvia	425	(4.6)	502	(2.8)	556	(9.1)	**77**	(4.8)	**54**	(9.0)	488	(2.7)	543	(11.0)	**55**	(6.5)
Liechtenstein	459	(10.0)	542	(4.7)	c	c	**83**	(11.2)	c	c	522	(4.2)	c	c	c	c
Macao-China	500	(1.3)	584	(1.5)	c	c	**83**	(2.0)	c	c	500	(1.3)	584	(1.5)	**84**	(7.6)
Russian Federation	434	(5.9)	482	(3.3)	506	(5.1)	**48**	(5.4)	**23**	(5.1)	477	(3.3)	506	(5.1)	**29**	(5.5)
Thailand	416	(6.8)	428	(3.7)	461	(11.7)	12	(7.1)	**32**	(11.8)	416	(6.8)	430	(3.6)	13	(4.4)
Tunisia	332	(3.0)	419	(4.3)	443	(5.9)	**87**	(5.4)	**25**	(4.9)	332	(3.0)	421	(4.2)	**89**	(4.9)
Uruguay	352	(4.5)	449	(2.8)	501	(10.7)	**96**	(5.1)	**52**	(11.1)	352	(4.5)	450	(2.7)	**97**	(4.2)

Notes: Values that are statistically significant are indicated in bold (see Annex A3).
Only countries and economies with comparable data from PISA 2003 and PISA 2012 are shown.
StatLink ⌐ᵐˢᴸ http://dx.doi.org/10.1787/888932957384

[Part 3/3]
Change between 2003 and 2012 in mathematics performance and students' grade level

Table IV.1.23 *Results based on students' self-reports*

	Change between 2003 and 2012 (PISA 2012 - PISA 2003)															
	Mathematics performance, by students in:										Mathematics performance, by students enrolled in:					
	Grades below the modal grade		The modal grade		Grades above the modal grade		Performance difference (modal - below modal)		Performance difference (above modal - modal)		Lower secondary education (ISCED 2)		Upper secondary education (ISCED 3)		Performance difference (ISCED 3 - ISCED 2)	
	Score dif.	S.E.	Score dif.	S.E.	Score dif.	S.E.	Score dif.	S.E.	Score dif.	S.E.	Score dif.	S.E.	Score dif.	S.E.	Score dif.	S.E.
OECD																
Australia	3	(7.1)	**-19**	(3.7)	**-32**	(4.4)	**-22**	(7.1)	**-13**	(4.3)	**-17**	(3.5)	**-31**	(4.4)	**-14**	(4.4)
Austria	-9	(5.3)	8	(5.7)	c	c	**17**	(6.2)	c	c	7	(13.5)	0	(4.4)	-7	(14.6)
Belgium	3	(5.1)	**-12**	(3.5)	**-53**	(15.7)	**-15**	(5.7)	**-41**	(15.8)	**17**	(8.7)	**-8**	(3.5)	**-25**	(8.9)
Canada	1	(4.9)	**-22**	(3.3)	-3	(11.7)	**-23**	(5.0)	20	(11.6)	1	(4.9)	**-22**	(3.3)	**-23**	(4.9)
Czech Republic	**-128**	(9.4)	**-44**	(5.7)	c	c	**84**	(10.4)	c	c	**-15**	(7.0)	**-13**	(5.7)	1	(7.5)
Denmark	10	(7.3)	**-10**	(4.1)	-26	(21.1)	**-20**	(7.4)	-15	(21.0)	**-13**	(4.1)	-48	(45.5)	-35	(45.6)
Finland	**-33**	(7.0)	**-23**	(3.2)	c	c	10	(6.0)	c	c	**-26**	(3.3)	c	c	c	c
France	**-43**	(5.9)	**-22**	(4.3)	-20	(16.0)	**22**	(6.2)	2	(14.7)	**-43**	(5.9)	**-21**	(4.5)	**23**	(6.3)
Germany	3	(6.6)	-6	(4.9)	-6	(5.4)	-9	(6.9)	0	(5.6)	**10**	(4.8)	25	(19.1)	14	(17.6)
Greece	-14	(10.4)	9	(5.4)	c	c	**22**	(11.7)	c	c	-14	(10.4)	6	(5.2)	**20**	(11.5)
Hungary	-3	(11.3)	-6	(5.2)	-4	(5.8)	-3	(12.1)	2	(4.3)	-3	(11.3)	-8	(5.0)	-5	(12.0)
Iceland	c	c	**-22**	(2.9)	c	c	c	c	c	c	**-22**	(2.9)	c	c	c	c
Ireland	**38**	(14.3)	2	(4.2)	**-13**	(5.4)	**-36**	(14.1)	**-15**	(5.3)	5	(4.3)	**-13**	(5.4)	**-17**	(5.4)
Italy	**26**	(6.5)	**21**	(4.0)	**36**	(10.8)	-6	(6.3)	15	(9.3)	**42**	(30.6)	**20**	(4.1)	-22	(31.1)
Japan	c	c	2	(5.7)	c	c	c	c	c	c	c	c	2	(5.7)	c	c
Korea	-13	(16.8)	**14**	(6.1)	c	c	26	(16.6)	c	c	-13	(16.8)	**14**	(6.1)	26	(16.6)
Luxembourg	**-29**	(4.4)	**-14**	(2.8)	-4	(3.4)	**16**	(4.5)	**9**	(3.5)	**-17**	(2.6)	-5	(3.4)	**12**	(3.5)
Mexico	**30**	(7.0)	**8**	(3.4)	-5	(11.1)	**-22**	(6.7)	-13	(11.3)	**28**	(6.9)	**8**	(3.4)	**-21**	(6.5)
Netherlands	**-64**	(9.4)	**-80**	(5.4)	c	c	**-16**	(9.5)	c	c	**-18**	(5.4)	**-26**	(4.8)	-8	(6.3)
New Zealand	-1	(9.6)	**-25**	(3.8)	**-46**	(12.5)	**-25**	(9.0)	-20	(11.3)	-1	(9.6)	**-26**	(3.8)	**-25**	(9.1)
Norway	c	c	-6	(4.1)	c	c	c	c	c	c	-6	(4.1)	c	c	c	c
Poland	**45**	(11.1)	**27**	(4.5)	c	c	-18	(11.0)	c	c	**27**	(4.6)	c	c	c	c
Portugal	**48**	(5.3)	**31**	(4.1)	c	c	**-17**	(6.0)	c	c	**33**	(5.3)	**31**	(4.1)	-3	(5.6)
Slovak Republic	**-27**	(7.4)	-6	(7.4)	**-46**	(18.3)	**21**	(9.5)	**-40**	(20.5)	**-20**	(7.6)	-7	(7.2)	12	(9.6)
Spain	-3	(4.0)	5	(3.6)	c	c	**8**	(3.6)	c	c	-1	(3.6)	c	c	c	c
Sweden	**-34**	(10.5)	**-29**	(3.7)	2	(22.1)	6	(10.3)	**30**	(22.2)	**-30**	(3.7)	-1	(21.4)	29	(21.5)
Switzerland	-4	(6.1)	-5	(4.7)	7	(13.4)	-1	(5.3)	12	(13.9)	-2	(4.7)	8	(16.2)	9	(15.6)
Turkey	**42**	(12.9)	**43**	(10.6)	**36**	(9.9)	1	(13.4)	-7	(10.0)	**56**	(17.7)	**21**	(8.6)	-36	(18.6)
United States	**-45**	(7.2)	**-10**	(5.0)	2	(9.0)	**36**	(6.8)	11	(8.7)	**-45**	(7.2)	-6	(4.9)	**39**	(6.7)
OECD average 2003	**-8**	(1.7)	**-7**	(0.9)	**-10**	(3.1)	1	(1.8)	**-4**	(3.1)	**-3**	(1.8)	**-4**	(2.5)	-2	(3.3)
Partners																
Brazil	**71**	(4.8)	**42**	(5.5)	15	(8.7)	**-29**	(6.2)	**-27**	(7.0)	**41**	(5.0)	11	(5.5)	**-30**	(7.1)
Hong Kong-China	11	(6.3)	2	(5.8)	c	c	-8	(4.7)	c	c	11	(6.3)	4	(5.9)	-7	(4.8)
Indonesia	**41**	(6.5)	**46**	(7.6)	-2	(10.4)	5	(8.7)	**-48**	(11.2)	**14**	(5.7)	-1	(10.0)	-15	(10.2)
Latvia	-1	(6.4)	**10**	(4.9)	20	(12.1)	12	(6.1)	9	(10.6)	**9**	(4.8)	7	(13.6)	-3	(12.3)
Liechtenstein	-7	(13.2)	-5	(6.9)	c	c	2	(13.8)	c	c	-7	(6.2)	c	c	c	c
Macao-China	**28**	(5.2)	**38**	(5.4)	c	c	10	(7.4)	c	c	**-8**	(4.0)	1	(7.0)	9	(8.0)
Russian Federation	-9	(7.3)	3	(6.8)	-22	(15.0)	11	(7.9)	**-24**	(14.1)	**34**	(5.4)	**25**	(7.9)	-9	(7.6)
Thailand	22	(8.1)	-5	(5.9)	**-63**	(19.8)	**-28**	(8.4)	**-57**	(20.3)	**22**	(8.1)	-7	(5.4)	**-29**	(8.4)
Tunisia	**11**	(4.2)	-1	(6.3)	0	(11.6)	-12	(6.9)	1	(9.8)	**11**	(4.2)	0	(6.4)	-11	(6.9)
Uruguay	7	(5.8)	**-9**	(4.5)	12	(12.1)	**-17**	(6.4)	22	(12.5)	7	(5.8)	**-12**	(4.4)	**-19**	(6.4)

Notes: Values that are statistically significant are indicated in bold (see Annex A3).
Only countries and economies with comparable data from PISA 2003 and PISA 2012 are shown.
StatLink ⌗ http://dx.doi.org/10.1787/888932957384

[Part 1/1]

Change between 2003 and 2012 in mathematics performance and ability grouping in mathematics classes

Table IV.1.24 · *Results based on school principals' reports*

	PISA 2003 — Mathematics performance, by use of ability grouping in mathematics classes								PISA 2012 — Mathematics performance, by use of ability grouping in mathematics classes								Change between 2003 and 2012 (PISA 2012 - PISA 2003) — Mathematics performance, by use of ability grouping in mathematics classes							
	No ability grouping for any class		One form of grouping for some classes		One form of grouping for all classes		Performance difference (not for any classes or for some classes - for all classes)		No ability grouping for any class		One form of grouping for some classes		One form of grouping for all classes		Performance difference (not for any classes or for some classes - for all classes)		No ability grouping for any class		One form of grouping for some classes		One form of grouping for all classes		Performance difference (not for any classes or for some classes - for all classes)
	Mean score	S.E.	Mean score	S.E.	Mean score	S.E.	Score dif.	S.E.	Mean score	S.E.	Mean score	S.E.	Mean score	S.E.	Score dif.	S.E.	Score dif.	S.E.	Score dif.	S.E.	Score dif.	S.E.	Score dif.	S.E.
OECD																								
Australia	529	(13.7)	524	(4.0)	524	(3.2)	0	(5.7)	538	(28.5)	502	(2.9)	506	(2.5)	-3	(4.3)	9	(31.7)	**-22**	(5.3)	**-19**	(4.5)	-3	(7.0)
Austria	531	(3.5)	461	(12.8)	437	(5.8)	**83**	(6.8)	529	(3.7)	467	(11.8)	435	(11.2)	**84**	(11.2)	-2	(5.4)	6	(17.6)	-2	(12.7)	1	(12.6)
Belgium	507	(7.7)	540	(4.8)	543	(8.1)	-15	(10.1)	521	(9.1)	522	(4.8)	497	(10.4)	25	(13.1)	15	(12.0)	**-18**	(7.1)	**-46**	(13.3)	**40**	(16.9)
Canada	522	(7.8)	532	(2.7)	533	(2.9)	-1	(4.0)	518	(6.8)	519	(2.7)	517	(3.4)	3	(4.5)	-4	(10.5)	**-13**	(4.3)	**-16**	(4.8)	4	(6.0)
Czech Republic	517	(5.1)	525	(7.0)	493	(12.2)	**27**	(13.1)	506	(5.5)	495	(8.4)	464	(16.0)	**38**	(17.3)	-11	(7.7)	**-30**	(11.1)	-29	(20.2)	12	(20.2)
Denmark	509	(4.7)	517	(5.1)	517	(4.9)	-5	(5.8)	505	(4.7)	497	(3.2)	508	(8.1)	-9	(8.5)	-4	(6.9)	**-21**	(6.3)	-9	(9.6)	-4	(10.1)
Finland	544	(2.9)	545	(2.8)	545	(4.4)	-1	(5.2)	523	(2.7)	517	(2.5)	513	(6.0)	6	(5.9)	**-21**	(4.4)	**-28**	(4.3)	**-32**	(7.7)	7	(8.1)
France	w	w	w	w	w	w	w	w	509	(6.1)	480	(8.8)	489	(11.1)	8	(13.7)	m	m	m	m	m	m	m	m
Germany	525	(6.3)	497	(11.8)	464	(10.8)	**53**	(10.8)	543	(6.8)	523	(8.3)	482	(7.4)	**51**	(9.1)	18	(9.5)	26	(14.6)	18	(11.2)	-2	(13.9)
Greece	442	(4.6)	458	(14.6)	437	(16.4)	8	(17.3)	459	(3.0)	421	(10.2)	444	(21.3)	10	(22.6)	**16**	(5.8)	**-37**	(17.9)	7	(26.9)	2	(29.2)
Hungary	474	(6.4)	509	(7.8)	488	(11.7)	3	(14.9)	470	(8.5)	499	(10.6)	467	(6.2)	20	(10.5)	-4	(10.8)	-9	(13.3)	-21	(13.4)	17	(18.1)
Iceland	505	(3.8)	517	(3.7)	518	(1.8)	-6	(3.4)	497	(4.8)	497	(2.5)	489	(2.3)	7	(3.1)	-9	(6.4)	**-20**	(4.9)	**-28**	(3.5)	**14**	(4.9)
Ireland	495	(19.2)	502	(6.1)	504	(3.4)	-3	(7.2)	c	c	498	(4.5)	506	(3.9)	-8	(6.6)	c	c	-4	(7.8)	1	(5.5)	-5	(9.3)
Italy	472	(6.7)	480	(8.6)	435	(8.6)	**42**	(10.4)	501	(6.2)	489	(2.9)	471	(5.5)	22	(6.6)	28	(9.3)	9	(6.8)	**37**	(10.4)	**-20**	(12.8)
Japan	550	(10.7)	514	(9.2)	519	(14.8)	18	(17.0)	548	(7.7)	528	(5.9)	534	(12.1)	3	(13.4)	-2	(10.6)	14	(11.1)	15	(19.2)	-15	(21.5)
Korea	535	(10.3)	542	(4.6)	563	(11.2)	-22	(12.1)	546	(27.4)	549	(7.0)	562	(6.6)	-14	(10.2)	10	(29.3)	6	(8.6)	-1	(13.1)	9	(16.4)
Luxembourg	503	(1.5)	503	(1.8)	460	(2.6)	**43**	(3.0)	522	(1.8)	467	(1.5)	485	(1.8)	**6**	(1.9)	**19**	(3.1)	**-36**	(3.0)	**25**	(3.7)	**-38**	(3.6)
Mexico	386	(7.6)	380	(5.7)	397	(8.9)	-16	(10.3)	423	(3.4)	408	(2.8)	412	(2.4)	3	(3.3)	**37**	(8.5)	**28**	(6.6)	15	(9.4)	19	(11.1)
Netherlands	562	(25.5)	537	(10.9)	533	(5.8)	10	(11.9)	540	(10.1)	525	(8.5)	516	(7.8)	11	(12.3)	-22	(27.4)	-12	(14.0)	-16	(10.0)	1	(17.5)
New Zealand	c	c	527	(3.7)	522	(5.3)	5	(7.6)	c	c	503	(3.4)	496	(5.8)	8	(7.5)	c	c	**-24**	(5.4)	**-27**	(8.1)	4	(10.2)
Norway	m	m	m	m	m	m	m	m	m	m	m	m	m	m	m	m	m	m	m	m	m	m	m	m
Poland	486	(6.5)	490	(4.5)	492	(3.9)	-3	(5.8)	513	(5.1)	511	(7.0)	524	(7.9)	-11	(9.2)	**27**	(8.5)	20	(8.5)	32	(9.1)	-8	(11.0)
Portugal	484	(5.6)	458	(7.7)	459	(7.2)	10	(10.0)	513	(5.2)	466	(5.9)	477	(9.1)	13	(10.4)	**29**	(7.9)	8	(9.9)	17	(11.7)	3	(15.5)
Slovak Republic	524	(5.9)	485	(7.1)	496	(6.4)	9	(9.2)	493	(9.0)	487	(7.6)	464	(9.6)	**26**	(11.7)	**-30**	(10.9)	2	(10.6)	**-32**	(11.7)	17	(16.1)
Spain	482	(14.1)	484	(3.8)	486	(4.8)	-2	(6.2)	496	(7.4)	486	(3.4)	481	(2.6)	7	(4.4)	14	(16.0)	2	(5.4)	-5	(5.8)	9	(7.4)
Sweden	492	(14.7)	509	(4.2)	510	(3.8)	-4	(5.9)	472	(6.6)	479	(5.8)	480	(3.1)	-3	(5.9)	**-20**	(16.2)	**-30**	(7.4)	**-31**	(5.3)	0	(7.5)
Switzerland	573	(9.7)	524	(5.6)	504	(6.1)	**35**	(9.9)	595	(7.3)	530	(5.9)	513	(4.1)	**34**	(8.4)	21	(12.3)	6	(8.4)	9	(7.6)	-1	(13.8)
Turkey	402	(7.9)	413	(9.5)	445	(13.4)	**-36**	(15.5)	483	(14.5)	438	(6.3)	437	(9.3)	18	(13.2)	**81**	(16.7)	26	(11.5)	-8	(16.5)	**53**	(21.0)
United States	452	(21.9)	485	(4.9)	488	(5.3)	-4	(7.4)	457	(12.5)	481	(5.0)	489	(7.3)	-10	(9.5)	4	(25.3)	-4	(7.3)	1	(9.2)	-6	(13.4)
OECD average 2003	500	(2.1)	498	(1.4)	493	(1.6)	**8**	(1.9)	508	(2.1)	493	(1.2)	488	(1.6)	**12**	(1.9)	**8**	(2.9)	**-6**	(1.9)	**-5**	(2.3)	4	(2.8)
Partners																								
Brazil	389	(10.5)	360	(11.9)	342	(7.8)	**31**	(11.9)	408	(8.6)	391	(4.5)	396	(3.5)	1	(6.2)	19	(13.8)	**30**	(12.9)	**54**	(8.8)	**-30**	(13.9)
Hong Kong-China	588	(13.6)	556	(5.7)	509	(13.8)	**52**	(15.3)	596	(17.2)	565	(5.4)	543	(9.4)	**26**	(12.3)	8	(22.0)	10	(8.0)	**35**	(16.8)	-26	(19.7)
Indonesia	375	(5.7)	365	(10.9)	352	(6.9)	**19**	(8.0)	378	(7.9)	386	(11.2)	368	(4.8)	14	(8.5)	4	(9.9)	21	(15.8)	16	(8.6)	-5	(11.7)
Latvia	474	(9.3)	482	(5.7)	492	(5.5)	-11	(7.4)	491	(8.2)	489	(4.6)	492	(4.7)	-2	(6.5)	17	(12.5)	7	(7.6)	0	(7.5)	9	(10.7)
Liechtenstein	c	c	549	(5.0)	c	c	c	c	c	c	c	c	508	(6.0)	**50**	(8.8)	c	c	c	c	c	c	c	c
Macao-China	525	(4.0)	523	(6.4)	537	(4.4)	**-13**	(5.2)	555	(1.7)	539	(1.3)	491	(2.6)	**55**	(2.8)	**30**	(4.7)	16	(6.8)	**-47**	(5.5)	**68**	(6.3)
Russian Federation	442	(11.0)	473	(5.8)	470	(7.1)	-2	(9.8)	481	(14.7)	474	(3.9)	488	(4.7)	**-14**	(6.2)	**39**	(18.5)	1	(7.3)	19	(8.7)	-13	(12.6)
Thailand	411	(7.7)	427	(5.9)	412	(5.1)	9	(7.7)	417	(6.8)	429	(4.6)	441	(21.5)	-15	(22.2)	7	(10.4)	2	(7.7)	28	(22.2)	-24	(22.7)
Tunisia	359	(6.2)	340	(9.9)	362	(5.0)	-7	(8.7)	403	(13.5)	392	(6.2)	380	(6.4)	16	(9.1)	**44**	(15.0)	**53**	(11.9)	18	(8.3)	23	(12.9)
Uruguay	448	(8.4)	418	(5.8)	406	(9.9)	21	(11.2)	425	(11.0)	405	(4.6)	417	(8.3)	-9	(10.9)	-23	(19.0)	-14	(7.7)	11	(13.0)	**-30**	(14.5)

Notes: Values that are statistically significant are indicated in bold (see Annex A3).
Only countries and economies with comparable data from PISA 2003 and PISA 2012 are shown.
StatLink ⊟⛁ http://dx.doi.org/10.1787/888932957384

[Part 1/1]
Change between 2003 and 2012 in mathematics performance and student-teacher ratio
Table IV.1.25   *Results based on school principals' reports*

| | | PISA 2003 | | PISA 2012 | | Change between 2003 and 2012 (PISA 2012 - PISA 2003) | |
| | | Correlation between mathematics performance and student-teacher ratio | | Correlation between mathematics performance and student-teacher ratio | | Correlation between mathematics performance and student-teacher ratio | |
		Corr.	S.E.	Corr.	S.E.	Corr. dif.	S.E.
OECD	Australia	0.06	(0.04)	0.00	(0.02)	-0.05	(0.05)
	Austria	**-0.14**	(0.03)	-0.07	(0.04)	0.07	(0.05)
	Belgium	**0.41**	(0.04)	**0.43**	(0.03)	0.02	(0.05)
	Canada	**0.09**	(0.03)	**0.10**	(0.02)	0.02	(0.04)
	Czech Republic	**-0.15**	(0.06)	0.06	(0.05)	**0.21**	(0.08)
	Denmark	**0.12**	(0.03)	0.07	(0.05)	-0.05	(0.06)
	Finland	**0.06**	(0.02)	0.05	(0.03)	-0.01	(0.03)
	France	w	w	**-0.10**	(0.05)	m	m
	Germany	-0.06	(0.09)	**0.14**	(0.04)	0.19	(0.10)
	Greece	**0.15**	(0.04)	**0.12**	(0.04)	-0.02	(0.06)
	Hungary	0.07	(0.07)	0.02	(0.06)	-0.05	(0.09)
	Iceland	0.03	(0.02)	**0.04**	(0.02)	0.01	(0.03)
	Ireland	0.07	(0.06)	**0.15**	(0.05)	0.08	(0.07)
	Italy	**0.16**	(0.04)	**0.34**	(0.03)	**0.19**	(0.05)
	Japan	**0.26**	(0.05)	**0.24**	(0.04)	-0.02	(0.06)
	Korea	**0.29**	(0.04)	0.10	(0.08)	**-0.19**	(0.09)
	Luxembourg	**0.19**	(0.01)	**0.11**	(0.01)	**-0.08**	(0.02)
	Mexico	m	m	0.03	(0.02)	m	m
	Netherlands	**0.46**	(0.05)	**0.41**	(0.08)	-0.05	(0.10)
	New Zealand	**0.16**	(0.04)	**0.08**	(0.04)	-0.08	(0.05)
	Norway	0.00	(0.03)	-0.02	(0.04)	-0.02	(0.05)
	Poland	-0.02	(0.03)	**0.13**	(0.04)	**0.15**	(0.05)
	Portugal	0.04	(0.04)	**0.23**	(0.04)	**0.19**	(0.05)
	Slovak Republic	**-0.13**	(0.04)	-0.05	(0.05)	0.08	(0.07)
	Spain	**0.14**	(0.03)	0.07	(0.05)	-0.07	(0.06)
	Sweden	**0.07**	(0.02)	**0.05**	(0.03)	-0.02	(0.03)
	Switzerland	-0.05	(0.04)	**0.07**	(0.03)	**0.12**	(0.05)
	Turkey	**-0.19**	(0.06)	**-0.29**	(0.04)	-0.10	(0.08)
	United States	-0.02	(0.03)	0.01	(0.04)	0.03	(0.05)
	OECD average 2003	**0.08**	(0.01)	**0.09**	(0.01)	0.02	(0.01)
Partners	Brazil	**-0.22**	(0.05)	**-0.15**	(0.02)	0.08	(0.06)
	Hong Kong-China	**0.37**	(0.06)	**0.34**	(0.05)	-0.03	(0.08)
	Indonesia	m	m	**-0.04**	(0.06)	m	m
	Latvia	**0.21**	(0.04)	**0.13**	(0.04)	-0.08	(0.06)
	Liechtenstein	**0.64**	(0.03)	**0.56**	(0.04)	-0.08	(0.04)
	Macao-China	**0.12**	(0.03)	**0.20**	(0.01)	**0.08**	(0.03)
	Russian Federation	**-0.13**	(0.06)	0.07	(0.04)	**0.20**	(0.07)
	Thailand	**-0.08**	(0.03)	0.00	(0.06)	0.08	(0.06)
	Tunisia	**-0.36**	(0.06)	**-0.07**	(0.02)	**0.29**	(0.06)
	Uruguay	0.08	(0.04)	-0.03	(0.03)	-0.11	(0.06)

Notes: Values that are statistically significant are indicated in bold (see Annex A3).
Only countries and economies with comparable data from PISA 2003 and PISA 2012 are shown.
StatLink ⬛️🔢🖳 http://dx.doi.org/10.1787/888932957384

[Part 1/1]

Change between 2003 and 2012 in mathematics performance and students' learning time at school

Table IV.1.26   *Results based on students' self-reports*

	PISA 2003				PISA 2012				Change between 2003 and 2012 (PISA 2012 - PISA 2003)			
	Correlation between mathematics performance and students' reports on the following:				Correlation between mathematics performance and students' reports on the following:				Correlation between mathematics performance and students' reports on the following:			
	Mathematics class periods per week (class periods)		Regular school lessons in mathematics per week (minutes)		Mathematics class periods per week (class periods)		Regular school lessons in mathematics per week (minutes)		Mathematics class periods per week (class periods)		Regular school lessons in mathematics per week (minutes)	
	Corr.	S.E.	Corr.	S.E.	Corr.	S.E.	Corr.	S.E.	Corr. dif.	S.E.	Corr. dif.	S.E.
Australia	**0.10**	(0.02)	**0.11**	(0.02)	**0.11**	(0.02)	**0.09**	(0.01)	0.01	(0.03)	-0.02	(0.02)
Austria	0.01	(0.03)	0.02	(0.03)	0.02	(0.04)	0.01	(0.04)	0.00	(0.05)	-0.01	(0.05)
Belgium	**0.38**	(0.03)	**0.37**	(0.03)	**0.31**	(0.01)	**0.21**	(0.03)	-0.06	(0.03)	**-0.17**	(0.04)
Canada	-0.02	(0.01)	-0.01	(0.02)	0.00	(0.02)	0.01	(0.02)	0.02	(0.02)	0.02	(0.02)
Czech Republic	**0.14**	(0.03)	**0.14**	(0.03)	0.05	(0.03)	0.05	(0.04)	-0.09	(0.05)	-0.09	(0.05)
Denmark	**-0.05**	(0.02)	**-0.06**	(0.03)	-0.04	(0.02)	**-0.08**	(0.02)	0.01	(0.03)	-0.02	(0.03)
Finland	**0.07**	(0.02)	**0.07**	(0.02)	0.04	(0.02)	0.03	(0.02)	-0.03	(0.03)	-0.04	(0.03)
France	0.06	(0.02)	0.06	(0.02)	0.12	(0.02)	0.17	(0.02)	0.06	(0.03)	0.11	(0.03)
Germany	**-0.15**	(0.02)	**-0.16**	(0.02)	**-0.16**	(0.03)	**-0.12**	(0.02)	0.00	(0.04)	0.03	(0.03)
Greece	**0.35**	(0.02)	**0.35**	(0.02)	**0.30**	(0.02)	**0.26**	(0.03)	-0.05	(0.03)	**-0.09**	(0.04)
Hungary	0.01	(0.03)	0.01	(0.03)	0.06	(0.04)	0.07	(0.04)	0.05	(0.05)	0.06	(0.05)
Iceland	-0.01	(0.02)	-0.03	(0.02)	0.03	(0.03)	-0.01	(0.03)	0.05	(0.04)	0.02	(0.03)
Ireland	-0.01	(0.02)	-0.01	(0.02)	0.03	(0.02)	0.02	(0.02)	0.05	(0.03)	0.03	(0.03)
Italy	-0.03	(0.02)	-0.02	(0.03)	0.17	(0.02)	0.14	(0.02)	0.20	(0.03)	0.16	(0.04)
Japan	**0.28**	(0.04)	**0.31**	(0.03)	**0.42**	(0.02)	**0.45**	(0.02)	**0.14**	(0.04)	**0.14**	(0.04)
Korea	**0.11**	(0.03)	**0.12**	(0.03)	**0.27**	(0.05)	**0.27**	(0.05)	**0.16**	(0.06)	**0.15**	(0.06)
Luxembourg	-0.03	(0.02)	**-0.04**	(0.02)	0.01	(0.02)	**-0.05**	(0.02)	0.04	(0.02)	0.00	(0.02)
Mexico	-0.01	(0.04)	0.13	(0.03)	**0.04**	(0.01)	**0.08**	(0.01)	0.05	(0.04)	-0.04	(0.03)
Netherlands	**0.07**	(0.03)	**0.08**	(0.03)	0.04	(0.05)	-0.07	(0.05)	-0.04	(0.06)	**-0.15**	(0.05)
New Zealand	**0.08**	(0.02)	**0.06**	(0.02)	**0.12**	(0.03)	0.06	(0.04)	0.04	(0.04)	0.00	(0.04)
Norway	0.01	(0.02)	0.01	(0.02)	0.01	(0.03)	-0.04	(0.02)	-0.01	(0.03)	-0.05	(0.03)
Poland	0.04	(0.02)	0.04	(0.02)	**0.10**	(0.03)	**0.10**	(0.03)	0.07	(0.04)	0.07	(0.04)
Portugal	**0.11**	(0.03)	-0.01	(0.03)	**0.09**	(0.04)	**0.10**	(0.03)	-0.02	(0.05)	**0.11**	(0.05)
Slovak Republic	-0.03	(0.03)	-0.03	(0.03)	0.06	(0.04)	0.06	(0.04)	0.10	(0.05)	0.10	(0.05)
Spain	-0.01	(0.02)	-0.01	(0.02)	**-0.06**	(0.02)	**-0.07**	(0.02)	-0.05	(0.03)	**-0.06**	(0.03)
Sweden	-0.04	(0.02)	-0.03	(0.02)	**-0.06**	(0.03)	-0.04	(0.03)	-0.02	(0.04)	-0.01	(0.04)
Switzerland	0.00	(0.02)	0.00	(0.02)	**-0.11**	(0.02)	**-0.13**	(0.02)	**-0.11**	(0.03)	**-0.12**	(0.03)
Turkey	**0.21**	(0.05)	**0.25**	(0.05)	**0.33**	(0.03)	**0.39**	(0.03)	**0.13**	(0.05)	**0.14**	(0.06)
United States	**0.18**	(0.03)	**0.16**	(0.02)	**0.17**	(0.04)	**0.16**	(0.03)	-0.01	(0.05)	0.00	(0.03)
OECD average 2003	**0.06**	(0.00)	**0.06**	(0.00)	**0.09**	(0.01)	**0.07**	(0.01)	**0.02**	(0.01)	0.01	(0.01)
Brazil	**-0.12**	(0.03)	**-0.11**	(0.03)	**0.04**	(0.02)	0.04	(0.02)	**0.17**	(0.03)	**0.14**	(0.04)
Hong Kong-China	**0.16**	(0.03)	**0.16**	(0.03)	0.05	(0.04)	0.00	(0.03)	-0.10	(0.05)	**-0.16**	(0.04)
Indonesia	**0.19**	(0.03)	**0.14**	(0.03)	**0.22**	(0.04)	**0.14**	(0.03)	0.03	(0.05)	0.00	(0.04)
Latvia	0.00	(0.05)	0.02	(0.05)	**0.13**	(0.03)	**0.11**	(0.03)	**0.13**	(0.06)	0.10	(0.06)
Liechtenstein	**-0.16**	(0.05)	**-0.16**	(0.05)	-0.10	(0.09)	-0.12	(0.09)	0.06	(0.11)	0.03	(0.11)
Macao-China	**0.09**	(0.04)	0.07	(0.04)	**0.21**	(0.02)	**0.18**	(0.02)	**0.12**	(0.04)	**0.11**	(0.04)
Russian Federation	**0.20**	(0.03)	**0.20**	(0.03)	**0.23**	(0.03)	**0.22**	(0.03)	0.03	(0.04)	0.02	(0.04)
Thailand	**0.14**	(0.03)	**0.15**	(0.03)	**0.41**	(0.03)	**0.40**	(0.03)	**0.27**	(0.04)	**0.25**	(0.04)
Tunisia	-0.02	(0.02)	-0.02	(0.03)	**-0.04**	(0.02)	**0.09**	(0.03)	-0.02	(0.03)	**0.11**	(0.03)
Uruguay	-0.01	(0.03)	**-0.06**	(0.03)	**0.13**	(0.03)	**0.09**	(0.03)	**0.15**	(0.04)	**0.15**	(0.04)

Notes: Values that are statistically significant are indicated in bold (see Annex A3).
Only countries and economies with comparable data from PISA 2003 and PISA 2012 are shown.
StatLink ᘻᘙᕫᓐ http://dx.doi.org/10.1787/888932957384

[Part 1/3]
Change between 2003 and 2012 in mathematics performance and pre-school attendance

Table IV.1.27 *Results based on students' self-reports*

	PISA 2003									
	Mathematics performance, by students who reported that they had attended pre-primary education (ISCED 0)					PISA index of economic, social and cultural status, by students who reported that they had attended pre-primary education (ISCED 0)				
	No attendance	For one year or less	For more than one year	Performance difference (more than one year or one year or less - no attendance)	Performance difference (more than one year - one year or less or no attendance)	No attendance	For one year or less	For more than one year	Mean index difference (more than one year or one year or less - no attendance)	Mean index difference (more than one year - one year or less or no attendance)
	Mean score	S.E.	Mean score	S.E.	Mean score	S.E.	Score dif.	S.E.	Score dif.	S.E.	Mean index	S.E.	Mean index	S.E.	Mean index	S.E.	Mean dif.	S.E.	Mean dif.	S.E.
Australia	501	(5.3)	521	(2.6)	535	(2.1)	**27**	(5.2)	**17**	(2.2)	-0.25	(0.03)	-0.03	(0.02)	0.18	(0.02)	**0.32**	(0.03)	**0.24**	(0.02)
Austria	470	(6.8)	490	(6.4)	513	(3.0)	**39**	(7.6)	**27**	(5.0)	-0.75	(0.07)	-0.59	(0.04)	-0.17	(0.02)	**0.52**	(0.06)	**0.46**	(0.04)
Belgium	447	(10.5)	445	(9.1)	540	(2.4)	**89**	(10.6)	**94**	(7.2)	-0.56	(0.09)	-0.43	(0.07)	0.02	(0.02)	**0.55**	(0.09)	**0.49**	(0.05)
Canada	512	(3.9)	529	(1.6)	549	(2.2)	**27**	(3.7)	**23**	(2.4)	-0.14	(0.03)	0.11	(0.02)	0.40	(0.02)	**0.39**	(0.03)	**0.33**	(0.03)
Czech Republic	511	(6.8)	515	(4.5)	525	(3.5)	**13**	(6.6)	**12**	(4.4)	-0.23	(0.06)	-0.15	(0.04)	-0.02	(0.02)	**0.19**	(0.06)	**0.16**	(0.04)
Denmark	462	(12.4)	502	(3.1)	524	(3.0)	**55**	(12.1)	**25**	(3.3)	-0.29	(0.14)	-0.03	(0.04)	0.15	(0.04)	**0.38**	(0.14)	**0.20**	(0.04)
Finland	535	(4.5)	538	(3.0)	549	(2.3)	**11**	(4.9)	**12**	(3.1)	-0.12	(0.05)	-0.12	(0.03)	0.15	(0.02)	**0.20**	(0.06)	**0.27**	(0.03)
France	423	(13.3)	464	(7.7)	516	(2.4)	**91**	(13.2)	**63**	(7.2)	-0.91	(0.16)	-0.55	(0.09)	-0.29	(0.03)	**0.61**	(0.15)	**0.35**	(0.08)
Germany	448	(9.7)	466	(6.5)	523	(3.3)	**67**	(10.0)	**61**	(4.4)	-0.64	(0.09)	-0.39	(0.06)	0.11	(0.03)	**0.68**	(0.09)	**0.56**	(0.05)
Greece	415	(8.8)	437	(4.6)	453	(4.1)	**33**	(8.8)	**19**	(4.1)	-0.66	(0.08)	-0.34	(0.05)	-0.24	(0.06)	**0.38**	(0.08)	**0.14**	(0.05)
Hungary	430	(17.0)	462	(8.1)	492	(2.8)	**61**	(17.2)	**36**	(7.1)	-0.64	(0.13)	-0.61	(0.07)	-0.29	(0.02)	**0.34**	(0.13)	**0.33**	(0.07)
Iceland	511	(6.6)	506	(7.2)	516	(1.6)	5	(7.0)	7	(5.4)	0.13	(0.06)	0.28	(0.08)	0.59	(0.01)	**0.45**	(0.06)	**0.41**	(0.05)
Ireland	490	(3.5)	517	(3.1)	500	(3.7)	**20**	(3.5)	-5	(3.8)	-0.55	(0.03)	-0.15	(0.03)	-0.11	(0.05)	**0.42**	(0.04)	**0.20**	(0.04)
Italy	448	(10.7)	434	(6.6)	470	(2.9)	19	(10.3)	31	(5.9)	-0.49	(0.08)	-0.38	(0.05)	-0.26	(0.02)	**0.21**	(0.08)	**0.15**	(0.04)
Japan	504	(13.3)	471	(15.0)	537	(4.0)	31	(13.1)	51	(9.6)	-0.54	(0.12)	-0.46	(0.09)	-0.41	(0.09)	0.12	(0.12)	0.08	(0.07)
Korea	531	(9.3)	535	(5.3)	544	(3.3)	12	(9.2)	10	(4.4)	-0.81	(0.08)	-0.58	(0.05)	-0.32	(0.03)	**0.47**	(0.08)	**0.33**	(0.05)
Luxembourg	481	(4.4)	471	(5.2)	500	(1.2)	**16**	(5.0)	**23**	(3.5)	-0.23	(0.05)	-0.16	(0.06)	-0.05	(0.02)	**0.17**	(0.05)	**0.15**	(0.04)
Mexico	340	(4.6)	383	(4.0)	398	(4.1)	**54**	(5.0)	**32**	(4.4)	-2.07	(0.04)	-1.50	(0.05)	-1.10	(0.06)	**0.88**	(0.04)	**0.63**	(0.05)
Netherlands	487	(13.2)	520	(9.9)	545	(2.8)	**58**	(12.6)	**42**	(8.0)	-0.40	(0.12)	-0.07	(0.10)	-0.08	(0.03)	**0.33**	(0.12)	**0.16**	(0.08)
New Zealand	480	(5.6)	517	(3.9)	532	(2.3)	**48**	(5.6)	**26**	(3.2)	-0.57	(0.05)	-0.26	(0.03)	-0.04	(0.03)	**0.48**	(0.05)	**0.31**	(0.03)
Norway	468	(5.6)	480	(3.9)	502	(2.6)	**31**	(5.6)	**27**	(3.8)	-0.15	(0.05)	0.01	(0.03)	0.26	(0.02)	**0.37**	(0.05)	**0.30**	(0.04)
Poland	469	(8.8)	479	(2.8)	506	(3.0)	**23**	(8.7)	**27**	(3.0)	-0.45	(0.08)	-0.64	(0.02)	-0.13	(0.03)	0.05	(0.08)	**0.49**	(0.03)
Portugal	457	(4.5)	462	(5.9)	473	(3.5)	**14**	(4.1)	**14**	(3.9)	-1.41	(0.04)	-0.86	(0.07)	-0.66	(0.06)	**0.70**	(0.06)	**0.54**	(0.05)
Slovak Republic	477	(7.5)	492	(6.6)	503	(3.1)	**25**	(6.9)	**16**	(5.1)	-0.53	(0.08)	-0.34	(0.07)	-0.19	(0.02)	**0.32**	(0.07)	**0.22**	(0.05)
Spain	464	(8.0)	458	(3.9)	491	(2.5)	**23**	(7.6)	**30**	(3.7)	-0.95	(0.08)	-0.70	(0.06)	-0.46	(0.05)	**0.47**	(0.08)	**0.33**	(0.06)
Sweden	476	(6.2)	508	(3.4)	518	(2.8)	**39**	(6.2)	**20**	(3.1)	-0.21	(0.05)	-0.02	(0.04)	0.20	(0.03)	**0.34**	(0.05)	**0.28**	(0.04)
Switzerland	420	(10.9)	533	(4.7)	529	(4.0)	**110**	(11.1)	7	(6.3)	-0.96	(0.10)	-0.25	(0.05)	-0.18	(0.04)	**0.76**	(0.10)	**0.14**	(0.05)
Turkey	407	(5.0)	477	(11.3)	505	(15.4)	**80**	(10.8)	**86**	(13.5)	-1.42	(0.04)	-0.37	(0.08)	0.08	(0.09)	**1.20**	(0.07)	**1.32**	(0.08)
United States	448	(11.0)	488	(3.0)	460	(6.0)	**38**	(10.3)	-27	(5.9)	-0.34	(0.09)	0.08	(0.03)	-0.03	(0.06)	**0.41**	(0.09)	-0.10	(0.05)
OECD average 2003	466	(1.6)	486	(1.2)	509	(0.8)	**40**	(1.7)	**28**	(1.0)	-0.59	(0.02)	-0.33	(0.01)	-0.10	(0.01)	**0.44**	(0.02)	**0.33**	(0.01)
Brazil	321	(4.4)	358	(5.4)	381	(5.7)	**51**	(4.6)	**38**	(4.8)	-2.03	(0.04)	-1.62	(0.06)	-1.24	(0.06)	**0.63**	(0.05)	**0.56**	(0.05)
Hong Kong-China	475	(8.1)	484	(7.5)	562	(4.0)	**82**	(7.3)	**82**	(5.5)	-1.95	(0.06)	-1.57	(0.06)	-1.20	(0.04)	**0.73**	(0.07)	**0.56**	(0.04)
Indonesia	341	(2.6)	377	(5.0)	389	(7.2)	**42**	(5.1)	**36**	(5.8)	-2.16	(0.03)	-1.68	(0.05)	-1.44	(0.06)	**0.60**	(0.05)	**0.55**	(0.06)
Latvia	481	(5.0)	483	(5.4)	486	(4.2)	4	(5.0)	4	(4.3)	-0.45	(0.04)	-0.35	(0.06)	-0.28	(0.03)	**0.15**	(0.04)	**0.13**	(0.04)
Liechtenstein	c	c	c	c	542	(4.6)	c	c	75	(21.3)	c	c	c	c	-0.26	(0.04)	c	c	**0.58**	(0.25)
Macao-China	496	(15.2)	510	(8.4)	532	(2.9)	**33**	(15.0)	25	(8.5)	-1.94	(0.12)	-1.67	(0.09)	-1.57	(0.03)	**0.35**	(0.12)	0.15	(0.08)
Russian Federation	454	(5.2)	447	(6.9)	474	(4.2)	17	(3.9)	23	(3.3)	-0.81	(0.05)	-0.66	(0.07)	-0.57	(0.03)	**0.23**	(0.05)	**0.18**	(0.04)
Thailand	392	(6.3)	397	(3.7)	425	(3.4)	27	(6.2)	29	(4.2)	-2.33	(0.07)	-2.30	(0.04)	-1.71	(0.04)	**0.49**	(0.07)	**0.60**	(0.05)
Tunisia	348	(2.4)	358	(3.9)	387	(5.4)	25	(4.7)	36	(5.2)	-2.25	(0.04)	-1.38	(0.05)	-0.95	(0.06)	**1.09**	(0.06)	**0.99**	(0.06)
Uruguay	389	(4.8)	404	(5.1)	442	(3.6)	**44**	(5.2)	45	(3.8)	-1.38	(0.06)	-1.05	(0.04)	-0.48	(0.04)	**0.76**	(0.05)	**0.71**	(0.04)

Notes: Values that are statistically significant are indicated in bold (see Annex A3).
Only countries and economies with comparable data from PISA 2003 and PISA 2012 are shown.
StatLink http://dx.doi.org/10.1787/888932957384

[Part 2/3]
Change between 2003 and 2012 in mathematics performance and pre-school attendance

Table IV.1.27   *Results based on students' self-reports*

	PISA 2012																		
	Mathematics performance, by students who reported that they had attended pre-primary education (ISCED 0)										PISA index of economic, social and cultural status, by students who reported that they had attended pre-primary education (ISCED 0)								
	No attendance		For one year or less		For more than one year		Performance difference (more than one year or one year or less - no attendance)		Performance difference (more than one year - one year or less or no attendance)		No attendance		For one year or less		For more than one year		Mean index difference (more than one year or one year or less - no attendance)		Mean index difference (more than one year - one year or less or no attendance)	
	Mean score	S.E.	Mean score	S.E.	Mean score	S.E.	Score dif.	S.E.	Score dif.	S.E.	Mean index	S.E.	Mean index	S.E.	Mean index	S.E.	Mean dif.	S.E.	Mean dif.	S.E.
Australia	462	(5.1)	499	(1.8)	515	(2.0)	**46**	(5.2)	**20**	(2.0)	-0.12	(0.05)	0.16	(0.01)	0.36	(0.01)	**0.39**	(0.05)	**0.23**	(0.02)
Austria	447	(14.3)	482	(5.9)	510	(2.6)	**59**	(14.1)	**33**	(6.0)	-0.76	(0.17)	-0.19	(0.05)	0.12	(0.02)	**0.85**	(0.17)	**0.40**	(0.06)
Belgium	448	(9.3)	455	(6.6)	521	(2.1)	**70**	(9.2)	**68**	(5.7)	-0.44	(0.09)	-0.20	(0.09)	0.18	(0.02)	**0.61**	(0.08)	**0.46**	(0.08)
Canada	499	(3.3)	512	(1.8)	532	(2.6)	**24**	(3.2)	**23**	(2.4)	0.12	(0.03)	0.33	(0.02)	0.54	(0.02)	**0.32**	(0.03)	**0.25**	(0.02)
Czech Republic	434	(15.1)	482	(7.1)	504	(2.7)	**67**	(15.0)	**34**	(7.3)	-0.40	(0.13)	-0.16	(0.05)	-0.04	(0.02)	**0.34**	(0.13)	**0.18**	(0.05)
Denmark	442	(10.9)	468	(3.3)	510	(2.2)	**60**	(10.4)	**44**	(3.0)	-0.03	(0.13)	0.25	(0.04)	0.48	(0.02)	**0.46**	(0.12)	**0.24**	(0.03)
Finland	471	(10.6)	512	(2.6)	527	(2.2)	**50**	(10.4)	**18**	(3.3)	-0.13	(0.12)	0.22	(0.02)	0.46	(0.02)	**0.50**	(0.12)	**0.26**	(0.02)
France	403	(13.1)	437	(5.6)	503	(2.5)	**96**	(13.0)	**73**	(5.6)	-0.73	(0.10)	-0.27	(0.05)	0.00	(0.02)	**0.71**	(0.10)	**0.37**	(0.05)
Germany	466	(8.2)	465	(4.7)	528	(3.1)	**55**	(7.8)	**62**	(4.7)	-0.11	(0.08)	-0.15	(0.06)	0.26	(0.02)	**0.32**	(0.08)	**0.40**	(0.05)
Greece	395	(7.9)	439	(3.9)	463	(2.5)	**61**	(7.8)	**30**	(3.7)	-0.79	(0.09)	-0.15	(0.04)	0.02	(0.03)	**0.76**	(0.09)	**0.26**	(0.04)
Hungary	c	c	432	(10.1)	480	(3.2)	c	c	**48**	(9.3)	c	c	-0.46	(0.11)	-0.25	(0.03)	c	c	**0.14**	(0.09)
Iceland	449	(12.0)	463	(9.4)	496	(1.7)	**47**	(12.3)	**39**	(7.0)	0.10	(0.13)	0.49	(0.10)	0.81	(0.01)	**0.69**	(0.13)	**0.47**	(0.07)
Ireland	491	(4.2)	506	(2.8)	502	(2.7)	**13**	(4.0)	0	(3.0)	-0.17	(0.04)	0.09	(0.02)	0.26	(0.03)	**0.35**	(0.04)	**0.23**	(0.02)
Italy	429	(4.5)	454	(3.3)	492	(2.1)	**60**	(4.5)	**46**	(2.9)	-0.41	(0.05)	-0.14	(0.03)	-0.03	(0.02)	**0.37**	(0.04)	**0.21**	(0.03)
Japan	502	(18.2)	484	(8.5)	540	(3.6)	**36**	(17.2)	**50**	(7.6)	-0.06	(0.13)	-0.33	(0.06)	-0.07	(0.02)	-0.01	(0.13)	**0.19**	(0.06)
Korea	533	(8.6)	541	(6.9)	557	(4.5)	**22**	(8.0)	**18**	(5.1)	-0.24	(0.06)	-0.06	(0.03)	0.04	(0.03)	**0.27**	(0.06)	**0.15**	(0.03)
Luxembourg	451	(6.4)	454	(4.0)	498	(1.4)	**42**	(6.7)	**45**	(3.8)	-0.42	(0.08)	-0.13	(0.05)	0.14	(0.02)	**0.52**	(0.08)	**0.34**	(0.04)
Mexico	378	(2.5)	411	(1.8)	419	(1.4)	**40**	(2.4)	**19**	(1.6)	-1.81	(0.04)	-1.31	(0.03)	-0.96	(0.03)	**0.78**	(0.04)	**0.52**	(0.03)
Netherlands	484	(12.1)	522	(10.1)	525	(3.5)	**41**	(11.5)	**21**	(8.1)	-0.10	(0.16)	0.13	(0.07)	0.25	(0.02)	**0.34**	(0.16)	**0.22**	(0.08)
New Zealand	451	(6.9)	489	(4.1)	511	(2.4)	**55**	(6.6)	**35**	(3.8)	-0.42	(0.05)	-0.07	(0.03)	0.13	(0.02)	**0.50**	(0.05)	**0.31**	(0.03)
Norway	463	(5.1)	459	(6.1)	495	(2.7)	**30**	(4.7)	**34**	(4.1)	0.08	(0.05)	0.13	(0.05)	0.52	(0.02)	**0.41**	(0.05)	**0.42**	(0.04)
Poland	471	(9.3)	504	(3.0)	532	(4.8)	**48**	(9.9)	**29**	(4.3)	-0.56	(0.08)	-0.54	(0.03)	0.11	(0.04)	**0.36**	(0.08)	**0.65**	(0.04)
Portugal	461	(5.0)	465	(5.0)	504	(4.0)	**34**	(4.8)	**41**	(3.9)	-0.93	(0.05)	-0.73	(0.06)	-0.30	(0.06)	**0.53**	(0.06)	**0.51**	(0.05)
Slovak Republic	390	(8.0)	462	(6.2)	494	(3.5)	**99**	(8.4)	**56**	(6.4)	-0.98	(0.09)	-0.49	(0.05)	-0.06	(0.02)	**0.86**	(0.09)	**0.60**	(0.06)
Spain	435	(3.2)	455	(3.9)	492	(1.8)	**54**	(3.0)	**46**	(2.8)	-0.64	(0.04)	-0.42	(0.04)	-0.13	(0.03)	**0.48**	(0.04)	**0.38**	(0.03)
Sweden	438	(6.3)	472	(3.0)	488	(2.3)	**46**	(6.0)	**26**	(3.3)	-0.07	(0.06)	0.15	(0.03)	0.35	(0.02)	**0.38**	(0.06)	**0.26**	(0.03)
Switzerland	456	(13.7)	536	(5.2)	532	(3.2)	**77**	(12.7)	1	(5.5)	-0.41	(0.11)	0.10	(0.05)	0.21	(0.02)	**0.59**	(0.10)	**0.14**	(0.05)
Turkey	433	(4.4)	480	(6.0)	495	(10.0)	**51**	(5.9)	**51**	(8.7)	-1.77	(0.03)	-0.91	(0.05)	-0.30	(0.08)	**1.03**	(0.05)	**1.27**	(0.08)
United States	450	(11.9)	472	(3.5)	486	(4.1)	**33**	(11.9)	**16**	(4.3)	-0.25	(0.19)	-0.19	(0.05)	0.30	(0.04)	**0.43**	(0.17)	**0.50**	(0.05)
OECD average 2003	451	(1.8)	476	(1.0)	505	(0.6)	**51**	(1.8)	**35**	(1.0)	-0.44	(0.02)	-0.17	(0.01)	0.12	(0.01)	**0.51**	(0.02)	**0.36**	(0.01)
Brazil	368	(2.4)	386	(2.0)	408	(2.8)	**31**	(2.6)	**28**	(2.3)	-1.57	(0.03)	-1.24	(0.03)	-0.94	(0.03)	**0.51**	(0.03)	**0.42**	(0.03)
Hong Kong-China	483	(15.5)	502	(8.2)	566	(3.1)	**81**	(15.3)	**70**	(7.9)	-1.30	(0.11)	-1.17	(0.08)	-0.77	(0.05)	**0.51**	(0.11)	**0.44**	(0.07)
Indonesia	351	(3.7)	390	(4.5)	405	(9.2)	**45**	(6.4)	**38**	(9.1)	-2.19	(0.04)	-1.56	(0.07)	-1.34	(0.11)	**0.72**	(0.07)	**0.60**	(0.11)
Latvia	485	(6.2)	483	(5.2)	494	(2.9)	6	(6.2)	**10**	(4.5)	-0.57	(0.06)	-0.53	(0.05)	-0.16	(0.03)	**0.36**	(0.06)	**0.39**	(0.04)
Liechtenstein	c	c	c	c	538	(4.8)	c	c	c	c	c	c	c	c	0.29	(0.06)	c	c	c	c
Macao-China	496	(8.6)	491	(4.0)	547	(1.1)	**44**	(8.7)	**55**	(4.1)	-0.79	(0.08)	-0.99	(0.03)	-0.87	(0.01)	-0.10	(0.08)	**0.09**	(0.03)
Russian Federation	461	(4.6)	464	(4.9)	491	(3.0)	**26**	(4.0)	**29**	(2.9)	-0.47	(0.04)	-0.22	(0.04)	0.01	(0.02)	**0.45**	(0.04)	**0.39**	(0.03)
Thailand	373	(11.2)	395	(4.8)	432	(3.5)	**54**	(11.0)	**40**	(4.1)	-1.75	(0.13)	-1.69	(0.06)	-1.30	(0.04)	**0.41**	(0.12)	**0.40**	(0.05)
Tunisia	373	(3.8)	394	(4.8)	408	(6.0)	**26**	(4.7)	**24**	(4.5)	-1.80	(0.05)	-0.88	(0.06)	-0.71	(0.06)	**0.98**	(0.06)	**0.62**	(0.06)
Uruguay	370	(3.2)	390	(4.7)	426	(3.2)	**50**	(4.0)	**47**	(3.8)	-1.35	(0.03)	-1.20	(0.05)	-0.69	(0.04)	**0.57**	(0.05)	**0.59**	(0.04)

Notes: Values that are statistically significant are indicated in bold (see Annex A3).
Only countries and economies with comparable data from PISA 2003 and PISA 2012 are shown.
StatLink http://dx.doi.org/10.1787/888932957384

[Part 3/3]
Change between 2003 and 2012 in mathematics performance and pre-school attendance
Table IV.1.27   *Results based on students' self-reports*

	Change between 2003 and 2012 (PISA 2012 - PISA 2003)																			
	Mathematics performance, by students who reported that they had attended pre-primary education (ISCED 0)										PISA index of economic, social and cultural status, by students who reported that they had attended pre-primary education (ISCED 0)									
	No attendance		For one year or less		For more than one year		Performance difference (more than one year or one year or less - no attendance)		Performance difference (more than one year - one year or less or no attendance)		No attendance		For one year or less		For more than one year		Mean index difference (more than one year or one year or less - no attendance)		Mean index difference (more than one year - one year or less or no attendance)	
	Score dif.	S.E.	Score dif.	S.E.	Score dif.	S.E.	Score dif.	S.E.	Score dif.	S.E.	Mean dif.	S.E.	Mean dif.	S.E.	Mean dif.	S.E.	Mean dif.	S.E.	Mean dif.	S.E.
Australia	**-39**	(7.6)	**-21**	(3.7)	**-20**	(3.5)	**19**	(7.4)	2	(3.1)	**0.13**	(0.06)	**0.19**	(0.03)	**0.18**	(0.03)	0.07	(0.06)	-0.02	(0.03)
Austria	-23	(16.0)	-8	(8.9)	-3	(4.4)	20	(13.9)	6	(7.9)	0.00	(0.18)	**0.40**	(0.07)	**0.29**	(0.03)	0.33	(0.18)	-0.06	(0.08)
Belgium	0	(14.2)	10	(11.4)	**-20**	(3.7)	-19	(14.6)	**-26**	(8.9)	0.11	(0.13)	0.23	(0.11)	**0.16**	(0.03)	0.05	(0.12)	-0.03	(0.09)
Canada	**-13**	(5.5)	**-17**	(3.1)	**-18**	(3.9)	-3	(4.6)	-1	(3.1)	**0.26**	(0.05)	**0.22**	(0.03)	**0.14**	(0.03)	-0.07	(0.04)	**-0.09**	(0.03)
Czech Republic	**-76**	(16.7)	**-33**	(8.6)	**-22**	(4.8)	**54**	(17.9)	**22**	(8.9)	-0.17	(0.14)	-0.01	(0.06)	-0.02	(0.03)	0.15	(0.15)	0.02	(0.07)
Denmark	-20	(16.6)	**-34**	(4.9)	**-13**	(4.2)	5	(16.0)	**19**	(4.5)	0.26	(0.19)	**0.28**	(0.05)	**0.33**	(0.04)	0.08	(0.19)	0.04	(0.05)
Finland	**-64**	(11.6)	**-26**	(4.4)	**-22**	(3.7)	**39**	(11.0)	6	(4.3)	0.00	(0.13)	**0.34**	(0.04)	**0.31**	(0.03)	**0.30**	(0.13)	0.00	(0.04)
France	-20	(18.8)	**-27**	(9.7)	**-14**	(4.0)	5	(17.2)	10	(8.9)	0.19	(0.19)	**0.28**	(0.10)	**0.29**	(0.03)	0.10	(0.18)	0.02	(0.09)
Germany	18	(12.8)	-1	(8.3)	5	(4.9)	-12	(13.8)	1	(6.3)	**0.53**	(0.12)	**0.24**	(0.08)	**0.15**	(0.04)	**-0.36**	(0.14)	**-0.16**	(0.07)
Greece	-20	(12.0)	2	(6.3)	10	(5.2)	28	(11.6)	11	(5.7)	-0.13	(0.12)	**0.19**	(0.07)	**0.26**	(0.07)	**0.38**	(0.11)	**0.12**	(0.06)
Hungary	c	c	**-30**	(13.1)	**-12**	(4.7)	c	c	12	(11.7)	c	c	**0.16**	(0.13)	0.04	(0.04)	c	c	-0.18	(0.12)
Iceland	**-63**	(13.8)	**-43**	(12.0)	**-20**	(3.0)	**42**	(14.3)	**32**	(9.0)	-0.02	(0.14)	0.21	(0.13)	**0.21**	(0.02)	0.24	(0.15)	0.06	(0.09)
Ireland	1	(5.8)	**-11**	(4.6)	2	(5.0)	-6	(5.2)	6	(5.0)	**0.38**	(0.05)	**0.24**	(0.04)	**0.37**	(0.06)	-0.08	(0.05)	0.03	(0.05)
Italy	-19	(11.8)	**20**	(7.6)	**22**	(4.1)	**41**	(11.3)	**15**	(6.3)	0.08	(0.09)	**0.24**	(0.06)	**0.24**	(0.03)	0.16	(0.09)	0.05	(0.05)
Japan	-2	(22.7)	14	(17.4)	3	(5.7)	5	(22.6)	-1	(12.9)	**0.47**	(0.17)	0.13	(0.11)	**0.35**	(0.04)	-0.13	(0.17)	0.11	(0.09)
Korea	2	(12.8)	7	(8.9)	**13**	(5.9)	10	(12.1)	7	(6.8)	**0.57**	(0.10)	**0.52**	(0.06)	**0.36**	(0.04)	**-0.20**	(0.09)	**-0.18**	(0.06)
Luxembourg	**-31**	(8.0)	**-17**	(6.8)	-2	(2.6)	**26**	(8.1)	**22**	(5.0)	**-0.19**	(0.09)	0.03	(0.08)	**0.18**	(0.02)	**0.34**	(0.11)	**0.19**	(0.06)
Mexico	**38**	(5.6)	**28**	(4.7)	**21**	(4.8)	**-15**	(5.6)	**-13**	(4.6)	**0.26**	(0.06)	**0.19**	(0.06)	**0.14**	(0.06)	-0.10	(0.07)	-0.11	(0.06)
Netherlands	-3	(17.9)	3	(14.2)	**-21**	(4.2)	-16	(18.7)	-21	(11.8)	0.31	(0.20)	0.20	(0.12)	**0.32**	(0.03)	0.01	(0.17)	0.06	(0.10)
New Zealand	**-29**	(9.1)	**-28**	(5.9)	**-21**	(3.9)	7	(9.2)	9	(5.7)	**0.15**	(0.07)	**0.19**	(0.05)	**0.17**	(0.03)	0.03	(0.07)	0.00	(0.05)
Norway	-5	(7.8)	**-21**	(7.5)	-7	(4.3)	-1	(7.2)	7	(5.9)	**0.23**	(0.07)	**0.12**	(0.06)	**0.26**	(0.03)	0.04	(0.07)	**0.12**	(0.05)
Poland	2	(12.9)	**25**	(4.6)	**26**	(6.0)	25	(14.0)	2	(5.0)	-0.11	(0.12)	**0.09**	(0.04)	**0.24**	(0.05)	**0.32**	(0.11)	**0.16**	(0.05)
Portugal	5	(7.0)	3	(7.9)	**31**	(5.7)	**20**	(5.9)	**27**	(5.8)	**0.48**	(0.06)	0.14	(0.09)	**0.37**	(0.08)	**-0.17**	(0.08)	-0.02	(0.07)
Slovak Republic	**-86**	(11.1)	**-30**	(9.2)	-10	(18.4)	**74**	(11.5)	**40**	(8.8)	**-0.45**	(0.12)	-0.15	(0.08)	**0.13**	(0.03)	**0.54**	(0.12)	**0.38**	(0.07)
Spain	**-29**	(8.8)	-3	(5.8)	2	(3.6)	**31**	(7.8)	**15**	(4.8)	**0.31**	(0.09)	**0.28**	(0.07)	**0.33**	(0.05)	0.02	(0.09)	0.05	(0.07)
Sweden	**-38**	(9.1)	**-36**	(5.0)	**-30**	(4.1)	7	(8.6)	6	(4.6)	0.14	(0.08)	**0.17**	(0.04)	**0.15**	(0.04)	0.04	(0.08)	-0.02	(0.07)
Switzerland	36	(17.6)	3	(7.3)	3	(5.5)	**-34**	(16.6)	-6	(8.2)	**0.56**	(0.15)	**0.36**	(0.07)	**0.39**	(0.04)	-0.17	(0.15)	0.00	(0.07)
Turkey	**26**	(6.9)	3	(12.9)	-10	(18.4)	**-28**	(12.5)	**-35**	(16.7)	**-0.34**	(0.05)	**-0.54**	(0.10)	**-0.38**	(0.12)	-0.17	(0.09)	-0.05	(0.12)
United States	2	(16.4)	**-17**	(5.0)	**26**	(7.5)	-5	(16.2)	**43**	(7.4)	0.09	(0.21)	**-0.28**	(0.05)	**0.33**	(0.07)	0.02	(0.19)	**0.60**	(0.07)
OECD average 2003	**-16**	(2.4)	**-10**	(1.6)	**-3**	(1.1)	**11**	(2.4)	**8**	(1.4)	**0.15**	(0.02)	**0.16**	(0.01)	**0.22**	(0.01)	**0.06**	(0.02)	**0.04**	(0.01)
Brazil	**47**	(5.3)	**27**	(6.1)	**27**	(6.6)	**-20**	(5.2)	-10	(5.1)	**0.45**	(0.05)	**0.37**	(0.06)	**0.29**	(0.07)	-0.13	(0.06)	**-0.13**	(0.06)
Hong Kong-China	9	(17.6)	18	(11.3)	5	(5.4)	-1	(17.6)	-12	(9.4)	**0.65**	(0.12)	**0.41**	(0.10)	**0.43**	(0.06)	-0.21	(0.15)	-0.12	(0.08)
Indonesia	**10**	(5.0)	12	(7.0)	16	(11.8)	3	(7.5)	2	(9.4)	-0.03	(0.05)	0.12	(0.08)	0.11	(0.13)	0.13	(0.07)	0.04	(0.10)
Latvia	5	(8.2)	0	(7.7)	8	(5.4)	2	(8.6)	5	(6.6)	-0.13	(0.07)	-0.07	(0.07)	**0.12**	(0.04)	**0.21**	(0.07)	**0.26**	(0.06)
Liechtenstein	c	c	c	c	-4	(6.9)	c	c	c	c	c	c	c	c	**0.56**	(0.07)	c	c	c	c
Macao-China	0	(17.6)	**-19**	(9.5)	**15**	(3.7)	12	(18.2)	**30**	(9.9)	**1.15**	(0.14)	**0.68**	(0.09)	**0.70**	(0.03)	**-0.45**	(0.16)	-0.07	(0.09)
Russian Federation	7	(7.2)	17	(8.7)	**17**	(5.5)	10	(6.2)	6	(4.5)	**0.34**	(0.06)	**0.44**	(0.08)	**0.57**	(0.04)	**0.22**	(0.07)	**0.21**	(0.05)
Thailand	-18	(13.0)	-2	(6.4)	7	(5.2)	**28**	(12.2)	11	(6.2)	**0.58**	(0.14)	**0.61**	(0.07)	**0.41**	(0.06)	-0.08	(0.13)	**-0.20**	(0.07)
Tunisia	**25**	(4.9)	**35**	(6.5)	**21**	(8.3)	1	(6.4)	-11	(6.1)	**0.44**	(0.06)	**0.50**	(0.07)	**0.24**	(0.09)	-0.10	(0.08)	**-0.37**	(0.08)
Uruguay	**-19**	(6.1)	-14	(7.2)	**-16**	(5.2)	2	(5.9)	7	(6.8)	0.03	(0.07)	**-0.15**	(0.06)	**-0.21**	(0.05)	**-0.19**	(0.07)	**-0.12**	(0.06)

Notes: Values that are statistically significant are indicated in bold (see Annex A3).
Only countries and economies with comparable data from PISA 2003 and PISA 2012 are shown.
StatLink ⬇ http://dx.doi.org/10.1787/888932957384

[Part 1/3]
Change between 2003 and 2012 in mathematics performance and arriving late for school
Table IV.1.28   *Results based on students' self-reports*

		PISA 2003								
		Mathematics performance, by students' reports on the number of times they had arrived late for school in the two weeks prior to the PISA test								
		None		One or two times		Three or four times		Five or more times		Performance difference (none - one or more)	
		Mean score	S.E.	Mean score	S.E.	Mean score	S.E.	Mean score	S.E.	Score dif.	S.E.
OECD	Australia	534	(2.4)	518	(2.8)	496	(4.8)	485	(4.7)	**24**	(2.3)
	Austria	508	(3.1)	506	(5.6)	508	(8.7)	503	(12.1)	2	(4.8)
	Belgium	549	(2.2)	510	(3.9)	468	(8.2)	444	(10.2)	**54**	(4.3)
	Canada	546	(1.9)	533	(2.2)	513	(3.6)	501	(4.0)	**22**	(2.0)
	Czech Republic	526	(3.2)	513	(4.6)	507	(10.5)	508	(9.9)	**14**	(3.6)
	Denmark	525	(2.6)	508	(4.0)	501	(6.6)	487	(6.3)	**22**	(3.4)
	Finland	554	(2.5)	536	(2.5)	532	(4.5)	518	(4.9)	**22**	(2.9)
	France	522	(2.8)	504	(3.6)	477	(7.2)	438	(8.8)	**29**	(3.9)
	Germany	516	(3.2)	501	(5.9)	479	(12.1)	476	(12.7)	**22**	(4.6)
	Greece	450	(4.1)	445	(5.1)	439	(5.1)	432	(7.2)	9	(3.7)
	Hungary	503	(3.0)	461	(4.4)	449	(9.8)	441	(11.5)	**45**	(5.1)
	Iceland	526	(2.0)	510	(2.9)	511	(4.6)	468	(7.1)	**22**	(3.0)
	Ireland	511	(2.5)	498	(3.9)	485	(7.6)	453	(9.7)	**20**	(3.6)
	Italy	479	(2.9)	455	(4.3)	442	(6.0)	434	(6.4)	**30**	(3.0)
	Japan	542	(3.9)	515	(7.2)	467	(14.3)	450	(13.7)	**43**	(7.3)
	Korea	551	(3.4)	527	(4.7)	514	(6.5)	491	(8.4)	**32**	(4.6)
	Luxembourg	494	(1.6)	496	(2.6)	489	(5.9)	482	(6.7)	1	(3.1)
	Mexico	390	(4.4)	381	(3.8)	388	(5.9)	379	(6.8)	7	(3.5)
	Netherlands	558	(2.7)	535	(3.8)	518	(7.2)	480	(8.5)	**33**	(3.6)
	New Zealand	539	(2.7)	519	(3.5)	509	(4.9)	475	(5.4)	**30**	(3.6)
	Norway	505	(2.5)	491	(3.7)	476	(6.5)	447	(5.7)	**23**	(3.1)
	Poland	494	(2.6)	489	(3.6)	486	(5.5)	460	(7.0)	11	(3.1)
	Portugal	465	(4.0)	469	(4.0)	471	(5.3)	451	(6.8)	-2	(3.6)
	Slovak Republic	503	(3.2)	487	(5.3)	469	(7.8)	481	(14.5)	**19**	(3.5)
	Spain	498	(2.7)	475	(3.1)	463	(5.2)	450	(5.9)	**29**	(2.8)
	Sweden	522	(2.7)	508	(3.7)	495	(5.0)	472	(7.5)	**24**	(3.2)
	Switzerland	530	(3.4)	525	(5.5)	511	(8.7)	491	(17.3)	10	(4.6)
	Turkey	431	(7.0)	408	(7.7)	392	(9.9)	402	(13.9)	**26**	(5.0)
	United States	496	(2.8)	472	(4.3)	440	(6.2)	434	(8.5)	**36**	(3.6)
	OECD average 2003	509	(0.6)	493	(0.8)	479	(1.4)	463	(1.7)	**23**	(0.7)
Partners	Brazil	361	(5.2)	356	(4.6)	349	(10.0)	334	(9.2)	9	(4.0)
	Hong Kong-China	559	(4.6)	521	(6.4)	473	(13.4)	446	(18.0)	**50**	(5.3)
	Indonesia	368	(4.0)	352	(4.7)	345	(6.8)	333	(9.2)	**18**	(3.4)
	Latvia	493	(3.3)	480	(4.7)	472	(7.0)	452	(10.1)	**19**	(4.1)
	Liechtenstein	537	(5.5)	518	(13.6)	c	c	c	c	4	(15.8)
	Macao-China	537	(3.0)	487	(9.3)	470	(13.7)	c	c	**54**	(8.1)
	Russian Federation	478	(4.2)	460	(5.4)	449	(6.4)	438	(7.9)	**23**	(3.7)
	Thailand	423	(3.4)	408	(3.7)	400	(7.9)	401	(6.9)	**17**	(3.6)
	Tunisia	361	(3.0)	359	(3.4)	352	(5.4)	369	(7.4)	2	(3.5)
	Uruguay	434	(3.9)	424	(4.1)	407	(5.9)	391	(5.9)	**19**	(3.5)

Notes: Values that are statistically significant are indicated in bold (see Annex A3).
Only countries and economies with comparable data from PISA 2003 and PISA 2012 are shown.
StatLink 🔗 http://dx.doi.org/10.1787/888932957384

[Part 2/3]
Change between 2003 and 2012 in mathematics performance and arriving late for school
Table IV.1.28 *Results based on students' self-reports*

		PISA 2012								
		Mathematics performance, by students' reports on the number of times they had arrived late for school in the two weeks prior to the PISA test									
		None		One or two times		Three or four times		Five or more times		Performance difference (none - one or more)	
		Mean score	S.E.	Mean score	S.E.	Mean score	S.E.	Mean score	S.E.	Score dif.	S.E.
OECD	Australia	517	(1.7)	495	(2.4)	469	(4.3)	456	(5.5)	**31**	(2.2)
	Austria	508	(2.8)	503	(5.7)	485	(9.5)	477	(12.3)	**10**	(5.2)
	Belgium	526	(2.2)	499	(3.8)	466	(7.2)	437	(8.5)	**38**	(3.5)
	Canada	534	(1.8)	510	(2.5)	491	(3.4)	471	(4.5)	**33**	(2.0)
	Czech Republic	508	(3.0)	481	(4.1)	467	(12.3)	447	(12.2)	**32**	(3.6)
	Denmark	509	(2.2)	494	(3.2)	480	(4.3)	471	(7.6)	**20**	(3.0)
	Finland	532	(2.6)	512	(2.3)	495	(3.3)	465	(7.1)	**27**	(2.8)
	France	509	(2.7)	480	(3.7)	445	(7.8)	421	(10.4)	**39**	(3.8)
	Germany	521	(3.2)	509	(4.7)	507	(10.1)	488	(13.6)	**15**	(4.3)
	Greece	456	(2.7)	452	(3.6)	458	(4.4)	440	(5.5)	5	(3.1)
	Hungary	490	(3.0)	443	(6.6)	446	(12.7)	409	(11.7)	**50**	(6.4)
	Iceland	505	(2.2)	479	(3.2)	467	(8.1)	446	(12.1)	**30**	(3.6)
	Ireland	510	(1.9)	485	(3.7)	474	(7.4)	450	(9.4)	**30**	(3.3)
	Italy	497	(2.2)	472	(2.3)	456	(4.4)	436	(5.1)	**31**	(2.1)
	Japan	541	(3.3)	512	(8.5)	479	(16.5)	468	(25.1)	**35**	(7.0)
	Korea	565	(4.4)	529	(5.1)	501	(7.3)	499	(12.3)	**45**	(3.9)
	Luxembourg	496	(1.4)	478	(3.0)	475	(6.0)	463	(7.2)	**20**	(3.1)
	Mexico	418	(1.6)	408	(1.5)	406	(2.5)	397	(4.7)	**10**	(1.5)
	Netherlands	535	(3.5)	509	(4.7)	477	(9.8)	461	(9.4)	**35**	(4.1)
	New Zealand	520	(2.6)	486	(3.3)	464	(5.7)	440	(6.4)	**44**	(3.7)
	Norway	502	(2.8)	472	(4.8)	456	(6.5)	420	(9.3)	**38**	(3.7)
	Poland	525	(3.6)	517	(4.6)	499	(6.1)	476	(6.2)	**17**	(3.6)
	Portugal	495	(4.2)	486	(3.7)	484	(5.9)	465	(7.6)	**11**	(3.0)
	Slovak Republic	490	(3.2)	472	(5.8)	433	(8.9)	406	(14.4)	**30**	(5.2)
	Spain	495	(2.0)	472	(2.8)	466	(4.5)	448	(5.7)	**27**	(2.6)
	Sweden	497	(2.7)	477	(2.8)	460	(4.0)	438	(5.6)	**30**	(3.3)
	Switzerland	533	(3.0)	530	(4.7)	512	(9.2)	503	(10.8)	**7**	(3.7)
	Turkey	454	(5.5)	442	(4.3)	433	(6.8)	444	(7.7)	**13**	(3.6)
	United States	494	(3.5)	465	(4.4)	427	(7.0)	427	(7.9)	**39**	(3.5)
	OECD average 2003	506	(0.5)	485	(0.8)	468	(1.4)	451	(1.9)	**27**	(0.7)
Partners	Brazil	394	(2.3)	391	(2.5)	388	(4.6)	372	(4.5)	**5**	(2.3)
	Hong Kong-China	569	(3.1)	533	(5.8)	494	(15.2)	469	(22.7)	**43**	(4.6)
	Indonesia	379	(4.3)	365	(4.0)	369	(11.1)	358	(9.6)	**14**	(3.6)
	Latvia	496	(3.5)	494	(3.3)	482	(4.5)	465	(5.9)	9	(3.5)
	Liechtenstein	541	(4.7)	514	(15.1)	c	c	c	c	**34**	(15.1)
	Macao-China	551	(1.2)	511	(2.7)	488	(9.1)	454	(9.7)	**46**	(3.1)
	Russian Federation	494	(3.2)	475	(3.6)	474	(4.3)	439	(5.8)	**26**	(3.2)
	Thailand	434	(3.9)	417	(3.7)	411	(6.2)	391	(6.6)	**21**	(3.2)
	Tunisia	391	(4.5)	388	(4.3)	382	(4.9)	383	(7.5)	5	(3.0)
	Uruguay	415	(3.9)	410	(2.8)	412	(4.7)	385	(5.4)	8	(3.8)

Notes: Values that are statistically significant are indicated in bold (see Annex A3).
Only countries and economies with comparable data from PISA 2003 and PISA 2012 are shown.
StatLink ⟨ms⟩ http://dx.doi.org/10.1787/888932957384

[Part 3/3]
Change between 2003 and 2012 in mathematics performance and arriving late for school
Table IV.1.28   *Results based on students' self-reports*

		Change between 2003 and 2012 (PISA 2012 - PISA 2003)									
		Mathematics performance, by students' reports on the number of times they had arrived late for school in the two weeks prior to the PISA test									
		None		One or two times		Three or four times		Five or more times		Performance difference (none - one or more)	
		Score dif.	S.E.	Score dif.	S.E.	Score dif.	S.E.	Score dif.	S.E.	Score dif.	S.E.
OECD	Australia	**-17**	(3.5)	**-23**	(4.2)	**-28**	(6.7)	**-29**	(7.5)	**7**	(3.1)
	Austria	0	(4.6)	-3	(8.2)	-23	(13.1)	-26	(17.3)	8	(6.8)
	Belgium	**-22**	(3.7)	**-11**	(5.8)	-1	(11.1)	-7	(13.4)	**-16**	(6.0)
	Canada	**-12**	(3.3)	**-24**	(3.9)	**-22**	(5.4)	**-30**	(6.3)	**11**	(2.8)
	Czech Republic	**-18**	(4.8)	**-32**	(6.4)	**-40**	(16.3)	**-61**	(15.9)	**18**	(5.4)
	Denmark	**-16**	(3.9)	**-14**	(5.4)	**-21**	(8.2)	-16	(10.1)	-2	(4.0)
	Finland	**-23**	(4.1)	**-23**	(3.9)	**-37**	(5.9)	**-53**	(8.8)	5	(4.0)
	France	**-13**	(4.3)	**-24**	(5.5)	**-31**	(10.8)	-17	(13.7)	10	(5.6)
	Germany	5	(4.9)	8	(7.8)	28	(15.9)	12	(18.7)	-7	(6.6)
	Greece	5	(5.3)	8	(6.6)	**19**	(7.0)	7	(9.2)	-4	(4.6)
	Hungary	**-13**	(4.7)	**-18**	(8.2)	-3	(16.1)	**-33**	(16.5)	4	(7.7)
	Iceland	**-21**	(3.5)	**-31**	(4.8)	**-44**	(9.5)	-22	(14.2)	8	(4.5)
	Ireland	-1	(3.7)	**-13**	(5.7)	-12	(10.8)	-3	(13.7)	**10**	(4.4)
	Italy	**17**	(4.1)	**17**	(5.2)	14	(7.7)	2	(8.4)	1	(3.7)
	Japan	-1	(5.5)	-3	(11.3)	12	(21.9)	18	(28.6)	-8	(10.4)
	Korea	14	(5.9)	2	(7.2)	-13	(9.9)	8	(15.0)	**13**	(5.6)
	Luxembourg	1	(2.9)	**-18**	(4.4)	-15	(8.6)	-19	(10.0)	**18**	(4.5)
	Mexico	**28**	(5.1)	**27**	(4.5)	**18**	(6.7)	**18**	(8.5)	3	(3.8)
	Netherlands	**-23**	(4.8)	**-26**	(6.4)	**-40**	(12.3)	-19	(12.8)	2	(5.7)
	New Zealand	**-19**	(4.2)	**-33**	(5.2)	**-45**	(7.8)	**-36**	(8.6)	**14**	(5.3)
	Norway	-3	(4.2)	**-19**	(6.3)	**-20**	(9.4)	**-27**	(11.1)	**15**	(4.5)
	Poland	**30**	(4.9)	**28**	(6.2)	13	(8.5)	15	(9.6)	6	(5.1)
	Portugal	**30**	(6.1)	**17**	(5.8)	14	(8.2)	14	(10.4)	**14**	(4.7)
	Slovak Republic	**-13**	(4.9)	-15	(8.1)	**-35**	(12.1)	**-75**	(20.5)	11	(5.6)
	Spain	-2	(3.9)	-3	(4.6)	3	(7.2)	-3	(8.4)	-2	(4.0)
	Sweden	**-25**	(4.3)	**-31**	(5.0)	**-35**	(6.7)	**-34**	(9.5)	6	(4.8)
	Switzerland	3	(4.9)	5	(7.5)	1	(12.8)	13	(20.5)	-3	(5.8)
	Turkey	**23**	(9.1)	**35**	(9.0)	**42**	(12.2)	**43**	(16.0)	**-13**	(5.9)
	United States	-2	(4.9)	-6	(6.5)	-13	(9.6)	-7	(11.7)	3	(5.4)
	OECD average 2003	**-3**	(0.9)	**-8**	(1.2)	**-11**	(2.0)	**-13**	(2.6)	**5**	(1.0)
Partners	Brazil	**32**	(6.0)	**35**	(5.6)	**38**	(11.2)	**38**	(10.4)	-4	(4.4)
	Hong Kong-China	10	(5.8)	12	(8.9)	21	(20.4)	23	(29.0)	-7	(6.9)
	Indonesia	11	(6.2)	**13**	(6.5)	24	(13.2)	25	(13.4)	-4	(4.4)
	Latvia	3	(5.2)	**14**	(6.1)	10	(8.5)	13	(11.8)	**-10**	(5.0)
	Liechtenstein	4	(7.4)	-5	(20.5)	c	c	c	c	29	(22.8)
	Macao-China	**13**	(3.8)	**24**	(9.9)	18	(16.6)	c	c	-8	(8.2)
	Russian Federation	**16**	(5.7)	**14**	(6.8)	**25**	(7.9)	1	(10.0)	3	(4.8)
	Thailand	**11**	(5.5)	9	(5.5)	11	(10.2)	-10	(9.8)	4	(4.8)
	Tunisia	**30**	(5.8)	**29**	(5.8)	**30**	(7.5)	13	(10.7)	3	(4.7)
	Uruguay	**-19**	(5.8)	**-14**	(5.3)	5	(7.8)	-6	(8.2)	**-11**	(5.0)

Notes: Values that are statistically significant are indicated in bold (see Annex A3).
Only countries and economies with comparable data from PISA 2003 and PISA 2012 are shown.
StatLink 🔗 http://dx.doi.org/10.1787/888932957384

[Part 1/3]

Change between 2003 and 2012 in mathematics performance and concentration of students arriving late for school

Table IV.1.29 *Results based on students' self-reports*

		PISA 2003								
		Mathematics performance, by schools where in the two weeks prior to the PISA test...								
		Over 50% of students arrived late at least once		More than 25% but 50% or less of students arrived late at least once		More than 10% but 25% or less of students arrived late at least once		10% of students or fewer arrived late at least once		Performance difference (25% or less - over 25%)	
		Mean score	S.E.	Mean score	S.E.	Mean score	S.E.	Mean score	S.E.	Score dif.	S.E.
OECD	Australia	502	(7.9)	528	(2.8)	525	(6.4)	c	c	2	(6.9)
	Austria	508	(21.4)	513	(7.6)	514	(6.3)	489	(7.8)	-8	(9.1)
	Belgium	428	(9.8)	515	(5.7)	561	(5.1)	608	(7.6)	**70**	(7.8)
	Canada	528	(3.7)	533	(2.3)	542	(5.3)	548	(10.3)	12	(5.1)
	Czech Republic	c	c	512	(7.0)	525	(5.3)	544	(10.1)	17	(9.5)
	Denmark	508	(5.8)	514	(3.3)	528	(5.6)	525	(7.4)	16	(5.7)
	Finland	543	(2.7)	543	(2.7)	559	(4.2)	541	(8.9)	13	(4.6)
	France	458	(13.4)	508	(5.4)	532	(7.3)	523	(27.0)	31	(10.0)
	Germany	459	(36.9)	496	(9.4)	516	(5.7)	521	(8.6)	26	(10.6)
	Greece	439	(7.7)	454	(6.4)	402	(13.8)	c	c	**-44**	(13.9)
	Hungary	399	(13.9)	472	(5.5)	514	(8.5)	540	(6.8)	**63**	(9.8)
	Iceland	517	(2.3)	512	(2.2)	519	(5.3)	511	(7.6)	2	(4.9)
	Ireland	483	(11.2)	496	(4.5)	513	(3.7)	c	c	19	(6.0)
	Italy	415	(6.3)	491	(4.3)	501	(15.7)	473	(26.6)	37	(15.8)
	Japan	c	c	483	(14.9)	540	(8.0)	560	(7.2)	**72**	(15.0)
	Korea	479	(20.6)	526	(6.6)	555	(6.7)	607	(13.3)	43	(10.1)
	Luxembourg	c	c	495	(1.1)	c	c	c	c	c	c
	Mexico	389	(4.4)	386	(6.1)	364	(11.6)	362	(26.4)	-24	(12.6)
	Netherlands	512	(6.9)	557	(6.5)	586	(11.9)	c	c	**50**	(13.5)
	New Zealand	511	(5.3)	528	(3.0)	541	(10.4)	c	c	20	(10.4)
	Norway	488	(6.3)	496	(2.9)	492	(4.5)	519	(12.3)	0	(4.8)
	Poland	493	(5.3)	492	(3.6)	482	(6.3)	488	(8.4)	-10	(6.4)
	Portugal	469	(4.7)	460	(7.8)	c	c	c	c	-3	(21.7)
	Slovak Republic	413	(26.5)	486	(6.9)	509	(4.3)	511	(8.1)	28	(7.9)
	Spain	468	(5.8)	494	(4.5)	496	(7.4)	484	(12.2)	11	(6.9)
	Sweden	503	(4.5)	516	(2.9)	500	(7.4)	c	c	-6	(7.0)
	Switzerland	527	(21.4)	529	(7.6)	524	(6.9)	527	(10.8)	-4	(10.5)
	Turkey	381	(36.3)	411	(11.0)	428	(8.5)	488	(24.2)	31	(11.8)
	United States	454	(6.1)	481	(5.0)	504	(5.1)	502	(6.7)	31	(4.9)
	OECD average 2003	472	(2.9)	498	(1.2)	510	(1.5)	518	(3.1)	**18**	(1.9)
Partners	Brazil	342	(10.5)	356	(6.7)	371	(10.9)	348	(23.0)	16	(11.6)
	Hong Kong-China	c	c	487	(10.0)	553	(8.2)	589	(8.7)	**86**	(10.9)
	Indonesia	325	(8.4)	364	(4.5)	371	(9.6)	382	(49.5)	15	(11.7)
	Latvia	476	(5.7)	492	(5.1)	472	(7.8)	c	c	-9	(9.9)
	Liechtenstein	c	c	c	c	544	(4.2)	c	c	c	c
	Macao-China	479	(6.9)	492	(7.4)	531	(3.6)	544	(5.9)	**48**	(6.9)
	Russian Federation	439	(8.0)	479	(5.2)	483	(13.0)	460	(17.1)	14	(12.8)
	Thailand	402	(7.0)	412	(4.4)	431	(8.1)	432	(17.7)	21	(8.8)
	Tunisia	363	(10.5)	358	(3.8)	350	(11.7)	c	c	-3	(14.5)
	Uruguay	408	(4.6)	448	(6.3)	c	c	c	c	0	(42.8)

Notes: Values that are statistically significant are indicated in bold (see Annex A3).
Only countries and economies with comparable data from PISA 2003 and PISA 2012 are shown.
StatLink ⟨⟨⟨ http://dx.doi.org/10.1787/888932957384

[Part 2/3]
Change between 2003 and 2012 in mathematics performance and concentration of students arriving late for school

Table IV.1.29   *Results based on students' self-reports*

		PISA 2012								
		Mathematics performance, by schools where in the two weeks prior to the PISA test...								
		Over 50% of students arrived late at least once		More than 25% but 50% or less of students arrived late at least once		More than 10% but 25% or less of students arrived late at least once		10% of students or fewer arrived late at least once		Performance difference (25% or less - over 25%)	
		Mean score	S.E.	Mean score	S.E.	Mean score	S.E.	Mean score	S.E.	Score dif.	S.E.
OECD	Australia	488	(4.9)	504	(2.3)	514	(3.8)	520	(10.0)	**15**	(4.3)
	Austria	507	(26.4)	493	(8.2)	521	(8.3)	500	(7.7)	15	(10.8)
	Belgium	403	(13.7)	503	(5.8)	538	(5.4)	562	(11.3)	**52**	(8.1)
	Canada	505	(4.1)	522	(2.7)	529	(4.9)	550	(15.2)	**15**	(5.7)
	Czech Republic	424	(12.2)	491	(5.8)	517	(5.0)	519	(8.8)	**39**	(7.9)
	Denmark	490	(6.8)	498	(2.9)	514	(4.9)	510	(12.2)	**18**	(5.9)
	Finland	512	(2.9)	522	(2.6)	522	(5.5)	527	(31.9)	4	(5.3)
	France	415	(10.9)	493	(5.4)	531	(6.5)	506	(12.8)	**51**	(8.1)
	Germany	484	(30.0)	509	(6.4)	522	(6.2)	511	(10.4)	13	(9.8)
	Greece	454	(4.9)	454	(5.2)	439	(31.4)	416	(25.2)	-25	(21.9)
	Hungary	391	(11.8)	448	(10.8)	501	(5.8)	510	(7.1)	**72**	(10.5)
	Iceland	469	(4.8)	496	(2.0)	498	(3.3)	497	(8.0)	6	(3.3)
	Ireland	434	(12.5)	499	(4.5)	511	(2.5)	506	(8.2)	**19**	(5.8)
	Italy	431	(5.3)	484	(2.9)	525	(4.6)	542	(12.9)	**56**	(5.1)
	Japan	c	c	468	(29.7)	514	(8.9)	553	(3.8)	**75**	(29.1)
	Korea	483	(15.0)	531	(5.7)	573	(8.7)	603	(13.3)	**56**	(8.9)
	Luxembourg	c	c	492	(1.6)	493	(1.3)	c	c	5	(1.9)
	Mexico	415	(2.6)	412	(1.7)	413	(4.8)	425	(12.3)	2	(4.9)
	Netherlands	450	(13.8)	512	(6.5)	551	(6.7)	591	(5.6)	**55**	(9.3)
	New Zealand	466	(5.0)	511	(3.7)	527	(9.1)	c	c	**34**	(10.5)
	Norway	481	(9.7)	488	(4.1)	488	(4.6)	513	(8.7)	5	(5.4)
	Poland	522	(6.1)	521	(5.4)	501	(6.3)	515	(19.9)	**-19**	(6.4)
	Portugal	484	(4.8)	493	(7.3)	c	c	c	c	c	c
	Slovak Republic	419	(16.4)	469	(7.9)	497	(7.3)	508	(11.3)	**37**	(11.5)
	Spain	474	(5.8)	485	(2.7)	488	(4.0)	506	(9.5)	8	(4.8)
	Sweden	473	(3.0)	489	(5.0)	c	c	c	c	10	(17.1)
	Switzerland	526	(17.0)	545	(6.2)	520	(4.7)	530	(7.4)	**-19**	(7.5)
	Turkey	418	(8.8)	451	(6.3)	530	(24.3)	c	c	**87**	(24.3)
	United States	414	(5.3)	474	(4.6)	508	(5.5)	491	(11.7)	**41**	(6.4)
	OECD average 2003	460	(2.3)	492	(1.4)	511	(1.8)	517	(2.7)	**26**	(2.1)
Partners	Brazil	394	(8.1)	387	(3.3)	397	(4.6)	402	(11.7)	10	(5.6)
	Hong Kong-China	c	c	503	(10.5)	554	(6.2)	593	(6.5)	**67**	(11.8)
	Indonesia	344	(7.7)	370	(6.6)	382	(6.5)	398	(17.5)	**20**	(8.4)
	Latvia	487	(3.1)	498	(5.5)	504	(18.0)	c	c	9	(16.1)
	Liechtenstein	c	c	c	c	558	(4.6)	c	c	c	c
	Macao-China	465	(3.9)	519	(1.8)	557	(1.6)	c	c	**51**	(2.0)
	Russian Federation	469	(4.6)	487	(4.6)	511	(8.0)	480	(11.4)	**26**	(8.1)
	Thailand	394	(5.0)	428	(5.7)	442	(7.1)	457	(17.0)	**28**	(7.7)
	Tunisia	387	(5.0)	390	(7.6)	c	c	c	c	c	c
	Uruguay	408	(3.4)	403	(9.5)	c	c	c	c	101	(25.7)

Notes: Values that are statistically significant are indicated in bold (see Annex A3).
Only countries and economies with comparable data from PISA 2003 and PISA 2012 are shown.
StatLink ﷽ http://dx.doi.org/10.1787/888932957384

[Part 3/3]
Change between 2003 and 2012 in mathematics performance and concentration of students arriving late for school

Table IV.1.29   *Results based on students' self-reports*

	Change between 2003 and 2012 (PISA 2012 - PISA 2003)									
	Mathematics performance, by schools where in the two weeks prior to the PISA test...									
	Over 50% of students arrived late at least once		More than 25% but 50% or less of students arrived late at least once		More than 10% but 25% or less of students arrived late at least once		10% of students or fewer arrived late at least once		Performance difference (25% or less - over 25%)	
	Score dif.	S.E.	Score dif.	S.E.	Score dif.	S.E.	Score dif.	S.E.	Score dif.	S.E.
Australia	-14	(9.5)	**-24**	(4.2)	-11	(7.6)	c	c	13	(8.4)
Austria	-1	(34.0)	-20	(11.3)	7	(10.6)	10	(11.1)	23	(13.9)
Belgium	-26	(16.9)	-12	(8.4)	**-23**	(7.6)	**-46**	(13.7)	-18	(10.9)
Canada	-23	(5.8)	**-11**	(4.1)	-13	(7.5)	1	(18.5)	3	(7.6)
Czech Republic	c	c	**-21**	(9.3)	-8	(7.5)	-25	(13.5)	22	(12.6)
Denmark	-17	(9.1)	**-17**	(4.8)	-14	(7.7)	-15	(14.4)	3	(7.9)
Finland	**-32**	(4.4)	**-20**	(4.2)	**-37**	(7.2)	-14	(33.2)	-9	(7.4)
France	**-43**	(17.4)	-15	(7.9)	-1	(10.0)	-17	(30.0)	20	(12.7)
Germany	26	(47.6)	12	(11.5)	6	(8.6)	-10	(13.6)	-13	(15.3)
Greece	15	(9.4)	0	(8.5)	37	(34.3)	c	c	19	(27.0)
Hungary	-8	(18.4)	**-24**	(12.2)	-13	(10.5)	**-30**	(10.0)	8	(13.7)
Iceland	**-48**	(5.7)	**-17**	(3.5)	**-22**	(6.5)	-15	(11.2)	4	(6.2)
Ireland	**-50**	(16.8)	4	(6.6)	-2	(4.8)	c	c	0	(8.7)
Italy	15	(8.5)	-7	(5.6)	24	(16.5)	69	(29.6)	19	(16.0)
Japan	c	c	-15	(33.3)	**-25**	(12.1)	-6	(8.3)	3	(34.0)
Korea	4	(25.6)	5	(8.9)	18	(11.2)	-4	(18.9)	13	(14.5)
Luxembourg	c	c	-3	(2.7)	c	c	c	c	c	c
Mexico	**25**	(5.5)	**26**	(6.6)	**50**	(12.7)	**63**	(29.1)	27	(13.8)
Netherlands	**-62**	(15.6)	**-45**	(9.4)	**-34**	(13.8)	c	c	5	(16.3)
New Zealand	**-45**	(7.6)	**-17**	(5.1)	-14	(14.0)	c	c	14	(15.1)
Norway	-7	(11.7)	-8	(5.4)	-4	(6.8)	-6	(15.2)	5	(7.0)
Poland	**29**	(8.3)	**29**	(6.8)	**20**	(9.1)	27	(21.7)	-9	(9.1)
Portugal	**15**	(7.0)	**33**	(10.9)	c	c	c	c	c	c
Slovak Republic	6	(31.2)	-17	(10.7)	-11	(8.7)	-3	(14.0)	9	(13.8)
Spain	6	(8.5)	-9	(5.6)	-8	(8.7)	22	(15.6)	-3	(9.0)
Sweden	**-30**	(5.7)	**-27**	(6.1)	c	c	c	c	16	(18.7)
Switzerland	-1	(27.4)	15	(10.0)	-3	(8.6)	3	(13.2)	-15	(11.5)
Turkey	37	(37.4)	**39**	(12.8)	**102**	(25.9)	c	c	**56**	(24.8)
United States	**-40**	(8.3)	-7	(7.1)	5	(7.7)	-11	(13.7)	11	(8.3)
OECD average 2003	**-10**	(3.8)	**-6**	(1.9)	1	(2.5)	0	(4.2)	**8**	(2.9)
Brazil	**51**	(13.4)	**31**	(7.7)	**26**	(12.0)	**54**	(25.9)	-6	(12.9)
Hong Kong-China	c	c	15	(14.6)	1	(10.5)	4	(11.1)	-19	(14.5)
Indonesia	18	(11.6)	5	(8.2)	11	(11.8)	16	(52.6)	5	(14.3)
Latvia	11	(6.8)	6	(7.7)	32	(19.7)	c	c	18	(18.1)
Liechtenstein	c	c	c	c	14	(6.5)	c	c	c	c
Macao-China	-14	(8.1)	**28**	(7.8)	**26**	(4.3)	c	c	3	(7.0)
Russian Federation	**30**	(9.4)	8	(7.2)	28	(15.4)	20	(20.7)	12	(15.2)
Thailand	-8	(8.8)	**16**	(7.5)	12	(10.9)	25	(24.6)	6	(12.0)
Tunisia	23	(11.8)	**32**	(8.7)	c	c	c	c	c	c
Uruguay	0	(6.1)	**-45**	(11.6)	c	c	c	c	**101**	(50.3)

Notes: Values that are statistically significant are indicated in bold (see Annex A3).
Only countries and economies with comparable data from PISA 2003 and PISA 2012 are shown.
StatLink ᴍᴸᴸ http://dx.doi.org/10.1787/888932957384

[Part 1/1]
Primary school starting age

Table IV.2.1   *Results based on students' self-reports*

| | | Age of entry into primary school | | | Percentage of students who started primary school at: | | | | | | | | | |
| | | | | | 4 years old | | 5 years old | | 6 years old | | 7 years old | | 8 years old or older | |
		Mean age	S.E.	S.D.	S.E.	%	S.E.	%	S.E.	%	S.E.	%	S.E.	%	S.E.
OECD	Australia	5.2	(0.0)	0.68	(0.01)	11.5	(0.3)	58.4	(0.4)	26.9	(0.5)	3.1	(0.2)	0.0	c
	Austria	6.2	(0.0)	0.52	(0.01)	0.0	c	4.2	(0.4)	73.6	(0.9)	20.8	(0.8)	1.4	(0.3)
	Belgium	5.9	(0.0)	0.60	(0.01)	1.3	(0.2)	18.9	(0.6)	70.3	(0.6)	8.3	(0.4)	1.1	(0.2)
	Canada	5.2	(0.0)	0.98	(0.03)	17.8	(0.6)	49.9	(0.7)	27.5	(0.6)	3.1	(0.2)	1.6	(0.1)
	Chile	6.0	(0.0)	0.63	(0.01)	1.0	(0.1)	15.1	(0.6)	69.1	(0.7)	13.5	(0.5)	1.2	(0.2)
	Czech Republic	6.4	(0.0)	0.55	(0.01)	0.0	c	1.2	(0.2)	61.9	(1.0)	34.9	(0.9)	1.9	(0.3)
	Denmark	6.6	(0.0)	0.68	(0.01)	0.1	(0.1)	3.2	(0.2)	36.1	(0.7)	53.6	(0.7)	7.0	(0.4)
	Estonia	6.9	(0.0)	0.44	(0.01)	0.0	c	0.5	(0.1)	15.3	(0.6)	80.3	(0.6)	3.9	(0.3)
	Finland	6.7	(0.0)	0.48	(0.00)	0.0	c	0.1	(0.0)	28.8	(0.7)	69.9	(0.7)	1.1	(0.1)
	France	5.9	(0.0)	0.80	(0.03)	3.5	(0.3)	15.9	(0.7)	68.9	(0.9)	9.4	(0.5)	2.3	(0.3)
	Germany	6.2	(0.0)	0.54	(0.01)	0.0	(0.0)	4.8	(0.4)	70.1	(0.8)	24.0	(0.7)	1.1	(0.2)
	Greece	6.3	(0.0)	0.77	(0.06)	0.1	(0.0)	4.4	(0.4)	70.5	(1.4)	23.0	(1.3)	2.1	(0.3)
	Hungary	6.7	(0.0)	0.59	(0.01)	0.1	(0.1)	0.4	(0.1)	36.1	(0.8)	57.8	(0.8)	5.6	(0.5)
	Iceland	5.8	(0.0)	0.51	(0.01)	1.7	(0.2)	19.5	(0.7)	75.7	(0.8)	3.0	(0.3)	0.1	(0.1)
	Ireland	4.5	(0.0)	0.58	(0.01)	56.0	(0.9)	39.5	(0.9)	4.5	(0.4)	0.0	c	0.0	c
	Israel	6.2	(0.0)	0.54	(0.01)	0.0	c	5.8	(0.5)	70.0	(1.2)	23.4	(1.3)	0.8	(0.1)
	Italy	5.9	(0.0)	0.44	(0.01)	0.0	c	13.0	(0.3)	81.9	(0.4)	4.6	(0.2)	0.5	(0.1)
	Japan	6.0	(0.0)	0.00	(0.00)	0.0	c	0.0	c	100.0	(0.0)	0.0	c	0.0	c
	Korea	6.6	(0.0)	0.61	(0.01)	0.3	(0.1)	1.2	(0.2)	38.3	(2.3)	55.5	(2.2)	4.7	(0.5)
	Luxembourg	6.2	(0.0)	0.59	(0.01)	0.0	c	6.5	(0.3)	67.6	(0.7)	23.3	(0.6)	2.6	(0.2)
	Mexico	6.1	(0.0)	0.73	(0.02)	0.8	(0.1)	8.2	(0.2)	73.5	(0.4)	15.8	(0.4)	1.7	(0.1)
	Netherlands	6.1	(0.0)	0.56	(0.01)	0.0	c	12.2	(0.6)	71.6	(0.9)	15.0	(0.6)	1.2	(0.2)
	New Zealand	5.1	(0.0)	0.56	(0.03)	5.3	(0.4)	84.3	(0.8)	7.7	(0.5)	2.0	(0.2)	0.8	(0.1)
	Norway	5.8	(0.0)	0.67	(0.05)	0.3	(0.1)	24.8	(0.7)	70.2	(0.7)	3.9	(0.3)	0.8	(0.2)
	Poland	7.0	(0.0)	0.07	(0.02)	0.0	c	0.0	c	0.5	(0.2)	99.5	(0.2)	0.0	c
	Portugal	5.9	(0.0)	0.83	(0.04)	0.0	c	24.9	(0.8)	64.9	(0.8)	7.7	(0.4)	2.5	(0.3)
	Slovak Republic	6.3	(0.0)	0.52	(0.01)	0.0	c	1.5	(0.2)	65.3	(1.1)	32.3	(1.0)	1.0	(0.1)
	Slovenia	6.2	(0.0)	0.60	(0.01)	0.0	c	8.2	(0.6)	60.8	(0.9)	30.1	(0.8)	0.9	(0.2)
	Spain	5.8	(0.0)	0.50	(0.01)	0.0	c	25.4	(0.7)	70.4	(0.8)	4.2	(0.4)	0.0	c
	Sweden	6.8	(0.0)	0.68	(0.05)	0.3	(0.1)	1.5	(0.3)	25.3	(1.3)	70.2	(1.5)	2.8	(0.3)
	Switzerland	6.5	(0.0)	1.03	(0.03)	2.8	(0.4)	6.4	(0.4)	44.2	(0.9)	41.4	(0.9)	5.1	(0.3)
	Turkey	6.9	(0.0)	0.54	(0.01)	0.0	c	1.1	(0.2)	17.5	(0.7)	74.7	(0.8)	6.7	(0.5)
	United Kingdom	5.0	(0.0)	0.63	(0.01)	19.9	(1.5)	64.2	(1.6)	14.6	(0.9)	1.2	(0.2)	0.0	c
	United States	5.9	(0.0)	1.05	(0.07)	3.5	(0.3)	24.5	(0.8)	57.5	(0.9)	12.6	(0.6)	1.9	(0.2)
	OECD average	6.1	(0.0)	0.60	(0.00)	3.7	(0.1)	16.2	(0.1)	51.1	(0.2)	27.1	(0.1)	1.9	(0.0)
Partners	Albania	6.4	(0.0)	0.75	(0.04)	0.1	(0.1)	1.9	(0.2)	61.9	(1.1)	32.2	(1.0)	3.8	(0.4)
	Argentina	5.9	(0.0)	0.50	(0.01)	0.0	c	16.3	(0.9)	74.6	(1.0)	9.1	(0.8)	0.0	c
	Brazil	7.2	(0.0)	2.28	(0.04)	3.6	(0.2)	9.2	(0.4)	32.4	(0.9)	34.3	(1.0)	20.5	(0.7)
	Bulgaria	6.9	(0.0)	0.54	(0.04)	0.1	(0.0)	0.2	(0.1)	13.4	(0.6)	82.8	(0.7)	3.5	(0.4)
	Colombia	6.0	(0.0)	0.80	(0.01)	0.0	c	27.5	(0.9)	52.0	(0.9)	16.4	(0.8)	4.0	(0.4)
	Costa Rica	6.6	(0.0)	0.60	(0.01)	0.0	c	2.9	(0.3)	40.6	(1.4)	54.6	(1.3)	1.8	(0.2)
	Croatia	6.7	(0.0)	0.50	(0.00)	0.0	c	0.2	(0.1)	34.5	(0.8)	63.9	(0.8)	1.4	(0.2)
	Cyprus*	6.1	(0.0)	0.61	(0.02)	1.1	(0.2)	7.6	(0.5)	76.1	(0.7)	14.4	(0.5)	0.8	(0.1)
	Hong Kong-China	6.1	(0.0)	0.61	(0.02)	0.0	c	11.1	(0.6)	73.3	(1.0)	13.3	(0.7)	2.3	(0.3)
	Indonesia	6.3	(0.0)	0.65	(0.01)	0.0	c	8.3	(0.9)	54.5	(1.4)	35.3	(1.6)	1.9	(0.3)
	Jordan	6.0	(0.0)	0.64	(0.02)	1.1	(0.2)	9.1	(0.5)	78.8	(0.9)	9.6	(0.5)	1.4	(0.2)
	Kazakhstan	6.5	(0.0)	0.60	(0.01)	0.0	c	3.3	(0.4)	42.5	(1.6)	52.0	(1.7)	2.2	(0.4)
	Latvia	6.8	(0.0)	0.56	(0.01)	0.0	c	1.8	(0.4)	25.0	(0.9)	69.4	(1.0)	3.8	(0.4)
	Liechtenstein	6.6	(0.1)	1.16	(0.21)	0.0	c	4.3	(1.2)	43.6	(3.0)	46.5	(2.9)	5.6	(1.4)
	Lithuania	6.6	(0.0)	0.57	(0.01)	0.0	c	2.0	(0.2)	34.1	(0.8)	61.1	(0.9)	2.8	(0.3)
	Macao-China	6.2	(0.0)	0.69	(0.01)	0.0	c	12.6	(0.5)	61.8	(0.7)	22.3	(0.7)	3.3	(0.2)
	Malaysia	7.0	(0.0)	0.99	(0.06)	0.7	(0.2)	1.0	(0.2)	4.9	(0.7)	90.4	(0.8)	3.0	(0.3)
	Montenegro	6.6	(0.0)	0.50	(0.00)	0.0	c	0.7	(0.1)	39.1	(0.6)	60.3	(0.6)	0.0	c
	Peru	6.1	(0.0)	1.29	(0.06)	2.2	(0.2)	17.4	(0.6)	60.8	(0.9)	15.3	(0.7)	4.3	(0.4)
	Qatar	5.8	(0.0)	0.86	(0.01)	10.0	(0.3)	19.5	(0.4)	51.8	(0.5)	18.7	(0.4)	0.0	c
	Romania	6.8	(0.0)	0.40	(0.01)	0.1	(0.0)	0.2	(0.1)	18.5	(0.9)	81.2	(0.9)	0.0	c
	Russian Federation	6.7	(0.0)	0.56	(0.01)	0.0	(0.0)	0.8	(0.2)	36.0	(1.6)	60.0	(1.6)	3.2	(0.2)
	Serbia	6.9	(0.0)	0.36	(0.01)	0.0	c	0.0	c	12.3	(0.6)	85.9	(0.6)	1.8	(0.3)
	Shanghai-China	6.7	(0.0)	0.82	(0.01)	1.3	(0.1)	3.7	(0.3)	31.0	(0.9)	51.1	(0.9)	13.0	(0.8)
	Singapore	6.7	(0.0)	0.59	(0.01)	0.7	(0.1)	2.2	(0.2)	23.2	(0.7)	71.8	(0.8)	2.1	(0.2)
	Chinese Taipei	6.8	(0.0)	0.67	(0.01)	0.0	c	3.0	(0.2)	26.5	(0.9)	59.1	(0.9)	11.4	(0.5)
	Thailand	6.2	(0.0)	0.47	(0.01)	0.0	c	4.4	(0.5)	76.5	(1.1)	18.9	(1.0)	0.2	(0.1)
	Tunisia	5.9	(0.0)	0.47	(0.03)	0.1	(0.1)	13.6	(0.5)	81.7	(0.7)	4.3	(0.5)	0.2	(0.1)
	United Arab Emirates	6.0	(0.0)	1.08	(0.04)	3.6	(0.2)	23.6	(0.6)	54.1	(0.7)	15.7	(0.5)	3.0	(0.3)
	Uruguay	5.9	(0.0)	0.54	(0.01)	1.5	(0.2)	11.9	(0.6)	78.0	(0.8)	8.0	(0.5)	0.6	(0.1)
	Viet Nam	6.2	(0.0)	0.43	(0.01)	0.0	c	2.5	(0.3)	78.5	(1.6)	19.0	(1.6)	0.0	c

* See notes at the beginning of this Annex.
StatLink ⌐司⌐ http://dx.doi.org/10.1787/888932957422

[Part 1/1]
Grade repetition
Table IV.2.2   *Results based on students' self-reports*

	Primary school						Lower secondary school						Upper secondary school						Primary, lower secondary or upper secondary school	
	Never		Once		Twice or more		Never		Once		Twice or more		Never		Once		Twice or more			
	%	S.E.	%	S.E.	%	S.E.	%	S.E.	%	S.E.	%	S.E.	%	S.E.	%	S.E.	%	S.E.	%	S.E.
Australia	93.3	(0.2)	6.4	(0.2)	0.3	(0.1)	98.7	(0.1)	1.2	(0.1)	0.1	(0.0)	99.7	(0.1)	0.3	(0.1)	0.0	(0.0)	7.5	(0.3)
Austria	94.9	(0.4)	5.0	(0.4)	0.1	(0.0)	95.1	(0.4)	4.6	(0.4)	0.3	(0.1)	96.4	(0.3)	3.6	(0.3)	0.0	c	11.9	(0.7)
Belgium	79.5	(0.7)	17.8	(0.6)	2.7	(0.2)	83.3	(0.6)	15.5	(0.6)	1.2	(0.1)	90.9	(0.4)	9.0	(0.4)	0.1	(0.0)	36.1	(0.6)
Canada	95.8	(0.2)	3.9	(0.2)	0.3	(0.1)	95.6	(0.2)	3.8	(0.2)	0.7	(0.1)	99.1	(0.1)	0.7	(0.1)	0.2	(0.1)	8.0	(0.3)
Chile	87.4	(0.9)	9.9	(0.6)	2.7	(0.5)	92.9	(0.6)	5.9	(0.6)	1.2	(0.3)	89.1	(0.7)	10.5	(0.7)	0.4	(0.1)	25.2	(1.2)
Czech Republic	97.9	(0.4)	1.9	(0.4)	0.3	(0.1)	96.7	(0.4)	3.0	(0.4)	0.3	(0.1)	100.0	c	0.0	c	0.0	c	4.9	(0.6)
Denmark	96.0	(0.4)	3.9	(0.4)	0.1	(0.0)	99.0	(0.2)	1.0	(0.2)	0.0	(0.0)	100.0	c	0.0	c	0.0	c	4.7	(0.4)
Estonia	98.0	(0.3)	1.7	(0.2)	0.2	(0.1)	98.2	(0.3)	1.6	(0.3)	0.2	(0.1)	100.0	c	0.0	c	0.0	c	3.5	(0.4)
Finland	96.8	(0.3)	3.1	(0.3)	0.1	(0.1)	99.3	(0.2)	0.7	(0.2)	0.0	(0.0)	c	c	c	c	c	c	3.8	(0.4)
France	83.0	(0.7)	16.5	(0.7)	0.5	(0.1)	85.6	(0.7)	13.9	(0.7)	0.5	(0.1)	99.5	(0.1)	0.5	(0.1)	0.0	(0.0)	28.4	(0.8)
Germany	89.8	(0.6)	9.6	(0.6)	0.7	(0.1)	87.2	(0.6)	12.3	(0.6)	0.5	(0.1)	100.0	c	0.0	c	0.0	c	20.3	(0.8)
Greece	98.5	(0.3)	0.9	(0.2)	0.7	(0.1)	96.1	(0.7)	2.8	(0.5)	1.2	(0.3)	100.0	c	0.0	c	0.0	c	4.5	(0.7)
Hungary	95.1	(0.6)	4.2	(0.5)	0.7	(0.2)	94.3	(0.7)	4.2	(0.5)	1.5	(0.4)	97.3	(0.3)	2.6	(0.3)	0.1	(0.0)	10.8	(0.9)
Iceland	99.3	(0.1)	0.5	(0.1)	0.2	(0.1)	99.2	(0.1)	0.6	(0.1)	0.2	(0.1)	100.0	c	0.0	c	0.0	c	1.2	(0.2)
Ireland	92.1	(0.4)	7.7	(0.4)	0.1	(0.1)	98.9	(0.2)	1.0	(0.1)	0.1	(0.0)	100.0	(0.0)	0.0	(0.0)	0.0	c	8.6	(0.4)
Israel	98.8	(0.2)	1.2	(0.2)	0.0	c	99.3	(0.2)	0.7	(0.2)	0.0	c	100.0	c	0.0	c	0.0	c	1.9	(0.3)
Italy	99.0	(0.1)	0.9	(0.1)	0.1	(0.0)	92.6	(0.3)	6.1	(0.3)	1.4	(0.2)	89.7	(0.4)	10.2	(0.4)	0.1	(0.0)	17.1	(0.5)
Japan	100.0	c	0.0	c	0.0	c	100.0	c	0.0	c	0.0	c	100.0	c	0.0	c	0.0	c	0.0	c
Korea	96.8	(0.2)	2.4	(0.2)	0.8	(0.0)	96.9	(0.2)	2.2	(0.2)	0.9	(0.1)	97.8	(0.2)	1.7	(0.2)	0.5	(0.1)	3.6	(0.3)
Luxembourg	78.5	(0.5)	19.3	(0.5)	2.2	(0.2)	80.7	(0.6)	18.5	(0.6)	0.8	(0.1)	99.1	(0.2)	0.7	(0.2)	0.3	(0.1)	34.5	(0.5)
Mexico	87.4	(0.5)	11.2	(0.4)	1.4	(0.1)	96.6	(0.3)	3.1	(0.3)	0.3	(0.0)	98.9	(0.1)	1.0	(0.1)	0.1	(0.0)	15.5	(0.6)
Netherlands	79.1	(1.1)	20.2	(1.0)	0.7	(0.1)	92.1	(0.6)	7.8	(0.6)	0.1	(0.0)	99.7	(0.1)	0.3	(0.1)	0.0	c	27.6	(0.9)
New Zealand	96.0	(0.3)	3.7	(0.3)	0.3	(0.1)	98.2	(0.2)	1.5	(0.2)	0.3	(0.1)	99.0	(0.2)	0.8	(0.2)	0.2	(0.1)	5.4	(0.3)
Norway	100.0	c	0.0	c	0.0	c	100.0	c	0.0	c	0.0	c	c	c	c	c	c	c	0.0	c
Poland	98.6	(0.2)	1.3	(0.2)	0.2	(0.1)	96.8	(0.3)	2.9	(0.3)	0.2	(0.1)	c	c	c	c	c	c	4.2	(0.4)
Portugal	76.7	(1.5)	17.9	(1.2)	5.4	(0.6)	80.2	(1.5)	17.5	(1.4)	2.4	(0.3)	99.9	(0.1)	0.1	(0.1)	0.0	c	34.3	(1.9)
Slovak Republic	95.1	(0.5)	3.5	(0.5)	1.4	(0.2)	96.6	(0.4)	2.9	(0.4)	0.5	(0.1)	99.5	(0.3)	0.2	(0.1)	0.3	(0.3)	7.6	(0.6)
Slovenia	100.0	c	0.0	c	0.0	c	97.1	(0.4)	2.5	(0.4)	0.4	(0.1)	99.4	(0.1)	0.5	(0.1)	0.1	(0.0)	3.4	(0.4)
Spain	86.2	(0.5)	12.9	(0.4)	0.8	(0.1)	72.3	(0.7)	25.0	(0.6)	2.7	(0.2)	c	c	c	c	c	c	32.9	(0.6)
Sweden	96.6	(0.3)	3.1	(0.3)	0.2	(0.1)	98.7	(0.2)	1.1	(0.2)	0.2	(0.1)	98.7	(1.1)	0.0	c	1.3	(1.1)	4.0	(0.4)
Switzerland	86.8	(0.7)	12.7	(0.7)	0.5	(0.1)	91.9	(0.5)	7.9	(0.5)	0.2	(0.0)	99.5	(0.2)	0.5	(0.2)	0.0	c	19.9	(0.9)
Turkey	97.7	(0.3)	2.3	(0.3)	0.1	(0.0)	100.0	c	0.0	c	0.0	c	87.0	(0.8)	12.9	(0.8)	0.1	(0.1)	14.2	(0.9)
United Kingdom	98.0	(0.2)	1.8	(0.2)	0.1	(0.1)	99.2	(0.1)	0.7	(0.1)	0.1	(0.0)	99.4	(0.1)	0.4	(0.1)	0.1	(0.1)	2.7	(0.3)
United States	88.9	(0.9)	10.7	(0.9)	0.4	(0.1)	96.0	(0.3)	4.0	(0.3)	0.1	(0.0)	97.9	(0.3)	2.0	(0.3)	0.0	(0.0)	13.3	(1.0)
OECD average	92.9	(0.1)	6.4	(0.1)	0.7	(0.0)	94.3	(0.1)	5.2	(0.1)	0.5	(0.0)	97.9	(0.1)	2.0	(0.1)	0.1	(0.1)	12.4	(0.1)
Albania	98.7	(0.2)	1.2	(0.2)	0.1	(0.0)	97.7	(0.3)	2.1	(0.3)	0.2	(0.1)	99.1	(0.2)	0.6	(0.2)	0.2	(0.1)	3.2	(0.3)
Argentina	80.1	(1.5)	14.7	(1.1)	5.2	(0.6)	74.4	(1.6)	20.9	(1.3)	4.7	(0.5)	96.2	(0.6)	2.7	(0.4)	1.1	(0.3)	36.2	(2.2)
Brazil	79.4	(0.7)	15.9	(0.6)	4.7	(0.4)	80.6	(0.8)	14.5	(0.6)	4.9	(0.4)	92.3	(0.4)	7.4	(0.4)	0.4	(0.1)	36.1	(1.0)
Bulgaria	98.1	(0.3)	1.7	(0.2)	0.2	(0.1)	96.5	(0.4)	2.9	(0.3)	0.6	(0.1)	99.4	(0.1)	0.4	(0.1)	0.2	(0.1)	4.8	(0.5)
Colombia	77.6	(0.9)	18.4	(0.8)	4.0	(0.4)	71.3	(1.2)	22.0	(0.9)	6.7	(0.5)	94.5	(0.5)	5.3	(0.5)	0.2	(0.1)	40.6	(1.1)
Costa Rica	83.6	(1.2)	13.0	(0.9)	3.4	(0.4)	74.5	(1.5)	20.3	(1.1)	5.2	(0.6)	99.6	(0.1)	0.4	(0.1)	0.1	(0.1)	33.5	(1.8)
Croatia	98.5	(0.2)	1.5	(0.2)	0.0	c	98.2	(0.2)	1.8	(0.2)	0.0	(0.0)	97.7	(0.3)	2.2	(0.3)	0.0	(0.0)	2.7	(0.3)
Cyprus*	97.3	(0.2)	2.2	(0.2)	0.4	(0.1)	98.0	(0.2)	1.4	(0.2)	0.6	(0.1)	98.7	(0.2)	0.6	(0.1)	0.7	(0.1)	4.0	(0.2)
Hong Kong-China	90.7	(0.5)	8.5	(0.5)	0.8	(0.1)	92.4	(0.5)	7.2	(0.5)	0.4	(0.1)	99.8	(0.1)	0.2	(0.1)	0.0	(0.0)	15.9	(0.7)
Indonesia	85.4	(1.2)	13.3	(1.1)	1.3	(0.0)	95.0	(0.6)	4.4	(0.5)	0.6	(0.2)	96.2	(0.6)	3.5	(0.6)	0.3	(0.1)	15.5	(1.3)
Jordan	95.1	(0.4)	4.3	(0.3)	0.6	(0.1)	94.2	(0.4)	4.9	(0.4)	1.0	(0.2)	100.0	c	0.0	c	0.0	c	7.9	(0.5)
Kazakhstan	98.9	(0.2)	1.0	(0.2)	0.1	(0.0)	99.2	(0.2)	0.7	(0.2)	0.1	(0.1)	100.0	c	0.0	c	0.0	c	1.6	(0.3)
Latvia	94.4	(0.4)	5.0	(0.4)	0.5	(0.2)	96.3	(0.5)	3.5	(0.5)	0.2	(0.1)	99.4	(0.6)	0.0	c	0.6	(0.6)	8.5	(0.6)
Liechtenstein	89.0	(1.7)	11.0	(1.7)	0.0	c	90.6	(1.5)	9.4	(1.5)	0.0	c	c	c	c	c	c	c	18.9	(1.9)
Lithuania	98.1	(0.2)	1.6	(0.2)	0.3	(0.1)	98.9	(0.2)	0.8	(0.1)	0.2	(0.1)	c	c	c	c	c	c	2.5	(0.2)
Macao-China	77.0	(0.4)	17.0	(0.4)	6.0	(0.3)	70.5	(0.5)	25.0	(0.5)	4.5	(0.2)	99.3	(0.2)	0.6	(0.2)	0.0	(0.0)	41.2	(0.4)
Malaysia	100.0	c	0.0	c	0.0	c	100.0	c	0.0	c	0.0	c	100.0	c	0.0	c	0.0	c	0.0	c
Montenegro	99.5	(0.1)	0.3	(0.1)	0.2	(0.1)	99.3	(0.1)	0.5	(0.1)	0.2	(0.1)	99.4	(0.1)	0.4	(0.1)	0.1	(0.1)	1.3	(0.2)
Peru	80.8	(1.0)	16.1	(0.9)	3.0	(0.2)	87.2	(0.9)	11.0	(0.8)	1.8	(0.2)	98.8	(0.2)	1.0	(0.2)	0.1	(0.1)	27.5	(1.3)
Qatar	91.2	(0.3)	7.4	(0.2)	1.3	(0.0)	93.8	(0.2)	5.0	(0.2)	1.2	(0.1)	96.5	(0.2)	2.2	(0.2)	1.4	(0.1)	13.3	(0.3)
Romania	97.0	(0.3)	2.4	(0.3)	0.6	(0.1)	97.3	(0.3)	2.1	(0.3)	0.7	(0.1)	100.0	c	0.0	c	0.0	c	4.5	(0.4)
Russian Federation	98.3	(0.2)	1.5	(0.2)	0.2	(0.1)	99.1	(0.2)	0.8	(0.2)	0.1	(0.1)	100.0	c	0.0	c	0.0	c	2.5	(0.3)
Serbia	99.6	(0.1)	0.4	(0.1)	0.0	(0.0)	98.7	(0.5)	1.1	(0.4)	0.2	(0.1)	99.4	(0.1)	0.6	(0.1)	0.1	(0.0)	1.6	(0.5)
Shanghai-China	93.3	(0.8)	6.1	(0.7)	0.6	(0.1)	97.2	(0.3)	2.7	(0.3)	0.1	(0.0)	100.0	(0.0)	0.0	c	0.0	c	9.1	(0.9)
Singapore	97.3	(0.2)	2.3	(0.2)	0.4	(0.1)	98.5	(0.1)	1.2	(0.1)	0.3	(0.1)	97.7	(0.2)	2.2	(0.2)	0.1	(0.0)	5.7	(0.2)
Chinese Taipei	99.5	(0.1)	0.5	(0.1)	0.1	(0.0)	99.7	(0.1)	0.3	(0.1)	0.1	(0.0)	99.8	(0.1)	0.1	(0.1)	0.1	(0.0)	0.8	(0.1)
Thailand	98.1	(0.2)	1.9	(0.2)	0.0	c	99.0	(0.2)	1.0	(0.2)	0.0	c	99.3	(0.1)	0.7	(0.1)	0.0	c	3.3	(0.3)
Tunisia	82.2	(1.8)	12.7	(1.2)	5.1	(0.7)	69.6	(2.4)	23.8	(1.8)	6.6	(0.7)	97.4	(0.3)	2.6	(0.3)	0.0	(0.0)	38.7	(2.8)
United Arab Emirates	92.0	(0.6)	7.0	(0.5)	1.0	(0.1)	93.9	(0.4)	5.2	(0.4)	0.9	(0.1)	98.4	(0.1)	1.3	(0.1)	0.3	(0.1)	12.0	(0.8)
Uruguay	78.4	(1.0)	17.4	(0.8)	4.2	(0.4)	72.9	(1.2)	20.7	(0.9)	6.4	(0.6)	99.7	(0.1)	0.3	(0.1)	0.0	(0.0)	37.9	(1.3)
Viet Nam	96.8	(0.7)	2.9	(0.6)	0.3	(0.1)	94.5	(1.2)	5.1	(1.1)	0.5	(0.1)	99.8	(0.1)	0.1	(0.1)	0.0	(0.0)	7.7	(1.5)

* See notes at the beginning of this Annex.
StatLink ⟨⟨⟨ http://dx.doi.org/10.1787/888932957422

[Part 1/1]
Relationship between grade repetition and students' socio-economic status

Table IV.2.3   *Logistic regression after accounting for mathematics performance*

			Logistic regression model estimating student reported to have repeated a grade at least once[1]			
		Intercept		Mathematics performance (1 score point increase)		PISA index of economic, social and cultural status (ESCS) (1 unit increase)	
		Intercept	S.E.	Logistic regression coef.	S.E.	Logistic regression coef.	S.E.
OECD	Australia	0.67	(0.22)	**-0.007**	(0.000)	0.03	(0.05)
	Austria	2.04	(0.39)	**-0.008**	(0.001)	-0.01	(0.08)
	Belgium	5.43	(0.21)	**-0.012**	(0.000)	**-0.32**	(0.04)
	Canada	2.29	(0.32)	**-0.010**	(0.001)	**-0.45**	(0.05)
	Chile	5.12	(0.30)	**-0.015**	(0.001)	0.00	(0.04)
	Czech Republic	4.20	(0.62)	**-0.017**	(0.001)	**-0.28**	(0.17)
	Denmark	2.64	(0.50)	**-0.012**	(0.001)	-0.18	(0.10)
	Estonia	4.26	(0.61)	**-0.016**	(0.001)	-0.19	(0.16)
	Finland	4.25	(0.54)	**-0.016**	(0.001)	**-0.36**	(0.13)
	France	7.90	(0.50)	**-0.019**	(0.001)	**-0.30**	(0.08)
	Germany	3.53	(0.35)	**-0.010**	(0.001)	-0.08	(0.06)
	Greece	2.86	(0.59)	**-0.016**	(0.001)	**-0.62**	(0.11)
	Hungary	3.81	(0.73)	**-0.014**	(0.002)	**-0.31**	(0.11)
	Iceland	-1.15	(0.88)	**-0.007**	(0.002)	-0.23	(0.25)
	Ireland	1.47	(0.29)	**-0.008**	(0.001)	**0.16**	(0.06)
	Israel	-0.50	(0.70)	**-0.008**	(0.002)	-0.18	(0.13)
	Italy	2.89	(0.18)	**-0.010**	(0.000)	**-0.25**	(0.03)
	Japan	a	a	a	a	a	a
	Korea	-1.40	(0.44)	**-0.004**	(0.001)	**0.26**	(0.10)
	Luxembourg	5.70	(0.24)	**-0.013**	(0.001)	**-0.20**	(0.03)
	Mexico	3.23	(0.21)	**-0.013**	(0.001)	**-0.21**	(0.03)
	Netherlands	3.24	(0.30)	**-0.008**	(0.001)	-0.07	(0.05)
	New Zealand	0.31	(0.39)	**-0.007**	(0.001)	0.07	(0.09)
	Norway	a	a	a	a	a	a
	Poland	4.02	(0.63)	**-0.016**	(0.001)	**-0.39**	(0.14)
	Portugal	8.93	(0.47)	**-0.021**	(0.001)	**-0.38**	(0.06)
	Slovak Republic	2.95	(0.65)	**-0.015**	(0.001)	**-0.96**	(0.15)
	Slovenia	2.82	(0.59)	**-0.014**	(0.001)	**-0.50**	(0.17)
	Spain	7.42	(0.23)	**-0.018**	(0.000)	**-0.41**	(0.04)
	Sweden	2.34	(0.41)	**-0.013**	(0.001)	**-0.38**	(0.10)
	Switzerland	3.84	(0.24)	**-0.010**	(0.000)	-0.03	(0.05)
	Turkey	4.34	(0.40)	**-0.014**	(0.001)	**0.16**	(0.04)
	United Kingdom	1.46	(0.48)	**-0.011**	(0.001)	0.22	(0.12)
	United States	2.96	(0.35)	**-0.011**	(0.001)	**-0.17**	(0.06)
	OECD average	3.25	(0.08)	**-0.012**	(0.000)	**-0.21**	(0.02)
Partners	Albania	m	m	m	m	m	m
	Argentina	4.59	(0.32)	**-0.014**	(0.001)	-0.12	(0.06)
	Brazil	4.24	(0.19)	**-0.013**	(0.000)	**-0.05**	(0.03)
	Bulgaria	2.15	(0.70)	**-0.015**	(0.002)	**-0.62**	(0.13)
	Colombia	2.80	(0.25)	**-0.009**	(0.001)	-0.04	(0.03)
	Costa Rica	5.14	(0.41)	**-0.015**	(0.001)	**-0.13**	(0.04)
	Croatia	-0.29	(0.56)	**-0.007**	(0.001)	0.06	(0.12)
	Cyprus*	1.03	(0.33)	**-0.011**	(0.001)	-0.12	(0.09)
	Hong Kong-China	2.31	(0.32)	**-0.008**	(0.001)	**-0.15**	(0.07)
	Indonesia	0.92	(0.47)	**-0.008**	(0.001)	**-0.20**	(0.06)
	Jordan	2.38	(0.56)	**-0.014**	(0.002)	-0.11	(0.07)
	Kazakhstan	-1.43	(0.94)	**-0.007**	(0.002)	-0.26	(0.18)
	Latvia	5.38	(0.78)	**-0.018**	(0.002)	**-0.56**	(0.13)
	Liechtenstein	1.52	(0.84)	**-0.006**	(0.002)	-0.30	(0.17)
	Lithuania	2.24	(0.67)	**-0.014**	(0.002)	**-0.44**	(0.12)
	Macao-China	6.43	(0.23)	**-0.013**	(0.000)	**-0.19**	(0.04)
	Malaysia	a	a	a	a	a	a
	Montenegro	-1.71	(0.80)	**-0.008**	(0.002)	**-0.45**	(0.17)
	Peru	2.28	(0.25)	**-0.010**	(0.001)	**-0.21**	(0.04)
	Qatar	0.67	(0.15)	**-0.007**	(0.000)	**-0.12**	(0.03)
	Romania	-0.53	(0.85)	**-0.007**	(0.002)	**-0.59**	(0.15)
	Russian Federation	0.63	(0.71)	**-0.011**	(0.002)	**-0.82**	(0.18)
	Serbia	1.45	(0.96)	**-0.015**	(0.002)	**-0.46**	(0.27)
	Shanghai-China	2.39	(0.41)	**-0.009**	(0.001)	**-0.63**	(0.08)
	Singapore	1.66	(0.36)	**-0.008**	(0.001)	0.10	(0.07)
	Chinese Taipei	-0.96	(0.92)	**-0.009**	(0.002)	**-0.50**	(0.19)
	Thailand	-1.19	(0.62)	**-0.005**	(0.001)	0.09	(0.08)
	Tunisia	7.09	(0.48)	**-0.021**	(0.001)	**-0.29**	(0.05)
	United Arab Emirates	2.75	(0.28)	**-0.012**	(0.001)	**-0.25**	(0.07)
	Uruguay	5.68	(0.35)	**-0.017**	(0.001)	**-0.37**	(0.04)
	Viet Nam	4.32	(0.91)	**-0.017**	(0.002)	**-0.49**	(0.14)

Note: Values that are statistically significant are indicated in bold (see Annex A3).
1. Logistic regression: Repeat = Intercept + variables listed in this table; where Repeat is equal to 0 if a student reported to have not repeated a grade and it is equal to 1 if a student reported to have repeated a grade.
* See notes at the beginning of this Annex.
StatLink ⟐ http://dx.doi.org/10.1787/888932957422

[Part 1/1]
Student grade level
Table IV.2.4 *Results based on students' self-reports*

| | Modal grade | Variation in student grade level | | Percentage of students at: | | | | | | Percentage of students enrolled in: | | | |
| | | | | Grades below the modal grade | | The modal grade | | Grades above the modal grade | | Lower secondary education (ISCED 2) | | Upper secondary education (ISCED 3) | |
		S.D.	S.E.	%	S.E.	%	S.E.	%	S.E.	%	S.E.	%	S.E.
Australia	10	0.55	(0.01)	10.9	(0.5)	70.0	(0.6)	19.1	(0.4)	80.9	(0.4)	19.1	(0.4)
Austria	10	0.61	(0.01)	49.0	(1.0)	51.0	(1.0)	0.1	(0.0)	5.6	(0.7)	94.4	(0.7)
Belgium	10	0.67	(0.01)	37.4	(0.6)	59.5	(0.6)	3.0	(0.3)	10.3	(0.6)	89.7	(0.6)
Canada	10	0.42	(0.01)	14.4	(0.6)	84.6	(0.6)	1.1	(0.1)	14.4	(0.6)	85.6	(0.6)
Chile	10	0.71	(0.02)	27.1	(1.2)	66.1	(1.2)	6.7	(0.3)	5.5	(0.8)	94.5	(0.8)
Czech Republic	9	0.59	(0.01)	4.9	(0.5)	51.1	(1.2)	44.1	(1.3)	56.1	(1.2)	43.9	(1.2)
Denmark	9	0.41	(0.01)	18.3	(0.9)	80.6	(0.8)	1.0	(0.2)	99.5	(0.1)	0.5	(0.1)
Estonia	9	0.47	(0.01)	22.7	(0.7)	75.4	(0.7)	1.9	(0.3)	98.1	(0.3)	1.9	(0.3)
Finland	9	0.39	(0.01)	14.9	(0.4)	85.0	(0.4)	0.1	(0.1)	99.9	(0.1)	0.1	(0.1)
France	10	0.57	(0.01)	29.8	(0.7)	66.6	(0.7)	3.6	(0.3)	29.8	(0.7)	70.2	(0.7)
Germany	9	0.67	(0.01)	10.6	(0.6)	51.9	(0.8)	37.5	(0.9)	97.6	(0.8)	2.4	(0.8)
Greece	10	0.33	(0.03)	5.5	(1.0)	94.5	(1.0)	0.0	c	5.5	(1.0)	94.5	(1.0)
Hungary	9	0.63	(0.02)	11.6	(0.9)	67.8	(0.9)	20.6	(0.6)	11.6	(0.9)	88.4	(0.9)
Iceland	10	0.00	(0.00)	0.0	c	100.0	c	0.0	c	100.0	c	0.0	c
Ireland	9	0.75	(0.01)	1.9	(0.2)	60.5	(0.8)	37.6	(0.8)	62.4	(0.8)	37.6	(0.8)
Israel	10	0.41	(0.01)	17.5	(0.9)	81.7	(0.9)	0.8	(0.3)	13.1	(1.1)	86.9	(1.1)
Italy	10	0.51	(0.01)	18.9	(0.6)	78.5	(0.7)	2.6	(0.2)	2.1	(0.2)	97.9	(0.2)
Japan	10	0.00	(0.00)	0.0	c	100.0	c	0.0	c	0.0	c	100.0	c
Korea	10	0.24	(0.02)	5.9	(0.8)	93.8	(0.8)	0.2	(0.1)	5.9	(0.8)	94.1	(0.8)
Luxembourg	9	0.67	(0.00)	10.9	(0.2)	50.7	(0.1)	38.5	(0.1)	60.0	(0.1)	40.0	(0.1)
Mexico	10	0.68	(0.01)	37.0	(1.1)	60.8	(1.1)	2.2	(0.3)	37.0	(1.1)	63.0	(1.1)
Netherlands	10	0.57	(0.01)	50.3	(1.1)	49.2	(1.1)	0.5	(0.1)	70.3	(1.6)	29.7	(1.6)
New Zealand	11	0.35	(0.01)	6.3	(0.4)	88.3	(0.5)	5.4	(0.4)	6.3	(0.4)	93.7	(0.4)
Norway	10	0.08	(0.01)	0.4	(0.1)	99.4	(0.1)	0.2	(0.0)	99.8	(0.0)	0.2	(0.0)
Poland	9	0.25	(0.01)	4.6	(0.4)	94.9	(0.4)	0.5	(0.2)	99.5	(0.2)	0.5	(0.2)
Portugal	10	0.75	(0.02)	35.6	(1.9)	54.9	(2.2)	9.5	(1.4)	44.9	(2.3)	55.1	(2.3)
Slovak Republic	10	0.69	(0.02)	45.7	(1.4)	52.7	(1.4)	1.6	(0.5)	45.2	(1.4)	54.8	(1.4)
Slovenia	10	0.32	(0.02)	5.4	(0.8)	90.7	(0.8)	3.9	(0.2)	5.4	(0.8)	94.6	(0.8)
Spain	10	0.67	(0.01)	34.0	(0.6)	66.0	(0.6)	0.0	(0.0)	100.0	(0.0)	0.0	(0.0)
Sweden	9	0.25	(0.01)	3.7	(0.3)	94.0	(0.6)	2.2	(0.5)	97.8	(0.6)	2.2	(0.6)
Switzerland	9	0.63	(0.01)	13.5	(0.8)	60.6	(1.0)	25.9	(1.0)	76.8	(1.2)	23.2	(1.2)
Turkey	10	0.61	(0.02)	30.3	(1.2)	65.5	(1.2)	4.3	(0.3)	2.7	(0.4)	97.3	(0.4)
United Kingdom	11	0.22	(0.01)	1.4	(0.3)	95.0	(0.3)	3.6	(0.1)	0.1	(0.0)	99.9	(0.0)
United States	10	0.55	(0.01)	12.0	(1.1)	71.2	(1.1)	16.8	(0.8)	12.0	(1.1)	88.0	(1.1)
OECD average	10	0.48	(0.00)	17.4	(0.1)	73.9	(0.2)	8.7	(0.1)	45.8	(0.2)	54.2	(0.2)
Albania	10	0.55	(0.01)	41.7	(2.5)	58.0	(2.5)	0.3	(0.1)	41.7	(2.5)	58.3	(2.5)
Argentina	10	0.86	(0.03)	36.6	(2.2)	59.4	(2.1)	4.0	(0.9)	36.6	(2.2)	63.4	(2.2)
Brazil	11	0.95	(0.02)	55.4	(1.0)	42.0	(1.0)	2.6	(0.2)	20.4	(1.1)	79.6	(1.1)
Bulgaria	9	0.36	(0.02)	5.5	(0.6)	89.5	(0.7)	4.9	(0.4)	4.8	(0.6)	95.2	(0.6)
Colombia	10	1.11	(0.02)	39.1	(1.2)	40.2	(0.9)	20.7	(1.0)	39.1	(1.2)	60.9	(1.2)
Costa Rica	9	0.91	(0.02)	21.1	(1.5)	39.6	(1.3)	39.4	(1.8)	60.6	(1.8)	39.4	(1.8)
Croatia	9	0.40	(0.00)	0.0	c	79.8	(0.4)	20.2	(0.4)	0.0	c	100.0	(0.0)
Cyprus*	10	0.27	(0.00)	5.0	(0.1)	94.3	(0.1)	0.7	(0.0)	5.0	(0.1)	95.0	(0.1)
Hong Kong-China	10	0.68	(0.02)	33.5	(1.0)	65.0	(0.9)	1.5	(1.4)	33.5	(1.0)	66.5	(1.0)
Indonesia	10	0.80	(0.03)	47.9	(3.3)	47.7	(3.0)	4.4	(0.8)	47.9	(3.3)	52.1	(3.3)
Jordan	10	0.32	(0.01)	7.1	(0.4)	92.9	(0.4)	0.0	c	100.0	c	0.0	c
Kazakhstan	9	0.55	(0.01)	5.1	(0.5)	67.2	(1.9)	27.7	(2.0)	72.3	(2.0)	27.7	(2.0)
Latvia	9	0.49	(0.02)	16.8	(0.8)	79.3	(0.8)	4.0	(0.6)	96.1	(0.7)	3.9	(0.7)
Liechtenstein	9	0.69	(0.02)	19.0	(1.4)	66.3	(1.3)	14.6	(0.2)	88.2	(0.2)	11.8	(0.2)
Lithuania	9	0.44	(0.01)	6.4	(0.5)	80.7	(0.7)	12.9	(0.7)	100.0	(0.0)	0.0	(0.0)
Macao-China	10	0.90	(0.00)	54.9	(0.1)	44.6	(0.1)	0.5	(0.1)	54.9	(0.1)	45.1	(0.1)
Malaysia	10	0.20	(0.01)	4.0	(0.5)	96.0	(0.5)	0.0	(0.0)	4.0	(0.5)	96.0	(0.5)
Montenegro	9	0.40	(0.00)	0.1	(0.0)	79.5	(0.1)	20.4	(0.1)	0.4	(0.2)	99.6	(0.2)
Peru	10	0.97	(0.02)	28.6	(1.3)	47.7	(0.9)	23.7	(0.8)	29.5	(1.4)	70.5	(1.4)
Qatar	10	0.72	(0.00)	17.8	(0.1)	64.8	(0.1)	17.4	(0.1)	17.8	(0.1)	82.2	(0.1)
Romania	9	0.37	(0.01)	7.7	(0.4)	87.2	(0.6)	5.1	(0.4)	100.0	c	0.0	c
Russian Federation	9	0.53	(0.01)	8.7	(0.5)	73.8	(1.6)	17.5	(1.8)	82.5	(1.8)	17.5	(1.8)
Serbia	9	0.19	(0.03)	1.6	(0.7)	96.7	(0.7)	1.7	(0.2)	1.6	(0.7)	98.4	(0.7)
Shanghai-China	10	0.65	(0.02)	45.1	(1.3)	54.2	(1.3)	0.7	(0.1)	44.4	(1.2)	55.6	(1.2)
Singapore	10	0.42	(0.01)	10.4	(0.3)	89.6	(0.3)	0.1	(0.1)	2.4	(0.2)	97.6	(0.2)
Chinese Taipei	10	0.48	(0.00)	36.4	(0.7)	63.6	(0.7)	0.0	c	36.4	(0.7)	63.6	(0.7)
Thailand	10	0.47	(0.01)	21.1	(1.0)	76.0	(1.1)	2.9	(0.5)	21.1	(1.0)	78.9	(1.0)
Tunisia	10	0.95	(0.02)	37.4	(3.0)	56.7	(2.7)	5.9	(0.5)	37.4	(3.0)	62.6	(3.0)
United Arab Emirates	10	0.75	(0.02)	15.0	(1.0)	61.9	(1.0)	23.0	(0.8)	15.0	(0.9)	85.0	(0.9)
Uruguay	10	0.95	(0.02)	41.4	(1.5)	57.3	(1.5)	1.3	(0.2)	41.4	(1.5)	58.6	(1.5)
Viet Nam	10	0.45	(0.04)	11.0	(2.2)	85.3	(2.6)	3.8	(1.6)	10.5	(2.2)	89.5	(2.2)

* See notes at the beginning of this Annex.
StatLink ⌘⑤ http://dx.doi.org/10.1787/888932957422

[Part 1/1]

Table IV.2.5   **Horizontal stratification of school systems**

		Source	Number of school types or distinct education programmes available to 15-year-old students	First age of selection in the education system
OECD	Australia	a	1.0	16.0
	Austria	a	4.0	10.0
	Belgium[1]	a	4.0	12.0
	Canada	a	1.0	16.0
	Chile	a	1.0	16.0
	Czech Republic	b	6.0	11.0
	Denmark	a	1.0	16.0
	Estonia	a	1.0	15.0
	Finland	a	1.0	16.0
	France	b	3.0	15.0
	Germany	a	4.0	10.0
	Greece	a	2.0	15.0
	Hungary	a	3.0	11.0
	Iceland	a	1.0	16.0
	Ireland	a	4.0	15.0
	Israel	a	2.0	15.0
	Italy	b	4.0	14.0
	Japan	a	2.0	15.0
	Korea	a	3.0	14.0
	Luxembourg	a	4.0	13.0
	Mexico	a	3.0	15.0
	Netherlands	a	7.0	12.0
	New Zealand	a	1.0	16.0
	Norway	a	1.0	16.0
	Poland	a	1.0	16.0
	Portugal	a	3.0	15.0
	Slovak Republic	a	5.0	11.0
	Slovenia	a	3.0	14.0
	Spain	a	1.0	16.0
	Sweden	a	1.0	16.0
	Switzerland	a	4.0	12.0
	Turkey	a	3.0	11.0
	United Kingdom	a	1.0	16.0
	United States	a	1.0	16.0
	OECD average		**2.6**	**14.0**
Partners	Albania	b	3.0	15.0
	Argentina	a	3.0	15.0
	Brazil	b	2.0	15.0
	Bulgaria	b	3.0	13.0
	Colombia	b	2.0	15.0
	Costa Rica		m	m
	Croatia	b	5.0	14.0
	Cyprus*	b	2.0	15.0
	Hong Kong-China	b	2.0	15.0
	Indonesia	a	1.0	15.0
	Jordan	b	1.0	16.0
	Kazakhstan		m	m
	Latvia	b	5.0	16.0
	Liechtenstein	b	3.0	15.0
	Lithuania	b	5.0	16.0
	Macao-China	b	2.0	15.0
	Malaysia	b	5.0	15.0
	Montenegro	b	6.0	15.0
	Peru	b	3.0	16.0
	Qatar	b	4.0	15.0
	Romania	b	2.0	14.0
	Russian Federation	b	3.0	15.5
	Serbia		m	m
	Shanghai-China	b	5.0	15.0
	Singapore	b	4.0	12.0
	Chinese Taipei	b	3.0	15.0
	Thailand	b	2.0	15.0
	Tunisia		m	m
	United Arab Emirates	b	5.0	15.0
	Uruguay	b	6.0	11.0
	Viet Nam	b	4.0	15.0

1. The first age of selection is 14 in Belgium (French Community) since 2008-09.
* See notes at the beginning of this Annex.
Sources: a) OECD (2010), *PISA 2009 Results: What Makes a School Successful*
     b) PISA system-level data collection in 2013.
StatLink ᐧᔑᓚ http://dx.doi.org/10.1787/888932957422

[Part 1/1]
Programme orientation
Table IV.2.6   *Results based on students' self-reports*

| | | Percentage of students who are enrolled in a programme whose curriculum is: | | | | | |
| | | General | | Pre-vocational or vocational | | Modular programmes | |
		%	S.E.	%	S.E.	%	S.E.
OECD	Australia	89.1	(0.5)	10.9	(0.5)	0.0	c
	Austria	30.7	(0.9)	69.3	(0.9)	0.0	c
	Belgium	56.0	(1.1)	44.0	(1.1)	0.0	c
	Canada	0.0	c	0.0	c	100.0	(0.0)
	Chile	97.2	(0.2)	2.8	(0.2)	0.0	c
	Czech Republic	69.0	(1.2)	31.0	(1.2)	0.0	c
	Denmark	100.0	c	0.0	c	0.0	c
	Estonia	99.6	(0.2)	0.4	(0.2)	0.0	c
	Finland	100.0	c	0.0	c	0.0	c
	France	84.7	(1.2)	15.3	(1.2)	0.0	c
	Germany	98.0	(0.9)	2.0	(0.9)	0.0	c
	Greece	86.5	(2.3)	13.5	(2.3)	0.0	c
	Hungary	85.7	(1.1)	14.3	(1.1)	0.0	c
	Iceland	100.0	c	0.0	c	0.0	c
	Ireland	99.2	(0.2)	0.8	(0.2)	0.0	c
	Israel	96.9	(0.2)	3.1	(0.2)	0.0	c
	Italy	50.4	(0.9)	49.6	(0.9)	0.0	c
	Japan	75.8	(0.8)	24.2	(0.8)	0.0	c
	Korea	80.1	(1.4)	19.9	(1.4)	0.0	c
	Luxembourg	78.6	(0.2)	14.5	(0.1)	6.9	(0.2)
	Mexico	74.8	(1.0)	25.2	(1.0)	0.0	c
	Netherlands	77.8	(1.7)	22.2	(1.7)	0.0	c
	New Zealand	100.0	c	0.0	c	0.0	c
	Norway	100.0	c	0.0	c	0.0	c
	Poland	99.9	(0.0)	0.1	(0.0)	0.0	c
	Portugal	83.3	(2.0)	16.7	(2.0)	0.0	c
	Slovak Republic	65.7	(1.5)	8.2	(1.4)	26.1	(1.3)
	Slovenia	46.8	(0.5)	53.2	(0.5)	0.0	c
	Spain	99.3	(0.1)	0.7	(0.1)	0.0	c
	Sweden	99.6	(0.1)	0.4	(0.1)	0.0	c
	Switzerland	89.3	(1.0)	10.7	(1.0)	0.0	c
	Turkey	61.9	(0.5)	38.1	(0.5)	0.0	c
	United Kingdom	98.9	(0.1)	1.1	(0.1)	0.0	c
	United States	100.0	c	0.0	c	0.0	c
	OECD average	**81.6**	**(0.2)**	**14.5**	**(0.2)**	**3.9**	**(0.5)**
Partners	Albania	91.6	(1.9)	8.4	(1.9)	0.0	c
	Argentina	85.5	(2.6)	14.5	(2.6)	0.0	c
	Brazil	100.0	(0.0)	0.0	(0.0)	0.0	c
	Bulgaria	59.2	(1.6)	40.8	(1.6)	0.0	c
	Colombia	74.8	(2.3)	25.2	(2.3)	0.0	c
	Costa Rica	90.9	(1.7)	9.1	(1.7)	0.0	c
	Croatia	29.9	(1.2)	70.1	(1.2)	0.0	c
	Cyprus*	89.2	(0.1)	10.8	(0.1)	0.0	c
	Hong Kong-China	100.0	c	0.0	c	0.0	c
	Indonesia	79.8	(3.1)	20.2	(3.1)	0.0	c
	Jordan	100.0	c	0.0	c	0.0	c
	Kazakhstan	92.3	(2.1)	7.7	(2.1)	0.0	c
	Latvia	99.1	(0.5)	0.9	(0.5)	0.0	c
	Liechtenstein	100.0	c	0.0	c	0.0	c
	Lithuania	99.4	(0.2)	0.6	(0.2)	0.0	c
	Macao-China	98.4	(0.1)	1.6	(0.1)	0.0	c
	Malaysia	86.7	(1.2)	13.3	(1.2)	0.0	c
	Montenegro	34.0	(0.2)	66.0	(0.2)	0.0	c
	Peru	100.0	c	0.0	c	0.0	c
	Qatar	100.0	c	0.0	c	0.0	c
	Romania	100.0	c	0.0	c	0.0	c
	Russian Federation	95.9	(1.1)	4.1	(1.1)	0.0	c
	Serbia	25.6	(1.0)	74.4	(1.0)	0.0	c
	Shanghai-China	78.8	(0.6)	21.2	(0.6)	0.0	c
	Singapore	100.0	c	0.0	c	0.0	c
	Chinese Taipei	65.5	(1.4)	34.5	(1.4)	0.0	c
	Thailand	80.4	(0.6)	19.6	(0.6)	0.0	c
	Tunisia	100.0	c	0.0	c	0.0	c
	United Arab Emirates	97.3	(0.0)	2.7	(0.0)	0.0	c
	Uruguay	97.3	(0.4)	1.4	(0.4)	1.3	(0.3)
	Viet Nam	99.3	(0.7)	0.0	c	0.7	(0.7)

* See notes at the beginning of this Annex.
StatLink ⟲ http://dx.doi.org/10.1787/888932957422

[Part 1/2]
School admissions policies
Table IV.2.7 *Results based on school principals' reports*

	Percentage of students in schools whose principal reported that the following factors are "never", "sometimes" or "always" considered for admission to school:																							
	Residence in a particular area						Students' records of academic performance						Recommendations of feeder schools						Parents' endorsement of the instructional or religious philosophy of the school					
	Never		Sometimes		Always		Never		Sometimes		Always		Never		Sometimes		Always		Never		Sometimes		Always	
	%	S.E.	%	S.E.	%	S.E.	%	S.E.	%	S.E.	%	S.E.	%	S.E.	%	S.E.	%	S.E.	%	S.E.	%	S.E.	%	S.E.
OECD																								
Australia	35.4	(1.5)	19.8	(1.6)	44.8	(1.5)	26.5	(1.8)	40.6	(1.7)	32.9	(1.8)	23.3	(1.5)	43.9	(2.2)	32.9	(2.0)	46.4	(1.9)	22.6	(1.7)	31.0	(1.4)
Austria	53.9	(3.9)	17.4	(2.8)	28.7	(3.2)	20.0	(1.5)	9.9	(2.2)	70.1	(2.1)	52.1	(3.5)	40.2	(3.9)	7.7	(1.9)	73.7	(3.8)	22.2	(3.6)	4.1	(1.8)
Belgium	82.2	(2.5)	16.3	(2.3)	1.5	(0.8)	45.1	(2.5)	29.2	(2.8)	25.7	(2.7)	56.0	(2.7)	38.1	(3.0)	5.9	(1.5)	42.3	(2.8)	16.8	(2.3)	40.9	(3.0)
Canada	17.8	(1.6)	12.8	(1.3)	69.4	(1.9)	41.6	(2.6)	31.8	(2.3)	26.6	(1.8)	34.5	(2.5)	35.6	(2.3)	29.9	(2.5)	67.0	(2.2)	20.7	(2.2)	12.3	(1.6)
Chile	63.9	(3.6)	24.3	(3.5)	11.8	(2.4)	30.1	(3.4)	35.7	(4.1)	34.2	(3.6)	41.5	(3.6)	44.7	(3.9)	13.8	(2.9)	61.8	(3.4)	12.7	(2.6)	25.6	(2.9)
Czech Republic	69.9	(3.2)	16.1	(3.1)	14.0	(2.1)	32.8	(2.5)	12.7	(2.6)	54.5	(2.5)	50.5	(3.2)	38.3	(3.2)	11.3	(2.6)	64.7	(3.7)	18.8	(3.3)	16.5	(2.9)
Denmark	33.2	(3.5)	25.6	(3.1)	41.2	(3.3)	70.1	(2.7)	23.0	(2.6)	7.0	(1.7)	57.1	(3.6)	31.0	(3.8)	11.9	(2.0)	59.0	(3.4)	21.6	(3.3)	19.3	(2.5)
Estonia	21.7	(2.6)	26.5	(2.3)	51.7	(3.0)	28.5	(2.3)	34.4	(2.3)	37.0	(2.6)	42.7	(2.8)	53.3	(2.8)	4.0	(1.2)	57.6	(2.8)	31.4	(2.9)	10.9	(1.8)
Finland	23.2	(3.2)	9.9	(2.0)	66.9	(3.3)	83.0	(2.1)	13.9	(1.8)	3.1	(1.0)	80.3	(2.4)	17.0	(2.2)	2.7	(0.8)	87.8	(2.1)	6.3	(1.5)	5.9	(1.5)
France	18.2	(2.1)	21.0	(2.8)	60.8	(2.7)	40.1	(3.0)	29.7	(3.6)	30.2	(2.9)	60.3	(2.9)	33.3	(3.0)	6.4	(1.6)	76.5	(2.2)	9.5	(2.3)	14.0	(1.8)
Germany	21.0	(2.9)	30.1	(3.3)	48.9	(3.5)	21.5	(3.0)	29.5	(3.3)	48.9	(3.7)	22.4	(2.9)	33.3	(3.4)	44.3	(3.9)	72.5	(3.2)	18.0	(2.7)	9.5	(1.9)
Greece	14.0	(2.8)	14.5	(3.3)	71.5	(4.0)	76.0	(2.8)	19.6	(2.6)	4.4	(1.7)	64.3	(3.7)	29.2	(3.4)	6.5	(2.0)	84.9	(2.5)	9.9	(2.2)	5.1	(1.5)
Hungary	51.1	(3.7)	29.0	(3.6)	19.9	(2.7)	7.5	(1.0)	9.6	(2.1)	82.9	(2.2)	50.8	(4.2)	39.6	(4.3)	9.6	(2.6)	52.2	(3.9)	24.9	(3.6)	22.9	(3.1)
Iceland	21.2	(0.2)	30.7	(0.2)	48.1	(0.2)	72.3	(0.2)	19.6	(0.2)	8.1	(0.2)	42.6	(0.2)	38.2	(0.3)	19.2	(0.2)	85.0	(0.2)	14.9	(0.2)	0.1	(0.0)
Ireland	38.3	(4.0)	17.4	(3.0)	44.4	(4.0)	64.5	(4.0)	13.8	(2.6)	21.6	(3.4)	53.0	(4.1)	22.6	(3.2)	24.4	(3.6)	49.8	(3.8)	24.6	(3.4)	25.6	(3.4)
Israel	29.4	(3.5)	31.8	(4.2)	38.8	(3.7)	26.8	(3.6)	30.6	(3.7)	42.6	(4.1)	23.9	(3.2)	34.0	(3.5)	42.1	(4.0)	39.8	(3.3)	19.0	(2.8)	41.1	(3.2)
Italy	36.8	(2.4)	36.2	(2.1)	27.0	(1.9)	21.9	(1.6)	21.7	(2.0)	56.5	(2.1)	20.6	(1.6)	30.6	(2.0)	48.8	(2.0)	37.1	(2.0)	23.1	(1.8)	39.8	(2.2)
Japan	76.7	(2.8)	13.7	(2.6)	9.5	(1.9)	0.9	(0.7)	6.0	(1.7)	93.1	(1.9)	32.1	(3.5)	37.9	(3.2)	30.0	(3.4)	76.7	(3.0)	12.7	(2.8)	10.7	(1.9)
Korea	61.5	(4.2)	20.6	(3.6)	17.8	(3.4)	25.7	(3.3)	7.7	(2.2)	66.6	(3.7)	53.6	(4.1)	28.5	(3.7)	17.9	(3.5)	64.3	(3.8)	21.2	(3.4)	14.4	(2.8)
Luxembourg	14.2	(0.1)	42.1	(0.1)	43.7	(0.1)	1.0	(0.0)	26.9	(0.1)	72.2	(0.1)	13.8	(0.1)	76.6	(0.1)	9.5	(0.1)	59.1	(0.1)	36.8	(0.1)	4.0	(0.0)
Mexico	66.1	(2.0)	24.6	(1.9)	9.2	(1.0)	31.8	(1.8)	20.5	(1.5)	47.7	(1.7)	63.8	(1.8)	24.5	(1.7)	11.7	(1.0)	69.9	(1.6)	15.6	(1.3)	14.5	(1.4)
Netherlands	56.9	(4.6)	21.6	(3.7)	21.4	(3.7)	1.3	(0.8)	6.7	(2.0)	92.0	(2.2)	0.7	(0.6)	6.7	(2.1)	92.7	(2.2)	38.7	(4.0)	32.3	(4.1)	29.0	(3.7)
New Zealand	32.7	(3.0)	17.4	(2.9)	49.9	(3.0)	34.6	(4.1)	14.0	(2.4)	51.4	(3.8)	31.7	(4.0)	17.9	(2.4)	50.4	(3.9)	54.3	(3.7)	21.7	(2.8)	24.1	(3.1)
Norway	29.8	(3.5)	6.9	(2.0)	63.3	(4.0)	88.9	(2.5)	4.3	(1.6)	6.7	(2.0)	84.5	(3.0)	11.1	(2.5)	4.4	(1.6)	93.0	(2.1)	5.1	(1.8)	1.9	(1.1)
Poland	12.0	(2.5)	11.3	(2.2)	76.7	(3.1)	40.5	(3.4)	42.2	(3.9)	17.3	(2.9)	44.3	(3.6)	51.1	(3.9)	4.5	(1.6)	75.5	(3.5)	20.9	(3.4)	3.6	(1.1)
Portugal	9.1	(2.7)	36.1	(4.7)	54.9	(4.6)	34.0	(4.6)	30.2	(4.2)	35.9	(4.3)	65.4	(4.5)	31.9	(4.3)	2.8	(1.2)	49.1	(4.5)	22.1	(3.7)	28.7	(3.8)
Slovak Republic	66.8	(3.3)	16.4	(2.8)	16.8	(2.6)	33.6	(2.4)	16.2	(2.5)	50.2	(2.4)	39.5	(3.7)	46.3	(3.8)	14.2	(3.0)	66.3	(3.8)	13.0	(2.6)	20.7	(3.9)
Slovenia	77.9	(0.7)	17.9	(0.8)	4.1	(0.7)	30.4	(0.7)	42.8	(0.5)	26.9	(0.7)	62.3	(0.9)	33.2	(0.9)	4.4	(0.2)	92.0	(0.3)	5.7	(0.3)	2.4	(0.1)
Spain	19.6	(2.2)	17.8	(2.3)	62.6	(3.0)	89.4	(1.9)	9.9	(1.9)	0.8	(0.3)	87.7	(1.8)	9.1	(1.6)	3.2	(1.0)	81.4	(1.8)	9.3	(1.7)	9.3	(1.1)
Sweden	37.4	(3.3)	12.6	(2.4)	50.1	(3.6)	89.9	(2.2)	2.9	(1.2)	7.1	(1.9)	84.1	(2.7)	9.0	(2.3)	6.8	(1.8)	86.9	(2.8)	9.3	(2.3)	3.9	(1.4)
Switzerland	28.6	(3.1)	14.8	(2.5)	56.6	(3.2)	21.4	(2.7)	15.2	(2.3)	63.5	(3.5)	29.6	(2.8)	23.6	(2.9)	46.8	(3.2)	82.5	(2.5)	14.3	(2.2)	3.2	(1.1)
Turkey	39.2	(3.2)	27.4	(3.9)	33.4	(3.4)	28.2	(3.3)	30.0	(3.0)	41.8	(3.3)	73.7	(4.1)	20.9	(3.4)	5.3	(1.8)	37.7	(3.6)	43.5	(3.8)	18.8	(2.8)
United Kingdom	21.1	(2.3)	30.4	(3.5)	48.4	(3.2)	68.4	(2.8)	8.6	(2.3)	23.0	(2.2)	57.5	(3.4)	22.1	(3.4)	20.4	(2.4)	69.8	(3.0)	17.7	(2.6)	12.4	(2.2)
United States	18.0	(3.4)	7.6	(2.0)	74.4	(3.7)	45.7	(4.0)	20.1	(3.3)	34.1	(3.5)	45.1	(4.3)	33.8	(4.4)	21.1	(3.4)	72.9	(4.2)	20.4	(3.9)	6.7	(2.0)
OECD average	38.2	(0.5)	21.1	(0.5)	40.7	(0.5)	40.4	(0.5)	20.9	(0.4)	38.7	(0.4)	48.4	(0.5)	32.0	(0.5)	19.6	(0.4)	65.5	(0.5)	18.8	(0.5)	15.7	(0.4)
Partners																								
Albania	26.8	(3.9)	34.9	(3.4)	38.3	(4.0)	28.5	(3.7)	25.0	(3.9)	46.5	(4.0)	24.2	(3.4)	36.8	(3.9)	39.1	(3.6)	52.8	(3.8)	19.3	(3.1)	27.9	(3.7)
Argentina	50.1	(3.9)	26.0	(3.9)	23.9	(3.0)	67.9	(3.4)	22.0	(3.2)	10.1	(2.5)	55.4	(3.7)	37.9	(3.7)	6.7	(1.5)	50.4	(3.8)	24.2	(3.5)	25.4	(3.7)
Brazil	33.0	(2.1)	28.1	(2.0)	38.8	(2.3)	70.1	(2.1)	12.7	(1.7)	17.2	(1.8)	70.3	(2.4)	22.7	(2.0)	7.0	(1.4)	61.9	(2.5)	20.4	(2.1)	17.7	(1.9)
Bulgaria	58.3	(3.4)	24.0	(3.0)	17.7	(2.3)	6.2	(1.6)	13.7	(2.7)	80.1	(2.9)	42.3	(3.5)	41.3	(3.4)	16.5	(2.8)	28.2	(3.0)	27.0	(3.4)	44.8	(3.9)
Colombia	45.0	(3.8)	29.9	(3.7)	25.1	(3.2)	28.8	(3.2)	33.3	(3.9)	37.9	(3.7)	49.2	(4.0)	34.1	(3.7)	16.7	(2.9)	56.7	(3.6)	19.6	(3.1)	23.7	(3.2)
Costa Rica	28.3	(2.9)	18.7	(3.5)	52.9	(3.8)	29.7	(3.3)	23.8	(3.2)	46.5	(3.6)	37.9	(3.5)	46.7	(3.8)	15.4	(2.3)	46.5	(3.5)	25.9	(3.4)	27.6	(3.0)
Croatia	69.7	(3.3)	23.8	(3.3)	6.6	(1.3)	0.3	(0.3)	4.1	(1.7)	95.6	(1.8)	45.1	(3.8)	47.7	(4.1)	7.2	(1.8)	58.6	(3.5)	23.5	(3.2)	17.8	(3.2)
Cyprus*	24.9	(0.1)	7.3	(0.1)	67.8	(0.1)	60.6	(0.1)	21.7	(0.1)	17.7	(0.1)	62.0	(0.1)	29.9	(0.1)	8.1	(0.1)	84.5	(0.1)	1.6	(0.0)	13.9	(0.1)
Hong Kong-China	49.8	(4.1)	35.4	(3.9)	14.8	(2.9)	0.0	c	8.0	(1.9)	92.0	(1.9)	6.1	(2.0)	65.1	(4.1)	28.7	(3.7)	25.0	(3.2)	44.7	(3.8)	30.4	(3.7)
Indonesia	30.9	(4.1)	27.2	(3.5)	41.9	(3.7)	24.4	(3.4)	19.6	(2.8)	56.0	(3.4)	37.7	(3.8)	25.2	(3.6)	37.1	(3.8)	43.0	(3.9)	18.5	(3.0)	38.5	(3.9)
Jordan	9.4	(2.1)	27.3	(3.6)	63.3	(3.3)	30.7	(3.2)	42.6	(3.6)	26.8	(3.1)	38.7	(3.1)	42.4	(3.4)	18.9	(2.8)	47.6	(2.8)	30.3	(3.0)	22.1	(2.6)
Kazakhstan	31.1	(3.9)	31.0	(3.8)	37.9	(3.9)	34.4	(4.0)	27.1	(3.8)	38.5	(4.1)	43.6	(3.9)	32.1	(3.8)	24.3	(3.4)	57.8	(4.2)	25.8	(3.5)	16.5	(3.1)
Latvia	60.8	(3.5)	18.7	(2.9)	20.5	(2.8)	47.0	(2.8)	25.4	(2.9)	27.6	(2.7)	60.7	(3.4)	35.2	(3.3)	4.1	(1.4)	86.0	(2.7)	11.5	(2.4)	2.5	(1.2)
Liechtenstein	37.9	(0.9)	5.4	(0.7)	56.7	(0.6)	19.9	(1.1)	7.4	(0.8)	72.8	(1.3)	12.8	(1.0)	13.4	(0.8)	73.8	(1.1)	72.5	(1.2)	21.4	(0.7)	6.1	(1.0)
Lithuania	25.1	(2.8)	14.0	(2.5)	60.8	(3.2)	53.0	(2.8)	28.0	(2.7)	19.0	(2.2)	51.2	(3.4)	44.7	(3.3)	4.1	(1.4)	49.3	(3.4)	27.7	(3.0)	23.0	(2.9)
Macao-China	71.1	(0.1)	22.9	(0.1)	6.0	(0.0)	4.1	(0.0)	27.2	(0.1)	68.8	(0.1)	9.5	(0.0)	45.4	(0.1)	45.1	(0.1)	23.4	(0.0)	66.3	(0.1)	10.3	(0.0)
Malaysia	33.5	(4.1)	35.4	(4.0)	31.1	(3.7)	27.1	(3.7)	27.1	(4.0)	45.7	(4.3)	30.6	(4.0)	43.0	(4.1)	26.4	(3.6)	36.3	(3.9)	36.9	(3.6)	26.8	(3.5)
Montenegro	66.0	(0.2)	26.4	(0.1)	7.6	(0.1)	34.8	(0.1)	12.9	(0.1)	52.4	(0.1)	32.4	(0.1)	39.6	(0.1)	27.9	(0.1)	61.2	(0.1)	22.5	(0.1)	16.3	(0.1)
Peru	64.1	(3.4)	29.4	(3.1)	6.6	(1.7)	50.8	(3.7)	23.2	(3.2)	26.0	(3.4)	62.2	(3.6)	30.1	(3.7)	7.7	(1.8)	59.5	(3.7)	24.6	(3.0)	16.0	(2.6)
Qatar	31.5	(0.1)	20.1	(0.1)	48.4	(0.1)	31.6	(0.1)	21.4	(0.1)	47.0	(0.1)	34.5	(0.1)	41.4	(0.1)	24.1	(0.1)	30.4	(0.1)	35.6	(0.1)	34.0	(0.1)
Romania	42.3	(3.9)	48.1	(3.8)	9.6	(2.3)	31.3	(3.9)	38.0	(4.0)	30.6	(3.3)	47.8	(3.8)	46.4	(3.8)	5.7	(1.8)	55.2	(3.9)	34.3	(3.5)	10.5	(2.2)
Russian Federation	30.4	(3.8)	23.1	(3.0)	46.5	(4.2)	54.1	(3.2)	31.0	(2.7)	15.0	(2.4)	49.1	(3.5)	40.4	(3.7)	10.5	(1.7)	17.3	(2.7)	43.9	(3.6)	38.8	(4.0)
Serbia	72.1	(3.8)	24.7	(3.7)	3.2	(1.5)	5.3	(1.9)	8.9	(2.3)	85.8	(2.6)	36.9	(4.5)	49.6	(4.7)	13.4	(3.2)	57.1	(4.4)	27.5	(3.6)	15.4	(3.3)
Shanghai-China	36.6	(3.9)	33.6	(3.6)	29.8	(3.6)	20.8	(2.8)	32.8	(3.6)	46.4	(3.2)	22.0	(3.2)	62.4	(3.7)	15.6	(2.7)	14.4	(2.8)	42.8	(4.3)	42.8	(4.1)
Singapore	34.0	(0.5)	58.2	(0.5)	7.8	(0.6)	1.8	(0.0)	18.9	(0.6)	79.2	(0.6)	31.7	(0.3)	52.5	(0.6)	15.8	(0.7)	66.4	(0.5)	28.8	(0.5)	4.9	(0.1)
Chinese Taipei	31.2	(3.9)	41.3	(3.5)	27.5	(3.2)	19.0	(2.1)	35.6	(3.3)	45.4	(3.2)	32.2	(3.6)	54.1	(3.8)	13.6	(2.6)	29.4	(3.5)	41.5	(4.1)	29.1	(3.8)
Thailand	26.4	(3.5)	31.0	(3.7)	42.6	(3.6)	3.1	(1.3)	15.8	(2.2)	81.1	(2.4)	2.7	(1.3)	26.2	(3.0)	71.0	(3.3)	12.3	(2.3)	33.4	(3.7)	54.3	(3.8)
Tunisia	19.4	(3.2)	25.3	(3.4)	55.3	(3.7)	23.5	(3.4)	33.4	(4.0)	43.1	(4.1)	40.1	(4.1)	36.9	(4.5)	23.0	(3.8)	83.4	(3.0)	14.1	(2.7)	2.4	(1.2)
United Arab Emirates	35.5	(2.5)	23.5	(1.9)	40.9	(2.1)	9.5	(1.6)	24.4	(2.0)	66.1	(2.1)	21.5	(2.4)	45.0	(2.3)	33.5	(2.3)	27.7	(2.4)	33.3	(2.4)	39.0	(2.6)
Uruguay	49.7	(3.3)	23.6	(2.9)	26.7	(2.6)	65.7	(3.1)	8.4	(2.3)	25.9	(3.1)	66.2	(3.3)	26.1	(3.1)	7.6	(1.6)	75.5	(2.6)	6.9	(1.5)	17.6	(2.3)
Viet Nam	33.3	(4.0)	25.4	(3.9)	41.3	(4.1)	4.0	(1.4)	9.8	(2.2)	86.2	(2.6)	22.8	(3.5)	41.4	(4.4)	35.8	(3.9)	12.9	(2.7)	32.4	(4.0)	54.7	(4.2)

* See notes at the beginning of this Annex.
StatLink http://dx.doi.org/10.1787/888932957422

[Part 2/2]
School admissions policies
Table IV.2.7 *Results based on school principals' reports*

		Percentage of students in schools whose principal reported that the following factors are "never", "sometimes" or "always" considered for admission to school:																	Percentage of students in schools whose principals reported whether "students' records of academic performance" or "recommendations of feeder schools" are considered for admission					
		Whether the student requires or is interested in a special programme						Preference given to family members of current or former students						Other											
		Never		Sometimes		Always		Never		Sometimes		Always		Never		Sometimes		Always		These two factors are "never" considered		At least one of these two factors is "sometimes" considered but neither factor is "always" considered		At least one of these two factors is "always" considered	
		%	S.E.	%	S.E.	%	S.E.	%	S.E.	%	S.E.	%	S.E.	%	S.E.	%	S.E.	%	S.E.	%	S.E.	%	S.E.	%	S.E.
OECD	Australia	20.7	(1.6)	56.0	(1.8)	23.3	(1.7)	26.8	(1.6)	31.2	(1.8)	42.0	(1.9)	33.9	(1.8)	56.1	(2.0)	10.0	(1.2)	15.8	(1.4)	39.8	(2.0)	44.4	(2.1)
	Austria	28.4	(3.2)	36.8	(3.8)	34.9	(3.5)	51.2	(3.7)	28.9	(3.8)	19.9	(2.9)	56.5	(3.9)	33.6	(3.7)	9.9	(2.4)	17.8	(1.1)	11.3	(2.0)	70.9	(2.0)
	Belgium	36.4	(3.2)	54.0	(3.2)	9.7	(1.8)	47.9	(3.1)	25.3	(3.1)	26.7	(3.2)	54.3	(4.2)	38.1	(4.1)	7.7	(1.9)	34.9	(2.6)	38.0	(3.3)	27.1	(2.8)
	Canada	19.9	(1.8)	54.6	(2.5)	25.5	(2.3)	55.8	(2.5)	29.5	(2.5)	14.6	(1.8)	41.5	(3.1)	45.4	(3.7)	13.1	(2.7)	26.5	(2.1)	34.4	(2.2)	39.0	(2.3)
	Chile	43.5	(3.8)	39.2	(3.8)	17.3	(2.7)	21.4	(2.5)	36.0	(3.6)	42.6	(3.7)	60.5	(3.9)	32.0	(3.8)	7.5	(2.0)	19.1	(2.6)	42.0	(4.3)	38.9	(3.8)
	Czech Republic	34.5	(3.7)	38.2	(3.5)	27.3	(3.4)	80.7	(3.0)	15.9	(2.8)	3.5	(1.3)	63.8	(3.1)	31.6	(3.4)	4.6	(1.3)	25.0	(2.2)	17.1	(2.4)	57.9	(2.4)
	Denmark	40.8	(3.5)	48.0	(3.6)	11.2	(2.2)	47.6	(3.4)	41.6	(3.4)	10.8	(1.9)	41.4	(4.0)	48.7	(4.0)	10.0	(2.1)	48.7	(3.2)	36.7	(3.5)	14.6	(2.2)
	Estonia	19.4	(2.1)	55.4	(2.8)	25.2	(2.5)	43.8	(2.2)	37.6	(2.2)	18.7	(2.1)	38.8	(2.5)	55.7	(2.6)	5.5	(1.3)	19.8	(1.8)	41.7	(2.7)	38.4	(2.6)
	Finland	62.4	(3.2)	34.9	(3.1)	2.8	(0.9)	77.2	(2.5)	16.7	(1.9)	6.1	(1.6)	41.8	(3.3)	54.0	(3.3)	4.2	(1.3)	75.2	(2.5)	21.2	(2.3)	3.6	(1.0)
	France	40.0	(3.6)	48.0	(3.8)	12.0	(2.4)	49.4	(3.1)	35.8	(3.0)	14.7	(2.4)	33.2	(3.9)	58.4	(4.3)	8.5	(2.1)	35.2	(2.8)	33.7	(3.6)	31.1	(2.8)
	Germany	24.3	(3.3)	41.1	(3.6)	34.6	(3.9)	59.9	(2.8)	20.6	(2.8)	19.5	(2.8)	34.4	(4.6)	59.9	(4.8)	5.7	(2.1)	15.3	(2.6)	23.1	(3.0)	61.6	(3.7)
	Greece	60.1	(3.8)	25.7	(3.2)	14.2	(2.8)	46.8	(4.0)	32.1	(3.7)	21.1	(3.2)	23.8	(3.2)	69.5	(3.5)	6.7	(2.1)	62.4	(3.8)	29.8	(3.5)	7.8	(2.2)
	Hungary	15.8	(2.8)	32.7	(4.0)	51.6	(4.1)	38.5	(3.6)	42.3	(4.2)	19.2	(3.1)	45.3	(4.2)	42.4	(4.2)	12.3	(2.1)	6.1	(1.0)	9.1	(2.0)	84.8	(2.0)
	Iceland	87.3	(0.2)	12.1	(0.2)	0.5	(0.0)	88.5	(0.1)	9.2	(0.1)	2.3	(0.0)	52.5	(0.2)	46.0	(0.2)	1.5	(0.1)	42.6	(0.2)	36.4	(0.3)	21.1	(0.2)
	Ireland	41.9	(3.8)	40.7	(4.1)	17.3	(3.0)	30.5	(3.2)	14.9	(3.1)	54.5	(3.6)	29.7	(3.7)	49.6	(4.0)	20.6	(3.6)	48.0	(4.4)	25.5	(3.5)	26.5	(3.7)
	Israel	19.3	(3.1)	54.3	(3.9)	26.5	(3.6)	51.0	(3.4)	35.1	(3.6)	13.9	(2.6)	45.0	(3.8)	47.5	(4.0)	7.5	(2.1)	19.7	(3.0)	24.0	(3.5)	56.3	(4.2)
	Italy	17.4	(1.7)	39.7	(2.0)	42.9	(2.1)	27.8	(2.0)	46.1	(2.0)	26.1	(1.7)	47.7	(2.5)	41.2	(2.6)	11.1	(1.5)	13.1	(1.3)	21.2	(1.9)	65.7	(2.0)
	Japan	33.4	(3.1)	35.1	(3.1)	31.4	(3.6)	81.6	(2.5)	15.6	(2.2)	2.8	(1.3)	66.5	(3.1)	30.8	(3.2)	2.6	(1.2)	0.9	(0.7)	5.1	(1.8)	94.0	(1.9)
	Korea	37.3	(3.8)	24.5	(3.7)	38.2	(4.1)	57.8	(4.4)	23.6	(3.7)	18.6	(3.4)	55.5	(4.0)	35.5	(4.2)	9.0	(2.5)	23.3	(3.2)	9.3	(2.3)	67.4	(3.6)
	Luxembourg	16.7	(0.1)	66.3	(0.1)	17.0	(0.1)	7.3	(0.1)	42.4	(0.1)	50.4	(0.1)	30.4	(0.1)	68.4	(0.1)	1.2	(0.0)	1.0	(0.0)	26.9	(0.1)	72.2	(0.1)
	Mexico	51.3	(2.0)	37.5	(1.8)	11.2	(1.2)	72.4	(1.7)	19.9	(1.6)	7.6	(0.9)	62.1	(2.5)	31.2	(2.2)	6.7	(1.5)	26.8	(1.8)	22.1	(1.5)	51.1	(1.8)
	Netherlands	13.2	(2.6)	67.5	(3.8)	19.3	(3.2)	62.8	(4.5)	16.3	(3.0)	20.9	(3.6)	52.7	(5.4)	43.3	(5.6)	4.0	(2.0)	0.0	c	2.6	(1.3)	97.4	(1.3)
	New Zealand	30.2	(3.8)	44.7	(4.2)	25.2	(3.5)	29.1	(2.9)	32.6	(4.2)	38.2	(4.0)	34.7	(5.3)	49.3	(4.8)	16.0	(3.8)	28.6	(4.0)	12.9	(2.3)	58.5	(3.8)
	Norway	82.0	(3.1)	15.9	(3.0)	2.1	(1.1)	85.2	(3.0)	11.8	(2.7)	3.0	(1.3)	48.9	(3.5)	45.4	(3.4)	5.7	(1.8)	83.8	(3.0)	9.4	(2.3)	6.7	(2.0)
	Poland	42.4	(3.4)	42.2	(3.6)	15.5	(2.5)	82.2	(2.9)	16.5	(3.0)	1.4	(0.9)	37.3	(4.0)	57.7	(4.2)	5.0	(1.6)	32.8	(3.5)	48.4	(4.2)	18.8	(2.9)
	Portugal	8.8	(2.3)	42.6	(4.9)	48.6	(4.3)	28.3	(4.1)	47.5	(4.3)	24.1	(3.9)	29.6	(4.1)	58.2	(4.4)	12.2	(2.8)	32.1	(4.5)	31.4	(4.1)	36.6	(4.3)
	Slovak Republic	32.5	(3.0)	35.7	(3.4)	31.8	(3.8)	85.1	(2.6)	12.2	(2.6)	2.7	(1.0)	48.4	(3.8)	43.7	(4.1)	8.0	(2.3)	22.4	(2.2)	24.5	(2.9)	53.0	(2.5)
	Slovenia	12.1	(0.8)	27.8	(0.8)	60.0	(0.7)	90.8	(0.8)	8.7	(0.6)	0.5	(0.5)	71.3	(0.6)	27.8	(0.6)	1.0	(0.0)	23.6	(0.9)	47.1	(0.8)	29.3	(0.8)
	Spain	57.8	(2.7)	31.0	(2.7)	11.2	(1.5)	33.6	(2.8)	28.5	(2.9)	37.9	(2.3)	35.9	(3.3)	34.9	(3.4)	29.2	(3.3)	81.3	(2.3)	15.0	(2.1)	3.7	(1.0)
	Sweden	69.3	(3.3)	20.3	(3.0)	10.4	(2.5)	69.2	(3.0)	18.7	(2.7)	12.1	(1.7)	51.5	(3.9)	38.1	(4.0)	10.4	(2.4)	80.1	(2.9)	9.6	(2.5)	10.3	(2.2)
	Switzerland	43.1	(3.6)	39.0	(3.7)	17.9	(2.9)	87.2	(2.1)	11.7	(2.1)	1.1	(0.5)	47.5	(3.1)	44.3	(3.3)	8.2	(2.0)	15.3	(2.0)	11.4	(2.0)	73.3	(2.9)
	Turkey	47.2	(3.4)	39.3	(3.7)	13.5	(2.8)	63.3	(4.0)	27.7	(4.0)	9.0	(2.1)	44.7	(4.8)	46.5	(4.7)	8.7	(2.8)	23.9	(3.3)	32.9	(2.9)	43.2	(3.5)
	United Kingdom	52.8	(3.4)	33.8	(3.1)	13.4	(2.1)	34.1	(3.1)	38.0	(3.0)	27.9	(3.0)	40.6	(4.3)	37.3	(4.2)	22.2	(3.9)	52.5	(3.1)	19.3	(3.3)	28.2	(2.7)
	United States	39.6	(4.2)	43.0	(4.2)	17.3	(3.4)	74.5	(3.2)	20.1	(3.1)	5.4	(1.9)	50.0	(6.3)	40.5	(5.6)	9.5	(3.8)	35.8	(4.1)	28.4	(4.0)	35.7	(3.5)
	OECD average	37.7	(0.5)	39.9	(0.6)	22.4	(0.5)	55.6	(0.5)	26.2	(0.5)	18.2	(0.4)	45.6	(0.6)	45.4	(0.6)	9.0	(0.4)	32.0	(0.5)	24.7	(0.5)	43.2	(0.5)
Partners	Albania	22.4	(3.6)	44.4	(4.1)	33.2	(4.1)	34.9	(4.0)	40.5	(3.5)	24.6	(3.5)	27.5	(4.0)	47.3	(4.2)	25.2	(3.9)	11.8	(2.6)	28.1	(4.1)	60.0	(4.3)
	Argentina	36.4	(4.1)	45.0	(4.1)	18.6	(3.3)	29.1	(3.5)	27.2	(3.5)	43.7	(3.8)	35.1	(4.0)	51.9	(4.3)	13.0	(3.2)	47.1	(3.4)	38.2	(3.7)	14.8	(2.6)
	Brazil	56.1	(2.5)	30.7	(2.4)	13.3	(1.6)	60.3	(2.6)	28.8	(2.4)	10.9	(1.8)	32.1	(3.2)	43.3	(3.2)	24.6	(2.9)	55.2	(2.4)	23.8	(2.3)	20.9	(2.0)
	Bulgaria	23.6	(3.1)	49.3	(3.9)	27.0	(3.6)	55.8	(3.2)	26.9	(3.2)	17.3	(2.2)	52.6	(3.9)	43.7	(4.2)	3.8	(1.2)	4.6	(1.4)	14.2	(2.8)	81.2	(2.9)
	Colombia	49.7	(3.9)	38.6	(3.8)	11.6	(2.7)	41.1	(3.5)	32.0	(3.7)	26.9	(3.8)	39.7	(4.7)	43.9	(5.2)	16.5	(3.2)	21.2	(2.8)	36.1	(3.7)	42.8	(3.9)
	Costa Rica	32.9	(3.4)	36.5	(4.1)	30.6	(3.7)	66.9	(2.8)	22.1	(2.7)	11.0	(2.0)	35.7	(5.4)	31.7	(4.2)	32.6	(4.9)	20.4	(3.0)	28.4	(3.3)	51.2	(3.6)
	Croatia	22.6	(3.2)	52.4	(4.1)	25.0	(3.6)	78.5	(3.6)	20.3	(3.5)	1.2	(0.9)	33.6	(3.9)	62.6	(4.0)	3.8	(1.5)	0.3	(0.3)	3.7	(1.7)	96.0	(1.7)
	Cyprus*	31.5	(0.1)	34.9	(0.1)	33.6	(0.1)	57.3	(0.1)	24.9	(0.1)	17.8	(0.1)	25.7	(0.1)	66.1	(0.1)	8.2	(0.1)	49.9	(0.1)	26.9	(0.1)	23.2	(0.1)
	Hong Kong-China	41.6	(3.8)	50.6	(4.1)	7.8	(2.3)	18.8	(3.3)	63.0	(4.2)	18.3	(3.6)	34.0	(8.6)	15.5	(6.5)	50.5	(9.6)	0.0	c	5.6	(1.5)	94.4	(1.5)
	Indonesia	24.3	(3.7)	26.5	(3.5)	49.2	(3.9)	34.5	(4.1)	37.3	(3.8)	28.2	(3.8)	26.7	(3.5)	54.7	(4.3)	18.5	(3.2)	17.5	(2.9)	15.6	(2.7)	67.0	(3.6)
	Jordan	40.5	(3.0)	41.9	(3.5)	17.6	(3.2)	46.2	(3.6)	29.7	(3.5)	24.1	(3.2)	27.1	(3.6)	50.4	(4.3)	22.5	(3.9)	24.7	(2.8)	39.3	(3.7)	35.9	(3.5)
	Kazakhstan	16.6	(3.1)	51.5	(3.9)	31.9	(3.6)	46.7	(4.5)	38.0	(4.2)	15.3	(3.2)	45.4	(4.5)	45.0	(4.1)	9.6	(2.5)	29.4	(3.8)	25.1	(3.7)	45.5	(4.0)
	Latvia	21.6	(2.8)	41.2	(3.4)	37.2	(3.2)	61.5	(3.8)	24.7	(3.6)	13.8	(2.4)	44.2	(3.9)	52.8	(4.1)	3.0	(1.4)	38.3	(2.9)	32.7	(3.3)	29.0	(2.9)
	Liechtenstein	37.8	(1.1)	46.8	(0.9)	15.3	(0.7)	93.9	(0.4)	6.1	(0.4)	0.0	c	45.8	(0.8)	50.3	(0.7)	3.9	(0.6)	12.8	(1.0)	8.1	(1.0)	79.2	(1.3)
	Lithuania	31.4	(3.3)	33.2	(3.5)	35.4	(3.4)	35.6	(2.9)	26.4	(2.7)	38.0	(3.4)	28.2	(4.2)	60.2	(4.3)	11.6	(2.9)	38.9	(2.9)	41.3	(3.0)	19.8	(2.3)
	Macao-China	20.4	(0.0)	67.9	(0.1)	11.7	(0.0)	4.5	(0.0)	45.1	(0.1)	50.4	(0.1)	14.2	(0.0)	85.8	(0.0)	0.0	c	4.1	(0.0)	18.1	(0.1)	77.8	(0.1)
	Malaysia	26.7	(3.7)	47.6	(4.4)	25.7	(3.5)	50.1	(3.9)	39.4	(3.8)	10.5	(2.4)	33.0	(3.8)	62.4	(4.0)	4.6	(1.7)	17.0	(3.2)	28.5	(3.9)	54.5	(4.4)
	Montenegro	10.2	(0.1)	48.9	(0.1)	40.9	(0.1)	62.0	(0.1)	35.5	(0.1)	2.5	(0.0)	31.2	(0.1)	63.1	(0.1)	5.7	(0.1)	20.5	(0.1)	20.1	(0.1)	59.4	(0.1)
	Peru	40.7	(3.4)	44.0	(3.4)	15.3	(2.7)	43.8	(3.8)	36.6	(3.5)	19.6	(2.6)	51.0	(3.8)	36.1	(4.1)	12.9	(2.3)	44.4	(3.5)	25.3	(3.1)	30.3	(3.3)
	Qatar	30.5	(0.1)	46.2	(0.1)	23.3	(0.1)	27.8	(0.1)	30.1	(0.1)	42.1	(0.1)	21.5	(0.1)	65.0	(0.1)	13.5	(0.1)	27.6	(0.1)	22.0	(0.1)	50.4	(0.1)
	Romania	38.7	(3.8)	45.9	(3.8)	15.4	(2.8)	44.3	(3.7)	47.9	(3.4)	7.8	(2.1)	38.4	(3.6)	52.1	(3.5)	9.5	(2.3)	19.9	(3.3)	45.1	(3.7)	35.0	(3.4)
	Russian Federation	18.3	(2.7)	37.3	(3.6)	44.4	(3.7)	59.3	(3.1)	31.4	(3.2)	9.3	(2.8)	30.5	(3.5)	65.1	(4.1)	4.4	(1.6)	38.6	(2.9)	38.4	(2.7)	23.1	(2.6)
	Serbia	4.7	(1.8)	33.7	(3.9)	61.6	(4.2)	70.2	(3.8)	25.0	(3.6)	4.8	(2.0)	55.6	(4.2)	44.4	(4.2)	0.0	c	3.2	(1.5)	9.6	(2.4)	87.2	(2.6)
	Shanghai-China	15.0	(3.0)	68.2	(3.7)	16.8	(3.0)	60.4	(3.8)	35.8	(3.7)	3.8	(1.6)	36.8	(4.2)	57.0	(4.4)	6.2	(2.2)	11.8	(2.5)	35.6	(3.5)	52.6	(3.1)
	Singapore	20.4	(0.5)	72.3	(0.5)	7.3	(0.1)	46.8	(0.6)	48.3	(0.5)	4.9	(0.6)	39.4	(0.6)	57.1	(0.4)	3.6	(0.5)	1.2	(0.0)	16.8	(0.2)	82.0	(0.2)
	Chinese Taipei	20.1	(3.5)	46.3	(4.2)	33.7	(3.5)	51.7	(3.5)	30.9	(3.7)	17.4	(3.0)	43.7	(4.4)	51.8	(4.3)	4.4	(1.9)	14.8	(2.1)	35.5	(3.4)	49.7	(3.5)
	Thailand	6.8	(1.7)	33.9	(3.6)	59.3	(3.6)	32.1	(3.5)	47.9	(3.8)	20.0	(3.2)	26.2	(4.6)	53.8	(4.7)	20.0	(4.3)	0.9	(0.7)	10.6	(2.1)	88.4	(2.2)
	Tunisia	58.4	(4.1)	35.6	(4.1)	6.1	(2.0)	50.6	(4.6)	39.5	(4.2)	10.0	(2.5)	19.5	(3.8)	76.3	(3.8)	4.2	(1.8)	17.5	(3.1)	31.8	(3.7)	50.7	(4.3)
	United Arab Emirates	29.3	(2.5)	46.0	(2.2)	24.7	(2.1)	21.6	(1.8)	34.8	(2.6)	43.6	(2.6)	28.1	(2.3)	60.9	(2.6)	11.0	(1.5)	6.1	(1.1)	23.8	(2.1)	70.1	(2.1)
	Uruguay	60.1	(3.7)	31.9	(3.6)	8.0	(2.1)	66.5	(2.8)	16.8	(2.6)	16.7	(2.3)	54.1	(4.0)	33.9	(4.0)	12.0	(2.7)	50.4	(3.6)	22.1	(3.3)	27.5	(3.2)
	Viet Nam	47.9	(4.1)	23.8	(3.7)	28.3	(3.8)	64.7	(3.9)	28.2	(3.6)	7.1	(2.1)	28.7	(3.8)	60.9	(4.0)	10.4	(2.5)	1.4	(0.6)	11.7	(2.5)	86.9	(2.5)

* See notes at the beginning of this Annex.
StatLink http://dx.doi.org/10.1787/888932957422

[Part 1/3]
School admissions policies, by level of education
Table IV.2.8   *Results based on school principals' reports*

	Lower secondary education (ISCED 2)														
	Percentage of students in schools whose principal reported that the following factors are "always" considered for admission to school:														Percentage of students in schools whose principals reported that at least either "students' records of academic performance" or "recommendations of feeder schools" is always considered for admission
	Residence in a particular area		Students' academic records		Recommendations of feeder schools		Parents' endorsement of the instructional or religious philosophy of the school		Students' needs or desires for a special programme		Attendance of other family members at the school		Other		
	%	S.E.	%	S.E.	%	S.E.	%	S.E.	%	S.E.	%	S.E.	%	S.E.	%	S.E.
Australia	46.7	(1.7)	33.1	(1.9)	34.0	(2.2)	31.5	(1.4)	22.6	(1.7)	42.3	(2.1)	9.6	(1.2)	45.2	(2.2)
Austria	56.9	(11.2)	29.8	(9.1)	8.0	(7.0)	0.9	(0.9)	38.6	(10.2)	18.7	(8.2)	16.5	(8.6)	31.4	(9.5)
Belgium	10.6	(6.0)	29.0	(5.4)	5.0	(2.8)	40.9	(5.6)	24.3	(7.5)	24.4	(4.9)	20.8	(6.3)	29.2	(5.3)
Canada	58.0	(3.9)	29.0	(3.7)	24.5	(3.9)	9.7	(2.3)	24.1	(3.4)	16.2	(3.2)	15.5	(5.7)	40.1	(4.0)
Chile	18.6	(7.2)	6.1	(2.7)	6.4	(2.9)	7.0	(2.8)	7.2	(5.0)	27.2	(7.4)	9.3	(5.9)	10.4	(3.5)
Czech Republic	23.7	(3.5)	18.7	(2.5)	9.6	(3.4)	16.6	(3.9)	29.5	(5.0)	4.1	(1.8)	4.6	(1.7)	25.0	(3.4)
Denmark	41.0	(3.3)	6.6	(1.7)	11.5	(2.0)	19.4	(2.5)	11.1	(2.2)	10.9	(1.9)	9.9	(2.1)	14.3	(2.2)
Estonia	52.2	(3.0)	36.7	(2.6)	4.0	(1.2)	11.0	(1.8)	25.2	(2.4)	18.8	(2.1)	5.4	(1.3)	38.2	(2.6)
Finland	67.0	(3.4)	2.9	(1.0)	2.7	(0.8)	5.8	(1.5)	2.8	(0.9)	6.1	(1.6)	4.2	(1.3)	3.4	(1.0)
France	72.9	(3.5)	16.7	(3.1)	2.2	(1.5)	14.0	(2.2)	9.2	(3.1)	19.4	(4.6)	7.5	(3.2)	16.7	(3.1)
Germany	48.6	(3.6)	49.2	(3.7)	45.4	(3.9)	9.6	(1.9)	34.9	(3.9)	19.8	(2.9)	5.8	(2.1)	62.2	(3.7)
Greece	68.9	(11.1)	0.0	c	8.4	(6.8)	12.0	(7.6)	3.5	(3.3)	8.1	(4.8)	6.8	(6.2)	8.4	(6.8)
Hungary	70.2	(6.8)	11.5	(6.0)	3.6	(2.1)	31.6	(7.7)	39.6	(8.7)	19.8	(8.0)	9.8	(6.2)	13.2	(6.0)
Iceland	48.1	(0.2)	8.1	(0.2)	19.2	(0.2)	0.1	(0.0)	0.5	(0.0)	2.3	(0.0)	1.5	(0.1)	21.1	(0.2)
Ireland	44.5	(4.0)	21.7	(3.5)	24.5	(3.7)	25.7	(3.4)	16.9	(3.0)	53.9	(3.6)	19.6	(3.5)	26.5	(3.8)
Israel	47.6	(6.3)	25.0	(4.7)	29.7	(5.1)	27.9	(4.7)	14.2	(3.6)	7.9	(2.8)	7.4	(3.9)	36.3	(5.6)
Italy	46.1	(7.5)	67.1	(7.6)	64.5	(7.5)	45.1	(6.8)	34.4	(5.4)	39.6	(6.9)	18.6	(5.0)	74.8	(7.6)
Japan	c	c	c	c	c	c	c	c	c	c	c	c	c	c	c	c
Korea	22.1	(12.0)	21.5	(12.2)	9.5	(3.4)	5.4	(5.3)	11.9	(8.2)	22.4	(11.6)	0.0	c	24.5	(11.2)
Luxembourg	47.2	(0.2)	73.2	(0.1)	10.0	(0.1)	3.6	(0.1)	17.3	(0.1)	50.7	(0.2)	0.9	(0.0)	73.2	(0.1)
Mexico	15.0	(2.3)	27.1	(3.1)	8.6	(1.5)	18.3	(3.1)	8.8	(2.4)	14.7	(2.5)	7.9	(2.7)	30.7	(3.2)
Netherlands	19.1	(3.8)	92.5	(2.3)	92.3	(2.6)	28.2	(4.0)	22.0	(3.4)	18.9	(3.5)	4.6	(2.5)	98.4	(0.9)
New Zealand	45.4	(3.9)	51.6	(4.5)	50.4	(4.5)	24.6	(3.7)	26.0	(4.6)	39.3	(5.0)	22.1	(5.3)	56.8	(4.5)
Norway	63.3	(4.0)	6.7	(2.0)	4.4	(1.6)	1.9	(1.1)	2.1	(1.1)	3.0	(1.3)	5.7	(1.8)	6.7	(2.0)
Poland	76.8	(3.1)	17.0	(2.8)	4.5	(1.6)	3.5	(1.1)	15.2	(2.5)	1.4	(0.9)	5.0	(1.6)	18.4	(2.8)
Portugal	59.1	(5.2)	34.9	(5.2)	3.6	(1.7)	18.7	(3.9)	41.7	(4.5)	19.3	(3.8)	10.8	(2.8)	36.4	(5.2)
Slovak Republic	32.8	(4.8)	7.9	(2.2)	8.9	(2.5)	14.5	(3.7)	17.3	(3.3)	4.3	(1.7)	3.2	(1.6)	13.9	(3.0)
Slovenia	58.9	(14.9)	13.6	(11.5)	5.3	(4.1)	0.0	c	10.5	(11.0)	10.9	(10.4)	0.0	c	18.9	(12.1)
Spain	62.7	(3.0)	0.8	(0.3)	3.2	(1.0)	9.3	(1.1)	11.2	(1.5)	37.9	(2.3)	29.2	(3.3)	3.8	(1.0)
Sweden	51.2	(3.6)	5.7	(1.9)	7.0	(1.9)	3.9	(1.4)	10.5	(2.5)	12.4	(1.8)	10.6	(2.5)	8.9	(2.2)
Switzerland	59.0	(3.5)	60.3	(3.6)	56.0	(3.5)	2.9	(1.1)	16.0	(2.9)	1.4	(0.6)	6.5	(1.8)	72.7	(2.7)
Turkey	c	c	c	c	c	c	c	c	c	c	c	c	c	c	c	c
United Kingdom	c	c	c	c	c	c	c	c	c	c	c	c	c	c	c	c
United States	79.1	(4.8)	30.0	(5.9)	19.5	(5.2)	4.6	(1.8)	17.3	(4.3)	6.0	(3.0)	1.9	(1.1)	31.4	(6.0)
OECD average	48.8	(1.1)	26.9	(0.9)	18.9	(0.6)	14.5	(0.7)	18.3	(0.9)	18.8	(0.8)	9.1	(0.7)	32.0	(0.9)
Albania	31.6	(5.8)	43.8	(5.2)	47.3	(5.9)	24.1	(5.5)	22.8	(4.7)	18.5	(4.8)	24.7	(6.0)	63.1	(5.9)
Argentina	30.8	(5.1)	5.1	(1.8)	3.6	(1.4)	19.7	(4.2)	16.5	(3.5)	32.7	(4.7)	15.5	(4.3)	7.9	(2.2)
Brazil	44.5	(3.7)	19.4	(3.0)	8.3	(1.6)	13.4	(2.9)	11.9	(2.4)	8.8	(1.5)	23.1	(4.0)	23.5	(3.0)
Bulgaria	51.6	(12.4)	24.6	(7.4)	12.6	(5.7)	21.5	(5.8)	26.5	(10.0)	28.5	(8.9)	3.8	(3.9)	31.6	(8.7)
Colombia	24.0	(3.0)	35.8	(3.6)	17.2	(2.9)	20.2	(2.9)	9.8	(2.4)	22.4	(3.5)	17.6	(3.7)	42.0	(4.0)
Costa Rica	55.9	(3.8)	42.6	(3.5)	15.1	(2.5)	22.8	(2.8)	26.5	(3.4)	10.9	(2.3)	30.8	(4.4)	47.2	(3.7)
Croatia	c	c	c	c	c	c	c	c	c	c	c	c	c	c	c	c
Cyprus*	81.9	(0.8)	16.2	(1.2)	17.5	(1.0)	9.1	(0.7)	11.5	(0.7)	14.2	(1.1)	10.6	(1.0)	26.7	(1.1)
Hong Kong-China	16.0	(3.2)	90.7	(2.4)	28.7	(3.7)	29.0	(3.5)	7.7	(2.4)	18.5	(3.3)	51.5	(9.8)	93.3	(1.9)
Indonesia	45.1	(5.6)	48.7	(4.8)	46.8	(4.8)	47.8	(5.2)	35.2	(5.4)	25.5	(4.5)	10.3	(3.7)	67.4	(4.7)
Jordan	63.3	(3.3)	26.8	(3.1)	18.9	(2.8)	22.1	(2.6)	17.6	(3.2)	24.1	(3.2)	22.5	(3.9)	35.9	(3.5)
Kazakhstan	40.3	(4.2)	35.3	(4.3)	24.0	(3.6)	15.9	(3.4)	31.7	(3.9)	15.3	(3.3)	9.8	(2.6)	40.2	(4.2)
Latvia	20.5	(2.9)	26.9	(2.7)	4.1	(1.4)	2.6	(1.3)	37.6	(3.2)	13.8	(2.4)	3.1	(1.4)	28.4	(2.8)
Liechtenstein	64.3	(0.6)	69.2	(1.4)	70.3	(1.2)	6.9	(1.1)	17.4	(0.8)	0.0	c	4.4	(0.7)	76.4	(1.4)
Lithuania	60.9	(3.2)	19.1	(2.2)	4.1	(1.4)	23.0	(2.9)	35.4	(3.4)	38.0	(3.4)	11.6	(2.9)	19.8	(2.3)
Macao-China	5.8	(0.1)	64.2	(0.1)	43.6	(0.2)	9.3	(0.1)	11.4	(0.1)	47.1	(0.2)	0.0	c	72.8	(0.1)
Malaysia	30.1	(6.6)	36.4	(8.2)	22.1	(7.2)	17.4	(5.8)	17.5	(5.9)	6.7	(3.6)	3.1	(3.1)	47.9	(9.7)
Montenegro	c	c	c	c	c	c	c	c	c	c	c	c	c	c	c	c
Peru	6.5	(1.8)	18.0	(3.1)	9.6	(2.2)	10.2	(2.2)	12.8	(2.7)	15.2	(2.5)	12.3	(2.4)	23.1	(3.0)
Qatar	45.6	(0.3)	57.1	(0.3)	24.8	(0.3)	34.2	(0.3)	19.8	(0.2)	31.1	(0.3)	4.6	(0.2)	58.2	(0.3)
Romania	9.6	(2.3)	30.6	(3.3)	5.7	(1.8)	10.5	(2.2)	15.4	(2.8)	7.8	(2.1)	9.5	(2.3)	35.0	(3.4)
Russian Federation	50.1	(4.3)	11.2	(2.0)	9.2	(1.8)	37.8	(3.9)	43.6	(4.1)	9.3	(2.8)	4.3	(1.7)	18.8	(2.4)
Serbia	c	c	c	c	c	c	c	c	c	c	c	c	c	c	c	c
Shanghai-China	49.7	(5.7)	17.4	(4.2)	14.6	(3.5)	39.6	(5.4)	15.5	(4.6)	3.9	(2.3)	4.2	(2.3)	24.9	(4.4)
Singapore	8.8	(2.0)	81.0	(2.6)	11.7	(2.3)	3.0	(1.0)	3.7	(1.5)	4.6	(1.1)	2.2	(0.6)	81.0	(2.6)
Chinese Taipei	47.7	(6.6)	21.7	(4.7)	13.3	(5.1)	24.3	(6.0)	11.5	(4.0)	11.5	(4.0)	4.4	(2.8)	27.7	(5.8)
Thailand	45.8	(5.1)	78.0	(4.5)	73.5	(4.4)	50.1	(5.0)	47.8	(5.1)	14.9	(3.8)	15.4	(4.8)	88.9	(2.9)
Tunisia	48.9	(5.5)	48.6	(6.6)	12.6	(3.6)	2.6	(1.8)	4.9	(2.9)	9.9	(3.1)	1.8	(1.8)	52.5	(6.5)
United Arab Emirates	42.6	(3.9)	66.7	(4.4)	31.0	(3.4)	36.5	(5.0)	23.9	(4.2)	42.0	(4.8)	16.9	(4.8)	69.8	(3.5)
Uruguay	33.2	(4.0)	15.9	(3.0)	6.9	(2.1)	8.3	(2.3)	7.5	(2.5)	12.2	(3.4)	8.5	(2.8)	18.2	(3.5)
Viet Nam	48.1	(10.7)	57.5	(11.2)	11.5	(6.8)	38.6	(11.9)	19.7	(8.9)	12.0	(8.1)	14.1	(9.0)	57.5	(11.2)

Note: Values that are statistically significant are indicated in bold (see Annex A3).
* See notes at the beginning of this Annex.
StatLink http://dx.doi.org/10.1787/888932957422

[Part 2/3]
School admissions policies, by level of education
Table IV.2.8 *Results based on school principals' reports*

	Upper secondary education (ISCED 3)														
	Percentage of students in schools whose principal reported that the following factors are "always" considered for admission to school:														Percentage of students in schools whose principals reported that at least either "students' records of academic performance" or "recommendations of feeder schools" is always considered for admission
	Residence in a particular area		Students' academic records		Recommendations of feeder schools		Parents' endorsement of the instructional or religious philosophy of the school		Students' needs or desires for a special programme		Attendance of other family members at the school		Other		
	%	S.E.	%	S.E.	%	S.E.	%	S.E.	%	S.E.	%	S.E.	%	S.E.	%	S.E.
Australia	36.6	(2.6)	31.6	(2.6)	28.4	(2.7)	29.3	(2.9)	26.3	(2.7)	41.0	(2.7)	11.9	(2.1)	40.6	(2.8)
Austria	27.1	(3.3)	72.4	(2.1)	7.7	(2.0)	4.3	(1.9)	34.7	(3.6)	19.9	(3.1)	9.5	(2.4)	73.1	(2.1)
Belgium	0.4	(0.3)	25.3	(2.8)	6.0	(1.6)	40.9	(3.1)	8.0	(1.7)	27.0	(3.3)	6.3	(1.9)	26.8	(2.9)
Canada	71.3	(1.9)	26.2	(2.0)	30.8	(2.7)	12.7	(1.8)	25.7	(2.5)	14.4	(1.8)	12.6	(2.8)	38.8	(2.5)
Chile	11.4	(2.5)	35.9	(3.8)	14.3	(3.1)	26.7	(3.0)	17.9	(2.8)	43.5	(3.8)	7.4	(2.1)	40.6	(3.9)
Czech Republic	2.3	(1.6)	97.5	(1.4)	13.2	(3.7)	16.4	(3.9)	24.6	(4.5)	2.8	(1.9)	4.6	(1.8)	97.5	(1.4)
Denmark	c	c	c	c	c	c	c	c	c	c	c	c	c	c	c	c
Estonia	29.2	(7.5)	53.9	(9.7)	6.4	(4.8)	10.2	(3.4)	28.6	(8.2)	13.1	(5.3)	13.9	(7.4)	53.9	(9.7)
Finland	c	c	c	c	c	c	c	c	c	c	c	c	c	c	c	c
France	55.5	(3.5)	36.2	(3.9)	8.2	(2.3)	14.0	(2.3)	13.2	(3.1)	12.7	(2.9)	8.9	(2.6)	37.3	(3.8)
Germany	60.4	(16.0)	39.4	(16.2)	7.1	(4.3)	4.5	(3.1)	22.7	(11.3)	7.0	(4.5)	0.0	c	40.3	(16.3)
Greece	71.6	(4.2)	4.7	(1.8)	6.4	(2.1)	4.7	(1.5)	14.8	(2.9)	21.9	(3.4)	6.7	(2.2)	7.8	(2.3)
Hungary	13.4	(2.8)	92.1	(2.2)	10.4	(2.9)	21.7	(3.1)	53.1	(4.5)	19.1	(3.3)	12.6	(2.2)	94.1	(1.9)
Iceland	c	c	c	c	c	c	c	c	c	c	c	c	c	c	c	c
Ireland	44.2	(4.2)	21.5	(3.5)	24.4	(3.7)	25.4	(3.7)	18.0	(3.2)	55.5	(4.0)	22.3	(3.9)	26.5	(3.8)
Israel	37.4	(3.7)	45.2	(4.3)	44.0	(4.3)	43.1	(3.3)	28.3	(3.8)	14.8	(2.7)	7.5	(2.2)	59.3	(4.4)
Italy	26.6	(1.9)	56.2	(2.1)	48.5	(2.1)	39.7	(2.2)	43.1	(2.1)	25.8	(1.7)	11.0	(1.5)	65.5	(2.0)
Japan	9.5	(1.9)	93.1	(1.9)	30.0	(3.4)	10.7	(1.9)	31.4	(3.6)	2.8	(1.3)	2.6	(1.2)	94.0	(1.9)
Korea	17.6	(3.5)	69.5	(3.9)	18.4	(3.7)	15.0	(3.0)	39.8	(4.3)	18.3	(3.5)	9.6	(2.7)	70.2	(3.8)
Luxembourg	38.3	(0.1)	70.6	(0.1)	8.9	(0.1)	4.7	(0.1)	16.6	(0.2)	49.8	(0.2)	1.7	(0.0)	70.6	(0.1)
Mexico	5.8	(1.1)	59.9	(2.2)	13.5	(1.3)	12.3	(1.5)	12.7	(1.4)	3.5	(0.9)	6.0	(1.9)	63.1	(2.3)
Netherlands	27.3	(6.1)	90.6	(4.1)	93.5	(3.4)	31.1	(5.5)	12.7	(5.2)	26.1	(5.7)	2.3	(2.2)	94.9	(3.1)
New Zealand	50.2	(3.0)	51.4	(3.9)	50.4	(3.9)	24.0	(3.1)	25.1	(3.5)	38.2	(4.0)	15.6	(3.7)	58.6	(3.8)
Norway	c	c	c	c	c	c	c	c	c	c	c	c	c	c	c	c
Poland	c	c	c	c	c	c	c	c	c	c	c	c	c	c	c	c
Portugal	51.4	(5.6)	36.6	(5.2)	2.0	(1.1)	37.1	(4.7)	54.2	(5.6)	28.1	(5.2)	13.3	(3.5)	36.6	(5.2)
Slovak Republic	3.9	(2.8)	83.4	(3.1)	18.3	(4.5)	25.5	(5.6)	43.2	(5.9)	1.4	(0.8)	11.6	(3.7)	84.0	(3.4)
Slovenia	1.3	(0.1)	27.5	(0.4)	4.4	(0.1)	2.5	(0.1)	62.5	(0.3)	0.0	c	1.0	(0.1)	29.8	(0.4)
Spain	c	c	c	c	c	c	c	c	c	c	c	c	c	c	c	c
Sweden	0.0	c	70.9	(9.5)	0.0	c	0.0	c	9.7	(4.9)	0.0	c	0.0	c	70.9	(9.5)
Switzerland	48.7	(7.7)	74.3	(7.8)	15.4	(4.7)	4.1	(2.7)	24.4	(6.2)	0.0	c	14.0	(6.0)	75.4	(7.7)
Turkey	32.1	(3.5)	42.7	(3.4)	5.4	(1.8)	19.1	(2.9)	13.8	(2.9)	9.1	(2.1)	8.9	(2.9)	44.1	(3.6)
United Kingdom	48.4	(3.2)	23.0	(2.2)	20.3	(2.4)	12.4	(2.2)	13.4	(2.1)	27.9	(3.0)	22.2	(3.9)	28.2	(2.7)
United States	73.8	(3.7)	34.7	(3.4)	21.3	(3.3)	7.0	(2.1)	17.3	(3.4)	5.3	(2.0)	10.6	(4.1)	36.4	(3.4)
OECD average	32.0	(0.9)	52.4	(1.0)	19.9	(0.6)	17.8	(0.6)	26.3	(0.8)	18.9	(0.6)	9.1	(0.6)	55.7	(1.0)
Albania	43.1	(5.3)	48.5	(5.1)	33.2	(4.3)	30.6	(4.8)	40.7	(5.5)	29.0	(4.8)	25.5	(5.3)	57.8	(5.3)
Argentina	20.0	(2.6)	12.9	(3.2)	8.5	(2.1)	28.6	(4.2)	19.8	(3.7)	49.8	(4.3)	11.5	(3.8)	18.6	(3.3)
Brazil	37.4	(2.5)	16.7	(1.9)	6.7	(1.5)	18.8	(2.1)	13.6	(1.8)	11.4	(2.0)	24.9	(3.0)	20.3	(2.1)
Bulgaria	16.1	(2.3)	82.7	(2.8)	16.6	(2.9)	45.9	(4.0)	27.1	(3.7)	16.8	(2.2)	3.8	(1.2)	83.5	(2.8)
Colombia	25.9	(3.7)	39.2	(4.2)	16.3	(3.3)	25.9	(3.8)	12.8	(3.1)	29.8	(4.4)	15.7	(3.3)	43.2	(4.3)
Costa Rica	48.5	(5.0)	52.4	(4.9)	15.8	(2.7)	35.0	(4.3)	36.9	(5.3)	11.2	(1.7)	35.4	(7.4)	57.4	(4.6)
Croatia	6.6	(1.3)	95.6	(1.8)	7.2	(1.8)	17.8	(3.2)	25.0	(3.6)	1.2	(0.9)	3.8	(1.5)	96.0	(1.7)
Cyprus*	67.1	(0.1)	17.8	(0.1)	7.6	(0.0)	14.1	(0.1)	34.8	(0.1)	18.0	(0.1)	8.1	(0.1)	23.1	(0.1)
Hong Kong-China	14.2	(2.9)	92.7	(1.9)	28.7	(3.9)	31.1	(4.1)	7.8	(2.3)	18.1	(3.9)	49.9	(9.7)	95.0	(1.3)
Indonesia	38.9	(5.6)	62.6	(4.7)	28.2	(5.5)	30.0	(6.1)	62.1	(5.1)	30.6	(5.6)	25.7	(4.7)	66.6	(4.9)
Jordan	c	c	c	c	c	c	c	c	c	c	c	c	c	c	c	c
Kazakhstan	31.5	(4.5)	46.6	(5.8)	25.1	(4.5)	17.9	(4.1)	32.2	(5.2)	15.3	(4.5)	9.2	(3.1)	54.7	(5.3)
Latvia	20.7	(5.9)	43.5	(10.6)	2.8	(1.6)	0.6	(0.5)	27.0	(7.4)	13.5	(5.0)	1.1	(1.1)	44.7	(10.6)
Liechtenstein	c	c	c	c	c	c	c	c	c	c	c	c	c	c	c	c
Lithuania	c	c	c	c	c	c	c	c	c	c	c	c	c	c	c	c
Macao-China	6.3	(0.1)	74.3	(0.1)	46.9	(0.1)	11.5	(0.1)	11.9	(0.1)	54.3	(0.1)	0.0	(0.1)	83.9	(0.1)
Malaysia	31.2	(3.7)	46.1	(4.3)	26.6	(3.6)	27.2	(3.5)	26.1	(3.5)	10.7	(2.4)	4.7	(1.7)	54.8	(4.4)
Montenegro	7.5	(0.1)	52.4	(0.1)	27.9	(0.1)	16.3	(0.1)	40.9	(0.1)	2.5	(0.0)	5.7	(0.1)	59.4	(0.1)
Peru	6.6	(1.8)	29.3	(4.1)	7.0	(1.9)	18.4	(3.0)	16.3	(3.1)	21.5	(3.0)	13.2	(2.6)	33.2	(4.0)
Qatar	49.0	(0.1)	44.8	(0.1)	23.9	(0.2)	34.0	(0.1)	24.0	(0.1)	44.3	(0.1)	15.3	(0.1)	48.7	(0.1)
Romania	c	c	c	c	c	c	c	c	c	c	c	c	c	c	c	c
Russian Federation	29.8	(4.4)	32.5	(5.2)	16.7	(3.6)	43.7	(6.2)	48.1	(4.4)	9.2	(3.6)	5.2	(2.0)	43.3	(5.4)
Serbia	3.2	(1.5)	85.8	(2.4)	13.1	(3.2)	15.5	(3.3)	61.5	(4.2)	4.8	(2.0)	0.0	c	87.2	(2.6)
Shanghai-China	13.7	(4.0)	69.5	(4.2)	16.4	(3.6)	45.2	(5.8)	17.9	(3.6)	3.8	(2.1)	7.8	(3.0)	74.4	(3.9)
Singapore	7.7	(0.6)	79.2	(0.6)	15.9	(0.7)	4.9	(0.1)	7.4	(0.1)	4.9	(0.6)	3.6	(0.5)	82.1	(0.2)
Chinese Taipei	15.8	(3.2)	59.2	(3.7)	13.8	(2.7)	31.9	(4.5)	46.5	(4.8)	20.8	(3.7)	4.4	(2.2)	62.5	(3.8)
Thailand	41.8	(3.9)	81.9	(2.5)	70.4	(3.5)	55.5	(4.1)	64.2	(3.9)	21.4	(3.6)	21.3	(4.7)	88.3	(2.4)
Tunisia	59.3	(5.0)	39.8	(5.4)	29.4	(5.3)	2.3	(1.3)	6.8	(2.6)	10.0	(3.5)	5.6	(2.6)	49.5	(5.7)
United Arab Emirates	40.6	(2.4)	66.1	(2.2)	33.9	(2.5)	39.4	(2.8)	24.9	(2.2)	43.9	(2.8)	9.9	(1.3)	70.1	(2.3)
Uruguay	22.3	(2.7)	32.9	(4.0)	8.1	(1.8)	24.2	(3.4)	8.3	(2.6)	19.9	(3.2)	14.6	(3.7)	34.0	(4.2)
Viet Nam	40.5	(4.3)	89.6	(2.8)	38.6	(4.3)	56.5	(4.5)	29.3	(4.1)	6.5	(2.2)	9.9	(2.5)	90.3	(2.7)

Note: Values that are statistically significant are indicated in bold (see Annex A3).
* See notes at the beginning of this Annex.
StatLink ᴍᴤᴸ http://dx.doi.org/10.1787/888932957422

[Part 3/3]

Table IV.2.8 **School admissions policies, by level of education**
Results based on school principals' reports

		Difference between upper and lower secondary education (ISCED 3 - ISCED 2)															
		Percentage of students in schools whose principal reported that the following factors are "always" considered for admission to school:														Percentage of students in schools whose principals reported that at least either "students' records of academic performance" or "recommendations of feeder schools" is always considered for admission	
		Residence in a particular area		Students' academic records		Recommendations of feeder schools		Parents' endorsement of the instructional or religious philosophy of the school		Students' needs or desires for a special programme		Attendance of other family members at the school		Other			
		% dif.	S.E.	% dif.	S.E.	% dif.	S.E.	% dif.	S.E.	% dif.	S.E.	% dif.	S.E.	% dif.	S.E.	% dif.	S.E.
OECD	Australia	**-10.1**	(2.8)	-1.5	(2.5)	**-5.6**	(2.5)	-2.1	(2.7)	3.8	(2.4)	-1.3	(2.7)	2.4	(2.0)	-4.6	(2.6)
	Austria	**-29.8**	(11.5)	**42.6**	(9.3)	-0.3	(7.2)	**3.4**	(1.7)	-4.0	(10.9)	1.2	(8.7)	-7.0	(8.8)	**41.7**	(9.7)
	Belgium	-10.2	(6.0)	-3.6	(5.2)	1.1	(2.9)	0.0	(5.5)	**-16.2**	(7.4)	2.7	(4.2)	**-14.5**	(6.4)	-2.4	(5.4)
	Canada	**13.3**	(3.8)	-2.7	(4.0)	6.3	(4.2)	3.0	(2.5)	1.6	(3.7)	-1.8	(3.2)	-2.9	(6.0)	-1.3	(4.4)
	Chile	-7.2	(7.3)	**29.8**	(4.0)	**7.9**	(4.0)	**19.6**	(3.5)	10.7	(5.6)	**16.3**	(7.5)	-1.9	(6.0)	**30.2**	(4.5)
	Czech Republic	**-21.4**	(3.8)	**78.8**	(3.0)	3.6	(4.7)	-0.3	(5.1)	-4.8	(6.7)	-1.3	(2.6)	0.0	(2.4)	**72.5**	(3.8)
	Denmark	c	c	c	c	c	c	c	c	c	c	c	c	c	c	c	c
	Estonia	**-23.0**	(6.6)	17.2	(9.1)	2.4	(4.2)	-0.8	(3.1)	3.4	(7.5)	-5.7	(4.7)	8.5	(6.7)	15.7	(9.1)
	Finland	c	c	c	c	c	c	c	c	c	c	c	c	c	c	c	c
	France	**-17.4**	(5.0)	**19.5**	(4.8)	**6.0**	(2.9)	0.0	(3.0)	4.0	(4.0)	-6.7	(5.6)	1.4	(4.2)	**20.6**	(4.7)
	Germany	11.8	(16.4)	-9.8	(16.3)	**-38.3**	(5.7)	-5.1	(3.6)	-12.3	(12.1)	**-12.8**	(4.8)	**-5.8**	(2.1)	-21.9	(16.3)
	Greece	2.7	(11.9)	**4.7**	(1.8)	-1.9	(7.1)	-7.3	(7.7)	**11.4**	(4.4)	**13.8**	(5.8)	-0.1	(6.5)	-0.6	(7.1)
	Hungary	**-56.8**	(7.2)	**80.6**	(6.1)	6.8	(3.5)	-9.9	(7.8)	13.5	(10.0)	-0.6	(8.7)	2.8	(6.5)	**80.8**	(6.1)
	Iceland	c	c	c	c	c	c	c	c	c	c	c	c	c	c	c	c
	Ireland	-0.3	(1.8)	-0.2	(1.5)	0.0	(1.6)	-0.3	(1.8)	1.1	(1.6)	1.6	(1.8)	2.7	(1.6)	0.0	(1.6)
	Israel	-10.2	(5.3)	**20.3**	(4.6)	**14.3**	(5.2)	**15.3**	(4.7)	**14.1**	(3.6)	**6.9**	(2.5)	0.2	(3.9)	**22.9**	(5.5)
	Italy	**-19.5**	(7.9)	-10.8	(7.9)	**-16.0**	(7.5)	-5.4	(7.1)	8.7	(5.7)	-13.8	(7.4)	-7.6	(5.2)	-9.3	(7.8)
	Japan	c	c	c	c	c	c	c	c	c	c	c	c	c	c	c	c
	Korea	-4.6	(12.5)	**47.9**	(12.8)	9.0	(5.0)	9.5	(6.0)	**28.0**	(9.2)	-4.0	(12.1)	**9.6**	(2.7)	**45.7**	(11.9)
	Luxembourg	**-9.0**	(0.2)	**-2.6**	(0.2)	**-1.1**	(0.2)	**1.2**	(0.2)	**-0.7**	(0.2)	**-0.9**	(0.3)	**0.8**	(0.0)	**-2.6**	(0.2)
	Mexico	**-9.2**	(2.6)	**32.8**	(3.9)	**4.9**	(1.8)	-6.0	(3.5)	3.9	(3.0)	**-11.2**	(2.9)	-1.9	(3.3)	**32.4**	(4.0)
	Netherlands	8.3	(5.9)	-1.9	(4.2)	1.2	(3.9)	2.9	(5.5)	-9.3	(5.3)	7.2	(5.1)	-2.3	(3.1)	-3.5	(3.0)
	New Zealand	4.8	(3.0)	-0.2	(3.1)	0.0	(3.1)	-0.6	(2.3)	-0.9	(2.4)	-1.1	(2.6)	**-6.5**	(3.0)	1.8	(3.1)
	Norway	c	c	c	c	c	c	c	c	c	c	c	c	c	c	c	c
	Poland	c	c	c	c	c	c	c	c	c	c	c	c	c	c	c	c
	Portugal	-7.7	(5.8)	1.7	(5.8)	-1.6	(1.5)	**18.4**	(4.6)	**12.5**	(5.4)	8.8	(5.1)	2.6	(3.2)	0.2	(5.7)
	Slovak Republic	**-28.8**	(5.6)	**75.5**	(3.2)	**9.4**	(4.6)	11.0	(6.0)	**25.9**	(6.4)	-2.9	(1.7)	**8.4**	(3.9)	**70.2**	(4.1)
	Slovenia	**-57.6**	(15.0)	13.9	(11.5)	-0.8	(4.1)	**2.5**	(0.1)	**52.0**	(11.0)	-10.9	(10.4)	**1.0**	(0.1)	10.9	(12.1)
	Spain	c	c	c	c	c	c	c	c	c	c	c	c	c	c	c	c
	Sweden	**-51.2**	(3.6)	**65.3**	(9.7)	**-7.0**	(1.9)	**-3.9**	(1.4)	-0.8	(5.5)	**-12.4**	(1.8)	**-10.6**	(2.5)	**62.0**	(9.7)
	Switzerland	-10.3	(8.3)	14.0	(8.2)	**-40.6**	(5.6)	1.2	(2.8)	8.4	(6.3)	**-1.4**	(0.6)	7.5	(6.3)	2.8	(7.9)
	Turkey	c	c	c	c	c	c	c	c	c	c	c	c	c	c	c	c
	United Kingdom	c	c	c	c	c	c	c	c	c	c	c	c	c	c	c	c
	United States	-5.3	(4.0)	4.8	(4.7)	1.8	(3.8)	2.4	(1.3)	0.0	(3.5)	-0.7	(2.9)	**8.6**	(3.3)	4.9	(4.7)
	OECD average	**-13.9**	(1.5)	**20.6**	(1.4)	-1.5	(0.9)	**1.9**	(0.9)	**6.2**	(1.3)	-1.3	(1.1)	-0.2	(0.9)	**18.8**	(1.4)
Partners	Albania	11.4	(7.5)	4.7	(6.6)	**-14.1**	(6.9)	6.5	(7.1)	**17.9**	(6.3)	10.5	(6.5)	0.8	(8.1)	-5.3	(7.1)
	Argentina	**-10.8**	(4.4)	**7.9**	(2.7)	**4.9**	(2.4)	**8.9**	(4.0)	3.3	(3.3)	**17.0**	(5.3)	-4.0	(4.9)	**10.7**	(3.2)
	Brazil	-7.1	(3.9)	-2.7	(2.9)	-1.5	(1.7)	5.4	(3.2)	1.8	(2.6)	2.6	(2.1)	1.8	(3.5)	-3.2	(3.0)
	Bulgaria	**-35.4**	(12.5)	**58.0**	(7.1)	4.0	(6.2)	**24.4**	(6.4)	0.6	(10.0)	-11.7	(8.9)	-0.1	(4.1)	**51.9**	(8.4)
	Colombia	1.9	(2.8)	3.4	(3.3)	-0.8	(2.7)	**5.7**	(2.8)	3.0	(1.7)	**7.4**	(3.1)	-1.9	(2.7)	1.3	(3.4)
	Costa Rica	-7.4	(4.2)	**9.9**	(4.0)	0.6	(2.4)	**12.2**	(3.9)	**10.3**	(4.5)	0.3	(1.6)	4.6	(6.6)	**10.3**	(4.0)
	Croatia	c	c	c	c	c	c	c	c	c	c	c	c	c	c	c	c
	Cyprus*	**-14.9**	(0.9)	1.6	(1.2)	**-9.9**	(1.1)	**5.0**	(0.7)	**23.3**	(0.7)	**3.8**	(1.1)	**-2.5**	(1.0)	**-3.6**	(1.1)
	Hong Kong-China	-1.8	(1.4)	2.0	(1.4)	0.0	(1.8)	2.1	(2.8)	0.1	(0.7)	-0.4	(2.1)	-1.6	(4.2)	1.7	(1.1)
	Indonesia	-6.2	(8.3)	**13.9**	(6.9)	**-18.6**	(7.2)	**-17.8**	(8.1)	**26.9**	(7.5)	5.2	(7.0)	**15.4**	(5.8)	-0.8	(6.5)
	Jordan	c	c	c	c	c	c	c	c	c	c	c	c	c	c	c	c
	Kazakhstan	**-8.8**	(4.3)	**11.3**	(5.4)	1.1	(4.0)	1.9	(4.0)	0.5	(5.3)	-0.1	(4.0)	-0.6	(2.6)	**12.7**	(5.1)
	Latvia	0.2	(6.1)	16.6	(10.3)	-1.3	(1.2)	-2.0	(1.2)	-10.6	(6.8)	-0.3	(4.4)	-2.0	(1.4)	16.3	(10.2)
	Liechtenstein	c	c	c	c	c	c	c	c	c	c	c	c	c	c	c	c
	Lithuania	c	c	c	c	c	c	c	c	c	c	c	c	c	c	c	c
	Macao-China	**0.5**	(0.2)	**10.1**	(0.2)	**3.3**	(0.2)	**2.2**	(0.1)	**0.5**	(0.1)	**7.2**	(0.2)	0.0	c	**11.2**	(0.2)
	Malaysia	1.0	(6.3)	9.7	(7.3)	4.5	(6.3)	9.7	(5.4)	8.6	(5.5)	4.0	(3.3)	1.6	(2.7)	7.0	(8.5)
	Montenegro	c	c	c	c	c	c	c	c	c	c	c	c	c	c	c	c
	Peru	0.1	(1.3)	**11.4**	(4.0)	-2.6	(2.0)	**8.2**	(2.4)	3.5	(2.5)	**6.3**	(2.5)	0.9	(2.3)	**10.1**	(4.1)
	Qatar	**3.4**	(0.3)	**-12.3**	(0.3)	**-0.9**	(0.3)	-0.2	(0.3)	**4.2**	(0.2)	**13.2**	(0.3)	**10.7**	(0.2)	**-9.6**	(0.3)
	Romania	c	c	c	c	c	c	c	c	c	c	c	c	c	c	c	c
	Russian Federation	**-20.3**	(3.7)	**21.3**	(4.5)	**7.5**	(3.7)	6.0	(4.6)	4.5	(4.5)	-0.2	(2.1)	0.9	(1.6)	**24.5**	(5.0)
	Serbia	c	c	c	c	c	c	c	c	c	c	c	c	c	c	c	c
	Shanghai-China	**-36.0**	(6.7)	**52.1**	(5.3)	1.8	(4.7)	5.6	(7.6)	2.4	(5.6)	-0.1	(3.0)	3.5	(3.2)	**49.5**	(5.4)
	Singapore	-1.1	(2.3)	-1.8	(2.7)	4.2	(2.5)	1.9	(1.0)	**3.7**	(1.5)	0.3	(1.3)	1.4	(0.8)	1.1	(2.6)
	Chinese Taipei	**-31.9**	(7.2)	**37.5**	(5.3)	0.5	(5.7)	7.6	(7.2)	**35.0**	(5.9)	9.3	(4.9)	0.0	(3.2)	**34.9**	(6.4)
	Thailand	-4.0	(5.3)	3.9	(4.5)	-3.1	(4.1)	5.4	(4.9)	**14.7**	(5.2)	6.5	(4.1)	5.8	(4.7)	-0.6	(2.8)
	Tunisia	10.4	(7.5)	-8.8	(8.5)	**16.8**	(6.0)	-0.3	(1.8)	1.9	(3.9)	0.1	(4.7)	3.8	(3.2)	-3.0	(8.7)
	United Arab Emirates	-2.0	(4.6)	-0.6	(4.7)	2.9	(3.7)	3.0	(5.2)	1.0	(4.3)	1.9	(4.9)	-7.0	(4.7)	0.3	(4.0)
	Uruguay	**-10.9**	(4.0)	**17.0**	(4.2)	1.2	(2.3)	**15.9**	(4.0)	0.9	(3.0)	7.7	(4.7)	6.1	(3.9)	**15.7**	(4.6)
	Viet Nam	-7.7	(11.4)	**32.0**	(12.0)	**27.1**	(8.2)	17.9	(13.2)	9.6	(9.7)	-5.5	(8.6)	-4.2	(9.1)	**32.8**	(12.0)

Note: Values that are statistically significant are indicated in bold (see Annex A3).
* See notes at the beginning of this Annex.
StatLink http://dx.doi.org/10.1787/888932957422

[Part 1/2]
Table IV.2.9 School transfer policies
Results based on school principals' reports

Percentage of students in schools whose principal reported that a student in the national modal grade for 15-year-olds would be transferred to another school for the following reasons:

		Low academic achievement						High academic achievement						Behavioural problems						Special learning needs					
		Not likely		Likely		Very likely		Not likely		Likely		Very likely		Not likely		Likely		Very likely		Not likely		Likely		Very likely	
		%	S.E.	%	S.E.	%	S.E.	%	S.E.	%	S.E.	%	S.E.	%	S.E.	%	S.E.	%	S.E.	%	S.E.	%	S.E.	%	S.E.
OECD	Australia	96.1	(0.7)	3.3	(0.7)	0.6	(0.3)	92.6	(1.2)	5.5	(1.0)	1.9	(0.6)	74.8	(1.7)	23.0	(1.6)	2.2	(0.6)	90.3	(1.2)	8.8	(1.1)	0.9	(0.4)
	Austria	17.6	(2.9)	22.1	(3.7)	60.3	(3.9)	95.0	(1.8)	4.6	(1.8)	0.4	(0.6)	45.6	(4.8)	47.2	(4.6)	7.2	(2.0)	57.9	(4.1)	36.1	(3.9)	6.0	(1.9)
	Belgium	45.1	(2.9)	38.2	(3.2)	16.7	(2.3)	92.5	(1.5)	5.9	(1.3)	1.6	(0.7)	36.6	(2.9)	50.1	(3.2)	13.3	(2.2)	53.7	(3.3)	41.1	(3.2)	5.2	(1.1)
	Canada	95.5	(0.8)	3.7	(0.7)	0.8	(0.4)	98.9	(0.3)	0.9	(0.3)	0.2	(0.2)	73.6	(2.2)	23.9	(2.1)	2.4	(0.5)	84.0	(1.7)	13.3	(1.6)	2.7	(0.7)
	Chile	62.9	(3.5)	30.5	(3.3)	6.6	(1.9)	67.9	(3.7)	23.5	(3.4)	8.6	(2.2)	24.7	(3.0)	59.2	(3.6)	16.1	(2.6)	58.9	(3.7)	32.2	(3.7)	8.9	(2.3)
	Czech Republic	75.7	(3.1)	18.0	(2.7)	6.4	(1.5)	92.8	(1.7)	6.3	(1.7)	0.9	(0.4)	76.9	(3.0)	18.8	(2.9)	4.3	(1.4)	92.7	(2.5)	3.4	(1.4)	3.9	(1.8)
	Denmark	90.3	(2.3)	9.5	(2.3)	0.2	(0.2)	87.5	(2.2)	12.5	(2.2)	0.1	(0.0)	55.2	(3.5)	42.6	(3.4)	2.1	(1.1)	72.6	(3.3)	25.5	(3.3)	1.9	(1.1)
	Estonia	90.0	(1.6)	8.6	(1.4)	1.4	(0.8)	84.4	(2.5)	12.2	(2.2)	3.4	(1.2)	74.3	(2.7)	25.0	(2.6)	0.8	(0.5)	56.7	(3.1)	40.0	(3.0)	3.3	(1.2)
	Finland	98.6	(0.1)	1.3	(0.1)	0.1	(0.0)	98.8	(0.8)	0.9	(0.7)	0.3	(0.3)	85.8	(2.5)	14.0	(2.5)	0.2	(0.0)	90.2	(1.9)	9.6	(1.9)	0.2	(0.0)
	France	77.8	(2.5)	18.0	(2.6)	4.2	(1.5)	90.1	(2.2)	9.5	(2.1)	0.5	(0.5)	48.5	(3.2)	43.4	(3.3)	8.1	(1.9)	44.6	(3.2)	47.2	(3.3)	8.2	(2.0)
	Germany	68.9	(3.1)	28.0	(3.0)	3.1	(1.3)	88.8	(2.3)	9.1	(2.1)	2.1	(1.0)	79.6	(2.9)	19.3	(2.8)	1.0	(0.8)	90.6	(2.1)	6.7	(1.7)	2.7	(1.1)
	Greece	40.4	(3.6)	48.1	(3.6)	11.5	(2.2)	82.8	(3.2)	11.0	(2.6)	6.2	(2.0)	19.9	(3.4)	68.2	(3.9)	11.8	(2.3)	45.9	(3.7)	45.2	(3.6)	8.9	(2.1)
	Hungary	52.3	(3.4)	41.1	(3.7)	6.6	(2.2)	91.9	(1.9)	5.8	(1.6)	2.4	(1.2)	42.5	(3.2)	47.3	(3.5)	10.2	(2.1)	91.0	(2.1)	5.9	(1.7)	3.1	(1.4)
	Iceland	99.9	(0.0)	0.1	(0.0)	0.0	c	94.1	(0.1)	3.7	(0.1)	2.2	(0.1)	79.2	(0.2)	20.8	(0.2)	0.0	c	91.0	(0.1)	8.3	(0.1)	0.8	(0.0)
	Ireland	94.1	(2.0)	4.1	(1.7)	1.8	(1.1)	97.1	(1.0)	2.9	(1.0)	0.0	c	87.6	(2.7)	11.2	(2.5)	1.2	(0.9)	93.8	(1.7)	4.5	(1.3)	1.7	(1.1)
	Israel	69.7	(4.1)	25.7	(3.9)	4.6	(1.9)	90.9	(1.9)	9.1	(1.9)	0.0	c	28.4	(3.7)	56.0	(4.1)	15.6	(3.0)	39.3	(4.3)	52.1	(4.3)	8.6	(2.2)
	Italy	37.7	(2.1)	49.4	(2.4)	13.0	(1.3)	97.6	(0.6)	2.4	(0.6)	0.0	(0.0)	62.5	(1.8)	34.3	(1.8)	3.2	(0.8)	70.1	(1.8)	27.2	(1.8)	2.7	(0.8)
	Japan	38.3	(3.4)	56.9	(3.7)	4.8	(1.5)	99.2	(0.6)	0.8	(0.6)	0.0	c	40.4	(3.2)	58.1	(3.4)	1.5	(0.9)	82.2	(2.7)	16.7	(2.6)	1.1	(0.8)
	Korea	70.3	(3.8)	18.9	(3.2)	10.9	(2.6)	88.7	(2.7)	8.6	(2.4)	2.7	(1.4)	37.0	(3.9)	43.4	(4.1)	19.6	(2.7)	74.1	(3.8)	24.5	(3.8)	1.3	(0.9)
	Luxembourg	72.8	(0.1)	20.5	(0.1)	6.7	(0.0)	87.9	(0.1)	9.2	(0.1)	2.9	(0.0)	46.4	(0.1)	40.2	(0.1)	13.4	(0.1)	59.4	(0.1)	39.7	(0.1)	0.8	(0.0)
	Mexico	58.6	(1.9)	36.0	(1.9)	5.4	(0.8)	75.2	(1.7)	18.5	(1.5)	6.3	(1.2)	37.7	(1.7)	50.5	(2.0)	11.8	(1.3)	50.6	(1.9)	39.9	(1.8)	9.5	(1.3)
	Netherlands	77.5	(3.8)	17.5	(3.4)	5.0	(1.8)	90.0	(2.4)	10.0	(2.4)	0.0	c	62.8	(3.8)	35.0	(3.7)	2.2	(1.2)	56.5	(4.5)	39.9	(4.6)	3.6	(1.4)
	New Zealand	97.1	(1.3)	1.6	(0.9)	1.3	(0.9)	97.3	(1.2)	1.5	(0.9)	1.1	(0.8)	83.2	(3.4)	14.4	(3.1)	2.4	(1.4)	95.8	(2.0)	1.4	(0.8)	2.9	(1.8)
	Norway	100.0	(0.0)	0.0	c	0.0	c	97.6	(1.1)	1.8	(1.0)	0.6	(0.5)	77.4	(2.9)	21.9	(2.9)	0.7	(0.7)	95.6	(1.6)	4.4	(1.6)	0.0	c
	Poland	90.2	(2.4)	9.1	(2.3)	0.7	(0.7)	93.7	(1.8)	6.3	(1.8)	0.0	c	58.1	(4.2)	39.5	(4.1)	2.5	(1.2)	50.8	(4.1)	47.5	(4.0)	1.7	(1.0)
	Portugal	85.6	(2.9)	13.0	(2.8)	1.4	(0.9)	93.0	(2.3)	7.0	(2.3)	0.0	c	64.9	(3.5)	33.0	(3.6)	2.1	(1.4)	89.7	(2.2)	10.0	(2.2)	0.3	(0.3)
	Slovak Republic	57.1	(3.4)	28.2	(2.9)	14.6	(2.5)	84.3	(2.9)	13.2	(2.4)	2.5	(1.7)	41.8	(3.4)	44.7	(3.9)	13.5	(2.9)	59.9	(3.9)	37.7	(3.8)	2.4	(1.0)
	Slovenia	21.0	(0.8)	61.1	(0.6)	17.9	(0.3)	81.9	(0.3)	15.8	(0.3)	2.3	(0.2)	22.5	(0.9)	70.4	(0.9)	7.1	(0.2)	65.2	(0.7)	34.4	(0.7)	0.4	(0.0)
	Spain	97.8	(0.6)	2.1	(0.6)	0.1	(0.1)	98.1	(0.5)	1.5	(0.4)	0.4	(0.2)	76.0	(2.2)	23.2	(2.2)	0.8	(0.4)	82.3	(1.8)	15.3	(1.7)	2.5	(0.7)
	Sweden	98.0	(0.9)	1.9	(0.9)	0.0	(0.0)	94.4	(1.8)	4.3	(1.5)	1.3	(0.9)	88.7	(2.5)	11.2	(2.5)	0.1	(0.1)	69.0	(3.0)	27.6	(2.8)	3.4	(1.4)
	Switzerland	78.8	(3.0)	15.1	(2.8)	6.1	(1.8)	73.1	(3.0)	14.1	(2.1)	12.7	(2.3)	59.2	(3.3)	37.7	(3.2)	3.0	(1.3)	63.2	(3.1)	33.4	(3.0)	3.4	(1.4)
	Turkey	58.5	(4.2)	32.1	(4.1)	9.3	(2.3)	74.6	(3.4)	20.6	(2.8)	4.7	(2.1)	37.2	(4.5)	45.0	(4.1)	17.8	(3.2)	60.8	(4.1)	30.3	(3.8)	8.9	(2.3)
	United Kingdom	95.9	(1.6)	2.4	(1.3)	1.7	(0.9)	96.7	(1.1)	3.2	(1.1)	0.1	(0.1)	71.7	(3.9)	25.6	(3.5)	2.7	(1.2)	95.7	(1.6)	4.1	(1.6)	0.2	(0.1)
	United States	91.5	(2.1)	8.0	(2.0)	0.5	(0.4)	96.4	(1.7)	3.2	(1.7)	0.5	(0.4)	65.1	(3.8)	31.2	(4.2)	3.7	(1.5)	88.6	(2.4)	10.4	(2.3)	0.9	(0.7)
	OECD average	73.6	(0.4)	19.8	(0.4)	6.6	(0.3)	90.2	(0.3)	7.8	(0.3)	2.0	(0.2)	57.8	(0.5)	36.2	(0.5)	6.0	(0.3)	72.4	(0.5)	24.2	(0.5)	3.3	(0.2)
Partners	Albania	72.0	(3.1)	26.1	(3.1)	1.9	(1.3)	82.9	(3.3)	14.2	(3.2)	2.8	(1.3)	56.7	(3.7)	36.2	(3.5)	7.1	(2.5)	56.5	(4.5)	41.0	(4.5)	2.5	(1.3)
	Argentina	80.2	(3.5)	17.6	(3.3)	2.2	(1.1)	90.8	(2.6)	8.5	(2.6)	0.7	(0.6)	39.2	(3.5)	55.0	(3.7)	5.8	(1.7)	47.9	(4.3)	46.1	(4.0)	6.0	(2.1)
	Brazil	77.6	(2.1)	16.9	(2.1)	5.5	(1.3)	92.6	(1.7)	4.3	(1.3)	3.1	(1.0)	41.3	(2.5)	48.2	(2.5)	10.5	(1.5)	73.1	(2.4)	24.2	(2.4)	2.7	(0.8)
	Bulgaria	65.2	(4.0)	29.5	(4.0)	5.3	(1.8)	80.8	(3.2)	18.5	(3.3)	0.6	(0.6)	6.8	(1.9)	67.5	(3.6)	25.7	(3.5)	47.7	(4.5)	46.4	(4.6)	6.0	(1.8)
	Colombia	58.4	(4.0)	38.9	(4.0)	2.7	(0.9)	72.8	(4.0)	23.7	(3.8)	3.5	(1.4)	28.3	(3.6)	60.5	(3.9)	11.2	(2.1)	44.2	(3.7)	48.5	(3.6)	7.3	(1.7)
	Costa Rica	33.1	(3.5)	56.1	(3.8)	10.7	(2.3)	67.7	(3.6)	26.4	(3.4)	5.8	(1.4)	26.4	(3.5)	59.7	(3.8)	13.9	(2.8)	55.4	(3.5)	37.5	(3.1)	7.2	(1.7)
	Croatia	47.1	(4.0)	42.5	(3.9)	10.4	(2.3)	88.9	(2.3)	10.6	(2.3)	0.5	(0.5)	59.1	(4.1)	38.4	(4.0)	2.6	(1.2)	58.1	(3.9)	36.0	(3.7)	5.9	(1.9)
	Cyprus*	59.5	(0.1)	35.9	(0.1)	4.6	(0.1)	90.6	(0.1)	8.0	(0.0)	1.4	(0.0)	10.9	(0.0)	64.2	(0.1)	24.9	(0.1)	53.2	(0.1)	37.2	(0.1)	9.6	(0.0)
	Hong Kong-China	32.0	(4.2)	62.0	(4.3)	6.0	(2.1)	68.0	(3.8)	30.5	(3.6)	1.5	(1.1)	35.8	(3.4)	60.2	(3.7)	4.1	(1.7)	48.2	(4.1)	49.9	(4.0)	1.9	(1.1)
	Indonesia	63.4	(4.3)	30.4	(3.9)	6.2	(2.0)	87.6	(2.7)	11.8	(2.7)	0.6	(0.5)	17.5	(3.3)	52.5	(4.0)	29.9	(3.8)	39.8	(3.9)	45.7	(4.1)	14.5	(2.9)
	Jordan	67.5	(3.6)	25.5	(3.4)	7.0	(1.9)	55.6	(3.6)	26.6	(3.5)	17.8	(2.9)	12.0	(2.4)	52.8	(3.7)	35.2	(3.6)	35.8	(3.5)	50.1	(3.5)	14.1	(2.6)
	Kazakhstan	73.1	(3.4)	23.0	(3.3)	3.9	(1.6)	58.0	(3.9)	34.0	(3.7)	8.0	(2.2)	68.0	(4.0)	27.4	(4.0)	4.5	(1.8)	39.1	(3.8)	55.9	(4.2)	5.0	(1.8)
	Latvia	75.6	(3.2)	23.4	(3.1)	1.1	(0.8)	76.2	(3.3)	21.2	(3.2)	2.6	(1.1)	65.9	(3.2)	31.2	(3.1)	2.8	(1.2)	31.3	(3.4)	58.7	(3.4)	10.0	(2.1)
	Liechtenstein	54.5	(0.6)	0.0	c	45.5	(0.6)	52.7	(1.2)	47.3	(1.2)	0.0	c	71.7	(1.0)	28.3	(1.0)	0.0	c	58.9	(0.8)	7.1	(0.8)	34.1	(0.4)
	Lithuania	81.0	(2.5)	19.0	(2.5)	0.0	c	74.0	(3.1)	19.6	(2.9)	6.3	(1.9)	58.5	(3.3)	38.7	(3.2)	2.7	(1.2)	76.6	(2.8)	22.0	(2.7)	1.4	(0.9)
	Macao-China	4.3	(0.0)	61.8	(0.1)	33.9	(0.1)	57.0	(0.1)	41.7	(0.1)	1.3	(0.0)	11.6	(0.0)	58.5	(0.1)	29.8	(0.0)	33.2	(0.1)	54.1	(0.1)	12.7	(0.0)
	Malaysia	87.4	(2.5)	12.0	(2.5)	0.6	(0.6)	62.7	(4.1)	23.6	(3.7)	13.7	(2.8)	33.1	(3.5)	49.7	(4.1)	17.2	(3.1)	31.9	(3.4)	57.0	(3.4)	11.1	(2.3)
	Montenegro	62.5	(0.1)	33.4	(0.1)	4.1	(0.0)	55.3	(0.2)	40.3	(0.2)	4.5	(0.0)	48.3	(0.1)	45.8	(0.2)	5.9	(0.0)	29.5	(0.1)	62.8	(0.1)	7.7	(0.1)
	Peru	74.6	(3.2)	22.4	(3.2)	3.0	(1.2)	69.1	(3.4)	21.9	(3.2)	9.0	(2.1)	36.6	(3.8)	48.9	(3.5)	14.5	(2.2)	56.2	(3.5)	34.6	(3.5)	9.2	(1.9)
	Qatar	93.2	(0.0)	6.0	(0.0)	0.8	(0.0)	88.0	(0.1)	8.6	(0.1)	3.4	(0.0)	40.2	(0.1)	48.8	(0.1)	11.0	(0.1)	65.3	(0.1)	32.6	(0.1)	2.1	(0.0)
	Romania	66.7	(3.3)	27.4	(3.2)	5.8	(1.7)	78.9	(3.1)	19.0	(3.0)	2.1	(1.1)	53.8	(3.4)	36.6	(3.6)	9.6	(2.3)	46.9	(3.3)	34.5	(3.6)	18.6	(3.2)
	Russian Federation	87.7	(2.1)	10.0	(1.9)	2.3	(1.0)	80.6	(2.9)	17.0	(2.8)	2.4	(0.8)	83.0	(2.8)	16.4	(2.9)	0.7	(0.6)	43.4	(3.9)	54.2	(4.1)	2.4	(1.2)
	Serbia	58.9	(4.1)	34.5	(4.0)	6.6	(2.2)	81.7	(3.4)	17.5	(3.3)	0.8	(0.9)	32.9	(4.1)	54.0	(4.8)	13.1	(2.7)	69.0	(3.7)	28.4	(3.8)	2.6	(1.4)
	Shanghai-China	72.7	(3.3)	22.4	(3.1)	4.9	(1.9)	77.4	(3.1)	21.4	(3.1)	1.2	(0.9)	62.2	(3.8)	35.1	(3.7)	2.8	(1.4)	28.7	(3.3)	68.9	(3.4)	2.4	(1.2)
	Singapore	97.0	(0.5)	1.5	(0.0)	1.5	(0.5)	92.3	(0.5)	7.1	(0.1)	0.6	(0.5)	92.4	(0.8)	7.0	(0.6)	0.6	(0.5)	87.2	(0.8)	12.2	(0.6)	0.6	(0.5)
	Chinese Taipei	26.5	(3.7)	63.6	(4.1)	9.9	(2.3)	70.5	(3.9)	29.5	(3.9)	0.0	c	5.2	(1.9)	73.8	(3.7)	21.0	(3.1)	19.6	(3.6)	71.1	(4.0)	9.3	(2.1)
	Thailand	56.8	(3.8)	41.3	(3.7)	2.0	(1.1)	76.0	(3.2)	23.0	(3.1)	1.0	(0.7)	21.2	(2.7)	68.5	(3.7)	10.3	(2.5)	48.4	(3.4)	47.1	(3.5)	4.5	(1.4)
	Tunisia	82.2	(2.9)	13.8	(2.6)	4.0	(1.6)	64.8	(4.3)	26.7	(3.7)	8.5	(2.3)	39.5	(3.8)	46.4	(3.9)	14.1	(3.1)	45.1	(4.1)	43.3	(4.1)	11.6	(2.6)
	United Arab Emirates	69.2	(2.5)	26.9	(2.4)	3.9	(0.7)	78.7	(2.1)	17.5	(1.9)	3.8	(0.9)	42.4	(2.8)	45.0	(2.7)	12.6	(1.8)	62.5	(2.5)	34.6	(2.4)	3.0	(0.6)
	Uruguay	93.6	(1.7)	6.4	(1.7)	0.0	c	97.4	(1.2)	1.5	(0.9)	1.0	(0.8)	64.7	(3.5)	33.6	(3.5)	1.7	(1.0)	72.3	(3.0)	25.6	(3.0)	2.0	(1.1)
	Viet Nam	74.6	(3.3)	18.7	(3.1)	6.7	(2.1)	89.5	(2.7)	8.4	(2.4)	2.1	(1.2)	72.0	(3.7)	25.8	(3.7)	2.2	(1.1)	45.1	(4.5)	41.5	(4.3)	13.4	(3.0)

* See notes at the beginning of this Annex.
StatLink http://dx.doi.org/10.1787/888932957422

[Part 2/2]
School transfer policies
Table IV.2.9   *Results based on school principals' reports*

		Percentage of students in schools whose principal reported that a student in the national modal grade for 15-year-olds would be transferred to another school for the following reasons:										Percentage of students in schools whose principal reported that a student in the national modal grade for 15-year-olds would be "very likely" transferred to another school because of "low academic achievement", "behavioural problems" or "special learning needs"	
		Parents' or guardians' request						Other							
		Not likely		Likely		Very likely		Not likely		Likely		Very likely			
		%	S.E.	%	S.E.	%	S.E.	%	S.E.	%	S.E.	%	S.E.	%	S.E.
OECD	Australia	60.1	(1.9)	34.4	(1.8)	5.5	(0.9)	84.0	(1.4)	14.5	(1.4)	1.5	(0.4)	2.9	(0.7)
	Austria	42.6	(3.9)	35.0	(3.8)	22.4	(3.6)	58.7	(4.3)	30.9	(4.0)	10.4	(2.5)	64.8	(4.0)
	Belgium	47.0	(2.9)	42.0	(2.8)	11.1	(2.0)	69.3	(3.6)	27.2	(3.6)	3.5	(1.3)	28.0	(3.0)
	Canada	61.0	(2.3)	33.1	(2.2)	6.0	(0.9)	76.2	(2.8)	22.3	(2.7)	1.5	(0.8)	4.7	(0.8)
	Chile	10.7	(2.2)	67.4	(3.7)	22.0	(3.4)	46.2	(4.0)	49.4	(3.9)	4.5	(1.6)	22.9	(3.1)
	Czech Republic	55.6	(3.9)	32.9	(3.2)	11.4	(2.7)	88.5	(2.7)	9.9	(2.7)	1.6	(0.9)	10.2	(2.0)
	Denmark	34.7	(3.7)	58.4	(3.9)	7.0	(1.9)	55.5	(3.4)	41.7	(3.4)	2.7	(1.3)	2.3	(1.1)
	Estonia	23.7	(2.5)	57.0	(2.6)	19.3	(2.3)	51.2	(2.8)	43.2	(2.8)	5.6	(1.5)	3.7	(1.3)
	Finland	55.9	(3.3)	40.9	(3.5)	3.2	(1.3)	82.4	(2.8)	17.5	(2.8)	0.1	(0.0)	0.4	(0.0)
	France	37.5	(3.2)	51.9	(3.5)	10.6	(2.0)	66.8	(3.6)	29.3	(3.4)	3.9	(1.5)	17.1	(2.6)
	Germany	66.3	(3.5)	28.2	(3.2)	5.6	(1.8)	81.1	(3.3)	18.9	(3.3)	0.0	c	6.5	(1.6)
	Greece	12.5	(2.9)	57.9	(3.6)	29.6	(3.9)	15.6	(2.8)	68.9	(3.4)	15.5	(3.0)	25.1	(3.5)
	Hungary	40.0	(3.7)	51.9	(3.8)	8.1	(1.8)	70.3	(3.8)	26.3	(3.5)	3.4	(1.3)	15.1	(2.7)
	Iceland	44.0	(0.2)	45.5	(0.2)	10.5	(0.2)	87.3	(0.2)	12.1	(0.2)	0.6	(0.1)	0.8	(0.0)
	Ireland	79.6	(3.2)	17.3	(3.0)	3.0	(1.4)	84.0	(3.1)	14.4	(3.0)	1.6	(1.1)	2.4	(1.3)
	Israel	27.8	(3.9)	57.4	(3.9)	14.8	(2.8)	41.0	(3.9)	50.2	(4.0)	8.7	(2.4)	20.4	(3.5)
	Italy	14.9	(1.8)	62.1	(2.6)	23.0	(2.0)	58.7	(2.8)	38.8	(2.8)	2.5	(0.7)	16.9	(1.6)
	Japan	49.4	(3.4)	48.7	(3.4)	1.9	(1.0)	23.3	(3.4)	74.4	(3.5)	2.3	(1.1)	5.8	(1.7)
	Korea	22.9	(3.5)	55.3	(3.9)	21.8	(3.4)	54.1	(4.2)	38.7	(4.1)	7.2	(2.2)	26.0	(3.3)
	Luxembourg	34.7	(0.1)	54.6	(0.1)	10.7	(0.1)	63.8	(0.1)	34.7	(0.1)	1.5	(0.0)	19.3	(0.1)
	Mexico	8.2	(0.9)	59.9	(1.9)	32.0	(1.7)	35.1	(2.3)	51.3	(2.3)	13.6	(1.5)	19.6	(1.5)
	Netherlands	54.5	(4.4)	36.5	(4.0)	9.0	(2.4)	82.0	(4.4)	17.1	(4.2)	1.0	(1.0)	10.1	(2.6)
	New Zealand	73.9	(4.0)	19.4	(3.4)	6.7	(2.2)	86.2	(3.6)	12.6	(3.5)	1.2	(0.9)	4.1	(1.9)
	Norway	55.7	(3.6)	38.5	(3.4)	5.8	(1.4)	79.8	(2.9)	19.4	(2.9)	0.8	(0.6)	0.7	(0.7)
	Poland	7.4	(2.2)	71.9	(3.7)	20.7	(3.2)	34.8	(4.6)	63.1	(4.7)	2.1	(1.2)	3.6	(1.4)
	Portugal	19.4	(3.1)	66.3	(3.8)	14.2	(2.4)	43.3	(4.6)	53.8	(4.6)	2.9	(1.2)	3.8	(1.7)
	Slovak Republic	16.3	(2.8)	57.0	(3.6)	26.7	(3.3)	51.1	(3.9)	42.7	(4.0)	6.3	(2.6)	24.2	(3.3)
	Slovenia	33.7	(0.9)	63.5	(0.9)	2.7	(0.1)	45.0	(0.8)	51.7	(0.8)	3.2	(0.2)	21.8	(0.3)
	Spain	53.9	(2.2)	40.0	(2.2)	6.1	(1.0)	80.6	(2.5)	18.8	(2.5)	0.6	(0.4)	3.2	(0.8)
	Sweden	35.3	(3.6)	46.3	(3.9)	18.4	(2.7)	86.1	(3.0)	12.5	(2.9)	1.4	(0.9)	3.5	(1.4)
	Switzerland	68.0	(3.1)	28.7	(2.9)	3.3	(1.4)	67.4	(3.7)	31.2	(3.4)	1.3	(0.8)	9.9	(2.3)
	Turkey	10.9	(2.5)	39.2	(3.9)	49.9	(3.7)	40.0	(4.4)	50.1	(4.4)	9.9	(2.5)	26.8	(3.6)
	United Kingdom	63.1	(3.9)	30.2	(3.6)	6.7	(1.8)	90.5	(2.1)	8.6	(2.0)	0.9	(0.7)	3.5	(1.7)
	United States	69.5	(3.5)	25.8	(3.6)	4.7	(1.7)	82.4	(3.8)	13.4	(3.5)	4.3	(2.0)	4.2	(1.6)
	OECD average	**40.9**	**(0.5)**	**45.7**	**(0.6)**	**13.4**	**(0.4)**	**63.6**	**(0.6)**	**32.6**	**(0.6)**	**3.8**	**(0.3)**	**12.8**	**(0.4)**
Partners	Albania	28.3	(3.9)	64.8	(4.3)	6.8	(1.9)	39.8	(4.3)	51.3	(4.3)	8.9	(3.0)	10.4	(2.9)
	Argentina	10.7	(2.4)	67.8	(3.5)	21.4	(3.4)	32.3	(5.0)	60.4	(5.2)	7.4	(2.3)	11.5	(2.6)
	Brazil	12.7	(2.0)	46.3	(3.1)	41.0	(2.8)	25.8	(2.7)	50.1	(3.2)	24.1	(2.5)	14.7	(1.9)
	Bulgaria	0.7	(0.6)	51.7	(3.6)	47.6	(3.7)	10.3	(2.3)	72.2	(3.5)	17.5	(3.6)	30.6	(3.6)
	Colombia	7.6	(2.1)	63.7	(4.1)	28.7	(4.0)	15.9	(3.0)	69.8	(3.5)	14.3	(2.5)	15.0	(2.5)
	Costa Rica	9.4	(2.7)	65.2	(3.9)	25.4	(3.4)	21.8	(4.1)	55.8	(5.4)	22.4	(4.5)	22.7	(2.8)
	Croatia	27.0	(3.5)	57.4	(3.9)	15.6	(2.7)	50.2	(4.5)	47.2	(4.4)	2.6	(1.4)	16.7	(2.7)
	Cyprus*	10.9	(0.0)	65.8	(0.1)	23.3	(0.1)	14.6	(0.1)	71.4	(0.1)	14.0	(0.1)	32.5	(0.1)
	Hong Kong-China	14.2	(3.0)	83.5	(3.1)	2.3	(1.2)	25.4	(9.2)	42.2	(13.1)	32.4	(14.5)	9.3	(2.6)
	Indonesia	2.0	(0.8)	54.7	(3.9)	43.4	(3.9)	7.9	(2.0)	74.1	(4.0)	18.0	(3.6)	34.9	(3.9)
	Jordan	9.0	(1.7)	57.1	(3.7)	33.9	(3.6)	20.6	(3.5)	60.5	(4.1)	18.9	(3.7)	42.5	(3.4)
	Kazakhstan	25.8	(2.9)	60.3	(3.5)	13.9	(2.6)	45.5	(4.4)	49.7	(4.3)	4.7	(2.0)	9.1	(2.3)
	Latvia	4.0	(1.3)	73.7	(3.0)	22.3	(3.0)	18.4	(2.9)	74.7	(3.0)	7.0	(2.2)	11.3	(2.3)
	Liechtenstein	36.0	(1.1)	64.0	(1.1)	0.0	c	53.5	(1.0)	46.5	(1.0)	0.0	c	45.5	(0.6)
	Lithuania	14.0	(2.5)	58.9	(3.3)	27.1	(2.9)	33.5	(4.0)	61.6	(4.1)	4.8	(2.3)	3.3	(1.3)
	Macao-China	21.6	(0.0)	76.3	(0.0)	2.0	(0.0)	16.5	(0.0)	83.5	(0.0)	0.0	c	36.0	(0.1)
	Malaysia	4.9	(1.7)	48.1	(4.2)	47.0	(4.1)	21.4	(3.7)	74.6	(4.0)	4.0	(1.8)	25.9	(3.6)
	Montenegro	3.0	(0.0)	80.8	(0.1)	16.2	(0.1)	4.9	(0.0)	89.1	(0.1)	6.0	(0.1)	9.5	(0.1)
	Peru	4.4	(1.4)	48.2	(3.8)	47.4	(3.8)	23.5	(3.0)	55.3	(3.4)	21.2	(2.8)	19.5	(2.7)
	Qatar	17.8	(0.1)	47.1	(0.1)	35.1	(0.1)	29.1	(0.1)	54.3	(0.1)	16.6	(0.1)	11.5	(0.1)
	Romania	29.2	(2.3)	33.4	(3.7)	37.4	(3.7)	81.7	(2.9)	15.7	(2.7)	2.6	(1.3)	22.3	(3.1)
	Russian Federation	30.2	(4.0)	57.3	(3.8)	12.5	(2.1)	51.4	(3.6)	44.5	(4.1)	4.1	(1.8)	4.7	(1.6)
	Serbia	6.2	(2.2)	60.0	(3.9)	33.8	(3.9)	29.2	(3.9)	63.8	(4.1)	7.0	(2.5)	19.5	(3.2)
	Shanghai-China	18.4	(3.2)	76.5	(3.2)	5.0	(1.8)	23.5	(3.4)	72.5	(3.5)	4.0	(1.7)	7.2	(2.1)
	Singapore	59.6	(0.7)	35.2	(0.5)	5.1	(0.5)	86.2	(0.5)	13.2	(0.6)	0.6	(0.5)	1.5	(0.5)
	Chinese Taipei	9.2	(2.4)	82.1	(2.9)	8.8	(2.0)	21.2	(3.5)	73.0	(3.3)	5.8	(1.8)	28.1	(3.5)
	Thailand	24.5	(3.3)	67.7	(3.9)	7.8	(2.1)	34.8	(5.0)	61.4	(5.1)	3.8	(1.8)	14.1	(2.6)
	Tunisia	11.7	(2.2)	46.0	(4.0)	42.4	(3.6)	34.6	(3.7)	58.1	(4.0)	7.4	(2.3)	24.2	(3.6)
	United Arab Emirates	13.9	(1.1)	54.6	(2.9)	31.6	(2.8)	27.7	(1.8)	58.0	(2.7)	14.3	(2.3)	16.0	(1.9)
	Uruguay	15.2	(2.8)	56.0	(3.9)	28.8	(3.2)	58.0	(4.2)	36.2	(4.2)	5.8	(2.0)	3.7	(1.0)
	Viet Nam	10.3	(2.5)	41.1	(3.8)	48.7	(4.0)	53.9	(4.1)	38.5	(3.8)	7.6	(2.2)	19.9	(3.3)

* See notes at the beginning of this Annex.
StatLink ⟨⟩ http://dx.doi.org/10.1787/888932957422

[Part 1/3]
School transfer policies, by level of education
Table IV.2.10 *Results based on school principals' reports*

		Lower secondary education (ISCED 2)												
		Percentage of students in schools whose principal reported that a student in the national modal grade for 15-year-olds would be "very likely" transferred to another school for the following reasons:												
		Low academic achievement		High academic achievement		Behavioural problems		Special learning needs		Parents' or guardians' request		Other		"low academic achievement", "behavioural problems" or "special learning needs"	
		%	S.E.	%	S.E.	%	S.E.	%	S.E.	%	S.E.	%	S.E.	%	S.E.
OECD	Australia	0.5	(0.3)	2.1	(0.7)	2.0	(0.5)	0.8	(0.4)	5.6	(1.0)	1.5	(0.4)	2.5	(0.6)
	Austria	31.0	(8.6)	7.7	(10.5)	26.2	(11.3)	15.4	(8.1)	15.2	(6.6)	12.1	(8.3)	52.5	(11.4)
	Belgium	8.1	(5.4)	4.4	(2.6)	22.9	(6.2)	15.9	(7.2)	19.1	(4.3)	1.6	(1.3)	29.6	(7.1)
	Canada	1.7	(0.8)	0.5	(0.5)	3.8	(1.2)	5.8	(1.8)	6.4	(1.5)	1.2	(0.8)	8.3	(2.0)
	Chile	3.1	(2.2)	15.7	(5.7)	21.6	(8.2)	4.7	(2.7)	21.5	(8.3)	9.7	(5.5)	26.0	(8.2)
	Czech Republic	2.4	(1.1)	1.6	(0.8)	3.3	(1.4)	5.5	(2.4)	10.1	(3.4)	1.8	(1.1)	6.5	(2.5)
	Denmark	0.2	(0.2)	0.1	(0.0)	2.1	(1.1)	1.9	(1.1)	7.0	(1.9)	2.7	(1.3)	2.3	(1.1)
	Estonia	1.4	(0.8)	3.4	(1.2)	0.8	(0.5)	3.3	(1.2)	19.4	(2.3)	5.7	(1.5)	3.7	(1.3)
	Finland	0.1	(0.0)	0.3	(0.3)	0.2	(0.0)	0.2	(0.0)	3.2	(1.3)	0.1	(0.0)	0.4	(0.0)
	France	0.0	c	1.6	(1.6)	20.8	(5.2)	8.8	(3.0)	5.8	(2.6)	2.1	(2.0)	24.8	(5.3)
	Germany	3.2	(1.3)	2.1	(1.0)	1.1	(0.8)	2.8	(1.1)	5.7	(1.9)	0.0	c	6.6	(1.7)
	Greece	0.0	c	1.9	(1.8)	6.0	(3.8)	9.9	(5.3)	10.4	(9.6)	7.4	(6.8)	13.2	(6.0)
	Hungary	0.0	c	9.9	(6.6)	4.0	(3.9)	1.2	(1.2)	2.3	(2.4)	0.8	(0.8)	5.2	(4.0)
	Iceland	0.0	c	2.2	(0.1)	0.0	c	0.8	(0.0)	10.5	(0.2)	0.6	(0.1)	0.8	(0.0)
	Ireland	1.8	(1.2)	0.0	c	1.4	(1.0)	2.0	(1.2)	2.8	(1.3)	1.5	(1.0)	2.4	(1.3)
	Israel	3.1	(2.4)	0.0	c	7.9	(3.3)	4.9	(2.2)	9.0	(3.2)	3.9	(1.8)	10.5	(3.6)
	Italy	2.2	(2.3)	0.0	c	4.0	(3.2)	0.0	c	11.8	(4.6)	4.3	(4.7)	6.2	(4.2)
	Japan	c	c	c	c	c	c	c	c	c	c	c	c	c	c
	Korea	0.0	c	0.0	c	15.9	(4.1)	0.0	c	35.6	(16.0)	10.0	(9.7)	15.9	(4.1)
	Luxembourg	4.6	(0.0)	3.8	(0.1)	17.1	(0.1)	0.5	(0.0)	10.6	(0.1)	0.8	(0.0)	21.2	(0.1)
	Mexico	3.0	(1.0)	3.4	(1.0)	12.9	(2.2)	9.3	(2.0)	35.8	(3.6)	19.6	(3.7)	19.2	(2.5)
	Netherlands	4.0	(1.7)	0.0	c	2.1	(1.1)	5.0	(1.9)	8.6	(2.5)	0.6	(0.6)	10.3	(2.8)
	New Zealand	1.7	(1.3)	0.9	(0.6)	2.2	(1.6)	1.9	(1.2)	6.0	(2.1)	1.9	(1.6)	3.1	(1.7)
	Norway	0.0	c	0.6	(0.5)	0.7	(0.7)	0.0	c	5.8	(1.4)	0.8	(0.6)	0.7	(0.7)
	Poland	0.7	(0.7)	0.0	c	2.5	(1.2)	1.7	(1.0)	20.5	(3.2)	1.8	(1.2)	3.6	(1.4)
	Portugal	1.0	(0.5)	0.0	c	2.3	(1.5)	0.2	(0.1)	19.2	(3.9)	2.3	(1.6)	3.4	(1.6)
	Slovak Republic	1.7	(1.2)	3.6	(1.7)	4.9	(2.0)	3.5	(1.5)	23.5	(3.6)	5.3	(2.3)	8.3	(2.6)
	Slovenia	0.0	c	0.0	c	0.0	c	0.0	c	0.0	c	0.0	c	0.0	c
	Spain	0.1	(0.1)	0.4	(0.2)	0.8	(0.4)	2.5	(0.7)	6.2	(1.0)	0.6	(0.4)	3.2	(0.8)
	Sweden	0.0	c	1.3	(0.9)	0.1	(0.1)	3.4	(1.4)	18.6	(2.7)	1.4	(0.9)	3.5	(1.4)
	Switzerland	3.7	(1.2)	16.2	(2.9)	3.1	(1.4)	2.8	(1.2)	1.9	(0.8)	1.7	(1.1)	8.2	(1.9)
	Turkey	c	c	c	c	c	c	c	c	c	c	c	c	c	c
	United Kingdom	c	c	c	c	c	c	c	c	c	c	c	c	c	c
	United States	3.2	(2.7)	3.2	(2.7)	5.5	(2.9)	3.6	(2.7)	6.6	(3.0)	7.9	(4.4)	5.9	(3.0)
	OECD average	2.7	(0.5)	2.8	(0.7)	6.4	(0.7)	3.8	(0.5)	11.8	(0.8)	3.6	(0.6)	9.9	(0.7)
Partners	Albania	0.0	c	1.9	(1.1)	5.5	(2.6)	2.3	(1.2)	7.3	(3.1)	6.7	(2.6)	7.8	(2.8)
	Argentina	0.7	(0.5)	0.4	(0.5)	8.8	(3.7)	4.4	(1.7)	24.9	(4.5)	7.4	(2.8)	12.7	(3.9)
	Brazil	3.9	(1.2)	1.8	(1.0)	10.8	(3.1)	3.0	(2.0)	39.2	(4.5)	20.4	(3.1)	13.6	(3.1)
	Bulgaria	0.8	(0.8)	0.0	c	20.6	(8.7)	9.9	(8.6)	64.9	(11.9)	24.9	(12.9)	30.5	(9.9)
	Colombia	2.7	(1.2)	3.6	(1.6)	11.7	(2.5)	8.6	(2.3)	29.7	(4.3)	14.7	(2.7)	16.7	(3.0)
	Costa Rica	9.7	(2.2)	7.0	(1.8)	13.5	(3.2)	7.5	(2.1)	27.6	(4.0)	23.4	(4.8)	21.8	(3.0)
	Croatia	c	c	c	c	c	c	c	c	c	c	c	c	c	c
	Cyprus*	0.0	c	3.7	(0.8)	20.8	(1.1)	8.1	(0.7)	20.9	(1.1)	16.7	(1.0)	23.6	(1.2)
	Hong Kong-China	5.8	(2.0)	1.5	(1.0)	3.7	(1.6)	1.9	(1.1)	2.4	(1.3)	23.9	(10.6)	8.8	(2.5)
	Indonesia	0.6	(0.7)	0.5	(0.5)	18.0	(5.4)	11.9	(3.7)	32.3	(5.1)	7.6	(2.6)	23.4	(5.6)
	Jordan	7.0	(1.9)	17.8	(2.9)	35.2	(3.6)	14.1	(2.6)	33.9	(3.6)	18.9	(3.7)	42.5	(3.4)
	Kazakhstan	3.1	(1.6)	9.0	(2.6)	4.3	(2.0)	5.5	(2.0)	15.5	(2.8)	5.0	(2.2)	8.9	(2.4)
	Latvia	0.9	(0.6)	2.7	(1.1)	2.9	(1.2)	10.0	(2.1)	22.6	(3.0)	6.6	(2.2)	11.3	(2.2)
	Liechtenstein	38.3	(0.6)	0.0	c	0.0	c	25.3	(0.4)	0.0	c	0.0	c	38.3	(0.6)
	Lithuania	0.0	c	6.3	(1.9)	2.7	(1.2)	1.4	(0.9)	27.2	(2.9)	4.8	(2.0)	3.3	(1.3)
	Macao-China	32.4	(0.1)	2.4	(0.0)	28.9	(0.1)	11.9	(0.1)	2.0	(0.0)	0.0	c	35.0	(0.1)
	Malaysia	0.0	c	13.7	(5.9)	28.8	(8.6)	8.2	(4.4)	41.1	(8.8)	1.8	(1.4)	35.1	(8.8)
	Montenegro	c	c	c	c	c	c	c	c	c	c	c	c	c	c
	Peru	3.0	(1.3)	7.9	(1.8)	11.7	(2.1)	9.5	(2.4)	45.5	(3.9)	16.5	(3.2)	18.0	(3.0)
	Qatar	0.1	(0.1)	12.4	(0.2)	11.7	(0.2)	2.7	(0.1)	32.4	(0.3)	26.8	(0.2)	11.9	(0.2)
	Romania	5.8	(1.7)	2.1	(1.1)	9.6	(2.3)	18.6	(3.2)	37.4	(3.7)	2.6	(1.3)	22.3	(3.1)
	Russian Federation	1.6	(0.8)	2.2	(0.7)	0.3	(0.5)	2.6	(1.3)	13.2	(2.3)	4.6	(2.1)	4.1	(1.6)
	Serbia	c	c	c	c	c	c	c	c	c	c	c	c	c	c
	Shanghai-China	5.4	(2.7)	1.3	(1.3)	2.9	(2.1)	3.6	(2.1)	7.4	(3.3)	4.9	(2.6)	7.4	(3.0)
	Singapore	0.3	(0.1)	0.0	c	0.0	c	0.0	c	4.1	(2.2)	0.0	c	0.3	(0.1)
	Chinese Taipei	1.1	(0.6)	0.0	c	13.9	(4.1)	13.0	(4.1)	17.4	(4.2)	9.4	(4.0)	21.0	(4.6)
	Thailand	0.3	(0.3)	1.5	(1.3)	7.4	(2.3)	1.5	(0.7)	7.4	(2.7)	4.4	(2.6)	8.7	(2.4)
	Tunisia	5.0	(2.9)	14.1	(4.7)	22.4	(6.4)	11.8	(3.7)	39.1	(5.8)	7.5	(3.8)	28.8	(6.1)
	United Arab Emirates	1.5	(0.2)	2.4	(1.3)	9.0	(3.1)	2.6	(0.3)	30.1	(4.8)	14.4	(2.9)	10.8	(3.0)
	Uruguay	0.0	c	1.4	(1.1)	1.9	(1.3)	3.0	(1.8)	30.7	(4.1)	7.5	(3.1)	4.9	(1.6)
	Viet Nam	3.2	(3.2)	0.0	c	5.5	(5.4)	7.3	(6.4)	40.7	(12.3)	0.0	c	15.5	(8.3)

Note: Values that are statistically significant are indicated in bold (see Annex A3).
* See notes at the beginning of this Annex.
StatLink ᵐˢᴾ http://dx.doi.org/10.1787/888932957422

[Part 2/3]
School transfer policies, by level of education
Table IV.2.10 *Results based on school principals' reports*

		Upper secondary education (ISCED 3)												
		Percentage of students in schools whose principal reported that a student in the national modal grade for 15-year-olds would be "very likely" transferred to another school for the following reasons:												
		Low academic achievement		High academic achievement		Behavioural problems		Special learning needs		Parents' or guardians' request		Other		"low academic achievement", "behavioural problems" or "special learning needs"	
		%	S.E.	%	S.E.	%	S.E.	%	S.E.	%	S.E.	%	S.E.	%	S.E.
OECD	Australia	1.0	(0.6)	1.4	(0.7)	3.4	(1.2)	1.4	(0.9)	5.0	(1.3)	1.5	(0.7)	4.4	(1.4)
	Austria	61.5	(4.0)	0.1	(0.2)	6.4	(2.0)	5.6	(2.0)	22.7	(3.7)	10.3	(2.6)	65.3	(4.2)
	Belgium	17.7	(2.5)	1.3	(0.6)	12.3	(2.1)	4.0	(1.0)	10.2	(1.9)	3.7	(1.4)	27.8	(3.0)
	Canada	0.7	(0.3)	0.1	(0.1)	2.2	(0.4)	2.2	(0.6)	5.9	(0.9)	1.6	(0.9)	4.1	(0.7)
	Chile	6.8	(2.0)	8.2	(2.2)	15.8	(2.7)	9.1	(2.4)	22.0	(3.5)	4.2	(1.6)	22.7	(3.2)
	Czech Republic	11.4	(3.2)	0.0	c	5.5	(2.5)	2.0	(2.8)	13.1	(4.2)	1.4	(1.4)	14.8	(3.3)
	Denmark	c	c	c	c	c	c	c	c	c	c	c	c	c	c
	Estonia	0.0	c	1.4	(1.4)	0.0	c	2.8	(2.9)	12.9	(4.7)	1.4	(1.0)	2.8	(2.9)
	Finland	c	c	c	c	c	c	c	c	c	c	c	c	c	c
	France	6.0	(2.1)	0.0	c	2.6	(1.2)	7.9	(2.4)	12.6	(2.6)	4.7	(2.0)	13.8	(2.8)
	Germany	0.0	c	0.0	c	0.0	c	0.0	c	0.0	c	0.0	c	0.0	c
	Greece	12.2	(2.3)	6.5	(2.1)	12.2	(2.5)	8.8	(2.2)	30.7	(4.0)	15.9	(3.2)	25.8	(3.7)
	Hungary	7.4	(2.5)	1.4	(1.0)	11.1	(2.4)	3.3	(1.5)	8.8	(2.1)	3.8	(1.5)	16.4	(3.0)
	Iceland	c	c	c	c	c	c	c	c	c	c	c	c	c	c
	Ireland	1.8	(1.3)	0.0	c	0.8	(0.7)	1.3	(0.9)	3.5	(1.7)	1.8	(1.2)	2.4	(1.4)
	Israel	4.8	(2.0)	0.0	c	16.8	(3.2)	9.1	(2.4)	15.7	(2.9)	9.5	(2.6)	21.9	(3.6)
	Italy	13.2	(1.4)	0.0	(0.0)	3.2	(0.8)	2.8	(0.8)	23.3	(2.0)	2.5	(0.7)	17.1	(1.6)
	Japan	4.8	(1.5)	0.0	c	1.5	(0.9)	1.1	(0.8)	1.9	(1.0)	2.3	(1.1)	5.8	(1.7)
	Korea	11.6	(2.8)	2.9	(1.4)	19.8	(2.8)	1.4	(1.0)	20.9	(3.4)	7.0	(2.2)	26.7	(3.5)
	Luxembourg	9.9	(0.1)	1.5	(0.1)	7.9	(0.1)	1.3	(0.1)	10.8	(0.1)	2.4	(0.1)	16.5	(0.1)
	Mexico	6.8	(1.1)	7.9	(1.8)	11.1	(1.6)	9.7	(1.7)	29.7	(2.0)	10.7	(1.4)	19.9	(2.0)
	Netherlands	7.6	(3.4)	0.0	c	2.5	(2.2)	0.0	c	9.9	(3.8)	1.8	(1.9)	9.7	(3.9)
	New Zealand	1.3	(0.9)	1.1	(0.8)	2.4	(1.4)	2.9	(1.8)	6.7	(2.2)	1.2	(0.9)	4.2	(2.0)
	Norway	c	c	c	c	c	c	c	c	c	c	c	c	c	c
	Poland	c	c	c	c	c	c	c	c	c	c	c	c	c	c
	Portugal	1.8	(1.3)	0.0	c	1.9	(1.6)	0.4	(0.4)	10.1	(2.8)	3.4	(1.6)	4.1	(2.1)
	Slovak Republic	25.3	(4.2)	1.5	(2.1)	20.4	(4.9)	1.4	(1.1)	29.4	(5.3)	7.1	(3.7)	37.2	(5.4)
	Slovenia	18.8	(0.3)	2.4	(0.2)	7.5	(0.2)	0.4	(0.0)	2.9	(0.1)	3.4	(0.2)	22.9	(0.3)
	Spain	c	c	c	c	c	c	c	c	c	c	c	c	c	c
	Sweden	1.3	(1.4)	1.3	(1.4)	1.3	(1.4)	1.3	(1.4)	8.1	(5.5)	1.4	(1.6)	1.3	(1.4)
	Switzerland	14.7	(6.5)	0.0	c	2.8	(2.0)	5.8	(4.7)	8.4	(5.7)	0.0	c	16.2	(6.7)
	Turkey	9.0	(2.3)	4.1	(2.1)	18.1	(3.3)	9.0	(2.3)	50.6	(3.8)	10.0	(2.5)	26.7	(3.6)
	United Kingdom	1.7	(0.9)	0.1	(0.1)	2.7	(1.2)	0.2	(0.1)	6.7	(1.8)	0.9	(0.7)	3.5	(1.7)
	United States	0.1	(0.1)	0.1	(0.1)	3.4	(1.5)	0.6	(0.6)	4.4	(1.7)	3.8	(1.9)	3.9	(1.6)
	OECD average	9.3	(0.5)	1.5	(0.3)	7.0	(0.4)	3.4	(0.4)	13.8	(0.6)	4.2	(0.3)	15.6	(0.6)
Partners	Albania	3.5	(2.4)	3.6	(2.2)	8.4	(3.5)	2.7	(2.0)	6.4	(2.4)	11.0	(4.5)	12.8	(4.2)
	Argentina	3.1	(1.6)	0.9	(0.8)	4.1	(1.5)	6.9	(2.5)	19.4	(3.6)	7.3	(2.5)	10.8	(2.9)
	Brazil	5.8	(1.4)	3.3	(1.1)	10.5	(1.6)	2.7	(0.8)	41.3	(2.9)	24.6	(2.7)	14.9	(2.0)
	Bulgaria	5.4	(1.8)	0.6	(0.7)	25.8	(3.5)	5.9	(1.8)	47.1	(3.7)	17.3	(3.6)	30.6	(3.7)
	Colombia	2.6	(0.8)	3.5	(1.4)	10.9	(2.0)	6.6	(1.6)	28.1	(4.2)	14.1	(2.6)	13.9	(2.3)
	Costa Rica	12.2	(3.0)	4.1	(1.1)	14.5	(3.0)	6.7	(2.4)	22.1	(3.4)	20.9	(4.9)	23.9	(3.7)
	Croatia	10.4	(2.3)	0.5	(0.5)	2.6	(1.2)	5.9	(1.9)	15.6	(2.7)	2.6	(1.4)	16.7	(2.7)
	Cyprus*	4.8	(0.1)	1.3	(0.0)	25.1	(0.1)	9.7	(0.0)	23.4	(0.1)	13.9	(0.0)	33.0	(0.1)
	Hong Kong-China	6.2	(2.1)	1.5	(1.1)	4.3	(1.9)	1.9	(1.1)	2.3	(1.2)	35.8	(15.6)	9.6	(2.6)
	Indonesia	11.3	(3.8)	0.7	(0.7)	40.7	(6.0)	17.0	(4.9)	53.5	(5.5)	28.8	(6.6)	45.5	(6.1)
	Jordan	c	c	c	c	c	c	c	c	c	c	c	c	c	c
	Kazakhstan	5.9	(2.2)	5.5	(1.9)	5.1	(2.0)	3.6	(1.8)	9.9	(2.5)	4.1	(2.1)	9.6	(3.0)
	Latvia	5.3	(5.1)	0.0	c	1.4	(1.4)	10.4	(5.8)	15.0	(5.7)	16.3	(8.0)	11.8	(5.9)
	Liechtenstein	c	c	c	c	c	c	c	c	c	c	c	c	c	c
	Lithuania	c	c	c	c	c	c	c	c	c	c	c	c	c	c
	Macao-China	35.7	(0.1)	0.0	c	31.0	(0.1)	13.6	(0.1)	2.1	(0.0)	0.0	c	37.2	(0.1)
	Malaysia	0.6	(0.6)	13.7	(2.7)	16.7	(3.0)	11.2	(2.4)	47.2	(4.1)	4.1	(1.8)	25.6	(3.6)
	Montenegro	4.1	(0.0)	4.5	(0.0)	5.9	(0.0)	7.7	(0.1)	16.2	(0.1)	6.0	(0.1)	9.6	(0.0)
	Peru	3.0	(1.2)	9.5	(2.4)	15.6	(2.5)	9.1	(2.0)	48.2	(4.1)	23.3	(3.2)	20.1	(2.8)
	Qatar	0.9	(0.0)	1.6	(0.0)	10.9	(0.0)	2.0	(0.0)	35.6	(0.1)	14.5	(0.1)	11.4	(0.1)
	Romania	c	c	c	c	c	c	c	c	c	c	c	c	c	c
	Russian Federation	5.4	(2.8)	3.1	(1.8)	2.2	(2.0)	1.8	(0.9)	9.0	(2.0)	2.0	(0.9)	7.2	(2.9)
	Serbia	6.6	(2.2)	0.8	(0.9)	13.1	(2.7)	2.6	(1.4)	33.8	(3.9)	7.0	(2.5)	19.5	(3.2)
	Shanghai-China	4.6	(2.3)	1.1	(1.1)	2.6	(1.9)	1.5	(0.8)	3.1	(1.8)	3.3	(2.0)	7.0	(2.7)
	Singapore	1.5	(0.5)	0.6	(0.5)	0.6	(0.5)	0.6	(0.5)	5.2	(0.6)	0.6	(0.6)	1.5	(0.5)
	Chinese Taipei	15.0	(3.5)	0.0	c	25.1	(4.2)	7.2	(2.2)	3.8	(1.6)	3.5	(1.4)	32.3	(4.6)
	Thailand	2.4	(1.3)	0.8	(0.8)	11.0	(2.7)	5.3	(1.7)	7.9	(2.3)	3.7	(2.0)	15.6	(2.9)
	Tunisia	3.4	(1.9)	5.4	(2.2)	9.1	(3.2)	11.5	(3.4)	44.3	(4.9)	7.3	(2.8)	21.4	(4.6)
	United Arab Emirates	4.2	(0.8)	4.0	(0.9)	13.0	(1.9)	3.0	(0.6)	31.8	(2.7)	14.3	(2.4)	16.6	(2.0)
	Uruguay	0.0	c	0.7	(0.7)	1.6	(0.9)	1.4	(0.9)	27.5	(4.0)	4.5	(1.9)	2.9	(1.3)
	Viet Nam	7.1	(2.4)	2.4	(1.4)	1.8	(1.1)	14.1	(3.2)	49.6	(4.2)	8.5	(2.5)	20.4	(3.6)

Note: Values that are statistically significant are indicated in bold (see Annex A3).
* See notes at the beginning of this Annex.
StatLink ⌕⌕ http://dx.doi.org/10.1787/888932957422

[Part 3/3]
School transfer policies, by level of education
Table IV.2.10 *Results based on school principals' reports*

		Difference between upper and lower secondary education (ISCED 3 - ISCED 2)												
		Percentage of students in schools whose principal reported that a student in the national modal grade for 15-year-olds would be "very likely" transferred to another school for the following reasons:												
		Low academic achievement		High academic achievement		Behavioural problems		Special learning needs		Parents' or guardians' request		Other		"low academic achievement", "behavioural problems" or "special learning needs"	
		% dif.	S.E.	% dif.	S.E.	% dif.	S.E.	% dif.	S.E.	% dif.	S.E.	% dif.	S.E.	% dif.	S.E.
OECD	Australia	0.5	(0.6)	-0.7	(0.8)	1.4	(1.1)	0.6	(0.8)	-0.6	(1.5)	0.0	(0.8)	1.9	(1.3)
	Austria	**30.5**	(8.9)	-7.6	(10.4)	-19.9	(11.4)	-9.8	(8.3)	7.6	(7.1)	-1.8	(8.7)	12.9	(12.2)
	Belgium	9.5	(5.6)	-3.2	(2.5)	-10.6	(6.0)	**-11.9**	(7.3)	**-9.0**	(3.8)	2.1	(1.4)	-1.7	(7.3)
	Canada	-1.1	(0.6)	-0.4	(0.4)	-1.5	(1.0)	**-3.7**	(1.6)	-0.5	(1.3)	0.3	(1.1)	**-4.2**	(1.8)
	Chile	3.6	(2.2)	-7.4	(5.6)	-5.7	(8.4)	4.4	(3.3)	0.4	(8.6)	-5.5	(5.8)	-3.2	(8.4)
	Czech Republic	**9.0**	(3.3)	**-1.6**	(0.8)	2.2	(2.9)	-3.4	(3.7)	3.0	(5.4)	-0.4	(1.8)	**8.4**	(4.1)
	Denmark	c	c	c	c	c	c	c	c	c	c	c	c	c	c
	Estonia	-1.4	(0.8)	-2.0	(1.3)	-0.8	(0.5)	-0.5	(2.8)	-6.5	(4.2)	**-4.2**	(1.8)	-0.9	(2.8)
	Finland	c	c	c	c	c	c	c	c	c	c	c	c	c	c
	France	**6.0**	(2.1)	-1.6	(1.6)	**-18.3**	(5.2)	-0.9	(3.6)	6.8	(3.6)	2.6	(2.9)	-11.0	(5.9)
	Germany	**-3.2**	(1.3)	**-2.1**	(1.0)	-1.1	(0.8)	**-2.8**	(1.1)	**-5.7**	(1.9)	0.0	c	**-6.6**	(1.7)
	Greece	12.2	(2.3)	4.6	(2.8)	6.2	(4.8)	-1.0	(5.8)	20.3	(10.4)	8.5	(7.8)	12.6	(7.2)
	Hungary	**7.4**	(2.5)	-8.5	(6.6)	7.0	(4.6)	2.2	(1.8)	**6.5**	(3.2)	3.0	(1.7)	**11.3**	(5.0)
	Iceland	c	c	c	c	c	c	c	c	c	c	c	c	c	c
	Ireland	0.0	(0.7)	0.0	c	-0.6	(0.4)	-0.6	(0.4)	0.7	(0.6)	0.3	(0.3)	-0.1	(0.7)
	Israel	1.7	(2.1)	0.0	c	**8.9**	(3.0)	4.3	(2.4)	**6.7**	(2.8)	**5.6**	(2.3)	**11.4**	(3.4)
	Italy	**11.1**	(2.6)	0.0	(0.0)	-0.9	(3.2)	**2.8**	(0.8)	**11.4**	(5.1)	-1.8	(4.7)	**10.9**	(4.4)
	Japan	c	c	c	c	c	c	c	c	c	c	c	c	c	c
	Korea	**11.6**	(2.8)	**2.9**	(1.4)	3.9	(5.0)	1.4	(1.0)	-14.7	(16.3)	-3.0	(10.0)	**10.8**	(5.4)
	Luxembourg	**5.4**	(0.1)	**-2.3**	(0.1)	**-9.2**	(0.2)	**0.8**	(0.1)	0.2	(0.2)	**1.6**	(0.1)	**-4.7**	(0.2)
	Mexico	**3.9**	(1.4)	**4.5**	(2.1)	-1.8	(2.7)	0.4	(2.7)	-6.1	(4.3)	**-8.9**	(4.1)	0.8	(3.3)
	Netherlands	3.6	(3.0)	0.0	c	0.4	(2.0)	**-5.0**	(1.9)	1.3	(3.7)	1.2	(1.4)	-0.5	(4.0)
	New Zealand	-0.4	(0.5)	0.2	(0.2)	0.2	(0.6)	1.0	(0.8)	0.8	(0.5)	-0.8	(0.9)	1.0	(1.0)
	Norway	c	c	c	c	c	c	c	c	c	c	c	c	c	c
	Poland	c	c	c	c	c	c	c	c	c	c	c	c	c	c
	Portugal	0.8	(0.9)	0.0	c	-0.4	(1.1)	0.2	(0.3)	-9.1	(4.7)	1.1	(2.1)	0.6	(1.5)
	Slovak Republic	**23.7**	(4.2)	**-2.1**	(1.6)	**15.6**	(5.2)	-2.1	(1.8)	5.9	(6.5)	1.9	(3.5)	**28.9**	(5.8)
	Slovenia	**18.8**	(0.3)	**2.4**	(0.2)	**7.5**	(0.2)	**0.4**	(0.0)	**2.9**	(0.1)	**3.4**	(0.2)	**22.9**	(0.3)
	Spain	c	c	c	c	c	c	c	c	c	c	c	c	c	c
	Sweden	1.3	(1.4)	0.0	(1.7)	1.2	(1.4)	-2.1	(2.0)	-10.5	(5.7)	0.0	(1.8)	-2.2	(2.0)
	Switzerland	11.0	(6.4)	**-16.2**	(2.9)	-0.3	(2.0)	3.0	(4.8)	6.5	(5.8)	-1.7	(1.1)	8.0	(6.7)
	Turkey	c	c	c	c	c	c	c	c	c	c	c	c	c	c
	United Kingdom	c	c	c	c	c	c	c	c	c	c	c	c	c	c
	United States	-3.1	(2.6)	-3.1	(2.6)	-2.0	(2.7)	-3.1	(2.6)	-2.2	(2.8)	-4.1	(4.1)	-2.0	(2.7)
	OECD average	**6.5**	(0.6)	**-1.8**	(0.7)	-0.7	(0.8)	-1.0	(0.7)	0.6	(1.1)	0.0	(0.8)	**4.2**	(1.0)
Partners	Albania	3.5	(2.4)	1.8	(2.4)	2.9	(3.7)	0.4	(2.0)	-0.9	(3.9)	4.4	(4.3)	5.0	(4.4)
	Argentina	2.4	(1.4)	0.4	(0.8)	-4.7	(4.0)	2.5	(1.8)	-5.5	(4.1)	-0.1	(2.6)	-1.9	(4.2)
	Brazil	1.9	(1.1)	1.5	(1.0)	-0.4	(3.1)	-0.3	(1.9)	2.1	(4.0)	4.3	(3.6)	1.2	(3.0)
	Bulgaria	4.7	(1.7)	0.6	(0.7)	5.2	(8.6)	-4.0	(8.4)	-17.8	(12.1)	-7.6	(12.5)	0.1	(10.2)
	Colombia	-0.1	(0.7)	-0.1	(0.7)	-0.7	(1.4)	-2.0	(1.6)	-1.6	(3.0)	-0.6	(1.8)	-2.8	(1.8)
	Costa Rica	2.5	(2.4)	**-2.8**	(1.2)	1.0	(2.8)	-0.9	(2.8)	-5.5	(3.4)	-2.6	(3.5)	2.1	(3.6)
	Croatia	c	c	c	c	c	c	c	c	c	c	c	c	c	c
	Cyprus*	**4.8**	(0.1)	**-2.4**	(0.8)	**4.3**	(1.1)	**1.6**	(0.7)	**2.4**	(1.1)	**-2.8**	(1.0)	**9.3**	(1.2)
	Hong Kong-China	0.4	(0.5)	0.1	(0.2)	0.6	(0.5)	0.0	(0.5)	0.0	(0.6)	11.9	(6.7)	0.7	(0.7)
	Indonesia	**10.7**	(3.8)	0.2	(0.9)	**22.7**	(8.6)	5.1	(6.5)	**21.1**	(7.4)	**21.2**	(7.3)	**22.1**	(8.7)
	Jordan	c	c	c	c	c	c	c	c	c	c	c	c	c	c
	Kazakhstan	2.7	(1.9)	-3.5	(2.2)	0.8	(1.8)	-1.9	(1.9)	**-5.5**	(2.3)	-0.9	(2.3)	0.7	(2.4)
	Latvia	4.4	(4.7)	**-2.7**	(1.1)	-1.5	(1.4)	0.5	(5.4)	-7.6	(5.4)	9.8	(7.8)	0.5	(5.4)
	Liechtenstein	c	c	c	c	c	c	c	c	c	c	c	c	c	c
	Lithuania	c	c	c	c	c	c	c	c	c	c	c	c	c	c
	Macao-China	**3.3**	(0.2)	**-2.4**	(0.0)	**2.1**	(0.2)	**1.7**	(0.1)	0.1	(0.1)	0.0	c	**2.2**	(0.2)
	Malaysia	0.6	(0.6)	0.0	(5.1)	-12.1	(7.7)	3.0	(4.7)	6.1	(7.8)	2.3	(1.4)	-9.5	(8.0)
	Montenegro	c	c	c	c	c	c	c	c	c	c	c	c	c	c
	Peru	0.0	(0.8)	1.6	(1.8)	**3.9**	(1.8)	-0.4	(1.8)	2.7	(3.2)	6.8	(3.6)	2.1	(2.3)
	Qatar	**0.8**	(0.1)	**-10.7**	(0.2)	**-0.8**	(0.2)	**-0.7**	(0.1)	**3.2**	(0.3)	**-12.3**	(0.2)	**-0.6**	(0.2)
	Romania	c	c	c	c	c	c	c	c	c	c	c	c	c	c
	Russian Federation	3.8	(2.4)	0.8	(1.4)	1.9	(2.0)	-0.8	(0.7)	-4.2	(2.3)	-2.6	(1.6)	3.1	(2.5)
	Serbia	c	c	c	c	c	c	c	c	c	c	c	c	c	c
	Shanghai-China	-0.8	(3.3)	-0.2	(1.7)	-0.3	(2.8)	-2.1	(2.0)	-4.3	(3.7)	-1.6	(3.1)	-0.3	(3.8)
	Singapore	**1.2**	(0.6)	0.6	(0.5)	0.6	(0.5)	0.6	(0.5)	1.1	(2.5)	0.6	(0.6)	**1.2**	(0.6)
	Chinese Taipei	**13.9**	(3.3)	0.0	c	**11.1**	(5.7)	-5.8	(4.6)	**-13.7**	(4.4)	-5.8	(4.1)	11.3	(6.2)
	Thailand	2.1	(1.2)	-0.7	(1.5)	3.6	(2.3)	**3.8**	(1.4)	0.4	(2.7)	-0.7	(2.7)	**6.9**	(2.4)
	Tunisia	-1.6	(3.4)	-8.7	(4.9)	-13.3	(7.1)	-0.3	(4.8)	5.3	(7.9)	-0.3	(4.6)	-7.4	(7.8)
	United Arab Emirates	**2.7**	(0.8)	1.6	(1.1)	4.0	(3.0)	0.4	(0.5)	1.6	(3.9)	-0.1	(2.6)	5.8	(3.0)
	Uruguay	0.0	c	-0.7	(0.9)	-0.3	(1.1)	-1.7	(1.5)	-3.2	(5.0)	-2.9	(2.9)	-2.0	(2.0)
	Viet Nam	4.0	(4.4)	2.4	(1.4)	-3.6	(5.5)	6.7	(7.0)	8.9	(13.0)	**8.5**	(2.5)	4.9	(9.2)

Note: Values that are statistically significant are indicated in bold (see Annex A3).
* See notes at the beginning of this Annex.
StatLink ⟨⟨⟩⟩ http://dx.doi.org/10.1787/888932957422

[Part 1/2]
Ability grouping for mathematics classes
Table IV.2.11 *Results based on school principals' reports*

		Percentage of students in schools whose principal reported:																	
		Mathematics classes study similar content, but at different levels of difficulty						Different classes study different content or sets of mathematics topics that have different levels of difficulty						Students are grouped by ability within their mathematics classes					
		For all classes		For some classes		Not for any classes		For all classes		For some classes		Not for any classes		For all classes		For some classes		Not for any classes	
		%	S.E.	%	S.E.	%	S.E.	%	S.E.	%	S.E.	%	S.E.	%	S.E.	%	S.E.	%	S.E.
OECD	Australia	37.6	(1.8)	56.3	(1.9)	6.2	(1.1)	26.4	(1.4)	60.1	(1.7)	13.5	(1.3)	43.6	(1.7)	45.4	(1.8)	10.9	(1.1)
	Austria	13.4	(1.8)	14.7	(2.3)	71.9	(2.3)	a	a	a	a	a	a	7.3	(1.4)	29.2	(3.7)	63.5	(3.8)
	Belgium	12.0	(2.1)	56.0	(3.3)	32.0	(3.2)	14.2	(2.1)	56.6	(3.4)	29.2	(3.1)	3.8	(0.9)	18.4	(2.5)	77.8	(2.5)
	Canada	24.2	(2.5)	57.7	(2.4)	18.2	(1.8)	30.4	(2.2)	49.6	(2.5)	20.0	(1.9)	19.9	(1.9)	44.5	(2.3)	35.6	(2.4)
	Chile	37.3	(4.3)	23.7	(3.4)	39.0	(3.8)	13.4	(2.9)	15.7	(2.9)	70.8	(3.8)	2.4	(1.0)	20.2	(3.3)	77.4	(3.5)
	Czech Republic	9.5	(2.7)	18.5	(2.9)	72.1	(3.5)	3.0	(1.1)	22.8	(3.3)	74.2	(3.4)	7.8	(1.7)	31.4	(3.5)	60.8	(3.3)
	Denmark	12.8	(2.6)	52.6	(4.0)	34.6	(3.7)	6.4	(1.7)	54.7	(3.5)	38.8	(3.5)	5.0	(1.5)	34.3	(3.9)	60.7	(3.7)
	Estonia	25.9	(2.7)	62.1	(2.9)	12.0	(2.1)	6.9	(1.5)	41.3	(3.1)	51.8	(3.0)	18.1	(2.3)	31.4	(2.6)	50.5	(3.1)
	Finland	14.5	(2.4)	34.8	(3.3)	50.7	(3.2)	6.5	(1.4)	45.4	(3.5)	48.2	(3.6)	7.4	(1.8)	41.0	(3.0)	51.6	(3.1)
	France	18.8	(2.9)	30.7	(3.2)	50.5	(3.6)	11.3	(2.2)	20.4	(2.8)	68.3	(3.1)	5.7	(1.3)	24.1	(3.0)	70.2	(3.3)
	Germany	32.8	(2.8)	28.9	(3.4)	38.4	(3.3)	11.1	(2.3)	26.6	(3.3)	62.4	(3.6)	19.6	(2.4)	31.5	(3.4)	48.9	(3.5)
	Greece	6.6	(1.7)	11.3	(3.0)	82.1	(3.1)	0.6	(0.6)	1.5	(0.9)	97.9	(1.1)	1.4	(0.8)	1.8	(1.1)	96.8	(1.3)
	Hungary	44.7	(3.8)	28.7	(3.6)	26.6	(3.5)	6.5	(1.9)	28.7	(4.1)	64.8	(4.1)	10.8	(2.6)	33.3	(3.4)	55.8	(3.9)
	Iceland	21.4	(0.2)	34.5	(0.3)	44.1	(0.2)	37.8	(0.3)	43.6	(0.3)	18.6	(0.2)	18.3	(0.2)	64.1	(0.2)	17.6	(0.2)
	Ireland	50.4	(4.0)	47.2	(4.0)	2.4	(1.3)	23.6	(3.5)	51.7	(3.9)	24.7	(3.4)	53.8	(3.9)	36.3	(3.9)	9.9	(2.5)
	Israel	32.4	(3.0)	50.2	(3.5)	17.4	(3.3)	39.4	(4.0)	49.6	(3.8)	10.9	(2.5)	72.1	(3.6)	22.3	(3.5)	5.7	(1.9)
	Italy	23.4	(1.9)	46.1	(2.3)	30.4	(1.9)	9.0	(1.4)	50.6	(2.3)	40.4	(2.1)	2.6	(0.6)	29.1	(1.9)	68.3	(2.0)
	Japan	17.5	(2.8)	43.3	(3.6)	39.2	(3.7)	3.1	(1.3)	27.8	(3.3)	69.1	(3.1)	16.6	(2.6)	29.5	(3.5)	53.9	(3.5)
	Korea	38.1	(4.0)	50.7	(3.9)	11.2	(2.5)	12.4	(2.8)	51.2	(4.0)	36.4	(4.1)	10.9	(2.7)	61.6	(4.0)	27.5	(3.7)
	Luxembourg	17.2	(0.1)	44.2	(0.1)	38.6	(0.1)	13.4	(0.1)	40.8	(0.1)	45.8	(0.1)	1.2	(0.0)	33.6	(0.1)	65.2	(0.1)
	Mexico	35.2	(1.7)	34.6	(1.8)	30.2	(1.7)	24.3	(1.8)	28.3	(2.4)	47.4	(2.0)	18.9	(1.8)	40.5	(1.9)	40.5	(2.0)
	Netherlands	35.4	(5.1)	47.2	(4.9)	17.4	(2.9)	31.5	(3.8)	48.4	(3.9)	20.1	(3.0)	10.7	(2.8)	50.9	(4.6)	38.4	(4.0)
	New Zealand	24.7	(4.0)	71.4	(4.1)	3.9	(1.4)	22.7	(2.9)	73.8	(3.0)	3.5	(1.3)	34.8	(4.3)	57.3	(4.4)	8.0	(2.2)
	Norway	17.6	(2.7)	18.1	(3.0)	64.3	(3.8)	8.3	(2.1)	16.1	(2.7)	75.5	(3.4)	7.9	(2.1)	19.8	(2.8)	72.3	(3.4)
	Poland	38.1	(4.4)	16.2	(3.2)	45.7	(4.2)	2.2	(1.1)	17.4	(3.4)	80.5	(3.5)	3.2	(1.4)	13.9	(3.2)	83.0	(3.3)
	Portugal	21.1	(3.7)	37.2	(3.8)	41.7	(4.0)	5.1	(1.9)	30.0	(3.6)	64.9	(4.0)	0.3	(0.3)	27.2	(3.5)	72.4	(3.5)
	Slovak Republic	29.8	(3.0)	36.3	(3.4)	33.8	(3.2)	6.6	(1.2)	29.3	(3.5)	64.1	(3.8)	7.9	(1.7)	24.8	(3.6)	67.3	(3.6)
	Slovenia	5.8	(1.0)	39.5	(0.7)	54.6	(0.8)	2.8	(0.1)	31.7	(0.8)	65.5	(0.8)	3.6	(0.2)	50.4	(0.7)	46.0	(0.7)
	Spain	39.4	(2.7)	46.4	(3.2)	14.2	(2.1)	17.7	(2.5)	46.2	(3.2)	36.1	(2.9)	7.3	(1.4)	20.0	(2.3)	72.7	(2.5)
	Sweden	53.2	(3.2)	27.8	(3.4)	19.0	(2.9)	10.5	(2.4)	34.5	(3.5)	54.9	(3.6)	9.2	(2.0)	36.0	(3.3)	54.7	(3.5)
	Switzerland	35.0	(2.8)	38.9	(3.5)	26.1	(3.0)	15.4	(2.3)	46.5	(3.4)	38.1	(3.1)	19.2	(2.7)	33.6	(2.6)	47.2	(3.4)
	Turkey	29.0	(3.9)	44.7	(4.1)	26.3	(3.2)	11.8	(2.6)	33.1	(3.7)	55.1	(4.1)	4.0	(1.5)	11.7	(2.5)	84.3	(3.1)
	United Kingdom	49.3	(3.7)	47.9	(3.8)	2.8	(1.0)	28.6	(3.2)	52.6	(3.6)	18.8	(3.0)	76.9	(2.6)	17.1	(2.4)	6.1	(1.5)
	United States	21.3	(3.6)	66.4	(4.7)	12.3	(3.5)	18.6	(2.7)	66.4	(4.0)	15.0	(3.6)	12.9	(2.7)	66.1	(4.3)	21.0	(4.1)
	OECD average	27.2	(0.5)	40.1	(0.6)	32.6	(0.5)	14.6	(0.4)	39.2	(0.5)	46.2	(0.5)	16.0	(0.4)	33.3	(0.5)	50.7	(0.5)
Partners	Albania	33.5	(4.2)	66.0	(4.2)	0.5	(0.4)	19.1	(2.8)	66.9	(3.6)	14.0	(2.9)	30.9	(4.0)	38.4	(4.2)	30.7	(3.8)
	Argentina	34.6	(3.4)	49.5	(4.0)	15.9	(3.2)	18.1	(2.9)	38.7	(4.4)	43.1	(3.7)	5.1	(2.1)	19.4	(2.9)	75.4	(3.5)
	Brazil	48.3	(2.6)	30.0	(2.3)	21.7	(2.4)	22.0	(2.5)	24.8	(2.4)	53.2	(3.0)	4.9	(1.2)	13.4	(2.0)	81.7	(2.1)
	Bulgaria	15.2	(2.9)	71.4	(3.7)	13.4	(2.6)	20.7	(3.2)	57.6	(4.3)	21.7	(3.9)	4.4	(1.6)	69.0	(3.7)	26.6	(3.4)
	Colombia	32.7	(3.7)	58.9	(4.0)	8.4	(2.1)	18.4	(3.0)	66.7	(3.8)	14.9	(2.4)	9.4	(2.3)	48.2	(3.7)	42.4	(3.8)
	Costa Rica	20.7	(3.4)	32.8	(3.6)	46.5	(4.1)	15.2	(2.9)	24.3	(3.3)	60.5	(3.7)	12.0	(2.3)	43.4	(4.1)	44.6	(4.0)
	Croatia	42.5	(4.2)	45.5	(4.0)	12.0	(2.8)	21.2	(2.8)	55.1	(3.8)	23.8	(3.3)	1.4	(1.0)	44.3	(4.1)	54.3	(4.1)
	Cyprus*	34.0	(0.1)	14.4	(0.1)	51.7	(0.1)	6.4	(0.0)	9.2	(0.1)	84.3	(0.1)	8.3	(0.0)	15.7	(0.1)	75.9	(0.1)
	Hong Kong-China	28.5	(3.9)	61.2	(4.4)	10.3	(2.4)	16.3	(3.0)	58.0	(4.0)	25.7	(3.9)	5.4	(1.7)	37.5	(4.1)	57.1	(4.3)
	Indonesia	45.0	(3.6)	24.8	(3.6)	30.2	(3.6)	23.5	(3.6)	36.3	(3.8)	40.2	(3.5)	13.1	(2.5)	14.7	(2.7)	72.2	(3.3)
	Jordan	49.9	(3.8)	30.5	(3.1)	19.5	(3.2)	15.3	(2.4)	41.0	(3.6)	43.7	(3.8)	11.7	(2.5)	13.5	(3.0)	74.8	(3.6)
	Kazakhstan	51.3	(3.8)	43.9	(3.8)	4.8	(1.6)	22.8	(3.8)	50.0	(4.1)	27.2	(3.5)	34.3	(4.0)	42.4	(4.1)	23.3	(3.3)
	Latvia	31.8	(3.3)	49.6	(3.8)	18.7	(3.1)	9.7	(2.3)	41.9	(4.1)	48.4	(3.6)	6.2	(2.0)	59.4	(3.4)	34.3	(3.3)
	Liechtenstein	39.0	(1.2)	20.8	(1.3)	40.1	(0.7)	10.6	(0.6)	19.4	(1.3)	70.1	(1.2)	50.5	(0.8)	14.5	(0.9)	35.1	(0.9)
	Lithuania	58.3	(3.4)	24.2	(3.1)	17.5	(2.8)	8.9	(2.0)	23.2	(3.1)	67.9	(3.6)	36.9	(3.7)	28.1	(3.6)	35.0	(3.3)
	Macao-China	10.8	(0.0)	55.3	(0.0)	33.9	(0.0)	11.6	(0.0)	50.1	(0.1)	38.3	(0.1)	1.1	(0.0)	36.7	(0.1)	62.2	(0.1)
	Malaysia	38.6	(3.9)	56.9	(3.8)	4.5	(1.6)	13.0	(2.2)	53.8	(3.6)	33.2	(3.5)	14.8	(2.6)	32.2	(3.3)	53.0	(3.7)
	Montenegro	19.4	(0.1)	70.5	(0.1)	10.1	(0.1)	14.2	(0.1)	75.1	(0.2)	10.7	(0.2)	0.6	(0.0)	7.7	(0.1)	91.7	(0.1)
	Peru	31.2	(3.0)	53.8	(3.4)	14.9	(2.4)	26.5	(3.4)	34.3	(3.3)	39.2	(3.5)	8.1	(1.9)	47.0	(3.3)	44.8	(3.3)
	Qatar	56.9	(0.1)	31.3	(0.1)	11.8	(0.0)	29.4	(0.1)	37.8	(0.1)	32.8	(0.1)	13.4	(0.1)	28.3	(0.1)	58.3	(0.1)
	Romania	35.9	(3.6)	45.6	(3.9)	18.5	(3.0)	26.3	(3.1)	57.4	(3.5)	16.2	(2.6)	25.1	(3.5)	40.2	(3.9)	34.7	(3.8)
	Russian Federation	48.4	(3.6)	46.4	(3.6)	5.2	(1.5)	14.5	(2.0)	21.3	(2.5)	64.2	(3.0)	5.2	(1.9)	79.2	(3.0)	15.5	(2.3)
	Serbia	38.5	(3.5)	51.3	(3.8)	10.1	(2.8)	22.4	(3.3)	54.5	(4.1)	23.1	(3.7)	6.3	(2.4)	33.7	(4.4)	60.0	(4.2)
	Shanghai-China	36.3	(4.2)	55.8	(4.1)	7.9	(2.2)	13.0	(2.6)	51.1	(3.6)	35.9	(3.7)	16.2	(3.2)	52.6	(4.4)	31.2	(3.9)
	Singapore	27.8	(0.2)	66.3	(0.6)	5.8	(0.6)	6.7	(0.6)	54.9	(0.6)	38.4	(0.3)	11.8	(0.5)	73.5	(0.5)	14.7	(0.1)
	Chinese Taipei	22.6	(3.5)	57.2	(3.9)	20.1	(2.7)	10.0	(2.4)	52.5	(4.0)	37.5	(3.9)	4.5	(1.6)	26.6	(3.9)	69.0	(4.1)
	Thailand	5.4	(1.9)	68.3	(3.3)	26.4	(3.3)	0.0	c	57.1	(3.4)	42.9	(3.4)	0.7	(0.7)	50.3	(3.8)	49.0	(3.8)
	Tunisia	40.6	(4.2)	36.0	(4.1)	23.5	(3.3)	28.9	(4.0)	32.6	(4.3)	38.6	(4.3)	4.8	(1.8)	11.0	(2.4)	84.2	(3.0)
	United Arab Emirates	57.1	(2.7)	25.1	(2.1)	17.8	(2.2)	31.6	(2.6)	22.8	(2.1)	45.7	(2.6)	42.2	(1.9)	37.6	(2.3)	20.2	(1.8)
	Uruguay	25.0	(3.2)	64.1	(3.5)	10.9	(2.4)	16.1	(2.8)	58.6	(3.7)	25.3	(3.4)	1.4	(1.0)	8.1	(2.1)	90.5	(2.1)
	Viet Nam	38.4	(4.1)	53.0	(4.6)	8.6	(2.2)	7.0	(1.9)	55.4	(4.2)	37.6	(4.3)	10.8	(2.6)	35.0	(4.3)	54.3	(4.1)

* See notes at the beginning of this Annex.
StatLink http://dx.doi.org/10.1787/888932957422

[Part 2/2]
Table IV.2.11 Ability grouping for mathematics classes
Results based on school principals' reports

	Percentage of students in schools whose principal reported:											
	In mathematics classes, teachers use pedagogy suitable for students with heterogeneous abilities (i.e. students are not grouped by ability)						No ability grouping for any class		One form of grouping for some classes		One form of grouping for all classes	
	For all classes		For some classes		Not for any classes							
	%	S.E.	%	S.E.	%	S.E.	%	S.E.	%	S.E.	%	S.E.
OECD												
Australia	21.3	(1.3)	50.2	(1.5)	28.5	(1.7)	1.6	(0.5)	48.6	(1.7)	49.8	(1.6)
Austria	31.4	(3.9)	51.8	(4.4)	16.9	(2.9)	71.9	(2.3)	14.7	(2.3)	13.4	(1.8)
Belgium	55.8	(3.3)	27.7	(2.8)	16.4	(2.2)	20.6	(2.9)	57.0	(3.1)	22.4	(2.7)
Canada	35.4	(2.8)	47.7	(2.7)	16.9	(2.0)	7.1	(1.2)	49.2	(2.5)	43.8	(2.7)
Chile	48.9	(3.8)	24.2	(3.7)	26.8	(3.5)	35.7	(3.8)	24.5	(3.6)	39.8	(4.2)
Czech Republic	49.8	(3.7)	37.4	(3.6)	12.8	(2.0)	58.8	(4.2)	30.6	(3.7)	10.6	(2.7)
Denmark	42.4	(3.6)	52.1	(3.7)	5.5	(1.7)	24.1	(3.2)	58.0	(3.8)	17.9	(2.8)
Estonia	47.6	(2.9)	44.8	(2.8)	7.6	(1.1)	10.9	(2.1)	61.1	(2.9)	28.0	(2.6)
Finland	51.7	(2.9)	37.2	(3.2)	11.1	(2.3)	35.5	(3.5)	46.4	(3.8)	18.0	(2.5)
France	67.6	(3.1)	22.6	(2.8)	9.7	(2.0)	43.8	(3.5)	31.4	(3.2)	24.8	(3.3)
Germany	40.9	(3.5)	33.4	(3.2)	25.7	(3.1)	31.9	(3.1)	32.9	(3.4)	35.3	(3.0)
Greece	63.7	(4.1)	18.8	(3.4)	17.5	(3.0)	81.4	(3.2)	11.3	(3.2)	7.3	(1.8)
Hungary	55.9	(4.0)	33.8	(3.7)	10.3	(2.4)	23.3	(2.9)	31.2	(3.8)	45.5	(3.8)
Iceland	67.9	(0.2)	29.1	(0.2)	2.9	(0.1)	12.9	(0.1)	40.8	(0.2)	46.3	(0.3)
Ireland	18.7	(3.0)	41.6	(3.8)	39.7	(4.1)	0.8	(0.7)	40.2	(4.0)	59.0	(4.0)
Israel	17.0	(3.0)	32.8	(3.9)	50.2	(4.1)	1.7	(1.0)	41.4	(3.8)	56.9	(3.9)
Italy	44.9	(2.2)	41.2	(2.1)	13.9	(1.6)	24.1	(1.7)	48.7	(1.9)	27.3	(1.9)
Japan	42.1	(3.7)	40.9	(3.7)	17.0	(2.6)	36.9	(3.7)	44.6	(3.6)	18.6	(2.9)
Korea	17.2	(3.1)	51.0	(4.0)	31.8	(3.6)	9.9	(2.3)	48.6	(3.8)	41.5	(3.9)
Luxembourg	44.4	(0.1)	39.3	(0.1)	16.3	(0.1)	32.1	(0.1)	41.4	(0.1)	26.5	(0.1)
Mexico	30.6	(1.9)	37.4	(1.9)	32.0	(1.8)	26.3	(1.6)	32.2	(1.9)	41.5	(1.9)
Netherlands	38.9	(4.2)	34.9	(3.7)	26.2	(4.2)	6.4	(1.7)	39.0	(4.6)	54.6	(4.9)
New Zealand	22.8	(3.4)	58.4	(3.6)	18.8	(3.1)	1.3	(0.9)	60.5	(3.7)	38.2	(3.6)
Norway	81.0	(2.8)	12.6	(2.3)	6.4	(1.9)	54.2	(4.0)	23.2	(3.3)	22.6	(3.1)
Poland	63.2	(4.4)	13.1	(2.9)	23.7	(3.7)	42.4	(4.1)	19.3	(3.5)	38.3	(4.3)
Portugal	60.9	(4.0)	32.3	(3.8)	6.7	(2.7)	38.3	(4.1)	38.1	(3.7)	23.6	(3.5)
Slovak Republic	55.9	(4.1)	25.7	(3.2)	18.3	(3.4)	28.4	(3.3)	39.1	(3.3)	32.5	(2.9)
Slovenia	27.3	(0.7)	64.3	(0.7)	8.4	(0.4)	50.5	(0.7)	42.1	(0.7)	7.4	(0.9)
Spain	59.2	(2.6)	26.0	(2.2)	14.8	(2.0)	7.6	(1.6)	43.8	(2.8)	48.6	(2.9)
Sweden	55.9	(4.0)	33.8	(3.3)	10.3	(2.3)	15.7	(2.8)	27.8	(3.3)	56.5	(3.3)
Switzerland	36.7	(3.2)	30.6	(3.2)	32.7	(2.8)	15.0	(2.3)	40.9	(3.4)	44.0	(3.0)
Turkey	43.0	(3.6)	21.7	(3.4)	35.3	(4.0)	24.2	(3.1)	42.1	(3.9)	33.7	(3.7)
United Kingdom	5.4	(1.4)	14.0	(2.0)	80.6	(2.2)	0.7	(0.5)	37.1	(3.4)	62.2	(3.5)
United States	33.6	(4.2)	56.0	(4.4)	10.4	(2.9)	6.1	(2.6)	62.9	(4.2)	31.0	(3.8)
OECD average	43.5	(0.6)	35.8	(0.5)	20.7	(0.5)	25.9	(0.5)	39.7	(0.6)	34.3	(0.5)
Partners												
Albania	50.1	(3.9)	39.2	(3.7)	10.7	(2.8)	0.1	(0.1)	51.8	(4.4)	48.2	(4.4)
Argentina	43.3	(3.5)	37.4	(4.1)	19.2	(3.3)	14.5	(3.0)	47.5	(4.1)	38.0	(3.6)
Brazil	37.5	(2.6)	20.4	(2.4)	42.1	(2.5)	18.4	(2.2)	28.1	(2.2)	53.5	(2.6)
Bulgaria	41.2	(3.8)	55.9	(3.8)	2.9	(1.3)	6.9	(2.1)	62.6	(4.1)	30.5	(3.6)
Colombia	38.9	(3.9)	42.2	(3.8)	18.9	(3.4)	6.4	(1.9)	52.6	(3.9)	41.0	(3.8)
Costa Rica	40.6	(3.8)	31.4	(3.8)	27.9	(4.1)	39.6	(4.2)	34.8	(3.8)	25.6	(3.8)
Croatia	39.3	(3.6)	47.2	(3.8)	13.4	(2.8)	8.0	(2.4)	37.8	(3.9)	54.2	(4.2)
Cyprus*	61.1	(0.1)	32.1	(0.1)	6.8	(0.0)	49.1	(0.1)	15.9	(0.1)	35.0	(0.1)
Hong Kong-China	41.0	(4.4)	50.0	(4.4)	9.0	(2.4)	9.0	(2.2)	60.1	(4.3)	31.0	(4.0)
Indonesia	52.6	(3.8)	22.2	(3.2)	25.2	(3.4)	24.6	(3.2)	27.7	(3.6)	47.6	(3.8)
Jordan	61.6	(3.0)	22.4	(3.0)	16.0	(2.7)	18.3	(3.2)	28.7	(2.9)	53.0	(3.7)
Kazakhstan	30.4	(3.9)	44.6	(4.4)	25.0	(3.4)	2.4	(1.2)	37.9	(4.0)	59.6	(4.1)
Latvia	41.7	(3.7)	53.0	(3.8)	5.2	(1.8)	17.8	(3.0)	46.1	(3.9)	36.1	(3.3)
Liechtenstein	43.3	(0.6)	32.1	(0.9)	24.5	(0.6)	40.1	(0.7)	13.2	(1.2)	46.7	(1.2)
Lithuania	48.7	(3.4)	25.3	(3.4)	26.0	(2.8)	15.9	(2.8)	24.7	(3.0)	59.4	(3.4)
Macao-China	49.2	(0.1)	29.4	(0.0)	21.4	(0.0)	33.9	(0.0)	52.9	(0.0)	13.3	(0.0)
Malaysia	41.6	(3.9)	49.2	(3.9)	9.2	(2.5)	4.1	(1.6)	56.0	(3.7)	39.9	(3.8)
Montenegro	38.9	(0.1)	54.6	(0.2)	6.5	(0.1)	6.9	(0.1)	66.4	(0.1)	26.7	(0.1)
Peru	34.9	(3.6)	36.4	(3.4)	28.7	(3.5)	13.2	(2.4)	45.3	(3.8)	41.5	(3.5)
Qatar	50.8	(0.1)	31.6	(0.1)	17.5	(0.1)	8.4	(0.0)	30.0	(0.1)	61.5	(0.1)
Romania	33.1	(3.7)	52.3	(3.8)	14.6	(2.5)	9.7	(2.2)	44.3	(3.6)	45.9	(3.5)
Russian Federation	35.4	(3.9)	60.5	(3.9)	4.1	(1.3)	4.0	(1.2)	39.2	(3.1)	56.8	(3.3)
Serbia	41.1	(4.8)	36.8	(4.3)	22.1	(3.6)	5.2	(2.1)	47.9	(4.1)	46.9	(3.9)
Shanghai-China	49.2	(3.8)	43.1	(3.8)	7.7	(2.0)	5.9	(1.9)	54.8	(4.1)	39.3	(4.3)
Singapore	32.5	(0.5)	63.5	(0.7)	4.0	(0.5)	2.8	(0.0)	66.6	(0.6)	30.5	(0.6)
Chinese Taipei	27.7	(3.6)	56.1	(4.2)	16.2	(3.0)	19.5	(2.6)	57.2	(3.9)	23.3	(3.5)
Thailand	21.1	(2.5)	74.4	(3.0)	4.4	(1.7)	23.7	(2.8)	71.0	(3.1)	5.4	(1.9)
Tunisia	51.7	(4.0)	18.5	(3.0)	29.8	(4.0)	17.7	(2.9)	32.1	(3.8)	50.2	(4.1)
United Arab Emirates	62.1	(2.4)	28.4	(2.5)	9.5	(1.3)	13.8	(2.2)	21.9	(1.8)	64.2	(2.7)
Uruguay	40.0	(3.9)	38.5	(3.5)	21.5	(3.3)	8.9	(2.2)	58.6	(3.8)	32.5	(3.5)
Viet Nam	46.5	(4.3)	41.5	(4.4)	12.0	(2.7)	6.9	(2.0)	51.6	(4.2)	41.5	(4.0)

* See notes at the beginning of this Annex.
StatLink http://dx.doi.org/10.1787/888932957422

[Part 1/2]
Correlation between stratification and students' motivation
Table IV.2.14 *System-level correlation*

		OECD countries							
		Index of vertical stratification							
		Index of vertical stratification =		Variability in students' grade levels +		Variability in students' primary school starting age +		Grade repetition	
				(a)		(b)		(c)	
		Corr.	p-value	Corr.	p-value	Corr.	p-value	Corr.	p-value
Index of instrumental motivation for mathematics	Mean index	0.06	(0.76)	-0.06	(0.72)	**0.39**	(0.02)	-0.20	(0.26)
	Variation in the index (standard deviation)	0.11	(0.52)	-0.07	(0.70)	0.05	(0.79)	*0.29*	(0.10)[1]
	10th percentile of the index	0.02	(0.93)	0.02	(0.90)	0.28	(0.11)	-0.27	(0.13)
	90th percentile of the index	0.12	(0.49)	-0.08	(0.65)	**0.43**	(0.01)	-0.06	(0.74)
Adjusted index of instrumental motivation for mathematics[2]	Mean index	0.05	(0.80)	-0.12	(0.49)	**0.40**	(0.02)	-0.17	(0.34)
	Variation in the index (standard deviation)	-0.04	(0.82)	-0.10	(0.58)	-0.06	(0.75)	0.06	(0.73)
	10th percentile of the index	0.02	(0.90)	-0.12	(0.48)	**0.38**	(0.03)	-0.20	(0.26)
	90th percentile of the index	-0.02	(0.93)	-0.11	(0.53)	0.07	(0.70)	0.01	(0.97)

		All participating countries and economies							
		Index of vertical stratification							
		Index of vertical stratification =		Variability in students' grade levels +		Variability in students' primary school starting age +		Grade repetition	
				(a)		(b)		(c)	
		Corr.	p-value	Corr.	p-value	Corr.	p-value	Corr.	p-value
Index of instrumental motivation for mathematics	Mean index	**0.27**	(0.03)	0.19	(0.14)	**0.38**	(0.00)	0.05	(0.71)
	Variation in the index (standard deviation)	-0.05	(0.72)	-0.13	(0.31)	-0.08	(0.51)	0.11	(0.38)
	10th percentile of the index	*0.21*	(0.09)	0.18	(0.14)	**0.33**	(0.01)	-0.04	(0.76)
	90th percentile of the index	*0.24*	(0.05)	0.13	(0.30)	**0.33**	(0.01)	0.09	(0.49)
Adjusted index of instrumental motivation for mathematics[2]	Mean index	*0.24*	(0.05)	0.14	(0.27)	**0.34**	(0.01)	0.07	(0.57)
	Variation in the index (standard deviation)	0.04	(0.76)	-0.03	(0.80)	0.03	(0.84)	0.10	(0.43)
	10th percentile of the index	*0.23*	(0.06)	0.16	(0.22)	**0.32**	(0.01)	0.05	(0.71)
	90th percentile of the index	0.20	(0.11)	0.14	(0.27)	0.16	(0.21)	0.19	(0.14)

Notes: Values that are statistically significant at the 10% level (p < 0.10) are indicated in italics and those at the 5% level (p < 0.05) are in bold. While Pearson's correlation coefficients are presented in this table, Spearman's rank correlation coefficients are also computed in order to examine the robustness of the results. When Pearson's correlation coefficient is significant at the 10% level but Spearman's rank correlation coefficient is not significant at the 10% level, the cell is shaded in grey.

(a) Standard deviation of students' grade levels (Table IV.2.4).

(b) Standard deviation of students' primary school starting age (Table IV.2.1).

(c) Percentage of students who have repeated a grade at least once in primary, lower secondary or upper secondary school (Table IV.2.2).

(d) Number of school types or distinct education programmes available to 15-year-old students (Table IV.2.5).

(e) Percentage of students who are enrolled in a programme whose curriculum is pre-vocational or vocational (Table IV.2.6).

(f) First age of selection in the education system (Table IV.2.5) is subtracted from 15. The negative values are set to 0.

(g) Percentage of students in schools whose principals reported both "students' records of academic performance" and "recommendations of feeder schools" are always considered for admission (Table IV.2.7).

(h) Percentage of students in schools whose principal reported that a student in the national modal grade for 15-year-olds would be "very likely" be transferred to another school because of "low academic achievement", "behavioural problems" or "special learning needs" (Table IV.2.9).

(i) Percentage of students in schools whose principals reported one form of ability grouping for all mathematics classes (Table IV.2.11)

1. While Pearson's correlation coefficients are presented in this table, Spearman's rank correlation coefficients are also computed in order to examine the robustness of the results. When Pearson's correlation coefficient is significant at least at the 10% level but Spearman's rank correlation coefficient is not significant at the 10% level, a 1 appears in the cell.

2. See Annex A6 for more details on the adjustment.

StatLink ᴍᴤᵽ http://dx.doi.org/10.1787/888932957441

[Part 2/2]
Correlation between stratification and students' motivation

Table IV.2.14 *System-level correlation*

OECD countries

		Index of horizontal stratification (between schools) =		Number of educational tracks (d)		Prevalence of vocational and pre-vocational programmes (e)		Early selection (f)		Academic selectivity (g)		School transfer rates (h)		Index of horizontal stratification (within schools) — Ability grouping for all mathematics classes (i)	
		Corr.	p-value	Corr.	p-value	Corr.	p-value	Corr.	p-value	Corr.	p-value	Corr.	p-value	Corr.	p-value
Index of instrumental motivation for mathematics	Mean index	**-0.65**	(0.00)	**-0.59**	(0.00)	**-0.54**	(0.00)	**-0.56**	(0.00)	**-0.45**	(0.01)	**-0.43**	(0.01)	**0.40**	(0.02)
	Variation in the index (standard deviation)	0.13	(0.45)	-0.02	(0.93)	0.09	(0.62)	0.05	(0.80)	0.13	(0.46)	0.28	(0.11)	-0.09	(0.60)
	10th percentile of the index	**-0.56**	(0.00)	**-0.45**	(0.01)	**-0.43**	(0.01)	**-0.41**	(0.02)	**-0.51**	(0.00)	**-0.41**	(0.02)	*0.29*	(0.10)
	90th percentile of the index	**-0.62**	(0.00)	**-0.61**	(0.00)	**-0.45**	(0.01)	**-0.54**	(0.00)	**-0.49**	(0.00)	*-0.33*	(0.05)	0.24	(0.17)
Adjusted index of instrumental motivation for mathematics[2]	Mean index	**-0.66**	(0.00)	**-0.57**	(0.00)	**-0.60**	(0.00)	**-0.57**	(0.00)	*-0.32*	(0.06)	**-0.53**	(0.00)	**0.47**	(0.01)
	Variation in the index (standard deviation)	0.23	(0.18)	0.12	(0.49)	0.20	(0.27)	*0.29*	(0.09)	-0.03	(0.88)	**0.34**	(0.05)	-0.18	(0.31)
	10th percentile of the index	**-0.57**	(0.00)	**-0.51**	(0.00)	**-0.51**	(0.00)	**-0.55**	(0.00)	-0.22	(0.21)	**-0.47**	(0.00)	**0.43**	(0.01)
	90th percentile of the index	**-0.50**	(0.00)	-0.16	(0.38)	**-0.53**	(0.00)	**-0.39**	(0.02)	-0.19	(0.28)	**-0.71**	(0.00)	0.24	(0.17)

All participating countries and economies

		Index of horizontal stratification (between schools) =		Number of educational tracks (d)		Prevalence of vocational and pre-vocational programmes (e)		Early selection (f)		Academic selectivity (g)		School transfer rates (h)		Index of horizontal stratification (within schools) — Ability grouping for all mathematics classes (i)	
		Corr.	p-value	Corr.	p-value	Corr.	p-value	Corr.	p-value	Corr.	p-value	Corr.	p-value	Corr.	p-value
Index of instrumental motivation for mathematics	Mean index	**-0.44**	(0.00)	*-0.25*	(0.05)	**-0.45**	(0.00)	**-0.41**	(0.00)	*-0.23*	(0.07)[1]	-0.17	(0.17)	**0.37**	(0.00)
	Variation in the index (standard deviation)	0.03	(0.78)	0.03	(0.81)	0.07	(0.56)	0.13	(0.30)	-0.17	(0.18)	0.07	(0.59)	0.02	(0.88)
	10th percentile of the index	**-0.34**	(0.01)	*-0.22*	(0.09)	**-0.35**	(0.00)	**-0.36**	(0.00)	-0.14	(0.28)	-0.14	(0.27)	*0.22*	(0.07)
	90th percentile of the index	**-0.48**	(0.00)	**-0.28**	(0.03)	**-0.44**	(0.00)	**-0.38**	(0.00)	**-0.34**	(0.01)	-0.19	(0.13)	**0.28**	(0.03)
Adjusted index of instrumental motivation for mathematics[2]	Mean index	**-0.49**	(0.00)	*-0.24*	(0.06)	**-0.48**	(0.00)	**-0.35**	(0.00)	-0.19	(0.13)	**-0.40**	(0.00)	**0.27**	(0.03)
	Variation in the index (standard deviation)	0.15	(0.24)	0.09	(0.47)	0.19	(0.12)	0.15	(0.23)	*-0.21*	(0.09)[1]	0.20	(0.12)	0.08	(0.51)
	10th percentile of the index	**-0.47**	(0.00)	**-0.30**	(0.02)	**-0.53**	(0.00)	**-0.37**	(0.00)	-0.04	(0.73)	**-0.32**	(0.01)	0.20	(0.11)
	90th percentile of the index	-0.10	(0.42)	0.11	(0.41)	-0.11	(0.40)	-0.12	(0.33)	-0.05	(0.70)	*-0.22*	(0.07)[1]	0.01	(0.92)

Notes: Values that are statistically significant at the 10% level (p<0.10) are indicated in italics and those at the 5% level (p<0.05) are in bold. While Pearson's correlation coefficients are presented in this table, Spearman's rank correlation coefficients are also computed in order to examine the robustness of the results. When Pearson's correlation coefficient is significant at least at the 10% level but Spearman's rank correlation coefficient is not significant at the 10% level, the cell is shaded in grey.

(a) Standard deviation of students' grade levels (Table IV.2.4).

(b) Standard deviation of students' primary school starting age (Table IV.2.1).

(c) Percentage of students who have repeated a grade at least once in primary, lower secondary or upper secondary school (Table IV.2.2).

(d) Number of school types or distinct education programmes available to 15-year-old students (Table IV.2.5).

(e) Percentage of students who are enrolled in a programme whose curriculum is pre-vocational or vocational (Table IV.2.6).

(f) First age of selection in the education system (Table IV.2.5) is subtracted from 15. The negative values are set to 0.

(g) Percentage of students in schools whose principals reported both "students' records of academic performance" and "recommendations of feeder schools" are always considered for admission (Table IV.2.7).

(h) Percentage of students in schools whose principal reported that a student in the national modal grade for 15-year-olds would be "very likely" be transferred to another school because of "low academic achievement", "behavioural problems" or "special learning needs" (Table IV.2.9).

(i) Percentage of students in schools whose principals reported one form of ability grouping for all mathematics classes (Table IV.2.11)

1. While Pearson's correlation coefficients are presented in this table, Spearman's rank correlation coefficients are also computed in order to examine the robustness of the results. When Pearson's correlation coefficient is significant at least at the 10% level but Spearman's rank correlation coefficient is not significant at the 10% level, a 1 appears in the cell.

2. See Annex A6 for more details on the adjustment.

StatLink ᘜᔒᖯ http://dx.doi.org/10.1787/888932957441

[Part 1/1]
Stratification, variation in socio-economic status and performance, and students' motivation
Table IV.2.16   *Results based on school principals' and students' reports and system-level data collection*

	Differentiation			Socio-economic profiles (ESCS)[1]		Academic profiles			Students' instrumental motivation			
	Vertical stratification	Horizontal stratification (between schools)	Horizontal stratification (within schools)	Variation in student socio-economic status	Socio-economic inclusion index (1-rho)	Mean mathematics performance	Variation in mathematics performance	Academic inclusion index (1-rho)	Index of instrumental motivation for mathematics		Adjusted index of instrumental motivation for mathematics	
	Mean index	Mean index	Mean index	S.D.	Ratio	Mean index	S.D.	Ratio	Mean index	S.E.	Mean index	S.E.
OECD												
Australia	0.09	-0.51	1.01	0.79	76.5	504.15	96.29	72.1	0.24	(0.01)	0.27	(0.01)
Austria	0.07	2.23	-1.37	0.85	71.2	505.54	92.48	51.6	-0.41	(0.03)	-0.22	(0.03)
Belgium	1.00	0.82	-0.78	0.91	72.4	514.75	102.29	49.5	-0.37	(0.02)	-0.22	(0.02)
Canada	0.38	-0.64	0.62	0.86	82.8	518.07	88.86	80.2	0.25	(0.01)	0.27	(0.02)
Chile	0.78	-0.33	0.36	1.13	47.2	422.63	80.75	56.6	0.32	(0.02)	0.15	(0.02)
Czech Republic	-0.13	1.00	-1.55	0.75	76.4	498.96	94.94	48.5	-0.17	(0.02)	-0.15	(0.03)
Denmark	-0.22	-0.87	-1.07	0.84	82.3	500.03	82.10	83.5	0.23	(0.02)	0.21	(0.02)
Estonia	-0.54	-0.66	-0.42	0.81	81.5	520.55	80.90	82.7	0.02	(0.02)	0.05	(0.02)
Finland	-0.59	-0.98	-1.06	0.77	91.1	518.75	85.29	92.5	-0.01	(0.02)	0.04	(0.02)
France	0.93	-0.03	-0.62	0.80	w	494.98	97.46	w	-0.16	(0.02)	-0.12	(0.03)
Germany	0.43	0.52	0.06	0.93	73.6	513.53	96.30	47.0	-0.13	(0.02)	-0.02	(0.03)
Greece	-0.19	-0.30	-1.77	1.00	73.5	452.97	87.79	67.9	0.02	(0.02)	-0.09	(0.03)
Hungary	0.17	0.73	0.73	0.96	62.6	477.04	93.62	38.1	-0.05	(0.02)	-0.15	(0.03)
Iceland	-1.23	-0.84	0.78	0.81	86.4	492.80	91.94	90.1	0.33	(0.02)	0.31	(0.02)
Ireland	0.28	-0.40	1.61	0.85	79.7	501.50	84.58	81.8	0.13	(0.02)	0.22	(0.02)
Israel	-0.53	-0.11	1.47	0.85	74.6	466.48	104.91	57.6	0.31	(0.02)	0.16	(0.03)
Italy	-0.06	0.78	-0.46	0.97	75.9	485.32	92.78	48.5	-0.19	(0.01)	-0.22	(0.01)
Japan	-2.08	0.19	-1.03	0.71	77.8	536.41	93.52	47.0	-0.50	(0.02)	-0.20	(0.02)
Korea	-0.61	0.49	0.47	0.74	78.3	553.77	99.08	60.4	-0.39	(0.03)	-0.22	(0.03)
Luxembourg	0.95	0.60	-0.51	1.10	73.6	489.85	95.40	61.1	-0.28	(0.02)	-0.21	(0.02)
Mexico	0.61	0.20	0.47	1.27	56.5	413.28	74.27	64.8	0.51	(0.01)	0.23	(0.01)
Netherlands	0.54	1.22	1.32	0.78	81.8	522.97	91.61	34.1	-0.36	(0.02)	-0.09	(0.03)
New Zealand	-0.48	-0.50	0.25	0.82	77.5	499.75	99.60	76.2	0.28	(0.02)	0.30	(0.03)
Norway	-0.88	-0.95	-0.77	0.76	91.0	489.37	90.48	87.1	0.19	(0.02)	0.07	(0.03)
Poland	-1.44	-0.81	0.26	0.90	76.4	517.50	90.37	79.5	-0.14	(0.02)	-0.23	(0.04)
Portugal	1.43	-0.25	-0.70	1.19	68.6	487.06	93.95	70.1	0.26	(0.02)	0.18	(0.02)
Slovak Republic	0.05	0.80	-0.12	0.92	64.4	481.64	100.84	50.1	-0.33	(0.02)	-0.42	(0.03)
Slovenia	-0.52	0.49	-1.76	0.87	74.6	501.13	91.66	41.3	-0.23	(0.02)	-0.38	(0.04)
Spain	0.75	-0.93	0.93	1.03	75.2	484.32	87.74	81.2	-0.02	(0.02)	-0.04	(0.02)
Sweden	-0.49	-0.88	1.45	0.82	86.9	478.26	91.75	87.5	0.18	(0.02)	0.15	(0.03)
Switzerland	1.15	0.53	0.63	0.89	82.7	530.93	94.29	64.4	-0.12	(0.02)	-0.08	(0.02)
Turkey	0.17	0.85	-0.04	1.10	72.3	447.98	91.07	38.2	0.06	(0.02)	-0.15	(0.03)
United Kingdom	-0.64	-0.73	1.82	0.80	79.4	493.93	94.52	71.8	0.32	(0.02)	0.30	(0.02)
United States	0.84	-0.68	-0.22	0.97	73.8	481.37	89.86	76.3	0.14	(0.02)	0.30	(0.02)
OECD average	0.00	0.00	0.00	0.90	75.7	494.05	91.86	64.8	0.00	(0.02)	0.00	(0.03)
Partners												
Albania	0.07	-0.05	0.90	m	m	394.33	91.49	95.4	0.55	(0.02)	0.20	(0.05)
Argentina	1.14	-0.32	0.24	1.11	66.5	388.43	76.74	55.6	0.16	(0.02)	-0.09	(0.03)
Brazil	4.11	-0.51	1.25	1.17	62.8	391.46	77.72	56.9	0.37	(0.01)	0.13	(0.02)
Bulgaria	-0.50	1.01	-0.25	1.05	59.6	438.74	93.91	47.2	-0.04	(0.02)	-0.25	(0.03)
Colombia	2.15	-0.05	0.44	1.18	63.2	376.49	74.33	64.9	0.42	(0.02)	0.21	(0.02)
Costa Rica	1.29	0.26	-0.57	1.24	61.8	407.00	68.36	57.6	0.30	(0.02)	0.19	(0.03)
Croatia	-0.56	1.36	1.30	0.85	75.9	471.13	88.47	55.7	-0.24	(0.02)	-0.18	(0.03)
Cyprus*	-0.57	-0.09	0.04	0.91	76.6	439.70	93.13	67.6	0.10	(0.02)	-0.03	(0.02)
Hong Kong-China	0.44	-0.02	-0.22	0.97	67.7	561.26	96.31	57.6	-0.23	(0.02)	-0.09	(0.02)
Indonesia	0.67	0.26	0.87	1.10	63.1	375.11	71.36	48.0	0.35	(0.02)	-0.13	(0.02)
Jordan	-0.33	-0.08	1.22	1.02	79.6	385.60	77.58	64.0	0.45	(0.02)	-0.09	(0.03)
Kazakhstan	-0.22	-0.19	1.65	0.75	76.8	431.80	71.18	63.5	0.41	(0.03)	0.25	(0.03)
Latvia	-0.18	-0.12	0.12	0.89	74.7	490.57	81.87	74.4	0.13	(0.02)	0.12	(0.03)
Liechtenstein	1.41	0.54	0.81	0.91	85.5	534.97	95.27	37.5	0.10	(0.07)	0.03	(0.10)
Lithuania	-0.41	-0.32	1.63	0.92	78.7	478.82	89.11	69.3	0.27	(0.02)	0.03	(0.03)
Macao-China	1.65	0.28	-1.38	0.87	73.7	538.13	94.50	58.2	-0.26	(0.02)	-0.07	(0.02)
Malaysia	-0.19	0.44	0.36	0.99	71.5	420.51	81.11	67.6	0.53	(0.02)	0.05	(0.03)
Montenegro	-0.60	0.93	-0.50	0.89	80.6	409.63	82.67	63.5	-0.29	(0.02)	-0.36	(0.03)
Peru	2.31	-0.24	0.47	1.23	54.2	368.10	84.36	54.4	0.56	(0.01)	0.36	(0.02)
Qatar	0.82	-0.08	1.78	0.89	75.5	376.45	99.86	53.8	0.29	(0.01)	-0.18	(0.02)
Romania	-0.73	-0.16	0.76	0.94	64.4	444.55	81.34	54.6	-0.57	(0.02)	-0.72	(0.03)
Russian Federation	-0.29	-0.48	1.47	0.76	75.0	482.17	86.37	73.2	-0.07	(0.02)	-0.02	(0.03)
Serbia	-1.16	1.84	0.82	0.90	78.0	448.86	90.68	54.0	-0.09	(0.02)	-0.19	(0.03)
Shanghai-China	0.52	0.23	0.32	0.96	66.8	612.68	100.98	53.1	0.01	(0.02)	0.33	(0.02)
Singapore	-0.30	0.35	-0.25	0.92	76.4	573.47	105.36	63.3	0.40	(0.02)	0.35	(0.02)
Chinese Taipei	-0.22	0.43	-0.72	0.84	76.7	559.82	115.61	57.9	-0.33	(0.02)	-0.29	(0.03)
Thailand	-0.49	0.23	-1.89	1.17	61.6	426.74	82.21	57.9	0.39	(0.01)	0.03	(0.02)
Tunisia	1.32	0.12	1.03	1.26	67.2	387.82	78.18	50.7	0.41	(0.02)	0.08	(0.04)
United Arab Emirates	1.18	0.29	1.95	0.85	73.9	434.01	89.51	55.6	0.37	(0.02)	0.12	(0.02)
Uruguay	1.40	0.34	-0.12	1.13	60.2	409.29	88.70	58.0	0.21	(0.02)	0.07	(0.03)
Viet Nam	-0.45	0.33	0.47	1.12	58.3	511.34	85.76	47.9	0.37	(0.02)	0.20	(0.02)

1. ESCS refers to the *PISA index of economic, social and cultural status.*
* See notes at the beginning of this Annex.
StatLink ᵃᵐˢ⁴ http://dx.doi.org/10.1787/888932957441

[Part 1/3]
Change between 2003 and 2012 in primary school starting age

Table IV.2.17 *Results based on students' self-reports*

		Average age of entry into primary school			Percentage of students who started primary school at:									
									PISA 2003					
					4 years old		5 years old		6 years old		7 years old		8 years old or older	
		Mean age	S.E.	S.D.	S.E.	%	S.E.	%	S.E.	%	S.E.	%	S.E.	%	S.E.
OECD	Australia	5.2	(0.0)	0.70	(0.01)	12.4	(0.5)	58.2	(0.8)	24.8	(0.7)	2.7	(0.2)	0.4	(0.1)
	Austria	6.2	(0.0)	0.54	(0.01)	0.2	(0.1)	4.9	(0.4)	70.6	(0.9)	22.9	(0.9)	1.1	(0.2)
	Belgium	5.9	(0.0)	0.60	(0.01)	1.7	(0.2)	15.2	(0.5)	68.1	(0.7)	9.5	(0.5)	0.6	(0.1)
	Canada	5.2	(0.0)	0.81	(0.01)	19.5	(0.6)	48.5	(0.7)	27.2	(0.6)	4.4	(0.3)	0.3	(0.1)
	Czech Republic	6.4	(0.0)	0.52	(0.00)	0.0	c	0.8	(0.1)	62.1	(0.9)	35.9	(0.9)	1.2	(0.2)
	Denmark	6.6	(0.0)	0.63	(0.01)	0.0	c	3.7	(0.3)	35.3	(1.1)	56.5	(1.0)	4.6	(0.4)
	Finland	6.7	(0.0)	0.48	(0.00)	0.0	c	0.3	(0.1)	27.7	(0.6)	71.0	(0.6)	1.1	(0.1)
	France	5.9	(0.0)	0.69	(0.02)	4.9	(0.5)	14.9	(0.9)	68.9	(1.2)	10.4	(0.7)	0.8	(0.2)
	Germany	6.3	(0.0)	0.55	(0.01)	0.1	(0.1)	2.3	(0.2)	62.4	(0.9)	34.0	(0.9)	1.2	(0.2)
	Greece	6.3	(0.0)	0.46	(0.01)	0.0	(0.0)	0.5	(0.1)	73.5	(1.1)	25.6	(1.1)	0.4	(0.1)
	Hungary	6.7	(0.0)	0.58	(0.01)	0.1	(0.1)	0.6	(0.1)	36.4	(0.8)	58.5	(0.8)	4.3	(0.3)
	Iceland	5.8	(0.0)	0.43	(0.01)	0.0	c	19.4	(0.7)	78.1	(0.8)	1.9	(0.2)	0.0	c
	Ireland	4.4	(0.0)	0.57	(0.01)	59.8	(1.2)	36.2	(1.2)	4.1	(0.3)	0.0	c	0.0	c
	Italy	5.9	(0.0)	0.42	(0.01)	0.2	(0.1)	12.9	(0.6)	82.8	(0.7)	3.9	(0.3)	0.2	(0.1)
	Japan	c	c	c	c	0.0	c	0.0	c	0.0	c	0.0	c	0.0	c
	Korea	6.1	(0.0)	0.30	(0.02)	0.0	(0.0)	1.1	(0.3)	91.6	(1.2)	6.9	(1.2)	0.4	(0.2)
	Luxembourg	6.0	(0.0)	0.73	(0.01)	4.6	(0.3)	8.6	(0.4)	64.8	(0.6)	17.8	(0.5)	1.6	(0.2)
	Mexico	6.1	(0.0)	0.64	(0.01)	0.9	(0.2)	11.0	(0.6)	68.5	(0.9)	17.6	(1.0)	2.0	(0.3)
	Netherlands	6.0	(0.0)	0.66	(0.01)	2.2	(0.3)	14.8	(0.7)	67.5	(1.0)	14.2	(1.0)	1.2	(0.2)
	New Zealand	5.0	(0.0)	0.47	(0.02)	5.7	(0.4)	85.6	(0.6)	5.0	(0.4)	2.2	(0.3)	0.3	(0.1)
	Norway	6.5	(0.0)	0.65	(0.01)	1.5	(0.2)	4.0	(0.4)	34.0	(1.2)	60.1	(1.4)	0.3	(0.1)
	Poland	7.0	(0.0)	0.35	(0.01)	0.0	c	0.2	(0.1)	5.2	(0.4)	89.1	(0.7)	5.5	(0.5)
	Portugal	5.9	(0.0)	0.59	(0.01)	0.4	(0.1)	22.4	(0.7)	66.7	(0.9)	10.0	(0.6)	0.5	(0.1)
	Slovak Republic	6.3	(0.0)	0.53	(0.01)	0.4	(0.1)	1.1	(0.1)	64.2	(1.2)	33.3	(1.2)	0.7	(0.2)
	Spain	5.8	(0.0)	0.47	(0.01)	0.0	c	20.4	(0.9)	76.1	(0.9)	3.1	(0.3)	0.4	(0.1)
	Sweden	6.7	(0.0)	0.55	(0.01)	0.3	(0.1)	2.3	(0.3)	26.2	(1.2)	67.6	(1.4)	1.1	(0.2)
	Switzerland	6.5	(0.0)	0.74	(0.02)	1.6	(0.3)	4.3	(0.4)	35.7	(1.0)	49.7	(1.3)	4.4	(0.3)
	Turkey	6.8	(0.0)	0.53	(0.02)	0.0	c	0.5	(0.1)	21.1	(1.0)	72.4	(1.2)	5.2	(1.0)
	United States	5.4	(0.0)	0.78	(0.01)	9.3	(0.6)	52.1	(0.9)	31.3	(0.7)	6.5	(0.5)	0.9	(0.2)
	OECD average 2003	6.1	(0.0)	0.57	(0.00)	4.3	(0.1)	15.4	(0.1)	47.6	(0.2)	27.2	(0.2)	1.4	(0.1)
Partners	Brazil	6.6	(0.0)	0.84	(0.02)	1.4	(0.2)	6.1	(0.5)	30.6	(1.0)	54.1	(1.2)	7.4	(0.8)
	Hong Kong-China	6.1	(0.0)	0.77	(0.02)	1.6	(0.2)	11.6	(0.6)	66.0	(1.1)	16.8	(0.8)	4.0	(0.4)
	Indonesia	6.3	(0.0)	0.73	(0.01)	1.1	(0.1)	10.0	(0.6)	48.9	(1.1)	37.8	(1.3)	2.2	(0.2)
	Latvia	6.8	(0.0)	0.58	(0.01)	0.1	(0.0)	1.1	(0.2)	26.5	(1.0)	66.5	(1.0)	5.8	(0.4)
	Liechtenstein	6.6	(0.0)	0.62	(0.03)	0.0	c	2.2	(0.8)	34.6	(2.7)	51.0	(2.9)	5.1	(1.2)
	Macao-China	6.2	(0.0)	0.89	(0.03)	3.0	(0.7)	14.4	(1.4)	50.7	(1.8)	26.2	(1.4)	5.7	(0.9)
	Russian Federation	6.8	(0.0)	0.54	(0.01)	0.0	c	0.4	(0.1)	24.1	(1.4)	68.5	(1.5)	6.1	(0.5)
	Thailand	6.7	(0.0)	0.50	(0.01)	0.0	c	0.5	(0.1)	29.4	(1.1)	68.4	(1.1)	1.6	(0.3)
	Tunisia	6.0	(0.0)	0.43	(0.01)	0.7	(0.1)	8.9	(0.6)	83.9	(0.8)	5.2	(0.4)	0.2	(0.1)
	Uruguay	5.8	(0.0)	0.65	(0.01)	3.4	(0.4)	25.8	(1.0)	63.7	(0.9)	6.5	(0.5)	0.6	(0.2)

Notes: Values that are statistically significant are indicated in bold (see Annex A3).
Only countries and economies with comparable data from PISA 2003 and PISA 2012 are shown.
StatLink http://dx.doi.org/10.1787/888932957441

[Part 2/3]
Change between 2003 and 2012 in primary school starting age
Table IV.2.17   *Results based on students' self-reports*

| | | Average age of entry into primary school | | | Percentage of students who started primary school at: | | | | | | | | | |
| | | | | | 4 years old | | 5 years old | | 6 years old | | 7 years old | | 8 years old or older | |
		Mean age	S.E.	S.D.	S.E.	%	S.E.	%	S.E.	%	S.E.	%	S.E.	%	S.E.
OECD	Australia	5.2	(0.0)	0.68	(0.01)	11.5	(0.3)	58.4	(0.4)	26.9	(0.5)	3.1	(0.2)	0.0	c
	Austria	6.2	(0.0)	0.52	(0.01)	0.0	c	4.2	(0.4)	73.6	(0.9)	20.8	(0.8)	1.4	(0.3)
	Belgium	5.9	(0.0)	0.60	(0.01)	1.3	(0.2)	18.9	(0.6)	70.3	(0.6)	8.3	(0.4)	1.1	(0.2)
	Canada	5.2	(0.0)	0.98	(0.03)	17.8	(0.6)	49.9	(0.7)	27.5	(0.6)	3.1	(0.2)	1.6	(0.1)
	Czech Republic	6.4	(0.0)	0.55	(0.01)	0.0	c	1.2	(0.2)	61.9	(1.0)	34.9	(0.9)	1.9	(0.3)
	Denmark	6.6	(0.0)	0.68	(0.01)	0.1	(0.1)	3.2	(0.2)	36.1	(0.7)	53.6	(0.7)	7.0	(0.4)
	Finland	6.7	(0.0)	0.48	(0.00)	0.0	(0.0)	0.1	(0.0)	28.8	(0.7)	69.9	(0.7)	1.1	(0.1)
	France	5.9	(0.0)	0.80	(0.03)	3.5	(0.3)	15.9	(0.7)	68.9	(0.9)	9.4	(0.5)	2.3	(0.3)
	Germany	6.2	(0.0)	0.54	(0.01)	0.0	(0.0)	4.8	(0.4)	70.1	(0.8)	24.0	(0.7)	1.1	(0.2)
	Greece	6.3	(0.0)	0.77	(0.06)	0.1	(0.0)	4.4	(0.4)	70.5	(1.4)	23.0	(1.3)	2.1	(0.3)
	Hungary	6.7	(0.0)	0.59	(0.01)	0.1	(0.1)	0.4	(0.1)	36.1	(0.8)	57.8	(0.8)	5.6	(0.5)
	Iceland	5.8	(0.0)	0.51	(0.01)	1.7	(0.2)	19.5	(0.7)	75.7	(0.8)	3.0	(0.3)	0.1	(0.1)
	Ireland	4.5	(0.0)	0.58	(0.01)	56.0	(0.9)	39.5	(0.9)	4.5	(0.4)	0.0	c	0.0	c
	Italy	5.9	(0.0)	0.44	(0.01)	0.0	c	13.0	(0.3)	81.9	(0.4)	4.6	(0.2)	0.5	(0.1)
	Japan	6.0	(0.0)	0.00	(0.00)	0.0	c	0.0	c	100.0	c	0.0	c	0.0	c
	Korea	6.6	(0.0)	0.61	(0.01)	0.3	(0.1)	1.2	(0.2)	38.3	(2.3)	55.5	(2.2)	4.7	(0.5)
	Luxembourg	6.2	(0.0)	0.59	(0.01)	0.0	c	6.5	(0.3)	67.6	(0.7)	23.3	(0.6)	2.6	(0.2)
	Mexico	6.1	(0.0)	0.73	(0.02)	0.8	(0.1)	8.2	(0.2)	73.5	(0.4)	15.8	(0.4)	1.7	(0.1)
	Netherlands	6.1	(0.0)	0.56	(0.01)	0.0	c	12.2	(0.6)	71.6	(0.9)	15.0	(0.6)	1.2	(0.2)
	New Zealand	5.1	(0.0)	0.56	(0.03)	5.3	(0.4)	84.3	(0.8)	7.7	(0.5)	2.0	(0.2)	0.8	(0.1)
	Norway	5.8	(0.0)	0.67	(0.05)	0.3	(0.1)	24.8	(0.7)	70.2	(0.7)	3.9	(0.3)	0.8	(0.2)
	Poland	7.0	(0.0)	0.07	(0.02)	0.0	c	0.0	c	0.5	(0.2)	99.5	(0.2)	0.0	c
	Portugal	5.9	(0.0)	0.83	(0.04)	0.0	c	24.9	(0.8)	64.9	(0.8)	7.7	(0.4)	2.5	(0.3)
	Slovak Republic	6.3	(0.0)	0.52	(0.01)	0.0	c	1.5	(0.2)	65.3	(1.1)	32.3	(1.0)	1.0	(0.1)
	Spain	5.8	(0.0)	0.50	(0.01)	0.0	c	25.4	(0.7)	70.4	(0.8)	4.2	(0.4)	0.0	c
	Sweden	6.8	(0.0)	0.68	(0.05)	0.3	(0.1)	1.5	(0.3)	25.3	(1.3)	70.2	(1.5)	2.8	(0.3)
	Switzerland	6.5	(0.0)	1.03	(0.03)	2.8	(0.4)	6.4	(0.4)	44.2	(0.9)	41.4	(0.9)	5.1	(0.3)
	Turkey	6.9	(0.0)	0.54	(0.01)	0.0	(0.0)	1.1	(0.2)	17.5	(0.7)	74.7	(0.8)	6.7	(0.5)
	United States	5.9	(0.0)	1.05	(0.07)	3.5	(0.3)	24.5	(0.8)	57.5	(0.9)	12.6	(0.6)	1.9	(0.2)
	OECD average 2003	6.1	(0.0)	0.61	(0.00)	3.6	(0.1)	15.7	(0.1)	52.0	(0.2)	26.7	(0.2)	2.0	(0.1)
Partners	Brazil	7.2	(0.0)	2.28	(0.04)	3.6	(0.2)	9.2	(0.4)	32.4	(0.9)	34.3	(1.0)	20.5	(0.7)
	Hong Kong-China	6.1	(0.0)	0.61	(0.02)	0.0	c	11.1	(0.6)	73.3	(1.0)	13.3	(0.7)	2.3	(0.3)
	Indonesia	6.3	(0.0)	0.65	(0.01)	0.0	c	8.3	(0.9)	54.5	(1.4)	35.3	(1.6)	1.9	(0.3)
	Latvia	6.8	(0.0)	0.56	(0.01)	0.0	c	1.8	(0.4)	25.0	(0.9)	69.4	(1.0)	3.8	(0.4)
	Liechtenstein	6.6	(0.1)	1.16	(0.21)	0.0	c	4.3	(1.2)	43.6	(3.0)	46.5	(2.9)	5.6	(1.4)
	Macao-China	6.2	(0.0)	0.69	(0.01)	0.0	c	12.6	(0.5)	61.8	(0.7)	22.3	(0.7)	3.3	(0.2)
	Russian Federation	6.7	(0.0)	0.56	(0.01)	0.0	(0.0)	0.8	(0.2)	36.0	(1.6)	60.0	(1.6)	3.2	(0.2)
	Thailand	6.2	(0.0)	0.47	(0.01)	0.0	c	4.4	(0.5)	76.5	(1.1)	18.9	(1.0)	0.2	(0.1)
	Tunisia	5.9	(0.0)	0.47	(0.03)	0.1	(0.1)	13.6	(0.5)	81.7	(0.7)	4.3	(0.5)	0.2	(0.1)
	Uruguay	5.9	(0.0)	0.54	(0.01)	1.5	(0.2)	11.9	(0.6)	78.0	(0.8)	8.0	(0.5)	0.6	(0.1)

Notes: Values that are statistically significant are indicated in bold (see Annex A3).
Only countries and economies with comparable data from PISA 2003 and PISA 2012 are shown.
StatLink ⟐⟐⟐ http://dx.doi.org/10.1787/888932957441

[Part 3/3]
Change between 2003 and 2012 in primary school starting age

Table IV.2.17   *Results based on students' self-reports*

		Change between 2003 and 2012 (PISA 2012 - PISA 2003)															
		Average age of entry into primary school				Percentage of students who started primary school at:											
						4 years old		5 years old		6 years old		7 years old		8 years old or older	
		Mean age	S.E.	S.D.	S.E.	% dif.	S.E.	% dif.	S.E.	% dif.	S.E.	% dif.	S.E.	% dif.	S.E.
OECD	Australia	0.0	(0.0)	-0.02	(0.01)	-0.9	(0.6)	0.2	(0.9)	**2.1**	(0.9)	0.4	(0.3)	-0.4	c
	Austria	0.0	(0.0)	-0.02	(0.02)	-0.2	c	-0.7	(0.6)	**3.1**	(1.3)	-2.2	(1.2)	0.3	(0.3)
	Belgium	0.0	(0.0)	0.00	(0.02)	-0.4	(0.3)	**3.7**	(0.8)	**2.2**	(0.9)	-1.1	(0.7)	**0.5**	(0.2)
	Canada	0.1	(0.0)	0.17	(0.03)	-1.7	(0.9)	1.4	(1.0)	0.3	(0.9)	**-1.3**	(0.3)	**1.3**	(0.2)
	Czech Republic	0.0	(0.0)	0.03	(0.01)	0.0	c	0.4	(0.2)	-0.2	(1.3)	-1.0	(1.3)	**0.8**	(0.3)
	Denmark	0.0	(0.0)	0.04	(0.01)	0.1	c	-0.5	(0.4)	0.8	(1.3)	-2.9	(1.2)	**2.4**	(0.6)
	Finland	0.0	(0.0)	0.00	(0.01)	0.0	c	**-0.2**	(0.1)	1.1	(0.9)	-1.1	(0.9)	0.1	(0.2)
	France	0.1	(0.0)	0.11	(0.03)	**-1.3**	(0.6)	0.9	(1.1)	0.0	(1.5)	-1.0	(0.8)	**1.4**	(0.3)
	Germany	-0.1	(0.0)	-0.02	(0.01)	-0.1	(0.1)	**2.5**	(0.4)	**7.7**	(1.2)	**-10.0**	(1.2)	-0.1	(0.3)
	Greece	0.0	(0.0)	0.31	(0.06)	0.1	(0.1)	**3.9**	(0.4)	-3.0	(1.7)	-2.6	(1.7)	**1.6**	(0.3)
	Hungary	0.0	(0.0)	0.01	(0.01)	0.0	(0.1)	-0.2	(0.1)	-0.3	(1.1)	-0.7	(1.1)	**1.3**	(0.6)
	Iceland	0.0	(0.0)	0.08	(0.01)	1.7	c	0.0	(1.0)	-2.4	(1.1)	1.1	(0.4)	0.1	c
	Ireland	0.0	(0.0)	0.01	(0.01)	**-3.8**	(1.5)	**3.4**	(1.5)	0.4	(0.5)	0.0	c	0.0	c
	Italy	0.0	(0.0)	0.02	(0.01)	-0.2	c	0.1	(0.7)	-0.8	(0.8)	0.7	(0.4)	**0.3**	(0.1)
	Japan	c	c	c	c	0.0	c	0.0	c	100.0	c	0.0	c	0.0	c
	Korea	0.6	(0.0)	0.31	(0.02)	**0.3**	(0.1)	0.1	(0.4)	**-53.3**	(2.6)	**48.7**	(2.5)	**4.3**	(0.5)
	Luxembourg	0.2	(0.0)	-0.14	(0.01)	-4.6	c	**-2.0**	(0.5)	**2.9**	(0.9)	**5.5**	(0.8)	**0.9**	(0.3)
	Mexico	0.0	(0.0)	0.09	(0.02)	-0.1	(0.2)	**-2.8**	(0.6)	**5.0**	(1.0)	-1.8	(1.1)	-0.3	(0.3)
	Netherlands	0.1	(0.0)	-0.10	(0.02)	-2.2	c	**-2.6**	(0.9)	**4.1**	(1.4)	0.8	(1.1)	0.0	(0.3)
	New Zealand	0.1	(0.0)	0.09	(0.03)	-0.5	(0.6)	-1.4	(1.0)	**2.7**	(0.6)	-0.2	(0.3)	**0.5**	(0.2)
	Norway	-0.7	(0.0)	0.03	(0.05)	**-1.2**	(0.2)	**20.9**	(0.8)	**36.2**	(1.4)	**-56.2**	(1.4)	**0.5**	(0.2)
	Poland	0.0	(0.0)	-0.28	(0.02)	0.0	c	-0.2	c	**-4.7**	(0.5)	**10.4**	(0.7)	-5.5	c
	Portugal	0.0	(0.0)	0.24	(0.04)	-0.4	c	**2.6**	(1.0)	-1.8	(1.2)	**-2.3**	(0.8)	**2.0**	(0.3)
	Slovak Republic	0.0	(0.0)	-0.01	(0.01)	-0.4	c	0.3	(0.2)	1.1	(1.6)	-1.1	(1.6)	0.3	(0.2)
	Spain	0.0	(0.0)	0.03	(0.01)	0.0	c	**5.0**	(1.1)	**-5.8**	(1.2)	1.1	(0.5)	-0.4	c
	Sweden	0.1	(0.0)	0.13	(0.05)	0.0	(0.1)	-0.8	(0.4)	-0.9	(1.8)	2.6	(2.0)	**1.7**	(0.3)
	Switzerland	-0.1	(0.0)	0.29	(0.04)	**1.2**	(0.5)	**2.1**	(0.5)	**8.5**	(1.4)	**-8.3**	(1.5)	0.7	(0.5)
	Turkey	0.0	(0.0)	0.01	(0.01)	0.0	c	**0.6**	(0.2)	**-3.6**	(1.2)	2.3	(1.4)	1.5	(1.1)
	United States	0.5	(0.0)	0.26	(0.07)	**-5.8**	(0.7)	**-27.5**	(1.2)	**26.3**	(1.1)	**6.1**	(0.8)	**0.9**	(0.3)
	OECD average 2003	0.0	(0.0)	0.06	(0.01)	**-0.7**	(0.1)	**0.3**	(0.1)	**4.4**	(0.2)	**-0.5**	(0.2)	**0.6**	(0.1)
Partners	Brazil	0.6	(0.0)	1.43	(0.05)	**2.2**	(0.3)	**3.1**	(0.6)	1.8	(1.4)	**-19.8**	(1.5)	**13.1**	(1.1)
	Hong Kong-China	0.0	(0.0)	-0.15	(0.03)	-1.6	c	-0.4	(0.8)	**7.3**	(1.5)	**-3.5**	(1.1)	**-1.8**	(0.5)
	Indonesia	0.0	(0.0)	-0.08	(0.01)	-1.1	c	-1.7	(1.0)	**5.6**	(1.8)	-2.4	(2.0)	-0.3	(0.3)
	Latvia	0.0	(0.0)	-0.02	(0.02)	-0.1	c	0.7	(0.4)	-1.5	(1.3)	**3.0**	(1.4)	**-2.0**	(0.6)
	Liechtenstein	0.0	(0.1)	0.54	(0.21)	0.0	c	2.1	(1.4)	**8.9**	(4.0)	-4.5	(4.1)	0.5	(1.8)
	Macao-China	0.0	(0.0)	-0.21	(0.03)	-3.0	c	-1.9	(1.4)	**11.2**	(1.9)	**-3.9**	(1.6)	**-2.4**	(0.9)
	Russian Federation	-0.2	(0.0)	0.02	(0.01)	0.0	c	**0.4**	(0.2)	**11.9**	(2.1)	**-8.6**	(2.2)	**-2.9**	(0.6)
	Thailand	-0.6	(0.0)	-0.03	(0.01)	0.0	c	**3.8**	(0.5)	**47.1**	(1.6)	**-49.6**	(1.5)	**-1.4**	(0.3)
	Tunisia	0.0	(0.0)	0.04	(0.03)	**-0.5**	(0.1)	**4.7**	(0.8)	**-2.2**	(1.1)	-0.9	(0.7)	0.0	(0.1)
	Uruguay	0.2	(0.0)	-0.12	(0.02)	**-1.9**	(0.4)	**-13.9**	(1.1)	**14.3**	(1.2)	**1.5**	(0.7)	0.0	(0.2)

Notes: Values that are statistically significant are indicated in bold (see Annex A3).
Only countries and economies with comparable data from PISA 2003 and PISA 2012 are shown.
StatLink ᵐˢ⁴ http://dx.doi.org/10.1787/888932957441

[Part 1/3]
Change between 2003 and 2012 in grade repetition
Table IV.2.18   *Results based on students' self-reports*

	PISA 2003																		
	Percentage of students reporting that they have repeated a grade in:																		
	Primary school						Lower secondary school						Upper secondary school						Primary, lower secondary or upper secondary school
	Never		Once		Twice or more		Never		Once		Twice or more		Never		Once		Twice or more		
	%	S.E.	%	S.E.	%	S.E.	%	S.E.	%	S.E.	%	S.E.	%	S.E.	%	S.E.	%	S.E.	%	S.E.
Australia	91.8	(0.4)	8.0	(0.4)	0.1	(0.0)	98.7	(0.1)	1.3	(0.1)	0.0	(0.0)	99.8	(0.1)	0.2	(0.1)	0.0	c	9.2	(0.5)
Austria	96.6	(0.6)	3.3	(0.6)	0.1	(0.1)	96.2	(0.6)	3.7	(0.6)	0.2	(0.1)	96.0	(0.6)	4.0	(0.6)	0.0	c	10.2	(1.0)
Belgium	82.3	(0.7)	16.1	(0.6)	1.6	(0.2)	91.3	(0.4)	8.4	(0.4)	0.3	(0.1)	90.6	(0.5)	9.4	(0.5)	0.1	(0.0)	30.3	(0.7)
Canada	94.1	(0.3)	5.3	(0.3)	0.7	(0.1)	94.2	(0.4)	5.0	(0.3)	0.8	(0.1)	99.3	(0.1)	0.7	(0.1)	0.0	(0.0)	10.9	(0.5)
Czech Republic	98.5	(0.2)	1.5	(0.2)	0.0	(0.0)	98.7	(0.2)	1.3	(0.2)	0.0	(0.0)	0.0	c	0.0	c	0.0	c	2.7	(0.3)
Denmark	97.1	(0.3)	2.8	(0.3)	0.1	(0.1)	99.2	(0.2)	0.8	(0.2)	0.0	(0.0)	100.0	c	0.0	c	0.0	c	3.6	(0.4)
Finland	97.6	(0.2)	2.3	(0.2)	0.0	(0.0)	99.5	(0.1)	0.5	(0.1)	0.0	c	0.0	c	0.0	c	0.0	c	2.8	(0.3)
France	82.7	(1.0)	16.3	(0.9)	1.0	(0.2)	70.4	(1.2)	28.6	(1.2)	1.1	(0.2)	0.0	c	0.0	c	0.0	c	39.5	(1.1)
Germany	90.2	(0.7)	9.5	(0.7)	0.2	(0.1)	84.9	(0.7)	14.4	(0.7)	0.7	(0.1)	0.0	c	0.0	c	0.0	c	21.6	(0.9)
Greece	99.3	(0.1)	0.7	(0.1)	0.0	(0.0)	94.0	(0.7)	5.2	(0.5)	0.8	(0.2)	99.1	(0.2)	0.9	(0.2)	0.0	c	7.1	(0.7)
Hungary	95.8	(0.4)	3.7	(0.4)	0.4	(0.1)	96.4	(0.4)	3.1	(0.3)	0.6	(0.1)	96.9	(0.3)	3.1	(0.3)	0.0	(0.0)	9.7	(0.5)
Iceland	100.0	c	0.0	c	0.0	c	100.0	c	0.0	c	0.0	c	0.0	c	0.0	c	0.0	c	0.0	c
Ireland	86.3	(0.7)	13.4	(0.7)	0.3	(0.1)	98.8	(0.2)	1.2	(0.2)	0.0	c	99.8	(0.1)	0.2	(0.1)	0.0	c	14.4	(0.7)
Italy	98.4	(0.4)	1.2	(0.3)	0.4	(0.2)	94.0	(0.6)	5.4	(0.5)	0.6	(0.2)	90.8	(0.5)	9.1	(0.5)	0.1	(0.1)	15.1	(0.7)
Japan	0.0	c	0.0	c	0.0	c	0.0	c	0.0	c	0.0	c	0.0	c	0.0	c	0.0	c	0.0	c
Korea	99.8	(0.1)	0.2	(0.1)	0.0	c	99.8	(0.1)	0.2	(0.1)	0.0	c	99.9	(0.0)	0.1	(0.0)	0.0	c	0.5	(0.1)
Luxembourg	82.3	(0.5)	15.0	(0.5)	2.7	(0.3)	71.0	(0.5)	28.4	(0.5)	0.7	(0.1)	99.9	(0.1)	0.1	(0.1)	0.0	c	38.6	(0.4)
Mexico	75.4	(1.6)	21.8	(1.4)	2.8	(0.3)	91.5	(0.9)	8.1	(0.9)	0.4	(0.1)	97.0	(0.5)	2.9	(0.5)	0.0	(0.0)	29.7	(1.7)
Netherlands	77.6	(1.0)	21.8	(1.0)	0.6	(0.2)	89.3	(0.8)	10.7	(0.8)	0.0	(0.0)	0.0	c	0.0	c	0.0	c	29.5	(1.1)
New Zealand	96.6	(0.3)	3.4	(0.3)	0.1	(0.0)	98.8	(0.2)	1.1	(0.2)	0.0	(0.0)	99.6	(0.1)	0.4	(0.1)	0.1	(0.0)	4.6	(0.3)
Norway	0.0	c	0.0	c	0.0	c	0.0	c	0.0	c	0.0	c	0.0	c	0.0	c	0.0	c	0.0	c
Poland	97.6	(0.3)	2.2	(0.3)	0.2	(0.1)	98.3	(0.3)	1.6	(0.2)	0.1	(0.1)	100.0	c	0.0	c	0.0	c	3.6	(0.4)
Portugal	80.7	(1.8)	15.0	(1.7)	4.3	(0.5)	80.8	(1.3)	15.8	(1.1)	3.4	(0.4)	99.8	(0.1)	0.2	(0.1)	0.0	c	30.2	(1.9)
Slovak Republic	98.4	(0.3)	1.3	(0.3)	0.3	(0.1)	98.8	(0.2)	1.0	(0.1)	0.2	(0.1)	0.0	c	0.0	c	0.0	c	2.5	(0.4)
Spain	93.6	(0.5)	6.2	(0.5)	0.2	(0.1)	74.7	(1.0)	25.1	(1.0)	0.2	(0.1)	0.0	c	0.0	c	0.0	c	29.0	(1.0)
Sweden	97.2	(0.4)	2.8	(0.4)	0.0	(0.0)	99.2	(0.2)	0.8	(0.2)	0.0	c	100.0	c	0.0	c	0.0	c	3.5	(0.4)
Switzerland	85.1	(0.8)	14.3	(0.8)	0.6	(0.1)	90.7	(0.7)	9.2	(0.7)	0.1	(0.0)	99.5	(0.2)	0.5	(0.2)	0.0	c	22.0	(1.1)
Turkey	94.1	(1.1)	5.3	(0.9)	0.6	(0.3)	95.2	(0.9)	4.6	(0.8)	0.2	(0.2)	88.5	(1.1)	11.5	(1.1)	0.0	c	18.0	(1.5)
United States	91.9	(0.6)	7.8	(0.6)	0.3	(0.1)	95.8	(0.6)	3.9	(0.6)	0.2	(0.1)	99.3	(0.2)	0.7	(0.2)	0.0	c	11.6	(0.8)
OECD average 2003	85.5	(0.1)	6.9	(0.1)	0.6	(0.0)	86.2	(0.1)	6.5	(0.1)	0.4	(0.0)	64.0	(0.1)	1.5	(0.1)	0.0	(0.0)	13.8	(0.2)
Brazil	77.5	(1.2)	19.5	(1.1)	3.1	(0.4)	81.0	(1.2)	15.6	(1.0)	3.4	(0.4)	97.6	(0.4)	2.4	(0.4)	0.0	c	33.1	(1.4)
Hong Kong-China	87.2	(0.6)	11.9	(0.6)	0.9	(0.1)	94.6	(0.4)	4.9	(0.4)	0.5	(0.1)	99.9	(0.1)	0.1	(0.1)	0.0	c	16.8	(0.6)
Indonesia	84.6	(0.9)	14.6	(0.9)	0.8	(0.1)	98.5	(0.2)	1.3	(0.2)	0.2	(0.1)	99.8	(0.1)	0.2	(0.1)	0.0	c	15.9	(0.9)
Latvia	94.2	(0.6)	5.5	(0.6)	0.3	(0.1)	98.4	(0.3)	1.4	(0.2)	0.2	(0.1)	100.0	c	0.0	c	0.0	c	7.0	(0.7)
Liechtenstein	91.5	(1.5)	8.5	(1.5)	0.0	c	88.0	(1.5)	11.7	(1.6)	0.3	(0.3)	100.0	c	0.0	c	0.0	c	18.7	(1.8)
Macao-China	67.6	(1.4)	24.6	(1.6)	7.8	(0.9)	67.0	(1.6)	27.3	(1.5)	5.6	(0.8)	98.1	(0.9)	1.9	(0.9)	0.0	c	49.8	(1.4)
Russian Federation	97.7	(0.3)	2.2	(0.3)	0.1	(0.0)	98.8	(0.2)	1.1	(0.2)	0.1	(0.1)	0.0	c	0.0	c	0.0	c	3.2	(0.3)
Thailand	99.6	(0.2)	0.4	(0.2)	0.0	c	98.8	(0.2)	1.0	(0.2)	0.1	(0.1)	99.3	(0.3)	0.7	(0.3)	0.0	c	1.8	(0.3)
Tunisia	47.5	(1.4)	34.0	(1.1)	18.4	(0.9)	58.5	(1.6)	36.1	(1.4)	5.3	(0.5)	98.8	(0.4)	1.2	(0.4)	0.0	c	61.8	(1.4)
Uruguay	79.6	(1.4)	15.8	(1.1)	4.6	(0.5)	78.0	(1.4)	17.8	(1.1)	4.2	(0.5)	98.6	(0.3)	1.4	(0.3)	0.0	c	33.6	(1.9)

Notes: Values that are statistically significant are indicated in bold (see Annex A3).
Only countries and economies with comparable data from PISA 2003 and PISA 2012 are shown.
StatLink http://dx.doi.org/10.1787/888932957441

[Part 2/3]
Change between 2003 and 2012 in grade repetition

Table IV.2.18 *Results based on students' self-reports*

	PISA 2012																				
	Percentage of students reporting that they have repeated a grade in:																				
	Primary school						Lower secondary school						Upper secondary school						Primary, lower secondary or upper secondary school	
	Never		Once		Twice or more		Never		Once		Twice or more		Never		Once		Twice or more			
	%	S.E.	%	S.E.	%	S.E.	%	S.E.	%	S.E.	%	S.E.	%	S.E.	%	S.E.	%	S.E.	%	S.E.
Australia	93.3	(0.2)	6.4	(0.2)	0.3	(0.1)	98.7	(0.1)	1.2	(0.1)	0.1	(0.0)	99.7	(0.1)	0.3	(0.1)	0.0	(0.0)	7.5	(0.3)
Austria	94.9	(0.4)	5.0	(0.4)	0.1	(0.0)	95.1	(0.4)	4.6	(0.4)	0.3	(0.1)	96.4	(0.3)	3.6	(0.3)	0.0	c	11.9	(0.7)
Belgium	79.5	(0.7)	17.8	(0.6)	2.7	(0.2)	83.3	(0.6)	15.5	(0.6)	1.2	(0.1)	90.9	(0.4)	9.0	(0.4)	0.1	(0.0)	36.1	(0.6)
Canada	95.8	(0.2)	3.9	(0.2)	0.3	(0.1)	95.6	(0.2)	3.8	(0.2)	0.7	(0.1)	99.1	(0.1)	0.7	(0.1)	0.2	(0.1)	8.0	(0.3)
Czech Republic	97.9	(0.4)	1.9	(0.4)	0.3	(0.1)	96.7	(0.4)	3.0	(0.4)	0.3	(0.1)	0.0	c	0.0	c	0.0	c	4.9	(0.6)
Denmark	96.0	(0.4)	3.9	(0.4)	0.1	(0.0)	99.0	(0.2)	1.0	(0.2)	0.0	(0.0)	100.0	c	0.0	c	0.0	c	4.7	(0.4)
Finland	96.8	(0.3)	3.1	(0.3)	0.1	(0.1)	99.3	(0.2)	0.7	(0.2)	0.0	(0.0)	100.0	c	0.0	c	0.0	c	3.8	(0.4)
France	83.0	(0.7)	16.5	(0.7)	0.5	(0.1)	85.6	(0.7)	13.9	(0.7)	0.5	(0.1)	99.5	(0.1)	0.5	(0.1)	0.0	(0.0)	28.4	(0.8)
Germany	89.8	(0.6)	9.6	(0.6)	0.7	(0.1)	87.2	(0.6)	12.3	(0.6)	0.5	(0.1)	0.0	c	0.0	c	0.0	c	20.3	(0.8)
Greece	98.5	(0.3)	0.9	(0.2)	0.7	(0.1)	96.1	(0.7)	2.8	(0.5)	1.2	(0.3)	0.0	c	0.0	c	0.0	c	4.5	(0.7)
Hungary	95.1	(0.6)	4.2	(0.5)	0.7	(0.2)	94.3	(0.7)	4.2	(0.5)	1.5	(0.4)	97.3	(0.3)	2.6	(0.3)	0.1	(0.0)	10.8	(0.9)
Iceland	99.3	(0.1)	0.5	(0.1)	0.2	(0.1)	99.2	(0.1)	0.6	(0.1)	0.2	(0.1)	0.0	c	0.0	c	0.0	c	1.2	(0.2)
Ireland	92.1	(0.4)	7.7	(0.4)	0.1	(0.1)	98.9	(0.2)	1.0	(0.1)	0.1	(0.0)	100.0	(0.0)	0.0	(0.0)	0.0	c	8.6	(0.4)
Italy	99.0	(0.1)	0.9	(0.1)	0.1	(0.0)	92.6	(0.3)	6.1	(0.3)	1.4	(0.2)	89.7	(0.4)	10.2	(0.4)	0.1	(0.0)	17.1	(0.5)
Japan	0.0	c	0.0	c	0.0	c	0.0	c	0.0	c	0.0	c	0.0	c	0.0	c	0.0	c	0.0	c
Korea	96.8	(0.2)	2.4	(0.2)	0.8	(0.1)	96.9	(0.2)	2.2	(0.2)	0.9	(0.1)	97.8	(0.2)	1.7	(0.2)	0.5	(0.1)	3.6	(0.3)
Luxembourg	78.5	(0.5)	19.3	(0.5)	2.2	(0.2)	80.7	(0.6)	18.5	(0.6)	0.8	(0.1)	99.1	(0.2)	0.7	(0.2)	0.3	(0.1)	34.5	(0.5)
Mexico	87.4	(0.5)	11.2	(0.4)	1.4	(0.1)	96.6	(0.3)	3.1	(0.3)	0.3	(0.0)	98.9	(0.1)	1.0	(0.1)	0.1	(0.0)	15.5	(0.6)
Netherlands	79.1	(1.1)	20.2	(1.0)	0.7	(0.1)	92.1	(0.6)	7.8	(0.6)	0.1	(0.0)	99.7	(0.1)	0.3	(0.1)	0.0	c	27.6	(0.9)
New Zealand	96.0	(0.3)	3.7	(0.3)	0.3	(0.1)	98.2	(0.2)	1.5	(0.2)	0.3	(0.1)	99.0	(0.2)	0.8	(0.2)	0.2	(0.1)	5.4	(0.3)
Norway	0.0	c	0.0	c	0.0	c	0.0	c	0.0	c	0.0	c	0.0	c	0.0	c	0.0	c	0.0	c
Poland	98.6	(0.2)	1.3	(0.2)	0.2	(0.1)	96.8	(0.3)	2.9	(0.3)	0.2	(0.1)	0.0	c	0.0	c	0.0	c	4.2	(0.4)
Portugal	76.7	(1.5)	17.9	(1.2)	5.4	(0.6)	80.2	(1.5)	17.5	(1.4)	2.4	(0.3)	99.9	(0.1)	0.1	(0.1)	0.0	c	34.3	(1.9)
Slovak Republic	95.1	(0.5)	3.5	(0.5)	1.4	(0.2)	96.6	(0.4)	2.9	(0.4)	0.5	(0.1)	99.5	(0.3)	0.2	(0.1)	0.3	(0.3)	7.6	(0.6)
Spain	86.2	(0.4)	12.9	(0.4)	0.8	(0.1)	72.3	(0.7)	25.0	(0.6)	2.7	(0.2)	0.0	c	0.0	c	0.0	c	32.9	(0.6)
Sweden	96.6	(0.3)	3.1	(0.3)	0.2	(0.1)	98.7	(0.2)	1.1	(0.2)	0.2	(0.1)	98.7	(1.1)	0.0	c	1.3	(1.1)	4.0	(0.4)
Switzerland	86.8	(0.7)	12.7	(0.7)	0.5	(0.1)	91.9	(0.5)	7.9	(0.5)	0.2	(0.0)	99.5	(0.2)	0.5	(0.2)	0.0	c	19.9	(0.9)
Turkey	97.7	(0.3)	2.3	(0.3)	0.1	(0.0)	0.0	c	0.0	c	0.0	c	87.0	(0.8)	12.9	(0.8)	0.1	(0.1)	14.2	(0.9)
United States	88.9	(0.9)	10.7	(0.9)	0.4	(0.1)	96.0	(0.3)	4.0	(0.3)	0.1	(0.0)	97.9	(0.3)	2.0	(0.3)	0.0	(0.0)	13.3	(1.0)
OECD average 2003	85.4	(0.1)	7.0	(0.0)	0.7	(0.0)	83.4	(0.1)	5.7	(0.1)	0.6	(0.0)	70.7	(0.1)	1.6	(0.1)	0.1	(0.1)	13.3	(0.1)
Brazil	79.4	(0.7)	15.9	(0.6)	4.7	(0.4)	80.6	(0.8)	14.5	(0.6)	4.9	(0.4)	92.3	(0.4)	7.4	(0.4)	0.4	(0.1)	36.1	(1.0)
Hong Kong-China	90.7	(0.5)	8.5	(0.5)	0.8	(0.1)	92.4	(0.5)	7.2	(0.5)	0.4	(0.1)	99.8	(0.1)	0.2	(0.1)	0.0	(0.0)	15.9	(0.9)
Indonesia	85.4	(1.2)	13.3	(1.1)	1.3	(0.2)	95.0	(0.6)	4.4	(0.5)	0.6	(0.2)	96.2	(0.6)	3.5	(0.6)	0.3	(0.1)	15.5	(1.3)
Latvia	94.4	(0.4)	5.0	(0.4)	0.5	(0.2)	96.3	(0.5)	3.5	(0.5)	0.2	(0.1)	99.4	(0.6)	0.0	c	0.6	(0.6)	8.5	(0.6)
Liechtenstein	89.0	(1.7)	11.0	(1.7)	0.0	c	90.6	(1.5)	9.4	(1.5)	0.0	c	100.0	c	0.0	c	0.0	c	18.9	(1.9)
Macao-China	77.0	(0.4)	17.0	(0.4)	6.0	(0.3)	70.5	(0.5)	25.0	(0.5)	4.5	(0.2)	99.3	(0.2)	0.6	(0.2)	0.0	(0.0)	41.2	(0.4)
Russian Federation	98.3	(0.2)	1.5	(0.2)	0.2	(0.1)	99.1	(0.2)	0.8	(0.2)	0.1	(0.1)	0.0	c	0.0	c	0.0	c	2.5	(0.3)
Thailand	98.1	(0.2)	1.9	(0.2)	0.0	c	99.0	(0.2)	1.0	(0.2)	0.0	(0.0)	99.3	(0.1)	0.7	(0.1)	0.0	(0.0)	3.3	(0.3)
Tunisia	82.2	(1.8)	12.7	(1.2)	5.1	(0.7)	69.6	(2.4)	23.8	(1.8)	6.6	(0.7)	97.4	(0.3)	2.6	(0.3)	0.0	(0.0)	38.7	(2.8)
Uruguay	78.4	(1.0)	17.4	(0.8)	4.2	(0.4)	72.9	(1.2)	20.7	(0.9)	6.4	(0.6)	99.7	(0.1)	0.3	(0.1)	0.0	(0.0)	37.9	(1.3)

Notes: Values that are statistically significant are indicated in bold (see Annex A3).
Only countries and economies with comparable data from PISA 2003 and PISA 2012 are shown.
StatLink http://dx.doi.org/10.1787/888932957441

[Part 3/3]
Change between 2003 and 2012 in grade repetition
Table IV.2.18   *Results based on students' self-reports*

	Primary school						Lower secondary school						Upper secondary school						Primary, lower secondary or upper secondary school	
	Never		Once		Twice or more		Never		Once		Twice or more		Never		Once		Twice or more			
	% dif.	S.E.	% dif.	S.E.	% dif.	S.E.	% dif.	S.E.	% dif.	S.E.	% dif.	S.E.	% dif.	S.E.	% dif.	S.E.	% dif.	S.E.	% dif.	S.E.
Australia	**1.5**	(0.5)	**-1.6**	(0.5)	**0.2**	(0.1)	0.0	(0.2)	-0.1	(0.2)	0.0	(0.0)	-0.1	(0.1)	0.1	(0.1)	0.0	c	**-1.7**	(0.5)
Austria	**-1.7**	(0.7)	**1.7**	(0.7)	0.0	(0.1)	-1.1	(0.7)	1.0	(0.7)	0.1	(0.1)	0.4	(0.7)	-0.4	(0.7)	0.0	c	1.7	(1.2)
Belgium	**-2.7**	(1.0)	**1.6**	(0.9)	**1.1**	(0.3)	**-8.0**	(0.7)	**7.2**	(0.7)	**0.8**	(0.2)	0.4	(0.6)	-0.4	(0.6)	0.0	(0.0)	**5.8**	(0.9)
Canada	**1.7**	(0.4)	**-1.4**	(0.4)	**-0.3**	(0.2)	**1.4**	(0.4)	**-1.3**	(0.4)	-0.1	(0.1)	-0.1	(0.1)	0.0	(0.1)	**0.2**	(0.1)	**-2.9**	(0.6)
Czech Republic	-0.6	(0.5)	0.3	(0.4)	0.2	(0.1)	**-2.0**	(0.5)	**1.7**	(0.5)	**0.3**	(0.1)	0.0	c	0.0	c	0.0	c	**2.1**	(0.7)
Denmark	**-1.1**	(0.5)	**1.1**	(0.5)	0.0	(0.1)	-0.2	(0.3)	0.2	(0.3)	0.0	(0.0)	0.0	c	0.0	c	0.0	c	1.2	(0.6)
Finland	**-0.8**	(0.4)	**0.7**	(0.4)	0.1	(0.1)	-0.3	(0.2)	0.3	(0.2)	0.0	c	100.0	c	0.0	c	0.0	c	**1.0**	(0.5)
France	0.3	(1.2)	0.2	(1.2)	**-0.5**	(0.2)	**15.2**	(1.4)	**-14.7**	(1.3)	**-0.6**	(0.2)	99.5	c	0.5	c	0.0	c	**-11.1**	(1.4)
Germany	-0.4	(0.9)	0.0	(0.9)	**0.4**	(0.1)	**2.2**	(0.9)	**-2.0**	(0.9)	-0.2	(0.2)	0.0	c	0.0	c	0.0	c	-1.4	(1.2)
Greece	**-0.8**	(0.3)	0.2	(0.2)	**0.6**	(0.1)	2.1	(1.0)	**-2.4**	(0.7)	0.3	(0.3)	-99.1	c	-0.9	c	0.0	c	**-2.6**	(1.0)
Hungary	-0.7	(0.7)	0.5	(0.7)	0.3	(0.2)	**-2.1**	(0.8)	**1.1**	(0.6)	**1.0**	(0.4)	0.4	(0.4)	-0.4	(0.4)	0.0	(0.0)	1.1	(1.0)
Iceland	-0.7	c	0.5	c	0.2	c	-0.8	c	0.6	c	0.2	c	0.0	c	0.0	c	0.0	c	1.2	c
Ireland	**5.8**	(0.8)	**-5.6**	(0.8)	-0.2	(0.1)	0.1	(0.3)	-0.2	(0.3)	0.1	c	0.1	(0.1)	-0.1	(0.1)	0.0	c	**-5.8**	(0.8)
Italy	0.6	(0.4)	-0.3	(0.3)	-0.3	(0.2)	**-1.4**	(0.7)	0.7	(0.6)	**0.8**	(0.3)	-1.1	(0.6)	1.1	(0.6)	0.0	(0.1)	**2.0**	(0.9)
Japan	0.0	c	0.0	c	0.0	c	0.0	c	0.0	c	0.0	c	0.0	c	0.0	c	0.0	c	0.0	c
Korea	**-3.0**	(0.2)	**2.2**	(0.2)	0.8	c	**-2.8**	(0.2)	**1.9**	(0.2)	0.9	c	**-2.1**	(0.2)	**1.6**	(0.2)	0.5	c	**3.2**	(0.3)
Luxembourg	**-3.8**	(0.7)	**4.3**	(0.7)	-0.4	(0.3)	**9.8**	(0.8)	**-9.9**	(0.8)	0.2	(0.2)	**-0.8**	(0.2)	**0.6**	(0.2)	0.3	c	**-4.0**	(0.7)
Mexico	**12.1**	(1.7)	**-10.7**	(1.5)	**-1.4**	(0.4)	**5.1**	(0.9)	**-5.0**	(0.9)	-0.1	(0.1)	**1.9**	(0.5)	**-2.0**	(0.5)	0.1	(0.0)	**-14.2**	(1.8)
Netherlands	1.6	(1.4)	-1.7	(1.4)	0.1	(0.2)	2.8	(1.0)	**-2.9**	(1.0)	0.1	(0.0)	99.7	c	0.3	c	0.0	c	-1.9	(1.4)
New Zealand	-0.6	(0.4)	0.3	(0.4)	**0.2**	(0.1)	-0.6	(0.3)	0.3	(0.3)	**0.3**	(0.1)	**-0.6**	(0.2)	**0.4**	(0.2)	**0.2**	(0.1)	0.7	(0.4)
Norway	0.0	c	0.0	c	0.0	c	0.0	c	0.0	c	0.0	c	0.0	c	0.0	c	0.0	c	0.0	c
Poland	**0.9**	(0.4)	**-0.9**	(0.3)	0.0	(0.1)	**-1.5**	(0.4)	**1.4**	(0.4)	0.1	(0.1)	-100.0	c	0.0	c	0.0	c	0.6	(0.5)
Portugal	-4.0	(2.4)	2.9	(2.0)	1.1	(0.8)	-0.6	(2.0)	1.7	(1.8)	**-1.1**	(0.5)	0.0	(0.1)	0.0	(0.1)	0.0	c	4.1	(2.7)
Slovak Republic	**-3.4**	(0.6)	**2.2**	(0.6)	**1.2**	(0.3)	**-2.2**	(0.5)	**1.9**	(0.4)	0.3	(0.2)	99.5	c	0.2	c	0.3	c	**5.0**	(0.7)
Spain	**-7.3**	(0.7)	**6.7**	(0.6)	**0.6**	(0.2)	-2.4	(1.2)	-0.1	(1.1)	**2.5**	(0.2)	0.0	c	0.0	c	0.0	c	**3.9**	(1.2)
Sweden	-0.5	(0.5)	0.3	(0.5)	**0.2**	(0.1)	**-0.5**	(0.3)	0.3	(0.3)	0.2	c	-1.3	c	0.0	c	1.3	c	0.4	(0.6)
Switzerland	1.7	(1.1)	-1.5	(1.1)	-0.1	(0.1)	1.3	(0.9)	-1.3	(0.9)	0.0	(0.1)	0.1	(0.3)	-0.1	(0.3)	0.0	c	-2.1	(1.4)
Turkey	**3.6**	(1.1)	**-3.0**	(0.9)	**-0.6**	(0.3)	-95.2	c	-4.6	c	-0.2	c	-1.5	(1.4)	1.4	(1.4)	0.1	c	**-3.8**	(1.7)
United States	**-3.0**	(1.1)	**2.9**	(1.1)	0.1	(0.2)	0.1	(0.7)	0.1	(0.7)	-0.2	(0.1)	**-1.4**	(0.3)	**1.4**	(0.3)	0.0	c	1.7	(1.3)
OECD average 2003	-0.2	(0.2)	0.1	(0.2)	**0.1**	(0.0)	**-2.8**	(0.2)	**-0.8**	(0.1)	**0.2**	(0.0)	**6.7**	(0.1)	0.1	(0.1)	**0.1**	(0.0)	**-0.5**	(0.2)
Brazil	1.9	(1.4)	**-3.6**	(1.2)	**1.7**	(0.6)	-0.5	(1.5)	-1.1	(1.2)	**1.6**	(0.5)	**-5.3**	(0.6)	**4.9**	(0.6)	0.4	c	2.9	(1.7)
Hong Kong-China	**3.5**	(0.8)	**-3.4**	(0.8)	-0.1	(0.2)	**-2.2**	(0.7)	**2.3**	(0.7)	-0.1	(0.1)	-0.2	(0.1)	0.1	(0.1)	0.0	c	-0.9	(1.0)
Indonesia	0.8	(1.5)	-1.4	(1.4)	**0.6**	(0.2)	**-3.5**	(0.7)	**3.1**	(0.5)	**0.4**	(0.1)	**-3.6**	(0.6)	**3.3**	(0.6)	0.3	c	-0.4	(1.6)
Latvia	0.2	(0.7)	-0.5	(0.7)	0.2	(0.2)	**-2.1**	(0.5)	**2.1**	(0.5)	0.1	(0.1)	-0.6	c	0.0	c	0.6	c	1.5	(0.9)
Liechtenstein	-2.5	(2.3)	2.5	(2.3)	0.0	c	2.7	(2.1)	-2.3	(2.2)	-0.3	c	0.0	c	0.0	c	0.0	c	0.2	(2.6)
Macao-China	**9.4**	(1.4)	**-7.6**	(1.6)	-1.8	(1.0)	3.4	(1.7)	-2.3	(1.6)	-1.1	(0.9)	1.3	(0.9)	-1.3	(0.9)	0.0	c	**-8.6**	(1.4)
Russian Federation	0.6	(0.4)	-0.7	(0.4)	0.1	(0.1)	0.3	(0.3)	-0.2	(0.3)	-0.1	(0.1)	0.0	c	0.0	c	0.0	c	-0.7	(0.5)
Thailand	**-1.5**	(0.3)	**1.5**	(0.3)	0.0	c	0.1	(0.2)	0.0	(0.2)	-0.1	(0.1)	-0.1	(0.3)	0.1	(0.3)	0.0	c	**1.5**	(0.4)
Tunisia	**34.7**	(2.3)	**-21.3**	(1.6)	**-13.4**	(1.1)	**11.1**	(2.9)	**-12.4**	(2.3)	1.3	(0.9)	**-1.4**	(0.5)	**1.4**	(0.5)	0.0	c	**-23.1**	(3.1)
Uruguay	-1.2	(1.7)	1.6	(1.4)	-0.4	(0.6)	**-5.1**	(1.9)	**2.9**	(1.4)	**2.1**	(0.8)	**1.1**	(0.3)	**-1.2**	(0.3)	0.0	c	4.3	(2.3)

Notes: Values that are statistically significant are indicated in bold (see Annex A3).
Only countries and economies with comparable data from PISA 2003 and PISA 2012 are shown.
StatLink ⌐ᴬ᠍⌐ http://dx.doi.org/10.1787/888932957441

[Part 1/1]
Change between 2003 and 2012 in the concentration of grade repetition
Table IV.2.19 *Results based on students' self-reports*

Percentage of students in schools where the following percentage of students have repeated a grade in primary, lower secondary or upper secondary school

	PISA 2003								PISA 2012								Change between 2003 and 2012 (PISA 2012 - PISA 2003)							
	Over 30%		More than 10% but 30% or less		More than 0% but 10% or less		0%		Over 30%		More than 10% but 30% or less		More than 0% but 10% or less		0%		Over 30%		More than 10% but 30% or less		More than 0% but 10% or less		0%	
	%	S.E.	%	S.E.	%	S.E.	%	S.E.	%	S.E.	%	S.E.	%	S.E.	%	S.E.	% dif.	S.E.	% dif.	S.E.	% dif.	S.E.	% dif.	S.E.
OECD																								
Australia	2.1	(1.6)	32.2	(2.7)	58.8	(3.1)	6.9	(1.7)	0.9	(0.3)	33.3	(1.9)	40.8	(1.7)	25.0	(1.5)	-1.2	(1.6)	1.1	(3.3)	**-18.0**	(3.6)	**18.1**	(2.3)
Austria	7.1	(1.7)	19.4	(2.8)	39.3	(3.4)	34.2	(2.8)	6.7	(1.3)	31.8	(3.8)	49.9	(4.0)	11.6	(2.2)	-0.5	(2.1)	**12.4**	(4.8)	**10.6**	(5.3)	**-22.5**	(3.6)
Belgium	46.8	(1.7)	31.6	(1.8)	15.7	(1.6)	5.8	(1.2)	55.7	(2.1)	27.0	(2.4)	14.6	(1.7)	2.7	(0.9)	**8.8**	(2.7)	-4.6	(3.0)	-1.1	(2.3)	**-3.2**	(1.5)
Canada	8.7	(1.2)	26.0	(2.1)	30.3	(2.1)	35.0	(2.3)	6.9	(1.0)	17.9	(1.4)	37.6	(2.3)	37.6	(2.2)	-1.8	(1.5)	**-8.1**	(2.5)	**7.3**	(3.1)	2.6	(3.2)
Czech Republic	0.7	(0.4)	8.5	(1.8)	16.7	(2.2)	74.2	(2.2)	3.2	(1.0)	14.3	(2.6)	18.1	(2.9)	64.4	(3.1)	**2.5**	(1.1)	5.9	(3.2)	1.5	(3.6)	**-9.8**	(3.8)
Denmark	0.5	(0.4)	9.2	(2.0)	35.9	(3.4)	54.4	(3.9)	0.7	(0.4)	14.3	(2.5)	44.5	(3.6)	40.6	(3.5)	0.2	(0.6)	5.1	(3.2)	8.6	(5.0)	**-13.8**	(5.3)
Finland	0.0	c	3.0	(1.4)	48.8	(4.0)	48.2	(4.0)	0.9	(0.5)	7.2	(1.8)	56.6	(3.0)	35.3	(2.9)	0.9	c	4.2	(2.3)	7.7	(5.0)	**-12.8**	(4.9)
France	42.3	(1.6)	5.3	(1.7)	10.0	(2.0)	42.5	(2.4)	31.6	(1.5)	5.7	(1.7)	14.9	(2.3)	47.7	(2.4)	**-10.6**	(2.2)	0.4	(2.4)	5.0	(3.1)	5.3	(3.4)
Germany	30.3	(2.9)	43.6	(3.1)	19.1	(2.9)	7.1	(1.2)	27.2	(2.1)	39.5	(2.5)	21.0	(2.5)	12.3	(2.1)	-3.1	(3.6)	-4.1	(4.3)	2.0	(3.8)	**5.2**	(2.4)
Greece	7.3	(1.1)	9.3	(2.6)	36.9	(5.1)	46.5	(4.8)	5.0	(1.1)	0.7	(0.4)	25.5	(3.8)	68.8	(3.8)	-2.3	(1.6)	**-8.7**	(2.7)	**-11.4**	(6.3)	**22.3**	(6.1)
Hungary	6.0	(0.6)	15.9	(2.5)	46.4	(3.4)	31.7	(2.8)	9.5	(1.0)	12.9	(1.8)	30.5	(3.5)	47.1	(3.6)	**3.5**	(1.2)	-3.0	(3.1)	**-15.8**	(4.8)	**15.3**	(4.6)
Iceland	0.0	c	0.0	c	0.0	c	100.0	c	0.0	c	0.6	(0.1)	35.2	(0.2)	64.3	(0.2)	0.0	c	0.6	c	35.2	c	-35.7	c
Ireland	9.0	(2.3)	54.3	(4.0)	28.5	(3.7)	8.2	(2.4)	0.1	(0.1)	39.5	(3.9)	46.8	(3.9)	13.6	(2.8)	**-8.9**	(2.3)	**-14.8**	(5.6)	**18.3**	(5.4)	5.4	(3.8)
Italy	14.8	(2.1)	37.5	(3.1)	29.1	(2.8)	18.7	(2.3)	17.1	(1.4)	37.9	(1.7)	29.4	(1.6)	15.6	(1.6)	2.3	(2.5)	0.4	(3.5)	0.3	(3.2)	-3.0	(2.8)
Japan	0.0	c	0.0	c	0.0	c	0.0	c	0.0	c	0.0	c	0.0	c	0.0	c	0.0	c	0.0	c	0.0	c	0.0	c
Korea	0.2	(0.1)	0.8	(0.4)	9.0	(2.2)	90.1	(2.2)	0.2	(0.2)	5.1	(1.3)	59.8	(3.7)	35.0	(3.8)	0.0	(0.2)	**4.3**	(1.4)	**50.8**	(4.3)	**-55.1**	(4.4)
Luxembourg	69.1	(0.0)	21.2	(0.0)	9.3	(0.0)	0.4	(0.0)	60.0	(0.1)	30.5	(0.1)	9.1	(0.1)	0.4	(0.0)	**-9.1**	(0.1)	**9.3**	(0.1)	**-0.2**	(0.1)	**0.0**	(0.0)
Mexico	43.9	(3.2)	15.3	(2.8)	16.7	(1.6)	24.0	(1.9)	22.1	(1.2)	13.8	(1.3)	17.7	(1.3)	46.4	(1.3)	**-21.8**	(3.5)	-1.6	(3.1)	1.0	(2.1)	**22.3**	(2.3)
Netherlands	52.4	(3.9)	35.6	(3.8)	8.0	(2.0)	4.0	(1.5)	40.8	(3.5)	48.6	(4.0)	10.6	(2.4)	0.0	c	**-11.6**	(5.3)	**13.0**	(5.5)	2.6	(3.1)	-4.0	c
New Zealand	0.2	(0.2)	10.6	(2.1)	63.2	(3.1)	26.0	(3.0)	0.1	(0.1)	13.1	(2.2)	61.1	(3.8)	25.7	(3.3)	-0.1	(0.2)	2.5	(3.1)	-2.1	(5.0)	-0.4	(4.5)
Norway	0.0	c	0.0	c	0.0	c	0.0	c	0.0	c	0.0	c	0.0	c	0.0	c	0.0	c	0.0	c	0.0	c	0.0	c
Poland	0.0	c	8.1	(2.3)	45.9	(3.6)	46.0	(3.8)	0.1	(0.1)	12.6	(2.5)	46.4	(3.9)	41.0	(4.1)	0.1	c	4.5	(3.4)	0.5	(5.3)	-5.0	(5.6)
Portugal	32.2	(3.1)	29.8	(3.7)	20.2	(3.8)	17.9	(3.3)	45.6	(3.6)	29.1	(4.1)	12.6	(2.9)	12.7	(2.8)	**13.4**	(4.7)	-0.7	(5.5)	-7.5	(4.8)	-5.1	(4.3)
Slovak Republic	1.7	(0.7)	5.5	(1.2)	14.1	(1.8)	78.6	(2.0)	6.8	(0.9)	16.3	(2.4)	19.1	(3.0)	57.8	(3.3)	**5.0**	(1.1)	**10.8**	(2.7)	5.0	(3.5)	**-20.8**	(3.9)
Spain	47.4	(3.2)	36.8	(3.4)	8.3	(1.7)	7.4	(1.7)	57.6	(2.2)	34.5	(2.5)	4.8	(1.0)	3.2	(0.9)	**10.1**	(3.9)	-2.4	(4.3)	-3.5	(2.0)	**-4.3**	(1.9)
Sweden	1.0	(0.6)	5.5	(1.8)	48.0	(3.7)	45.5	(3.8)	1.1	(0.7)	7.3	(2.0)	44.2	(3.7)	47.5	(3.7)	0.1	(0.9)	1.8	(2.7)	-3.9	(5.2)	2.0	(5.3)
Switzerland	25.9	(2.9)	46.2	(3.5)	13.5	(2.9)	14.4	(1.9)	26.5	(2.4)	36.3	(2.7)	17.0	(2.7)	20.2	(2.0)	0.6	(3.8)	**-9.8**	(4.4)	3.4	(4.0)	**5.8**	(2.8)
Turkey	16.6	(3.1)	44.5	(4.1)	22.4	(3.3)	16.5	(3.3)	11.2	(2.6)	46.7	(3.5)	21.1	(3.2)	21.1	(3.2)	-5.5	(4.0)	2.2	(5.4)	-1.3	(4.6)	4.6	(4.6)
United States	8.0	(1.6)	33.9	(3.0)	32.8	(3.2)	25.3	(2.5)	7.9	(2.9)	40.9	(4.6)	43.5	(4.7)	7.7	(2.1)	-0.1	(3.3)	7.0	(5.5)	10.7	(5.6)	**-17.6**	(3.3)
OECD average 2003	16.4	(0.4)	20.3	(0.5)	25.1	(0.6)	31.4	(0.5)	15.4	(0.3)	21.3	(0.5)	28.7	(0.6)	27.8	(0.5)	-1.0	(0.5)	1.0	(0.7)	**3.6**	(0.8)	**-3.6**	(0.8)
Partners																								
Brazil	48.1	(3.0)	30.7	(2.8)	14.5	(2.5)	6.7	(1.8)	52.4	(2.6)	37.7	(2.7)	7.6	(1.3)	2.3	(1.1)	4.3	(4.0)	7.0	(3.8)	**-6.9**	(2.9)	**-4.4**	(2.1)
Hong Kong-China	7.7	(2.7)	61.8	(4.1)	29.9	(3.2)	0.6	(0.6)	9.8	(2.6)	59.0	(4.1)	25.5	(3.7)	5.7	(1.9)	2.1	(3.8)	-2.8	(5.8)	-4.4	(4.9)	**5.1**	(2.0)
Indonesia	21.3	(3.0)	30.6	(3.8)	23.6	(2.9)	24.4	(2.6)	17.5	(2.9)	25.6	(3.6)	41.0	(3.8)	15.8	(2.4)	-3.8	(4.2)	-5.0	(5.2)	**17.4**	(4.8)	**-8.6**	(3.5)
Latvia	3.2	(1.3)	23.8	(4.0)	38.3	(3.9)	34.7	(4.0)	5.6	(1.5)	22.6	(3.1)	34.3	(3.4)	37.5	(2.9)	2.5	(2.0)	-1.2	(5.0)	-4.0	(5.2)	2.7	(4.9)
Liechtenstein	15.7	(0.4)	44.7	(0.5)	37.6	(0.4)	2.1	(0.0)	31.0	(0.9)	31.1	(1.3)	34.1	(0.4)	3.9	(0.6)	**15.3**	(1.0)	**-13.6**	(1.4)	**-3.5**	(0.6)	**1.8**	(0.6)
Macao-China	84.3	(0.1)	15.7	(0.1)	0.0	c	0.0	c	67.5	(0.0)	31.7	(0.0)	0.8	(0.0)	0.0	c	**-16.8**	(0.1)	**16.0**	(0.1)	0.8	c	0.0	c
Russian Federation	0.6	(0.6)	8.2	(1.9)	36.8	(3.4)	54.3	(3.2)	0.4	(0.3)	7.3	(2.2)	26.7	(2.9)	65.6	(2.9)	-0.3	(0.6)	-1.0	(2.9)	**-10.1**	(4.5)	**11.3**	(4.3)
Thailand	0.0	c	2.9	(1.2)	29.1	(3.6)	68.0	(3.7)	0.5	(0.4)	7.5	(1.9)	44.1	(3.9)	47.9	(3.6)	0.5	c	**4.7**	(2.2)	**14.9**	(5.3)	**-20.1**	(5.1)
Tunisia	67.2	(1.7)	7.4	(2.2)	17.6	(3.0)	7.8	(2.4)	38.2	(3.1)	11.2	(2.5)	39.0	(3.8)	11.6	(2.6)	**-29.0**	(3.6)	3.8	(3.4)	**21.4**	(4.9)	3.8	(3.5)
Uruguay	35.5	(2.3)	16.9	(3.6)	31.1	(3.5)	16.4	(3.6)	48.6	(2.4)	18.8	(2.4)	10.5	(2.0)	22.0	(2.3)	**13.1**	(3.3)	1.8	(4.3)	**-20.5**	(4.0)	5.6	(4.3)

Notes: Values that are statistically significant are indicated in bold (see Annex A3).
Only countries and economies with comparable data from PISA 2003 and PISA 2012 are shown.
StatLink ᛖᛗᛋᛚ http://dx.doi.org/10.1787/888932957441

[Part 1/3]
Change between 2003 and 2012 in student grade level

Table IV.2.20   *Results based on students' self-reports*

		PISA 2003									
		Percentage of students at:						Percentage of students enrolled in:			
		Grades below the modal grade		The modal grade		Grades above the modal grade		Lower secondary education (ISCED 2)		Upper secondary education (ISCED 3)	
		%	S.E.	%	S.E.	%	S.E.	%	S.E.	%	S.E.
OECD	Australia	8.5	(0.4)	72.3	(0.7)	19.3	(0.7)	80.7	(0.7)	19.3	(0.7)
	Austria	48.5	(1.6)	51.5	(1.6)	0.0	c	5.6	(1.0)	94.4	(1.0)
	Belgium	33.7	(0.7)	65.5	(0.7)	0.8	(0.1)	4.4	(0.4)	95.6	(0.4)
	Canada	16.8	(0.6)	82.0	(0.6)	1.2	(0.1)	16.8	(0.6)	83.2	(0.6)
	Czech Republic	47.6	(1.1)	52.4	(1.1)	0.0	c	48.3	(1.2)	51.7	(1.2)
	Denmark	9.2	(0.6)	87.0	(0.8)	3.9	(0.7)	98.4	(0.4)	1.6	(0.4)
	Finland	12.7	(0.5)	87.3	(0.5)	0.0	c	100.0	c	0.0	c
	France	40.4	(1.1)	57.3	(1.1)	2.3	(0.3)	40.4	(1.1)	59.6	(1.1)
	Germany	16.7	(0.8)	59.9	(0.7)	23.4	(0.6)	98.3	(0.2)	1.7	(0.2)
	Greece	8.9	(1.3)	76.1	(1.4)	15.0	(0.9)	8.9	(1.3)	91.1	(1.3)
	Hungary	6.1	(0.5)	65.1	(0.7)	28.8	(0.6)	6.1	(0.5)	93.9	(0.5)
	Iceland	0.0	c	100.0	c	0.0	c	100.0	c	0.0	c
	Ireland	2.8	(0.3)	60.9	(1.3)	36.3	(1.4)	63.7	(1.4)	36.3	(1.4)
	Italy	15.8	(0.7)	80.0	(0.8)	4.3	(0.5)	1.6	(0.4)	98.4	(0.4)
	Japan	0.0	c	100.0	c	0.0	c	0.0	c	100.0	c
	Korea	1.6	(0.2)	98.3	(0.2)	0.1	(0.0)	1.6	(0.2)	98.4	(0.2)
	Luxembourg	14.9	(0.2)	55.8	(0.2)	29.4	(0.2)	70.6	(0.2)	29.4	(0.2)
	Mexico	55.3	(2.9)	43.7	(2.8)	1.0	(0.5)	56.3	(2.7)	43.7	(2.7)
	Netherlands	50.2	(1.3)	49.3	(1.3)	0.5	(0.1)	74.8	(1.2)	25.2	(1.2)
	New Zealand	6.9	(0.5)	89.4	(0.5)	3.8	(0.2)	6.9	(0.5)	93.1	(0.5)
	Norway	0.6	(0.1)	98.7	(0.3)	0.7	(0.2)	99.3	(0.2)	0.7	(0.2)
	Poland	3.8	(0.4)	95.7	(0.4)	0.5	(0.2)	99.5	(0.2)	0.5	(0.2)
	Portugal	35.1	(2.4)	64.3	(2.4)	0.6	(0.1)	35.1	(2.4)	64.9	(2.4)
	Slovak Republic	38.6	(1.5)	60.9	(1.5)	0.5	(0.2)	35.7	(1.5)	64.3	(1.5)
	Spain	30.2	(1.0)	69.7	(1.0)	0.0	(0.0)	100.0	(0.0)	0.0	(0.0)
	Sweden	2.4	(0.2)	93.0	(1.0)	4.6	(0.9)	95.5	(0.9)	4.5	(0.9)
	Switzerland	17.7	(1.1)	62.8	(2.1)	19.6	(2.5)	82.9	(2.7)	17.1	(2.7)
	Turkey	8.4	(1.9)	52.1	(2.2)	39.4	(2.4)	5.2	(1.8)	94.8	(1.8)
	United States	32.4	(1.6)	60.6	(1.3)	7.0	(0.9)	32.4	(1.6)	67.6	(1.6)
	OECD average 2003	19.5	(0.2)	72.1	(0.2)	8.4	(0.2)	50.7	(0.2)	49.3	(0.2)
Partners	Brazil	38.5	(2.6)	42.9	(1.9)	18.6	(1.1)	38.5	(2.6)	61.5	(2.6)
	Hong Kong-China	41.6	(1.0)	58.4	(1.0)	0.1	(0.0)	41.6	(1.0)	58.4	(1.0)
	Indonesia	15.1	(1.0)	48.8	(1.7)	36.1	(2.0)	63.9	(2.0)	36.1	(2.0)
	Latvia	17.8	(0.8)	76.0	(0.8)	6.2	(0.5)	93.8	(0.5)	6.2	(0.5)
	Liechtenstein	21.0	(0.9)	71.3	(0.9)	7.8	(0.2)	94.3	(0.2)	5.7	(0.2)
	Macao-China	38.2	(0.6)	36.8	(0.7)	25.0	(0.5)	75.0	(0.5)	25.0	(0.5)
	Russian Federation	31.7	(2.1)	67.2	(2.2)	1.1	(0.2)	31.7	(2.1)	68.3	(2.1)
	Thailand	45.3	(1.3)	53.3	(1.2)	1.4	(0.3)	45.3	(1.3)	54.7	(1.3)
	Tunisia	62.5	(1.4)	34.5	(1.4)	2.9	(0.2)	62.5	(1.4)	37.5	(1.4)
	Uruguay	33.6	(2.0)	59.4	(1.7)	7.1	(1.0)	33.6	(2.0)	66.4	(2.0)

Notes: Values that are statistically significant are indicated in bold (see Annex A3).
Only countries and economies with comparable data from PISA 2003 and PISA 2012 are shown.
StatLink ⌁ http://dx.doi.org/10.1787/888932957441

[Part 2/3]
Change between 2003 and 2012 in student grade level
Table IV.2.20   *Results based on students' self-reports*

	PISA 2012									
	Percentage of students at:						Percentage of students enrolled in:			
	Grades below the modal grade		The modal grade		Grades above the modal grade		Lower secondary education (ISCED 2)		Upper secondary education (ISCED 3)	
	%	S.E.	%	S.E.	%	S.E.	%	S.E.	%	S.E.
Australia	10.9	(0.5)	70.0	(0.6)	19.1	(0.4)	80.9	(0.4)	19.1	(0.4)
Austria	49.0	(1.0)	51.0	(1.0)	0.1	(0.0)	5.6	(0.7)	94.4	(0.7)
Belgium	38.2	(0.6)	60.8	(0.6)	1.0	(0.1)	10.3	(0.6)	89.7	(0.6)
Canada	14.4	(0.6)	84.6	(0.6)	1.1	(0.1)	14.4	(0.6)	85.6	(0.6)
Czech Republic	4.9	(0.5)	51.1	(1.2)	44.1	(1.3)	56.1	(1.2)	43.9	(1.2)
Denmark	18.3	(0.9)	80.6	(0.8)	1.0	(0.2)	99.5	(0.1)	0.5	(0.1)
Finland	14.9	(0.4)	85.0	(0.4)	0.1	(0.1)	99.9	(0.1)	0.1	(0.1)
France	29.8	(0.7)	66.6	(0.7)	3.6	(0.3)	29.8	(0.7)	70.2	(0.7)
Germany	10.6	(0.6)	51.9	(0.8)	37.5	(0.9)	97.6	(0.8)	2.4	(0.8)
Greece	5.5	(1.0)	94.5	(1.0)	0.0	c	5.5	(1.0)	94.5	(1.0)
Hungary	11.6	(0.9)	67.8	(0.9)	20.6	(0.6)	11.6	(0.9)	88.4	(0.9)
Iceland	0.0	c	100.0	c	0.0	c	100.0	c	0.0	c
Ireland	1.9	(0.2)	60.5	(0.8)	37.6	(0.8)	62.4	(0.8)	37.6	(0.8)
Italy	18.9	(0.6)	78.5	(0.7)	2.6	(0.2)	2.1	(0.2)	97.9	(0.2)
Japan	0.0	c	100.0	c	0.0	c	0.0	c	100.0	c
Korea	5.9	(0.8)	93.8	(0.8)	0.2	(0.1)	5.9	(0.8)	94.1	(0.8)
Luxembourg	10.9	(0.2)	50.7	(0.1)	38.5	(0.1)	60.0	(0.1)	40.0	(0.1)
Mexico	37.0	(1.1)	60.8	(1.1)	2.2	(0.3)	37.0	(1.1)	63.0	(1.1)
Netherlands	3.6	(0.4)	46.7	(1.0)	49.7	(1.1)	70.3	(1.6)	29.7	(1.6)
New Zealand	6.3	(0.4)	88.3	(0.5)	5.4	(0.4)	6.3	(0.4)	93.7	(0.4)
Norway	0.4	(0.1)	99.4	(0.1)	0.2	(0.0)	99.8	(0.0)	0.2	(0.0)
Poland	4.6	(0.4)	94.9	(0.4)	0.5	(0.2)	99.5	(0.2)	0.5	(0.2)
Portugal	39.2	(2.1)	60.5	(2.1)	0.3	(0.1)	44.9	(2.3)	55.1	(2.3)
Slovak Republic	45.7	(1.4)	52.7	(1.4)	1.6	(0.5)	45.2	(1.4)	54.8	(1.4)
Spain	34.0	(0.6)	66.0	(0.6)	0.0	(0.0)	100.0	(0.0)	0.0	(0.0)
Sweden	3.7	(0.3)	94.0	(0.6)	2.2	(0.5)	97.8	(0.6)	2.2	(0.6)
Switzerland	13.5	(0.8)	60.6	(1.0)	25.9	(1.0)	76.8	(1.2)	23.2	(1.2)
Turkey	30.3	(1.2)	65.5	(1.2)	4.3	(0.3)	2.7	(0.4)	97.3	(0.4)
United States	12.0	(1.1)	71.2	(1.1)	16.8	(0.8)	12.0	(1.1)	88.0	(1.1)
OECD average 2003	16.4	(0.2)	72.7	(0.2)	10.9	(0.1)	49.4	(0.2)	50.6	(0.2)
Brazil	20.4	(1.1)	34.9	(1.0)	44.6	(1.0)	20.4	(1.1)	79.6	(1.1)
Hong Kong-China	33.5	(1.0)	65.0	(0.9)	1.5	(1.4)	33.5	(1.0)	66.5	(1.0)
Indonesia	47.9	(3.3)	47.7	(3.0)	4.4	(0.8)	47.9	(3.3)	52.1	(3.3)
Latvia	16.9	(0.8)	80.0	(0.8)	3.0	(0.4)	96.1	(0.7)	3.9	(0.7)
Liechtenstein	19.0	(1.4)	66.3	(1.3)	14.6	(0.2)	88.2	(0.2)	11.8	(0.2)
Macao-China	21.7	(0.1)	33.2	(0.2)	45.1	(0.1)	54.9	(0.1)	45.1	(0.1)
Russian Federation	8.7	(0.5)	73.8	(1.6)	17.5	(1.8)	82.5	(1.8)	17.5	(1.8)
Thailand	21.1	(1.0)	76.0	(1.1)	2.9	(0.5)	21.1	(1.0)	78.9	(1.0)
Tunisia	37.4	(3.0)	56.7	(2.7)	5.9	(0.5)	37.4	(3.0)	62.6	(3.0)
Uruguay	41.4	(1.5)	57.3	(1.5)	1.3	(0.2)	41.4	(1.5)	58.6	(1.5)

Notes: Values that are statistically significant are indicated in bold (see Annex A3).
Only countries and economies with comparable data from PISA 2003 and PISA 2012 are shown.
StatLink ⌐⌐⌐⌐ http://dx.doi.org/10.1787/888932957441

[Part 3/3]
Change between 2003 and 2012 in student grade level

Table IV.2.20   *Results based on students' self-reports*

		Change between 2003 and 2012 (PISA 2012 - PISA 2003)								
		Percentage of students at:						Percentage of students enrolled in:			
		Grades below the modal grade		The modal grade		Grades above the modal grade		Lower secondary education (ISCED 2)		Upper secondary education (ISCED 3)	
		% dif.	S.E.	% dif.	S.E.	% dif.	S.E.	% dif.	S.E.	% dif.	S.E.
OECD	Australia	**2.4**	(0.7)	**-2.3**	(0.9)	-0.1	(0.8)	0.2	(0.8)	-0.2	(0.8)
	Austria	0.4	(1.9)	-0.5	(1.9)	0.1	c	0.0	(1.3)	0.0	(1.3)
	Belgium	**4.5**	(0.9)	**-4.7**	(0.9)	0.2	(0.2)	**5.9**	(0.8)	**-5.9**	(0.8)
	Canada	**-2.4**	(0.8)	**2.5**	(0.8)	-0.1	(0.2)	**-2.4**	(0.8)	**2.4**	(0.8)
	Czech Republic	**-42.8**	(1.2)	-1.3	(1.7)	**44.1**	c	**7.9**	(1.7)	**-7.9**	(1.7)
	Denmark	**9.2**	(1.0)	**-6.3**	(1.2)	**-2.8**	(0.7)	**1.1**	(0.5)	**-1.1**	(0.5)
	Finland	**2.2**	(0.7)	**-2.3**	(0.7)	0.1	c	-0.1	c	0.1	c
	France	**-10.6**	(1.4)	**9.3**	(1.3)	**1.3**	(0.4)	**-10.6**	(1.4)	**10.6**	(1.4)
	Germany	**-6.1**	(1.0)	**-8.0**	(1.1)	**14.1**	(1.1)	-0.7	(0.8)	0.7	(0.8)
	Greece	-3.4	(1.6)	**18.4**	(1.7)	-15.0	c	-3.4	(1.6)	3.4	(1.6)
	Hungary	**5.5**	(1.1)	**2.7**	(1.1)	**-8.1**	(0.9)	**5.5**	(1.1)	**-5.5**	(1.1)
	Iceland	0.0	c	0.0	c	0.0	c	0.0	c	0.0	c
	Ireland	**-0.9**	(0.4)	-0.4	(1.5)	1.3	(1.6)	-1.3	(1.6)	1.3	(1.6)
	Italy	**3.1**	(0.9)	-1.4	(1.1)	**-1.7**	(0.5)	0.5	(0.5)	-0.5	(0.5)
	Japan	0.0	c	0.0	c	0.0	c	0.0	c	0.0	c
	Korea	**4.4**	(0.9)	**-4.5**	(0.9)	0.1	(0.1)	**4.4**	(0.9)	**-4.4**	(0.9)
	Luxembourg	**-4.0**	(0.3)	**-5.1**	(0.3)	**9.1**	(0.2)	**-10.6**	(0.2)	**10.6**	(0.2)
	Mexico	**-18.3**	(3.1)	**17.1**	(3.0)	**1.2**	(0.6)	**-19.2**	(2.9)	**19.2**	(2.9)
	Netherlands	**-46.6**	(1.4)	-2.6	(1.6)	**49.2**	(1.1)	**-4.5**	(2.0)	**4.5**	(2.0)
	New Zealand	-0.5	(0.6)	-1.1	(0.7)	**1.6**	(0.5)	-0.5	(0.6)	0.5	(0.6)
	Norway	-0.2	(0.2)	**0.7**	(0.3)	**-0.5**	(0.2)	**0.5**	(0.2)	**-0.5**	(0.2)
	Poland	0.8	(0.6)	0.0	(0.6)	0.0	(0.3)	0.0	(0.3)	0.0	(0.3)
	Portugal	4.2	(3.2)	-3.9	(3.2)	**-0.3**	(0.1)	**9.8**	(3.3)	**-9.8**	(3.3)
	Slovak Republic	**7.1**	(2.1)	**-8.2**	(2.1)	**1.2**	(0.5)	**9.5**	(2.0)	**-9.5**	(2.0)
	Spain	**3.7**	(1.2)	**-3.8**	(1.2)	0.0	(0.0)	0.0	(0.0)	0.0	(0.0)
	Sweden	**1.3**	(0.4)	1.1	(1.2)	**-2.4**	(1.1)	**2.3**	(1.1)	**-2.3**	(1.1)
	Switzerland	**-4.2**	(1.3)	-2.2	(2.3)	**6.3**	(2.7)	**-6.1**	(3.0)	**6.1**	(3.0)
	Turkey	**21.8**	(2.2)	**13.4**	(2.5)	**-35.2**	(2.4)	-2.6	(1.9)	2.6	(1.9)
	United States	**-20.4**	(1.9)	**10.6**	(1.7)	**9.8**	(1.2)	**-20.4**	(1.9)	**20.4**	(1.9)
	OECD average 2003	**-3.1**	(0.3)	0.6	(0.3)	**2.5**	(0.2)	**-1.2**	(0.3)	**1.2**	(0.3)
Partners	Brazil	**-18.1**	(2.8)	**-8.0**	(2.1)	**26.1**	(1.5)	**-18.1**	(2.8)	**18.1**	(2.8)
	Hong Kong-China	**-8.1**	(1.4)	**6.6**	(1.3)	1.4	(1.4)	**-8.1**	(1.4)	**8.1**	(1.4)
	Indonesia	**32.8**	(3.4)	-1.1	(3.5)	**-31.7**	(2.2)	**-16.0**	(3.9)	**16.0**	(3.9)
	Latvia	-0.9	(1.1)	**4.1**	(1.2)	**-3.2**	(0.7)	**2.3**	(0.9)	**-2.3**	(0.9)
	Liechtenstein	-1.9	(1.7)	**-5.0**	(1.6)	**6.9**	(0.3)	**-6.1**	(0.3)	**6.1**	(0.3)
	Macao-China	**-16.4**	(0.6)	**-3.6**	(0.8)	**20.1**	(0.5)	**-20.1**	(0.5)	**20.1**	(0.5)
	Russian Federation	**-23.0**	(2.2)	**6.5**	(2.7)	**16.4**	(1.8)	**50.8**	(2.8)	**-50.8**	(2.8)
	Thailand	**-24.2**	(1.6)	**22.7**	(1.7)	**1.5**	(0.5)	**-24.2**	(1.6)	**24.2**	(1.6)
	Tunisia	**-25.2**	(3.3)	**22.2**	(3.0)	**3.0**	(0.5)	**-25.2**	(3.3)	**25.2**	(3.3)
	Uruguay	**7.8**	(2.5)	-2.0	(2.3)	**-5.8**	(1.0)	**7.8**	(2.5)	**-7.8**	(2.5)

Notes: Values that are statistically significant are indicated in bold (see Annex A3).
Only countries and economies with comparable data from PISA 2003 and PISA 2012 are shown.
StatLink ᴍ㈱ http://dx.doi.org/10.1787/888932957441

[Part 1/6]

Change between 2003 and 2012 in ability grouping for mathematics classes

Table IV.2.21 *Results based on school principals' reports*

	PISA 2003																	
	Percentage of students in schools whose principal reported:																	
	Mathematics classes study similar content, but at different levels of difficulty						Different classes study different content or sets of mathematics topics that have different levels of difficulty						Students are grouped by ability within their mathematics classes					
	For all classes		For some classes		Not for any classes		For all classes		For some classes		Not for any classes		For all classes		For some classes		Not for any classes	
	%	S.E.	%	S.E.	%	S.E.	%	S.E.	%	S.E.	%	S.E.	%	S.E.	%	S.E.	%	S.E.
Australia	32.2	(3.1)	56.8	(2.9)	11.0	(2.0)	22.9	(2.8)	60.4	(3.2)	16.7	(2.6)	49.6	(3.1)	34.4	(2.9)	16.1	(2.3)
Austria	16.3	(1.9)	13.7	(2.7)	70.1	(2.1)	a	a	a	a	a	a	7.7	(2.0)	19.7	(3.0)	72.5	(2.7)
Belgium	4.4	(1.3)	46.8	(3.1)	48.8	(3.0)	16.8	(1.8)	44.1	(2.9)	39.1	(3.1)	2.1	(0.7)	16.7	(2.5)	81.1	(2.5)
Canada	26.6	(2.2)	54.4	(2.2)	19.1	(2.0)	33.4	(1.9)	52.5	(2.1)	14.0	(1.6)	18.4	(2.0)	34.6	(2.4)	47.0	(2.5)
Czech Republic	7.6	(1.7)	17.6	(2.5)	74.7	(2.8)	8.7	(2.3)	23.7	(3.1)	67.6	(3.5)	13.1	(2.2)	28.8	(3.2)	58.2	(3.1)
Denmark	23.0	(3.4)	23.3	(3.7)	53.7	(4.1)	14.7	(2.8)	23.6	(3.5)	61.8	(3.3)	5.4	(1.8)	15.2	(2.8)	79.3	(2.9)
Finland	10.9	(2.2)	27.6	(3.7)	61.5	(3.8)	1.4	(0.9)	32.7	(3.5)	66.0	(3.5)	7.0	(2.0)	36.2	(3.9)	56.8	(4.3)
France	w	w	w	w	w	w	w	w	w	w	w	w	w	w	w	w	w	w
Germany	24.2	(2.9)	18.2	(2.8)	57.5	(3.2)	12.2	(2.5)	16.6	(2.6)	71.2	(2.9)	11.2	(2.3)	34.6	(3.6)	54.2	(3.5)
Greece	6.2	(3.0)	12.8	(3.6)	80.9	(3.5)	0.0	c	4.7	(2.2)	95.3	(2.2)	0.6	(0.5)	1.3	(1.1)	98.1	(1.3)
Hungary	19.3	(3.5)	37.3	(4.0)	43.4	(4.0)	5.7	(2.0)	24.1	(3.4)	70.1	(3.7)	15.2	(2.9)	38.9	(4.2)	45.9	(4.3)
Iceland	52.7	(0.2)	19.2	(0.1)	28.2	(0.2)	22.9	(0.1)	34.7	(0.2)	42.4	(0.2)	23.3	(0.1)	46.4	(0.2)	30.4	(0.2)
Ireland	60.9	(4.4)	34.4	(4.4)	4.7	(1.9)	27.0	(4.0)	45.8	(4.3)	27.1	(4.0)	49.3	(4.2)	28.1	(4.2)	22.6	(3.7)
Italy	21.5	(2.7)	34.0	(3.5)	44.5	(3.1)	9.8	(2.2)	45.6	(3.4)	44.6	(3.6)	2.7	(1.4)	21.4	(3.2)	75.8	(3.5)
Japan	13.7	(2.6)	29.8	(3.8)	56.6	(4.4)	3.4	(1.5)	23.9	(3.3)	72.7	(3.5)	13.8	(2.7)	22.4	(3.5)	63.7	(4.2)
Korea	10.9	(2.8)	60.2	(4.5)	28.9	(3.8)	2.3	(1.3)	55.0	(4.1)	42.7	(4.0)	5.9	(1.9)	64.6	(3.9)	29.5	(3.8)
Luxembourg	4.3	(0.0)	41.8	(0.1)	54.0	(0.1)	19.0	(0.0)	41.3	(0.1)	39.7	(0.1)	0.0	c	6.9	(0.0)	93.1	(0.0)
Mexico	15.6	(2.4)	56.3	(3.7)	28.0	(3.3)	13.5	(1.8)	57.2	(3.3)	29.3	(3.0)	8.1	(1.7)	40.5	(3.5)	51.4	(3.3)
Netherlands	34.8	(4.4)	42.4	(4.2)	22.7	(3.6)	39.7	(4.2)	38.7	(4.1)	21.6	(3.8)	11.5	(2.5)	44.8	(4.4)	43.8	(4.7)
New Zealand	37.0	(3.5)	59.8	(3.4)	3.2	(1.2)	14.6	(2.4)	76.8	(3.0)	8.7	(2.1)	19.3	(2.9)	66.1	(3.4)	14.6	(2.5)
Norway	m	m	m	m	m	m	m	m	m	m	m	m	m	m	m	m	m	m
Poland	41.9	(3.8)	38.2	(3.9)	20.0	(3.2)	1.0	(0.7)	21.1	(3.1)	78.0	(3.2)	3.5	(1.5)	17.7	(3.1)	78.9	(3.4)
Portugal	32.3	(4.1)	39.5	(4.3)	28.2	(4.3)	0.7	(0.5)	9.8	(2.2)	89.5	(2.2)	0.5	(0.5)	13.8	(2.8)	85.8	(2.9)
Slovak Republic	44.2	(3.7)	25.8	(3.1)	30.0	(3.4)	11.8	(2.9)	21.7	(2.6)	66.5	(3.5)	8.0	(1.6)	26.8	(3.5)	65.2	(3.4)
Spain	33.3	(3.6)	58.3	(3.5)	8.4	(2.4)	6.9	(1.8)	50.5	(3.9)	42.5	(3.9)	8.3	(1.4)	33.7	(3.2)	58.1	(3.1)
Sweden	50.7	(3.9)	39.6	(3.9)	9.7	(2.2)	12.4	(2.6)	45.2	(4.0)	42.4	(3.7)	22.3	(3.4)	44.8	(3.5)	33.0	(3.6)
Switzerland	19.9	(2.3)	46.6	(4.1)	33.5	(3.9)	20.7	(3.3)	34.9	(3.9)	44.4	(3.6)	13.9	(2.6)	27.5	(3.6)	58.6	(3.3)
Turkey	33.2	(4.4)	41.9	(4.7)	24.9	(3.6)	23.5	(4.0)	39.9	(4.1)	36.6	(4.2)	8.0	(2.7)	16.9	(3.6)	75.1	(4.3)
United States	25.4	(3.0)	65.5	(3.3)	9.1	(2.0)	31.4	(3.2)	56.2	(3.3)	12.4	(2.3)	21.9	(3.3)	45.7	(3.6)	32.4	(3.1)
OECD average 2003	26.0	(0.6)	38.6	(0.7)	35.4	(0.6)	14.5	(0.5)	37.7	(0.6)	47.8	(0.6)	13.0	(0.4)	30.7	(0.6)	56.3	(0.6)
Brazil	44.3	(3.5)	28.7	(3.3)	27.0	(3.4)	29.8	(3.3)	27.4	(3.7)	42.8	(3.7)	5.8	(1.7)	8.9	(2.4)	85.3	(2.6)
Hong Kong-China	15.9	(3.2)	70.3	(4.0)	13.8	(3.2)	14.1	(2.9)	54.7	(4.3)	31.2	(4.1)	3.7	(1.6)	32.0	(3.9)	64.4	(3.9)
Indonesia	46.9	(3.1)	24.4	(3.5)	28.7	(3.3)	31.0	(3.3)	17.8	(2.8)	51.2	(3.7)	9.3	(2.3)	12.3	(2.1)	78.4	(3.1)
Latvia	34.3	(4.9)	52.4	(5.1)	13.3	(3.3)	13.1	(3.2)	47.0	(4.8)	39.8	(4.7)	5.1	(1.8)	71.2	(3.3)	23.7	(3.1)
Liechtenstein	21.6	(0.5)	37.0	(0.4)	41.4	(0.4)	11.2	(0.5)	70.4	(0.5)	18.3	(0.2)	25.4	(0.5)	35.8	(0.4)	38.8	(0.4)
Macao-China	7.2	(0.0)	40.6	(0.2)	52.2	(0.2)	17.9	(0.2)	32.2	(0.2)	49.9	(0.2)	0.0	c	12.7	(0.2)	87.3	(0.2)
Russian Federation	33.4	(3.4)	56.1	(3.9)	10.6	(2.6)	24.7	(3.4)	40.5	(3.8)	34.8	(4.1)	8.3	(2.1)	71.4	(4.1)	20.3	(4.0)
Thailand	27.6	(3.8)	41.9	(4.0)	30.5	(4.2)	36.6	(4.6)	34.1	(4.1)	29.3	(4.0)	13.2	(2.6)	43.5	(3.6)	43.3	(3.6)
Tunisia	36.1	(3.9)	11.4	(2.3)	52.5	(3.9)	17.7	(3.6)	12.7	(2.7)	69.6	(4.1)	6.3	(2.0)	11.1	(2.8)	82.6	(3.1)
Uruguay	13.3	(2.5)	56.9	(4.1)	29.8	(4.3)	7.6	(1.8)	35.6	(4.6)	56.9	(4.5)	0.0	c	11.9	(2.5)	88.1	(2.5)

Notes: Values that are statistically significant are indicated in bold (see Annex A3).
Only countries and economies with comparable data from PISA 2003 and PISA 2012 are shown.
StatLink ⟐ http://dx.doi.org/10.1787/888932957441

[Part 2/6]
Change between 2003 and 2012 in ability grouping for mathematics classes
Table IV.2.21   *Results based on school principals' reports*

		PISA 2003											
		Percentage of students in schools whose principal reported:											
		In mathematics classes, teachers use pedagogy suitable for students with heterogeneous abilities (i.e. students are not grouped by ability)						No ability grouping for any class		One form of grouping for some classes		One form of grouping for all classes	
		For all classes		For some classes		Not for any classes							
		%	S.E.	%	S.E.	%	S.E.	%	S.E.	%	S.E.	%	S.E.
OECD	Australia	18.1	(2.5)	44.5	(3.0)	37.4	(3.0)	3.1	(1.1)	50.0	(3.5)	46.8	(3.5)
	Austria	23.7	(3.2)	40.0	(3.2)	36.3	(3.8)	70.1	(2.1)	13.7	(2.7)	16.3	(1.9)
	Belgium	50.2	(3.2)	31.3	(3.1)	18.5	(2.1)	29.2	(2.9)	51.5	(3.2)	19.2	(1.9)
	Canada	37.0	(2.2)	38.8	(2.1)	24.2	(2.1)	2.6	(0.5)	48.8	(1.9)	48.6	(2.0)
	Czech Republic	53.4	(3.5)	30.7	(3.0)	15.8	(2.4)	58.9	(3.2)	27.1	(2.9)	14.1	(2.5)
	Denmark	73.8	(3.1)	18.2	(3.1)	8.0	(1.6)	42.7	(3.7)	24.6	(3.7)	32.7	(3.8)
	Finland	39.9	(3.9)	45.7	(4.3)	14.4	(2.9)	47.5	(4.0)	41.0	(4.0)	11.5	(2.3)
	France	w	w	w	w	w	w	w	w	w	w	w	w
	Germany	35.2	(3.6)	17.0	(2.4)	47.8	(3.6)	53.6	(3.0)	20.0	(2.9)	26.4	(3.3)
	Greece	62.0	(4.7)	12.6	(3.9)	25.4	(4.1)	77.9	(3.7)	15.9	(3.9)	6.2	(3.0)
	Hungary	49.2	(4.4)	38.6	(4.0)	12.1	(2.5)	40.8	(4.0)	38.6	(3.9)	20.6	(3.6)
	Iceland	47.9	(0.2)	39.2	(0.2)	12.9	(0.1)	20.0	(0.2)	22.7	(0.2)	57.3	(0.2)
	Ireland	27.1	(4.2)	42.7	(4.6)	30.3	(4.1)	3.2	(1.5)	34.4	(4.4)	62.5	(4.4)
	Italy	39.1	(3.3)	37.3	(3.6)	23.7	(2.8)	32.8	(2.9)	42.6	(3.4)	24.7	(2.9)
	Japan	19.6	(3.5)	18.7	(3.3)	61.7	(3.9)	54.6	(4.2)	31.8	(3.6)	13.5	(2.6)
	Korea	14.9	(2.7)	69.4	(4.0)	15.7	(3.1)	26.1	(3.6)	63.1	(4.3)	10.9	(2.8)
	Luxembourg	46.2	(0.1)	34.0	(0.1)	19.7	(0.0)	38.8	(0.1)	38.3	(0.1)	22.9	(0.0)
	Mexico	32.1	(3.4)	41.5	(3.3)	26.4	(3.2)	18.0	(2.5)	60.9	(3.5)	21.1	(2.6)
	Netherlands	29.7	(4.1)	39.1	(4.4)	31.2	(4.0)	8.4	(2.5)	30.9	(4.0)	60.7	(4.3)
	New Zealand	23.5	(2.9)	57.5	(3.5)	19.0	(2.9)	0.6	(0.6)	55.6	(3.5)	43.7	(3.6)
	Norway	m	m	m	m	m	m	m	m	m	m	m	m
	Poland	73.3	(3.3)	18.9	(3.0)	7.8	(2.2)	18.8	(3.1)	38.8	(3.9)	42.4	(3.8)
	Portugal	67.5	(4.2)	16.9	(3.0)	15.6	(3.1)	28.2	(4.3)	38.8	(4.3)	33.0	(4.1)
	Slovak Republic	53.3	(3.5)	22.5	(3.2)	24.3	(2.8)	25.6	(3.3)	25.4	(2.7)	48.9	(3.7)
	Spain	51.0	(3.6)	32.7	(3.1)	16.3	(2.9)	5.4	(2.0)	57.2	(3.8)	37.4	(3.7)
	Sweden	34.0	(4.0)	45.2	(3.7)	20.8	(3.1)	6.3	(1.8)	38.8	(4.0)	55.0	(3.9)
	Switzerland	42.2	(3.8)	28.9	(3.8)	28.9	(3.5)	19.5	(2.7)	45.7	(4.2)	34.8	(3.2)
	Turkey	12.4	(3.0)	27.5	(4.2)	60.1	(5.1)	20.3	(3.3)	40.2	(5.0)	39.5	(4.7)
	United States	14.2	(2.3)	46.6	(3.8)	39.2	(3.8)	2.6	(1.0)	56.4	(3.4)	41.0	(3.3)
	OECD average 2003	39.6	(0.6)	34.7	(0.7)	25.7	(0.6)	28.0	(0.5)	39.0	(0.7)	33.0	(0.6)
Partners	Brazil	30.4	(3.2)	16.5	(3.0)	53.1	(3.7)	21.6	(2.8)	26.5	(3.1)	51.9	(3.3)
	Hong Kong-China	34.5	(3.9)	47.1	(4.5)	18.4	(3.1)	13.1	(3.1)	66.4	(4.2)	20.5	(3.5)
	Indonesia	76.3	(3.3)	10.0	(2.3)	13.8	(2.7)	26.3	(3.1)	17.5	(2.8)	56.3	(3.6)
	Latvia	43.7	(4.4)	52.1	(4.3)	4.2	(1.7)	8.5	(2.6)	53.1	(5.1)	38.4	(5.1)
	Liechtenstein	33.1	(0.4)	33.7	(0.4)	33.1	(0.5)	7.7	(0.1)	70.7	(0.5)	21.6	(0.5)
	Macao-China	63.4	(0.2)	17.2	(0.2)	19.4	(0.2)	43.3	(0.2)	31.7	(0.2)	25.0	(0.2)
	Russian Federation	43.1	(4.3)	53.6	(4.6)	3.3	(1.6)	8.3	(2.4)	47.8	(3.7)	43.9	(3.3)
	Thailand	35.5	(3.6)	48.6	(3.8)	16.0	(2.7)	19.1	(3.2)	36.5	(4.0)	44.4	(4.3)
	Tunisia	63.6	(4.3)	7.9	(2.4)	28.5	(3.8)	44.3	(4.1)	10.6	(2.2)	45.2	(4.0)
	Uruguay	44.3	(3.6)	44.2	(3.6)	11.5	(2.4)	24.2	(4.1)	59.3	(4.7)	16.5	(2.6)

Notes: Values that are statistically significant are indicated in bold (see Annex A3).
Only countries and economies with comparable data from PISA 2003 and PISA 2012 are shown.
StatLink ⟐ http://dx.doi.org/10.1787/888932957441

[Part 3/6]
Change between 2003 and 2012 in ability grouping for mathematics classes
Table IV.2.21 *Results based on school principals' reports*

	PISA 2012																	
	Percentage of students in schools whose principal reported:																	
	Mathematics classes study similar content, but at different levels of difficulty						Different classes study different content or sets of mathematics topics that have different levels of difficulty						Students are grouped by ability within their mathematics classes					
	For all classes		For some classes		Not for any classes		For all classes		For some classes		Not for any classes		For all classes		For some classes		Not for any classes	
	%	S.E.	%	S.E.	%	S.E.	%	S.E.	%	S.E.	%	S.E.	%	S.E.	%	S.E.	%	S.E.
Australia	37.6	(1.8)	56.3	(1.9)	6.2	(1.1)	26.4	(1.4)	60.1	(1.7)	13.5	(1.3)	43.6	(1.7)	45.4	(1.8)	10.9	(1.1)
Austria	13.4	(1.8)	14.7	(2.3)	71.9	(2.3)	a	a	a	a	a	a	7.3	(1.4)	29.2	(3.7)	63.5	(3.8)
Belgium	12.0	(2.1)	56.0	(3.3)	32.0	(3.2)	14.2	(2.1)	56.6	(3.4)	29.2	(3.1)	3.8	(0.9)	18.4	(2.5)	77.8	(2.5)
Canada	24.2	(2.5)	57.7	(2.4)	18.2	(1.8)	30.4	(2.2)	49.6	(2.5)	20.0	(1.9)	19.9	(1.9)	44.5	(2.3)	35.6	(2.4)
Czech Republic	9.5	(2.7)	18.5	(2.9)	72.1	(3.5)	3.0	(1.1)	22.8	(3.3)	74.2	(3.4)	7.8	(1.7)	31.4	(3.5)	60.8	(3.3)
Denmark	12.8	(2.6)	52.6	(4.0)	34.6	(3.7)	6.4	(1.7)	54.7	(3.5)	38.8	(3.5)	5.0	(1.5)	34.3	(3.9)	60.7	(3.7)
Finland	14.5	(2.4)	34.8	(3.3)	50.7	(3.2)	6.5	(1.4)	45.4	(3.5)	48.2	(3.6)	7.4	(1.8)	41.0	(3.0)	51.6	(3.1)
France	18.8	(2.9)	30.7	(3.2)	50.5	(3.6)	11.3	(2.2)	20.4	(2.8)	68.3	(3.1)	5.7	(1.3)	24.1	(3.0)	70.2	(3.3)
Germany	32.8	(2.8)	28.9	(3.4)	38.4	(3.3)	11.1	(2.3)	26.6	(3.3)	62.4	(3.6)	19.6	(2.4)	31.5	(3.4)	48.9	(3.5)
Greece	6.6	(1.7)	11.3	(3.0)	82.1	(3.1)	0.6	(0.6)	1.5	(0.9)	97.9	(1.1)	1.4	(0.8)	1.8	(1.1)	96.8	(1.3)
Hungary	44.7	(3.8)	28.7	(3.6)	26.6	(3.5)	6.5	(1.9)	28.7	(4.1)	64.8	(4.1)	10.8	(2.6)	33.3	(3.4)	55.8	(3.9)
Iceland	21.4	(0.2)	34.5	(0.3)	44.1	(0.2)	37.8	(0.3)	43.6	(0.3)	18.6	(0.2)	18.3	(0.2)	64.1	(0.2)	17.6	(0.2)
Ireland	50.4	(4.0)	47.2	(4.0)	2.4	(1.3)	23.6	(3.5)	51.7	(3.9)	24.7	(3.4)	53.8	(3.9)	36.3	(3.9)	9.9	(2.5)
Italy	23.4	(1.9)	46.1	(2.3)	30.4	(1.9)	9.0	(1.4)	50.6	(2.3)	40.4	(2.1)	2.6	(0.6)	29.1	(1.9)	68.3	(2.0)
Japan	17.5	(2.8)	43.3	(3.6)	39.2	(3.7)	3.1	(1.3)	27.8	(3.3)	69.1	(3.1)	16.6	(2.6)	29.5	(3.5)	53.9	(3.5)
Korea	38.1	(4.0)	50.7	(3.9)	11.2	(2.5)	12.4	(2.8)	51.2	(4.0)	36.4	(4.1)	10.9	(2.7)	61.6	(4.0)	27.5	(3.7)
Luxembourg	17.2	(0.1)	44.2	(0.1)	38.6	(0.1)	13.4	(0.1)	40.8	(0.1)	45.8	(0.1)	1.2	(0.0)	33.6	(0.1)	65.2	(0.1)
Mexico	35.2	(1.7)	34.6	(1.8)	30.2	(1.7)	24.3	(1.8)	28.3	(2.4)	47.4	(2.0)	18.9	(1.8)	40.5	(1.9)	40.5	(2.0)
Netherlands	35.4	(5.1)	47.2	(4.9)	17.4	(2.9)	31.5	(3.8)	48.4	(3.9)	20.1	(3.0)	10.7	(2.8)	50.9	(4.6)	38.4	(4.0)
New Zealand	24.7	(4.0)	71.4	(4.1)	3.9	(1.4)	22.7	(2.9)	73.8	(3.0)	3.5	(1.3)	34.8	(4.3)	57.3	(4.4)	8.0	(2.2)
Norway	m	m	m	m	m	m	m	m	m	m	m	m	m	m	m	m	m	m
Poland	38.1	(4.4)	16.2	(3.2)	45.7	(4.2)	2.2	(1.1)	17.4	(3.4)	80.5	(3.5)	3.2	(1.4)	13.9	(3.2)	83.0	(3.3)
Portugal	21.1	(3.7)	37.2	(3.8)	41.7	(4.0)	5.1	(1.9)	30.0	(3.6)	64.9	(4.0)	0.3	(0.3)	27.2	(3.5)	72.4	(3.5)
Slovak Republic	29.8	(3.0)	36.3	(3.4)	33.8	(3.2)	6.6	(1.2)	29.3	(3.5)	64.1	(3.8)	7.9	(1.7)	24.8	(3.6)	67.3	(3.6)
Spain	39.4	(2.7)	46.4	(3.2)	14.2	(2.1)	17.7	(2.5)	46.2	(3.2)	36.1	(2.9)	7.3	(1.4)	20.0	(2.3)	72.7	(2.5)
Sweden	53.2	(3.2)	27.8	(3.4)	19.0	(2.9)	10.5	(2.4)	34.5	(3.5)	54.9	(3.6)	9.2	(2.0)	36.0	(3.3)	54.7	(3.5)
Switzerland	35.0	(2.8)	38.9	(3.5)	26.1	(3.0)	15.4	(2.3)	46.5	(3.4)	38.1	(3.1)	19.2	(2.7)	33.6	(2.6)	47.2	(3.4)
Turkey	29.0	(3.9)	44.7	(4.1)	26.3	(3.2)	11.8	(2.6)	33.1	(3.7)	55.1	(4.1)	4.0	(1.5)	11.7	(2.5)	84.3	(3.1)
United States	21.3	(3.6)	66.4	(4.7)	12.3	(3.5)	18.6	(2.7)	66.4	(4.0)	15.0	(3.6)	12.9	(2.7)	66.1	(4.3)	21.0	(4.1)
OECD average 2003	27.3	(0.6)	40.5	(0.6)	32.2	(0.5)	14.3	(0.4)	41.0	(0.6)	44.8	(0.6)	13.3	(0.4)	35.1	(0.6)	51.6	(0.6)
Brazil	48.3	(2.6)	30.0	(2.3)	21.7	(2.4)	22.0	(2.5)	24.8	(2.4)	53.2	(3.0)	4.9	(1.2)	13.4	(2.0)	81.7	(2.1)
Hong Kong-China	28.5	(3.9)	61.2	(4.4)	10.3	(2.4)	16.3	(3.0)	58.0	(4.0)	25.7	(3.9)	5.4	(1.7)	37.5	(4.1)	57.1	(4.3)
Indonesia	45.0	(3.6)	24.8	(3.6)	30.2	(3.6)	23.5	(3.6)	36.3	(3.8)	40.2	(3.5)	13.1	(2.5)	14.7	(2.7)	72.2	(3.3)
Latvia	31.8	(3.3)	49.6	(3.8)	18.7	(3.1)	9.7	(2.3)	41.9	(4.1)	48.4	(3.6)	6.2	(2.0)	59.4	(3.4)	34.3	(3.3)
Liechtenstein	39.0	(1.2)	20.8	(1.3)	40.1	(0.7)	10.6	(0.6)	19.4	(1.3)	70.1	(1.2)	50.5	(0.8)	14.5	(0.9)	35.1	(0.9)
Macao-China	10.8	(0.0)	55.3	(0.0)	33.9	(0.0)	11.6	(0.0)	50.1	(0.1)	38.3	(0.1)	1.1	(0.0)	36.7	(0.1)	62.2	(0.1)
Russian Federation	48.4	(3.6)	46.4	(3.6)	5.2	(1.5)	14.5	(2.0)	21.3	(2.5)	64.2	(3.0)	5.2	(1.9)	79.2	(3.0)	15.5	(2.3)
Thailand	5.4	(1.9)	68.3	(3.3)	26.4	(3.3)	0.0	c	57.1	(3.4)	42.9	(3.4)	0.7	(0.7)	50.3	(3.8)	49.0	(3.8)
Tunisia	40.6	(4.2)	36.0	(4.1)	23.5	(3.3)	28.9	(4.3)	32.6	(4.3)	38.6	(4.3)	4.8	(1.8)	11.0	(2.4)	84.2	(3.0)
Uruguay	25.0	(3.2)	64.1	(3.5)	10.9	(2.4)	16.1	(2.8)	58.6	(3.7)	25.3	(3.4)	1.4	(1.0)	8.1	(2.1)	90.5	(2.1)

Notes: Values that are statistically significant are indicated in bold (see Annex A3).
Only countries and economies with comparable data from PISA 2003 and PISA 2012 are shown.
StatLink ⌨ http://dx.doi.org/10.1787/888932957441

[Part 4/6]
Change between 2003 and 2012 in ability grouping for mathematics classes
Table IV.2.21   *Results based on school principals' reports*

	PISA 2012											
	Percentage of students in schools whose principal reported:											
	In mathematics classes, teachers use pedagogy suitable for students with heterogeneous abilities (i.e. students are not grouped by ability)						No ability grouping for any class		One form of grouping for some classes		One form of grouping for all classes	
	For all classes		For some classes		Not for any classes							
	%	S.E.	%	S.E.	%	S.E.	%	S.E.	%	S.E.	%	S.E.
Australia	21.3	(1.3)	50.2	(1.5)	28.5	(1.7)	1.6	(0.5)	48.6	(1.7)	49.8	(1.6)
Austria	31.4	(3.9)	51.8	(4.4)	16.9	(2.9)	71.9	(2.3)	14.7	(2.3)	13.4	(1.8)
Belgium	55.8	(3.3)	27.7	(2.8)	16.4	(2.2)	20.6	(2.9)	57.0	(3.1)	22.4	(2.7)
Canada	35.4	(2.8)	47.7	(2.7)	16.9	(2.0)	7.1	(1.2)	49.2	(2.5)	43.8	(2.7)
Czech Republic	49.8	(3.7)	37.4	(3.6)	12.8	(2.0)	58.8	(4.2)	30.6	(3.7)	10.6	(2.7)
Denmark	42.4	(3.6)	52.1	(3.7)	5.5	(1.7)	24.1	(3.2)	58.0	(3.8)	17.9	(2.8)
Finland	51.7	(2.9)	37.2	(3.2)	11.1	(2.3)	35.5	(3.5)	46.4	(3.8)	18.0	(2.5)
France	67.6	(3.1)	22.6	(2.8)	9.7	(2.0)	43.8	(3.5)	31.4	(3.2)	24.8	(3.3)
Germany	40.9	(3.5)	33.4	(3.2)	25.7	(3.1)	31.9	(3.1)	32.9	(3.4)	35.3	(3.0)
Greece	63.7	(4.1)	18.8	(3.4)	17.5	(3.0)	81.4	(3.2)	11.3	(3.2)	7.3	(1.8)
Hungary	55.9	(4.0)	33.8	(3.7)	10.3	(2.4)	23.3	(2.9)	31.2	(3.8)	45.5	(3.8)
Iceland	67.9	(0.2)	29.1	(0.2)	2.9	(0.1)	12.9	(0.1)	40.8	(0.2)	46.3	(0.3)
Ireland	18.7	(3.0)	41.6	(3.8)	39.7	(4.1)	0.8	(0.7)	40.2	(4.0)	59.0	(4.0)
Italy	44.9	(2.2)	41.2	(2.1)	13.9	(1.6)	24.1	(1.7)	48.7	(1.9)	27.3	(1.9)
Japan	42.1	(3.7)	40.9	(3.7)	17.0	(2.6)	36.9	(3.7)	44.6	(3.6)	18.6	(2.9)
Korea	17.2	(3.1)	51.0	(4.0)	31.8	(3.6)	9.9	(2.3)	48.6	(3.8)	41.5	(3.9)
Luxembourg	44.4	(0.1)	39.3	(0.1)	16.3	(0.1)	32.1	(0.1)	41.4	(0.1)	26.5	(0.1)
Mexico	30.6	(1.9)	37.4	(1.9)	32.0	(1.8)	26.3	(1.6)	32.2	(1.9)	41.5	(1.9)
Netherlands	38.9	(4.2)	34.9	(3.7)	26.2	(4.2)	6.4	(1.7)	39.0	(4.6)	54.6	(4.9)
New Zealand	22.8	(3.4)	58.4	(3.6)	18.8	(3.1)	1.3	(0.9)	60.5	(3.7)	38.2	(3.6)
Norway	m	m	m	m	m	m	m	m	m	m	m	m
Poland	63.2	(4.4)	13.1	(2.9)	23.7	(3.7)	42.4	(4.1)	19.3	(3.5)	38.3	(4.3)
Portugal	60.9	(4.0)	32.3	(3.8)	6.7	(2.7)	38.3	(4.1)	38.1	(3.7)	23.6	(3.5)
Slovak Republic	55.9	(4.1)	25.7	(3.2)	18.3	(3.4)	28.4	(3.3)	39.1	(3.3)	32.5	(2.9)
Spain	59.2	(2.6)	26.0	(2.2)	14.8	(2.0)	7.6	(1.6)	43.8	(2.8)	48.6	(2.9)
Sweden	55.9	(4.0)	33.8	(3.3)	10.3	(2.3)	15.7	(2.8)	27.8	(3.3)	56.5	(3.3)
Switzerland	36.7	(3.2)	30.6	(3.2)	32.7	(2.8)	15.0	(2.3)	40.9	(3.4)	44.0	(3.0)
Turkey	43.0	(3.6)	21.7	(3.4)	35.3	(4.0)	24.2	(3.1)	42.1	(3.4)	33.7	(3.7)
United States	33.6	(4.2)	56.0	(4.4)	10.4	(2.9)	6.1	(2.6)	62.9	(4.2)	31.0	(3.8)
OECD average 2003	43.9	(0.6)	37.2	(0.6)	19.0	(0.5)	25.4	(0.5)	40.4	(0.6)	34.3	(0.6)
Brazil	37.5	(2.6)	20.4	(2.4)	42.1	(2.5)	18.4	(2.2)	28.1	(2.2)	53.5	(2.6)
Hong Kong-China	41.0	(4.4)	50.0	(4.4)	9.0	(2.4)	9.0	(2.2)	60.1	(4.3)	31.0	(4.0)
Indonesia	52.6	(3.8)	22.2	(3.2)	25.2	(3.4)	24.6	(3.2)	27.7	(3.6)	47.6	(3.8)
Latvia	41.7	(3.7)	53.0	(3.8)	5.2	(1.8)	17.8	(3.0)	46.1	(3.9)	36.1	(3.3)
Liechtenstein	43.3	(0.6)	32.1	(0.9)	24.5	(0.6)	40.1	(0.7)	13.2	(1.2)	46.7	(1.2)
Macao-China	49.2	(0.1)	29.4	(0.0)	21.4	(0.0)	33.9	(0.0)	52.9	(0.0)	13.3	(0.0)
Russian Federation	35.4	(3.9)	60.5	(3.9)	4.1	(1.3)	4.0	(1.2)	39.2	(3.1)	56.8	(3.3)
Thailand	21.1	(2.5)	74.4	(3.0)	4.4	(1.7)	23.7	(2.8)	71.0	(3.1)	5.4	(1.9)
Tunisia	51.7	(4.0)	18.5	(3.0)	29.8	(4.0)	17.7	(2.9)	32.1	(3.8)	50.2	(4.1)
Uruguay	40.0	(3.9)	38.5	(3.5)	21.5	(3.3)	8.9	(2.2)	58.6	(3.8)	32.5	(3.5)

Notes: Values that are statistically significant are indicated in bold (see Annex A3).
Only countries and economies with comparable data from PISA 2003 and PISA 2012 are shown.
StatLink ᐁᔑᓈ http://dx.doi.org/10.1787/888932957441

[Part 5/6]
Change between 2003 and 2012 in ability grouping for mathematics classes
Table IV.2.21 *Results based on school principals' reports*

	Change between 2003 and 2012 (PISA 2012 - PISA 2003)																	
	Percentage of students in schools whose principal reported:																	
	Mathematics classes study similar content, but at different levels of difficulty						Different classes study different content or sets of mathematics topics that have different levels of difficulty						Students are grouped by ability within their mathematics classes					
	For all classes		For some classes		Not for any classes		For all classes		For some classes		Not for any classes		For all classes		For some classes		Not for any classes	
	% dif.	S.E.	% dif.	S.E.	% dif.	S.E.	% dif.	S.E.	% dif.	S.E.	% dif.	S.E.	% dif.	S.E.	% dif.	S.E.	% dif.	S.E.
Australia	5.4	(3.6)	-0.6	(3.5)	**-4.8**	(2.2)	3.5	(3.2)	-0.3	(3.6)	-3.2	(2.9)	**-5.9**	(3.5)	**11.1**	(3.4)	**-5.1**	(2.6)
Austria	-2.9	(2.7)	1.0	(3.5)	1.9	(3.1)	a	a	a	a	a	a	-0.4	(2.4)	**9.5**	(4.7)	**-9.1**	(4.7)
Belgium	**7.6**	(2.5)	**9.2**	(4.5)	**-16.8**	(4.4)	-2.6	(2.8)	**12.5**	(4.5)	**-9.9**	(4.4)	1.7	(1.1)	1.7	(3.5)	-3.4	(3.5)
Canada	-2.4	(3.3)	3.3	(3.3)	-0.9	(2.7)	-3.0	(3.0)	-2.9	(3.3)	**5.9**	(2.5)	1.5	(2.8)	**9.8**	(3.3)	**-11.3**	(3.5)
Czech Republic	1.9	(3.2)	0.8	(3.8)	-2.7	(4.5)	**-5.8**	(2.5)	-0.9	(4.5)	6.7	(4.9)	**-5.3**	(2.8)	2.7	(4.7)	2.6	(4.5)
Denmark	**-10.1**	(4.3)	**29.3**	(5.5)	**-19.2**	(5.5)	**-8.2**	(3.3)	**31.1**	(4.9)	**-22.9**	(4.8)	-0.4	(2.4)	**19.1**	(4.8)	**-18.7**	(4.6)
Finland	3.6	(3.3)	7.1	(5.0)	**-10.7**	(5.0)	**5.1**	(1.7)	**12.7**	(4.9)	**-17.8**	(5.0)	0.4	(2.6)	4.7	(4.9)	-5.2	(5.3)
France	m	m	m	m	m	m	m	m	m	m	m	m	m	m	m	m	m	m
Germany	**8.5**	(4.1)	**10.6**	(4.4)	**-19.2**	(4.6)	-1.1	(3.4)	**10.0**	(4.2)	-8.8	(4.6)	**8.4**	(3.3)	-3.0	(5.0)	-5.3	(4.9)
Greece	0.4	(3.5)	-1.6	(4.7)	1.2	(4.6)	0.6	c	-3.3	(2.3)	2.6	(2.4)	0.8	(1.0)	0.5	(1.5)	-1.3	(1.8)
Hungary	**25.4**	(5.1)	-8.6	(5.4)	**-16.8**	(5.4)	0.7	(2.8)	4.6	(5.3)	-5.3	(5.5)	-4.4	(3.9)	-5.6	(5.4)	10.0	(5.8)
Iceland	**-31.3**	(0.3)	**15.4**	(0.3)	**15.9**	(0.3)	**15.0**	(0.3)	**8.9**	(0.3)	**-23.9**	(0.2)	**-5.0**	(0.2)	**17.7**	(0.3)	**-12.7**	(0.3)
Ireland	**-10.5**	(5.9)	**12.8**	(6.0)	-2.3	(2.2)	-3.4	(5.3)	5.8	(5.8)	-2.4	(5.3)	4.5	(5.8)	8.2	(5.7)	**-12.7**	(4.5)
Italy	1.9	(3.3)	**12.2**	(4.2)	**-14.1**	(3.7)	-0.8	(2.6)	5.0	(4.1)	-4.2	(4.2)	-0.1	(1.5)	**7.6**	(3.3)	-7.5	(4.0)
Japan	3.8	(3.8)	**13.5**	(5.2)	**-17.4**	(5.7)	-0.3	(1.9)	3.9	(4.6)	-3.6	(4.7)	2.7	(3.8)	7.1	(4.9)	-9.8	(5.5)
Korea	**27.2**	(4.9)	-9.5	(6.0)	**-17.7**	(4.5)	**10.1**	(3.1)	-3.9	(5.7)	-6.2	(5.8)	5.0	(3.3)	-3.0	(5.6)	-2.0	(5.3)
Luxembourg	**12.9**	(0.1)	**2.5**	(0.1)	**-15.4**	(0.1)	**-5.6**	(0.1)	**-0.5**	(0.1)	**6.1**	(0.1)	1.2	c	**26.7**	(0.1)	**-27.9**	(0.1)
Mexico	**19.5**	(3.0)	**-21.7**	(4.1)	2.2	(3.7)	**10.8**	(2.5)	**-28.9**	(4.1)	**18.1**	(3.6)	**10.8**	(2.5)	0.0	(4.0)	**-10.9**	(3.9)
Netherlands	0.6	(6.7)	4.7	(6.4)	-5.3	(4.6)	-8.2	(5.7)	9.7	(5.1)	-1.5	(4.9)	-0.8	(3.8)	6.2	(6.4)	-5.4	(6.2)
New Zealand	**-12.3**	(5.3)	**11.6**	(5.3)	0.7	(1.8)	**8.1**	(3.7)	-3.0	(4.2)	**-5.2**	(2.4)	**15.4**	(5.2)	-8.8	(5.6)	-6.6	(3.4)
Norway	m	m	m	m	m	m	m	m	m	m	m	m	m	m	m	m	m	m
Poland	-3.8	(5.8)	**-22.0**	(5.1)	**25.7**	(5.3)	1.2	(1.4)	-3.7	(4.6)	2.5	(4.8)	-0.3	(2.1)	-3.8	(4.4)	4.1	(4.7)
Portugal	**-11.2**	(5.5)	-2.2	(5.7)	**13.5**	(5.9)	**4.4**	(2.0)	**20.2**	(4.2)	**-24.7**	(4.6)	-0.2	(0.6)	**13.5**	(4.5)	**-13.3**	(4.5)
Slovak Republic	**-14.4**	(4.8)	**10.5**	(4.6)	3.8	(4.7)	-5.2	(3.1)	7.6	(4.4)	-2.4	(5.3)	-0.1	(2.4)	-1.9	(5.1)	2.0	(5.0)
Spain	6.1	(4.5)	**-11.9**	(4.7)	5.8	(3.2)	**10.8**	(3.1)	-4.4	(5.1)	-6.4	(4.9)	-1.0	(1.9)	**-13.6**	(3.9)	**14.7**	(4.0)
Sweden	2.5	(5.0)	**-11.7**	(5.2)	**9.3**	(3.6)	-1.8	(3.5)	**-10.7**	(5.4)	**12.6**	(5.2)	**-13.0**	(3.9)	-8.7	(4.8)	**21.8**	(5.0)
Switzerland	**15.2**	(3.6)	-7.7	(5.4)	-7.4	(5.0)	-5.3	(4.0)	**11.6**	(5.1)	-6.3	(4.8)	5.3	(3.7)	6.1	(4.4)	**-11.4**	(4.7)
Turkey	-4.2	(5.9)	2.8	(6.2)	1.4	(4.8)	**-11.6**	(4.8)	-6.9	(5.5)	**18.5**	(5.8)	-4.0	(3.1)	-5.2	(4.4)	9.2	(5.3)
United States	-4.2	(4.7)	1.0	(5.8)	3.2	(4.0)	**-12.8**	(4.2)	**10.2**	(5.2)	2.6	(4.2)	**-9.0**	(4.3)	**20.4**	(5.6)	**-11.4**	(5.1)
OECD average 2003	1.3	(0.8)	1.9	(0.9)	**-3.2**	(0.8)	-0.2	(0.6)	**3.3**	(0.9)	**-3.0**	(0.9)	0.3	(0.6)	**4.4**	(0.9)	**-4.7**	(0.8)
Brazil	4.0	(4.4)	1.3	(4.0)	-5.3	(4.2)	-7.7	(4.1)	-2.6	(4.4)	**10.4**	(4.7)	-1.0	(2.1)	4.5	(3.1)	-3.5	(3.3)
Hong Kong-China	**12.6**	(5.1)	-9.1	(5.9)	-3.5	(4.0)	2.2	(4.2)	3.4	(5.9)	-5.5	(5.7)	1.7	(2.3)	5.5	(5.6)	-7.2	(5.8)
Indonesia	-1.9	(4.8)	0.3	(5.0)	1.5	(4.9)	-7.5	(4.9)	**18.5**	(4.7)	**-11.0**	(5.1)	3.8	(3.4)	2.4	(3.4)	-6.2	(4.5)
Latvia	-2.5	(5.9)	-2.8	(6.3)	5.3	(4.5)	-3.5	(4.0)	-5.1	(6.3)	8.6	(5.9)	1.1	(2.7)	**-11.8**	(4.7)	10.6	(4.5)
Liechtenstein	**17.4**	(1.3)	**-16.1**	(1.3)	-1.3	(0.8)	-0.7	(0.8)	**-51.0**	(1.4)	**51.7**	(1.2)	**25.0**	(0.9)	**-21.3**	(1.0)	**-3.7**	(0.9)
Macao-China	**3.5**	(0.0)	**14.7**	(0.2)	**-18.3**	(0.3)	**-6.3**	(0.2)	**17.9**	(0.2)	**-11.7**	(0.2)	1.1	c	**24.0**	(0.2)	**-25.1**	(0.2)
Russian Federation	**15.0**	(5.0)	-9.6	(5.3)	-5.4	(3.0)	**-10.2**	(3.9)	**-19.2**	(4.6)	**29.4**	(5.1)	-3.1	(2.9)	7.9	(5.1)	-4.8	(4.6)
Thailand	**-22.3**	(4.3)	**26.4**	(5.2)	-4.1	(5.3)	-36.6	c	**23.0**	(5.4)	**13.6**	(5.3)	**-12.5**	(5.2)	6.8	(5.3)	5.7	(5.3)
Tunisia	4.5	(5.7)	**24.6**	(4.7)	**-29.1**	(5.1)	**11.2**	(5.4)	**19.9**	(5.1)	**-31.1**	(5.9)	-1.5	(2.7)	-0.1	(3.6)	1.6	(4.3)
Uruguay	**11.7**	(4.0)	7.2	(5.4)	**-18.9**	(4.9)	**8.6**	(3.3)	**23.0**	(5.9)	**-31.6**	(5.7)	1.4	c	-3.8	(3.3)	2.4	(3.3)

OECD (rows Australia through OECD average 2003); *Partners* (rows Brazil through Uruguay)

Notes: Values that are statistically significant are indicated in bold (see Annex A3).
Only countries and economies with comparable data from PISA 2003 and PISA 2012 are shown.
StatLink ⟐ http://dx.doi.org/10.1787/888932957441

[Part 6/6]
Change between 2003 and 2012 in ability grouping for mathematics classes

Table IV.2.21 *Results based on school principals' reports*

	Change between 2003 and 2012 (PISA 2012 - PISA 2003)												
	Percentage of students in schools whose principal reported:												
	In mathematics classes. teachers use pedagogy suitable for students with heterogeneous abilities (i.e. students are not grouped by ability)						No ability grouping for any class		One form of grouping for some classes		One form of grouping for all classes	
	For all classes		For some classes		Not for any classes							
	% dif.	S.E.	% dif.	S.E.	% dif.	S.E.	% dif.	S.E.	% dif.	S.E.	% dif.	S.E.
Australia	3.2	(2.9)	5.6	(3.3)	**-8.9**	(3.4)	-1.5	(1.2)	-1.4	(3.9)	3.0	(3.9)
Austria	7.6	(5.0)	**11.8**	(5.4)	**-19.4**	(4.8)	1.9	(3.1)	1.0	(3.5)	-2.9	(2.7)
Belgium	5.7	(4.5)	-3.6	(4.2)	-2.1	(3.1)	**-8.6**	(4.1)	5.5	(4.4)	3.1	(3.3)
Canada	-1.6	(3.6)	**8.9**	(3.4)	**-7.3**	(2.9)	**4.5**	(1.3)	0.3	(3.2)	-4.8	(3.3)
Czech Republic	-3.6	(5.1)	6.7	(4.7)	-3.1	(3.2)	-0.1	(5.2)	3.5	(4.7)	-3.4	(3.7)
Denmark	**-31.4**	(4.7)	**33.9**	(4.8)	-2.4	(2.3)	**-18.6**	(4.9)	**33.4**	(5.3)	**-14.8**	(4.7)
Finland	**11.8**	(4.9)	-8.5	(5.4)	-3.2	(3.7)	**-12.0**	(5.3)	5.4	(5.5)	6.6	(3.4)
France	m	m	m	m	m	m	m	m	m	m	m	m
Germany	5.7	(5.0)	**16.4**	(4.0)	**-22.1**	(4.8)	**-21.7**	(4.3)	**12.9**	(4.5)	**8.8**	(4.4)
Greece	1.7	(6.2)	6.2	(5.1)	-7.9	(5.1)	3.5	(4.9)	-4.6	(5.0)	1.1	(3.5)
Hungary	6.7	(6.0)	-4.9	(5.5)	-1.8	(3.5)	**-17.5**	(4.9)	-7.4	(5.5)	**24.9**	(5.2)
Iceland	**20.1**	(0.3)	**-10.1**	(0.3)	**-10.0**	(0.1)	**-7.1**	(0.2)	**18.1**	(0.3)	**-10.9**	(0.3)
Ireland	-8.4	(5.1)	-1.0	(6.0)	9.4	(5.8)	-2.4	(1.6)	5.9	(5.9)	-3.5	(5.9)
Italy	5.9	(4.0)	3.9	(4.2)	**-9.8**	(3.3)	**-8.7**	(3.3)	6.1	(3.9)	2.6	(3.5)
Japan	**22.5**	(5.1)	**22.2**	(4.9)	**-44.7**	(4.7)	**-17.8**	(5.6)	**12.7**	(5.1)	5.0	(3.9)
Korea	2.3	(4.1)	**-18.4**	(5.6)	**16.1**	(4.8)	**-16.2**	(4.3)	**-14.5**	(5.8)	**30.7**	(4.8)
Luxembourg	**-1.8**	(0.1)	**5.3**	(0.1)	**-3.5**	(0.1)	**-6.7**	(0.1)	**3.1**	(0.1)	**3.6**	(0.1)
Mexico	-1.4	(3.9)	-4.1	(3.8)	5.6	(3.7)	**8.3**	(3.0)	**-28.7**	(3.9)	**20.4**	(3.2)
Netherlands	9.2	(5.9)	-4.2	(5.7)	-4.9	(5.8)	-2.0	(3.0)	8.1	(6.1)	-6.1	(6.5)
New Zealand	-0.7	(4.5)	0.9	(5.0)	-0.1	(4.2)	0.7	(1.1)	4.9	(5.1)	-5.5	(5.0)
Norway	m	m	m	m	m	m	m	m	m	m	m	m
Poland	-10.1	(5.5)	-5.8	(4.2)	**15.9**	(4.3)	**23.6**	(5.1)	**-19.5**	(5.3)	-4.1	(5.8)
Portugal	-6.5	(5.8)	**15.5**	(4.8)	**-8.9**	(4.1)	10.1	(6.0)	-0.7	(5.7)	-9.4	(5.4)
Slovak Republic	2.7	(5.4)	3.3	(4.5)	-5.9	(4.5)	2.8	(4.7)	**13.7**	(4.3)	**-16.4**	(4.7)
Spain	**8.2**	(4.5)	-6.8	(3.8)	-1.5	(3.5)	2.2	(2.5)	**-13.4**	(4.7)	**11.2**	(4.7)
Sweden	**21.8**	(5.7)	**-11.3**	(4.9)	**-10.5**	(3.8)	**9.4**	(3.3)	**-11.0**	(5.2)	1.5	(5.1)
Switzerland	-5.5	(5.0)	1.8	(4.9)	3.7	(4.5)	-4.5	(3.6)	-4.8	(5.4)	**9.3**	(4.4)
Turkey	**30.6**	(4.7)	-5.8	(5.4)	**-24.8**	(6.5)	3.9	(4.5)	1.9	(6.4)	-5.8	(6.0)
United States	**19.4**	(4.8)	9.4	(5.8)	**-28.8**	(4.8)	3.5	(2.8)	6.6	(5.4)	**-10.0**	(5.0)
OECD average 2003	**4.2**	(0.9)	**2.5**	(0.9)	**-6.7**	(0.8)	**-2.6**	(0.7)	**1.4**	(0.9)	**1.3**	(0.9)
Brazil	**7.1**	(4.1)	3.9	(3.9)	**-10.9**	(4.4)	-3.3	(3.6)	1.7	(3.8)	1.6	(4.2)
Hong Kong-China	6.5	(5.9)	3.0	(6.2)	**-9.5**	(3.9)	-4.2	(3.8)	-6.4	(6.0)	**10.5**	(5.3)
Indonesia	**-23.6**	(5.0)	**12.2**	(3.9)	**11.4**	(4.3)	-1.6	(4.4)	**10.3**	(4.6)	-8.6	(5.2)
Latvia	-2.0	(5.8)	0.9	(5.7)	1.0	(2.4)	**9.3**	(3.9)	-7.0	(6.4)	-2.3	(6.1)
Liechtenstein	**10.2**	(0.7)	-1.6	(1.0)	**-8.6**	(0.8)	**32.4**	(0.7)	**-57.6**	(1.3)	**25.1**	(1.3)
Macao-China	**-14.1**	(0.2)	**12.2**	(0.2)	**2.0**	(0.2)	**-9.4**	(0.2)	**21.1**	(0.2)	**-11.7**	(0.2)
Russian Federation	-7.7	(5.8)	6.9	(6.0)	0.8	(2.1)	-4.3	(2.7)	-8.7	(4.9)	**12.9**	(4.6)
Thailand	**-14.3**	(4.4)	**25.9**	(4.9)	**-11.5**	(3.1)	4.5	(4.3)	**34.4**	(5.1)	**-39.0**	(4.7)
Tunisia	**-11.9**	(5.8)	**10.6**	(3.9)	1.3	(5.5)	**-26.5**	(5.1)	**21.6**	(4.4)	5.0	(5.8)
Uruguay	-4.3	(5.3)	-5.7	(5.0)	**10.0**	(4.1)	**-15.3**	(4.7)	-0.6	(6.0)	**16.0**	(4.4)

Notes: Values that are statistically significant are indicated in bold (see Annex A3).
Only countries and economies with comparable data from PISA 2003 and PISA 2012 are shown.
StatLink ⌗ http://dx.doi.org/10.1787/888932957441

[Part 1/1]
Cumulative expenditure by educational institutions
Table IV.3.1   *In equivalent USD converted using PPPs for GDP, based on full-time equivalents*

		PISA 2003			PISA 2012	
			Cumulative expenditure by educational institutions per student aged 6 to 15			Cumulative expenditure by educational institutions per student aged 6 to 15
	Source	Year of reference	In equivalent USD converted using PPPs	Source	Year of reference	In equivalent USD converted using PPPs
Australia	a	2001	83 341	b	2010	98 025
Austria	a	2001	89 518	b	2010	116 603
Belgium	a	2001	76 412	b	2010	97 126
Canada	a	2001	74 137	b	2009	80 397
Chile			m	b	2011	32 250
Czech Republic	a	2001	29 814	b	2010	54 519
Denmark	a	2001	91 130	b	2010	109 746
Estonia			m	b	2010	55 520
Finland	a	2001	60 148	b	2010	86 233
France	a	2001	74 110	b	2010	83 582
Germany	a	2001	53 768	b	2010	80 796
Greece	a	2001	43 019			m
Hungary[1]	a	2001	38 524	b	2010	46 598
Iceland	a	2001	109 957	b	2010	93 986
Ireland[1]	a	2001	44 968	b	2010	93 117
Israel			m	b	2010	57 013
Italy[1]	a	2001	91 876	b	2010	84 416
Japan	a	2001	53 296	b	2010	89 724
Korea	a	2001	52 100	b	2010	69 037
Luxembourg			m	b	2010	197 598
Mexico	a	2001	26 262	b	2010	23 913
Netherlands	a	2001	64 951	b	2010	95 072
New Zealand			m	b	2010	70 650
Norway	a	2001	98 866	b	2010	123 591
Poland[1]	a	2001	29 353	b	2010	57 644
Portugal[1]	a	2001	59 995	b	2010	70 370
Slovak Republic	a	2001	18 748	b	2010	53 160
Slovenia[1]			m	b	2010	91 785
Spain	a	2001	61 070	b	2010	82 178
Sweden	a	2001	69 920	b	2010	95 831
Switzerland[1]	a	2001	88 092	b	2010	127 322
Turkey			m	b	2010	19 821
United Kingdom			m	b	2010	98 023
United States	a	2001	97 517	b	2010	115 961
Albania			m	c	2010	m
Argentina			m	b	2010	m
Brazil[1]			m	b	2010	26 765
Bulgaria			m	c	2009	31 944
Colombia			m	c	2010	20 362
Costa Rica			m			m
Croatia[2]			m	c	2012	38 992
Cyprus*,[1]			m	c	2010	109 575
Hong Kong-China			m	c	2010	m
Indonesia			m	b	2010	m
Jordan			m	c	2010	7 125
Kazakhstan			m			m
Latvia			m	c	2010	45 342
Liechtenstein			m			m
Lithuania			m	c	2010	44 963
Macao-China			m			m
Malaysia[1]			m	c	2010	16 816
Montenegro			m	c	2011	23 913
Peru			m	c	2011	12 431
Qatar			m			m
Romania[1]			m			m
Russian Federation			m			m
Serbia			m			m
Shanghai-China			m	c	2010	49 006
Singapore[1]			m	c	2010/2011	85 284
Chinese Taipei			m			m
Thailand			m	c	2010	13 964
Tunisia[1]			m	d	2010	21 504
United Arab Emirates			m			m
Uruguay[1]			m	c	2010	19 068
Viet Nam[1]			m	c	2010	6 969

1. Public institutions only. For Ireland and Portugal, this applies only to the PISA 2012 columns.
2. Only for students aged 7 to 15.
Sources: *a. Education at a Glance 2004: OECD Indicators* (OECD, 2004a). For further notes, see *Education at a Glance 2004: OECD Indicators* (OECD, 2004a) Annex 3, available on line: *www.oecd.org/education/skills-beyond-school/educationataglance2004-home.htm*. Values reported in *Education at a Glance 2004: OECD Indicators* (2004a) have been updated with the GDP deflator to allow for comparisons with data from 2010.
  b. Education at a Glance 2013: OECD Indicators (OECD, 2013a). For further notes, see *Education at a Glance 2013: OECD Indicators* (OECD, 2013a) Annex 3, available on line: *www.oecd.org/edu/eag.htm*.
  c. PISA system-level data collection in 2013.
  d. UNESCO Institute for Statistics (World Education Indicators Programme).
* See notes at the beginning of this Annex.
StatLink http://dx.doi.org/10.1787/888932957460

[Part 1/1]
Per capita GDP
Table IV.3.2   *In equivalent USD converted using PPPs*

		PISA 2003			PISA 2012		
		Per capita GDP			Per capita GDP		
	Source	Year of reference	In equivalent USD converted using PPPs	Source	Year of reference	In equivalent USD converted using PPPs	
OECD	Australia	a	2001	37 844	b	2010	40 801
	Austria	a	2001	33 503	b	2010	40 411
	Belgium	a	2001	32 541	b	2010	37 878
	Canada	a	2001	34 695	b	2009	40 136
	Chile	a	2001	15 793	b	2011	17 312
	Czech Republic	a	2001	22 788	b	2010	25 364
	Denmark	a	2001	31 071	b	2010	40 600
	Estonia	a	2001	14 319	b	2010	20 093
	Finland	a	2001	30 797	b	2010	36 030
	France	a	2001	29 188	b	2010	34 395
	Germany	a	2001	29 001	b	2010	37 661
	Greece	a	2001	23 191	b	2010	27 539
	Hungary	a	2001	15 704	b	2010	20 625
	Iceland	a	2001	36 369	b	2010	35 509
	Ireland	a	2001	37 954	b	2010	41 000
	Israel	a	2001	32 134	b	2010	26 552
	Italy	a	2001	27 803	b	2010	32 110
	Japan	a	2001	28 429	b	2010	35 238
	Korea	a	2001	26 230	b	2010	28 829
	Luxembourg	a	2001	68 631	b	2010	84 672
	Mexico	a	2001	12 100	b	2010	15 195
	Netherlands	a	2001	34 548	b	2010	41 682
	New Zealand	a	2001	27 119	b	2010	29 629
	Norway[1]	a	2001	35 884	b	2010	44 825
	Poland	a	2001	15 857	b	2010	20 034
	Portugal	a	2001	19 342	b	2010	25 519
	Slovak Republic	a	2001	18 622	b	2010	23 194
	Slovenia	a	2001	23 373	b	2010	26 649
	Spain	a	2001	26 668	b	2010	31 574
	Sweden	a	2001	34 510	b	2010	39 251
	Switzerland	a	2001	38 767	b	2010	48 962
	Turkey	a	2001	13 353	b	2010	15 775
	United Kingdom	a	2001	31 870	b	2010	35 299
	United States	a	2001	41 326	b	2010	46 548
	OECD average		2001	28 862		2010	33 732
Partners	Albania			m	d	2010	8 631
	Argentina			m	b	2010	15 868
	Brazil			m	b	2010	12 537
	Bulgaria			m	c	2010	14 203
	Colombia			m	c	2011	9 555
	Costa Rica			m	d	2010	11 579
	Croatia			m	c	2010	19 026
	Cyprus*			m	c	2010	30 307
	Hong Kong-China			m	c	2010	47 274
	Indonesia			m	b	2010	4 638
	Jordan			m	c	2010	5 752
	Kazakhstan			m	d	2010	12 092
	Latvia			m	c	2010	16 902
	Liechtenstein			m			m
	Lithuania			m	c	2010	18 022
	Macao-China			m	c	2010	60 397
	Malaysia			m	c	2010	15 077
	Montenegro			m	c	2010	13 147
	Peru			m	d	2010	9 350
	Qatar			m	c	2010	77 265
	Romania			m	c	2010	14 531
	Russian Federation			m	b	2010	19 811
	Serbia			m	d	2010	11 421
	Shanghai-China			m	c	2010	18 805
	Singapore			m	c	2010	57 799
	Chinese Taipei			m	c	2010	29 255
	Thailand			m	c	2010	9 748
	Tunisia			m	c	2010	9 410
	United Arab Emirates			m	d	2010	46 916
	Uruguay			m	c	2010	14 004
	Viet Nam			m	c	2010	4 098

1. The GDP mainland market value is used for Norway.
Sources: *a.* OECD National Accounts Database, 2013.
  b. Education at a Glance 2013: OECD Indicators (OECD, 2013a). For further notes, see *Education at a Glance 2013: OECD Indicators* (OECD, 2013a) Annex 3, available on line: *www.oecd.org/edu/eag.htm.*
  c. PISA system-level data collection in 2013.
  d. UNESCO Institute for Statistics (World Education Indicators Programme).
* See notes at the beginning of this Annex.
StatLink ⣏⣶⣭⣤ http://dx.doi.org/10.1787/888932957460

[Part 1/1]
Teachers' salaries
Annual statutory teachers' salaries in public institutions at starting salary, after 10 and 15 years of experience and at the top of the scale, by level of education (2011)

Table IV.3.3

	Source	Ratio of salaries after 15 years of experience/minimum training to per capita GDP		Ratio of salary at top of scale to starting salary		Years from starting to top salary (lower secondary education)	Outstanding performance in teaching used as a criteria for the base salary and additional payments in public institutions.		
		Lower secondary education	Upper secondary education	Lower secondary education	Upper secondary education		Decisions on position in base salary scale	Decisions on supplemental payments which are paid every year	Decisions on supplemental incidental payments
		(1)	(2)	(3)	(4)	(5)	(6)	(7)	(8)
OECD									
Australia	a	1.22	1.22	1.41	1.41	9	No	No	No
Austria	a	1.11	1.14	1.96	2.02	34	No	No	Yes
Belgium (Fl.)	a	1.24	1.59	1.73	1.76	27	No	No	No
Belgium (Fr.)	a	1.21	1.55	1.72	1.75	27	No	No	No
Canada	a	1.50	1.51	1.59	1.59	11	No	No	No
Chile	a	1.31	1.39	1.79	1.83	30	No	Yes	Yes
Czech Republic	a	0.87	0.93	1.36	1.40	27	Yes	Yes	Yes
Denmark	a	1.36	1.58	1.16	1.31	8	No	Yes	Yes
England	a	1.32	1.32	1.46	1.46	12	Yes	Yes	Yes
Estonia	a	0.68	0.68	1.46	1.46	7	Yes	Yes	Yes
Finland	a	1.21	1.28	1.31	1.35	20	No	Yes	No
France	a	1.07	1.08	1.82	1.81	34	No	No	No
Germany	a	1.75	1.89	1.33	1.38	28	No	No	No
Greece	a	1.15	1.15	1.49	1.49	33	No	No	No
Hungary	a	0.70	0.83	1.64	1.90	40	No	Yes	No
Iceland	a	0.80	0.81	1.17	1.26	18	No	No	No
Ireland	a	1.51	1.51	1.80	1.80	22	No	No	No
Israel	a	1.02	0.87	1.88	2.24	36	No	No	No
Italy	a	1.17	1.21	1.50	1.57	35	No	No	No
Japan	a	1.47	1.47	2.21	2.27	34	No	No	No
Korea	a	1.82	1.82	2.78	2.78	37	No	No	No
Luxembourg	a	1.24	1.24	1.74	1.74	30	No	No	No
Mexico	a	1.78	m	2.12	m	14	Yes	Yes	No
Netherlands	a	1.57	1.57	1.70	1.70	15	Yes	Yes	Yes
New Zealand	a	1.50	1.52	1.50	1.51	8	No	Yes	No
Norway[1]	a	0.89	0.96	1.26	1.21	16	No	Yes	No
Poland	a	0.98	1.12	1.68	1.70	20	No	Yes	Yes
Portugal	a	1.74	1.74	1.69	1.69	34	No	No	No
Scotland	a	1.43	1.43	1.60	1.60	6	No	No	No
Slovak Republic	a	0.61	0.61	1.35	1.35	32	No	Yes	Yes
Slovenia	a	1.29	1.29	1.28	1.28	13	No	No	Yes
Spain	a	1.58	1.60	1.40	1.40	38	No	No	No
Sweden	a	0.92	0.97	1.31	1.34	a	Yes	No	No
Switzerland	a	m	m	1.55	1.53	27	No	No	No
Turkey	a	a	1.87	a	1.15	a	Yes	No	Yes
United States	a	0.97	1.04	1.50	1.48	m	No	No	Yes
OECD average		1.24	1.29	1.61	1.62	24			
Partners									
Albania	a	m	m	m	m	m	m	m	m
Argentina	c	0.79	0.79	1.60	1.60	25	m	m	m
Brazil	b	m	m	m	m	m	m	m	m
Bulgaria	b	0.95	0.95	2.22	2.22	20	Yes	No	No
Colombia	b	1.60	1.69	1.55	1.81	13	No	Yes	No
Costa Rica		m	m	m	m	m	m	m	m
Croatia	b	1.28	1.28	1.36	1.36	35	No	Yes	No
Cyprus*	b	2.19	2.19	2.19	2.19	22	No	No	No
Hong Kong-China	b	1.48	2.23	1.62	1.91	10	No	No	No
Indonesia	a	0.44	0.49	1.45	1.41	32	No	No	No
Jordan	b	2.15	2.15	2.75	2.75	40	No	No	No
Kazakhstan		m	m	m	m	m	m	m	m
Latvia	b	0.52	0.52	a	a	15	No	Yes	Yes
Liechtenstein	b	m	m	1.62	1.62	a	Yes	No	No
Lithuania[2]	b	1.01	1.01	m	m	a	No	No	No
Macao-China	b	1.13	1.13	1.74	1.74	33	No	No	No
Malaysia	b	2.09	2.09	3.25	3.25	20	No	No	No
Montenegro	b	1.55	1.55	1.12	1.13	40	No	No	m
Peru	b	0.92	0.92	1.05	1.05	20	No	No	No
Qatar	b	1.41	1.41	1.67	1.67	20	Yes	Yes	Yes
Romania	b	0.44	0.44	2.54	2.54	40	No	No	No
Russian Federation	a	m	m	m	m	m	No	No	Yes
Serbia		m	m	m	m	m	m	m	m
Shanghai-China	b	0.94	1.15	4.51	5.58	35	No	Yes	Yes
Singapore	b	1.33	1.33	2.69	2.69	m	Yes	Yes	Yes
Chinese Taipei	b	m	m	1.64	1.64	20	No	No	No
Thailand	b	1.24	1.24	2.12	2.12	14	No	No	No
Tunisia	c	1.88	1.88	m	m	m	m	m	m
United Arab Emirates	b	m	m	1.76	1.76	5	No	No	No
Uruguay	b	0.76	0.79	1.66	1.64	32	No	No	No
Viet Nam	b	m	m	2.13	2.13	m	Yes	Yes	Yes

1. The GDP mainland market value is used for columns 1 and 2.
2. Average actual teachers' salaries for all teachers, irrespective of the level of education they teach.
Sources: *a. Education at a Glance 2013: OECD Indicators* (OECD, 2013a). For further notes, see *Education at a Glance 2013: OECD Indicators* (OECD, 2013a) Annex 3, available on line: *www.oecd.org/edu/eag.htm*
b. PISA system-level data collection in 2013.
c. UNESCO Institute for Statistics (World Education Indicators Programme).
* See notes at the beginning of this Annex.
StatLink http://dx.doi.org/10.1787/888932957460

[Part 1/2]

Table IV.3.4 Pre-service teacher training requirements in public institutions

	Source	Year of reference	Competitive examination required to enter pre-service teacher training				Duration of teacher-training programme in years				Teaching practicum required as part of pre-service training			
			Pre-primary education	Primary education	Lower secondary education	Upper secondary education	Pre-primary education	Primary education	Lower secondary education	Upper secondary education	Pre-primary education	Primary education	Lower secondary education	Upper secondary education
			(1)	(2)	(3)	(4)	(5)	(6)	(7)	(8)	(9)	(10)	(11)	(12)
OECD														
Australia	a	2010	m	Yes	Yes	Yes	m	4	4	4	m	Yes	Yes	Yes
Austria[2]	a	2010	Yes	Yes	a	No	3	3	5.5	5.5	Yes	Yes	a	No
Belgium (Fl.)	a	2010	No	No	No	No	3	3	3	5	Yes	Yes	Yes	Yes
Belgium (Fr.)	a	2010	No	No	No	No	3	3	3	5	Yes	Yes	Yes	Yes
Canada	a	2010	m	No	No	No	m	5	5	5	m	Yes	Yes	Yes
Chile	a	2010	m	No	No	No	m	m	m	m	m	No	No	No
Czech Republic	a	2010	No	No	No	No	3	5	5	5	Yes	Yes	Yes	Yes
Denmark	a	2010	Yes	No	No	No	4	4	4	6	Yes	Yes	Yes	No
England	a	2010	No	No	No	No	3, 4	3, 4	3, 4	3, 4	No	No	No	No
Estonia	a	2010	No	No	No	No	4, 5	4, 5	4, 5	4, 5	No	Yes	Yes	Yes
Finland	a	2010	Yes	Yes	Yes	Yes	3	5	5	5	Yes	Yes	Yes	Yes
France	a	2010	No	No	No	No	5	5	5	5, 6	Yes	Yes	Yes	Yes
Germany	a	2010	a	Yes	Yes	Yes	3	5.5	5.5, 6.5	6.5	a	Yes	Yes	Yes
Greece	a	2010	Yes	Yes	Yes	Yes	4	4	4	4, 5	Yes	Yes	a	a
Hungary	a	2010	m	Yes	Yes	Yes	m	4	4	5	m	Yes	Yes	Yes
Iceland	a	2010	m	No	No	No	m	3, 4	3, 4	4	m	Yes	Yes	Yes
Ireland	a	2010	Yes	Yes	Yes	Yes	3	3, 5.5	4, 5	4, 5	Yes	Yes	Yes	Yes
Israel[3]	a	2010	Yes	Yes	Yes	Yes	3, 4	3, 4	3, 4	3, 4	Yes	Yes	Yes	Yes
Italy	a	2010	m	No	No	No	m	4	4-6	4-6	m	Yes	Yes	Yes
Japan[4]	a	2010	No	No	No	No	2, 4, 6	2, 4, 6	2, 4, 6	4, 6	Yes	Yes	Yes	Yes
Korea	a	2010	Yes	Yes	Yes	Yes	2, 4, 6.5	4	4, 6.5	4, 6.5	Yes	Yes	Yes	Yes
Luxembourg	a	2010	Yes	No	No	No	4	3, 4	5	5	Yes	Yes	Yes	Yes
Mexico	a	2010	m	Yes	Yes	Yes	m	4	4, 6	4, 6	m	Yes	Yes	No
Netherlands[5]	a	2010	No	No	No	No	4	4	4	5, 6	Yes	Yes	Yes	Yes
New Zealand	a	2010	No	No	No	No	3, 4	3, 4	3, 4	4	Yes	Yes	Yes	Yes
Norway	a	2010	No	No	No	No	3	4	4, 6	4, 6	Yes	Yes	Yes	Yes
Poland	a	2010	No	No	No	No	3, 5	3, 5	3, 5	3, 5	Yes	Yes	Yes	Yes
Portugal	a	2010	No	No	No	No	5	5	5	5	Yes	Yes	Yes	Yes
Scotland	a	2010	No	No	No	No	4, 5	4, 5	4, 5	4, 5	Yes	Yes	Yes	Yes
Slovak Republic	a	2010	m	No	No	No	m	5	5	5	m	Yes	Yes	Yes
Slovenia	a	2010	m	m	m	m	m	5	5-6	5-6	m	m	m	m
Spain	a	2010	No	No	No	No	3	3	6	6	Yes	Yes	Yes	Yes
Sweden	a	2010	No	No	No	No	3.5	3.5	4.5	4.5	Yes	Yes	Yes	Yes
Switzerland	a	2010	m	No	No	No	m	3	5	6	m	Yes	Yes	Yes
Turkey	a	2010	Yes	Yes	a	Yes	4-5	4-5	a	4-5	Yes	Yes	a	Yes
United States	a	2010	No	No	No	No	2-4	4	4	4	Yes	Yes	Yes	Yes
Partners														
Albania	a	2010	m	m	m	m	m	m	m	m	m	m	m	m
Argentina	a	2010	m	m	m	m	m	m	m	m	m	m	m	m
Brazil	a	2010	No	No	No	No	m	m	m	m	No	No	No	No
Bulgaria	b	2010	Yes	Yes	Yes	Yes	3	3	3	3	Yes	Yes	Yes	Yes
Colombia	b	2010	Yes	Yes	Yes	Yes	4	4	5	5	Yes	Yes	Yes	Yes
Costa Rica			m	m	m	m	m	m	m	m	m	m	m	m
Croatia	b	2011	Yes	Yes	Yes	Yes	4	4	4	4	Yes	Yes	Yes	Yes
Cyprus*	b	2010	Yes	Yes	Yes	Yes	4	4	4	4	Yes	Yes	No	No
Hong Kong-China	b	2010	No	No	No	No	2	4	4	4	Yes	Yes	Yes	Yes
Indonesia	a	2010	m	Yes	Yes	Yes	m	4-5	4-5	4-5	m	Yes	Yes	Yes
Jordan	b	2010	No	No	No	No	a	a	a	a	No	No	No	No
Kazakhstan			m	m	m	m	m	m	m	m	m	m	m	m
Latvia	b	2010	No	No	No	No	2	4	4	4	Yes	Yes	Yes	Yes
Liechtenstein	b	2010	No	No	No	No	3	4	4	5	Yes	Yes	Yes	Yes
Lithuania	b	2010	Yes	Yes	Yes	Yes	3	3	4	4	Yes	Yes	Yes	Yes
Macao-China	b	2010	Yes	Yes	Yes	Yes	4	4	4	4	Yes	Yes	No	No
Malaysia	b	2010	No	No	No	No	5	5	5	5	Yes	Yes	Yes	Yes
Montenegro	b	2010	No	No	No	No	3	4	4	4	Yes	Yes	Yes	Yes
Peru	b	2010	No	No	No	No	5	5	5	5	Yes	Yes	Yes	Yes
Qatar	b	2010	No	No	No	No	2	4	4	4	Yes	Yes	Yes	Yes
Romania	b	2010	Yes	Yes	Yes	Yes	4	4	4	4	Yes	Yes	No	No
Russian Federation	a	2010	m	m	m	m	m	m	m	m	m	m	m	m
Serbia			m	m	m	m	m	m	m	m	m	m	m	m
Shanghai-China	b	2010	Yes	Yes	Yes	Yes	3	3	4	4	Yes	Yes	Yes	Yes
Singapore	b	2010	No	No	No	No	2	4	4	4	Yes	Yes	Yes	Yes
Chinese Taipei	b	2011	Yes	Yes	Yes	Yes	4	4	4	4	Yes	Yes	Yes	Yes
Thailand	b	2010	a	a	a	a	a	a	a	a	a	a	a	a
Tunisia	b	2010	No	No	m	m	m	m	m	m	No	No	m	m
United Arab Emirates	b	2010	Yes	Yes	Yes	Yes	m	m	m	m	Yes	Yes	Yes	Yes
Uruguay	b	2010	No	No	No	No	4	4	4	4	Yes	Yes	Yes	Yes
Viet Nam	b	2010	Yes	Yes	Yes	Yes	3	3	4	4	Yes	Yes	Yes	Yes

1. Tertiary-type A programmes are largely theory-based and are designed to provide qualifications for entry into advanced research programmes and professions with high knowledge and skill requirements. Tertiary-type B programmes are classified at the same level of competence as tertiary-type A programmes but are more occupationally oriented and usually lead directly to the labour market.
2. Refers to pre-primary education provided in primary schools only, for columns 1, 5, 9, 13 and 17.
3. Year of reference 2012 for column 7.
4. Year of reference 2007 for columns 17, 18, 19 and 20.
5. Refers to pre-primary education provided in primary schools for 4-5 year-olds only, for columns 1, 5, 9, 13 and 17.
6. Refers to full-time teachers only.
Sources: a. *Education at a Glance 2012: OECD Indicators* (OECD, 2012). For further notes, see *Education at a Glance 2012: OECD Indicators* (OECD, 2012) Annex 3, available on line: *www.oecd.org/edu/eag2012*
b. PISA system-level data collection in 2013.
* See notes at the beginning of this Annex.
StatLink ⓘ http://dx.doi.org/10.1787/888932957460

[Part 2/2]

Table IV.3.4 **Pre-service teacher training requirements in public institutions**

	ISCED type of final qualification[1]				Percentage of current teacher stock with this type of qualification			
	Pre-primary education	Primary education	Lower secondary education	Upper secondary education	Pre-primary education	Primary education	Lower secondary education	Upper secondary education
	(13)	(14)	(15)	(16)	(17)	(18)	(19)	(20)
OECD								
Australia	m	5A	5A	5A	m	87%	91%	x(19)
Austria[2]	5A	5A	5A	5A	94%	94%	95%	78%
Belgium (Fl.)	5B	5B	5B	5A, 5B	99%	98%	97%	96%
Belgium (Fr.)	5B	5B	5B	5A	100%	100%	m	m
Canada	m	5A	5A	5A	m	m	m	m
Chile	m	5A, 5B	5A, 5B	5A, 5B	m	m	m	m
Czech Republic	5B, 5A	5A	5A	5A	12%	87%	88%	87%
Denmark	5B	5A	5A	5A	100%	100%	100%	100%
England	5A	5A	5A	5A	100%	100%	100%	100%
Estonia	4, 5A, 5B	5A	5A	5A	70%	66%	75%	84%
Finland	5A	5A	5A	5A	m	90%	90%	95%
France	5A	5A	5A	5A	m	m	m	m
Germany	5B	5A	5A	5A	m	m	m	m
Greece	5A	5A	5A	5A	97%	94%	97%	98%
Hungary	m	5A	5A	5A	m	95%	100%	100%
Iceland	m	5A	5A	5A	m	92%	x(18)	82%
Ireland	3, 4, 5A, 5B	5A, 5B	5A, 5B	5A, 5B	m	m	m	m
Israel[3]	5A	5A	5A	5A	74%	83%	92%	87%
Italy	m	5A	5A	5A	m	86%	90%	99%
Japan[4]	5A+5B, 5A, 5A	5A+5B, 5A, 5A	5A+5B, 5A, 5A	5A	74%, 21%, 0.4%	15%, 80%, 3%	5%, 89%, 5%	75%, 24%
Korea	5B, 5A, 5A	5A	5A	5A	100%	100%	100%	100%
Luxembourg	5B	5B	5A	5A	86%	95.6%, 4.5%	100%	100%
Mexico	m	5A	5A, 5B	5A, 5B	m	96%	90%	91%
Netherlands[5]	5A	5A	5A	5A	100%	100%	100%	100%
New Zealand	5B, 5A	5B, 5A	5B, 5A	5A	m	m	m	m
Norway	5A	5A	5A, 5A	5A, 5A	83%	47%	46.8%, m	20.5%, m
Poland	5B, 5A	5B, 5A	5A	5A	0.9%, 91.5%	0.8%, 98%	99%	98%
Portugal	5A	5A	5A	5A	100%	100%	100%	100%
Scotland	5A	5A	5A	5A	m	m	m	m
Slovak Republic	m	5A	5A	5A	m	93%, 7%	91%, 9%	87%, 13%
Slovenia	m	5A	5A	5A, 5B	m	m	m	m
Spain	5B, 5A	5A	5A	5A	100%	100%	100%	100%
Sweden	5A	5A	5A	5A	54%[6]	82%	x(18)	72%
Switzerland	m	5A	5A	5A	m	m	m	m
Turkey	5A	5A	a	5A	94%	91%	a	98%
United States	5B, 5A	5A	5A	5A	99%	99%	99%	99%
Partners								
Albania	m	m	m	m	m	m	m	m
Argentina	m	m	m	m	m	m	m	m
Brazil	3B, 5A	3B	5A	5A	87%	99%	84%	91%
Bulgaria	5A	5A	5A	5A	100%	100%	100%	100%
Colombia	4	4	5A, 5B	5A, 5B	6%	49%	32%	13%
Costa Rica	m	m	m	m	m	m	m	m
Croatia	5A, 5B	5A, 5B	5A	5A	100%	100%	100%	100%
Cyprus*	5A	5A	5A	5A	100%	100%	100%	100%
Hong Kong-China	5B	5A	5A	5A	100%	100%	100%	100%
Indonesia	m	5A	5A	5A	m	m	m	m
Jordan	5A	5A	5A	5A	85%	90%	96%	98%
Kazakhstan	m	m	m	m	m	m	m	m
Latvia	5A, 5B	5A, 5B	5A, 5B	5A, 5B	88%	88%	96%	96%
Liechtenstein	5A	5A	5A	5A	30%	100%	100%	95%
Lithuania	5B	5A, 5B	5A	5A	m	m	m	m
Macao-China	5A	5A	5A	5A	m	m	m	m
Malaysia	4	5A	5B	5A, 5B	2%	53%	24%	21%
Montenegro	5B	5B	5B	5B	m	64%	66%	92%
Peru	5A, 5B	5A, 5B	5A, 5B	5A, 5B	m	m	m	m
Qatar	4	5A	5B	5B	40%	35%	65%	80%
Romania	4	4	5A, 5B	5A, 5B	95%	98%	95%	95%
Russian Federation	m	m	m	m	m	m	m	m
Serbia	m	m	m	m	m	m	m	m
Shanghai-China	5B	5B	5A	5A	94%	92%	93%	99%
Singapore	5B	5A	5A	5A	85%	62%	93%	x(19)
Chinese Taipei	5A	5A	5A	5A	80%	85%	90%	100%
Thailand	5A	5A	5A	5A	a	a	a	a
Tunisia	5A	5A	m	m	50%	50%	m	m
United Arab Emirates	4	4	4	4	80%	80%	80%	80%
Uruguay	5B	5B	5B	5B	100%	100%	59%	59%
Viet Nam	5A	5A	5A	5A	100%	100%	100%	100%

1. Tertiary-type A programmes are largely theory-based and are designed to provide qualifications for entry into advanced research programmes and professions with high knowledge and skill requirements. Tertiary-type B programmes are classified at the same level of competence as tertiary-type A programmes but are more occupationally oriented and usually lead directly to the labour market.
2. Refers to pre-primary education provided in primary schools only, for columns 1, 5, 9, 13 and 17.
3. Year of reference 2012 for column 7.
4. Year of reference 2007 for columns 17, 18, 19 and 20.
5. Refers to pre-primary education provided in primary schools for 4-5 year-olds only, for columns 1, 5, 9, 13 and 17.
6. Refers to full-time teachers only.
Sources: a. *Education at a Glance 2012: OECD Indicators* (OECD, 2012). For further notes, see *Education at a Glance 2012: OECD Indicators* (OECD, 2012) Annex 3, available on line: *www.oecd.org/edu/eag2012*.
b. PISA system-level data collection in 2013.
* See notes at the beginning of this Annex.
StatLink ᵐˢᴸ http://dx.doi.org/10.1787/888932957460

[Part 1/2]

Table IV.3.5 **Requirements to enter the teaching profession, public institutions**

	Source	Year of reference	Competitive examination required to enter the teaching profession				Credential or license, in addition to the education diploma, required to start teaching				Credential or license, in addition to the education diploma, required to become a fully qualified teacher			
			Pre-primary education	Primary education	Lower secondary education	Upper secondary education	Pre-primary education	Primary education	Lower secondary education	Upper secondary education	Pre-primary education	Primary education	Lower secondary education	Upper secondary education
			(1)	(2)	(3)	(4)	(5)	(6)	(7)	(8)	(9)	(10)	(11)	(12)
OECD														
Australia¹	a	2010	m	No	No	No	m	Yes	Yes	Yes	m	Yes	Yes	Yes
Austria²	a	2010	No	No	a	No	No	No	No	No	No	No	No	No
Belgium (Fl.)	a	2010	No	No	No	No	No	No	No	No	No	No	No	No
Belgium (Fr.)	a	2010	No	No	No	No	No	No	No	No	No	No	No	No
Canada	a	2010	m	No	No	No	m	Yes	Yes	Yes	m	Yes	Yes	Yes
Chile	a	2010	No	No	No	No	m	No	No	No	m	No	No	No
Czech Republic	a	2010	No	No	No	No	No	No	No	No	No	No	No	No
Denmark	a	2010	Yes	No	No	No	No	No	No	No	No	No	No	Yes
England	a	2010	No	No	No	No	Yes	Yes	Yes	Yes	No	No	No	No
Estonia	a	2010	No	No	No	No	No	No	No	No	No	No	No	No
Finland	a	2010	No	No	No	No	No	No	No	No	No	No	No	No
France	a	2010	Yes	Yes	Yes	Yes	No	No	No	No	No	No	No	No
Germany	a	2010	a	Yes	Yes	Yes	a	Yes	Yes	Yes	a	Yes	Yes	Yes
Greece	a	2010	Yes	Yes	Yes	Yes	No	No	No	No	No	No	No	No
Hungary	a	2010	m	No	No	No	m	No	No	No	m	No	No	No
Iceland	a	2010	No	No	No	No	m	No	No	No	m	Yes	Yes	Yes
Ireland	a	2010	No	No	No	No	Yes	Yes	Yes	Yes	Yes	Yes	Yes	Yes
Israel	a	2010	Yes	Yes	Yes	Yes	Yes	Yes	Yes	Yes	Yes	Yes	Yes	Yes
Italy	a	2010	m	Yes	Yes	Yes	m	No	Yes	Yes	m	No	Yes	Yes
Japan	a	2010	Yes	Yes	Yes	Yes	Yes	Yes	Yes	Yes	Yes	Yes	Yes	Yes
Korea	a	2010	Yes	Yes	Yes	Yes	No	No	No	No	Yes	Yes	Yes	Yes
Luxembourg	a	2010	Yes	Yes	Yes	Yes	No	No	No	No	No	No	No	No
Mexico	a	2010	m	Yes	Yes	Yes	m	No	No	Yes	m	No	No	No
Netherlands³	a	2010	No	No	No	No	No	No	No	No	No	No	No	No
New Zealand	a	2010	No	No	No	No	No	Yes	Yes	Yes	No	Yes	Yes	Yes
Norway	a	2010	No	No	No	No	No	No	No	No	No	No	No	No
Poland	a	2010	No	No	No	No	No	No	No	No	No	No	No	No
Portugal	a	2010	No	No	No	No	No	No	No	No	No	No	No	No
Scotland	a	2010	No	No	No	No	Yes	Yes	Yes	Yes	Yes	Yes	Yes	Yes
Slovak Republic	a	2010	m	No	No	No	m	No	No	No	m	No	No	No
Slovenia	a	2010	m	m	m	m	m	m	m	m	m	m	m	m
Spain	a	2010	Yes	Yes	Yes	Yes	No	No	No	No	No	No	No	No
Sweden	a	2010	No	No	No	No	No	No	No	No	No	No	No	No
Switzerland	a	2010	m	No	No	No	m	Yes	Yes	Yes	m	No	No	No
Turkey	a	2010	Yes	Yes	a	Yes	No	No	a	No	No	No	a	No
United States	a	2010	Yes	Yes	Yes	Yes	Yes	Yes	Yes	Yes	Yes	Yes	Yes	Yes
Partners														
Albania	b	2010	m	m	m	m	m	m	m	m	m	m	m	m
Argentina	a	2010	m	m	m	m	m	m	m	m	m	m	m	m
Brazil	a	2010	Yes	Yes	Yes	Yes	No	No	No	No	No	No	No	No
Bulgaria	b	2010	No	No	No	No	No	No	Yes	Yes	No	No	Yes	Yes
Colombia	b	2010	Yes	Yes	Yes	Yes	No	No	No	No	No	No	No	No
Costa Rica			m	m	m	m	m	m	m	m	m	m	m	m
Croatia	b	2011	No	No	No	No	No	No	No	No	Yes	Yes	Yes	Yes
Cyprus*	b	2010	No	No	No	No	No	No	Yes	Yes	Yes	Yes	Yes	Yes
Hong Kong-China	b	2010	No	No	No	No	Yes	Yes	Yes	Yes	Yes	Yes	Yes	Yes
Indonesia	a	2010	m	No	No	No	m	No	No	No	m	Yes	Yes	Yes
Jordan	b	2010	No	No	No	No	No	No	No	No	No	No	No	No
Kazakhstan			m	m	m	m	m	m	m	m	m	m	m	m
Latvia	b	2010	No	No	No	No	No	No	No	No	No	No	No	No
Liechtenstein	b	2010	No	No	No	No	No	No	No	No	No	No	No	No
Lithuania	b	2010	No	No	No	No	No	No	No	No	No	No	No	No
Macao-China	b	2010	Yes	Yes	Yes	Yes	No	No	No	No	No	No	No	No
Malaysia	b	2010	No	No	No	No	Yes	Yes	Yes	Yes	Yes	Yes	Yes	Yes
Montenegro	b	2010	No	No	No	No	No	No	No	No	Yes	Yes	Yes	Yes
Peru	b	2010	Yes	Yes	Yes	Yes	No	No	No	No	No	No	No	No
Qatar	b	2010	No	Yes	Yes	Yes	No	No	No	No	No	No	No	No
Romania	b	2010	Yes	Yes	Yes	Yes	No	No	No	No	No	No	No	No
Russian Federation	a	2010	m	m	m	m	m	m	m	m	m	m	m	m
Serbia			m	m	m	m	m	m	m	m	m	m	m	m
Shanghai-China	b	2010	Yes	Yes	Yes	Yes	Yes	Yes	Yes	Yes	No	No	No	No
Singapore	b	2010	No	No	No	No	No	No	No	No	No	No	No	No
Chinese Taipei	b	2011	Yes	Yes	Yes	Yes	Yes	Yes	Yes	Yes	No	No	No	No
Thailand	b	2010	Yes	Yes	Yes	Yes	Yes	Yes	Yes	Yes	Yes	Yes	Yes	Yes
Tunisia	b	2010	No	No	m	m	No	No	m	m	No	No	m	m
United Arab Emirates	b	2010	Yes	Yes	Yes	Yes	Yes	Yes	Yes	Yes	No	No	No	No
Uruguay	b	2010	No	No	No	No	No	No	No	No	Yes	Yes	No	No
Viet Nam	b	2010	Yes	Yes	Yes	Yes	Yes	Yes	Yes	Yes	Yes	Yes	Yes	Yes

1. The data of *Education at a Glance 2012: OECD Indicators* (OECD, 2012) have been updated in columns 2 to 4.
2. Refers to pre-primary education provided in primary schools only, for columns 1, 5, 9, 13, 17, 21 and 25.
3. Refers to pre-primary education provided in primary schools for 4-5 year-olds only, for columns 1, 5, 9, 13, 17, 21 and 25.
Sources: a. *Education at a Glance 2012: OECD Indicators* (OECD, 2012). For further notes, see *Education at a Glance 2012: OECD Indicators* (OECD, 2012) Annex 3, available on line: *www.oecd.org/edu/eag2012*.
b. PISA system-level data collection in 2013.
* See notes at the beginning of this Annex.
StatLink http://dx.doi.org/10.1787/888932957460

[Part 2/2]

Table IV.3.5 **Requirements to enter the teaching profession, public institutions**

	Teaching practicum required to obtain credential/licence				Teaching practicum required after being recruited, as an induction/probation period				Existence of a register for teachers				Compulsory requirement for continuing education to maintain employment in the teaching profession			
	Pre-primary education	Primary education	Lower secondary education	Upper secondary education	Pre-primary education	Primary education	Lower secondary education	Upper secondary education	Pre-primary education	Primary education	Lower secondary education	Upper secondary education	Pre-primary education	Primary education	Lower secondary education	Upper secondary education
	(13)	(14)	(15)	(16)	(17)	(18)	(19)	(20)	(21)	(22)	(23)	(24)	(25)	(26)	(27)	(28)
OECD																
Australia[1]	m	No	No	No	m	No	No	No	m	Yes	Yes	Yes	m	m	m	m
Austria[2]	No	No	No	No	No	No	a	Yes	Yes	Yes	Yes	Yes	No	No	No	No
Belgium (Fl.)	No	No	No	No	No	No	No	No	Yes	Yes	Yes	Yes	No	No	No	No
Belgium (Fr.)	No	No	No	No	No	No	No	No	Yes	Yes	Yes	Yes	Yes	Yes	Yes	Yes
Canada	m	Yes	Yes	Yes	m	No	No	No	m	Yes	Yes	Yes	No	No	No	No
Chile	m	No	No	No	m	No	No	No	m	No	No	No	m	No	No	No
Czech Republic	No	No	No	No	No	No	No	No	No	No	No	No	No	No	No	No
Denmark	No	No	No	No	No	No	No	Yes	No	No	No	No	No	No	No	No
England	Yes	Yes	Yes	Yes	No	No	No	No	Yes	Yes	Yes	Yes	Yes	Yes	Yes	Yes
Estonia	No	No	No	No	No	No	No	No	Yes	Yes	Yes	Yes	Yes	Yes	Yes	Yes
Finland	No	No	No	No	No	No	No	No	No	No	No	No	Yes	Yes	Yes	Yes
France	No	No	No	No	No	No	No	No	No	No	No	No	Yes	Yes	No	No
Germany	a	Yes	Yes	Yes	a	No	No	No	a	No	No	No	a	No	No	No
Greece	No	No	No	No	Yes	Yes	Yes	Yes	Yes	Yes	Yes	Yes	No	No	No	No
Hungary	m	No	No	No	m	Yes	Yes	Yes	m	No	No	No	m	Yes	Yes	Yes
Iceland	m	No	No	No	m	No	No	No	m	Yes	Yes	Yes	m	Yes	Yes	No
Ireland	m	m	m	m	Yes	Yes	Yes	Yes	Yes	Yes	Yes	Yes	No	No	No	No
Israel	Yes	Yes	Yes	Yes	Yes	Yes	Yes	Yes	Yes	Yes	Yes	Yes	Yes	Yes	Yes	Yes
Italy	m	No	No	No	m	No	No	No	m	No	No	No	m	No	No	No
Japan	Yes	Yes	Yes	Yes	No	No	No	No	No	No	No	No	Yes	Yes	Yes	Yes
Korea	Yes	Yes	Yes	Yes	No	No	No	No	Yes	Yes	Yes	Yes	No	No	No	No
Luxembourg	No	No	No	No	Yes	Yes	Yes	Yes	Yes	Yes	Yes	Yes	Yes	Yes	Yes	Yes
Mexico	m	No	No	No	m	No	No	No	m	No	No	No	m	No	No	No
Netherlands[3]	No	No	No	No	No	No	No	No	Yes	Yes	Yes	Yes	Yes	Yes	Yes	Yes
New Zealand	No	Yes	Yes	Yes	No	Yes	Yes	Yes	Yes	Yes	Yes	Yes	m	m	m	m
Norway	No	No	No	No	No	No	No	No	Yes	No	No	No	No	No	No	No
Poland	No	No	No	No	No	No	No	No	No	No	No	No	No	No	No	No
Portugal	No	No	No	No	No	No	No	No	Yes	Yes	Yes	Yes	No	No	No	No
Scotland	Yes	Yes	Yes	Yes	Yes	Yes	Yes	Yes	Yes	Yes	Yes	Yes	Yes	Yes	Yes	Yes
Slovak Republic	m	No	No	No	m	No	No	No	m	No	No	No	m	No	No	No
Slovenia	m	m	m	m	m	m	m	m	m	m	m	m	m	m	m	m
Spain	No	No	No	No	Yes	Yes	Yes	Yes	No	No	No	No	No	No	No	No
Sweden	No	No	No	No	No	No	No	No	Yes	Yes	Yes	Yes	No	No	No	No
Switzerland	m	No	No	No	m	No	No	No	m	No	No	No	m	No	No	No
Turkey	No	No	a	No	Yes	Yes	a	Yes	No	No	a	No	No	No	a	No
United States	Yes	Yes	Yes	Yes	No	No	No	No	No	No	No	No	Yes	Yes	Yes	Yes
Partners																
Albania	m	m	m	m	m	m	m	m	m	m	m	m	m	m	m	m
Argentina	m	m	m	m	m	m	m	m	m	m	m	m	m	m	m	m
Brazil	No	No	No	No	No	No	No	No	Yes	Yes	Yes	Yes	No	No	No	No
Bulgaria	No	No	No	No	No	No	No	No	No	No	No	No	No	No	No	No
Colombia	No	No	No	No	Yes	Yes	Yes	Yes	Yes	Yes	Yes	Yes	No	No	No	No
Costa Rica	m	m	m	m	m	m	m	m	m	m	m	m	m	m	m	m
Croatia	Yes	Yes	Yes	Yes	Yes	Yes	Yes	Yes	No	No	No	No	Yes	Yes	Yes	Yes
Cyprus*	Yes	Yes	Yes	Yes	Yes	Yes	Yes	Yes	No	No	No	No	Yes	Yes	Yes	Yes
Hong Kong-China	No	No	No	No	No	No	No	No	Yes	Yes	Yes	Yes	No	No	No	No
Indonesia	m	No	No	No	m	No	No	No	m	Yes	Yes	Yes	m	No	No	No
Jordan	No	No	No	No	No	No	No	No	m	No	No	No	No	No	No	No
Kazakhstan	m	m	m	m	m	m	m	m	m	m	m	m	m	m	m	m
Latvia	No	No	No	No	No	No	No	No	No	No	No	No	No	No	No	No
Liechtenstein	No	No	No	No	No	No	No	No	Yes	Yes	Yes	Yes	Yes	Yes	Yes	Yes
Lithuania	No	No	No	No	No	No	No	No	No	No	No	No	No	No	No	No
Macao-China	No	No	No	No	No	No	No	No	Yes	Yes	Yes	Yes	No	No	No	No
Malaysia	Yes	Yes	Yes	Yes	No	No	No	No	Yes	Yes	Yes	Yes	No	No	No	No
Montenegro	Yes	Yes	Yes	Yes	Yes	Yes	Yes	Yes	Yes	Yes	Yes	Yes	Yes	Yes	Yes	Yes
Peru	No	No	No	No	No	No	No	No	No	No	No	No	No	No	No	No
Qatar	Yes	Yes	Yes	Yes	Yes	Yes	Yes	Yes	Yes	Yes	Yes	Yes	No	No	No	No
Romania	No	No	No	No	Yes	Yes	Yes	Yes	a	a	a	a	Yes	Yes	Yes	Yes
Russian Federation	m	m	m	m	m	m	m	m	m	m	m	m	m	m	m	m
Serbia	m	m	m	m	m	m	m	m	m	m	m	m	m	m	m	m
Shanghai-China	No	No	No	No	Yes	Yes	Yes	Yes	No	No	No	No	Yes	Yes	Yes	Yes
Singapore	No	No	No	No	No	No	No	No	Yes	Yes	Yes	Yes	No	No	No	No
Chinese Taipei	Yes	Yes	Yes	Yes	No	No	No	No	No	No	No	No	No	No	No	No
Thailand	No	No	No	No	No	No	No	No	No	No	No	No	Yes	Yes	Yes	Yes
Tunisia	No	No	m	m	Yes	Yes	m	m	Yes	Yes	m	m	Yes	Yes	m	m
United Arab Emirates	Yes	Yes	Yes	Yes	Yes	Yes	Yes	Yes	No	No	No	No	Yes	Yes	Yes	Yes
Uruguay	No	No	No	No	No	No	No	No	Yes	Yes	Yes	Yes	No	No	No	No
Viet Nam	Yes	Yes	Yes	Yes	Yes	Yes	Yes	Yes	a	a	a	a	Yes	Yes	Yes	Yes

1. The data of *Education at a Glance 2012: OECD Indicators* (OECD, 2012) have been updated in columns 2 to 4.
2. Refers to pre-primary education provided in primary schools only, for columns 1, 5, 9, 13, 17, 21 and 25.
3. Refers to pre-primary education provided in primary schools for 4-5 year-olds only, for columns 1, 5, 9, 13, 17, 21 and 25.
Sources: a. *Education at a Glance 2012: OECD Indicators* (OECD, 2012). For further notes, see *Education at a Glance 2012: OECD Indicators* (OECD, 2012) Annex 3, available
on line: *www.oecd.org/edu/eag2012*.
b. PISA system-level data collection in 2013.
* See notes at the beginning of this Annex.
StatLink ᵐˢᵖ http://dx.doi.org/10.1787/888932957460

[Part 1/1]
Composition and qualifications of teaching staff
Table IV.3.6 *Results based on school principals' reports*

| | School principals' report on the following: | | | | | | | |
| | Percentage of certified teachers in the school | | Percentage of teachers with ISCED 5A in the school | | Percentage of mathematics teachers in the school | | Percentage of mathematics teachers with ISCED 5A in the school | |
	Mean %	S.E.	Mean %	S.E.	Mean %	S.E.	Mean %	S.E.
OECD								
Australia	97.8	(0.5)	97.0	(0.7)	17.1	(0.3)	62.8	(1.1)
Austria	87.0	(1.8)	52.6	(1.8)	20.6	(1.2)	46.3	(4.2)
Belgium	87.0	(1.7)	39.1	(1.0)	11.9	(0.2)	23.2	(1.1)
Canada	96.7	(0.8)	95.3	(0.7)	15.2	(0.3)	63.5	(1.6)
Chile	19.5	(2.5)	92.2	(1.4)	10.7	(0.3)	55.3	(2.8)
Czech Republic	91.6	(0.7)	91.8	(0.7)	16.5	(0.9)	81.5	(2.2)
Denmark	m	m	88.6	(1.8)	35.8	(0.9)	72.0	(2.6)
Estonia	94.9	(0.4)	m	m	9.1	(0.3)	73.6	(2.4)
Finland	91.5	(0.9)	91.5	(0.9)	14.4	(0.3)	63.5	(2.0)
France	81.4	(1.6)	65.7	(3.1)	11.3	(0.2)	83.0	(2.7)
Germany	93.4	(1.3)	m	m	27.6	(0.8)	60.0	(2.6)
Greece	81.8	(3.1)	93.5	(1.3)	13.9	(0.2)	98.3	(1.1)
Hungary	m	m	99.3	(0.2)	12.5	(0.5)	83.2	(3.2)
Iceland	97.6	(0.0)	81.8	(0.2)	38.1	(0.1)	6.5	(0.1)
Ireland	99.6	(0.1)	99.7	(0.2)	19.7	(0.5)	67.4	(2.5)
Israel	75.2	(2.9)	85.9	(1.8)	13.5	(0.3)	61.6	(2.6)
Italy	85.5	(0.9)	89.6	(0.8)	11.9	(0.2)	68.8	(1.1)
Japan	99.9	(0.1)	99.9	(0.0)	13.0	(0.3)	m	m
Korea	99.6	(0.2)	99.7	(0.1)	13.8	(0.6)	72.2	(2.3)
Luxembourg	69.4	(0.0)	91.6	(0.0)	10.1	(0.0)	76.1	(0.1)
Mexico	27.7	(1.9)	88.1	(1.0)	23.1	(0.8)	27.6	(1.7)
Netherlands	79.7	(2.8)	32.0	(1.7)	11.1	(0.3)	16.9	(1.6)
New Zealand	95.5	(0.6)	93.1	(1.1)	14.0	(0.4)	59.0	(2.2)
Norway	89.2	(1.8)	100.0	c	32.4	(0.9)	55.2	(2.0)
Poland	99.3	(0.4)	93.2	(1.8)	10.6	(0.2)	86.6	(2.3)
Portugal	95.8	(0.2)	71.5	(4.1)	11.8	(0.3)	74.8	(2.8)
Slovak Republic	94.6	(1.1)	90.4	(1.2)	16.1	(0.8)	43.4	(3.4)
Slovenia	95.3	(0.1)	88.3	(0.2)	9.6	(0.1)	71.3	(0.6)
Spain	100.0	c	94.6	(1.2)	14.6	(0.6)	46.9	(1.5)
Sweden	88.8	(1.3)	76.5	(3.3)	25.7	(0.8)	60.7	(2.1)
Switzerland	85.4	(1.7)	64.8	(2.8)	26.2	(0.9)	35.9	(2.4)
Turkey	92.1	(1.3)	93.3	(1.5)	12.1	(0.3)	13.4	(2.9)
United Kingdom	95.2	(1.1)	95.8	(1.2)	11.8	(0.2)	71.7	(1.9)
United States	95.5	(0.8)	98.7	(0.2)	14.6	(0.7)	65.8	(3.4)
OECD average	87.0	(0.3)	85.5	(0.3)	16.8	(0.1)	59.0	(0.4)
Partners								
Albania	93.9	(2.2)	83.9	(1.5)	11.6	(0.3)	15.4	(2.3)
Argentina	88.3	(2.2)	17.5	(1.5)	9.5	(0.4)	9.9	(1.9)
Brazil	m	m	87.1	(1.0)	16.3	(0.6)	72.8	(1.9)
Bulgaria	m	m	m	m	9.9	(0.9)	86.0	(2.3)
Colombia	10.0	(1.2)	90.8	(1.3)	13.3	(0.6)	19.8	(2.6)
Costa Rica	78.7	(2.0)	84.0	(2.2)	10.3	(0.4)	71.2	(3.7)
Croatia	100.0	c	94.2	(0.6)	8.1	(0.2)	81.2	(3.1)
Cyprus*	96.7	(0.0)	95.7	(0.0)	9.9	(0.0)	92.9	(0.1)
Hong Kong-China	96.0	(0.7)	97.4	(0.6)	16.4	(0.3)	56.1	(1.7)
Indonesia	60.2	(2.6)	82.1	(1.6)	10.4	(0.3)	76.6	(2.7)
Jordan	73.7	(3.2)	84.8	(1.8)	10.8	(0.2)	89.5	(1.6)
Kazakhstan	91.2	(2.1)	85.3	(2.1)	9.2	(1.0)	87.9	(2.3)
Latvia	80.2	(2.4)	49.7	(2.4)	9.6	(0.2)	40.4	(3.6)
Liechtenstein	80.8	(0.7)	76.5	(0.6)	24.9	(0.3)	42.7	(0.6)
Lithuania	96.3	(0.6)	89.9	(1.7)	10.2	(0.7)	78.8	(2.9)
Macao-China	99.6	(0.0)	92.1	(0.0)	17.8	(0.0)	60.3	(0.0)
Malaysia	97.6	(1.0)	88.8	(1.6)	14.0	(0.3)	23.5	(2.2)
Montenegro	96.1	(0.0)	89.0	(0.1)	8.6	(0.0)	66.6	(0.3)
Peru	89.1	(1.9)	77.3	(3.3)	17.5	(0.6)	25.3	(3.1)
Qatar	75.1	(0.1)	97.0	(0.0)	16.1	(0.0)	39.1	(0.1)
Romania	99.4	(0.2)	95.9	(0.7)	9.3	(0.2)	92.8	(1.4)
Russian Federation	97.3	(0.5)	87.9	(1.2)	10.1	(0.2)	88.0	(2.0)
Serbia	91.1	(1.9)	6.8	(1.7)	8.2	(0.2)	83.1	(3.4)
Shanghai-China	96.7	(0.5)	95.1	(0.5)	15.1	(0.2)	85.0	(1.3)
Singapore	96.9	(0.0)	95.1	(0.0)	18.2	(0.0)	67.7	(0.2)
Chinese Taipei	92.9	(0.8)	90.6	(2.2)	12.2	(0.2)	75.4	(2.2)
Thailand	93.7	(0.7)	99.2	(0.2)	11.3	(0.3)	79.0	(2.1)
Tunisia	56.9	(3.9)	87.3	(1.7)	11.3	(0.6)	87.7	(1.9)
United Arab Emirates	m	m	91.2	(0.8)	14.1	(0.4)	85.5	(1.0)
Uruguay	57.0	(1.3)	8.3	(0.6)	10.3	(0.4)	1.5	(0.5)
Viet Nam	78.5	(3.4)	87.2	(2.6)	16.1	(0.3)	62.4	(3.8)

* See notes at the beginning of this Annex.
StatLink ⌐⌐ http://dx.doi.org/10.1787/888932957460

[Part 1/1]
Student-teacher ratio
Table IV.3.8 *Results based on school principals' reports*

		School principals' report on the following:			
		Student-teacher ratio in the school		Student-mathematics teacher ratio in the school	
		Mean ratio	S.E.	Mean ratio	S.E.
OECD	Australia	13.2	(0.1)	91.3	(1.7)
	Austria	11.0	(0.4)	96.6	(5.6)
	Belgium	9.3	(0.1)	86.7	(2.3)
	Canada	15.6	(0.2)	122.5	(4.5)
	Chile	22.1	(0.5)	223.5	(6.0)
	Czech Republic	13.1	(0.3)	110.6	(5.8)
	Denmark	12.1	(0.2)	37.5	(1.1)
	Estonia	11.4	(0.1)	140.8	(2.5)
	Finland	10.6	(0.1)	83.1	(2.3)
	France	11.8	(0.2)	111.1	(2.4)
	Germany	15.1	(0.3)	68.6	(3.6)
	Greece	9.1	(0.3)	67.6	(1.6)
	Hungary	12.4	(0.3)	117.2	(4.4)
	Iceland	10.5	(0.0)	33.8	(0.1)
	Ireland	14.3	(0.2)	78.1	(2.9)
	Israel	10.8	(0.2)	85.8	(2.7)
	Italy	10.3	(0.1)	96.8	(2.5)
	Japan	11.6	(0.2)	96.5	(2.6)
	Korea	16.1	(0.2)	132.6	(2.9)
	Luxembourg	9.0	(0.0)	110.8	(0.1)
	Mexico	30.6	(0.7)	187.0	(6.0)
	Netherlands	16.8	(0.4)	157.5	(4.7)
	New Zealand	15.2	(0.2)	119.3	(3.2)
	Norway	10.4	(0.1)	35.7	(0.9)
	Poland	9.4	(0.2)	94.6	(2.3)
	Portugal	8.9	(0.2)	81.3	(2.3)
	Slovak Republic	13.3	(0.3)	127.5	(6.1)
	Slovenia	10.5	(0.0)	121.1	(0.6)
	Spain	12.5	(0.4)	114.0	(6.7)
	Sweden	12.5	(0.2)	57.0	(2.8)
	Switzerland	12.1	(0.3)	88.3	(16.7)
	Turkey	17.4	(0.5)	181.9	(9.0)
	United Kingdom	14.8	(0.2)	129.5	(2.2)
	United States	17.4	(1.1)	121.2	(4.5)
	OECD average	13.3	(0.1)	106.1	(0.8)
Partners	Albania	c	c	c	c
	Argentina	10.5	(1.2)	100.0	(4.2)
	Brazil	28.2	(0.7)	223.8	(12.5)
	Bulgaria	14.6	(1.4)	161.3	(5.5)
	Colombia	27.0	(0.6)	246.8	(8.6)
	Costa Rica	20.4	(2.5)	197.8	(9.7)
	Croatia	12.6	(0.2)	164.8	(3.8)
	Cyprus*	7.9	(0.0)	81.1	(0.0)
	Hong Kong-China	15.4	(0.1)	96.6	(1.8)
	Indonesia	16.9	(0.6)	166.6	(6.4)
	Jordan	17.0	(0.4)	157.1	(3.8)
	Kazakhstan	10.0	(0.2)	149.8	(6.7)
	Latvia	10.0	(0.2)	117.2	(3.1)
	Liechtenstein	8.0	(0.0)	40.7	(0.4)
	Lithuania	11.4	(0.6)	121.8	(1.9)
	Macao-China	15.7	(0.0)	95.9	(0.0)
	Malaysia	13.4	(0.2)	100.8	(2.5)
	Montenegro	15.7	(0.0)	222.7	(0.6)
	Peru	18.5	(0.6)	131.8	(7.6)
	Qatar	13.9	(0.0)	108.5	(0.2)
	Romania	16.1	(0.4)	182.9	(4.6)
	Russian Federation	14.3	(0.2)	156.9	(5.0)
	Serbia	11.5	(0.3)	157.2	(6.3)
	Shanghai-China	12.1	(0.4)	118.3	(8.7)
	Singapore	14.6	(0.3)	85.8	(1.5)
	Chinese Taipei	17.4	(0.2)	183.9	(8.4)
	Thailand	20.3	(0.4)	289.1	(14.8)
	Tunisia	12.2	(0.7)	107.4	(1.8)
	United Arab Emirates	12.2	(0.3)	101.0	(3.3)
	Uruguay	15.5	(0.3)	160.5	(4.4)
	Viet Nam	18.8	(0.4)	119.3	(3.3)

* See notes at the beginning of this Annex.
StatLink ᵐˢᵖ http://dx.doi.org/10.1787/888932957460

[Part 1/4]
Student-teacher ratio, by school features
Table IV.3.9   *Results based on school principals' reports*

	Bottom quarter of ESCS		Second quarter of ESCS		Third quarter of ESCS		Top quarter of ESCS		Socio-economically disadvantaged schools[1]		Socio-economically average schools[1]		Socio-economically advantaged schools[1]	
	Mean ratio	S.E.	Mean ratio	S.E.	Mean ratio	S.E.	Mean ratio	S.E.	Mean ratio	S.E.	Mean ratio	S.E.	Mean ratio	S.E.
Australia	13.1	(0.1)	13.4	(0.1)	13.3	(0.1)	12.9	(0.1)	12.7	(0.2)	13.7	(0.1)	12.4	(0.2)
Austria	11.5	(0.7)	11.5	(0.6)	10.6	(0.5)	10.4	(0.3)	12.7	(1.3)	10.4	(0.5)	10.0	(0.4)
Belgium	8.0	(0.2)	9.0	(0.2)	9.7	(0.2)	10.5	(0.2)	6.9	(0.2)	9.1	(0.3)	11.5	(0.2)
Canada	15.0	(0.2)	15.7	(0.2)	15.8	(0.2)	16.1	(0.3)	14.7	(0.4)	15.3	(0.3)	16.9	(0.3)
Chile	21.1	(0.6)	23.1	(0.7)	23.5	(0.6)	20.6	(0.6)	21.4	(0.7)	23.2	(1.5)	22.3	(0.8)
Czech Republic	12.8	(0.4)	13.3	(0.4)	13.2	(0.3)	13.2	(0.3)	12.4	(0.8)	13.6	(0.4)	12.5	(0.5)
Denmark	11.6	(0.3)	12.0	(0.3)	12.3	(0.3)	12.5	(0.3)	11.0	(0.6)	12.0	(0.3)	13.4	(0.5)
Estonia	10.4	(0.2)	11.1	(0.2)	11.8	(0.2)	12.2	(0.1)	9.7	(0.4)	11.2	(0.2)	13.2	(0.2)
Finland	10.2	(0.2)	10.6	(0.1)	10.7	(0.1)	10.9	(0.1)	9.2	(0.3)	10.8	(0.2)	11.4	(0.2)
France	11.8	(0.2)	11.9	(0.2)	11.7	(0.2)	11.9	(0.3)	12.3	(0.4)	11.3	(0.3)	12.2	(0.4)
Germany	14.3	(0.3)	15.1	(0.4)	15.4	(0.4)	15.6	(0.5)	13.5	(0.5)	15.7	(0.3)	16.0	(0.9)
Greece	8.5	(0.3)	9.1	(0.4)	9.5	(0.3)	9.4	(0.3)	7.7	(0.3)	9.8	(0.5)	9.3	(0.4)
Hungary	12.8	(0.5)	12.3	(0.4)	12.2	(0.4)	12.4	(0.3)	13.4	(0.7)	11.4	(0.5)	12.6	(0.3)
Iceland	10.1	(0.1)	10.4	(0.1)	10.6	(0.1)	11.0	(0.1)	9.8	(0.0)	10.3	(0.0)	11.7	(0.0)
Ireland	13.7	(0.2)	14.4	(0.2)	14.5	(0.2)	14.7	(0.2)	12.6	(0.5)	14.5	(0.2)	15.0	(0.4)
Israel	11.0	(0.3)	10.8	(0.3)	10.6	(0.2)	11.0	(0.2)	11.1	(0.5)	10.6	(0.4)	10.8	(0.4)
Italy	9.4	(0.1)	10.0	(0.1)	10.6	(0.1)	11.3	(0.2)	8.7	(0.2)	9.9	(0.2)	12.3	(0.2)
Japan	10.6	(0.2)	11.6	(0.3)	12.1	(0.3)	12.4	(0.3)	10.0	(0.4)	12.0	(0.5)	13.0	(0.5)
Korea	15.3	(0.3)	16.1	(0.3)	16.4	(0.3)	16.6	(0.4)	14.0	(0.5)	17.0	(0.4)	16.6	(0.7)
Luxembourg	8.9	(0.0)	8.9	(0.0)	9.0	(0.0)	9.3	(0.0)	9.0	(0.0)	8.6	(0.0)	9.3	(0.0)
Mexico	28.2	(0.8)	31.5	(1.0)	32.4	(0.9)	30.1	(0.8)	27.3	(0.7)	34.0	(1.9)	30.5	(1.0)
Netherlands	15.7	(0.4)	16.6	(0.4)	17.1	(0.4)	17.7	(0.5)	14.1	(0.4)	17.6	(0.5)	18.1	(0.8)
New Zealand	14.8	(0.3)	15.1	(0.3)	15.4	(0.2)	15.4	(0.3)	14.1	(0.6)	15.3	(0.3)	15.5	(0.5)
Norway	10.2	(0.2)	10.4	(0.1)	10.4	(0.2)	10.9	(0.2)	10.7	(0.4)	10.1	(0.2)	11.6	(0.3)
Poland	9.4	(0.2)	9.2	(0.2)	9.5	(0.3)	9.6	(0.2)	8.7	(0.3)	9.8	(0.3)	9.7	(0.4)
Portugal	8.2	(0.3)	8.5	(0.2)	8.8	(0.2)	9.9	(0.2)	7.7	(0.4)	9.0	(0.3)	10.4	(0.4)
Slovak Republic	13.2	(0.3)	13.0	(0.4)	13.4	(0.3)	13.4	(0.3)	12.8	(0.6)	13.6	(0.4)	13.1	(0.4)
Slovenia	9.8	(0.1)	10.4	(0.1)	10.6	(0.1)	11.4	(0.1)	9.5	(0.1)	10.2	(0.1)	12.0	(0.0)
Spain	11.7	(0.6)	12.1	(0.5)	12.7	(0.3)	13.6	(0.3)	11.6	(1.3)	11.8	(0.2)	14.7	(0.4)
Sweden	12.1	(0.2)	12.2	(0.2)	12.7	(0.3)	12.9	(0.3)	11.4	(0.5)	12.2	(0.3)	14.0	(0.5)
Switzerland	12.3	(0.4)	12.2	(0.3)	12.1	(0.3)	11.7	(0.2)	12.1	(0.6)	12.3	(0.5)	11.6	(0.5)
Turkey	19.3	(0.9)	18.0	(0.6)	17.4	(0.6)	15.1	(0.7)	20.7	(1.4)	16.9	(0.8)	14.2	(1.0)
United Kingdom	14.9	(0.2)	15.1	(0.2)	15.0	(0.2)	14.2	(0.2)	14.5	(0.4)	15.4	(0.1)	13.8	(0.4)
United States	17.4	(1.0)	17.4	(1.2)	17.1	(0.9)	17.7	(1.5)	16.8	(1.1)	17.1	(1.1)	18.5	(2.4)
OECD average	12.9	(0.1)	13.3	(0.1)	13.5	(0.1)	13.5	(0.1)	12.5	(0.1)	13.4	(0.1)	13.8	(0.1)
Albania	m		m		m		m		m		m		m	
Argentina	9.6	(1.2)	10.4	(1.1)	11.1	(1.5)	10.8	(1.2)	9.6	(0.7)	10.7	(3.2)	11.3	(1.3)
Brazil	29.7	(0.8)	29.5	(0.8)	28.6	(1.0)	24.7	(1.0)	31.3	(1.2)	28.6	(1.1)	22.9	(1.5)
Bulgaria	14.7	(2.0)	14.5	(1.6)	15.5	(2.0)	14.0	(0.7)	13.8	(2.8)	16.5	(3.3)	13.7	(0.7)
Colombia	26.3	(0.9)	28.2	(0.7)	28.3	(0.7)	25.3	(0.8)	26.0	(1.4)	28.8	(1.0)	25.4	(0.9)
Costa Rica	17.8	(0.8)	18.3	(0.9)	20.1	(1.6)	25.4	(9.1)	16.5	(1.0)	19.7	(1.4)	25.3	(9.1)
Croatia	12.3	(0.2)	12.5	(0.2)	12.5	(0.2)	13.1	(0.3)	12.2	(0.3)	12.2	(0.3)	14.0	(0.4)
Cyprus*	7.4	(0.0)	7.8	(0.0)	8.1	(0.0)	8.5	(0.0)	7.0	(0.0)	8.1	(0.0)	8.9	(0.0)
Hong Kong-China	15.1	(0.2)	15.6	(0.1)	15.7	(0.1)	15.3	(0.3)	14.5	(0.2)	16.4	(0.2)	15.1	(0.4)
Indonesia	17.1	(0.7)	17.4	(0.7)	16.7	(0.7)	16.2	(0.8)	17.9	(0.9)	15.6	(1.1)	16.7	(1.0)
Jordan	17.3	(0.4)	17.3	(0.4)	17.4	(0.5)	16.2	(0.6)	16.7	(0.8)	17.8	(0.6)	15.0	(1.0)
Kazakhstan	9.5	(0.3)	9.9	(0.2)	10.2	(0.2)	10.4	(0.4)	9.2	(0.5)	9.8	(0.4)	10.8	(0.5)
Latvia	9.0	(0.2)	10.1	(0.2)	10.1	(0.2)	10.6	(0.3)	8.1	(0.4)	10.4	(0.3)	10.4	(0.4)
Liechtenstein	7.7	(0.2)	8.1	(0.2)	8.1	(0.2)	8.3	(0.1)	c	c	7.7	(0.1)	c	c
Lithuania	11.1	(0.9)	11.5	(0.8)	11.4	(0.4)	11.7	(0.6)	11.1	(1.8)	11.4	(0.8)	11.6	(0.3)
Macao-China	15.7	(0.1)	16.0	(0.1)	15.7	(0.1)	15.4	(0.1)	16.4	(0.0)	14.3	(0.0)	15.2	(0.0)
Malaysia	13.2	(0.2)	13.3	(0.2)	13.6	(0.3)	13.6	(0.3)	13.3	(0.3)	13.3	(0.4)	13.7	(0.5)
Montenegro	15.0	(0.1)	15.4	(0.1)	15.7	(0.1)	16.6	(0.1)	14.6	(0.0)	15.7	(0.0)	16.8	(0.0)
Peru	16.8	(0.6)	18.3	(0.6)	19.5	(0.8)	19.4	(0.7)	17.0	(0.7)	18.3	(0.9)	20.1	(1.1)
Qatar	13.2	(0.2)	14.8	(0.2)	14.3	(0.2)	13.8	(0.2)	12.5	(0.0)	11.8	(0.0)	16.0	(0.0)
Romania	17.2	(0.6)	16.0	(0.4)	15.7	(0.5)	15.4	(0.4)	18.1	(0.9)	15.4	(0.5)	15.0	(0.7)
Russian Federation	12.7	(0.3)	14.5	(0.3)	14.9	(0.2)	14.9	(0.3)	12.2	(0.8)	14.4	(0.4)	15.5	(0.3)
Serbia	11.0	(0.3)	11.2	(0.3)	11.5	(0.3)	12.3	(0.4)	10.5	(0.4)	11.3	(0.6)	13.3	(0.6)
Shanghai-China	13.3	(0.7)	12.5	(0.5)	11.6	(0.3)	11.2	(0.3)	14.7	(0.8)	11.5	(0.6)	10.5	(0.3)
Singapore	14.2	(0.1)	14.4	(0.1)	14.8	(0.3)	15.0	(1.0)	14.0	(0.0)	14.3	(0.1)	15.9	(1.3)
Chinese Taipei	17.4	(0.4)	17.5	(0.3)	17.4	(0.3)	17.3	(0.3)	18.0	(0.4)	16.6	(0.5)	18.0	(0.5)
Thailand	19.5	(0.5)	20.3	(0.5)	20.5	(0.5)	20.8	(0.6)	19.8	(0.7)	20.0	(0.8)	21.1	(0.7)
Tunisia	11.6	(0.3)	12.2	(0.6)	12.4	(1.0)	12.7	(1.3)	11.4	(0.3)	11.7	(0.3)	14.1	(2.9)
United Arab Emirates	12.2	(0.3)	12.4	(0.3)	12.1	(0.4)	11.9	(0.4)	12.0	(0.4)	12.4	(0.4)	12.0	(0.5)
Uruguay	15.2	(0.5)	16.3	(0.4)	16.2	(0.4)	14.3	(0.6)	15.5	(0.6)	16.9	(0.6)	13.2	(0.7)
Viet Nam	17.6	(0.4)	19.0	(0.4)	19.5	(0.5)	19.1	(0.8)	18.0	(0.5)	19.4	(0.6)	19.2	(1.2)

Notes: Values that are statistically significant are indicated in bold (see Annex A3).
ESCS refers to the *PISA index of economic, social and cultural status.*
1. A socio-economically disadvantaged school is one whose students' mean socio-economic status (ESCS) is statistically significantly below the mean socio-economic status of the country/economy; an average school is one where there is no difference from the country's/economy's mean; and an advantaged school is one whose students' mean socio-economic status is statistically significantly above the country/economy mean.
* See notes at the beginning of this Annex.
StatLink ᵃᵇᵖ http://dx.doi.org/10.1787/888932957460

[Part 2/4]
Student-teacher ratio, by school features
Table IV.3.9   *Results based on school principals' reports*

		Public schools		Private schools		Lower secondary education (ISCED 2)		Upper secondary education (ISCED 3)		Schools located in a village, hamlet or rural area (fewer than 3 000 people)		Schools located in a small town or town (3 000 to about 100 000 people)		Schools located in a city or a large city (over 100 000 people)	
		Mean ratio	S.E.	Mean ratio	S.E.	Mean ratio	S.E.	Mean ratio	S.E.	Mean ratio	S.E.	Mean ratio	S.E.	Mean ratio	S.E.
OECD	Australia	13.5	(0.1)	12.6	(0.2)	13.1	(0.1)	13.3	(0.1)	11.5	(0.4)	13.5	(0.1)	13.2	(0.1)
	Austria	11.2	(0.5)	9.3	(0.7)	8.1	(0.5)	11.2	(0.5)	7.6	(0.6)	11.7	(0.7)	10.9	(0.8)
	Belgium	8.4	(0.3)	9.5	(0.2)	7.5	(0.2)	9.5	(0.1)	7.8	(1.4)	9.2	(0.2)	9.6	(0.5)
	Canada	15.5	(0.2)	16.6	(0.8)	15.9	(0.3)	15.6	(0.2)	15.5	(1.1)	15.3	(0.3)	15.8	(0.3)
	Chile	19.6	(0.7)	23.5	(0.7)	19.9	(2.1)	22.2	(0.5)	15.2	(1.1)	21.7	(0.6)	22.7	(0.8)
	Czech Republic	13.3	(0.3)	10.9	(0.8)	14.6	(0.3)	11.3	(0.1)	13.5	(1.4)	13.0	(0.3)	13.3	(0.6)
	Denmark	12.5	(0.3)	10.8	(0.5)	12.1	(0.2)	8.5	(0.5)	10.4	(0.5)	12.5	(0.3)	13.2	(0.7)
	Estonia	11.4	(0.1)	9.5	(0.9)	11.4	(0.1)	12.5	(1.1)	8.4	(0.3)	11.9	(0.2)	13.0	(0.2)
	Finland	10.6	(0.1)	10.7	(0.5)	10.6	(0.1)	c	c	9.1	(0.4)	10.5	(0.2)	11.3	(0.2)
	France	11.8	(0.2)	12.4	(0.7)	13.6	(0.3)	11.0	(0.2)	11.7	(0.9)	11.9	(0.2)	11.4	(0.5)
	Germany	15.1	(0.3)	15.7	(0.9)	15.0	(0.3)	19.9	(2.4)	c	c	14.9	(0.3)	15.7	(0.9)
	Greece	9.1	(0.3)	c	c	9.1	(0.6)	9.1	(0.3)	7.9	(0.9)	9.6	(0.4)	8.6	(0.4)
	Hungary	12.5	(0.3)	12.2	(1.0)	10.9	(0.4)	12.6	(0.4)	9.0	(0.2)	12.6	(0.4)	12.4	(0.6)
	Iceland	10.5	(0.0)	c	c	10.5	(0.0)	c	c	8.4	(0.0)	11.0	(0.0)	11.2	(0.2)
	Ireland	13.8	(0.3)	14.7	(0.2)	14.3	(0.2)	14.2	(0.2)	13.8	(0.4)	14.8	(0.2)	13.8	(0.5)
	Israel	10.8	(0.2)	c	c	10.8	(0.3)	10.8	(0.2)	10.0	(0.4)	11.4	(0.4)	10.6	(0.4)
	Italy	10.3	(0.1)	11.9	(0.7)	8.8	(0.6)	10.3	(0.1)	9.2	(0.8)	10.2	(0.1)	10.8	(0.2)
	Japan	11.7	(0.2)	11.6	(0.6)	c	c	11.6	(0.2)	c	c	10.5	(0.5)	12.1	(0.3)
	Korea	16.1	(0.4)	16.2	(0.4)	18.3	(0.8)	16.0	(0.2)	c	c	14.4	(0.9)	16.5	(0.3)
	Luxembourg	8.9	(0.2)	9.7	(0.0)	8.9	(0.0)	9.3	(0.0)	c	c	9.1	(0.0)	c	c
	Mexico	32.1	(0.8)	18.4	(1.3)	26.0	(1.0)	33.4	(1.1)	22.1	(1.0)	33.7	(1.7)	30.5	(0.9)
	Netherlands	16.7	(0.8)	16.8	(0.3)	16.0	(0.4)	18.7	(0.6)	c	c	16.4	(0.4)	17.6	(0.6)
	New Zealand	15.4	(0.2)	12.1	(0.6)	15.2	(0.3)	15.2	(0.2)	11.8	(0.4)	14.7	(0.4)	15.8	(0.3)
	Norway	10.5	(0.1)	c	c	10.4	(0.1)	c	c	8.9	(0.3)	10.6	(0.2)	11.5	(0.3)
	Poland	9.5	(0.2)	5.8	(0.6)	9.4	(0.2)	c	c	9.0	(0.3)	9.8	(0.3)	9.3	(0.5)
	Portugal	8.2	(0.2)	13.8	(0.6)	8.1	(0.2)	9.4	(0.2)	9.1	(2.1)	8.6	(0.2)	9.4	(0.5)
	Slovak Republic	13.4	(0.2)	11.4	(0.6)	13.5	(0.2)	13.1	(0.4)	12.8	(0.4)	13.2	(0.3)	14.0	(0.8)
	Slovenia	10.5	(0.0)	11.7	(0.1)	9.7	(0.3)	10.6	(0.0)	9.1	(0.5)	10.0	(0.0)	11.5	(0.1)
	Spain	10.8	(0.6)	16.2	(0.3)	12.5	(0.4)	c	c	7.9	(0.4)	11.4	(0.2)	14.7	(1.0)
	Sweden	12.2	(0.2)	14.3	(0.7)	12.5	(0.2)	11.7	(0.6)	11.7	(0.6)	12.2	(0.3)	13.6	(0.5)
	Switzerland	12.1	(0.3)	11.5	(1.2)	11.4	(0.3)	14.4	(0.7)	11.5	(0.7)	12.2	(0.4)	11.5	(0.8)
	Turkey	17.5	(0.5)	c	c	31.9	(3.4)	17.0	(0.5)	23.4	(5.7)	15.2	(0.7)	18.7	(0.8)
	United Kingdom	15.4	(0.1)	14.3	(0.3)	c	c	14.8	(0.2)	14.4	(0.7)	14.8	(0.2)	14.8	(0.3)
	United States	17.7	(1.1)	13.3	(0.7)	17.3	(1.9)	17.4	(1.1)	17.5	(4.7)	16.4	(0.5)	19.0	(2.2)
	OECD average	**13.2**	**(0.1)**	**13.0**	**(0.1)**	**13.4**	**(0.1)**	**14.0**	**(0.1)**	**11.7**	**(0.3)**	**13.2**	**(0.1)**	**13.9**	**(0.1)**
Partners	Albania	m	m	m	m	m	m	m	m	m	m	m	m	m	m
	Argentina	9.9	(1.8)	11.3	(1.2)	10.1	(1.4)	10.7	(1.2)	5.0	(0.6)	9.4	(0.6)	13.8	(3.3)
	Brazil	28.9	(0.8)	23.3	(2.3)	30.1	(1.9)	27.7	(0.7)	18.6	(3.2)	29.0	(0.8)	27.6	(1.1)
	Bulgaria	14.7	(1.5)	c	c	20.4	(8.6)	14.3	(1.5)	21.0	(11.1)	15.4	(2.4)	12.7	(0.4)
	Colombia	27.2	(0.7)	27.4	(1.9)	27.2	(0.7)	26.9	(0.6)	24.3	(2.5)	25.3	(1.0)	28.5	(0.8)
	Costa Rica	18.5	(0.9)	30.0	(14.6)	20.6	(2.3)	20.0	(3.0)	17.9	(2.5)	17.5	(0.6)	34.6	(13.8)
	Croatia	12.6	(0.2)	c	c	c	c	12.6	(0.2)	c	c	12.2	(0.2)	13.3	(0.3)
	Cyprus*	7.6	(0.0)	9.9	(0.0)	7.8	(0.0)	7.9	(0.0)	6.7	(0.0)	8.0	(0.0)	7.9	(0.0)
	Hong Kong-China	17.0	(0.3)	15.4	(0.1)	15.3	(0.1)	15.5	(0.2)	c	c	c	c	15.4	(0.1)
	Indonesia	17.4	(0.7)	16.2	(1.0)	17.2	(0.7)	16.6	(0.8)	15.6	(1.1)	17.0	(0.7)	18.2	(1.5)
	Jordan	17.0	(0.5)	17.2	(1.0)	17.0	(0.4)	c	c	13.1	(0.8)	16.6	(0.7)	18.3	(0.6)
	Kazakhstan	9.8	(0.2)	15.7	(2.0)	9.6	(0.3)	10.9	(0.4)	7.5	(0.4)	10.2	(0.4)	11.7	(0.4)
	Latvia	10.1	(0.2)	c	c	9.9	(0.2)	11.4	(0.7)	7.5	(0.2)	10.5	(0.3)	11.1	(0.4)
	Liechtenstein	8.1	(0.0)	c	c	7.9	(0.0)	8.9	(0.0)	c	c	8.0	(0.0)	c	c
	Lithuania	11.4	(0.6)	c	c	11.4	(0.6)	c	c	12.2	(2.9)	11.6	(0.2)	10.8	(0.3)
	Macao-China	c	c	16.0	(0.0)	15.4	(0.0)	16.0	(0.0)	c	c	c	c	15.7	(0.0)
	Malaysia	13.3	(0.2)	17.5	(1.5)	15.0	(0.4)	13.3	(0.2)	13.1	(0.5)	13.4	(0.3)	13.7	(0.4)
	Montenegro	15.7	(0.0)	c	c	c	c	15.7	(0.0)	c	c	15.2	(0.0)	16.7	(0.0)
	Peru	17.7	(0.5)	22.3	(2.5)	17.6	(0.8)	18.9	(0.6)	13.8	(0.8)	19.1	(0.7)	19.8	(1.1)
	Qatar	12.9	(0.0)	15.6	(0.0)	12.5	(0.0)	14.3	(0.0)	11.8	(0.0)	12.0	(0.0)	16.2	(0.0)
	Romania	16.1	(0.4)	c	c	16.1	(0.4)	c	c	16.6	(1.4)	16.5	(0.6)	15.3	(0.5)
	Russian Federation	14.3	(0.2)	c	c	14.2	(0.2)	14.4	(0.5)	8.0	(0.7)	15.1	(0.6)	16.3	(0.2)
	Serbia	11.5	(0.3)	c	c	c	c	11.5	(0.3)	c	c	11.2	(0.4)	11.8	(0.4)
	Shanghai-China	11.7	(0.4)	16.1	(1.0)	11.5	(0.5)	12.6	(0.5)	c	c	c	c	12.1	(0.4)
	Singapore	14.5	(0.0)	c	c	14.5	(0.3)	14.6	(0.3)	c	c	c	c	14.6	(0.3)
	Chinese Taipei	14.6	(0.2)	22.5	(0.6)	14.7	(0.2)	18.9	(0.3)	c	c	16.5	(0.4)	18.0	(0.4)
	Thailand	20.3	(0.5)	20.2	(1.2)	17.3	(0.5)	21.0	(0.5)	15.2	(0.8)	21.0	(0.6)	21.5	(0.7)
	Tunisia	12.2	(0.7)	c	c	14.1	(1.9)	11.1	(0.3)	11.7	(1.0)	12.5	(1.0)	11.5	(0.4)
	United Arab Emirates	11.2	(0.2)	12.5	(0.6)	13.0	(0.6)	12.0	(0.3)	11.3	(0.5)	12.8	(0.5)	11.9	(0.4)
	Uruguay	16.0	(0.4)	12.8	(0.9)	14.6	(0.5)	16.1	(0.4)	13.6	(1.7)	15.3	(0.4)	16.1	(0.6)
	Viet Nam	18.5	(0.4)	21.7	(1.9)	15.4	(0.7)	19.2	(0.5)	18.4	(0.6)	19.2	(0.8)	19.1	(1.1)

Notes: Values that are statistically significant are indicated in bold (see Annex A3).
ESCS refers to the *PISA index of economic, social and cultural status.*
1. A socio-economically disadvantaged school is one whose students' mean socio-economic status (ESCS) is statistically significantly below the mean socio-economic status of the country/economy; an average school is one where there is no difference from the country's/economy's mean; and an advantaged school is one whose students' mean socio-economic status is statistically significantly above the country/economy mean.
* See notes at the beginning of this Annex.
StatLink 🔗 http://dx.doi.org/10.1787/888932957460

[Part 3/4]
Student-teacher ratio, by school features
Table IV.3.9 *Results based on school principals' reports*

	Bottom quarter of ESCS		Second quarter of ESCS		Third quarter of ESCS		Top quarter of ESCS		Socio-economically disadvantaged schools[1]		Socio-economically average schools[1]		Socio-economically advantaged schools[1]	
	Mean ratio	S.E.	Mean ratio	S.E.	Mean ratio	S.E.	Mean ratio	S.E.	Mean ratio	S.E.	Mean ratio	S.E.	Mean ratio	S.E.
OECD														
Australia	88.8	(3.0)	90.2	(2.1)	91.2	(1.5)	94.6	(2.0)	86.8	(4.8)	89.6	(1.9)	98.2	(3.0)
Austria	81.2	(7.2)	101.7	(6.3)	103.0	(6.3)	100.2	(6.6)	64.8	(11.9)	114.5	(8.8)	103.0	(12.7)
Belgium	91.0	(4.9)	88.8	(2.4)	83.8	(1.9)	83.2	(2.2)	96.0	(7.6)	85.9	(3.3)	80.3	(3.2)
Canada	118.7	(6.9)	121.4	(4.0)	126.0	(6.3)	123.8	(3.2)	128.1	(17.2)	116.2	(4.1)	130.6	(4.5)
Chile	213.8	(7.2)	230.0	(7.7)	230.1	(8.2)	219.9	(7.9)	219.4	(7.4)	226.3	(14.4)	227.4	(11.1)
Czech Republic	110.0	(6.2)	117.9	(7.2)	111.6	(6.7)	102.5	(5.1)	119.2	(9.6)	117.3	(9.5)	83.8	(5.3)
Denmark	35.3	(1.4)	37.2	(1.3)	36.9	(1.3)	40.2	(1.4)	37.0	(2.9)	35.0	(1.3)	44.0	(2.3)
Estonia	124.2	(3.8)	136.2	(3.0)	147.1	(3.3)	156.2	(2.9)	111.7	(7.5)	134.4	(3.9)	180.6	(4.1)
Finland	80.7	(2.6)	83.1	(2.4)	83.3	(2.8)	85.1	(2.4)	77.6	(5.4)	82.8	(3.1)	89.5	(5.4)
France	111.8	(2.5)	114.9	(2.7)	111.8	(3.1)	106.4	(3.2)	108.0	(3.2)	118.7	(4.3)	101.9	(3.9)
Germany	63.7	(6.0)	67.6	(4.1)	67.8	(2.7)	72.1	(2.2)	66.1	(11.4)	65.7	(4.8)	77.1	(2.0)
Greece	68.4	(2.0)	68.8	(2.5)	68.2	(1.8)	64.7	(1.6)	70.8	(2.8)	68.0	(2.9)	63.9	(2.3)
Hungary	133.7	(7.3)	119.2	(5.0)	112.5	(5.0)	102.1	(4.7)	143.4	(10.0)	117.0	(9.6)	94.4	(4.2)
Iceland	29.5	(0.8)	32.3	(0.8)	35.3	(0.8)	38.3	(0.9)	24.7	(0.1)	30.0	(0.2)	48.9	(0.3)
Ireland	76.7	(3.4)	78.5	(3.4)	78.1	(2.7)	79.0	(2.9)	71.8	(3.8)	80.1	(4.3)	78.2	(3.9)
Israel	84.7	(3.6)	85.4	(3.0)	84.2	(2.8)	90.4	(2.9)	86.4	(6.0)	83.8	(4.4)	88.0	(3.9)
Italy	100.2	(1.8)	98.8	(2.0)	96.1	(2.3)	92.1	(5.1)	105.5	(2.7)	96.1	(1.7)	89.7	(7.9)
Japan	99.5	(2.9)	100.6	(3.2)	96.6	(2.9)	89.0	(2.9)	106.1	(5.5)	99.4	(4.7)	82.0	(3.8)
Korea	149.1	(4.1)	135.2	(3.5)	126.6	(3.2)	119.3	(3.8)	172.6	(8.4)	122.5	(4.4)	110.7	(6.0)
Luxembourg	124.6	(1.5)	118.5	(2.1)	108.0	(2.2)	91.1	(1.2)	127.5	(0.2)	116.4	(0.4)	88.9	(0.1)
Mexico	150.4	(5.0)	194.6	(6.2)	204.1	(5.3)	189.4	(5.0)	144.2	(6.2)	210.5	(9.9)	198.6	(6.1)
Netherlands	152.3	(5.9)	156.1	(5.3)	161.6	(4.5)	161.2	(5.3)	138.4	(8.9)	162.1	(6.4)	166.2	(8.1)
New Zealand	116.8	(4.4)	120.0	(3.9)	121.1	(3.2)	119.2	(3.2)	110.6	(7.6)	124.0	(4.6)	115.6	(3.9)
Norway	33.6	(0.9)	34.6	(0.9)	35.2	(1.1)	39.9	(1.3)	31.8	(2.8)	33.7	(1.0)	46.3	(2.7)
Poland	89.6	(2.8)	92.6	(2.8)	97.0	(2.7)	99.3	(2.6)	81.5	(4.8)	96.3	(3.3)	108.1	(4.8)
Portugal	72.2	(2.9)	76.4	(2.4)	79.6	(2.2)	97.6	(4.8)	66.7	(5.0)	80.3	(2.5)	107.0	(7.8)
Slovak Republic	128.1	(9.7)	139.5	(8.4)	129.5	(6.4)	112.8	(4.5)	149.2	(19.1)	129.5	(8.3)	102.6	(5.9)
Slovenia	123.6	(1.7)	123.3	(2.1)	119.4	(1.8)	117.9	(1.2)	126.9	(1.4)	120.8	(1.3)	116.2	(0.3)
Spain	100.4	(3.6)	107.6	(4.7)	119.7	(8.7)	128.8	(13.5)	93.8	(3.5)	105.3	(4.4)	149.7	(22.4)
Sweden	55.1	(3.6)	56.0	(2.9)	57.4	(3.2)	59.6	(2.6)	49.9	(3.9)	56.7	(4.4)	63.2	(3.5)
Switzerland	80.2	(19.6)	91.3	(20.3)	93.9	(18.8)	86.9	(11.0)	102.4	(48.0)	69.8	(18.0)	105.6	(19.7)
Turkey	218.2	(14.2)	192.7	(11.3)	179.8	(10.9)	133.8	(7.8)	237.5	(20.0)	189.1	(18.1)	97.2	(8.1)
United Kingdom	128.0	(3.0)	129.8	(2.7)	130.3	(2.1)	130.9	(3.2)	123.3	(6.9)	132.4	(1.7)	129.0	(5.2)
United States	120.7	(6.0)	121.5	(5.2)	121.8	(5.1)	121.0	(3.7)	118.2	(8.4)	122.1	(8.1)	122.1	(4.5)
OECD average	104.6	(1.0)	107.7	(1.0)	107.3	(0.9)	104.4	(0.8)	105.8	(2.0)	106.8	(1.2)	105.5	(1.3)
Partners														
Albania	m	m	m	m	m	m	m	m	m	m	m	m	m	m
Argentina	95.0	(5.2)	98.6	(4.5)	104.6	(4.7)	103.7	(6.6)	97.1	(6.5)	95.5	(7.3)	108.2	(8.5)
Brazil	215.7	(12.8)	222.9	(13.7)	232.7	(15.5)	223.7	(17.3)	202.1	(12.8)	235.5	(17.6)	231.2	(33.6)
Bulgaria	165.6	(7.3)	161.2	(6.3)	163.8	(7.3)	155.3	(5.6)	164.8	(9.8)	160.6	(6.1)	159.0	(10.6)
Colombia	257.4	(12.4)	258.1	(10.3)	250.2	(9.0)	221.3	(10.5)	272.6	(18.9)	255.9	(13.1)	211.1	(12.1)
Costa Rica	182.0	(9.9)	205.7	(11.0)	204.1	(9.8)	200.0	(19.1)	171.1	(11.2)	219.6	(16.8)	190.6	(20.7)
Croatia	175.5	(4.4)	169.3	(4.5)	164.0	(4.4)	150.1	(4.0)	188.3	(5.9)	159.8	(7.1)	140.0	(5.4)
Cyprus*	80.7	(0.2)	82.0	(0.3)	81.5	(0.3)	80.3	(0.3)	80.2	(0.1)	83.5	(0.0)	79.0	(0.1)
Hong Kong-China	92.5	(1.7)	96.2	(1.9)	98.1	(1.9)	99.9	(2.9)	87.5	(2.2)	101.1	(3.0)	101.9	(3.6)
Indonesia	168.3	(8.2)	169.5	(7.9)	165.3	(7.5)	163.2	(8.9)	175.6	(11.5)	152.5	(11.3)	168.6	(11.4)
Jordan	158.9	(4.2)	159.9	(3.6)	158.6	(4.6)	151.8	(4.9)	160.9	(9.5)	161.1	(4.3)	142.2	(9.3)
Kazakhstan	142.9	(7.1)	151.6	(6.9)	156.2	(8.2)	148.7	(8.0)	136.3	(9.8)	158.8	(12.7)	147.5	(8.1)
Latvia	102.3	(2.9)	120.0	(4.0)	120.1	(3.7)	125.4	(5.0)	84.1	(5.2)	127.3	(5.7)	119.9	(6.7)
Liechtenstein	34.3	(1.9)	39.0	(2.2)	43.4	(2.2)	47.7	(1.9)	c	c	33.4	(0.6)	c	c
Lithuania	118.9	(2.8)	124.4	(2.1)	123.3	(2.5)	120.2	(2.6)	122.6	(5.9)	123.0	(2.9)	118.6	(4.7)
Macao-China	93.9	(0.9)	95.7	(0.9)	96.3	(1.0)	98.1	(1.0)	99.3	(0.1)	79.2	(0.1)	99.8	(0.1)
Malaysia	99.5	(2.9)	101.2	(2.6)	100.8	(2.8)	101.8	(3.3)	97.4	(4.3)	104.1	(3.7)	99.2	(5.1)
Montenegro	242.1	(6.7)	230.0	(6.0)	209.2	(5.2)	210.9	(6.4)	200.0	(0.3)	362.5	(2.4)	164.4	(0.1)
Peru	120.9	(8.7)	135.8	(11.2)	136.5	(8.2)	134.8	(8.8)	124.2	(13.9)	139.4	(12.7)	132.7	(11.5)
Qatar	98.1	(1.2)	116.9	(1.5)	115.5	(1.3)	106.6	(0.9)	112.4	(0.4)	91.1	(0.2)	114.5	(0.1)
Romania	193.5	(6.2)	188.5	(6.4)	183.0	(4.8)	166.9	(4.8)	203.1	(9.0)	179.1	(6.6)	165.9	(8.0)
Russian Federation	139.5	(6.6)	159.0	(5.7)	165.7	(5.8)	163.6	(5.4)	127.7	(8.4)	167.1	(8.7)	161.1	(5.2)
Serbia	158.0	(6.2)	159.9	(6.6)	156.9	(6.4)	155.0	(9.9)	150.7	(7.9)	163.7	(9.9)	153.2	(19.2)
Shanghai-China	151.1	(19.2)	135.3	(13.4)	104.0	(7.9)	81.8	(4.2)	199.7	(27.1)	100.5	(15.2)	65.0	(3.0)
Singapore	82.6	(0.7)	83.7	(0.9)	86.1	(1.7)	91.2	(4.2)	85.2	(0.1)	79.3	(0.6)	99.2	(5.8)
Chinese Taipei	202.9	(8.7)	207.5	(18.8)	173.3	(5.2)	152.4	(8.0)	225.6	(18.5)	191.8	(28.0)	122.2	(3.7)
Thailand	305.8	(20.8)	313.8	(20.3)	300.8	(23.4)	234.3	(14.4)	339.6	(31.7)	315.6	(45.1)	192.9	(15.2)
Tunisia	109.3	(2.3)	109.0	(1.9)	106.9	(2.0)	103.9	(2.2)	110.7	(3.6)	109.0	(2.7)	101.3	(3.1)
United Arab Emirates	93.0	(2.6)	98.9	(3.3)	103.9	(4.9)	108.1	(5.1)	89.8	(3.6)	95.3	(4.4)	114.7	(7.2)
Uruguay	159.3	(4.9)	168.3	(5.2)	167.2	(5.1)	147.2	(7.6)	166.7	(7.4)	166.7	(7.9)	140.1	(11.3)
Viet Nam	115.7	(4.1)	123.4	(4.4)	123.0	(4.0)	115.3	(4.2)	122.8	(6.0)	116.5	(3.5)	117.7	(7.5)

Notes: Values that are statistically significant are indicated in bold (see Annex A3).
ESCS refers to the *PISA index of economic, social and cultural status*.
1. A socio-economically disadvantaged school is one whose students' mean socio-economic status (ESCS) is statistically significantly below the mean socio-economic status of the country/economy; an average school is one where there is no difference from the country's/economy's mean; and an advantaged school is one whose students' mean socio-economic status is statistically significantly above the country/economy mean.
* See notes at the beginning of this Annex.
StatLink http://dx.doi.org/10.1787/888932957460

[Part 4/4]
Student-teacher ratio, by school features
Table IV.3.9 *Results based on school principals' reports*

	School principals' report on the following:													
	Student-mathematics teacher ratio in the school													
	Public schools		Private schools		Lower secondary education (ISCED 2)		Upper secondary education (ISCED 3)		Schools located in a village, hamlet or rural area (fewer than 3 000 people)		Schools located in a small town or town (3 000 to about 100 000 people)		Schools located in a city or a large city (over 100 000 people)	
	Mean ratio	S.E.	Mean ratio	S.E.	Mean ratio	S.E.	Mean ratio	S.E.	Mean ratio	S.E.	Mean ratio	S.E.	Mean ratio	S.E.
Australia	90.3	(2.1)	92.6	(2.8)	90.9	(1.7)	92.8	(2.7)	68.8	(5.5)	92.3	(4.3)	92.9	(1.7)
Austria	94.4	(5.9)	118.1	(21.0)	36.6	(2.9)	100.3	(5.7)	62.2	(11.6)	107.0	(8.2)	91.4	(9.3)
Belgium	94.1	(4.6)	84.5	(3.0)	79.0	(8.1)	87.5	(2.3)	96.1	(18.4)	84.0	(2.8)	94.3	(5.9)
Canada	124.9	(4.9)	96.4	(5.8)	117.6	(12.5)	123.3	(3.7)	80.3	(4.4)	116.9	(5.6)	131.7	(7.1)
Chile	200.1	(8.8)	236.9	(8.2)	209.1	(23.9)	224.4	(6.2)	158.7	(23.7)	226.1	(11.3)	227.2	(8.3)
Czech Republic	111.1	(6.3)	105.5	(13.7)	110.1	(9.1)	111.1	(6.3)	91.2	(12.6)	111.6	(7.8)	113.6	(6.9)
Denmark	38.3	(1.3)	35.1	(2.7)	37.2	(1.1)	c	c	31.7	(3.0)	38.1	(1.2)	43.9	(2.4)
Estonia	140.5	(2.6)	153.6	(10.8)	139.4	(2.4)	210.7	(31.3)	85.8	(4.2)	146.5	(3.5)	175.0	(6.0)
Finland	83.1	(2.4)	82.4	(1.2)	83.1	(2.3)	c	c	80.9	(7.7)	75.9	(2.4)	102.6	(4.4)
France	114.1	(2.6)	101.5	(6.8)	115.6	(3.1)	109.2	(3.1)	111.2	(11.4)	113.0	(2.9)	105.2	(4.9)
Germany	68.6	(3.9)	71.5	(6.1)	62.7	(1.4)	309.0	(82.0)	c	c	69.4	(5.2)	66.5	(3.5)
Greece	67.8	(1.7)	c	c	87.5	(6.1)	66.5	(1.7)	58.8	(6.3)	70.9	(2.4)	63.6	(2.3)
Hungary	119.0	(5.0)	108.0	(9.6)	141.6	(10.5)	113.9	(5.3)	88.3	(11.9)	120.2	(6.8)	114.6	(6.8)
Iceland	33.8	(0.1)	c	c	33.8	(0.1)	c	c	20.5	(0.1)	33.7	(0.1)	43.1	(0.3)
Ireland	83.0	(6.4)	74.4	(2.6)	78.4	(2.9)	77.7	(2.9)	77.0	(9.1)	78.0	(3.1)	79.4	(4.5)
Israel	85.8	(2.7)	c	c	86.2	(3.7)	85.8	(2.9)	80.9	(5.7)	88.7	(4.6)	84.3	(3.8)
Italy	97.5	(2.6)	90.8	(7.9)	70.1	(7.5)	97.4	(2.6)	113.8	(11.3)	97.5	(3.7)	93.9	(2.5)
Japan	101.2	(2.6)	85.3	(6.1)	c	c	96.5	(2.6)	c	c	92.0	(5.4)	98.1	(3.0)
Korea	132.5	(4.5)	132.6	(5.7)	161.0	(9.0)	130.8	(3.1)	c	c	124.2	(12.5)	135.2	(3.1)
Luxembourg	111.7	(0.2)	105.8	(0.2)	114.6	(0.2)	105.0	(0.4)	c	c	111.0	(0.1)	c	c
Mexico	194.2	(6.6)	129.2	(11.2)	155.4	(8.5)	205.0	(8.1)	81.8	(8.1)	196.7	(11.0)	208.5	(7.4)
Netherlands	151.5	(10.8)	161.0	(4.9)	152.5	(5.1)	169.4	(6.2)	c	c	156.4	(6.0)	160.3	(5.3)
New Zealand	120.4	(3.3)	102.2	(8.3)	123.3	(4.2)	119.1	(3.2)	79.8	(6.6)	115.2	(5.2)	126.8	(4.2)
Norway	36.0	(0.9)	c	c	35.7	(0.9)	c	c	22.1	(2.0)	37.1	(1.1)	44.1	(2.3)
Poland	95.6	(2.4)	52.9	(5.4)	94.4	(2.3)	c	c	80.3	(4.0)	101.7	(3.6)	101.0	(4.9)
Portugal	76.3	(2.4)	121.1	(7.5)	70.7	(3.0)	90.0	(2.8)	67.9	(12.5)	77.0	(2.3)	97.9	(7.6)
Slovak Republic	130.7	(6.6)	93.5	(14.7)	87.2	(4.7)	160.3	(10.1)	70.4	(7.9)	136.4	(8.1)	136.5	(10.6)
Slovenia	121.0	(0.6)	128.0	(0.6)	140.5	(4.7)	120.1	(0.5)	126.1	(8.3)	114.4	(0.7)	131.4	(1.0)
Spain	102.0	(3.1)	141.2	(20.6)	114.0	(6.7)	c	c	71.6	(5.3)	104.2	(4.7)	132.7	(15.8)
Sweden	55.2	(3.2)	69.4	(5.5)	56.1	(2.9)	97.8	(7.0)	61.2	(14.5)	56.6	(2.3)	55.2	(2.5)
Switzerland	86.8	(17.4)	108.5	(60.7)	47.4	(2.0)	237.5	(67.1)	42.9	(8.4)	87.2	(20.8)	118.7	(34.6)
Turkey	179.5	(8.8)	c	c	650.4	(101.7)	169.2	(8.7)	250.7	(83.4)	158.9	(13.5)	195.6	(14.7)
United Kingdom	129.9	(1.6)	130.5	(4.7)	c	c	129.5	(2.2)	134.9	(4.5)	130.2	(2.9)	126.4	(4.2)
United States	122.2	(4.7)	114.0	(15.6)	127.2	(13.1)	120.4	(3.8)	126.4	(32.5)	116.8	(4.7)	126.3	(4.6)
OECD average	105.7	(0.9)	107.8	(2.5)	115.9	(3.3)	134.3	(3.9)	87.0	(3.3)	105.5	(1.2)	112.7	(1.5)
Albania	c	c	c	c	c	c	c	c	c	c	c	c	c	c
Argentina	96.1	(5.4)	107.7	(6.7)	99.7	(6.1)	100.2	(5.0)	58.3	(9.7)	101.9	(5.8)	107.9	(7.1)
Brazil	217.4	(12.6)	271.0	(44.7)	187.1	(9.2)	231.7	(14.4)	119.6	(27.7)	221.4	(19.2)	229.0	(16.4)
Bulgaria	162.3	(5.6)	c	c	176.4	(14.7)	160.6	(5.7)	175.5	(17.9)	159.7	(8.4)	162.6	(7.2)
Colombia	253.4	(9.1)	222.1	(22.5)	248.0	(9.9)	246.0	(8.7)	260.7	(26.9)	231.3	(17.5)	252.2	(11.1)
Costa Rica	200.6	(10.0)	191.7	(35.2)	190.6	(9.1)	209.1	(14.6)	189.8	(24.9)	195.9	(9.3)	224.2	(36.5)
Croatia	165.3	(3.8)	c	c	c	c	164.8	(3.8)	c	c	166.0	(4.0)	163.9	(8.2)
Cyprus*	82.1	(0.0)	75.8	(0.1)	81.1	(0.5)	81.1	(0.0)	74.3	(0.3)	83.4	(0.0)	77.5	(0.1)
Hong Kong-China	109.8	(4.0)	96.1	(1.9)	95.2	(1.7)	97.3	(1.8)	c	c	c	c	96.6	(1.8)
Indonesia	168.8	(6.2)	164.2	(13.9)	152.7	(7.8)	180.3	(9.7)	153.5	(12.3)	165.7	(8.4)	186.0	(14.9)
Jordan	156.3	(3.5)	160.8	(12.1)	157.1	(3.8)	c	c	125.2	(8.0)	153.9	(6.4)	167.7	(5.2)
Kazakhstan	144.4	(5.8)	338.4	(137.2)	138.1	(4.4)	180.0	(19.5)	105.9	(5.7)	142.4	(6.9)	187.5	(14.3)
Latvia	118.0	(3.1)	c	c	114.9	(2.8)	171.4	(39.8)	77.1	(3.7)	119.9	(4.0)	142.3	(7.8)
Liechtenstein	40.3	(0.4)	c	c	38.2	(0.5)	58.6	c	40.4	(0.4)	c	c	c	c
Lithuania	122.2	(1.9)	c	c	121.8	(1.9)	c	c	101.6	(3.9)	124.4	(2.6)	129.2	(3.9)
Macao-China	c	c	97.7	(0.1)	94.3	(0.2)	97.9	(0.2)	c	c	c	c	96.1	(0.0)
Malaysia	99.6	(2.6)	125.3	(12.3)	109.4	(4.6)	100.5	(2.5)	92.3	(6.2)	100.4	(3.7)	106.2	(3.9)
Montenegro	223.3	(0.6)	c	c	c	c	222.5	(0.6)	c	c	171.4	(0.3)	339.5	(1.7)
Peru	136.5	(8.7)	119.7	(18.6)	125.3	(8.8)	134.7	(7.7)	78.0	(5.2)	126.7	(9.3)	162.1	(15.0)
Qatar	78.1	(0.0)	163.8	(0.3)	114.0	(0.6)	107.4	(0.2)	101.8	(0.3)	108.5	(0.3)	110.1	(0.1)
Romania	183.4	(4.5)	c	c	182.9	(4.6)	c	c	191.2	(8.8)	188.7	(7.5)	171.3	(5.8)
Russian Federation	157.6	(5.0)	c	c	151.6	(4.4)	182.1	(18.2)	78.5	(7.1)	167.7	(11.2)	183.6	(7.5)
Serbia	157.5	(6.3)	c	c	c	c	156.6	(6.3)	c	c	154.6	(6.9)	159.4	(12.2)
Shanghai-China	109.0	(8.8)	206.3	(48.0)	61.7	(1.9)	162.0	(15.4)	c	c	c	c	118.3	(8.7)
Singapore	85.3	(0.1)	c	c	85.7	(2.3)	85.8	(1.5)	c	c	c	c	85.8	(1.5)
Chinese Taipei	117.4	(1.8)	297.0	(34.5)	102.2	(2.2)	232.9	(13.6)	c	c	170.3	(18.5)	194.5	(19.9)
Thailand	275.4	(16.4)	358.3	(33.9)	163.2	(10.0)	322.7	(18.6)	153.7	(11.9)	329.0	(34.0)	290.2	(33.7)
Tunisia	107.3	(1.8)	c	c	111.6	(2.2)	105.0	(2.4)	120.7	(12.5)	106.8	(2.2)	107.3	(3.0)
United Arab Emirates	77.8	(1.6)	106.0	(7.3)	104.6	(4.4)	100.4	(3.7)	79.3	(3.7)	99.3	(6.4)	104.4	(4.5)
Uruguay	166.6	(4.8)	131.3	(11.3)	163.7	(5.8)	158.2	(5.6)	156.5	(18.8)	161.4	(5.2)	159.8	(8.8)
Viet Nam	117.7	(3.6)	132.3	(7.4)	97.2	(8.6)	122.0	(3.5)	119.9	(5.1)	124.8	(7.5)	111.7	(5.3)

Notes: Values that are statistically significant are indicated in bold (see Annex A3).
ESCS refers to the *PISA index of economic, social and cultural status.*
1. A socio-economically disadvantaged school is one whose students' mean socio-economic status (ESCS) is statistically significantly below the mean socio-economic status of the country/economy; an average school is one where there is no difference from the country's/economy's mean; and an advantaged school is one whose students' mean socio-economic status is statistically significantly above the country/economy mean.
* See notes at the beginning of this Annex.
StatLink http://dx.doi.org/10.1787/888932957460

[Part 1/2]
Index of teacher shortage and mathematics performance

Table IV.3.10   *Results based on school principals' reports*

| | | Index of teacher shortage | | | | | | | | | Variability in this index | |
| | | All students | | Bottom quarter | | Second quarter | | Third quarter | | Top quarter | | | |
		Mean index	S.E.	Mean index	S.E.	Mean index	S.E.	Mean index	S.E.	Mean index	S.E.	Standard deviation	S.E.
OECD	Australia	0.20	(0.04)	-1.09	(0.00)	-0.31	(0.09)	0.68	(0.04)	1.51	(0.05)	1.04	(0.02)
	Austria	-0.13	(0.09)	-1.09	(0.00)	-0.86	(0.13)	0.21	(0.13)	1.22	(0.14)	0.99	(0.06)
	Belgium	0.26	(0.06)	-1.05	(0.07)	-0.06	(0.08)	0.71	(0.06)	1.45	(0.08)	0.96	(0.03)
	Canada	-0.30	(0.04)	-1.09	(0.00)	-0.95	(0.08)	-0.08	(0.06)	0.92	(0.05)	0.85	(0.02)
	Chile	0.62	(0.10)	-0.99	(0.10)	0.25	(0.16)	1.14	(0.11)	2.06	(0.12)	1.19	(0.05)
	Czech Republic	-0.42	(0.05)	-1.09	(0.00)	-0.96	(0.10)	-0.16	(0.05)	0.52	(0.07)	0.70	(0.03)
	Denmark	-0.18	(0.05)	-1.09	(0.00)	-0.45	(0.12)	0.09	(0.08)	0.74	(0.06)	0.71	(0.02)
	Estonia	0.00	(0.05)	-1.03	(0.07)	-0.24	(0.05)	0.28	(0.03)	1.00	(0.08)	0.78	(0.03)
	Finland	-0.44	(0.04)	-1.09	(0.00)	-0.93	(0.10)	-0.19	(0.05)	0.46	(0.05)	0.67	(0.02)
	France	-0.18	(0.06)	-1.09	(0.00)	-0.67	(0.10)	0.07	(0.11)	0.98	(0.08)	0.85	(0.04)
	Germany	0.42	(0.06)	-0.81	(0.09)	0.25	(0.08)	0.79	(0.06)	1.44	(0.07)	0.87	(0.04)
	Greece	-0.42	(0.07)	-1.09	(0.00)	-1.01	(0.12)	-0.28	(0.02)	0.72	(0.21)	0.94	(0.10)
	Hungary	-0.65	(0.05)	-1.09	(0.00)	-1.09	(0.00)	-0.72	(0.13)	0.31	(0.11)	0.66	(0.05)
	Iceland	0.18	(0.00)	-0.95	(0.01)	-0.07	(0.00)	0.56	(0.01)	1.18	(0.01)	0.83	(0.00)
	Ireland	-0.15	(0.06)	-1.09	(0.00)	-0.65	(0.14)	0.19	(0.08)	0.95	(0.10)	0.84	(0.04)
	Israel	0.69	(0.09)	-0.82	(0.12)	0.43	(0.12)	1.09	(0.09)	2.05	(0.12)	1.11	(0.05)
	Italy	0.25	(0.04)	-1.06	(0.05)	0.05	(0.08)	0.68	(0.04)	1.33	(0.04)	0.92	(0.02)
	Japan	-0.29	(0.07)	-1.09	(0.00)	-1.00	(0.12)	-0.01	(0.11)	0.94	(0.10)	0.89	(0.05)
	Korea	0.06	(0.08)	-1.09	(0.00)	-0.61	(0.19)	0.63	(0.08)	1.32	(0.12)	1.03	(0.04)
	Luxembourg	1.12	(0.00)	-0.23	(0.00)	1.11	(0.00)	1.46	(0.00)	2.13	(0.00)	0.92	(0.00)
	Mexico	0.53	(0.04)	-0.91	(0.04)	0.36	(0.06)	0.90	(0.03)	1.77	(0.05)	1.03	(0.02)
	Netherlands	0.60	(0.08)	-0.65	(0.14)	0.48	(0.09)	0.94	(0.07)	1.61	(0.08)	0.88	(0.05)
	New Zealand	0.08	(0.07)	-1.09	(0.01)	-0.33	(0.17)	0.45	(0.09)	1.30	(0.09)	0.93	(0.04)
	Norway	0.31	(0.07)	-0.94	(0.09)	0.17	(0.10)	0.71	(0.07)	1.29	(0.07)	0.87	(0.04)
	Poland	-1.02	(0.02)	-1.09	(0.00)	-1.09	(0.00)	-1.09	(0.00)	-0.80	(0.09)	0.25	(0.04)
	Portugal	-0.80	(0.06)	-1.09	(0.00)	-1.09	(0.00)	-1.09	(0.03)	0.05	(0.21)	0.65	(0.12)
	Slovak Republic	-0.34	(0.05)	-1.09	(0.00)	-0.81	(0.13)	-0.03	(0.06)	0.56	(0.06)	0.71	(0.02)
	Slovenia	-0.68	(0.01)	-1.09	(0.00)	-1.09	(0.00)	-0.68	(0.02)	0.15	(0.02)	0.59	(0.01)
	Spain	-0.73	(0.03)	-1.09	(0.00)	-1.09	(0.00)	-0.99	(0.07)	0.24	(0.06)	0.64	(0.03)
	Sweden	-0.06	(0.07)	-1.09	(0.00)	-0.47	(0.14)	0.29	(0.10)	1.05	(0.08)	0.85	(0.04)
	Switzerland	0.05	(0.06)	-1.09	(0.01)	-0.29	(0.14)	0.43	(0.07)	1.17	(0.06)	0.89	(0.03)
	Turkey	0.88	(0.06)	-0.38	(0.12)	0.64	(0.04)	1.08	(0.10)	2.17	(0.11)	1.03	(0.06)
	United Kingdom	-0.18	(0.06)	-1.09	(0.00)	-0.78	(0.11)	0.14	(0.10)	0.99	(0.08)	0.88	(0.03)
	United States	-0.42	(0.07)	-1.09	(0.00)	-1.09	(0.00)	-0.44	(0.21)	0.94	(0.10)	0.91	(0.06)
	OECD average	-0.03	(0.01)	-0.99	(0.01)	-0.42	(0.02)	0.23	(0.01)	1.05	(0.02)	0.85	(0.01)
Partners	Albania	-0.23	(0.07)	-1.09	(0.00)	-0.91	(0.12)	0.00	(0.10)	1.06	(0.13)	0.94	(0.06)
	Argentina	-0.10	(0.08)	-1.09	(0.00)	-0.82	(0.12)	0.23	(0.14)	1.27	(0.11)	1.01	(0.05)
	Brazil	0.19	(0.05)	-1.09	(0.00)	-0.28	(0.11)	0.60	(0.08)	1.55	(0.06)	1.04	(0.03)
	Bulgaria	-0.80	(0.04)	-1.09	(0.00)	-1.09	(0.00)	-0.99	(0.10)	-0.05	(0.06)	0.48	(0.03)
	Colombia	0.67	(0.12)	-1.09	(0.08)	0.17	(0.20)	1.00	(0.12)	2.58	(0.21)	1.40	(0.07)
	Costa Rica	-0.01	(0.06)	-1.09	(0.01)	-0.35	(0.13)	0.33	(0.10)	1.06	(0.09)	0.84	(0.04)
	Croatia	-0.43	(0.06)	-1.09	(0.00)	-1.09	(0.00)	-0.22	(0.18)	0.66	(0.08)	0.77	(0.03)
	Cyprus*	-0.52	(0.00)	-1.09	(0.00)	-1.09	(0.00)	-0.88	(0.00)	0.99	(0.01)	1.16	(0.00)
	Hong Kong-China	-0.23	(0.07)	-1.09	(0.00)	-0.81	(0.12)	0.02	(0.11)	0.97	(0.12)	0.89	(0.06)
	Indonesia	0.27	(0.08)	-0.82	(0.11)	-0.13	(0.09)	0.58	(0.07)	1.43	(0.14)	0.93	(0.07)
	Jordan	1.02	(0.09)	-0.85	(0.10)	0.40	(0.14)	1.54	(0.13)	2.99	(0.12)	1.48	(0.06)
	Kazakhstan	0.29	(0.10)	-1.09	(0.00)	-0.57	(0.20)	0.81	(0.14)	2.00	(0.16)	1.29	(0.06)
	Latvia	-0.41	(0.06)	-1.09	(0.00)	-1.00	(0.12)	-0.19	(0.07)	0.63	(0.11)	0.76	(0.05)
	Liechtenstein	0.05	(0.02)	c	c	c	c	c	c	c	c	0.73	(0.00)
	Lithuania	-0.66	(0.04)	-1.09	(0.00)	-1.09	(0.00)	-0.64	(0.11)	0.19	(0.08)	0.59	(0.03)
	Macao-China	0.00	(0.00)	-1.09	(0.00)	-1.09	(0.00)	0.50	(0.00)	1.69	(0.00)	1.25	(0.00)
	Malaysia	0.22	(0.06)	-0.75	(0.09)	0.04	(0.06)	0.48	(0.08)	1.10	(0.11)	0.76	(0.06)
	Montenegro	-0.50	(0.00)	-1.09	(0.00)	-1.09	(0.00)	-0.38	(0.01)	0.54	(0.00)	0.72	(0.00)
	Peru	0.62	(0.08)	-0.85	(0.11)	0.44	(0.11)	0.99	(0.07)	1.88	(0.10)	1.06	(0.04)
	Qatar	-0.14	(0.00)	-1.09	(0.00)	-1.03	(0.00)	0.17	(0.00)	1.41	(0.00)	1.10	(0.00)
	Romania	-0.54	(0.05)	-1.09	(0.00)	-1.09	(0.00)	-0.47	(0.14)	0.48	(0.09)	0.72	(0.06)
	Russian Federation	0.35	(0.07)	-1.09	(0.03)	-0.03	(0.14)	0.74	(0.10)	1.80	(0.12)	1.13	(0.05)
	Serbia	-0.74	(0.05)	-1.09	(0.00)	-1.09	(0.00)	-0.96	(0.12)	0.18	(0.12)	0.60	(0.05)
	Shanghai-China	0.75	(0.09)	-0.91	(0.12)	0.50	(0.11)	1.09	(0.12)	2.32	(0.16)	1.24	(0.07)
	Singapore	0.13	(0.01)	-1.09	(0.01)	-0.08	(0.02)	0.59	(0.00)	1.09	(0.00)	0.84	(0.00)
	Chinese Taipei	-0.15	(0.09)	-1.09	(0.00)	-1.04	(0.11)	0.01	(0.14)	1.53	(0.19)	1.17	(0.09)
	Thailand	0.94	(0.08)	-0.57	(0.14)	0.67	(0.12)	1.46	(0.09)	2.21	(0.08)	1.10	(0.05)
	Tunisia	-0.11	(0.07)	-1.09	(0.00)	-0.71	(0.13)	0.19	(0.13)	1.18	(0.09)	0.93	(0.03)
	United Arab Emirates	0.14	(0.08)	-1.09	(0.00)	-0.85	(0.09)	0.34	(0.12)	2.17	(0.13)	1.40	(0.04)
	Uruguay	0.35	(0.07)	-1.03	(0.09)	0.02	(0.11)	0.79	(0.09)	1.61	(0.08)	1.02	(0.04)
	Viet Nam	0.41	(0.09)	-1.09	(0.00)	-0.12	(0.22)	0.98	(0.11)	1.87	(0.10)	1.18	(0.05)

Note: Values that are statistically significant are indicated in bold (see Annex A3).
* See notes at the beginning of this Annex.
StatLink ᴍᴤᴸ http://dx.doi.org/10.1787/888932957460

[Part 2/2]
Index of teacher shortage and mathematics performance

Table IV.3.10   *Results based on school principals' reports*

| | | Performance on the mathematics scale, by national quarters of this index | | | | | | | | Change in the mathematics score per unit of this index | | Increased likelihood of students in the bottom quarter of this index scoring in the bottom quarter of the national mathematics performance distribution | | Explained variance in student performance (r-squared x 100) | |
| | | Bottom quarter | | Second quarter | | Third quarter | | Top quarter | | | | | | | |
		Mean score	S.E.	Mean score	S.E.	Mean score	S.E.	Mean score	S.E.	Score dif.	S.E.	Ratio	S.E.	%	S.E.
OECD	Australia	**525**	(3.6)	514	(4.2)	497	(3.7)	**481**	(2.8)	**-15.5**	(1.67)	**0.7**	(0.05)	2.8	(0.58)
	Austria	**522**	(7.1)	520	(7.5)	495	(10.3)	**489**	(10.4)	**-12.9**	(5.51)	**0.7**	(0.11)	1.9	(1.61)
	Belgium	**539**	(7.9)	511	(7.7)	513	(9.2)	**497**	(6.5)	**-17.4**	(4.12)	**0.7**	(0.12)	2.7	(1.20)
	Canada	521	(3.9)	520	(3.8)	514	(3.7)	517	(4.0)	-2.4	(2.77)	1.0	(0.06)	0.1	(0.14)
	Chile	**439**	(6.9)	423	(7.6)	424	(6.1)	**405**	(8.4)	**-11.4**	(3.12)	**0.7**	(0.11)	2.8	(1.53)
	Czech Republic	**530**	(6.2)	522	(6.0)	486	(7.8)	**456**	(7.5)	**-44.6**	(6.12)	**0.6**	(0.10)	10.7	(2.81)
	Denmark	**509**	(6.0)	503	(4.8)	499	(5.0)	**491**	(4.5)	**-9.6**	(3.64)	0.9	(0.10)	0.7	(0.52)
	Estonia	520	(4.8)	520	(4.5)	524	(4.1)	518	(4.3)	-1.4	(3.05)	1.0	(0.11)	0.0	(0.10)
	Finland	520	(4.7)	522	(3.4)	517	(3.8)	515	(3.7)	-5.5	(3.20)	0.9	(0.07)	0.2	(0.22)
	France	504	(7.2)	496	(6.8)	490	(7.9)	495	(10.2)	-5.5	(5.66)	0.8	(0.12)	0.2	(0.51)
	Germany	**539**	(7.3)	523	(8.0)	513	(9.2)	**481**	(10.3)	**-24.1**	(5.18)	**0.6**	(0.10)	4.7	(2.14)
	Greece	459	(5.6)	461	(5.3)	447	(6.9)	445	(6.8)	-5.7	(4.49)	**0.8**	(0.10)	0.4	(0.55)
	Hungary	482	(6.9)	484	(6.7)	480	(7.8)	464	(10.4)	-15.3	(10.71)	0.9	(0.12)	1.1	(1.62)
	Iceland	**502**	(3.4)	494	(3.6)	488	(3.3)	**490**	(3.2)	**-7.2**	(1.74)	0.9	(0.07)	0.4	(0.21)
	Ireland	**515**	(5.3)	509	(5.9)	490	(6.6)	**495**	(5.6)	**-11.1**	(3.20)	**0.7**	(0.12)	1.2	(0.72)
	Israel	460	(9.8)	460	(11.4)	476	(8.5)	467	(12.3)	3.1	(5.92)	1.1	(0.18)	0.1	(0.53)
	Italy	481	(5.8)	493	(4.7)	490	(5.0)	485	(4.8)	1.2	(2.91)	1.1	(0.11)	0.0	(0.10)
	Japan	537	(6.8)	538	(6.5)	539	(9.5)	531	(8.6)	-3.6	(5.18)	0.9	(0.12)	0.1	(0.39)
	Korea	555	(9.4)	550	(9.3)	551	(9.6)	559	(7.9)	1.7	(5.11)	1.0	(0.14)	0.0	(0.33)
	Luxembourg	**514**	(2.0)	483	(2.3)	471	(2.8)	**491**	(1.9)	**-14.4**	(1.02)	**0.6**	(0.04)	1.9	(0.27)
	Mexico	**428**	(3.1)	418	(3.3)	406	(2.8)	**401**	(2.9)	**-10.2**	(1.59)	**0.7**	(0.06)	2.0	(0.60)
	Netherlands	519	(11.1)	525	(10.8)	509	(10.2)	529	(11.6)	4.6	(6.75)	1.2	(0.22)	0.2	(0.64)
	New Zealand	**526**	(7.1)	504	(6.0)	488	(5.9)	**490**	(6.7)	**-15.7**	(3.35)	**0.7**	(0.10)	2.2	(0.93)
	Norway	**499**	(5.3)	496	(7.5)	484	(5.8)	**483**	(4.2)	**-7.1**	(2.88)	0.9	(0.08)	0.5	(0.38)
	Poland	519	(5.5)	517	(5.6)	518	(4.8)	516	(5.8)	-9.8	(13.36)	1.0	(0.10)	0.1	(0.22)
	Portugal	488	(5.8)	487	(5.6)	488	(6.6)	483	(8.1)	-9.6	(6.87)	1.0	(0.11)	0.4	(0.70)
	Slovak Republic	**509**	(8.2)	496	(7.8)	475	(7.6)	**447**	(7.8)	**-36.3**	(7.36)	**0.6**	(0.10)	6.5	(2.62)
	Slovenia	503	(3.4)	498	(4.3)	503	(4.3)	511	(4.0)	8.8	(2.19)	1.0	(0.08)	0.3	(0.15)
	Spain	486	(2.8)	486	(2.7)	486	(3.3)	480	(4.3)	-4.4	(3.33)	1.0	(0.07)	0.1	(0.14)
	Sweden	**486**	(5.0)	490	(5.1)	468	(6.2)	**469**	(5.9)	**-9.8**	(3.82)	0.9	(0.10)	0.8	(0.64)
	Switzerland	**546**	(8.4)	531	(8.0)	524	(7.0)	**527**	(7.2)	**-9.5**	(4.41)	**0.7**	(0.10)	0.8	(0.79)
	Turkey	455	(14.0)	461	(10.7)	441	(9.7)	435	(9.8)	-10.3	(5.00)	1.1	(0.15)	1.4	(1.31)
	United Kingdom	**514**	(5.6)	506	(6.0)	491	(6.1)	**469**	(10.0)	**-19.5**	(4.10)	**0.7**	(0.09)	3.2	(1.31)
	United States	492	(6.1)	491	(6.0)	485	(7.4)	460	(7.3)	-14.9	(3.75)	0.8	(0.09)	2.3	(1.23)
	OECD average	**504**	(1.1)	499	(1.1)	490	(1.2)	**484**	(1.3)	**-10.2**	(0.88)	**0.8**	(0.02)	1.6	(0.18)
Partners	Albania	392	(4.4)	396	(4.6)	393	(5.4)	396	(3.6)	0.1	(1.96)	1.0	(0.08)	0.0	(0.04)
	Argentina	388	(7.2)	393	(6.6)	394	(7.1)	379	(5.8)	-3.0	(3.84)	1.0	(0.14)	0.2	(0.41)
	Brazil	**409**	(5.7)	393	(4.2)	383	(4.2)	**381**	(4.7)	**-11.2**	(2.30)	**0.8**	(0.08)	2.2	(0.94)
	Bulgaria	442	(6.0)	443	(6.8)	440	(6.3)	430	(9.3)	-12.1	(10.15)	1.0	(0.11)	0.4	(0.77)
	Colombia	385	(7.6)	378	(5.8)	367	(7.1)	377	(6.0)	-1.8	(2.91)	1.0	(0.16)	0.1	(0.44)
	Costa Rica	412	(6.3)	407	(7.3)	395	(9.6)	414	(6.1)	-0.9	(3.71)	0.8	(0.13)	0.0	(0.17)
	Croatia	481	(6.2)	479	(5.9)	459	(6.8)	465	(12.9)	-9.3	(7.37)	0.8	(0.10)	0.7	(1.05)
	Cyprus*	441	(3.3)	438	(3.0)	437	(4.9)	440	(3.6)	1.9	(1.05)	1.0	(0.07)	0.1	(0.06)
	Hong Kong-China	568	(7.4)	568	(6.2)	561	(9.6)	548	(10.6)	-9.3	(5.84)	0.9	(0.12)	0.7	(0.97)
	Indonesia	**399**	(11.1)	379	(6.4)	373	(8.4)	**349**	(6.7)	**-20.5**	(5.45)	**0.6**	(0.12)	7.1	(3.22)
	Jordan	**401**	(7.1)	388	(8.8)	376	(7.4)	**375**	(6.0)	**-6.5**	(2.40)	**0.7**	(0.09)	1.5	(1.09)
	Kazakhstan	425	(5.9)	432	(7.6)	441	(6.6)	430	(5.8)	1.8	(2.61)	1.2	(0.12)	0.1	(0.41)
	Latvia	488	(5.1)	491	(5.6)	499	(6.0)	483	(6.4)	-1.2	(4.62)	1.0	(0.12)	0.0	(0.18)
	Liechtenstein	c	c	c	c	c	c	c	c	-35.9	(5.53)	0.5	(0.19)	7.5	(2.15)
	Lithuania	479	(4.8)	480	(4.7)	483	(5.3)	473	(6.9)	-3.7	(6.49)	0.9	(0.10)	0.1	(0.23)
	Macao-China	542	(3.4)	542	(3.5)	536	(2.1)	533	(2.0)	-3.0	(0.74)	1.0	(0.06)	0.2	(0.08)
	Malaysia	424	(6.7)	417	(5.5)	418	(6.9)	423	(7.3)	2.7	(7.76)	1.0	(0.12)	0.1	(0.61)
	Montenegro	**423**	(4.1)	422	(4.8)	398	(2.4)	**396**	(2.2)	**-17.2**	(1.56)	**0.8**	(0.09)	2.3	(0.41)
	Peru	**389**	(9.1)	367	(8.4)	362	(8.1)	**355**	(6.3)	**-12.9**	(3.70)	**0.7**	(0.12)	2.6	(1.50)
	Qatar	**395**	(2.0)	394	(2.2)	376	(1.9)	**341**	(1.4)	**-18.4**	(0.60)	0.9	(0.04)	4.1	(0.26)
	Romania	**454**	(5.7)	454	(6.0)	439	(8.0)	**431**	(7.0)	**-11.2**	(6.54)	**0.8**	(0.09)	1.0	(1.09)
	Russian Federation	492	(7.1)	477	(6.6)	473	(6.4)	488	(8.0)	-1.7	(3.31)	0.8	(0.10)	0.0	(0.24)
	Serbia	**460**	(6.6)	462	(6.8)	455	(7.7)	**417**	(7.5)	**-32.4**	(7.64)	0.8	(0.11)	4.8	(2.25)
	Shanghai-China	**644**	(9.1)	599	(11.4)	599	(8.7)	**608**	(10.5)	**-11.5**	(3.98)	**0.5**	(0.10)	2.0	(1.37)
	Singapore	**583**	(2.9)	566	(2.4)	579	(3.0)	**571**	(2.9)	**-4.3**	(1.41)	0.9	(0.05)	0.1	(0.08)
	Chinese Taipei	**586**	(7.9)	585	(7.1)	557	(12.9)	**513**	(8.3)	**-25.1**	(4.24)	**0.7**	(0.09)	6.4	(1.87)
	Thailand	427	(8.4)	419	(7.1)	429	(8.0)	432	(6.0)	3.0	(3.54)	1.1	(0.15)	0.2	(0.41)
	Tunisia	391	(9.4)	390	(6.9)	380	(7.0)	388	(7.0)	-2.5	(5.03)	1.0	(0.15)	0.1	(0.47)
	United Arab Emirates	**437**	(4.8)	442	(5.2)	439	(5.7)	**421**	(6.1)	**-6.5**	(1.72)	1.0	(0.10)	1.0	(0.56)
	Uruguay	**435**	(10.0)	407	(8.9)	403	(6.2)	**392**	(6.6)	**-17.3**	(4.14)	**0.7**	(0.12)	3.9	(1.83)
	Viet Nam	506	(9.4)	504	(8.8)	523	(10.0)	513	(11.8)	2.0	(4.37)	1.1	(0.20)	0.1	(0.41)

Note: Values that are statistically significant are indicated in bold (see Annex A3).
* See notes at the beginning of this Annex.
StatLink http://dx.doi.org/10.1787/888932957460

[Part 1/2]
Index of teacher shortage, by school features
Table IV.3.11   *Results based on school principals' reports*

	Index of teacher shortage												
	Bottom quarter of ESCS		Second quarter of ESCS		Third quarter of ESCS		Top quarter of ESCS		Socio-economically disadvantaged schools[1]		Socio-economically average schools[1]		Socio-economically advantaged schools[1]	
	Mean index	S.E.	Mean index	S.E.	Mean index	S.E.	Mean index	S.E.	Mean index	S.E.	Mean index	S.E.	Mean index	S.E.
OECD														
Australia	**0.38**	(0.05)	0.29	(0.04)	0.14	(0.04)	**-0.04**	(0.05)	**0.53**	(0.07)	0.27	(0.05)	**-0.27**	(0.06)
Austria	**0.00**	(0.09)	-0.15	(0.09)	-0.15	(0.10)	**-0.23**	(0.11)	0.03	(0.14)	-0.18	(0.12)	-0.24	(0.19)
Belgium	**0.32**	(0.07)	0.34	(0.06)	0.19	(0.07)	**0.18**	(0.07)	**0.53**	(0.10)	0.25	(0.10)	**0.05**	(0.10)
Canada	**-0.22**	(0.05)	-0.28	(0.04)	-0.30	(0.05)	**-0.40**	(0.04)	**-0.15**	(0.10)	-0.29	(0.05)	**-0.44**	(0.08)
Chile	**0.77**	(0.13)	0.70	(0.11)	0.61	(0.12)	**0.37**	(0.12)	**0.80**	(0.15)	0.87	(0.17)	**0.21**	(0.15)
Czech Republic	**-0.28**	(0.08)	-0.37	(0.05)	-0.41	(0.05)	**-0.64**	(0.04)	**-0.27**	(0.12)	-0.32	(0.06)	**-0.87**	(0.07)
Denmark	**-0.08**	(0.06)	-0.17	(0.06)	-0.20	(0.06)	**-0.28**	(0.06)	**-0.05**	(0.12)	-0.12	(0.06)	**-0.44**	(0.12)
Estonia	-0.02	(0.05)	-0.03	(0.05)	0.02	(0.06)	0.04	(0.05)	0.02	(0.09)	-0.08	(0.07)	0.21	(0.09)
Finland	**-0.40**	(0.05)	-0.45	(0.04)	-0.44	(0.04)	**-0.48**	(0.04)	-0.22	(0.11)	-0.52	(0.05)	-0.33	(0.07)
France	-0.19	(0.07)	-0.14	(0.07)	-0.17	(0.07)	-0.22	(0.08)	-0.18	(0.10)	-0.11	(0.09)	-0.28	(0.11)
Germany	**0.53**	(0.07)	0.44	(0.07)	0.37	(0.08)	**0.30**	(0.09)	0.54	(0.10)	0.44	(0.09)	0.21	(0.13)
Greece	-0.37	(0.08)	-0.34	(0.09)	-0.45	(0.07)	-0.51	(0.08)	-0.30	(0.12)	-0.43	(0.11)	-0.50	(0.12)
Hungary	**-0.55**	(0.08)	-0.62	(0.06)	-0.70	(0.05)	**-0.74**	(0.06)	**-0.38**	(0.11)	-0.76	(0.07)	**-0.78**	(0.07)
Iceland	**0.30**	(0.03)	0.23	(0.03)	0.08	(0.03)	**0.12**	(0.03)	**0.38**	(0.01)	0.27	(0.00)	**-0.11**	(0.01)
Ireland	**-0.02**	(0.07)	-0.11	(0.07)	-0.16	(0.07)	**-0.30**	(0.07)	**0.07**	(0.13)	-0.07	(0.09)	**-0.47**	(0.11)
Israel	0.64	(0.11)	0.69	(0.11)	0.67	(0.09)	0.76	(0.10)	0.66	(0.20)	0.63	(0.14)	0.80	(0.13)
Italy	0.26	(0.06)	0.25	(0.05)	0.25	(0.04)	0.24	(0.05)	0.21	(0.10)	0.26	(0.05)	0.27	(0.07)
Japan	-0.22	(0.08)	-0.28	(0.07)	-0.29	(0.08)	-0.34	(0.07)	-0.15	(0.12)	-0.30	(0.11)	-0.41	(0.10)
Korea	-0.01	(0.09)	0.03	(0.08)	0.09	(0.09)	0.13	(0.11)	-0.13	(0.11)	0.14	(0.12)	0.11	(0.19)
Luxembourg	**1.31**	(0.02)	1.22	(0.02)	1.09	(0.02)	**0.87**	(0.02)	**1.34**	(0.00)	0.94	(0.00)	**0.90**	(0.00)
Mexico	**0.78**	(0.04)	0.62	(0.04)	0.49	(0.05)	**0.23**	(0.05)	**0.83**	(0.05)	0.54	(0.07)	**0.18**	(0.07)
Netherlands	0.59	(0.09)	0.62	(0.08)	0.61	(0.08)	0.59	(0.10)	0.56	(0.15)	0.66	(0.08)	0.51	(0.18)
New Zealand	**0.24**	(0.08)	0.10	(0.09)	0.05	(0.07)	**-0.09**	(0.10)	**0.55**	(0.17)	0.06	(0.09)	**-0.25**	(0.13)
Norway	**0.37**	(0.07)	0.32	(0.07)	0.32	(0.08)	**0.22**	(0.08)	0.37	(0.22)	0.34	(0.07)	0.12	(0.14)
Poland	-1.01	(0.03)	-1.02	(0.02)	-1.02	(0.02)	-1.02	(0.02)	-0.99	(0.05)	-1.03	(0.03)	-1.01	(0.04)
Portugal	-0.79	(0.08)	-0.79	(0.06)	-0.79	(0.06)	-0.86	(0.07)	-0.75	(0.14)	-0.85	(0.05)	-0.80	(0.11)
Slovak Republic	**-0.13**	(0.06)	-0.31	(0.05)	-0.40	(0.05)	**-0.52**	(0.08)	**0.06**	(0.08)	-0.40	(0.05)	**-0.65**	(0.12)
Slovenia	**-0.73**	(0.02)	-0.68	(0.02)	-0.67	(0.02)	**-0.63**	(0.02)	**-0.73**	(0.01)	-0.66	(0.02)	**-0.66**	(0.01)
Spain	**-0.70**	(0.04)	-0.70	(0.04)	-0.75	(0.03)	**-0.79**	(0.03)	**-0.68**	(0.06)	-0.69	(0.06)	**-0.86**	(0.06)
Sweden	**0.06**	(0.09)	-0.04	(0.07)	-0.07	(0.07)	**-0.20**	(0.08)	**0.38**	(0.17)	-0.06	(0.09)	**-0.39**	(0.13)
Switzerland	0.06	(0.07)	0.09	(0.05)	0.07	(0.07)	0.01	(0.08)	0.05	(0.11)	0.17	(0.07)	-0.15	(0.12)
Turkey	**1.04**	(0.08)	0.95	(0.07)	0.86	(0.08)	**0.66**	(0.10)	**1.07**	(0.14)	1.00	(0.13)	**0.42**	(0.17)
United Kingdom	**-0.07**	(0.08)	-0.13	(0.07)	-0.19	(0.06)	**-0.37**	(0.06)	**-0.08**	(0.14)	-0.08	(0.09)	**-0.51**	(0.08)
United States	**-0.28**	(0.12)	-0.42	(0.08)	-0.47	(0.06)	**-0.52**	(0.07)	**-0.04**	(0.17)	-0.52	(0.09)	**-0.61**	(0.11)
OECD average	**0.05**	(0.01)	0.00	(0.01)	-0.05	(0.01)	**-0.13**	(0.01)	**0.11**	(0.02)	-0.02	(0.01)	**-0.21**	(0.02)
Partners														
Albania	m	m	m	m	m	m	m	m	m	m	m	m	m	m
Argentina	-0.08	(0.09)	-0.08	(0.10)	-0.07	(0.09)	-0.16	(0.10)	-0.11	(0.12)	-0.04	(0.14)	-0.16	(0.14)
Brazil	**0.42**	(0.06)	0.28	(0.06)	0.12	(0.06)	**-0.05**	(0.07)	**0.53**	(0.08)	0.20	(0.08)	**-0.27**	(0.13)
Bulgaria	-0.77	(0.05)	-0.80	(0.04)	-0.80	(0.04)	-0.86	(0.04)	-0.78	(0.06)	-0.78	(0.07)	-0.85	(0.06)
Colombia	0.65	(0.13)	0.77	(0.11)	0.72	(0.15)	0.52	(0.22)	0.57	(0.17)	0.84	(0.12)	0.52	(0.32)
Costa Rica	0.06	(0.07)	-0.01	(0.07)	-0.03	(0.07)	-0.07	(0.09)	-0.03	(0.10)	0.03	(0.10)	-0.08	(0.15)
Croatia	**-0.35**	(0.07)	-0.44	(0.06)	-0.41	(0.06)	**-0.54**	(0.08)	-0.32	(0.10)	-0.43	(0.09)	-0.60	(0.13)
Cyprus*	-0.52	(0.03)	-0.50	(0.04)	-0.55	(0.03)	-0.50	(0.03)	-0.53	(0.00)	-0.58	(0.00)	-0.41	(0.00)
Hong Kong-China	**-0.10**	(0.10)	-0.16	(0.08)	-0.27	(0.07)	**-0.36**	(0.10)	**0.08**	(0.14)	-0.40	(0.09)	**-0.39**	(0.16)
Indonesia	**0.48**	(0.10)	0.34	(0.10)	0.28	(0.08)	**-0.04**	(0.12)	**0.53**	(0.15)	0.30	(0.10)	**-0.16**	(0.13)
Jordan	1.15	(0.12)	1.04	(0.11)	0.98	(0.10)	0.89	(0.12)	1.25	(0.24)	1.02	(0.13)	0.76	(0.26)
Kazakhstan	0.31	(0.12)	0.23	(0.11)	0.32	(0.12)	0.28	(0.12)	0.34	(0.23)	0.14	(0.14)	0.45	(0.21)
Latvia	-0.48	(0.07)	-0.39	(0.07)	-0.43	(0.07)	-0.33	(0.09)	-0.41	(0.11)	-0.46	(0.05)	-0.32	(0.13)
Liechtenstein	0.17	(0.09)	-0.14	(0.09)	0.12	(0.09)	0.05	(0.07)	c	c	-0.27	(0.03)	c	c
Lithuania	-0.63	(0.05)	-0.64	(0.05)	-0.69	(0.05)	-0.68	(0.05)	-0.58	(0.10)	-0.67	(0.05)	-0.71	(0.08)
Macao-China	0.00	(0.03)	0.02	(0.03)	0.05	(0.03)	-0.07	(0.02)	0.01	(0.00)	0.17	(0.00)	-0.12	(0.00)
Malaysia	0.23	(0.07)	0.21	(0.06)	0.25	(0.06)	0.19	(0.11)	0.19	(0.10)	0.20	(0.09)	0.27	(0.15)
Montenegro	**-0.43**	(0.02)	-0.47	(0.02)	-0.48	(0.02)	**-0.64**	(0.02)	**-0.51**	(0.00)	-0.04	(0.00)	**-0.79**	(0.00)
Peru	**0.84**	(0.10)	0.72	(0.09)	0.54	(0.09)	**0.36**	(0.12)	**0.81**	(0.12)	0.73	(0.12)	**0.30**	(0.15)
Qatar	0.04	(0.02)	-0.24	(0.02)	-0.20	(0.02)	-0.14	(0.02)	-0.09	(0.00)	-0.06	(0.00)	-0.21	(0.00)
Romania	-0.49	(0.06)	-0.50	(0.05)	-0.54	(0.06)	-0.65	(0.07)	-0.48	(0.08)	-0.48	(0.08)	-0.70	(0.12)
Russian Federation	0.42	(0.08)	0.32	(0.08)	0.36	(0.09)	0.32	(0.11)	0.64	(0.15)	0.21	(0.07)	0.39	(0.18)
Serbia	**-0.61**	(0.08)	-0.69	(0.06)	-0.76	(0.05)	**-0.90**	(0.03)	**-0.40**	(0.12)	-0.85	(0.07)	**-1.02**	(0.04)
Shanghai-China	**0.98**	(0.12)	0.77	(0.10)	0.65	(0.11)	**0.60**	(0.12)	**1.11**	(0.18)	0.77	(0.15)	**0.41**	(0.17)
Singapore	**0.14**	(0.02)	0.15	(0.02)	0.17	(0.02)	**0.04**	(0.04)	0.14	(0.00)	0.14	(0.01)	0.10	(0.04)
Chinese Taipei	**0.11**	(0.11)	-0.02	(0.10)	-0.23	(0.09)	**-0.47**	(0.08)	**0.33**	(0.19)	-0.04	(0.17)	**-0.83**	(0.08)
Thailand	0.99	(0.10)	1.01	(0.09)	0.90	(0.10)	0.88	(0.11)	1.05	(0.12)	0.86	(0.16)	0.90	(0.17)
Tunisia	-0.12	(0.10)	-0.06	(0.08)	-0.05	(0.08)	-0.20	(0.12)	-0.14	(0.15)	0.00	(0.11)	-0.26	(0.18)
United Arab Emirates	**0.28**	(0.09)	0.16	(0.09)	0.12	(0.09)	**0.02**	(0.10)	0.27	(0.11)	0.22	(0.13)	-0.03	(0.14)
Uruguay	**0.55**	(0.10)	0.43	(0.07)	0.39	(0.07)	**0.01**	(0.11)	**0.58**	(0.13)	0.38	(0.10)	**-0.12**	(0.14)
Viet Nam	**0.55**	(0.13)	0.51	(0.12)	0.35	(0.10)	**0.22**	(0.11)	**0.64**	(0.16)	0.36	(0.15)	**0.12**	(0.15)

Notes: Values that are statistically significant are indicated in bold (see Annex A3).
ESCS refers to the *PISA index of economic, social and cultural status*.
1. A socio-economically disadvantaged school is one whose students' mean socio-economic status (ESCS) is statistically significantly below the mean socio-economic status of the country/economy; an average school is one where there is no difference from the country's/economy's mean; and an advantaged school is one whose students' mean socio-economic status is statistically significantly above the country/economy mean.
* See notes at the beginning of this Annex.
StatLink ᵃᵐˢ⌐ http://dx.doi.org/10.1787/888932957460

[Part 2/2]
Index of teacher shortage, by school features
Table IV.3.11 *Results based on school principals' reports*

		Index of teacher shortage												
		Public schools		Private schools		Lower secondary education (ISCED 2)		Upper secondary education (ISCED 3)		Schools located in a village, hamlet or rural area (fewer than 3 000 people)		Schools located in a small town or town (3 000 to about 100 000 people)		Schools located in a city or a large city (over 100 000 people)
		Mean index	S.E.	Mean index	S.E.	Mean index	S.E.	Mean index	S.E.	Mean index	S.E.	Mean index	S.E.	Mean index	S.E.
OECD	Australia	**0.41**	(0.04)	**-0.09**	(0.06)	0.18	(0.04)	0.28	(0.07)	0.49	(0.17)	0.58	(0.08)	**-0.01**	(0.04)
	Austria	-0.11	(0.09)	-0.37	(0.25)	**0.26**	(0.17)	**-0.15**	(0.09)	-0.13	(0.20)	-0.10	(0.12)	-0.18	(0.14)
	Belgium	0.33	(0.12)	0.24	(0.08)	**0.56**	(0.10)	**0.23**	(0.06)	0.01	(0.31)	0.24	(0.07)	0.37	(0.12)
	Canada	-0.30	(0.04)	-0.37	(0.14)	**0.03**	(0.06)	**-0.35**	(0.04)	-0.17	(0.11)	-0.18	(0.07)	**-0.40**	(0.06)
	Chile	0.88	(0.17)	0.40	(0.11)	1.00	(0.21)	0.59	(0.10)	1.46	(0.46)	0.49	(0.15)	0.62	(0.13)
	Czech Republic	-0.39	(0.05)	-0.79	(0.12)	-0.21	(0.07)	-0.69	(0.05)	0.03	(0.16)	-0.48	(0.05)	-0.41	(0.11)
	Denmark	**-0.11**	(0.06)	-0.39	(0.11)	-0.18	(0.05)	c	c	-0.09	(0.08)	-0.21	(0.07)	-0.19	(0.13)
	Estonia	0.01	(0.05)	-0.35	(0.28)	**0.01**	(0.05)	**-0.18**	(0.08)	0.06	(0.11)	-0.07	(0.06)	0.07	(0.08)
	Finland	-0.44	(0.04)	-0.35	(0.16)	-0.44	(0.04)	c	c	-0.58	(0.15)	-0.35	(0.05)	**-0.62**	(0.05)
	France	-0.22	(0.06)	0.05	(0.19)	-0.24	(0.08)	-0.15	(0.07)	-0.09	(0.21)	-0.17	(0.06)	-0.24	(0.17)
	Germany	0.44	(0.06)	0.03	(0.23)	0.42	(0.06)	0.30	(0.37)	c	c	0.48	(0.08)	0.29	(0.12)
	Greece	-0.37	(0.07)	c	c	-0.41	(0.13)	-0.42	(0.07)	-0.24	(0.16)	-0.41	(0.09)	-0.49	(0.14)
	Hungary	-0.68	(0.06)	-0.47	(0.12)	-0.59	(0.14)	-0.66	(0.05)	**0.03**	(0.16)	-0.61	(0.07)	-0.75	(0.07)
	Iceland	0.18	(0.00)	c	c	0.18	(0.00)	c	c	0.51	(0.01)	0.15	(0.01)	0.01	(0.01)
	Ireland	-0.15	(0.11)	-0.10	(0.09)	-0.14	(0.07)	-0.15	(0.07)	-0.11	(0.15)	-0.05	(0.08)	-0.35	(0.12)
	Israel	0.69	(0.09)	c	c	**0.90**	(0.11)	**0.66**	(0.09)	0.78	(0.18)	0.76	(0.15)	0.55	(0.14)
	Italy	**0.29**	(0.04)	**-0.27**	(0.18)	0.21	(0.16)	0.25	(0.04)	0.01	(0.24)	0.28	(0.05)	0.20	(0.06)
	Japan	-0.27	(0.08)	-0.33	(0.10)	c	c	-0.29	(0.07)	c	c	-0.38	(0.13)	-0.25	(0.07)
	Korea	0.03	(0.11)	0.10	(0.12)	-0.19	(0.29)	0.08	(0.08)	c	c	0.30	(0.18)	0.04	(0.09)
	Luxembourg	**1.33**	(0.00)	**-0.08**	(0.00)	**1.22**	(0.00)	**0.97**	(0.00)	c	c	1.12	(0.00)	c	c
	Mexico	**0.63**	(0.04)	**-0.07**	(0.09)	**0.72**	(0.05)	**0.42**	(0.05)	**0.84**	(0.07)	0.62	(0.06)	**0.34**	(0.06)
	Netherlands	0.59	(0.15)	0.59	(0.09)	0.57	(0.08)	0.67	(0.12)	c	c	0.60	(0.09)	0.59	(0.16)
	New Zealand	0.12	(0.08)	-0.40	(0.32)	0.09	(0.09)	0.08	(0.07)	0.44	(0.18)	0.35	(0.13)	-0.14	(0.08)
	Norway	0.32	(0.07)	c	c	0.31	(0.07)	c	c	0.62	(0.12)	0.32	(0.09)	**0.00**	(0.13)
	Poland	-1.02	(0.02)	-1.06	(0.03)	-1.02	(0.02)	c	c	-1.01	(0.04)	-1.03	(0.03)	-1.00	(0.05)
	Portugal	-0.79	(0.06)	-0.91	(0.09)	-0.77	(0.09)	-0.83	(0.06)	-0.83	(0.26)	-0.79	(0.07)	-0.84	(0.10)
	Slovak Republic	-0.34	(0.05)	-0.40	(0.22)	-0.13	(0.07)	-0.51	(0.07)	0.26	(0.12)	-0.44	(0.06)	-0.42	(0.14)
	Slovenia	**-0.69**	(0.01)	**-0.38**	(0.03)	-0.72	(0.15)	-0.68	(0.01)	-0.32	(0.29)	-0.73	(0.01)	-0.62	(0.02)
	Spain	-0.70	(0.04)	-0.79	(0.04)	-0.73	(0.03)	c	c	-0.49	(0.16)	-0.74	(0.04)	-0.75	(0.06)
	Sweden	-0.05	(0.07)	-0.06	(0.19)	-0.05	(0.07)	-0.34	(0.19)	0.21	(0.17)	-0.10	(0.08)	-0.14	(0.13)
	Switzerland	0.07	(0.05)	-0.13	(0.29)	0.12	(0.05)	-0.19	(0.16)	0.03	(0.18)	0.07	(0.06)	-0.01	(0.19)
	Turkey	0.89	(0.06)	c	c	0.87	(0.13)	0.88	(0.07)	1.03	(0.20)	0.94	(0.11)	0.83	(0.10)
	United Kingdom	-0.09	(0.07)	-0.32	(0.11)	c	c	-0.18	(0.06)	-0.04	(0.16)	-0.13	(0.08)	-0.34	(0.10)
	United States	-0.42	(0.07)	-0.24	(0.24)	-0.21	(0.12)	-0.45	(0.07)	-0.37	(0.29)	-0.47	(0.09)	-0.37	(0.12)
	OECD average	**0.00**	(0.01)	**-0.25**	(0.03)	**0.05**	(0.02)	**-0.03**	(0.02)	**0.08**	(0.03)	**0.00**	(0.01)	**-0.14**	(0.02)
Partners	Albania	-0.22	(0.07)	-0.43	(0.33)	-0.14	(0.10)	-0.30	(0.09)	-0.09	(0.13)	-0.38	(0.09)	-0.08	(0.15)
	Argentina	-0.02	(0.10)	-0.24	(0.14)	0.02	(0.11)	-0.18	(0.09)	-0.08	(0.14)	-0.11	(0.11)	-0.07	(0.13)
	Brazil	**0.34**	(0.06)	**-0.42**	(0.15)	0.19	(0.08)	0.20	(0.06)	0.57	(0.20)	0.35	(0.08)	**0.03**	(0.07)
	Bulgaria	-0.80	(0.04)	c	c	-0.77	(0.09)	-0.81	(0.04)	-0.49	(0.22)	-0.80	(0.05)	-0.85	(0.05)
	Colombia	0.74	(0.11)	0.35	(0.51)	0.64	(0.12)	0.68	(0.14)	0.69	(0.24)	1.08	(0.26)	**0.43**	(0.11)
	Costa Rica	0.03	(0.07)	-0.26	(0.19)	-0.05	(0.06)	0.04	(0.09)	-0.01	(0.13)	0.03	(0.09)	-0.22	(0.15)
	Croatia	-0.43	(0.06)	c	c	c	c	-0.43	(0.06)	c	c	-0.38	(0.07)	-0.54	(0.10)
	Cyprus*	**-0.44**	(0.00)	**-0.93**	(0.00)	-0.49	(0.03)	-0.52	(0.00)	**-0.41**	(0.01)	-0.51	(0.00)	**-0.54**	(0.00)
	Hong Kong-China	-0.34	(0.37)	-0.21	(0.07)	-0.20	(0.07)	-0.24	(0.07)	c	c	c	c	-0.23	(0.07)
	Indonesia	0.16	(0.09)	0.41	(0.13)	**0.55**	(0.11)	**0.01**	(0.09)	0.55	(0.18)	0.32	(0.10)	-0.26	(0.13)
	Jordan	1.12	(0.10)	0.54	(0.28)	1.02	(0.09)	c	c	1.08	(0.28)	1.09	(0.17)	0.93	(0.17)
	Kazakhstan	0.28	(0.11)	0.55	(0.23)	0.26	(0.11)	0.35	(0.13)	0.27	(0.19)	0.07	(0.21)	0.42	(0.15)
	Latvia	-0.39	(0.06)	c	c	-0.42	(0.06)	-0.10	(0.24)	-0.46	(0.11)	-0.51	(0.08)	-0.23	(0.14)
	Liechtenstein	0.04	(0.02)	c	c	**0.04**	(0.02)	**0.15**	(0.00)	c	c	0.05	(0.02)	c	c
	Lithuania	-0.66	(0.04)	c	c	-0.66	(0.04)	c	c	-0.57	(0.08)	-0.62	(0.06)	-0.75	(0.06)
	Macao-China	c	c	0.05	(0.00)	**0.09**	(0.00)	-0.11	(0.00)	c	c	c	c	0.00	(0.00)
	Malaysia	0.20	(0.06)	0.84	(0.37)	0.29	(0.12)	0.22	(0.06)	0.27	(0.18)	0.15	(0.07)	0.33	(0.13)
	Montenegro	-0.51	(0.00)	c	c	c	c	-0.50	(0.00)	c	c	-0.36	(0.00)	-0.84	(0.00)
	Peru	**0.81**	(0.08)	**-0.18**	(0.19)	0.73	(0.09)	0.57	(0.09)	0.65	(0.15)	0.79	(0.11)	**0.44**	(0.12)
	Qatar	**0.19**	(0.00)	**-0.66**	(0.00)	**-0.24**	(0.01)	**-0.11**	(0.00)	0.75	(0.01)	0.06	(0.00)	**-0.49**	(0.00)
	Romania	-0.54	(0.05)	c	c	-0.54	(0.05)	c	c	**-0.81**	(0.12)	-0.44	(0.08)	-0.66	(0.08)
	Russian Federation	0.36	(0.08)	c	c	0.33	(0.08)	0.46	(0.13)	0.35	(0.13)	0.28	(0.14)	0.41	(0.12)
	Serbia	-0.74	(0.05)	c	c	c	c	-0.75	(0.05)	c	c	-0.66	(0.08)	-0.86	(0.07)
	Shanghai-China	0.74	(0.10)	0.86	(0.42)	0.87	(0.14)	0.66	(0.11)	c	c	c	c	0.75	(0.09)
	Singapore	0.15	(0.00)	c	c	0.18	(0.06)	0.13	(0.01)	c	c	c	c	0.13	(0.01)
	Chinese Taipei	-0.19	(0.12)	-0.01	(0.15)	**0.10**	(0.16)	**-0.29**	(0.09)	c	c	0.13	(0.15)	**-0.31**	(0.11)
	Thailand	0.99	(0.08)	0.70	(0.25)	1.09	(0.11)	0.91	(0.09)	1.23	(0.18)	0.93	(0.11)	0.83	(0.13)
	Tunisia	-0.10	(0.07)	c	c	-0.11	(0.11)	-0.10	(0.10)	-0.48	(0.26)	-0.05	(0.09)	-0.19	(0.17)
	United Arab Emirates	**0.49**	(0.11)	**-0.31**	(0.10)	0.20	(0.16)	0.13	(0.08)	0.35	(0.17)	0.41	(0.16)	**-0.02**	(0.09)
	Uruguay	**0.49**	(0.08)	**-0.34**	(0.16)	**0.51**	(0.10)	**0.23**	(0.08)	0.63	(0.35)	0.54	(0.10)	**-0.01**	(0.13)
	Viet Nam	**0.47**	(0.09)	**-0.66**	(0.20)	0.52	(0.26)	0.40	(0.10)	0.47	(0.15)	0.61	(0.18)	**0.06**	(0.15)

Notes: Values that are statistically significant are indicated in bold (see Annex A3).
ESCS refers to the *PISA index of economic, social and cultural status*.
1. A socio-economically disadvantaged school is one whose students' mean socio-economic status (ESCS) is statistically significantly below the mean socio-economic status of the country/economy; an average school is one where there is no difference from the country's/economy's mean; and an advantaged school is one whose students' mean socio-economic status is statistically significantly above the country/economy mean.
* See notes at the beginning of this Annex.
StatLink http://dx.doi.org/10.1787/888932957460

[Part 1/1]
Teacher professional development
Table IV.3.12 *Results based on school principals' reports*

		Principal's report on the percentage of mathematics teachers in the school who have attended a programme of professional development with a focus on mathematics during the previous three months	
		Mean %	S.E.
OECD	Australia	52.6	(1.5)
	Austria	53.1	(2.6)
	Belgium	36.1	(2.3)
	Canada	59.0	(1.8)
	Chile	28.0	(2.6)
	Czech Republic	24.0	(2.3)
	Denmark	25.4	(2.3)
	Estonia	61.9	(2.2)
	Finland	31.7	(2.4)
	France	33.8	(2.6)
	Germany	23.3	(1.8)
	Greece	24.8	(2.9)
	Hungary	21.1	(2.2)
	Iceland	34.4	(0.2)
	Ireland	88.0	(2.4)
	Israel	60.7	(2.6)
	Italy	28.4	(1.3)
	Japan	21.5	(1.8)
	Korea	31.3	(2.9)
	Luxembourg	47.4	(0.1)
	Mexico	46.6	(1.3)
	Netherlands	29.2	(2.8)
	New Zealand	61.2	(3.0)
	Norway	24.1	(2.2)
	Poland	45.9	(3.6)
	Portugal	35.4	(2.8)
	Slovak Republic	24.2	(2.5)
	Slovenia	58.2	(0.6)
	Spain	25.3	(1.6)
	Sweden	43.9	(3.3)
	Switzerland	23.4	(1.8)
	Turkey	18.4	(2.3)
	United Kingdom	51.7	(2.8)
	United States	61.5	(3.3)
	OECD average	**39.3**	**(0.4)**
Partners	Albania	48.1	(3.5)
	Argentina	48.3	(3.0)
	Brazil	36.3	(2.1)
	Bulgaria	36.2	(2.6)
	Colombia	21.9	(2.1)
	Costa Rica	46.0	(3.0)
	Croatia	68.5	(2.6)
	Cyprus*	33.0	(0.1)
	Hong Kong-China	33.6	(3.0)
	Indonesia	42.3	(3.1)
	Jordan	32.6	(3.1)
	Kazakhstan	35.8	(2.9)
	Latvia	37.4	(2.8)
	Liechtenstein	35.6	(0.7)
	Lithuania	47.7	(2.8)
	Macao-China	59.0	(0.0)
	Malaysia	42.5	(3.1)
	Montenegro	45.6	(0.1)
	Peru	33.1	(2.4)
	Qatar	77.3	(0.1)
	Romania	45.0	(3.2)
	Russian Federation	26.0	(2.6)
	Serbia	47.8	(3.9)
	Shanghai-China	72.3	(2.7)
	Singapore	66.7	(0.4)
	Chinese Taipei	57.2	(3.3)
	Thailand	73.3	(2.7)
	Tunisia	39.7	(3.4)
	United Arab Emirates	58.0	(1.7)
	Uruguay	33.1	(3.1)
	Viet Nam	49.6	(3.7)

* See notes at the beginning of this Annex.
StatLink ⟨⟩ http://dx.doi.org/10.1787/888932957460

[Part 1/2]
Teacher professional development, by school features
Table IV.3.13 *Results based on school principals' reports*

		Principal's report on the percentage of mathematics teachers in the school who have attended a programme of professional development with a focus on mathematics during the previous three months													
		Bottom quarter of ESCS		Second quarter of ESCS		Third quarter of ESCS		Top quarter of ESCS		Socio-economically disadvantaged schools[1]		Socio-economically average schools[1]		Socio-economically advantaged schools[1]	
		Mean %	S.E.	Mean %	S.E.	Mean %	S.E.	Mean %	S.E.	Mean %	S.E.	Mean %	S.E.	Mean %	S.E.
OECD	Australia	53.8	(1.7)	51.5	(1.8)	52.2	(1.7)	52.8	(1.9)	50.3	(3.0)	54.9	(2.2)	49.8	(3.0)
	Austria	**44.7**	(3.0)	49.4	(3.0)	56.7	(3.1)	**61.8**	(3.8)	**31.5**	(4.7)	59.4	(3.9)	**66.3**	(5.8)
	Belgium	35.0	(3.0)	37.3	(2.6)	35.5	(2.5)	36.2	(2.7)	32.7	(4.7)	37.1	(4.2)	37.7	(3.9)
	Canada	60.4	(2.2)	59.5	(1.8)	58.1	(2.1)	57.5	(2.0)	**60.4**	(3.3)	62.5	(2.5)	**51.1**	(3.4)
	Chile	**25.2**	(3.4)	23.6	(2.7)	25.9	(3.1)	**37.5**	(4.4)	**26.2**	(3.7)	13.5	(4.3)	**39.6**	(5.5)
	Czech Republic	22.7	(2.6)	27.9	(3.1)	24.8	(2.7)	20.7	(2.4)	27.9	(5.4)	24.3	(3.1)	19.1	(3.5)
	Denmark	23.0	(2.7)	25.2	(2.4)	26.9	(2.7)	27.4	(3.5)	19.9	(6.2)	24.4	(2.5)	33.4	(6.9)
	Estonia	59.8	(3.0)	60.9	(2.7)	62.6	(2.4)	64.0	(2.6)	64.7	(6.0)	60.0	(2.9)	64.3	(4.3)
	Finland	31.3	(2.5)	30.5	(2.6)	31.6	(2.3)	33.1	(2.6)	23.3	(5.5)	34.4	(3.0)	28.4	(4.9)
	France	35.1	(3.3)	33.4	(3.1)	34.8	(2.9)	31.6	(3.0)	36.6	(5.5)	31.5	(3.6)	35.4	(4.4)
	Germany	21.4	(2.0)	22.8	(2.0)	25.1	(2.2)	24.8	(2.6)	24.9	(3.7)	21.7	(3.0)	24.5	(3.2)
	Greece	26.8	(3.9)	22.6	(3.2)	23.1	(3.0)	26.7	(4.0)	33.3	(6.0)	20.1	(3.7)	25.4	(5.0)
	Hungary	**17.6**	(2.5)	19.8	(2.3)	22.4	(2.7)	**24.3**	(3.1)	**17.8**	(3.1)	14.8	(3.9)	**30.5**	(4.3)
	Iceland	**30.9**	(1.1)	33.5	(1.2)	36.1	(1.3)	**37.6**	(1.3)	**22.2**	(0.5)	37.6	(0.3)	**35.3**	(0.3)
	Ireland	86.0	(3.2)	88.4	(2.4)	87.9	(2.7)	89.5	(2.7)	85.3	(5.1)	88.4	(3.2)	88.7	(4.9)
	Israel	63.4	(3.1)	61.1	(3.0)	57.4	(2.9)	61.8	(3.1)	64.8	(4.7)	55.0	(4.7)	63.4	(4.1)
	Italy	**26.5**	(1.7)	28.2	(1.5)	28.3	(1.4)	**31.0**	(1.8)	27.2	(3.0)	27.5	(2.0)	30.9	(2.2)
	Japan	22.2	(2.4)	21.0	(1.9)	21.1	(1.7)	21.9	(2.1)	24.2	(3.6)	17.3	(2.8)	25.1	(2.9)
	Korea	31.3	(3.9)	30.6	(2.9)	31.3	(3.0)	32.0	(3.3)	32.5	(6.2)	30.8	(3.6)	31.3	(5.4)
	Luxembourg	**38.3**	(0.9)	39.8	(1.2)	47.4	(1.1)	**64.0**	(0.9)	**35.2**	(0.1)	22.5	(0.1)	**70.8**	(0.1)
	Mexico	**40.1**	(1.9)	45.9	(1.4)	48.6	(1.6)	**51.1**	(1.7)	**39.4**	(2.6)	45.7	(2.4)	**55.1**	(2.7)
	Netherlands	29.7	(3.6)	27.4	(3.1)	29.4	(2.9)	30.7	(3.0)	24.9	(6.4)	30.0	(3.4)	31.4	(5.0)
	New Zealand	57.5	(4.1)	64.8	(3.1)	62.0	(3.2)	60.4	(4.1)	50.4	(7.7)	68.6	(3.8)	53.0	(6.1)
	Norway	**21.2**	(2.1)	25.0	(2.5)	22.5	(2.3)	**27.5**	(2.8)	**17.3**	(4.3)	22.7	(2.6)	**34.0**	(6.0)
	Poland	48.7	(4.7)	49.4	(4.0)	42.1	(3.9)	43.1	(3.9)	**57.7**	(7.1)	44.1	(4.7)	**35.2**	(7.3)
	Portugal	38.1	(4.3)	34.4	(3.2)	33.4	(2.9)	35.7	(3.8)	38.3	(6.7)	32.3	(4.1)	38.0	(7.8)
	Slovak Republic	19.9	(2.7)	26.2	(3.3)	24.8	(2.7)	25.6	(2.9)	18.7	(4.6)	24.5	(3.5)	30.0	(5.1)
	Slovenia	**56.8**	(1.2)	56.3	(1.4)	58.4	(1.6)	**61.4**	(1.2)	**58.2**	(0.9)	50.3	(1.2)	**68.5**	(0.5)
	Spain	25.4	(1.8)	24.6	(1.7)	24.8	(1.7)	26.5	(2.7)	27.2	(3.1)	22.3	(2.1)	28.0	(4.2)
	Sweden	42.2	(3.6)	45.6	(3.5)	45.8	(3.8)	41.8	(4.1)	45.5	(7.2)	43.6	(4.1)	43.2	(7.5)
	Switzerland	24.8	(2.4)	22.8	(1.9)	22.8	(2.1)	23.3	(2.0)	24.9	(4.1)	21.4	(2.6)	25.4	(3.6)
	Turkey	**12.2**	(2.6)	14.8	(2.2)	17.9	(2.7)	**28.9**	(4.3)	**8.3**	(3.3)	12.2	(3.5)	**41.4**	(7.3)
	United Kingdom	53.8	(3.4)	52.7	(3.4)	50.8	(2.9)	48.9	(3.1)	56.4	(6.4)	52.2	(3.7)	46.0	(5.1)
	United States	63.4	(3.8)	63.8	(3.6)	59.9	(3.9)	58.6	(4.0)	63.2	(6.8)	64.3	(5.3)	55.6	(6.6)
	OECD average	**37.9**	(0.5)	38.8	(0.5)	39.2	(0.4)	**41.2**	(0.5)	**37.4**	(0.8)	37.4	(0.6)	**42.2**	(0.8)
Partners	Albania	m	m	m	m	m	m	m	m	m	m	m	m	m	m
	Argentina	**44.6**	(3.6)	46.8	(3.0)	48.0	(3.6)	**53.9**	(4.4)	46.6	(4.3)	40.1	(4.8)	58.4	(6.8)
	Brazil	38.0	(2.9)	33.5	(2.3)	35.8	(2.4)	38.1	(2.7)	38.2	(4.0)	33.4	(3.0)	38.7	(3.9)
	Bulgaria	33.6	(3.1)	34.8	(2.9)	35.2	(2.8)	41.9	(4.1)	34.1	(4.7)	31.3	(5.3)	43.0	(4.6)
	Colombia	**18.8**	(3.3)	19.8	(2.0)	23.7	(2.4)	**25.4**	(2.7)	**13.0**	(3.4)	23.8	(4.5)	**27.9**	(3.2)
	Costa Rica	42.6	(3.6)	47.6	(3.8)	46.3	(3.3)	47.7	(4.9)	38.3	(5.0)	49.7	(4.4)	48.4	(6.8)
	Croatia	71.5	(2.9)	68.6	(3.0)	67.1	(2.9)	66.9	(3.1)	69.5	(4.4)	70.3	(4.3)	63.6	(5.8)
	Cyprus*	**40.7**	(1.1)	34.2	(1.2)	31.8	(1.2)	**24.6**	(0.9)	**43.5**	(0.2)	33.0	(0.2)	**19.1**	(0.1)
	Hong Kong-China	31.2	(3.2)	30.7	(2.9)	33.9	(3.1)	39.0	(6.4)	30.9	(4.4)	31.0	(4.1)	41.7	(7.5)
	Indonesia	**38.6**	(3.7)	41.6	(3.6)	39.3	(3.2)	**49.6**	(4.7)	39.4	(4.5)	39.9	(6.2)	49.6	(5.4)
	Jordan	31.9	(3.6)	33.1	(3.3)	31.9	(3.1)	34.2	(5.0)	31.6	(6.5)	30.9	(4.1)	38.6	(7.9)
	Kazakhstan	32.7	(3.0)	36.6	(3.4)	36.5	(3.2)	37.5	(3.5)	**23.3**	(4.4)	40.6	(4.0)	**38.1**	(5.4)
	Latvia	35.9	(3.4)	38.8	(3.4)	36.9	(3.3)	37.8	(3.5)	24.0	(5.3)	45.3	(4.3)	33.1	(5.4)
	Liechtenstein	**23.3**	(4.0)	35.6	(4.2)	41.2	(4.1)	**43.4**	(3.6)	c	c	23.0	(1.1)	c	c
	Lithuania	45.7	(3.3)	46.5	(3.1)	49.5	(2.8)	49.3	(3.7)	42.4	(5.3)	47.0	(3.9)	54.4	(5.6)
	Macao-China	**60.6**	(1.0)	61.2	(1.2)	60.5	(1.2)	**54.0**	(1.0)	**68.8**	(0.1)	31.3	(0.1)	**58.3**	(0.1)
	Malaysia	40.5	(3.4)	41.9	(3.4)	41.8	(3.7)	45.6	(3.9)	35.4	(4.8)	44.9	(5.0)	45.7	(5.7)
	Montenegro	**43.9**	(1.0)	42.6	(1.0)	44.1	(1.1)	**52.5**	(0.9)	**42.8**	(0.2)	33.3	(0.2)	**56.1**	(0.1)
	Peru	**24.5**	(2.9)	29.8	(2.7)	36.6	(2.7)	**41.7**	(4.2)	**23.9**	(3.9)	31.2	(3.9)	**44.4**	(4.8)
	Qatar	**81.0**	(0.5)	75.9	(0.6)	74.1	(0.6)	**77.5**	(0.6)	**77.1**	(0.1)	84.2	(0.1)	**73.8**	(0.1)
	Romania	42.2	(4.2)	45.9	(3.7)	45.1	(3.6)	46.9	(4.0)	39.4	(6.1)	48.9	(4.8)	45.4	(5.7)
	Russian Federation	22.8	(2.5)	25.6	(2.7)	25.1	(2.8)	30.3	(4.2)	**19.8**	(2.9)	25.0	(3.5)	**32.7**	(5.3)
	Serbia	**40.3**	(4.3)	46.0	(4.3)	49.7	(4.2)	**55.0**	(4.3)	**26.5**	(5.5)	58.9	(5.9)	**57.2**	(6.8)
	Shanghai-China	**66.5**	(3.9)	69.3	(3.0)	74.4	(2.9)	**78.9**	(3.1)	**55.7**	(5.7)	77.2	(4.1)	**81.0**	(4.4)
	Singapore	**65.2**	(1.0)	66.5	(1.1)	66.2	(1.0)	**68.8**	(1.4)	**62.2**	(0.2)	68.7	(0.5)	**68.4**	(0.9)
	Chinese Taipei	**49.3**	(3.6)	55.2	(3.7)	59.8	(3.6)	**64.5**	(4.2)	**43.9**	(5.2)	58.3	(5.5)	**70.1**	(5.8)
	Thailand	77.0	(3.3)	70.5	(3.5)	70.7	(3.3)	74.9	(2.7)	77.1	(4.5)	66.1	(5.5)	76.1	(3.7)
	Tunisia	37.6	(4.7)	38.9	(3.9)	40.3	(3.7)	42.2	(5.2)	38.6	(7.2)	35.8	(5.1)	47.9	(7.1)
	United Arab Emirates	**64.2**	(2.7)	58.1	(1.9)	54.5	(1.8)	**55.2**	(2.3)	**70.8**	(4.1)	56.1	(2.8)	**51.1**	(3.1)
	Uruguay	34.3	(4.2)	34.9	(3.6)	34.1	(3.3)	29.5	(3.9)	35.1	(5.2)	32.3	(4.5)	30.8	(5.9)
	Viet Nam	53.2	(4.7)	51.2	(4.2)	49.8	(4.3)	44.4	(5.6)	52.3	(5.9)	49.5	(6.3)	45.8	(7.8)

Notes: Values that are statistically significant are indicated in bold (see Annex A3).
ESCS refers to the *PISA index of economic, social and cultural status*.
1. A socio-economically disadvantaged school is one whose students' mean socio-economic status (ESCS) is statistically significantly below the mean socio-economic status of the country/economy; an average school is one where there is no difference from the country's/economy's mean; and an advantaged school is one whose students' mean socio-economic status is statistically significantly above the country/economy mean.
* See notes at the beginning of this Annex.
StatLink http://dx.doi.org/10.1787/888932957460

[Part 2/2]
Teacher professional development, by school features
Table IV.3.13 *Results based on school principals' reports*

	Principal's report on the percentage of mathematics teachers in the school who have attended a programme of professional development with a focus on mathematics during the previous three months												
	Public schools		Private schools		Lower secondary education (ISCED 2)		Upper secondary education (ISCED 3)		Schools located in a village, hamlet or rural area (fewer than 3 000 people)		Schools located in a small town or town (3 000 to about 100 000 people)		Schools located in a city or a large city (over 100 000 people)	
	Mean %	S.E.	Mean %	S.E.	Mean %	S.E.	Mean %	S.E.	Mean %	S.E.	Mean %	S.E.	Mean %	S.E.
Australia	53.6	(2.0)	50.7	(2.2)	52.3	(1.6)	53.4	(2.3)	42.1	(6.3)	53.4	(2.9)	53.7	(1.9)
Austria	53.5	(2.8)	49.7	(10.7)	46.6	(5.2)	53.5	(2.8)	50.0	(10.7)	53.2	(3.8)	53.8	(5.2)
Belgium	32.0	(4.2)	40.1	(2.8)	39.8	(4.7)	35.6	(2.3)	31.9	(17.3)	38.5	(2.9)	28.0	(4.8)
Canada	**60.7**	(1.9)	40.4	(6.4)	56.6	(2.7)	59.4	(1.9)	55.4	(6.0)	60.0	(3.1)	58.9	(2.7)
Chile	26.2	(3.5)	28.7	(3.7)	19.7	(4.2)	28.5	(2.7)	47.5	(15.4)	29.6	(3.8)	26.4	(3.5)
Czech Republic	23.8	(2.3)	26.5	(9.7)	22.7	(2.8)	25.6	(3.6)	29.5	(7.4)	22.9	(2.7)	25.3	(4.9)
Denmark	26.3	(2.9)	23.7	(4.8)	25.5	(2.3)	c	c	**13.0**	(3.4)	31.8	(3.3)	22.4	(4.8)
Estonia	62.0	(2.2)	41.1	(17.5)	61.9	(2.2)	57.8	(8.5)	54.8	(4.9)	61.2	(3.3)	68.6	(4.2)
Finland	**32.0**	(2.4)	**23.7**	(0.9)	31.6	(2.4)	c	c	26.8	(10.2)	30.9	(2.9)	34.8	(3.7)
France	37.1	(3.1)	22.7	(4.0)	31.2	(3.8)	35.0	(3.2)	43.8	(12.5)	30.6	(3.0)	39.7	(5.7)
Germany	**24.3**	(1.9)	**10.8**	(4.1)	23.4	(1.8)	19.8	(10.7)	c	c	23.6	(2.3)	22.0	(3.7)
Greece	24.2	(3.0)	c	c	18.8	(5.9)	25.1	(3.0)	34.1	(9.5)	24.2	(3.6)	23.7	(4.9)
Hungary	20.9	(2.3)	22.1	(7.2)	20.7	(6.2)	21.1	(2.3)	**4.5**	(3.5)	20.9	(3.1)	22.5	(4.0)
Iceland	34.6	(0.2)	c	c	34.4	(0.2)	c	c	**17.5**	(0.5)	43.8	(0.3)	**30.6**	(0.3)
Ireland	90.4	(3.3)	85.3	(3.5)	88.4	(2.3)	87.3	(2.6)	88.1	(5.6)	84.9	(3.7)	92.8	(2.7)
Israel	60.7	(2.6)	c	c	**68.1**	(4.3)	59.5	(2.6)	51.5	(5.9)	62.8	(3.7)	62.0	(5.0)
Italy	28.1	(1.3)	32.0	(9.4)	**18.3**	(3.5)	28.7	(1.4)	18.6	(10.3)	28.4	(1.5)	29.2	(2.8)
Japan	20.7	(2.0)	23.5	(3.5)	c	c	21.5	(1.8)	c	c	25.0	(4.0)	20.2	(2.1)
Korea	35.0	(4.1)	26.8	(4.0)	47.5	(11.7)	30.3	(3.0)	c	c	37.8	(10.7)	30.4	(3.0)
Luxembourg	**45.5**	(0.1)	**58.6**	(0.2)	**43.4**	(0.1)	**53.1**	(0.1)	c	c	47.3	(0.1)	c	c
Mexico	46.3	(1.3)	47.0	(4.0)	49.5	(2.3)	44.9	(1.7)	**34.2**	(3.7)	47.0	(2.5)	50.5	(2.1)
Netherlands	35.2	(6.0)	26.2	(2.8)	27.6	(3.2)	32.8	(3.8)	c	c	30.1	(3.5)	26.9	(4.9)
New Zealand	61.1	(3.0)	55.7	(15.6)	55.5	(3.5)	61.6	(3.0)	53.0	(10.9)	64.8	(4.9)	59.7	(4.1)
Norway	24.4	(2.2)	c	c	24.1	(2.2)	c	c	**12.4**	(2.2)	25.3	(3.0)	31.8	(5.4)
Poland	46.1	(3.7)	39.8	(10.3)	45.9	(3.6)	c	c	45.4	(6.9)	47.9	(5.1)	42.0	(6.9)
Portugal	35.1	(3.0)	38.3	(8.1)	35.5	(3.9)	35.2	(3.3)	59.9	(20.2)	34.0	(3.9)	32.7	(6.1)
Slovak Republic	24.3	(2.6)	24.1	(7.3)	19.1	(3.0)	28.6	(4.0)	**12.1**	(3.4)	25.2	(3.1)	31.6	(6.2)
Slovenia	58.3	(0.6)	54.9	(2.1)	52.7	(9.7)	58.5	(0.3)	**25.7**	(16.4)	58.2	(0.5)	59.2	(1.1)
Spain	26.5	(1.6)	22.3	(3.2)	25.3	(1.6)	c	c	34.6	(6.2)	28.5	(2.1)	**19.7**	(2.8)
Sweden	45.2	(5.5)	35.6	(7.1)	44.7	(3.4)	52.6	(11.7)	47.5	(7.4)	44.3	(4.5)	40.4	(6.9)
Switzerland	**24.3**	(1.9)	**10.3**	(3.4)	24.4	(1.9)	19.9	(3.9)	22.8	(4.9)	22.9	(2.3)	26.0	(4.8)
Turkey	17.3	(2.2)	c	c	14.6	(9.0)	18.5	(2.4)	8.9	(5.2)	18.9	(4.6)	18.5	(3.8)
United Kingdom	50.3	(3.4)	53.6	(5.2)	c	c	51.7	(2.8)	40.0	(8.1)	52.5	(4.1)	53.2	(5.5)
United States	62.0	(3.5)	55.4	(13.8)	63.5	(7.1)	61.2	(3.2)	48.0	(15.7)	62.5	(4.5)	63.9	(5.0)
OECD average	**39.6**	(0.5)	**36.9**	(1.3)	38.5	(0.8)	41.5	(0.8)	**36.3**	(1.7)	40.4	(0.6)	39.4	(0.7)
Albania	47.2	(3.8)	49.6	(12.8)	45.4	(5.1)	50.0	(4.4)	40.9	(8.1)	41.1	(5.1)	**63.0**	(6.8)
Argentina	48.4	(3.5)	48.0	(6.1)	**43.7**	(3.4)	**51.0**	(3.4)	33.4	(8.5)	50.5	(4.7)	49.0	(3.8)
Brazil	34.9	(2.3)	43.3	(7.2)	**46.5**	(3.2)	33.7	(2.4)	23.7	(11.2)	38.8	(3.2)	34.1	(3.0)
Bulgaria	35.8	(2.5)	c	c	29.1	(4.1)	36.6	(2.6)	19.3	(13.7)	39.0	(3.2)	33.4	(4.6)
Colombia	21.5	(2.4)	23.8	(4.5)	22.2	(2.6)	21.7	(2.1)	15.7	(5.9)	21.9	(5.7)	23.2	(2.4)
Costa Rica	46.2	(3.2)	49.7	(8.8)	44.6	(2.9)	48.3	(4.2)	50.0	(6.2)	44.9	(3.7)	44.4	(6.6)
Croatia	69.2	(2.7)	c	c	c	c	68.5	(2.6)	c	c	70.5	(3.2)	65.8	(4.6)
Cyprus*	**35.4**	(0.1)	**20.0**	(0.2)	53.7	(1.0)	31.9	(0.1)	**35.0**	(0.5)	39.3	(0.1)	**21.1**	(0.1)
Hong Kong-China	29.1	(9.1)	33.0	(3.0)	32.2	(2.8)	34.3	(3.2)	c	c	c	c	33.6	(3.0)
Indonesia	46.9	(3.5)	36.8	(5.2)	43.8	(4.5)	40.7	(4.3)	40.1	(6.4)	40.6	(4.0)	49.5	(5.5)
Jordan	30.3	(3.1)	43.3	(10.9)	32.6	(3.1)	c	c	28.2	(7.8)	30.2	(4.7)	36.4	(5.0)
Kazakhstan	36.3	(2.9)	19.1	(12.7)	36.3	(3.1)	34.5	(4.3)	30.4	(4.4)	43.3	(6.8)	35.8	(4.0)
Latvia	37.9	(2.9)	c	c	37.3	(2.8)	40.7	(7.1)	34.5	(4.2)	39.1	(4.8)	37.5	(4.9)
Liechtenstein	36.5	(0.7)	c	c	**31.0**	(0.7)	**70.0**	(0.0)	c	c	35.6	(0.7)	c	c
Lithuania	48.0	(2.8)	c	c	47.7	(2.8)	c	c	37.1	(4.5)	47.5	(4.7)	53.7	(4.2)
Macao-China	c	c	61.1	(0.0)	61.4	(0.1)	56.0	(0.1)	c	c	c	c	59.2	(0.0)
Malaysia	43.3	(3.3)	27.6	(14.9)	39.4	(5.9)	42.6	(3.1)	35.8	(6.7)	44.4	(4.2)	41.4	(5.8)
Montenegro	45.4	(0.1)	c	c	c	c	45.7	(0.1)	c	c	47.4	(0.2)	**41.4**	(0.2)
Peru	28.7	(2.7)	39.1	(5.9)	**28.7**	(2.9)	34.9	(2.7)	23.5	(6.0)	28.6	(3.1)	**41.6**	(4.4)
Qatar	**91.7**	(0.0)	52.2	(0.1)	68.4	(0.2)	79.1	(0.1)	88.5	(0.1)	80.4	(0.1)	72.2	(0.1)
Romania	44.6	(3.2)	c	c	45.0	(3.2)	c	c	35.0	(10.6)	43.9	(4.0)	49.2	(5.6)
Russian Federation	25.7	(2.6)	c	c	26.9	(2.8)	21.8	(3.5)	22.3	(2.9)	25.2	(4.7)	28.3	(3.9)
Serbia	48.0	(3.9)	c	c	c	c	47.9	(3.8)	c	c	37.1	(5.2)	**63.6**	(5.1)
Shanghai-China	**70.7**	(2.9)	86.9	(6.0)	74.5	(4.5)	70.5	(3.3)	c	c	c	c	72.3	(2.7)
Singapore	66.3	(0.1)	c	c	64.3	(2.5)	66.7	(0.4)	c	c	c	c	66.7	(0.4)
Chinese Taipei	61.1	(4.5)	50.8	(5.2)	**66.3**	(6.3)	51.9	(3.5)	c	c	53.6	(6.1)	58.9	(4.2)
Thailand	76.2	(2.7)	56.6	(9.5)	74.5	(3.6)	72.9	(3.0)	80.5	(5.5)	74.0	(3.9)	68.6	(5.2)
Tunisia	40.0	(3.5)	c	c	33.6	(5.7)	43.3	(4.4)	56.4	(22.6)	35.7	(3.6)	50.0	(9.4)
United Arab Emirates	**74.5**	(2.6)	46.8	(3.2)	53.9	(4.8)	58.7	(1.7)	50.1	(6.6)	60.9	(4.2)	57.4	(2.4)
Uruguay	34.8	(3.6)	25.0	(6.0)	33.7	(4.4)	32.6	(3.4)	49.5	(14.8)	32.5	(4.0)	30.8	(4.7)
Viet Nam	51.0	(3.9)	27.9	(19.2)	70.4	(10.8)	47.2	(4.0)	54.5	(5.7)	51.1	(6.3)	39.4	(8.3)

Notes: Values that are statistically significant are indicated in bold (see Annex A3).
ESCS refers to the *PISA index of economic, social and cultural status*.
1. A socio-economically disadvantaged school is one whose students' mean socio-economic status (ESCS) is statistically significantly below the mean socio-economic status of the country/economy; an average school is one where there is no difference from the country's/economy's mean; and an advantaged school is one whose students' mean socio-economic status is statistically significantly above the country/economy mean.
* See notes at the beginning of this Annex.
StatLink ⟟ http://dx.doi.org/10.1787/888932957460

[Part 1/2]
Index of quality of physical infrastructure and mathematics performance
Table IV.3.14   *Results based on school principals' reports*

| | | Index of quality of physical infrastructure | | | | | | | | | Variability in this index | |
| | | All students | | Bottom quarter | | Second quarter | | Third quarter | | Top quarter | | | |
		Mean index	S.E.	Mean index	S.E.	Mean index	S.E.	Mean index	S.E.	Mean index	S.E.	Standard deviation	S.E.
OECD	Australia	0.17	(0.04)	-1.07	(0.06)	-0.19	(0.04)	0.63	(0.08)	1.31	(0.00)	0.95	(0.02)
	Austria	-0.16	(0.09)	-1.51	(0.15)	-0.50	(0.10)	0.10	(0.16)	1.30	(0.07)	1.07	(0.06)
	Belgium	-0.15	(0.06)	-1.31	(0.09)	-0.52	(0.07)	0.09	(0.09)	1.15	(0.08)	0.96	(0.04)
	Canada	0.32	(0.04)	-0.81	(0.07)	-0.02	(0.04)	0.78	(0.10)	1.31	(0.00)	0.86	(0.03)
	Chile	-0.12	(0.07)	-1.60	(0.16)	-0.32	(0.07)	0.28	(0.09)	1.17	(0.09)	1.10	(0.07)
	Czech Republic	0.45	(0.06)	-0.58	(0.10)	0.22	(0.09)	0.84	(0.10)	1.31	(0.00)	0.78	(0.04)
	Denmark	-0.17	(0.05)	-1.22	(0.06)	-0.40	(0.07)	-0.01	(0.07)	0.96	(0.08)	0.86	(0.04)
	Estonia	0.10	(0.06)	-1.19	(0.08)	-0.25	(0.08)	0.52	(0.11)	1.31	(0.00)	0.99	(0.03)
	Finland	-0.32	(0.07)	-1.52	(0.09)	-0.67	(0.08)	-0.10	(0.09)	1.02	(0.10)	0.99	(0.05)
	France	0.19	(0.07)	-1.00	(0.09)	-0.18	(0.08)	0.66	(0.15)	1.31	(0.00)	0.93	(0.03)
	Germany	-0.03	(0.06)	-1.23	(0.12)	-0.30	(0.06)	0.24	(0.08)	1.18	(0.07)	0.94	(0.05)
	Greece	-0.19	(0.08)	-1.60	(0.16)	-0.49	(0.07)	0.13	(0.08)	1.20	(0.09)	1.09	(0.05)
	Hungary	0.21	(0.07)	-0.87	(0.11)	-0.05	(0.07)	0.44	(0.13)	1.31	(0.06)	0.84	(0.04)
	Iceland	0.34	(0.00)	-0.73	(0.00)	-0.05	(0.01)	0.84	(0.01)	1.31	(0.00)	0.83	(0.00)
	Ireland	-0.03	(0.09)	-1.58	(0.12)	-0.42	(0.16)	0.57	(0.18)	1.31	(0.00)	1.14	(0.06)
	Israel	-0.54	(0.09)	-1.86	(0.12)	-0.91	(0.08)	-0.29	(0.12)	0.90	(0.13)	1.06	(0.05)
	Italy	-0.33	(0.04)	-1.64	(0.05)	-0.66	(0.06)	-0.05	(0.05)	1.04	(0.05)	1.04	(0.03)
	Japan	-0.13	(0.07)	-1.31	(0.10)	-0.42	(0.08)	0.10	(0.08)	1.11	(0.10)	0.94	(0.05)
	Korea	-0.18	(0.08)	-1.34	(0.13)	-0.47	(0.09)	0.02	(0.09)	1.08	(0.11)	0.94	(0.06)
	Luxembourg	-0.49	(0.00)	-1.57	(0.00)	-0.75	(0.00)	-0.27	(0.00)	0.63	(0.00)	0.88	(0.00)
	Mexico	-0.40	(0.04)	-1.73	(0.07)	-0.74	(0.04)	-0.11	(0.04)	0.97	(0.06)	1.06	(0.03)
	Netherlands	-0.29	(0.08)	-1.56	(0.10)	-0.56	(0.10)	0.03	(0.10)	0.95	(0.11)	0.97	(0.05)
	New Zealand	0.03	(0.09)	-1.21	(0.14)	-0.34	(0.10)	0.38	(0.15)	1.31	(0.06)	0.97	(0.05)
	Norway	-0.31	(0.08)	-1.53	(0.11)	-0.66	(0.10)	-0.02	(0.12)	0.99	(0.09)	0.99	(0.05)
	Poland	0.50	(0.07)	-0.61	(0.15)	0.32	(0.07)	0.97	(0.12)	1.31	(0.00)	0.82	(0.07)
	Portugal	-0.26	(0.09)	-1.38	(0.12)	-0.62	(0.14)	-0.02	(0.09)	0.96	(0.13)	0.91	(0.04)
	Slovak Republic	-0.13	(0.07)	-1.40	(0.11)	-0.45	(0.08)	0.15	(0.10)	1.18	(0.08)	1.00	(0.05)
	Slovenia	0.05	(0.01)	-1.11	(0.02)	-0.29	(0.01)	0.31	(0.02)	1.29	(0.02)	0.93	(0.01)
	Spain	0.01	(0.05)	-1.33	(0.12)	-0.28	(0.05)	0.36	(0.09)	1.31	(0.03)	1.03	(0.05)
	Sweden	0.21	(0.08)	-1.14	(0.12)	-0.13	(0.09)	0.83	(0.18)	1.31	(0.00)	1.01	(0.05)
	Switzerland	0.29	(0.05)	-0.83	(0.08)	-0.03	(0.06)	0.73	(0.14)	1.31	(0.00)	0.87	(0.04)
	Turkey	-0.25	(0.07)	-1.51	(0.10)	-0.47	(0.13)	-0.03	(0.06)	1.00	(0.11)	0.97	(0.05)
	United Kingdom	0.04	(0.07)	-1.36	(0.10)	-0.33	(0.11)	0.55	(0.14)	1.31	(0.00)	1.07	(0.04)
	United States	0.46	(0.06)	-0.61	(0.09)	0.16	(0.10)	0.99	(0.12)	1.31	(0.00)	0.80	(0.04)
	OECD average	-0.03	(0.01)	-1.26	(0.02)	-0.35	(0.01)	0.31	(0.02)	1.17	(0.01)	0.96	(0.01)
Partners	Albania	-0.42	(0.07)	-1.64	(0.09)	-0.75	(0.08)	-0.19	(0.09)	0.91	(0.12)	1.00	(0.04)
	Argentina	-0.38	(0.10)	-2.04	(0.16)	-0.77	(0.11)	0.03	(0.16)	1.27	(0.07)	1.25	(0.06)
	Brazil	-0.35	(0.05)	-1.84	(0.08)	-0.77	(0.06)	0.05	(0.08)	1.15	(0.06)	1.16	(0.03)
	Bulgaria	0.19	(0.06)	-1.02	(0.10)	-0.09	(0.07)	0.57	(0.13)	1.31	(0.00)	0.91	(0.04)
	Colombia	-0.78	(0.09)	-2.24	(0.14)	-1.12	(0.11)	-0.41	(0.08)	0.67	(0.12)	1.13	(0.05)
	Costa Rica	-0.71	(0.07)	-2.25	(0.12)	-0.98	(0.07)	-0.34	(0.06)	0.73	(0.13)	1.15	(0.05)
	Croatia	-0.57	(0.07)	-1.72	(0.09)	-0.90	(0.10)	-0.18	(0.08)	0.52	(0.07)	0.89	(0.04)
	Cyprus*	-0.02	(0.00)	-1.12	(0.00)	-0.29	(0.00)	0.22	(0.00)	1.09	(0.00)	0.88	(0.00)
	Hong Kong-China	-0.02	(0.07)	-1.08	(0.11)	-0.30	(0.05)	0.13	(0.10)	1.14	(0.10)	0.85	(0.04)
	Indonesia	-0.52	(0.08)	-1.57	(0.13)	-0.72	(0.10)	-0.32	(0.05)	0.52	(0.14)	0.85	(0.06)
	Jordan	-0.56	(0.09)	-2.08	(0.13)	-0.97	(0.11)	-0.18	(0.11)	0.98	(0.12)	1.18	(0.05)
	Kazakhstan	-0.21	(0.09)	-1.70	(0.14)	-0.66	(0.12)	0.23	(0.18)	1.31	(0.04)	1.17	(0.06)
	Latvia	0.38	(0.06)	-0.61	(0.09)	0.12	(0.10)	0.70	(0.10)	1.31	(0.00)	0.77	(0.04)
	Liechtenstein	0.11	(0.02)	c	c	c	c	c	c	c	c	0.79	(0.01)
	Lithuania	-0.01	(0.06)	-1.16	(0.12)	-0.28	(0.05)	0.28	(0.08)	1.15	(0.08)	0.91	(0.05)
	Macao-China	-0.11	(0.00)	-1.36	(0.00)	-0.46	(0.00)	0.11	(0.00)	1.27	(0.00)	1.00	(0.02)
	Malaysia	0.08	(0.08)	-1.31	(0.11)	-0.29	(0.11)	0.60	(0.16)	1.31	(0.00)	1.04	(0.05)
	Montenegro	-0.07	(0.00)	-1.03	(0.00)	-0.42	(0.00)	0.12	(0.00)	1.05	(0.00)	0.82	(0.00)
	Peru	-0.47	(0.08)	-1.94	(0.10)	-0.85	(0.10)	-0.14	(0.09)	1.06	(0.11)	1.15	(0.05)
	Qatar	0.46	(0.00)	-0.91	(0.00)	0.14	(0.01)	1.31	(0.00)	1.31	(0.00)	0.98	(0.00)
	Romania	0.18	(0.05)	-0.65	(0.08)	-0.11	(0.05)	0.33	(0.06)	1.15	(0.09)	0.71	(0.03)
	Russian Federation	0.17	(0.07)	-1.07	(0.12)	-0.13	(0.08)	0.56	(0.15)	1.31	(0.00)	0.95	(0.05)
	Serbia	-0.34	(0.09)	-1.47	(0.12)	-0.65	(0.09)	-0.16	(0.10)	0.90	(0.14)	0.94	(0.06)
	Shanghai-China	-0.19	(0.09)	-1.67	(0.11)	-0.53	(0.10)	0.18	(0.14)	1.28	(0.08)	1.13	(0.04)
	Singapore	0.40	(0.01)	-0.65	(0.01)	0.08	(0.01)	0.88	(0.02)	1.31	(0.00)	0.80	(0.00)
	Chinese Taipei	0.05	(0.08)	-1.34	(0.14)	-0.29	(0.11)	0.53	(0.17)	1.31	(0.00)	1.04	(0.06)
	Thailand	-0.87	(0.08)	-2.34	(0.12)	-1.23	(0.09)	-0.49	(0.10)	0.56	(0.12)	1.13	(0.05)
	Tunisia	-1.25	(0.08)	-2.35	(0.09)	-1.53	(0.07)	-1.08	(0.11)	-0.04	(0.15)	0.93	(0.06)
	United Arab Emirates	0.14	(0.05)	-1.53	(0.10)	-0.15	(0.09)	0.91	(0.08)	1.31	(0.00)	1.18	(0.04)
	Uruguay	-0.41	(0.08)	-2.04	(0.16)	-0.81	(0.10)	0.08	(0.12)	1.15	(0.08)	1.24	(0.05)
	Viet Nam	-0.40	(0.09)	-1.70	(0.15)	-0.64	(0.08)	-0.11	(0.11)	0.84	(0.12)	1.01	(0.06)

Note: Values that are statistically significant are indicated in bold (see Annex A3).
* See notes at the beginning of this Annex.
StatLink ᐅ http://dx.doi.org/10.1787/888932957460

[Part 2/2]
Index of quality of physical infrastructure and mathematics performance

Table IV.3.14   *Results based on school principals' reports*

		Performance on the mathematics scale by national quarters of this index								Change in the mathematics score per unit of this index		Increased likelihood of students in the bottom quarter of this index scoring in the bottom quarter of the national mathematics performance distribution		Explained variance in student performance (r-squared x 100)	
		Bottom quarter		Second quarter		Third quarter		Top quarter							
		Mean score	S.E.	Mean score	S.E.	Mean score	S.E.	Mean score	S.E.	Score dif.	S.E.	Ratio	S.E.	%	S.E.
OECD	Australia	**494**	(4.6)	498	(4.7)	511	(3.7)	**517**	(3.5)	**9.4**	(2.60)	**1.2**	(0.08)	0.8	(0.47)
	Austria	517	(9.7)	491	(10.9)	511	(8.7)	509	(9.5)	1.5	(5.15)	0.9	(0.20)	0.0	(0.33)
	Belgium	**505**	(8.5)	513	(9.1)	514	(9.1)	**530**	(7.9)	8.3	(5.30)	1.1	(0.17)	0.6	(0.80)
	Canada	520	(4.5)	515	(3.8)	518	(3.5)	519	(3.3)	0.4	(2.37)	0.9	(0.07)	0.0	(0.06)
	Chile	**394**	(5.1)	415	(7.1)	430	(6.8)	**451**	(8.3)	**17.7**	(3.01)	**1.7**	(0.20)	5.8	(1.78)
	Czech Republic	507	(9.0)	492	(7.4)	500	(7.6)	496	(8.2)	-6.1	(5.88)	0.9	(0.15)	0.3	(0.44)
	Denmark	497	(5.8)	499	(4.8)	506	(5.8)	502	(5.4)	1.5	(3.37)	1.1	(0.14)	0.0	(0.15)
	Estonia	527	(4.2)	524	(5.1)	513	(4.9)	522	(4.0)	-4.1	(1.92)	0.9	(0.09)	0.3	(0.25)
	Finland	517	(4.1)	518	(4.2)	520	(4.4)	520	(4.0)	0.5	(2.06)	1.0	(0.08)	0.0	(0.05)
	France	516	(9.2)	488	(9.7)	482	(9.2)	500	(8.3)	-7.4	(5.97)	**0.7**	(0.15)	0.5	(0.82)
	Germany	518	(7.6)	515	(9.8)	512	(8.2)	510	(9.6)	-3.9	(5.11)	0.8	(0.13)	0.1	(0.43)
	Greece	440	(7.3)	456	(5.9)	464	(6.2)	453	(8.1)	4.9	(3.38)	1.3	(0.17)	0.4	(0.50)
	Hungary	472	(10.3)	474	(10.3)	497	(13.7)	469	(10.6)	0.7	(6.69)	1.1	(0.22)	0.0	(0.28)
	Iceland	500	(3.1)	490	(4.0)	487	(3.4)	493	(4.9)	-3.1	(2.14)	**0.8**	(0.06)	0.1	(0.11)
	Ireland	502	(5.0)	502	(6.9)	499	(7.4)	507	(6.6)	0.1	(2.69)	1.0	(0.12)	0.0	(0.10)
	Israel	448	(11.8)	482	(11.9)	467	(11.3)	477	(11.8)	5.6	(6.44)	1.3	(0.25)	0.3	(0.75)
	Italy	**481**	(5.1)	489	(5.3)	483	(5.5)	**496**	(5.1)	5.4	(2.57)	1.1	(0.11)	0.4	(0.35)
	Japan	538	(9.7)	532	(10.2)	526	(8.2)	549	(7.5)	4.7	(4.95)	1.0	(0.19)	0.2	(0.53)
	Korea	557	(9.1)	554	(9.3)	550	(9.1)	555	(9.9)	-1.9	(5.21)	1.0	(0.14)	0.0	(0.28)
	Luxembourg	502	(2.5)	477	(2.1)	471	(2.9)	510	(2.6)	3.4	(1.10)	**0.8**	(0.04)	0.1	(0.06)
	Mexico	**394**	(2.87)	407	(2.86)	421	(2.55)	**432**	(3.8)	**13.6**	(1.84)	**1.6**	(0.10)	3.8	(0.98)
	Netherlands	528	(12.3)	512	(12.8)	512	(10.1)	526	(12.9)	2.3	(6.83)	0.9	(0.21)	0.1	(0.56)
	New Zealand	502	(7.7)	508	(6.0)	495	(8.6)	503	(7.9)	-1.6	(4.22)	1.0	(0.14)	0.0	(0.19)
	Norway	493	(6.2)	491	(5.3)	486	(6.4)	496	(5.5)	0.3	(2.79)	1.0	(0.12)	0.0	(0.08)
	Poland	525	(8.8)	519	(6.4)	512	(4.8)	513	(5.9)	-8.4	(4.69)	0.9	(0.11)	0.6	(0.66)
	Portugal	**462**	(7.7)	489	(7.7)	484	(9.7)	**512**	(6.9)	**19.2**	(4.19)	**1.6**	(0.21)	3.4	(1.48)
	Slovak Republic	479	(8.4)	483	(9.3)	488	(10.3)	477	(10.8)	-1.5	(5.29)	1.0	(0.14)	0.0	(0.24)
	Slovenia	**512**	(3.7)	507	(4.1)	505	(3.1)	**496**	(2.4)	-2.9	(1.40)	1.0	(0.10)	0.1	(0.09)
	Spain	**474**	(3.6)	480	(4.6)	489	(4.0)	**495**	(4.4)	7.8	(2.06)	**1.2**	(0.09)	0.8	(0.41)
	Sweden	472	(6.3)	479	(5.1)	477	(5.1)	484	(5.8)	4.2	(3.33)	1.1	(0.14)	0.2	(0.35)
	Switzerland	535	(7.4)	523	(8.6)	536	(7.7)	534	(5.2)	0.4	(3.64)	0.9	(0.11)	0.0	(0.11)
	Turkey	**414**	(7.4)	442	(9.3)	457	(9.9)	**479**	(13.7)	**22.3**	(5.83)	**1.6**	(0.20)	5.7	(2.76)
	United Kingdom	**497**	(5.7)	501	(5.6)	502	(8.0)	481	(10.0)	-4.7	(4.24)	0.9	(0.12)	0.3	(0.57)
	United States	**467**	(7.1)	486	(5.9)	485	(6.8)	491	(6.9)	**11.4**	(4.62)	1.3	(0.17)	1.0	(0.87)
	OECD average	**491**	(1.2)	493	(1.3)	494	(1.3)	**500**	(1.3)	**2.9**	(0.72)	**1.1**	(0.03)	0.8	(0.13)
Partners	Albania	394	(4.4)	391	(4.7)	395	(4.6)	396	(4.6)	1.7	(2.15)	1.0	(0.09)	0.0	(0.11)
	Argentina	355	(7.5)	393	(7.4)	393	(7.0)	412	(8.3)	**16.6**	(3.02)	**2.0**	(0.27)	7.4	(2.63)
	Brazil	**369**	(3.6)	381	(3.2)	396	(6.5)	**419**	(4.9)	**16.4**	(2.09)	**1.4**	(0.11)	6.0	(1.38)
	Bulgaria	**464**	(9.2)	428	(9.2)	438	(8.2)	**425**	(9.1)	**-14.6**	(5.80)	**0.7**	(0.12)	2.0	(1.59)
	Colombia	**363**	(7.0)	372	(5.8)	379	(5.6)	**392**	(6.5)	**11.0**	(2.84)	1.3	(0.17)	2.8	(1.44)
	Costa Rica	**385**	(6.8)	398	(6.1)	413	(6.5)	**433**	(7.5)	**16.7**	(3.51)	**1.7**	(0.23)	7.8	(3.13)
	Croatia	472	(8.2)	470	(8.9)	465	(9.1)	477	(9.1)	0.5	(4.81)	0.9	(0.14)	0.0	(0.16)
	Cyprus*	**442**	(2.5)	453	(2.7)	447	(2.9)	**424**	(2.6)	-6.8	(1.24)	1.0	(0.07)	0.4	(0.15)
	Hong Kong-China	570	(8.6)	549	(10.4)	557	(7.9)	569	(9.1)	0.8	(5.81)	0.8	(0.13)	0.0	(0.25)
	Indonesia	**358**	(6.8)	366	(6.7)	378	(7.2)	**398**	(10.0)	**21.4**	(5.91)	1.3	(0.20)	6.4	(3.34)
	Jordan	380	(7.4)	383	(6.3)	383	(8.0)	397	(7.2)	4.6	(3.09)	1.1	(0.16)	0.5	(0.64)
	Kazakhstan	437	(6.5)	432	(7.9)	425	(7.5)	435	(7.1)	-0.3	(2.99)	0.9	(0.13)	0.0	(0.22)
	Latvia	487	(7.8)	491	(5.7)	493	(5.1)	489	(5.9)	-1.1	(5.10)	1.1	(0.16)	0.0	(0.23)
	Liechtenstein	c	c	c	c	c	c	c	c	-51.6	(5.06)	**0.5**	(0.23)	19.4	(3.23)
	Lithuania	**491**	(6.5)	481	(6.4)	475	(5.6)	**469**	(6.8)	-8.6	(3.83)	0.8	(0.12)	0.8	(0.71)
	Macao-China	**533**	(2.4)	548	(2.0)	521	(2.4)	**550**	(1.9)	6.8	(0.98)	1.1	(0.05)	0.5	(0.15)
	Malaysia	415	(6.5)	426	(7.5)	425	(8.0)	416	(7.0)	-0.0	(3.22)	1.1	(0.14)	0.0	(0.15)
	Montenegro	**401**	(2.5)	429	(3.4)	401	(2.7)	**408**	(2.4)	2.0	(1.16)	**1.2**	(0.07)	0.0	(0.05)
	Peru	**341**	(6.3)	353	(6.4)	374	(9.0)	**403**	(9.6)	**18.6**	(3.74)	**1.6**	(0.22)	6.4	(2.31)
	Qatar	**387**	(1.5)	389	(1.5)	365	(2.0)	**365**	(1.8)	**-10.3**	(0.83)	0.9	(0.04)	1.0	(0.16)
	Romania	443	(7.6)	440	(7.2)	448	(8.4)	448	(7.5)	4.5	(5.17)	1.0	(0.15)	0.2	(0.43)
	Russian Federation	484	(5.6)	489	(5.3)	474	(5.5)	481	(7.5)	-2.6	(3.66)	1.0	(0.09)	0.1	(0.26)
	Serbia	442	(9.0)	449	(8.9)	457	(10.2)	446	(9.3)	1.0	(5.30)	1.1	(0.20)	0.0	(0.32)
	Shanghai-China	606	(9.1)	612	(9.4)	604	(10.1)	629	(11.3)	7.2	(5.19)	1.0	(0.18)	0.7	(1.04)
	Singapore	**570**	(2.6)	566	(3.0)	577	(3.6)	**581**	(4.2)	**7.5**	(1.80)	1.0	(0.06)	0.3	(0.17)
	Chinese Taipei	556	(11.2)	552	(11.8)	574	(10.4)	554	(9.5)	2.5	(5.81)	1.1	(0.16)	0.1	(0.36)
	Thailand	422	(8.0)	430	(8.0)	434	(7.3)	421	(6.5)	-0.4	(3.42)	1.0	(0.14)	0.0	(0.21)
	Tunisia	389	(6.6)	393	(7.7)	379	(7.1)	392	(11.4)	-1.6	(4.71)	0.8	(0.15)	0.0	(0.42)
	United Arab Emirates	**408**	(4.2)	436	(5.2)	447	(4.4)	**449**	(5.8)	**14.6**	(2.15)	**1.5**	(0.15)	3.7	(1.08)
	Uruguay	**378**	(5.8)	383	(9.3)	434	(8.2)	**442**	(8.1)	**21.8**	(2.97)	**1.6**	(0.17)	9.3	(2.32)
	Viet Nam	500	(13.8)	510	(7.9)	523	(9.7)	512	(10.6)	7.0	(6.39)	1.4	(0.28)	0.7	(1.23)

Note: Values that are statistically significant are indicated in bold (see Annex A3).
* See notes at the beginning of this Annex.
StatLink ⌐⌐⌐ http://dx.doi.org/10.1787/888932957460

[Part 1/2]
Index of quality of physical infrastructure, by school features

Table IV.3.15 *Results based on school principals' reports*

| | Index of quality of physical infrastructure | | | | | | | | | | | | | |
| | Bottom quarter of ESCS | | Second quarter of ESCS | | Third quarter of ESCS | | Top quarter of ESCS | | Socio-economically disadvantaged schools[1] | | Socio-economically average schools[1] | | Socio-economically advantaged schools[1] | |
	Mean index	S.E.	Mean index	S.E.	Mean index	S.E.	Mean index	S.E.	Mean index	S.E.	Mean index	S.E.	Mean index	S.E.
Australia	**0.02**	(0.05)	0.10	(0.04)	0.21	(0.04)	**0.35**	(0.04)	**0.02**	(0.07)	0.05	(0.05)	**0.53**	(0.06)
Austria	-0.14	(0.11)	-0.08	(0.10)	-0.19	(0.11)	-0.21	(0.10)	-0.19	(0.19)	-0.07	(0.14)	-0.26	(0.11)
Belgium	-0.16	(0.07)	-0.19	(0.07)	-0.13	(0.07)	-0.12	(0.08)	-0.17	(0.11)	-0.24	(0.09)	-0.03	(0.13)
Canada	0.31	(0.05)	0.33	(0.04)	0.29	(0.05)	0.33	(0.05)	0.25	(0.09)	0.36	(0.06)	0.29	(0.08)
Chile	**-0.46**	(0.11)	-0.26	(0.09)	-0.08	(0.09)	**0.34**	(0.09)	**-0.51**	(0.11)	-0.18	(0.18)	**0.41**	(0.12)
Czech Republic	0.48	(0.07)	0.47	(0.08)	0.48	(0.06)	0.36	(0.07)	0.39	(0.16)	0.53	(0.07)	0.27	(0.12)
Denmark	-0.15	(0.06)	-0.17	(0.06)	-0.16	(0.06)	-0.19	(0.07)	-0.22	(0.11)	-0.11	(0.07)	-0.26	(0.12)
Estonia	**0.24**	(0.08)	0.11	(0.07)	0.04	(0.06)	**0.00**	(0.05)	0.15	(0.16)	0.18	(0.07)	-0.15	(0.08)
Finland	**-0.26**	(0.08)	-0.32	(0.08)	-0.33	(0.07)	**-0.35**	(0.07)	-0.01	(0.18)	-0.37	(0.08)	-0.39	(0.11)
France	0.27	(0.07)	0.21	(0.07)	0.14	(0.07)	0.15	(0.10)	0.40	(0.11)	0.07	(0.10)	0.22	(0.14)
Germany	0.02	(0.06)	0.00	(0.07)	0.00	(0.08)	-0.02	(0.09)	0.01	(0.11)	0.03	(0.09)	-0.12	(0.15)
Greece	**-0.31**	(0.11)	-0.24	(0.10)	-0.16	(0.09)	-0.04	(0.08)	**-0.39**	(0.19)	-0.26	(0.12)	**0.14**	(0.14)
Hungary	0.24	(0.09)	0.21	(0.08)	0.19	(0.08)	0.19	(0.09)	0.23	(0.12)	0.25	(0.10)	0.13	(0.11)
Iceland	**0.37**	(0.03)	0.33	(0.03)	0.36	(0.03)	**0.29**	(0.03)	**0.06**	(0.01)	0.49	(0.01)	**0.24**	(0.00)
Ireland	-0.06	(0.10)	-0.06	(0.10)	-0.04	(0.11)	0.03	(0.11)	0.15	(0.20)	-0.12	(0.12)	0.04	(0.22)
Israel	-0.56	(0.12)	-0.54	(0.11)	-0.48	(0.10)	-0.53	(0.11)	-0.67	(0.21)	-0.36	(0.14)	-0.60	(0.13)
Italy	**-0.37**	(0.06)	-0.34	(0.04)	-0.31	(0.04)	-0.30	(0.05)	-0.38	(0.09)	-0.28	(0.07)	-0.34	(0.07)
Japan	**-0.22**	(0.08)	-0.13	(0.07)	-0.12	(0.07)	**-0.04**	(0.08)	**-0.23**	(0.12)	-0.25	(0.09)	**0.16**	(0.12)
Korea	-0.13	(0.08)	-0.16	(0.08)	-0.21	(0.09)	-0.21	(0.10)	-0.17	(0.12)	-0.10	(0.10)	-0.35	(0.19)
Luxembourg	**-0.61**	(0.02)	-0.52	(0.02)	-0.45	(0.02)	**-0.39**	(0.02)	**-0.59**	(0.00)	-0.44	(0.00)	**-0.39**	(0.00)
Mexico	**-0.76**	(0.05)	-0.48	(0.05)	-0.34	(0.05)	**-0.02**	(0.06)	**-0.80**	(0.06)	-0.37	(0.06)	0.02	(0.08)
Netherlands	-0.30	(0.09)	-0.31	(0.08)	-0.25	(0.09)	-0.26	(0.11)	-0.28	(0.13)	-0.35	(0.11)	-0.17	(0.17)
New Zealand	0.10	(0.10)	0.02	(0.10)	-0.04	(0.09)	0.05	(0.12)	0.34	(0.16)	-0.11	(0.11)	0.11	(0.16)
Norway	-0.31	(0.10)	-0.35	(0.08)	-0.30	(0.08)	-0.26	(0.09)	-0.15	(0.24)	-0.38	(0.09)	-0.10	(0.21)
Poland	0.50	(0.08)	0.54	(0.07)	0.52	(0.08)	0.42	(0.10)	0.58	(0.12)	0.53	(0.09)	0.33	(0.18)
Portugal	**-0.50**	(0.10)	-0.30	(0.10)	-0.20	(0.09)	**-0.05**	(0.11)	**-0.57**	(0.15)	-0.23	(0.11)	**0.15**	(0.17)
Slovak Republic	-0.09	(0.08)	-0.07	(0.08)	-0.19	(0.07)	-0.19	(0.10)	-0.14	(0.11)	-0.05	(0.12)	-0.27	(0.16)
Slovenia	0.09	(0.03)	0.08	(0.03)	-0.01	(0.04)	0.06	(0.03)	0.19	(0.02)	0.01	(0.03)	-0.01	(0.01)
Spain	**-0.13**	(0.07)	-0.02	(0.06)	0.04	(0.06)	**0.17**	(0.06)	**-0.19**	(0.11)	-0.09	(0.08)	**0.39**	(0.08)
Sweden	**0.14**	(0.10)	0.18	(0.09)	0.22	(0.08)	**0.32**	(0.08)	**-0.01**	(0.22)	0.13	(0.10)	**0.60**	(0.14)
Switzerland	0.35	(0.06)	0.29	(0.06)	0.25	(0.06)	0.28	(0.07)	0.31	(0.09)	0.25	(0.09)	0.34	(0.10)
Turkey	**-0.47**	(0.09)	-0.30	(0.08)	-0.30	(0.08)	0.06	(0.09)	**-0.57**	(0.14)	-0.29	(0.12)	**0.21**	(0.12)
United Kingdom	0.12	(0.08)	0.07	(0.09)	-0.07	(0.08)	0.01	(0.09)	**0.57**	(0.11)	-0.22	(0.10)	**0.12**	(0.15)
United States	0.33	(0.09)	0.47	(0.07)	0.54	(0.06)	0.50	(0.08)	**0.10**	(0.14)	0.60	(0.09)	**0.57**	(0.11)
OECD average	**-0.07**	(0.01)	-0.04	(0.01)	-0.03	(0.01)	**0.02**	(0.01)	**-0.07**	(0.02)	-0.04	(0.02)	**0.05**	(0.02)
Albania	m	m	m	m	m	m	m	m	m	m	m	m	m	m
Argentina	**-0.77**	(0.12)	-0.50	(0.11)	-0.27	(0.12)	**0.06**	(0.12)	**-0.90**	(0.15)	-0.54	(0.18)	**0.35**	(0.14)
Brazil	**-0.70**	(0.07)	-0.55	(0.06)	-0.28	(0.07)	**0.12**	(0.06)	**-0.83**	(0.09)	-0.45	(0.08)	**0.46**	(0.10)
Bulgaria	0.32	(0.07)	0.25	(0.06)	0.17	(0.06)	0.02	(0.10)	0.41	(0.09)	0.15	(0.09)	0.02	(0.13)
Colombia	**-1.00**	(0.13)	-0.86	(0.08)	-0.76	(0.10)	**-0.48**	(0.14)	**-1.12**	(0.18)	-0.71	(0.11)	**-0.54**	(0.20)
Costa Rica	**-1.01**	(0.10)	-0.88	(0.08)	-0.72	(0.08)	**-0.23**	(0.11)	**-1.09**	(0.15)	-0.84	(0.10)	0.03	(0.18)
Croatia	**-0.49**	(0.06)	-0.55	(0.08)	-0.58	(0.08)	**-0.66**	(0.09)	**-0.51**	(0.11)	-0.53	(0.10)	-0.74	(0.16)
Cyprus*	-0.04	(0.02)	-0.02	(0.02)	0.02	(0.02)	-0.06	(0.02)	**-0.13**	(0.00)	0.10	(0.00)	-0.08	(0.00)
Hong Kong-China	-0.07	(0.08)	-0.07	(0.08)	0.00	(0.07)	0.03	(0.09)	-0.17	(0.10)	0.01	(0.11)	0.12	(0.14)
Indonesia	**-0.71**	(0.09)	-0.65	(0.08)	-0.52	(0.09)	**-0.21**	(0.15)	**-0.76**	(0.10)	-0.58	(0.13)	**-0.10**	(0.15)
Jordan	**-0.68**	(0.11)	-0.59	(0.10)	-0.58	(0.09)	**-0.39**	(0.11)	**-0.82**	(0.19)	-0.56	(0.12)	-0.28	(0.21)
Kazakhstan	-0.28	(0.10)	-0.15	(0.10)	-0.15	(0.10)	-0.25	(0.11)	-0.39	(0.18)	-0.04	(0.13)	-0.31	(0.18)
Latvia	**0.50**	(0.06)	0.36	(0.07)	0.34	(0.07)	**0.29**	(0.09)	**0.60**	(0.11)	0.37	(0.08)	**0.20**	(0.15)
Liechtenstein	0.31	(0.10)	-0.05	(0.09)	0.01	(0.11)	0.11	(0.09)	c	c	0.31	(0.03)	c	c
Lithuania	**0.11**	(0.07)	0.04	(0.06)	-0.06	(0.07)	**-0.12**	(0.07)	**0.22**	(0.11)	0.02	(0.08)	**-0.28**	(0.12)
Macao-China	**-0.29**	(0.02)	-0.23	(0.02)	-0.10	(0.02)	**0.18**	(0.02)	**-0.27**	(0.00)	-0.51	(0.00)	**0.38**	(0.00)
Malaysia	0.10	(0.10)	0.12	(0.09)	0.03	(0.09)	0.06	(0.09)	0.26	(0.15)	-0.06	(0.14)	0.10	(0.14)
Montenegro	-0.11	(0.02)	-0.05	(0.02)	-0.05	(0.03)	-0.06	(0.02)	**-0.21**	(0.01)	-0.02	(0.00)	**0.04**	(0.00)
Peru	**-0.87**	(0.11)	-0.60	(0.09)	-0.35	(0.09)	**-0.05**	(0.11)	**-0.87**	(0.12)	-0.58	(0.12)	**0.07**	(0.12)
Qatar	0.47	(0.01)	0.41	(0.02)	0.41	(0.02)	0.57	(0.02)	0.36	(0.00)	0.37	(0.00)	0.58	(0.00)
Romania	0.11	(0.07)	0.20	(0.06)	0.18	(0.05)	0.23	(0.07)	0.02	(0.09)	0.28	(0.09)	0.20	(0.10)
Russian Federation	0.19	(0.07)	0.21	(0.08)	0.12	(0.08)	0.15	(0.10)	0.13	(0.11)	0.29	(0.09)	-0.03	(0.16)
Serbia	**-0.32**	(0.10)	-0.32	(0.10)	-0.35	(0.10)	-0.36	(0.09)	**-0.52**	(0.16)	-0.17	(0.12)	-0.42	(0.14)
Shanghai-China	-0.25	(0.12)	-0.17	(0.10)	-0.17	(0.10)	-0.16	(0.11)	-0.27	(0.19)	-0.31	(0.16)	0.02	(0.16)
Singapore	**0.36**	(0.02)	0.36	(0.02)	0.38	(0.02)	**0.52**	(0.03)	**0.36**	(0.00)	0.34	(0.00)	**0.61**	(0.03)
Chinese Taipei	0.01	(0.10)	0.01	(0.09)	0.07	(0.09)	0.11	(0.09)	-0.04	(0.16)	-0.04	(0.14)	0.29	(0.14)
Thailand	**-1.01**	(0.09)	-0.94	(0.09)	-0.81	(0.09)	**-0.74**	(0.10)	**-1.11**	(0.12)	-0.76	(0.16)	**-0.69**	(0.16)
Tunisia	-1.24	(0.11)	-1.30	(0.09)	-1.28	(0.08)	-1.16	(0.09)	-1.26	(0.16)	-1.35	(0.12)	-1.08	(0.12)
United Arab Emirates	**-0.11**	(0.08)	0.12	(0.06)	0.23	(0.05)	**0.30**	(0.06)	**-0.17**	(0.11)	-0.01	(0.08)	**0.52**	(0.09)
Uruguay	**-0.76**	(0.13)	-0.54	(0.11)	-0.43	(0.09)	**0.12**	(0.09)	**-0.88**	(0.17)	-0.39	(0.13)	**0.43**	(0.13)
Viet Nam	**-0.61**	(0.11)	-0.45	(0.10)	-0.34	(0.11)	**-0.21**	(0.12)	**-0.69**	(0.13)	-0.22	(0.12)	**-0.22**	(0.20)

Notes: Values that are statistically significant are indicated in bold (see Annex A3).
ESCS refers to the *PISA index of economic, social and cultural status.*
1. A socio-economically disadvantaged school is one whose students' mean socio-economic status (ESCS) is statistically significantly below the mean socio-economic status of the country/economy; an average school is one where there is no difference from the country's/economy's mean; and an advantaged school is one whose students' mean socio-economic status is statistically significantly above the country/economy mean.
* See notes at the beginning of this Annex.
StatLink ᴍᔕ᷍ http://dx.doi.org/10.1787/888932957460

[Part 2/2]
Index of quality of physical infrastructure, by school features
Table IV.3.15   *Results based on school principals' reports*

| | Index of quality of physical infrastructure | | | | | | | | | | | | |
| | Public schools | | Private schools | | Lower secondary education (ISCED 2) | | Upper secondary education (ISCED 3) | | Schools located in a village, hamlet or rural area (fewer than 3 000 people) | | Schools located in a small town or town (3 000 to about 100 000 people) | | Schools located in a city or a large city (over 100 000 people) | |
	Mean index	S.E.	Mean index	S.E.	Mean index	S.E.	Mean index	S.E.	Mean index	S.E.	Mean index	S.E.	Mean index	S.E.
Australia	**-0.08**	(0.05)	**0.53**	(0.05)	**0.14**	(0.04)	**0.29**	(0.06)	-0.21	(0.14)	-0.01	(0.07)	**0.28**	(0.04)
Austria	-0.16	(0.10)	-0.13	(0.25)	-0.07	(0.15)	-0.16	(0.09)	0.30	(0.25)	-0.01	(0.12)	**-0.54**	(0.16)
Belgium	-0.09	(0.12)	-0.21	(0.08)	**-0.35**	(0.10)	**-0.12**	(0.07)	0.25	(0.41)	-0.13	(0.07)	-0.27	(0.13)
Canada	0.30	(0.04)	0.45	(0.11)	0.37	(0.05)	0.31	(0.05)	0.52	(0.12)	0.35	(0.07)	0.26	(0.06)
Chile	**-0.65**	(0.12)	**0.27**	(0.09)	-0.47	(0.19)	-0.10	(0.08)	0.00	(0.39)	-0.33	(0.12)	**0.05**	(0.10)
Czech Republic	0.45	(0.06)	0.41	(0.19)	0.40	(0.08)	0.51	(0.07)	0.43	(0.27)	0.39	(0.07)	0.59	(0.09)
Denmark	-0.23	(0.05)	0.03	(0.13)	-0.17	(0.05)	c	c	0.05	(0.11)	-0.16	(0.07)	**-0.51**	(0.14)
Estonia	**0.06**	(0.06)	**1.10**	(0.16)	0.09	(0.06)	0.23	(0.21)	**0.46**	(0.13)	-0.07	(0.08)	0.05	(0.10)
Finland	**-0.34**	(0.07)	**0.33**	(0.23)	-0.32	(0.07)	c	c	-0.03	(0.21)	-0.37	(0.09)	-0.26	(0.08)
France	0.20	(0.07)	0.16	(0.19)	0.37	(0.10)	0.12	(0.09)	0.41	(0.28)	0.19	(0.08)	0.14	(0.13)
Germany	-0.05	(0.06)	0.28	(0.23)	-0.03	(0.06)	-0.04	(0.28)	c	c	0.09	(0.07)	**-0.31**	(0.11)
Greece	-0.23	(0.08)	c	c	-0.08	(0.26)	-0.19	(0.08)	-0.18	(0.35)	-0.37	(0.10)	**0.19**	(0.13)
Hungary	0.20	(0.07)	0.24	(0.20)	0.13	(0.15)	0.22	(0.07)	0.64	(0.30)	0.18	(0.10)	0.21	(0.10)
Iceland	0.35	(0.00)	c	c	0.34	(0.00)	c	c	**0.11**	(0.02)	0.39	(0.01)	0.41	(0.01)
Ireland	-0.04	(0.16)	-0.05	(0.12)	-0.04	(0.09)	-0.02	(0.10)	0.12	(0.21)	-0.28	(0.13)	0.28	(0.21)
Israel	-0.54	(0.09)	c	c	-0.50	(0.14)	-0.54	(0.10)	-0.57	(0.13)	-0.60	(0.15)	-0.45	(0.17)
Italy	**-0.38**	(0.04)	**0.52**	(0.14)	**-0.69**	(0.13)	**-0.32**	(0.04)	0.01	(0.32)	-0.36	(0.05)	-0.30	(0.08)
Japan	**-0.30**	(0.08)	**0.26**	(0.11)	c	c	-0.13	(0.07)	c	c	-0.33	(0.12)	-0.06	(0.08)
Korea	-0.21	(0.09)	-0.13	(0.12)	-0.18	(0.23)	-0.18	(0.08)	c	c	-0.11	(0.17)	-0.19	(0.09)
Luxembourg	**-0.53**	(0.00)	**-0.28**	(0.00)	**-0.47**	(0.00)	**-0.53**	(0.00)	c	c	-0.49	(0.00)	c	c
Mexico	**-0.54**	(0.04)	**0.59**	(0.09)	**-0.65**	(0.06)	**-0.26**	(0.05)	**-0.91**	(0.07)	-0.50	(0.06)	**-0.12**	(0.06)
Netherlands	-0.15	(0.15)	-0.33	(0.11)	-0.31	(0.08)	-0.22	(0.13)	c	c	-0.23	(0.09)	-0.44	(0.15)
New Zealand	**-0.04**	(0.09)	**1.09**	(0.12)	0.03	(0.10)	0.03	(0.09)	0.47	(0.17)	0.16	(0.16)	-0.10	(0.11)
Norway	-0.32	(0.08)	c	c	-0.31	(0.08)	c	c	**-0.65**	(0.16)	-0.23	(0.11)	-0.27	(0.19)
Poland	0.50	(0.07)	0.44	(0.17)	0.50	(0.07)	c	c	0.57	(0.10)	0.45	(0.11)	0.48	(0.16)
Portugal	**-0.35**	(0.10)	**0.47**	(0.14)	**-0.48**	(0.09)	**-0.09**	(0.11)	-0.19	(0.20)	-0.35	(0.11)	-0.02	(0.15)
Slovak Republic	-0.11	(0.07)	-0.39	(0.20)	0.06	(0.09)	**-0.29**	(0.10)	-0.06	(0.15)	-0.07	(0.08)	**-0.55**	(0.20)
Slovenia	**0.04**	(0.01)	**0.46**	(0.03)	-0.13	(0.22)	0.06	(0.01)	**-0.72**	(0.34)	0.17	(0.01)	**-0.10**	(0.03)
Spain	**-0.25**	(0.07)	**0.54**	(0.07)	0.01	(0.05)	c	c	-0.05	(0.12)	-0.06	(0.08)	0.14	(0.08)
Sweden	0.16	(0.08)	0.52	(0.18)	0.20	(0.08)	0.61	(0.24)	0.29	(0.16)	0.18	(0.09)	0.23	(0.19)
Switzerland	0.28	(0.06)	0.56	(0.17)	**0.36**	(0.06)	0.06	(0.12)	**0.65**	(0.15)	0.30	(0.06)	0.10	(0.13)
Turkey	-0.26	(0.07)	c	c	-0.66	(0.33)	-0.24	(0.07)	0.09	(0.42)	-0.21	(0.10)	-0.30	(0.10)
United Kingdom	-0.04	(0.08)	0.13	(0.12)	c	c	0.04	(0.07)	-0.34	(0.22)	0.03	(0.10)	0.17	(0.12)
United States	0.46	(0.07)	0.55	(0.24)	0.43	(0.12)	0.46	(0.06)	0.43	(0.25)	0.60	(0.09)	**0.27**	(0.10)
OECD average	**-0.09**	(0.01)	**0.29**	(0.03)	**-0.08**	(0.02)	**-0.02**	(0.02)	**0.07**	(0.04)	-0.05	(0.02)	-0.03	(0.02)
Albania	**-0.57**	(0.07)	**1.02**	(0.24)	-0.51	(0.09)	-0.35	(0.10)	-0.39	(0.12)	**-0.65**	(0.12)	-0.15	(0.14)
Argentina	**-0.74**	(0.13)	**0.30**	(0.14)	**-0.70**	(0.14)	**-0.19**	(0.11)	**-1.06**	(0.25)	-0.36	(0.14)	-0.24	(0.14)
Brazil	**-0.60**	(0.05)	**0.76**	(0.12)	**-0.55**	(0.08)	**-0.30**	(0.06)	-0.46	(0.23)	-0.64	(0.08)	**-0.06**	(0.08)
Bulgaria	0.19	(0.06)	c	c	0.21	(0.15)	0.19	(0.06)	0.29	(0.34)	0.20	(0.06)	0.17	(0.11)
Colombia	**-0.95**	(0.10)	**0.20**	(0.31)	**-0.87**	(0.10)	-0.71	(0.09)	-1.38	(0.19)	-0.98	(0.19)	**-0.52**	(0.10)
Costa Rica	**-0.93**	(0.07)	**0.61**	(0.18)	**-0.81**	(0.07)	-0.56	(0.09)	-0.89	(0.20)	-0.67	(0.08)	-0.62	(0.22)
Croatia	**-0.56**	(0.07)	c	c	c	c	-0.57	(0.07)	c	c	-0.47	(0.07)	**-0.76**	(0.13)
Cyprus*	**-0.09**	(0.00)	**0.37**	(0.00)	**-0.47**	(0.03)	**0.00**	(0.00)	**0.14**	(0.01)	-0.07	(0.00)	**0.05**	(0.00)
Hong Kong-China	0.31	(0.29)	-0.05	(0.07)	-0.04	(0.07)	-0.02	(0.07)	c	c	c	c	-0.02	(0.07)
Indonesia	**-0.65**	(0.11)	**-0.33**	(0.11)	-0.62	(0.11)	-0.43	(0.12)	-0.74	(0.17)	-0.65	(0.10)	**0.11**	(0.10)
Jordan	**-0.69**	(0.10)	**0.08**	(0.22)	-0.56	(0.09)	c	c	-0.81	(0.22)	-0.69	(0.14)	-0.35	(0.12)
Kazakhstan	-0.23	(0.09)	0.56	(0.45)	-0.18	(0.10)	-0.27	(0.12)	-0.28	(0.15)	-0.31	(0.20)	-0.10	(0.17)
Latvia	0.37	(0.06)	c	c	0.38	(0.06)	0.38	(0.18)	0.55	(0.09)	0.31	(0.09)	0.33	(0.12)
Liechtenstein	0.04	(0.01)	c	c	**0.19**	(0.02)	**-0.46**	(0.00)	c	c	0.11	(0.02)	c	c
Lithuania	-0.01	(0.06)	c	c	-0.01	(0.06)	c	c	0.11	(0.11)	0.07	(0.09)	-0.15	(0.10)
Macao-China	c	c	-0.11	(0.00)	**-0.23**	(0.00)	**0.04**	(0.00)	c	c	c	c	-0.11	(0.00)
Malaysia	0.07	(0.08)	0.33	(0.49)	-0.03	(0.23)	0.08	(0.07)	0.05	(0.26)	0.09	(0.11)	0.06	(0.14)
Montenegro	-0.07	(0.00)	c	c	c	c	-0.07	(0.00)	c	c	-0.15	(0.00)	0.13	(0.00)
Peru	**-0.69**	(0.09)	**0.32**	(0.16)	-0.69	(0.10)	-0.37	(0.08)	**-1.08**	(0.14)	-0.53	(0.12)	**-0.12**	(0.12)
Qatar	0.60	(0.00)	0.24	(0.00)	0.54	(0.01)	0.44	(0.00)	0.84	(0.00)	0.46	(0.00)	0.39	(0.00)
Romania	0.18	(0.05)	c	c	0.18	(0.05)	c	c	0.22	(0.18)	0.09	(0.06)	0.31	(0.09)
Russian Federation	0.17	(0.07)	c	c	0.19	(0.07)	0.03	(0.11)	0.22	(0.12)	0.20	(0.13)	0.11	(0.09)
Serbia	-0.35	(0.09)	c	c	c	c	-0.34	(0.09)	c	c	-0.32	(0.12)	-0.40	(0.12)
Shanghai-China	-0.18	(0.10)	-0.28	(0.41)	-0.33	(0.11)	-0.07	(0.13)	c	c	c	c	-0.19	(0.09)
Singapore	0.39	(0.00)	c	c	0.44	(0.05)	0.40	(0.01)	c	c	c	c	0.40	(0.01)
Chinese Taipei	-0.03	(0.11)	0.24	(0.13)	**-0.16**	(0.14)	0.17	(0.10)	c	c	0.00	(0.13)	0.06	(0.11)
Thailand	**-1.03**	(0.08)	**-0.10**	(0.22)	-0.97	(0.09)	-0.85	(0.09)	-0.90	(0.11)	-0.99	(0.12)	-0.67	(0.16)
Tunisia	-1.26	(0.08)	c	c	-1.26	(0.13)	-1.25	(0.10)	-1.43	(0.26)	-1.28	(0.10)	-1.12	(0.14)
United Arab Emirates	**-0.30**	(0.10)	**0.47**	(0.07)	0.07	(0.12)	0.15	(0.05)	0.01	(0.14)	-0.03	(0.12)	0.24	(0.07)
Uruguay	**-0.60**	(0.10)	**0.57**	(0.13)	**-0.73**	(0.12)	**-0.18**	(0.10)	-1.13	(0.34)	-0.57	(0.14)	**-0.02**	(0.12)
Viet Nam	-0.45	(0.09)	0.19	(0.34)	**-1.04**	(0.28)	**-0.33**	(0.09)	-0.61	(0.14)	-0.37	(0.14)	-0.07	(0.17)

Notes: Values that are statistically significant are indicated in bold (see Annex A3).
ESCS refers to the *PISA index of economic, social and cultural status.*
1. A socio-economically disadvantaged school is one whose students' mean socio-economic status (ESCS) is statistically significantly below the mean socio-economic status of the country/economy; an average school is one where there is no difference from the country's/economy's mean; and an advantaged school is one whose students' mean socio-economic status is statistically significantly above the country/economy mean.
* See notes at the beginning of this Annex.
StatLink ⟐ http://dx.doi.org/10.1787/888932957460

[Part 1/2]
Index of quality of schools' educational resources and mathematics performance
Table IV.3.16 *Results based on school principals' reports*

		All students		Bottom quarter		Second quarter		Third quarter		Top quarter		Variability in this index	
		Mean index	S.E.	Mean index	S.E.	Mean index	S.E.	Mean index	S.E.	Mean index	S.E.	Standard deviation	S.E.
OECD	Australia	0.68	(0.03)	-0.53	(0.04)	0.22	(0.04)	1.05	(0.08)	1.98	(0.01)	0.97	(0.02)
	Austria	0.22	(0.09)	-1.21	(0.14)	-0.20	(0.08)	0.56	(0.14)	1.74	(0.11)	1.16	(0.07)
	Belgium	0.30	(0.06)	-0.87	(0.08)	-0.09	(0.06)	0.55	(0.08)	1.62	(0.10)	0.98	(0.04)
	Canada	0.27	(0.04)	-0.85	(0.07)	-0.14	(0.04)	0.45	(0.04)	1.62	(0.09)	0.97	(0.03)
	Chile	-0.38	(0.07)	-1.60	(0.14)	-0.61	(0.07)	-0.12	(0.07)	0.82	(0.12)	1.00	(0.07)
	Czech Republic	0.05	(0.06)	-0.83	(0.07)	-0.25	(0.04)	0.15	(0.07)	1.13	(0.13)	0.80	(0.05)
	Denmark	-0.15	(0.05)	-1.05	(0.09)	-0.38	(0.06)	0.02	(0.05)	0.83	(0.11)	0.78	(0.05)
	Estonia	-0.17	(0.04)	-1.00	(0.05)	-0.44	(0.05)	-0.05	(0.04)	0.80	(0.07)	0.74	(0.03)
	Finland	-0.20	(0.06)	-1.13	(0.07)	-0.51	(0.05)	-0.05	(0.07)	0.88	(0.11)	0.82	(0.05)
	France	0.38	(0.07)	-0.75	(0.08)	-0.03	(0.06)	0.52	(0.10)	1.80	(0.09)	0.98	(0.04)
	Germany	0.09	(0.07)	-0.92	(0.07)	-0.25	(0.06)	0.22	(0.09)	1.31	(0.12)	0.89	(0.05)
	Greece	-0.35	(0.07)	-1.45	(0.16)	-0.61	(0.05)	-0.17	(0.05)	0.83	(0.12)	0.96	(0.07)
	Hungary	0.17	(0.06)	-0.90	(0.09)	-0.05	(0.08)	0.40	(0.07)	1.25	(0.10)	0.84	(0.05)
	Iceland	-0.34	(0.00)	-1.33	(0.01)	-0.62	(0.00)	-0.21	(0.01)	0.79	(0.01)	0.85	(0.00)
	Ireland	0.11	(0.08)	-1.04	(0.09)	-0.26	(0.07)	0.28	(0.09)	1.46	(0.15)	0.97	(0.05)
	Israel	-0.35	(0.09)	-1.61	(0.10)	-0.80	(0.08)	-0.12	(0.13)	1.14	(0.14)	1.10	(0.06)
	Italy	0.05	(0.04)	-0.95	(0.05)	-0.30	(0.03)	0.19	(0.04)	1.25	(0.08)	0.89	(0.03)
	Japan	0.44	(0.08)	-0.81	(0.10)	0.03	(0.07)	0.66	(0.12)	1.87	(0.10)	1.02	(0.04)
	Korea	0.06	(0.08)	-1.00	(0.13)	-0.25	(0.06)	0.22	(0.09)	1.28	(0.15)	0.92	(0.07)
	Luxembourg	0.04	(0.00)	-0.76	(0.00)	-0.31	(0.00)	0.05	(0.00)	1.17	(0.00)	0.78	(0.00)
	Mexico	-0.86	(0.04)	-2.26	(0.05)	-1.23	(0.06)	-0.52	(0.05)	0.57	(0.07)	1.14	(0.03)
	Netherlands	0.19	(0.08)	-0.92	(0.08)	-0.22	(0.07)	0.37	(0.10)	1.51	(0.15)	0.95	(0.05)
	New Zealand	0.20	(0.08)	-0.85	(0.09)	-0.28	(0.08)	0.29	(0.10)	1.63	(0.13)	0.98	(0.05)
	Norway	-0.19	(0.06)	-1.04	(0.06)	-0.57	(0.05)	-0.08	(0.07)	0.93	(0.14)	0.82	(0.05)
	Poland	0.36	(0.08)	-0.68	(0.07)	-0.03	(0.08)	0.53	(0.08)	1.62	(0.15)	0.90	(0.05)
	Portugal	0.17	(0.08)	-0.91	(0.11)	-0.15	(0.07)	0.38	(0.11)	1.36	(0.14)	0.91	(0.06)
	Slovak Republic	-0.54	(0.05)	-1.36	(0.06)	-0.75	(0.06)	-0.37	(0.05)	0.30	(0.09)	0.69	(0.04)
	Slovenia	0.43	(0.01)	-0.50	(0.01)	0.05	(0.01)	0.52	(0.01)	1.65	(0.03)	0.84	(0.01)
	Spain	0.02	(0.05)	-0.98	(0.06)	-0.31	(0.04)	0.18	(0.05)	1.17	(0.09)	0.86	(0.03)
	Sweden	0.05	(0.06)	-0.92	(0.10)	-0.22	(0.06)	0.25	(0.06)	1.09	(0.11)	0.83	(0.06)
	Switzerland	0.55	(0.07)	-0.57	(0.06)	0.11	(0.08)	0.88	(0.11)	1.78	(0.09)	0.93	(0.03)
	Turkey	-0.40	(0.06)	-1.52	(0.10)	-0.64	(0.08)	-0.17	(0.06)	0.73	(0.12)	0.92	(0.06)
	United Kingdom	0.51	(0.08)	-0.74	(0.08)	0.01	(0.05)	0.81	(0.21)	1.98	(0.01)	1.06	(0.03)
	United States	0.38	(0.08)	-0.89	(0.10)	-0.13	(0.08)	0.63	(0.15)	1.92	(0.09)	1.07	(0.05)
	OECD average	0.05	(0.01)	-1.02	(0.01)	-0.30	(0.01)	0.25	(0.02)	1.29	(0.02)	0.92	(0.01)
Partners	Albania	-0.41	(0.06)	-1.37	(0.08)	-0.69	(0.06)	-0.27	(0.05)	0.68	(0.13)	0.83	(0.05)
	Argentina	-0.54	(0.09)	-1.87	(0.13)	-0.80	(0.09)	-0.26	(0.07)	0.77	(0.15)	1.07	(0.06)
	Brazil	-0.54	(0.05)	-1.76	(0.06)	-0.92	(0.05)	-0.33	(0.06)	0.86	(0.10)	1.05	(0.04)
	Bulgaria	-0.04	(0.07)	-1.05	(0.07)	-0.38	(0.08)	0.15	(0.08)	1.14	(0.11)	0.88	(0.04)
	Colombia	-1.38	(0.07)	-2.84	(0.11)	-1.68	(0.14)	-1.05	(0.07)	0.06	(0.09)	1.17	(0.06)
	Costa Rica	-1.08	(0.08)	-2.58	(0.12)	-1.48	(0.10)	-0.77	(0.09)	0.52	(0.12)	1.24	(0.06)
	Croatia	-0.50	(0.05)	-1.32	(0.09)	-0.68	(0.06)	-0.33	(0.06)	0.33	(0.07)	0.66	(0.04)
	Cyprus*	0.25	(0.00)	-0.85	(0.00)	-0.28	(0.00)	0.47	(0.01)	1.67	(0.00)	1.00	(0.00)
	Hong Kong-China	0.44	(0.07)	-0.62	(0.08)	0.01	(0.07)	0.61	(0.09)	1.78	(0.13)	0.93	(0.04)
	Indonesia	-0.76	(0.10)	-2.13	(0.16)	-1.09	(0.12)	-0.48	(0.10)	0.67	(0.16)	1.12	(0.08)
	Jordan	-0.45	(0.08)	-1.68	(0.12)	-0.73	(0.07)	-0.23	(0.10)	0.85	(0.13)	1.02	(0.06)
	Kazakhstan	-0.68	(0.07)	-1.80	(0.11)	-0.98	(0.08)	-0.48	(0.07)	0.54	(0.12)	0.96	(0.06)
	Latvia	0.04	(0.05)	-0.83	(0.07)	-0.20	(0.06)	0.20	(0.06)	0.98	(0.12)	0.73	(0.05)
	Liechtenstein	0.77	(0.01)	c	c	c	c	c	c	c	c	0.51	(0.01)
	Lithuania	0.15	(0.05)	-0.62	(0.05)	-0.13	(0.05)	0.27	(0.06)	1.07	(0.10)	0.69	(0.04)
	Macao-China	0.36	(0.00)	-0.86	(0.00)	-0.15	(0.00)	0.75	(0.00)	1.70	(0.00)	1.02	(0.00)
	Malaysia	-0.21	(0.07)	-1.26	(0.07)	-0.53	(0.09)	-0.02	(0.06)	0.97	(0.14)	0.90	(0.05)
	Montenegro	-0.48	(0.00)	-1.23	(0.00)	-0.77	(0.00)	-0.37	(0.00)	0.43	(0.00)	0.65	(0.00)
	Peru	-1.16	(0.08)	-2.73	(0.10)	-1.53	(0.08)	-0.74	(0.10)	0.38	(0.14)	1.24	(0.06)
	Qatar	0.78	(0.00)	-0.40	(0.00)	0.28	(0.00)	1.25	(0.00)	1.98	(0.00)	0.98	(0.00)
	Romania	0.22	(0.06)	-0.71	(0.07)	-0.11	(0.06)	0.38	(0.06)	1.33	(0.14)	0.82	(0.05)
	Russian Federation	-0.48	(0.07)	-1.56	(0.09)	-0.76	(0.05)	-0.28	(0.07)	0.67	(0.13)	0.91	(0.05)
	Serbia	-0.56	(0.07)	-1.61	(0.10)	-0.79	(0.06)	-0.31	(0.08)	0.47	(0.13)	0.86	(0.06)
	Shanghai-China	0.13	(0.09)	-1.46	(0.16)	-0.27	(0.11)	0.55	(0.12)	1.68	(0.11)	1.24	(0.08)
	Singapore	1.19	(0.01)	-0.06	(0.01)	0.94	(0.02)	1.93	(0.01)	1.98	(0.00)	0.87	(0.00)
	Chinese Taipei	0.58	(0.09)	-0.96	(0.18)	0.13	(0.11)	1.16	(0.18)	1.98	(0.00)	1.20	(0.09)
	Thailand	-0.68	(0.07)	-2.00	(0.13)	-1.00	(0.07)	-0.37	(0.08)	0.66	(0.12)	1.07	(0.06)
	Tunisia	-1.34	(0.08)	-2.42	(0.12)	-1.58	(0.09)	-1.17	(0.07)	-0.20	(0.17)	0.93	(0.08)
	United Arab Emirates	0.37	(0.05)	-1.14	(0.05)	-0.22	(0.07)	0.85	(0.10)	1.98	(0.03)	1.21	(0.03)
	Uruguay	0.12	(0.04)	-1.15	(0.04)	-0.23	(0.08)	0.46	(0.08)	1.39	(0.11)	1.03	(0.07)
	Viet Nam	-0.48	(0.07)	-1.72	(0.13)	-0.78	(0.07)	-0.16	(0.11)	0.73	(0.11)	0.99	(0.07)

Note: Values that are statistically significant are indicated in bold (see Annex A3).
* See notes at the beginning of this Annex.
StatLink ᴍˢ⌐ http://dx.doi.org/10.1787/888932957460

[Part 2/2]
Index of quality of schools' educational resources and mathematics performance

Table IV.3.16 *Results based on school principals' reports*

| | Performance on the mathematics scale by national quarters of this index | | | | | | | | Change in the mathematics score per unit of this index | | Increased likelihood of students in the bottom quarter of this index scoring in the bottom quarter of the national mathematics performance distribution | | Explained variance in student performance (r-squared x 100) | |
| | Bottom quarter | | Second quarter | | Third quarter | | Top quarter | | | | | | | |
	Mean score	S.E.	Mean score	S.E.	Mean score	S.E.	Mean score	S.E.	Score dif.	S.E.	Ratio	S.E.	%	S.E.
Australia	**483**	(3.6)	496	(4.7)	514	(4.3)	**525**	(4.3)	**16.8**	(2.05)	**1.5**	(0.09)	2.9	(0.69)
Austria	500	(10.8)	496	(9.0)	505	(8.3)	524	(9.1)	8.4	(4.15)	1.3	(0.23)	1.1	(1.11)
Belgium	**494**	(8.6)	516	(6.8)	522	(7.9)	**528**	(9.8)	**11.5**	(5.36)	**1.4**	(0.19)	1.2	(1.18)
Canada	510	(4.2)	520	(3.9)	523	(4.2)	519	(4.0)	3.7	(2.19)	1.1	(0.08)	0.2	(0.21)
Chile	**400**	(6.2)	416	(6.0)	438	(8.2)	**436**	(7.3)	**16.2**	(2.72)	**1.5**	(0.18)	4.0	(1.31)
Czech Republic	503	(10.5)	488	(9.0)	496	(9.4)	507	(9.3)	3.3	(6.13)	1.0	(0.15)	0.1	(0.35)
Denmark	**494**	(5.3)	499	(5.3)	498	(5.0)	**512**	(4.7)	**7.1**	(3.32)	1.2	(0.12)	0.5	(0.41)
Estonia	523	(4.5)	515	(4.6)	521	(5.4)	522	(4.4)	1.4	(2.67)	0.9	(0.09)	0.0	(0.08)
Finland	521	(3.6)	510	(5.5)	523	(5.0)	520	(3.7)	0.5	(1.80)	0.9	(0.07)	0.0	(0.03)
France	492	(9.0)	491	(9.8)	493	(10.6)	510	(9.6)	9.2	(4.51)	1.0	(0.19)	0.8	(0.90)
Germany	506	(8.3)	511	(9.8)	514	(8.1)	525	(8.6)	6.0	(4.72)	1.1	(0.15)	0.3	(0.50)
Greece	445	(8.6)	454	(7.1)	455	(5.4)	457	(5.2)	6.5	(3.97)	1.2	(0.18)	0.5	(0.60)
Hungary	475	(9.2)	469	(10.1)	484	(10.7)	482	(10.3)	5.5	(7.52)	1.0	(0.18)	0.2	(0.56)
Iceland	496	(3.3)	491	(4.0)	492	(3.3)	494	(3.1)	0.9	(2.11)	0.9	(0.08)	0.0	(0.05)
Ireland	498	(5.6)	489	(7.8)	512	(6.2)	511	(6.3)	5.3	(3.38)	1.0	(0.13)	0.4	(0.48)
Israel	465	(7.7)	465	(12.4)	454	(14.2)	481	(13.4)	6.2	(4.89)	0.9	(0.16)	0.4	(0.69)
Italy	**472**	(4.7)	488	(5.2)	491	(4.5)	**498**	(4.7)	**9.6**	(2.87)	**1.3**	(0.11)	0.8	(0.49)
Japan	539	(11.3)	538	(10.1)	522	(9.0)	547	(9.4)	2.5	(6.20)	1.1	(0.22)	0.1	(0.46)
Korea	553	(12.7)	552	(11.0)	563	(10.5)	547	(10.8)	-2.3	(6.13)	1.1	(0.19)	0.0	(0.33)
Luxembourg	478	(2.1)	469	(2.6)	505	(2.5)	507	(2.2)	**18.5**	(1.31)	1.2	(0.06)	2.3	(0.32)
Mexico	**389**	(3.0)	408	(2.9)	420	(2.8)	**436**	(3.7)	**16.6**	(1.50)	**1.7**	(0.11)	6.5	(1.24)
Netherlands	520	(10.1)	505	(12.0)	531	(18.0)	522	(14.9)	3.3	(6.73)	0.9	(0.21)	0.1	(0.58)
New Zealand	**486**	(7.2)	499	(6.6)	497	(7.8)	**526**	(9.1)	**13.8**	(4.51)	**1.3**	(0.18)	1.8	(1.17)
Norway	492	(5.6)	488	(6.1)	486	(6.0)	495	(5.5)	1.8	(3.85)	1.0	(0.10)	0.0	(0.16)
Poland	510	(6.0)	520	(7.7)	521	(6.6)	518	(7.0)	4.3	(3.82)	1.1	(0.12)	0.2	(0.37)
Portugal	**470**	(9.8)	484	(8.7)	488	(8.8)	**504**	(6.8)	**15.0**	(3.71)	**1.3**	(0.18)	2.1	(1.08)
Slovak Republic	480	(9.3)	494	(9.7)	472	(11.6)	480	(9.5)	0.0	(7.72)	1.0	(0.18)	0.0	(0.24)
Slovenia	**483**	(3.1)	509	(3.2)	513	(3.1)	510	(3.5)	**7.2**	(1.57)	**1.4**	(0.11)	0.4	(0.19)
Spain	**478**	(4.2)	481	(4.6)	484	(5.6)	**495**	(3.5)	**6.5**	(2.35)	1.1	(0.11)	0.4	(0.28)
Sweden	474	(5.3)	482	(5.7)	475	(5.2)	482	(4.8)	3.5	(3.25)	1.0	(0.10)	0.1	(0.18)
Switzerland	**514**	(5.5)	527	(7.6)	536	(8.8)	**551**	(6.5)	**14.3**	(3.25)	**1.3**	(0.13)	2.0	(0.87)
Turkey	**424**	(10.7)	438	(8.3)	448	(11.8)	**482**	(14.2)	**24.2**	(6.84)	**1.5**	(0.21)	5.9	(3.20)
United Kingdom	491	(6.8)	500	(6.1)	488	(7.2)	502	(11.6)	3.2	(5.51)	1.0	(0.14)	0.1	(0.48)
United States	**470**	(7.1)	474	(10.4)	490	(10.3)	**496**	(6.6)	**9.6**	(3.17)	**1.3**	(0.18)	1.3	(0.86)
OECD average	**486**	(1.3)	491	(1.3)	496	(1.4)	**504**	(1.4)	**7.7**	(0.75)	**1.2**	(0.03)	1.1	(0.15)
Albania	**389**	(4.0)	389	(5.2)	395	(4.0)	**404**	(3.7)	4.5	(2.52)	1.0	(0.10)	0.2	(0.18)
Argentina	366	(9.0)	393	(6.5)	385	(7.0)	409	(7.2)	**15.4**	(3.57)	**1.6**	(0.24)	4.6	(2.02)
Brazil	**372**	(3.3)	381	(3.4)	386	(4.5)	**425**	(6.0)	**20.7**	(2.32)	**1.3**	(0.08)	7.7	(1.63)
Bulgaria	409	(10.2)	436	(9.1)	455	(10.2)	455	(10.8)	**20.8**	(6.53)	**1.6**	(0.23)	3.8	(2.31)
Colombia	**356**	(5.5)	370	(6.2)	381	(6.8)	**398**	(7.4)	**13.4**	(3.04)	**1.5**	(0.19)	4.4	(1.96)
Costa Rica	**386**	(7.9)	393	(5.6)	412	(8.0)	**436**	(8.2)	**17.9**	(3.03)	**1.6**	(0.24)	10.4	(3.24)
Croatia	472	(7.8)	465	(9.9)	458	(8.7)	488	(10.5)	4.3	(6.58)	1.0	(0.17)	0.1	(0.34)
Cyprus*	**428**	(2.7)	449	(2.7)	422	(2.5)	**457**	(2.2)	**7.7**	(1.09)	1.2	(0.07)	0.7	(0.19)
Hong Kong-China	570	(9.2)	556	(13.0)	556	(10.8)	563	(9.3)	1.0	(5.55)	0.9	(0.16)	0.0	(0.27)
Indonesia	**351**	(6.0)	365	(11.7)	384	(8.0)	**399**	(11.0)	**20.5**	(4.19)	**1.5**	(0.22)	10.4	(4.12)
Jordan	385	(5.8)	378	(6.8)	379	(5.7)	400	(8.4)	9.0	(4.66)	1.0	(0.13)	1.4	(1.41)
Kazakhstan	439	(6.5)	428	(8.0)	424	(7.0)	438	(6.6)	4.5	(3.66)	0.8	(0.12)	0.4	(0.57)
Latvia	489	(6.8)	481	(6.6)	501	(4.8)	490	(7.4)	4.7	(4.52)	1.0	(0.14)	0.2	(0.35)
Liechtenstein	c	c	c	c	c	c	c	c	-75.4	(8.19)	0.1	(0.04)	16.5	(3.27)
Lithuania	**462**	(5.6)	483	(5.7)	486	(6.1)	**485**	(6.6)	**13.2**	(4.93)	**1.3**	(0.14)	1.1	(0.82)
Macao-China	**538**	(2.3)	529	(2.5)	528	(2.2)	**558**	(2.3)	**9.3**	(0.97)	1.1	(0.05)	1.0	(0.21)
Malaysia	409	(6.7)	414	(5.2)	421	(6.8)	438	(9.1)	**14.9**	(4.79)	1.2	(0.16)	2.7	(1.79)
Montenegro	**397**	(1.7)	442	(2.4)	395	(2.5)	**404**	(2.2)	-5.3	(1.48)	1.2	(0.07)	0.2	(0.17)
Peru	**332**	(6.3)	348	(5.8)	378	(7.6)	**414**	(10.6)	**24.2**	(3.57)	**2.0**	(0.21)	12.6	(3.07)
Qatar	**380**	(1.5)	388	(1.6)	369	(2.2)	**369**	(1.9)	-6.1	(0.82)	0.9	(0.05)	0.4	(0.09)
Romania	437	(7.9)	435	(9.0)	442	(10.1)	464	(9.3)	**16.8**	(4.32)	1.1	(0.19)	2.9	(1.53)
Russian Federation	471	(4.6)	477	(5.3)	487	(5.6)	494	(9.1)	6.8	(3.93)	1.2	(0.11)	0.5	(0.59)
Serbia	447	(9.4)	449	(10.3)	452	(9.7)	447	(13.2)	-1.6	(6.44)	1.0	(0.17)	0.0	(0.32)
Shanghai-China	598	(9.8)	609	(10.0)	618	(11.2)	626	(9.7)	8.6	(4.29)	1.2	(0.20)	1.1	(1.09)
Singapore	**565**	(2.3)	563	(3.5)	585	(3.2)	**585**	(3.0)	**6.3**	(1.45)	1.0	(0.06)	0.3	(0.13)
Chinese Taipei	**545**	(9.3)	575	(13.7)	542	(10.6)	**579**	(9.8)	9.7	(4.79)	1.3	(0.16)	1.0	(1.07)
Thailand	416	(6.7)	422	(6.7)	434	(9.7)	435	(7.2)	**8.1**	(3.27)	1.1	(0.15)	1.1	(0.88)
Tunisia	388	(7.1)	382	(8.7)	391	(10.6)	391	(9.9)	0.9	(4.41)	0.9	(0.16)	0.0	(0.27)
United Arab Emirates	**408**	(3.9)	421	(4.8)	452	(4.7)	**457**	(6.7)	**16.2**	(2.19)	**1.5**	(0.13)	4.8	(1.23)
Uruguay	**388**	(6.4)	399	(6.3)	418	(6.9)	**432**	(8.7)	**13.8**	(4.22)	**1.4**	(0.17)	2.6	(1.45)
Viet Nam	503	(13.3)	510	(7.9)	522	(10.7)	510	(11.2)	6.1	(5.79)	1.3	(0.27)	0.5	(0.95)

Note: Values that are statistically significant are indicated in bold (see Annex A3).
* See notes at the beginning of this Annex.
StatLink http://dx.doi.org/10.1787/888932957460

[Part 1/2]
Index of quality of schools' educational resources, by school features

Table IV.3.17   *Results based on school principals' reports*

| | Index of quality of schools' educational resources | | | | | | | | | | | | | |
| | Bottom quarter of ESCS | | Second quarter of ESCS | | Third quarter of ESCS | | Top quarter of ESCS | | Socio-economically disadvantaged schools[1] | | Socio-economically average schools[1] | | Socio-economically advantaged schools[1] | |
	Mean index	S.E.	Mean index	S.E.	Mean index	S.E.	Mean index	S.E.	Mean index	S.E.	Mean index	S.E.	Mean index	S.E.
Australia	**0.49**	(0.05)	0.60	(0.04)	0.73	(0.04)	**0.92**	(0.05)	**0.41**	(0.08)	0.59	(0.05)	**1.13**	(0.07)
Austria	0.20	(0.10)	0.30	(0.09)	0.25	(0.11)	0.16	(0.13)	0.04	(0.18)	0.45	(0.13)	0.10	(0.19)
Belgium	0.25	(0.08)	0.28	(0.07)	0.35	(0.08)	0.34	(0.08)	0.13	(0.11)	0.34	(0.10)	0.40	(0.13)
Canada	**0.19**	(0.06)	0.25	(0.04)	0.28	(0.04)	0.37	(0.05)	0.02	(0.12)	0.28	(0.06)	**0.45**	(0.08)
Chile	**-0.64**	(0.11)	**-0.45**	(0.09)	**-0.39**	(0.08)	**-0.03**	(0.08)	**-0.71**	(0.12)	-0.29	(0.18)	**-0.02**	(0.10)
Czech Republic	0.05	(0.08)	0.04	(0.07)	0.02	(0.06)	0.09	(0.08)	0.00	(0.14)	0.03	(0.08)	0.14	(0.14)
Denmark	-0.21	(0.07)	-0.14	(0.06)	-0.12	(0.06)	-0.08	(0.06)	-0.36	(0.14)	-0.08	(0.07)	-0.15	(0.11)
Estonia	-0.20	(0.05)	-0.18	(0.05)	-0.17	(0.04)	-0.13	(0.04)	-0.28	(0.09)	-0.14	(0.05)	-0.17	(0.05)
Finland	-0.17	(0.07)	-0.22	(0.06)	-0.21	(0.05)	-0.21	(0.07)	0.01	(0.15)	-0.22	(0.07)	**-0.35**	(0.09)
France	0.36	(0.08)	0.35	(0.08)	0.38	(0.07)	0.47	(0.08)	0.31	(0.11)	0.30	(0.11)	0.57	(0.11)
Germany	0.11	(0.08)	0.06	(0.07)	0.12	(0.08)	0.08	(0.08)	0.12	(0.10)	0.09	(0.11)	0.09	(0.13)
Greece	**-0.45**	(0.08)	**-0.44**	(0.09)	-0.33	(0.08)	**-0.17**	(0.07)	**-0.52**	(0.17)	-0.42	(0.10)	-0.06	(0.12)
Hungary	0.15	(0.09)	0.16	(0.07)	0.17	(0.07)	0.22	(0.09)	0.08	(0.11)	0.25	(0.09)	0.18	(0.12)
Iceland	-0.35	(0.02)	-0.31	(0.03)	-0.32	(0.03)	-0.37	(0.03)	**-0.43**	(0.01)	-0.41	(0.00)	-0.16	(0.01)
Ireland	**-0.01**	(0.09)	0.11	(0.08)	0.14	(0.08)	**0.20**	(0.10)	-0.11	(0.17)	0.07	(0.10)	0.35	(0.16)
Israel	**-0.50**	(0.11)	-0.38	(0.11)	-0.26	(0.10)	**-0.26**	(0.10)	**-0.64**	(0.18)	-0.31	(0.15)	-0.13	(0.12)
Italy	**-0.01**	(0.04)	0.03	(0.05)	0.07	(0.05)	0.10	(0.04)	-0.07	(0.07)	0.11	(0.07)	0.08	(0.06)
Japan	0.36	(0.09)	0.41	(0.08)	0.44	(0.08)	0.53	(0.11)	0.33	(0.13)	0.32	(0.11)	0.72	(0.19)
Korea	0.06	(0.08)	0.07	(0.08)	0.05	(0.09)	0.06	(0.11)	0.03	(0.11)	0.10	(0.12)	0.02	(0.18)
Luxembourg	**-0.10**	(0.02)	-0.01	(0.02)	0.05	(0.02)	**0.22**	(0.02)	**-0.14**	(0.00)	0.26	(0.00)	**0.17**	(0.00)
Mexico	**-1.38**	(0.04)	**-0.99**	(0.05)	**-0.76**	(0.05)	**-0.30**	(0.08)	**-1.43**	(0.06)	**-0.91**	(0.06)	**-0.15**	(0.10)
Netherlands	0.19	(0.09)	0.11	(0.08)	0.23	(0.09)	0.22	(0.10)	0.11	(0.12)	0.21	(0.11)	0.22	(0.18)
New Zealand	**0.06**	(0.10)	0.11	(0.08)	0.21	(0.09)	**0.43**	(0.11)	**-0.03**	(0.16)	0.03	(0.10)	**0.76**	(0.17)
Norway	-0.17	(0.07)	-0.21	(0.07)	-0.22	(0.07)	-0.16	(0.07)	0.09	(0.20)	-0.26	(0.07)	-0.01	(0.17)
Poland	**0.23**	(0.09)	0.34	(0.09)	0.39	(0.09)	**0.48**	(0.09)	**0.16**	(0.13)	0.36	(0.10)	**0.60**	(0.15)
Portugal	**0.07**	(0.10)	0.13	(0.09)	0.20	(0.09)	**0.28**	(0.09)	0.17	(0.14)	0.07	(0.12)	0.40	(0.14)
Slovak Republic	-0.58	(0.05)	-0.53	(0.05)	-0.56	(0.06)	-0.51	(0.07)	-0.58	(0.08)	-0.50	(0.06)	-0.58	(0.10)
Slovenia	0.38	(0.03)	0.45	(0.02)	0.39	(0.03)	0.50	(0.03)	0.45	(0.02)	0.32	(0.02)	0.54	(0.01)
Spain	-0.03	(0.05)	0.01	(0.05)	0.02	(0.05)	0.07	(0.06)	-0.02	(0.07)	-0.08	(0.07)	0.20	(0.09)
Sweden	**-0.01**	(0.06)	0.00	(0.06)	0.05	(0.06)	**0.17**	(0.07)	**-0.15**	(0.12)	-0.02	(0.07)	0.37	(0.15)
Switzerland	**0.49**	(0.08)	0.52	(0.07)	0.55	(0.08)	**0.62**	(0.08)	0.46	(0.12)	0.51	(0.11)	0.71	(0.10)
Turkey	**-0.64**	(0.06)	-0.44	(0.07)	-0.40	(0.07)	**-0.11**	(0.11)	**-0.81**	(0.10)	-0.31	(0.08)	**-0.03**	(0.17)
United Kingdom	0.52	(0.09)	0.52	(0.09)	0.42	(0.09)	0.58	(0.10)	0.71	(0.14)	0.37	(0.10)	0.64	(0.19)
United States	**0.20**	(0.10)	0.36	(0.09)	0.46	(0.10)	0.51	(0.10)	-0.04	(0.17)	0.42	(0.13)	0.70	(0.15)
OECD average	**-0.03**	(0.01)	0.03	(0.01)	0.06	(0.01)	**0.16**	(0.01)	**-0.08**	(0.02)	0.05	(0.02)	**0.23**	(0.02)
Albania	m	m	m	m	m	m	m	m	m	m	m	m	m	m
Argentina	**-0.82**	(0.09)	-0.65	(0.09)	-0.46	(0.10)	**-0.18**	(0.13)	**-0.85**	(0.12)	-0.65	(0.12)	**-0.08**	(0.17)
Brazil	**-0.80**	(0.04)	**-0.74**	(0.05)	-0.54	(0.06)	**-0.06**	(0.08)	**-0.85**	(0.07)	-0.74	(0.07)	**0.24**	(0.11)
Bulgaria	**-0.21**	(0.08)	-0.08	(0.08)	-0.01	(0.07)	0.16	(0.09)	**-0.21**	(0.10)	-0.18	(0.13)	0.28	(0.11)
Colombia	**-1.70**	(0.11)	**-1.50**	(0.08)	**-1.35**	(0.08)	**-0.97**	(0.10)	**-1.87**	(0.16)	**-1.33**	(0.10)	**-0.96**	(0.18)
Costa Rica	**-1.51**	(0.12)	**-1.21**	(0.10)	**-1.08**	(0.10)	**-0.50**	(0.13)	**-1.54**	(0.16)	-1.21	(0.13)	-0.21	(0.17)
Croatia	-0.49	(0.06)	-0.47	(0.06)	-0.54	(0.06)	-0.50	(0.07)	-0.46	(0.09)	-0.50	(0.08)	-0.57	(0.13)
Cyprus*	0.10	(0.02)	0.15	(0.03)	0.34	(0.03)	0.42	(0.02)	-0.04	(0.00)	0.27	(0.00)	0.61	(0.00)
Hong Kong-China	0.39	(0.09)	0.39	(0.08)	0.48	(0.07)	0.52	(0.10)	0.34	(0.13)	0.46	(0.11)	0.57	(0.15)
Indonesia	**-1.03**	(0.11)	-0.96	(0.10)	-0.78	(0.11)	**-0.25**	(0.19)	**-1.14**	(0.14)	-0.84	(0.16)	-0.10	(0.19)
Jordan	**-0.59**	(0.10)	-0.50	(0.08)	-0.47	(0.08)	**-0.24**	(0.10)	**-0.62**	(0.15)	-0.54	(0.10)	**0.00**	(0.18)
Kazakhstan	**-0.78**	(0.07)	-0.68	(0.08)	-0.68	(0.08)	**-0.58**	(0.10)	-0.90	(0.12)	-0.53	(0.11)	-0.73	(0.13)
Latvia	0.00	(0.08)	0.04	(0.06)	0.06	(0.06)	0.04	(0.07)	-0.13	(0.11)	0.18	(0.08)	-0.10	(0.10)
Liechtenstein	0.95	(0.04)	0.80	(0.06)	0.67	(0.06)	0.65	(0.05)	c	c	1.08	(0.02)	c	c
Lithuania	0.11	(0.06)	0.10	(0.05)	0.17	(0.05)	0.22	(0.06)	0.06	(0.09)	0.12	(0.06)	0.28	(0.10)
Macao-China	0.24	(0.02)	0.26	(0.02)	0.34	(0.02)	0.60	(0.02)	0.28	(0.00)	0.08	(0.00)	0.66	(0.00)
Malaysia	**-0.37**	(0.08)	-0.28	(0.07)	-0.17	(0.07)	**-0.03**	(0.10)	**-0.46**	(0.11)	-0.19	(0.11)	0.01	(0.14)
Montenegro	-0.46	(0.02)	-0.47	(0.02)	-0.50	(0.02)	-0.50	(0.02)	-0.53	(0.00)	-0.34	(0.00)	-0.53	(0.00)
Peru	**-1.78**	(0.10)	**-1.36**	(0.09)	**-0.92**	(0.10)	**-0.54**	(0.13)	**-1.83**	(0.12)	-1.29	(0.12)	**-0.32**	(0.14)
Qatar	0.73	(0.01)	0.73	(0.02)	0.73	(0.02)	0.90	(0.02)	0.68	(0.00)	0.53	(0.00)	0.98	(0.00)
Romania	0.09	(0.07)	0.21	(0.07)	0.19	(0.07)	0.41	(0.10)	**-0.06**	(0.11)	0.26	(0.09)	0.47	(0.14)
Russian Federation	**-0.60**	(0.08)	-0.46	(0.08)	-0.51	(0.08)	**-0.35**	(0.09)	-0.58	(0.12)	-0.54	(0.10)	-0.30	(0.13)
Serbia	**-0.54**	(0.10)	-0.53	(0.08)	-0.60	(0.08)	-0.58	(0.08)	-0.62	(0.15)	-0.45	(0.09)	-0.67	(0.13)
Shanghai-China	-0.06	(0.12)	0.11	(0.10)	0.18	(0.11)	0.27	(0.14)	**-0.21**	(0.20)	0.16	(0.15)	**0.39**	(0.19)
Singapore	1.19	(0.02)	1.18	(0.02)	1.17	(0.02)	1.24	(0.03)	1.18	(0.00)	1.19	(0.01)	1.22	(0.02)
Chinese Taipei	0.47	(0.11)	0.51	(0.10)	0.61	(0.10)	0.73	(0.11)	0.38	(0.19)	0.54	(0.14)	0.85	(0.15)
Thailand	**-1.03**	(0.08)	**-0.82**	(0.08)	-0.56	(0.09)	**-0.31**	(0.10)	**-1.08**	(0.10)	-0.73	(0.11)	-0.09	(0.14)
Tunisia	-1.42	(0.11)	-1.42	(0.08)	-1.34	(0.08)	-1.18	(0.11)	**-1.58**	(0.17)	-1.31	(0.10)	-1.13	(0.16)
United Arab Emirates	0.14	(0.07)	0.34	(0.06)	0.44	(0.05)	0.55	(0.06)	0.11	(0.09)	0.25	(0.09)	0.69	(0.10)
Uruguay	-0.04	(0.09)	0.02	(0.09)	0.05	(0.09)	0.44	(0.10)	**-0.07**	(0.14)	0.00	(0.11)	0.66	(0.13)
Viet Nam	**-0.68**	(0.10)	-0.57	(0.09)	-0.47	(0.08)	**-0.21**	(0.11)	**-0.76**	(0.13)	-0.45	(0.13)	-0.11	(0.16)

Notes: Values that are statistically significant are indicated in bold (see Annex A3).
ESCS refers to the *PISA index of economic, social and cultural status*.
1. A socio-economically disadvantaged school is one whose students' mean socio-economic status (ESCS) is statistically significantly below the mean socio-economic status of the country/economy; an average school is one where there is no difference from the country's/economy's mean; and an advantaged school is one whose students' mean socio-economic status is statistically significantly above the country/economy mean.
* See notes at the beginning of this Annex.
StatLink ￼ http://dx.doi.org/10.1787/888932957460

[Part 2/2]
Index of quality of schools' educational resources, by school features
Table IV.3.17   *Results based on school principals' reports*

| | Index of quality of schools' educational resources | | | | | | | | | | | | | |
| | Public schools | | Private schools | | Lower secondary education (ISCED 2) | | Upper secondary education (ISCED 3) | | Schools located in a village, hamlet or rural area (fewer than 3 000 people) | | Schools located in a small town or town (3 000 to about 100 000 people) | | Schools located in a city or a large city (over 100 000 people) | |
	Mean index	S.E.	Mean index	S.E.	Mean index	S.E.	Mean index	S.E.	Mean index	S.E.	Mean index	S.E.	Mean index	S.E.
Australia	**0.43**	(0.05)	**1.03**	(0.05)	0.69	(0.04)	0.65	(0.06)	0.33	(0.14)	0.47	(0.08)	**0.81**	(0.04)
Austria	0.23	(0.09)	0.07	(0.31)	-0.02	(0.24)	0.24	(0.09)	0.56	(0.27)	0.36	(0.13)	-0.08	(0.15)
Belgium	0.19	(0.12)	0.36	(0.08)	0.07	(0.14)	0.33	(0.07)	-0.19	(0.43)	0.41	(0.07)	0.01	(0.15)
Canada	**0.24**	(0.05)	**0.62**	(0.14)	0.16	(0.06)	0.29	(0.05)	0.40	(0.12)	0.32	(0.07)	0.22	(0.07)
Chile	**-0.77**	(0.13)	**-0.10**	(0.08)	-0.59	(0.16)	-0.37	(0.07)	**-1.07**	(0.29)	-0.42	(0.13)	-0.30	(0.09)
Czech Republic	0.05	(0.07)	0.03	(0.13)	-0.01	(0.08)	0.12	(0.08)	0.10	(0.21)	-0.02	(0.07)	0.20	(0.11)
Denmark	**-0.30**	(0.05)	0.26	(0.12)	-0.15	(0.05)	c	c	-0.13	(0.11)	-0.11	(0.07)	-0.28	(0.16)
Estonia	-0.18	(0.04)	0.01	(0.13)	-0.17	(0.04)	-0.02	(0.09)	-0.26	(0.08)	-0.21	(0.05)	-0.03	(0.09)
Finland	**-0.21**	(0.06)	**0.14**	(0.16)	-0.20	(0.06)	c	c	-0.16	(0.14)	-0.29	(0.06)	**-0.01**	(0.12)
France	0.42	(0.08)	0.24	(0.17)	0.25	(0.10)	0.44	(0.08)	0.29	(0.22)	0.36	(0.08)	0.49	(0.14)
Germany	0.10	(0.07)	0.06	(0.20)	0.09	(0.06)	0.08	(0.36)	c	c	0.18	(0.09)	**-0.16**	(0.11)
Greece	-0.45	(0.07)	c	c	-0.47	(0.12)	-0.34	(0.07)	-0.18	(0.17)	-0.43	(0.09)	-0.23	(0.14)
Hungary	0.14	(0.07)	0.35	(0.19)	0.14	(0.20)	0.18	(0.07)	0.25	(0.36)	0.09	(0.09)	0.29	(0.10)
Iceland	-0.34	(0.00)	c	c	-0.34	(0.00)	c	c	**-0.19**	(0.01)	-0.33	(0.01)	**-0.46**	(0.01)
Ireland	0.24	(0.14)	0.00	(0.09)	0.10	(0.08)	0.13	(0.08)	0.20	(0.16)	-0.13	(0.09)	**0.45**	(0.19)
Israel	-0.35	(0.09)	c	c	-0.45	(0.13)	-0.33	(0.09)	-0.29	(0.21)	-0.37	(0.14)	-0.34	(0.13)
Italy	0.03	(0.04)	0.30	(0.15)	**-0.54**	(0.11)	**0.06**	(0.04)	-0.14	(0.22)	0.02	(0.04)	0.12	(0.08)
Japan	**0.31**	(0.09)	**0.73**	(0.15)	c	c	0.44	(0.08)	c	c	0.33	(0.13)	0.48	(0.09)
Korea	0.06	(0.10)	0.06	(0.12)	0.01	(0.22)	0.06	(0.08)	c	c	-0.09	(0.21)	0.08	(0.09)
Luxembourg	**-0.06**	(0.00)	**0.58**	(0.00)	**-0.01**	(0.00)	**0.10**	(0.00)	c	c	0.04	(0.00)	c	c
Mexico	**-1.03**	(0.04)	**0.27**	(0.13)	**-1.20**	(0.07)	**-0.66**	(0.05)	**-1.69**	(0.07)	**-0.96**	(0.07)	**-0.47**	(0.06)
Netherlands	0.25	(0.13)	0.19	(0.10)	0.15	(0.08)	0.27	(0.12)	c	c	0.20	(0.09)	0.15	(0.13)
New Zealand	0.12	(0.08)	**1.46**	(0.25)	0.14	(0.10)	0.20	(0.08)	0.04	(0.18)	0.02	(0.10)	0.33	(0.12)
Norway	-0.20	(0.06)	c	c	-0.19	(0.06)	c	c	-0.39	(0.11)	-0.22	(0.08)	0.09	(0.16)
Poland	0.36	(0.08)	0.36	(0.32)	0.36	(0.08)	c	c	0.28	(0.15)	0.31	(0.10)	0.60	(0.16)
Portugal	**0.10**	(0.08)	**0.80**	(0.17)	**0.02**	(0.08)	0.29	(0.10)	0.64	(0.52)	0.05	(0.10)	0.40	(0.16)
Slovak Republic	**-0.58**	(0.05)	**-0.14**	(0.19)	-0.53	(0.06)	-0.56	(0.06)	-0.65	(0.08)	-0.51	(0.06)	-0.61	(0.10)
Slovenia	**0.41**	(0.01)	**1.17**	(0.05)	0.26	(0.22)	0.44	(0.01)	0.14	(0.30)	0.44	(0.01)	0.42	(0.02)
Spain	**-0.06**	(0.05)	**0.16**	(0.09)	0.02	(0.05)	c	c	-0.02	(0.27)	-0.01	(0.06)	0.06	(0.07)
Sweden	0.01	(0.06)	0.28	(0.18)	0.04	(0.06)	0.62	(0.35)	-0.13	(0.12)	0.04	(0.08)	0.19	(0.14)
Switzerland	0.56	(0.08)	0.32	(0.22)	**0.47**	(0.15)	**0.82**	(0.15)	0.50	(0.20)	0.56	(0.08)	0.52	(0.19)
Turkey	-0.42	(0.06)	c	c	**-0.83**	(0.21)	**-0.39**	(0.07)	-0.40	(0.21)	-0.49	(0.10)	-0.33	(0.10)
United Kingdom	**0.33**	(0.09)	**0.72**	(0.13)	c	c	0.51	(0.08)	0.15	(0.18)	0.52	(0.09)	0.61	(0.15)
United States	0.36	(0.09)	0.94	(0.29)	**0.23**	(0.11)	0.41	(0.08)	0.12	(0.26)	0.48	(0.11)	0.32	(0.14)
OECD average	**0.00**	(0.01)	**0.39**	(0.03)	**-0.08**	(0.02)	**0.14**	(0.02)	**-0.07**	(0.04)	0.02	(0.02)	**0.11**	(0.02)
Albania	**-0.50**	(0.06)	**0.46**	(0.11)	-0.49	(0.07)	-0.36	(0.08)	**-0.92**	(0.06)	-0.34	(0.08)	-0.14	(0.13)
Argentina	-0.64	(0.11)	-0.38	(0.15)	-0.78	(0.10)	-0.40	(0.10)	**-1.31**	(0.25)	-0.54	(0.12)	-0.36	(0.14)
Brazil	**-0.79**	(0.04)	**0.59**	(0.16)	**-0.70**	(0.07)	**-0.50**	(0.05)	-0.77	(0.38)	-0.75	(0.07)	**-0.32**	(0.07)
Bulgaria	-0.04	(0.07)	c	c	-0.29	(0.15)	-0.02	(0.07)	-0.11	(0.21)	-0.10	(0.08)	0.07	(0.13)
Colombia	**-1.63**	(0.08)	**0.00**	(0.24)	**-1.52**	(0.09)	**-1.28**	(0.07)	-1.91	(0.22)	-1.64	(0.14)	**-1.10**	(0.10)
Costa Rica	**-1.30**	(0.09)	**0.45**	(0.20)	**-1.22**	(0.10)	**-0.85**	(0.08)	-1.31	(0.20)	-1.05	(0.11)	-0.84	(0.17)
Croatia	-0.50	(0.05)	c	c	c	c	-0.50	(0.05)	c	c	-0.53	(0.06)	-0.46	(0.11)
Cyprus*	**0.11**	(0.00)	**0.98**	(0.01)	-0.30	(0.03)	0.28	(0.00)	1.03	(0.01)	0.12	(0.00)	0.41	(0.00)
Hong Kong-China	0.50	(0.11)	0.45	(0.08)	0.43	(0.07)	0.45	(0.07)	c	c	c	c	0.44	(0.07)
Indonesia	-0.80	(0.11)	-0.66	(0.18)	**-0.95**	(0.12)	**-0.58**	(0.14)	-1.09	(0.22)	-0.87	(0.13)	-0.02	(0.15)
Jordan	**-0.60**	(0.09)	**0.31**	(0.19)	-0.45	(0.08)	c	c	-0.66	(0.19)	-0.55	(0.12)	-0.29	(0.12)
Kazakhstan	**-0.71**	(0.07)	**0.34**	(0.21)	-0.67	(0.08)	-0.70	(0.10)	-0.83	(0.09)	-0.80	(0.18)	-0.50	(0.11)
Latvia	0.02	(0.06)	c	c	0.04	(0.05)	-0.06	(0.18)	0.03	(0.12)	0.11	(0.08)	-0.06	(0.09)
Liechtenstein	0.76	(0.01)	c	c	0.84	(0.01)	0.22	(0.00)	c	c	0.77	(0.01)	c	c
Lithuania	0.13	(0.05)	c	c	0.15	(0.05)	c	c	0.09	(0.08)	0.19	(0.08)	0.13	(0.07)
Macao-China	c	c	0.39	(0.00)	0.23	(0.00)	0.52	(0.00)	c	c	c	c	0.36	(0.00)
Malaysia	-0.24	(0.07)	0.67	(0.54)	-0.06	(0.16)	-0.22	(0.07)	**-0.71**	(0.16)	-0.17	(0.09)	-0.04	(0.16)
Montenegro	-0.48	(0.00)	c	c	c	c	-0.48	(0.00)	c	c	-0.56	(0.00)	-0.30	(0.00)
Peru	**-1.46**	(0.08)	**-0.17**	(0.18)	**-1.48**	(0.09)	**-1.02**	(0.09)	-2.01	(0.13)	-1.38	(0.12)	**-0.54**	(0.13)
Qatar	**0.95**	(0.00)	**0.49**	(0.00)	0.74	(0.01)	0.79	(0.00)	0.62	(0.01)	0.83	(0.00)	0.76	(0.00)
Romania	0.21	(0.06)	c	c	0.22	(0.06)	c	c	-0.23	(0.23)	0.19	(0.07)	0.38	(0.13)
Russian Federation	-0.49	(0.07)	c	c	-0.45	(0.07)	-0.62	(0.12)	-0.60	(0.12)	-0.56	(0.12)	-0.37	(0.08)
Serbia	-0.57	(0.07)	c	c	c	c	-0.56	(0.07)	c	c	-0.54	(0.11)	-0.57	(0.10)
Shanghai-China	0.14	(0.10)	0.02	(0.48)	0.09	(0.14)	0.15	(0.12)	c	c	c	c	0.13	(0.09)
Singapore	1.19	(0.00)	c	c	1.22	(0.06)	1.19	(0.01)	c	c	c	c	1.19	(0.01)
Chinese Taipei	0.54	(0.11)	0.67	(0.17)	0.45	(0.13)	0.65	(0.12)	c	c	0.41	(0.15)	0.66	(0.12)
Thailand	**-0.80**	(0.08)	**-0.09**	(0.19)	**-0.99**	(0.08)	**-0.59**	(0.08)	-1.39	(0.16)	-0.75	(0.11)	**-0.21**	(0.12)
Tunisia	-1.35	(0.08)	c	c	-1.29	(0.12)	-1.37	(0.10)	-1.72	(0.33)	-1.39	(0.10)	-1.13	(0.18)
United Arab Emirates	**-0.01**	(0.08)	**0.71**	(0.09)	0.27	(0.12)	0.38	(0.05)	-0.03	(0.17)	0.09	(0.10)	**0.57**	(0.06)
Uruguay	**-0.02**	(0.08)	**0.80**	(0.16)	0.13	(0.09)	0.11	(0.09)	-0.48	(0.23)	-0.07	(0.11)	**0.52**	(0.11)
Viet Nam	**-0.53**	(0.07)	**0.22**	(0.23)	-0.87	(0.26)	-0.44	(0.07)	-0.70	(0.13)	-0.61	(0.13)	**0.07**	(0.14)

Notes: Values that are statistically significant are indicated in bold (see Annex A3).
ESCS refers to the *PISA index of economic, social and cultural status*.
1. A socio-economically disadvantaged school is one whose students' mean socio-economic status (ESCS) is statistically significantly below the mean socio-economic status of the country/economy; an average school is one where there is no difference from the country's/economy's mean; and an advantaged school is one whose students' mean socio-economic status is statistically significantly above the country/economy mean.
* See notes at the beginning of this Annex.
StatLink ⏹🖳 http://dx.doi.org/10.1787/888932957460

[Part 1/1]
Availability of computers at school
Table IV.3.18   *Results based on school principals' reports*

		School principals' report on the following:			
		Computers for educational purposes per student in the school		Proportion of computers connected to the Internet in the school	
		Mean ratio	S.E.	Mean ratio	S.E.
OECD	Australia	1.53	(0.05)	1.00	(0.00)
	Austria	1.47	(0.16)	0.99	(0.01)
	Belgium	0.72	(0.03)	0.97	(0.01)
	Canada	0.84	(0.03)	1.00	(0.00)
	Chile	0.49	(0.03)	0.95	(0.01)
	Czech Republic	0.92	(0.04)	0.99	(0.01)
	Denmark	0.83	(0.04)	0.99	(0.01)
	Estonia	0.69	(0.02)	1.00	(0.00)
	Finland	0.46	(0.02)	1.00	(0.00)
	France	0.60	(0.04)	0.96	(0.01)
	Germany	0.65	(0.07)	0.98	(0.01)
	Greece	0.24	(0.01)	0.99	(0.01)
	Hungary	0.64	(0.03)	0.99	(0.01)
	Iceland	0.63	(0.00)	1.00	(0.00)
	Ireland	0.64	(0.04)	1.00	(0.00)
	Israel	0.38	(0.02)	0.91	(0.01)
	Italy	0.48	(0.01)	0.96	(0.01)
	Japan	0.56	(0.04)	0.97	(0.01)
	Korea	0.40	(0.03)	0.97	(0.01)
	Luxembourg	0.87	(0.00)	1.00	(0.00)
	Mexico	0.28	(0.03)	0.73	(0.01)
	Netherlands	0.68	(0.04)	1.00	(0.00)
	New Zealand	1.10	(0.04)	0.99	(0.00)
	Norway	0.79	(0.03)	0.99	(0.01)
	Poland	0.36	(0.01)	0.98	(0.01)
	Portugal	0.46	(0.05)	0.97	(0.01)
	Slovak Republic	0.77	(0.03)	0.99	(0.00)
	Slovenia	0.62	(0.01)	1.00	(0.00)
	Spain	0.67	(0.02)	0.99	(0.01)
	Sweden	0.63	(0.03)	0.99	(0.00)
	Switzerland	0.68	(0.05)	0.99	(0.00)
	Turkey	0.14	(0.01)	0.96	(0.01)
	United Kingdom	1.02	(0.04)	0.99	(0.00)
	United States	0.95	(0.06)	0.94	(0.01)
	OECD average	0.68	(0.01)	0.97	(0.00)
Partners	Albania	0.36	(0.08)	0.70	(0.03)
	Argentina	0.49	(0.04)	0.71	(0.03)
	Brazil	0.20	(0.02)	0.92	(0.01)
	Bulgaria	0.56	(0.02)	0.97	(0.01)
	Colombia	0.48	(0.03)	0.71	(0.03)
	Costa Rica	0.53	(0.18)	0.83	(0.03)
	Croatia	0.32	(0.03)	0.96	(0.01)
	Cyprus*	0.74	(0.00)	0.90	(0.00)
	Hong Kong-China	0.73	(0.03)	1.00	(0.00)
	Indonesia	0.16	(0.01)	0.56	(0.04)
	Jordan	0.35	(0.01)	0.84	(0.02)
	Kazakhstan	0.80	(0.05)	0.57	(0.03)
	Latvia	0.98	(0.07)	0.99	(0.00)
	Liechtenstein	0.62	(0.01)	1.00	(0.00)
	Lithuania	0.85	(0.13)	0.99	(0.00)
	Macao-China	1.02	(0.00)	0.99	(0.00)
	Malaysia	0.19	(0.01)	0.87	(0.02)
	Montenegro	0.18	(0.01)	0.94	(0.00)
	Peru	0.40	(0.02)	0.65	(0.03)
	Qatar	0.61	(0.00)	0.90	(0.00)
	Romania	0.54	(0.13)	0.95	(0.01)
	Russian Federation	0.58	(0.03)	0.82	(0.02)
	Serbia	0.24	(0.01)	0.83	(0.03)
	Shanghai-China	0.51	(0.03)	0.95	(0.01)
	Singapore	0.67	(0.01)	0.99	(0.00)
	Chinese Taipei	0.34	(0.03)	1.00	(0.00)
	Thailand	0.48	(0.02)	0.95	(0.01)
	Tunisia	0.51	(0.11)	0.63	(0.04)
	United Arab Emirates	0.69	(0.04)	0.83	(0.01)
	Uruguay	0.40	(0.05)	0.96	(0.01)
	Viet Nam	0.24	(0.03)	0.80	(0.03)

* See notes at the beginning of this Annex.
StatLink ᘓᗑᔊ http://dx.doi.org/10.1787/888932957460

[Part 1/1]

Table IV.3.19 **Instructional use of Internet**

Results based on school principals' reports

School principals' report on how much of the work, in all subjects combined, expected from 15-year-olds in the national modal grade requires Internet access:

		Work during lessons								Homework								Assignments or projects							
		<10%		10-50%		51-75%		>75%		<10%		10-50%		51-75%		>75%		<10%		10-50%		51-75%		>75%	
		%	S.E.	%	S.E.	%	S.E.	%	S.E.	%	S.E.	%	S.E.	%	S.E.	%	S.E.	%	S.E.	%	S.E.	%	S.E.	%	S.E.
OECD	Australia	8.5	(1.1)	78.0	(1.6)	10.8	(1.2)	2.7	(0.6)	8.3	(1.0)	71.7	(1.7)	15.4	(1.3)	4.5	(0.7)	1.6	(0.5)	47.1	(1.5)	33.2	(1.6)	18.0	(1.4)
	Austria	25.0	(3.3)	60.8	(4.4)	8.7	(2.5)	5.4	(1.9)	31.2	(3.5)	53.7	(4.5)	8.3	(2.6)	6.9	(2.3)	6.7	(2.1)	37.3	(3.6)	26.4	(3.4)	29.6	(3.9)
	Belgium	44.1	(2.8)	51.9	(2.8)	2.6	(0.9)	1.4	(0.8)	38.1	(3.1)	52.4	(3.5)	5.1	(1.6)	4.4	(1.2)	17.7	(2.3)	51.9	(3.5)	21.1	(2.6)	9.3	(1.8)
	Canada	38.3	(2.7)	56.7	(2.9)	4.1	(1.1)	0.8	(0.4)	19.6	(1.9)	66.3	(2.3)	11.0	(1.7)	3.1	(0.7)	6.0	(1.1)	51.2	(2.4)	28.6	(2.3)	14.3	(1.6)
	Chile	15.5	(2.6)	56.8	(3.5)	14.6	(3.1)	13.1	(2.8)	5.8	(1.5)	40.4	(3.8)	32.9	(3.6)	21.0	(2.9)	5.8	(1.7)	36.9	(3.7)	31.3	(3.7)	26.0	(3.0)
	Czech Republic	32.3	(3.5)	66.3	(3.5)	0.2	(0.2)	1.2	(0.8)	32.7	(3.3)	63.3	(3.5)	3.2	(1.1)	0.7	(0.6)	29.6	(3.5)	58.1	(3.3)	8.1	(1.9)	4.2	(1.4)
	Denmark	7.0	(1.7)	75.2	(3.4)	10.2	(2.3)	7.6	(2.3)	8.4	(1.9)	66.7	(3.6)	18.1	(3.0)	6.8	(2.2)	1.1	(0.4)	19.1	(3.3)	33.9	(3.6)	45.9	(4.1)
	Estonia	25.8	(2.4)	70.7	(2.6)	2.3	(1.0)	1.1	(0.8)	16.7	(2.4)	76.5	(2.7)	4.8	(1.5)	2.0	(1.1)	10.0	(2.0)	53.4	(3.3)	22.6	(2.8)	14.0	(2.2)
	Finland	47.1	(3.5)	51.0	(3.5)	0.4	(0.0)	1.5	(1.0)	48.1	(3.2)	48.1	(3.3)	2.6	(1.4)	1.2	(0.7)	8.5	(1.5)	51.2	(3.1)	27.5	(2.7)	12.8	(2.3)
	France	49.0	(3.3)	50.5	(3.3)	0.0	c	0.6	(0.5)	28.4	(3.2)	66.9	(3.5)	4.3	(1.5)	0.4	(0.5)	10.3	(2.0)	63.6	(2.9)	15.4	(2.4)	10.7	(1.8)
	Germany	41.0	(3.5)	54.7	(3.4)	2.8	(1.2)	1.5	(0.9)	32.6	(3.2)	60.8	(3.4)	3.8	(1.4)	2.8	(1.3)	9.9	(2.0)	43.9	(3.8)	29.4	(3.0)	16.7	(2.6)
	Greece	45.0	(3.8)	48.2	(3.9)	2.5	(0.8)	4.3	(1.6)	24.8	(3.6)	60.2	(4.2)	12.4	(3.1)	2.7	(1.3)	2.4	(1.2)	18.9	(2.9)	26.0	(3.4)	52.7	(4.0)
	Hungary	39.5	(3.7)	59.5	(3.8)	0.0	c	1.0	(0.9)	27.0	(3.6)	69.1	(3.7)	2.6	(1.2)	1.3	(0.9)	20.1	(3.1)	53.2	(3.6)	17.4	(3.0)	9.3	(2.1)
	Iceland	60.0	(0.2)	40.0	(0.2)	0.0	c	0.0	c	46.8	(0.2)	52.0	(0.3)	0.0	c	1.2	(0.1)	25.5	(0.2)	71.9	(0.2)	1.4	(0.0)	1.2	(0.1)
	Ireland	67.4	(3.9)	31.9	(3.8)	0.0	c	0.7	(0.7)	45.6	(3.9)	47.8	(3.8)	5.4	(1.8)	1.3	(1.1)	24.0	(3.5)	46.1	(3.9)	16.6	(3.0)	13.4	(2.7)
	Israel	50.4	(4.0)	44.1	(3.9)	4.9	(2.2)	0.6	(0.6)	25.8	(3.1)	61.2	(3.9)	8.8	(2.4)	4.3	(1.8)	12.5	(2.4)	55.6	(4.1)	19.4	(3.2)	12.5	(2.8)
	Italy	23.8	(1.8)	60.0	(2.4)	10.6	(1.3)	5.6	(1.0)	16.6	(1.9)	59.2	(2.1)	16.1	(1.5)	8.1	(1.2)	6.2	(1.2)	35.8	(2.2)	27.6	(1.9)	30.4	(2.1)
	Japan	32.8	(3.6)	50.3	(4.0)	4.1	(1.5)	12.8	(2.7)	30.8	(3.4)	54.9	(4.1)	5.0	(1.6)	9.4	(2.3)	8.0	(2.0)	45.5	(4.0)	18.5	(2.9)	28.1	(3.5)
	Korea	57.3	(3.4)	31.7	(3.2)	6.1	(2.0)	5.0	(1.9)	20.4	(3.4)	50.1	(4.4)	11.2	(2.7)	18.2	(3.5)	17.2	(3.1)	39.1	(4.0)	20.1	(3.1)	23.5	(3.5)
	Luxembourg	54.0	(0.1)	46.0	(0.1)	0.0	c	0.0	c	45.4	(0.1)	54.1	(0.1)	0.4	(0.0)	0.0	c	17.7	(0.1)	70.5	(0.1)	7.0	(0.1)	4.8	(0.0)
	Mexico	36.2	(1.9)	50.0	(2.4)	9.6	(1.3)	4.1	(0.7)	12.8	(1.2)	52.0	(1.9)	23.7	(1.5)	11.4	(1.2)	12.4	(1.4)	46.0	(2.0)	25.7	(1.7)	15.9	(1.5)
	Netherlands	48.3	(3.6)	47.0	(3.7)	2.6	(1.5)	2.2	(1.2)	20.3	(3.0)	62.0	(4.3)	13.3	(3.8)	4.4	(1.9)	9.3	(2.3)	41.9	(4.5)	30.5	(3.9)	18.3	(3.6)
	New Zealand	29.2	(3.5)	66.1	(3.8)	3.7	(1.5)	1.0	(0.5)	16.3	(3.2)	72.6	(4.0)	4.8	(1.6)	6.3	(1.9)	5.3	(1.9)	60.5	(3.9)	22.9	(4.0)	11.3	(2.4)
	Norway	4.1	(1.5)	39.8	(3.6)	10.8	(2.2)	45.2	(3.6)	2.4	(1.1)	27.8	(3.7)	17.6	(3.1)	52.2	(4.1)	0.5	(0.5)	12.3	(2.6)	23.6	(3.2)	63.5	(3.7)
	Poland	53.3	(3.8)	45.8	(3.8)	0.9	(0.8)	0.0	c	22.1	(3.0)	70.5	(3.6)	6.4	(2.1)	0.9	(0.9)	8.2	(2.1)	41.6	(3.9)	31.8	(3.8)	18.4	(3.1)
	Portugal	42.5	(4.3)	54.9	(4.1)	2.4	(1.2)	0.2	(0.1)	21.9	(4.1)	65.4	(4.6)	10.4	(2.9)	2.4	(1.2)	15.8	(3.5)	59.7	(4.2)	19.1	(3.2)	5.4	(2.1)
	Slovak Republic	11.9	(2.8)	75.6	(3.0)	7.5	(1.9)	5.1	(1.2)	30.8	(3.8)	60.7	(3.8)	6.2	(1.9)	2.3	(1.0)	8.3	(2.3)	52.6	(3.8)	23.4	(3.0)	15.7	(2.2)
	Slovenia	20.0	(0.5)	66.7	(0.7)	7.7	(0.6)	5.6	(0.2)	7.8	(0.4)	68.2	(0.7)	15.6	(0.7)	8.4	(0.2)	9.9	(0.4)	45.5	(0.7)	23.7	(0.7)	20.9	(0.4)
	Spain	29.6	(2.6)	61.6	(2.6)	6.3	(1.5)	2.4	(0.8)	15.0	(1.8)	67.7	(2.6)	12.8	(2.6)	4.5	(1.1)	4.8	(0.8)	42.2	(2.9)	27.0	(2.7)	25.9	(2.2)
	Sweden	11.0	(2.1)	56.8	(3.6)	7.8	(1.9)	24.4	(3.1)	32.2	(3.1)	38.2	(4.0)	11.2	(2.1)	18.5	(2.9)	7.8	(2.1)	41.6	(3.7)	19.2	(2.6)	31.4	(3.2)
	Switzerland	44.5	(3.5)	53.2	(3.7)	1.2	(0.8)	1.1	(0.7)	46.4	(3.2)	51.1	(3.2)	1.3	(0.8)	1.2	(0.7)	10.8	(2.2)	55.4	(3.8)	20.8	(2.3)	13.0	(2.4)
	Turkey	24.6	(3.4)	62.0	(4.0)	7.8	(2.1)	5.7	(1.8)	7.1	(2.0)	49.9	(4.0)	28.1	(3.5)	14.9	(2.8)	4.3	(1.5)	36.0	(3.3)	24.3	(3.5)	35.4	(4.2)
	United Kingdom	34.0	(4.0)	62.0	(4.0)	3.8	(1.5)	0.2	(0.1)	11.1	(2.2)	64.6	(3.4)	20.5	(3.2)	3.8	(1.3)	5.1	(2.4)	51.6	(3.4)	30.6	(3.2)	12.7	(2.6)
	United States	33.3	(4.1)	58.4	(4.3)	5.6	(2.1)	2.7	(1.4)	21.8	(3.4)	70.1	(3.8)	5.9	(2.0)	2.2	(1.2)	4.4	(1.5)	56.1	(4.0)	28.8	(3.8)	10.7	(2.2)
	OECD average	34.9	(0.5)	55.4	(0.6)	4.8	(0.3)	4.9	(0.3)	24.2	(0.5)	58.7	(0.6)	10.3	(0.4)	6.9	(0.3)	10.2	(0.3)	46.9	(0.6)	23.0	(0.5)	19.9	(0.5)
Partners	Albania	56.4	(4.1)	32.9	(3.6)	8.8	(2.6)	1.9	(1.1)	19.6	(3.3)	63.0	(4.4)	10.7	(2.6)	6.6	(2.9)	12.0	(2.5)	33.3	(3.9)	23.2	(3.6)	31.5	(3.8)
	Argentina	34.2	(3.8)	51.1	(4.3)	9.5	(2.3)	5.2	(1.7)	15.6	(2.6)	59.2	(3.9)	16.8	(3.0)	8.3	(2.5)	10.7	(2.2)	50.3	(4.0)	23.5	(3.8)	15.6	(2.4)
	Brazil	44.4	(3.3)	44.6	(3.2)	8.0	(1.8)	3.0	(1.0)	12.8	(2.0)	52.0	(2.9)	26.0	(2.5)	9.1	(1.6)	5.8	(1.2)	32.8	(2.4)	33.8	(2.5)	27.6	(2.0)
	Bulgaria	11.5	(2.2)	59.6	(4.0)	11.5	(2.6)	17.5	(3.0)	9.6	(2.2)	43.5	(4.0)	22.9	(3.6)	24.0	(2.9)	10.3	(2.6)	40.9	(3.8)	22.1	(3.0)	26.7	(3.1)
	Colombia	29.3	(3.9)	46.6	(3.9)	15.4	(3.1)	8.7	(2.1)	9.7	(1.7)	53.2	(4.4)	23.6	(4.1)	13.5	(2.4)	10.6	(2.4)	49.5	(4.2)	24.4	(3.9)	15.4	(3.1)
	Costa Rica	48.2	(3.5)	37.5	(3.5)	9.6	(2.4)	4.7	(1.4)	13.6	(2.9)	43.0	(3.9)	29.4	(3.8)	14.0	(2.5)	11.4	(2.4)	35.6	(4.0)	28.3	(3.8)	24.7	(3.1)
	Croatia	15.8	(2.8)	67.3	(3.4)	8.5	(1.7)	8.3	(2.2)	8.7	(2.2)	64.9	(3.9)	20.6	(2.8)	5.8	(1.8)	5.0	(1.7)	35.8	(3.6)	31.2	(3.8)	27.9	(3.4)
	Cyprus*	43.7	(0.1)	45.0	(0.1)	4.9	(0.0)	6.3	(0.1)	15.8	(0.1)	56.5	(0.1)	18.1	(0.1)	9.6	(0.1)	12.0	(0.1)	48.9	(0.1)	18.9	(0.1)	20.2	(0.1)
	Hong Kong-China	61.4	(4.1)	36.4	(4.2)	1.6	(0.9)	0.7	(0.6)	24.7	(3.5)	70.6	(3.7)	4.7	(1.7)	0.0	c	9.5	(2.6)	61.0	(4.4)	21.9	(3.5)	7.6	(2.3)
	Indonesia	40.7	(4.1)	46.1	(4.5)	6.5	(2.0)	6.7	(2.0)	22.0	(3.8)	62.9	(4.4)	10.6	(1.9)	4.4	(1.8)	24.5	(4.0)	53.2	(4.9)	13.8	(3.0)	8.5	(2.2)
	Jordan	29.4	(3.5)	47.6	(3.9)	13.0	(2.6)	10.0	(2.2)	25.1	(3.2)	48.7	(4.0)	16.6	(2.8)	9.6	(2.6)	19.8	(2.9)	44.8	(3.9)	18.1	(2.9)	17.3	(2.8)
	Kazakhstan	17.6	(3.0)	45.6	(4.5)	22.2	(3.7)	14.5	(2.9)	18.5	(2.7)	49.5	(3.8)	20.7	(2.9)	11.3	(2.2)	13.4	(2.5)	36.7	(4.1)	29.7	(4.2)	20.3	(3.3)
	Latvia	34.2	(3.4)	59.8	(3.2)	4.2	(1.5)	1.8	(1.1)	15.2	(2.7)	74.5	(3.0)	6.3	(1.3)	4.0	(1.6)	7.3	(1.8)	58.2	(3.7)	23.7	(3.0)	10.8	(2.4)
	Liechtenstein	14.1	(0.7)	85.9	(0.7)	0.0	c	0.0	c	80.4	(1.1)	19.6	(1.1)	0.0	c	0.0	c	1.0	(0.6)	79.6	(0.8)	19.4	(1.0)	0.0	c
	Lithuania	36.9	(3.6)	55.4	(3.8)	4.2	(1.4)	3.6	(1.3)	20.2	(2.9)	63.5	(3.3)	11.9	(2.1)	4.3	(1.5)	9.4	(1.8)	46.2	(3.1)	25.5	(2.9)	18.9	(2.6)
	Macao-China	34.4	(0.1)	55.9	(0.1)	3.7	(0.0)	6.1	(0.0)	7.0	(0.0)	77.6	(0.0)	9.4	(0.0)	6.1	(0.0)	2.5	(0.0)	43.0	(0.1)	34.0	(0.1)	20.5	(0.0)
	Malaysia	56.0	(4.0)	34.8	(3.9)	7.0	(2.2)	2.3	(1.2)	38.1	(3.6)	45.2	(3.7)	15.2	(3.0)	1.5	(0.9)	20.7	(3.1)	39.7	(4.2)	22.5	(3.4)	17.1	(3.3)
	Montenegro	16.7	(0.1)	51.8	(0.1)	14.0	(0.1)	17.5	(0.1)	19.0	(0.2)	42.1	(0.1)	38.9	(0.2)	0.0	(0.0)	13.7	(0.1)	43.9	(0.1)	14.6	(0.1)	27.8	(0.1)
	Peru	22.6	(2.9)	57.0	(3.6)	13.3	(2.4)	7.1	(2.1)	19.8	(2.7)	59.0	(3.4)	16.1	(2.6)	5.2	(1.6)	18.4	(2.7)	49.2	(4.0)	19.7	(3.3)	12.7	(2.5)
	Qatar	20.8	(0.1)	53.4	(0.1)	17.3	(0.1)	8.5	(0.0)	10.1	(0.1)	61.9	(0.1)	15.7	(0.1)	12.2	(0.1)	5.5	(0.0)	30.2	(0.1)	31.6	(0.1)	32.7	(0.1)
	Romania	12.5	(2.1)	36.1	(3.9)	12.7	(2.7)	38.6	(3.9)	25.1	(3.4)	37.4	(3.8)	17.7	(3.2)	19.7	(3.0)	17.4	(2.6)	31.8	(3.6)	18.9	(3.4)	31.8	(3.7)
	Russian Federation	31.2	(3.5)	59.2	(3.7)	5.0	(1.5)	4.5	(1.5)	16.4	(2.4)	68.2	(3.0)	10.2	(2.3)	5.2	(1.6)	13.3	(2.3)	47.5	(3.4)	22.7	(3.3)	16.5	(3.3)
	Serbia	29.0	(4.1)	62.9	(4.2)	2.6	(1.3)	5.5	(1.6)	35.4	(4.5)	59.1	(4.7)	3.6	(1.7)	1.9	(1.3)	47.1	(4.5)	35.2	(4.2)	10.7	(2.5)	7.0	(2.5)
	Shanghai-China	30.9	(3.6)	65.1	(3.8)	0.7	(0.7)	3.3	(1.3)	25.8	(3.8)	70.1	(3.9)	2.0	(1.3)	2.1	(1.1)	11.2	(2.5)	51.6	(3.9)	21.2	(3.5)	16.1	(3.2)
	Singapore	31.0	(0.3)	66.5	(0.5)	2.5	(0.6)	0.0	c	23.8	(0.2)	70.2	(0.5)	4.4	(0.1)	1.6	(0.6)	9.8	(0.1)	73.7	(0.6)	9.2	(0.8)	7.2	(0.5)
	Chinese Taipei	48.3	(4.1)	44.4	(3.9)	5.4	(1.5)	2.0	(1.2)	37.0	(4.1)	52.9	(4.0)	7.8	(2.0)	2.3	(1.3)	21.9	(3.3)	41.5	(3.9)	16.0	(3.2)	20.6	(3.2)
	Thailand	8.7	(2.4)	59.4	(3.7)	18.7	(3.0)	13.3	(2.4)	6.3	(1.7)	58.3	(4.1)	19.1	(3.0)	16.3	(3.1)	5.0	(1.6)	44.2	(3.3)	23.2	(2.8)	27.5	(3.2)
	Tunisia	61.8	(4.0)	25.4	(4.0)	3.6	(1.6)	9.2	(2.4)	63.6	(4.1)	27.3	(3.9)	2.3	(1.4)	6.8	(2.2)	45.3	(4.0)	34.7	(4.0)	8.4	(2.5)	11.7	(2.9)
	United Arab Emirates	28.8	(2.0)	54.0	(2.5)	9.9	(1.3)	7.3	(1.0)	11.3	(2.3)	57.4	(2.8)	16.9	(1.5)	14.4	(1.7)	5.2	(1.9)	30.3	(2.4)	26.0	(1.9)	38.5	(2.2)
	Uruguay	23.6	(2.6)	54.2	(3.5)	14.5	(2.5)	7.7	(1.9)	6.8	(1.4)	46.4	(3.7)	25.7	(3.1)	21.1	(2.6)	14.1	(2.4)	38.5	(3.7)	17.1	(2.7)	30.3	(3.2)
	Viet Nam	70.1	(3.8)	23.8	(3.4)	3.6	(1.6)	2.5	(1.3)	51.3	(3.5)	40.3	(4.0)	6.2	(2.0)	2.3	(1.3)	75.6	(3.6)	15.0	(3.1)	6.5	(1.8)	2.9	(1.4)

* See notes at the beginning of this Annex.

StatLink http://dx.doi.org/10.1787/888932957460

[Part 1/1]

Table IV.3.20 Compulsory and intended instruction time, by age

Number of hours per year for 5-15 year-olds in public institutions (2011)

		Source	Number of hours per year of total intended instruction time											
			Age 5[1]	Age 6[1]	Age 7	Age 8	Age 9	Age 10	Age 11	Age 12	Age 13	Age 14	Age 15 (typical programme)	Age 15 (least demanding programme)
OECD	Australia	a	714	991	991	992	993	997	995	1 026	1 002	1 003	1 004	949
	Austria	a	a	a	735	735	765	765	905	935	940	1 000	1 050	1 005
	Belgium (Fl.)	a	a	831	831	831	831	831	831	955	955	955	955	448
	Belgium (Fr.)	a	a	930	930	930	930	930	930	1 020	1 020	m	m	a
	Canada	a	a	913	913	921	921	921	922	928	927	915	920	a
	Chile	a	a	855	855	1 083	1 083	1 083	1 083	1 083	1 083	1 197	1 197	1 197
	Czech Republic[2]	a	a	526	526	644	644	644	819	819	878	878	790	585
	Denmark	a	a	a	690	713	803	803	833	840	870	990	930	900
	England	a	798	798	893	893	893	893	912	912	912	950	950	a
	Estonia	a	a	a	608	608	608	691	691	691	770	770	770	m
	Finland	a	a	a	608	608	671	671	707	660	913	913	913	a
	France	a	a	864	864	864	864	864	964	982	1 234	1 144	1 036	a
	Germany	a	m	m	627	655	754	770	856	873	887	900	933	m
	Greece	a	a	1 188	1 188	1 170	1 170	1 164	1 164	796	796	796	773	a
	Hungary	a	a	a	611	617	611	780	780	853	902	902	1 106	1 106
	Iceland	a	a	800	800	800	800	933	933	933	987	987	987	a
	Ireland	a	732	732	915	915	915	915	915	915	935	935	935	935
	Israel	a	a	906	910	946	1 001	985	991	960	983	1 000	1 102	m
	Italy	a	a	891	891	891	891	891	990	990	990	979	1 089	m
	Japan	a	a	663	707	760	797	797	797	866	866	866	m	a
	Korea	a	a	560	560	635	635	703	703	842	842	867	963	a
	Luxembourg	a	a	924	924	924	924	924	924	900	900	900	900	900
	Mexico	a	a	800	800	800	800	800	800	1 167	1 167	1 167	864	a
	Netherlands	a	a	940	940	940	940	940	940	1 000	1 000	1 000	1 000	a
	New Zealand		m	m	m	m	m	m	m	m	m	m	m	m
	Norway	a	a	678	694	713	735	797	808	809	853	854	859	a
	Poland	a	a	a	618	618	644	779	779	779	783	783	832	a
	Portugal	a	a	1 004	915	915	915	898	898	950	950	950	950	m
	Scotland	a	a	a	a	a	a	a	a	a	a	a	a	a
	Slovak Republic	a	a	627	656	713	798	770	827	855	855	855	941	941
	Slovenia	a	a	581	608	634	686	739	739	831	844	776	908	888
	Spain	a	a	875	875	875	875	875	875	1 050	1 050	1 050	1 050	1 050
	Sweden[3]	a	a	a	741	741	741	741	741	741	741	741	741	a
	Switzerland		m	m	m	m	m	m	m	m	m	m	m	m
	Turkey	a	a	864	864	864	864	864	864	864	864	810	810	a
	United States	a	m	m	m	m	m	m	m	m	m	m	m	a
	OECD average			823	790	811	828	849	872	901	928	930	942	
Partners	Albania	b	a	525	525	578	604	604	709	761	761	761	761	761
	Argentina[4]	c	m	m	m	m	720	720	720	896	896	896	m	m
	Brazil	a	m	m	m	m	m	m	m	m	m	m	m	m
	Bulgaria	b	a	a	438	455	587	587	848	848	848	848	1 080	855
	Colombia	b	a	1 000	1 000	1 000	1 000	1 000	1 200	1 200	1 200	1 200	1 200	1 200
	Costa Rica		m	m	m	m	m	m	m	m	m	m	m	m
	Croatia	b	a	a	525	525	525	578	735	761	840	840	840	698
	Cyprus*	b	a	863	817	817	817	817	817	919	919	919	889	a
	Hong Kong-China	b	a	554	554	554	554	554	554	697	697	697	697	a
	Indonesia	a	a	a	455	473	653	793	793	793	1 020	1 020	1 020	a
	Jordan	b	a	731	878	878	907	907	936	1 024	1 024	995	1 053	1 024
	Kazakhstan		m	m	m	m	m	m	m	m	m	m	m	m
	Latvia	b	a	a	499	537	560	607	653	700	747	793	839	839
	Liechtenstein	b	a	673	761	772	878	878	878	995	995	995	1 024	0
	Lithuania	b	a	a	411	552	528	552	624	756	783	810	810	m
	Macao-China	b	a	587	587	587	587	622	622	833	833	833	800	800
	Malaysia	b	m	m	m	m	m	m	m	m	m	m	m	m
	Montenegro	b	a	510	510	510	599	650	663	765	765	698	919	840
	Peru	b	a	900	900	900	900	900	900	1 050	1 050	1 050	1 050	1 050
	Qatar	b	a	720	720	1 056	1 056	1 056	1 056	1 056	1 056	1 056	1 152	m
	Romania	b	m	m	m	m	m	m	m	m	m	m	m	m
	Russian Federation	a	a	a	385	499	499	499	814	840	893	919	919	m
	Serbia		m	m	m	m	m	m	m	m	m	m	m	m
	Shanghai-China	b	a	635	635	655	674	674	771	771	771	680	793	227
	Singapore	b	a	754	780	803	803	803	624	793	820	838	703	618
	Chinese Taipei	b	a	624	624	624	780	780	858	858	1 141	1 141	1 170	1 300
	Thailand	b	a	a	833	833	833	833	833	833	1 000	1 000	1 000	1 000
	Tunisia	c	m	m	m	m	800	960	992	992	992	992	m	m
	United Arab Emirates	b	a	919	919	919	919	919	1 021	1 021	1 021	1 021	1 021	1 021
	Uruguay	b	850	850	850	850	850	850	850	589	589	589	589	589
	Viet Nam	b	m	m	m	m	m	m	m	m	m	m	m	m

1. Only if applicable to primary education.
2. Minimum number of hours per year.
3. Estimated minimum numbers of hours per year because breakdown by age not available.
4. Year of reference 2010.

Sources: *a. Education at a Glance 2013: OECD Indicators* (OECD, 2013). For further notes, see *Education at a Glance 2013: OECD Indicators* (OECD, 2013) Annex 3, available on line: *www.oecd.org/edu/eag.htm*
b. PISA system-level data collection in 2013.
c. UNESCO Institute for Statistics (World Education Indicators Programme).

* See notes at the beginning of this Annex.

StatLink http://dx.doi.org/10.1787/888932957460

[Part 1/1]
Table IV.3.21 Students' learning time in school
Results based on students' self-reports

	Total class periods per week				Regular mathematics lessons				Regular language-of-instruction lessons				Regular science lessons				Regular mathematics, language-of-instruction and science lessons			
	Number of all class periods in a normal full week of school (class periods)		Variability in total class periods		Time per week spent learning (minutes)		Variability in learning time		Time per week spent learning (minutes)		Variability in learning time		Time per week spent learning (minutes)		Variability in learning time		Time per week spent learning (minutes)		Variability in learning time	
	Mean	S.E.	S.D.	S.E.	Mean	S.E.	S.D.	S.E.	Mean	S.E.	S.D.	S.E.	Mean	S.E.	S.D.	S.E.	Mean	S.E.	S.D.	S.E.
OECD																				
Australia	26.5	(0.2)	9.5	(0.2)	236.3	(0.9)	60.2	(1.3)	233.3	(1.0)	56.2	(1.3)	227.2	(1.3)	65.8	(1.6)	693.5	(2.9)	157.8	(3.8)
Austria	33.2	(0.3)	7.9	(0.2)	156.4	(2.4)	69.7	(2.3)	144.3	(1.7)	48.5	(1.4)	199.8	(4.8)	146.8	(5.1)	499.7	(5.2)	182.0	(4.7)
Belgium	31.8	(0.1)	6.1	(0.2)	216.9	(1.4)	70.6	(2.2)	217.8	(1.4)	61.6	(2.7)	192.2	(2.6)	109.4	(3.3)	633.7	(3.7)	171.6	(4.6)
Canada	19.4	(0.1)	7.8	(0.1)	313.8	(2.8)	122.0	(1.6)	316.1	(2.9)	126.2	(1.8)	306.2	(2.7)	132.1	(1.7)	936.8	(7.9)	330.0	(4.7)
Chile	30.1	(0.5)	15.0	(0.2)	397.6	(6.3)	189.7	(4.0)	374.4	(6.2)	179.5	(3.9)	295.7	(5.4)	194.7	(4.1)	1 066.6	(15.6)	490.1	(9.9)
Czech Republic	32.6	(0.1)	2.9	(0.1)	182.3	(1.9)	43.1	(1.5)	179.1	(1.5)	40.0	(1.3)	216.4	(3.2)	131.9	(3.8)	578.2	(4.4)	155.6	(4.2)
Denmark	29.2	(0.2)	6.3	(0.2)	224.4	(3.0)	90.5	(4.6)	314.5	(4.1)	126.1	(6.2)	176.8	(2.3)	92.2	(3.5)	713.3	(7.0)	235.7	(8.8)
Estonia	32.8	(0.1)	5.4	(0.2)	222.8	(1.0)	31.3	(1.4)	198.2	(1.2)	42.5	(4.8)	196.1	(2.5)	106.3	(2.2)	616.6	(3.4)	127.1	(3.3)
Finland	29.3	(0.2)	3.9	(0.3)	175.5	(1.5)	38.8	(0.8)	152.2	(1.2)	37.1	(1.0)	188.6	(1.6)	70.0	(1.3)	513.6	(3.4)	104.7	(2.5)
France	23.3	(0.3)	10.6	(0.1)	207.0	(2.2)	88.4	(3.0)	214.8	(1.9)	89.4	(2.6)	173.8	(2.7)	120.5	(3.1)	597.0	(5.1)	227.5	(6.0)
Germany	32.9	(0.1)	3.7	(0.1)	196.8	(2.6)	75.7	(6.2)	190.8	(2.1)	67.5	(4.6)	254.8	(3.6)	106.8	(4.4)	639.8	(6.8)	187.5	(10.8)
Greece	32.6	(0.0)	1.1	(0.0)	209.0	(0.7)	24.7	(0.6)	170.5	(0.6)	16.4	(0.6)	229.2	(1.6)	46.7	(0.9)	623.3	(2.4)	62.0	(1.7)
Hungary	31.3	(0.2)	3.0	(0.1)	149.9	(1.7)	37.2	(1.1)	164.2	(1.6)	45.0	(1.4)	193.1	(3.7)	84.7	(2.9)	512.0	(5.1)	123.0	(4.1)
Iceland	33.8	(0.2)	7.8	(0.2)	243.9	(1.9)	84.2	(4.0)	238.1	(2.0)	85.9	(5.0)	141.2	(1.5)	68.4	(2.4)	619.3	(4.2)	178.1	(6.6)
Ireland	42.6	(0.2)	7.6	(0.2)	188.8	(1.2)	32.9	(0.8)	180.7	(1.2)	31.4	(0.7)	145.4	(1.9)	58.4	(2.4)	515.3	(3.3)	96.4	(2.3)
Israel	35.2	(0.5)	10.9	(0.3)	254.2	(2.5)	89.6	(1.9)	192.4	(2.7)	84.5	(2.3)	196.5	(3.4)	124.4	(3.5)	628.6	(5.6)	196.1	(4.9)
Italy	30.2	(0.1)	3.1	(0.0)	232.0	(1.7)	59.5	(0.8)	277.4	(1.3)	80.0	(0.9)	135.5	(1.2)	61.5	(1.8)	645.9	(2.8)	130.7	(1.9)
Japan	31.9	(0.2)	3.7	(0.2)	234.7	(3.0)	74.7	(1.9)	204.8	(2.1)	58.3	(1.9)	165.4	(3.1)	65.6	(2.4)	604.9	(6.3)	164.1	(5.0)
Korea	34.9	(0.2)	10.0	(0.3)	213.3	(3.2)	64.5	(3.0)	203.8	(2.6)	57.8	(3.5)	199.4	(6.5)	96.1	(19.9)	616.5	(9.3)	171.6	(14.8)
Luxembourg	27.6	(0.1)	6.8	(0.1)	204.7	(0.8)	57.4	(1.0)	188.4	(0.8)	56.4	(1.1)	156.6	(1.1)	79.2	(1.0)	553.6	(1.9)	143.7	(2.8)
Mexico	23.6	(0.2)	13.9	(0.1)	253.2	(1.7)	113.6	(3.1)	232.1	(1.8)	120.9	(5.2)	251.8	(1.8)	141.5	(3.6)	734.4	(4.0)	286.2	(5.6)
Netherlands	30.9	(0.3)	6.1	(0.3)	170.7	(2.9)	100.0	(15.2)	168.8	(2.3)	82.9	(8.1)	164.7	(4.5)	152.2	(6.6)	500.6	(6.6)	243.3	(9.6)
New Zealand	24.5	(0.2)	7.2	(0.2)	240.8	(2.0)	49.3	(2.6)	242.6	(2.0)	53.6	(4.4)	247.9	(3.5)	103.0	(8.3)	731.2	(6.4)	166.8	(9.4)
Norway	27.5	(0.3)	9.4	(0.7)	199.0	(2.4)	93.3	(13.8)	217.9	(2.2)	78.3	(5.6)	144.3	(1.7)	59.7	(3.3)	554.4	(4.4)	160.2	(8.4)
Poland	33.5	(0.1)	2.1	(0.1)	198.1	(1.7)	26.1	(1.1)	219.7	(1.6)	25.0	(1.1)	169.3	(2.5)	37.6	(1.3)	587.1	(3.7)	55.5	(2.3)
Portugal	24.5	(0.4)	9.7	(0.2)	288.0	(4.9)	110.3	(5.7)	237.6	(3.7)	94.8	(3.2)	237.9	(9.3)	194.6	(14.8)	788.2	(14.3)	297.0	(21.3)
Slovak Republic	31.8	(0.1)	3.0	(0.1)	180.8	(2.7)	62.6	(1.9)	179.3	(1.7)	49.1	(0.9)	161.6	(4.6)	129.8	(2.9)	510.7	(8.1)	184.8	(4.8)
Slovenia	32.0	(0.1)	7.9	(0.2)	160.3	(0.5)	25.7	(0.3)	168.9	(0.4)	22.3	(0.5)	184.9	(1.6)	76.0	(0.5)	513.7	(2.2)	98.6	(0.9)
Spain	30.9	(0.0)	1.5	(0.0)	210.3	(0.9)	46.0	(2.0)	203.3	(1.1)	49.3	(1.9)	184.3	(1.8)	96.0	(2.2)	598.1	(3.1)	143.6	(6.6)
Sweden	24.0	(0.3)	7.2	(0.2)	182.2	(2.2)	65.6	(4.9)	178.8	(2.9)	71.8	(5.1)	188.5	(2.6)	74.8	(3.9)	547.6	(6.2)	162.4	(13.0)
Switzerland	32.1	(0.3)	9.9	(0.6)	207.0	(2.6)	93.1	(6.2)	206.6	(3.1)	120.7	(9.8)	164.3	(3.7)	147.4	(12.2)	575.6	(5.5)	212.6	(10.6)
Turkey	34.7	(0.2)	4.3	(0.1)	171.9	(2.2)	72.1	(2.0)	198.9	(2.5)	72.0	(1.3)	166.9	(6.3)	125.0	(5.6)	537.3	(9.2)	197.9	(6.7)
United Kingdom	27.2	(0.3)	7.6	(0.3)	230.0	(2.2)	88.9	(4.8)	231.8	(2.6)	86.4	(4.0)	295.0	(3.7)	126.7	(5.3)	746.2	(6.5)	223.9	(9.4)
United States	19.7	(0.4)	14.0	(0.3)	254.1	(4.9)	131.9	(5.4)	257.7	(5.0)	145.0	(8.2)	254.9	(4.9)	137.2	(6.1)	764.6	(13.5)	349.2	(13.3)
OECD average	29.9	(0.0)	7.0	(0.0)	217.8	(0.4)	73.0	(0.8)	214.7	(0.4)	72.4	(0.7)	200.2	(0.6)	104.8	(1.0)	632.3	(1.2)	188.7	(1.4)
Partners																				
Albania	25.5	(0.3)	9.6	(0.2)	170.8	(1.3)	47.9	(1.4)	176.2	(1.9)	57.5	(1.1)	148.8	(1.8)	85.8	(1.4)	496.0	(3.7)	135.8	(4.1)
Argentina	14.2	(0.3)	8.6	(0.2)	268.6	(6.3)	142.6	(3.2)	262.4	(7.0)	147.4	(4.2)	216.5	(6.2)	160.1	(6.8)	701.1	(13.3)	341.2	(9.2)
Brazil	21.6	(0.2)	11.1	(0.1)	214.7	(1.7)	94.4	(3.0)	208.0	(1.9)	91.8	(2.0)	161.6	(3.0)	106.2	(4.1)	582.5	(5.3)	227.1	(6.3)
Bulgaria	30.7	(0.2)	8.8	(0.2)	133.9	(3.0)	56.0	(3.9)	140.6	(1.5)	43.9	(2.1)	257.5	(3.3)	98.6	(7.5)	530.9	(5.1)	135.0	(7.0)
Colombia	22.6	(0.4)	10.6	(0.2)	262.6	(3.8)	136.0	(5.0)	231.7	(3.5)	113.2	(3.4)	205.0	(4.0)	122.7	(4.7)	702.0	(9.5)	309.3	(9.9)
Costa Rica	41.5	(0.8)	17.2	(0.4)	207.7	(2.5)	54.4	(1.9)	188.9	(1.9)	45.2	(1.5)	202.9	(2.4)	66.2	(1.9)	596.9	(5.0)	125.8	(3.8)
Croatia	32.4	(0.1)	3.9	(0.1)	147.1	(2.1)	44.8	(1.3)	164.4	(1.2)	34.3	(0.9)	182.2	(5.4)	119.9	(2.3)	494.7	(6.9)	157.7	(3.2)
Cyprus*	35.5	(0.0)	1.4	(0.0)	189.1	(0.4)	24.0	(0.7)	198.1	(0.5)	31.6	(0.7)	186.1	(0.6)	23.0	(1.0)	567.5	(1.4)	57.3	(2.4)
Hong Kong-China	40.7	(0.4)	5.8	(0.3)	267.6	(2.6)	72.7	(2.5)	279.7	(2.6)	75.4	(2.9)	235.4	(4.2)	158.0	(3.8)	781.9	(7.0)	230.5	(6.3)
Indonesia	17.8	(0.7)	13.9	(0.3)	209.4	(4.5)	136.8	(4.4)	181.9	(4.5)	138.2	(9.4)	198.9	(6.7)	165.4	(8.9)	584.5	(13.6)	382.2	(13.6)
Jordan	27.2	(0.3)	13.3	(0.2)	227.1	(2.0)	85.6	(11.0)	264.9	(2.5)	85.8	(6.9)	277.6	(3.1)	126.0	(8.8)	767.8	(4.4)	202.6	(10.6)
Kazakhstan	31.1	(0.4)	11.7	(0.2)	182.5	(4.1)	79.4	(8.1)	109.0	(2.4)	80.5	(7.0)	209.0	(6.8)	191.6	(10.2)	497.1	(10.6)	237.8	(14.3)
Latvia	35.5	(0.1)	1.9	(0.1)	224.4	(1.5)	42.2	(2.6)	157.7	(1.5)	44.8	(2.4)	229.6	(3.5)	113.7	(1.6)	610.1	(4.8)	136.3	(4.0)
Liechtenstein	36.2	(0.5)	7.5	(1.3)	210.7	(4.5)	64.4	(6.1)	201.5	(10.2)	147.9	(64.0)	166.5	(11.7)	168.2	(49.1)	579.4	(18.5)	266.5	(69.3)
Lithuania	32.4	(0.1)	1.4	(0.0)	171.8	(1.5)	36.8	(3.3)	203.4	(1.3)	34.6	(3.0)	320.7	(1.4)	58.5	(2.5)	694.8	(2.5)	73.2	(2.6)
Macao-China	40.8	(0.1)	3.6	(0.1)	275.0	(0.9)	58.4	(0.9)	265.2	(0.6)	46.6	(0.6)	188.7	(2.2)	131.9	(2.7)	726.5	(3.0)	172.7	(3.8)
Malaysia	30.7	(0.7)	17.4	(0.2)	201.2	(3.7)	97.3	(3.4)	202.2	(2.7)	77.8	(1.8)	188.6	(2.7)	91.0	(2.8)	579.9	(7.9)	229.2	(6.9)
Montenegro	26.9	(0.2)	10.0	(0.3)	142.2	(0.8)	50.8	(5.8)	149.6	(0.8)	45.7	(5.7)	105.2	(1.1)	64.0	(2.0)	398.0	(2.1)	121.5	(9.0)
Peru	25.0	(0.4)	14.1	(0.1)	287.0	(4.3)	152.6	(5.6)	259.3	(4.0)	138.0	(4.5)	215.0	(3.8)	125.0	(7.0)	750.1	(9.6)	333.2	(11.8)
Qatar	22.0	(0.2)	13.6	(0.1)	258.6	(0.7)	48.9	(0.8)	227.8	(0.8)	50.5	(0.6)	263.6	(1.3)	88.2	(1.2)	743.9	(2.3)	138.8	(1.8)
Romania	31.5	(0.1)	2.8	(0.1)	169.4	(1.9)	57.5	(2.2)	178.9	(1.4)	43.1	(1.1)	161.6	(5.0)	123.9	(2.3)	513.1	(6.7)	163.9	(3.1)
Russian Federation	35.2	(0.1)	2.7	(0.1)	222.5	(2.5)	63.1	(2.4)	135.1	(2.1)	55.2	(2.1)	279.5	(4.3)	150.4	(4.1)	635.9	(6.6)	192.0	(5.7)
Serbia	30.9	(0.2)	7.6	(0.2)	154.4	(1.2)	39.3	(1.4)	145.3	(1.0)	30.8	(0.8)	149.7	(3.9)	129.5	(6.4)	451.3	(4.9)	147.0	(5.8)
Shanghai-China	41.3	(0.3)	7.0	(0.2)	269.5	(2.9)	94.4	(2.2)	248.1	(2.7)	84.8	(1.7)	264.1	(5.6)	160.6	(3.6)	770.9	(9.5)	283.5	(6.0)
Singapore	45.6	(0.2)	13.5	(0.2)	287.8	(1.3)	80.8	(0.7)	223.6	(1.4)	45.7	(5.2)	302.2	(2.3)	127.5	(1.9)	813.4	(3.7)	181.2	(3.0)
Chinese Taipei	39.6	(0.2)	5.9	(0.2)	242.7	(2.4)	76.8	(2.0)	253.1	(2.5)	72.3	(1.8)	190.7	(2.9)	110.6	(3.1)	692.4	(6.9)	219.0	(5.5)
Thailand	35.9	(0.2)	5.8	(0.2)	205.9	(3.1)	85.6	(1.8)	138.6	(1.7)	48.4	(1.1)	262.4	(5.4)	180.0	(4.6)	609.0	(7.9)	240.1	(5.1)
Tunisia	26.3	(0.3)	12.3	(0.6)	275.9	(4.0)	140.8	(10.0)	305.8	(4.3)	156.9	(7.5)	179.9	(3.7)	140.2	(7.5)	739.7	(9.2)	286.6	(9.8)
United Arab Emirates	27.5	(0.2)	13.8	(0.1)	311.0	(3.2)	144.9	(5.2)	269.5	(2.1)	101.1	(2.7)	306.5	(3.8)	209.3	(7.2)	886.3	(6.6)	326.8	(7.8)
Uruguay	21.3	(0.6)	16.7	(0.7)	155.8	(1.9)	63.1	(1.5)	137.9	(1.7)	56.9	(1.1)	152.5	(3.6)	109.5	(3.3)	443.9	(6.6)	187.6	(3.9)
Viet Nam	30.9	(0.3)	5.0	(0.3)	226.6	(3.3)	81.8	(3.5)	193.1	(3.0)	69.2	(3.2)	238.3	(6.5)	153.2	(3.5)	650.2	(9.4)	199.2	(6.0)

* See notes at the beginning of this Annex.
StatLink http://dx.doi.org/10.1787/888932957460

[Part 1/10]
Students' learning time in school, by school features
Table IV.3.22 *Results based on students' self-reports*

| | Total class periods in a normal full week of school (class periods) | | | | | | | | | | | | | |
| | Bottom quarter of ESCS | | Second quarter of ESCS | | Third quarter of ESCS | | Top quarter of ESCS | | Socio-economically disadvantaged schools[1] | | Socio-economically average schools[1] | | Socio-economically advantaged schools[1] | |
	Mean	S.E.	Mean	S.E.	Mean	S.E.	Mean	S.E.	Mean	S.E.	Mean	S.E.	Mean	S.E.
Australia	**25.2**	(0.4)	26.0	(0.3)	26.7	(0.3)	**28.0**	(0.2)	**24.0**	(0.4)	26.5	(0.3)	**28.6**	(0.4)
Austria	**31.7**	(0.6)	34.0	(0.3)	33.7	(0.5)	**33.6**	(0.3)	32.7	(0.7)	33.5	(0.6)	33.3	(0.5)
Belgium	**31.3**	(0.3)	31.7	(0.2)	31.9	(0.2)	**32.1**	(0.2)	**30.8**	(0.4)	32.0	(0.2)	**32.2**	(0.2)
Canada	**18.9**	(0.2)	19.2	(0.3)	19.6	(0.2)	**19.9**	(0.3)	18.7	(0.5)	19.5	(0.2)	19.7	(0.3)
Chile	**27.8**	(0.8)	30.2	(0.8)	30.0	(0.7)	**32.6**	(0.7)	**27.9**	(0.9)	30.4	(1.0)	**32.4**	(0.6)
Czech Republic	**32.5**	(0.2)	32.5	(0.2)	32.6	(0.1)	**32.9**	(0.1)	32.6	(0.3)	32.4	(0.1)	**33.4**	(0.1)
Denmark	**28.9**	(0.4)	28.8	(0.3)	29.4	(0.3)	**29.8**	(0.3)	29.1	(0.6)	28.9	(0.3)	30.1	(0.5)
Estonia	**32.3**	(0.3)	32.9	(0.2)	32.6	(0.2)	**33.4**	(0.2)	32.4	(0.4)	32.7	(0.1)	**33.4**	(0.2)
Finland	**29.6**	(0.3)	29.4	(0.3)	29.0	(0.3)	**29.2**	(0.3)	**30.1**	(0.2)	29.2	(0.3)	**28.9**	(0.5)
France	**21.2**	(0.5)	22.4	(0.5)	24.1	(0.4)	**25.4**	(0.5)	**21.3**	(0.7)	22.7	(0.5)	**25.3**	(0.4)
Germany	**32.2**	(0.2)	32.3	(0.2)	33.1	(0.2)	**33.7**	(0.2)	32.3	(0.2)	32.2	(0.2)	**34.3**	(0.3)
Greece	**32.8**	(0.1)	32.6	(0.1)	32.5	(0.0)	**32.5**	(0.1)	33.3	(0.2)	32.3	(0.0)	32.5	(0.1)
Hungary	**30.7**	(0.2)	31.1	(0.2)	31.5	(0.2)	**32.0**	(0.2)	**30.5**	(0.3)	31.2	(0.3)	**32.1**	(0.2)
Iceland	**33.3**	(0.4)	33.8	(0.4)	33.8	(0.4)	**34.4**	(0.3)	33.3	(0.4)	33.4	(0.3)	**34.7**	(0.3)
Ireland	**41.7**	(0.3)	42.7	(0.3)	42.9	(0.3)	**42.9**	(0.3)	41.3	(0.6)	43.1	(0.2)	42.2	(0.3)
Israel	**33.7**	(0.6)	34.8	(0.7)	36.0	(0.8)	**36.5**	(0.6)	33.0	(0.6)	35.2	(0.9)	**36.8**	(0.7)
Italy	**30.9**	(0.1)	30.5	(0.1)	30.0	(0.1)	**29.2**	(0.1)	**31.7**	(0.1)	30.4	(0.1)	**28.5**	(0.1)
Japan	**31.0**	(0.3)	31.9	(0.2)	32.1	(0.2)	**32.7**	(0.2)	**30.2**	(0.4)	32.4	(0.3)	**32.9**	(0.4)
Korea	**33.9**	(0.4)	34.6	(0.4)	34.9	(0.4)	**36.4**	(0.4)	32.5	(0.4)	35.8	(0.4)	**35.9**	(0.6)
Luxembourg	**26.1**	(0.3)	27.3	(0.3)	28.2	(0.2)	**28.6**	(0.2)	26.5	(0.2)	28.6	(0.3)	28.5	(0.1)
Mexico	**20.9**	(0.3)	23.7	(0.3)	23.9	(0.3)	**25.8**	(0.4)	**21.4**	(0.4)	23.6	(0.3)	**26.0**	(0.3)
Netherlands	**30.2**	(0.4)	30.7	(0.5)	31.1	(0.3)	**31.4**	(0.4)	29.7	(0.8)	31.0	(0.4)	31.5	(0.5)
New Zealand	**22.6**	(0.4)	24.4	(0.4)	24.9	(0.4)	**26.0**	(0.3)	**21.9**	(0.6)	24.4	(0.3)	**27.1**	(0.5)
Norway	26.8	(0.5)	28.0	(0.5)	27.6	(0.5)	27.4	(0.4)	28.3	(0.6)	27.4	(0.3)	27.1	(0.6)
Poland	**33.5**	(0.1)	33.5	(0.1)	33.3	(0.1)	**33.6**	(0.2)	33.8	(0.2)	33.1	(0.2)	33.8	(0.2)
Portugal	24.7	(0.6)	24.8	(0.5)	24.9	(0.5)	23.6	(0.8)	**26.7**	(0.7)	23.6	(0.6)	**23.3**	(1.2)
Slovak Republic	**31.6**	(0.2)	31.8	(0.2)	31.9	(0.2)	**31.7**	(0.2)	31.9	(0.3)	31.4	(0.2)	32.1	(0.2)
Slovenia	**30.6**	(0.4)	31.9	(0.4)	32.9	(0.4)	**32.7**	(0.3)	**30.7**	(0.3)	32.3	(0.3)	**33.4**	(0.2)
Spain	**30.6**	(0.1)	30.8	(0.0)	30.9	(0.1)	**31.1**	(0.1)	30.6	(0.1)	30.7	(0.1)	**31.3**	(0.2)
Sweden	23.9	(0.4)	23.7	(0.4)	24.1	(0.4)	24.4	(0.3)	24.0	(0.6)	24.4	(0.4)	23.5	(0.6)
Switzerland	**31.7**	(0.5)	31.4	(0.3)	31.6	(0.5)	**33.6**	(0.4)	31.9	(0.9)	31.7	(0.6)	33.0	(0.8)
Turkey	**34.0**	(0.3)	34.6	(0.3)	34.8	(0.3)	**35.4**	(0.3)	33.5	(0.4)	35.1	(0.3)	35.3	(0.3)
United Kingdom	**26.5**	(0.4)	26.8	(0.5)	27.3	(0.4)	**28.3**	(0.4)	**25.8**	(0.8)	27.1	(0.4)	**28.9**	(0.6)
United States	**16.4**	(0.7)	18.9	(0.6)	20.7	(0.8)	**23.0**	(0.6)	**15.5**	(0.7)	20.1	(0.7)	**22.8**	(0.8)
OECD average	**29.1**	(0.1)	29.8	(0.1)	30.1	(0.1)	**30.7**	(0.1)	29.1	(0.1)	30.0	(0.1)	**30.7**	(0.1)
Albania	m	m	m	m	m	m	m	m	m	m	m	m	m	m
Argentina	**12.5**	(0.4)	13.3	(0.5)	14.8	(0.5)	**16.1**	(0.5)	**11.8**	(0.4)	13.7	(0.5)	**16.9**	(0.5)
Brazil	**20.0**	(0.4)	20.2	(0.3)	22.2	(0.4)	**24.2**	(0.5)	**19.7**	(0.4)	20.7	(0.3)	**25.1**	(0.5)
Bulgaria	**28.9**	(0.4)	30.6	(0.4)	30.8	(0.4)	**32.4**	(0.3)	**28.3**	(0.3)	30.8	(0.3)	**32.8**	(0.3)
Colombia	22.3	(0.6)	22.0	(0.6)	22.1	(0.6)	23.9	(0.8)	22.4	(0.4)	21.9	(0.6)	23.8	(0.8)
Costa Rica	**38.8**	(1.5)	41.8	(1.1)	41.8	(1.0)	**43.7**	(1.0)	39.4	(1.8)	41.2	(1.2)	44.5	(1.2)
Croatia	**31.5**	(0.2)	32.1	(0.2)	32.6	(0.2)	**33.1**	(0.1)	31.6	(0.3)	32.3	(0.2)	**33.4**	(0.1)
Cyprus*	**35.3**	(0.0)	35.5	(0.1)	35.5	(0.1)	**35.9**	(0.1)	35.3	(0.0)	35.2	(0.0)	**36.2**	(0.1)
Hong Kong-China	40.1	(0.6)	40.4	(0.5)	41.0	(0.4)	41.4	(0.5)	40.6	(0.8)	40.3	(0.6)	41.6	(0.6)
Indonesia	17.8	(1.0)	17.4	(1.2)	17.0	(1.1)	18.8	(0.9)	18.0	(1.0)	15.9	(1.0)	20.0	(1.4)
Jordan	**26.7**	(0.5)	25.2	(0.5)	27.6	(0.5)	**29.4**	(0.5)	**27.0**	(0.6)	26.2	(0.3)	**30.2**	(0.5)
Kazakhstan	**29.8**	(0.5)	30.4	(0.5)	31.5	(0.6)	**32.6**	(0.8)	**30.8**	(0.6)	29.4	(0.7)	**33.7**	(0.8)
Latvia	**35.3**	(0.1)	35.4	(0.1)	35.6	(0.1)	**35.8**	(0.1)	**35.1**	(0.3)	35.5	(0.1)	**36.1**	(0.2)
Liechtenstein	35.8	(0.9)	36.4	(0.5)	35.7	(1.5)	36.4	(1.3)	c	c	36.7	(0.8)	c	c
Lithuania	**32.4**	(0.1)	32.3	(0.1)	32.5	(0.1)	**32.4**	(0.1)	32.2	(0.1)	32.4	(0.1)	**32.5**	(0.1)
Macao-China	**40.5**	(0.1)	40.8	(0.1)	40.6	(0.1)	**41.5**	(0.1)	40.3	(0.1)	41.2	(0.1)	**41.5**	(0.1)
Malaysia	**28.5**	(1.0)	28.7	(0.9)	32.5	(0.9)	**33.2**	(1.0)	**27.7**	(1.3)	29.3	(1.0)	**35.5**	(1.5)
Montenegro	**25.5**	(0.4)	26.4	(0.4)	27.6	(0.4)	**28.3**	(0.4)	**25.3**	(0.3)	26.1	(0.4)	**28.9**	(0.3)
Peru	**23.0**	(0.7)	23.7	(0.6)	25.3	(0.7)	**28.0**	(0.8)	**22.9**	(0.7)	23.1	(0.7)	**28.2**	(0.6)
Qatar	**20.3**	(0.4)	22.9	(0.5)	22.9	(0.4)	**22.1**	(0.3)	22.6	(0.4)	20.7	(0.4)	22.2	(0.2)
Romania	**31.7**	(0.2)	31.4	(0.2)	31.2	(0.1)	**31.5**	(0.2)	31.7	(0.2)	31.4	(0.1)	31.4	(0.2)
Russian Federation	**35.1**	(0.2)	34.9	(0.1)	35.3	(0.2)	**35.6**	(0.2)	35.3	(0.2)	34.8	(0.2)	35.9	(0.2)
Serbia	**30.0**	(0.4)	31.0	(0.3)	30.9	(0.3)	**31.6**	(0.3)	**29.9**	(0.4)	31.2	(0.3)	**31.5**	(0.2)
Shanghai-China	**39.4**	(0.5)	40.7	(0.4)	42.3	(0.4)	**42.7**	(0.3)	**37.2**	(0.6)	42.5	(0.6)	**43.5**	(0.4)
Singapore	45.0	(0.4)	45.4	(0.4)	45.7	(0.5)	46.3	(0.8)	**46.1**	(0.2)	43.9	(0.3)	**48.1**	(1.0)
Chinese Taipei	**38.2**	(0.3)	39.2	(0.3)	40.2	(0.2)	**41.0**	(0.3)	**38.2**	(0.3)	39.7	(0.3)	**41.0**	(0.3)
Thailand	**34.7**	(0.2)	35.7	(0.3)	36.2	(0.3)	**37.0**	(0.3)	**34.4**	(0.4)	36.1	(0.4)	**37.6**	(0.5)
Tunisia	25.3	(0.7)	25.7	(0.7)	27.2	(0.7)	27.2	(0.6)	23.8	(0.7)	26.9	(0.6)	27.9	(0.6)
United Arab Emirates	**25.6**	(0.6)	27.6	(0.4)	28.4	(0.5)	**28.5**	(0.4)	**26.2**	(0.6)	27.9	(0.4)	**27.9**	(0.4)
Uruguay	**17.5**	(0.8)	19.2	(0.8)	20.7	(0.8)	**27.6**	(1.3)	**17.5**	(0.8)	19.8	(0.7)	**29.0**	(1.5)
Viet Nam	**30.4**	(0.3)	30.6	(0.2)	31.1	(0.3)	**31.4**	(0.6)	**30.2**	(0.2)	30.7	(0.4)	**32.0**	(0.9)

Note: Values that are statistically significant are indicated in bold (see Annex A3).
1. A socio-economically disadvantaged school is one whose students' mean socio-economic status (ESCS) is statistically significantly below the mean socio-economic status of the country/economy; an average school is one where there is no difference from the country's/economy's mean; and an advantaged school is one whose students' mean socio-economic status is statistically significantly above the country/economy mean.
* See notes at the beginning of this Annex.
StatLink ⌼⌼⌼ http://dx.doi.org/10.1787/888932957460

[Part 2/10]
Students' learning time in school, by school features
Table IV.3.22   *Results based on students' self-reports*

| | | Total class periods in a normal full week of school (class periods) | | | | | | | | | | | | | | |
| | | Public schools | | Private schools | | Lower secondary education (ISCED 2) | | Upper secondary education (ISCED 3) | | Schools located in a village, hamlet or rural area (fewer than 3 000 people) | | Schools located in a small town or town (3 000 to about 100 000 people) | | Schools located in a city or a large city (over 100 000 people) | |
		Mean	S.E.	Mean	S.E.	Mean	S.E.	Mean	S.E.	Mean	S.E.	Mean	S.E.	Mean	S.E.
OECD	Australia	24.7	(0.2)	28.9	(0.3)	26.9	(0.2)	24.9	(0.3)	25.8	(0.8)	26.3	(0.4)	26.6	(0.2)
	Austria	33.1	(0.3)	34.6	(1.2)	28.6	(1.5)	33.4	(0.3)	34.7	(1.1)	33.7	(0.4)	32.0	(0.5)
	Belgium	31.6	(0.3)	31.9	(0.2)	26.3	(0.7)	32.1	(0.1)	28.3	(1.3)	32.0	(0.1)	31.1	(0.3)
	Canada	19.1	(0.1)	22.1	(0.6)	21.5	(0.3)	19.1	(0.2)	21.1	(0.4)	20.1	(0.2)	18.6	(0.2)
	Chile	27.3	(1.0)	31.6	(0.5)	18.3	(1.6)	30.7	(0.4)	25.3	(2.0)	30.5	(0.8)	30.1	(0.6)
	Czech Republic	32.6	(0.1)	33.0	(0.4)	32.1	(0.1)	33.3	(0.2)	32.0	(0.4)	32.7	(0.1)	32.7	(0.3)
	Denmark	29.2	(0.2)	28.8	(0.7)	29.2	(0.2)	c	c	27.8	(0.7)	29.5	(0.3)	29.3	(0.7)
	Estonia	32.8	(0.3)	32.4	(1.3)	32.7	(0.1)	35.8	(0.6)	32.2	(0.3)	32.9	(0.3)	33.2	(0.2)
	Finland	29.4	(0.2)	26.7	(1.8)	29.3	(0.2)	c	c	30.4	(0.3)	29.3	(0.3)	29.0	(0.3)
	France	23.0	(0.3)	24.4	(0.6)	21.0	(0.6)	24.1	(0.3)	23.0	(0.8)	23.1	(0.3)	23.8	(0.7)
	Germany	32.7	(0.1)	33.8	(1.1)	32.9	(0.1)	33.0	(0.7)	c	c	32.5	(0.2)	33.5	(0.3)
	Greece	32.5	(0.0)	c	c	34.5	(0.1)	32.5	(0.0)	32.5	(0.2)	32.5	(0.1)	32.6	(0.1)
	Hungary	31.2	(0.2)	32.3	(0.4)	28.9	(0.3)	31.6	(0.2)	28.3	(0.9)	31.1	(0.3)	31.9	(0.3)
	Iceland	33.8	(0.2)	c	c	33.8	(0.2)	c	c	33.0	(0.4)	33.9	(0.3)	34.1	(0.3)
	Ireland	42.7	(0.3)	42.6	(0.2)	42.5	(0.2)	42.6	(0.3)	43.0	(0.3)	43.1	(0.2)	41.2	(0.4)
	Israel	35.2	(0.5)	c	c	32.5	(0.9)	35.6	(0.5)	33.9	(1.1)	34.9	(0.7)	36.1	(0.9)
	Italy	30.1	(0.1)	30.6	(0.3)	30.9	(0.3)	30.1	(0.1)	32.0	(0.4)	30.0	(0.1)	30.1	(0.1)
	Japan	31.1	(0.2)	33.8	(0.4)	c	c	31.9	(0.2)	c	c	31.5	(0.2)	32.1	(0.2)
	Korea	34.3	(0.4)	35.8	(0.4)	30.3	(0.5)	35.2	(0.3)	c	c	36.3	(0.7)	34.8	(0.3)
	Luxembourg	27.7	(0.1)	26.9	(0.4)	26.6	(0.2)	28.8	(0.1)	c	c	27.5	(0.1)	c	c
	Mexico	23.1	(0.2)	26.8	(0.9)	22.3	(0.4)	24.3	(0.2)	18.5	(0.5)	24.5	(0.3)	24.5	(0.3)
	Netherlands	30.8	(0.6)	30.9	(0.4)	30.9	(0.4)	30.8	(0.4)	c	c	30.8	(0.3)	31.1	(0.8)
	New Zealand	24.2	(0.2)	27.8	(1.4)	23.5	(0.7)	24.5	(0.2)	22.5	(1.0)	23.8	(0.3)	25.2	(0.4)
	Norway	27.4	(0.3)	c	c	27.4	(0.3)	c	c	27.5	(0.9)	27.4	(0.3)	27.8	(0.5)
	Poland	33.4	(0.1)	35.8	(0.6)	33.5	(0.1)	c	c	33.7	(0.2)	33.3	(0.2)	33.6	(0.1)
	Portugal	24.6	(0.5)	23.7	(1.6)	26.3	(0.4)	23.2	(0.6)	27.3	(1.6)	24.6	(0.3)	23.1	(1.0)
	Slovak Republic	31.7	(0.1)	32.2	(0.5)	30.4	(0.1)	32.7	(0.1)	30.1	(0.4)	31.9	(0.1)	32.1	(0.2)
	Slovenia	32.1	(0.1)	32.1	(1.0)	24.8	(1.5)	32.5	(0.1)	25.9	(2.7)	32.3	(0.2)	32.1	(0.3)
	Spain	30.6	(0.0)	31.4	(0.1)	30.9	(0.0)	c	c	30.7	(0.1)	30.8	(0.1)	30.9	(0.1)
	Sweden	24.8	(0.3)	19.8	(1.1)	24.2	(0.3)	17.6	(0.8)	24.4	(0.6)	24.0	(0.4)	23.9	(0.5)
	Switzerland	32.1	(0.3)	31.0	(2.3)	33.6	(0.2)	27.4	(0.6)	31.9	(1.0)	32.4	(0.4)	30.6	(1.4)
	Turkey	34.6	(0.2)	c	c	30.6	(0.4)	34.8	(0.2)	33.7	(0.8)	34.8	(0.4)	34.6	(0.3)
	United Kingdom	27.3	(0.3)	27.5	(0.7)	c	c	27.2	(0.3)	26.8	(1.1)	27.6	(0.5)	27.0	(0.7)
	United States	19.6	(0.4)	23.2	(2.1)	14.0	(0.9)	20.5	(0.4)	22.0	(2.0)	20.2	(0.6)	18.5	(0.7)
	OECD average	**29.7**	**(0.1)**	**30.1**	**(0.2)**	**28.5**	**(0.1)**	**29.7**	**(0.1)**	**28.9**	**(0.2)**	**30.1**	**(0.1)**	**29.9**	**(0.1)**
Partners	Albania	25.3	(0.3)	26.9	(1.1)	25.6	(0.4)	25.5	(0.4)	23.9	(0.7)	26.2	(0.3)	25.7	(0.3)
	Argentina	13.1	(0.4)	16.2	(0.5)	12.5	(0.5)	15.1	(0.4)	14.0	(1.5)	13.9	(0.4)	14.6	(0.4)
	Brazil	20.6	(0.2)	25.5	(0.6)	18.1	(0.4)	22.4	(0.2)	20.3	(1.4)	20.7	(0.3)	22.6	(0.3)
	Bulgaria	30.7	(0.2)	c	c	25.8	(1.3)	30.9	(0.2)	27.9	(1.4)	30.4	(0.3)	31.5	(0.3)
	Colombia	22.2	(0.3)	25.1	(1.5)	21.2	(0.4)	23.4	(0.4)	22.7	(0.7)	23.0	(0.6)	22.4	(0.5)
	Costa Rica	41.1	(0.9)	45.2	(1.3)	37.0	(0.9)	47.5	(0.9)	42.2	(1.5)	41.0	(1.2)	42.3	(1.8)
	Croatia	32.3	(0.1)	c	c	c	c	32.4	(0.1)	c	c	32.1	(0.2)	32.7	(0.2)
	Cyprus*	35.2	(0.0)	37.4	(0.1)	36.7	(0.1)	35.5	(0.0)	35.7	(0.1)	35.5	(0.0)	35.7	(0.1)
	Hong Kong-China	39.8	(1.1)	40.7	(0.4)	40.3	(0.5)	40.9	(0.4)	c	c	c	c	40.7	(0.4)
	Indonesia	18.9	(0.8)	16.3	(1.1)	17.8	(0.9)	17.7	(0.9)	15.8	(1.0)	18.6	(0.9)	19.0	(1.7)
	Jordan	26.5	(0.3)	30.5	(0.7)	27.2	(0.3)	c	c	28.0	(1.0)	26.4	(0.4)	27.9	(0.4)
	Kazakhstan	31.4	(0.4)	20.7	(2.1)	31.6	(0.4)	29.6	(0.8)	30.0	(0.6)	31.5	(0.6)	31.8	(0.8)
	Latvia	35.5	(0.1)	c	c	35.5	(0.1)	36.1	(0.3)	35.2	(0.1)	35.6	(0.1)	35.7	(0.2)
	Liechtenstein	35.9	(0.6)	c	c	36.1	(0.5)	c	c	c	c	36.2	(0.5)	c	c
	Lithuania	32.4	(0.1)	c	c	32.4	(0.1)	c	c	32.2	(0.1)	32.3	(0.1)	32.6	(0.1)
	Macao-China	c	c	40.9	(0.1)	40.5	(0.1)	41.2	(0.1)	c	c	c	c	40.8	(0.1)
	Malaysia	30.1	(0.7)	49.3	(3.7)	33.8	(2.0)	30.7	(0.7)	26.6	(2.2)	30.8	(1.0)	32.5	(1.4)
	Montenegro	26.9	(0.2)	c	c	c	c	26.9	(0.2)	c	c	26.8	(0.2)	27.0	(0.4)
	Peru	24.0	(0.4)	27.3	(1.1)	20.7	(0.8)	26.4	(0.4)	22.9	(0.9)	24.3	(0.6)	26.4	(0.6)
	Qatar	19.3	(0.2)	25.3	(0.3)	19.5	(0.5)	22.5	(0.2)	18.3	(0.5)	21.1	(0.3)	23.5	(0.3)
	Romania	31.5	(0.1)	c	c	31.5	(0.1)	c	c	31.8	(0.3)	31.5	(0.1)	31.4	(0.1)
	Russian Federation	35.2	(0.1)	c	c	35.1	(0.1)	35.9	(0.2)	34.9	(0.3)	35.0	(0.2)	35.5	(0.2)
	Serbia	30.8	(0.2)	c	c	c	c	30.9	(0.2)	c	c	30.8	(0.3)	31.0	(0.3)
	Shanghai-China	41.2	(0.3)	42.4	(1.2)	43.7	(0.5)	39.5	(0.3)	c	c	c	c	41.3	(0.3)
	Singapore	46.4	(0.2)	c	c	42.9	(1.1)	45.7	(0.2)	c	c	c	c	45.9	(0.2)
	Chinese Taipei	39.5	(0.2)	39.9	(0.4)	41.1	(0.3)	38.9	(0.2)	c	c	39.8	(0.4)	39.5	(0.2)
	Thailand	35.9	(0.2)	36.1	(0.6)	34.4	(0.3)	36.3	(0.2)	34.3	(0.5)	36.2	(0.3)	36.2	(0.5)
	Tunisia	26.4	(0.3)	c	c	23.7	(0.7)	27.6	(0.4)	23.6	(1.4)	26.4	(0.4)	26.7	(0.6)
	United Arab Emirates	27.9	(0.4)	27.3	(0.4)	20.6	(0.6)	28.6	(0.2)	29.8	(0.7)	27.4	(0.5)	27.3	(0.3)
	Uruguay	19.0	(0.5)	30.6	(1.9)	17.6	(1.0)	23.3	(0.7)	16.5	(2.2)	19.4	(0.7)	24.7	(1.1)
	Viet Nam	30.7	(0.2)	33.4	(1.9)	29.2	(0.4)	31.0	(0.3)	30.9	(0.3)	30.2	(0.5)	31.6	(0.8)

Note: Values that are statistically significant are indicated in bold (see Annex A3).
1. A socio-economically disadvantaged school is one whose students' mean socio-economic status (ESCS) is statistically significantly below the mean socio-economic status of the country/economy; an average school is one where there is no difference from the country's/economy's mean; and an advantaged school is one whose students' mean socio-economic status is statistically significantly above the country/economy mean.
* See notes at the beginning of this Annex.
StatLink ⫘ http://dx.doi.org/10.1787/888932957460

[Part 3/10]
Students' learning time in school, by school features
Table IV.3.22   *Results based on students' self-reports*

	Time spent per week in regular school lessons in mathematics (minutes)															
	Bottom quarter of ESCS		Second quarter of ESCS		Third quarter of ESCS		Top quarter of ESCS		Socio-economically disadvantaged schools[1]		Socio-economically average schools[1]		Socio-economically advantaged schools[1]	
	Mean	S.E.	Mean	S.E.	Mean	S.E.	Mean	S.E.	Mean	S.E.	Mean	S.E.	Mean	S.E.
OECD														
Australia	234.9	(1.7)	234.1	(1.6)	238.6	(1.7)	237.6	(1.6)	234.5	(2.3)	237.3	(1.3)	236.0	(2.2)
Austria	157.6	(3.9)	157.8	(3.1)	154.4	(3.4)	155.3	(2.7)	**173.0**	(6.8)	144.4	(5.7)	**156.3**	(2.9)
Belgium	**202.6**	(2.5)	209.0	(2.9)	224.6	(2.7)	**232.0**	(2.0)	**195.0**	(3.8)	212.9	(3.2)	**233.9**	(2.3)
Canada	307.2	(4.5)	311.3	(3.8)	319.1	(4.0)	317.5	(4.6)	300.4	(7.9)	321.4	(3.3)	308.6	(6.5)
Chile	399.0	(9.9)	402.5	(8.4)	414.2	(10.2)	375.5	(9.1)	405.4	(9.0)	397.5	(12.8)	388.9	(11.6)
Czech Republic	179.7	(3.1)	182.1	(2.7)	184.3	(2.1)	183.1	(2.4)	171.2	(7.1)	187.7	(2.7)	177.8	(3.1)
Denmark	226.1	(5.3)	219.3	(4.0)	228.3	(4.3)	223.5	(3.3)	221.9	(5.9)	223.7	(4.3)	228.3	(4.3)
Estonia	221.1	(1.5)	222.1	(1.6)	222.7	(1.5)	225.3	(1.6)	221.8	(2.0)	222.3	(1.6)	225.4	(1.7)
Finland	**172.9**	(1.7)	175.6	(1.9)	176.1	(2.0)	**177.2**	(2.1)	173.6	(3.2)	175.6	(2.1)	176.4	(2.9)
France	**199.2**	(4.0)	197.7	(4.0)	213.2	(4.2)	**218.3**	(3.6)	**197.5**	(5.8)	203.0	(3.6)	**218.4**	(3.6)
Germany	**200.7**	(3.7)	202.9	(4.3)	195.6	(3.5)	**188.8**	(3.7)	**217.4**	(5.6)	194.2	(3.3)	**185.3**	(4.6)
Greece	**204.5**	(1.9)	208.5	(1.2)	210.1	(1.0)	**212.9**	(1.1)	**197.5**	(2.9)	210.2	(1.0)	**213.1**	(1.0)
Hungary	148.2	(2.5)	149.4	(2.7)	150.4	(2.2)	151.6	(2.4)	145.0	(3.7)	155.2	(2.8)	148.3	(2.8)
Iceland	241.5	(4.0)	239.9	(3.9)	248.9	(3.7)	246.8	(3.7)	247.2	(4.3)	243.9	(2.6)	242.0	(3.1)
Ireland	187.5	(1.9)	188.4	(1.6)	189.9	(1.9)	188.8	(1.8)	189.4	(2.6)	188.6	(1.5)	188.7	(2.5)
Israel	**245.2**	(4.1)	252.0	(4.6)	256.2	(4.4)	**263.8**	(4.6)	**240.3**	(4.3)	261.2	(4.0)	**257.1**	(4.6)
Italy	230.3	(1.5)	230.8	(1.6)	232.1	(2.0)	234.9	(3.2)	232.7	(1.8)	225.6	(2.0)	240.0	(4.4)
Japan	**207.6**	(4.5)	227.5	(3.7)	241.9	(3.7)	**262.3**	(4.8)	**183.4**	(5.4)	236.5	(5.1)	**283.7**	(4.8)
Korea	**201.8**	(3.4)	210.4	(3.7)	215.0	(3.9)	**226.1**	(6.0)	**181.4**	(5.2)	219.9	(4.7)	**233.6**	(9.5)
Luxembourg	206.7	(2.0)	199.8	(2.2)	202.3	(2.2)	209.4	(1.6)	**202.4**	(1.3)	199.8	(2.2)	**209.4**	(1.1)
Mexico	**248.5**	(2.9)	254.2	(2.2)	251.1	(2.6)	**259.4**	(3.0)	253.4	(2.9)	252.2	(2.7)	254.2	(2.8)
Netherlands	176.4	(4.9)	165.0	(4.1)	173.6	(5.3)	167.8	(3.7)	188.2	(8.2)	164.1	(2.2)	171.0	(8.7)
New Zealand	240.6	(3.8)	239.2	(2.3)	239.3	(2.8)	244.9	(2.2)	245.5	(4.5)	237.3	(2.6)	244.8	(3.2)
Norway	198.0	(4.4)	200.2	(5.9)	197.4	(6.0)	200.3	(4.0)	207.8	(9.2)	198.1	(3.0)	198.5	(3.9)
Poland	**193.9**	(1.8)	196.7	(2.0)	199.1	(2.3)	**202.4**	(2.2)	**191.5**	(2.6)	198.0	(2.7)	**206.6**	(3.4)
Portugal	280.9	(8.3)	282.8	(7.3)	288.9	(5.7)	299.5	(7.9)	287.3	(11.2)	282.9	(4.4)	299.7	(12.7)
Slovak Republic	182.0	(4.9)	172.7	(4.1)	181.3	(4.1)	187.3	(2.9)	167.7	(8.7)	187.5	(4.9)	180.9	(4.1)
Slovenia	151.4	(1.1)	155.9	(1.2)	163.3	(1.0)	170.8	(0.9)	144.1	(1.2)	158.1	(0.9)	178.0	(0.3)
Spain	214.0	(1.7)	208.4	(1.3)	208.9	(1.4)	209.7	(1.6)	215.5	(2.4)	205.9	(1.7)	211.9	(2.3)
Sweden	186.3	(4.2)	179.0	(2.9)	183.5	(3.0)	179.3	(3.3)	184.9	(3.8)	180.7	(2.9)	180.3	(5.7)
Switzerland	**217.2**	(4.6)	205.0	(3.9)	202.8	(4.1)	**203.0**	(3.2)	**218.8**	(4.1)	207.8	(4.8)	**194.1**	(4.5)
Turkey	**155.8**	(3.0)	166.5	(3.5)	172.7	(3.6)	**192.5**	(4.5)	**152.1**	(4.0)	161.4	(3.5)	**207.7**	(5.6)
United Kingdom	233.0	(3.1)	236.5	(4.2)	225.3	(3.1)	223.4	(4.1)	**242.1**	(4.6)	226.4	(3.0)	**225.7**	(5.3)
United States	**245.3**	(8.5)	244.2	(7.0)	255.9	(6.9)	**270.7**	(5.9)	239.0	(11.2)	259.1	(6.3)	259.6	(6.9)
OECD average	**214.6**	(0.7)	215.5	(0.7)	219.4	(0.7)	**221.8**	(0.7)	**213.8**	(1.0)	217.1	(0.7)	**222.5**	(0.9)
Partners														
Albania	m	m	m	m	m	m	m	m	m	m	m	m	m	m
Argentina	233.1	(8.3)	264.2	(8.9)	277.4	(7.2)	**299.9**	(12.1)	229.1	(8.7)	264.4	(8.7)	**305.3**	(13.1)
Brazil	**205.9**	(2.7)	211.5	(2.8)	214.0	(3.1)	**226.7**	(3.0)	**205.9**	(2.6)	214.8	(3.5)	**224.7**	(3.2)
Bulgaria	**127.7**	(2.6)	129.9	(3.1)	132.9	(3.8)	**144.4**	(5.8)	**126.5**	(3.3)	124.4	(4.4)	**146.5**	(7.0)
Colombia	254.0	(7.3)	257.5	(6.0)	267.8	(6.3)	271.2	(6.7)	263.3	(8.0)	251.6	(6.2)	275.7	(7.2)
Costa Rica	**201.1**	(3.2)	198.3	(3.6)	208.9	(4.0)	**222.3**	(3.8)	**200.1**	(2.9)	198.5	(4.0)	**236.3**	(4.6)
Croatia	**134.9**	(2.5)	140.8	(2.3)	147.4	(3.1)	**165.5**	(3.3)	**133.3**	(2.7)	141.2	(3.3)	**177.7**	(4.7)
Cyprus*	**187.1**	(1.0)	187.6	(1.0)	189.1	(1.0)	**192.6**	(1.0)	**188.5**	(0.9)	186.3	(0.5)	**193.5**	(0.9)
Hong Kong-China	265.5	(3.4)	265.8	(3.5)	264.9	(3.0)	273.5	(5.3)	264.3	(4.2)	271.6	(3.8)	265.5	(3.3)
Indonesia	199.2	(6.7)	202.3	(5.5)	209.0	(7.9)	**227.1**	(9.9)	198.4	(5.3)	205.4	(7.8)	**229.6**	(10.1)
Jordan	227.6	(4.3)	224.9	(4.8)	228.1	(3.2)	227.6	(3.6)	222.8	(2.9)	227.0	(3.0)	231.9	(5.0)
Kazakhstan	**168.2**	(3.0)	174.2	(3.4)	182.9	(5.6)	**204.9**	(9.0)	**164.5**	(3.8)	170.0	(2.6)	**213.7**	(11.1)
Latvia	**218.5**	(2.1)	221.8	(2.3)	224.5	(2.6)	**232.5**	(2.0)	**217.7**	(3.6)	220.4	(2.2)	**235.3**	(2.5)
Liechtenstein	225.8	(16.3)	216.8	(9.1)	191.2	(7.1)	207.2	(10.0)	c	c	229.1	(6.8)	c	c
Lithuania	169.7	(1.7)	171.2	(2.1)	171.2	(1.6)	175.4	(2.9)	168.4	(2.7)	170.7	(1.9)	177.4	(3.5)
Macao-China	**269.2**	(2.2)	278.1	(2.2)	275.0	(1.8)	**277.9**	(1.9)	**267.2**	(1.3)	285.0	(2.0)	**282.6**	(1.4)
Malaysia	**190.3**	(4.4)	188.0	(4.4)	203.9	(5.9)	**222.8**	(6.9)	**185.4**	(5.4)	191.3	(4.8)	**231.3**	(9.4)
Montenegro	**131.7**	(1.8)	137.3	(2.0)	146.8	(2.4)	**153.1**	(1.5)	**127.9**	(1.1)	138.6	(1.9)	**158.8**	(1.5)
Peru	282.8	(8.2)	269.4	(7.2)	290.2	(10.0)	305.7	(8.4)	267.4	(6.5)	276.3	(7.0)	313.4	(8.5)
Qatar	**257.8**	(1.5)	261.8	(1.7)	262.2	(1.5)	**253.0**	(1.6)	**263.7**	(1.4)	252.1	(1.4)	**258.4**	(1.0)
Romania	**168.5**	(2.3)	165.2	(2.5)	164.9	(3.2)	**179.2**	(3.9)	167.5	(3.0)	168.8	(3.4)	172.1	(4.4)
Russian Federation	**211.7**	(3.3)	223.0	(3.3)	223.3	(3.6)	**232.4**	(4.0)	222.3	(5.1)	216.7	(3.6)	232.8	(4.8)
Serbia	**148.4**	(2.0)	151.6	(1.7)	153.6	(1.9)	**164.3**	(2.3)	**148.7**	(2.6)	149.1	(2.2)	**171.4**	(2.7)
Shanghai-China	263.9	(5.2)	264.0	(4.8)	274.8	(5.0)	274.9	(4.5)	245.0	(9.3)	281.0	(6.9)	278.1	(6.3)
Singapore	**270.0**	(2.8)	285.1	(3.0)	295.9	(3.4)	**300.2**	(3.4)	**272.3**	(2.0)	291.3	(2.3)	**300.7**	(3.4)
Chinese Taipei	**213.6**	(3.3)	236.7	(3.7)	250.5	(3.5)	**270.3**	(4.0)	**204.7**	(6.2)	242.1	(5.3)	**283.5**	(4.9)
Thailand	**194.3**	(4.2)	196.4	(4.0)	204.1	(4.6)	**229.7**	(5.8)	**189.7**	(4.7)	197.2	(5.1)	**236.0**	(6.5)
Tunisia	261.5	(6.4)	273.6	(8.2)	283.1	(8.2)	285.0	(7.9)	262.3	(6.4)	277.0	(7.1)	288.0	(7.1)
United Arab Emirates	311.0	(5.9)	314.6	(4.4)	315.1	(6.3)	304.0	(6.2)	327.2	(9.8)	318.3	(5.4)	292.2	(5.9)
Uruguay	154.7	(3.0)	152.6	(3.3)	155.7	(3.2)	160.0	(3.4)	152.9	(2.9)	159.6	(3.5)	154.4	(3.9)
Viet Nam	**219.5**	(5.1)	218.5	(5.1)	229.3	(5.1)	**239.0**	(5.3)	**217.8**	(5.0)	229.0	(7.5)	**236.6**	(7.1)

Note: Values that are statistically significant are indicated in bold (see Annex A3).
1. A socio-economically disadvantaged school is one whose students' mean socio-economic status (ESCS) is statistically significantly below the mean socio-economic status of the country/economy; an average school is one where there is no difference from the country's/economy's mean; and an advantaged school is one whose students' mean socio-economic status is statistically significantly above the country/economy mean.
* See notes at the beginning of this Annex.
StatLink http://dx.doi.org/10.1787/888932957460

[Part 4/10]
Students' learning time in school, by school features
Table IV.3.22 *Results based on students' self-reports*

| | Time spent per week in regular school lessons in mathematics (minutes) | | | | | | | | | | | | | |
| | Public schools | | Private schools | | Lower secondary education (ISCED 2) | | Upper secondary education (ISCED 3) | | Schools located in a village, hamlet or rural area (fewer than 3 000 people) | | Schools located in a small town or town (3 000 to about 100 000 people) | | Schools located in a city or a large city (over 100 000 people) | |
	Mean	S.E.	Mean	S.E.	Mean	S.E.	Mean	S.E.	Mean	S.E.	Mean	S.E.	Mean	S.E.
OECD														
Australia	237.8	(1.4)	233.6	(1.6)	**234.4**	(1.0)	**244.4**	(2.6)	237.1	(3.6)	236.6	(2.1)	236.1	(1.2)
Austria	**158.0**	(2.6)	139.8	(6.9)	**191.5**	(4.9)	155.0	(2.5)	143.9	(8.9)	157.4	(3.6)	158.6	(5.1)
Belgium	218.2	(2.8)	214.2	(2.4)	**246.0**	(7.0)	**214.9**	(1.4)	213.8	(13.8)	215.2	(2.0)	220.5	(4.7)
Canada	**317.9**	(2.8)	**271.3**	(13.2)	**297.4**	(4.6)	**316.5**	(3.1)	311.6	(6.3)	313.1	(3.8)	314.7	(4.2)
Chile	407.8	(10.0)	394.9	(8.2)	354.1	(32.6)	399.3	(6.4)	385.1	(23.1)	423.3	(9.0)	**382.0**	(9.1)
Czech Republic	**184.0**	(2.4)	**150.5**	(6.4)	**201.6**	(1.7)	**159.5**	(3.4)	**217.2**	(5.5)	176.8	(2.7)	182.2	(4.5)
Denmark	221.7	(3.3)	235.8	(8.0)	224.2	(3.0)	c	c	233.1	(10.1)	222.2	(2.9)	225.6	(4.5)
Estonia	222.8	(1.1)	224.7	(4.0)	223.3	(1.1)	195.6	(12.1)	223.8	(2.2)	223.5	(1.3)	220.8	(2.3)
Finland	**175.0**	(1.6)	**191.6**	(3.0)	175.4	(1.5)	c	c	169.3	(4.7)	174.8	(2.1)	178.9	(2.5)
France	206.6	(2.5)	207.6	(4.5)	202.4	(4.4)	208.6	(2.3)	198.7	(6.8)	208.0	(2.8)	207.1	(5.4)
Germany	196.6	(2.7)	184.6	(11.8)	197.5	(2.4)	169.8	(30.8)	c	c	195.7	(3.1)	196.6	(5.1)
Greece	209.0	(0.7)	c	c	**173.3**	(3.6)	**210.2**	(0.6)	208.6	(2.5)	208.8	(1.1)	209.8	(1.4)
Hungary	149.4	(1.8)	151.1	(5.9)	**167.4**	(3.9)	**147.7**	(2.0)	156.3	(8.7)	150.6	(2.6)	148.0	(2.9)
Iceland	243.6	(1.9)	c	c	243.9	(1.9)	c	c	237.6	(3.3)	242.1	(2.6)	250.2	(3.9)
Ireland	189.7	(1.6)	187.5	(1.7)	**195.3**	(1.2)	**178.0**	(2.0)	188.4	(2.1)	189.0	(1.8)	188.7	(2.0)
Israel	254.9	(2.4)	c	c	260.5	(6.4)	253.2	(2.6)	**242.7**	(5.6)	256.8	(3.7)	257.6	(4.4)
Italy	**232.9**	(1.8)	**218.5**	(6.7)	**289.8**	(6.0)	**231.1**	(1.8)	219.4	(8.4)	233.0	(2.1)	231.9	(3.2)
Japan	226.3	(3.1)	254.6	(7.9)	c	c	234.7	(3.0)	c	c	217.3	(6.3)	**241.3**	(4.2)
Korea	211.9	(4.0)	215.2	(5.3)	**163.5**	(5.1)	**216.4**	(3.3)	c	c	209.7	(6.1)	214.0	(3.6)
Luxembourg	204.2	(0.9)	207.6	(2.4)	**216.9**	(1.0)	**187.4**	(1.3)	c	c	204.8	(0.8)	c	c
Mexico	252.9	(1.6)	260.9	(6.9)	250.3	(2.6)	254.9	(2.2)	253.6	(3.9)	256.4	(2.7)	250.2	(2.6)
Netherlands	169.2	(4.1)	172.3	(5.1)	**175.0**	(4.1)	**161.4**	(3.0)	c	c	168.0	(3.2)	179.9	(9.6)
New Zealand	239.9	(2.1)	256.1	(12.6)	**215.6**	(3.5)	**242.5**	(2.1)	240.6	(8.4)	235.6	(2.5)	**243.7**	(3.0)
Norway	199.5	(2.5)	c	c	199.1	(2.4)	c	c	196.4	(5.1)	198.4	(3.7)	204.8	(4.8)
Poland	**197.2**	(1.7)	**220.9**	(3.3)	198.2	(1.7)	c	c	192.1	(3.3)	195.4	(2.2)	**212.2**	(3.8)
Portugal	287.9	(5.4)	286.6	(11.2)	290.5	(5.7)	286.0	(7.3)	330.7	(39.6)	286.8	(4.6)	278.6	(10.1)
Slovak Republic	182.4	(2.8)	164.4	(16.2)	**230.1**	(1.7)	**141.7**	(3.5)	**230.1**	(2.9)	174.2	(3.9)	168.3	(9.1)
Slovenia	**160.2**	(0.5)	**178.3**	(0.7)	**176.3**	(1.8)	**159.3**	(0.5)	**175.6**	(1.7)	161.7	(0.5)	**158.5**	(0.9)
Spain	208.7	(1.0)	212.8	(1.8)	210.3	(0.9)	c	c	202.2	(6.0)	209.2	(1.5)	212.0	(2.4)
Sweden	182.3	(1.9)	181.6	(11.7)	**180.9**	(2.1)	239.5	(20.8)	180.0	(2.7)	181.5	(3.3)	185.2	(4.6)
Switzerland	207.7	(2.7)	203.0	(14.5)	**220.9**	(2.2)	161.5	(6.9)	217.4	(9.3)	210.7	(3.0)	**188.5**	(8.1)
Turkey	171.0	(2.2)	c	c	170.1	(8.4)	171.9	(2.2)	189.7	(8.3)	175.1	(5.0)	168.3	(4.0)
United Kingdom	228.7	(2.6)	230.6	(4.3)	c	c	230.0	(2.2)	**239.9**	(6.6)	225.6	(2.7)	235.7	(5.6)
United States	255.4	(5.2)	245.1	(21.4)	239.4	(11.2)	255.9	(4.9)	**228.1**	(6.1)	266.7	(6.8)	**245.2**	(7.7)
OECD average	218.0	(0.5)	217.1	(1.5)	**219.2**	(1.2)	**215.3**	(1.5)	222.9	(1.8)	217.8	(0.6)	218.0	(0.6)
Partners														
Albania	171.0	(1.3)	165.2	(5.8)	**175.3**	(1.8)	**167.5**	(1.4)	170.2	(3.0)	173.3	(1.7)	166.9	(2.6)
Argentina	**246.1**	(6.3)	**306.9**	(12.2)	**240.1**	(6.9)	**280.4**	(7.6)	246.7	(19.8)	264.9	(9.3)	275.5	(8.4)
Brazil	**211.3**	(1.8)	**230.5**	(4.2)	**227.9**	(3.5)	**212.0**	(2.0)	207.3	(7.0)	207.6	(2.3)	221.6	(2.5)
Bulgaria	133.6	(3.1)	c	c	**180.5**	(7.7)	**132.4**	(3.1)	153.1	(9.2)	135.8	(3.9)	129.0	(5.2)
Colombia	**257.6**	(4.0)	**286.2**	(10.7)	266.7	(5.9)	260.2	(5.0)	**276.2**	(13.5)	242.7	(6.2)	**270.8**	(5.6)
Costa Rica	**200.6**	(2.5)	**246.0**	(7.1)	**216.7**	(1.8)	**195.0**	(5.1)	210.3	(3.3)	205.6	(3.8)	212.6	(8.9)
Croatia	146.7	(2.1)	c	c	c	c	147.1	(2.1)	c	c	143.1	(2.1)	**153.9**	(4.6)
Cyprus*	**186.4**	(0.5)	**206.2**	(1.5)	**195.0**	(2.7)	**188.9**	(0.4)	**193.2**	(1.9)	185.9	(0.5)	**194.1**	(0.8)
Hong Kong-China	260.9	(7.0)	267.6	(2.8)	**258.8**	(3.4)	**271.9**	(2.8)	c	c	c	c	267.6	(2.6)
Indonesia	210.8	(5.5)	209.2	(7.5)	212.3	(6.2)	206.7	(6.4)	198.1	(9.9)	212.9	(5.9)	216.0	(8.6)
Jordan	226.7	(2.1)	229.3	(5.3)	227.1	(2.0)	c	c	232.0	(4.4)	226.9	(2.5)	226.2	(3.8)
Kazakhstan	182.4	(4.2)	186.6	(16.5)	181.4	(3.8)	185.4	(7.5)	162.7	(2.7)	178.2	(3.4)	200.7	(9.5)
Latvia	224.5	(1.6)	c	c	224.6	(1.5)	219.8	(12.7)	216.1	(2.6)	228.0	(2.4)	226.2	(2.6)
Liechtenstein	215.3	(3.9)	c	c	217.1	(4.8)	c	c	c	c	210.7	(4.5)	c	c
Lithuania	171.1	(1.4)	c	c	171.8	(1.5)	c	c	168.7	(2.6)	172.1	(2.4)	173.1	(2.2)
Macao-China	c	c	276.1	(0.9)	267.7	(1.2)	283.9	(1.3)	c	c	c	c	275.1	(0.9)
Malaysia	198.5	(3.3)	273.0	(39.7)	187.9	(9.4)	201.7	(3.7)	191.6	(10.0)	199.4	(4.4)	209.7	(9.5)
Montenegro	142.0	(0.8)	c	c	c	c	142.1	(0.8)	c	c	145.7	(1.1)	**134.1**	(1.2)
Peru	**272.3**	(4.4)	**351.1**	(13.7)	**263.0**	(8.5)	**294.8**	(4.8)	280.1	(8.0)	288.8	(6.6)	288.2	(6.8)
Qatar	253.7	(0.9)	266.1	(1.3)	266.5	(2.1)	257.1	(0.8)	261.5	(2.6)	252.6	(1.1)	263.0	(1.2)
Romania	169.4	(1.9)	c	c	169.4	(1.9)	c	c	186.0	(7.0)	165.9	(3.0)	171.4	(3.3)
Russian Federation	221.9	(2.4)	c	c	**218.2**	(2.6)	**242.7**	(5.2)	206.7	(5.3)	222.9	(4.3)	229.0	(3.8)
Serbia	153.6	(1.3)	c	c	c	c	153.9	(1.1)	c	c	153.2	(1.8)	154.2	(2.8)
Shanghai-China	267.2	(3.3)	291.1	(17.2)	**331.3**	(3.7)	**222.4**	(3.6)	c	c	c	c	269.5	(2.9)
Singapore	287.5	(1.1)	c	c	**203.4**	(3.9)	**289.8**	(1.3)	c	c	c	c	288.4	(1.4)
Chinese Taipei	**253.4**	(2.5)	**224.4**	(6.3)	**266.8**	(3.3)	**229.5**	(3.1)	c	c	245.7	(6.3)	241.0	(4.4)
Thailand	**210.4**	(2.9)	**182.1**	(11.9)	201.3	(4.1)	207.1	(3.5)	**216.4**	(5.6)	196.4	(4.5)	**216.1**	(7.3)
Tunisia	276.2	(4.0)	c	c	**246.2**	(5.0)	**291.4**	(5.2)	294.3	(31.1)	275.6	(4.8)	273.3	(7.2)
United Arab Emirates	**351.4**	(5.6)	**283.6**	(4.5)	**246.5**	(4.6)	**320.4**	(3.5)	325.2	(14.7)	336.4	(8.4)	**296.7**	(4.0)
Uruguay	155.7	(2.1)	156.0	(5.0)	160.0	(3.1)	153.4	(2.5)	148.0	(5.9)	154.3	(3.2)	159.2	(2.9)
Viet Nam	**223.2**	(3.4)	**268.8**	(17.9)	213.3	(8.3)	228.0	(3.7)	220.8	(6.1)	223.4	(6.5)	241.2	(7.3)

Note: Values that are statistically significant are indicated in bold (see Annex A3).
1. A socio-economically disadvantaged school is one whose students' mean socio-economic status (ESCS) is statistically significantly below the mean socio-economic status of the country/economy; an average school is one where there is no difference from the country's/economy's mean; and an advantaged school is one whose students' mean socio-economic status is statistically significantly above the country/economy mean.
* See notes at the beginning of this Annex.
StatLink ᴪ᷉ᵴ᷇ᵹ᷇᷾ http://dx.doi.org/10.1787/888932957460

[Part 5/10]
Students' learning time in school, by school features
Table IV.3.22 *Results based on students' self-reports*

	Time spent per week in regular school lessons in the language of instruction (minutes)													
	Bottom quarter of ESCS		Second quarter of ESCS		Third quarter of ESCS		Top quarter of ESCS		Socio-economically disadvantaged schools[1]		Socio-economically average schools[1]		Socio-economically advantaged schools[1]	
	Mean	S.E.	Mean	S.E.	Mean	S.E.	Mean	S.E.	Mean	S.E.	Mean	S.E.	Mean	S.E.
OECD														
Australia	233.6	(1.5)	232.7	(1.8)	234.6	(1.5)	232.7	(1.7)	234.0	(2.3)	234.4	(1.3)	230.6	(2.0)
Austria	144.6	(3.1)	141.6	(3.3)	143.3	(2.5)	147.3	(1.9)	149.2	(4.2)	134.9	(3.3)	153.2	(2.4)
Belgium	215.6	(2.9)	215.9	(2.2)	219.7	(1.8)	220.3	(2.0)	**209.1**	(3.6)	216.8	(2.8)	**223.8**	(2.0)
Canada	317.6	(4.8)	309.0	(4.2)	317.9	(4.4)	319.5	(4.4)	302.8	(7.7)	324.6	(3.6)	308.8	(6.4)
Chile	**376.7**	(9.4)	379.4	(7.9)	390.3	(10.1)	351.6	(7.9)	378.9	(7.6)	375.4	(11.9)	368.8	(10.6)
Czech Republic	181.5	(2.0)	178.2	(2.5)	177.5	(2.0)	178.9	(2.2)	173.6	(4.5)	184.2	(1.4)	170.2	(2.9)
Denmark	318.5	(7.6)	304.8	(4.9)	323.1	(6.0)	311.4	(5.3)	311.2	(5.4)	318.7	(6.0)	307.4	(6.4)
Estonia	197.6	(2.3)	198.7	(1.8)	197.5	(1.9)	199.5	(1.4)	195.8	(3.6)	198.7	(1.7)	199.2	(1.7)
Finland	**149.6**	(1.5)	152.0	(1.9)	152.7	(1.7)	**154.3**	(1.6)	150.8	(3.3)	152.3	(1.8)	152.6	(2.4)
France	212.0	(4.1)	210.8	(4.1)	215.9	(3.7)	220.1	(3.5)	216.4	(5.2)	209.7	(3.2)	220.6	(2.9)
Germany	**201.1**	(4.2)	194.3	(3.2)	186.8	(3.3)	**181.0**	(3.0)	**207.8**	(4.9)	188.6	(2.9)	**180.8**	(4.5)
Greece	**167.0**	(1.1)	170.8	(1.1)	171.2	(1.2)	**172.9**	(1.0)	166.5	(1.5)	170.8	(0.8)	172.1	(1.1)
Hungary	**159.5**	(2.6)	164.0	(2.3)	166.9	(2.7)	**166.3**	(2.2)	155.4	(3.2)	168.8	(2.9)	167.0	(2.4)
Iceland	239.9	(4.5)	236.2	(3.9)	238.7	(3.6)	238.6	(3.7)	251.9	(5.9)	235.6	(2.6)	234.6	(3.2)
Ireland	182.1	(1.6)	182.3	(1.4)	179.9	(1.9)	178.1	(1.7)	182.2	(2.9)	181.3	(1.5)	178.4	(2.5)
Israel	195.5	(4.3)	191.5	(3.7)	190.2	(5.5)	191.9	(4.3)	199.6	(4.3)	189.0	(4.8)	190.7	(5.2)
Italy	**285.9**	(2.0)	281.6	(2.2)	274.6	(2.1)	**267.5**	(2.3)	**290.3**	(2.4)	281.2	(2.4)	**261.2**	(2.9)
Japan	**189.2**	(3.3)	201.6	(3.1)	209.2	(2.7)	**220.0**	(2.9)	**172.4**	(4.1)	205.9	(3.7)	**236.0**	(4.1)
Korea	**195.6**	(3.4)	203.0	(3.3)	202.7	(2.9)	**214.1**	(4.9)	**177.9**	(5.0)	211.8	(3.3)	**215.4**	(7.7)
Luxembourg	193.6	(1.7)	182.1	(2.1)	186.1	(1.8)	192.0	(1.8)	**188.4**	(1.3)	173.0	(2.4)	**194.4**	(1.2)
Mexico	**226.6**	(2.4)	231.5	(2.5)	232.1	(3.1)	**238.3**	(2.8)	230.7	(3.0)	234.5	(3.0)	231.0	(3.5)
Netherlands	**177.0**	(4.3)	170.7	(3.5)	169.5	(3.2)	**158.1**	(3.5)	**193.7**	(6.0)	167.2	(2.5)	**154.2**	(5.0)
New Zealand	243.7	(4.1)	241.4	(2.2)	240.0	(2.7)	246.0	(2.3)	246.1	(4.3)	240.0	(2.7)	245.6	(3.2)
Norway	222.5	(5.2)	215.9	(3.1)	214.7	(3.2)	218.5	(3.8)	233.2	(8.8)	215.0	(2.8)	222.2	(4.1)
Poland	**216.7**	(2.5)	218.7	(2.1)	220.5	(1.7)	**223.0**	(1.8)	216.1	(3.7)	218.8	(2.3)	226.8	(2.7)
Portugal	**251.6**	(6.2)	241.6	(5.0)	234.3	(5.2)	**222.9**	(5.0)	**256.2**	(8.3)	235.2	(4.7)	**215.6**	(6.9)
Slovak Republic	**189.8**	(2.9)	178.0	(2.8)	178.0	(2.5)	**171.4**	(2.5)	**181.2**	(5.6)	194.6	(2.9)	**150.6**	(2.5)
Slovenia	**162.1**	(1.0)	167.4	(1.0)	170.8	(1.2)	**175.4**	(1.0)	**155.8**	(1.0)	170.6	(0.7)	**178.6**	(0.3)
Spain	**210.5**	(2.2)	203.7	(1.5)	200.0	(1.3)	**198.7**	(1.8)	**208.3**	(2.7)	201.4	(2.2)	201.1	(2.8)
Sweden	**185.5**	(5.0)	177.1	(3.0)	177.8	(3.8)	**173.9**	(3.5)	177.6	(3.7)	179.3	(3.5)	174.9	(6.0)
Switzerland	211.1	(4.0)	208.2	(5.3)	201.2	(4.8)	205.1	(5.1)	207.0	(7.1)	212.0	(3.9)	196.9	(7.0)
Turkey	**188.5**	(4.3)	191.5	(4.1)	197.6	(4.0)	**218.2**	(3.0)	**178.9**	(3.3)	196.8	(4.8)	**223.9**	(4.6)
United Kingdom	**239.1**	(4.1)	231.9	(3.6)	228.8	(3.4)	**226.4**	(4.3)	**245.2**	(5.5)	227.2	(3.3)	228.6	(5.6)
United States	260.8	(9.2)	246.9	(7.9)	257.9	(6.1)	264.7	(5.6)	250.8	(11.2)	261.8	(6.7)	257.6	(7.6)
OECD average	215.9	(0.7)	213.4	(0.6)	214.8	(0.6)	214.7	(0.6)	214.6	(0.9)	215.0	(0.7)	213.9	(0.8)
Partners														
Albania	m	m	m	m	m	m	m	m	m	m	m	m	m	m
Argentina	**223.8**	(7.7)	263.0	(11.2)	271.2	(10.3)	**292.0**	(12.3)	219.9	(8.2)	253.1	(7.6)	305.4	(14.9)
Brazil	207.7	(2.8)	210.2	(2.6)	208.7	(3.5)	204.8	(3.8)	206.9	(2.8)	212.9	(3.1)	201.8	(4.3)
Bulgaria	**144.6**	(2.1)	141.3	(2.4)	137.3	(2.2)	**137.8**	(2.5)	**143.7**	(3.0)	142.9	(3.1)	**135.3**	(2.9)
Colombia	224.3	(5.6)	233.3	(5.3)	233.9	(5.6)	235.3	(6.7)	232.9	(5.5)	229.3	(5.8)	233.3	(6.4)
Costa Rica	**187.2**	(2.2)	182.8	(3.0)	190.2	(2.9)	**195.4**	(3.1)	**185.0**	(1.9)	184.2	(3.0)	**203.8**	(3.7)
Croatia	**159.5**	(2.3)	160.7	(1.6)	164.6	(1.6)	**172.9**	(1.2)	**160.2**	(2.7)	159.6	(1.8)	**179.5**	(1.4)
Cyprus*	198.2	(1.4)	194.7	(1.1)	198.9	(1.2)	200.3	(1.2)	**198.3**	(1.2)	193.3	(0.9)	**204.7**	(1.1)
Hong Kong-China	280.6	(3.9)	282.7	(3.7)	279.4	(4.1)	275.4	(4.9)	281.9	(4.8)	285.2	(4.0)	268.2	(5.0)
Indonesia	177.9	(7.7)	177.4	(7.7)	182.9	(6.7)	189.3	(7.2)	176.0	(8.1)	177.5	(6.6)	195.2	(7.3)
Jordan	264.5	(3.2)	265.9	(4.2)	265.9	(4.5)	263.1	(6.3)	267.0	(3.8)	264.3	(2.9)	264.5	(8.2)
Kazakhstan	108.1	(4.2)	102.9	(3.2)	107.8	(3.6)	117.0	(4.9)	104.8	(6.6)	106.5	(3.5)	115.5	(4.8)
Latvia	**152.4**	(2.7)	156.8	(2.4)	159.4	(3.0)	**161.9**	(2.1)	155.0	(3.5)	157.7	(2.1)	159.9	(2.3)
Liechtenstein	220.1	(10.2)	192.7	(7.0)	170.1	(6.2)	186.8	(7.5)	c	c	227.7	(19.0)	c	c
Lithuania	202.2	(1.9)	202.7	(1.8)	204.6	(1.8)	204.4	(1.8)	202.7	(2.3)	202.1	(1.8)	207.1	(2.7)
Macao-China	262.5	(1.4)	266.5	(1.4)	265.9	(1.5)	265.8	(1.6)	261.0	(0.9)	274.3	(1.5)	267.1	(1.2)
Malaysia	201.0	(4.1)	196.0	(3.6)	203.1	(3.7)	208.9	(4.4)	198.8	(5.0)	200.6	(4.5)	207.6	(5.2)
Montenegro	**143.1**	(2.0)	146.0	(1.8)	149.9	(1.3)	**159.6**	(1.6)	**138.7**	(1.5)	148.4	(2.0)	**161.4**	(1.0)
Peru	267.7	(6.8)	252.5	(7.7)	258.3	(8.1)	258.6	(7.1)	261.1	(6.6)	258.6	(7.9)	258.3	(5.1)
Qatar	225.6	(1.7)	230.3	(1.6)	232.3	(1.5)	222.7	(1.5)	228.7	(1.2)	220.1	(1.6)	230.8	(1.1)
Romania	**174.9**	(2.4)	176.1	(2.1)	176.7	(2.6)	**187.8**	(2.1)	**171.7**	(3.3)	176.6	(3.0)	**188.9**	(3.1)
Russian Federation	**139.7**	(2.8)	136.9	(3.4)	131.5	(2.4)	**132.0**	(3.0)	**146.6**	(4.7)	130.9	(2.3)	**133.6**	(3.6)
Serbia	**140.7**	(1.2)	142.8	(1.4)	143.2	(2.0)	**154.4**	(2.0)	**138.8**	(1.5)	139.1	(1.5)	**164.5**	(3.4)
Shanghai-China	252.0	(4.8)	246.7	(4.2)	248.7	(4.2)	245.0	(4.1)	237.2	(7.6)	259.2	(7.1)	245.4	(5.6)
Singapore	**231.9**	(2.0)	227.8	(2.9)	218.9	(2.0)	**215.7**	(1.6)	**233.7**	(1.0)	223.3	(3.4)	**211.5**	(2.0)
Chinese Taipei	**230.4**	(3.5)	249.9	(3.9)	259.1	(3.3)	**273.2**	(3.9)	**223.3**	(6.3)	255.4	(5.1)	**281.1**	(4.9)
Thailand	**144.1**	(2.2)	141.9	(2.4)	135.9	(2.4)	**132.6**	(2.7)	**143.0**	(2.6)	138.4	(3.6)	**133.0**	(3.2)
Tunisia	309.7	(8.9)	307.6	(7.9)	308.8	(8.0)	297.3	(8.4)	300.3	(8.4)	306.4	(6.0)	310.6	(8.1)
United Arab Emirates	274.2	(3.3)	267.4	(3.2)	268.4	(3.5)	268.2	(3.8)	**287.3**	(4.7)	262.8	(3.4)	**264.9**	(4.7)
Uruguay	136.8	(3.0)	135.7	(2.8)	136.4	(2.8)	142.7	(2.7)	137.4	(2.7)	138.2	(2.7)	138.3	(3.2)
Viet Nam	**202.0**	(4.8)	191.3	(4.4)	191.0	(4.1)	**188.0**	(4.2)	**201.7**	(5.0)	191.8	(5.9)	**182.0**	(4.0)

Note: Values that are statistically significant are indicated in bold (see Annex A3).
1. A socio-economically disadvantaged school is one whose students' mean socio-economic status (ESCS) is statistically significantly below the mean socio-economic status of the country/economy; an average school is one where there is no difference from the country's/economy's mean; and an advantaged school is one whose students' mean socio-economic status is statistically significantly above the country/economy mean.
* See notes at the beginning of this Annex.
StatLink ᠊᠊ᇬᐨ http://dx.doi.org/10.1787/888932957460

[Part 6/10]
Students' learning time in school, by school features
Table IV.3.22   *Results based on students' self-reports*

| | Time spent per week in regular school lessons in the language of instruction (minutes) | | | | | | | | | | | | | |
| | Public schools | | Private schools | | Lower secondary education (ISCED 2) | | Upper secondary education (ISCED 3) | | Schools located in a village, hamlet or rural area (fewer than 3 000 people) | | Schools located in a small town or town (3 000 to about 100 000 people) | | Schools located in a city or a large city (over 100 000 people) | |
	Mean	S.E.	Mean	S.E.	Mean	S.E.	Mean	S.E.	Mean	S.E.	Mean	S.E.	Mean	S.E.
Australia	235.3	(1.4)	230.1	(1.5)	232.9	(1.1)	235.2	(2.3)	235.5	(4.1)	234.1	(1.8)	232.7	(1.3)
Austria	144.4	(1.8)	142.8	(4.6)	191.3	(6.2)	142.4	(1.8)	140.5	(6.1)	145.0	(2.7)	144.3	(2.6)
Belgium	223.9	(2.7)	212.5	(2.2)	256.4	(8.4)	215.2	(1.4)	239.9	(12.8)	212.7	(1.9)	230.0	(3.5)
Canada	320.2	(2.9)	273.6	(13.1)	329.5	(6.5)	313.9	(3.1)	308.0	(6.9)	314.3	(3.6)	318.4	(4.4)
Chile	379.6	(9.0)	373.2	(8.0)	360.4	(32.1)	375.0	(6.2)	393.7	(34.9)	395.4	(8.0)	360.5	(8.6)
Czech Republic	181.3	(1.8)	148.4	(5.4)	197.3	(2.0)	157.6	(2.4)	205.2	(5.3)	176.4	(2.2)	176.6	(3.4)
Denmark	315.6	(4.3)	313.6	(10.2)	314.8	(4.1)	c	c	315.5	(11.6)	314.1	(4.2)	316.5	(7.1)
Estonia	197.8	(1.2)	205.1	(5.8)	198.5	(1.2)	183.7	(7.8)	199.8	(3.2)	197.9	(1.5)	197.4	(2.0)
Finland	151.7	(1.3)	171.5	(4.4)	152.1	(1.2)	c	c	146.4	(3.7)	150.7	(1.8)	157.8	(2.0)
France	215.3	(2.4)	212.8	(4.3)	213.8	(4.2)	215.1	(2.1)	209.6	(7.2)	213.0	(2.6)	220.4	(4.7)
Germany	192.0	(2.4)	180.8	(10.2)	191.9	(2.2)	149.2	(14.4)	c	c	191.6	(3.0)	190.5	(4.5)
Greece	170.4	(0.6)	c	c	c	c	170.8	(0.6)	171.3	(2.2)	169.7	(0.7)	171.7	(1.1)
Hungary	162.5	(1.6)	171.8	(6.0)	169.6	(3.9)	163.5	(1.8)	161.1	(14.2)	166.1	(2.2)	160.9	(2.9)
Iceland	237.6	(2.0)	c	c	238.1	(2.0)	c	c	232.1	(4.0)	236.7	(2.4)	242.9	(3.9)
Ireland	181.6	(1.8)	180.5	(1.6)	186.0	(1.3)	171.9	(1.9)	181.0	(2.4)	181.9	(1.9)	178.1	(2.2)
Israel	192.5	(2.7)	c	c	172.4	(6.4)	195.5	(2.8)	188.4	(9.0)	196.4	(4.2)	189.6	(4.7)
Italy	277.3	(1.5)	260.2	(10.1)	396.0	(13.8)	275.6	(1.3)	288.2	(14.4)	276.0	(1.7)	276.4	(2.4)
Japan	199.4	(2.7)	217.9	(4.2)	c	c	204.8	(2.1)	c	c	189.3	(4.3)	210.7	(2.6)
Korea	200.4	(3.1)	207.8	(4.5)	178.5	(4.9)	205.4	(2.7)	c	c	204.7	(5.7)	204.2	(2.9)
Luxembourg	187.3	(0.9)	194.3	(2.1)	194.8	(1.2)	179.5	(1.3)	c	c	188.4	(0.8)	c	c
Mexico	232.4	(1.9)	233.2	(4.6)	238.7	(2.3)	228.5	(2.4)	222.7	(3.8)	233.9	(2.2)	233.3	(3.2)
Netherlands	167.0	(3.1)	170.4	(3.6)	173.7	(2.8)	158.3	(3.1)	c	c	168.3	(2.6)	171.5	(6.4)
New Zealand	241.8	(1.9)	257.8	(13.7)	216.8	(4.3)	244.4	(2.1)	241.7	(7.3)	237.7	(2.5)	245.6	(2.8)
Norway	217.7	(2.2)	c	c	218.0	(2.2)	c	c	215.2	(6.2)	214.7	(2.8)	229.5	(5.3)
Poland	219.2	(2.7)	234.6	(4.1)	219.8	(1.6)	c	c	216.2	(4.2)	220.7	(1.6)	222.5	(3.0)
Portugal	240.6	(4.2)	213.1	(4.7)	280.4	(5.6)	206.9	(3.8)	278.3	(20.3)	237.5	(4.4)	226.7	(6.2)
Slovak Republic	181.7	(1.9)	156.1	(7.1)	220.2	(1.8)	147.4	(1.6)	223.3	(3.0)	174.5	(2.6)	163.2	(4.7)
Slovenia	168.9	(0.5)	178.7	(0.7)	174.7	(3.7)	168.6	(0.4)	180.0	(0.0)	169.1	(0.5)	168.9	(0.8)
Spain	203.0	(1.1)	202.6	(2.2)	203.3	(1.1)	c	c	197.6	(2.7)	201.7	(1.5)	205.3	(2.1)
Sweden	179.8	(2.2)	172.6	(15.0)	179.1	(3.0)	163.9	(7.6)	185.0	(5.1)	179.7	(4.7)	172.5	(3.3)
Switzerland	207.4	(3.0)	189.3	(21.0)	215.5	(2.9)	178.0	(7.0)	217.7	(9.9)	208.5	(3.8)	192.0	(8.9)
Turkey	198.6	(2.5)	c	c	203.7	(10.5)	198.8	(2.5)	237.7	(13.7)	205.3	(5.1)	191.8	(3.1)
United Kingdom	232.1	(3.5)	230.4	(4.3)	c	c	231.8	(2.6)	238.8	(8.4)	227.5	(3.3)	238.3	(6.0)
United States	259.0	(5.4)	246.3	(10.4)	247.8	(14.1)	259.0	(5.1)	230.3	(5.6)	272.8	(7.1)	245.7	(7.9)
OECD average	215.2	(0.5)	213.2	(1.4)	224.7	(1.4)	205.0	(0.8)	224.2	(1.8)	214.9	(0.6)	214.7	(0.8)
Albania	176.0	(1.9)	177.8	(9.9)	184.0	(2.4)	170.5	(2.4)	176.9	(3.5)	179.5	(2.9)	169.8	(3.2)
Argentina	235.0	(5.9)	311.0	(14.3)	232.3	(6.8)	275.0	(8.9)	233.4	(16.1)	265.5	(10.2)	262.4	(10.0)
Brazil	210.4	(1.8)	203.2	(7.1)	221.6	(4.8)	205.2	(2.0)	211.7	(9.8)	208.2	(2.6)	207.7	(2.9)
Bulgaria	140.4	(1.5)	c	c	206.1	(8.8)	138.5	(1.5)	169.2	(11.4)	141.9	(1.8)	135.8	(2.6)
Colombia	228.9	(3.7)	248.2	(8.7)	238.6	(5.7)	227.8	(4.5)	233.7	(12.9)	227.8	(7.2)	233.4	(4.8)
Costa Rica	185.3	(1.9)	211.0	(6.5)	193.3	(1.5)	182.9	(3.6)	191.4	(2.5)	186.5	(2.4)	195.7	(7.9)
Croatia	164.1	(1.2)	c	c	c	c	164.4	(1.2)	c	c	162.0	(1.8)	168.5	(1.6)
Cyprus*	196.0	(0.6)	212.4	(1.6)	225.4	(2.7)	196.9	(0.6)	201.3	(3.4)	195.2	(0.7)	202.8	(1.0)
Hong Kong-China	279.3	(5.6)	279.5	(2.8)	277.5	(3.3)	280.8	(2.9)	c	c	c	c	279.7	(2.6)
Indonesia	189.4	(6.6)	172.8	(5.8)	204.4	(6.6)	161.8	(4.4)	177.9	(6.9)	187.2	(7.2)	174.2	(7.8)
Jordan	265.2	(2.2)	263.5	(9.5)	264.9	(2.5)	c	c	273.6	(6.1)	266.2	(3.4)	261.5	(4.3)
Kazakhstan	107.8	(2.4)	211.9	(30.9)	108.0	(2.7)	111.6	(4.4)	103.1	(4.2)	102.4	(4.7)	117.6	(4.6)
Latvia	157.6	(1.5)	c	c	156.9	(1.4)	183.0	(19.8)	149.2	(2.9)	162.8	(2.1)	157.8	(2.9)
Liechtenstein	204.7	(11.0)	c	c	209.9	(11.5)	c	c	c	c	201.5	(10.2)	c	c
Lithuania	203.0	(1.4)	c	c	203.4	(1.3)	c	c	202.3	(3.1)	205.3	(2.0)	201.8	(2.1)
Macao-China	c	c	265.7	(0.6)	261.4	(0.9)	269.7	(1.0)	c	c	c	c	265.2	(0.6)
Malaysia	200.5	(2.5)	262.1	(10.8)	198.7	(6.4)	202.3	(2.7)	205.3	(8.8)	202.4	(3.7)	200.5	(5.5)
Montenegro	149.6	(0.8)	c	c	c	c	149.6	(0.8)	c	c	152.4	(1.0)	143.3	(1.3)
Peru	262.7	(4.0)	271.6	(11.0)	246.5	(9.5)	263.2	(3.9)	252.6	(6.5)	269.9	(5.9)	252.6	(5.9)
Qatar	213.5	(0.9)	249.5	(1.2)	252.4	(2.2)	223.4	(0.8)	230.9	(2.2)	220.4	(1.1)	233.2	(1.1)
Romania	178.8	(1.4)	c	c	178.9	(1.4)	c	c	186.9	(6.6)	176.9	(2.0)	180.2	(3.2)
Russian Federation	135.1	(2.1)	c	c	137.0	(2.1)	125.8	(4.7)	132.3	(3.3)	135.8	(3.1)	135.7	(3.3)
Serbia	145.0	(1.1)	c	c	c	c	144.7	(0.9)	c	c	144.1	(1.1)	146.2	(2.7)
Shanghai-China	246.2	(3.0)	267.0	(15.6)	314.4	(3.3)	199.9	(2.7)	c	c	c	c	248.1	(2.7)
Singapore	220.1	(0.4)	c	c	221.6	(2.9)	223.7	(1.5)	c	c	c	c	222.4	(1.5)
Chinese Taipei	264.1	(2.6)	234.4	(5.5)	292.0	(3.2)	231.8	(3.1)	c	c	259.5	(5.9)	249.8	(4.1)
Thailand	139.5	(1.7)	133.9	(6.1)	178.2	(2.9)	128.1	(1.9)	164.6	(5.7)	134.5	(2.1)	132.2	(3.0)
Tunisia	306.7	(4.1)	c	c	295.7	(5.7)	311.1	(5.7)	298.0	(18.0)	305.8	(4.8)	307.3	(9.4)
United Arab Emirates	289.9	(3.1)	253.6	(3.8)	257.3	(5.5)	271.2	(2.3)	298.8	(6.7)	287.2	(4.1)	257.0	(3.0)
Uruguay	137.5	(1.9)	139.6	(4.0)	142.2	(3.3)	135.7	(1.7)	134.9	(6.4)	137.6	(2.4)	139.0	(2.2)
Viet Nam	190.3	(3.1)	225.6	(12.5)	233.5	(9.1)	188.8	(3.2)	199.3	(5.3)	181.3	(4.3)	196.7	(7.6)

Note: Values that are statistically significant are indicated in bold (see Annex A3).
1. A socio-economically disadvantaged school is one whose students' mean socio-economic status (ESCS) is statistically significantly below the mean socio-economic status of the country/economy; an average school is one where there is no difference from the country's/economy's mean; and an advantaged school is one whose students' mean socio-economic status is statistically significantly above the country/economy mean.
* See notes at the beginning of this Annex.
StatLink http://dx.doi.org/10.1787/888932957460

[Part 7/10]
Students' learning time in school, by school features

Table IV.3.22   *Results based on students' self-reports*

| | Time spent per week in regular school lessons in science (minutes) | | | | | | | | | | | | | |
| | Bottom quarter of ESCS | | Second quarter of ESCS | | Third quarter of ESCS | | Top quarter of ESCS | | Socio-economically disadvantaged schools[1] | | Socio-economically average schools[1] | | Socio-economically advantaged schools[1] | |
	Mean	S.E.	Mean	S.E.	Mean	S.E.	Mean	S.E.	Mean	S.E.	Mean	S.E.	Mean	S.E.
OECD														
Australia	224.3	(2.1)	225.3	(2.1)	229.2	(2.1)	229.9	(2.3)	229.2	(2.8)	226.2	(1.5)	227.3	(2.8)
Austria	193.0	(7.9)	189.8	(7.5)	203.9	(6.3)	212.2	(7.4)	**181.8**	(12.3)	197.2	(6.3)	**221.7**	(9.5)
Belgium	**173.2**	(3.4)	184.9	(4.5)	200.1	(4.9)	**211.1**	(4.6)	**164.6**	(6.8)	193.5	(5.1)	**204.8**	(4.1)
Canada	**294.8**	(4.9)	300.0	(4.2)	313.1	(4.4)	**316.5**	(4.6)	**278.9**	(7.4)	315.6	(3.7)	**308.2**	(6.2)
Chile	**264.6**	(9.5)	287.9	(9.4)	303.4	(9.1)	**327.4**	(8.7)	**267.2**	(7.9)	293.2	(9.6)	**329.9**	(10.5)
Czech Republic	**195.4**	(7.2)	207.8	(6.4)	222.9	(6.7)	**238.7**	(5.6)	**204.3**	(9.7)	200.6	(4.5)	**268.2**	(8.1)
Denmark	178.5	(3.6)	169.5	(3.8)	177.3	(3.7)	181.4	(4.2)	180.7	(5.2)	175.0	(3.2)	178.1	(4.1)
Estonia	191.9	(4.7)	192.0	(4.9)	196.8	(3.4)	203.4	(5.2)	199.4	(6.4)	194.0	(3.7)	198.8	(5.6)
Finland	**180.5**	(2.1)	187.9	(3.0)	191.8	(2.7)	**194.6**	(2.5)	186.3	(3.8)	188.3	(1.9)	191.5	(3.5)
France	**152.8**	(5.3)	157.2	(5.8)	180.2	(5.4)	**205.2**	(5.3)	**131.3**	(5.1)	169.5	(4.3)	**204.6**	(4.7)
Germany	**236.8**	(5.2)	251.8	(6.0)	259.0	(6.9)	**271.4**	(4.3)	**237.0**	(7.6)	241.3	(5.5)	**288.7**	(6.5)
Greece	**220.5**	(3.3)	226.7	(2.8)	232.5	(2.8)	**237.3**	(2.7)	**213.3**	(5.3)	229.9	(1.5)	**238.2**	(2.5)
Hungary	191.2	(6.5)	188.5	(4.9)	189.9	(4.7)	203.0	(5.1)	188.4	(8.5)	190.6	(6.0)	200.1	(5.0)
Iceland	139.9	(3.1)	138.7	(3.2)	141.4	(3.1)	145.7	(3.2)	136.6	(3.7)	141.7	(2.0)	142.9	(3.2)
Ireland	**137.7**	(3.3)	142.7	(2.7)	152.1	(2.8)	**149.3**	(2.2)	**130.9**	(7.0)	149.3	(2.1)	145.8	(2.9)
Israel	**179.0**	(5.4)	191.0	(5.5)	197.0	(6.9)	**219.5**	(6.0)	185.3	(6.0)	198.3	(5.5)	203.1	(6.5)
Italy	133.6	(1.6)	134.7	(1.4)	138.4	(1.8)	135.5	(1.9)	136.0	(2.7)	137.2	(1.8)	132.8	(2.7)
Japan	151.1	(3.4)	158.8	(4.0)	168.3	(4.0)	**183.6**	(3.9)	**130.7**	(3.8)	163.7	(5.2)	**203.2**	(6.0)
Korea	**181.2**	(4.2)	197.6	(5.2)	202.3	(9.0)	**216.7**	(11.9)	**161.3**	(5.9)	199.7	(3.4)	**238.0**	(23.8)
Luxembourg	**144.7**	(2.5)	143.2	(2.6)	158.7	(3.0)	**180.8**	(2.5)	148.2	(1.6)	134.2	(3.2)	**174.8**	(1.5)
Mexico	**239.5**	(3.2)	251.5	(3.6)	257.2	(3.7)	**259.2**	(2.8)	**245.6**	(4.2)	251.8	(2.8)	**258.2**	(3.1)
Netherlands	159.9	(8.2)	156.6	(6.9)	175.2	(6.9)	167.7	(7.9)	159.8	(7.4)	163.3	(7.8)	170.9	(6.7)
New Zealand	**231.0**	(5.0)	241.0	(4.1)	242.2	(4.9)	**277.5**	(7.6)	234.9	(5.3)	234.4	(3.3)	**288.9**	(10.2)
Norway	147.5	(3.4)	144.4	(2.5)	142.1	(2.4)	143.6	(2.9)	150.2	(5.3)	142.3	(1.9)	146.6	(3.7)
Poland	169.8	(2.9)	169.4	(2.7)	165.8	(2.8)	172.2	(3.7)	172.4	(4.7)	167.1	(3.7)	169.8	(5.9)
Portugal	**185.3**	(16.7)	220.1	(10.6)	258.9	(12.9)	**289.5**	(12.9)	197.0	(21.4)	238.7	(8.7)	**308.3**	(23.6)
Slovak Republic	**132.3**	(7.3)	134.2	(7.6)	165.0	(6.3)	**215.7**	(6.7)	**107.4**	(10.3)	146.1	(8.5)	**233.9**	(9.4)
Slovenia	**167.0**	(3.7)	176.1	(3.7)	191.8	(3.8)	**204.9**	(3.7)	**150.1**	(2.3)	182.2	(2.8)	**220.7**	(2.9)
Spain	**168.5**	(2.6)	179.2	(3.7)	186.1	(2.6)	**203.6**	(3.4)	**172.1**	(3.8)	180.2	(2.8)	**202.8**	(3.4)
Sweden	184.5	(4.4)	187.3	(3.3)	189.1	(3.3)	192.7	(4.5)	182.8	(4.8)	186.4	(2.9)	196.1	(7.5)
Switzerland	162.3	(6.2)	161.0	(5.3)	157.9	(5.7)	176.3	(8.4)	**159.9**	(5.3)	149.6	(4.7)	**194.1**	(9.9)
Turkey	**140.0**	(4.9)	152.4	(8.0)	170.9	(8.9)	**205.1**	(13.2)	**134.6**	(4.5)	142.2	(5.2)	**231.1**	(13.9)
United Kingdom	**273.1**	(4.5)	289.2	(5.5)	297.1	(5.9)	**321.5**	(6.6)	**275.2**	(6.2)	285.3	(3.7)	**335.7**	(12.1)
United States	**245.9**	(8.1)	243.7	(8.0)	258.1	(7.3)	**272.4**	(6.1)	241.8	(11.0)	253.8	(5.9)	267.6	(8.1)
OECD average	**187.4**	(1.0)	193.6	(0.9)	203.4	(1.0)	**216.6**	(1.1)	**184.6**	(1.2)	196.0	(0.8)	**221.3**	(1.5)
Partners														
Albania	m	m	m	m	m	m	m	m	m	m	m	m	m	m
Argentina	**190.5**	(10.4)	204.2	(9.3)	222.9	(8.1)	**248.6**	(11.3)	**179.7**	(8.0)	208.2	(10.9)	**257.6**	(9.5)
Brazil	**137.9**	(2.5)	142.4	(2.9)	164.2	(4.5)	**201.9**	(8.2)	**138.3**	(2.4)	145.5	(2.6)	**210.5**	(8.2)
Bulgaria	**268.3**	(4.6)	261.3	(5.8)	248.8	(3.7)	**248.6**	(5.6)	**276.7**	(5.2)	258.3	(6.2)	**240.6**	(5.3)
Colombia	**191.8**	(6.2)	204.1	(5.3)	205.1	(5.1)	**218.5**	(10.2)	199.6	(6.4)	198.2	(5.5)	217.8	(9.1)
Costa Rica	**192.8**	(2.7)	197.9	(3.4)	202.1	(3.3)	**218.9**	(5.6)	193.5	(3.1)	197.3	(2.4)	228.3	(9.2)
Croatia	**139.6**	(6.5)	163.6	(6.4)	191.6	(6.6)	**234.6**	(7.5)	**125.1**	(8.0)	175.3	(9.1)	**274.6**	(6.6)
Cyprus*	**184.4**	(1.1)	185.5	(1.0)	186.0	(1.3)	**188.6**	(1.3)	185.0	(0.8)	185.1	(0.7)	188.8	(1.4)
Hong Kong-China	**220.6**	(7.0)	221.9	(6.4)	228.4	(7.7)	**270.0**	(8.9)	**208.1**	(5.1)	237.7	(5.6)	**267.6**	(8.4)
Indonesia	**175.4**	(5.8)	175.9	(7.4)	195.6	(9.2)	**248.7**	(16.5)	**166.5**	(6.2)	174.2	(9.3)	**279.3**	(15.5)
Jordan	**262.4**	(4.4)	274.8	(5.7)	285.4	(5.0)	**287.9**	(6.9)	**261.0**	(5.8)	276.2	(3.7)	**297.9**	(9.3)
Kazakhstan	206.3	(9.7)	188.0	(7.9)	213.3	(9.6)	228.3	(11.2)	222.8	(11.6)	204.6	(9.8)	206.7	(13.4)
Latvia	**215.0**	(6.8)	213.1	(5.8)	236.9	(6.3)	**256.6**	(5.6)	**220.7**	(10.2)	220.8	(4.7)	**251.7**	(5.5)
Liechtenstein	138.9	(7.4)	150.1	(12.7)	172.5	(34.8)	201.8	(32.2)	c	c	173.7	(22.0)	c	c
Lithuania	321.0	(2.8)	321.6	(2.9)	319.9	(2.5)	320.5	(2.3)	321.8	(3.2)	318.0	(2.0)	325.7	(2.8)
Macao-China	**166.4**	(3.9)	185.2	(4.4)	188.2	(5.0)	**216.5**	(5.6)	**165.3**	(2.8)	198.6	(5.6)	**223.0**	(4.6)
Malaysia	**183.7**	(4.4)	175.8	(4.7)	186.8	(4.6)	**208.0**	(5.4)	**180.6**	(4.0)	186.3	(4.4)	**201.5**	(7.4)
Montenegro	104.1	(2.6)	102.7	(2.6)	106.4	(2.6)	107.6	(2.6)	**100.5**	(1.7)	111.4	(2.4)	**105.9**	(1.7)
Peru	**200.3**	(4.7)	201.4	(6.1)	223.3	(8.7)	**235.1**	(8.6)	198.9	(4.6)	208.3	(5.2)	232.8	(7.6)
Qatar	**250.6**	(2.2)	264.3	(3.2)	275.0	(3.1)	**265.5**	(2.8)	261.6	(2.3)	254.3	(2.5)	269.7	(2.1)
Romania	**132.5**	(6.7)	152.4	(6.0)	155.4	(6.9)	**206.6**	(8.3)	**137.0**	(7.7)	147.1	(7.2)	**204.0**	(9.0)
Russian Federation	**253.3**	(6.2)	269.4	(6.5)	285.1	(7.5)	**311.3**	(8.2)	**257.2**	(8.6)	272.7	(6.7)	**308.2**	(8.8)
Serbia	**155.3**	(7.7)	158.2	(6.6)	146.1	(4.7)	**139.1**	(4.8)	**166.7**	(9.3)	145.3	(5.4)	**136.7**	(4.2)
Shanghai-China	**225.8**	(9.5)	250.7	(7.4)	280.8	(8.1)	**298.9**	(6.9)	**195.0**	(12.2)	282.5	(13.4)	**303.9**	(8.4)
Singapore	**253.0**	(4.1)	286.1	(4.9)	320.1	(5.8)	**350.5**	(5.2)	**260.5**	(3.1)	286.9	(3.4)	**383.2**	(6.3)
Chinese Taipei	**164.8**	(4.2)	185.4	(4.3)	192.2	(4.7)	**220.4**	(4.6)	**148.9**	(7.8)	193.3	(6.4)	**229.0**	(6.6)
Thailand	**250.4**	(9.9)	244.9	(6.8)	258.8	(7.9)	**296.6**	(10.6)	**243.7**	(10.3)	248.4	(8.6)	**300.2**	(12.2)
Tunisia	**165.0**	(6.6)	185.7	(7.9)	185.0	(7.8)	**184.2**	(5.4)	158.8	(5.6)	187.4	(5.7)	189.2	(6.8)
United Arab Emirates	**263.7**	(6.8)	308.1	(6.6)	334.5	(7.0)	**320.9**	(7.7)	**263.9**	(7.5)	311.4	(8.3)	**330.6**	(7.8)
Uruguay	145.2	(4.2)	144.3	(5.5)	155.0	(6.8)	165.7	(5.6)	142.4	(4.3)	157.9	(5.1)	160.2	(9.4)
Viet Nam	**209.0**	(8.9)	228.1	(8.8)	234.9	(10.0)	**281.4**	(11.9)	**210.4**	(9.2)	236.3	(9.0)	**281.2**	(14.0)

Note: Values that are statistically significant are indicated in bold (see Annex A3).
1. A socio-economically disadvantaged school is one whose students' mean socio-economic status (ESCS) is statistically significantly below the mean socio-economic status of the country/economy; an average school is one where there is no difference from the country's/economy's mean; and an advantaged school is one whose students' mean socio-economic status is statistically significantly above the country/economy mean.
* See notes at the beginning of this Annex.
StatLink ᶆᶊᶈ http://dx.doi.org/10.1787/888932957460

[Part 8/10]
Students' learning time in school, by school features
Table IV.3.22 *Results based on students' self-reports*

		Time spent per week in regular school lessons in science (minutes)													
		Public schools		Private schools		Lower secondary education (ISCED 2)		Upper secondary education (ISCED 3)		Schools located in a village, hamlet or rural area (fewer than 3 000 people)		Schools located in a small town or town (3 000 to about 100 000 people)		Schools located in a city or a large city (over 100 000 people)	
		Mean	S.E.	Mean	S.E.	Mean	S.E.	Mean	S.E.	Mean	S.E.	Mean	S.E.	Mean	S.E.
OECD	Australia	**231.1**	(1.6)	**221.4**	(2.0)	**222.2**	(1.3)	**262.1**	(4.1)	222.2	(5.2)	225.6	(2.3)	228.1	(1.7)
	Austria	199.2	(5.4)	199.8	(14.6)	**326.8**	(14.5)	**194.6**	(4.9)	210.8	(27.4)	193.9	(7.8)	205.6	(7.8)
	Belgium	190.2	(5.6)	193.6	(3.6)	**155.2**	(6.8)	**194.9**	(2.7)	195.9	(22.6)	194.3	(3.4)	187.3	(6.5)
	Canada	**309.6**	(2.9)	**269.5**	(13.7)	**249.4**	(5.0)	**315.2**	(3.0)	**287.9**	(7.0)	305.6	(4.2)	309.2	(4.0)
	Chile	285.9	(10.0)	303.1	(7.1)	283.8	(31.4)	296.1	(5.4)	**245.7**	(13.9)	295.2	(9.8)	297.6	(6.6)
	Czech Republic	216.9	(4.1)	206.2	(20.8)	219.7	(3.9)	212.5	(6.0)	203.1	(15.6)	215.9	(5.2)	219.3	(9.1)
	Denmark	173.6	(2.6)	182.0	(6.1)	176.6	(2.3)	c	c	170.2	(5.4)	177.6	(2.9)	174.9	(4.9)
	Estonia	196.3	(2.5)	193.8	(20.3)	195.8	(2.5)	210.7	(15.5)	**202.0**	(6.3)	187.1	(2.9)	**204.7**	(4.8)
	Finland	**188.3**	(1.6)	**205.7**	(6.0)	188.5	(1.6)	c	c	187.6	(6.4)	186.9	(1.8)	193.5	(2.9)
	France	174.7	(3.1)	169.6	(5.7)	**125.0**	(4.9)	**190.9**	(2.9)	**139.4**	(10.5)	174.1	(3.8)	185.4	(6.4)
	Germany	254.7	(4.1)	259.3	(14.0)	255.9	(3.5)	204.8	(47.9)	c	c	252.2	(4.6)	262.5	(9.3)
	Greece	228.9	(1.6)	c	c	**189.2**	(8.4)	**230.5**	(1.6)	231.3	(3.4)	227.3	(2.2)	232.2	(2.5)
	Hungary	193.0	(4.1)	191.8	(12.2)	**249.2**	(6.8)	**185.9**	(4.1)	203.6	(31.1)	194.9	(5.0)	188.7	(6.1)
	Iceland	141.3	(1.6)	c	c	141.2	(1.5)	c	c	139.7	(3.2)	142.1	(2.0)	141.1	(2.9)
	Ireland	143.4	(2.9)	146.0	(2.7)	**150.2**	(1.1)	**137.2**	(4.1)	152.5	(3.3)	146.7	(2.3)	**136.4**	(3.9)
	Israel	196.6	(3.5)	c	c	205.4	(7.6)	195.1	(3.7)	182.7	(10.0)	202.7	(4.5)	194.9	(6.0)
	Italy	135.6	(1.2)	143.1	(10.9)	124.9	(8.4)	135.7	(1.2)	133.3	(5.4)	135.9	(1.6)	135.1	(2.0)
	Japan	**157.3**	(3.1)	**184.9**	(7.1)	c	c	165.4	(3.1)	c	c	154.3	(5.9)	**169.7**	(4.0)
	Korea	209.0	(11.8)	189.1	(4.4)	**176.6**	(4.7)	**200.9**	(6.9)	c	c	200.0	(10.7)	199.4	(7.4)
	Luxembourg	**154.5**	(1.1)	**167.2**	(3.6)	**140.4**	(1.2)	**181.3**	(2.0)	c	c	156.2	(1.1)	c	c
	Mexico	**252.8**	(2.1)	**240.9**	(5.3)	**261.2**	(2.9)	**246.5**	(2.3)	**238.1**	(5.5)	253.8	(3.3)	254.4	(2.9)
	Netherlands	162.4	(8.8)	162.5	(4.0)	**171.7**	(4.3)	**149.4**	(7.2)	c	c	160.7	(4.5)	166.8	(7.8)
	New Zealand	244.4	(3.2)	311.0	(37.7)	**200.4**	(6.6)	**251.3**	(3.7)	229.7	(8.3)	233.6	(4.1)	**259.4**	(6.0)
	Norway	143.3	(1.6)	c	c	143.8	(1.7)	c	c	141.5	(2.8)	141.5	(2.1)	**152.2**	(4.5)
	Poland	**168.5**	(2.6)	**198.0**	(13.3)	168.7	(2.5)	c	c	165.9	(4.5)	172.7	(3.6)	167.2	(5.3)
	Portugal	**234.3**	(9.9)	**277.0**	(19.7)	**129.7**	(3.1)	**360.7**	(14.7)	254.5	(83.9)	245.0	(10.7)	**208.6**	(13.3)
	Slovak Republic	154.1	(4.6)	234.8	(42.1)	**195.2**	(5.5)	**141.3**	(5.9)	**188.8**	(8.2)	154.5	(6.0)	179.1	(12.9)
	Slovenia	**186.3**	(1.6)	**205.5**	(8.7)	**206.8**	(9.5)	**183.4**	(1.5)	197.4	(10.0)	184.7	(1.7)	189.4	(3.3)
	Spain	**174.4**	(2.1)	**201.6**	(3.1)	184.2	(1.8)	c	c	**161.4**	(8.2)	181.6	(2.6)	189.7	(3.4)
	Sweden	190.1	(2.6)	178.5	(12.8)	187.3	(2.4)	250.3	(34.8)	178.0	(4.4)	187.2	(3.8)	198.6	(6.0)
	Switzerland	160.8	(3.3)	226.7	(38.2)	**158.4**	(3.6)	**184.6**	(11.3)	164.8	(10.0)	162.3	(4.7)	174.4	(10.5)
	Turkey	164.7	(6.2)	c	c	166.8	(8.9)	166.9	(6.5)	193.7	(16.7)	176.2	(12.2)	158.0	(7.4)
	United Kingdom	**286.0**	(3.8)	**306.9**	(8.1)	c	c	295.0	(3.7)	304.4	(11.9)	289.7	(4.0)	307.9	(9.9)
	United States	256.9	(5.2)	241.3	(17.0)	**233.2**	(9.9)	**257.6**	(4.9)	**227.3**	(6.9)	271.1	(6.5)	**241.4**	(8.0)
	OECD average	**198.8**	(0.8)	**214.2**	(2.9)	**193.2**	(1.4)	**214.3**	(2.3)	198.4	(3.4)	199.5	(0.9)	203.4	(1.1)
Partners	Albania	148.6	(2.0)	151.5	(7.4)	148.7	(2.6)	148.9	(2.5)	143.7	(3.4)	151.4	(3.3)	149.1	(3.1)
	Argentina	**194.2**	(7.7)	**260.6**	(9.5)	**182.9**	(10.0)	**234.4**	(6.3)	200.4	(24.0)	212.5	(7.9)	222.7	(9.0)
	Brazil	**144.0**	(2.1)	**228.0**	(13.3)	156.8	(2.6)	162.7	(3.6)	142.0	(10.5)	150.9	(4.8)	**171.8**	(4.4)
	Bulgaria	257.2	(3.3)	c	c	280.1	(19.1)	256.8	(3.2)	276.0	(18.0)	256.3	(4.0)	257.7	(5.6)
	Colombia	**200.7**	(3.8)	**232.1**	(12.9)	209.2	(4.9)	202.4	(5.8)	208.8	(10.7)	194.4	(8.0)	210.1	(6.3)
	Costa Rica	**197.9**	(2.5)	**243.4**	(11.2)	**194.1**	(1.9)	**216.0**	(5.1)	202.3	(5.6)	201.5	(3.4)	209.9	(7.4)
	Croatia	180.3	(5.6)	c	c	c	c	182.2	(5.4)	c	c	162.6	(5.9)	**215.6**	(11.0)
	Cyprus*	**184.9**	(0.5)	**196.3**	(2.9)	**214.1**	(3.7)	**185.2**	(0.5)	189.2	(2.8)	185.2	(0.7)	187.3	(1.0)
	Hong Kong-China	239.2	(12.2)	235.7	(4.5)	**208.5**	(4.2)	**249.8**	(5.8)	c	c	c	c	235.4	(4.2)
	Indonesia	**211.3**	(9.2)	**182.4**	(9.5)	194.7	(6.2)	202.9	(11.5)	180.8	(10.7)	198.5	(8.9)	223.8	(20.0)
	Jordan	274.2	(2.8)	294.0	(11.5)	277.6	(3.1)	c	c	272.0	(7.0)	272.9	(3.8)	283.6	(5.9)
	Kazakhstan	209.1	(7.0)	204.2	(24.3)	**190.9**	(6.6)	**258.8**	(14.5)	226.0	(9.5)	206.4	(17.3)	196.6	(11.4)
	Latvia	228.0	(3.6)	c	c	229.0	(3.4)	243.5	(12.3)	229.3	(7.8)	229.5	(5.3)	229.5	(5.9)
	Liechtenstein	166.4	(12.4)	c	c	154.6	(13.2)	c	c	c	c	166.5	(11.7)	c	c
	Lithuania	320.8	(1.4)	c	c	320.7	(1.4)	c	c	324.5	(3.8)	321.2	(1.8)	318.1	(2.5)
	Macao-China	c	c	190.9	(2.2)	**157.7**	(2.0)	**231.7**	(4.2)	c	c	c	c	188.8	(2.2)
	Malaysia	189.0	(2.7)	172.9	(21.8)	**170.2**	(8.2)	**189.2**	(2.7)	186.4	(7.3)	191.4	(3.9)	182.9	(5.5)
	Montenegro	105.0	(1.1)	c	c	c	c	105.1	(1.1)	c	c	108.9	(1.4)	**96.5**	(1.8)
	Peru	**204.3**	(3.1)	**255.0**	(16.1)	209.1	(7.4)	216.8	(4.0)	203.5	(7.3)	214.3	(6.5)	219.9	(5.9)
	Qatar	**253.9**	(1.6)	**278.8**	(2.2)	264.2	(2.4)	263.4	(1.4)	**263.6**	(4.3)	252.6	(2.1)	**272.9**	(2.1)
	Romania	161.1	(5.0)	c	c	161.6	(5.0)	c	c	154.2	(14.5)	154.9	(6.4)	173.9	(9.2)
	Russian Federation	278.9	(4.2)	c	c	279.0	(4.5)	281.8	(9.1)	264.4	(9.4)	268.6	(7.2)	**293.5**	(6.6)
	Serbia	150.2	(4.1)	c	c	c	c	150.3	(3.9)	c	c	150.9	(6.1)	150.1	(5.1)
	Shanghai-China	259.9	(6.1)	303.4	(21.4)	**339.9**	(10.1)	**203.9**	(4.2)	c	c	c	c	264.1	(5.6)
	Singapore	303.4	(2.1)	c	c	**199.4**	(3.7)	**304.7**	(2.3)	c	c	c	c	304.1	(2.3)
	Chinese Taipei	**205.7**	(2.9)	**157.6**	(6.4)	**261.1**	(4.3)	**148.7**	(3.5)	c	c	197.7	(6.9)	187.3	(4.7)
	Thailand	**275.8**	(6.3)	**190.1**	(7.3)	**178.2**	(2.7)	**284.7**	(6.5)	276.7	(19.7)	250.9	(7.5)	273.9	(12.7)
	Tunisia	180.5	(3.8)	c	c	**144.9**	(5.4)	**198.0**	(4.6)	176.2	(23.9)	180.7	(4.6)	178.1	(7.4)
	United Arab Emirates	**277.0**	(4.3)	**329.5**	(8.2)	**221.0**	(7.8)	**319.9**	(4.1)	276.1	(8.4)	282.8	(8.2)	**322.2**	(5.5)
	Uruguay	149.6	(3.4)	164.7	(12.2)	**143.8**	(3.5)	**157.9**	(4.9)	154.7	(9.1)	150.9	(4.6)	154.5	(6.3)
	Viet Nam	236.5	(6.4)	270.3	(35.8)	**166.3**	(11.3)	**245.8**	(7.0)	**205.9**	(8.1)	254.2	(10.9)	277.1	(14.0)

Note: Values that are statistically significant are indicated in bold (see Annex A3).
1. A socio-economically disadvantaged school is one whose students' mean socio-economic status (ESCS) is statistically significantly below the mean socio-economic status of the country/economy; an average school is one where there is no difference from the country's/economy's mean; and an advantaged school is one whose students' mean socio-economic status is statistically significantly above the country/economy mean.
* See notes at the beginning of this Annex.
StatLink http://dx.doi.org/10.1787/888932957460

[Part 9/10]
Students' learning time in school, by school features
Table IV.3.22 *Results based on students' self-reports*

		Time spent per week in regular school lessons in mathematics, language-of-instruction and science (minutes)														
		Bottom quarter of ESCS		Second quarter of ESCS		Third quarter of ESCS		Top quarter of ESCS		Socio-economically disadvantaged schools[1]		Socio-economically average schools[1]		Socio-economically advantaged schools[1]	
		Mean	S.E.	Mean	S.E.	Mean	S.E.	Mean	S.E.	Mean	S.E.	Mean	S.E.	Mean	S.E.
OECD	Australia	689.1	(5.2)	688.3	(5.3)	701.7	(4.8)	695.2	(5.0)	695.7	(6.8)	693.9	(3.5)	691.1	(6.0)
	Austria	492.8	(11.4)	487.3	(7.8)	500.9	(7.8)	516.3	(7.7)	501.7	(14.4)	476.4	(9.9)	531.4	(10.5)
	Belgium	602.1	(5.6)	616.7	(6.6)	650.5	(7.6)	666.5	(6.7)	574.7	(10.1)	631.1	(8.6)	664.9	(6.2)
	Canada	918.4	(12.9)	920.8	(10.8)	951.6	(12.2)	955.8	(13.1)	881.2	(22.2)	962.3	(9.8)	927.9	(18.5)
	Chile	1 039.3	(26.2)	1 062.4	(23.3)	1 112.4	(28.8)	1 053.9	(24.0)	1 050.1	(21.8)	1 063.4	(31.2)	1 087.8	(27.8)
	Czech Republic	557.2	(9.1)	569.6	(8.3)	585.3	(8.0)	599.6	(6.8)	549.1	(15.9)	573.2	(7.0)	616.0	(9.9)
	Denmark	716.7	(12.6)	692.1	(8.7)	727.5	(11.5)	716.2	(10.6)	713.7	(10.7)	713.8	(10.1)	711.7	(11.8)
	Estonia	610.6	(6.2)	612.5	(6.1)	616.9	(4.7)	626.7	(5.7)	616.6	(8.0)	614.7	(4.7)	622.4	(6.0)
	Finland	498.3	(3.8)	513.6	(5.1)	518.8	(4.4)	524.3	(5.0)	507.7	(7.3)	513.6	(4.3)	518.6	(7.2)
	France	565.5	(10.8)	564.0	(10.3)	612.1	(11.2)	646.8	(9.0)	543.4	(12.3)	586.9	(8.8)	641.7	(8.7)
	Germany	636.9	(8.9)	643.2	(10.9)	641.3	(11.4)	638.8	(8.8)	653.3	(13.4)	623.9	(9.2)	655.3	(14.4)
	Greece	608.3	(5.1)	621.3	(4.7)	629.3	(5.1)	633.8	(4.6)	602.7	(9.2)	621.8	(3.0)	633.7	(4.3)
	Hungary	503.3	(8.8)	507.1	(6.2)	510.1	(7.6)	527.5	(7.6)	491.8	(12.3)	519.5	(7.8)	521.3	(7.3)
	Iceland	617.7	(9.3)	610.7	(8.4)	621.1	(8.6)	624.5	(7.6)	626.7	(11.2)	619.2	(5.6)	614.8	(6.9)
	Ireland	506.7	(5.5)	514.6	(4.3)	522.8	(5.3)	517.2	(4.2)	502.4	(10.1)	519.4	(4.1)	514.2	(6.0)
	Israel	610.2	(10.2)	615.9	(10.0)	619.1	(8.9)	668.8	(10.3)	613.8	(12.1)	626.9	(9.4)	641.4	(10.6)
	Italy	652.3	(3.7)	648.0	(3.3)	645.7	(4.0)	638.0	(4.9)	662.7	(4.3)	644.0	(4.4)	634.3	(6.3)
	Japan	547.7	(9.2)	588.3	(8.5)	619.3	(8.3)	665.8	(9.1)	486.7	(10.6)	606.3	(11.4)	722.7	(11.3)
	Korea	578.4	(8.7)	610.2	(9.0)	622.0	(12.5)	656.2	(17.7)	519.4	(11.7)	613.9	(9.6)	685.7	(32.2)
	Luxembourg	548.7	(4.6)	530.0	(5.0)	551.9	(5.1)	584.7	(4.4)	544.8	(3.1)	512.1	(6.3)	579.2	(2.9)
	Mexico	714.4	(5.7)	733.8	(6.5)	736.3	(7.2)	753.6	(6.8)	728.0	(6.4)	732.3	(6.1)	743.0	(7.4)
	Netherlands	506.1	(12.8)	488.2	(10.3)	516.6	(9.5)	492.4	(10.8)	534.6	(17.7)	494.5	(10.7)	488.4	(9.1)
	New Zealand	713.2	(9.6)	722.8	(7.2)	721.4	(9.8)	768.0	(11.2)	726.3	(12.1)	711.9	(7.5)	778.6	(15.3)
	Norway	556.1	(9.1)	553.7	(7.0)	548.9	(7.1)	558.8	(9.0)	581.9	(15.8)	548.8	(5.6)	560.9	(8.5)
	Poland	580.3	(5.0)	585.0	(4.2)	585.4	(4.1)	597.6	(4.9)	579.9	(7.7)	584.0	(5.4)	603.0	(6.2)
	Portugal	755.7	(31.0)	775.6	(17.4)	799.1	(15.7)	824.6	(21.4)	775.3	(33.9)	781.3	(11.2)	825.4	(35.9)
	Slovak Republic	485.0	(13.6)	474.3	(12.9)	513.8	(11.5)	570.4	(9.4)	441.5	(23.4)	511.4	(15.2)	567.3	(14.2)
	Slovenia	479.0	(5.0)	495.8	(4.9)	527.7	(5.3)	552.4	(4.5)	447.9	(3.4)	510.4	(4.1)	578.7	(3.2)
	Spain	592.4	(5.0)	591.2	(4.4)	595.4	(4.1)	612.8	(5.6)	596.6	(7.2)	587.9	(5.4)	615.2	(7.1)
	Sweden	552.1	(11.6)	543.4	(7.1)	549.5	(8.0)	543.9	(9.7)	540.3	(9.2)	544.7	(6.9)	550.9	(16.9)
	Switzerland	581.6	(8.3)	573.7	(9.1)	558.6	(9.7)	587.4	(10.4)	579.6	(10.1)	567.1	(8.8)	586.3	(14.3)
	Turkey	480.7	(9.6)	518.8	(13.5)	542.2	(13.1)	608.8	(19.1)	466.9	(9.0)	496.6	(8.9)	657.2	(20.4)
	United Kingdom	731.7	(8.8)	745.7	(9.4)	742.1	(9.9)	763.0	(10.6)	746.9	(12.1)	730.6	(7.7)	779.3	(18.4)
	United States	746.2	(23.2)	731.8	(22.6)	773.6	(17.0)	807.0	(15.2)	723.8	(31.0)	773.7	(16.1)	785.4	(20.0)
	OECD average	616.9	(2.0)	622.1	(1.7)	637.6	(1.8)	652.9	(1.8)	612.0	(2.5)	627.3	(1.7)	656.9	(2.5)
Partners	Albania	m	m	m	m	m	m	m	m	m	m	m	m	m	m
	Argentina	620.3	(21.0)	685.8	(22.3)	737.0	(18.9)	760.6	(25.3)	613.3	(19.9)	690.8	(20.4)	789.7	(25.3)
	Brazil	548.4	(6.8)	560.8	(6.6)	586.1	(9.8)	633.4	(11.3)	548.1	(6.8)	571.4	(8.5)	634.1	(11.7)
	Bulgaria	539.8	(7.6)	530.4	(8.0)	520.5	(6.3)	530.3	(8.5)	545.2	(9.1)	526.0	(10.5)	522.3	(9.2)
	Colombia	675.7	(16.7)	697.4	(14.1)	706.9	(13.1)	727.8	(20.4)	695.2	(16.8)	687.0	(15.6)	724.9	(19.4)
	Costa Rica	581.4	(6.0)	577.8	(7.9)	600.7	(7.3)	627.6	(8.9)	579.0	(6.3)	579.4	(6.9)	661.3	(12.7)
	Croatia	435.4	(8.0)	465.9	(8.1)	504.4	(9.3)	573.6	(9.9)	419.8	(9.8)	476.4	(11.2)	632.4	(10.4)
	Cyprus*	564.9	(3.3)	563.9	(2.6)	567.6	(2.8)	573.4	(3.1)	568.0	(2.7)	559.9	(2.0)	579.8	(3.1)
	Hong Kong-China	763.5	(10.3)	773.9	(10.1)	768.6	(10.3)	818.4	(14.3)	752.8	(10.8)	793.2	(9.9)	800.5	(15.7)
	Indonesia	548.3	(16.7)	549.4	(17.2)	578.8	(20.7)	660.9	(29.2)	532.0	(15.3)	558.3	(22.1)	696.0	(29.1)
	Jordan	755.0	(10.0)	759.8	(9.3)	776.8	(8.7)	779.2	(8.5)	744.2	(10.6)	767.0	(6.5)	793.9	(8.5)
	Kazakhstan	482.4	(11.3)	461.6	(10.0)	499.6	(13.8)	544.7	(19.8)	488.8	(13.2)	479.8	(10.9)	528.8	(23.6)
	Latvia	582.6	(7.6)	569.3	(7.6)	601.8	(7.6)	650.3	(7.7)	590.1	(11.5)	598.1	(5.9)	646.5	(8.0)
	Liechtenstein	577.4	(23.2)	558.5	(14.5)	543.1	(39.6)	596.5	(44.3)	c	c	632.7	(35.1)	c	c
	Lithuania	692.5	(3.6)	694.3	(4.0)	694.9	(4.2)	698.0	(4.0)	690.8	(4.0)	690.0	(3.4)	708.8	(6.1)
	Macao-China	698.4	(5.6)	728.8	(5.9)	726.5	(6.2)	754.1	(6.6)	693.9	(4.0)	756.2	(7.3)	765.6	(5.4)
	Malaysia	577.0	(12.2)	547.2	(13.1)	576.9	(11.7)	618.5	(15.6)	556.3	(13.8)	573.5	(13.8)	615.6	(17.4)
	Montenegro	379.3	(4.8)	388.5	(5.1)	404.1	(4.9)	420.4	(3.8)	367.3	(3.5)	399.3	(5.0)	427.1	(3.1)
	Peru	757.2	(18.5)	710.8	(17.8)	755.3	(20.8)	777.2	(16.9)	736.1	(16.3)	730.2	(17.6)	778.7	(14.1)
	Qatar	731.7	(4.2)	744.6	(5.0)	763.9	(5.4)	737.0	(4.5)	743.0	(4.2)	724.6	(4.2)	754.5	(3.4)
	Romania	478.0	(8.7)	495.1	(8.2)	501.1	(9.3)	578.8	(11.6)	479.6	(11.0)	495.7	(11.1)	566.6	(13.9)
	Russian Federation	602.7	(9.7)	625.4	(8.2)	640.1	(10.3)	676.7	(10.3)	624.1	(14.1)	618.7	(9.3)	674.9	(11.0)
	Serbia	444.6	(8.6)	454.8	(7.5)	444.8	(6.8)	461.3	(7.0)	455.2	(10.5)	434.8	(6.8)	475.6	(7.4)
	Shanghai-China	734.4	(16.5)	747.8	(14.9)	791.0	(14.3)	810.3	(12.2)	665.2	(25.0)	809.6	(24.5)	820.6	(16.0)
	Singapore	754.9	(6.3)	798.5	(7.4)	835.0	(9.0)	866.3	(8.3)	766.6	(4.1)	801.2	(7.2)	895.4	(9.7)
	Chinese Taipei	622.9	(9.5)	678.6	(11.0)	705.9	(9.9)	762.0	(10.0)	585.2	(19.2)	696.0	(14.8)	793.6	(13.5)
	Thailand	591.4	(13.6)	583.5	(9.8)	602.1	(11.6)	694.1	(14.6)	579.3	(14.7)	586.2	(14.0)	669.6	(16.5)
	Tunisia	709.2	(14.5)	743.0	(16.8)	752.5	(16.1)	754.5	(19.1)	694.8	(13.6)	746.1	(13.9)	773.9	(17.3)
	United Arab Emirates	851.5	(12.8)	894.2	(10.2)	916.5	(10.7)	885.4	(13.5)	886.5	(19.0)	891.7	(12.1)	880.8	(11.0)
	Uruguay	436.9	(9.7)	427.8	(9.9)	443.8	(11.6)	466.9	(10.3)	429.7	(9.6)	452.8	(9.3)	451.9	(14.8)
	Viet Nam	633.6	(13.0)	628.6	(14.3)	644.7	(13.7)	694.1	(16.7)	627.0	(14.3)	648.0	(16.1)	687.4	(19.4)

Note: Values that are statistically significant are indicated in bold (see Annex A3).
1. A socio-economically disadvantaged school is one whose students' mean socio-economic status (ESCS) is statistically significantly below the mean socio-economic status of the country/economy; an average school is one where there is no difference from the country's/economy's mean; and an advantaged school is one whose students' mean socio-economic status is statistically significantly above the country/economy mean.
* See notes at the beginning of this Annex.
StatLink ⧉ http://dx.doi.org/10.1787/888932957460

[Part 10/10]
Students' learning time in school, by school features
Table IV.3.22 *Results based on students' self-reports*

| | Time spent per week in regular school lessons in mathematics, language-of-instruction and science (minutes) | | | | | | | | | | | | | |
| | Public schools | | Private schools | | Lower secondary education (ISCED 2) | | Upper secondary education (ISCED 3) | | Schools located in a village, hamlet or rural area (fewer than 3 000 people) | | Schools located in a small town or town (3 000 to about 100 000 people) | | Schools located in a city or a large city (over 100 000 people) | |
	Mean	S.E.	Mean	S.E.	Mean	S.E.	Mean	S.E.	Mean	S.E.	Mean	S.E.	Mean	S.E.
Australia	**701.4**	(3.7)	**680.8**	(4.5)	**686.3**	(2.9)	**744.1**	(9.0)	695.2	(12.0)	690.6	(5.5)	694.3	(3.5)
Austria	500.8	(6.1)	482.5	(21.0)	**709.5**	(18.0)	491.0	(5.3)	491.9	(31.3)	495.3	(8.5)	508.6	(10.0)
Belgium	635.4	(8.6)	628.7	(5.9)	663.9	(18.0)	631.5	(3.5)	666.3	(42.8)	629.2	(5.4)	642.0	(10.9)
Canada	948.6	(8.2)	814.5	(38.9)	873.9	(14.5)	946.8	(8.8)	904.3	(18.4)	933.9	(10.8)	943.7	(11.9)
Chile	1 073.6	(23.9)	1 070.6	(20.5)	1 018.0	(95.8)	1 068.4	(15.6)	**987.9**	(38.8)	1 115.4	(23.0)	**1 039.2**	(21.5)
Czech Republic	**582.6**	(5.7)	**503.0**	(26.0)	619.7	(5.7)	530.1	(7.2)	624.5	(22.0)	569.2	(7.6)	579.1	(9.7)
Denmark	711.2	(8.7)	719.3	(12.4)	713.1	(7.1)	c	c	707.4	(19.0)	714.3	(8.3)	716.2	(13.0)
Estonia	616.4	(3.4)	623.4	(20.1)	617.1	(3.4)	590.0	(28.4)	625.3	(8.1)	608.2	(3.6)	622.2	(6.6)
Finland	**512.4**	(3.4)	**567.6**	(7.9)	513.5	(3.4)	c	c	501.6	(6.6)	509.6	(4.5)	**527.9**	(5.7)
France	598.8	(6.4)	593.2	(9.9)	**537.3**	(9.9)	617.8	(5.5)	548.2	(19.3)	596.9	(6.6)	612.3	(13.2)
Germany	641.2	(7.3)	626.8	(30.4)	642.0	(6.7)	537.7	(68.4)	c	c	637.0	(8.6)	649.5	(14.3)
Greece	623.1	(2.2)	c	c	c	c	625.5	(2.3)	624.8	(5.0)	619.9	(3.0)	628.7	(4.3)
Hungary	509.3	(5.6)	521.9	(18.6)	**586.4**	(11.3)	502.4	(5.8)	522.8	(48.9)	515.6	(7.0)	503.5	(9.3)
Iceland	619.0	(4.3)	c	c	619.3	(4.2)	c	c	608.8	(8.6)	616.1	(5.2)	630.6	(8.3)
Ireland	516.0	(4.0)	513.9	(5.1)	**532.2**	(2.5)	**486.5**	(6.5)	521.9	(5.3)	518.0	(5.0)	504.1	(6.1)
Israel	629.5	(5.6)	c	c	631.4	(13.8)	628.1	(5.9)	603.9	(15.5)	643.7	(7.5)	622.7	(10.5)
Italy	646.7	(3.0)	628.3	(21.6)	809.1	(20.0)	643.6	(2.9)	646.7	(23.2)	645.8	(3.9)	644.3	(5.2)
Japan	**583.0**	(6.6)	**657.3**	(16.4)	c	c	604.9	(6.3)	c	c	561.0	(14.0)	**621.7**	(8.6)
Korea	620.7	(14.6)	612.9	(11.6)	**510.5**	(9.6)	**623.3**	(9.8)	c	c	614.4	(19.4)	617.6	(10.5)
Luxembourg	549.8	(2.0)	573.2	(6.6)	549.9	(2.3)	559.2	(3.8)	c	c	553.3	(1.9)	c	c
Mexico	735.2	(4.2)	734.8	(13.8)	753.8	(6.7)	723.6	(5.0)	712.8	(10.4)	740.1	(5.5)	735.9	(6.5)
Netherlands	498.1	(10.4)	499.0	(8.4)	515.2	(7.5)	469.2	(9.5)	c	c	495.8	(7.5)	506.3	(12.7)
New Zealand	726.3	(5.9)	824.1	(61.6)	**633.4**	(12.8)	738.1	(6.6)	710.7	(20.7)	708.0	(7.7)	**748.4**	(10.2)
Norway	553.6	(4.5)	c	c	554.1	(4.4)	c	c	547.5	(8.2)	550.4	(6.3)	571.2	(11.0)
Poland	**584.9**	(3.8)	**653.6**	(13.8)	586.6	(3.6)	c	c	574.0	(8.1)	588.9	(4.0)	601.9	(7.2)
Portugal	789.5	(15.8)	784.1	(26.2)	722.4	(10.6)	857.5	(25.8)	882.1	(130.8)	791.2	(12.1)	746.9	(17.4)
Slovak Republic	506.1	(7.9)	553.8	(60.6)	641.8	(6.2)	432.3	(9.2)	640.7	(9.5)	494.1	(11.3)	502.7	(22.3)
Slovenia	**514.7**	(2.3)	**561.7**	(8.6)	c	c	511.1	(2.0)	531.8	(27.1)	515.0	(2.5)	516.7	(4.4)
Spain	**586.0**	(3.3)	**617.7**	(6.0)	598.1	(3.1)	c	c	561.1	(16.0)	593.2	(4.9)	606.7	(6.1)
Sweden	550.2	(4.9)	531.3	(36.4)	545.2	(6.2)	666.1	(51.6)	536.8	(9.1)	546.8	(10.3)	556.7	(11.3)
Switzerland	572.8	(5.2)	623.4	(48.4)	**589.9**	(5.7)	526.1	(13.5)	607.5	(18.9)	576.4	(6.6)	558.1	(18.2)
Turkey	534.4	(9.1)	c	c	539.4	(27.4)	537.2	(9.5)	623.1	(27.9)	558.5	(19.6)	514.8	(12.9)
United Kingdom	738.0	(7.7)	755.2	(12.5)	c	c	746.2	(6.5)	770.4	(24.8)	734.6	(7.5)	766.7	(16.9)
United States	768.9	(14.3)	733.5	(47.3)	718.4	(28.7)	770.3	(13.5)	688.8	(17.6)	807.3	(17.9)	730.3	(21.6)
OECD average	631.7	(1.4)	644.5	(4.7)	641.1	(3.7)	636.0	(3.5)	643.7	(5.6)	632.0	(1.7)	635.5	(2.0)
Albania	494.9	(4.0)	504.3	(9.5)	505.4	(5.3)	489.0	(4.7)	489.0	(6.2)	502.4	(6.5)	490.6	(6.5)
Argentina	**647.1**	(13.9)	**802.7**	(23.1)	650.2	(19.4)	725.9	(14.6)	631.6	(40.7)	695.0	(18.3)	715.3	(19.3)
Brazil	**563.3**	(4.8)	**662.5**	(17.4)	601.3	(9.5)	578.4	(6.1)	550.8	(33.3)	566.0	(7.3)	**598.2**	(7.3)
Bulgaria	530.0	(5.2)	c	c	648.9	(25.0)	527.3	(5.0)	603.3	(25.3)	531.9	(6.5)	522.6	(8.8)
Colombia	690.3	(9.5)	766.2	(27.9)	720.0	(14.4)	691.4	(12.4)	723.2	(35.9)	668.8	(18.1)	716.3	(14.0)
Costa Rica	583.2	(4.8)	689.1	(19.8)	605.2	(4.6)	584.6	(9.7)	605.2	(9.4)	590.3	(6.4)	611.6	(20.4)
Croatia	492.1	(7.1)	c	c	c	c	494.7	(6.9)	c	c	468.6	(7.1)	**539.0**	(14.1)
Cyprus*	**562.6**	(1.4)	**610.0**	(6.3)	645.7	(8.7)	565.0	(1.4)	**580.0**	(6.7)	563.6	(1.8)	572.8	(2.9)
Hong Kong-China	782.3	(12.1)	782.1	(7.6)	748.2	(7.9)	799.4	(8.5)	c	c	c	c	781.9	(7.0)
Indonesia	604.8	(18.1)	560.4	(19.4)	606.0	(17.0)	564.0	(19.4)	554.7	(25.3)	589.0	(18.6)	612.2	(30.7)
Jordan	764.8	(4.9)	782.6	(10.3)	767.8	(4.4)	c	c	772.9	(13.6)	764.6	(7.1)	770.0	(6.3)
Kazakhstan	496.5	(10.7)	561.4	(37.6)	**476.3**	(9.5)	556.4	(21.5)	489.8	(11.6)	484.9	(19.2)	510.4	(20.7)
Latvia	608.3	(4.8)	c	c	609.3	(4.7)	643.1	(18.4)	**593.7**	(8.4)	618.6	(7.4)	611.3	(8.2)
Liechtenstein	582.6	(19.5)	c	c	582.7	(20.9)	c	c	c	c	579.4	(18.5)	c	c
Lithuania	694.1	(2.6)	c	c	694.7	(2.5)	c	c	691.8	(4.7)	698.2	(3.9)	692.5	(4.0)
Macao-China	c	c	730.3	(3.0)	**686.8**	(3.3)	781.4	(5.1)	c	c	c	c	726.7	(3.0)
Malaysia	578.6	(7.9)	651.4	(65.9)	557.5	(18.5)	580.7	(8.1)	575.7	(23.0)	583.5	(11.0)	573.6	(15.5)
Montenegro	397.5	(2.1)	c	c	c	c	397.7	(2.1)	c	c	407.5	(2.8)	**375.8**	(3.1)
Peru	739.6	(10.4)	839.3	(22.4)	720.4	(24.9)	758.9	(9.0)	748.1	(19.2)	767.8	(15.0)	735.5	(13.7)
Qatar	722.7	(2.6)	781.1	(4.0)	781.1	(6.4)	737.0	(2.3)	749.8	(7.2)	722.0	(3.5)	761.8	(3.7)
Romania	512.5	(6.7)	c	c	513.1	(6.7)	c	c	538.8	(15.4)	501.6	(9.1)	526.3	(14.2)
Russian Federation	634.7	(6.4)	c	c	633.0	(7.0)	649.8	(12.2)	599.8	(14.7)	626.8	(10.9)	657.7	(10.3)
Serbia	450.8	(5.3)	c	c	c	c	450.9	(4.9)	c	c	449.4	(7.4)	453.8	(6.8)
Shanghai-China	763.2	(10.6)	845.9	(49.4)	965.6	(15.2)	629.1	(8.0)	c	c	c	c	770.9	(9.5)
Singapore	811.1	(2.5)	c	c	**624.3**	(7.0)	818.1	(3.8)	c	c	c	c	814.9	(3.8)
Chinese Taipei	725.9	(6.8)	624.8	(17.6)	819.4	(9.8)	617.3	(8.4)	c	c	705.8	(17.2)	686.1	(12.4)
Thailand	628.0	(8.2)	507.1	(22.7)	558.5	(8.0)	622.6	(9.1)	658.0	(21.6)	584.3	(11.8)	624.4	(18.3)
Tunisia	741.2	(9.3)	c	c	669.3	(12.1)	776.8	(12.3)	722.3	(47.8)	743.2	(11.0)	731.8	(17.8)
United Arab Emirates	921.8	(10.7)	862.2	(10.5)	734.3	(13.2)	909.6	(7.0)	900.2	(28.2)	909.8	(14.5)	873.3	(8.0)
Uruguay	439.7	(6.8)	460.5	(19.2)	444.9	(9.6)	443.2	(7.8)	424.1	(19.1)	440.8	(9.4)	451.4	(9.8)
Viet Nam	643.8	(9.3)	744.6	(47.6)	617.2	(17.6)	653.5	(10.2)	618.7	(14.8)	653.5	(14.1)	703.9	(19.0)

Note: Values that are statistically significant are indicated in bold (see Annex A3).
1. A socio-economically disadvantaged school is one whose students' mean socio-economic status (ESCS) is statistically significantly below the mean socio-economic status of the country/economy; an average school is one where there is no difference from the country's/economy's mean; and an advantaged school is one whose students' mean socio-economic status is statistically significantly above the country/economy mean.
* See notes at the beginning of this Annex.
StatLink ⟨⟨⟨ http://dx.doi.org/10.1787/888932957460

[Part 1/1]

Table IV.3.25 Percentage of students attending after-school lessons, by hours per week

Results based on students' self-reports

		Mathematics						Language of instruction						Science						Other subjects					
		No attendance		Less than 4 a week		Four a week or more		No attendance		Less than 4 a week		Four a week or more		No attendance		Less than 4 a week		Four a week or more		No attendance		Less than 4 a week		Four a week or more	
		%	S.E.	%	S.E.	%	S.E.	%	S.E.	%	S.E.	%	S.E.	%	S.E.	%	S.E.	%	S.E.	%	S.E.	%	S.E.	%	S.E.
OECD	Australia	72.9	(0.6)	23.0	(0.6)	4.1	(0.2)	80.2	(0.5)	16.5	(0.5)	3.3	(0.2)	84.5	(0.5)	12.6	(0.5)	2.8	(0.2)	74.3	(0.6)	19.1	(0.5)	6.5	(0.3)
	Austria	76.9	(1.0)	20.8	(1.0)	2.3	(0.3)	91.6	(0.7)	7.6	(0.6)	0.8	(0.2)	94.6	(0.6)	4.7	(0.5)	0.7	(0.2)	82.2	(0.8)	16.0	(0.8)	1.7	(0.3)
	Belgium	65.5	(0.8)	27.8	(0.7)	6.7	(0.4)	75.9	(0.6)	19.2	(0.6)	4.9	(0.3)	75.1	(0.8)	21.1	(0.8)	3.8	(0.3)	68.8	(0.7)	24.4	(0.6)	6.8	(0.4)
	Canada	72.7	(0.7)	22.0	(0.6)	5.3	(0.3)	80.4	(0.5)	15.2	(0.4)	4.4	(0.2)	80.3	(0.6)	15.6	(0.5)	4.1	(0.3)	72.3	(0.6)	19.7	(0.5)	8.0	(0.4)
	Chile	62.4	(1.1)	22.9	(0.9)	14.7	(0.7)	72.3	(1.0)	14.3	(0.8)	13.4	(0.7)	71.4	(0.9)	21.2	(0.8)	7.4	(0.5)	68.7	(1.0)	23.2	(0.9)	8.1	(0.5)
	Czech Republic	63.2	(1.1)	31.0	(0.9)	5.7	(0.6)	69.0	(1.0)	27.1	(0.9)	3.9	(0.5)	67.2	(1.2)	27.3	(1.1)	5.5	(0.5)	58.0	(1.1)	34.3	(1.2)	7.6	(0.5)
	Denmark	59.0	(0.9)	32.9	(0.9)	8.0	(0.5)	60.7	(0.8)	28.2	(0.9)	11.1	(0.6)	63.7	(0.9)	33.1	(0.8)	3.2	(0.3)	57.9	(0.9)	32.7	(0.8)	9.3	(0.5)
	Estonia	63.2	(1.0)	27.2	(0.9)	9.6	(0.6)	74.9	(0.9)	20.3	(0.8)	4.9	(0.5)	70.7	(0.9)	24.9	(0.9)	4.5	(0.4)	60.6	(1.0)	30.5	(1.1)	8.9	(0.5)
	Finland	52.6	(0.9)	37.8	(1.0)	9.6	(0.5)	53.1	(0.9)	41.4	(1.0)	5.4	(0.5)	54.0	(0.9)	41.4	(1.0)	4.7	(0.4)	42.4	(0.9)	42.3	(0.9)	15.3	(0.6)
	France	64.4	(1.1)	29.7	(1.0)	5.9	(0.4)	72.1	(0.9)	22.1	(0.8)	5.8	(0.4)	73.7	(0.9)	22.9	(0.9)	3.4	(0.3)	69.4	(0.9)	24.3	(0.9)	6.4	(0.4)
	Germany	71.4	(0.9)	25.6	(0.8)	3.0	(0.3)	84.0	(0.8)	14.3	(0.8)	1.7	(0.2)	84.7	(0.7)	13.4	(0.7)	1.9	(0.3)	72.0	(0.8)	24.4	(0.8)	3.6	(0.4)
	Greece	44.7	(1.3)	39.8	(1.3)	15.6	(0.8)	64.1	(0.9)	31.4	(0.9)	4.6	(0.5)	52.3	(1.2)	35.9	(1.1)	11.8	(0.7)	56.0	(0.9)	29.2	(0.8)	14.8	(0.7)
	Hungary	69.4	(0.9)	28.3	(0.9)	2.3	(0.3)	88.0	(0.6)	10.5	(0.6)	1.5	(0.2)	87.1	(0.7)	11.2	(0.7)	1.7	(0.2)	73.5	(0.9)	22.9	(0.9)	3.6	(0.4)
	Iceland	68.1	(1.0)	24.9	(0.9)	7.1	(0.6)	80.6	(0.9)	13.4	(0.7)	6.0	(0.5)	85.1	(0.8)	12.8	(0.7)	2.1	(0.3)	73.9	(0.9)	18.9	(0.8)	7.2	(0.6)
	Ireland	75.9	(0.8)	21.2	(0.8)	2.9	(0.3)	87.6	(0.8)	10.3	(0.7)	2.1	(0.3)	88.1	(0.7)	10.2	(0.6)	1.7	(0.2)	76.5	(0.9)	19.4	(0.8)	4.1	(0.3)
	Israel	48.2	(1.3)	41.7	(1.2)	10.1	(0.7)	73.4	(1.1)	23.1	(1.0)	3.5	(0.3)	77.5	(0.9)	17.7	(0.8)	4.8	(0.4)	57.6	(1.1)	33.9	(0.8)	8.5	(0.5)
	Italy	48.8	(0.5)	39.8	(0.5)	11.4	(0.3)	61.9	(0.6)	26.9	(0.5)	11.2	(0.4)	63.7	(0.5)	30.8	(0.5)	5.5	(0.2)	50.3	(0.5)	36.3	(0.5)	13.4	(0.4)
	Japan	30.2	(1.2)	55.7	(1.2)	14.1	(1.0)	42.4	(1.1)	53.5	(1.0)	4.1	(0.4)	45.8	(1.1)	50.3	(1.0)	3.9	(0.4)	30.5	(1.2)	57.1	(0.9)	12.3	(0.8)
	Korea	34.0	(1.6)	39.7	(1.6)	26.3	(1.1)	47.5	(2.0)	42.8	(2.0)	9.8	(0.8)	60.8	(2.1)	32.3	(1.9)	6.9	(0.8)	35.4	(1.7)	44.3	(1.6)	20.2	(1.0)
	Luxembourg	63.0	(0.8)	29.1	(0.8)	7.9	(0.4)	77.3	(0.7)	17.8	(0.7)	5.0	(0.4)	77.2	(0.7)	19.1	(0.6)	3.8	(0.3)	66.9	(0.7)	26.3	(0.6)	6.8	(0.4)
	Mexico	55.9	(0.6)	30.8	(0.5)	13.4	(0.3)	61.6	(0.5)	27.1	(0.5)	11.3	(0.3)	59.7	(0.5)	28.3	(0.5)	12.1	(0.3)	58.8	(0.6)	29.2	(0.5)	11.9	(0.4)
	Netherlands	71.8	(1.1)	24.3	(1.0)	3.9	(0.5)	79.3	(1.2)	17.6	(1.0)	3.1	(0.4)	80.7	(1.0)	16.0	(0.9)	3.3	(0.4)	74.6	(1.0)	19.7	(0.8)	5.7	(0.5)
	New Zealand	72.6	(1.2)	20.9	(1.1)	6.5	(0.5)	79.0	(1.1)	14.6	(0.9)	6.3	(0.6)	81.3	(0.9)	13.1	(0.7)	5.6	(0.5)	71.0	(0.8)	19.1	(0.8)	9.9	(0.7)
	Norway	77.3	(0.8)	18.3	(0.8)	4.4	(0.4)	82.9	(0.6)	12.9	(0.6)	4.2	(0.4)	83.9	(0.7)	14.3	(0.6)	1.8	(0.3)	80.7	(0.7)	14.0	(0.7)	5.3	(0.4)
	Poland	52.4	(1.3)	44.1	(1.4)	3.5	(0.5)	65.0	(1.5)	32.1	(1.5)	3.0	(0.4)	64.3	(1.3)	33.2	(1.3)	2.6	(0.3)	40.4	(1.1)	48.2	(1.0)	11.4	(0.8)
	Portugal	46.4	(1.0)	39.3	(1.0)	14.2	(0.7)	57.2	(1.0)	33.8	(0.9)	8.9	(0.7)	69.2	(1.0)	24.7	(0.9)	6.2	(0.5)	55.8	(1.0)	36.1	(1.0)	8.2	(0.5)
	Slovak Republic	69.5	(1.1)	26.7	(1.1)	3.9	(0.5)	77.3	(0.9)	19.1	(0.8)	3.5	(0.4)	82.0	(0.9)	15.1	(0.8)	2.9	(0.3)	69.8	(1.0)	24.8	(0.9)	5.4	(0.4)
	Slovenia	72.6	(1.0)	24.9	(1.0)	2.5	(0.3)	87.8	(0.7)	10.7	(0.6)	1.5	(0.2)	84.8	(0.9)	13.7	(0.9)	1.5	(0.2)	78.5	(0.8)	18.3	(0.8)	3.2	(0.2)
	Spain	61.3	(0.9)	30.5	(0.7)	8.1	(0.5)	81.2	(0.6)	15.0	(0.6)	3.7	(0.2)	76.1	(0.7)	19.2	(0.6)	4.6	(0.3)	62.0	(0.7)	31.0	(0.6)	7.0	(0.4)
	Sweden	60.4	(1.0)	33.6	(1.0)	6.0	(0.6)	63.7	(1.0)	30.6	(0.9)	5.7	(0.5)	64.0	(0.9)	29.9	(0.9)	6.0	(0.5)	54.4	(1.0)	34.2	(0.9)	11.4	(0.7)
	Switzerland	71.3	(0.9)	24.2	(0.8)	4.5	(0.4)	80.5	(0.6)	16.2	(0.6)	3.3	(0.3)	82.8	(0.7)	15.4	(0.6)	1.9	(0.2)	70.5	(0.8)	24.4	(0.7)	5.0	(0.4)
	Turkey	66.1	(1.3)	24.0	(1.0)	9.9	(0.6)	75.1	(1.1)	19.6	(1.0)	5.3	(0.4)	76.0	(1.1)	16.5	(0.7)	7.5	(0.7)	73.4	(1.1)	19.1	(0.9)	7.5	(0.5)
	United Kingdom	58.3	(1.2)	32.8	(1.3)	8.9	(0.7)	66.6	(1.0)	24.9	(1.1)	8.5	(0.7)	65.1	(1.0)	24.4	(1.1)	10.5	(0.8)	49.6	(1.0)	36.7	(1.0)	13.7	(0.6)
	United States	70.3	(1.0)	23.8	(1.0)	5.9	(0.4)	74.7	(0.9)	20.2	(0.9)	5.1	(0.4)	75.4	(0.9)	19.5	(0.9)	5.0	(0.4)	67.2	(1.0)	23.1	(0.9)	9.7	(0.5)
	OECD average	62.1	(0.2)	30.0	(0.2)	7.9	(0.1)	72.6	(0.2)	22.1	(0.1)	5.3	(0.1)	73.6	(0.2)	21.8	(0.1)	4.6	(0.1)	63.4	(0.2)	28.2	(0.1)	8.5	(0.1)
Partners	Albania	40.8	(1.1)	48.6	(1.1)	10.6	(0.7)	52.9	(1.3)	38.7	(1.2)	8.4	(0.6)	56.0	(1.1)	37.6	(1.0)	6.4	(0.5)	52.7	(1.0)	36.0	(0.9)	11.3	(0.8)
	Argentina	63.4	(1.1)	33.0	(1.0)	3.6	(0.5)	74.7	(0.9)	22.4	(0.8)	2.9	(0.3)	73.2	(1.0)	23.1	(0.8)	3.8	(0.5)	63.4	(1.1)	29.6	(0.9)	6.9	(0.7)
	Brazil	41.8	(0.9)	42.1	(0.6)	16.1	(0.5)	46.0	(0.8)	40.6	(0.7)	13.5	(0.5)	50.6	(0.8)	42.5	(0.8)	7.0	(0.3)	40.7	(0.7)	46.8	(0.6)	12.4	(0.5)
	Bulgaria	60.1	(0.9)	33.9	(0.8)	6.0	(0.5)	69.3	(1.0)	25.8	(0.9)	5.0	(0.4)	64.7	(1.1)	21.5	(0.8)	13.8	(0.7)	58.5	(1.0)	30.5	(0.9)	11.0	(0.6)
	Colombia	34.5	(1.4)	42.9	(1.4)	22.6	(1.0)	42.6	(1.7)	40.7	(1.5)	16.8	(1.0)	36.5	(1.3)	45.2	(1.1)	18.2	(1.0)	45.3	(1.4)	31.0	(1.4)	23.7	(1.2)
	Costa Rica	57.0	(1.4)	33.9	(1.3)	9.0	(0.5)	78.2	(1.0)	16.2	(0.9)	5.6	(0.4)	72.4	(0.9)	19.7	(0.8)	7.9	(0.4)	70.1	(1.0)	22.0	(0.9)	7.9	(0.6)
	Croatia	65.2	(1.2)	31.4	(1.1)	3.4	(0.3)	88.5	(0.7)	9.1	(0.6)	2.4	(0.3)	85.8	(0.8)	13.1	(0.7)	1.1	(0.2)	81.5	(0.8)	15.6	(0.7)	3.0	(0.4)
	Cyprus*	37.5	(0.9)	57.8	(0.9)	4.7	(0.4)	82.0	(0.7)	15.3	(0.7)	2.7	(0.3)	81.0	(0.7)	15.8	(0.7)	3.1	(0.3)	35.0	(0.7)	51.3	(0.8)	13.7	(0.5)
	Hong Kong-China	53.3	(1.2)	40.7	(1.1)	6.0	(0.4)	75.5	(1.1)	22.5	(1.2)	2.0	(0.3)	71.0	(1.0)	24.3	(0.8)	4.7	(0.5)	58.4	(1.2)	36.6	(1.2)	5.0	(0.4)
	Indonesia	54.0	(1.7)	37.4	(1.5)	8.7	(0.7)	65.0	(1.6)	28.5	(1.4)	6.5	(0.6)	56.6	(1.6)	34.9	(1.3)	8.5	(0.7)	57.9	(1.4)	34.0	(1.2)	8.1	(0.7)
	Jordan	51.3	(0.9)	33.4	(0.9)	15.3	(0.6)	62.8	(1.0)	24.8	(0.9)	12.5	(0.6)	55.2	(1.0)	30.2	(1.0)	14.7	(0.6)	56.0	(0.9)	30.5	(0.9)	13.5	(0.6)
	Kazakhstan	29.6	(1.3)	53.9	(1.3)	16.5	(0.9)	42.1	(1.4)	50.5	(1.4)	7.4	(0.5)	41.6	(1.3)	44.4	(1.1)	14.0	(0.9)	30.5	(1.1)	48.9	(1.1)	20.6	(0.9)
	Latvia	55.6	(1.3)	39.8	(1.2)	4.6	(0.5)	73.0	(1.2)	24.7	(1.2)	2.2	(0.3)	82.0	(1.1)	15.9	(0.9)	2.1	(0.3)	49.3	(1.1)	41.5	(1.1)	9.3	(0.7)
	Liechtenstein	74.0	(3.3)	21.7	(3.3)	4.3	(1.3)	84.1	(2.6)	13.9	(2.5)	2.0	(1.0)	85.0	(2.5)	13.3	(2.5)	1.7	(0.9)	74.9	(3.2)	23.1	(3.1)	2.0	(1.0)
	Lithuania	59.6	(1.2)	33.6	(1.3)	6.8	(0.5)	66.7	(1.1)	25.2	(1.0)	8.1	(0.5)	67.1	(1.0)	27.1	(0.9)	5.7	(0.4)	56.3	(1.0)	31.9	(0.9)	11.7	(0.6)
	Macao-China	59.5	(0.9)	29.9	(0.8)	10.6	(0.5)	75.5	(0.7)	20.2	(0.7)	4.4	(0.4)	73.8	(0.7)	21.1	(0.7)	5.1	(0.4)	58.1	(0.8)	32.0	(0.8)	9.9	(0.5)
	Malaysia	28.0	(1.0)	55.7	(1.0)	16.3	(0.8)	37.0	(0.9)	53.1	(0.9)	10.0	(0.6)	31.2	(0.9)	54.0	(0.9)	14.9	(0.7)	27.3	(0.8)	57.7	(0.8)	15.0	(0.7)
	Montenegro	62.2	(1.0)	31.6	(1.0)	6.2	(0.4)	85.4	(0.6)	10.7	(0.6)	3.9	(0.4)	81.6	(0.7)	14.8	(0.7)	3.6	(0.4)	75.2	(0.8)	19.0	(0.7)	5.8	(0.4)
	Peru	28.1	(0.9)	43.2	(0.9)	28.6	(0.8)	33.7	(1.0)	42.8	(0.9)	23.5	(0.8)	32.8	(1.1)	49.4	(1.0)	17.8	(0.8)	31.1	(0.9)	50.0	(0.8)	18.9	(0.7)
	Qatar	42.2	(0.6)	39.3	(0.6)	18.5	(0.4)	60.2	(0.5)	30.8	(0.4)	9.0	(0.3)	46.4	(0.5)	34.9	(0.5)	18.7	(0.4)	49.5	(0.6)	34.5	(0.6)	16.0	(0.5)
	Romania	57.8	(1.0)	35.1	(1.0)	7.1	(0.5)	62.6	(1.2)	30.3	(1.1)	7.1	(0.6)	68.2	(1.1)	26.5	(1.0)	5.2	(0.5)	57.2	(1.0)	33.6	(1.0)	9.2	(0.5)
	Russian Federation	30.0	(1.6)	59.1	(1.4)	10.9	(0.6)	37.9	(1.8)	55.9	(1.7)	6.2	(0.4)	55.7	(1.5)	37.8	(1.5)	6.5	(0.4)	47.3	(1.4)	43.1	(1.3)	9.7	(0.6)
	Serbia	55.3	(1.1)	38.1	(1.0)	6.6	(0.5)	74.4	(1.0)	21.4	(0.7)	4.2	(0.5)	71.4	(0.9)	23.2	(0.9)	5.4	(0.5)	64.4	(1.1)	26.3	(0.9)	9.3	(0.6)
	Shanghai-China	29.3	(1.1)	55.1	(1.1)	15.6	(0.6)	48.8	(0.9)	40.6	(0.9)	10.6	(0.6)	44.8	(1.1)	43.5	(1.1)	11.6	(0.6)	43.2	(1.0)	47.0	(0.9)	9.8	(0.6)
	Singapore	32.5	(1.0)	49.6	(0.8)	18.0	(0.6)	54.4	(0.9)	37.5	(0.9)	8.2	(0.5)	45.9	(1.0)	41.1	(0.9)	13.0	(0.5)	48.6	(1.0)	40.7	(0.9)	10.7	(0.5)
	Chinese Taipei	42.9	(0.9)	40.5	(0.9)	16.6	(0.7)	56.3	(0.8)	34.8	(0.8)	8.9	(0.5)	53.0	(0.8)	35.7	(0.7)	11.2	(0.6)	43.3	(0.9)	42.3	(0.9)	14.5	(0.7)
	Thailand	41.2	(1.0)	48.7	(1.0)	10.1	(0.6)	74.2	(1.1)	23.3	(1.0)	2.5	(0.2)	54.6	(1.3)	34.6	(1.2)	10.8	(0.7)	61.9	(1.3)	30.9	(1.2)	7.1	(0.5)
	Tunisia	21.8	(1.0)	50.1	(1.1)	28.2	(1.1)	37.9	(1.2)	47.5	(1.1)	14.6	(0.7)	30.3	(1.0)	52.0	(0.9)	17.7	(0.7)	26.8	(0.9)	51.4	(1.0)	21.8	(1.0)
	United Arab Emirates	50.2	(0.7)	32.6	(0.6)	17.1	(0.6)	67.6	(0.9)	23.0	(0.7)	9.3	(0.4)	58.2	(0.9)	26.1	(0.6)	15.7	(0.6)	58.0	(0.8)	29.1	(0.7)	12.9	(0.4)
	Uruguay	65.5	(1.0)	26.1	(0.8)	8.4	(0.6)	76.8	(0.8)	18.0	(0.7)	5.2	(0.4)	70.9	(0.9)	23.9	(0.8)	5.2	(0.4)	64.7	(0.9)	25.9	(0.7)	9.4	(0.6)
	Viet Nam	17.2	(1.1)	47.2	(1.1)	35.6	(1.6)	47.2	(1.2)	41.5	(1.1)	11.3	(0.7)	32.7	(1.5)	46.3	(1.2)	21.0	(1.1)	36.1	(1.1)	52.8	(1.1)	11.1	(0.6)

* See notes at the beginning of this Annex.

StatLink http://dx.doi.org/10.1787/888932957460

[Part 1/1]
Hours of after-school study time per week
Table IV.3.27 *Results based on students' self-reports*

	Average number of hours per week spent on the following, all school subjects combined:												
	Homework or other study set by teachers		Homework or other study set by teachers, with somebody overlooking and providing help if necessary, either at school or elsewhere		Work with a personal tutor whether paid or not		Attend after-school classes organised by a commercial company, and paid for by parents		Study with a parent or other family member		Work on a computer for practice (e.g. learn vocabulary with training software)	
	Mean	S.E.	Mean	S.E.	Mean	S.E.	Mean	S.E.	Mean	S.E.	Mean	S.E.
OECD												
Australia	6.0	(0.1)	1.3	(0.0)	0.5	(0.0)	0.4	(0.0)	1.0	(0.0)	1.2	(0.0)
Austria	4.5	(0.1)	1.0	(0.0)	0.4	(0.0)	0.2	(0.0)	1.1	(0.0)	1.0	(0.0)
Belgium	5.5	(0.1)	0.7	(0.0)	0.3	(0.0)	0.2	(0.0)	0.7	(0.0)	0.9	(0.0)
Canada	5.5	(0.1)	1.2	(0.0)	0.4	(0.0)	0.3	(0.0)	0.9	(0.0)	0.8	(0.0)
Chile	3.5	(0.1)	1.7	(0.0)	0.6	(0.0)	0.4	(0.0)	1.4	(0.0)	1.4	(0.0)
Czech Republic	3.1	(0.1)	0.8	(0.0)	0.4	(0.0)	0.4	(0.0)	0.9	(0.0)	1.3	(0.1)
Denmark	4.3	(0.1)	0.9	(0.0)	0.2	(0.0)	0.1	(0.0)	1.0	(0.0)	0.7	(0.0)
Estonia	6.9	(0.1)	1.5	(0.0)	0.6	(0.0)	0.8	(0.0)	0.9	(0.0)	1.5	(0.0)
Finland	2.8	(0.1)	0.5	(0.0)	0.1	(0.0)	0.1	(0.0)	0.4	(0.0)	0.4	(0.0)
France	5.1	(0.1)	1.0	(0.0)	0.4	(0.0)	0.2	(0.0)	0.9	(0.0)	0.9	(0.0)
Germany	4.7	(0.1)	0.2	(0.0)	0.5	(0.0)	0.6	(0.0)	1.0	(0.0)	1.3	(0.0)
Greece	5.3	(0.1)	2.0	(0.1)	2.1	(0.1)	3.0	(0.1)	0.9	(0.0)	1.2	(0.0)
Hungary	6.2	(0.1)	2.1	(0.1)	0.9	(0.1)	0.3	(0.0)	1.3	(0.0)	1.3	(0.0)
Iceland	4.1	(0.1)	1.3	(0.0)	0.5	(0.0)	0.2	(0.0)	1.1	(0.0)	0.8	(0.0)
Ireland	7.3	(0.1)	1.6	(0.1)	0.4	(0.0)	0.3	(0.0)	0.7	(0.0)	0.7	(0.0)
Israel	4.6	(0.1)	1.4	(0.0)	1.3	(0.0)	0.8	(0.0)	1.1	(0.0)	1.2	(0.1)
Italy	8.7	(0.1)	1.9	(0.0)	1.0	(0.0)	0.5	(0.0)	1.2	(0.0)	1.8	(0.0)
Japan	3.8	(0.1)	0.8	(0.0)	0.1	(0.0)	0.6	(0.1)	0.3	(0.0)	0.1	(0.0)
Korea	2.9	(0.1)	0.9	(0.0)	1.4	(0.1)	3.6	(0.2)	0.4	(0.0)	1.1	(0.0)
Luxembourg	4.6	(0.1)	1.1	(0.0)	0.5	(0.0)	0.4	(0.0)	1.0	(0.0)	1.1	(0.0)
Mexico	5.2	(0.1)	2.3	(0.0)	1.1	(0.0)	0.7	(0.0)	1.7	(0.0)	2.7	(0.0)
Netherlands	5.8	(0.1)	1.0	(0.0)	0.4	(0.0)	0.3	(0.0)	1.0	(0.0)	1.4	(0.1)
New Zealand	4.2	(0.1)	1.0	(0.0)	0.4	(0.0)	0.2	(0.0)	0.8	(0.0)	0.7	(0.0)
Norway	4.7	(0.1)	0.9	(0.0)	0.2	(0.0)	0.2	(0.0)	1.0	(0.0)	1.1	(0.0)
Poland	6.6	(0.1)	1.9	(0.1)	1.1	(0.0)	0.7	(0.0)	1.2	(0.0)	1.9	(0.1)
Portugal	3.8	(0.1)	1.3	(0.0)	1.1	(0.0)	0.4	(0.0)	0.8	(0.0)	1.1	(0.0)
Slovak Republic	3.2	(0.1)	1.0	(0.0)	0.5	(0.0)	0.5	(0.0)	0.8	(0.0)	1.5	(0.0)
Slovenia	3.7	(0.1)	1.2	(0.1)	0.6	(0.0)	0.5	(0.0)	1.0	(0.1)	1.4	(0.0)
Spain	6.5	(0.1)	1.7	(0.1)	1.3	(0.0)	1.1	(0.0)	1.0	(0.0)	1.2	(0.0)
Sweden	3.6	(0.1)	1.2	(0.0)	0.2	(0.0)	0.2	(0.0)	1.2	(0.0)	0.9	(0.0)
Switzerland	4.0	(0.1)	0.9	(0.0)	0.4	(0.0)	0.3	(0.0)	1.0	(0.0)	0.9	(0.0)
Turkey	4.2	(0.1)	2.1	(0.0)	1.3	(0.1)	1.9	(0.1)	1.7	(0.1)	2.3	(0.1)
United Kingdom	4.9	(0.1)	1.0	(0.0)	0.4	(0.0)	0.3	(0.0)	0.9	(0.0)	1.2	(0.0)
United States	6.1	(0.2)	1.5	(0.1)	0.4	(0.0)	0.3	(0.0)	1.2	(0.1)	1.2	(0.1)
OECD average	4.9	(0.0)	1.3	(0.0)	0.7	(0.0)	0.6	(0.0)	1.0	(0.0)	1.2	(0.0)
Partners												
Albania	5.1	(0.1)	3.2	(0.1)	2.2	(0.1)	2.2	(0.1)	2.9	(0.1)	3.6	(0.1)
Argentina	3.7	(0.1)	1.8	(0.1)	1.4	(0.1)	1.1	(0.1)	1.5	(0.0)	2.1	(0.1)
Brazil	3.3	(0.1)	1.6	(0.0)	1.0	(0.0)	1.5	(0.1)	1.3	(0.0)	1.6	(0.0)
Bulgaria	5.6	(0.2)	1.9	(0.1)	1.0	(0.0)	1.5	(0.1)	1.1	(0.0)	2.0	(0.1)
Colombia	5.3	(0.1)	2.5	(0.1)	1.2	(0.0)	1.4	(0.1)	1.8	(0.1)	2.1	(0.1)
Costa Rica	3.5	(0.2)	1.5	(0.0)	1.1	(0.0)	0.8	(0.0)	1.1	(0.0)	1.6	(0.1)
Croatia	5.9	(0.1)	1.3	(0.0)	0.9	(0.0)	0.3	(0.0)	1.1	(0.0)	1.5	(0.1)
Cyprus*	3.8	(0.1)	1.2	(0.0)	2.0	(0.1)	2.2	(0.0)	0.7	(0.0)	1.2	(0.0)
Hong Kong-China	6.0	(0.2)	1.2	(0.0)	0.7	(0.0)	1.0	(0.1)	0.5	(0.0)	0.9	(0.0)
Indonesia	4.9	(0.2)	3.2	(0.1)	2.5	(0.1)	2.7	(0.1)	3.0	(0.1)	3.0	(0.1)
Jordan	4.2	(0.1)	2.0	(0.1)	1.5	(0.1)	1.2	(0.1)	1.9	(0.1)	2.3	(0.1)
Kazakhstan	8.8	(0.2)	4.1	(0.1)	2.8	(0.1)	2.1	(0.1)	3.4	(0.1)	4.1	(0.1)
Latvia	6.2	(0.1)	1.8	(0.1)	0.8	(0.0)	1.6	(0.1)	1.1	(0.1)	2.0	(0.1)
Liechtenstein	3.3	(0.2)	1.1	(0.2)	0.2	(0.00)	0.1	(0.0)	1.1	(0.2)	1.3	(0.2)
Lithuania	6.7	(0.1)	1.5	(0.0)	0.6	(0.0)	0.6	(0.0)	1.1	(0.0)	1.8	(0.0)
Macao-China	5.9	(0.1)	2.0	(0.1)	1.0	(0.0)	0.6	(0.0)	0.6	(0.0)	1.2	(0.0)
Malaysia	4.8	(0.1)	2.5	(0.1)	1.9	(0.1)	2.8	(0.1)	1.9	(0.0)	2.0	(0.1)
Montenegro	4.3	(0.1)	1.4	(0.0)	1.2	(0.0)	0.7	(0.0)	1.3	(0.0)	2.0	(0.1)
Peru	5.5	(0.1)	2.4	(0.1)	1.2	(0.1)	1.9	(0.1)	1.8	(0.1)	2.0	(0.1)
Qatar	4.3	(0.0)	1.7	(0.0)	1.7	(0.0)	1.0	(0.0)	1.5	(0.0)	1.6	(0.0)
Romania	7.3	(0.2)	1.7	(0.1)	0.8	(0.0)	0.6	(0.0)	1.1	(0.1)	2.0	(0.1)
Russian Federation	9.7	(0.2)	2.7	(0.1)	1.8	(0.1)	1.5	(0.0)	2.2	(0.1)	3.2	(0.1)
Serbia	4.4	(0.1)	1.6	(0.0)	1.3	(0.1)	0.6	(0.0)	1.2	(0.1)	2.0	(0.1)
Shanghai-China	13.8	(0.3)	2.5	(0.1)	1.2	(0.0)	2.1	(0.1)	0.8	(0.0)	1.2	(0.1)
Singapore	9.4	(0.2)	2.4	(0.1)	2.0	(0.1)	1.0	(0.0)	0.9	(0.0)	0.9	(0.0)
Chinese Taipei	5.3	(0.1)	1.3	(0.0)	0.7	(0.0)	1.5	(0.1)	0.9	(0.0)	0.7	(0.0)
Thailand	5.6	(0.1)	2.3	(0.1)	1.5	(0.0)	1.7	(0.1)	1.6	(0.1)	2.5	(0.1)
Tunisia	3.5	(0.1)	1.7	(0.1)	2.2	(0.1)	1.5	(0.1)	2.0	(0.1)	2.4	(0.1)
United Arab Emirates	6.2	(0.1)	2.3	(0.1)	2.0	(0.1)	1.5	(0.1)	2.1	(0.1)	3.2	(0.1)
Uruguay	4.7	(0.1)	1.6	(0.1)	1.1	(0.1)	1.1	(0.1)	1.3	(0.1)	1.6	(0.1)
Viet Nam	5.8	(0.2)	2.9	(0.1)	1.6	(0.1)	4.9	(0.2)	1.7	(0.1)	1.8	(0.1)

* See notes at the beginning of this Annex.
StatLink ⟦▉⟧ http://dx.doi.org/10.1787/888932957460

[Part 1/1]
Additional mathematics lessons at school
Table IV.3.29   *Results based on school principals' reports*

		School offers mathematics lessons in addition to those offered during regular school hours				Percentage of students in schools offering additional mathematics lessons whose principal reported that additional mathematics lessons are organised for the following purpose:							
		Yes		No		Enrichment mathematics only		Remedial mathematics only		Both enrichment and remedial mathematics		Without differentiation, depending on the prior achievement of the students	
		%	S.E.	%	S.E.	%	S.E.	%	S.E.	%	S.E.	%	S.E.
OECD	Australia	64.1	(1.9)	35.9	(1.9)	6.0	(1.0)	10.8	(1.6)	66.9	(2.2)	16.3	(1.8)
	Austria	47.8	(4.1)	52.2	(4.1)	1.8	(1.3)	68.4	(4.4)	24.8	(4.1)	5.1	(2.4)
	Belgium	61.0	(3.0)	39.0	(3.0)	1.4	(1.0)	61.7	(4.0)	35.5	(4.1)	1.4	(0.8)
	Canada	66.0	(2.4)	34.0	(2.4)	0.5	(0.2)	44.3	(2.7)	47.2	(2.8)	8.0	(1.9)
	Chile	72.7	(3.3)	27.3	(3.3)	1.9	(1.2)	60.0	(4.3)	32.4	(4.1)	5.6	(2.2)
	Czech Republic	51.4	(3.8)	48.6	(3.8)	10.6	(2.9)	29.4	(5.0)	51.2	(5.3)	8.8	(2.3)
	Denmark	38.9	(3.4)	61.1	(3.4)	0.0	c	51.2	(5.4)	32.5	(5.2)	16.3	(3.8)
	Estonia	70.8	(2.7)	29.2	(2.7)	6.2	(1.6)	21.8	(2.9)	58.2	(3.2)	13.7	(2.5)
	Finland	59.3	(3.3)	40.7	(3.3)	1.5	(0.5)	41.7	(3.6)	53.2	(3.6)	3.7	(1.2)
	France	64.7	(3.0)	35.3	(3.0)	2.9	(1.5)	34.9	(4.0)	59.4	(4.0)	2.8	(1.4)
	Germany	63.3	(3.2)	36.7	(3.2)	2.0	(1.4)	48.8	(4.2)	47.6	(4.4)	1.6	(1.1)
	Greece	28.2	(2.7)	71.8	(2.7)	11.9	(4.9)	38.4	(6.7)	49.7	(6.2)	0.0	c
	Hungary	84.9	(2.9)	15.1	(2.9)	6.7	(2.1)	13.4	(2.7)	78.5	(3.5)	1.4	(1.0)
	Iceland	50.5	(0.3)	49.5	(0.3)	6.7	(0.1)	26.4	(0.3)	57.3	(0.3)	9.6	(0.3)
	Ireland	53.9	(4.1)	46.1	(4.1)	18.8	(4.1)	34.0	(5.2)	45.5	(5.7)	1.7	(1.3)
	Israel	84.4	(2.8)	15.6	(2.8)	12.7	(2.7)	23.8	(3.5)	56.5	(4.6)	6.9	(2.3)
	Italy	89.0	(1.5)	11.0	(1.5)	0.7	(0.3)	23.2	(1.8)	71.9	(2.1)	4.2	(0.8)
	Japan	74.2	(3.1)	25.8	(3.1)	14.0	(2.7)	12.0	(2.9)	72.4	(4.0)	1.6	(1.1)
	Korea	91.8	(2.3)	8.2	(2.3)	2.1	(1.2)	12.5	(2.6)	80.0	(2.8)	5.5	(1.7)
	Luxembourg	95.7	(0.0)	4.3	(0.0)	4.6	(0.0)	71.4	(0.1)	24.0	(0.1)	0.0	c
	Mexico	61.4	(1.8)	38.6	(1.8)	1.4	(0.5)	35.8	(2.6)	50.8	(2.6)	12.1	(1.4)
	Netherlands	56.2	(3.8)	43.8	(3.8)	4.1	(2.2)	58.9	(5.7)	29.8	(5.8)	7.2	(2.7)
	New Zealand	87.4	(2.1)	12.6	(2.1)	3.5	(1.9)	4.8	(1.6)	75.5	(3.9)	16.2	(3.7)
	Norway	30.7	(3.3)	69.3	(3.3)	14.8	(4.2)	38.5	(6.8)	23.5	(5.9)	23.2	(4.6)
	Poland	87.3	(2.9)	12.7	(2.9)	1.6	(1.1)	6.6	(2.1)	91.0	(2.4)	0.8	(0.8)
	Portugal	89.5	(2.2)	10.5	(2.2)	0.9	(0.7)	7.7	(2.4)	86.5	(3.1)	4.9	(1.8)
	Slovak Republic	65.2	(3.2)	34.8	(3.2)	20.9	(3.9)	11.7	(3.1)	64.7	(4.1)	2.6	(1.4)
	Slovenia	79.2	(0.4)	20.8	(0.4)	8.3	(0.3)	19.9	(0.4)	60.8	(0.5)	11.0	(0.3)
	Spain	40.0	(2.4)	60.0	(2.4)	10.3	(2.5)	57.3	(4.6)	29.0	(3.5)	3.4	(1.4)
	Sweden	66.8	(3.8)	33.2	(3.8)	3.6	(1.7)	39.4	(4.5)	40.6	(4.6)	16.4	(3.0)
	Switzerland	56.8	(3.3)	43.2	(3.3)	7.3	(3.4)	43.4	(3.8)	37.8	(4.0)	11.5	(3.1)
	Turkey	46.9	(4.1)	53.1	(4.1)	25.8	(5.7)	4.6	(3.3)	62.9	(5.8)	6.7	(2.7)
	United Kingdom	92.2	(1.9)	7.8	(1.9)	2.1	(1.4)	11.0	(2.4)	74.4	(3.0)	12.5	(2.3)
	United States	63.6	(3.7)	36.4	(3.7)	3.1	(1.5)	36.1	(5.5)	53.6	(6.0)	7.2	(2.9)
	OECD average	65.8	(0.5)	34.2	(0.5)	6.5	(0.4)	32.5	(0.7)	53.7	(0.7)	7.3	(0.4)
Partners	Albania	81.3	(3.2)	18.7	(3.2)	12.0	(2.4)	13.1	(2.5)	66.5	(3.7)	8.4	(2.7)
	Argentina	57.0	(3.4)	43.0	(3.4)	3.8	(2.1)	50.4	(5.3)	42.1	(5.6)	3.7	(1.7)
	Brazil	53.4	(2.9)	46.6	(2.9)	18.0	(2.8)	3.0	(1.2)	78.2	(3.3)	0.8	(0.5)
	Bulgaria	60.0	(4.0)	40.0	(4.0)	9.2	(2.9)	22.9	(3.9)	56.6	(4.8)	11.3	(3.2)
	Colombia	34.3	(3.2)	65.7	(3.2)	13.0	(4.8)	1.4	(1.1)	60.9	(7.3)	24.7	(6.2)
	Costa Rica	47.3	(3.8)	52.7	(3.8)	6.2	(3.0)	38.1	(5.3)	48.9	(5.3)	6.8	(2.9)
	Croatia	89.0	(2.2)	11.0	(2.2)	8.3	(2.7)	13.3	(2.9)	74.1	(3.7)	4.3	(1.8)
	Cyprus*	63.9	(0.1)	36.1	(0.1)	4.8	(0.1)	75.0	(0.1)	19.0	(0.1)	1.1	(0.0)
	Hong Kong-China	95.9	(1.7)	4.1	(1.7)	8.1	(2.2)	9.6	(2.4)	80.2	(3.1)	2.1	(0.8)
	Indonesia	75.7	(3.7)	24.3	(3.7)	17.8	(3.6)	11.8	(3.4)	54.4	(5.3)	16.0	(3.3)
	Jordan	68.5	(3.3)	31.5	(3.3)	6.3	(2.0)	42.1	(4.3)	44.0	(4.8)	7.6	(2.7)
	Kazakhstan	91.8	(1.9)	8.2	(1.9)	7.2	(2.2)	3.9	(1.3)	63.0	(3.3)	25.9	(3.0)
	Latvia	73.9	(3.0)	26.1	(3.0)	11.2	(2.4)	8.7	(2.2)	76.0	(3.4)	4.1	(1.7)
	Liechtenstein	51.9	(0.9)	48.1	(0.9)	0.0	c	35.7	(1.4)	39.0	(1.6)	25.2	(1.7)
	Lithuania	78.6	(2.7)	21.4	(2.7)	3.3	(1.6)	2.5	(1.1)	85.5	(2.9)	8.7	(2.3)
	Macao-China	92.3	(0.0)	7.7	(0.0)	0.0	c	24.7	(0.1)	74.5	(0.1)	0.8	(0.0)
	Malaysia	91.4	(2.2)	8.6	(2.2)	5.8	(1.8)	1.4	(0.9)	87.8	(2.6)	5.0	(1.8)
	Montenegro	82.9	(0.1)	17.1	(0.1)	15.4	(0.1)	29.9	(0.2)	52.3	(0.2)	2.4	(0.0)
	Peru	45.6	(3.4)	54.4	(3.4)	9.5	(2.8)	46.6	(5.2)	40.4	(5.9)	3.4	(1.7)
	Qatar	81.2	(0.1)	18.8	(0.1)	8.0	(0.1)	13.3	(0.1)	71.3	(0.1)	7.4	(0.1)
	Romania	77.1	(3.2)	22.9	(3.2)	34.8	(3.6)	30.2	(3.6)	35.0	(3.4)	0.0	c
	Russian Federation	96.8	(1.3)	3.2	(1.3)	1.2	(0.9)	1.7	(0.9)	80.9	(2.7)	16.2	(2.3)
	Serbia	93.5	(2.1)	6.5	(2.1)	0.0	c	12.3	(2.9)	53.3	(4.5)	34.5	(4.4)
	Shanghai-China	49.2	(3.4)	50.8	(3.4)	19.5	(5.8)	18.4	(4.4)	54.8	(5.6)	7.3	(2.8)
	Singapore	91.2	(0.7)	8.8	(0.7)	1.3	(0.0)	12.5	(0.1)	86.2	(0.1)	0.0	c
	Chinese Taipei	85.1	(3.0)	14.9	(3.0)	5.3	(2.0)	15.3	(3.0)	75.7	(3.7)	3.7	(1.7)
	Thailand	90.3	(2.4)	9.7	(2.4)	2.1	(1.2)	3.7	(1.7)	85.0	(2.7)	9.2	(2.3)
	Tunisia	79.4	(3.5)	20.6	(3.5)	2.7	(1.5)	43.4	(4.9)	47.9	(5.2)	5.9	(2.2)
	United Arab Emirates	65.7	(2.4)	34.3	(2.4)	4.2	(0.7)	23.6	(3.0)	63.3	(3.6)	8.9	(2.0)
	Uruguay	82.2	(2.6)	17.8	(2.6)	0.9	(0.0)	46.3	(3.8)	46.5	(3.8)	6.4	(1.5)
	Viet Nam	95.2	(1.5)	4.8	(1.5)	3.5	(1.6)	12.3	(2.6)	83.5	(2.9)	0.7	(0.7)

* See notes at the beginning of this Annex.
StatLink ᴬᴹˢᴸ http://dx.doi.org/10.1787/888932957460

[Part 1/1]
Table IV.3.30 Extracurricular activities at school
Results based on school principals' reports

Percentage of students in schools whose principal reported that the school offers the following activities to students in the national modal grade for 15-year-olds:

		Band, orchestra, or choir		School play or school musical		School yearbook, newspaper or magazine		Volunteering or service activities		Mathematics club		Mathematics competitions		Chess club		Club with a focus on computers and ICT		Art club or art activities		Sporting team or sporting activities	
		%	S.E.	%	S.E.	%	S.E.	%	S.E.	%	S.E.	%	S.E.	%	S.E.	%	S.E.	%	S.E.	%	S.E.
OECD	Australia	90.5	(1.2)	68.2	(1.7)	67.7	(1.9)	83.5	(1.3)	27.3	(1.8)	95.2	(0.9)	55.9	(2.0)	29.7	(2.1)	64.0	(2.1)	99.1	(0.3)
	Austria	51.9	(2.8)	35.5	(3.1)	49.7	(3.3)	92.0	(2.1)	1.5	(0.9)	32.9	(3.1)	16.6	(3.0)	19.7	(3.3)	28.2	(4.4)	86.3	(2.8)
	Belgium	31.3	(2.5)	52.3	(3.2)	42.9	(2.8)	77.8	(2.7)	1.5	(0.7)	70.5	(2.3)	16.1	(2.2)	9.2	(1.9)	40.2	(3.1)	89.0	(1.8)
	Canada	88.1	(1.2)	91.3	(1.3)	89.8	(1.5)	96.3	(0.8)	41.5	(2.4)	77.2	(1.4)	51.1	(2.1)	54.0	(2.2)	88.6	(1.4)	98.9	(0.5)
	Chile	68.6	(3.8)	48.3	(3.7)	18.9	(2.8)	62.0	(3.6)	12.5	(2.7)	41.9	(3.9)	32.4	(4.0)	49.2	(3.9)	80.1	(3.1)	98.4	(0.9)
	Czech Republic	40.7	(3.5)	24.5	(2.9)	54.1	(3.2)	57.9	(3.2)	33.3	(3.4)	85.5	(2.1)	14.2	(2.6)	37.6	(3.1)	51.6	(3.5)	86.3	(2.1)
	Denmark	45.8	(3.6)	39.4	(3.2)	36.5	(3.4)	14.5	(2.4)	7.3	(1.8)	10.6	(2.1)	9.2	(1.7)	9.2	(1.9)	30.3	(3.5)	69.3	(3.4)
	Estonia	82.8	(2.0)	58.3	(3.1)	59.2	(2.9)	83.7	(2.4)	30.3	(2.4)	92.0	(1.7)	18.4	(2.2)	41.8	(3.1)	75.1	(2.5)	96.5	(0.8)
	Finland	80.0	(2.7)	43.4	(3.8)	38.6	(3.2)	29.4	(3.2)	8.2	(1.9)	88.3	(2.0)	10.1	(1.9)	11.7	(2.1)	37.1	(3.5)	75.4	(2.9)
	France	42.1	(3.4)	71.8	(3.0)	27.7	(3.3)	61.7	(3.5)	11.0	(2.1)	73.5	(2.7)	21.4	(2.9)	23.8	(3.2)	82.7	(2.6)	96.9	(1.3)
	Germany	83.5	(2.5)	64.4	(3.1)	59.7	(3.5)	94.4	(1.8)	21.2	(3.3)	58.2	(3.2)	30.5	(2.7)	59.9	(3.3)	78.6	(3.6)	94.4	(1.7)
	Greece	56.6	(3.9)	45.5	(4.2)	25.5	(3.5)	51.8	(4.4)	8.9	(1.8)	74.9	(3.0)	14.1	(2.9)	16.7	(3.0)	42.7	(3.5)	78.7	(2.6)
	Hungary	68.5	(3.2)	50.9	(3.5)	65.6	(3.6)	60.9	(3.6)	50.7	(3.7)	78.8	(2.6)	18.8	(2.9)	56.8	(3.9)	65.4	(3.9)	99.2	(0.7)
	Iceland	53.7	(0.2)	73.5	(0.2)	62.2	(0.2)	36.8	(0.3)	6.6	(0.1)	66.7	(0.2)	30.3	(0.2)	22.7	(0.2)	67.7	(0.3)	63.7	(0.2)
	Ireland	66.5	(3.7)	38.6	(3.5)	37.1	(4.0)	39.6	(3.8)	19.1	(3.3)	61.1	(3.8)	40.3	(3.7)	26.2	(3.8)	56.8	(3.8)	99.8	(0.0)
	Israel	60.2	(3.5)	51.9	(3.9)	55.6	(3.8)	91.9	(2.4)	10.1	(2.3)	48.1	(3.4)	7.0	(2.3)	47.3	(4.3)	55.5	(3.6)	84.0	(2.6)
	Italy	29.7	(1.9)	72.2	(1.6)	61.2	(2.2)	68.5	(1.7)	5.7	(0.9)	66.6	(2.1)	11.1	(1.3)	21.2	(1.8)	36.5	(1.9)	95.0	(0.9)
	Japan	85.5	(2.4)	42.5	(3.3)	42.2	(3.3)	89.9	(2.4)	6.5	(1.7)	12.0	(2.3)	35.9	(3.6)	55.6	(3.7)	94.9	(1.4)	100.0	c
	Korea	73.4	(3.6)	43.4	(4.0)	89.1	(2.3)	99.7	(0.3)	76.4	(3.0)	75.9	(2.5)	92.8	(2.2)	85.4	(2.9)	92.7	(2.2)	94.6	(2.0)
	Luxembourg	74.2	(0.1)	79.0	(0.1)	63.8	(0.1)	94.1	(0.1)	19.5	(0.1)	78.7	(0.1)	46.7	(0.1)	34.1	(0.1)	79.1	(0.1)	97.9	(0.0)
	Mexico	55.8	(1.9)	56.0	(1.9)	38.5	(1.8)	64.4	(1.8)	34.4	(1.9)	81.8	(1.2)	45.1	(1.7)	31.2	(2.2)	72.5	(1.9)	94.5	(0.8)
	Netherlands	58.3	(4.1)	63.0	(4.3)	66.2	(4.1)	95.4	(1.6)	2.7	(1.2)	46.5	(3.5)	9.7	(2.6)	5.0	(1.5)	65.3	(4.0)	91.1	(2.5)
	New Zealand	98.6	(0.7)	84.0	(2.7)	86.0	(2.2)	97.9	(1.0)	25.0	(3.8)	96.5	(1.2)	69.2	(4.0)	53.4	(4.0)	84.7	(2.9)	99.9	(0.1)
	Norway	28.7	(3.3)	31.8	(3.3)	29.7	(3.4)	59.3	(3.7)	5.6	(1.8)	32.2	(3.4)	2.7	(1.2)	19.1	(2.9)	7.9	(2.1)	37.7	(3.5)
	Poland	81.5	(2.9)	87.5	(2.7)	67.2	(3.3)	99.8	(0.1)	94.2	(1.9)	99.8	(0.2)	21.4	(3.4)	78.2	(3.2)	86.5	(2.6)	98.5	(0.9)
	Portugal	29.8	(3.9)	54.4	(3.9)	77.3	(3.3)	83.2	(3.4)	44.9	(4.5)	97.8	(0.9)	33.0	(3.9)	12.2	(2.4)	52.0	(3.9)	97.7	(1.2)
	Slovak Republic	31.1	(3.8)	47.7	(4.3)	74.4	(2.7)	83.9	(2.5)	84.8	(2.7)	91.4	(2.1)	24.9	(3.5)	92.6	(1.6)	56.9	(4.0)	99.3	(0.5)
	Slovenia	73.9	(0.4)	75.4	(0.6)	88.1	(0.4)	77.7	(0.7)	63.7	(0.7)	99.1	(0.0)	31.0	(0.8)	58.8	(0.6)	74.0	(0.4)	98.5	(0.1)
	Spain	28.9	(2.0)	45.4	(2.8)	48.2	(2.6)	54.4	(2.5)	8.4	(1.8)	66.0	(2.1)	15.0	(2.1)	13.3	(2.0)	22.2	(2.3)	79.6	(2.5)
	Sweden	68.1	(3.2)	46.5	(3.7)	23.4	(3.2)	46.3	(3.6)	9.5	(2.2)	58.2	(3.7)	5.9	(1.7)	2.6	(1.1)	29.7	(3.1)	81.0	(2.6)
	Switzerland	71.2	(3.1)	60.0	(3.3)	32.5	(3.0)	54.5	(3.2)	5.3	(1.5)	27.7	(2.3)	10.0	(2.1)	17.5	(2.9)	68.2	(3.4)	89.1	(1.9)
	Turkey	52.3	(3.6)	67.2	(4.1)	50.5	(3.6)	78.7	(3.4)	18.6	(3.0)	23.0	(3.1)	86.4	(2.8)	56.6	(4.0)	51.3	(4.0)	96.8	(1.3)
	United Kingdom	95.9	(1.3)	89.6	(1.8)	80.0	(2.4)	93.0	(1.6)	72.8	(2.8)	93.7	(1.5)	53.8	(3.7)	77.3	(3.1)	91.5	(1.8)	99.6	(0.4)
	United States	92.2	(1.9)	85.8	(3.2)	87.6	(2.4)	93.4	(2.7)	56.1	(3.7)	67.7	(3.7)	42.9	(4.2)	55.1	(4.1)	88.4	(3.0)	99.6	(0.4)
	OECD average	62.9	(0.5)	58.5	(0.5)	55.8	(0.5)	72.6	(0.4)	27.2	(0.4)	66.8	(0.4)	30.1	(0.5)	37.8	(0.5)	61.7	(0.5)	90.2	(0.3)
Partners	Albania	45.0	(4.0)	61.6	(3.7)	39.1	(4.1)	68.9	(3.6)	67.3	(3.6)	90.9	(2.3)	19.0	(2.9)	48.2	(4.2)	78.6	(3.6)	91.0	(2.2)
	Argentina	26.6	(2.9)	33.2	(3.6)	29.6	(3.4)	50.6	(3.4)	41.1	(3.6)	42.1	(4.0)	16.9	(3.0)	51.4	(4.1)	46.1	(3.5)	82.7	(3.5)
	Brazil	23.0	(2.4)	57.8	(2.7)	23.6	(2.5)	44.8	(2.8)	8.3	(1.4)	92.4	(1.4)	24.1	(2.5)	17.5	(2.1)	45.5	(3.0)	90.8	(1.8)
	Bulgaria	49.2	(3.6)	51.5	(4.0)	69.2	(3.5)	89.7	(2.3)	36.1	(3.8)	79.9	(2.8)	22.5	(3.4)	58.2	(3.6)	61.7	(3.6)	99.0	(0.7)
	Colombia	51.8	(3.9)	54.0	(3.8)	46.0	(4.0)	96.3	(1.4)	28.9	(3.4)	60.7	(3.9)	21.8	(3.0)	24.0	(3.2)	68.0	(3.6)	96.3	(1.3)
	Costa Rica	83.3	(2.5)	75.8	(3.2)	15.2	(2.4)	39.1	(3.5)	32.1	(3.0)	61.5	(3.4)	27.1	(3.3)	21.9	(3.0)	75.6	(3.4)	95.9	(1.7)
	Croatia	44.7	(3.9)	62.3	(3.8)	66.2	(3.8)	95.1	(1.5)	20.4	(3.1)	71.5	(2.8)	16.2	(2.9)	39.7	(3.9)	48.1	(3.7)	99.3	(0.5)
	Cyprus*	98.2	(0.0)	89.8	(0.1)	95.9	(0.0)	99.9	(0.0)	48.4	(0.1)	93.6	(0.1)	48.4	(0.1)	82.7	(0.1)	91.3	(0.1)	97.5	(0.0)
	Hong Kong-China	92.8	(2.1)	86.0	(2.8)	88.0	(2.9)	100.0	c	90.1	(2.6)	91.0	(2.6)	78.2	(3.5)	96.9	(1.4)	98.1	(1.1)	100.0	c
	Indonesia	50.5	(4.0)	53.6	(4.5)	40.4	(4.1)	93.1	(2.1)	37.4	(3.9)	67.8	(3.8)	23.7	(3.8)	45.6	(3.9)	61.4	(4.5)	92.8	(2.2)
	Jordan	25.3	(3.4)	54.0	(3.1)	62.6	(3.5)	86.2	(2.8)	33.2	(3.1)	38.5	(3.5)	43.0	(3.3)	44.5	(3.3)	54.7	(3.6)	92.4	(1.8)
	Kazakhstan	62.6	(3.5)	51.3	(4.1)	81.9	(3.0)	97.1	(1.5)	63.8	(3.6)	97.5	(1.1)	71.6	(3.6)	63.8	(3.8)	89.3	(2.5)	99.1	(0.8)
	Latvia	76.4	(2.8)	66.9	(3.6)	60.4	(3.5)	89.3	(2.3)	35.3	(3.6)	91.6	(1.7)	16.3	(2.5)	29.4	(3.4)	90.8	(2.1)	95.0	(1.7)
	Liechtenstein	78.5	(0.8)	59.6	(0.8)	32.5	(1.0)	74.1	(0.8)	2.9	(0.0)	34.1	(0.4)	0.0	c	29.0	(1.0)	72.2	(0.8)	100.0	c
	Lithuania	92.3	(1.7)	58.8	(3.0)	66.2	(2.9)	65.6	(3.1)	19.7	(2.5)	93.2	(1.8)	12.5	(2.5)	34.1	(3.4)	87.9	(2.2)	98.1	(0.9)
	Macao-China	87.5	(0.0)	96.1	(0.0)	88.8	(0.0)	99.8	(0.0)	61.6	(0.1)	87.8	(0.0)	50.2	(0.1)	76.5	(0.0)	94.1	(0.0)	99.9	(0.0)
	Malaysia	42.3	(3.5)	41.8	(3.7)	90.0	(2.5)	79.3	(3.2)	96.7	(1.5)	80.4	(3.1)	89.9	(2.4)	86.0	(2.7)	93.6	(1.8)	99.3	(0.7)
	Montenegro	38.5	(0.2)	86.9	(0.1)	89.1	(0.2)	81.7	(0.1)	40.5	(0.2)	54.7	(0.1)	30.7	(0.1)	69.0	(0.1)	62.8	(0.1)	95.3	(0.1)
	Peru	55.3	(3.7)	59.0	(3.2)	38.9	(3.3)	47.0	(3.4)	30.1	(3.3)	80.8	(2.6)	31.5	(3.2)	31.4	(3.3)	61.4	(3.5)	87.7	(2.1)
	Qatar	28.3	(0.1)	77.7	(0.1)	89.4	(0.1)	97.8	(0.0)	72.1	(0.1)	91.5	(0.0)	36.2	(0.1)	72.5	(0.1)	79.8	(0.1)	100.0	(0.0)
	Romania	51.2	(3.8)	56.2	(3.9)	79.7	(2.9)	73.6	(3.4)	43.5	(3.8)	68.1	(3.6)	52.9	(3.5)	49.3	(3.9)	63.0	(3.5)	70.1	(3.4)
	Russian Federation	66.2	(2.9)	40.3	(3.6)	74.5	(3.3)	92.8	(1.7)	65.6	(3.3)	96.6	(1.1)	33.3	(3.3)	51.2	(3.1)	65.1	(3.9)	99.9	(0.1)
	Serbia	69.9	(3.9)	81.0	(3.4)	56.2	(4.2)	76.3	(3.7)	18.4	(3.4)	75.1	(3.5)	30.1	(4.0)	46.1	(4.2)	50.7	(4.8)	98.8	(0.8)
	Shanghai-China	74.4	(3.1)	67.3	(3.8)	78.2	(3.0)	95.4	(1.8)	68.0	(3.3)	67.3	(2.6)	61.0	(4.0)	69.7	(3.6)	86.7	(2.5)	99.4	(0.6)
	Singapore	98.0	(0.0)	70.3	(0.3)	92.8	(0.1)	100.0	c	20.7	(0.6)	86.9	(0.1)	27.6	(0.6)	94.8	(0.7)	85.9	(0.2)	99.7	(0.0)
	Chinese Taipei	74.1	(3.4)	49.7	(3.9)	91.1	(2.1)	91.1	(2.1)	41.7	(4.5)	59.2	(3.4)	56.4	(3.8)	67.8	(3.6)	88.6	(2.8)	95.3	(1.9)
	Thailand	67.6	(2.9)	72.4	(3.1)	83.2	(3.0)	90.9	(1.7)	79.7	(2.2)	53.2	(3.6)	44.3	(3.8)	90.9	(2.1)	87.1	(2.1)	100.0	(0.0)
	Tunisia	32.6	(4.3)	54.9	(4.0)	59.6	(4.3)	82.7	(3.0)	52.1	(4.0)	56.0	(4.1)	40.9	(3.7)	59.3	(3.9)	62.2	(4.4)	86.0	(2.7)
	United Arab Emirates	21.5	(1.6)	63.7	(2.1)	79.4	(2.1)	79.6	(1.7)	57.9	(2.6)	86.4	(1.6)	33.3	(2.1)	64.9	(2.7)	67.7	(2.2)	96.4	(0.8)
	Uruguay	69.9	(2.9)	52.1	(3.8)	11.9	(2.4)	35.5	(2.9)	6.1	(1.6)	25.8	(3.1)	8.5	(2.1)	24.0	(3.3)	27.4	(3.5)	92.7	(1.9)
	Viet Nam	18.2	(3.5)	85.0	(2.7)	50.1	(3.1)	84.4	(2.7)	26.5	(3.6)	82.3	(2.8)	21.5	(3.2)	16.6	(3.0)	47.1	(4.0)	99.1	(0.7)

* See notes at the beginning of this Annex.
StatLink http://dx.doi.org/10.1787/888932957460

[Part 1/2]
Index of creative extracurricular activities at school and mathematics performance

Table IV.3.31   *Results based on school principals' reports*

		Index of creative extracurricular activities at school										Variability in this index	
		All students		Bottom quarter		Second quarter		Third quarter		Top quarter			
		Mean index	S.E.	Mean index	S.E.	Mean index	S.E.	Mean index	S.E.	Mean index	S.E.	Standard deviation	S.E.
OECD	Australia	2.18	(0.03)	1.10	(0.09)	2.00	(0.00)	2.62	(0.07)	3.00	(0.00)	0.82	(0.03)
	Austria	1.12	(0.06)	0.00	(0.00)	0.55	(0.10)	1.55	(0.13)	2.37	(0.10)	1.01	(0.04)
	Belgium	1.22	(0.05)	0.00	(0.02)	0.94	(0.10)	1.61	(0.12)	2.34	(0.07)	0.93	(0.03)
	Canada	2.68	(0.02)	1.72	(0.06)	2.99	(0.06)	3.00	(0.00)	3.00	(0.00)	0.62	(0.03)
	Chile	1.94	(0.07)	0.77	(0.08)	1.67	(0.14)	2.32	(0.14)	3.00	(0.00)	0.91	(0.04)
	Czech Republic	1.16	(0.07)	0.00	(0.00)	0.70	(0.13)	1.47	(0.14)	2.49	(0.08)	1.02	(0.03)
	Denmark	1.14	(0.07)	0.00	(0.00)	0.59	(0.13)	1.44	(0.13)	2.53	(0.10)	1.04	(0.04)
	Estonia	2.09	(0.05)	0.86	(0.13)	2.00	(0.01)	2.50	(0.11)	3.00	(0.00)	0.88	(0.04)
	Finland	1.59	(0.07)	0.48	(0.11)	1.17	(0.15)	2.00	(0.00)	2.71	(0.11)	0.92	(0.04)
	France	1.96	(0.06)	0.83	(0.06)	1.84	(0.14)	2.19	(0.13)	3.00	(0.00)	0.85	(0.04)
	Germany	2.26	(0.06)	1.03	(0.17)	2.00	(0.10)	3.00	(0.08)	3.00	(0.00)	0.89	(0.05)
	Greece	1.41	(0.08)	0.00	(0.08)	1.00	(0.10)	1.80	(0.15)	2.87	(0.12)	1.09	(0.04)
	Hungary	1.84	(0.07)	0.52	(0.11)	1.73	(0.13)	2.13	(0.13)	3.00	(0.01)	0.97	(0.05)
	Iceland	1.87	(0.00)	0.73	(0.01)	1.70	(0.01)	2.06	(0.01)	3.00	(0.00)	0.88	(0.00)
	Ireland	1.56	(0.07)	0.46	(0.11)	1.14	(0.15)	2.00	(0.02)	2.65	(0.12)	0.92	(0.04)
	Israel	1.63	(0.07)	0.31	(0.10)	1.19	(0.14)	2.03	(0.09)	3.00	(0.04)	1.05	(0.04)
	Italy	1.37	(0.03)	0.22	(0.06)	1.00	(0.00)	1.78	(0.07)	2.47	(0.05)	0.93	(0.02)
	Japan	2.23	(0.05)	1.29	(0.12)	2.00	(0.00)	2.62	(0.13)	3.00	(0.00)	0.76	(0.04)
	Korea	2.06	(0.07)	0.82	(0.17)	2.00	(0.04)	2.41	(0.16)	3.00	(0.00)	0.88	(0.05)
	Luxembourg	2.32	(0.00)	1.13	(0.00)	2.16	(0.00)	3.00	(0.00)	3.00	(0.00)	0.87	(0.00)
	Mexico	1.82	(0.04)	0.48	(0.05)	1.52	(0.08)	2.30	(0.07)	3.00	(0.00)	1.03	(0.02)
	Netherlands	1.85	(0.08)	0.51	(0.10)	1.63	(0.15)	2.26	(0.15)	3.00	(0.00)	1.00	(0.04)
	New Zealand	2.66	(0.04)	1.79	(0.07)	2.86	(0.13)	3.00	(0.00)	3.00	(0.00)	0.57	(0.04)
	Norway	0.68	(0.06)	0.00	(0.00)	0.05	(0.12)	1.00	(0.05)	1.66	(0.13)	0.78	(0.05)
	Poland	2.51	(0.04)	1.74	(0.08)	2.30	(0.14)	3.00	(0.00)	3.00	(0.00)	0.62	(0.03)
	Portugal	1.36	(0.07)	0.32	(0.12)	1.00	(0.00)	1.73	(0.17)	2.38	(0.09)	0.87	(0.04)
	Slovak Republic	1.34	(0.09)	0.00	(0.06)	0.98	(0.12)	1.76	(0.17)	2.64	(0.12)	1.03	(0.04)
	Slovenia	2.19	(0.01)	0.94	(0.02)	2.00	(0.00)	2.80	(0.03)	3.00	(0.00)	0.88	(0.00)
	Spain	0.95	(0.04)	0.00	(0.00)	0.56	(0.11)	1.08	(0.07)	2.17	(0.03)	0.87	(0.02)
	Sweden	1.43	(0.07)	0.34	(0.10)	1.00	(0.00)	1.84	(0.15)	2.56	(0.08)	0.92	(0.03)
	Switzerland	1.96	(0.06)	0.63	(0.08)	1.78	(0.11)	2.42	(0.13)	3.00	(0.00)	0.97	(0.04)
	Turkey	1.71	(0.08)	0.39	(0.12)	1.25	(0.15)	2.19	(0.14)	3.00	(0.00)	1.05	(0.03)
	United Kingdom	2.75	(0.04)	2.01	(0.14)	3.00	(0.00)	3.00	(0.00)	3.00	(0.00)	0.55	(0.05)
	United States	2.66	(0.05)	1.73	(0.12)	2.92	(0.12)	3.00	(0.00)	3.00	(0.00)	0.61	(0.06)
	OECD average	1.81	(0.01)	0.68	(0.02)	1.56	(0.02)	2.20	(0.02)	2.79	(0.01)	0.88	(0.01)
Partners	Albania	1.83	(0.07)	0.64	(0.08)	1.43	(0.15)	2.25	(0.15)	3.00	(0.00)	0.97	(0.04)
	Argentina	1.04	(0.07)	0.00	(0.00)	0.59	(0.16)	1.19	(0.11)	2.40	(0.09)	0.97	(0.04)
	Brazil	1.25	(0.06)	0.01	(0.07)	1.00	(0.06)	1.65	(0.12)	2.36	(0.07)	0.93	(0.03)
	Bulgaria	1.61	(0.08)	0.18	(0.12)	1.17	(0.16)	2.08	(0.12)	3.00	(0.02)	1.09	(0.03)
	Colombia	1.69	(0.08)	0.38	(0.11)	1.34	(0.16)	2.04	(0.12)	3.00	(0.06)	1.02	(0.04)
	Costa Rica	2.31	(0.06)	1.10	(0.15)	2.16	(0.15)	3.00	(0.00)	3.00	(0.00)	0.87	(0.05)
	Croatia	1.54	(0.08)	0.19	(0.13)	1.00	(0.08)	1.97	(0.15)	2.99	(0.09)	1.07	(0.04)
	Cyprus*	2.78	(0.00)	2.10	(0.00)	3.00	(0.00)	3.00	(0.00)	3.00	(0.00)	0.48	(0.00)
	Hong Kong-China	2.77	(0.04)	2.08	(0.15)	3.00	(0.00)	3.00	(0.00)	3.00	(0.00)	0.48	(0.05)
	Indonesia	1.65	(0.10)	0.05	(0.12)	1.17	(0.20)	2.38	(0.16)	3.00	(0.00)	1.18	(0.04)
	Jordan	1.32	(0.07)	0.00	(0.00)	0.84	(0.12)	1.82	(0.14)	2.63	(0.11)	1.06	(0.04)
	Kazakhstan	2.02	(0.06)	0.79	(0.06)	1.91	(0.11)	2.37	(0.16)	3.00	(0.00)	0.88	(0.03)
	Latvia	2.33	(0.05)	1.43	(0.10)	2.00	(0.02)	2.91	(0.12)	3.00	(0.00)	0.72	(0.03)
	Liechtenstein	2.05	(0.02)	c	c	c	c	c	c	c	c	1.12	(0.01)
	Lithuania	2.35	(0.05)	1.43	(0.10)	2.00	(0.05)	2.96	(0.10)	3.00	(0.00)	0.74	(0.04)
	Macao-China	2.78	(0.00)	2.11	(0.00)	3.00	(0.00)	3.00	(0.00)	3.00	(0.00)	0.61	(0.00)
	Malaysia	1.76	(0.07)	0.76	(0.07)	1.09	(0.13)	2.18	(0.14)	3.00	(0.00)	0.95	(0.03)
	Montenegro	1.88	(0.00)	0.76	(0.00)	1.52	(0.00)	2.25	(0.01)	3.00	(0.00)	0.92	(0.00)
	Peru	1.71	(0.07)	0.54	(0.09)	1.29	(0.14)	2.02	(0.09)	3.00	(0.07)	0.97	(0.03)
	Qatar	1.83	(0.00)	0.74	(0.00)	1.54	(0.00)	2.05	(0.00)	3.00	(0.00)	0.89	(0.00)
	Romania	1.70	(0.07)	0.57	(0.10)	1.45	(0.14)	2.00	(0.00)	2.79	(0.13)	0.91	(0.04)
	Russian Federation	1.71	(0.07)	0.50	(0.09)	1.38	(0.15)	2.00	(0.05)	2.96	(0.10)	0.97	(0.04)
	Serbia	2.00	(0.08)	0.77	(0.08)	1.76	(0.15)	2.46	(0.17)	3.00	(0.00)	0.92	(0.04)
	Shanghai-China	2.27	(0.06)	1.05	(0.16)	2.04	(0.11)	3.00	(0.06)	3.00	(0.00)	0.88	(0.05)
	Singapore	2.47	(0.01)	1.72	(0.00)	2.18	(0.02)	3.00	(0.00)	3.00	(0.00)	0.65	(0.00)
	Chinese Taipei	2.08	(0.07)	0.78	(0.15)	2.00	(0.06)	2.56	(0.16)	3.00	(0.00)	0.90	(0.05)
	Thailand	2.26	(0.06)	0.77	(0.11)	2.29	(0.16)	3.00	(0.00)	3.00	(0.00)	0.97	(0.04)
	Tunisia	1.43	(0.09)	0.06	(0.12)	1.00	(0.05)	1.89	(0.15)	2.77	(0.14)	1.05	(0.04)
	United Arab Emirates	1.51	(0.04)	0.29	(0.08)	1.08	(0.09)	2.00	(0.01)	2.65	(0.05)	0.96	(0.02)
	Uruguay	1.48	(0.07)	0.30	(0.10)	1.02	(0.08)	2.00	(0.09)	2.62	(0.12)	0.96	(0.04)
	Viet Nam	1.50	(0.06)	0.65	(0.09)	1.00	(0.02)	1.90	(0.15)	2.46	(0.11)	0.81	(0.04)

Note: Values that are statistically significant are indicated in bold (see Annex A3).
* See notes at the beginning of this Annex.
StatLink ᵐᵖ http://dx.doi.org/10.1787/888932957460

[Part 2/2]
Index of creative extracurricular activities at school and mathematics performance
Table IV.3.31   *Results based on school principals' reports*

| | | Performance on the mathematics scale by national quarters of this index | | | | | | | | Change in the mathematics score per unit of this index | | Increased likelihood of students in the bottom quarter of this index scoring in the bottom quarter of the national mathematics performance distribution | | Explained variance in student performance (r-squared x 100) | |
| | | Bottom quarter | | Second quarter | | Third quarter | | Top quarter | | | | | | | |
		Mean score	S.E.	Mean score	S.E.	Mean score	S.E.	Mean score	S.E.	Score dif.	S.E.	Ratio	S.E.	%	S.E.
OECD	Australia	487	(3.7)	500	(3.8)	513	(3.0)	519	(3.4)	16.4	(2.54)	1.3	(0.07)	2.0	(0.59)
	Austria	472	(5.5)	499	(7.4)	524	(5.4)	528	(7.0)	22.6	(3.92)	1.8	(0.17)	6.0	(2.06)
	Belgium	484	(7.8)	520	(7.2)	527	(5.6)	532	(7.4)	18.8	(4.84)	1.6	(0.20)	3.0	(1.56)
	Canada	510	(3.2)	520	(4.1)	521	(4.2)	521	(2.9)	9.7	(2.49)	1.2	(0.07)	0.5	(0.23)
	Chile	405	(6.3)	414	(5.9)	427	(6.1)	445	(6.0)	17.1	(3.77)	1.4	(0.15)	3.7	(1.61)
	Czech Republic	488	(6.1)	483	(7.6)	496	(8.4)	527	(7.9)	16.6	(3.87)	1.0	(0.13)	3.1	(1.41)
	Denmark	501	(4.9)	501	(4.4)	498	(4.1)	502	(5.1)	0.7	(2.52)	1.0	(0.09)	0.0	(0.11)
	Estonia	506	(4.5)	525	(4.4)	524	(3.5)	525	(3.8)	9.8	(2.59)	1.3	(0.14)	1.1	(0.62)
	Finland	514	(5.2)	517	(4.9)	523	(4.0)	519	(2.7)	2.6	(2.30)	1.1	(0.09)	0.1	(0.16)
	France	498	(8.0)	503	(6.8)	499	(6.2)	486	(10.2)	-6.0	(6.11)	0.9	(0.15)	0.3	(0.58)
	Germany	469	(7.5)	497	(9.1)	543	(7.8)	545	(6.9)	35.0	(5.07)	2.1	(0.29)	10.2	(2.65)
	Greece	448	(5.4)	455	(6.1)	447	(7.8)	462	(6.3)	3.9	(2.99)	1.0	(0.14)	0.2	(0.40)
	Hungary	443	(6.2)	479	(6.4)	485	(7.8)	503	(11.0)	24.9	(4.28)	1.9	(0.21)	6.6	(2.27)
	Iceland	490	(3.7)	493	(3.1)	493	(3.3)	498	(3.6)	4.2	(1.92)	1.1	(0.09)	0.2	(0.15)
	Ireland	502	(5.9)	504	(5.9)	501	(6.4)	503	(5.6)	0.2	(3.65)	1.0	(0.13)	0.0	(0.15)
	Israel	419	(9.9)	464	(8.9)	481	(9.5)	500	(7.3)	30.3	(3.95)	2.2	(0.26)	9.1	(2.35)
	Italy	473	(4.6)	484	(4.8)	494	(3.8)	498	(4.4)	11.1	(2.80)	1.2	(0.11)	1.2	(0.65)
	Japan	502	(7.7)	531	(7.7)	550	(6.6)	562	(6.1)	36.3	(5.53)	1.8	(0.21)	8.6	(2.64)
	Korea	540	(10.9)	543	(7.8)	557	(8.0)	575	(7.4)	17.0	(5.84)	1.4	(0.23)	2.3	(1.64)
	Luxembourg	465	(2.8)	506	(2.9)	494	(2.7)	494	(3.3)	16.1	(1.64)	1.5	(0.08)	2.2	(0.29)
	Mexico	399	(2.8)	407	(2.6)	419	(2.4)	429	(3.1)	11.5	(1.65)	1.4	(0.08)	2.5	(0.71)
	Netherlands	485	(10.9)	522	(9.4)	537	(7.5)	535	(9.4)	21.7	(5.75)	1.9	(0.29)	5.6	(3.17)
	New Zealand	470	(6.9)	510	(8.2)	514	(5.2)	513	(5.2)	32.6	(7.39)	1.8	(0.19)	3.5	(1.55)
	Norway	487	(4.5)	488	(5.0)	492	(5.3)	494	(5.4)	4.1	(3.59)	1.1	(0.10)	0.1	(0.22)
	Poland	515	(6.1)	519	(5.5)	518	(5.3)	517	(5.4)	1.5	(5.52)	1.0	(0.12)	0.0	(0.12)
	Portugal	488	(6.9)	478	(7.6)	489	(6.5)	493	(7.0)	3.2	(3.95)	0.9	(0.14)	0.1	(0.25)
	Slovak Republic	484	(10.6)	477	(10.8)	481	(8.3)	486	(9.9)	1.6	(6.20)	0.9	(0.17)	0.0	(0.41)
	Slovenia	469	(2.6)	484	(2.4)	525	(5.1)	536	(4.0)	32.3	(1.47)	1.7	(0.11)	9.6	(0.83)
	Spain	485	(3.0)	484	(3.5)	483	(3.8)	488	(4.0)	1.3	(1.92)	1.0	(0.08)	0.0	(0.05)
	Sweden	476	(4.8)	474	(4.6)	478	(5.0)	485	(4.8)	3.7	(2.97)	1.1	(0.09)	0.1	(0.23)
	Switzerland	525	(6.3)	527	(5.4)	533	(5.8)	543	(7.4)	6.8	(4.12)	1.1	(0.14)	0.5	(0.67)
	Turkey	421	(6.0)	443	(10.5)	463	(8.7)	468	(9.8)	18.8	(4.00)	1.4	(0.13)	4.7	(2.05)
	United Kingdom	481	(5.7)	500	(6.4)	498	(7.3)	501	(5.7)	18.7	(6.44)	1.3	(0.17)	1.1	(0.82)
	United States	450	(8.5)	492	(6.3)	493	(5.6)	494	(4.8)	35.4	(5.12)	1.8	(0.22)	5.7	(1.72)
	OECD average	**478**	**(1.1)**	**492**	**(1.1)**	**501**	**(1.0)**	**507**	**(1.1)**	**14.1**	**(0.72)**	**1.4**	**(0.03)**	**2.8**	**(0.23)**
Partners	Albania	387	(3.7)	391	(5.1)	393	(5.7)	398	(3.7)	5.1	(2.02)	1.1	(0.08)	0.3	(0.24)
	Argentina	390	(6.8)	392	(5.6)	387	(6.4)	386	(5.8)	-0.5	(3.58)	0.9	(0.15)	0.0	(0.21)
	Brazil	386	(3.6)	400	(5.1)	400	(3.8)	405	(4.8)	7.4	(2.34)	1.2	(0.10)	0.8	(0.53)
	Bulgaria	419	(9.0)	425	(10.4)	457	(9.0)	464	(9.6)	17.6	(5.34)	1.5	(0.21)	4.3	(2.58)
	Colombia	365	(5.8)	377	(5.5)	381	(5.6)	389	(5.9)	8.8	(3.11)	1.4	(0.15)	1.5	(1.03)
	Costa Rica	399	(7.3)	404	(7.1)	411	(5.1)	413	(5.7)	6.3	(3.62)	1.3	(0.16)	0.6	(0.69)
	Croatia	435	(7.3)	469	(10.8)	474	(7.1)	506	(7.8)	23.3	(3.81)	1.8	(0.22)	7.9	(2.79)
	Cyprus*	410	(2.2)	449	(2.9)	450	(3.4)	448	(3.1)	33.0	(2.40)	1.8	(0.09)	2.8	(0.41)
	Hong Kong-China	537	(7.7)	569	(5.1)	567	(5.2)	572	(5.5)	32.4	(8.29)	1.5	(0.20)	2.6	(1.36)
	Indonesia	342	(6.6)	363	(6.3)	390	(7.6)	408	(8.2)	22.4	(3.36)	2.1	(0.28)	13.7	(3.16)
	Jordan	370	(5.3)	376	(6.4)	388	(5.2)	408	(8.8)	14.7	(3.58)	1.4	(0.14)	4.0	(1.84)
	Kazakhstan	439	(6.4)	432	(5.9)	429	(4.4)	425	(5.3)	-6.1	(3.71)	0.8	(0.11)	0.6	(0.72)
	Latvia	479	(5.9)	482	(5.9)	498	(6.0)	501	(4.5)	13.6	(4.24)	1.3	(0.16)	1.4	(0.91)
	Liechtenstein	c	c	c	c	c	c	c	c	35.6	(3.93)	2.6	(0.71)	17.6	(3.48)
	Lithuania	459	(4.7)	470	(5.9)	491	(5.4)	495	(5.2)	20.9	(4.13)	1.5	(0.14)	3.0	(1.19)
	Macao-China	513	(2.5)	548	(2.9)	546	(4.2)	546	(4.1)	31.0	(1.73)	1.6	(0.07)	4.0	(0.37)
	Malaysia	408	(5.3)	408	(4.5)	424	(6.7)	443	(7.8)	15.1	(4.09)	1.2	(0.13)	3.1	(1.57)
	Montenegro	393	(2.4)	401	(3.8)	413	(4.0)	436	(3.4)	18.4	(1.39)	1.3	(0.10)	4.3	(0.60)
	Peru	349	(6.0)	358	(5.3)	362	(6.6)	404	(9.4)	20.3	(4.12)	1.4	(0.15)	5.5	(2.09)
	Qatar	346	(1.9)	356	(2.0)	364	(2.0)	440	(1.6)	37.3	(0.84)	1.4	(0.08)	11.1	(0.44)
	Romania	434	(8.3)	435	(7.3)	451	(5.8)	457	(8.5)	10.6	(5.53)	1.3	(0.17)	1.4	(1.43)
	Russian Federation	465	(4.6)	476	(5.1)	481	(5.7)	506	(6.4)	15.4	(3.00)	1.3	(0.13)	3.0	(1.13)
	Serbia	431	(7.6)	441	(7.3)	455	(7.6)	468	(9.3)	15.0	(5.32)	1.2	(0.18)	2.4	(1.62)
	Shanghai-China	577	(8.3)	596	(8.8)	638	(6.0)	639	(5.6)	32.0	(4.41)	1.8	(0.18)	7.8	(2.20)
	Singapore	553	(3.8)	564	(3.6)	591	(3.5)	590	(3.7)	27.3	(1.87)	1.3	(0.08)	2.8	(0.38)
	Chinese Taipei	537	(7.8)	554	(10.1)	568	(6.5)	580	(8.4)	18.0	(5.54)	1.4	(0.15)	2.0	(1.14)
	Thailand	401	(5.6)	420	(7.1)	443	(6.0)	444	(5.9)	19.1	(3.12)	1.6	(0.19)	5.0	(1.65)
	Tunisia	383	(6.6)	383	(7.6)	392	(9.6)	393	(10.2)	4.2	(4.68)	1.0	(0.18)	0.3	(0.77)
	United Arab Emirates	416	(5.0)	423	(4.2)	442	(5.8)	482	(4.2)	27.5	(2.45)	1.4	(0.13)	9.1	(1.50)
	Uruguay	400	(8.0)	407	(5.8)	421	(7.4)	411	(6.8)	4.9	(4.59)	1.3	(0.16)	0.3	(0.53)
	Viet Nam	499	(7.5)	503	(9.5)	512	(7.7)	531	(7.5)	16.7	(5.45)	1.3	(0.15)	2.5	(1.66)

Note: Values that are statistically significant are indicated in bold (see Annex A3).
* See notes at the beginning of this Annex.
StatLink ⌧📊 http://dx.doi.org/10.1787/888932957460

[Part 1/2]
Index of extracurricular mathematics activities at school and mathematics performance
Table IV.3.32   *Results based on school principals' reports*

| | | Index of extracurricular mathematics activities at school | | | | | | | | | Variability in this index | |
| | | All students | | Bottom quarter | | Second quarter | | Third quarter | | Top quarter | | | |
		Mean index	S.E.	Mean index	S.E.	Mean index	S.E.	Mean index	S.E.	Mean index	S.E.	Standard deviation	S.E.
OECD	Australia	2.64	(0.06)	0.92	(0.06)	2.23	(0.11)	3.11	(0.08)	4.31	(0.04)	1.30	(0.03)
	Austria	1.14	(0.07)	0.00	(0.01)	0.79	(0.14)	1.25	(0.13)	2.52	(0.13)	1.04	(0.07)
	Belgium	1.61	(0.06)	0.37	(0.07)	1.08	(0.11)	2.00	(0.03)	3.00	(0.14)	1.06	(0.04)
	Canada	2.67	(0.07)	0.77	(0.09)	2.11	(0.10)	3.25	(0.09)	4.55	(0.07)	1.46	(0.03)
	Chile	2.01	(0.11)	0.44	(0.11)	1.63	(0.13)	2.28	(0.15)	3.70	(0.15)	1.30	(0.06)
	Czech Republic	2.34	(0.10)	0.84	(0.04)	1.73	(0.14)	2.63	(0.14)	4.15	(0.18)	1.32	(0.05)
	Denmark	0.87	(0.07)	0.00	(0.00)	0.26	(0.15)	1.00	(0.00)	2.20	(0.17)	0.95	(0.05)
	Estonia	2.74	(0.07)	1.15	(0.11)	2.12	(0.11)	3.23	(0.09)	4.45	(0.07)	1.31	(0.04)
	Finland	2.16	(0.07)	0.79	(0.06)	1.80	(0.13)	2.67	(0.12)	3.36	(0.09)	1.06	(0.05)
	France	2.08	(0.07)	0.56	(0.08)	1.60	(0.12)	2.53	(0.12)	3.62	(0.12)	1.25	(0.05)
	Germany	2.32	(0.10)	0.68	(0.08)	1.85	(0.11)	2.56	(0.12)	4.20	(0.20)	1.38	(0.06)
	Greece	1.45	(0.08)	0.54	(0.09)	1.00	(0.00)	1.21	(0.13)	3.05	(0.18)	1.13	(0.07)
	Hungary	3.39	(0.11)	1.28	(0.17)	3.16	(0.24)	4.12	(0.13)	5.00	(0.01)	1.47	(0.07)
	Iceland	1.81	(0.01)	0.56	(0.01)	1.00	(0.00)	2.17	(0.02)	3.52	(0.01)	1.24	(0.00)
	Ireland	1.81	(0.11)	0.29	(0.13)	1.18	(0.15)	2.22	(0.15)	3.54	(0.14)	1.31	(0.07)
	Israel	2.35	(0.10)	0.73	(0.19)	2.00	(0.03)	2.74	(0.15)	3.92	(0.14)	1.24	(0.05)
	Italy	2.45	(0.05)	1.05	(0.10)	2.16	(0.10)	3.00	(0.00)	3.60	(0.05)	1.08	(0.03)
	Japan	2.02	(0.08)	0.56	(0.11)	1.70	(0.13)	2.40	(0.12)	3.43	(0.11)	1.17	(0.06)
	Korea	4.08	(0.08)	2.32	(0.17)	4.01	(0.15)	5.00	(0.07)	5.00	(0.00)	1.17	(0.07)
	Luxembourg	2.49	(0.00)	1.48	(0.00)	2.00	(0.00)	2.47	(0.00)	4.01	(0.00)	1.09	(0.00)
	Mexico	2.42	(0.05)	0.70	(0.03)	1.79	(0.05)	2.86	(0.07)	4.33	(0.10)	1.42	(0.03)
	Netherlands	1.24	(0.07)	0.05	(0.10)	1.00	(0.03)	1.42	(0.17)	2.49	(0.12)	0.96	(0.06)
	New Zealand	3.23	(0.09)	1.68	(0.17)	3.00	(0.02)	3.71	(0.16)	4.52	(0.14)	1.15	(0.06)
	Norway	0.99	(0.07)	0.00	(0.00)	0.49	(0.14)	1.08	(0.12)	2.41	(0.15)	1.02	(0.07)
	Poland	4.31	(0.08)	2.85	(0.19)	4.37	(0.16)	5.00	(0.00)	5.00	(0.00)	0.98	(0.06)
	Portugal	3.26	(0.08)	2.19	(0.18)	3.00	(0.00)	3.64	(0.18)	4.20	(0.07)	0.91	(0.06)
	Slovak Republic	3.69	(0.09)	2.02	(0.17)	3.33	(0.13)	4.41	(0.13)	5.00	(0.00)	1.25	(0.06)
	Slovenia	3.78	(0.01)	2.70	(0.01)	3.42	(0.02)	4.00	(0.02)	5.00	(0.03)	0.91	(0.01)
	Spain	1.36	(0.06)	0.14	(0.08)	1.00	(0.00)	1.55	(0.10)	2.75	(0.11)	1.06	(0.04)
	Sweden	1.62	(0.09)	0.56	(0.10)	1.00	(0.00)	1.81	(0.17)	3.10	(0.18)	1.08	(0.05)
	Switzerland	1.38	(0.06)	0.23	(0.11)	1.00	(0.00)	1.70	(0.13)	2.59	(0.09)	0.97	(0.04)
	Turkey	1.76	(0.12)	0.27	(0.14)	1.05	(0.13)	2.13	(0.20)	3.61	(0.13)	1.32	(0.06)
	United Kingdom	3.96	(0.07)	2.57	(0.09)	3.65	(0.13)	4.63	(0.14)	5.00	(0.00)	1.05	(0.04)
	United States	2.71	(0.12)	0.78	(0.21)	2.26	(0.16)	3.18	(0.15)	4.62	(0.12)	1.48	(0.07)
	OECD average	2.36	(0.01)	0.94	(0.02)	1.94	(0.02)	2.73	(0.02)	3.82	(0.02)	1.17	(0.01)
Partners	Albania	3.30	(0.09)	1.37	(0.12)	2.89	(0.21)	4.00	(0.09)	4.94	(0.10)	1.37	(0.05)
	Argentina	2.13	(0.10)	0.58	(0.11)	1.44	(0.14)	2.56	(0.15)	3.94	(0.15)	1.38	(0.06)
	Brazil	2.10	(0.07)	0.92	(0.03)	1.36	(0.12)	2.60	(0.13)	3.51	(0.09)	1.13	(0.04)
	Bulgaria	2.62	(0.11)	0.69	(0.13)	2.08	(0.17)	3.26	(0.16)	4.45	(0.09)	1.46	(0.05)
	Colombia	1.65	(0.10)	0.00	(0.08)	1.00	(0.10)	1.92	(0.20)	3.69	(0.20)	1.43	(0.08)
	Costa Rica	1.86	(0.10)	0.33	(0.12)	1.12	(0.13)	2.33	(0.15)	3.65	(0.15)	1.36	(0.07)
	Croatia	2.78	(0.09)	1.00	(0.14)	2.59	(0.13)	3.15	(0.13)	4.38	(0.10)	1.32	(0.06)
	Cyprus*	2.98	(0.00)	1.76	(0.00)	2.77	(0.00)	3.13	(0.00)	4.28	(0.00)	1.00	(0.00)
	Hong Kong-China	4.44	(0.07)	3.34	(0.15)	4.43	(0.17)	5.00	(0.00)	5.00	(0.00)	0.79	(0.05)
	Indonesia	2.62	(0.13)	0.75	(0.16)	2.11	(0.19)	3.19	(0.18)	4.44	(0.11)	1.42	(0.06)
	Jordan	2.07	(0.09)	0.43	(0.11)	1.67	(0.15)	2.34	(0.12)	3.85	(0.12)	1.35	(0.06)
	Kazakhstan	3.77	(0.08)	2.28	(0.14)	3.67	(0.12)	4.15	(0.15)	5.00	(0.00)	1.08	(0.06)
	Latvia	2.78	(0.09)	1.03	(0.13)	2.38	(0.13)	3.27	(0.14)	4.46	(0.10)	1.34	(0.05)
	Liechtenstein	1.36	(0.02)	0.71	(0.03)	1.00	(0.00)	1.00	(0.00)	2.75	(0.08)	0.95	(0.01)
	Lithuania	2.86	(0.10)	1.21	(0.14)	2.73	(0.14)	3.19	(0.14)	4.31	(0.07)	1.21	(0.05)
	Macao-China	3.87	(0.00)	1.98	(0.00)	3.62	(0.00)	4.88	(0.00)	5.00	(0.00)	1.31	(0.00)
	Malaysia	4.25	(0.07)	2.93	(0.14)	4.08	(0.15)	5.00	(0.04)	5.00	(0.00)	0.90	(0.04)
	Montenegro	3.00	(0.00)	1.58	(0.00)	2.26	(0.01)	3.44	(0.01)	4.73	(0.01)	1.29	(0.00)
	Peru	2.07	(0.09)	0.70	(0.07)	1.28	(0.13)	2.29	(0.12)	4.02	(0.16)	1.37	(0.06)
	Qatar	3.72	(0.00)	2.11	(0.00)	3.32	(0.00)	4.45	(0.00)	5.00	(0.00)	1.27	(0.00)
	Romania	2.92	(0.09)	1.63	(0.10)	2.50	(0.15)	3.18	(0.15)	4.39	(0.09)	1.11	(0.05)
	Russian Federation	3.87	(0.07)	2.45	(0.12)	3.62	(0.12)	4.41	(0.12)	5.00	(0.00)	1.08	(0.06)
	Serbia	2.78	(0.09)	1.35	(0.11)	2.42	(0.16)	3.03	(0.10)	4.31	(0.12)	1.16	(0.05)
	Shanghai-China	2.81	(0.09)	0.85	(0.14)	2.30	(0.14)	3.31	(0.13)	4.77	(0.11)	1.50	(0.06)
	Singapore	3.66	(0.01)	2.46	(0.03)	3.61	(0.02)	4.00	(0.00)	4.58	(0.01)	0.92	(0.01)
	Chinese Taipei	3.19	(0.11)	1.45	(0.15)	2.87	(0.14)	3.77	(0.16)	4.66	(0.13)	1.28	(0.08)
	Thailand	3.89	(0.08)	1.90	(0.19)	3.84	(0.10)	4.84	(0.14)	5.00	(0.00)	1.35	(0.08)
	Tunisia	2.73	(0.13)	0.60	(0.11)	2.20	(0.27)	3.44	(0.15)	4.69	(0.12)	1.60	(0.05)
	United Arab Emirates	3.15	(0.07)	1.40	(0.09)	2.71	(0.09)	3.55	(0.11)	4.93	(0.09)	1.38	(0.04)
	Uruguay	1.76	(0.08)	0.45	(0.10)	1.29	(0.14)	2.00	(0.05)	3.29	(0.16)	1.13	(0.05)
	Viet Nam	2.99	(0.08)	1.62	(0.08)	2.87	(0.13)	3.07	(0.11)	4.40	(0.12)	1.08	(0.05)

Note: Values that are statistically significant are indicated in bold (see Annex A3).
* See notes at the beginning of this Annex.
StatLink http://dx.doi.org/10.1787/888932957460

[Part 2/2]
Index of extracurricular mathematics activities at school and mathematics performance
Table IV.3.32 *Results based on school principals' reports*

| | Performance on the mathematics scale by national quarters of this index | | | | | | | | Change in the mathematics score per unit of this index | | Increased likelihood of students in the bottom quarter of this index scoring in the bottom quarter of the national mathematics performance distribution | | Explained variance in student performance (r-squared x 100) | |
| | Bottom quarter | | Second quarter | | Third quarter | | Top quarter | | | | | | | |
	Mean score	S.E.	Mean score	S.E.	Mean score	S.E.	Mean score	S.E.	Score dif.	S.E.	Ratio	S.E.	%	S.E.
Australia	**495**	(3.4)	502	(3.5)	502	(3.5)	**519**	(4.1)	**6.8**	(1.55)	**1.2**	(0.06)	0.8	(0.38)
Austria	482	(8.2)	500	(6.9)	510	(6.3)	**529**	(7.9)	**18.3**	(3.60)	**1.5**	(0.19)	4.2	(1.82)
Belgium	474	(6.1)	524	(6.0)	535	(7.4)	**530**	(6.6)	**21.2**	(3.22)	**2.0**	(0.20)	4.8	(1.46)
Canada	510	(3.2)	514	(3.5)	521	(4.2)	**528**	(4.3)	**4.8**	(1.11)	**1.1**	(0.07)	0.6	(0.29)
Chile	**404**	(5.9)	413	(5.7)	424	(5.5)	**450**	(6.5)	**13.2**	(2.63)	**1.4**	(0.15)	4.6	(1.75)
Czech Republic	479	(9.8)	504	(9.4)	511	(7.0)	500	(6.4)	5.2	(3.26)	**1.4**	(0.18)	0.5	(0.66)
Denmark	497	(3.8)	502	(3.9)	505	(5.3)	499	(7.1)	-0.6	(3.30)	1.0	(0.10)	0.0	(0.12)
Estonia	521	(4.3)	520	(5.0)	523	(4.0)	517	(4.2)	0.1	(1.67)	1.0	(0.09)	0.0	(0.06)
Finland	517	(5.0)	518	(4.2)	520	(3.2)	519	(2.9)	0.9	(1.80)	1.0	(0.10)	0.0	(0.07)
France	493	(7.8)	498	(6.3)	490	(7.3)	504	(8.3)	4.1	(3.98)	1.0	(0.15)	0.3	(0.54)
Germany	474	(9.3)	510	(7.2)	527	(7.5)	**544**	(8.9)	**20.3**	(3.39)	**2.1**	(0.30)	8.3	(2.83)
Greece	443	(5.9)	458	(4.5)	452	(5.2)	459	(7.0)	8.1	(2.93)	1.2	(0.15)	1.1	(0.78)
Hungary	**453**	(10.5)	469	(9.4)	490	(9.0)	**499**	(7.9)	**13.2**	(3.66)	**1.6**	(0.27)	4.3	(2.35)
Iceland	485	(3.5)	487	(3.5)	499	(3.2)	503	(3.3)	5.9	(1.33)	1.2	(0.13)	0.6	(0.29)
Ireland	499	(4.1)	502	(5.4)	498	(6.3)	511	(5.9)	3.8	(2.21)	1.0	(0.10)	0.3	(0.42)
Israel	453	(13.4)	467	(9.1)	463	(8.0)	481	(8.2)	7.3	(4.99)	1.3	(0.23)	0.7	(1.04)
Italy	**464**	(5.2)	474	(5.3)	502	(4.1)	**508**	(4.2)	**18.1**	(2.59)	**1.5**	(0.14)	4.4	(1.21)
Japan	513	(8.3)	529	(6.1)	538	(5.1)	**566**	(8.9)	**18.7**	(4.02)	1.3	(0.18)	5.4	(2.29)
Korea	508	(10.4)	553	(10.7)	578	(6.7)	**577**	(7.0)	**27.9**	(3.28)	**2.4**	(0.33)	10.9	(2.84)
Luxembourg	468	(2.4)	494	(3.0)	488	(3.4)	510	(2.0)	**17.6**	(0.76)	**1.4**	(0.07)	4.1	(0.35)
Mexico	392	(2.7)	412	(3.0)	417	(2.9)	433	(3.6)	**10.1**	(1.18)	**1.6**	(0.09)	3.7	(0.80)
Netherlands	471	(8.9)	522	(8.7)	536	(8.7)	553	(8.3)	**30.3**	(4.72)	**2.3**	(0.37)	9.9	(3.04)
New Zealand	**489**	(5.6)	490	(7.1)	509	(6.9)	**519**	(7.7)	**9.3**	(3.45)	**1.3**	(0.12)	1.2	(0.84)
Norway	480	(6.6)	489	(4.9)	497	(4.7)	495	(4.8)	5.9	(3.07)	1.2	(0.11)	0.4	(0.45)
Poland	514	(5.9)	525	(7.5)	516	(5.5)	514	(5.5)	2.2	(2.96)	1.0	(0.11)	0.1	(0.19)
Portugal	486	(6.6)	484	(7.6)	490	(6.2)	487	(7.7)	2.4	(4.12)	1.0	(0.12)	0.1	(0.22)
Slovak Republic	467	(9.3)	482	(6.4)	490	(6.4)	488	(10.3)	8.9	(4.59)	1.2	(0.17)	1.2	(1.30)
Slovenia	**476**	(2.9)	498	(4.2)	519	(4.1)	**520**	(3.5)	**21.5**	(1.70)	**1.5**	(0.11)	4.6	(0.68)
Spain	486	(3.5)	484	(4.8)	483	(3.5)	486	(4.6)	0.1	(2.37)	0.9	(0.08)	0.0	(0.07)
Sweden	472	(5.4)	476	(4.9)	477	(5.5)	489	(4.9)	**6.2**	(2.73)	1.1	(0.11)	0.5	(0.47)
Switzerland	519	(6.6)	537	(6.3)	536	(6.1)	538	(6.3)	7.4	(3.63)	1.2	(0.12)	0.6	(0.59)
Turkey	425	(8.1)	428	(6.8)	452	(11.4)	**488**	(11.6)	**20.1**	(3.95)	1.3	(0.18)	8.5	(3.11)
United Kingdom	510	(6.7)	501	(6.0)	486	(6.1)	483	(6.8)	**-9.5**	(3.84)	**0.8**	(0.08)	1.1	(0.84)
United States	463	(9.0)	475	(7.7)	491	(6.1)	500	(7.2)	**10.2**	(2.82)	**1.5**	(0.22)	2.8	(1.53)
OECD average	**479**	(1.2)	**492**	(1.1)	**499**	(1.0)	**507**	(1.1)	**10.0**	(0.54)	**1.3**	(0.03)	2.7	(0.24)
Albania	402	(4.4)	390	(5.8)	391	(4.9)	394	(4.6)	-2.2	(1.56)	0.9	(0.07)	0.1	(0.16)
Argentina	395	(8.4)	391	(6.1)	380	(5.8)	389	(5.8)	-2.1	(2.68)	0.9	(0.16)	0.2	(0.41)
Brazil	**385**	(3.6)	384	(3.3)	399	(5.4)	409	(4.9)	9.2	(2.19)	1.1	(0.08)	1.8	(0.83)
Bulgaria	411	(8.9)	432	(9.4)	447	(8.8)	473	(8.0)	17.0	(2.82)	1.7	(0.26)	7.1	(2.42)
Colombia	356	(6.3)	373	(6.6)	383	(5.5)	398	(4.2)	10.5	(2.00)	1.7	(0.22)	4.1	(1.53)
Costa Rica	407	(6.1)	401	(5.8)	401	(5.2)	419	(8.4)	4.0	(3.71)	0.9	(0.13)	0.6	(1.18)
Croatia	**434**	(6.0)	471	(6.8)	485	(7.5)	**495**	(7.8)	**19.6**	(2.70)	**2.0**	(0.22)	8.5	(2.27)
Cyprus*	**424**	(2.4)	440	(3.5)	443	(3.2)	449	(2.2)	**10.9**	(1.10)	1.3	(0.09)	1.4	(0.27)
Hong Kong-China	557	(8.2)	560	(6.0)	564	(6.8)	564	(6.5)	3.0	(6.51)	1.1	(0.17)	0.1	(0.39)
Indonesia	356	(6.8)	368	(5.1)	374	(8.1)	**402**	(10.4)	**12.8**	(3.22)	**1.5**	(0.23)	6.5	(2.98)
Jordan	373	(4.9)	379	(5.6)	387	(5.5)	403	(7.8)	8.6	(2.67)	1.2	(0.14)	2.2	(1.29)
Kazakhstan	439	(5.7)	437	(6.6)	433	(5.8)	418	(4.6)	-6.5	(2.70)	0.9	(0.10)	1.0	(0.81)
Latvia	**481**	(6.0)	489	(5.4)	490	(5.1)	501	(5.2)	5.9	(2.10)	1.3	(0.15)	0.9	(0.65)
Liechtenstein	545	(15.3)	555	(20.1)	544	(18.8)	495	(11.7)	-26.7	(3.91)	0.5	(0.27)	7.0	(1.99)
Lithuania	**464**	(6.8)	476	(6.5)	486	(5.6)	491	(6.2)	9.4	(2.85)	1.3	(0.13)	1.6	(0.99)
Macao-China	525	(2.4)	534	(3.8)	545	(3.5)	548	(2.5)	6.5	(0.68)	1.3	(0.06)	0.8	(0.17)
Malaysia	428	(7.2)	420	(7.8)	417	(5.6)	417	(6.0)	-4.8	(4.11)	0.9	(0.13)	0.3	(0.58)
Montenegro	415	(2.6)	407	(3.0)	391	(2.9)	426	(2.2)	2.9	(0.78)	**0.8**	(0.07)	0.2	(0.11)
Peru	359	(7.1)	359	(4.9)	367	(6.9)	386	(8.1)	8.3	(3.34)	1.2	(0.14)	1.8	(1.55)
Qatar	375	(2.1)	389	(2.2)	369	(3.2)	373	(1.6)	0.0	(0.53)	1.0	(0.04)	0.0	(0.00)
Romania	430	(7.7)	440	(6.8)	450	(7.0)	459	(6.8)	10.9	(3.97)	1.3	(0.18)	2.2	(1.72)
Russian Federation	475	(6.1)	477	(5.9)	484	(5.7)	492	(6.4)	6.8	(3.72)	1.2	(0.11)	0.7	(0.79)
Serbia	**430**	(8.5)	445	(6.3)	449	(8.3)	**468**	(11.0)	11.4	(4.67)	**1.4**	(0.21)	2.2	(1.85)
Shanghai-China	547	(7.9)	610	(8.4)	635	(8.0)	**659**	(7.2)	**27.6**	(2.40)	**2.8**	(0.30)	16.9	(2.90)
Singapore	559	(3.3)	564	(3.9)	572	(3.6)	**603**	(2.8)	**19.2**	(1.49)	1.2	(0.07)	2.8	(0.43)
Chinese Taipei	537	(9.1)	540	(9.5)	569	(10.8)	**593**	(11.1)	**18.6**	(4.09)	**1.4**	(0.17)	4.3	(1.96)
Thailand	**393**	(4.5)	415	(6.5)	446	(7.0)	**453**	(5.9)	**17.7**	(2.18)	**1.8**	(0.21)	8.5	(1.81)
Tunisia	379	(7.3)	394	(10.1)	390	(7.0)	388	(8.6)	1.6	(2.92)	1.2	(0.21)	0.1	(0.49)
United Arab Emirates	**422**	(4.6)	441	(4.3)	436	(5.7)	**453**	(6.3)	**7.1**	(2.17)	**1.4**	(0.12)	1.2	(0.69)
Uruguay	398	(7.4)	407	(5.6)	406	(6.9)	426	(10.7)	11.1	(4.80)	1.3	(0.17)	2.0	(1.71)
Viet Nam	487	(8.3)	506	(8.5)	512	(9.5)	**540**	(8.1)	**15.9**	(3.89)	**1.5**	(0.25)	4.0	(1.95)

Note: Values that are statistically significant are indicated in bold (see Annex A3).
* See notes at the beginning of this Annex.
StatLink ⌘⫘ http://dx.doi.org/10.1787/888932957460

[Part 1/1]
Pre-school attendance
Table IV.3.33 *Results based on students' self-reports*

		Percentage of students reporting that they had attended pre-primary education (ISCED 0)					
		No attendance		For one year or less		For more than one year	
		%	S.E.	%	S.E.	%	S.E.
OECD	Australia	4.6	(0.2)	43.7	(0.6)	51.7	(0.6)
	Austria	1.8	(0.3)	10.5	(0.6)	87.7	(0.7)
	Belgium	2.4	(0.2)	4.6	(0.3)	93.0	(0.4)
	Canada	9.1	(0.3)	40.4	(0.7)	50.5	(0.6)
	Chile	9.2	(0.7)	56.5	(0.9)	34.3	(0.8)
	Czech Republic	3.2	(0.5)	8.8	(0.6)	88.0	(0.8)
	Denmark	1.1	(0.1)	20.1	(0.6)	78.9	(0.6)
	Estonia	7.3	(0.6)	8.7	(0.5)	83.9	(0.8)
	Finland	2.5	(0.2)	34.8	(1.0)	62.7	(1.0)
	France	1.8	(0.3)	6.4	(0.3)	91.8	(0.4)
	Germany	3.3	(0.3)	11.5	(0.6)	85.2	(0.7)
	Greece	4.6	(0.5)	27.4	(0.9)	68.0	(1.0)
	Hungary	0.5	(0.1)	4.0	(0.4)	95.5	(0.4)
	Iceland	2.1	(0.2)	3.2	(0.3)	94.7	(0.4)
	Ireland	13.6	(0.7)	43.6	(0.9)	42.8	(0.9)
	Israel	2.1	(0.2)	16.5	(0.8)	81.4	(0.9)
	Italy	4.3	(0.2)	8.0	(0.2)	87.7	(0.3)
	Japan	0.9	(0.1)	2.2	(0.2)	96.9	(0.2)
	Korea	4.5	(0.4)	12.6	(0.7)	82.9	(0.9)
	Luxembourg	4.6	(0.3)	12.8	(0.4)	82.6	(0.5)
	Mexico	9.5	(0.3)	18.7	(0.3)	71.8	(0.5)
	Netherlands	2.3	(0.3)	2.7	(0.3)	95.0	(0.3)
	New Zealand	9.3	(0.6)	19.5	(0.7)	71.2	(0.8)
	Norway	7.9	(0.4)	5.8	(0.4)	86.3	(0.6)
	Poland	2.5	(0.3)	46.4	(1.5)	51.1	(1.5)
	Portugal	15.0	(0.8)	20.7	(0.8)	64.4	(1.1)
	Slovak Republic	6.8	(0.7)	13.2	(0.8)	80.0	(1.0)
	Slovenia	14.7	(0.5)	12.8	(0.6)	72.5	(0.7)
	Spain	5.9	(0.3)	8.3	(0.2)	85.8	(0.4)
	Sweden	8.2	(0.5)	20.4	(0.8)	71.4	(0.8)
	Switzerland	1.8	(0.2)	25.0	(1.8)	73.1	(1.8)
	Turkey	70.3	(1.4)	21.0	(1.0)	8.6	(0.8)
	United Kingdom	5.0	(0.4)	26.1	(0.5)	68.9	(0.7)
	United States	1.5	(0.2)	24.0	(0.9)	74.6	(0.9)
	OECD average	7.2	(0.1)	18.8	(0.1)	74.0	(0.1)
Partners	Albania	25.4	(0.9)	21.8	(0.8)	52.8	(1.1)
	Argentina	6.2	(0.9)	22.6	(0.9)	71.2	(1.4)
	Brazil	18.9	(0.6)	33.4	(0.7)	47.7	(0.8)
	Bulgaria	10.2	(0.7)	13.0	(0.5)	76.7	(1.0)
	Colombia	14.2	(0.8)	52.5	(0.8)	33.3	(1.1)
	Costa Rica	15.4	(0.9)	39.6	(1.1)	45.0	(1.2)
	Croatia	26.8	(1.1)	22.4	(0.8)	50.8	(1.1)
	Cyprus*	3.6	(0.3)	23.5	(0.6)	73.0	(0.7)
	Hong Kong-China	1.6	(0.2)	3.3	(0.3)	95.1	(0.4)
	Indonesia	46.2	(2.2)	31.4	(2.0)	22.5	(1.5)
	Jordan	24.2	(1.0)	49.3	(0.9)	26.5	(1.0)
	Kazakhstan	65.0	(1.7)	11.3	(0.6)	23.8	(1.4)
	Latvia	11.3	(0.8)	13.3	(0.7)	75.4	(0.9)
	Liechtenstein	0.7	(0.5)	8.8	(1.8)	90.5	(1.9)
	Lithuania	30.5	(1.0)	13.2	(0.6)	56.3	(1.0)
	Macao-China	2.4	(0.2)	11.9	(0.4)	85.6	(0.5)
	Malaysia	23.8	(1.3)	28.6	(1.0)	47.6	(1.4)
	Montenegro	32.8	(0.6)	24.8	(0.6)	42.4	(0.7)
	Peru	13.8	(0.7)	25.0	(0.7)	61.1	(1.1)
	Qatar	30.7	(0.5)	41.5	(0.5)	27.8	(0.4)
	Romania	4.5	(0.5)	9.0	(0.5)	86.5	(0.8)
	Russian Federation	18.9	(1.1)	10.2	(0.6)	71.0	(1.4)
	Serbia	20.3	(0.9)	28.9	(1.1)	50.7	(1.2)
	Shanghai-China	3.6	(0.6)	8.6	(0.6)	87.8	(1.0)
	Singapore	2.3	(0.2)	7.1	(0.4)	90.6	(0.4)
	Chinese Taipei	1.5	(0.2)	14.7	(0.6)	83.8	(0.6)
	Thailand	1.7	(0.3)	10.5	(0.6)	87.8	(0.6)
	Tunisia	37.6	(1.6)	39.3	(1.1)	23.1	(1.0)
	United Arab Emirates	23.7	(0.7)	26.6	(0.6)	49.7	(0.9)
	Uruguay	16.2	(0.8)	14.1	(0.7)	69.7	(1.0)
	Viet Nam	9.3	(1.0)	22.5	(1.2)	68.2	(1.5)

* See notes at the beginning of this Annex.
StatLink http://dx.doi.org/10.1787/888932957460

[Part 1/2]
Pre-school attendance, by school features
Table IV.3.34 *Results based on students' self-reports*

		Percentage of students reporting that they had attended pre-primary education (ISCED 0) for more than one year												
		Bottom quarter of ESCS		Second quarter of ESCS		Third quarter of ESCS		Top quarter of ESCS		Socio-economically disadvantaged schools[1]		Socio-economically average schools[1]		Socio-economically advantaged schools[1]
		%	S.E.	%	S.E.	%	S.E.	%	S.E.	%	S.E.	%	S.E.	%	S.E.
OECD	Australia	42.7	(1.2)	49.0	(1.1)	54.2	(1.1)	61.5	(1.3)	42.3	(1.1)	49.9	(0.8)	64.3	(1.3)
	Austria	80.7	(1.9)	86.4	(1.3)	90.7	(1.1)	93.2	(0.9)	82.1	(1.6)	88.7	(0.9)	93.2	(1.0)
	Belgium	89.2	(0.9)	92.1	(0.7)	95.3	(0.5)	96.1	(0.5)	87.3	(0.9)	94.6	(0.6)	96.0	(0.5)
	Canada	42.6	(1.1)	46.8	(1.2)	52.0	(1.2)	61.2	(1.1)	46.6	(2.3)	48.1	(1.2)	58.8	(1.4)
	Chile	27.9	(1.3)	30.9	(1.6)	31.1	(1.6)	47.6	(1.5)	29.9	(1.3)	31.2	(1.3)	42.0	(1.7)
	Czech Republic	84.4	(1.9)	87.4	(1.3)	91.0	(1.2)	89.5	(1.1)	84.0	(2.3)	88.8	(0.9)	89.8	(1.1)
	Denmark	72.6	(1.1)	78.2	(1.4)	80.0	(1.2)	85.2	(1.1)	73.1	(1.5)	78.3	(0.9)	85.5	(1.3)
	Estonia	76.7	(1.7)	84.0	(1.2)	86.4	(1.3)	88.9	(1.0)	75.9	(2.4)	84.5	(0.8)	89.0	(0.9)
	Finland	51.4	(1.4)	61.3	(1.7)	66.3	(1.6)	72.0	(1.6)	47.6	(3.1)	62.4	(1.9)	78.2	(1.8)
	France	87.5	(1.1)	90.6	(0.8)	94.5	(0.7)	95.2	(0.7)	83.9	(1.3)	93.2	(0.7)	96.0	(0.6)
	Germany	79.2	(1.6)	84.3	(1.2)	88.2	(1.1)	91.2	(1.1)	75.8	(1.7)	86.7	(0.9)	92.0	(0.9)
	Greece	59.9	(1.9)	67.1	(1.8)	70.3	(1.5)	74.8	(1.6)	61.8	(2.6)	68.3	(1.5)	73.4	(1.6)
	Hungary	94.8	(0.8)	95.8	(0.7)	95.3	(0.7)	96.3	(0.8)	94.2	(0.7)	95.4	(0.6)	96.9	(0.5)
	Iceland	90.2	(1.0)	95.4	(0.7)	96.7	(0.7)	96.6	(0.7)	93.3	(1.0)	94.1	(0.5)	96.7	(0.6)
	Ireland	34.2	(1.6)	40.2	(1.8)	44.4	(1.7)	52.4	(1.6)	41.2	(2.1)	38.5	(1.1)	53.3	(1.6)
	Israel	73.0	(1.7)	80.9	(1.4)	86.4	(1.3)	85.7	(1.3)	71.7	(1.9)	81.8	(1.6)	89.6	(0.9)
	Italy	84.2	(0.7)	87.5	(0.6)	89.4	(0.5)	89.9	(0.6)	84.0	(0.8)	87.8	(0.5)	91.1	(0.5)
	Japan	95.8	(0.6)	97.2	(0.5)	97.1	(0.4)	97.7	(0.4)	94.9	(0.9)	97.5	(0.3)	98.0	(0.3)
	Korea	79.8	(1.5)	80.7	(1.4)	85.2	(1.1)	85.7	(1.3)	82.1	(1.8)	82.4	(1.3)	84.6	(1.3)
	Luxembourg	74.8	(1.2)	83.3	(1.1)	87.2	(0.9)	85.1	(1.0)	78.4	(0.8)	87.9	(1.1)	85.7	(0.8)
	Mexico	61.3	(1.2)	68.6	(0.9)	74.2	(0.7)	83.3	(0.6)	64.4	(1.2)	71.3	(0.7)	80.6	(0.6)
	Netherlands	92.7	(1.0)	96.2	(0.7)	95.3	(0.8)	95.9	(0.6)	93.3	(1.0)	95.5	(0.4)	95.6	(0.7)
	New Zealand	60.3	(1.9)	70.8	(1.7)	74.6	(1.5)	80.6	(1.4)	61.9	(2.7)	71.6	(1.3)	78.8	(1.6)
	Norway	78.0	(1.3)	84.9	(1.3)	88.1	(1.2)	94.6	(0.8)	79.0	(1.9)	85.5	(0.7)	93.9	(1.0)
	Poland	28.4	(2.2)	42.8	(2.5)	56.7	(2.4)	76.6	(1.7)	31.9	(3.2)	50.7	(2.2)	75.9	(1.7)
	Portugal	52.5	(1.7)	60.3	(1.7)	65.8	(2.0)	78.9	(1.4)	59.5	(1.8)	62.6	(1.6)	75.9	(2.2)
	Slovak Republic	63.9	(2.4)	80.1	(1.6)	85.5	(1.3)	89.8	(1.0)	63.6	(2.6)	84.2	(1.0)	89.4	(1.5)
	Slovenia	61.4	(1.6)	69.3	(1.3)	77.1	(1.3)	82.6	(1.4)	63.5	(1.4)	73.2	(1.1)	80.2	(1.2)
	Spain	80.1	(0.9)	84.1	(0.9)	87.9	(0.9)	91.3	(0.5)	82.7	(1.1)	85.6	(0.6)	89.5	(0.7)
	Sweden	61.9	(1.5)	70.7	(1.5)	76.2	(1.5)	77.3	(1.2)	70.5	(2.4)	68.3	(1.1)	80.5	(1.7)
	Switzerland	68.2	(2.4)	71.7	(2.0)	77.0	(2.2)	75.6	(2.6)	63.2	(4.3)	76.1	(1.9)	77.8	(3.8)
	Turkey	1.7	(0.5)	3.4	(0.7)	6.7	(1.2)	22.9	(1.9)	4.8	(0.7)	5.4	(0.6)	19.2	(1.9)
	United Kingdom	61.1	(1.6)	67.4	(1.3)	71.9	(1.3)	76.9	(1.1)	60.3	(1.5)	70.3	(1.0)	74.3	(1.3)
	United States	61.1	(2.0)	72.2	(1.6)	79.7	(1.5)	85.3	(1.1)	63.9	(1.6)	75.6	(1.2)	82.8	(1.3)
	OECD average	66.3	(0.3)	72.4	(0.2)	76.4	(0.2)	81.1	(0.2)	67.4	(0.3)	74.0	(0.2)	80.8	(0.2)
Partners	Albania	m	m	m	m	m	m	m	m	m	m	m	m	m	m
	Argentina	56.3	(2.5)	68.9	(2.2)	76.4	(1.8)	83.8	(1.6)	54.1	(2.1)	73.6	(2.3)	85.9	(1.4)
	Brazil	36.8	(1.1)	44.7	(1.0)	49.2	(1.5)	60.5	(1.6)	38.8	(1.3)	46.8	(1.1)	61.4	(1.9)
	Bulgaria	66.2	(2.3)	79.6	(1.5)	81.4	(1.2)	80.4	(1.1)	69.0	(2.1)	80.0	(1.4)	81.7	(0.9)
	Colombia	23.9	(1.6)	28.6	(1.6)	33.6	(1.6)	47.3	(2.5)	27.0	(1.8)	29.6	(1.4)	44.8	(1.9)
	Costa Rica	33.1	(2.1)	37.9	(2.0)	46.7	(2.0)	62.5	(2.3)	35.5	(2.3)	42.1	(1.3)	62.8	(3.0)
	Croatia	27.4	(1.8)	44.4	(1.8)	58.1	(1.9)	73.5	(1.6)	32.3	(1.9)	53.8	(2.1)	71.2	(1.7)
	Cyprus*	66.9	(1.5)	72.0	(1.3)	76.0	(1.2)	77.4	(1.2)	68.3	(1.2)	75.1	(1.0)	75.9	(1.0)
	Hong Kong-China	91.2	(0.9)	95.6	(0.8)	96.4	(0.7)	97.2	(0.6)	92.2	(0.9)	95.7	(0.5)	98.2	(0.4)
	Indonesia	13.7	(1.7)	15.5	(2.0)	24.3	(2.0)	36.6	(3.5)	16.7	(2.3)	20.0	(2.6)	33.8	(4.0)
	Jordan	15.5	(1.4)	22.2	(1.7)	30.0	(1.7)	38.3	(1.6)	18.4	(1.8)	24.1	(1.2)	41.5	(2.7)
	Kazakhstan	9.6	(1.2)	19.9	(2.5)	26.2	(1.8)	39.4	(2.1)	9.2	(1.8)	18.2	(1.6)	42.2	(2.2)
	Latvia	60.6	(2.4)	75.7	(1.8)	81.2	(1.8)	83.3	(1.3)	58.5	(3.5)	77.2	(1.4)	83.3	(1.1)
	Liechtenstein	91.0	(3.6)	93.2	(2.7)	94.6	(2.9)	83.8	(4.8)	c	c	88.9	(2.8)	c	c
	Lithuania	38.6	(1.7)	47.9	(1.7)	66.3	(1.6)	72.4	(1.4)	32.6	(2.4)	57.4	(1.8)	76.3	(1.6)
	Macao-China	83.7	(1.0)	86.1	(0.9)	86.6	(0.8)	86.4	(1.0)	84.9	(0.7)	85.6	(1.0)	86.8	(0.8)
	Malaysia	33.4	(2.0)	43.1	(2.1)	51.7	(2.3)	62.2	(2.1)	34.9	(1.9)	44.2	(2.1)	65.0	(2.3)
	Montenegro	22.6	(1.2)	36.7	(1.5)	48.1	(1.8)	61.9	(1.5)	30.4	(1.1)	37.5	(1.6)	57.5	(1.3)
	Peru	45.7	(1.8)	56.8	(1.7)	66.4	(2.2)	75.7	(1.8)	48.4	(1.8)	58.8	(1.7)	76.2	(1.7)
	Qatar	15.8	(0.7)	28.9	(0.8)	31.6	(1.0)	35.4	(1.0)	21.8	(0.6)	23.2	(1.0)	34.7	(0.6)
	Romania	79.3	(1.8)	86.7	(1.2)	87.9	(1.3)	92.3	(1.0)	80.8	(1.8)	86.3	(1.1)	92.8	(0.8)
	Russian Federation	55.9	(2.6)	70.4	(2.2)	77.1	(1.4)	80.9	(1.5)	54.5	(3.9)	72.0	(2.5)	82.0	(1.2)
	Serbia	35.9	(1.9)	44.1	(1.6)	54.9	(2.2)	68.2	(1.7)	41.2	(2.3)	48.3	(1.9)	67.5	(1.8)
	Shanghai-China	73.9	(2.8)	89.7	(1.2)	92.2	(0.8)	95.4	(0.7)	76.0	(2.5)	90.8	(0.9)	94.8	(0.7)
	Singapore	88.5	(0.9)	90.6	(0.8)	91.5	(0.9)	91.9	(0.8)	88.4	(0.8)	90.8	(0.6)	92.8	(0.9)
	Chinese Taipei	78.2	(1.4)	83.5	(1.0)	86.2	(0.9)	87.3	(1.1)	81.9	(1.2)	83.6	(1.0)	86.0	(1.2)
	Thailand	83.9	(1.2)	86.3	(1.2)	87.9	(1.1)	93.2	(0.7)	84.3	(1.3)	87.3	(0.9)	93.0	(0.7)
	Tunisia	10.9	(1.1)	21.4	(2.2)	28.2	(1.5)	32.3	(1.9)	12.8	(1.1)	23.8	(1.5)	33.2	(1.7)
	United Arab Emirates	38.2	(1.6)	48.6	(1.6)	54.6	(1.3)	57.8	(1.3)	40.2	(1.4)	48.5	(1.8)	58.2	(1.9)
	Uruguay	57.7	(1.8)	65.0	(2.0)	70.8	(1.7)	85.2	(1.2)	60.5	(1.6)	68.6	(1.7)	87.5	(1.3)
	Viet Nam	49.8	(2.7)	66.5	(2.0)	73.7	(2.5)	82.7	(1.7)	59.4	(2.7)	67.3	(2.7)	82.4	(1.9)

Notes: Values that are statistically significant are indicated in bold (see Annex A3).
ESCS refers to the *PISA index of economic, social and cultural status*.
1. A socio-economically disadvantaged school is one whose students' mean socio-economic status (ESCS) is statistically significantly below the mean socio-economic status of the country/economy; an average school is one where there is no difference from the country's/economy's mean; and an advantaged school is one whose students' mean socio-economic status is statistically significantly above the country/economy mean.
* See notes at the beginning of this Annex.
StatLink ⋯ http://dx.doi.org/10.1787/888932957460

[Part 2/2]
Pre-school attendance, by school features
Table IV.3.34 *Results based on students' self-reports*

	Percentage of students reporting that they had attended pre-primary education (ISCED 0) for more than one year													
	Public schools		Private schools		Lower secondary education (ISCED 2)		Upper secondary education (ISCED 3)		Schools located in a village, hamlet or rural area (fewer than 3 000 people)		Schools located in a small town or town (3 000 to about 100 000 people)		Schools located in a city or a large city (over 100 000 people)	
	%	S.E.	%	S.E.	%	S.E.	%	S.E.	%	S.E.	%	S.E.	%	S.E.
Australia	**48.6**	(0.8)	**56.7**	(1.1)	**54.0**	(0.7)	**42.0**	(1.3)	46.4	(2.2)	49.5	(1.3)	**53.3**	(0.9)
Austria	87.3	(0.8)	92.1	(2.2)	79.3	(4.9)	88.2	(0.7)	85.1	(3.0)	88.1	(1.0)	87.9	(1.1)
Belgium	**90.0**	(1.0)	**94.3**	(0.4)	74.5	(1.9)	**95.0**	(0.3)	88.3	(5.2)	93.7	(0.4)	91.4	(1.1)
Canada	50.4	(0.7)	52.1	(2.7)	37.3	(1.3)	52.7	(0.7)	47.3	(2.4)	43.6	(1.4)	55.9	(1.0)
Chile	**30.8**	(1.0)	**36.1**	(1.1)	30.1	(2.8)	34.5	(0.8)	30.8	(2.9)	31.5	(1.4)	**36.5**	(1.1)
Czech Republic	87.8	(1.0)	85.9	(2.5)	87.5	(1.3)	88.6	(0.8)	88.1	(4.6)	87.8	(1.1)	87.3	(1.8)
Denmark	**77.8**	(0.7)	**82.4**	(1.3)	78.8	(0.6)	89.6	(5.1)	77.7	(1.4)	79.5	(0.9)	78.8	(1.5)
Estonia	83.8	(0.8)	86.1	(4.9)	84.0	(0.8)	81.5	(5.0)	74.6	(2.3)	86.7	(0.9)	87.2	(0.9)
Finland	**62.0**	(1.1)	**81.1**	(3.9)	62.7	(1.0)	c	c	49.1	(6.5)	58.0	(1.2)	**77.3**	(1.2)
France	91.7	(0.6)	91.2	(0.9)	83.1	(1.3)	95.4	(0.4)	87.8	(2.0)	92.3	(0.7)	91.2	(1.4)
Germany	84.8	(0.8)	89.2	(3.5)	85.2	(0.6)	84.2	(5.8)	c	c	85.2	(0.9)	85.0	(1.6)
Greece	68.3	(1.0)	c	c	42.4	(3.9)	69.5	(1.0)	69.6	(4.3)	67.8	(1.3)	67.9	(1.9)
Hungary	95.6	(0.4)	95.7	(1.1)	**90.2**	(1.6)	96.2	(0.3)	95.4	(2.3)	96.2	(0.5)	94.8	(0.5)
Iceland	94.7	(0.4)	c	c	94.7	(0.4)	c	c	**92.4**	(0.9)	96.5	(0.5)	**93.6**	(0.9)
Ireland	40.8	(1.3)	43.1	(1.3)	**48.0**	(1.1)	34.2	(1.3)	38.4	(2.0)	40.5	(1.2)	**50.9**	(1.7)
Israel	81.3	(0.9)	c	c	83.5	(2.3)	81.0	(0.9)	**87.2**	(2.1)	76.8	(1.5)	84.3	(1.5)
Italy	87.8	(0.3)	86.1	(1.6)	56.7	(3.9)	**88.4**	(0.3)	85.0	(2.6)	89.0	(0.4)	85.4	(0.7)
Japan	96.7	(0.3)	97.4	(0.3)	c	c	96.9	(0.2)	c	c	96.4	(0.5)	97.0	(0.3)
Korea	82.5	(1.2)	83.2	(1.4)	78.2	(5.2)	83.2	(0.9)	c	c	81.2	(3.9)	83.0	(0.8)
Luxembourg	83.2	(0.6)	79.1	(1.5)	80.2	(0.7)	86.1	(0.7)	c	c	82.6	(0.5)	c	c
Mexico	**70.4**	(0.6)	**82.2**	(0.9)	67.6	(0.9)	74.3	(0.7)	**66.0**	(1.4)	70.6	(1.1)	**75.0**	(0.7)
Netherlands	94.8	(0.7)	94.7	(0.4)	94.7	(0.4)	95.8	(0.7)	c	c	95.1	(0.4)	93.9	(0.9)
New Zealand	71.3	(0.9)	79.4	(2.3)	57.4	(3.4)	72.1	(0.8)	67.0	(3.5)	73.8	(1.6)	70.1	(1.4)
Norway	86.4	(0.6)	c	c	86.3	(0.6)	c	c	83.1	(1.6)	87.0	(0.8)	86.7	(1.6)
Poland	**50.4**	(1.6)	**76.5**	(3.5)	51.0	(1.5)	c	c	32.4	(3.0)	54.4	(2.1)	72.9	(2.5)
Portugal	62.8	(1.0)	78.1	(3.7)	57.6	(1.4)	69.7	(1.3)	58.9	(5.9)	64.4	(1.2)	65.9	(3.4)
Slovak Republic	79.9	(1.1)	81.0	(5.1)	75.7	(2.0)	83.5	(1.2)	66.7	(4.0)	80.8	(1.2)	**88.9**	(1.6)
Slovenia	72.8	(0.7)	65.9	(5.2)	64.6	(5.1)	73.0	(0.7)	60.2	(11.8)	69.9	(0.8)	77.0	(1.1)
Spain	**83.9**	(0.6)	**89.9**	(0.6)	85.8	(0.4)	c	c	**90.4**	(1.1)	85.4	(0.6)	86.0	(1.0)
Sweden	70.8	(0.9)	75.2	(2.4)	71.9	(0.9)	49.2	(5.7)	71.5	(1.6)	70.9	(1.3)	72.3	(1.6)
Switzerland	71.8	(2.0)	86.3	(2.4)	74.3	(2.0)	69.4	(4.1)	69.7	(7.4)	70.9	(2.4)	81.8	(2.2)
Turkey	8.2	(0.7)	c	c	3.8	(2.3)	8.8	(0.8)	10.7	(4.5)	8.0	(1.3)	9.0	(1.0)
United Kingdom	**67.5**	(0.9)	**71.1**	(1.5)	c	c	68.9	(0.7)	66.7	(2.8)	69.9	(1.0)	67.8	(1.4)
United States	**74.2**	(1.0)	**84.1**	(2.9)	69.2	(2.5)	75.3	(0.9)	72.6	(3.5)	76.6	(1.3)	73.3	(1.3)
OECD average	**73.3**	(0.2)	**79.2**	(0.4)	**68.4**	(0.4)	**73.4**	(0.4)	**67.6**	(0.7)	**73.5**	(0.2)	**76.0**	(0.2)
Albania	52.0	(1.1)	61.8	(6.2)	51.2	(1.5)	54.0	(1.3)	48.8	(2.8)	54.0	(1.2)	53.6	(2.3)
Argentina	**65.5**	(1.8)	**81.9**	(1.8)	62.7	(2.1)	76.0	(1.6)	61.2	(6.2)	71.6	(2.3)	72.5	(1.9)
Brazil	**44.1**	(0.7)	**63.9**	(2.5)	37.2	(1.5)	50.4	(0.9)	43.4	(7.3)	42.4	(0.9)	53.1	(1.1)
Bulgaria	76.8	(1.0)	c	c	35.0	(5.6)	78.8	(0.8)	59.3	(6.6)	75.5	(1.5)	80.6	(1.0)
Colombia	30.3	(1.0)	48.2	(4.0)	30.7	(1.3)	35.0	(1.4)	23.5	(2.1)	33.0	(2.4)	35.8	(1.3)
Costa Rica	40.3	(1.2)	71.0	(3.4)	44.8	(1.4)	45.3	(1.8)	33.7	(2.3)	46.8	(1.8)	55.2	(4.0)
Croatia	50.2	(1.2)	c	c	c	c	50.8	(1.1)	c	c	41.3	(1.4)	66.9	(1.9)
Cyprus*	**73.7**	(0.7)	**67.2**	(1.5)	66.6	(2.3)	73.3	(0.7)	67.3	(2.9)	71.6	(0.9)	**76.0**	(1.0)
Hong Kong-China	96.1	(1.5)	95.1	(0.5)	90.6	(0.9)	97.3	(0.3)	c	c	c	c	95.1	(0.4)
Indonesia	21.5	(1.8)	24.3	(2.8)	22.5	(2.2)	22.5	(2.3)	19.1	(3.7)	21.2	(2.1)	30.5	(4.9)
Jordan	23.9	(1.0)	39.2	(3.3)	26.5	(1.0)	c	c	21.6	(2.7)	24.7	(1.6)	29.6	(1.5)
Kazakhstan	23.8	(1.4)	21.2	(3.0)	25.2	(1.4)	19.9	(1.9)	8.7	(1.5)	21.0	(2.4)	36.7	(2.3)
Latvia	75.3	(1.0)	c	c	76.1	(1.0)	56.6	(4.5)	59.9	(3.2)	80.7	(1.0)	80.2	(1.3)
Liechtenstein	90.4	(1.8)	c	c	90.0	(2.1)	94.4	(3.9)	c	c	90.5	(1.9)	c	c
Lithuania	56.0	(1.0)	c	c	56.3	(1.0)	c	c	26.8	(2.8)	54.8	(1.7)	73.8	(1.2)
Macao-China	c	c	85.6	(0.4)	82.4	(0.7)	89.5	(0.6)	c	c	c	c	85.7	(0.5)
Malaysia	46.3	(1.5)	81.4	(5.3)	45.2	(3.6)	47.6	(1.5)	30.7	(3.0)	46.2	(2.0)	59.0	(2.3)
Montenegro	42.3	(0.7)	c	c	c	c	42.4	(0.7)	c	c	38.6	(0.7)	51.0	(1.6)
Peru	**57.3**	(1.3)	**73.5**	(2.9)	47.9	(1.4)	66.4	(1.3)	52.8	(2.3)	56.4	(1.8)	69.4	(2.0)
Qatar	**20.1**	(0.5)	**40.2**	(0.7)	22.1	(1.0)	29.0	(0.5)	20.7	(1.1)	21.8	(0.6)	34.5	(0.6)
Romania	86.5	(0.8)	c	c	86.5	(0.8)	c	c	76.7	(3.3)	87.3	(1.1)	87.4	(1.1)
Russian Federation	71.0	(1.4)	c	c	72.5	(1.4)	63.7	(2.4)	50.5	(3.1)	71.0	(2.6)	80.0	(1.1)
Serbia	50.1	(1.3)	c	c	c	c	51.1	(1.2)	c	c	45.3	(2.0)	56.9	(2.1)
Shanghai-China	87.5	(1.0)	90.9	(2.3)	84.8	(2.0)	90.1	(0.7)	c	c	c	c	87.8	(1.0)
Singapore	90.9	(0.4)	c	c	67.8	(4.1)	91.1	(0.4)	c	c	c	c	90.8	(0.4)
Chinese Taipei	84.5	(0.8)	82.7	(0.9)	83.8	(1.3)	83.7	(0.7)	c	c	84.0	(1.0)	84.0	(0.8)
Thailand	87.9	(0.7)	87.0	(1.3)	82.5	(1.6)	89.2	(0.6)	84.2	(2.3)	87.1	(0.9)	90.7	(0.8)
Tunisia	23.2	(1.0)	c	c	17.5	(1.4)	26.4	(1.2)	18.5	(3.6)	21.6	(1.2)	28.5	(2.0)
United Arab Emirates	**47.1**	(1.3)	**52.1**	(1.8)	32.2	(1.7)	52.7	(0.9)	46.3	(2.3)	47.2	(2.2)	51.6	(1.2)
Uruguay	**65.6**	(1.1)	**89.3**	(1.4)	58.0	(1.7)	77.6	(1.0)	61.3	(6.1)	65.2	(1.5)	78.1	(1.3)
Viet Nam	66.8	(1.5)	82.2	(3.5)	40.6	(6.7)	71.4	(1.5)	64.9	(2.2)	63.7	(3.2)	79.6	(2.7)

Notes: Values that are statistically significant are indicated in bold (see Annex A3).
ESCS refers to the *PISA index of economic, social and cultural status*.
1. A socio-economically disadvantaged school is one whose students' mean socio-economic status (ESCS) is statistically significantly below the mean socio-economic status of the country/economy; an average school is one where there is no difference from the country's/economy's mean; and an advantaged school is one whose students' mean socio-economic status is statistically significantly above the country/economy mean.
* See notes at the beginning of this Annex.
StatLink ⏹⏺ http://dx.doi.org/10.1787/888932957460

[Part 1/1]
Change between 2003 and 2012 in student-teacher ratio
Table IV.3.35   *Results based on school principals' reports*

| | PISA 2003 | | PISA 2012 | | Change between 2003 and 2012 (PISA 2012 - PISA 2003) | |
| | Student-teacher ratio in the school | | Student-teacher ratio in the school | | Student-teacher ratio in the school | |
	Mean ratio	S.E.	Mean ratio	S.E.	Dif.	S.E.
Australia	13.55	(0.2)	13.15	(0.1)	**-0.40**	(0.2)
Austria	13.04	(0.5)	11.02	(0.4)	**-2.02**	(0.6)
Belgium	9.40	(0.2)	9.27	(0.1)	-0.13	(0.2)
Canada	17.00	(0.1)	15.60	(0.2)	**-1.40**	(0.3)
Czech Republic	15.15	(0.2)	13.13	(0.3)	**-2.03**	(0.4)
Denmark	11.28	(0.2)	12.09	(0.2)	**0.81**	(0.3)
Finland	10.75	(0.2)	10.61	(0.1)	-0.15	(0.2)
France	w	w	11.80	(0.2)	m	m
Germany	17.62	(0.3)	15.13	(0.3)	**-2.49**	(0.5)
Greece	9.69	(0.2)	9.11	(0.3)	-0.58	(0.4)
Hungary	10.26	(0.4)	12.41	(0.3)	**2.15**	(0.5)
Iceland	11.37	(0.0)	10.53	(0.0)	**-0.84**	(0.0)
Ireland	14.31	(0.4)	14.30	(0.2)	-0.01	(0.5)
Italy	10.04	(0.4)	10.31	(0.1)	0.27	(0.4)
Japan	14.00	(0.2)	11.64	(0.2)	**-2.36**	(0.3)
Korea	16.36	(0.1)	16.11	(0.2)	-0.24	(0.3)
Luxembourg	10.25	(0.0)	9.05	(0.0)	**-1.21**	(0.0)
Mexico	m	m	30.59	(0.7)	m	m
Netherlands	15.37	(0.3)	16.76	(0.4)	**1.39**	(0.5)
New Zealand	16.46	(0.2)	15.16	(0.2)	**-1.30**	(0.3)
Norway	10.32	(0.1)	10.44	(0.1)	0.12	(0.2)
Poland	13.30	(0.2)	9.43	(0.2)	**-3.87**	(0.3)
Portugal	10.99	(0.5)	8.85	(0.2)	**-2.14**	(0.5)
Slovak Republic	14.80	(0.2)	13.25	(0.3)	**-1.55**	(0.3)
Spain	13.61	(0.3)	12.54	(0.4)	**-1.08**	(0.5)
Sweden	12.40	(0.3)	12.46	(0.2)	0.06	(0.4)
Switzerland	12.64	(0.4)	12.07	(0.3)	-0.57	(0.5)
Turkey	21.79	(1.5)	17.44	(0.5)	**-4.35**	(1.6)
United States	15.66	(0.3)	17.42	(1.1)	1.76	(1.1)
OECD average 2003	13.39	(0.1)	12.57	(0.1)	**-0.82**	(0.1)
Brazil	33.90	(1.2)	28.16	(0.7)	**-5.74**	(1.4)
Hong Kong-China	18.20	(0.2)	15.42	(0.1)	**-2.78**	(0.2)
Indonesia	m	m	16.87	(0.6)	m	m
Latvia	12.71	(0.2)	9.96	(0.2)	**-2.75**	(0.3)
Indonesia	m	m	16.87	(0.6)	m	m
Liechtenstein	7.47	(0.0)	8.04	(0.0)	**0.58**	(0.0)
Macao-China	24.51	(0.0)	15.68	(0.0)	**-8.84**	(0.0)
Russian Federation	16.28	(1.0)	14.26	(0.2)	-2.03	(1.1)
Thailand	22.79	(0.6)	20.25	(0.4)	**-2.54**	(0.7)
Tunisia	19.42	(0.3)	12.21	(0.7)	**-7.21**	(0.8)
Uruguay	17.84	(0.8)	15.48	(0.3)	**-2.37**	(0.9)

Notes: Values that are statistically significant are indicated in bold (see Annex A3).
Only countries and economies with comparable data from PISA 2003 and PISA 2012 are shown.
StatLink ᵐˢ┑ http://dx.doi.org/10.1787/888932957479

[Part 1/1]
Change between 2003 and 2012 in teacher shortage
Table IV.3.37 *Results based on school principals' reports*

| | PISA 2003 | | | | | | | | PISA 2012 | | | | | | | | Change between 2003 and 2012 (PISA 2012 - PISA 2003) | | | | | | | |
| | Index of teacher shortage | | Qualified mathematics teachers | | Qualified science teachers | | Qualified language-of-assessment teachers | | Index of teacher shortage | | Qualified mathematics teachers | | Qualified science teachers | | Qualified language-of-assessment teachers | | Index of teacher shortage | | Qualified mathematics teachers | | Qualified science teachers | | Qualified language-of-assessment teachers | |
	Mean index	S.E.	%	S.E.	%	S.E.	%	S.E.	Mean index	S.E.	%	S.E.	%	S.E.	%	S.E.	Dif.	S.E.	% dif.	S.E.	% dif.	S.E.	% dif.	S.E.
OECD																								
Australia	0.28	(0.05)	30.1	(3.0)	25.6	(2.8)	13.7	(2.2)	0.20	(0.04)	24.9	(1.5)	31.8	(1.7)	12.4	(1.2)	-0.08	(0.06)	-5.3	(3.4)	6.2	(3.2)	-1.3	(2.5)
Austria	-0.50	(0.06)	6.1	(1.8)	10.9	(2.3)	4.5	(1.6)	-0.13	(0.09)	16.4	(3.2)	13.5	(3.1)	13.8	(2.8)	**0.37**	(0.11)	**10.3**	(3.7)	2.6	(3.8)	**9.4**	(3.3)
Belgium	0.42	(0.07)	36.0	(3.0)	26.4	(2.6)	20.3	(2.8)	0.26	(0.06)	20.9	(2.9)	24.8	(2.8)	9.5	(1.9)	-0.16	(0.09)	**-15.1**	(4.1)	-1.6	(3.8)	**-10.8**	(3.4)
Canada	0.00	(0.05)	19.0	(2.0)	17.7	(1.4)	7.3	(1.0)	-0.30	(0.04)	7.1	(0.8)	12.8	(1.7)	3.7	(0.7)	**-0.29**	(0.06)	**-11.9**	(2.1)	**-4.9**	(2.2)	**-3.6**	(1.2)
Czech Republic	0.18	(0.08)	10.4	(2.2)	15.2	(2.4)	6.3	(1.7)	-0.42	(0.05)	3.9	(0.9)	5.4	(1.6)	1.2	(0.7)	**-0.61**	(0.06)	**-6.5**	(2.4)	**-9.8**	(2.9)	**-5.2**	(1.9)
Denmark	-0.12	(0.06)	3.7	(1.5)	13.5	(2.9)	4.2	(1.7)	-0.18	(0.05)	7.1	(1.8)	3.2	(1.0)	2.1	(1.1)	-0.06	(0.08)	3.4	(2.3)	**-10.3**	(3.0)	-2.1	(2.0)
Finland	-0.56	(0.05)	6.5	(1.5)	4.0	(1.3)	6.5	(2.0)	-0.44	(0.04)	3.9	(1.3)	4.3	(1.3)	1.3	(0.4)	**0.12**	(0.06)	-2.6	(1.9)	0.4	(1.8)	**-5.2**	(2.0)
France	w	w	w	w	w	w	w	w	-0.18	(0.06)	4.8	(1.7)	8.2	(2.3)	7.4	(1.9)	m	m	m	m	m	m	m	m
Germany	0.40	(0.08)	27.7	(3.2)	40.5	(3.2)	20.7	(2.8)	0.42	(0.06)	38.4	(3.3)	18.1	(2.8)	6.8	(1.8)	0.02	(0.10)	**10.7**	(4.6)	**-22.4**	(4.3)	**-14.0**	(3.3)
Greece	0.33	(0.19)	30.4	(5.8)	31.6	(5.8)	29.6	(5.7)	-0.42	(0.07)	9.3	(2.3)	5.3	(1.5)	6.8	(1.8)	**-0.75**	(0.20)	**-21.1**	(6.2)	**-26.3**	(6.0)	**-22.9**	(6.0)
Hungary	-0.41	(0.06)	7.4	(2.0)	7.2	(2.1)	3.0	(1.4)	-0.65	(0.05)	7.0	(1.9)	2.7	(1.3)	1.2	(0.9)	**-0.24**	(0.08)	-0.4	(2.8)	-4.5	(2.5)	-1.8	(1.7)
Iceland	0.27	(0.00)	29.0	(0.2)	42.7	(0.2)	14.3	(0.1)	0.18	(0.00)	28.0	(0.2)	23.4	(0.2)	9.3	(0.1)	**-0.09**	(0.01)	**-1.0**	(0.3)	**-19.3**	(0.3)	**-5.0**	(0.2)
Ireland	-0.08	(0.08)	13.4	(2.9)	10.4	(2.6)	4.8	(1.9)	-0.15	(0.06)	5.6	(1.9)	14.0	(3.0)	4.6	(1.8)	-0.07	(0.10)	**-7.8**	(3.4)	3.6	(3.9)	-0.2	(2.6)
Italy	0.26	(0.08)	19.6	(2.5)	18.8	(2.9)	17.3	(2.6)	0.25	(0.04)	14.4	(1.8)	15.6	(1.7)	14.7	(1.5)	-0.01	(0.09)	-5.2	(3.1)	-3.2	(3.4)	-2.6	(3.0)
Japan	-0.03	(0.13)	20.6	(3.8)	21.2	(3.8)	18.7	(3.5)	-0.29	(0.07)	9.4	(2.3)	8.3	(1.9)	3.5	(1.1)	-0.25	(0.15)	**-11.2**	(4.4)	**-12.9**	(4.3)	**-15.2**	(3.7)
Korea	-0.57	(0.07)	2.7	(1.3)	4.0	(1.6)	1.5	(1.0)	0.06	(0.08)	13.6	(2.4)	12.1	(2.4)	13.2	(2.7)	**0.64**	(0.11)	**10.9**	(2.7)	**8.0**	(2.9)	**11.7**	(2.9)
Luxembourg	0.91	(0.01)	59.7	(0.1)	13.2	(0.1)	63.6	(0.1)	1.12	(0.00)	71.1	(0.1)	68.9	(0.1)	17.9	(0.1)	**0.21**	(0.00)	**11.5**	(0.1)	**55.6**	(0.1)	**-45.7**	(0.1)
Mexico	0.77	(0.07)	35.8	(3.0)	36.3	(3.4)	36.6	(3.4)	0.53	(0.04)	22.9	(1.6)	28.3	(1.7)	25.5	(1.7)	**-0.24**	(0.08)	**-12.9**	(3.4)	**-8.1**	(3.8)	**-11.2**	(3.8)
Netherlands	0.22	(0.08)	21.9	(3.2)	25.6	(3.9)	15.6	(3.1)	0.60	(0.08)	32.0	(3.6)	45.3	(4.0)	22.8	(3.3)	**0.38**	(0.11)	**10.1**	(4.8)	**19.7**	(5.6)	7.2	(4.5)
New Zealand	0.63	(0.06)	41.1	(3.1)	32.3	(2.9)	27.6	(2.7)	0.08	(0.07)	14.7	(2.4)	21.7	(3.0)	7.3	(2.0)	**-0.55**	(0.09)	**-26.4**	(3.9)	**-10.6**	(4.2)	**-20.3**	(3.3)
Norway	0.32	(0.06)	14.7	(2.9)	19.7	(3.3)	10.7	(2.3)	0.31	(0.07)	13.3	(2.7)	18.8	(2.9)	20.1	(3.3)	-0.01	(0.09)	-1.4	(4.0)	-0.9	(4.4)	**9.5**	(4.0)
Poland	0.13	(0.09)	14.9	(3.1)	10.6	(2.5)	9.3	(2.4)	-1.02	(0.02)	0.7	(0.7)	0.0	c	0.0	c	**-1.15**	(0.10)	**-14.1**	(3.1)	-10.6	c	-9.3	c
Portugal	-0.72	(0.07)	5.9	(2.3)	4.0	(1.5)	4.8	(1.7)	-0.80	(0.06)	1.2	(0.8)	0.8	(0.8)	0.8	(0.8)	-0.09	(0.09)	-4.7	(2.5)	-3.2	(1.7)	**-4.0**	(1.9)
Slovak Republic	-0.18	(0.04)	5.7	(1.5)	9.8	(1.9)	4.9	(1.2)	-0.34	(0.05)	5.0	(1.2)	5.3	(1.4)	2.2	(0.8)	**-0.16**	(0.07)	-0.7	(1.9)	-4.4	(2.4)	-2.7	(1.4)
Spain	-0.44	(0.09)	10.1	(2.3)	9.1	(2.5)	9.7	(2.4)	-0.73	(0.03)	2.2	(0.6)	2.2	(0.8)	1.3	(0.6)	**-0.29**	(0.09)	**-8.0**	(2.3)	**-6.9**	(2.6)	**-8.3**	(2.5)
Sweden	0.24	(0.08)	16.8	(2.9)	21.7	(2.6)	17.9	(2.8)	-0.06	(0.05)	20.0	(2.6)	14.2	(2.6)	4.1	(1.6)	**-0.30**	(0.10)	3.3	(3.8)	-7.5	(3.7)	**-13.8**	(3.2)
Switzerland	-0.18	(0.08)	8.8	(2.1)	15.7	(2.9)	9.6	(2.3)	0.05	(0.06)	23.2	(2.6)	14.2	(2.4)	3.6	(1.0)	**0.23**	(0.09)	**14.4**	(3.4)	-1.5	(3.8)	**-6.0**	(2.5)
Turkey	2.21	(0.10)	84.4	(3.0)	77.0	(3.8)	77.6	(4.0)	0.88	(0.06)	41.9	(4.0)	30.6	(3.5)	27.6	(3.5)	**-1.33**	(0.12)	**-42.4**	(5.0)	**-46.4**	(5.1)	**-50.0**	(5.3)
United States	-0.01	(0.07)	22.0	(2.8)	22.3	(2.9)	5.8	(1.6)	-0.42	(0.07)	9.4	(2.1)	9.2	(2.1)	2.3	(1.0)	**-0.41**	(0.10)	**-12.6**	(3.5)	**-13.1**	(3.6)	-3.5	(1.9)
OECD average 2003	0.13	(0.01)	21.6	(0.5)	21.0	(0.5)	16.7	(0.5)	-0.05	(0.01)	16.7	(0.4)	16.2	(0.4)	8.5	(0.3)	**-0.18**	(0.02)	**-4.9**	(0.6)	**-4.7**	(0.7)	**-8.1**	(0.6)
Partners																								
Brazil	0.47	(0.11)	33.3	(3.4)	29.6	(3.2)	24.4	(3.3)	0.19	(0.05)	21.8	(2.2)	18.3	(1.9)	12.8	(1.7)	**-0.27**	(0.12)	**-11.5**	(4.0)	**-11.3**	(3.8)	**-11.7**	(3.7)
Hong Kong-China	-0.01	(0.07)	15.8	(3.0)	7.1	(2.0)	10.0	(2.6)	-0.23	(0.07)	3.9	(1.5)	10.6	(2.5)	5.8	(1.7)	**-0.22**	(0.10)	**-11.9**	(3.3)	3.5	(3.2)	-4.2	(3.1)
Indonesia	1.61	(0.11)	54.3	(4.1)	54.1	(4.4)	48.4	(4.1)	0.27	(0.08)	16.2	(2.9)	12.8	(2.4)	13.1	(2.7)	**-1.35**	(0.14)	**-38.0**	(5.0)	**-41.4**	(5.0)	**-35.3**	(4.9)
Latvia	-0.06	(0.06)	13.7	(3.0)	12.0	(2.9)	8.1	(2.2)	-0.41	(0.06)	6.4	(1.9)	3.3	(1.5)	4.6	(1.6)	**-0.35**	(0.08)	**-7.3**	(3.6)	**-8.7**	(3.2)	-3.5	(2.7)
Liechtenstein	-0.39	(0.01)	0.0	c	0.0	c	0.0	c	0.05	(0.02)	0.0	c	0.0	c	7.1	(0.8)	**0.44**	(0.02)	0.0	c	0.0	c	7.1	c
Macao-China	0.34	(0.00)	18.3	(0.2)	27.4	(0.2)	8.3	(0.1)	0.00	(0.00)	24.1	(0.0)	27.5	(0.1)	15.4	(0.0)	**-0.34**	(0.00)	**5.8**	(0.2)	0.1	(0.2)	**7.1**	(0.1)
Russian Federation	0.59	(0.10)	35.5	(3.8)	33.4	(3.4)	31.0	(3.8)	0.35	(0.07)	24.3	(3.4)	26.5	(3.3)	21.5	(3.4)	**-0.24**	(0.12)	**-11.2**	(5.1)	-6.9	(4.7)	-9.5	(5.1)
Thailand	0.54	(0.10)	37.1	(4.0)	34.3	(3.9)	26.6	(3.6)	0.94	(0.08)	47.4	(3.6)	45.5	(4.1)	44.4	(3.9)	**0.40**	(0.13)	10.3	(5.4)	11.2	(5.6)	17.9	(5.3)
Tunisia	0.23	(0.07)	28.9	(3.8)	16.6	(3.0)	6.3	(2.1)	-0.11	(0.07)	12.3	(2.6)	10.0	(2.6)	9.3	(2.4)	**-0.33**	(0.10)	**-16.6**	(4.6)	-6.6	(3.9)	3.0	(3.2)
Uruguay	0.79	(0.09)	55.9	(3.8)	43.5	(3.8)	27.7	(3.2)	0.35	(0.07)	26.3	(3.1)	33.9	(3.4)	12.6	(2.3)	**-0.45**	(0.12)	**-29.6**	(4.9)	-9.6	(5.1)	**-15.2**	(3.9)

Notes: Values that are statistically significant are indicated in bold (see Annex A3).
Only countries and economies with comparable data from PISA 2003 and PISA 2012 are shown.
For comparability over time, PISA 2003 values on the *index of teacher shortage* have been rescaled to the PISA 2012 scale of the index. PISA 2003 results reported in this table may thus differ from those presented in *Learning for Tomorrow's World: First Results from PISA 2003* (OECD, 2004) (see Annex A5 for more details).
StatLink ᵃᵗˢ⌐ http://dx.doi.org/10.1787/888932957479

[Part 1/1]
Change between 2003 and 2012 in the quality of physical infrastructure
Table IV.3.40 *Results based on school principals' reports*

	PISA 2003								PISA 2012								Change between 2003 and 2012 (PISA 2012 - PISA 2003)							
	Index of quality of physical infrastructure		Percentage of students in schools whose principal reported that the school's capacity to provide instruction is hindered to some extent or a lot by a shortage or inadequacy of the following:						Index of quality of physical infrastructure		Percentage of students in schools whose principal reported that the school's capacity to provide instruction is hindered to some extent or a lot by a shortage or inadequacy of the following:						Index of quality of physical infrastructure		Percentage of students in schools whose principal reported that the school's capacity to provide instruction is hindered to some extent or a lot by a shortage or inadequacy of the following:					
			School buildings and grounds		Heating/cooling and lighting systems		Instructional space (e.g. classrooms)				School buildings and grounds		Heating/cooling and lighting systems		Instructional space (e.g. classrooms)				School buildings and grounds		Heating/cooling and lighting systems		Instructional space (e.g. classrooms)	
	Mean index	S.E.	%	S.E.	%	S.E.	%	S.E.	Mean index	S.E.	%	S.E.	%	S.E.	%	S.E.	Dif.	S.E.	% dif.	S.E.	% dif.	S.E.	% dif.	S.E.
Australia	-0.11	(0.06)	10.7	(2.0)	4.7	(1.1)	5.9	(1.4)	0.17	(0.04)	5.7	(1.0)	3.8	(0.6)	4.0	(0.8)	**0.28**	(0.07)	-5.0	(2.2)	-0.8	(1.3)	-1.9	(1.6)
Austria	-0.15	(0.10)	22.0	(3.7)	6.9	(2.1)	15.7	(3.0)	-0.16	(0.09)	10.2	(2.4)	6.3	(2.3)	17.7	(3.5)	0.00	(0.14)	**-11.8**	(4.5)	-0.7	(3.1)	2.0	(4.7)
Belgium	-0.21	(0.07)	16.2	(2.6)	6.6	(1.7)	11.4	(2.0)	-0.15	(0.06)	12.5	(2.0)	4.1	(1.2)	7.5	(1.7)	0.06	(0.09)	-4.0	(1.4)	-2.0	(1.2)	**-3.3**	(1.5)
Canada	-0.10	(0.04)	7.2	(1.3)	4.6	(0.9)	6.4	(1.1)	0.32	(0.04)	3.2	(0.7)	2.6	(0.8)	3.2	(0.9)	**0.42**	(0.06)	**-4.0**	(1.4)	-2.0	(1.2)	**-3.3**	(1.5)
Czech Republic	0.30	(0.06)	3.2	(1.3)	0.7	(0.5)	1.1	(0.7)	0.45	(0.06)	1.6	(0.9)	3.1	(1.3)	2.3	(1.2)	0.14	(0.08)	-1.6	(1.6)	2.4	(1.4)	1.2	(1.4)
Denmark	-0.48	(0.07)	13.0	(2.5)	6.9	(2.1)	16.2	(3.0)	-0.17	(0.05)	6.4	(1.6)	2.2	(0.9)	6.8	(1.5)	**0.31**	(0.09)	**-6.6**	(3.0)	**-4.6**	(2.3)	**-9.4**	(3.4)
Finland	-0.55	(0.08)	14.3	(2.9)	13.9	(2.9)	9.2	(2.2)	-0.32	(0.07)	11.7	(2.3)	7.3	(1.7)	8.1	(2.0)	**0.24**	(0.10)	-2.7	(3.7)	**-6.6**	(3.4)	-1.1	(3.0)
France	w	w	w	w	w	w	w	w	0.19	(0.07)	6.1	(1.7)	3.1	(1.4)	2.7	(1.1)	m	m	m	m	m	m	m	m
Germany	-0.15	(0.09)	15.8	(2.6)	8.6	(1.8)	14.5	(2.6)	-0.03	(0.06)	7.9	(2.0)	3.7	(1.5)	10.6	(2.3)	0.12	(0.11)	**-7.9**	(3.3)	**-4.9**	(2.4)	-3.9	(3.5)
Greece	-0.74	(0.14)	33.3	(4.7)	19.8	(3.8)	30.8	(5.1)	-0.19	(0.08)	18.1	(3.6)	6.0	(1.8)	12.1	(2.6)	**0.56**	(0.16)	**-15.2**	(5.9)	**-13.8**	(4.2)	**-18.6**	(5.7)
Hungary	-0.49	(0.08)	17.2	(3.1)	10.2	(2.3)	27.6	(3.3)	0.21	(0.07)	3.0	(1.3)	2.6	(1.3)	4.2	(1.5)	**0.70**	(0.11)	**-14.2**	(3.3)	**-7.5**	(2.7)	**-23.4**	(3.6)
Iceland	0.05	(0.00)	10.3	(0.1)	2.1	(0.0)	10.5	(0.1)	0.34	(0.00)	7.5	(0.1)	0.0	c	2.2	(0.0)	**0.29**	(0.00)	-2.8	(0.1)	-2.1	c	**-8.3**	(0.1)
Ireland	-0.59	(0.10)	36.0	(4.0)	12.3	(3.0)	27.2	(4.0)	-0.03	(0.09)	26.1	(3.8)	5.8	(2.1)	18.2	(3.4)	**0.56**	(0.14)	-9.9	(5.6)	-6.5	(3.8)	-8.9	(5.2)
Italy	-0.33	(0.08)	19.7	(2.8)	8.3	(2.2)	18.1	(2.8)	-0.33	(0.04)	17.9	(1.6)	10.0	(1.1)	13.0	(1.4)	0.00	(0.09)	-1.8	(3.2)	1.8	(2.5)	-5.1	(3.2)
Japan	-0.39	(0.10)	16.7	(3.5)	13.8	(3.1)	14.1	(3.1)	-0.13	(0.07)	14.9	(2.4)	8.1	(1.8)	9.4	(2.3)	**0.26**	(0.12)	-1.8	(4.2)	-5.7	(3.6)	-4.7	(3.9)
Korea	0.31	(0.07)	4.3	(1.7)	4.2	(1.7)	3.2	(0.9)	-0.18	(0.08)	10.1	(2.6)	4.3	(1.8)	14.7	(2.9)	**-0.49**	(0.10)	5.8	(3.2)	0.1	(2.5)	**11.5**	(3.1)
Luxembourg	-0.46	(0.00)	24.8	(0.1)	4.9	(0.0)	16.2	(0.1)	-0.49	(0.00)	25.7	(0.1)	2.1	(0.0)	19.1	(0.1)	**-0.03**	(0.00)	0.9	(0.1)	**-2.9**	(0.1)	**2.9**	(0.1)
Mexico	-0.40	(0.07)	17.1	(2.2)	17.8	(2.4)	15.0	(2.3)	-0.40	(0.04)	14.7	(1.5)	21.9	(1.3)	11.3	(1.3)	0.00	(0.08)	-2.4	(2.6)	4.1	(2.7)	-3.7	(2.6)
Netherlands	0.00	(0.10)	15.0	(3.3)	7.7	(2.1)	12.2	(2.8)	-0.29	(0.08)	10.1	(2.3)	12.5	(2.3)	13.3	(3.1)	**-0.28**	(0.12)	-4.8	(4.0)	4.8	(3.1)	1.1	(4.2)
New Zealand	-0.04	(0.05)	6.5	(1.8)	1.8	(0.9)	6.3	(1.3)	0.03	(0.09)	10.4	(3.3)	1.2	(0.7)	9.8	(3.1)	0.07	(0.10)	4.0	(3.8)	-0.6	(1.1)	3.5	(3.3)
Norway	-0.83	(0.07)	22.8	(3.5)	20.7	(3.0)	15.3	(2.6)	-0.31	(0.08)	9.3	(2.1)	12.4	(2.5)	6.8	(2.1)	**0.52**	(0.10)	**-13.5**	(4.0)	**-8.3**	(4.0)	**-8.5**	(3.3)
Poland	0.00	(0.08)	15.0	(2.8)	2.6	(1.3)	7.2	(2.2)	0.50	(0.07)	4.2	(1.7)	2.2	(1.2)	2.8	(1.4)	**0.50**	(0.10)	**-10.8**	(3.3)	-0.4	(1.8)	-4.4	(2.6)
Portugal	-0.27	(0.08)	12.1	(3.2)	9.7	(2.3)	7.7	(2.6)	-0.26	(0.09)	7.8	(2.3)	12.3	(2.9)	5.8	(1.8)	0.00	(0.10)	-4.3	(3.9)	2.6	(3.7)	-1.9	(3.2)
Slovak Republic	-0.63	(0.05)	23.4	(3.0)	11.1	(2.4)	17.1	(2.3)	-0.13	(0.07)	12.9	(2.4)	8.4	(2.1)	4.3	(1.3)	**0.50**	(0.09)	**-10.5**	(3.8)	-2.7	(3.2)	**-12.7**	(2.6)
Spain	-0.16	(0.07)	14.2	(2.7)	9.3	(2.5)	12.3	(2.1)	0.01	(0.05)	10.2	(1.8)	6.7	(1.5)	10.7	(1.8)	0.17	(0.09)	-3.9	(3.3)	-2.6	(2.9)	-1.5	(2.7)
Sweden	-0.27	(0.07)	16.1	(2.6)	3.6	(1.4)	9.5	(2.0)	0.21	(0.08)	6.8	(1.9)	4.5	(1.6)	4.6	(1.4)	**0.48**	(0.11)	**-9.3**	(3.3)	0.9	(2.1)	**-4.9**	(2.5)
Switzerland	0.11	(0.06)	5.7	(1.6)	2.5	(1.2)	6.1	(1.7)	0.29	(0.05)	4.6	(1.4)	1.0	(0.4)	3.7	(1.2)	0.19	(0.08)	-1.1	(2.1)	-1.5	(1.3)	-2.4	(2.1)
Turkey	-1.48	(0.10)	48.2	(4.9)	50.0	(5.1)	45.2	(5.1)	-0.25	(0.07)	22.8	(3.2)	7.5	(2.0)	17.4	(2.7)	**1.22**	(0.12)	**-25.3**	(5.8)	**-42.5**	(5.5)	**-27.9**	(5.7)
United States	0.01	(0.07)	6.8	(1.7)	2.7	(1.1)	7.9	(2.0)	0.46	(0.06)	2.4	(1.2)	0.0	c	5.1	(2.2)	**0.45**	(0.09)	**-4.5**	(2.1)	-2.7	c	-2.8	(2.9)
OECD average 2003	-0.29	(0.01)	16.7	(0.5)	9.6	(0.4)	13.9	(0.5)	-0.03	(0.01)	10.7	(0.4)	5.8	(0.3)	8.9	(0.4)	**0.26**	(0.02)	**-6.0**	(0.7)	**-3.8**	(0.6)	**-5.0**	(0.6)
Brazil	-0.35	(0.10)	23.6	(3.5)	21.9	(3.2)	19.8	(3.3)	-0.35	(0.05)	17.8	(1.9)	26.8	(2.2)	9.5	(1.5)	0.00	(0.11)	-5.7	(4.0)	4.9	(3.9)	**-10.3**	(3.6)
Hong Kong-China	-0.31	(0.07)	20.4	(3.5)	1.6	(1.1)	18.7	(3.4)	-0.02	(0.07)	13.5	(3.1)	0.5	(0.5)	10.3	(2.7)	**0.28**	(0.10)	-6.9	(4.7)	-1.0	(1.2)	-8.4	(4.4)
Indonesia	-0.86	(0.08)	38.6	(4.3)	18.9	(3.0)	46.4	(4.1)	-0.52	(0.08)	10.3	(2.8)	40.5	(4.6)	5.2	(1.8)	**0.34**	(0.12)	**-28.3**	(5.1)	**21.6**	(5.5)	**-41.2**	(4.5)
Latvia	-0.24	(0.08)	6.9	(2.1)	9.3	(2.5)	7.7	(2.2)	0.38	(0.06)	3.5	(1.4)	2.4	(1.2)	1.6	(1.0)	**0.61**	(0.10)	-3.4	(2.5)	**-7.0**	(2.8)	**-6.1**	(2.4)
Liechtenstein	0.27	(0.01)	1.2	(0.0)	0.0	c	0.0	c	0.11	(0.02)	0.0	c	0.0	c	0.0	c	**-0.16**	(0.02)	-1.2	c	0.0	c	0.0	c
Macao-China	-0.57	(0.00)	32.5	(0.2)	3.9	(0.1)	21.0	(0.2)	-0.11	(0.00)	17.2	(0.1)	3.5	(0.0)	15.2	(0.0)	**0.46**	(0.00)	**-15.2**	(0.2)	**-0.4**	(0.1)	**-5.8**	(0.2)
Russian Federation	-0.40	(0.11)	15.3	(3.3)	19.3	(3.0)	10.8	(2.5)	0.17	(0.07)	8.2	(1.9)	3.8	(1.3)	4.4	(1.6)	**0.56**	(0.13)	-7.2	(3.8)	**-15.4**	(3.2)	**-6.4**	(3.0)
Thailand	-0.30	(0.08)	14.6	(2.4)	10.4	(2.3)	8.1	(1.9)	-0.87	(0.08)	31.4	(3.6)	16.7	(2.8)	31.4	(3.6)	**-0.58**	(0.11)	**16.8**	(4.3)	6.2	(3.7)	**23.3**	(4.1)
Tunisia	-0.66	(0.07)	25.2	(3.8)	32.4	(3.9)	6.0	(2.0)	-1.25	(0.08)	33.1	(4.0)	63.7	(3.9)	20.4	(3.3)	**-0.59**	(0.11)	7.9	(5.5)	**31.4**	(5.5)	**14.3**	(3.9)
Uruguay	-0.98	(0.07)	25.1	(4.0)	43.0	(3.8)	28.5	(3.7)	-0.41	(0.09)	18.4	(2.9)	20.8	(3.0)	19.8	(2.9)	**0.57**	(0.12)	-6.6	(4.9)	**-22.2**	(4.9)	-8.8	(4.7)

Notes: Values that are statistically significant are indicated in bold (see Annex A3).
Only countries and economies with comparable data from PISA 2003 and PISA 2012 are shown.
For comparability over time, PISA 2003 values on the *index of quality of physical infrastructure* have been rescaled to the PISA 2012 scale of the index. PISA 2003 results reported in this table may thus differ from those presented in *Learning for Tomorrow's World: First Results from PISA 2003* (OECD, 2004) (see Annex A5 for more details).
StatLink ⟐ http://dx.doi.org/10.1787/888932957479

[Part 1/3]

Change between 2003 and 2012 in the quality of schools' educational resources

Table IV.3.43 *Results based on school principals' reports*

		Index of quality of schools' educational resources		PISA 2003 Percentage of students in schools whose principal reported that the school's capacity to provide instruction is hindered a lot by a shortage or inadequacy of the following:									
				Science laboratory equipment		Instructional materials (e.g. textbooks)		Computers for instruction		Computer software for instruction		Library materials	
		Mean index	S.E.	%	S.E.	%	S.E.	%	S.E.	%	S.E.	%	S.E.
OECD	Australia	0.27	(0.07)	9.5	(1.7)	2.2	(0.9)	13.1	(1.8)	0.7	(0.5)	3.1	(0.9)
	Austria	0.06	(0.08)	1.4	(0.9)	0.9	(0.7)	11.6	(2.7)	2.9	(1.4)	6.5	(2.1)
	Belgium	-0.12	(0.06)	8.2	(1.9)	11.2	(2.2)	25.0	(3.0)	4.0	(1.3)	10.5	(2.1)
	Canada	-0.34	(0.05)	8.0	(1.1)	2.5	(0.8)	14.6	(1.5)	4.5	(1.1)	10.8	(1.3)
	Czech Republic	-0.41	(0.06)	19.8	(2.0)	0.6	(0.6)	5.0	(1.4)	3.8	(1.2)	22.9	(3.0)
	Denmark	-0.32	(0.07)	0.9	(0.7)	1.4	(1.0)	5.0	(1.7)	2.7	(1.2)	4.0	(1.6)
	Finland	-0.37	(0.06)	0.7	(0.7)	0.0	(0.0)	7.9	(2.0)	0.8	(0.7)	4.6	(1.7)
	France	w	w	w	w	w	w	w	w	w	w	w	w
	Germany	-0.13	(0.08)	10.6	(2.4)	4.6	(1.4)	44.1	(3.9)	6.5	(1.6)	8.3	(1.9)
	Greece	-0.78	(0.13)	11.0	(3.2)	21.5	(5.0)	10.7	(3.9)	23.3	(4.5)	21.2	(4.2)
	Hungary	-0.24	(0.08)	1.0	(0.6)	0.0	c	9.4	(2.4)	1.5	(1.1)	28.5	(3.6)
	Iceland	-0.03	(0.00)	2.2	(0.1)	0.6	(0.1)	7.5	(0.1)	3.4	(0.0)	1.9	(0.0)
	Ireland	-0.36	(0.08)	1.3	(0.9)	2.6	(0.9)	50.5	(4.6)	0.8	(0.8)	21.7	(3.7)
	Italy	-0.16	(0.07)	4.1	(1.5)	4.5	(1.3)	10.3	(2.2)	6.5	(1.9)	6.8	(2.1)
	Japan	-0.25	(0.10)	8.2	(2.3)	5.5	(1.9)	0.0	c	8.9	(2.4)	9.6	(2.5)
	Korea	0.38	(0.06)	3.8	(1.6)	2.0	(1.2)	2.4	(1.2)	0.6	(0.7)	0.6	(0.7)
	Luxembourg	-0.04	(0.00)	13.1	(0.0)	10.9	(0.0)	15.3	(0.0)	0.0	c	4.3	(0.0)
	Mexico	-0.69	(0.09)	8.6	(1.9)	9.3	(2.2)	20.8	(2.8)	11.3	(2.1)	15.4	(2.4)
	Netherlands	0.15	(0.06)	5.6	(2.1)	8.0	(2.5)	27.1	(3.7)	1.0	(0.7)	2.8	(1.9)
	New Zealand	0.00	(0.06)	6.2	(1.4)	7.8	(1.5)	8.2	(1.6)	2.7	(1.4)	5.7	(1.8)
	Norway	-0.70	(0.05)	3.1	(1.3)	0.7	(0.7)	4.9	(1.7)	2.7	(1.3)	5.5	(1.6)
	Poland	-1.02	(0.07)	19.0	(3.3)	5.3	(1.8)	8.5	(2.1)	18.4	(2.8)	16.5	(2.8)
	Portugal	-0.35	(0.07)	1.2	(0.8)	5.2	(1.9)	5.4	(1.9)	1.1	(0.9)	3.8	(1.6)
	Slovak Republic	-1.10	(0.05)	11.4	(1.9)	0.8	(0.6)	5.1	(1.5)	19.9	(2.7)	53.9	(3.3)
	Spain	-0.41	(0.07)	5.6	(1.8)	6.4	(2.1)	16.8	(2.5)	6.3	(1.8)	7.5	(1.5)
	Sweden	-0.31	(0.07)	8.9	(2.2)	3.9	(1.4)	8.2	(2.1)	4.9	(1.7)	3.9	(1.5)
	Switzerland	0.20	(0.07)	3.1	(1.5)	3.9	(1.6)	7.0	(1.4)	2.6	(1.3)	2.3	(1.0)
	Turkey	-1.91	(0.11)	41.7	(4.2)	51.1	(4.4)	22.2	(4.3)	51.4	(4.4)	42.1	(3.8)
	United States	0.25	(0.09)	2.8	(1.0)	2.3	(1.2)	8.2	(1.5)	2.0	(0.9)	6.9	(2.1)
	OECD average 2003	-0.31	(0.01)	7.9	(0.4)	6.3	(0.4)	13.4	(0.5)	7.0	(0.4)	11.8	(0.4)
Partners	Brazil	-1.17	(0.10)	17.9	(3.3)	11.4	(2.4)	31.9	(3.5)	20.3	(2.7)	29.5	(3.1)
	Hong Kong-China	0.03	(0.08)	2.2	(2.2)	1.4	(1.0)	3.4	(1.5)	0.8	(0.8)	1.5	(1.0)
	Indonesia	-1.08	(0.09)	36.2	(3.8)	43.0	(4.0)	13.2	(2.3)	47.9	(3.9)	38.9	(3.7)
	Latvia	-0.80	(0.07)	4.3	(1.7)	1.0	(1.0)	9.9	(2.7)	9.4	(2.3)	16.1	(2.8)
	Liechtenstein	0.52	(0.01)	0.0	c	0.0	c	9.5	(0.1)	0.0	c	1.2	(0.0)
	Macao-China	-0.46	(0.00)	2.4	(0.0)	13.0	(0.2)	3.2	(0.0)	0.3	(0.0)	0.0	c
	Russian Federation	-1.58	(0.08)	16.3	(2.7)	10.3	(2.8)	24.3	(3.9)	27.6	(3.6)	27.0	(3.2)
	Thailand	-0.82	(0.10)	11.7	(2.7)	3.0	(1.4)	16.4	(2.9)	15.8	(3.0)	13.5	(2.9)
	Tunisia	-0.68	(0.07)	6.8	(2.1)	6.3	(1.9)	24.5	(3.0)	5.1	(1.8)	3.1	(1.4)
	Uruguay	-1.21	(0.09)	18.5	(3.4)	14.3	(3.2)	29.7	(4.5)	31.8	(3.8)	46.2	(4.0)

Notes: Values that are statistically significant are indicated in bold (see Annex A3).
Only countries and economies with comparable data from PISA 2003 and PISA 2012 are shown.
For comparability over time, PISA 2003 values on the *index of quality of schools' educational resources* have been rescaled to the PISA 2012 scale of the index. PISA 2003 results reported in this table may thus differ from those presented in *Learning for Tomorrow's World: First Results from PISA 2003* (OECD, 2004) (see Annex A5 for more details).
StatLink http://dx.doi.org/10.1787/888932957479

[Part 2/3]
Change between 2003 and 2012 in the quality of schools' educational resources
Table IV.3.43   *Results based on school principals' reports*

		Index of quality of schools' educational resources		Science laboratory equipment		Instructional materials (e.g. textbooks)		Computers for instruction		Computer software for instruction		Library materials	
		Mean index	S.E.	%	S.E.	%	S.E.	%	S.E.	%	S.E.	%	S.E.
OECD	Australia	0.68	(0.03)	1.7	(0.5)	0.9	(0.4)	0.7	(0.3)	0.8	(0.3)	0.8	(0.4)
	Austria	0.22	(0.09)	18.5	(3.3)	1.7	(1.0)	10.2	(2.5)	2.9	(1.3)	2.4	(1.1)
	Belgium	0.30	(0.06)	3.2	(1.1)	0.7	(0.5)	6.1	(1.6)	2.9	(1.1)	4.6	(1.2)
	Canada	0.27	(0.04)	2.1	(0.9)	1.0	(0.6)	5.8	(1.4)	2.7	(0.8)	1.6	(0.6)
	Czech Republic	0.05	(0.06)	7.4	(2.0)	1.6	(0.8)	2.5	(1.2)	1.7	(0.9)	6.3	(1.9)
	Denmark	-0.15	(0.05)	2.5	(1.3)	1.8	(1.5)	10.8	(2.2)	1.2	(0.8)	1.0	(0.7)
	Finland	-0.20	(0.06)	1.5	(0.3)	3.6	(1.4)	11.4	(2.3)	6.2	(1.5)	5.4	(1.4)
	France	0.38	(0.07)	2.6	(1.1)	0.8	(0.6)	3.7	(1.2)	2.8	(1.1)	2.4	(0.9)
	Germany	0.09	(0.07)	5.8	(1.8)	0.0	c	4.3	(1.4)	2.0	(0.8)	2.4	(1.1)
	Greece	-0.35	(0.07)	13.0	(2.7)	11.7	(2.6)	17.8	(3.2)	10.4	(2.5)	20.1	(3.3)
	Hungary	0.17	(0.06)	11.8	(2.7)	2.8	(1.3)	3.2	(1.3)	3.5	(1.5)	2.8	(1.6)
	Iceland	-0.34	(0.00)	14.4	(0.2)	0.0	c	20.0	(0.1)	5.4	(0.1)	3.0	(0.1)
	Ireland	0.11	(0.08)	9.4	(2.4)	1.3	(0.9)	8.8	(2.4)	4.8	(1.9)	13.7	(2.9)
	Italy	0.05	(0.04)	8.5	(1.1)	1.2	(0.4)	3.5	(0.7)	5.0	(0.9)	5.5	(0.9)
	Japan	0.44	(0.08)	5.1	(1.7)	0.5	(0.5)	5.6	(1.9)	7.7	(2.0)	2.3	(1.0)
	Korea	0.06	(0.08)	6.5	(2.2)	0.6	(0.6)	3.1	(1.4)	2.9	(1.5)	7.6	(2.4)
	Luxembourg	0.04	(0.00)	5.6	(0.1)	0.0	c	6.1	(0.0)	3.2	(0.0)	5.2	(0.1)
	Mexico	-0.86	(0.04)	31.0	(1.7)	11.1	(1.2)	30.9	(1.9)	26.5	(1.6)	14.5	(1.0)
	Netherlands	0.19	(0.08)	4.6	(1.8)	0.0	c	12.4	(2.6)	7.1	(2.0)	1.3	(1.0)
	New Zealand	0.20	(0.08)	1.2	(0.7)	0.8	(0.1)	6.4	(2.1)	0.4	(0.4)	0.1	(0.1)
	Norway	-0.19	(0.06)	7.8	(1.9)	1.1	(0.8)	5.0	(1.6)	1.8	(1.1)	10.9	(2.3)
	Poland	0.36	(0.08)	4.1	(1.6)	0.0	c	6.3	(1.7)	4.8	(1.5)	2.5	(1.3)
	Portugal	0.17	(0.08)	4.5	(1.5)	0.8	(0.8)	8.7	(2.2)	4.6	(1.8)	2.2	(1.2)
	Slovak Republic	-0.54	(0.05)	15.4	(2.5)	18.4	(2.7)	3.3	(1.1)	5.8	(1.8)	5.2	(1.6)
	Spain	0.02	(0.05)	5.4	(1.3)	0.4	(0.2)	9.9	(1.4)	4.2	(1.0)	2.5	(0.7)
	Sweden	0.05	(0.06)	2.7	(1.2)	0.0	c	15.9	(2.7)	5.2	(1.7)	4.0	(1.2)
	Switzerland	0.55	(0.07)	1.6	(0.5)	1.2	(0.7)	4.8	(1.6)	1.5	(0.7)	2.4	(1.0)
	Turkey	-0.40	(0.06)	22.1	(3.1)	8.3	(2.2)	15.0	(2.6)	9.8	(2.4)	9.8	(2.2)
	United States	0.38	(0.08)	4.2	(1.7)	3.3	(1.5)	5.5	(1.9)	2.2	(1.2)	1.1	(0.6)
	OECD average 2003	0.05	(0.01)	7.9	(0.3)	2.7	(0.3)	8.7	(0.4)	4.9	(0.3)	5.0	(0.3)
Partners	Brazil	-0.54	(0.05)	41.2	(1.9)	2.9	(0.7)	21.6	(2.2)	25.6	(2.3)	12.5	(1.6)
	Hong Kong-China	0.44	(0.07)	1.0	(0.8)	0.9	(0.7)	2.4	(1.2)	1.9	(1.1)	1.3	(0.9)
	Indonesia	-0.76	(0.10)	28.8	(3.7)	9.6	(2.2)	23.1	(3.5)	21.0	(3.6)	13.8	(3.1)
	Latvia	0.04	(0.05)	7.4	(1.9)	4.1	(1.6)	7.5	(2.0)	3.0	(1.3)	4.8	(1.7)
	Liechtenstein	0.77	(0.01)	0.0	c	0.0	c	0.0	c	0.0	c	0.0	c
	Macao-China	0.36	(0.00)	0.0	c	2.4	(0.0)	0.1	(0.0)	0.3	(0.0)	4.0	(0.0)
	Russian Federation	-0.48	(0.07)	17.1	(2.5)	3.4	(1.1)	12.8	(2.7)	12.0	(1.7)	5.0	(1.2)
	Thailand	-0.68	(0.07)	26.2	(3.4)	2.7	(1.2)	14.3	(2.5)	15.1	(2.6)	19.9	(2.5)
	Tunisia	-1.34	(0.08)	30.8	(3.7)	17.3	(3.1)	37.0	(4.6)	25.3	(3.9)	47.9	(3.6)
	Uruguay	0.12	(0.08)	8.2	(2.2)	6.9	(1.9)	12.3	(2.3)	13.1	(2.6)	6.7	(1.9)

Notes: Values that are statistically significant are indicated in bold (see Annex A3).
Only countries and economies with comparable data from PISA 2003 and PISA 2012 are shown.
For comparability over time, PISA 2003 values on the *index of quality of schools' educational resources* have been rescaled to the PISA 2012 scale of the index. PISA 2003 results reported in this table may thus differ from those presented in *Learning for Tomorrow's World: First Results from PISA 2003* (OECD, 2004) (see Annex A5 for more details).
StatLink http://dx.doi.org/10.1787/888932957479

[Part 3/3]
Change between 2003 and 2012 in the quality of schools' educational resources

Table IV.3.43   *Results based on school principals' reports*

		Change between 2003 and 2012 (PISA 2012 - PISA 2003)										
		Index of quality of schools' educational resources		Percentage of students in schools whose principal reported that the school's capacity to provide instruction is hindered a lot by a shortage or inadequacy of the following:									
				Science laboratory equipment		Instructional materials (e.g. textbooks)		Computers for instruction		Computer software for instruction		Library materials	
		Dif.	S.E.	% dif.	S.E.	% dif.	S.E.	% dif.	S.E.	% dif.	S.E.	% dif.	S.E.
OECD	Australia	**0.41**	(0.08)	**-7.8**	(1.8)	-1.3	(1.0)	**-12.4**	(1.8)	0.1	(0.6)	**-2.3**	(0.9)
	Austria	0.16	(0.12)	**17.1**	(3.4)	0.8	(1.2)	-1.4	(3.6)	0.0	(1.9)	-4.1	(2.3)
	Belgium	**0.42**	(0.09)	**-5.0**	(2.3)	**-10.6**	(2.2)	**-18.9**	(3.4)	-1.1	(1.7)	**-5.9**	(2.4)
	Canada	**0.61**	(0.06)	**-5.8**	(1.4)	-1.5	(1.0)	**-8.8**	(2.0)	-1.9	(1.3)	**-9.2**	(1.4)
	Czech Republic	**0.46**	(0.09)	**-12.4**	(2.8)	1.0	(1.0)	-2.6	(1.8)	-2.1	(1.5)	**-16.6**	(3.5)
	Denmark	**0.18**	(0.09)	1.6	(1.4)	0.4	(1.8)	5.8	(2.8)	-1.5	(1.4)	-3.0	(1.8)
	Finland	**0.17**	(0.08)	0.8	(0.7)	**3.6**	(1.4)	3.5	(3.0)	**5.5**	(1.6)	0.8	(2.2)
	France	m	m	m	m	m	m	m	m	m	m	m	m
	Germany	**0.22**	(0.10)	-4.9	(3.0)	-4.6	c	**-39.9**	(4.1)	**-4.5**	(1.8)	**-5.8**	(2.2)
	Greece	**0.43**	(0.15)	1.9	(4.1)	-9.8	(5.6)	7.1	(5.1)	**-13.0**	(5.1)	-1.1	(5.4)
	Hungary	**0.41**	(0.10)	**10.8**	(2.7)	2.8	c	**-6.2**	(2.7)	2.0	(1.8)	**-25.7**	(4.0)
	Iceland	**-0.31**	(0.01)	**12.2**	(0.2)	-0.6	c	**12.4**	(0.2)	**2.0**	(0.1)	**1.2**	(0.1)
	Ireland	**0.47**	(0.11)	**8.1**	(2.6)	-1.3	(1.3)	**-41.7**	(5.2)	4.0	(2.0)	-8.0	(4.7)
	Italy	**0.20**	(0.08)	**4.4**	(1.9)	**-3.3**	(1.4)	**-6.8**	(2.3)	-1.5	(2.1)	-1.2	(2.3)
	Japan	**0.69**	(0.13)	-3.1	(2.9)	**-5.0**	(2.0)	5.6	c	-1.2	(3.1)	**-7.2**	(2.7)
	Korea	**-0.32**	(0.10)	2.8	(2.7)	-1.4	(1.3)	0.7	(1.9)	2.2	(1.6)	**7.0**	(2.5)
	Luxembourg	**0.07**	(0.00)	**-7.6**	(0.1)	**-10.9**	c	**-9.2**	(0.1)	**3.2**	c	**0.9**	(0.1)
	Mexico	-0.16	(0.10)	**22.3**	(2.6)	1.8	(2.5)	**10.1**	(3.4)	**15.2**	(2.6)	-0.9	(2.6)
	Netherlands	0.04	(0.10)	-1.0	(2.8)	**-8.0**	c	**-14.8**	(4.5)	**6.1**	(2.1)	-1.5	(2.1)
	New Zealand	**0.20**	(0.10)	**-5.0**	(1.6)	**-6.9**	(1.5)	-1.8	(2.7)	-2.4	(1.5)	**-5.6**	(1.8)
	Norway	**0.51**	(0.08)	**4.7**	(2.3)	0.4	(1.0)	0.2	(2.3)	-0.8	(1.7)	5.4	(2.8)
	Poland	**1.38**	(0.10)	**-14.9**	(3.7)	-5.3	c	-2.2	(2.7)	**-13.6**	(3.2)	**-14.1**	(3.1)
	Portugal	**0.52**	(0.11)	3.3	(1.7)	**-4.3**	(2.0)	3.2	(2.9)	3.5	(2.0)	-1.6	(2.0)
	Slovak Republic	**0.55**	(0.07)	4.0	(3.2)	**17.6**	(2.8)	-1.7	(1.9)	**-14.0**	(3.2)	**-48.7**	(3.7)
	Spain	**0.43**	(0.09)	-0.2	(2.2)	**-6.0**	(2.1)	**-6.9**	(2.8)	-2.1	(2.1)	**-5.0**	(1.7)
	Sweden	**0.36**	(0.09)	**-6.2**	(2.5)	-3.9	c	**7.7**	(3.5)	0.3	(2.4)	0.2	(1.9)
	Switzerland	**0.35**	(0.10)	-1.5	(1.6)	-2.7	(1.7)	-2.3	(2.1)	-1.1	(1.4)	0.0	(1.4)
	Turkey	**1.51**	(0.13)	**-19.5**	(5.2)	**-42.7**	(4.9)	-7.3	(5.1)	**-41.7**	(5.0)	**-32.2**	(4.4)
	United States	0.13	(0.12)	1.4	(2.0)	1.0	(1.9)	-2.7	(2.4)	0.2	(1.5)	**-5.8**	(2.1)
	OECD average 2003	**0.36**	(0.02)	0.0	(0.5)	**-3.6**	(0.5)	**-4.7**	(0.6)	**-2.1**	(0.5)	**-6.8**	(0.5)
Partners	Brazil	**0.63**	(0.11)	**23.2**	(3.8)	**-8.5**	(2.5)	**-10.2**	(4.1)	5.3	(3.5)	**-17.0**	(3.5)
	Hong Kong-China	**0.41**	(0.10)	-1.2	(2.3)	-0.4	(1.2)	-1.0	(1.9)	1.1	(1.4)	-0.2	(1.3)
	Indonesia	**0.33**	(0.14)	-7.5	(5.3)	**-33.3**	(4.6)	**10.0**	(4.1)	**-27.0**	(5.3)	**-25.1**	(4.9)
	Latvia	**0.83**	(0.08)	3.1	(2.6)	3.0	(1.9)	-2.3	(3.4)	**-6.4**	(2.6)	**-11.3**	(3.3)
	Liechtenstein	**0.24**	(0.01)	0.0	c	0.0	c	-9.5	c	0.0	c	-1.2	c
	Macao-China	**0.82**	(0.00)	-2.4	c	**-10.6**	(0.2)	-3.1	(0.0)	0.0	(0.0)	4.0	c
	Russian Federation	**1.10**	(0.11)	0.8	(3.7)	**-6.9**	(3.0)	**-11.5**	(4.7)	**-15.6**	(4.0)	**-21.9**	(3.4)
	Thailand	0.14	(0.12)	**14.5**	(4.3)	-0.3	(1.8)	-2.1	(3.8)	-0.7	(3.9)	6.4	(3.8)
	Tunisia	**-0.66**	(0.11)	**24.0**	(4.3)	**11.0**	(3.6)	**12.5**	(5.5)	**20.1**	(4.3)	**44.7**	(3.9)
	Uruguay	**1.33**	(0.12)	**-10.3**	(4.0)	-7.4	(3.7)	**-17.4**	(5.0)	**-18.7**	(4.6)	**-39.6**	(4.5)

Notes: Values that are statistically significant are indicated in bold (see Annex A3).
Only countries and economies with comparable data from PISA 2003 and PISA 2012 are shown.
For comparability over time, PISA 2003 values on the *index of quality of schools' educational resources* have been rescaled to the PISA 2012 scale of the index. PISA 2003 results reported in this table may thus differ from those presented in *Learning for Tomorrow's World: First Results from PISA 2003* (OECD, 2004) (see Annex A5 for more details).

StatLink ᴍᴧᴤᴨ http://dx.doi.org/10.1787/888932957479

[Part 1/1]
Change between 2003 and 2012 in students' learning time in school
Table IV.3.46   *Results based on students' self-reports*

		PISA 2003				PISA 2012				Change between 2003 and 2012 (PISA 2012 - PISA 2003)			
		Number of mathematics class periods in a normal full week of school (class periods)		Time spent per week in regular school lessons in mathematics (minutes)		Number of mathematics class periods in a normal full week of school (class periods)		Time spent per week in regular school lessons in mathematics (minutes)		Number of mathematics class periods in a normal full week of school (class periods)		Time spent per week in regular school lessons in mathematics (minutes)	
		Mean	S.E.	Mean	S.E.	Mean	S.E.	Mean	S.E.	Dif.	S.E.	Dif.	S.E.
OECD	Australia	4.5	(0.1)	230.3	(1.7)	4.3	(0.0)	236.3	(0.9)	**-0.2**	(0.1)	**6.0**	(1.9)
	Austria	3.4	(0.1)	166.4	(4.0)	3.1	(0.0)	156.4	(2.4)	**-0.2**	(0.1)	**-9.9**	(4.7)
	Belgium	3.9	(0.0)	196.4	(2.0)	4.0	(0.0)	216.9	(1.4)	**0.1**	(0.0)	**20.5**	(2.5)
	Canada	3.2	(0.0)	222.8	(2.0)	4.3	(0.0)	313.8	(2.8)	**1.1**	(0.0)	**91.0**	(3.5)
	Czech Republic	3.7	(0.1)	168.8	(2.3)	4.0	(0.0)	182.3	(1.9)	**0.3**	(0.1)	**13.5**	(3.0)
	Denmark	4.3	(0.0)	206.4	(2.4)	4.4	(0.0)	224.4	(3.0)	0.1	(0.1)	**18.1**	(3.8)
	Finland	3.5	(0.1)	156.1	(2.6)	3.7	(0.0)	175.5	(1.5)	**0.2**	(0.1)	**19.3**	(3.0)
	France	3.8	(0.0)	208.1	(1.7)	3.5	(0.0)	207.0	(2.2)	**-0.3**	(0.0)	-1.0	(2.8)
	Germany	4.0	(0.0)	182.3	(1.9)	4.0	(0.0)	196.8	(2.6)	-0.1	(0.1)	**14.5**	(3.2)
	Greece	4.1	(0.0)	186.7	(2.0)	4.7	(0.0)	209.0	(0.7)	**0.6**	(0.0)	**22.3**	(2.2)
	Hungary	3.6	(0.0)	162.9	(2.0)	3.4	(0.0)	149.9	(1.7)	**-0.3**	(0.1)	**-13.0**	(2.6)
	Iceland	5.8	(0.0)	254.2	(1.0)	5.5	(0.0)	243.9	(1.9)	**-0.4**	(0.0)	**-10.4**	(2.2)
	Ireland	4.8	(0.0)	190.3	(1.6)	4.8	(0.0)	188.8	(1.2)	0.0	(0.0)	-1.6	(2.0)
	Italy	4.0	(0.1)	213.3	(3.1)	4.1	(0.0)	232.0	(1.7)	0.1	(0.1)	**18.7**	(3.6)
	Japan	4.3	(0.1)	216.3	(4.3)	4.6	(0.1)	234.7	(3.0)	**0.4**	(0.1)	**18.4**	(5.3)
	Korea	4.9	(0.1)	245.8	(3.6)	4.3	(0.1)	213.3	(3.2)	**-0.6**	(0.1)	**-32.5**	(4.8)
	Luxembourg	4.0	(0.0)	200.3	(1.5)	4.0	(0.0)	204.7	(0.8)	0.0	(0.0)	**4.4**	(1.7)
	Mexico	4.8	(0.1)	235.4	(4.9)	4.4	(0.0)	253.2	(1.7)	**-0.4**	(0.1)	**17.8**	(5.2)
	Netherlands	3.1	(0.1)	149.3	(2.5)	3.2	(0.0)	170.7	(2.9)	0.1	(0.1)	**21.4**	(3.8)
	New Zealand	4.3	(0.0)	239.6	(1.7)	4.3	(0.0)	240.8	(2.0)	0.0	(0.1)	1.3	(2.7)
	Norway	3.7	(0.1)	165.6	(4.3)	3.9	(0.0)	199.0	(2.4)	0.2	(0.1)	**33.4**	(4.9)
	Poland	4.6	(0.0)	205.5	(1.6)	4.4	(0.0)	198.1	(1.7)	**-0.2**	(0.1)	**-7.4**	(2.3)
	Portugal	3.6	(0.1)	195.0	(3.2)	3.6	(0.1)	288.0	(4.9)	0.1	(0.1)	**93.0**	(5.9)
	Slovak Republic	4.4	(0.1)	198.4	(3.0)	4.0	(0.1)	180.8	(2.7)	**-0.4**	(0.1)	**-17.6**	(4.0)
	Spain	3.3	(0.0)	176.0	(1.4)	3.8	(0.0)	210.3	(0.9)	**0.6**	(0.0)	**34.4**	(1.7)
	Sweden	3.2	(0.1)	165.0	(2.4)	3.1	(0.0)	182.2	(2.2)	-0.1	(0.1)	**17.2**	(3.2)
	Switzerland	4.4	(0.1)	198.6	(5.2)	4.4	(0.1)	207.0	(2.6)	0.0	(0.1)	8.4	(5.8)
	Turkey	4.8	(0.1)	200.0	(3.2)	3.9	(0.1)	171.9	(2.2)	**-0.8**	(0.1)	**-28.2**	(3.8)
	United States	3.7	(0.1)	221.0	(3.3)	4.0	(0.1)	254.1	(4.9)	**0.4**	(0.1)	**33.1**	(6.0)
	OECD average 2003	4.1	(0.0)	198.5	(0.5)	4.1	(0.0)	211.8	(0.5)	0.0	(0.0)	**13.3**	(0.7)
Partners	Brazil	4.3	(0.1)	210.6	(4.2)	4.1	(0.0)	214.7	(1.7)	**-0.2**	(0.1)	4.1	(4.6)
	Hong Kong-China	7.5	(0.1)	269.7	(3.6)	6.5	(0.1)	267.6	(2.6)	**-1.0**	(0.1)	-2.1	(4.4)
	Indonesia	4.9	(0.1)	232.5	(4.5)	3.8	(0.1)	209.4	(4.5)	**-1.1**	(0.1)	**-23.2**	(6.4)
	Latvia	5.3	(0.1)	214.1	(3.0)	5.5	(0.0)	224.4	(1.5)	0.2	(0.1)	**10.3**	(3.4)
	Liechtenstein	4.8	(0.0)	215.7	(1.8)	4.6	(0.1)	210.7	(4.5)	**-0.2**	(0.1)	-5.0	(4.8)
	Macao-China	6.7	(0.1)	271.8	(2.7)	6.7	(0.0)	275.0	(0.9)	0.0	(0.1)	3.3	(2.9)
	Russian Federation	4.8	(0.1)	207.3	(4.0)	5.0	(0.1)	222.5	(2.5)	0.2	(0.1)	**15.2**	(4.7)
	Thailand	4.3	(0.1)	223.7	(2.7)	3.9	(0.1)	205.9	(3.1)	**-0.4**	(0.1)	**-17.8**	(4.1)
	Tunisia	4.2	(0.0)	249.5	(1.4)	3.9	(0.0)	275.9	(4.0)	**-0.2**	(0.0)	**26.4**	(4.2)
	Uruguay	4.3	(0.1)	182.9	(3.5)	3.6	(0.0)	155.8	(1.9)	**-0.8**	(0.1)	**-27.1**	(4.0)

Notes: Values that are statistically significant are indicated in bold (see Annex A3).
Only countries and economies with comparable data from PISA 2003 and PISA 2012 are shown.
StatLink 🖳 http://dx.doi.org/10.1787/888932957479

[Part 1/1]
Change between 2003 and 2012 in hours of after-school study time per week
Table IV.3.48   *Results based on students' self-reports*

		PISA 2003		PISA 2012		Change between 2003 and 2012 (PISA 2012 - PISA 2003)	
		Homework or other study set by teachers per week (hours)		Homework or other study set by teachers per week (hours)		Homework or other study set by teachers per week (hours)	
		Mean	S.E.	Mean	S.E.	Dif.	S.E.
OECD	Australia	5.7	(0.1)	6.0	(0.1)	**0.3**	(0.1)
	Austria	4.0	(0.1)	4.5	(0.1)	**0.6**	(0.1)
	Belgium	6.2	(0.1)	5.5	(0.1)	**-0.7**	(0.2)
	Canada	5.6	(0.1)	5.5	(0.1)	-0.2	(0.1)
	Czech Republic	3.8	(0.1)	3.1	(0.1)	**-0.7**	(0.1)
	Denmark	5.4	(0.1)	4.3	(0.1)	**-1.1**	(0.1)
	Finland	3.7	(0.1)	2.8	(0.1)	**-0.9**	(0.1)
	France	6.8	(0.1)	5.1	(0.1)	**-1.7**	(0.1)
	Germany	6.3	(0.1)	4.7	(0.1)	**-1.6**	(0.1)
	Greece	8.3	(0.2)	5.3	(0.1)	**-3.0**	(0.2)
	Hungary	10.0	(0.2)	6.2	(0.1)	**-3.7**	(0.2)
	Iceland	4.6	(0.1)	4.1	(0.1)	**-0.5**	(0.1)
	Ireland	7.7	(0.2)	7.3	(0.1)	**-0.4**	(0.2)
	Italy	10.5	(0.2)	8.7	(0.1)	**-1.8**	(0.2)
	Japan	3.8	(0.2)	3.8	(0.1)	0.0	(0.3)
	Korea	3.5	(0.1)	2.9	(0.1)	**-0.6**	(0.2)
	Luxembourg	6.1	(0.1)	4.6	(0.1)	**-1.5**	(0.1)
	Mexico	5.8	(0.1)	5.2	(0.1)	**-0.6**	(0.2)
	Netherlands	5.7	(0.1)	5.8	(0.1)	0.1	(0.2)
	New Zealand	4.5	(0.1)	4.2	(0.1)	**-0.3**	(0.1)
	Norway	4.8	(0.1)	4.7	(0.1)	-0.1	(0.1)
	Poland	8.1	(0.2)	6.6	(0.1)	**-1.5**	(0.2)
	Portugal	4.9	(0.1)	3.8	(0.1)	**-1.1**	(0.2)
	Slovak Republic	8.4	(0.2)	3.2	(0.1)	**-5.2**	(0.2)
	Spain	7.4	(0.1)	6.5	(0.1)	**-0.9**	(0.2)
	Sweden	3.9	(0.1)	3.6	(0.1)	**-0.3**	(0.1)
	Switzerland	4.6	(0.1)	4.0	(0.1)	**-0.6**	(0.1)
	Turkey	5.9	(0.2)	4.2	(0.1)	**-1.6**	(0.2)
	United States	5.7	(0.1)	6.1	(0.2)	0.4	(0.3)
	OECD average 2003	5.9	(0.0)	4.9	(0.0)	**-1.0**	(0.0)
Partners	Brazil	4.9	(0.1)	3.3	(0.1)	**-1.5**	(0.1)
	Hong Kong-China	6.8	(0.2)	6.0	(0.2)	**-0.7**	(0.2)
	Indonesia	c	c	4.9	(0.2)	c	c
	Latvia	9.4	(0.2)	6.2	(0.1)	**-3.2**	(0.2)
	Liechtenstein	4.4	(0.2)	3.3	(0.2)	**-1.1**	(0.3)
	Macao-China	7.8	(0.2)	5.9	(0.1)	**-1.9**	(0.2)
	Russian Federation	12.7	(0.3)	9.7	(0.2)	**-3.0**	(0.3)
	Thailand	6.9	(0.2)	5.6	(0.1)	**-1.3**	(0.2)
	Tunisia	4.9	(0.2)	3.5	(0.1)	**-1.4**	(0.2)
	Uruguay	6.8	(0.1)	4.7	(0.1)	**-2.1**	(0.2)

Notes: Values that are statistically significant are indicated in bold (see Annex A3).
Only countries and economies with comparable data from PISA 2003 and PISA 2012 are shown.
StatLink ᴍᴙᴘ http://dx.doi.org/10.1787/888932957479

[Part 1/1]
Change between 2003 and 2012 in pre-school attendance

Table IV.3.50 *Results based on students' self-reports*

		PISA 2003						PISA 2012						Change between 2003 and 2012 (PISA 2012 - PISA 2003)					
		Percentage of students reporting that they had attended pre-primary education (ISCED 0)						Percentage of students reporting that they had attended pre-primary education (ISCED 0)						Percentage of students reporting that they had attended pre-primary education (ISCED 0)					
		No attendance		For one year or less		For more than one year		No attendance		For one year or less		For more than one year		No attendance		For one year or less		For more than one year	
		%	S.E.	%	S.E.	%	S.E.	%	S.E.	%	S.E.	%	S.E.	% dif.	S.E.	% dif.	S.E.	% dif.	S.E.
OECD	Australia	7.4	(0.4)	46.8	(0.6)	45.8	(0.7)	4.6	(0.2)	43.7	(0.6)	51.7	(0.6)	-2.8	(0.5)	-3.1	(0.8)	6.0	(0.9)
	Austria	4.3	(0.5)	15.5	(0.9)	80.2	(1.2)	1.8	(0.3)	10.5	(0.6)	87.7	(0.7)	-2.5	(0.5)	-5.0	(1.1)	7.6	(1.4)
	Belgium	2.4	(0.2)	3.8	(0.3)	93.8	(0.3)	2.4	(0.2)	4.6	(0.3)	93.0	(0.4)	0.0	(0.3)	0.8	(0.4)	-0.8	(0.5)
	Canada	9.0	(0.4)	45.3	(0.6)	45.7	(0.7)	9.1	(0.3)	40.4	(0.7)	50.5	(0.6)	0.1	(0.5)	-4.9	(0.9)	4.8	(0.9)
	Czech Republic	7.3	(0.4)	13.9	(0.6)	78.8	(0.7)	3.2	(0.5)	8.8	(0.6)	88.0	(0.8)	-4.1	(0.6)	-5.1	(0.8)	9.2	(1.1)
	Denmark	2.3	(0.3)	32.0	(1.0)	65.7	(1.0)	1.1	(0.1)	20.1	(0.6)	78.9	(0.6)	-1.3	(0.3)	-11.9	(1.1)	13.2	(1.2)
	Finland	7.9	(0.5)	25.3	(0.8)	66.8	(0.9)	2.5	(0.2)	34.8	(1.0)	62.7	(1.0)	-5.4	(0.6)	9.5	(1.3)	-4.1	(1.4)
	France	1.6	(0.3)	4.5	(0.4)	93.9	(0.5)	1.8	(0.3)	6.4	(0.3)	91.8	(0.4)	0.2	(0.4)	1.9	(0.5)	-2.1	(0.6)
	Germany	4.4	(0.3)	13.0	(0.5)	82.6	(0.6)	3.3	(0.3)	11.5	(0.6)	85.2	(0.7)	-1.1	(0.4)	-1.5	(0.8)	2.6	(0.9)
	Greece	5.4	(0.5)	32.7	(1.3)	62.0	(1.4)	4.6	(0.5)	27.4	(0.9)	68.0	(1.0)	-0.8	(0.7)	-5.3	(1.6)	6.1	(1.7)
	Hungary	1.0	(0.2)	4.7	(0.3)	94.2	(0.4)	0.5	(0.1)	4.0	(0.4)	95.5	(0.4)	-0.5	(0.2)	-0.7	(0.5)	1.3	(0.6)
	Iceland	6.6	(0.4)	4.5	(0.3)	88.9	(0.5)	2.1	(0.3)	3.2	(0.3)	94.7	(0.4)	-4.6	(0.5)	-1.3	(0.4)	5.8	(0.6)
	Ireland	27.7	(1.3)	39.8	(1.1)	32.5	(1.3)	13.6	(0.7)	43.6	(0.9)	42.8	(0.9)	-14.1	(1.5)	3.8	(1.4)	10.3	(1.5)
	Italy	4.8	(0.4)	8.4	(0.5)	86.7	(0.7)	4.3	(0.2)	8.0	(0.2)	87.7	(0.3)	-0.5	(0.4)	-0.4	(0.6)	1.0	(0.7)
	Japan	1.3	(0.2)	1.7	(0.2)	97.0	(0.3)	0.9	(0.1)	2.2	(0.2)	96.9	(0.2)	-0.4	(0.2)	0.6	(0.3)	-0.2	(0.4)
	Korea	3.8	(0.3)	9.7	(0.5)	86.5	(0.6)	4.5	(0.4)	12.6	(0.7)	82.9	(0.9)	0.7	(0.5)	3.0	(0.8)	-3.7	(1.1)
	Luxembourg	11.9	(0.5)	8.7	(0.4)	79.3	(0.7)	4.6	(0.3)	12.8	(0.4)	82.6	(0.5)	-7.3	(0.6)	4.1	(0.6)	3.3	(0.9)
	Mexico	13.5	(0.9)	20.6	(0.9)	65.8	(1.2)	9.5	(0.3)	18.7	(0.3)	71.8	(0.5)	-4.1	(0.9)	-1.9	(0.9)	6.0	(1.3)
	Netherlands	2.9	(0.3)	3.1	(0.3)	93.9	(0.4)	2.3	(0.3)	2.7	(0.3)	95.0	(0.3)	-0.6	(0.4)	-0.4	(0.4)	1.1	(0.5)
	New Zealand	8.3	(0.4)	20.0	(0.7)	71.7	(0.8)	9.3	(0.6)	19.5	(0.7)	71.2	(0.8)	1.1	(0.7)	-0.6	(1.0)	-0.5	(1.1)
	Norway	7.6	(0.6)	14.0	(0.8)	78.3	(1.0)	7.9	(0.4)	5.8	(0.4)	86.3	(0.6)	0.3	(0.7)	-8.3	(0.9)	8.0	(1.2)
	Poland	3.9	(0.3)	51.7	(1.2)	44.4	(1.2)	2.5	(0.3)	46.4	(1.5)	51.1	(1.5)	-1.4	(0.4)	-5.3	(1.9)	6.7	(2.0)
	Portugal	27.7	(1.3)	17.4	(0.8)	54.9	(1.3)	15.0	(0.8)	20.7	(0.8)	64.4	(1.1)	-12.7	(1.5)	3.3	(1.1)	9.4	(1.7)
	Slovak Republic	8.1	(0.5)	15.6	(0.7)	76.3	(0.9)	6.8	(0.7)	13.2	(0.8)	80.0	(1.0)	-1.3	(0.8)	-2.4	(1.1)	3.7	(1.4)
	Spain	5.4	(0.5)	10.2	(0.5)	84.4	(0.7)	5.9	(0.3)	8.3	(0.2)	85.8	(0.4)	0.5	(0.6)	-1.9	(0.5)	1.5	(0.8)
	Sweden	11.8	(0.6)	28.6	(0.8)	59.5	(1.1)	8.2	(0.5)	20.4	(0.8)	71.4	(0.8)	-3.6	(0.8)	-8.2	(1.1)	11.8	(1.4)
	Switzerland	3.1	(0.3)	30.2	(1.8)	66.7	(1.8)	1.8	(0.2)	25.0	(1.8)	73.1	(1.8)	-1.3	(0.4)	-5.2	(2.5)	6.5	(2.6)
	Turkey	76.7	(1.7)	15.5	(1.1)	7.8	(0.7)	70.3	(1.4)	21.0	(1.0)	8.6	(0.8)	-6.3	(2.2)	5.5	(1.5)	0.8	(1.0)
	United States	2.7	(0.3)	87.1	(0.5)	10.3	(0.5)	1.5	(0.2)	24.0	(0.9)	74.6	(0.9)	-1.2	(0.3)	-63.1	(1.0)	64.3	(1.0)
	OECD average 2003	9.7	(0.1)	21.5	(0.1)	68.8	(0.2)	7.1	(0.1)	17.9	(0.1)	75.0	(0.2)	-2.6	(0.1)	-3.6	(0.2)	6.2	(0.2)
Partners	Brazil	23.6	(1.1)	31.4	(0.9)	45.1	(1.2)	18.9	(0.6)	33.4	(0.7)	47.7	(0.8)	-4.7	(1.2)	2.0	(1.1)	2.7	(1.4)
	Hong Kong-China	6.1	(0.6)	6.8	(0.5)	87.1	(0.9)	1.6	(0.2)	3.3	(0.3)	95.1	(0.4)	-4.6	(0.6)	-3.4	(0.6)	8.0	(1.0)
	Indonesia	49.5	(1.6)	25.1	(0.9)	25.4	(1.4)	46.2	(2.2)	31.4	(2.0)	22.5	(1.5)	-3.3	(2.7)	6.3	(2.2)	-3.0	(2.0)
	Latvia	29.2	(1.0)	15.1	(0.6)	55.7	(1.1)	11.3	(0.8)	13.3	(0.7)	75.4	(0.9)	-17.9	(1.3)	-1.8	(0.9)	19.6	(1.4)
	Liechtenstein	3.3	(0.9)	6.1	(1.3)	90.6	(1.5)	0.7	(0.5)	8.8	(1.8)	90.5	(1.9)	-2.6	(1.0)	2.7	(2.2)	-0.1	(2.4)
	Macao-China	3.8	(0.7)	16.2	(1.2)	80.0	(1.4)	2.4	(0.2)	11.9	(0.4)	85.6	(0.5)	-1.4	(0.8)	-4.3	(1.3)	5.7	(1.4)
	Russian Federation	11.8	(0.9)	9.8	(0.5)	78.4	(1.1)	18.9	(1.1)	10.2	(0.5)	71.0	(1.4)	7.1	(1.4)	0.3	(0.8)	-7.5	(1.8)
	Thailand	4.8	(0.4)	20.9	(0.9)	74.3	(1.1)	1.7	(0.3)	10.5	(0.6)	87.8	(0.6)	-3.1	(0.5)	-10.4	(1.1)	13.5	(1.3)
	Tunisia	46.8	(1.7)	26.2	(1.1)	27.0	(1.2)	37.6	(1.6)	39.3	(1.1)	23.1	(1.0)	-9.2	(2.3)	13.1	(1.5)	-3.9	(1.5)
	Uruguay	15.6	(0.9)	20.6	(0.9)	63.8	(1.1)	16.2	(0.8)	14.1	(0.7)	69.7	(1.0)	0.6	(1.2)	-6.5	(1.1)	5.9	(1.5)

Notes: Values that are statistically significant are indicated in bold (see Annex A3).
Only countries and economies with comparable data from PISA 2003 and PISA 2012 are shown.
StatLink ᵐˢᴾ http://dx.doi.org/10.1787/888932957479

[Part 1/6]
Change between 2003 and 2012 in years in pre-school, by school features

Table IV.3.51 *Results based on students' self-reports*

		PISA 2003												
		Percentage of students reporting that they had attended pre-primary education (ISCED 0) for more than one year												
		Bottom quarter of ESCS		Second quarter of ESCS		Third quarter of ESCS		Top quarter of ESCS		Socio-economically disadvantaged schools[1]		Socio-economically average schools[1]		Socio-economically advantaged schools[1]	
		%	S.E.	%	S.E.	%	S.E.	%	S.E.	%	S.E.	%	S.E.	%	S.E.
OECD	Australia	37.6	(1.3)	42.5	(1.3)	47.2	(1.3)	55.6	(1.0)	38.9	(1.4)	44.4	(1.3)	55.4	(1.0)
	Austria	66.1	(2.2)	79.0	(1.7)	86.1	(1.5)	89.5	(1.3)	73.3	(2.1)	80.7	(1.8)	88.8	(1.4)
	Belgium	90.1	(0.9)	92.6	(0.6)	95.9	(0.5)	96.7	(0.4)	90.3	(0.8)	94.8	(0.5)	96.1	(0.4)
	Canada	35.4	(1.2)	40.5	(1.1)	49.5	(1.1)	57.4	(1.4)	32.8	(1.7)	46.7	(1.0)	56.2	(1.9)
	Czech Republic	74.7	(1.6)	77.7	(1.1)	80.9	(1.2)	81.9	(1.1)	74.6	(1.7)	80.5	(1.1)	80.0	(1.3)
	Denmark	57.9	(1.9)	67.7	(1.9)	65.9	(1.5)	71.3	(1.7)	62.4	(2.8)	64.5	(1.2)	72.7	(1.8)
	Finland	58.1	(1.6)	65.4	(1.4)	69.6	(1.4)	73.9	(1.5)	55.5	(2.3)	66.9	(1.0)	78.9	(1.8)
	France	91.1	(0.9)	93.3	(0.9)	94.1	(0.7)	97.0	(0.8)	90.5	(1.1)	94.5	(0.6)	96.3	(0.6)
	Germany	71.3	(1.5)	82.3	(1.4)	86.3	(1.2)	90.3	(0.9)	73.6	(1.3)	83.8	(1.1)	91.2	(0.9)
	Greece	58.7	(2.3)	59.5	(2.0)	62.1	(1.7)	67.6	(2.1)	58.6	(2.4)	61.0	(2.2)	66.5	(2.6)
	Hungary	92.0	(1.0)	94.1	(0.7)	93.8	(0.8)	97.1	(0.5)	92.3	(0.8)	94.9	(0.8)	95.7	(0.6)
	Iceland	82.2	(1.2)	88.6	(1.1)	91.0	(0.9)	93.8	(0.9)	81.9	(1.7)	89.6	(0.7)	91.9	(0.8)
	Ireland	25.6	(1.9)	30.7	(1.7)	34.9	(1.6)	38.5	(2.2)	28.8	(2.6)	29.4	(1.4)	44.4	(2.7)
	Italy	84.4	(1.2)	87.6	(1.0)	86.0	(1.1)	89.0	(0.8)	82.7	(1.5)	88.7	(0.9)	88.8	(0.7)
	Japan	96.6	(0.6)	96.9	(0.5)	97.5	(0.5)	97.2	(0.5)	95.8	(0.5)	97.2	(0.5)	98.1	(0.4)
	Korea	79.8	(1.2)	86.6	(1.1)	89.4	(0.9)	90.4	(0.9)	82.3	(1.2)	87.8	(0.9)	89.7	(0.9)
	Luxembourg	75.7	(1.5)	79.2	(1.4)	81.2	(1.2)	81.0	(1.3)	77.4	(0.9)	c	c	82.0	(1.0)
	Mexico	49.6	(1.8)	59.3	(1.6)	72.1	(1.4)	82.0	(1.2)	53.0	(2.1)	67.8	(1.3)	79.4	(1.5)
	Netherlands	93.3	(1.0)	93.7	(0.9)	93.7	(0.8)	95.0	(0.7)	92.5	(1.0)	94.6	(0.6)	94.5	(0.8)
	New Zealand	63.8	(1.3)	67.8	(1.5)	75.1	(1.5)	79.9	(1.5)	66.1	(1.6)	71.3	(1.1)	77.4	(1.7)
	Norway	68.2	(1.8)	77.8	(1.7)	80.7	(1.2)	86.4	(1.6)	75.5	(3.2)	77.4	(1.2)	86.0	(1.9)
	Poland	29.4	(2.0)	36.8	(1.8)	47.3	(1.8)	64.2	(1.5)	32.5	(2.9)	44.0	(1.4)	60.3	(1.8)
	Portugal	45.3	(2.0)	48.6	(1.8)	54.7	(1.5)	71.2	(1.6)	50.5	(2.3)	54.3	(1.9)	62.2	(2.0)
	Slovak Republic	67.7	(2.1)	78.6	(0.9)	79.5	(1.0)	79.3	(1.5)	72.5	(2.0)	76.2	(1.3)	80.0	(0.9)
	Spain	79.9	(1.7)	82.2	(1.0)	85.6	(1.0)	89.6	(0.7)	81.3	(1.6)	83.4	(1.0)	88.9	(0.8)
	Sweden	51.0	(1.9)	56.0	(1.7)	63.9	(1.7)	67.1	(1.7)	53.1	(2.4)	58.6	(1.2)	68.2	(2.6)
	Switzerland	63.3	(2.5)	66.6	(2.3)	66.0	(2.1)	70.9	(2.4)	58.6	(3.8)	69.4	(2.1)	70.4	(3.8)
	Turkey	0.8	(0.3)	2.7	(0.6)	5.4	(0.6)	22.1	(1.4)	2.5	(0.5)	5.5	(0.7)	18.2	(1.3)
	United States	11.5	(1.0)	10.1	(1.1)	9.5	(0.8)	10.1	(0.8)	11.9	(1.1)	9.7	(0.6)	10.1	(1.0)
	OECD average 2003	62.1	(0.3)	67.0	(0.3)	70.5	(0.2)	75.4	(0.2)	63.5	(0.4)	68.5	(0.2)	74.8	(0.3)
Partners	Brazil	31.3	(1.9)	39.8	(1.7)	48.8	(1.6)	59.8	(2.0)	34.4	(2.2)	42.2	(1.4)	64.4	(2.1)
	Hong Kong-China	76.0	(1.3)	85.6	(1.9)	92.3	(1.0)	94.5	(0.7)	80.1	(2.2)	88.8	(1.1)	93.8	(0.9)
	Indonesia	12.6	(1.4)	22.1	(1.6)	27.8	(1.7)	38.9	(3.0)	13.6	(2.0)	26.8	(2.7)	37.5	(3.6)
	Latvia	47.8	(1.9)	57.1	(2.1)	61.1	(1.6)	56.9	(1.9)	41.0	(3.4)	56.5	(1.5)	63.5	(2.1)
	Liechtenstein	79.3	(4.2)	97.6	(1.7)	92.7	(2.9)	92.7	(2.9)	c	c	92.5	(1.8)	c	c
	Macao-China	75.4	(3.3)	79.4	(2.9)	83.4	(2.6)	81.7	(2.5)	73.6	(2.7)	84.0	(1.9)	84.7	(2.4)
	Russian Federation	72.0	(2.1)	79.4	(1.6)	82.3	(1.3)	80.0	(1.3)	72.8	(2.4)	80.3	(1.3)	81.2	(1.5)
	Thailand	63.5	(2.4)	69.0	(1.6)	76.3	(1.5)	88.2	(1.1)	66.5	(2.2)	72.0	(1.8)	88.2	(1.2)
	Tunisia	7.8	(0.9)	17.3	(1.3)	32.9	(1.7)	48.8	(2.2)	11.5	(1.2)	27.0	(1.5)	47.0	(2.7)
	Uruguay	43.8	(1.9)	60.3	(2.2)	69.1	(1.3)	80.8	(1.2)	47.6	(1.8)	65.0	(1.9)	78.8	(1.6)

Notes: Values that are statistically significant are indicated in bold (see Annex A3).
ESCS refers to the *PISA index of economic, social and cultural status*.
Only countries and economies with comparable data from PISA 2003 and PISA 2012 are shown.
1. A socio-economically disadvantaged school is one whose students' mean socio-economic status (ESCS) is statistically significantly below the mean socio-economic status of the country/economy; an average school is one where there is no difference from the country's/economy's mean; and an advantaged school is one whose students' mean socio-economic status is statistically significantly above the country/economy mean.
StatLink ᴬᴵˢᴾ http://dx.doi.org/10.1787/888932957479

[Part 2/6]
Change between 2003 and 2012 in years in pre-school, by school features
Table IV.3.51   *Results based on students' self-reports*

		PISA 2003												
		Percentage of students reporting that they had attended pre-primary education (ISCED 0) for more than one year												
		Public schools		Private schools		Lower secondary education (ISCED 2)		Upper secondary education (ISCED 3)		Schools located in a village, hamlet or rural area (fewer than 3 000 people)		Schools located in a small town or town (3 000 to about 100 000 people)		Schools located in a city or a large city (over 100 000 people)	
		%	S.E.	%	S.E.	%	S.E.	%	S.E.	%	S.E.	%	S.E.	%	S.E.
OECD	Australia	w	w	w	w	**47.2**	(0.8)	**39.8**	(1.3)	41.3	(3.7)	43.7	(1.2)	47.3	(1.0)
	Austria	79.6	(1.2)	**86.2**	(3.0)	71.1	(3.5)	80.6	(1.2)	76.1	(3.3)	81.0	(1.6)	79.7	(1.9)
	Belgium	91.8	(0.9)	95.0	(0.4)	70.4	(3.2)	94.5	(0.3)	90.5	(2.7)	94.6	(0.4)	92.1	(1.0)
	Canada	44.9	(0.8)	48.1	(2.9)	31.9	(1.2)	48.5	(0.8)	**40.9**	(2.4)	42.1	(1.2)	**50.8**	(1.3)
	Czech Republic	78.8	(0.7)	78.7	(3.6)	79.1	(1.2)	78.5	(0.9)	80.4	(3.1)	79.2	(0.9)	77.0	(1.6)
	Denmark	66.0	(1.2)	65.9	(1.9)	65.8	(1.0)	57.9	(5.4)	**60.7**	(2.4)	66.5	(1.4)	**70.7**	(2.4)
	Finland	**66.2**	(0.9)	**74.4**	(3.5)	66.8	(0.9)	c	c	**53.3**	(2.9)	65.9	(1.1)	**76.9**	(1.6)
	France	c	c	c	c	89.8	(1.0)	96.6	(0.4)	c	c	c	c	c	c
	Germany	82.1	(0.7)	89.1	(2.6)	82.8	(0.6)	75.7	(3.5)	80.9	(1.8)	83.4	(0.9)	80.9	(1.7)
	Greece	**61.7**	(1.5)	**73.5**	(3.6)	47.5	(2.9)	63.4	(1.5)	55.8	(6.5)	62.8	(1.6)	60.6	(3.1)
	Hungary	94.4	(0.5)	93.6	(1.0)	87.7	(2.1)	94.7	(0.4)	88.8	(3.3)	94.3	(0.5)	94.5	(0.6)
	Iceland	88.9	(0.6)	c	c	88.9	(0.5)	c	c	81.4	(1.3)	90.7	(0.7)	**92.8**	(1.1)
	Ireland	**28.8**	(1.8)	**34.3**	(1.6)	35.1	(1.4)	27.9	(1.5)	22.3	(1.9)	30.2	(1.5)	**44.1**	(2.3)
	Italy	86.7	(0.7)	89.9	(1.8)	55.1	(8.4)	87.2	(0.6)	90.4	(6.8)	87.5	(0.7)	84.9	(1.2)
	Japan	96.9	(0.4)	97.7	(0.4)	c	c	97.0	(0.3)	c	c	96.2	(0.5)	97.5	(0.3)
	Korea	85.7	(1.1)	87.2	(0.7)	86.5	(4.5)	86.5	(0.6)	c	c	81.8	(2.2)	87.6	(0.6)
	Luxembourg	**78.4**	(0.8)	**84.8**	(1.5)	79.0	(0.8)	80.0	(1.2)	c	c	79.3	(0.7)	c	c
	Mexico	**63.3**	(1.2)	**77.4**	(2.3)	62.6	(2.2)	70.0	(0.9)	51.8	(3.1)	67.0	(1.3)	72.7	(1.5)
	Netherlands	91.8	(1.2)	**94.4**	(0.5)	93.5	(0.5)	95.2	(0.7)	c	c	94.3	(0.5)	93.0	(0.8)
	New Zealand	72.0	(0.8)	74.9	(5.4)	70.5	(2.5)	71.8	(0.8)	69.4	(3.2)	73.0	(1.1)	70.7	(1.3)
	Norway	78.5	(1.1)	c	c	78.3	(1.1)	c	c	**77.0**	(1.9)	77.7	(1.4)	**82.9**	(2.3)
	Poland	44.0	(1.2)	c	c	44.5	(1.2)	c	c	35.4	(2.6)	43.6	(1.4)	60.0	(1.8)
	Portugal	54.5	(1.4)	60.9	(4.2)	52.1	(1.9)	56.5	(1.6)	54.2	(3.7)	54.3	(1.6)	57.5	(2.7)
	Slovak Republic	76.2	(1.0)	76.3	(2.1)	74.5	(1.5)	77.2	(0.9)	71.3	(3.4)	76.6	(1.0)	78.0	(1.6)
	Spain	82.4	(0.9)	87.7	(0.7)	84.4	(0.7)	c	c	85.5	(2.9)	84.5	(0.8)	84.4	(1.2)
	Sweden	59.4	(1.1)	61.0	(1.8)	59.7	(1.1)	55.9	(8.4)	58.0	(2.3)	58.6	(1.4)	63.4	(2.0)
	Switzerland	66.1	(1.9)	70.7	(6.4)	65.5	(2.0)	72.4	(3.0)	**61.0**	(5.1)	65.3	(2.4)	**78.9**	(2.9)
	Turkey	7.0	(0.7)	c	c	2.2	(1.4)	8.1	(0.7)	c	c	5.6	(0.9)	9.8	(0.9)
	United States	10.0	(0.6)	7.2	(1.8)	**13.8**	(1.1)	8.6	(0.6)	8.5	(1.7)	9.9	(0.7)	9.8	(0.9)
	OECD average 2003	**68.0**	(0.2)	**74.3**	(0.6)	**63.8**	(0.5)	**67.7**	(0.5)	**62.4**	(0.7)	67.5	(0.2)	70.3	(0.3)
Partners	Brazil	**42.3**	(1.5)	60.7	(2.3)	34.2	(1.7)	51.4	(1.4)	36.4	(7.2)	42.1	(1.8)	49.8	(1.8)
	Hong Kong-China	89.4	(1.2)	86.9	(1.0)	75.2	(1.9)	95.6	(0.4)	c	c	c	c	87.1	(0.9)
	Indonesia	25.2	(1.5)	25.7	(2.4)	22.9	(1.6)	29.9	(2.3)	22.8	(3.5)	24.7	(3.2)	29.6	(2.8)
	Latvia	55.6	(1.2)	c	c	55.4	(1.1)	60.1	(3.1)	**39.2**	(2.7)	60.3	(1.8)	**65.0**	(1.5)
	Liechtenstein	90.4	(1.6)	c	c	90.7	(1.5)	c	c	c	c	90.6	(1.5)	c	c
	Macao-China	c	c	80.2	(1.4)	**77.1**	(1.6)	88.7	(2.5)	c	c	c	c	80.0	(1.4)
	Russian Federation	78.3	(1.2)	c	c	73.8	(2.0)	80.5	(1.2)	67.2	(3.6)	78.8	(1.6)	81.5	(1.1)
	Thailand	74.0	(1.2)	76.9	(2.9)	72.7	(1.7)	75.6	(1.1)	68.9	(2.5)	71.6	(2.0)	84.3	(1.7)
	Tunisia	c	c	c	c	**19.8**	(1.2)	38.4	(2.3)	17.1	(6.2)	24.7	(1.4)	40.5	(4.0)
	Uruguay	60.1	(1.3)	85.1	(1.3)	51.8	(1.3)	69.4	(1.4)	44.9	(6.0)	58.5	(1.6)	72.9	(1.6)

Notes: Values that are statistically significant are indicated in bold (see Annex A3).
ESCS refers to the *PISA index of economic, social and cultural status.*
Only countries and economies with comparable data from PISA 2003 and PISA 2012 are shown.
1. A socio-economically disadvantaged school is one whose students' mean socio-economic status (ESCS) is statistically significantly below the mean socio-economic status of the country/economy; an average school is one where there is no difference from the country's/economy's mean; and an advantaged school is one whose students' mean socio-economic status is statistically significantly above the country/economy mean.
StatLink ⫘ http://dx.doi.org/10.1787/888932957479

[Part 3/6]
Change between 2003 and 2012 in years in pre-school, by school features

Table IV.3.51   *Results based on students' self-reports*

	PISA 2012													
	Percentage of students reporting that they had attended pre-primary education (ISCED 0) for more than one year													
	Bottom quarter of ESCS		Second quarter of ESCS		Third quarter of ESCS		Top quarter of ESCS		Socio-economically disadvantaged schools[1]		Socio-economically average schools[1]		Socio-economically advantaged schools[1]	
	%	S.E.	%	S.E.	%	S.E.	%	S.E.	%	S.E.	%	S.E.	%	S.E.
Australia	42.7	(1.1)	49.0	(1.0)	54.1	(1.0)	61.6	(1.1)	42.3	(1.1)	49.9	(0.8)	64.3	(1.3)
Austria	80.8	(1.8)	86.5	(1.3)	90.6	(1.0)	93.1	(0.9)	82.1	(1.6)	88.7	(0.9)	93.2	(1.0)
Belgium	89.2	(0.9)	92.1	(0.7)	95.3	(0.4)	96.1	(0.5)	87.3	(0.9)	94.6	(0.6)	96.0	(0.5)
Canada	42.5	(1.1)	46.9	(1.2)	52.1	(1.1)	61.0	(1.0)	46.6	(2.3)	48.1	(1.2)	58.8	(1.4)
Czech Republic	84.5	(1.8)	87.3	(1.3)	91.0	(1.1)	89.5	(1.1)	84.0	(2.3)	88.8	(0.9)	89.8	(1.1)
Denmark	72.4	(1.2)	78.4	(1.2)	80.0	(1.1)	85.2	(1.1)	73.1	(1.5)	78.3	(0.9)	85.5	(1.3)
Finland	51.4	(1.3)	61.2	(1.7)	66.3	(1.4)	72.1	(1.6)	47.6	(3.1)	62.4	(1.3)	78.2	(1.8)
France	87.4	(1.1)	90.6	(0.8)	94.6	(0.7)	95.2	(0.7)	83.9	(1.3)	93.2	(0.7)	96.0	(0.6)
Germany	79.1	(1.6)	84.4	(1.2)	88.1	(1.0)	91.2	(1.0)	75.8	(1.7)	86.7	(0.9)	92.0	(0.9)
Greece	59.9	(1.9)	67.1	(1.6)	70.3	(1.5)	74.8	(1.5)	61.8	(2.6)	68.3	(1.5)	73.4	(1.6)
Hungary	94.8	(0.8)	95.8	(0.7)	95.3	(0.6)	96.3	(0.7)	94.2	(0.7)	95.4	(0.6)	96.9	(0.5)
Iceland	90.2	(1.0)	95.4	(0.6)	96.7	(0.7)	96.6	(0.6)	93.3	(1.0)	94.1	(0.5)	96.7	(0.6)
Ireland	34.2	(1.5)	40.1	(1.7)	44.4	(1.5)	52.3	(1.5)	41.2	(2.1)	38.5	(1.1)	53.3	(1.6)
Italy	84.2	(0.7)	87.5	(0.6)	89.4	(0.4)	89.9	(0.6)	84.0	(0.8)	87.8	(0.5)	91.1	(0.5)
Japan	95.8	(0.5)	97.2	(0.5)	97.1	(0.4)	97.7	(0.3)	94.9	(0.6)	97.5	(0.3)	98.0	(0.3)
Korea	79.8	(1.4)	80.6	(1.4)	85.2	(1.1)	85.7	(1.4)	82.1	(1.8)	82.4	(1.3)	84.6	(1.3)
Luxembourg	74.7	(1.3)	83.2	(1.1)	87.2	(0.9)	85.1	(1.0)	78.4	(0.8)	87.9	(1.1)	85.7	(0.8)
Mexico	61.3	(1.1)	68.6	(0.8)	74.2	(0.7)	83.3	(0.5)	64.4	(1.2)	71.3	(0.7)	80.6	(0.6)
Netherlands	92.7	(1.0)	96.3	(0.6)	95.2	(0.7)	95.9	(0.6)	93.3	(1.0)	95.5	(0.4)	95.6	(0.7)
New Zealand	60.2	(1.9)	70.9	(1.6)	74.5	(1.6)	80.6	(1.4)	61.9	(2.7)	71.6	(1.3)	78.8	(1.6)
Norway	78.0	(1.2)	85.0	(1.2)	88.1	(0.9)	94.5	(0.7)	79.0	(1.9)	85.5	(0.7)	93.9	(1.0)
Poland	28.4	(2.2)	42.7	(2.1)	56.7	(1.8)	76.6	(1.6)	31.9	(3.2)	50.7	(2.2)	75.9	(1.7)
Portugal	52.4	(1.5)	60.3	(1.7)	65.6	(1.7)	78.9	(1.3)	59.5	(1.8)	62.6	(1.6)	75.9	(2.2)
Slovak Republic	63.8	(2.3)	81.0	(1.5)	85.5	(1.2)	89.7	(0.9)	63.6	(2.6)	84.2	(1.0)	89.4	(1.5)
Spain	80.1	(0.9)	84.1	(1.0)	87.8	(0.7)	91.3	(0.5)	82.7	(1.1)	85.6	(0.6)	89.5	(0.7)
Sweden	61.9	(1.5)	70.6	(1.4)	76.3	(1.4)	77.2	(1.1)	70.5	(2.4)	68.3	(1.1)	80.5	(1.7)
Switzerland	68.2	(2.3)	71.7	(1.9)	77.0	(2.1)	75.7	(2.6)	63.2	(4.3)	76.1	(1.9)	77.8	(3.8)
Turkey	1.7	(0.5)	3.5	(0.6)	6.7	(0.9)	22.9	(1.7)	4.8	(0.7)	5.4	(0.6)	19.2	(1.9)
United States	61.2	(1.9)	72.1	(1.4)	79.7	(1.3)	85.4	(1.1)	63.9	(1.6)	75.6	(1.2)	82.8	(1.3)
OECD average 2003	67.4	(0.3)	73.5	(0.2)	77.4	(0.2)	81.9	(0.2)	68.7	(0.4)	75.0	(0.2)	81.8	(0.3)
Brazil	36.7	(1.1)	44.7	(1.0)	49.1	(1.3)	60.5	(1.6)	38.8	(1.3)	46.8	(1.1)	61.4	(1.9)
Hong Kong-China	91.2	(0.9)	95.7	(0.7)	96.4	(0.6)	97.2	(0.5)	92.2	(0.9)	95.7	(0.5)	98.2	(0.4)
Indonesia	13.7	(1.6)	15.4	(1.9)	24.3	(1.9)	36.7	(3.0)	16.7	(2.3)	20.0	(2.6)	33.8	(4.0)
Latvia	60.7	(2.3)	75.5	(1.5)	81.4	(1.3)	83.2	(1.3)	58.5	(3.5)	77.2	(1.4)	83.3	(1.1)
Liechtenstein	90.9	(3.6)	93.2	(2.3)	94.6	(2.7)	83.8	(5.0)	c	c	88.9	(2.8)	c	c
Macao-China	83.7	(1.0)	86.2	(0.8)	86.6	(0.8)	86.3	(1.0)	84.9	(0.7)	85.6	(1.0)	86.8	(0.8)
Russian Federation	56.0	(2.2)	70.1	(2.0)	77.3	(1.3)	80.9	(1.6)	54.5	(3.9)	72.0	(2.5)	82.0	(1.2)
Thailand	84.0	(1.1)	86.3	(1.2)	87.9	(1.0)	93.2	(0.7)	84.3	(1.3)	87.3	(0.9)	93.0	(0.7)
Tunisia	10.9	(1.1)	21.3	(1.8)	28.2	(1.5)	32.3	(1.8)	12.8	(1.3)	23.8	(1.5)	33.2	(1.7)
Uruguay	57.5	(1.8)	65.0	(1.9)	70.6	(1.4)	85.1	(1.1)	60.5	(1.6)	68.6	(1.7)	87.5	(1.3)

Notes: Values that are statistically significant are indicated in bold (see Annex A3).
ESCS refers to the *PISA index of economic, social and cultural status*.
Only countries and economies with comparable data from PISA 2003 and PISA 2012 are shown.
1. A socio-economically disadvantaged school is one whose students' mean socio-economic status (ESCS) is statistically significantly below the mean socio-economic status of the country/economy; an average school is one where there is no difference from the country's/economy's mean; and an advantaged school is one whose students' mean socio-economic status is statistically significantly above the country/economy mean.
StatLink ᴍᴤ▪ http://dx.doi.org/10.1787/888932957479

[Part 4/6]
Change between 2003 and 2012 in years in pre-school, by school features

Table IV.3.51   *Results based on students' self-reports*

		PISA 2012												
		Percentage of students reporting that they had attended pre-primary education (ISCED 0) for more than one year												
		Public schools		Private schools		Lower secondary education (ISCED 2)		Upper secondary education (ISCED 3)		Schools located in a village, hamlet or rural area (fewer than 3 000 people)		Schools located in a small town or town (3 000 to about 100 000 people)		Schools located in a city or a large city (over 100 000 people)	
		%	S.E.	%	S.E.	%	S.E.	%	S.E.	%	S.E.	%	S.E.	%	S.E.
OECD	Australia	48.6	(0.8)	56.7	(1.1)	54.0	(0.7)	42.0	(1.3)	46.4	(2.2)	49.5	(1.3)	53.3	(0.9)
	Austria	87.3	(0.8)	92.1	(2.2)	79.3	(4.9)	88.2	(0.7)	85.1	(3.0)	88.1	(1.0)	87.9	(1.1)
	Belgium	90.0	(1.0)	94.3	(0.4)	74.5	(1.9)	95.0	(0.3)	88.3	(5.2)	93.7	(0.4)	91.4	(1.1)
	Canada	50.4	(0.7)	52.1	(2.7)	37.3	(1.3)	52.7	(0.7)	47.3	(2.4)	43.6	(1.4)	55.9	(1.0)
	Czech Republic	87.8	(1.0)	85.9	(2.5)	87.5	(1.3)	88.6	(0.8)	88.1	(4.6)	87.8	(1.1)	87.3	(1.8)
	Denmark	77.8	(0.7)	82.4	(1.3)	78.8	(0.6)	89.6	(5.1)	77.7	(1.4)	79.5	(0.9)	78.8	(1.5)
	Finland	62.0	(1.1)	81.1	(3.9)	62.7	(1.0)	c	c	49.1	(6.5)	58.0	(1.2)	77.3	(1.2)
	France	91.7	(0.6)	91.2	(0.9)	83.1	(1.3)	95.4	(0.4)	87.8	(2.0)	92.3	(0.7)	91.2	(1.4)
	Germany	84.8	(0.8)	89.2	(3.5)	85.2	(0.6)	84.2	(5.8)	c	c	85.2	(0.9)	85.0	(1.6)
	Greece	68.3	(1.0)	c	c	42.4	(3.9)	69.5	(1.0)	69.6	(4.3)	67.8	(1.3)	67.9	(1.9)
	Hungary	95.6	(0.4)	95.7	(1.1)	90.2	(1.6)	96.2	(0.3)	95.4	(2.3)	96.2	(0.5)	94.8	(0.5)
	Iceland	94.7	(0.4)	c	c	94.7	(0.4)	c	c	92.4	(0.9)	96.5	(0.5)	93.6	(0.9)
	Ireland	40.8	(1.3)	43.1	(1.3)	48.0	(1.1)	34.2	(1.3)	38.4	(2.0)	40.5	(1.2)	50.9	(1.7)
	Italy	87.8	(0.3)	86.1	(1.6)	56.7	(3.9)	88.4	(0.3)	85.0	(2.6)	89.0	(0.4)	85.4	(0.7)
	Japan	96.7	(0.3)	97.4	(0.3)	c	c	96.9	(0.2)	c	c	96.4	(0.5)	97.0	(0.3)
	Korea	82.5	(1.2)	83.2	(1.4)	78.2	(5.2)	83.2	(0.9)	c	c	81.2	(3.9)	83.0	(0.8)
	Luxembourg	83.2	(0.6)	79.1	(1.5)	80.2	(0.7)	86.1	(0.7)	c	c	82.6	(0.5)	c	c
	Mexico	70.4	(0.6)	82.2	(0.9)	67.6	(0.9)	74.3	(0.7)	66.0	(1.4)	70.6	(1.1)	75.0	(0.7)
	Netherlands	94.8	(0.7)	94.7	(0.4)	94.7	(0.4)	95.8	(0.7)	c	c	95.1	(0.4)	93.9	(0.9)
	New Zealand	71.3	(0.9)	79.4	(2.3)	57.4	(3.4)	72.1	(0.8)	67.0	(3.5)	73.8	(1.6)	70.1	(1.4)
	Norway	86.4	(0.6)	c	c	86.3	(0.6)	c	c	83.1	(1.6)	87.0	(0.8)	86.7	(1.6)
	Poland	50.4	(1.6)	76.5	(3.5)	51.0	(1.5)	c	c	32.4	(3.0)	54.4	(2.1)	72.9	(2.5)
	Portugal	62.8	(1.0)	78.1	(3.7)	57.6	(1.4)	69.7	(1.3)	58.9	(5.9)	64.4	(1.2)	65.9	(3.4)
	Slovak Republic	79.9	(1.1)	81.0	(5.1)	75.7	(2.0)	83.5	(1.2)	66.7	(4.0)	80.8	(1.2)	88.9	(1.6)
	Spain	83.9	(0.6)	89.9	(0.6)	85.8	(0.4)	c	c	90.4	(1.1)	85.4	(0.6)	86.0	(1.0)
	Sweden	70.8	(0.9)	75.2	(2.4)	71.9	(0.9)	49.2	(5.7)	71.5	(1.6)	70.9	(1.3)	72.3	(1.6)
	Switzerland	71.8	(2.0)	86.3	(2.4)	74.3	(2.0)	69.4	(4.1)	69.7	(7.4)	70.9	(2.4)	81.8	(2.2)
	Turkey	8.2	(0.7)	c	c	3.8	(2.3)	8.8	(0.8)	10.7	(4.5)	8.0	(1.3)	9.0	(1.0)
	United States	74.2	(1.0)	84.1	(2.9)	69.2	(2.5)	75.3	(0.9)	72.6	(3.5)	76.6	(1.3)	73.3	(1.3)
	OECD average 2003	73.7	(0.2)	81.1	(0.5)	68.9	(0.4)	74.5	(0.5)	67.5	(0.8)	74.1	(0.3)	76.5	(0.3)
Partners	Brazil	44.1	(0.7)	63.9	(2.5)	37.2	(1.5)	50.4	(0.9)	43.4	(7.3)	42.4	(0.9)	53.1	(1.1)
	Hong Kong-China	96.1	(1.5)	95.1	(0.5)	90.6	(0.9)	97.3	(0.3)	c	c	c	c	95.1	(0.4)
	Indonesia	21.5	(1.8)	24.3	(2.8)	22.5	(2.2)	22.5	(2.3)	19.1	(3.7)	21.2	(2.1)	30.5	(4.9)
	Latvia	75.3	(1.0)	c	c	76.1	(1.0)	56.6	(4.5)	59.9	(3.2)	80.7	(1.0)	80.2	(1.3)
	Liechtenstein	90.4	(1.8)	c	c	90.0	(2.1)	c	c	c	c	90.5	(1.9)	c	c
	Macao-China	c	c	85.6	(0.4)	82.4	(0.7)	89.5	(0.6)	c	c	c	c	85.7	(0.5)
	Russian Federation	71.0	(1.4)	c	c	72.5	(1.4)	63.7	(2.4)	50.5	(3.1)	71.0	(2.6)	80.0	(1.1)
	Thailand	87.9	(0.7)	87.0	(1.3)	82.5	(1.6)	89.2	(1.6)	84.2	(2.3)	87.1	(0.9)	90.7	(0.8)
	Tunisia	23.2	(1.0)	c	c	17.5	(1.4)	26.4	(1.2)	18.5	(3.6)	21.6	(1.2)	28.5	(2.0)
	Uruguay	65.6	(1.1)	89.3	(1.4)	58.0	(1.7)	77.6	(1.0)	61.3	(6.1)	65.2	(1.5)	78.1	(1.3)

Notes: Values that are statistically significant are indicated in bold (see Annex A3).
ESCS refers to the *PISA index of economic, social and cultural status*.
Only countries and economies with comparable data from PISA 2003 and PISA 2012 are shown.
1. A socio-economically disadvantaged school is one whose students' mean socio-economic status (ESCS) is statistically significantly below the mean socio-economic status of the country/economy; an average school is one where there is no difference from the country's/economy's mean; and an advantaged school is one whose students' mean socio-economic status is statistically significantly above the country/economy mean.
StatLink ⟐ http://dx.doi.org/10.1787/888932957479

[Part 5/6]
Change between 2003 and 2012 in years in pre-school, by school features
Table IV.3.51 *Results based on students' self-reports*

	Change between 2003 and 2012 (PISA 2012 - PISA 2003)																
	Percentage of students reporting that they had attended pre-primary education (ISCED 0) for more than one year																
	Bottom quarter of ESCS		Second quarter of ESCS		Third quarter of ESCS		Top quarter of ESCS		Difference between top and bottom quarters of ESCS (top - bottom)		Socio-economically disadvantaged schools[1]		Socio-economically average schools[1]		Socio-economically advantaged schools[1]		Difference between advantaged and disadvantaged schools (advantaged - disadvantaged)	
	% dif.	S.E.	% dif.	S.E.	% dif.	S.E.	% dif.	S.E.	Dif. in % dif.	S.E.	% dif.	S.E.	% dif.	S.E.	% dif.	S.E.	Dif. in % dif.	S.E.
Australia	5.0	(1.7)	6.5	(1.6)	6.9	(1.6)	6.0	(1.5)	1.0	(2.3)	3.4	(1.8)	5.5	(1.5)	8.9	(1.7)	5.5	(2.4)
Austria	14.7	(2.8)	7.5	(2.2)	4.5	(1.8)	3.6	(1.6)	-11.1	(3.6)	8.8	(2.6)	8.0	(2.0)	4.4	(1.7)	-4.4	(3.3)
Belgium	-0.9	(1.3)	-0.4	(1.0)	-0.6	(0.6)	-0.6	(0.6)	0.3	(1.3)	-3.0	(1.2)	-0.2	(0.8)	-0.1	(0.6)	2.9	(1.4)
Canada	7.1	(1.6)	6.3	(1.6)	2.6	(1.6)	3.5	(1.7)	-3.6	(2.1)	13.8	(2.9)	1.4	(1.6)	2.6	(2.3)	-11.2	(3.6)
Czech Republic	9.8	(2.4)	9.6	(1.7)	10.1	(1.6)	7.5	(1.6)	-2.3	(1.9)	9.4	(2.9)	8.4	(1.4)	9.8	(1.7)	0.4	(3.6)
Denmark	14.5	(2.2)	10.7	(2.2)	14.0	(1.9)	14.0	(2.0)	-0.5	(2.8)	10.7	(3.2)	13.8	(1.5)	12.8	(2.2)	2.1	(4.0)
Finland	-6.7	(2.1)	-4.1	(2.2)	-3.4	(2.0)	-1.8	(2.2)	4.8	(2.6)	-7.9	(3.9)	-4.5	(1.7)	-0.7	(2.6)	7.2	(4.8)
France	-3.7	(1.4)	-2.7	(1.2)	0.5	(1.0)	-1.8	(1.0)	1.9	(1.8)	-6.6	(1.7)	-1.3	(0.9)	-0.3	(0.8)	6.3	(1.9)
Germany	7.7	(2.1)	2.1	(1.8)	1.8	(1.6)	0.9	(1.4)	-6.9	(2.7)	2.3	(2.1)	3.0	(1.4)	0.7	(1.3)	-1.5	(2.7)
Greece	1.2	(3.0)	7.6	(2.6)	8.3	(2.2)	7.2	(2.5)	6.0	(3.6)	3.2	(3.6)	7.3	(2.7)	7.0	(3.0)	3.8	(4.5)
Hungary	2.9	(1.2)	1.7	(0.9)	1.5	(1.0)	-0.8	(0.9)	-3.7	(1.5)	1.9	(1.1)	0.5	(1.0)	1.1	(0.8)	-0.8	(1.3)
Iceland	8.1	(1.6)	6.9	(1.3)	5.7	(1.1)	2.7	(1.1)	-5.3	(1.9)	11.4	(2.0)	4.6	(0.9)	4.8	(1.0)	-6.6	(2.1)
Ireland	8.7	(2.4)	9.4	(2.4)	9.5	(2.3)	13.8	(2.7)	5.1	(3.1)	12.4	(3.3)	9.1	(1.8)	9.0	(3.1)	-3.4	(4.7)
Italy	-0.2	(1.4)	-0.1	(1.1)	3.4	(1.2)	0.9	(1.0)	1.1	(1.5)	1.3	(1.7)	-0.9	(1.0)	2.2	(0.9)	0.9	(2.0)
Japan	-0.8	(0.8)	0.2	(0.7)	-0.4	(0.7)	0.6	(0.6)	1.3	(0.9)	-1.0	(0.8)	0.3	(0.6)	0.0	(0.5)	0.9	(0.9)
Korea	0.0	(1.8)	-5.9	(1.8)	-4.2	(1.4)	-4.6	(1.7)	-4.6	(2.3)	-0.2	(2.2)	-5.5	(1.6)	-5.1	(1.6)	-4.9	(2.5)
Luxembourg	-1.0	(1.9)	4.0	(1.8)	6.1	(1.5)	4.1	(1.6)	5.1	(2.4)	1.1	(1.2)	c	c	3.7	(1.3)	2.7	(1.6)
Mexico	11.8	(2.1)	9.2	(1.7)	2.1	(1.5)	1.3	(1.3)	-10.5	(2.2)	11.4	(2.4)	3.4	(1.5)	1.2	(1.6)	-10.2	(3.1)
Netherlands	-0.7	(1.4)	2.7	(1.1)	1.5	(1.1)	0.9	(0.9)	1.6	(1.6)	0.8	(1.4)	0.9	(0.7)	1.1	(1.1)	0.3	(1.8)
New Zealand	-3.6	(2.3)	3.0	(2.2)	-0.6	(2.2)	0.7	(2.0)	4.3	(3.1)	-4.2	(3.1)	0.3	(1.7)	1.4	(2.3)	5.6	(4.5)
Norway	9.7	(2.1)	7.2	(2.1)	7.3	(1.5)	8.2	(1.7)	-1.6	(2.5)	3.5	(3.7)	8.1	(1.4)	7.8	(2.1)	4.4	(4.0)
Poland	-0.9	(2.9)	6.0	(2.8)	9.4	(2.6)	12.4	(2.2)	13.3	(3.7)	-0.6	(4.4)	6.7	(2.6)	15.5	(2.5)	16.1	(5.4)
Portugal	7.1	(2.5)	11.7	(2.5)	10.9	(2.3)	7.8	(2.1)	0.6	(2.8)	9.1	(2.9)	8.3	(2.5)	13.8	(3.0)	4.7	(4.0)
Slovak Republic	-3.9	(3.1)	2.4	(1.8)	6.0	(1.6)	10.5	(1.7)	14.3	(2.9)	-8.9	(3.3)	8.0	(1.6)	9.4	(1.8)	18.3	(3.6)
Spain	0.2	(1.9)	1.9	(1.4)	2.2	(1.2)	1.7	(0.9)	1.5	(2.5)	1.4	(2.0)	2.2	(1.2)	0.6	(1.1)	-0.8	(2.5)
Sweden	10.9	(2.4)	14.6	(2.2)	12.4	(2.2)	10.1	(2.0)	-0.8	(2.9)	17.4	(3.4)	9.7	(1.6)	12.3	(3.1)	-5.1	(4.8)
Switzerland	4.9	(3.4)	5.2	(3.0)	11.0	(3.0)	4.8	(3.6)	-0.1	(3.9)	4.6	(5.7)	6.7	(2.8)	7.4	(5.4)	2.9	(7.3)
Turkey	0.8	(0.5)	0.8	(0.9)	1.3	(1.1)	0.8	(2.2)	0.0	(2.4)	2.3	(0.8)	-0.1	(0.9)	1.0	(2.3)	-1.2	(2.6)
United States	49.7	(2.1)	62.0	(1.7)	70.1	(1.5)	75.3	(1.3)	25.6	(2.6)	52.0	(1.9)	65.9	(1.4)	72.7	(1.6)	20.7	(2.6)
OECD average 2003	5.3	(0.4)	6.4	(0.3)	6.9	(0.3)	6.5	(0.3)	1.3	(0.5)	5.2	(0.5)	6.1	(0.3)	7.1	(0.4)	1.9	(0.7)
Brazil	5.4	(2.2)	4.9	(1.9)	0.4	(2.0)	0.8	(2.5)	-4.6	(3.1)	4.4	(2.6)	4.7	(1.8)	-3.0	(2.8)	-7.5	(3.9)
Hong Kong-China	15.2	(1.6)	10.1	(2.0)	4.2	(1.2)	2.7	(0.9)	-12.5	(1.7)	12.1	(2.4)	7.0	(1.2)	4.5	(1.0)	-7.6	(2.6)
Indonesia	1.1	(2.2)	-6.7	(2.4)	-3.5	(2.5)	-2.3	(4.3)	-3.4	(3.9)	3.1	(3.1)	-6.8	(3.7)	-3.8	(5.3)	-6.9	(5.4)
Latvia	12.9	(3.0)	18.4	(2.6)	20.3	(2.1)	26.4	(2.3)	13.5	(3.7)	17.5	(4.9)	20.7	(2.0)	19.8	(2.3)	2.3	(5.7)
Liechtenstein	11.6	(5.5)	-4.4	(2.8)	1.9	(4.0)	-8.9	(5.8)	-20.5	(8.3)	c	c	-3.6	(3.3)	c	c	c	c
Macao-China	8.3	(3.5)	6.8	(3.0)	3.2	(2.8)	4.6	(2.7)	-3.7	(4.5)	11.3	(2.8)	1.6	(2.2)	2.2	(2.5)	-9.2	(3.7)
Russian Federation	-16.0	(3.1)	-9.3	(2.6)	-5.0	(1.9)	0.9	(2.1)	16.9	(3.3)	-18.3	(4.6)	-8.3	(2.8)	0.8	(1.9)	19.1	(4.8)
Thailand	20.5	(2.7)	17.2	(2.0)	11.6	(1.9)	5.0	(1.2)	-15.5	(2.9)	17.8	(2.6)	15.2	(2.0)	4.8	(1.3)	-13.0	(2.9)
Tunisia	3.1	(1.4)	4.0	(2.2)	-4.7	(2.2)	-16.5	(2.9)	-19.6	(2.9)	1.3	(1.8)	-3.2	(2.1)	-13.8	(3.2)	-15.1	(3.4)
Uruguay	13.7	(2.7)	4.8	(2.9)	1.5	(1.9)	4.3	(1.6)	-9.4	(2.8)	12.9	(2.4)	3.6	(2.6)	8.8	(2.1)	-4.2	(3.6)

Notes: Values that are statistically significant are indicated in bold (see Annex A3).
ESCS refers to the *PISA index of economic, social and cultural status*.
Only countries and economies with comparable data from PISA 2003 and PISA 2012 are shown.
1. A socio-economically disadvantaged school is one whose students' mean socio-economic status (ESCS) is statistically significantly below the mean socio-economic status of the country/economy; an average school is one where there is no difference from the country's/economy's mean; and an advantaged school is one whose students' mean socio-economic status is statistically significantly above the country/economy mean.
StatLink http://dx.doi.org/10.1787/888932957479

[Part 6/6]
Change between 2003 and 2012 in years in pre-school, by school features
Table IV.3.51   *Results based on students' self-reports*

	Change between 2003 and 2012 (PISA 2012 - PISA 2003)																	
	Percentage of students reporting that they had attended pre-primary education (ISCED 0) for more than one year																	
	Public schools		Private schools		Difference between private and public schools (priv. - pub.)		Lower secondary education (ISCED 2)		Upper secondary education (ISCED 3)		Difference between ISCED 3 and ISCED 2 (ISCED 3 - ISCED 2)		Schools located in a village, hamlet or rural area (fewer than 3 000 people)		Schools located in a small town or town (3 000 to about 100 000 people)		Schools located in a city or a large city (over 100 000 people)		Difference between rural area and town (town - rural)		Difference between town and a city (town - city)	
	% dif.	S.E.	% dif.	S.E.	Dif. in % dif.	S.E.	% dif.	S.E.	% dif.	S.E.	Dif. in % dif.	S.E.	% dif.	S.E.	% dif.	S.E.	% dif.	S.E.	Dif. in % dif.	S.E.	Dif. in % dif.	S.E.
Australia	c	c	c	c	c	c	6.8	(1.0)	2.2	(1.9)	-4.6	(2.0)	5.2	(4.3)	5.8	(1.8)	6.0	(1.3)	0.6	(4.6)	-0.2	(2.5)
Austria	7.7	(1.4)	5.8	(3.7)	-1.8	(4.0)	8.3	(6.0)	7.6	(1.4)	-0.6	(5.4)	9.0	(4.4)	7.1	(1.9)	8.3	(2.2)	-1.9	(5.0)	-1.2	(2.7)
Belgium	-1.8	(1.3)	-0.7	(0.6)	1.1	(1.5)	4.1	(3.7)	0.5	(0.4)	-3.6	(3.6)	-2.2	(5.8)	-0.9	(0.6)	-0.7	(1.5)	1.2	(4.8)	-0.3	(1.7)
Canada	5.4	(1.0)	4.0	(4.0)	-1.4	(4.1)	5.3	(1.8)	4.3	(1.1)	-1.0	(2.1)	6.4	(3.4)	1.6	(1.9)	5.1	(1.6)	-4.8	(3.9)	-3.5	(2.9)
Czech Republic	9.0	(1.2)	7.2	(4.4)	-1.8	(4.2)	8.3	(1.8)	10.1	(1.2)	1.8	(2.1)	7.7	(5.5)	8.6	(1.4)	10.3	(2.4)	0.9	(5.5)	-1.7	(2.6)
Denmark	11.9	(1.4)	16.5	(2.4)	4.6	(3.1)	13.0	(1.2)	31.6	(7.4)	18.7	(7.5)	17.0	(2.8)	13.0	(1.7)	8.1	(2.9)	-4.1	(3.6)	4.9	(3.5)
Finland	-4.2	(1.4)	6.6	(5.2)	10.8	(5.4)	-4.1	(1.4)	c	c	c	c	-4.2	(7.1)	-7.9	(1.6)	0.4	(2.0)	-3.7	(7.1)	-8.3	(2.6)
France	c	c	c	c	c	c	-6.7	(1.6)	-1.1	(0.5)	5.6	(1.5)	c	c	c	c	c	c	c	c	c	c
Germany	2.7	(1.1)	0.2	(4.4)	-2.6	(4.2)	2.5	(0.9)	8.6	(6.8)	6.1	(6.7)	c	c	1.8	(1.3)	4.2	(2.3)	c	c	-2.4	(2.5)
Greece	6.6	(1.8)	c	c	c	c	-5.1	(4.8)	6.1	(1.8)	11.2	(5.3)	13.8	(7.8)	5.0	(2.1)	7.3	(3.7)	-8.8	(8.4)	-2.3	(4.4)
Hungary	1.3	(0.6)	2.1	(1.5)	0.8	(1.6)	2.5	(2.6)	1.5	(0.5)	-0.9	(2.8)	6.6	(4.0)	1.9	(0.8)	0.2	(0.8)	-4.7	(4.6)	1.6	(1.1)
Iceland	5.9	(0.7)	c	c	c	c	5.8	(0.6)	c	c	c	c	11.0	(1.6)	5.7	(0.8)	0.8	(1.4)	-5.3	(1.7)	4.9	(1.6)
Ireland	12.1	(2.2)	8.9	(2.1)	-3.2	(3.2)	12.9	(1.8)	6.3	(2.0)	-6.7	(2.3)	16.2	(2.8)	10.3	(1.9)	6.8	(2.8)	-5.9	(3.2)	3.5	(3.1)
Italy	1.1	(0.8)	-3.8	(2.5)	-4.9	(2.5)	1.6	(9.2)	1.1	(0.7)	-0.5	(9.8)	-5.4	(7.3)	1.4	(0.8)	0.6	(1.3)	6.8	(7.1)	0.9	(1.6)
Japan	-0.2	(0.5)	-0.3	(0.5)	-0.1	(0.8)	c	c	-0.2	(0.4)	c	c	c	c	0.2	(0.7)	-0.4	(0.4)	c	c	0.6	(0.8)
Korea	-3.1	(1.6)	-4.0	(1.5)	-0.9	(2.2)	-8.3	(6.9)	-3.4	(1.1)	4.9	(7.1)	c	c	-0.6	(4.5)	-4.6	(1.0)	c	c	4.0	(4.9)
Luxembourg	4.8	(1.0)	-5.7	(2.1)	-10.4	(2.3)	1.2	(1.1)	6.1	(1.4)	4.9	(1.9)	c	c	3.3	(0.9)	c	c	c	c	c	c
Mexico	7.1	(1.4)	4.8	(2.4)	-2.3	(2.8)	5.1	(2.4)	4.3	(1.1)	-0.8	(2.7)	14.3	(3.4)	3.6	(1.7)	2.3	(1.6)	-10.6	(3.8)	1.3	(2.6)
Netherlands	3.0	(1.4)	0.3	(0.6)	-2.7	(1.7)	1.2	(0.6)	0.6	(1.0)	-0.6	(1.1)	c	c	0.8	(0.7)	0.9	(1.2)	c	c	-0.1	(1.3)
New Zealand	-0.7	(1.2)	4.5	(5.9)	5.3	(5.9)	-13.1	(4.2)	0.4	(1.1)	13.5	(4.5)	-2.4	(4.7)	0.9	(2.0)	-0.6	(1.9)	3.3	(5.5)	1.5	(2.8)
Norway	7.9	(1.2)	c	c	c	c	7.9	(1.2)	c	c	c	c	6.1	(2.5)	9.3	(1.6)	3.8	(2.8)	3.2	(2.7)	5.5	(3.3)
Poland	6.3	(2.0)	c	c	c	c	6.5	(2.0)	c	c	c	c	-3.0	(4.0)	10.8	(2.6)	12.8	(3.0)	13.8	(4.7)	-2.1	(3.7)
Portugal	8.3	(1.7)	17.2	(5.6)	8.9	(6.4)	5.5	(2.4)	13.3	(2.1)	7.8	(3.1)	4.7	(7.0)	10.1	(2.0)	8.4	(4.3)	5.4	(7.0)	1.7	(5.2)
Slovak Republic	3.7	(1.5)	4.7	(5.5)	1.0	(5.8)	1.2	(2.5)	6.3	(1.5)	5.0	(2.8)	-4.6	(5.2)	4.2	(1.5)	10.9	(2.2)	8.8	(4.5)	-6.7	(2.9)
Spain	1.5	(1.1)	2.2	(0.9)	0.6	(1.5)	1.5	(0.8)	c	c	c	c	4.9	(3.1)	0.9	(1.0)	1.6	(1.6)	-4.0	(3.4)	-0.7	(2.0)
Sweden	11.3	(1.5)	14.2	(3.0)	2.9	(3.2)	12.2	(1.4)	-6.7	(10.2)	-18.9	(10.6)	13.5	(2.8)	12.3	(1.9)	8.9	(2.5)	-1.2	(3.2)	3.5	(3.1)
Switzerland	5.7	(2.8)	15.6	(6.9)	9.9	(7.3)	8.7	(2.8)	-2.9	(5.1)	-11.6	(6.2)	8.7	(9.0)	5.6	(3.4)	3.0	(3.7)	-3.2	(10.8)	2.6	(5.5)
Turkey	1.2	(1.0)	c	c	c	c	1.7	(2.7)	0.6	(1.1)	-1.0	(3.2)	c	c	2.4	(1.5)	-0.7	(1.4)	c	c	3.1	(2.2)
United States	64.3	(1.1)	76.9	(3.4)	12.7	(4.5)	55.5	(2.8)	66.7	(1.1)	11.2	(2.9)	64.1	(3.8)	66.7	(1.5)	63.4	(1.6)	2.5	(4.1)	3.2	(2.1)
OECD average 2003	6.6	(0.3)	8.1	(0.8)	1.2	(0.8)	5.1	(0.6)	6.8	(0.7)	1.7	(1.0)	8.5	(1.1)	6.6	(0.3)	6.2	(0.4)	-0.5	(1.1)	0.5	(0.6)
Brazil	1.8	(1.7)	3.2	(3.4)	1.5	(3.9)	3.0	(2.3)	-1.1	(1.7)	-4.0	(2.9)	7.1	(10.2)	0.3	(2.0)	3.3	(2.1)	-6.7	(10.2)	-3.0	(3.0)
Hong Kong-China	6.7	(1.9)	8.2	(1.1)	1.5	(2.6)	15.4	(2.1)	1.8	(0.5)	-13.7	(2.1)	c	c	c	c	8.0	(1.0)	c	c	c	c
Indonesia	-3.8	(2.4)	-1.4	(3.7)	2.4	(4.2)	-0.4	(2.7)	-7.4	(3.2)	-7.0	(3.6)	-3.7	(5.1)	-3.5	(3.9)	0.9	(5.6)	0.2	(7.1)	-4.4	(7.2)
Latvia	19.7	(1.5)	c	c	c	c	20.7	(1.5)	-3.5	(5.4)	-24.2	(5.7)	20.7	(4.2)	20.4	(2.1)	15.2	(2.0)	-0.3	(4.7)	5.2	(2.8)
Liechtenstein	0.0	(2.4)	c	c	c	c	-0.7	(2.6)	c	c	c	c	c	c	-0.1	(2.4)	c	c	c	c	c	c
Macao-China	c	c	5.5	(1.5)	c	c	5.4	(1.8)	0.9	(2.5)	-4.5	(3.1)	c	c	c	c	5.7	(1.4)	c	c	c	c
Russian Federation	-7.3	(1.9)	c	c	c	c	-1.3	(2.4)	-16.9	(2.6)	-15.6	(2.8)	-16.7	(4.7)	-7.8	(3.0)	-1.5	(1.6)	8.9	(5.1)	-6.3	(3.4)
Thailand	14.0	(1.4)	10.1	(3.2)	-3.8	(3.5)	9.7	(2.3)	13.6	(1.3)	3.9	(2.3)	15.2	(3.4)	15.5	(2.2)	6.4	(1.8)	0.2	(4.3)	9.1	(3.0)
Tunisia	c	c	c	c	c	c	-2.3	(1.8)	-12.1	(2.6)	-9.8	(2.7)	1.4	(7.2)	-3.1	(1.9)	-12.0	(4.4)	-4.5	(7.7)	8.9	(5.5)
Uruguay	5.5	(1.7)	4.2	(1.9)	-1.3	(2.8)	6.2	(2.1)	8.2	(1.7)	2.0	(2.6)	16.5	(8.6)	6.7	(2.2)	5.1	(2.1)	-9.8	(9.0)	1.6	(3.2)

Notes: Values that are statistically significant are indicated in bold (see Annex A3).
ESCS refers to the *PISA index of economic, social and cultural status*.
Only countries and economies with comparable data from PISA 2003 and PISA 2012 are shown.
1. A socio-economically disadvantaged school is one whose students' mean socio-economic status (ESCS) is statistically significantly below the mean socio-economic status of the country/economy; an average school is one where there is no difference from the country's/economy's mean; and an advantaged school is one whose students' mean socio-economic status is statistically significantly above the country/economy mean.
StatLink ⌸ http://dx.doi.org/10.1787/888932957479

[Part 1/2]
Index of school responsibility for resource allocation and mathematics performance
Table IV.4.1   *Results based on school principals' reports*

| | | Index of school responsibility for resource allocation | | | | | | | | | | Variability in this index | |
| | | All students | | Bottom quarter | | Second quarter | | Third quarter | | Top quarter | | | |
		Mean index	S.E.	Mean index	S.E.	Mean index	S.E.	Mean index	S.E.	Mean index	S.E.	Standard deviation	S.E.
OECD	Australia	0.06	(0.03)	-0.61	(0.01)	-0.43	(0.01)	-0.15	(0.02)	1.44	(0.10)	1.00	(0.03)
	Austria	-0.56	(0.03)	-0.72	(0.01)	-0.67	(0.01)	-0.58	(0.01)	-0.26	(0.12)	0.37	(0.14)
	Belgium	-0.29	(0.01)	-0.67	(0.02)	-0.40	(0.02)	-0.10	(0.02)	0.01	(0.02)	0.29	(0.02)
	Canada	-0.35	(0.03)	-0.67	(0.01)	-0.55	(0.00)	-0.45	(0.01)	0.26	(0.10)	0.61	(0.06)
	Chile	0.57	(0.07)	-0.75	(0.01)	-0.34	(0.06)	0.91	(0.17)	2.46	(0.11)	1.29	(0.04)
	Czech Republic	1.22	(0.10)	-0.36	(0.02)	0.28	(0.14)	2.26	(0.25)	2.71	(0.00)	1.36	(0.02)
	Denmark	0.18	(0.06)	-0.40	(0.01)	-0.21	(0.04)	-0.01	(0.02)	1.34	(0.22)	0.88	(0.07)
	Estonia	0.14	(0.04)	-0.34	(0.01)	-0.13	(0.02)	-0.01	(0.01)	1.05	(0.16)	0.75	(0.06)
	Finland	-0.28	(0.02)	-0.63	(0.01)	-0.44	(0.02)	-0.34	(0.01)	0.29	(0.07)	0.55	(0.04)
	France	-0.54	(0.01)	-0.77	(0.01)	-0.62	(0.02)	-0.53	(0.01)	-0.25	(0.05)	0.31	(0.06)
	Germany	-0.58	(0.01)	-0.74	(0.01)	-0.65	(0.01)	-0.56	(0.01)	-0.38	(0.01)	0.14	(0.01)
	Greece	-0.70	(0.01)	-0.79	(0.00)	-0.77	(0.00)	-0.71	(0.01)	-0.53	(0.02)	0.16	(0.02)
	Hungary	0.46	(0.10)	-0.50	(0.03)	-0.22	(0.05)	0.26	(0.14)	2.31	(0.23)	1.15	(0.07)
	Iceland	-0.04	(0.00)	-0.42	(0.00)	-0.24	(0.00)	-0.04	(0.00)	0.54	(0.02)	0.61	(0.01)
	Ireland	-0.43	(0.02)	-0.72	(0.01)	-0.54	(0.03)	-0.35	(0.02)	-0.09	(0.02)	0.25	(0.01)
	Israel	-0.24	(0.04)	-0.61	(0.01)	-0.46	(0.02)	-0.33	(0.02)	0.44	(0.15)	0.60	(0.09)
	Italy	-0.59	(0.02)	-0.79	(0.00)	-0.76	(0.01)	-0.69	(0.00)	-0.10	(0.07)	0.57	(0.05)
	Japan	-0.27	(0.04)	-0.73	(0.01)	-0.70	(0.00)	-0.53	(0.03)	0.89	(0.13)	0.76	(0.06)
	Korea	-0.44	(0.05)	-0.77	(0.01)	-0.67	(0.02)	-0.49	(0.04)	0.19	(0.18)	0.58	(0.12)
	Luxembourg	-0.20	(0.00)	-0.65	(0.00)	-0.54	(0.00)	-0.44	(0.00)	0.84	(0.01)	0.78	(0.00)
	Mexico	-0.31	(0.02)	-0.79	(0.00)	-0.70	(0.01)	-0.51	(0.01)	0.75	(0.08)	0.84	(0.04)
	Netherlands	1.26	(0.10)	-0.21	(0.07)	0.64	(0.15)	1.91	(0.22)	2.71	(0.01)	1.16	(0.03)
	New Zealand	0.11	(0.05)	-0.33	(0.02)	-0.14	(0.03)	0.00	(0.03)	0.90	(0.17)	0.67	(0.08)
	Norway	-0.18	(0.03)	-0.50	(0.02)	-0.36	(0.01)	-0.16	(0.04)	0.29	(0.10)	0.43	(0.08)
	Poland	-0.34	(0.02)	-0.59	(0.01)	-0.48	(0.03)	-0.36	(0.01)	0.08	(0.06)	0.44	(0.03)
	Portugal	-0.48	(0.03)	-0.78	(0.01)	-0.65	(0.03)	-0.51	(0.02)	0.03	(0.11)	0.50	(0.09)
	Slovak Republic	0.78	(0.09)	-0.38	(0.04)	-0.04	(0.04)	0.83	(0.30)	2.71	(0.03)	1.25	(0.04)
	Slovenia	-0.11	(0.02)	-0.48	(0.00)	-0.35	(0.00)	-0.19	(0.00)	0.57	(0.06)	0.66	(0.03)
	Spain	-0.42	(0.03)	-0.78	(0.00)	-0.72	(0.01)	-0.52	(0.02)	0.32	(0.11)	0.61	(0.08)
	Sweden	0.63	(0.07)	-0.35	(0.02)	-0.10	(0.03)	0.46	(0.10)	2.50	(0.19)	1.16	(0.05)
	Switzerland	-0.13	(0.04)	-0.57	(0.02)	-0.37	(0.01)	-0.20	(0.03)	0.60	(0.14)	0.63	(0.06)
	Turkey	-0.72	(0.01)	-0.80	(0.00)	-0.77	(0.00)	-0.74	(0.01)	-0.59	(0.02)	0.09	(0.01)
	United Kingdom	1.10	(0.08)	-0.37	(0.03)	0.40	(0.10)	1.68	(0.22)	2.71	(0.00)	1.24	(0.03)
	United States	0.08	(0.06)	-0.56	(0.02)	-0.40	(0.02)	-0.17	(0.12)	1.47	(0.15)	0.86	(0.05)
	OECD average	-0.05	(0.01)	-0.59	(0.00)	-0.39	(0.01)	-0.04	(0.02)	0.83	(0.02)	0.69	(0.01)
Partners	Albania	-0.60	(0.04)	-0.79	(0.00)	-0.77	(0.00)	-0.70	(0.02)	-0.13	(0.14)	0.50	(0.11)
	Argentina	m	m	m	m	m	m	m	m	m	m	m	m
	Brazil	-0.32	(0.04)	-0.80	(0.00)	-0.80	(0.00)	-0.72	(0.02)	1.02	(0.16)	1.02	(0.05)
	Bulgaria	0.86	(0.10)	-0.22	(0.03)	0.25	(0.09)	0.84	(0.14)	2.58	(0.20)	1.08	(0.05)
	Colombia	-0.36	(0.04)	-0.79	(0.00)	-0.76	(0.01)	-0.64	(0.02)	0.75	(0.14)	0.92	(0.06)
	Costa Rica	-0.36	(0.04)	-0.78	(0.00)	-0.72	(0.02)	-0.58	(0.01)	0.66	(0.16)	0.89	(0.07)
	Croatia	-0.34	(0.03)	-0.60	(0.02)	-0.42	(0.02)	-0.31	(0.02)	0.00	(0.08)	0.32	(0.10)
	Cyprus*	-0.35	(0.00)	-0.80	(0.00)	-0.79	(0.00)	-0.66	(0.00)	0.86	(0.00)	0.94	(0.00)
	Hong Kong-China	0.42	(0.09)	-0.33	(0.02)	-0.03	(0.02)	0.17	(0.05)	1.87	(0.31)	0.99	(0.09)
	Indonesia	0.33	(0.09)	-0.70	(0.02)	-0.53	(0.03)	0.25	(0.20)	2.32	(0.15)	1.26	(0.05)
	Jordan	-0.51	(0.03)	-0.79	(0.00)	-0.77	(0.01)	-0.63	(0.02)	0.14	(0.10)	0.65	(0.05)
	Kazakhstan	-0.33	(0.04)	-0.61	(0.01)	-0.56	(0.00)	-0.43	(0.03)	0.28	(0.17)	0.56	(0.12)
	Latvia	0.60	(0.08)	-0.30	(0.02)	-0.04	(0.02)	0.46	(0.11)	2.26	(0.21)	1.06	(0.05)
	Liechtenstein	-0.08	(0.02)	c	c	c	c	-0.38	(0.01)	1.19	(0.06)	0.89	(0.02)
	Lithuania	0.78	(0.08)	-0.38	(0.03)	-0.02	(0.06)	0.89	(0.21)	2.62	(0.06)	1.20	(0.04)
	Macao-China	1.64	(0.00)	-0.25	(0.00)	1.41	(0.00)	2.68	(0.00)	2.71	(0.00)	1.25	(0.00)
	Malaysia	-0.49	(0.03)	-0.75	(0.01)	-0.60	(0.02)	-0.56	(0.00)	-0.04	(0.12)	0.52	(0.10)
	Montenegro	-0.33	(0.00)	-0.58	(0.00)	-0.47	(0.00)	-0.36	(0.00)	0.07	(0.00)	0.50	(0.00)
	Peru	0.18	(0.07)	-0.78	(0.01)	-0.61	(0.02)	-0.41	(0.07)	2.50	(0.22)	1.38	(0.04)
	Qatar	-0.37	(0.00)	-0.68	(0.00)	-0.41	(0.00)	-0.36	(0.00)	-0.04	(0.00)	0.36	(0.00)
	Romania	-0.57	(0.02)	-0.79	(0.01)	-0.70	(0.02)	-0.57	(0.02)	-0.23	(0.06)	0.28	(0.06)
	Russian Federation	0.03	(0.07)	-0.52	(0.02)	-0.34	(0.03)	-0.07	(0.04)	1.04	(0.22)	0.77	(0.08)
	Serbia	-0.39	(0.02)	-0.64	(0.02)	-0.50	(0.02)	-0.37	(0.01)	-0.07	(0.06)	0.30	(0.06)
	Shanghai-China	-0.28	(0.05)	-0.75	(0.01)	-0.58	(0.03)	-0.37	(0.03)	0.56	(0.18)	0.67	(0.10)
	Singapore	-0.36	(0.01)	-0.70	(0.00)	-0.57	(0.00)	-0.46	(0.00)	0.29	(0.06)	0.69	(0.03)
	Chinese Taipei	0.07	(0.06)	-0.64	(0.02)	-0.39	(0.02)	-0.18	(0.04)	1.50	(0.20)	1.01	(0.06)
	Thailand	0.70	(0.08)	-0.47	(0.03)	-0.04	(0.06)	0.74	(0.17)	2.59	(0.11)	1.20	(0.04)
	Tunisia	-0.20	(0.06)	-0.75	(0.01)	-0.66	(0.02)	-0.41	(0.09)	1.01	(0.18)	0.82	(0.08)
	United Arab Emirates	0.39	(0.05)	-0.78	(0.01)	-0.52	(0.02)	0.57	(0.14)	2.27	(0.07)	1.25	(0.03)
	Uruguay	-0.46	(0.04)	-0.80	(0.00)	-0.79	(0.01)	-0.69	(0.01)	0.42	(0.15)	0.72	(0.07)
	Viet Nam	-0.43	(0.06)	-0.80	(0.01)	-0.72	(0.02)	-0.58	(0.03)	0.39	(0.21)	0.72	(0.11)

Note: Values that are statistically significant are indicated in bold (see Annex A3).
* See notes at the beginning of this Annex.
StatLink ⫸ http://dx.doi.org/10.1787/888932957498

[Part 2/2]
Index of school responsibility for resource allocation and mathematics performance

Table IV.4.1 — *Results based on school principals' reports*

	Performance on the mathematics scale by national quarters of this index								Change in the mathematics score per unit of this index		Increased likelihood of students in the bottom quarter of this index scoring in the bottom quarter of the national mathematics performance distribution		Explained variance in student performance (r-squared x 100)	
	Bottom quarter		Second quarter		Third quarter		Top quarter							
	Mean score	S.E.	Mean score	S.E.	Mean score	S.E.	Mean score	S.E.	Score dif.	S.E.	Ratio	S.E.	%	S.E.
Australia	**489**	(3.9)	491	(4.6)	507	(3.2)	**531**	(3.3)	**17.0**	(1.6)	**1.4**	(0.1)	3.2	(0.6)
Austria	522	(7.7)	482	(7.4)	519	(7.4)	500	(9.1)	0.8	(10.1)	0.7	(0.1)	0.0	(0.1)
Belgium	**485**	(6.9)	511	(6.9)	532	(5.6)	**531**	(6.4)	**65.8**	(13.9)	**1.5**	(0.2)	3.5	(1.3)
Canada	**506**	(3.8)	520	(4.3)	513	(3.7)	**533**	(3.6)	**19.1**	(3.2)	1.2	(0.1)	1.7	(0.6)
Chile	**382**	(4.5)	418	(7.6)	428	(6.8)	**463**	(5.8)	**22.0**	(2.4)	**2.1**	(0.2)	12.4	(2.5)
Czech Republic	507	(8.9)	508	(8.7)	493	(6.2)	487	(7.1)	-7.1	(3.3)	0.8	(0.1)	1.0	(0.9)
Denmark	504	(3.9)	495	(4.7)	494	(5.2)	510	(5.4)	**5.3**	(2.6)	0.9	(0.1)	0.3	(0.3)
Estonia	509	(4.6)	526	(4.0)	524	(4.5)	522	(4.5)	2.3	(3.8)	1.2	(0.1)	0.1	(0.2)
Finland	515	(4.0)	516	(5.0)	526	(3.5)	517	(3.5)	7.5	(3.1)	1.0	(0.1)	0.2	(0.2)
France	497	(8.8)	491	(8.3)	499	(7.0)	493	(7.2)	**-23.9**	(11.2)	1.0	(0.2)	0.6	(0.5)
Germany	516	(8.8)	514	(7.6)	510	(7.2)	514	(8.5)	-7.2	(31.7)	1.0	(0.2)	0.0	(0.2)
Greece	449	(7.0)	447	(5.5)	452	(5.8)	464	(6.3)	34.9	(27.2)	1.1	(0.2)	0.4	(0.6)
Hungary	467	(9.3)	479	(9.5)	485	(10.8)	477	(11.9)	0.3	(5.4)	1.2	(0.2)	0.0	(0.4)
Iceland	496	(3.4)	495	(3.2)	491	(3.4)	493	(3.4)	-0.4	(2.2)	1.0	(0.1)	0.0	(0.0)
Ireland	487	(7.1)	512	(8.0)	508	(6.2)	502	(6.0)	**23.1**	(12.9)	**1.4**	(0.2)	0.5	(0.5)
Israel	459	(9.1)	459	(11.3)	476	(9.0)	471	(12.5)	-3.7	(10.8)	1.1	(0.2)	0.0	(0.4)
Italy	**488**	(4.2)	495	(3.8)	486	(4.8)	**473**	(4.6)	-5.3	(3.7)	0.9	(0.1)	0.1	(0.2)
Japan	535	(6.6)	527	(5.8)	544	(9.3)	539	(11.3)	10.7	(6.2)	1.0	(0.1)	0.8	(0.9)
Korea	540	(8.2)	550	(9.6)	557	(9.8)	568	(11.2)	7.7	(13.5)	1.2	(0.2)	0.2	(0.8)
Luxembourg	507	(1.8)	503	(2.1)	483	(2.4)	466	(2.0)	**-8.2**	(1.2)	0.8	(0.0)	0.4	(0.1)
Mexico	**393**	(2.79)	398	(3.05)	418	(3.4)	**444**	(2.8)	**18.6**	(1.9)	**1.6**	(0.1)	4.5	(0.9)
Netherlands	524	(12.3)	517	(9.8)	516	(8.3)	536	(10.9)	1.6	(5.7)	0.9	(0.2)	0.0	(0.4)
New Zealand	488	(6.5)	498	(7.5)	503	(6.4)	510	(8.6)	**11.9**	(5.8)	1.2	(0.1)	0.6	(0.6)
Norway	488	(5.7)	484	(5.5)	491	(5.4)	495	(5.3)	**14.3**	(5.4)	1.0	(0.1)	0.5	(0.5)
Poland	519	(6.5)	525	(9.6)	516	(6.4)	511	(5.4)	3.7	(4.6)	0.9	(0.1)	0.0	(0.1)
Portugal	482	(9.1)	482	(7.7)	484	(10.6)	500	(7.9)	**29.4**	(5.7)	1.1	(0.2)	2.4	(0.9)
Slovak Republic	484	(9.6)	480	(11.9)	491	(14.3)	471	(10.6)	-3.4	(4.5)	0.8	(0.1)	0.2	(0.4)
Slovenia	510	(3.1)	484	(3.4)	508	(2.7)	502	(2.7)	**5.3**	(2.5)	0.9	(0.1)	0.1	(0.1)
Spain	**471**	(3.3)	471	(4.0)	479	(3.7)	**516**	(2.8)	**24.2**	(4.5)	**1.3**	(0.1)	2.8	(0.6)
Sweden	475	(4.7)	475	(6.5)	478	(4.6)	485	(4.8)	3.5	(2.1)	1.0	(0.1)	0.2	(0.2)
Switzerland	520	(5.0)	551	(7.9)	533	(7.7)	523	(7.6)	**-11.2**	(5.4)	1.2	(0.1)	0.6	(0.6)
Turkey	454	(12.9)	450	(8.9)	447	(8.7)	440	(8.1)	-51.2	(57.9)	1.0	(0.1)	0.3	(0.7)
United Kingdom	**484**	(3.8)	485	(6.4)	494	(10.1)	**513**	(7.0)	**8.0**	(3.0)	1.1	(0.1)	1.1	(0.8)
United States	469	(9.8)	481	(8.1)	489	(7.6)	486	(6.4)	5.5	(4.1)	1.3	(0.2)	0.3	(0.5)
OECD average	**489**	(1.2)	492	(1.2)	496	(1.2)	**500**	(1.2)	**6.5**	(2.4)	**1.1**	(0.0)	1.1	(0.1)
Albania	394	(4.4)	396	(4.6)	389	(3.5)	398	(4.5)	7.6	(3.4)	0.9	(0.1)	0.2	(0.1)
Argentina	m	m	m	m	m	m	m	m	m	m	m	m	m	m
Brazil	**375**	(3.5)	374	(2.8)	382	(3.7)	**433**	(5.9)	**27.8**	(2.9)	1.2	(0.1)	13.3	(2.0)
Bulgaria	**430**	(8.9)	423	(10.4)	442	(10.4)	**460**	(9.9)	**11.9**	(4.5)	1.2	(0.2)	1.9	(1.4)
Colombia	375	(4.1)	369	(4.7)	362	(5.6)	399	(8.0)	**17.3**	(4.8)	0.9	(0.1)	4.6	(2.5)
Costa Rica	397	(5.4)	393	(6.5)	392	(4.8)	446	(8.8)	**24.9**	(3.1)	1.2	(0.2)	10.3	(3.1)
Croatia	474	(9.2)	477	(7.0)	469	(9.6)	465	(8.9)	-8.5	(14.2)	0.9	(0.2)	0.1	(0.3)
Cyprus*	**431**	(2.7)	420	(2.5)	434	(2.3)	**471**	(2.3)	**24.3**	(1.1)	1.1	(0.1)	6.1	(0.6)
Hong Kong-China	570	(10.8)	565	(11.5)	560	(8.5)	550	(12.4)	-4.7	(6.5)	0.9	(0.2)	0.2	(0.7)
Indonesia	391	(9.1)	369	(5.8)	358	(6.4)	383	(11.3)	1.5	(4.2)	0.7	(0.1)	0.1	(0.6)
Jordan	**373**	(5.6)	371	(5.0)	385	(4.8)	**413**	(9.2)	**29.8**	(9.5)	1.3	(0.1)	6.2	(3.5)
Kazakhstan	434	(5.4)	431	(5.4)	429	(7.1)	433	(8.3)	6.9	(9.1)	0.9	(0.1)	0.3	(0.9)
Latvia	492	(6.5)	483	(5.6)	489	(5.7)	498	(6.1)	3.3	(2.7)	1.1	(0.1)	0.2	(0.3)
Liechtenstein	c	c	c	c	514	(9.2)	**479**	(8.9)	-33.2	(4.8)	1.1	(0.2)	9.7	(2.7)
Lithuania	474	(7.2)	481	(7.5)	483	(7.2)	478	(6.9)	0.2	(2.8)	1.1	(0.1)	0.0	(0.1)
Macao-China	543	(1.9)	545	(2.4)	534	(2.4)	530	(2.2)	-3.4	(0.1)	1.0	(0.1)	0.2	(0.1)
Malaysia	428	(7.0)	415	(7.2)	413	(5.7)	426	(8.2)	**27.9**	(8.4)	0.9	(0.1)	3.2	(2.6)
Montenegro	**411**	(2.6)	421	(3.3)	408	(2.4)	**399**	(2.3)	**-14.8**	(2.1)	0.9	(0.1)	0.8	(0.2)
Peru	**345**	(6.4)	351	(6.1)	353	(6.4)	**423**	(9.4)	**24.0**	(2.7)	**1.4**	(0.2)	15.4	(3.1)
Qatar	337	(1.4)	394	(2.2)	398	(2.1)	376	(2.0)	**20.2**	(2.0)	**1.6**	(0.1)	0.5	(0.1)
Romania	431	(7.3)	437	(9.8)	465	(8.8)	446	(8.9)	16.8	(16.3)	1.2	(0.2)	0.3	(0.6)
Russian Federation	470	(5.8)	476	(8.7)	489	(5.9)	495	(7.0)	8.6	(5.3)	1.2	(0.2)	0.6	(0.7)
Serbia	447	(10.7)	456	(8.8)	450	(7.2)	441	(7.8)	-0.4	(13.2)	1.1	(0.2)	0.0	(0.2)
Shanghai-China	605	(10.1)	603	(12.3)	623	(10.8)	620	(9.7)	3.5	(6.7)	1.1	(0.2)	0.1	(0.2)
Singapore	**567**	(2.6)	554	(2.7)	567	(3.2)	**605**	(3.3)	**34.3**	(5.4)	1.0	(0.1)	5.0	(1.1)
Chinese Taipei	**570**	(11.1)	581	(8.8)	568	(9.1)	**515**	(9.6)	**-28.3**	(4.9)	0.9	(0.1)	6.2	(2.0)
Thailand	417	(7.9)	446	(8.9)	424	(8.4)	421	(6.8)	-2.5	(2.8)	1.3	(0.2)	0.1	(0.3)
Tunisia	393	(8.9)	403	(10.6)	380	(7.8)	376	(9.1)	-4.9	(5.6)	0.9	(0.2)	0.3	(0.6)
United Arab Emirates	**395**	(3.1)	414	(4.8)	455	(6.9)	**473**	(5.9)	**22.8**	(2.1)	**1.9**	(0.1)	10.1	(1.6)
Uruguay	**391**	(4.9)	390	(6.6)	394	(6.2)	**462**	(9.0)	**43.1**	(6.8)	**1.3**	(0.1)	12.3	(2.6)
Viet Nam	503	(9.4)	496	(12.1)	526	(9.6)	520	(9.5)	8.5	(4.7)	1.1	(0.2)	0.5	(0.6)

Note: Values that are statistically significant are indicated in bold (see Annex A3).
* See notes at the beginning of this Annex.
StatLink http://dx.doi.org/10.1787/888932957498

WHAT MAKES SCHOOLS SUCCESSFUL? RESOURCES, POLICIES AND PRACTICES – VOLUME IV

[Part 1/1]
School responsibility for resource allocation, curriculum and assessment, by type of school and education level

Table IV.4.2   *Results based on school principals' reports*

	Index of school responsibility for resource allocation								Index of school responsibility for curriculum and assessment							
	Public schools		Private schools		Lower secondary education (ISCED 2)		Upper secondary education (ISCED 3)		Public schools		Private schools		Lower secondary education (ISCED 2)		Upper secondary education (ISCED 3)	
	Mean index	S.E.	Mean index	S.E.	Mean index	S.E.	Mean index	S.E.	Mean index	S.E.	Mean index	S.E.	Mean index	S.E.	Mean index	S.E.
Australia	-0.43	(0.02)	0.77	(0.06)	0.05	(0.03)	0.11	(0.05)	-0.06	(0.04)	0.40	(0.06)	0.14	(0.04)	0.08	(0.05)
Austria	-0.57	(0.03)	-0.41	(0.06)	-0.63	(0.02)	-0.55	(0.03)	-0.29	(0.07)	-0.34	(0.16)	-0.11	(0.17)	-0.31	(0.07)
Belgium	-0.38	(0.03)	-0.23	(0.01)	-0.44	(0.02)	-0.27	(0.01)	-0.19	(0.09)	-0.05	(0.06)	-0.11	(0.08)	-0.11	(0.05)
Canada	-0.48	(0.01)	1.11	(0.22)	-0.39	(0.03)	-0.35	(0.05)	-0.56	(0.03)	0.25	(0.14)	-0.37	(0.05)	-0.51	(0.03)
Chile	-0.65	(0.02)	1.31	(0.11)	-0.21	(0.08)	0.62	(0.08)	-0.35	(0.11)	0.39	(0.10)	-0.31	(0.13)	0.15	(0.07)
Czech Republic	1.47	(0.10)	2.01	(0.27)	1.22	(0.12)	1.23	(0.14)	1.03	(0.06)	1.05	(0.15)	0.72	(0.08)	0.78	(0.11)
Denmark	-0.04	(0.04)	1.10	(0.22)	0.18	(0.06)	0.70	(0.69)	-0.11	(0.07)	0.43	(0.14)	-0.05	(0.06)	-0.72	(0.08)
Estonia	0.12	(0.05)	0.83	(0.47)	0.14	(0.04)	0.42	(0.25)	0.50	(0.05)	-0.08	(0.24)	0.49	(0.05)	0.20	(0.20)
Finland	-0.34	(0.02)	1.68	(0.39)	-0.28	(0.02)	c	c	-0.06	(0.07)	0.72	(0.17)	-0.05	(0.07)	c	c
France	-0.62	(0.01)	-0.26	(0.08)	-0.49	(0.05)	-0.57	(0.01)	-0.19	(0.06)	0.48	(0.21)	-0.02	(0.11)	-0.14	(0.07)
Germany	-0.62	(0.01)	-0.49	(0.05)	-0.58	(0.01)	-0.58	(0.04)	-0.14	(0.05)	0.26	(0.29)	-0.19	(0.05)	-0.35	(0.16)
Greece	-0.72	(0.01)	c	c	-0.75	(0.01)	-0.70	(0.01)	-1.17	(0.01)	c	c	-1.19	(0.03)	-1.14	(0.02)
Hungary	0.26	(0.08)	1.57	(0.27)	0.16	(0.15)	0.50	(0.10)	-0.07	(0.07)	0.53	(0.19)	0.14	(0.15)	0.00	(0.07)
Iceland	-0.05	(0.00)	c	c	-0.04	(0.00)	c	c	0.16	(0.00)	c	c	0.15	(0.00)	c	c
Ireland	-0.58	(0.02)	-0.33	(0.02)	-0.43	(0.02)	-0.42	(0.02)	0.10	(0.10)	0.13	(0.08)	0.10	(0.06)	0.11	(0.06)
Israel	-0.24	(0.04)	c	c	-0.32	(0.05)	-0.23	(0.04)	0.01	(0.06)	c	c	-0.06	(0.10)	0.01	(0.07)
Italy	-0.70	(0.01)	1.06	(0.22)	-0.69	(0.01)	-0.59	(0.02)	0.41	(0.04)	0.55	(0.15)	0.69	(0.12)	0.35	(0.04)
Japan	-0.64	(0.03)	0.61	(0.11)	c	c	-0.27	(0.04)	1.04	(0.07)	1.43	(0.01)	c	c	1.15	(0.05)
Korea	-0.68	(0.01)	-0.17	(0.09)	-0.57	(0.06)	-0.43	(0.05)	0.72	(0.11)	0.69	(0.11)	0.96	(0.15)	0.69	(0.08)
Luxembourg	-0.51	(0.00)	1.54	(0.00)	-0.22	(0.00)	-0.17	(0.00)	-0.89	(0.00)	-0.54	(0.01)	-0.88	(0.00)	-0.79	(0.00)
Mexico	-0.55	(0.00)	1.39	(0.15)	-0.56	(0.02)	-0.17	(0.03)	-0.94	(0.01)	-0.30	(0.11)	-0.89	(0.02)	-0.86	(0.02)
Netherlands	1.16	(0.15)	1.65	(0.12)	1.21	(0.11)	1.38	(0.17)	1.30	(0.07)	1.18	(0.07)	1.00	(0.08)	0.88	(0.13)
New Zealand	0.10	(0.05)	1.56	(0.42)	0.06	(0.06)	0.11	(0.05)	0.66	(0.07)	0.26	(0.31)	0.41	(0.09)	0.47	(0.07)
Norway	-0.21	(0.03)	c	c	-0.18	(0.03)	c	c	-0.55	(0.05)	c	c	-0.55	(0.05)	c	c
Poland	-0.39	(0.02)	1.50	(0.36)	-0.34	(0.02)	c	c	0.36	(0.07)	0.83	(0.25)	0.37	(0.07)	c	c
Portugal	-0.58	(0.02)	0.40	(0.25)	-0.52	(0.02)	-0.44	(0.04)	-0.72	(0.03)	-0.27	(0.21)	-0.63	(0.05)	-0.71	(0.04)
Slovak Republic	0.77	(0.09)	0.90	(0.28)	0.81	(0.10)	0.75	(0.14)	0.53	(0.08)	-0.03	(0.20)	0.39	(0.10)	0.55	(0.12)
Slovenia	-0.13	(0.02)	1.03	(0.08)	-0.06	(0.27)	-0.12	(0.01)	-0.31	(0.01)	-0.79	(0.00)	-0.48	(0.19)	-0.34	(0.01)
Spain	-0.69	(0.01)	0.14	(0.10)	-0.42	(0.03)	c	c	-0.66	(0.04)	-0.06	(0.09)	-0.47	(0.04)	c	c
Sweden	0.40	(0.08)	2.06	(0.17)	0.63	(0.07)	0.63	(0.28)	-0.27	(0.06)	-0.09	(0.10)	-0.25	(0.06)	-0.26	(0.17)
Switzerland	-0.22	(0.04)	1.31	(0.24)	-0.09	(0.05)	-0.27	(0.04)	-0.67	(0.04)	0.48	(0.25)	-0.64	(0.05)	-0.49	(0.06)
Turkey	-0.73	(0.01)	c	c	-0.70	(0.04)	-0.72	(0.01)	-1.14	(0.02)	c	c	-1.01	(0.14)	-1.12	(0.02)
United Kingdom	0.80	(0.09)	1.73	(0.11)	c	c	1.10	(0.08)	0.93	(0.06)	1.25	(0.06)	c	c	0.93	(0.05)
United States	0.01	(0.06)	1.26	(0.35)	-0.08	(0.07)	0.10	(0.07)	-0.49	(0.07)	0.87	(0.27)	-0.57	(0.10)	-0.36	(0.08)
OECD average	-0.20	(0.01)	0.92	(0.04)	-0.14	(0.01)	0.03	(0.03)	-0.06	(0.01)	0.33	(0.03)	-0.10	(0.02)	-0.06	(0.02)
Albania	-0.70	(0.01)	0.37	(0.48)	-0.69	(0.03)	-0.53	(0.05)	-0.30	(0.07)	0.13	(0.36)	-0.35	(0.09)	-0.21	(0.10)
Argentina	c	c	c	c	c	c	c	c	-0.57	(0.05)	-0.37	(0.14)	-0.50	(0.07)	-0.51	(0.07)
Brazil	-0.73	(0.01)	1.74	(0.16)	-0.58	(0.04)	-0.26	(0.05)	-0.59	(0.03)	0.39	(0.14)	-0.52	(0.04)	-0.39	(0.04)
Bulgaria	0.83	(0.09)	c	c	**0.41**	(0.12)	**0.88**	(0.10)	-0.84	(0.03)	c	c	-0.81	(0.08)	-0.84	(0.02)
Colombia	-0.68	(0.01)	1.39	(0.30)	-0.44	(0.05)	-0.31	(0.05)	-0.20	(0.07)	0.61	(0.14)	-0.07	(0.08)	-0.09	(0.07)
Costa Rica	-0.66	(0.01)	1.21	(0.27)	-0.43	(0.03)	-0.25	(0.08)	-0.88	(0.04)	0.57	(0.20)	-0.70	(0.05)	-0.57	(0.07)
Croatia	-0.36	(0.02)	c	c	c	c	-0.34	(0.03)	-0.85	(0.03)	c	c	c	c	-0.86	(0.03)
Cyprus*	-0.69	(0.00)	1.46	(0.00)	-0.59	(0.01)	-0.33	(0.00)	-1.11	(0.00)	0.55	(0.00)	-0.95	(0.01)	-0.84	(0.00)
Hong Kong-China	-0.48	(0.04)	0.48	(0.10)	0.40	(0.08)	0.43	(0.10)	0.98	(0.32)	0.99	(0.07)	0.98	(0.07)	0.95	(0.07)
Indonesia	-0.31	(0.10)	1.27	(0.14)	0.39	(0.12)	0.28	(0.12)	0.49	(0.11)	0.86	(0.12)	0.77	(0.11)	0.54	(0.12)
Jordan	-0.67	(0.02)	0.26	(0.14)	-0.51	(0.03)	c	c	-1.12	(0.04)	-0.61	(0.13)	-1.04	(0.04)	c	c
Kazakhstan	-0.38	(0.04)	1.34	(0.45)	-0.37	(0.04)	-0.23	(0.10)	-0.77	(0.05)	-0.21	(0.34)	-0.81	(0.04)	-0.62	(0.09)
Latvia	0.56	(0.08)	c	c	0.58	(0.08)	0.92	(0.26)	-0.21	(0.06)	c	c	-0.20	(0.06)	0.06	(0.21)
Liechtenstein	-0.27	(0.01)	c	c	**-0.02**	(0.02)	**-0.53**	(0.00)	-0.45	(0.02)	c	c	-0.24	(0.02)	-0.95	(0.00)
Lithuania	0.76	(0.08)	c	c	0.78	(0.08)	c	c	0.65	(0.05)	c	c	0.66	(0.05)	c	c
Macao-China	c	c	1.73	(0.00)	**1.69**	(0.00)	**1.58**	(0.00)	c	c	0.81	(0.00)	**0.87**	(0.00)	0.67	(0.00)
Malaysia	-0.58	(0.01)	2.09	(0.45)	-0.43	(0.06)	-0.49	(0.03)	-0.95	(0.04)	1.07	(0.30)	-0.79	(0.05)	-0.88	(0.04)
Montenegro	-0.34	(0.00)	c	c	c	c	-0.33	(0.00)	-0.84	(0.00)	c	c	c	c	-0.83	(0.00)
Peru	-0.51	(0.05)	2.32	(0.18)	-0.11	(0.10)	0.29	(0.08)	-0.41	(0.07)	0.99	(0.13)	-0.21	(0.06)	-0.04	(0.06)
Qatar	-0.39	(0.00)	-0.33	(0.00)	-0.37	(0.00)	-0.37	(0.00)	-0.94	(0.00)	-0.84	(0.00)	-0.93	(0.00)	-0.90	(0.00)
Romania	-0.57	(0.02)	c	c	-0.57	(0.02)	c	c	-0.52	(0.05)	c	c	-0.52	(0.05)	c	c
Russian Federation	0.01	(0.06)	c	c	0.02	(0.07)	0.08	(0.08)	-0.22	(0.05)	c	c	-0.22	(0.06)	-0.26	(0.09)
Serbia	-0.41	(0.02)	c	c	c	c	-0.39	(0.02)	-0.87	(0.02)	c	c	c	c	-0.86	(0.02)
Shanghai-China	-0.38	(0.04)	0.67	(0.30)	-0.32	(0.08)	-0.26	(0.06)	-0.55	(0.05)	-0.57	(0.23)	-0.77	(0.07)	-0.39	(0.06)
Singapore	-0.40	(0.00)	c	c	-0.43	(0.05)	-0.36	(0.01)	-0.24	(0.00)	c	c	-0.31	(0.06)	-0.25	(0.01)
Chinese Taipei	-0.41	(0.03)	0.93	(0.17)	-0.34	(0.04)	0.31	(0.06)	0.15	(0.09)	0.34	(0.12)	0.10	(0.11)	0.28	(0.09)
Thailand	0.46	(0.08)	1.94	(0.20)	0.58	(0.11)	0.74	(0.08)	0.95	(0.06)	1.15	(0.11)	1.05	(0.08)	0.96	(0.06)
Tunisia	-0.20	(0.06)	c	c	-0.29	(0.07)	-0.15	(0.09)	-0.58	(0.08)	c	c	-0.62	(0.12)	-0.56	(0.10)
United Arab Emirates	-0.56	(0.03)	1.09	(0.10)	0.28	(0.10)	0.40	(0.05)	-1.07	(0.04)	0.03	(0.07)	-0.39	(0.08)	-0.44	(0.04)
Uruguay	-0.73	(0.01)	0.89	(0.20)	-0.64	(0.04)	-0.34	(0.05)	-1.02	(0.02)	0.11	(0.21)	-0.96	(0.03)	-0.74	(0.06)
Viet Nam	-0.54	(0.02)	1.03	(0.58)	-0.71	(0.01)	-0.40	(0.06)	-1.05	(0.03)	-0.48	(0.38)	-1.16	(0.04)	-0.96	(0.04)

Note: Values that are statistically significant are indicated in bold (see Annex A3).
* See notes at the beginning of this Annex.
StatLink 🔗 http://dx.doi.org/10.1787/888932957498

[Part 1/2]
Index of school responsibility for curriculum and assessment and mathematics performance
Table IV.4.3 *Results based on school principals' reports*

		Index of school responsibility for curriculum and assessment										Variability in this index	
		All students		Bottom quarter		Second quarter		Third quarter		Top quarter			
		Mean index	S.E.	Mean index	S.E.	Mean index	S.E.	Mean index	S.E.	Mean index	S.E.	Standard deviation	S.E.
OECD	Australia	0.13	(0.04)	-0.78	(0.01)	-0.42	(0.03)	0.27	(0.13)	1.44	(0.00)	0.90	(0.02)
	Austria	-0.30	(0.06)	-0.97	(0.03)	-0.77	(0.03)	-0.35	(0.09)	0.91	(0.16)	0.79	(0.05)
	Belgium	-0.11	(0.05)	-0.85	(0.02)	-0.52	(0.02)	-0.23	(0.05)	1.17	(0.14)	0.82	(0.03)
	Canada	-0.49	(0.03)	-0.98	(0.02)	-0.80	(0.01)	-0.57	(0.02)	0.39	(0.11)	0.66	(0.04)
	Chile	0.12	(0.07)	-0.93	(0.03)	-0.53	(0.07)	0.52	(0.22)	1.44	(0.00)	0.99	(0.03)
	Czech Republic	0.75	(0.06)	-0.74	(0.05)	0.85	(0.22)	1.44	(0.00)	1.44	(0.00)	0.96	(0.03)
	Denmark	-0.05	(0.06)	-0.88	(0.02)	-0.66	(0.04)	-0.09	(0.17)	1.44	(0.05)	0.92	(0.03)
	Estonia	0.49	(0.05)	-0.71	(0.03)	-0.10	(0.07)	1.32	(0.14)	1.44	(0.00)	0.94	(0.01)
	Finland	-0.05	(0.07)	-0.85	(0.01)	-0.59	(0.04)	-0.17	(0.17)	1.43	(0.12)	0.90	(0.03)
	France	-0.10	(0.06)	-0.88	(0.02)	-0.61	(0.04)	-0.17	(0.06)	1.26	(0.17)	0.86	(0.04)
	Germany	-0.19	(0.05)	-0.87	(0.02)	-0.65	(0.05)	-0.27	(0.05)	1.03	(0.13)	0.79	(0.03)
	Greece	-1.15	(0.02)	-1.26	(0.00)	-1.26	(0.00)	-1.16	(0.03)	-0.91	(0.07)	0.26	(0.09)
	Hungary	0.02	(0.07)	-0.85	(0.03)	-0.52	(0.04)	0.08	(0.17)	1.35	(0.07)	0.87	(0.03)
	Iceland	0.15	(0.00)	-0.83	(0.00)	-0.58	(0.00)	0.56	(0.02)	1.44	(0.00)	1.00	(0.00)
	Ireland	0.10	(0.06)	-0.76	(0.03)	-0.35	(0.04)	0.11	(0.16)	1.41	(0.06)	0.84	(0.03)
	Israel	0.00	(0.06)	-0.85	(0.01)	-0.58	(0.05)	0.02	(0.16)	1.42	(0.08)	0.89	(0.03)
	Italy	0.36	(0.04)	-0.75	(0.02)	-0.25	(0.04)	0.98	(0.11)	1.44	(0.00)	0.92	(0.01)
	Japan	1.15	(0.05)	0.30	(0.21)	1.44	(0.00)	1.44	(0.00)	1.44	(0.00)	0.69	(0.06)
	Korea	0.71	(0.08)	-0.72	(0.08)	0.66	(0.25)	1.44	(0.00)	1.44	(0.00)	0.94	(0.03)
	Luxembourg	-0.84	(0.00)	-1.11	(0.00)	-0.90	(0.00)	-0.81	(0.00)	-0.54	(0.00)	0.36	(0.00)
	Mexico	-0.87	(0.02)	-1.24	(0.01)	-1.09	(0.01)	-0.90	(0.02)	-0.24	(0.05)	0.52	(0.02)
	Netherlands	0.96	(0.08)	-0.43	(0.23)	1.41	(0.12)	1.44	(0.00)	1.44	(0.00)	0.84	(0.06)
	New Zealand	0.47	(0.07)	-0.68	(0.04)	-0.09	(0.07)	1.20	(0.20)	1.44	(0.00)	0.92	(0.01)
	Norway	-0.55	(0.05)	-1.03	(0.03)	-0.81	(0.00)	-0.69	(0.05)	0.33	(0.16)	0.65	(0.06)
	Poland	0.37	(0.07)	-0.49	(0.05)	-0.14	(0.04)	0.65	(0.21)	1.44	(0.00)	0.82	(0.02)
	Portugal	-0.68	(0.03)	-1.06	(0.02)	-0.85	(0.02)	-0.74	(0.03)	-0.06	(0.11)	0.50	(0.06)
	Slovak Republic	0.48	(0.08)	-0.76	(0.02)	-0.20	(0.26)	1.44	(0.11)	1.44	(0.00)	1.00	(0.02)
	Slovenia	-0.35	(0.01)	-0.86	(0.00)	-0.77	(0.00)	-0.50	(0.01)	0.73	(0.04)	0.73	(0.01)
	Spain	-0.47	(0.04)	-1.04	(0.03)	-0.80	(0.01)	-0.55	(0.04)	0.51	(0.12)	0.71	(0.04)
	Sweden	-0.25	(0.06)	-0.86	(0.01)	-0.67	(0.02)	-0.42	(0.05)	0.97	(0.17)	0.79	(0.04)
	Switzerland	-0.60	(0.04)	-1.08	(0.03)	-0.83	(0.02)	-0.71	(0.03)	0.21	(0.12)	0.62	(0.05)
	Turkey	-1.12	(0.02)	-1.26	(0.00)	-1.25	(0.00)	-1.18	(0.02)	-0.79	(0.09)	0.32	(0.07)
	United Kingdom	0.93	(0.05)	-0.45	(0.07)	1.27	(0.15)	1.44	(0.00)	1.44	(0.00)	0.84	(0.03)
	United States	-0.39	(0.08)	-1.06	(0.03)	-0.82	(0.01)	-0.61	(0.07)	0.94	(0.23)	0.86	(0.06)
	OECD average	-0.04	(0.01)	-0.84	(0.01)	-0.38	(0.01)	0.12	(0.02)	0.93	(0.02)	0.78	(0.01)
Partners	Albania	-0.27	(0.07)	-1.01	(0.03)	-0.81	(0.01)	-0.42	(0.11)	1.17	(0.18)	0.90	(0.05)
	Argentina	-0.51	(0.06)	-1.02	(0.03)	-0.81	(0.00)	-0.59	(0.07)	0.40	(0.16)	0.66	(0.06)
	Brazil	-0.42	(0.03)	-1.09	(0.01)	-0.86	(0.02)	-0.48	(0.05)	0.75	(0.09)	0.79	(0.03)
	Bulgaria	-0.84	(0.03)	-1.12	(0.02)	-0.99	(0.01)	-0.83	(0.02)	-0.43	(0.09)	0.35	(0.06)
	Colombia	-0.08	(0.07)	-1.02	(0.04)	-0.63	(0.08)	0.14	(0.15)	1.18	(0.06)	0.88	(0.03)
	Costa Rica	-0.65	(0.05)	-1.18	(0.02)	-1.06	(0.02)	-0.84	(0.03)	0.50	(0.17)	0.81	(0.06)
	Croatia	-0.86	(0.03)	-1.12	(0.01)	-1.00	(0.02)	-0.87	(0.02)	-0.44	(0.08)	0.38	(0.05)
	Cyprus*	-0.84	(0.00)	-1.26	(0.00)	-1.23	(0.00)	-1.10	(0.00)	0.22	(0.00)	0.81	(0.00)
	Hong Kong-China	0.96	(0.07)	-0.35	(0.11)	1.32	(0.21)	1.44	(0.00)	1.44	(0.00)	0.80	(0.04)
	Indonesia	0.65	(0.08)	-0.76	(0.08)	0.48	(0.26)	1.44	(0.00)	1.44	(0.00)	0.97	(0.03)
	Jordan	-1.04	(0.04)	-1.26	(0.00)	-1.26	(0.00)	-1.22	(0.02)	-0.40	(0.15)	0.61	(0.08)
	Kazakhstan	-0.76	(0.05)	-1.21	(0.02)	-1.02	(0.04)	-0.79	(0.03)	0.00	(0.15)	0.55	(0.06)
	Latvia	-0.19	(0.06)	-0.89	(0.02)	-0.66	(0.04)	-0.29	(0.06)	1.08	(0.16)	0.82	(0.04)
	Liechtenstein	-0.33	(0.02)	c	c	c	c	c	c	c	c	0.90	(0.01)
	Lithuania	0.66	(0.05)	-0.57	(0.05)	0.34	(0.15)	1.42	(0.06)	1.44	(0.00)	0.87	(0.02)
	Macao-China	0.78	(0.00)	-0.60	(0.00)	0.84	(0.00)	1.44	(0.00)	1.44	(0.00)	0.90	(0.00)
	Malaysia	-0.88	(0.04)	-1.23	(0.01)	-1.11	(0.01)	-0.96	(0.04)	-0.22	(0.12)	0.58	(0.06)
	Montenegro	-0.83	(0.00)	-1.26	(0.00)	-1.10	(0.00)	-0.91	(0.00)	-0.06	(0.00)	0.62	(0.00)
	Peru	-0.09	(0.05)	-1.09	(0.03)	-0.75	(0.04)	0.03	(0.18)	1.44	(0.01)	1.02	(0.03)
	Qatar	-0.90	(0.00)	-1.26	(0.00)	-1.18	(0.00)	-0.83	(0.00)	-0.34	(0.00)	0.50	(0.00)
	Romania	-0.52	(0.05)	-1.15	(0.02)	-0.87	(0.03)	-0.57	(0.06)	0.50	(0.15)	0.71	(0.05)
	Russian Federation	-0.22	(0.05)	-0.97	(0.02)	-0.69	(0.05)	-0.25	(0.06)	1.02	(0.14)	0.82	(0.04)
	Serbia	-0.86	(0.02)	-1.09	(0.02)	-0.94	(0.02)	-0.82	(0.01)	-0.61	(0.05)	0.21	(0.02)
	Shanghai-China	-0.56	(0.05)	-1.22	(0.02)	-0.97	(0.05)	-0.71	(0.05)	0.68	(0.13)	0.82	(0.04)
	Singapore	-0.25	(0.01)	-0.87	(0.00)	-0.77	(0.00)	-0.33	(0.01)	0.97	(0.03)	0.80	(0.01)
	Chinese Taipei	0.21	(0.07)	-0.86	(0.03)	-0.40	(0.10)	0.67	(0.19)	1.44	(0.00)	0.94	(0.02)
	Thailand	0.98	(0.05)	-0.20	(0.09)	1.24	(0.15)	1.44	(0.00)	1.44	(0.00)	0.73	(0.04)
	Tunisia	-0.58	(0.08)	-1.26	(0.00)	-1.22	(0.02)	-0.89	(0.10)	1.04	(0.21)	1.01	(0.06)
	United Arab Emirates	-0.44	(0.04)	-1.26	(0.00)	-1.12	(0.02)	-0.61	(0.06)	1.25	(0.09)	1.03	(0.03)
	Uruguay	-0.83	(0.04)	-1.26	(0.01)	-1.09	(0.02)	-0.90	(0.02)	-0.08	(0.15)	0.61	(0.07)
	Viet Nam	-0.98	(0.03)	-1.26	(0.00)	-1.23	(0.02)	-1.07	(0.03)	-0.37	(0.11)	0.50	(0.05)

Note: Values that are statistically significant are indicated in bold (see Annex A3).
* See notes at the beginning of this Annex.
StatLink http://dx.doi.org/10.1787/888932957498

[Part 2/2]
Index of school responsibility for curriculum and assessment and mathematics performance
Table IV.4.3   *Results based on school principals' reports*

| | Performance on the mathematics scale by national quarters of this index | | | | | | | | Change in the mathematics score per unit of this index | | Increased likelihood of students in the bottom quarter of this index scoring in the bottom quarter of the national mathematics performance distribution | | Explained variance in student performance (r-squared x 100) | |
| | Bottom quarter | | Second quarter | | Third quarter | | Top quarter | | | | | | | |
	Mean score	S.E.	Mean score	S.E.	Mean score	S.E.	Mean score	S.E.	Score dif.	S.E.	Ratio	S.E.	%	S.E.
OECD														
Australia	**495**	(3.6)	505	(4.6)	508	(3.2)	**510**	(4.6)	5.1	(2.7)	1.1	(0.1)	0.2	(0.2)
Austria	512	(9.4)	508	(13.6)	503	(12.4)	499	(8.4)	-9.2	(6.0)	0.9	(0.1)	0.6	(0.8)
Belgium	**493**	(7.1)	527	(7.4)	523	(7.6)	**517**	(6.9)	5.5	(5.0)	1.4	(0.1)	0.2	(0.4)
Canada	**510**	(2.9)	517	(4.5)	519	(4.5)	**526**	(3.4)	10.2	(2.7)	1.1	(0.1)	0.6	(0.3)
Chile	**404**	(6.3)	422	(5.7)	429	(8.1)	**435**	(5.8)	11.4	(3.5)	1.4	(0.2)	2.0	(1.2)
Czech Republic	504	(8.6)	495	(6.6)	497	(6.2)	499	(6.3)	-1.8	(5.1)	0.9	(0.1)	0.0	(0.2)
Denmark	501	(3.8)	503	(5.9)	494	(5.9)	505	(4.4)	1.9	(2.3)	1.0	(0.1)	0.0	(0.1)
Estonia	521	(4.1)	518	(4.2)	520	(3.4)	523	(3.8)	0.8	(2.1)	1.0	(0.1)	0.0	(0.1)
Finland	**514**	(4.0)	516	(3.8)	517	(3.8)	**528**	(4.0)	5.9	(2.1)	1.1	(0.1)	0.4	(0.3)
France	483	(9.7)	492	(7.7)	507	(8.7)	498	(9.9)	6.0	(6.8)	1.2	(0.2)	0.3	(0.7)
Germany	**525**	(8.0)	529	(6.6)	512	(6.4)	**488**	(9.0)	-18.5	(6.2)	0.7	(0.1)	2.3	(1.5)
Greece	451	(5.4)	452	(6.2)	453	(4.8)	456	(5.8)	7.6	(8.8)	1.1	(0.1)	0.1	(0.1)
Hungary	477	(11.4)	473	(9.7)	478	(11.4)	480	(13.8)	1.1	(7.6)	1.0	(0.2)	0.0	(0.4)
Iceland	496	(3.8)	489	(3.4)	497	(3.9)	492	(4.0)	-0.8	(1.5)	0.9	(0.1)	0.0	(0.0)
Ireland	508	(5.6)	500	(6.3)	498	(5.9)	505	(5.7)	0.3	(3.4)	0.9	(0.1)	0.0	(0.1)
Israel	466	(7.8)	452	(12.2)	477	(9.9)	470	(12.6)	4.7	(7.1)	1.0	(0.1)	0.2	(0.5)
Italy	485	(5.1)	493	(5.1)	483	(4.3)	481	(4.8)	-2.7	(3.2)	1.0	(0.1)	0.1	(0.2)
Japan	536	(7.0)	536	(5.8)	538	(5.8)	536	(6.1)	-0.6	(8.1)	1.0	(0.1)	0.0	(0.3)
Korea	548	(10.8)	557	(10.0)	554	(7.0)	556	(5.9)	1.1	(5.6)	1.1	(0.2)	0.0	(0.2)
Luxembourg	496	(2.1)	497	(2.3)	474	(3.5)	493	(2.6)	34.8	(2.6)	0.8	(0.1)	1.7	(0.2)
Mexico	**409**	(3.11)	401	(2.74)	419	(3.3)	**424**	(3.2)	14.1	(3.9)	1.1	(0.1)	1.0	(0.5)
Netherlands	538	(10.9)	518	(6.7)	520	(5.7)	516	(5.9)	-12.1	(7.1)	0.6	(0.1)	1.2	(1.4)
New Zealand	501	(7.0)	511	(5.1)	495	(6.8)	492	(6.2)	-5.7	(3.8)	1.0	(0.1)	0.3	(0.4)
Norway	496	(5.7)	484	(4.7)	491	(5.6)	487	(5.7)	-5.8	(5.2)	0.9	(0.1)	0.2	(0.3)
Poland	521	(6.7)	515	(4.6)	518	(6.0)	516	(7.2)	-0.9	(4.6)	1.0	(0.1)	0.0	(0.2)
Portugal	491	(9.5)	489	(7.0)	485	(8.2)	482	(9.1)	-6.7	(11.9)	0.9	(0.2)	0.1	(0.6)
Slovak Republic	480	(11.1)	493	(9.8)	477	(7.7)	478	(7.1)	-2.6	(5.9)	1.1	(0.2)	0.1	(0.4)
Slovenia	**508**	(4.1)	503	(4.2)	500	(2.9)	**493**	(2.4)	-8.5	(1.7)	0.9	(0.1)	0.5	(0.2)
Spain	469	(4.6)	488	(3.7)	484	(6.3)	497	(3.2)	13.0	(2.0)	1.4	(0.1)	1.1	(0.3)
Sweden	480	(4.9)	482	(5.5)	475	(6.3)	475	(5.3)	-3.2	(3.1)	0.9	(0.1)	0.1	(0.2)
Switzerland	**513**	(5.8)	525	(7.1)	537	(6.1)	**552**	(7.5)	7.8	(5.6)	1.3	(0.1)	0.3	(0.4)
Turkey	447	(10.0)	446	(8.5)	454	(11.7)	445	(9.9)	-10.3	(17.7)	1.0	(0.1)	0.1	(0.5)
United Kingdom	**478**	(5.1)	494	(6.2)	502	(5.1)	**502**	(6.0)	12.3	(3.4)	1.3	(0.1)	1.2	(0.7)
United States	464	(8.1)	474	(8.8)	495	(6.3)	493	(4.3)	11.6	(4.3)	1.4	(0.2)	1.2	(1.0)
OECD average	**492**	(1.2)	494	(1.2)	495	(1.2)	496	(1.2)	1.9	(1.0)	1.0	(0.0)	0.5	(0.1)
Partners														
Albania	390	(4.5)	399	(5.3)	393	(4.6)	396	(4.3)	-0.4	(2.3)	1.2	(0.1)	0.0	(0.0)
Argentina	373	(8.0)	396	(6.9)	394	(6.3)	390	(7.6)	9.4	(4.7)	1.4	(0.2)	0.7	(0.6)
Brazil	**377**	(3.8)	386	(4.9)	391	(4.8)	**410**	(5.1)	17.9	(3.0)	1.2	(0.1)	3.3	(1.1)
Bulgaria	439	(7.7)	453	(9.6)	434	(10.4)	429	(9.5)	-27.1	(16.6)	0.9	(0.2)	1.0	(1.4)
Colombia	370	(5.6)	382	(4.5)	372	(6.1)	382	(8.1)	3.6	(4.4)	1.1	(0.1)	0.2	(0.5)
Costa Rica	393	(6.4)	397	(4.8)	400	(6.1)	443	(8.2)	28.1	(4.4)	1.3	(0.2)	11.1	(3.3)
Croatia	487	(10.7)	467	(8.3)	467	(8.2)	464	(8.1)	-13.8	(10.2)	0.7	(0.1)	0.4	(0.6)
Cyprus*	**432**	(3.0)	429	(3.3)	430	(2.4)	**466**	(2.5)	34.0	(1.3)	1.0	(0.1)	8.7	(0.6)
Hong Kong-China	563	(10.8)	564	(6.1)	560	(6.0)	558	(5.0)	-3.8	(7.5)	1.0	(0.2)	0.1	(0.5)
Indonesia	**393**	(9.6)	367	(9.2)	369	(6.2)	**370**	(6.1)	-8.8	(4.4)	0.7	(0.1)	1.4	(1.5)
Jordan	378	(4.6)	381	(4.7)	383	(6.8)	400	(7.5)	18.4	(11.9)	1.1	(0.1)	2.1	(2.6)
Kazakhstan	436	(6.1)	432	(6.4)	431	(6.2)	426	(8.2)	-6.5	(8.4)	0.9	(0.1)	0.3	(0.7)
Latvia	483	(5.3)	494	(5.2)	493	(6.6)	492	(6.3)	2.0	(3.4)	1.3	(0.2)	0.0	(0.2)
Liechtenstein	c	c	c	c	c	c	c	c	-37.7	(4.6)	0.7	(0.2)	12.7	(3.0)
Lithuania	481	(6.6)	482	(7.1)	475	(4.8)	477	(4.3)	-3.9	(3.9)	0.9	(0.1)	0.1	(0.3)
Macao-China	555	(2.4)	557	(3.3)	520	(3.0)	521	(3.0)	-18.8	(1.3)	0.7	(0.0)	3.2	(0.4)
Malaysia	423	(6.3)	404	(4.4)	421	(6.8)	435	(8.4)	15.6	(10.6)	1.0	(0.1)	1.2	(1.5)
Montenegro	**406**	(1.9)	419	(3.2)	420	(2.5)	**394**	(2.5)	-10.9	(1.7)	1.1	(0.1)	0.7	(0.2)
Peru	**361**	(5.9)	352	(6.3)	366	(8.7)	**394**	(8.8)	16.8	(4.3)	1.0	(0.1)	4.1	(2.0)
Qatar	352	(2.3)	362	(1.7)	403	(2.4)	388	(1.8)	28.4	(1.6)	1.3	(0.1)	2.0	(0.2)
Romania	441	(8.3)	456	(7.9)	434	(8.3)	446	(7.9)	-1.8	(5.6)	1.1	(0.2)	0.0	(0.3)
Russian Federation	482	(7.2)	492	(5.7)	485	(5.3)	470	(5.8)	-6.9	(4.1)	1.0	(0.1)	0.4	(0.5)
Serbia	447	(9.2)	461	(9.5)	446	(9.2)	441	(7.7)	-6.3	(20.3)	1.0	(0.2)	0.0	(0.2)
Shanghai-China	**620**	(8.9)	627	(8.8)	622	(10.1)	**582**	(9.6)	-24.1	(5.4)	0.8	(0.1)	3.9	(1.6)
Singapore	561	(3.3)	571	(3.5)	571	(2.9)	590	(2.8)	15.0	(1.5)	1.3	(0.1)	1.3	(0.3)
Chinese Taipei	570	(10.0)	566	(10.7)	558	(10.6)	541	(13.0)	-11.8	(6.9)	0.8	(0.1)	0.9	(1.1)
Thailand	422	(8.7)	424	(7.7)	430	(6.2)	431	(6.1)	6.1	(5.6)	1.1	(0.2)	0.3	(0.6)
Tunisia	**412**	(8.4)	388	(9.2)	374	(9.7)	**377**	(9.7)	-5.1	(4.2)	0.5	(0.1)	0.4	(0.7)
United Arab Emirates	398	(2.9)	415	(4.9)	453	(6.2)	470	(5.5)	24.9	(2.4)	1.9	(0.1)	8.3	(1.5)
Uruguay	387	(5.6)	397	(7.3)	408	(7.9)	445	(8.5)	43.2	(6.1)	1.3	(0.2)	8.7	(2.8)
Viet Nam	501	(9.3)	513	(11.1)	505	(11.3)	526	(9.6)	8.0	(7.5)	1.2	(0.2)	0.2	(0.5)

Note: Values that are statistically significant are indicated in bold (see Annex A3).
* See notes at the beginning of this Annex.
StatLink ⫶⫶⫶ http://dx.doi.org/10.1787/888932957498

[Part 1/1]
School choice
Table IV.4.4   *Results based on school principals' reports*

| | Percentage of students in schools whose principal reported on the number of schools competing for students in the same area | | | | | |
| | Two or more other schools | | One other school | | No other schools | |
	%	S.E.	%	S.E.	%	S.E.
Australia	88.6	(1.4)	5.9	(0.9)	5.5	(0.9)
Austria	42.1	(3.6)	18.4	(3.1)	39.5	(3.2)
Belgium	80.2	(2.2)	14.3	(2.0)	5.5	(1.5)
Canada	67.2	(2.2)	14.6	(1.8)	18.2	(1.6)
Chile	65.8	(3.7)	18.5	(3.0)	15.8	(2.5)
Czech Republic	72.8	(3.2)	12.4	(2.7)	14.8	(2.3)
Denmark	65.4	(2.8)	19.2	(2.8)	15.4	(2.6)
Estonia	61.8	(2.2)	19.6	(2.0)	18.6	(2.0)
Finland	30.7	(2.6)	16.1	(2.9)	53.2	(3.3)
France	43.8	(3.5)	19.0	(2.9)	37.2	(3.4)
Germany	58.8	(3.2)	24.9	(3.0)	16.3	(2.5)
Greece	43.4	(3.6)	24.1	(3.2)	32.5	(3.0)
Hungary	54.2	(3.7)	23.0	(3.3)	22.8	(3.3)
Iceland	32.3	(0.2)	15.6	(0.1)	52.1	(0.2)
Ireland	74.8	(3.3)	11.6	(2.7)	13.5	(2.5)
Israel	58.5	(3.9)	20.0	(3.2)	21.5	(3.4)
Italy	35.3	(1.9)	21.8	(1.6)	42.9	(1.8)
Japan	85.0	(2.5)	5.3	(1.7)	9.8	(1.8)
Korea	70.9	(3.4)	19.9	(3.1)	9.1	(2.5)
Luxembourg	63.1	(0.1)	11.8	(0.1)	25.2	(0.1)
Mexico	72.4	(1.6)	16.1	(1.4)	11.5	(1.0)
Netherlands	76.6	(3.4)	13.8	(2.8)	9.5	(2.1)
New Zealand	85.7	(2.7)	7.5	(2.1)	6.9	(2.1)
Norway	17.9	(2.9)	17.0	(2.9)	65.1	(3.4)
Poland	54.1	(3.6)	18.2	(3.1)	27.7	(3.0)
Portugal	56.4	(3.7)	21.0	(3.6)	22.6	(2.9)
Slovak Republic	75.7	(2.9)	10.0	(2.1)	14.3	(1.9)
Slovenia	62.5	(0.5)	13.5	(0.4)	24.0	(0.5)
Spain	67.6	(2.7)	16.5	(2.5)	15.9	(1.9)
Sweden	55.2	(3.1)	14.5	(2.8)	30.3	(3.0)
Switzerland	25.5	(2.4)	16.8	(2.4)	57.6	(3.0)
Turkey	69.1	(3.0)	9.7	(1.9)	21.1	(2.8)
United Kingdom	82.1	(2.4)	9.6	(2.0)	8.3	(1.6)
United States	68.6	(4.1)	7.3	(2.4)	24.2	(3.9)
OECD average	60.7	(0.5)	15.5	(0.4)	23.8	(0.4)
Albania	44.5	(4.1)	22.1	(3.7)	33.4	(3.7)
Argentina	77.9	(3.5)	8.1	(1.8)	14.0	(3.1)
Brazil	51.7	(2.1)	22.0	(2.1)	26.4	(2.1)
Bulgaria	74.5	(3.0)	12.6	(2.2)	12.9	(2.5)
Colombia	69.4	(3.3)	16.8	(3.1)	13.8	(2.7)
Costa Rica	65.6	(3.4)	15.8	(3.0)	18.7	(2.8)
Croatia	70.1	(3.7)	9.4	(2.4)	20.4	(3.2)
Cyprus*	38.3	(0.1)	17.9	(0.1)	43.8	(0.1)
Hong Kong-China	93.7	(2.1)	5.1	(1.9)	1.3	(0.9)
Indonesia	85.9	(2.9)	11.0	(2.6)	3.2	(1.5)
Jordan	50.3	(3.3)	22.1	(3.4)	27.5	(3.2)
Kazakhstan	48.1	(3.7)	18.2	(3.5)	33.6	(3.6)
Latvia	74.0	(3.2)	19.5	(3.2)	6.5	(1.7)
Liechtenstein	9.2	(0.4)	31.3	(0.8)	59.5	(0.8)
Lithuania	52.1	(3.2)	21.9	(2.9)	26.0	(2.7)
Macao-China	87.3	(0.0)	8.8	(0.0)	3.9	(0.0)
Malaysia	61.1	(3.8)	22.2	(3.6)	16.7	(2.9)
Montenegro	24.7	(0.2)	22.0	(0.1)	53.4	(0.2)
Peru	67.8	(2.8)	12.5	(2.1)	19.7	(2.6)
Qatar	57.1	(0.1)	17.0	(0.1)	25.9	(0.1)
Romania	56.5	(4.2)	17.1	(3.0)	26.4	(3.4)
Russian Federation	56.7	(3.6)	20.0	(2.9)	23.3	(2.7)
Serbia	63.1	(4.0)	14.9	(2.6)	21.9	(3.7)
Shanghai-China	72.5	(3.5)	10.8	(2.8)	16.8	(2.9)
Singapore	92.7	(0.1)	6.7	(0.1)	0.7	(0.0)
Chinese Taipei	83.7	(2.3)	12.3	(2.4)	4.0	(1.5)
Thailand	74.7	(3.0)	14.3	(2.7)	11.0	(2.2)
Tunisia	38.5	(3.5)	29.4	(3.3)	32.1	(3.5)
United Arab Emirates	75.9	(1.9)	14.4	(1.7)	9.7	(1.6)
Uruguay	40.6	(3.2)	15.7	(2.7)	43.7	(3.3)
Viet Nam	50.3	(4.0)	28.2	(3.9)	21.5	(3.3)

* See notes at the beginning of this Annex.
StatLink http://dx.doi.org/10.1787/888932957498

[Part 1/1]
School choice, by level of education

Table IV.4.5   *Results based on school principals' reports*

	Percentage of students in schools whose principal reported on the number of schools competing for students in the same area						Difference between the percentage of upper secondary students in schools that compete for students, and the percentage of lower secondary students in schools that compete for students	
	Lower secondary education (ISCED 2)			Upper secondary education (ISCED 3)				
	Two or more other schools	One other school	No other schools	Two or more other schools	One other school	No other schools		
	%	S.E.	%	S.E.	%	S.E.	%	S.E.	%	S.E.	%	S.E.	% dif.	S.E.
---	---	---	---	---	---	---	---	---	---	---	---	---	---	---
OECD Australia	88.2	(1.5)	6.0	(0.9)	5.9	(1.0)	90.8	(1.6)	5.6	(1.4)	3.6	(0.9)	**2.3**	(1.0)
Austria	61.8	(10.5)	18.5	(9.9)	19.7	(8.8)	40.9	(3.6)	18.4	(3.2)	40.7	(3.3)	**-21.0**	(9.4)
Belgium	75.3	(7.4)	16.3	(6.5)	8.5	(4.5)	80.7	(2.3)	14.1	(2.1)	5.2	(1.5)	3.3	(4.5)
Canada	62.7	(3.8)	11.6	(2.0)	25.8	(3.7)	68.0	(2.4)	15.1	(2.0)	16.9	(1.6)	**8.8**	(3.5)
Chile	69.5	(8.0)	17.9	(7.0)	12.6	(5.2)	65.6	(3.8)	18.5	(3.1)	15.9	(2.5)	-3.3	(5.5)
Czech Republic	58.0	(5.1)	17.5	(4.3)	24.5	(4.1)	91.3	(3.0)	5.9	(2.5)	2.7	(1.7)	**21.8**	(4.7)
Denmark	65.5	(2.8)	19.3	(2.8)	15.2	(2.6)	48.3	(25.7)	0.0	c	51.7	(25.7)	-36.5	(25.8)
Estonia	61.5	(2.3)	19.8	(2.0)	18.8	(2.0)	79.0	(7.0)	9.4	(5.0)	11.5	(5.6)	7.3	(5.7)
Finland	30.6	(2.6)	16.1	(2.9)	53.3	(3.3)	c	c	c	c	c	c	c	c
France	34.5	(4.9)	17.3	(4.2)	48.2	(5.8)	47.9	(4.3)	19.7	(3.4)	32.4	(3.6)	**15.8**	(6.1)
Germany	59.2	(3.2)	24.8	(3.1)	16.0	(2.5)	44.8	(17.2)	30.5	(18.5)	24.7	(15.8)	-8.7	(15.6)
Greece	36.8	(9.9)	10.2	(4.9)	53.0	(9.8)	43.8	(3.8)	25.0	(3.4)	31.3	(3.1)	**21.8**	(10.4)
Hungary	65.5	(6.1)	14.3	(5.2)	20.2	(5.3)	52.7	(4.3)	24.1	(3.7)	23.1	(3.6)	-3.0	(6.2)
Iceland	32.3	(0.2)	15.6	(0.1)	52.1	(0.2)	c	c	c	c	c	c	c	c
Ireland	74.1	(3.4)	11.8	(2.8)	14.0	(2.4)	76.0	(3.4)	11.2	(2.6)	12.7	(2.7)	1.3	(1.1)
Israel	63.6	(6.9)	17.7	(4.6)	18.7	(5.9)	57.7	(4.0)	20.3	(3.3)	22.0	(3.6)	-3.3	(5.9)
Italy	44.4	(7.7)	23.1	(7.0)	32.5	(6.9)	35.1	(1.9)	21.7	(1.7)	43.2	(1.9)	-10.7	(7.4)
Japan	c	c	c	c	c	c	85.0	(2.5)	5.3	(1.7)	9.8	(1.8)	c	c
Korea	76.5	(12.5)	23.5	(12.5)	0.0	c	70.6	(3.6)	19.7	(3.2)	9.7	(2.6)	**-9.7**	(2.6)
Luxembourg	65.1	(0.1)	5.4	(0.1)	29.5	(0.1)	60.0	(0.2)	21.3	(0.1)	18.7	(0.1)	**10.7**	(0.2)
Mexico	64.6	(2.9)	18.9	(2.5)	16.4	(1.8)	77.0	(2.0)	14.4	(1.6)	8.7	(1.1)	**7.8**	(2.0)
Netherlands	74.6	(3.8)	16.5	(3.5)	8.9	(2.1)	81.8	(5.0)	7.1	(3.2)	11.1	(3.9)	-2.2	(3.8)
New Zealand	86.3	(2.9)	7.5	(2.3)	6.2	(2.0)	85.6	(2.7)	7.5	(2.1)	6.9	(2.1)	-0.7	(0.9)
Norway	17.9	(2.9)	17.0	(2.9)	65.1	(3.4)	c	c	c	c	c	c	c	c
Poland	54.1	(3.6)	18.1	(3.1)	27.8	(3.0)	c	c	c	c	c	c	c	c
Portugal	44.7	(4.6)	25.7	(4.0)	29.6	(4.4)	65.9	(4.2)	17.2	(4.2)	16.9	(2.9)	**12.7**	(4.7)
Slovak Republic	58.5	(4.2)	14.4	(2.8)	27.1	(3.3)	89.9	(3.9)	6.3	(3.0)	3.9	(1.9)	**23.2**	(3.8)
Slovenia	68.7	(8.8)	14.1	(7.1)	17.2	(7.7)	62.2	(0.3)	13.5	(0.3)	24.3	(0.3)	-7.2	(7.8)
Spain	67.6	(2.7)	16.6	(2.5)	15.9	(1.9)	c	c	c	c	c	c	c	c
Sweden	54.3	(3.1)	14.8	(2.8)	30.9	(3.1)	93.1	(4.4)	2.2	(2.3)	4.7	(3.6)	**26.2**	(4.7)
Switzerland	27.4	(2.8)	13.7	(2.3)	58.8	(3.3)	19.1	(5.1)	27.3	(6.1)	53.5	(6.6)	5.3	(7.2)
Turkey	c	c	c	c	c	c	69.4	(3.1)	9.7	(2.0)	20.9	(2.9)	c	c
United Kingdom	c	c	c	c	c	c	82.1	(2.4)	9.6	(2.0)	8.3	(1.6)	c	c
United States	56.8	(7.5)	9.7	(4.6)	33.5	(7.8)	70.2	(3.8)	6.9	(2.2)	22.9	(3.7)	10.6	(6.1)
OECD average	58.1	(1.0)	15.9	(0.9)	26.0	(0.8)	66.7	(1.2)	14.1	(0.9)	19.2	(1.2)	**2.8**	(1.6)
Partners Albania	47.9	(6.0)	22.4	(5.5)	29.7	(4.9)	42.1	(5.3)	21.9	(4.9)	36.0	(4.8)	-6.4	(6.4)
Argentina	75.0	(4.8)	7.4	(2.1)	17.6	(4.6)	79.6	(3.6)	8.4	(2.1)	12.0	(3.1)	5.6	(4.3)
Brazil	48.5	(3.8)	26.0	(3.5)	25.6	(3.3)	52.5	(2.4)	20.9	(2.2)	26.6	(2.3)	-1.0	(3.6)
Bulgaria	38.8	(8.9)	11.4	(4.7)	49.8	(9.0)	76.3	(2.9)	12.7	(2.3)	11.0	(2.4)	**38.8**	(9.0)
Colombia	65.7	(3.5)	19.1	(3.5)	15.2	(3.2)	71.8	(3.7)	15.3	(3.2)	12.9	(2.6)	2.3	(1.9)
Costa Rica	64.1	(3.4)	16.7	(3.4)	19.2	(2.9)	67.8	(4.3)	14.4	(3.3)	17.9	(3.3)	1.3	(2.2)
Croatia	c	c	c	c	c	c	70.1	(3.7)	9.4	(2.4)	20.4	(3.2)	c	c
Cyprus*	25.8	(1.1)	20.9	(1.1)	53.3	(1.2)	39.0	(0.1)	17.8	(0.1)	43.3	(0.1)	**10.0**	(1.2)
Hong Kong-China	95.4	(1.6)	3.6	(1.5)	0.9	(0.7)	92.8	(2.4)	5.8	(2.1)	1.4	(1.0)	-0.5	(0.3)
Indonesia	81.0	(4.6)	13.6	(4.0)	5.5	(2.8)	90.4	(3.3)	8.5	(3.2)	1.0	(1.0)	4.4	(3.0)
Jordan	50.3	(3.3)	22.1	(3.4)	27.5	(3.2)	c	c	c	c	c	c	c	c
Kazakhstan	48.5	(3.9)	16.3	(3.5)	35.3	(3.9)	47.2	(5.6)	23.4	(5.2)	29.4	(4.4)	5.9	(4.0)
Latvia	73.9	(3.2)	19.3	(3.2)	6.8	(1.8)	75.3	(8.3)	23.7	(8.3)	1.0	(0.7)	**5.8**	(1.7)
Liechtenstein	10.5	(0.5)	35.5	(0.9)	54.1	(0.9)	c	c	c	c	c	c	c	c
Lithuania	52.1	(3.2)	21.8	(2.9)	26.0	(2.7)	c	c	c	c	c	c	c	c
Macao-China	92.1	(0.1)	5.9	(0.1)	2.0	(0.0)	81.3	(0.1)	12.4	(0.1)	6.3	(0.0)	**-4.3**	(0.1)
Malaysia	66.8	(8.5)	17.7	(6.4)	15.5	(6.6)	60.9	(3.8)	22.4	(3.6)	16.7	(2.9)	-1.2	(5.7)
Montenegro	c	c	c	c	c	c	24.4	(0.1)	22.0	(0.1)	53.6	(0.1)	c	c
Peru	57.2	(3.9)	13.8	(2.5)	29.0	(3.8)	72.3	(2.8)	12.0	(2.1)	15.8	(2.4)	**13.3**	(3.1)
Qatar	66.3	(0.3)	8.8	(0.2)	24.8	(0.3)	55.1	(0.1)	18.8	(0.1)	26.1	(0.1)	**-1.3**	(0.3)
Romania	56.5	(4.2)	17.1	(3.0)	26.4	(3.4)	c	c	c	c	c	c	c	c
Russian Federation	56.9	(3.6)	19.7	(3.1)	23.4	(2.6)	55.8	(4.7)	21.2	(3.3)	23.0	(4.8)	0.4	(3.8)
Serbia	c	c	c	c	c	c	63.3	(4.0)	14.7	(2.7)	22.0	(3.8)	c	c
Shanghai-China	67.1	(5.0)	10.5	(5.0)	22.4	(4.1)	76.7	(4.5)	11.0	(2.9)	12.3	(3.8)	10.1	(5.5)
Singapore	92.4	(2.2)	7.6	(2.2)	0.0	c	92.7	(0.1)	6.7	(0.1)	0.7	(0.0)	**-0.7**	(0.0)
Chinese Taipei	74.2	(4.8)	20.8	(5.3)	5.0	(2.7)	89.2	(2.4)	7.4	(2.1)	3.4	(1.7)	1.6	(3.2)
Thailand	67.9	(4.4)	17.8	(3.9)	14.3	(3.7)	76.5	(3.4)	13.4	(2.9)	10.1	(2.3)	4.2	(3.5)
Tunisia	34.7	(4.7)	26.9	(4.5)	38.4	(5.6)	40.7	(5.0)	30.8	(4.1)	28.4	(4.3)	10.0	(7.0)
United Arab Emirates	73.0	(3.9)	16.8	(4.0)	10.2	(2.8)	76.4	(1.9)	14.0	(1.7)	9.7	(1.5)	0.6	(2.3)
Uruguay	38.4	(4.3)	18.8	(3.7)	42.7	(4.5)	42.1	(3.7)	13.5	(3.0)	44.4	(4.0)	-1.7	(5.3)
Viet Nam	25.1	(9.8)	13.0	(7.9)	61.9	(11.2)	53.2	(4.1)	30.0	(4.2)	16.8	(3.2)	**45.1**	(11.6)

Note: Values that are statistically significant are indicated in bold (see Annex A3).
* See notes at the beginning of this Annex.
StatLink http://dx.doi.org/10.1787/888932957498

[Part 1/1]
School admissions policies and school competition
Table IV.4.6 *Results based on school principals' reports*

	Percentage of students in schools whose principal reported that residence in a particular area is:												Difference between the percentage of students where residence is "always" considered for admission to school and there is school competition, and the percentage of students where residence is "never" or "sometimes" considered for admission and there is school competition	
	"always" considered for admission to school:		Among these students, percentage of students in schools whose principal reported on the number of schools competing for students in the same area				"never" or "sometimes" considered for admission to school:		Among these students, percentage of students in schools whose principal reported on the number of schools competing for students in the same area					
			No other school		One or more schools				No other school		One or more schools			
	%	S.E.	%	S.E.	%	S.E.	%	S.E.	%	S.E.	%	S.E.	% dif.	S.E.
OECD														
Australia	44.8	(1.5)	5.2	(1.3)	94.8	(1.3)	55.2	(1.5)	5.8	(1.2)	94.2	(1.2)	-0.6	(1.6)
Austria	28.7	(3.2)	46.2	(6.5)	53.8	(6.5)	71.3	(3.2)	36.2	(4.3)	63.8	(4.3)	10.0	(8.5)
Belgium	1.5	(0.8)	0.7	(0.4)	99.3	(0.4)	98.5	(0.8)	5.7	(1.5)	94.3	(1.5)	**-5.1**	(1.6)
Canada	69.4	(1.9)	16.0	(1.9)	84.0	(1.9)	30.6	(1.9)	22.4	(2.6)	77.6	(2.6)	-6.4	(3.2)
Chile	11.8	(2.4)	29.5	(11.0)	70.5	(11.0)	88.2	(2.4)	14.0	(2.5)	86.0	(2.5)	15.4	(11.5)
Czech Republic	14.0	(2.1)	28.0	(9.8)	72.0	(9.8)	86.0	(2.1)	13.1	(2.1)	86.9	(2.1)	14.9	(9.8)
Denmark	41.2	(3.3)	16.8	(4.1)	83.2	(4.1)	58.8	(3.3)	12.8	(3.4)	87.2	(3.4)	4.1	(5.5)
Estonia	51.7	(3.0)	19.6	(2.6)	80.4	(2.6)	48.3	(3.0)	17.7	(3.7)	82.3	(3.7)	1.9	(5.0)
Finland	66.9	(3.3)	47.9	(3.9)	52.1	(3.9)	33.1	(3.3)	64.2	(5.7)	35.8	(5.7)	**-16.4**	(6.9)
France	60.8	(2.7)	42.6	(4.8)	57.4	(4.8)	39.2	(2.7)	28.7	(4.9)	71.3	(4.9)	13.9	(7.2)
Germany	48.9	(3.5)	20.2	(3.6)	79.8	(3.6)	51.1	(3.5)	12.5	(3.5)	87.5	(3.5)	7.7	(5.0)
Greece	71.5	(4.0)	30.5	(3.7)	69.5	(3.7)	28.5	(4.0)	36.3	(6.9)	63.7	(6.9)	-5.8	(8.3)
Hungary	19.9	(2.7)	23.6	(6.7)	76.4	(6.7)	80.1	(2.7)	22.4	(4.0)	77.6	(4.0)	1.1	(8.2)
Iceland	48.1	(0.2)	56.7	(0.3)	43.3	(0.3)	51.9	(0.2)	44.1	(0.4)	55.9	(0.4)	**12.6**	(0.5)
Ireland	44.4	(4.6)	21.9	(4.7)	78.1	(4.7)	55.6	(4.0)	7.0	(2.5)	93.0	(2.5)	**14.9**	(5.3)
Israel	38.8	(3.7)	23.9	(5.0)	76.1	(5.0)	61.2	(3.7)	19.7	(4.6)	80.3	(4.6)	4.2	(6.6)
Italy	27.0	(1.9)	39.6	(4.0)	60.4	(4.0)	73.0	(1.9)	44.1	(2.0)	55.9	(2.0)	-4.6	(4.2)
Japan	9.5	(1.9)	0.0	c	100.0	c	90.5	(1.9)	10.8	(2.0)	89.2	(2.0)	**-10.8**	(2.0)
Korea	17.8	(3.4)	7.4	(5.1)	92.6	(5.1)	82.2	(3.4)	9.5	(2.7)	90.5	(2.7)	-2.2	(5.6)
Luxembourg	43.7	(0.1)	41.4	(0.1)	58.6	(0.1)	56.3	(0.1)	12.7	(0.1)	87.3	(0.1)	**28.6**	(0.2)
Mexico	9.2	(1.0)	7.4	(2.0)	92.6	(2.0)	90.8	(1.0)	12.0	(1.1)	88.0	(1.1)	**-4.5**	(2.2)
Netherlands	21.4	(3.7)	5.1	(3.7)	94.9	(3.7)	78.6	(3.7)	10.8	(2.4)	89.2	(2.4)	-5.7	(4.2)
New Zealand	49.9	(3.0)	6.1	(3.4)	93.9	(3.4)	50.1	(3.0)	7.8	(2.5)	92.2	(2.5)	-1.6	(4.1)
Norway	63.3	(4.0)	63.8	(4.5)	36.2	(4.5)	36.7	(4.0)	69.9	(6.0)	30.1	(6.0)	-6.1	(7.6)
Poland	76.7	(3.1)	25.3	(3.7)	74.7	(3.7)	23.3	(3.1)	35.9	(6.8)	64.1	(6.8)	-10.6	(8.3)
Portugal	54.9	(4.6)	24.4	(4.4)	75.6	(4.4)	45.1	(4.6)	18.3	(4.5)	81.7	(4.5)	6.1	(6.8)
Slovak Republic	16.8	(2.6)	25.1	(7.0)	74.9	(7.0)	83.2	(2.6)	12.4	(2.0)	87.6	(2.0)	12.7	(7.6)
Slovenia	4.1	(0.7)	14.0	(7.3)	86.0	(7.3)	95.9	(0.7)	24.7	(0.4)	75.3	(0.4)	-10.7	(7.3)
Spain	62.6	(3.0)	14.9	(2.2)	85.1	(2.2)	37.4	(3.0)	17.7	(3.5)	82.3	(3.5)	-2.8	(4.2)
Sweden	50.1	(3.6)	27.7	(4.4)	72.3	(4.4)	49.9	(3.6)	34.2	(4.6)	65.8	(4.6)	-6.5	(6.7)
Switzerland	56.6	(3.2)	60.2	(3.9)	39.8	(3.9)	43.4	(3.2)	52.1	(4.9)	47.9	(4.9)	8.1	(6.2)
Turkey	33.4	(3.4)	27.5	(5.6)	72.5	(5.6)	66.6	(3.4)	17.5	(2.8)	82.5	(2.8)	10.0	(6.0)
United Kingdom	48.4	(3.2)	12.5	(2.9)	87.5	(2.9)	51.6	(3.2)	4.6	(1.5)	95.4	(1.5)	**7.8**	(3.2)
United States	74.4	(3.7)	27.2	(5.0)	72.8	(5.0)	25.6	(3.7)	15.6	(6.1)	84.4	(6.1)	11.6	(8.3)
OECD average	40.7	(0.5)	25.2	(0.8)	74.8	(0.8)	59.3	(0.5)	22.7	(0.6)	77.3	(0.6)	**2.5**	(1.1)
Partners														
Albania	38.3	(4.0)	32.9	(5.1)	67.1	(5.1)	61.7	(4.0)	34.0	(4.9)	66.0	(4.9)	-1.1	(6.9)
Argentina	23.9	(3.0)	19.4	(6.3)	80.6	(6.3)	76.1	(3.0)	12.8	(3.4)	87.2	(3.4)	6.6	(6.7)
Brazil	38.8	(2.3)	30.2	(3.9)	69.8	(3.9)	61.2	(2.3)	24.1	(2.7)	75.9	(2.7)	6.1	(5.0)
Bulgaria	17.7	(2.3)	10.1	(6.0)	89.9	(6.0)	82.3	(2.3)	13.4	(2.8)	86.6	(2.8)	-3.3	(6.7)
Colombia	25.1	(3.2)	13.6	(5.5)	86.4	(5.5)	74.9	(3.2)	13.9	(3.3)	86.1	(3.3)	-0.3	(6.5)
Costa Rica	52.9	(3.8)	21.6	(4.3)	78.4	(4.3)	47.1	(3.8)	14.5	(3.2)	85.5	(3.2)	7.1	(5.1)
Croatia	6.6	(1.3)	19.0	(14.3)	81.0	(14.3)	93.4	(1.3)	20.1	(3.1)	79.9	(3.1)	-1.1	(14.4)
Cyprus*	67.8	(0.1)	52.3	(0.1)	47.7	(0.1)	32.2	(0.1)	26.0	(0.1)	74.0	(0.1)	**26.3**	(0.2)
Hong Kong-China	14.8	(2.9)	0.0	c	100.0	c	85.2	(2.9)	1.5	(1.0)	98.5	(1.0)	-1.5	(1.0)
Indonesia	41.9	(3.7)	6.6	(3.4)	93.4	(3.4)	58.1	(3.7)	0.7	(0.8)	99.3	(0.8)	5.9	(3.5)
Jordan	63.3	(3.3)	30.6	(3.6)	69.4	(3.6)	36.7	(3.3)	22.5	(5.8)	77.5	(5.8)	8.1	(6.4)
Kazakhstan	37.9	(3.9)	27.8	(5.4)	72.2	(5.4)	62.1	(3.9)	36.4	(5.2)	63.6	(5.2)	-8.6	(7.9)
Latvia	20.5	(2.8)	7.9	(5.3)	92.1	(5.3)	79.5	(2.8)	6.4	(2.0)	93.6	(2.0)	1.5	(5.8)
Liechtenstein	56.7	(0.6)	44.8	(1.5)	55.2	(1.5)	43.3	(0.6)	c	c	c	c	c	c
Lithuania	60.8	(3.2)	28.0	(3.7)	72.0	(3.7)	39.2	(3.2)	22.5	(4.6)	77.5	(4.6)	5.6	(6.2)
Macao-China	6.0	(0.0)	c	c	c	c	94.0	(0.0)	4.2	(0.0)	95.8	(0.0)	c	c
Malaysia	31.1	(3.7)	10.8	(4.2)	89.2	(4.2)	68.9	(3.7)	19.3	(3.8)	80.7	(3.8)	-8.5	(5.8)
Montenegro	7.6	(0.1)	70.2	(1.3)	29.8	(1.3)	92.4	(0.1)	52.1	(0.1)	47.9	(0.1)	**18.0**	(1.3)
Peru	6.6	(1.7)	46.5	(12.5)	53.5	(12.5)	93.4	(1.7)	17.9	(2.7)	82.1	(2.7)	**28.6**	(13.1)
Qatar	48.4	(0.1)	23.4	(0.1)	76.6	(0.1)	51.6	(0.1)	28.4	(0.1)	71.6	(0.1)	**-5.0**	(0.2)
Romania	9.6	(2.3)	27.0	(11.3)	73.0	(11.3)	90.4	(2.3)	26.1	(3.5)	73.9	(3.5)	0.9	(11.6)
Russian Federation	46.5	(4.2)	20.8	(3.6)	79.2	(3.6)	53.5	(4.2)	25.5	(3.6)	74.5	(3.6)	-4.7	(4.7)
Serbia	3.2	(1.5)	c	c	c	c	96.8	(1.5)	21.6	(3.8)	78.4	(3.8)	c	c
Shanghai-China	29.8	(3.6)	28.3	(6.1)	71.7	(6.1)	70.2	(3.6)	12.2	(3.2)	87.8	(3.2)	**16.0**	(6.6)
Singapore	7.8	(0.6)	0.0	c	100.0	c	92.2	(0.6)	0.7	(0.0)	99.3	(0.0)	**-0.7**	(0.0)
Chinese Taipei	27.5	(3.2)	4.5	(2.9)	95.5	(2.9)	72.5	(3.2)	3.8	(1.7)	96.2	(1.7)	0.7	(3.3)
Thailand	42.6	(3.6)	13.0	(3.9)	87.0	(3.9)	57.4	(3.6)	9.5	(2.7)	90.5	(2.7)	3.5	(4.8)
Tunisia	55.3	(3.7)	32.8	(4.5)	67.2	(4.5)	44.7	(3.7)	31.4	(5.9)	68.6	(5.9)	1.3	(7.7)
United Arab Emirates	40.9	(2.1)	13.2	(2.5)	86.8	(2.5)	59.1	(2.1)	7.1	(2.0)	92.9	(2.0)	6.2	(3.2)
Uruguay	26.7	(2.6)	43.9	(6.7)	56.1	(6.7)	73.3	(2.6)	43.6	(3.7)	56.4	(3.7)	0.3	(7.6)
Viet Nam	41.3	(4.1)	24.8	(5.7)	75.2	(5.7)	58.7	(4.1)	19.2	(4.5)	80.8	(4.5)	5.6	(7.9)

Note: Values that are statistically significant are indicated in bold (see Annex A3).
* See notes at the beginning of this Annex.
StatLink ᴍᴤᴸ http://dx.doi.org/10.1787/888932957498

[Part 1/2]
School type and performance in mathematics, reading and science
Table IV.4.7   *Results based on school principals' reports*

	Government or public schools[1]								Government-dependent private schools[2]							
	Percentage of students		Performance on the mathematics scale		Performance on the reading scale		Performance on the science scale		Percentage of students		Performance on the mathematics scale		Performance on the reading scale		Performance on the science scale	
	%	S.E.	Mean score	S.E.	Mean score	S.E.	Mean score	S.E.	%	S.E.	Mean score	S.E.	Mean score	S.E.	Mean score	S.E.
Australia	61.0	(0.7)	489	(2.3)	495	(2.4)	506	(2.5)	26.5	(1.0)	510	(2.9)	520	(2.9)	527	(3.2)
Austria	91.4	(2.3)	502	(3.2)	486	(3.4)	502	(3.2)	7.5	(2.1)	546	(15.9)	532	(13.7)	550	(13.1)
Belgium	w	w	w	w	w	w	w	w	w	w	w	w	w	w	w	w
Canada	92.2	(0.8)	514	(2.2)	519	(2.2)	523	(2.2)	4.3	(0.6)	570	(8.1)	567	(9.4)	550	(6.7)
Chile	37.5	(1.6)	390	(5.0)	410	(5.0)	412	(4.5)	48.1	(2.7)	424	(4.9)	444	(4.5)	447	(4.7)
Czech Republic	91.8	(1.9)	498	(3.8)	491	(3.9)	507	(3.7)	6.9	(1.6)	493	(17.3)	502	(17.2)	511	(15.9)
Denmark	77.0	(1.8)	494	(2.5)	489	(3.1)	491	(2.9)	18.9	(2.0)	517	(6.2)	520	(6.3)	519	(7.1)
Estonia	97.5	(1.0)	520	(2.0)	516	(2.1)	541	(2.0)	1.9	(1.0)	509	(36.3)	522	(39.7)	531	(44.0)
Finland	97.0	(0.7)	518	(2.0)	523	(2.5)	545	(2.3)	3.0	(0.7)	542	(7.2)	555	(8.0)	561	(8.0)
France	82.8	(1.4)	490	(3.2)	503	(3.4)	495	(3.2)	17.2	(1.4)	521	(6.6)	529	(9.3)	521	(7.3)
Germany	94.5	(1.6)	511	(3.5)	506	(3.6)	521	(3.8)	5.0	(1.6)	549	(19.4)	541	(18.8)	549	(18.6)
Greece	97.7	(0.7)	450	(2.7)	474	(3.5)	464	(3.3)	0.0	c	c	c	c	c	c	c
Hungary	84.0	(2.9)	475	(3.4)	485	(3.8)	493	(3.4)	16.0	(2.9)	489	(14.1)	507	(10.7)	505	(11.6)
Iceland	99.5	(0.1)	493	(1.7)	483	(1.8)	478	(2.1)	0.5	(0.1)	c	c	c	c	c	c
Ireland	43.8	(0.9)	492	(3.9)	510	(4.5)	511	(4.2)	54.0	(1.1)	502	(3.0)	527	(3.1)	524	(3.2)
Israel	100.0	c	466	(4.7)	485	(5.0)	469	(4.9)	0.0	c	c	c	c	c	c	c
Italy	95.3	(0.7)	487	(2.3)	492	(2.3)	495	(2.1)	1.8	(0.4)	437	(7.1)	433	(10.9)	454	(8.7)
Japan	70.1	(1.2)	535	(3.3)	537	(3.8)	548	(3.5)	0.0	c	c	c	c	c	c	c
Korea	52.7	(4.1)	546	(7.1)	529	(6.2)	532	(5.6)	31.4	(3.8)	539	(7.2)	525	(6.0)	527	(5.8)
Luxembourg	84.9	(0.1)	492	(1.3)	487	(1.7)	493	(1.4)	13.4	(0.0)	464	(2.4)	478	(3.2)	467	(2.5)
Mexico	90.7	(0.9)	408	(1.5)	418	(1.7)	410	(1.5)	0.1	(0.1)	c	c	c	c	c	c
Netherlands	33.6	(4.4)	516	(10.0)	508	(9.8)	519	(9.2)	66.4	(4.4)	523	(5.6)	511	(5.5)	521	(5.6)
New Zealand	94.7	(1.4)	496	(2.5)	509	(2.9)	512	(2.6)	0.0	c	c	c	c	c	c	c
Norway	98.3	(1.0)	489	(2.8)	504	(3.2)	494	(3.2)	1.7	(1.0)	c	c	c	c	c	c
Poland	97.1	(0.4)	516	(3.6)	517	(3.1)	524	(3.1)	1.9	(0.4)	566	(22.1)	562	(29.3)	567	(24.9)
Portugal	89.9	(2.0)	481	(3.8)	482	(3.7)	484	(3.8)	5.8	(1.9)	516	(7.3)	517	(9.1)	513	(8.6)
Slovak Republic	91.0	(2.4)	478	(4.1)	458	(5.0)	468	(4.4)	8.6	(2.5)	520	(20.2)	513	(21.0)	508	(18.0)
Slovenia	97.6	(0.1)	501	(1.3)	481	(1.2)	514	(1.4)	2.4	(0.1)	589	(6.9)	571	(6.5)	601	(6.7)
Spain	68.2	(0.8)	471	(2.5)	476	(2.5)	485	(2.5)	24.4	(1.1)	506	(3.6)	507	(3.9)	515	(3.3)
Sweden	86.0	(0.7)	476	(2.4)	480	(3.3)	482	(3.3)	14.0	(0.7)	491	(7.9)	505	(9.2)	501	(8.3)
Switzerland	93.7	(1.3)	532	(3.3)	509	(2.9)	515	(3.0)	1.5	(0.8)	567	(18.4)	540	(18.4)	529	(10.6)
Turkey	100.0	c	447	(4.9)	475	(4.2)	463	(3.9)	0.0	c	c	c	c	c	c	c
United Kingdom	56.2	(3.1)	485	(3.6)	492	(4.1)	506	(4.1)	36.0	(3.2)	494	(7.6)	499	(8.8)	515	(8.0)
United States	94.9	(0.9)	482	(4.0)	497	(4.1)	498	(4.2)	0.0	c	c	c	c	c	c	c
OECD average	81.7	(0.3)	489	(0.7)	491	(0.7)	496	(0.6)	14.2	(0.4)	517	(2.6)	518	(2.8)	521	(2.7)
Albania	91.7	(2.1)	393	(2.2)	393	(3.3)	397	(2.6)	0.0	c	c	c	c	c	c	c
Argentina	67.7	(2.3)	368	(4.1)	370	(4.2)	382	(4.4)	25.6	(2.9)	428	(5.7)	448	(7.5)	454	(5.3)
Brazil	86.5	(1.3)	376	(2.0)	396	(2.3)	390	(2.2)	0.6	(0.4)	c	c	c	c	c	c
Bulgaria	98.8	(0.9)	438	(4.1)	435	(6.1)	446	(4.9)	0.0	c	c	c	c	c	c	c
Colombia	85.9	(1.4)	369	(2.8)	394	(3.5)	392	(3.0)	4.0	(0.8)	362	(8.0)	393	(8.2)	375	(8.1)
Costa Rica	86.9	(1.4)	396	(3.3)	430	(3.8)	419	(3.2)	3.6	(0.9)	465	(17.1)	498	(15.2)	490	(14.2)
Croatia	98.2	(1.1)	471	(3.6)	484	(3.4)	491	(3.2)	0.8	(0.8)	c	c	c	c	c	c
Cyprus*	83.9	(0.0)	430	(1.3)	444	(1.4)	429	(1.3)	0.0	c	c	c	c	c	c	c
Hong Kong-China	7.0	(0.2)	597	(9.5)	571	(9.1)	582	(7.7)	91.9	(0.8)	560	(3.5)	543	(3.0)	554	(2.8)
Indonesia	58.9	(2.6)	377	(5.0)	399	(5.5)	385	(4.8)	17.5	(2.3)	342	(5.6)	362	(7.0)	352	(5.7)
Jordan	83.3	(1.5)	376	(3.1)	390	(4.0)	400	(3.3)	0.9	(0.6)	c	c	c	c	c	c
Kazakhstan	97.2	(1.0)	432	(3.0)	392	(2.8)	425	(3.0)	0.7	(0.5)	c	c	c	c	c	c
Latvia	97.7	(1.5)	490	(2.9)	488	(2.5)	501	(2.9)	0.4	(0.4)	c	c	c	c	c	c
Liechtenstein	93.6	(0.4)	541	(3.9)	519	(4.3)	528	(3.6)	0.0	c	c	c	c	c	c	c
Lithuania	98.6	(0.7)	478	(2.7)	476	(2.5)	495	(2.6)	1.1	(0.6)	c	c	c	c	c	c
Macao-China	4.2	(0.0)	c	c	c	c	c	c	81.3	(0.0)	537	(1.1)	509	(0.9)	520	(0.9)
Malaysia	96.6	(0.7)	418	(3.2)	397	(3.2)	418	(2.9)	0.0	c	c	c	c	c	c	c
Montenegro	99.6	(0.0)	410	(1.1)	422	(1.2)	410	(1.1)	0.0	c	c	c	c	c	c	c
Peru	85.3	(1.8)	350	(3.2)	366	(3.8)	358	(3.2)	0.0	c	c	c	c	c	c	c
Qatar	61.9	(0.1)	335	(1.0)	350	(1.0)	341	(0.9)	0.9	(0.0)	c	c	c	c	c	c
Romania	99.4	(0.6)	444	(3.7)	437	(3.9)	438	(3.2)	0.0	c	c	c	c	c	c	c
Russian Federation	99.4	(0.6)	482	(3.0)	474	(3.0)	486	(2.9)	0.0	c	c	c	c	c	c	c
Serbia	99.6	(0.4)	448	(3.9)	446	(3.8)	444	(3.8)	0.0	c	c	c	c	c	c	c
Shanghai-China	90.7	(1.8)	609	(3.4)	567	(2.8)	578	(3.1)	0.0	c	c	c	c	c	c	c
Singapore	97.6	(0.7)	574	(1.2)	542	(1.2)	552	(1.3)	0.0	c	c	c	c	c	c	c
Chinese Taipei	67.6	(1.4)	581	(3.7)	538	(3.3)	539	(2.7)	4.6	(1.3)	469	(9.5)	465	(10.6)	458	(9.4)
Thailand	83.5	(0.6)	433	(3.8)	447	(3.3)	450	(3.2)	11.6	(1.5)	396	(5.1)	412	(4.7)	417	(4.6)
Tunisia	99.4	(0.4)	389	(3.9)	405	(4.5)	399	(3.5)	0.0	c	c	c	c	c	c	c
United Arab Emirates	54.5	(1.7)	399	(2.6)	413	(2.8)	419	(2.9)	0.6	(0.4)	c	c	c	c	c	c
Uruguay	83.3	(1.2)	393	(2.6)	394	(3.2)	399	(2.8)	0.0	c	c	c	c	c	c	c
Viet Nam	92.6	(1.1)	513	(5.1)	510	(4.7)	530	(4.6)	0.0	c	c	c	c	c	c	c

Note: Values that are statistically significant are indicated in bold (see Annex A3).
1. Schools which are directly controlled or managed by: *i)* a public education authority or agency or *ii)* a government agency directly or a governing body, most of whose members are either appointed by a public authority or elected by public franchise.
2. Schools which receive 50% or more of their core funding (i.e. funding that supports the basic educational services of the institution) from government agencies.
3. Schools which receive less than 50% of their core funding (i.e. funding that supports the basic educational services of the institution) from government agencies.
* See notes at the beginning of this Annex.
StatLink ⟶ http://dx.doi.org/10.1787/888932957498

[Part 2/2]
School type and performance in mathematics, reading and science
Table IV.4.7   *Results based on school principals' reports*

| | Government-independent private schools[3] | | | | | | | Difference in performance on the mathematics scale between public and private schools (government-dependent and government-independent schools combined) | | PISA index of economic, social and cultural status | | | | | | Difference in performance on the mathematics scale between public and private schools after accounting for the PISA index of economic, social and cultural status of: | | | |
| | Percentage of students | | Performance on the mathematics scale | | Performance on the reading scale | | Performance on the science scale | | | | Public schools | | Private schools (government-dependent and government-independent) | | Difference | | Students | | Students and schools | |
	%	S.E.	Mean score	S.E.	Mean score	S.E.	Mean score	S.E.	Dif. (Pub.- Priv.)	S.E.	Mean index	S.E.	Mean index	S.E.	Dif. (Pub.- Priv.)	S.E.	Dif. (Pub.- Priv.)	S.E.	Dif. (Pub.- Priv.)	S.E.
OECD																				
Australia	12.5	(0.9)	559	(3.6)	567	(3.8)	576	(3.9)	-37	(3.4)	0.06	(0.0)	0.52	(0.0)	-0.46	(0.0)	-17	(3.4)	8	(4.3)
Austria	1.1	(0.9)	559	(14.5)	548	(11.2)	560	(11.4)	-45	(14.9)	0.02	(0.0)	0.64	(0.1)	-0.62	(0.1)	-18	(13.3)	21	(15.7)
Belgium	w	w	w	w	w	w	w	w	w	w	w	w	w	w	w	w	w	w	w	w
Canada	3.5	(0.8)	566	(10.1)	566	(9.5)	565	(9.9)	-54	(6.7)	0.37	(0.0)	0.85	(0.1)	-0.48	(0.1)	-38	(6.5)	-25	(6.6)
Chile	14.5	(2.2)	503	(6.6)	511	(5.9)	520	(6.4)	-53	(6.1)	-1.09	(0.1)	-0.26	(0.0)	-0.84	(0.1)	-27	(6.0)	-8	(6.7)
Czech Republic	1.3	(0.9)	c	c	c	c	c	c	-6	(17.3)	-0.08	(0.0)	0.07	(0.1)	-0.15	(0.1)	3	(14.0)	16	(12.5)
Denmark	4.2	(1.5)	527	(13.0)	519	(14.5)	526	(17.7)	-25	(6.4)	0.35	(0.0)	0.69	(0.1)	-0.34	(0.1)	-11	(5.0)	0	(4.6)
Estonia	0.5	(0.5)	c	c	c	c	c	c	-9	(30.5)	0.10	(0.0)	0.48	(0.2)	-0.38	(0.2)	3	(26.7)	15	(22.0)
Finland	0.0	c	c	c	c	c	c	c	-24	(7.7)	0.35	(0.0)	0.69	(0.1)	-0.34	(0.1)	-13	(6.9)	-5	(6.7)
France	0.0	c	c	c	c	c	c	c	-31	(7.4)	-0.11	(0.0)	0.28	(0.0)	-0.38	(0.0)			26	(7.9)
Germany	0.5	(0.4)	c	c	c	c	c	c	-44	(19.7)	0.15	(0.0)	0.65	(0.2)	-0.51	(0.2)	-17	(16.0)	23	(15.7)
Greece	2.3	(0.7)	c	c	c	c	c	c	c	c	-0.12	(0.0)	c	c	c	c	c	c	c	c
Hungary	0.0	c	c	c	c	c	c	c	-15	(15.1)	-0.27	(0.0)	-0.12	(0.1)	-0.15	(0.1)	-8	(10.8)	1	(8.6)
Iceland	0.0	c	c	c	c	c	c	c	c	c	0.79	(0.0)	c	c	c	c	c	c	c	c
Ireland	2.2	(1.1)	c	c	c	c	c	c	-12	(5.0)	0.03	(0.0)	0.13	(0.0)	-0.10	(0.0)	-8	(4.1)	-4	(3.7)
Israel	0.0	c	c	c	c	c	c	c	c	c	0.17	(0.0)	c	c	c	c	c	c	c	c
Italy	2.9	(0.5)	515	(8.9)	522	(9.3)	526	(9.0)	3	(7.7)	-0.07	(0.0)	0.23	(0.1)	-0.30	(0.1)	12	(6.1)	31	(7.8)
Japan	29.9	(1.2)	540	(9.6)	541	(9.3)	544	(9.4)	-5	(10.3)	-0.15	(0.0)	0.12	(0.0)	-0.28	(0.0)	6	(8.7)	43	(6.7)
Korea	15.9	(3.1)	609	(10.5)	582	(8.9)	579	(7.6)	-17	(10.1)	0.00	(0.0)	0.03	(0.0)	-0.04	(0.1)	-15	(8.4)	-12	(6.9)
Luxembourg	1.8	(0.0)	c	c	c	c	c	c	13	(2.7)	0.06	(0.0)	0.12	(0.0)	-0.06	(0.0)	15	(3.0)	18	(2.8)
Mexico	9.2	(0.8)	452	(6.0)	466	(6.3)	451	(4.7)	-43	(6.5)	-1.30	(0.0)	0.29	(0.1)	-1.59	(0.1)	-16	(5.4)	18	(4.6)
Netherlands	0.0	c	c	c	c	c	c	c	-7	(12.5)	0.22	(0.1)	0.21	(0.0)	0.01	(0.1)	-8	(10.6)	-9	(7.8)
New Zealand	5.3	(1.4)	583	(6.8)	593	(6.8)	593	(6.2)	-87	(6.9)	0.00	(0.0)	0.84	(0.1)	-0.84	(0.1)	-43	(7.2)	0	(9.4)
Norway	0.0	c	c	c	c	c	c	c	c	c	0.47	(0.0)	c	c	c	c	c	c	c	c
Poland	1.0	(0.2)	581	(14.9)	577	(14.3)	583	(14.3)	-56	(12.9)	-0.24	(0.0)	0.77	(0.1)	-1.01	(0.1)	-15	(11.3)	15	(12.9)
Portugal	4.2	(1.4)	581	(5.2)	572	(5.8)	574	(8.4)	-62	(9.4)	-0.58	(0.0)	0.37	(0.2)	-0.95	(0.2)	-29	(4.8)	-7	(7.2)
Slovak Republic	0.5	(0.3)	c	c	c	c	c	c	-42	(20.4)	-0.23	(0.0)	0.25	(0.1)	-0.47	(0.2)	-17	(14.8)	7	(11.9)
Slovenia	0.0	c	c	c	c	c	c	c	-87	(6.9)	0.07	(0.0)	0.74	(0.1)	-0.67	(0.1)	-60	(7.4)	-3	(7.0)
Spain	7.4	(1.0)	523	(4.8)	528	(5.2)	530	(3.7)	-39	(3.3)	-0.39	(0.0)	0.20	(0.1)	-0.59	(0.1)	-21	(3.3)	-10	(4.1)
Sweden	0.0	c	c	c	c	c	c	c	-15	(8.4)	0.24	(0.0)	0.48	(0.1)	-0.24	(0.1)	-7	(6.4)	2	(5.0)
Switzerland	4.8	(1.0)	505	(13.0)	493	(10.2)	509	(9.8)	12	(14.8)	0.13	(0.0)	0.71	(0.1)	-0.57	(0.1)	34	(14.3)	71	(15.5)
Turkey	0.0	c	c	c	c	c	c	c	c	c	-1.48	(0.0)	c	c	c	c	c	c	c	c
United Kingdom	7.8	(0.7)	569	(12.7)	577	(11.7)	592	(11.0)	-23	(8.1)	0.18	(0.0)	0.40	(0.0)	-0.21	(0.0)	-13	(5.9)	-1	(5.2)
United States	5.1	(0.9)	496	(10.0)	527	(13.1)	518	(13.8)	-14	(11.4)	0.15	(0.0)	0.73	(0.1)	-0.58	(0.1)	7	(8.1)	27	(6.4)
OECD average	4.1	(0.2)	542	(2.5)	543	(2.4)	547	(2.5)	-28	(2.1)	-0.07	(0.0)	0.39	(0.0)	-0.46	(0.0)	-12	(1.7)	7	(1.6)
Partners																				
Albania	8.3	(2.1)	403	(6.4)	392	(15.1)	402	(12.0)	-10	(6.8)	c	c	c	c	c	c	c	c	c	c
Argentina	6.7	(2.2)	428	(14.3)	442	(12.9)	443	(19.0)	-60	(7.3)	-0.95	(0.0)	-0.30	(0.1)	-0.65	(0.1)	-45	(6.3)	-27	(8.3)
Brazil	12.8	(1.3)	461	(6.9)	479	(6.1)	471	(6.2)	-83	(6.7)	-1.42	(0.0)	-0.03	(0.1)	-1.39	(0.1)	-60	(6.0)	-19	(7.1)
Bulgaria	1.2	(0.9)	c	c	c	c	c	c	c	c	-0.29	(0.0)	c	c	c	c	c	c	c	c
Colombia	10.1	(1.4)	441	(12.7)	476	(12.2)	455	(13.0)	-50	(11.0)	-1.42	(0.0)	-0.44	(0.1)	-0.99	(0.1)	-28	(9.0)	-7	(8.2)
Costa Rica	9.5	(1.5)	478	(9.5)	510	(9.8)	496	(9.3)	-78	(8.6)	-1.22	(0.0)	0.38	(0.1)	-1.61	(0.1)	-48	(8.4)	-10	(10.8)
Croatia	0.9	(0.7)	c	c	c	c	c	c	c	c	-0.35	(0.0)	c	c	c	c	c	c	c	c
Cyprus*	16.1	(0.0)	486	(2.5)	472	(3.1)	477	(3.2)	-56	(2.9)	-0.04	(0.0)	0.69	(0.0)	-0.72	(0.0)	-31	(3.3)	16	(3.7)
Hong Kong-China	1.2	(0.7)	c	c	c	c	c	c	37	(10.1)	-0.77	(0.1)	-0.79	(0.1)	0.02	(0.1)	34	(10.0)	33	(12.0)
Indonesia	23.7	(2.7)	395	(10.7)	413	(8.8)	394	(8.8)	5	(8.9)	-1.78	(0.0)	-1.81	(0.1)	0.03	(0.1)	4	(7.6)	4	(6.8)
Jordan	15.8	(1.2)	440	(10.8)	447	(10.4)	457	(9.9)	-60	(10.0)	-0.51	(0.0)	0.04	(0.1)	-0.55	(0.1)	-48	(8.4)	-33	(8.4)
Kazakhstan	2.1	(0.9)	436	(14.7)	412	(9.5)	442	(14.0)	-2	(12.4)	-0.32	(0.0)	-0.16	(0.1)	-0.16	(0.1)	2	(11.3)	8	(10.6)
Latvia	1.9	(1.3)	c	c	c	c	c	c	c	c	-0.27	(0.0)	c	c	c	c	c	c	c	c
Liechtenstein	6.4	(0.4)	c	c	c	c	c	c	c	c	0.27	(0.1)	c	c	c	c	c	c	c	c
Lithuania	0.4	(0.4)	c	c	c	c	c	c	c	c	-0.15	(0.0)	c	c	c	c	c	c	c	c
Macao-China	14.5	(0.0)	559	(2.9)	523	(2.5)	534	(2.5)	c	c	-0.87	(0.0)	c	c	c	c	c	c	c	c
Malaysia	3.4	(0.7)	505	(27.3)	432	(36.7)	465	(31.6)	-87	(27.8)	-0.75	(0.0)	0.04	(0.2)	-0.79	(0.2)	-65	(23.2)	-39	(18.9)
Montenegro	0.4	(0.0)	c	c	c	c	c	c	c	c	-0.25	(0.0)	c	c	c	c	c	c	c	c
Peru	14.7	(1.8)	424	(11.3)	437	(11.4)	419	(9.5)	-74	(12.0)	-1.52	(0.0)	-0.31	(0.1)	-1.21	(0.1)	-42	(9.0)	-7	(7.4)
Qatar	37.2	(0.1)	442	(1.3)	447	(1.5)	451	(1.4)	-108	(1.7)	0.32	(0.0)	0.62	(0.0)	-0.30	(0.0)	-102	(1.7)	-93	(1.6)
Romania	0.6	(0.6)	c	c	c	c	c	c	c	c	-0.48	(0.0)	c	c	c	c	c	c	c	c
Russian Federation	0.6	(0.6)	c	c	c	c	c	c	c	c	-0.11	(0.0)	c	c	c	c	c	c	c	c
Serbia	0.4	(0.4)	c	c	c	c	c	c	c	c	-0.31	(0.0)	c	c	c	c	c	c	c	c
Shanghai-China	9.3	(1.8)	644	(9.3)	599	(9.3)	600	(8.5)	-35	(10.1)	-0.40	(0.0)	0.05	(0.1)	-0.45	(0.1)	-16	(7.7)	10	(9.4)
Singapore	2.4	(0.7)	c	c	c	c	c	c	c	c	-0.28	(0.0)	c	c	c	c	c	c	c	c
Chinese Taipei	27.9	(1.9)	529	(7.9)	501	(7.4)	501	(5.5)	60	(7.3)	-0.36	(0.0)	-0.47	(0.0)	0.12	(0.1)	54	(5.0)	44	(4.4)
Thailand	4.9	(1.3)	398	(23.2)	417	(25.1)	410	(22.0)	36	(8.9)	-1.37	(0.0)	-1.23	(0.1)	-0.14	(0.1)	39	(6.4)	42	(5.2)
Tunisia	0.6	(0.4)	c	c	c	c	c	c	c	c	-1.20	(0.0)	c	c	c	c	c	c	c	c
United Arab Emirates	44.9	(1.7)	461	(4.3)	464	(4.6)	469	(5.3)	-62	(4.9)	0.05	(0.0)	0.56	(0.0)	-0.51	(0.0)	-50	(4.5)	-28	(4.4)
Uruguay	16.7	(1.2)	492	(6.6)	497	(6.8)	501	(6.9)	-100	(7.1)	-1.15	(0.0)	0.46	(0.1)	-1.61	(0.1)	-55	(5.9)	28	(8.8)
Viet Nam	7.4	(1.1)	499	(11.6)	493	(7.6)	515	(11.1)	14	(12.4)	-1.86	(0.0)	-1.15	(0.2)	-0.71	(0.2)	36	(12.9)	58	(16.3)

Note: Values that are statistically significant are indicated in bold (see Annex A3).
1. Schools which are directly controlled or managed by: *i)* a public education authority or agency or *ii)* a government agency directly or a governing body, most of whose members are either appointed by a public authority or elected by public franchise.
2. Schools which receive 50% or more of their core funding (i.e. funding that supports the basic educational services of the institution) from government agencies.
3. Schools which receive less than 50% of their core funding (i.e. funding that supports the basic educational services of the institution) from government agencies.
* See notes at the beginning of this Annex.
StatLink ᐧᒥᔑᐸ http://dx.doi.org/10.1787/888932957498

[Part 1/7]
School management and leadership
Table IV.4.8 *Results based on school principals' reports*

Percentage of students in schools whose principal reported that he/she engaged in the following actions during the previous academic year:

	Use student performance results to develop the school's educational goals								Make sure that professional development activities for teachers are in accordance with the teaching goals of the school							
	Never or 1-2 times during the year		3-4 times during the year		Once a month to once a week		More than once a week		Never or 1-2 times during the year		3-4 times during the year		Once a month to once a week		More than once a week	
	%	S.E.	%	S.E.	%	S.E.	%	S.E.	%	S.E.	%	S.E.	%	S.E.	%	S.E.
Australia	12.9	(1.3)	35.8	(1.7)	34.7	(1.9)	16.5	(1.5)	5.9	(1.0)	20.1	(1.7)	48.5	(1.7)	25.5	(1.5)
Austria	31.2	(3.5)	22.4	(3.4)	37.3	(3.3)	9.1	(2.4)	28.1	(3.7)	35.4	(4.3)	29.0	(3.6)	7.5	(2.2)
Belgium	63.1	(3.0)	24.7	(2.7)	9.1	(1.8)	3.1	(1.0)	26.6	(2.6)	30.9	(2.9)	29.9	(3.0)	12.7	(2.3)
Canada	22.3	(1.6)	42.8	(2.3)	28.9	(2.1)	6.0	(1.1)	14.0	(1.6)	32.2	(2.4)	42.0	(2.4)	11.8	(1.5)
Chile	27.1	(3.5)	22.9	(3.3)	37.3	(3.8)	12.7	(2.6)	14.6	(2.8)	52.0	(3.2)	17.8	(3.2)	15.8	(2.8)
Czech Republic	19.3	(3.0)	44.7	(3.8)	28.8	(3.4)	7.3	(2.0)	21.0	(3.0)	36.3	(3.7)	36.1	(4.0)	6.6	(1.9)
Denmark	47.0	(3.6)	25.1	(3.3)	22.9	(2.8)	4.9	(1.5)	38.2	(3.6)	26.9	(3.0)	29.5	(3.1)	5.3	(1.5)
Estonia	27.3	(2.7)	32.1	(3.0)	31.5	(2.9)	9.1	(2.1)	31.5	(3.0)	25.6	(2.7)	37.3	(2.9)	5.5	(1.5)
Finland	51.7	(3.3)	31.0	(3.1)	14.3	(2.5)	3.0	(1.0)	42.3	(2.9)	29.6	(3.0)	20.6	(2.8)	7.6	(1.8)
France	30.0	(3.1)	48.5	(3.2)	13.8	(2.6)	7.7	(1.7)	54.2	(3.7)	29.7	(3.2)	10.5	(2.2)	5.6	(1.7)
Germany	25.1	(3.2)	35.0	(3.5)	33.2	(3.5)	6.7	(1.7)	24.4	(3.2)	31.0	(3.4)	42.6	(3.5)	2.0	(1.0)
Greece	47.9	(3.9)	28.3	(4.0)	13.8	(2.8)	10.0	(1.9)	43.5	(3.8)	30.7	(3.7)	20.8	(3.4)	5.0	(1.4)
Hungary	26.8	(3.0)	34.5	(3.8)	29.4	(3.4)	9.3	(2.2)	27.5	(3.9)	23.0	(3.0)	41.1	(3.7)	8.5	(2.0)
Iceland	26.9	(0.2)	47.9	(0.2)	21.0	(0.2)	4.3	(0.1)	29.0	(0.2)	30.5	(0.2)	31.9	(0.2)	8.6	(0.1)
Ireland	33.7	(4.2)	42.4	(4.1)	17.1	(3.1)	6.9	(2.0)	25.3	(3.5)	30.2	(3.4)	32.5	(3.6)	12.0	(2.4)
Israel	16.8	(2.9)	30.8	(3.5)	42.8	(4.3)	9.5	(2.3)	28.2	(3.6)	34.3	(3.9)	29.9	(3.8)	7.6	(2.0)
Italy	28.9	(1.6)	30.7	(2.0)	23.6	(1.6)	16.8	(1.6)	20.5	(1.7)	30.2	(2.0)	30.6	(2.1)	18.7	(1.8)
Japan	80.4	(2.7)	16.4	(2.6)	2.7	(1.2)	0.6	(0.6)	55.9	(3.5)	34.4	(3.3)	8.0	(2.0)	1.7	(1.0)
Korea	24.2	(3.3)	52.6	(4.2)	18.7	(3.3)	4.5	(1.4)	26.0	(3.3)	38.2	(3.7)	29.9	(4.0)	5.8	(2.0)
Luxembourg	57.2	(0.1)	30.1	(0.1)	12.8	(0.1)	0.0	c	31.2	(0.1)	53.0	(0.1)	14.4	(0.1)	1.4	(0.0)
Mexico	21.0	(1.6)	38.5	(1.9)	28.7	(1.7)	11.8	(1.3)	26.3	(1.8)	34.6	(1.9)	28.0	(1.6)	11.1	(1.1)
Netherlands	20.5	(3.1)	35.5	(4.2)	35.4	(4.0)	8.5	(2.2)	22.4	(3.4)	33.5	(4.0)	34.3	(3.7)	9.9	(2.7)
New Zealand	26.4	(3.5)	36.0	(4.0)	25.6	(3.1)	12.1	(2.8)	10.3	(2.2)	31.9	(3.8)	42.9	(4.7)	14.8	(3.1)
Norway	23.6	(3.1)	29.7	(3.3)	36.5	(3.7)	10.2	(2.3)	25.2	(3.3)	30.6	(3.3)	34.2	(3.7)	10.1	(2.2)
Poland	51.9	(3.6)	29.5	(2.9)	12.4	(2.7)	6.2	(1.7)	76.0	(3.5)	16.0	(3.1)	7.7	(2.3)	0.2	(0.1)
Portugal	17.6	(3.4)	33.1	(4.2)	26.0	(3.5)	23.4	(3.4)	41.1	(4.6)	33.5	(4.1)	16.2	(2.8)	9.2	(2.2)
Slovak Republic	25.9	(3.6)	42.2	(4.5)	24.6	(3.3)	7.2	(1.9)	30.2	(3.5)	25.1	(3.5)	36.7	(3.6)	8.0	(1.8)
Slovenia	33.1	(0.8)	30.0	(0.8)	30.6	(0.5)	6.3	(0.2)	12.9	(0.6)	24.9	(0.5)	44.4	(0.7)	17.9	(0.4)
Spain	43.0	(2.5)	44.5	(2.8)	8.3	(1.2)	4.2	(1.3)	51.7	(2.8)	31.2	(2.4)	12.7	(1.8)	4.3	(1.4)
Sweden	14.5	(2.6)	31.7	(3.5)	46.3	(3.6)	7.6	(1.8)	33.2	(3.8)	30.2	(3.4)	28.0	(3.4)	8.6	(1.8)
Switzerland	68.3	(3.4)	21.7	(3.4)	8.6	(1.8)	1.5	(0.9)	57.7	(3.3)	26.5	(3.0)	14.3	(2.6)	1.5	(0.9)
Turkey	13.1	(2.5)	29.1	(3.4)	42.6	(3.6)	15.2	(2.8)	35.5	(4.0)	21.3	(3.4)	28.5	(4.0)	14.7	(3.0)
United Kingdom	9.6	(2.0)	20.3	(2.4)	39.3	(3.4)	30.8	(3.4)	11.5	(2.2)	19.9	(2.3)	43.6	(3.7)	25.0	(3.3)
United States	10.0	(2.4)	24.0	(3.7)	44.6	(4.9)	21.4	(3.9)	7.2	(2.1)	18.5	(3.8)	52.9	(4.0)	21.3	(3.7)
OECD average	31.7	(0.5)	33.1	(0.5)	26.0	(0.5)	9.2	(0.4)	30.4	(0.5)	29.3	(0.5)	30.6	(0.5)	9.8	(0.3)
Albania	25.2	(3.3)	18.6	(3.2)	39.8	(3.5)	16.3	(3.2)	5.3	(1.8)	15.7	(2.7)	53.1	(4.1)	25.9	(3.6)
Argentina	30.2	(3.3)	37.4	(3.6)	21.3	(3.6)	11.1	(2.7)	28.5	(3.8)	28.9	(3.5)	30.0	(3.8)	12.6	(2.9)
Brazil	17.6	(2.3)	33.3	(2.7)	27.6	(2.4)	21.5	(2.2)	2.8	(0.7)	10.5	(1.6)	29.3	(2.3)	57.4	(2.3)
Bulgaria	33.0	(3.8)	36.0	(3.6)	19.4	(2.8)	11.6	(2.6)	14.7	(2.7)	38.7	(3.7)	31.7	(3.3)	14.9	(2.5)
Colombia	19.3	(2.9)	41.0	(4.0)	20.7	(3.6)	19.1	(3.1)	27.7	(3.2)	26.4	(3.4)	34.0	(3.1)	11.9	(3.0)
Costa Rica	31.6	(3.6)	44.9	(3.9)	15.7	(2.7)	7.8	(1.8)	29.7	(3.3)	30.3	(3.5)	28.1	(3.5)	12.0	(2.2)
Croatia	25.1	(3.5)	38.9	(4.0)	23.4	(3.2)	12.6	(2.6)	21.9	(3.3)	32.2	(3.9)	36.2	(3.6)	9.7	(2.3)
Cyprus*	14.9	(0.1)	32.0	(0.1)	24.7	(0.1)	28.4	(0.1)	12.9	(0.1)	27.3	(0.1)	34.7	(0.1)	25.0	(0.1)
Hong Kong-China	33.4	(4.1)	42.3	(3.5)	20.3	(3.8)	4.0	(1.3)	17.4	(3.0)	57.3	(4.3)	21.2	(3.7)	4.2	(1.7)
Indonesia	26.9	(3.7)	33.6	(3.6)	24.6	(3.6)	14.9	(2.9)	19.4	(2.7)	28.4	(4.0)	36.9	(3.8)	15.3	(2.6)
Jordan	18.9	(2.9)	19.6	(2.9)	43.5	(3.5)	18.0	(3.2)	24.1	(3.4)	15.9	(2.7)	40.1	(3.7)	19.9	(3.3)
Kazakhstan	3.8	(1.2)	26.6	(3.5)	39.5	(4.0)	30.1	(3.6)	5.4	(1.4)	10.4	(2.3)	40.8	(4.0)	43.3	(3.8)
Latvia	27.9	(3.5)	33.8	(3.6)	24.7	(3.3)	13.6	(2.3)	21.0	(3.0)	34.9	(3.3)	28.3	(3.3)	15.8	(2.6)
Liechtenstein	68.2	(0.8)	17.5	(0.5)	8.9	(1.0)	5.4	(0.7)	44.9	(0.9)	34.1	(0.4)	15.7	(0.9)	5.4	(0.7)
Lithuania	72.8	(2.9)	19.5	(2.6)	6.2	(1.7)	1.4	(0.8)	35.2	(3.0)	24.9	(3.0)	34.5	(3.2)	5.4	(1.7)
Macao-China	41.6	(0.1)	48.6	(0.1)	8.7	(0.0)	1.1	(0.0)	19.2	(0.0)	53.0	(0.1)	24.2	(0.1)	3.7	(0.0)
Malaysia	5.3	(1.8)	39.0	(4.0)	27.3	(3.7)	28.5	(3.4)	4.0	(1.6)	29.9	(3.6)	38.8	(3.8)	27.4	(3.3)
Montenegro	10.3	(0.1)	45.4	(0.2)	25.1	(0.1)	19.2	(0.1)	19.9	(0.1)	19.1	(0.1)	41.0	(0.1)	20.0	(0.1)
Peru	38.7	(3.1)	34.0	(3.0)	18.7	(2.6)	8.5	(2.1)	30.0	(3.5)	30.9	(3.4)	26.2	(3.2)	12.9	(2.4)
Qatar	9.8	(0.1)	32.6	(0.1)	32.6	(0.1)	25.0	(0.1)	10.1	(0.1)	25.0	(0.1)	32.8	(0.1)	32.0	(0.1)
Romania	62.8	(3.3)	15.7	(2.4)	13.9	(2.7)	7.6	(2.2)	60.9	(3.2)	20.2	(3.0)	11.2	(2.4)	7.7	(1.8)
Russian Federation	42.7	(3.2)	26.8	(2.9)	19.6	(2.5)	10.9	(2.3)	10.9	(2.1)	25.0	(2.9)	50.6	(3.6)	13.6	(2.5)
Serbia	22.9	(3.4)	33.9	(4.4)	28.7	(3.5)	14.6	(3.1)	16.7	(2.9)	28.5	(3.8)	32.7	(3.5)	22.1	(3.7)
Shanghai-China	75.1	(3.4)	16.9	(3.1)	7.3	(2.1)	0.7	(0.4)	21.8	(3.2)	40.8	(3.9)	33.2	(3.6)	4.3	(1.7)
Singapore	13.1	(0.6)	52.3	(0.5)	21.6	(0.5)	13.0	(0.1)	13.6	(0.6)	35.6	(0.5)	34.5	(0.6)	16.3	(0.2)
Chinese Taipei	34.7	(3.6)	22.8	(3.1)	25.3	(3.6)	17.2	(3.1)	12.8	(2.6)	36.2	(3.8)	34.8	(3.9)	16.2	(3.0)
Thailand	27.8	(2.8)	26.9	(3.2)	26.0	(3.3)	19.3	(3.1)	19.8	(3.0)	28.8	(3.3)	36.3	(3.0)	15.1	(3.1)
Tunisia	44.6	(4.3)	49.1	(4.2)	2.9	(1.4)	3.5	(1.5)	64.4	(3.6)	19.3	(3.5)	11.4	(2.5)	4.9	(1.9)
United Arab Emirates	11.2	(1.6)	37.8	(2.6)	32.5	(2.5)	18.5	(2.0)	10.6	(1.9)	26.3	(2.5)	43.5	(2.8)	19.5	(2.1)
Uruguay	27.4	(3.3)	31.9	(3.4)	28.1	(3.0)	12.6	(2.5)	30.7	(3.4)	16.8	(2.9)	34.5	(3.3)	18.0	(3.0)
Viet Nam	45.0	(4.2)	32.5	(3.9)	19.4	(3.2)	3.1	(1.4)	31.1	(4.2)	34.8	(3.7)	33.3	(3.9)	0.7	(0.7)

* See notes at the beginning of this Annex.
StatLink http://dx.doi.org/10.1787/888932957498

[Part 2/7]
School management and leadership
Table IV.4.8 *Results based on school principals' reports*

Percentage of students in schools whose principal reported that he/she engaged in the following actions during the previous academic year:

	Ensure that teachers work according to the school's educational goals								Discuss the school's academic goals with teachers at faculty meetings							
	Never or 1-2 times during the year		3-4 times during the year		Once a month to once a week		More than once a week		Never or 1-2 times during the year		3-4 times during the year		Once a month to once a week		More than once a week	
	%	S.E.	%	S.E.	%	S.E.	%	S.E.	%	S.E.	%	S.E.	%	S.E.	%	S.E.
OECD																
Australia	4.8	(0.8)	18.2	(1.6)	41.1	(1.8)	35.8	(1.8)	12.3	(1.3)	19.2	(1.6)	62.4	(2.0)	6.1	(0.9)
Austria	19.7	(3.3)	28.3	(3.1)	40.7	(4.1)	11.3	(2.8)	21.3	(3.8)	55.6	(4.2)	22.0	(2.7)	1.1	(0.8)
Belgium	19.7	(2.6)	27.6	(2.6)	30.7	(3.0)	21.9	(2.6)	35.2	(3.4)	41.6	(3.3)	18.5	(2.6)	4.7	(1.3)
Canada	9.1	(1.4)	21.1	(2.1)	42.5	(2.4)	27.3	(2.3)	5.7	(1.0)	13.8	(1.4)	75.1	(2.0)	5.5	(1.0)
Chile	3.9	(1.4)	19.1	(2.8)	58.1	(3.7)	18.9	(3.1)	10.3	(2.6)	18.2	(2.9)	60.9	(3.2)	10.6	(2.7)
Czech Republic	9.0	(2.3)	30.8	(3.3)	45.8	(3.6)	14.4	(3.2)	14.3	(2.8)	52.4	(4.1)	33.1	(3.7)	0.2	(0.2)
Denmark	38.1	(3.7)	26.8	(3.8)	28.7	(3.3)	6.4	(1.5)	27.2	(3.2)	35.5	(3.8)	35.2	(3.3)	2.1	(1.0)
Estonia	17.5	(2.5)	22.8	(2.6)	42.2	(2.6)	17.5	(2.7)	24.9	(2.7)	42.8	(3.0)	30.9	(2.7)	1.4	(1.2)
Finland	32.7	(3.0)	32.5	(3.4)	24.0	(2.9)	10.8	(2.1)	22.1	(3.2)	25.2	(3.0)	50.0	(3.3)	2.6	(1.4)
France	17.8	(2.5)	40.7	(3.3)	26.9	(3.1)	14.6	(2.6)	9.5	(2.1)	57.5	(3.5)	27.8	(2.9)	5.2	(1.7)
Germany	18.6	(3.2)	28.2	(3.4)	44.8	(3.4)	8.4	(2.2)	28.0	(3.7)	40.5	(3.7)	28.8	(3.4)	2.7	(1.2)
Greece	17.8	(3.1)	14.7	(2.5)	47.3	(4.1)	20.2	(3.1)	16.6	(2.7)	45.9	(3.9)	29.7	(3.8)	7.9	(2.0)
Hungary	1.2	(0.7)	9.4	(2.3)	48.9	(3.7)	40.6	(3.6)	36.3	(3.7)	34.5	(4.3)	27.5	(3.7)	1.6	(0.8)
Iceland	32.5	(0.2)	30.4	(0.2)	28.2	(0.2)	9.0	(0.1)	3.9	(0.1)	29.2	(0.2)	63.8	(0.2)	3.1	(0.0)
Ireland	15.4	(3.3)	28.1	(3.7)	27.9	(3.5)	28.6	(3.7)	32.7	(3.9)	39.7	(3.9)	20.5	(3.2)	7.1	(1.9)
Israel	6.2	(1.9)	34.4	(3.6)	45.1	(4.3)	14.2	(3.0)	11.5	(2.5)	31.4	(3.6)	51.0	(3.9)	6.1	(1.9)
Italy	7.7	(1.2)	27.2	(1.9)	37.7	(2.1)	27.4	(2.0)	7.3	(1.4)	56.0	(2.2)	25.5	(1.8)	11.2	(1.3)
Japan	45.6	(3.9)	38.2	(3.6)	11.4	(2.0)	4.7	(1.6)	44.3	(4.0)	30.3	(3.5)	23.8	(3.3)	1.6	(0.9)
Korea	33.7	(3.2)	31.8	(3.9)	29.5	(3.7)	5.1	(1.8)	22.4	(3.4)	12.9	(2.8)	60.2	(3.9)	4.5	(1.4)
Luxembourg	14.9	(0.1)	26.0	(0.1)	32.5	(0.1)	26.6	(0.1)	20.2	(0.1)	36.3	(0.1)	35.3	(0.1)	8.1	(0.1)
Mexico	9.4	(1.1)	26.5	(2.0)	45.9	(2.2)	18.2	(1.4)	14.4	(1.2)	36.4	(2.0)	41.4	(1.9)	7.7	(0.9)
Netherlands	16.7	(3.2)	24.5	(4.1)	40.3	(4.0)	18.5	(3.4)	50.8	(4.2)	33.1	(4.3)	14.6	(2.7)	1.5	(1.1)
New Zealand	14.7	(2.8)	31.8	(4.2)	38.6	(4.3)	14.9	(3.2)	11.2	(2.6)	29.8	(4.3)	56.8	(4.7)	2.3	(1.4)
Norway	11.8	(2.2)	32.3	(3.2)	41.7	(3.3)	14.2	(2.5)	5.6	(1.9)	29.0	(3.7)	63.6	(3.8)	1.9	(1.1)
Poland	21.2	(3.1)	40.9	(3.6)	34.3	(3.7)	3.6	(1.6)	15.4	(2.9)	63.0	(3.8)	20.1	(3.2)	1.4	(1.0)
Portugal	13.3	(2.7)	26.4	(4.2)	33.6	(3.7)	26.7	(3.8)	1.7	(0.8)	10.7	(2.8)	81.7	(3.3)	5.9	(2.1)
Slovak Republic	10.6	(2.4)	15.4	(3.2)	50.1	(4.2)	23.9	(3.0)	1.9	(1.2)	36.3	(3.2)	61.8	(3.1)	0.0	c
Slovenia	10.2	(0.4)	12.1	(0.4)	47.3	(0.8)	30.4	(0.7)	6.4	(0.4)	25.5	(0.8)	63.9	(0.8)	4.2	(0.2)
Spain	11.4	(1.9)	35.3	(2.2)	38.7	(2.8)	14.6	(2.2)	6.7	(1.0)	64.2	(2.6)	24.8	(2.3)	4.2	(1.4)
Sweden	13.2	(2.6)	29.2	(3.2)	43.1	(3.7)	14.6	(2.6)	8.7	(2.0)	26.1	(3.3)	59.9	(3.7)	5.3	(1.7)
Switzerland	48.0	(3.1)	24.7	(3.2)	21.7	(2.7)	5.6	(1.4)	47.8	(3.5)	35.4	(3.6)	14.9	(2.2)	2.0	(1.2)
Turkey	10.9	(2.4)	11.0	(2.8)	38.3	(4.1)	39.9	(4.0)	9.7	(2.4)	51.9	(3.6)	18.5	(3.4)	20.0	(2.8)
United Kingdom	2.9	(0.9)	12.7	(2.0)	34.5	(2.9)	49.9	(3.1)	6.8	(1.5)	24.8	(2.6)	54.2	(3.5)	14.2	(2.3)
United States	5.6	(1.9)	3.0	(1.3)	41.2	(4.4)	50.2	(4.5)	7.7	(2.3)	9.2	(2.1)	74.3	(3.9)	8.9	(2.3)
OECD average	16.6	(0.4)	25.4	(0.5)	37.7	(0.6)	20.3	(0.5)	17.7	(0.4)	35.1	(0.5)	42.1	(0.5)	5.1	(0.3)
Partners																
Albania	1.2	(0.4)	9.3	(2.4)	58.0	(3.4)	31.5	(3.6)	22.7	(3.4)	27.6	(3.6)	44.2	(4.5)	5.5	(1.8)
Argentina	9.7	(2.2)	31.0	(3.8)	36.3	(3.9)	23.0	(4.0)	19.5	(2.9)	42.6	(3.9)	27.0	(3.7)	10.9	(2.4)
Brazil	2.2	(0.5)	8.7	(1.4)	28.4	(2.6)	60.7	(2.5)	4.4	(1.1)	21.0	(2.0)	52.9	(2.4)	21.8	(2.2)
Bulgaria	3.3	(1.4)	4.3	(1.6)	42.8	(4.2)	49.5	(4.0)	7.8	(1.9)	26.5	(3.6)	62.0	(3.9)	3.7	(1.3)
Colombia	23.0	(2.8)	27.9	(3.4)	31.6	(3.4)	17.5	(3.4)	10.7	(2.8)	30.6	(3.5)	43.3	(3.9)	15.3	(2.7)
Costa Rica	11.7	(2.3)	31.8	(3.7)	37.7	(3.8)	18.7	(3.0)	11.1	(2.2)	20.5	(3.3)	57.5	(3.6)	10.9	(2.2)
Croatia	13.1	(2.5)	25.2	(3.2)	43.8	(3.7)	17.9	(2.9)	7.1	(1.9)	24.2	(3.4)	65.3	(3.7)	3.4	(1.6)
Cyprus*	6.3	(0.0)	6.7	(0.1)	37.8	(0.1)	49.2	(0.1)	3.1	(0.0)	34.0	(0.1)	55.0	(0.1)	7.9	(0.1)
Hong Kong-China	21.1	(3.1)	26.9	(3.7)	41.2	(4.1)	10.7	(2.3)	29.7	(3.6)	41.4	(4.2)	28.8	(3.9)	0.1	(0.1)
Indonesia	6.4	(1.7)	26.3	(3.6)	46.9	(3.8)	20.3	(3.0)	7.4	(2.3)	29.3	(3.9)	56.5	(3.4)	6.8	(2.2)
Jordan	3.8	(1.4)	8.1	(2.0)	53.9	(3.5)	34.2	(3.6)	13.9	(2.9)	12.0	(2.6)	51.5	(3.8)	22.5	(2.9)
Kazakhstan	3.0	(1.3)	8.5	(2.1)	19.7	(3.2)	68.9	(3.9)	4.0	(1.5)	31.1	(3.7)	62.5	(3.8)	2.4	(1.2)
Latvia	10.3	(2.2)	17.4	(3.0)	29.1	(3.3)	43.2	(3.3)	29.5	(3.3)	28.8	(3.3)	37.9	(3.6)	3.7	(1.3)
Liechtenstein	43.9	(0.8)	35.1	(0.9)	15.7	(0.9)	5.4	(0.7)	57.3	(0.9)	24.5	(0.9)	18.2	(0.8)	0.0	c
Lithuania	10.9	(2.3)	17.8	(2.8)	44.8	(3.3)	26.5	(3.0)	17.5	(2.8)	53.4	(3.2)	28.6	(3.2)	0.5	(0.3)
Macao-China	14.6	(0.0)	49.5	(0.1)	23.6	(0.1)	12.4	(0.0)	16.8	(0.0)	40.5	(0.1)	38.5	(0.1)	4.2	(0.0)
Malaysia	0.9	(0.9)	13.7	(2.7)	39.9	(3.9)	45.5	(4.3)	1.4	(0.9)	28.5	(4.0)	47.7	(4.4)	22.4	(3.2)
Montenegro	10.1	(0.1)	12.5	(0.1)	45.2	(0.2)	32.2	(0.2)	5.8	(0.1)	41.7	(0.2)	37.1	(0.1)	15.4	(0.1)
Peru	18.3	(3.0)	29.0	(3.0)	32.7	(3.6)	20.1	(2.8)	18.2	(2.6)	42.2	(3.8)	34.6	(3.6)	5.0	(1.6)
Qatar	3.0	(0.0)	11.4	(0.1)	36.2	(0.1)	49.4	(0.1)	3.3	(0.0)	15.1	(0.1)	59.8	(0.1)	21.7	(0.1)
Romania	40.5	(2.8)	9.7	(1.9)	24.2	(2.6)	25.6	(2.8)	47.3	(3.2)	12.0	(2.4)	32.8	(3.4)	7.9	(2.2)
Russian Federation	2.9	(1.1)	10.5	(2.7)	52.5	(3.3)	34.1	(3.3)	11.7	(2.1)	38.4	(3.8)	48.1	(3.9)	1.8	(0.9)
Serbia	4.8	(1.5)	14.2	(3.1)	35.3	(4.0)	45.6	(4.3)	17.0	(3.3)	41.3	(3.4)	37.3	(3.8)	4.4	(1.9)
Shanghai-China	11.7	(2.4)	29.3	(3.3)	54.7	(3.9)	4.4	(1.8)	24.1	(3.0)	36.6	(4.0)	37.4	(3.8)	1.9	(0.8)
Singapore	6.1	(0.6)	29.4	(0.3)	33.2	(0.7)	31.2	(0.0)	8.9	(0.6)	30.1	(0.5)	57.4	(0.5)	3.5	(0.1)
Chinese Taipei	17.8	(3.2)	29.6	(3.8)	34.6	(3.8)	17.9	(3.1)	29.6	(3.8)	41.3	(3.9)	22.6	(3.5)	6.5	(1.9)
Thailand	14.8	(2.4)	23.3	(3.0)	44.0	(3.2)	18.0	(3.1)	6.6	(1.9)	7.8	(1.7)	73.7	(3.8)	11.9	(2.6)
Tunisia	26.2	(3.7)	32.0	(3.8)	21.6	(3.5)	20.2	(3.5)	27.9	(3.8)	51.2	(3.9)	15.2	(3.2)	5.6	(2.0)
United Arab Emirates	8.2	(1.9)	13.3	(1.7)	44.7	(2.4)	33.8	(2.6)	5.6	(1.0)	23.7	(2.3)	56.6	(2.2)	14.0	(1.9)
Uruguay	12.6	(2.6)	18.6	(2.9)	43.8	(3.4)	25.0	(3.3)	2.8	(1.2)	9.2	(2.1)	69.2	(3.6)	18.8	(2.9)
Viet Nam	8.8	(2.2)	12.0	(2.6)	56.7	(4.0)	22.4	(3.3)	7.6	(2.3)	13.1	(2.4)	77.0	(3.3)	2.2	(1.2)

* See notes at the beginning of this Annex.
StatLink ᵃᵢˢᴸ http://dx.doi.org/10.1787/888932957498

[Part 3/7]
School management and leadership
Table IV.4.8   *Results based on school principals' reports*

Percentage of students in schools whose principal reported that he/she engaged in the following actions during the previous academic year:

	Promote teaching practices based on recent educational research								Praise teachers whose students are actively participating in learning							
	Never or 1-2 times during the year		3-4 times during the year		Once a month to once a week		More than once a week		Never or 1-2 times during the year		3-4 times during the year		Once a month to once a week		More than once a week	
	%	S.E.	%	S.E.	%	S.E.	%	S.E.	%	S.E.	%	S.E.	%	S.E.	%	S.E.
Australia	8.6	(1.2)	18.2	(1.5)	46.6	(1.7)	26.6	(1.6)	4.0	(0.8)	7.3	(1.1)	53.4	(2.0)	35.3	(1.9)
Austria	21.3	(3.3)	31.0	(4.4)	34.7	(4.2)	12.9	(2.9)	7.5	(2.2)	20.1	(3.4)	44.6	(3.6)	27.7	(3.8)
Belgium	48.5	(3.4)	27.0	(3.0)	18.1	(2.3)	6.4	(1.8)	21.8	(2.4)	25.3	(2.7)	38.1	(3.0)	14.9	(2.1)
Canada	16.3	(1.8)	21.5	(2.1)	39.0	(2.4)	23.2	(2.2)	4.0	(0.8)	7.8	(1.3)	48.2	(2.6)	40.1	(2.3)
Chile	38.1	(3.3)	24.8	(3.3)	30.2	(3.3)	6.9	(2.0)	9.9	(2.2)	16.6	(3.1)	52.3	(3.8)	21.2	(3.2)
Czech Republic	18.7	(3.1)	28.5	(3.4)	35.4	(3.4)	17.4	(3.2)	6.8	(2.3)	31.6	(3.6)	46.0	(3.6)	15.6	(2.8)
Denmark	27.4	(3.0)	32.6	(3.7)	33.3	(3.5)	6.6	(1.6)	15.5	(2.6)	24.0	(3.2)	48.9	(3.7)	11.6	(2.4)
Estonia	48.2	(2.9)	27.9	(2.5)	14.8	(2.3)	9.1	(1.8)	10.8	(1.5)	15.8	(2.2)	60.9	(2.6)	12.5	(1.9)
Finland	46.9	(4.1)	28.1	(3.3)	23.2	(3.2)	1.8	(0.1)	22.2	(3.1)	26.7	(3.4)	39.6	(3.6)	11.5	(2.3)
France	66.0	(3.6)	20.9	(2.9)	8.9	(2.2)	4.2	(1.5)	23.0	(2.9)	34.2	(3.3)	31.9	(3.3)	10.9	(2.2)
Germany	23.2	(3.1)	23.6	(3.0)	42.1	(3.7)	11.0	(2.5)	6.5	(1.6)	19.0	(2.8)	52.3	(3.6)	22.2	(3.0)
Greece	17.1	(3.5)	24.1	(3.5)	42.5	(4.1)	16.3	(2.7)	12.3	(2.4)	19.6	(3.1)	48.1	(3.9)	19.9	(2.7)
Hungary	23.9	(3.2)	28.2	(3.5)	35.7	(3.9)	12.3	(2.7)	6.2	(1.8)	15.6	(2.9)	56.1	(4.4)	22.1	(3.5)
Iceland	50.4	(0.2)	33.2	(0.2)	14.4	(0.2)	2.1	(0.1)	4.6	(0.1)	13.5	(0.2)	62.7	(0.2)	19.3	(0.2)
Ireland	21.9	(3.4)	34.7	(3.6)	28.0	(3.4)	15.5	(2.7)	11.5	(2.8)	17.5	(3.3)	39.3	(4.1)	31.7	(3.8)
Israel	51.8	(4.0)	24.6	(3.5)	20.6	(3.0)	3.0	(1.3)	10.6	(2.3)	22.7	(3.2)	44.8	(3.9)	21.8	(3.3)
Italy	29.6	(2.1)	31.1	(2.2)	24.9	(1.9)	14.5	(1.5)	13.8	(1.5)	21.7	(1.7)	34.9	(2.0)	29.5	(1.9)
Japan	54.2	(3.3)	33.8	(3.5)	10.4	(2.1)	1.6	(1.0)	56.6	(4.0)	35.6	(3.7)	5.6	(1.4)	2.2	(1.1)
Korea	30.4	(3.7)	36.6	(4.2)	27.8	(3.7)	5.3	(1.9)	16.6	(3.3)	28.4	(4.1)	47.9	(4.3)	7.1	(2.0)
Luxembourg	54.4	(0.1)	21.4	(0.1)	11.8	(0.1)	12.4	(0.1)	10.6	(0.1)	36.0	(0.1)	39.1	(0.1)	14.3	(0.1)
Mexico	38.1	(1.9)	26.2	(1.7)	27.7	(1.8)	7.9	(0.9)	31.6	(1.9)	29.2	(1.6)	29.3	(1.8)	9.9	(1.1)
Netherlands	48.4	(4.6)	23.9	(4.1)	24.1	(3.7)	3.5	(1.5)	22.1	(3.4)	30.2	(4.7)	40.9	(3.9)	6.8	(2.2)
New Zealand	7.3	(1.8)	31.6	(4.1)	46.5	(4.3)	14.5	(2.7)	4.4	(1.4)	9.6	(2.4)	60.4	(3.9)	25.7	(3.8)
Norway	17.2	(2.6)	36.5	(3.7)	37.1	(3.7)	9.2	(2.3)	21.0	(2.9)	20.0	(3.3)	45.1	(4.0)	13.9	(3.0)
Poland	47.9	(3.7)	34.2	(3.4)	14.9	(3.1)	3.0	(1.4)	12.6	(2.8)	33.0	(4.1)	39.0	(4.3)	15.4	(2.8)
Portugal	34.9	(4.1)	27.1	(3.9)	26.0	(3.4)	11.9	(2.8)	13.5	(3.1)	25.9	(4.0)	33.0	(3.9)	27.5	(3.7)
Slovak Republic	17.7	(3.3)	24.6	(3.5)	35.2	(3.4)	22.5	(3.3)	25.1	(3.4)	33.4	(3.5)	38.1	(3.9)	3.4	(1.3)
Slovenia	5.2	(0.2)	17.3	(0.4)	53.9	(0.7)	23.6	(0.6)	7.8	(0.4)	13.2	(0.4)	56.6	(0.6)	22.3	(0.5)
Spain	55.5	(2.0)	23.5	(1.8)	16.4	(1.7)	4.5	(1.4)	21.4	(2.1)	32.3	(2.4)	33.4	(2.4)	12.9	(2.2)
Sweden	22.0	(2.5)	28.0	(3.4)	39.5	(4.0)	10.5	(2.1)	8.4	(1.9)	17.1	(2.8)	59.0	(3.6)	15.4	(2.6)
Switzerland	60.7	(3.3)	28.4	(3.3)	8.5	(1.8)	2.4	(1.1)	26.0	(3.2)	23.7	(2.8)	39.5	(3.4)	10.8	(2.4)
Turkey	12.5	(2.7)	21.8	(3.7)	43.0	(4.2)	22.7	(3.2)	4.7	(1.7)	15.4	(3.0)	40.7	(4.3)	39.1	(4.0)
United Kingdom	11.3	(1.4)	24.8	(2.8)	42.9	(3.3)	21.0	(2.8)	1.6	(0.6)	8.1	(1.6)	44.7	(3.7)	45.7	(3.5)
United States	6.7	(2.3)	10.9	(2.9)	40.0	(4.6)	42.4	(4.4)	1.8	(1.1)	12.0	(3.0)	35.8	(4.1)	50.3	(4.6)
OECD average	31.8	(0.5)	26.8	(0.5)	29.3	(0.5)	12.0	(0.4)	14.0	(0.4)	21.8	(0.5)	43.8	(0.6)	20.3	(0.5)
Albania	12.1	(2.4)	26.8	(3.5)	50.9	(4.0)	10.2	(2.9)	5.7	(1.8)	21.7	(3.1)	54.0	(4.3)	18.6	(3.4)
Argentina	33.7	(3.8)	26.0	(3.6)	23.1	(3.6)	17.1	(3.4)	17.9	(3.1)	25.6	(3.3)	36.8	(4.2)	19.8	(3.5)
Brazil	19.0	(2.0)	17.0	(2.0)	39.2	(2.5)	24.8	(2.2)	5.5	(1.0)	10.1	(1.5)	34.2	(2.9)	50.1	(3.0)
Bulgaria	9.3	(2.2)	27.8	(3.0)	43.5	(3.4)	19.4	(3.3)	2.3	(1.2)	13.1	(2.5)	63.9	(3.4)	20.7	(3.2)
Colombia	36.4	(3.9)	28.7	(3.5)	26.5	(3.5)	8.4	(2.5)	23.1	(3.3)	35.7	(3.7)	24.4	(3.3)	16.7	(3.4)
Costa Rica	39.9	(3.7)	27.2	(3.7)	26.1	(3.2)	6.7	(1.7)	30.7	(3.5)	27.6	(3.7)	29.4	(3.5)	12.3	(2.5)
Croatia	24.5	(3.5)	29.4	(3.8)	36.0	(3.9)	10.1	(2.3)	11.5	(2.7)	34.5	(3.8)	35.3	(3.6)	18.7	(3.0)
Cyprus*	20.5	(0.1)	15.0	(0.1)	37.6	(0.1)	27.0	(0.1)	0.1	(0.0)	8.4	(0.1)	41.1	(0.1)	50.4	(0.1)
Hong Kong-China	60.5	(4.0)	27.2	(3.9)	10.2	(2.5)	2.0	(1.2)	12.9	(2.8)	34.5	(4.1)	45.7	(4.2)	6.9	(2.2)
Indonesia	27.8	(3.6)	34.8	(3.6)	27.8	(3.4)	9.7	(2.4)	12.9	(2.5)	23.5	(3.7)	41.8	(4.0)	21.8	(3.5)
Jordan	14.5	(2.6)	17.7	(2.3)	39.7	(3.7)	28.1	(3.3)	6.3	(2.1)	4.6	(1.5)	36.5	(3.8)	52.5	(3.7)
Kazakhstan	13.1	(2.5)	10.0	(2.3)	39.7	(3.4)	37.2	(3.3)	35.7	(4.1)	32.3	(3.8)	23.4	(3.7)	8.6	(1.7)
Latvia	10.9	(2.2)	17.3	(2.9)	26.1	(3.2)	45.7	(3.7)	6.3	(1.7)	15.4	(2.3)	46.6	(3.8)	31.7	(3.5)
Liechtenstein	65.6	(0.9)	12.4	(0.6)	16.6	(1.1)	5.4	(0.7)	40.8	(0.7)	13.4	(0.8)	35.3	(0.9)	10.5	(1.0)
Lithuania	34.8	(3.7)	33.1	(3.4)	22.0	(3.2)	10.2	(2.3)	6.9	(1.6)	17.2	(2.8)	53.5	(3.4)	22.4	(3.0)
Macao-China	38.1	(0.1)	42.1	(0.1)	15.6	(0.0)	4.2	(0.0)	11.6	(0.0)	28.5	(0.0)	55.7	(0.1)	4.2	(0.0)
Malaysia	14.6	(3.0)	28.3	(3.9)	33.7	(4.0)	23.4	(3.2)	3.0	(1.3)	10.2	(2.6)	36.9	(3.8)	49.9	(3.8)
Montenegro	17.4	(0.1)	20.7	(0.1)	41.6	(0.1)	20.3	(0.2)	13.1	(0.1)	25.3	(0.2)	35.2	(0.1)	26.4	(0.2)
Peru	61.5	(3.1)	18.3	(2.7)	15.8	(2.7)	4.4	(1.4)	31.6	(3.2)	28.4	(2.9)	26.7	(3.1)	13.3	(2.5)
Qatar	14.5	(0.1)	16.8	(0.1)	34.4	(0.1)	34.3	(0.1)	0.4	(0.0)	11.1	(0.1)	37.2	(0.1)	51.3	(0.1)
Romania	43.3	(3.0)	13.2	(2.5)	20.6	(3.0)	22.8	(2.9)	43.6	(2.9)	7.4	(2.1)	26.2	(3.3)	22.9	(2.9)
Russian Federation	23.4	(3.2)	28.9	(2.9)	34.8	(4.0)	13.0	(2.6)	1.7	(0.7)	14.8	(2.0)	58.5	(3.4)	25.1	(3.3)
Serbia	31.3	(3.9)	28.6	(4.1)	29.9	(3.7)	10.1	(2.8)	6.2	(2.1)	29.0	(3.2)	38.5	(4.4)	26.2	(4.2)
Shanghai-China	41.4	(4.2)	37.0	(3.8)	19.7	(3.5)	2.0	(1.1)	7.4	(2.4)	33.3	(3.8)	46.8	(4.1)	12.5	(2.9)
Singapore	22.9	(0.2)	33.4	(0.7)	38.2	(0.6)	5.5	(0.1)	3.8	(0.1)	21.5	(0.2)	54.3	(0.5)	20.3	(0.6)
Chinese Taipei	31.2	(4.1)	31.0	(4.1)	27.7	(3.9)	10.2	(2.3)	10.4	(2.4)	19.3	(3.5)	50.7	(4.4)	19.5	(3.2)
Thailand	37.5	(3.5)	23.1	(3.1)	26.7	(3.3)	12.7	(2.6)	15.4	(2.8)	14.5	(3.0)	45.7	(3.3)	24.4	(3.3)
Tunisia	53.0	(4.6)	23.1	(3.5)	12.3	(2.9)	11.6	(2.7)	37.0	(3.9)	35.2	(3.9)	15.8	(2.8)	11.9	(3.0)
United Arab Emirates	18.0	(2.1)	23.6	(2.3)	39.4	(2.4)	19.0	(1.9)	4.7	(1.4)	12.0	(1.5)	36.7	(2.1)	46.6	(2.5)
Uruguay	32.5	(3.3)	20.8	(3.1)	35.5	(3.5)	11.2	(2.1)	14.5	(2.7)	19.7	(2.7)	41.1	(3.7)	24.7	(3.3)
Viet Nam	28.2	(4.2)	23.5	(3.8)	37.0	(4.1)	11.2	(2.3)	18.3	(3.5)	19.9	(3.3)	50.6	(4.5)	11.1	(2.5)

* See notes at the beginning of this Annex.
StatLink 🔢 http://dx.doi.org/10.1787/888932957498

[Part 4/7]
School management and leadership
Table IV.4.8   *Results based on school principals' reports*

Percentage of students in schools whose principal reported that he/she engaged in the following actions during the previous academic year:

| | Draw teachers' attention to the importance of developing students' critical and social capacities | | | | | | | | When a teacher has problems in his/her classroom, take the initiative to discuss matters | | | | | | | |
| | Never or 1-2 times during the year | | 3-4 times during the year | | Once a month to once a week | | More than once a week | | Never or 1-2 times during the year | | 3-4 times during the year | | Once a month to once a week | | More than once a week | |
	%	S.E.	%	S.E.	%	S.E.	%	S.E.	%	S.E.	%	S.E.	%	S.E.	%	S.E.
Australia	7.1	(1.0)	17.5	(1.5)	55.7	(1.7)	19.7	(1.6)	8.4	(1.1)	14.8	(1.4)	54.4	(1.8)	22.5	(1.7)
Austria	21.2	(3.2)	28.1	(3.6)	37.4	(3.6)	13.3	(2.7)	12.0	(2.7)	26.7	(3.9)	44.5	(3.8)	16.8	(3.2)
Belgium	17.9	(2.5)	28.4	(2.9)	38.2	(3.4)	15.5	(2.4)	6.6	(1.4)	25.8	(2.7)	49.5	(3.0)	18.0	(2.6)
Canada	12.2	(1.2)	13.4	(1.2)	48.9	(2.4)	25.5	(2.2)	4.3	(0.9)	10.7	(1.4)	48.0	(3.2)	37.1	(2.5)
Chile	9.4	(2.2)	16.6	(2.8)	57.2	(3.7)	16.8	(3.2)	11.9	(2.7)	11.2	(2.4)	52.3	(3.8)	24.6	(3.5)
Czech Republic	21.0	(3.3)	38.5	(3.7)	32.8	(3.3)	7.7	(2.0)	8.4	(1.7)	20.9	(2.7)	56.0	(3.5)	14.7	(2.7)
Denmark	26.1	(3.1)	24.7	(3.0)	40.5	(3.5)	8.7	(1.9)	6.7	(1.7)	12.5	(2.0)	63.8	(3.2)	17.0	(2.6)
Estonia	17.9	(2.1)	30.0	(2.7)	46.5	(3.2)	5.6	(1.3)	12.6	(2.1)	23.4	(2.6)	56.7	(3.1)	7.3	(1.6)
Finland	16.1	(1.7)	27.3	(3.2)	44.4	(4.0)	12.2	(2.4)	11.3	(1.7)	32.3	(3.6)	47.2	(3.8)	9.1	(2.2)
France	32.0	(3.4)	37.1	(3.5)	24.5	(2.7)	6.3	(1.7)	10.3	(2.4)	38.1	(3.0)	35.2	(3.3)	16.4	(2.4)
Germany	13.9	(2.5)	26.3	(2.8)	48.3	(3.4)	11.4	(2.4)	9.2	(2.2)	22.8	(2.6)	54.9	(3.8)	13.0	(2.6)
Greece	16.4	(3.0)	33.9	(4.1)	39.3	(3.9)	10.5	(2.3)	10.5	(2.5)	21.2	(3.5)	46.8	(4.2)	21.5	(3.2)
Hungary	25.3	(3.9)	29.5	(3.8)	38.4	(3.7)	6.9	(1.7)	4.2	(1.6)	17.5	(3.2)	60.1	(3.8)	18.2	(3.1)
Iceland	11.1	(0.2)	25.8	(0.2)	45.2	(0.2)	17.9	(0.2)	10.8	(0.1)	22.2	(0.2)	50.9	(0.2)	16.0	(0.2)
Ireland	26.2	(3.9)	30.9	(4.0)	25.3	(4.0)	17.6	(3.0)	13.7	(3.0)	30.2	(3.8)	34.0	(4.3)	22.2	(3.6)
Israel	13.9	(2.9)	27.5	(3.4)	47.8	(3.9)	10.8	(2.3)	4.5	(1.4)	16.6	(2.9)	59.8	(3.7)	19.2	(3.0)
Italy	6.4	(1.0)	27.9	(1.8)	36.8	(1.8)	28.9	(1.8)	5.5	(0.9)	13.6	(1.7)	45.2	(2.0)	35.8	(2.1)
Japan	52.1	(3.3)	29.2	(3.4)	17.7	(2.7)	1.0	(0.7)	33.9	(3.6)	30.7	(3.3)	29.5	(3.3)	5.9	(1.9)
Korea	22.6	(3.6)	30.1	(4.0)	42.2	(4.2)	5.1	(1.8)	16.1	(3.1)	25.4	(3.5)	50.5	(4.1)	8.0	(2.1)
Luxembourg	10.4	(0.1)	62.3	(0.1)	17.7	(0.0)	9.6	(0.1)	0.0	c	3.1	(0.0)	68.3	(0.1)	28.6	(0.1)
Mexico	22.2	(1.6)	29.4	(2.0)	36.2	(1.8)	12.2	(1.4)	17.3	(1.5)	23.0	(1.6)	39.9	(2.1)	19.9	(1.7)
Netherlands	31.3	(4.1)	27.6	(3.6)	36.4	(4.1)	4.7	(2.1)	21.3	(4.1)	30.8	(4.2)	41.1	(4.7)	6.8	(2.2)
New Zealand	18.2	(2.6)	23.7	(3.5)	46.3	(4.4)	11.9	(2.8)	21.8	(3.4)	24.5	(3.6)	44.0	(4.2)	9.7	(3.0)
Norway	17.7	(3.1)	32.9	(3.7)	40.2	(3.8)	9.2	(2.2)	12.4	(2.6)	24.7	(3.5)	54.8	(4.1)	8.2	(2.1)
Poland	23.3	(3.5)	32.1	(3.8)	36.8	(3.5)	7.8	(2.0)	10.4	(2.4)	14.7	(3.0)	59.0	(4.0)	15.9	(3.2)
Portugal	12.0	(3.1)	29.8	(4.4)	36.2	(3.8)	22.0	(3.0)	9.6	(2.6)	30.1	(4.0)	33.7	(4.3)	26.6	(4.0)
Slovak Republic	14.2	(2.4)	33.5	(3.4)	45.6	(3.3)	6.7	(1.8)	17.0	(2.9)	29.2	(3.8)	48.7	(3.7)	5.1	(1.7)
Slovenia	9.3	(0.4)	17.4	(0.7)	54.7	(0.8)	18.5	(0.7)	14.5	(0.6)	22.4	(0.5)	57.6	(0.7)	5.5	(0.3)
Spain	25.9	(2.5)	34.0	(2.3)	27.4	(2.4)	12.7	(2.2)	19.7	(2.2)	21.0	(2.3)	36.0	(2.3)	23.3	(2.8)
Sweden	19.1	(2.6)	24.9	(3.5)	43.1	(3.8)	12.9	(2.3)	7.9	(2.1)	24.5	(2.8)	56.2	(3.4)	11.4	(2.3)
Switzerland	35.6	(3.5)	28.5	(2.3)	29.4	(3.5)	6.6	(2.0)	15.7	(2.5)	27.4	(3.5)	47.2	(3.5)	9.7	(2.3)
Turkey	8.2	(1.9)	9.5	(2.9)	45.5	(3.8)	36.8	(3.1)	4.5	(1.2)	9.0	(2.4)	39.6	(3.4)	47.0	(3.9)
United Kingdom	11.6	(2.0)	15.7	(2.7)	48.5	(3.4)	24.2	(3.0)	7.8	(1.5)	15.9	(2.6)	51.9	(3.5)	24.4	(3.3)
United States	6.3	(1.9)	15.2	(3.7)	48.4	(4.3)	30.2	(4.1)	2.4	(1.2)	7.7	(2.7)	52.4	(4.7)	37.6	(4.3)
OECD average	18.7	(0.5)	27.6	(0.5)	40.0	(0.6)	13.7	(0.4)	11.3	(0.4)	21.3	(0.5)	49.1	(0.6)	18.3	(0.5)
Albania	5.1	(1.8)	13.4	(2.3)	51.7	(4.2)	29.7	(3.9)	2.7	(1.1)	7.8	(2.2)	44.5	(4.2)	45.0	(4.0)
Argentina	14.2	(2.5)	21.8	(3.0)	32.0	(3.3)	32.0	(3.7)	11.0	(2.3)	16.9	(2.7)	34.1	(3.7)	38.0	(3.8)
Brazil	6.0	(1.1)	10.4	(1.5)	40.7	(2.2)	42.9	(2.3)	4.7	(1.1)	4.8	(0.8)	29.0	(2.1)	61.6	(2.5)
Bulgaria	2.9	(1.0)	12.2	(2.3)	61.5	(3.7)	23.5	(3.5)	1.6	(1.0)	14.0	(2.6)	56.5	(3.3)	27.9	(3.2)
Colombia	14.6	(3.0)	26.9	(3.3)	33.7	(3.5)	24.8	(3.6)	14.0	(2.1)	19.2	(3.2)	40.9	(3.8)	25.9	(3.4)
Costa Rica	17.8	(2.8)	22.2	(3.3)	45.7	(3.9)	14.4	(2.5)	16.7	(3.1)	23.1	(3.4)	35.0	(3.7)	25.2	(2.9)
Croatia	10.5	(2.5)	31.3	(3.2)	37.6	(3.6)	20.5	(3.1)	5.1	(1.7)	27.1	(3.6)	44.9	(3.8)	22.9	(3.4)
Cyprus*	0.1	(0.0)	11.5	(0.1)	46.4	(0.1)	42.0	(0.1)	4.0	(0.0)	12.3	(0.1)	48.0	(0.1)	35.6	(0.1)
Hong Kong-China	25.0	(3.8)	35.7	(4.6)	33.9	(4.1)	5.5	(1.9)	16.6	(3.0)	36.9	(4.3)	41.6	(3.9)	4.9	(1.8)
Indonesia	6.1	(2.0)	23.5	(3.1)	54.8	(3.6)	15.6	(2.2)	5.1	(2.1)	19.5	(3.4)	58.3	(3.7)	17.1	(3.0)
Jordan	2.6	(1.3)	8.2	(2.2)	53.2	(4.2)	36.0	(3.7)	3.3	(1.4)	2.2	(1.2)	41.4	(3.7)	53.2	(3.7)
Kazakhstan	3.0	(1.7)	16.1	(2.7)	48.0	(4.1)	32.8	(3.9)	11.3	(2.4)	10.4	(1.9)	48.8	(4.1)	29.5	(3.6)
Latvia	12.8	(2.5)	25.3	(2.7)	48.4	(3.6)	13.6	(2.9)	6.4	(1.4)	18.2	(3.0)	57.8	(3.8)	17.6	(3.1)
Liechtenstein	25.2	(0.6)	40.1	(0.7)	34.6	(0.9)	0.0	c	31.5	(0.8)	40.4	(0.6)	28.1	(0.9)	0.0	c
Lithuania	19.6	(2.6)	30.3	(3.3)	40.0	(3.3)	10.1	(2.0)	9.7	(1.8)	14.8	(2.9)	64.7	(3.6)	10.8	(2.3)
Macao-China	14.7	(0.0)	27.1	(0.1)	46.1	(0.1)	12.1	(0.0)	5.8	(0.0)	27.2	(0.0)	41.9	(0.1)	25.0	(0.0)
Malaysia	5.7	(1.8)	19.8	(3.2)	44.1	(3.5)	30.4	(3.6)	5.3	(1.8)	17.5	(3.2)	43.3	(4.1)	33.9	(3.8)
Montenegro	10.9	(0.1)	21.2	(0.2)	29.1	(0.1)	38.8	(0.2)	2.3	(0.0)	16.4	(0.1)	26.8	(0.1)	54.5	(0.2)
Peru	25.9	(2.8)	28.5	(3.0)	29.8	(2.8)	15.8	(2.8)	31.3	(3.0)	26.5	(2.8)	30.1	(3.0)	12.1	(2.5)
Qatar	4.1	(0.0)	9.5	(0.0)	40.6	(0.1)	45.8	(0.1)	2.5	(0.0)	9.6	(0.1)	30.4	(0.1)	57.4	(0.1)
Romania	43.1	(2.8)	8.8	(1.8)	33.2	(3.1)	14.9	(2.7)	40.0	(2.5)	15.5	(2.8)	20.4	(2.6)	24.0	(3.2)
Russian Federation	4.4	(1.4)	28.2	(2.4)	55.2	(2.9)	12.2	(2.4)	4.7	(1.3)	10.5	(1.9)	60.9	(3.3)	24.0	(3.1)
Serbia	10.0	(2.7)	20.9	(3.7)	47.1	(4.5)	22.0	(3.9)	4.1	(1.6)	20.3	(3.6)	47.0	(4.5)	28.6	(4.1)
Shanghai-China	22.2	(3.3)	28.6	(3.6)	34.1	(3.7)	15.0	(3.1)	5.1	(1.7)	18.1	(3.1)	53.3	(4.2)	23.6	(3.5)
Singapore	0.8	(0.0)	19.5	(0.6)	62.1	(0.5)	17.6	(0.2)	2.9	(0.6)	20.4	(0.2)	55.4	(0.5)	21.2	(0.2)
Chinese Taipei	16.8	(3.0)	23.5	(3.3)	50.4	(4.2)	9.3	(2.1)	9.0	(1.6)	23.5	(3.8)	49.5	(4.5)	18.0	(2.9)
Thailand	13.3	(2.9)	12.8	(2.7)	50.6	(3.9)	23.3	(3.3)	18.2	(2.9)	13.3	(2.5)	51.7	(3.9)	16.8	(2.6)
Tunisia	24.9	(3.7)	40.0	(4.1)	15.1	(3.1)	20.1	(3.6)	12.7	(2.9)	18.3	(3.2)	36.5	(4.2)	32.5	(4.1)
United Arab Emirates	6.1	(1.4)	14.6	(2.0)	48.0	(2.7)	31.4	(2.4)	11.5	(1.8)	10.5	(1.7)	41.2	(2.4)	36.9	(2.1)
Uruguay	17.7	(2.4)	17.6	(2.8)	46.8	(3.5)	17.9	(3.0)	10.3	(2.2)	15.1	(2.8)	39.6	(3.6)	35.0	(3.6)
Viet Nam	22.4	(3.2)	19.7	(3.6)	49.7	(3.9)	8.2	(1.7)	12.7	(2.8)	22.1	(3.6)	53.3	(3.9)	12.0	(2.6)

* See notes at the beginning of this Annex.
StatLink http://dx.doi.org/10.1787/888932957498

[Part 5/7]
School management and leadership
Table IV.4.8   *Results based on school principals' reports*

		Percentage of students in schools whose principal reported that he/she engaged in the following actions during the previous academic year:															
		Pay attention to disruptive behaviour in classrooms								When a teacher discusses a classroom problem, solve the problem together							
		Never or 1-2 times during the year		3-4 times during the year		Once a month to once a week		More than once a week		Never or 1-2 times during the year		3-4 times during the year		Once a month to once a week		More than once a week	
		%	S.E.	%	S.E.	%	S.E.	%	S.E.	%	S.E.	%	S.E.	%	S.E.	%	S.E.
OECD	Australia	6.1	(0.8)	7.4	(0.9)	41.7	(1.8)	44.8	(1.7)	9.8	(1.2)	11.1	(1.2)	54.3	(1.8)	24.8	(1.6)
	Austria	9.8	(2.4)	18.8	(2.9)	48.9	(3.9)	22.5	(3.3)	11.3	(2.7)	24.2	(3.2)	48.1	(4.0)	16.4	(2.8)
	Belgium	1.6	(0.8)	16.9	(2.7)	44.5	(3.3)	37.0	(3.1)	3.8	(1.4)	21.4	(2.9)	48.3	(3.4)	26.5	(3.1)
	Canada	2.9	(0.8)	5.6	(1.2)	31.2	(2.3)	60.3	(2.5)	2.3	(0.7)	8.2	(1.3)	42.9	(2.5)	46.6	(2.5)
	Chile	3.8	(1.4)	8.6	(2.5)	43.3	(3.5)	44.4	(3.9)	7.0	(2.0)	13.0	(2.6)	47.6	(3.7)	32.4	(3.7)
	Czech Republic	13.8	(2.0)	25.4	(3.2)	48.3	(3.6)	12.5	(2.4)	6.6	(1.7)	17.4	(2.3)	61.2	(3.4)	14.9	(2.7)
	Denmark	8.4	(2.1)	13.7	(2.6)	57.4	(3.5)	20.6	(2.8)	8.1	(1.7)	12.8	(2.5)	65.2	(3.4)	13.9	(2.5)
	Estonia	7.4	(1.6)	20.8	(2.3)	58.4	(3.0)	13.4	(2.1)	10.3	(2.0)	23.0	(2.5)	59.8	(3.4)	7.0	(2.0)
	Finland	3.7	(0.8)	19.8	(2.6)	57.9	(3.7)	18.6	(3.2)	2.2	(0.5)	11.3	(2.2)	65.2	(3.1)	21.3	(3.0)
	France	1.2	(0.7)	13.1	(2.9)	54.3	(3.6)	31.5	(3.5)	6.7	(1.9)	19.7	(3.0)	54.2	(3.5)	19.4	(3.1)
	Germany	4.7	(1.7)	11.7	(2.3)	63.2	(3.4)	20.4	(2.8)	3.6	(1.4)	18.1	(3.1)	61.3	(3.7)	17.0	(2.9)
	Greece	6.8	(1.8)	14.4	(2.6)	52.9	(3.6)	25.9	(3.2)	11.3	(2.5)	25.5	(3.6)	40.1	(3.9)	23.1	(3.3)
	Hungary	5.0	(1.6)	6.9	(2.2)	53.7	(3.9)	34.3	(3.6)	7.8	(1.9)	23.1	(3.9)	47.4	(3.9)	21.6	(3.2)
	Iceland	3.2	(0.1)	9.0	(0.1)	55.0	(0.2)	32.8	(0.2)	3.0	(0.1)	7.4	(0.2)	47.2	(0.2)	42.4	(0.3)
	Ireland	5.4	(1.9)	11.6	(2.7)	39.7	(4.2)	43.3	(4.2)	11.3	(2.5)	18.5	(3.3)	36.7	(4.0)	33.5	(4.1)
	Israel	1.7	(1.1)	11.3	(2.1)	48.5	(4.6)	38.5	(4.4)	4.1	(1.4)	10.9	(2.7)	54.9	(3.9)	30.2	(3.9)
	Italy	2.7	(0.6)	8.8	(1.3)	44.0	(2.2)	44.5	(2.1)	3.3	(0.8)	9.4	(1.5)	45.0	(1.8)	42.3	(2.2)
	Japan	17.4	(2.8)	19.3	(3.0)	44.3	(3.7)	19.0	(3.1)	14.0	(2.8)	30.0	(3.5)	42.7	(3.7)	13.3	(2.8)
	Korea	8.7	(2.2)	16.2	(2.9)	53.3	(4.4)	21.8	(3.4)	12.6	(2.8)	22.9	(3.2)	54.3	(4.3)	10.2	(2.4)
	Luxembourg	0.0	c	2.5	(0.0)	52.5	(0.1)	44.9	(0.1)	0.2	(0.0)	6.5	(0.0)	66.8	(0.1)	26.5	(0.1)
	Mexico	4.8	(0.6)	14.3	(1.4)	36.6	(1.8)	44.2	(1.7)	12.0	(1.0)	21.1	(1.7)	38.2	(2.0)	28.7	(1.7)
	Netherlands	18.9	(3.2)	23.9	(3.3)	47.4	(4.2)	9.8	(2.5)	16.4	(3.3)	31.2	(3.8)	43.1	(4.4)	9.3	(2.6)
	New Zealand	9.9	(2.2)	11.9	(2.9)	59.6	(4.0)	18.6	(3.8)	14.1	(2.8)	33.0	(3.9)	44.7	(4.4)	8.3	(2.4)
	Norway	4.9	(1.4)	14.3	(2.7)	54.6	(4.2)	26.2	(3.6)	4.9	(1.9)	12.2	(2.7)	64.0	(3.6)	18.9	(3.1)
	Poland	7.5	(2.2)	18.0	(3.0)	56.3	(4.3)	18.2	(3.1)	3.2	(1.4)	17.2	(3.2)	58.8	(3.7)	20.8	(2.8)
	Portugal	0.9	(0.6)	3.4	(1.9)	26.2	(3.6)	69.4	(3.9)	5.9	(1.7)	15.0	(3.0)	40.9	(4.4)	38.2	(4.2)
	Slovak Republic	3.3	(1.2)	22.3	(3.1)	59.0	(3.4)	15.4	(2.5)	0.6	(0.4)	12.8	(2.5)	64.7	(3.2)	21.9	(3.1)
	Slovenia	3.3	(0.2)	15.2	(0.4)	55.8	(0.7)	25.6	(0.5)	9.2	(0.4)	31.0	(0.6)	51.4	(0.7)	8.4	(0.3)
	Spain	2.3	(0.7)	9.2	(1.6)	31.1	(2.6)	57.3	(3.0)	5.5	(1.1)	21.7	(2.3)	39.7	(2.2)	33.1	(2.8)
	Sweden	5.3	(1.7)	20.7	(3.0)	58.4	(3.5)	15.6	(2.2)	3.7	(1.4)	18.2	(2.8)	62.1	(3.4)	16.0	(2.6)
	Switzerland	10.2	(1.9)	18.1	(2.7)	57.6	(3.4)	14.1	(2.6)	11.8	(2.1)	30.4	(3.3)	49.6	(3.4)	8.2	(2.1)
	Turkey	0.7	(0.7)	6.0	(2.3)	37.1	(4.0)	56.2	(4.0)	4.1	(1.8)	5.3	(2.1)	35.1	(4.0)	55.5	(4.1)
	United Kingdom	5.8	(1.3)	5.0	(1.4)	34.7	(3.9)	54.5	(3.5)	8.9	(1.9)	10.0	(1.6)	54.9	(3.5)	26.2	(3.3)
	United States	5.3	(2.1)	2.4	(1.3)	34.6	(4.4)	57.6	(4.3)	2.3	(1.2)	8.8	(2.4)	52.6	(4.4)	36.3	(4.5)
	OECD average	5.8	(0.3)	13.1	(0.4)	48.3	(0.6)	32.8	(0.5)	7.1	(0.3)	17.7	(0.5)	51.3	(0.6)	23.9	(0.5)
Partners	Albania	5.5	(1.6)	3.9	(1.5)	28.7	(3.8)	61.9	(3.9)	7.5	(2.6)	7.0	(1.6)	34.6	(3.3)	51.0	(3.7)
	Argentina	1.3	(0.7)	8.9	(2.1)	23.1	(3.3)	66.6	(3.6)	4.0	(1.4)	9.0	(2.0)	33.6	(4.1)	53.4	(4.1)
	Brazil	2.0	(0.8)	2.2	(0.6)	11.7	(1.4)	84.1	(1.7)	0.9	(0.4)	3.2	(0.9)	18.1	(1.7)	77.7	(2.0)
	Bulgaria	0.0	c	0.0	c	17.2	(2.8)	82.8	(2.8)	3.9	(1.6)	10.4	(2.3)	50.4	(4.0)	35.3	(3.6)
	Colombia	4.5	(1.2)	10.1	(2.1)	33.8	(3.8)	51.6	(3.9)	9.5	(2.8)	14.2	(2.4)	41.3	(4.1)	35.0	(3.6)
	Costa Rica	11.2	(2.3)	14.3	(2.9)	39.0	(3.7)	35.5	(3.5)	12.8	(2.4)	22.5	(3.3)	32.2	(3.7)	32.5	(3.6)
	Croatia	2.6	(1.3)	11.7	(2.4)	56.2	(3.7)	29.6	(3.6)	1.4	(0.9)	13.4	(3.0)	52.2	(4.0)	33.0	(4.0)
	Cyprus*	0.7	(0.0)	3.9	(0.0)	47.7	(0.1)	47.7	(0.1)	1.9	(0.0)	9.3	(0.1)	53.9	(0.1)	35.0	(0.1)
	Hong Kong-China	7.9	(2.4)	21.8	(3.5)	49.7	(4.2)	20.7	(2.9)	15.2	(3.3)	36.7	(4.3)	43.2	(4.6)	4.9	(1.8)
	Indonesia	1.8	(1.0)	3.1	(1.4)	44.9	(4.1)	50.2	(4.2)	4.1	(1.5)	10.8	(2.5)	58.0	(4.2)	27.1	(3.9)
	Jordan	4.6	(1.8)	2.6	(1.1)	39.5	(3.7)	53.3	(4.1)	3.2	(1.2)	5.3	(1.5)	35.5	(3.4)	56.0	(3.7)
	Kazakhstan	8.1	(2.3)	6.5	(1.9)	33.0	(3.0)	52.5	(3.6)	8.8	(2.1)	9.1	(2.1)	43.5	(3.9)	38.5	(3.3)
	Latvia	9.9	(2.2)	13.6	(2.7)	47.0	(3.8)	29.5	(3.6)	4.5	(1.5)	13.2	(2.5)	59.0	(3.6)	23.3	(3.1)
	Liechtenstein	18.2	(0.5)	54.2	(0.9)	17.2	(1.1)	10.5	(1.0)	0.0	c	69.4	(1.0)	30.6	(1.0)	0.0	c
	Lithuania	12.8	(2.1)	17.4	(2.9)	52.0	(3.5)	17.8	(2.6)	9.5	(2.1)	23.4	(3.1)	51.6	(3.2)	15.5	(2.7)
	Macao-China	6.6	(0.1)	27.2	(0.0)	44.7	(0.1)	21.5	(0.0)	2.9	(0.0)	19.6	(0.0)	47.9	(0.1)	29.6	(0.0)
	Malaysia	2.4	(1.2)	5.8	(2.0)	37.2	(3.9)	54.5	(3.9)	0.7	(0.7)	12.9	(2.4)	47.0	(4.3)	39.4	(4.0)
	Montenegro	4.0	(0.0)	2.6	(0.0)	23.1	(0.1)	70.4	(0.1)	2.1	(0.0)	5.0	(0.0)	25.9	(0.2)	67.1	(0.2)
	Peru	10.7	(2.2)	21.2	(2.9)	35.4	(3.2)	32.7	(3.4)	26.8	(3.2)	20.9	(3.0)	34.8	(3.6)	17.6	(3.0)
	Qatar	13.5	(0.1)	6.8	(0.1)	19.6	(0.1)	60.0	(0.1)	4.4	(0.0)	7.2	(0.1)	39.4	(0.1)	49.0	(0.1)
	Romania	46.2	(3.3)	9.8	(2.9)	22.3	(3.4)	21.7	(3.0)	46.1	(3.0)	9.4	(2.4)	21.3	(2.6)	23.2	(2.8)
	Russian Federation	5.1	(1.6)	10.1	(2.0)	64.4	(4.1)	20.4	(3.0)	3.5	(1.1)	13.4	(2.6)	53.9	(4.4)	29.2	(4.1)
	Serbia	1.6	(1.1)	7.9	(2.3)	45.5	(4.1)	45.0	(4.3)	5.2	(1.7)	17.7	(3.5)	45.3	(4.7)	31.8	(4.0)
	Shanghai-China	17.8	(3.0)	14.1	(2.8)	47.5	(4.0)	20.6	(3.5)	6.7	(2.1)	30.8	(3.8)	49.0	(3.8)	13.5	(2.8)
	Singapore	4.6	(0.6)	8.1	(0.6)	45.6	(0.4)	41.7	(0.4)	2.6	(0.0)	16.4	(0.2)	57.0	(0.4)	24.0	(0.3)
	Chinese Taipei	5.5	(1.9)	10.4	(2.5)	47.0	(4.3)	37.2	(3.9)	8.9	(2.1)	21.8	(3.7)	55.7	(4.1)	13.6	(2.7)
	Thailand	10.5	(2.0)	15.3	(2.6)	44.3	(3.4)	30.0	(3.4)	6.1	(1.5)	12.4	(2.2)	50.5	(3.7)	31.0	(3.5)
	Tunisia	3.6	(1.6)	9.6	(2.3)	24.5	(3.4)	62.4	(3.8)	7.7	(2.2)	19.2	(3.3)	33.4	(4.0)	39.7	(4.2)
	United Arab Emirates	5.0	(1.3)	8.2	(1.5)	35.1	(2.1)	51.7	(2.7)	4.3	(1.0)	8.0	(1.7)	40.9	(2.4)	46.8	(3.0)
	Uruguay	1.7	(0.7)	5.6	(2.0)	40.9	(3.9)	51.8	(3.9)	5.8	(2.0)	11.0	(2.3)	42.4	(3.7)	40.8	(3.5)
	Viet Nam	9.5	(2.3)	7.6	(2.3)	51.2	(4.0)	31.7	(3.6)	5.7	(2.0)	13.6	(2.5)	61.3	(3.7)	19.5	(3.1)

* See notes at the beginning of this Annex.
StatLink ⟡ http://dx.doi.org/10.1787/888932957498

[Part 6/7]
School management and leadership
Table IV.4.8 *Results based on school principals' reports*

Percentage of students in schools whose principal reported that he/she engaged in the following actions during the previous academic year:

	Provide staff with opportunities to make decisions concerning the school								Engage teachers to help build a culture of continuous improvement in the school							
	Never or 1-2 times during the year		3-4 times during the year		Once a month to once a week		More than once a week		Never or 1-2 times during the year		3-4 times during the year		Once a month to once a week		More than once a week	
	%	S.E.	%	S.E.	%	S.E.	%	S.E.	%	S.E.	%	S.E.	%	S.E.	%	S.E.
Australia	2.1	(0.6)	12.0	(1.3)	61.6	(1.9)	24.3	(1.8)	1.7	(0.5)	11.0	(1.3)	49.2	(2.1)	38.1	(2.0)
Austria	7.8	(2.0)	26.6	(3.5)	46.3	(4.4)	19.4	(3.1)	11.2	(2.7)	23.8	(3.4)	49.7	(4.0)	15.2	(2.9)
Belgium	6.2	(1.7)	30.3	(2.9)	49.5	(3.0)	14.0	(1.9)	14.1	(2.2)	31.1	(3.1)	36.0	(3.3)	18.8	(2.6)
Canada	1.5	(0.5)	8.3	(1.4)	67.3	(2.1)	22.9	(2.0)	4.7	(1.0)	13.0	(1.4)	46.1	(2.7)	36.1	(2.3)
Chile	2.1	(1.0)	13.2	(3.0)	53.3	(3.6)	31.3	(3.5)	2.4	(1.0)	8.5	(1.9)	57.3	(3.8)	31.8	(3.4)
Czech Republic	8.8	(2.2)	36.5	(3.4)	38.7	(3.3)	16.0	(3.1)	8.5	(2.3)	26.9	(3.4)	46.2	(3.4)	18.4	(3.3)
Denmark	3.2	(1.3)	12.3	(2.3)	71.6	(3.3)	12.8	(2.6)	3.9	(1.4)	14.7	(2.5)	58.1	(3.5)	23.3	(3.2)
Estonia	4.2	(1.0)	34.6	(2.8)	44.0	(3.0)	17.3	(2.6)	4.1	(1.0)	22.1	(2.5)	51.0	(2.8)	22.7	(2.7)
Finland	3.6	(1.4)	9.1	(1.9)	70.4	(3.3)	16.8	(2.8)	6.7	(1.6)	18.6	(2.9)	53.9	(3.7)	20.9	(2.9)
France	8.7	(1.9)	46.9	(3.4)	36.6	(3.1)	7.8	(2.0)	17.3	(2.5)	46.7	(3.4)	25.8	(3.1)	10.3	(2.2)
Germany	0.6	(0.6)	15.4	(2.3)	52.8	(3.3)	31.3	(3.1)	1.9	(1.0)	14.5	(2.6)	51.7	(3.5)	31.9	(3.3)
Greece	4.3	(1.3)	21.1	(3.2)	56.8	(3.3)	17.9	(2.8)	2.5	(1.2)	20.0	(3.2)	48.4	(3.7)	29.2	(3.6)
Hungary	5.1	(1.7)	29.7	(3.4)	59.9	(3.6)	5.3	(1.7)	19.6	(3.7)	23.5	(3.2)	44.4	(3.6)	12.4	(2.6)
Iceland	1.0	(0.1)	13.0	(0.2)	68.1	(0.2)	17.9	(0.2)	5.6	(0.1)	18.7	(0.2)	62.8	(0.2)	12.8	(0.2)
Ireland	3.0	(1.5)	25.7	(4.1)	48.9	(4.1)	22.4	(3.8)	7.0	(2.2)	25.4	(3.8)	37.7	(4.3)	29.9	(3.9)
Israel	7.6	(2.3)	25.1	(3.6)	51.9	(4.2)	15.4	(2.8)	10.8	(2.6)	23.6	(3.1)	46.3	(3.3)	19.3	(3.2)
Italy	4.6	(1.0)	30.9	(2.3)	42.9	(2.4)	21.6	(1.6)	3.2	(0.7)	20.5	(2.0)	38.4	(2.0)	38.0	(2.0)
Japan	19.5	(2.7)	13.5	(2.7)	59.5	(3.5)	7.5	(1.7)	23.8	(3.0)	34.9	(3.4)	36.5	(3.6)	4.8	(1.5)
Korea	9.2	(2.5)	16.6	(2.9)	62.4	(3.9)	11.8	(2.1)	13.9	(3.1)	21.2	(3.3)	58.5	(4.2)	6.4	(1.9)
Luxembourg	4.7	(0.0)	46.8	(0.1)	36.8	(0.1)	11.7	(0.1)	21.8	(0.1)	43.4	(0.1)	20.9	(0.1)	14.0	(0.1)
Mexico	17.8	(1.4)	27.7	(1.8)	34.4	(1.7)	20.1	(1.3)	7.8	(0.8)	27.5	(1.7)	41.8	(1.8)	23.0	(1.5)
Netherlands	4.5	(1.6)	35.9	(4.5)	45.2	(4.5)	14.3	(3.6)	6.4	(1.9)	22.3	(3.2)	56.8	(4.3)	14.5	(3.5)
New Zealand	2.5	(0.8)	12.6	(2.6)	67.3	(3.3)	17.6	(3.1)	5.4	(1.8)	14.5	(3.0)	57.8	(4.0)	22.3	(3.7)
Norway	3.9	(1.7)	11.1	(2.5)	67.8	(3.6)	17.2	(3.0)	7.6	(1.9)	18.4	(2.9)	58.7	(3.8)	15.3	(2.9)
Poland	13.1	(2.9)	42.5	(4.2)	33.3	(4.1)	11.0	(2.5)	14.7	(2.7)	33.4	(3.5)	39.8	(4.1)	12.0	(2.5)
Portugal	5.8	(2.3)	7.0	(2.1)	56.9	(4.6)	30.3	(4.1)	2.5	(1.1)	17.3	(3.5)	38.9	(4.1)	41.3	(4.4)
Slovak Republic	8.6	(2.5)	27.8	(3.7)	55.2	(3.6)	8.5	(2.1)	3.3	(1.2)	25.4	(3.6)	54.8	(4.2)	16.5	(3.2)
Slovenia	6.6	(0.7)	21.8	(0.4)	53.4	(0.8)	18.2	(0.5)	3.7	(0.6)	13.3	(0.4)	57.3	(0.7)	25.8	(0.5)
Spain	4.2	(1.1)	22.4	(2.3)	54.7	(2.6)	18.7	(2.0)	4.4	(1.1)	31.0	(2.1)	43.3	(2.4)	21.3	(2.5)
Sweden	1.8	(1.0)	10.2	(2.5)	70.7	(3.3)	17.3	(2.6)	3.0	(1.2)	15.9	(2.6)	55.5	(3.9)	25.6	(3.4)
Switzerland	10.7	(2.1)	34.7	(3.2)	48.8	(3.4)	5.8	(1.9)	13.3	(2.0)	34.1	(3.0)	41.0	(3.5)	11.6	(2.4)
Turkey	2.1	(1.0)	13.6	(2.8)	40.7	(3.7)	43.6	(3.4)	2.8	(1.0)	9.2	(2.3)	42.3	(4.3)	45.6	(3.9)
United Kingdom	3.4	(1.4)	22.8	(3.0)	53.0	(3.9)	20.8	(3.3)	1.8	(0.8)	13.6	(2.7)	41.9	(3.2)	42.7	(3.5)
United States	3.5	(1.5)	8.9	(2.4)	58.9	(4.5)	28.6	(4.1)	1.9	(1.1)	4.5	(1.7)	53.9	(4.4)	39.6	(4.5)
OECD average	5.8	(0.3)	22.5	(0.5)	53.5	(0.6)	18.2	(0.5)	7.7	(0.3)	21.8	(0.5)	47.1	(0.6)	23.3	(0.5)
Albania	9.3	(1.9)	28.6	(3.4)	48.2	(3.9)	13.8	(3.3)	10.7	(2.2)	21.1	(3.0)	39.7	(4.1)	28.5	(3.8)
Argentina	11.5	(2.2)	21.7	(3.3)	36.1	(3.8)	30.7	(4.0)	4.2	(1.2)	17.5	(3.4)	32.0	(3.7)	46.3	(3.9)
Brazil	3.0	(0.8)	11.6	(1.6)	38.0	(2.4)	47.4	(2.5)	5.6	(0.9)	11.8	(1.5)	36.8	(2.2)	45.8	(2.7)
Bulgaria	6.7	(2.0)	18.2	(2.6)	59.0	(3.8)	16.2	(2.8)	3.9	(1.3)	21.2	(3.2)	52.8	(3.7)	22.2	(2.9)
Colombia	5.6	(1.6)	9.6	(1.9)	47.3	(3.7)	37.5	(3.5)	6.9	(1.9)	14.4	(2.6)	37.6	(3.7)	41.0	(3.6)
Costa Rica	14.1	(2.3)	19.8	(3.3)	48.0	(3.6)	18.0	(2.7)	11.8	(2.3)	20.0	(3.4)	44.2	(3.6)	24.0	(3.2)
Croatia	6.4	(2.0)	18.7	(2.7)	59.4	(3.5)	15.5	(2.9)	3.6	(1.2)	19.4	(2.8)	43.1	(3.6)	33.9	(3.7)
Cyprus*	3.3	(0.0)	6.2	(0.1)	71.6	(0.1)	18.9	(0.1)	1.8	(0.0)	4.1	(0.1)	51.3	(0.1)	42.7	(0.1)
Hong Kong-China	7.4	(2.2)	33.4	(4.3)	51.4	(4.0)	7.9	(2.1)	11.2	(2.6)	33.5	(4.1)	42.9	(4.0)	12.4	(2.7)
Indonesia	11.3	(2.3)	20.3	(3.3)	49.4	(4.1)	19.0	(3.2)	5.7	(1.6)	11.9	(2.6)	49.5	(4.5)	32.9	(4.0)
Jordan	6.3	(1.8)	8.3	(2.2)	48.9	(3.7)	36.6	(3.7)	8.2	(1.6)	11.5	(2.1)	41.7	(3.7)	38.6	(3.8)
Kazakhstan	5.2	(2.0)	23.2	(2.8)	50.0	(4.4)	21.5	(3.5)	5.3	(1.7)	15.4	(2.9)	48.8	(4.3)	30.5	(3.6)
Latvia	6.1	(1.9)	25.2	(3.2)	49.5	(3.6)	19.1	(3.2)	3.7	(1.4)	15.8	(2.5)	54.0	(3.5)	26.5	(3.3)
Liechtenstein	0.0	c	56.2	(0.8)	42.7	(0.9)	1.1	(0.7)	0.0	c	0.0	c	95.9	(0.7)	4.1	(0.7)
Lithuania	6.1	(1.9)	29.3	(3.1)	50.0	(3.7)	14.6	(2.6)	11.8	(2.3)	26.1	(2.9)	39.5	(3.3)	22.6	(2.6)
Macao-China	23.6	(0.0)	45.8	(0.0)	24.0	(0.1)	6.6	(0.0)	15.1	(0.0)	46.0	(0.1)	34.7	(0.1)	4.2	(0.0)
Malaysia	5.1	(1.8)	24.6	(3.5)	46.0	(3.8)	24.2	(3.3)	1.6	(0.9)	14.3	(2.7)	49.8	(4.0)	34.3	(3.6)
Montenegro	10.9	(0.1)	30.5	(0.2)	26.9	(0.1)	31.7	(0.2)	4.8	(0.0)	18.6	(0.1)	26.2	(0.1)	50.4	(0.2)
Peru	14.3	(2.7)	33.4	(3.2)	34.5	(3.7)	17.8	(2.7)	19.4	(3.2)	24.7	(3.2)	32.6	(3.3)	23.3	(3.0)
Qatar	14.1	(0.1)	17.0	(0.1)	44.5	(0.1)	24.4	(0.1)	5.9	(0.0)	18.7	(0.1)	42.1	(0.1)	33.3	(0.1)
Romania	40.3	(2.7)	13.9	(2.3)	28.6	(2.9)	17.3	(2.4)	43.4	(2.7)	9.8	(2.4)	20.0	(3.2)	26.8	(3.1)
Russian Federation	2.7	(1.4)	36.1	(3.9)	52.6	(3.9)	8.6	(2.0)	12.7	(2.2)	19.6	(2.8)	53.0	(3.7)	14.8	(2.0)
Serbia	3.0	(1.5)	30.5	(4.1)	45.5	(4.5)	21.0	(3.3)	4.5	(1.8)	26.3	(3.5)	40.0	(4.3)	29.2	(4.1)
Shanghai-China	48.3	(4.3)	37.6	(4.0)	12.5	(2.4)	1.6	(0.7)	17.4	(3.1)	41.6	(4.1)	32.1	(4.1)	8.8	(2.3)
Singapore	2.9	(0.1)	19.1	(0.2)	59.6	(0.4)	18.4	(0.2)	2.3	(0.0)	14.1	(0.1)	58.4	(0.4)	25.2	(0.3)
Chinese Taipei	11.3	(2.7)	25.2	(3.3)	51.2	(4.1)	12.3	(2.4)	12.6	(2.5)	26.5	(3.5)	48.3	(4.2)	12.6	(2.8)
Thailand	5.0	(1.7)	11.5	(2.1)	50.2	(3.5)	33.2	(3.6)	4.8	(1.5)	12.9	(2.6)	46.2	(4.0)	36.0	(3.8)
Tunisia	13.8	(2.8)	34.6	(3.4)	26.0	(3.8)	25.6	(3.4)	15.6	(2.9)	34.2	(3.6)	25.6	(3.6)	24.6	(3.4)
United Arab Emirates	7.1	(1.3)	21.1	(2.4)	52.3	(2.6)	19.5	(2.0)	6.0	(1.8)	8.8	(1.4)	50.3	(2.7)	34.8	(2.9)
Uruguay	7.4	(2.1)	12.8	(2.6)	51.9	(3.9)	28.0	(3.5)	6.6	(2.1)	9.6	(2.3)	53.3	(3.9)	30.5	(3.6)
Viet Nam	19.2	(3.3)	16.0	(3.0)	60.2	(3.9)	4.6	(1.6)	14.2	(2.9)	19.9	(3.5)	56.3	(4.1)	9.7	(2.4)

* See notes at the beginning of this Annex.
StatLink ⓘ http://dx.doi.org/10.1787/888932957498

[Part 7/7]
Table IV.4.8 School management and leadership
Results based on school principals' reports

Percentage of students in schools whose principal reported that he/she engaged in the following actions during the previous academic year:

Ask teachers to participate in reviewing management practices

		Never or 1-2 times during the year		3-4 times during the year		Once a month to once a week		More than once a week	
		%	S.E.	%	S.E.	%	S.E.	%	S.E.
OECD	Australia	22.4	(1.8)	26.0	(1.6)	41.7	(2.0)	9.9	(1.3)
	Austria	75.4	(3.4)	10.7	(2.6)	12.6	(2.5)	1.3	(0.9)
	Belgium	69.9	(3.0)	15.9	(2.1)	12.0	(2.3)	2.2	(0.9)
	Canada	35.5	(2.0)	20.9	(1.7)	38.5	(2.3)	5.1	(1.1)
	Chile	41.0	(3.9)	16.8	(3.0)	35.5	(3.8)	6.8	(1.9)
	Czech Republic	52.1	(4.3)	27.0	(3.2)	17.5	(3.1)	3.4	(1.5)
	Denmark	62.2	(3.6)	18.9	(3.1)	16.5	(2.8)	2.3	(1.0)
	Estonia	71.1	(2.9)	12.0	(2.0)	13.2	(1.9)	3.6	(1.5)
	Finland	62.8	(3.6)	17.7	(2.5)	15.8	(2.5)	3.6	(1.6)
	France	74.2	(3.4)	19.6	(3.0)	3.6	(1.1)	2.6	(1.3)
	Germany	78.9	(3.1)	10.0	(2.5)	10.2	(2.3)	0.9	(0.6)
	Greece	51.1	(3.9)	19.1	(3.1)	23.9	(3.4)	5.9	(1.6)
	Hungary	82.4	(2.8)	11.3	(2.4)	6.2	(1.9)	0.1	(0.1)
	Iceland	68.1	(0.2)	16.5	(0.2)	14.1	(0.1)	1.2	(0.0)
	Ireland	37.7	(4.0)	29.6	(4.0)	21.6	(3.2)	11.0	(2.4)
	Israel	59.8	(4.3)	20.8	(3.3)	15.8	(3.0)	3.5	(1.4)
	Italy	21.0	(1.8)	32.7	(2.1)	33.8	(2.2)	12.5	(1.3)
	Japan	35.0	(3.6)	18.7	(3.0)	44.2	(3.5)	2.1	(1.0)
	Korea	28.7	(4.1)	19.6	(3.1)	43.1	(4.3)	8.7	(2.3)
	Luxembourg	64.8	(0.1)	29.7	(0.1)	2.3	(0.0)	3.2	(0.0)
	Mexico	42.3	(1.9)	22.9	(1.9)	27.6	(1.6)	7.1	(0.7)
	Netherlands	56.9	(4.4)	23.9	(3.8)	17.7	(3.3)	1.4	(1.0)
	New Zealand	30.5	(3.7)	26.0	(3.9)	38.1	(3.9)	5.4	(2.1)
	Norway	64.6	(3.5)	21.4	(2.9)	11.9	(2.6)	2.1	(1.2)
	Poland	35.6	(3.8)	41.9	(4.0)	20.0	(3.2)	2.4	(1.3)
	Portugal	26.5	(3.5)	27.7	(4.1)	33.4	(4.0)	12.4	(3.0)
	Slovak Republic	35.1	(3.2)	32.7	(3.7)	30.2	(3.3)	2.0	(1.0)
	Slovenia	40.1	(0.8)	24.6	(0.8)	30.2	(0.7)	5.1	(0.3)
	Spain	38.5	(2.6)	36.7	(3.1)	19.0	(2.0)	5.8	(1.5)
	Sweden	64.5	(3.6)	17.1	(2.8)	16.1	(2.7)	2.3	(1.2)
	Switzerland	81.9	(2.6)	10.6	(2.2)	7.1	(1.8)	0.4	(0.3)
	Turkey	6.5	(2.5)	19.1	(3.0)	45.4	(4.3)	29.1	(3.3)
	United Kingdom	22.3	(2.9)	27.5	(2.6)	39.8	(3.5)	10.3	(2.2)
	United States	26.2	(4.0)	18.7	(3.9)	43.5	(4.9)	11.5	(2.8)
	OECD average	49.0	(0.6)	21.9	(0.5)	23.6	(0.5)	5.5	(0.3)
Partners	Albania	9.5	(2.3)	23.8	(3.6)	43.4	(4.1)	23.3	(4.0)
	Argentina	45.9	(3.5)	21.7	(2.8)	18.7	(2.9)	13.6	(2.4)
	Brazil	23.4	(2.1)	19.0	(1.8)	38.7	(2.5)	18.9	(2.0)
	Bulgaria	6.9	(2.0)	33.7	(3.8)	50.5	(3.7)	8.9	(2.3)
	Colombia	33.8	(3.6)	19.8	(3.1)	32.8	(3.3)	13.6	(2.6)
	Costa Rica	34.8	(3.5)	22.4	(3.0)	31.3	(4.0)	11.5	(2.2)
	Croatia	42.5	(3.7)	26.3	(3.9)	23.8	(3.1)	7.3	(2.3)
	Cyprus*	17.1	(0.1)	21.7	(0.1)	41.2	(0.1)	20.0	(0.1)
	Hong Kong-China	15.8	(3.1)	43.0	(4.7)	39.7	(4.3)	1.5	(1.0)
	Indonesia	16.0	(3.3)	23.1	(3.4)	48.5	(4.0)	12.3	(2.5)
	Jordan	22.7	(3.0)	8.6	(2.2)	42.9	(3.9)	25.8	(3.4)
	Kazakhstan	13.0	(2.7)	29.7	(3.7)	45.2	(4.2)	12.0	(2.5)
	Latvia	43.7	(3.8)	27.6	(3.7)	24.0	(3.5)	4.7	(1.5)
	Liechtenstein	74.1	(0.7)	12.3	(0.2)	12.5	(1.0)	1.1	(0.7)
	Lithuania	61.2	(3.5)	24.6	(2.6)	10.0	(2.3)	4.2	(1.5)
	Macao-China	27.5	(0.0)	48.0	(0.1)	18.1	(0.0)	6.3	(0.0)
	Malaysia	10.0	(2.1)	20.0	(3.4)	46.3	(3.6)	23.8	(3.4)
	Montenegro	20.4	(0.1)	28.5	(0.2)	35.1	(0.2)	16.1	(0.2)
	Peru	47.0	(3.8)	28.8	(3.5)	20.4	(3.0)	3.8	(1.4)
	Qatar	32.1	(0.1)	29.6	(0.1)	27.5	(0.1)	10.9	(0.1)
	Romania	46.8	(3.5)	18.7	(2.5)	22.9	(3.0)	11.5	(2.1)
	Russian Federation	16.9	(2.6)	39.2	(3.2)	42.1	(3.3)	1.8	(0.8)
	Serbia	53.2	(3.9)	24.5	(3.7)	17.1	(3.5)	5.2	(2.0)
	Shanghai-China	47.5	(4.0)	41.8	(4.1)	7.8	(2.1)	2.9	(1.1)
	Singapore	32.9	(0.3)	33.2	(0.6)	28.2	(0.5)	5.7	(0.1)
	Chinese Taipei	25.4	(3.5)	29.1	(3.6)	39.2	(4.2)	6.2	(2.0)
	Thailand	14.0	(2.5)	12.2	(2.4)	53.6	(3.8)	20.2	(3.2)
	Tunisia	31.0	(3.6)	34.8	(3.9)	24.2	(3.5)	9.9	(2.4)
	United Arab Emirates	29.1	(2.5)	18.0	(2.0)	37.1	(2.4)	15.8	(2.0)
	Uruguay	25.8	(3.1)	15.5	(2.9)	44.9	(3.7)	13.8	(2.7)
	Viet Nam	39.7	(3.9)	22.5	(3.8)	34.1	(4.3)	3.7	(1.6)

* See notes at the beginning of this Annex.
StatLink http://dx.doi.org/10.1787/888932957498

[Part 1/1]
School competition reported by principals and parents
Table IV.4.9   *Results based on school principals' and parents' reports*

		Students in schools whose principal reported on the number of schools competing for students in the same area								Difference between the percentage of students whose principals and parents reported that schools compete for students, and the percentage of students whose principals reported that schools DO NOT compete for students but whose parents reported that schools DO compete for students	
		No other school				One school or more					
		Among these students, percentage of students whose parents reported on the number of schools competing for students in the same area				Among these students, percentage of students whose parents reported on the number of schools competing for students in the same area					
		No other school		One school or more		No other school		One school or more			
		%	S.E.	%	S.E.	%	S.E.	%	S.E.	% dif.	S.E.
OECD	Belgium (Flemish community)	55.8	(9.5)	44.2	(9.5)	26.0	(1.2)	74.0	(1.2)	**29.8**	(9.7)
	Chile	75.2	(3.9)	24.8	(3.9)	45.0	(2.0)	55.0	(2.0)	**30.2**	(4.5)
	Germany	53.0	(3.4)	47.0	(3.4)	28.8	(2.2)	71.2	(2.2)	**24.2**	(4.0)
	Hungary	53.8	(2.8)	46.2	(2.8)	33.3	(1.4)	66.7	(1.4)	**20.5**	(3.2)
	Italy	60.9	(1.2)	39.1	(1.2)	41.1	(1.1)	58.9	(1.1)	**19.8**	(1.7)
	Korea	42.8	(5.9)	57.2	(5.9)	20.0	(1.4)	80.0	(1.4)	**22.8**	(6.2)
	Mexico	65.5	(2.8)	34.5	(2.8)	31.2	(0.8)	68.8	(0.8)	**34.3**	(3.1)
	Portugal	73.9	(3.2)	26.1	(3.2)	43.3	(2.3)	56.7	(2.3)	**30.6**	(4.0)
Partners	Croatia	57.6	(3.4)	42.4	(3.4)	41.2	(1.2)	58.8	(1.2)	**16.5**	(3.7)
	Hong Kong-China	28.1	(2.4)	71.9	(2.4)	20.8	(0.9)	79.2	(0.9)	**7.2**	(2.5)
	Macao-China	41.2	(3.2)	58.8	(3.2)	33.2	(0.7)	66.8	(0.7)	**8.0**	(3.3)

Notes: Values that are statistically significant are indicated in bold (see Annex A3).
Only countries and economies with data from the parent questionnaire are shown.
StatLink ᵃⁱˢᵖ http://dx.doi.org/10.1787/888932957498

[Part 1/1]
Parents' reports on their criteria for choosing schools for their children
Table IV.4.10   *Results based on parents' reports*

Percentage of parents reporting the following reasons in choosing a school for their child:

		The school is at a short distance to home				The school has a good reputation				The school offers particular courses or school subjects			
		Not important	Somewhat important	Important	Very important	Not important	Somewhat important	Important	Very important	Not important	Somewhat important	Important	Very important
		% S.E.	% S.E.	% S.E.	% S.E.	% S.E.	% S.E.	% S.E.	% S.E.	% S.E.	% S.E.	% S.E.	% S.E.
OECD	Belgium (Flemish community)	8.7 (0.7)	32.7 (1.0)	45.7 (1.0)	12.9 (0.7)	0.6 (0.1)	5.0 (0.4)	51.1 (0.9)	43.2 (1.1)	1.3 (0.2)	5.9 (0.4)	54.9 (1.0)	37.9 (1.1)
	Chile	25.0 (1.1)	23.8 (0.6)	27.4 (0.7)	23.8 (1.0)	2.2 (0.3)	10.4 (0.7)	33.2 (1.0)	54.2 (1.4)	4.8 (0.4)	13.8 (0.5)	44.5 (0.7)	37.0 (0.8)
	Germany	13.1 (0.8)	30.8 (1.1)	38.7 (1.0)	17.3 (0.9)	1.2 (0.2)	11.1 (0.6)	46.3 (1.2)	41.4 (1.3)	4.6 (0.4)	18.2 (0.9)	50.9 (0.9)	26.2 (0.9)
	Hungary	15.7 (0.9)	33.3 (1.0)	34.5 (0.9)	16.5 (1.0)	2.5 (0.3)	13.5 (0.8)	52.7 (1.0)	31.4 (1.2)	6.9 (0.5)	17.5 (1.0)	48.3 (1.2)	27.3 (1.1)
	Italy	37.4 (0.7)	31.1 (0.4)	22.3 (0.5)	9.2 (0.3)	3.0 (0.1)	18.0 (0.4)	44.0 (0.4)	35.1 (0.4)	9.4 (0.3)	23.0 (0.4)	48.4 (0.4)	19.2 (0.4)
	Korea	4.5 (0.4)	27.4 (0.8)	45.0 (0.8)	23.1 (0.9)	1.2 (0.2)	9.9 (0.6)	48.6 (0.8)	40.4 (0.9)	3.1 (0.3)	17.8 (0.7)	54.6 (0.6)	24.5 (0.7)
	Mexico	16.1 (0.4)	18.8 (0.4)	32.8 (0.4)	32.3 (0.5)	2.7 (0.2)	10.6 (0.3)	35.2 (0.5)	51.5 (0.6)	5.9 (0.2)	15.1 (0.3)	45.0 (0.4)	34.0 (0.5)
	Portugal	7.5 (0.6)	23.0 (1.0)	29.9 (0.9)	39.6 (1.2)	1.7 (0.2)	9.6 (0.6)	34.5 (1.1)	54.3 (1.4)	3.1 (0.3)	11.2 (0.6)	41.3 (0.9)	44.4 (1.2)
Partners	Croatia	25.2 (1.0)	24.9 (0.6)	35.1 (0.9)	14.8 (0.7)	5.1 (0.3)	17.6 (0.7)	49.6 (0.8)	27.7 (1.0)	2.1 (0.2)	14.8 (0.6)	52.4 (0.8)	30.7 (0.9)
	Hong Kong-China	14.4 (0.7)	40.0 (0.9)	35.8 (0.8)	9.8 (0.5)	0.7 (0.1)	6.7 (0.4)	41.3 (0.8)	51.2 (1.0)	8.2 (0.5)	24.9 (0.6)	50.8 (0.7)	16.1 (0.8)
	Macao-China	21.5 (0.6)	33.0 (0.6)	32.8 (0.6)	12.7 (0.5)	5.0 (0.3)	15.9 (0.5)	45.7 (0.7)	33.4 (0.6)	7.0 (0.4)	21.4 (0.5)	55.0 (0.6)	16.6 (0.5)

Percentage of parents reporting the following reasons in choosing a school for their child:

		The school adheres to a particular religious philosophy				The school has a particular approach to pedagogy				Other family members attend the school			
		Not important	Somewhat important	Important	Very important	Not important	Somewhat important	Important	Very important	Not important	Somewhat important	Important	Very important
		% S.E.	% S.E.	% S.E.	% S.E.	% S.E.	% S.E.	% S.E.	% S.E.	% S.E.	% S.E.	% S.E.	% S.E.
OECD	Belgium (Flemish community)	41.9 (0.9)	31.9 (0.7)	22.3 (0.8)	3.9 (0.4)	65.2 (1.0)	20.3 (0.6)	12.6 (0.7)	1.9 (0.3)	57.4 (1.1)	19.6 (0.7)	18.4 (0.9)	4.6 (0.4)
	Chile	38.8 (1.4)	20.6 (0.7)	23.5 (0.8)	17.1 (1.1)	28.2 (0.9)	27.5 (0.7)	32.3 (0.8)	12.0 (0.5)	49.9 (1.0)	12.1 (0.5)	18.9 (0.7)	19.1 (0.7)
	Germany	62.8 (1.4)	20.2 (0.6)	12.9 (0.9)	4.0 (0.6)	52.5 (1.0)	29.1 (0.8)	14.3 (0.6)	4.1 (0.5)	66.0 (1.0)	14.7 (0.6)	14.8 (0.6)	4.5 (0.4)
	Hungary	71.9 (1.8)	15.0 (0.8)	8.9 (0.9)	4.1 (0.9)	67.3 (0.8)	21.0 (0.7)	9.9 (0.4)	1.8 (0.2)	64.0 (1.1)	15.3 (0.6)	15.2 (0.8)	5.5 (0.4)
	Italy	61.0 (0.5)	16.3 (0.3)	17.8 (0.4)	5.0 (0.2)	48.3 (0.5)	24.9 (0.4)	22.0 (0.4)	4.7 (0.2)	67.9 (0.5)	11.6 (0.3)	14.1 (0.3)	6.4 (0.2)
	Korea	58.0 (0.9)	22.1 (0.6)	13.8 (0.6)	6.1 (0.5)	20.0 (0.8)	31.5 (0.7)	37.4 (0.8)	11.1 (0.5)	69.6 (0.8)	17.7 (0.7)	10.1 (0.5)	2.5 (0.2)
	Mexico	72.6 (0.6)	12.6 (0.3)	9.7 (0.2)	5.0 (0.4)	17.2 (0.3)	23.6 (0.3)	38.2 (0.4)	21.0 (0.4)	43.2 (0.5)	14.5 (0.3)	24.2 (0.4)	18.1 (0.3)
	Portugal	46.3 (1.2)	28.3 (0.7)	20.2 (0.8)	5.2 (0.5)	34.6 (0.8)	34.5 (0.7)	25.3 (0.8)	5.5 (0.4)	38.7 (1.0)	20.0 (0.7)	26.8 (0.8)	14.4 (0.7)
Partners	Croatia	49.4 (1.0)	14.8 (0.5)	27.9 (0.7)	7.8 (0.6)	a a	a a	a a	a a	81.1 (0.7)	6.0 (0.4)	10.1 (0.5)	2.8 (0.2)
	Hong Kong-China	43.6 (1.2)	25.5 (0.6)	23.6 (0.7)	7.3 (0.6)	12.7 (0.7)	30.3 (1.0)	47.4 (0.9)	9.6 (0.8)	60.6 (0.8)	20.4 (0.6)	15.6 (0.7)	3.4 (0.3)
	Macao-China	55.1 (0.7)	23.0 (0.6)	18.3 (0.5)	3.6 (0.3)	9.5 (0.4)	28.6 (0.6)	47.2 (0.7)	14.6 (0.5)	44.9 (0.7)	24.9 (0.5)	24.5 (0.7)	5.7 (0.3)

Percentage of parents reporting the following reasons in choosing a school for their child:

		Expenses are low (e.g. tuition, books, room and board)				The school has financial aid available, such as a school loan, scholarship, or grant				The school has an active and pleasant school climate			
		Not important	Somewhat important	Important	Very important	Not important	Somewhat important	Important	Very important	Not important	Somewhat important	Important	Very important
		% S.E.	% S.E.	% S.E.	% S.E.	% S.E.	% S.E.	% S.E.	% S.E.	% S.E.	% S.E.	% S.E.	% S.E.
OECD	Belgium (Flemish community)	43.6 (0.9)	32.9 (0.7)	18.4 (0.8)	5.1 (0.4)	55.7 (1.0)	21.2 (0.7)	18.1 (0.8)	5.0 (0.4)	1.9 (0.2)	8.9 (0.5)	59.8 (0.8)	29.4 (1.0)
	Chile	16.5 (0.6)	23.5 (0.6)	31.0 (0.7)	29.0 (0.8)	19.9 (0.7)	17.8 (0.6)	27.4 (0.7)	34.9 (0.9)	2.3 (0.3)	9.6 (0.5)	30.5 (0.8)	57.6 (1.0)
	Germany	41.4 (0.9)	29.8 (0.8)	20.5 (0.8)	8.4 (0.5)	55.9 (1.2)	23.1 (0.8)	14.9 (0.9)	6.1 (0.4)	1.3 (0.3)	7.4 (0.6)	41.7 (1.2)	49.6 (1.3)
	Hungary	25.1 (0.7)	34.2 (0.8)	28.9 (0.8)	11.9 (0.6)	45.6 (0.9)	25.1 (0.7)	21.2 (0.6)	8.0 (0.6)	7.3 (0.6)	21.2 (0.8)	53.3 (0.8)	18.2 (0.7)
	Italy	39.7 (0.6)	27.3 (0.4)	22.9 (0.4)	10.1 (0.3)	a a	a a	a a	a a	3.2 (0.2)	17.7 (0.3)	45.7 (0.4)	33.4 (0.4)
	Korea	16.3 (0.6)	30.4 (0.7)	38.6 (0.8)	14.6 (0.6)	20.1 (0.7)	25.3 (0.7)	36.0 (0.7)	18.6 (0.6)	0.9 (0.2)	7.1 (0.4)	41.1 (0.7)	50.9 (0.8)
	Mexico	13.9 (0.3)	22.4 (0.4)	34.8 (0.4)	29.0 (0.4)	16.1 (0.4)	17.5 (0.3)	31.9 (0.4)	34.4 (0.5)	2.8 (0.1)	11.5 (0.3)	36.4 (0.5)	49.2 (0.5)
	Portugal	14.8 (0.9)	24.0 (0.7)	34.2 (1.1)	27.0 (0.9)	26.4 (1.1)	21.1 (0.6)	28.0 (0.8)	24.6 (0.9)	1.5 (0.2)	9.9 (0.5)	38.9 (0.8)	49.7 (0.9)
Partners	Croatia	39.7 (0.9)	18.7 (0.6)	26.8 (0.8)	14.8 (0.6)	52.9 (0.8)	12.6 (0.5)	22.3 (0.6)	12.2 (0.6)	3.7 (0.3)	16.9 (0.6)	46.1 (0.8)	33.2 (0.8)
	Hong Kong-China	34.0 (0.8)	34.0 (1.1)	23.5 (0.8)	8.5 (0.5)	39.9 (1.2)	27.0 (0.7)	23.6 (0.8)	9.5 (0.6)	2.7 (0.3)	12.0 (0.6)	46.4 (0.8)	38.9 (1.0)
	Macao-China	33.1 (0.6)	29.2 (0.6)	25.5 (0.6)	12.2 (0.4)	28.5 (0.6)	25.0 (0.6)	28.2 (0.6)	18.3 (0.5)	3.1 (0.3)	13.6 (0.5)	48.4 (0.8)	34.9 (0.6)

Percentage of parents reporting the following reasons in choosing a school for their child:

		The academic achievements of students in the school are high				There is a safe school environment			
		Not important	Somewhat important	Important	Very important	Not important	Somewhat important	Important	Very important
		% S.E.	% S.E.	% S.E.	% S.E.	% S.E.	% S.E.	% S.E.	% S.E.
OECD	Belgium (Flemish community)	5.2 (0.4)	19.5 (0.7)	60.1 (0.7)	15.2 (0.7)	1.7 (0.2)	8.8 (0.5)	53.2 (0.9)	36.4 (0.9)
	Chile	3.2 (0.4)	13.1 (0.6)	36.1 (0.9)	47.6 (1.2)	2.1 (0.2)	7.9 (0.5)	24.8 (0.7)	65.3 (0.9)
	Germany	4.1 (0.4)	16.8 (0.8)	51.8 (1.1)	27.2 (1.0)	1.7 (0.3)	6.8 (0.5)	37.7 (1.0)	53.8 (1.2)
	Hungary	4.6 (0.4)	19.3 (0.8)	53.3 (1.0)	22.8 (1.0)	1.2 (0.2)	5.8 (0.4)	45.5 (1.0)	47.6 (0.9)
	Italy	8.0 (0.3)	23.7 (0.3)	45.4 (0.4)	22.9 (0.3)	2.2 (0.1)	10.2 (0.3)	33.2 (0.4)	54.3 (0.5)
	Korea	1.4 (0.2)	8.3 (0.5)	40.0 (0.8)	50.4 (1.0)	0.9 (0.2)	4.4 (0.3)	28.4 (0.6)	66.2 (0.7)
	Mexico	3.5 (0.2)	13.1 (0.4)	38.4 (0.4)	45.0 (0.5)	2.7 (0.1)	9.6 (0.3)	30.3 (0.4)	57.4 (0.6)
	Portugal	2.5 (0.3)	12.2 (0.7)	40.2 (0.9)	45.2 (1.0)	1.4 (0.2)	5.3 (0.4)	24.3 (0.8)	68.9 (1.0)
Partners	Croatia	5.9 (0.4)	16.8 (0.6)	46.4 (0.9)	31.0 (0.8)	1.4 (0.2)	10.3 (0.5)	32.7 (0.7)	55.6 (0.8)
	Hong Kong-China	3.3 (0.3)	16.4 (0.5)	50.7 (0.8)	29.6 (0.8)	0.6 (0.1)	4.3 (0.3)	32.5 (0.9)	62.6 (0.9)
	Macao-China	5.1 (0.3)	17.3 (0.5)	46.6 (0.7)	31.0 (0.7)	1.2 (0.1)	5.6 (0.3)	31.9 (0.6)	61.3 (0.7)

Note: Only countries and economies with data from the parent questionnaire are shown.
StatLink ᐃᓯᐊᔭ http://dx.doi.org/10.1787/888932957498

[Part 1/1]

Parents' reports on their criteria for choosing schools for their children, by socio-economic status of students

Table IV.4.11   *Results based on parents' reports*

Percentage of parents reporting the following reasons are "very important" in choosing a school for their child:

	The school is at a short distance to home				The school has a good reputation				The school offers particular courses or school subjects			
	Bottom ESCS quarter	Second ESCS quarter	Third ESCS quarter	Top ESCS quarter	Bottom ESCS quarter	Second ESCS quarter	Third ESCS quarter	Top ESCS quarter	Bottom ESCS quarter	Second ESCS quarter	Third ESCS quarter	Top ESCS quarter
	% S.E.	% S.E.	% S.E.	% S.E.	% S.E.	% S.E.	% S.E.	% S.E.	% S.E.	% S.E.	% S.E.	% S.E.
OECD												
Belgium (Flemish community)	12.2 (1.0)	12.7 (0.9)	12.8 (1.3)	14.0 (1.5)	37.4 (1.8)	41.9 (1.7)	47.4 (2.0)	47.2 (1.9)	36.6 (1.8)	37.7 (1.9)	37.7 (1.7)	39.6 (1.6)
Chile	29.5 (2.0)	22.9 (1.6)	24.2 (1.8)	18.2 (1.5)	46.5 (2.3)	56.8 (2.2)	60.3 (2.0)	53.5 (1.5)	32.9 (1.5)	41.0 (1.5)	40.9 (1.5)	33.2 (1.4)
Germany	21.1 (1.9)	17.0 (1.4)	17.0 (1.5)	14.8 (1.5)	43.0 (1.9)	43.9 (2.4)	39.8 (2.1)	39.4 (2.2)	25.0 (1.9)	25.8 (1.7)	25.6 (1.8)	28.8 (1.9)
Hungary	21.6 (2.0)	16.4 (1.7)	15.5 (1.6)	12.3 (1.6)	23.5 (1.8)	30.4 (2.1)	31.5 (2.2)	40.5 (2.0)	17.3 (1.4)	26.8 (1.9)	31.0 (1.9)	34.2 (2.1)
Italy	12.3 (0.6)	8.9 (0.6)	8.5 (0.5)	7.0 (0.5)	31.9 (0.8)	34.7 (0.9)	36.3 (0.9)	37.6 (0.9)	18.2 (0.6)	19.1 (0.6)	20.6 (0.7)	18.8 (0.8)
Korea	20.3 (1.4)	23.1 (1.5)	24.1 (1.4)	24.9 (1.6)	30.8 (1.4)	36.8 (1.6)	44.6 (1.7)	49.3 (1.8)	22.1 (1.2)	24.6 (1.5)	23.5 (1.4)	27.6 (1.5)
Mexico	35.4 (1.0)	36.1 (0.8)	33.9 (0.8)	23.8 (1.0)	41.4 (1.2)	50.5 (0.9)	54.7 (1.0)	59.5 (1.0)	28.6 (0.8)	31.0 (0.8)	36.9 (1.0)	39.6 (0.9)
Portugal	40.2 (1.9)	42.8 (2.2)	43.7 (2.3)	31.9 (2.3)	40.6 (2.1)	51.4 (2.3)	56.0 (2.7)	69.7 (2.4)	36.5 (1.7)	45.0 (1.7)	46.8 (1.9)	48.8 (2.2)
Partners												
Croatia	19.9 (1.4)	15.3 (1.2)	12.9 (1.3)	11.1 (1.1)	24.4 (1.4)	26.0 (1.5)	27.2 (1.5)	33.2 (1.7)	23.5 (1.3)	26.9 (1.4)	32.9 (1.5)	39.7 (1.9)
Hong Kong-China	12.5 (1.1)	9.5 (1.0)	8.9 (0.9)	8.1 (1.0)	40.2 (1.7)	47.7 (1.9)	56.4 (1.9)	62.1 (1.9)	15.2 (1.1)	15.2 (1.1)	16.6 (1.2)	17.3 (2.5)
Macao-China	14.0 (1.1)	11.2 (0.8)	12.7 (1.0)	12.7 (0.9)	26.4 (1.3)	31.0 (1.2)	33.7 (1.4)	42.5 (1.5)	15.3 (1.0)	15.2 (0.9)	16.4 (1.0)	19.4 (1.1)

Percentage of parents reporting the following reasons are "very important" in choosing a school for their child:

	The school adheres to a particular religious philosophy				The school has a particular approach to pedagogy				Other family members attend the school			
	Bottom ESCS quarter	Second ESCS quarter	Third ESCS quarter	Top ESCS quarter	Bottom ESCS quarter	Second ESCS quarter	Third ESCS quarter	Top ESCS quarter	Bottom ESCS quarter	Second ESCS quarter	Third ESCS quarter	Top ESCS quarter
	% S.E.	% S.E.	% S.E.	% S.E.	% S.E.	% S.E.	% S.E.	% S.E.	% S.E.	% S.E.	% S.E.	% S.E.
OECD												
Belgium (Flemish community)	4.1 (0.7)	2.8 (0.6)	3.3 (0.7)	5.7 (0.9)	2.6 (0.5)	1.5 (0.5)	1.6 (0.6)	1.8 (0.5)	4.2 (0.7)	3.9 (0.7)	4.1 (0.7)	6.2 (1.0)
Chile	15.4 (1.4)	17.2 (1.5)	17.1 (1.9)	18.7 (1.8)	10.2 (1.3)	13.3 (1.1)	12.6 (1.0)	12.3 (0.9)	23.8 (1.6)	19.1 (1.4)	17.4 (1.3)	16.3 (1.0)
Germany	5.4 (1.1)	3.2 (0.9)	3.9 (0.8)	3.8 (1.0)	3.2 (0.6)	4.4 (0.9)	4.7 (1.0)	4.6 (1.2)	4.8 (0.8)	5.1 (0.8)	4.9 (0.9)	3.6 (0.9)
Hungary	2.9 (0.8)	2.3 (0.7)	3.7 (1.1)	7.6 (2.0)	1.8 (0.3)	1.4 (0.4)	2.1 (0.6)	1.9 (0.5)	6.1 (1.0)	5.4 (0.9)	4.8 (0.9)	5.8 (1.0)
Italy	6.7 (0.4)	5.0 (0.4)	3.7 (0.3)	4.5 (0.6)	5.4 (0.4)	4.7 (0.4)	4.5 (0.4)	4.4 (0.3)	7.9 (0.6)	6.8 (0.5)	5.8 (0.4)	5.1 (0.4)
Korea	4.1 (0.7)	5.6 (0.7)	7.2 (0.9)	7.6 (1.1)	9.4 (0.9)	9.7 (1.0)	11.5 (1.1)	13.7 (1.2)	2.5 (0.4)	2.9 (0.5)	2.8 (0.5)	1.9 (0.4)
Mexico	3.9 (0.3)	3.7 (0.3)	4.3 (0.4)	8.2 (1.0)	14.3 (0.6)	19.3 (0.6)	22.8 (0.7)	27.6 (0.9)	20.4 (0.8)	17.9 (0.6)	17.8 (0.6)	16.4 (0.6)
Portugal	7.6 (0.9)	5.7 (1.0)	3.7 (0.9)	3.9 (0.9)	5.5 (0.8)	4.3 (0.7)	5.2 (0.8)	7.2 (1.1)	11.5 (1.2)	13.5 (1.3)	13.7 (1.3)	13.5 (1.1)
Partners												
Croatia	8.2 (0.9)	9.2 (1.1)	8.0 (0.9)	5.8 (0.9)	a a	a a	a a	a a	2.9 (0.5)	2.3 (0.5)	2.3 (0.4)	3.7 (0.5)
Hong Kong-China	6.0 (0.6)	5.9 (0.9)	6.1 (0.9)	10.9 (1.8)	9.8 (1.0)	8.2 (1.0)	8.6 (1.0)	11.9 (2.9)	4.5 (0.7)	3.3 (0.6)	2.7 (0.5)	2.8 (0.5)
Macao-China	3.5 (0.5)	2.9 (0.5)	3.2 (0.5)	4.6 (0.6)	13.0 (1.0)	12.9 (0.9)	14.8 (1.2)	17.9 (1.2)	5.7 (0.7)	4.2 (0.6)	6.3 (0.7)	6.5 (0.6)

Percentage of parents reporting the following reasons are "very important" in choosing a school for their child:

	Expenses are low (e.g. tuition, books, room and board)				The school has financial aid available, such as a school loan, scholarship, or grant				The school has an active and pleasant school climate			
	Bottom ESCS quarter	Second ESCS quarter	Third ESCS quarter	Top ESCS quarter	Bottom ESCS quarter	Second ESCS quarter	Third ESCS quarter	Top ESCS quarter	Bottom ESCS quarter	Second ESCS quarter	Third ESCS quarter	Top ESCS quarter
	% S.E.	% S.E.	% S.E.	% S.E.	% S.E.	% S.E.	% S.E.	% S.E.	% S.E.	% S.E.	% S.E.	% S.E.
OECD												
Belgium (Flemish community)	11.2 (1.2)	5.8 (0.9)	2.5 (0.7)	0.6 (0.2)	10.8 (1.1)	6.0 (0.9)	2.2 (0.6)	0.8 (0.3)	21.6 (1.4)	28.6 (1.7)	32.7 (1.5)	35.4 (1.9)
Chile	38.8 (2.0)	32.6 (1.4)	30.0 (1.5)	14.2 (1.2)	41.0 (1.8)	38.4 (1.6)	37.8 (1.5)	22.3 (1.5)	47.1 (1.9)	59.0 (1.7)	60.0 (1.7)	64.6 (1.3)
Germany	14.3 (1.2)	9.8 (1.3)	5.7 (1.0)	3.6 (0.8)	12.4 (1.3)	5.4 (0.9)	3.8 (0.7)	2.5 (0.6)	45.6 (1.7)	49.0 (2.2)	49.6 (2.0)	54.4 (2.4)
Hungary	21.2 (1.5)	14.1 (1.4)	8.5 (1.2)	3.8 (0.6)	15.8 (1.3)	8.3 (1.2)	5.6 (1.1)	2.5 (0.5)	15.7 (1.3)	18.2 (1.8)	19.6 (1.3)	19.6 (1.2)
Italy	14.2 (0.6)	11.2 (0.6)	9.5 (0.5)	5.7 (0.4)	a a	a a	a a	a a	31.4 (0.9)	33.0 (0.9)	34.4 (0.8)	35.0 (0.8)
Korea	20.5 (1.4)	15.8 (1.1)	12.7 (0.9)	9.2 (1.1)	26.9 (1.4)	22.3 (1.3)	15.4 (1.3)	9.7 (0.9)	44.2 (1.5)	51.3 (1.4)	53.3 (1.4)	54.7 (1.8)
Mexico	31.3 (0.9)	31.6 (0.9)	29.9 (0.8)	23.0 (0.8)	34.8 (1.0)	37.1 (0.8)	36.2 (0.8)	29.5 (0.9)	41.2 (0.9)	47.0 (0.9)	51.4 (1.1)	57.4 (0.8)
Portugal	32.2 (1.7)	33.3 (1.8)	26.2 (2.0)	16.1 (1.5)	31.1 (1.7)	32.6 (1.6)	24.7 (1.6)	9.9 (1.5)	40.6 (2.0)	50.1 (1.5)	51.8 (2.4)	56.5 (2.1)
Partners												
Croatia	22.7 (1.3)	15.2 (1.1)	14.0 (1.1)	7.3 (0.8)	18.6 (1.1)	12.7 (1.1)	12.0 (1.4)	5.7 (0.7)	31.0 (1.2)	31.0 (1.3)	31.9 (1.6)	39.1 (1.6)
Hong Kong-China	13.5 (1.0)	10.2 (1.1)	7.0 (1.1)	2.9 (0.7)	14.7 (1.1)	11.3 (1.1)	8.2 (1.1)	3.3 (0.8)	31.6 (1.4)	35.9 (1.8)	42.8 (1.6)	45.2 (2.1)
Macao-China	18.0 (1.1)	12.7 (1.0)	11.3 (1.0)	6.9 (0.7)	25.5 (1.3)	20.9 (1.2)	15.7 (1.0)	10.7 (0.8)	30.9 (1.2)	31.2 (1.3)	36.5 (1.5)	41.2 (1.2)

Percentage of parents reporting the following reasons are "very important" in choosing a school for their child:

	The academic achievements of students in the school are high				There is a safe school environment			
	Bottom ESCS quarter	Second ESCS quarter	Third ESCS quarter	Top ESCS quarter	Bottom ESCS quarter	Second ESCS quarter	Third ESCS quarter	Top ESCS quarter
	% S.E.	% S.E.	% S.E.	% S.E.	% S.E.	% S.E.	% S.E.	% S.E.
OECD								
Belgium (Flemish community)	12.2 (1.1)	13.2 (1.2)	15.1 (1.3)	20.9 (1.7)	37.7 (2.0)	38.3 (2.0)	33.6 (1.6)	36.1 (1.7)
Chile	41.2 (2.0)	47.7 (2.1)	52.3 (2.2)	48.8 (1.6)	55.9 (1.7)	63.8 (1.7)	68.1 (1.6)	73.2 (1.0)
Germany	31.4 (1.8)	29.4 (2.1)	26.8 (2.0)	21.3 (1.8)	56.5 (1.9)	56.4 (1.8)	53.0 (2.2)	48.6 (2.4)
Hungary	16.0 (1.3)	20.5 (1.4)	21.8 (2.1)	33.6 (2.0)	48.5 (2.0)	47.1 (1.6)	47.5 (2.1)	47.3 (1.8)
Italy	21.0 (0.7)	22.7 (0.7)	23.7 (0.7)	24.4 (0.7)	52.7 (0.8)	55.2 (0.8)	56.1 (0.9)	53.3 (0.9)
Korea	38.9 (1.7)	46.2 (1.7)	55.9 (2.0)	60.4 (1.8)	58.1 (1.4)	64.3 (1.5)	70.2 (1.5)	72.3 (1.5)
Mexico	35.3 (0.7)	42.7 (0.8)	47.8 (1.1)	54.0 (1.0)	48.3 (1.0)	55.3 (0.9)	60.0 (1.0)	66.1 (0.9)
Portugal	34.6 (2.2)	45.3 (1.8)	48.2 (2.1)	53.2 (1.9)	59.1 (2.1)	68.8 (1.8)	70.4 (2.3)	77.4 (1.8)
Partners								
Croatia	29.1 (1.4)	28.3 (1.4)	29.7 (1.4)	37.0 (1.3)	56.0 (1.5)	54.2 (1.4)	58.6 (1.6)	55.3 (1.5)
Hong Kong-China	26.2 (1.6)	29.3 (1.4)	31.5 (1.6)	31.3 (1.5)	58.9 (1.6)	58.0 (1.8)	65.2 (1.8)	68.6 (1.6)
Macao-China	28.6 (1.3)	30.6 (1.4)	32.5 (1.3)	32.6 (1.1)	57.6 (1.2)	60.4 (1.5)	62.7 (1.5)	64.3 (1.3)

Notes: Values that are statistically significant are indicated in bold (see Annex A3).
ESCS refers to the *PISA index of economic, social and cultural status* of students.
Only countries and economies with data from the parent questionnaire are shown.
StatLink ⛓ http://dx.doi.org/10.1787/888932957498

[Part 1/2]
Index of school management: Teacher participation and mathematics performance
Table IV.4.12   *Results based on school principals' reports*

		Index of school management: Teacher participation										Variability in this index	
		All students		Bottom quarter		Second quarter		Third quarter		Top quarter			
		Mean index	S.E.	Mean index	S.E.	Mean index	S.E.	Mean index	S.E.	Mean index	S.E.	Standard deviation	S.E.
OECD	Australia	0.51	(0.04)	-0.56	(0.05)	0.26	(0.04)	0.74	(0.04)	1.62	(0.07)	0.87	(0.03)
	Austria	-0.32	(0.07)	-1.47	(0.09)	-0.61	(0.10)	0.01	(0.07)	0.80	(0.12)	0.91	(0.05)
	Belgium	-0.39	(0.06)	-1.54	(0.08)	-0.78	(0.08)	-0.08	(0.07)	0.84	(0.09)	0.96	(0.04)
	Canada	0.28	(0.04)	-0.83	(0.06)	0.05	(0.04)	0.56	(0.05)	1.35	(0.07)	0.87	(0.03)
	Chile	0.39	(0.07)	-0.74	(0.11)	0.11	(0.08)	0.68	(0.08)	1.50	(0.11)	0.89	(0.05)
	Czech Republic	-0.26	(0.08)	-1.46	(0.15)	-0.53	(0.07)	-0.01	(0.11)	0.95	(0.13)	0.99	(0.09)
	Denmark	-0.01	(0.06)	-0.95	(0.11)	-0.22	(0.04)	0.23	(0.07)	0.93	(0.09)	0.77	(0.05)
	Estonia	-0.08	(0.05)	-0.98	(0.05)	-0.40	(0.05)	0.11	(0.06)	0.95	(0.11)	0.78	(0.05)
	Finland	0.03	(0.06)	-1.03	(0.11)	-0.21	(0.07)	0.32	(0.06)	1.03	(0.12)	0.85	(0.06)
	France	-0.78	(0.07)	-1.84	(0.06)	-1.16	(0.07)	-0.60	(0.08)	0.50	(0.16)	0.96	(0.05)
	Germany	0.03	(0.05)	-0.94	(0.09)	-0.14	(0.08)	0.32	(0.05)	0.87	(0.06)	0.72	(0.04)
	Greece	0.07	(0.07)	-1.08	(0.09)	-0.31	(0.09)	0.36	(0.08)	1.31	(0.10)	0.96	(0.05)
	Hungary	-0.48	(0.06)	-1.36	(0.09)	-0.77	(0.09)	-0.24	(0.05)	0.44	(0.09)	0.73	(0.05)
	Iceland	-0.04	(0.00)	-0.86	(0.00)	-0.32	(0.01)	0.14	(0.00)	0.89	(0.00)	0.70	(0.00)
	Ireland	0.09	(0.10)	-1.26	(0.15)	-0.29	(0.10)	0.43	(0.13)	1.49	(0.12)	1.10	(0.07)
	Israel	-0.24	(0.07)	-1.53	(0.13)	-0.48	(0.09)	0.17	(0.09)	0.90	(0.08)	0.95	(0.06)
	Italy	0.30	(0.04)	-0.92	(0.07)	-0.05	(0.05)	0.52	(0.05)	1.65	(0.06)	1.01	(0.03)
	Japan	-0.42	(0.07)	-1.80	(0.18)	-0.50	(0.07)	-0.01	(0.06)	0.64	(0.08)	1.00	(0.07)
	Korea	0.06	(0.09)	-1.27	(0.15)	-0.14	(0.13)	0.37	(0.08)	1.26	(0.11)	1.03	(0.07)
	Luxembourg	-0.56	(0.00)	-1.65	(0.00)	-0.81	(0.00)	-0.29	(0.00)	0.50	(0.00)	0.92	(0.00)
	Mexico	-0.11	(0.04)	-1.52	(0.04)	-0.52	(0.06)	0.28	(0.05)	1.32	(0.05)	1.12	(0.02)
	Netherlands	-0.19	(0.07)	-1.20	(0.10)	-0.40	(0.08)	0.05	(0.06)	0.80	(0.13)	0.80	(0.06)
	New Zealand	0.22	(0.07)	-0.89	(0.10)	0.02	(0.07)	0.47	(0.07)	1.30	(0.12)	0.90	(0.05)
	Norway	-0.02	(0.06)	-1.02	(0.13)	-0.18	(0.04)	0.20	(0.07)	0.92	(0.11)	0.80	(0.06)
	Poland	-0.34	(0.07)	-1.37	(0.06)	-0.65	(0.10)	-0.14	(0.06)	0.78	(0.13)	0.85	(0.05)
	Portugal	0.39	(0.09)	-0.81	(0.13)	0.05	(0.08)	0.63	(0.12)	1.69	(0.16)	1.01	(0.08)
	Slovak Republic	-0.14	(0.06)	-1.11	(0.08)	-0.38	(0.09)	0.09	(0.04)	0.82	(0.10)	0.77	(0.04)
	Slovenia	0.12	(0.01)	-1.00	(0.04)	-0.11	(0.01)	0.38	(0.01)	1.21	(0.02)	0.89	(0.02)
	Spain	0.00	(0.05)	-1.13	(0.05)	-0.33	(0.05)	0.26	(0.06)	1.21	(0.09)	0.94	(0.04)
	Sweden	0.06	(0.06)	-0.87	(0.09)	-0.16	(0.05)	0.29	(0.07)	1.00	(0.09)	0.75	(0.04)
	Switzerland	-0.60	(0.06)	-1.66	(0.08)	-0.85	(0.05)	-0.35	(0.07)	0.45	(0.08)	0.83	(0.03)
	Turkey	0.92	(0.08)	-0.38	(0.13)	0.49	(0.10)	1.29	(0.15)	2.26	(0.02)	1.03	(0.05)
	United Kingdom	0.39	(0.07)	-0.80	(0.10)	0.15	(0.09)	0.65	(0.07)	1.56	(0.11)	0.92	(0.05)
	United States	0.54	(0.09)	-0.63	(0.15)	0.23	(0.09)	0.78	(0.11)	1.77	(0.11)	0.99	(0.08)
	OECD average	-0.02	(0.01)	-1.13	(0.02)	-0.29	(0.01)	0.25	(0.01)	1.10	(0.02)	0.90	(0.01)
Partners	Albania	0.26	(0.08)	-0.99	(0.14)	0.01	(0.07)	0.54	(0.11)	1.47	(0.11)	0.99	(0.08)
	Argentina	0.17	(0.08)	-1.28	(0.13)	-0.12	(0.10)	0.50	(0.10)	1.60	(0.12)	1.12	(0.05)
	Brazil	0.65	(0.06)	-0.82	(0.09)	0.38	(0.07)	1.05	(0.06)	2.00	(0.07)	1.12	(0.04)
	Bulgaria	0.26	(0.06)	-0.69	(0.08)	0.04	(0.06)	0.40	(0.06)	1.31	(0.11)	0.81	(0.05)
	Colombia	0.46	(0.08)	-0.98	(0.13)	0.22	(0.11)	0.83	(0.07)	1.75	(0.12)	1.10	(0.07)
	Costa Rica	-0.06	(0.08)	-1.64	(0.13)	-0.27	(0.12)	0.28	(0.07)	1.39	(0.12)	1.20	(0.07)
	Croatia	0.09	(0.07)	-1.02	(0.11)	-0.17	(0.07)	0.30	(0.05)	1.24	(0.15)	0.90	(0.05)
	Cyprus*	0.63	(0.00)	-0.40	(0.00)	0.35	(0.00)	0.75	(0.00)	1.81	(0.00)	0.89	(0.00)
	Hong Kong-China	-0.12	(0.07)	-1.11	(0.10)	-0.42	(0.09)	0.12	(0.06)	0.95	(0.12)	0.83	(0.05)
	Indonesia	0.31	(0.08)	-0.94	(0.14)	0.12	(0.06)	0.46	(0.07)	1.58	(0.15)	1.02	(0.07)
	Jordan	0.64	(0.09)	-0.87	(0.14)	0.27	(0.10)	1.02	(0.12)	2.14	(0.08)	1.17	(0.05)
	Kazakhstan	0.41	(0.07)	-0.70	(0.08)	0.09	(0.10)	0.68	(0.06)	1.59	(0.12)	0.91	(0.05)
	Latvia	0.11	(0.07)	-0.95	(0.07)	-0.21	(0.08)	0.40	(0.09)	1.21	(0.09)	0.86	(0.04)
	Liechtenstein	-0.14	(0.01)	c	c	c	c	c	c	c	c	0.58	(0.03)
	Lithuania	-0.18	(0.06)	-1.23	(0.08)	-0.53	(0.05)	0.06	(0.08)	0.97	(0.10)	0.87	(0.05)
	Macao-China	-0.48	(0.00)	-1.28	(0.00)	-0.70	(0.00)	-0.41	(0.00)	0.46	(0.00)	0.75	(0.00)
	Malaysia	0.62	(0.08)	-0.53	(0.09)	0.22	(0.08)	0.82	(0.11)	1.99	(0.12)	0.98	(0.05)
	Montenegro	0.46	(0.00)	-1.01	(0.00)	0.07	(0.00)	0.82	(0.01)	1.95	(0.01)	1.14	(0.00)
	Peru	-0.32	(0.09)	-1.69	(0.12)	-0.72	(0.11)	0.04	(0.10)	1.09	(0.12)	1.10	(0.05)
	Qatar	0.22	(0.00)	-1.18	(0.00)	-0.14	(0.00)	0.48	(0.00)	1.72	(0.00)	1.12	(0.00)
	Romania	-0.73	(0.09)	-2.94	(0.15)	-1.45	(0.13)	0.04	(0.11)	1.44	(0.13)	1.73	(0.07)
	Russian Federation	-0.03	(0.05)	-1.04	(0.09)	-0.22	(0.06)	0.22	(0.06)	0.93	(0.07)	0.78	(0.03)
	Serbia	-0.01	(0.07)	-1.00	(0.07)	-0.37	(0.09)	0.15	(0.07)	1.18	(0.16)	0.87	(0.06)
	Shanghai-China	-0.79	(0.06)	-1.67	(0.05)	-1.12	(0.10)	-0.55	(0.08)	0.19	(0.09)	0.77	(0.04)
	Singapore	0.19	(0.00)	-0.74	(0.00)	-0.13	(0.01)	0.32	(0.00)	1.31	(0.01)	0.82	(0.00)
	Chinese Taipei	-0.06	(0.08)	-1.37	(0.14)	-0.36	(0.09)	0.26	(0.07)	1.24	(0.14)	1.04	(0.06)
	Thailand	0.59	(0.08)	-0.74	(0.14)	0.28	(0.05)	0.88	(0.10)	1.93	(0.11)	1.04	(0.05)
	Tunisia	-0.19	(0.10)	-1.65	(0.13)	-0.74	(0.10)	0.22	(0.16)	1.43	(0.12)	1.23	(0.06)
	United Arab Emirates	0.34	(0.06)	-0.93	(0.09)	0.07	(0.05)	0.56	(0.07)	1.65	(0.09)	1.05	(0.03)
	Uruguay	0.50	(0.08)	-1.01	(0.15)	0.27	(0.10)	0.90	(0.08)	1.82	(0.11)	1.11	(0.06)
	Viet Nam	-0.27	(0.07)	-1.46	(0.15)	-0.42	(0.08)	0.08	(0.06)	0.70	(0.12)	0.91	(0.07)

Note: Values that are statistically significant are indicated in bold (see Annex A3).
* See notes at the beginning of this Annex.
StatLink ⟨⟩ http://dx.doi.org/10.1787/888932957498

[Part 2/2]
Index of school management: Teacher participation and mathematics performance
Table IV.4.12   *Results based on school principals' reports*

| | Performance on the mathematics scale by national quarters of this index | | | | | | | | Change in the mathematics score per unit of this index | | Increased likelihood of students in the bottom quarter of this index scoring in the bottom quarter of the national mathematics performance distribution | | Explained variance in student performance (r-squared x 100) | |
| | Bottom quarter | | Second quarter | | Third quarter | | Top quarter | | | | | | | |
	Mean score	S.E.	Mean score	S.E.	Mean score	S.E.	Mean score	S.E.	Score dif.	S.E.	Ratio	S.E.	%	S.E.
Australia	**513**	(4.0)	508	(4.6)	500	(3.8)	**496**	(4.2)	**-6.3**	(2.6)	**0.8**	(0.1)	0.3	(0.3)
Austria	511	(10.4)	509	(8.3)	503	(8.5)	498	(8.8)	-5.0	(6.1)	1.0	(0.2)	0.2	(0.6)
Belgium	515	(8.3)	508	(7.3)	532	(8.9)	507	(7.6)	-3.2	(4.9)	1.1	(0.1)	0.1	(0.3)
Canada	522	(3.6)	517	(3.7)	521	(4.7)	513	(3.7)	**-4.7**	(2.2)	0.9	(0.1)	0.2	(0.2)
Chile	415	(6.9)	432	(7.9)	416	(7.2)	426	(7.0)	1.1	(4.0)	1.1	(0.1)	0.0	(0.2)
Czech Republic	504	(8.9)	490	(8.6)	503	(9.6)	496	(9.5)	2.0	(5.3)	0.9	(0.2)	0.0	(0.3)
Denmark	502	(5.3)	500	(4.0)	498	(5.6)	497	(6.0)	-2.7	(3.7)	1.0	(0.1)	0.1	(0.2)
Estonia	516	(4.3)	518	(4.8)	527	(5.4)	522	(5.0)	2.6	(2.7)	1.0	(0.1)	0.1	(0.1)
Finland	**526**	(3.6)	520	(3.2)	516	(3.9)	**512**	(4.5)	**-5.7**	(2.0)	**0.9**	(0.1)	0.3	(0.2)
France	481	(8.6)	502	(8.9)	520	(8.9)	480	(11.7)	-0.4	(6.7)	1.2	(0.2)	0.0	(0.4)
Germany	510	(10.9)	509	(8.2)	511	(11.8)	525	(8.8)	5.6	(7.1)	1.1	(0.2)	0.2	(0.5)
Greece	**463**	(5.8)	456	(6.3)	453	(6.8)	**440**	(7.9)	**-10.6**	(3.7)	0.8	(0.1)	1.3	(0.9)
Hungary	**488**	(9.5)	478	(12.8)	492	(11.3)	**453**	(7.2)	**-17.1**	(6.2)	0.8	(0.1)	1.8	(1.4)
Iceland	486	(3.7)	490	(3.5)	494	(3.3)	**504**	(3.4)	8.7	(2.1)	**1.2**	(0.1)	0.4	(0.2)
Ireland	508	(5.7)	504	(6.7)	492	(7.2)	500	(7.7)	-3.2	(3.4)	0.8	(0.1)	0.2	(0.5)
Israel	471	(12.4)	478	(10.6)	458	(12.5)	464	(11.1)	-5.0	(7.5)	1.0	(0.2)	0.2	(0.7)
Italy	487	(5.9)	488	(4.8)	492	(5.6)	481	(5.1)	-1.8	(2.7)	1.0	(0.1)	0.0	(0.2)
Japan	542	(9.9)	516	(9.3)	545	(9.5)	544	(7.1)	5.3	(4.3)	0.9	(0.1)	0.3	(0.5)
Korea	552	(9.3)	561	(9.1)	555	(10.1)	544	(8.8)	-3.0	(6.0)	1.0	(0.2)	0.1	(0.5)
Luxembourg	482	(2.5)	498	(3.5)	489	(2.8)	497	(2.4)	9.0	(1.1)	1.1	(0.1)	0.8	(0.2)
Mexico	**428**	(3.16)	414	(2.96)	407	(3.1)	405	(3.1)	-7.4	(1.3)	**0.6**	(0.1)	1.2	(0.5)
Netherlands	519	(12.3)	514	(9.9)	518	(10.6)	534	(15.1)	1.5	(8.5)	1.1	(0.3)	0.0	(0.5)
New Zealand	507	(11.3)	502	(7.2)	500	(7.1)	497	(7.5)	-7.7	(6.4)	1.0	(0.2)	0.5	(0.8)
Norway	488	(6.8)	494	(5.7)	494	(5.9)	486	(4.1)	-1.9	(3.5)	1.1	(0.1)	0.0	(0.1)
Poland	526	(5.7)	511	(6.9)	518	(10.5)	517	(7.3)	-1.3	(3.4)	0.9	(0.1)	0.0	(0.1)
Portugal	486	(7.6)	479	(8.3)	504	(7.3)	476	(10.0)	-1.7	(5.5)	1.0	(0.1)	0.0	(0.3)
Slovak Republic	487	(9.6)	481	(8.4)	486	(10.9)	472	(10.3)	-4.8	(8.3)	0.9	(0.1)	0.1	(0.5)
Slovenia	**515**	(3.2)	514	(4.0)	504	(3.9)	**485**	(3.0)	**-13.0**	(2.1)	0.8	(0.1)	1.6	(0.5)
Spain	**490**	(3.6)	485	(4.0)	490	(4.0)	**473**	(5.3)	**-6.5**	(2.4)	0.9	(0.1)	0.5	(0.4)
Sweden	478	(5.1)	474	(4.9)	475	(5.4)	488	(6.2)	1.6	(3.4)	1.1	(0.1)	0.0	(0.1)
Switzerland	531	(7.0)	549	(7.3)	533	(9.6)	517	(5.9)	-6.6	(4.1)	1.0	(0.1)	0.3	(0.4)
Turkey	439	(9.1)	455	(9.8)	462	(12.5)	438	(9.1)	-0.9	(5.3)	1.1	(0.1)	0.0	(0.4)
United Kingdom	**507**	(8.1)	498	(8.6)	485	(12.0)	**487**	(5.7)	**-11.0**	(3.3)	0.8	(0.1)	1.2	(0.7)
United States	483	(8.4)	475	(8.3)	481	(9.6)	492	(7.4)	3.7	(4.2)	0.9	(0.1)	0.2	(0.3)
OECD average	**496**	(1.3)	495	(1.2)	496	(1.4)	**490**	(1.3)	**-2.7**	(0.8)	1.0	(0.0)	0.4	(0.1)
Albania	395	(4.6)	399	(5.3)	389	(4.9)	394	(4.8)	0.2	(2.4)	1.0	(0.1)	0.0	(0.1)
Argentina	394	(7.5)	397	(6.4)	388	(8.3)	383	(8.0)	-2.8	(3.5)	0.9	(0.1)	0.2	(0.5)
Brazil	396	(5.1)	386	(4.3)	390	(5.1)	394	(5.0)	1.0	(2.6)	1.0	(0.1)	0.0	(0.2)
Bulgaria	434	(9.9)	450	(9.9)	442	(8.2)	432	(10.4)	-1.7	(5.9)	1.0	(0.2)	0.0	(0.3)
Colombia	373	(6.8)	381	(8.1)	375	(7.4)	377	(6.5)	1.3	(3.0)	1.1	(0.1)	0.0	(0.2)
Costa Rica	413	(8.0)	401	(6.6)	409	(7.4)	406	(8.3)	-0.7	(3.3)	0.9	(0.2)	0.0	(0.2)
Croatia	474	(7.5)	479	(8.2)	470	(12.7)	463	(8.5)	-5.5	(4.9)	0.9	(0.1)	0.3	(0.6)
Cyprus*	**460**	(2.0)	450	(2.8)	421	(2.5)	**427**	(2.7)	**-17.6**	(1.2)	0.7	(0.0)	2.8	(0.4)
Hong Kong-China	558	(7.8)	563	(9.8)	569	(9.4)	555	(10.0)	6.0	(6.5)	1.1	(0.2)	0.3	(0.7)
Indonesia	374	(11.2)	367	(7.1)	364	(5.7)	398	(10.5)	10.6	(4.6)	1.2	(0.2)	2.3	(2.1)
Jordan	398	(6.5)	378	(6.3)	386	(10.9)	378	(7.6)	-4.0	(3.1)	**0.7**	(0.1)	0.4	(0.6)
Kazakhstan	430	(7.0)	425	(6.0)	435	(8.6)	438	(6.8)	2.2	(4.4)	1.0	(0.1)	0.1	(0.5)
Latvia	483	(6.7)	487	(5.1)	499	(6.7)	485	(5.9)	2.2	(4.1)	1.1	(0.2)	0.1	(0.3)
Liechtenstein	c	c	c	c	c	c	c	c	**-75.0**	(8.2)	0.3	(0.2)	22.4	(3.3)
Lithuania	481	(6.0)	485	(6.4)	469	(7.2)	481	(6.4)	0.3	(3.9)	0.9	(0.1)	0.0	(0.1)
Macao-China	541	(2.0)	542	(2.3)	563	(2.1)	507	(2.0)	-7.8	(1.3)	0.9	(0.1)	0.4	(0.1)
Malaysia	**436**	(7.4)	420	(7.6)	412	(5.4)	**412**	(6.9)	**-8.1**	(3.6)	**0.7**	(0.1)	1.0	(0.9)
Montenegro	**411**	(2.4)	419	(2.4)	417	(2.2)	**391**	(2.2)	-2.6	(1.0)	0.8	(0.1)	0.1	(0.1)
Peru	362	(6.4)	366	(6.3)	373	(7.9)	371	(9.6)	3.3	(3.9)	1.1	(0.1)	0.2	(0.4)
Qatar	**397**	(1.3)	355	(1.6)	377	(1.4)	377	(1.6)	-7.7	(0.6)	**0.6**	(0.0)	0.8	(0.1)
Romania	448	(8.5)	444	(8.1)	436	(8.3)	451	(9.4)	0.0	(2.7)	0.9	(0.1)	0.0	(0.3)
Russian Federation	477	(7.1)	476	(5.5)	492	(7.6)	485	(5.1)	4.3	(4.0)	1.1	(0.1)	0.2	(0.3)
Serbia	455	(9.0)	446	(11.0)	453	(8.6)	441	(9.5)	-4.1	(5.6)	0.9	(0.2)	0.2	(0.5)
Shanghai-China	598	(9.8)	617	(9.0)	611	(10.7)	625	(9.2)	8.4	(7.0)	1.3	(0.2)	0.4	(0.7)
Singapore	573	(2.6)	568	(3.0)	572	(2.8)	573	(2.5)	1.8	(1.4)	1.0	(0.1)	0.0	(0.0)
Chinese Taipei	567	(8.7)	556	(11.9)	548	(12.8)	561	(10.4)	-4.2	(5.4)	**0.8**	(0.1)	0.1	(0.3)
Thailand	**411**	(6.8)	424	(7.5)	432	(9.0)	**440**	(7.3)	11.0	(3.4)	**1.4**	(0.2)	1.9	(1.3)
Tunisia	395	(9.8)	395	(10.0)	388	(8.4)	370	(6.4)	-3.8	(3.5)	0.9	(0.2)	0.4	(0.7)
United Arab Emirates	**447**	(5.9)	446	(6.4)	422	(5.6)	**422**	(4.2)	**-10.4**	(2.2)	**0.8**	(0.1)	1.5	(0.7)
Uruguay	**437**	(9.0)	418	(9.3)	391	(7.2)	**392**	(8.6)	**-17.5**	(3.7)	**0.6**	(0.1)	4.8	(2.0)
Viet Nam	511	(9.3)	516	(10.2)	516	(9.5)	502	(9.0)	-0.3	(6.1)	1.0	(0.2)	0.0	(0.4)

Note: Values that are statistically significant are indicated in bold (see Annex A3).
* See notes at the beginning of this Annex.
StatLink ⇒ http://dx.doi.org/10.1787/888932957498

[Part 1/1]

Table IV.4.16 Correlation between indices of school management

Results based on school principals' reports

		Correlation between:											
		Index of school management: Framing and communicating the school's goals and curricular development and…						Index of school management: Instructional leadership and…				Index of school management: Promoting instructional improvements and professional development and…	
		Index of school management: Instructional leadership		Index of school management: Promoting instructional improvements and professional development		Index of school management: Teacher participation		Index of school management: Promoting instructional improvements and professional development		Index of school management: Teacher participation		Index of school management: Teacher participation	
		Corr.	S.E.	Corr.	S.E.	Corr.	S.E.	Corr.	S.E.	Corr.	S.E.	Corr.	S.E.
OECD	Australia	**0.68**	(0.02)	**0.49**	(0.03)	**0.64**	(0.03)	**0.57**	(0.02)	**0.64**	(0.02)	**0.55**	(0.02)
	Austria	**0.67**	(0.05)	**0.42**	(0.07)	**0.64**	(0.05)	**0.58**	(0.07)	**0.69**	(0.05)	**0.53**	(0.05)
	Belgium	**0.68**	(0.04)	**0.52**	(0.04)	**0.51**	(0.05)	**0.59**	(0.05)	**0.62**	(0.03)	**0.51**	(0.05)
	Canada	**0.58**	(0.03)	**0.35**	(0.04)	**0.54**	(0.04)	**0.54**	(0.04)	**0.63**	(0.03)	**0.45**	(0.04)
	Chile	**0.69**	(0.05)	**0.59**	(0.05)	**0.61**	(0.05)	**0.67**	(0.04)	**0.67**	(0.04)	**0.68**	(0.03)
	Czech Republic	**0.68**	(0.04)	**0.50**	(0.06)	**0.60**	(0.05)	**0.51**	(0.06)	**0.49**	(0.06)	**0.38**	(0.07)
	Denmark	**0.63**	(0.06)	**0.36**	(0.05)	**0.42**	(0.07)	**0.46**	(0.05)	**0.46**	(0.06)	0.21	(0.11)
	Estonia	**0.66**	(0.03)	**0.43**	(0.07)	**0.44**	(0.04)	**0.61**	(0.04)	**0.53**	(0.04)	**0.38**	(0.05)
	Finland	**0.66**	(0.04)	**0.58**	(0.05)	**0.55**	(0.05)	**0.60**	(0.04)	**0.58**	(0.05)	**0.50**	(0.06)
	France	**0.59**	(0.06)	**0.54**	(0.05)	**0.62**	(0.05)	**0.50**	(0.05)	**0.58**	(0.05)	**0.50**	(0.06)
	Germany	**0.70**	(0.03)	**0.41**	(0.06)	**0.52**	(0.05)	**0.53**	(0.05)	**0.53**	(0.05)	**0.43**	(0.06)
	Greece	**0.73**	(0.04)	**0.56**	(0.06)	**0.66**	(0.05)	**0.59**	(0.05)	**0.70**	(0.04)	**0.57**	(0.05)
	Hungary	**0.67**	(0.05)	**0.36**	(0.07)	**0.59**	(0.05)	**0.51**	(0.06)	**0.56**	(0.05)	**0.45**	(0.05)
	Iceland	**0.70**	(0.00)	**0.54**	(0.00)	**0.65**	(0.00)	**0.54**	(0.00)	**0.66**	(0.00)	**0.48**	(0.00)
	Ireland	**0.70**	(0.06)	**0.54**	(0.06)	**0.56**	(0.06)	**0.60**	(0.05)	**0.62**	(0.05)	**0.58**	(0.06)
	Israel	**0.61**	(0.04)	**0.35**	(0.07)	**0.45**	(0.07)	**0.52**	(0.05)	**0.53**	(0.05)	**0.43**	(0.06)
	Italy	**0.71**	(0.02)	**0.49**	(0.03)	**0.58**	(0.03)	**0.66**	(0.03)	**0.70**	(0.03)	**0.53**	(0.04)
	Japan	**0.72**	(0.04)	**0.39**	(0.07)	**0.52**	(0.07)	**0.53**	(0.05)	**0.47**	(0.07)	**0.50**	(0.06)
	Korea	**0.80**	(0.03)	**0.68**	(0.04)	**0.66**	(0.06)	**0.78**	(0.03)	**0.62**	(0.09)	**0.68**	(0.06)
	Luxembourg	**0.62**	(0.00)	**0.52**	(0.00)	**0.28**	(0.00)	**0.25**	(0.00)	**0.37**	(0.00)	**0.12**	(0.00)
	Mexico	**0.75**	(0.01)	**0.56**	(0.02)	**0.62**	(0.03)	**0.62**	(0.02)	**0.60**	(0.03)	**0.58**	(0.03)
	Netherlands	**0.71**	(0.05)	**0.40**	(0.08)	**0.57**	(0.07)	**0.50**	(0.05)	**0.68**	(0.04)	**0.43**	(0.07)
	New Zealand	**0.75**	(0.03)	**0.52**	(0.06)	**0.64**	(0.04)	**0.59**	(0.05)	**0.69**	(0.04)	**0.53**	(0.06)
	Norway	**0.62**	(0.05)	**0.56**	(0.04)	**0.58**	(0.06)	**0.65**	(0.04)	**0.56**	(0.06)	**0.48**	(0.05)
	Poland	**0.54**	(0.07)	**0.31**	(0.08)	**0.58**	(0.06)	**0.49**	(0.06)	**0.55**	(0.06)	**0.40**	(0.08)
	Portugal	**0.59**	(0.09)	**0.54**	(0.09)	**0.63**	(0.07)	**0.67**	(0.05)	**0.62**	(0.05)	**0.63**	(0.05)
	Slovak Republic	**0.67**	(0.04)	**0.42**	(0.05)	**0.59**	(0.06)	**0.56**	(0.04)	**0.61**	(0.06)	**0.44**	(0.07)
	Slovenia	**0.63**	(0.01)	**0.45**	(0.01)	**0.65**	(0.01)	**0.59**	(0.01)	**0.70**	(0.02)	**0.59**	(0.01)
	Spain	**0.64**	(0.04)	**0.38**	(0.06)	**0.60**	(0.04)	**0.53**	(0.05)	**0.65**	(0.03)	**0.52**	(0.04)
	Sweden	**0.66**	(0.05)	**0.48**	(0.06)	**0.56**	(0.05)	**0.50**	(0.06)	**0.58**	(0.05)	**0.43**	(0.05)
	Switzerland	**0.53**	(0.05)	**0.50**	(0.05)	**0.27**	(0.07)	**0.49**	(0.06)	**0.48**	(0.04)	**0.28**	(0.07)
	Turkey	**0.74**	(0.03)	**0.59**	(0.05)	**0.71**	(0.04)	**0.65**	(0.05)	**0.69**	(0.05)	**0.63**	(0.07)
	United Kingdom	**0.74**	(0.03)	**0.55**	(0.07)	**0.65**	(0.05)	**0.56**	(0.07)	**0.66**	(0.04)	**0.55**	(0.06)
	United States	**0.75**	(0.06)	**0.53**	(0.10)	**0.71**	(0.07)	**0.64**	(0.10)	**0.69**	(0.06)	**0.60**	(0.08)
	OECD average	**0.67**	(0.01)	**0.48**	(0.01)	**0.57**	(0.01)	**0.56**	(0.01)	**0.60**	(0.01)	**0.49**	(0.01)
Partners	Albania	**0.54**	(0.06)	**0.38**	(0.07)	**0.52**	(0.09)	**0.44**	(0.08)	**0.46**	(0.14)	**0.56**	(0.06)
	Argentina	**0.68**	(0.04)	**0.47**	(0.08)	**0.57**	(0.05)	**0.58**	(0.05)	**0.55**	(0.05)	**0.40**	(0.07)
	Brazil	**0.68**	(0.03)	**0.47**	(0.04)	**0.61**	(0.03)	**0.53**	(0.04)	**0.63**	(0.03)	**0.48**	(0.04)
	Bulgaria	**0.57**	(0.06)	**0.28**	(0.07)	**0.45**	(0.06)	**0.27**	(0.08)	**0.50**	(0.07)	**0.25**	(0.09)
	Colombia	**0.76**	(0.04)	**0.53**	(0.06)	**0.62**	(0.07)	**0.65**	(0.05)	**0.67**	(0.04)	**0.59**	(0.07)
	Costa Rica	**0.82**	(0.02)	**0.68**	(0.03)	**0.72**	(0.04)	**0.70**	(0.03)	**0.74**	(0.03)	**0.73**	(0.03)
	Croatia	**0.61**	(0.07)	**0.51**	(0.06)	**0.52**	(0.07)	**0.55**	(0.07)	**0.66**	(0.05)	**0.56**	(0.08)
	Cyprus*	**0.72**	(0.00)	**0.57**	(0.00)	**0.50**	(0.00)	**0.47**	(0.00)	**0.59**	(0.00)	**0.48**	(0.00)
	Hong Kong-China	**0.64**	(0.06)	**0.58**	(0.06)	**0.61**	(0.05)	**0.66**	(0.08)	**0.66**	(0.06)	**0.68**	(0.05)
	Indonesia	**0.77**	(0.04)	**0.65**	(0.05)	**0.71**	(0.04)	**0.71**	(0.04)	**0.72**	(0.04)	**0.73**	(0.04)
	Jordan	**0.71**	(0.04)	**0.49**	(0.07)	**0.60**	(0.05)	**0.63**	(0.06)	**0.67**	(0.05)	**0.66**	(0.06)
	Kazakhstan	**0.61**	(0.04)	**0.28**	(0.07)	**0.54**	(0.05)	**0.35**	(0.06)	**0.60**	(0.05)	**0.47**	(0.06)
	Latvia	**0.62**	(0.05)	**0.32**	(0.06)	**0.65**	(0.04)	**0.52**	(0.06)	**0.67**	(0.03)	**0.46**	(0.05)
	Liechtenstein	**0.60**	(0.02)	**0.70**	(0.02)	**0.28**	(0.02)	**0.79**	(0.01)	**0.81**	(0.02)	**0.53**	(0.02)
	Lithuania	**0.55**	(0.05)	**0.35**	(0.07)	**0.46**	(0.06)	**0.53**	(0.04)	**0.58**	(0.05)	**0.42**	(0.06)
	Macao-China	**0.63**	(0.00)	**0.50**	(0.00)	**0.56**	(0.00)	**0.47**	(0.00)	**0.57**	(0.00)	**0.40**	(0.00)
	Malaysia	**0.73**	(0.04)	**0.72**	(0.04)	**0.72**	(0.04)	**0.73**	(0.05)	**0.69**	(0.04)	**0.70**	(0.04)
	Montenegro	**0.69**	(0.00)	**0.42**	(0.00)	**0.75**	(0.00)	**0.65**	(0.00)	**0.81**	(0.00)	**0.71**	(0.00)
	Peru	**0.78**	(0.03)	**0.59**	(0.05)	**0.70**	(0.03)	**0.68**	(0.04)	**0.73**	(0.03)	**0.72**	(0.04)
	Qatar	**0.75**	(0.00)	**0.52**	(0.00)	**0.47**	(0.00)	**0.62**	(0.00)	**0.66**	(0.00)	**0.67**	(0.00)
	Romania	**0.88**	(0.01)	**0.81**	(0.02)	**0.87**	(0.02)	**0.83**	(0.02)	**0.87**	(0.02)	**0.83**	(0.02)
	Russian Federation	**0.59**	(0.05)	**0.45**	(0.06)	**0.52**	(0.05)	**0.58**	(0.05)	**0.56**	(0.06)	**0.48**	(0.05)
	Serbia	**0.70**	(0.05)	**0.53**	(0.08)	**0.68**	(0.04)	**0.58**	(0.06)	**0.71**	(0.04)	**0.62**	(0.06)
	Shanghai-China	**0.52**	(0.05)	**0.51**	(0.05)	**0.56**	(0.06)	**0.70**	(0.05)	**0.57**	(0.03)	**0.51**	(0.05)
	Singapore	**0.69**	(0.01)	**0.54**	(0.01)	**0.55**	(0.02)	**0.67**	(0.00)	**0.63**	(0.00)	**0.52**	(0.01)
	Chinese Taipei	**0.75**	(0.05)	**0.50**	(0.09)	**0.59**	(0.07)	**0.76**	(0.04)	**0.75**	(0.04)	**0.73**	(0.05)
	Thailand	**0.83**	(0.03)	**0.64**	(0.06)	**0.77**	(0.04)	**0.72**	(0.05)	**0.80**	(0.03)	**0.74**	(0.04)
	Tunisia	**0.62**	(0.06)	**0.32**	(0.08)	**0.56**	(0.06)	**0.47**	(0.07)	**0.58**	(0.06)	**0.44**	(0.08)
	United Arab Emirates	**0.78**	(0.02)	**0.48**	(0.05)	**0.55**	(0.03)	**0.54**	(0.05)	**0.61**	(0.03)	**0.39**	(0.05)
	Uruguay	**0.51**	(0.07)	**0.34**	(0.07)	**0.53**	(0.07)	**0.47**	(0.06)	**0.53**	(0.06)	**0.44**	(0.07)
	Viet Nam	**0.66**	(0.05)	**0.52**	(0.06)	**0.56**	(0.08)	**0.58**	(0.06)	**0.63**	(0.06)	**0.44**	(0.07)

Note: Values that are statistically significant are indicated in bold (see Annex A3).
* See notes at the beginning of this Annex.

StatLink http://dx.doi.org/10.1787/888932957498

[Part 1/1]

Table IV.4.17 Parental involvement

Results based on school principals' reports

		School principals' report on the percentage of students' parents who participated in the following school-related activities during the previous academic year:																									
		Discussed their child's behaviour with a teacher on their own initiative		Discussed their child's behaviour on the initiative of one of their child's teachers		Discussed their child's progress with a teacher on their own initiative		Discussed their child's progress on the initiative of one of their child's teachers		Volunteered in physical activities, e.g. building maintenance, carpentry, gardening or yard work		Volunteered in extracurricular activities, e.g. book club, school play, sports, field trip		Volunteered in the school library or media centre		Assisted a teacher in the school		Appeared as a guest speaker		Participated in local school government, e.g. parent council or school-management committee		Assisted in fundraising for the school		Volunteered in the school canteen	
		Mean %	S.E.	Mean %	S.E.	Mean %	S.E.	Mean %	S.E.	Mean %	S.E.	Mean %	S.E.	Mean %	S.E.	Mean %	S.E.	Mean %	S.E.	Mean %	S.E.	Mean %	S.E.	Mean %	S.E.
OECD	Australia	18.8	(0.8)	29.7	(0.9)	25.6	(1.0)	40.7	(1.1)	4.8	(0.4)	6.9	(0.4)	1.6	(0.2)	5.0	(0.4)	1.9	(0.2)	4.8	(0.4)	13.5	(0.9)	4.1	(0.3)
	Austria	17.2	(1.9)	22.1	(1.8)	26.4	(1.8)	28.9	(1.8)	1.8	(0.5)	4.9	(1.0)	0.9	(0.5)	4.2	(0.7)	1.4	(0.2)	6.0	(0.9)	7.7	(1.6)	0.7	(0.4)
	Belgium	20.4	(1.4)	28.1	(2.0)	23.9	(1.5)	34.9	(2.1)	1.1	(0.4)	2.3	(0.6)	0.2	(0.1)	1.4	(0.5)	0.6	(0.2)	3.3	(0.4)	1.5	(0.3)	0.1	(0.0)
	Canada	24.3	(1.1)	35.7	(1.4)	31.6	(1.0)	41.5	(1.3)	3.2	(0.3)	8.9	(0.7)	0.8	(0.1)	4.0	(0.4)	1.9	(0.2)	5.3	(0.5)	9.0	(0.6)	1.2	(0.6)
	Chile	29.3	(2.2)	58.0	(2.3)	28.5	(2.3)	58.6	(2.4)	9.1	(1.9)	14.1	(1.9)	4.9	(1.4)	15.3	(1.8)	6.3	(1.3)	33.8	(2.7)	29.5	(2.5)	1.9	(0.8)
	Czech Republic	17.8	(1.7)	30.5	(2.2)	23.9	(1.9)	40.2	(2.1)	0.9	(0.3)	1.7	(0.2)	0.1	(0.1)	0.3	(0.1)	0.4	(0.1)	4.9	(0.8)	4.7	(1.0)	a	a
	Denmark	17.1	(1.7)	40.9	(2.8)	19.8	(2.0)	73.6	(2.7)	5.2	(1.0)	17.3	(2.1)	0.4	(0.2)	5.7	(0.9)	1.8	(0.4)	7.8	(0.9)	2.0	(0.7)	0.5	(0.4)
	Estonia	17.4	(1.3)	27.3	(1.9)	21.9	(1.4)	39.6	(2.1)	5.5	(0.6)	16.0	(1.2)	1.0	(0.4)	9.6	(0.9)	6.4	(0.8)	9.2	(0.6)	3.3	(0.9)	0.3	(0.2)
	Finland	25.6	(2.0)	44.9	(2.2)	28.0	(1.8)	54.6	(2.2)	1.2	(0.3)	4.3	(0.3)	0.0	(0.0)	0.3	(0.1)	1.1	(0.2)	4.4	(0.4)	9.8	(1.1)	0.8	(0.2)
	France	25.5	(1.7)	40.3	(2.3)	24.6	(1.8)	40.6	(2.4)	0.8	(0.5)	3.0	(0.7)	1.2	(0.6)	0.7	(0.2)	2.2	(0.8)	8.5	(1.1)	3.4	(0.8)	0.1	(0.1)
	Germany	21.6	(1.7)	30.1	(2.1)	27.1	(1.6)	34.7	(1.8)	3.7	(0.4)	6.7	(0.8)	1.4	(0.2)	5.6	(0.7)	1.5	(0.3)	5.5	(0.5)	4.0	(0.6)	0.5	(0.1)
	Greece	32.7	(2.2)	33.1	(2.1)	51.0	(2.3)	38.6	(2.2)	4.8	(1.0)	6.8	(1.4)	1.5	(0.4)	a	a	2.9	(0.8)	20.4	(2.0)	14.2	(1.9)	0.7	(0.4)
	Hungary	17.0	(1.8)	19.8	(1.5)	22.0	(1.9)	23.5	(1.5)	6.6	(1.2)	12.1	(1.8)	0.8	(0.2)	9.1	(1.3)	1.4	(0.3)	5.4	(1.0)	11.5	(1.6)	0.1	(0.1)
	Iceland	15.9	(0.1)	40.8	(0.2)	18.6	(0.1)	56.9	(0.2)	1.7	(0.0)	8.1	(0.1)	0.0	(0.0)	2.0	(0.0)	1.8	(0.0)	3.6	(0.0)	12.7	(0.1)	3.5	(0.1)
	Ireland	11.4	(1.4)	23.6	(2.1)	15.2	(1.8)	28.5	(2.7)	1.5	(0.3)	4.4	(0.7)	0.7	(0.2)	2.0	(0.3)	1.9	(0.3)	6.4	(0.7)	13.0	(1.6)	0.5	(0.3)
	Israel	24.4	(2.0)	40.9	(2.1)	27.9	(1.7)	49.2	(2.2)	4.7	(0.8)	7.5	(1.4)	1.4	(0.6)	5.4	(1.1)	5.8	(1.2)	11.0	(1.4)	3.4	(0.6)	0.2	(0.1)
	Italy	43.2	(1.6)	46.1	(1.5)	47.7	(1.2)	46.8	(1.6)	1.0	(0.2)	9.0	(0.5)	2.2	(0.3)	a	a	2.1	(0.3)	36.0	(1.5)	11.2	(1.2)	a	a
	Japan	10.1	(1.5)	63.2	(3.1)	10.9	(1.7)	69.7	(3.0)	7.2	(1.3)	6.7	(1.1)	0.4	(0.2)	1.3	(0.5)	0.4	(0.1)	8.7	(1.5)	4.4	(1.0)	a	a
	Korea	25.5	(2.0)	45.4	(2.6)	29.7	(2.0)	47.3	(2.7)	1.9	(0.8)	7.0	(1.2)	3.7	(0.9)	5.6	(0.8)	2.9	(0.9)	13.4	(1.8)	2.6	(0.8)	0.2	(0.2)
	Luxembourg	26.3	(0.0)	43.5	(0.1)	32.5	(0.1)	47.8	(0.1)	0.5	(0.0)	4.2	(0.0)	0.9	(0.0)	0.8	(0.0)	2.1	(0.0)	5.5	(0.0)	6.1	(0.0)	0.1	(0.0)
	Mexico	27.9	(1.2)	45.4	(1.1)	29.3	(1.1)	47.8	(1.1)	17.9	(1.2)	17.5	(1.2)	6.5	(0.7)	12.9	(1.2)	6.3	(0.7)	34.0	(1.5)	25.2	(1.5)	5.1	(0.6)
	Netherlands	16.8	(1.7)	31.0	(2.5)	27.1	(2.4)	42.6	(2.9)	0.9	(0.2)	3.5	(0.7)	1.7	(1.0)	0.9	(0.2)	1.1	(0.2)	3.4	(0.3)	0.3	(0.1)	0.7	(0.6)
	New Zealand	17.9	(1.8)	25.8	(2.0)	23.2	(1.8)	41.9	(2.2)	3.6	(0.5)	9.7	(0.7)	0.6	(0.1)	5.3	(0.6)	1.4	(0.2)	2.8	(0.4)	14.3	(1.6)	0.5	(0.2)
	Norway	13.0	(1.4)	51.7	(2.8)	17.3	(1.5)	86.6	(1.8)	5.9	(1.2)	12.1	(1.3)	0.0	(0.0)	0.6	(0.1)	0.6	(0.2)	7.2	(0.4)	9.9	(1.7)	0.1	(0.0)
	Poland	27.7	(2.2)	52.8	(2.5)	31.8	(2.2)	58.6	(2.7)	5.3	(1.2)	19.8	(2.0)	3.7	(1.1)	11.7	(1.5)	2.7	(0.8)	17.5	(1.7)	15.9	(2.0)	a	a
	Portugal	35.3	(2.4)	46.6	(2.3)	37.8	(2.5)	52.9	(2.7)	0.7	(0.2)	3.8	(0.6)	0.5	(0.1)	1.0	(0.2)	2.3	(0.4)	6.7	(0.9)	4.0	(1.1)	0.2	(0.1)
	Slovak Republic	25.9	(2.0)	32.1	(1.6)	18.7	(1.6)	23.2	(1.6)	3.7	(0.6)	10.0	(1.1)	1.0	(0.3)	1.4	(0.4)	1.3	(0.3)	17.4	(1.7)	13.3	(1.6)	0.1	(0.0)
	Slovenia	30.3	(0.3)	35.6	(0.5)	38.4	(0.4)	34.3	(0.4)	2.3	(0.2)	4.1	(0.2)	2.2	(0.1)	4.1	(0.2)	2.5	(0.1)	15.1	(0.3)	26.3	(0.6)	0.5	(0.0)
	Spain	34.6	(1.3)	51.9	(1.7)	40.5	(1.1)	61.6	(1.4)	1.9	(0.4)	6.1	(0.6)	1.3	(0.3)	5.0	(0.5)	2.3	(0.3)	14.1	(0.9)	9.0	(1.4)	0.2	(0.0)
	Sweden	15.3	(1.8)	36.0	(2.4)	27.2	(2.1)	80.3	(2.4)	3.4	(1.1)	8.2	(1.1)	0.2	(0.1)	0.6	(0.1)	2.3	(0.7)	6.6	(0.8)	4.6	(1.1)	1.5	(0.8)
	Switzerland	18.2	(1.5)	41.6	(2.3)	20.2	(1.7)	47.1	(2.4)	0.9	(0.2)	4.2	(0.5)	0.5	(0.2)	4.3	(0.8)	1.1	(0.1)	3.2	(0.5)	1.6	(0.6)	0.3	(0.1)
	Turkey	32.3	(1.8)	41.3	(2.4)	30.1	(1.5)	35.8	(2.4)	10.2	(1.5)	12.6	(1.6)	8.1	(1.5)	11.6	(1.5)	6.6	(1.3)	22.1	(2.1)	11.1	(1.7)	1.6	(0.8)
	United Kingdom	15.0	(1.3)	28.9	(2.3)	18.8	(1.3)	52.6	(2.6)	1.3	(0.2)	4.2	(0.7)	0.5	(0.1)	2.4	(0.4)	1.5	(0.2)	2.3	(0.3)	10.3	(1.4)	0.1	(0.0)
	United States	23.8	(2.1)	33.3	(2.5)	31.6	(1.9)	41.0	(2.5)	7.5	(1.2)	13.6	(1.3)	2.7	(0.6)	5.9	(1.0)	3.4	(0.6)	10.6	(1.7)	23.2	(2.6)	0.7	(0.3)
	OECD average	22.8	(0.3)	38.2	(0.4)	27.3	(0.3)	47.1	(0.4)	3.9	(0.1)	8.3	(0.2)	1.6	(0.1)	4.6	(0.1)	2.4	(0.1)	10.8	(0.2)	9.9	(0.2)	0.9	(0.1)
Partners	Albania	42.1	(2.4)	57.9	(2.7)	45.2	(2.5)	57.5	(2.6)	10.2	(1.4)	19.1	(2.1)	8.8	(1.6)	13.6	(2.0)	17.8	(2.2)	48.2	(2.7)	19.0	(2.3)	4.6	(1.4)
	Argentina	22.4	(2.2)	42.9	(2.4)	20.2	(1.8)	44.2	(2.5)	8.8	(1.6)	11.2	(2.0)	6.1	(1.7)	9.9	(2.0)	4.7	(0.9)	17.8	(2.0)	17.5	(2.2)	6.0	(1.9)
	Brazil	23.9	(1.2)	41.0	(1.5)	24.9	(1.5)	42.4	(1.6)	2.5	(0.4)	6.2	(0.7)	2.0	(0.5)	2.8	(0.7)	2.8	(0.5)	21.4	(1.7)	4.7	(0.9)	1.0	(0.5)
	Bulgaria	30.1	(1.6)	47.6	(2.4)	30.1	(1.8)	44.3	(2.4)	8.5	(1.1)	9.6	(1.2)	1.9	(0.7)	24.0	(1.9)	3.1	(0.7)	12.9	(1.6)	9.5	(1.5)	0.0	(0.0)
	Colombia	37.3	(2.6)	59.4	(2.3)	38.7	(2.5)	58.3	(2.3)	12.9	(1.6)	15.7	(1.9)	9.7	(1.3)	14.4	(1.4)	12.3	(2.1)	50.6	(2.6)	28.3	(2.6)	5.8	(1.4)
	Costa Rica	26.0	(1.9)	39.5	(2.3)	30.7	(1.9)	40.2	(2.2)	6.8	(1.4)	10.1	(1.5)	3.3	(0.9)	8.2	(1.4)	5.4	(1.0)	21.1	(2.2)	22.5	(2.3)	2.9	(0.8)
	Croatia	30.8	(2.6)	27.2	(2.3)	32.3	(2.6)	26.7	(2.6)	2.3	(0.9)	7.4	(1.7)	0.7	(0.2)	a	a	1.5	(0.6)	18.1	(2.6)	11.0	(2.4)	a	a
	Cyprus*	32.0	(0.1)	31.9	(0.1)	40.2	(0.1)	36.6	(0.1)	3.3	(0.0)	7.7	(0.0)	1.5	(0.0)	4.1	(0.0)	2.9	(0.0)	12.7	(0.0)	20.5	(0.0)	a	a
	Hong Kong-China	38.2	(2.7)	65.6	(2.9)	39.3	(2.8)	66.5	(3.0)	1.8	(0.3)	6.7	(0.9)	2.3	(0.6)	2.9	(0.4)	1.4	(0.3)	8.9	(1.8)	12.3	(2.1)	0.5	(0.2)
	Indonesia	31.2	(2.4)	48.6	(2.5)	32.2	(2.2)	43.4	(2.3)	21.3	(2.3)	20.6	(2.3)	12.1	(2.1)	18.1	(2.3)	10.9	(1.9)	53.4	(3.0)	22.9	(3.0)	5.7	(1.8)
	Jordan	28.8	(1.9)	33.1	(2.1)	27.7	(2.0)	30.3	(2.1)	12.4	(1.7)	14.2	(1.8)	8.0	(1.3)	10.9	(1.6)	12.6	(1.8)	31.3	(2.3)	5.2	(1.2)	4.7	(1.2)
	Kazakhstan	56.8	(2.8)	55.7	(2.5)	61.1	(2.8)	64.7	(2.5)	41.3	(2.7)	52.4	(2.7)	33.4	(3.0)	45.5	(3.1)	33.8	(2.7)	50.6	(3.0)	15.1	(2.4)	10.6	(2.1)
	Latvia	25.6	(1.8)	35.1	(2.3)	32.8	(1.7)	42.0	(1.9)	8.8	(1.2)	22.1	(1.5)	1.1	(0.2)	1.8	(0.3)	1.8	(0.2)	11.4	(1.4)	9.0	(1.3)	1.1	(0.6)
	Liechtenstein	11.4	(0.3)	42.1	(0.7)	10.8	(0.3)	56.8	(0.4)	0.8	(0.2)	1.8	(0.2)	0.0	c	4.5	(0.1)	0.5	(0.0)	3.0	(0.2)	0.4	(0.1)	3.2	(0.3)
	Lithuania	31.6	(1.6)	37.9	(2.1)	36.2	(1.8)	44.2	(2.2)	7.3	(0.9)	13.7	(0.9)	1.8	(0.4)	11.0	(1.1)	3.9	(0.4)	9.5	(0.8)	16.0	(1.4)	0.3	(0.1)
	Macao-China	31.4	(0.0)	80.2	(0.0)	34.2	(0.0)	75.5	(0.0)	1.2	(0.0)	8.4	(0.0)	1.4	(0.0)	4.4	(0.0)	2.9	(0.0)	13.2	(0.0)	24.6	(0.0)	0.1	(0.0)
	Malaysia	16.8	(1.8)	24.5	(2.3)	16.0	(1.7)	30.6	(2.4)	7.0	(1.0)	7.1	(1.0)	3.3	(0.8)	7.9	(1.0)	3.8	(0.8)	18.7	(2.0)	31.9	(2.9)	3.3	(0.9)
	Montenegro	49.2	(0.1)	42.8	(0.1)	38.8	(0.1)	38.1	(0.1)	2.8	(0.0)	7.1	(0.0)	1.7	(0.0)	3.4	(0.0)	0.9	(0.0)	22.2	(0.1)	2.4	(0.0)	a	a
	Peru	33.4	(2.1)	41.1	(2.3)	33.3	(2.1)	44.0	(2.4)	16.2	(1.8)	15.6	(1.8)	5.2	(1.2)	18.2	(2.0)	5.4	(1.1)	48.1	(2.6)	30.2	(2.7)	2.8	(0.8)
	Qatar	39.8	(0.1)	46.5	(0.1)	42.7	(0.1)	51.7	(0.1)	9.9	(0.0)	21.7	(0.1)	16.6	(0.0)	17.9	(0.0)	19.7	(0.1)	27.8	(0.1)	15.8	(0.0)	4.1	(0.0)
	Romania	39.2	(2.3)	46.2	(2.7)	40.1	(2.3)	49.2	(2.5)	15.9	(1.6)	22.0	(2.0)	13.1	(1.8)	12.3	(2.0)	10.7	(1.3)	35.4	(2.9)	31.2	(2.9)	1.8	(0.8)
	Russian Federation	28.0	(1.8)	39.3	(1.9)	38.6	(1.9)	48.7	(2.4)	30.9	(2.3)	31.8	(1.9)	4.7	(0.9)	26.0	(1.7)	18.4	(1.6)	26.6	(1.5)	27.2	(2.0)	7.6	(1.4)
	Serbia	39.3	(2.4)	50.3	(2.5)	36.1	(2.4)	44.7	(2.6)	2.1	(0.5)	3.9	(1.2)	0.2	(0.1)	0.6	(0.2)	1.8	(0.9)	23.1	(3.0)	19.9	(2.9)	0.1	(0.1)
	Shanghai-China	49.1	(2.8)	58.5	(3.0)	45.9	(2.8)	55.1	(3.1)	8.2	(2.0)	13.5	(1.9)	5.5	(1.4)	12.1	(2.0)	7.5	(1.4)	12.1	(1.4)	13.4	(2.3)	2.6	(1.0)
	Singapore	20.0	(0.1)	49.1	(0.4)	23.6	(0.1)	66.0	(0.4)	2.0	(0.0)	5.3	(0.3)	0.8	(0.0)	2.6	(0.0)	1.0	(0.0)	4.5	(0.0)	14.4	(0.1)	0.3	(0.0)
	Chinese Taipei	39.1	(2.2)	41.5	(2.5)	33.9	(2.2)	38.3	(2.6)	6.2	(1.3)	9.8	(1.8)	4.2	(1.2)	4.8	(0.9)	2.7	(0.7)	12.9	(2.1)	9.3	(1.7)	1.4	(0.7)
	Thailand	37.7	(2.9)	53.1	(2.9)	40.5	(2.6)	56.3	(2.9)	12.5	(1.4)	17.7	(1.5)	9.4	(1.3)	9.3	(1.3)	12.0	(1.2)	18.3	(1.5)	50.8	(2.9)	7.1	(1.0)
	Tunisia	19.4	(2.4)	33.1	(3.0)	15.3	(2.1)	17.6	(2.3)	2.2	(0.8)	4.3	(1.2)	1.1	(0.4)	1.6	(0.8)	1.1	(0.6)	7.3	(1.8)	2.9	(0.8)	0.5	(0.3)
	United Arab Emirates	34.6	(1.8)	38.0	(1.8)	38.9	(1.5)	41.5	(1.4)	11.7	(1.5)	21.4	(1.9)	15.1	(1.5)	15.3	(1.6)	14.6	(1.6)	25.3	(1.7)	9.0	(1.0)	3.7	(0.8)
	Uruguay	10.1	(0.9)	22.6	(1.6)	18.1	(1.6)	27.3	(1.7)	2.5	(0.6)	5.4	(0.8)	2.7	(0.7)	2.9	(0.6)	1.9	(0.5)	9.8	(1.4)	8.3	(1.2)	0.3	(0.3)
	Viet Nam	45.0	(3.3)	49.4	(3.1)	49.2	(3.2)	51.8	(2.9)	12.9	(1.9)	14.4	(1.8)	12.4	(2.2)	40.6	(3.5)	17.9	(2.3)	24.2	(2.9)	61.0	(3.5)	1.7	(1.0)

* See notes at the beginning of this Annex.

StatLink http://dx.doi.org/10.1787/888932957498

[Part 1/1]
Parents' expectations of high academic performance
Table IV.4.18   *Results based on school principals' reports*

	Pressure on the school to meet high academic standards comes from:					
	Many parents		A minority of parents		Very few parents	
	%	S.E.	%	S.E.	%	S.E.
OECD Australia	35.7	(1.7)	55.3	(2.0)	9.0	(1.1)
Austria	7.3	(2.3)	31.0	(3.6)	61.7	(4.0)
Belgium	9.4	(1.9)	34.3	(2.9)	56.3	(3.1)
Canada	32.6	(2.3)	50.9	(2.6)	16.5	(1.8)
Chile	30.3	(3.6)	42.5	(3.9)	27.2	(3.6)
Czech Republic	32.8	(3.0)	58.3	(3.2)	8.9	(2.4)
Denmark	26.6	(3.2)	44.5	(3.4)	28.9	(3.2)
Estonia	17.0	(2.0)	45.9	(2.5)	37.1	(2.7)
Finland	4.3	(1.4)	23.9	(2.8)	71.8	(3.0)
France	15.8	(2.2)	35.0	(3.1)	49.1	(3.3)
Germany	5.6	(1.7)	50.0	(3.8)	44.4	(3.9)
Greece	20.8	(3.0)	28.2	(3.7)	51.0	(4.0)
Hungary	20.2	(3.3)	52.8	(4.2)	27.0	(3.2)
Iceland	14.4	(0.2)	47.4	(0.2)	38.2	(0.2)
Ireland	48.1	(4.0)	36.1	(3.9)	15.8	(2.5)
Israel	26.3	(3.3)	52.0	(3.7)	21.7	(3.1)
Italy	14.9	(1.4)	60.3	(1.8)	24.9	(1.5)
Japan	23.7	(2.7)	50.4	(3.5)	25.9	(3.1)
Korea	9.2	(2.5)	62.7	(3.5)	28.1	(3.4)
Luxembourg	11.1	(0.1)	31.0	(0.1)	57.9	(0.1)
Mexico	20.3	(1.2)	45.9	(1.6)	33.8	(1.7)
Netherlands	12.2	(2.8)	58.6	(4.3)	29.2	(3.9)
New Zealand	47.2	(4.0)	44.3	(3.8)	8.4	(2.4)
Norway	19.2	(2.7)	43.9	(4.1)	36.9	(4.0)
Poland	19.2	(3.2)	44.5	(4.3)	36.3	(3.9)
Portugal	18.5	(3.1)	60.7	(4.5)	20.9	(4.1)
Slovak Republic	10.2	(2.3)	58.9	(4.0)	30.9	(3.6)
Slovenia	18.1	(0.6)	45.0	(0.8)	36.9	(0.8)
Spain	7.3	(1.4)	30.8	(2.5)	61.9	(2.7)
Sweden	45.6	(3.8)	51.7	(3.7)	2.7	(1.2)
Switzerland	9.8	(2.0)	41.6	(3.4)	48.6	(3.4)
Turkey	6.7	(1.6)	46.4	(4.0)	46.8	(4.1)
United Kingdom	42.5	(3.1)	49.2	(3.2)	8.3	(1.7)
United States	37.1	(4.4)	42.0	(4.3)	20.9	(4.3)
OECD average	21.2	(0.5)	45.8	(0.6)	33.1	(0.5)
Partners Albania	31.7	(3.1)	55.6	(3.4)	12.8	(2.5)
Argentina	7.8	(2.4)	32.6	(4.0)	59.6	(4.7)
Brazil	14.7	(1.6)	46.5	(2.6)	38.7	(2.7)
Bulgaria	29.3	(2.4)	38.2	(3.3)	32.6	(3.4)
Colombia	14.0	(3.2)	30.4	(3.6)	55.6	(4.2)
Costa Rica	20.1	(3.3)	32.8	(3.5)	47.1	(4.0)
Croatia	4.6	(1.7)	39.3	(3.8)	56.1	(3.9)
Cyprus*	23.5	(0.1)	38.3	(0.1)	38.2	(0.1)
Hong Kong-China	2.0	(1.1)	56.9	(3.8)	41.2	(3.9)
Indonesia	31.3	(3.6)	49.7	(4.4)	19.0	(3.7)
Jordan	22.7	(2.7)	44.3	(4.2)	32.9	(3.9)
Kazakhstan	9.8	(2.0)	43.8	(4.0)	46.4	(3.8)
Latvia	4.3	(1.6)	33.0	(3.2)	62.7	(3.4)
Liechtenstein	12.5	(0.7)	34.3	(1.1)	53.2	(0.9)
Lithuania	7.2	(1.8)	48.1	(3.2)	44.8	(3.5)
Macao-China	1.8	(0.0)	42.3	(0.1)	55.8	(0.1)
Malaysia	20.2	(3.1)	65.8	(3.8)	14.1	(2.6)
Montenegro	11.0	(0.1)	40.0	(0.2)	49.1	(0.1)
Peru	29.4	(3.5)	44.9	(3.5)	25.6	(3.4)
Qatar	42.3	(0.1)	41.1	(0.1)	16.6	(0.1)
Romania	16.5	(2.6)	40.2	(3.7)	43.3	(3.7)
Russian Federation	20.0	(3.1)	60.3	(3.6)	19.6	(2.4)
Serbia	7.3	(1.8)	43.7	(4.4)	49.0	(4.5)
Shanghai-China	19.5	(3.1)	62.9	(3.9)	17.6	(3.3)
Singapore	60.1	(0.5)	36.4	(0.5)	3.5	(0.1)
Chinese Taipei	22.0	(3.5)	71.4	(4.0)	6.6	(1.8)
Thailand	39.0	(3.5)	48.1	(3.4)	12.9	(2.7)
Tunisia	13.5	(2.8)	42.9	(4.3)	43.6	(4.1)
United Arab Emirates	36.9	(2.3)	41.8	(2.4)	21.3	(2.1)
Uruguay	6.4	(2.2)	43.7	(3.6)	49.9	(3.7)
Viet Nam	39.8	(4.0)	51.1	(3.7)	9.0	(2.3)

* See notes at the beginning of this Annex.
StatLink ⟐⟐⟐ http://dx.doi.org/10.1787/888932957498

[Part 1/6]
Change between 2003 and 2012 in school type and performance in mathematics
Table IV.4.19   *Results based on school principals' reports*

		PISA 2003												
		Government or public schools[1]				Government-dependent private schools[2]				Government-independent private schools[3]				Difference in performance on the mathematics scale between public and private schools (government-dependent and government-independent schools combined)	
		Percentage of students		Performance on the mathematics scale		Percentage of students		Performance on the mathematics scale		Percentage of students		Performance on the mathematics scale		Dif. (Pub. - Priv.)	
		%	S.E.	Mean score	S.E.	%	S.E.	Mean score	S.E.	%	S.E.	Mean score	S.E.	Dif. (Pub. - Priv.)	S.E.
OECD	Australia	w	w	w	w	w	w	w	w	w	w	w	w	w	w
	Austria	92.0	(1.9)	504	(3.4)	6.7	(1.6)	518	(12.6)	1.3	(0.6)	c	c	-18	(12.0)
	Belgium	w	w	w	w	w	w	w	w	w	w	w	w	w	w
	Canada	94.2	(0.7)	529	(1.8)	3.8	(0.6)	573	(10.8)	1.9	(0.3)	563	(11.1)	**-41**	(8.3)
	Czech Republic	93.3	(1.7)	517	(3.8)	5.8	(1.6)	505	(13.5)	0.9	(0.5)	c	c	3	(13.5)
	Denmark	77.8	(2.5)	515	(3.1)	21.7	(2.6)	511	(6.3)	0.5	(0.5)	c	c	4	(7.1)
	Finland	93.3	(1.6)	545	(1.8)	6.7	(1.6)	539	(12.2)	0.0	c	c	c	5	(12.3)
	France	w	w	w	w	w	w	w	w	w	w	w	w	w	w
	Germany	92.2	(1.7)	497	(3.7)	7.5	(1.8)	566	(12.7)	0.4	(0.4)	c	c	**-66**	(13.7)
	Greece	97.4	(1.9)	442	(3.6)	0.0	c	c	c	2.6	(1.9)	507	(30.1)	**-65**	(30.4)
	Hungary	88.9	(2.5)	489	(3.6)	9.8	(2.3)	504	(16.8)	1.2	(0.8)	c	c	-17	(18.1)
	Iceland	99.5	(0.1)	515	(1.6)	0.0	c	c	c	0.5	(0.1)	c	c	c	c
	Ireland	41.6	(1.6)	486	(3.8)	57.6	(1.8)	516	(3.3)	0.8	(0.9)	c	c	**-31**	(5.0)
	Italy	96.1	(1.2)	468	(3.1)	0.4	(0.2)	392	(61.4)	3.5	(1.3)	452	(35.4)	22	(22.4)
	Japan	73.0	(1.7)	544	(4.7)	0.6	(0.6)	c	c	26.4	(1.8)	513	(7.5)	**31**	(8.6)
	Korea	42.3	(3.7)	527	(6.1)	36.0	(4.1)	532	(7.5)	21.7	(3.4)	593	(9.6)	**-28**	(10.1)
	Luxembourg	85.9	(0.1)	498	(1.1)	14.1	(0.1)	463	(2.9)	0.0	c	c	c	**35**	(3.3)
	Mexico	86.7	(1.9)	375	(3.5)	0.1	(0.1)	c	c	13.2	(1.9)	430	(8.9)	**-55**	(9.8)
	Netherlands	23.3	(4.2)	516	(14.0)	76.7	(4.2)	541	(4.5)	0.0	c	c	c	-25	(16.4)
	New Zealand	95.4	(0.5)	522	(2.3)	0.0	c	c	c	4.6	(0.5)	579	(17.1)	**-57**	(17.3)
	Norway	99.1	(0.7)	494	(2.4)	0.9	(0.7)	c	c	0.0	c	c	c	c	c
	Poland	99.2	(0.4)	489	(2.5)	0.4	(0.4)	c	c	0.4	(0.3)	c	c	c	c
	Portugal	93.7	(1.3)	465	(3.6)	4.2	(1.2)	459	(8.5)	2.1	(1.2)	c	c	-19	(16.9)
	Slovak Republic	87.4	(2.7)	495	(3.7)	12.6	(2.7)	523	(9.3)	0.0	c	c	c	-27	(10.3)
	Spain	64.2	(1.5)	472	(3.4)	28.1	(2.1)	505	(4.2)	7.7	(1.7)	520	(9.7)	**-35**	(5.4)
	Sweden	95.7	(0.5)	509	(2.6)	4.3	(0.5)	516	(11.0)	0.0	c	c	c	-8	(11.3)
	Switzerland	95.3	(1.0)	528	(3.8)	0.9	(0.7)	546	(34.2)	3.8	(0.7)	497	(23.2)	21	(22.3)
	Turkey	99.0	(1.0)	420	(6.6)	0.0	c	c	c	1.0	(1.0)	c	c	c	c
	United States	94.3	(1.0)	483	(3.6)	0.0	c	c	c	5.7	(1.0)	507	(9.1)	**-24**	(9.9)
	OECD average 2003	82.7	(0.3)	494	(0.9)	13.6	(0.4)	514	(4.5)	3.7	(0.3)	516	(5.9)	**-19**	(3.0)
Partners	Brazil	87.4	(2.3)	342	(6.2)	0.0	c	c	c	12.6	(2.3)	454	(11.3)	**-112**	(13.5)
	Hong Kong-China	9.5	(0.4)	571	(11.4)	90.1	(0.5)	548	(4.8)	0.4	(0.3)	c	c	23	(12.3)
	Indonesia	51.4	(2.3)	373	(4.9)	4.1	(1.5)	326	(19.3)	44.5	(2.6)	345	(7.0)	**29**	(8.1)
	Latvia	99.0	(0.7)	485	(3.7)	0.0	c	c	c	1.0	(0.7)	c	c	c	c
	Liechtenstein	95.0	(0.3)	539	(4.1)	0.0	c	c	c	5.0	(0.3)	c	c	c	c
	Macao-China	5.0	(0.1)	c	c	49.3	(0.2)	528	(3.5)	45.8	(0.2)	529	(5.2)	c	c
	Russian Federation	99.7	(0.2)	468	(4.3)	0.0	c	c	c	0.3	(0.2)	c	c	c	c
	Thailand	88.0	(1.2)	416	(3.0)	6.0	(1.1)	419	(18.8)	6.0	(1.6)	428	(13.7)	-7	(12.7)
	Tunisia	m	m	m	m	m	m	m	m	m	m	m	m	m	m
	Uruguay	85.9	(0.8)	409	(3.7)	0.0	c	c	c	14.1	(0.8)	501	(6.1)	**-92**	(6.8)

Notes: Values that are statistically significant are indicated in bold (see Annex A3).
Only countries and economies with comparable data from PISA 2003 and PISA 2012 are shown.
1. Schools which are directly controlled or managed by: *i)* a public education authority or agency or *ii)* a government agency directly or a governing body, most of whose members are either appointed by a public authority or elected by public franchise.
2. Schools which receive 50% or more of their core funding (i.e. funding that supports the basic educational services of the institution) from government agencies.
3. Schools which receive less than 50% of their core funding (i.e. funding that supports the basic educational services of the institution) from government agencies.
StatLink ⌁ http://dx.doi.org/10.1787/888932957498

[Part 2/6]
Change between 2003 and 2012 in school type and performance in mathematics
Table IV.4.19   *Results based on school principals' reports*

	PISA 2003										
	PISA index of economic, social and cultural status						Difference in performance on the mathematics scale between public and private schools after accounting for the PISA index of economic, social and cultural status of:				
	Public schools		Private schools (government-dependent and government-independent)		Difference		Students		Students and schools		
	Mean index	S.E.	Mean index	S.E.	Dif. (Pub. - Priv.)	S.E.	Dif. (Pub. - Priv.)	S.E.	Dif. (Pub. - Priv.)	S.E.	
Australia	w	w	w	w	w	w	w	w	w	w	
Austria	-0.28	(0.03)	-0.04	(0.11)	**-0.24**	(0.12)	-6	(10.3)	10	(11.9)	
Belgium	w	w	w	w	w	w	w	w	w	w	
Canada	0.18	(0.02)	0.67	(0.08)	**-0.50**	(0.08)	**-27**	(6.4)	**-14**	(6.6)	
Czech Republic	-0.06	(0.02)	0.01	(0.13)	-0.07	(0.13)	12	(9.8)	17	(10.5)	
Denmark	0.07	(0.04)	0.09	(0.07)	-0.02	(0.08)	5	(5.2)	5	(4.8)	
Finland	0.04	(0.02)	0.34	(0.14)	**-0.30**	(0.14)	13	(11.0)	14	(11.2)	
France	w	w	w	w	w	w	w	w	w	w	
Germany	-0.05	(0.03)	0.74	(0.08)	**-0.79**	(0.09)	**-29**	(10.7)	17	(11.7)	
Greece	-0.35	(0.04)	0.95	(0.44)	**-1.30**	(0.44)	-19	(15.5)	**42**	(9.0)	
Hungary	-0.34	(0.03)	-0.09	(0.11)	-0.24	(0.13)	-4	(13.1)	8	(9.8)	
Iceland	0.54	(0.02)	c	c	c	c	c	c	c	c	
Ireland	-0.49	(0.03)	-0.08	(0.05)	**-0.41**	(0.06)	**-16**	(3.9)	-3	(4.0)	
Italy	-0.30	(0.03)	-0.01	(0.07)	**-0.29**	(0.08)	31	(22.5)	46	(23.5)	
Japan	-0.47	(0.03)	-0.25	(0.05)	**-0.22**	(0.06)	**41**	(6.8)	**62**	(5.6)	
Korea	-0.59	(0.05)	-0.21	(0.05)	**-0.39**	(0.08)	-14	(8.2)	10	(7.1)	
Luxembourg	-0.06	(0.02)	-0.30	(0.04)	**0.25**	(0.04)	**27**	(3.5)	**13**	(3.4)	
Mexico	-1.52	(0.04)	-0.37	(0.13)	**-1.15**	(0.14)	**-25**	(8.0)	**19**	(8.1)	
Netherlands	-0.18	(0.08)	-0.09	(0.04)	-0.10	(0.10)	-10	(10.7)	-2	(8.6)	
New Zealand	-0.16	(0.02)	0.60	(0.11)	**-0.76**	(0.11)	-23	(12.8)	12	(9.7)	
Norway	0.18	(0.02)	c	c	c	c	c	c	c	c	
Poland	-0.42	(0.02)	c	c	c	c	c	c	c	c	
Portugal	-0.93	(0.04)	-0.62	(0.36)	-0.31	(0.36)	-11	(9.9)	-2	(10.6)	
Slovak Republic	-0.27	(0.03)	-0.02	(0.08)	**-0.25**	(0.09)	-15	(7.8)	-2	(7.3)	
Spain	-0.76	(0.06)	-0.13	(0.07)	**-0.63**	(0.09)	**-20**	(4.4)	-6	(4.3)	
Sweden	0.07	(0.03)	0.44	(0.11)	**-0.38**	(0.11)	6	(8.2)	**17**	(7.0)	
Switzerland	-0.26	(0.03)	0.17	(0.12)	**-0.43**	(0.12)	**40**	(20.1)	**62**	(19.6)	
Turkey	-1.20	(0.06)	c	c	c	c	c	c	c	c	
United States	0.05	(0.03)	0.48	(0.11)	**-0.43**	(0.12)	-6	(8.3)	11	(9.7)	
OECD average 2003	-0.29	(0.01)	0.10	(0.03)	**-0.40**	(0.03)	-4	(2.2)	**14**	(2.1)	
Brazil	-1.77	(0.05)	-0.10	(0.09)	**-1.68**	(0.11)	**-73**	(14.0)	12	(20.3)	
Hong Kong-China	-1.25	(0.11)	-1.27	(0.04)	0.03	(0.12)	**22**	(10.0)	**20**	(8.9)	
Indonesia	-1.82	(0.05)	-1.92	(0.06)	0.10	(0.08)	**27**	(7.2)	**23**	(6.1)	
Latvia	-0.35	(0.03)	c	c	c	c	c	c	c	c	
Liechtenstein	-0.31	(0.04)	c	c	c	c	c	c	c	c	
Macao-China	c	c	-1.58	(0.03)	c	c	c	c	c	c	
Russian Federation	-0.62	(0.03)	c	c	c	c	c	c	c	c	
Thailand	-1.92	(0.04)	-1.45	(0.09)	**-0.47**	(0.10)	3	(11.9)	13	(11.5)	
Tunisia	m	m	m	m	m	m	m	m	m	m	
Uruguay	-0.95	(0.04)	0.39	(0.07)	**-1.34**	(0.08)	**-55**	(6.7)	16	(11.4)	

Notes: Values that are statistically significant are indicated in bold (see Annex A3).
Only countries and economies with comparable data from PISA 2003 and PISA 2012 are shown.
1. Schools which are directly controlled or managed by: *i)* a public education authority or agency or *ii)* a government agency directly or a governing body, most of whose members are either appointed by a public authority or elected by public franchise.
2. Schools which receive 50% or more of their core funding (i.e. funding that supports the basic educational services of the institution) from government agencies.
3. Schools which receive less than 50% of their core funding (i.e. funding that supports the basic educational services of the institution) from government agencies.
StatLink ⌨🖳⤷ http://dx.doi.org/10.1787/888932957498

[Part 3/6]
Change between 2003 and 2012 in school type and performance in mathematics

Table IV.4.19   *Results based on school principals' reports*

	Government or public schools[1]				Government-dependent private schools[2]				Government-independent private schools[3]				Difference in performance on the mathematics scale between public and private schools (government-dependent and government-independent schools combined)	
	Percentage of students		Performance on the mathematics scale		Percentage of students		Performance on the mathematics scale		Percentage of students		Performance on the mathematics scale		Dif. (Pub. - Priv.)	S.E.
	%	S.E.	Mean score	S.E.	%	S.E.	Mean score	S.E.	%	S.E.	Mean score	S.E.		
Australia	61.0	(0.7)	489	(2.3)	26.5	(1.0)	510	(2.9)	12.5	(0.9)	559	(3.6)	**-37**	(3.4)
Austria	91.4	(2.3)	502	(3.2)	7.5	(2.1)	546	(15.9)	1.1	(0.9)	559	(14.5)	**-45**	(14.9)
Belgium	w	w	w	w	w	w	w	w	w	w	w	w	w	w
Canada	92.2	(0.8)	514	(2.0)	4.3	(0.6)	570	(8.1)	3.5	(0.8)	566	(10.1)	**-54**	(6.7)
Czech Republic	91.8	(1.9)	498	(3.8)	6.9	(1.6)	493	(17.3)	1.3	(0.9)	c	c	-6	(17.3)
Denmark	77.0	(1.8)	494	(2.5)	18.9	(2.0)	517	(6.2)	4.2	(1.5)	527	(13.0)	**-25**	(6.4)
Finland	97.0	(0.7)	518	(2.0)	3.0	(0.7)	542	(7.2)	0.0	c	c	c	**-24**	(7.7)
France	82.8	(1.4)	490	(3.2)	17.2	(1.4)	521	(6.6)	0.0	c	c	c	**-31**	(7.4)
Germany	94.5	(1.6)	511	(3.5)	5.0	(1.6)	549	(19.4)	0.5	(0.4)	c	c	**-44**	(19.7)
Greece	97.7	(0.7)	450	(2.7)	0.0	c	c	c	2.3	(0.7)	c	c	c	c
Hungary	84.0	(2.9)	475	(3.4)	16.0	(2.9)	489	(14.1)	0.0	c	c	c	-15	(15.1)
Iceland	99.5	(0.1)	493	(1.7)	0.5	(0.1)	c	c	0.0	c	c	c	c	c
Ireland	43.8	(0.9)	492	(3.9)	54.0	(1.1)	502	(3.0)	2.2	(1.1)	c	c	**-12**	(5.0)
Italy	95.3	(0.7)	487	(2.3)	1.8	(0.4)	437	(7.1)	2.9	(0.5)	515	(8.9)	3	(7.7)
Japan	70.1	(1.2)	535	(3.3)	0.0	c	c	c	29.9	(1.2)	540	(9.6)	-5	(10.3)
Korea	52.7	(4.1)	546	(7.1)	31.4	(3.8)	539	(7.2)	15.9	(3.1)	609	(10.5)	-17	(10.1)
Luxembourg	84.9	(0.1)	492	(1.3)	13.4	(0.0)	464	(2.4)	1.8	(0.0)	c	c	**13**	(2.7)
Mexico	90.7	(0.9)	408	(1.5)	0.1	(0.1)	c	c	9.2	(0.8)	452	(6.0)	**-43**	(6.5)
Netherlands	33.6	(4.4)	516	(10.0)	66.4	(4.4)	523	(5.6)	0.0	c	c	c	-7	(12.5)
New Zealand	94.7	(1.4)	496	(2.5)	0.0	c	c	c	5.3	(1.4)	583	(6.8)	**-87**	(6.9)
Norway	98.3	(1.0)	489	(2.8)	1.7	(1.0)	c	c	0.0	c	c	c	c	c
Poland	97.1	(0.4)	516	(3.6)	1.9	(0.4)	566	(22.1)	1.0	(0.2)	581	(14.9)	**-56**	(12.9)
Portugal	89.9	(2.0)	481	(3.8)	5.8	(1.9)	516	(7.3)	4.2	(1.4)	581	(5.2)	**-62**	(9.4)
Slovak Republic	91.0	(2.4)	478	(4.1)	8.6	(2.5)	520	(20.2)	0.5	(0.3)	c	c	**-42**	(20.4)
Spain	68.2	(0.8)	471	(2.5)	24.4	(1.1)	506	(3.6)	7.4	(1.0)	523	(4.8)	**-39**	(3.3)
Sweden	86.0	(0.7)	476	(2.4)	14.0	(0.7)	491	(7.9)	0.0	c	c	c	-15	(8.4)
Switzerland	93.7	(1.3)	532	(3.3)	1.5	(0.8)	567	(18.4)	4.8	(1.0)	505	(13.0)	12	(14.8)
Turkey	100.0	c	447	(4.9)	0.0	c	c	c	0.0	c	c	c	c	c
United States	94.9	(0.9)	482	(4.0)	0.0	c	c	c	5.1	(0.9)	496	(10.0)	-14	(11.4)
OECD average 2003	83.1	(0.4)	492	(0.7)	13.0	(0.4)	519	(2.8)	3.9	(0.3)	541	(2.9)	**-28**	(2.4)
Brazil	86.5	(1.3)	376	(2.0)	0.6	(0.4)	c	c	12.8	(1.3)	461	(6.9)	**-83**	(6.7)
Hong Kong-China	7.0	(0.2)	597	(9.5)	91.9	(0.8)	560	(3.5)	1.2	(0.7)	c	c	**37**	(10.1)
Indonesia	58.9	(2.6)	377	(5.0)	17.5	(2.3)	342	(5.6)	23.7	(2.7)	395	(10.7)	5	(8.9)
Latvia	97.7	(1.5)	490	(2.9)	0.4	(0.4)	c	c	1.9	(1.3)	c	c	c	c
Liechtenstein	93.6	(0.4)	541	(3.9)	0.0	c	c	c	6.4	(0.4)	c	c	c	c
Macao-China	4.2	(0.0)	c	c	81.3	(0.0)	537	(1.1)	14.5	(0.0)	559	(2.9)	c	c
Russian Federation	99.4	(0.6)	482	(3.0)	0.0	c	c	c	0.6	(0.6)	c	c	c	c
Thailand	83.5	(0.6)	433	(3.8)	11.6	(1.5)	396	(5.1)	4.9	(1.3)	398	(23.2)	**36**	(8.9)
Tunisia	99.4	(0.4)	389	(3.9)	0.0	c	c	c	0.6	(0.4)	c	c	c	c
Uruguay	83.3	(1.2)	393	(2.6)	0.0	c	c	c	16.7	(1.2)	492	(6.6)	**-100**	(7.1)

Notes: Values that are statistically significant are indicated in bold (see Annex A3).
Only countries and economies with comparable data from PISA 2003 and PISA 2012 are shown.
1. Schools which are directly controlled or managed by: *i)* a public education authority or agency or *ii)* a government agency directly or a governing body, most of whose members are either appointed by a public authority or elected by public franchise.
2. Schools which receive 50% or more of their core funding (i.e. funding that supports the basic educational services of the institution) from government agencies.
3. Schools which receive less than 50% of their core funding (i.e. funding that supports the basic educational services of the institution) from government agencies.

StatLink ᵐˢᵖ http://dx.doi.org/10.1787/888932957498

[Part 4/6]
Change between 2003 and 2012 in school type and performance in mathematics

Table IV.4.19   *Results based on school principals' reports*

		PISA 2012									
		PISA index of economic, social and cultural status						Difference in performance on the mathematics scale between public and private schools after accounting for the PISA index of economic, social and cultural status of:			
		Public schools		Private schools (government-dependent and government-independent)		Difference		Students		Students and schools	
		Mean index	S.E.	Mean index	S.E.	Dif. (Pub. - Priv.)	S.E.	Dif. (Pub. - Priv.)	S.E.	Dif. (Pub. - Priv.)	S.E.
OECD	Australia	0.06	(0.01)	0.52	(0.02)	**-0.46**	(0.02)	**-17**	(3.4)	8	(4.3)
	Austria	0.02	(0.02)	0.64	(0.13)	**-0.62**	(0.14)	-18	(13.3)	21	(15.7)
	Belgium	w	w	w	w	w	w	w	w	w	w
	Canada	0.37	(0.02)	0.85	(0.07)	**-0.48**	(0.07)	**-38**	(6.5)	**-25**	(6.6)
	Czech Republic	-0.08	(0.02)	0.07	(0.10)	-0.15	(0.11)	3	(14.0)	16	(12.5)
	Denmark	0.35	(0.03)	0.69	(0.05)	**-0.34**	(0.05)	**-11**	(5.0)	0	(4.6)
	Finland	0.35	(0.02)	0.69	(0.08)	**-0.34**	(0.08)	-13	(6.9)	-5	(6.7)
	France	-0.11	(0.02)	0.28	(0.04)	**-0.38**	(0.05)	-8	(6.6)	26	(7.9)
	Germany	0.15	(0.03)	0.65	(0.16)	**-0.51**	(0.17)	-17	(16.0)	23	(15.7)
	Greece	-0.12	(0.03)	c	c	c	c	c	c	c	c
	Hungary	-0.27	(0.03)	-0.12	(0.11)	-0.15	(0.12)	-8	(10.8)	1	(8.6)
	Iceland	0.79	(0.01)	c	c	c	c	c	c	c	c
	Ireland	0.03	(0.03)	0.13	(0.03)	-0.10	(0.04)	-8	(4.1)	-4	(3.7)
	Italy	-0.07	(0.02)	0.23	(0.10)	**-0.30**	(0.11)	**12**	(6.1)	**31**	(7.8)
	Japan	-0.15	(0.02)	0.12	(0.04)	**-0.28**	(0.04)	6	(8.7)	**43**	(6.7)
	Korea	0.00	(0.04)	0.03	(0.04)	-0.04	(0.06)	-15	(8.4)	-12	(6.9)
	Luxembourg	0.06	(0.02)	0.12	(0.03)	-0.06	(0.03)	**15**	(3.0)	**18**	(2.8)
	Mexico	-1.30	(0.02)	0.29	(0.08)	**-1.59**	(0.08)	**-16**	(5.4)	**18**	(4.6)
	Netherlands	0.22	(0.06)	0.21	(0.03)	0.01	(0.07)	-8	(10.6)	-9	(7.8)
	New Zealand	0.00	(0.02)	0.84	(0.07)	**-0.84**	(0.07)	**-43**	(7.2)	0	(9.4)
	Norway	0.47	(0.02)	c	c	c	c	c	c	c	c
	Poland	-0.24	(0.03)	0.77	(0.09)	**-1.01**	(0.09)	-15	(11.3)	15	(12.9)
	Portugal	-0.58	(0.05)	0.37	(0.21)	**-0.95**	(0.22)	**-29**	(4.8)	-7	(7.2)
	Slovak Republic	-0.23	(0.03)	0.25	(0.14)	**-0.47**	(0.16)	-17	(14.8)	7	(11.9)
	Spain	-0.39	(0.03)	0.20	(0.05)	**-0.59**	(0.06)	**-21**	(3.3)	**-10**	(4.1)
	Sweden	0.24	(0.02)	0.48	(0.08)	**-0.24**	(0.08)	-7	(6.4)	2	(5.0)
	Switzerland	0.13	(0.02)	0.71	(0.06)	**-0.57**	(0.06)	**34**	(14.3)	**71**	(15.5)
	Turkey	-1.48	(0.03)	c	c	c	c	c	c	c	c
	United States	0.15	(0.04)	0.73	(0.11)	**-0.58**	(0.12)	7	(8.1)	**27**	(6.4)
	OECD average 2003	-0.06	(0.01)	0.40	(0.02)	**-0.45**	(0.02)	**-11**	(1.9)	**8**	(1.9)
Partners	Brazil	-1.42	(0.02)	-0.03	(0.09)	**-1.39**	(0.09)	**-60**	(6.0)	**-19**	(7.1)
	Hong Kong-China	-0.77	(0.12)	-0.79	(0.05)	0.02	(0.13)	**34**	(10.0)	**33**	(12.0)
	Indonesia	-1.78	(0.06)	-1.81	(0.09)	0.03	(0.11)	4	(7.6)	4	(6.8)
	Latvia	-0.27	(0.03)	c	c	c	c	c	c	c	c
	Liechtenstein	0.27	(0.05)	c	c	c	c	c	c	c	c
	Macao-China	c	c	-0.87	(0.01)	c	c	c	c	c	c
	Russian Federation	-0.11	(0.02)	c	c	c	c	c	c	c	c
	Thailand	-1.37	(0.04)	-1.23	(0.15)	-0.14	(0.15)	**39**	(6.4)	**42**	(5.2)
	Tunisia	-1.20	(0.05)	c	c	c	c	c	c	c	c
	Uruguay	-1.15	(0.03)	0.46	(0.07)	**-1.61**	(0.07)	**-55**	(5.9)	**28**	(8.8)

Notes: Values that are statistically significant are indicated in bold (see Annex A3).
Only countries and economies with comparable data from PISA 2003 and PISA 2012 are shown.
1. Schools which are directly controlled or managed by: *i)* a public education authority or agency or *ii)* a government agency directly or a governing body, most of whose members are either appointed by a public authority or elected by public franchise.
2. Schools which receive 50% or more of their core funding (i.e. funding that supports the basic educational services of the institution) from government agencies.
3. Schools which receive less than 50% of their core funding (i.e. funding that supports the basic educational services of the institution) from government agencies.

StatLink 🔗 http://dx.doi.org/10.1787/888932957498

[Part 5/6]
Change between 2003 and 2012 in school type and performance in mathematics
Table IV.4.19   *Results based on school principals' reports*

	Government or public schools[1]				Government-dependent private schools[2]				Government-independent private schools[3]				Difference in performance on the mathematics scale between public and private schools (government-dependent and government-independent schools combined)	
	Percentage of students		Performance on the mathematics scale		Percentage of students		Performance on the mathematics scale		Percentage of students		Performance on the mathematics scale		Dif.	
	%	S.E.	Mean score	S.E.	%	S.E.	Mean score	S.E.	%	S.E.	Mean score	S.E.	(Pub. - Priv.)	S.E.
Australia	w	w	w	w	w	w	w	w	w	w	w	w	w	w
Austria	-0.6	(3.0)	-2	(5.0)	0.8	(2.7)	27	(20.3)	-0.2	(1.1)	c	c	-27	(19.4)
Belgium	w	w	w	w	w	w	w	w	w	w	w	w	w	w
Canada	**-2.1**	(1.0)	**-16**	(3.3)	0.5	(0.9)	-4	(13.7)	1.6	(0.9)	3	(15.2)	-14	(11.0)
Czech Republic	-1.6	(2.6)	**-19**	(5.7)	1.2	(2.3)	-12	(22.0)	0.4	(1.1)	c	c	-8	(21.9)
Denmark	-0.9	(3.1)	**-22**	(4.5)	-2.8	(3.3)	6	(9.1)	**3.7**	(1.6)	c	c	**-29**	(10.3)
Finland	**3.6**	(1.7)	**-27**	(3.3)	**-3.6**	(1.7)	2	(14.3)	0.0	c	c	c	**-29**	(14.7)
France	w	w	w	w	w	w	w	w	w	w	w	w	w	w
Germany	2.4	(2.3)	**14**	(5.5)	-2.5	(2.4)	-16	(23.3)	0.1	(0.6)	c	c	22	(24.4)
Greece	0.3	(2.0)	7	(4.9)	0.0	c	c	c	-0.3	(2.0)	c	c	c	c
Hungary	-4.9	(3.8)	**-14**	(5.4)	6.2	(3.7)	-14	(22.1)	-1.2	c	c	c	2	(23.6)
Iceland	-0.1	(0.1)	**-22**	(3.0)	0.5	c	c	c	-0.5	c	c	c	c	c
Ireland	2.2	(1.8)	6	(5.8)	-3.6	(2.1)	-14	(4.9)	1.4	(1.4)	c	c	**18**	(7.1)
Italy	-0.8	(1.4)	**19**	(4.4)	**1.4**	(0.5)	45	(61.9)	-0.7	(1.4)	63	(36.5)	-20	(24.4)
Japan	-2.9	(2.0)	-9	(6.1)	-0.6	c	c	c	3.5	(2.1)	27	(12.4)	**-35**	(13.7)
Korea	10.4	(5.5)	**19**	(9.6)	-4.6	(5.6)	7	(10.6)	-5.8	(4.6)	16	(14.3)	11	(13.9)
Luxembourg	**-1.0**	(0.1)	**-6**	(2.6)	**-0.8**	(0.1)	1	(4.3)	1.8	c	c	c	**-22**	(5.0)
Mexico	4.0	(2.1)	**33**	(4.3)	0.0	(0.2)	c	c	-4.0	(2.1)	22	(10.9)	12	(11.8)
Netherlands	10.3	(6.1)	0	(17.3)	-10.3	(6.1)	**-18**	(7.4)	0.0	c	c	c	18	(21.0)
New Zealand	-0.8	(1.5)	**-26**	(3.9)	0.0	c	c	c	0.8	(1.5)	4	(18.5)	-30	(18.7)
Norway	-0.8	(1.2)	-5	(4.1)	0.8	(1.2)	c	c	0.0	c	c	c	c	c
Poland	**-2.2**	(0.5)	26	(4.8)	1.5	(0.6)	c	c	0.7	(0.4)	c	c	c	c
Portugal	-3.8	(2.3)	**16**	(5.6)	1.6	(2.2)	57	(11.4)	2.2	(1.9)	c	c	**-43**	(19.2)
Slovak Republic	3.5	(3.6)	**-18**	(5.9)	-4.0	(3.7)	-2	(22.3)	0.5	c	c	c	-15	(24.5)
Spain	**4.0**	(1.7)	-1	(4.7)	-3.7	(2.4)	2	(5.9)	-0.3	(2.0)	3	(11.0)	-3	(6.5)
Sweden	**-9.7**	(0.9)	**-33**	(4.1)	**9.7**	(0.9)	-25	(13.7)	0.0	c	c	c	-7	(14.7)
Switzerland	-1.6	(1.7)	4	(5.4)	0.6	(1.1)	21	(38.9)	1.0	(1.3)	7	(26.7)	-9	(26.0)
Turkey	1.0	c	**28**	(8.4)	0.0	c	c	c	-1.0	c	c	c	c	c
United States	0.6	(1.3)	-1	(5.7)	0.0	c	c	c	-0.6	(1.3)	-11	(13.6)	9	(14.7)
OECD average 2003	0.5	(0.5)	**-2**	(1.2)	-0.6	(0.6)	3	(5.2)	0.1	(0.4)	**15**	(6.5)	**-9**	(3.7)
Brazil	-0.9	(2.7)	**35**	(6.8)	0.6	c	c	c	0.3	(2.7)	6	(13.4)	**29**	(14.6)
Hong Kong-China	**-2.5**	(0.4)	26	(15.0)	1.7	(0.9)	12	(6.3)	0.8	(0.8)	c	c	14	(15.5)
Indonesia	7.5	(3.5)	5	(7.2)	**13.4**	(2.8)	16	(20.2)	**-20.8**	(3.8)	49	(12.9)	**-24**	(12.2)
Latvia	-1.3	(1.7)	5	(5.1)	0.4	c	c	c	0.9	(1.5)	c	c	c	c
Liechtenstein	**-1.3**	(0.5)	2	(6.0)	0.0	c	c	c	**1.3**	(0.5)	c	c	c	c
Macao-China	**-0.8**	(0.1)	c	c	**32.0**	(0.2)	9	(4.1)	**-31.3**	(0.2)	29	(6.3)	c	c
Russian Federation	-0.4	(0.7)	**14**	(5.6)	0.0	c	c	c	0.4	(0.7)	c	c	c	c
Thailand	**-4.6**	(1.3)	17	(5.2)	5.7	(1.9)	-23	(19.6)	-1.1	(2.0)	-30	(27.0)	**43**	(15.2)
Tunisia	m	m	m	m	m	m	m	m	m	m	m	m	m	m
Uruguay	-2.6	(1.5)	**-17**	(4.9)	0.0	c	c	c	2.6	(1.5)	-9	(9.2)	-8	(10.2)

Notes: Values that are statistically significant are indicated in bold (see Annex A3).
Only countries and economies with comparable data from PISA 2003 and PISA 2012 are shown.
1. Schools which are directly controlled or managed by: *i)* a public education authority or agency or *ii)* a government agency directly or a governing body, most of whose members are either appointed by a public authority or elected by public franchise.
2. Schools which receive 50% or more of their core funding (i.e. funding that supports the basic educational services of the institution) from government agencies.
3. Schools which receive less than 50% of their core funding (i.e. funding that supports the basic educational services of the institution) from government agencies.
StatLink 🔗 http://dx.doi.org/10.1787/888932957498

[Part 6/6]
Change between 2003 and 2012 in school type and performance in mathematics

Table IV.4.19   *Results based on school principals' reports*

		Change between 2003 and 2012 (PISA 2012 - PISA 2003)								
		PISA index of economic, social and cultural status						Difference in performance on the mathematics scale between public and private schools after accounting for the PISA index of economic, social and cultural status of:		
		Public schools		Private schools (government-dependent and government-independent)		Difference		Students		Students and schools	
		Mean index	S.E.	Mean index	S.E.	Dif. (Pub. - Priv.)	S.E.	Dif. (Pub. - Priv.)	S.E.	Dif. (Pub. - Priv.)	S.E.
OECD	Australia	w	w	w	w	w	w	w	w	w	w
	Austria	**0.30**	(0.04)	**0.68**	(0.17)	**-0.38**	(0.18)	-12	(16.8)	13	(19.5)
	Belgium	w	w	w	w	w	w	w	w	w	w
	Canada	**0.20**	(0.02)	0.18	(0.10)	0.02	(0.10)	-12	(9.5)	-12	(9.7)
	Czech Republic	-0.02	(0.03)	0.05	(0.17)	-0.07	(0.17)	-11	(17.2)	-5	(17.1)
	Denmark	**0.27**	(0.04)	**0.60**	(0.09)	**-0.32**	(0.10)	**-16**	(7.7)	-7	(7.0)
	Finland	**0.31**	(0.03)	**0.35**	(0.16)	-0.04	(0.17)	**-28**	(13.1)	**-27**	(12.9)
	France	w	w	w	w	w	w	w	w	w	w
	Germany	**0.20**	(0.04)	-0.09	(0.18)	0.29	(0.19)	12	(20.4)	-6	(20.8)
	Greece	**0.23**	(0.05)	c	c	c	c	c	c	c	c
	Hungary	0.06	(0.05)	-0.03	(0.16)	0.10	(0.19)	-3	(16.3)	-8	(11.6)
	Iceland	**0.24**	(0.02)	c	c	c	c	c	c	c	c
	Ireland	**0.52**	(0.04)	**0.21**	(0.06)	**0.31**	(0.06)	8	(6.0)	-4	(5.5)
	Italy	**0.23**	(0.03)	0.24	(0.13)	-0.01	(0.13)	-19	(23.9)	-19	(24.8)
	Japan	**0.32**	(0.03)	**0.37**	(0.07)	-0.05	(0.08)	**-34**	(11.3)	**-28**	(8.6)
	Korea	**0.59**	(0.06)	**0.24**	(0.06)	**0.35**	(0.10)	-3	(11.7)	**-27**	(10.3)
	Luxembourg	**0.12**	(0.02)	**0.42**	(0.05)	**-0.30**	(0.05)	**-11**	(5.2)	5	(5.0)
	Mexico	**0.22**	(0.05)	**0.66**	(0.15)	**-0.44**	(0.16)	21	(9.3)	**33**	(7.5)
	Netherlands	**0.40**	(0.10)	**0.30**	(0.05)	0.10	(0.12)	2	(16.3)	-8	(13.3)
	New Zealand	**0.16**	(0.03)	0.24	(0.13)	-0.08	(0.13)	-25	(14.4)	-21	(11.8)
	Norway	**0.29**	(0.03)	c	c	c	c	c	c	c	c
	Poland	**0.18**	(0.04)	c	c	c	c	c	c	c	c
	Portugal	**0.35**	(0.07)	**0.99**	(0.41)	-0.64	(0.43)	-21	(10.8)	-5	(13.9)
	Slovak Republic	0.05	(0.05)	0.27	(0.17)	-0.22	(0.18)	-4	(18.6)	7	(16.0)
	Spain	**0.37**	(0.07)	**0.33**	(0.08)	0.04	(0.11)	-5	(5.3)	-5	(5.4)
	Sweden	**0.17**	(0.03)	0.04	(0.13)	0.14	(0.14)	-13	(10.8)	**-17**	(8.6)
	Switzerland	**0.39**	(0.04)	**0.53**	(0.13)	-0.14	(0.14)	-4	(24.4)	4	(24.6)
	Turkey	**-0.28**	(0.07)	c	c	c	c	c	c	c	c
	United States	0.10	(0.05)	0.25	(0.16)	-0.15	(0.19)	16	(11.5)	21	(12.4)
	OECD average 2003	**0.23**	(0.01)	**0.32**	(0.03)	-0.06	(0.04)	**-8**	(3.0)	**-6**	(2.9)
Partners	Brazil	**0.35**	(0.05)	0.06	(0.13)	**0.29**	(0.15)	24	(12.9)	13	(11.0)
	Hong Kong-China	**0.48**	(0.17)	**0.49**	(0.07)	-0.01	(0.17)	12	(13.8)	13	(14.9)
	Indonesia	0.03	(0.08)	0.11	(0.11)	-0.07	(0.14)	**-23**	(10.4)	**-21**	(8.9)
	Latvia	**0.08**	(0.04)	c	c	c	c	c	c	c	c
	Liechtenstein	**0.58**	(0.07)	c	c	c	c	c	c	c	c
	Macao-China	c	c	c	c	c	c	c	c	c	c
	Russian Federation	**0.50**	(0.04)	c	c	c	c	c	c	c	c
	Thailand	**0.55**	(0.06)	0.22	(0.17)	0.33	(0.18)	35	(13.5)	29	(13.0)
	Tunisia	m	m	m	m	m	m	m	m	m	m
	Uruguay	**-0.20**	(0.05)	0.07	(0.10)	**-0.27**	(0.11)	0	(8.8)	14	(8.9)

Notes: Values that are statistically significant are indicated in bold (see Annex A3).
Only countries and economies with comparable data from PISA 2003 and PISA 2012 are shown.
1. Schools which are directly controlled or managed by: *i)* a public education authority or agency or *ii)* a government agency directly or a governing body, most of whose members are either appointed by a public authority or elected by public franchise.
2. Schools which receive 50% or more of their core funding (i.e. funding that supports the basic educational services of the institution) from government agencies.
3. Schools which receive less than 50% of their core funding (i.e. funding that supports the basic educational services of the institution) from government agencies.

StatLink ᴹˢˡ http://dx.doi.org/10.1787/888932957498

Table IV.4.20

[Part 1/1]
National assessments at the lower secondary level

	Source	Year of reference	Type of programme	Existence
OECD				
Australia	a	2009	All programmes	Yes
Austria	a	2009	All programmes	No
Belgium (Fl.)	a	2009	All programmes	Yes
Belgium (Fr.)¹	a	2009	All programmes	No
Canada	a	2009	All programmes	m
Chile	a	2009	All programmes	Yes
Czech Republic	a	2009	All programmes	No
Denmark	a	2009	All programmes	Yes
England	a	2009	All programmes	No
Estonia	a	2009	All programmes	No
Finland	a	2009	All programmes	Yes
France	a	2009	All programmes	No
Germany	a	2009	All programmes	Yes
Greece	a	2009	All programmes	No
Hungary	a	2009	All programmes	Yes
Iceland	a	2009	All programmes	Yes
Ireland	a	2009	All programmes	No
Israel	a	2009	All programmes	Yes
Italy	a	2009	All programmes	Yes
Japan	a	2009	All programmes	Yes
Korea	a	2009	All programmes	Yes
Luxembourg	a	2009	All programmes	Yes
Mexico	a	2009	All programmes	Yes
Netherlands	a	2009	All programmes	No
New Zealand	a	2009	All programmes	m
Norway	a	2009	All programmes	Yes
Poland	a	2009	All programmes	No
Portugal	a	2009	All programmes	No
Scotland	a	2009	All programmes	No
Slovak Republic	a	2009	General	Yes
	a	2009	Pre-voc. and voc.	No
Slovenia	a	2009	All programmes	m
Spain	a	2009	All programmes	Yes
Sweden	a	2009	All programmes	Yes
Switzerland	a	2009	All programmes	m
Turkey	a	2009	All programmes	a
United States	a	2009	All programmes	Yes
Partners				
Albania	b	2011	All programmes	No
Argentina				m
Brazil	a	2009	All programmes	Yes
Bulgaria	b	2011	All programmes	Yes
Colombia	b	2011	All programmes	Yes
Costa Rica				m
Croatia	b	2011	All programmes	No
Cyprus*	b	2011	All programmes	No
Hong Kong-China	b	2011	All programmes	Yes
Indonesia	a	2009	All programmes	Yes
Jordan	b	2012	All programmes	Yes
Kazakhstan				m
Latvia	b	2011	All programmes	No
Liechtenstein	b	2011	All programmes	Yes
Lithuania	b	2011	All programmes	Yes
Macao-China	b	2011	All programmes	No
Malaysia	b	2011	All programmes	Yes
Montenegro	b	2011	All programmes	Yes
Peru	b	2011	General	Yes
			Pre-voc. and voc.	No
Qatar	b	2011	All programmes	Yes
Romania	b	2011	All programmes	Yes
Russian Federation	a	2009	All programmes	Yes
Serbia				m
Shanghai-China	b	2011	General	Yes
			Pre-voc. and voc.	No
Singapore	b	2011	All programmes	No
Chinese Taipei	b	2011	All programmes	No
Thailand	b	2011	All programmes	Yes
Tunisia	b	2011	All programmes	Yes
United Arab Emirates	b	2011	All programmes	Yes
Uruguay	b	2011	All programmes	No
Viet Nam	b	2011	General	Yes
			Pre-voc. and voc.	No

Table IV.4.21

[Part 1/1]
National assessments at the upper secondary level

	Source	Year of reference	Type of programme	Existence
OECD				
Australia	a	2009	All programmes	No
Austria	a	2009	All programmes	No
Belgium (Fl.)	a	2010	All programmes	Yes
Belgium (Fr.)¹	a	2009	All programmes	No
Canada				m
Chile	a	2009	All programmes	Yes
Czech Republic	a	2009	All programmes	No
Denmark	a	2009	All programmes	No
England	a	2009	All programmes	No
Estonia	a	2009	All programmes	No
Finland	a	2009	All programmes	No
France	a	2009	All programmes	No
Germany	a	2009	All programmes	No
Greece	a	2009	All programmes	No
Hungary	a	2009	All programmes	Yes
Iceland	a	2009	All programmes	No
Ireland	a	2009	All programmes	No
Israel	a	2009	All programmes	No
Italy	a	2009	All programmes	No
Japan	a	2009	All programmes	No
Korea	a	2009	All programmes	Yes
Luxembourg	a	2009	All programmes	No
Mexico	a	2009	All programmes	Yes
Netherlands	a	2009	All programmes	No
New Zealand				m
Norway	a	2009	All programmes	No
Poland	a	2009	All programmes	No
Portugal	a	2009	All programmes	No
Scotland	a	2009	All programmes	No
Slovak Republic	a	2009	All programmes	No
Slovenia				m
Spain	a	2009	All programmes	No
Sweden	a	2009	All programmes	Yes
Switzerland				m
Turkey	a	2009	All programmes	Yes
United States	a	2009	All programmes	Yes
Partners				
Albania	b	2011	All programmes	No
Argentina				m
Brazil	a	2009	General	Yes
			Pre-voc. and voc.	No
Bulgaria	b	2011	All programmes	No
Colombia	b	2011	All programmes	No
Costa Rica				m
Croatia	b	2011	All programmes	No
Cyprus*	b	2011	All programmes	Yes
Hong Kong-China	b	2011	All programmes	No
Indonesia	a	2009	All programmes	Yes
Jordan	b	2012	All programmes	Yes
Kazakhstan				m
Latvia	b	2011	All programmes	No
Liechtenstein	b	2011	All programmes	Yes
Lithuania	b	2011	All programmes	No
Macao-China	b	2011	All programmes	No
Malaysia	b	2011	All programmes	Yes
Montenegro	b	2011	All programmes	No
Peru	b	2011	General	Yes
			Pre-voc. and voc.	No
Qatar	b	2011	All programmes	Yes
Romania	b	2011	All programmes	Yes
Russian Federation	a	2009	All programmes	Yes
Serbia				m
Shanghai-China	b	2011	All programmes	No
Singapore	b	2011	All programmes	No
Chinese Taipei	b	2011	All programmes	Yes
Thailand	b	2011	All programmes	Yes
Tunisia	b	2011	All programmes	Yes
United Arab Emirates	b	2011	All programmes	Yes
Uruguay	b	2011	All programmes	No
Viet Nam	b	2011	General	Yes
			Pre-voc. and voc.	No

Note: Federal states or countries with highly decentralised school systems may experience regulatory differences between states, provinces or regions.
1. A national assessment has been organised every year up to 2013, but exceptionally not in 2009.
* See notes at the beginning of this Annex.
Sources: a. *Education at a Glance 2011: OECD Indicators* (OECD, 2011). For further notes, see Annex 3, available on line: www.oecd.org/edu/eag2011.
 b. PISA system-level data collection in 2013.
StatLink http://dx.doi.org/10.1787/888932957498

Note: Federal states or countries with highly decentralised school systems may experience regulatory differences between states, provinces or regions.
1. A national assessment has been organised every year up to 2013, but exceptionally not in 2009.
* See notes at the beginning of this Annex.
Sources: a. *Education at a Glance 2011: OECD Indicators* (OECD, 2011). For further notes, see Annex 3, available on line: www.oecd.org/edu/eag2011.
 b. PISA system-level data collection in 2013.
StatLink http://dx.doi.org/10.1787/888932957498

[Part 1/2]
Table IV.4.22 National examinations at the lower secondary level

	Source	Year of reference	Type of programme	Existence (1)	Level of government at which they are devised and graded (2)	Standardised at the national level (3)	Compulsory for students (4)	Percentage of students taking them (5)	Student certification/graduation/grade completion (6)	Student promotion/entry to higher grade (7)	Student entry to upper secondary education (8)	Student access to selective upper secondary schools (9)	Student selection for programme/course/tracks at the upper secondary level (10)	Student expulsion from school (11)	Decisions about scholarships/financial assistance for students (12)	Other (13)	Shared with external audience in addition to education authorities (14)	Shared directly with school administrators (15)	Shared directly with classroom teachers (16)	Shared directly with parents (17)	Shared directly with students (18)	Shared directly with media (19)
Australia	a	2011	All programmes	No	a	a	a	a	a	a	a	a	a	a	a	a	a	a	a	a	a	a
Austria	a	2011	All programmes	No	a	a	a	a	a	a	a	a	a	a	a	a	a	a	a	a	a	a
Belgium (Fl.)	a	2011	All programmes	No	a	a	a	a	a	a	a	a	a	a	a	a	a	a	a	a	a	a
Belgium (Fr.)	a	2011	All programmes	No	a	a	a	a	a	a	a	a	a	a	a	a	a	a	a	a	a	a
Canada				m	m	m	m	m	m	m	m	m	m	m	m	m	m	m	m	m	m	m
Chile	a	2011	All programmes	No	a	a	a	a	a	a	a	a	a	a	a	a	a	a	a	a	a	a
Czech Republic	a	2011	All programmes	No	a	a	a	a	a	a	a	a	a	a	a	a	a	a	a	a	a	a
Denmark	a	2011	All programmes	Yes	1	Yes	Yes	2	Yes	No	Yes	No	No	No	No	No	Yes	Yes	Yes	Yes	Yes	Yes
England	a	2011	All programmes	No	a	a	a	a	a	a	a	a	a	a	a	a	a	a	a	a	a	a
Estonia	a	2011	General	Yes	1; 6	Yes	Yes	1	Yes	Yes	Yes	No	No	No	No	No	Yes	Yes	Yes	Yes	Yes	Yes
	a	2011	Pre-voc. and voc.	No	a	a	a	a	a	a	a	a	a	a	a	a	a	a	a	a	a	a
Finland	a	2011	All programmes	No	a	a	a	a	a	a	a	a	a	a	a	a	a	a	a	a	a	a
France	a	2011	All programmes	Yes	1; 6	Yes	Yes	1	Yes	No	No	No	No	No	No	No	Yes	Yes	Yes	Yes	Yes	Yes
Germany	a	2011	General	Yes	2	No	Yes	1	Yes	Yes	Yes	No	No	No	No	No	Yes	Yes	Yes	No	Yes	No
	a	2011	Pre-voc. and voc.	No	a	a	a	a	a	a	a	a	a	a	a	a	a	a	a	a	a	a
Greece	a	2011	All programmes	No	a	a	a	a	a	a	a	a	a	a	a	a	a	a	a	a	a	a
Hungary	a	2011	All programmes	No	a	a	a	a	a	a	a	a	a	a	a	a	a	a	a	a	a	a
Iceland	a	2011	All programmes	No	a	a	a	a	a	a	a	a	a	a	a	a	a	a	a	a	a	a
Ireland	a	2011	All programmes	Yes	1	Yes	Yes	2	Yes	No	No	No	Yes	No	No	No	Yes	Yes	No	Yes	Yes	No
Israel	a	2011	All programmes	No	a	a	a	a	a	a	a	a	a	a	a	a	a	a	a	a	a	a
Italy	a	2011	All programmes	Yes	1; 6	No	Yes	1	Yes	Yes	Yes	No	No	No	No	No	Yes	No	Yes	Yes	Yes	No
Japan	a	2011	All programmes	No	a	a	a	a	a	a	a	a	a	a	a	a	a	a	a	a	a	a
Korea	a	2011	All programmes	No	a	a	a	a	a	a	a	a	a	a	a	a	a	a	a	a	a	a
Luxembourg	a	2011	All programmes	No	a	a	a	a	a	a	a	a	a	a	a	a	a	a	a	a	a	a
Mexico	a	2011	All programmes	No	a	a	a	a	a	a	a	a	a	a	a	a	a	a	a	a	a	a
Netherlands	a	2011	General	Yes	1; 6	Yes	Yes	1	Yes	No	Yes	No	No	No	No	No	Yes	Yes	Yes	Yes	Yes	No
	a	2011	Pre-voc. and voc.	Yes	1; 6	Yes	Yes	1	Yes	No	Yes	No	No	No	No	No	Yes	Yes	Yes	Yes	Yes	No
New Zealand				m	m	m	m	m	m	m	m	m	m	m	m	m	m	m	m	m	m	m
Norway	a	2011	All programmes	Yes	1	Yes	Yes	1	Yes	Yes	Yes	Yes	Yes	No	No	No	Yes	Yes	No	Yes	Yes	Yes
Poland	a	2011	All programmes	Yes	1; 3	Yes	Yes	1	Yes	Yes	Yes	Yes	No	No	No	m	Yes	Yes	Yes	Yes	Yes	Yes
Portugal	a	2011	General	Yes	1	Yes	Yes	1	Yes	Yes	Yes	No	No	No	No	No	Yes	Yes	Yes	Yes	Yes	Yes
	a	2011	Pre-voc. and voc.	No	a	a	a	a	a	a	a	a	a	a	a	a	a	a	a	a	a	a
Scotland	a	2011	All programmes	Yes	1	Yes	No	5	Yes	Yes	No	No	Yes	No	No	No	Yes	Yes	Yes	Yes	Yes	Yes
Slovak Republic	a	2011	All programmes	No	a	a	a	a	a	a	a	a	a	a	a	a	a	a	a	a	a	a
Slovenia				m	m	m	m	m	m	m	m	m	m	m	m	m	m	m	m	m	m	m
Spain	a	2011	All programmes	No	a	a	a	a	a	a	a	a	a	a	a	a	a	a	a	a	a	a
Sweden	a	2011	All programmes	No	a	a	a	a	a	a	a	a	a	a	a	a	a	a	a	a	a	a
Switzerland	a	2011	All programmes	No	a	a	a	a	a	a	a	a	a	a	a	a	a	a	a	a	a	a
Turkey	a	2011	All programmes	a	a	a	a	a	a	a	a	a	a	a	a	a	a	a	a	a	a	a
United States	a	2011	All programmes	Yes	2	No	Yes	2	Yes	m	m	m	m	No	No	Yes	Yes	Yes	Yes	Yes	Yes	No

Levels of government (Column 2)
1: Central authority or government
2: State authorities or governments
3: Provincial/regional authorities or governments
4: Sub-regional or inter-municipal authorities or governments
5: Local authorities or governments
6: School, school board or committee

Percentage of students taking national examinations (Column 5)
1: All students
2: Between 76% and 99% of students
3: Between 51% and 75% of students
4: Between 26% and 50% of students
5: Between 11% and 25% of students
6: 10% or less of students

Note: Federal states or countries with highly decentralised school systems may experience regulatory differences between states, provinces or regions.
* See notes at the beginning of this Annex.
Sources: *a. Education at a Glance 2012: OECD Indicators* (OECD, 2012). For further notes, see Annex 3, available on line: *www.oecd.org/edu/eag2012.*
  b. PISA system-level data collection in 2013.
StatLink ⟨📊⟩ http://dx.doi.org/10.1787/888932957498

[Part 2/2]

Table IV.4.22 National examinations at the lower secondary level

	Source	Year of reference	Type of programme	(1) Existence	(2) Level of government at which they are devised and graded	(3) Standardised at the national level	(4) Compulsory for students	(5) Percentage of students taking them	(6) Student certification/graduation/grade completion	(7) Student promotion/entry to higher grade	(8) Student entry to upper secondary education	(9) Student access to selective upper secondary schools	(10) Student selection for programme/course/tracks at the upper secondary level	(11) Student expulsion from school	(12) Decisions about scholarships/financial assistance for students	(13) Other	(14) Shared with external audience in addition to education authorities	(15) Shared directly with school administrators	(16) Shared directly with classroom teachers	(17) Shared directly with parents	(18) Shared directly with students	(19) Shared directly with media
Albania	b	2011	All programmes	Yes	3	Yes	Yes	1	Yes	a	Yes	No	No	a	No	No	No	No	No	No	No	No
Argentina				m	m	m	m	m	m	m	m	m	m	m	m	m	m	m	m	m	m	m
Brazil	a	2011	All programmes	No	a	a	a	a	a	a	a	a	a	a	a	a	a	a	a	a	a	a
Bulgaria	b	2011	All programmes	Yes	1	Yes	Yes	1	No	No	No	Yes	Yes	No	No	No	Yes	a	a	a	a	a
Colombia	b	2011	All programmes	No	a	a	a	a	a	a	a	a	a	a	a	a	a	a	a	a	a	a
Costa Rica				m	m	m	m	m	m	m	m	m	m	m	m	m	m	m	m	m	m	m
Croatia	b	2011	All programmes	No	a	a	a	a	a	a	a	a	a	a	a	a	a	a	a	a	a	a
Cyprus*	b	2011	All programmes	No	a	a	a	a	a	a	a	a	a	a	a	a	a	a	a	a	a	a
Hong Kong-China	b	2011	All programmes	No	a	a	a	a	a	a	a	a	a	a	a	a	a	a	a	a	a	a
Indonesia	a	2011	All programmes	Yes	1	Yes	Yes	1	Yes	Yes	Yes	No	No	No	No	No	Yes	Yes	Yes	Yes	Yes	No
Jordan	b	2012	All programmes	Yes	6	No	Yes	1	Yes	Yes	a	Yes	Yes	No	Yes	No	Yes	Yes	Yes	Yes	Yes	Yes
Kazakhstan				m	m	m	m	m	m	m	m	m	m	m	m	m	m	m	m	m	m	m
Latvia	b	2011	All programmes	Yes	1	Yes	Yes	1	Yes	No	Yes	Yes	Yes	No	No	No	Yes	Yes	Yes	No	Yes	No
Liechtenstein	b	2011	All programmes	No	a	a	a	a	a	a	a	a	a	a	a	a	a	a	a	a	a	a
Lithuania	b	2011	All programmes	Yes	1	Yes	Yes	1	Yes	No	No	Yes	No	No	No	a	Yes	Yes	Yes	No	Yes	No
Macao-China	b	2011	All programmes	No	a	a	a	a	a	a	a	a	a	a	a	a	a	a	a	a	a	a
Malaysia	b	2011	All programmes	Yes	1	Yes	Yes	1	Yes	Yes	Yes	Yes	No	Yes	m	Yes	Yes	Yes	Yes	Yes	Yes	No
Montenegro	b	2011	All programmes	No	a	a	a	a	a	a	a	a	a	No	No	a	a	a	a	a	a	a
Peru	b	2011	All programmes	No	a	a	a	a	a	a	a	a	a	a	a	a	a	a	a	a	a	a
Qatar	b	2011	General	Yes	2	Yes	Yes	2	Yes	Yes	Yes	Yes	No	No	No	No	Yes	Yes	Yes	Yes	Yes	Yes
			Pre-voc. and voc.	Yes	2	Yes	Yes	1	Yes	Yes	Yes	Yes	No	No	No	No	Yes	Yes	Yes	Yes	Yes	Yes
Romania	b	2011	All programmes	Yes	1	Yes	Yes	1	Yes	Yes	Yes	Yes	No	No	No	m	Yes	Yes	No	No	No	Yes
Russian Federation	a	2011	All programmes	Yes	1	Yes	Yes	1	Yes	Yes	Yes	No	No	a	No	No	Yes	Yes	Yes	No	Yes	No
Serbia				m	m	m	m	m	m	m	m	m	m	m	m	m	m	m	m	m	m	m
Shanghai-China	b	2011	General	Yes	3	Yes	Yes	1	Yes	No	Yes	Yes	Yes	No	No	No	Yes	No	No	No	Yes	No
			Pre-voc. and voc.	No	a	a	a	a	a	a	a	a	a	a	a	a	a	a	a	a	a	a
Singapore	b	2011	All programmes	No	a	a	a	a	a	a	a	a	a	a	a	a	a	a	a	a	a	a
Chinese Taipei	b	2011	All programmes	Yes	1	Yes	Yes	2	No	No	Yes	Yes	No	No	No	No	Yes	Yes	Yes	Yes	Yes	Yes
Thailand	b	2011	All programmes	Yes	1	Yes	Yes	1	No	Yes	Yes	No	No	No	No	No	Yes	Yes	No	No	No	No
Tunisia	b	2011	All programmes	Yes	1	Yes	No	4	Yes	Yes	Yes	Yes	No	No	a	No	a	a	a	a	a	a
United Arab Emirates	b	2011	All programmes	No	a	a	a	a	a	a	a	a	a	a	a	a	a	a	a	a	a	a
Uruguay	b	2011	All programmes	No	a	a	a	a	a	a	a	a	a	a	a	a	a	a	a	a	a	a
Viet Nam	b	2011	General	Yes	1	Yes	Yes	m	Yes	No	No	No	No	No	No	No	Yes	Yes	Yes	Yes	Yes	Yes
			Pre-voc. and voc.	Yes	1	Yes	Yes	m	Yes	No	No	No	No	No	No	No	Yes	Yes	Yes	Yes	Yes	Yes

(Left margin group label: Partners)

Levels of government (Column 2)
1: Central authority or government
2: State authorities or governments
3: Provincial/regional authorities or governments
4: Sub-regional or inter-municipal authorities or governments
5: Local authorities or governments
6: School, school board or committee

Percentage of students taking national examinations (Column 5)
1: All students
2: Between 76% and 99% of students
3: Between 51% and 75% of students
4: Between 26% and 50% of students
5: Between 11% and 25% of students
6: 10% or less of students

Note: Federal states or countries with highly decentralised school systems may experience regulatory differences between states, provinces or regions.
* See notes at the beginning of this Annex.
Sources: a. *Education at a Glance 2012: OECD Indicators* (OECD, 2012). For further notes, see Annex 3, available on line: *www.oecd.org/edu/eag2012*.
b. PISA system-level data collection in 2013.
StatLink ⟐ http://dx.doi.org/10.1787/888932957498

[Part 1/2]

Table IV.4.23 National examinations at the upper secondary level

	Source	Year of reference	Type of programme	(1) Existence	(2) Level of government at which they are devised and graded	(3) Standardised at the national level	(4) Compulsory for students	(5) Percentage of students taking them	(6) Student certification/graduation/grade completion	(7) Student promotion/entry to higher grade	(8) Student entry to tertiary education	(9) Student access to selective tertiary institutions	(10) Student selection for programme/course/tracks at the upper secondary level	(11) Student selection for programme/faculty/discipline/field/specialisation at tertiary level	(12) Student expulsion from school	(13) Decisions about scholarships/financial assistance for students	(14) Other	(15) Shared with external audience in addition to education authorities	(16) Shared directly with school administrators	(17) Shared directly with classroom teachers	(18) Shared directly with parents	(19) Shared directly with students	(20) Shared directly with media
Australia	a	2011	All programmes	Yes	2	No	No	m	Yes	No	Yes	Yes	No	Yes	No	Yes	No	Yes	Yes	No	No	Yes	No
Austria	a	2011	All programmes	No	a	a	a	a	a	a	a	a	a	a	a	a	a	a	a	a	a	a	a
Belgium (Fl.)	a	2011	All programmes	No	a	a	a	a	a	a	a	a	a	a	a	a	a	a	a	a	a	a	a
Belgium (Fr.)	a	2011	All programmes	No	a	a	a	a	a	a	a	a	a	a	a	a	a	a	a	a	a	a	a
Canada				m	m	m	m	m	m	m	m	m	m	m	m	m	m	m	m	m	m	m	m
Chile	a	2011	All programmes	No	a	a	a	a	a	a	a	a	a	a	a	a	a	a	a	a	a	a	a
Czech Republic[1]	a	2011	General	Yes	1; 6	Yes	Yes	3	Yes	Yes	Yes	Yes	No	Yes	No	No	No	Yes	Yes	Yes	No	Yes	No
			Pre-voc. and voc.	Yes	1; 6	Yes	Yes	3	Yes	Yes	Yes	Yes	No	Yes	No	No	No	Yes	Yes	Yes	No	Yes	No
Denmark	a	2011	General	Yes	1	Yes	Yes	1	Yes	No	Yes	Yes	No	No	No	No	No	Yes	Yes	Yes	Yes	Yes	Yes
			Pre-voc. and voc.	Yes	1	Yes	Yes	1	Yes	No	No	No	No	No	No	No	No	Yes	Yes	Yes	Yes	Yes	Yes
England	a	2011	All programmes	Yes	1	Yes	Yes	2	Yes	No	Yes	Yes	Yes	Yes	No	No	No	Yes	Yes	Yes	Yes	Yes	Yes
Estonia	a	2011	General	Yes	1	Yes	Yes	2	Yes	No	Yes	No	No	Yes	No	No	No	Yes	Yes	Yes	Yes	Yes	Yes
			Pre-voc. and voc.	Yes	1	Yes	No	2	Yes	No	Yes	No	No	Yes	No	No	No	Yes	Yes	Yes	Yes	Yes	No
Finland	a	2011	General	Yes	1; 6	Yes	Yes	1	Yes	No	Yes	Yes	No	Yes	No	No	No	Yes	Yes	Yes	No	Yes	Yes
			Pre-voc. and voc.	No	a	a	a	a	a	a	a	a	a	a	a	a	a	a	a	a	a	a	a
France	a	2011	All programmes	Yes	1	Yes	Yes	1	Yes	Yes	Yes	Yes	Yes	Yes	No	No	No	Yes	Yes	Yes	Yes	Yes	Yes
Germany	a	2011	General	Yes	2	No	Yes	1	Yes	Yes	Yes	No	No	No	No	No	No	Yes	Yes	Yes	No	Yes	No
			Pre-voc. and voc.	No	a	a	a	a	a	a	a	a	a	a	a	a	a	a	a	a	a	a	a
Greece	a	2011	All programmes	No	a	a	a	a	a	a	a	a	a	a	a	a	a	a	a	a	a	a	a
Hungary	a	2011	General	Yes	1	Yes	Yes	2	Yes	Yes	Yes	Yes	No	Yes	No	No	No	Yes	Yes	Yes	Yes	Yes	Yes
			Pre-voc. and voc.	Yes	1	Yes	Yes	2	Yes	No	No	No	No	No	No	No	No	Yes	Yes	Yes	Yes	Yes	Yes
Iceland	a	2011	All programmes	No	a	a	a	a	a	a	a	a	a	a	a	a	a	a	a	a	a	a	a
Ireland	a	2011	All programmes	Yes	1	Yes	Yes	2	Yes	No	Yes	Yes	No	Yes	No	No	No	Yes	Yes	No	Yes	Yes	No
Israel	a	2011	All programmes	Yes	1; 6	Yes	No	2	Yes	No	Yes	No	No	Yes	No	No	No	Yes	Yes	No	No	Yes	Yes
Italy	a	2011	All programmes	Yes	1; 6	No	Yes	1	Yes	No	No	No	No	No	Yes	No	No	Yes	No	Yes	Yes	Yes	No
Japan	a	2011	All programmes	No	a	a	a	a	a	a	a	a	a	a	a	a	a	a	a	a	a	a	a
Korea	a	2011	All programmes	No	a	a	a	a	a	a	a	a	a	a	a	a	a	a	a	a	a	a	a
Luxembourg	a	2011	All programmes	Yes	1	Yes	Yes	2	Yes	Yes	Yes	a	No	No	No	No	No	Yes	Yes	Yes	Yes	Yes	Yes
Mexico	a	2011	All programmes	No	a	a	a	a	a	a	a	a	a	a	a	a	a	a	a	a	a	a	a
Netherlands	a	2011	General	Yes	1; 6	Yes	Yes	1	Yes	No	Yes	Yes	No	Yes	No	No	No	Yes	Yes	Yes	Yes	Yes	No
			Pre-voc. and voc.	No	a	a	a	a	a	a	a	a	a	a	a	a	a	a	a	a	a	a	a
New Zealand				m	m	m	m	m	m	m	m	m	m	m	m	m	m	m	m	m	m	m	m
Norway	a	2011	General	Yes	1	Yes	Yes	1	Yes	Yes	Yes	Yes	Yes	Yes	No	No	No	Yes	Yes	No	No	No	Yes
			Pre-voc. and voc.	Yes	1; 3	Yes	Yes	1	Yes	Yes	Yes	Yes	No	Yes	No	No	No	Yes	Yes	No	No	No	Yes
Poland[1]	a	2011	General	Yes	1; 3	Yes	No	2	No	No	No	No	Yes	No	No	m		Yes	Yes	Yes	Yes	Yes	Yes
			Pre-voc. and voc.	Yes	1; 3	Yes	No	2	No	No	No	No	Yes	No	No	Yes		Yes	Yes	Yes	Yes	Yes	Yes
Portugal	a	2011	General	Yes	1	Yes	Yes	1	Yes	Yes	Yes	No	Yes	No	No	No	No	Yes	Yes	Yes	Yes	Yes	Yes
			Pre-voc. and voc.	No	a	a	a	a	a	a	a	a	a	a	a	a	a	a	a	a	a	a	a
Scotland	a	2011	General	Yes	1	Yes	Yes	2	Yes	Yes	Yes	No	No	Yes	No	No	No	Yes	Yes	Yes	Yes	Yes	Yes
			Pre-voc. and voc.	Yes	1	Yes	No	6	Yes	Yes	Yes	No	No	Yes	No	No	No	Yes	Yes	Yes	Yes	Yes	Yes
Slovak Republic[1]	a	2011	General	Yes	1; 6	Yes	Yes	1	Yes	No	Yes	Yes	No	Yes	No	No	No	Yes	No	No	No	Yes	No
			Pre-voc. and voc.	Yes	1; 6	Yes	Yes	3	Yes	No	Yes	No	No	Yes	No	No	No	Yes	No	No	No	Yes	No
Slovenia				m	m	m	m	m	m	m	m	m	m	m	m	m	m	m	m	m	m	m	m
Spain	a	2011	General	No	a	a	a	a	a	a	a	a	a	a	a	a	a	a	a	a	a	a	a
			Pre-voc. and voc.	Yes	2	No	No	6	No	No	No	No	No	No	No	No	No	Yes	Yes	No	Yes	Yes	No
Sweden	a	2011	All programmes	No	a	a	a	a	a	a	a	a	a	a	a	a	a	a	a	a	a	a	a
Switzerland	a	2011	All programmes	No	a	a	a	a	a	a	a	a	a	a	a	a	a	a	a	a	a	a	a
Turkey	a	2011	All programmes	No	a	a	a	a	a	a	a	a	a	a	a	a	a	a	a	a	a	a	a
United States	a	2011	All programmes	Yes	2	No	Yes	2	Yes	m	No	m	m	m	No	No	Yes	Yes	Yes	Yes	Yes	Yes	No

OECD

Levels of government (Column 2)
1: Central authority or government
2: State authorities or governments
3: Provincial/regional authorities or governments
4: Sub-regional or inter-municipal authorities or governments
5: Local authorities or governments
6: School, school board or committee

Percentage of students taking national examinations (Column 5)
1: All students
2: Between 76% and 99% of students
3: Between 51% and 75% of students
4: Between 26% and 50% of students
5: Between 11% and 25% of students
6: 10% or less of students

Note: Federal states or countries with highly decentralised school systems may have different regulations in states, provinces or regions.
1. Excludes ISCED 3C programmes, includes ISCED 3A vocational programmes only.
* See notes at the beginning of this Annex.
Sources: a. *Education at a Glance 2012: OECD Indicators* (OECD, 2012). For further notes, see Annex 3, available on line: *www.oecd.org/edu/eag2012.*
b. PISA system-level data collection in 2013.
StatLink http://dx.doi.org/10.1787/888932957498

[Part 2/2]

Table IV.4.23 National examinations at the upper secondary level

	Source	Year of reference	Type of programme	(1) Existence	(2) Level of government at which they are devised and graded	(3) Standardised at the national level	(4) Compulsory for students	(5) Percentage of students taking them	(6) Student certification/graduation/grade completion	(7) Student promotion/entry to higher grade	(8) Student entry to tertiary education	(9) Student access to selective tertiary institutions	(10) Student selection for programme/course/tracks at the upper secondary level	(11) Student selection for programme/faculty/discipline/field/specialisation at tertiary level	(12) Student expulsion from school	(13) Decisions about scholarships/financial assistance for students	(14) Other	(15) Shared with external audience in addition to education authorities	(16) Shared directly with school administrators	(17) Shared directly with classroom teachers	(18) Shared directly with parents	(19) Shared directly with students	(20) Shared directly with media
Albania	b	2011	All programmes	Yes	1	Yes	Yes	2	Yes	No	Yes	Yes	No	Yes	a	Yes	No	Yes	No	No	No	No	Yes
Argentina	m			m	m	m	m	m	m	m	m	m	m	m	m	m	m	m	m	m	m	m	m
Brazil	a	2011	All programmes	No	a	a	a	a	a	a	a	a	a	a	a	a	a	a	a	a	a	a	a
Bulgaria	b	2011	All programmes	Yes	1	Yes	Yes	2	Yes	Yes	Yes	Yes	No	Yes	No	No	No	Yes	a	a	a	a	a
Colombia	b	2011	All programmes	No	a	a	a	a	a	a	a	a	a	a	a	a	a	a	a	a	a	a	a
Costa Rica	m			m	m	m	m	m	m	m	m	m	m	m	m	m	m	m	m	m	m	m	m
Croatia	b	2011	All programmes	Yes	2	Yes	No	3	Yes	No	Yes	Yes	No	Yes	No	No	No	Yes	No	No	No	Yes	Yes
			Pre-voc. and voc.	Yes	1	Yes	Yes	1	Yes	No	Yes	Yes	No	Yes	No	Yes	a	Yes	Yes	Yes	Yes	Yes	Yes
Cyprus*	b	2011	General	Yes	1	Yes	Yes	1	Yes	No	Yes	Yes	No	Yes	No	Yes	a	Yes	Yes	Yes	Yes	Yes	Yes
			Pre-voc. and voc.	Yes	1	Yes	Yes	1	Yes	No	Yes	Yes	No	Yes	No	Yes	a	Yes	Yes	Yes	Yes	Yes	Yes
Hong Kong-China	b	2011	All programmes	Yes	1	Yes	No	2	Yes	Yes	Yes	Yes	Yes	Yes	No	No	a	Yes	Yes	Yes	Yes	No	No
Indonesia	a	2011	All programmes	Yes	1	Yes	Yes	1	Yes	Yes	No	No	No	No	No	No	No	Yes	Yes	Yes	Yes	Yes	No
Jordan	b	2012	All programmes	Yes	1	Yes	Yes	1	Yes	Yes	Yes	Yes	Yes	Yes	No	Yes	No	Yes	Yes	Yes	Yes	Yes	Yes
Kazakhstan	m			m	m	m	m	m	m	m	m	m	m	m	m	m	m	m	m	m	m	m	m
Latvia	b	2011	All programmes	Yes	1	Yes	Yes	1	Yes	No	Yes	Yes	No	Yes	No	No	No	Yes	No	No	Yes	No	No
Liechtenstein	b	2011	All programmes	Yes	2	Yes	Yes	5	Yes	Yes	Yes	No	Yes	No	No	No	No	Yes	Yes	Yes	Yes	Yes	No
Lithuania	b	2011	All programmes	Yes	1	Yes	Yes	1	Yes	No	Yes	Yes	No	Yes	a	Yes	a	Yes	No	No	Yes	Yes	No
Macao-China	b	2011	All programmes	No	a	a	a	a	a	a	a	a	a	a	a	a	a	a	a	a	a	a	a
Malaysia	b	2011	All programmes	Yes	1	Yes	Yes	1	Yes	Yes	Yes	Yes	Yes	Yes	No	Yes	m	Yes	Yes	Yes	Yes	Yes	No
Montenegro	b	2011	General	Yes	1	Yes	Yes	2	Yes	No	Yes	Yes	No	Yes	No	Yes	No	Yes	Yes	Yes	Yes	Yes	No
			Pre-voc. and voc.	Yes	1	Yes	Yes	2	Yes	No	Yes	Yes	No	Yes	No	Yes	No	Yes	Yes	Yes	Yes	Yes	No
Peru	b	2011	All programmes	No	a	a	a	a	a	a	a	a	a	a	a	a	a	a	a	a	a	a	a
Qatar	b	2011	General	Yes	2	Yes	Yes	2	Yes	Yes	Yes	Yes	Yes	Yes	No	No	No	Yes	Yes	Yes	Yes	Yes	Yes
			Pre-voc. and voc.	Yes	2	Yes	Yes	1	Yes	Yes	Yes	Yes	Yes	Yes	No	No	No	Yes	Yes	Yes	Yes	Yes	Yes
Romania	b	2011	All programmes	Yes	1	Yes	Yes	1	Yes	Yes	Yes	Yes	No	No	No	No	m	Yes	Yes	No	No	No	Yes
Russian Federation	a	2011	All programmes	Yes	1	Yes	Yes	1	Yes	Yes	Yes	No	No	No	a	No	a	Yes	Yes	Yes	Yes	No	No
Serbia	m			m	m	m	m	m	m	m	m	m	m	m	m	m	m	m	m	m	m	m	m
Shanghai-China	b	2011	General	Yes	3	Yes	Yes	1	Yes	No	Yes	No	Yes	No	No	No	No	Yes	No	No	No	No	No
			Pre-voc. and voc.	No	a	a	a	a	a	a	a	a	a	a	a	a	a	a	a	a	a	a	a
Singapore	b	2011	All programmes	Yes	1	Yes	No	2	Yes	Yes	Yes	Yes	Yes	Yes	No	Yes	a	Yes	Yes	Yes	Yes	Yes	Yes
Chinese Taipei	b	2011	General	Yes	1	Yes	Yes	2	No	No	Yes	Yes	Yes	Yes	No	No	No	Yes	Yes	Yes	Yes	Yes	Yes
			Pre-voc. and voc.	Yes	1	Yes	Yes	2	No	No	Yes	Yes	Yes	Yes	No	No	No	Yes	Yes	Yes	Yes	Yes	Yes
Thailand	b	2011	General	Yes	1	Yes	Yes	1	No	Yes	Yes	No	No	No	No	No	No	Yes	Yes	No	No	No	No
			Pre-voc. and voc.	No	a	a	a	a	a	a	a	a	a	a	a	a	a	a	a	a	a	a	a
Tunisia	b	2011	All programmes	Yes	1	Yes	Yes	1	Yes	Yes	Yes	Yes	Yes	Yes	Yes	No	a	No	a	a	a	a	a
United Arab Emirates	b	2011	General	Yes	1	Yes	Yes	1	Yes	Yes	Yes	Yes	No	Yes	No	Yes	No	Yes	Yes	Yes	Yes	Yes	Yes
			Pre-voc. and voc.	Yes	1	Yes	Yes	1	Yes	Yes	Yes	Yes	No	Yes	No	Yes	No	Yes	Yes	Yes	Yes	Yes	Yes
Uruguay	b	2011	All programmes	No	a	a	a	a	a	a	a	a	a	a	a	a	a	a	a	a	a	a	a
Viet Nam	b	2011	General	Yes	1	Yes	Yes	m	Yes	No	No	No	No	No	No	No	No	Yes	Yes	Yes	Yes	Yes	Yes
			Pre-voc. and voc.	Yes	1	Yes	Yes	m	Yes	No	No	No	No	No	No	No	No	Yes	Yes	Yes	Yes	Yes	Yes

Partners

Main purposes or uses = columns (6)–(14). **How results are shared** = columns (15)–(20).

Levels of government (Column 2)
1: Central authority or government
2: State authorities or governments
3: Provincial/regional authorities or governments
4: Sub-regional or inter-municipal authorities or governments
5: Local authorities or governments
6: School, school board or committee

Percentage of students taking national examinations (Column 5)
1: All students
2: Between 76% and 99% of students
3: Between 51% and 75% of students
4: Between 26% and 50% of students
5: Between 11% and 25% of students
6: 10% or less of students

Note: Federal states or countries with highly decentralised school systems may have different regulations in states, provinces or regions.
1. Excludes ISCED 3C programmes, includes ISCED 3A vocational programmes only.
* See notes at the beginning of this Annex.
Sources: a. *Education at a Glance 2012: OECD Indicators* (OECD, 2012). For further notes, see Annex 3, available on line: *www.oecd.org/edu/eag2012.*
b. PISA system-level data collection in 2013.
StatLink ᵐˢᵖ http://dx.doi.org/10.1787/888932957498

[Part 1/2]

Table IV.4.24 **Other (non-national) standardised examinations administered in multiple lower secondary schools**

	Source	Year of reference	Type of programme	(1) Existence	(2) Level of government at which they are devised and graded	(3) Compulsory for students	(4) Percentage of students taking them	Main purposes or uses (5) Student certification/graduation/grade completion	(6) Student promotion/entry to higher grade	(7) Student entry to upper secondary education	(8) Student access to selective upper secondary schools	(9) Student selection for programme/course/tracks at the upper secondary level	(10) Student expulsion from school	(11) Decisions about scholarships/financial assistance for students	(12) Other	How results are shared (13) Shared with external audience in addition to education authorities	(14) Shared directly with school administrators	(15) Shared directly with classroom teachers	(16) Shared directly with parents	(17) Shared directly with students	(18) Shared directly with media
OECD Australia				m	m	m	m	m	m	m	m	m	m	m	m	m	m	m	m	m	m
Austria	a	2011	All programmes	No	a	a	a	a	a	a	a	a	a	a	a	a	a	a	a	a	a
Belgium (Fl.)	a	2011	All programmes	No	a	a	a	a	a	a	a	a	a	a	a	a	a	a	a	a	a
Belgium (Fr.)	a	2011	All programmes	Yes	2	No	3	Yes	Yes	No	No	Yes	No	No	No	Yes	Yes	Yes	Yes	Yes	Yes
Canada				m	m	m	m	m	m	m	m	m	m	m	m	m	m	m	m	m	m
Chile	a	2011	All programmes	No	a	a	a	a	a	a	a	a	a	a	a	a	a	a	a	a	a
Czech Republic	a	2011	All programmes	No	a	a	a	a	a	a	a	a	a	a	a	a	a	a	a	a	a
Denmark	a	2011	All programmes	No	a	a	a	a	a	a	a	a	a	a	a	a	a	a	a	a	a
England	a	2011	All programmes	No	a	a	a	a	a	a	a	a	a	a	a	a	a	a	a	a	a
Estonia	a	2011	All programmes	No	a	a	a	a	a	a	a	a	a	a	a	a	a	a	a	a	a
Finland	a	2011	All programmes	No	a	a	a	a	a	a	a	a	a	a	a	a	a	a	a	a	a
France	a	2011	All programmes	No	a	a	a	a	a	a	a	a	a	a	a	a	a	a	a	a	a
Germany	a	2011	General	No	a	a	a	a	a	a	a	a	a	a	a	a	a	a	a	a	a
			Pre-voc. and voc.	m	m	m	m	m	m	m	m	m	m	m	m	m	m	m	m	m	m
Greece	a	2011	All programmes	No	a	a	a	a	a	a	a	a	a	a	a	a	a	a	a	a	a
Hungary	a	2011	All programmes	No	a	a	a	a	a	a	a	a	a	a	a	a	a	a	a	a	a
Iceland	a	2011	All programmes	No	a	a	a	a	a	a	a	a	a	a	a	a	a	a	a	a	a
Ireland	a	2011	All programmes	No	a	a	a	a	a	a	a	a	a	a	a	a	a	a	a	a	a
Israel	a	2011	All programmes	No	a	a	a	a	a	a	a	a	a	a	a	a	a	a	a	a	a
Italy	a	2011	All programmes	No	a	a	a	a	a	a	a	a	a	a	a	a	a	a	a	a	a
Japan	a	2011	All programmes	Yes	3	No	m	No	No	Yes	Yes	No	No	No	No	Yes	No	No	No	Yes	No
Korea				m	m	m	m	m	m	m	m	m	m	m	m	m	m	m	m	m	m
Luxembourg	a	2011	All programmes	No	a	a	a	a	a	a	a	a	a	a	a	a	a	a	a	a	a
Mexico	a	2011	All programmes	No	a	a	a	a	a	a	a	a	a	a	a	a	a	a	a	a	a
Netherlands	a	2011	All programmes	No	a	a	a	a	a	a	a	a	a	a	a	a	a	a	a	a	a
New Zealand				m	m	m	m	m	m	m	m	m	m	m	m	m	m	m	m	m	m
Norway	a	2011	All programmes	Yes	5	Yes	1	Yes	Yes	Yes	Yes	Yes	No	No	No	Yes	Yes	Yes	Yes	Yes	Yes
Poland	a	2011	All programmes	No	a	a	a	a	a	a	a	a	a	a	a	a	a	a	a	a	a
Portugal	a	2011	All programmes	No	a	a	a	a	a	a	a	a	a	a	a	a	a	a	a	a	a
Scotland	a	2011	All programmes	No	a	a	a	a	a	a	a	a	a	a	a	a	a	a	a	a	a
Slovak Republic	a	2011	All programmes	No	a	a	a	a	a	a	a	a	a	a	a	a	a	a	a	a	a
Slovenia				m	m	m	m	m	m	m	m	m	m	m	m	m	m	m	m	m	m
Spain	a	2011	All programmes	No	a	a	a	a	a	a	a	a	a	a	a	a	a	a	a	a	a
Sweden	a	2011	All programmes	No	a	a	a	a	a	a	a	a	a	a	a	a	a	a	a	a	a
Switzerland	a	2011	All programmes	Yes	2; 6	m	m	m	m	m	m	m	m	m	m	m	m	m	m	m	m
Turkey	a	2011	All programmes	a	a	a	a	a	a	a	a	a	a	a	a	a	a	a	a	a	a
United States	a	2011	All programmes	Yes	m	m	m	Yes	m	m	m	m	No	No	Yes	No	a	a	a	a	a

Levels of government (Column 2)
1: Central authority or government
2: State authorities or governments
3: Provincial/regional authorities or governments
4: Sub-regional or inter-municipal authorities or governments
5: Local authorities or governments
6: School, school board or committee
7: Private company

Percentage of students taking non-national examinations (Column 4)
1: All students
2: Between 76% and 99% of students
3: Between 51% and 75% of students
4: Between 26% and 50% of students
5: Between 11% and 25% of students
6: 10% or less of students

Note: Federal states or countries with highly decentralised school systems may have different regulations in states, provinces or regions.
* See notes at the beginning of this Annex.
Sources: a. *Education at a Glance 2012: OECD Indicators* (OECD, 2012). For further notes, see Annex 3, available on line: *www.oecd.org/edu/eag2012*.
b. PISA system-level data collection in 2013.
StatLink ᵃᵗᵍˢᵖ http://dx.doi.org/10.1787/888932957498

[Part 2/2]

Table IV.4.24 **Other (non-national) standardised examinations administered in multiple lower secondary schools**

		Source	Year of reference	Type of programme	Existence (1)	Level of government at which they are devised and graded (2)	Compulsory for students (3)	Percentage of students taking them (4)	Student certification/graduation/grade completion (5)	Student promotion/entry to higher grade (6)	Student entry to upper secondary education (7)	Student access to selective upper secondary schools (8)	Student selection for programme/course/tracks at the upper secondary level (9)	Student expulsion from school (10)	Decisions about scholarships/financial assistance for students (11)	Other (12)	Shared with external audience in addition to education authorities (13)	Shared directly with school administrators (14)	Shared directly with classroom teachers (15)	Shared directly with parents (16)	Shared directly with students (17)	Shared directly with media (18)
Partners	Albania	b	2011	All programmes	No	a	a	a	a	a	a	a	a	a	a	a	a	a	a	a	a	a
	Argentina				m	m	m	m	m	m	m	m	m	m	m	m	m	m	m	m	m	m
	Brazil	a	2011	All programmes	No	a	a	a	a	a	a	a	a	a	a	a	a	a	a	a	a	a
	Bulgaria	b	2011	All programmes	No	a	a	a	a	a	a	a	a	a	a	a	a	a	a	a	a	a
	Colombia	b	2011	All programmes	No	a	a	a	a	a	a	a	a	a	a	a	a	a	a	a	a	a
	Costa Rica				m	m	m	m	m	m	m	m	m	m	m	m	m	m	m	m	m	m
	Croatia	b	2011	All programmes	No	a	a	a	a	a	a	a	a	a	a	a	a	a	a	a	a	a
	Cyprus*	b	2011	All programmes	No	a	a	a	a	a	a	a	a	a	a	a	a	a	a	a	a	a
	Hong Kong-China	b	2011	All programmes	No	a	a	a	a	a	a	a	a	a	a	a	a	a	a	a	a	a
	Indonesia	a	2011	All programmes	No	a	a	a	a	a	a	a	a	a	a	a	a	a	a	a	a	a
	Jordan	b	2012	All programmes	No	a	a	a	a	a	a	a	a	a	a	a	a	a	a	a	a	a
	Kazakhstan				m	m	m	m	m	m	m	m	m	m	m	m	m	m	m	m	m	m
	Latvia	b	2011	All programmes	No	a	a	a	a	a	a	a	a	a	a	a	a	a	a	a	a	a
	Liechtenstein	b	2011	All programmes	Yes	6	Yes	1	Yes	Yes	Yes	Yes	Yes	Yes	No	No	No	a	a	a	a	a
	Lithuania	b	2011	All programmes	No	a	a	a	a	a	a	a	a	a	a	a	a	a	a	a	a	a
	Macao-China	b	2011	All programmes	No	a	a	a	a	a	a	a	a	a	a	a	a	a	a	a	a	a
	Malaysia	b	2011	All programmes	No	a	a	a	a	a	a	a	a	a	a	a	a	a	a	a	a	a
	Montenegro	b	2011	All programmes	No	a	a	a	a	a	a	a	a	a	a	a	a	a	a	a	a	a
	Peru	b	2011	All programmes	No	a	a	a	a	a	a	a	a	a	a	a	a	a	a	a	a	a
	Qatar	b	2011	General	Yes	m	Yes	4	Yes	Yes	Yes	Yes	Yes	No	No	No	Yes	Yes	Yes	Yes	Yes	Yes
				Pre-voc. and voc.	a	a	a	a	a	a	a	a	a	a	a	a	a	a	a	a	a	a
	Romania	b	2011	All programmes	m	m	m	m	m	m	m	m	m	m	m	m	m	m	m	m	m	m
	Russian Federation	a	2011	All programmes	No	a	a	a	a	a	a	a	a	a	a	a	a	a	a	a	a	a
	Serbia				m	m	m	m	m	m	m	m	m	m	m	m	m	m	m	m	m	m
	Shanghai-China	b	2011	All programmes	No	a	a	a	a	a	a	a	a	a	a	a	a	a	a	a	a	a
	Singapore	b	2011	All programmes	No	a	a	a	a	a	a	a	a	a	a	a	a	a	a	a	a	a
	Chinese Taipei	b	2011	All programmes	No	a	a	a	a	a	a	a	a	a	a	a	a	a	a	a	a	a
	Thailand	b	2011	All programmes	No	a	a	a	a	a	a	a	a	a	a	a	a	a	a	a	a	a
	Tunisia	b	2011	All programmes	m	m	m	m	m	m	m	m	m	m	m	m	m	m	m	m	m	m
	United Arab Emirates	b	2011	All programmes	Yes	3	Yes	1	Yes	Yes	No	Yes	No	No	No	No	Yes	Yes	Yes	Yes	Yes	No
	Uruguay	b	2011	All programmes	No	a	a	a	a	a	a	a	a	a	a	a	a	a	a	a	a	a
	Viet Nam	b	2011	General	m	m	m	m	m	m	m	m	m	m	m	m	m	m	m	m	m	m
				Pre-voc. and voc.	m	m	m	m	m	m	m	m	m	m	m	m	m	m	m	m	m	m

Levels of government (Column 2)
1: Central authority or government
2: State authorities or governments
3: Provincial/regional authorities or governments
4: Sub-regional or inter-municipal authorities or governments
5: Local authorities or governments
6: School, school board or committee
7: Private company

Percentage of students taking non-national examinations (Column 4)
1: All students
2: Between 76% and 99% of students
3: Between 51% and 75% of students
4: Between 26% and 50% of students
5: Between 11% and 25% of students
6: 10% or less of students

Note: Federal states or countries with highly decentralised school systems may have different regulations in states, provinces or regions.
* See notes at the beginning of this Annex.
Sources: a. *Education at a Glance 2012: OECD Indicators* (OECD, 2012). For further notes, see Annex 3, available on line: *www.oecd.org/edu/eag2012*.
    b. PISA system-level data collection in 2013.
StatLink ⌦ http://dx.doi.org/10.1787/888932957498

[Part 1/2]

Table IV.4.25 Other (non-national) standardised examinations administered in multiple upper secondary schools

	Source	Year of reference	Type of programme	(1) Existence	(2) Level of government at which they are devised and graded	(3) Compulsory for students	(4) Percentage of students taking them	(5) Student certification/graduation/grade completion	(6) Student promotion/entry to higher grade	(7) Student entry to tertiary education	(8) Student access to selective tertiary institutions	(9) Student selection for programme/course/tracks at the upper secondary level	(10) Student selection for programme/faculty/discipline/field/specialisation at tertiary level	(11) Student expulsion from school	(12) Decisions about scholarships/financial assistance for students	(13) Other	(14) Shared with external audience in addition to education authorities	(15) Shared directly with school administrators	(16) Shared directly with classroom teachers	(17) Shared directly with parents	(18) Shared directly with students	(19) Shared directly with media
Australia	a	2011	All programmes	m	m	m	m	m	m	m	m	m	m	m	m	m	m	m	m	m	m	m
Austria	a	2011	All programmes	No	a	a	a	a	a	a	a	a	a	a	a	a	a	a	a	a	a	a
Belgium (Fl.)	a	2011	All programmes	No	a	a	a	a	a	a	a	a	a	a	a	a	a	a	a	a	a	a
Belgium (Fr.)	a	2011	All programmes	Yes	2	No	3	Yes	Yes	Yes	No	No	No	No	No	No	Yes	Yes	Yes	Yes	Yes	Yes
Canada			All programmes	m	m	m	m	m	m	m	m	m	m	m	m	m	m	m	m	m	m	m
Chile	a	2011	All programmes	No	a	a	a	a	a	a	a	a	a	a	a	a	a	a	a	a	a	a
Czech Republic[1]	a	2011	General	No	a	a	a	a	a	a	a	a	a	a	a	a	a	a	a	a	a	a
			Pre-voc. and voc.	Yes	1; 6	Yes	4	Yes	Yes	No	No	No	No	No	No	No	Yes	Yes	Yes	Yes	Yes	No
Denmark	a	2011	All programmes	No	a	a	a	a	a	a	a	a	a	a	a	a	a	a	a	a	a	a
England	a	2011	All programmes	No	a	a	a	a	a	a	a	a	a	a	a	a	a	a	a	a	a	a
Estonia	a	2011	General	No	a	a	a	a	a	a	a	a	a	a	a	a	a	a	a	a	a	a
			Pre-voc. and voc.	Yes	7	No	3	Yes	No	No	No	No	No	No	No	No	Yes	Yes	Yes	Yes	Yes	Yes
Finland	a	2011	All programmes	No	a	a	a	a	a	a	a	a	a	a	a	a	a	a	a	a	a	a
France	a	2011	All programmes	No	a	a	a	a	a	a	a	a	a	a	a	a	a	a	a	a	a	a
Germany	a	2011	General	No	a	a	a	a	a	a	a	a	a	a	a	a	a	a	a	a	a	a
			Pre-voc. and voc.	m	m	m	m	m	m	m	m	m	m	m	m	m	m	m	m	m	m	m
Greece	a	2011	All programmes	No	a	a	a	a	a	a	a	a	a	a	a	a	a	a	a	a	a	a
Hungary	a	2011	All programmes	No	a	a	a	a	a	a	a	a	a	a	a	a	a	a	a	a	a	a
Iceland	a	2011	All programmes	No	a	a	a	a	a	a	a	a	a	a	a	a	a	a	a	a	a	a
Ireland	a	2011	All programmes	No	a	a	a	a	a	a	a	a	a	a	a	a	a	a	a	a	a	a
Israel	a	2011	All programmes	No	a	a	a	a	a	a	a	a	a	a	a	a	a	a	a	a	a	a
Italy	a	2011	All programmes	No	a	a	a	a	a	a	a	a	a	a	a	a	a	a	a	a	a	a
Japan	a	2011	All programmes	No	a	a	a	a	a	a	a	a	a	a	a	a	a	a	a	a	a	a
Korea	a	2011	All programmes	No	a	a	a	a	a	a	a	a	a	a	a	a	a	a	a	a	a	a
Luxembourg	a	2011	All programmes	No	a	a	a	a	a	a	a	a	a	a	a	a	a	a	a	a	a	a
Mexico	a	2011	All programmes	No	a	a	a	a	a	a	a	a	a	a	a	a	a	a	a	a	a	a
Netherlands	a	2011	General	No	a	a	a	a	a	a	a	a	a	a	a	a	a	a	a	a	a	a
			Pre-voc. and voc.	Yes	6; 1	Yes	1	Yes	a	Yes	No	No	Yes	No	No	No	No	a	a	a	a	a
New Zealand	a	2011	All programmes	m	m	m	m	m	m	m	m	m	m	m	m	m	m	m	m	m	m	m
Norway	a	2011	General	Yes	3	Yes	1	Yes	Yes	Yes	Yes	Yes	Yes	No	No	No	Yes	Yes	Yes	No	Yes	Yes
			Pre-voc. and voc.	Yes	3	Yes	1	Yes	Yes	Yes	Yes	Yes	Yes	No	No	No	Yes	Yes	Yes	No	Yes	Yes
Poland	a	2011	General	No	a	a	a	a	a	a	a	a	a	a	a	a	a	a	a	a	a	a
			Pre-voc. and voc.	m	m	m	m	m	m	m	m	m	m	m	m	m	m	m	m	m	m	m
Portugal	a	2011	All programmes	No	a	a	a	a	a	a	a	a	a	a	a	a	a	a	a	a	a	a
Scotland	a	2011	All programmes	No	a	a	a	a	a	a	a	a	a	a	a	a	a	a	a	a	a	a
Slovak Republic	a	2011	All programmes	No	a	a	a	a	a	a	a	a	a	a	a	a	a	a	a	a	a	a
Slovenia	a	2011	All programmes	m	m	m	m	m	m	m	m	m	m	m	m	m	m	m	m	m	m	m
Spain	a	2011	All programmes	No	a	a	a	a	a	a	a	a	a	a	a	a	a	a	a	a	a	a
Sweden	a	2011	All programmes	No	a	a	a	a	a	a	a	a	a	a	a	a	a	a	a	a	a	a
Switzerland	a	2011	All programmes	Yes	1; 2; 5; 6; 7	m	m	m	m	m	m	m	m	m	m	m	m	m	m	m	m	m
Turkey	a	2011	All programmes	No	a	a	a	a	a	a	a	a	a	a	a	a	a	a	a	a	a	a
United States	a	2011	All programmes	Yes	m	m	m	Yes	m	m	m	m	m	No	No	Yes	No	a	a	a	a	a

Main purposes or uses: columns (5)–(13). How results are shared: columns (14)–(19). OECD countries.

Levels of government (Column 2)
1: Central authority or government
2: State authorities or governments
3: Provincial/regional authorities or governments
4: Sub-regional or inter-municipal authorities or governments
5: Local authorities or governments
6: School, school board or committee
7: Private company

Percentage of students taking non-national examinations (Column 4)
1: All students
2: Between 76% and 99% of students
3: Between 51% and 75% of students
4: Between 26% and 50% of students
5: Between 11% and 25% of students
6: 10% or less of students

Note: Federal states or countries with highly decentralised school systems may have different regulations in states, provinces or regions.
1. Includes ISCED 3C programmes only.
* See notes at the beginning of this Annex.
Sources: *a. Education at a Glance 2012: OECD Indicators* (OECD, 2012). For further notes, see Annex 3, available on line: *www.oecd.org/edu/eag2012*.
   b. PISA system-level data collection in 2013.
StatLink ⌸⌸⌸ http://dx.doi.org/10.1787/888932957498

[Part 2/2]
Table IV.4.25 Other (non-national) standardised examinations administered in multiple upper secondary schools

		Source	Year of reference	Type of programme	Existence (1)	Level of government at which they are devised and graded (2)	Compulsory for students (3)	Percentage of students taking them (4)	Student certification/graduation/grade completion (5)	Student promotion/entry to higher grade (6)	Student entry to tertiary education (7)	Student access to selective tertiary institutions (8)	Student selection for programme/course/tracks at the upper secondary level (9)	Student selection for programme/faculty/discipline/field/specialisation at tertiary level (10)	Student expulsion from school (11)	Decisions about scholarships/financial assistance for students (12)	Other (13)	Shared with external audience in addition to education authorities (14)	Shared directly with school administrators (15)	Shared directly with classroom teachers (16)	Shared directly with parents (17)	Shared directly with students (18)	Shared directly with media (19)
Partners	Albania	b	2011	All programmes	No	a	a	a	a	a	a	a	a	a	a	a	a	a	a	a	a	a	a
	Argentina				m	m	m	m	m	m	m	m	m	m	m	m	m	m	m	m	m	m	m
	Brazil	a	2011	All programmes	No	a	a	a	a	a	a	a	a	a	a	a	a	a	a	a	a	a	a
	Bulgaria	b	2011	All programmes	No	a	a	a	a	a	a	a	a	a	a	a	a	a	a	a	a	a	a
	Colombia	b	2011	All programmes	No	a	a	a	a	a	a	a	a	a	a	a	a	a	a	a	a	a	a
	Costa Rica				m	m	m	m	m	m	m	m	m	m	m	m	m	m	m	m	m	m	m
	Croatia	b	2011	All programmes	No	a	a	a	a	a	a	a	a	a	a	a	a	a	a	a	a	a	a
	Cyprus*	b	2011	All programmes	No	a	a	a	a	a	a	a	a	a	a	a	a	a	a	a	a	a	a
	Hong Kong-China	b	2011	All programmes	No	a	a	a	a	a	a	a	a	a	a	a	a	a	a	a	a	a	a
	Indonesia	a	2011	All programmes	No	a	a	a	a	a	a	a	a	a	a	a	a	a	a	a	a	a	a
	Jordan	b	2012	All programmes	No	a	a	a	a	a	a	a	a	a	a	a	a	a	a	a	a	a	a
	Kazakhstan				m	m	m	m	m	m	m	m	m	m	m	m	m	m	m	m	m	m	m
	Latvia	b	2011	All programmes	No	a	a	a	a	a	a	a	a	a	a	a	a	a	a	a	a	a	a
	Liechtenstein	b	2011	All programmes	Yes	6	Yes	1	Yes	Yes	Yes	No	No	Yes	Yes	No	No	No	a	a	a	a	a
	Lithuania	b	2011	All programmes	No	a	a	a	a	a	a	a	a	a	a	a	a	a	a	a	a	a	a
	Macao-China	b	2011	All programmes	No	a	a	a	a	a	a	a	a	a	a	a	a	a	a	a	a	a	a
	Malaysia	b	2011	All programmes	No	a	a	a	a	a	a	a	a	a	a	a	a	a	a	a	a	a	a
	Montenegro	b	2011	General	Yes	6	Yes	2	Yes	No	Yes	Yes	No	Yes	Yes	Yes	No	Yes	Yes	Yes	Yes	Yes	No
				Pre-voc. and voc.	Yes	6	Yes	2	Yes	No	No	No	No	No	Yes	Yes	No	Yes	Yes	Yes	Yes	Yes	No
	Peru	b	2011	All programmes	No	a	a	a	a	a	a	a	a	a	a	a	a	a	a	a	a	a	a
	Qatar	b	2011	General	Yes	m	Yes	1	Yes	Yes	Yes	Yes	Yes	Yes	No	No	No	Yes	Yes	Yes	Yes	Yes	Yes
				Pre-voc. and voc.	No	a	a	a	a	a	a	a	a	a	a	a	a	a	a	a	a	a	a
	Romania	b	2011	All programmes	m	m	m	m	m	m	m	m	m	m	m	m	m	m	m	m	m	m	m
	Russian Federation	a	2011	All programmes	No	a	a	a	a	a	a	a	a	a	a	a	a	a	a	a	a	a	a
	Serbia				m	m	m	m	m	m	m	m	m	m	m	m	m	m	m	m	m	m	m
	Shanghai-China	b	2011	All programmes	No	a	a	a	a	a	a	a	a	a	a	a	a	a	a	a	a	a	a
	Singapore	b	2011	All programmes	No	a	a	a	a	a	a	a	a	a	a	a	a	a	a	a	a	a	a
	Chinese Taipei	b	2011	All programmes	No	a	a	a	a	a	a	a	a	a	a	a	a	a	a	a	a	a	a
	Thailand	b	2011	All programmes	No	a	a	a	a	a	a	a	a	a	a	a	a	a	a	a	a	a	a
	Tunisia	b	2011	All programmes	m	m	m	m	m	m	m	m	m	m	m	m	m	m	m	m	m	m	m
	United Arab Emirates	b	2011	General	Yes	3	Yes	1	Yes	Yes	Yes	Yes	No	No	No	Yes	No	Yes	Yes	Yes	Yes	Yes	No
				Pre-voc. and voc.	Yes	1	Yes	1	Yes	Yes	Yes	Yes	No	No	No	Yes	No	Yes	Yes	Yes	Yes	Yes	No
	Uruguay	b	2011	All programmes	No	a	a	a	a	a	a	a	a	a	a	a	a	a	a	a	a	a	a
	Viet Nam	b	2011	General	m	m	m	m	m	m	m	m	m	m	m	m	m	m	m	m	m	m	m
				Pre-voc. and voc.	m	m	m	m	m	m	m	m	m	m	m	m	m	m	m	m	m	m	m

Levels of government (Column 2)
1: Central authority or government
2: State authorities or governments
3: Provincial/regional authorities or governments
4: Sub-regional or inter-municipal authorities or governments
5: Local authorities or governments
6: School, school board or committee
7: Private company

Percentage of students taking non-national examinations (Column 4)
1: All students
2: Between 76% and 99% of students
3: Between 51% and 75% of students
4: Between 26% and 50% of students
5: Between 11% and 25% of students
6: 10% or less of students

Note: Federal states or countries with highly decentralised school systems may have different regulations in states, provinces or regions.
1. Includes ISCED 3C programmes only.
* See notes at the beginning of this Annex.
Sources: a. *Education at a Glance 2012: OECD Indicators* (OECD, 2012). For further notes, see Annex 3, available on line: *www.oecd.org/edu/eag2012*.
 b. PISA system-level data collection in 2013.
StatLink ⟶ http://dx.doi.org/10.1787/888932957498

[Part 1/2]
Entrance examinations to enter the first stage of tertiary education
Entrance examinations that are not administered by upper secondary schools to access tertiary-type A and tertiary-type B programmes

Table IV.4.26

	Source	Year of reference	(1) Existence of tertiary entrance examinations (not administered by secondary schools)	(2) Level of government at which they are devised and graded	(3) Standardised/comparable	(4) Compulsory for students to gain access to tertiary-type A and B programmes	(5) Percentage of students taking them	Main purposes or uses						How results are shared					
								(6) Only available route into tertiary education	(7) Only available route into some fields of study	(8) Student access to selective tertiary institutions	(9) Student access to programme/faculty/discipline/field/specialisation	(10) Decisions about scholarships/financial assistance for students	(11) Other	(12) Shared with external audience in addition to education authorities	(13) Shared directly with school administrators	(14) Shared directly with classroom teachers	(15) Shared directly with parents	(16) Shared directly with students	(17) Shared directly with media
Australia	a	2011	3	1	Yes	No	m	No	Yes	No	Yes	No	No	Yes	Yes	No	No	Yes	No
Austria	a	2011	3	6	No	No	5	No	Yes	Yes	Yes	No	No	No	a	a	a	a	a
Belgium (Fl.)	a	2011	3	2; 6	Yes	No	m	No	Yes	No	Yes	No	No	Yes	No	No	No	Yes	No
Belgium (Fr.)	a	2011	3	6	No	No	6	No	Yes	No	Yes	No	No	Yes	No	No	No	Yes	No
Canada			m	m	m	m	m	m	m	m	m	m	m	m	m	m	m	m	m
Chile	a	2011	1	6	Yes	Yes	2	Yes	Yes	Yes	Yes	Yes	No	Yes	Yes	Yes	Yes	Yes	Yes
Czech Republic	a	2011	2	6	No	No	m	No	No	No	Yes	No	No	Yes	No	No	No	Yes	No
Denmark	a	2011	3	6	No	No	6	No	Yes	No	No	No	No	No	a	a	a	a	a
England	a	2011	3	6	No	No	6	No	Yes	No	Yes	No	No	Yes	No	No	No	Yes	No
Estonia	a	2011	2	6	No	No	m	No	No	No	Yes	No	No	Yes	m	m	m	Yes	m
Finland	a	2011	2	6	No	No	2	No	Yes	Yes	Yes	No	No	Yes	No	No	No	Yes	No
France	a	2011	3	6	No	No	6	No	Yes	Yes	Yes	No	No	Yes	No	No	No	Yes	No
Germany	a	2011	3	6	No	No	m	No	Yes	Yes	Yes	No	No	Yes	No	No	No	Yes	No
Greece	a	2011	1	1	Yes	Yes	2	No	Yes	No	No	Yes	No	Yes	Yes	No	No	Yes	No
Hungary	a	2011	3	6	No	No	6	No	Yes	No	No	No	No	Yes	No	No	No	Yes	No
Iceland	a	2011	4	a	a	a	a	a	a	a	a	a	a	a	a	a	a	a	a
Ireland	a	2011	3	6	Yes	No	6	No	Yes	No	Yes	No	m	Yes	No	No	No	Yes	No
Israel	a	2011	2	6	Yes	Yes[1]	2	No	Yes	Yes	Yes	Yes	No	Yes	No	No	No	Yes	No
Italy	a	2011	2	1; 6	No	No	2	Yes	Yes	No	Yes	No	No	Yes	No	No	No	Yes	No
Japan	a	2011	1	6	No	Yes	3	Yes	Yes	Yes	Yes	m	m	Yes	No	No	No	Yes	No
Korea	a	2011	1	1	Yes	No	2	No	No	Yes	Yes	Yes	No	Yes	Yes	Yes	No	Yes	No
Luxembourg	a	2011	3	6	No	Yes	6	No	Yes	No	Yes	No	No	Yes	Yes	No	No	Yes	No
Mexico	a	2011	1	6	No	Yes	m	No	Yes	Yes	Yes	No	No	No	a	a	a	a	a
Netherlands	a	2011	4	a	a	a	a	a	a	a	a	a	a	a	a	a	a	a	a
New Zealand			m	m	m	m	m	m	m	m	m	m	m	m	m	m	m	m	m
Norway	a	2011	3	6	No	No	6	No	Yes	No	Yes	No	No	Yes	No	No	No	Yes	No
Poland	a	2011	3	6	No	No	6	No	Yes	No	Yes	No	m	Yes	No	No	No	Yes	No
Portugal	a	2011	4	a	a	a	a	a	a	a	a	a	a	a	a	a	a	a	a
Scotland	a	2011	3	6	No	No	m	No	No	No	Yes	No	No	m	m	m	m	m	m
Slovak Republic	a	2011	3	6	No	No	m	No	No	No	Yes	No	No	Yes	No	No	No	Yes	No
Slovenia			m	m	m	m	m	m	m	m	m	m	m	m	m	m	m	m	m
Spain	a	2011	2	2	Yes	Yes[2]	3	No	Yes	Yes	Yes	No	No	Yes	Yes	Yes	Yes	Yes	Yes
Sweden	a	2011	1	1	Yes	No	m	No	No	No	Yes	No	m	Yes	No	No	No	Yes	No
Switzerland	a	2011	3	2; 6	No	No	m	m	m	m	m	m	m	m	m	m	m	m	m
Turkey	a	2011	1	1	Yes	Yes	3	Yes	Yes	Yes	Yes	No	No	Yes	Yes	Yes	Yes	Yes	Yes
United States	a	2011	2	7	Yes	No	4	No	No	Yes	Yes	Yes	No	Yes	Yes	Yes	Yes	Yes	Yes

Existence of tertiary entrance examinations (Column 1)
1: Yes, for all fields of study
2: Yes, for most (more than half) fields of study
3: Yes, for some fields of study
4: No

Levels of government (Column 2)
1: Central authority or government
2: State authorities or governments
3: Provincial/regional authorities or governments
4: Sub-regional or inter-municipal authorities or governments
5: Local authorities or governments
6: Individual tertiary institute or consortium of tertiary institutes
7: Private company

Percentage of students taking entrance examinations (Column 5)
1: All students
2: Between 76% and 99% of students
3: Between 51% and 75% of students
4: Between 26% and 50% of students
5: Between 11% and 25% of students
6: 10% or less of students

Notes: Federal states or countries with highly decentralised school systems may have different regulations in states, provinces or regions.
Tertiary-type A programmes refer to university-level education (ISCED 5A) and tertiary-type B programmes refer to vocationally oriented tertiary education (ISCED 5B).
1. Except to access ISCED 5B tertiary programmes.
2. Except to access ISCED 5B tertiary programmes after completion of general upper secondary education.
* See notes at the beginning of this Annex.
Sources: a. *Education at a Glance 2012: OECD Indicators* (OECD, 2012). For further notes, see Annex 3, available on line: *www.oecd.org/edu/eag2012*.
b. PISA system-level data collection in 2013.
StatLink ⟱ http://dx.doi.org/10.1787/888932957498

[Part 2/2]
Entrance examinations to enter the first stage of tertiary education
Entrance examinations that are not administered by upper secondary schools to access tertiary-type A and tertiary-type B programmes

Table IV.4.26

	Source	Year of reference	(1) Existence of tertiary entrance examinations (not administered by secondary schools)	(2) Level of government at which they are devised and graded	(3) Standardised/comparable	(4) Compulsory for students to gain access to tertiary-type A and B programmes	(5) Percentage of students taking them	Main purposes or uses						How results are shared					
								(6) Only available route into tertiary education	(7) Only available route into some fields of study	(8) Student access to selective tertiary institutions	(9) Student access to programme/faculty/discipline/field/specialisation	(10) Decisions about scholarships/financial assistance for students	(11) Other	(12) Shared with external audience in addition to education authorities	(13) Shared directly with school administrators	(14) Shared directly with classroom teachers	(15) Shared directly with parents	(16) Shared directly with students	(17) Shared directly with media
Albania	b	2011	3	6	Yes	No	6	No	Yes	Yes	Yes	No	a	Yes	Yes	m	m	Yes	Yes
Argentina			m	m	m	m	m	m	m	m	m	m	m	m	m	m	m	m	m
Brazil	a	2011	1	1; 6	Yes	No	2	No	No	Yes	Yes	Yes	No	Yes	Yes	No	No	Yes	Yes
Bulgaria	b	2011	1	6	No	Yes	m	Yes	Yes	No	Yes	No	No	Yes	a	a	a	a	a
Colombia	b	2011	1	1	Yes	Yes	2	Yes	Yes	Yes	Yes	Yes	No	Yes	Yes	No	No	Yes	Yes
Costa Rica			m	m	m	m	m	m	m	m	m	m	m	m	m	m	m	m	m
Croatia	b	2011	3	6	Yes	No	3	No	Yes	Yes	Yes	No	No	Yes	No	No	No	Yes	Yes
Cyprus*	b	2011	4	a	a	a	a	a	a	a	a	a	a	a	a	a	a	a	a
Hong Kong- China	b	2011	4	a	a	a	a	a	a	a	a	a	a	a	a	a	a	a	a
Indonesia	a	2011	1	6	No	Yes	3	Yes	Yes	Yes	Yes	Yes	No	Yes	Yes	No	No	Yes	No
Jordan	b	2011	1	1	Yes	Yes	1	Yes	Yes	Yes	Yes	Yes	No	Yes	Yes	Yes	Yes	Yes	Yes
Kazakhstan			m	m	m	m	m	m	m	m	m	m	m	m	m	m	m	m	m
Latvia	b	2011	3	6	No	a	6	No	Yes	No	Yes	No	No	Yes	Yes	No	No	Yes	No
Liechtenstein	b	2011	3	6	Yes	No	6	No	Yes	Yes	Yes	No	No	No	a	a	a	a	a
Lithuania	b	2011	3	6	Yes	Yes	5	No	Yes	No	Yes	Yes	a	Yes	No	No	No	Yes	No
Macao-China	b	2011	1	6	No	Yes	m	No	No	Yes	Yes	Yes	No	Yes	No	No	No	Yes	No
Malaysia	b	2011	4	a	a	a	a	a	a	a	a	a	a	a	a	a	a	a	a
Montenegro	b	2011	3	1	No	4	4	No	Yes	No	No	No	No	Yes	No	No	No	Yes	No
Peru	b	2011	2	6	No	Yes	m	Yes	Yes	Yes	Yes	Yes	No	Yes	Yes	Yes	Yes	Yes	Yes
Qatar	b	2011	1	2	Yes	Yes	1	Yes	Yes	Yes	Yes	Yes	No	Yes	Yes	Yes	Yes	Yes	Yes
Romania	b	2011	2	6	m	Yes	m	Yes	a	Yes	Yes	No	a	Yes	No	No	No	Yes	Yes
Russian Federation	a	2011	4	a	a	a	a	a	a	a	a	a	a	a	a	a	a	a	a
Serbia			m	m	m	m	m	m	m	m	m	m	m	m	m	m	m	m	m
Shanghai-China	b	2011	1	3	Yes	Yes	2	No	No	Yes	Yes	Yes	No	Yes	No	No	No	Yes	No
Singapore	b	2011	4	a	a	a	a	a	a	a	a	a	a	a	a	a	a	a	a
Chinese Taipei	b	2011	1	1	Yes	Yes	2	Yes	Yes	Yes	Yes	No	No	Yes	Yes	Yes	Yes	Yes	Yes
Thailand	b	2011	1	1	Yes	No	3	Yes	Yes	No	Yes	No	No	Yes	No	No	No	Yes	No
Tunisia	b	2011	m	m	m	m	m	m	m	m	m	m	m	m	m	m	m	m	m
United Arab Emirates	b	2011	1	1	Yes	Yes	1	No	No	Yes	Yes	No	No	Yes	No	No	Yes	Yes	Yes
Uruguay	b	2011	3	6	No	No	6	No	Yes	No	Yes	No	a	Yes	No	No	No	Yes	No
Viet Nam	b	2011	1	1	Yes	Yes	2	Yes	No	No	Yes	No	No	Yes	Yes	Yes	Yes	Yes	Yes

Existence of tertiary entrance examinations (Column 1)
1: Yes, for all fields of study
2: Yes, for most (more than half) fields of study
3: Yes, for some fields of study
4: No

Levels of government (Column 2)
1: Central authority or government
2: State authorities or governments
3: Provincial/regional authorities or governments
4: Sub-regional or inter-municipal authorities or governments
5: Local authorities or governments
6: Individual tertiary institute or consortium of tertiary institutes
7: Private company

Percentage of students taking entrance examinations (Column 5)
1: All students
2: Between 76% and 99% of students
3: Between 51% and 75% of students
4: Between 26% and 50% of students
5: Between 11% and 25% of students
6: 10% or less of students

Notes: Federal states or countries with highly decentralised school systems may have different regulations in states, provinces or regions.
Tertiary-type A programmes refer to university-level education (ISCED 5A) and tertiary-type B programmes refer to vocationally oriented tertiary education (ISCED 5B).
1. Except to access ISCED 5B tertiary programmes.
2. Except to access ISCED 5B tertiary programmes after completion of general upper secondary education.
* See notes at the beginning of this Annex.
Sources: *a. Education at a Glance 2012: OECD Indicators* (OECD, 2012). For further notes, see Annex 3, available on line: *www.oecd.org/edu/eag2012.*
    b. PISA system-level data collection in 2013.
StatLink ⛁ http://dx.doi.org/10.1787/888932957498

[Part 1/2]
Factors, criteria or special circumstances used by tertiary institutions to determine admission
Factors, criteria or special circumstances (other than examinations) used by tertiary institutions to determine access to tertiary-type A and tertiary-type B programmes

Table IV.4.27

	Source	Year of reference	Existence of additional criteria or special circumstances for entry into tertiary education	Grade point average from secondary schools		Ethnicity of applicant		Family income of applicant		Previous work experience		Past service or volunteer work		Recommendations		Applicant letter or written rationale to justify admission		Other	
				Factor used	Level of importance	Factor used	Level of importance	Factor used	Level of importance	Factor used	Level of importance	Factor used	Level of importance	Factor used	Level of importance	Factor used	Level of importance	Factor used	Level of importance
			(1)	(2)	(3)	(4)	(5)	(6)	(7)	(8)	(9)	(10)	(11)	(12)	(13)	(14)	(15)	(16)	(17)
Australia	a	2011	Yes	No	a	Yes	m	Yes	m	Yes	m	m	m	m	m	Yes	m	Yes	m
Austria	a	2011	No	a	a	a	a	a	a	a	a	a	a	a	a	a	a	a	a
Belgium (Fl.)	a	2011	Yes	No	a	No	a	No	a	No	a	No	a	No	a	No	a	Yes	4
Belgium (Fr.)	a	2011	Yes	No	a	No	a	No	a	No	a	No	a	a	a	No	a	Yes	4
Canada			m	m	m	m	m	m	m	m	m	m	m	m	m	m	m	m	m
Chile	a	2011	Yes	Yes	3	No	a	No	a	No	a	No	a	No	a	No	a	Yes	3
Czech Republic	a	2011	Yes	Yes	m	No	a	No	a	No	a	No	a	No	a	No	a	Yes	m
Denmark	a	2011	Yes	Yes	4	No	a	No	a	Yes	3	Yes	2	No	a	Yes	3	m	m
England	a	2011	Yes	a	a	No	a	No	a	Yes	2	Yes	2	Yes	4	Yes	4	Yes	4
Estonia	a	2011	Yes	m	m	m	m	m	m	m	m	m	m	m	m	m	m	m	m
Finland	a	2011	Yes	Yes	m	No	a	No	a	Yes	m	Yes	m	No	a	Yes	m	Yes	m
France	a	2011	Yes	Yes	4	No	a	Yes	3	Yes	3	No	a	No	a	Yes	3	Yes	3
Germany	a	2011	Yes	Yes	m	Yes	m	No	a	Yes	m	Yes	m	Yes	m	Yes	m	No	a
Greece	a	2011	Yes	No	a	No	a	No	a	No	a	No	a	No	a	No	a	Yes	2
Hungary	a	2011	Yes	Yes	4	No	a	Yes	2	No	a	No	a	No	a	No	a	Yes	2
Iceland	a	2011	Yes	a	a	No	a	No	a	No	a	No	a	No	a	No	a	Yes	4
Ireland	a	2011	Yes	No	a	No	a	Yes	m	Yes	m	No	a	No	a	No	a	No	a
Israel	a	2011	Yes	Yes	4	Yes	4	Yes	m	Yes	m	Yes	m	Yes	3	No	a	Yes	m
Italy	a	2011	Yes	Yes	2	Yes	m	No	a	No	a	No	a	No	a	No	a	No	a
Japan	a	2011	Yes	Yes	m	No	a	No	a	m	m	m	m	m	m	Yes	4	m	m
Korea	a	2011	Yes	Yes	4	No	a	Yes	2	Yes	2	Yes	2	Yes	2	Yes	2	Yes	2
Luxembourg	a	2011	Yes	Yes	3	No	a	No	a	No	a	No	a	No	a	No	a	Yes	4
Mexico	a	2011	Yes	Yes	4	No	a	Yes	3	No	a	No	a	No	a	No	a	Yes	3
Netherlands	a	2011	Yes	Yes	2	No	a	No	a	No	a	No	a	No	a	No	a	Yes	2
New Zealand			m	m	m	m	m	m	m	m	m	m	m	m	m	m	m	m	m
Norway	a	2011	Yes	Yes	4	Yes	2	No	a	Yes	2	Yes	2	No	a	No	a	Yes	3
Poland	a	2011	Yes	Yes	4	No	a	No	a	No	a	No	a	No	a	No	a	Yes	3
Portugal	a	2011	Yes	Yes	4	No	a	No	a	No	a	No	a	No	a	No	a	Yes	4
Scotland	a	2011	Yes	a	a	No	a	No	a	Yes	m	Yes	m	Yes	m	Yes	2	Yes	4
Slovak Republic	a	2011	Yes	Yes	m	No	a	No	a	Yes	m	m	m	m	m	m	m	m	m
Slovenia			m	m	m	m	m	m	m	m	m	m	m	m	m	m	m	m	m
Spain	a	2011	Yes	Yes	4	No	a	No	a	No	a	No	a	No	a	No	a	No	a
Sweden	a	2011	Yes	Yes	4	No	a	No	a	Yes	2	Yes	2	No	a	Yes	2	Yes	m
Switzerland			m	m	m	m	m	m	m	m	m	m	m	m	m	m	m	m	m
Turkey	a	2011	No	a	a	a	a	a	a	a	a	a	a	a	a	a	a	a	a
United States	a	2011	Yes	Yes	3	No	a	No	a	Yes	2	Yes	2	Yes	2	Yes	3	Yes	3

Levels of importance (Columns 3, 5, 7, 9, 11, 13, 15 and 17)

1: No importance
2: Low level of importance
3: Moderate level of importance
4: High level of importance

Notes: Federal states or countries with highly decentralised school systems may have different regulations in states, provinces or regions.
Tertiary-type A programmes refer to university-level education (ISCED 5A) and tertiary-type B programmes refer to vocationally oriented tertiary education (ISCED 5B).
* See notes at the beginning of this Annex.
Sources: a. *Education at a Glance 2012: OECD Indicators* (OECD, 2012). For further notes, see Annex 3, available on line: *www.oecd.org/edu/eag2012*.
 b. PISA system-level data collection in 2013.
StatLink ⌨ http://dx.doi.org/10.1787/888932957498

[Part 2/2]
Factors, criteria or special circumstances used by tertiary institutions to determine admission
Factors, criteria or special circumstances (other than examinations) used by tertiary institutions to determine access to tertiary-type A and tertiary-type B programmes

Table IV.4.27

	Source	Year of reference	Existence of additional criteria or special circumstances for entry into tertiary education	Grade point average from secondary schools		Ethnicity of applicant		Family income of applicant		Previous work experience		Past service or volunteer work		Recommendations		Applicant letter or written rationale to justify admission		Other	
				Factor used	Level of importance	Factor used	Level of importance	Factor used	Level of importance	Factor used	Level of importance	Factor used	Level of importance	Factor used	Level of importance	Factor used	Level of importance	Factor used	Level of importance
			(1)	(2)	(3)	(4)	(5)	(6)	(7)	(8)	(9)	(10)	(11)	(12)	(13)	(14)	(15)	(16)	(17)
Albania	b	2011	No	a	a	a	a	a	a	a	a	a	a	a	a	a	a	a	a
Argentina			m	m	m	m	m	m	m	m	m	m	m	m	m	m	m	m	m
Brazil	a	2011	Yes	No	a	Yes	3	Yes	4	No	a	No	a	No	a	No	a	Yes	m
Bulgaria	b	2011	Yes	Yes	4	No	a	No	a	No	a	No	a	No	a	No	a	No	a
Colombia	b	2011	Yes	No	a	Yes	3	m	a	No	a	No	a	No	a	Yes	3	Yes	4
Costa Rica			m	m	m	m	m	m	m	m	m	m	m	m	m	m	m	m	m
Croatia	b	2011	Yes	Yes	4	No	a	No	a	No	a	No	a	No	a	No	a	a	a
Cyprus*	b	2011	Yes	Yes	4	No	a	Yes	4	No	a	No	a	No	a	No	a	No	a
Hong Kong-China	b	2011	Yes	No	a	No	a	No	a	No	a	No	a	Yes	3	Yes	2	Yes	3
Indonesia	a	2011	No	a	a	a	a	a	a	a	a	a	a	a	a	a	a	a	a
Jordan	b	2011	Yes	Yes	4	Yes	4	No	1	No	a	No	a	No	a	No	a	No	a
Kazakhstan			m	m	m	m	m	m	m	m	m	m	m	m	m	m	m	m	m
Latvia	b	2011	Yes	Yes	4	No	a	No	a	No	a	No	a	No	a	Yes	3	No	a
Liechtenstein	b	2011	No	a	a	a	a	a	a	a	a	a	a	a	a	a	a	a	a
Lithuania	b	2011	Yes	Yes	2	No	a	No	a	Yes	2	Yes	2	No	a	No	a	No	a
Macao-China	b	2011	Yes	Yes	4	Yes	4	No	a	No	a	Yes	3	Yes	3	Yes	2	No	a
Malaysia	b	2011	Yes	No	a	No	a	Yes	3	Yes	3	Yes	3	No	a	No	a	Yes	3
Montenegro	b	2011	Yes	Yes	3	No	1	No	1	Yes	4	No	1	Yes	2	Yes	2	No	a
Peru	b	2011	Yes	Yes	3	No	a	No	a	Yes	3	Yes	3	Yes	3	No	a	No	a
Qatar	b	2011	Yes	Yes	4	No	a	Yes	3	No	a	Yes	2	Yes	3	Yes	2	No	a
Romania	b	2011	No	a	a	a	a	a	a	a	a	a	a	a	a	a	a	a	a
Russian Federation	a	2011	Yes	No	a	No	a	No	a	No	a	No	a	No	a	No	a	Yes	4
Serbia			m	m	m	m	m	m	m	m	m	m	m	m	m	m	m	m	m
Shanghai-China	b	2011	Yes	Yes	2	Yes	3	No	a	No	a	Yes	1	Yes	3	Yes	1	Yes	4
Singapore	b	2011	Yes	No	a	No	a	No	a	No	a	Yes	2	Yes	2	Yes	2	Yes	4
Chinese Taipei	b	2011	Yes	No	a	No	a	No	a	No	a	No	a	No	a	No	a	Yes	2
Thailand	b	2011	Yes	Yes	2	No	a	No	a	No	a	No	a	No	a	No	a	No	a
Tunisia	b	2011	m	m	m	m	m	m	m	m	m	m	m	m	m	m	m	m	m
United Arab Emirates	b	2011	No	a	a	a	a	a	a	a	a	a	a	a	a	a	a	a	a
Uruguay	b	2011	No	a	a	a	a	a	a	a	a	a	a	a	a	a	a	a	a
Viet Nam	b	2011	Yes	Yes	4	Yes	2	No	a	No	a	No	a	No	a	No	a	No	a

Levels of importance (Columns 3, 5, 7, 9, 11, 13, 15 and 17)

1: No importance
2: Low level of importance
3: Moderate level of importance
4: High level of importance

Notes: Federal states or countries with highly decentralised school systems may have different regulations in states, provinces or regions.
Tertiary-type A programmes refer to university-level education (ISCED 5A) and tertiary-type B programmes refer to vocationally oriented tertiary education (ISCED 5B).
* See notes at the beginning of this Annex.
Sources: *a. Education at a Glance 2012: OECD Indicators* (OECD, 2012). For further notes, see Annex 3, available on line: *www.oecd.org/edu/eag2012*.
    b. PISA system-level data collection in 2013.
StatLink ᠁ http://dx.doi.org/10.1787/888932957498

[Part 1/2]
Assessment practices
Table IV.4.30   *Results based on school principals' reports*

Percentage of students in schools whose principal reported that assessments of students in the national modal grade for 15-year-olds are used

	To inform parents about their child's progress		To make decisions about students' retention or promotion		To group students for instructional purposes		To compare the school to district or national performance		To monitor the school's progress from year to year		To make judgements about teachers' effectiveness		To identify aspects of instruction or the curriculum that could be improved		To compare the school with other schools	
	%	S.E.	%	S.E.	%	S.E.	%	S.E.	%	S.E.	%	S.E.	%	S.E.	%	S.E.
Australia	100.0	(0.0)	62.8	(1.8)	83.5	(1.3)	56.4	(1.9)	87.6	(1.3)	49.8	(1.8)	90.9	(1.1)	44.3	(2.0)
Austria	95.5	(1.7)	94.2	(1.7)	30.5	(2.4)	28.5	(4.0)	62.6	(4.2)	39.1	(4.1)	69.6	(3.6)	30.0	(4.1)
Belgium	96.6	(1.3)	96.2	(1.3)	17.2	(2.3)	23.3	(2.6)	59.8	(3.2)	35.2	(3.0)	73.1	(3.0)	18.3	(2.3)
Canada	99.7	(0.2)	95.0	(1.2)	74.1	(2.1)	82.3	(1.5)	92.3	(1.0)	30.2	(1.9)	86.6	(1.5)	62.0	(2.3)
Chile	100.0	c	88.9	(2.5)	43.6	(4.1)	53.7	(4.1)	93.6	(1.8)	61.3	(3.5)	91.7	(2.0)	38.5	(4.2)
Czech Republic	93.1	(1.7)	79.4	(2.9)	32.8	(3.3)	58.2	(3.2)	86.2	(2.7)	62.8	(3.4)	86.3	(2.7)	63.1	(3.2)
Denmark	99.2	(0.4)	10.3	(1.9)	52.3	(3.4)	54.9	(3.5)	56.8	(3.3)	27.1	(3.1)	84.7	(2.4)	55.9	(3.5)
Estonia	99.5	(0.5)	82.0	(2.4)	20.7	(2.6)	64.7	(2.8)	78.0	(2.4)	65.5	(3.0)	83.1	(2.2)	58.9	(2.8)
Finland	98.7	(0.3)	93.3	(1.6)	17.0	(2.5)	45.8	(3.4)	59.5	(3.5)	15.5	(2.2)	60.5	(3.6)	21.1	(2.7)
France	97.2	(1.1)	96.4	(1.3)	42.7	(3.4)	62.2	(2.9)	73.2	(3.1)	22.6	(3.0)	50.4	(3.5)	40.6	(3.4)
Germany	95.9	(1.5)	95.8	(1.5)	39.5	(3.2)	43.4	(3.3)	57.2	(3.7)	24.2	(3.2)	60.8	(3.6)	27.7	(3.1)
Greece	100.0	c	98.2	(1.0)	8.1	(2.4)	17.0	(2.4)	55.9	(3.6)	14.0	(2.4)	49.4	(3.6)	21.9	(2.8)
Hungary	93.9	(1.8)	69.2	(3.7)	47.1	(3.6)	78.5	(3.3)	92.6	(2.0)	57.8	(3.9)	77.4	(3.0)	71.3	(3.9)
Iceland	100.0	c	15.0	(0.2)	42.4	(0.3)	77.1	(0.2)	89.2	(0.1)	39.1	(0.2)	92.8	(0.1)	73.2	(0.2)
Ireland	100.0	c	62.0	(4.0)	81.4	(2.9)	77.3	(3.3)	86.4	(2.7)	46.5	(4.1)	68.4	(3.9)	35.2	(4.0)
Israel	100.0	c	81.5	(2.9)	97.2	(1.3)	65.5	(3.4)	95.3	(1.7)	81.7	(3.2)	91.7	(2.4)	53.7	(4.1)
Italy	99.3	(0.4)	86.6	(1.8)	53.4	(2.0)	65.1	(2.2)	82.0	(1.6)	29.6	(1.9)	91.7	(1.2)	36.6	(2.1)
Japan	99.2	(0.6)	90.4	(2.1)	45.3	(3.5)	17.3	(2.5)	51.6	(3.5)	75.7	(3.0)	79.2	(2.9)	14.9	(2.6)
Korea	94.7	(1.9)	56.3	(4.2)	85.6	(2.8)	70.2	(3.6)	89.9	(2.6)	85.3	(3.0)	96.3	(1.6)	66.8	(3.8)
Luxembourg	95.4	(0.0)	94.2	(0.1)	41.2	(0.1)	74.2	(0.1)	72.3	(0.1)	22.3	(0.1)	73.8	(0.1)	39.8	(0.1)
Mexico	99.0	(0.3)	91.5	(1.2)	72.8	(1.7)	77.1	(1.5)	92.3	(1.0)	76.7	(1.3)	88.4	(1.2)	70.6	(1.6)
Netherlands	99.3	(0.9)	97.7	(1.1)	61.0	(3.7)	69.7	(4.1)	88.8	(2.7)	68.4	(3.9)	78.1	(3.5)	64.1	(4.2)
New Zealand	100.0	c	76.7	(3.3)	93.6	(2.1)	92.8	(2.7)	100.0	c	67.7	(3.8)	99.4	(0.5)	87.5	(3.4)
Norway	98.3	(1.0)	1.5	(0.9)	47.9	(3.3)	68.2	(3.0)	83.8	(2.7)	30.2	(3.3)	73.8	(3.2)	51.9	(3.3)
Poland	99.2	(0.7)	97.7	(1.2)	55.0	(3.8)	58.2	(3.6)	96.3	(1.5)	78.9	(3.0)	95.4	(1.7)	59.4	(3.9)
Portugal	100.0	c	98.2	(1.1)	40.3	(4.6)	85.0	(3.5)	95.9	(1.6)	50.5	(3.6)	93.5	(2.1)	63.2	(4.2)
Slovak Republic	100.0	c	93.4	(1.4)	38.2	(3.4)	64.2	(3.5)	70.7	(3.9)	69.0	(3.3)	83.0	(2.6)	69.3	(3.3)
Slovenia	98.0	(0.1)	92.7	(0.3)	26.2	(0.9)	58.7	(0.6)	91.5	(0.3)	38.2	(0.9)	72.1	(0.6)	46.9	(0.6)
Spain	99.5	(0.4)	94.6	(0.9)	47.2	(3.3)	44.0	(2.5)	88.5	(1.8)	50.1	(2.8)	93.7	(1.2)	36.9	(2.4)
Sweden	93.9	(1.8)	43.0	(4.0)	25.2	(3.3)	89.8	(2.3)	96.2	(1.4)	43.6	(3.6)	83.9	(2.6)	84.9	(2.8)
Switzerland	93.7	(1.8)	85.7	(2.4)	40.1	(3.1)	41.1	(3.2)	48.0	(3.4)	36.4	(3.8)	50.7	(3.7)	27.5	(3.6)
Turkey	97.1	(1.5)	55.3	(4.1)	44.1	(4.0)	74.9	(3.7)	92.6	(1.9)	70.8	(3.7)	68.5	(3.6)	84.9	(2.9)
United Kingdom	99.4	(0.7)	68.9	(3.5)	96.3	(0.9)	96.0	(1.3)	99.7	(0.2)	88.2	(2.1)	96.2	(1.4)	90.3	(2.2)
United States	98.7	(1.0)	56.8	(4.2)	74.3	(3.7)	93.6	(2.6)	95.2	(2.0)	59.9	(4.2)	94.1	(1.6)	86.3	(2.9)
OECD average	98.1	(0.2)	76.5	(0.4)	50.5	(0.5)	62.6	(0.5)	81.2	(0.4)	50.4	(0.5)	80.3	(0.4)	52.9	(0.5)
Albania	99.3	(0.6)	77.5	(2.8)	73.9	(3.3)	76.7	(3.5)	91.0	(2.3)	86.8	(3.1)	87.4	(2.8)	78.1	(3.3)
Argentina	91.0	(2.5)	87.2	(2.7)	24.3	(3.1)	22.3	(3.4)	73.9	(3.6)	50.7	(3.7)	94.0	(1.4)	7.2	(2.2)
Brazil	97.0	(0.9)	91.2	(1.6)	47.0	(2.4)	83.2	(1.9)	97.0	(0.8)	79.9	(2.0)	88.7	(1.5)	56.4	(2.5)
Bulgaria	99.1	(0.7)	65.1	(3.8)	39.3	(3.6)	86.1	(2.9)	94.9	(1.8)	93.2	(2.0)	71.8	(3.6)	85.4	(2.9)
Colombia	99.5	(0.6)	92.9	(2.1)	43.6	(3.9)	68.1	(4.0)	94.0	(1.8)	59.6	(3.9)	95.1	(1.8)	63.7	(3.8)
Costa Rica	97.6	(0.9)	91.1	(2.1)	37.1	(3.5)	65.1	(3.5)	86.1	(2.4)	71.2	(3.7)	84.7	(3.0)	50.3	(3.7)
Croatia	100.0	c	88.3	(2.4)	51.5	(4.4)	65.7	(3.9)	94.6	(1.7)	55.9	(3.8)	84.5	(3.0)	62.2	(3.9)
Cyprus*	100.0	c	98.8	(0.0)	28.0	(0.1)	15.4	(0.1)	66.7	(0.1)	38.1	(0.1)	61.9	(0.1)	14.3	(0.1)
Hong Kong-China	98.1	(1.1)	98.1	(1.1)	86.4	(2.9)	44.1	(4.7)	96.1	(1.7)	80.0	(3.5)	99.4	(0.6)	30.5	(3.7)
Indonesia	97.1	(1.7)	92.8	(2.1)	79.6	(3.2)	69.0	(4.3)	98.1	(1.3)	95.8	(2.1)	97.1	(1.6)	86.9	(2.9)
Jordan	97.3	(1.4)	92.1	(2.1)	80.7	(2.9)	70.2	(3.0)	85.4	(2.4)	72.3	(3.4)	88.8	(2.4)	55.3	(3.6)
Kazakhstan	99.8	(0.2)	95.3	(1.6)	65.5	(3.8)	91.8	(2.3)	99.8	(0.2)	100.0	c	98.8	(0.8)	90.6	(2.1)
Latvia	100.0	c	96.9	(1.2)	38.1	(3.5)	92.5	(1.6)	99.8	(0.2)	92.5	(1.8)	99.6	(0.5)	85.5	(2.3)
Liechtenstein	100.0	c	71.8	(1.4)	49.1	(1.2)	68.1	(1.4)	66.8	(1.0)	20.2	(1.2)	69.5	(1.5)	59.4	(0.8)
Lithuania	99.5	(0.6)	84.6	(2.6)	53.1	(3.5)	61.4	(3.4)	94.1	(1.8)	73.9	(3.0)	82.1	(2.6)	59.7	(3.2)
Macao-China	99.4	(0.0)	94.9	(0.0)	65.2	(0.1)	31.9	(0.0)	86.7	(0.1)	75.3	(0.1)	96.5	(0.0)	21.4	(0.0)
Malaysia	98.8	(0.9)	52.8	(3.7)	87.2	(2.7)	80.8	(3.0)	97.7	(1.0)	92.0	(2.2)	96.7	(1.5)	67.3	(3.6)
Montenegro	97.3	(0.0)	81.0	(0.1)	38.9	(0.2)	78.6	(0.1)	96.3	(0.0)	91.5	(0.1)	89.3	(0.1)	64.9	(0.1)
Peru	97.8	(1.1)	88.2	(2.2)	45.0	(3.4)	40.9	(3.4)	84.5	(2.7)	77.9	(2.8)	93.1	(2.0)	37.6	(3.9)
Qatar	96.9	(0.0)	87.7	(0.1)	86.4	(0.1)	82.6	(0.1)	96.1	(0.0)	87.0	(0.1)	97.4	(0.0)	81.0	(0.1)
Romania	77.2	(2.8)	70.3	(3.7)	57.4	(3.8)	67.6	(3.8)	72.4	(3.5)	74.8	(3.2)	76.5	(3.0)	69.1	(3.9)
Russian Federation	99.4	(0.6)	94.4	(1.9)	56.7	(4.4)	93.2	(1.5)	99.7	(0.3)	99.2	(0.7)	99.2	(0.8)	97.8	(1.0)
Serbia	98.5	(1.1)	83.8	(3.2)	35.5	(4.3)	34.2	(4.0)	95.5	(1.8)	57.3	(4.4)	86.0	(2.9)	57.1	(4.1)
Shanghai-China	98.0	(1.0)	50.9	(3.4)	55.0	(4.0)	50.1	(4.2)	87.5	(2.5)	86.4	(2.7)	95.8	(1.6)	56.7	(3.9)
Singapore	100.0	c	88.4	(0.1)	96.0	(0.0)	95.5	(0.8)	99.4	(0.6)	87.7	(0.8)	98.2	(0.6)	88.2	(0.6)
Chinese Taipei	95.6	(1.7)	45.4	(3.2)	35.0	(3.9)	36.6	(3.9)	78.2	(3.4)	47.9	(3.6)	94.2	(1.7)	41.7	(3.8)
Thailand	99.5	(0.5)	86.1	(2.8)	79.4	(2.9)	85.2	(2.1)	97.3	(1.2)	91.0	(2.1)	95.8	(1.5)	75.6	(3.3)
Tunisia	80.0	(3.4)	95.4	(1.9)	51.6	(4.4)	70.7	(4.0)	89.1	(2.6)	67.1	(4.1)	55.9	(4.3)	69.1	(4.4)
United Arab Emirates	100.0	(0.0)	90.5	(1.5)	87.2	(2.0)	77.1	(2.6)	96.4	(1.4)	94.3	(1.1)	97.1	(0.7)	72.3	(2.7)
Uruguay	95.0	(1.6)	92.1	(1.7)	25.2	(3.3)	16.5	(2.8)	87.5	(2.3)	31.2	(3.6)	86.3	(2.5)	12.2	(2.3)
Viet Nam	99.3	(0.7)	95.5	(1.6)	74.2	(3.6)	88.7	(2.7)	98.3	(1.0)	99.2	(0.7)	91.2	(2.2)	87.5	(2.7)

* See notes at the beginning of this Annex.
StatLink ᕫᑐᓯ http://dx.doi.org/10.1787/888932957498

[Part 2/2]
Assessment practices
Table IV.4.30 *Results based on school principals' reports*

	Index of assessment practices (sum of "yes" responses to the eight purposes)		None of the eight purposes		One of the eight purposes		Two of the eight purposes		Three of the eight purposes		Four of the eight purposes		Five of the eight purposes		Six or more of the eight purposes	
	Mean index	S.E.	%	S.E.	%	S.E.	%	S.E.	%	S.E.	%	S.E.	%	S.E.	%	S.E.
OECD																
Australia	4.7	(0.1)	0.0	(0.0)	0.8	(0.3)	3.7	(0.8)	12.6	(1.6)	21.7	(2.0)	28.3	(2.1)	32.9	(2.3)
Austria	4.0	(0.1)	1.7	(1.2)	2.6	(1.4)	14.7	(3.1)	18.0	(3.3)	23.0	(3.6)	21.8	(3.8)	18.2	(3.7)
Belgium	3.8	(0.1)	0.0	c	0.0	c	17.8	(2.6)	23.5	(3.2)	27.0	(3.0)	19.8	(2.6)	12.0	(2.3)
Canada	5.1	(0.1)	0.1	(0.0)	0.3	(0.0)	3.0	(1.4)	6.2	(1.0)	12.1	(2.0)	29.5	(3.1)	48.8	(3.4)
Chile	4.9	(0.1)	0.0	c	0.0	c	2.4	(1.5)	8.0	(2.5)	27.3	(4.2)	25.5	(4.4)	36.8	(4.4)
Czech Republic	4.5	(0.2)	4.8	(1.6)	1.0	(0.8)	4.1	(1.7)	12.5	(3.8)	14.6	(3.0)	29.9	(4.3)	33.1	(5.0)
Denmark	3.9	(0.1)	0.6	(0.3)	3.8	(1.5)	9.4	(2.2)	28.0	(3.0)	20.5	(3.3)	21.9	(2.8)	15.8	(2.9)
Estonia	4.4	(0.1)	0.0	c	1.7	(1.0)	9.4	(2.2)	20.7	(3.2)	12.5	(2.6)	25.3	(3.1)	30.4	(3.2)
Finland	3.9	(0.1)	0.0	(0.0)	0.4	(0.0)	15.8	(3.0)	26.4	(3.8)	24.2	(3.0)	19.9	(3.0)	13.2	(2.3)
France	4.2	(0.1)	0.7	(0.7)	1.4	(0.8)	8.1	(2.0)	22.5	(3.3)	23.9	(3.3)	24.8	(3.4)	18.7	(2.9)
Germany	4.0	(0.1)	0.8	(0.8)	1.6	(0.9)	13.2	(2.7)	21.1	(2.4)	25.5	(3.5)	18.1	(3.0)	19.7	(2.9)
Greece	3.4	(0.1)	0.0	c	1.2	(0.8)	29.2	(3.8)	29.2	(3.5)	19.6	(2.8)	12.1	(2.7)	8.8	(1.5)
Hungary	4.9	(0.1)	0.0	c	0.0	c	0.2	(0.2)	13.3	(3.5)	23.6	(4.7)	26.8	(4.8)	36.0	(4.7)
Iceland	4.8	(0.0)	0.0	c	1.1	(0.1)	3.1	(0.1)	10.4	(0.2)	19.5	(0.2)	35.6	(0.3)	30.4	(0.2)
Ireland	4.9	(0.1)	0.0	c	1.7	(1.5)	2.3	(1.3)	8.2	(2.7)	19.3	(3.6)	30.2	(4.1)	38.3	(4.3)
Israel	5.2	(0.1)	0.0	c	0.0	c	3.6	(2.5)	3.7	(2.2)	16.9	(4.0)	19.2	(4.8)	56.5	(6.1)
Italy	4.8	(0.1)	0.0	c	0.0	(0.0)	2.5	(0.6)	11.6	(1.5)	23.5	(2.0)	30.0	(2.5)	32.3	(2.2)
Japan	4.3	(0.1)	0.0	c	1.9	(1.0)	9.2	(2.4)	14.1	(2.7)	25.3	(3.2)	30.6	(3.9)	18.8	(2.8)
Korea	4.8	(0.2)	0.0	c	4.7	(2.7)	3.7	(2.6)	7.2	(2.5)	11.4	(4.1)	33.1	(5.9)	39.8	(6.6)
Luxembourg	4.4	(0.0)	0.0	c	0.0	c	14.7	(0.1)	0.3	(0.0)	31.7	(0.1)	33.4	(0.1)	19.9	(0.1)
Mexico	5.0	(0.1)	0.1	(0.1)	0.7	(0.5)	1.9	(0.6)	5.9	(1.2)	19.6	(2.4)	28.0	(3.1)	43.8	(3.0)
Netherlands	4.7	(0.1)	0.0	c	2.5	(1.8)	2.7	(1.8)	14.9	(4.2)	16.3	(4.9)	26.0	(4.9)	37.6	(5.8)
New Zealand	5.5	(0.2)	0.0	c	0.0	c	0.0	c	5.8	(5.7)	0.0	c	30.6	(9.0)	63.6	(9.5)
Norway	4.2	(0.1)	1.2	(0.9)	7.5	(2.2)	6.8	(2.1)	11.2	(2.1)	22.7	(3.3)	27.3	(3.3)	23.2	(3.3)
Poland	5.0	(0.1)	0.0	c	0.0	c	0.0	c	4.7	(2.6)	23.0	(5.2)	35.4	(5.9)	36.9	(5.3)
Portugal	5.2	(0.1)	0.0	c	0.0	c	1.7	(1.3)	3.1	(1.9)	14.2	(4.2)	31.3	(5.6)	49.6	(5.3)
Slovak Republic	4.6	(0.1)	0.0	c	2.8	(1.5)	5.8	(2.4)	11.6	(3.4)	20.2	(4.3)	28.8	(4.7)	30.7	(4.6)
Slovenia	4.6	(0.0)	0.0	c	2.8	(0.2)	3.3	(0.1)	12.4	(0.4)	27.5	(0.7)	22.7	(0.6)	31.4	(0.8)
Spain	4.8	(0.1)	0.1	(0.1)	0.6	(0.5)	2.9	(1.1)	6.6	(1.7)	28.5	(2.9)	30.8	(2.5)	30.5	(2.6)
Sweden	5.0	(0.1)	0.0	c	1.7	(1.2)	0.6	(0.6)	9.8	(2.6)	14.7	(3.2)	32.6	(4.4)	40.6	(4.6)
Switzerland	3.7	(0.1)	1.3	(0.8)	3.3	(1.3)	15.4	(2.8)	23.8	(3.1)	26.4	(3.5)	16.5	(2.6)	13.4	(2.7)
Turkey	4.9	(0.1)	0.0	c	1.1	(1.6)	3.2	(1.6)	12.2	(3.1)	18.2	(5.0)	21.7	(5.3)	43.5	(5.6)
United Kingdom	5.2	(0.2)	0.0	c	1.6	(1.7)	0.0	c	8.0	(5.8)	9.5	(5.2)	28.7	(8.3)	52.1	(9.1)
United States	5.1	(0.2)	2.5	(2.6)	0.0	c	0.9	(0.9)	6.3	(4.8)	15.5	(5.2)	23.0	(7.4)	51.7	(7.1)
OECD average	4.6	(0.0)	0.4	(0.3)	1.4	(0.2)	6.3	(0.3)	12.8	(0.5)	20.0	(0.6)	26.4	(0.7)	32.6	(0.8)
Partners																
Albania	4.6	(0.3)	0.0	c	15.9	(5.6)	5.5	(3.1)	0.0	c	7.4	(4.2)	27.4	(6.3)	43.7	(7.1)
Argentina	4.2	(0.1)	0.8	(0.6)	3.1	(1.2)	3.4	(1.1)	18.7	(3.5)	29.5	(4.1)	29.2	(3.4)	15.4	(2.7)
Brazil	5.0	(0.1)	3.5	(1.7)	0.3	(0.2)	0.7	(0.3)	3.8	(1.3)	16.0	(3.1)	34.7	(4.4)	41.0	(3.9)
Bulgaria	5.2	(0.1)	1.3	(1.3)	0.0	c	0.5	(0.5)	4.9	(1.7)	11.3	(3.1)	27.7	(5.1)	54.2	(5.5)
Colombia	5.0	(0.1)	0.0	c	0.1	(0.1)	2.0	(1.6)	7.2	(3.1)	18.6	(3.9)	31.1	(5.7)	41.0	(5.3)
Costa Rica	4.8	(0.1)	0.8	(0.8)	2.9	(1.5)	5.0	(1.9)	9.0	(2.6)	11.9	(2.5)	29.8	(5.0)	40.5	(4.3)
Croatia	4.9	(0.1)	0.0	c	0.0	c	4.6	(2.0)	10.2	(3.3)	16.7	(4.1)	25.0	(4.7)	43.5	(5.2)
Cyprus*	3.9	(0.0)	0.0	c	0.0	c	24.3	(0.1)	16.9	(0.1)	22.2	(0.1)	21.8	(0.1)	14.8	(0.1)
Hong Kong-China	5.4	(0.1)	0.0	c	0.0	c	0.0	c	2.7	(1.7)	13.1	(3.9)	26.4	(4.9)	57.7	(5.2)
Indonesia	5.4	(0.2)	0.0	c	4.4	(4.5)	0.0	c	0.0	c	9.6	(5.6)	23.1	(7.2)	62.9	(8.7)
Jordan	5.0	(0.1)	0.0	c	0.0	c	0.2	(0.1)	12.2	(3.3)	17.3	(3.6)	29.8	(4.7)	40.5	(5.0)
Kazakhstan	5.6	(0.1)	0.0	c	0.0	c	0.0	c	0.0	c	1.8	(2.0)	33.4	(13.3)	64.8	(13.5)
Latvia	5.5	(0.1)	0.0	c	0.0	c	0.0	c	1.2	(1.2)	2.4	(2.4)	39.7	(9.3)	56.7	(9.1)
Liechtenstein	5.0	(0.0)	0.0	c	0.0	c	9.8	(0.8)	8.5	(1.0)	6.8	(0.9)	23.8	(1.5)	51.1	(1.0)
Lithuania	5.0	(0.1)	0.9	(1.0)	1.1	(0.9)	2.2	(1.1)	6.1	(2.2)	13.7	(3.2)	33.5	(4.2)	42.4	(4.0)
Macao-China	5.1	(0.0)	0.0	c	0.0	c	0.0	c	16.1	(0.1)	3.9	(0.0)	32.5	(0.1)	47.5	(0.1)
Malaysia	5.0	(0.1)	0.0	c	1.6	(1.6)	0.0	c	2.7	(2.4)	19.6	(5.4)	42.4	(7.4)	33.7	(7.3)
Montenegro	5.0	(0.0)	0.0	c	0.0	c	10.9	(0.1)	3.3	(0.1)	7.2	(0.3)	35.1	(0.2)	43.5	(0.2)
Peru	4.8	(0.1)	0.0	c	1.9	(1.3)	3.1	(1.4)	10.4	(2.6)	17.6	(3.6)	32.3	(4.1)	34.7	(4.2)
Qatar	4.8	(0.0)	0.0	c	1.3	(0.0)	8.8	(0.1)	6.5	(0.1)	13.9	(0.1)	32.2	(0.2)	37.3	(0.1)
Romania	3.9	(0.2)	7.0	(2.8)	1.4	(1.1)	6.3	(1.9)	10.2	(3.3)	42.9	(5.0)	20.2	(3.9)	12.1	(3.3)
Russian Federation	5.8	(0.1)	0.0	c	0.0	c	0.0	c	6.1	(3.8)	0.0	c	2.8	(2.4)	91.2	(3.9)
Serbia	4.7	(0.1)	0.0	c	0.4	(0.4)	2.9	(1.4)	12.7	(3.4)	26.2	(4.4)	29.9	(4.8)	27.9	(4.7)
Shanghai-China	4.8	(0.1)	0.0	c	2.2	(1.5)	3.7	(1.9)	4.1	(1.7)	25.1	(4.3)	35.8	(4.8)	29.1	(3.8)
Singapore	5.5	(0.1)	0.0	c	0.0	c	0.0	c	0.0	c	12.5	(4.8)	28.2	(2.0)	59.3	(3.8)
Chinese Taipei	4.1	(0.1)	0.0	c	1.4	(1.0)	9.2	(2.8)	21.3	(4.0)	27.7	(3.7)	24.9	(3.8)	15.5	(3.3)
Thailand	5.3	(0.2)	0.0	c	0.0	c	0.0	c	12.2	(4.8)	5.6	(3.1)	21.2	(6.4)	61.1	(9.0)
Tunisia	4.8	(0.1)	0.0	c	2.2	(1.6)	5.8	(2.5)	7.0	(2.6)	23.3	(4.2)	20.9	(4.1)	40.7	(5.1)
United Arab Emirates	5.4	(0.1)	0.0	(0.0)	0.0	c	4.4	(2.1)	1.6	(1.3)	8.8	(4.2)	15.9	(4.1)	69.2	(5.8)
Uruguay	4.2	(0.1)	0.0	c	0.1	(0.1)	4.5	(1.4)	19.5	(2.9)	37.5	(3.9)	22.8	(3.1)	15.5	(2.7)
Viet Nam	5.6	(0.1)	0.0	c	0.0	c	0.0	c	2.8	(2.9)	2.1	(2.1)	29.6	(9.1)	65.4	(9.3)

* See notes at the beginning of this Annex.
StatLink 🔗 http://dx.doi.org/10.1787/888932957498

[Part 1/1]
Use of achievement data for accountability purposes
Table IV.4.31   *Results based on school principals' reports*

		Percentage of students in schools that use achievement data in the following ways:			
		Posted publicly		Tracked over time by an administrative authority	
		%	S.E.	%	S.E.
OECD	Australia	69.0	(2.0)	91.7	(0.9)
	Austria	5.7	(1.9)	58.8	(3.8)
	Belgium	3.1	(1.1)	51.3	(2.7)
	Canada	61.0	(2.3)	92.7	(0.8)
	Chile	64.5	(3.6)	84.9	(3.0)
	Czech Republic	44.1	(2.8)	57.5	(2.9)
	Denmark	39.7	(3.6)	69.9	(3.2)
	Estonia	34.8	(2.8)	78.2	(2.0)
	Finland	1.6	(0.8)	47.6	(3.4)
	France	45.9	(3.8)	75.2	(3.0)
	Germany	10.4	(2.2)	36.3	(3.3)
	Greece	27.0	(3.4)	57.2	(4.8)
	Hungary	48.0	(3.8)	57.7	(4.0)
	Iceland	31.4	(0.2)	78.2	(0.2)
	Ireland	20.2	(3.0)	48.4	(4.0)
	Israel	48.0	(3.9)	92.7	(2.0)
	Italy	40.4	(2.1)	30.0	(2.0)
	Japan	5.5	(1.5)	7.0	(1.7)
	Korea	71.0	(3.2)	89.9	(2.6)
	Luxembourg	14.0	(0.0)	68.2	(0.1)
	Mexico	43.5	(1.6)	92.7	(0.9)
	Netherlands	90.5	(2.4)	82.1	(3.2)
	New Zealand	80.3	(3.4)	95.4	(1.8)
	Norway	53.6	(3.8)	84.2	(2.6)
	Poland	47.8	(3.8)	78.1	(3.2)
	Portugal	52.4	(4.1)	88.7	(2.6)
	Slovak Republic	77.1	(2.7)	80.6	(2.9)
	Slovenia	52.9	(0.7)	63.4	(0.7)
	Spain	12.8	(1.7)	81.0	(2.1)
	Sweden	80.4	(2.8)	w	w
	Switzerland	5.8	(2.0)	52.8	(3.3)
	Turkey	67.0	(3.5)	95.5	(1.7)
	United Kingdom	87.1	(2.2)	89.9	(2.0)
	United States	92.0	(1.8)	98.4	(0.7)
	OECD average	**45.0**	**(0.5)**	**72.1**	**(0.4)**
Partners	Albania	24.6	(3.0)	86.5	(2.6)
	Argentina	8.0	(1.9)	75.5	(2.8)
	Brazil	40.9	(2.7)	92.3	(1.1)
	Bulgaria	55.4	(3.5)	89.2	(2.5)
	Colombia	51.2	(4.1)	83.8	(3.3)
	Costa Rica	12.2	(2.3)	96.1	(1.5)
	Croatia	25.3	(3.4)	87.5	(2.6)
	Cyprus*	16.7	(0.1)	79.9	(0.1)
	Hong Kong-China	32.7	(3.8)	66.3	(4.5)
	Indonesia	21.3	(3.7)	63.7	(3.6)
	Jordan	20.4	(3.3)	84.4	(2.5)
	Kazakhstan	79.9	(2.9)	100.0	c
	Latvia	32.5	(3.0)	57.7	(3.8)
	Liechtenstein	34.1	(0.4)	50.9	(0.8)
	Lithuania	31.8	(3.4)	75.6	(2.8)
	Macao-China	8.3	(0.0)	54.0	(0.0)
	Malaysia	35.1	(3.5)	96.9	(1.4)
	Montenegro	79.9	(0.1)	93.6	(0.1)
	Peru	10.4	(2.2)	62.9	(3.3)
	Qatar	48.4	(0.1)	96.6	(0.0)
	Romania	67.9	(4.0)	69.8	(3.5)
	Russian Federation	77.7	(3.0)	99.5	(0.5)
	Serbia	57.1	(4.3)	56.9	(4.3)
	Shanghai-China	3.4	(1.2)	61.1	(4.1)
	Singapore	50.8	(0.5)	98.8	(0.6)
	Chinese Taipei	14.5	(2.7)	47.6	(4.0)
	Thailand	76.4	(3.2)	98.1	(1.1)
	Tunisia	16.9	(2.7)	76.4	(3.6)
	United Arab Emirates	46.7	(2.8)	91.5	(1.9)
	Uruguay	9.8	(2.2)	72.5	(3.2)
	Viet Nam	75.3	(3.5)	82.0	(3.5)

* See notes at the beginning of this Annex.
StatLink ᴍᔿᴾ http://dx.doi.org/10.1787/888932957498

[Part 1/1]
Quality assurance and school improvement
Table IV.4.32   *Results based on school principals' reports*

Percentage of students in schools whose principal reported that their schools have the following measures aimed at quality assurance and improvement:

	Written specification of the school's curriculum and educational goals		Written specification of student-performance standards		Systematic recording of data, including teacher and student attendance and graduation rates, test results and professional development of teachers		Internal evaluation/self-evaluation		External evaluation		Seeking written feed-back from students (e.g. regarding lessons, teachers or resources)		Teacher mentoring		Regular consultation with one or more experts over a period of at least six months with the aim of improving the school		Implementation of a standardised policy for mathematics (i.e. school curriculum with shared instructional materials accompanied by staff development and training)	
	%	S.E.	%	S.E.	%	S.E.	%	S.E.	%	S.E.	%	S.E.	%	S.E.	%	S.E.	%	S.E.
Australia	96.5	(0.6)	90.0	(1.2)	98.1	(0.4)	94.5	(0.9)	69.9	(1.7)	69.1	(1.7)	92.5	(1.0)	72.2	(1.8)	76.6	(1.7)
Austria	76.2	(3.1)	55.9	(3.9)	75.1	(3.5)	86.5	(2.7)	20.3	(2.9)	81.0	(3.2)	88.5	(2.8)	54.9	(4.2)	61.5	(3.3)
Belgium	82.4	(2.4)	48.4	(3.7)	76.8	(2.3)	79.5	(2.5)	69.2	(2.8)	35.6	(2.7)	72.2	(2.5)	40.1	(3.3)	42.0	(2.6)
Canada	94.7	(0.9)	85.3	(1.7)	89.8	(1.1)	80.9	(1.7)	62.0	(2.1)	41.8	(2.4)	86.0	(1.5)	68.8	(1.5)	80.1	(1.9)
Chile	83.4	(2.6)	76.5	(2.9)	86.8	(2.4)	89.9	(2.6)	55.3	(3.8)	49.3	(4.3)	20.9	(3.2)	40.3	(3.9)	49.5	(3.7)
Czech Republic	98.5	(0.7)	77.1	(3.0)	84.7	(2.7)	97.9	(1.1)	62.9	(3.8)	62.6	(4.1)	95.9	(0.8)	27.3	(3.0)	90.2	(2.4)
Denmark	65.6	(3.6)	37.8	(3.5)	80.2	(3.2)	87.6	(2.4)	58.3	(3.7)	36.6	(3.3)	51.7	(3.5)	49.7	(3.2)	23.9	(2.8)
Estonia	92.5	(1.6)	88.3	(1.8)	95.5	(1.2)	99.4	(0.1)	77.1	(2.3)	83.4	(2.0)	79.9	(2.4)	39.2	(2.9)	88.0	(1.9)
Finland	94.1	(1.8)	75.3	(3.3)	74.0	(2.9)	95.9	(1.1)	51.4	(3.0)	74.4	(3.0)	55.2	(3.5)	10.3	(2.0)	63.2	(2.6)
France	71.8	(3.4)	24.7	(3.2)	74.9	(2.8)	60.8	(3.7)	51.9	(3.9)	13.3	(2.6)	17.2	(2.6)	20.7	(3.1)	43.9	(3.4)
Germany	86.1	(2.9)	71.4	(3.3)	76.8	(3.0)	73.9	(3.0)	60.0	(3.4)	48.0	(3.3)	32.9	(3.4)	19.2	(2.6)	55.1	(3.8)
Greece	57.2	(3.6)	38.2	(4.4)	68.5	(3.4)	32.5	(3.9)	5.7	(1.9)	28.8	(3.3)	87.0	(2.3)	76.7	(3.2)	69.9	(3.7)
Hungary	96.4	(1.4)	90.6	(2.4)	79.9	(3.5)	96.9	(1.3)	57.4	(3.8)	80.3	(3.3)	71.5	(3.5)	17.3	(3.2)	69.4	(4.0)
Iceland	64.5	(0.2)	84.2	(0.2)	95.0	(0.1)	99.3	(0.1)	79.4	(0.2)	54.4	(0.2)	19.3	(0.2)	46.1	(0.2)	46.6	(0.2)
Ireland	74.7	(3.4)	48.3	(3.6)	89.4	(2.5)	82.9	(3.0)	81.8	(3.1)	23.7	(3.5)	64.3	(3.8)	52.9	(4.4)	81.4	(3.3)
Israel	96.4	(1.5)	77.7	(3.2)	95.8	(1.2)	81.8	(3.3)	60.0	(3.4)	41.9	(3.6)	94.1	(1.7)	54.0	(3.8)	86.7	(2.7)
Italy	98.4	(0.4)	84.5	(1.7)	52.2	(2.0)	76.1	(2.0)	34.0	(2.2)	40.3	(2.0)	77.5	(1.8)	23.0	(1.7)	56.5	(1.9)
Japan	97.7	(1.3)	48.6	(3.2)	53.7	(3.8)	96.2	(1.5)	77.3	(3.1)	75.3	(3.3)	87.9	(2.4)	4.8	(1.5)	38.1	(3.3)
Korea	99.4	(0.6)	95.0	(1.6)	93.7	(1.9)	97.3	(1.4)	78.6	(3.0)	84.2	(2.8)	87.8	(2.9)	59.3	(3.8)	65.0	(4.1)
Luxembourg	64.1	(0.1)	44.7	(0.1)	70.9	(0.1)	75.5	(0.1)	40.4	(0.1)	19.4	(0.1)	64.8	(0.1)	41.7	(0.1)	59.9	(0.1)
Mexico	93.1	(0.8)	82.5	(1.7)	94.3	(0.8)	93.9	(0.8)	74.7	(1.7)	72.6	(1.7)	53.9	(1.9)	52.3	(1.4)	67.9	(1.5)
Netherlands	91.5	(2.5)	85.5	(2.9)	99.1	(0.6)	91.4	(2.2)	81.2	(3.3)	89.2	(2.3)	97.5	(1.2)	46.7	(4.9)	46.8	(4.5)
New Zealand	99.5	(0.5)	88.0	(2.7)	98.1	(0.7)	99.7	(0.3)	89.0	(2.2)	95.7	(1.0)	97.2	(1.2)	63.4	(3.8)	80.8	(2.6)
Norway	96.7	(1.3)	73.0	(3.0)	83.7	(2.8)	61.1	(3.7)	52.5	(3.9)	46.4	(3.7)	69.7	(3.7)	33.2	(3.4)	28.9	(3.4)
Poland	67.6	(3.6)	82.8	(3.1)	99.2	(0.3)	97.4	(1.2)	78.6	(3.4)	69.6	(3.5)	86.6	(2.2)	39.4	(4.0)	81.8	(3.2)
Portugal	92.8	(2.3)	74.0	(4.0)	96.5	(1.0)	97.6	(1.3)	85.5	(2.8)	76.9	(3.3)	77.8	(3.7)	28.9	(3.8)	74.6	(3.7)
Slovak Republic	86.5	(2.9)	79.9	(3.4)	93.4	(1.8)	94.5	(1.5)	37.7	(3.4)	52.6	(4.0)	87.9	(2.9)	53.7	(3.8)	61.2	(3.8)
Slovenia	93.7	(0.6)	95.3	(0.2)	86.4	(0.3)	92.2	(0.6)	32.4	(0.8)	74.9	(0.8)	67.2	(0.7)	41.0	(0.8)	67.1	(0.6)
Spain	95.8	(1.1)	78.7	(2.1)	92.0	(1.4)	82.2	(1.7)	78.5	(2.1)	62.9	(2.0)	26.1	(1.9)	27.2	(2.4)	38.2	(3.0)
Sweden	69.9	(3.6)	94.5	(1.7)	95.2	(1.6)	89.9	(2.6)	65.1	(3.6)	78.6	(3.0)	68.2	(3.5)	31.8	(3.3)	29.5	(3.1)
Switzerland	69.7	(3.0)	42.9	(2.6)	63.0	(3.1)	84.3	(2.4)	62.8	(2.2)	72.1	(2.9)	71.0	(3.2)	27.5	(3.2)	53.6	(2.7)
Turkey	89.4	(2.3)	93.7	(2.1)	96.3	(1.8)	98.6	(1.3)	79.5	(3.9)	90.8	(2.3)	86.3	(2.2)	59.7	(3.6)	74.4	(3.2)
United Kingdom	97.5	(1.0)	93.0	(1.7)	99.6	(0.2)	100.0	c	91.4	(2.0)	73.1	(3.3)	96.4	(0.9)	80.2	(2.3)	74.3	(3.1)
United States	98.1	(0.9)	95.1	(1.8)	98.1	(1.1)	92.5	(2.3)	86.1	(3.2)	58.6	(4.8)	98.4	(1.0)	73.5	(3.8)	88.1	(3.0)
OECD average	86.2	(0.4)	73.6	(0.5)	85.5	(0.4)	87.1	(0.4)	63.2	(0.5)	60.5	(0.5)	71.5	(0.4)	43.4	(0.5)	62.2	(0.5)
Albania	95.7	(1.5)	96.6	(1.4)	96.9	(1.4)	94.8	(1.6)	68.2	(3.7)	69.4	(3.8)	92.0	(2.0)	68.3	(3.9)	90.7	(2.1)
Argentina	90.8	(2.5)	65.7	(3.9)	78.6	(3.5)	83.1	(3.5)	36.3	(3.9)	42.6	(3.7)	48.3	(4.3)	43.5	(4.0)	40.1	(3.3)
Brazil	93.5	(1.2)	74.1	(2.5)	82.6	(1.9)	95.7	(0.6)	82.1	(1.5)	69.3	(2.9)	92.7	(1.1)	50.2	(2.7)	72.4	(2.5)
Bulgaria	93.0	(1.8)	78.6	(3.1)	98.3	(1.0)	97.9	(1.1)	95.2	(1.2)	82.0	(3.1)	69.3	(3.5)	69.6	(3.6)	52.8	(3.7)
Colombia	96.0	(1.4)	95.3	(1.6)	88.4	(2.5)	98.0	(1.1)	82.3	(2.9)	71.2	(3.6)	67.4	(3.9)	54.6	(4.1)	49.7	(4.4)
Costa Rica	87.4	(2.6)	80.3	(2.7)	87.2	(2.5)	85.2	(3.1)	48.4	(3.8)	55.9	(3.8)	28.0	(3.5)	48.0	(3.9)	51.4	(4.0)
Croatia	92.9	(1.9)	68.1	(4.0)	95.1	(1.6)	91.6	(2.4)	81.3	(3.1)	60.1	(4.2)	98.4	(1.1)	57.6	(4.1)	79.3	(3.5)
Cyprus*	97.5	(0.0)	77.6	(0.1)	94.7	(0.0)	78.3	(0.1)	75.5	(0.1)	42.7	(0.1)	94.5	(0.0)	56.4	(0.1)	93.9	(0.0)
Hong Kong-China	98.1	(1.1)	90.7	(2.3)	100.0	c	99.9	(0.1)	91.3	(2.4)	81.1	(3.2)	91.0	(2.3)	45.1	(4.1)	85.6	(3.1)
Indonesia	98.7	(0.8)	91.5	(1.8)	100.0	c	91.5	(2.4)	84.8	(3.2)	84.7	(2.8)	100.0	c	73.5	(3.3)	81.6	(2.9)
Jordan	90.8	(2.2)	91.6	(1.9)	93.1	(1.9)	90.4	(2.3)	71.0	(3.2)	72.4	(3.1)	68.4	(3.8)	57.0	(3.8)	75.8	(3.3)
Kazakhstan	97.1	(1.5)	98.6	(1.0)	100.0	c	99.0	(0.8)	94.9	(1.7)	81.5	(3.3)	97.4	(1.1)	86.8	(2.6)	92.4	(1.9)
Latvia	96.4	(1.4)	87.7	(2.4)	99.8	(0.2)	100.0	c	84.2	(2.6)	76.5	(3.2)	71.9	(3.3)	23.5	(3.5)	51.7	(3.8)
Liechtenstein	81.1	(0.9)	59.2	(0.7)	37.1	(1.0)	93.6	(0.4)	83.2	(0.7)	93.8	(0.6)	81.8	(0.5)	67.5	(0.9)	56.7	(0.6)
Lithuania	72.7	(3.4)	78.6	(2.9)	98.0	(1.0)	95.0	(1.3)	56.5	(3.8)	75.2	(2.9)	53.5	(3.5)	40.2	(3.0)	30.3	(3.0)
Macao-China	90.4	(0.0)	93.5	(0.0)	98.6	(0.0)	87.7	(0.0)	63.7	(0.1)	70.3	(0.1)	91.3	(0.0)	44.0	(0.1)	57.0	(0.1)
Malaysia	97.4	(1.3)	100.0	c	98.8	(0.7)	98.6	(0.7)	82.7	(2.6)	70.1	(3.4)	88.7	(2.5)	82.1	(2.8)	93.2	(2.2)
Montenegro	94.9	(0.1)	81.4	(0.1)	97.3	(0.0)	100.0	c	93.1	(0.1)	59.2	(0.2)	97.8	(0.0)	73.9	(0.1)	89.5	(0.1)
Peru	89.1	(2.2)	66.6	(3.6)	67.3	(3.1)	86.7	(2.1)	41.6	(3.7)	66.9	(3.3)	97.5	(1.5)	41.7	(3.5)	44.4	(3.5)
Qatar	99.7	(0.0)	97.9	(0.0)	99.5	(0.0)	99.3	(0.0)	86.8	(0.0)	89.5	(0.1)	100.0	c	90.0	(0.0)	98.0	(0.0)
Romania	87.5	(2.6)	86.6	(2.5)	88.6	(2.4)	87.6	(2.0)	83.6	(2.8)	82.9	(2.7)	84.6	(2.9)	66.2	(3.5)	73.7	(3.3)
Russian Federation	93.1	(2.1)	89.4	(1.8)	98.2	(0.8)	94.8	(1.7)	96.0	(1.1)	83.0	(2.8)	96.0	(1.4)	54.2	(3.5)	86.1	(2.6)
Serbia	81.9	(3.4)	54.6	(4.0)	96.5	(1.7)	95.9	(1.5)	52.6	(4.4)	48.0	(4.3)	97.7	(1.1)	58.1	(4.6)	41.3	(4.4)
Shanghai-China	100.0	c	86.2	(2.7)	97.5	(1.2)	100.0	c	88.4	(2.7)	91.4	(2.1)	98.5	(0.7)	93.2	(1.9)	94.1	(2.1)
Singapore	98.9	(0.0)	97.7	(0.8)	99.4	(0.6)	100.0	c	93.4	(0.5)	87.4	(0.1)	99.7	(0.0)	63.4	(0.3)	92.1	(0.7)
Chinese Taipei	94.1	(1.4)	87.9	(2.8)	92.3	(1.8)	83.7	(3.2)	53.5	(3.9)	62.0	(3.4)	73.2	(3.5)	32.3	(3.6)	57.3	(4.3)
Thailand	97.6	(1.1)	93.9	(1.9)	98.4	(1.0)	100.0	c	99.3	(0.3)	80.3	(3.1)	98.2	(1.1)	88.8	(2.4)	86.1	(2.6)
Tunisia	50.2	(4.0)	33.5	(4.0)	71.4	(3.6)	91.5	(2.0)	48.7	(4.5)	29.3	(3.8)	80.3	(3.3)	21.4	(3.1)	60.6	(3.7)
United Arab Emirates	95.4	(1.2)	95.7	(1.0)	99.0	(0.4)	91.6	(0.7)	94.0	(1.1)	77.5	(2.0)	92.0	(0.9)	73.1	(2.0)	82.0	(2.2)
Uruguay	75.2	(3.4)	59.1	(3.5)	96.0	(1.5)	84.9	(2.3)	44.8	(3.8)	52.6	(3.9)	74.5	(2.9)	27.4	(3.3)	29.3	(3.4)
Viet Nam	98.1	(1.1)	92.2	(2.1)	97.8	(1.3)	96.1	(1.7)	49.4	(3.9)	84.9	(3.1)	98.5	(1.0)	45.2	(4.3)	93.2	(2.1)

OECD (rows Australia–OECD average), Partners (rows Albania–Viet Nam)

* See notes at the beginning of this Annex.
StatLink ⟨⟩ http://dx.doi.org/10.1787/888932957498

[Part 1/1]
Internal or external evaluations and feedback from students
Table IV.4.33 *Results based on school principals' reports*

		Percentage of students in schools whose principal reported that there are...							
		...neither internal nor external evaluations...				...internal or external evaluations...			
		...and no written feedback from students is sought (regarding lessons, teachers or resources)		...but written feedback from students is sought (regarding lessons, teachers or resources)		...but no written feedback from students is sought (regarding lessons, teachers or resources)		...and written feedback from students is sought (regarding lessons, teachers or resources)	
		%	S.E.	%	S.E.	%	S.E.	%	S.E.
OECD	Australia	2.4	(0.6)	1.6	(0.5)	28.5	(1.7)	67.5	(1.8)
	Austria	6.0	(1.9)	5.9	(1.6)	12.9	(2.7)	75.1	(3.3)
	Belgium	7.9	(1.6)	1.4	(0.6)	56.3	(3.0)	34.4	(2.7)
	Canada	11.8	(1.4)	1.8	(0.5)	46.3	(2.3)	40.1	(2.4)
	Chile	4.4	(1.6)	1.4	(1.0)	46.4	(4.3)	47.8	(4.5)
	Czech Republic	0.6	(0.4)	0.5	(0.4)	36.9	(4.1)	62.0	(4.0)
	Denmark	5.0	(1.5)	0.5	(0.3)	58.4	(3.3)	36.1	(3.3)
	Estonia	0.6	(0.1)	0.0	c	16.0	(2.0)	83.4	(2.0)
	Finland	0.8	(0.5)	1.1	(0.7)	24.6	(2.9)	73.5	(3.0)
	France	20.5	(2.8)	1.4	(0.8)	66.1	(2.9)	12.0	(2.5)
	Germany	12.6	(2.2)	1.4	(0.8)	39.3	(3.2)	46.6	(3.3)
	Greece	51.0	(3.8)	14.5	(2.9)	20.0	(2.9)	14.4	(2.9)
	Hungary	0.2	(0.2)	1.7	(0.9)	19.6	(3.3)	78.5	(3.5)
	Iceland	0.3	(0.0)	0.0	c	45.3	(0.2)	54.4	(0.2)
	Ireland	2.7	(1.4)	0.0	c	74.2	(3.8)	23.2	(3.5)
	Israel	9.0	(2.3)	1.8	(1.0)	49.1	(4.2)	40.2	(3.7)
	Italy	16.4	(1.8)	3.2	(0.6)	43.3	(2.3)	37.2	(2.0)
	Japan	3.0	(1.4)	0.0	c	21.8	(3.0)	75.3	(3.3)
	Korea	0.0	c	1.3	(0.9)	15.8	(2.8)	82.9	(2.9)
	Luxembourg	17.2	(0.1)	0.3	(0.0)	63.3	(0.1)	19.1	(0.1)
	Mexico	1.1	(0.4)	1.0	(0.3)	26.2	(1.6)	71.7	(1.7)
	Netherlands	2.2	(1.3)	2.3	(1.2)	8.1	(1.9)	87.5	(2.4)
	New Zealand	0.3	(0.3)	0.0	c	3.9	(0.9)	95.7	(1.0)
	Norway	11.0	(2.4)	8.9	(2.2)	42.6	(3.6)	37.5	(3.6)
	Poland	0.6	(0.5)	0.1	(0.1)	29.8	(3.5)	69.6	(3.5)
	Portugal	0.2	(0.2)	0.7	(0.8)	22.9	(3.3)	76.1	(3.2)
	Slovak Republic	0.8	(0.5)	1.1	(0.6)	46.6	(4.0)	51.5	(4.0)
	Slovenia	3.7	(0.2)	2.2	(0.1)	21.4	(0.8)	72.7	(0.8)
	Spain	6.0	(1.6)	1.3	(0.3)	31.0	(2.3)	61.6	(2.0)
	Sweden	2.8	(1.2)	3.4	(1.4)	18.6	(3.0)	75.2	(3.2)
	Switzerland	11.8	(2.3)	1.4	(0.4)	16.1	(2.2)	70.7	(2.8)
	Turkey	0.0	c	1.4	(1.3)	9.2	(2.3)	89.4	(2.6)
	United Kingdom	0.0	c	0.0	c	26.9	(3.3)	73.1	(3.3)
	United States	2.0	(1.2)	0.9	(0.9)	39.4	(4.7)	57.7	(4.7)
	OECD average	6.3	(0.3)	1.9	(0.2)	33.1	(0.5)	58.6	(0.5)
Partners	Albania	2.6	(1.1)	0.0	c	28.2	(3.8)	69.2	(3.9)
	Argentina	7.3	(2.5)	4.3	(1.7)	50.0	(3.8)	38.4	(3.4)
	Brazil	1.6	(0.4)	0.5	(0.2)	29.1	(2.9)	68.7	(2.9)
	Bulgaria	0.0	c	0.0	c	18.0	(3.1)	82.0	(3.1)
	Colombia	1.9	(1.1)	0.1	(0.1)	26.9	(3.6)	71.1	(3.6)
	Costa Rica	8.6	(1.9)	1.6	(1.1)	34.9	(3.7)	54.8	(3.9)
	Croatia	0.3	(0.3)	1.8	(1.1)	39.6	(4.2)	58.2	(4.2)
	Cyprus*	3.6	(0.0)	3.8	(0.0)	53.7	(0.1)	38.9	(0.1)
	Hong Kong-China	0.0	c	0.0	c	18.9	(3.2)	81.1	(3.2)
	Indonesia	1.0	(0.8)	1.2	(0.9)	14.3	(2.7)	83.5	(2.8)
	Jordan	2.8	(1.2)	1.3	(0.9)	24.8	(3.0)	71.1	(3.1)
	Kazakhstan	0.0	c	0.0	c	18.5	(3.3)	81.5	(3.3)
	Latvia	0.0	c	0.0	c	23.5	(3.2)	76.5	(3.2)
	Liechtenstein	0.0	c	0.0	c	6.2	(0.6)	93.8	(0.6)
	Lithuania	0.8	(0.5)	1.7	(1.0)	23.9	(2.9)	73.5	(2.9)
	Macao-China	0.0	c	2.7	(0.0)	29.7	(0.1)	67.7	(0.1)
	Malaysia	0.7	(0.5)	0.7	(0.5)	29.3	(3.4)	69.3	(3.5)
	Montenegro	0.0	c	0.0	c	40.8	(0.2)	59.2	(0.2)
	Peru	6.6	(1.6)	2.6	(1.0)	26.9	(3.0)	63.9	(3.4)
	Qatar	0.0	c	0.2	(0.0)	10.5	(0.1)	89.3	(0.1)
	Romania	2.6	(0.8)	2.8	(1.3)	14.5	(2.7)	80.1	(2.9)
	Russian Federation	0.3	(0.3)	0.0	c	16.7	(2.8)	83.0	(2.8)
	Serbia	3.1	(1.5)	0.0	c	48.5	(4.4)	48.4	(4.4)
	Shanghai-China	0.0	c	0.0	c	8.6	(2.1)	91.4	(2.1)
	Singapore	0.0	c	0.0	c	12.6	(0.1)	87.4	(0.1)
	Chinese Taipei	8.4	(2.5)	1.6	(1.0)	29.6	(2.9)	60.4	(3.4)
	Thailand	0.0	c	0.0	c	19.7	(3.1)	80.3	(3.1)
	Tunisia	5.6	(1.8)	1.5	(1.0)	64.9	(3.9)	28.0	(3.7)
	United Arab Emirates	0.3	(0.2)	0.0	c	22.2	(2.0)	77.5	(2.0)
	Uruguay	4.5	(1.5)	6.3	(1.5)	43.2	(4.2)	46.0	(4.0)
	Viet Nam	1.4	(1.0)	2.5	(1.4)	13.6	(3.0)	82.4	(3.4)

* See notes at the beginning of this Annex.
StatLink ⟪⟫ http://dx.doi.org/10.1787/888932957498

[Part 1/1]
Monitoring mathematics teachers' practice
Table IV.4.34 *Results based on school principals' reports*

		Percentage of students in schools whose principal reported that the following methods have been used to monitor the practice of mathematics teachers at their schools:							
		Tests or assessments of student achievement		Teacher peer review of lesson plans, assessment instruments and lessons		Principal or senior staff observations of lessons		Observation of classes by inspectors or other persons external to the school	
		%	S.E.	%	S.E.	%	S.E.	%	S.E.
OECD	Australia	78.8	(1.5)	77.4	(1.5)	70.0	(1.8)	10.9	(1.3)
	Austria	91.0	(2.1)	78.6	(3.4)	73.9	(3.5)	29.2	(3.1)
	Belgium	65.6	(3.2)	76.3	(2.4)	65.0	(3.2)	48.0	(2.8)
	Canada	72.9	(2.3)	60.0	(2.1)	81.9	(1.6)	20.6	(2.2)
	Chile	76.9	(3.2)	80.3	(3.2)	91.0	(2.1)	25.2	(3.2)
	Czech Republic	92.0	(2.3)	66.6	(3.7)	98.0	(0.8)	32.7	(3.8)
	Denmark	75.1	(2.8)	40.9	(3.6)	64.3	(3.8)	16.8	(2.5)
	Estonia	71.3	(2.8)	48.8	(2.7)	89.6	(1.5)	7.6	(1.7)
	Finland	39.6	(3.2)	19.1	(2.9)	31.3	(2.5)	2.2	(0.8)
	France	60.5	(3.4)	42.5	(3.5)	12.3	(2.3)	72.9	(3.3)
	Germany	72.1	(3.3)	44.6	(3.0)	66.9	(3.3)	22.1	(3.0)
	Greece	59.7	(3.7)	26.0	(3.5)	8.3	(2.3)	20.6	(3.0)
	Hungary	74.3	(3.6)	74.5	(3.1)	96.7	(1.3)	13.0	(2.4)
	Iceland	84.2	(0.2)	12.1	(0.2)	46.4	(0.2)	25.3	(0.2)
	Ireland	65.3	(3.9)	33.7	(3.6)	12.7	(2.4)	48.5	(3.9)
	Israel	96.0	(1.4)	51.3	(3.8)	74.8	(3.6)	34.0	(3.4)
	Italy	74.1	(1.8)	87.4	(1.7)	17.2	(1.4)	0.6	(0.2)
	Japan	69.4	(3.3)	54.2	(3.4)	81.0	(2.6)	26.5	(3.1)
	Korea	84.1	(3.1)	98.7	(0.9)	96.0	(1.7)	68.5	(3.8)
	Luxembourg	80.6	(0.1)	63.3	(0.1)	47.9	(0.1)	6.4	(0.0)
	Mexico	92.5	(0.9)	76.4	(1.7)	76.6	(1.3)	41.1	(1.7)
	Netherlands	83.2	(3.6)	54.0	(4.6)	86.6	(3.1)	41.9	(4.5)
	New Zealand	84.1	(3.5)	91.7	(2.3)	96.6	(1.1)	32.3	(3.4)
	Norway	72.4	(2.7)	53.9	(4.1)	47.7	(3.7)	10.9	(2.2)
	Poland	100.0	c	64.4	(4.0)	94.4	(1.8)	16.2	(3.1)
	Portugal	98.2	(1.1)	71.3	(4.6)	60.2	(3.4)	4.2	(2.2)
	Slovak Republic	74.6	(3.2)	84.2	(3.0)	98.2	(0.8)	27.0	(3.4)
	Slovenia	72.1	(0.7)	62.4	(0.8)	94.1	(0.5)	4.7	(0.3)
	Spain	78.0	(2.5)	21.9	(2.2)	9.6	(1.4)	15.5	(2.4)
	Sweden	67.5	(3.5)	58.7	(3.7)	79.7	(3.2)	26.9	(3.4)
	Switzerland	60.6	(3.0)	62.9	(3.3)	83.0	(2.2)	28.7	(2.7)
	Turkey	91.6	(2.7)	51.8	(3.8)	93.9	(1.9)	22.1	(3.6)
	United Kingdom	94.7	(1.2)	92.9	(1.5)	96.6	(1.0)	68.0	(2.9)
	United States	89.4	(2.7)	65.9	(3.7)	99.7	(0.3)	42.0	(4.5)
	OECD average	77.7	(0.5)	60.3	(0.5)	68.9	(0.4)	26.9	(0.5)
Partners	Albania	98.3	(0.9)	91.9	(2.2)	99.2	(0.7)	62.2	(3.6)
	Argentina	82.0	(3.0)	73.5	(3.9)	85.0	(2.8)	21.5	(3.7)
	Brazil	88.3	(1.4)	74.8	(2.2)	49.8	(2.1)	22.8	(2.4)
	Bulgaria	90.8	(2.1)	29.4	(3.7)	97.1	(1.3)	48.8	(3.8)
	Colombia	83.7	(2.9)	60.4	(4.0)	43.0	(3.8)	10.7	(2.5)
	Costa Rica	83.3	(2.8)	80.9	(2.6)	86.5	(2.2)	45.1	(3.5)
	Croatia	72.4	(3.5)	62.0	(3.7)	93.0	(2.0)	33.7	(3.3)
	Cyprus*	89.5	(0.1)	63.5	(0.1)	92.0	(0.1)	86.8	(0.1)
	Hong Kong-China	94.9	(1.8)	85.0	(3.1)	96.7	(1.5)	39.0	(4.1)
	Indonesia	91.3	(2.4)	91.3	(1.6)	95.4	(1.5)	77.1	(3.6)
	Jordan	93.9	(1.9)	93.0	(1.8)	97.9	(1.0)	96.6	(1.6)
	Kazakhstan	98.9	(0.7)	98.9	(0.7)	99.9	(0.1)	81.9	(3.0)
	Latvia	83.2	(2.8)	89.3	(2.3)	100.0	c	41.0	(3.1)
	Liechtenstein	82.4	(0.7)	69.6	(1.0)	49.4	(0.8)	86.9	(0.6)
	Lithuania	95.6	(1.3)	74.7	(3.1)	98.2	(1.0)	37.7	(3.3)
	Macao-China	89.9	(0.0)	88.0	(0.1)	96.0	(0.0)	47.9	(0.0)
	Malaysia	98.7	(0.9)	91.0	(2.4)	98.9	(0.8)	69.5	(3.8)
	Montenegro	80.9	(0.1)	72.3	(0.1)	99.0	(0.0)	55.6	(0.1)
	Peru	71.4	(3.2)	79.7	(2.6)	84.4	(2.5)	53.8	(3.3)
	Qatar	96.6	(0.0)	98.0	(0.0)	99.7	(0.0)	82.0	(0.1)
	Romania	67.6	(3.1)	69.4	(3.1)	73.3	(3.3)	57.7	(3.7)
	Russian Federation	98.9	(0.5)	95.9	(1.1)	99.5	(0.3)	43.8	(4.2)
	Serbia	50.1	(4.2)	58.8	(4.5)	94.5	(2.3)	34.0	(4.3)
	Shanghai-China	92.4	(2.0)	91.3	(2.2)	97.4	(1.2)	89.8	(1.8)
	Singapore	96.2	(0.6)	85.5	(0.1)	99.8	(0.0)	23.3	(0.6)
	Chinese Taipei	81.9	(3.2)	60.8	(3.8)	61.0	(3.8)	7.7	(1.9)
	Thailand	97.9	(1.1)	92.5	(2.1)	95.1	(1.6)	44.7	(4.3)
	Tunisia	75.0	(3.8)	39.6	(3.9)	50.1	(4.1)	86.9	(2.7)
	United Arab Emirates	96.5	(1.0)	84.8	(2.2)	99.7	(0.2)	84.2	(2.1)
	Uruguay	57.8	(3.9)	63.3	(3.6)	88.4	(2.2)	66.2	(3.2)
	Viet Nam	97.7	(1.4)	83.0	(2.7)	96.7	(1.6)	85.2	(3.1)

* See notes at the beginning of this Annex.
StatLink ᵐˢᵖ http://dx.doi.org/10.1787/888932957498

[Part 1/2]
Consequences of teacher appraisals
Table IV.4.35 *Results based on school principals' reports*

		Percentage of students in schools whose principal reported that appraisals of and/or feedback to teachers lead directly to the following:																							
		A change in salary						A financial bonus or another kind of monetary reward						Opportunities for professional-development activities						A change in the likelihood of career advancement					
		No change		A small or moderate change		A large change		No change		A small or moderate change		A large change		No change		A small or moderate change		A large change		No change		A small or moderate change		A large change	
		%	S.E.	%	S.E.	%	S.E.	%	S.E.	%	S.E.	%	S.E.	%	S.E.	%	S.E.	%	S.E.	%	S.E.	%	S.E.	%	S.E.
OECD	Australia	87.2	(1.3)	12.0	(1.3)	0.8	(0.3)	93.7	(0.9)	5.9	(0.9)	0.4	(0.2)	14.3	(1.5)	76.1	(1.6)	9.5	(1.2)	31.5	(1.8)	66.6	(1.8)	1.8	(0.6)
	Austria	96.7	(1.5)	1.9	(1.1)	1.4	(1.0)	91.9	(2.4)	6.7	(2.2)	1.4	(1.0)	64.5	(4.0)	31.9	(3.8)	3.6	(1.8)	69.7	(3.4)	25.4	(3.0)	4.8	(1.9)
	Belgium	99.6	(0.4)	0.4	(0.4)	0.0	c	98.9	(0.6)	1.1	(0.6)	0.0	c	32.3	(3.2)	64.8	(3.2)	2.9	(1.0)	76.7	(2.1)	22.5	(2.1)	0.8	(0.5)
	Canada	96.9	(0.6)	2.7	(0.6)	0.3	(0.2)	97.1	(0.6)	2.9	(0.6)	0.0	(0.0)	21.4	(2.2)	71.8	(2.6)	6.8	(1.4)	56.0	(2.4)	42.5	(2.3)	1.5	(0.7)
	Chile	62.3	(3.8)	33.2	(3.5)	4.5	(1.8)	59.5	(3.9)	34.9	(3.9)	5.6	(2.0)	23.9	(3.3)	64.7	(3.7)	11.4	(2.5)	33.4	(3.5)	60.4	(3.5)	6.2	(2.1)
	Czech Republic	27.8	(3.2)	70.3	(3.2)	2.0	(0.8)	14.5	(2.3)	78.7	(2.9)	6.9	(1.8)	16.1	(3.0)	81.3	(3.0)	2.6	(0.7)	41.4	(3.9)	58.2	(4.0)	0.4	(0.3)
	Denmark	95.7	(1.9)	4.3	(1.9)	0.0	c	92.8	(2.3)	7.1	(2.3)	0.1	(0.1)	33.5	(3.3)	61.0	(3.5)	5.5	(1.6)	85.5	(2.5)	12.9	(2.4)	1.6	(0.9)
	Estonia	61.8	(3.2)	33.8	(3.0)	4.4	(1.5)	29.7	(2.7)	63.6	(2.7)	6.6	(1.3)	20.6	(2.2)	70.1	(2.6)	9.3	(1.8)	42.1	(2.7)	53.0	(2.7)	4.9	(1.1)
	Finland	80.8	(2.5)	19.2	(2.5)	0.0	c	77.1	(2.8)	22.9	(2.8)	0.0	c	28.9	(3.0)	68.3	(3.3)	2.8	(1.4)	73.1	(3.3)	26.9	(3.3)	0.0	c
	France	58.1	(3.9)	40.9	(3.9)	1.0	(0.7)	79.8	(3.0)	19.7	(3.0)	0.5	(0.5)	37.2	(3.3)	60.8	(3.3)	2.1	(1.1)	36.2	(3.6)	60.7	(3.8)	3.1	(1.2)
	Germany	93.2	(1.6)	6.8	(1.6)	0.0	c	91.8	(1.5)	8.2	(1.5)	0.0	c	43.6	(3.6)	56.4	(3.6)	0.0	c	55.7	(3.3)	42.9	(3.3)	1.4	(1.0)
	Greece	75.9	(3.1)	17.9	(3.1)	6.2	(1.9)	76.2	(3.4)	20.7	(3.2)	3.0	(1.4)	48.3	(4.3)	38.9	(4.3)	12.8	(2.6)	58.1	(4.1)	31.8	(3.0)	10.1	(2.5)
	Hungary	77.9	(3.6)	21.4	(3.6)	0.7	(0.7)	18.0	(2.8)	61.2	(3.9)	20.8	(3.5)	32.6	(3.3)	61.8	(3.6)	5.7	(1.6)	25.8	(3.5)	59.3	(4.0)	15.0	(2.9)
	Iceland	81.1	(0.2)	18.9	(0.2)	0.0	c	82.3	(0.2)	16.8	(0.2)	0.9	(0.1)	16.8	(0.2)	75.8	(0.2)	7.4	(0.2)	70.8	(0.2)	28.2	(0.2)	1.0	(0.1)
	Ireland	98.7	(0.9)	0.8	(0.7)	0.5	(0.5)	98.8	(0.9)	1.2	(0.9)	0.0	c	46.7	(4.0)	46.5	(4.1)	6.8	(2.1)	72.3	(3.5)	27.2	(3.4)	0.5	(0.5)
	Israel	77.0	(3.0)	20.0	(3.1)	3.0	(1.4)	73.8	(3.2)	20.8	(3.1)	5.4	(1.8)	18.9	(2.8)	71.5	(3.2)	9.5	(2.5)	21.3	(2.9)	67.9	(3.4)	10.8	(2.6)
	Italy	83.9	(1.9)	14.8	(1.9)	1.3	(0.5)	61.9	(2.3)	36.8	(2.3)	1.3	(0.5)	33.2	(2.2)	63.6	(2.3)	3.2	(0.8)	65.7	(2.2)	32.2	(2.2)	2.1	(0.7)
	Japan	72.7	(3.1)	23.9	(3.1)	3.4	(1.4)	65.9	(3.5)	30.1	(3.3)	3.9	(1.4)	33.0	(3.1)	65.0	(3.3)	2.0	(1.0)	46.5	(3.4)	48.3	(3.6)	5.2	(1.6)
	Korea	52.6	(4.3)	44.4	(4.3)	2.9	(1.3)	31.2	(4.0)	62.4	(4.2)	6.4	(2.0)	10.5	(2.3)	78.0	(3.4)	11.5	(2.6)	37.2	(3.9)	59.7	(4.0)	3.1	(1.4)
	Luxembourg	97.7	(0.0)	2.3	(0.0)	0.0	c	97.7	(0.0)	0.0	c	2.3	(0.0)	50.9	(0.1)	48.6	(0.1)	0.4	(0.0)	81.1	(0.1)	18.9	(0.1)	0.0	c
	Mexico	58.3	(1.9)	34.5	(1.8)	7.2	(0.9)	48.8	(1.9)	42.8	(1.8)	8.3	(0.9)	26.6	(1.7)	61.8	(1.8)	11.6	(1.0)	22.0	(1.2)	66.6	(1.5)	11.4	(1.0)
	Netherlands	77.9	(3.2)	20.6	(3.1)	1.5	(1.0)	73.3	(4.1)	26.7	(4.1)	0.0	c	9.0	(2.6)	74.0	(3.9)	17.0	(3.5)	30.3	(3.9)	61.2	(4.2)	8.5	(2.4)
	New Zealand	79.5	(2.8)	20.2	(2.8)	0.3	(0.3)	93.0	(1.9)	6.7	(1.9)	0.3	(0.3)	2.4	(1.1)	86.0	(2.6)	11.6	(2.5)	17.9	(3.0)	78.7	(3.1)	3.4	(1.7)
	Norway	91.3	(2.2)	8.7	(2.2)	0.0	c	96.7	(1.5)	3.3	(1.5)	0.0	c	15.6	(2.7)	78.2	(2.7)	6.2	(1.7)	49.1	(3.6)	46.9	(3.6)	4.0	(1.5)
	Poland	65.6	(3.8)	32.3	(3.8)	2.1	(1.1)	17.3	(3.0)	73.7	(3.4)	9.0	(2.2)	25.5	(3.5)	67.4	(3.9)	7.2	(2.1)	43.5	(3.8)	48.5	(3.5)	8.0	(2.3)
	Portugal	78.7	(3.3)	17.5	(3.1)	3.8	(1.9)	88.9	(2.6)	9.9	(2.6)	1.2	(0.6)	54.4	(4.5)	43.9	(4.8)	1.7	(0.8)	58.5	(4.3)	35.9	(4.3)	5.6	(1.6)
	Slovak Republic	50.6	(4.2)	47.5	(4.3)	1.9	(1.0)	16.7	(2.9)	72.2	(3.3)	11.1	(2.1)	15.5	(2.7)	70.9	(3.7)	13.6	(2.7)	28.1	(3.5)	64.9	(3.7)	7.0	(1.7)
	Slovenia	57.2	(0.7)	39.4	(0.7)	3.4	(0.3)	46.6	(0.6)	50.9	(0.6)	2.4	(0.3)	14.3	(0.6)	76.6	(0.6)	9.1	(0.3)	14.7	(0.4)	74.2	(0.7)	11.1	(0.7)
	Spain	91.1	(1.7)	7.1	(1.5)	1.7	(0.8)	90.7	(1.5)	7.9	(1.3)	1.4	(0.7)	54.1	(2.7)	42.6	(2.7)	3.3	(0.9)	77.3	(1.8)	21.5	(1.8)	1.2	(0.5)
	Sweden	12.9	(2.4)	76.2	(3.4)	10.9	(2.5)	81.2	(3.3)	17.6	(3.2)	1.1	(0.7)	7.2	(1.9)	74.1	(3.3)	18.7	(2.9)	39.5	(3.9)	54.6	(4.0)	5.9	(1.6)
	Switzerland	88.1	(2.4)	11.9	(2.4)	0.0	(0.0)	82.8	(3.0)	17.2	(3.0)	0.0	(0.0)	42.5	(3.5)	56.4	(3.6)	1.1	(0.9)	78.7	(3.5)	21.1	(3.5)	0.1	(0.0)
	Turkey	43.5	(3.9)	35.1	(3.5)	21.4	(3.6)	39.1	(4.0)	41.2	(3.9)	19.7	(3.2)	14.3	(2.6)	71.3	(3.1)	14.4	(2.4)	16.8	(3.0)	63.6	(3.8)	19.7	(3.0)
	United Kingdom	34.2	(2.8)	63.9	(3.0)	1.8	(0.9)	84.3	(3.7)	15.6	(3.7)	0.1	(0.1)	1.7	(0.7)	78.8	(2.7)	19.5	(2.7)	12.7	(2.2)	81.5	(2.2)	5.8	(1.8)
	United States	88.5	(3.1)	10.9	(3.0)	0.6	(0.7)	85.3	(3.3)	14.0	(3.2)	0.7	(0.7)	11.9	(2.9)	78.4	(3.2)	9.8	(2.2)	43.5	(3.6)	54.4	(3.6)	2.1	(1.2)
	OECD average	73.4	(0.5)	24.0	(0.5)	2.6	(0.3)	69.9	(0.5)	26.5	(0.5)	3.6	(0.3)	27.1	(0.5)	65.2	(0.5)	7.7	(0.3)	47.4	(0.5)	47.6	(0.5)	4.9	(0.3)
Partners	Albania	61.3	(3.7)	33.1	(3.7)	5.7	(1.6)	77.8	(3.2)	20.7	(3.0)	1.4	(0.8)	24.6	(3.5)	69.5	(3.4)	5.9	(1.6)	33.7	(3.9)	61.6	(3.8)	4.7	(1.6)
	Argentina	90.5	(2.0)	9.5	(2.0)	0.0	c	94.2	(1.6)	5.7	(1.6)	0.1	(0.2)	38.0	(4.0)	53.1	(4.3)	8.9	(2.2)	32.9	(3.8)	54.7	(4.0)	12.4	(2.7)
	Brazil	64.1	(2.5)	32.6	(2.6)	3.4	(1.1)	57.0	(2.6)	37.5	(2.5)	5.4	(1.3)	34.5	(2.4)	57.2	(3.0)	8.3	(1.6)	42.6	(2.3)	49.7	(2.8)	7.7	(1.5)
	Bulgaria	70.7	(3.4)	29.0	(3.4)	0.3	(0.2)	14.7	(2.3)	79.4	(2.7)	5.9	(1.6)	10.1	(2.2)	83.4	(2.6)	6.6	(1.8)	15.1	(2.7)	78.6	(3.1)	6.3	(2.0)
	Colombia	60.9	(3.9)	35.7	(3.9)	3.4	(1.0)	79.3	(2.9)	18.0	(2.8)	2.7	(1.0)	26.5	(3.5)	58.4	(3.8)	15.1	(2.6)	26.2	(3.5)	57.0	(3.9)	16.7	(2.6)
	Costa Rica	67.2	(3.5)	29.0	(3.3)	3.8	(1.5)	83.0	(2.6)	14.6	(2.5)	2.4	(1.2)	28.2	(3.7)	59.5	(4.1)	12.3	(2.3)	26.8	(3.1)	62.2	(3.6)	11.0	(2.2)
	Croatia	84.7	(2.9)	12.1	(2.5)	3.2	(1.5)	73.5	(3.7)	20.9	(3.3)	5.6	(1.8)	12.4	(2.6)	74.7	(3.5)	12.9	(2.6)	9.5	(2.4)	76.7	(3.3)	13.8	(2.7)
	Cyprus*	78.5	(0.1)	20.4	(0.1)	1.2	(0.0)	83.5	(0.1)	16.5	(0.1)	0.0	c	23.3	(0.1)	73.1	(0.1)	3.6	(0.1)	14.8	(0.1)	75.1	(0.1)	10.1	(0.1)
	Hong Kong-China	69.7	(4.2)	28.3	(4.1)	2.1	(1.2)	83.9	(2.9)	15.2	(2.7)	0.9	(0.9)	38.7	(4.3)	59.1	(4.4)	2.2	(1.2)	2.0	(1.1)	84.2	(3.1)	13.8	(3.0)
	Indonesia	15.0	(2.8)	78.7	(3.7)	6.3	(1.9)	19.8	(3.1)	79.5	(3.1)	0.6	(0.4)	3.2	(1.3)	76.1	(3.2)	20.8	(3.1)	2.9	(1.1)	78.7	(3.3)	18.4	(3.2)
	Jordan	41.0	(3.2)	39.4	(3.7)	19.6	(3.1)	39.9	(3.3)	33.8	(3.5)	26.3	(3.1)	18.6	(2.8)	66.1	(3.4)	15.3	(3.1)	20.7	(2.8)	59.1	(3.5)	20.2	(2.8)
	Kazakhstan	37.7	(4.1)	56.5	(4.2)	5.8	(1.7)	33.5	(3.3)	55.5	(3.9)	11.1	(2.4)	4.9	(1.3)	69.0	(3.8)	26.1	(3.7)	16.6	(2.7)	68.9	(3.6)	14.5	(3.0)
	Latvia	56.3	(3.2)	37.4	(3.0)	6.3	(1.6)	64.9	(3.6)	28.8	(3.5)	6.4	(1.9)	13.2	(2.5)	77.7	(3.2)	9.1	(2.3)	35.6	(3.1)	60.2	(3.2)	4.3	(1.1)
	Liechtenstein	93.8	(0.6)	6.2	(0.6)	0.0	c	93.8	(0.6)	6.2	(0.6)	0.0	c	12.1	(1.1)	87.9	(1.1)	0.0	c	74.3	(0.9)	25.7	(0.9)	0.0	c
	Lithuania	55.0	(3.5)	41.4	(3.3)	3.6	(1.3)	52.5	(3.4)	40.9	(3.4)	6.7	(2.0)	12.2	(2.0)	70.9	(3.3)	16.9	(2.8)	36.9	(3.2)	57.0	(3.5)	6.1	(1.7)
	Macao-China	38.4	(0.0)	60.5	(0.0)	1.1	(0.0)	31.0	(0.0)	68.8	(0.0)	0.2	(0.0)	20.1	(0.1)	78.8	(0.1)	1.1	(0.0)	11.3	(0.0)	79.8	(0.0)	8.9	(0.0)
	Malaysia	25.1	(3.8)	52.5	(4.1)	22.4	(3.7)	14.9	(3.0)	63.3	(3.8)	21.8	(3.5)	6.5	(2.0)	67.5	(3.9)	26.0	(3.7)	7.1	(2.1)	64.5	(4.1)	28.5	(3.9)
	Montenegro	82.3	(0.1)	15.8	(0.1)	1.9	(0.0)	77.8	(0.1)	16.7	(0.1)	5.5	(0.1)	15.3	(0.1)	65.1	(0.1)	19.6	(0.1)	30.2	(0.1)	59.2	(0.1)	10.7	(0.1)
	Peru	51.4	(3.3)	44.0	(3.6)	4.6	(1.7)	58.8	(3.6)	39.2	(3.6)	2.1	(1.2)	26.5	(3.0)	67.2	(3.2)	6.3	(1.8)	30.7	(3.2)	61.8	(3.5)	7.5	(2.1)
	Qatar	45.9	(0.1)	48.4	(0.1)	5.8	(0.1)	33.7	(0.1)	56.2	(0.1)	10.1	(0.1)	4.6	(0.0)	51.5	(0.1)	43.9	(0.1)	10.7	(0.1)	68.1	(0.1)	21.2	(0.1)
	Romania	70.2	(3.1)	29.2	(3.2)	0.6	(0.6)	66.9	(3.6)	32.4	(3.6)	0.6	(0.6)	34.0	(3.4)	57.0	(3.9)	9.0	(2.3)	28.4	(3.4)	67.5	(3.5)	4.1	(1.6)
	Russian Federation	5.7	(1.7)	79.4	(3.0)	14.9	(2.7)	9.8	(1.8)	70.6	(2.6)	19.6	(2.3)	8.0	(2.2)	67.3	(3.7)	24.7	(3.1)	7.5	(1.6)	77.0	(2.8)	15.5	(2.6)
	Serbia	87.3	(3.0)	11.7	(2.9)	0.9	(0.8)	76.1	(4.0)	23.1	(4.0)	0.8	(0.7)	34.7	(4.2)	61.3	(4.2)	4.0	(1.8)	54.6	(4.5)	42.6	(4.4)	2.8	(1.6)
	Shanghai-China	58.9	(4.3)	35.4	(4.1)	5.6	(1.6)	7.7	(2.0)	85.2	(2.6)	7.1	(1.6)	6.4	(2.0)	72.5	(3.8)	21.1	(3.4)	3.0	(1.4)	78.9	(3.3)	18.1	(3.0)
	Singapore	39.2	(0.5)	56.4	(0.5)	4.4	(0.1)	6.3	(0.8)	65.2	(0.5)	28.5	(0.3)	6.7	(0.6)	77.9	(0.6)	15.4	(0.2)	3.7	(0.6)	79.1	(0.6)	17.1	(0.2)
	Chinese Taipei	72.5	(3.4)	19.4	(3.2)	8.1	(2.5)	60.9	(3.8)	32.3	(3.7)	6.8	(2.3)	16.9	(3.1)	71.8	(3.8)	11.3	(2.6)	48.3	(3.7)	43.5	(3.7)	8.2	(2.3)
	Thailand	11.9	(2.2)	77.2	(3.0)	11.0	(2.4)	26.2	(3.0)	65.8	(3.2)	8.0	(2.2)	14.3	(3.0)	71.0	(3.4)	14.6	(2.4)	14.0	(2.9)	74.8	(3.1)	11.3	(2.3)
	Tunisia	28.4	(3.9)	54.0	(4.8)	17.6	(3.3)	33.8	(4.2)	49.5	(4.7)	16.7	(3.4)	9.7	(2.7)	72.6	(4.1)	17.7	(3.2)	12.9	(2.9)	62.4	(3.9)	24.7	(3.4)
	United Arab Emirates	41.6	(2.1)	43.0	(2.0)	15.4	(1.9)	50.4	(2.5)	38.3	(2.4)	11.3	(1.7)	7.2	(1.9)	61.0	(2.1)	31.8	(2.1)	11.3	(2.1)	67.3	(2.3)	21.4	(2.1)
	Uruguay	72.5	(3.7)	24.7	(3.4)	2.8	(1.5)	75.5	(3.1)	20.1	(2.9)	4.4	(1.8)	32.4	(3.6)	58.1	(3.7)	9.5	(2.0)	44.2	(3.6)	50.0	(3.8)	5.9	(1.9)
	Viet Nam	28.1	(3.5)	64.6	(3.8)	7.3	(1.9)	8.3	(2.0)	80.8	(2.9)	10.9	(2.3)	1.8	(1.1)	87.2	(2.6)	11.0	(2.4)	4.8	(1.3)	87.5	(2.2)	7.7	(2.0)

* See notes at the beginning of this Annex.
StatLink http://dx.doi.org/10.1787/888932957498

[Part 2/2]
Consequences of teacher appraisals
Table IV.4.35 *Results based on school principals' reports*

Percentage of students in schools whose principal reported that appraisals of and/or feedback to teachers lead directly to the following:

| | Public recognition from the principal | | | | | | Changes in work responsibilities that make the job more attractive | | | | | | A role in school-development initiatives (e.g. curriculum-development group, development of school objectives) | | | | | |
| | No change | | A small or moderate change | | A large change | | No change | | A small or moderate change | | A large change | | No change | | A small or moderate change | | A large change | |
	%	S.E.	%	S.E.	%	S.E.	%	S.E.	%	S.E.	%	S.E.	%	S.E.	%	S.E.	%	S.E.
Australia	16.9	(1.5)	76.4	(1.6)	6.6	(1.1)	36.7	(1.9)	62.6	(1.9)	0.7	(0.3)	12.9	(1.2)	81.4	(1.4)	5.8	(0.9)
Austria	25.3	(3.3)	64.8	(3.9)	9.8	(2.4)	55.9	(4.2)	41.5	(3.9)	2.6	(1.4)	27.5	(3.3)	61.8	(3.8)	10.8	(2.7)
Belgium	34.0	(3.0)	59.8	(3.2)	6.2	(1.5)	49.0	(2.9)	49.0	(2.8)	2.0	(0.9)	36.3	(3.0)	57.9	(3.3)	5.8	(1.7)
Canada	27.4	(2.2)	65.9	(2.4)	6.8	(1.3)	55.8	(2.2)	42.6	(2.3)	1.6	(0.7)	16.1	(1.8)	75.0	(2.1)	8.9	(1.7)
Chile	13.0	(2.5)	60.3	(4.0)	26.7	(3.7)	17.1	(2.8)	66.7	(3.6)	16.2	(3.0)	18.7	(2.8)	68.5	(3.6)	12.9	(2.8)
Czech Republic	7.1	(2.2)	82.0	(3.4)	10.9	(2.7)	38.1	(3.5)	61.9	(3.5)	0.0	c	14.0	(2.6)	80.2	(3.1)	5.8	(2.2)
Denmark	22.0	(2.8)	69.2	(3.3)	8.8	(2.0)	44.5	(4.0)	51.6	(3.9)	3.9	(1.5)	38.2	(3.5)	56.7	(3.4)	5.0	(1.4)
Estonia	7.4	(1.6)	76.3	(2.7)	16.4	(2.3)	29.9	(2.6)	61.9	(3.0)	8.2	(1.8)	10.5	(1.6)	78.4	(2.1)	11.1	(1.8)
Finland	24.0	(2.7)	73.9	(2.6)	2.1	(0.8)	32.0	(3.1)	65.9	(3.0)	2.1	(1.0)	19.5	(2.5)	77.0	(2.5)	3.5	(0.8)
France	21.3	(2.9)	60.4	(3.8)	18.4	(3.0)	41.1	(3.3)	54.6	(3.5)	4.3	(1.4)	26.8	(2.8)	63.9	(3.4)	9.3	(2.2)
Germany	46.7	(3.8)	52.8	(3.8)	0.5	(0.5)	51.2	(3.8)	47.7	(3.7)	1.1	(0.8)	32.1	(3.6)	64.6	(3.7)	3.3	(1.4)
Greece	27.0	(3.2)	52.0	(3.9)	21.0	(3.3)	46.6	(4.3)	36.8	(4.0)	16.6	(2.9)	39.8	(3.6)	46.5	(3.9)	13.8	(2.9)
Hungary	2.2	(1.2)	30.0	(3.5)	67.9	(3.8)	13.8	(2.8)	72.1	(3.7)	14.1	(2.9)	6.6	(1.9)	62.5	(3.7)	31.0	(3.5)
Iceland	23.9	(0.2)	64.5	(0.2)	11.6	(0.2)	18.2	(0.2)	74.5	(0.2)	7.4	(0.2)	31.0	(0.2)	61.7	(0.3)	7.3	(0.2)
Ireland	29.1	(3.8)	61.0	(3.8)	9.9	(2.2)	59.3	(3.9)	38.9	(3.8)	1.8	(1.1)	21.5	(3.7)	71.9	(3.9)	6.6	(2.0)
Israel	4.9	(1.6)	56.6	(3.6)	38.5	(3.7)	9.6	(1.9)	67.3	(3.0)	23.1	(3.4)	16.4	(3.1)	68.5	(3.3)	15.1	(3.0)
Italy	37.2	(2.1)	56.9	(2.3)	5.9	(1.1)	19.2	(1.9)	71.1	(2.2)	9.7	(1.1)	16.5	(1.7)	75.8	(2.0)	7.7	(0.9)
Japan	35.1	(3.6)	61.8	(3.7)	3.1	(1.3)	12.9	(2.3)	80.5	(2.8)	6.6	(1.9)	7.6	(1.7)	74.8	(3.1)	17.6	(2.8)
Korea	4.8	(1.8)	85.5	(2.9)	9.8	(2.3)	22.1	(3.7)	68.2	(4.0)	9.7	(2.5)	17.5	(3.1)	69.2	(3.9)	13.4	(2.8)
Luxembourg	19.8	(0.1)	71.0	(0.1)	9.1	(0.1)	40.4	(0.1)	57.1	(0.1)	2.5	(0.0)	17.9	(0.1)	75.1	(0.1)	7.0	(0.0)
Mexico	13.7	(1.3)	63.6	(1.8)	22.8	(1.3)	19.7	(1.2)	68.3	(1.6)	12.0	(1.2)	22.0	(1.3)	67.9	(1.6)	10.2	(1.1)
Netherlands	8.3	(2.4)	74.2	(4.1)	17.4	(3.4)	26.1	(3.6)	64.0	(3.8)	9.9	(2.7)	14.1	(3.0)	73.9	(3.8)	12.0	(2.6)
New Zealand	17.8	(2.8)	76.5	(3.3)	5.7	(1.9)	20.7	(3.4)	77.9	(3.4)	1.4	(0.8)	10.7	(2.6)	85.5	(2.9)	3.9	(1.4)
Norway	21.4	(3.1)	73.5	(3.6)	5.1	(1.9)	22.5	(3.0)	71.5	(3.4)	6.0	(1.7)	14.9	(2.6)	74.7	(3.4)	10.4	(2.6)
Poland	7.5	(2.2)	70.5	(3.8)	22.0	(3.4)	39.5	(4.0)	56.8	(4.0)	3.7	(1.5)	12.8	(2.3)	73.9	(3.2)	13.3	(2.7)
Portugal	42.0	(4.3)	51.5	(4.3)	6.5	(1.9)	36.8	(4.4)	55.1	(4.0)	8.1	(2.5)	27.4	(4.2)	67.1	(4.2)	5.5	(2.3)
Slovak Republic	5.5	(2.1)	70.5	(3.3)	24.0	(3.1)	19.4	(3.2)	72.2	(3.0)	8.4	(2.1)	5.9	(2.2)	72.1	(3.7)	22.0	(3.0)
Slovenia	4.2	(0.2)	77.8	(0.7)	18.0	(0.7)	8.9	(0.4)	80.4	(0.5)	10.7	(0.3)	6.2	(0.4)	74.3	(0.5)	19.5	(0.4)
Spain	32.6	(2.5)	59.9	(2.5)	7.5	(1.5)	45.4	(2.9)	50.7	(3.1)	3.9	(1.1)	36.5	(2.1)	59.1	(2.3)	4.3	(1.2)
Sweden	10.8	(2.4)	68.5	(3.8)	20.6	(3.0)	17.7	(2.8)	67.8	(3.0)	14.6	(2.6)	5.6	(1.8)	67.6	(3.5)	26.7	(3.3)
Switzerland	56.8	(3.7)	40.4	(3.6)	2.8	(1.1)	61.4	(3.6)	36.9	(3.5)	1.7	(1.0)	41.5	(3.4)	57.1	(3.4)	1.4	(0.6)
Turkey	15.6	(3.0)	63.3	(3.7)	21.0	(2.8)	10.3	(2.3)	63.9	(3.7)	25.9	(3.4)	7.7	(2.3)	77.9	(3.8)	14.4	(3.1)
United Kingdom	12.4	(2.1)	71.6	(3.0)	16.1	(2.5)	18.5	(2.5)	77.3	(2.6)	4.2	(1.3)	3.1	(1.0)	85.7	(1.9)	11.1	(2.1)
United States	20.2	(3.7)	72.2	(4.2)	7.6	(2.3)	40.4	(4.7)	59.0	(4.7)	0.7	(0.6)	10.0	(2.1)	77.0	(3.7)	12.9	(3.2)
OECD average	20.5	(0.4)	65.2	(0.6)	14.3	(0.4)	31.8	(0.5)	61.0	(0.6)	7.2	(0.3)	19.0	(0.4)	70.1	(0.5)	10.9	(0.4)
Albania	27.7	(3.7)	65.2	(4.0)	7.1	(1.9)	19.3	(3.0)	69.9	(3.7)	10.8	(2.8)	10.9	(2.1)	74.9	(3.3)	14.1	(3.0)
Argentina	37.2	(3.9)	48.0	(3.8)	14.8	(2.5)	37.3	(4.1)	52.5	(4.2)	10.2	(2.3)	22.2	(3.5)	64.7	(4.1)	13.0	(2.7)
Brazil	20.7	(2.1)	61.9	(2.4)	17.4	(2.3)	17.1	(2.1)	71.3	(2.3)	11.6	(1.9)	23.0	(2.3)	67.8	(2.4)	9.2	(1.6)
Bulgaria	6.5	(1.9)	77.8	(2.9)	15.7	(2.4)	18.8	(2.9)	75.7	(3.1)	5.5	(1.7)	7.8	(2.1)	78.6	(3.3)	13.6	(2.7)
Colombia	20.0	(3.2)	59.7	(3.8)	20.3	(3.0)	26.4	(3.6)	63.2	(4.0)	10.4	(2.5)	18.2	(3.3)	61.7	(3.9)	20.1	(2.5)
Costa Rica	25.9	(3.1)	52.1	(3.9)	22.1	(3.3)	33.7	(3.6)	55.5	(3.8)	10.8	(2.1)	20.3	(3.1)	56.4	(4.0)	23.3	(3.3)
Croatia	2.2	(1.1)	64.0	(4.0)	33.7	(3.8)	19.2	(3.6)	70.5	(3.9)	10.4	(2.3)	9.1	(2.4)	73.0	(3.6)	17.9	(3.1)
Cyprus*	7.8	(0.1)	66.1	(0.1)	26.2	(0.1)	16.7	(0.1)	70.4	(0.1)	13.0	(0.1)	16.0	(0.1)	66.4	(0.1)	17.5	(0.1)
Hong Kong-China	7.5	(2.1)	87.6	(2.6)	4.9	(1.9)	6.2	(1.9)	91.0	(2.1)	2.8	(1.4)	1.2	(0.9)	93.4	(1.7)	5.4	(1.4)
Indonesia	8.0	(1.7)	76.2	(3.1)	15.8	(3.2)	2.7	(1.2)	80.4	(3.1)	16.9	(2.9)	1.3	(0.8)	81.1	(3.0)	17.5	(2.9)
Jordan	4.0	(1.0)	45.7	(4.3)	50.3	(4.2)	5.5	(1.6)	56.0	(4.0)	38.5	(3.7)	10.2	(2.3)	67.1	(3.1)	22.7	(3.1)
Kazakhstan	2.7	(1.0)	68.3	(3.7)	28.9	(3.4)	9.6	(2.0)	74.3	(3.4)	16.1	(2.8)	4.4	(1.2)	76.9	(3.6)	18.7	(3.2)
Latvia	6.5	(1.7)	87.6	(2.2)	5.9	(1.3)	21.2	(2.8)	71.8	(3.3)	7.0	(1.9)	8.8	(1.9)	81.2	(3.1)	10.0	(2.4)
Liechtenstein	72.7	(1.0)	27.3	(1.0)	0.0	c	40.3	(0.8)	54.6	(0.9)	5.1	(0.8)	5.4	(0.7)	83.2	(1.1)	11.5	(0.9)
Lithuania	4.3	(1.4)	69.7	(3.2)	26.0	(3.0)	36.4	(3.2)	58.1	(3.5)	5.5	(1.7)	5.8	(1.3)	76.8	(2.8)	17.4	(2.8)
Macao-China	9.3	(0.0)	71.4	(0.0)	19.4	(0.0)	7.7	(0.0)	89.6	(0.0)	2.7	(0.0)	4.7	(0.0)	76.8	(0.0)	18.5	(0.0)
Malaysia	4.6	(1.7)	58.6	(4.3)	36.8	(4.1)	4.7	(1.7)	65.3	(4.0)	30.0	(3.9)	3.6	(1.6)	66.5	(4.0)	30.0	(4.0)
Montenegro	5.7	(0.1)	72.4	(0.2)	21.9	(0.1)	15.3	(0.1)	78.3	(0.1)	6.4	(0.1)	8.8	(0.1)	74.6	(0.1)	16.6	(0.1)
Peru	11.6	(2.3)	72.5	(3.4)	15.9	(2.5)	9.0	(1.9)	80.3	(2.8)	10.7	(2.1)	11.8	(2.1)	79.1	(2.4)	9.1	(2.0)
Qatar	11.1	(0.1)	45.8	(0.1)	43.1	(0.1)	7.2	(0.0)	55.1	(0.1)	37.7	(0.1)	5.9	(0.0)	55.4	(0.1)	38.7	(0.1)
Romania	23.8	(2.7)	54.6	(3.5)	21.6	(3.1)	27.2	(3.4)	69.7	(3.4)	3.1	(1.3)	26.8	(3.2)	64.1	(3.7)	9.1	(2.2)
Russian Federation	4.3	(1.1)	55.6	(4.6)	40.0	(4.5)	16.6	(3.0)	72.3	(3.2)	11.1	(1.8)	5.0	(1.5)	72.1	(3.2)	23.0	(2.6)
Serbia	15.6	(3.1)	72.4	(4.2)	12.0	(3.1)	30.3	(3.9)	64.2	(4.0)	5.5	(2.1)	29.9	(4.0)	65.7	(3.9)	4.5	(1.8)
Shanghai-China	3.2	(1.4)	75.5	(3.8)	21.3	(3.5)	5.1	(1.8)	78.3	(3.4)	16.6	(3.0)	2.7	(1.3)	79.6	(3.5)	17.7	(3.2)
Singapore	9.7	(0.6)	76.9	(0.6)	13.5	(0.2)	6.2	(0.8)	81.5	(0.7)	12.3	(0.1)	4.0	(0.1)	80.3	(0.2)	15.6	(0.2)
Chinese Taipei	44.5	(3.4)	51.4	(3.1)	4.1	(1.7)	26.7	(3.3)	60.8	(3.9)	12.5	(2.6)	10.5	(2.6)	77.4	(3.5)	12.1	(2.7)
Thailand	5.3	(1.6)	72.0	(3.2)	22.6	(3.0)	6.6	(2.0)	76.0	(3.8)	17.4	(3.2)	5.4	(1.8)	76.0	(3.5)	18.6	(3.3)
Tunisia	9.5	(2.7)	63.0	(3.9)	27.5	(3.8)	12.2	(2.9)	65.4	(4.2)	22.4	(3.7)	26.4	(3.8)	51.2	(3.9)	22.4	(3.9)
United Arab Emirates	4.4	(1.1)	49.7	(2.3)	46.0	(2.5)	6.2	(1.2)	61.6	(2.4)	32.2	(2.3)	3.5	(1.1)	61.4	(2.5)	35.2	(2.3)
Uruguay	30.3	(3.3)	59.9	(3.5)	9.8	(2.1)	25.8	(3.5)	67.1	(3.8)	7.2	(2.0)	29.9	(3.5)	63.3	(3.6)	6.8	(1.8)
Viet Nam	0.7	(0.7)	76.1	(3.6)	23.2	(3.5)	0.7	(0.7)	84.1	(2.8)	15.2	(2.7)	7.8	(2.0)	87.0	(2.7)	5.2	(1.9)

* See notes at the beginning of this Annex.
StatLink ᴍˢ◖ http://dx.doi.org/10.1787/888932957498

[Part 1/3]
Change between 2003 and 2012 in assessment practices
Table IV.4.36   *Results based on school principals' reports*

		PISA 2003																
		Percentage of students in schools whose principal reported that assessments of students in national modal grade for 15-year-olds are used for the following purposes:																**Index of assessment practices (sum of "yes" for these eight practices)**
		To inform parents about their child's progress		To make decisions about students' retention or promotion		To group students for instructional purposes		To compare the school to district or national performance		To monitor the school's progress from year to year		To make judgements about teachers' effectiveness		To identify aspects of instruction or the curriculum that could be improved		To compare the school with other schools		
		%	S.E.	%	S.E.	%	S.E.	%	S.E.	%	S.E.	%	S.E.	%	S.E.	%	S.E.	Mean index	S.E.
OECD	Australia	100.0	c	61.5	(2.9)	77.8	(2.6)	54.9	(2.4)	76.5	(2.7)	34.0	(2.9)	81.5	(2.5)	38.7	(2.7)	5.2	(0.1)
	Austria	92.2	(2.2)	93.2	(2.3)	31.8	(2.3)	12.4	(2.8)	59.2	(3.9)	35.6	(3.5)	65.6	(3.7)	38.0	(3.9)	4.2	(0.1)
	Belgium	99.6	(0.4)	99.1	(0.6)	19.9	(2.4)	9.6	(2.2)	37.6	(2.8)	19.4	(2.4)	66.1	(3.0)	6.9	(1.7)	3.6	(0.1)
	Canada	99.4	(0.3)	95.5	(1.0)	72.0	(2.1)	70.1	(2.2)	79.5	(1.8)	31.4	(2.4)	84.1	(1.8)	53.0	(2.4)	5.8	(0.1)
	Czech Republic	98.3	(0.9)	91.8	(1.9)	35.2	(3.3)	50.0	(3.3)	85.6	(2.4)	61.7	(3.4)	88.7	(2.1)	55.3	(3.7)	5.6	(0.1)
	Denmark	67.6	(3.5)	3.8	(0.9)	14.1	(2.6)	5.9	(1.7)	8.4	(2.0)	3.7	(1.4)	46.7	(3.9)	2.9	(1.3)	1.5	(0.1)
	Finland	100.0	(0.0)	95.2	(0.9)	17.1	(3.0)	56.3	(4.0)	65.0	(4.1)	32.1	(3.5)	65.6	(3.6)	34.9	(3.5)	4.6	(0.1)
	France	w	w	w	w	w	w	w	w	w	w	w	w	w	w	w	w	w	w
	Germany	96.1	(1.4)	96.3	(1.2)	35.8	(3.0)	21.2	(3.2)	44.0	(3.2)	11.8	(2.3)	44.8	(3.9)	17.1	(2.7)	3.6	(0.1)
	Greece	96.6	(2.0)	99.4	(0.5)	11.1	(2.1)	12.2	(2.8)	35.6	(5.7)	15.2	(4.4)	40.5	(5.3)	15.8	(3.0)	3.2	(0.2)
	Hungary	99.1	(0.9)	94.7	(1.9)	34.8	(3.5)	86.4	(2.6)	95.8	(1.4)	77.0	(3.5)	93.7	(2.1)	77.5	(3.2)	6.6	(0.1)
	Iceland	99.7	(0.0)	14.8	(0.1)	56.1	(0.2)	84.1	(0.1)	88.1	(0.1)	30.9	(0.2)	96.6	(0.0)	65.6	(0.2)	5.3	(0.0)
	Ireland	99.3	(0.7)	43.7	(4.2)	78.1	(3.3)	17.2	(3.2)	49.5	(4.0)	16.9	(3.2)	42.2	(4.3)	8.8	(2.6)	3.5	(0.1)
	Italy	96.0	(1.3)	83.7	(2.8)	51.5	(3.9)	32.8	(3.4)	69.3	(3.0)	23.3	(3.2)	83.8	(2.9)	29.1	(3.2)	4.6	(0.1)
	Japan	98.3	(1.0)	89.5	(2.6)	44.7	(4.5)	17.8	(3.4)	47.7	(4.4)	81.5	(3.3)	78.9	(3.4)	11.8	(2.8)	4.7	(0.1)
	Korea	95.5	(1.8)	24.8	(3.8)	62.6	(4.0)	62.0	(3.7)	58.6	(4.0)	54.5	(4.3)	90.2	(2.7)	54.9	(3.9)	5.0	(0.2)
	Luxembourg	100.0	c	100.0	c	29.7	(0.1)	21.8	(0.0)	26.1	(0.1)	21.0	(0.0)	62.9	(0.1)	10.3	(0.0)	3.7	(0.0)
	Mexico	96.7	(0.9)	92.9	(1.8)	59.4	(3.2)	55.5	(3.1)	91.2	(1.6)	77.3	(3.1)	89.2	(2.2)	50.5	(3.5)	6.1	(0.1)
	Netherlands	99.5	(0.5)	96.8	(1.6)	88.7	(2.7)	63.5	(4.1)	63.3	(4.2)	42.2	(4.4)	71.8	(3.9)	47.0	(4.4)	5.7	(0.2)
	New Zealand	98.4	(1.0)	77.9	(2.8)	73.7	(3.0)	86.7	(2.3)	95.6	(1.6)	53.0	(3.4)	95.8	(1.2)	73.5	(3.2)	6.5	(0.1)
	Norway	100.0	c	0.0	c	37.8	(4.0)	63.8	(3.6)	67.7	(3.3)	19.5	(3.0)	70.1	(3.5)	47.1	(3.8)	4.1	(0.1)
	Poland	98.0	(1.1)	84.2	(2.8)	33.0	(4.1)	71.1	(3.7)	96.6	(1.5)	73.2	(3.2)	87.8	(2.8)	62.3	(3.6)	6.1	(0.1)
	Portugal	98.8	(0.7)	96.6	(1.6)	26.1	(3.8)	32.9	(4.2)	78.5	(3.1)	34.7	(4.4)	84.3	(3.2)	22.3	(3.4)	4.7	(0.1)
	Slovak Republic	98.7	(0.7)	96.7	(1.0)	54.9	(3.8)	45.9	(3.7)	95.0	(1.5)	75.0	(2.7)	89.0	(2.2)	47.7	(3.1)	6.0	(0.1)
	Spain	99.7	(0.3)	99.5	(0.3)	47.6	(3.5)	18.2	(2.1)	68.6	(3.2)	35.9	(3.5)	88.5	(2.3)	17.2	(2.1)	4.7	(0.1)
	Sweden	96.4	(1.5)	38.9	(4.1)	45.2	(4.0)	73.0	(3.1)	85.4	(2.7)	21.2	(3.1)	80.7	(3.0)	64.8	(3.5)	5.0	(0.1)
	Switzerland	94.1	(1.6)	95.2	(1.5)	28.1	(3.2)	18.5	(2.0)	24.9	(4.5)	36.8	(3.5)	51.9	(3.6)	15.9	(3.7)	3.6	(0.1)
	Turkey	84.8	(3.0)	71.1	(4.2)	50.8	(4.3)	58.7	(4.4)	76.3	(3.3)	33.8	(4.4)	34.0	(3.7)	58.9	(4.4)	4.6	(0.2)
	United States	98.4	(0.8)	76.3	(2.8)	65.9	(3.3)	90.7	(1.9)	93.5	(1.6)	54.7	(3.1)	92.0	(1.9)	80.3	(2.8)	6.5	(0.1)
	OECD average 2003	96.5	(0.3)	75.5	(0.5)	45.8	(0.6)	46.2	(0.6)	66.5	(0.6)	39.5	(0.6)	73.8	(0.6)	39.6	(0.6)	4.8	(0.0)
Partners	Brazil	87.9	(2.6)	83.4	(2.5)	44.7	(4.1)	37.5	(3.5)	75.7	(3.5)	55.5	(3.5)	92.1	(2.1)	23.3	(2.9)	5.0	(0.1)
	Hong Kong-China	98.7	(0.9)	96.3	(1.5)	63.3	(4.2)	22.7	(4.0)	90.5	(2.5)	63.9	(4.0)	96.9	(1.2)	18.9	(3.1)	5.5	(0.1)
	Indonesia	89.2	(2.4)	84.3	(2.6)	46.4	(3.8)	50.6	(3.8)	86.0	(2.7)	87.3	(2.5)	78.8	(3.2)	77.2	(2.9)	6.0	(0.2)
	Latvia	100.0	c	94.1	(2.7)	40.1	(4.3)	79.7	(4.1)	99.2	(0.6)	86.5	(2.8)	96.7	(1.4)	65.1	(4.2)	6.6	(0.1)
	Liechtenstein	100.0	c	96.7	(0.0)	57.7	(0.4)	28.7	(0.3)	17.5	(0.3)	39.1	(0.5)	21.3	(0.5)	39.3	(0.4)	4.0	(0.0)
	Macao-China	96.5	(0.1)	96.5	(0.1)	43.4	(0.2)	3.1	(0.1)	81.4	(0.2)	81.5	(0.3)	97.5	(0.1)	14.5	(0.1)	5.0	(0.0)
	Russian Federation	100.0	c	96.7	(1.3)	55.7	(4.0)	69.9	(4.1)	96.9	(1.3)	98.7	(0.8)	98.8	(0.7)	81.3	(3.2)	7.0	(0.1)
	Thailand	89.6	(2.6)	71.9	(4.0)	77.2	(3.5)	59.3	(3.6)	88.0	(3.0)	70.6	(3.6)	76.9	(3.8)	56.8	(4.0)	5.9	(0.2)
	Tunisia	74.8	(3.4)	84.3	(2.9)	43.6	(4.3)	73.1	(3.6)	81.8	(3.4)	62.7	(3.7)	71.9	(3.2)	71.7	(3.4)	5.6	(0.2)
	Uruguay	94.2	(1.7)	90.6	(2.4)	29.0	(3.1)	18.1	(3.2)	76.5	(4.0)	40.7	(4.5)	68.8	(3.7)	10.5	(2.4)	4.3	(0.1)

Notes: Values that are statistically significant are indicated in bold (see Annex A3).
Only countries and economies with comparable data from PISA 2003 and PISA 2012 are shown.
StatLink [logo] http://dx.doi.org/10.1787/888932957498

[Part 2/3]
Change between 2003 and 2012 in assessment practices

Table IV.4.36 · *Results based on school principals' reports*

	PISA 2012																
	Percentage of students in schools whose principal reported that assessments of students in national modal grade for 15-year-olds are used for the following purposes:																Index of assessment practices (sum of "yes" for these eight practices)
	To inform parents about their child's progress		To make decisions about students' retention or promotion		To group students for instructional purposes		To compare the school to district or national performance		To monitor the school's progress from year to year		To make judgements about teachers' effectiveness		To identify aspects of instruction or the curriculum that could be improved		To compare the school with other schools		
	%	S.E.	%	S.E.	%	S.E.	%	S.E.	%	S.E.	%	S.E.	%	S.E.	%	S.E.	Mean index	S.E.
OECD																		
Australia	100.0	(0.0)	62.8	(1.8)	83.5	(1.3)	56.4	(1.9)	87.6	(1.3)	49.8	(1.8)	90.9	(1.1)	44.3	(2.0)	4.7	(0.1)
Austria	95.5	(1.7)	94.2	(1.7)	30.5	(2.4)	28.5	(4.0)	62.6	(4.2)	39.1	(4.1)	69.6	(3.6)	30.0	(4.1)	4.0	(0.1)
Belgium	96.6	(1.3)	96.2	(1.3)	17.2	(2.3)	23.3	(2.6)	59.8	(3.2)	35.2	(3.0)	73.1	(3.0)	18.3	(2.3)	3.8	(0.1)
Canada	99.7	(0.2)	95.0	(1.2)	74.1	(2.1)	82.3	(1.5)	92.3	(1.0)	30.2	(1.9)	86.6	(1.5)	62.0	(2.3)	5.1	(0.1)
Czech Republic	93.1	(1.7)	79.4	(2.9)	32.8	(3.3)	58.2	(3.2)	86.2	(2.7)	62.8	(3.4)	86.3	(2.7)	63.1	(3.2)	4.5	(0.2)
Denmark	99.2	(0.4)	10.3	(1.9)	52.3	(3.4)	54.9	(3.5)	56.8	(3.3)	27.1	(3.1)	84.7	(2.4)	55.9	(3.5)	3.9	(0.1)
Finland	98.7	(0.3)	93.3	(1.6)	17.0	(2.5)	45.8	(3.4)	59.5	(3.5)	15.5	(2.2)	60.5	(3.6)	21.1	(2.7)	3.9	(0.1)
France	97.2	(1.1)	96.4	(1.3)	42.7	(3.4)	62.2	(2.9)	73.2	(3.1)	22.6	(3.0)	50.4	(3.5)	40.6	(3.4)	4.2	(0.1)
Germany	95.9	(1.5)	95.8	(1.5)	39.5	(3.2)	43.4	(3.3)	57.2	(3.7)	24.2	(3.2)	60.8	(3.6)	27.7	(3.1)	4.0	(0.1)
Greece	100.0	c	98.2	(1.0)	8.1	(2.4)	17.0	(2.4)	55.9	(3.6)	14.0	(2.4)	49.4	(3.6)	21.9	(2.8)	3.4	(0.1)
Hungary	93.9	(1.8)	69.2	(3.7)	47.1	(3.6)	78.5	(3.3)	92.6	(2.0)	57.8	(3.9)	77.4	(3.0)	71.3	(3.9)	4.9	(0.1)
Iceland	100.0	c	15.0	(0.2)	42.4	(0.3)	77.1	(0.2)	89.2	(0.1)	39.1	(0.2)	92.8	(0.1)	73.2	(0.2)	4.8	(0.0)
Ireland	100.0	c	62.0	(4.0)	81.4	(2.9)	77.3	(3.3)	86.4	(2.7)	46.5	(4.1)	68.4	(3.9)	35.2	(4.0)	4.9	(0.1)
Italy	99.3	(0.4)	86.6	(1.8)	53.4	(2.0)	65.1	(2.2)	82.0	(1.6)	29.6	(1.9)	91.7	(1.2)	36.6	(2.1)	4.8	(0.1)
Japan	99.2	(0.6)	90.4	(2.1)	45.3	(3.5)	17.3	(2.5)	51.6	(3.5)	75.7	(3.0)	79.2	(2.9)	14.9	(2.6)	4.3	(0.1)
Korea	94.7	(1.9)	56.3	(4.2)	85.6	(2.8)	70.2	(3.6)	89.9	(2.6)	85.3	(3.0)	96.3	(1.6)	66.8	(3.8)	4.8	(0.2)
Luxembourg	95.4	(0.0)	94.2	(0.1)	41.2	(0.1)	74.2	(0.1)	72.3	(0.1)	22.3	(0.2)	73.8	(0.1)	39.8	(0.2)	4.4	(0.0)
Mexico	99.0	(0.3)	91.5	(0.2)	72.8	(1.7)	77.1	(1.5)	92.3	(1.0)	76.7	(1.3)	88.4	(1.2)	70.6	(1.6)	5.0	(0.1)
Netherlands	99.3	(0.9)	97.7	(1.1)	61.0	(3.7)	69.7	(4.1)	88.8	(2.7)	68.4	(3.9)	78.1	(3.5)	64.1	(4.2)	4.7	(0.2)
New Zealand	100.0	c	76.7	(3.3)	93.6	(2.1)	92.8	(2.7)	100.0	c	67.7	(3.8)	99.4	(0.5)	87.5	(3.4)	5.5	(0.2)
Norway	98.3	(1.0)	1.5	(0.9)	47.9	(3.3)	68.2	(3.0)	83.8	(2.7)	30.2	(3.3)	73.8	(3.2)	51.9	(3.3)	4.2	(0.1)
Poland	99.2	(0.7)	97.7	(1.2)	55.0	(3.8)	58.2	(3.6)	96.3	(1.5)	78.9	(3.0)	95.4	(1.7)	59.4	(3.9)	5.0	(0.1)
Portugal	100.0	c	98.2	(1.1)	40.3	(4.6)	85.0	(3.5)	95.9	(1.6)	50.5	(3.6)	93.5	(2.1)	63.2	(4.2)	5.2	(0.1)
Slovak Republic	100.0	c	93.4	(1.4)	38.2	(3.4)	64.2	(3.5)	70.7	(3.9)	69.0	(3.3)	83.0	(2.6)	69.3	(3.3)	4.6	(0.1)
Spain	99.5	(0.4)	94.6	(0.9)	47.2	(3.3)	44.0	(2.5)	88.5	(1.8)	50.1	(2.8)	93.7	(1.2)	36.9	(2.4)	4.8	(0.1)
Sweden	93.9	(1.8)	43.0	(4.0)	25.2	(3.3)	89.8	(2.3)	96.2	(1.4)	43.6	(3.6)	83.9	(2.6)	84.9	(2.8)	5.0	(0.1)
Switzerland	93.7	(1.8)	85.7	(2.4)	40.1	(3.1)	41.1	(3.2)	48.0	(3.4)	36.4	(3.8)	50.7	(3.7)	27.5	(3.6)	3.7	(0.1)
Turkey	97.1	(1.5)	55.3	(4.1)	44.1	(4.0)	74.9	(3.7)	92.6	(1.9)	70.8	(3.7)	68.5	(3.6)	84.9	(2.9)	4.9	(0.1)
United States	98.7	(1.0)	56.8	(4.2)	74.3	(3.7)	93.6	(2.6)	95.2	(2.0)	59.9	(4.2)	94.1	(1.6)	86.3	(2.9)	5.1	(0.2)
OECD average 2003	97.9	(0.2)	74.7	(0.4)	49.7	(0.6)	61.7	(0.6)	79.6	(0.5)	48.4	(0.6)	80.1	(0.5)	52.5	(0.6)	4.6	(0.0)
Partners																		
Brazil	97.0	(0.9)	91.2	(1.6)	47.0	(2.4)	83.2	(1.9)	97.0	(0.8)	79.9	(2.0)	88.7	(1.5)	56.4	(2.5)	5.0	(0.1)
Hong Kong-China	98.1	(1.1)	98.1	(1.1)	86.4	(2.9)	44.1	(4.7)	96.1	(1.7)	80.0	(3.5)	99.4	(0.6)	30.5	(3.7)	5.4	(0.1)
Indonesia	97.1	(1.7)	92.8	(2.1)	79.6	(3.2)	69.0	(4.3)	98.1	(1.3)	95.8	(2.1)	97.1	(1.6)	86.9	(2.9)	5.4	(0.2)
Latvia	100.0	c	96.9	(1.2)	38.1	(3.5)	92.5	(1.6)	99.8	(0.2)	92.5	(1.8)	99.6	(0.5)	85.5	(2.3)	5.5	(0.1)
Liechtenstein	100.0	c	71.8	(1.4)	49.1	(1.2)	68.1	(1.4)	66.8	(1.0)	20.2	(1.2)	69.5	(1.5)	59.4	(0.8)	5.0	(0.0)
Macao-China	99.4	(0.0)	94.9	(0.0)	65.2	(0.1)	31.9	(0.0)	86.7	(0.1)	75.3	(0.1)	96.5	(0.0)	21.4	(0.0)	5.1	(0.0)
Russian Federation	99.4	(0.6)	94.4	(1.9)	56.7	(4.4)	93.2	(1.5)	99.7	(0.3)	99.2	(0.7)	99.2	(0.8)	97.8	(1.0)	5.8	(0.1)
Thailand	99.5	(0.5)	86.1	(2.8)	79.4	(2.9)	85.2	(2.1)	97.3	(1.2)	91.0	(2.1)	95.8	(1.5)	75.6	(3.3)	5.3	(0.2)
Tunisia	80.0	(3.4)	95.4	(1.9)	51.6	(4.4)	70.7	(4.0)	89.1	(2.6)	67.1	(4.1)	55.9	(4.3)	69.1	(4.4)	4.8	(0.1)
Uruguay	95.0	(1.6)	92.1	(1.7)	25.2	(3.3)	16.5	(2.8)	87.5	(2.3)	31.2	(3.6)	86.3	(2.5)	12.2	(2.3)	4.2	(0.1)

Notes: Values that are statistically significant are indicated in bold (see Annex A3).
Only countries and economies with comparable data from PISA 2003 and PISA 2012 are shown.
StatLink ᴍsᴘ http://dx.doi.org/10.1787/888932957498

[Part 3/3]
Change between 2003 and 2012 in assessment practices
Table IV.4.36 — *Results based on school principals' reports*

	Change between 2003 and 2012 (PISA 2012 - PISA 2003)																
	Percentage of students in schools whose principal reported that assessments of students in national modal grade for 15-year-olds are used for the following purposes:																Index of assessment practices (sum of "yes" for these eight practices)
	To inform parents about their child's progress		To make decisions about students' retention or promotion		To group students for instructional purposes		To compare the school to district or national performance		To monitor the school's progress from year to year		To make judgements about teachers' effectiveness		To identify aspects of instruction or the curriculum that could be improved		To compare the school with other schools		
	% dif.	S.E.	% dif.	S.E.	% dif.	S.E.	% dif.	S.E.	% dif.	S.E.	% dif.	S.E.	% dif.	S.E.	% dif.	S.E.	Dif.	S.E.
OECD																		
Australia	0.0	c	1.3	(3.4)	5.7	(2.9)	1.4	(3.0)	**11.1**	(3.0)	**15.8**	(3.4)	**9.3**	(2.7)	5.5	(3.3)	**-0.5**	(0.1)
Austria	3.4	(2.8)	1.0	(2.9)	-1.3	(3.4)	**16.1**	(4.9)	3.4	(5.8)	3.5	(5.3)	4.0	(5.2)	-8.0	(5.7)	-0.3	(0.2)
Belgium	**-3.0**	(1.4)	**-2.9**	(1.4)	-2.7	(3.3)	**13.7**	(3.4)	**22.2**	(4.2)	**15.8**	(3.8)	7.0	(4.3)	**11.4**	(2.8)	**0.3**	(0.1)
Canada	0.3	(0.4)	-0.5	(1.5)	2.1	(3.0)	**12.2**	(2.7)	**12.8**	(2.0)	-1.2	(3.0)	2.5	(2.4)	**9.0**	(3.3)	**-0.6**	(0.1)
Czech Republic	**-5.2**	(1.9)	**-12.4**	(3.5)	-2.4	(4.7)	8.2	(4.6)	0.6	(3.6)	1.2	(4.8)	-2.4	(3.4)	7.9	(4.9)	**-1.1**	(0.2)
Denmark	**31.5**	(3.5)	**6.5**	(2.1)	**38.2**	(4.3)	**48.9**	(3.8)	**48.3**	(3.9)	**23.4**	(3.4)	**38.0**	(4.5)	**53.0**	(3.7)	**2.4**	(0.1)
Finland	-1.3	(0.3)	-2.0	(1.8)	-0.2	(3.9)	**-10.5**	(5.3)	-5.5	(5.4)	**-16.6**	(4.1)	-5.1	(5.1)	**-13.8**	(4.4)	**-0.8**	(0.2)
France	m	m	m	m	m	m	m	m	m	m	m	m	m	m	m	m	m	m
Germany	-0.1	(2.0)	-0.5	(1.9)	3.7	(4.4)	**22.2**	(4.6)	**13.1**	(4.9)	**12.4**	(4.0)	**16.0**	(5.3)	**10.7**	(4.1)	**0.4**	(0.2)
Greece	3.4	c	-1.2	(1.2)	-3.0	(3.2)	4.8	(3.7)	**20.4**	(6.8)	-1.1	(5.0)	8.9	(6.4)	6.0	(4.1)	0.1	(0.2)
Hungary	**-5.2**	(2.0)	**-25.6**	(4.2)	**12.2**	(5.1)	-7.9	(4.2)	-3.2	(2.5)	**-19.2**	(5.2)	**-16.3**	(3.7)	-6.2	(5.1)	**-1.7**	(0.1)
Iceland	0.3	c	0.2	(0.3)	**-13.7**	(0.3)	**-7.0**	(0.2)	**1.2**	(0.2)	**8.2**	(0.3)	**-3.8**	(0.1)	**7.6**	(0.3)	**-0.6**	(0.0)
Ireland	0.7	c	**18.3**	(5.8)	3.3	(4.4)	**60.1**	(4.6)	**36.9**	(4.8)	**29.6**	(5.2)	**26.2**	(5.8)	**26.4**	(4.7)	**1.3**	(0.2)
Italy	**3.3**	(1.4)	3.0	(3.3)	1.9	(4.4)	**32.3**	(4.1)	**12.7**	(3.4)	6.2	(3.7)	7.9	(3.2)	7.5	(3.8)	0.1	(0.1)
Japan	0.9	(1.2)	0.8	(3.3)	0.6	(5.7)	-0.5	(4.3)	3.9	(5.7)	-5.8	(4.4)	0.3	(4.5)	3.1	(3.9)	-0.4	(0.2)
Korea	-0.8	(2.6)	**31.5**	(5.6)	**22.9**	(4.9)	8.2	(5.2)	**31.3**	(4.7)	**30.8**	(5.2)	6.2	(3.2)	**11.9**	(5.4)	-0.2	(0.2)
Luxembourg	**-4.6**	c	**-5.8**	c	**11.5**	(0.1)	**52.4**	(0.1)	**46.2**	(0.1)	**1.3**	(0.1)	**10.9**	(0.1)	**29.5**	(0.1)	**0.7**	(0.0)
Mexico	**2.3**	(0.9)	-1.5	(2.1)	**13.4**	(3.6)	**21.6**	(3.5)	1.2	(1.9)	-0.6	(3.4)	-0.8	(2.5)	**20.1**	(3.9)	**-1.0**	(0.1)
Netherlands	-0.2	(1.1)	0.9	(2.0)	**-27.7**	(4.6)	6.2	(5.8)	**25.5**	(5.0)	**26.2**	(5.9)	6.4	(5.3)	**17.1**	(6.1)	**-1.0**	(0.2)
New Zealand	1.6	c	-1.2	(4.3)	19.9	(3.7)	6.1	(3.6)	4.4	c	**14.8**	(5.1)	**3.6**	(1.3)	**13.9**	(4.7)	**-1.0**	(0.2)
Norway	-1.7	c	1.5	c	10.1	(5.2)	4.4	(4.7)	**16.1**	(4.3)	**10.7**	(4.5)	3.7	(4.7)	4.7	(5.1)	0.2	(0.2)
Poland	1.2	(1.4)	**13.5**	(3.1)	**22.0**	(5.6)	**-12.9**	(5.2)	-0.3	(2.1)	5.6	(4.4)	7.7	(3.3)	-2.9	(5.3)	**-1.0**	(0.1)
Portugal	1.2	c	1.6	(1.9)	**14.2**	(5.9)	**52.1**	(5.5)	**17.4**	(3.5)	**15.8**	(5.7)	9.2	(3.8)	**40.9**	(5.4)	**0.5**	(0.2)
Slovak Republic	1.3	c	-3.2	(1.8)	**-16.8**	(5.2)	**18.3**	(5.1)	**-24.3**	(4.2)	-6.0	(4.2)	-6.0	(3.4)	**21.7**	(4.5)	**-1.4**	(0.2)
Spain	-0.2	(0.5)	**-4.9**	(1.0)	-0.4	(4.8)	**25.8**	(3.3)	**19.9**	(3.7)	**14.2**	(4.5)	**5.2**	(2.6)	**19.7**	(3.3)	0.0	(0.1)
Sweden	-2.5	(2.3)	4.1	(5.7)	**-20.1**	(5.1)	**16.8**	(3.9)	**10.8**	(3.1)	**22.4**	(4.8)	3.2	(3.9)	**20.2**	(4.5)	0.0	(0.2)
Switzerland	-0.4	(2.3)	**-9.5**	(2.8)	**12.0**	(4.5)	**22.5**	(3.4)	**23.0**	(5.7)	-0.3	(5.1)	-1.2	(5.2)	**11.5**	(5.1)	0.1	(0.2)
Turkey	**12.4**	(3.3)	**-15.7**	(5.8)	-6.7	(5.9)	**16.2**	(5.7)	**16.3**	(3.8)	**36.9**	(5.7)	**34.5**	(5.2)	**26.0**	(5.3)	0.2	(0.2)
United States	0.3	(1.3)	**-19.6**	(5.0)	8.4	(4.9)	2.9	(3.2)	1.7	(2.6)	5.2	(5.2)	2.1	(2.5)	6.0	(4.1)	**-1.4**	(0.2)
OECD average 2003	**1.4**	(0.4)	-0.8	(0.7)	**3.8**	(0.8)	**15.5**	(0.8)	**13.1**	(0.6)	**8.9**	(0.8)	**6.3**	(0.8)	**12.9**	(0.8)	**-0.2**	(0.0)
Partners																		
Brazil	**9.2**	(2.8)	**7.8**	(3.0)	2.3	(4.7)	**45.6**	(4.0)	**21.3**	(3.6)	**24.3**	(4.0)	-3.4	(2.5)	**33.2**	(3.8)	0.0	(0.2)
Hong Kong-China	-0.6	(1.4)	1.9	(1.9)	**23.1**	(5.0)	**21.3**	(6.1)	5.5	(3.0)	**16.1**	(5.3)	2.5	(1.3)	**11.5**	(4.9)	-0.1	(0.2)
Indonesia	**7.9**	(3.0)	**8.5**	(3.3)	**33.2**	(5.0)	**18.4**	(5.7)	**12.1**	(3.0)	**8.5**	(3.3)	**18.3**	(3.5)	**9.6**	(4.1)	**-0.6**	(0.3)
Latvia	0.0	c	2.8	(2.9)	-1.9	(5.5)	**12.7**	(4.4)	0.6	(0.7)	6.1	(3.4)	2.8	(1.5)	**20.4**	(4.8)	**-1.1**	(0.1)
Liechtenstein	0.0	c	**-25.0**	(1.4)	**-8.6**	(1.3)	**39.4**	(1.4)	**49.4**	(1.0)	**-18.9**	(1.3)	**48.2**	(1.6)	**20.1**	(0.9)	**1.0**	(0.0)
Macao-China	**2.8**	(0.1)	**-1.6**	(0.1)	**21.9**	(0.2)	**28.8**	(0.1)	**5.2**	(0.2)	**-6.2**	(0.3)	**-1.0**	(0.1)	**6.9**	(0.2)	**0.1**	(0.0)
Russian Federation	-0.6	c	-2.3	(2.4)	1.0	(5.9)	**23.3**	(4.4)	2.7	(1.3)	0.5	(1.1)	0.4	(1.1)	**16.5**	(3.4)	**-1.2**	(0.1)
Thailand	**9.8**	(2.6)	**14.1**	(4.9)	2.2	(4.5)	**25.9**	(4.2)	**9.3**	(3.2)	**20.3**	(4.1)	**18.9**	(4.0)	**18.8**	(5.2)	**-0.6**	(0.3)
Tunisia	5.1	(4.8)	**11.1**	(3.5)	8.0	(6.2)	-2.4	(5.4)	7.2	(4.2)	4.4	(5.5)	**-16.0**	(5.4)	-2.7	(5.5)	**-0.8**	(0.2)
Uruguay	0.7	(2.4)	1.5	(2.9)	-3.8	(4.5)	-1.7	(4.2)	**11.0**	(4.6)	-9.5	(5.7)	**17.5**	(4.5)	1.7	(3.4)	0.0	(0.1)

Notes: Values that are statistically significant are indicated in bold (see Annex A3).
Only countries and economies with comparable data from PISA 2003 and PISA 2012 are shown.
StatLink ⟨⟩ http://dx.doi.org/10.1787/888932957498

[Part 1/1]
Change between 2003 and 2012 in monitoring mathematics teachers' practice

Table IV.4.37 *Results based on school principals' reports*

	PISA 2003								PISA 2012								Change between 2003 and 2012 (PISA 2012 - PISA 2003)							
	Percentage of students in schools whose principal reported that the following methods have been used to monitor the practice of mathematics teachers at their schools:								Percentage of students in schools whose principal reported that the following methods have been used to monitor the practice of mathematics teachers at their schools:								Percentage of students in schools whose principal reported that the following methods have been used to monitor the practice of mathematics teachers at their schools:							
	Tests or assessments of student achievement		Teacher peer review of lesson plans, assessment instruments and lessons		Principal or senior staff observations of lessons		Observation of classes by inspectors or other persons external to the school		Tests or assessments of student achievement		Teacher peer review of lesson plans, assessment instruments and lessons		Principal or senior staff observations of lessons		Observation of classes by inspectors or other persons external to the school		Tests or assessments of student achievement		Teacher peer review of lesson plans, assessment instruments and lessons		Principal or senior staff observations of lessons		Observation of classes by inspectors or other persons external to the school	
	%	S.E.	%	S.E.	%	S.E.	%	S.E.	%	S.E.	%	S.E.	%	S.E.	%	S.E.	% dif.	S.E.	% dif.	S.E.	% dif.	S.E.	% dif.	S.E.
Australia	58.7	(3.1)	65.0	(3.3)	63.4	(2.6)	7.8	(1.9)	78.8	(1.5)	77.4	(1.5)	70.0	(1.8)	10.9	(1.3)	**20.0**	(3.5)	**12.4**	(3.6)	**6.6**	(3.1)	3.1	(2.3)
Austria	25.3	(3.7)	78.5	(3.6)	77.9	(3.3)	37.1	(3.4)	91.0	(2.1)	78.6	(3.4)	73.9	(3.5)	29.2	(3.1)	**65.7**	(4.3)	0.1	(4.9)	-4.0	(4.8)	-7.8	(4.6)
Belgium	40.9	(3.0)	61.7	(3.0)	57.8	(3.2)	47.5	(3.1)	65.6	(3.2)	76.3	(2.4)	65.0	(3.2)	48.0	(2.8)	**24.7**	(4.3)	**14.5**	(3.9)	7.2	(4.5)	0.5	(4.2)
Canada	m	m	m	m	86.9	(1.2)	10.1	(1.2)	72.9	(2.3)	60.0	(2.1)	81.9	(1.6)	20.6	(2.2)	m	m	m	m	**-5.0**	(2.0)	**10.5**	(2.5)
Czech Republic	73.4	(3.1)	63.0	(2.9)	99.3	(0.4)	31.5	(2.9)	92.0	(2.3)	66.6	(3.7)	98.0	(0.8)	32.7	(3.8)	**18.5**	(3.9)	3.6	(4.7)	-1.3	(0.9)	1.3	(4.8)
Denmark	12.8	(2.6)	31.1	(3.5)	63.0	(3.3)	11.3	(2.3)	75.1	(2.8)	40.9	(3.6)	64.3	(3.8)	16.8	(2.5)	**62.2**	(3.8)	9.7	(5.0)	1.3	(5.1)	5.6	(3.4)
Finland	47.2	(3.8)	35.0	(3.8)	34.4	(3.4)	3.8	(1.6)	39.6	(3.2)	19.1	(2.9)	31.3	(2.5)	2.2	(0.8)	-7.6	(5.0)	**-15.9**	(4.8)	-3.1	(4.2)	-1.6	(1.8)
France	w	w	w	w	w	w	w	w	60.5	(3.4)	42.5	(3.5)	12.3	(2.3)	72.9	(3.3)	m	m	m	m	m	m	m	m
Germany	61.6	(3.2)	25.3	(3.1)	69.4	(3.3)	25.7	(2.8)	72.1	(3.3)	44.6	(3.0)	66.9	(3.3)	22.1	(3.0)	**10.5**	(4.7)	**19.3**	(4.3)	-2.5	(4.7)	-3.6	(4.1)
Greece	34.5	(5.7)	4.6	(1.9)	7.2	(3.4)	16.1	(4.1)	59.7	(3.7)	26.0	(3.5)	8.3	(2.3)	20.6	(3.0)	**25.2**	(6.8)	**21.4**	(4.0)	1.0	(4.1)	4.5	(5.1)
Hungary	62.6	(4.1)	83.1	(3.0)	95.8	(1.5)	26.0	(3.9)	74.3	(3.6)	74.5	(3.1)	96.7	(1.3)	13.0	(2.4)	**11.7**	(5.4)	**-8.6**	(4.3)	0.9	(2.0)	**-12.9**	(4.5)
Iceland	80.3	(0.2)	12.6	(0.1)	46.7	(0.2)	1.8	(0.1)	84.2	(0.2)	12.1	(0.2)	46.4	(0.2)	25.3	(0.2)	**3.9**	(0.2)	-0.5	(0.2)	-0.2	(0.3)	**23.5**	(0.2)
Ireland	42.0	(4.3)	9.2	(2.7)	6.6	(2.3)	4.7	(1.6)	65.3	(3.9)	33.7	(3.6)	12.7	(2.4)	48.5	(3.9)	**23.3**	(5.8)	**24.4**	(4.5)	6.1	(3.4)	**43.8**	(4.2)
Italy	44.4	(3.8)	84.0	(2.8)	16.1	(2.8)	1.2	(0.8)	74.1	(1.8)	87.4	(1.7)	17.2	(1.4)	0.6	(0.2)	**29.7**	(4.1)	3.3	(3.3)	1.1	(3.1)	-0.5	(0.8)
Japan	56.9	(4.0)	51.2	(4.3)	55.9	(4.4)	15.1	(3.0)	69.4	(3.3)	54.2	(3.4)	81.0	(2.6)	26.5	(3.1)	**12.5**	(5.2)	3.1	(5.4)	**25.1**	(5.1)	**11.4**	(4.3)
Korea	70.6	(3.2)	73.2	(3.7)	90.1	(2.6)	61.9	(3.4)	84.1	(3.1)	98.7	(0.9)	96.0	(1.7)	68.5	(3.8)	**13.5**	(4.5)	**25.5**	(3.8)	5.9	(3.1)	6.6	(5.1)
Luxembourg	58.9	(0.1)	27.2	(0.1)	42.2	(0.1)	7.3	(0.0)	80.6	(0.1)	63.3	(0.1)	47.9	(0.1)	6.4	(0.0)	**21.7**	(0.1)	**36.1**	(0.1)	**5.7**	(0.1)	**-0.9**	(0.0)
Mexico	92.2	(1.6)	62.8	(3.3)	72.1	(2.6)	36.3	(3.2)	92.5	(0.9)	76.4	(1.7)	76.6	(1.3)	41.1	(1.7)	0.3	(1.8)	**13.6**	(3.7)	4.5	(2.9)	4.7	(3.7)
Netherlands	54.1	(4.2)	52.0	(4.9)	58.4	(4.8)	33.3	(4.3)	83.2	(3.6)	54.0	(4.6)	86.6	(3.1)	41.9	(4.5)	**29.1**	(5.6)	2.0	(6.7)	**28.3**	(5.7)	8.6	(6.2)
New Zealand	73.0	(3.1)	91.2	(2.2)	94.3	(1.7)	52.4	(3.2)	84.1	(3.5)	91.7	(2.3)	96.6	(1.1)	32.3	(3.4)	**11.1**	(4.6)	0.5	(3.2)	2.3	(2.0)	**-20.2**	(4.7)
Norway	49.1	(3.9)	35.3	(3.8)	25.9	(3.3)	6.9	(2.2)	72.4	(2.7)	53.9	(4.1)	47.7	(3.7)	10.9	(2.2)	**23.3**	(4.7)	**18.7**	(5.6)	**21.8**	(5.0)	4.0	(3.1)
Poland	94.9	(1.8)	71.9	(3.6)	97.4	(1.3)	13.7	(2.6)	100.0	c	64.4	(4.0)	94.4	(1.8)	16.2	(3.1)	5.1	c	-7.5	(5.4)	-3.0	(2.2)	2.5	(4.0)
Portugal	32.9	(4.7)	58.0	(4.7)	4.9	(1.6)	9.6	(2.8)	98.2	(1.1)	71.3	(4.6)	60.2	(3.4)	4.2	(2.2)	**65.2**	(4.8)	**13.3**	(6.6)	**55.3**	(3.8)	-5.4	(3.6)
Slovak Republic	70.1	(3.0)	87.9	(2.2)	97.8	(1.0)	24.6	(3.0)	74.6	(3.2)	84.2	(3.0)	98.2	(0.8)	27.0	(3.4)	4.5	(4.4)	-3.7	(3.7)	0.4	(1.3)	2.4	(4.5)
Spain	71.9	(3.2)	39.1	(3.5)	14.8	(2.6)	14.1	(2.5)	78.0	(2.5)	21.9	(2.2)	9.6	(1.4)	15.5	(2.4)	6.2	(4.1)	**-17.2**	(4.2)	-5.2	(3.0)	1.3	(3.5)
Sweden	41.4	(4.0)	21.3	(3.0)	58.4	(3.4)	15.7	(2.4)	67.5	(3.5)	58.7	(3.7)	79.7	(3.2)	26.9	(3.4)	**26.1**	(5.3)	**37.4**	(4.8)	**21.3**	(4.6)	**11.3**	(4.1)
Switzerland	42.7	(3.6)	45.7	(3.9)	41.8	(4.3)	58.8	(4.0)	60.6	(3.0)	62.9	(3.3)	83.0	(2.2)	28.7	(2.7)	**17.9**	(4.7)	**17.2**	(5.1)	**41.2**	(4.9)	**-30.0**	(4.8)
Turkey	72.3	(4.2)	77.0	(4.0)	89.3	(2.6)	39.5	(4.3)	91.6	(2.7)	51.8	(3.8)	93.9	(1.9)	22.1	(3.6)	**19.3**	(5.0)	**-25.2**	(5.5)	4.6	(3.2)	**-17.4**	(5.6)
United States	89.2	(2.2)	59.6	(3.2)	99.7	(0.3)	37.2	(3.6)	89.4	(2.7)	65.9	(3.7)	99.7	(0.3)	42.0	(4.5)	0.2	(3.5)	6.4	(4.9)	0.0	(0.5)	4.8	(5.8)
OECD average 2003	57.5	(0.7)	51.6	(0.6)	59.6	(0.5)	23.2	(0.5)	77.5	(0.6)	59.0	(0.6)	67.3	(0.4)	25.0	(0.5)	**20.1**	(0.9)	**7.4**	(0.9)	**7.7**	(0.7)	**1.8**	(0.8)
Brazil	75.4	(3.3)	53.8	(3.3)	49.6	(3.7)	11.5	(2.2)	88.3	(1.4)	74.8	(2.2)	49.8	(2.1)	22.8	(2.4)	**12.8**	(3.6)	**21.0**	(4.0)	0.2	(4.2)	**11.3**	(3.3)
Hong Kong-China	82.4	(3.5)	86.0	(2.8)	92.2	(2.4)	26.2	(3.5)	94.9	(1.8)	85.0	(3.1)	96.7	(1.5)	39.0	(4.1)	**12.5**	(3.9)	-1.0	(4.2)	4.5	(2.8)	**12.9**	(5.4)
Indonesia	91.3	(1.9)	66.9	(4.0)	91.6	(2.2)	75.0	(3.4)	91.3	(2.4)	91.3	(1.6)	95.4	(1.5)	77.1	(3.6)	-0.1	(3.1)	**24.5**	(4.3)	3.9	(2.7)	2.1	(4.9)
Latvia	94.8	(2.3)	97.5	(1.3)	99.5	(0.5)	41.4	(4.9)	83.2	(2.8)	89.3	(2.3)	100.0	c	41.0	(3.1)	**-11.6**	(3.6)	**-8.2**	(2.7)	0.5	c	-0.3	(5.8)
Liechtenstein	59.2	(0.5)	52.7	(0.5)	5.0	(0.3)	96.2	(0.3)	82.4	(0.7)	69.6	(1.0)	49.4	(0.8)	86.9	(0.6)	**23.2**	(0.8)	**16.9**	(1.1)	**44.3**	(0.8)	**-9.2**	(0.7)
Macao-China	87.5	(0.1)	95.5	(0.2)	95.0	(0.0)	29.9	(0.3)	89.9	(0.0)	88.0	(0.1)	96.0	(0.0)	47.9	(0.0)	**2.4**	(0.1)	**-7.5**	(0.2)	**1.1**	(0.1)	**18.0**	(0.3)
Russian Federation	95.5	(1.6)	98.4	(1.0)	100.0	c	73.8	(3.3)	98.9	(0.5)	95.9	(1.1)	99.5	(0.3)	43.8	(4.2)	**3.5**	(1.7)	-2.5	(1.5)	-0.5	c	**-30.0**	(5.3)
Thailand	91.1	(2.0)	85.4	(2.5)	87.1	(2.7)	49.3	(3.7)	97.9	(1.1)	92.5	(2.1)	95.1	(1.6)	44.7	(4.3)	**6.8**	(2.3)	**7.1**	(3.3)	**8.0**	(3.2)	-4.6	(5.7)
Tunisia	79.0	(3.6)	60.1	(4.0)	74.2	(3.6)	80.4	(3.4)	75.0	(3.8)	39.6	(3.9)	50.1	(4.1)	86.9	(2.7)	-4.0	(5.2)	**-20.5**	(5.6)	**-24.1**	(5.5)	6.5	(4.3)
Uruguay	50.7	(4.0)	63.2	(3.2)	92.4	(1.6)	51.9	(3.7)	57.8	(3.9)	63.3	(3.6)	88.4	(2.2)	66.2	(3.2)	7.0	(5.6)	0.1	(4.8)	-4.1	(2.7)	**14.2**	(4.8)

Notes: Values that are statistically significant are indicated in bold (see Annex A3).
Only countries and economies with comparable data from PISA 2003 and PISA 2012 are shown.
StatLink 🔗 http://dx.doi.org/10.1787/888932957498

[Part 1/1]
Arriving late for school
Table IV.5.1 *Results based on students' self-reports*

| | | Percentage of students who reported having arrived late for school in the two weeks prior to the PISA test: | | | | | | | |
| | | Not at all | | One or two times | | Three or four times | | Five or more times | |
		%	S.E.	%	S.E.	%	S.E.	%	S.E.
OECD	Australia	64.5	(0.6)	25.4	(0.5)	6.6	(0.3)	3.5	(0.2)
	Austria	79.1	(0.9)	15.6	(0.7)	3.2	(0.3)	2.0	(0.3)
	Belgium	72.7	(0.7)	20.8	(0.6)	3.7	(0.3)	2.8	(0.2)
	Canada	56.9	(0.7)	28.6	(0.5)	9.2	(0.4)	5.4	(0.3)
	Chile	47.0	(1.1)	35.0	(0.7)	10.5	(0.5)	7.5	(0.5)
	Czech Republic	73.0	(0.8)	20.7	(0.7)	3.3	(0.3)	3.0	(0.3)
	Denmark	61.5	(1.1)	26.3	(0.7)	7.5	(0.4)	4.6	(0.4)
	Estonia	58.9	(0.9)	29.1	(0.7)	7.8	(0.4)	4.2	(0.4)
	Finland	57.0	(0.9)	30.8	(0.7)	8.2	(0.5)	4.0	(0.3)
	France	67.7	(0.9)	24.4	(0.7)	5.0	(0.4)	2.8	(0.3)
	Germany	77.3	(0.8)	17.8	(0.7)	3.0	(0.3)	1.9	(0.2)
	Greece	50.7	(1.0)	29.3	(0.7)	10.5	(0.5)	9.4	(0.4)
	Hungary	75.9	(1.2)	18.6	(1.0)	2.9	(0.4)	2.6	(0.3)
	Iceland	65.0	(0.8)	26.8	(0.8)	5.7	(0.4)	2.5	(0.2)
	Ireland	72.6	(1.0)	20.1	(0.7)	4.8	(0.4)	2.5	(0.3)
	Israel	45.7	(1.1)	35.7	(0.8)	11.0	(0.6)	7.7	(0.5)
	Italy	64.8	(0.6)	26.3	(0.5)	5.4	(0.3)	3.5	(0.2)
	Japan	91.1	(0.6)	7.5	(0.5)	1.0	(0.1)	0.5	(0.1)
	Korea	74.9	(1.0)	17.3	(0.7)	4.6	(0.4)	3.2	(0.3)
	Luxembourg	70.9	(0.5)	21.4	(0.5)	4.6	(0.3)	3.1	(0.2)
	Mexico	60.1	(0.6)	31.9	(0.5)	5.9	(0.2)	2.1	(0.1)
	Netherlands	69.7	(1.0)	23.4	(0.8)	3.7	(0.3)	3.2	(0.3)
	New Zealand	57.9	(1.3)	28.0	(0.8)	8.9	(0.6)	5.2	(0.3)
	Norway	70.8	(1.0)	21.2	(0.7)	4.9	(0.4)	3.1	(0.3)
	Poland	57.6	(1.2)	28.2	(0.7)	8.0	(0.5)	6.2	(0.5)
	Portugal	44.8	(1.0)	39.0	(0.7)	10.2	(0.5)	6.0	(0.4)
	Slovak Republic	73.8	(0.9)	20.1	(0.8)	3.7	(0.3)	2.5	(0.3)
	Slovenia	60.4	(0.8)	29.1	(0.7)	5.9	(0.4)	4.5	(0.3)
	Spain	64.7	(0.8)	24.3	(0.6)	6.5	(0.2)	4.4	(0.2)
	Sweden	44.4	(1.0)	34.3	(0.7)	12.9	(0.5)	8.4	(0.5)
	Switzerland	75.7	(0.8)	19.4	(0.6)	3.4	(0.3)	1.5	(0.1)
	Turkey	56.2	(1.0)	30.1	(0.7)	8.4	(0.5)	5.3	(0.4)
	United Kingdom	68.2	(0.8)	24.0	(0.6)	5.1	(0.3)	2.7	(0.2)
	United States	69.9	(1.2)	21.8	(0.8)	5.1	(0.4)	3.2	(0.4)
	OECD average	64.7	(0.2)	25.1	(0.1)	6.2	(0.1)	4.0	(0.1)
Partners	Albania	64.7	(0.7)	27.8	(0.6)	4.9	(0.4)	2.6	(0.3)
	Argentina	53.0	(1.3)	28.6	(0.8)	9.9	(0.6)	8.5	(0.6)
	Brazil	66.3	(0.8)	24.8	(0.6)	5.5	(0.3)	3.4	(0.2)
	Bulgaria	41.0	(1.1)	37.0	(0.7)	12.7	(0.6)	9.3	(0.7)
	Colombia	64.1	(1.4)	29.0	(1.1)	4.8	(0.4)	2.2	(0.3)
	Costa Rica	42.5	(1.1)	37.9	(0.9)	12.2	(0.7)	7.3	(0.6)
	Croatia	66.1	(0.9)	26.0	(0.7)	5.4	(0.3)	2.5	(0.3)
	Cyprus*	52.3	(0.7)	28.0	(0.6)	10.6	(0.5)	9.1	(0.4)
	Hong Kong-China	85.4	(0.6)	12.5	(0.5)	1.3	(0.2)	0.8	(0.1)
	Indonesia	73.0	(1.0)	22.2	(0.8)	3.0	(0.3)	1.7	(0.3)
	Jordan	64.6	(0.8)	25.1	(0.6)	5.5	(0.4)	4.8	(0.4)
	Kazakhstan	71.8	(1.2)	23.6	(0.9)	3.3	(0.3)	1.3	(0.2)
	Latvia	43.7	(1.2)	35.0	(0.9)	12.7	(0.6)	8.6	(0.7)
	Liechtenstein	81.3	(2.3)	16.5	(2.1)	1.0	(0.6)	1.1	(0.6)
	Lithuania	56.3	(1.2)	31.2	(0.9)	7.5	(0.4)	5.0	(0.4)
	Macao-China	74.9	(0.5)	20.9	(0.5)	2.7	(0.2)	1.5	(0.2)
	Malaysia	66.4	(1.0)	23.3	(0.8)	6.2	(0.3)	4.1	(0.3)
	Montenegro	60.6	(0.9)	29.7	(0.8)	5.4	(0.3)	4.4	(0.3)
	Peru	47.2	(1.2)	36.2	(0.9)	11.0	(0.5)	5.7	(0.5)
	Qatar	60.5	(0.5)	26.9	(0.4)	7.5	(0.2)	5.1	(0.2)
	Romania	54.2	(1.1)	31.4	(0.8)	7.8	(0.5)	6.6	(0.5)
	Russian Federation	53.3	(1.3)	30.9	(0.8)	8.2	(0.5)	7.6	(0.5)
	Serbia	58.2	(1.0)	30.4	(0.8)	6.6	(0.4)	4.8	(0.4)
	Shanghai-China	83.4	(0.7)	13.1	(0.6)	2.1	(0.3)	1.3	(0.2)
	Singapore	79.4	(0.5)	16.9	(0.5)	2.4	(0.2)	1.3	(0.2)
	Chinese Taipei	77.7	(0.8)	14.7	(0.6)	4.5	(0.3)	3.1	(0.3)
	Thailand	65.9	(1.2)	24.0	(0.8)	6.3	(0.5)	3.8	(0.3)
	Tunisia	48.2	(0.9)	38.4	(0.8)	7.6	(0.4)	5.8	(0.5)
	United Arab Emirates	68.5	(0.7)	22.8	(0.5)	5.0	(0.2)	3.8	(0.3)
	Uruguay	40.7	(0.9)	38.1	(0.7)	12.6	(0.5)	8.6	(0.5)
	Viet Nam	83.8	(0.8)	14.2	(0.7)	1.4	(0.2)	0.7	(0.2)

* See notes at the beginning of this Annex.
StatLink ᵃᵐˢᴸ http://dx.doi.org/10.1787/888932957517

[Part 1/1]
Concentration of students arriving late for school
Table IV.5.2   *Results based on students' self-reports*

| | | Percentage of students who are in schools where, in the two weeks prior to the PISA test... | | | | | | | |
| | | Over 50% of students arrived late at least once | | More than 25% but 50% of students or fewer arrived late at least once | | More than 10% but 25% of students or fewer arrived late at least once | | 10% of students or fewer arrived late at least once | |
		%	S.E.	%	S.E.	%	S.E.	%	S.E.
OECD	Australia	17.2	(1.4)	57.0	(1.9)	22.9	(1.7)	2.9	(0.7)
	Austria	5.4	(1.8)	29.2	(3.3)	34.6	(4.1)	30.8	(3.2)
	Belgium	6.7	(1.3)	46.1	(3.0)	38.9	(3.2)	8.2	(1.7)
	Canada	31.6	(2.3)	53.7	(2.7)	13.5	(1.3)	1.3	(0.4)
	Chile	53.4	(3.5)	44.9	(3.4)	1.4	(0.5)	0.3	(0.2)
	Czech Republic	8.2	(1.6)	39.7	(2.8)	39.2	(3.2)	12.8	(2.2)
	Denmark	23.0	(2.8)	52.3	(3.3)	20.6	(2.8)	4.1	(1.5)
	Estonia	27.4	(2.5)	54.7	(3.1)	12.7	(1.8)	5.2	(1.3)
	Finland	33.3	(3.3)	52.6	(3.7)	13.0	(2.4)	1.0	(0.5)
	France	13.9	(2.3)	47.5	(3.3)	31.6	(3.0)	6.9	(1.6)
	Germany	4.2	(1.3)	35.2	(3.4)	42.4	(3.2)	18.2	(2.4)
	Greece	51.7	(4.0)	44.4	(4.1)	2.3	(1.1)	1.6	(0.9)
	Hungary	10.2	(1.9)	28.9	(3.5)	34.0	(3.5)	26.9	(2.8)
	Iceland	12.2	(0.1)	65.9	(0.2)	18.4	(0.2)	3.5	(0.1)
	Ireland	5.6	(1.7)	43.3	(3.5)	45.5	(3.5)	5.6	(1.8)
	Israel	59.1	(3.8)	37.6	(3.8)	3.3	(1.4)	0.0	(0.0)
	Italy	17.7	(1.6)	56.7	(2.0)	22.2	(1.6)	3.3	(0.8)
	Japan	0.2	(0.2)	6.2	(1.7)	28.4	(3.3)	65.2	(3.7)
	Korea	5.1	(1.5)	44.9	(3.7)	34.9	(3.7)	15.0	(2.8)
	Luxembourg	3.5	(0.1)	51.9	(0.1)	44.1	(0.1)	0.5	(0.0)
	Mexico	27.0	(1.7)	54.4	(1.8)	15.5	(1.4)	3.1	(0.6)
	Netherlands	11.9	(2.3)	44.4	(3.8)	40.8	(3.9)	3.0	(1.2)
	New Zealand	30.1	(3.5)	56.2	(4.3)	13.3	(3.0)	0.4	(0.3)
	Norway	7.4	(1.9)	55.2	(3.6)	30.8	(3.4)	6.6	(1.7)
	Poland	32.6	(3.5)	45.7	(3.9)	19.2	(3.2)	2.4	(1.2)
	Portugal	64.8	(4.0)	34.1	(3.9)	1.0	(0.8)	0.1	(0.1)
	Slovak Republic	6.0	(1.2)	43.1	(3.7)	39.9	(3.8)	11.1	(2.2)
	Slovenia	23.4	(0.5)	65.9	(0.7)	7.9	(0.2)	2.8	(0.6)
	Spain	17.5	(2.0)	55.1	(3.2)	24.6	(2.7)	2.7	(0.8)
	Sweden	65.7	(3.4)	31.9	(3.3)	2.1	(1.1)	0.3	(0.2)
	Switzerland	5.2	(1.3)	36.1	(2.8)	42.6	(3.4)	16.1	(2.3)
	Turkey	27.0	(4.2)	66.3	(4.3)	6.6	(1.8)	0.1	(0.0)
	United Kingdom	7.7	(1.6)	59.5	(3.2)	28.5	(2.8)	4.3	(1.4)
	United States	9.5	(2.2)	49.2	(4.3)	34.5	(4.3)	6.8	(2.0)
	OECD average	**21.3**	**(0.4)**	**46.8**	**(0.6)**	**23.9**	**(0.5)**	**8.0**	**(0.3)**
Partners	Albania	7.3	(1.6)	75.8	(3.0)	14.7	(2.6)	2.2	(0.9)
	Argentina	47.3	(4.0)	41.2	(3.6)	11.3	(2.5)	0.2	(0.2)
	Brazil	14.8	(1.8)	50.9	(2.7)	32.0	(2.4)	2.3	(0.8)
	Bulgaria	71.2	(3.6)	28.0	(3.8)	0.7	(0.7)	0.1	(0.1)
	Colombia	17.3	(2.8)	58.0	(3.7)	18.0	(2.9)	6.7	(2.3)
	Costa Rica	70.0	(3.0)	25.4	(3.0)	4.5	(1.5)	0.0	c
	Croatia	13.5	(2.2)	59.3	(3.5)	22.5	(2.8)	4.6	(1.8)
	Cyprus*	47.0	(0.1)	49.4	(0.1)	3.5	(0.1)	0.1	(0.0)
	Hong Kong-China	0.1	(0.1)	11.4	(2.4)	54.1	(3.7)	34.4	(3.3)
	Indonesia	9.0	(1.9)	39.2	(3.5)	41.9	(3.5)	9.9	(2.3)
	Jordan	15.7	(2.5)	59.9	(3.7)	21.7	(3.0)	2.6	(1.3)
	Kazakhstan	10.5	(2.3)	44.2	(3.9)	32.5	(3.6)	12.7	(2.1)
	Latvia	65.9	(3.4)	29.7	(3.2)	3.4	(1.3)	1.0	(0.6)
	Liechtenstein	1.0	(0.6)	18.8	(0.9)	73.5	(1.0)	6.7	(0.5)
	Lithuania	35.4	(3.4)	50.7	(3.7)	10.8	(2.0)	3.1	(0.8)
	Macao-China	8.2	(0.1)	34.0	(0.0)	46.8	(0.1)	10.9	(0.0)
	Malaysia	10.9	(2.3)	61.5	(3.7)	25.0	(3.3)	2.5	(1.4)
	Montenegro	10.2	(0.1)	83.1	(0.1)	6.3	(0.1)	0.4	(0.0)
	Peru	56.8	(3.5)	39.0	(3.3)	4.2	(1.5)	0.0	c
	Qatar	18.3	(0.1)	68.6	(0.1)	11.5	(0.1)	1.6	(0.0)
	Romania	40.0	(3.6)	47.6	(3.9)	11.3	(2.5)	1.0	(0.5)
	Russian Federation	39.6	(4.0)	48.9	(4.6)	9.2	(2.3)	2.3	(0.4)
	Serbia	31.6	(3.6)	52.5	(4.2)	14.7	(2.8)	1.3	(0.9)
	Shanghai-China	0.0	c	17.9	(2.5)	55.8	(3.5)	26.2	(3.6)
	Singapore	1.0	(0.0)	32.0	(0.5)	48.9	(0.5)	18.0	(0.1)
	Chinese Taipei	1.4	(0.8)	38.8	(3.7)	45.7	(4.4)	14.1	(2.8)
	Thailand	20.9	(2.6)	43.0	(3.7)	31.0	(3.8)	5.1	(1.7)
	Tunisia	55.9	(4.0)	43.2	(4.1)	0.9	(0.8)	0.0	c
	United Arab Emirates	11.5	(1.9)	52.9	(2.7)	31.4	(2.1)	4.2	(0.6)
	Uruguay	79.1	(2.6)	18.6	(2.5)	1.5	(0.9)	0.8	(0.8)
	Viet Nam	1.3	(0.6)	18.6	(2.9)	43.8	(4.2)	36.3	(4.0)

* See notes at the beginning of this Annex.
StatLink ⟲⟲ http://dx.doi.org/10.1787/888932957517

[Part 1/1]
Skipping a day of school or some classes
Table IV.5.3   *Results based on students' self-reports*

	Percentage of students who reported having skipped a day of school in the two weeks prior to the PISA test:								Percentage of students who reported having skipped some classes in the two weeks prior to the PISA test:							
	Not at all		One or two times		Three or four times		Five or more times		Not at all		One or two times		Three or four times		Five or more times	
	%	S.E.	%	S.E.	%	S.E.	%	S.E.	%	S.E.	%	S.E.	%	S.E.	%	S.E.
Australia	68.2	(0.6)	25.7	(0.5)	4.3	(0.2)	1.8	(0.1)	86.5	(0.4)	10.4	(0.3)	1.9	(0.1)	1.2	(0.1)
Austria	92.0	(0.5)	7.1	(0.5)	0.4	(0.1)	0.5	(0.1)	87.2	(0.8)	11.4	(0.7)	1.0	(0.2)	0.3	(0.1)
Belgium	94.4	(0.4)	4.2	(0.3)	0.7	(0.1)	0.6	(0.1)	91.8	(0.4)	6.8	(0.3)	0.7	(0.1)	0.7	(0.1)
Canada	77.9	(0.4)	18.9	(0.4)	2.3	(0.2)	0.9	(0.1)	75.4	(0.5)	19.1	(0.4)	3.7	(0.2)	1.8	(0.2)
Chile	92.3	(0.5)	6.5	(0.5)	0.8	(0.1)	0.5	(0.1)	84.6	(0.8)	13.8	(0.7)	1.2	(0.2)	0.5	(0.1)
Czech Republic	94.1	(0.5)	4.1	(0.4)	0.7	(0.1)	1.1	(0.2)	92.6	(0.5)	6.5	(0.5)	0.5	(0.1)	0.4	(0.1)
Denmark	90.4	(0.6)	7.8	(0.5)	1.3	(0.2)	0.6	(0.1)	83.7	(0.9)	13.7	(0.7)	1.8	(0.3)	0.9	(0.2)
Estonia	84.7	(0.7)	11.9	(0.6)	2.0	(0.2)	1.4	(0.2)	70.1	(0.9)	23.2	(0.7)	4.5	(0.3)	2.3	(0.3)
Finland	89.6	(0.5)	8.9	(0.4)	0.8	(0.1)	0.7	(0.2)	84.4	(0.6)	13.1	(0.5)	1.7	(0.2)	0.8	(0.2)
France	90.5	(0.5)	7.3	(0.5)	1.1	(0.1)	1.0	(0.2)	83.2	(0.8)	13.8	(0.7)	2.0	(0.2)	1.1	(0.2)
Germany	94.9	(0.4)	4.2	(0.3)	0.5	(0.1)	0.5	(0.1)	90.3	(0.5)	8.6	(0.4)	0.7	(0.1)	0.4	(0.1)
Greece	78.3	(0.8)	16.7	(0.7)	3.0	(0.3)	2.0	(0.2)	58.0	(1.2)	30.3	(0.9)	7.7	(0.5)	4.0	(0.3)
Hungary	93.2	(0.5)	5.5	(0.5)	0.8	(0.1)	0.5	(0.1)	90.8	(0.6)	7.7	(0.4)	1.1	(0.2)	0.4	(0.1)
Iceland	97.9	(0.2)	1.7	(0.2)	0.1	(0.1)	0.3	(0.1)	88.3	(0.5)	9.6	(0.4)	1.6	(0.2)	0.5	(0.1)
Ireland	96.0	(0.3)	3.3	(0.3)	0.4	(0.1)	0.3	(0.1)	87.6	(0.8)	9.9	(0.6)	1.7	(0.2)	0.8	(0.2)
Israel	69.5	(0.7)	25.0	(0.7)	3.4	(0.3)	2.2	(0.2)	68.8	(1.1)	23.5	(0.8)	4.5	(0.4)	3.2	(0.3)
Italy	51.8	(0.5)	41.3	(0.5)	4.6	(0.2)	2.2	(0.1)	65.5	(0.5)	29.0	(0.4)	3.6	(0.2)	2.0	(0.1)
Japan	98.5	(0.2)	1.3	(0.2)	0.2	(0.1)	0.1	(0.1)	97.1	(0.5)	2.3	(0.4)	0.3	(0.1)	0.3	(0.1)
Korea	98.2	(0.3)	1.3	(0.2)	0.2	(0.1)	0.3	(0.1)	97.1	(0.4)	2.3	(0.3)	0.3	(0.1)	0.3	(0.1)
Luxembourg	93.0	(0.3)	5.3	(0.3)	0.7	(0.1)	1.0	(0.1)	93.0	(0.4)	5.6	(0.3)	0.6	(0.1)	0.8	(0.1)
Mexico	79.1	(0.4)	18.7	(0.4)	1.6	(0.1)	0.6	(0.1)	78.2	(0.4)	18.9	(0.4)	2.2	(0.1)	0.7	(0.1)
Netherlands	97.3	(0.2)	2.2	(0.2)	0.2	(0.1)	0.3	(0.1)	89.0	(0.7)	9.5	(0.6)	1.1	(0.2)	0.4	(0.1)
New Zealand	82.9	(0.6)	12.9	(0.5)	2.6	(0.3)	1.5	(0.2)	84.7	(0.7)	11.8	(0.6)	2.1	(0.3)	1.4	(0.2)
Norway	92.9	(0.4)	5.9	(0.4)	0.6	(0.1)	0.6	(0.1)	88.2	(0.5)	9.7	(0.5)	1.3	(0.2)	0.9	(0.2)
Poland	84.1	(0.8)	13.3	(0.8)	1.6	(0.2)	1.1	(0.2)	79.6	(0.9)	16.4	(0.7)	2.4	(0.2)	1.5	(0.2)
Portugal	80.7	(0.7)	15.2	(0.7)	2.4	(0.3)	1.7	(0.2)	71.4	(0.9)	23.2	(0.8)	3.4	(0.3)	2.1	(0.2)
Slovak Republic	90.6	(0.5)	7.3	(0.4)	1.4	(0.2)	0.7	(0.2)	88.2	(0.8)	10.0	(0.7)	1.1	(0.2)	0.7	(0.1)
Slovenia	85.8	(0.5)	10.8	(0.5)	2.0	(0.2)	1.4	(0.1)	74.4	(0.6)	20.4	(0.6)	3.2	(0.3)	1.9	(0.2)
Spain	72.0	(0.9)	24.2	(0.7)	2.6	(0.2)	1.2	(0.1)	67.7	(0.8)	25.5	(0.6)	3.9	(0.3)	2.9	(0.2)
Sweden	92.8	(0.4)	5.8	(0.4)	0.8	(0.1)	0.6	(0.1)	79.5	(0.8)	16.1	(0.7)	3.0	(0.3)	1.4	(0.2)
Switzerland	95.0	(0.3)	4.3	(0.3)	0.4	(0.1)	0.3	(0.1)	89.4	(0.6)	9.0	(0.5)	0.9	(0.1)	0.7	(0.1)
Turkey	45.8	(1.0)	33.7	(1.0)	12.7	(0.6)	7.8	(0.4)	54.8	(1.1)	30.5	(0.8)	8.9	(0.5)	5.8	(0.4)
United Kingdom	82.1	(0.6)	15.2	(0.5)	1.9	(0.2)	0.8	(0.1)	88.0	(0.5)	9.5	(0.4)	1.4	(0.1)	1.1	(0.2)
United States	78.9	(0.8)	17.9	(0.7)	2.4	(0.3)	0.8	(0.1)	87.1	(0.6)	10.4	(0.6)	1.8	(0.2)	0.7	(0.1)
OECD average	85.5	(0.1)	11.6	(0.1)	1.8	(0.0)	1.1	(0.0)	82.2	(0.1)	14.2	(0.1)	2.3	(0.0)	1.3	(0.0)
Albania	85.3	(0.6)	12.0	(0.6)	2.0	(0.3)	0.7	(0.1)	80.6	(0.6)	16.6	(0.6)	2.2	(0.2)	0.7	(0.2)
Argentina	41.9	(1.0)	41.9	(0.8)	8.7	(0.6)	7.6	(0.4)	55.7	(1.1)	33.0	(0.9)	6.7	(0.4)	4.6	(0.4)
Brazil	79.7	(0.5)	16.6	(0.4)	2.3	(0.2)	1.4	(0.1)	81.2	(0.5)	15.8	(0.4)	1.9	(0.1)	1.1	(0.1)
Bulgaria	74.8	(1.2)	18.0	(0.8)	3.9	(0.4)	3.2	(0.4)	66.2	(1.2)	24.7	(0.8)	5.3	(0.5)	3.8	(0.4)
Colombia	95.6	(0.4)	4.1	(0.4)	0.2	(0.1)	0.2	(0.1)	84.3	(0.7)	14.5	(0.7)	0.8	(0.1)	0.4	(0.1)
Costa Rica	68.5	(1.0)	25.1	(0.9)	4.0	(0.4)	2.4	(0.3)	57.0	(1.4)	33.5	(1.1)	6.3	(0.4)	3.2	(0.4)
Croatia	87.3	(0.6)	9.4	(0.4)	1.7	(0.2)	1.6	(0.1)	76.4	(0.7)	18.5	(0.6)	3.2	(0.3)	1.8	(0.2)
Cyprus*	77.3	(0.6)	16.0	(0.6)	3.8	(0.3)	2.9	(0.2)	64.0	(0.7)	26.0	(0.6)	6.1	(0.4)	3.9	(0.3)
Hong Kong-China	96.0	(0.3)	3.4	(0.3)	0.4	(0.1)	0.2	(0.1)	96.9	(0.3)	2.8	(0.3)	0.2	(0.1)	0.1	(0.0)
Indonesia	88.0	(0.7)	10.0	(0.6)	1.4	(0.2)	0.6	(0.1)	75.0	(0.9)	21.5	(0.8)	2.2	(0.2)	1.3	(0.1)
Jordan	56.6	(0.9)	36.6	(0.8)	4.6	(0.3)	2.1	(0.2)	70.3	(0.9)	23.8	(0.8)	3.8	(0.3)	2.1	(0.2)
Kazakhstan	80.3	(0.9)	17.2	(0.8)	1.8	(0.2)	0.8	(0.1)	82.5	(0.8)	15.2	(0.7)	1.6	(0.2)	0.7	(0.1)
Latvia	77.3	(0.8)	18.2	(0.7)	2.7	(0.3)	1.8	(0.2)	36.8	(1.0)	45.7	(1.1)	10.2	(0.6)	7.2	(0.6)
Liechtenstein	98.0	(0.8)	1.3	(0.7)	0.0	c	0.7	(0.5)	96.3	(1.0)	2.3	(0.9)	0.4	(0.4)	1.0	(0.6)
Lithuania	81.0	(0.9)	16.1	(0.8)	1.8	(0.2)	1.1	(0.2)	67.3	(1.1)	26.4	(0.9)	4.3	(0.3)	1.9	(0.3)
Macao-China	95.1	(0.3)	4.3	(0.3)	0.4	(0.1)	0.1	(0.0)	94.6	(0.4)	4.7	(0.3)	0.4	(0.1)	0.3	(0.1)
Malaysia	71.6	(1.2)	22.0	(0.9)	4.1	(0.4)	2.3	(0.3)	74.6	(1.0)	20.5	(0.7)	3.2	(0.3)	1.7	(0.2)
Montenegro	75.3	(0.8)	18.4	(0.7)	3.3	(0.3)	2.9	(0.2)	67.9	(0.7)	25.9	(0.6)	4.1	(0.3)	2.2	(0.2)
Peru	85.8	(0.8)	11.3	(0.6)	2.2	(0.3)	0.7	(0.1)	88.0	(0.8)	10.5	(0.7)	1.1	(0.2)	0.4	(0.1)
Qatar	83.6	(0.4)	12.7	(0.4)	2.4	(0.1)	1.3	(0.1)	79.7	(0.4)	15.9	(0.3)	2.7	(0.1)	1.7	(0.1)
Romania	65.7	(1.1)	25.9	(0.8)	4.7	(0.4)	3.6	(0.4)	55.8	(1.3)	34.1	(1.0)	6.1	(0.4)	4.0	(0.4)
Russian Federation	78.7	(0.7)	15.7	(0.6)	3.1	(0.3)	2.5	(0.2)	69.6	(1.1)	23.4	(0.8)	4.5	(0.4)	2.4	(0.3)
Serbia	87.1	(0.4)	10.3	(0.6)	1.5	(0.2)	1.2	(0.2)	73.3	(1.0)	21.9	(0.8)	3.2	(0.3)	1.6	(0.2)
Shanghai-China	99.3	(0.1)	0.6	(0.1)	0.0	(0.0)	0.1	(0.1)	96.6	(0.4)	2.9	(0.3)	0.2	(0.1)	0.3	(0.1)
Singapore	85.5	(0.4)	12.5	(0.4)	1.5	(0.2)	0.5	(0.1)	87.5	(0.5)	10.6	(0.5)	1.4	(0.1)	0.5	(0.1)
Chinese Taipei	95.7	(0.3)	3.2	(0.2)	0.6	(0.1)	0.6	(0.1)	90.7	(0.6)	7.1	(0.5)	1.2	(0.2)	1.0	(0.2)
Thailand	81.8	(0.7)	14.2	(0.6)	2.4	(0.3)	1.5	(0.2)	73.4	(0.8)	23.0	(0.7)	2.5	(0.2)	1.0	(0.2)
Tunisia	79.3	(1.0)	16.3	(0.7)	2.4	(0.3)	2.0	(0.3)	74.5	(0.9)	21.1	(0.8)	2.6	(0.3)	1.7	(0.3)
United Arab Emirates	60.8	(0.8)	31.6	(0.7)	5.4	(0.2)	2.1	(0.2)	77.2	(0.7)	17.2	(0.6)	3.5	(0.3)	2.2	(0.2)
Uruguay	76.4	(0.9)	18.4	(0.7)	3.0	(0.3)	2.2	(0.2)	76.2	(0.9)	19.0	(0.8)	3.1	(0.2)	1.6	(0.2)
Viet Nam	90.8	(0.8)	7.9	(0.6)	1.0	(0.2)	0.3	(0.1)	93.4	(0.5)	5.6	(0.4)	0.7	(0.1)	0.3	(0.1)

* See notes at the beginning of this Annex.
StatLink ⌧ http://dx.doi.org/10.1787/888932957517

[Part 1/1]
Concentration of students skipping a day of school or some classes

Table IV.5.4   *Results based on students' self-reports*

		Percentage of students who are in schools where, in the two weeks prior to the PISA test...							
		Over 50% of students skipped a day or a class at least once		More than 25% but 50% of students or fewer skipped a day or a class at least once		More than 10% but 25% of students or fewer skipped a day or a class at least once		10% of students or fewer skipped a day or a class at least once	
		%	S.E.	%	S.E.	%	S.E.	%	S.E.
OECD	Australia	24.0	(1.6)	53.5	(2.0)	18.8	(1.6)	3.7	(0.7)
	Austria	1.5	(0.7)	24.3	(3.5)	41.4	(4.1)	32.8	(3.3)
	Belgium	1.2	(0.4)	9.1	(1.6)	29.3	(2.5)	60.4	(2.3)
	Canada	15.3	(1.8)	60.0	(2.4)	23.2	(1.6)	1.6	(0.5)
	Chile	2.2	(1.0)	32.1	(2.9)	36.5	(3.7)	29.2	(3.4)
	Czech Republic	1.1	(0.6)	9.0	(1.8)	35.3	(3.5)	54.6	(3.5)
	Denmark	4.1	(1.2)	31.6	(3.1)	42.5	(3.5)	21.9	(3.2)
	Estonia	18.5	(2.4)	55.2	(2.6)	23.0	(1.9)	3.3	(1.1)
	Finland	0.3	(0.2)	31.2	(3.2)	54.5	(3.4)	14.0	(2.1)
	France	4.2	(1.2)	31.6	(3.1)	38.7	(3.8)	25.6	(3.0)
	Germany	0.5	(0.4)	10.4	(2.1)	45.2	(3.2)	43.9	(3.1)
	Greece	45.9	(4.2)	43.2	(4.1)	10.0	(1.8)	0.8	(0.4)
	Hungary	2.0	(0.8)	13.1	(2.2)	26.6	(3.5)	58.3	(3.3)
	Iceland	0.0	c	6.1	(0.2)	54.7	(0.2)	39.2	(0.2)
	Ireland	0.0	c	15.9	(2.8)	45.2	(4.1)	38.9	(3.9)
	Israel	39.1	(3.5)	57.9	(3.6)	2.9	(1.2)	0.0	(0.0)
	Italy	77.5	(1.6)	21.4	(1.6)	0.8	(0.2)	0.2	(0.1)
	Japan	0.5	(0.5)	2.6	(1.2)	4.2	(1.5)	92.7	(1.8)
	Korea	0.0	c	1.6	(1.0)	7.3	(1.8)	91.0	(2.1)
	Luxembourg	0.0	c	8.3	(0.1)	27.3	(0.1)	64.4	(0.1)
	Mexico	15.0	(1.2)	54.0	(1.7)	25.4	(1.4)	5.6	(0.7)
	Netherlands	0.8	(0.7)	9.2	(2.0)	43.0	(4.1)	47.1	(3.7)
	New Zealand	6.0	(1.1)	43.4	(3.8)	41.2	(3.6)	9.5	(2.0)
	Norway	0.1	(0.1)	14.9	(2.5)	52.4	(3.6)	32.6	(3.2)
	Poland	10.0	(2.3)	45.1	(3.8)	29.6	(3.7)	15.3	(2.6)
	Portugal	14.6	(3.2)	67.4	(4.2)	16.5	(3.2)	1.5	(1.3)
	Slovak Republic	3.1	(1.1)	18.4	(2.7)	42.6	(3.7)	35.9	(3.5)
	Slovenia	12.8	(0.4)	47.5	(0.8)	30.4	(0.6)	9.3	(0.8)
	Spain	37.7	(2.8)	50.9	(2.9)	9.7	(1.4)	1.8	(0.3)
	Sweden	4.5	(1.6)	32.7	(3.6)	52.9	(3.5)	9.8	(2.0)
	Switzerland	1.1	(0.5)	8.5	(1.8)	42.2	(3.1)	48.3	(3.2)
	Turkey	86.3	(2.6)	12.8	(2.4)	0.9	(0.5)	0.1	(0.1)
	United Kingdom	3.3	(1.0)	41.3	(3.2)	48.8	(3.3)	6.7	(1.8)
	United States	4.1	(1.5)	53.2	(3.7)	39.8	(3.5)	2.9	(1.4)
	OECD average	12.9	(0.3)	29.9	(0.5)	30.7	(0.5)	26.6	(0.4)
Partners	Albania	2.3	(1.0)	47.8	(3.7)	44.5	(3.9)	5.3	(1.3)
	Argentina	89.4	(2.1)	9.4	(2.0)	1.2	(1.0)	0.0	c
	Brazil	8.9	(1.1)	51.5	(2.3)	35.1	(2.5)	4.5	(1.0)
	Bulgaria	31.7	(3.0)	39.3	(3.9)	24.3	(3.3)	4.6	(1.5)
	Colombia	1.3	(0.7)	23.3	(3.5)	51.4	(4.1)	24.0	(3.5)
	Costa Rica	67.5	(3.6)	28.5	(3.5)	4.0	(1.6)	0.0	c
	Croatia	12.1	(1.8)	41.1	(3.3)	39.1	(3.4)	7.7	(2.1)
	Cyprus*	29.1	(0.1)	56.6	(0.1)	13.7	(0.1)	0.7	(0.0)
	Hong Kong-China	0.0	c	0.2	(0.0)	19.0	(3.0)	80.7	(3.0)
	Indonesia	8.7	(2.0)	51.1	(4.0)	35.7	(3.7)	4.4	(1.3)
	Jordan	71.8	(3.2)	27.3	(3.1)	0.9	(0.7)	0.0	c
	Kazakhstan	10.8	(2.3)	42.4	(4.1)	31.3	(3.6)	15.5	(2.4)
	Latvia	87.7	(2.4)	11.0	(2.4)	1.2	(0.7)	0.1	(0.1)
	Liechtenstein	0.0	c	0.0	c	19.2	(1.1)	80.8	(1.1)
	Lithuania	23.4	(3.1)	52.8	(3.5)	18.9	(2.9)	4.9	(1.4)
	Macao-China	0.9	(0.0)	3.2	(0.0)	31.2	(0.1)	64.7	(0.1)
	Malaysia	33.9	(3.8)	53.6	(4.1)	10.1	(2.2)	2.4	(1.3)
	Montenegro	20.4	(0.1)	65.6	(0.2)	13.8	(0.1)	0.2	(0.0)
	Peru	1.9	(0.8)	29.6	(3.1)	48.3	(3.6)	20.2	(3.0)
	Qatar	9.3	(0.1)	48.6	(0.1)	40.9	(0.1)	1.1	(0.0)
	Romania	70.4	(3.6)	25.5	(3.4)	3.6	(1.4)	0.5	(0.4)
	Russian Federation	21.5	(2.8)	57.3	(3.0)	15.7	(2.3)	5.5	(1.2)
	Serbia	9.9	(2.2)	50.2	(3.9)	31.0	(3.8)	8.9	(2.3)
	Shanghai-China	0.0	c	0.0	c	5.8	(1.8)	94.2	(1.8)
	Singapore	1.4	(0.0)	32.3	(0.2)	58.8	(0.2)	7.4	(0.1)
	Chinese Taipei	0.5	(0.6)	9.3	(1.9)	31.0	(3.9)	59.2	(3.8)
	Thailand	16.3	(2.0)	48.9	(3.4)	29.4	(3.0)	5.4	(1.7)
	Tunisia	13.9	(3.0)	59.6	(4.3)	24.4	(3.6)	2.1	(1.3)
	United Arab Emirates	52.8	(2.3)	41.0	(2.4)	6.1	(1.0)	0.2	(0.1)
	Uruguay	12.4	(2.3)	64.6	(3.1)	18.1	(2.3)	4.9	(1.4)
	Viet Nam	1.2	(0.6)	10.2	(2.6)	38.2	(4.0)	50.4	(4.2)

* See notes at the beginning of this Annex.

StatLink ᴍᴄ▨ http://dx.doi.org/10.1787/888932957517

[Part 1/2]
Index of teacher-student relations and mathematics performance
Table IV.5.5   *Results based on students' self-reports*

		Index of teacher-student relations									Variability in this index		School variability in the distribution of this index
		All students		Bottom quarter		Second quarter		Third quarter		Top quarter				
		Mean index	S.E.	Mean index	S.E.	Mean index	S.E.	Mean index	S.E.	Mean index	S.E.	Standard deviation	S.E.	Percentage of the index variance between schools
OECD	Australia	0.15	(0.01)	-0.96	(0.01)	-0.12	(0.01)	0.23	(0.02)	1.45	(0.02)	0.95	(0.01)	10.29
	Austria	-0.14	(0.03)	-1.40	(0.03)	-0.59	(0.04)	0.17	(0.02)	1.27	(0.03)	1.05	(0.01)	6.56
	Belgium	-0.11	(0.02)	-1.16	(0.02)	-0.37	(0.02)	0.01	(0.01)	1.09	(0.02)	0.91	(0.01)	5.39
	Canada	0.28	(0.01)	-0.90	(0.02)	-0.06	(0.01)	0.45	(0.02)	1.64	(0.02)	1.00	(0.01)	4.11
	Chile	0.19	(0.02)	-1.10	(0.03)	-0.21	(0.02)	0.48	(0.03)	1.60	(0.03)	1.06	(0.01)	3.57
	Czech Republic	-0.16	(0.03)	-1.23	(0.03)	-0.46	(0.04)	0.01	(0.02)	1.05	(0.04)	0.92	(0.01)	6.95
	Denmark	0.15	(0.02)	-0.95	(0.02)	-0.12	(0.02)	0.27	(0.04)	1.40	(0.03)	0.92	(0.01)	8.22
	Estonia	-0.08	(0.02)	-1.13	(0.02)	-0.33	(0.03)	0.05	(0.02)	1.10	(0.04)	0.89	(0.02)	6.10
	Finland	-0.09	(0.02)	-1.17	(0.02)	-0.31	(0.03)	0.01	(0.02)	1.10	(0.03)	0.90	(0.01)	5.58
	France	-0.17	(0.02)	-1.29	(0.03)	-0.55	(0.03)	0.03	(0.02)	1.11	(0.04)	0.96	(0.02)	4.88
	Germany	-0.22	(0.02)	-1.44	(0.03)	-0.62	(0.02)	0.06	(0.04)	1.13	(0.04)	1.02	(0.01)	11.44
	Greece	-0.13	(0.02)	-1.30	(0.02)	-0.54	(0.04)	0.09	(0.02)	1.22	(0.03)	1.00	(0.01)	7.37
	Hungary	-0.02	(0.02)	-1.19	(0.03)	-0.33	(0.03)	0.15	(0.02)	1.32	(0.02)	0.99	(0.01)	9.02
	Iceland	0.21	(0.02)	-1.03	(0.03)	-0.11	(0.02)	0.28	(0.03)	1.71	(0.04)	1.06	(0.02)	8.69
	Ireland	0.03	(0.02)	-1.08	(0.03)	-0.26	(0.02)	0.13	(0.02)	1.33	(0.04)	0.95	(0.01)	5.68
	Israel	0.08	(0.03)	-1.28	(0.03)	-0.33	(0.03)	0.34	(0.04)	1.60	(0.05)	1.13	(0.02)	6.22
	Italy	-0.16	(0.01)	-1.34	(0.01)	-0.55	(0.02)	0.09	(0.01)	1.16	(0.02)	1.00	(0.01)	6.84
	Japan	-0.17	(0.02)	-1.38	(0.03)	-0.51	(0.03)	0.01	(0.02)	1.19	(0.04)	1.02	(0.01)	4.43
	Korea	-0.12	(0.03)	-1.16	(0.02)	-0.35	(0.04)	-0.02	(0.00)	1.06	(0.06)	0.89	(0.02)	6.05
	Luxembourg	-0.05	(0.02)	-1.38	(0.03)	-0.44	(0.03)	0.21	(0.02)	1.41	(0.03)	1.10	(0.01)	2.54
	Mexico	0.47	(0.01)	-0.79	(0.02)	0.04	(0.01)	0.79	(0.01)	1.85	(0.02)	1.03	(0.01)	8.57
	Netherlands	-0.15	(0.02)	-1.08	(0.03)	-0.32	(0.03)	-0.02	(0.00)	0.81	(0.04)	0.78	(0.01)	9.11
	New Zealand	0.11	(0.02)	-0.97	(0.03)	-0.16	(0.02)	0.16	(0.03)	1.40	(0.04)	0.93	(0.01)	7.38
	Norway	-0.14	(0.02)	-1.33	(0.03)	-0.44	(0.03)	0.03	(0.02)	1.20	(0.04)	1.01	(0.02)	3.42
	Poland	-0.42	(0.02)	-1.53	(0.03)	-0.79	(0.02)	-0.19	(0.02)	0.82	(0.04)	0.97	(0.02)	7.77
	Portugal	0.32	(0.02)	-0.80	(0.04)	-0.02	(0.00)	0.44	(0.04)	1.67	(0.03)	0.96	(0.01)	7.41
	Slovak Republic	-0.18	(0.02)	-1.23	(0.03)	-0.48	(0.04)	-0.02	(0.00)	1.01	(0.05)	0.91	(0.01)	9.34
	Slovenia	-0.24	(0.02)	-1.30	(0.03)	-0.61	(0.01)	-0.06	(0.02)	1.01	(0.04)	0.93	(0.01)	3.68
	Spain	0.00	(0.02)	-1.20	(0.02)	-0.37	(0.02)	0.19	(0.02)	1.37	(0.02)	1.01	(0.01)	6.80
	Sweden	0.08	(0.03)	-1.12	(0.04)	-0.23	(0.02)	0.18	(0.03)	1.51	(0.04)	1.03	(0.02)	6.49
	Switzerland	0.11	(0.02)	-1.15	(0.03)	-0.22	(0.02)	0.39	(0.03)	1.44	(0.03)	1.02	(0.01)	6.94
	Turkey	0.19	(0.02)	-1.12	(0.03)	-0.24	(0.02)	0.50	(0.03)	1.62	(0.03)	1.08	(0.01)	3.80
	United Kingdom	0.15	(0.02)	-0.99	(0.03)	-0.15	(0.02)	0.27	(0.03)	1.47	(0.03)	0.97	(0.01)	7.22
	United States	0.21	(0.03)	-0.94	(0.03)	-0.12	(0.02)	0.34	(0.04)	1.55	(0.04)	0.98	(0.02)	8.70
	OECD average	0.00	(0.00)	-1.16	(0.00)	-0.33	(0.00)	0.18	(0.00)	1.31	(0.01)	0.98	(0.00)	6.87
Partners	Albania	0.71	(0.02)	-0.51	(0.03)	0.35	(0.03)	1.05	(0.03)	1.95	(0.02)	0.96	(0.01)	2.47
	Argentina	0.18	(0.03)	-1.10	(0.03)	-0.21	(0.03)	0.42	(0.03)	1.60	(0.03)	1.06	(0.01)	3.87
	Brazil	0.25	(0.02)	-1.00	(0.02)	-0.17	(0.01)	0.47	(0.03)	1.69	(0.03)	1.05	(0.01)	6.62
	Bulgaria	0.24	(0.02)	-1.07	(0.03)	-0.17	(0.02)	0.47	(0.04)	1.74	(0.03)	1.09	(0.01)	3.55
	Colombia	0.45	(0.02)	-0.82	(0.03)	0.03	(0.03)	0.78	(0.03)	1.82	(0.03)	1.03	(0.01)	6.73
	Costa Rica	0.47	(0.02)	-0.86	(0.02)	0.03	(0.04)	0.83	(0.03)	1.88	(0.03)	1.06	(0.02)	8.33
	Croatia	-0.15	(0.02)	-1.31	(0.02)	-0.50	(0.03)	0.03	(0.03)	1.20	(0.04)	1.00	(0.01)	8.35
	Cyprus*	-0.22	(0.02)	-1.43	(0.03)	-0.59	(0.03)	-0.01	(0.01)	1.16	(0.03)	1.03	(0.02)	0.46
	Hong Kong-China	0.03	(0.02)	-1.06	(0.03)	-0.21	(0.02)	0.11	(0.02)	1.29	(0.04)	0.94	(0.01)	1.67
	Indonesia	0.42	(0.02)	-0.58	(0.03)	0.00	(0.02)	0.67	(0.02)	1.61	(0.03)	0.87	(0.01)	10.25
	Jordan	0.39	(0.02)	-1.08	(0.03)	0.01	(0.03)	0.82	(0.02)	1.81	(0.02)	1.13	(0.01)	5.05
	Kazakhstan	0.75	(0.03)	-0.41	(0.03)	0.30	(0.04)	1.09	(0.03)	2.01	(0.02)	0.96	(0.01)	4.80
	Latvia	0.16	(0.02)	-0.87	(0.02)	-0.15	(0.02)	0.29	(0.04)	1.36	(0.04)	0.89	(0.01)	6.53
	Liechtenstein	0.05	(0.07)	-1.24	(0.11)	-0.37	(0.08)	0.36	(0.10)	1.49	(0.11)	1.09	(0.06)	10.27
	Lithuania	0.43	(0.02)	-0.92	(0.03)	0.05	(0.03)	0.81	(0.03)	1.79	(0.03)	1.05	(0.01)	8.87
	Macao-China	-0.04	(0.02)	-1.15	(0.02)	-0.31	(0.03)	0.06	(0.01)	1.22	(0.03)	0.95	(0.01)	6.06
	Malaysia	0.23	(0.02)	-0.88	(0.02)	-0.14	(0.02)	0.51	(0.04)	1.42	(0.04)	0.91	(0.01)	5.42
	Montenegro	0.12	(0.02)	-1.22	(0.03)	-0.23	(0.02)	0.32	(0.03)	1.63	(0.04)	1.11	(0.01)	1.61
	Peru	0.38	(0.02)	-0.82	(0.02)	-0.02	(0.03)	0.66	(0.03)	1.71	(0.03)	0.98	(0.01)	3.79
	Qatar	0.08	(0.01)	-1.28	(0.02)	-0.33	(0.02)	0.36	(0.02)	1.58	(0.02)	1.13	(0.01)	5.86
	Romania	0.37	(0.02)	-0.89	(0.03)	-0.04	(0.03)	0.67	(0.04)	1.76	(0.03)	1.03	(0.01)	4.70
	Russian Federation	0.14	(0.03)	-1.03	(0.03)	-0.25	(0.02)	0.32	(0.03)	1.53	(0.05)	1.01	(0.02)	7.03
	Serbia	0.08	(0.03)	-1.12	(0.03)	-0.26	(0.02)	0.24	(0.03)	1.48	(0.04)	1.02	(0.02)	7.82
	Shanghai-China	0.46	(0.03)	-0.73	(0.03)	-0.02	(0.00)	0.67	(0.05)	1.92	(0.04)	1.04	(0.01)	6.84
	Singapore	0.36	(0.02)	-0.74	(0.03)	-0.02	(0.00)	0.50	(0.03)	1.72	(0.02)	0.96	(0.01)	4.20
	Chinese Taipei	0.03	(0.02)	-1.19	(0.02)	-0.35	(0.03)	0.13	(0.03)	1.51	(0.03)	1.06	(0.01)	2.54
	Thailand	0.30	(0.02)	-0.76	(0.02)	-0.02	(0.00)	0.41	(0.03)	1.57	(0.03)	0.92	(0.01)	4.81
	Tunisia	-0.02	(0.03)	-1.37	(0.03)	-0.49	(0.03)	0.32	(0.03)	1.45	(0.03)	1.11	(0.01)	6.97
	United Arab Emirates	0.35	(0.02)	-0.99	(0.02)	-0.08	(0.03)	0.71	(0.02)	1.78	(0.02)	1.08	(0.01)	3.18
	Uruguay	0.19	(0.02)	-1.03	(0.03)	-0.19	(0.02)	0.41	(0.03)	1.57	(0.04)	1.02	(0.01)	7.08
	Viet Nam	0.02	(0.02)	-1.04	(0.02)	-0.30	(0.03)	0.19	(0.02)	1.22	(0.03)	0.89	(0.01)	8.13

Note: Values that are statistically significant are indicated in bold (see Annex A3).
* See notes at the beginning of this Annex.
StatLink ⫘⫘⫘ http://dx.doi.org/10.1787/888932957517

[Part 2/2]
Index of teacher-student relations and mathematics performance
Table IV.5.5   *Results based on students' self-reports*

| | Performance on the mathematics scale by national quarters of this index | | | | | | | | Change in the mathematics score per unit of this index | | Increased likelihood of students in the bottom quarter of this index scoring in the bottom quarter of the national mathematics performance distribution | | Explained variance in student performance (r-squared x 100) | |
| | Bottom quarter | | Second quarter | | Third quarter | | Top quarter | | | | | | | |
	Mean score	S.E.	Mean score	S.E.	Mean score	S.E.	Mean score	S.E.	Score dif.	S.E.	Ratio	S.E.	%	S.E.
OECD														
Australia	471	(2.6)	506	(2.8)	513	(3.3)	527	(3.0)	21.8	(1.3)	1.74	(0.1)	4.8	(0.5)
Austria	503	(4.3)	514	(4.1)	513	(4.6)	503	(4.2)	-0.9	(1.5)	1.06	(0.1)	0.0	(0.0)
Belgium	508	(3.9)	530	(3.7)	537	(4.1)	512	(3.6)	2.1	(1.9)	1.23	(0.1)	0.0	(0.1)
Canada	503	(3.4)	521	(2.8)	528	(2.9)	530	(2.9)	10.8	(1.2)	1.43	(0.1)	1.5	(0.4)
Chile	422	(4.0)	427	(4.3)	426	(4.6)	417	(4.5)	-1.2	(1.5)	0.98	(0.1)	0.0	(0.1)
Czech Republic	496	(4.8)	503	(5.1)	521	(4.2)	498	(4.4)	1.4	(2.2)	1.21	(0.1)	0.0	(0.1)
Denmark	480	(3.5)	505	(3.9)	516	(3.8)	520	(4.1)	16.3	(2.0)	1.60	(0.1)	3.4	(0.8)
Estonia	511	(3.2)	524	(3.4)	527	(4.2)	519	(4.7)	3.5	(2.3)	1.15	(0.1)	0.2	(0.2)
Finland	505	(2.8)	526	(3.6)	531	(4.3)	529	(3.3)	9.2	(1.5)	1.44	(0.1)	1.0	(0.3)
France	491	(4.4)	503	(4.4)	508	(5.2)	489	(4.7)	-1.2	(2.1)	1.06	(0.1)	0.0	(0.1)
Germany	514	(3.9)	529	(4.8)	532	(5.1)	515	(5.1)	-0.1	(2.1)	1.12	(0.1)	0.0	(0.1)
Greece	457	(4.3)	461	(4.5)	458	(4.2)	445	(4.1)	-4.9	(1.7)	0.88	(0.1)	0.3	(0.2)
Hungary	473	(6.1)	481	(5.2)	486	(4.9)	472	(4.9)	-2.2	(2.7)	1.03	(0.1)	0.1	(0.2)
Iceland	474	(4.7)	496	(4.9)	504	(5.2)	512	(4.1)	13.5	(2.2)	1.52	(0.1)	2.4	(0.8)
Ireland	488	(3.9)	505	(4.3)	507	(4.0)	504	(4.1)	6.2	(1.9)	1.32	(0.1)	0.5	(0.3)
Israel	473	(5.7)	481	(6.9)	478	(6.6)	463	(7.6)	-4.1	(2.3)	0.94	(0.1)	0.2	(0.3)
Italy	494	(2.8)	497	(3.1)	488	(3.0)	469	(2.9)	-9.1	(1.3)	0.84	(0.0)	1.0	(0.3)
Japan	520	(5.2)	543	(4.6)	544	(5.1)	542	(4.3)	8.4	(2.0)	1.39	(0.1)	0.9	(0.4)
Korea	538	(5.7)	552	(5.0)	546	(6.1)	580	(7.7)	16.4	(3.0)	1.28	(0.1)	2.2	(0.8)
Luxembourg	484	(3.2)	494	(4.2)	500	(3.8)	482	(3.2)	0.4	(1.5)	1.12	(0.1)	0.0	(0.0)
Mexico	422	(1.9)	417	(1.9)	411	(2.0)	407	(2.1)	-5.6	(0.8)	0.83	(0.0)	0.6	(0.2)
Netherlands	512	(4.3)	530	(5.3)	544	(5.2)	526	(6.6)	5.7	(2.9)	1.31	(0.1)	0.3	(0.3)
New Zealand	475	(4.1)	501	(5.0)	511	(5.4)	511	(4.3)	13.9	(2.4)	1.43	(0.1)	1.7	(0.6)
Norway	465	(5.5)	496	(4.3)	504	(5.2)	498	(5.1)	13.2	(2.4)	1.56	(0.1)	2.1	(0.8)
Poland	517	(5.6)	524	(4.7)	526	(6.0)	508	(5.6)	-4.4	(2.0)	1.00	(0.1)	0.2	(0.2)
Portugal	480	(5.2)	487	(4.7)	497	(5.5)	494	(5.8)	6.2	(2.5)	1.17	(0.1)	0.4	(0.3)
Slovak Republic	487	(6.4)	492	(5.0)	498	(4.8)	459	(6.4)	-11.7	(3.4)	0.93	(0.1)	1.1	(0.6)
Slovenia	498	(4.1)	509	(4.8)	511	(4.4)	498	(4.2)	-0.3	(2.1)	1.10	(0.1)	0.0	(0.0)
Spain	477	(3.0)	492	(3.2)	492	(3.0)	483	(3.0)	1.5	(1.3)	1.23	(0.1)	0.0	(0.1)
Sweden	465	(3.8)	484	(4.1)	489	(5.0)	492	(4.4)	9.9	(2.1)	1.30	(0.1)	1.3	(0.5)
Switzerland	521	(4.3)	541	(4.3)	538	(5.0)	527	(4.7)	1.7	(1.6)	1.12	(0.1)	0.0	(0.1)
Turkey	449	(6.2)	456	(6.5)	449	(5.7)	443	(5.7)	-3.3	(1.8)	1.09	(0.1)	0.2	(0.2)
United Kingdom	472	(4.6)	504	(4.6)	506	(4.6)	509	(5.2)	13.3	(1.9)	1.51	(0.1)	1.9	(0.5)
United States	466	(4.1)	479	(4.9)	492	(6.4)	499	(5.1)	13.9	(1.9)	1.41	(0.1)	2.3	(0.6)
OECD average	**486**	(0.8)	**500**	(0.8)	**504**	(0.8)	**497**	(0.8)	**4.1**	(0.4)	**1.22**	(0.0)	**0.9**	(0.1)
Partners														
Albania	395	(4.6)	392	(5.0)	397	(4.9)	391	(4.5)	-1.0	(2.0)	0.97	(0.1)	0.0	(0.1)
Argentina	401	(4.6)	395	(4.6)	390	(4.5)	374	(5.2)	-9.6	(1.7)	0.78	(0.1)	1.8	(0.6)
Brazil	397	(3.0)	399	(3.1)	393	(3.2)	383	(3.1)	-4.6	(1.2)	0.84	(0.1)	0.4	(0.2)
Bulgaria	456	(4.5)	440	(5.4)	445	(5.1)	424	(5.9)	-10.3	(2.0)	0.68	(0.1)	1.5	(0.6)
Colombia	390	(4.1)	383	(3.9)	379	(4.2)	372	(4.1)	-7.0	(1.5)	0.81	(0.1)	1.0	(0.4)
Costa Rica	415	(4.5)	413	(4.2)	406	(4.4)	393	(4.1)	-7.2	(1.4)	0.80	(0.1)	1.3	(0.5)
Croatia	475	(3.9)	480	(4.6)	475	(4.8)	460	(7.2)	-7.2	(2.6)	0.90	(0.1)	0.7	(0.5)
Cyprus*	432	(3.3)	446	(3.5)	452	(3.9)	445	(3.1)	5.5	(1.6)	1.15	(0.1)	0.4	(0.2)
Hong Kong-China	553	(5.1)	565	(4.5)	570	(5.5)	567	(4.9)	4.1	(2.6)	1.16	(0.1)	0.2	(0.2)
Indonesia	372	(5.7)	372	(4.4)	378	(4.7)	380	(4.7)	2.7	(1.8)	1.13	(0.1)	0.1	(0.1)
Jordan	387	(4.3)	392	(3.9)	392	(3.8)	383	(4.9)	-0.5	(1.5)	1.07	(0.1)	0.0	(0.1)
Kazakhstan	430	(4.3)	432	(4.4)	433	(4.2)	434	(4.2)	1.7	(1.8)	1.07	(0.1)	0.1	(0.1)
Latvia	485	(4.5)	496	(4.8)	496	(4.8)	484	(4.6)	-1.6	(2.7)	1.06	(0.1)	0.0	(0.1)
Liechtenstein	555	(13.7)	536	(17.6)	533	(18.6)	526	(16.2)	-5.6	(6.5)	0.59	(0.3)	0.5	(1.1)
Lithuania	469	(3.9)	480	(4.4)	479	(5.0)	485	(4.8)	5.7	(1.8)	1.15	(0.1)	0.5	(0.3)
Macao-China	533	(2.9)	542	(4.8)	538	(4.4)	546	(3.6)	4.0	(1.8)	1.12	(0.1)	0.2	(0.1)
Malaysia	423	(4.8)	428	(4.7)	422	(4.0)	414	(4.0)	-3.3	(1.8)	1.10	(0.1)	0.1	(0.2)
Montenegro	431	(3.9)	420	(3.9)	410	(3.6)	386	(3.2)	-15.5	(1.5)	0.66	(0.1)	4.4	(0.8)
Peru	379	(5.8)	378	(4.5)	373	(4.6)	364	(5.0)	-6.2	(1.8)	0.91	(0.1)	0.5	(0.3)
Qatar	371	(2.6)	383	(2.6)	389	(2.9)	385	(2.6)	4.7	(1.2)	1.16	(0.1)	0.3	(0.1)
Romania	453	(5.7)	446	(4.5)	445	(4.8)	435	(4.3)	-5.8	(1.7)	0.89	(0.1)	0.6	(0.3)
Russian Federation	479	(3.7)	485	(5.0)	488	(4.9)	479	(4.5)	-0.5	(2.0)	1.01	(0.1)	0.0	(0.1)
Serbia	457	(4.2)	459	(5.2)	452	(4.9)	429	(5.3)	-10.4	(2.0)	0.79	(0.1)	1.3	(0.5)
Shanghai-China	585	(5.1)	613	(4.9)	618	(5.2)	635	(5.2)	16.9	(2.2)	1.53	(0.1)	3.0	(0.8)
Singapore	556	(3.6)	581	(4.3)	587	(4.4)	579	(3.4)	8.3	(1.6)	1.36	(0.1)	0.6	(0.2)
Chinese Taipei	554	(4.8)	563	(5.7)	555	(5.8)	567	(4.5)	3.9	(1.9)	0.98	(0.1)	0.1	(0.1)
Thailand	432	(5.2)	425	(4.1)	429	(4.5)	424	(4.4)	-2.8	(1.9)	0.94	(0.1)	0.1	(0.2)
Tunisia	403	(5.5)	396	(5.3)	383	(5.4)	373	(4.3)	-10.2	(1.6)	0.76	(0.1)	2.2	(0.6)
United Arab Emirates	432	(3.6)	439	(3.7)	432	(3.7)	439	(3.9)	2.2	(1.3)	1.03	(0.1)	0.1	(0.1)
Uruguay	426	(3.7)	423	(3.7)	412	(5.0)	387	(4.6)	-13.1	(1.9)	0.71	(0.1)	2.3	(0.7)
Viet Nam	530	(5.3)	508	(6.6)	507	(6.0)	501	(6.0)	-10.7	(2.0)	0.58	(0.1)	1.2	(0.5)

Note: Values that are statistically significant are indicated in bold (see Annex A3).
* See notes at the beginning of this Annex.
StatLink ᴍ𝒮🖳 http://dx.doi.org/10.1787/888932957517

[Part 1/2]
Index of disciplinary climate and mathematics performance
Table IV.5.6 *Results based on students' self-reports*

		Index of disciplinary climate										Variability in this index		School variability in the distribution of this index
		All students		Bottom quarter		Second quarter		Third quarter		Top quarter				
		Mean index	S.E.	Mean index	S.E.	Mean index	S.E.	Mean index	S.E.	Mean index	S.E.	Standard deviation	S.E.	Percentage of the index variance between schools
OECD	Australia	-0.14	(0.02)	-1.45	(0.02)	-0.45	(0.02)	0.18	(0.02)	1.17	(0.02)	1.03	(0.01)	9.59
	Austria	0.21	(0.03)	-1.22	(0.04)	-0.15	(0.04)	0.65	(0.04)	1.55	(0.02)	1.08	(0.02)	17.68
	Belgium	0.04	(0.03)	-1.27	(0.03)	-0.31	(0.04)	0.37	(0.04)	1.37	(0.03)	1.04	(0.01)	10.95
	Canada	0.01	(0.01)	-1.21	(0.02)	-0.28	(0.01)	0.28	(0.02)	1.25	(0.02)	0.97	(0.01)	12.09
	Chile	-0.25	(0.03)	-1.35	(0.03)	-0.56	(0.03)	0.00	(0.03)	0.91	(0.03)	0.90	(0.01)	10.03
	Czech Republic	0.10	(0.04)	-1.30	(0.04)	-0.27	(0.05)	0.48	(0.04)	1.48	(0.04)	1.09	(0.02)	23.06
	Denmark	-0.01	(0.03)	-1.13	(0.04)	-0.27	(0.02)	0.25	(0.03)	1.11	(0.05)	0.89	(0.02)	14.37
	Estonia	0.20	(0.03)	-1.02	(0.03)	-0.13	(0.04)	0.52	(0.03)	1.43	(0.03)	0.96	(0.01)	15.74
	Finland	-0.33	(0.02)	-1.38	(0.03)	-0.59	(0.02)	-0.09	(0.02)	0.76	(0.03)	0.86	(0.02)	8.49
	France	-0.29	(0.03)	-1.59	(0.03)	-0.69	(0.03)	0.03	(0.04)	1.08	(0.03)	1.05	(0.01)	13.77
	Germany	-0.02	(0.02)	-1.30	(0.03)	-0.38	(0.03)	0.30	(0.04)	1.29	(0.03)	1.02	(0.01)	9.01
	Greece	-0.24	(0.03)	-1.33	(0.03)	-0.54	(0.03)	-0.03	(0.03)	0.92	(0.04)	0.90	(0.02)	12.22
	Hungary	0.05	(0.04)	-1.26	(0.04)	-0.26	(0.04)	0.41	(0.05)	1.33	(0.03)	1.02	(0.03)	12.30
	Iceland	-0.03	(0.02)	-1.14	(0.03)	-0.25	(0.01)	0.15	(0.02)	1.13	(0.03)	0.91	(0.02)	22.23
	Ireland	0.13	(0.03)	-1.31	(0.04)	-0.23	(0.04)	0.55	(0.03)	1.50	(0.03)	1.10	(0.02)	15.52
	Israel	0.26	(0.03)	-1.12	(0.04)	-0.11	(0.03)	0.66	(0.04)	1.61	(0.02)	1.07	(0.01)	9.77
	Italy	-0.04	(0.02)	-1.30	(0.02)	-0.39	(0.02)	0.30	(0.02)	1.22	(0.01)	0.99	(0.01)	14.37
	Japan	0.67	(0.03)	-0.52	(0.04)	0.41	(0.04)	1.02	(0.02)	1.75	(0.02)	0.90	(0.02)	17.16
	Korea	0.19	(0.03)	-0.88	(0.03)	-0.13	(0.03)	0.44	(0.03)	1.33	(0.04)	0.87	(0.01)	15.63
	Luxembourg	-0.02	(0.02)	-1.40	(0.03)	-0.39	(0.02)	0.32	(0.02)	1.38	(0.02)	1.09	(0.01)	3.95
	Mexico	0.06	(0.01)	-1.08	(0.01)	-0.24	(0.01)	0.33	(0.02)	1.22	(0.02)	0.91	(0.01)	1.78
	Netherlands	-0.16	(0.03)	-1.27	(0.03)	-0.49	(0.03)	0.08	(0.03)	1.04	(0.04)	0.92	(0.02)	14.24
	New Zealand	-0.25	(0.03)	-1.49	(0.04)	-0.56	(0.02)	0.04	(0.03)	1.03	(0.03)	1.00	(0.02)	14.14
	Norway	-0.08	(0.03)	-1.14	(0.04)	-0.29	(0.02)	0.12	(0.03)	1.02	(0.04)	0.87	(0.02)	7.82
	Poland	0.08	(0.04)	-1.30	(0.06)	-0.23	(0.04)	0.48	(0.04)	1.36	(0.03)	1.05	(0.02)	19.54
	Portugal	0.00	(0.03)	-1.22	(0.04)	-0.30	(0.03)	0.28	(0.04)	1.25	(0.03)	0.97	(0.01)	16.56
	Slovak Republic	-0.13	(0.03)	-1.29	(0.04)	-0.44	(0.03)	0.14	(0.03)	1.05	(0.04)	0.93	(0.02)	15.94
	Slovenia	0.06	(0.02)	-1.26	(0.02)	-0.30	(0.02)	0.43	(0.04)	1.39	(0.03)	1.04	(0.01)	14.67
	Spain	-0.04	(0.02)	-1.35	(0.03)	-0.37	(0.02)	0.29	(0.02)	1.26	(0.03)	1.03	(0.01)	14.53
	Sweden	-0.20	(0.03)	-1.29	(0.03)	-0.49	(0.03)	0.02	(0.02)	0.96	(0.04)	0.89	(0.01)	11.83
	Switzerland	0.07	(0.03)	-1.17	(0.04)	-0.27	(0.02)	0.41	(0.04)	1.32	(0.03)	0.98	(0.01)	6.30
	Turkey	-0.09	(0.02)	-1.22	(0.03)	-0.35	(0.02)	0.13	(0.02)	1.08	(0.03)	0.91	(0.01)	10.89
	United Kingdom	0.15	(0.02)	-1.24	(0.03)	-0.17	(0.03)	0.55	(0.03)	1.45	(0.03)	1.07	(0.01)	11.52
	United States	0.06	(0.03)	-1.19	(0.04)	-0.25	(0.02)	0.36	(0.05)	1.35	(0.03)	1.00	(0.02)	8.38
	OECD average	0.00	(0.00)	-1.24	(0.01)	-0.32	(0.00)	0.31	(0.01)	1.25	(0.01)	0.98	(0.00)	13.99
Partners	Albania	0.39	(0.03)	-0.86	(0.03)	0.09	(0.04)	0.76	(0.04)	1.58	(0.02)	0.96	(0.01)	4.96
	Argentina	-0.51	(0.03)	-1.57	(0.03)	-0.80	(0.03)	-0.28	(0.03)	0.63	(0.05)	0.88	(0.02)	7.73
	Brazil	-0.34	(0.02)	-1.49	(0.02)	-0.66	(0.02)	-0.10	(0.02)	0.86	(0.03)	0.94	(0.01)	16.04
	Bulgaria	-0.20	(0.03)	-1.36	(0.04)	-0.45	(0.04)	0.11	(0.03)	0.90	(0.03)	0.91	(0.01)	17.07
	Colombia	-0.05	(0.02)	-1.12	(0.03)	-0.28	(0.02)	0.19	(0.03)	1.01	(0.03)	0.85	(0.02)	10.34
	Costa Rica	0.04	(0.03)	-1.04	(0.03)	-0.25	(0.02)	0.28	(0.03)	1.17	(0.05)	0.88	(0.02)	12.14
	Croatia	-0.12	(0.03)	-1.43	(0.04)	-0.43	(0.04)	0.21	(0.04)	1.17	(0.04)	1.02	(0.01)	15.84
	Cyprus*	-0.19	(0.02)	-1.32	(0.03)	-0.46	(0.02)	0.03	(0.01)	0.99	(0.03)	0.92	(0.01)	9.77
	Hong Kong-China	0.29	(0.02)	-0.93	(0.04)	-0.02	(0.02)	0.55	(0.03)	1.55	(0.03)	0.97	(0.01)	6.41
	Indonesia	0.12	(0.02)	-0.96	(0.03)	-0.17	(0.02)	0.36	(0.03)	1.27	(0.03)	0.88	(0.02)	13.89
	Jordan	-0.23	(0.03)	-1.51	(0.03)	-0.64	(0.03)	0.03	(0.04)	1.20	(0.04)	1.07	(0.01)	15.44
	Kazakhstan	0.72	(0.03)	-0.64	(0.04)	0.45	(0.05)	1.20	(0.06)	1.85	(0.00)	0.99	(0.01)	11.06
	Latvia	0.08	(0.04)	-1.11	(0.05)	-0.24	(0.03)	0.38	(0.06)	1.30	(0.04)	0.95	(0.02)	22.38
	Liechtenstein	0.25	(0.07)	-1.03	(0.12)	-0.07	(0.08)	0.59	(0.11)	1.53	(0.08)	1.01	(0.05)	20.05
	Lithuania	0.28	(0.03)	-1.09	(0.03)	-0.09	(0.03)	0.66	(0.04)	1.63	(0.03)	1.06	(0.01)	15.51
	Macao-China	0.10	(0.01)	-0.86	(0.02)	-0.14	(0.01)	0.29	(0.02)	1.11	(0.02)	0.79	(0.01)	18.09
	Malaysia	-0.21	(0.02)	-1.21	(0.03)	-0.49	(0.02)	0.00	(0.02)	0.85	(0.02)	0.83	(0.01)	12.15
	Montenegro	-0.02	(0.02)	-1.31	(0.03)	-0.34	(0.02)	0.35	(0.03)	1.23	(0.02)	1.01	(0.01)	3.58
	Peru	-0.04	(0.02)	-1.01	(0.03)	-0.26	(0.02)	0.20	(0.03)	0.93	(0.03)	0.78	(0.01)	9.14
	Qatar	-0.32	(0.01)	-1.67	(0.02)	-0.77	(0.02)	-0.01	(0.02)	1.17	(0.02)	1.12	(0.01)	10.78
	Romania	0.01	(0.04)	-1.22	(0.04)	-0.36	(0.04)	0.30	(0.05)	1.34	(0.04)	1.00	(0.02)	10.28
	Russian Federation	0.35	(0.03)	-0.98	(0.04)	0.01	(0.04)	0.74	(0.04)	1.62	(0.03)	1.02	(0.02)	17.92
	Serbia	-0.16	(0.03)	-1.45	(0.04)	-0.46	(0.04)	0.16	(0.03)	1.13	(0.04)	1.02	(0.02)	15.43
	Shanghai-China	0.57	(0.03)	-0.64	(0.03)	0.25	(0.03)	0.94	(0.03)	1.75	(0.03)	0.95	(0.01)	14.37
	Singapore	0.21	(0.02)	-1.09	(0.03)	-0.09	(0.02)	0.56	(0.02)	1.46	(0.02)	1.00	(0.01)	11.10
	Chinese Taipei	-0.01	(0.03)	-1.23	(0.03)	-0.28	(0.02)	0.19	(0.04)	1.28	(0.04)	0.98	(0.01)	10.04
	Thailand	0.07	(0.02)	-0.88	(0.03)	-0.14	(0.01)	0.26	(0.02)	1.02	(0.03)	0.77	(0.01)	6.25
	Tunisia	-0.43	(0.02)	-1.47	(0.03)	-0.74	(0.02)	-0.23	(0.03)	0.71	(0.03)	0.87	(0.01)	18.00
	United Arab Emirates	0.02	(0.02)	-1.29	(0.02)	-0.36	(0.02)	0.37	(0.03)	1.37	(0.02)	1.04	(0.01)	10.97
	Uruguay	-0.16	(0.02)	-1.40	(0.03)	-0.48	(0.04)	0.15	(0.03)	1.07	(0.03)	0.98	(0.01)	11.37
	Viet Nam	0.36	(0.02)	-0.49	(0.03)	0.11	(0.02)	0.58	(0.02)	1.25	(0.02)	0.70	(0.01)	18.65

Note: Values that are statistically significant are indicated in bold (see Annex A3).
* See notes at the beginning of this Annex.
StatLink ⧉ http://dx.doi.org/10.1787/888932957517

[Part 2/2]
Index of disciplinary climate and mathematics performance
Table IV.5.6 *Results based on students' self-reports*

| | Performance on the mathematics scale by national quarters of this index | | | | | | | | Change in the mathematics score per unit of this index | | Increased likelihood of students in the bottom quarter of this index scoring in the bottom quarter of the national mathematics performance distribution | | Explained variance in student performance (r-squared x 100) | |
| | Bottom quarter | | Second quarter | | Third quarter | | Top quarter | | | | | | | |
	Mean score	S.E.	Mean score	S.E.	Mean score	S.E.	Mean score	S.E.	Score dif.	S.E.	Ratio	S.E.	%	S.E.
Australia	465	(2.6)	491	(2.7)	515	(2.9)	546	(3.1)	**29.7**	(1.4)	**1.89**	(0.1)	10.4	(0.9)
Austria	487	(5.4)	502	(4.2)	513	(4.8)	531	(4.9)	**14.6**	(2.3)	**1.53**	(0.1)	3.0	(0.9)
Belgium	496	(4.0)	518	(3.7)	530	(3.7)	544	(3.9)	**17.2**	(1.9)	**1.52**	(0.1)	3.3	(0.7)
Canada	496	(2.9)	514	(3.5)	528	(3.1)	545	(2.9)	**18.0**	(1.2)	**1.59**	(0.1)	4.0	(0.5)
Chile	412	(5.0)	424	(4.1)	423	(4.0)	432	(4.1)	**8.2**	(2.1)	**1.30**	(0.1)	0.8	(0.5)
Czech Republic	474	(5.5)	494	(4.8)	516	(5.2)	534	(5.4)	**20.3**	(2.3)	**1.81**	(0.2)	6.0	(1.3)
Denmark	489	(3.7)	500	(4.1)	507	(4.2)	524	(3.4)	**13.8**	(2.0)	**1.40**	(0.1)	2.2	(0.6)
Estonia	498	(3.6)	515	(4.5)	529	(3.8)	540	(3.7)	**16.8**	(1.9)	**1.55**	(0.1)	4.0	(0.9)
Finland	509	(3.7)	523	(4.0)	523	(3.4)	534	(3.6)	**8.6**	(2.0)	**1.32**	(0.1)	0.8	(0.4)
France	482	(4.2)	482	(4.9)	503	(4.3)	526	(4.3)	**16.4**	(1.8)	**1.25**	(0.1)	3.2	(0.7)
Germany	499	(5.4)	515	(4.8)	530	(5.8)	548	(4.3)	**17.5**	(2.1)	**1.65**	(0.2)	3.8	(0.9)
Greece	430	(4.1)	446	(4.5)	459	(3.8)	486	(3.9)	**21.6**	(2.0)	**1.75**	(0.1)	5.0	(0.9)
Hungary	451	(4.6)	461	(4.8)	484	(5.6)	517	(6.7)	**25.2**	(2.7)	**1.60**	(0.2)	8.0	(1.5)
Iceland	481	(4.8)	496	(5.0)	501	(4.8)	507	(4.3)	**12.4**	(2.6)	**1.32**	(0.1)	1.5	(0.6)
Ireland	472	(4.4)	493	(4.7)	514	(4.0)	526	(4.2)	**19.6**	(1.8)	**1.82**	(0.2)	6.5	(1.1)
Israel	426	(6.5)	470	(5.8)	497	(6.1)	502	(6.1)	**26.2**	(2.2)	**2.07**	(0.1)	7.4	(1.1)
Italy	464	(2.6)	477	(2.6)	497	(3.0)	511	(3.1)	**17.9**	(1.3)	**1.50**	(0.1)	3.7	(0.5)
Japan	504	(5.6)	539	(5.1)	548	(4.5)	557	(5.1)	**22.7**	(2.6)	**1.84**	(0.1)	4.9	(1.0)
Korea	531	(6.1)	541	(5.0)	563	(6.2)	581	(7.3)	**22.2**	(3.2)	**1.50**	(0.1)	3.9	(1.1)
Luxembourg	469	(3.6)	480	(4.0)	499	(3.3)	513	(3.1)	**15.2**	(1.4)	**1.41**	(0.1)	3.1	(0.6)
Mexico	401	(2.1)	411	(1.6)	417	(1.8)	428	(2.0)	**11.3**	(1.0)	**1.41**	(0.1)	1.9	(0.3)
Netherlands	507	(5.5)	529	(5.6)	534	(5.5)	548	(5.6)	**15.5**	(2.9)	**1.44**	(0.1)	2.7	(0.9)
New Zealand	463	(3.6)	486	(4.9)	507	(4.7)	543	(4.8)	**29.8**	(2.3)	**1.80**	(0.2)	9.2	(1.4)
Norway	470	(4.7)	490	(4.3)	497	(4.9)	507	(4.8)	**15.5**	(2.2)	**1.44**	(0.1)	2.2	(0.6)
Poland	502	(5.2)	513	(4.3)	525	(5.3)	534	(6.7)	**11.8**	(2.3)	**1.35**	(0.1)	1.9	(0.7)
Portugal	475	(5.6)	483	(5.9)	488	(5.4)	513	(4.5)	**14.5**	(2.3)	**1.34**	(0.1)	2.3	(0.7)
Slovak Republic	453	(6.0)	479	(5.7)	495	(5.2)	510	(4.8)	**22.7**	(2.8)	**1.82**	(0.1)	4.5	(1.1)
Slovenia	474	(3.3)	487	(3.7)	519	(5.3)	536	(4.8)	**23.5**	(1.8)	**1.61**	(0.1)	7.3	(1.1)
Spain	467	(3.6)	480	(3.4)	492	(2.6)	505	(3.2)	**13.6**	(1.6)	**1.51**	(0.1)	2.6	(0.6)
Sweden	464	(4.0)	483	(4.5)	484	(4.3)	497	(4.1)	**11.5**	(2.3)	**1.37**	(0.1)	1.3	(0.5)
Switzerland	512	(4.4)	528	(4.0)	539	(4.5)	546	(5.0)	**12.6**	(2.2)	**1.40**	(0.1)	1.8	(0.6)
Turkey	425	(4.9)	435	(5.2)	458	(7.3)	479	(7.7)	**21.8**	(2.8)	**1.45**	(0.1)	4.9	(1.1)
United Kingdom	466	(4.2)	485	(4.6)	513	(4.7)	526	(5.1)	**23.0**	(1.9)	**1.80**	(0.1)	6.9	(1.1)
United States	447	(4.9)	477	(4.8)	499	(5.5)	515	(4.7)	**25.3**	(1.9)	**1.91**	(0.1)	8.1	(1.1)
OECD average	472	(0.8)	490	(0.8)	504	(0.8)	520	(0.8)	**18.1**	(0.4)	**1.57**	(0.0)	4.2	(0.2)
Albania	389	(4.6)	399	(4.6)	395	(5.3)	392	(4.9)	0.8	(2.6)	1.09	(0.1)	0.0	(0.1)
Argentina	380	(4.9)	386	(4.9)	393	(4.5)	403	(5.2)	9.2	(2.5)	1.35	(0.1)	1.2	(0.6)
Brazil	376	(2.9)	391	(3.0)	397	(2.9)	407	(3.0)	11.6	(1.4)	1.43	(0.1)	2.0	(0.5)
Bulgaria	407	(5.6)	438	(5.1)	452	(5.5)	469	(6.0)	25.8	(3.1)	1.92	(0.2)	6.4	(1.4)
Colombia	368	(4.2)	378	(4.3)	381	(4.1)	394	(3.9)	11.6	(1.9)	1.44	(0.1)	1.8	(0.6)
Costa Rica	400	(3.4)	406	(3.8)	404	(5.9)	416	(5.2)	7.1	(2.6)	1.09	(0.1)	0.8	(0.6)
Croatia	438	(3.9)	460	(4.6)	480	(5.3)	513	(7.4)	26.7	(2.8)	1.83	(0.1)	9.6	(1.7)
Cyprus*	423	(3.4)	438	(3.4)	450	(3.3)	465	(3.4)	15.3	(1.9)	1.58	(0.1)	2.4	(0.6)
Hong Kong-China	542	(5.7)	559	(4.4)	575	(4.4)	578	(4.5)	14.1	(2.3)	1.49	(0.1)	2.1	(0.7)
Indonesia	360	(5.9)	386	(4.9)	387	(5.5)	369	(4.1)	3.8	(2.1)	1.54	(0.1)	0.2	(0.2)
Jordan	367	(4.3)	378	(3.9)	400	(4.1)	407	(5.9)	14.4	(2.2)	1.55	(0.1)	4.1	(1.1)
Kazakhstan	411	(3.8)	429	(4.9)	442	(4.8)	446	(4.5)	14.7	(1.7)	1.65	(0.1)	4.3	(0.9)
Latvia	478	(4.6)	485	(4.8)	494	(5.5)	503	(5.3)	10.6	(2.1)	1.41	(0.1)	1.5	(0.6)
Liechtenstein	520	(14.1)	536	(18.5)	536	(15.0)	554	(15.4)	14.4	(6.7)	1.14	(0.4)	2.4	(2.2)
Lithuania	445	(3.8)	471	(5.1)	491	(4.0)	506	(4.5)	21.1	(2.0)	1.99	(0.1)	6.3	(1.1)
Macao-China	524	(3.3)	533	(3.5)	544	(3.2)	559	(3.1)	16.2	(2.1)	1.38	(0.1)	1.9	(0.5)
Malaysia	388	(4.7)	415	(4.5)	432	(4.1)	452	(4.6)	29.4	(2.1)	2.06	(0.2)	9.3	(1.4)
Montenegro	390	(3.5)	406	(3.2)	420	(3.7)	428	(4.2)	13.3	(1.7)	1.54	(0.1)	2.6	(0.7)
Peru	359	(5.2)	369	(5.5)	376	(4.7)	382	(4.7)	11.1	(2.7)	1.50	(0.1)	1.1	(0.5)
Qatar	353	(2.9)	353	(2.3)	399	(2.8)	422	(2.8)	23.1	(1.2)	1.56	(0.1)	6.8	(0.7)
Romania	424	(5.1)	431	(4.8)	452	(4.9)	474	(5.8)	20.5	(2.2)	1.56	(0.1)	6.5	(1.3)
Russian Federation	462	(3.6)	478	(5.0)	491	(4.4)	500	(4.7)	14.6	(1.7)	1.52	(0.1)	3.1	(0.7)
Serbia	422	(5.6)	444	(4.4)	457	(5.6)	475	(5.6)	19.7	(2.3)	1.65	(0.1)	4.8	(1.1)
Shanghai-China	572	(5.4)	598	(5.8)	631	(4.5)	649	(4.4)	33.4	(2.5)	1.96	(0.1)	9.9	(1.2)
Singapore	527	(3.6)	564	(3.7)	598	(3.6)	614	(3.3)	33.7	(1.9)	2.38	(0.1)	10.7	(1.1)
Chinese Taipei	527	(4.9)	551	(5.5)	564	(5.4)	598	(5.9)	26.7	(2.6)	1.61	(0.1)	5.3	(1.0)
Thailand	404	(4.6)	425	(4.7)	441	(4.3)	440	(4.7)	17.6	(2.2)	1.60	(0.2)	2.8	(0.7)
Tunisia	382	(4.4)	383	(5.0)	391	(5.3)	400	(5.1)	6.4	(1.9)	1.13	(0.1)	0.5	(0.3)
United Arab Emirates	402	(3.2)	432	(3.6)	451	(4.3)	458	(4.6)	19.7	(1.8)	1.85	(0.1)	5.5	(0.9)
Uruguay	386	(3.8)	405	(4.7)	422	(5.1)	435	(4.2)	19.0	(2.2)	1.64	(0.1)	4.5	(1.0)
Viet Nam	499	(6.4)	513	(5.6)	519	(5.6)	516	(7.2)	8.4	(3.3)	1.25	(0.1)	0.5	(0.4)

Note: Values that are statistically significant are indicated in bold (see Annex A3).
* See notes at the beginning of this Annex.
StatLink ⟨ms⟩ http://dx.doi.org/10.1787/888932957517

[Part 1/2]
Index of teacher-related factors affecting school climate and mathematics performance
Table IV.5.7   *Results based on school principals' reports*

		Index of teacher-related factors affecting school climate										Variability in this index	
		All students		Bottom quarter		Second quarter		Third quarter		Top quarter			
		Mean index	S.E.	Mean index	S.E.	Mean index	S.E.	Mean index	S.E.	Mean index	S.E.	Standard deviation	S.E.
OECD	Australia	-0.15	(0.03)	-1.18	(0.04)	-0.54	(0.03)	-0.07	(0.03)	1.21	(0.09)	0.99	(0.04)
	Austria	-0.16	(0.07)	-1.18	(0.09)	-0.48	(0.07)	0.01	(0.08)	1.01	(0.13)	0.88	(0.05)
	Belgium	-0.26	(0.05)	-1.19	(0.04)	-0.62	(0.04)	-0.09	(0.08)	0.89	(0.09)	0.83	(0.04)
	Canada	0.10	(0.04)	-0.99	(0.05)	-0.31	(0.04)	0.30	(0.06)	1.40	(0.08)	0.97	(0.04)
	Chile	-0.55	(0.08)	-1.80	(0.13)	-0.84	(0.08)	-0.29	(0.09)	0.74	(0.16)	1.02	(0.07)
	Czech Republic	0.19	(0.05)	-0.67	(0.05)	-0.15	(0.06)	0.27	(0.06)	1.31	(0.12)	0.81	(0.04)
	Denmark	0.13	(0.06)	-0.89	(0.06)	-0.32	(0.05)	0.24	(0.10)	1.48	(0.13)	0.94	(0.05)
	Estonia	0.14	(0.05)	-0.94	(0.06)	-0.20	(0.06)	0.38	(0.07)	1.31	(0.10)	0.89	(0.04)
	Finland	-0.08	(0.05)	-0.95	(0.04)	-0.43	(0.05)	0.04	(0.08)	1.03	(0.09)	0.78	(0.03)
	France	-0.17	(0.06)	-1.14	(0.06)	-0.54	(0.06)	0.00	(0.08)	1.02	(0.11)	0.88	(0.06)
	Germany	-0.31	(0.05)	-1.02	(0.05)	-0.58	(0.04)	-0.27	(0.05)	0.64	(0.14)	0.71	(0.06)
	Greece	-0.16	(0.09)	-1.57	(0.13)	-0.56	(0.08)	0.10	(0.10)	1.39	(0.16)	1.19	(0.07)
	Hungary	0.37	(0.07)	-0.64	(0.06)	0.01	(0.07)	0.54	(0.08)	1.57	(0.15)	0.89	(0.06)
	Iceland	0.05	(0.01)	-0.99	(0.00)	-0.35	(0.01)	0.28	(0.01)	1.28	(0.01)	0.92	(0.01)
	Ireland	0.10	(0.08)	-1.02	(0.08)	-0.31	(0.07)	0.30	(0.12)	1.44	(0.16)	0.99	(0.07)
	Israel	-0.37	(0.08)	-1.60	(0.13)	-0.67	(0.08)	-0.09	(0.09)	0.88	(0.14)	1.02	(0.08)
	Italy	-0.29	(0.04)	-1.35	(0.05)	-0.62	(0.04)	-0.15	(0.04)	0.98	(0.09)	0.95	(0.04)
	Japan	-0.31	(0.06)	-1.15	(0.06)	-0.59	(0.05)	-0.23	(0.05)	0.74	(0.14)	0.81	(0.06)
	Korea	0.04	(0.10)	-1.14	(0.17)	-0.35	(0.06)	0.04	(0.08)	1.60	(0.23)	1.14	(0.12)
	Luxembourg	-0.29	(0.00)	-1.10	(0.00)	-0.65	(0.00)	-0.10	(0.00)	0.68	(0.00)	0.73	(0.00)
	Mexico	-0.27	(0.04)	-1.39	(0.05)	-0.63	(0.04)	-0.10	(0.04)	1.05	(0.05)	0.99	(0.02)
	Netherlands	-0.85	(0.04)	-1.50	(0.06)	-1.03	(0.05)	-0.72	(0.05)	-0.17	(0.08)	0.53	(0.04)
	New Zealand	-0.16	(0.07)	-1.03	(0.06)	-0.53	(0.07)	-0.02	(0.11)	0.92	(0.11)	0.79	(0.05)
	Norway	-0.45	(0.06)	-1.22	(0.05)	-0.80	(0.04)	-0.38	(0.06)	0.61	(0.15)	0.80	(0.07)
	Poland	0.47	(0.06)	-0.51	(0.07)	0.08	(0.07)	0.69	(0.10)	1.62	(0.08)	0.86	(0.04)
	Portugal	0.11	(0.09)	-0.96	(0.14)	-0.23	(0.08)	0.27	(0.10)	1.37	(0.14)	0.95	(0.07)
	Slovak Republic	0.04	(0.06)	-0.82	(0.04)	-0.28	(0.06)	0.18	(0.08)	1.08	(0.11)	0.76	(0.04)
	Slovenia	-0.08	(0.01)	-1.06	(0.02)	-0.42	(0.01)	0.00	(0.01)	1.17	(0.02)	0.92	(0.01)
	Spain	-0.19	(0.05)	-1.28	(0.05)	-0.56	(0.06)	0.01	(0.06)	1.06	(0.12)	0.94	(0.05)
	Sweden	-0.09	(0.07)	-1.18	(0.08)	-0.48	(0.06)	-0.02	(0.08)	1.31	(0.15)	1.02	(0.07)
	Switzerland	0.01	(0.05)	-0.87	(0.06)	-0.29	(0.05)	0.19	(0.07)	1.02	(0.08)	0.77	(0.04)
	Turkey	-0.23	(0.08)	-1.48	(0.09)	-0.68	(0.09)	0.00	(0.12)	1.25	(0.11)	1.12	(0.05)
	United Kingdom	0.38	(0.07)	-0.72	(0.05)	-0.12	(0.06)	0.45	(0.09)	1.90	(0.14)	1.05	(0.05)
	United States	0.13	(0.10)	-1.09	(0.10)	-0.39	(0.07)	0.20	(0.13)	1.80	(0.20)	1.16	(0.08)
	OECD average	-0.09	(0.01)	-1.11	(0.01)	-0.46	(0.01)	0.06	(0.01)	1.13	(0.02)	0.91	(0.01)
Partners	Albania	0.55	(0.08)	-0.70	(0.12)	0.18	(0.08)	0.79	(0.10)	1.94	(0.15)	1.06	(0.07)
	Argentina	-0.39	(0.07)	-1.47	(0.07)	-0.79	(0.08)	-0.20	(0.12)	0.92	(0.10)	0.93	(0.04)
	Brazil	-0.33	(0.06)	-1.78	(0.09)	-0.78	(0.07)	-0.15	(0.06)	1.41	(0.13)	1.27	(0.06)
	Bulgaria	0.37	(0.10)	-1.29	(0.10)	-0.13	(0.12)	0.76	(0.15)	2.13	(0.13)	1.33	(0.05)
	Colombia	-0.53	(0.08)	-1.89	(0.12)	-0.89	(0.08)	-0.26	(0.09)	0.92	(0.14)	1.13	(0.06)
	Costa Rica	-0.45	(0.06)	-1.45	(0.06)	-0.78	(0.06)	-0.33	(0.08)	0.76	(0.15)	0.91	(0.08)
	Croatia	-0.31	(0.08)	-1.25	(0.08)	-0.68	(0.06)	-0.18	(0.10)	0.89	(0.14)	0.87	(0.05)
	Cyprus*	-0.43	(0.00)	-1.36	(0.00)	-0.70	(0.00)	-0.25	(0.00)	0.59	(0.00)	0.83	(0.00)
	Hong Kong-China	-0.37	(0.07)	-1.23	(0.06)	-0.69	(0.04)	-0.33	(0.06)	0.76	(0.18)	0.86	(0.08)
	Indonesia	0.30	(0.08)	-0.83	(0.09)	-0.04	(0.08)	0.49	(0.09)	1.60	(0.17)	0.99	(0.07)
	Jordan	-0.48	(0.09)	-2.00	(0.15)	-0.92	(0.07)	-0.23	(0.11)	1.22	(0.17)	1.28	(0.08)
	Kazakhstan	-0.57	(0.13)	-2.51	(0.12)	-1.37	(0.18)	0.01	(0.20)	1.59	(0.15)	1.61	(0.07)
	Latvia	0.13	(0.07)	-0.87	(0.09)	-0.25	(0.06)	0.33	(0.10)	1.30	(0.13)	0.89	(0.05)
	Liechtenstein	-0.12	(0.01)	c	c	c	c	c	c	c	c	0.66	(0.01)
	Lithuania	0.54	(0.05)	-0.38	(0.07)	0.29	(0.06)	0.72	(0.06)	1.54	(0.09)	0.76	(0.04)
	Macao-China	-0.09	(0.00)	-1.52	(0.00)	-0.60	(0.00)	-0.01	(0.00)	1.77	(0.00)	1.31	(0.00)
	Malaysia	0.05	(0.08)	-1.07	(0.12)	-0.30	(0.08)	0.24	(0.10)	1.33	(0.14)	0.98	(0.07)
	Montenegro	0.08	(0.00)	-0.84	(0.00)	-0.15	(0.00)	0.18	(0.00)	1.14	(0.00)	0.79	(0.00)
	Peru	-0.32	(0.06)	-1.61	(0.11)	-0.70	(0.08)	-0.05	(0.07)	1.06	(0.12)	1.08	(0.06)
	Qatar	0.45	(0.00)	-1.21	(0.00)	0.13	(0.00)	0.85	(0.00)	2.03	(0.00)	1.33	(0.00)
	Romania	0.58	(0.08)	-0.53	(0.08)	0.23	(0.07)	0.72	(0.09)	1.92	(0.15)	0.99	(0.05)
	Russian Federation	-0.27	(0.08)	-1.94	(0.11)	-0.64	(0.10)	0.17	(0.08)	1.32	(0.14)	1.27	(0.07)
	Serbia	-0.01	(0.09)	-1.09	(0.08)	-0.41	(0.07)	0.10	(0.10)	1.35	(0.19)	0.98	(0.07)
	Shanghai-China	-0.64	(0.12)	-2.60	(0.15)	-1.15	(0.21)	-0.04	(0.11)	1.25	(0.18)	1.52	(0.08)
	Singapore	0.06	(0.00)	-1.00	(0.00)	-0.45	(0.00)	0.05	(0.01)	1.64	(0.01)	1.09	(0.01)
	Chinese Taipei	0.02	(0.11)	-1.49	(0.16)	-0.44	(0.09)	0.26	(0.12)	1.74	(0.17)	1.28	(0.07)
	Thailand	-0.08	(0.07)	-1.10	(0.08)	-0.35	(0.07)	0.13	(0.08)	0.98	(0.12)	0.83	(0.05)
	Tunisia	-0.70	(0.07)	-1.62	(0.09)	-0.98	(0.05)	-0.58	(0.07)	0.37	(0.15)	0.81	(0.07)
	United Arab Emirates	0.04	(0.06)	-1.65	(0.10)	-0.39	(0.09)	0.44	(0.07)	1.76	(0.11)	1.38	(0.05)
	Uruguay	-0.67	(0.06)	-1.88	(0.10)	-1.01	(0.07)	-0.37	(0.07)	0.59	(0.13)	1.01	(0.07)
	Viet Nam	-0.10	(0.06)	-0.96	(0.08)	-0.35	(0.08)	0.05	(0.05)	0.87	(0.09)	0.72	(0.04)

Note: Values that are statistically significant are indicated in bold (see Annex A3).
* See notes at the beginning of this Annex.
StatLink ᴀ╤╘ http://dx.doi.org/10.1787/888932957517

[Part 2/2]
Index of teacher-related factors affecting school climate and mathematics performance

Table IV.5.7 *Results based on school principals' reports*

| | Performance on the mathematics scale by national quarters of this index | | | | | | | | Change in the mathematics score per unit of this index | | Increased likelihood of students in the bottom quarter of this index scoring in the bottom quarter of the national mathematics performance distribution | | Explained variance in student performance (r-squared x 100) | |
| | Bottom quarter | | Second quarter | | Third quarter | | Top quarter | | | | | | | |
	Mean score	S.E.	Mean score	S.E.	Mean score	S.E.	Mean score	S.E.	Score dif.	S.E.	Ratio	S.E.	%	S.E.
Australia	**480**	(3.3)	502	(4.2)	514	(4.5)	**522**	(3.9)	**15.9**	(1.9)	**1.51**	(0.1)	2.7	(0.7)
Austria	493	(9.8)	498	(8.2)	512	(10.0)	517	(10.1)	9.1	(5.3)	1.16	(0.2)	0.7	(0.9)
Belgium	**474**	(8.0)	521	(8.4)	535	(8.7)	**531**	(7.9)	**24.4**	(4.9)	**1.92**	(0.2)	3.9	(1.6)
Canada	**510**	(5.0)	516	(3.6)	520	(4.6)	**527**	(4.1)	**6.1**	(2.5)	**1.19**	(0.1)	0.4	(0.4)
Chile	**392**	(5.8)	416	(7.0)	433	(7.6)	**451**	(7.4)	**21.4**	(3.8)	**1.78**	(0.2)	7.4	(2.2)
Czech Republic	486	(8.5)	502	(8.9)	500	(9.8)	**511**	(8.5)	7.6	(4.5)	1.25	(0.2)	0.4	(0.5)
Denmark	**485**	(4.7)	501	(5.4)	507	(5.7)	510	(6.2)	**8.6**	(2.4)	**1.47**	(0.1)	1.0	(0.5)
Estonia	**512**	(4.4)	514	(3.5)	521	(5.7)	**532**	(6.1)	**8.2**	(2.9)	1.15	(0.1)	0.8	(0.6)
Finland	514	(3.9)	520	(3.5)	521	(4.7)	520	(3.9)	1.9	(2.3)	1.07	(0.1)	0.0	(0.1)
France	**468**	(9.1)	489	(8.9)	521	(8.9)	508	(8.6)	**16.0**	(6.0)	**1.61**	(0.2)	2.1	(1.5)
Germany	485	(8.3)	530	(9.5)	527	(11.0)	**512**	(10.1)	12.1	(6.8)	**1.57**	(0.2)	0.8	(0.9)
Greece	**440**	(6.6)	443	(7.6)	467	(6.9)	**462**	(7.3)	3.8	(2.7)	1.28	(0.2)	0.3	(0.4)
Hungary	**452**	(8.0)	488	(10.1)	473	(9.4)	**499**	(9.1)	**19.5**	(5.7)	**1.48**	(0.3)	3.4	(2.3)
Iceland	488	(3.1)	498	(3.7)	490	(3.5)	496	(3.2)	-0.5	(1.6)	1.07	(0.1)	0.0	(0.0)
Ireland	**485**	(7.6)	503	(6.9)	502	(5.7)	**518**	(6.1)	**11.2**	(3.3)	**1.47**	(0.2)	1.7	(1.0)
Israel	459	(12.1)	470	(11.0)	473	(11.1)	470	(11.8)	6.7	(6.3)	1.17	(0.2)	0.4	(0.8)
Italy	482	(5.9)	495	(5.0)	488	(5.9)	488	(5.3)	0.8	(3.2)	1.10	(0.1)	0.0	(0.1)
Japan	**511**	(8.0)	529	(11.2)	542	(8.8)	**563**	(9.6)	**22.2**	(6.0)	**1.50**	(0.2)	3.7	(2.0)
Korea	544	(8.9)	560	(9.4)	541	(10.9)	568	(12.2)	7.4	(4.7)	1.23	(0.2)	0.7	(1.0)
Luxembourg	494	(2.0)	474	(2.2)	512	(2.1)	486	(2.6)	2.7	(1.4)	0.86	(0.1)	0.0	(0.0)
Mexico	**404**	(2.8)	412	(3.1)	419	(2.5)	419	(3.4)	**6.3**	(1.6)	**1.19**	(0.1)	0.7	(0.4)
Netherlands	515	(10.7)	523	(12.5)	520	(11.0)	520	(13.7)	-10.0	(12.4)	0.99	(0.2)	0.3	(0.8)
New Zealand	**474**	(7.4)	510	(6.8)	513	(8.9)	**509**	(8.5)	**16.0**	(5.0)	**1.55**	(0.2)	1.6	(1.0)
Norway	**476**	(6.5)	489	(5.2)	493	(5.1)	503	(6.0)	**15.8**	(3.3)	**1.26**	(0.1)	2.0	(0.9)
Poland	513	(6.2)	521	(7.3)	514	(6.0)	522	(9.5)	5.2	(6.0)	1.04	(0.1)	0.2	(0.6)
Portugal	477	(10.4)	485	(12.3)	483	(8.2)	500	(8.2)	11.8	(4.3)	1.17	(0.2)	1.4	(1.1)
Slovak Republic	482	(9.2)	484	(9.6)	476	(13.1)	484	(9.1)	4.3	(7.5)	0.92	(0.1)	0.1	(0.5)
Slovenia	**476**	(2.9)	515	(4.0)	519	(3.2)	**509**	(2.9)	**17.6**	(1.3)	**1.55**	(0.1)	3.2	(0.5)
Spain	**471**	(4.1)	486	(5.2)	485	(4.0)	**498**	(3.4)	**10.2**	(1.8)	**1.36**	(0.1)	1.2	(0.5)
Sweden	477	(5.9)	471	(5.5)	477	(5.5)	489	(5.7)	6.0	(2.5)	1.05	(0.1)	0.5	(0.4)
Switzerland	520	(8.5)	533	(6.3)	537	(9.4)	542	(8.5)	10.6	(5.4)	1.33	(0.2)	0.7	(0.8)
Turkey	**431**	(7.9)	432	(9.6)	450	(12.5)	**481**	(15.2)	**19.5**	(6.6)	1.21	(0.2)	5.8	(3.6)
United Kingdom	**479**	(7.9)	499	(6.3)	487	(9.9)	**515**	(8.9)	**12.6**	(4.8)	1.26	(0.2)	1.9	(1.5)
United States	451	(7.0)	491	(8.4)	489	(8.8)	498	(7.6)	**13.0**	(3.0)	**1.78**	(0.2)	2.8	(1.2)
OECD average	**479**	(1.2)	495	(1.3)	499	(1.4)	**505**	(1.4)	**10.1**	(0.8)	**1.31**	(0.0)	1.6	(0.2)
Albania	395	(4.3)	395	(4.5)	396	(9.8)	392	(5.1)	-0.9	(2.1)	1.04	(0.1)	0.0	(0.1)
Argentina	372	(7.4)	382	(7.9)	392	(9.8)	396	(9.3)	13.5	(4.0)	1.29	(0.2)	2.7	(1.7)
Brazil	**380**	(3.5)	385	(4.1)	388	(4.8)	**413**	(7.1)	**11.0**	(2.7)	1.10	(0.1)	3.3	(1.6)
Bulgaria	429	(9.9)	438	(9.6)	437	(10.0)	447	(9.8)	6.6	(4.1)	1.19	(0.2)	0.9	(1.1)
Colombia	**367**	(5.2)	375	(5.9)	370	(5.9)	**391**	(6.9)	**7.9**	(3.1)	1.15	(0.2)	1.5	(1.1)
Costa Rica	**395**	(5.4)	405	(6.6)	405	(7.2)	**422**	(9.0)	**13.4**	(4.2)	1.19	(0.1)	3.2	(2.0)
Croatia	463	(7.9)	462	(9.2)	481	(8.7)	478	(11.7)	7.5	(6.3)	1.13	(0.2)	0.5	(0.9)
Cyprus*	**436**	(2.6)	444	(2.8)	433	(2.8)	**448**	(2.3)	6.7	(1.4)	1.07	(0.1)	0.4	(0.1)
Hong Kong-China	**532**	(9.3)	553	(10.5)	575	(8.4)	**585**	(9.7)	**22.7**	(5.4)	**1.66**	(0.3)	4.1	(2.0)
Indonesia	374	(9.1)	354	(8.7)	385	(8.6)	386	(10.2)	7.7	(4.9)	0.91	(0.2)	1.2	(1.4)
Jordan	**376**	(6.9)	374	(6.3)	391	(8.8)	**405**	(8.4)	**7.3**	(3.0)	**1.22**	(0.1)	1.4	(1.1)
Kazakhstan	428	(6.3)	434	(7.8)	435	(7.6)	427	(6.3)	-1.2	(1.9)	1.09	(0.1)	0.1	(0.3)
Latvia	493	(5.3)	489	(5.0)	483	(7.1)	495	(8.6)	2.3	(4.3)	0.87	(0.1)	0.1	(0.3)
Liechtenstein	c	c	c	c	c	c	c	c	-6.0	(5.7)	0.90	(0.3)	0.2	(0.4)
Lithuania	**465**	(5.9)	475	(6.2)	479	(6.5)	**496**	(5.8)	**15.4**	(4.5)	1.22	(0.1)	1.7	(1.0)
Macao-China	**524**	(2.0)	538	(1.7)	539	(2.0)	**552**	(2.2)	**11.7**	(0.8)	**1.22**	(0.1)	2.7	(0.3)
Malaysia	**408**	(4.7)	420	(7.8)	411	(9.0)	**444**	(7.1)	**13.2**	(3.5)	1.25	(0.1)	2.5	(1.3)
Montenegro	**394**	(2.0)	401	(2.8)	408	(3.0)	**436**	(2.7)	**20.3**	(1.3)	**1.25**	(0.1)	3.8	(0.5)
Peru	**347**	(5.7)	364	(7.0)	383	(10.1)	**379**	(8.2)	**9.0**	(3.3)	**1.34**	(0.2)	1.3	(1.0)
Qatar	**361**	(1.7)	362	(1.6)	399	(1.8)	**384**	(1.7)	**8.5**	(0.6)	1.06	(0.1)	1.3	(0.2)
Romania	441	(7.6)	447	(8.7)	440	(8.3)	451	(8.4)	6.1	(4.2)	1.07	(0.2)	0.5	(0.8)
Russian Federation	476	(6.2)	473	(6.2)	492	(7.8)	485	(5.4)	4.1	(2.3)	1.10	(0.1)	0.4	(0.4)
Serbia	434	(10.1)	451	(9.6)	445	(12.2)	463	(11.5)	10.4	(6.1)	1.28	(0.2)	1.3	(1.5)
Shanghai-China	608	(8.9)	597	(11.3)	610	(12.0)	636	(10.9)	5.6	(3.8)	1.09	(0.2)	0.7	(1.1)
Singapore	**553**	(2.4)	566	(3.1)	562	(3.3)	**607**	(2.9)	**19.0**	(1.1)	**1.25**	(0.1)	3.9	(0.5)
Chinese Taipei	**536**	(8.7)	556	(12.2)	559	(10.2)	**583**	(9.3)	**13.5**	(3.9)	1.25	(0.2)	2.3	(1.3)
Thailand	**401**	(4.8)	428	(7.8)	439	(8.1)	**439**	(9.2)	**17.4**	(4.5)	**1.56**	(0.2)	3.1	(1.5)
Tunisia	379	(7.2)	393	(7.5)	397	(11.0)	371	(9.6)	-8.1	(4.6)	1.07	(0.2)	0.8	(1.0)
United Arab Emirates	**413**	(5.2)	428	(4.6)	433	(5.6)	**463**	(5.8)	**12.6**	(1.9)	**1.36**	(0.1)	3.8	(1.0)
Uruguay	**385**	(6.8)	401	(8.3)	400	(7.9)	**451**	(8.5)	**26.8**	(3.7)	**1.39**	(0.2)	9.3	(2.5)
Viet Nam	515	(10.4)	512	(8.5)	511	(9.2)	507	(10.2)	-7.5	(7.7)	0.96	(0.2)	0.4	(0.8)

Note: Values that are statistically significant are indicated in bold (see Annex A3).
* See notes at the beginning of this Annex.
StatLink ⟨⟩ http://dx.doi.org/10.1787/888932957517

[Part 1/2]
Index of student-related factors affecting school climate and mathematics performance
Table IV.5.8 *Results based on school principals' reports*

| | Index of student-related factors affecting school climate | | | | | | | | | | Variability in this index | |
| | All students | | Bottom quarter | | Second quarter | | Third quarter | | Top quarter | | | |
	Mean index	S.E.	Mean index	S.E.	Mean index	S.E.	Mean index	S.E.	Mean index	S.E.	Standard deviation	S.E.
Australia	-0.18	(0.04)	-1.39	(0.04)	-0.51	(0.04)	0.04	(0.04)	1.14	(0.08)	1.02	(0.03)
Austria	-0.30	(0.08)	-1.49	(0.13)	-0.60	(0.07)	0.07	(0.10)	0.83	(0.11)	0.95	(0.06)
Belgium	-0.08	(0.06)	-1.29	(0.06)	-0.44	(0.06)	0.09	(0.06)	1.30	(0.13)	1.04	(0.05)
Canada	-0.47	(0.04)	-1.42	(0.05)	-0.78	(0.04)	-0.31	(0.04)	0.64	(0.07)	0.85	(0.03)
Chile	0.03	(0.09)	-1.52	(0.15)	-0.36	(0.07)	0.40	(0.12)	1.62	(0.14)	1.24	(0.08)
Czech Republic	0.20	(0.06)	-0.96	(0.08)	-0.17	(0.08)	0.47	(0.09)	1.49	(0.10)	0.96	(0.05)
Denmark	0.07	(0.07)	-1.04	(0.10)	-0.18	(0.06)	0.26	(0.07)	1.25	(0.12)	0.91	(0.06)
Estonia	-0.05	(0.05)	-1.12	(0.05)	-0.38	(0.06)	0.18	(0.07)	1.10	(0.08)	0.88	(0.03)
Finland	-0.50	(0.04)	-1.30	(0.05)	-0.74	(0.05)	-0.29	(0.08)	0.33	(0.05)	0.65	(0.03)
France	0.01	(0.06)	-1.16	(0.08)	-0.32	(0.05)	0.15	(0.08)	1.40	(0.11)	1.01	(0.05)
Germany	-0.18	(0.04)	-1.03	(0.07)	-0.40	(0.05)	-0.01	(0.05)	0.72	(0.07)	0.69	(0.03)
Greece	0.03	(0.08)	-1.37	(0.16)	-0.16	(0.08)	0.38	(0.07)	1.26	(0.10)	1.05	(0.07)
Hungary	0.13	(0.05)	-1.22	(0.10)	-0.09	(0.09)	0.47	(0.05)	1.38	(0.11)	1.04	(0.06)
Iceland	0.31	(0.01)	-0.63	(0.01)	-0.08	(0.01)	0.48	(0.01)	1.49	(0.01)	0.86	(0.00)
Ireland	-0.09	(0.06)	-1.15	(0.10)	-0.40	(0.06)	0.09	(0.07)	1.11	(0.12)	0.91	(0.06)
Israel	-0.15	(0.08)	-1.46	(0.12)	-0.40	(0.09)	0.11	(0.08)	1.13	(0.15)	1.04	(0.07)
Italy	0.01	(0.04)	-1.15	(0.05)	-0.31	(0.05)	0.31	(0.04)	1.19	(0.07)	0.94	(0.03)
Japan	0.31	(0.07)	-0.81	(0.11)	0.04	(0.06)	0.52	(0.07)	1.50	(0.11)	0.94	(0.06)
Korea	0.07	(0.09)	-1.32	(0.13)	-0.27	(0.09)	0.35	(0.08)	1.53	(0.18)	1.13	(0.07)
Luxembourg	-0.27	(0.00)	-1.11	(0.00)	-0.43	(0.00)	-0.09	(0.00)	0.53	(0.00)	0.67	(0.00)
Mexico	0.01	(0.03)	-1.18	(0.06)	-0.28	(0.05)	0.33	(0.03)	1.17	(0.05)	0.95	(0.03)
Netherlands	-0.40	(0.05)	-1.28	(0.08)	-0.59	(0.05)	-0.21	(0.06)	0.48	(0.09)	0.70	(0.04)
New Zealand	-0.25	(0.06)	-1.25	(0.10)	-0.47	(0.07)	-0.12	(0.04)	0.85	(0.15)	0.91	(0.07)
Norway	-0.12	(0.05)	-0.96	(0.06)	-0.35	(0.06)	0.00	(0.05)	0.84	(0.11)	0.74	(0.05)
Poland	0.05	(0.06)	-0.89	(0.06)	-0.31	(0.08)	0.24	(0.10)	1.17	(0.09)	0.84	(0.04)
Portugal	-0.14	(0.09)	-1.39	(0.12)	-0.59	(0.10)	0.11	(0.12)	1.29	(0.14)	1.07	(0.06)
Slovak Republic	-0.22	(0.06)	-1.24	(0.06)	-0.58	(0.07)	0.01	(0.10)	0.94	(0.10)	0.85	(0.05)
Slovenia	-0.38	(0.01)	-1.28	(0.01)	-0.73	(0.01)	-0.22	(0.01)	0.72	(0.02)	0.80	(0.01)
Spain	0.19	(0.05)	-0.98	(0.07)	-0.12	(0.05)	0.43	(0.07)	1.43	(0.07)	0.96	(0.04)
Sweden	-0.19	(0.05)	-1.15	(0.07)	-0.44	(0.08)	-0.03	(0.03)	0.85	(0.11)	0.81	(0.05)
Switzerland	-0.04	(0.06)	-0.96	(0.07)	-0.26	(0.06)	0.17	(0.06)	0.89	(0.10)	0.76	(0.05)
Turkey	-0.30	(0.07)	-1.57	(0.11)	-0.66	(0.10)	0.07	(0.09)	0.97	(0.12)	1.01	(0.06)
United Kingdom	0.40	(0.06)	-0.53	(0.06)	0.00	(0.03)	0.47	(0.08)	1.65	(0.12)	0.91	(0.05)
United States	-0.14	(0.08)	-1.22	(0.08)	-0.46	(0.10)	-0.03	(0.05)	1.16	(0.16)	0.94	(0.06)
OECD average	-0.08	(0.01)	-1.17	(0.01)	-0.38	(0.01)	0.14	(0.01)	1.10	(0.02)	0.91	(0.01)
Albania	0.91	(0.07)	-0.23	(0.11)	0.63	(0.08)	1.14	(0.09)	2.11	(0.11)	0.93	(0.05)
Argentina	0.21	(0.10)	-1.28	(0.12)	-0.19	(0.12)	0.59	(0.12)	1.72	(0.14)	1.16	(0.06)
Brazil	-0.49	(0.06)	-1.88	(0.08)	-0.92	(0.07)	-0.23	(0.07)	1.08	(0.11)	1.17	(0.05)
Bulgaria	0.12	(0.10)	-1.50	(0.14)	-0.20	(0.12)	0.57	(0.10)	1.61	(0.14)	1.24	(0.06)
Colombia	-0.59	(0.06)	-1.82	(0.09)	-0.94	(0.06)	-0.39	(0.09)	0.77	(0.12)	1.03	(0.06)
Costa Rica	-0.66	(0.06)	-1.75	(0.06)	-1.08	(0.07)	-0.47	(0.08)	0.68	(0.13)	0.98	(0.05)
Croatia	-0.53	(0.07)	-1.70	(0.07)	-0.87	(0.09)	-0.27	(0.09)	0.73	(0.14)	0.96	(0.06)
Cyprus*	-0.12	(0.00)	-1.28	(0.00)	-0.32	(0.00)	0.03	(0.00)	1.10	(0.00)	0.99	(0.00)
Hong Kong-China	0.37	(0.06)	-0.65	(0.09)	0.06	(0.06)	0.57	(0.07)	1.48	(0.13)	0.88	(0.06)
Indonesia	0.78	(0.06)	-0.05	(0.10)	0.52	(0.06)	0.97	(0.06)	1.68	(0.09)	0.71	(0.05)
Jordan	-0.12	(0.10)	-1.92	(0.15)	-0.54	(0.12)	0.34	(0.10)	1.63	(0.17)	1.38	(0.08)
Kazakhstan	-0.61	(0.13)	-2.54	(0.12)	-1.54	(0.19)	0.02	(0.23)	1.64	(0.12)	1.66	(0.06)
Latvia	-0.19	(0.06)	-1.29	(0.08)	-0.48	(0.08)	0.08	(0.07)	0.95	(0.10)	0.89	(0.04)
Liechtenstein	0.12	(0.02)	c	c	c	c	c	c	c	c	0.63	(0.02)
Lithuania	0.27	(0.05)	-0.61	(0.08)	-0.01	(0.03)	0.40	(0.06)	1.30	(0.12)	0.80	(0.06)
Macao-China	0.53	(0.00)	-1.22	(0.00)	0.02	(0.00)	1.17	(0.00)	2.15	(0.00)	1.41	(0.00)
Malaysia	0.00	(0.09)	-1.34	(0.10)	-0.38	(0.13)	0.27	(0.07)	1.46	(0.14)	1.11	(0.06)
Montenegro	-0.01	(0.00)	-0.93	(0.00)	-0.44	(0.00)	0.20	(0.00)	1.11	(0.01)	0.81	(0.01)
Peru	0.30	(0.06)	-0.93	(0.08)	-0.01	(0.10)	0.64	(0.07)	1.48	(0.09)	0.95	(0.04)
Qatar	0.53	(0.00)	-0.80	(0.00)	0.24	(0.00)	0.69	(0.00)	2.00	(0.00)	1.15	(0.00)
Romania	0.60	(0.07)	-0.56	(0.10)	0.33	(0.09)	0.85	(0.06)	1.77	(0.13)	0.93	(0.05)
Russian Federation	-0.19	(0.11)	-2.11	(0.16)	-0.60	(0.12)	0.39	(0.12)	1.55	(0.14)	1.44	(0.06)
Serbia	-0.50	(0.06)	-1.48	(0.07)	-0.82	(0.06)	-0.29	(0.10)	0.58	(0.10)	0.81	(0.05)
Shanghai-China	0.26	(0.13)	-2.19	(0.11)	-0.44	(0.25)	1.13	(0.21)	2.54	(0.10)	1.82	(0.07)
Singapore	0.47	(0.01)	-0.45	(0.01)	0.09	(0.00)	0.38	(0.01)	1.87	(0.02)	0.97	(0.00)
Chinese Taipei	0.72	(0.11)	-0.99	(0.18)	0.26	(0.12)	1.14	(0.16)	2.47	(0.11)	1.35	(0.07)
Thailand	0.02	(0.06)	-1.05	(0.07)	-0.25	(0.09)	0.28	(0.07)	1.08	(0.10)	0.84	(0.05)
Tunisia	-0.73	(0.08)	-1.86	(0.09)	-1.04	(0.11)	-0.42	(0.07)	0.43	(0.12)	0.90	(0.05)
United Arab Emirates	0.39	(0.06)	-1.35	(0.14)	0.18	(0.06)	0.85	(0.05)	1.89	(0.06)	1.31	(0.05)
Uruguay	0.00	(0.08)	-1.48	(0.11)	-0.56	(0.08)	0.37	(0.11)	1.69	(0.13)	1.26	(0.06)
Viet Nam	0.03	(0.06)	-0.82	(0.08)	-0.21	(0.07)	0.23	(0.07)	0.93	(0.08)	0.69	(0.04)

Note: Values that are statistically significant are indicated in bold (see Annex A3).
* See notes at the beginning of this Annex.
StatLink ⟨⟨⟩⟩ http://dx.doi.org/10.1787/888932957517

[Part 2/2]
Index of student-related factors affecting school climate and mathematics performance

Table IV.5.8 *Results based on school principals' reports*

| | | Performance on the mathematics scale by national quarters of this index | | | | | | | Change in the mathematics score per unit of this index | | Increased likelihood of students in the bottom quarter of this index scoring in the bottom quarter of the national mathematics performance distribution | | Explained variance in student performance (r-squared x 100) | |
| | | Bottom quarter | | Second quarter | | Third quarter | | Top quarter | | | | | | | |
		Mean score	S.E.	Mean score	S.E.	Mean score	S.E.	Mean score	S.E.	Score dif.	S.E.	Ratio	S.E.	%	S.E.
OECD	Australia	468	(2.9)	493	(4.5)	517	(3.7)	540	(3.7)	25.8	(1.4)	1.80	(0.1)	7.5	(0.7)
	Austria	482	(7.9)	514	(10.5)	508	(9.9)	518	(8.4)	15.5	(4.2)	1.52	(0.2)	2.6	(1.4)
	Belgium	453	(7.7)	511	(9.9)	534	(6.1)	563	(6.7)	37.9	(3.9)	2.68	(0.3)	14.8	(2.7)
	Canada	497	(3.6)	509	(4.2)	523	(4.1)	543	(3.8)	22.4	(2.0)	1.43	(0.1)	4.6	(0.9)
	Chile	389	(6.3)	404	(5.4)	441	(8.0)	458	(6.9)	21.4	(2.9)	1.85	(0.3)	10.8	(2.5)
	Czech Republic	464	(10.3)	499	(9.1)	504	(8.8)	532	(6.6)	23.6	(4.0)	1.96	(0.3)	5.8	(1.9)
	Denmark	480	(4.0)	496	(5.2)	512	(5.2)	514	(5.4)	15.1	(2.2)	1.54	(0.1)	2.7	(0.8)
	Estonia	513	(3.9)	517	(4.6)	527	(4.5)	525	(5.0)	7.3	(2.3)	1.14	(0.1)	0.6	(0.4)
	Finland	509	(3.8)	514	(4.7)	523	(4.3)	528	(3.8)	11.5	(2.7)	1.19	(0.1)	0.8	(0.4)
	France	469	(8.2)	490	(8.3)	500	(8.8)	526	(8.7)	23.4	(4.2)	1.53	(0.2)	5.8	(2.1)
	Germany	481	(9.9)	501	(7.6)	518	(7.2)	555	(8.0)	42.0	(5.9)	1.72	(0.3)	8.9	(2.6)
	Greece	439	(6.1)	442	(6.2)	467	(6.1)	464	(6.0)	5.5	(3.5)	1.27	(0.2)	0.4	(0.5)
	Hungary	410	(7.2)	498	(7.2)	503	(10.0)	501	(10.0)	33.3	(4.2)	3.24	(0.4)	13.6	(3.5)
	Iceland	486	(3.5)	500	(3.4)	493	(3.3)	495	(3.2)	5.4	(1.8)	1.17	(0.1)	0.3	(0.2)
	Ireland	476	(5.9)	500	(6.4)	516	(6.0)	519	(4.0)	19.8	(2.7)	1.80	(0.2)	4.6	(1.2)
	Israel	454	(11.6)	457	(9.9)	471	(10.8)	482	(12.3)	12.3	(5.4)	1.21	(0.2)	1.5	(1.3)
	Italy	449	(4.1)	481	(4.7)	498	(4.5)	524	(5.7)	31.0	(2.4)	1.92	(0.1)	9.8	(1.6)
	Japan	497	(10.3)	530	(9.4)	552	(9.1)	567	(7.0)	27.5	(6.1)	2.15	(0.3)	7.6	(3.2)
	Korea	514	(9.9)	544	(10.4)	570	(8.4)	588	(9.2)	25.5	(4.3)	2.02	(0.3)	8.5	(2.7)
	Luxembourg	465	(1.9)	497	(2.5)	482	(2.2)	522	(2.2)	32.1	(1.4)	1.55	(0.1)	5.1	(0.4)
	Mexico	400	(2.3)	416	(3.0)	418	(2.9)	419	(3.7)	8.5	(1.7)	1.29	(0.1)	1.2	(0.5)
	Netherlands	473	(10.9)	530	(9.5)	527	(10.2)	549	(9.0)	35.5	(7.1)	2.30	(0.4)	7.1	(2.9)
	New Zealand	459	(5.7)	495	(9.6)	531	(5.9)	521	(6.3)	29.1	(3.5)	2.06	(0.2)	7.1	(1.4)
	Norway	478	(5.5)	487	(4.6)	492	(5.4)	503	(6.5)	18.1	(3.8)	1.17	(0.1)	2.2	(0.9)
	Poland	513	(6.9)	507	(5.7)	527	(6.4)	523	(9.6)	6.9	(7.0)	1.04	(0.1)	0.4	(0.8)
	Portugal	466	(9.4)	485	(7.2)	487	(6.9)	508	(8.2)	14.2	(3.8)	1.44	(0.2)	2.6	(1.3)
	Slovak Republic	440	(9.5)	490	(9.4)	499	(11.2)	498	(7.7)	22.6	(5.2)	1.87	(0.2)	3.7	(1.7)
	Slovenia	468	(2.7)	494	(4.7)	522	(4.4)	530	(2.9)	30.8	(1.7)	1.92	(0.1)	7.3	(0.8)
	Spain	461	(4.2)	481	(4.8)	488	(4.0)	509	(3.6)	18.4	(2.0)	1.59	(0.1)	4.0	(0.9)
	Sweden	464	(5.2)	475	(4.7)	482	(4.9)	493	(4.8)	14.4	(3.6)	1.32	(0.1)	1.6	(0.8)
	Switzerland	515	(7.3)	531	(7.8)	533	(7.9)	549	(7.7)	14.1	(5.5)	1.32	(0.2)	1.3	(1.0)
	Turkey	426	(4.9)	409	(6.6)	463	(10.2)	495	(15.9)	30.7	(6.4)	1.20	(0.1)	11.7	(4.5)
	United Kingdom	477	(6.3)	484	(9.0)	498	(7.4)	521	(9.0)	20.2	(5.1)	1.37	(0.1)	3.7	(1.8)
	United States	447	(5.7)	476	(11.4)	502	(5.7)	504	(9.3)	18.5	(4.9)	1.88	(0.2)	3.8	(1.8)
	OECD average	467	(1.2)	490	(1.2)	504	(1.2)	517	(1.3)	21.2	(0.7)	1.66	(0.0)	5.1	(0.3)
Partners	Albania	398	(3.8)	396	(4.9)	391	(6.0)	392	(5.0)	-2.4	(2.1)	0.97	(0.1)	0.1	(0.1)
	Argentina	351	(7.8)	380	(7.0)	396	(8.0)	415	(7.4)	20.2	(3.1)	2.06	(0.3)	9.5	(2.7)
	Brazil	381	(3.8)	376	(3.2)	384	(4.8)	424	(6.4)	15.0	(2.6)	1.09	(0.1)	5.1	(1.6)
	Bulgaria	410	(8.4)	426	(10.6)	441	(10.7)	478	(8.6)	19.4	(3.7)	1.58	(0.2)	6.4	(2.5)
	Colombia	361	(6.1)	378	(6.6)	367	(6.4)	397	(6.9)	13.3	(3.1)	1.39	(0.2)	3.5	(1.7)
	Costa Rica	387	(4.4)	393	(6.2)	408	(7.4)	440	(7.3)	22.6	(3.5)	1.51	(0.2)	10.5	(3.0)
	Croatia	451	(9.8)	455	(7.5)	472	(9.9)	507	(9.3)	20.8	(5.2)	1.45	(0.2)	5.1	(2.5)
	Cyprus*	437	(2.7)	438	(3.0)	434	(3.4)	449	(2.1)	3.3	(1.2)	1.03	(0.1)	0.1	(0.1)
	Hong Kong-China	542	(9.4)	548	(8.5)	563	(11.0)	591	(9.0)	23.6	(5.2)	1.45	(0.2)	4.7	(2.1)
	Indonesia	370	(6.2)	360	(7.3)	376	(8.0)	392	(9.7)	15.9	(7.1)	1.03	(0.2)	2.5	(2.2)
	Jordan	380	(7.4)	379	(6.4)	387	(6.2)	400	(10.4)	6.7	(3.3)	1.16	(0.1)	1.4	(1.3)
	Kazakhstan	426	(5.5)	440	(7.7)	431	(8.2)	429	(6.5)	-0.5	(2.1)	1.12	(0.1)	0.0	(0.3)
	Latvia	478	(5.1)	489	(6.9)	501	(5.1)	493	(7.3)	6.4	(3.4)	1.24	(0.1)	0.5	(0.5)
	Liechtenstein	c	c	c	c	c	c	c	c	17.4	(6.7)	2.98	(0.7)	1.4	(1.0)
	Lithuania	462	(5.9)	466	(5.4)	490	(6.1)	497	(6.2)	18.6	(4.4)	1.39	(0.1)	2.8	(1.2)
	Macao-China	506	(2.1)	530	(2.2)	541	(1.8)	575	(2.2)	17.5	(0.7)	1.77	(0.1)	6.8	(0.5)
	Malaysia	399	(5.5)	410	(5.4)	417	(8.6)	456	(7.7)	18.6	(3.1)	1.45	(0.1)	6.6	(2.0)
	Montenegro	392	(2.6)	419	(2.7)	400	(2.2)	427	(2.5)	13.4	(1.9)	1.46	(0.1)	1.7	(0.5)
	Peru	350	(4.9)	353	(7.1)	375	(9.2)	395	(8.8)	18.9	(4.1)	1.21	(0.2)	4.5	(1.8)
	Qatar	358	(1.4)	397	(1.8)	357	(1.6)	394	(1.6)	8.7	(0.6)	1.25	(0.0)	1.0	(0.1)
	Romania	416	(6.7)	449	(7.9)	450	(9.0)	463	(7.7)	17.3	(4.0)	1.65	(0.2)	3.9	(1.8)
	Russian Federation	471	(6.6)	466	(7.1)	486	(5.0)	502	(7.0)	8.8	(2.3)	1.15	(0.1)	2.2	(1.2)
	Serbia	422	(8.3)	443	(8.3)	452	(8.4)	476	(10.1)	22.8	(5.7)	1.53	(0.2)	4.2	(2.0)
	Shanghai-China	589	(10.0)	604	(13.1)	604	(12.8)	656	(8.8)	11.7	(2.8)	1.45	(0.2)	4.5	(2.1)
	Singapore	544	(2.6)	567	(3.0)	555	(3.1)	633	(2.6)	38.4	(3.2)	1.40	(0.1)	12.4	(0.7)
	Chinese Taipei	527	(6.8)	540	(11.0)	580	(10.4)	591	(11.1)	18.6	(3.5)	1.49	(0.2)	4.7	(1.8)
	Thailand	397	(4.7)	435	(9.9)	434	(7.9)	442	(9.2)	19.7	(4.6)	1.65	(0.2)	4.0	(1.7)
	Tunisia	401	(7.2)	378	(7.4)	376	(8.0)	385	(10.0)	-5.9	(5.2)	0.63	(0.1)	0.5	(1.1)
	United Arab Emirates	414	(5.8)	425	(4.7)	431	(6.4)	467	(5.9)	14.8	(2.0)	1.36	(0.1)	4.7	(1.2)
	Uruguay	376	(5.3)	393	(5.5)	416	(7.9)	453	(7.9)	25.1	(2.9)	1.81	(0.2)	12.8	(2.9)
	Viet Nam	487	(9.9)	513	(9.0)	523	(7.7)	523	(11.5)	21.3	(8.2)	1.62	(0.3)	3.0	(2.2)

Note: Values that are statistically significant are indicated in bold (see Annex A3).
* See notes at the beginning of this Annex.
StatLink ⟨⟩ http://dx.doi.org/10.1787/888932957517

[Part 1/1]
Principals' views on student truancy
Table IV.5.9   *Results based on school principals' reports*

		Percentage of students in schools whose principals reported that the following hinders learning:														
		Students skipping classes								Students arriving late for school							
		Not at all		Very little		To some extent		A lot		Not at all		Very little		To some extent		A lot	
		%	S.E.	%	S.E.	%	S.E.	%	S.E.	%	S.E.	%	S.E.	%	S.E.	%	S.E.
OECD	Australia	21.0	(1.6)	54.4	(2.1)	22.2	(1.6)	2.4	(0.6)	8.7	(1.1)	56.9	(1.5)	31.2	(1.4)	3.3	(0.7)
	Austria	13.7	(2.6)	45.6	(3.6)	29.5	(3.6)	11.3	(2.6)	8.9	(2.4)	51.1	(3.9)	30.1	(3.6)	9.8	(2.2)
	Belgium	24.3	(2.8)	55.6	(3.2)	17.6	(2.3)	2.5	(0.8)	12.8	(2.3)	55.7	(2.8)	25.9	(2.5)	5.7	(1.2)
	Canada	6.8	(0.7)	36.4	(2.5)	48.8	(2.7)	8.0	(1.3)	4.5	(0.4)	42.1	(2.2)	47.7	(2.3)	5.7	(1.3)
	Chile	39.0	(3.0)	40.3	(3.4)	11.9	(2.4)	8.8	(2.0)	7.6	(2.0)	41.4	(4.0)	35.6	(3.6)	15.4	(2.7)
	Czech Republic	12.1	(2.2)	48.1	(4.3)	34.1	(3.7)	5.7	(1.5)	36.8	(3.6)	53.1	(3.6)	10.0	(2.4)	0.1	(0.1)
	Denmark	23.8	(3.3)	54.8	(3.6)	19.8	(2.9)	1.6	(0.8)	17.2	(2.7)	56.6	(3.6)	24.5	(3.1)	1.7	(0.8)
	Estonia	8.7	(1.7)	54.0	(2.8)	34.5	(2.8)	2.8	(1.1)	17.2	(2.3)	52.7	(2.8)	29.1	(2.6)	1.0	(0.6)
	Finland	6.9	(1.9)	58.1	(3.1)	33.0	(2.8)	2.0	(0.8)	2.1	(0.9)	46.9	(3.5)	49.2	(3.3)	1.9	(0.7)
	France	23.6	(2.4)	48.1	(3.5)	26.2	(2.9)	2.1	(1.1)	12.0	(2.1)	61.3	(3.3)	24.4	(2.7)	2.3	(1.2)
	Germany	18.2	(2.4)	65.3	(3.1)	16.0	(2.5)	0.5	(0.5)	4.2	(1.5)	64.9	(3.4)	30.5	(3.4)	0.4	(0.4)
	Greece	19.5	(2.6)	58.3	(3.4)	16.8	(2.7)	5.3	(1.8)	12.5	(2.0)	60.4	(3.8)	21.2	(3.1)	5.8	(2.1)
	Hungary	18.4	(2.6)	60.0	(3.7)	16.4	(2.9)	5.1	(1.7)	8.8	(1.7)	58.4	(3.1)	26.3	(3.1)	6.5	(1.7)
	Iceland	24.8	(0.2)	66.8	(0.3)	7.9	(0.2)	0.6	(0.0)	20.3	(0.2)	63.2	(0.3)	15.9	(0.2)	0.6	(0.0)
	Ireland	19.5	(3.0)	65.9	(3.8)	13.3	(2.7)	1.4	(1.1)	9.6	(2.1)	65.6	(3.9)	22.8	(3.2)	2.0	(1.1)
	Israel	10.6	(2.6)	47.3	(3.3)	31.8	(3.4)	10.4	(2.4)	11.2	(2.6)	51.4	(3.7)	30.1	(3.5)	7.3	(2.1)
	Italy	8.2	(1.2)	55.2	(2.3)	32.0	(2.1)	4.5	(0.9)	10.1	(1.2)	51.3	(1.8)	34.1	(1.9)	4.5	(1.0)
	Japan	37.5	(3.6)	52.5	(3.7)	9.0	(1.8)	0.9	(0.7)	4.6	(1.6)	58.1	(3.3)	33.6	(3.2)	3.7	(1.4)
	Korea	41.2	(3.8)	44.1	(4.1)	10.6	(2.5)	4.1	(1.6)	17.0	(3.3)	57.4	(4.1)	21.8	(3.2)	3.8	(1.6)
	Luxembourg	9.8	(0.1)	78.5	(0.1)	11.6	(0.1)	0.0	c	3.1	(0.0)	69.4	(0.1)	25.1	(0.1)	2.4	(0.0)
	Mexico	13.0	(1.1)	54.3	(1.8)	26.7	(2.0)	6.0	(1.0)	7.3	(1.0)	59.7	(2.0)	26.2	(1.7)	6.8	(0.9)
	Netherlands	2.8	(1.2)	67.9	(3.5)	27.3	(3.4)	2.1	(1.2)	3.6	(1.4)	57.3	(4.1)	35.2	(3.7)	3.9	(1.6)
	New Zealand	11.1	(1.8)	56.0	(3.7)	28.4	(3.4)	4.5	(1.9)	7.7	(1.9)	61.2	(4.2)	28.0	(3.9)	3.1	(1.6)
	Norway	10.5	(2.4)	59.7	(3.4)	27.6	(3.3)	2.2	(1.0)	6.8	(1.9)	68.1	(3.4)	24.6	(3.0)	0.5	(0.5)
	Poland	5.1	(1.5)	54.8	(4.2)	38.9	(4.0)	1.3	(0.8)	11.0	(2.3)	62.5	(3.9)	24.4	(3.4)	2.0	(1.1)
	Portugal	9.8	(2.5)	48.9	(3.8)	35.3	(3.9)	6.0	(2.7)	19.5	(3.5)	51.7	(4.4)	24.1	(3.2)	4.7	(1.7)
	Slovak Republic	2.1	(1.1)	26.1	(2.9)	57.8	(3.4)	14.0	(2.4)	24.7	(3.2)	44.4	(3.4)	27.8	(3.5)	3.1	(1.5)
	Slovenia	1.6	(0.1)	32.3	(0.6)	55.7	(0.6)	10.4	(0.3)	5.8	(0.2)	58.8	(0.6)	31.9	(0.6)	3.5	(0.1)
	Spain	21.7	(2.3)	52.9	(3.1)	23.3	(2.5)	2.1	(0.7)	24.4	(2.1)	59.6	(2.8)	15.5	(2.0)	0.5	(0.3)
	Sweden	3.9	(1.2)	56.0	(3.7)	38.7	(3.6)	1.4	(0.8)	5.6	(1.5)	63.9	(3.5)	29.2	(3.1)	1.3	(1.0)
	Switzerland	18.2	(2.3)	64.3	(2.8)	16.7	(2.8)	0.8	(0.4)	10.9	(2.2)	69.3	(3.3)	19.3	(2.9)	0.5	(0.3)
	Turkey	7.1	(2.0)	38.8	(3.5)	35.8	(3.8)	18.3	(2.7)	5.6	(2.1)	51.4	(4.6)	32.5	(4.2)	10.5	(2.5)
	United Kingdom	32.3	(3.0)	62.2	(3.3)	5.3	(1.5)	0.2	(0.1)	14.5	(2.2)	70.2	(2.9)	14.9	(2.2)	0.3	(0.1)
	United States	11.6	(2.5)	57.4	(3.9)	28.0	(3.4)	2.9	(1.4)	5.0	(1.7)	60.9	(4.6)	30.0	(4.0)	4.1	(1.6)
	OECD average	15.8	(0.4)	53.6	(0.6)	26.1	(0.5)	4.5	(0.2)	11.2	(0.4)	57.6	(0.6)	27.4	(0.5)	3.8	(0.2)
Partners	Albania	37.0	(3.3)	53.4	(3.6)	8.3	(1.7)	1.3	(0.9)	32.3	(4.2)	58.7	(4.5)	9.0	(1.8)	0.0	c
	Argentina	25.9	(4.2)	38.9	(4.4)	28.8	(3.8)	6.3	(2.1)	26.2	(4.1)	37.5	(4.0)	25.9	(3.8)	10.5	(2.3)
	Brazil	16.5	(1.6)	35.6	(2.3)	29.8	(2.4)	18.0	(2.3)	9.9	(1.6)	47.6	(2.9)	33.2	(2.3)	9.4	(1.7)
	Bulgaria	14.4	(2.7)	43.5	(4.1)	31.7	(3.6)	10.3	(2.3)	16.4	(2.9)	56.1	(4.2)	23.0	(3.2)	4.4	(1.5)
	Colombia	14.7	(2.1)	42.2	(4.0)	29.6	(3.8)	13.4	(2.5)	5.4	(1.4)	39.2	(4.1)	42.0	(4.1)	13.4	(2.4)
	Costa Rica	7.3	(1.6)	28.0	(3.5)	34.4	(3.5)	30.3	(3.6)	6.2	(1.7)	33.8	(3.6)	38.6	(4.0)	21.5	(3.3)
	Croatia	2.2	(1.1)	22.7	(3.3)	50.1	(4.2)	25.1	(3.4)	9.8	(2.4)	50.0	(3.9)	35.1	(3.5)	5.1	(1.8)
	Cyprus*	14.8	(0.1)	54.6	(0.1)	28.0	(0.1)	2.6	(0.1)	9.8	(0.1)	61.5	(0.1)	23.5	(0.1)	5.2	(0.0)
	Hong Kong-China	51.2	(3.6)	43.0	(3.6)	4.9	(1.8)	0.9	(0.7)	10.0	(2.4)	65.6	(4.1)	23.8	(3.5)	0.6	(0.6)
	Indonesia	37.1	(3.5)	59.9	(3.4)	3.0	(1.5)	0.0	c	15.7	(3.1)	77.8	(3.6)	6.5	(2.1)	0.0	c
	Jordan	33.4	(3.5)	29.7	(3.2)	24.3	(2.8)	12.6	(2.7)	24.6	(3.5)	37.0	(3.6)	25.4	(3.4)	13.0	(3.0)
	Kazakhstan	9.1	(1.8)	29.4	(4.0)	39.2	(4.0)	22.3	(3.3)	16.1	(2.4)	34.0	(4.2)	40.1	(3.8)	9.8	(2.6)
	Latvia	10.0	(2.3)	48.8	(3.6)	34.1	(3.5)	7.1	(1.9)	8.9	(1.8)	49.9	(4.0)	37.0	(3.7)	4.2	(1.3)
	Liechtenstein	35.7	(0.9)	57.2	(0.9)	7.1	(0.8)	0.0	c	0.0	c	92.9	(0.8)	7.1	(0.8)	0.0	c
	Lithuania	18.2	(2.7)	70.8	(3.5)	10.5	(2.2)	0.5	(0.5)	15.0	(2.2)	73.9	(2.7)	10.8	(2.0)	0.4	(0.4)
	Macao-China	46.2	(0.1)	46.8	(0.1)	2.3	(0.0)	4.6	(0.0)	19.0	(0.0)	63.9	(0.1)	14.6	(0.1)	2.6	(0.0)
	Malaysia	18.3	(2.9)	49.6	(3.7)	23.6	(3.1)	8.6	(2.1)	19.0	(3.1)	55.6	(3.6)	20.0	(2.7)	5.4	(1.8)
	Montenegro	1.2	(0.1)	54.9	(0.2)	39.7	(0.2)	4.3	(0.1)	7.2	(0.1)	70.5	(0.2)	22.3	(0.1)	0.0	c
	Peru	27.3	(3.0)	49.5	(3.4)	18.2	(2.3)	4.9	(1.8)	12.8	(2.2)	52.7	(3.2)	25.6	(3.2)	8.9	(2.0)
	Qatar	25.0	(0.1)	50.3	(0.1)	19.1	(0.1)	5.6	(0.0)	21.9	(0.1)	49.6	(0.1)	26.0	(0.1)	2.5	(0.0)
	Romania	32.9	(3.2)	42.4	(4.0)	23.5	(3.2)	1.3	(0.9)	27.8	(3.7)	58.1	(3.5)	13.4	(2.4)	0.7	(0.7)
	Russian Federation	4.7	(1.7)	25.0	(2.6)	46.5	(2.8)	23.8	(2.7)	18.1	(3.0)	37.6	(2.8)	36.2	(3.2)	8.0	(1.8)
	Serbia	2.5	(1.2)	30.1	(4.0)	55.3	(4.4)	12.1	(2.5)	5.7	(2.0)	42.0	(4.4)	43.1	(4.3)	9.2	(2.2)
	Shanghai-China	43.8	(3.5)	22.6	(3.3)	12.2	(2.6)	21.3	(3.2)	38.0	(4.0)	35.2	(4.1)	24.4	(3.1)	2.4	(1.0)
	Singapore	26.8	(0.7)	68.5	(0.6)	4.1	(0.1)	0.6	(0.0)	16.3	(0.6)	71.8	(0.6)	11.4	(0.1)	0.6	(0.0)
	Chinese Taipei	52.1	(4.4)	36.7	(4.2)	8.5	(2.3)	2.7	(1.3)	25.0	(3.6)	54.4	(4.4)	20.6	(3.1)	0.0	c
	Thailand	9.1	(1.7)	61.2	(4.0)	29.6	(3.6)	0.1	(0.1)	4.0	(1.4)	56.8	(3.9)	37.7	(3.7)	1.4	(0.7)
	Tunisia	8.6	(2.4)	38.8	(4.1)	38.6	(4.0)	14.1	(3.2)	1.4	(0.9)	34.6	(3.8)	42.5	(4.5)	21.6	(3.5)
	United Arab Emirates	39.6	(2.3)	42.1	(2.8)	11.1	(1.6)	7.2	(1.0)	14.5	(1.5)	59.5	(2.2)	21.2	(1.8)	4.7	(0.7)
	Uruguay	28.7	(3.0)	35.6	(3.6)	27.4	(3.3)	8.3	(2.2)	10.6	(2.0)	38.8	(3.5)	35.7	(3.5)	15.0	(2.6)
	Viet Nam	10.5	(2.6)	66.2	(3.7)	22.8	(3.5)	0.5	(0.5)	3.4	(1.5)	67.7	(4.0)	27.4	(3.9)	1.6	(0.9)

* See notes at the beginning of this Annex.
StatLink ⏳ http://dx.doi.org/10.1787/888932957517

[Part 1/2]
Index of teacher morale and mathematics performance
Table IV.5.10   *Results based on school principals' reports*

| | Index of teacher morale | | | | | | | | | | Variability in this index | |
| | All students | | Bottom quarter | | Second quarter | | Third quarter | | Top quarter | | | |
	Mean index	S.E.	Mean index	S.E.	Mean index	S.E.	Mean index	S.E.	Mean index	S.E.	Standard deviation	S.E.
OECD												
Australia	0.14	(0.03)	-0.96	(0.04)	-0.22	(0.05)	0.48	(0.05)	1.28	(0.03)	0.90	(0.02)
Austria	0.54	(0.07)	-0.54	(0.11)	0.26	(0.07)	1.01	(0.16)	1.45	(0.00)	0.81	(0.03)
Belgium	-0.27	(0.06)	-1.27	(0.09)	-0.74	(0.02)	0.01	(0.11)	0.93	(0.10)	0.90	(0.03)
Canada	0.18	(0.04)	-1.02	(0.05)	-0.21	(0.09)	0.59	(0.04)	1.36	(0.05)	0.95	(0.02)
Chile	-0.31	(0.08)	-1.49	(0.15)	-0.74	(0.11)	0.13	(0.12)	0.88	(0.09)	0.98	(0.06)
Czech Republic	-0.10	(0.05)	-1.01	(0.06)	-0.44	(0.12)	0.21	(0.05)	0.84	(0.07)	0.78	(0.03)
Denmark	0.40	(0.06)	-0.86	(0.04)	0.07	(0.14)	0.94	(0.11)	1.45	(0.00)	0.92	(0.03)
Estonia	0.05	(0.05)	-0.96	(0.06)	-0.37	(0.08)	0.32	(0.05)	1.20	(0.07)	0.87	(0.03)
Finland	0.33	(0.06)	-0.83	(0.12)	0.21	(0.06)	0.62	(0.05)	1.31	(0.06)	0.83	(0.04)
France	-0.39	(0.07)	-1.66	(0.14)	-0.74	(0.02)	0.02	(0.12)	0.82	(0.08)	0.98	(0.04)
Germany	0.01	(0.06)	-1.06	(0.09)	-0.47	(0.12)	0.39	(0.09)	1.18	(0.06)	0.92	(0.04)
Greece	-0.41	(0.09)	-1.87	(0.11)	-0.76	(0.09)	0.06	(0.17)	0.95	(0.09)	1.09	(0.05)
Hungary	-0.02	(0.07)	-1.15	(0.08)	-0.35	(0.12)	0.38	(0.07)	1.07	(0.08)	0.90	(0.03)
Iceland	0.53	(0.00)	-0.72	(0.01)	0.27	(0.00)	1.10	(0.01)	1.45	(0.00)	0.91	(0.00)
Ireland	0.49	(0.08)	-0.90	(0.08)	0.25	(0.17)	1.18	(0.12)	1.45	(0.00)	0.96	(0.05)
Israel	0.17	(0.07)	-1.17	(0.12)	0.11	(0.16)	0.56	(0.06)	1.19	(0.07)	0.95	(0.06)
Italy	-0.60	(0.03)	-1.80	(0.03)	-0.81	(0.05)	-0.34	(0.07)	0.56	(0.05)	0.92	(0.02)
Japan	-0.49	(0.07)	-1.60	(0.10)	-0.74	(0.03)	-0.49	(0.15)	0.88	(0.09)	0.94	(0.04)
Korea	-0.32	(0.09)	-1.59	(0.12)	-0.74	(0.00)	-0.05	(0.19)	1.12	(0.12)	1.06	(0.04)
Luxembourg	0.00	(0.00)	-0.85	(0.00)	-0.41	(0.00)	0.35	(0.00)	0.92	(0.00)	0.76	(0.00)
Mexico	-0.05	(0.04)	-1.20	(0.05)	-0.59	(0.07)	0.33	(0.05)	1.27	(0.03)	1.01	(0.02)
Netherlands	-0.19	(0.07)	-1.01	(0.07)	-0.74	(0.00)	-0.01	(0.18)	0.99	(0.11)	0.85	(0.04)
New Zealand	0.36	(0.06)	-0.88	(0.05)	0.04	(0.14)	0.81	(0.12)	1.45	(0.00)	0.91	(0.04)
Norway	0.26	(0.06)	-0.91	(0.06)	-0.10	(0.14)	0.61	(0.09)	1.43	(0.06)	0.91	(0.03)
Poland	-0.14	(0.08)	-1.15	(0.12)	-0.57	(0.13)	0.16	(0.06)	0.99	(0.10)	0.90	(0.06)
Portugal	-0.17	(0.08)	-1.42	(0.13)	-0.51	(0.13)	0.24	(0.06)	1.01	(0.10)	0.98	(0.05)
Slovak Republic	-0.27	(0.06)	-1.28	(0.12)	-0.68	(0.10)	0.14	(0.07)	0.75	(0.06)	0.84	(0.04)
Slovenia	-0.18	(0.01)	-1.22	(0.02)	-0.63	(0.03)	0.24	(0.01)	0.90	(0.01)	0.89	(0.01)
Spain	-0.43	(0.05)	-1.70	(0.08)	-0.74	(0.06)	-0.12	(0.06)	0.86	(0.09)	0.98	(0.03)
Sweden	0.39	(0.07)	-0.81	(0.14)	0.20	(0.06)	0.74	(0.09)	1.45	(0.05)	0.87	(0.04)
Switzerland	0.31	(0.06)	-0.95	(0.10)	0.17	(0.09)	0.68	(0.05)	1.35	(0.07)	0.89	(0.04)
Turkey	-0.23	(0.08)	-1.50	(0.15)	-0.74	(0.03)	0.20	(0.17)	1.12	(0.10)	1.06	(0.05)
United Kingdom	0.45	(0.06)	-0.87	(0.13)	0.30	(0.06)	0.93	(0.11)	1.45	(0.00)	0.92	(0.04)
United States	-0.03	(0.08)	-1.18	(0.10)	-0.53	(0.12)	0.38	(0.06)	1.20	(0.13)	0.99	(0.05)
OECD average	0.00	(0.01)	-1.16	(0.02)	-0.34	(0.02)	0.38	(0.02)	1.13	(0.01)	0.92	(0.01)
Partners												
Albania	0.35	(0.07)	-0.70	(0.13)	0.16	(0.07)	0.60	(0.06)	1.34	(0.07)	0.78	(0.04)
Argentina	-0.07	(0.07)	-1.11	(0.10)	-0.47	(0.13)	0.29	(0.06)	1.01	(0.09)	0.89	(0.04)
Brazil	-0.50	(0.05)	-1.91	(0.07)	-0.75	(0.05)	-0.25	(0.08)	0.90	(0.09)	1.07	(0.04)
Bulgaria	0.21	(0.07)	-0.98	(0.07)	-0.03	(0.17)	0.53	(0.06)	1.30	(0.07)	0.88	(0.04)
Colombia	0.11	(0.07)	-1.03	(0.08)	-0.29	(0.14)	0.45	(0.08)	1.32	(0.07)	0.94	(0.04)
Costa Rica	-0.02	(0.07)	-1.23	(0.10)	-0.53	(0.11)	0.43	(0.10)	1.25	(0.07)	1.02	(0.04)
Croatia	-0.29	(0.07)	-1.31	(0.10)	-0.74	(0.02)	-0.04	(0.13)	0.94	(0.11)	0.92	(0.05)
Cyprus*	-0.07	(0.00)	-1.18	(0.00)	-0.63	(0.00)	0.25	(0.00)	1.28	(0.00)	0.99	(0.00)
Hong Kong-China	-0.42	(0.07)	-1.43	(0.12)	-0.74	(0.00)	-0.29	(0.13)	0.79	(0.13)	0.89	(0.05)
Indonesia	0.59	(0.07)	-0.77	(0.11)	0.39	(0.11)	1.27	(0.09)	1.45	(0.00)	0.91	(0.04)
Jordan	-0.21	(0.08)	-1.51	(0.11)	-0.73	(0.09)	0.25	(0.14)	1.14	(0.11)	1.08	(0.05)
Kazakhstan	0.51	(0.07)	-0.65	(0.16)	0.33	(0.07)	0.92	(0.15)	1.45	(0.00)	0.89	(0.08)
Latvia	0.09	(0.06)	-0.78	(0.03)	-0.30	(0.11)	0.28	(0.08)	1.16	(0.08)	0.78	(0.03)
Liechtenstein	0.08	(0.01)	c	c	c	c	c	c	c	c	0.70	(0.01)
Lithuania	0.34	(0.06)	-0.76	(0.15)	0.26	(0.06)	0.66	(0.05)	1.22	(0.06)	0.83	(0.06)
Macao-China	-0.50	(0.00)	-1.35	(0.00)	-0.74	(0.00)	-0.49	(0.00)	0.56	(0.00)	0.83	(0.00)
Malaysia	0.46	(0.08)	-0.86	(0.15)	0.16	(0.08)	1.11	(0.16)	1.45	(0.00)	0.95	(0.05)
Montenegro	0.10	(0.00)	-0.96	(0.00)	-0.49	(0.01)	0.52	(0.00)	1.34	(0.00)	0.94	(0.00)
Peru	-0.17	(0.07)	-1.28	(0.11)	-0.73	(0.08)	0.19	(0.11)	1.15	(0.10)	0.99	(0.04)
Qatar	0.77	(0.00)	-0.54	(0.00)	0.73	(0.00)	1.45	(0.00)	1.45	(0.00)	0.87	(0.00)
Romania	-0.04	(0.07)	-1.16	(0.10)	-0.27	(0.13)	0.31	(0.06)	0.94	(0.10)	0.87	(0.05)
Russian Federation	-0.04	(0.05)	-1.07	(0.07)	-0.40	(0.10)	0.25	(0.05)	1.05	(0.08)	0.87	(0.03)
Serbia	-0.37	(0.08)	-1.47	(0.14)	-0.74	(0.05)	0.01	(0.15)	0.70	(0.09)	0.87	(0.05)
Shanghai-China	-0.01	(0.07)	-1.07	(0.09)	-0.53	(0.13)	0.33	(0.10)	1.24	(0.06)	0.95	(0.04)
Singapore	0.13	(0.01)	-1.00	(0.00)	-0.26	(0.02)	0.38	(0.02)	1.40	(0.01)	0.95	(0.00)
Chinese Taipei	-0.14	(0.08)	-1.06	(0.09)	-0.74	(0.00)	0.01	(0.19)	1.25	(0.12)	0.97	(0.05)
Thailand	0.06	(0.08)	-1.24	(0.12)	-0.25	(0.11)	0.47	(0.11)	1.28	(0.07)	1.01	(0.05)
Tunisia	-0.66	(0.09)	-2.09	(0.13)	-1.02	(0.11)	-0.41	(0.12)	0.90	(0.14)	1.16	(0.05)
United Arab Emirates	0.39	(0.05)	-0.96	(0.03)	0.04	(0.11)	1.02	(0.09)	1.45	(0.00)	0.99	(0.02)
Uruguay	-0.28	(0.07)	-1.49	(0.13)	-0.64	(0.11)	0.13	(0.05)	0.90	(0.09)	0.96	(0.05)
Viet Nam	-0.30	(0.06)	-1.15	(0.10)	-0.74	(0.00)	-0.16	(0.11)	0.84	(0.11)	0.85	(0.05)

Note: Values that are statistically significant are indicated in bold (see Annex A3).
* See notes at the beginning of this Annex.
StatLink ⊞≋⊐ http://dx.doi.org/10.1787/888932957517

[Part 2/2]
Index of teacher morale and mathematics performance
Table IV.5.10 *Results based on school principals' reports*

		Performance on the mathematics scale by national quarters of this index								Change in the mathematics score per unit of this index		Increased likelihood of students in the bottom quarter of this index scoring in the bottom quarter of the national mathematics performance distribution		Explained variance in student performance (r-squared x 100)	
		Bottom quarter		Second quarter		Third quarter		Top quarter							
		Mean score	S.E.	Mean score	S.E.	Mean score	S.E.	Mean score	S.E.	Score dif.	S.E.	Ratio	S.E.	%	S.E.
OECD	Australia	**490**	(3.1)	496	(2.7)	511	(3.8)	**520**	(3.9)	**14.3**	(1.7)	**1.30**	(0.1)	1.8	(0.4)
	Austria	497	(8.3)	518	(9.2)	499	(9.5)	509	(7.7)	3.3	(6.5)	1.10	(0.2)	0.1	(0.4)
	Belgium	485	(6.9)	515	(6.8)	528	(7.8)	536	(9.1)	**23.9**	(5.7)	**1.66**	(0.2)	4.5	(2.2)
	Canada	508	(4.0)	514	(3.6)	520	(3.7)	531	(4.5)	9.0	(2.1)	1.19	(0.1)	0.9	(0.4)
	Chile	395	(6.0)	412	(6.2)	435	(7.1)	448	(7.1)	**20.5**	(3.8)	**1.66**	(0.2)	6.2	(2.0)
	Czech Republic	498	(7.4)	495	(7.9)	501	(7.5)	506	(8.0)	4.9	(5.4)	1.00	(0.1)	0.2	(0.4)
	Denmark	493	(3.9)	497	(6.4)	500	(7.1)	512	(5.4)	7.4	(2.5)	1.15	(0.1)	0.7	(0.5)
	Estonia	512	(3.7)	512	(4.5)	526	(4.5)	531	(4.4)	10.1	(2.3)	1.18	(0.1)	1.2	(0.5)
	Finland	518	(3.7)	515	(4.7)	520	(4.0)	522	(4.4)	2.4	(2.2)	1.00	(0.1)	0.1	(0.1)
	France	478	(9.3)	477	(8.5)	500	(10.6)	532	(8.2)	**19.6**	(4.8)	**1.31**	(0.2)	3.9	(1.8)
	Germany	489	(7.5)	516	(9.5)	526	(8.6)	522	(9.2)	**14.9**	(4.8)	**1.41**	(0.2)	2.0	(1.4)
	Greece	439	(6.5)	451	(7.2)	461	(7.4)	461	(7.7)	8.5	(3.6)	**1.35**	(0.2)	1.1	(1.0)
	Hungary	453	(10.8)	474	(7.1)	485	(8.9)	500	(10.3)	**19.5**	(7.2)	**1.74**	(0.3)	3.6	(2.7)
	Iceland	487	(4.0)	496	(3.6)	491	(5.1)	499	(3.6)	5.7	(1.8)	1.17	(0.1)	0.3	(0.2)
	Ireland	493	(7.1)	503	(5.7)	506	(5.5)	509	(5.5)	6.1	(3.6)	1.28	(0.2)	0.5	(0.6)
	Israel	443	(10.9)	466	(7.5)	479	(9.8)	476	(11.9)	**16.5**	(7.1)	**1.41**	(0.3)	2.2	(2.1)
	Italy	474	(4.9)	486	(4.2)	492	(4.2)	497	(4.9)	9.4	(3.2)	**1.25**	(0.1)	0.9	(0.6)
	Japan	496	(8.2)	544	(7.0)	542	(8.3)	564	(10.7)	**26.8**	(4.4)	**1.82**	(0.2)	7.3	(2.4)
	Korea	519	(11.7)	549	(8.2)	563	(8.2)	583	(9.1)	**23.7**	(5.0)	**1.93**	(0.3)	6.4	(2.8)
	Luxembourg	469	(2.8)	488	(2.4)	503	(2.7)	500	(2.4)	**21.0**	(1.4)	**1.38**	(0.1)	2.8	(0.4)
	Mexico	408	(2.5)	413	(2.5)	410	(3.3)	422	(3.7)	4.9	(1.9)	1.10	(0.1)	0.4	(0.3)
	Netherlands	524	(7.3)	512	(8.9)	516	(10.4)	527	(10.0)	3.2	(7.0)	0.90	(0.1)	0.1	(0.5)
	New Zealand	487	(5.1)	491	(7.1)	512	(7.3)	517	(7.6)	**15.6**	(3.7)	1.20	(0.1)	2.0	(1.0)
	Norway	478	(5.8)	485	(6.2)	495	(4.9)	503	(5.8)	11.4	(3.8)	1.24	(0.1)	1.3	(0.9)
	Poland	506	(5.4)	515	(6.0)	521	(8.9)	528	(6.1)	10.9	(3.0)	1.20	(0.1)	1.2	(0.7)
	Portugal	471	(8.5)	483	(7.0)	487	(8.2)	505	(7.5)	13.3	(4.2)	1.29	(0.2)	1.9	(1.2)
	Slovak Republic	480	(8.2)	486	(8.4)	479	(8.6)	481	(10.5)	-0.2	(6.6)	0.99	(0.1)	0.0	(0.3)
	Slovenia	500	(3.9)	495	(4.1)	506	(3.9)	513	(4.9)	5.7	(1.8)	0.99	(0.1)	0.3	(0.2)
	Spain	467	(4.5)	478	(4.4)	492	(4.1)	500	(4.9)	12.1	(2.6)	**1.39**	(0.1)	1.8	(0.8)
	Sweden	465	(5.1)	477	(4.8)	484	(5.3)	487	(5.1)	9.4	(3.2)	**1.31**	(0.1)	0.8	(0.5)
	Switzerland	537	(6.2)	529	(5.6)	526	(5.7)	537	(8.0)	-1.4	(4.1)	0.85	(0.1)	0.0	(0.2)
	Turkey	427	(8.1)	429	(6.4)	456	(10.1)	481	(13.5)	**20.5**	(4.9)	**1.31**	(0.2)	5.7	(2.7)
	United Kingdom	470	(10.0)	497	(7.4)	506	(6.6)	504	(6.7)	**16.7**	(4.4)	**1.57**	(0.2)	2.6	(1.4)
	United States	465	(6.9)	472	(6.5)	492	(5.7)	500	(9.4)	**14.4**	(4.9)	**1.49**	(0.2)	2.5	(1.6)
	OECD average	**480**	(1.2)	**491**	(1.1)	**499**	(1.2)	**508**	(1.3)	**11.9**	(0.7)	**1.30**	(0.0)	2.0	(0.2)
Partners	Albania	394	(5.1)	396	(5.3)	393	(4.0)	394	(4.5)	-0.9	(2.8)	1.00	(0.1)	0.0	(0.1)
	Argentina	381	(6.4)	384	(6.3)	387	(7.5)	406	(5.9)	10.3	(5.3)	1.29	(0.2)	1.5	(1.4)
	Brazil	382	(2.8)	382	(4.1)	389	(5.2)	413	(5.4)	**12.8**	(1.8)	1.04	(0.1)	3.1	(0.9)
	Bulgaria	413	(8.3)	434	(8.6)	452	(10.1)	456	(10.2)	**20.0**	(5.5)	**1.47**	(0.2)	3.5	(2.0)
	Colombia	369	(4.5)	367	(6.0)	375	(6.2)	395	(5.7)	10.3	(2.7)	1.17	(0.1)	1.7	(0.9)
	Costa Rica	395	(5.6)	401	(5.6)	409	(8.0)	423	(7.3)	10.9	(3.4)	1.31	(0.2)	2.6	(1.8)
	Croatia	456	(5.9)	478	(6.9)	467	(7.1)	483	(11.9)	10.5	(5.3)	**1.38**	(0.1)	1.2	(1.2)
	Cyprus*	424	(2.5)	432	(4.1)	450	(2.9)	451	(2.3)	**12.1**	(1.1)	1.26	(0.1)	1.6	(0.3)
	Hong Kong-China	535	(7.5)	564	(7.9)	563	(8.7)	583	(9.8)	**21.2**	(5.0)	**1.58**	(0.2)	3.9	(1.9)
	Indonesia	361	(8.8)	368	(8.4)	384	(7.6)	387	(6.0)	11.9	(4.5)	1.32	(0.2)	2.3	(1.7)
	Jordan	373	(6.7)	379	(6.5)	389	(6.9)	402	(8.9)	11.3	(3.9)	1.32	(0.1)	2.4	(1.6)
	Kazakhstan	431	(5.4)	432	(6.7)	436	(6.2)	428	(5.9)	-1.0	(3.4)	0.96	(0.1)	0.0	(0.2)
	Latvia	490	(5.5)	487	(5.0)	485	(6.4)	493	(6.9)	0.6	(4.4)	0.94	(0.1)	0.0	(0.1)
	Liechtenstein	c	c	c	c	c	c	c	c	-0.3	(5.4)	1.40	(0.3)	0.0	(0.2)
	Lithuania	454	(5.8)	476	(6.4)	491	(5.1)	494	(5.3)	**18.1**	(3.7)	**1.62**	(0.2)	2.8	(1.0)
	Macao-China	520	(2.9)	535	(2.6)	538	(3.5)	559	(2.8)	**21.6**	(1.2)	**1.37**	(0.1)	3.6	(0.4)
	Malaysia	422	(7.1)	421	(5.8)	416	(6.7)	423	(6.5)	1.5	(3.8)	0.98	(0.1)	0.0	(0.1)
	Montenegro	401	(2.7)	389	(2.3)	404	(2.2)	445	(2.4)	**17.0**	(1.2)	1.16	(0.1)	3.7	(0.5)
	Peru	350	(5.2)	355	(5.5)	373	(9.1)	394	(9.0)	**17.7**	(4.3)	1.23	(0.1)	4.3	(2.0)
	Qatar	369	(1.4)	374	(1.8)	381	(2.6)	382	(2.4)	6.1	(0.8)	1.04	(0.1)	0.3	(0.1)
	Romania	429	(6.6)	443	(5.9)	451	(7.4)	455	(8.2)	13.1	(4.9)	1.32	(0.2)	2.0	(1.4)
	Russian Federation	462	(4.2)	480	(5.9)	490	(5.8)	496	(7.0)	**17.2**	(3.1)	**1.41**	(0.1)	3.0	(1.1)
	Serbia	439	(9.0)	437	(9.2)	447	(9.8)	468	(10.0)	13.8	(6.7)	1.16	(0.2)	1.8	(1.7)
	Shanghai-China	591	(8.7)	609	(7.8)	620	(8.4)	631	(9.5)	16.0	(5.7)	**1.49**	(0.2)	2.3	(1.5)
	Singapore	553	(2.9)	565	(4.1)	579	(4.0)	602	(2.8)	**21.0**	(1.4)	1.21	(0.1)	3.5	(0.5)
	Chinese Taipei	540	(7.1)	545	(8.8)	569	(10.5)	586	(13.5)	**21.1**	(6.7)	**1.30**	(0.1)	3.1	(2.1)
	Thailand	403	(5.1)	416	(6.2)	441	(9.1)	447	(8.0)	**16.1**	(3.2)	**1.47**	(0.2)	4.0	(1.5)
	Tunisia	381	(6.8)	387	(6.5)	390	(7.5)	394	(10.6)	4.0	(4.0)	1.03	(0.2)	0.3	(0.7)
	United Arab Emirates	414	(4.9)	427	(5.9)	443	(4.5)	455	(5.0)	**16.7**	(2.9)	**1.42**	(0.1)	3.4	(1.1)
	Uruguay	385	(5.0)	395	(6.4)	421	(6.6)	436	(8.5)	**21.6**	(3.7)	**1.39**	(0.1)	5.5	(1.9)
	Viet Nam	503	(7.0)	508	(8.4)	506	(9.4)	529	(9.5)	9.6	(5.9)	1.17	(0.2)	0.9	(1.1)

Note: Values that are statistically significant are indicated in bold (see Annex A3).
* See notes at the beginning of this Annex.
StatLink ᓀᓂᔅᒪ http://dx.doi.org/10.1787/888932957517

[Part 1/2]

Table IV.5.11 Correlation between learning environment indicators at the school level

Results based on students' and school principals' reports

		Correlation between:																			
		Percentage of students who arrived late for school at least once in the two weeks prior to the PISA test (at the school level) and...												Percentage of students who skipped a day or a class at least once in the two weeks prior to the PISA test (at the school level) and...							
		Percentage of students who skipped a day or a class at least once in the two weeks prior to the PISA test (at the school level)		School average index of teacher-student relations		School average index of disciplinary climate		Index of student-related factors affecting school climate		Index of teacher-related factors affecting school climate		Index of teacher morale		School average index of teacher-student relations		School average index of disciplinary climate		Index of student-related factors affecting school climate		Index of teacher-related factors affecting school climate		Index of teacher morale	
		Corr.	S.E.	Corr.	S.E.	Corr.	S.E.	Corr.	S.E.	Corr.	S.E.	Corr.	S.E.	Corr.	S.E.	Corr.	S.E.	Corr.	S.E.	Corr.	S.E.	Corr.	S.E.
OECD	Australia	**0.23**	(0.03)	**-0.09**	(0.04)	**-0.15**	(0.04)	**-0.16**	(0.04)	-0.06	(0.04)	-0.04	(0.03)	**-0.22**	(0.03)	**-0.20**	(0.04)	**-0.29**	(0.03)	**-0.19**	(0.05)	**-0.17**	(0.04)
	Austria	**0.62**	(0.06)	**-0.23**	(0.08)	**-0.27**	(0.07)	-0.11	(0.07)	0.06	(0.08)	-0.04	(0.08)	**-0.30**	(0.08)	-0.14	(0.07)	-0.07	(0.07)	0.05	(0.08)	-0.04	(0.08)
	Belgium	**0.63**	(0.04)	0.08	(0.06)	**-0.24**	(0.05)	**-0.30**	(0.04)	**-0.15**	(0.06)	**-0.19**	(0.06)	0.09	(0.06)	**-0.31**	(0.05)	**-0.25**	(0.05)	**-0.18**	(0.06)	**-0.31**	(0.06)
	Canada	**0.39**	(0.05)	**-0.23**	(0.05)	**-0.13**	(0.04)	**-0.27**	(0.04)	**-0.11**	(0.04)	-0.09	(0.05)	**-0.17**	(0.05)	**-0.12**	(0.04)	**-0.22**	(0.05)	-0.06	(0.05)	-0.06	(0.04)
	Chile	**0.45**	(0.06)	-0.07	(0.07)	**-0.29**	(0.07)	**-0.24**	(0.06)	**-0.12**	(0.06)	**-0.15**	(0.06)	**-0.22**	(0.08)	**-0.21**	(0.07)	**-0.31**	(0.06)	**-0.25**	(0.07)	**-0.28**	(0.07)
	Czech Republic	**0.33**	(0.07)	**-0.25**	(0.06)	**-0.26**	(0.05)	**-0.22**	(0.05)	-0.07	(0.05)	0.08	(0.06)	**-0.16**	(0.06)	-0.11	(0.07)	-0.10	(0.07)	-0.03	(0.06)	0.04	(0.06)
	Denmark	**0.50**	(0.05)	-0.06	(0.09)	**-0.25**	(0.08)	**-0.23**	(0.06)	**-0.18**	(0.07)	-0.07	(0.06)	-0.06	(0.09)	**-0.19**	(0.06)	**-0.15**	(0.07)	**-0.13**	(0.06)	-0.04	(0.06)
	Estonia	**0.50**	(0.05)	-0.04	(0.07)	-0.06	(0.07)	0.04	(0.06)	0.02	(0.07)	-0.04	(0.06)	**-0.21**	(0.07)	**-0.17**	(0.06)	**-0.21**	(0.06)	-0.10	(0.06)	**-0.11**	(0.05)
	Finland	**0.34**	(0.04)	**-0.13**	(0.06)	**-0.29**	(0.06)	**-0.21**	(0.06)	-0.01	(0.05)	**0.15**	(0.07)	**-0.20**	(0.06)	**-0.13**	(0.05)	**-0.14**	(0.06)	0.00	(0.05)	-0.10	(0.06)
	France	**0.59**	(0.04)	0.00	(0.06)	**-0.33**	(0.05)	**-0.34**	(0.05)	**-0.25**	(0.06)	**-0.21**	(0.07)	-0.05	(0.06)	**-0.39**	(0.06)	**-0.41**	(0.05)	**-0.30**	(0.07)	**-0.19**	(0.07)
	Germany	**0.31**	(0.09)	-0.06	(0.07)	**-0.20**	(0.10)	**-0.24**	(0.07)	-0.03	(0.07)	-0.05	(0.07)	-0.03	(0.06)	**-0.22**	(0.09)	**-0.25**	(0.06)	0.00	(0.07)	-0.05	(0.07)
	Greece	**0.39**	(0.06)	**-0.29**	(0.08)	**-0.21**	(0.09)	**-0.16**	(0.08)	-0.10	(0.08)	-0.06	(0.09)	**-0.20**	(0.06)	**-0.28**	(0.08)	**-0.24**	(0.08)	**-0.23**	(0.07)	**-0.23**	(0.09)
	Hungary	**0.57**	(0.06)	-0.09	(0.07)	**-0.42**	(0.06)	**-0.39**	(0.06)	**-0.16**	(0.06)	**-0.19**	(0.08)	-0.05	(0.06)	**-0.48**	(0.05)	**-0.51**	(0.06)	**-0.25**	(0.05)	**-0.31**	(0.07)
	Iceland	**0.28**	(0.01)	**-0.05**	(0.01)	**-0.12**	(0.01)	**-0.29**	(0.01)	**-0.13**	(0.01)	**-0.03**	(0.01)	**-0.23**	(0.01)	**-0.25**	(0.00)	**-0.23**	(0.01)	**-0.07**	(0.01)	**-0.06**	(0.01)
	Ireland	**0.46**	(0.06)	0.07	(0.09)	**-0.32**	(0.06)	**-0.28**	(0.07)	-0.14	(0.08)	-0.05	(0.08)	-0.06	(0.07)	**-0.22**	(0.07)	**-0.18**	(0.07)	-0.13	(0.07)	-0.13	(0.09)
	Israel	**0.21**	(0.09)	-0.05	(0.07)	0.01	(0.08)	-0.09	(0.08)	0.03	(0.09)	-0.08	(0.09)	-0.08	(0.08)	-0.08	(0.07)	-0.16	(0.08)	-0.06	(0.08)	-0.01	(0.07)
	Italy	**0.50**	(0.03)	**0.14**	(0.04)	**-0.21**	(0.04)	**-0.23**	(0.04)	-0.04	(0.05)	-0.04	(0.05)	**0.12**	(0.05)	**-0.18**	(0.03)	**-0.29**	(0.04)	-0.01	(0.05)	**-0.10**	(0.05)
	Japan	**0.47**	(0.07)	-0.15	(0.08)	**-0.36**	(0.06)	**-0.30**	(0.07)	**-0.14**	(0.06)	-0.10	(0.06)	-0.13	(0.07)	**-0.35**	(0.07)	-0.23	(0.14)	-0.03	(0.12)	-0.07	(0.07)
	Korea	**0.47**	(0.05)	**-0.32**	(0.06)	**-0.48**	(0.07)	**-0.45**	(0.05)	**-0.13**	(0.06)	**-0.29**	(0.08)	**-0.31**	(0.07)	**-0.51**	(0.05)	**-0.40**	(0.06)	-0.11	(0.06)	**-0.28**	(0.07)
	Luxembourg	**0.70**	(0.00)	**0.10**	(0.00)	**-0.20**	(0.00)	**-0.10**	(0.00)	**0.01**	(0.00)	**-0.20**	(0.00)	**0.08**	(0.00)	**-0.25**	(0.00)	**-0.25**	(0.00)	**-0.04**	(0.00)	**-0.07**	(0.00)
	Mexico	**0.45**	(0.03)	**-0.22**	(0.04)	**-0.13**	(0.03)	**-0.21**	(0.04)	-0.08	(0.04)	**-0.10**	(0.04)	**-0.17**	(0.04)	**-0.22**	(0.03)	**-0.21**	(0.04)	**-0.11**	(0.03)	-0.07	(0.04)
	Netherlands	**0.38**	(0.06)	**-0.15**	(0.07)	**-0.29**	(0.09)	**-0.20**	(0.07)	0.07	(0.08)	-0.01	(0.08)	**-0.21**	(0.08)	-0.09	(0.09)	-0.14	(0.07)	-0.04	(0.09)	-0.03	(0.08)
	New Zealand	**0.50**	(0.05)	-0.02	(0.08)	**-0.28**	(0.06)	**-0.40**	(0.05)	**-0.18**	(0.08)	-0.09	(0.08)	-0.11	(0.08)	**-0.42**	(0.07)	**-0.42**	(0.06)	**-0.17**	(0.07)	-0.05	(0.08)
	Norway	**0.48**	(0.06)	-0.03	(0.08)	**-0.14**	(0.06)	**-0.20**	(0.06)	-0.06	(0.07)	0.03	(0.07)	**-0.24**	(0.06)	**-0.28**	(0.07)	**-0.17**	(0.07)	-0.07	(0.08)	0.01	(0.07)
	Poland	**0.64**	(0.04)	**-0.33**	(0.07)	**-0.33**	(0.06)	**-0.18**	(0.07)	0.01	(0.08)	0.03	(0.09)	**-0.25**	(0.06)	**-0.30**	(0.07)	-0.14	(0.08)	-0.04	(0.09)	-0.16	(0.09)
	Portugal	**0.46**	(0.06)	**-0.37**	(0.08)	**-0.20**	(0.08)	-0.12	(0.07)	-0.12	(0.07)	0.00	(0.09)	**-0.34**	(0.07)	**-0.24**	(0.07)	**-0.27**	(0.07)	-0.15	(0.07)	-0.15	(0.08)
	Slovak Republic	**0.46**	(0.07)	-0.08	(0.07)	**-0.37**	(0.05)	**-0.27**	(0.06)	-0.06	(0.06)	-0.06	(0.06)	0.00	(0.07)	**-0.44**	(0.05)	**-0.19**	(0.07)	-0.01	(0.07)	0.07	(0.06)
	Slovenia	**0.56**	(0.04)	**-0.23**	(0.06)	**-0.35**	(0.02)	**-0.24**	(0.02)	**-0.06**	(0.01)	**-0.04**	(0.02)	**-0.19**	(0.04)	**-0.45**	(0.03)	**-0.33**	(0.02)	**-0.14**	(0.01)	0.01	(0.01)
	Spain	**0.32**	(0.05)	**-0.19**	(0.04)	**-0.13**	(0.06)	**-0.20**	(0.05)	-0.10	(0.06)	**-0.11**	(0.05)	0.01	(0.06)	-0.08	(0.05)	**-0.25**	(0.04)	**-0.13**	(0.07)	**-0.22**	(0.05)
	Sweden	**0.41**	(0.06)	-0.13	(0.07)	-0.12	(0.07)	-0.07	(0.06)	0.03	(0.07)	-0.03	(0.08)	-0.13	(0.08)	**-0.26**	(0.07)	**-0.16**	(0.07)	0.00	(0.07)	**-0.18**	(0.08)
	Switzerland	**0.52**	(0.05)	**-0.30**	(0.05)	**-0.26**	(0.05)	**-0.22**	(0.06)	0.00	(0.06)	**-0.22**	(0.06)	**-0.37**	(0.05)	**-0.28**	(0.05)	**-0.18**	(0.06)	-0.04	(0.06)	**-0.22**	(0.06)
	Turkey	**0.32**	(0.07)	0.10	(0.07)	**-0.29**	(0.07)	**-0.18**	(0.08)	-0.08	(0.07)	-0.05	(0.08)	0.11	(0.06)	-0.01	(0.10)	-0.05	(0.09)	-0.06	(0.08)	0.12	(0.08)
	United Kingdom	**0.23**	(0.06)	**-0.11**	(0.05)	-0.07	(0.06)	-0.08	(0.06)	-0.05	(0.06)	-0.09	(0.07)	0.01	(0.08)	**-0.16**	(0.06)	-0.02	(0.08)	0.06	(0.09)	-0.05	(0.07)
	United States	**0.35**	(0.06)	**-0.25**	(0.07)	**-0.34**	(0.08)	**-0.21**	(0.08)	**-0.19**	(0.06)	**-0.18**	(0.09)	**-0.34**	(0.07)	**-0.36**	(0.07)	**-0.12**	(0.06)	-0.09	(0.07)	-0.02	(0.08)
	OECD average	**0.44**	(0.01)	**-0.12**	(0.01)	**-0.24**	(0.01)	**-0.22**	(0.01)	**-0.08**	(0.01)	**-0.08**	(0.01)	**-0.14**	(0.01)	**-0.25**	(0.01)	**-0.22**	(0.01)	**-0.09**	(0.01)	**-0.10**	(0.01)
Partners	Albania	**0.29**	(0.06)	-0.04	(0.07)	**-0.22**	(0.08)	0.08	(0.07)	-0.05	(0.07)	0.03	(0.07)	**-0.14**	(0.06)	**-0.20**	(0.07)	-0.04	(0.07)	-0.10	(0.07)	0.09	(0.08)
	Argentina	**0.43**	(0.06)	-0.02	(0.08)	**-0.16**	(0.08)	**-0.33**	(0.08)	-0.08	(0.07)	-0.12	(0.07)	-0.03	(0.07)	**-0.32**	(0.08)	**-0.38**	(0.05)	**-0.22**	(0.06)	-0.13	(0.08)
	Brazil	**0.20**	(0.05)	-0.03	(0.05)	-0.05	(0.05)	-0.01	(0.07)	**0.13**	(0.06)	0.05	(0.05)	-0.04	(0.05)	**-0.15**	(0.04)	-0.03	(0.05)	0.00	(0.05)	-0.03	(0.05)
	Bulgaria	**0.63**	(0.04)	0.11	(0.08)	**-0.35**	(0.08)	**-0.24**	(0.08)	-0.10	(0.08)	**-0.13**	(0.07)	**0.16**	(0.07)	**-0.42**	(0.06)	**-0.34**	(0.07)	-0.10	(0.07)	**-0.19**	(0.07)
	Colombia	**0.35**	(0.07)	-0.15	(0.10)	**-0.26**	(0.07)	-0.12	(0.06)	0.05	(0.09)	-0.07	(0.07)	-0.09	(0.09)	**-0.22**	(0.08)	-0.11	(0.07)	0.04	(0.08)	-0.02	(0.08)
	Costa Rica	**0.24**	(0.06)	**-0.16**	(0.07)	**-0.24**	(0.06)	**-0.28**	(0.08)	**-0.15**	(0.07)	-0.05	(0.08)	-0.06	(0.07)	**-0.27**	(0.08)	**-0.32**	(0.08)	**-0.24**	(0.09)	**-0.19**	(0.07)
	Croatia	**0.61**	(0.04)	**-0.17**	(0.08)	**-0.35**	(0.06)	**-0.37**	(0.07)	0.04	(0.10)	-0.04	(0.07)	-0.03	(0.09)	**-0.55**	(0.05)	**-0.35**	(0.06)	-0.07	(0.07)	-0.12	(0.07)
	Cyprus*	**0.25**	(0.00)	**-0.37**	(0.00)	**-0.37**	(0.00)	**-0.14**	(0.00)	**-0.02**	(0.00)	**-0.08**	(0.00)	**-0.18**	(0.01)	**-0.20**	(0.00)	**-0.15**	(0.00)	**0.07**	(0.00)	**0.02**	(0.00)
	Hong Kong-China	**0.35**	(0.07)	-0.04	(0.07)	**-0.17**	(0.08)	**-0.19**	(0.08)	-0.06	(0.07)	-0.15	(0.08)	0.02	(0.09)	-0.13	(0.07)	**-0.16**	(0.07)	-0.13	(0.07)	**-0.16**	(0.06)
	Indonesia	**0.40**	(0.06)	0.05	(0.07)	-0.12	(0.07)	-0.08	(0.08)	0.02	(0.06)	-0.12	(0.09)	-0.08	(0.08)	**-0.22**	(0.08)	-0.12	(0.07)	0.01	(0.08)	-0.14	(0.08)
	Jordan	0.07	(0.08)	0.02	(0.07)	**-0.29**	(0.07)	**-0.23**	(0.07)	-0.08	(0.07)	-0.08	(0.08)	-0.07	(0.07)	**-0.27**	(0.08)	0.02	(0.08)	-0.03	(0.07)	0.02	(0.08)
	Kazakhstan	**0.70**	(0.04)	**-0.46**	(0.05)	**-0.47**	(0.07)	-0.11	(0.07)	-0.04	(0.08)	-0.03	(0.06)	**-0.38**	(0.05)	**-0.49**	(0.07)	-0.10	(0.07)	-0.03	(0.08)	-0.03	(0.07)
	Latvia	**0.43**	(0.06)	-0.09	(0.07)	**-0.34**	(0.06)	**-0.28**	(0.06)	-0.10	(0.08)	**-0.16**	(0.07)	-0.02	(0.06)	-0.09	(0.07)	**-0.17**	(0.06)	-0.08	(0.06)	0.00	(0.07)
	Liechtenstein	**-0.26**	(0.02)	0.23	(0.17)	**-0.52**	(0.03)	**0.12**	(0.02)	**0.32**	(0.02)	**0.53**	(0.01)	**0.28**	(0.02)	**0.11**	(0.03)	**0.18**	(0.05)	**0.13**	(0.03)	-0.07	(0.05)
	Lithuania	**0.53**	(0.04)	**-0.23**	(0.06)	**-0.29**	(0.05)	**-0.28**	(0.05)	**-0.14**	(0.06)	-0.11	(0.07)	**-0.34**	(0.07)	**-0.37**	(0.06)	**-0.31**	(0.06)	-0.09	(0.06)	-0.15	(0.08)
	Macao-China	**0.69**	(0.00)	**0.05**	(0.00)	**-0.49**	(0.00)	**-0.31**	(0.00)	**-0.03**	(0.00)	**0.08**	(0.00)	**0.18**	(0.00)	**-0.35**	(0.00)	**-0.25**	(0.00)	**-0.08**	(0.00)	**0.17**	(0.00)
	Malaysia	**0.29**	(0.08)	**0.26**	(0.08)	**-0.19**	(0.09)	**-0.26**	(0.06)	0.02	(0.07)	0.12	(0.06)	-0.12	(0.07)	**-0.20**	(0.07)	0.00	(0.08)	0.10	(0.08)	**0.19**	(0.08)
	Montenegro	**0.32**	(0.00)	**0.06**	(0.01)	**-0.43**	(0.01)	**-0.29**	(0.00)	**-0.12**	(0.00)	**-0.23**	(0.00)	**-0.08**	(0.00)	**-0.25**	(0.00)	**-0.17**	(0.00)	**-0.21**	(0.00)	**-0.08**	(0.00)
	Peru	**0.31**	(0.07)	0.04	(0.06)	-0.09	(0.07)	**-0.19**	(0.07)	-0.09	(0.07)	-0.09	(0.07)	**0.12**	(0.06)	**-0.22**	(0.07)	**-0.24**	(0.07)	**-0.15**	(0.05)	**-0.26**	(0.06)
	Qatar	**0.09**	(0.00)	**-0.25**	(0.00)	**-0.29**	(0.00)	**-0.23**	(0.00)	**-0.25**	(0.00)	**-0.21**	(0.00)	**-0.12**	(0.00)	**-0.01**	(0.00)	**-0.02**	(0.00)	**0.02**	(0.00)	**-0.03**	(0.00)
	Romania	**0.64**	(0.05)	0.09	(0.07)	**-0.14**	(0.07)	**-0.15**	(0.07)	-0.10	(0.07)	-0.04	(0.08)	0.04	(0.07)	**-0.27**	(0.07)	-0.10	(0.08)	-0.07	(0.06)	-0.08	(0.06)
	Russian Federation	**0.54**	(0.05)	**-0.29**	(0.08)	**-0.35**	(0.06)	**-0.16**	(0.05)	-0.08	(0.05)	**-0.15**	(0.07)	**-0.17**	(0.09)	**-0.28**	(0.06)	-0.08	(0.08)	-0.03	(0.08)	**-0.14**	(0.05)
	Serbia	**0.61**	(0.06)	-0.01	(0.09)	**-0.28**	(0.07)	**-0.38**	(0.07)	-0.11	(0.09)	-0.11	(0.08)	0.09	(0.08)	**-0.30**	(0.08)	**-0.39**	(0.07)	-0.14	(0.08)	-0.08	(0.10)
	Shanghai-China	**0.24**	(0.09)	**-0.21**	(0.07)	**-0.44**	(0.07)	**-0.28**	(0.07)	-0.12	(0.08)	**-0.14**	(0.06)	**-0.19**	(0.08)	**-0.29**	(0.10)	-0.14	(0.08)	-0.07	(0.07)	-0.10	(0.07)
	Singapore	**0.23**	(0.01)	**-0.19**	(0.03)	**-0.40**	(0.02)	**-0.28**	(0.01)	**-0.14**	(0.00)	**-0.06**	(0.01)	**-0.12**	(0.01)	**-0.20**	(0.01)	**-0.02**	(0.01)	**-0.01**	(0.00)	**0.05**	(0.01)
	Chinese Taipei	**0.29**	(0.10)	**-0.19**	(0.08)	**-0.33**	(0.07)	**-0.22**	(0.08)	**-0.17**	(0.07)	**-0.21**	(0.08)	**-0.22**	(0.07)	**-0.49**	(0.04)	**-0.31**	(0.06)	**-0.17**	(0.07)	**-0.17**	(0.08)
	Thailand	**0.58**	(0.04)	-0.03	(0.07)	**-0.50**	(0.06)	-0.06	(0.06)	0.02	(0.06)	-0.12	(0.07)	-0.03	(0.06)	**-0.46**	(0.05)	-0.10	(0.07)	-0.04	(0.08)	**-0.17**	(0.07)
	Tunisia	**0.34**	(0.07)	-0.13	(0.08)	**-0.17**	(0.08)	-0.12	(0.07)	-0.06	(0.06)	-0.12	(0.09)	0.02	(0.08)	**-0.28**	(0.08)	**-0.19**	(0.08)	-0.01	(0.09)	-0.07	(0.08)
	United Arab Emirates	**0.26**	(0.04)	-0.04	(0.05)	**-0.24**	(0.04)	**-0.26**	(0.06)	-0.12	(0.08)	**-0.21**	(0.04)	-0.09	(0.05)	**-0.37**	(0.05)	**-0.14**	(0.04)	**-0.12**	(0.05)	-0.09	(0.05)
	Uruguay	**0.36**	(0.07)	-0.06	(0.06)	**-0.24**	(0.10)	**-0.27**	(0.08)	-0.05	(0.07)	-0.03	(0.07)	**0.18**	(0.07)	**-0.37**	(0.08)	**-0.42**	(0.06)	**-0.33**	(0.06)	**-0.15**	(0.07)
	Viet Nam	**0.59**	(0.07)	0.02	(0.07)	**-0.19**	(0.09)	**-0.15**	(0.07)	0.13	(0.08)	-0.12	(0.07)	0.09	(0.07)	-0.10	(0.10)	-0.11	(0.08)	0.13	(0.09)	-0.04	(0.08)

Note: Values that are statistically significant are indicated in bold (see Annex A3).

* See notes at the beginning of this Annex.

StatLink http://dx.doi.org/10.1787/888932957517

[Part 2/2]

Table IV.5.11 Correlation between learning environment indicators at the school level

Results based on students' and school principals' reports

		Correlation between:																			
		School average index of teacher-student relations and...								School average index of disciplinary climate and...						Index of student-related factors affecting school climate and...				Index of teacher-related factors affecting school climate and...	
		School average index of disciplinary climate		Index of student-related factors affecting school climate		Index of teacher-related factors affecting school climate		Index of teacher morale		Index of student-related factors affecting school climate		Index of teacher-related factors affecting school climate		Index of teacher morale		Index of teacher-related factors affecting school climate		Index of teacher morale		Index of teacher morale	
		Corr.	S.E.	Corr.	S.E.	Corr.	S.E.	Corr.	S.E.	Corr.	S.E.	Corr.	S.E.	Corr.	S.E.	Corr.	S.E.	Corr.	S.E.	Corr.	S.E.
OECD	Australia	**0.39**	(0.04)	**0.36**	(0.03)	**0.19**	(0.04)	**0.26**	(0.03)	**0.34**	(0.03)	**0.16**	(0.04)	**0.21**	(0.04)	**0.66**	(0.03)	**0.39**	(0.03)	**0.46**	(0.03)
	Austria	**0.19**	(0.08)	0.13	(0.07)	0.05	(0.07)	**0.21**	(0.08)	**0.14**	(0.06)	0.06	(0.06)	0.08	(0.08)	**0.48**	(0.07)	**0.37**	(0.07)	**0.44**	(0.06)
	Belgium	0.04	(0.07)	-0.09	(0.07)	-0.09	(0.07)	**-0.17**	(0.06)	**0.21**	(0.06)	-0.02	(0.07)	0.07	(0.07)	**0.59**	(0.04)	**0.28**	(0.05)	**0.42**	(0.05)
	Canada	**0.19**	(0.05)	**0.23**	(0.05)	0.10	(0.06)	**0.12**	(0.04)	**0.14**	(0.05)	-0.03	(0.04)	**0.15**	(0.05)	**0.47**	(0.04)	**0.27**	(0.04)	**0.42**	(0.05)
	Chile	**0.22**	(0.07)	**0.19**	(0.08)	**0.19**	(0.06)	**0.21**	(0.08)	**0.16**	(0.08)	0.10	(0.07)	0.13	(0.08)	**0.75**	(0.03)	**0.47**	(0.06)	**0.56**	(0.06)
	Czech Republic	**0.26**	(0.06)	**0.21**	(0.07)	0.09	(0.07)	-0.02	(0.06)	**0.24**	(0.07)	0.11	(0.07)	**0.13**	(0.06)	**0.59**	(0.05)	**0.35**	(0.06)	**0.44**	(0.05)
	Denmark	**0.37**	(0.05)	**0.17**	(0.08)	**0.16**	(0.08)	0.07	(0.07)	**0.31**	(0.06)	**0.16**	(0.08)	**0.16**	(0.05)	**0.57**	(0.10)	**0.39**	(0.06)	**0.55**	(0.04)
	Estonia	**0.13**	(0.06)	**0.16**	(0.06)	0.14	(0.07)	0.05	(0.06)	0.10	(0.05)	**0.16**	(0.06)	0.05	(0.06)	**0.59**	(0.04)	**0.31**	(0.05)	**0.39**	(0.05)
	Finland	**0.17**	(0.06)	**0.17**	(0.05)	0.06	(0.06)	0.05	(0.06)	**0.17**	(0.07)	0.05	(0.06)	-0.09	(0.07)	**0.45**	(0.05)	**0.22**	(0.06)	**0.45**	(0.05)
	France	0.00	(0.07)	-0.03	(0.08)	0.02	(0.06)	0.04	(0.07)	**0.34**	(0.06)	**0.26**	(0.07)	**0.21**	(0.07)	**0.59**	(0.05)	**0.44**	(0.05)	**0.44**	(0.07)
	Germany	0.09	(0.07)	0.02	(0.08)	0.07	(0.06)	-0.01	(0.08)	**0.35**	(0.06)	**0.19**	(0.06)	0.10	(0.07)	**0.44**	(0.05)	**0.28**	(0.06)	**0.40**	(0.05)
	Greece	0.13	(0.08)	**0.17**	(0.08)	**0.22**	(0.07)	0.04	(0.08)	**0.24**	(0.07)	0.13	(0.07)	**0.20**	(0.08)	**0.71**	(0.04)	**0.40**	(0.08)	**0.39**	(0.07)
	Hungary	0.13	(0.08)	0.06	(0.07)	0.02	(0.06)	0.10	(0.07)	**0.38**	(0.08)	**0.15**	(0.07)	**0.14**	(0.07)	**0.52**	(0.06)	**0.36**	(0.06)	**0.47**	(0.06)
	Iceland	**0.31**	(0.01)	**-0.03**	(0.01)	**-0.03**	(0.01)	**0.09**	(0.00)	**0.13**	(0.01)	**0.03**	(0.01)	**0.23**	(0.01)	**0.69**	(0.00)	**0.23**	(0.00)	**0.37**	(0.00)
	Ireland	0.11	(0.07)	**0.25**	(0.08)	0.11	(0.07)	**0.19**	(0.08)	**0.33**	(0.08)	**0.22**	(0.08)	0.04	(0.08)	**0.55**	(0.07)	**0.36**	(0.07)	**0.47**	(0.05)
	Israel	0.05	(0.08)	-0.06	(0.08)	0.07	(0.08)	**0.16**	(0.07)	0.15	(0.08)	**0.25**	(0.08)	**0.27**	(0.07)	**0.71**	(0.04)	**0.36**	(0.06)	**0.44**	(0.06)
	Italy	0.04	(0.04)	-0.02	(0.05)	**0.13**	(0.05)	0.03	(0.04)	**0.27**	(0.04)	-0.03	(0.05)	0.08	(0.04)	**0.46**	(0.04)	**0.33**	(0.04)	**0.32**	(0.04)
	Japan	**0.33**	(0.09)	0.15	(0.08)	**0.20**	(0.06)	0.14	(0.08)	**0.42**	(0.08)	**0.28**	(0.06)	**0.21**	(0.07)	**0.61**	(0.05)	**0.21**	(0.07)	**0.49**	(0.06)
	Korea	**0.46**	(0.09)	**0.34**	(0.07)	**0.20**	(0.07)	**0.17**	(0.08)	**0.44**	(0.07)	0.12	(0.07)	**0.38**	(0.08)	**0.65**	(0.06)	**0.51**	(0.07)	**0.39**	(0.10)
	Luxembourg	**0.10**	(0.00)	**0.35**	(0.00)	**0.44**	(0.00)	**0.03**	(0.00)	**0.10**	(0.00)	0.01	(0.00)	**-0.12**	(0.00)	**0.69**	(0.00)	**0.51**	(0.00)	**0.50**	(0.00)
	Mexico	**0.15**	(0.03)	**0.11**	(0.04)	**0.11**	(0.03)	**0.09**	(0.03)	**0.14**	(0.03)	**0.10**	(0.03)	0.06	(0.03)	**0.67**	(0.02)	**0.38**	(0.03)	**0.54**	(0.03)
	Netherlands	**0.24**	(0.08)	0.07	(0.09)	0.12	(0.08)	0.09	(0.08)	**0.27**	(0.07)	0.14	(0.09)	**0.14**	(0.07)	**0.52**	(0.06)	**0.30**	(0.07)	**0.33**	(0.08)
	New Zealand	**0.32**	(0.07)	**0.24**	(0.07)	**0.23**	(0.07)	**0.16**	(0.07)	**0.42**	(0.06)	**0.26**	(0.06)	0.05	(0.06)	**0.61**	(0.07)	**0.30**	(0.07)	**0.37**	(0.07)
	Norway	**0.28**	(0.08)	**0.17**	(0.06)	0.13	(0.08)	**0.17**	(0.06)	**0.20**	(0.08)	**0.16**	(0.07)	0.12	(0.08)	**0.61**	(0.07)	**0.44**	(0.05)	**0.49**	(0.06)
	Poland	**0.26**	(0.07)	0.13	(0.08)	0.01	(0.07)	-0.02	(0.08)	0.09	(0.07)	-0.03	(0.07)	-0.02	(0.08)	**0.63**	(0.05)	**0.29**	(0.06)	**0.46**	(0.07)
	Portugal	**0.35**	(0.06)	0.16	(0.09)	0.13	(0.09)	0.10	(0.08)	**0.28**	(0.08)	**0.23**	(0.08)	**0.28**	(0.07)	**0.58**	(0.06)	**0.31**	(0.08)	**0.42**	(0.07)
	Slovak Republic	0.04	(0.08)	-0.09	(0.08)	-0.10	(0.07)	0.02	(0.08)	**0.25**	(0.08)	-0.02	(0.08)	-0.05	(0.06)	**0.56**	(0.06)	**0.35**	(0.08)	**0.56**	(0.05)
	Slovenia	**0.11**	(0.03)	**0.17**	(0.01)	**0.08**	(0.02)	0.00	(0.02)	**0.37**	(0.01)	**0.27**	(0.01)	**0.15**	(0.01)	**0.53**	(0.01)	**0.23**	(0.01)	**0.40**	(0.01)
	Spain	**0.20**	(0.07)	**0.19**	(0.04)	**0.23**	(0.04)	**0.20**	(0.05)	**0.26**	(0.05)	**0.16**	(0.06)	0.06	(0.06)	**0.60**	(0.03)	**0.37**	(0.05)	**0.45**	(0.05)
	Sweden	**0.37**	(0.05)	0.07	(0.07)	0.04	(0.06)	0.13	(0.07)	**0.31**	(0.06)	**0.26**	(0.07)	**0.24**	(0.06)	**0.67**	(0.05)	**0.40**	(0.06)	**0.54**	(0.04)
	Switzerland	**0.32**	(0.05)	0.10	(0.06)	0.10	(0.06)	**0.23**	(0.06)	**0.18**	(0.08)	0.07	(0.07)	0.09	(0.07)	**0.53**	(0.04)	**0.31**	(0.05)	**0.31**	(0.05)
	Turkey	**0.15**	(0.06)	0.10	(0.07)	0.05	(0.08)	0.04	(0.09)	**0.36**	(0.06)	**0.17**	(0.06)	0.13	(0.08)	**0.64**	(0.04)	**0.26**	(0.09)	**0.41**	(0.08)
	United Kingdom	**0.35**	(0.06)	**0.14**	(0.06)	**0.19**	(0.08)	**0.27**	(0.06)	**0.18**	(0.06)	0.09	(0.08)	0.08	(0.08)	**0.68**	(0.04)	**0.43**	(0.05)	**0.48**	(0.04)
	United States	**0.42**	(0.06)	**0.40**	(0.07)	**0.36**	(0.08)	**0.31**	(0.09)	**0.44**	(0.05)	**0.29**	(0.07)	**0.31**	(0.07)	**0.76**	(0.04)	**0.50**	(0.07)	**0.50**	(0.08)
	OECD average	**0.21**	(0.01)	**0.14**	(0.01)	**0.12**	(0.01)	**0.10**	(0.01)	**0.26**	(0.01)	**0.13**	(0.01)	**0.13**	(0.01)	**0.60**	(0.01)	**0.35**	(0.01)	**0.44**	(0.01)
Partners	Albania	**0.24**	(0.07)	-0.02	(0.07)	0.06	(0.06)	0.01	(0.06)	-0.01	(0.07)	-0.02	(0.07)	-0.07	(0.06)	**0.48**	(0.07)	**0.36**	(0.07)	**0.32**	(0.09)
	Argentina	**0.19**	(0.07)	0.04	(0.07)	0.07	(0.07)	**0.15**	(0.06)	**0.34**	(0.08)	**0.28**	(0.07)	0.14	(0.08)	**0.55**	(0.05)	**0.44**	(0.07)	**0.52**	(0.06)
	Brazil	0.10	(0.05)	**0.15**	(0.05)	**0.14**	(0.05)	**0.16**	(0.05)	**0.13**	(0.06)	0.10	(0.06)	**0.13**	(0.05)	**0.70**	(0.03)	**0.34**	(0.05)	**0.51**	(0.05)
	Bulgaria	0.04	(0.09)	-0.03	(0.08)	0.00	(0.08)	-0.01	(0.07)	**0.26**	(0.07)	0.13	(0.08)	0.07	(0.06)	**0.65**	(0.05)	**0.32**	(0.07)	**0.34**	(0.07)
	Colombia	**0.13**	(0.07)	0.08	(0.05)	0.09	(0.06)	0.01	(0.09)	**0.19**	(0.09)	0.08	(0.08)	0.09	(0.07)	**0.65**	(0.06)	**0.40**	(0.06)	**0.39**	(0.06)
	Costa Rica	0.00	(0.07)	-0.10	(0.06)	-0.04	(0.06)	0.00	(0.07)	**0.19**	(0.09)	**0.19**	(0.08)	0.06	(0.08)	**0.60**	(0.05)	**0.42**	(0.07)	**0.51**	(0.05)
	Croatia	0.01	(0.10)	**0.24**	(0.06)	**0.18**	(0.09)	**0.26**	(0.07)	**0.28**	(0.08)	0.13	(0.08)	0.13	(0.07)	**0.54**	(0.06)	**0.32**	(0.07)	**0.41**	(0.08)
	Cyprus*	**0.20**	(0.01)	**0.39**	(0.00)	**0.16**	(0.00)	**0.12**	(0.00)	**0.07**	(0.00)	**0.01**	(0.01)	**0.12**	(0.00)	**0.70**	(0.00)	**0.30**	(0.00)	**0.34**	(0.00)
	Hong Kong-China	**0.23**	(0.08)	0.04	(0.09)	-0.03	(0.09)	-0.11	(0.08)	0.09	(0.09)	0.05	(0.10)	-0.03	(0.08)	**0.63**	(0.06)	**0.25**	(0.07)	**0.56**	(0.07)
	Indonesia	0.05	(0.06)	0.11	(0.06)	0.01	(0.07)	0.06	(0.07)	0.11	(0.07)	0.03	(0.07)	**-0.15**	(0.07)	**0.46**	(0.06)	**0.27**	(0.08)	**0.20**	(0.10)
	Jordan	0.11	(0.06)	0.01	(0.08)	0.02	(0.08)	0.01	(0.08)	**0.19**	(0.07)	0.13	(0.07)	0.11	(0.08)	**0.71**	(0.04)	**0.24**	(0.08)	**0.36**	(0.07)
	Kazakhstan	**0.51**	(0.06)	0.06	(0.08)	0.05	(0.08)	0.06	(0.07)	0.02	(0.07)	0.01	(0.08)	0.09	(0.07)	**0.85**	(0.02)	**0.17**	(0.08)	**0.18**	(0.09)
	Latvia	**0.28**	(0.06)	**0.18**	(0.08)	0.12	(0.06)	0.08	(0.06)	**0.17**	(0.07)	0.13	(0.07)	**0.21**	(0.07)	**0.56**	(0.05)	**0.28**	(0.06)	**0.41**	(0.07)
	Liechtenstein	**0.25**	(0.07)	-0.06	(0.03)	**0.24**	(0.04)	**0.32**	(0.06)	**-0.33**	(0.02)	**-0.21**	(0.03)	**-0.32**	(0.02)	**0.57**	(0.01)	**0.55**	(0.01)	**0.76**	(0.01)
	Lithuania	**0.37**	(0.05)	**0.16**	(0.07)	0.09	(0.06)	**0.17**	(0.06)	**0.31**	(0.05)	**0.14**	(0.06)	**0.19**	(0.07)	**0.46**	(0.06)	**0.31**	(0.07)	**0.41**	(0.08)
	Macao-China	**0.14**	(0.00)	**0.03**	(0.00)	**0.03**	(0.00)	**0.39**	(0.00)	**0.40**	(0.00)	**0.29**	(0.00)	**0.05**	(0.00)	**0.74**	(0.00)	**0.24**	(0.00)	**0.41**	(0.00)
	Malaysia	**0.21**	(0.08)	-0.15	(0.08)	0.03	(0.08)	0.12	(0.09)	**0.21**	(0.09)	**0.15**	(0.07)	0.09	(0.08)	**0.63**	(0.05)	**0.26**	(0.06)	**0.38**	(0.07)
	Montenegro	**-0.06**	(0.01)	**-0.20**	(0.01)	**-0.19**	(0.00)	**-0.21**	(0.00)	**0.08**	(0.01)	**0.15**	(0.00)	**0.18**	(0.01)	**0.68**	(0.00)	**0.41**	(0.00)	**0.36**	(0.00)
	Peru	**0.15**	(0.07)	0.04	(0.07)	0.08	(0.06)	0.09	(0.06)	0.13	(0.08)	-0.01	(0.07)	0.04	(0.06)	**0.62**	(0.05)	**0.42**	(0.07)	**0.41**	(0.08)
	Qatar	**0.13**	(0.00)	**0.26**	(0.00)	**0.29**	(0.00)	**0.35**	(0.00)	**0.13**	(0.00)	**0.10**	(0.00)	**0.02**	(0.00)	**0.75**	(0.00)	**0.32**	(0.00)	**0.34**	(0.00)
	Romania	**0.22**	(0.08)	**-0.17**	(0.06)	-0.06	(0.08)	-0.13	(0.07)	**0.17**	(0.07)	-0.04	(0.06)	0.05	(0.06)	**0.37**	(0.07)	0.08	(0.09)	0.15	(0.09)
	Russian Federation	**0.25**	(0.07)	-0.10	(0.07)	0.03	(0.09)	0.10	(0.07)	0.06	(0.06)	-0.04	(0.06)	**0.19**	(0.08)	**0.74**	(0.03)	**0.27**	(0.07)	**0.28**	(0.07)
	Serbia	-0.13	(0.09)	-0.05	(0.07)	-0.04	(0.08)	0.00	(0.09)	**0.24**	(0.07)	0.10	(0.07)	**0.22**	(0.08)	**0.61**	(0.06)	**0.42**	(0.07)	**0.51**	(0.06)
	Shanghai-China	**0.58**	(0.04)	**0.15**	(0.07)	0.01	(0.08)	**0.20**	(0.08)	**0.36**	(0.07)	0.14	(0.08)	**0.24**	(0.06)	**0.80**	(0.03)	**0.30**	(0.07)	**0.30**	(0.07)
	Singapore	**0.15**	(0.01)	**0.13**	(0.01)	**0.04**	(0.00)	**0.15**	(0.02)	**0.37**	(0.00)	**0.15**	(0.00)	**0.21**	(0.01)	**0.74**	(0.00)	**0.30**	(0.01)	**0.30**	(0.00)
	Chinese Taipei	**0.39**	(0.06)	0.07	(0.06)	**0.18**	(0.06)	0.05	(0.09)	**0.21**	(0.08)	0.13	(0.08)	**0.30**	(0.07)	**0.69**	(0.05)	**0.35**	(0.08)	**0.25**	(0.09)
	Thailand	0.04	(0.08)	0.00	(0.06)	0.04	(0.06)	-0.03	(0.08)	0.15	(0.08)	-0.05	(0.07)	0.09	(0.08)	**0.57**	(0.05)	**0.39**	(0.07)	**0.51**	(0.05)
	Tunisia	0.08	(0.10)	-0.08	(0.08)	0.07	(0.08)	-0.07	(0.07)	0.06	(0.10)	0.09	(0.08)	0.09	(0.08)	**0.50**	(0.07)	**0.35**	(0.10)	**0.47**	(0.08)
	United Arab Emirates	**0.19**	(0.04)	-0.03	(0.04)	**-0.08**	(0.04)	-0.02	(0.04)	**0.20**	(0.04)	**0.12**	(0.04)	**0.16**	(0.05)	**0.74**	(0.02)	**0.30**	(0.05)	**0.42**	(0.05)
	Uruguay	0.02	(0.06)	**-0.19**	(0.07)	**-0.15**	(0.07)	**-0.15**	(0.07)	**0.38**	(0.07)	**0.33**	(0.06)	**0.23**	(0.06)	**0.64**	(0.05)	**0.32**	(0.07)	**0.59**	(0.04)
	Viet Nam	**0.42**	(0.07)	0.02	(0.08)	0.04	(0.07)	0.02	(0.07)	0.16	(0.08)	0.03	(0.09)	0.04	(0.07)	**0.54**	(0.06)	**0.41**	(0.07)	**0.33**	(0.07)

Note: Values that are statistically significant are indicated in bold (see Annex A3).
* See notes at the beginning of this Annex.
StatLink http://dx.doi.org/10.1787/888932957517

[Part 1/1]
Correlation between learning environment indicators and school average socio-economic status at the school level

Table IV.5.12 *Results based on students' and school principals' reports*

	Correlation between:												
	School average PISA index of economic, social and cultural status (ESCS) and...												
	Percentage of students who arrived late for school at least once in the two weeks prior to the PISA test (at the school level)		Percentage of students who skipped a day or a class at least once in the two weeks prior to the PISA test (at the school level)		School average index of teacher-student relations		School average index of disciplinary climate		Index of student-related factors affecting school climate		Index of teacher-related factors affecting school climate		Index of teacher morale	
	Corr.	S.E.	Corr.	S.E.	Corr.	S.E.	Corr.	S.E.	Corr.	S.E.	Corr.	S.E.	Corr.	S.E.
OECD														
Australia	**-0.11**	(0.04)	**-0.36**	(0.03)	**0.38**	(0.03)	**0.34**	(0.03)	**0.52**	(0.02)	**0.38**	(0.04)	**0.31**	(0.03)
Austria	0.13	(0.07)	0.13	(0.07)	**-0.13**	(0.06)	**0.34**	(0.07)	**0.23**	(0.07)	0.16	(0.08)	0.09	(0.08)
Belgium	**-0.34**	(0.06)	**-0.41**	(0.05)	-0.06	(0.06)	**0.35**	(0.06)	**0.56**	(0.04)	**0.30**	(0.05)	**0.30**	(0.05)
Canada	-0.09	(0.06)	**-0.14**	(0.06)	**0.13**	(0.05)	**0.13**	(0.04)	**0.36**	(0.05)	**0.21**	(0.06)	**0.17**	(0.05)
Chile	**-0.30**	(0.05)	**-0.27**	(0.06)	-0.10	(0.06)	**0.19**	(0.06)	**0.45**	(0.05)	**0.33**	(0.06)	**0.33**	(0.06)
Czech Republic	**-0.28**	(0.06)	**-0.18**	(0.07)	-0.07	(0.06)	**0.25**	(0.06)	**0.31**	(0.06)	**0.12**	(0.06)	**0.14**	(0.07)
Denmark	-0.03	(0.07)	**-0.15**	(0.06)	**0.21**	(0.06)	**0.31**	(0.06)	**0.35**	(0.05)	**0.22**	(0.06)	**0.25**	(0.05)
Estonia	0.09	(0.05)	-0.01	(0.06)	0.03	(0.07)	-0.03	(0.05)	0.09	(0.05)	0.04	(0.05)	**0.10**	(0.04)
Finland	**0.16**	(0.05)	-0.06	(0.06)	0.10	(0.06)	0.06	(0.07)	0.01	(0.06)	0.04	(0.05)	**0.15**	(0.06)
France	**-0.29**	(0.06)	**-0.28**	(0.05)	**-0.20**	(0.08)	**0.39**	(0.04)	**0.34**	(0.05)	**0.24**	(0.08)	**0.29**	(0.06)
Germany	0.03	(0.08)	**-0.15**	(0.07)	**-0.20**	(0.06)	**0.22**	(0.07)	**0.29**	(0.06)	0.12	(0.07)	**0.19**	(0.07)
Greece	0.16	(0.09)	**-0.13**	(0.06)	**-0.22**	(0.05)	**0.39**	(0.06)	0.14	(0.05)	**0.15**	(0.05)	**0.22**	(0.09)
Hungary	**-0.39**	(0.08)	**-0.60**	(0.05)	-0.09	(0.08)	**0.50**	(0.06)	**0.47**	(0.06)	**0.22**	(0.06)	**0.20**	(0.09)
Iceland	0.03	(0.01)	**-0.21**	(0.01)	**0.28**	(0.01)	**0.03**	(0.01)	-0.01	(0.01)	**0.01**	(0.01)	**0.25**	(0.01)
Ireland	**-0.28**	(0.07)	-0.04	(0.07)	-0.05	(0.08)	**0.28**	(0.06)	**0.42**	(0.06)	**0.27**	(0.07)	**0.24**	(0.09)
Israel	-0.09	(0.07)	**0.18**	(0.06)	**-0.16**	(0.08)	**0.22**	(0.08)	0.14	(0.07)	0.03	(0.08)	**0.17**	(0.08)
Italy	**-0.28**	(0.04)	**-0.34**	(0.03)	**-0.23**	(0.05)	**0.34**	(0.04)	**0.41**	(0.04)	0.03	(0.05)	**0.18**	(0.04)
Japan	**-0.24**	(0.08)	**-0.43**	(0.06)	**0.30**	(0.07)	**0.47**	(0.07)	**0.34**	(0.08)	**0.26**	(0.07)	**0.38**	(0.06)
Korea	**-0.33**	(0.07)	**-0.31**	(0.06)	**0.23**	(0.08)	**0.36**	(0.07)	**0.25**	(0.07)	0.06	(0.09)	**0.32**	(0.07)
Luxembourg	-0.02	(0.00)	**-0.35**	(0.00)	**-0.18**	(0.00)	**0.16**	(0.00)	**0.47**	(0.00)	**0.13**	(0.00)	**0.34**	(0.00)
Mexico	**0.17**	(0.04)	**0.25**	(0.03)	**-0.15**	(0.04)	0.04	(0.04)	**0.12**	(0.03)	**0.13**	(0.03)	**0.14**	(0.04)
Netherlands	**-0.23**	(0.06)	0.04	(0.08)	0.01	(0.09)	0.18	(0.08)	**0.21**	(0.07)	-0.06	(0.09)	-0.01	(0.09)
New Zealand	**-0.37**	(0.07)	**-0.59**	(0.05)	**0.18**	(0.06)	**0.43**	(0.07)	**0.53**	(0.05)	**0.30**	(0.07)	**0.27**	(0.07)
Norway	0.10	(0.07)	0.06	(0.06)	0.08	(0.08)	0.00	(0.07)	**0.28**	(0.06)	**0.20**	(0.07)	**0.29**	(0.07)
Poland	**0.43**	(0.05)	**0.17**	(0.06)	**-0.22**	(0.08)	-0.09	(0.08)	0.04	(0.09)	0.07	(0.08)	**0.19**	(0.07)
Portugal	-0.02	(0.07)	**-0.20**	(0.08)	0.00	(0.08)	0.01	(0.09)	**0.17**	(0.09)	0.13	(0.10)	0.17	(0.09)
Slovak Republic	**-0.20**	(0.08)	**-0.37**	(0.05)	**-0.36**	(0.07)	**0.36**	(0.06)	**0.25**	(0.05)	0.05	(0.07)	0.01	(0.08)
Slovenia	**-0.16**	(0.03)	**-0.38**	(0.03)	**-0.14**	(0.03)	**0.52**	(0.02)	**0.27**	(0.01)	**0.25**	(0.01)	**0.06**	(0.01)
Spain	**-0.11**	(0.06)	**-0.27**	(0.04)	-0.05	(0.04)	**0.20**	(0.04)	**0.45**	(0.04)	**0.27**	(0.04)	**0.33**	(0.06)
Sweden	-0.01	(0.08)	**-0.16**	(0.07)	0.11	(0.07)	**0.32**	(0.07)	**0.43**	(0.06)	**0.33**	(0.06)	**0.30**	(0.06)
Switzerland	**0.32**	(0.06)	**0.23**	(0.05)	-0.02	(0.06)	0.03	(0.07)	0.08	(0.07)	0.09	(0.07)	-0.07	(0.06)
Turkey	**-0.22**	(0.06)	**0.24**	(0.07)	-0.12	(0.08)	**0.36**	(0.06)	**0.31**	(0.07)	**0.34**	(0.08)	**0.36**	(0.08)
United Kingdom	**-0.19**	(0.05)	**-0.16**	(0.06)	**0.20**	(0.07)	**0.20**	(0.09)	**0.35**	(0.06)	**0.23**	(0.08)	**0.25**	(0.07)
United States	**-0.47**	(0.06)	**-0.46**	(0.06)	**0.32**	(0.09)	**0.44**	(0.05)	**0.42**	(0.06)	**0.35**	(0.07)	**0.26**	(0.09)
OECD average	**-0.10**	(0.01)	**-0.17**	(0.01)	-0.01	(0.01)	**0.24**	(0.01)	**0.30**	(0.01)	**0.18**	(0.01)	**0.21**	(0.01)
Partners														
Albania	m	m	m	m	m	m	m	m	m	m	m	m	m	m
Argentina	**-0.25**	(0.08)	**-0.20**	(0.10)	**-0.48**	(0.06)	0.03	(0.09)	**0.33**	(0.08)	**0.20**	(0.07)	0.13	(0.08)
Brazil	0.10	(0.05)	-0.03	(0.06)	-0.06	(0.05)	**0.12**	(0.05)	**0.38**	(0.04)	**0.31**	(0.05)	**0.32**	(0.05)
Bulgaria	**-0.32**	(0.07)	**-0.44**	(0.05)	**-0.38**	(0.06)	**0.34**	(0.09)	**0.23**	(0.06)	0.10	(0.08)	**0.18**	(0.07)
Colombia	-0.03	(0.07)	0.06	(0.06)	**-0.19**	(0.05)	0.11	(0.06)	**0.25**	(0.06)	**0.21**	(0.07)	**0.26**	(0.06)
Costa Rica	-0.02	(0.08)	**-0.23**	(0.08)	**-0.36**	(0.06)	0.07	(0.10)	**0.43**	(0.07)	**0.19**	(0.08)	**0.19**	(0.08)
Croatia	0.03	(0.06)	**-0.39**	(0.05)	**-0.25**	(0.10)	**0.49**	(0.05)	**0.20**	(0.08)	**0.17**	(0.08)	**0.16**	(0.08)
Cyprus*	**-0.19**	(0.00)	-0.05	(0.00)	**0.23**	(0.01)	**0.21**	(0.00)	**0.15**	(0.00)	**0.19**	(0.00)	**0.18**	(0.00)
Hong Kong-China	**-0.22**	(0.07)	-0.11	(0.08)	-0.14	(0.09)	0.08	(0.09)	**0.21**	(0.09)	**0.25**	(0.09)	**0.26**	(0.08)
Indonesia	0.11	(0.10)	0.06	(0.07)	**0.13**	(0.06)	**-0.24**	(0.07)	0.17	(0.08)	0.09	(0.08)	**0.24**	(0.05)
Jordan	0.09	(0.07)	-0.03	(0.07)	-0.02	(0.08)	0.01	(0.09)	0.06	(0.08)	**0.15**	(0.08)	**0.19**	(0.07)
Kazakhstan	-0.14	(0.09)	**-0.25**	(0.07)	0.01	(0.08)	**0.22**	(0.08)	-0.04	(0.07)	-0.02	(0.07)	0.09	(0.07)
Latvia	0.01	(0.08)	0.03	(0.07)	**-0.32**	(0.06)	-0.04	(0.07)	0.01	(0.08)	-0.03	(0.08)	-0.03	(0.08)
Liechtenstein	**-0.35**	(0.02)	0.10	(0.03)	-0.08	(0.02)	0.08	(0.02)	**0.45**	(0.02)	**0.20**	(0.02)	**0.41**	(0.02)
Lithuania	-0.02	(0.06)	**-0.22**	(0.07)	0.08	(0.06)	**0.24**	(0.06)	**0.24**	(0.06)	**0.21**	(0.06)	**0.24**	(0.06)
Macao-China	-0.02	(0.00)	**0.14**	(0.00)	**0.16**	(0.00)	**0.13**	(0.00)	**0.26**	(0.00)	**0.35**	(0.00)	**0.34**	(0.00)
Malaysia	**-0.31**	(0.07)	0.09	(0.09)	**-0.26**	(0.06)	**0.24**	(0.08)	**0.41**	(0.06)	**0.25**	(0.09)	0.10	(0.09)
Montenegro	**-0.16**	(0.01)	**-0.11**	(0.01)	**-0.80**	(0.00)	**0.23**	(0.01)	**0.20**	(0.01)	**0.28**	(0.01)	**0.30**	(0.01)
Peru	-0.14	(0.08)	**-0.43**	(0.06)	-0.17	(0.07)	0.07	(0.08)	**0.29**	(0.06)	0.14	(0.07)	**0.29**	(0.07)
Qatar	0.05	(0.00)	**0.23**	(0.00)	**-0.15**	(0.00)	**0.29**	(0.00)	-0.02	(0.00)	**0.02**	(0.00)	**-0.05**	(0.00)
Romania	-0.14	(0.08)	**-0.26**	(0.08)	**-0.30**	(0.06)	**0.39**	(0.06)	**0.27**	(0.06)	0.12	(0.08)	**0.19**	(0.07)
Russian Federation	0.04	(0.07)	-0.01	(0.07)	**-0.20**	(0.06)	0.08	(0.07)	**0.21**	(0.09)	0.04	(0.08)	**0.30**	(0.07)
Serbia	0.02	(0.08)	-0.20	(0.11)	**-0.38**	(0.06)	**0.38**	(0.07)	**0.24**	(0.08)	0.14	(0.10)	**0.19**	(0.09)
Shanghai-China	**-0.29**	(0.07)	-0.10	(0.08)	**0.47**	(0.05)	**0.41**	(0.06)	**0.17**	(0.07)	0.02	(0.09)	**0.20**	(0.07)
Singapore	**-0.32**	(0.01)	**-0.15**	(0.00)	**0.10**	(0.01)	**0.46**	(0.01)	**0.47**	(0.01)	**0.25**	(0.01)	**0.18**	(0.02)
Chinese Taipei	**-0.22**	(0.08)	**-0.53**	(0.05)	0.12	(0.08)	**0.54**	(0.07)	**0.36**	(0.07)	**0.22**	(0.06)	**0.28**	(0.09)
Thailand	-0.05	(0.05)	-0.10	(0.06)	**-0.14**	(0.06)	-0.09	(0.06)	**0.12**	(0.06)	**0.20**	(0.07)	**0.29**	(0.05)
Tunisia	**0.17**	(0.07)	-0.10	(0.07)	**-0.41**	(0.08)	**-0.29**	(0.09)	-0.08	(0.08)	-0.14	(0.09)	0.03	(0.09)
United Arab Emirates	0.04	(0.04)	**-0.26**	(0.05)	**-0.20**	(0.04)	**0.31**	(0.05)	**0.11**	(0.04)	**0.20**	(0.04)	**0.09**	(0.05)
Uruguay	-0.13	(0.08)	**-0.43**	(0.05)	**-0.48**	(0.07)	**0.27**	(0.07)	**0.54**	(0.05)	**0.51**	(0.06)	**0.34**	(0.06)
Viet Nam	**-0.24**	(0.06)	**-0.38**	(0.05)	**-0.27**	(0.07)	**-0.19**	(0.09)	**0.20**	(0.08)	-0.06	(0.09)	0.11	(0.07)

Note: Values that are statistically significant are indicated in bold (see Annex A3).
* See notes at the beginning of this Annex.
StatLink http://dx.doi.org/10.1787/888932957517

[Part 1/2]
Table IV.5.13 Relationship between disciplinary climate and school features
Results based on students' and school principals' reports

	Regression model estimating the average index of disciplinary climate at the school level[1]													
	Intercept		School average PISA index of economic, social and cultural status (ESCS) (1 unit increase)		School size (per 100 students)		School size (per 100 students) (squared)		School in a small town or village (15 000 or less people)		School in a city or a large city (100 000 or more people)		Private school	
	Intercept	S.E.	Coef.	S.E.	Coef.	S.E.	Coef.	S.E.	Coef.	S.E.	Coef.	S.E.	Coef.	S.E.
OECD														
Australia	-0.21	(0.13)	**0.25**	(0.06)	0.00	(0.01)	0.00	(0.00)	0.03	(0.06)	0.05	(0.04)	**0.13**	(0.05)
Austria	0.15	(0.28)	**0.29**	(0.10)	**0.04**	(0.02)	0.00	(0.00)	0.17	(0.09)	-0.01	(0.10)	-0.02	(0.17)
Belgium	-0.01	(0.25)	**0.24**	(0.07)	0.02	(0.04)	0.00	(0.00)	-0.04	(0.06)	-0.03	(0.07)	**0.20**	(0.06)
Canada	-0.18	(0.17)	0.04	(0.05)	**-0.04**	(0.01)	**0.00**	(0.00)	-0.06	(0.05)	0.03	(0.04)	0.10	(0.06)
Chile	-0.12	(0.24)	**0.10**	(0.05)	0.02	(0.01)	0.00	(0.00)	0.09	(0.09)	-0.05	(0.08)	0.03	(0.06)
Czech Republic	0.42	(0.29)	**0.46**	(0.14)	-0.03	(0.07)	0.00	(0.01)	-0.09	(0.10)	-0.20	(0.10)	-0.15	(0.16)
Denmark	-0.72	(0.26)	**0.31**	(0.07)	0.01	(0.04)	0.00	(0.00)	-0.10	(0.07)	0.00	(0.06)	**0.31**	(0.10)
Estonia	0.40	(0.26)	0.06	(0.10)	-0.06	(0.04)	0.00	(0.00)	-0.09	(0.07)	-0.06	(0.07)	-0.03	(0.19)
Finland	-0.45	(0.25)	**0.21**	(0.09)	-0.08	(0.05)	0.01	(0.00)	0.04	(0.06)	**-0.08**	(0.04)	**0.28**	(0.08)
France	-0.20	(0.25)	**0.41**	(0.08)	-0.03	(0.03)	0.00	(0.00)	0.09	(0.06)	-0.03	(0.07)	0.01	(0.09)
Germany	-0.24	(0.26)	**0.18**	(0.08)	0.01	(0.03)	0.00	(0.00)	0.04	(0.08)	-0.01	(0.07)	-0.04	(0.12)
Greece	-0.34	(0.21)	**0.23**	(0.08)	-0.03	(0.05)	0.00	(0.00)	0.09	(0.08)	0.02	(0.06)	c	c
Hungary	0.44	(0.21)	**0.39**	(0.06)	0.02	(0.02)	**0.00**	(0.00)	-0.04	(0.09)	-0.05	(0.09)	-0.02	(0.13)
Iceland	0.00	(0.06)	-0.01	(0.01)	**0.02**	(0.01)	**0.00**	(0.00)	**0.11**	(0.01)	**0.12**	(0.01)	c	c
Ireland	0.09	(0.32)	**0.30**	(0.09)	-0.07	(0.04)	0.00	(0.00)	0.13	(0.09)	-0.13	(0.11)	**0.16**	(0.07)
Israel	0.51	(0.34)	0.10	(0.14)	0.01	(0.03)	0.00	(0.00)	-0.08	(0.09)	0.08	(0.07)	c	c
Italy	-0.03	(0.17)	**0.31**	(0.04)	0.01	(0.01)	0.00	(0.00)	-0.04	(0.05)	**-0.10**	(0.05)	-0.13	(0.10)
Japan	1.16	(0.27)	**0.66**	(0.11)	-0.02	(0.02)	0.00	(0.00)	c	c	-0.06	(0.07)	**-0.24**	(0.08)
Korea	0.53	(0.30)	**0.37**	(0.09)	**-0.10**	(0.03)	**0.00**	(0.00)	**-0.47**	(0.11)	-0.02	(0.08)	**0.16**	(0.06)
Luxembourg	0.10	(0.01)	**-0.05**	(0.00)	0.00	(0.00)	**0.00**	(0.00)	**0.09**	(0.00)	c	c	**0.13**	(0.00)
Mexico	0.28	(0.10)	0.01	(0.02)	**0.01**	(0.00)	0.00	(0.00)	0.00	(0.04)	**-0.10**	(0.03)	0.01	(0.06)
Netherlands	-0.12	(0.26)	0.11	(0.11)	-0.03	(0.02)	0.00	(0.00)	-0.11	(0.09)	**-0.19**	(0.06)	-0.07	(0.05)
New Zealand	-0.17	(0.29)	**0.35**	(0.09)	-0.01	(0.02)	0.00	(0.00)	0.10	(0.07)	0.00	(0.08)	0.32	(0.23)
Norway	0.33	(0.29)	-0.04	(0.12)	-0.07	(0.08)	0.01	(0.01)	0.06	(0.08)	0.12	(0.08)	c	c
Poland	-0.12	(0.39)	0.05	(0.15)	**-0.12**	(0.06)	**0.01**	(0.01)	0.17	(0.12)	-0.07	(0.13)	-0.14	(0.21)
Portugal	0.01	(0.26)	0.00	(0.06)	-0.03	(0.02)	0.00	(0.00)	0.00	(0.07)	**-0.16**	(0.07)	**0.31**	(0.11)
Slovak Republic	0.00	(0.19)	**0.40**	(0.08)	-0.07	(0.05)	0.00	(0.00)	0.14	(0.07)	-0.15	(0.08)	0.06	(0.12)
Slovenia	-0.14	(0.18)	**0.54**	(0.03)	0.01	(0.02)	0.00	(0.00)	0.07	(0.04)	0.01	(0.02)	**0.10**	(0.03)
Spain	-0.23	(0.18)	**0.11**	(0.04)	0.00	(0.01)	0.00	(0.00)	-0.01	(0.06)	-0.03	(0.05)	**0.18**	(0.07)
Sweden	-0.08	(0.19)	**0.27**	(0.08)	0.00	(0.03)	0.00	(0.00)	-0.03	(0.06)	-0.02	(0.07)	0.12	(0.07)
Switzerland	0.50	(0.16)	0.02	(0.06)	0.00	(0.02)	0.00	(0.00)	0.09	(0.05)	**-0.16**	(0.07)	-0.09	(0.13)
Turkey	0.03	(0.21)	**0.19**	(0.05)	-0.01	(0.01)	0.00	(0.00)	0.18	(0.10)	-0.07	(0.06)	c	c
United Kingdom	0.44	(0.25)	0.15	(0.13)	-0.06	(0.03)	0.00	(0.00)	-0.10	(0.06)	-0.04	(0.08)	-0.01	(0.08)
United States	0.19	(0.31)	**0.28**	(0.06)	-0.01	(0.01)	0.00	(0.00)	-0.10	(0.08)	-0.01	(0.07)	0.22	(0.15)
OECD average	0.06	(0.04)	**0.21**	(0.01)	**-0.02**	(0.01)	**0.00**	(0.00)	0.01	(0.01)	**-0.04**	(0.01)	**0.07**	(0.02)
Partners														
Albania	m	m	m	m	m	m	m	m	m	m	m	m	m	m
Argentina	-1.10	(0.22)	-0.01	(0.08)	**-0.06**	(0.03)	**0.00**	(0.00)	0.15	(0.09)	0.05	(0.08)	0.01	(0.09)
Brazil	-0.52	(0.19)	0.03	(0.04)	-0.01	(0.00)	0.00	(0.00)	0.00	(0.05)	-0.04	(0.04)	**0.20**	(0.08)
Bulgaria	0.08	(0.20)	0.07	(0.07)	**0.08**	(0.03)	**0.00**	(0.00)	0.03	(0.08)	**-0.17**	(0.06)	c	c
Colombia	0.24	(0.22)	0.02	(0.03)	0.00	(0.01)	0.00	(0.00)	-0.03	(0.08)	-0.08	(0.07)	0.15	(0.08)
Costa Rica	-0.06	(0.26)	-0.11	(0.07)	0.00	(0.01)	0.00	(0.00)	-0.04	(0.07)	0.01	(0.08)	**0.50**	(0.19)
Croatia	0.66	(0.27)	**0.66**	(0.09)	**0.13**	(0.05)	**-0.01**	(0.00)	-0.01	(0.08)	**-0.29**	(0.09)	c	c
Cyprus*	-0.59	(0.03)	**0.20**	(0.01)	**-0.04**	(0.00)	**0.00**	(0.00)	**0.03**	(0.00)	**-0.11**	(0.00)	**0.05**	(0.00)
Hong Kong-China	1.17	(0.33)	-0.07	(0.05)	0.05	(0.05)	0.00	(0.00)	c	c	c	c	0.12	(0.11)
Indonesia	0.52	(0.27)	-0.08	(0.05)	0.00	(0.02)	0.00	(0.00)	0.03	(0.07)	0.00	(0.07)	-0.10	(0.06)
Jordan	0.12	(0.24)	**-0.23**	(0.10)	-0.03	(0.02)	0.00	(0.00)	0.04	(0.07)	0.14	(0.08)	**0.32**	(0.15)
Kazakhstan	0.89	(0.32)	**0.38**	(0.10)	-0.03	(0.02)	0.00	(0.00)	0.01	(0.13)	-0.08	(0.12)	-0.16	(0.14)
Latvia	0.21	(0.28)	0.09	(0.11)	-0.08	(0.05)	**0.01**	(0.00)	0.16	(0.14)	-0.14	(0.11)	c	c
Liechtenstein	c	c	c	c	c	c	c	c	c	c	c	c	c	c
Lithuania	0.24	(0.30)	**0.36**	(0.10)	-0.04	(0.05)	0.00	(0.00)	-0.01	(0.11)	-0.01	(0.09)	c	c
Macao-China	2.32	(0.01)	**0.21**	(0.00)	**0.03**	(0.00)	**0.00**	(0.00)	c	c	c	c	c	c
Malaysia	0.02	(0.25)	**0.15**	(0.05)	-0.01	(0.01)	0.00	(0.00)	-0.04	(0.06)	0.01	(0.07)	0.00	(0.16)
Montenegro	-0.78	(0.06)	**0.25**	(0.01)	**-0.06**	(0.00)	**0.00**	(0.00)	**0.02**	(0.00)	**-0.23**	(0.00)	c	c
Peru	0.18	(0.21)	0.03	(0.04)	0.00	(0.01)	0.00	(0.00)	-0.04	(0.07)	-0.03	(0.06)	-0.11	(0.08)
Qatar	-0.33	(0.01)	**0.05**	(0.00)	**0.00**	(0.00)	**0.00**	(0.00)	**-0.05**	(0.00)	**-0.13**	(0.00)	**0.45**	(0.00)
Romania	-0.03	(0.26)	**0.47**	(0.06)	-0.03	(0.02)	0.00	(0.00)	0.13	(0.08)	**-0.16**	(0.08)	c	c
Russian Federation	0.56	(0.25)	**0.30**	(0.11)	**-0.06**	(0.02)	**0.00**	(0.00)	**0.25**	(0.10)	0.07	(0.06)	c	c
Serbia	-0.39	(0.36)	**0.32**	(0.12)	0.02	(0.03)	0.00	(0.00)	0.08	(0.11)	-0.02	(0.08)	c	c
Shanghai-China	0.40	(0.32)	**0.39**	(0.07)	-0.01	(0.01)	0.00	(0.00)	c	c	c	c	0.01	(0.12)
Singapore	0.74	(0.02)	**0.34**	(0.01)	**0.03**	(0.01)	**0.00**	(0.00)	c	c	c	c	c	c
Chinese Taipei	0.40	(0.30)	**0.46**	(0.09)	**-0.01**	(0.00)	0.00	(0.00)	-0.02	(0.12)	-0.03	(0.07)	-0.05	(0.07)
Thailand	-0.03	(0.18)	0.01	(0.03)	0.00	(0.01)	0.00	(0.00)	**0.14**	(0.06)	-0.02	(0.05)	-0.07	(0.06)
Tunisia	-0.15	(0.30)	-0.05	(0.04)	0.04	(0.03)	0.00	(0.00)	0.07	(0.07)	-0.01	(0.05)	c	c
United Arab Emirates	-0.10	(0.22)	**0.15**	(0.08)	-0.01	(0.01)	0.00	(0.00)	0.02	(0.07)	0.00	(0.07)	**0.20**	(0.09)
Uruguay	-0.03	(0.27)	**0.15**	(0.07)	0.00	(0.01)	0.00	(0.00)	0.09	(0.09)	-0.07	(0.07)	0.09	(0.20)
Viet Nam	0.24	(0.25)	0.00	(0.05)	-0.02	(0.01)	**0.00**	(0.00)	0.04	(0.08)	-0.15	(0.10)	-0.08	(0.08)

Note: Values that are statistically significant are indicated in bold (see Annex A3).
1. Regression: School average disciplinary climate = Intercept + variables listed in this table.
* See notes at the beginning of this Annex.
StatLink http://dx.doi.org/10.1787/888932957517

[Part 2/2]
Relationship between disciplinary climate and school features

Table IV.5.13   *Results based on students' and school principals' reports*

	Regression model estimating the average index of disciplinary climate at the school level[1]													
	School receives pressure from parents to achieve high academic standards		Index of quality of physical infrastructure (1 unit increase)		Index of quality of schools' educational resources (1 unit increase)		Index of teacher shortage (1 unit increase)		Socio-economic heterogeneity of school intake (standard deviation of ESCS within school)		Academic heterogeneity of school intake (standard deviation of mathematics performance within school)		Variance accounted for by this model	
	Coef.	S.E.	Coef.	S.E.	Coef.	S.E.	Coef.	S.E.	Coef.	S.E.	Coef.	S.E.	%	S.E.
OECD														
Australia	-0.01	(0.06)	0.01	(0.02)	-0.02	(0.02)	**-0.04**	(0.02)	0.06	(0.14)	0.00	(0.00)	15.0	(3.0)
Austria	-0.10	(0.08)	0.05	(0.03)	-0.01	(0.04)	-0.03	(0.05)	-0.11	(0.24)	0.00	(0.00)	18.4	(7.2)
Belgium	-0.05	(0.06)	0.05	(0.03)	-0.04	(0.03)	-0.03	(0.03)	-0.03	(0.24)	0.00	(0.00)	20.3	(5.6)
Canada	0.04	(0.05)	-0.01	(0.02)	0.00	(0.02)	-0.02	(0.02)	0.10	(0.12)	0.00	(0.00)	8.9	(2.8)
Chile	-0.01	(0.07)	0.05	(0.03)	-0.06	(0.04)	-0.02	(0.02)	0.13	(0.17)	0.00	(0.00)	8.7	(5.1)
Czech Republic	0.02	(0.12)	0.03	(0.05)	-0.02	(0.07)	-0.07	(0.07)	-0.38	(0.27)	0.00	(0.00)	11.2	(5.0)
Denmark	-0.03	(0.05)	-0.01	(0.04)	-0.01	(0.04)	0.04	(0.04)	0.38	(0.25)	**0.00**	(0.00)	25.9	(6.1)
Estonia	-0.01	(0.06)	-0.05	(0.03)	**0.09**	(0.03)	**-0.07**	(0.04)	-0.22	(0.27)	0.00	(0.00)	6.1	(4.1)
Finland	0.02	(0.04)	0.00	(0.02)	0.01	(0.03)	-0.03	(0.04)	0.00	(0.19)	0.00	(0.00)	7.7	(3.8)
France	-0.03	(0.06)	0.00	(0.04)	-0.02	(0.03)	-0.07	(0.04)	-0.34	(0.23)	0.00	(0.00)	21.7	(6.0)
Germany	-0.03	(0.06)	0.02	(0.04)	0.03	(0.04)	-0.05	(0.04)	0.26	(0.23)	0.00	(0.00)	9.4	(5.2)
Greece	0.06	(0.06)	0.00	(0.03)	-0.01	(0.05)	-0.01	(0.04)	-0.24	(0.16)	0.00	(0.00)	20.7	(6.3)
Hungary	**0.28**	(0.09)	0.04	(0.06)	-0.05	(0.06)	-0.02	(0.06)	-0.24	(0.22)	0.00	(0.00)	32.9	(6.6)
Iceland	**0.25**	(0.01)	**0.04**	(0.01)	**-0.03**	(0.01)	**-0.04**	(0.00)	**-0.28**	(0.03)	0.00	(0.00)	13.8	(0.4)
Ireland	-0.02	(0.12)	0.00	(0.04)	0.05	(0.05)	0.05	(0.05)	-0.01	(0.28)	0.00	(0.00)	18.8	(6.5)
Israel	-0.02	(0.09)	0.00	(0.04)	-0.01	(0.03)	-0.04	(0.03)	-0.32	(0.25)	0.00	(0.00)	10.6	(5.5)
Italy	**0.09**	(0.04)	0.00	(0.02)	0.00	(0.02)	0.00	(0.02)	0.10	(0.15)	0.00	(0.00)	18.5	(2.5)
Japan	**0.11**	(0.05)	**0.07**	(0.03)	0.00	(0.03)	0.03	(0.04)	0.19	(0.32)	**-0.01**	(0.00)	39.3	(5.5)
Korea	0.00	(0.07)	**0.12**	(0.04)	-0.04	(0.05)	0.01	(0.04)	-0.45	(0.32)	**-0.01**	(0.00)	36.8	(7.7)
Luxembourg	**-0.12**	(0.00)	**-0.07**	(0.00)	**0.09**	(0.00)	**0.02**	(0.00)	**-0.83**	(0.00)	**0.01**	(0.00)	35.0	(0.2)
Mexico	-0.03	(0.03)	0.02	(0.02)	0.01	(0.01)	0.00	(0.01)	**-0.16**	(0.07)	0.00	(0.00)	2.9	(1.3)
Netherlands	0.13	(0.08)	-0.05	(0.04)	0.00	(0.04)	**-0.08**	(0.04)	-0.17	(0.29)	0.00	(0.00)	15.5	(6.1)
New Zealand	-0.12	(0.09)	0.01	(0.04)	-0.03	(0.04)	-0.03	(0.03)	-0.15	(0.20)	0.00	(0.00)	26.3	(8.6)
Norway	-0.03	(0.07)	-0.02	(0.03)	**0.10**	(0.04)	0.01	(0.04)	**-0.49**	(0.20)	0.00	(0.00)	16.0	(5.6)
Poland	0.00	(0.09)	-0.03	(0.06)	-0.01	(0.05)	-0.03	(0.18)	0.06	(0.34)	0.00	(0.00)	7.8	(5.3)
Portugal	-0.03	(0.07)	0.02	(0.04)	**0.08**	(0.04)	0.01	(0.03)	-0.06	(0.20)	0.00	(0.00)	18.9	(5.9)
Slovak Republic	0.01	(0.08)	-0.02	(0.03)	-0.03	(0.04)	0.00	(0.04)	-0.28	(0.19)	0.00	(0.00)	21.3	(5.7)
Slovenia	**-0.05**	(0.02)	0.02	(0.01)	**0.03**	(0.01)	**0.05**	(0.02)	-0.11	(0.16)	**0.00**	(0.00)	31.3	(2.5)
Spain	-0.06	(0.05)	**-0.07**	(0.02)	**0.09**	(0.03)	0.00	(0.02)	-0.08	(0.14)	0.00	(0.00)	9.5	(3.1)
Sweden	-0.06	(0.11)	-0.02	(0.03)	-0.01	(0.04)	-0.04	(0.03)	-0.10	(0.21)	0.00	(0.00)	12.9	(6.2)
Switzerland	-0.06	(0.04)	-0.02	(0.03)	0.02	(0.03)	0.03	(0.03)	**-0.35**	(0.16)	0.00	(0.00)	9.3	(4.6)
Turkey	-0.01	(0.05)	0.03	(0.03)	-0.04	(0.03)	0.01	(0.02)	**0.32**	(0.15)	0.00	(0.00)	29.9	(6.3)
United Kingdom	0.04	(0.11)	0.02	(0.03)	-0.04	(0.04)	-0.04	(0.04)	-0.42	(0.29)	0.00	(0.00)	10.8	(5.7)
United States	-0.03	(0.07)	-0.01	(0.05)	-0.01	(0.03)	-0.04	(0.03)	-0.02	(0.24)	0.00	(0.00)	24.9	(6.5)
OECD average	0.00	(0.01)	0.01	(0.01)	0.00	(0.01)	**-0.02**	(0.01)	**-0.12**	(0.04)	0.00	(0.00)	18.2	(0.9)
Partners														
Albania	m	m	m	m	m	m	m	m	m	m	m	m	m	m
Argentina	**0.14**	(0.07)	0.01	(0.03)	0.03	(0.04)	-0.04	(0.02)	0.07	(0.18)	0.01	(0.00)	13.8	(6.5)
Brazil	**0.08**	(0.03)	-0.01	(0.02)	-0.03	(0.03)	-0.01	(0.02)	0.03	(0.13)	0.00	(0.00)	7.0	(3.0)
Bulgaria	**0.10**	(0.05)	-0.05	(0.03)	0.01	(0.04)	**-0.11**	(0.05)	**-0.39**	(0.17)	0.00	(0.00)	27.5	(7.4)
Colombia	-0.04	(0.04)	0.00	(0.03)	0.02	(0.03)	0.02	(0.02)	-0.22	(0.17)	0.00	(0.00)	9.2	(4.5)
Costa Rica	-0.07	(0.06)	0.00	(0.03)	-0.02	(0.03)	0.04	(0.03)	0.06	(0.16)	0.00	(0.00)	13.2	(6.5)
Croatia	-0.06	(0.07)	0.03	(0.04)	-0.01	(0.06)	-0.02	(0.04)	-0.08	(0.35)	0.00	(0.00)	34.4	(6.7)
Cyprus*	0.01	(0.00)	0.01	(0.00)	-0.01	(0.00)	0.00	(0.00)	**0.57**	(0.02)	**0.00**	(0.00)	14.4	(0.3)
Hong Kong-China	-0.03	(0.05)	0.04	(0.04)	-0.04	(0.04)	0.01	(0.03)	**-0.55**	(0.23)	**-0.01**	(0.00)	16.2	(5.9)
Indonesia	0.04	(0.06)	-0.04	(0.03)	0.05	(0.03)	0.04	(0.04)	**-0.31**	(0.13)	-0.01	(0.00)	13.8	(6.5)
Jordan	0.02	(0.07)	-0.07	(0.04)	0.00	(0.05)	**-0.07**	(0.03)	**-0.59**	(0.26)	0.00	(0.00)	20.3	(8.5)
Kazakhstan	0.07	(0.06)	0.03	(0.03)	0.04	(0.04)	0.05	(0.03)	0.16	(0.33)	0.00	(0.00)	17.8	(6.8)
Latvia	-0.06	(0.08)	0.01	(0.06)	-0.01	(0.06)	-0.04	(0.06)	-0.23	(0.25)	0.00	(0.00)	9.8	(4.5)
Liechtenstein	c	c	c	c	c	c	c	c	c	c	c	c	c	c
Lithuania	0.05	(0.07)	-0.01	(0.04)	0.09	(0.05)	-0.04	(0.06)	-0.05	(0.24)	0.00	(0.00)	10.2	(3.9)
Macao-China	**-0.10**	(0.00)	0.00	(0.00)	**-0.05**	(0.00)	**-0.04**	(0.00)	**-1.20**	(0.00)	**-0.01**	(0.00)	45.0	(0.1)
Malaysia	0.09	(0.06)	0.04	(0.03)	0.04	(0.03)	**0.11**	(0.04)	0.23	(0.15)	**-0.01**	(0.00)	27.5	(7.9)
Montenegro	**0.14**	(0.00)	**-0.02**	(0.00)	**0.04**	(0.00)	**-0.04**	(0.00)	**1.11**	(0.05)	**-0.01**	(0.00)	40.2	(0.6)
Peru	-0.09	(0.05)	0.02	(0.02)	0.03	(0.03)	0.00	(0.02)	-0.11	(0.12)	0.00	(0.00)	6.4	(4.5)
Qatar	**0.20**	(0.00)	**-0.03**	(0.00)	**-0.02**	(0.00)	**-0.03**	(0.00)	**-0.28**	(0.01)	0.00	(0.00)	39.8	(0.2)
Romania	0.10	(0.07)	0.01	(0.06)	-0.05	(0.05)	**0.08**	(0.04)	0.04	(0.21)	0.00	(0.00)	26.7	(6.2)
Russian Federation	-0.02	(0.08)	-0.01	(0.04)	0.00	(0.05)	-0.02	(0.04)	-0.30	(0.25)	0.00	(0.00)	14.1	(4.8)
Serbia	0.01	(0.08)	0.07	(0.04)	-0.01	(0.04)	-0.03	(0.05)	**0.75**	(0.37)	0.00	(0.00)	19.7	(7.7)
Shanghai-China	-0.12	(0.10)	0.04	(0.04)	-0.01	(0.04)	0.04	(0.03)	0.55	(0.31)	0.00	(0.00)	33.7	(7.1)
Singapore	**0.12**	(0.01)	**0.01**	(0.00)	**0.06**	(0.00)	**-0.02**	(0.00)	**-0.25**	(0.01)	**0.00**	(0.00)	27.2	(0.3)
Chinese Taipei	-0.02	(0.13)	0.00	(0.05)	-0.01	(0.04)	-0.01	(0.04)	0.01	(0.34)	0.00	(0.00)	39.1	(8.6)
Thailand	0.10	(0.07)	-0.04	(0.02)	0.02	(0.03)	0.02	(0.02)	-0.06	(0.14)	0.00	(0.00)	15.0	(5.3)
Tunisia	-0.01	(0.05)	0.03	(0.03)	0.01	(0.03)	0.02	(0.03)	0.02	(0.16)	0.00	(0.00)	13.9	(8.1)
United Arab Emirates	0.01	(0.05)	-0.02	(0.03)	0.03	(0.02)	-0.02	(0.02)	-0.24	(0.19)	0.00	(0.00)	19.6	(4.3)
Uruguay	-0.08	(0.05)	0.03	(0.02)	-0.03	(0.03)	-0.04	(0.03)	**0.44**	(0.20)	**0.00**	(0.00)	17.8	(4.7)
Viet Nam	-0.01	(0.08)	0.03	(0.02)	-0.01	(0.03)	0.01	(0.02)	0.15	(0.12)	0.00	(0.00)	15.0	(7.7)

Note: Values that are statistically significant are indicated in bold (see Annex A3).
1. Regression: School average disciplinary climate = Intercept + variables listed in this table.
* See notes at the beginning of this Annex.
StatLink � http://dx.doi.org/10.1787/888932957517

[Part 1/1]
Probability of having skipped a class or a day of school, by students having arrived late for school
Table IV.5.14   *Results based on students' self-reports*

| | Logistic regression model estimating student having skipped a class or a day of school in the two weeks prior to the PISA test[1] | | | | Probability of a student to have skipped a class or a day of school at least once in the two weeks prior to the PISA test for a student... | |
| | Intercept | | Student having arrived late for school in the two weeks prior to the PISA test | | ...who did not arrive late for school in the two weeks prior to the PISA test | ...who arrived late for school at least once in the two weeks prior to the PISA test |
	Intercept	S.E.	Logistic regression coef.	S.E.	Probability	Probability
Australia	-0.80	(0.03)	**0.82**	(0.04)	0.31	0.51
Austria	-2.01	(0.08)	**1.57**	(0.12)	0.12	0.39
Belgium	-2.72	(0.06)	**1.54**	(0.08)	0.06	0.23
Canada	-1.13	(0.03)	**1.16**	(0.05)	0.24	0.51
Chile	-2.02	(0.07)	**1.03**	(0.09)	0.12	0.27
Czech Republic	-2.65	(0.09)	**1.37**	(0.10)	0.07	0.22
Denmark	-1.89	(0.07)	**1.25**	(0.08)	0.13	0.34
Estonia	-1.12	(0.06)	**1.16**	(0.07)	0.25	0.51
Finland	-2.14	(0.06)	**1.42**	(0.06)	0.11	0.33
France	-1.94	(0.07)	**1.49**	(0.08)	0.13	0.39
Germany	-2.49	(0.08)	**1.53**	(0.11)	0.08	0.28
Greece	-0.54	(0.05)	**0.95**	(0.06)	0.37	0.60
Hungary	-2.57	(0.09)	**1.73**	(0.13)	0.07	0.30
Iceland	-2.76	(0.09)	**1.60**	(0.11)	0.06	0.24
Ireland	-2.18	(0.08)	**1.13**	(0.11)	0.10	0.26
Israel	-0.63	(0.06)	**0.94**	(0.07)	0.35	0.58
Italy	0.15	(0.03)	**0.95**	(0.04)	0.54	0.75
Japan	-3.72	(0.15)	**2.22**	(0.13)	0.02	0.18
Korea	-4.24	(0.14)	**2.14**	(0.16)	0.01	0.11
Luxembourg	-2.63	(0.06)	**1.36**	(0.10)	0.07	0.22
Mexico	-1.13	(0.03)	**1.03**	(0.04)	0.24	0.47
Netherlands	-2.59	(0.10)	**1.43**	(0.11)	0.07	0.24
New Zealand	-1.65	(0.05)	**1.24**	(0.08)	0.16	0.40
Norway	-2.44	(0.08)	**1.68**	(0.10)	0.08	0.32
Poland	-1.79	(0.07)	**1.59**	(0.09)	0.14	0.45
Portugal	-1.21	(0.06)	**1.05**	(0.06)	0.23	0.46
Slovak Republic	-2.13	(0.07)	**1.42**	(0.10)	0.11	0.33
Slovenia	-1.67	(0.05)	**1.78**	(0.07)	0.16	0.53
Spain	-0.63	(0.04)	**1.04**	(0.05)	0.35	0.60
Sweden	-2.11	(0.08)	**1.40**	(0.09)	0.11	0.33
Switzerland	-2.44	(0.06)	**1.43**	(0.09)	0.08	0.27
Turkey	0.22	(0.05)	**1.06**	(0.07)	0.55	0.78
United Kingdom	-1.44	(0.05)	**0.94**	(0.06)	0.19	0.38
United States	-1.24	(0.05)	**0.86**	(0.06)	0.23	0.41
OECD average	**-1.83**	**(0.01)**	**1.33**	**(0.02)**	**0.14**	**0.38**
Albania	-1.73	(0.05)	**1.49**	(0.07)	0.15	0.44
Argentina	0.41	(0.06)	**0.59**	(0.07)	0.60	0.73
Brazil	-1.11	(0.04)	**0.72**	(0.05)	0.25	0.40
Bulgaria	-1.35	(0.07)	**1.44**	(0.07)	0.21	0.52
Colombia	-1.83	(0.06)	**0.79**	(0.08)	0.14	0.26
Costa Rica	-0.16	(0.06)	**0.76**	(0.07)	0.46	0.65
Croatia	-1.61	(0.06)	**1.70**	(0.07)	0.17	0.52
Cyprus*	-0.91	(0.05)	**1.14**	(0.06)	0.29	0.56
Hong Kong-China	-3.07	(0.08)	**1.41**	(0.14)	0.04	0.16
Indonesia	-1.21	(0.06)	**1.22**	(0.09)	0.23	0.50
Jordan	0.13	(0.05)	**0.45**	(0.07)	0.53	0.64
Kazakhstan	-1.50	(0.06)	**1.53**	(0.08)	0.18	0.51
Latvia	0.22	(0.06)	**0.89**	(0.07)	0.56	0.75
Liechtenstein	-3.87	(0.50)	**2.38**	(0.60)	0.02	0.18
Lithuania	-0.97	(0.06)	**1.09**	(0.07)	0.28	0.53
Macao-China	-2.84	(0.08)	**1.46**	(0.10)	0.05	0.20
Malaysia	-0.62	(0.06)	**0.92**	(0.07)	0.35	0.58
Montenegro	-0.96	(0.04)	**1.20**	(0.07)	0.28	0.56
Peru	-1.90	(0.08)	**0.91**	(0.07)	0.13	0.27
Qatar	-1.27	(0.03)	**0.85**	(0.04)	0.22	0.39
Romania	-0.32	(0.06)	**1.46**	(0.07)	0.42	0.76
Russian Federation	-1.22	(0.06)	**1.43**	(0.08)	0.23	0.55
Serbia	-1.56	(0.06)	**1.45**	(0.07)	0.17	0.47
Shanghai-China	-3.88	(0.14)	**1.78**	(0.18)	0.02	0.11
Singapore	-1.47	(0.04)	**0.95**	(0.08)	0.19	0.37
Chinese Taipei	-2.76	(0.09)	**1.75**	(0.11)	0.06	0.27
Thailand	-1.16	(0.05)	**1.23**	(0.07)	0.24	0.52
Tunisia	-1.20	(0.07)	**1.00**	(0.08)	0.23	0.45
United Arab Emirates	-0.24	(0.03)	**0.83**	(0.05)	0.44	0.64
Uruguay	-1.33	(0.06)	**1.03**	(0.07)	0.21	0.43
Viet Nam	-2.22	(0.07)	**1.43**	(0.12)	0.10	0.31

Note: Values that are statistically significant are indicated in bold (see Annex A3).
1. Logistic regression: SKIP = Intercept + LATE; where SKIP (0=did not skip; and 1=skipped) and LATE (0=did not arrive late; and 1=arrived late).
* See notes at the beginning of this Annex.
StatLink ⌨️📊 http://dx.doi.org/10.1787/888932957517

[Part 1/1]
Students arriving late for school and student gender and immigrant backgrounds

Table IV.5.15   *Results based on students' self-reports*

		Increased likelihood that:			
		Boys reported having arrived late at least once in the two weeks prior to the PISA test		Students with an immigrant background reported having arrived late at least once in the two weeks prior to the PISA test	
		Ratio	S.E.	Ratio	S.E.
OECD	Australia	**0.95**	(0.03)	1.04	(0.04)
	Austria	0.98	(0.07)	**1.93**	(0.16)
	Belgium	1.08	(0.04)	**1.65**	(0.09)
	Canada	1.04	(0.02)	**1.18**	(0.04)
	Chile	0.96	(0.03)	**1.29**	(0.12)
	Czech Republic	**1.22**	(0.07)	1.28	(0.19)
	Denmark	**1.19**	(0.05)	**1.36**	(0.06)
	Estonia	**1.20**	(0.05)	**1.31**	(0.07)
	Finland	**1.16**	(0.03)	**1.43**	(0.06)
	France	1.08	(0.04)	**1.55**	(0.10)
	Germany	1.03	(0.06)	**1.57**	(0.13)
	Greece	0.99	(0.03)	0.99	(0.05)
	Hungary	1.10	(0.08)	0.93	(0.27)
	Iceland	**1.25**	(0.06)	1.23	(0.14)
	Ireland	**1.20**	(0.08)	1.14	(0.10)
	Israel	0.95	(0.03)	1.06	(0.05)
	Italy	**1.10**	(0.03)	**1.12**	(0.06)
	Japan	**1.40**	(0.13)	c	c
	Korea	1.06	(0.07)	c	c
	Luxembourg	1.03	(0.04)	**1.37**	(0.06)
	Mexico	1.00	(0.02)	1.04	(0.08)
	Netherlands	1.06	(0.06)	**1.39**	(0.13)
	New Zealand	0.94	(0.05)	0.97	(0.05)
	Norway	1.07	(0.05)	**1.30**	(0.08)
	Poland	**1.27**	(0.05)	c	c
	Portugal	0.97	(0.03)	**1.18**	(0.06)
	Slovak Republic	**1.19**	(0.07)	0.79	(0.30)
	Slovenia	0.98	(0.04)	**1.19**	(0.08)
	Spain	0.96	(0.02)	**1.53**	(0.06)
	Sweden	**1.10**	(0.03)	**1.28**	(0.04)
	Switzerland	1.01	(0.05)	**1.40**	(0.09)
	Turkey	**1.20**	(0.04)	1.14	(0.18)
	United Kingdom	1.02	(0.04)	**1.23**	(0.08)
	United States	1.06	(0.05)	**1.27**	(0.09)
	OECD average	**1.08**	(0.01)	**1.26**	(0.02)
Partners	Albania	1.03	(0.04)	c	c
	Argentina	0.97	(0.04)	**1.25**	(0.07)
	Brazil	1.01	(0.03)	**1.67**	(0.23)
	Bulgaria	1.03	(0.03)	c	c
	Colombia	1.06	(0.04)	c	c
	Costa Rica	0.97	(0.03)	0.96	(0.07)
	Croatia	**1.25**	(0.05)	**1.17**	(0.07)
	Cyprus*	**1.09**	(0.03)	1.03	(0.06)
	Hong Kong-China	1.15	(0.08)	0.95	(0.08)
	Indonesia	**1.23**	(0.07)	c	c
	Jordan	**1.24**	(0.06)	1.01	(0.06)
	Kazakhstan	**1.21**	(0.06)	1.00	(0.07)
	Latvia	**1.13**	(0.04)	0.96	(0.07)
	Liechtenstein	1.44	(0.37)	1.60	(0.38)
	Lithuania	**1.31**	(0.05)	**1.36**	(0.14)
	Macao-China	**1.12**	(0.05)	0.97	(0.05)
	Malaysia	**1.20**	(0.06)	**1.38**	(0.18)
	Montenegro	**1.13**	(0.04)	1.10	(0.09)
	Peru	1.03	(0.03)	c	c
	Qatar	**1.11**	(0.03)	**0.55**	(0.01)
	Romania	**1.13**	(0.04)	c	c
	Russian Federation	**1.13**	(0.03)	1.12	(0.07)
	Serbia	**1.20**	(0.05)	0.99	(0.08)
	Shanghai-China	**1.27**	(0.09)	1.30	(0.41)
	Singapore	**1.18**	(0.06)	**0.85**	(0.06)
	Chinese Taipei	**1.28**	(0.08)	c	c
	Thailand	**1.40**	(0.05)	0.68	(0.23)
	Tunisia	**1.09**	(0.04)	c	c
	United Arab Emirates	**1.19**	(0.06)	**0.61**	(0.03)
	Uruguay	0.95	(0.03)	c	c
	Viet Nam	**1.26**	(0.08)	c	c

Note: Values that are statistically significant are indicated in bold (see Annex A3).
* See notes at the beginning of this Annex.
StatLink ⌷⌷⌷ http://dx.doi.org/10.1787/888932957517

[Part 1/2]
Relationship between student having arrived late for school and student and school features

Table IV.5.16 · *Results based on students' and school principals' reports*

| | Logistic regression model estimating student having arrived late for school in the two weeks prior to the PISA test[1] | | | | | | | | | | | | | |
| | Intercept | | PISA index of economic, social and cultural status (ESCS) (1 unit increase) | | Student is a female | | Student's language at home is the same as the language of assessment | | Student without an immigrant background | | School average PISA index of economic, social and cultural status (1 unit increase) | | School size (per 100 students) | |
	Intercept	S.E.	Logistic regression coef.	S.E.	Logistic regression coef.	S.E.	Logistic regression coef.	S.E.	Logistic regression coef.	S.E.	Logistic regression coef.	S.E.	Logistic regression coef.	S.E.
OECD														
Australia	-0.85	(0.10)	**-0.13**	(0.03)	0.09	(0.05)	0.11	(0.08)	0.02	(0.08)	0.06	(0.09)	-0.01	(0.01)
Austria	-0.42	(0.23)	**0.16**	(0.07)	-0.11	(0.11)	-0.21	(0.22)	**-0.76**	(0.21)	**0.55**	(0.20)	**-0.05**	(0.02)
Belgium	-0.42	(0.11)	0.09	(0.05)	-0.02	(0.06)	-0.04	(0.08)	**-0.61**	(0.10)	-0.10	(0.12)	-0.01	(0.01)
Canada	-0.24	(0.11)	**-0.11**	(0.03)	-0.06	(0.04)	**0.19**	(0.08)	**-0.21**	(0.08)	0.11	(0.10)	0.00	(0.01)
Chile	0.44	(0.49)	-0.02	(0.05)	0.11	(0.07)	-0.11	(0.36)	**-0.68**	(0.30)	**-0.19**	(0.07)	**-0.03**	(0.01)
Czech Republic	-0.90	(0.28)	0.08	(0.08)	**-0.21**	(0.09)	0.10	(0.38)	-0.34	(0.39)	**-0.51**	(0.18)	-0.01	(0.03)
Denmark	-0.07	(0.17)	-0.01	(0.05)	**-0.34**	(0.07)	-0.14	(0.16)	**-0.30**	(0.11)	**0.41**	(0.15)	**-0.05**	(0.02)
Estonia	0.18	(0.20)	-0.08	(0.05)	**-0.30**	(0.07)	0.06	(0.15)	**-0.39**	(0.12)	-0.11	(0.16)	0.03	(0.03)
Finland	0.20	(0.14)	**-0.16**	(0.04)	**-0.24**	(0.06)	-0.18	(0.13)	**-0.27**	(0.13)	-0.03	(0.16)	**0.08**	(0.03)
France	-0.20	(0.19)	0.05	(0.06)	-0.12	(0.07)	-0.08	(0.17)	**-0.54**	(0.17)	-0.13	(0.18)	-0.03	(0.02)
Germany	-1.03	(0.21)	0.04	(0.06)	-0.05	(0.10)	0.10	(0.19)	**-0.53**	(0.14)	0.23	(0.17)	-0.02	(0.02)
Greece	0.16	(0.18)	**0.11**	(0.04)	0.01	(0.06)	0.00	(0.19)	-0.20	(0.19)	-0.26	(0.16)	**0.12**	(0.04)
Hungary	-1.66	(0.65)	0.04	(0.06)	0.02	(0.11)	-0.19	(0.47)	0.10	(0.41)	**-0.66**	(0.16)	-0.04	(0.03)
Iceland	-0.30	(0.26)	**-0.15**	(0.05)	**-0.42**	(0.07)	-0.23	(0.32)	-0.12	(0.35)	0.28	(0.15)	0.05	(0.03)
Ireland	-0.82	(0.22)	-0.08	(0.05)	**-0.26**	(0.10)	0.08	(0.23)	-0.15	(0.19)	-0.22	(0.16)	-0.05	(0.03)
Israel	0.14	(0.18)	-0.08	(0.04)	0.07	(0.08)	-0.07	(0.11)	-0.03	(0.12)	0.10	(0.12)	**-0.06**	(0.01)
Italy	-0.40	(0.11)	**0.08**	(0.02)	**-0.11**	(0.04)	-0.08	(0.06)	-0.09	(0.11)	**-0.35**	(0.08)	-0.01	(0.01)
Japan	0.39	(0.64)	-0.07	(0.07)	**-0.37**	(0.10)	c	c	c	c	-0.07	(0.30)	-0.02	(0.02)
Korea	2.12	(0.45)	-0.10	(0.06)	0.00	(0.08)	c	c	c	c	-0.23	(0.17)	-0.02	(0.01)
Luxembourg	-0.87	(0.08)	0.01	(0.04)	-0.01	(0.07)	0.16	(0.12)	**-0.30**	(0.08)	0.14	(0.08)	**0.03**	(0.01)
Mexico	-0.48	(0.22)	**0.06**	(0.02)	-0.01	(0.03)	**0.24**	(0.12)	-0.11	(0.13)	-0.05	(0.05)	0.01	(0.01)
Netherlands	-0.33	(0.23)	0.11	(0.07)	-0.09	(0.09)	0.08	(0.25)	**-0.69**	(0.15)	-0.29	(0.20)	-0.01	(0.01)
New Zealand	-0.56	(0.15)	**-0.19**	(0.05)	0.06	(0.09)	-0.20	(0.12)	**0.30**	(0.10)	**-0.48**	(0.17)	0.00	(0.01)
Norway	-0.54	(0.17)	**-0.15**	(0.05)	-0.09	(0.08)	-0.28	(0.19)	-0.05	(0.19)	0.24	(0.20)	0.01	(0.04)
Poland	0.18	(0.91)	-0.04	(0.04)	**-0.48**	(0.07)	-0.20	(0.68)	c	c	0.23	(0.16)	0.06	(0.05)
Portugal	0.49	(0.28)	-0.01	(0.03)	0.05	(0.08)	0.31	(0.27)	**-0.41**	(0.16)	0.04	(0.10)	0.00	(0.01)
Slovak Republic	-1.29	(0.66)	-0.03	(0.05)	**-0.21**	(0.08)	**-0.52**	(0.17)	c	c	-0.14	(0.17)	0.04	(0.03)
Slovenia	-0.29	(0.18)	**0.10**	(0.05)	0.11	(0.07)	-0.13	(0.21)	-0.16	(0.19)	-0.16	(0.12)	0.00	(0.01)
Spain	0.26	(0.12)	**-0.06**	(0.02)	0.07	(0.05)	**-0.20**	(0.09)	**-0.62**	(0.09)	0.07	(0.08)	-0.02	(0.01)
Sweden	0.74	(0.15)	**-0.11**	(0.05)	**-0.24**	(0.07)	0.10	(0.18)	**-0.53**	(0.16)	0.02	(0.18)	0.03	(0.03)
Switzerland	-0.79	(0.12)	0.05	(0.04)	-0.04	(0.08)	**-0.18**	(0.09)	**-0.38**	(0.08)	**0.63**	(0.13)	**0.04**	(0.01)
Turkey	-0.02	(0.39)	**0.06**	(0.03)	**-0.28**	(0.06)	-0.23	(0.16)	-0.20	(0.33)	**-0.20**	(0.08)	-0.01	(0.01)
United Kingdom	-0.69	(0.16)	**-0.14**	(0.04)	-0.09	(0.06)	**0.36**	(0.16)	**-0.42**	(0.14)	-0.10	(0.10)	-0.01	(0.01)
United States	-0.99	(0.17)	**-0.17**	(0.05)	-0.09	(0.06)	0.23	(0.16)	-0.12	(0.14)	-0.29	(0.16)	-0.01	(0.01)
OECD average	**-0.26**	(0.06)	**-0.03**	(0.01)	**-0.11**	(0.01)	-0.04	(0.04)	**-0.29**	(0.04)	-0.03	(0.03)	0.00	(0.00)
Partners														
Albania	m	m	m	m	m	m	m	m	m	m	m	m	m	m
Argentina	-0.15	(0.27)	-0.02	(0.04)	0.04	(0.07)	0.31	(0.26)	**-0.35**	(0.14)	**-0.24**	(0.12)	0.00	(0.02)
Brazil	0.19	(0.44)	**0.09**	(0.03)	-0.01	(0.04)	-0.03	(0.20)	**-0.87**	(0.29)	-0.05	(0.10)	-0.01	(0.01)
Bulgaria	0.73	(0.60)	**-0.12**	(0.04)	0.00	(0.06)	0.02	(0.17)	c	c	-0.07	(0.10)	**-0.04**	(0.02)
Colombia	-2.25	(0.96)	0.05	(0.04)	-0.09	(0.07)	-0.28	(0.38)	c	c	**-0.26**	(0.11)	-0.01	(0.01)
Costa Rica	0.36	(0.42)	**0.12**	(0.04)	0.11	(0.07)	0.31	(0.38)	-0.06	(0.18)	0.03	(0.13)	0.01	(0.01)
Croatia	-0.60	(0.37)	0.07	(0.04)	**-0.32**	(0.07)	-0.05	(0.34)	-0.13	(0.10)	-0.07	(0.16)	**-0.04**	(0.02)
Cyprus*	0.01	(0.14)	-0.06	(0.04)	**-0.15**	(0.06)	-0.15	(0.11)	0.00	(0.13)	-0.16	(0.10)	0.01	(0.02)
Hong Kong-China	-1.61	(0.29)	-0.04	(0.07)	-0.16	(0.09)	**-0.61**	(0.16)	0.15	(0.10)	**-0.36**	(0.14)	-0.02	(0.01)
Indonesia	0.24	(0.69)	**0.11**	(0.05)	**-0.31**	(0.07)	**0.22**	(0.10)	c	c	-0.02	(0.12)	**-0.05**	(0.02)
Jordan	-0.16	(0.20)	-0.03	(0.04)	**-0.27**	(0.08)	**-0.28**	(0.14)	0.04	(0.10)	0.04	(0.11)	0.01	(0.01)
Kazakhstan	0.26	(0.26)	**-0.22**	(0.05)	**-0.27**	(0.10)	**-0.42**	(0.10)	0.10	(0.10)	-0.09	(0.20)	0.01	(0.01)
Latvia	0.61	(0.21)	-0.01	(0.05)	**-0.32**	(0.09)	-0.17	(0.14)	0.13	(0.14)	-0.09	(0.16)	0.01	(0.03)
Liechtenstein	-0.52	(1.02)	-0.26	(0.20)	-0.38	(0.36)	c	c	-0.39	(0.41)	-1.49	(1.00)	0.14	(0.23)
Lithuania	0.44	(0.33)	0.02	(0.04)	**-0.45**	(0.06)	0.05	(0.16)	-0.43	(0.26)	-0.21	(0.18)	0.02	(0.03)
Macao-China	-1.49	(0.23)	**-0.11**	(0.04)	-0.04	(0.07)	**0.77**	(0.13)	0.02	(0.07)	**0.54**	(0.10)	**-0.05**	(0.01)
Malaysia	-0.42	(0.30)	-0.01	(0.04)	**-0.26**	(0.07)	**0.23**	(0.10)	-0.47	(0.25)	-0.14	(0.10)	0.00	(0.01)
Montenegro	-0.36	(0.38)	**0.11**	(0.04)	**-0.16**	(0.06)	0.00	(0.32)	-0.16	(0.15)	-0.29	(0.15)	-0.02	(0.01)
Peru	0.05	(0.53)	0.04	(0.04)	-0.05	(0.07)	-0.18	(0.21)	c	c	**-0.25**	(0.11)	-0.02	(0.01)
Qatar	-0.59	(0.10)	0.04	(0.03)	**-0.18**	(0.05)	-0.08	(0.06)	**0.86**	(0.06)	0.06	(0.07)	-0.01	(0.01)
Romania	-0.55	(0.95)	-0.01	(0.04)	**-0.19**	(0.07)	0.18	(0.25)	c	c	**-0.30**	(0.12)	-0.01	(0.01)
Russian Federation	0.07	(0.25)	**-0.17**	(0.06)	**-0.22**	(0.06)	0.08	(0.20)	-0.11	(0.11)	0.10	(0.19)	**0.06**	(0.02)
Serbia	-0.31	(0.29)	**0.15**	(0.04)	**-0.33**	(0.08)	-0.05	(0.22)	0.00	(0.15)	-0.07	(0.16)	-0.03	(0.02)
Shanghai-China	-1.08	(0.56)	0.06	(0.05)	**-0.28**	(0.09)	-0.12	(0.33)	-0.10	(0.45)	-0.22	(0.11)	0.00	(0.01)
Singapore	-1.19	(0.11)	**-0.16**	(0.04)	**-0.22**	(0.07)	-0.12	(0.09)	0.12	(0.10)	0.12	(0.13)	**-0.05**	(0.01)
Chinese Taipei	-0.71	(0.46)	-0.08	(0.05)	**-0.24**	(0.08)	0.06	(0.11)	c	c	-0.02	(0.17)	-0.01	(0.01)
Thailand	-1.47	(0.64)	0.06	(0.04)	**-0.38**	(0.07)	**0.21**	(0.09)	0.62	(0.61)	**-0.28**	(0.09)	-0.01	(0.01)
Tunisia	-0.07	(0.57)	-0.01	(0.03)	**-0.18**	(0.08)	0.14	(0.36)	c	c	0.00	(0.08)	0.01	(0.01)
United Arab Emirates	-1.32	(0.18)	0.00	(0.05)	**-0.18**	(0.07)	0.12	(0.14)	**0.75**	(0.07)	0.04	(0.11)	-0.01	(0.01)
Uruguay	-0.52	(0.46)	0.05	(0.04)	0.12	(0.08)	-0.04	(0.24)	c	c	-0.12	(0.13)	0.01	(0.01)
Viet Nam	-1.28	(1.40)	0.01	(0.04)	**-0.16**	(0.08)	-0.55	(0.31)	c	c	**-0.36**	(0.13)	**-0.04**	(0.01)

Note: Values that are statistically significant are indicated in bold (see Annex A3).
1. Logistic regression: LATE = Intercept + variables listed in this table; where LATE (0=did not arrive late; and 1=arrived late).
* See notes at the beginning of this Annex.
StatLink ⌸𝖘⌸ http://dx.doi.org/10.1787/888932957517

[Part 2/2]
Relationship between student having arrived late for school and student and school features
Table IV.5.16   *Results based on students' and school principals' reports*

	Logistic regression model estimating student having arrived late for school in the two weeks prior to the PISA test[1]											
	School size (per 100 students) (squared)		School in a small town or village (15 000 or less people)		School in a city or a large city (100 000 or more people)		School average index of disciplinary climate (1 unit increase)		School average index of teacher-student relations (1 unit increase)		Private school	
	Logistic regression coef.	S.E.	Logistic regression coef.	S.E.	Logistic regression coef.	S.E.	Logistic regression coef.	S.E.	Logistic regression coef.	S.E.	Logistic regression coef.	S.E.
Australia	0.00	(0.00)	**-0.31**	(0.09)	**0.24**	(0.07)	**-0.18**	(0.07)	-0.10	(0.08)	-0.11	(0.07)
Austria	0.00	(0.00)	**-0.61**	(0.23)	0.23	(0.19)	**-0.58**	(0.21)	-0.25	(0.19)	-0.17	(0.37)
Belgium	0.00	(0.00)	0.03	(0.11)	**0.49**	(0.10)	-0.22	(0.13)	0.24	(0.15)	**-0.28**	(0.09)
Canada	0.00	(0.00)	-0.13	(0.10)	**0.27**	(0.08)	**-0.23**	(0.08)	**-0.39**	(0.10)	**-0.39**	(0.12)
Chile	**0.00**	(0.00)	-0.10	(0.14)	0.15	(0.11)	**-0.43**	(0.13)	0.02	(0.15)	0.01	(0.12)
Czech Republic	0.00	(0.01)	-0.16	(0.12)	0.23	(0.13)	-0.15	(0.10)	**-0.56**	(0.17)	0.38	(0.20)
Denmark	0.00	(0.00)	-0.10	(0.12)	**0.39**	(0.11)	**-0.51**	(0.16)	0.10	(0.18)	**-0.41**	(0.18)
Estonia	**-0.01**	(0.00)	-0.18	(0.13)	0.21	(0.12)	-0.08	(0.10)	-0.10	(0.16)	**0.86**	(0.24)
Finland	**-0.03**	(0.01)	-0.14	(0.12)	**0.28**	(0.09)	**-0.49**	(0.13)	-0.21	(0.15)	**0.48**	(0.17)
France	**0.00**	(0.00)	**-0.37**	(0.10)	0.06	(0.14)	**-0.34**	(0.12)	0.07	(0.14)	**-0.34**	(0.17)
Germany	0.00	(0.00)	-0.20	(0.14)	0.27	(0.14)	-0.16	(0.16)	-0.08	(0.16)	-0.11	(0.19)
Greece	-0.01	(0.00)	**-0.22**	(0.09)	0.15	(0.09)	**-0.43**	(0.13)	0.13	(0.11)	c	c
Hungary	0.00	(0.00)	-0.01	(0.15)	**0.67**	(0.14)	**-0.55**	(0.16)	-0.07	(0.24)	0.31	(0.21)
Iceland	-0.02	(0.01)	**0.22**	(0.10)	0.16	(0.11)	-0.16	(0.10)	0.00	(0.12)	c	c
Ireland	0.00	(0.00)	-0.03	(0.15)	**0.33**	(0.15)	**-0.41**	(0.14)	0.13	(0.20)	-0.04	(0.11)
Israel	0.00	(0.00)	-0.21	(0.13)	**0.29**	(0.10)	-0.01	(0.11)	**-0.24**	(0.11)	c	c
Italy	0.00	(0.00)	-0.24	(0.14)	**0.12**	(0.06)	**-0.14**	(0.07)	**0.28**	(0.09)	-0.18	(0.15)
Japan	0.00	(0.00)	c	c	-0.22	(0.16)	**-0.64**	(0.19)	-0.14	(0.22)	**0.35**	(0.15)
Korea	**0.01**	(0.00)	-0.50	(0.35)	0.17	(0.22)	**-0.80**	(0.21)	-0.41	(0.23)	-0.14	(0.11)
Luxembourg	**0.00**	(0.00)	-0.08	(0.09)	c	c	-0.21	(0.16)	**0.46**	(0.20)	-0.20	(0.12)
Mexico	0.00	(0.00)	-0.04	(0.08)	**0.22**	(0.06)	**-0.21**	(0.06)	**-0.25**	(0.08)	-0.02	(0.17)
Netherlands	0.00	(0.00)	-0.13	(0.16)	0.01	(0.13)	**-0.49**	(0.18)	-0.40	(0.21)	-0.15	(0.11)
New Zealand	0.00	(0.00)	**-0.39**	(0.17)	0.17	(0.13)	-0.18	(0.13)	0.09	(0.17)	-0.26	(0.26)
Norway	-0.01	(0.02)	-0.25	(0.14)	0.20	(0.12)	-0.17	(0.12)	-0.01	(0.18)	c	c
Poland	-0.01	(0.01)	**-0.40**	(0.15)	0.26	(0.18)	**-0.31**	(0.11)	**-0.36**	(0.15)	0.27	(0.26)
Portugal	0.00	(0.00)	0.03	(0.11)	0.03	(0.12)	-0.05	(0.17)	**-0.50**	(0.19)	-0.13	(0.16)
Slovak Republic	0.00	(0.01)	-0.25	(0.15)	0.10	(0.19)	**-0.51**	(0.12)	-0.17	(0.16)	0.19	(0.17)
Slovenia	0.00	(0.00)	-0.10	(0.11)	0.18	(0.10)	**-0.34**	(0.07)	**-0.27**	(0.11)	-0.08	(0.24)
Spain	0.00	(0.00)	**-0.30**	(0.10)	-0.11	(0.07)	-0.06	(0.10)	**-0.20**	(0.09)	**-0.24**	(0.09)
Sweden	0.00	(0.00)	**-0.30**	(0.11)	0.16	(0.12)	-0.21	(0.15)	-0.16	(0.15)	0.07	(0.17)
Switzerland	**0.00**	(0.00)	0.02	(0.10)	**0.44**	(0.15)	**-0.37**	(0.14)	**-0.49**	(0.12)	-0.41	(0.26)
Turkey	0.00	(0.00)	-0.05	(0.14)	0.16	(0.09)	-0.27	(0.14)	**0.25**	(0.12)	c	c
United Kingdom	**0.00**	(0.00)	-0.08	(0.10)	0.03	(0.10)	-0.06	(0.11)	-0.19	(0.14)	0.05	(0.08)
United States	0.00	(0.00)	-0.21	(0.17)	**0.34**	(0.14)	-0.38	(0.20)	-0.08	(0.23)	-0.32	(0.33)
OECD average	**0.00**	(0.00)	**-0.18**	(0.02)	**0.20**	(0.02)	**-0.30**	(0.02)	**-0.11**	(0.03)	-0.03	(0.04)
Albania	m	m	m	m	m	m	m	m	m	m	m	m
Argentina	0.00	(0.00)	-0.31	(0.19)	-0.01	(0.14)	-0.17	(0.15)	-0.25	(0.17)	**-0.36**	(0.15)
Brazil	0.00	(0.00)	-0.07	(0.11)	0.05	(0.11)	-0.16	(0.10)	-0.05	(0.10)	0.17	(0.21)
Bulgaria	**0.01**	(0.00)	-0.17	(0.14)	0.14	(0.09)	**-0.35**	(0.13)	0.07	(0.14)	c	c
Colombia	0.00	(0.00)	-0.14	(0.19)	**0.31**	(0.16)	**-0.55**	(0.18)	-0.25	(0.20)	0.13	(0.15)
Costa Rica	0.00	(0.00)	0.17	(0.12)	0.19	(0.19)	**-0.32**	(0.15)	**-0.45**	(0.19)	**-0.78**	(0.24)
Croatia	0.01	(0.01)	**-0.36**	(0.14)	**0.45**	(0.12)	**-0.46**	(0.12)	-0.17	(0.16)	c	c
Cyprus*	0.01	(0.01)	**-0.29**	(0.08)	**0.17**	(0.08)	**-0.45**	(0.12)	**-0.26**	(0.11)	**-0.49**	(0.14)
Hong Kong-China	**0.01**	(0.00)	c	c	c	c	**-0.41**	(0.17)	-0.11	(0.25)	0.07	(0.23)
Indonesia	0.00	(0.00)	-0.06	(0.19)	0.13	(0.28)	-0.29	(0.16)	0.14	(0.23)	-0.16	(0.13)
Jordan	0.00	(0.00)	**-0.28**	(0.13)	0.05	(0.11)	**-0.30**	(0.11)	-0.06	(0.13)	-0.17	(0.12)
Kazakhstan	0.00	(0.00)	-0.11	(0.22)	0.07	(0.19)	**-0.55**	(0.21)	**-0.70**	(0.20)	0.30	(0.26)
Latvia	0.00	(0.00)	**-0.28**	(0.14)	-0.08	(0.13)	**-0.46**	(0.10)	0.08	(0.18)	c	c
Liechtenstein	0.04	(0.10)	c	c	c	c	-1.45	(0.86)	0.36	(0.39)	c	c
Lithuania	**-0.02**	(0.01)	-0.03	(0.13)	**0.40**	(0.11)	**-0.43**	(0.10)	-0.12	(0.11)	c	c
Macao-China	**0.00**	(0.00)	c	c	c	c	**-1.28**	(0.19)	-0.11	(0.19)	c	c
Malaysia	0.00	(0.00)	0.02	(0.12)	-0.04	(0.11)	-0.30	(0.17)	0.29	(0.22)	-0.57	(0.29)
Montenegro	0.00	(0.00)	-0.13	(0.08)	**0.47**	(0.10)	-0.25	(0.17)	-0.10	(0.18)	c	c
Peru	0.00	(0.00)	**-0.30**	(0.12)	0.16	(0.13)	-0.29	(0.16)	-0.02	(0.13)	0.23	(0.17)
Qatar	**0.00**	(0.00)	**-0.22**	(0.07)	**-0.26**	(0.07)	-0.05	(0.06)	-0.16	(0.08)	0.11	(0.07)
Romania	0.00	(0.00)	-0.13	(0.12)	**0.46**	(0.13)	-0.06	(0.11)	0.12	(0.16)	c	c
Russian Federation	0.00	(0.00)	0.29	(0.17)	0.10	(0.12)	**-0.47**	(0.14)	**-0.34**	(0.17)	c	c
Serbia	0.00	(0.00)	-0.25	(0.17)	**0.36**	(0.13)	**-0.48**	(0.14)	-0.14	(0.19)	c	c
Shanghai-China	0.00	(0.00)	c	c	c	c	**-0.68**	(0.17)	0.21	(0.23)	0.10	(0.18)
Singapore	0.00	(0.00)	c	c	c	c	**-0.54**	(0.10)	-0.23	(0.14)	c	c
Chinese Taipei	0.00	(0.00)	-0.08	(0.25)	0.08	(0.14)	**-0.51**	(0.19)	-0.31	(0.19)	**-0.25**	(0.12)
Thailand	0.00	(0.00)	-0.17	(0.14)	0.19	(0.14)	**-1.17**	(0.21)	-0.12	(0.19)	**0.34**	(0.14)
Tunisia	0.00	(0.00)	-0.04	(0.11)	0.15	(0.10)	-0.26	(0.16)	-0.21	(0.15)	c	c
United Arab Emirates	0.00	(0.00)	-0.10	(0.11)	0.05	(0.12)	**-0.31**	(0.09)	-0.10	(0.13)	**0.41**	(0.12)
Uruguay	0.00	(0.00)	-0.01	(0.11)	-0.03	(0.11)	**-0.34**	(0.16)	-0.18	(0.13)	-0.06	(0.28)
Viet Nam	**0.00**	(0.00)	0.00	(0.27)	0.21	(0.30)	**-0.74**	(0.32)	-0.07	(0.24)	**0.53**	(0.19)

OECD (left margin label for upper block)
Partners (left margin label for lower block)

Note: Values that are statistically significant are indicated in bold (see Annex A3).
1. Logistic regression: LATE = Intercept + variables listed in this table; where LATE (0=did not arrive late; and 1=arrived late).
* See notes at the beginning of this Annex.
StatLink ᴍ٫ٱ http://dx.doi.org/10.1787/888932957517

[Part 1/3]
Change between 2003 and 2012 in teacher-student relations

Table IV.5.17 *Results based on students' self-reports*

		Index of teacher-student relations		Students get along well with most teachers		Most teachers are interested in my well-being		Most of my teachers really listen to what I have to say		If I need extra help, I will receive it from my teachers		Most of my teachers treat me fairly	
		Mean index	S.E.	%	S.E.	%	S.E.	%	S.E.	%	S.E.	%	S.E.
OECD	Australia	-0.17	(0.01)	78.0	(0.6)	81.8	(0.5)	71.9	(0.6)	86.6	(0.5)	86.3	(0.4)
	Austria	-0.32	(0.02)	72.7	(1.1)	63.9	(1.0)	57.8	(1.1)	67.1	(1.0)	77.6	(0.8)
	Belgium	-0.40	(0.01)	68.7	(0.7)	68.6	(0.7)	65.6	(0.7)	80.8	(0.5)	75.7	(0.6)
	Canada	-0.16	(0.01)	73.5	(0.5)	78.0	(0.4)	72.5	(0.4)	90.2	(0.3)	84.3	(0.4)
	Czech Republic	-0.51	(0.02)	63.7	(1.0)	65.8	(0.9)	55.8	(1.0)	77.7	(0.7)	73.7	(0.7)
	Denmark	-0.11	(0.02)	77.7	(0.9)	79.6	(0.7)	71.3	(1.0)	82.0	(0.6)	90.4	(0.5)
	Finland	-0.38	(0.02)	72.8	(0.9)	64.3	(0.9)	64.2	(0.8)	85.9	(0.6)	80.9	(0.7)
	France	-0.45	(0.02)	62.1	(1.1)	65.6	(1.0)	66.0	(1.0)	81.0	(0.7)	65.6	(0.8)
	Germany	-0.38	(0.02)	65.5	(0.9)	59.7	(1.1)	58.0	(0.9)	67.2	(0.9)	75.1	(0.7)
	Greece	-0.44	(0.03)	68.2	(1.2)	60.3	(1.2)	66.3	(1.0)	68.0	(1.3)	70.6	(0.9)
	Hungary	-0.46	(0.02)	63.2	(1.2)	59.2	(1.0)	74.5	(0.9)	71.8	(0.9)	68.1	(1.0)
	Iceland	-0.34	(0.02)	70.2	(0.7)	69.5	(0.7)	65.3	(0.8)	76.8	(0.7)	76.1	(0.7)
	Ireland	-0.36	(0.02)	71.6	(1.0)	78.2	(0.9)	59.9	(0.9)	76.8	(0.9)	82.0	(0.7)
	Italy	-0.61	(0.02)	59.4	(0.9)	65.2	(0.9)	59.2	(0.9)	58.2	(1.0)	64.7	(0.8)
	Japan	-0.71	(0.02)	64.0	(1.1)	44.9	(1.0)	53.7	(1.0)	57.5	(0.8)	67.0	(0.8)
	Korea	-0.42	(0.02)	84.4	(0.7)	65.0	(0.9)	54.8	(0.9)	85.3	(0.6)	69.9	(0.7)
	Luxembourg	-0.69	(0.02)	56.3	(0.8)	52.5	(0.9)	50.1	(0.8)	53.4	(0.7)	66.9	(0.7)
	Mexico	0.12	(0.02)	85.2	(0.6)	85.3	(0.6)	76.9	(0.7)	79.8	(0.8)	83.9	(0.6)
	Netherlands	-0.41	(0.02)	69.9	(1.2)	67.6	(1.0)	64.2	(1.2)	84.0	(0.9)	84.2	(0.8)
	New Zealand	-0.26	(0.02)	71.9	(0.7)	78.5	(0.7)	67.7	(0.9)	85.0	(0.6)	84.3	(0.6)
	Norway	-0.43	(0.02)	74.5	(1.0)	66.5	(1.1)	55.4	(1.0)	75.3	(0.8)	73.9	(0.9)
	Poland	-0.60	(0.02)	66.7	(1.0)	47.4	(1.0)	61.8	(1.1)	67.8	(1.1)	68.6	(0.9)
	Portugal	-0.14	(0.02)	83.5	(0.8)	80.4	(0.8)	76.4	(0.8)	84.4	(0.7)	84.0	(0.6)
	Slovak Republic	-0.57	(0.02)	64.6	(1.0)	47.3	(1.0)	62.0	(1.1)	66.7	(0.8)	76.2	(0.9)
	Spain	-0.46	(0.02)	62.5	(1.0)	69.9	(0.8)	65.8	(0.8)	65.4	(0.9)	75.0	(0.7)
	Sweden	-0.17	(0.02)	80.5	(0.8)	78.3	(0.7)	71.9	(0.9)	81.1	(0.7)	83.3	(0.6)
	Switzerland	-0.08	(0.02)	69.7	(1.1)	74.3	(0.9)	70.2	(0.9)	82.2	(0.6)	81.7	(0.6)
	Turkey	-0.19	(0.03)	79.7	(1.1)	60.3	(1.2)	74.0	(0.9)	74.7	(0.8)	66.4	(0.9)
	United States	-0.18	(0.02)	71.0	(0.8)	75.3	(0.7)	69.8	(0.8)	88.4	(0.5)	87.2	(0.5)
	OECD average 2003	**-0.35**	**(0.00)**	**70.8**	**(0.2)**	**67.4**	**(0.2)**	**64.9**	**(0.2)**	**75.9**	**(0.1)**	**76.7**	**(0.1)**
Partners	Brazil	0.16	(0.02)	79.6	(0.8)	82.3	(0.8)	79.2	(0.7)	88.1	(0.6)	85.2	(0.6)
	Hong Kong-China	-0.30	(0.02)	84.4	(1.0)	65.3	(1.1)	66.2	(1.0)	82.6	(0.7)	75.4	(0.8)
	Indonesia	0.22	(0.01)	91.3	(0.5)	93.2	(0.4)	71.6	(0.8)	94.2	(0.4)	91.1	(0.6)
	Latvia	-0.33	(0.02)	74.1	(1.0)	76.2	(1.4)	69.7	(1.1)	71.2	(1.0)	78.7	(0.7)
	Liechtenstein	-0.33	(0.04)	66.0	(2.4)	65.9	(2.5)	60.4	(2.1)	71.7	(2.5)	78.7	(2.3)
	Macao-China	-0.43	(0.03)	80.6	(1.3)	57.7	(1.7)	57.9	(1.7)	75.2	(1.3)	72.6	(1.5)
	Russian Federation	-0.36	(0.02)	76.3	(0.8)	58.6	(1.1)	73.6	(0.8)	61.3	(1.4)	77.3	(0.8)
	Thailand	0.12	(0.02)	93.5	(0.4)	91.1	(0.5)	83.6	(0.7)	85.6	(0.6)	91.3	(0.5)
	Tunisia	-0.05	(0.03)	63.8	(1.0)	59.8	(1.0)	78.1	(0.8)	77.6	(0.9)	75.1	(0.8)
	Uruguay	-0.12	(0.02)	81.1	(0.9)	77.2	(1.2)	77.7	(0.7)	76.9	(0.8)	76.5	(0.7)

PISA 2003 — Percentage of students reporting that they agree or strongly agree with the following statements:

Notes: Values that are statistically significant are indicated in bold (see Annex A3).
Only countries and economies with comparable data from PISA 2003 and PISA 2012 are shown.
For comparability over time, PISA 2003 values on the *index of teacher-student relations* have been rescaled to the PISA 2012 scale of the index. PISA 2003 results reported in this table may thus differ from those presented in *Learning for Tomorrow's World: First Results from PISA 2003* (OECD, 2004) (see Annex A5 for more details).
StatLink ⌨️ http://dx.doi.org/10.1787/888932957517

[Part 2/3]
Change between 2003 and 2012 in teacher-student relations
Table IV.5.17   *Results based on students' self-reports*

			PISA 2012									
			Percentage of students reporting that they agree or strongly agree with the following statements:									
		Index of teacher-student relations		Students get along well with most teachers		Most teachers are interested in my well-being		Most of my teachers really listen to what I have to say		If I need extra help, I will receive it from my teachers		Most of my teachers treat me fairly	
		Mean index	S.E.	%	S.E.	%	S.E.	%	S.E.	%	S.E.	%	S.E.
OECD	Australia	0.15	(0.01)	84.1	(0.4)	87.3	(0.4)	79.5	(0.4)	89.5	(0.3)	86.8	(0.4)
	Austria	-0.14	(0.03)	81.1	(1.0)	70.2	(1.1)	61.5	(1.1)	63.8	(1.2)	80.2	(1.1)
	Belgium	-0.11	(0.02)	79.8	(0.6)	77.4	(0.7)	74.1	(0.7)	85.1	(0.6)	79.1	(0.6)
	Canada	0.28	(0.01)	85.5	(0.5)	86.1	(0.4)	80.7	(0.5)	91.8	(0.3)	89.8	(0.4)
	Czech Republic	-0.16	(0.03)	80.8	(1.1)	72.0	(1.2)	68.4	(1.1)	87.4	(0.8)	78.9	(1.1)
	Denmark	0.15	(0.02)	88.7	(0.6)	85.3	(0.7)	80.1	(0.8)	84.6	(0.7)	87.4	(0.7)
	Finland	-0.09	(0.02)	79.6	(0.9)	73.0	(0.8)	73.8	(0.8)	88.6	(0.7)	83.4	(0.6)
	France	-0.17	(0.02)	78.0	(0.7)	70.7	(1.0)	72.2	(0.9)	81.9	(0.7)	69.1	(1.0)
	Germany	-0.22	(0.02)	76.3	(1.0)	66.9	(1.1)	66.6	(1.0)	66.3	(1.1)	75.6	(0.8)
	Greece	-0.13	(0.02)	74.1	(1.0)	76.5	(0.9)	70.2	(0.9)	74.0	(0.9)	73.3	(0.9)
	Hungary	-0.02	(0.02)	83.4	(0.8)	73.0	(0.9)	82.7	(0.8)	76.8	(0.9)	76.7	(0.8)
	Iceland	0.21	(0.02)	84.1	(0.7)	85.1	(0.8)	82.0	(0.8)	87.4	(0.7)	84.4	(0.8)
	Ireland	0.03	(0.02)	82.2	(0.9)	83.9	(0.8)	73.3	(0.9)	83.8	(0.9)	86.7	(0.6)
	Italy	-0.16	(0.01)	74.9	(0.5)	71.4	(0.5)	69.5	(0.5)	70.7	(0.5)	81.4	(0.4)
	Japan	-0.17	(0.02)	79.9	(0.8)	58.8	(1.0)	73.0	(0.9)	81.5	(0.7)	79.3	(0.8)
	Korea	-0.12	(0.03)	89.9	(0.8)	71.9	(1.0)	68.8	(1.0)	89.0	(0.7)	79.8	(0.8)
	Luxembourg	-0.05	(0.02)	85.8	(0.6)	66.2	(0.8)	70.0	(0.8)	72.6	(0.9)	78.0	(0.8)
	Mexico	0.47	(0.01)	90.8	(0.3)	89.6	(0.3)	83.9	(0.4)	85.0	(0.4)	88.7	(0.3)
	Netherlands	-0.15	(0.02)	83.5	(0.9)	78.3	(0.8)	74.1	(0.9)	82.8	(1.1)	85.5	(0.9)
	New Zealand	0.11	(0.02)	84.1	(0.9)	85.1	(0.8)	78.1	(0.9)	88.5	(0.7)	87.6	(0.7)
	Norway	-0.14	(0.02)	81.6	(0.8)	74.8	(1.0)	67.2	(1.0)	80.6	(0.9)	77.0	(0.8)
	Poland	-0.42	(0.02)	74.1	(1.0)	53.8	(1.1)	62.5	(1.1)	75.5	(1.0)	66.0	(1.0)
	Portugal	0.32	(0.02)	90.9	(0.6)	91.6	(0.6)	85.3	(0.7)	91.5	(0.6)	83.7	(0.7)
	Slovak Republic	-0.18	(0.02)	76.9	(1.2)	77.6	(1.0)	73.6	(1.0)	75.2	(1.0)	76.7	(1.0)
	Spain	0.00	(0.02)	78.4	(0.7)	78.9	(0.6)	73.7	(0.5)	76.3	(0.7)	81.3	(0.5)
	Sweden	0.08	(0.03)	84.6	(0.9)	81.5	(0.8)	76.6	(1.1)	83.0	(0.9)	83.1	(0.9)
	Switzerland	0.11	(0.02)	81.9	(0.8)	78.3	(0.8)	75.7	(0.7)	84.4	(0.7)	82.5	(0.8)
	Turkey	0.19	(0.02)	88.4	(0.6)	75.4	(0.9)	84.0	(0.7)	76.8	(0.9)	71.9	(0.9)
	United States	0.21	(0.03)	82.6	(0.8)	86.1	(0.8)	78.3	(1.0)	89.9	(0.6)	89.7	(0.6)
	OECD average 2003	0.00	(0.00)	82.3	(0.1)	76.8	(0.2)	74.5	(0.2)	81.5	(0.1)	80.8	(0.1)
Partners	Brazil	0.25	(0.02)	84.0	(0.7)	81.8	(0.5)	75.8	(0.6)	85.6	(0.4)	85.5	(0.5)
	Hong Kong-China	0.03	(0.02)	92.4	(0.5)	78.9	(0.9)	70.5	(1.1)	91.3	(0.6)	82.7	(0.8)
	Indonesia	0.42	(0.02)	94.5	(0.5)	94.4	(0.5)	78.1	(0.7)	93.4	(0.5)	88.1	(0.7)
	Latvia	0.16	(0.02)	83.9	(0.8)	91.8	(0.6)	74.6	(1.1)	89.9	(0.8)	85.3	(0.8)
	Liechtenstein	0.05	(0.07)	81.5	(2.8)	74.4	(3.0)	70.6	(3.2)	78.7	(3.0)	83.7	(2.7)
	Macao-China	-0.04	(0.02)	91.4	(0.5)	81.9	(0.7)	65.9	(0.8)	86.5	(0.6)	74.8	(0.9)
	Russian Federation	0.14	(0.03)	87.8	(0.7)	66.1	(0.9)	80.3	(0.9)	86.4	(0.9)	83.2	(0.9)
	Thailand	0.30	(0.02)	90.2	(0.5)	89.1	(0.6)	86.6	(0.6)	90.4	(0.5)	86.6	(0.6)
	Tunisia	-0.02	(0.03)	78.1	(0.9)	64.2	(1.1)	71.9	(1.1)	73.8	(0.8)	71.7	(0.9)
	Uruguay	0.19	(0.03)	87.4	(0.8)	83.8	(0.8)	80.1	(0.8)	83.4	(0.8)	75.5	(0.8)

Notes: Values that are statistically significant are indicated in bold (see Annex A3).
Only countries and economies with comparable data from PISA 2003 and PISA 2012 are shown.
For comparability over time, PISA 2003 values on the *index of teacher-student relations* have been rescaled to the PISA 2012 scale of the index. PISA 2003 results reported in this table may thus differ from those presented in *Learning for Tomorrow's World: First Results from PISA 2003* (OECD, 2004) (see Annex A5 for more details).
StatLink ⤷ http://dx.doi.org/10.1787/888932957517

[Part 3/3]
Change between 2003 and 2012 in teacher-student relations

Table IV.5.17   *Results based on students' self-reports*

		Change between 2003 and 2012 (PISA 2012 - PISA 2003)										
				Percentage of students reporting that they agree or strongly agree with the following statements:								
		Index of teacher-student relations		Students get along well with most teachers		Most teachers are interested in my well-being		Most of my teachers really listen to what I have to say		If I need extra help, I will receive it from my teachers		Most of my teachers treat me fairly	
		Dif.	S.E.	% dif.	S.E.	% dif.	S.E.	% dif.	S.E.	% dif.	S.E.	% dif.	S.E.
OECD	Australia	**0.32**	(0.02)	**6.1**	(0.7)	**5.5**	(0.6)	**7.6**	(0.8)	**2.9**	(0.6)	0.5	(0.6)
	Austria	**0.18**	(0.04)	**8.3**	(1.5)	**6.3**	(1.5)	**3.7**	(1.6)	**-3.3**	(1.6)	2.6	(1.3)
	Belgium	**0.29**	(0.02)	**11.1**	(1.0)	**8.7**	(0.9)	**8.5**	(1.0)	**4.3**	(0.8)	**3.4**	(0.9)
	Canada	**0.44**	(0.02)	**12.0**	(0.7)	**8.0**	(0.6)	**8.2**	(0.7)	**1.6**	(0.4)	**5.5**	(0.6)
	Czech Republic	**0.34**	(0.03)	**17.1**	(1.5)	**6.2**	(1.5)	**12.6**	(1.5)	**9.7**	(1.1)	**5.2**	(1.4)
	Denmark	**0.26**	(0.03)	**11.0**	(1.1)	**5.7**	(1.0)	**8.8**	(1.3)	2.6	(0.9)	**-3.0**	(0.9)
	Finland	**0.28**	(0.02)	**6.8**	(1.2)	**8.8**	(1.2)	**9.7**	(1.2)	**2.7**	(0.9)	**2.5**	(0.9)
	France	**0.28**	(0.03)	**15.9**	(1.3)	**5.1**	(1.4)	**6.3**	(1.4)	0.9	(1.0)	**3.5**	(1.3)
	Germany	**0.16**	(0.03)	**10.8**	(1.3)	**7.2**	(1.5)	**8.6**	(1.3)	-0.9	(1.4)	0.5	(1.1)
	Greece	**0.31**	(0.04)	**5.8**	(1.5)	**16.2**	(1.5)	**3.9**	(1.4)	**6.0**	(1.6)	2.6	(1.3)
	Hungary	**0.44**	(0.03)	**20.3**	(1.4)	**13.8**	(1.4)	**8.3**	(1.2)	**5.0**	(1.3)	**8.5**	(1.3)
	Iceland	**0.55**	(0.03)	**13.9**	(1.0)	**15.5**	(1.1)	**16.7**	(1.1)	**10.5**	(1.0)	**8.4**	(1.1)
	Ireland	**0.39**	(0.03)	**10.6**	(1.3)	**5.7**	(1.2)	**13.4**	(1.3)	**7.0**	(1.2)	**4.7**	(0.9)
	Italy	**0.45**	(0.02)	**15.5**	(1.1)	**6.2**	(1.0)	**10.3**	(1.0)	**12.4**	(1.1)	**16.8**	(0.9)
	Japan	**0.54**	(0.03)	**16.0**	(1.3)	**13.9**	(1.5)	**19.3**	(1.3)	**24.0**	(1.1)	**12.4**	(1.2)
	Korea	**0.30**	(0.03)	**5.5**	(1.1)	**7.0**	(1.4)	**14.0**	(1.3)	**3.7**	(0.9)	**10.0**	(1.1)
	Luxembourg	**0.64**	(0.03)	**29.5**	(1.0)	**13.6**	(1.2)	**19.9**	(1.2)	**19.2**	(1.2)	**11.1**	(1.0)
	Mexico	**0.35**	(0.02)	**5.6**	(0.6)	**4.3**	(0.7)	**7.0**	(0.8)	**5.2**	(0.9)	**4.7**	(0.7)
	Netherlands	**0.26**	(0.03)	**13.7**	(1.5)	**10.8**	(1.3)	**9.9**	(1.5)	-1.2	(1.4)	1.2	(1.2)
	New Zealand	**0.36**	(0.03)	**12.2**	(1.2)	**6.6**	(1.1)	**10.4**	(1.3)	**3.5**	(0.9)	**3.2**	(0.9)
	Norway	**0.29**	(0.03)	**7.1**	(1.3)	**8.3**	(1.5)	**11.9**	(1.4)	**5.3**	(1.2)	**3.0**	(1.2)
	Poland	**0.18**	(0.03)	**7.4**	(1.4)	**6.4**	(1.5)	0.7	(1.5)	**7.7**	(1.5)	-2.6	(1.3)
	Portugal	**0.46**	(0.03)	**7.5**	(1.0)	**11.1**	(1.0)	**8.9**	(1.1)	**7.1**	(1.0)	-0.3	(0.9)
	Slovak Republic	**0.39**	(0.03)	**12.3**	(1.6)	**30.3**	(1.4)	**11.6**	(1.5)	**8.5**	(1.3)	0.5	(1.3)
	Spain	**0.46**	(0.02)	**16.0**	(1.2)	**9.0**	(1.0)	**7.9**	(1.0)	**10.8**	(1.1)	**6.2**	(0.9)
	Sweden	**0.25**	(0.03)	**4.1**	(1.2)	**3.3**	(1.0)	**4.7**	(1.4)	1.9	(1.1)	-0.2	(1.1)
	Switzerland	**0.19**	(0.03)	**12.2**	(1.4)	**4.1**	(1.2)	**5.5**	(1.1)	**2.2**	(0.9)	0.9	(1.0)
	Turkey	**0.38**	(0.03)	**8.7**	(1.2)	**15.1**	(1.5)	**10.0**	(1.1)	2.1	(1.2)	**5.4**	(1.2)
	United States	**0.38**	(0.03)	**11.6**	(1.2)	**10.9**	(1.1)	**8.5**	(1.2)	1.4	(0.8)	**2.5**	(0.8)
	OECD average 2003	**0.35**	(0.01)	**11.5**	(0.2)	**9.4**	(0.2)	**9.5**	(0.2)	**5.6**	(0.2)	**4.1**	(0.2)
Partners	Brazil	0.08	(0.03)	**4.4**	(1.0)	-0.5	(0.9)	**-3.4**	(0.9)	**-2.5**	(0.7)	0.3	(0.8)
	Hong Kong-China	**0.33**	(0.03)	**8.0**	(1.1)	**13.7**	(1.5)	**4.3**	(1.5)	**8.7**	(1.0)	**7.2**	(1.1)
	Indonesia	**0.21**	(0.02)	**3.2**	(0.7)	1.2	(0.6)	**6.5**	(1.0)	-0.8	(0.6)	**-3.0**	(0.9)
	Latvia	**0.49**	(0.03)	**9.8**	(1.3)	**15.6**	(1.5)	**4.9**	(1.5)	**18.7**	(1.3)	**6.6**	(1.0)
	Liechtenstein	**0.38**	(0.08)	**15.6**	(3.7)	**8.5**	(3.9)	**10.2**	(3.8)	6.9	(3.9)	5.0	(3.5)
	Macao-China	**0.38**	(0.03)	**10.8**	(1.4)	**24.2**	(1.8)	**8.0**	(1.9)	**11.3**	(1.4)	2.2	(1.7)
	Russian Federation	**0.50**	(0.04)	**11.5**	(1.0)	**7.5**	(1.4)	**6.7**	(1.2)	**25.1**	(1.6)	**5.9**	(1.2)
	Thailand	0.17	(0.03)	**-3.3**	(0.7)	-1.9	(0.9)	**3.0**	(0.9)	**4.8**	(0.8)	**-4.7**	(0.8)
	Tunisia	0.03	(0.04)	**14.3**	(1.3)	**4.3**	(1.5)	**-6.2**	(1.3)	**-3.8**	(1.2)	**-3.3**	(1.2)
	Uruguay	**0.31**	(0.03)	**6.3**	(1.2)	**6.6**	(1.4)	2.4	(1.1)	**6.5**	(1.2)	-1.0	(1.1)

Notes: Values that are statistically significant are indicated in bold (see Annex A3).
Only countries and economies with comparable data from PISA 2003 and PISA 2012 are shown.
For comparability over time, PISA 2003 values on the *index of teacher-student relations* have been rescaled to the PISA 2012 scale of the index. PISA 2003 results reported in this table may thus differ from those presented in *Learning for Tomorrow's World: First Results from PISA 2003* (OECD, 2004) (see Annex A5 for more details).
StatLink ⫘⫘⪦ http://dx.doi.org/10.1787/888932957517

[Part 1/3]
Change between 2003 and 2012 in disciplinary climate
Table IV.5.18 *Results based on students' self-reports*

		Index of disciplinary climate		PISA 2003									
				Percentage of students reporting that the following phenomena occur "never or hardly ever" or "some lessons" in their mathematics lessons									
				Students don't listen to what the teacher says		There is noise and disorder		The teacher has to wait a long time for students to quiet down		Students cannot work well		Student don't start working for a long time after the lessons begins	
		Mean index	S.E.	%	S.E.	%	S.E.	%	S.E.	%	S.E.	%	S.E.
OECD	Australia	-0.16	(0.02)	66.5	(0.7)	58.2	(0.8)	68.1	(0.7)	80.3	(0.7)	73.3	(0.6)
	Austria	0.03	(0.03)	69.1	(1.0)	72.8	(1.1)	67.0	(1.2)	73.3	(1.0)	69.6	(0.9)
	Belgium	-0.12	(0.02)	72.4	(0.7)	62.6	(0.9)	65.9	(0.8)	80.6	(0.6)	66.9	(0.8)
	Canada	-0.14	(0.01)	71.1	(0.5)	61.2	(0.7)	72.2	(0.6)	82.3	(0.4)	69.0	(0.6)
	Czech Republic	-0.17	(0.03)	64.0	(1.2)	66.3	(1.4)	66.4	(1.4)	75.3	(0.9)	75.1	(1.0)
	Denmark	-0.22	(0.02)	67.9	(0.9)	56.8	(1.3)	72.4	(1.2)	80.3	(0.9)	73.1	(0.9)
	Finland	-0.28	(0.02)	63.8	(0.9)	51.8	(1.1)	65.2	(1.1)	81.2	(0.7)	68.0	(0.9)
	France	-0.26	(0.02)	66.9	(0.8)	54.5	(1.1)	62.0	(1.1)	75.1	(0.9)	58.1	(0.9)
	Germany	0.11	(0.02)	77.8	(0.8)	74.7	(1.0)	68.5	(1.1)	74.5	(0.8)	74.4	(0.9)
	Greece	-0.35	(0.02)	65.0	(1.3)	57.0	(1.4)	64.7	(1.3)	71.3	(1.2)	60.7	(1.1)
	Hungary	-0.01	(0.03)	72.3	(1.1)	71.5	(1.1)	70.2	(1.3)	77.7	(0.8)	81.2	(0.9)
	Iceland	-0.28	(0.01)	69.4	(0.7)	59.2	(0.8)	63.9	(0.8)	74.8	(0.7)	73.9	(0.7)
	Ireland	0.08	(0.03)	67.8	(0.9)	68.4	(1.2)	74.6	(1.0)	80.8	(0.9)	78.8	(0.8)
	Italy	-0.24	(0.02)	63.3	(1.0)	58.3	(1.3)	61.4	(1.2)	75.1	(1.0)	67.5	(1.0)
	Japan	0.23	(0.03)	80.9	(0.9)	83.1	(1.0)	86.3	(0.8)	75.2	(1.0)	84.5	(1.0)
	Korea	-0.04	(0.02)	72.7	(0.9)	0.0	c	81.1	(0.7)	82.1	(0.7)	79.1	(0.8)
	Luxembourg	-0.33	(0.01)	64.8	(0.7)	51.6	(0.8)	57.2	(0.8)	60.7	(0.8)	64.7	(0.8)
	Mexico	-0.15	(0.02)	71.5	(0.7)	73.2	(0.8)	73.7	(1.0)	76.0	(0.7)	65.7	(1.0)
	Netherlands	-0.26	(0.02)	72.8	(1.0)	58.4	(1.3)	63.7	(1.3)	80.9	(0.9)	61.5	(1.1)
	New Zealand	-0.30	(0.02)	61.6	(0.7)	52.6	(0.9)	62.9	(0.9)	77.2	(0.7)	68.7	(0.8)
	Norway	-0.36	(0.02)	66.0	(0.9)	58.8	(1.2)	64.1	(1.1)	71.7	(1.0)	63.9	(1.0)
	Poland	-0.07	(0.03)	66.9	(1.2)	73.1	(1.3)	69.6	(1.3)	78.6	(1.0)	77.7	(0.9)
	Portugal	-0.14	(0.02)	71.9	(0.8)	64.9	(1.1)	69.8	(1.0)	77.6	(0.9)	72.8	(1.1)
	Slovak Republic	-0.24	(0.02)	60.9	(0.9)	65.8	(0.9)	65.9	(0.9)	74.9	(0.7)	71.6	(0.7)
	Spain	-0.18	(0.03)	70.4	(1.0)	64.9	(1.2)	64.3	(1.2)	76.1	(1.0)	65.5	(1.1)
	Sweden	-0.19	(0.02)	74.1	(0.9)	64.1	(1.2)	67.3	(1.1)	80.1	(0.9)	71.6	(1.2)
	Switzerland	-0.07	(0.03)	72.4	(0.9)	67.3	(1.1)	67.6	(1.0)	74.1	(0.9)	68.9	(0.9)
	Turkey	-0.26	(0.02)	76.1	(1.1)	67.2	(1.1)	64.5	(1.1)	69.1	(1.3)	69.0	(1.3)
	United States	-0.05	(0.02)	68.0	(0.8)	66.0	(0.9)	73.9	(0.8)	81.1	(0.7)	73.1	(0.8)
	OECD average 2003	-0.15	(0.00)	69.3	(0.2)	61.5	(0.2)	68.1	(0.2)	76.5	(0.2)	70.6	(0.2)
Partners	Brazil	-0.46	(0.02)	65.4	(1.1)	62.0	(1.1)	61.8	(1.0)	70.3	(0.8)	37.0	(1.0)
	Hong Kong-China	-0.02	(0.02)	79.5	(0.8)	82.7	(0.8)	81.1	(0.9)	80.5	(0.8)	80.2	(0.8)
	Indonesia	-0.10	(0.02)	74.8	(0.8)	67.7	(0.9)	62.5	(1.0)	78.4	(0.7)	70.4	(0.8)
	Latvia	0.11	(0.03)	73.3	(1.0)	80.0	(1.2)	79.6	(1.1)	81.7	(1.0)	79.4	(1.1)
	Liechtenstein	0.05	(0.04)	73.8	(2.5)	72.2	(2.1)	67.0	(2.5)	71.8	(2.4)	75.0	(2.1)
	Macao-China	-0.07	(0.02)	81.6	(1.3)	84.5	(1.1)	82.5	(1.1)	79.4	(1.5)	80.3	(1.2)
	Russian Federation	0.27	(0.03)	78.1	(0.9)	84.0	(0.9)	81.5	(1.0)	81.2	(0.8)	84.9	(0.8)
	Thailand	-0.15	(0.02)	77.8	(0.9)	73.3	(0.9)	68.2	(1.0)	76.6	(0.9)	72.1	(1.0)
	Tunisia	-0.22	(0.02)	74.3	(0.7)	63.3	(1.1)	63.6	(1.2)	67.4	(0.9)	48.4	(1.0)
	Uruguay	-0.18	(0.02)	67.9	(1.0)	62.6	(1.3)	68.0	(1.0)	76.0	(1.0)	68.9	(1.0)

Notes: Values that are statistically significant are indicated in bold (see Annex A3).
Only countries and economies with comparable data from PISA 2003 and PISA 2012 are shown.
For comparability over time, PISA 2003 values on the *index of disciplinary climate* have been rescaled to the PISA 2012 scale of the index. PISA 2003 results reported in this table may thus differ from those presented in *Learning for Tomorrow's World: First Results from PISA 2003* (OECD, 2004) (see Annex A5 for more details).
StatLink ⟐ http://dx.doi.org/10.1787/888932957517

[Part 2/3]
Change between 2003 and 2012 in disciplinary climate
Table IV.5.18   *Results based on students' self-reports*

		Index of disciplinary climate		Students don't listen to what the teacher says		There is noise and disorder		The teacher has to wait a long time for students to quiet down		Students cannot work well		Student don't start working for a long time after the lessons begins	
		Mean index	S.E.	%	S.E.	%	S.E.	%	S.E.	%	S.E.	%	S.E.
OECD	Australia	-0.14	(0.02)	61.6	(0.7)	56.9	(0.7)	68.2	(0.7)	77.7	(0.6)	72.9	(0.6)
	Austria	0.21	(0.03)	73.2	(1.0)	74.9	(1.1)	72.4	(1.2)	78.2	(1.0)	73.8	(1.1)
	Belgium	0.04	(0.03)	72.3	(0.8)	66.5	(1.0)	70.9	(1.0)	81.1	(0.8)	70.9	(0.9)
	Canada	0.01	(0.01)	71.2	(0.6)	65.8	(0.7)	74.9	(0.6)	81.5	(0.5)	71.8	(0.7)
	Czech Republic	0.10	(0.04)	63.5	(1.4)	70.1	(1.4)	73.2	(1.2)	80.1	(1.1)	77.0	(1.1)
	Denmark	-0.01	(0.03)	69.9	(0.9)	66.8	(1.1)	77.1	(1.0)	81.9	(0.9)	75.4	(1.0)
	Finland	-0.33	(0.02)	57.4	(1.0)	50.9	(1.1)	64.5	(1.2)	77.9	(0.8)	65.0	(1.0)
	France	-0.29	(0.03)	59.7	(1.1)	51.9	(1.1)	60.6	(1.0)	69.5	(1.0)	57.8	(1.1)
	Germany	-0.02	(0.02)	64.4	(1.1)	70.8	(1.0)	68.0	(1.1)	73.0	(1.0)	70.8	(1.0)
	Greece	-0.24	(0.03)	59.2	(1.3)	61.4	(1.4)	67.7	(1.4)	66.4	(1.1)	67.3	(0.9)
	Hungary	0.05	(0.04)	64.4	(1.4)	71.8	(1.4)	72.6	(1.4)	77.5	(1.1)	79.8	(1.3)
	Iceland	-0.03	(0.02)	75.3	(0.8)	65.6	(0.8)	75.3	(0.9)	82.6	(0.7)	77.1	(0.8)
	Ireland	0.13	(0.03)	63.6	(1.2)	69.2	(1.3)	75.1	(1.1)	81.0	(1.0)	77.6	(1.0)
	Italy	-0.04	(0.02)	67.0	(0.7)	63.9	(0.7)	69.1	(0.7)	73.1	(0.6)	73.1	(0.6)
	Japan	0.67	(0.03)	90.5	(0.6)	89.9	(0.7)	92.8	(0.6)	83.7	(0.9)	90.5	(0.7)
	Korea	0.19	(0.03)	81.2	(1.0)	69.7	(1.1)	83.5	(0.8)	85.1	(0.9)	81.0	(0.9)
	Luxembourg	-0.02	(0.02)	64.3	(0.8)	68.5	(0.8)	69.8	(0.9)	72.7	(0.8)	66.9	(0.8)
	Mexico	0.06	(0.01)	71.1	(0.5)	72.6	(0.5)	79.0	(0.4)	79.0	(0.4)	73.7	(0.4)
	Netherlands	-0.16	(0.03)	71.1	(1.2)	63.3	(1.3)	66.1	(1.5)	79.7	(1.0)	56.5	(1.2)
	New Zealand	-0.25	(0.03)	57.2	(1.2)	55.4	(1.2)	65.5	(1.1)	75.0	(0.9)	68.6	(1.0)
	Norway	-0.08	(0.03)	72.0	(1.0)	70.7	(1.1)	75.9	(1.2)	78.8	(1.1)	71.4	(1.2)
	Poland	0.08	(0.04)	63.1	(1.5)	74.3	(1.5)	74.6	(1.4)	78.1	(1.3)	78.3	(1.2)
	Portugal	0.00	(0.03)	67.5	(1.2)	68.0	(1.2)	73.3	(1.1)	78.2	(1.0)	74.1	(1.1)
	Slovak Republic	-0.13	(0.03)	60.9	(1.0)	71.0	(1.1)	68.2	(1.2)	73.8	(1.0)	69.0	(1.1)
	Spain	-0.04	(0.02)	65.7	(0.8)	68.3	(0.9)	66.6	(1.1)	77.4	(0.7)	69.7	(0.8)
	Sweden	-0.20	(0.03)	65.7	(1.2)	61.9	(1.2)	65.8	(1.3)	74.6	(0.9)	67.7	(1.1)
	Switzerland	0.07	(0.03)	72.3	(0.9)	69.3	(1.2)	74.7	(1.1)	79.0	(0.8)	72.5	(1.1)
	Turkey	-0.09	(0.02)	75.5	(1.0)	74.6	(1.0)	72.1	(0.9)	67.9	(0.9)	70.6	(0.9)
	United States	0.06	(0.03)	66.6	(1.1)	69.8	(1.0)	75.6	(1.1)	82.2	(1.0)	77.9	(0.9)
	OECD average 2003	-0.01	(0.00)	67.8	(0.2)	67.4	(0.2)	72.2	(0.2)	77.5	(0.2)	72.4	(0.2)
Partners	Brazil	-0.34	(0.02)	58.2	(0.8)	58.5	(0.8)	62.4	(0.9)	67.9	(0.7)	55.8	(0.8)
	Hong Kong-China	0.29	(0.02)	79.6	(0.8)	81.3	(0.9)	85.7	(0.8)	84.8	(0.7)	82.8	(0.9)
	Indonesia	0.12	(0.02)	83.2	(0.8)	74.5	(1.0)	74.9	(1.0)	84.4	(0.8)	84.3	(0.8)
	Latvia	0.08	(0.04)	64.3	(1.5)	72.8	(1.5)	75.9	(1.4)	78.4	(1.3)	82.6	(1.1)
	Liechtenstein	0.25	(0.07)	75.5	(3.1)	75.4	(2.9)	79.0	(3.0)	80.3	(2.9)	79.8	(2.8)
	Macao-China	0.10	(0.01)	75.6	(0.7)	84.5	(0.6)	85.4	(0.6)	84.2	(0.6)	79.1	(0.7)
	Russian Federation	0.35	(0.03)	73.1	(1.1)	81.6	(1.0)	81.3	(1.0)	82.7	(0.8)	86.0	(0.8)
	Thailand	0.07	(0.02)	84.5	(0.7)	73.9	(0.9)	77.8	(0.8)	84.6	(0.8)	84.6	(0.8)
	Tunisia	-0.43	(0.02)	64.3	(1.0)	52.9	(1.3)	59.6	(1.0)	59.0	(1.3)	49.6	(1.0)
	Uruguay	-0.16	(0.03)	66.0	(1.0)	62.5	(1.2)	60.0	(1.3)	75.6	(0.9)	71.7	(1.1)

Notes: Values that are statistically significant are indicated in bold (see Annex A3).
Only countries and economies with comparable data from PISA 2003 and PISA 2012 are shown.
For comparability over time, PISA 2003 values on the *index of disciplinary climate* have been rescaled to the PISA 2012 scale of the index. PISA 2003 results reported in this table may thus differ from those presented in *Learning for Tomorrow's World: First Results from PISA 2003* (OECD, 2004) (see Annex A5 for more details).
StatLink ⟲ http://dx.doi.org/10.1787/888932957517

[Part 3/3]
Change between 2003 and 2012 in disciplinary climate
Table IV.5.18   *Results based on students' self-reports*

	Index of disciplinary climate		Students don't listen to what the teacher says		There is noise and disorder		The teacher has to wait a long time for students to quiet down		Students cannot work well		Student don't start working for a long time after the lessons begins	
	Dif.	S.E.	% dif.	S.E.	% dif.	S.E.	% dif.	S.E.	% dif.	S.E.	% dif.	S.E.
Australia	0.03	(0.02)	**-4.9**	(1.0)	-1.3	(1.1)	0.1	(1.0)	**-2.6**	(0.9)	-0.4	(0.9)
Austria	**0.18**	(0.04)	**4.1**	(1.4)	2.1	(1.6)	**5.4**	(1.7)	**4.9**	(1.4)	**4.2**	(1.4)
Belgium	**0.16**	(0.03)	-0.1	(1.1)	**4.0**	(1.4)	**5.0**	(1.3)	0.6	(1.0)	**4.0**	(1.2)
Canada	**0.15**	(0.02)	0.0	(0.8)	**4.6**	(0.9)	**2.7**	(0.8)	-0.7	(0.6)	**2.8**	(0.9)
Czech Republic	**0.26**	(0.05)	-0.5	(1.8)	3.8	(2.0)	**6.8**	(1.8)	**4.8**	(1.4)	2.0	(1.4)
Denmark	**0.21**	(0.03)	2.0	(1.3)	**10.0**	(1.7)	**4.6**	(1.6)	1.6	(1.3)	2.3	(1.3)
Finland	-0.04	(0.03)	**-6.4**	(1.3)	-0.9	(1.6)	-0.7	(1.6)	**-3.3**	(1.0)	**-3.0**	(1.4)
France	-0.03	(0.04)	**-7.2**	(1.4)	-2.6	(1.5)	-1.4	(1.5)	**-5.5**	(1.3)	-0.3	(1.4)
Germany	**-0.13**	(0.03)	**-13.5**	(1.4)	**-3.9**	(1.4)	-0.5	(1.5)	-1.5	(1.2)	**-3.6**	(1.3)
Greece	**0.10**	(0.04)	**-5.8**	(1.8)	4.4	(2.0)	3.0	(1.9)	**-4.8**	(1.6)	**6.6**	(1.4)
Hungary	0.06	(0.04)	**-7.9**	(1.8)	0.3	(1.7)	2.4	(1.9)	-0.2	(1.3)	-1.4	(1.6)
Iceland	**0.26**	(0.02)	**5.9**	(1.1)	**6.3**	(1.1)	**11.4**	(1.2)	**7.8**	(1.0)	**3.2**	(1.1)
Ireland	0.05	(0.04)	**-4.2**	(1.5)	0.9	(1.7)	0.5	(1.5)	0.1	(1.3)	-1.2	(1.3)
Italy	**0.20**	(0.03)	**3.7**	(1.2)	**5.6**	(1.4)	**7.7**	(1.3)	-2.0	(1.2)	**5.7**	(1.2)
Japan	**0.44**	(0.04)	**9.7**	(1.1)	**6.8**	(1.2)	**6.5**	(1.0)	**8.5**	(1.3)	**6.0**	(1.2)
Korea	**0.23**	(0.03)	**8.6**	(1.3)	69.7	c	**2.4**	(1.0)	**3.1**	(1.1)	2.0	(1.3)
Luxembourg	**0.31**	(0.02)	-0.5	(1.1)	**16.9**	(1.1)	**12.7**	(1.2)	**12.0**	(1.1)	**2.2**	(1.1)
Mexico	**0.21**	(0.02)	-0.4	(0.8)	-0.6	(0.9)	**5.3**	(1.0)	**2.9**	(0.8)	**8.0**	(1.1)
Netherlands	**0.10**	(0.04)	-1.6	(1.6)	**4.9**	(1.9)	2.4	(2.0)	-1.2	(1.4)	**-5.0**	(1.6)
New Zealand	0.05	(0.03)	**-4.4**	(1.4)	2.8	(1.5)	2.6	(1.4)	-2.2	(1.1)	0.0	(1.2)
Norway	**0.28**	(0.03)	**6.1**	(1.4)	**11.9**	(1.6)	**11.8**	(1.6)	**7.0**	(1.5)	**7.5**	(1.6)
Poland	**0.14**	(0.05)	-3.8	(1.9)	1.2	(2.0)	**4.9**	(1.9)	-0.5	(1.6)	0.6	(1.5)
Portugal	**0.15**	(0.03)	**-4.3**	(1.5)	3.1	(1.7)	**3.5**	(1.5)	0.6	(1.4)	1.3	(1.5)
Slovak Republic	**0.10**	(0.03)	-0.1	(1.3)	**5.2**	(1.4)	2.3	(1.5)	-1.0	(1.3)	**-2.7**	(1.3)
Spain	**0.14**	(0.04)	**-4.7**	(1.3)	**3.4**	(1.5)	2.3	(1.6)	1.3	(1.2)	**4.2**	(1.4)
Sweden	-0.01	(0.04)	**-8.5**	(1.5)	-2.2	(1.7)	-1.5	(1.7)	**-5.4**	(1.3)	**-3.8**	(1.7)
Switzerland	**0.14**	(0.04)	-0.1	(1.3)	1.9	(1.6)	**7.0**	(1.5)	**4.9**	(1.2)	**3.5**	(1.4)
Turkey	**0.17**	(0.03)	-0.6	(1.5)	**7.3**	(1.5)	**7.5**	(1.4)	-1.2	(1.5)	1.6	(1.6)
United States	**0.11**	(0.04)	-1.4	(1.4)	**3.8**	(1.3)	1.7	(1.3)	1.1	(1.2)	**4.7**	(1.2)
OECD average 2003	**0.14**	(0.01)	**-1.4**	(0.3)	**5.8**	(0.3)	**4.1**	(0.3)	**1.0**	(0.2)	**1.8**	(0.2)
Brazil	**0.11**	(0.03)	**-7.2**	(1.3)	**-3.5**	(1.3)	0.6	(1.4)	**-2.3**	(1.1)	**18.8**	(1.2)
Hong Kong-China	**0.31**	(0.03)	0.1	(1.2)	-1.4	(1.2)	**4.6**	(1.2)	**4.3**	(1.1)	**2.6**	(1.2)
Indonesia	**0.22**	(0.03)	**8.4**	(1.2)	**6.8**	(1.3)	**12.4**	(1.5)	**6.0**	(1.1)	**14.0**	(1.1)
Latvia	-0.03	(0.05)	**-9.1**	(1.8)	**-7.2**	(1.9)	**-3.6**	(1.7)	**-3.3**	(1.7)	**3.2**	(1.6)
Liechtenstein	**0.20**	(0.09)	1.7	(4.0)	3.2	(3.6)	**12.0**	(3.9)	**8.5**	(3.7)	4.8	(3.5)
Macao-China	**0.17**	(0.02)	**-6.0**	(1.5)	0.0	(1.5)	**2.9**	(1.3)	**4.8**	(1.6)	-1.3	(1.4)
Russian Federation	0.08	(0.05)	**-5.0**	(1.4)	-2.4	(1.4)	-0.3	(1.4)	1.6	(1.2)	1.1	(1.1)
Thailand	**0.22**	(0.03)	**6.8**	(1.2)	0.6	(1.2)	**9.6**	(1.3)	**8.0**	(1.2)	**12.5**	(1.3)
Tunisia	**-0.21**	(0.03)	**-9.9**	(1.2)	**-10.4**	(1.7)	**-4.0**	(1.6)	**-8.4**	(1.5)	1.2	(1.4)
Uruguay	0.02	(0.03)	-1.9	(1.5)	-0.1	(1.8)	**-8.0**	(1.6)	-0.4	(1.3)	2.8	(1.5)

Change between 2003 and 2012 (PISA 2012 - PISA 2003). Percentage of students reporting that the following phenomena occur "never or hardly ever" or "some lessons" in their mathematics lessons.

Notes: Values that are statistically significant are indicated in bold (see Annex A3).
Only countries and economies with comparable data from PISA 2003 and PISA 2012 are shown.
For comparability over time, PISA 2003 values on the *index of disciplinary climate* have been rescaled to the PISA 2012 scale of the index. PISA 2003 results reported in this table may thus differ from those presented in *Learning for Tomorrow's World: First Results from PISA 2003* (OECD, 2004) (see Annex A5 for more details).
StatLink ᴍ︎ᴱ︎ http://dx.doi.org/10.1787/888932957517

[Part 1/3]
Change between 2003 and 2012 in teacher-related factors affecting school climate
Table IV.5.19   *Results based on school principals' reports*

		PISA 2003														
			Percentage of students in schools whose principals reported that the following phenomena hindered learning "not at all" or "very little"													
		Index of teacher-related factors affecting school climate		Teachers' low expectations of students		Teachers not meeting individual students' needs		Teacher absenteeism		Staff resisting change		Teacher being too strict with students		Students not being encouraged to achieve their full potential		Poor teacher-student relations	
		Mean index	S.E.	%	S.E.	%	S.E.	%	S.E.	%	S.E.	%	S.E.	%	S.E.	%	S.E.
OECD	Australia	-0.48	(0.05)	68.6	(2.8)	51.9	(3.3)	84.2	(2.2)	65.9	(3.0)	92.5	(1.6)	81.4	(2.3)	85.4	(1.9)
	Austria	-0.07	(0.08)	84.3	(3.5)	78.6	(2.9)	86.0	(2.9)	83.5	(2.9)	92.8	(2.0)	78.0	(3.6)	90.6	(2.3)
	Belgium	-0.01	(0.06)	91.8	(1.6)	78.2	(3.0)	77.7	(2.6)	73.4	(2.6)	96.9	(1.2)	85.0	(2.3)	91.0	(1.7)
	Canada	-0.29	(0.05)	89.2	(1.6)	67.2	(2.5)	92.0	(1.4)	67.2	(2.2)	91.6	(1.4)	84.1	(1.8)	87.8	(1.6)
	Czech Republic	-0.13	(0.04)	91.2	(1.9)	86.9	(2.1)	77.3	(2.5)	89.8	(2.2)	90.1	(2.0)	79.7	(2.7)	93.0	(1.3)
	Denmark	0.12	(0.07)	90.9	(2.0)	81.1	(2.7)	86.0	(2.6)	83.9	(2.8)	97.4	(1.1)	93.1	(2.0)	95.1	(1.7)
	Finland	-0.24	(0.06)	93.3	(1.8)	65.4	(3.5)	79.6	(3.2)	86.6	(2.4)	94.2	(1.7)	83.7	(3.2)	86.0	(2.6)
	France	w	w	w	w	w	w	w	w	w	w	w	w	w	w	w	w
	Germany	-0.36	(0.06)	90.5	(2.1)	68.9	(3.4)	76.8	(3.3)	75.4	(3.2)	97.1	(1.2)	77.0	(3.3)	86.1	(2.6)
	Greece	-0.61	(0.22)	54.8	(5.1)	57.0	(6.0)	60.1	(5.6)	68.5	(4.9)	76.6	(5.1)	70.9	(5.4)	59.2	(5.6)
	Hungary	0.09	(0.09)	90.9	(2.6)	77.0	(3.6)	78.6	(3.5)	95.5	(1.2)	88.0	(2.8)	77.4	(3.8)	83.5	(3.4)
	Iceland	0.03	(0.00)	85.6	(0.1)	60.5	(0.2)	67.8	(0.2)	87.1	(0.1)	98.7	(0.1)	88.7	(0.1)	91.8	(0.1)
	Ireland	-0.47	(0.08)	70.5	(4.0)	52.6	(4.8)	70.2	(4.0)	72.2	(3.9)	91.3	(2.5)	79.0	(3.8)	84.5	(3.5)
	Italy	-0.25	(0.08)	87.6	(2.3)	72.1	(3.3)	89.6	(2.3)	63.3	(3.5)	86.7	(2.5)	75.3	(3.3)	65.7	(3.2)
	Japan	-0.53	(0.07)	68.3	(3.6)	66.1	(4.1)	96.3	(1.6)	58.5	(4.4)	79.4	(3.6)	62.9	(3.9)	76.6	(3.4)
	Korea	0.08	(0.11)	68.1	(4.0)	72.0	(3.2)	89.1	(2.9)	82.7	(3.2)	92.3	(2.3)	73.0	(4.0)	85.9	(3.2)
	Luxembourg	-0.65	(0.00)	91.2	(0.0)	43.8	(0.1)	95.0	(0.0)	81.1	(0.1)	86.2	(0.0)	63.2	(0.1)	71.1	(0.1)
	Mexico	-0.57	(0.09)	59.3	(3.6)	64.8	(3.1)	73.4	(3.1)	59.6	(3.4)	72.6	(3.1)	54.3	(3.6)	76.3	(2.9)
	Netherlands	-1.02	(0.06)	61.1	(4.8)	44.1	(4.8)	54.4	(3.9)	39.9	(4.6)	81.8	(3.6)	59.6	(4.3)	79.9	(3.5)
	New Zealand	-0.49	(0.05)	60.3	(3.2)	53.9	(3.4)	92.1	(1.8)	76.6	(3.3)	93.8	(1.8)	76.2	(2.8)	82.4	(2.9)
	Norway	-0.68	(0.06)	79.6	(3.3)	28.5	(3.9)	75.5	(3.5)	64.9	(3.6)	96.5	(1.5)	76.3	(3.5)	77.7	(3.4)
	Poland	0.08	(0.09)	87.9	(2.7)	81.1	(3.1)	89.7	(2.5)	90.0	(2.4)	95.1	(1.7)	81.5	(3.4)	89.7	(2.5)
	Portugal	-0.69	(0.06)	55.5	(4.6)	55.4	(4.5)	70.5	(4.1)	56.4	(4.7)	98.0	(1.2)	65.0	(4.3)	84.1	(3.0)
	Slovak Republic	0.22	(0.05)	83.0	(2.8)	89.8	(1.8)	81.2	(2.9)	92.5	(1.6)	94.2	(1.2)	87.9	(2.2)	93.1	(2.1)
	Spain	0.00	(0.08)	78.9	(3.0)	79.4	(3.3)	87.2	(2.6)	73.4	(3.4)	93.1	(2.1)	78.9	(2.6)	90.3	(2.4)
	Sweden	-0.19	(0.07)	88.5	(2.6)	67.4	(3.4)	84.3	(2.8)	68.6	(3.4)	97.8	(1.1)	84.0	(3.0)	89.1	(2.2)
	Switzerland	0.09	(0.06)	92.2	(1.8)	79.5	(2.8)	95.2	(1.4)	77.4	(3.1)	97.2	(1.0)	88.5	(2.1)	89.2	(2.0)
	Turkey	-1.14	(0.14)	39.2	(4.7)	53.7	(4.1)	62.6	(3.9)	53.6	(4.7)	65.7	(4.5)	37.5	(4.7)	41.9	(4.8)
	United States	-0.36	(0.06)	75.7	(3.3)	67.9	(3.0)	86.7	(2.3)	66.0	(3.4)	95.0	(1.5)	86.5	(2.5)	85.9	(2.5)
	OECD average 2003	-0.30	(0.02)	77.8	(0.6)	65.9	(0.6)	80.7	(0.6)	73.3	(0.6)	90.5	(0.4)	76.0	(0.6)	82.6	(0.5)
Partners	Brazil	-0.10	(0.10)	72.5	(3.3)	73.1	(3.5)	73.0	(3.5)	75.9	(3.2)	87.2	(2.6)	72.2	(3.4)	81.0	(3.2)
	Hong Kong-China	-0.67	(0.10)	56.6	(3.9)	56.3	(3.8)	79.0	(3.5)	80.4	(3.4)	60.1	(3.5)	76.3	(3.2)		
	Indonesia	-2.46	(0.11)	24.9	(2.8)	24.4	(3.2)	21.6	(3.1)	39.0	(3.6)	28.2	(3.6)	25.8	(3.0)	26.7	(3.9)
	Latvia	-0.04	(0.08)	87.3	(2.7)	75.5	(4.0)	93.2	(1.7)	87.8	(2.9)	93.5	(2.2)	75.9	(4.0)	84.7	(3.5)
	Liechtenstein	-0.37	(0.01)	73.4	(0.4)	73.7	(0.3)	100.0	c	46.5	(0.4)	100.0	c	94.4	(0.3)	89.3	(0.4)
	Macao-China	-1.18	(0.01)	40.8	(0.3)	39.7	(0.2)	62.6	(0.3)	52.1	(0.3)	54.9	(0.2)	44.0	(0.3)	55.9	(0.3)
	Russian Federation	-0.98	(0.09)	47.7	(4.4)	60.2	(3.5)	48.8	(4.2)	61.5	(3.7)	44.5	(3.4)	58.4	(3.7)	55.1	(3.9)
	Thailand	-0.30	(0.09)	62.0	(4.0)	63.5	(4.0)	88.2	(2.9)	90.2	(2.3)	74.2	(3.8)	82.9	(3.1)	87.0	(2.7)
	Tunisia	-1.66	(0.08)	16.1	(3.1)	25.4	(3.7)	26.3	(3.4)	54.5	(4.0)	54.9	(4.4)	40.3	(3.6)	33.8	(4.0)
	Uruguay	-0.78	(0.10)	50.3	(4.3)	66.5	(4.2)	35.9	(3.2)	59.2	(3.8)	79.4	(4.0)	53.2	(4.8)	78.2	(3.6)

Notes: Values that are statistically significant are indicated in bold (see Annex A3).
Only countries and economies with comparable data from PISA 2003 and PISA 2012 are shown.
For comparability over time, PISA 2003 values on the *index of teacher-related factors affecting school climate* have been rescaled to the PISA 2012 scale of the index. PISA 2003 results reported in this table may thus differ from those presented in *Learning for Tomorrow's World: First Results from PISA 2003* (OECD, 2004) (see Annex A5 for more details).
StatLink ᛗᛃᛌᛁ http://dx.doi.org/10.1787/888932957517

[Part 2/3]
Change between 2003 and 2012 in teacher-related factors affecting school climate
Table IV.5.19   *Results based on school principals' reports*

| | Index of teacher-related factors affecting school climate | | Percentage of students in schools whose principals reported that the following phenomena hindered learning "not at all" or "very little" | | | | | | | | | | | | | |
| | | | Teachers' low expectations of students | | Teachers not meeting individual students' needs | | Teacher absenteeism | | Staff resisting change | | Teacher being too strict with students | | Students not being encouraged to achieve their full potential | | Poor teacher-student relations | |
	Mean index	S.E.	%	S.E.	%	S.E.	%	S.E.	%	S.E.	%	S.E.	%	S.E.	%	S.E.
Australia	-0.15	(0.03)	80.6	(1.4)	65.0	(1.8)	87.4	(1.4)	63.5	(2.0)	93.9	(0.9)	84.7	(1.4)	91.2	(1.0)
Austria	-0.16	(0.07)	85.1	(3.0)	80.6	(3.3)	80.3	(3.1)	73.0	(3.4)	88.4	(2.6)	85.5	(2.9)	93.9	(1.9)
Belgium	-0.26	(0.05)	91.5	(1.6)	84.1	(2.4)	75.0	(2.7)	65.7	(3.0)	85.7	(2.1)	81.6	(2.2)	96.7	(0.9)
Canada	0.10	(0.04)	94.3	(1.3)	78.1	(1.9)	91.0	(1.5)	65.7	(2.5)	92.0	(1.4)	89.8	(1.5)	94.9	(0.9)
Czech Republic	0.19	(0.05)	93.2	(2.0)	96.3	(1.4)	90.7	(2.7)	93.4	(1.7)	90.8	(1.9)	81.6	(2.8)	96.0	(1.7)
Denmark	0.13	(0.06)	91.2	(2.1)	85.8	(2.6)	84.7	(2.7)	83.5	(2.9)	98.8	(0.6)	86.2	(2.6)	97.0	(1.1)
Finland	-0.08	(0.05)	96.8	(0.8)	80.5	(3.1)	82.7	(3.0)	77.7	(3.1)	95.5	(1.0)	92.8	(1.4)	95.1	(1.3)
France	-0.17	(0.06)	92.4	(1.6)	65.8	(2.8)	91.3	(1.8)	57.9	(3.4)	76.8	(2.8)	78.1	(2.8)	92.1	(1.8)
Germany	-0.31	(0.05)	91.7	(2.0)	84.5	(2.8)	70.3	(3.5)	75.5	(2.9)	92.9	(1.9)	86.8	(2.3)	97.9	(1.0)
Greece	-0.16	(0.09)	69.5	(3.4)	79.5	(3.0)	88.4	(2.6)	77.2	(3.1)	87.0	(2.4)	74.3	(3.1)	85.4	(3.1)
Hungary	0.37	(0.07)	96.3	(1.5)	86.2	(2.4)	99.5	(0.5)	95.4	(1.7)	91.7	(2.1)	71.2	(3.5)	93.3	(2.1)
Iceland	0.05	(0.01)	91.5	(0.1)	75.5	(0.2)	85.3	(0.2)	69.1	(0.2)	96.9	(0.1)	85.7	(0.2)	98.5	(0.0)
Ireland	0.10	(0.08)	86.3	(2.8)	82.1	(3.0)	88.3	(2.7)	81.3	(3.3)	88.5	(2.8)	86.7	(2.9)	98.1	(1.3)
Italy	-0.29	(0.04)	78.7	(2.1)	75.7	(2.0)	88.9	(1.7)	46.7	(2.1)	79.6	(1.7)	72.1	(2.4)	74.5	(1.8)
Japan	-0.31	(0.06)	79.7	(3.0)	73.9	(3.3)	97.0	(1.2)	68.9	(3.5)	81.3	(2.7)	71.6	(3.2)	90.4	(2.1)
Korea	0.04	(0.10)	75.3	(3.8)	73.8	(3.1)	99.1	(0.9)	86.3	(2.9)	83.9	(3.4)	79.8	(3.6)	86.4	(3.0)
Luxembourg	-0.29	(0.00)	95.8	(0.0)	83.3	(0.1)	93.6	(0.1)	79.9	(0.1)	91.4	(0.0)	78.7	(0.1)	92.2	(0.1)
Mexico	-0.27	(0.04)	74.1	(2.0)	74.6	(1.9)	82.6	(1.4)	64.6	(1.7)	77.5	(1.6)	60.9	(1.9)	94.0	(0.9)
Netherlands	-0.85	(0.04)	75.4	(3.5)	28.7	(3.8)	59.8	(4.0)	54.1	(4.6)	89.0	(2.4)	35.5	(3.7)	93.3	(1.7)
New Zealand	-0.16	(0.07)	85.7	(2.7)	66.9	(4.2)	92.6	(2.4)	73.3	(3.9)	97.2	(1.7)	91.5	(2.5)	96.0	(1.6)
Norway	-0.45	(0.06)	81.6	(3.3)	56.2	(4.0)	70.0	(3.6)	74.5	(3.4)	98.7	(1.0)	75.2	(3.1)	90.3	(1.9)
Poland	0.47	(0.06)	95.8	(1.5)	90.3	(2.3)	93.0	(2.2)	89.2	(2.4)	96.6	(1.1)	92.8	(2.1)	98.6	(1.0)
Portugal	0.11	(0.09)	82.7	(3.8)	87.9	(3.4)	97.8	(1.7)	81.7	(3.7)	97.5	(1.5)	76.4	(3.4)	96.8	(2.0)
Slovak Republic	0.04	(0.06)	87.8	(2.3)	92.0	(1.9)	92.0	(2.1)	84.1	(3.2)	76.1	(3.1)	78.8	(3.1)	97.5	(1.0)
Spain	-0.19	(0.05)	77.9	(2.2)	75.9	(2.0)	95.3	(0.8)	68.1	(2.5)	85.4	(1.8)	71.0	(2.4)	93.7	(0.9)
Sweden	-0.09	(0.07)	81.2	(3.0)	74.5	(3.3)	79.1	(2.7)	79.1	(3.4)	97.3	(1.0)	79.0	(2.8)	93.3	(1.6)
Switzerland	0.01	(0.05)	95.9	(1.5)	87.2	(2.4)	94.6	(1.7)	75.4	(3.2)	93.6	(1.6)	89.4	(2.2)	97.9	(0.7)
Turkey	-0.23	(0.08)	67.8	(3.4)	46.5	(4.3)	89.0	(2.5)	75.9	(3.2)	93.5	(2.3)	68.0	(3.4)	82.2	(3.2)
United States	0.13	(0.10)	83.4	(3.3)	75.9	(3.9)	90.6	(2.4)	71.9	(4.1)	94.6	(2.1)	89.0	(2.5)	94.3	(1.8)
OECD average 2003	-0.09	(0.01)	85.2	(0.5)	76.5	(0.5)	87.1	(0.4)	74.8	(0.6)	90.5	(0.4)	79.2	(0.5)	93.2	(0.3)
Brazil	-0.33	(0.06)	60.8	(2.8)	59.4	(2.5)	66.5	(2.5)	63.9	(2.8)	83.2	(2.2)	63.0	(2.5)	81.4	(1.8)
Hong Kong-China	-0.37	(0.07)	69.6	(3.3)	55.2	(4.0)	88.8	(2.6)	81.5	(3.0)	94.1	(2.0)	63.3	(4.1)	95.5	(1.7)
Indonesia	0.30	(0.08)	94.1	(1.8)	97.2	(1.3)	97.3	(1.2)	97.6	(1.3)	96.3	(1.6)	58.5	(3.7)	99.2	(0.8)
Latvia	0.13	(0.07)	85.9	(2.8)	87.0	(2.5)	94.7	(1.6)	90.7	(2.3)	91.0	(2.3)	82.5	(3.0)	93.4	(1.7)
Liechtenstein	-0.12	(0.01)	100.0	c	93.3	(0.6)	87.8	(1.0)	74.4	(1.2)	93.3	(0.6)	100.0	c	93.3	(0.6)
Macao-China	-0.09	(0.00)	78.1	(0.0)	56.7	(0.1)	84.1	(0.0)	81.9	(0.0)	84.4	(0.0)	61.6	(0.1)	83.3	(0.0)
Russian Federation	-0.27	(0.08)	68.2	(2.8)	63.5	(3.8)	74.1	(3.1)	65.0	(3.3)	75.7	(3.2)	45.2	(3.5)	80.1	(2.4)
Thailand	-0.08	(0.07)	86.7	(2.7)	85.8	(2.5)	89.1	(2.5)	88.7	(2.4)	66.5	(3.9)	92.6	(1.9)	97.3	(1.0)
Tunisia	-0.70	(0.07)	59.4	(4.1)	65.8	(4.0)	36.1	(3.7)	61.0	(4.5)	70.9	(3.6)	40.7	(3.8)	75.9	(3.6)
Uruguay	-0.67	(0.06)	63.0	(3.7)	63.4	(3.3)	35.1	(3.0)	65.8	(3.6)	89.4	(2.2)	44.9	(3.4)	86.2	(2.4)

Notes: Values that are statistically significant are indicated in bold (see Annex A3).
Only countries and economies with comparable data from PISA 2003 and PISA 2012 are shown.
For comparability over time, PISA 2003 values on the *index of teacher-related factors affecting school climate* have been rescaled to the PISA 2012 scale of the index. PISA 2003 results reported in this table may thus differ from those presented in *Learning for Tomorrow's World: First Results from PISA 2003* (OECD, 2004) (see Annex A5 for more details).
StatLink ⟐ http://dx.doi.org/10.1787/888932957517

[Part 3/3]
Change between 2003 and 2012 in teacher-related factors affecting school climate
Table IV.5.19   *Results based on school principals' reports*

		Change between 2003 and 2012 (PISA 2012 - PISA 2003)														
				Percentage of students in schools whose principals reported that the following phenomena hindered learning "not at all" or "very little"												
		Index of teacher-related factors affecting school climate		Teachers' low expectations of students		Teachers not meeting individual students' needs		Teacher absenteeism		Staff resisting change		Teacher being too strict with students		Students not being encouraged to achieve their full potential		Poor teacher-student relations	
		Dif.	S.E.	% dif.	S.E.	% dif.	S.E.	% dif.	S.E.	% dif.	S.E.	% dif.	S.E.	% dif.	S.E.	% dif.	S.E.
OECD	Australia	**0.33**	(0.06)	**12.1**	(3.1)	**13.1**	(3.7)	3.3	(2.6)	-2.4	(3.6)	1.4	(1.8)	3.3	(2.7)	**5.8**	(2.2)
	Austria	-0.09	(0.11)	0.8	(4.6)	2.0	(4.4)	-5.7	(4.3)	**-10.5**	(4.4)	-4.5	(3.3)	7.5	(4.6)	3.3	(3.0)
	Belgium	**-0.25**	(0.07)	-0.3	(2.3)	5.8	(3.9)	-2.8	(3.8)	-7.7	(4.0)	**-11.2**	(2.4)	-3.4	(3.2)	**5.7**	(1.9)
	Canada	**0.39**	(0.06)	**5.1**	(2.0)	**10.9**	(3.2)	-0.9	(2.0)	-1.5	(3.3)	0.4	(1.9)	**5.7**	(2.3)	**7.1**	(1.8)
	Czech Republic	**0.32**	(0.07)	2.0	(2.7)	**9.4**	(2.5)	**13.4**	(3.7)	3.6	(2.8)	0.7	(2.7)	2.0	(3.9)	3.0	(2.2)
	Denmark	0.00	(0.09)	0.3	(2.9)	4.7	(3.7)	-1.3	(3.7)	-0.4	(4.0)	1.4	(1.2)	**-6.9**	(3.3)	2.0	(2.0)
	Finland	**0.17**	(0.08)	3.5	(2.0)	**15.1**	(4.7)	3.1	(4.4)	**-8.9**	(3.9)	1.3	(1.9)	**9.1**	(3.5)	**9.0**	(2.9)
	France	m	m	m	m	m	m	m	m	m	m	m	m	m	m	m	m
	Germany	0.05	(0.08)	1.3	(2.9)	**15.6**	(4.4)	-6.5	(4.8)	0.0	(4.3)	-4.2	(2.3)	**9.8**	(4.0)	**11.7**	(2.7)
	Greece	0.45	(0.24)	**14.7**	(6.1)	**22.6**	(6.7)	**28.3**	(6.2)	8.6	(5.8)	10.4	(5.6)	3.4	(6.2)	**26.2**	(6.4)
	Hungary	**0.28**	(0.11)	5.5	(3.0)	**9.1**	(4.3)	**20.9**	(3.5)	-0.1	(2.1)	3.7	(3.5)	-6.1	(5.2)	**9.8**	(4.0)
	Iceland	**0.02**	(0.01)	**5.9**	(0.2)	**14.9**	(0.3)	**17.5**	(0.3)	**-18.0**	(0.3)	**-1.8**	(0.1)	**-3.0**	(0.2)	**6.7**	(0.1)
	Ireland	**0.58**	(0.11)	**15.8**	(4.9)	**29.5**	(5.7)	**18.1**	(4.9)	9.1	(5.1)	-2.8	(3.7)	7.6	(4.7)	**13.6**	(3.7)
	Italy	-0.04	(0.09)	**-8.9**	(3.1)	3.7	(3.8)	-0.6	(2.8)	**-16.7**	(4.1)	**-7.0**	(3.1)	-3.2	(4.1)	**8.8**	(3.7)
	Japan	**0.22**	(0.09)	**11.4**	(4.7)	7.8	(5.3)	0.7	(2.1)	10.4	(5.6)	1.9	(4.5)	8.7	(5.1)	**13.8**	(4.0)
	Korea	-0.04	(0.15)	7.3	(5.5)	1.8	(4.5)	**10.1**	(3.0)	3.6	(4.3)	**-8.5**	(4.1)	6.8	(5.4)	0.5	(4.4)
	Luxembourg	**0.36**	(0.00)	**4.6**	(0.0)	**39.5**	(0.1)	**-1.5**	(0.1)	**-1.2**	(0.1)	**5.2**	(0.1)	**15.5**	(0.1)	**21.2**	(0.1)
	Mexico	**0.30**	(0.10)	**14.8**	(4.1)	**9.8**	(3.7)	**9.1**	(3.4)	5.0	(3.8)	4.8	(3.5)	6.5	(4.1)	**17.7**	(3.0)
	Netherlands	**0.16**	(0.07)	**14.3**	(6.0)	**-15.5**	(6.2)	5.4	(5.6)	**14.2**	(6.5)	7.2	(4.3)	**-24.1**	(5.7)	**13.4**	(3.9)
	New Zealand	**0.32**	(0.08)	**25.4**	(4.2)	**13.0**	(5.4)	0.5	(3.0)	-3.3	(5.1)	3.4	(2.5)	**15.3**	(3.8)	**13.6**	(3.3)
	Norway	**0.22**	(0.08)	2.0	(4.6)	**27.8**	(5.6)	-5.6	(5.0)	9.5	(5.0)	2.2	(1.8)	-1.1	(4.6)	**12.6**	(3.9)
	Poland	**0.39**	(0.11)	**7.9**	(3.1)	**9.2**	(3.8)	3.2	(3.3)	-0.9	(3.4)	1.5	(2.1)	**11.3**	(4.0)	**8.9**	(2.7)
	Portugal	**0.80**	(0.11)	**27.2**	(5.9)	**32.5**	(5.6)	**27.3**	(4.4)	**25.3**	(6.0)	-0.5	(1.9)	**11.4**	(5.5)	**12.7**	(3.6)
	Slovak Republic	**-0.18**	(0.08)	4.8	(3.7)	2.3	(2.6)	**10.9**	(3.6)	**-8.4**	(3.6)	**-18.0**	(3.3)	**-9.1**	(3.9)	4.5	(2.3)
	Spain	-0.19	(0.10)	-1.0	(3.8)	-3.5	(3.9)	8.0	(2.8)	-5.3	(4.2)	**-7.7**	(2.7)	**-8.0**	(3.5)	3.3	(2.5)
	Sweden	0.10	(0.09)	-7.3	(3.9)	7.0	(4.7)	-5.2	(3.9)	**10.5**	(4.8)	-0.5	(1.5)	-5.0	(4.1)	4.2	(2.8)
	Switzerland	-0.08	(0.08)	3.7	(2.3)	7.8	(3.7)	-0.6	(2.2)	-2.0	(4.5)	-3.6	(1.8)	0.9	(3.1)	**8.7**	(2.2)
	Turkey	**0.91**	(0.16)	**28.6**	(5.8)	-7.2	(5.9)	**26.4**	(4.7)	**22.3**	(5.6)	**27.8**	(5.1)	**30.5**	(5.8)	**40.3**	(5.7)
	United States	**0.48**	(0.11)	7.8	(4.7)	8.0	(5.0)	3.9	(3.4)	5.9	(5.3)	-0.4	(2.6)	2.5	(3.5)	**8.5**	(3.1)
	OECD average 2003	**0.21**	(0.02)	**7.5**	(0.8)	**10.6**	(0.8)	**6.4**	(0.7)	1.5	(0.8)	0.1	(0.6)	**3.1**	(0.8)	**10.6**	(0.6)
Partners	Brazil	-0.23	(0.12)	**-11.7**	(4.4)	**-13.7**	(4.3)	-6.5	(4.3)	**-12.0**	(4.2)	-3.9	(3.4)	**-9.3**	(4.2)	0.5	(3.7)
	Hong Kong-China	**0.30**	(0.12)	**12.9**	(5.2)	-1.1	(5.6)	**9.7**	(4.4)	**12.6**	(4.6)	**13.7**	(4.0)	3.2	(5.4)	**19.2**	(3.7)
	Indonesia	**2.76**	(0.14)	**69.2**	(3.3)	**72.8**	(3.4)	**75.8**	(3.3)	**58.6**	(3.8)	**68.1**	(4.0)	**32.7**	(4.8)	**72.4**	(4.0)
	Latvia	0.16	(0.11)	-1.4	(3.9)	**11.6**	(4.7)	1.5	(2.3)	2.9	(3.7)	-2.5	(3.2)	6.7	(5.0)	**8.7**	(3.9)
	Liechtenstein	**0.25**	(0.02)	26.6	c	**19.6**	(0.7)	-12.2	c	**28.0**	(1.3)	-6.7	c	5.6	c	**3.9**	(0.7)
	Macao-China	**1.09**	(0.01)	**37.3**	(0.3)	**16.9**	(0.2)	**21.6**	(0.3)	**29.8**	(0.3)	**29.5**	(0.2)	**17.6**	(0.3)	**27.4**	(0.3)
	Russian Federation	**0.71**	(0.13)	**20.6**	(5.2)	3.4	(5.2)	**25.3**	(5.2)	3.5	(5.0)	**31.2**	(4.7)	**-13.1**	(5.1)	**25.0**	(4.6)
	Thailand	0.22	(0.12)	**24.7**	(4.8)	**22.3**	(4.7)	0.9	(3.8)	-1.5	(3.3)	-7.7	(5.5)	**9.7**	(3.7)	**10.3**	(2.9)
	Tunisia	**0.96**	(0.10)	**43.3**	(5.1)	**40.4**	(5.4)	**9.8**	(5.0)	6.5	(6.0)	**16.0**	(5.7)	0.4	(5.3)	**42.1**	(5.4)
	Uruguay	0.11	(0.12)	**12.7**	(5.7)	-3.0	(5.9)	-0.8	(4.4)	6.6	(5.2)	**10.0**	(4.6)	-8.3	(5.9)	8.0	(4.3)

Notes: Values that are statistically significant are indicated in bold (see Annex A3).
Only countries and economies with comparable data from PISA 2003 and PISA 2012 are shown.
For comparability over time, PISA 2003 values on the *index of teacher-related factors affecting school climate* have been rescaled to the PISA 2012 scale of the index. PISA 2003 results reported in this table may thus differ from those presented in *Learning for Tomorrow's World: First Results from PISA 2003* (OECD, 2004) (see Annex A5 for more details).
StatLink ⌐⌐⌐ http://dx.doi.org/10.1787/888932957517

[Part 1/3]
Change between 2003 and 2012 in student-related factors affecting school climate

Table IV.5.20 *Results based on school principals' reports*

		PISA 2003											
			Percentage of students in schools whose principals reported that the following phenomena hindered learning "not at all" or "very little"										
		Index of student-related factors affecting school climate		Students skipping classes		Students lacking respect for teachers		Disruption of classes by students		Student use of alcohol or illegal drugs		Students intimidating or bullying other students	
		Mean index	S.E.	%	S.E.	%	S.E.	%	S.E.	%	S.E.	%	S.E.
OECD	Australia	-0.27	(0.05)	80.2	(2.2)	78.2	(2.4)	62.9	(3.0)	94.2	(1.3)	76.2	(2.6)
	Austria	-0.27	(0.06)	57.5	(3.8)	82.9	(3.1)	61.6	(4.2)	91.4	(2.2)	85.2	(2.5)
	Belgium	0.14	(0.07)	78.8	(2.4)	82.4	(2.3)	73.7	(2.4)	92.7	(1.9)	85.9	(2.4)
	Canada	-0.68	(0.04)	42.4	(2.4)	75.2	(2.4)	66.0	(2.7)	68.0	(2.1)	81.9	(2.0)
	Czech Republic	-0.07	(0.05)	75.8	(2.8)	83.6	(2.4)	63.8	(2.9)	98.1	(0.9)	97.9	(0.9)
	Denmark	0.01	(0.05)	85.6	(2.3)	87.5	(2.3)	58.3	(3.2)	99.2	(0.6)	93.1	(1.7)
	Finland	-0.37	(0.05)	65.9	(3.8)	87.6	(2.5)	61.5	(3.8)	96.2	(1.6)	92.6	(2.0)
	France	w	w	w	w	w	w	w	w	w	w	w	w
	Germany	-0.33	(0.06)	74.6	(3.1)	77.8	(3.2)	49.3	(3.5)	91.0	(1.8)	76.0	(2.9)
	Greece	-0.57	(0.18)	53.5	(5.2)	52.7	(5.4)	47.9	(5.9)	68.7	(5.7)	76.6	(5.3)
	Hungary	0.09	(0.08)	74.0	(3.9)	86.0	(3.2)	58.4	(3.8)	94.3	(2.0)	91.8	(2.3)
	Iceland	-0.19	(0.00)	72.2	(0.2)	77.9	(0.2)	38.0	(0.2)	94.8	(0.1)	75.4	(0.1)
	Ireland	-0.54	(0.09)	78.6	(3.8)	77.2	(4.2)	53.2	(4.2)	75.9	(4.0)	79.2	(3.6)
	Italy	-0.25	(0.06)	36.7	(3.2)	83.0	(2.8)	59.2	(3.3)	99.3	(0.3)	92.2	(1.7)
	Japan	0.23	(0.07)	77.5	(3.0)	68.3	(3.2)	87.4	(2.6)	99.3	(0.7)	92.7	(2.3)
	Korea	0.76	(0.13)	87.1	(2.9)	76.6	(3.6)	82.2	(3.1)	86.9	(3.2)	86.5	(3.2)
	Luxembourg	-0.40	(0.00)	74.9	(0.1)	84.2	(0.1)	54.8	(0.1)	91.3	(0.0)	84.8	(0.0)
	Mexico	-0.01	(0.07)	67.7	(3.4)	86.5	(1.8)	73.3	(3.3)	92.2	(1.1)	76.0	(3.2)
	Netherlands	-0.45	(0.07)	69.9	(4.0)	71.6	(4.3)	56.7	(4.3)	92.9	(2.9)	78.2	(3.9)
	New Zealand	-0.65	(0.04)	62.0	(2.9)	75.6	(3.1)	58.7	(3.0)	79.9	(2.4)	85.0	(2.6)
	Norway	-0.42	(0.05)	79.7	(3.0)	64.5	(3.8)	26.2	(3.6)	96.6	(1.4)	87.8	(2.7)
	Poland	-0.30	(0.06)	55.4	(3.6)	79.2	(3.2)	60.1	(4.2)	90.4	(2.3)	92.5	(2.2)
	Portugal	-0.38	(0.04)	50.0	(4.0)	84.0	(3.0)	65.4	(4.1)	97.3	(1.3)	90.7	(2.6)
	Slovak Republic	-0.01	(0.05)	c	c	87.6	(1.9)	60.1	(3.6)	96.1	(1.8)	94.9	(1.3)
	Spain	-0.26	(0.07)	61.6	(3.2)	66.2	(3.4)	40.7	(2.9)	95.3	(1.4)	86.8	(2.4)
	Sweden	-0.35	(0.05)	71.8	(3.3)	74.8	(3.4)	49.6	(3.8)	95.4	(1.6)	83.4	(2.6)
	Switzerland	-0.26	(0.08)	89.3	(2.0)	82.6	(3.6)	48.3	(4.2)	80.7	(2.8)	75.6	(3.9)
	Turkey	-0.56	(0.14)	55.4	(4.6)	62.9	(5.0)	54.3	(4.9)	77.7	(3.9)	68.0	(4.7)
	United States	-0.52	(0.06)	64.3	(3.2)	77.9	(2.8)	72.8	(2.7)	78.7	(3.1)	85.8	(2.4)
	OECD average 2003	**-0.25**	**(0.01)**	**68.2**	**(0.6)**	**77.7**	**(0.6)**	**58.7**	**(0.7)**	**89.8**	**(0.4)**	**84.7**	**(0.5)**
Partners	Brazil	-0.39	(0.10)	55.0	(3.9)	70.3	(3.5)	55.5	(3.6)	79.2	(3.1)	74.0	(3.9)
	Hong Kong-China	0.17	(0.13)	79.2	(3.4)	72.2	(3.5)	68.7	(3.7)	82.2	(3.3)	75.2	(3.3)
	Indonesia	-1.90	(0.13)	27.8	(3.6)	31.5	(3.5)	21.1	(3.6)	32.6	(4.0)	36.2	(3.8)
	Latvia	-0.37	(0.08)	42.8	(4.2)	85.8	(3.1)	75.6	(3.8)	89.3	(2.7)	92.5	(2.3)
	Liechtenstein	-0.72	(0.00)	51.8	(0.4)	80.8	(0.2)	6.5	(0.1)	100.0	c	45.6	(0.5)
	Macao-China	-0.74	(0.01)	48.8	(0.3)	43.8	(0.2)	45.5	(0.3)	60.8	(0.3)	68.2	(0.3)
	Russian Federation	-1.25	(0.11)	14.1	(2.5)	51.2	(4.0)	58.6	(3.7)	58.7	(4.3)	59.3	(4.0)
	Thailand	0.05	(0.07)	81.2	(3.3)	92.0	(2.2)	81.2	(2.5)	98.2	(1.0)	95.9	(1.5)
	Tunisia	-1.40	(0.11)	33.1	(4.0)	41.9	(4.2)	21.8	(3.3)	54.9	(3.8)	57.4	(4.0)
	Uruguay	0.29	(0.07)	58.0	(4.1)	83.3	(2.5)	87.9	(2.5)	92.6	(2.0)	88.5	(2.0)

Notes: Values that are statistically significant are indicated in bold (see Annex A3).
Only countries and economies with comparable data from PISA 2003 and PISA 2012 are shown.
For comparability over time, PISA 2003 values on the *index of student-related factors affecting school climate* have been rescaled to the PISA 2012 scale of the index. PISA 2003 results reported in this table may thus differ from those presented in *Learning for Tomorrow's World: First Results from PISA 2003* (OECD, 2004) (see Annex A5 for more details).
StatLink ⌦ http://dx.doi.org/10.1787/888932957517

[Part 2/3]
Change between 2003 and 2012 in student-related factors affecting school climate
Table IV.5.20   *Results based on school principals' reports*

| | | Index of student-related factors affecting school climate | | Percentage of students in schools whose principals reported that the following phenomena hindered learning "not at all" or "very little" | | | | | | | | | |
| | | | | Students skipping classes | | Students lacking respect for teachers | | Disruption of classes by students | | Student use of alcohol or illegal drugs | | Students intimidating or bullying other students | |
		Mean index	S.E.	%	S.E.	%	S.E.	%	S.E.	%	S.E.	%	S.E.
OECD	Australia	-0.18	(0.04)	75.4	(1.6)	76.9	(1.5)	67.9	(1.9)	95.5	(0.7)	81.3	(1.3)
	Austria	-0.30	(0.08)	59.2	(3.8)	78.4	(3.3)	62.5	(3.7)	94.5	(1.8)	82.8	(3.0)
	Belgium	-0.08	(0.06)	79.9	(2.2)	82.0	(2.5)	69.5	(2.4)	94.3	(1.5)	85.2	(1.9)
	Canada	-0.47	(0.04)	43.2	(2.5)	89.2	(1.5)	81.2	(2.1)	79.6	(1.9)	84.9	(1.9)
	Czech Republic	0.20	(0.06)	60.2	(3.8)	83.9	(2.8)	66.4	(3.5)	97.9	(1.1)	94.9	(1.9)
	Denmark	0.07	(0.07)	78.6	(3.0)	81.4	(2.9)	65.8	(3.3)	97.0	(1.1)	94.8	(1.5)
	Finland	-0.50	(0.04)	65.0	(2.8)	67.7	(3.3)	41.2	(3.6)	98.1	(0.7)	70.1	(3.3)
	France	0.01	(0.06)	71.7	(2.9)	85.7	(2.0)	72.8	(2.6)	87.7	(2.2)	94.6	(1.5)
	Germany	-0.18	(0.04)	83.5	(2.6)	82.4	(2.6)	58.1	(3.2)	98.1	(1.1)	85.4	(2.6)
	Greece	0.03	(0.08)	77.9	(3.0)	82.4	(2.8)	58.5	(3.9)	92.0	(2.2)	88.7	(2.4)
	Hungary	0.13	(0.05)	78.5	(2.6)	82.7	(2.3)	71.9	(2.8)	93.4	(1.9)	94.2	(1.6)
	Iceland	0.31	(0.01)	91.6	(0.2)	87.1	(0.2)	64.4	(0.2)	95.9	(0.1)	95.2	(0.2)
	Ireland	-0.09	(0.06)	85.4	(3.0)	80.6	(3.0)	77.0	(3.0)	88.9	(2.6)	85.8	(3.0)
	Italy	0.01	(0.04)	63.4	(2.1)	84.3	(1.5)	65.9	(2.1)	97.0	(0.7)	94.4	(1.2)
	Japan	0.31	(0.07)	90.0	(1.9)	82.2	(2.7)	94.8	(1.7)	98.5	(0.8)	95.7	(1.5)
	Korea	0.07	(0.09)	85.3	(2.9)	61.7	(3.8)	69.4	(3.5)	93.1	(1.9)	79.6	(3.5)
	Luxembourg	-0.27	(0.00)	88.4	(0.1)	84.1	(0.1)	59.5	(0.1)	99.0	(0.0)	89.3	(0.1)
	Mexico	0.01	(0.03)	67.3	(1.9)	89.6	(1.3)	87.4	(1.3)	90.7	(1.2)	86.8	(1.3)
	Netherlands	-0.40	(0.05)	70.6	(3.3)	77.6	(3.8)	62.9	(4.2)	88.9	(2.6)	76.4	(2.8)
	New Zealand	-0.25	(0.06)	67.1	(3.5)	87.9	(2.7)	77.1	(3.2)	93.3	(2.3)	88.4	(2.4)
	Norway	-0.12	(0.05)	70.2	(3.2)	72.3	(3.2)	50.4	(3.7)	100.0	c	91.3	(2.3)
	Poland	0.05	(0.06)	59.8	(4.1)	83.6	(3.3)	70.0	(3.9)	99.3	(0.6)	93.3	(2.1)
	Portugal	-0.14	(0.09)	58.7	(3.9)	69.3	(4.2)	46.1	(4.2)	92.5	(2.1)	90.8	(2.6)
	Slovak Republic	-0.22	(0.06)	28.2	(3.2)	68.2	(3.5)	53.5	(4.0)	98.6	(0.8)	97.6	(0.9)
	Spain	0.19	(0.05)	74.6	(2.4)	76.4	(2.1)	62.3	(2.6)	96.2	(1.2)	96.0	(1.0)
	Sweden	-0.19	(0.05)	59.9	(3.7)	77.6	(3.2)	66.0	(3.4)	95.3	(1.7)	89.9	(2.3)
	Switzerland	-0.04	(0.06)	82.5	(2.8)	84.5	(2.4)	60.5	(3.7)	91.2	(2.0)	91.6	(1.7)
	Turkey	-0.30	(0.07)	45.9	(3.4)	79.4	(3.5)	72.1	(4.0)	94.4	(1.8)	90.7	(2.6)
	United States	-0.14	(0.08)	69.0	(3.7)	84.7	(3.0)	83.9	(3.3)	82.6	(3.1)	88.0	(2.7)
	OECD average 2003	**-0.09**	**(0.01)**	**70.0**	**(0.6)**	**79.9**	**(0.5)**	**66.7**	**(0.6)**	**94.1**	**(0.3)**	**88.7**	**(0.4)**
Partners	Brazil	-0.49	(0.06)	52.1	(2.6)	58.4	(2.6)	39.8	(2.4)	82.2	(2.0)	77.4	(2.2)
	Hong Kong-China	0.37	(0.06)	94.2	(1.9)	85.5	(2.8)	86.6	(2.7)	98.8	(0.9)	94.0	(1.8)
	Indonesia	0.78	(0.06)	97.0	(1.5)	97.0	(1.4)	94.3	(1.9)	98.9	(0.9)	99.2	(0.8)
	Latvia	-0.19	(0.06)	58.8	(3.3)	79.5	(3.1)	69.4	(3.6)	95.7	(1.5)	97.5	(1.0)
	Liechtenstein	0.12	(0.02)	92.9	(0.8)	86.7	(0.9)	38.2	(0.8)	93.3	(0.6)	94.5	(0.9)
	Macao-China	0.53	(0.00)	93.1	(0.0)	79.4	(0.0)	76.5	(0.0)	89.5	(0.0)	83.2	(0.0)
	Russian Federation	-0.19	(0.11)	29.7	(3.0)	65.4	(2.8)	75.9	(3.2)	79.7	(3.2)	80.5	(3.0)
	Thailand	0.02	(0.06)	70.3	(3.6)	91.2	(2.1)	87.2	(2.5)	92.9	(2.1)	93.5	(1.7)
	Tunisia	-0.73	(0.08)	47.4	(4.3)	64.4	(3.9)	53.2	(3.6)	94.1	(2.1)	79.9	(3.2)
	Uruguay	0.00	(0.08)	64.3	(3.5)	80.5	(2.3)	64.3	(3.0)	94.4	(1.6)	80.9	(2.8)

Notes: Values that are statistically significant are indicated in bold (see Annex A3).
Only countries and economies with comparable data from PISA 2003 and PISA 2012 are shown.
For comparability over time, PISA 2003 values on the *index of student-related factors affecting school climate* have been rescaled to the PISA 2012 scale of the index. PISA 2003 results reported in this table may thus differ from those presented in *Learning for Tomorrow's World: First Results from PISA 2003* (OECD, 2004) (see Annex A5 for more details).
StatLink ᵐˢᵖ http://dx.doi.org/10.1787/888932957517

[Part 3/3]
Change between 2003 and 2012 in student-related factors affecting school climate
Table IV.5.20 *Results based on school principals' reports*

		Change between 2003 and 2012 (PISA 2012 - PISA 2003)											
		Percentage of students in schools whose principals reported that the following phenomena hindered learning "not at all" or "very little"											
		Index of student-related factors affecting school climate		Students skipping classes		Students lacking respect for teachers		Disruption of classes by students		Student use of alcohol or illegal drugs		Students intimidating or bullying other students	
		Dif.	S.E.	% dif.	S.E.	% dif.	S.E.	% dif.	S.E.	% dif.	S.E.	% dif.	S.E.
OECD	Australia	0.09	(0.06)	-4.9	(2.8)	-1.3	(2.9)	5.0	(3.5)	1.3	(1.4)	5.1	(2.9)
	Austria	-0.03	(0.10)	1.8	(5.3)	-4.5	(4.5)	0.9	(5.5)	3.1	(2.8)	-2.3	(3.9)
	Belgium	**-0.22**	(0.09)	1.1	(3.3)	-0.4	(3.4)	-4.2	(3.4)	1.6	(2.4)	-0.7	(3.1)
	Canada	0.21	(0.06)	0.8	(3.5)	13.9	(2.8)	15.3	(3.4)	11.5	(2.8)	3.1	(2.8)
	Czech Republic	0.27	(0.08)	-15.6	(4.7)	0.2	(3.6)	2.6	(4.5)	-0.3	(1.4)	-2.9	(2.1)
	Denmark	0.07	(0.08)	-7.0	(3.8)	-6.0	(3.7)	7.5	(4.6)	-2.2	(1.2)	1.7	(2.2)
	Finland	**-0.13**	(0.06)	-0.9	(4.7)	**-20.0**	(4.2)	**-20.2**	(5.2)	1.9	(1.7)	**-22.4**	(3.9)
	France	m	m	m	m	m	m	m	m	m	m	m	m
	Germany	0.15	(0.08)	**8.8**	(4.0)	4.6	(4.1)	8.8	(4.8)	**7.1**	(2.1)	**9.4**	(3.9)
	Greece	0.60	(0.19)	24.3	(6.0)	29.7	(6.1)	10.6	(7.1)	23.3	(6.0)	12.0	(5.8)
	Hungary	0.04	(0.10)	4.5	(4.7)	-3.3	(4.0)	13.6	(4.7)	-0.9	(2.8)	2.4	(2.8)
	Iceland	0.51	(0.01)	19.4	(0.2)	9.3	(0.2)	26.4	(0.3)	1.1	(0.1)	19.8	(0.2)
	Ireland	0.46	(0.11)	6.8	(4.8)	3.4	(5.2)	23.8	(5.2)	13.0	(4.8)	6.6	(4.7)
	Italy	0.26	(0.07)	26.7	(3.8)	1.3	(3.2)	6.7	(3.9)	-2.3	(0.8)	2.1	(2.1)
	Japan	0.08	(0.10)	12.5	(3.6)	13.9	(4.2)	7.4	(3.1)	-0.8	(1.1)	3.0	(2.7)
	Korea	-0.69	(0.16)	-1.8	(4.1)	-14.9	(5.2)	-12.8	(4.7)	6.2	(3.7)	-6.9	(4.8)
	Luxembourg	0.13	(0.00)	13.4	(0.1)	-0.1	(0.1)	4.8	(0.1)	7.7	(0.0)	4.5	(0.1)
	Mexico	0.02	(0.08)	-0.5	(3.9)	3.1	(2.2)	14.1	(3.5)	-1.5	(1.6)	10.8	(3.4)
	Netherlands	0.05	(0.09)	0.7	(5.2)	6.0	(5.7)	6.3	(6.0)	-4.0	(3.9)	-1.7	(4.8)
	New Zealand	0.40	(0.07)	5.1	(4.5)	12.3	(4.1)	18.5	(4.4)	13.4	(3.3)	3.4	(3.5)
	Norway	0.30	(0.08)	-9.5	(4.4)	7.8	(5.0)	24.2	(5.2)	3.4	c	3.5	(3.5)
	Poland	0.35	(0.09)	4.4	(5.4)	4.4	(4.6)	9.9	(5.7)	8.9	(2.4)	0.8	(3.1)
	Portugal	0.24	(0.12)	8.6	(5.6)	-14.7	(5.2)	-19.3	(5.9)	-4.8	(2.5)	0.1	(3.7)
	Slovak Republic	-0.21	(0.08)	c	c	-19.5	(4.0)	-6.5	(5.4)	2.5	(2.0)	2.8	(1.6)
	Spain	0.45	(0.08)	13.0	(4.0)	10.3	(4.0)	21.5	(3.9)	0.9	(1.9)	9.2	(2.6)
	Sweden	0.15	(0.07)	-11.9	(4.9)	2.8	(4.6)	16.4	(5.0)	-0.2	(2.3)	6.5	(3.4)
	Switzerland	0.22	(0.10)	-6.8	(3.4)	1.9	(4.4)	12.2	(5.6)	10.5	(3.4)	16.0	(4.3)
	Turkey	0.26	(0.16)	-9.5	(5.7)	16.5	(6.1)	17.8	(6.3)	16.8	(4.3)	22.7	(5.3)
	United States	0.38	(0.10)	4.7	(4.8)	6.8	(4.1)	11.1	(4.3)	4.0	(4.4)	2.2	(3.6)
	OECD average 2003	0.16	(0.02)	3.3	(0.8)	2.3	(0.8)	7.9	(0.9)	4.3	(0.5)	4.0	(0.7)
Partners	Brazil	-0.09	(0.12)	-2.8	(4.7)	-11.9	(4.4)	-15.7	(4.3)	3.0	(3.7)	3.4	(4.5)
	Hong Kong-China	0.19	(0.15)	15.0	(3.9)	13.3	(4.5)	17.8	(4.6)	16.6	(3.4)	18.7	(3.8)
	Indonesia	2.68	(0.14)	69.2	(3.9)	65.5	(3.7)	73.2	(4.0)	66.2	(4.1)	63.0	(3.9)
	Latvia	0.18	(0.10)	16.0	(5.3)	-6.3	(4.4)	-6.2	(5.2)	6.4	(3.1)	5.1	(2.5)
	Liechtenstein	0.85	(0.02)	41.2	(0.9)	5.9	(0.9)	31.7	(0.8)	-6.7	c	49.0	(1.0)
	Macao-China	1.28	(0.01)	44.2	(0.3)	35.6	(0.2)	31.0	(0.3)	28.7	(0.3)	15.1	(0.3)
	Russian Federation	1.06	(0.15)	15.6	(3.9)	14.1	(4.9)	17.4	(4.9)	21.0	(5.4)	21.2	(5.0)
	Thailand	-0.04	(0.09)	-10.9	(4.9)	-0.7	(3.0)	5.9	(3.5)	-5.3	(2.3)	-2.5	(2.3)
	Tunisia	0.67	(0.13)	14.3	(5.8)	22.5	(5.7)	31.3	(4.9)	39.2	(4.4)	22.5	(5.2)
	Uruguay	-0.29	(0.11)	6.3	(5.4)	-2.7	(3.4)	-23.6	(3.9)	1.8	(2.6)	-7.6	(3.4)

Notes: Values that are statistically significant are indicated in bold (see Annex A3).
Only countries and economies with comparable data from PISA 2003 and PISA 2012 are shown.
For comparability over time, PISA 2003 values on the *index of student-related factors affecting school climate* have been rescaled to the PISA 2012 scale of the index. PISA 2003 results reported in this table may thus differ from those presented in *Learning for Tomorrow's World: First Results from PISA 2003* (OECD, 2004) (see Annex A5 for more details).
StatLink http://dx.doi.org/10.1787/888932957517

[Part 1/2]
Change between 2003 and 2012 in teacher morale
Table IV.5.21 *Results based on school principals' reports*

		PISA 2003										PISA 2012									
				Percentage of students in schools whose principals agree or strongly agree with the following statements:										Percentage of students in schools whose principals agree or strongly agree with the following statements:						
		Index of teacher morale		The morale of teachers in this school is high		Teachers work with enthusiasm		Teachers take pride in this school		Teachers value academic achievement		Index of teacher morale		The morale of teachers in this school is high		Teachers work with enthusiasm		Teachers take pride in this school		Teachers value academic achievement	
		Mean index	S.E.	%	S.E.	%	S.E.	%	S.E.	%	S.E.	Mean index	S.E.	%	S.E.	%	S.E.	%	S.E.	%	S.E.
OECD	Australia	0.02	(0.06)	90.1	(1.8)	96.9	(1.6)	97.5	(1.0)	99.8	(0.2)	0.14	(0.03)	93.5	(1.0)	97.5	(0.6)	97.8	(0.6)	99.2	(0.3)
	Austria	0.31	(0.07)	98.2	(1.0)	98.8	(0.9)	97.1	(1.6)	99.0	(0.8)	0.54	(0.07)	99.9	(0.1)	100.0	c	98.0	(0.9)	98.7	(0.9)
	Belgium	-0.54	(0.05)	87.4	(2.1)	93.4	(1.4)	95.0	(1.1)	90.5	(1.6)	-0.27	(0.06)	88.7	(2.0)	95.3	(1.4)	94.5	(1.5)	94.6	(1.5)
	Canada	-0.04	(0.05)	87.7	(1.7)	95.3	(1.1)	97.5	(0.7)	99.0	(0.4)	0.18	(0.04)	90.2	(1.3)	96.2	(1.0)	98.9	(0.4)	99.6	(0.2)
	Czech Republic	-0.32	(0.05)	96.4	(1.2)	85.7	(2.5)	96.9	(1.1)	99.3	(0.5)	-0.10	(0.05)	99.6	(0.3)	92.0	(1.7)	97.6	(0.9)	99.7	(0.3)
	Denmark	0.14	(0.06)	98.8	(0.9)	100.0	c	99.2	(0.5)	97.6	(0.7)	0.40	(0.06)	98.7	(0.7)	99.4	(0.5)	96.4	(1.4)	99.4	(0.4)
	Finland	0.14	(0.06)	97.9	(1.1)	96.2	(1.2)	95.9	(1.3)	99.4	(0.6)	0.33	(0.06)	99.2	(0.6)	97.0	(1.2)	93.8	(2.1)	99.6	(0.4)
	France	w	w	w	w	w	w	w	w	w	w	-0.39	(0.07)	79.8	(3.1)	86.5	(2.5)	94.3	(1.7)	91.8	(1.9)
	Germany	-0.12	(0.06)	96.6	(1.4)	96.1	(1.2)	89.6	(2.0)	97.4	(1.2)	0.01	(0.06)	96.7	(1.4)	99.1	(0.6)	93.0	(1.9)	95.8	(1.5)
	Greece	-0.08	(0.12)	87.1	(3.3)	83.7	(3.6)	87.3	(3.0)	99.3	(0.7)	-0.41	(0.09)	83.5	(2.8)	84.0	(2.7)	85.5	(3.5)	91.8	(2.6)
	Hungary	-0.06	(0.08)	96.4	(1.8)	86.6	(3.0)	95.9	(1.6)	100.0	(0.0)	-0.02	(0.07)	96.5	(1.1)	87.6	(2.4)	95.3	(1.5)	99.0	(0.8)
	Iceland	0.45	(0.00)	98.7	(0.0)	98.8	(0.0)	98.4	(0.0)	99.0	(0.0)	0.53	(0.00)	97.5	(0.1)	95.3	(0.1)	97.9	(0.1)	99.0	(0.1)
	Ireland	0.09	(0.08)	87.6	(2.6)	96.8	(1.6)	95.0	(1.8)	98.8	(0.9)	0.49	(0.08)	93.6	(2.0)	96.5	(1.5)	98.7	(0.9)	100.0	c
	Italy	-0.76	(0.05)	75.4	(2.4)	81.2	(2.8)	87.4	(2.0)	94.0	(1.4)	-0.60	(0.03)	73.1	(1.7)	79.8	(1.7)	91.7	(1.1)	96.6	(0.6)
	Japan	-0.52	(0.08)	90.1	(2.5)	93.6	(1.9)	79.7	(3.0)	75.4	(3.2)	-0.49	(0.07)	96.6	(1.5)	97.7	(1.3)	89.8	(2.3)	75.6	(2.6)
	Korea	-0.56	(0.08)	80.2	(3.4)	93.4	(2.0)	85.2	(3.1)	86.8	(2.7)	-0.32	(0.09)	79.3	(3.0)	96.5	(1.6)	90.8	(2.2)	93.4	(1.8)
	Luxembourg	-0.54	(0.00)	92.2	(0.0)	92.2	(0.0)	85.6	(0.0)	100.0	c	0.00	(0.00)	97.2	(0.0)	100.0	c	96.1	(0.1)	100.0	c
	Mexico	-0.17	(0.07)	91.1	(1.9)	89.9	(1.9)	87.2	(2.7)	92.4	(1.9)	-0.05	(0.04)	95.0	(0.9)	93.5	(0.9)	94.2	(0.9)	95.3	(0.9)
	Netherlands	-0.35	(0.05)	98.2	(1.0)	100.0	c	96.7	(1.6)	96.9	(1.5)	-0.19	(0.07)	97.5	(1.1)	100.0	c	96.0	(1.5)	94.9	(1.6)
	New Zealand	-0.01	(0.07)	91.2	(2.0)	97.9	(1.1)	97.8	(1.1)	97.3	(1.2)	0.36	(0.06)	94.3	(1.3)	99.5	(0.5)	98.7	(0.4)	100.0	c
	Norway	-0.11	(0.07)	98.2	(1.1)	94.8	(1.7)	91.1	(2.3)	100.0	c	0.26	(0.06)	98.9	(0.8)	97.7	(1.1)	96.1	(1.5)	99.6	(0.5)
	Poland	-0.08	(0.07)	81.4	(3.1)	96.9	(1.1)	94.9	(1.8)	99.4	(0.6)	-0.14	(0.08)	86.1	(2.8)	96.5	(1.4)	99.2	(0.7)	98.5	(1.0)
	Portugal	-0.57	(0.07)	70.7	(4.1)	84.6	(3.3)	96.6	(1.3)	98.6	(1.0)	-0.17	(0.08)	76.3	(3.3)	89.2	(2.8)	96.4	(2.1)	99.6	(0.2)
	Slovak Republic	-0.33	(0.06)	98.0	(0.9)	81.5	(2.4)	94.5	(1.7)	99.0	(0.6)	-0.27	(0.04)	97.9	(1.1)	85.2	(2.7)	96.5	(1.7)	97.6	(1.5)
	Spain	-0.51	(0.06)	79.0	(2.9)	89.8	(2.5)	93.4	(1.8)	97.0	(1.1)	-0.43	(0.05)	76.3	(2.0)	85.4	(2.4)	94.3	(1.2)	93.9	(1.6)
	Sweden	0.32	(0.06)	99.5	(0.5)	99.5	(0.5)	95.9	(1.5)	99.0	(0.7)	0.39	(0.07)	96.9	(1.3)	96.9	(1.3)	93.9	(1.9)	100.0	c
	Switzerland	0.04	(0.07)	94.2	(1.5)	99.3	(0.1)	93.9	(1.7)	98.2	(0.5)	0.31	(0.06)	96.2	(1.3)	98.4	(0.9)	98.6	(0.8)	97.2	(1.3)
	Turkey	-0.54	(0.11)	81.6	(3.4)	81.0	(3.9)	84.5	(3.0)	83.7	(3.4)	-0.23	(0.08)	88.4	(2.6)	88.8	(3.0)	86.8	(2.7)	98.2	(1.1)
	United States	0.07	(0.07)	88.5	(2.4)	95.3	(1.3)	96.5	(1.1)	99.4	(0.5)	-0.03	(0.08)	81.4	(3.2)	95.2	(1.8)	97.9	(0.9)	99.5	(0.5)
	OECD average 2003	-0.17	(0.01)	90.4	(0.4)	92.8	(0.4)	93.1	(0.3)	96.3	(0.3)	0.01	(0.01)	91.7	(0.3)	94.3	(0.3)	95.2	(0.3)	97.0	(0.3)
Partners	Brazil	-0.26	(0.08)	89.9	(2.7)	83.2	(3.2)	93.7	(2.4)	94.1	(2.3)	-0.50	(0.05)	75.6	(2.5)	77.7	(2.3)	92.8	(1.2)	94.5	(1.1)
	Hong Kong-China	-0.51	(0.07)	85.9	(2.8)	94.8	(1.8)	87.1	(2.4)	94.9	(1.5)	-0.42	(0.07)	78.2	(3.5)	98.0	(1.1)	88.8	(2.4)	100.0	c
	Indonesia	0.41	(0.07)	97.6	(1.1)	93.9	(1.6)	96.1	(1.5)	99.1	(0.6)	0.59	(0.07)	100.0	c	97.9	(0.9)	98.5	(1.0)	100.0	c
	Latvia	-0.02	(0.07)	98.9	(0.8)	97.9	(1.1)	98.2	(1.0)	95.8	(1.7)	0.09	(0.06)	100.0	c	98.2	(1.1)	99.6	(0.4)	98.8	(0.7)
	Liechtenstein	-0.35	(0.01)	100.0	c	100.0	c	100.0	c	100.0	c	0.08	(0.01)	100.0	c	100.0	c	100.0	c	100.0	c
	Macao-China	-0.77	(0.00)	82.4	(0.2)	96.7	(0.1)	83.4	(0.1)	91.7	(0.1)	-0.50	(0.00)	92.7	(0.0)	92.7	(0.0)	88.8	(0.0)	91.4	(0.0)
	Russian Federation	-0.37	(0.06)	93.4	(1.8)	86.8	(2.0)	97.4	(1.5)	98.1	(0.8)	-0.04	(0.05)	97.8	(0.9)	91.6	(1.7)	96.8	(1.1)	98.1	(1.0)
	Thailand	-0.33	(0.09)	88.8	(2.7)	86.8	(3.1)	92.4	(2.3)	91.0	(2.6)	0.06	(0.08)	90.1	(2.5)	93.9	(1.9)	96.8	(1.4)	95.9	(1.5)
	Tunisia	-0.10	(0.08)	93.2	(2.1)	90.3	(2.2)	95.2	(1.5)	91.7	(2.4)	-0.66	(0.09)	74.3	(3.5)	67.7	(3.4)	82.2	(3.3)	92.0	(2.4)
	Uruguay	-0.28	(0.06)	98.0	(0.7)	91.3	(2.1)	95.0	(1.4)	98.0	(1.1)	-0.28	(0.07)	91.3	(2.1)	88.0	(2.3)	91.6	(2.1)	93.2	(1.9)

Notes: Values that are statistically significant are indicated in bold (see Annex A3).
Only countries and economies with comparable data from PISA 2003 and PISA 2012 are shown.
For comparability over time, PISA 2003 values on the *index of teacher morale* have been rescaled to the PISA 2012 scale of the index. PISA 2003 results reported in this table may thus differ from those presented in *Learning for Tomorrow's World: First Results from PISA 2003* (OECD, 2004) (see Annex A5 for more details).
StatLink ⟨⟩ http://dx.doi.org/10.1787/888932957517

[Part 2/2]
Change between 2003 and 2012 in teacher morale
Table IV.5.21   *Results based on school principals' reports*

		Change between 2003 and 2012 (PISA 2012 - PISA 2003)								
				Percentage of students in schools whose principals agree or strongly agree with the following statements:						
		Index of teacher morale		The morale of teachers in this school is high		Teachers work with enthusiasm		Teachers take pride in this school		Teachers value academic achievement	
		Dif.	S.E.	% dif.	S.E.	% dif.	S.E.	% dif.	S.E.	% dif.	S.E.
OECD	Australia	0.13	(0.07)	3.4	(2.1)	0.6	(1.7)	0.3	(1.1)	-0.6	(0.4)
	Austria	**0.23**	(0.10)	1.7	(1.0)	1.2	c	0.9	(1.8)	-0.3	(1.2)
	Belgium	**0.28**	(0.08)	1.3	(2.9)	1.8	(2.0)	-0.4	(1.9)	4.1	(2.2)
	Canada	**0.22**	(0.06)	2.5	(2.1)	1.0	(1.4)	1.4	(0.8)	0.6	(0.5)
	Czech Republic	**0.22**	(0.07)	**3.1**	(1.2)	**6.3**	(3.0)	0.8	(1.4)	0.4	(0.5)
	Denmark	**0.26**	(0.09)	0.0	(1.1)	-0.6	c	-2.8	(1.5)	**1.8**	(0.8)
	Finland	**0.19**	(0.08)	1.3	(1.2)	0.8	(1.7)	-2.1	(2.4)	0.2	(0.7)
	France	m	m	m	m	m	m	m	m	m	m
	Germany	0.13	(0.09)	0.0	(2.0)	**3.0**	(1.4)	3.4	(2.8)	-1.5	(1.9)
	Greece	**-0.33**	(0.15)	-3.6	(4.3)	0.3	(4.5)	-1.9	(4.6)	**-7.5**	(2.7)
	Hungary	0.04	(0.10)	0.2	(2.1)	0.9	(3.8)	-0.6	(2.2)	-1.0	(0.8)
	Iceland	**0.08**	(0.01)	**-1.2**	(0.1)	**-3.5**	(0.1)	**-0.6**	(0.1)	-0.1	(0.1)
	Ireland	**0.41**	(0.12)	5.9	(3.3)	-0.3	(2.1)	3.7	(2.1)	1.2	c
	Italy	**0.16**	(0.06)	-2.3	(3.0)	-1.4	(3.2)	4.3	(2.3)	2.6	(1.6)
	Japan	0.04	(0.11)	**6.4**	(2.9)	4.1	(2.3)	**10.1**	(3.8)	0.2	(4.1)
	Korea	**0.24**	(0.12)	-0.9	(4.5)	3.1	(2.6)	5.5	(3.8)	**6.6**	(3.2)
	Luxembourg	**0.55**	(0.00)	**5.0**	(0.0)	7.8	c	**10.6**	(0.1)	0.0	c
	Mexico	0.12	(0.08)	3.9	(2.1)	3.6	(2.1)	**7.0**	(2.8)	2.9	(2.1)
	Netherlands	0.16	(0.09)	-0.8	(1.5)	0.0	c	-0.8	(2.2)	-2.1	(2.2)
	New Zealand	**0.36**	(0.09)	3.1	(2.4)	1.7	(1.2)	0.9	(1.2)	2.7	c
	Norway	**0.37**	(0.09)	0.7	(1.4)	2.9	(2.1)	5.1	(2.7)	-0.4	c
	Poland	-0.06	(0.10)	4.7	(4.2)	-0.3	(1.8)	**4.3**	(1.9)	-0.8	(1.2)
	Portugal	**0.40**	(0.11)	5.6	(5.3)	4.6	(4.4)	-0.2	(2.4)	1.0	(1.0)
	Slovak Republic	0.07	(0.09)	0.0	(1.4)	3.7	(3.6)	2.0	(2.4)	-1.4	(1.6)
	Spain	0.08	(0.08)	-2.6	(3.5)	-4.4	(3.4)	0.9	(2.1)	-3.1	(2.0)
	Sweden	0.07	(0.09)	-2.6	(1.4)	-2.6	(1.4)	-2.0	(2.4)	1.0	c
	Switzerland	**0.27**	(0.09)	2.0	(2.0)	-0.9	(0.9)	**4.7**	(1.9)	-0.9	(1.4)
	Turkey	**0.31**	(0.14)	6.8	(4.3)	7.8	(4.9)	2.2	(4.0)	**14.4**	(3.6)
	United States	-0.10	(0.10)	-7.0	(4.1)	-0.1	(2.2)	1.4	(1.4)	0.1	(0.7)
	OECD average 2003	**0.18**	(0.02)	**1.3**	(0.5)	**1.5**	(0.5)	**2.1**	(0.5)	0.7	(0.4)
Partners	Brazil	**-0.24**	(0.10)	**-14.2**	(3.7)	-5.5	(3.9)	-0.9	(2.7)	0.4	(2.5)
	Hong Kong-China	0.09	(0.10)	-7.7	(4.4)	3.2	(2.2)	1.7	(3.4)	5.1	c
	Indonesia	0.18	(0.10)	2.4	c	**4.0**	(1.9)	2.4	(1.8)	0.9	c
	Latvia	0.11	(0.09)	1.1	c	0.3	(1.6)	1.3	(1.1)	3.0	(1.8)
	Liechtenstein	**0.42**	(0.01)	0.0	c	0.0	c	0.0	c	0.0	c
	Macao-China	**0.26**	(0.00)	10.3	(0.2)	**-4.0**	(0.1)	5.4	(0.2)	**-0.3**	(0.1)
	Russian Federation	**0.33**	(0.08)	**4.4**	(2.0)	4.9	(2.7)	-0.6	(1.9)	0.0	(1.2)
	Thailand	**0.40**	(0.12)	1.3	(3.7)	7.0	(3.6)	4.4	(2.7)	4.9	(3.0)
	Tunisia	**-0.55**	(0.12)	**-19.0**	(4.1)	**-22.6**	(4.0)	**-13.0**	(3.7)	0.3	(3.4)
	Uruguay	0.01	(0.09)	**-6.7**	(2.2)	-3.3	(3.2)	-3.4	(2.5)	**-4.8**	(2.1)

Notes: Values that are statistically significant are indicated in bold (see Annex A3).
Only countries and economies with comparable data from PISA 2003 and PISA 2012 are shown.
For comparability over time, PISA 2003 values on the *index of teacher morale* have been rescaled to the PISA 2012 scale of the index. PISA 2003 results reported in this table may thus differ from those presented in *Learning for Tomorrow's World: First Results from PISA 2003* (OECD, 2004) (see Annex A5 for more details).
StatLink ⫴ http://dx.doi.org/10.1787/888932957517

[Part 1/1]
Change between 2003 and 2012 in arriving late for school

Table IV.5.22   *Results based on students' self-reports*

	PISA 2003								PISA 2012								Change between 2003 and 2012 (PISA 2012 - PISA 2003)							
	Percentage of students who reported having arrived late for school in the two weeks prior to the PISA test:								Percentage of students who reported having arrived late for school in the two weeks prior to the PISA test:								Percentage of students who reported having arrived late for school in the two weeks prior to the PISA test:							
	Not at all		One or two times		Three or four times		Five or more times		Not at all		One or two times		Three or four times		Five or more times		Not at all		One or two times		Three or four times		Five or more times	
	%	S.E.	%	S.E.	%	S.E.	%	S.E.	%	S.E.	%	S.E.	%	S.E.	%	S.E.	% dif.	S.E.	% dif.	S.E.	% dif.	S.E.	% dif.	S.E.
Australia	63.5	(0.7)	25.5	(0.5)	6.5	(0.3)	4.5	(0.2)	64.5	(0.6)	25.4	(0.5)	6.6	(0.3)	3.5	(0.2)	1.0	(0.9)	-0.1	(0.7)	0.1	(0.4)	**-0.9**	(0.3)
Austria	76.9	(1.1)	16.5	(0.8)	3.6	(0.3)	2.9	(0.3)	79.1	(0.9)	15.6	(0.7)	3.2	(0.3)	2.0	(0.3)	2.2	(1.4)	-0.9	(1.1)	-0.4	(0.4)	**-0.9**	(0.4)
Belgium	71.9	(0.8)	20.1	(0.6)	4.3	(0.3)	3.8	(0.3)	72.7	(0.7)	20.8	(0.6)	3.7	(0.3)	2.8	(0.2)	0.7	(1.1)	0.7	(0.8)	-0.6	(0.5)	**-0.9**	(0.4)
Canada	56.2	(0.6)	27.8	(0.5)	9.3	(0.3)	6.8	(0.3)	56.9	(0.7)	28.6	(0.5)	9.2	(0.4)	5.4	(0.3)	0.7	(0.9)	0.8	(0.7)	-0.1	(0.5)	**-1.4**	(0.4)
Czech Republic	76.9	(0.7)	17.6	(0.6)	3.0	(0.3)	2.5	(0.2)	73.0	(0.8)	20.7	(0.7)	3.3	(0.3)	3.0	(0.3)	**-3.9**	(1.1)	**3.2**	(0.9)	0.3	(0.4)	0.5	(0.4)
Denmark	56.9	(1.3)	26.8	(0.8)	9.6	(0.6)	6.7	(0.6)	61.5	(1.1)	26.3	(0.7)	7.5	(0.4)	4.6	(0.4)	**4.6**	(1.7)	-0.5	(1.1)	**-2.0**	(0.8)	**-2.1**	(0.7)
Finland	55.5	(1.1)	29.7	(0.7)	8.9	(0.5)	5.9	(0.4)	57.0	(0.9)	30.8	(0.7)	8.2	(0.5)	4.0	(0.3)	1.5	(1.5)	1.1	(1.0)	-0.7	(0.7)	**-1.9**	(0.5)
France	67.6	(1.2)	24.1	(0.9)	4.9	(0.4)	3.5	(0.3)	67.7	(0.9)	24.4	(0.7)	5.0	(0.4)	2.8	(0.3)	0.2	(1.5)	0.3	(1.2)	0.2	(0.5)	-0.6	(0.4)
Germany	78.6	(1.0)	15.5	(0.7)	3.4	(0.3)	2.4	(0.3)	77.3	(0.8)	17.8	(0.7)	3.0	(0.3)	1.9	(0.2)	-1.3	(1.2)	**2.3**	(0.9)	-0.5	(0.5)	-0.6	(0.4)
Greece	51.8	(1.1)	30.4	(0.8)	9.4	(0.4)	8.3	(0.5)	50.7	(1.0)	29.3	(0.7)	10.5	(0.5)	9.4	(0.4)	-1.1	(1.4)	-1.1	(1.1)	1.1	(0.6)	1.1	(0.6)
Hungary	72.4	(1.0)	20.7	(0.8)	3.8	(0.3)	3.2	(0.4)	75.9	(1.2)	18.6	(1.0)	2.9	(0.4)	2.6	(0.3)	**3.5**	(1.6)	-2.1	(1.3)	-0.8	(0.5)	-0.6	(0.5)
Iceland	54.4	(0.9)	29.3	(0.8)	9.9	(0.5)	6.4	(0.4)	65.0	(0.8)	26.8	(0.8)	5.7	(0.4)	2.5	(0.2)	**10.6**	(1.2)	**-2.5**	(1.1)	**-4.2**	(0.6)	**-4.0**	(0.5)
Ireland	71.3	(1.0)	21.0	(0.8)	4.3	(0.4)	3.4	(0.4)	72.6	(1.0)	20.1	(0.7)	4.8	(0.4)	2.5	(0.3)	1.4	(1.5)	-0.9	(1.1)	0.4	(0.6)	**-0.9**	(0.5)
Italy	55.4	(1.0)	29.6	(0.8)	7.9	(0.4)	7.1	(0.4)	64.8	(0.6)	26.3	(0.5)	5.4	(0.3)	3.5	(0.2)	**9.4**	(1.2)	**-3.3**	(0.9)	**-2.5**	(0.5)	**-3.7**	(0.5)
Japan	83.7	(1.0)	11.7	(0.6)	2.6	(0.4)	2.0	(0.3)	91.1	(0.6)	7.5	(0.5)	1.0	(0.1)	0.5	(0.1)	**7.4**	(1.1)	**-4.1**	(0.8)	**-1.7**	(0.4)	**-1.5**	(0.3)
Korea	73.0	(1.0)	17.8	(0.7)	5.3	(0.4)	3.8	(0.3)	74.9	(1.0)	17.3	(0.7)	4.6	(0.4)	3.2	(0.3)	1.9	(1.5)	-0.5	(1.0)	-0.7	(0.5)	-0.7	(0.5)
Luxembourg	64.3	(0.6)	24.5	(0.6)	5.5	(0.4)	5.7	(0.4)	70.9	(0.5)	21.4	(0.5)	4.6	(0.3)	3.1	(0.2)	**6.6**	(0.8)	**-3.1**	(0.8)	**-0.9**	(0.5)	**-2.6**	(0.4)
Mexico	54.5	(1.0)	33.5	(0.9)	7.4	(0.3)	4.5	(0.3)	60.1	(0.6)	31.9	(0.5)	5.9	(0.2)	2.1	(0.1)	**5.6**	(1.2)	-1.6	(1.0)	**-1.6**	(0.4)	**-2.4**	(0.3)
Netherlands	55.5	(1.1)	31.5	(0.8)	7.3	(0.5)	5.7	(0.6)	69.7	(1.0)	23.4	(0.8)	3.7	(0.3)	3.2	(0.3)	**14.2**	(1.5)	**-8.1**	(1.1)	**-3.6**	(0.6)	**-2.4**	(0.6)
New Zealand	54.3	(1.1)	28.1	(0.8)	9.3	(0.4)	8.3	(0.5)	57.9	(1.3)	28.0	(0.8)	8.9	(0.6)	5.2	(0.3)	**3.7**	(1.7)	-0.1	(1.2)	-0.4	(0.7)	**-3.2**	(0.6)
Norway	64.4	(0.9)	24.3	(0.7)	6.0	(0.4)	5.3	(0.4)	70.8	(1.0)	21.2	(0.7)	4.9	(0.4)	3.1	(0.3)	**6.4**	(1.3)	**-3.1**	(1.0)	**-1.1**	(0.5)	**-2.2**	(0.5)
Poland	63.5	(0.9)	23.2	(0.7)	7.3	(0.5)	6.0	(0.4)	57.6	(1.2)	28.2	(0.7)	8.0	(0.5)	6.2	(0.5)	**-5.9**	(1.5)	**5.0**	(1.0)	0.6	(0.7)	0.2	(0.7)
Portugal	46.0	(1.1)	39.4	(0.8)	9.0	(0.6)	5.5	(0.4)	44.8	(1.0)	39.0	(0.7)	10.2	(0.5)	6.0	(0.4)	-1.3	(1.5)	-0.4	(1.1)	1.2	(0.8)	0.5	(0.5)
Slovak Republic	77.1	(1.0)	17.9	(0.7)	3.0	(0.3)	2.0	(0.2)	73.8	(0.9)	20.1	(0.8)	3.7	(0.3)	2.5	(0.3)	**-3.4**	(1.3)	**2.2**	(1.1)	0.7	(0.4)	0.4	(0.4)
Spain	58.8	(0.9)	26.3	(0.6)	7.2	(0.4)	7.7	(0.5)	64.7	(0.8)	24.3	(0.6)	6.5	(0.2)	4.4	(0.2)	**5.9**	(1.2)	**-1.9**	(0.9)	-0.7	(0.4)	**-3.3**	(0.5)
Sweden	49.2	(1.2)	29.0	(0.9)	11.8	(0.6)	10.1	(0.5)	44.4	(1.0)	34.3	(0.7)	12.9	(0.5)	8.4	(0.5)	**-4.8**	(1.6)	**5.4**	(1.2)	1.1	(0.8)	-1.6	(0.7)
Switzerland	73.4	(0.8)	20.4	(0.7)	3.5	(0.2)	2.6	(0.2)	75.7	(0.8)	19.4	(0.6)	3.4	(0.3)	1.5	(0.1)	2.2	(1.2)	-1.0	(0.9)	-0.1	(0.4)	**-1.1**	(0.3)
Turkey	73.3	(1.1)	20.1	(0.7)	4.0	(0.4)	2.6	(0.4)	56.2	(1.0)	30.1	(0.7)	8.4	(0.5)	5.3	(0.4)	**-17.1**	(1.5)	**10.0**	(1.0)	**4.4**	(0.6)	**2.8**	(0.6)
United States	65.4	(1.0)	23.3	(0.8)	6.3	(0.4)	5.0	(0.4)	69.9	(1.2)	21.8	(0.8)	5.1	(0.4)	3.2	(0.4)	**4.5**	(1.5)	-1.5	(1.1)	-1.1	(0.6)	**-1.9**	(0.6)
OECD average 2003	64.3	(0.2)	24.3	(0.1)	6.4	(0.1)	5.0	(0.1)	66.2	(0.2)	24.1	(0.1)	5.9	(0.1)	3.7	(0.1)	**1.9**	(0.2)	-0.2	(0.2)	**-0.5**	(0.1)	**-1.2**	(0.1)
Brazil	63.0	(1.2)	25.8	(0.8)	7.0	(0.5)	4.2	(0.4)	66.3	(0.8)	24.8	(0.6)	5.5	(0.3)	3.4	(0.2)	**3.3**	(1.5)	-0.9	(1.0)	**-1.6**	(0.6)	-0.8	(0.5)
Hong Kong-China	83.0	(0.8)	13.4	(0.6)	2.1	(0.2)	1.4	(0.2)	85.4	(0.6)	12.5	(0.5)	1.3	(0.2)	0.8	(0.1)	**2.3**	(1.0)	-0.9	(0.8)	**-0.8**	(0.3)	**-0.6**	(0.3)
Indonesia	64.0	(1.1)	28.4	(0.8)	4.9	(0.4)	2.7	(0.3)	73.0	(1.0)	22.2	(0.8)	3.0	(0.3)	1.7	(0.3)	**9.0**	(1.5)	**-6.2**	(1.1)	**-1.9**	(0.5)	**-0.9**	(0.4)
Latvia	51.8	(1.5)	30.0	(1.0)	9.9	(0.5)	8.3	(0.7)	43.7	(1.2)	35.0	(0.9)	12.7	(0.6)	8.6	(0.7)	**-8.0**	(1.9)	**5.0**	(1.4)	**2.8**	(0.8)	0.3	(1.0)
Liechtenstein	79.3	(2.4)	14.0	(2.1)	4.9	(1.1)	1.8	(0.8)	81.3	(2.3)	16.5	(2.1)	1.0	(0.6)	1.1	(0.6)	2.1	(3.3)	2.5	(2.9)	**-3.9**	(1.2)	-0.7	(1.0)
Macao-China	81.4	(1.1)	14.4	(1.1)	3.2	(0.5)	1.0	(0.2)	74.9	(0.5)	20.9	(0.5)	2.7	(0.2)	1.5	(0.2)	**-6.5**	(1.2)	**6.5**	(1.2)	-0.5	(0.6)	0.5	(0.3)
Russian Federation	59.4	(1.2)	27.2	(1.1)	7.1	(0.5)	6.3	(0.4)	53.3	(1.3)	30.9	(0.8)	8.2	(0.5)	7.6	(0.5)	**-6.1**	(1.8)	**3.7**	(1.4)	1.1	(0.7)	**1.3**	(0.6)
Thailand	66.0	(1.2)	23.7	(0.8)	5.7	(0.5)	4.6	(0.4)	65.9	(1.2)	24.0	(0.8)	6.3	(0.5)	3.8	(0.3)	-0.1	(1.7)	0.3	(1.1)	0.6	(0.7)	-0.7	(0.5)
Tunisia	62.1	(1.1)	27.5	(0.9)	5.7	(0.4)	4.6	(0.4)	48.2	(0.9)	38.4	(0.8)	7.6	(0.4)	5.8	(0.5)	**-13.9**	(1.4)	**10.9**	(1.2)	**1.9**	(0.5)	1.1	(0.7)
Uruguay	43.5	(1.1)	36.2	(0.8)	11.7	(0.6)	8.6	(0.4)	40.7	(0.9)	38.1	(0.7)	12.6	(0.5)	8.6	(0.5)	-2.8	(1.4)	1.9	(1.1)	0.9	(0.8)	0.0	(0.7)

Notes: Values that are statistically significant are indicated in bold (see Annex A3).
Only countries and economies with comparable data from PISA 2003 and PISA 2012 are shown.
StatLink ⇲ http://dx.doi.org/10.1787/888932957517

[Part 1/1]
Change between 2003 and 2012 in the concentration of students arriving late for school

Table IV.5.23   *Results based on students' self-reports*

	PISA 2003 Percentage of students who are in schools where, in the two weeks prior to the PISA test...								PISA 2012 Percentage of students who are in schools where, in the two weeks prior to the PISA test...								Change between 2003 and 2012 (PISA 2012 - PISA 2003) Percentage of students who are in schools where, in the two weeks prior to the PISA test...							
	Over 50% of students arrived late at least once		More than 25% but 50% of students or fewer arrived late at least once		More than 10% but 25% of students or fewer arrived late at least once		10% of students or fewer arrived late at least once		Over 50% of students arrived late at least once		More than 25% but 50% of students or fewer arrived late at least once		More than 10% but 25% of students or fewer arrived late at least once		10% of students or fewer arrived late at least once		Over 50% of students arrived late at least once		More than 25% but 50% of students or fewer arrived late at least once		More than 10% but 25% of students or fewer arrived late at least once		10% of students or fewer arrived late at least once	
	%	S.E.	%	S.E.	%	S.E.	%	S.E.	%	S.E.	%	S.E.	%	S.E.	%	S.E.	% dif.	S.E.	% dif.	S.E.	% dif.	S.E.	% dif.	S.E.
OECD																								
Australia	13.3	(1.9)	71.2	(2.8)	15.5	(2.3)	0.0	c	17.1	(1.4)	57.1	(1.9)	25.8	(1.7)	0.0	(0.0)	3.8	(2.4)	**-14.1**	(3.4)	**10.3**	(2.8)	0.0	c
Austria	6.2	(1.7)	33.0	(3.3)	57.4	(3.6)	3.4	(1.0)	6.1	(1.9)	28.5	(3.2)	59.6	(3.7)	5.8	(1.7)	-0.1	(2.6)	-4.5	(4.6)	2.2	(5.2)	2.5	(1.9)
Belgium	10.2	(1.7)	41.4	(3.2)	48.0	(3.1)	0.4	(0.4)	6.7	(1.3)	46.1	(3.0)	46.9	(2.8)	0.3	(0.2)	-3.5	(2.2)	4.7	(4.4)	-1.1	(4.2)	-0.1	(0.4)
Canada	32.1	(2.2)	55.4	(2.3)	11.8	(1.3)	0.7	(0.4)	31.5	(2.3)	53.7	(2.7)	14.5	(1.4)	0.2	(0.1)	-0.6	(3.2)	-1.7	(3.5)	2.7	(1.9)	-0.5	(0.5)
Czech Republic	1.2	(0.6)	38.9	(3.4)	57.7	(3.5)	2.2	(0.9)	8.6	(1.7)	39.3	(2.8)	47.2	(2.8)	4.9	(1.3)	**7.4**	(1.8)	0.5	(4.4)	**-10.6**	(4.5)	2.7	(1.6)
Denmark	32.7	(3.0)	51.7	(3.0)	15.5	(2.6)	0.1	(0.1)	23.0	(2.8)	52.0	(3.3)	23.9	(2.9)	1.1	(0.8)	**-9.7**	(4.1)	0.3	(4.5)	**8.4**	(3.9)	1.0	(0.8)
Finland	38.7	(3.9)	50.9	(4.1)	10.4	(1.9)	0.0	(0.0)	33.3	(3.3)	52.6	(3.7)	13.5	(2.4)	0.5	(0.4)	-5.3	(5.1)	1.7	(5.5)	3.1	(3.1)	0.5	(0.4)
France	9.8	(2.4)	56.2	(4.0)	33.4	(3.9)	0.6	(0.5)	13.9	(2.3)	47.5	(3.3)	37.3	(3.0)	1.2	(0.7)	4.1	(3.3)	-8.7	(5.2)	3.9	(4.9)	0.6	(0.8)
Germany	3.4	(1.3)	28.7	(3.1)	64.8	(3.3)	3.1	(1.1)	4.2	(1.3)	35.2	(3.4)	57.2	(3.3)	3.4	(1.2)	0.8	(1.8)	6.5	(4.6)	-7.6	(4.7)	0.3	(1.7)
Greece	44.1	(4.7)	51.3	(4.6)	4.4	(1.2)	0.2	(0.1)	51.1	(4.0)	44.9	(4.1)	3.6	(1.4)	0.4	(0.2)	7.1	(6.1)	-6.4	(6.2)	-0.8	(1.8)	0.1	(0.3)
Hungary	9.0	(1.9)	43.2	(3.2)	43.3	(3.4)	4.4	(1.5)	10.2	(1.9)	28.9	(3.5)	55.5	(3.6)	5.4	(1.1)	1.2	(2.7)	**-14.4**	(4.8)	**12.2**	(5.0)	1.0	(1.9)
Iceland	45.3	(0.2)	44.6	(0.2)	8.1	(0.1)	1.9	(0.1)	12.2	(0.1)	65.9	(0.2)	19.6	(0.2)	2.3	(0.1)	**-33.1**	(0.2)	**21.3**	(0.3)	**11.4**	(0.2)	0.4	(0.1)
Ireland	8.9	(2.3)	41.2	(4.5)	49.8	(4.4)	0.0	c	5.6	(1.7)	43.3	(3.5)	51.1	(3.6)	0.0	c	-3.3	(2.8)	2.0	(5.6)	1.3	(5.7)	0.0	c
Italy	34.2	(3.4)	55.7	(3.2)	9.9	(1.9)	0.2	(0.2)	17.7	(1.6)	56.8	(2.0)	24.8	(1.7)	0.7	(0.3)	**-16.5**	(3.7)	1.1	(3.7)	**14.9**	(2.6)	0.5	(0.3)
Japan	2.3	(1.2)	20.2	(3.3)	71.4	(3.5)	6.1	(1.9)	0.2	(0.2)	6.2	(1.7)	80.8	(2.9)	12.7	(2.4)	-2.1	(1.2)	**-14.0**	(3.7)	**9.5**	(4.6)	**6.6**	(3.1)
Korea	5.0	(1.9)	48.1	(4.5)	46.8	(4.2)	0.2	(0.1)	5.1	(1.5)	45.5	(3.6)	47.4	(3.5)	2.0	(1.2)	0.1	(2.4)	-2.5	(5.8)	0.5	(5.5)	1.9	(1.2)
Luxembourg	10.2	(0.2)	77.6	(0.1)	12.1	(0.1)	0.0	c	3.5	(0.1)	51.9	(0.1)	44.6	(0.1)	0.0	c	**-6.8**	(0.2)	**-25.7**	(0.1)	**32.5**	(0.1)	0.0	c
Mexico	36.8	(3.1)	53.5	(3.3)	7.8	(1.6)	1.9	(0.8)	27.1	(1.7)	54.3	(1.8)	17.8	(1.4)	0.8	(0.1)	**-9.7**	(3.5)	0.8	(3.8)	**10.0**	(2.2)	-1.1	(0.8)
Netherlands	40.9	(3.7)	45.2	(4.1)	13.9	(2.8)	0.0	c	11.9	(2.3)	44.4	(3.8)	43.7	(3.7)	0.0	c	**-29.1**	(4.4)	-0.8	(5.5)	**29.8**	(4.6)	0.0	c
New Zealand	34.5	(3.0)	56.7	(2.9)	8.8	(1.9)	0.0	(0.0)	30.1	(3.5)	57.2	(4.1)	12.7	(2.8)	0.1	(0.1)	-4.4	(4.6)	0.4	(5.0)	3.9	(3.4)	0.1	(0.1)
Norway	12.6	(2.6)	67.3	(3.5)	18.2	(2.9)	2.0	(0.7)	7.6	(2.0)	55.0	(3.6)	35.5	(3.6)	1.8	(0.7)	-4.9	(3.2)	**-12.3**	(5.0)	**17.4**	(4.6)	-0.1	(1.0)
Poland	17.6	(3.0)	58.3	(3.6)	23.9	(2.8)	0.2	(0.1)	33.3	(3.5)	45.0	(4.0)	21.1	(2.9)	0.5	(0.3)	**15.7**	(4.6)	**-13.3**	(5.3)	-2.7	(4.0)	0.3	(0.3)
Portugal	65.2	(3.5)	31.2	(3.2)	3.6	(1.6)	0.0	c	64.7	(4.0)	34.2	(4.0)	1.0	(0.8)	0.1	(0.1)	-0.5	(5.3)	3.0	(5.1)	-2.6	(1.8)	0.1	c
Slovak Republic	2.2	(0.9)	38.4	(3.2)	55.3	(3.4)	4.0	(1.2)	6.0	(1.2)	43.1	(3.7)	46.5	(4.0)	4.5	(1.1)	**3.8**	(1.5)	4.6	(4.9)	-8.8	(5.2)	0.5	(1.6)
Spain	33.9	(2.9)	51.3	(3.2)	14.8	(2.2)	0.0	(0.0)	17.5	(2.0)	55.2	(3.2)	27.2	(2.9)	0.1	(0.0)	**-16.4**	(3.5)	3.9	(4.6)	**12.4**	(3.6)	0.0	(0.0)
Sweden	48.2	(3.7)	45.7	(3.7)	5.9	(1.6)	0.2	(0.2)	65.5	(3.4)	32.1	(3.2)	2.1	(1.1)	0.3	(0.2)	**17.2**	(5.0)	**-13.6**	(4.9)	**-3.8**	(1.9)	0.1	(0.2)
Switzerland	8.0	(1.3)	38.0	(4.0)	51.0	(4.0)	3.0	(0.5)	5.1	(1.3)	36.1	(2.8)	55.7	(3.0)	3.1	(0.9)	-2.9	(1.8)	-1.9	(4.9)	4.7	(5.0)	0.1	(1.1)
Turkey	5.6	(1.9)	44.7	(4.6)	49.6	(4.4)	0.1	(0.1)	24.9	(3.8)	68.5	(3.9)	6.6	(1.8)	0.1	(0.0)	**19.3**	(4.3)	**23.7**	(6.1)	**-42.9**	(4.8)	-0.1	(0.1)
United States	19.4	(2.2)	47.8	(3.4)	31.5	(2.7)	1.3	(0.6)	9.5	(2.2)	49.2	(4.3)	40.8	(4.2)	0.5	(0.3)	**-9.9**	(3.1)	1.3	(5.5)	**9.4**	(5.0)	-0.7	(0.6)
OECD average 2003	21.8	(0.5)	47.8	(0.6)	29.1	(0.5)	1.2	(0.1)	19.1	(0.4)	45.9	(0.6)	33.2	(0.5)	1.8	(0.2)	**-2.7**	(0.6)	**-2.0**	(0.9)	**4.1**	(0.7)	**0.6**	(0.2)
Partners																								
Brazil	19.8	(3.1)	55.1	(3.9)	24.3	(3.3)	0.8	(0.4)	14.8	(1.8)	50.9	(2.7)	34.0	(2.4)	0.3	(0.1)	-5.0	(3.5)	-4.2	(4.7)	**9.7**	(4.1)	-0.5	(0.4)
Hong Kong-China	0.6	(0.6)	24.8	(3.1)	72.0	(3.2)	2.6	(1.3)	0.2	(0.0)	11.3	(2.4)	84.6	(2.5)	3.8	(1.3)	-0.4	(0.6)	**-13.5**	(3.9)	**12.6**	(4.0)	1.3	(1.8)
Indonesia	14.8	(2.4)	65.3	(3.5)	19.2	(2.9)	0.6	(0.6)	9.0	(1.9)	39.2	(3.5)	50.0	(3.2)	1.7	(1.0)	-5.8	(3.0)	**-26.1**	(4.9)	**30.9**	(4.4)	1.1	(1.2)
Latvia	44.3	(4.2)	45.6	(4.5)	8.9	(2.5)	1.2	(0.7)	65.9	(3.4)	29.7	(3.2)	4.0	(1.4)	0.4	(0.2)	**21.6**	(5.4)	**-15.9**	(5.6)	-4.9	(2.9)	-0.8	(0.8)
Liechtenstein	0.0	c	15.1	(0.5)	84.9	(0.5)	0.0	c	1.0	(0.6)	18.8	(0.9)	80.2	(1.1)	0.0	c	1.0	c	**3.8**	(1.0)	**-4.7**	(1.2)	0.0	c
Macao-China	5.1	(0.1)	14.0	(0.2)	80.9	(0.3)	0.0	c	8.2	(0.1)	34.0	(0.0)	57.8	(0.1)	0.0	c	**3.1**	(0.2)	**20.0**	(0.2)	**-23.1**	(0.3)	0.0	c
Russian Federation	27.3	(3.6)	60.4	(4.0)	10.9	(2.8)	1.4	(0.5)	39.7	(4.0)	48.6	(4.5)	9.9	(2.5)	1.9	(0.4)	**12.4**	(5.4)	**-11.8**	(6.1)	-1.0	(3.7)	0.5	(0.6)
Thailand	17.5	(2.7)	47.7	(4.1)	34.5	(3.6)	0.4	(0.3)	21.1	(2.6)	42.8	(3.7)	34.7	(4.0)	1.4	(0.8)	3.6	(3.8)	-4.9	(5.6)	0.2	(5.3)	1.0	(0.8)
Tunisia	19.2	(3.2)	64.9	(3.8)	15.9	(2.8)	0.0	c	55.9	(4.0)	43.2	(4.1)	0.9	(0.8)	0.0	c	**36.7**	(5.1)	**-21.7**	(5.6)	**-15.0**	(2.9)	0.0	c
Uruguay	63.4	(3.7)	35.6	(3.7)	0.7	(0.3)	0.3	(0.3)	79.8	(2.7)	18.0	(2.5)	2.2	(1.2)	0.0	c	**16.4**	(4.6)	**-17.6**	(4.5)	1.5	(1.2)	-0.3	c

Notes: Values that are statistically significant are indicated in bold (see Annex A3).
Only countries and economies with comparable data from PISA 2003 and PISA 2012 are shown.
StatLink http://dx.doi.org/10.1787/888932957517

ANNEX B2

RESULTS FOR REGIONS WITHIN COUNTRIES

[Part 1/2]
Grade repetition, by region
Table B2.IV.1 *Results based on students' self-reports*

OECD

	Percentage of students reporting that they have repeated a grade in:																		Primary, lower secondary or upper secondary school	
	Primary school						Lower secondary school						Upper secondary school							
	Never		Once		Twice or more		Never		Once		Twice or more		Never		Once		Twice or more			
	%	S.E.	%	S.E.	%	S.E.	%	S.E.	%	S.E.	%	S.E.	%	S.E.	%	S.E.	%	S.E.	%	S.E.
Australia																				
Australian Capital Territory	94.4	(0.8)	5.6	(0.8)	0.0	c	99.6	(0.3)	0.4	(0.3)	0.0	c	100.0	c	0.0	c	0.0	c	6.1	(0.9)
New South Wales	94.0	(0.4)	5.7	(0.4)	0.3	(0.1)	99.0	(0.2)	1.0	(0.2)	0.0	(0.0)	100.0	c	0.0	c	0.0	c	6.7	(0.5)
Northern Territory	90.9	(1.5)	8.4	(1.6)	0.7	(0.3)	98.1	(0.4)	1.5	(0.4)	0.5	(0.2)	97.1	(1.8)	0.0	c	2.9	(1.8)	10.5	(1.5)
Queensland	91.8	(0.5)	7.9	(0.5)	0.3	(0.1)	98.6	(0.3)	1.3	(0.3)	0.2	(0.1)	99.7	(0.2)	0.3	(0.2)	0.0	c	9.2	(0.6)
South Australia	90.6	(0.8)	8.8	(0.7)	0.6	(0.2)	98.7	(0.3)	1.1	(0.3)	0.2	(0.1)	100.0	c	0.0	c	0.0	c	9.9	(0.8)
Tasmania	94.3	(0.8)	5.3	(0.8)	0.5	(0.3)	98.0	(0.5)	1.8	(0.5)	0.3	(0.2)	c	c	c	c	c	c	6.7	(0.9)
Victoria	93.5	(0.5)	6.3	(0.5)	0.2	(0.1)	98.8	(0.3)	1.2	(0.3)	0.0	c	100.0	c	0.0	c	0.0	c	7.2	(0.6)
Western Australia	95.2	(0.5)	4.6	(0.5)	0.2	(0.1)	98.2	(0.4)	1.7	(0.4)	0.1	(0.1)	99.5	(0.3)	0.5	(0.3)	0.0	c	6.1	(0.6)
Belgium																				
Flemish community•	82.4	(0.8)	16.5	(0.7)	1.1	(0.2)	91.4	(0.6)	8.2	(0.6)	0.4	(0.1)	94.9	(0.4)	5.1	(0.4)	0.1	(0.0)	27.4	(0.8)
French community	75.3	(1.2)	19.7	(1.0)	4.9	(0.5)	72.1	(1.1)	25.7	(1.1)	2.2	(0.3)	84.5	(0.8)	15.3	(0.8)	0.1	(0.1)	47.8	(1.1)
German-speaking community	85.6	(1.0)	12.9	(1.0)	1.5	(0.3)	85.2	(1.2)	14.0	(1.2)	0.8	(0.3)	91.6	(0.9)	8.4	(0.9)	0.0	c	31.7	(1.1)
Canada																				
Alberta	94.8	(0.9)	5.0	(0.9)	0.1	(0.1)	98.2	(0.7)	1.7	(0.6)	0.1	(0.1)	99.4	(0.2)	0.6	(0.2)	0.1	(0.1)	6.6	(1.2)
British Columbia	98.7	(0.4)	1.2	(0.3)	0.1	(0.1)	98.5	(0.3)	1.2	(0.3)	0.3	(0.2)	99.2	(0.2)	0.6	(0.2)	0.2	(0.1)	2.8	(0.5)
Manitoba	95.1	(0.9)	4.7	(1.0)	0.2	(0.1)	97.6	(0.3)	2.1	(0.3)	0.2	(0.1)	98.5	(0.3)	1.2	(0.3)	0.3	(0.1)	7.1	(0.9)
New Brunswick	92.8	(0.6)	7.1	(0.6)	0.1	(0.1)	97.1	(0.5)	2.8	(0.5)	0.1	(0.1)	99.0	(0.3)	0.7	(0.3)	0.3	(0.2)	9.6	(0.7)
Newfoundland and Labrador	97.6	(0.7)	2.4	(0.7)	0.1	(0.1)	99.2	(0.4)	0.7	(0.4)	0.1	(0.1)	99.7	(0.1)	0.2	(0.1)	0.1	(0.1)	3.1	(0.5)
Nova Scotia	95.8	(2.0)	4.0	(2.0)	0.2	(0.1)	96.3	(2.0)	3.5	(2.0)	0.2	(0.1)	99.9	(0.1)	0.0	c	0.1	(0.1)	6.9	(3.3)
Ontario	97.5	(0.4)	2.3	(0.4)	0.2	(0.1)	98.6	(0.2)	1.2	(0.2)	0.2	(0.1)	99.0	(0.2)	0.7	(0.2)	0.3	(0.1)	3.7	(0.4)
Prince Edward Island	95.5	(0.4)	4.4	(0.4)	0.1	(0.1)	99.1	(0.3)	0.9	(0.3)	0.0	c	99.6	(0.2)	0.3	(0.2)	0.1	(0.1)	5.0	(0.4)
Quebec	91.5	(0.8)	7.5	(0.7)	1.0	(0.3)	86.0	(0.9)	11.8	(0.8)	2.2	(0.4)	99.1	(0.3)	0.7	(0.2)	0.1	(0.1)	20.4	(1.1)
Saskatchewan	96.2	(0.4)	3.6	(0.4)	0.3	(0.1)	98.3	(0.3)	1.5	(0.3)	0.2	(0.0)	99.3	(0.2)	0.5	(0.2)	0.2	(0.1)	5.2	(0.6)
Italy																				
Abruzzo	99.7	(0.2)	0.1	(0.1)	0.2	(0.1)	92.6	(0.9)	6.8	(0.7)	0.7	(0.3)	91.6	(0.9)	8.1	(0.9)	0.3	(0.2)	14.8	(1.4)
Basilicata	99.5	(0.2)	0.5	(0.2)	0.0	(0.0)	96.3	(0.8)	3.5	(0.7)	0.2	(0.2)	92.6	(0.9)	7.4	(0.9)	0.0	c	10.9	(1.0)
Bolzano	97.8	(0.6)	2.1	(0.6)	0.1	(0.1)	91.9	(1.1)	7.5	(0.8)	0.6	(0.3)	86.2	(0.7)	13.8	(0.7)	0.0	(0.0)	21.3	(0.9)
Calabria	98.5	(0.5)	1.3	(0.5)	0.3	(0.1)	93.7	(1.1)	4.9	(1.1)	1.3	(0.4)	95.4	(0.8)	4.6	(0.8)	0.0	c	10.9	(1.3)
Campania	99.5	(0.3)	0.2	(0.1)	0.4	(0.3)	95.4	(1.0)	3.6	(0.8)	0.9	(0.6)	91.4	(1.0)	8.6	(1.0)	0.0	c	12.2	(1.3)
Emilia Romagna	98.1	(0.3)	1.8	(0.3)	0.1	(0.1)	91.2	(0.8)	7.6	(0.7)	1.2	(0.5)	87.7	(0.9)	12.3	(0.9)	0.1	(0.1)	20.6	(1.2)
Friuli Venezia Giulia	98.7	(0.5)	1.2	(0.5)	0.1	(0.1)	90.2	(1.6)	7.7	(1.0)	2.0	(2.0)	89.0	(0.9)	10.9	(0.9)	0.1	(0.1)	20.4	(2.1)
Lazio	98.9	(0.3)	0.8	(0.3)	0.2	(0.1)	93.0	(1.0)	5.0	(0.7)	2.0	(0.7)	90.4	(1.0)	9.5	(1.1)	0.1	(0.1)	16.3	(1.5)
Liguria	97.8	(0.6)	2.0	(0.6)	0.2	(0.1)	89.4	(1.6)	8.7	(1.5)	1.9	(0.6)	90.0	(1.6)	9.9	(1.6)	0.1	(0.1)	20.3	(2.5)
Lombardia	99.4	(0.2)	0.6	(0.2)	0.0	c	94.1	(0.8)	5.3	(0.8)	0.6	(0.2)	87.2	(1.3)	12.8	(1.3)	0.0	c	17.9	(1.6)
Marche	98.7	(0.5)	1.1	(0.5)	0.2	(0.1)	91.6	(1.2)	6.8	(1.0)	1.6	(0.7)	90.2	(1.4)	9.3	(1.3)	0.4	(0.2)	17.4	(2.0)
Molise	99.5	(0.2)	0.5	(0.2)	0.1	(0.1)	93.9	(0.7)	5.3	(0.7)	0.8	(0.1)	93.4	(0.8)	6.5	(0.8)	0.1	(0.1)	12.2	(0.8)
Piemonte	99.0	(0.4)	0.9	(0.3)	0.1	(0.1)	89.4	(1.0)	8.7	(0.8)	1.9	(0.3)	88.7	(1.0)	11.3	(1.0)	0.0	c	21.1	(1.6)
Puglia	99.3	(0.3)	0.6	(0.3)	0.0	(0.0)	95.5	(0.7)	3.6	(0.6)	0.9	(0.5)	93.2	(0.9)	6.7	(0.9)	0.0	(0.0)	10.7	(1.1)
Sardegna	99.1	(0.3)	0.6	(0.3)	0.3	(0.2)	86.0	(2.0)	8.9	(1.8)	5.1	(1.1)	84.2	(2.2)	15.4	(2.0)	0.4	(0.3)	26.9	(2.9)
Sicilia	98.7	(0.5)	1.2	(0.5)	0.1	(0.0)	90.7	(1.7)	6.2	(1.0)	3.1	(0.9)	90.8	(1.0)	8.9	(1.0)	0.3	(0.1)	17.7	(1.9)
Toscana	98.7	(0.2)	1.2	(0.2)	0.0	(0.0)	91.2	(1.2)	7.6	(1.2)	1.1	(0.3)	87.0	(1.1)	13.0	(1.1)	0.0	c	20.7	(1.5)
Trento	99.1	(0.4)	0.9	(0.4)	0.0	c	93.8	(1.0)	6.1	(1.0)	0.1	(0.1)	88.8	(1.0)	11.2	(1.0)	0.0	c	16.8	(1.5)
Umbria	99.0	(0.5)	0.9	(0.5)	0.1	(0.1)	92.6	(1.4)	6.4	(1.2)	1.0	(0.4)	93.2	(0.8)	6.8	(0.8)	0.0	c	14.0	(1.5)
Valle d'Aosta	96.8	(0.7)	2.6	(0.6)	0.6	(0.2)	82.4	(1.1)	13.8	(1.2)	3.8	(0.5)	81.7	(1.2)	18.3	(1.2)	0.0	c	33.9	(1.1)
Veneto	98.7	(0.4)	1.2	(0.5)	0.1	(0.1)	91.5	(1.9)	7.9	(1.8)	0.6	(0.2)	89.1	(1.3)	10.9	(1.3)	0.0	(0.0)	19.1	(2.3)
Mexico																				
Aguascalientes	87.1	(3.9)	11.8	(3.5)	1.1	(0.5)	96.0	(1.4)	3.6	(1.2)	0.5	(0.4)	99.4	(0.3)	0.6	(0.3)	0.0	c	15.9	(4.4)
Baja California	89.3	(2.3)	10.1	(2.4)	0.6	(0.2)	98.3	(0.6)	1.7	(0.6)	0.0	c	98.2	(0.8)	1.8	(0.8)	0.0	c	12.9	(2.1)
Baja California Sur	87.3	(2.5)	11.6	(2.2)	1.0	(0.5)	96.5	(0.9)	3.2	(1.0)	0.2	(0.2)	99.4	(0.3)	0.5	(0.2)	0.1	(0.1)	15.1	(2.7)
Campeche	76.8	(2.2)	19.3	(2.1)	4.0	(0.7)	94.1	(1.4)	5.6	(1.4)	0.4	(0.3)	98.8	(0.5)	0.9	(0.4)	0.3	(0.3)	26.6	(2.0)
Chiapas	80.5	(3.1)	16.5	(2.9)	3.0	(0.6)	96.6	(1.0)	2.9	(0.8)	0.5	(0.3)	98.2	(0.9)	1.5	(0.6)	0.3	(0.3)	22.0	(3.3)
Chihuahua	83.5	(2.5)	15.1	(2.3)	1.4	(0.3)	96.0	(0.8)	3.8	(0.9)	0.1	(0.1)	98.7	(0.6)	1.3	(0.6)	0.0	c	19.9	(2.3)
Coahuila	93.7	(1.7)	6.1	(1.6)	0.2	(0.2)	97.3	(1.0)	2.5	(1.0)	0.2	(0.2)	98.4	(0.7)	1.5	(0.7)	0.1	(0.1)	9.5	(2.2)
Colima	82.3	(2.1)	15.1	(1.8)	2.6	(0.4)	94.3	(1.4)	4.8	(1.1)	0.9	(0.4)	99.4	(0.2)	0.6	(0.2)	0.0	c	21.5	(2.0)
Distrito Federal	94.7	(1.8)	4.7	(1.5)	0.7	(0.4)	94.6	(0.5)	5.0	(0.6)	0.3	(0.2)	99.2	(0.4)	0.8	(0.4)	0.0	c	10.9	(1.9)
Durango	89.7	(2.3)	9.1	(1.9)	1.1	(0.7)	97.6	(1.2)	1.8	(1.1)	0.6	(0.5)	99.2	(0.6)	0.8	(0.6)	0.0	c	12.3	(2.5)
Guanajuato	84.9	(2.6)	13.1	(2.2)	1.9	(0.7)	98.6	(0.5)	1.2	(0.6)	0.2	(0.2)	99.2	(0.4)	0.7	(0.3)	0.1	(0.1)	16.2	(2.7)
Guerrero	76.8	(2.7)	19.7	(2.2)	3.5	(0.8)	95.5	(1.2)	3.2	(0.9)	1.3	(0.5)	97.3	(1.2)	2.2	(1.1)	0.6	(0.3)	26.0	(2.8)
Hidalgo	82.6	(3.0)	14.5	(2.6)	3.0	(0.7)	97.3	(0.9)	2.3	(0.8)	0.3	(0.3)	98.4	(0.5)	1.6	(0.5)	0.0	c	20.1	(3.3)
Jalisco	87.4	(2.1)	11.0	(1.8)	1.6	(0.4)	97.0	(0.7)	2.8	(0.7)	0.2	(0.2)	98.2	(0.5)	1.6	(0.5)	0.2	(0.0)	15.5	(2.0)
Mexico	90.5	(2.2)	9.3	(2.1)	0.2	(0.2)	93.5	(2.0)	6.2	(1.8)	0.3	(0.2)	99.2	(0.3)	0.7	(0.4)	0.1	(0.1)	15.1	(2.9)
Morelos	94.6	(1.1)	5.1	(1.0)	0.3	(0.2)	97.6	(0.7)	2.2	(0.6)	0.1	(0.1)	99.2	(0.4)	0.7	(0.4)	0.1	(0.1)	7.7	(1.5)
Nayarit	92.8	(1.7)	6.6	(1.7)	0.6	(0.3)	97.4	(0.8)	2.2	(0.8)	0.4	(0.2)	98.7	(0.6)	1.1	(0.5)	0.2	(0.2)	8.7	(2.0)
Nuevo León	92.2	(1.8)	7.2	(1.8)	0.6	(0.2)	98.9	(0.5)	1.1	(0.5)	0.0	c	98.2	(0.4)	1.8	(0.4)	0.0	(0.0)	9.7	(1.9)
Puebla	85.8	(2.6)	11.2	(1.9)	3.0	(1.0)	98.7	(0.4)	1.3	(0.4)	0.0	c	99.7	(0.2)	0.3	(0.2)	0.0	c	15.3	(2.7)
Querétaro	88.8	(2.6)	9.6	(1.9)	1.5	(0.9)	95.3	(1.5)	4.6	(1.4)	0.1	(0.2)	99.5	(0.2)	0.5	(0.2)	0.0	c	15.0	(3.2)
Quintana Roo	81.2	(2.0)	15.1	(1.6)	3.7	(1.0)	96.6	(0.7)	3.3	(0.7)	0.2	(0.1)	98.1	(0.6)	1.8	(0.6)	0.1	(0.1)	21.2	(2.0)
San Luis Potosí	84.0	(2.8)	14.4	(2.5)	1.6	(0.8)	96.4	(0.8)	2.7	(0.7)	0.9	(0.5)	99.6	(0.3)	0.4	(0.3)	0.0	c	18.0	(2.8)
Sinaloa	87.5	(1.9)	11.6	(1.7)	0.9	(0.2)	96.0	(1.0)	3.9	(1.1)	0.1	(0.1)	99.3	(0.3)	0.7	(0.3)	0.0	c	15.6	(2.1)
Tabasco	85.2	(1.9)	13.4	(1.8)	1.5	(0.4)	96.4	(1.2)	3.2	(0.9)	0.4	(0.4)	99.3	(0.4)	0.7	(0.4)	0.0	c	17.2	(2.4)
Tamaulipas	92.3	(1.8)	7.3	(1.7)	0.4	(0.4)	97.2	(0.4)	2.1	(0.6)	0.6	(0.5)	99.1	(0.4)	0.7	(0.3)	0.1	(0.1)	10.2	(1.8)
Tlaxcala	93.5	(1.0)	6.3	(1.0)	0.2	(0.1)	97.7	(0.5)	2.3	(0.5)	0.0	c	99.7	(0.2)	0.3	(0.2)	0.0	c	8.6	(0.9)
Veracruz	77.1	(2.1)	20.6	(1.9)	2.2	(0.3)	96.4	(1.1)	3.4	(1.0)	0.2	(0.2)	99.5	(0.3)	0.5	(0.3)	0.0	c	25.0	(2.5)
Yucatán	73.3	(2.6)	24.2	(2.4)	2.5	(0.7)	95.3	(0.8)	4.3	(0.6)	0.3	(0.2)	97.7	(0.6)	2.1	(0.6)	0.1	(0.1)	29.4	(2.2)
Zacatecas	87.2	(1.6)	11.8	(1.3)	1.0	(0.4)	96.0	(0.9)	4.0	(0.9)	0.0	c	99.4	(0.3)	0.6	(0.3)	0.0	c	15.9	(1.7)

• PISA adjudicated region.
Note: See Table IV.2.2 for national data.
StatLink http://dx.doi.org/10.1787/888932957536

[Part 2/2]
Grade repetition, by region
Table B2.IV.1   *Results based on students' self-reports*

	Percentage of students reporting that they have repeated a grade in:									Primary, lower secondary or upper secondary school	
	Primary school			Lower secondary school			Upper secondary school				
	Never	Once	Twice or more	Never	Once	Twice or more	Never	Once	Twice or more		
	% S.E.	% S.E.	% S.E.	% S.E.	% S.E.	% S.E.	% S.E.	% S.E.	% S.E.	%	S.E.
Portugal											
Alentejo	79.1 (4.3)	15.5 (3.2)	5.4 (1.2)	83.3 (3.5)	15.0 (3.0)	1.8 (0.8)	100.0 c	0.0 c	0.0 c	29.9	(5.5)
Spain											
Andalusia●	83.9 (1.4)	14.8 (1.2)	1.2 (0.4)	69.1 (1.6)	27.3 (1.4)	3.7 (0.8)	100.0 c	0.0 c	0.0 c	36.7	(1.4)
Aragon●	83.6 (1.4)	15.4 (1.4)	1.1 (0.2)	69.4 (1.7)	27.9 (1.4)	2.7 (0.6)	100.0 c	0.0 c	0.0 c	36.1	(1.9)
Asturias●	88.9 (1.0)	10.6 (1.0)	0.5 (0.2)	76.6 (1.5)	22.4 (1.4)	0.9 (0.3)	c c	c c	c c	27.4	(1.5)
Balearic Islands●	79.2 (1.4)	19.6 (1.4)	1.1 (0.3)	69.1 (1.7)	28.1 (1.5)	2.8 (0.6)	c c	c c	c c	39.1	(1.8)
Basque Country●	90.9 (0.6)	8.5 (0.5)	0.6 (0.1)	84.0 (0.7)	15.0 (0.7)	1.0 (0.2)	100.0 c	0.0 c	0.0 c	20.8	(0.9)
Cantabria●	86.3 (1.2)	13.1 (1.1)	0.6 (0.2)	72.4 (1.8)	26.2 (1.6)	1.4 (0.3)	100.0 c	0.0 c	0.0 c	32.3	(1.9)
Castile and Leon●	86.7 (1.1)	12.3 (0.9)	1.0 (0.3)	69.7 (1.8)	27.5 (1.6)	2.8 (0.5)	100.0 c	0.0 c	0.0 c	34.5	(1.7)
Catalonia●	93.6 (1.0)	6.0 (1.0)	0.3 (0.1)	83.0 (1.9)	16.3 (1.9)	0.7 (0.2)	c c	c c	c c	20.6	(2.0)
Extremadura●	82.1 (1.4)	16.4 (1.4)	1.4 (0.4)	61.5 (1.6)	34.1 (1.5)	4.4 (0.6)	c c	c c	c c	42.9	(1.6)
Galicia●	86.8 (1.2)	12.1 (1.1)	1.1 (0.2)	71.8 (1.8)	25.5 (1.5)	2.8 (0.5)	100.0 c	0.0 c	0.0 c	33.0	(1.9)
La Rioja●	90.1 (0.7)	9.0 (0.8)	0.9 (0.3)	68.9 (0.7)	27.9 (0.8)	3.2 (0.5)	c c	c c	c c	34.0	(0.6)
Madrid●	86.9 (1.3)	12.6 (1.3)	0.6 (0.2)	71.6 (1.5)	25.8 (1.4)	2.7 (0.4)	100.0 c	0.0 c	0.0 c	32.4	(1.6)
Murcia●	77.3 (1.3)	21.6 (1.2)	1.1 (0.3)	64.5 (1.3)	32.2 (1.1)	3.3 (0.7)	100.0 c	0.0 c	0.0 c	42.5	(1.3)
Navarre●	88.4 (0.9)	11.3 (0.9)	0.3 (0.2)	80.1 (1.3)	19.1 (1.2)	0.7 (0.2)	c c	c c	c c	25.3	(1.2)
United Kingdom											
England	98.0 (0.3)	1.9 (0.2)	0.1 (0.1)	99.2 (0.1)	0.7 (0.1)	0.1 (0.0)	99.4 (0.1)	0.4 (0.1)	0.1 (0.1)	2.7	(0.3)
Northern Ireland	98.2 (0.3)	1.6 (0.4)	0.2 (0.2)	99.0 (0.3)	0.8 (0.2)	0.2 (0.1)	99.1 (0.2)	0.8 (0.2)	0.1 (0.1)	2.7	(0.5)
Scotland●	98.2 (0.2)	1.6 (0.2)	0.2 (0.1)	99.1 (0.2)	0.6 (0.1)	0.2 (0.1)	99.2 (0.2)	0.6 (0.2)	0.2 (0.1)	2.8	(0.3)
Wales	98.0 (0.1)	1.8 (0.3)	0.2 (0.1)	99.2 (0.2)	0.6 (0.1)	0.2 (0.1)	99.4 (0.2)	0.4 (0.1)	0.2 (0.1)	2.7	(0.3)
United States											
Connecticut●	90.6 (1.0)	9.0 (0.9)	0.4 (0.2)	96.3 (0.6)	3.6 (0.6)	0.1 (0.1)	98.4 (0.3)	1.6 (0.3)	0.1 (0.1)	11.4	(1.2)
Florida●	80.9 (1.2)	17.8 (1.0)	1.3 (0.3)	94.3 (0.6)	5.4 (0.5)	0.3 (0.2)	98.0 (0.3)	2.0 (0.3)	0.0 c	22.0	(1.1)
Massachusetts●	95.5 (0.6)	4.4 (0.6)	0.1 (0.1)	96.4 (0.6)	3.5 (0.5)	0.2 (0.1)	98.1 (0.4)	1.8 (0.4)	0.1 (0.1)	6.6	(0.7)
Argentina											
Ciudad Autónoma de Buenos Aires●	88.7 (1.6)	9.4 (1.4)	1.9 (0.5)	80.4 (2.2)	17.4 (1.9)	2.1 (0.6)	97.9 (0.5)	1.5 (0.5)	0.6 (0.3)	25.4	(2.8)
Brazil											
Acre	69.8 (3.4)	26.7 (2.7)	3.5 (1.0)	90.1 (2.0)	8.6 (1.5)	1.3 (0.6)	96.4 (1.4)	3.6 (1.4)	0.0 c	35.7	(3.5)
Alagoas	63.3 (3.1)	26.0 (1.8)	10.7 (2.4)	75.1 (3.9)	17.1 (2.0)	7.7 (2.4)	93.5 (1.3)	6.5 (1.3)	0.0 c	50.1	(3.7)
Amapá	69.0 (4.2)	25.1 (2.6)	5.9 (1.9)	86.6 (2.6)	11.6 (2.1)	1.7 (0.7)	95.7 (1.1)	4.3 (1.1)	0.0 c	37.3	(3.7)
Amazonas	70.7 (3.0)	23.2 (2.5)	6.1 (0.9)	77.1 (3.2)	17.6 (2.7)	5.3 (1.2)	94.5 (1.6)	4.1 (1.0)	1.4 (0.8)	42.7	(3.8)
Bahia	67.7 (3.9)	24.9 (2.9)	7.5 (2.2)	77.5 (5.8)	20.2 (5.4)	2.4 (1.1)	95.4 (1.6)	4.4 (1.5)	0.2 (0.2)	46.3	(4.6)
Ceará	76.2 (3.5)	20.7 (3.4)	3.1 (0.7)	83.4 (2.3)	12.7 (1.9)	3.9 (0.9)	92.9 (1.5)	6.8 (1.4)	0.3 (0.3)	36.4	(4.0)
Espírito Santo	85.2 (2.3)	11.5 (2.3)	3.3 (0.8)	79.0 (2.8)	15.5 (2.4)	5.5 (1.3)	87.8 (1.9)	12.2 (1.9)	0.0 c	36.0	(3.0)
Federal District	77.5 (3.6)	15.0 (2.2)	7.5 (2.2)	79.9 (2.0)	15.1 (1.6)	5.0 (0.7)	92.7 (1.1)	7.1 (1.0)	0.2 (0.2)	37.9	(3.2)
Goiás	80.3 (3.7)	13.4 (2.3)	6.3 (2.5)	79.0 (3.7)	14.9 (2.6)	6.1 (1.4)	93.1 (1.2)	6.4 (1.3)	0.5 (0.3)	37.0	(4.7)
Maranhão	75.0 (3.7)	21.0 (3.3)	3.9 (1.5)	78.1 (4.2)	17.7 (3.7)	4.1 (1.3)	91.9 (1.9)	7.6 (1.8)	0.5 (0.4)	39.9	(4.5)
Mato Grosso	74.1 (3.0)	20.8 (2.5)	5.2 (1.5)	85.2 (2.8)	11.7 (1.7)	3.1 (1.4)	89.7 (1.5)	10.1 (1.5)	0.2 (0.2)	37.5	(3.2)
Mato Grosso do Sul	77.2 (3.1)	15.9 (2.1)	6.9 (1.3)	74.1 (3.3)	17.1 (1.6)	8.8 (2.0)	88.3 (1.8)	11.7 (1.8)	0.0 c	43.7	(3.7)
Minas Gerais	78.6 (3.1)	16.2 (2.6)	5.2 (1.3)	78.4 (3.2)	16.4 (2.1)	5.2 (1.4)	95.9 (1.0)	3.9 (1.0)	0.2 (0.2)	36.9	(4.1)
Pará	67.4 (4.0)	25.0 (2.9)	7.6 (1.6)	74.6 (2.8)	19.4 (2.4)	5.9 (1.6)	97.1 (0.8)	2.9 (0.8)	0.0 c	44.7	(4.1)
Paraíba	80.4 (2.2)	15.5 (1.8)	4.1 (0.9)	79.1 (3.1)	15.3 (2.3)	5.6 (1.2)	92.5 (1.3)	7.3 (1.3)	0.2 (0.2)	36.7	(2.6)
Paraná	76.2 (3.0)	18.1 (2.0)	5.7 (1.2)	76.6 (2.8)	15.3 (2.2)	8.1 (1.5)	88.8 (1.9)	11.0 (2.0)	0.2 (0.2)	42.0	(3.4)
Pernambuco	67.7 (2.3)	26.4 (2.2)	5.9 (1.5)	77.8 (1.9)	17.3 (2.0)	4.9 (1.0)	93.6 (1.0)	6.1 (1.1)	0.3 (0.3)	45.8	(2.7)
Piauí	75.4 (2.7)	20.6 (2.6)	4.0 (1.0)	75.4 (2.8)	20.5 (2.5)	4.1 (0.8)	93.6 (0.9)	6.4 (0.9)	0.0 c	41.4	(2.8)
Rio de Janeiro	86.0 (2.9)	11.1 (2.4)	2.8 (0.8)	78.3 (3.5)	16.5 (3.0)	5.2 (1.6)	92.8 (1.1)	6.7 (1.2)	0.5 (0.4)	32.4	(4.1)
Rio Grande do Norte	70.1 (3.3)	22.3 (2.5)	7.6 (1.6)	68.7 (4.2)	19.6 (2.2)	11.8 (2.4)	92.5 (1.4)	6.2 (1.5)	1.3 (0.7)	49.2	(4.4)
Rio Grande do Sul	78.4 (3.5)	13.9 (1.9)	7.7 (1.9)	76.6 (3.6)	15.2 (1.5)	8.2 (2.6)	87.2 (2.3)	12.5 (2.3)	0.2 (0.2)	40.5	(3.4)
Rondônia	73.2 (2.8)	20.2 (2.2)	6.5 (1.2)	66.6 (3.9)	23.0 (2.9)	10.4 (1.5)	92.1 (1.2)	7.9 (1.2)	0.0 c	48.3	(3.5)
Roraima	71.2 (4.2)	20.6 (3.4)	8.2 (1.4)	73.6 (1.8)	18.7 (1.5)	7.7 (1.0)	91.2 (1.7)	8.0 (1.6)	0.8 (0.5)	45.8	(3.3)
Santa Catarina	79.7 (3.4)	13.8 (2.2)	6.4 (1.5)	80.0 (2.4)	15.7 (2.2)	4.3 (0.9)	93.1 (1.2)	6.3 (1.2)	0.5 (0.3)	35.1	(3.7)
São Paulo	87.5 (1.3)	10.1 (0.9)	2.4 (0.7)	87.7 (1.3)	9.3 (0.9)	3.0 (0.6)	91.7 (1.0)	7.8 (1.0)	0.4 (0.2)	25.9	(2.0)
Sergipe	72.5 (4.4)	18.2 (2.5)	9.4 (2.6)	67.8 (4.8)	21.2 (3.2)	11.0 (2.2)	93.0 (1.8)	7.0 (1.8)	0.0 c	49.4	(5.1)
Tocantins	79.0 (2.4)	16.5 (1.7)	4.6 (1.5)	78.9 (2.9)	15.2 (2.2)	5.9 (1.4)	89.4 (1.6)	9.0 (1.6)	1.7 (0.5)	36.4	(3.1)
Colombia											
Bogota	83.9 (1.2)	13.9 (1.2)	2.2 (0.5)	71.3 (1.8)	21.3 (1.4)	7.4 (0.8)	94.2 (0.8)	5.4 (0.8)	0.4 (0.2)	37.4	(1.7)
Cali	79.2 (1.9)	17.4 (1.7)	3.3 (0.6)	75.1 (1.6)	21.1 (1.3)	3.9 (0.6)	97.7 (0.6)	2.2 (0.6)	0.1 (0.1)	35.8	(2.0)
Manizales	77.4 (1.5)	17.9 (1.5)	4.7 (0.8)	71.8 (1.5)	21.5 (1.5)	6.8 (0.9)	94.2 (0.8)	5.8 (0.8)	0.0 c	41.0	(1.7)
Medellin	81.9 (2.3)	14.2 (1.9)	3.9 (0.8)	70.9 (2.3)	21.8 (1.9)	7.4 (1.1)	95.6 (0.7)	4.0 (0.6)	0.4 (0.3)	38.4	(2.5)
Russian Federation											
Perm Territory region●	97.3 (0.5)	2.6 (0.5)	0.1 (0.1)	98.4 (0.3)	1.0 (0.3)	0.6 (0.2)	100.0 c	0.0 c	0.0 c	3.8	(0.7)
United Arab Emirates											
Abu Dhabi●	91.1 (0.7)	7.9 (0.7)	1.0 (0.2)	92.4 (0.7)	6.4 (0.6)	1.3 (0.2)	98.2 (0.3)	1.4 (0.3)	0.4 (0.1)	13.3	(0.9)
Ajman	88.7 (4.6)	9.6 (3.8)	1.7 (0.8)	92.5 (3.5)	6.9 (3.3)	0.6 (0.3)	97.9 (0.8)	1.8 (0.7)	0.3 (0.2)	15.6	(6.5)
Dubai●	94.1 (0.3)	5.2 (0.3)	0.7 (0.1)	95.1 (0.3)	4.5 (0.2)	0.4 (0.1)	98.8 (0.2)	1.1 (0.2)	0.1 (0.1)	9.8	(0.4)
Fujairah	88.8 (1.7)	10.1 (1.5)	1.1 (0.5)	94.3 (1.3)	4.3 (1.0)	1.4 (0.5)	98.0 (0.9)	1.2 (0.7)	0.7 (0.4)	13.9	(2.1)
Ras Al Khaimah	91.7 (2.1)	7.0 (1.9)	1.3 (0.4)	92.2 (2.7)	6.6 (2.3)	1.3 (0.4)	98.0 (0.4)	1.7 (0.5)	0.3 (0.2)	14.3	(3.3)
Sharjah	93.0 (2.4)	6.2 (2.1)	0.8 (0.4)	96.7 (1.4)	2.9 (1.2)	0.4 (0.3)	98.4 (0.4)	1.4 (0.3)	0.2 (0.2)	9.7	(3.1)
Umm Al Quwain	82.7 (1.6)	13.7 (1.5)	3.6 (0.9)	85.9 (1.4)	11.3 (1.5)	2.8 (0.6)	98.0 (0.9)	1.7 (0.9)	0.3 (0.3)	23.9	(1.5)

● PISA adjudicated region.
Note: See Table IV.2.2 for national data.
StatLink ⫘ http://dx.doi.org/10.1787/888932957536

[Part 1/6]
School admissions policies, by region
Table B2.IV.2 · *Results based on school principals' reports*

	Residence in a particular area						Students' records of academic performance						Recommendations of feeder schools					
	Never		Sometimes		Always		Never		Sometimes		Always		Never		Sometimes		Always	
	%	S.E.	%	S.E.	%	S.E.	%	S.E.	%	S.E.	%	S.E.	%	S.E.	%	S.E.	%	S.E.
Australia																		
Australian Capital Territory	24.9	(0.8)	22.3	(0.8)	52.8	(0.9)	33.2	(0.9)	42.3	(1.1)	24.5	(0.9)	43.8	(1.1)	38.6	(1.2)	17.6	(0.8)
New South Wales	28.8	(2.9)	17.4	(2.9)	53.8	(2.8)	26.3	(3.6)	32.5	(3.1)	41.2	(3.6)	18.1	(3.1)	39.9	(4.4)	42.1	(3.8)
Northern Territory	54.3	(3.4)	6.0	(0.7)	39.7	(3.0)	31.3	(5.5)	44.8	(9.8)	23.9	(8.9)	24.5	(5.9)	52.4	(9.9)	23.2	(8.8)
Queensland	49.1	(3.7)	24.1	(3.8)	26.8	(3.4)	28.3	(3.7)	41.5	(3.9)	30.3	(4.0)	28.0	(3.2)	47.1	(4.1)	24.9	(3.6)
South Australia	36.3	(4.1)	22.7	(4.0)	41.0	(3.0)	30.9	(4.0)	40.7	(4.9)	28.3	(4.8)	24.0	(4.4)	41.8	(5.3)	34.2	(4.7)
Tasmania	32.9	(1.1)	13.5	(0.9)	53.6	(1.3)	64.0	(2.1)	16.3	(1.3)	19.8	(1.8)	31.2	(1.9)	40.3	(1.7)	28.6	(1.5)
Victoria	29.1	(3.4)	22.2	(3.4)	48.8	(3.9)	19.4	(3.6)	52.0	(4.9)	28.6	(3.6)	21.3	(3.1)	47.7	(4.1)	31.0	(3.8)
Western Australia	44.2	(3.9)	13.8	(3.1)	42.1	(3.6)	28.0	(4.4)	40.9	(4.2)	31.0	(4.2)	28.8	(4.8)	42.7	(5.0)	28.6	(4.2)
Belgium																		
Flemish community*	91.9	(2.6)	6.5	(2.3)	1.5	(1.2)	36.7	(3.6)	30.9	(3.8)	32.4	(3.7)	48.6	(3.8)	42.8	(4.0)	8.7	(2.2)
French community	69.0	(4.7)	29.7	(4.6)	1.4	(0.8)	57.3	(4.8)	26.6	(4.3)	16.2	(3.2)	66.6	(4.2)	31.4	(4.2)	2.0	(1.4)
German-speaking community	71.1	(0.3)	27.6	(0.2)	1.3	(0.3)	20.3	(0.2)	42.5	(0.3)	37.2	(0.2)	34.5	(0.3)	52.1	(0.3)	13.3	(0.2)
Canada																		
Alberta	18.8	(4.3)	20.0	(4.2)	61.1	(5.0)	40.9	(6.0)	39.0	(5.3)	20.1	(4.5)	30.3	(4.9)	43.8	(5.4)	25.9	(4.9)
British Columbia	26.4	(4.2)	9.7	(3.7)	63.9	(4.7)	47.4	(5.8)	34.1	(5.8)	18.5	(4.7)	34.7	(5.8)	39.5	(6.1)	25.8	(5.8)
Manitoba	10.8	(2.3)	15.7	(2.8)	73.5	(3.0)	38.9	(2.8)	44.0	(3.1)	17.1	(2.1)	27.8	(3.2)	48.1	(3.3)	24.1	(2.2)
New Brunswick	15.2	(3.4)	17.9	(1.3)	66.9	(3.0)	69.5	(3.1)	19.3	(1.6)	11.1	(3.3)	58.0	(2.9)	27.1	(1.7)	14.9	(3.2)
Newfoundland and Labrador	43.6	(3.0)	5.4	(0.3)	51.1	(2.8)	69.0	(4.3)	4.2	(0.7)	26.8	(4.3)	49.7	(4.5)	23.1	(1.9)	27.3	(3.7)
Nova Scotia	22.6	(11.3)	4.7	(1.3)	72.6	(10.6)	47.2	(8.0)	20.6	(4.5)	32.2	(10.2)	40.9	(7.6)	24.2	(5.3)	34.9	(9.6)
Ontario	8.0	(2.7)	5.3	(2.3)	86.7	(3.5)	41.6	(5.4)	30.1	(4.5)	28.3	(4.2)	31.8	(5.4)	28.7	(4.4)	39.5	(5.5)
Prince Edward Island	30.7	(0.4)	3.8	(0.1)	65.5	(0.4)	62.4	(0.4)	4.9	(0.2)	32.7	(0.4)	32.0	(0.5)	24.2	(0.4)	43.9	(0.4)
Quebec	26.0	(3.6)	22.3	(3.4)	51.7	(4.0)	32.9	(4.3)	32.2	(3.9)	34.9	(2.7)	38.1	(4.5)	42.9	(4.3)	19.0	(3.2)
Saskatchewan	38.1	(3.3)	32.5	(2.4)	29.4	(3.6)	45.9	(3.4)	34.8	(2.2)	19.3	(2.6)	36.2	(3.8)	37.7	(2.8)	26.1	(2.8)
Italy																		
Abruzzo	41.4	(6.2)	32.3	(6.1)	26.3	(5.7)	13.6	(4.8)	12.4	(4.8)	74.0	(6.2)	18.2	(4.4)	31.0	(5.6)	50.7	(6.4)
Basilicata	39.1	(6.1)	38.6	(5.3)	22.2	(5.3)	23.4	(4.3)	22.0	(4.4)	54.6	(5.0)	25.8	(5.3)	36.9	(5.1)	37.3	(4.5)
Bolzano	62.0	(0.8)	25.8	(0.7)	12.2	(1.3)	69.9	(1.0)	14.8	(0.5)	15.4	(1.1)	77.0	(0.6)	13.8	(0.4)	9.1	(0.4)
Calabria	27.1	(8.0)	35.9	(7.9)	37.0	(6.7)	24.9	(6.0)	25.8	(5.5)	49.3	(6.9)	28.1	(7.7)	34.9	(6.3)	36.9	(8.6)
Campania	44.2	(9.4)	27.8	(9.4)	28.0	(6.8)	20.3	(5.8)	23.4	(6.6)	56.3	(9.1)	29.8	(6.1)	32.8	(7.3)	37.4	(9.0)
Emilia Romagna	45.7	(7.3)	26.3	(7.3)	28.0	(6.6)	19.6	(6.9)	17.7	(6.5)	62.6	(8.7)	12.1	(5.6)	13.4	(4.7)	74.5	(6.4)
Friuli Venezia Giulia	38.0	(5.8)	31.7	(4.6)	30.4	(5.9)	10.7	(4.2)	31.0	(5.9)	58.3	(6.7)	12.3	(4.6)	25.0	(4.9)	62.7	(5.1)
Lazio	34.0	(8.7)	25.6	(7.1)	40.4	(6.8)	17.6	(6.1)	12.1	(3.6)	70.3	(6.8)	21.9	(6.8)	36.2	(6.8)	41.9	(6.7)
Liguria	37.2	(5.7)	43.5	(6.5)	19.2	(5.6)	23.3	(6.4)	22.6	(5.5)	54.1	(6.9)	17.5	(4.1)	46.3	(6.3)	36.2	(6.5)
Lombardia	23.2	(6.7)	43.3	(7.7)	33.4	(5.4)	25.4	(5.8)	27.7	(7.5)	46.9	(7.6)	18.2	(5.7)	19.9	(7.4)	62.0	(7.7)
Marche	42.4	(7.3)	36.8	(6.8)	20.8	(5.6)	17.1	(4.2)	27.1	(5.2)	55.8	(6.6)	13.8	(2.9)	35.1	(6.1)	51.1	(6.3)
Molise	41.5	(0.9)	29.2	(0.8)	29.3	(0.8)	7.9	(0.6)	31.8	(0.9)	60.3	(0.9)	20.0	(0.9)	44.8	(1.0)	35.2	(0.9)
Piemonte	36.8	(6.2)	46.4	(6.6)	16.8	(5.6)	29.8	(9.3)	22.6	(6.8)	47.6	(8.6)	15.2	(5.1)	34.0	(6.9)	50.7	(8.4)
Puglia	32.1	(5.7)	39.3	(5.7)	28.7	(6.3)	17.8	(5.4)	24.7	(6.4)	57.5	(7.8)	24.9	(6.5)	38.2	(7.2)	36.9	(5.2)
Sardegna	33.9	(6.6)	34.6	(7.7)	31.5	(7.0)	26.5	(5.5)	10.0	(4.2)	63.4	(6.5)	31.1	(5.8)	29.8	(7.7)	39.1	(6.6)
Sicilia	40.8	(7.0)	34.3	(6.6)	24.9	(4.8)	23.6	(5.1)	19.2	(6.1)	57.1	(6.2)	20.2	(5.0)	36.1	(6.9)	43.6	(7.7)
Toscana	36.5	(6.1)	39.6	(6.3)	23.9	(7.0)	26.2	(6.7)	22.9	(5.5)	50.9	(7.9)	19.1	(6.1)	29.9	(8.0)	51.0	(8.2)
Trento	38.1	(4.3)	34.5	(4.3)	27.4	(4.6)	31.7	(3.8)	28.1	(4.7)	40.2	(4.1)	12.8	(2.9)	31.2	(4.1)	56.0	(4.9)
Umbria	31.7	(5.7)	40.4	(6.1)	27.9	(6.4)	11.1	(4.2)	32.1	(5.6)	56.8	(5.2)	9.0	(2.9)	41.6	(5.4)	49.3	(5.3)
Valle d'Aosta	56.0	(1.1)	35.2	(1.0)	8.7	(0.6)	51.1	(0.9)	11.9	(0.6)	36.9	(0.9)	22.7	(0.8)	53.4	(0.8)	24.0	(0.9)
Veneto	45.1	(7.4)	42.9	(7.5)	12.0	(4.5)	13.1	(4.8)	17.7	(6.2)	69.2	(6.4)	12.5	(5.4)	31.1	(7.5)	56.4	(8.4)
Mexico																		
Aguascalientes	55.8	(5.3)	27.3	(6.8)	17.0	(4.9)	14.0	(5.2)	19.9	(6.7)	66.1	(6.8)	30.9	(5.7)	58.0	(6.5)	11.1	(4.7)
Baja California	43.9	(8.4)	29.1	(9.1)	27.0	(4.8)	22.7	(12.2)	30.7	(14.1)	46.6	(7.0)	40.7	(11.0)	53.9	(11.3)	5.5	(2.8)
Baja California Sur	47.8	(5.7)	27.2	(7.9)	24.9	(7.9)	35.9	(8.8)	13.7	(4.9)	50.3	(7.7)	57.2	(9.3)	30.5	(7.8)	12.3	(5.0)
Campeche	69.9	(7.9)	28.1	(7.6)	2.0	(2.0)	41.3	(7.0)	15.7	(7.6)	43.0	(9.0)	66.1	(8.1)	13.8	(7.7)	20.1	(4.9)
Chiapas	81.4	(8.0)	14.2	(7.6)	4.4	(3.1)	29.9	(7.2)	33.4	(6.0)	36.7	(8.9)	65.2	(8.8)	18.0	(6.6)	16.8	(6.4)
Chihuahua	49.2	(10.9)	45.8	(11.5)	5.0	(3.6)	25.3	(8.0)	34.3	(9.6)	40.4	(6.5)	51.3	(11.5)	36.3	(9.3)	12.4	(7.0)
Coahuila	75.7	(8.5)	16.0	(6.7)	8.3	(6.0)	20.0	(6.2)	19.4	(9.5)	60.5	(9.3)	52.6	(9.5)	25.9	(8.3)	21.5	(7.6)
Colima	63.3	(5.9)	21.9	(6.1)	14.8	(5.6)	19.8	(4.9)	23.0	(6.3)	57.2	(6.2)	80.5	(5.3)	16.6	(5.2)	2.8	(2.0)
Distrito Federal	59.3	(9.0)	32.4	(10.1)	8.3	(6.9)	37.8	(8.4)	24.0	(8.0)	38.2	(8.1)	69.0	(8.7)	22.3	(6.8)	8.7	(5.4)
Durango	66.5	(9.7)	14.6	(3.3)	18.9	(10.7)	17.4	(6.5)	23.8	(8.2)	58.9	(7.9)	53.9	(9.2)	32.8	(7.8)	13.3	(6.3)
Guanajuato	70.1	(6.8)	28.0	(7.0)	1.9	(1.8)	36.8	(6.5)	7.6	(2.6)	55.7	(6.7)	61.4	(9.0)	24.3	(7.7)	14.3	(5.8)
Guerrero	60.7	(9.8)	31.5	(8.5)	7.8	(5.7)	30.5	(8.8)	24.8	(7.8)	44.8	(7.4)	56.9	(8.7)	28.7	(9.0)	14.4	(5.0)
Hidalgo	80.4	(5.5)	13.9	(4.8)	5.7	(2.8)	26.4	(6.4)	15.3	(5.2)	58.3	(7.1)	66.6	(8.5)	26.1	(7.6)	7.3	(4.0)
Jalisco	54.9	(7.7)	37.3	(8.1)	7.8	(3.8)	41.4	(7.6)	8.6	(4.3)	50.0	(6.5)	77.1	(6.1)	14.0	(2.7)	8.9	(5.0)
Mexico	72.8	(7.8)	22.4	(7.0)	4.8	(3.7)	31.3	(8.0)	22.7	(6.4)	46.1	(8.2)	79.6	(5.0)	16.6	(6.0)	3.8	(2.8)
Morelos	63.5	(5.0)	19.7	(4.9)	16.8	(5.4)	22.8	(7.2)	20.0	(7.0)	57.1	(8.1)	50.6	(9.4)	21.7	(6.9)	27.7	(8.4)
Nayarit	58.2	(5.8)	24.1	(5.3)	17.6	(6.0)	32.3	(4.5)	14.1	(3.6)	53.6	(5.8)	55.2	(6.6)	36.9	(6.9)	7.8	(3.3)
Nuevo León	63.5	(9.0)	23.1	(8.3)	13.4	(5.2)	36.5	(9.7)	8.2	(4.0)	55.2	(9.5)	62.1	(10.2)	27.7	(7.7)	10.2	(6.6)
Puebla	74.5	(7.7)	22.4	(7.2)	3.1	(3.0)	33.4	(6.1)	26.9	(6.5)	39.7	(4.2)	59.6	(7.8)	23.3	(6.9)	17.1	(4.6)
Querétaro	40.2	(10.8)	31.1	(10.3)	28.8	(6.6)	26.6	(8.7)	13.7	(3.2)	59.7	(10.0)	70.3	(8.3)	19.2	(7.5)	10.5	(3.1)
Quintana Roo	55.7	(8.2)	24.9	(8.8)	19.4	(7.5)	24.3	(4.0)	27.8	(4.6)	47.9	(7.0)	40.6	(7.6)	46.5	(7.0)	13.0	(4.7)
San Luis Potosí	74.4	(5.6)	10.2	(5.4)	15.5	(2.9)	39.2	(9.9)	13.5	(5.5)	47.3	(11.0)	60.3	(8.4)	33.8	(8.2)	5.8	(2.0)
Sinaloa	64.2	(9.0)	22.8	(7.4)	13.0	(5.3)	24.6	(7.4)	21.7	(7.1)	53.7	(8.1)	42.6	(9.4)	37.7	(6.8)	19.7	(6.8)
Tabasco	51.3	(9.9)	42.5	(9.2)	6.2	(3.7)	28.9	(8.9)	25.3	(8.6)	45.8	(8.3)	64.2	(9.1)	22.8	(8.5)	13.0	(5.7)
Tamaulipas	67.2	(11.8)	21.5	(10.1)	11.3	(7.3)	13.7	(5.7)	26.1	(6.5)	60.2	(7.8)	43.0	(11.2)	37.1	(11.1)	19.9	(7.9)
Tlaxcala	63.2	(6.0)	31.1	(6.2)	5.7	(2.4)	34.0	(6.3)	12.0	(5.0)	54.1	(7.5)	67.4	(6.1)	24.3	(5.4)	8.3	(3.9)
Veracruz	70.1	(6.7)	21.9	(4.3)	8.0	(5.5)	49.5	(9.2)	21.5	(8.0)	29.0	(5.4)	74.7	(6.7)	15.0	(6.4)	10.3	(3.2)
Yucatán	64.8	(9.7)	15.5	(5.7)	19.8	(8.8)	23.3	(7.1)	26.8	(9.5)	49.9	(10.2)	87.0	(4.8)	9.1	(2.8)	3.9	(3.9)
Zacatecas	80.6	(5.0)	10.7	(4.4)	8.7	(3.2)	28.9	(7.8)	21.4	(6.2)	49.7	(7.2)	64.5	(6.6)	20.5	(5.0)	14.9	(5.1)

* PISA adjudicated region.
Note: See Table IV.2.7 for national data.
StatLink ᕫᕤᓬ http://dx.doi.org/10.1787/888932957536

[Part 2/6]
School admissions policies, by region
Table B2.IV.2 *Results based on school principals' reports*

Percentage of students in schools whose principal reported that the following factors are "never", "sometimes" or "always" considered for admission to school:

	Residence in a particular area						Students' records of academic performance						Recommendations of feeder schools					
	Never		Sometimes		Always		Never		Sometimes		Always		Never		Sometimes		Always	
	%	S.E.	%	S.E.	%	S.E.	%	S.E.	%	S.E.	%	S.E.	%	S.E.	%	S.E.	%	S.E.
Portugal																		
Alentejo	16.4	(9.0)	44.1	(12.3)	39.6	(10.7)	56.5	(13.1)	22.8	(10.6)	20.8	(7.7)	83.1	(6.6)	10.7	(5.6)	6.2	(4.5)
Spain																		
Andalusia•	19.5	(5.7)	12.3	(4.1)	68.1	(6.5)	94.1	(3.4)	5.9	(3.4)	0.0	c	84.8	(4.6)	7.4	(3.7)	7.8	(3.9)
Aragon•	36.3	(7.6)	19.6	(5.8)	44.2	(7.8)	95.5	(3.1)	4.5	(3.1)	0.0	c	93.4	(3.8)	4.5	(3.1)	2.1	(2.1)
Asturias•	16.3	(5.3)	26.7	(5.6)	57.0	(6.3)	91.1	(4.4)	8.9	(4.4)	0.0	c	91.9	(2.5)	8.1	(2.5)	0.0	c
Balearic Islands•	20.3	(5.3)	18.3	(5.3)	61.4	(6.5)	92.3	(3.9)	4.4	(3.1)	3.3	(2.4)	92.3	(3.6)	5.9	(3.1)	1.9	(1.9)
Basque Country•	23.8	(3.2)	22.2	(3.0)	54.0	(3.7)	82.4	(3.0)	14.0	(2.7)	3.7	(1.5)	66.0	(4.0)	22.3	(3.5)	11.7	(2.3)
Cantabria•	19.2	(4.7)	22.3	(5.2)	58.6	(5.5)	95.8	(3.0)	1.9	(2.0)	2.3	(2.2)	93.9	(3.6)	3.9	(2.8)	2.3	(2.2)
Castile and Leon•	22.8	(5.8)	25.4	(6.6)	51.8	(6.8)	93.1	(3.7)	6.0	(3.5)	1.0	(1.0)	90.0	(4.1)	10.0	(4.1)	0.0	c
Catalonia•	20.6	(6.5)	8.1	(4.1)	71.3	(7.2)	93.3	(4.0)	6.7	(4.0)	0.0	c	93.0	(2.3)	7.0	(2.3)	0.0	c
Extremadura•	35.8	(7.4)	12.3	(4.9)	51.9	(7.7)	93.7	(3.6)	4.3	(3.0)	2.0	(2.0)	94.0	(3.5)	3.9	(2.8)	2.1	(2.1)
Galicia•	24.9	(5.5)	8.9	(4.1)	66.2	(5.8)	96.8	(2.3)	0.0	c	3.2	(2.3)	94.5	(3.3)	5.5	(3.3)	0.0	c
La Rioja•	10.9	(0.3)	29.2	(0.5)	59.9	(0.6)	76.9	(0.4)	22.2	(0.4)	0.9	(0.1)	89.5	(0.3)	9.6	(0.3)	0.9	(0.1)
Madrid•	17.9	(6.1)	18.7	(5.9)	63.5	(5.8)	77.1	(6.7)	21.1	(6.4)	1.8	(1.8)	87.4	(5.1)	10.7	(4.8)	1.9	(1.9)
Murcia•	14.7	(4.8)	24.3	(5.7)	61.0	(5.7)	92.5	(3.8)	7.5	(3.8)	0.0	c	85.4	(4.6)	12.7	(4.2)	1.9	(1.9)
Navarre•	31.1	(5.0)	34.8	(5.6)	34.2	(6.5)	85.4	(3.3)	14.6	(3.3)	0.0	c	87.1	(4.5)	9.3	(3.6)	3.7	(2.6)
United Kingdom																		
England	20.4	(2.7)	31.7	(4.2)	47.9	(3.8)	68.4	(3.2)	9.1	(2.8)	22.5	(2.6)	57.8	(4.0)	22.6	(4.1)	19.6	(2.9)
Northern Ireland	29.4	(5.7)	37.1	(4.9)	33.5	(5.3)	38.9	(4.0)	8.7	(2.2)	52.3	(3.5)	43.5	(5.1)	26.9	(5.2)	29.6	(4.5)
Scotland•	22.0	(3.6)	17.2	(4.0)	60.8	(4.7)	76.4	(3.8)	4.3	(3.0)	19.4	(3.9)	59.7	(5.0)	17.1	(3.9)	23.1	(4.1)
Wales	27.5	(3.6)	26.4	(3.5)	46.1	(3.6)	74.7	(3.8)	7.1	(2.2)	18.2	(3.1)	58.3	(4.0)	19.4	(3.4)	22.4	(3.5)
United States																		
Connecticut•	28.0	(7.2)	5.7	(3.3)	66.3	(7.8)	48.7	(6.2)	0.0	c	51.3	(6.2)	48.4	(6.6)	19.1	(6.2)	32.4	(7.0)
Florida•	8.0	(3.3)	8.8	(4.1)	83.2	(5.3)	36.7	(8.0)	34.7	(7.6)	28.6	(7.1)	48.0	(7.3)	34.7	(6.7)	17.3	(5.9)
Massachusetts•	30.9	(6.1)	8.2	(4.2)	61.0	(7.4)	55.2	(8.0)	8.9	(4.1)	36.0	(7.5)	52.4	(8.6)	19.3	(5.4)	28.3	(7.7)
Argentina																		
Ciudad Autónoma de Buenos Aires•	57.6	(8.3)	19.4	(7.3)	23.0	(7.1)	33.3	(6.5)	35.0	(7.6)	31.8	(7.6)	42.0	(7.6)	39.5	(7.5)	18.5	(6.2)
Brazil																		
Acre	34.6	(13.3)	21.0	(9.0)	44.4	(13.6)	67.2	(11.0)	6.4	(4.7)	26.4	(11.1)	76.7	(8.2)	13.2	(5.1)	10.0	(6.2)
Alagoas	59.1	(9.8)	20.3	(7.2)	20.5	(9.8)	46.6	(12.5)	9.5	(6.9)	43.9	(13.1)	73.0	(10.8)	15.1	(7.9)	11.9	(7.8)
Amapá	20.4	(8.0)	36.1	(6.8)	43.5	(10.0)	49.0	(9.3)	25.5	(10.1)	25.5	(11.2)	43.9	(11.0)	41.8	(9.7)	14.3	(8.1)
Amazonas	19.9	(9.4)	31.6	(9.9)	48.5	(7.8)	67.5	(9.5)	20.2	(8.8)	12.2	(2.6)	70.6	(9.5)	23.5	(9.9)	5.9	(4.1)
Bahia	47.6	(9.8)	14.4	(9.0)	38.0	(8.9)	73.0	(13.2)	14.9	(10.6)	12.2	(7.8)	48.1	(11.3)	25.2	(11.1)	26.7	(13.3)
Ceará	34.4	(10.3)	29.4	(10.2)	36.2	(10.3)	51.1	(7.0)	20.0	(7.9)	28.9	(7.7)	77.2	(8.5)	15.7	(7.9)	7.1	(2.0)
Espírito Santo	26.3	(14.9)	31.0	(15.3)	42.6	(8.8)	92.4	(6.9)	7.6	(6.9)	0.0	c	74.8	(6.9)	19.7	(8.9)	5.6	(3.9)
Federal District	28.1	(6.8)	40.7	(9.8)	31.2	(11.0)	70.4	(10.1)	17.5	(7.6)	12.1	(6.8)	90.5	(5.8)	2.1	(2.1)	7.4	(5.2)
Goiás	36.8	(8.3)	26.0	(9.7)	37.3	(9.6)	71.6	(7.8)	1.4	(1.4)	27.0	(7.5)	65.8	(9.1)	29.5	(10.0)	4.7	(4.6)
Maranhão	32.0	(12.3)	34.4	(9.4)	33.6	(13.7)	50.3	(10.8)	14.2	(8.5)	35.5	(11.4)	57.6	(14.4)	38.5	(14.3)	3.8	(4.0)
Mato Grosso	48.3	(10.7)	39.9	(10.0)	11.8	(3.3)	55.2	(11.7)	23.8	(10.5)	21.0	(8.2)	61.4	(8.4)	26.0	(8.7)	12.6	(7.5)
Mato Grosso do Sul	23.4	(8.8)	40.6	(10.4)	36.0	(7.5)	79.2	(6.7)	6.6	(5.1)	14.2	(7.1)	67.8	(9.2)	25.4	(9.6)	6.9	(4.9)
Minas Gerais	48.2	(9.9)	16.0	(6.8)	35.9	(9.6)	70.9	(7.8)	9.5	(5.0)	19.5	(6.5)	73.4	(8.1)	19.3	(7.9)	7.3	(4.9)
Pará	32.5	(6.0)	40.9	(11.2)	26.5	(11.5)	49.7	(9.3)	36.9	(6.9)	13.4	(6.9)	69.7	(8.1)	21.3	(5.1)	9.0	(6.4)
Paraíba	46.6	(11.3)	31.1	(9.6)	22.3	(5.8)	71.6	(6.7)	13.7	(7.1)	14.7	(7.1)	65.2	(12.9)	23.4	(10.7)	11.4	(5.9)
Paraná	13.6	(8.8)	36.5	(11.0)	49.9	(8.7)	82.3	(9.5)	11.7	(8.5)	6.0	(4.4)	69.7	(10.8)	21.8	(8.0)	8.5	(8.3)
Pernambuco	33.5	(11.4)	39.9	(12.4)	26.6	(10.2)	50.8	(11.3)	5.3	(5.2)	44.0	(12.3)	69.4	(9.6)	28.5	(9.2)	2.2	(2.2)
Piauí	30.9	(9.4)	50.2	(12.0)	19.0	(6.0)	19.6	(7.7)	29.9	(9.9)	50.5	(10.0)	36.7	(13.1)	49.7	(13.6)	13.6	(5.1)
Rio de Janeiro	39.4	(9.3)	36.0	(8.7)	24.6	(9.1)	69.5	(9.2)	10.9	(4.2)	19.6	(9.2)	73.0	(9.4)	27.0	(9.4)	0.0	c
Rio Grande do Norte	36.8	(9.7)	27.2	(8.1)	36.0	(12.5)	62.0	(10.5)	23.4	(8.4)	14.6	(6.3)	67.5	(10.8)	29.1	(10.2)	3.4	(3.5)
Rio Grande do Sul	37.5	(10.8)	31.3	(11.1)	31.3	(10.1)	75.1	(8.7)	4.8	(3.5)	20.1	(8.1)	92.9	(4.9)	3.9	(3.9)	3.2	(3.1)
Rondônia	21.5	(7.0)	49.0	(11.9)	29.5	(10.2)	70.6	(9.1)	8.3	(5.8)	21.1	(7.9)	69.0	(6.9)	18.5	(5.4)	12.6	(4.4)
Roraima	17.3	(8.4)	42.6	(8.5)	40.1	(8.2)	61.7	(9.5)	20.9	(6.0)	17.4	(9.8)	70.8	(5.5)	16.1	(5.4)	13.1	(4.5)
Santa Catarina	36.9	(8.0)	34.8	(8.4)	28.4	(7.1)	91.4	(5.2)	8.6	(5.2)	0.0	c	87.1	(6.2)	10.8	(5.9)	2.0	(2.1)
São Paulo	23.6	(4.1)	21.1	(5.8)	55.2	(5.3)	78.8	(5.4)	12.1	(4.3)	9.2	(3.4)	68.9	(6.5)	25.4	(5.7)	5.7	(3.3)
Sergipe	34.1	(11.0)	40.8	(12.7)	25.0	(12.4)	45.5	(10.0)	20.5	(12.5)	33.9	(12.9)	71.3	(9.1)	20.2	(11.0)	8.5	(10.5)
Tocantins	44.1	(8.6)	44.1	(9.0)	11.8	(6.8)	33.3	(8.3)	18.1	(6.4)	48.7	(8.5)	65.3	(7.2)	24.3	(6.4)	10.5	(5.6)
Colombia																		
Bogota	47.2	(7.0)	21.2	(5.8)	31.7	(4.8)	55.0	(5.9)	20.9	(5.5)	24.1	(5.0)	76.9	(3.9)	20.6	(4.9)	2.5	(2.6)
Cali	44.8	(6.0)	30.4	(7.0)	24.9	(6.2)	26.4	(5.8)	30.7	(6.9)	42.9	(7.0)	37.3	(6.2)	41.7	(7.5)	21.0	(5.4)
Manizales	48.8	(8.2)	31.7	(6.8)	19.6	(5.0)	24.3	(6.5)	28.4	(7.4)	47.3	(8.4)	43.3	(8.9)	42.0	(8.3)	14.7	(5.3)
Medellín	52.5	(8.2)	30.2	(7.5)	17.3	(5.6)	32.1	(6.9)	36.0	(8.2)	32.0	(6.7)	49.0	(7.5)	34.6	(7.4)	16.3	(4.8)
Russian Federation																		
Perm Territory region•	23.8	(5.6)	18.0	(5.0)	58.2	(7.0)	43.4	(5.8)	37.4	(6.5)	19.2	(5.6)	43.0	(5.7)	44.8	(6.6)	12.2	(4.6)
United Arab Emirates																		
Abu Dhabi•	33.0	(3.5)	15.9	(2.9)	51.2	(3.1)	14.0	(2.9)	28.4	(3.6)	57.6	(3.4)	26.2	(3.7)	40.5	(3.7)	33.3	(3.8)
Ajman	16.2	(4.7)	28.7	(8.5)	55.2	(7.4)	0.0	c	36.9	(6.6)	63.1	(6.6)	17.3	(8.5)	42.1	(7.3)	40.6	(5.7)
Dubai•	43.8	(0.3)	35.0	(0.3)	21.2	(0.2)	2.5	(0.0)	12.2	(0.1)	85.3	(0.1)	13.2	(0.2)	48.5	(0.2)	38.3	(0.2)
Fujairah	44.0	(2.1)	12.9	(3.3)	43.1	(4.2)	15.2	(4.7)	25.0	(5.8)	59.8	(6.1)	16.6	(5.8)	39.1	(6.3)	44.3	(3.8)
Ras Al Khaimah	24.8	(7.4)	6.0	(3.7)	69.2	(8.4)	22.2	(7.0)	38.4	(8.5)	39.4	(8.5)	34.3	(10.4)	43.1	(9.5)	22.6	(8.5)
Sharjah	37.4	(10.6)	30.9	(7.7)	31.7	(8.9)	4.1	(5.7)	26.0	(6.1)	69.9	(7.6)	21.1	(9.2)	50.7	(8.6)	28.2	(8.8)
Umm Al Quwain	7.7	(0.5)	24.9	(0.4)	67.3	(0.5)	43.3	(0.2)	10.7	(0.3)	46.0	(0.3)	22.9	(0.3)	69.7	(0.3)	7.4	(0.1)

• PISA adjudicated region.
Note: See Table IV.2.7 for national data.
StatLink ⍟ http://dx.doi.org/10.1787/888932957536

[Part 3/6]
School admissions policies, by region
Table B2.IV.2   *Results based on school principals' reports*

	Percentage of students in schools whose principal reported that the following factors are "never", "sometimes" or "always" considered for admission to school:								
	Parents' endorsement of the instructional or religious philosophy of the school			Whether the student requires or is interested in a special programme			Preference given to family members of current or former students		
	Never	Sometimes	Always	Never	Sometimes	Always	Never	Sometimes	Always
	% S.E.	% S.E.	% S.E.	% S.E.	% S.E.	% S.E.	% S.E.	% S.E.	% S.E.
Australia									
Australian Capital Territory	33.1 (1.0)	37.6 (1.0)	29.3 (1.0)	17.5 (0.7)	66.9 (0.8)	15.6 (0.7)	3.6 (0.3)	31.2 (0.9)	65.2 (0.9)
New South Wales	49.9 (3.0)	17.3 (2.8)	32.9 (2.4)	26.2 (3.2)	47.1 (3.1)	26.6 (3.0)	26.6 (3.4)	39.2 (4.0)	34.2 (4.0)
Northern Territory	42.7 (4.9)	24.6 (2.5)	32.7 (3.2)	24.0 (5.9)	49.1 (4.4)	26.9 (2.6)	63.2 (3.7)	13.4 (8.5)	23.4 (9.7)
Queensland	44.7 (3.7)	25.6 (3.7)	29.7 (3.6)	15.7 (3.1)	57.7 (4.4)	26.5 (4.1)	39.4 (2.7)	18.1 (3.3)	42.5 (3.4)
South Australia	44.6 (3.6)	26.8 (4.4)	28.7 (4.5)	14.8 (2.9)	59.2 (5.2)	26.0 (4.7)	22.6 (2.9)	29.3 (4.9)	48.1 (4.5)
Tasmania	51.2 (1.2)	18.2 (1.0)	30.5 (1.1)	29.8 (1.4)	44.3 (1.7)	25.8 (1.0)	27.6 (1.7)	30.3 (1.1)	42.1 (1.6)
Victoria	44.0 (3.6)	24.8 (3.6)	31.2 (2.9)	21.4 (3.6)	63.3 (3.9)	15.3 (3.3)	20.3 (3.3)	31.0 (4.2)	48.7 (3.9)
Western Australia	47.5 (5.3)	23.3 (4.4)	29.2 (4.7)	13.9 (3.6)	60.9 (4.5)	25.2 (3.6)	22.2 (3.8)	35.9 (5.1)	41.9 (4.6)
Belgium									
Flemish community●	59.5 (4.1)	15.9 (2.9)	24.6 (3.8)	41.3 (4.1)	54.9 (4.2)	3.8 (1.6)	54.9 (3.9)	20.7 (3.5)	24.4 (3.4)
French community	18.6 (4.1)	17.5 (3.8)	63.8 (4.8)	30.1 (4.7)	52.7 (5.2)	17.2 (3.7)	37.4 (4.5)	32.1 (4.9)	30.5 (4.8)
German-speaking community	29.2 (0.3)	46.1 (0.3)	24.7 (0.3)	0.0 c	49.6 (0.3)	50.4 (0.3)	89.8 (0.0)	10.2 (0.0)	0.0 c
Canada									
Alberta	47.5 (5.2)	29.3 (4.4)	23.2 (4.7)	15.9 (4.2)	60.5 (5.0)	23.6 (4.5)	43.4 (4.5)	36.9 (4.3)	19.7 (4.1)
British Columbia	69.4 (5.1)	22.4 (5.2)	8.1 (2.6)	20.2 (5.0)	65.9 (5.3)	13.9 (4.2)	37.0 (5.0)	36.0 (5.8)	27.0 (4.9)
Manitoba	78.4 (2.4)	12.2 (2.3)	9.4 (0.9)	21.8 (2.9)	55.2 (3.4)	23.0 (2.2)	56.4 (2.6)	36.9 (2.8)	6.7 (0.9)
New Brunswick	91.7 (1.2)	8.2 (1.2)	0.1 (0.1)	47.8 (2.4)	40.8 (2.2)	11.4 (3.2)	88.8 (1.6)	11.2 (1.6)	0.1 (0.1)
Newfoundland and Labrador	87.7 (1.9)	6.0 (1.2)	6.3 (1.4)	50.6 (4.3)	34.1 (4.1)	15.3 (2.2)	73.8 (1.4)	15.5 (1.0)	10.7 (1.2)
Nova Scotia	72.1 (10.7)	25.5 (11.0)	2.4 (0.4)	24.0 (5.9)	45.9 (8.1)	30.2 (10.1)	83.5 (3.5)	15.9 (3.4)	0.6 (0.5)
Ontario	65.1 (4.8)	21.2 (4.2)	13.7 (3.6)	17.5 (3.9)	50.4 (5.5)	32.1 (5.1)	60.1 (5.2)	28.5 (4.8)	11.4 (3.3)
Prince Edward Island	73.8 (0.3)	24.7 (0.3)	1.4 (0.2)	16.9 (0.4)	59.2 (0.5)	24.0 (0.4)	82.6 (0.3)	17.4 (0.3)	0.0 c
Quebec	73.9 (3.3)	16.7 (3.2)	9.4 (2.1)	18.4 (3.1)	57.9 (4.4)	23.7 (3.9)	51.4 (3.8)	30.7 (4.0)	17.9 (3.3)
Saskatchewan	56.7 (2.4)	23.9 (2.3)	19.4 (1.4)	36.2 (3.8)	44.1 (2.7)	19.7 (2.4)	88.4 (1.6)	8.7 (1.5)	3.0 (1.7)
Italy									
Abruzzo	28.1 (6.0)	25.8 (6.1)	46.1 (6.0)	7.5 (3.8)	38.5 (5.6)	54.0 (6.3)	25.2 (5.3)	34.7 (6.0)	40.1 (6.1)
Basilicata	33.9 (5.8)	22.6 (3.2)	43.5 (5.6)	16.7 (4.9)	45.8 (4.9)	37.4 (4.7)	20.0 (5.9)	63.4 (7.4)	16.6 (5.0)
Bolzano	77.0 (0.7)	19.0 (0.7)	4.1 (0.2)	37.1 (1.2)	26.4 (0.7)	36.5 (0.8)	65.7 (0.9)	31.9 (0.8)	2.5 (0.2)
Calabria	28.3 (6.9)	26.3 (8.0)	45.4 (7.5)	16.3 (5.5)	20.5 (6.7)	63.1 (7.8)	17.2 (6.0)	46.9 (7.8)	35.9 (7.9)
Campania	32.5 (6.5)	18.2 (8.5)	49.4 (8.7)	28.3 (7.9)	30.2 (9.1)	41.4 (7.5)	20.3 (6.1)	41.6 (7.9)	38.0 (7.2)
Emilia Romagna	50.9 (8.1)	17.5 (6.5)	31.6 (7.2)	16.6 (6.3)	29.8 (6.4)	53.6 (8.3)	44.5 (7.5)	24.8 (6.7)	30.7 (6.5)
Friuli Venezia Giulia	39.8 (4.6)	23.5 (6.9)	36.8 (7.5)	2.2 (2.2)	37.3 (6.0)	60.5 (5.7)	26.1 (4.2)	60.1 (5.9)	13.8 (4.5)
Lazio	34.8 (7.5)	19.5 (6.0)	45.7 (8.9)	18.0 (5.9)	56.0 (8.2)	26.0 (7.0)	25.2 (5.5)	37.7 (7.1)	37.1 (8.0)
Liguria	42.9 (6.5)	18.3 (5.5)	38.9 (7.7)	13.3 (3.8)	34.5 (7.6)	52.2 (7.8)	33.7 (6.9)	49.1 (6.7)	17.2 (5.1)
Lombardia	38.8 (6.8)	23.4 (5.6)	37.8 (6.6)	13.7 (5.4)	35.6 (7.8)	50.7 (7.8)	30.3 (7.2)	46.5 (7.7)	23.3 (5.1)
Marche	39.2 (7.3)	14.0 (5.2)	46.8 (5.2)	12.8 (5.2)	29.6 (7.7)	57.6 (8.0)	35.3 (6.8)	44.0 (7.5)	20.7 (6.4)
Molise	22.3 (0.7)	25.1 (0.8)	52.6 (1.0)	11.4 (0.7)	46.1 (1.0)	42.5 (0.9)	24.6 (0.9)	52.3 (0.9)	23.2 (0.7)
Piemonte	38.4 (6.5)	31.5 (7.3)	30.1 (6.5)	18.3 (5.2)	39.4 (7.3)	42.3 (7.8)	24.2 (5.9)	55.2 (5.5)	20.6 (4.2)
Puglia	31.7 (6.5)	33.7 (7.0)	34.6 (6.7)	18.0 (4.5)	50.9 (7.0)	31.1 (6.0)	22.6 (5.4)	50.9 (7.3)	26.5 (6.0)
Sardegna	42.7 (7.3)	21.7 (6.7)	35.6 (6.7)	24.5 (4.6)	31.9 (7.0)	43.6 (7.7)	30.8 (5.2)	35.1 (6.7)	34.1 (6.9)
Sicilia	27.2 (6.8)	23.0 (6.2)	49.8 (6.0)	15.3 (4.7)	49.3 (6.9)	35.4 (5.4)	25.7 (6.0)	51.4 (7.7)	22.9 (5.4)
Toscana	42.6 (7.3)	20.8 (7.2)	36.6 (7.8)	21.1 (6.5)	30.8 (7.3)	48.0 (8.4)	34.1 (7.1)	42.2 (7.3)	23.7 (6.9)
Trento	57.5 (4.9)	17.1 (3.0)	25.4 (4.2)	9.3 (1.4)	51.6 (4.5)	39.0 (4.8)	58.2 (5.9)	24.3 (5.4)	17.5 (2.5)
Umbria	25.7 (4.5)	28.2 (4.2)	46.1 (5.1)	5.0 (2.3)	58.7 (6.5)	36.3 (6.1)	30.0 (5.9)	48.5 (4.5)	21.5 (3.9)
Valle d'Aosta	90.7 (0.6)	0.9 (0.1)	8.4 (0.6)	43.2 (1.0)	39.9 (0.8)	17.0 (0.8)	76.7 (0.8)	21.6 (0.7)	1.7 (0.3)
Veneto	39.8 (6.2)	25.6 (6.7)	34.6 (6.8)	12.6 (4.6)	49.3 (6.8)	38.1 (6.1)	22.4 (6.6)	65.4 (7.5)	12.2 (4.7)
Mexico									
Aguascalientes	56.5 (6.9)	9.3 (5.1)	34.3 (6.7)	33.4 (8.1)	51.3 (7.9)	15.3 (3.7)	52.9 (7.1)	30.1 (6.9)	17.1 (4.3)
Baja California	80.4 (6.7)	8.7 (6.3)	10.9 (3.5)	63.6 (8.9)	25.4 (7.8)	11.1 (5.1)	55.4 (6.9)	18.4 (5.9)	26.3 (6.0)
Baja California Sur	78.6 (7.8)	9.2 (5.9)	12.2 (5.3)	46.6 (7.1)	43.7 (5.7)	9.7 (5.8)	60.4 (8.9)	21.5 (7.5)	18.1 (5.6)
Campeche	86.1 (5.3)	9.3 (4.9)	4.7 (1.9)	67.9 (8.6)	26.3 (8.5)	5.8 (1.8)	80.0 (9.4)	20.0 (9.4)	0.0 c
Chiapas	71.3 (7.1)	9.0 (4.7)	19.8 (6.7)	51.4 (8.6)	42.8 (7.8)	5.8 (4.3)	83.9 (5.5)	15.6 (5.4)	0.5 (0.5)
Chihuahua	61.7 (11.5)	15.8 (6.6)	22.6 (10.8)	43.2 (9.9)	46.5 (9.6)	10.3 (4.7)	43.8 (9.8)	44.1 (11.3)	12.2 (7.2)
Coahuila	79.3 (4.9)	14.9 (4.3)	5.9 (3.1)	56.1 (8.4)	32.9 (8.2)	11.0 (2.6)	71.0 (8.9)	20.7 (7.9)	8.2 (4.9)
Colima	80.3 (7.2)	8.9 (4.7)	10.8 (5.8)	61.0 (5.9)	33.7 (5.6)	5.3 (2.5)	82.7 (4.4)	17.3 (4.4)	0.0 c
Distrito Federal	59.5 (8.7)	16.0 (7.3)	24.5 (9.2)	42.1 (8.0)	40.3 (7.8)	17.6 (8.8)	64.0 (7.2)	23.4 (8.6)	12.5 (7.2)
Durango	74.8 (5.5)	8.3 (3.3)	16.9 (3.7)	49.7 (9.8)	19.3 (5.4)	31.0 (10.5)	71.4 (10.7)	25.7 (10.7)	3.0 (2.2)
Guanajuato	69.5 (6.6)	21.2 (5.4)	9.4 (4.0)	48.5 (8.5)	37.1 (7.8)	14.3 (5.3)	71.9 (8.8)	26.8 (8.7)	1.4 (1.3)
Guerrero	72.9 (4.9)	15.8 (4.5)	11.3 (5.4)	44.6 (6.4)	47.9 (6.6)	7.5 (4.1)	76.6 (6.1)	17.0 (7.0)	6.5 (4.5)
Hidalgo	80.0 (6.8)	14.0 (5.7)	5.9 (3.8)	49.1 (7.6)	38.3 (7.8)	12.6 (4.7)	80.7 (6.8)	12.5 (6.0)	6.8 (3.6)
Jalisco	64.8 (7.4)	25.6 (8.1)	9.6 (6.0)	54.4 (10.3)	41.5 (10.1)	4.1 (2.8)	70.1 (8.4)	26.5 (9.3)	3.5 (2.5)
Mexico	66.8 (7.4)	18.5 (4.6)	14.7 (6.0)	60.7 (9.1)	26.9 (8.7)	12.4 (5.5)	77.8 (6.3)	12.2 (5.5)	10.0 (4.6)
Morelos	74.3 (8.9)	11.5 (6.1)	14.2 (6.5)	51.7 (9.8)	41.5 (9.1)	6.8 (2.9)	73.1 (7.9)	24.8 (7.8)	2.1 (1.5)
Nayarit	65.4 (6.1)	14.7 (5.3)	19.9 (6.8)	51.0 (6.5)	30.9 (6.9)	18.1 (5.8)	64.6 (6.3)	21.8 (4.6)	13.6 (5.2)
Nuevo León	64.4 (8.8)	16.4 (4.5)	19.2 (7.5)	44.9 (9.5)	43.2 (9.2)	11.9 (6.1)	65.2 (7.5)	13.2 (6.4)	21.6 (9.3)
Puebla	59.5 (8.9)	23.5 (8.1)	16.9 (6.2)	43.5 (9.0)	54.2 (8.8)	2.3 (1.9)	73.0 (6.0)	23.4 (5.5)	3.6 (2.3)
Querétaro	77.3 (5.8)	14.1 (3.5)	8.6 (4.0)	58.6 (5.9)	24.9 (5.9)	16.5 (4.7)	70.1 (5.5)	16.5 (6.2)	13.3 (5.4)
Quintana Roo	55.6 (9.2)	28.1 (8.9)	16.3 (7.6)	34.1 (6.7)	49.5 (10.5)	16.4 (7.3)	48.2 (8.7)	41.6 (9.0)	10.1 (5.6)
San Luis Potosí	67.5 (10.5)	9.4 (4.8)	23.0 (9.8)	59.5 (10.0)	33.9 (10.1)	6.6 (2.4)	76.1 (9.8)	10.6 (8.4)	13.3 (6.5)
Sinaloa	79.5 (5.1)	12.1 (5.0)	8.4 (4.8)	47.4 (8.2)	40.9 (6.3)	11.7 (5.4)	59.3 (10.0)	28.8 (8.1)	11.9 (6.3)
Tabasco	68.6 (8.0)	19.9 (6.2)	11.4 (6.8)	40.3 (10.4)	45.2 (10.2)	14.6 (5.7)	68.4 (8.6)	30.6 (8.4)	1.0 (1.0)
Tamaulipas	74.0 (10.4)	8.8 (4.5)	17.2 (9.7)	37.7 (10.3)	32.7 (9.3)	29.7 (10.8)	56.6 (11.8)	32.1 (10.8)	11.3 (7.3)
Tlaxcala	64.1 (6.8)	21.4 (5.4)	14.5 (5.5)	34.7 (7.1)	43.6 (7.5)	21.7 (4.4)	78.9 (6.4)	21.1 (6.4)	0.0 c
Veracruz	79.2 (4.3)	11.9 (3.7)	8.9 (2.3)	56.8 (8.7)	35.9 (8.8)	7.3 (4.4)	86.1 (3.5)	13.9 (3.5)	0.0 c
Yucatán	85.0 (6.2)	11.2 (5.7)	3.7 (2.3)	68.0 (7.6)	25.9 (6.8)	6.1 (3.2)	68.3 (9.1)	23.8 (6.8)	8.0 (7.7)
Zacatecas	73.9 (6.3)	9.2 (4.6)	16.9 (7.9)	58.3 (7.1)	26.3 (5.5)	15.3 (4.9)	92.1 (3.4)	7.9 (3.4)	0.0 c

● PISA adjudicated region.
Note: See Table IV.2.7 for national data.
StatLink ⟍⟍ http://dx.doi.org/10.1787/888932957536

[Part 4/6]
School admissions policies, by region
Table B2.IV.2 *Results based on school principals' reports*

	Parents' endorsement of the instructional or religious philosophy of the school						Whether the student requires or is interested in a special programme						Preference given to family members of current or former students					
	Never		Sometimes		Always		Never		Sometimes		Always		Never		Sometimes		Always	
	%	S.E.	%	S.E.	%	S.E.	%	S.E.	%	S.E.	%	S.E.	%	S.E.	%	S.E.	%	S.E.
Portugal																		
Alentejo	60.8	(9.3)	9.0	(2.7)	30.2	(9.7)	3.2	(2.6)	47.6	(11.5)	49.2	(11.1)	28.6	(10.7)	48.8	(13.5)	22.6	(9.7)
Spain																		
Andalusia●	93.7	(3.6)	4.4	(3.1)	1.8	(1.9)	66.0	(6.8)	20.7	(6.4)	13.3	(4.2)	42.2	(7.8)	21.7	(6.0)	36.1	(6.4)
Aragon●	89.9	(4.6)	6.7	(3.8)	3.4	(2.5)	65.0	(6.9)	33.7	(6.9)	1.2	(1.2)	61.3	(6.7)	27.4	(6.1)	11.3	(3.3)
Asturias●	85.3	(4.3)	3.7	(2.6)	11.0	(3.4)	57.3	(6.5)	32.4	(5.4)	10.2	(4.2)	31.3	(5.4)	39.8	(5.0)	28.9	(4.3)
Balearic Islands●	77.2	(5.7)	10.4	(4.3)	12.4	(4.2)	57.7	(7.8)	37.0	(7.9)	5.4	(3.1)	30.3	(5.2)	35.5	(6.0)	34.2	(5.1)
Basque Country●	61.9	(3.7)	16.3	(2.6)	21.8	(3.3)	54.4	(3.7)	30.0	(3.4)	15.7	(3.0)	30.5	(3.0)	29.4	(3.0)	40.1	(3.7)
Cantabria●	88.7	(4.0)	5.7	(2.9)	5.6	(3.3)	51.5	(6.3)	36.4	(6.2)	12.2	(4.3)	46.9	(5.7)	34.1	(5.9)	19.0	(5.4)
Castile and Leon●	75.0	(6.0)	16.9	(5.0)	8.1	(3.8)	50.6	(7.3)	36.9	(6.5)	12.5	(4.9)	37.3	(7.2)	23.2	(6.2)	39.5	(7.1)
Catalonia●	86.5	(3.2)	2.0	(2.0)	11.5	(3.9)	74.7	(6.7)	20.4	(6.4)	4.9	(3.5)	30.8	(6.9)	18.3	(6.4)	50.8	(7.8)
Extremadura●	87.2	(2.8)	6.1	(2.0)	6.7	(1.9)	59.8	(6.7)	25.9	(6.5)	14.3	(5.2)	55.9	(7.3)	22.3	(6.7)	21.8	(5.0)
Galicia●	86.5	(4.7)	2.0	(2.1)	11.4	(4.2)	70.9	(5.0)	23.2	(4.6)	5.9	(3.4)	68.9	(5.0)	13.6	(5.2)	17.6	(4.9)
La Rioja●	78.2	(0.5)	14.1	(0.5)	7.7	(0.1)	46.5	(0.6)	46.8	(0.6)	6.7	(0.3)	27.0	(0.6)	36.8	(0.5)	36.1	(0.4)
Madrid●	73.4	(5.5)	13.7	(5.3)	12.9	(5.2)	46.4	(6.7)	43.5	(7.6)	10.0	(4.5)	14.6	(4.7)	35.7	(6.8)	49.7	(7.6)
Murcia●	78.4	(3.7)	16.6	(3.8)	4.9	(3.0)	46.5	(5.7)	32.3	(5.8)	21.2	(5.3)	19.6	(6.1)	38.7	(7.1)	41.7	(6.8)
Navarre●	75.6	(4.0)	14.9	(4.9)	9.6	(4.4)	54.6	(5.0)	34.9	(4.5)	10.6	(3.7)	41.1	(3.9)	28.6	(4.0)	30.4	(4.9)
United Kingdom																		
England	69.8	(3.5)	18.2	(3.1)	12.1	(2.6)	53.4	(4.0)	32.7	(3.8)	13.9	(2.5)	30.6	(3.7)	39.6	(3.6)	29.8	(3.5)
Northern Ireland	53.1	(5.1)	24.8	(4.6)	22.1	(3.5)	44.2	(5.4)	47.6	(5.8)	8.1	(2.6)	18.8	(4.6)	50.1	(4.5)	31.1	(4.8)
Scotland●	78.9	(4.3)	9.9	(2.8)	11.2	(3.3)	50.4	(4.5)	38.7	(4.7)	10.9	(3.5)	60.2	(5.1)	23.5	(4.1)	16.4	(3.7)
Wales	67.5	(4.0)	18.9	(3.2)	13.5	(2.8)	51.7	(3.8)	34.7	(4.0)	13.6	(2.5)	58.7	(3.5)	27.8	(3.7)	13.4	(2.5)
United States																		
Connecticut●	81.1	(5.6)	10.7	(3.6)	8.2	(4.2)	50.4	(6.7)	24.0	(5.0)	25.6	(6.2)	83.2	(4.9)	13.0	(5.1)	3.8	(2.8)
Florida●	69.2	(7.2)	25.4	(7.4)	5.5	(3.2)	21.9	(7.2)	44.7	(8.5)	33.3	(8.3)	70.8	(6.7)	22.9	(6.5)	6.3	(6.1)
Massachusetts●	80.4	(6.4)	17.7	(6.0)	1.9	(1.9)	54.7	(7.4)	30.8	(6.5)	14.5	(5.7)	93.0	(3.6)	5.0	(3.0)	2.0	(2.0)
Argentina																		
Ciudad Autónoma de Buenos Aires●	25.7	(7.7)	36.1	(8.4)	38.2	(7.5)	37.3	(6.8)	36.1	(5.9)	26.6	(6.8)	15.5	(6.1)	19.8	(5.8)	64.7	(8.3)
Brazil																		
Acre	71.3	(9.3)	22.5	(9.3)	6.2	(4.6)	64.8	(9.5)	24.7	(8.6)	10.4	(6.3)	76.4	(8.5)	18.5	(8.4)	5.1	(4.0)
Alagoas	73.0	(10.2)	12.9	(7.6)	14.1	(7.7)	60.6	(9.9)	21.7	(8.2)	17.7	(8.1)	86.1	(5.8)	13.9	(5.8)	0.0	c
Amapá	46.3	(11.1)	29.4	(9.4)	24.3	(7.8)	25.5	(11.1)	49.1	(8.3)	25.4	(10.0)	49.6	(9.2)	39.2	(11.3)	11.2	(7.8)
Amazonas	50.5	(11.5)	44.9	(11.0)	4.5	(3.0)	68.2	(9.6)	28.0	(9.7)	3.8	(3.5)	54.0	(10.9)	41.7	(11.3)	4.3	(4.2)
Bahia	52.5	(11.9)	23.0	(9.7)	24.5	(9.7)	52.4	(15.7)	40.3	(16.0)	7.3	(6.4)	46.7	(15.7)	40.6	(15.5)	12.7	(8.0)
Ceará	58.8	(9.2)	13.5	(7.2)	27.7	(10.4)	47.2	(11.7)	34.2	(9.1)	18.7	(8.1)	51.1	(12.3)	30.6	(10.1)	18.3	(9.1)
Espírito Santo	83.4	(9.3)	12.0	(8.3)	4.6	(4.7)	75.2	(8.1)	19.7	(6.4)	5.2	(4.9)	62.7	(12.7)	11.7	(5.5)	25.6	(11.4)
Federal District	55.1	(6.9)	31.6	(12.8)	13.3	(9.6)	47.8	(11.4)	43.7	(14.8)	8.6	(8.7)	71.6	(13.2)	14.4	(11.2)	13.9	(7.3)
Goiás	64.4	(6.6)	25.9	(8.1)	9.7	(6.4)	53.2	(12.4)	38.9	(11.9)	7.9	(5.2)	64.3	(9.9)	33.1	(9.8)	2.6	(2.6)
Maranhão	37.5	(8.8)	34.0	(13.0)	28.5	(14.2)	35.6	(9.2)	44.6	(13.7)	19.8	(9.6)	31.2	(9.5)	50.3	(10.3)	18.5	(8.9)
Mato Grosso	50.1	(8.8)	28.4	(8.7)	21.5	(8.3)	38.9	(10.3)	35.7	(11.3)	25.4	(7.9)	52.1	(6.0)	16.6	(7.8)	31.3	(5.4)
Mato Grosso do Sul	48.8	(10.7)	16.9	(6.8)	34.3	(11.8)	49.4	(10.2)	44.1	(10.4)	6.5	(4.0)	40.7	(10.5)	35.4	(10.1)	23.9	(8.2)
Minas Gerais	69.4	(8.5)	27.2	(8.4)	3.4	(2.7)	75.3	(8.2)	22.3	(7.9)	2.4	(2.4)	73.9	(7.7)	17.3	(4.8)	8.8	(5.4)
Pará	41.3	(8.5)	25.0	(6.1)	33.7	(6.4)	41.1	(9.2)	41.0	(13.8)	17.9	(11.7)	52.5	(6.7)	20.5	(5.2)	27.0	(4.2)
Paraíba	49.1	(12.1)	19.5	(7.5)	31.4	(10.3)	38.8	(10.0)	56.4	(13.2)	4.8	(5.5)	28.4	(11.4)	41.3	(12.0)	30.3	(14.3)
Paraná	80.3	(9.7)	12.0	(6.3)	7.8	(7.7)	60.1	(10.4)	34.3	(11.3)	5.6	(5.2)	56.0	(10.2)	44.0	(10.2)	0.0	c
Pernambuco	35.9	(12.5)	27.6	(10.5)	36.5	(13.6)	29.0	(9.1)	33.4	(11.1)	37.7	(13.7)	47.1	(13.7)	45.1	(13.7)	7.8	(5.1)
Piauí	50.2	(8.7)	18.5	(8.3)	31.3	(10.3)	31.0	(10.2)	42.2	(14.2)	26.8	(10.2)	29.0	(10.6)	28.4	(8.7)	42.5	(13.4)
Rio de Janeiro	61.0	(10.5)	15.1	(7.6)	23.9	(9.0)	47.2	(8.6)	31.5	(7.5)	21.3	(7.5)	55.3	(11.5)	38.9	(10.1)	5.8	(5.1)
Rio Grande do Norte	50.0	(11.1)	13.9	(6.9)	36.1	(9.0)	47.2	(11.5)	21.9	(7.3)	31.0	(8.8)	38.3	(10.9)	48.2	(10.5)	13.4	(6.7)
Rio Grande do Sul	73.6	(6.3)	6.9	(5.0)	19.6	(4.0)	64.2	(8.9)	27.4	(8.0)	8.4	(5.1)	71.5	(10.0)	24.9	(8.8)	3.6	(5.1)
Rondônia	58.5	(11.1)	27.8	(10.9)	13.7	(7.4)	47.5	(9.9)	46.7	(10.1)	5.7	(5.5)	64.9	(11.2)	15.5	(6.9)	19.6	(9.9)
Roraima	59.0	(4.7)	25.1	(7.1)	15.9	(6.6)	54.4	(10.7)	28.5	(9.8)	17.1	(4.2)	42.0	(11.1)	43.5	(7.4)	14.5	(9.7)
Santa Catarina	61.5	(9.0)	32.1	(9.3)	6.4	(4.7)	58.6	(6.7)	31.0	(5.9)	10.5	(6.4)	69.7	(8.5)	17.5	(4.7)	12.9	(6.2)
São Paulo	66.2	(5.7)	18.3	(4.6)	15.6	(3.5)	61.4	(6.0)	23.5	(5.1)	15.1	(4.3)	68.7	(6.0)	22.4	(4.9)	8.9	(4.5)
Sergipe	50.1	(13.2)	24.4	(10.8)	25.4	(11.1)	40.0	(8.8)	56.3	(7.7)	3.7	(3.8)	44.8	(10.3)	48.5	(10.8)	6.7	(5.1)
Tocantins	55.6	(10.7)	19.0	(8.8)	25.4	(9.5)	63.6	(10.2)	28.9	(9.8)	7.5	(5.1)	71.5	(9.7)	14.8	(6.4)	13.7	(7.4)
Colombia																		
Bogota	70.4	(6.2)	10.4	(3.3)	19.2	(5.4)	57.9	(6.9)	36.1	(7.1)	6.0	(3.5)	38.9	(6.8)	39.9	(8.2)	21.2	(6.2)
Cali	53.6	(9.2)	18.0	(5.3)	28.4	(7.6)	44.2	(8.5)	36.5	(6.9)	19.3	(7.6)	27.4	(6.9)	38.2	(9.1)	34.4	(6.4)
Manizales	51.2	(7.6)	13.5	(3.0)	35.2	(6.9)	49.3	(7.6)	40.9	(7.8)	9.8	(3.9)	56.4	(9.4)	27.2	(5.2)	16.4	(6.5)
Medellin	48.3	(7.5)	19.0	(6.0)	32.7	(6.7)	51.1	(7.8)	28.8	(7.6)	20.2	(6.5)	27.2	(6.6)	39.0	(8.4)	33.8	(6.7)
Russian Federation																		
Perm Territory region●	21.5	(5.2)	43.9	(6.0)	34.6	(5.6)	13.8	(4.0)	37.7	(6.2)	48.5	(5.8)	55.5	(5.5)	41.2	(5.5)	3.4	(2.4)
United Arab Emirates																		
Abu Dhabi●	31.9	(4.1)	33.2	(4.3)	34.9	(3.9)	28.5	(3.7)	43.6	(3.8)	27.9	(3.9)	26.0	(3.1)	22.1	(3.4)	51.9	(4.0)
Ajman	12.8	(4.0)	27.0	(2.6)	60.2	(4.4)	23.1	(6.2)	35.9	(6.3)	41.0	(5.6)	21.2	(6.0)	54.1	(7.3)	24.7	(7.6)
Dubai●	18.1	(0.3)	38.6	(0.2)	43.3	(0.2)	26.1	(0.3)	47.2	(0.3)	26.7	(0.1)	8.0	(0.1)	37.0	(0.2)	55.0	(0.2)
Fujairah	21.8	(6.5)	21.7	(7.2)	56.5	(6.1)	7.9	(3.6)	60.6	(6.4)	31.5	(4.8)	54.8	(2.7)	18.8	(1.4)	26.4	(2.5)
Ras Al Khaimah	37.0	(8.4)	27.1	(9.1)	35.8	(5.9)	50.2	(10.0)	30.3	(7.5)	19.5	(8.6)	52.8	(10.6)	33.5	(9.8)	13.8	(4.6)
Sharjah	34.2	(9.3)	32.2	(8.3)	33.6	(10.6)	34.7	(10.4)	53.4	(8.0)	11.9	(7.0)	10.3	(5.9)	58.4	(11.1)	31.3	(10.7)
Umm Al Quwain	27.1	(0.2)	37.7	(0.3)	35.2	(0.3)	28.3	(0.2)	51.8	(0.2)	19.9	(0.1)	60.1	(0.2)	26.9	(0.3)	13.0	(0.3)

● PISA adjudicated region.
Note: See Table IV.2.7 for national data.
StatLink ᴍᴤ█ http://dx.doi.org/10.1787/888932957536

[Part 5/6]
School admissions policies, by region
Table B2.IV.2 *Results based on school principals' reports*

	Percentage of students in schools whose principal reported that the following factors are "never", "sometimes" or "always" considered for admission to school: Other						Percentage of students in schools whose principals reported whether "students' records of academic performance" and "recommendations of feeder schools" are considered for admission					
	Never		Sometimes		Always		These two factors are "never" considered		At least one of these two factors is "sometimes" considered but neither factor is "always" considered		At least one of these two factors is "always" considered	
	%	S.E.	%	S.E.	%	S.E.	%	S.E.	%	S.E.	%	S.E.
Australia												
Australian Capital Territory	21.9	(0.9)	74.4	(1.0)	3.7	(0.4)	23.5	(0.9)	49.6	(1.2)	26.9	(1.0)
New South Wales	29.9	(3.5)	57.3	(3.7)	12.8	(2.5)	12.1	(2.5)	32.1	(3.5)	55.7	(3.8)
Northern Territory	65.0	(9.2)	27.4	(2.3)	7.6	(8.4)	21.0	(6.1)	54.8	(9.9)	24.3	(8.9)
Queensland	43.9	(3.6)	44.4	(4.1)	11.7	(3.1)	20.7	(3.2)	40.8	(4.2)	38.5	(4.2)
South Australia	30.9	(4.5)	64.1	(4.8)	5.0	(2.3)	15.5	(3.2)	42.7	(5.2)	41.8	(4.9)
Tasmania	38.1	(1.4)	50.2	(1.4)	11.7	(0.9)	26.5	(1.9)	41.1	(1.5)	32.5	(1.7)
Victoria	31.7	(4.0)	63.0	(4.5)	5.3	(2.0)	12.3	(2.8)	45.4	(4.6)	42.3	(4.1)
Western Australia	32.0	(4.6)	54.5	(4.9)	13.5	(3.7)	22.0	(4.3)	42.0	(4.1)	36.0	(4.2)
Belgium												
Flemish community•	54.8	(5.2)	40.0	(5.2)	5.2	(1.9)	26.2	(3.3)	39.1	(4.0)	34.7	(3.9)
French community	53.7	(7.4)	34.1	(6.9)	12.2	(4.0)	47.3	(4.9)	36.5	(4.7)	16.2	(3.2)
German-speaking community	37.8	(0.3)	60.8	(0.3)	1.4	(0.3)	20.3	(0.2)	42.5	(0.3)	37.2	(0.2)
Canada												
Alberta	41.7	(5.9)	48.3	(6.6)	10.0	(3.9)	27.7	(5.2)	43.0	(5.6)	29.3	(5.2)
British Columbia	45.0	(9.7)	48.5	(9.3)	6.4	(3.5)	28.2	(5.8)	36.9	(5.7)	34.8	(5.9)
Manitoba	26.9	(5.3)	44.1	(5.0)	29.0	(4.6)	22.3	(3.0)	47.1	(3.2)	30.6	(2.4)
New Brunswick	30.0	(3.3)	70.0	(3.3)	0.0	c	50.7	(2.8)	34.4	(2.0)	14.9	(3.2)
Newfoundland and Labrador	59.8	(5.0)	36.1	(4.9)	4.1	(0.4)	49.7	(4.5)	18.9	(1.0)	31.4	(4.0)
Nova Scotia	35.1	(10.1)	30.4	(9.2)	34.5	(17.1)	38.8	(7.1)	20.9	(5.0)	40.3	(9.1)
Ontario	28.1	(7.2)	54.2	(8.9)	17.8	(6.1)	23.7	(4.5)	32.5	(4.6)	43.8	(5.1)
Prince Edward Island	77.9	(0.4)	22.1	(0.4)	0.0	c	31.4	(0.5)	24.8	(0.4)	43.9	(0.4)
Quebec	60.8	(5.8)	32.0	(5.5)	7.2	(3.1)	24.1	(4.0)	32.6	(3.6)	43.2	(3.5)
Saskatchewan	63.7	(4.6)	29.1	(4.2)	7.3	(1.8)	34.4	(4.1)	38.2	(3.0)	27.3	(2.8)
Italy												
Abruzzo	24.6	(8.3)	65.4	(9.6)	10.0	(7.5)	9.4	(3.7)	11.3	(4.6)	79.3	(5.9)
Basilicata	39.1	(7.4)	56.2	(6.6)	4.7	(4.6)	17.8	(3.3)	21.9	(5.1)	60.3	(4.8)
Bolzano	62.6	(0.7)	29.9	(0.8)	7.5	(0.4)	64.9	(0.9)	19.3	(0.6)	15.7	(1.1)
Calabria	43.1	(9.6)	42.9	(9.7)	14.0	(5.8)	14.0	(5.5)	28.3	(6.0)	57.7	(7.2)
Campania	64.7	(9.7)	26.8	(8.2)	8.4	(5.9)	11.3	(3.4)	26.2	(7.7)	62.5	(8.8)
Emilia Romagna	70.0	(9.5)	22.4	(8.5)	7.5	(5.3)	10.1	(5.2)	12.9	(4.3)	76.9	(6.2)
Friuli Venezia Giulia	31.3	(5.3)	61.3	(6.4)	7.4	(3.6)	8.3	(3.6)	17.5	(3.4)	74.2	(4.7)
Lazio	49.8	(8.8)	30.6	(8.6)	19.7	(7.0)	13.5	(5.3)	10.6	(3.2)	75.9	(6.2)
Liguria	57.9	(8.6)	32.2	(7.3)	9.9	(6.3)	8.7	(4.2)	29.1	(6.0)	62.1	(7.3)
Lombardia	45.6	(9.1)	47.3	(8.9)	7.1	(4.4)	15.1	(4.9)	22.1	(7.8)	62.8	(7.6)
Marche	38.3	(9.0)	47.8	(7.9)	13.9	(6.5)	13.8	(2.9)	6.9	(3.5)	79.3	(4.5)
Molise	38.3	(1.2)	40.5	(1.2)	21.2	(0.9)	0.0	c	39.7	(0.9)	60.3	(0.9)
Piemonte	45.0	(6.6)	46.5	(7.3)	8.5	(4.4)	12.3	(4.9)	31.3	(6.1)	56.4	(8.5)
Puglia	42.9	(8.2)	44.8	(9.0)	12.3	(6.1)	12.7	(5.0)	25.6	(6.6)	61.7	(7.2)
Sardegna	31.7	(9.8)	49.9	(11.8)	18.4	(7.6)	18.3	(3.6)	13.9	(5.5)	67.8	(6.2)
Sicilia	42.3	(8.4)	48.8	(9.0)	8.9	(4.7)	15.0	(4.1)	17.9	(5.7)	67.1	(6.6)
Toscana	47.3	(10.6)	43.3	(11.2)	9.3	(3.5)	16.8	(5.7)	27.1	(6.7)	56.0	(8.1)
Trento	53.9	(4.5)	31.2	(5.1)	14.9	(4.0)	10.4	(1.3)	30.8	(4.9)	58.8	(4.9)
Umbria	36.3	(8.7)	47.1	(7.7)	16.6	(3.4)	3.2	(2.1)	23.5	(3.9)	73.3	(4.2)
Valle d'Aosta	70.5	(1.0)	28.7	(1.0)	0.8	(0.0)	22.7	(0.8)	38.7	(0.8)	38.6	(0.9)
Veneto	43.5	(9.3)	40.1	(9.3)	16.4	(4.9)	7.0	(3.7)	18.3	(4.2)	74.8	(5.5)
Mexico												
Aguascalientes	45.4	(7.0)	50.8	(7.6)	3.8	(2.3)	11.0	(4.5)	19.0	(4.4)	70.1	(5.4)
Baja California	35.8	(12.7)	50.9	(13.1)	13.3	(8.2)	10.8	(7.8)	41.6	(10.8)	47.6	(6.6)
Baja California Sur	48.4	(8.2)	42.4	(7.6)	9.2	(4.2)	29.6	(9.7)	16.3	(6.6)	54.0	(8.6)
Campeche	55.0	(8.4)	32.3	(11.4)	12.7	(9.7)	39.3	(6.9)	16.6	(7.9)	44.1	(9.1)
Chiapas	71.9	(11.0)	23.8	(10.6)	4.2	(4.0)	27.9	(7.4)	24.5	(6.5)	47.6	(9.5)
Chihuahua	49.3	(10.2)	46.9	(13.2)	3.8	(4.4)	12.9	(3.5)	36.3	(9.6)	50.7	(9.1)
Coahuila	70.1	(10.3)	29.9	(10.3)	0.0	c	15.2	(5.9)	23.3	(8.4)	61.5	(9.5)
Colima	75.3	(6.5)	17.5	(6.7)	7.3	(1.9)	18.3	(5.1)	24.5	(6.5)	57.2	(6.2)
Distrito Federal	43.5	(11.6)	42.1	(10.9)	14.4	(9.9)	34.1	(10.0)	27.7	(9.3)	38.2	(8.1)
Durango	71.4	(8.6)	22.7	(7.4)	6.0	(4.5)	16.5	(6.1)	19.6	(7.2)	63.8	(7.6)
Guanajuato	48.8	(9.4)	51.2	(9.4)	0.0	c	35.9	(6.7)	5.4	(2.8)	58.7	(7.0)
Guerrero	74.5	(11.2)	25.5	(11.2)	0.0	c	24.0	(7.2)	28.4	(8.9)	47.6	(7.0)
Hidalgo	88.3	(3.0)	8.5	(3.7)	3.2	(3.2)	22.1	(6.7)	15.4	(5.0)	62.5	(7.5)
Jalisco	75.7	(7.7)	17.2	(6.0)	7.1	(4.3)	37.1	(7.0)	12.8	(2.8)	50.0	(6.5)
Mexico	55.4	(8.8)	36.9	(7.8)	7.7	(7.0)	28.6	(7.9)	24.0	(6.4)	47.4	(8.3)
Morelos	62.7	(8.9)	29.3	(8.7)	8.0	(4.3)	17.4	(5.9)	18.0	(6.8)	64.6	(8.0)
Nayarit	67.6	(8.5)	23.0	(8.4)	9.4	(5.3)	27.9	(4.5)	18.1	(4.5)	54.0	(5.8)
Nuevo León	54.0	(10.6)	42.0	(10.3)	4.1	(4.1)	26.1	(8.7)	18.7	(5.5)	55.2	(9.5)
Puebla	80.4	(7.2)	16.8	(6.5)	2.8	(2.8)	25.6	(6.4)	28.3	(7.0)	46.2	(5.1)
Querétaro	47.7	(9.8)	39.8	(10.5)	12.5	(3.2)	26.6	(8.7)	13.7	(3.2)	59.7	(10.0)
Quintana Roo	34.4	(11.6)	52.4	(8.5)	13.3	(9.1)	20.9	(5.4)	31.2	(5.9)	47.9	(7.0)
San Luis Potosí	60.9	(7.0)	31.9	(11.5)	7.2	(7.0)	34.3	(9.6)	16.5	(5.6)	49.2	(10.8)
Sinaloa	56.9	(10.1)	29.2	(9.9)	13.9	(8.0)	11.6	(4.2)	23.9	(7.2)	64.6	(7.7)
Tabasco	42.8	(10.2)	55.7	(10.0)	1.5	(1.5)	28.4	(8.9)	25.8	(8.5)	45.8	(8.3)
Tamaulipas	60.3	(14.3)	38.0	(14.4)	1.7	(1.7)	10.1	(4.9)	27.8	(6.1)	62.1	(7.4)
Tlaxcala	76.3	(7.6)	17.7	(5.7)	6.0	(4.7)	34.0	(6.3)	8.1	(4.1)	57.9	(7.4)
Veracruz	91.5	(4.9)	5.9	(4.2)	2.7	(2.6)	43.1	(9.0)	23.8	(8.5)	33.0	(6.1)
Yucatán	61.5	(8.8)	35.6	(9.6)	2.9	(2.9)	21.8	(6.9)	28.2	(9.6)	49.9	(10.2)
Zacatecas	61.8	(10.2)	31.6	(10.1)	6.5	(3.0)	28.1	(7.8)	18.8	(5.5)	53.1	(7.1)

• PISA adjudicated region.
Note: See Table IV.2.7 for national data.
StatLink ᴍᴤᴸ http://dx.doi.org/10.1787/888932957536

[Part 6/6]
School admissions policies, by region
Table B2.IV.2   *Results based on school principals' reports*

| | | Percentage of students in schools whose principal reported that the following factors are "never", "sometimes" or "always" considered for admission to school: Other | | | | | | Percentage of students in schools whose principals reported whether "students' records of academic performance" and "recommendations of feeder schools" are considered for admission | | | | | |
| | | Never | | Sometimes | | Always | | These two factors are "never" considered | | At least one of these two factors is "sometimes" considered but neither factor is "always" considered | | At least one of these two factors is "always" considered | |
		%	S.E.	%	S.E.	%	S.E.	%	S.E.	%	S.E.	%	S.E.
OECD	**Portugal**												
	Alentejo	37.1	(13.6)	54.2	(14.8)	8.6	(7.3)	53.8	(12.9)	22.8	(10.6)	23.4	(8.0)
	Spain												
	Andalusia•	45.1	(8.0)	26.7	(6.9)	28.2	(7.4)	80.8	(5.4)	11.4	(4.7)	7.8	(3.9)
	Aragon•	59.9	(6.6)	19.6	(6.8)	20.5	(5.1)	89.0	(4.9)	8.9	(4.4)	2.1	(2.1)
	Asturias•	40.0	(7.9)	43.9	(8.4)	16.2	(7.0)	88.2	(3.6)	11.8	(3.6)	0.0	c
	Balearic Islands•	45.3	(9.4)	32.6	(8.0)	22.1	(6.5)	90.1	(4.2)	6.6	(3.5)	3.3	(2.4)
	Basque Country•	32.7	(4.3)	38.5	(4.2)	28.8	(4.1)	62.8	(4.2)	24.3	(3.7)	12.9	(2.4)
	Cantabria•	38.7	(8.4)	33.4	(8.3)	27.9	(8.0)	93.9	(3.6)	3.9	(2.8)	2.3	(2.2)
	Castile and Leon•	45.9	(7.1)	38.0	(7.6)	16.2	(5.5)	84.6	(5.3)	14.4	(5.2)	1.0	(1.0)
	Catalonia•	44.1	(6.2)	23.4	(7.0)	32.6	(8.6)	88.1	(4.2)	11.9	(4.2)	0.0	c
	Extremadura•	57.0	(7.4)	18.0	(6.6)	25.0	(5.3)	89.8	(4.5)	6.1	(3.5)	4.2	(2.9)
	Galicia•	31.3	(6.1)	34.9	(7.2)	33.8	(7.3)	92.4	(3.9)	4.3	(3.0)	3.3	(2.4)
	La Rioja•	32.1	(0.6)	63.7	(0.7)	4.3	(0.2)	70.2	(0.5)	28.9	(0.5)	0.9	(0.1)
	Madrid•	15.1	(6.5)	52.3	(10.3)	32.6	(8.6)	70.9	(7.0)	25.4	(6.5)	3.8	(2.7)
	Murcia•	37.6	(8.0)	36.5	(8.4)	25.9	(7.8)	81.8	(5.2)	16.3	(4.9)	1.9	(1.9)
	Navarre•	49.6	(6.9)	36.0	(5.3)	14.4	(4.8)	78.1	(4.5)	18.2	(3.6)	3.7	(2.6)
	United Kingdom												
	England	40.2	(5.1)	35.1	(5.0)	24.7	(4.7)	52.7	(3.7)	20.0	(4.0)	27.3	(3.3)
	Northern Ireland	37.7	(5.6)	52.6	(5.7)	9.7	(3.9)	23.6	(4.6)	18.9	(4.6)	57.5	(4.0)
	Scotland•	41.5	(5.9)	52.0	(5.8)	6.4	(2.3)	58.8	(5.1)	13.6	(3.4)	27.6	(4.3)
	Wales	46.0	(4.7)	38.4	(4.4)	15.6	(3.3)	57.5	(4.1)	17.1	(3.3)	25.3	(3.6)
	United States												
	Connecticut•	57.2	(10.3)	20.3	(7.6)	22.5	(9.1)	43.9	(6.4)	3.1	(2.3)	53.0	(5.8)
	Florida•	54.9	(9.5)	34.9	(8.6)	10.2	(5.9)	33.9	(8.1)	34.8	(7.6)	31.3	(7.3)
	Massachusetts•	63.3	(9.1)	19.2	(9.0)	17.5	(8.3)	47.0	(8.6)	11.0	(4.7)	42.0	(7.7)
Partners	**Argentina**												
	Ciudad Autónoma de Buenos Aires•	34.5	(10.3)	45.9	(10.7)	19.6	(8.3)	25.4	(5.1)	33.3	(6.9)	41.3	(7.7)
	Brazil												
	Acre	46.0	(13.0)	42.8	(13.5)	11.2	(11.8)	60.6	(11.3)	7.4	(4.1)	32.0	(10.8)
	Alagoas	50.1	(12.1)	34.8	(11.6)	15.0	(10.7)	39.5	(11.7)	13.0	(7.9)	47.5	(12.9)
	Amapá	16.3	(5.8)	67.0	(10.8)	16.7	(8.3)	28.6	(7.8)	39.2	(9.3)	32.2	(11.6)
	Amazonas	22.1	(10.1)	58.7	(11.4)	19.2	(9.5)	61.4	(9.1)	22.4	(9.2)	16.3	(4.7)
	Bahia	13.2	(8.6)	44.1	(13.9)	42.6	(16.5)	44.6	(11.1)	25.2	(11.1)	30.2	(13.0)
	Ceará	30.2	(10.1)	39.0	(13.1)	30.8	(13.4)	43.6	(9.5)	25.9	(9.3)	30.5	(8.1)
	Espírito Santo	35.7	(16.7)	25.2	(16.4)	39.2	(8.1)	72.2	(7.6)	22.3	(9.5)	5.6	(3.9)
	Federal District	25.2	(13.7)	62.8	(11.6)	12.0	(9.5)	66.8	(10.8)	17.5	(7.6)	15.7	(7.8)
	Goiás	42.2	(10.7)	32.6	(9.2)	25.2	(10.3)	51.1	(10.0)	21.9	(7.8)	27.0	(7.5)
	Maranhão	28.7	(15.8)	68.4	(16.2)	2.9	(2.8)	36.3	(12.8)	24.4	(13.5)	39.3	(11.5)
	Mato Grosso	38.3	(9.2)	33.2	(10.6)	28.5	(13.0)	47.0	(10.9)	19.4	(8.9)	33.6	(9.8)
	Mato Grosso do Sul	21.1	(9.0)	57.7	(11.3)	21.2	(7.6)	59.9	(9.8)	23.0	(9.2)	17.1	(7.7)
	Minas Gerais	24.3	(9.6)	48.3	(9.6)	27.5	(10.7)	62.4	(7.7)	15.2	(5.5)	22.4	(7.1)
	Pará	24.3	(8.9)	49.7	(15.7)	26.0	(14.0)	38.7	(8.8)	42.9	(4.4)	18.3	(8.3)
	Paraíba	27.6	(10.0)	40.6	(13.7)	31.8	(14.7)	54.8	(12.2)	23.4	(10.7)	21.8	(6.1)
	Paraná	38.8	(12.3)	45.9	(10.8)	15.3	(6.6)	55.3	(13.0)	30.2	(10.6)	14.5	(9.2)
	Pernambuco	49.3	(17.4)	41.5	(14.7)	9.2	(8.6)	34.7	(10.1)	19.2	(7.0)	46.1	(11.5)
	Piauí	22.2	(11.6)	67.1	(14.2)	10.7	(7.7)	11.1	(5.3)	30.4	(10.1)	58.5	(10.0)
	Rio de Janeiro	19.8	(10.7)	43.1	(11.9)	37.1	(13.6)	52.4	(11.2)	28.0	(8.7)	19.6	(9.2)
	Rio Grande do Norte	22.1	(11.6)	54.8	(13.1)	23.1	(11.4)	62.0	(10.5)	20.0	(7.7)	18.1	(8.8)
	Rio Grande do Sul	57.9	(11.3)	24.9	(9.7)	17.2	(8.8)	71.2	(9.3)	8.7	(5.2)	20.1	(8.1)
	Rondônia	19.5	(9.7)	30.1	(12.0)	50.4	(14.0)	57.1	(8.9)	17.4	(5.0)	25.4	(8.8)
	Roraima	20.1	(9.5)	48.6	(12.4)	31.3	(11.9)	51.9	(8.9)	20.6	(6.5)	27.5	(10.1)
	Santa Catarina	44.2	(11.9)	44.3	(12.7)	11.5	(6.6)	80.5	(7.3)	17.4	(7.1)	2.0	(2.1)
	São Paulo	34.0	(7.8)	41.7	(7.4)	24.2	(5.5)	60.9	(6.3)	28.5	(5.2)	10.6	(3.7)
	Sergipe	29.8	(13.8)	27.1	(14.5)	43.2	(17.7)	35.6	(8.5)	22.0	(10.6)	42.4	(11.2)
	Tocantins	60.9	(11.3)	26.8	(10.7)	12.3	(6.1)	31.4	(7.9)	17.6	(4.9)	51.1	(8.6)
	Colombia												
	Bogota	47.1	(8.3)	35.4	(8.7)	17.4	(8.0)	50.1	(5.9)	25.8	(6.2)	24.1	(5.0)
	Cali	32.0	(7.7)	55.7	(8.2)	12.2	(5.0)	18.7	(5.8)	36.7	(8.0)	44.6	(6.6)
	Manizales	25.5	(7.4)	48.7	(9.2)	25.8	(11.7)	24.3	(6.5)	28.4	(7.4)	47.3	(8.4)
	Medellin	34.0	(8.6)	54.1	(9.0)	12.0	(6.7)	21.0	(5.7)	44.4	(8.0)	34.7	(6.5)
	Russian Federation												
	Perm Territory region•	23.6	(5.7)	72.1	(6.2)	4.3	(2.7)	28.0	(5.4)	47.5	(6.7)	24.5	(5.7)
	United Arab Emirates												
	Abu Dhabi•	22.7	(3.7)	59.6	(4.4)	17.7	(3.5)	10.4	(2.6)	27.1	(3.3)	62.5	(3.3)
	Ajman	16.6	(6.7)	72.0	(8.1)	11.3	(6.3)	0.0	c	26.5	(4.2)	73.5	(4.2)
	Dubai•	42.9	(0.3)	46.6	(0.3)	10.4	(0.1)	1.6	(0.0)	10.7	(0.1)	87.7	(0.1)
	Fujairah	39.4	(12.5)	57.4	(12.5)	3.2	(0.2)	5.8	(3.6)	24.1	(6.1)	70.1	(6.2)
	Ras Al Khaimah	20.7	(11.3)	72.6	(12.9)	6.6	(6.3)	17.5	(7.0)	34.7	(7.4)	47.8	(10.1)
	Sharjah	20.5	(8.1)	77.0	(8.1)	2.5	(1.7)	0.0	c	30.1	(7.6)	69.9	(7.6)
	Umm Al Quwain	29.4	(0.5)	70.3	(0.6)	0.3	(0.3)	17.7	(0.2)	36.3	(0.4)	46.0	(0.3)

• PISA adjudicated region.
Note: See Table IV.2.7 for national data.
StatLink ⫘⫘⫘ http://dx.doi.org/10.1787/888932957536

[Part 1/4]
Table B2.IV.3 **School transfer policies, by region**
Results based on school principals' reports

OECD	Percentage of students in schools whose principal reported that a student in the national modal grade for 15-year-olds would be transferred to another school for the following reasons:																							
	Low academic achievement						High academic achievement						Behavioural problems						Special learning needs					
	Not likely		Likely		Very likely		Not likely		Likely		Very likely		Not likely		Likely		Very likely		Not likely		Likely		Very likely	
	%	S.E.	%	S.E.	%	S.E.	%	S.E.	%	S.E.	%	S.E.	%	S.E.	%	S.E.	%	S.E.	%	S.E.	%	S.E.	%	S.E.
Australia																								
Australian Capital Territory	100.0	c	0.0	c	0.0	c	96.0	(0.4)	4.0	(0.4)	0.0	c	89.8	(0.7)	10.2	(0.7)	0.0	c	95.2	(0.4)	4.8	(0.4)	0.0	c
New South Wales	96.8	(1.4)	2.5	(1.2)	0.6	(0.7)	92.0	(2.1)	5.6	(1.7)	2.4	(1.2)	75.2	(3.2)	22.9	(3.1)	1.9	(1.1)	88.6	(2.4)	10.2	(2.2)	1.2	(0.9)
Northern Territory	84.4	(8.6)	15.6	(8.6)	0.0	c	90.7	(1.1)	9.3	(1.1)	0.0	c	88.7	(1.1)	8.9	(0.9)	2.4	(0.3)	100.0	c	0.0	c	0.0	c
Queensland	98.7	(1.0)	0.7	(0.7)	0.6	(0.7)	96.6	(1.7)	3.4	(1.7)	0.0	c	73.1	(4.1)	22.3	(3.8)	4.6	(2.0)	96.2	(1.8)	3.8	(1.8)	0.0	c
South Australia	97.6	(1.6)	2.4	(1.6)	0.0	c	94.7	(2.8)	5.3	(2.8)	0.0	c	75.8	(4.4)	21.6	(4.3)	2.6	(0.7)	97.2	(1.5)	2.8	(1.5)	0.0	c
Tasmania	100.0	c	0.0	c	0.0	c	98.5	(1.6)	1.5	(1.6)	0.0	c	93.2	(1.1)	6.8	(1.1)	0.0	c	92.8	(0.7)	7.2	(0.7)	0.0	c
Victoria	92.1	(2.0)	7.3	(2.1)	0.6	(0.6)	88.7	(3.1)	7.7	(2.5)	3.5	(1.8)	68.0	(4.5)	30.7	(4.4)	1.3	(0.9)	84.4	(3.5)	15.0	(3.6)	0.7	(0.7)
Western Australia	96.7	(1.9)	2.0	(1.3)	1.3	(1.3)	92.6	(2.8)	4.9	(2.2)	2.6	(1.8)	84.4	(4.2)	13.8	(4.0)	1.7	(1.4)	91.1	(3.4)	5.6	(2.5)	3.2	(2.3)
Belgium																								
Flemish community•	34.9	(3.2)	41.4	(3.9)	23.7	(3.5)	95.0	(1.7)	3.0	(1.5)	2.0	(0.9)	45.3	(4.0)	43.9	(4.1)	10.8	(2.3)	57.7	(4.1)	38.7	(3.8)	3.6	(1.6)
French community	59.4	(5.4)	34.1	(5.7)	6.5	(2.7)	89.3	(2.9)	9.7	(2.7)	1.0	(1.1)	24.6	(4.8)	58.4	(5.5)	17.0	(3.8)	48.9	(5.5)	44.4	(5.2)	6.7	(1.9)
German-speaking community	23.8	(0.2)	29.2	(0.3)	47.0	(0.3)	85.4	(0.3)	14.6	(0.3)	0.0	c	27.0	(0.3)	68.6	(0.4)	4.5	(0.3)	13.8	(0.2)	46.2	(0.2)	40.0	(0.3)
Canada																								
Alberta	97.2	(1.8)	1.7	(1.5)	1.1	(1.0)	97.1	(1.6)	2.9	(1.6)	0.0	(0.0)	74.1	(4.7)	23.4	(4.6)	2.6	(1.1)	85.5	(4.3)	13.4	(4.2)	1.1	(1.0)
British Columbia	95.2	(2.6)	4.7	(2.6)	0.1	(0.1)	100.0	c	0.0	c	0.0	c	65.1	(5.8)	30.4	(6.0)	4.5	(2.5)	93.5	(2.7)	4.7	(2.5)	1.8	(1.2)
Manitoba	97.7	(1.6)	2.3	(1.6)	0.0	c	98.2	(1.1)	1.8	(1.1)	0.0	c	94.1	(2.3)	5.9	(2.3)	0.0	c	96.1	(1.9)	3.9	(1.9)	0.0	c
New Brunswick	98.9	(0.1)	1.1	(0.1)	0.0	c	99.6	(0.0)	0.4	(0.0)	0.0	c	85.4	(1.2)	10.8	(1.1)	3.8	(0.3)	91.9	(0.4)	8.1	(0.4)	0.0	c
Newfoundland and Labrador	100.0	c	0.0	c	0.0	c	100.0	c	0.0	c	0.0	c	94.8	(0.4)	5.2	(0.4)	0.0	c	98.4	(1.1)	0.0	c	1.6	(1.1)
Nova Scotia	99.6	(0.1)	0.4	(0.1)	0.0	c	97.1	(0.5)	2.9	(0.5)	0.0	c	89.6	(2.6)	10.4	(2.6)	0.0	c	92.0	(1.8)	8.0	(1.8)	0.0	c
Ontario	99.8	(0.0)	0.2	(0.0)	0.0	c	100.0	c	0.0	c	0.0	c	84.6	(4.0)	15.4	(4.0)	0.0	c	90.3	(3.2)	8.6	(3.0)	1.1	(1.0)
Prince Edward Island	100.0	c	0.0	c	0.0	c	100.0	c	0.0	c	0.0	c	88.8	(0.3)	11.2	(0.3)	0.0	c	100.0	c	0.0	c	0.0	c
Quebec	85.1	(3.3)	11.8	(3.0)	3.1	(1.5)	97.5	(1.3)	1.7	(1.0)	0.9	(0.8)	48.2	(4.5)	45.2	(4.3)	6.6	(1.9)	60.0	(4.6)	31.9	(4.3)	8.1	(2.5)
Saskatchewan	97.1	(0.2)	2.9	(0.2)	0.0	c	99.7	(0.3)	0.3	(0.3)	0.0	c	88.1	(1.3)	11.0	(1.3)	0.9	(0.1)	94.5	(1.0)	3.4	(1.0)	2.1	(0.1)
Italy																								
Abruzzo	21.0	(5.0)	62.0	(5.9)	17.0	(4.8)	97.9	(2.1)	2.1	(2.1)	0.0	c	52.7	(6.7)	42.0	(6.7)	5.3	(3.8)	75.6	(5.6)	22.1	(6.1)	2.3	(2.3)
Basilicata	47.4	(5.8)	47.7	(6.4)	4.9	(2.3)	96.5	(2.4)	2.2	(2.1)	1.3	(1.3)	71.4	(5.2)	25.0	(6.1)	3.6	(2.3)	74.5	(6.6)	25.5	(6.6)	0.0	c
Bolzano	22.0	(0.6)	48.2	(0.8)	29.9	(0.6)	89.7	(0.4)	9.7	(0.4)	0.6	(0.1)	57.4	(0.8)	34.4	(0.9)	8.2	(0.3)	46.5	(0.9)	43.1	(0.9)	10.4	(0.3)
Calabria	46.9	(5.8)	44.9	(6.2)	8.2	(4.1)	99.5	(0.5)	0.5	(0.5)	0.0	c	53.9	(7.0)	45.2	(7.0)	0.9	(0.9)	71.9	(8.0)	25.7	(7.6)	2.4	(2.5)
Campania	34.9	(7.1)	53.7	(7.4)	11.4	(2.9)	100.0	c	0.0	c	0.0	c	54.3	(6.1)	42.0	(5.9)	3.8	(2.6)	72.7	(6.2)	27.3	(6.2)	0.0	c
Emilia Romagna	40.6	(6.9)	41.3	(7.5)	18.0	(4.6)	96.7	(2.4)	3.3	(2.4)	0.0	c	62.2	(7.0)	33.6	(7.6)	4.2	(3.0)	65.9	(6.7)	29.9	(6.7)	4.2	(3.0)
Friuli Venezia Giulia	32.9	(6.0)	57.9	(5.6)	9.2	(4.4)	100.0	c	0.0	c	0.0	c	69.7	(4.9)	26.2	(4.8)	4.1	(2.5)	69.0	(5.4)	28.6	(5.0)	2.4	(1.9)
Lazio	35.9	(6.6)	50.9	(7.5)	13.3	(4.4)	100.0	c	0.0	c	0.0	c	67.2	(5.3)	29.4	(5.0)	3.3	(2.7)	63.6	(8.1)	33.6	(7.7)	2.8	(2.7)
Liguria	32.7	(6.3)	46.3	(6.6)	21.0	(5.9)	100.0	c	0.0	c	0.0	c	61.4	(8.8)	38.4	(8.8)	0.1	(0.1)	66.3	(6.6)	31.7	(7.0)	1.9	(1.9)
Lombardia	35.2	(7.3)	48.9	(8.0)	15.9	(6.1)	98.9	(1.1)	1.1	(1.1)	0.0	c	64.9	(6.9)	31.1	(6.3)	4.0	(2.8)	55.1	(7.1)	38.0	(7.9)	6.8	(4.0)
Marche	39.9	(4.7)	47.6	(6.6)	12.5	(4.9)	96.9	(3.1)	3.1	(3.1)	0.0	c	62.8	(6.5)	34.9	(6.9)	2.3	(2.3)	71.7	(3.7)	23.6	(4.4)	4.7	(2.8)
Molise	33.8	(0.9)	61.2	(0.9)	5.0	(0.3)	97.9	(0.2)	2.1	(0.2)	0.0	c	69.0	(0.8)	31.0	(0.8)	0.0	c	66.9	(0.9)	31.2	(0.9)	1.9	(0.2)
Piemonte	43.3	(6.6)	45.8	(7.2)	10.9	(4.6)	92.0	(4.2)	8.0	(4.2)	0.0	c	72.8	(6.1)	27.2	(6.1)	0.0	c	81.3	(6.2)	18.7	(6.2)	0.0	c
Puglia	42.5	(7.5)	43.6	(7.7)	13.9	(4.8)	94.8	(3.2)	5.2	(3.2)	0.0	c	61.3	(7.0)	32.0	(6.4)	6.7	(3.4)	79.6	(6.1)	18.4	(5.7)	2.0	(2.1)
Sardegna	28.7	(5.9)	57.6	(7.7)	13.7	(5.5)	98.4	(1.6)	1.6	(1.6)	0.0	c	44.4	(7.7)	50.6	(6.8)	5.0	(3.6)	61.1	(5.6)	36.6	(6.2)	2.3	(2.4)
Sicilia	48.8	(5.8)	41.2	(6.5)	10.1	(3.4)	97.3	(2.6)	2.7	(2.6)	0.0	c	71.7	(6.1)	24.3	(5.4)	4.0	(2.6)	83.7	(3.8)	16.3	(3.8)	0.0	c
Toscana	27.3	(5.8)	62.8	(6.7)	9.9	(4.8)	100.0	c	0.0	c	0.0	c	59.1	(6.3)	38.7	(6.7)	2.2	(2.2)	69.8	(6.2)	28.0	(6.6)	2.3	(2.3)
Trento	42.5	(4.3)	46.4	(3.6)	11.1	(3.9)	92.6	(3.7)	7.4	(3.7)	0.0	c	66.7	(5.0)	26.6	(4.4)	6.7	(3.5)	65.1	(4.4)	29.9	(4.4)	5.0	(0.4)
Umbria	42.4	(5.1)	41.6	(5.5)	15.9	(5.0)	96.8	(3.1)	3.2	(3.1)	0.0	c	60.5	(6.3)	39.5	(6.3)	0.0	c	74.2	(4.1)	14.7	(4.2)	11.1	(2.7)
Valle d'Aosta	38.4	(0.8)	47.0	(0.9)	14.6	(0.7)	87.9	(0.7)	12.1	(0.7)	0.0	c	68.1	(1.0)	31.9	(1.0)	0.0	c	80.8	(0.6)	19.2	(0.6)	0.0	c
Veneto	34.5	(7.5)	54.3	(8.5)	11.2	(4.8)	96.5	(3.3)	3.5	(3.3)	0.0	c	58.7	(7.4)	41.2	(7.4)	0.1	(0.0)	73.6	(6.6)	24.1	(6.2)	2.2	(2.0)
Mexico																								
Aguascalientes	51.3	(6.6)	42.6	(5.9)	6.1	(3.6)	76.5	(5.3)	17.4	(6.8)	6.1	(3.7)	39.0	(5.4)	44.1	(6.7)	16.8	(5.7)	41.5	(6.6)	44.7	(5.5)	13.8	(4.2)
Baja California	49.1	(12.0)	43.6	(11.8)	7.3	(4.4)	77.7	(8.1)	12.4	(4.0)	9.9	(7.2)	15.0	(5.7)	68.6	(7.2)	16.4	(4.6)	44.3	(11.4)	42.6	(7.1)	13.0	(7.1)
Baja California Sur	67.7	(5.3)	26.7	(5.1)	5.5	(0.4)	84.4	(5.6)	10.3	(3.8)	5.3	(3.9)	47.0	(7.8)	48.5	(7.6)	4.5	(1.4)	33.4	(6.3)	53.5	(7.1)	13.1	(5.8)
Campeche	62.0	(5.8)	32.9	(6.4)	5.1	(2.6)	74.1	(5.3)	19.1	(3.9)	6.8	(3.7)	38.8	(8.6)	44.9	(10.6)	16.3	(8.2)	45.7	(8.3)	45.5	(8.8)	8.8	(3.7)
Chiapas	60.7	(8.9)	32.9	(8.0)	6.4	(3.8)	58.1	(6.8)	35.0	(7.8)	6.9	(4.4)	31.4	(6.6)	55.2	(8.4)	13.3	(6.4)	49.4	(8.3)	37.5	(7.5)	13.1	(5.1)
Chihuahua	52.2	(7.0)	40.9	(7.4)	6.9	(3.5)	84.7	(7.1)	15.3	(7.1)	0.0	c	25.1	(5.3)	57.1	(9.9)	17.8	(8.1)	31.8	(6.3)	60.4	(6.5)	7.9	(3.9)
Coahuila	46.8	(7.0)	43.2	(7.0)	10.0	(3.8)	74.9	(6.8)	15.4	(6.1)	9.6	(4.9)	18.7	(6.1)	65.3	(8.6)	16.0	(6.9)	48.8	(8.4)	44.8	(7.7)	6.4	(3.2)
Colima	69.1	(4.7)	29.4	(5.0)	1.5	(1.5)	70.9	(6.4)	17.9	(5.0)	11.2	(5.0)	48.9	(6.5)	47.0	(5.7)	4.2	(3.1)	52.3	(6.1)	38.0	(7.9)	9.7	(5.3)
Distrito Federal	68.4	(6.6)	25.3	(7.8)	6.3	(3.7)	75.5	(7.9)	15.0	(6.8)	9.5	(5.4)	43.9	(8.7)	46.7	(8.9)	9.4	(4.8)	54.5	(7.4)	39.7	(8.2)	5.8	(3.5)
Durango	51.9	(9.3)	43.2	(9.7)	4.9	(3.0)	78.1	(7.2)	19.6	(6.8)	2.3	(2.0)	28.5	(7.0)	58.6	(7.8)	12.9	(5.3)	50.6	(8.0)	45.0	(7.9)	4.5	(2.6)
Guanajuato	61.1	(7.9)	34.0	(7.6)	4.9	(2.9)	83.0	(5.7)	10.8	(4.6)	6.2	(3.4)	44.2	(7.1)	43.4	(8.4)	12.3	(6.1)	52.2	(7.9)	47.8	(7.9)	0.0	c
Guerrero	56.9	(8.9)	34.3	(8.7)	8.8	(3.4)	47.3	(10.0)	34.0	(10.4)	18.7	(8.2)	37.6	(8.9)	43.7	(7.8)	18.7	(7.8)	45.8	(9.0)	39.3	(8.5)	14.9	(6.5)
Hidalgo	50.2	(7.1)	43.7	(7.6)	6.1	(3.9)	74.7	(7.0)	22.5	(6.3)	2.9	(2.9)	41.5	(7.7)	47.5	(8.0)	11.0	(5.9)	71.7	(6.1)	24.4	(6.5)	3.9	(2.3)
Jalisco	83.0	(6.1)	14.6	(5.7)	2.3	(2.3)	89.2	(5.3)	10.6	(5.3)	0.2	(0.2)	54.2	(10.2)	41.8	(10.0)	3.9	(2.8)	54.7	(9.9)	38.0	(8.2)	7.3	(5.0)
Mexico	42.9	(8.6)	52.4	(8.5)	4.7	(3.3)	72.8	(9.1)	15.4	(6.2)	11.8	(7.2)	40.4	(7.9)	45.7	(6.7)	13.9	(6.8)	50.3	(8.8)	37.9	(7.8)	11.8	(7.2)
Morelos	66.6	(8.0)	29.3	(8.8)	4.1	(3.1)	66.5	(8.1)	24.3	(7.9)	9.2	(3.8)	32.2	(8.3)	59.7	(9.3)	8.1	(3.6)	42.4	(9.6)	47.9	(9.6)	9.7	(4.0)
Nayarit	63.1	(4.9)	30.1	(6.4)	6.8	(4.1)	72.2	(6.2)	25.2	(5.8)	2.6	(2.5)	25.2	(3.9)	43.1	(5.2)	31.7	(5.0)	52.9	(6.9)	39.5	(6.9)	7.6	(3.6)
Nuevo León	70.6	(8.6)	27.7	(8.5)	1.7	(1.8)	84.4	(5.0)	15.6	(5.0)	0.0	c	39.2	(8.4)	50.7	(8.5)	10.1	(4.4)	54.1	(9.6)	42.5	(9.6)	3.4	(2.4)
Puebla	62.7	(7.4)	37.3	(7.4)	0.0	c	73.6	(8.2)	24.5	(7.8)	2.0	(2.8)	33.9	(6.6)	55.9	(8.5)	10.3	(4.6)	58.9	(7.2)	25.6	(6.4)	15.5	(7.4)
Querétaro	55.1	(6.6)	35.7	(7.8)	9.2	(5.5)	77.4	(9.4)	16.1	(8.1)	6.5	(5.1)	26.9	(5.8)	66.2	(7.4)	6.9	(5.2)	66.7	(8.7)	21.7	(6.9)	11.7	(6.1)
Quintana Roo	52.1	(9.5)	41.1	(10.2)	6.7	(1.7)	83.5	(4.8)	11.8	(3.5)	4.8	(2.0)	22.0	(5.3)	70.4	(5.7)	7.6	(2.8)	49.8	(9.6)	39.1	(8.0)	11.1	(5.0)
San Luis Potosí	57.5	(9.5)	35.1	(8.9)	7.3	(4.6)	82.9	(4.9)	13.6	(5.0)	3.5	(2.4)	41.8	(9.2)	50.1	(9.3)	8.1	(5.1)	52.1	(5.5)	40.1	(5.8)	7.8	(3.9)
Sinaloa	57.2	(8.9)	41.7	(9.0)	1.2	(1.6)	89.9	(4.8)	8.6	(4.9)	1.5	(1.5)	43.3	(8.5)	52.4	(9.3)	4.3	(3.6)	57.8	(8.9)	26.1	(7.2)	16.1	(7.7)
Tabasco	68.1	(9.3)	31.4	(9.3)	0.5	(0.7)	72.0	(9.8)	22.9	(9.1)	5.1	(3.7)	25.7	(6.1)	53.0	(9.8)	21.3	(9.1)	57.9	(10.5)	26.4	(8.1)	15.7	(8.4)
Tamaulipas	45.2	(9.2)	47.0	(7.9)	7.9	(4.8)	81.5	(7.2)	12.9	(6.0)	5.7	(3.8)	29.9	(8.1)	53.6	(10.5)	16.5	(7.4)	34.7	(7.5)	55.5	(9.8)	9.8	(5.9)
Tlaxcala	46.2	(6.9)	42.3	(8.0)	11.4	(4.4)	88.5	(4.3)	8.9	(3.7)	2.6	(2.1)	27.4	(5.7)	53.8	(7.3)	18.8	(7.5)	30.7	(7.5)	50.9	(6.4)	18.4	(7.3)
Veracruz	67.3	(6.2)	21.4	(5.0)	11.3	(4.7)	72.4	(5.7)	17.8	(5.0)	9.7	(4.2)	34.6	(7.4)	54.8	(7.1)	10.6	(3.8)	56.4	(4.9)	36.6	(5.4)	7.0	(3.1)
Yucatán	64.9	(9.4)	31.9	(9.0)	3.2	(2.5)	73.0	(8.1)	20.8	(8.1)	6.2	(3.6)	40.0	(7.5)	41.3	(8.5)	18.7	(8.8)	52.9	(9.5)	35.4	(8.5)	11.8	(6.1)
Zacatecas	67.5	(8.3)	26.7	(7.4)	5.8	(3.8)	77.7	(5.7)	13.0	(4.5)	9.3	(4.6)	37.4	(5.9)	47.5	(8.5)	15.1	(6.2)	49.7	(7.7)	33.6	(7.9)	16.6	(4.3)

• PISA adjudicated region.
Note: See Table IV.2.9 for national data.
StatLink http://dx.doi.org/10.1787/888932957536

[Part 2/4]
Table B2.IV.3 School transfer policies, by region
Results based on school principals' reports

Percentage of students in schools whose principal reported that a student in the national modal grade for 15-year-olds would be transferred to another school for the following reasons:

	Low academic achievement						High academic achievement						Behavioural problems						Special learning needs					
	Not likely		Likely		Very likely		Not likely		Likely		Very likely		Not likely		Likely		Very likely		Not likely		Likely		Very likely	
	%	S.E.	%	S.E.	%	S.E.	%	S.E.	%	S.E.	%	S.E.	%	S.E.	%	S.E.	%	S.E.	%	S.E.	%	S.E.	%	S.E.
OECD																								
Portugal																								
Alentejo	93.1	(4.5)	6.9	(4.5)	0.0	c	100.0	c	0.0	c	0.0	c	81.3	(7.0)	18.7	(7.0)	0.0	c	84.9	(7.0)	10.7	(5.9)	4.4	(3.9)
Spain																								
Andalusia•	100.0	(0.0)	0.0	c	0.0	c	100.0	c	0.0	c	0.0	c	76.8	(5.4)	23.2	(5.4)	0.0	c	89.6	(3.7)	10.4	(3.7)	0.0	c
Aragon•	98.7	(1.2)	1.3	(1.2)	0.0	c	98.4	(1.5)	0.0	c	1.6	(1.5)	87.8	(5.0)	12.2	(5.0)	0.0	c	73.5	(6.4)	26.5	(6.4)	0.0	c
Asturias•	100.0	(0.0)	0.0	c	0.0	c	99.0	(0.7)	1.0	(0.7)	0.0	c	62.9	(7.0)	37.1	(7.0)	0.0	c	93.1	(3.5)	6.9	(3.5)	0.0	c
Balearic Islands•	98.3	(1.8)	1.7	(1.8)	0.0	c	100.0	c	0.0	c	0.0	c	84.3	(5.5)	15.7	(5.5)	0.0	c	88.2	(4.9)	9.4	(4.3)	2.4	(2.4)
Basque Country•	86.1	(2.6)	12.1	(2.4)	1.9	(1.1)	94.3	(1.7)	5.0	(1.6)	0.6	(0.6)	77.1	(3.2)	20.9	(3.0)	2.0	(1.1)	71.3	(3.4)	23.0	(3.2)	5.7	(1.5)
Cantabria•	96.0	(2.8)	4.0	(2.8)	0.0	c	100.0	c	0.0	c	0.0	c	63.2	(5.8)	32.5	(5.9)	4.3	(3.0)	80.2	(5.4)	19.8	(5.4)	0.0	c
Castile and Leon•	95.9	(2.9)	4.1	(2.9)	0.0	c	100.0	c	0.0	c	0.0	c	81.7	(5.0)	15.6	(4.6)	2.8	(2.3)	82.1	(5.6)	12.7	(4.8)	5.3	(3.0)
Catalonia•	100.0	c	0.0	c	0.0	c	100.0	c	0.0	c	0.0	c	72.3	(7.0)	25.3	(6.6)	2.4	(2.4)	70.4	(6.5)	27.0	(6.1)	2.6	(2.5)
Extremadura•	97.9	(2.1)	0.0	c	2.1	(2.1)	100.0	c	0.0	c	0.0	c	88.3	(4.7)	9.6	(4.1)	2.1	(2.1)	86.9	(5.2)	8.8	(4.2)	4.3	(3.0)
Galicia•	95.9	(2.9)	4.1	(2.9)	0.0	c	92.7	(3.7)	5.4	(3.1)	1.9	(1.9)	78.8	(5.0)	21.2	(5.0)	0.0	c	90.8	(3.1)	7.3	(3.7)	1.9	(1.9)
La Rioja•	100.0	c	0.0	c	0.0	c	93.1	(0.3)	6.9	(0.3)	0.0	c	66.1	(0.6)	33.9	(0.6)	0.0	c	83.5	(0.5)	16.5	(0.5)	0.0	c
Madrid•	93.1	(3.9)	6.9	(3.9)	0.0	c	95.3	(2.9)	2.4	(2.4)	2.3	(1.6)	78.2	(5.5)	21.8	(5.5)	0.0	c	73.2	(6.0)	16.9	(5.8)	9.9	(4.6)
Murcia•	97.7	(2.3)	2.3	(2.3)	0.0	c	93.7	(3.7)	6.3	(3.7)	0.0	c	60.5	(6.4)	37.5	(6.2)	2.1	(2.0)	88.8	(5.0)	11.2	(5.0)	0.0	c
Navarre•	92.4	(3.7)	7.6	(3.7)	0.0	c	94.8	(2.0)	5.2	(2.0)	0.0	c	70.1	(4.3)	28.2	(3.9)	1.7	(1.7)	75.5	(4.9)	19.5	(4.6)	5.0	(1.9)
United Kingdom																								
England	95.6	(1.9)	2.5	(1.6)	1.8	(1.1)	96.7	(1.3)	3.3	(1.3)	0.0	c	69.8	(4.7)	27.5	(4.2)	2.7	(1.4)	95.5	(1.9)	4.5	(1.9)	0.0	c
Northern Ireland	92.3	(2.7)	5.3	(2.1)	2.4	(1.7)	92.3	(2.5)	7.1	(2.4)	0.5	(0.5)	83.6	(3.8)	15.0	(3.8)	1.4	(0.1)	96.4	(1.5)	2.5	(1.0)	1.1	(1.1)
Scotland•	98.5	(1.1)	0.7	(0.8)	0.7	(0.8)	98.7	(1.1)	0.6	(0.9)	0.7	(0.8)	86.1	(3.4)	10.6	(3.2)	3.3	(1.7)	97.5	(1.5)	0.7	(0.8)	1.7	(1.3)
Wales	97.8	(1.3)	1.5	(1.1)	0.7	(0.7)	96.3	(1.7)	3.0	(1.5)	0.7	(0.7)	71.5	(3.2)	26.6	(3.3)	1.9	(1.2)	94.4	(1.9)	4.9	(1.8)	0.7	(0.7)
United States																								
Connecticut•	100.0	c	0.0	c	0.0	c	98.1	(1.9)	1.9	(1.9)	0.0	c	88.8	(3.8)	11.2	(3.8)	0.0	c	92.2	(2.6)	7.8	(2.6)	0.0	c
Florida•	95.9	(2.4)	4.1	(2.4)	0.0	c	100.0	c	0.0	c	0.0	c	52.6	(7.8)	47.4	(7.8)	0.0	c	85.9	(5.4)	11.7	(4.9)	2.3	(2.3)
Massachusetts•	97.5	(2.6)	2.5	(2.6)	0.0	c	100.0	c	0.0	c	0.0	c	87.4	(5.1)	12.6	(5.1)	0.0	c	83.1	(5.9)	16.9	(5.9)	0.0	c
Partners																								
Argentina																								
Ciudad Autónoma de Buenos Aires•	65.9	(7.3)	29.2	(6.4)	4.8	(3.6)	96.6	(2.6)	3.4	(2.6)	0.0	c	19.1	(6.8)	70.4	(7.9)	10.5	(4.9)	32.7	(7.2)	52.9	(7.5)	14.4	(5.8)
Brazil																								
Acre	93.6	(2.7)	6.4	(2.7)	0.0	c	100.0	c	0.0	c	0.0	c	43.7	(7.9)	36.7	(8.9)	19.6	(11.2)	83.2	(8.4)	16.8	(8.4)	0.0	c
Alagoas	82.6	(6.1)	17.4	(6.1)	0.0	c	92.5	(5.1)	7.5	(5.1)	0.0	c	36.7	(11.0)	63.3	(11.0)	0.0	c	80.6	(12.3)	5.1	(4.1)	14.2	(12.2)
Amapá	90.7	(5.9)	9.3	(5.9)	0.0	c	93.5	(4.5)	6.5	(4.5)	0.0	c	24.2	(10.5)	71.5	(10.5)	4.3	(3.4)	86.9	(6.7)	13.1	(6.7)	0.0	c
Amazonas	86.4	(8.5)	10.9	(8.0)	2.7	(2.7)	100.0	c	0.0	c	0.0	c	25.3	(7.3)	49.7	(11.5)	25.0	(9.9)	51.3	(9.3)	47.6	(9.2)	1.0	(1.0)
Bahia	71.5	(8.2)	18.7	(10.4)	9.8	(10.7)	96.8	(3.0)	3.2	(3.0)	0.0	c	42.3	(16.8)	57.7	(16.8)	0.0	c	77.5	(16.2)	22.5	(16.2)	0.0	c
Ceará	88.6	(6.9)	11.4	(6.9)	0.0	c	88.5	(8.5)	11.5	(8.5)	0.0	c	39.2	(9.7)	52.8	(9.9)	8.0	(7.4)	71.5	(11.5)	28.5	(11.5)	0.0	c
Espírito Santo	73.3	(8.4)	20.8	(7.5)	5.8	(4.1)	100.0	c	0.0	c	0.0	c	35.9	(8.3)	46.6	(14.1)	17.6	(9.8)	88.5	(6.9)	11.5	(6.9)	0.0	c
Federal District	83.9	(8.7)	5.5	(5.4)	10.6	(7.1)	100.0	c	0.0	c	0.0	c	16.8	(12.2)	60.5	(7.3)	22.8	(12.6)	68.8	(11.4)	23.2	(10.6)	8.0	(5.5)
Goiás	74.0	(9.5)	23.1	(9.2)	2.8	(2.8)	100.0	c	0.0	c	0.0	c	24.4	(9.8)	52.2	(11.4)	23.4	(10.8)	67.6	(11.6)	29.9	(11.2)	2.5	(2.4)
Maranhão	63.9	(14.8)	25.2	(12.6)	10.9	(9.9)	100.0	c	0.0	c	0.0	c	18.2	(9.9)	76.5	(11.0)	5.3	(5.2)	49.4	(15.0)	50.6	(15.0)	0.0	c
Mato Grosso	72.7	(8.8)	14.9	(8.6)	12.5	(6.8)	91.0	(6.8)	6.0	(6.1)	2.9	(2.9)	40.7	(11.3)	40.3	(9.8)	19.0	(10.3)	74.5	(9.2)	22.4	(8.7)	3.1	(3.1)
Mato Grosso do Sul	62.0	(9.3)	22.6	(9.2)	15.3	(3.0)	97.3	(2.9)	2.7	(2.9)	0.0	c	35.4	(9.4)	62.6	(8.6)	2.1	(2.2)	71.2	(8.3)	23.1	(8.4)	5.7	(3.4)
Minas Gerais	71.0	(8.1)	23.6	(9.6)	5.5	(4.2)	93.4	(4.6)	6.6	(4.6)	0.0	c	39.3	(9.4)	52.2	(9.0)	8.6	(5.3)	66.4	(7.5)	33.6	(7.5)	0.0	c
Pará	85.5	(13.0)	14.5	(13.0)	0.0	c	97.6	(1.2)	0.0	c	2.4	(1.2)	34.9	(12.8)	60.7	(13.3)	4.4	(3.7)	82.5	(9.8)	17.5	(9.8)	0.0	c
Paraíba	79.8	(11.2)	15.9	(9.2)	4.3	(4.8)	100.0	c	0.0	c	0.0	c	18.2	(10.3)	57.0	(12.2)	24.9	(15.6)	78.0	(9.3)	17.7	(7.1)	4.3	(4.8)
Paraná	87.7	(8.8)	12.3	(8.8)	0.0	c	91.1	(8.7)	0.0	c	8.9	(8.7)	48.8	(7.9)	51.2	(7.9)	0.0	c	66.2	(13.1)	33.8	(13.1)	0.0	c
Pernambuco	90.0	(5.7)	4.6	(3.3)	5.4	(4.3)	100.0	c	0.0	c	0.0	c	35.3	(9.2)	45.8	(10.6)	18.9	(7.8)	57.8	(12.0)	25.7	(10.5)	16.5	(9.3)
Piauí	58.8	(10.5)	25.6	(9.9)	15.6	(4.4)	91.0	(6.1)	9.0	(6.1)	0.0	c	25.2	(12.5)	56.4	(9.5)	18.5	(11.7)	56.3	(13.5)	38.2	(14.6)	5.5	(4.5)
Rio de Janeiro	72.4	(9.4)	18.7	(7.8)	8.9	(7.3)	84.0	(8.8)	4.5	(4.5)	11.5	(7.2)	45.7	(8.4)	28.4	(9.9)	25.9	(9.3)	71.7	(9.6)	23.3	(9.6)	5.0	(5.9)
Rio Grande do Norte	72.6	(9.8)	17.9	(11.5)	9.5	(6.9)	91.9	(8.3)	8.1	(8.3)	0.0	c	36.4	(11.7)	48.1	(13.7)	15.5	(9.6)	88.5	(6.1)	11.5	(6.1)	0.0	c
Rio Grande do Sul	72.9	(11.3)	22.0	(9.0)	5.2	(3.8)	85.6	(8.8)	5.2	(3.8)	9.3	(5.9)	43.4	(11.9)	45.8	(9.0)	10.8	(5.5)	73.4	(10.1)	26.6	(10.1)	0.0	c
Rondônia	81.1	(10.2)	18.9	(10.2)	0.0	c	94.9	(5.3)	5.1	(5.3)	0.0	c	42.8	(11.8)	57.2	(11.8)	0.0	c	74.6	(7.9)	25.4	(7.9)	0.0	c
Roraima	55.3	(9.1)	36.7	(10.6)	8.0	(7.7)	94.9	(5.1)	0.0	c	5.1	(5.1)	30.7	(9.2)	64.5	(10.4)	4.7	(4.6)	57.1	(11.7)	30.0	(8.2)	12.9	(9.0)
Santa Catarina	67.0	(10.4)	28.3	(8.9)	4.7	(4.9)	95.0	(5.0)	0.0	c	5.0	(5.0)	32.0	(9.9)	50.5	(11.8)	17.4	(8.8)	95.0	(5.0)	0.0	c	5.0	(5.0)
São Paulo	82.5	(4.5)	12.8	(4.4)	4.7	(2.8)	91.8	(3.7)	5.5	(3.2)	2.7	(2.0)	51.4	(6.3)	42.2	(6.1)	6.3	(3.3)	80.7	(5.5)	16.4	(5.2)	2.9	(2.0)
Sergipe	50.3	(12.0)	30.2	(11.1)	19.5	(9.0)	76.7	(12.9)	16.4	(10.2)	6.9	(6.7)	26.0	(12.1)	46.1	(16.4)	27.9	(14.5)	42.7	(12.1)	57.3	(12.1)	0.0	c
Tocantins	70.1	(10.7)	24.1	(10.7)	5.8	(1.0)	88.7	(6.6)	11.3	(6.6)	0.0	c	27.4	(11.4)	63.6	(9.6)	9.0	(5.1)	56.6	(11.3)	28.4	(8.2)	15.0	(6.8)
Colombia																								
Bogota	75.7	(5.5)	22.9	(5.6)	1.5	(1.6)	78.7	(4.8)	15.1	(4.1)	6.3	(3.3)	34.8	(6.9)	56.9	(7.7)	8.3	(4.8)	24.5	(6.9)	72.3	(6.8)	3.1	(2.2)
Cali	76.6	(5.4)	19.8	(5.8)	3.6	(2.1)	76.9	(7.5)	20.5	(7.3)	2.5	(2.0)	34.6	(8.0)	61.7	(7.6)	3.7	(2.8)	26.0	(6.0)	63.4	(7.2)	10.6	(5.4)
Manizales	49.8	(7.7)	42.9	(7.8)	7.3	(4.0)	84.4	(5.8)	15.6	(5.8)	0.0	c	32.8	(8.0)	61.3	(7.2)	6.0	(3.7)	41.5	(6.8)	43.5	(7.5)	15.0	(4.6)
Medellin	54.1	(7.8)	42.3	(7.7)	3.6	(2.6)	78.9	(6.1)	15.5	(4.9)	5.6	(5.4)	26.7	(7.8)	66.4	(8.4)	6.8	(3.4)	40.9	(7.3)	54.7	(7.8)	4.4	(2.8)
Russian Federation																								
Perm Territory region•	87.7	(4.7)	11.0	(4.5)	1.3	(1.3)	69.3	(4.7)	21.3	(5.0)	9.4	(3.2)	85.5	(3.5)	14.5	(3.5)	0.0	c	38.0	(7.5)	53.8	(7.1)	8.2	(3.8)
United Arab Emirates																								
Abu Dhabi•	62.2	(4.1)	33.8	(3.6)	4.1	(1.8)	75.8	(3.3)	20.1	(2.8)	4.0	(2.0)	35.8	(4.7)	50.3	(4.9)	13.9	(2.9)	55.4	(3.9)	42.4	(3.6)	2.2	(1.5)
Ajman	65.5	(5.5)	34.5	(5.5)	0.0	c	53.1	(8.4)	41.4	(8.0)	5.5	(5.2)	34.7	(7.1)	44.0	(7.2)	21.3	(6.2)	55.5	(6.9)	44.5	(6.9)	0.0	c
Dubai•	73.4	(0.1)	21.1	(0.1)	5.5	(0.0)	85.5	(0.3)	10.5	(0.1)	3.9	(0.3)	54.3	(0.2)	35.7	(0.2)	9.9	(0.1)	73.6	(0.1)	18.3	(0.1)	8.1	(0.1)
Fujairah	87.2	(0.6)	7.3	(0.3)	5.5	(0.3)	69.0	(2.8)	31.0	(2.8)	0.0	c	51.3	(6.7)	32.6	(6.6)	16.0	(0.8)	64.9	(2.9)	35.1	(2.9)	0.0	c
Ras Al Khaimah	70.8	(7.6)	23.8	(6.8)	5.4	(5.1)	78.7	(5.2)	9.8	(3.5)	11.4	(4.9)	40.2	(9.4)	39.7	(7.4)	20.1	(8.9)	76.0	(7.8)	24.0	(7.8)	0.0	c
Sharjah	73.9	(10.2)	26.1	(10.2)	0.0	c	82.0	(8.5)	16.5	(8.3)	1.5	(1.1)	37.7	(10.8)	53.3	(9.3)	9.0	(6.5)	58.2	(9.8)	41.8	(9.8)	0.0	c
Umm Al Quwain	66.3	(0.3)	5.4	(0.3)	28.2	(0.2)	87.4	(0.4)	12.6	(0.4)	0.0	c	63.6	(0.3)	35.6	(0.3)	0.8	(0.2)	43.7	(0.3)	55.5	(0.2)	0.8	(0.2)

• PISA adjudicated region.
Note: See Table IV.2.9 for national data.
StatLink http://dx.doi.org/10.1787/888932957536

[Part 3/4]
School transfer policies, by region
Table B2.IV.3 *Results based on school principals' reports*

	Percentage of students in schools whose principal reported that a student in the national modal grade for 15-year-olds would be transferred to another school for the following reasons:												Percentage of students in schools whose principal reported that a student in the national modal grade for 15-year-olds would be "very likely" transferred to another school because of "low academic achievement", "behavioural problems" or "special learning needs"	
	Parents' or guardians' request						Other							
	Not likely		Likely		Very likely		Not likely		Likely		Very likely			
	%	S.E.	%	S.E.	%	S.E.	%	S.E.	%	S.E.	%	S.E.	%	S.E.
Australia														
Australian Capital Territory	69.6	(1.0)	25.7	(0.9)	4.6	(0.5)	84.6	(0.8)	14.8	(0.8)	0.6	(0.1)	0.0	c
New South Wales	59.3	(3.8)	36.4	(3.5)	4.2	(1.6)	83.7	(2.8)	14.1	(2.7)	2.2	(1.1)	1.9	(1.1)
Northern Territory	68.4	(9.2)	31.6	(9.2)	0.0	c	89.1	(1.2)	10.9	(1.2)	0.0	c	2.4	(0.3)
Queensland	62.9	(4.3)	30.2	(4.0)	6.9	(2.1)	91.0	(2.3)	8.1	(2.1)	0.9	(0.9)	5.1	(2.1)
South Australia	62.6	(5.0)	32.8	(5.2)	4.6	(1.9)	82.2	(3.8)	17.8	(3.8)	0.0	c	2.6	(0.7)
Tasmania	70.9	(1.8)	27.9	(1.8)	1.2	(0.5)	87.4	(1.3)	12.6	(1.3)	0.0	c	0.0	c
Victoria	55.9	(4.3)	36.4	(4.1)	7.7	(2.4)	80.3	(3.3)	18.4	(3.2)	1.2	(0.9)	2.6	(1.3)
Western Australia	61.1	(5.0)	35.6	(5.2)	3.3	(1.8)	80.4	(3.7)	16.7	(3.3)	2.9	(1.7)	3.7	(2.4)
Belgium														
Flemish community*	54.7	(4.1)	38.2	(3.7)	7.1	(1.8)	77.8	(3.9)	17.7	(3.8)	4.5	(1.8)	30.2	(3.7)
French community	36.5	(4.5)	46.9	(4.9)	16.7	(4.2)	56.0	(7.0)	42.1	(7.0)	1.9	(1.9)	24.7	(4.5)
German-speaking community	41.7	(0.4)	53.8	(0.4)	4.5	(0.3)	47.4	(0.4)	52.6	(0.4)	0.0	c	47.0	(0.3)
Canada														
Alberta	55.1	(5.1)	33.0	(4.8)	11.9	(3.7)	73.4	(6.4)	26.6	(6.4)	0.0	c	3.6	(1.5)
British Columbia	55.2	(5.0)	31.3	(5.6)	13.5	(4.3)	86.6	(6.2)	13.4	(6.2)	0.0	c	6.3	(2.7)
Manitoba	73.5	(2.4)	23.8	(2.2)	2.8	(1.0)	86.3	(5.0)	13.7	(5.0)	0.0	c	0.0	c
New Brunswick	58.6	(2.7)	36.1	(2.7)	5.3	(0.8)	74.2	(4.6)	21.2	(4.8)	4.5	(0.5)	3.7	(0.3)
Newfoundland and Labrador	74.2	(1.9)	24.1	(1.9)	1.6	(1.1)	82.0	(1.8)	18.0	(1.8)	0.0	c	1.6	(1.1)
Nova Scotia	48.5	(8.4)	48.7	(8.6)	2.9	(1.9)	83.1	(3.4)	10.6	(3.1)	6.3	(0.9)	0.0	c
Ontario	69.0	(4.7)	29.9	(4.6)	1.1	(1.0)	74.9	(6.6)	22.8	(6.5)	2.3	(2.1)	1.1	(1.0)
Prince Edward Island	53.0	(0.4)	36.8	(0.4)	10.2	(0.2)	98.5	(0.2)	1.1	(0.2)	0.4	(0.0)	0.0	c
Quebec	53.2	(3.7)	39.6	(3.5)	7.2	(2.0)	72.3	(5.0)	26.3	(4.9)	1.4	(1.0)	12.9	(3.0)
Saskatchewan	52.1	(3.1)	30.9	(2.3)	17.0	(1.9)	74.0	(3.2)	23.5	(3.0)	2.4	(1.1)	2.9	(0.1)
Italy														
Abruzzo	13.8	(3.6)	58.8	(6.6)	27.4	(6.5)	31.5	(7.4)	68.5	(7.4)	0.0	c	19.2	(4.2)
Basilicata	11.8	(3.9)	75.3	(4.4)	12.9	(3.9)	49.5	(7.8)	48.1	(7.9)	2.4	(0.2)	6.3	(2.4)
Bolzano	29.2	(0.6)	45.1	(0.8)	25.7	(0.9)	44.3	(0.8)	51.6	(0.8)	4.2	(0.3)	38.4	(0.7)
Calabria	6.5	(3.8)	55.5	(7.3)	38.0	(7.0)	54.6	(10.4)	45.4	(10.4)	0.0	c	11.5	(4.8)
Campania	13.1	(5.2)	63.7	(7.4)	23.3	(5.6)	64.0	(9.7)	36.0	(9.7)	0.0	c	15.2	(4.1)
Emilia Romagna	23.8	(7.5)	56.5	(7.7)	19.7	(6.8)	65.4	(13.2)	34.6	(13.2)	0.0	c	21.4	(5.1)
Friuli Venezia Giulia	18.0	(5.4)	68.8	(5.2)	13.1	(3.3)	53.5	(8.2)	40.1	(7.5)	6.4	(3.6)	9.2	(4.4)
Lazio	10.2	(4.5)	69.0	(7.6)	20.8	(6.7)	37.9	(8.9)	55.9	(8.9)	6.3	(5.1)	16.6	(5.2)
Liguria	12.0	(4.1)	59.5	(6.7)	28.5	(6.1)	60.2	(11.3)	39.5	(11.3)	0.3	(0.3)	21.2	(5.9)
Lombardia	15.3	(5.8)	54.6	(8.5)	30.1	(7.1)	56.1	(9.0)	43.9	(9.0)	0.0	c	23.3	(6.7)
Marche	14.2	(4.3)	66.2	(7.5)	19.7	(6.3)	62.1	(10.7)	31.7	(9.5)	6.2	(6.0)	12.5	(4.9)
Molise	14.1	(0.5)	69.0	(0.7)	16.9	(0.5)	42.2	(1.5)	57.8	(1.5)	0.0	c	6.9	(0.3)
Piemonte	10.0	(4.3)	66.4	(6.8)	23.5	(7.0)	65.6	(7.5)	28.7	(6.7)	5.7	(4.1)	10.9	(4.6)
Puglia	25.4	(7.9)	58.7	(8.9)	15.8	(4.9)	63.6	(8.0)	30.6	(7.6)	5.8	(0.8)	20.6	(6.0)
Sardegna	13.1	(5.0)	58.0	(5.9)	28.9	(6.4)	66.8	(9.7)	29.3	(9.6)	3.9	(3.9)	21.0	(6.0)
Sicilia	8.8	(3.8)	65.4	(7.8)	25.8	(7.1)	57.4	(7.9)	39.6	(7.3)	3.0	(3.0)	14.1	(4.3)
Toscana	16.0	(6.2)	73.2	(7.7)	10.9	(4.7)	69.8	(10.6)	27.7	(10.0)	2.6	(2.8)	12.1	(5.3)
Trento	16.4	(4.7)	69.5	(5.4)	14.0	(3.1)	62.6	(5.7)	37.4	(5.7)	0.0	c	16.1	(3.8)
Umbria	22.2	(4.5)	61.0	(4.8)	16.8	(4.7)	59.5	(10.0)	35.6	(9.7)	4.8	(4.6)	23.1	(5.5)
Valle d'Aosta	26.6	(1.0)	53.6	(1.0)	19.7	(0.7)	60.1	(1.3)	28.1	(1.1)	11.9	(0.6)	14.6	(0.7)
Veneto	17.4	(6.0)	61.5	(8.2)	21.2	(6.7)	66.1	(10.0)	33.9	(10.0)	0.0	c	13.4	(5.3)
Mexico														
Aguascalientes	4.6	(2.5)	61.8	(5.4)	33.5	(5.3)	19.0	(5.8)	62.8	(7.5)	18.2	(4.5)	24.9	(4.5)
Baja California	3.5	(2.8)	45.4	(8.2)	51.1	(8.1)	12.3	(10.3)	64.7	(8.2)	23.0	(5.2)	24.9	(6.0)
Baja California Sur	3.1	(2.3)	61.9	(6.6)	35.0	(6.0)	26.7	(6.0)	61.0	(8.2)	12.3	(7.3)	23.1	(5.8)
Campeche	7.6	(2.7)	41.3	(7.6)	51.1	(7.1)	21.9	(5.2)	60.7	(8.3)	17.4	(7.3)	20.8	(8.2)
Chiapas	9.3	(4.3)	47.4	(9.9)	43.4	(9.3)	45.8	(10.8)	31.9	(9.4)	22.3	(10.4)	24.3	(7.6)
Chihuahua	5.4	(3.1)	52.9	(10.8)	41.7	(10.4)	30.8	(9.1)	56.0	(11.1)	13.2	(8.0)	27.0	(9.2)
Coahuila	7.5	(3.2)	53.7	(8.9)	38.8	(8.0)	28.9	(11.2)	59.4	(11.3)	11.7	(6.3)	21.7	(7.5)
Colima	2.8	(0.2)	64.4	(6.8)	32.9	(6.7)	47.7	(6.5)	45.5	(6.9)	6.8	(4.2)	12.4	(6.0)
Distrito Federal	6.5	(4.0)	69.2	(8.5)	24.3	(7.7)	38.4	(12.1)	55.3	(12.5)	6.2	(4.3)	13.3	(5.6)
Durango	19.4	(10.4)	64.1	(9.5)	16.4	(5.1)	31.0	(7.6)	62.4	(7.7)	6.7	(3.9)	17.3	(6.1)
Guanajuato	16.0	(6.3)	69.8	(7.9)	14.2	(6.6)	37.6	(8.0)	62.4	(8.0)	0.0	c	13.9	(6.2)
Guerrero	10.2	(4.9)	58.4	(8.3)	31.4	(9.4)	66.7	(13.0)	25.5	(10.7)	7.8	(7.2)	29.6	(8.3)
Hidalgo	12.9	(4.8)	69.4	(8.5)	17.8	(6.9)	49.5	(11.0)	45.0	(11.1)	5.5	(4.8)	17.2	(6.8)
Jalisco	3.8	(2.1)	59.8	(9.3)	36.4	(9.1)	55.6	(9.4)	27.4	(7.4)	17.1	(7.4)	11.3	(5.8)
Mexico	4.3	(2.7)	74.8	(5.9)	20.9	(6.1)	32.0	(9.7)	65.5	(9.5)	2.4	(2.3)	19.2	(7.6)
Morelos	7.2	(4.1)	62.7	(7.9)	30.1	(6.0)	36.5	(11.3)	50.5	(10.8)	13.0	(5.2)	16.9	(5.3)
Nayarit	7.7	(3.7)	48.4	(6.6)	43.9	(7.0)	40.1	(7.3)	47.1	(7.9)	12.8	(5.5)	37.2	(5.7)
Nuevo León	21.6	(8.0)	63.3	(9.9)	15.1	(7.5)	36.4	(9.0)	50.5	(9.0)	13.1	(8.0)	11.5	(4.8)
Puebla	8.4	(3.4)	59.0	(7.9)	32.7	(7.6)	42.8	(9.2)	41.2	(10.0)	15.9	(9.1)	24.4	(7.2)
Querétaro	10.2	(4.3)	44.1	(9.5)	45.8	(9.7)	35.9	(6.8)	48.4	(10.5)	15.7	(8.2)	23.7	(6.1)
Quintana Roo	2.0	(1.0)	42.8	(7.5)	55.2	(7.4)	24.7	(8.5)	65.0	(8.1)	10.3	(3.5)	19.0	(4.8)
San Luis Potosí	10.7	(4.4)	59.7	(9.9)	29.6	(9.1)	30.4	(8.4)	59.1	(11.7)	10.5	(7.8)	21.8	(7.2)
Sinaloa	5.0	(2.7)	45.7	(8.9)	49.3	(9.1)	30.5	(11.8)	40.8	(12.9)	28.7	(9.2)	19.8	(8.2)
Tabasco	2.3	(1.4)	61.1	(9.2)	36.6	(9.2)	23.1	(9.4)	71.4	(10.7)	5.5	(5.7)	23.8	(9.3)
Tamaulipas	1.1	(0.7)	58.9	(10.1)	40.0	(10.0)	36.2	(10.7)	57.5	(9.9)	6.3	(5.0)	22.3	(8.8)
Tlaxcala	9.9	(2.6)	51.6	(8.7)	38.5	(8.6)	39.7	(7.3)	56.4	(7.5)	3.9	(3.1)	31.1	(8.4)
Veracruz	8.3	(3.7)	52.7	(10.1)	38.9	(9.7)	18.4	(6.2)	38.0	(12.4)	43.6	(12.9)	17.8	(4.3)
Yucatán	22.8	(6.0)	54.2	(9.2)	23.0	(7.0)	40.9	(9.1)	53.9	(9.3)	5.2	(3.8)	25.4	(9.4)
Zacatecas	8.6	(3.6)	40.5	(7.5)	50.9	(8.1)	23.3	(6.7)	38.3	(8.4)	38.4	(9.7)	30.1	(6.3)

* PISA adjudicated region.
Note: See Table IV.2.9 for national data.
StatLink ᴹˢᴾ http://dx.doi.org/10.1787/888932957536

[Part 4/4]
School transfer policies, by region
Table B2.IV.3   *Results based on school principals' reports*

	Parents' or guardians' request						Other						Percentage of students in schools whose principal reported that a student in the national modal grade for 15-year-olds would be "very likely" transferred to another school because of "low academic achievement", "behavioural problems" or "special learning needs"	
	Not likely		Likely		Very likely		Not likely		Likely		Very likely			
	%	S.E.	%	S.E.	%	S.E.	%	S.E.	%	S.E.	%	S.E.	%	S.E.
Portugal														
Alentejo	22.0	(8.7)	63.1	(12.7)	14.9	(9.8)	48.1	(13.0)	51.9	(13.0)	0.0	c	4.4	(3.9)
Spain														
Andalusia•	54.1	(7.9)	40.1	(8.4)	5.8	(3.3)	80.8	(7.1)	19.2	(7.1)	0.0	c	0.0	c
Aragon•	55.8	(6.1)	39.3	(6.0)	4.9	(3.4)	76.1	(7.9)	23.9	(7.9)	0.0	c	0.0	c
Asturias•	50.2	(6.5)	42.5	(6.1)	7.3	(3.6)	86.0	(5.8)	14.0	(5.8)	0.0	c	0.0	c
Balearic Islands•	52.1	(7.1)	37.5	(6.7)	10.5	(4.7)	82.0	(7.2)	18.0	(7.2)	0.0	c	2.4	(2.4)
Basque Country•	48.8	(3.7)	35.0	(3.5)	16.1	(2.5)	73.3	(4.6)	21.2	(4.1)	5.5	(2.7)	9.5	(2.0)
Cantabria•	36.9	(6.3)	45.2	(6.7)	17.9	(5.4)	76.4	(7.4)	20.4	(7.1)	3.2	(3.1)	4.2	(2.9)
Castile and Leon•	53.8	(6.6)	37.5	(6.5)	8.7	(4.2)	84.9	(4.7)	15.1	(4.7)	0.0	c	6.3	(3.3)
Catalonia•	56.7	(7.5)	36.6	(6.6)	6.6	(3.8)	88.9	(5.7)	11.1	(5.7)	0.0	c	4.9	(3.4)
Extremadura•	52.4	(8.4)	35.0	(7.1)	12.6	(4.8)	90.9	(4.3)	9.1	(4.3)	0.0	c	4.3	(3.0)
Galicia•	64.1	(5.8)	30.1	(5.5)	5.8	(1.9)	60.2	(8.3)	39.8	(8.3)	0.0	c	1.9	(1.9)
La Rioja•	49.1	(0.6)	48.3	(0.6)	2.6	(0.1)	74.7	(0.8)	25.3	(0.8)	0.0	c	0.0	c
Madrid•	50.5	(6.2)	47.3	(5.8)	2.2	(2.2)	86.2	(6.2)	10.3	(5.5)	3.5	(3.4)	9.9	(4.6)
Murcia•	41.2	(7.9)	45.9	(7.3)	13.0	(5.1)	72.0	(9.3)	28.0	(9.3)	0.0	c	2.1	(2.0)
Navarre•	51.1	(4.9)	42.2	(4.4)	6.7	(2.4)	83.7	(1.5)	16.3	(1.5)	0.0	c	6.7	(2.6)
United Kingdom														
England	61.9	(4.6)	31.0	(4.3)	7.0	(2.1)	90.7	(2.5)	8.4	(2.4)	0.9	(0.9)	3.5	(2.0)
Northern Ireland	70.2	(5.3)	20.8	(4.6)	8.9	(3.5)	88.3	(4.3)	11.7	(4.3)	0.0	c	4.9	(2.0)
Scotland•	73.6	(4.1)	23.7	(4.0)	2.7	(1.6)	89.7	(3.4)	9.3	(3.7)	1.0	(1.1)	3.3	(1.7)
Wales	61.1	(3.7)	32.3	(3.8)	6.6	(2.2)	90.0	(2.9)	8.0	(2.5)	2.0	(1.4)	2.6	(1.3)
United States														
Connecticut•	73.9	(6.4)	19.5	(5.9)	6.6	(4.1)	90.2	(5.3)	7.5	(4.7)	2.4	(2.6)	0.0	c
Florida•	72.2	(6.5)	25.0	(6.5)	2.8	(2.1)	78.7	(8.2)	18.2	(7.5)	3.1	(3.2)	2.3	(2.3)
Massachusetts•	71.5	(7.1)	25.9	(6.7)	2.6	(2.6)	86.9	(7.2)	9.2	(6.4)	3.9	(3.9)	0.0	c
Argentina														
Ciudad Autónoma de Buenos Aires•	13.9	(5.3)	72.8	(6.7)	13.4	(4.7)	23.3	(10.6)	67.8	(11.7)	8.9	(6.4)	24.4	(7.5)
Brazil														
Acre	0.0	c	24.4	(8.7)	75.6	(8.7)	20.3	(7.2)	56.9	(10.9)	22.8	(13.3)	19.6	(11.2)
Alagoas	5.7	(5.9)	65.2	(14.2)	29.1	(14.1)	26.8	(12.7)	54.7	(18.4)	18.5	(13.4)	13.7	(11.8)
Amapá	3.9	(4.2)	36.8	(11.9)	59.2	(10.9)	13.4	(8.6)	46.9	(9.3)	39.7	(10.8)	4.3	(3.4)
Amazonas	0.0	c	38.5	(13.2)	61.5	(13.2)	18.6	(8.3)	62.5	(7.1)	18.9	(10.6)	28.7	(9.8)
Bahia	7.8	(7.1)	54.0	(10.4)	38.2	(14.3)	19.5	(15.1)	57.6	(18.1)	22.9	(10.4)	9.8	(10.7)
Ceará	11.1	(6.3)	16.6	(9.1)	72.3	(9.0)	24.6	(12.4)	38.0	(9.1)	37.4	(14.7)	8.0	(7.4)
Espírito Santo	4.8	(6.8)	37.3	(11.8)	57.9	(9.0)	28.0	(5.6)	50.6	(16.8)	21.4	(15.3)	17.6	(9.8)
Federal District	5.3	(5.2)	33.5	(9.1)	61.2	(9.9)	22.4	(14.1)	50.0	(13.0)	27.6	(10.9)	35.0	(14.1)
Goiás	15.7	(7.6)	56.2	(12.2)	28.1	(10.3)	30.1	(10.9)	57.2	(12.6)	12.8	(8.2)	28.7	(11.3)
Maranhão	8.7	(6.7)	55.6	(16.5)	35.7	(14.2)	19.0	(11.8)	68.6	(14.4)	12.4	(9.4)	15.9	(10.5)
Mato Grosso	5.1	(4.9)	54.9	(8.7)	40.0	(8.4)	40.3	(11.9)	34.0	(12.9)	25.7	(12.1)	29.5	(9.9)
Mato Grosso do Sul	5.5	(3.6)	62.2	(9.6)	32.3	(9.6)	24.0	(10.6)	39.3	(12.0)	36.6	(11.7)	21.0	(3.9)
Minas Gerais	16.6	(8.2)	46.2	(9.2)	37.2	(9.8)	27.3	(8.1)	62.5	(7.8)	10.2	(2.6)	14.0	(6.9)
Pará	20.8	(12.2)	25.6	(8.1)	53.6	(11.8)	18.5	(9.9)	67.5	(15.3)	14.0	(15.5)	4.4	(3.7)
Paraíba	9.6	(8.4)	58.8	(13.2)	31.7	(15.4)	41.4	(11.9)	46.0	(12.8)	12.6	(6.3)	24.9	(15.6)
Paraná	16.0	(8.2)	34.1	(11.4)	49.8	(9.6)	29.1	(11.8)	40.0	(12.6)	30.9	(10.6)	0.0	c
Pernambuco	8.4	(7.0)	57.9	(15.5)	33.7	(13.6)	37.2	(14.8)	29.9	(13.5)	32.9	(15.8)	18.9	(7.8)
Piauí	19.3	(9.2)	67.2	(12.9)	13.5	(8.3)	31.0	(13.7)	33.1	(12.6)	35.9	(14.1)	27.9	(10.4)
Rio de Janeiro	35.9	(9.0)	34.8	(10.1)	29.3	(9.1)	31.3	(11.1)	41.9	(13.4)	26.7	(11.0)	29.8	(11.4)
Rio Grande do Norte	18.5	(10.3)	39.6	(13.5)	41.9	(13.7)	6.2	(5.8)	75.4	(11.8)	18.4	(10.3)	24.4	(11.8)
Rio Grande do Sul	17.0	(6.3)	58.8	(9.8)	24.2	(10.8)	20.9	(8.3)	57.1	(15.0)	22.0	(12.6)	10.8	(5.5)
Rondônia	6.2	(5.2)	37.6	(10.1)	56.2	(9.8)	12.1	(4.4)	39.6	(11.5)	48.3	(11.6)	0.0	c
Roraima	0.0	c	50.8	(9.4)	49.2	(9.4)	16.4	(9.1)	55.0	(13.5)	28.6	(10.3)	17.6	(10.0)
Santa Catarina	0.0	c	43.7	(14.2)	56.3	(14.2)	51.1	(12.7)	19.1	(8.6)	29.8	(13.1)	27.1	(11.7)
São Paulo	8.1	(3.7)	50.0	(7.9)	41.9	(7.3)	20.5	(5.1)	52.3	(6.6)	27.2	(6.2)	9.2	(3.9)
Sergipe	11.7	(8.5)	36.5	(8.3)	51.8	(11.2)	32.4	(16.5)	47.6	(14.8)	20.0	(12.5)	35.1	(14.8)
Tocantins	3.3	(3.3)	54.1	(11.9)	42.5	(11.3)	50.4	(13.3)	33.6	(10.9)	15.9	(8.3)	24.9	(9.5)
Colombia														
Bogota	3.0	(2.2)	58.5	(7.0)	38.4	(6.7)	19.3	(5.7)	62.2	(7.5)	18.5	(7.5)	11.8	(5.0)
Cali	3.8	(2.6)	72.7	(7.3)	23.5	(7.3)	10.9	(4.5)	65.8	(8.4)	23.2	(7.7)	16.8	(6.1)
Manizales	7.3	(2.6)	64.3	(6.9)	28.4	(6.2)	6.3	(3.4)	61.0	(10.5)	32.7	(10.8)	19.6	(5.4)
Medellin	4.8	(3.1)	62.9	(6.9)	32.3	(6.3)	14.0	(4.8)	68.3	(7.7)	17.7	(6.1)	9.3	(3.2)
Russian Federation														
Perm Territory region•	38.9	(7.1)	40.0	(7.0)	21.1	(5.8)	44.9	(7.7)	49.1	(8.0)	6.0	(3.2)	9.3	(3.9)
United Arab Emirates														
Abu Dhabi•	7.6	(1.9)	57.1	(4.5)	35.3	(4.0)	27.6	(3.5)	60.0	(4.6)	12.4	(3.7)	16.6	(3.3)
Ajman	0.0	c	59.2	(9.6)	40.8	(9.6)	3.3	(3.1)	57.1	(7.5)	39.6	(8.2)	21.3	(6.2)
Dubai•	30.4	(0.2)	45.8	(0.2)	23.8	(0.2)	40.9	(0.3)	49.8	(0.3)	9.3	(0.1)	17.0	(0.1)
Fujairah	4.6	(3.5)	55.6	(6.4)	39.8	(7.9)	19.3	(3.8)	54.8	(7.3)	25.9	(8.6)	21.6	(1.0)
Ras Al Khaimah	3.0	(0.3)	62.0	(5.4)	35.0	(5.4)	3.6	(3.7)	74.5	(10.4)	21.9	(9.7)	20.1	(8.9)
Sharjah	11.0	(3.8)	60.2	(12.3)	28.8	(11.7)	23.4	(6.2)	63.5	(10.7)	13.1	(8.8)	9.0	(6.5)
Umm Al Quwain	29.5	(0.2)	19.4	(0.3)	51.1	(0.2)	40.1	(0.2)	33.1	(0.4)	26.9	(0.3)	29.0	(0.1)

• PISA adjudicated region.
Note: See Table IV.2.9 for national data.
StatLink ᵃᵢₛₚ http://dx.doi.org/10.1787/888932957536

[Part 1/4]
Ability grouping for mathematics classes, by region
Table B2.IV.4   *Results based on school principals' reports*

	Percentage of students in schools whose principal reported:																	
	Mathematics classes study similar content, but at different levels of difficulty						Different classes study different content or sets of mathematics topics that have different levels of difficulty						Students are grouped by ability within their mathematics classes					
	For all classes		For some classes		Not for any class		For all classes		For some classes		Not for any class		For all classes		For some classes		Not for any class	
	%	S.E.	%	S.E.	%	S.E.	%	S.E.	%	S.E.	%	S.E.	%	S.E.	%	S.E.	%	S.E.
Australia																		
Australian Capital Territory	67.2	(0.9)	29.2	(0.9)	3.6	(0.3)	24.8	(0.7)	61.4	(0.9)	13.7	(0.6)	55.3	(1.1)	39.3	(1.1)	5.4	(0.5)
New South Wales	44.2	(3.9)	49.6	(4.0)	6.2	(1.7)	35.4	(3.4)	53.8	(3.6)	10.8	(2.2)	63.2	(3.2)	31.2	(3.2)	5.7	(1.2)
Northern Territory	43.3	(4.3)	55.6	(4.3)	1.1	(1.1)	31.2	(3.0)	44.2	(4.7)	24.6	(2.9)	72.9	(2.8)	25.1	(2.5)	2.0	(1.3)
Queensland	40.5	(4.5)	58.0	(4.4)	1.4	(1.0)	15.0	(3.0)	62.4	(4.0)	22.6	(3.5)	27.2	(4.6)	62.5	(4.9)	10.3	(2.6)
South Australia	28.7	(4.7)	66.5	(5.1)	4.8	(2.3)	16.5	(3.0)	71.5	(4.2)	12.1	(3.5)	33.9	(4.4)	49.4	(4.8)	16.7	(4.2)
Tasmania	46.2	(1.5)	49.3	(1.6)	4.5	(1.6)	25.2	(1.9)	65.4	(1.9)	9.3	(0.8)	46.8	(1.6)	44.1	(1.2)	9.2	(1.1)
Victoria	29.3	(4.1)	62.4	(4.3)	8.3	(2.5)	21.1	(3.7)	64.6	(4.3)	14.3	(3.0)	24.5	(3.4)	56.2	(4.0)	19.3	(3.2)
Western Australia	29.8	(5.0)	58.3	(5.7)	11.9	(4.1)	39.8	(5.3)	56.8	(5.5)	3.4	(2.3)	61.8	(5.5)	31.5	(5.2)	6.7	(2.3)
Belgium																		
Flemish community•	9.1	(2.5)	66.8	(4.0)	24.1	(3.7)	18.5	(3.2)	66.7	(4.2)	14.8	(3.0)	2.8	(1.1)	24.1	(3.2)	73.1	(3.5)
French community	16.5	(4.1)	40.7	(5.6)	42.8	(6.0)	8.0	(2.5)	42.2	(5.8)	49.8	(5.8)	5.3	(1.9)	10.8	(3.4)	83.9	(3.8)
German-speaking community	0.0	c	43.1	(0.4)	56.9	(0.4)	33.3	(0.2)	66.7	(0.2)	0.0	c	1.3	(0.3)	0.0	c	98.7	(0.3)
Canada																		
Alberta	28.1	(4.2)	62.8	(4.6)	9.1	(3.0)	41.4	(3.7)	51.9	(4.4)	6.8	(3.2)	28.5	(4.7)	48.8	(5.3)	22.6	(4.5)
British Columbia	13.8	(4.4)	61.1	(5.3)	25.1	(4.8)	27.2	(5.1)	46.5	(5.6)	26.3	(3.8)	13.2	(3.5)	46.5	(5.2)	40.3	(4.6)
Manitoba	30.1	(3.2)	50.7	(3.5)	19.2	(2.4)	32.0	(3.1)	45.8	(3.3)	22.2	(3.6)	5.2	(1.6)	50.3	(3.4)	44.5	(3.0)
New Brunswick	30.5	(3.0)	53.6	(2.5)	15.8	(1.2)	5.9	(1.5)	45.1	(2.5)	49.1	(2.5)	3.0	(0.2)	59.3	(2.9)	37.6	(3.0)
Newfoundland and Labrador	10.0	(1.5)	59.7	(5.1)	30.2	(5.4)	16.3	(3.8)	64.2	(2.8)	19.5	(5.7)	16.7	(1.3)	21.3	(3.4)	62.0	(3.5)
Nova Scotia	8.8	(2.6)	84.5	(3.9)	6.7	(2.7)	22.2	(4.7)	69.2	(6.1)	8.6	(3.1)	15.7	(4.1)	56.1	(7.5)	28.2	(5.8)
Ontario	31.9	(5.7)	57.5	(5.4)	10.6	(2.8)	34.2	(5.2)	47.8	(5.5)	18.0	(4.3)	21.4	(3.8)	46.6	(5.0)	32.0	(4.8)
Prince Edward Island	26.0	(0.4)	55.7	(0.5)	18.3	(0.3)	13.2	(0.2)	84.0	(0.3)	2.8	(0.3)	38.6	(0.4)	19.6	(0.3)	41.8	(0.4)
Quebec	17.2	(3.0)	48.7	(4.5)	34.2	(4.6)	26.4	(4.0)	49.2	(4.0)	24.4	(3.2)	23.8	(3.5)	32.8	(3.3)	43.4	(4.6)
Saskatchewan	13.9	(2.6)	75.4	(3.3)	10.6	(2.0)	17.3	(1.2)	57.6	(4.2)	25.1	(4.1)	5.0	(2.5)	58.6	(3.4)	36.4	(3.5)
Italy																		
Abruzzo	16.6	(5.3)	54.6	(6.4)	28.7	(6.5)	12.0	(5.0)	54.8	(6.9)	33.2	(6.5)	0.0	(0.0)	32.7	(4.9)	67.3	(4.9)
Basilicata	16.5	(3.4)	51.9	(5.0)	31.6	(5.2)	7.9	(2.2)	47.7	(6.3)	44.4	(6.1)	6.8	(2.7)	25.1	(6.5)	68.1	(6.6)
Bolzano	12.3	(0.5)	41.3	(0.8)	46.3	(0.8)	7.6	(0.3)	44.4	(0.8)	48.0	(0.9)	2.4	(0.1)	45.2	(0.9)	52.4	(0.9)
Calabria	19.4	(6.2)	50.9	(7.8)	29.6	(6.5)	2.9	(2.1)	59.7	(8.2)	37.4	(8.3)	0.5	(0.5)	41.1	(7.1)	58.4	(7.0)
Campania	36.1	(8.3)	46.7	(7.9)	17.2	(5.3)	18.6	(8.9)	45.8	(7.7)	35.6	(8.0)	4.2	(2.6)	25.0	(5.2)	70.8	(5.8)
Emilia Romagna	31.0	(6.0)	35.2	(7.9)	33.9	(7.6)	7.6	(3.9)	45.0	(6.7)	47.4	(7.3)	0.0	c	38.3	(7.0)	61.7	(7.0)
Friuli Venezia Giulia	16.0	(3.1)	62.1	(5.6)	21.9	(5.0)	1.9	(1.6)	72.0	(3.8)	26.1	(3.5)	0.3	(0.3)	54.0	(5.4)	45.7	(5.4)
Lazio	23.7	(8.1)	38.1	(8.8)	38.2	(7.9)	11.8	(6.9)	41.8	(8.8)	46.4	(8.0)	4.7	(3.3)	33.6	(8.8)	61.7	(8.5)
Liguria	28.1	(6.8)	40.7	(7.0)	31.2	(7.6)	19.1	(5.5)	44.9	(7.1)	36.0	(6.8)	9.5	(5.2)	30.0	(6.8)	60.5	(7.2)
Lombardia	22.3	(5.9)	39.6	(9.0)	38.2	(8.0)	3.5	(3.0)	57.1	(8.0)	39.4	(7.7)	0.0	c	27.0	(6.6)	73.0	(6.6)
Marche	10.6	(4.9)	54.0	(6.2)	35.4	(5.8)	5.5	(3.6)	50.2	(7.5)	44.3	(6.6)	0.0	c	18.4	(5.2)	81.6	(5.2)
Molise	11.5	(0.6)	55.1	(0.8)	33.4	(0.8)	12.1	(0.7)	55.5	(0.8)	32.5	(0.8)	4.8	(0.4)	33.7	(1.0)	61.5	(1.0)
Piemonte	20.5	(4.8)	53.0	(7.4)	26.4	(6.8)	15.4	(5.7)	49.1	(7.9)	35.6	(6.1)	2.5	(2.4)	29.5	(7.1)	68.0	(7.5)
Puglia	16.7	(4.7)	49.0	(6.8)	34.2	(6.7)	8.0	(4.0)	39.2	(7.4)	52.8	(7.8)	6.3	(1.9)	30.0	(8.2)	63.6	(8.6)
Sardegna	9.9	(4.5)	59.3	(5.9)	30.8	(7.0)	8.0	(4.2)	44.3	(6.9)	47.7	(7.9)	2.3	(2.2)	30.5	(7.0)	67.3	(7.2)
Sicilia	30.9	(6.3)	40.8	(6.9)	28.4	(6.4)	7.6	(3.5)	53.3	(7.1)	39.1	(6.9)	4.0	(2.7)	26.0	(6.8)	69.9	(7.3)
Toscana	20.6	(7.0)	49.3	(7.5)	30.0	(8.0)	0.0	c	50.6	(7.8)	49.4	(7.8)	0.0	c	25.6	(6.3)	74.4	(6.3)
Trento	22.1	(4.1)	51.5	(3.5)	26.4	(3.9)	18.5	(2.7)	52.6	(5.2)	28.9	(5.0)	1.7	(1.2)	34.0	(4.8)	64.4	(4.7)
Umbria	17.2	(4.2)	56.7	(5.4)	26.1	(4.9)	6.6	(4.6)	48.2	(4.8)	45.2	(5.8)	0.0	c	18.7	(3.6)	81.3	(3.6)
Valle d'Aosta	1.7	(0.1)	28.6	(1.0)	69.7	(1.0)	1.0	(0.1)	28.8	(0.8)	70.2	(0.8)	0.9	(0.2)	41.4	(1.0)	57.6	(1.0)
Veneto	19.4	(5.2)	53.5	(6.4)	27.1	(5.7)	7.2	(3.6)	63.1	(6.0)	29.7	(6.0)	2.8	(2.7)	22.2	(6.0)	75.1	(5.6)
Mexico																		
Aguascalientes	36.7	(5.2)	31.0	(7.6)	32.3	(7.3)	19.1	(5.0)	18.6	(7.1)	62.4	(8.5)	10.5	(4.7)	39.4	(6.0)	50.1	(6.8)
Baja California	24.8	(6.3)	35.9	(8.9)	39.3	(7.7)	20.0	(5.3)	35.3	(10.0)	44.6	(9.7)	25.4	(8.5)	46.6	(14.9)	28.0	(10.1)
Baja California Sur	29.3	(6.8)	41.9	(7.9)	28.8	(6.1)	16.8	(5.5)	32.1	(8.5)	51.1	(8.2)	13.6	(8.0)	42.7	(6.4)	43.7	(6.0)
Campeche	45.4	(6.4)	18.5	(7.5)	36.1	(8.1)	26.4	(6.2)	27.7	(7.5)	46.0	(8.6)	24.4	(7.3)	49.9	(6.8)	25.7	(7.1)
Chiapas	41.0	(8.2)	39.0	(8.1)	20.0	(6.2)	43.0	(7.3)	24.6	(5.8)	32.3	(7.0)	32.5	(8.3)	36.4	(8.9)	31.1	(7.1)
Chihuahua	40.7	(8.1)	40.5	(8.8)	18.9	(5.0)	17.7	(6.7)	34.5	(11.5)	47.8	(8.9)	24.2	(4.9)	40.8	(8.8)	35.0	(9.3)
Coahuila	37.3	(8.7)	25.9	(7.9)	36.8	(9.4)	21.2	(7.7)	22.8	(7.7)	56.0	(10.0)	8.7	(3.9)	40.9	(10.1)	50.4	(9.7)
Colima	27.4	(3.7)	28.8	(5.4)	43.8	(5.0)	14.2	(4.5)	20.1	(6.3)	65.7	(4.8)	14.6	(4.3)	45.0	(7.9)	40.3	(7.4)
Distrito Federal	38.8	(7.4)	37.3	(8.9)	23.8	(6.4)	20.5	(7.6)	36.8	(10.5)	42.7	(9.4)	17.8	(5.6)	40.2	(8.6)	42.0	(7.4)
Durango	54.4	(9.0)	20.8	(7.5)	24.9	(6.7)	23.7	(6.5)	28.6	(8.1)	47.7	(8.8)	22.2	(6.3)	47.7	(9.2)	30.1	(7.2)
Guanajuato	40.4	(8.2)	17.2	(6.2)	42.4	(8.9)	28.1	(7.2)	18.9	(6.0)	53.0	(8.7)	21.0	(7.2)	35.4	(7.1)	43.6	(5.4)
Guerrero	31.1	(8.1)	37.5	(8.6)	31.4	(9.2)	26.1	(8.1)	40.4	(8.8)	33.5	(9.0)	26.2	(7.6)	37.8	(10.3)	36.0	(9.4)
Hidalgo	36.6	(8.4)	35.8	(7.4)	27.5	(5.9)	23.4	(6.8)	19.4	(6.8)	57.2	(7.9)	13.4	(4.7)	48.5	(7.6)	38.1	(7.1)
Jalisco	25.2	(5.4)	42.1	(10.5)	32.6	(9.2)	13.5	(4.9)	34.5	(10.2)	51.9	(9.3)	19.1	(9.1)	38.2	(9.9)	42.7	(9.5)
Mexico	30.2	(6.6)	38.4	(7.1)	31.4	(6.5)	20.2	(6.8)	29.8	(8.1)	50.0	(7.4)	23.3	(9.2)	29.7	(6.3)	47.0	(9.0)
Morelos	23.7	(7.0)	33.1	(9.0)	43.2	(8.4)	23.9	(8.2)	34.3	(8.1)	41.7	(9.7)	6.7	(2.6)	64.8	(6.4)	28.5	(6.4)
Nayarit	40.0	(7.4)	28.0	(5.7)	32.0	(6.0)	16.2	(4.7)	26.9	(6.3)	57.0	(5.9)	18.1	(5.7)	28.1	(6.4)	53.8	(7.1)
Nuevo León	46.0	(6.6)	22.8	(7.1)	31.2	(7.0)	33.6	(7.6)	13.9	(4.1)	52.6	(6.9)	23.1	(7.8)	29.3	(7.0)	47.7	(8.3)
Puebla	26.9	(7.6)	50.0	(7.4)	23.1	(5.1)	28.7	(7.6)	43.7	(10.0)	27.7	(7.7)	18.0	(5.5)	43.0	(7.4)	39.0	(7.2)
Querétaro	19.2	(7.4)	34.5	(10.2)	46.3	(12.6)	24.7	(6.1)	16.1	(7.7)	59.2	(10.5)	7.0	(3.1)	46.0	(9.8)	47.0	(9.8)
Quintana Roo	37.4	(5.7)	36.7	(4.4)	25.9	(6.6)	38.2	(9.5)	17.5	(6.3)	44.3	(10.7)	8.0	(4.2)	40.8	(9.7)	51.1	(8.8)
San Luis Potosí	33.7	(5.5)	37.3	(6.6)	29.0	(6.4)	28.9	(6.4)	22.8	(9.0)	48.3	(10.0)	18.4	(5.3)	37.1	(5.9)	44.5	(6.2)
Sinaloa	40.7	(9.3)	35.4	(9.9)	24.0	(8.0)	23.1	(8.8)	23.2	(8.0)	53.8	(9.5)	19.7	(8.2)	55.8	(8.2)	24.5	(5.6)
Tabasco	46.0	(9.4)	29.0	(7.1)	25.1	(8.1)	20.9	(7.0)	25.4	(8.0)	53.7	(8.6)	13.7	(7.4)	42.7	(9.4)	43.6	(9.8)
Tamaulipas	38.5	(5.9)	30.3	(10.7)	31.2	(7.6)	20.6	(7.7)	22.8	(10.3)	56.7	(7.1)	17.8	(7.5)	33.7	(9.9)	48.5	(8.3)
Tlaxcala	43.1	(9.2)	31.8	(8.0)	25.1	(5.7)	27.4	(5.8)	21.2	(7.2)	51.4	(6.7)	19.3	(7.2)	45.6	(8.0)	35.1	(8.0)
Veracruz	31.8	(7.1)	36.6	(8.1)	31.6	(6.7)	24.1	(7.0)	26.1	(6.3)	49.9	(7.1)	10.8	(4.2)	43.3	(9.4)	46.0	(9.7)
Yucatán	39.5	(9.8)	23.9	(8.3)	36.6	(9.3)	20.8	(7.0)	25.3	(8.3)	53.9	(7.8)	12.1	(5.8)	48.3	(8.5)	39.6	(8.3)
Zacatecas	43.2	(7.9)	33.0	(7.6)	23.8	(6.4)	26.8	(6.0)	28.6	(6.7)	44.6	(6.8)	19.2	(5.2)	47.7	(7.3)	33.2	(4.7)

• PISA adjudicated region.
Note: See Table IV.2.11 for national data.
StatLink ⟨ms⟩ http://dx.doi.org/10.1787/888932957536

[Part 2/4]
Ability grouping for mathematics classes, by region
Table B2.IV.4 *Results based on school principals' reports*

	Percentage of students in schools whose principal reported:																	
	Mathematics classes study similar content, but at different levels of difficulty						Different classes study different content or sets of mathematics topics that have different levels of difficulty						Students are grouped by ability within their mathematics classes					
	For all classes		For some classes		Not for any class		For all classes		For some classes		Not for any class		For all classes		For some classes		Not for any class	
	%	S.E.	%	S.E.	%	S.E.	%	S.E.	%	S.E.	%	S.E.	%	S.E.	%	S.E.	%	S.E.
OECD																		
Portugal																		
Alentejo	9.9	(6.3)	37.0	(9.5)	53.1	(9.3)	0.0	c	33.8	(10.3)	66.2	(10.3)	0.0	c	20.9	(8.7)	79.1	(8.7)
Spain																		
Andalusia•	45.3	(7.8)	40.1	(7.4)	14.6	(5.4)	24.1	(5.5)	47.2	(6.4)	28.7	(5.8)	7.0	(3.5)	18.2	(6.1)	74.9	(7.1)
Aragon•	31.1	(5.0)	49.3	(6.9)	19.6	(6.5)	21.5	(5.1)	41.7	(7.9)	36.8	(7.7)	1.8	(1.8)	19.8	(5.9)	78.4	(5.5)
Asturias•	41.9	(6.9)	52.4	(7.1)	5.6	(1.7)	27.5	(7.4)	41.6	(7.7)	30.9	(6.9)	3.5	(2.4)	25.0	(6.1)	71.6	(5.5)
Balearic Islands•	41.1	(7.8)	48.6	(7.0)	10.3	(4.6)	18.0	(5.2)	40.7	(6.9)	41.3	(5.5)	11.2	(4.6)	22.8	(6.2)	66.0	(7.6)
Basque Country•	19.9	(2.8)	51.9	(4.2)	28.2	(3.4)	3.8	(1.3)	38.3	(3.7)	57.9	(3.8)	4.7	(1.6)	17.6	(3.1)	77.7	(3.5)
Cantabria•	35.4	(6.6)	54.8	(6.9)	9.8	(4.5)	11.3	(4.6)	37.7	(5.8)	51.0	(5.9)	1.7	(1.7)	20.1	(5.5)	78.2	(5.2)
Castile and Leon•	33.1	(7.1)	41.8	(5.1)	25.0	(6.9)	25.2	(5.2)	39.8	(5.9)	35.0	(6.2)	5.0	(2.9)	12.5	(4.9)	82.5	(5.7)
Catalonia•	38.0	(7.0)	52.9	(7.7)	9.1	(4.2)	12.0	(4.7)	48.8	(7.3)	39.2	(7.6)	26.6	(6.2)	35.0	(7.1)	38.4	(5.7)
Extremadura•	31.0	(5.7)	45.6	(7.3)	23.4	(6.3)	29.8	(6.0)	43.4	(6.5)	26.8	(6.2)	1.9	(1.9)	5.7	(3.3)	92.4	(3.8)
Galicia•	31.4	(6.1)	39.0	(7.5)	29.6	(6.0)	16.7	(4.8)	31.0	(7.2)	52.3	(7.1)	7.3	(3.6)	9.5	(4.0)	83.3	(5.4)
La Rioja•	36.7	(0.5)	48.3	(0.5)	14.9	(0.4)	28.3	(0.4)	35.6	(0.5)	36.1	(0.5)	13.1	(0.3)	11.0	(0.3)	75.9	(0.4)
Madrid•	37.1	(7.1)	46.7	(7.4)	16.2	(6.0)	16.2	(6.2)	48.5	(8.4)	35.3	(7.2)	3.1	(2.3)	23.1	(5.2)	73.8	(5.7)
Murcia•	28.8	(6.7)	57.2	(8.3)	14.0	(5.6)	23.2	(7.2)	50.6	(7.8)	26.2	(6.1)	4.0	(2.8)	24.5	(6.3)	71.5	(6.3)
Navarre•	37.4	(5.2)	48.4	(7.0)	14.2	(4.7)	15.3	(5.4)	65.0	(5.5)	19.6	(4.5)	5.2	(3.0)	29.7	(4.7)	65.1	(5.5)
United Kingdom																		
England	50.6	(4.3)	47.3	(4.5)	2.2	(1.2)	28.5	(3.7)	52.0	(4.3)	19.5	(3.6)	79.1	(3.0)	16.0	(2.8)	4.9	(1.6)
Northern Ireland	52.2	(5.0)	41.1	(4.6)	6.8	(2.9)	15.8	(3.6)	67.8	(4.6)	16.4	(4.2)	59.5	(5.0)	29.1	(5.0)	11.4	(3.3)
Scotland•	32.8	(4.8)	59.1	(5.1)	8.1	(2.6)	35.7	(4.8)	54.0	(4.9)	10.3	(2.4)	62.3	(4.9)	24.1	(4.4)	13.6	(3.5)
Wales	53.2	(4.1)	44.6	(4.1)	2.2	(1.3)	26.9	(3.5)	50.9	(3.8)	22.2	(3.2)	74.4	(3.5)	15.8	(3.1)	9.8	(2.5)
United States																		
Connecticut•	30.0	(6.8)	67.4	(7.0)	2.6	(2.5)	29.5	(7.1)	56.4	(8.4)	14.1	(5.6)	32.5	(7.0)	44.2	(6.9)	23.3	(6.1)
Florida•	12.6	(4.7)	82.6	(5.4)	4.8	(2.7)	26.1	(6.4)	61.9	(7.6)	12.0	(4.7)	25.5	(6.2)	65.1	(6.2)	9.4	(4.2)
Massachusetts•	37.2	(7.8)	60.5	(8.1)	2.3	(2.6)	17.8	(6.1)	69.7	(6.4)	12.6	(5.1)	35.9	(7.5)	44.7	(7.8)	19.4	(5.6)
Partners																		
Argentina																		
Ciudad Autónoma de Buenos Aires•	23.6	(6.6)	47.5	(8.0)	28.9	(8.1)	8.1	(3.8)	39.8	(8.1)	52.1	(8.7)	7.4	(4.3)	7.6	(3.9)	85.1	(5.7)
Brazil																		
Acre	67.1	(7.5)	22.9	(8.0)	10.1	(6.9)	35.5	(12.8)	25.8	(7.2)	38.7	(11.0)	1.9	(2.0)	9.8	(7.3)	88.4	(7.8)
Alagoas	34.0	(13.5)	55.7	(14.7)	10.2	(9.7)	4.8	(5.1)	61.7	(12.9)	33.5	(14.4)	12.5	(8.8)	13.9	(9.4)	73.7	(6.9)
Amapá	49.7	(9.1)	39.1	(8.5)	11.2	(6.6)	9.1	(6.4)	25.8	(10.2)	65.1	(11.6)	5.2	(5.1)	6.9	(1.4)	87.9	(5.2)
Amazonas	44.0	(14.3)	30.6	(11.1)	25.4	(12.1)	14.0	(9.4)	18.9	(10.2)	67.1	(10.4)	0.0	c	12.7	(8.2)	87.3	(8.2)
Bahia	49.3	(18.6)	30.8	(12.8)	19.9	(14.3)	7.3	(6.7)	27.9	(12.4)	64.8	(12.5)	7.3	(6.7)	16.0	(10.8)	76.7	(11.8)
Ceará	28.2	(10.7)	34.6	(11.2)	37.2	(9.2)	3.4	(3.8)	30.7	(9.3)	65.9	(10.1)	0.0	c	16.3	(10.9)	83.7	(10.9)
Espírito Santo	48.1	(18.7)	34.4	(9.6)	17.5	(12.6)	11.6	(6.6)	26.5	(10.3)	62.0	(9.9)	0.0	c	3.7	(3.3)	96.3	(3.3)
Federal District	43.1	(17.1)	21.2	(10.4)	35.7	(14.9)	4.3	(4.5)	12.9	(9.2)	82.8	(6.9)	4.3	(4.5)	18.7	(13.5)	77.0	(12.2)
Goiás	45.2	(8.1)	41.9	(10.0)	12.9	(7.2)	32.9	(10.0)	38.8	(10.3)	28.2	(9.7)	10.9	(7.2)	7.1	(5.4)	82.0	(8.8)
Maranhão	32.2	(13.7)	32.1	(12.5)	35.8	(13.0)	20.5	(11.3)	26.6	(11.3)	52.9	(14.2)	4.3	(4.5)	4.8	(4.7)	90.9	(6.3)
Mato Grosso	19.6	(6.8)	51.3	(11.7)	29.1	(10.5)	17.0	(6.2)	41.7	(10.2)	41.3	(11.8)	5.8	(5.8)	19.5	(5.9)	74.7	(7.9)
Mato Grosso do Sul	49.8	(13.2)	15.2	(8.0)	35.0	(10.7)	33.8	(9.9)	19.9	(7.3)	46.3	(9.6)	4.9	(4.5)	0.0	c	95.1	(4.5)
Minas Gerais	62.9	(7.4)	23.7	(8.0)	13.4	(6.5)	34.7	(10.2)	31.0	(9.0)	34.3	(10.3)	0.0	c	11.4	(7.6)	88.6	(7.6)
Pará	30.4	(8.5)	27.8	(8.3)	41.7	(7.8)	26.6	(11.6)	20.2	(5.7)	53.1	(13.1)	0.0	c	6.1	(5.8)	93.9	(5.8)
Paraíba	74.8	(10.2)	19.1	(8.9)	6.1	(4.5)	23.4	(14.4)	31.7	(11.8)	44.8	(15.2)	5.4	(6.2)	14.2	(8.6)	80.4	(11.8)
Paraná	36.2	(10.1)	42.4	(11.0)	21.4	(7.7)	7.4	(5.2)	22.9	(10.9)	69.8	(11.3)	4.6	(4.2)	17.8	(9.2)	77.6	(10.0)
Pernambuco	54.5	(9.3)	30.9	(9.0)	14.5	(8.2)	28.1	(9.3)	19.7	(11.7)	52.2	(14.0)	6.0	(6.0)	0.0	c	94.0	(6.0)
Piauí	45.9	(11.2)	36.3	(12.5)	17.8	(6.1)	12.1	(2.1)	34.8	(13.1)	53.1	(12.1)	3.8	(2.0)	27.7	(11.1)	68.5	(10.9)
Rio de Janeiro	53.8	(6.6)	24.5	(7.4)	21.7	(7.9)	24.2	(11.7)	15.0	(7.8)	60.8	(13.2)	2.7	(4.1)	15.0	(8.6)	82.3	(10.1)
Rio Grande do Norte	25.8	(11.1)	44.5	(11.1)	29.7	(11.1)	21.6	(10.6)	34.3	(12.4)	44.1	(11.2)	7.9	(7.6)	13.0	(8.8)	79.1	(11.2)
Rio Grande do Sul	53.1	(11.7)	20.8	(11.2)	26.1	(9.7)	29.1	(11.9)	17.5	(9.0)	53.4	(12.0)	12.5	(8.3)	5.1	(4.9)	82.4	(9.2)
Rondônia	7.9	(5.2)	44.2	(11.6)	47.9	(12.4)	9.9	(6.4)	40.8	(10.7)	49.3	(11.1)	0.0	c	14.0	(8.9)	86.0	(8.9)
Roraima	27.1	(10.0)	47.7	(11.9)	25.3	(11.6)	18.7	(9.6)	32.9	(10.9)	48.4	(10.7)	9.4	(6.7)	7.8	(5.8)	82.8	(9.1)
Santa Catarina	44.3	(11.2)	16.8	(6.5)	38.9	(11.6)	8.5	(4.7)	31.8	(10.8)	59.7	(11.5)	0.0	c	0.0	c	100.0	c
São Paulo	51.6	(7.1)	29.2	(6.2)	19.2	(5.2)	26.8	(6.8)	19.2	(5.5)	54.0	(6.7)	6.8	(3.4)	18.7	(5.3)	74.5	(5.3)
Sergipe	46.5	(10.5)	35.1	(9.2)	18.4	(10.4)	5.1	(4.2)	68.3	(13.1)	26.5	(12.8)	0.0	c	23.1	(14.5)	76.9	(14.5)
Tocantins	41.0	(9.8)	43.5	(9.5)	15.5	(6.1)	26.3	(8.7)	33.3	(9.3)	40.4	(8.8)	4.1	(4.2)	0.0	c	95.9	(4.2)
Colombia																		
Bogota	35.9	(7.8)	59.6	(6.9)	4.4	(3.1)	25.6	(7.1)	57.7	(8.6)	16.6	(6.3)	9.3	(4.6)	49.2	(8.3)	41.4	(7.7)
Cali	45.7	(9.1)	40.0	(9.2)	14.3	(6.0)	41.2	(9.0)	33.3	(7.6)	25.5	(8.1)	6.8	(3.3)	53.2	(8.3)	40.1	(8.8)
Manizales	36.4	(7.9)	52.9	(8.2)	10.6	(4.3)	27.6	(7.4)	40.2	(6.2)	32.1	(7.8)	15.2	(6.1)	59.1	(8.4)	25.6	(7.1)
Medellin	21.5	(6.3)	72.7	(5.6)	5.7	(3.4)	18.3	(5.9)	47.9	(7.4)	33.8	(7.8)	1.6	(1.5)	62.8	(7.9)	35.6	(7.6)
Russian Federation																		
Perm Territory region•	43.0	(6.0)	53.7	(5.5)	3.3	(2.4)	19.3	(5.4)	33.9	(5.9)	46.8	(7.5)	12.4	(4.5)	75.1	(5.4)	12.5	(4.5)
United Arab Emirates																		
Abu Dhabi•	57.5	(4.5)	27.4	(4.3)	15.1	(3.1)	38.6	(4.0)	23.2	(4.1)	38.2	(4.3)	47.8	(4.3)	35.7	(4.3)	16.5	(3.3)
Ajman	75.2	(7.4)	8.5	(7.1)	16.2	(2.0)	19.5	(5.6)	12.5	(6.2)	67.9	(4.8)	50.0	(7.8)	34.6	(7.5)	15.3	(3.6)
Dubai•	55.6	(0.3)	28.6	(0.2)	15.8	(0.2)	22.3	(0.2)	30.1	(0.2)	47.6	(0.3)	54.1	(0.3)	32.6	(0.3)	13.3	(0.1)
Fujairah	41.2	(5.6)	56.3	(6.6)	2.6	(3.6)	46.3	(3.7)	38.7	(6.5)	14.9	(5.6)	38.1	(3.9)	61.3	(3.9)	0.6	(0.2)
Ras Al Khaimah	68.2	(8.8)	18.3	(7.7)	13.5	(5.3)	37.6	(10.1)	29.6	(10.8)	32.8	(11.5)	59.1	(11.0)	26.8	(9.7)	14.2	(6.9)
Sharjah	52.7	(10.4)	15.6	(6.3)	31.7	(9.4)	27.1	(10.5)	7.8	(4.8)	65.1	(9.4)	7.8	(3.4)	47.3	(7.6)	44.8	(7.4)
Umm Al Quwain	94.6	(0.3)	4.7	(0.2)	0.8	(0.2)	48.0	(0.3)	29.8	(0.3)	22.1	(0.5)	39.9	(0.2)	47.0	(0.4)	13.1	(0.3)

• PISA adjudicated region.
Note: See Table IV.2.11 for national data.
StatLink ᴍˢᴾ http://dx.doi.org/10.1787/888932957536

[Part 3/4]
Ability grouping for mathematics classes, by region
Table B2.IV.4   *Results based on school principals' reports*

| | In mathematics classes, teachers use pedagogy suitable for students with heterogeneous abilities (i.e. students are not grouped by ability) | | | | | | No ability grouping for any class | | One form of grouping for some classes | | One form of grouping for all classes | |
| | For all classes | | For some classes | | Not for any class | | | | | | | |
	%	S.E.	%	S.E.	%	S.E.	%	S.E.	%	S.E.	%	S.E.
Australia												
Australian Capital Territory	18.4	(0.8)	49.2	(0.9)	32.4	(1.0)	1.1	(0.1)	26.0	(0.9)	72.8	(0.9)
New South Wales	16.4	(2.6)	43.0	(3.4)	40.6	(3.7)	1.8	(1.0)	38.9	(3.6)	59.3	(3.5)
Northern Territory	3.8	(0.9)	47.5	(9.7)	48.8	(9.7)	0.0	c	39.6	(4.9)	60.4	(4.9)
Queensland	23.8	(3.8)	57.1	(4.3)	19.1	(3.4)	0.0	c	54.3	(4.3)	45.7	(4.3)
South Australia	22.4	(4.2)	55.6	(5.1)	22.0	(4.3)	1.1	(0.9)	59.7	(5.1)	39.2	(4.9)
Tasmania	12.5	(0.9)	54.9	(1.7)	32.6	(1.4)	0.5	(0.5)	46.2	(1.6)	53.3	(1.7)
Victoria	30.0	(3.5)	52.6	(4.0)	17.4	(3.1)	3.6	(1.6)	56.5	(4.5)	39.9	(4.3)
Western Australia	14.4	(3.5)	48.4	(5.6)	37.2	(5.4)	0.0	c	46.4	(5.9)	53.6	(5.9)
Belgium												
Flemish community*	51.3	(4.5)	34.0	(4.3)	14.8	(2.8)	9.9	(2.3)	66.8	(3.9)	23.3	(3.5)
French community	63.2	(5.1)	18.6	(4.0)	18.3	(3.5)	36.3	(5.7)	42.8	(5.9)	20.9	(4.5)
German-speaking community	0.0	c	56.5	(0.3)	43.5	(0.3)	0.0	c	66.7	(0.2)	33.3	(0.2)
Canada												
Alberta	38.4	(5.0)	49.3	(5.4)	12.3	(3.9)	1.8	(1.3)	45.9	(4.2)	52.3	(4.1)
British Columbia	39.8	(6.0)	47.9	(5.5)	12.3	(4.0)	10.4	(3.3)	54.7	(6.0)	34.9	(5.2)
Manitoba	47.9	(3.1)	46.9	(3.0)	5.2	(1.4)	8.2	(1.7)	40.7	(3.1)	51.1	(3.1)
New Brunswick	35.0	(2.8)	62.3	(2.7)	2.7	(0.2)	14.0	(1.1)	55.4	(2.6)	30.5	(3.0)
Newfoundland and Labrador	51.0	(5.1)	30.2	(4.6)	18.9	(0.8)	14.1	(5.8)	65.0	(2.8)	20.9	(4.0)
Nova Scotia	32.5	(6.3)	64.9	(6.6)	2.6	(2.0)	2.8	(1.7)	68.6	(6.0)	28.5	(5.7)
Ontario	40.1	(5.9)	44.8	(5.9)	15.1	(3.8)	3.0	(1.7)	44.9	(5.8)	52.0	(6.0)
Prince Edward Island	49.6	(0.4)	47.7	(0.4)	2.7	(0.3)	1.7	(0.2)	72.3	(0.5)	26.0	(0.4)
Quebec	18.7	(3.8)	49.3	(4.3)	32.0	(4.2)	14.5	(3.0)	49.3	(4.6)	36.2	(4.5)
Saskatchewan	45.5	(4.0)	46.3	(3.7)	8.3	(1.5)	6.7	(2.1)	68.8	(3.5)	24.5	(2.7)
Italy												
Abruzzo	48.1	(6.5)	39.8	(5.8)	12.1	(4.4)	24.3	(5.7)	54.3	(7.1)	21.4	(6.1)
Basilicata	26.5	(5.9)	45.5	(5.9)	28.0	(4.1)	30.2	(5.2)	53.3	(5.0)	16.5	(3.4)
Bolzano	20.3	(0.5)	73.9	(0.5)	5.8	(0.2)	31.4	(1.0)	49.7	(0.9)	18.9	(0.6)
Calabria	50.5	(9.3)	33.8	(8.7)	15.7	(5.3)	14.8	(5.5)	64.9	(8.4)	20.3	(6.2)
Campania	51.0	(9.9)	38.1	(9.5)	10.9	(4.7)	14.9	(4.8)	34.5	(6.7)	50.6	(8.9)
Emilia Romagna	51.0	(7.2)	42.0	(7.5)	7.0	(3.8)	22.5	(5.4)	46.6	(7.3)	31.0	(6.0)
Friuli Venezia Giulia	47.7	(4.4)	50.6	(4.4)	1.7	(0.2)	14.0	(3.5)	70.0	(4.4)	16.0	(3.1)
Lazio	45.6	(7.4)	37.3	(6.9)	17.1	(5.1)	33.9	(7.3)	40.2	(8.1)	26.0	(8.2)
Liguria	50.4	(7.6)	34.5	(6.3)	15.0	(6.0)	19.5	(5.5)	52.3	(7.4)	28.2	(6.8)
Lombardia	32.2	(7.7)	46.9	(8.2)	20.9	(7.3)	29.8	(6.9)	47.9	(8.4)	22.3	(5.9)
Marche	42.7	(6.8)	47.1	(7.1)	10.3	(4.4)	32.8	(6.1)	53.8	(6.9)	13.5	(5.5)
Molise	33.8	(0.9)	33.3	(1.0)	32.9	(1.0)	19.8	(0.7)	59.1	(0.9)	21.1	(0.8)
Piemonte	42.1	(6.5)	48.3	(7.4)	9.5	(4.3)	23.9	(6.4)	52.1	(7.9)	24.0	(5.4)
Puglia	47.2	(7.5)	42.4	(6.2)	10.5	(4.5)	27.9	(6.3)	51.3	(7.2)	20.9	(5.5)
Sardegna	52.2	(7.2)	34.6	(6.8)	13.2	(5.5)	28.5	(6.6)	56.7	(6.5)	14.7	(4.6)
Sicilia	53.4	(6.2)	32.1	(5.7)	14.5	(4.3)	19.5	(5.6)	49.0	(6.6)	31.5	(6.2)
Toscana	49.8	(8.8)	33.8	(7.9)	16.3	(6.0)	24.6	(7.8)	54.8	(7.4)	20.6	(7.0)
Trento	51.0	(4.6)	38.9	(4.9)	10.1	(2.3)	19.0	(3.6)	49.1	(3.9)	31.9	(4.7)
Umbria	48.9	(6.3)	36.4	(5.4)	14.7	(4.0)	22.1	(3.7)	54.3	(4.9)	23.6	(5.9)
Valle d'Aosta	31.3	(1.0)	33.8	(0.9)	34.9	(1.1)	65.2	(0.9)	33.1	(0.9)	1.7	(0.1)
Veneto	40.0	(6.3)	46.5	(6.4)	13.5	(4.1)	22.0	(4.8)	51.7	(6.0)	26.3	(6.2)
Mexico												
Aguascalientes	19.4	(6.0)	46.0	(7.3)	34.6	(5.9)	30.7	(7.4)	28.5	(7.3)	40.8	(5.9)
Baja California	24.7	(9.4)	41.2	(6.9)	34.1	(9.3)	29.6	(8.5)	38.5	(9.2)	32.0	(7.5)
Baja California Sur	22.2	(7.2)	53.0	(6.5)	24.7	(2.3)	23.4	(4.6)	40.0	(7.9)	36.6	(7.7)
Campeche	19.8	(5.9)	55.0	(8.7)	25.2	(9.7)	31.8	(8.1)	13.1	(6.4)	55.1	(6.9)
Chiapas	33.3	(7.5)	36.4	(7.2)	30.3	(7.4)	14.8	(5.0)	31.6	(6.8)	53.6	(8.1)
Chihuahua	35.8	(9.9)	37.0	(7.9)	27.2	(10.0)	18.9	(5.0)	38.6	(8.7)	42.6	(8.0)
Coahuila	37.1	(8.1)	32.3	(7.4)	30.7	(8.2)	34.1	(9.6)	28.2	(8.2)	37.7	(8.5)
Colima	22.0	(5.1)	41.0	(8.8)	37.0	(7.2)	42.2	(5.3)	24.7	(6.9)	33.1	(5.8)
Distrito Federal	21.9	(5.6)	32.7	(7.9)	45.4	(9.0)	22.0	(6.1)	35.2	(7.8)	42.9	(8.6)
Durango	26.3	(6.2)	44.6	(9.3)	29.1	(6.1)	16.6	(6.0)	21.0	(8.4)	62.4	(9.2)
Guanajuato	40.1	(7.8)	25.9	(7.3)	34.0	(8.1)	41.7	(9.0)	16.0	(6.0)	42.3	(8.4)
Guerrero	32.6	(6.3)	28.7	(8.2)	38.7	(9.1)	28.9	(9.0)	35.5	(7.9)	35.6	(7.4)
Hidalgo	21.0	(7.3)	36.0	(8.0)	43.0	(8.6)	26.5	(6.2)	31.1	(7.7)	42.3	(8.5)
Jalisco	31.6	(9.7)	41.6	(10.1)	26.8	(6.6)	32.6	(9.2)	41.5	(10.5)	25.9	(5.5)
Mexico	41.5	(8.6)	30.6	(6.9)	27.9	(6.6)	28.1	(5.7)	30.9	(7.5)	41.0	(7.6)
Morelos	31.4	(7.6)	41.0	(9.1)	27.6	(7.6)	31.3	(7.9)	34.4	(8.7)	34.4	(9.5)
Nayarit	18.8	(6.6)	44.3	(7.5)	36.9	(4.7)	28.3	(5.2)	26.3	(5.1)	45.4	(6.8)
Nuevo León	35.5	(6.7)	27.0	(5.9)	37.4	(7.6)	27.3	(6.5)	21.4	(6.5)	51.3	(7.3)
Puebla	28.1	(6.0)	48.8	(7.3)	23.1	(7.6)	15.4	(5.6)	44.5	(8.6)	40.0	(8.7)
Querétaro	14.2	(5.0)	33.1	(7.9)	52.7	(8.7)	39.2	(12.1)	30.1	(10.4)	30.6	(7.2)
Quintana Roo	41.9	(8.3)	30.3	(8.9)	27.9	(8.1)	8.8	(2.8)	29.6	(6.5)	61.6	(7.3)
San Luis Potosí	36.6	(7.1)	32.6	(9.8)	30.9	(9.0)	23.8	(6.2)	35.5	(6.4)	40.7	(5.9)
Sinaloa	16.1	(5.5)	50.2	(9.4)	33.7	(8.5)	24.0	(8.0)	35.0	(9.9)	41.0	(9.3)
Tabasco	18.3	(6.0)	31.3	(9.1)	50.4	(8.9)	24.0	(8.2)	27.1	(6.9)	48.9	(9.2)
Tamaulipas	38.0	(9.8)	41.5	(10.2)	20.5	(8.0)	31.2	(7.6)	28.3	(10.5)	40.6	(9.8)
Tlaxcala	25.7	(6.6)	53.7	(7.7)	20.6	(5.9)	22.9	(5.6)	29.5	(7.8)	47.5	(8.7)
Veracruz	33.8	(7.5)	43.7	(9.3)	22.5	(7.4)	28.8	(7.1)	34.3	(7.8)	36.9	(7.8)
Yucatán	22.5	(7.1)	33.7	(8.8)	43.8	(8.9)	26.0	(6.6)	31.1	(8.8)	42.9	(9.6)
Zacatecas	23.3	(5.9)	42.4	(7.5)	34.3	(6.8)	20.4	(6.2)	33.6	(7.7)	46.0	(7.9)

* PISA adjudicated region.
Note: See Table IV.2.11 for national data.
StatLink ⌐ᵓᵖ http://dx.doi.org/10.1787/888932957536

[Part 4/4]
Ability grouping for mathematics classes, by region
Table B2.IV.4   *Results based on school principals' reports*

	Percentage of students in schools whose principal reported:											
	In mathematics classes, teachers use pedagogy suitable for students with heterogeneous abilities (i.e. students are not grouped by ability)						No ability grouping for any class		One form of grouping for some classes		One form of grouping for all classes	
	For all classes		For some classes		Not for any class							
	%	S.E.	%	S.E.	%	S.E.	%	S.E.	%	S.E.	%	S.E.
Portugal												
Alentejo	60.9	(10.3)	30.6	(10.8)	8.5	(4.9)	51.3	(9.5)	38.8	(9.6)	9.9	(6.3)
Spain												
Andalusia•	61.0	(7.6)	22.7	(6.8)	16.3	(4.7)	4.7	(2.9)	37.6	(6.7)	57.6	(7.3)
Aragon•	71.3	(5.8)	19.0	(4.8)	9.7	(3.3)	8.4	(4.2)	43.3	(6.0)	48.3	(5.9)
Asturias•	58.8	(5.6)	30.6	(6.1)	10.6	(4.3)	3.8	(2.6)	41.9	(7.6)	54.4	(7.7)
Balearic Islands•	61.5	(6.7)	24.3	(6.8)	14.1	(5.3)	5.7	(3.3)	40.4	(7.5)	53.9	(8.2)
Basque Country•	52.3	(4.0)	36.4	(4.1)	11.3	(2.5)	24.2	(3.2)	54.2	(4.0)	21.5	(3.0)
Cantabria•	73.0	(5.2)	15.6	(4.7)	11.4	(4.7)	9.8	(4.5)	47.1	(6.5)	43.1	(6.2)
Castile and Leon•	52.0	(7.1)	32.4	(6.9)	15.6	(4.8)	3.9	(2.8)	45.9	(5.9)	50.2	(6.4)
Catalonia•	41.0	(7.4)	29.5	(5.9)	29.5	(7.2)	6.0	(3.5)	49.4	(7.9)	44.5	(7.6)
Extremadura•	76.1	(6.1)	11.6	(4.6)	12.3	(4.9)	9.0	(4.2)	40.8	(6.9)	50.2	(6.3)
Galicia•	62.3	(7.4)	27.3	(7.2)	10.3	(4.2)	18.9	(5.7)	40.9	(7.1)	40.2	(6.7)
La Rioja•	60.7	(0.6)	19.6	(0.5)	19.7	(0.4)	6.4	(0.3)	43.7	(0.5)	49.9	(0.5)
Madrid•	48.1	(7.4)	35.8	(5.9)	16.1	(4.8)	9.5	(4.1)	44.7	(7.2)	45.8	(7.6)
Murcia•	61.7	(6.5)	26.2	(6.4)	12.1	(5.2)	0.0	c	57.0	(8.6)	43.0	(8.6)
Navarre•	44.9	(4.8)	32.7	(4.3)	22.4	(4.4)	1.2	(1.2)	52.8	(5.8)	46.1	(6.0)
United Kingdom												
England	4.6	(1.6)	12.3	(2.3)	83.0	(2.6)	0.7	(0.7)	36.2	(4.1)	63.1	(4.1)
Northern Ireland	15.6	(3.9)	19.6	(3.9)	64.8	(5.1)	2.8	(2.1)	40.0	(4.8)	57.2	(4.9)
Scotland•	9.3	(3.1)	26.6	(4.3)	64.1	(5.1)	0.9	(0.8)	44.1	(4.7)	55.1	(4.6)
Wales	5.0	(1.7)	17.9	(3.1)	77.1	(3.2)	0.0	c	38.5	(3.8)	61.5	(3.8)
United States												
Connecticut•	21.8	(6.9)	66.1	(8.3)	12.1	(5.3)	0.0	c	52.7	(7.9)	47.3	(7.9)
Florida•	23.9	(6.1)	57.4	(7.7)	18.8	(7.0)	3.6	(2.5)	66.7	(7.0)	29.7	(7.0)
Massachusetts•	33.2	(6.8)	47.6	(7.7)	19.2	(6.4)	0.0	c	54.4	(8.1)	45.6	(8.1)
Argentina												
Ciudad Autónoma de Buenos Aires•	56.8	(9.1)	26.8	(7.3)	16.4	(6.2)	26.7	(7.9)	49.7	(8.0)	23.6	(6.6)
Brazil												
Acre	38.2	(13.3)	4.4	(4.7)	57.4	(14.3)	5.2	(5.2)	22.9	(8.0)	71.9	(6.9)
Alagoas	15.5	(10.9)	31.9	(12.0)	52.6	(12.7)	10.2	(9.7)	50.9	(13.5)	38.9	(12.0)
Amapá	24.9	(9.4)	21.7	(9.3)	53.4	(11.5)	11.2	(6.6)	39.1	(8.5)	49.7	(9.1)
Amazonas	34.3	(12.0)	17.8	(10.8)	47.8	(13.0)	25.4	(12.1)	30.6	(11.1)	44.0	(14.3)
Bahia	66.7	(12.9)	6.6	(4.5)	26.7	(13.0)	19.9	(14.3)	30.8	(12.8)	49.3	(18.6)
Ceará	36.6	(9.2)	12.0	(8.3)	51.4	(11.7)	35.9	(9.3)	33.4	(10.7)	30.7	(10.8)
Espírito Santo	60.7	(18.6)	6.4	(4.4)	32.9	(18.1)	17.5	(12.6)	28.0	(9.8)	54.5	(18.9)
Federal District	20.1	(12.6)	28.6	(15.2)	51.3	(9.3)	35.7	(14.9)	21.2	(10.4)	43.1	(17.1)
Goiás	40.3	(8.3)	12.6	(7.4)	47.1	(9.6)	9.1	(6.1)	32.6	(9.8)	58.4	(9.3)
Maranhão	10.5	(7.4)	31.5	(13.0)	58.0	(14.4)	24.5	(14.3)	33.4	(9.5)	42.1	(14.8)
Mato Grosso	36.3	(10.2)	20.6	(7.1)	43.1	(12.4)	25.2	(11.7)	46.1	(12.7)	28.7	(7.0)
Mato Grosso do Sul	38.1	(11.1)	29.4	(9.1)	32.4	(6.0)	24.3	(7.5)	14.5	(7.7)	61.2	(11.0)
Minas Gerais	56.7	(11.3)	23.9	(9.6)	19.4	(6.4)	12.0	(6.3)	19.6	(7.9)	68.4	(7.1)
Pará	41.6	(18.8)	11.3	(7.5)	47.1	(17.8)	33.1	(13.8)	27.8	(8.3)	39.0	(12.5)
Paraíba	36.2	(16.0)	36.9	(16.4)	26.9	(10.6)	6.1	(4.5)	19.1	(8.9)	74.8	(10.2)
Paraná	29.5	(11.3)	30.7	(9.6)	39.8	(11.7)	21.4	(7.7)	42.4	(11.0)	36.2	(10.1)
Pernambuco	46.6	(13.3)	9.6	(7.2)	43.7	(10.6)	8.6	(6.6)	30.9	(9.0)	60.4	(8.7)
Piauí	10.8	(8.0)	33.5	(13.6)	55.7	(11.5)	17.8	(6.1)	36.3	(12.5)	45.9	(11.2)
Rio de Janeiro	26.9	(10.7)	26.3	(9.1)	46.8	(11.0)	16.0	(6.7)	24.5	(7.4)	59.5	(6.1)
Rio Grande do Norte	10.5	(6.7)	26.2	(11.0)	63.3	(9.2)	24.3	(11.4)	36.4	(13.7)	39.3	(12.6)
Rio Grande do Sul	36.9	(10.3)	8.4	(7.0)	54.7	(10.1)	26.1	(9.7)	14.8	(8.1)	59.1	(12.5)
Rondônia	17.7	(9.1)	30.3	(12.0)	52.0	(13.5)	39.5	(11.8)	47.3	(11.1)	13.2	(7.0)
Roraima	19.8	(9.7)	30.7	(12.0)	49.5	(12.1)	14.0	(9.8)	47.7	(11.9)	38.4	(11.2)
Santa Catarina	14.3	(8.2)	10.2	(6.9)	75.5	(10.2)	26.1	(10.0)	23.5	(4.9)	50.5	(11.8)
São Paulo	36.0	(5.9)	22.0	(5.2)	42.1	(5.7)	15.1	(4.4)	26.8	(5.8)	58.0	(6.8)
Sergipe	25.3	(11.6)	14.5	(13.0)	60.2	(11.9)	15.6	(10.0)	37.9	(8.5)	46.5	(10.5)
Tocantins	35.2	(11.9)	16.7	(8.1)	48.1	(10.2)	15.5	(6.1)	43.5	(9.5)	41.0	(9.8)
Colombia												
Bogota	41.2	(7.5)	44.1	(6.6)	14.7	(5.4)	4.4	(3.1)	47.1	(7.0)	48.4	(7.7)
Cali	47.5	(8.2)	32.2	(8.8)	20.2	(7.0)	12.8	(5.8)	22.8	(6.8)	64.4	(8.4)
Manizales	26.7	(8.5)	59.5	(6.4)	13.8	(4.9)	10.6	(4.3)	39.8	(7.1)	49.6	(7.0)
Medellin	24.0	(6.7)	53.0	(7.4)	23.0	(6.5)	4.1	(3.0)	67.2	(6.7)	28.8	(7.1)
Russian Federation												
Perm Territory region•	27.3	(6.2)	67.3	(6.9)	5.4	(3.2)	0.0	c	45.4	(5.9)	54.6	(5.9)
United Arab Emirates												
Abu Dhabi•	65.1	(4.0)	24.5	(4.3)	10.4	(3.1)	10.2	(2.5)	27.3	(4.2)	62.5	(4.5)
Ajman	70.1	(5.3)	27.6	(5.2)	2.3	(0.4)	16.2	(2.0)	8.5	(7.1)	75.2	(7.4)
Dubai•	52.6	(0.3)	29.7	(0.2)	17.8	(0.3)	12.2	(0.2)	26.9	(0.2)	60.9	(0.2)
Fujairah	75.6	(7.0)	23.8	(6.9)	0.6	(0.1)	0.0	c	38.7	(6.5)	61.3	(6.5)
Ras Al Khaimah	82.8	(8.1)	10.7	(7.4)	6.5	(3.1)	7.0	(5.5)	18.3	(7.7)	74.7	(8.9)
Sharjah	59.8	(9.0)	39.4	(9.3)	0.8	(0.8)	28.9	(10.1)	5.3	(3.5)	65.9	(10.0)
Umm Al Quwain	34.4	(0.4)	64.8	(0.5)	0.9	(0.3)	0.8	(0.2)	4.7	(0.2)	94.6	(0.3)

• PISA adjudicated region.
Note: See Table IV.2.11 for national data.
StatLink ⧉ http://dx.doi.org/10.1787/888932957536

[Part 1/2]
Composition and qualifications of teaching staff, by region
Table B2.IV.5   *Results based on school principals' reports*

	School principals' report on the following:							
	Percentage of certified teachers in the school		Percentage of teachers with ISCED 5A in the school		Percentage of mathematics teachers in the school		Percentage of mathematics teachers with ISCED 5A in the school	
	Mean %	S.E.	Mean %	S.E.	Mean %	S.E.	Mean %	S.E.
Australia								
Australian Capital Territory	99.6	(0.0)	99.7	(0.0)	16.8	(0.2)	64.5	(0.7)
New South Wales	95.4	(1.5)	96.4	(1.4)	12.3	(0.3)	74.9	(2.0)
Northern Territory	99.3	(0.2)	99.9	(0.1)	21.2	(2.7)	46.9	(3.9)
Queensland	97.9	(1.0)	96.2	(1.6)	21.9	(1.1)	47.6	(2.8)
South Australia	99.7	(0.2)	99.1	(0.8)	19.6	(0.8)	53.8	(3.3)
Tasmania	99.3	(0.1)	96.0	(0.4)	26.9	(0.5)	34.2	(0.6)
Victoria	99.4	(0.2)	97.5	(1.2)	20.1	(0.6)	64.0	(2.7)
Western Australia	98.3	(1.2)	97.1	(1.4)	12.2	(0.5)	66.3	(3.4)
Belgium								
Flemish community•	89.8	(2.3)	39.0	(1.0)	11.4	(0.3)	24.6	(1.4)
French community	83.6	(2.5)	39.2	(1.7)	12.6	(0.4)	20.7	(1.8)
German-speaking community	74.9	(0.3)	39.3	(0.2)	12.4	(0.0)	46.5	(0.3)
Canada								
Alberta	99.4	(0.2)	95.9	(2.2)	16.8	(1.7)	62.1	(3.7)
British Columbia	98.7	(0.7)	94.6	(2.4)	12.3	(0.6)	61.6	(3.9)
Manitoba	99.1	(0.1)	93.8	(1.6)	17.3	(1.7)	61.3	(2.9)
New Brunswick	93.0	(0.3)	97.2	(0.2)	18.5	(0.6)	46.3	(2.2)
Newfoundland and Labrador	99.8	(0.1)	98.6	(0.6)	16.6	(0.9)	79.1	(1.9)
Nova Scotia	98.7	(0.3)	96.6	(1.7)	17.0	(0.6)	71.0	(5.1)
Ontario	98.5	(1.1)	96.7	(1.1)	14.0	(0.5)	60.6	(3.4)
Prince Edward Island	98.4	(0.1)	97.4	(0.1)	20.7	(0.1)	41.6	(0.2)
Quebec	88.9	(2.9)	92.8	(2.1)	16.0	(0.5)	73.3	(3.1)
Saskatchewan	99.4	(0.4)	90.2	(2.4)	22.6	(1.4)	54.1	(2.3)
Italy								
Abruzzo	91.8	(1.4)	93.6	(1.1)	10.5	(0.5)	67.4	(3.6)
Basilicata	88.9	(3.0)	90.6	(3.1)	11.8	(0.4)	51.5	(3.1)
Bolzano	54.9	(0.4)	72.1	(0.4)	9.9	(0.1)	42.6	(0.5)
Calabria	89.1	(3.1)	89.2	(3.1)	11.2	(0.5)	75.7	(3.7)
Campania	93.0	(2.0)	91.4	(2.9)	12.7	(1.0)	72.3	(4.1)
Emilia Romagna	84.6	(1.3)	90.9	(1.1)	10.8	(0.6)	66.6	(4.7)
Friuli Venezia Giulia	79.8	(2.2)	90.9	(1.9)	11.7	(0.3)	56.4	(4.7)
Lazio	90.5	(1.5)	92.7	(1.2)	12.9	(0.7)	74.2	(4.3)
Liguria	87.8	(2.1)	90.9	(1.7)	11.8	(0.7)	76.3	(3.8)
Lombardia	80.5	(3.9)	86.6	(3.3)	11.7	(0.8)	73.3	(3.5)
Marche	88.1	(2.3)	92.0	(1.3)	11.7	(0.6)	71.5	(3.8)
Molise	90.9	(0.2)	94.2	(0.1)	12.1	(0.1)	62.2	(0.5)
Piemonte	70.8	(6.0)	83.8	(3.5)	10.3	(0.8)	68.3	(4.7)
Puglia	87.4	(4.9)	89.1	(4.9)	12.8	(0.6)	63.5	(3.8)
Sardegna	88.4	(2.2)	90.6	(2.3)	12.8	(0.7)	33.6	(4.4)
Sicilia	95.0	(1.1)	95.5	(1.1)	11.8	(0.6)	73.7	(3.1)
Toscana	88.4	(1.2)	89.2	(1.8)	12.1	(0.7)	71.0	(5.0)
Trento	73.6	(3.5)	84.9	(2.8)	11.5	(0.3)	67.6	(3.7)
Umbria	90.2	(1.0)	92.6	(0.9)	11.4	(0.4)	78.0	(4.7)
Valle d'Aosta	74.1	(0.4)	91.2	(0.2)	10.4	(0.1)	70.6	(0.8)
Veneto	77.3	(1.4)	86.1	(1.0)	12.0	(0.5)	62.9	(4.0)
Mexico								
Aguascalientes	29.4	(8.0)	95.5	(1.0)	21.0	(1.7)	28.6	(4.3)
Baja California	16.6	(6.0)	81.3	(8.6)	21.6	(3.8)	24.0	(5.9)
Baja California Sur	25.6	(7.3)	87.8	(2.7)	18.9	(2.0)	19.3	(5.8)
Campeche	42.9	(12.4)	78.1	(8.4)	17.0	(1.8)	38.5	(9.3)
Chiapas	33.1	(8.6)	85.2	(7.2)	26.7	(3.2)	26.8	(8.6)
Chihuahua	31.4	(12.3)	91.2	(3.1)	20.7	(1.5)	38.1	(8.1)
Coahuila	27.7	(8.0)	90.0	(3.8)	18.7	(2.5)	22.8	(8.3)
Colima	19.9	(4.5)	92.3	(0.7)	25.2	(3.7)	30.7	(5.1)
Distrito Federal	24.0	(8.1)	79.5	(4.3)	11.7	(0.4)	24.2	(6.2)
Durango	16.0	(3.5)	85.6	(5.1)	22.0	(2.3)	25.0	(6.5)
Guanajuato	43.9	(5.1)	90.7	(2.5)	39.0	(4.6)	24.7	(5.4)
Guerrero	4.6	(2.3)	85.2	(4.4)	22.1	(3.3)	38.8	(9.6)
Hidalgo	17.2	(5.7)	89.2	(2.4)	17.0	(2.3)	30.4	(6.1)
Jalisco	17.3	(4.5)	91.7	(3.3)	18.0	(1.3)	23.8	(8.0)
Mexico	20.4	(6.1)	91.9	(1.3)	22.2	(3.8)	23.3	(7.3)
Morelos	30.8	(9.1)	85.8	(4.6)	21.8	(2.7)	18.6	(8.6)
Nayarit	17.8	(4.2)	97.9	(0.8)	19.9	(2.6)	29.4	(5.0)
Nuevo León	40.0	(11.0)	91.3	(4.8)	18.0	(1.3)	43.9	(7.5)
Puebla	33.4	(10.8)	86.0	(5.2)	28.1	(4.1)	23.1	(8.4)
Querétaro	39.4	(10.8)	93.6	(2.7)	21.1	(2.9)	34.5	(6.3)
Quintana Roo	37.5	(10.2)	86.9	(5.9)	20.1	(2.1)	34.5	(9.8)
San Luis Potosí	36.9	(9.2)	91.2	(3.2)	22.0	(2.7)	43.4	(10.6)
Sinaloa	17.3	(5.0)	94.5	(1.8)	18.6	(1.9)	33.2	(8.6)
Tabasco	29.8	(8.4)	95.1	(3.1)	26.1	(5.1)	23.2	(6.1)
Tamaulipas	30.5	(8.9)	86.8	(5.2)	17.5	(1.4)	23.6	(5.2)
Tlaxcala	22.6	(6.6)	90.9	(4.5)	22.8	(3.8)	28.4	(5.2)
Veracruz	38.7	(11.2)	85.9	(6.2)	40.2	(5.4)	26.0	(7.8)
Yucatán	52.8	(10.4)	89.4	(5.3)	20.1	(2.8)	50.3	(9.3)
Zacatecas	34.0	(6.4)	94.7	(1.8)	27.1	(2.8)	26.9	(8.7)

• PISA adjudicated region.
Note: See Table IV.3.6 for national data.
StatLink ⫘⫘ http://dx.doi.org/10.1787/888932957536

[Part 2/2]
Composition and qualifications of teaching staff, by region
Table B2.IV.5   *Results based on school principals' reports*

	School principals' report on the following:							
	Percentage of certified teachers in the school		Percentage of teachers with ISCED 5A in the school		Percentage of mathematics teachers in the school		Percentage of mathematics teachers with ISCED 5A in the school	
	Mean %	S.E.	Mean %	S.E.	Mean %	S.E.	Mean %	S.E.
Portugal								
Alentejo	92.4	(2.5)	75.5	(6.1)	12.5	(0.3)	70.9	(4.9)
Spain								
Andalusia•	100.0	c	96.2	(2.3)	15.3	(1.1)	54.0	(4.1)
Aragon•	100.0	c	96.7	(1.5)	15.6	(1.4)	53.6	(3.4)
Asturias•	100.0	c	97.6	(1.0)	13.6	(1.3)	35.3	(3.0)
Balearic Islands•	100.0	c	84.8	(2.8)	12.2	(1.4)	35.8	(2.7)
Basque Country•	100.0	c	99.0	(0.4)	15.1	(0.8)	23.5	(2.2)
Cantabria•	100.0	c	97.1	(1.4)	15.2	(1.3)	43.5	(4.0)
Castile and Leon•	100.0	c	96.7	(1.4)	15.0	(1.4)	41.7	(4.2)
Catalonia•	100.0	c	91.3	(2.7)	12.9	(1.1)	29.8	(3.8)
Extremadura•	100.0	c	95.9	(1.9)	11.5	(0.5)	58.8	(3.8)
Galicia•	100.0	c	76.1	(4.2)	14.6	(1.2)	57.7	(3.5)
La Rioja•	100.0	c	96.5	(0.1)	16.4	(0.1)	59.2	(0.3)
Madrid•	100.0	c	96.1	(1.8)	17.6	(2.5)	47.7	(4.3)
Murcia•	100.0	c	98.1	(1.4)	15.5	(1.7)	62.0	(3.2)
Navarre•	100.0	c	95.7	(2.4)	13.7	(1.0)	48.6	(4.5)
United Kingdom								
England	94.5	(1.3)	95.5	(1.4)	11.8	(0.2)	69.3	(2.2)
Northern Ireland	98.6	(1.2)	97.3	(1.9)	11.5	(0.3)	80.1	(2.9)
Scotland•	98.2	(0.3)	96.4	(1.6)	11.1	(0.2)	90.8	(2.2)
Wales	99.0	(0.6)	97.1	(1.2)	12.0	(0.2)	75.0	(2.2)
United States								
Connecticut•	99.3	(0.2)	98.2	(1.0)	12.6	(0.3)	86.6	(4.2)
Florida•	94.1	(2.0)	98.6	(0.9)	16.4	(1.9)	55.3	(5.2)
Massachusetts•	94.8	(2.3)	95.3	(1.8)	14.2	(0.4)	80.6	(4.4)
Argentina								
Ciudad Autónoma de Buenos Aires•	88.2	(4.5)	19.8	(2.8)	7.1	(0.7)	11.1	(3.8)
Brazil								
Acre	m	m	93.1	(3.8)	17.7	(2.3)	81.1	(9.9)
Alagoas	m	m	82.2	(8.6)	22.2	(4.1)	46.2	(14.1)
Amapá	m	m	91.9	(3.9)	13.0	(0.8)	88.2	(3.5)
Amazonas	m	m	84.1	(9.2)	25.8	(5.5)	80.4	(10.5)
Bahia	m	m	74.7	(5.8)	18.1	(2.3)	47.1	(11.0)
Ceará	m	m	88.1	(3.2)	18.8	(1.9)	72.9	(10.7)
Espírito Santo	m	m	74.2	(10.2)	19.2	(3.4)	83.5	(14.1)
Federal District	m	m	98.5	(0.6)	11.7	(1.4)	82.4	(8.2)
Goiás	m	m	88.4	(4.2)	18.8	(1.7)	75.5	(9.2)
Maranhão	m	m	92.5	(3.1)	17.0	(2.4)	70.4	(10.9)
Mato Grosso	m	m	81.7	(5.9)	19.4	(2.5)	85.9	(4.7)
Mato Grosso do Sul	m	m	92.7	(5.3)	15.4	(2.2)	64.4	(8.5)
Minas Gerais	m	m	87.7	(3.1)	14.1	(1.9)	81.1	(5.5)
Pará	m	m	90.8	(4.3)	18.2	(1.8)	50.9	(10.4)
Paraíba	m	m	85.6	(5.2)	13.2	(2.4)	78.4	(9.0)
Paraná	m	m	87.8	(4.3)	14.2	(1.4)	69.5	(6.5)
Pernambuco	m	m	90.9	(3.9)	25.2	(3.2)	63.0	(11.2)
Piauí	m	m	92.1	(3.8)	15.0	(1.2)	53.2	(9.3)
Rio de Janeiro	m	m	79.2	(6.6)	13.4	(1.5)	63.2	(9.8)
Rio Grande do Norte	m	m	78.9	(8.4)	13.4	(2.2)	49.4	(10.8)
Rio Grande do Sul	m	m	86.0	(3.7)	15.7	(1.4)	72.2	(6.0)
Rondônia	m	m	86.5	(6.2)	23.9	(3.7)	82.9	(6.1)
Roraima	m	m	74.3	(7.0)	15.2	(1.3)	79.5	(6.8)
Santa Catarina	m	m	83.1	(5.6)	16.9	(1.7)	80.6	(5.9)
São Paulo	m	m	90.8	(2.2)	15.2	(1.7)	81.6	(4.0)
Sergipe	m	m	90.4	(4.1)	11.2	(1.3)	62.8	(14.6)
Tocantins	m	m	91.6	(3.5)	27.1	(2.7)	81.3	(6.6)
Colombia								
Bogota	11.1	(2.5)	94.2	(1.7)	12.4	(1.0)	23.9	(3.5)
Cali	25.0	(4.8)	75.9	(4.3)	14.5	(1.2)	24.8	(5.9)
Manizales	17.8	(3.8)	85.3	(3.7)	10.6	(0.7)	10.5	(3.9)
Medellin	8.5	(2.9)	91.9	(3.1)	16.0	(3.1)	23.6	(4.9)
Russian Federation								
Perm Territory region•	96.2	(1.0)	80.5	(1.5)	11.0	(0.5)	92.6	(1.6)
United Arab Emirates								
Abu Dhabi•	m	m	90.7	(1.4)	14.5	(0.4)	89.8	(1.8)
Ajman	m	m	90.8	(2.7)	13.6	(0.5)	80.5	(4.6)
Dubai•	m	m	90.3	(0.1)	14.3	(0.1)	76.5	(0.2)
Fujairah	m	m	96.3	(1.1)	11.8	(0.2)	95.2	(4.5)
Ras Al Khaimah	m	m	95.1	(2.3)	12.9	(0.5)	96.1	(0.4)
Sharjah	m	m	91.3	(3.0)	13.9	(2.2)	84.9	(3.5)
Umm Al Quwain	m	m	89.2	(0.2)	12.3	(0.0)	87.2	(0.2)

• PISA adjudicated region.
Note: See Table IV.3.6 for national data
StatLink 🔗 http://dx.doi.org/10.1787/888932957536

[Part 1/4]
Index of teacher shortage and mathematics performance, by region

Table B2.IV.6 *Results based on school principals' reports*

	Index of teacher shortage										Variability in this index	
	All students		Bottom quarter		Second quarter		Third quarter		Top quarter			
	Mean index	S.E.	Mean index	S.E.	Mean index	S.E.	Mean index	S.E.	Mean index	S.E.	Standard deviation	S.E.
Australia												
Australian Capital Territory	0.38	(0.02)	-1.09	(0.00)	0.16	(0.07)	0.86	(0.02)	1.60	(0.02)	1.03	(0.01)
New South Wales	-0.06	(0.07)	-1.09	(0.00)	-0.74	(0.12)	0.39	(0.12)	1.20	(0.09)	0.97	(0.04)
Northern Territory	0.83	(0.28)	-0.12	(0.51)	0.71	(0.19)	0.98	(0.06)	1.74	(0.37)	0.77	(0.10)
Queensland	0.60	(0.08)	-0.95	(0.11)	0.42	(0.14)	1.12	(0.10)	1.80	(0.09)	1.07	(0.05)
South Australia	0.31	(0.10)	-1.04	(0.10)	-0.03	(0.18)	0.76	(0.11)	1.54	(0.12)	1.00	(0.06)
Tasmania	0.61	(0.04)	-0.85	(0.05)	0.46	(0.07)	1.10	(0.02)	1.73	(0.05)	1.03	(0.02)
Victoria	0.20	(0.07)	-1.09	(0.05)	-0.13	(0.19)	0.68	(0.07)	1.32	(0.07)	0.93	(0.04)
Western Australia	0.00	(0.12)	-1.09	(0.00)	-0.79	(0.15)	0.31	(0.17)	1.57	(0.26)	1.15	(0.12)
Belgium												
Flemish community*	-0.02	(0.08)	-1.09	(0.00)	-0.58	(0.18)	0.38	(0.10)	1.24	(0.10)	0.95	(0.04)
French community	-0.06	(0.07)	-1.09	(0.00)	-0.74	(0.12)	0.39	(0.12)	1.20	(0.09)	0.97	(0.04)
German-speaking community	0.20	(0.07)	-1.09	(0.05)	-0.13	(0.19)	0.68	(0.07)	1.32	(0.07)	0.93	(0.04)
Canada												
Alberta	-0.32	(0.09)	-1.09	(0.00)	-1.02	(0.15)	-0.09	(0.18)	0.93	(0.09)	0.86	(0.04)
British Columbia	-0.42	(0.11)	-1.09	(0.00)	-1.09	(0.00)	-0.26	(0.33)	0.79	(0.15)	0.83	(0.06)
Manitoba	-0.26	(0.06)	-1.09	(0.00)	-0.88	(0.11)	0.08	(0.08)	0.85	(0.07)	0.82	(0.03)
New Brunswick	-0.08	(0.02)	-1.09	(0.00)	-0.41	(0.06)	0.25	(0.04)	0.93	(0.02)	0.80	(0.02)
Newfoundland and Labrador	-0.59	(0.04)	-1.09	(0.00)	-1.09	(0.00)	-0.91	(0.10)	0.72	(0.09)	0.85	(0.05)
Nova Scotia	-0.24	(0.12)	-1.09	(0.00)	-0.74	(0.21)	0.04	(0.28)	0.82	(0.14)	0.82	(0.06)
Ontario	-0.52	(0.07)	-1.09	(0.00)	-1.09	(0.03)	-0.37	(0.18)	0.45	(0.13)	0.67	(0.04)
Prince Edward Island	0.34	(0.01)	-0.52	(0.02)	c	c	0.57	(0.00)	1.14	(0.01)	0.65	(0.00)
Quebec	0.16	(0.08)	-1.09	(0.01)	-0.27	(0.17)	0.61	(0.11)	1.41	(0.09)	0.98	(0.04)
Saskatchewan	-0.38	(0.06)	-1.09	(0.00)	-0.95	(0.12)	-0.21	(0.06)	0.73	(0.13)	0.77	(0.05)
Italy												
Abruzzo	0.30	(0.09)	-0.81	(0.11)	0.10	(0.14)	0.66	(0.11)	1.27	(0.14)	0.81	(0.06)
Basilicata	0.26	(0.09)	-1.01	(0.14)	0.13	(0.19)	0.68	(0.08)	1.23	(0.06)	0.86	(0.06)
Bolzano	0.48	(0.02)	-0.74	(0.02)	0.17	(0.04)	0.90	(0.02)	1.58	(0.02)	0.92	(0.01)
Calabria	0.09	(0.12)	-1.09	(0.05)	-0.37	(0.28)	0.57	(0.16)	1.27	(0.19)	0.96	(0.08)
Campania	0.25	(0.17)	-1.09	(0.08)	0.16	(0.49)	0.75	(0.07)	1.20	(0.13)	0.92	(0.06)
Emilia Romagna	0.10	(0.16)	-1.09	(0.00)	-0.56	(0.43)	0.75	(0.19)	1.32	(0.12)	1.02	(0.05)
Friuli Venezia Giulia	0.27	(0.10)	-1.04	(0.10)	0.09	(0.19)	0.72	(0.10)	1.31	(0.10)	0.90	(0.03)
Lazio	0.18	(0.14)	-1.09	(0.04)	-0.08	(0.38)	0.66	(0.08)	1.23	(0.20)	0.93	(0.08)
Liguria	0.34	(0.12)	-0.86	(0.19)	0.08	(0.23)	0.70	(0.06)	1.46	(0.17)	0.90	(0.07)
Lombardia	0.28	(0.15)	-0.87	(0.19)	0.04	(0.20)	0.58	(0.14)	1.37	(0.20)	0.88	(0.07)
Marche	-0.02	(0.10)	-1.09	(0.00)	-0.42	(0.27)	0.54	(0.12)	0.89	(0.09)	0.83	(0.05)
Molise	0.21	(0.02)	-1.09	(0.00)	0.07	(0.06)	0.73	(0.01)	1.15	(0.02)	0.92	(0.01)
Piemonte	0.15	(0.13)	-0.98	(0.15)	-0.13	(0.14)	0.50	(0.14)	1.24	(0.18)	0.86	(0.06)
Puglia	0.21	(0.14)	-1.09	(0.14)	0.06	(0.34)	0.68	(0.07)	1.17	(0.23)	0.93	(0.13)
Sardegna	0.31	(0.16)	-1.01	(0.15)	0.07	(0.32)	0.74	(0.12)	1.45	(0.18)	0.94	(0.06)
Sicilia	0.08	(0.13)	-1.09	(0.00)	-0.44	(0.28)	0.46	(0.17)	1.38	(0.13)	1.00	(0.06)
Toscana	0.45	(0.15)	-0.84	(0.21)	0.20	(0.24)	0.89	(0.18)	1.55	(0.11)	0.93	(0.07)
Trento	0.17	(0.08)	-1.06	(0.11)	-0.03	(0.15)	0.67	(0.11)	1.10	(0.01)	0.84	(0.03)
Umbria	0.37	(0.09)	-0.86	(0.14)	0.11	(0.18)	0.78	(0.06)	1.46	(0.13)	0.91	(0.06)
Valle d'Aosta	0.06	(0.02)	-1.09	(0.00)	-0.15	(0.05)	0.57	(0.01)	0.90	(0.01)	0.79	(0.01)
Veneto	0.60	(0.12)	-0.50	(0.26)	0.63	(0.09)	0.87	(0.09)	1.41	(0.16)	0.78	(0.10)
Mexico												
Aguascalientes	0.64	(0.11)	-0.49	(0.22)	0.57	(0.11)	0.88	(0.11)	1.59	(0.19)	0.84	(0.10)
Baja California	0.57	(0.15)	-0.68	(0.13)	0.38	(0.19)	0.88	(0.21)	1.70	(0.24)	0.95	(0.09)
Baja California Sur	0.39	(0.18)	-0.75	(0.16)	0.14	(0.19)	0.65	(0.12)	1.54	(0.33)	0.92	(0.07)
Campeche	0.43	(0.10)	-0.69	(0.19)	0.33	(0.12)	0.77	(0.08)	1.31	(0.18)	0.81	(0.07)
Chiapas	0.33	(0.18)	-1.09	(0.04)	-0.15	(0.48)	0.78	(0.16)	1.77	(0.18)	1.11	(0.07)
Chihuahua	0.39	(0.17)	-1.02	(0.14)	0.11	(0.23)	0.96	(0.37)	1.53	(0.10)	0.99	(0.08)
Coahuila	0.41	(0.22)	-1.09	(0.07)	-0.02	(0.58)	0.99	(0.18)	1.78	(0.27)	1.16	(0.11)
Colima	0.07	(0.09)	-1.09	(0.00)	-0.56	(0.27)	0.61	(0.10)	1.31	(0.11)	1.02	(0.05)
Distrito Federal	0.56	(0.14)	-0.84	(0.20)	0.34	(0.18)	0.91	(0.16)	1.85	(0.24)	1.03	(0.10)
Durango	0.72	(0.17)	-0.64	(0.24)	0.57	(0.14)	1.03	(0.23)	1.95	(0.24)	1.01	(0.09)
Guanajuato	0.43	(0.15)	-0.82	(0.25)	0.41	(0.27)	0.71	(0.05)	1.42	(0.23)	0.87	(0.10)
Guerrero	0.86	(0.13)	0.07	(0.21)	0.68	(0.10)	1.05	(0.19)	1.67	(0.18)	0.66	(0.10)
Hidalgo	0.27	(0.21)	-1.09	(0.01)	-0.30	(0.43)	0.63	(0.24)	1.86	(0.28)	1.15	(0.09)
Jalisco	0.66	(0.19)	-0.48	(0.44)	0.56	(0.16)	0.82	(0.14)	1.75	(0.26)	0.89	(0.15)
Mexico	0.47	(0.13)	-0.94	(0.22)	0.35	(0.19)	0.90	(0.19)	1.59	(0.15)	0.97	(0.09)
Morelos	0.31	(0.14)	-1.09	(0.09)	0.27	(0.43)	0.78	(0.05)	1.28	(0.09)	0.94	(0.06)
Nayarit	0.69	(0.13)	-0.46	(0.18)	0.51	(0.14)	1.02	(0.14)	1.70	(0.17)	0.85	(0.06)
Nuevo León	0.31	(0.18)	-1.09	(0.14)	-0.15	(0.21)	0.64	(0.23)	1.83	(0.45)	1.17	(0.19)
Puebla	1.02	(0.11)	-0.30	(0.25)	0.84	(0.11)	1.39	(0.13)	2.14	(0.14)	0.98	(0.10)
Querétaro	0.35	(0.27)	-1.09	(0.07)	-0.14	(0.48)	0.65	(0.35)	2.01	(0.53)	1.24	(0.21)
Quintana Roo	0.20	(0.16)	-1.05	(0.15)	-0.13	(0.23)	0.60	(0.20)	1.38	(0.21)	0.93	(0.08)
San Luis Potosí	0.52	(0.19)	-0.92	(0.27)	0.34	(0.37)	0.86	(0.12)	1.80	(0.28)	1.08	(0.14)
Sinaloa	0.41	(0.20)	-1.02	(0.21)	0.29	(0.45)	0.86	(0.23)	1.52	(0.10)	0.97	(0.09)
Tabasco	0.54	(0.21)	-0.89	(0.31)	0.45	(0.24)	0.84	(0.16)	1.78	(0.28)	0.99	(0.08)
Tamaulipas	0.49	(0.18)	-1.09	(0.16)	0.18	(0.39)	1.01	(0.23)	1.86	(0.22)	1.14	(0.10)
Tlaxcala	0.33	(0.12)	-1.02	(0.17)	0.07	(0.18)	0.67	(0.19)	1.60	(0.14)	0.98	(0.08)
Veracruz	0.72	(0.13)	-0.72	(0.25)	0.69	(0.20)	1.09	(0.07)	1.81	(0.22)	0.99	(0.10)
Yucatán	0.42	(0.13)	-0.93	(0.19)	0.22	(0.25)	0.85	(0.13)	1.56	(0.15)	0.96	(0.08)
Zacatecas	0.78	(0.15)	-0.67	(0.27)	0.62	(0.16)	1.08	(0.19)	2.09	(0.21)	1.04	(0.11)

* PISA adjudicated region.
Notes: Values that are statistically significant are indicated in bold (see Annex A3).
See Table IV.3.10 for national data.
StatLink ⬛ᵐˢᴸ http://dx.doi.org/10.1787/888932957536

[Part 2/4]
Index of teacher shortage and mathematics performance, by region

Table B2.IV.6   *Results based on school principals' reports*

| | Index of teacher shortage | | | | | | | | | | Variability in this index | |
| | All students | | Bottom quarter | | Second quarter | | Third quarter | | Top quarter | | | |
	Mean index	S.E.	Mean index	S.E.	Mean index	S.E.	Mean index	S.E.	Mean index	S.E.	Standard deviation	S.E.
Portugal												
Alentejo	-0.66	(0.12)	-1.09	(0.00)	-1.09	(0.05)	-0.54	(0.38)	0.09	(0.17)	0.58	(0.07)
Spain												
Andalusia•	-0.82	(0.06)	-1.09	(0.00)	-1.09	(0.00)	-1.09	(0.11)	-0.01	(0.19)	0.51	(0.06)
Aragon•	-0.90	(0.06)	-1.09	(0.00)	-1.09	(0.00)	-1.09	(0.00)	-0.34	(0.23)	0.42	(0.07)
Asturias•	-0.89	(0.06)	-1.09	(0.00)	-1.09	(0.00)	-1.09	(0.01)	-0.30	(0.23)	0.41	(0.06)
Balearic Islands•	-0.71	(0.09)	-1.09	(0.00)	-1.09	(0.00)	-0.91	(0.23)	0.26	(0.17)	0.62	(0.06)
Basque Country•	-0.72	(0.05)	-1.09	(0.00)	-1.09	(0.00)	-0.97	(0.11)	0.27	(0.13)	0.66	(0.08)
Cantabria•	-0.84	(0.07)	-1.09	(0.00)	-1.09	(0.00)	-1.09	(0.01)	-0.08	(0.28)	0.54	(0.09)
Castile and Leon•	-0.79	(0.07)	-1.09	(0.00)	-1.09	(0.00)	-1.07	(0.17)	0.10	(0.16)	0.57	(0.05)
Catalonia•	-0.42	(0.11)	-1.09	(0.00)	-1.09	(0.07)	-0.21	(0.34)	0.70	(0.12)	0.78	(0.05)
Extremadura•	-0.66	(0.10)	-1.09	(0.00)	-1.09	(0.00)	-0.72	(0.27)	0.27	(0.16)	0.61	(0.06)
Galicia•	-0.58	(0.10)	-1.09	(0.00)	-1.09	(0.00)	-0.68	(0.24)	0.53	(0.22)	0.73	(0.08)
La Rioja•	-0.92	(0.01)	-1.09	(0.00)	-1.09	(0.00)	-1.09	(0.00)	-0.40	(0.02)	0.45	(0.01)
Madrid•	-0.77	(0.08)	-1.09	(0.00)	-1.09	(0.00)	-1.09	(0.01)	0.21	(0.33)	0.71	(0.08)
Murcia•	-0.82	(0.09)	-1.09	(0.00)	-1.09	(0.00)	-1.09	(0.00)	0.00	(0.37)	0.61	(0.11)
Navarre•	-0.68	(0.07)	-1.09	(0.00)	-1.09	(0.00)	-0.86	(0.15)	0.32	(0.17)	0.66	(0.06)
United Kingdom												
England	-0.17	(0.07)	-1.09	(0.00)	-0.73	(0.12)	0.18	(0.11)	0.97	(0.10)	0.86	(0.04)
Northern Ireland	-0.53	(0.09)	-1.09	(0.00)	-1.09	(0.00)	-0.75	(0.20)	0.81	(0.23)	0.89	(0.12)
Scotland•	-0.15	(0.09)	-1.09	(0.00)	-0.79	(0.17)	0.10	(0.14)	1.18	(0.11)	0.94	(0.04)
Wales	-0.29	(0.08)	-1.09	(0.00)	-1.06	(0.08)	-0.06	(0.16)	1.04	(0.12)	0.92	(0.05)
United States												
Connecticut•	-0.67	(0.11)	-1.09	(0.00)	-1.09	(0.00)	-0.84	(0.26)	0.36	(0.20)	0.66	(0.07)
Florida•	0.08	(0.14)	-1.09	(0.01)	-0.55	(0.34)	0.59	(0.20)	1.37	(0.15)	1.01	(0.07)
Massachusetts•	-0.62	(0.10)	-1.09	(0.00)	-1.09	(0.00)	-0.82	(0.23)	0.51	(0.21)	0.74	(0.08)
Argentina												
Ciudad Autónoma de Buenos Aires•	-0.08	(0.18)	-1.09	(0.00)	-1.03	(0.17)	0.19	(0.37)	1.62	(0.33)	1.20	(0.15)
Brazil												
Acre	0.66	(0.20)	-0.64	(0.32)	0.60	(0.29)	0.98	(0.25)	1.73	(0.16)	0.91	(0.10)
Alagoas	-0.08	(0.25)	-1.09	(0.00)	-0.76	(0.41)	0.38	(0.46)	1.16	(0.20)	0.94	(0.07)
Amapá	-0.09	(0.12)	-1.09	(0.00)	-0.77	(0.24)	0.04	(0.29)	1.47	(0.11)	1.07	(0.07)
Amazonas	0.29	(0.23)	-1.09	(0.10)	-0.31	(0.36)	0.75	(0.49)	1.82	(0.23)	1.17	(0.12)
Bahia	0.91	(0.31)	-0.58	(0.59)	0.59	(0.35)	c	c	2.35	(0.55)	1.18	(0.26)
Ceará	0.32	(0.13)	-1.09	(0.15)	0.15	(0.29)	0.79	(0.17)	1.43	(0.06)	0.96	(0.06)
Espírito Santo	-0.20	(0.08)	-1.09	(0.00)	-0.92	(0.14)	0.12	(0.16)	1.10	(0.16)	0.92	(0.07)
Federal District	-0.07	(0.19)	-1.09	(0.00)	-0.81	(0.23)	0.27	(0.33)	1.34	(0.34)	1.03	(0.11)
Goiás	0.34	(0.22)	-1.07	(0.19)	-0.08	(0.44)	0.82	(0.26)	1.70	(0.27)	1.09	(0.11)
Maranhão	0.81	(0.24)	-0.49	(0.36)	0.65	(0.46)	c	c	1.92	(0.25)	0.95	(0.14)
Mato Grosso	0.38	(0.19)	-0.73	(0.28)	0.13	(0.19)	0.64	(0.14)	1.50	(0.41)	0.89	(0.17)
Mato Grosso do Sul	-0.16	(0.20)	-1.09	(0.00)	-1.09	(0.40)	0.36	(0.38)	1.16	(0.14)	0.99	(0.05)
Minas Gerais	0.35	(0.21)	-1.09	(0.18)	-0.10	(0.40)	0.92	(0.29)	1.68	(0.17)	1.06	(0.09)
Pará	-0.52	(0.15)	-1.09	(0.00)	-1.09	(0.02)	-0.53	(0.26)	0.63	(0.38)	0.78	(0.11)
Paraíba	-0.02	(0.19)	-1.09	(0.14)	-0.33	(0.39)	0.19	(0.17)	1.16	(0.35)	0.88	(0.13)
Paraná	-0.07	(0.20)	-1.09	(0.03)	-0.54	(0.30)	0.26	(0.46)	1.11	(0.16)	0.88	(0.08)
Pernambuco	0.43	(0.20)	-0.64	(0.23)	0.12	(0.10)	0.59	(0.50)	1.66	(0.30)	0.91	(0.14)
Piauí	0.06	(0.21)	-1.09	(0.00)	-0.76	(0.37)	0.54	(0.29)	1.58	(0.37)	1.13	(0.13)
Rio de Janeiro	-0.41	(0.17)	-1.09	(0.00)	-1.09	(0.02)	-0.39	(0.46)	0.94	(0.29)	0.88	(0.10)
Rio Grande do Norte	0.28	(0.24)	-1.09	(0.03)	-0.24	(0.48)	0.85	(0.33)	1.59	(0.25)	1.09	(0.09)
Rio Grande do Sul	0.02	(0.19)	-1.09	(0.00)	-0.47	(0.42)	0.23	(0.17)	1.43	(0.38)	1.02	(0.15)
Rondônia	1.07	(0.16)	0.20	(0.15)	0.89	(0.29)	1.28	(0.12)	1.89	(0.24)	0.68	(0.08)
Roraima	-0.07	(0.18)	-1.09	(0.01)	-0.64	(0.38)	0.23	(0.30)	1.22	(0.15)	0.96	(0.06)
Santa Catarina	0.30	(0.15)	-0.76	(0.26)	0.03	(0.21)	0.61	(0.19)	1.31	(0.21)	0.81	(0.11)
São Paulo	0.25	(0.12)	-1.00	(0.16)	-0.22	(0.12)	0.66	(0.21)	1.54	(0.14)	0.99	(0.06)
Sergipe	0.03	(0.17)	-0.94	(0.21)	-0.34	(0.12)	0.17	(0.34)	1.24	(0.31)	0.85	(0.13)
Tocantins	0.04	(0.16)	-1.09	(0.09)	-0.24	(0.38)	0.32	(0.17)	1.16	(0.24)	0.86	(0.09)
Colombia												
Bogota	0.19	(0.20)	-1.09	(0.00)	-0.59	(0.36)	0.52	(0.21)	1.94	(0.40)	1.27	(0.13)
Cali	0.36	(0.20)	-1.09	(0.00)	-0.81	(0.44)	0.70	(0.21)	2.66	(0.46)	1.61	(0.15)
Manizales	0.05	(0.18)	-1.09	(0.00)	-0.81	(0.40)	0.48	(0.21)	1.62	(0.27)	1.15	(0.10)
Medellin	0.69	(0.24)	-1.09	(0.00)	-0.33	(0.43)	1.35	(0.28)	2.85	(0.41)	1.62	(0.13)
Russian Federation												
Perm Territory region•	0.66	(0.16)	-0.80	(0.20)	0.43	(0.20)	1.09	(0.11)	1.93	(0.28)	1.09	(0.10)
United Arab Emirates												
Abu Dhabi•	0.19	(0.12)	-1.09	(0.00)	-0.68	(0.14)	0.34	(0.16)	2.18	(0.25)	1.39	(0.08)
Ajman	0.13	(0.14)	-1.09	(0.00)	-0.70	(0.38)	0.48	(0.16)	1.84	(0.16)	1.31	(0.07)
Dubai•	0.05	(0.00)	-1.09	(0.00)	-0.95	(0.01)	0.31	(0.01)	1.93	(0.01)	1.34	(0.00)
Fujairah	-0.20	(0.15)	-1.09	(0.00)	-1.09	(0.03)	-0.19	(0.50)	1.60	(0.07)	1.25	(0.03)
Ras Al Khaimah	0.63	(0.35)	-1.09	(0.03)	-0.66	(0.39)	0.87	(0.78)	3.41	(0.46)	1.82	(0.16)
Sharjah	0.13	(0.30)	-1.09	(0.00)	-1.02	(0.32)	0.48	(0.77)	2.15	(0.29)	1.38	(0.12)
Umm Al Quwain	-0.18	(0.01)	-1.09	(0.00)	-0.73	(0.03)	0.17	(0.01)	0.94	(0.02)	0.89	(0.01)

• PISA adjudicated region.
Notes: Values that are statistically significant are indicated in bold (see Annex A3).
See Table IV.3.10 for national data.
StatLink http://dx.doi.org/10.1787/888932957536

[Part 3/4]
Index of teacher shortage and mathematics performance, by region

Table B2.IV.6   *Results based on school principals' reports*

	Performance on the mathematics scale, by national quarters of this index								Change in the mathematics score per unit of this index		Increased likelihood of students in the bottom quarter of this index scoring in the bottom quarter of the national mathematics performance distribution		Explained variance in student performance (r-squared x 100)	
	Bottom quarter		Second quarter		Third quarter		Top quarter							
	Mean score	S.E.	Mean score	S.E.	Mean score	S.E.	Mean score	S.E.	Score dif.	S.E.	Ratio	S.E.	%	S.E.
Australia														
Australian Capital Territory	530	(7.0)	525	(9.2)	500	(8.8)	508	(8.8)	**-10.0**	(3.7)	**0.7**	(0.13)	1.1	(0.89)
New South Wales	**527**	(7.4)	524	(8.6)	500	(8.3)	**488**	(7.0)	**-16.9**	(4.1)	**0.7**	(0.09)	2.6	(1.24)
Northern Territory	461	(24.2)	475	(34.9)	450	(22.7)	421	(23.0)	-14.1	(22.0)	0.9	(0.46)	1.0	(3.55)
Queensland	**540**	(7.4)	502	(6.8)	486	(7.3)	**487**	(6.5)	**-19.7**	(2.9)	**0.5**	(0.09)	5.1	(1.46)
South Australia	**501**	(8.8)	483	(10.7)	500	(9.4)	**474**	(8.2)	-7.9	(4.2)	0.7	(0.16)	0.7	(0.84)
Tasmania	483	(8.0)	498	(6.9)	471	(7.1)	466	(8.4)	**-9.3**	(3.5)	0.8	(0.14)	1.0	(0.77)
Victoria	**511**	(10.0)	518	(8.2)	493	(10.1)	**481**	(5.1)	**-12.0**	(4.6)	0.8	(0.14)	1.5	(1.08)
Western Australia	**531**	(7.2)	534	(9.2)	518	(11.0)	**483**	(8.4)	**-14.5**	(5.1)	**0.7**	(0.12)	3.1	(1.79)
Belgium														
Flemish community*	544	(10.2)	534	(8.8)	527	(14.7)	524	(13.3)	-7.6	(7.1)	0.8	(0.17)	0.5	(0.76)
French community	**529**	(7.7)	523	(9.3)	499	(8.3)	**488**	(7.1)	**-16.9**	(4.1)	**0.7**	(0.11)	2.6	(1.24)
German-speaking community	**511**	(10.1)	518	(8.1)	494	(9.7)	**481**	(5.1)	**-12.0**	(4.6)	0.8	(0.14)	1.5	(1.08)
Canada														
Alberta	519	(9.2)	519	(9.6)	520	(7.2)	511	(6.5)	-3.5	(5.3)	1.0	(0.19)	0.1	(0.41)
British Columbia	530	(7.4)	523	(7.6)	524	(8.9)	512	(9.8)	-7.1	(5.6)	0.9	(0.14)	0.5	(0.90)
Manitoba	500	(6.2)	498	(5.9)	488	(10.1)	484	(6.9)	**-9.7**	(4.8)	0.9	(0.16)	0.8	(0.80)
New Brunswick	503	(6.7)	504	(7.0)	499	(4.9)	503	(5.4)	-2.0	(3.4)	1.1	(0.17)	0.0	(0.17)
Newfoundland and Labrador	**503**	(7.8)	503	(7.6)	498	(6.9)	456	(11.6)	**-23.9**	(7.2)	**0.7**	(0.12)	5.4	(2.60)
Nova Scotia	495	(6.8)	500	(7.0)	503	(15.6)	490	(10.3)	-1.8	(5.0)	1.2	(0.16)	0.0	(0.22)
Ontario	518	(6.9)	519	(6.9)	511	(8.3)	509	(8.6)	-5.5	(7.6)	1.0	(0.12)	0.2	(0.61)
Prince Edward Island	489	(5.1)	c	c	458	(4.5)	490	(5.1)	0.3	(3.6)	1.0	(0.12)	0.0	(0.07)
Quebec	549	(6.6)	532	(9.8)	533	(7.7)	531	(7.4)	-7.4	(4.0)	**0.8**	(0.11)	0.6	(0.63)
Saskatchewan	**495**	(5.3)	500	(5.4)	506	(6.5)	**522**	(8.0)	**12.2**	(4.4)	1.1	(0.12)	1.3	(0.88)
Italy														
Abruzzo	464	(18.2)	485	(16.8)	488	(12.8)	467	(17.8)	4.6	(11.6)	1.2	(0.35)	0.2	(1.18)
Basilicata	452	(13.4)	448	(18.4)	481	(8.2)	478	(13.6)	**15.2**	(6.9)	1.2	(0.33)	2.3	(2.02)
Bolzano	506	(5.1)	527	(4.4)	501	(4.2)	498	(3.9)	**-7.3**	(2.1)	1.1	(0.14)	0.6	(0.34)
Calabria	430	(16.0)	442	(13.2)	425	(12.6)	428	(11.0)	-4.3	(7.9)	1.1	(0.36)	0.2	(0.87)
Campania	450	(17.7)	476	(19.7)	442	(15.1)	455	(24.3)	-0.9	(10.9)	1.1	(0.38)	0.0	(1.08)
Emilia Romagna	525	(16.7)	514	(16.0)	492	(17.9)	486	(22.4)	-17.2	(11.2)	0.6	(0.23)	3.4	(3.81)
Friuli Venezia Giulia	**539**	(14.7)	546	(11.6)	506	(9.9)	**488**	(11.7)	**-18.1**	(6.2)	0.8	(0.20)	3.4	(2.19)
Lazio	504	(19.9)	454	(21.6)	485	(21.9)	474	(12.9)	-9.8	(10.3)	0.6	(0.26)	1.0	(2.23)
Liguria	467	(22.3)	485	(14.8)	510	(17.9)	491	(10.8)	12.4	(8.5)	1.3	(0.40)	1.5	(2.14)
Lombardia	513	(16.4)	529	(14.6)	520	(21.2)	518	(15.1)	-1.2	(12.2)	1.3	(0.37)	0.0	(1.23)
Marche	**478**	(10.8)	498	(12.0)	499	(22.8)	**522**	(10.2)	**17.4**	(6.3)	1.6	(0.37)	2.9	(2.10)
Molise	**465**	(5.6)	454	(6.9)	475	(7.3)	**440**	(5.9)	**-4.6**	(2.3)	**0.7**	(0.12)	0.3	(0.26)
Piemonte	504	(16.7)	486	(12.5)	511	(20.0)	493	(15.7)	-2.2	(9.9)	0.8	(0.25)	0.1	(0.87)
Puglia	491	(19.0)	454	(16.1)	473	(14.9)	502	(16.2)	4.3	(9.6)	0.9	(0.35)	0.2	(1.22)
Sardegna	459	(16.5)	446	(14.5)	457	(13.0)	485	(19.3)	8.7	(10.8)	1.2	(0.37)	0.9	(2.39)
Sicilia	432	(15.8)	455	(9.5)	459	(11.5)	445	(19.5)	5.0	(9.8)	1.4	(0.40)	0.4	(1.89)
Toscana	486	(24.3)	520	(21.3)	531	(25.9)	451	(17.8)	-8.3	(14.5)	1.2	(0.46)	0.7	(3.07)
Trento	518	(13.8)	533	(12.8)	509	(7.1)	545	(11.7)	8.6	(8.1)	1.1	(0.34)	0.7	(1.51)
Umbria	507	(15.4)	481	(18.1)	485	(15.8)	492	(7.7)	-5.3	(7.7)	0.8	(0.29)	0.3	(1.02)
Valle d'Aosta	**467**	(5.7)	510	(7.4)	504	(6.1)	**493**	(6.1)	**9.1**	(3.6)	**1.7**	(0.25)	0.7	(0.54)
Veneto	511	(14.6)	528	(13.9)	544	(25.0)	509	(16.8)	8.0	(11.0)	1.1	(0.39)	0.5	(1.51)
Mexico														
Aguascalientes	**458**	(10.4)	458	(8.4)	415	(16.6)	**418**	(8.0)	**-20.0**	(5.9)	0.6	(0.20)	5.2	(2.41)
Baja California	424	(9.9)	416	(14.0)	402	(15.4)	419	(22.0)	-3.3	(7.7)	0.8	(0.15)	0.2	(1.33)
Baja California Sur	425	(13.2)	426	(10.5)	401	(17.6)	405	(7.6)	-10.0	(5.2)	0.8	(0.29)	1.6	(1.81)
Campeche	394	(7.5)	415	(8.8)	389	(9.8)	384	(9.4)	-2.8	(4.9)	1.0	(0.22)	0.1	(0.43)
Chiapas	376	(14.5)	366	(15.2)	389	(14.9)	361	(17.1)	-2.6	(6.6)	0.9	(0.31)	0.2	(0.96)
Chihuahua	435	(8.1)	412	(13.0)	437	(27.3)	430	(22.6)	-2.8	(8.7)	0.8	(0.23)	0.1	(1.40)
Coahuila	442	(21.0)	422	(14.6)	403	(10.7)	406	(13.7)	**-14.8**	(7.3)	0.6	(0.27)	5.7	(5.74)
Colima	444	(10.9)	439	(9.8)	416	(14.8)	417	(14.6)	-10.4	(6.4)	0.7	(0.22)	1.9	(2.25)
Distrito Federal	**453**	(13.0)	441	(15.3)	422	(16.8)	**395**	(11.3)	**-17.7**	(5.2)	**0.5**	(0.19)	6.2	(3.34)
Durango	450	(11.2)	420	(10.6)	407	(14.0)	420	(23.3)	**-13.6**	(6.9)	**0.4**	(0.18)	3.6	(3.58)
Guanajuato	419	(11.9)	426	(16.0)	404	(17.0)	398	(9.6)	-10.5	(6.5)	0.6	(0.20)	1.5	(1.86)
Guerrero	375	(13.4)	378	(13.1)	366	(12.1)	354	(11.7)	-13.3	(8.0)	0.9	(0.27)	1.7	(2.04)
Hidalgo	**434**	(10.6)	426	(14.0)	383	(20.6)	**387**	(14.7)	**-17.1**	(5.6)	**0.4**	(0.17)	7.1	(4.40)
Jalisco	455	(12.8)	431	(11.2)	429	(17.2)	425	(11.4)	**-12.2**	(5.1)	**0.5**	(0.22)	2.3	(2.08)
Mexico	432	(12.4)	423	(14.7)	404	(11.2)	410	(10.2)	-9.6	(5.1)	0.7	(0.21)	1.9	(2.03)
Morelos	449	(20.3)	417	(17.3)	404	(16.0)	416	(12.9)	-17.6	(10.3)	0.6	(0.25)	4.4	(4.92)
Nayarit	418	(12.4)	420	(11.6)	401	(20.0)	420	(11.7)	-3.4	(6.4)	0.9	(0.24)	0.2	(0.68)
Nuevo León	**466**	(17.9)	424	(17.3)	450	(17.3)	**403**	(15.6)	**-15.4**	(5.4)	**0.4**	(0.13)	6.0	(4.20)
Puebla	435	(12.0)	417	(11.1)	408	(14.0)	402	(10.9)	**-12.5**	(5.3)	**0.6**	(0.18)	2.7	(2.24)
Querétaro	433	(10.9)	437	(11.5)	436	(12.8)	432	(21.1)	-4.1	(6.7)	1.0	(0.24)	0.5	(1.70)
Quintana Roo	418	(16.7)	413	(10.1)	404	(12.8)	407	(8.4)	-7.1	(7.2)	0.9	(0.40)	0.9	(2.02)
San Luis Potosí	429	(23.6)	418	(28.3)	402	(14.3)	399	(10.6)	-12.1	(6.3)	0.7	(0.26)	3.0	(2.44)
Sinaloa	423	(16.9)	411	(10.8)	417	(11.0)	397	(10.8)	-8.4	(7.4)	0.9	(0.35)	1.4	(2.27)
Tabasco	381	(16.9)	379	(13.6)	381	(11.4)	372	(10.3)	-1.6	(8.5)	1.1	(0.33)	0.1	(1.19)
Tamaulipas	423	(13.3)	417	(22.2)	393	(13.1)	411	(20.5)	-9.0	(6.4)	0.6	(0.21)	1.9	(2.69)
Tlaxcala	416	(7.7)	421	(7.2)	400	(17.9)	407	(12.1)	-5.2	(4.9)	1.0	(0.23)	0.5	(0.98)
Veracruz	415	(20.3)	402	(11.8)	398	(12.3)	394	(9.9)	-4.5	(8.0)	1.0	(0.33)	0.4	(1.63)
Yucatán	407	(7.5)	406	(16.0)	404	(13.7)	422	(9.9)	4.3	(3.8)	0.9	(0.21)	0.3	(0.60)
Zacatecas	408	(8.6)	413	(11.8)	402	(10.4)	413	(11.9)	-1.5	(5.2)	1.1	(0.23)	0.1	(0.50)

* PISA adjudicated region.

Notes: Values that are statistically significant are indicated in bold (see Annex A3).
See Table IV.3.10 for national data.
StatLink ᵃˢˡ http://dx.doi.org/10.1787/888932957536

[Part 4/4]
Index of teacher shortage and mathematics performance, by region
Table B2.IV.6 *Results based on school principals' reports*

	Performance on the mathematics scale, by national quarters of this index								Change in the mathematics score per unit of this index		Increased likelihood of students in the bottom quarter of this index scoring in the bottom quarter of the national mathematics performance distribution		Explained variance in student performance (r-squared x 100)	
	Bottom quarter		Second quarter		Third quarter		Top quarter							
	Mean score	S.E.	Mean score	S.E.	Mean score	S.E.	Mean score	S.E.	Score dif.	S.E.	Ratio	S.E.	%	S.E.
Portugal														
Alentejo	490	(14.3)	491	(14.8)	494	(19.8)	490	(19.5)	-5.2	(18.6)	1.0	(0.23)	0.1	(1.26)
Spain														
Andalusia●	475	(7.0)	476	(8.3)	473	(8.3)	465	(7.8)	-12.0	(7.7)	0.9	(0.19)	0.5	(0.65)
Aragon●	495	(8.3)	495	(10.1)	496	(9.1)	499	(13.9)	-3.4	(22.2)	1.1	(0.19)	0.0	(0.77)
Asturias●	499	(11.4)	494	(11.1)	498	(10.0)	506	(9.6)	5.3	(11.4)	1.0	(0.20)	0.1	(0.31)
Balearic Islands●	476	(8.1)	477	(8.4)	477	(9.1)	470	(10.1)	-5.1	(9.2)	0.9	(0.21)	0.1	(0.51)
Basque Country●	506	(4.7)	502	(4.5)	505	(4.0)	508	(5.9)	2.5	(4.6)	1.1	(0.08)	0.0	(0.20)
Cantabria●	488	(8.2)	492	(7.4)	493	(8.4)	493	(7.0)	-0.6	(9.1)	1.0	(0.14)	0.0	(0.24)
Castile and Leon●	513	(6.6)	508	(7.3)	510	(8.8)	504	(14.9)	1.2	(12.3)	0.9	(0.16)	0.0	(0.58)
Catalonia●	503	(9.3)	503	(9.4)	488	(9.9)	479	(10.7)	-15.5	(6.4)	0.9	(0.15)	2.1	(1.74)
Extremadura●	460	(8.1)	458	(9.3)	466	(13.1)	465	(9.9)	5.1	(7.5)	1.1	(0.18)	0.1	(0.37)
Galicia●	492	(8.4)	493	(8.6)	497	(7.8)	474	(10.3)	-8.6	(6.9)	0.9	(0.18)	0.5	(1.03)
La Rioja●	501	(7.4)	502	(6.7)	503	(8.6)	508	(5.4)	1.9	(4.6)	1.0	(0.27)	0.0	(0.05)
Madrid●	505	(7.1)	507	(7.8)	505	(9.2)	499	(6.8)	-1.2	(4.2)	0.9	(0.17)	0.0	(0.12)
Murcia●	460	(7.4)	458	(10.0)	464	(9.5)	465	(9.3)	4.0	(6.1)	1.1	(0.17)	0.1	(0.27)
Navarre●	516	(6.7)	513	(6.9)	517	(9.1)	521	(5.4)	4.8	(4.5)	1.1	(0.16)	0.1	(0.27)
United Kingdom														
England	**520**	(6.6)	509	(7.4)	490	(6.7)	**468**	(11.8)	-22.5	(5.0)	**0.7**	(0.10)	4.1	(1.74)
Northern Ireland	**496**	(8.1)	495	(8.8)	490	(9.2)	**455**	(11.8)	-21.9	(6.0)	0.8	(0.14)	4.5	(2.48)
Scotland●	**504**	(5.5)	506	(5.8)	499	(7.7)	**484**	(6.4)	**-8.6**	(3.6)	0.9	(0.13)	0.9	(0.76)
Wales	468	(4.2)	469	(5.0)	474	(5.4)	464	(5.4)	-0.8	(3.0)	1.0	(0.10)	0.0	(0.14)
United States														
Connecticut●	508	(11.9)	507	(11.5)	508	(12.7)	500	(16.7)	-8.1	(11.6)	1.0	(0.15)	0.3	(1.26)
Florida●	479	(10.5)	483	(12.2)	458	(12.8)	457	(7.1)	**-10.3**	(4.5)	0.8	(0.14)	1.5	(1.17)
Massachusetts●	517	(11.9)	517	(10.3)	528	(13.5)	492	(16.0)	**-19.1**	(8.1)	0.9	(0.15)	2.1	(2.03)
Argentina														
Ciudad Autónoma de Buenos Aires●	439	(14.6)	437	(14.9)	412	(27.0)	382	(22.7)	-14.6	(9.1)	0.7	(0.27)	3.3	(3.96)
Brazil														
Acre	356	(9.7)	369	(19.4)	356	(13.5)	354	(18.0)	-1.1	(5.9)	1.0	(0.25)	0.0	(0.56)
Alagoas	353	(15.0)	347	(15.3)	348	(12.4)	326	(14.7)	-10.6	(8.7)	1.0	(0.37)	2.0	(3.19)
Amapá	372	(14.4)	370	(19.1)	351	(20.1)	348	(8.6)	-3.8	(4.3)	0.7	(0.26)	0.4	(0.93)
Amazonas	373	(21.4)	358	(10.4)	352	(9.3)	340	(7.4)	**-10.5**	(5.3)	0.8	(0.33)	3.6	(3.44)
Bahia	392	(36.7)	363	(36.3)	c	c	359	(18.7)	**-15.5**	(7.3)	0.6	(0.43)	5.2	(7.29)
Ceará	360	(11.6)	403	(21.8)	389	(26.3)	361	(6.6)	1.3	(5.4)	1.2	(0.42)	0.1	(0.43)
Espírito Santo	420	(13.6)	427	(22.5)	412	(21.2)	398	(13.4)	-11.4	(9.0)	1.1	(0.24)	1.5	(2.51)
Federal District	**446**	(20.4)	419	(16.2)	408	(29.6)	**372**	(21.2)	**-25.3**	(11.3)	**0.5**	(0.22)	9.9	(9.86)
Goiás	406	(19.4)	378	(13.4)	370	(12.2)	362	(13.9)	-16.5	(8.3)	0.9	(0.38)	6.3	(6.08)
Maranhão	356	(35.1)	322	(35.9)	c	c	306	(24.0)	-8.3	(13.4)	0.8	(0.46)	1.1	(3.72)
Mato Grosso	377	(32.1)	374	(22.7)	358	(10.7)	372	(10.6)	-7.7	(12.0)	1.1	(0.37)	0.9	(2.57)
Mato Grosso do Sul	428	(15.0)	426	(17.5)	399	(16.7)	380	(19.4)	**-19.4**	(8.2)	0.7	(0.22)	6.8	(5.59)
Minas Gerais	**445**	(18.6)	396	(16.6)	388	(8.7)	**394**	(10.5)	-16.5	(7.0)	**0.5**	(0.24)	6.2	(4.98)
Pará	**375**	(10.7)	374	(13.6)	349	(16.4)	341	(10.4)	-20.9	(5.1)	0.8	(0.22)	5.8	(3.43)
Paraíba	398	(20.7)	426	(13.6)	408	(27.5)	350	(22.0)	-25.3	(14.4)	0.9	(0.42)	7.9	(9.41)
Paraná	370	(9.7)	388	(15.6)	413	(12.4)	442	(53.2)	32.1	(15.5)	1.7	(0.50)	12.1	(11.94)
Pernambuco	359	(16.0)	379	(12.2)	363	(13.8)	352	(12.2)	-4.6	(8.4)	1.5	(0.42)	0.4	(2.06)
Piauí	**433**	(19.4)	403	(27.0)	333	(17.4)	**371**	(14.1)	**-26.9**	(9.1)	**0.3**	(0.14)	14.1	(6.21)
Rio de Janeiro	395	(12.1)	398	(15.4)	387	(22.8)	367	(21.5)	-11.5	(8.8)	0.8	(0.25)	2.1	(3.62)
Rio Grande do Norte	433	(28.1)	372	(23.2)	348	(9.9)	368	(24.3)	**-25.6**	(11.0)	**0.4**	(0.20)	11.0	(8.63)
Rio Grande do Sul	418	(15.5)	413	(11.5)	405	(16.1)	401	(12.1)	-6.9	(6.8)	0.7	(0.30)	1.1	(2.25)
Rondônia	399	(15.0)	376	(15.9)	392	(13.2)	362	(18.1)	-18.9	(10.8)	0.7	(0.28)	4.1	(3.91)
Roraima	366	(15.6)	375	(20.9)	362	(24.8)	344	(9.1)	-7.6	(7.7)	0.9	(0.35)	1.0	(2.21)
Santa Catarina	418	(16.1)	401	(25.5)	418	(21.5)	424	(11.6)	3.5	(8.2)	1.0	(0.48)	0.1	(0.84)
São Paulo	**434**	(17.7)	399	(11.2)	390	(10.4)	**392**	(7.1)	**-16.3**	(6.7)	0.7	(0.21)	4.2	(3.20)
Sergipe	390	(13.8)	404	(24.5)	374	(19.3)	369	(14.6)	-9.2	(9.1)	0.7	(0.25)	1.2	(2.36)
Tocantins	377	(21.5)	351	(13.9)	364	(13.2)	370	(15.4)	3.1	(10.8)	0.8	(0.27)	0.1	(1.53)
Colombia														
Bogota	402	(9.1)	392	(8.8)	392	(8.3)	385	(7.4)	-5.8	(3.1)	0.8	(0.15)	1.3	(1.30)
Cali	399	(11.8)	390	(17.4)	362	(9.6)	374	(11.7)	-5.8	(3.4)	0.7	(0.22)	1.8	(2.20)
Manizales	**417**	(11.1)	408	(11.0)	411	(18.4)	**378**	(13.1)	-11.5	(5.1)	**0.6**	(0.14)	3.4	(3.63)
Medellin	416	(18.7)	390	(12.1)	391	(16.7)	377	(13.4)	-8.4	(4.4)	0.8	(0.23)	2.7	(2.59)
Russian Federation														
Perm Territory region●	512	(19.3)	477	(14.9)	472	(14.3)	478	(12.7)	-6.3	(9.5)	0.7	(0.20)	0.6	(1.77)
United Arab Emirates														
Abu Dhabi●	410	(7.5)	437	(12.9)	429	(12.0)	414	(6.6)	-1.5	(3.0)	1.3	(0.17)	0.1	(0.29)
Ajman	389	(18.7)	393	(12.5)	420	(11.7)	411	(19.7)	7.0	(11.0)	1.4	(0.48)	1.6	(5.10)
Dubai●	**484**	(2.9)	480	(4.3)	471	(3.0)	**425**	(3.2)	-20.7	(0.9)	**0.7**	(0.05)	8.7	(0.77)
Fujairah	413	(13.1)	415	(14.1)	395	(23.7)	422	(19.0)	3.1	(5.1)	1.0	(0.22)	0.2	(0.88)
Ras Al Khaimah	416	(10.6)	427	(12.0)	416	(21.0)	402	(20.9)	-5.0	(3.9)	0.8	(0.21)	1.4	(2.29)
Sharjah	437	(16.0)	443	(14.5)	442	(13.2)	435	(19.0)	-1.5	(5.8)	0.9	(0.20)	0.1	(0.74)
Umm Al Quwain	387	(7.0)	381	(7.6)	426	(10.3)	397	(9.1)	2.4	(3.9)	1.6	(0.34)	0.1	(0.30)

● PISA adjudicated region.
Notes: Values that are statistically significant are indicated in bold (see Annex A3).
See Table IV.3.10 for national data.
StatLink ᴍˢᴾ http://dx.doi.org/10.1787/888932957536

[Part 1/1]
Teacher professional development, by region
Table B2.IV.7   *Results based on school principals' reports*

	Principal's report on the percentage of mathematics teachers in the school who have attended a programme of professional development with a focus on mathematics during the previous three months					
	Mean %	S.E.			Mean %	S.E.
Australia				**Portugal**		
Australian Capital Territory	10.1	(0.3)		Alentejo	8.4	(3.3)
New South Wales	16.8	(2.1)		**Spain**		
Northern Territory	15.3	(8.4)		Andalusia•	10.6	(3.3)
Queensland	21.7	(2.2)		Aragon•	7.0	(3.8)
South Australia	17.6	(2.8)		Asturias•	10.8	(3.2)
Tasmania	19.6	(0.9)		Balearic Islands•	5.9	(1.8)
Victoria	14.7	(2.2)		Basque Country•	9.7	(1.5)
Western Australia	10.2	(1.7)		Cantabria•	7.3	(2.7)
Belgium				Castile and Leon•	5.1	(1.8)
Flemish community•	9.3	(1.3)		Catalonia•	5.0	(1.9)
French community	14.3	(3.1)		Extremadura•	2.4	(0.7)
German-speaking community	6.0	(0.1)		Galicia•	7.4	(2.4)
Canada				La Rioja•	6.9	(0.1)
Alberta	16.7	(2.9)		Madrid•	8.7	(2.4)
British Columbia	7.8	(0.9)		Murcia•	5.2	(1.2)
Manitoba	16.5	(2.0)		Navarre•	9.9	(3.3)
New Brunswick	16.7	(3.5)		**United Kingdom**		
Newfoundland and Labrador	18.7	(4.2)		England	15.1	(3.3)
Nova Scotia	19.4	(3.6)		Northern Ireland	18.6	(3.4)
Ontario	17.9	(2.8)		Scotland•	13.6	(3.0)
Prince Edward Island	8.7	(0.2)		Wales	24.2	(2.9)
Quebec	25.8	(2.5)		**United States**		
Saskatchewan	14.2	(2.4)		Connecticut•	21.8	(4.5)
Italy				Florida•	20.7	(3.5)
Abruzzo	11.3	(2.1)		Massachusetts•	14.0	(2.8)
Basilicata	16.8	(4.4)				
Bolzano	9.3	(0.3)		**Argentina**		
Calabria	14.3	(3.9)		Ciudad Autónoma de Buenos Aires•	13.6	(3.7)
Campania	11.6	(2.7)		**Brazil**		
Emilia Romagna	9.6	(2.0)		Acre	76.9	(9.1)
Friuli Venezia Giulia	11.8	(4.2)		Alagoas	26.8	(11.2)
Lazio	11.7	(2.8)		Amapá	29.4	(11.0)
Liguria	20.1	(4.4)		Amazonas	45.3	(7.8)
Lombardia	15.2	(3.3)		Bahia	28.2	(9.8)
Marche	11.6	(2.2)		Ceará	17.8	(7.8)
Molise	18.8	(0.7)		Espírito Santo	32.5	(5.3)
Piemonte	13.7	(3.7)		Federal District	25.4	(9.9)
Puglia	13.5	(3.1)		Goiás	32.4	(7.6)
Sardegna	8.6	(2.9)		Maranhão	37.1	(11.7)
Sicilia	13.2	(2.3)		Mato Grosso	24.5	(8.0)
Toscana	8.3	(2.5)		Mato Grosso do Sul	34.1	(8.7)
Trento	27.7	(2.7)		Minas Gerais	31.7	(7.2)
Umbria	8.1	(1.6)		Pará	22.2	(9.5)
Valle d'Aosta	12.7	(0.6)		Paraíba	49.0	(13.0)
Veneto	15.1	(3.8)		Paraná	68.1	(9.1)
Mexico				Pernambuco	33.8	(9.7)
Aguascalientes	21.1	(5.5)		Piauí	12.4	(4.9)
Baja California	27.8	(5.5)		Rio de Janeiro	22.2	(7.3)
Baja California Sur	27.8	(4.4)		Rio Grande do Norte	21.6	(5.4)
Campeche	21.4	(4.5)		Rio Grande do Sul	19.5	(7.2)
Chiapas	24.8	(6.7)		Rondônia	12.0	(5.8)
Chihuahua	26.5	(7.9)		Roraima	29.8	(7.6)
Coahuila	20.8	(4.5)		Santa Catarina	12.2	(2.9)
Colima	22.8	(2.3)		São Paulo	23.9	(4.4)
Distrito Federal	16.7	(4.3)		Sergipe	14.0	(6.8)
Durango	16.4	(3.5)		Tocantins	13.8	(4.3)
Guanajuato	15.0	(4.6)		**Colombia**		
Guerrero	25.8	(4.2)		Bogota	20.3	(4.6)
Hidalgo	10.3	(3.2)		Cali	15.3	(4.3)
Jalisco	26.0	(6.5)		Manizales	3.0	(1.4)
Mexico	20.3	(5.8)		Medellin	10.0	(3.7)
Morelos	15.5	(4.0)		**Russian Federation**		
Nayarit	15.7	(4.3)		Perm Territory region•	10.4	(1.8)
Nuevo León	39.4	(7.5)		**United Arab Emirates**		
Puebla	35.1	(5.4)		Abu Dhabi•	37.2	(4.1)
Querétaro	23.6	(4.7)		Ajman	60.8	(6.3)
Quintana Roo	13.9	(2.9)		Dubai•	40.8	(0.3)
San Luis Potosí	32.5	(8.5)		Fujairah	46.7	(5.0)
Sinaloa	27.6	(7.1)		Ras Al Khaimah	28.8	(8.8)
Tabasco	12.2	(3.2)		Sharjah	16.7	(7.8)
Tamaulipas	24.2	(5.1)		Umm Al Quwain	26.5	(0.5)
Tlaxcala	48.1	(5.6)				
Veracruz	31.3	(6.9)				
Yucatán	31.5	(6.9)				
Zacatecas	25.0	(5.4)				

• PISA adjudicated region.
Note: See Table IV.3.12 for national data.
StatLink http://dx.doi.org/10.1787/888932957536

[Part 1/4]
Index of quality of physical infrastructure and mathematics performance, by region

Table B2.IV.8   *Results based on school principals' reports*

| | Index of quality of physical infrastructure | | | | | | | | | | Variability in this index | |
| | All students | | Bottom quarter | | Second quarter | | Third quarter | | Top quarter | | | |
	Mean index	S.E.	Mean index	S.E.	Mean index	S.E.	Mean index	S.E.	Mean index	S.E.	Standard deviation	S.E.
Australia												
Australian Capital Territory	-0.04	(0.02)	-1.04	(0.02)	-0.51	(0.03)	0.16	(0.03)	1.25	(0.03)	0.89	(0.01)
New South Wales	-0.02	(0.08)	-1.29	(0.10)	-0.37	(0.09)	0.29	(0.13)	1.29	(0.07)	0.98	(0.04)
Northern Territory	-0.01	(0.14)	-1.26	(0.11)	-0.49	(0.07)	0.42	(0.47)	c	c	1.01	(0.06)
Queensland	0.39	(0.08)	-0.89	(0.10)	0.11	(0.16)	1.03	(0.14)	1.31	(0.00)	0.93	(0.05)
South Australia	0.14	(0.08)	-0.84	(0.13)	-0.14	(0.09)	0.37	(0.08)	1.15	(0.14)	0.79	(0.05)
Tasmania	0.12	(0.03)	-0.90	(0.02)	-0.25	(0.01)	0.32	(0.11)	1.31	(0.01)	0.84	(0.02)
Victoria	0.21	(0.08)	-1.05	(0.13)	-0.15	(0.10)	0.75	(0.19)	1.31	(0.00)	0.97	(0.06)
Western Australia	0.27	(0.09)	-0.86	(0.13)	-0.15	(0.10)	0.78	(0.21)	1.31	(0.00)	0.89	(0.05)
Belgium												
Flemish community*	-0.04	(0.08)	-1.20	(0.11)	-0.44	(0.09)	0.18	(0.12)	1.29	(0.10)	0.97	(0.05)
French community	-0.02	(0.08)	-1.29	(0.10)	-0.37	(0.09)	0.29	(0.13)	1.29	(0.07)	0.98	(0.04)
German-speaking community	0.21	(0.08)	-1.05	(0.13)	-0.15	(0.10)	0.75	(0.19)	1.31	(0.00)	0.97	(0.06)
Canada												
Alberta	0.42	(0.08)	-0.66	(0.12)	0.10	(0.12)	0.96	(0.15)	1.31	(0.00)	0.83	(0.05)
British Columbia	0.32	(0.10)	-0.75	(0.12)	-0.08	(0.15)	0.80	(0.21)	1.31	(0.00)	0.84	(0.05)
Manitoba	0.07	(0.06)	-1.03	(0.06)	-0.23	(0.05)	0.31	(0.08)	1.21	(0.10)	0.89	(0.03)
New Brunswick	0.09	(0.05)	-0.89	(0.04)	-0.14	(0.02)	0.28	(0.04)	1.10	(0.10)	0.83	(0.02)
Newfoundland and Labrador	0.51	(0.08)	-0.80	(0.11)	0.27	(0.16)	1.26	(0.12)	1.31	(0.00)	0.92	(0.04)
Nova Scotia	0.34	(0.07)	-0.76	(0.12)	0.05	(0.07)	0.79	(0.27)	1.31	(0.00)	0.84	(0.06)
Ontario	0.26	(0.09)	-0.87	(0.13)	-0.06	(0.11)	0.66	(0.22)	1.31	(0.00)	0.88	(0.07)
Prince Edward Island	-0.03	(0.01)	-0.55	(0.02)	-0.17	(0.00)	-0.12	(0.00)	0.73	(0.01)	0.65	(0.01)
Quebec	0.39	(0.06)	-0.72	(0.10)	0.07	(0.11)	0.90	(0.11)	1.31	(0.00)	0.85	(0.04)
Saskatchewan	0.52	(0.05)	-0.50	(0.03)	0.18	(0.09)	1.11	(0.10)	1.31	(0.00)	0.77	(0.01)
Italy												
Abruzzo	-0.36	(0.17)	-1.94	(0.30)	-0.63	(0.14)	0.02	(0.22)	1.11	(0.20)	1.18	(0.12)
Basilicata	-0.08	(0.09)	-1.42	(0.22)	-0.45	(0.09)	0.26	(0.17)	1.31	(0.06)	1.07	(0.10)
Bolzano	0.23	(0.02)	-1.04	(0.02)	-0.02	(0.02)	0.68	(0.05)	1.31	(0.00)	0.91	(0.01)
Calabria	-0.43	(0.16)	-2.08	(0.28)	-0.82	(0.13)	-0.01	(0.27)	1.19	(0.18)	1.25	(0.12)
Campania	-0.49	(0.16)	-1.82	(0.24)	-0.77	(0.12)	-0.22	(0.20)	0.84	(0.28)	1.04	(0.11)
Emilia Romagna	-0.23	(0.16)	-1.30	(0.12)	-0.64	(0.20)	-0.10	(0.17)	1.11	(0.25)	0.92	(0.07)
Friuli Venezia Giulia	-0.48	(0.09)	-1.51	(0.10)	-0.70	(0.09)	-0.30	(0.07)	0.59	(0.25)	0.86	(0.08)
Lazio	-0.53	(0.16)	-1.81	(0.18)	-0.74	(0.21)	-0.30	(0.16)	0.75	(0.26)	1.00	(0.09)
Liguria	-0.66	(0.13)	-2.00	(0.13)	-1.06	(0.19)	-0.33	(0.18)	0.76	(0.19)	1.08	(0.08)
Lombardia	0.04	(0.12)	-1.28	(0.19)	-0.28	(0.21)	0.44	(0.25)	1.31	(0.03)	0.98	(0.08)
Marche	-0.16	(0.08)	-1.06	(0.16)	-0.21	(0.06)	0.04	(0.09)	0.61	(0.15)	0.68	(0.07)
Molise	-0.41	(0.02)	-1.83	(0.04)	-0.73	(0.02)	-0.07	(0.02)	0.99	(0.03)	1.12	(0.01)
Piemonte	-0.04	(0.10)	-1.23	(0.14)	-0.44	(0.16)	0.28	(0.14)	1.25	(0.12)	0.95	(0.06)
Puglia	-0.68	(0.15)	-2.13	(0.18)	-1.06	(0.24)	-0.23	(0.16)	0.69	(0.21)	1.11	(0.09)
Sardegna	-0.15	(0.12)	-1.34	(0.13)	-0.52	(0.12)	0.01	(0.19)	1.24	(0.21)	0.99	(0.09)
Sicilia	-0.42	(0.15)	-1.74	(0.26)	-0.72	(0.21)	-0.08	(0.12)	0.86	(0.21)	1.04	(0.11)
Toscana	-0.52	(0.15)	-1.78	(0.31)	-0.63	(0.20)	-0.17	(0.07)	0.51	(0.23)	0.95	(0.12)
Trento	0.02	(0.07)	-1.09	(0.12)	-0.31	(0.06)	0.16	(0.17)	1.31	(0.08)	0.93	(0.05)
Umbria	-0.49	(0.12)	-2.03	(0.08)	-0.71	(0.14)	-0.15	(0.15)	0.95	(0.20)	1.17	(0.05)
Valle d'Aosta	0.13	(0.02)	-1.11	(0.03)	0.00	(0.04)	0.56	(0.00)	1.10	(0.02)	0.89	(0.01)
Veneto	-0.40	(0.12)	-1.52	(0.16)	-0.73	(0.15)	-0.27	(0.17)	0.94	(0.19)	0.96	(0.09)
Mexico												
Aguascalientes	-0.27	(0.16)	-1.56	(0.22)	-0.67	(0.17)	0.02	(0.18)	1.13	(0.18)	1.04	(0.08)
Baja California	-0.40	(0.15)	-1.46	(0.23)	-0.77	(0.18)	-0.19	(0.20)	0.83	(0.17)	0.91	(0.09)
Baja California Sur	-0.32	(0.15)	-1.74	(0.23)	-0.51	(0.22)	0.04	(0.19)	0.94	(0.13)	1.05	(0.10)
Campeche	-0.43	(0.20)	-1.85	(0.22)	-0.78	(0.37)	0.03	(0.23)	0.90	(0.18)	1.07	(0.11)
Chiapas	-0.89	(0.19)	-2.30	(0.28)	-1.10	(0.24)	-0.63	(0.16)	0.47	(0.27)	1.06	(0.11)
Chihuahua	-0.30	(0.14)	-1.30	(0.20)	-0.55	(0.19)	-0.17	(0.14)	0.85	(0.29)	0.85	(0.12)
Coahuila	-0.11	(0.13)	-1.20	(0.18)	-0.44	(0.14)	0.19	(0.24)	1.02	(0.16)	0.87	(0.09)
Colima	-0.03	(0.13)	-1.30	(0.25)	-0.19	(0.08)	0.18	(0.17)	1.18	(0.12)	1.01	(0.08)
Distrito Federal	0.01	(0.17)	-1.22	(0.22)	-0.38	(0.24)	0.36	(0.43)	1.31	(0.03)	1.04	(0.10)
Durango	-0.73	(0.17)	-1.89	(0.21)	-1.14	(0.27)	-0.37	(0.18)	0.46	(0.18)	0.94	(0.09)
Guanajuato	-0.62	(0.10)	-1.58	(0.11)	-0.96	(0.14)	-0.39	(0.17)	0.44	(0.16)	0.83	(0.07)
Guerrero	-0.74	(0.14)	-2.15	(0.25)	-1.07	(0.11)	-0.33	(0.20)	0.58	(0.19)	1.08	(0.10)
Hidalgo	-0.36	(0.11)	-1.55	(0.17)	-0.72	(0.16)	-0.05	(0.22)	0.89	(0.16)	0.95	(0.10)
Jalisco	-0.51	(0.12)	-1.61	(0.27)	-0.60	(0.18)	-0.17	(0.09)	0.33	(0.12)	0.81	(0.11)
Mexico	-0.10	(0.23)	-1.73	(0.42)	-0.43	(0.20)	0.44	(0.39)	1.31	(0.09)	1.22	(0.14)
Morelos	-0.66	(0.20)	-2.30	(0.44)	-0.92	(0.15)	-0.22	(0.18)	0.83	(0.29)	1.21	(0.14)
Nayarit	-0.76	(0.14)	-1.98	(0.17)	-0.98	(0.10)	-0.61	(0.13)	0.55	(0.32)	1.00	(0.11)
Nuevo León	0.10	(0.21)	-1.51	(0.38)	-0.26	(0.29)	0.85	(0.31)	1.31	(0.00)	1.18	(0.15)
Puebla	-0.41	(0.12)	-1.54	(0.17)	-0.79	(0.21)	-0.09	(0.14)	0.79	(0.19)	0.95	(0.09)
Querétaro	-0.60	(0.20)	-1.95	(0.39)	-0.79	(0.18)	-0.32	(0.24)	0.66	(0.21)	1.01	(0.12)
Quintana Roo	-0.24	(0.11)	-1.29	(0.11)	-0.49	(0.19)	-0.03	(0.14)	0.86	(0.14)	0.84	(0.06)
San Luis Potosí	-0.52	(0.18)	-1.82	(0.27)	-0.94	(0.16)	-0.20	(0.20)	0.88	(0.22)	1.07	(0.06)
Sinaloa	-0.29	(0.15)	-1.19	(0.13)	-0.66	(0.15)	-0.08	(0.18)	0.76	(0.24)	0.77	(0.07)
Tabasco	-0.71	(0.15)	-1.91	(0.24)	-1.07	(0.12)	-0.42	(0.19)	0.58	(0.28)	1.00	(0.12)
Tamaulipas	-0.21	(0.15)	-1.53	(0.33)	-0.54	(0.18)	-0.04	(0.30)	1.29	(0.12)	1.08	(0.14)
Tlaxcala	-0.07	(0.13)	-1.13	(0.19)	-0.26	(0.12)	-0.03	(0.14)	1.12	(0.22)	0.85	(0.08)
Veracruz	-0.66	(0.12)	-1.83	(0.26)	-0.90	(0.10)	-0.34	(0.19)	0.43	(0.11)	0.89	(0.10)
Yucatán	-0.45	(0.13)	-1.78	(0.16)	-0.75	(0.16)	-0.10	(0.18)	0.87	(0.22)	1.05	(0.08)
Zacatecas	-0.77	(0.16)	-1.98	(0.13)	-1.17	(0.22)	-0.38	(0.20)	0.45	(0.25)	1.00	(0.08)

* PISA adjudicated region.
Notes: Values that are statistically significant are indicated in bold (see Annex A3).
See Table IV.3.14 for national data.
StatLink ⬛ http://dx.doi.org/10.1787/888932957536

[Part 2/4]
Index of quality of physical infrastructure and mathematics performance, by region

Table B2.IV.8   *Results based on school principals' reports*

| | | Index of quality of physical infrastructure | | | | | | | | | | Variability in this index | |
| | | All students | | Bottom quarter | | Second quarter | | Third quarter | | Top quarter | | | |
		Mean index	S.E.	Mean index	S.E.	Mean index	S.E.	Mean index	S.E.	Mean index	S.E.	Standard deviation	S.E.
OECD	**Portugal**												
	Alentejo	0.18	(0.24)	-0.73	(0.15)	-0.32	(0.24)	0.48	(0.61)	1.31	(0.11)	0.82	(0.07)
	Spain												
	Andalusia●	-0.17	(0.15)	-1.52	(0.30)	-0.40	(0.14)	0.20	(0.14)	1.03	(0.16)	1.03	(0.12)
	Aragon●	0.13	(0.13)	-1.00	(0.18)	-0.30	(0.16)	0.51	(0.30)	1.31	(0.03)	0.91	(0.07)
	Asturias●	0.13	(0.10)	-1.06	(0.17)	-0.09	(0.14)	0.37	(0.16)	1.28	(0.12)	0.89	(0.08)
	Balearic Islands●	-0.35	(0.11)	-1.52	(0.19)	-0.74	(0.15)	-0.03	(0.14)	0.88	(0.16)	0.95	(0.10)
	Basque Country●	0.21	(0.07)	-1.05	(0.10)	-0.11	(0.07)	0.68	(0.16)	1.31	(0.00)	0.94	(0.04)
	Cantabria●	0.04	(0.12)	-1.01	(0.20)	-0.31	(0.08)	0.20	(0.22)	1.27	(0.12)	0.89	(0.07)
	Castile and Leon●	0.12	(0.12)	-1.38	(0.26)	-0.11	(0.14)	0.66	(0.22)	1.31	(0.00)	1.08	(0.10)
	Catalonia●	0.19	(0.14)	-0.92	(0.17)	-0.33	(0.15)	0.72	(0.35)	1.31	(0.00)	0.94	(0.06)
	Extremadura●	0.08	(0.17)	-1.74	(0.24)	-0.24	(0.29)	1.02	(0.24)	1.31	(0.00)	1.27	(0.09)
	Galicia●	0.07	(0.14)	-1.21	(0.18)	-0.26	(0.21)	0.43	(0.29)	1.31	(0.03)	0.98	(0.07)
	La Rioja●	0.13	(0.01)	-1.24	(0.02)	-0.03	(0.01)	0.48	(0.01)	1.31	(0.00)	0.96	(0.01)
	Madrid●	0.30	(0.12)	-0.79	(0.23)	-0.02	(0.12)	0.70	(0.29)	1.31	(0.00)	0.88	(0.12)
	Murcia●	0.01	(0.14)	-1.51	(0.24)	-0.41	(0.16)	0.67	(0.30)	1.31	(0.00)	1.14	(0.09)
	Navarre●	0.05	(0.09)	-1.43	(0.20)	-0.28	(0.12)	0.61	(0.19)	1.31	(0.00)	1.11	(0.09)
	United Kingdom												
	England	0.04	(0.09)	-1.37	(0.12)	-0.33	(0.13)	0.56	(0.17)	1.31	(0.00)	1.07	(0.05)
	Northern Ireland	-0.28	(0.14)	-1.89	(0.27)	-0.59	(0.12)	0.11	(0.21)	1.26	(0.13)	1.21	(0.09)
	Scotland●	0.36	(0.08)	-0.84	(0.15)	0.01	(0.09)	0.96	(0.14)	1.31	(0.00)	0.91	(0.06)
	Wales	-0.25	(0.09)	-1.52	(0.16)	-0.56	(0.07)	0.04	(0.12)	1.02	(0.10)	1.00	(0.06)
	United States												
	Connecticut●	0.39	(0.11)	-0.67	(0.18)	0.11	(0.08)	0.79	(0.32)	1.31	(0.00)	0.82	(0.07)
	Florida●	0.44	(0.16)	-0.81	(0.25)	0.20	(0.23)	1.06	(0.25)	1.31	(0.00)	0.89	(0.08)
	Massachusetts●	0.07	(0.14)	-1.09	(0.22)	-0.29	(0.14)	0.36	(0.25)	1.31	(0.09)	0.95	(0.09)
Partners	**Argentina**												
	Ciudad Autónoma de Buenos Aires●	0.07	(0.12)	-1.53	(0.20)	-0.47	(0.19)	0.98	(0.26)	1.31	(0.00)	1.20	(0.09)
	Brazil												
	Acre	-1.01	(0.12)	-1.78	(0.11)	-1.40	(0.16)	-0.85	(0.27)	-0.01	(0.08)	0.77	(0.05)
	Alagoas	-0.29	(0.21)	-1.29	(0.26)	-0.73	(0.16)	-0.25	(0.33)	1.14	(0.41)	0.96	(0.14)
	Amapá	-0.90	(0.08)	-2.07	(0.16)	-1.21	(0.14)	-0.81	(0.13)	0.52	(0.14)	1.05	(0.07)
	Amazonas	-0.41	(0.21)	-1.72	(0.38)	-0.73	(0.26)	-0.10	(0.32)	0.94	(0.24)	1.05	(0.16)
	Bahia	-0.66	(0.30)	-2.43	(0.50)	-0.95	(0.44)	-0.11	(0.46)	c	c	1.28	(0.18)
	Ceará	-0.60	(0.16)	-1.78	(0.24)	-0.90	(0.15)	-0.34	(0.28)	0.65	(0.32)	0.98	(0.14)
	Espírito Santo	-0.43	(0.21)	-1.63	(0.47)	-0.61	(0.11)	-0.33	(0.19)	0.87	(0.46)	1.02	(0.20)
	Federal District	-0.20	(0.18)	-1.51	(0.35)	-0.40	(0.15)	0.04	(0.19)	1.06	(0.42)	1.00	(0.19)
	Goiás	-0.53	(0.21)	-2.23	(0.47)	-0.62	(0.28)	-0.14	(0.15)	0.90	(0.24)	1.19	(0.16)
	Maranhão	-1.11	(0.26)	-2.24	(0.33)	-1.52	(0.19)	-0.99	(0.37)	0.30	(0.40)	0.98	(0.15)
	Mato Grosso	-0.66	(0.23)	-2.02	(0.35)	-0.86	(0.31)	-0.22	(0.25)	0.49	(0.20)	1.00	(0.13)
	Mato Grosso do Sul	-0.52	(0.19)	-1.72	(0.22)	-0.96	(0.34)	-0.22	(0.15)	0.84	(0.32)	1.03	(0.12)
	Minas Gerais	-0.40	(0.15)	-1.95	(0.23)	-0.84	(0.30)	0.04	(0.19)	1.13	(0.13)	1.19	(0.10)
	Pará	-0.76	(0.18)	-2.34	(0.20)	-1.49	(0.34)	-0.49	(0.37)	c	c	1.42	(0.09)
	Paraíba	0.08	(0.22)	-1.57	(0.27)	-0.43	(0.31)	1.02	(0.50)	1.31	(0.00)	1.24	(0.11)
	Paraná	-0.63	(0.24)	-1.92	(0.28)	-1.20	(0.23)	-0.30	(0.26)	0.90	(0.37)	1.12	(0.12)
	Pernambuco	-0.71	(0.25)	-2.14	(0.50)	-0.91	(0.22)	-0.40	(0.29)	0.61	(0.36)	1.09	(0.18)
	Piauí	-0.60	(0.22)	-2.13	(0.29)	-1.21	(0.26)	-0.18	(0.48)	1.14	(0.17)	1.27	(0.12)
	Rio de Janeiro	0.23	(0.25)	-1.22	(0.34)	-0.29	(0.41)	1.16	(0.44)	1.31	(0.00)	1.12	(0.13)
	Rio Grande do Norte	-0.35	(0.19)	-1.90	(0.14)	-0.92	(0.40)	0.17	(0.33)	1.27	(0.17)	1.22	(0.11)
	Rio Grande do Sul	-0.34	(0.21)	-1.64	(0.31)	-0.75	(0.29)	-0.07	(0.23)	1.10	(0.28)	1.08	(0.14)
	Rondônia	-0.92	(0.20)	-2.01	(0.27)	-1.12	(0.28)	-0.57	(0.18)	0.01	(0.27)	0.83	(0.12)
	Roraima	-0.71	(0.23)	-2.18	(0.31)	-1.01	(0.33)	-0.25	(0.20)	0.60	(0.29)	1.10	(0.14)
	Santa Catarina	-0.50	(0.25)	-1.94	(0.31)	-1.10	(0.34)	0.06	(0.37)	1.02	(0.27)	1.19	(0.15)
	São Paulo	-0.06	(0.10)	-1.45	(0.17)	-0.43	(0.15)	0.39	(0.16)	1.28	(0.12)	1.05	(0.09)
	Sergipe	-0.55	(0.22)	-1.92	(0.34)	-0.89	(0.48)	0.00	(0.20)	0.63	(0.21)	1.06	(0.15)
	Tocantins	-0.75	(0.17)	-1.93	(0.24)	-0.88	(0.27)	-0.59	(0.11)	0.40	(0.30)	0.94	(0.11)
	Colombia												
	Bogota	-0.37	(0.15)	-1.75	(0.28)	-0.48	(0.23)	-0.01	(0.14)	0.74	(0.14)	0.99	(0.10)
	Cali	-0.36	(0.20)	-2.47	(0.28)	-0.80	(0.35)	0.55	(0.35)	1.31	(0.02)	1.49	(0.12)
	Manizales	-0.14	(0.19)	-2.19	(0.35)	-0.35	(0.29)	0.68	(0.27)	1.31	(0.04)	1.37	(0.13)
	Medellin	-0.39	(0.16)	-2.01	(0.16)	-0.91	(0.27)	0.13	(0.23)	1.23	(0.16)	1.26	(0.08)
	Russian Federation												
	Perm Territory region●	0.21	(0.15)	-1.04	(0.22)	-0.12	(0.17)	0.70	(0.31)	1.31	(0.00)	0.96	(0.09)
	United Arab Emirates												
	Abu Dhabi●	-0.02	(0.10)	-1.72	(0.17)	-0.35	(0.15)	0.71	(0.17)	1.31	(0.00)	1.23	(0.06)
	Ajman●	0.11	(0.17)	-1.67	(0.23)	-0.18	(0.23)	0.99	(0.36)	1.31	(0.00)	1.22	(0.07)
	Dubai●	0.37	(0.00)	-1.28	(0.01)	0.25	(0.01)	1.22	(0.01)	1.31	(0.00)	1.13	(0.00)
	Fujairah●	0.17	(0.15)	-1.12	(0.14)	-0.22	(0.26)	0.74	(0.28)	1.31	(0.02)	0.97	(0.06)
	Ras Al Khaimah	-0.04	(0.20)	-1.48	(0.45)	-0.25	(0.15)	0.38	(0.25)	1.20	(0.19)	1.08	(0.16)
	Sharjah●	0.20	(0.16)	-1.32	(0.34)	-0.18	(0.31)	1.02	(0.28)	1.31	(0.00)	1.13	(0.15)
	Umm Al Quwain	-0.32	(0.01)	-2.15	(0.02)	c	c	0.16	(0.02)	c	c	1.34	(0.00)

● PISA adjudicated region.
Notes: Values that are statistically significant are indicated in bold (see Annex A3).
See Table IV.3.14 for national data.
StatLink ⟨≡⟩ http://dx.doi.org/10.1787/888932957536

[Part 3/4]
Index of quality of physical infrastructure and mathematics performance, by region

Table B2.IV.8   *Results based on school principals' reports*

	Performance on the mathematics scale, by national quarters of this index								Change in the mathematics score per unit of this index		Increased likelihood of students in the bottom quarter of this index scoring in the bottom quarter of the national mathematics performance distribution		Explained variance in student performance (r-squared x 100)	
	Bottom quarter		Second quarter		Third quarter		Top quarter							
	Mean score	S.E.	Mean score	S.E.	Mean score	S.E.	Mean score	S.E.	Score dif.	S.E.	Ratio	S.E.	%	S.E.
Australia														
Australian Capital Territory	515	(9.8)	513	(11.6)	498	(9.5)	545	(9.1)	**13.1**	(4.3)	1.2	(0.20)	1.4	(0.91)
New South Wales	**508**	(10.9)	504	(11.4)	514	(10.0)	**516**	(7.1)	2.8	(5.6)	1.2	(0.16)	0.1	(0.39)
Northern Territory	401	(30.5)	481	(28.9)	429	(24.3)	c	c	19.3	(10.4)	1.4	(0.56)	3.0	(2.95)
Queensland	**481**	(7.1)	505	(9.3)	510	(7.9)	519	(6.8)	**14.6**	(3.2)	**1.4**	(0.17)	2.1	(0.93)
South Australia	**467**	(7.3)	485	(11.6)	497	(9.8)	**501**	(9.8)	**15.7**	(5.1)	**1.4**	(0.19)	1.9	(1.28)
Tasmania	464	(7.0)	471	(7.7)	517	(7.5)	468	(7.8)	6.1	(4.0)	1.2	(0.17)	0.3	(0.41)
Victoria	**486**	(6.7)	496	(11.7)	512	(7.4)	**517**	(8.4)	**13.4**	(4.2)	**1.4**	(0.18)	2.0	(1.28)
Western Australia	**500**	(6.2)	512	(9.8)	533	(10.1)	**526**	(8.8)	**11.0**	(4.4)	1.3	(0.20)	1.1	(0.83)
Belgium														
Flemish community[*]	525	(10.4)	528	(13.0)	536	(12.8)	543	(12.1)	4.6	(7.1)	1.0	(0.20)	0.2	(0.73)
French community	**507**	(10.9)	504	(11.6)	514	(9.5)	**517**	(7.1)	2.8	(5.6)	1.2	(0.16)	0.1	(0.39)
German-speaking community	**486**	(7.0)	497	(11.7)	510	(6.7)	**517**	(8.4)	**13.4**	(4.2)	**1.4**	(0.19)	2.0	(1.28)
Canada														
Alberta	521	(10.6)	508	(9.5)	519	(9.6)	521	(8.2)	-1.3	(6.5)	1.0	(0.16)	0.0	(0.33)
British Columbia	519	(7.4)	523	(9.5)	517	(8.2)	529	(9.4)	1.3	(4.8)	1.0	(0.17)	0.0	(0.29)
Manitoba	499	(7.5)	502	(5.7)	487	(9.6)	481	(9.5)	-8.6	(4.7)	0.8	(0.15)	0.7	(0.85)
New Brunswick	511	(6.5)	509	(7.5)	499	(5.1)	490	(6.2)	-3.8	(3.4)	0.9	(0.18)	0.2	(0.29)
Newfoundland and Labrador	**496**	(10.1)	488	(10.1)	491	(13.2)	**485**	(11.4)	-4.2	(7.5)	0.8	(0.22)	0.2	(0.78)
Nova Scotia	513	(5.3)	486	(11.7)	494	(10.0)	496	(6.8)	-6.9	(3.6)	**0.7**	(0.10)	0.5	(0.56)
Ontario	519	(9.4)	511	(9.8)	514	(6.7)	514	(6.7)	-0.6	(4.6)	0.9	(0.15)	0.0	(0.19)
Prince Edward Island	488	(5.6)	486	(5.3)	481	(7.3)	470	(5.5)	-3.6	(3.6)	0.9	(0.14)	0.1	(0.18)
Quebec	527	(7.0)	544	(9.2)	538	(7.0)	535	(7.7)	2.6	(4.4)	1.2	(0.16)	0.1	(0.25)
Saskatchewan	**505**	(4.6)	508	(8.7)	503	(6.3)	**508**	(7.5)	0.0	(3.3)	1.0	(0.12)	0.0	(0.08)
Italy														
Abruzzo	474	(16.9)	496	(14.3)	462	(17.5)	470	(28.7)	-1.4	(8.7)	1.1	(0.33)	0.0	(0.96)
Basilicata	470	(8.4)	460	(13.2)	466	(17.1)	462	(13.4)	2.3	(5.2)	1.1	(0.21)	0.1	(0.51)
Bolzano	505	(3.7)	501	(4.8)	524	(4.4)	501	(5.5)	1.2	(2.4)	1.0	(0.10)	0.0	(0.08)
Calabria	406	(19.7)	444	(17.0)	424	(24.2)	451	(16.0)	**14.3**	(6.5)	1.6	(0.59)	4.0	(3.57)
Campania	460	(20.8)	453	(25.4)	449	(15.4)	462	(19.6)	3.6	(9.1)	0.9	(0.31)	0.2	(1.25)
Emilia Romagna	523	(20.9)	492	(20.7)	491	(22.2)	510	(17.0)	-4.1	(13.2)	0.8	(0.32)	0.2	(1.70)
Friuli Venezia Giulia	**513**	(19.9)	539	(16.8)	533	(14.3)	**493**	(15.2)	-11.8	(8.2)	1.1	(0.47)	1.3	(1.91)
Lazio	482	(18.9)	483	(26.8)	469	(22.1)	482	(20.7)	-2.6	(11.5)	0.9	(0.33)	0.1	(1.52)
Liguria	494	(15.9)	485	(15.5)	481	(12.2)	493	(20.9)	-1.8	(8.8)	1.0	(0.32)	0.1	(0.99)
Lombardia	500	(16.3)	530	(17.8)	519	(20.4)	531	(13.4)	10.7	(7.0)	1.4	(0.46)	1.5	(2.10)
Marche	**512**	(11.7)	516	(15.0)	507	(11.0)	**463**	(20.8)	**-22.0**	(11.2)	0.7	(0.20)	3.1	(2.88)
Molise	**441**	(5.7)	453	(5.0)	474	(7.2)	**467**	(5.3)	10.7	(2.3)	**1.4**	(0.19)	2.0	(0.84)
Piemonte	508	(17.4)	515	(15.8)	488	(17.8)	482	(8.8)	-12.1	(7.3)	0.8	(0.27)	1.7	(2.01)
Puglia	476	(16.8)	488	(18.5)	470	(15.2)	486	(17.8)	0.3	(6.9)	1.0	(0.23)	0.0	(0.58)
Sardegna	444	(13.9)	458	(14.7)	457	(12.8)	480	(13.5)	**15.0**	(7.3)	1.4	(0.30)	3.0	(3.09)
Sicilia	444	(18.2)	444	(10.6)	441	(14.3)	463	(12.2)	2.6	(9.0)	1.3	(0.44)	0.1	(1.20)
Toscana	484	(20.2)	492	(19.3)	511	(14.8)	501	(13.9)	2.5	(9.0)	1.3	(0.49)	0.1	(0.70)
Trento	521	(10.8)	524	(14.0)	526	(12.9)	536	(10.9)	4.1	(5.0)	1.1	(0.31)	0.2	(0.57)
Umbria	508	(12.6)	497	(11.4)	481	(25.4)	479	(28.2)	-13.1	(7.0)	0.7	(0.25)	3.0	(3.08)
Valle d'Aosta	**538**	(5.8)	450	(6.9)	504	(6.3)	**482**	(5.5)	**-25.3**	(2.9)	**0.5**	(0.13)	6.7	(1.46)
Veneto	500	(20.7)	513	(32.0)	548	(21.2)	530	(13.1)	7.0	(8.5)	1.8	(0.47)	0.5	(1.41)
Mexico														
Aguascalientes	**402**	(17.8)	430	(10.0)	447	(14.7)	**469**	(5.0)	**25.2**	(5.0)	**2.4**	(0.54)	12.9	(4.42)
Baja California	390	(5.1)	421	(11.7)	429	(16.4)	429	(10.9)	**15.5**	(4.9)	1.9	(0.47)	3.8	(2.80)
Baja California Sur	398	(15.1)	423	(8.4)	406	(13.3)	427	(9.5)	**9.5**	(4.1)	1.3	(0.30)	1.9	(1.66)
Campeche	376	(12.8)	389	(17.7)	408	(14.4)	409	(9.7)	**14.4**	(5.1)	1.7	(0.42)	4.7	(3.36)
Chiapas	363	(12.6)	361	(20.3)	388	(13.1)	379	(15.0)	9.9	(6.3)	1.0	(0.28)	2.0	(2.59)
Chihuahua	407	(13.2)	445	(25.6)	418	(21.0)	443	(14.0)	8.3	(8.5)	1.5	(0.48)	0.8	(1.83)
Coahuila	401	(13.2)	406	(14.7)	426	(13.3)	441	(22.9)	**19.6**	(9.6)	1.6	(0.44)	5.7	(5.64)
Colima	419	(12.3)	398	(14.3)	437	(13.2)	464	(13.5)	**15.8**	(6.8)	1.1	(0.30)	4.3	(3.27)
Distrito Federal	**411**	(8.6)	429	(16.5)	440	(12.9)	**432**	(18.3)	6.2	(9.5)	1.4	(0.47)	0.8	(3.38)
Durango	419	(23.6)	402	(9.1)	421	(12.3)	455	(11.0)	15.7	(8.8)	1.2	(0.47)	4.1	(4.45)
Guanajuato	374	(15.9)	415	(13.5)	426	(11.0)	431	(10.5)	**21.6**	(8.4)	**2.4**	(0.64)	5.7	(3.85)
Guerrero	345	(12.7)	374	(10.2)	368	(9.3)	385	(11.0)	**15.7**	(4.7)	1.8	(0.43)	6.5	(3.94)
Hidalgo	**400**	(10.3)	381	(16.1)	418	(15.1)	**428**	(14.7)	**14.8**	(6.6)	1.1	(0.35)	3.7	(3.04)
Jalisco	431	(14.5)	415	(13.9)	445	(10.2)	448	(12.2)	4.9	(8.8)	1.1	(0.35)	0.3	(1.39)
Mexico	404	(11.4)	415	(13.0)	422	(9.4)	429	(16.1)	4.1	(6.1)	1.3	(0.42)	0.6	(1.95)
Morelos	420	(15.7)	408	(11.5)	400	(22.7)	458	(20.8)	8.7	(8.5)	1.0	(0.36)	1.8	(3.62)
Nayarit	403	(12.3)	423	(11.3)	422	(11.4)	413	(13.4)	4.2	(5.3)	1.4	(0.35)	0.3	(0.89)
Nuevo León	**421**	(17.8)	434	(12.2)	440	(14.8)	**449**	(19.6)	9.9	(7.0)	1.5	(0.49)	2.5	(3.87)
Puebla	392	(13.2)	412	(14.7)	425	(8.8)	433	(11.4)	**16.7**	(6.1)	1.7	(0.43)	4.6	(3.00)
Querétaro	410	(13.3)	452	(13.9)	414	(18.4)	462	(15.2)	**13.1**	(6.6)	1.6	(0.42)	3.1	(3.06)
Quintana Roo	376	(13.1)	414	(16.3)	427	(7.6)	425	(8.8)	**22.7**	(5.6)	**2.1**	(0.50)	7.2	(3.52)
San Luis Potosí	385	(13.2)	393	(14.6)	432	(9.5)	438	(17.1)	**23.5**	(6.6)	**1.9**	(0.43)	11.1	(5.72)
Sinaloa	407	(9.4)	418	(13.7)	408	(13.8)	415	(13.2)	8.1	(6.7)	1.1	(0.24)	0.8	(1.63)
Tabasco	367	(8.2)	363	(9.3)	381	(12.3)	403	(9.2)	**14.6**	(3.7)	1.3	(0.26)	4.3	(2.13)
Tamaulipas	368	(10.4)	421	(22.6)	418	(10.5)	437	(15.2)	**21.4**	(5.2)	**2.5**	(0.47)	9.5	(5.32)
Tlaxcala	377	(13.6)	417	(14.3)	422	(8.7)	428	(10.2)	**18.8**	(7.5)	**2.2**	(0.48)	4.9	(3.68)
Veracruz	396	(13.7)	401	(12.0)	393	(9.6)	419	(20.1)	10.9	(8.0)	1.1	(0.30)	1.7	(2.55)
Yucatán	409	(9.0)	411	(14.3)	402	(9.2)	418	(12.8)	7.5	(5.1)	1.0	(0.26)	1.1	(1.60)
Zacatecas	401	(12.8)	405	(8.8)	413	(11.9)	417	(11.4)	5.0	(6.5)	1.3	(0.30)	0.5	(0.71)

[*] PISA adjudicated region.

Notes: Values that are statistically significant are indicated in bold (see Annex A3).
See Table IV.3.14 for national data.
StatLink http://dx.doi.org/10.1787/888932957536

[Part 4/4]

Index of quality of physical infrastructure and mathematics performance, by region

Table B2.IV.8 *Results based on school principals' reports*

| | Performance on the mathematics scale, by national quarters of this index | | | | | | | | Change in the mathematics score per unit of this index | | Increased likelihood of students in the bottom quarter of this index scoring in the bottom quarter of the national mathematics performance distribution | | Explained variance in student performance (r-squared x 100) | |
| | Bottom quarter | | Second quarter | | Third quarter | | Top quarter | | | | | | | |
	Mean score	S.E.	Mean score	S.E.	Mean score	S.E.	Mean score	S.E.	Score dif.	S.E.	Ratio	S.E.	%	S.E.
Portugal														
Alentejo	491	(13.7)	474	(35.5)	479	(29.5)	521	(20.7)	16.9	(11.3)	0.9	(0.32)	2.4	(3.40)
Spain														
Andalusia•	476	(6.3)	456	(7.6)	482	(11.1)	474	(10.4)	1.4	(3.8)	1.0	(0.14)	0.0	(0.24)
Aragon•	485	(13.5)	503	(10.9)	491	(10.7)	507	(13.4)	7.1	(6.8)	1.2	(0.26)	0.5	(1.00)
Asturias•	483	(15.3)	499	(8.6)	509	(8.4)	508	(10.0)	10.5	(5.9)	1.4	(0.28)	1.0	(1.12)
Balearic Islands•	458	(12.0)	467	(8.2)	491	(9.6)	484	(9.5)	**13.0**	(5.2)	1.5	(0.25)	2.0	(1.49)
Basque Country•	499	(5.9)	503	(5.9)	510	(5.5)	508	(4.3)	2.4	(2.6)	1.1	(0.11)	0.1	(0.17)
Cantabria•	486	(8.5)	488	(8.9)	488	(8.5)	502	(10.8)	5.7	(7.1)	1.0	(0.19)	0.3	(0.85)
Castile and Leon•	520	(9.4)	508	(11.8)	506	(6.4)	502	(9.9)	-7.1	(4.5)	0.9	(0.14)	0.8	(1.04)
Catalonia•	486	(14.5)	481	(11.6)	500	(10.6)	508	(10.0)	**14.9**	(6.6)	1.3	(0.29)	2.7	(2.41)
Extremadura•	457	(9.7)	473	(11.5)	467	(13.7)	450	(9.8)	-2.0	(3.5)	1.1	(0.19)	0.1	(0.32)
Galicia•	481	(10.8)	493	(10.3)	491	(7.6)	491	(10.0)	1.2	(4.8)	1.2	(0.21)	0.0	(0.28)
La Rioja•	489	(6.9)	511	(6.5)	505	(5.8)	510	(4.3)	**6.9**	(2.8)	1.2	(0.16)	0.5	(0.36)
Madrid•	498	(9.2)	493	(10.6)	502	(10.2)	524	(8.5)	**13.6**	(4.8)	1.1	(0.21)	1.9	(1.33)
Murcia•	442	(9.3)	459	(12.7)	473	(10.1)	473	(12.3)	**11.0**	(4.8)	1.4	(0.22)	2.0	(1.62)
Navarre•	498	(7.3)	519	(5.9)	517	(8.0)	533	(5.0)	**9.8**	(2.6)	**1.4**	(0.18)	1.6	(0.80)
United Kingdom														
England	**499**	(6.7)	506	(6.6)	502	(10.1)	**480**	(12.1)	-6.9	(5.0)	0.9	(0.13)	0.6	(0.93)
Northern Ireland	**477**	(12.0)	461	(17.0)	510	(13.5)	**487**	(13.7)	8.0	(5.4)	1.1	(0.23)	1.1	(1.47)
Scotland•	**493**	(7.2)	498	(5.3)	498	(6.4)	**503**	(6.2)	2.0	(4.4)	1.2	(0.17)	0.0	(0.26)
Wales	470	(5.8)	468	(5.1)	465	(5.4)	473	(5.8)	2.9	(3.2)	0.9	(0.12)	0.1	(0.29)
United States														
Connecticut•	502	(15.3)	506	(10.7)	501	(13.8)	514	(14.7)	8.0	(9.3)	1.2	(0.28)	0.4	(1.10)
Florida•	486	(11.5)	473	(10.8)	458	(8.7)	460	(10.1)	-12.7	(5.8)	**0.6**	(0.16)	1.8	(1.68)
Massachusetts•	514	(10.6)	490	(17.6)	531	(20.9)	519	(15.1)	3.3	(6.7)	0.9	(0.17)	0.1	(0.57)
Argentina														
Ciudad Autónoma de Buenos Aires•	342	(21.9)	413	(18.8)	456	(9.8)	461	(11.3)	**39.0**	(7.3)	**3.8**	(0.86)	23.9	(6.02)
Brazil														
Acre	345	(7.5)	355	(10.4)	355	(8.7)	381	(17.5)	**24.1**	(9.8)	1.4	(0.28)	7.6	(5.55)
Alagoas	**323**	(8.6)	324	(16.7)	332	(23.5)	**392**	(23.6)	**25.5**	(9.9)	1.4	(0.45)	12.2	(6.43)
Amapá	346	(9.5)	355	(19.7)	359	(12.1)	380	(21.6)	15.5	(8.5)	1.3	(0.42)	6.3	(7.09)
Amazonas	353	(10.2)	347	(9.2)	351	(11.3)	372	(15.7)	5.1	(7.8)	0.9	(0.28)	0.7	(2.20)
Bahia	341	(21.2)	354	(31.8)	375	(25.5)	c	c	**23.4**	(8.6)	1.6	(0.76)	14.1	(8.26)
Ceará	**345**	(13.0)	369	(20.2)	393	(13.5)	**406**	(26.0)	**26.8**	(11.8)	2.0	(0.68)	10.8	(8.08)
Espírito Santo	404	(16.1)	419	(22.8)	397	(24.8)	436	(49.4)	17.4	(13.8)	1.0	(0.32)	4.2	(7.01)
Federal District	370	(19.6)	397	(12.8)	433	(42.1)	446	(31.6)	24.5	(16.7)	2.2	(1.01)	8.9	(9.56)
Goiás	**347**	(11.6)	368	(9.1)	376	(11.2)	**427**	(13.5)	**25.1**	(4.8)	1.7	(0.46)	17.4	(6.31)
Maranhão	315	(14.9)	350	(27.0)	347	(18.1)	361	(43.8)	17.8	(15.0)	1.3	(0.37)	5.2	(7.81)
Mato Grosso	355	(12.7)	356	(10.7)	369	(19.8)	400	(24.4)	17.0	(10.0)	1.1	(0.41)	5.4	(5.70)
Mato Grosso do Sul	**389**	(10.5)	381	(11.3)	425	(23.8)	**439**	(11.6)	**21.9**	(7.8)	1.2	(0.39)	9.3	(4.89)
Minas Gerais	**384**	(10.6)	398	(13.0)	415	(19.9)	**415**	(8.6)	**10.4**	(5.1)	1.5	(0.38)	3.0	(2.45)
Pará	349	(6.7)	328	(12.6)	343	(18.2)	c	c	**19.5**	(3.3)	1.0	(0.21)	16.8	(4.14)
Paraíba	**354**	(19.1)	374	(12.8)	415	(22.6)	**439**	(15.2)	**27.3**	(7.2)	2.1	(0.67)	18.5	(7.17)
Paraná	384	(9.9)	396	(17.1)	413	(34.2)	420	(49.7)	10.2	(10.0)	1.2	(0.28)	2.0	(3.66)
Pernambuco	350	(12.4)	368	(14.2)	364	(17.9)	375	(20.9)	13.5	(5.9)	1.3	(0.39)	4.9	(3.75)
Piauí	**355**	(10.8)	367	(17.9)	369	(26.8)	**455**	(15.5)	**28.3**	(4.7)	1.5	(0.51)	19.2	(3.98)
Rio de Janeiro	377	(14.1)	366	(31.7)	410	(26.9)	393	(15.8)	10.2	(7.5)	1.1	(0.39)	2.6	(3.82)
Rio Grande do Norte	**355**	(9.2)	349	(7.9)	352	(17.8)	**465**	(31.5)	**31.0**	(8.9)	1.3	(0.34)	20.3	(8.14)
Rio Grande do Sul	395	(16.1)	427	(18.3)	384	(18.6)	422	(14.2)	7.4	(6.9)	1.2	(0.44)	1.4	(2.97)
Rondônia	**362**	(12.1)	373	(15.5)	391	(9.5)	**402**	(11.6)	16.2	(8.3)	1.7	(0.59)	4.4	(4.36)
Roraima	**330**	(10.1)	358	(10.7)	358	(12.4)	**401**	(28.4)	**25.3**	(6.8)	**1.9**	(0.41)	14.7	(9.21)
Santa Catarina	410	(14.5)	393	(14.8)	425	(16.5)	433	(30.0)	6.8	(10.5)	0.9	(0.31)	1.2	(4.10)
São Paulo	**387**	(5.4)	391	(6.8)	412	(11.4)	**425**	(16.5)	**13.5**	(5.3)	1.2	(0.18)	3.3	(2.40)
Sergipe	378	(14.6)	367	(17.0)	370	(13.9)	422	(30.0)	17.8	(10.2)	1.0	(0.44)	7.1	(7.58)
Tocantins	359	(11.2)	341	(14.3)	374	(23.7)	388	(18.4)	**18.4**	(6.1)	1.0	(0.35)	5.2	(3.40)
Colombia														
Bogota	375	(7.7)	398	(7.6)	401	(6.2)	395	(10.6)	**9.4**	(4.7)	**1.6**	(0.22)	2.0	(2.02)
Cali	385	(17.5)	366	(9.4)	372	(14.8)	396	(12.2)	2.8	(5.0)	0.8	(0.32)	0.3	(1.45)
Manizales	**381**	(6.1)	379	(7.2)	423	(16.4)	**430**	(17.2)	**14.5**	(3.5)	**1.6**	(0.29)	7.6	(3.50)
Medellin	369	(9.6)	383	(12.6)	387	(20.8)	435	(19.9)	**19.3**	(6.7)	1.4	(0.35)	8.4	(4.90)
Russian Federation														
Perm Territory region•	484	(11.3)	474	(9.5)	495	(18.2)	487	(13.1)	0.2	(9.5)	1.0	(0.26)	0.0	(0.77)
United Arab Emirates														
Abu Dhabi•	405	(7.5)	418	(14.5)	438	(9.4)	430	(9.1)	**9.9**	(3.6)	1.3	(0.17)	1.9	(1.32)
Ajman	416	(17.8)	395	(24.2)	409	(15.4)	393	(8.4)	-7.6	(4.5)	0.8	(0.24)	1.6	(2.01)
Dubai•	**426**	(2.4)	486	(3.1)	473	(3.8)	**475**	(4.2)	**18.2**	(1.1)	**2.0**	(0.12)	4.8	(0.58)
Fujairah	390	(6.5)	390	(27.5)	423	(15.0)	441	(18.1)	**25.0**	(6.0)	1.5	(0.42)	8.7	(4.51)
Ras Al Khaimah	398	(21.0)	432	(10.0)	408	(18.8)	423	(10.4)	11.7	(8.0)	1.8	(0.68)	2.8	(4.10)
Sharjah	419	(15.5)	423	(12.9)	456	(16.6)	460	(24.6)	16.4	(8.4)	1.4	(0.42)	5.0	(5.03)
Umm Al Quwain	401	(10.2)	c	c	395	(9.8)	c	c	-1.5	(2.4)	1.1	(0.29)	0.1	(0.29)

• PISA adjudicated region.

Notes: Values that are statistically significant are indicated in bold (see Annex A3).

See Table IV.3.14 for national data.

StatLink ᴍˢᴸ http://dx.doi.org/10.1787/888932957536

[Part 1/4]
Index of quality of schools' educational resources and mathematics performance, by region

Table B2.IV.9 *Results based on school principals' reports*

	Index of quality of schools' educational resources										Variability in this index	
	All students		Bottom quarter		Second quarter		Third quarter		Top quarter			
	Mean index	S.E.	Mean index	S.E.	Mean index	S.E.	Mean index	S.E.	Mean index	S.E.	Standard deviation	S.E.
Australia												
Australian Capital Territory	0.28	(0.02)	-0.97	(0.02)	-0.29	(0.02)	0.63	(0.05)	1.75	(0.01)	1.06	(0.01)
New South Wales	0.71	(0.07)	-0.56	(0.08)	0.25	(0.08)	1.18	(0.18)	1.98	(0.00)	1.00	(0.03)
Northern Territory	0.14	(0.13)	-0.89	(0.05)	-0.27	(0.19)	0.48	(0.30)	1.26	(0.09)	0.87	(0.02)
Queensland	0.54	(0.07)	-0.50	(0.07)	0.13	(0.10)	0.79	(0.10)	1.75	(0.11)	0.88	(0.04)
South Australia	0.42	(0.08)	-0.52	(0.07)	-0.01	(0.08)	0.57	(0.15)	1.63	(0.12)	0.84	(0.05)
Tasmania	0.42	(0.04)	-0.52	(0.06)	0.11	(0.01)	0.45	(0.03)	1.63	(0.06)	0.83	(0.01)
Victoria	0.81	(0.08)	-0.42	(0.12)	0.38	(0.12)	1.32	(0.17)	1.98	(0.00)	0.97	(0.06)
Western Australia	0.87	(0.08)	-0.47	(0.10)	0.37	(0.13)	1.58	(0.18)	1.98	(0.00)	1.01	(0.04)
Belgium												
Flemish community●	0.54	(0.07)	-0.49	(0.07)	0.17	(0.09)	0.82	(0.11)	1.66	(0.10)	0.85	(0.04)
French community	0.71	(0.07)	-0.56	(0.08)	0.25	(0.08)	1.18	(0.18)	1.98	(0.00)	1.00	(0.03)
German-speaking community	0.81	(0.08)	-0.42	(0.12)	0.38	(0.12)	1.32	(0.17)	1.98	(0.00)	0.97	(0.06)
Canada												
Alberta	0.55	(0.08)	-0.36	(0.06)	0.13	(0.10)	0.62	(0.13)	1.81	(0.12)	0.84	(0.04)
British Columbia	0.28	(0.12)	-0.82	(0.14)	-0.21	(0.13)	0.50	(0.15)	1.65	(0.17)	0.97	(0.06)
Manitoba	0.16	(0.06)	-0.85	(0.05)	-0.16	(0.05)	0.26	(0.07)	1.37	(0.14)	0.87	(0.05)
New Brunswick	-0.25	(0.02)	-1.21	(0.04)	-0.40	(0.01)	-0.08	(0.02)	0.71	(0.06)	0.81	(0.03)
Newfoundland and Labrador	0.69	(0.12)	-0.39	(0.06)	0.20	(0.12)	0.99	(0.32)	1.98	(0.00)	0.95	(0.03)
Nova Scotia	0.12	(0.16)	-0.92	(0.05)	-0.45	(0.23)	0.19	(0.21)	1.66	(0.22)	1.02	(0.05)
Ontario	0.23	(0.10)	-0.98	(0.14)	-0.19	(0.09)	0.44	(0.12)	1.66	(0.18)	1.03	(0.07)
Prince Edward Island	-0.05	(0.00)	-0.42	(0.00)	-0.22	(0.00)	-0.08	(0.00)	0.52	(0.01)	0.40	(0.00)
Quebec	0.24	(0.08)	-0.81	(0.11)	-0.11	(0.08)	0.42	(0.07)	1.47	(0.15)	0.91	(0.06)
Saskatchewan	0.48	(0.08)	-0.52	(0.02)	0.05	(0.07)	0.57	(0.10)	1.81	(0.17)	0.90	(0.04)
Italy												
Abruzzo	-0.24	(0.10)	-1.33	(0.13)	-0.58	(0.12)	0.07	(0.10)	0.88	(0.20)	0.89	(0.08)
Basilicata	-0.23	(0.14)	-1.40	(0.14)	-0.67	(0.12)	0.06	(0.13)	1.08	(0.30)	1.01	(0.10)
Bolzano	0.43	(0.02)	-0.60	(0.02)	0.00	(0.01)	0.69	(0.03)	1.65	(0.05)	0.88	(0.01)
Calabria	0.08	(0.12)	-0.82	(0.11)	-0.31	(0.09)	0.14	(0.23)	1.33	(0.21)	0.86	(0.08)
Campania	-0.02	(0.13)	-0.95	(0.16)	-0.33	(0.11)	0.11	(0.10)	1.09	(0.30)	0.84	(0.11)
Emilia Romagna	0.18	(0.12)	-0.83	(0.13)	-0.27	(0.12)	0.32	(0.15)	1.52	(0.26)	0.94	(0.09)
Friuli Venezia Giulia	0.04	(0.08)	-0.82	(0.09)	-0.33	(0.11)	0.24	(0.11)	1.09	(0.12)	0.78	(0.05)
Lazio	-0.13	(0.14)	-1.21	(0.26)	-0.39	(0.13)	0.08	(0.11)	0.98	(0.30)	0.94	(0.16)
Liguria	-0.08	(0.08)	-1.10	(0.14)	-0.36	(0.16)	0.23	(0.09)	0.94	(0.11)	0.82	(0.07)
Lombardia	0.31	(0.16)	-0.85	(0.25)	-0.08	(0.10)	0.51	(0.23)	1.68	(0.20)	0.99	(0.09)
Marche	-0.13	(0.07)	-0.87	(0.09)	-0.35	(0.08)	0.05	(0.15)	0.63	(0.07)	0.59	(0.04)
Molise	-0.13	(0.02)	-1.13	(0.03)	-0.37	(0.02)	-0.02	(0.01)	1.01	(0.04)	0.85	(0.01)
Piemonte	0.10	(0.08)	-0.72	(0.13)	-0.14	(0.08)	0.27	(0.10)	1.00	(0.12)	0.67	(0.06)
Puglia	0.04	(0.13)	-0.85	(0.11)	-0.38	(0.10)	0.07	(0.20)	1.30	(0.25)	0.86	(0.09)
Sardegna	-0.40	(0.14)	-1.62	(0.31)	-0.66	(0.09)	-0.17	(0.21)	0.83	(0.20)	1.01	(0.14)
Sicilia	0.11	(0.13)	-0.88	(0.12)	-0.20	(0.19)	0.31	(0.11)	1.23	(0.20)	0.83	(0.07)
Toscana	-0.19	(0.10)	-0.89	(0.17)	-0.37	(0.08)	-0.12	(0.07)	0.63	(0.22)	0.64	(0.11)
Trento	0.51	(0.10)	-0.47	(0.09)	-0.01	(0.10)	0.66	(0.17)	1.88	(0.10)	0.91	(0.03)
Umbria	-0.25	(0.10)	-1.37	(0.10)	-0.55	(0.13)	0.01	(0.18)	0.90	(0.11)	0.90	(0.05)
Valle d'Aosta	0.51	(0.02)	-0.41	(0.02)	0.16	(0.01)	0.60	(0.04)	1.68	(0.02)	0.84	(0.01)
Veneto	0.03	(0.13)	-0.91	(0.10)	-0.42	(0.08)	0.06	(0.15)	1.38	(0.33)	0.92	(0.11)
Mexico												
Aguascalientes	-0.97	(0.09)	-2.23	(0.21)	-1.28	(0.10)	-0.61	(0.17)	0.24	(0.17)	1.00	(0.11)
Baja California	-0.73	(0.15)	-2.11	(0.22)	-1.04	(0.28)	-0.32	(0.13)	0.57	(0.18)	1.09	(0.12)
Baja California Sur	-1.09	(0.14)	-2.47	(0.27)	-1.44	(0.15)	-0.68	(0.23)	0.25	(0.11)	1.14	(0.10)
Campeche	-1.01	(0.14)	-2.37	(0.25)	-1.31	(0.21)	-0.62	(0.18)	0.28	(0.08)	1.08	(0.10)
Chiapas	-1.44	(0.17)	-2.83	(0.21)	-1.75	(0.27)	-0.95	(0.20)	-0.23	(0.22)	1.04	(0.11)
Chihuahua	-1.14	(0.17)	-2.26	(0.13)	-1.57	(0.28)	-0.91	(0.25)	0.20	(0.23)	1.00	(0.10)
Coahuila	-0.98	(0.17)	-2.37	(0.31)	-1.26	(0.22)	-0.72	(0.15)	0.43	(0.28)	1.12	(0.15)
Colima	-0.31	(0.14)	-1.75	(0.24)	-0.62	(0.21)	-0.12	(0.07)	1.24	(0.19)	1.18	(0.10)
Distrito Federal	-0.42	(0.16)	-1.72	(0.27)	-0.94	(0.20)	-0.03	(0.31)	1.02	(0.11)	1.12	(0.11)
Durango	-0.96	(0.09)	-1.86	(0.14)	-1.34	(0.06)	-0.86	(0.18)	0.24	(0.20)	0.91	(0.11)
Guanajuato	-1.03	(0.17)	-2.70	(0.36)	-1.38	(0.13)	-0.59	(0.25)	0.56	(0.27)	1.30	(0.15)
Guerrero	-1.00	(0.12)	-2.47	(0.25)	-1.23	(0.15)	-0.56	(0.22)	0.28	(0.17)	1.08	(0.13)
Hidalgo	-0.95	(0.14)	-2.49	(0.29)	-1.17	(0.22)	-0.56	(0.14)	0.45	(0.12)	1.17	(0.12)
Jalisco	-0.74	(0.19)	-2.27	(0.25)	-1.03	(0.30)	-0.39	(0.22)	0.73	(0.28)	1.17	(0.14)
Mexico	-0.52	(0.17)	-1.61	(0.22)	-0.81	(0.16)	-0.23	(0.17)	0.58	(0.35)	0.92	(0.15)
Morelos	-0.82	(0.16)	-2.26	(0.24)	-1.26	(0.20)	-0.39	(0.19)	0.63	(0.23)	1.11	(0.11)
Nayarit	-1.29	(0.16)	-2.52	(0.13)	-1.75	(0.20)	-1.04	(0.14)	0.13	(0.33)	1.07	(0.14)
Nuevo León	-0.04	(0.26)	-1.56	(0.40)	-0.40	(0.16)	0.11	(0.35)	1.71	(0.36)	1.27	(0.16)
Puebla	-1.11	(0.10)	-1.96	(0.08)	-1.61	(0.08)	-1.08	(0.14)	0.20	(0.27)	0.94	(0.13)
Querétaro	-0.93	(0.16)	-2.17	(0.22)	-1.18	(0.33)	-0.77	(0.11)	0.39	(0.34)	1.02	(0.14)
Quintana Roo	-0.86	(0.14)	-1.96	(0.18)	-1.26	(0.15)	-0.61	(0.17)	0.41	(0.21)	0.98	(0.07)
San Luis Potosí	-1.07	(0.17)	-2.28	(0.20)	-1.35	(0.26)	-0.78	(0.11)	0.15	(0.30)	0.99	(0.11)
Sinaloa	-0.48	(0.11)	-1.36	(0.15)	-0.74	(0.15)	-0.21	(0.13)	0.38	(0.15)	0.69	(0.07)
Tabasco	-1.24	(0.16)	-2.40	(0.23)	-1.60	(0.14)	-1.04	(0.15)	0.09	(0.33)	1.02	(0.14)
Tamaulipas	-0.51	(0.19)	-1.85	(0.18)	-1.02	(0.36)	-0.25	(0.15)	1.09	(0.34)	1.16	(0.14)
Tlaxcala	-0.71	(0.13)	-2.11	(0.21)	-0.98	(0.17)	-0.28	(0.12)	0.54	(0.24)	1.07	(0.13)
Veracruz	-1.04	(0.18)	-2.24	(0.15)	-1.57	(0.14)	-0.67	(0.32)	0.33	(0.24)	1.03	(0.10)
Yucatán	-1.10	(0.16)	-2.13	(0.18)	-1.40	(0.15)	-0.93	(0.14)	0.07	(0.43)	0.96	(0.20)
Zacatecas	-1.38	(0.19)	-2.90	(0.28)	-1.74	(0.20)	-1.11	(0.26)	0.24	(0.30)	1.24	(0.14)

● PISA adjudicated region.
Notes: Values that are statistically significant are indicated in bold (see Annex A3).
See Table IV.3.16 for national data.
StatLink ⌐⌐⌐ http://dx.doi.org/10.1787/888932957536

[Part 2/4]
Index of quality of schools' educational resources and mathematics performance, by region
Table B2.IV.9   *Results based on school principals' reports*

		Index of quality of schools' educational resources									Variability in this index	
		All students		Bottom quarter		Second quarter		Third quarter		Top quarter			
		Mean index	S.E.	Mean index	S.E.	Mean index	S.E.	Mean index	S.E.	Mean index	S.E.	Standard deviation	S.E.
Portugal													
	Alentejo	0.30	(0.23)	-0.69	(0.12)	-0.06	(0.25)	0.55	(0.28)	1.41	(0.46)	0.85	(0.15)
Spain													
	Andalusia•	0.10	(0.11)	-0.69	(0.11)	-0.14	(0.10)	0.19	(0.12)	1.03	(0.22)	0.69	(0.09)
	Aragon•	0.24	(0.15)	-0.94	(0.16)	-0.13	(0.20)	0.40	(0.17)	1.65	(0.19)	0.99	(0.07)
	Asturias•	0.28	(0.13)	-0.65	(0.09)	-0.12	(0.15)	0.47	(0.15)	1.43	(0.25)	0.84	(0.08)
	Balearic Islands•	-0.24	(0.11)	-1.18	(0.30)	-0.45	(0.08)	-0.14	(0.09)	0.82	(0.19)	0.86	(0.17)
	Basque Country•	0.14	(0.07)	-0.98	(0.15)	-0.20	(0.06)	0.37	(0.07)	1.38	(0.12)	0.97	(0.09)
	Cantabria•	0.15	(0.12)	-0.83	(0.08)	-0.20	(0.16)	0.29	(0.12)	1.36	(0.23)	0.87	(0.07)
	Castile and Leon•	-0.26	(0.11)	-1.30	(0.10)	-0.70	(0.10)	-0.09	(0.18)	1.07	(0.24)	0.95	(0.10)
	Catalonia•	0.09	(0.14)	-1.05	(0.17)	-0.27	(0.13)	0.30	(0.15)	1.38	(0.28)	0.96	(0.10)
	Extremadura•	0.52	(0.17)	-0.91	(0.28)	0.19	(0.22)	0.93	(0.19)	1.88	(0.17)	1.10	(0.11)
	Galicia•	-0.12	(0.12)	-0.99	(0.12)	-0.37	(0.08)	-0.04	(0.08)	0.91	(0.29)	0.78	(0.10)
	La Rioja•	0.46	(0.01)	-0.62	(0.01)	-0.03	(0.01)	0.66	(0.01)	1.82	(0.01)	0.95	(0.01)
	Madrid•	0.02	(0.13)	-0.93	(0.16)	-0.26	(0.07)	0.15	(0.14)	1.14	(0.26)	0.83	(0.09)
	Murcia•	-0.04	(0.12)	-1.00	(0.11)	-0.48	(0.07)	0.12	(0.21)	1.21	(0.22)	0.88	(0.08)
	Navarre•	-0.04	(0.06)	-0.93	(0.09)	-0.34	(0.06)	0.14	(0.10)	0.97	(0.09)	0.75	(0.04)
United Kingdom													
	England	0.55	(0.09)	-0.68	(0.09)	0.03	(0.06)	0.89	(0.24)	1.98	(0.00)	1.05	(0.03)
	Northern Ireland	-0.01	(0.10)	-1.14	(0.12)	-0.32	(0.08)	0.15	(0.10)	1.29	(0.22)	0.97	(0.08)
	Scotland•	0.56	(0.10)	-0.79	(0.11)	0.13	(0.13)	0.92	(0.23)	1.98	(0.01)	1.07	(0.05)
	Wales	0.14	(0.08)	-1.09	(0.10)	-0.29	(0.07)	0.29	(0.09)	1.64	(0.15)	1.06	(0.06)
United States													
	Connecticut•	0.76	(0.18)	-0.58	(0.15)	0.07	(0.20)	1.59	(0.43)	1.98	(0.00)	1.11	(0.05)
	Florida•	0.09	(0.17)	-1.00	(0.20)	-0.31	(0.12)	0.16	(0.23)	1.51	(0.27)	0.99	(0.10)
	Massachusetts•	0.33	(0.17)	-1.08	(0.13)	-0.41	(0.24)	0.84	(0.37)	1.98	(0.09)	1.21	(0.06)
Argentina													
	Ciudad Autónoma de Buenos Aires•	0.38	(0.17)	-1.47	(0.24)	-0.31	(0.25)	1.32	(0.39)	1.98	(0.00)	1.45	(0.12)
Brazil													
	Acre	-1.08	(0.11)	-1.84	(0.11)	-1.29	(0.18)	-0.85	(0.14)	-0.33	(0.17)	0.59	(0.07)
	Alagoas	-0.93	(0.23)	-2.16	(0.35)	-1.20	(0.21)	-0.83	(0.21)	0.48	(0.52)	1.05	(0.22)
	Amapá	-0.82	(0.08)	-1.56	(0.07)	-1.27	(0.09)	-0.86	(0.15)	0.41	(0.25)	0.91	(0.16)
	Amazonas	-0.95	(0.18)	-1.88	(0.12)	-1.44	(0.20)	-0.71	(0.34)	0.24	(0.22)	0.91	(0.11)
	Bahia	-0.44	(0.24)	-1.68	(0.41)	-0.72	(0.17)	c	c	c	c	1.03	(0.15)
	Ceará	-0.36	(0.13)	-1.57	(0.36)	-0.60	(0.18)	-0.13	(0.12)	0.89	(0.11)	1.03	(0.14)
	Espírito Santo	-0.57	(0.16)	-1.36	(0.16)	-0.97	(0.09)	-0.57	(0.15)	0.63	(0.47)	0.89	(0.18)
	Federal District	-0.68	(0.25)	-2.23	(0.65)	-1.02	(0.14)	-0.23	(0.35)	c	c	1.26	(0.24)
	Goiás	-1.29	(0.25)	-2.41	(0.31)	-1.77	(0.20)	-1.13	(0.23)	0.17	(0.45)	1.11	(0.11)
	Maranhão	-1.21	(0.13)	-1.96	(0.14)	-1.44	(0.21)	-1.01	(0.19)	-0.42	(0.23)	0.69	(0.15)
	Mato Grosso	-0.87	(0.18)	-1.95	(0.12)	-1.27	(0.24)	-0.63	(0.08)	0.38	(0.46)	0.99	(0.17)
	Mato Grosso do Sul	-0.98	(0.18)	-1.90	(0.24)	-1.28	(0.06)	-0.95	(0.16)	0.22	(0.47)	0.96	(0.20)
	Minas Gerais	-0.76	(0.12)	-1.96	(0.18)	-1.06	(0.15)	-0.58	(0.20)	0.56	(0.16)	1.01	(0.09)
	Pará	-0.74	(0.18)	-2.01	(0.05)	-1.55	(0.31)	-0.80	(0.10)	1.41	(0.48)	1.38	(0.17)
	Paraíba	-0.46	(0.17)	-1.77	(0.17)	-0.88	(0.24)	-0.06	(0.35)	c	c	1.05	(0.15)
	Paraná	-0.45	(0.10)	-1.31	(0.19)	-0.77	(0.12)	-0.37	(0.13)	0.68	(0.21)	0.79	(0.10)
	Pernambuco	-0.53	(0.16)	-1.46	(0.22)	-0.90	(0.17)	-0.39	(0.21)	0.65	(0.28)	0.83	(0.12)
	Piauí	-0.98	(0.23)	-2.20	(0.41)	-1.42	(0.18)	-0.78	(0.29)	0.50	(0.48)	1.15	(0.23)
	Rio de Janeiro	-0.22	(0.14)	-1.11	(0.15)	-0.57	(0.18)	-0.01	(0.18)	0.80	(0.23)	0.75	(0.08)
	Rio Grande do Norte	-0.64	(0.25)	-2.28	(0.30)	-1.04	(0.24)	-0.45	(0.31)	1.23	(0.59)	1.39	(0.21)
	Rio Grande do Sul	-0.46	(0.27)	-2.16	(0.58)	-0.90	(0.25)	-0.04	(0.34)	1.25	(0.24)	1.38	(0.22)
	Rondônia	-1.18	(0.10)	-1.97	(0.22)	-1.42	(0.07)	-0.98	(0.12)	-0.35	(0.18)	0.67	(0.10)
	Roraima	-0.98	(0.22)	-2.43	(0.39)	-1.19	(0.27)	-0.53	(0.19)	0.24	(0.28)	1.04	(0.15)
	Santa Catarina	-0.53	(0.17)	-1.48	(0.16)	-0.80	(0.19)	-0.46	(0.11)	0.64	(0.44)	0.86	(0.18)
	São Paulo	-0.28	(0.12)	-1.47	(0.13)	-0.72	(0.15)	0.01	(0.13)	1.07	(0.24)	1.02	(0.10)
	Sergipe	-0.90	(0.18)	-1.98	(0.30)	-1.00	(0.22)	-0.50	(0.26)	-0.13	(0.08)	0.73	(0.09)
	Tocantins	-0.84	(0.09)	-1.49	(0.06)	-1.11	(0.14)	-0.67	(0.13)	-0.07	(0.14)	0.56	(0.05)
Colombia													
	Bogota	-0.94	(0.12)	-2.37	(0.22)	-1.11	(0.17)	-0.59	(0.14)	0.31	(0.16)	1.07	(0.11)
	Cali	-0.70	(0.23)	-2.68	(0.23)	-1.43	(0.32)	-0.13	(0.37)	1.44	(0.26)	1.60	(0.13)
	Manizales	-0.75	(0.17)	-2.22	(0.19)	-1.29	(0.25)	-0.27	(0.26)	0.78	(0.17)	1.16	(0.09)
	Medellin	-0.55	(0.19)	-2.25	(0.33)	-1.14	(0.17)	-0.25	(0.23)	1.47	(0.23)	1.43	(0.11)
Russian Federation													
	Perm Territory region•	-0.53	(0.13)	-1.78	(0.23)	-0.72	(0.18)	-0.22	(0.11)	0.60	(0.19)	0.98	(0.12)
United Arab Emirates													
	Abu Dhabi•	0.25	(0.09)	-1.28	(0.09)	-0.40	(0.10)	0.70	(0.23)	1.98	(0.03)	1.28	(0.04)
	Ajman	0.26	(0.11)	-1.42	(0.23)	-0.04	(0.15)	0.64	(0.10)	1.85	(0.13)	1.27	(0.06)
	Dubai•	0.61	(0.01)	-1.04	(0.00)	0.30	(0.01)	1.21	(0.01)	1.98	(0.00)	1.17	(0.00)
	Fujairah	0.21	(0.10)	-0.87	(0.05)	0.02	(0.08)	0.37	(0.05)	1.35	(0.33)	0.88	(0.09)
	Ras Al Khaimah	0.38	(0.22)	-1.07	(0.24)	-0.13	(0.27)	0.75	(0.44)	1.98	(0.14)	1.17	(0.11)
	Sharjah	0.34	(0.14)	-0.94	(0.16)	-0.35	(0.17)	0.75	(0.26)	1.92	(0.20)	1.13	(0.10)
	Umm Al Quwain	0.22	(0.01)	-0.88	(0.03)	c	c	0.25	(0.02)	c	c	1.06	(0.01)

OECD (left margin, vertical)
Partners (left margin, vertical)

• PISA adjudicated region.
Notes: Values that are statistically significant are indicated in bold (see Annex A3).
See Table IV.3.16 for national data.
StatLink ⧉ http://dx.doi.org/10.1787/888932957536

[Part 3/4]
Index of quality of schools' educational resources and mathematics performance, by region
Table B2.IV.9   *Results based on school principals' reports*

| | Performance on the mathematics scale, by national quarters of this index | | | | | | | | Change in the mathematics score per unit of this index | | Increased likelihood of students in the bottom quarter of this index scoring in the bottom quarter of the national mathematics performance distribution | | Explained variance in student performance (r-squared x 100) | |
| | Bottom quarter | | Second quarter | | Third quarter | | Top quarter | | | | | | | |
	Mean score	S.E.	Mean score	S.E.	Mean score	S.E.	Mean score	S.E.	Score dif.	S.E.	Ratio	S.E.	%	S.E.
Australia														
Australian Capital Territory	510	(8.9)	504	(7.6)	495	(7.4)	554	(6.7)	**17.2**	(3.5)	1.2	(0.20)	3.5	(1.42)
New South Wales	**491**	(8.0)	494	(7.1)	527	(10.2)	527	(9.9)	**16.5**	(4.8)	1.3	(0.16)	2.7	(1.45)
Northern Territory	446	(12.9)	431	(42.0)	447	(56.9)	485	(18.1)	18.1	(10.4)	1.1	(0.30)	2.1	(2.14)
Queensland	**478**	(6.9)	506	(8.5)	510	(7.6)	**521**	(7.7)	**17.5**	(4.6)	**1.6**	(0.20)	2.7	(1.47)
South Australia	**494**	(9.6)	478	(10.8)	487	(10.4)	**499**	(10.7)	6.9	(5.6)	1.0	(0.15)	0.4	(0.71)
Tasmania	455	(6.5)	471	(8.6)	493	(8.3)	500	(6.2)	**18.0**	(4.6)	**1.6**	(0.20)	2.5	(1.24)
Victoria	**475**	(6.9)	503	(10.8)	508	(7.1)	**518**	(7.1)	**15.3**	(3.9)	**1.7**	(0.24)	2.7	(1.32)
Western Australia	**490**	(7.1)	504	(10.2)	529	(8.4)	**542**	(9.2)	**20.6**	(4.2)	**1.6**	(0.23)	4.9	(1.90)
Belgium														
Flemish community●	521	(12.2)	534	(10.0)	539	(11.1)	536	(12.2)	8.4	(8.8)	1.2	(0.23)	0.5	(1.13)
French community	**490**	(8.0)	495	(7.4)	526	(10.6)	**527**	(9.7)	**16.5**	(4.8)	1.3	(0.15)	2.7	(1.45)
German-speaking community	**475**	(6.9)	504	(11.0)	508	(7.2)	**517**	(7.5)	**15.3**	(3.9)	**1.7**	(0.23)	2.7	(1.32)
Canada														
Alberta	523	(12.3)	514	(8.3)	513	(10.0)	520	(6.3)	1.5	(5.1)	1.0	(0.21)	0.0	(0.23)
British Columbia	515	(7.6)	519	(11.9)	528	(9.8)	526	(8.6)	3.0	(4.3)	1.1	(0.15)	0.1	(0.50)
Manitoba	489	(7.1)	497	(7.8)	493	(7.1)	492	(10.3)	2.8	(5.4)	1.0	(0.16)	0.1	(0.36)
New Brunswick	494	(5.3)	503	(4.8)	510	(5.6)	501	(7.8)	3.3	(3.7)	1.2	(0.14)	0.1	(0.26)
Newfoundland and Labrador	**499**	(11.1)	503	(6.6)	482	(9.9)	**476**	(17.0)	-9.6	(9.2)	0.8	(0.27)	1.1	(2.19)
Nova Scotia	486	(21.2)	507	(13.6)	505	(6.9)	490	(7.2)	-1.9	(4.5)	1.1	(0.20)	0.1	(0.40)
Ontario	508	(8.4)	515	(9.2)	517	(7.7)	518	(7.5)	4.6	(4.1)	1.1	(0.17)	0.3	(0.54)
Prince Edward Island	490	(4.9)	481	(5.4)	486	(5.6)	468	(5.3)	**-23.1**	(6.6)	0.9	(0.12)	1.2	(0.71)
Quebec	520	(6.9)	543	(8.5)	545	(9.5)	535	(8.9)	6.1	(4.8)	**1.3**	(0.17)	0.4	(0.54)
Saskatchewan	**508**	(5.6)	509	(7.1)	510	(7.8)	498	(7.1)	-4.1	(3.1)	0.9	(0.12)	0.2	(0.28)
Italy														
Abruzzo	426	(17.2)	483	(25.1)	499	(10.0)	494	(13.2)	**25.7**	(7.8)	**2.4**	(0.61)	6.5	(3.24)
Basilicata	452	(9.3)	448	(11.9)	501	(14.9)	457	(18.2)	3.7	(7.5)	1.2	(0.28)	0.2	(0.99)
Bolzano	500	(4.3)	498	(4.3)	511	(4.2)	522	(5.6)	**13.4**	(3.3)	1.0	(0.13)	1.8	(0.85)
Calabria	405	(19.1)	433	(21.2)	440	(16.2)	447	(15.9)	16.6	(10.3)	1.8	(0.45)	2.6	(2.70)
Campania	416	(16.3)	448	(20.6)	490	(15.7)	469	(11.0)	**21.7**	(8.8)	2.0	(0.56)	4.3	(3.38)
Emilia Romagna	446	(19.5)	492	(14.9)	537	(20.9)	542	(9.2)	**36.5**	(6.7)	**3.0**	(0.76)	12.6	(4.00)
Friuli Venezia Giulia	**509**	(15.1)	509	(10.2)	521	(21.3)	**540**	(8.9)	15.3	(8.3)	1.3	(0.44)	1.8	(2.12)
Lazio	451	(15.9)	479	(23.6)	482	(19.1)	504	(17.4)	9.9	(13.3)	1.5	(0.43)	1.1	(2.89)
Liguria	504	(14.0)	470	(22.7)	501	(15.4)	477	(13.8)	-5.5	(8.0)	0.9	(0.31)	0.3	(0.81)
Lombardia	525	(14.0)	526	(21.8)	518	(25.0)	512	(22.5)	-4.2	(9.2)	0.8	(0.31)	0.2	(1.33)
Marche	**510**	(12.3)	507	(12.9)	480	(23.5)	**501**	(11.6)	-4.2	(9.4)	0.9	(0.29)	0.1	(0.46)
Molise	**432**	(5.8)	462	(4.8)	453	(4.6)	**487**	(7.2)	**17.2**	(3.6)	**1.7**	(0.25)	3.0	(1.16)
Piemonte	508	(12.6)	498	(12.6)	489	(17.6)	498	(12.6)	-5.2	(10.1)	0.7	(0.19)	0.2	(0.79)
Puglia	471	(9.6)	487	(18.4)	474	(20.5)	490	(22.4)	11.7	(8.6)	1.1	(0.21)	1.4	(2.17)
Sardegna	440	(21.2)	456	(18.2)	475	(13.9)	468	(9.5)	**16.5**	(6.0)	1.6	(0.49)	3.8	(3.19)
Sicilia	458	(13.4)	435	(12.1)	468	(15.8)	430	(10.5)	-10.2	(7.5)	0.8	(0.21)	1.1	(1.59)
Toscana	509	(23.3)	503	(25.8)	504	(23.9)	472	(29.8)	-2.9	(15.4)	0.8	(0.29)	0.0	(1.03)
Trento	508	(14.4)	516	(13.5)	540	(10.3)	541	(10.2)	**15.2**	(7.7)	1.5	(0.37)	2.7	(2.74)
Umbria	501	(7.4)	493	(13.8)	503	(15.4)	468	(24.9)	-11.2	(10.3)	0.8	(0.25)	1.3	(2.29)
Valle d'Aosta	**510**	(7.1)	504	(8.2)	474	(8.5)	**486**	(7.1)	-5.3	(3.3)	0.9	(0.16)	0.3	(0.33)
Veneto	523	(20.1)	533	(20.6)	509	(17.5)	527	(17.4)	2.9	(11.7)	1.1	(0.42)	0.1	(1.55)
Mexico														
Aguascalientes	**426**	(8.9)	419	(16.0)	430	(10.3)	**473**	(9.7)	**16.1**	(4.2)	1.2	(0.29)	4.9	(2.49)
Baja California	389	(8.2)	403	(12.6)	430	(10.7)	439	(16.6)	**14.9**	(5.3)	1.8	(0.45)	5.1	(2.93)
Baja California Sur	412	(20.5)	421	(16.1)	408	(12.3)	415	(12.2)	4.8	(5.2)	1.1	(0.26)	0.6	(1.27)
Campeche	374	(11.9)	390	(11.5)	394	(7.5)	424	(7.4)	**16.8**	(5.0)	1.8	(0.39)	6.6	(3.85)
Chiapas	349	(14.7)	366	(20.9)	396	(20.2)	381	(16.5)	11.1	(6.5)	1.6	(0.44)	2.4	(2.78)
Chihuahua	400	(17.3)	424	(18.3)	440	(14.5)	449	(12.8)	**20.2**	(9.5)	1.7	(0.46)	6.7	(5.86)
Coahuila	400	(20.9)	413	(16.2)	417	(11.6)	442	(19.1)	13.9	(7.7)	1.5	(0.41)	4.7	(5.24)
Colima	386	(14.9)	417	(15.0)	448	(11.8)	466	(12.1)	**24.8**	(5.7)	**2.6**	(0.52)	14.6	(6.35)
Distrito Federal	**405**	(11.2)	418	(10.8)	437	(14.8)	**452**	(19.3)	**16.2**	(6.3)	1.6	(0.54)	6.2	(5.42)
Durango	397	(11.2)	415	(21.2)	430	(10.4)	456	(10.5)	**22.1**	(5.9)	1.8	(0.45)	7.7	(3.88)
Guanajuato	364	(11.3)	405	(17.2)	446	(10.1)	432	(10.6)	**19.9**	(4.2)	**3.0**	(0.79)	11.9	(4.32)
Guerrero	358	(7.3)	371	(12.9)	376	(14.6)	367	(15.7)	3.4	(4.1)	1.2	(0.24)	0.3	(0.92)
Hidalgo	**370**	(12.2)	403	(14.0)	424	(18.0)	**429**	(10.3)	**16.9**	(6.7)	**2.2**	(0.53)	7.2	(4.42)
Jalisco	428	(11.1)	432	(18.9)	434	(13.4)	445	(14.0)	4.6	(5.4)	1.1	(0.26)	0.6	(1.35)
Mexico	406	(10.6)	409	(8.2)	408	(14.5)	446	(14.9)	**19.8**	(7.0)	1.4	(0.42)	7.4	(5.71)
Morelos	405	(13.6)	395	(23.0)	426	(18.9)	460	(21.4)	**20.0**	(8.4)	1.5	(0.46)	8.0	(6.00)
Nayarit	410	(14.2)	398	(17.4)	417	(9.2)	435	(9.5)	**15.1**	(5.0)	1.1	(0.30)	4.5	(3.25)
Nuevo León	**413**	(15.3)	415	(18.3)	454	(11.5)	**463**	(12.7)	**15.6**	(4.8)	1.6	(0.36)	7.2	(4.10)
Puebla	393	(11.0)	395	(13.8)	412	(11.0)	462	(6.9)	**28.0**	(5.1)	1.7	(0.43)	12.8	(3.26)
Querétaro	403	(10.2)	429	(23.7)	452	(14.1)	455	(11.1)	**18.1**	(6.0)	**1.8**	(0.41)	6.1	(3.65)
Quintana Roo	383	(14.9)	396	(10.3)	428	(9.2)	436	(10.0)	**23.0**	(4.1)	1.8	(0.48)	10.1	(3.25)
San Luis Potosí	385	(12.9)	403	(14.4)	416	(13.5)	444	(15.8)	**25.3**	(6.0)	1.8	(0.43)	11.1	(5.65)
Sinaloa	405	(10.1)	410	(14.6)	418	(13.8)	415	(14.9)	7.2	(9.7)	1.1	(0.25)	0.5	(1.56)
Tabasco	346	(10.0)	360	(10.6)	393	(13.5)	414	(12.5)	**20.6**	(3.8)	2.0	(0.57)	8.8	(3.07)
Tamaulipas	410	(23.5)	402	(13.8)	396	(13.8)	437	(15.0)	10.5	(7.2)	1.2	(0.33)	2.7	(3.71)
Tlaxcala	397	(16.3)	418	(13.5)	417	(8.6)	412	(14.9)	9.2	(6.9)	1.5	(0.43)	1.9	(2.89)
Veracruz	398	(9.7)	390	(14.0)	411	(19.9)	410	(25.6)	8.9	(9.3)	0.8	(0.21)	1.5	(3.41)
Yucatán	370	(8.9)	412	(10.4)	429	(10.1)	429	(11.6)	**23.9**	(4.9)	**2.2**	(0.37)	9.5	(3.28)
Zacatecas	404	(7.9)	411	(13.3)	402	(11.6)	419	(10.8)	4.6	(4.0)	1.1	(0.23)	0.6	(0.80)

● PISA adjudicated region.
Notes: Values that are statistically significant are indicated in bold (see Annex A3).
See Table IV.3.16 for national data.
StatLink ◫◱ http://dx.doi.org/10.1787/888932957536

[Part 4/4]
Index of quality of schools' educational resources and mathematics performance, by region
Table B2.IV.9   *Results based on school principals' reports*

| | Performance on the mathematics scale, by national quarters of this index | | | | | | | | Change in the mathematics score per unit of this index | | Increased likelihood of students in the bottom quarter of this index scoring in the bottom quarter of the national mathematics performance distribution | | Explained variance in student performance (r-squared x 100) | |
| | Bottom quarter | | Second quarter | | Third quarter | | Top quarter | | | | | | | |
	Mean score	S.E.	Mean score	S.E.	Mean score	S.E.	Mean score	S.E.	Score dif.	S.E.	Ratio	S.E.	%	S.E.
OECD														
Portugal														
Alentejo	488	(15.9)	493	(28.8)	475	(29.8)	508	(23.3)	7.8	(13.5)	0.9	(0.35)	0.6	(2.23)
Spain														
Andalusia•	468	(9.1)	475	(11.4)	472	(10.7)	473	(8.7)	1.7	(5.6)	1.1	(0.18)	0.0	(0.22)
Aragon•	503	(11.1)	499	(16.2)	497	(13.8)	486	(10.7)	-5.0	(4.6)	0.8	(0.17)	0.3	(0.54)
Asturias•	490	(14.4)	486	(12.0)	507	(10.7)	515	(8.8)	**15.0**	(7.4)	1.2	(0.26)	1.8	(1.98)
Balearic Islands•	471	(8.2)	467	(9.0)	459	(10.9)	503	(8.4)	**12.8**	(5.5)	1.1	(0.21)	1.6	(1.08)
Basque Country•	512	(5.5)	494	(7.5)	508	(5.2)	508	(6.3)	-2.3	(3.1)	0.9	(0.09)	0.1	(0.23)
Cantabria•	496	(8.5)	488	(9.3)	488	(8.4)	493	(10.9)	0.8	(7.2)	0.9	(0.19)	0.0	(0.41)
Castile and Leon•	501	(12.1)	517	(9.5)	517	(8.7)	501	(8.4)	-1.6	(6.4)	1.3	(0.24)	0.0	(0.49)
Catalonia•	472	(14.4)	493	(15.7)	506	(9.0)	502	(13.2)	9.7	(7.0)	1.6	(0.34)	1.2	(1.67)
Extremadura•	476	(11.6)	461	(10.9)	459	(11.5)	451	(9.6)	-6.0	(6.1)	0.8	(0.15)	0.5	(0.76)
Galicia•	491	(10.6)	491	(11.5)	493	(9.0)	481	(10.3)	-7.5	(7.1)	1.0	(0.20)	0.5	(0.92)
La Rioja•	503	(6.1)	490	(6.8)	512	(4.8)	509	(5.1)	**5.6**	(2.6)	0.9	(0.11)	0.3	(0.28)
Madrid•	507	(8.6)	490	(10.8)	504	(14.2)	515	(15.1)	5.3	(7.8)	0.9	(0.14)	0.3	(0.78)
Murcia•	454	(8.4)	450	(10.6)	468	(15.1)	474	(11.1)	6.1	(6.2)	1.1	(0.19)	0.4	(0.75)
Navarre•	512	(5.3)	516	(8.9)	522	(8.3)	516	(6.0)	4.3	(3.5)	1.1	(0.12)	0.1	(0.23)
United Kingdom														
England	**495**	(8.3)	500	(7.1)	489	(7.8)	**504**	(13.8)	2.8	(6.7)	1.0	(0.17)	0.1	(0.57)
Northern Ireland	**471**	(9.0)	491	(13.9)	485	(13.2)	**488**	(13.7)	8.0	(6.5)	1.2	(0.19)	0.7	(1.23)
Scotland•	**500**	(6.2)	501	(6.0)	487	(8.5)	**503**	(6.9)	-0.7	(3.3)	0.9	(0.13)	0.0	(0.17)
Wales	464	(5.5)	467	(7.3)	483	(5.9)	462	(5.7)	0.1	(2.8)	1.1	(0.13)	0.0	(0.11)
United States														
Connecticut•	480	(9.7)	491	(13.9)	521	(15.2)	531	(10.5)	**20.9**	(5.5)	**1.6**	(0.28)	5.5	(3.00)
Florida•	476	(15.9)	474	(15.4)	457	(15.1)	471	(15.0)	-1.0	(6.8)	0.8	(0.19)	0.0	(0.47)
Massachusetts•	505	(12.3)	496	(18.2)	531	(18.9)	522	(15.8)	7.5	(6.5)	1.0	(0.23)	0.9	(1.47)
Partners														
Argentina														
Ciudad Autónoma de Buenos Aires•	341	(24.0)	411	(12.9)	455	(12.4)	463	(11.1)	**35.9**	(6.5)	**3.9**	(0.98)	29.4	(9.73)
Brazil														
Acre	360	(11.8)	358	(10.8)	349	(12.2)	368	(19.0)	3.3	(9.8)	0.9	(0.25)	0.1	(0.91)
Alagoas	328	(18.6)	333	(20.7)	323	(17.0)	387	(22.2)	**19.7**	(7.5)	1.1	(0.35)	8.7	(4.97)
Amapá	**341**	(10.0)	373	(19.9)	340	(20.9)	**387**	(17.1)	17.2	(12.7)	1.5	(0.50)	5.9	(6.46)
Amazonas	351	(9.7)	357	(10.7)	350	(14.5)	365	(18.5)	15.8	(11.6)	1.1	(0.32)	4.9	(7.10)
Bahia	345	(16.8)	353	(23.0)	c	c	c	c	**28.8**	(11.6)	1.6	(0.73)	13.8	(7.65)
Ceará	353	(12.8)	388	(23.4)	386	(22.1)	386	(21.3)	18.8	(10.0)	1.6	(0.55)	5.9	(6.30)
Espírito Santo	**383**	(12.5)	409	(20.3)	394	(16.9)	471	(19.4)	**31.8**	(14.7)	1.6	(0.51)	10.9	(9.89)
Federal District	388	(26.0)	383	(19.6)	389	(24.9)	c	c	20.2	(12.7)	1.5	(0.78)	9.5	(9.15)
Goiás	**366**	(15.5)	365	(9.5)	361	(14.9)	**424**	(16.9)	**25.2**	(7.6)	1.2	(0.53)	15.4	(10.25)
Maranhão	337	(17.9)	334	(32.1)	341	(37.3)	361	(36.8)	5.7	(18.4)	1.1	(0.49)	0.3	(2.63)
Mato Grosso	342	(14.4)	366	(8.9)	368	(12.7)	405	(30.6)	**33.3**	(10.3)	1.7	(0.57)	20.2	(13.76)
Mato Grosso do Sul	405	(11.9)	416	(21.5)	385	(17.2)	427	(17.7)	13.9	(10.7)	0.9	(0.32)	3.3	(6.14)
Minas Gerais	**388**	(8.8)	394	(6.0)	396	(19.9)	**435**	(19.9)	**18.6**	(7.4)	1.3	(0.29)	6.8	(5.39)
Pará	**333**	(10.6)	341	(9.9)	358	(15.1)	**407**	(8.8)	**20.3**	(4.5)	1.4	(0.46)	17.2	(3.57)
Paraíba	345	(26.3)	393	(15.4)	395	(22.5)	c	c	**38.9**	(6.8)	**3.0**	(0.96)	27.1	(8.01)
Paraná	406	(9.7)	384	(9.7)	382	(16.7)	442	(43.9)	18.4	(21.2)	**0.6**	(0.14)	3.2	(6.48)
Pernambuco	361	(11.0)	370	(14.0)	362	(15.1)	361	(18.5)	5.7	(11.1)	0.9	(0.29)	0.5	(1.65)
Piauí	361	(11.3)	370	(12.1)	394	(49.8)	416	(26.9)	24.5	(7.0)	1.2	(0.48)	12.0	(9.57)
Rio de Janeiro	**364**	(15.8)	370	(7.9)	394	(34.5)	**419**	(16.6)	29.2	(9.9)	1.7	(0.56)	9.6	(5.98)
Rio Grande do Norte	**354**	(7.8)	348	(14.5)	360	(13.6)	**460**	(36.6)	**31.4**	(8.0)	1.1	(0.31)	27.3	(12.56)
Rio Grande do Sul	372	(17.8)	430	(20.6)	409	(12.9)	417	(14.2)	12.9	(5.1)	**2.2**	(0.57)	6.9	(6.34)
Rondônia	380	(6.9)	390	(19.2)	376	(9.3)	383	(10.7)	2.4	(8.9)	1.1	(0.29)	0.1	(1.05)
Roraima	344	(9.5)	340	(10.8)	372	(18.0)	392	(30.2)	**21.7**	(8.0)	1.4	(0.42)	9.7	(7.47)
Santa Catarina	411	(12.3)	422	(24.0)	380	(15.9)	449	(28.0)	**20.0**	(8.4)	1.0	(0.28)	5.3	(5.25)
São Paulo	**388**	(7.2)	386	(7.7)	402	(10.4)	**438**	(13.8)	18.4	(6.4)	1.1	(0.20)	5.8	(4.03)
Sergipe	407	(33.0)	370	(15.7)	388	(19.9)	371	(13.0)	-18.2	(13.5)	0.6	(0.34)	3.6	(5.50)
Tocantins	373	(11.3)	333	(8.3)	355	(20.5)	401	(20.2)	**31.8**	(14.9)	0.7	(0.23)	5.4	(5.12)
Colombia														
Bogota	383	(6.5)	387	(7.3)	401	(9.7)	400	(10.3)	3.6	(4.5)	1.4	(0.21)	0.3	(0.83)
Cali	383	(14.1)	362	(9.9)	375	(15.1)	398	(15.5)	3.5	(4.3)	0.7	(0.24)	0.6	(1.65)
Manizales	**375**	(5.7)	382	(9.3)	405	(15.4)	**451**	(15.4)	**23.1**	(4.9)	**1.8**	(0.35)	13.9	(4.44)
Medellin	373	(8.7)	373	(13.2)	390	(15.3)	437	(19.2)	**19.7**	(5.1)	1.2	(0.31)	11.5	(4.98)
Russian Federation														
Perm Territory region•	472	(11.6)	479	(13.2)	482	(12.9)	506	(20.1)	9.3	(7.2)	1.2	(0.26)	1.1	(1.52)
United Arab Emirates														
Abu Dhabi•	404	(7.9)	415	(9.9)	429	(10.1)	441	(11.3)	**11.3**	(3.9)	1.3	(0.21)	2.8	(1.82)
Ajman	404	(22.0)	389	(20.4)	411	(15.7)	410	(8.3)	-0.1	(4.4)	1.0	(0.30)	0.0	(0.43)
Dubai•	**422**	(2.4)	474	(2.8)	467	(3.0)	**496**	(3.0)	**24.1**	(1.2)	**2.1**	(0.13)	9.0	(0.86)
Fujairah	380	(6.5)	422	(16.5)	411	(20.6)	431	(25.8)	**23.1**	(10.9)	1.8	(0.48)	6.1	(6.35)
Ras Al Khaimah	397	(22.2)	399	(19.3)	431	(12.3)	435	(10.2)	**12.6**	(5.2)	1.6	(0.71)	3.9	(3.31)
Sharjah	416	(15.2)	439	(17.2)	450	(18.4)	451	(24.2)	12.8	(9.2)	1.4	(0.35)	3.0	(3.97)
Umm Al Quwain	389	(9.8)	c	c	379	(6.1)	c	c	2.9	(3.3)	1.0	(0.26)	0.2	(0.49)

• PISA adjudicated region.
Notes: Values that are statistically significant are indicated in bold (see Annex A3).
See Table IV.3.16 for national data.
StatLink ᴍ𝖘ᴸ http://dx.doi.org/10.1787/888932957536

[Part 1/4]
Students' learning time in school, by region
Table B2.IV.10   *Results based on students' self-reports*

	Total class periods per week				Regular mathematics lessons				Regular language-of-instruction lessons			
	Number of all class periods in a normal full week of school (class periods)		Variability in total class periods		Time per week spent learning (minutes)		Variability in learning time		Time per week spent learning (minutes)		Variability in learning time	
	Mean	S.E.	Standard deviation	S.E.	Mean	S.E.	Standard deviation	S.E.	Mean	S.E.	Standard deviation	S.E.
Australia												
Australian Capital Territory	28.1	(0.4)	7.7	(0.6)	219.1	(2.4)	51.5	(2.9)	217.3	(2.6)	48.5	(3.1)
New South Wales	28.6	(0.3)	8.0	(0.3)	233.8	(1.7)	58.4	(1.8)	231.0	(1.6)	56.8	(1.6)
Northern Territory	26.3	(0.8)	7.5	(0.8)	251.1	(4.1)	48.9	(6.1)	252.2	(4.0)	52.5	(5.8)
Queensland	24.8	(0.5)	8.9	(0.4)	227.3	(3.0)	61.3	(4.0)	222.0	(2.7)	50.7	(4.4)
South Australia	30.4	(0.6)	8.0	(0.5)	233.2	(3.5)	63.0	(4.5)	230.9	(3.5)	59.3	(5.0)
Tasmania	26.1	(0.4)	8.7	(0.5)	245.0	(3.5)	79.7	(4.3)	237.9	(2.8)	78.5	(3.8)
Victoria	28.2	(0.5)	8.1	(0.4)	241.9	(2.5)	59.0	(3.0)	240.7	(2.6)	58.7	(3.0)
Western Australia	27.4	(0.4)	7.7	(0.5)	248.9	(2.8)	58.2	(3.6)	245.0	(2.3)	46.5	(3.2)
Belgium												
Flemish community*	32.9	(0.1)	3.5	(0.2)	206.1	(2.1)	66.8	(2.4)	199.2	(1.6)	53.7	(4.3)
French community	31.4	(0.2)	6.3	(0.3)	230.7	(2.2)	73.0	(3.9)	241.2	(2.1)	63.0	(4.0)
German-speaking community	33.3	(0.2)	4.7	(0.4)	216.6	(2.9)	64.1	(2.0)	232.6	(2.5)	59.0	(4.1)
Canada												
Alberta	22.5	(0.5)	7.3	(0.5)	364.3	(7.9)	146.1	(6.3)	360.0	(8.1)	150.7	(7.4)
British Columbia	20.5	(0.3)	5.9	(0.3)	294.5	(11.3)	131.3	(3.7)	292.9	(10.6)	131.7	(3.7)
Manitoba	23.4	(0.5)	8.6	(0.5)	293.5	(5.2)	127.1	(4.3)	295.6	(5.5)	126.2	(5.3)
New Brunswick	25.2	(0.2)	4.4	(0.4)	292.7	(2.7)	57.2	(5.1)	291.1	(2.6)	58.9	(5.9)
Newfoundland and Labrador	26.4	(0.2)	4.6	(0.3)	256.6	(5.0)	112.6	(11.3)	229.4	(3.2)	60.0	(4.4)
Nova Scotia	23.9	(0.4)	5.7	(0.5)	321.3	(6.2)	89.1	(5.7)	293.2	(7.4)	112.4	(4.3)
Ontario	19.7	(0.2)	5.7	(0.2)	325.4	(5.0)	122.9	(2.7)	324.6	(4.9)	127.3	(3.3)
Prince Edward Island	20.8	(0.2)	5.7	(0.3)	338.1	(4.8)	121.0	(4.2)	347.8	(3.5)	106.6	(4.4)
Quebec	22.1	(0.2)	5.4	(0.3)	292.9	(3.7)	102.7	(3.1)	311.8	(4.5)	115.8	(3.8)
Saskatchewan	25.2	(0.3)	6.0	(0.3)	277.4	(2.8)	85.9	(6.3)	280.5	(2.3)	62.4	(4.0)
Italy												
Abruzzo	29.9	(0.2)	3.3	(0.1)	237.6	(5.6)	63.6	(2.7)	284.8	(4.1)	79.0	(3.8)
Basilicata	29.9	(0.2)	2.8	(0.1)	243.3	(4.0)	60.5	(3.2)	281.4	(3.2)	71.8	(1.7)
Bolzano	35.5	(0.1)	2.3	(0.3)	188.1	(2.2)	60.1	(2.0)	217.0	(1.9)	58.8	(2.5)
Calabria	30.2	(0.3)	3.3	(0.1)	237.4	(4.4)	55.1	(2.4)	295.9	(4.0)	78.9	(2.7)
Campania	29.6	(0.1)	3.1	(0.1)	243.2	(7.0)	64.3	(3.8)	302.4	(5.0)	85.9	(2.6)
Emilia Romagna	30.5	(0.2)	2.8	(0.1)	225.1	(4.7)	54.0	(2.6)	271.0	(4.1)	76.4	(4.6)
Friuli Venezia Giulia	31.0	(0.2)	3.3	(0.1)	227.9	(3.7)	56.7	(2.1)	267.3	(5.2)	75.9	(3.5)
Lazio	29.8	(0.3)	3.1	(0.1)	239.2	(5.4)	56.6	(3.2)	289.4	(4.8)	83.7	(3.2)
Liguria	30.1	(0.3)	3.2	(0.2)	224.4	(6.7)	60.9	(2.9)	262.0	(3.8)	69.0	(3.4)
Lombardia	30.0	(0.1)	2.7	(0.1)	224.9	(5.4)	55.8	(3.1)	259.0	(3.9)	66.2	(2.9)
Marche	31.2	(0.3)	3.4	(0.2)	224.8	(4.7)	58.5	(2.2)	276.9	(4.9)	72.7	(2.6)
Molise	29.9	(0.1)	2.9	(0.1)	239.7	(2.1)	56.7	(2.3)	282.0	(3.0)	73.8	(2.5)
Piemonte	30.3	(0.2)	2.9	(0.1)	231.3	(5.0)	61.1	(4.9)	273.4	(4.2)	78.3	(4.1)
Puglia	29.6	(0.1)	2.9	(0.1)	243.8	(5.2)	62.8	(2.5)	286.1	(3.6)	78.6	(2.7)
Sardegna	29.8	(0.2)	3.2	(0.1)	241.6	(5.8)	67.0	(3.9)	276.6	(4.3)	78.1	(3.9)
Sicilia	30.0	(0.2)	3.1	(0.1)	234.4	(5.3)	61.2	(2.2)	295.8	(5.3)	92.2	(3.3)
Toscana	30.7	(0.3)	3.2	(0.2)	235.5	(4.5)	56.7	(2.1)	274.6	(6.0)	79.7	(3.9)
Trento	33.2	(0.3)	2.6	(0.2)	205.1	(2.3)	50.4	(1.4)	252.8	(5.2)	74.4	(3.9)
Umbria	30.0	(0.2)	3.3	(0.1)	233.6	(3.8)	56.7	(2.9)	275.8	(4.2)	78.1	(3.6)
Valle d'Aosta	34.5	(0.1)	2.9	(0.1)	197.6	(1.8)	48.5	(3.1)	227.2	(2.5)	59.4	(3.2)
Veneto	30.2	(0.2)	2.8	(0.1)	218.0	(5.4)	52.3	(2.0)	253.0	(3.9)	71.5	(4.2)
Mexico												
Aguascalientes	31.7	(0.5)	9.5	(0.5)	245.1	(4.8)	101.3	(8.9)	219.2	(5.1)	90.2	(6.0)
Baja California	31.5	(1.5)	10.0	(1.1)	260.3	(5.9)	108.6	(18.4)	240.8	(4.8)	98.7	(9.2)
Baja California Sur	30.3	(0.7)	10.3	(0.7)	238.9	(3.5)	103.5	(8.2)	233.3	(9.4)	167.9	(38.6)
Campeche	28.2	(0.8)	11.7	(0.6)	264.5	(7.3)	115.6	(8.7)	237.2	(7.0)	114.4	(9.6)
Chiapas	27.8	(1.0)	13.2	(0.6)	238.1	(3.5)	95.3	(4.7)	211.6	(6.0)	88.5	(5.2)
Chihuahua	32.0	(0.6)	10.4	(1.5)	248.2	(4.9)	90.3	(8.9)	223.9	(5.0)	95.0	(10.9)
Coahuila	31.1	(1.5)	12.0	(0.7)	250.3	(9.1)	124.1	(15.5)	229.9	(9.8)	112.6	(10.0)
Colima	29.7	(0.7)	12.9	(0.7)	262.2	(5.9)	105.7	(6.6)	226.4	(3.6)	93.2	(5.0)
Distrito Federal	26.6	(1.4)	12.7	(0.8)	247.9	(9.8)	110.0	(11.2)	236.6	(9.1)	128.6	(19.1)
Durango	31.7	(0.6)	10.7	(1.0)	250.5	(4.6)	98.8	(11.7)	236.8	(7.3)	123.0	(19.2)
Guanajuato	27.3	(0.8)	11.6	(0.6)	232.1	(4.9)	95.6	(7.3)	222.5	(5.5)	105.0	(7.4)
Guerrero	27.8	(1.0)	14.5	(2.1)	250.6	(6.4)	134.2	(9.2)	235.6	(7.6)	157.3	(22.9)
Hidalgo	26.4	(1.0)	10.9	(0.6)	254.2	(8.7)	110.4	(8.6)	227.0	(7.1)	119.6	(12.6)
Jalisco	28.2	(0.7)	11.3	(0.5)	245.0	(5.0)	99.0	(6.4)	233.9	(5.2)	127.4	(22.9)
Mexico	30.1	(0.6)	11.7	(0.4)	275.9	(6.1)	132.0	(10.6)	266.9	(8.0)	157.6	(25.6)
Morelos	29.8	(0.9)	12.1	(0.9)	262.1	(7.1)	129.1	(13.7)	238.0	(5.5)	113.4	(9.2)
Nayarit	29.1	(0.6)	10.1	(0.4)	252.5	(5.8)	119.5	(9.6)	227.2	(7.2)	140.6	(14.3)
Nuevo León	33.6	(0.8)	10.0	(0.6)	244.5	(7.3)	127.4	(14.0)	212.7	(6.2)	104.7	(15.7)
Puebla	28.7	(0.5)	9.6	(0.5)	250.2	(7.4)	109.9	(18.3)	213.3	(6.0)	100.3	(13.2)
Querétaro	32.0	(0.8)	10.7	(1.2)	262.7	(6.4)	98.6	(11.1)	243.8	(5.9)	86.2	(8.9)
Quintana Roo	30.4	(0.8)	14.5	(2.0)	249.5	(3.7)	96.4	(7.0)	233.2	(3.9)	107.8	(11.3)
San Luis Potosí	30.7	(1.0)	10.3	(0.6)	247.3	(4.0)	84.1	(6.8)	223.6	(5.1)	87.3	(6.1)
Sinaloa	29.7	(0.7)	8.8	(0.4)	235.4	(4.5)	97.3	(12.0)	210.6	(5.9)	106.7	(19.0)
Tabasco	26.6	(0.9)	12.8	(0.9)	273.1	(6.0)	161.1	(14.9)	237.6	(9.1)	156.0	(22.3)
Tamaulipas	29.7	(0.8)	10.8	(0.4)	241.9	(5.4)	94.8	(8.6)	227.0	(6.9)	115.2	(16.3)
Tlaxcala	27.5	(1.0)	10.8	(0.4)	275.9	(7.2)	165.6	(22.9)	250.6	(7.0)	167.5	(21.2)
Veracruz	29.5	(0.7)	11.2	(1.2)	255.9	(9.5)	127.6	(11.7)	225.9	(6.4)	101.3	(10.9)
Yucatán	30.1	(0.7)	10.6	(1.1)	256.4	(4.8)	118.1	(13.5)	225.2	(6.0)	94.5	(8.0)
Zacatecas	30.0	(0.7)	10.4	(0.8)	241.6	(6.2)	103.8	(14.0)	217.6	(5.2)	101.8	(12.4)

* PISA adjudicated region.
Note: See Table IV.3.21 for national data.
StatLink ᴍⁱˢᴾ http://dx.doi.org/10.1787/888932957536

[Part 2/4]
Students' learning time in school, by region
Table B2.IV.10   *Results based on students' self-reports*

	Total class periods per week				Regular mathematics lessons				Regular language-of-instruction lessons			
	Number of all class periods in a normal full week of school (class periods)		Variability in total class periods		Time per week spent learning (minutes)		Variability in learning time		Time per week spent learning (minutes)		Variability in learning time	
	Mean	S.E.	Standard deviation	S.E.	Mean	S.E.	Standard deviation	S.E.	Mean	S.E.	Standard deviation	S.E.
Portugal												
Alentejo	24.8	(1.1)	9.6	(0.4)	299.9	(8.7)	118.0	(7.9)	250.7	(11.1)	104.7	(7.7)
Spain												
Andalusia•	30.2	(0.1)	0.9	(0.1)	237.0	(2.2)	52.4	(6.4)	215.2	(3.5)	67.8	(5.9)
Aragon•	30.3	(0.1)	1.0	(0.1)	208.4	(2.1)	40.6	(4.8)	213.5	(2.1)	38.6	(5.2)
Asturias•	30.4	(0.1)	1.1	(0.1)	188.3	(2.1)	41.8	(2.6)	220.9	(1.1)	31.3	(2.0)
Balearic Islands•	32.3	(0.1)	1.1	(0.0)	206.8	(1.2)	28.7	(0.9)	180.1	(1.5)	36.0	(3.8)
Basque Country•	30.8	(0.1)	1.5	(0.1)	212.5	(1.3)	34.3	(1.0)	198.4	(1.4)	36.1	(0.9)
Cantabria•	30.3	(0.1)	1.0	(0.1)	209.4	(1.8)	45.2	(5.4)	217.4	(1.7)	38.7	(2.7)
Castile and Leon•	30.3	(0.1)	1.2	(0.2)	211.7	(1.5)	31.0	(2.6)	215.8	(1.4)	31.6	(1.7)
Catalonia•	31.3	(0.1)	1.8	(0.1)	182.7	(2.4)	27.8	(2.6)	180.7	(2.0)	28.0	(3.2)
Extremadura•	30.2	(0.1)	0.9	(0.1)	218.8	(1.7)	38.2	(2.2)	219.0	(1.9)	41.9	(4.2)
Galicia•	31.8	(0.1)	1.2	(0.1)	174.7	(1.9)	38.9	(3.6)	159.4	(1.5)	35.2	(4.2)
La Rioja•	30.3	(0.0)	1.0	(0.1)	216.6	(1.1)	37.2	(2.5)	215.6	(1.5)	39.4	(3.0)
Madrid•	31.2	(0.2)	1.8	(0.2)	213.7	(4.2)	60.4	(6.7)	227.1	(3.1)	49.4	(6.3)
Murcia•	30.4	(0.1)	1.1	(0.1)	214.1	(1.2)	44.3	(6.0)	227.3	(1.4)	42.8	(6.2)
Navarre•	30.5	(0.1)	1.3	(0.1)	211.7	(1.4)	31.0	(1.4)	216.1	(1.8)	34.2	(3.3)
United Kingdom												
England	27.2	(0.4)	6.3	(0.4)	229.8	(2.6)	87.0	(5.5)	231.9	(3.0)	84.8	(4.7)
Northern Ireland	40.5	(0.9)	10.8	(0.3)	261.6	(7.2)	164.4	(14.3)	261.2	(6.5)	155.9	(11.5)
Scotland•	30.8	(0.2)	5.2	(0.3)	227.1	(3.2)	68.6	(8.5)	229.7	(3.4)	67.1	(8.9)
Wales	26.3	(0.2)	4.5	(0.3)	216.8	(2.4)	72.0	(4.3)	213.9	(2.4)	70.0	(3.1)
United States												
Connecticut•	28.9	(1.0)	11.4	(0.4)	233.2	(6.2)	103.1	(11.7)	231.8	(5.3)	89.3	(8.3)
Florida•	25.7	(1.0)	13.9	(0.6)	251.5	(7.7)	126.7	(7.4)	250.9	(6.9)	161.9	(20.7)
Massachusetts•	27.4	(0.8)	10.9	(0.8)	292.7	(15.5)	164.1	(22.0)	287.2	(14.3)	163.9	(21.3)
Argentina												
Ciudad Autónoma de Buenos Aires•	23.6	(1.0)	10.3	(0.5)	327.0	(14.4)	183.6	(8.8)	300.4	(13.7)	175.2	(9.3)
Brazil												
Acre	20.3	(0.5)	8.8	(0.5)	222.6	(10.2)	133.0	(16.0)	211.9	(5.6)	113.7	(12.4)
Alagoas	21.2	(0.8)	9.4	(0.5)	238.1	(8.9)	117.2	(8.5)	225.8	(10.9)	128.4	(14.2)
Amapá	22.7	(1.3)	10.9	(0.7)	209.7	(8.0)	117.0	(10.6)	227.5	(9.3)	130.0	(9.7)
Amazonas	21.6	(0.7)	9.3	(0.6)	199.7	(6.9)	85.3	(8.1)	203.3	(4.9)	82.5	(6.4)
Bahia	23.8	(1.1)	9.1	(0.9)	184.3	(4.5)	80.8	(4.5)	177.3	(8.8)	79.6	(7.7)
Ceará	22.8	(1.4)	10.7	(1.3)	239.2	(10.4)	130.0	(7.8)	224.7	(9.7)	124.3	(6.1)
Espírito Santo	24.8	(0.5)	7.4	(0.5)	208.7	(5.8)	50.7	(3.1)	203.4	(5.7)	53.6	(3.7)
Federal District	27.9	(0.7)	9.7	(0.5)	207.5	(7.6)	92.2	(5.3)	210.3	(14.2)	112.3	(14.4)
Goiás	25.3	(0.7)	10.0	(0.5)	199.3	(5.0)	66.8	(3.6)	194.6	(6.1)	79.4	(6.6)
Maranhão	24.3	(1.5)	11.3	(0.5)	196.3	(8.2)	94.4	(12.0)	202.7	(12.1)	88.8	(9.6)
Mato Grosso	19.9	(1.1)	8.2	(0.5)	216.8	(9.9)	136.3	(17.4)	223.8	(8.1)	131.3	(12.0)
Mato Grosso do Sul	23.7	(0.6)	7.8	(0.4)	179.6	(5.5)	75.0	(5.2)	180.4	(7.0)	86.7	(7.8)
Minas Gerais	24.4	(0.6)	8.3	(0.7)	210.3	(4.9)	56.9	(2.8)	202.2	(6.8)	59.6	(3.5)
Pará	23.2	(0.8)	10.5	(0.4)	225.7	(6.6)	122.6	(12.2)	214.2	(13.1)	111.6	(7.9)
Paraíba	28.3	(0.8)	8.3	(0.8)	211.5	(5.1)	64.5	(5.0)	206.5	(2.6)	72.7	(4.3)
Paraná	24.3	(1.0)	8.6	(0.7)	188.4	(6.6)	70.0	(5.6)	179.7	(5.3)	73.9	(3.5)
Pernambuco	26.2	(1.3)	10.0	(1.2)	244.1	(11.1)	118.7	(9.5)	243.0	(10.1)	116.9	(12.7)
Piauí	27.7	(0.9)	11.9	(0.5)	219.4	(8.1)	95.9	(6.5)	202.9	(7.3)	84.9	(7.4)
Rio de Janeiro	25.8	(0.7)	9.3	(0.6)	245.1	(8.1)	142.0	(16.4)	228.8	(10.4)	129.2	(6.8)
Rio Grande do Norte	24.5	(1.0)	8.8	(0.7)	198.2	(10.2)	94.3	(8.1)	210.4	(9.0)	98.7	(7.0)
Rio Grande do Sul	24.9	(0.3)	6.1	(0.3)	193.9	(4.0)	71.8	(8.0)	180.1	(5.4)	68.3	(5.9)
Rondônia	19.8	(0.9)	6.5	(0.4)	176.7	(7.5)	85.3	(7.0)	188.5	(5.1)	72.9	(4.0)
Roraima	21.0	(0.8)	8.1	(0.5)	214.7	(8.1)	92.8	(11.2)	200.6	(2.9)	76.2	(4.0)
Santa Catarina	24.9	(0.6)	8.5	(0.7)	163.6	(7.6)	86.5	(23.9)	148.9	(4.3)	61.6	(10.0)
São Paulo	26.5	(0.4)	9.3	(0.4)	230.4	(3.7)	86.7	(5.4)	225.2	(4.3)	83.2	(4.1)
Sergipe	25.8	(1.2)	8.9	(0.5)	206.2	(6.7)	92.0	(9.3)	201.0	(12.1)	93.4	(14.6)
Tocantins	22.9	(0.6)	9.6	(0.7)	213.8	(3.4)	79.9	(2.9)	221.9	(5.5)	77.2	(4.2)
Colombia												
Bogota	21.1	(0.6)	9.7	(0.4)	283.3	(14.0)	162.4	(10.1)	235.0	(9.0)	120.8	(4.9)
Cali	22.4	(0.7)	10.8	(0.4)	265.8	(11.3)	153.8	(8.9)	234.4	(6.8)	129.4	(5.8)
Manizales	25.5	(0.5)	9.3	(0.3)	268.9	(8.1)	125.2	(9.7)	229.7	(5.4)	98.8	(5.8)
Medellin	25.3	(0.7)	9.9	(0.3)	255.7	(6.4)	127.0	(6.1)	232.6	(7.2)	109.0	(4.7)
Russian Federation												
Perm Territory region•	33.1	(0.2)	3.5	(0.1)	220.7	(4.8)	63.8	(3.7)	142.2	(4.1)	53.5	(3.4)
United Arab Emirates												
Abu Dhabi•	35.3	(0.5)	10.2	(0.3)	364.5	(7.2)	183.2	(7.9)	283.1	(4.7)	119.6	(4.7)
Ajman	32.1	(0.6)	8.9	(0.7)	268.4	(3.5)	75.7	(5.9)	285.6	(3.6)	76.7	(4.8)
Dubai•	32.4	(0.2)	9.6	(0.2)	271.2	(2.4)	100.4	(3.8)	248.3	(1.4)	83.5	(2.3)
Fujairah	31.3	(0.8)	10.3	(0.5)	278.8	(5.2)	100.2	(6.0)	273.6	(9.4)	109.3	(9.8)
Ras Al Khaimah	32.2	(0.6)	8.7	(0.5)	278.5	(6.2)	110.7	(13.0)	263.9	(7.2)	85.1	(7.3)
Sharjah	31.9	(0.7)	9.3	(0.7)	291.1	(8.3)	107.2	(17.7)	270.7	(6.9)	86.5	(7.3)
Umm Al Quwain	30.7	(0.8)	9.2	(0.7)	273.4	(4.5)	76.2	(5.2)	273.3	(5.6)	79.3	(6.1)

• PISA adjudicated region.
Note: See Table IV.3.21 for national data.
StatLink ᗧ᠍ᓯᓬ http://dx.doi.org/10.1787/888932957536

[Part 3/4]
Students' learning time in school, by region
Table B2.IV.10   *Results based on students' self-reports*

	Regular science lessons				Regular mathematics, language-of-instruction and science lessons			
	Time per week spent learning (minutes)		Variability in learning time		Time per week spent learning (minutes)		Variability in learning time	
	Mean	S.E.	Standard deviation	S.E.	Mean	S.E.	Standard deviation	S.E.
Australia								
Australian Capital Territory	217.9	(2.8)	56.3	(4.1)	653.0	(7.5)	144.2	(9.1)
New South Wales	223.6	(1.7)	59.6	(1.9)	686.0	(4.6)	157.8	(4.6)
Northern Territory	243.5	(6.4)	72.9	(6.0)	736.3	(12.0)	134.9	(18.9)
Queensland	231.5	(3.1)	71.2	(3.1)	677.4	(8.3)	153.8	(11.9)
South Australia	229.9	(3.8)	63.7	(5.0)	692.4	(11.1)	176.3	(14.1)
Tasmania	219.7	(3.7)	78.7	(4.9)	682.9	(8.4)	173.8	(10.6)
Victoria	219.6	(3.1)	64.2	(3.2)	698.2	(6.5)	150.6	(7.3)
Western Australia	252.4	(3.7)	73.6	(6.1)	747.0	(9.1)	155.9	(11.2)
Belgium								
Flemish community*	196.6	(4.2)	119.3	(4.2)	608.2	(5.4)	164.7	(6.4)
French community	187.9	(3.0)	97.0	(4.4)	661.7	(5.5)	174.6	(7.9)
German-speaking community	162.5	(4.8)	113.8	(15.2)	617.8	(6.8)	164.9	(10.3)
Canada								
Alberta	365.6	(8.7)	149.8	(5.8)	1091.1	(23.8)	392.5	(18.6)
British Columbia	295.1	(10.5)	136.4	(4.0)	882.3	(32.2)	369.3	(11.5)
Manitoba	287.5	(5.5)	134.5	(5.2)	877.0	(13.8)	324.9	(12.8)
New Brunswick	277.1	(3.4)	81.7	(4.3)	861.1	(8.1)	162.7	(14.6)
Newfoundland and Labrador	261.0	(6.7)	126.8	(14.6)	747.3	(11.5)	244.1	(23.5)
Nova Scotia	277.2	(15.2)	130.0	(4.3)	889.6	(27.9)	275.3	(10.4)
Ontario	321.2	(4.7)	131.2	(3.3)	974.6	(14.1)	329.3	(9.0)
Prince Edward Island	338.0	(4.4)	120.0	(4.7)	1024.7	(10.8)	286.9	(10.4)
Quebec	278.3	(4.1)	114.5	(2.9)	880.4	(10.5)	272.8	(7.9)
Saskatchewan	242.0	(4.0)	97.9	(3.0)	798.8	(6.8)	182.1	(7.4)
Italy								
Abruzzo	127.7	(1.7)	41.8	(3.2)	649.9	(7.0)	121.8	(6.3)
Basilicata	141.2	(3.3)	65.8	(6.9)	666.1	(5.3)	130.0	(4.2)
Bolzano	138.6	(2.9)	98.3	(2.6)	547.8	(5.4)	159.2	(3.7)
Calabria	130.8	(2.3)	44.8	(3.4)	662.6	(7.5)	115.0	(3.9)
Campania	135.4	(3.6)	55.4	(4.6)	682.1	(8.2)	129.1	(7.4)
Emilia Romagna	137.7	(4.6)	73.1	(7.3)	635.6	(7.0)	126.6	(6.8)
Friuli Venezia Giulia	144.4	(6.2)	75.9	(5.3)	642.2	(11.7)	137.1	(6.9)
Lazio	135.5	(4.0)	55.0	(6.1)	664.5	(8.6)	122.5	(4.2)
Liguria	128.8	(3.7)	58.8	(5.2)	615.3	(10.3)	121.4	(6.2)
Lombardia	137.7	(4.2)	67.2	(6.2)	624.5	(10.5)	123.1	(6.9)
Marche	135.9	(4.2)	68.3	(8.1)	637.1	(8.0)	135.3	(7.2)
Molise	132.2	(1.9)	44.3	(2.8)	653.8	(4.3)	111.2	(3.4)
Piemonte	139.0	(5.7)	69.0	(8.9)	644.6	(10.4)	144.0	(10.6)
Puglia	141.2	(4.8)	69.1	(10.5)	671.7	(9.0)	140.7	(9.9)
Sardegna	132.5	(3.1)	50.8	(3.9)	650.8	(7.4)	128.3	(10.2)
Sicilia	129.5	(3.0)	47.1	(3.9)	659.2	(6.5)	127.0	(4.5)
Toscana	134.4	(1.9)	50.0	(2.8)	644.0	(9.9)	123.7	(5.8)
Trento	144.9	(3.8)	69.8	(4.0)	601.3	(5.6)	120.8	(3.6)
Umbria	131.8	(2.8)	51.5	(6.0)	640.9	(6.8)	118.5	(5.6)
Valle d'Aosta	124.6	(2.2)	57.5	(2.6)	550.1	(4.8)	110.4	(7.0)
Veneto	131.9	(5.0)	62.5	(4.2)	606.1	(10.9)	126.8	(6.6)
Mexico								
Aguascalientes	238.1	(5.1)	131.0	(17.7)	701.7	(11.1)	265.9	(27.5)
Baja California	255.5	(9.7)	112.4	(12.9)	758.8	(11.1)	254.8	(27.4)
Baja California Sur	252.4	(5.2)	126.1	(7.5)	723.6	(13.9)	299.7	(33.3)
Campeche	270.1	(10.5)	159.2	(18.9)	770.5	(19.8)	297.1	(22.9)
Chiapas	234.6	(5.1)	128.0	(9.7)	685.9	(11.2)	245.2	(9.7)
Chihuahua	254.1	(7.9)	127.0	(23.4)	729.0	(16.2)	247.8	(26.0)
Coahuila	263.6	(11.9)	158.6	(17.6)	741.5	(27.2)	319.6	(24.5)
Colima	279.7	(9.0)	154.8	(12.3)	771.8	(17.6)	294.0	(20.5)
Distrito Federal	253.9	(7.5)	144.4	(21.4)	741.6	(23.5)	301.9	(24.6)
Durango	250.6	(6.4)	126.5	(15.9)	739.5	(11.0)	242.3	(14.8)
Guanajuato	228.5	(5.1)	131.4	(6.4)	685.3	(11.7)	261.5	(12.1)
Guerrero	263.6	(8.1)	172.2	(14.9)	747.4	(17.9)	357.5	(19.1)
Hidalgo	241.3	(7.8)	111.2	(6.3)	725.7	(20.5)	274.9	(18.9)
Jalisco	281.9	(9.9)	161.7	(19.1)	755.5	(13.0)	289.4	(16.2)
Mexico	240.0	(11.6)	163.7	(13.3)	771.2	(16.6)	330.7	(27.1)
Morelos	256.3	(7.2)	128.4	(9.7)	747.7	(16.9)	317.1	(28.8)
Nayarit	226.5	(9.2)	156.7	(15.9)	715.6	(19.6)	348.8	(31.6)
Nuevo León	250.5	(6.5)	152.6	(13.5)	707.1	(15.5)	279.1	(21.2)
Puebla	251.2	(6.3)	105.3	(6.7)	710.2	(16.0)	224.3	(14.4)
Querétaro	272.0	(6.8)	127.9	(11.7)	778.6	(15.6)	251.8	(23.8)
Quintana Roo	251.5	(5.4)	125.2	(21.3)	730.5	(11.6)	240.5	(13.7)
San Luis Potosí	251.6	(7.0)	110.5	(8.0)	728.1	(13.5)	236.8	(17.9)
Sinaloa	260.7	(7.2)	139.4	(16.1)	704.5	(14.4)	258.5	(27.0)
Tabasco	274.6	(11.9)	202.6	(29.6)	778.0	(24.3)	384.7	(21.8)
Tamaulipas	245.5	(8.3)	131.6	(13.7)	712.3	(17.0)	279.7	(25.1)
Tlaxcala	273.7	(9.5)	157.8	(13.0)	790.2	(17.3)	359.2	(17.1)
Veracruz	244.8	(8.7)	127.1	(10.2)	726.9	(20.4)	287.5	(17.6)
Yucatán	267.2	(7.0)	136.1	(12.9)	749.9	(13.3)	265.5	(11.6)
Zacatecas	246.4	(5.4)	124.1	(14.6)	709.7	(13.2)	251.0	(21.7)

* PISA adjudicated region.
Note: See Table IV.3.21 for national data.
StatLink ⧉ http://dx.doi.org/10.1787/888932957536

 WHAT MAKES SCHOOLS SUCCESSFUL? RESOURCES, POLICIES AND PRACTICES – VOLUME IV

[Part 4/4]
Students' learning time in school, by region
Table B2.IV.10   *Results based on students' self-reports*

| | | Regular science lessons | | | Regular mathematics, language-of-instruction and science lessons | | | |
| | Time per week spent learning (minutes) | | Variability in learning time | | Time per week spent learning (minutes) | | Variability in learning time | |
	Mean	S.E.	Standard deviation	S.E.	Mean	S.E.	Standard deviation	S.E.
Portugal								
Alentejo	248.3	(13.8)	207.9	(17.5)	813.4	(26.6)	333.8	(19.8)
Spain								
Andalusia•	206.6	(4.3)	109.2	(6.0)	663.3	(8.2)	175.8	(20.3)
Aragon•	168.9	(3.6)	87.0	(4.9)	590.0	(6.2)	131.7	(17.4)
Asturias•	180.9	(4.2)	84.1	(2.4)	590.7	(5.1)	111.8	(4.4)
Balearic Islands•	182.4	(3.5)	85.6	(3.1)	570.6	(5.3)	106.7	(3.3)
Basque Country•	193.7	(2.3)	81.8	(2.3)	605.4	(3.5)	105.4	(2.5)
Cantabria•	180.1	(3.3)	82.2	(3.4)	606.2	(5.4)	120.7	(6.1)
Castile and Leon•	180.4	(3.7)	93.7	(2.9)	609.8	(5.9)	118.3	(5.0)
Catalonia•	178.5	(4.0)	100.0	(3.5)	542.4	(6.5)	115.4	(5.5)
Extremadura•	185.2	(3.0)	85.0	(4.0)	624.1	(5.3)	133.1	(7.8)
Galicia•	160.0	(2.9)	78.6	(2.5)	492.7	(4.2)	106.4	(6.2)
La Rioja•	171.2	(3.4)	97.3	(2.9)	602.3	(4.7)	126.4	(5.4)
Madrid•	200.8	(3.2)	104.2	(4.2)	641.8	(8.5)	159.9	(15.0)
Murcia•	181.1	(4.7)	103.8	(4.4)	624.9	(5.9)	151.0	(17.6)
Navarre•	192.0	(3.3)	100.6	(3.2)	621.0	(4.5)	120.4	(3.9)
United Kingdom								
England	300.9	(4.3)	121.3	(6.3)	752.5	(7.6)	218.0	(11.2)
Northern Ireland	321.4	(6.2)	198.6	(8.6)	809.2	(13.1)	379.9	(20.6)
Scotland•	232.0	(4.5)	135.1	(5.9)	678.5	(7.3)	197.3	(16.6)
Wales	279.7	(3.5)	112.9	(4.9)	706.2	(7.0)	202.6	(10.5)
United States								
Connecticut•	255.1	(6.2)	144.2	(25.8)	716.2	(14.7)	248.5	(18.2)
Florida•	236.4	(5.0)	115.2	(8.1)	734.9	(16.9)	315.6	(16.3)
Massachusetts•	286.2	(11.2)	155.3	(12.8)	863.3	(35.3)	405.6	(48.1)
Argentina								
Ciudad Autónoma de Buenos Aires•	244.6	(10.8)	182.6	(20.5)	786.5	(28.5)	420.1	(23.1)
Brazil								
Acre	127.3	(4.9)	81.4	(8.2)	542.0	(13.2)	247.5	(25.3)
Alagoas	148.8	(6.9)	80.0	(8.1)	592.6	(17.5)	234.2	(24.4)
Amapá	142.0	(8.1)	86.6	(7.4)	561.6	(16.7)	260.1	(26.6)
Amazonas	144.1	(8.3)	96.5	(18.4)	543.2	(15.8)	187.6	(15.6)
Bahia	143.1	(5.7)	91.1	(7.5)	491.3	(18.8)	189.2	(22.4)
Ceará	166.4	(14.4)	135.4	(22.8)	621.6	(31.7)	291.1	(20.7)
Espírito Santo	179.7	(13.0)	122.3	(16.8)	590.9	(10.9)	149.8	(10.6)
Federal District	198.1	(17.2)	132.2	(14.2)	617.4	(30.5)	264.4	(18.4)
Goiás	155.5	(7.6)	100.1	(10.3)	544.4	(13.6)	177.6	(12.8)
Maranhão	149.6	(12.0)	87.8	(5.8)	540.4	(22.7)	210.4	(26.4)
Mato Grosso	150.7	(11.8)	102.8	(13.5)	576.9	(25.8)	284.7	(21.8)
Mato Grosso do Sul	160.8	(10.1)	107.0	(15.8)	519.2	(18.6)	204.1	(9.8)
Minas Gerais	169.9	(7.9)	95.7	(10.4)	582.4	(13.1)	162.9	(14.4)
Pará	154.3	(5.1)	100.3	(9.6)	597.2	(15.7)	276.1	(22.2)
Paraíba	176.3	(4.3)	103.0	(7.4)	595.9	(9.8)	185.0	(9.7)
Paraná	178.7	(13.8)	113.4	(22.2)	544.0	(21.4)	197.1	(20.2)
Pernambuco	158.7	(7.9)	109.5	(12.4)	643.7	(23.8)	280.6	(30.1)
Piauí	167.1	(5.6)	103.2	(8.5)	584.7	(17.7)	216.7	(14.2)
Rio de Janeiro	176.5	(8.1)	125.2	(7.9)	647.7	(19.2)	334.2	(30.9)
Rio Grande do Norte	171.0	(7.9)	118.7	(11.9)	586.1	(17.9)	256.4	(20.1)
Rio Grande do Sul	145.5	(5.6)	75.2	(6.7)	516.5	(10.4)	160.7	(15.3)
Rondônia	139.1	(4.4)	75.3	(5.3)	495.1	(16.2)	181.6	(11.8)
Roraima	143.5	(7.2)	76.9	(10.7)	552.2	(15.2)	188.8	(11.9)
Santa Catarina	126.5	(8.5)	76.5	(12.6)	435.8	(15.3)	154.7	(16.9)
São Paulo	161.7	(8.0)	108.3	(10.2)	616.3	(11.9)	213.0	(10.4)
Sergipe	152.4	(9.4)	91.1	(9.7)	557.9	(15.3)	211.8	(29.1)
Tocantins	141.5	(5.9)	91.2	(8.9)	575.6	(11.7)	203.1	(12.3)
Colombia								
Bogota	209.2	(8.5)	137.4	(7.8)	725.6	(28.5)	344.2	(18.0)
Cali	196.6	(9.3)	132.9	(8.2)	689.0	(25.5)	357.3	(24.0)
Manizales	208.1	(11.1)	119.3	(6.9)	712.8	(17.6)	267.5	(14.7)
Medellin	202.5	(7.8)	119.2	(5.7)	687.2	(16.8)	299.1	(17.1)
Russian Federation								
Perm Territory region•	258.5	(7.3)	133.5	(2.9)	618.7	(9.3)	167.8	(5.3)
United Arab Emirates								
Abu Dhabi•	308.8	(6.8)	213.0	(12.7)	956.1	(14.9)	376.9	(13.8)
Ajman	270.2	(13.9)	183.3	(37.9)	823.9	(15.3)	243.5	(29.5)
Dubai•	316.5	(5.0)	213.8	(13.2)	835.8	(6.2)	292.7	(11.5)
Fujairah	260.9	(11.8)	165.8	(8.0)	816.0	(21.6)	276.8	(17.3)
Ras Al Khaimah	271.3	(13.2)	177.8	(14.5)	815.2	(17.5)	276.9	(19.9)
Sharjah	324.2	(12.1)	219.8	(16.7)	879.0	(18.2)	278.5	(16.7)
Umm Al Quwain	252.1	(12.7)	158.2	(17.3)	809.8	(15.3)	215.9	(11.5)

• PISA adjudicated region.
Note: See Table IV.3.21 for national data.
StatLink ⟨⟨MSL⟩⟩ http://dx.doi.org/10.1787/888932957536

[Part 1/2]
Table B2.IV.11 Percentage of students attending after-school lessons (hours per week), by region
Results based on students' self-reports

		Mathematics						Language of instruction						Science						Other subjects					
		No attendance		Less than 4 hours a week		4 hours a week or more		No attendance		Less than 4 hours a week		4 hours a week or more		No attendance		Less than 4 hours a week		4 hours a week or more		No attendance		Less than 4 hours a week		4 hours a week or more	
		%	S.E.	%	S.E.	%	S.E.	%	S.E.	%	S.E.	%	S.E.	%	S.E.	%	S.E.	%	S.E.	%	S.E.	%	S.E.	%	S.E.
OECD	**Australia**																								
	Australian Capital Territory	75.8	(2.0)	20.8	(1.7)	3.4	(0.9)	83.2	(1.8)	14.2	(1.6)	2.7	(0.8)	86.5	(1.7)	11.4	(1.6)	2.0	(0.5)	74.8	(2.2)	19.1	(2.0)	6.0	(1.1)
	New South Wales	69.0	(1.5)	25.8	(1.4)	5.1	(0.5)	78.5	(1.1)	17.2	(1.1)	4.3	(0.5)	84.5	(1.0)	12.4	(0.9)	3.1	(0.4)	77.2	(1.1)	16.9	(1.0)	5.8	(0.5)
	Northern Territory	79.9	(3.3)	17.0	(3.2)	3.1	(1.3)	78.9	(2.5)	16.7	(2.4)	4.3	(1.6)	82.5	(3.7)	15.4	(4.0)	2.1	(1.0)	74.8	(2.7)	19.3	(3.0)	5.9	(2.4)
	Queensland	72.1	(1.2)	24.5	(1.2)	3.4	(0.4)	80.3	(1.0)	17.9	(1.0)	1.8	(0.3)	83.8	(0.9)	13.6	(0.9)	2.7	(0.4)	70.2	(1.1)	22.2	(1.1)	7.6	(0.7)
	South Australia	82.3	(1.5)	13.8	(1.3)	3.9	(0.6)	85.8	(1.3)	10.3	(1.1)	3.9	(0.7)	86.2	(1.2)	10.0	(1.0)	3.7	(0.6)	77.2	(1.4)	16.0	(1.2)	6.8	(0.9)
	Tasmania	77.7	(1.9)	16.5	(1.7)	5.8	(1.0)	81.5	(1.7)	14.1	(1.6)	4.4	(0.8)	84.4	(1.6)	11.8	(1.4)	3.8	(0.7)	69.5	(2.0)	21.8	(1.5)	8.7	(1.4)
	Victoria	74.8	(1.4)	21.7	(1.2)	3.6	(0.4)	80.9	(1.2)	16.3	(1.2)	2.9	(0.4)	85.9	(1.0)	12.0	(0.9)	2.1	(0.4)	74.3	(1.3)	19.7	(1.2)	5.9	(0.6)
	Western Australia	72.7	(1.4)	23.3	(1.4)	4.0	(0.6)	78.7	(1.3)	17.8	(1.2)	3.5	(0.7)	81.6	(1.2)	15.1	(1.1)	3.3	(0.6)	72.9	(1.8)	19.8	(1.6)	7.3	(0.9)
	Belgium																								
	Flemish community•	68.6	(1.0)	25.8	(0.9)	5.6	(0.4)	77.9	(0.9)	19.4	(0.8)	2.7	(0.3)	77.6	(1.0)	19.2	(0.9)	3.2	(0.4)	69.9	(1.0)	23.8	(0.9)	6.3	(0.5)
	French community	61.0	(1.1)	30.7	(1.1)	8.4	(0.8)	72.9	(0.8)	19.2	(0.9)	7.9	(0.6)	71.4	(1.1)	23.9	(1.2)	4.7	(0.5)	67.1	(1.1)	25.4	(1.1)	7.5	(0.7)
	German-speaking community	80.0	(1.7)	17.3	(1.5)	2.7	(0.8)	91.3	(1.3)	7.0	(1.2)	1.8	(0.6)	90.1	(1.4)	8.4	(1.2)	1.5	(0.6)	84.6	(1.8)	13.1	(1.7)	2.3	(0.8)
	Canada																								
	Alberta	74.7	(1.1)	20.5	(1.2)	4.8	(0.6)	78.3	(1.1)	17.9	(1.0)	3.7	(0.6)	76.2	(1.3)	18.8	(1.2)	5.0	(0.6)	70.6	(1.4)	22.6	(1.4)	6.7	(0.8)
	British Columbia	72.5	(1.5)	22.4	(1.5)	5.1	(0.6)	79.5	(1.3)	15.1	(1.2)	5.3	(0.7)	80.2	(1.2)	15.1	(1.1)	4.8	(0.7)	71.4	(1.5)	18.8	(1.1)	9.8	(0.9)
	Manitoba	76.5	(1.7)	17.6	(1.5)	5.9	(0.9)	81.8	(1.5)	13.3	(1.3)	5.0	(0.9)	81.6	(1.6)	13.3	(1.2)	5.1	(0.9)	71.3	(1.7)	19.2	(1.6)	9.5	(1.3)
	New Brunswick	76.8	(1.6)	18.7	(1.5)	4.5	(0.8)	82.2	(1.3)	14.1	(1.2)	3.6	(0.6)	81.8	(1.4)	15.1	(1.4)	3.2	(0.4)	73.5	(1.6)	20.1	(1.5)	6.4	(0.8)
	Newfoundland and Labrador	66.3	(2.5)	28.4	(2.4)	5.3	(1.0)	79.6	(1.3)	17.6	(1.3)	2.8	(0.6)	72.9	(1.6)	22.0	(1.6)	5.1	(0.8)	72.0	(1.7)	23.1	(1.8)	4.9	(0.9)
	Nova Scotia	73.7	(2.6)	22.7	(2.2)	3.6	(0.7)	83.2	(1.9)	12.8	(1.5)	4.0	(0.7)	82.2	(1.3)	12.9	(1.5)	4.8	(1.3)	75.3	(1.5)	15.4	(1.7)	9.3	(1.7)
	Ontario	72.1	(1.5)	22.3	(1.5)	5.6	(0.6)	80.3	(1.1)	14.8	(1.0)	4.8	(0.5)	80.6	(1.2)	15.4	(1.2)	4.0	(0.6)	70.6	(1.2)	19.6	(1.0)	9.7	(0.8)
	Prince Edward Island	71.2	(1.7)	24.6	(1.5)	4.3	(0.6)	77.2	(1.5)	18.6	(1.4)	4.2	(0.7)	74.1	(1.6)	21.4	(1.3)	4.5	(0.8)	69.7	(1.7)	23.3	(1.5)	7.0	(1.0)
	Quebec	71.5	(1.4)	23.0	(1.1)	5.5	(0.6)	81.3	(1.0)	15.3	(0.9)	3.4	(0.4)	81.5	(1.0)	15.1	(0.8)	3.4	(0.4)	76.2	(1.1)	19.4	(1.0)	4.3	(0.5)
	Saskatchewan	77.7	(1.5)	17.8	(1.4)	4.6	(0.7)	80.3	(1.4)	15.2	(1.5)	4.4	(0.7)	81.4	(1.2)	15.4	(1.3)	3.2	(0.5)	72.0	(1.2)	19.3	(1.4)	8.7	(0.8)
	Italy																								
	Abruzzo	50.7	(1.9)	37.4	(1.5)	11.9	(1.3)	60.9	(1.6)	26.8	(1.4)	12.3	(1.0)	64.2	(1.8)	30.8	(1.6)	5.0	(0.6)	52.1	(2.0)	35.8	(1.9)	12.0	(0.9)
	Basilicata	41.1	(1.8)	41.7	(1.6)	17.2	(1.3)	48.5	(1.5)	34.8	(1.3)	16.7	(1.0)	52.2	(1.5)	41.4	(1.4)	6.4	(0.8)	44.4	(1.7)	38.6	(1.4)	16.9	(1.1)
	Bolzano	70.6	(1.1)	26.7	(1.2)	2.7	(0.6)	84.5	(1.1)	12.6	(1.0)	2.9	(0.5)	88.0	(0.9)	10.7	(0.8)	1.4	(0.4)	67.4	(1.3)	28.3	(1.1)	4.2	(0.6)
	Calabria	41.5	(2.1)	41.8	(1.9)	16.8	(1.4)	46.8	(2.3)	33.2	(1.6)	20.0	(1.5)	47.2	(2.2)	43.5	(2.0)	9.2	(1.2)	40.6	(1.9)	39.8	(1.8)	19.7	(1.8)
	Campania	35.9	(1.4)	44.7	(1.1)	19.4	(1.2)	44.9	(1.8)	33.0	(1.5)	22.1	(2.0)	47.7	(1.6)	44.8	(1.5)	7.5	(1.0)	38.5	(1.2)	40.0	(2.2)	21.5	(2.2)
	Emilia Romagna	54.1	(1.8)	37.6	(1.4)	8.3	(1.1)	71.9	(1.4)	20.1	(1.5)	8.0	(1.1)	71.8	(1.4)	23.5	(1.3)	4.8	(0.6)	56.5	(1.5)	33.1	(1.5)	10.4	(0.9)
	Friuli Venezia Giulia	60.0	(2.2)	32.6	(2.1)	7.4	(1.1)	74.1	(1.7)	20.1	(1.5)	5.8	(0.8)	73.6	(1.6)	21.4	(1.7)	4.9	(0.9)	56.9	(1.8)	33.3	(1.5)	9.8	(1.1)
	Lazio	53.0	(1.5)	38.2	(1.5)	8.7	(1.1)	67.6	(1.8)	24.0	(1.5)	8.4	(1.3)	70.3	(1.8)	25.5	(1.5)	4.2	(1.0)	53.9	(1.9)	36.7	(1.7)	9.4	(1.3)
	Liguria	49.8	(1.4)	42.5	(1.5)	7.7	(1.0)	69.3	(1.5)	24.5	(1.7)	6.2	(1.1)	69.7	(1.5)	26.9	(1.3)	3.3	(0.6)	54.9	(2.3)	35.6	(2.1)	9.6	(1.0)
	Lombardia	54.2	(1.7)	38.8	(1.6)	7.0	(0.8)	70.3	(1.6)	23.2	(1.5)	6.5	(0.7)	71.0	(1.6)	24.5	(1.5)	4.5	(0.7)	56.3	(1.8)	34.5	(1.5)	9.2	(0.9)
	Marche	54.1	(2.1)	37.7	(1.8)	8.3	(0.9)	70.7	(2.4)	22.1	(2.0)	7.2	(1.1)	71.9	(2.0)	24.5	(2.0)	3.7	(0.7)	56.0	(2.4)	34.9	(1.9)	9.1	(0.9)
	Molise	47.0	(2.2)	39.9	(2.1)	13.1	(1.5)	58.2	(2.0)	27.9	(1.6)	14.0	(1.5)	61.9	(2.2)	32.1	(2.0)	5.9	(1.0)	51.9	(2.0)	35.9	(2.0)	12.1	(1.4)
	Piemonte	55.9	(1.9)	36.2	(1.5)	7.9	(1.1)	68.5	(2.0)	25.4	(1.8)	6.1	(0.7)	70.7	(2.0)	25.5	(1.8)	3.7	(0.8)	57.1	(1.8)	31.9	(1.2)	11.0	(1.0)
	Puglia	41.7	(2.2)	39.4	(1.9)	18.9	(1.4)	53.5	(2.0)	30.7	(1.6)	15.8	(1.5)	56.8	(1.6)	35.0	(1.7)	8.2	(0.9)	44.3	(1.8)	36.3	(1.3)	19.5	(1.5)
	Sardegna	55.2	(1.7)	36.4	(1.6)	8.5	(1.0)	62.7	(1.6)	28.3	(1.5)	9.0	(0.9)	65.1	(1.6)	29.8	(1.5)	5.0	(0.7)	52.0	(1.6)	35.8	(1.6)	12.2	(1.2)
	Sicilia	44.3	(1.8)	41.6	(1.4)	14.1	(1.2)	55.4	(1.8)	28.8	(1.7)	15.8	(1.1)	58.4	(1.7)	34.5	(1.6)	7.2	(1.0)	45.8	(1.7)	37.0	(1.4)	17.1	(1.1)
	Toscana	43.0	(1.8)	44.0	(1.9)	12.9	(1.1)	59.0	(1.6)	30.1	(1.7)	11.0	(1.1)	58.9	(2.1)	35.3	(2.1)	5.8	(0.8)	45.5	(1.5)	40.8	(1.8)	13.7	(1.1)
	Trento	60.5	(1.6)	33.5	(1.7)	6.0	(0.9)	71.0	(1.4)	24.3	(1.3)	4.7	(0.7)	69.8	(1.3)	27.3	(1.4)	2.8	(0.6)	57.6	(1.5)	32.8	(1.6)	9.6	(0.9)
	Umbria	52.5	(1.7)	38.9	(1.7)	8.6	(1.2)	70.4	(1.7)	21.7	(1.4)	7.9	(1.0)	71.2	(1.8)	25.1	(1.6)	3.7	(0.7)	57.0	(1.9)	32.9	(1.9)	10.1	(0.8)
	Valle d'Aosta	62.3	(2.0)	31.8	(2.0)	6.0	(0.9)	70.8	(1.9)	24.6	(2.1)	4.6	(1.0)	72.5	(1.8)	24.3	(1.7)	3.3	(0.7)	57.9	(2.1)	32.8	(2.1)	9.3	(1.2)
	Veneto	50.1	(1.9)	41.3	(2.1)	8.6	(1.2)	64.2	(2.0)	29.6	(1.7)	6.2	(1.1)	65.9	(1.9)	29.9	(1.9)	4.2	(0.6)	50.3	(2.2)	37.8	(2.0)	11.9	(1.2)
	Mexico																								
	Aguascalientes	60.8	(1.3)	25.4	(1.3)	13.8	(1.0)	64.6	(1.7)	24.0	(1.7)	11.4	(1.0)	64.3	(1.7)	25.0	(1.8)	10.6	(1.2)	61.1	(1.8)	27.0	(1.4)	12.0	(1.0)
	Baja California	60.5	(2.1)	23.7	(2.0)	15.8	(1.5)	64.6	(1.6)	22.3	(1.1)	13.1	(1.3)	64.7	(2.8)	21.5	(2.8)	13.8	(1.3)	65.5	(1.8)	21.0	(1.5)	13.4	(1.0)
	Baja California Sur	66.8	(2.0)	23.6	(1.8)	9.6	(1.0)	74.7	(1.8)	16.1	(1.8)	9.2	(1.2)	70.0	(1.9)	20.2	(1.7)	9.8	(1.1)	69.9	(1.7)	20.3	(1.5)	9.8	(1.0)
	Campeche	52.8	(1.6)	33.7	(1.6)	13.5	(0.9)	59.1	(2.5)	27.9	(2.0)	13.0	(1.1)	53.2	(2.2)	33.0	(2.3)	13.8	(1.1)	57.5	(1.5)	30.6	(1.4)	12.0	(1.3)
	Chiapas	48.5	(3.4)	38.3	(3.5)	13.2	(1.5)	56.4	(2.9)	32.1	(2.6)	11.4	(1.4)	53.4	(2.7)	34.9	(2.5)	11.6	(1.4)	52.5	(2.3)	34.3	(2.0)	13.3	(2.0)
	Chihuahua	59.8	(2.2)	26.7	(1.8)	13.5	(1.3)	64.2	(2.4)	23.7	(1.9)	12.1	(1.1)	61.3	(2.1)	26.6	(1.6)	12.1	(1.3)	59.8	(1.9)	29.8	(1.9)	10.4	(1.6)
	Coahuila	59.9	(2.3)	26.7	(1.9)	13.4	(1.3)	66.3	(2.7)	20.3	(1.9)	13.4	(2.1)	62.0	(1.6)	24.0	(2.0)	14.0	(1.9)	62.2	(2.6)	25.6	(2.0)	12.2	(1.4)
	Colima	61.4	(1.9)	27.6	(1.8)	11.1	(1.1)	68.9	(1.9)	21.7	(1.5)	9.4	(1.0)	68.7	(2.0)	22.2	(1.7)	9.0	(1.0)	65.0	(1.9)	25.2	(1.6)	9.8	(1.0)
	Distrito Federal	53.8	(2.6)	32.5	(1.8)	13.7	(1.7)	60.8	(2.6)	27.2	(1.6)	12.0	(2.0)	60.0	(3.1)	26.4	(1.9)	13.5	(1.9)	55.5	(2.8)	30.0	(3.2)	14.5	(1.6)
	Durango	56.1	(3.0)	28.0	(2.9)	16.0	(1.7)	61.5	(3.0)	26.4	(2.4)	12.2	(1.8)	58.8	(2.7)	28.2	(2.6)	13.0	(1.7)	60.1	(3.3)	27.7	(1.8)	12.2	(2.2)
	Guanajuato	55.2	(2.0)	34.2	(2.4)	10.6	(1.3)	64.9	(2.2)	26.5	(2.5)	8.6	(1.3)	60.6	(2.2)	31.3	(2.4)	8.1	(1.2)	60.0	(2.8)	31.6	(2.5)	8.4	(1.5)
	Guerrero	52.4	(2.5)	35.7	(2.5)	11.9	(1.7)	55.6	(2.5)	35.2	(2.0)	9.2	(1.6)	52.3	(2.7)	33.1	(2.6)	14.6	(1.8)	52.9	(2.4)	35.9	(2.0)	11.2	(1.3)
	Hidalgo	51.7	(2.5)	35.7	(2.4)	12.6	(1.3)	60.0	(2.1)	29.6	(1.8)	10.4	(1.3)	53.4	(2.2)	34.2	(2.0)	12.4	(1.6)	57.0	(2.5)	31.3	(2.2)	11.7	(1.7)
	Jalisco	61.2	(1.8)	28.6	(1.4)	10.3	(1.7)	63.5	(2.3)	25.7	(1.8)	10.8	(2.0)	63.8	(2.2)	23.8	(2.0)	12.4	(1.9)	61.7	(3.0)	27.5	(2.6)	10.8	(1.5)
	Mexico	54.7	(1.8)	31.9	(1.7)	13.5	(1.4)	62.4	(2.1)	25.3	(1.9)	12.3	(1.7)	62.7	(1.7)	27.8	(2.0)	9.6	(1.3)	58.4	(2.3)	24.9	(2.0)	16.7	(1.5)
	Morelos	63.2	(2.4)	23.3	(1.9)	13.5	(1.4)	66.4	(2.3)	21.9	(1.7)	11.6	(1.6)	66.3	(2.4)	20.1	(1.9)	13.5	(1.5)	61.4	(2.5)	25.6	(1.7)	13.1	(1.8)
	Nayarit	60.4	(2.8)	25.3	(1.9)	14.3	(1.5)	62.0	(2.3)	24.6	(2.3)	13.3	(1.4)	64.1	(2.8)	23.7	(2.0)	12.2	(1.5)	62.5	(1.9)	23.8	(1.9)	13.7	(1.6)
	Nuevo León	60.6	(2.7)	24.4	(1.8)	15.0	(1.8)	66.0	(2.8)	21.0	(1.7)	13.1	(1.8)	61.7	(2.6)	25.1	(1.8)	13.3	(2.2)	62.3	(2.7)	26.7	(2.3)	11.0	(1.4)
	Puebla	57.0	(3.1)	31.3	(2.7)	11.7	(1.4)	57.8	(2.5)	32.9	(2.1)	9.3	(1.1)	58.9	(2.2)	29.7	(2.0)	11.4	(1.4)	59.1	(2.6)	32.0	(2.3)	8.9	(1.0)
	Querétaro	63.7	(2.5)	25.8	(1.6)	10.5	(1.7)	71.4	(2.1)	20.4	(2.0)	8.1	(1.2)	68.0	(2.0)	22.2	(1.7)	9.8	(1.1)	65.4	(1.3)	24.6	(1.3)	10.0	(1.4)
	Quintana Roo	58.4	(2.2)	28.6	(1.3)	13.0	(1.7)	63.4	(2.1)	25.6	(2.0)	10.9	(1.3)	60.5	(2.4)	29.3	(1.8)	10.2	(1.1)	58.8	(2.2)	30.5	(1.5)	10.7	(1.3)
	San Luis Potosí	55.3	(2.5)	31.7	(2.0)	12.9	(1.4)	62.7	(3.1)	27.9	(2.8)	9.4	(1.6)	60.4	(2.8)	28.0	(2.6)	11.5	(1.5)	59.1	(2.9)	32.4	(2.6)	8.5	(1.5)
	Sinaloa	57.5	(2.1)	29.4	(2.1)	13.1	(1.5)	61.5	(2.2)	27.6	(1.9)	11.0	(1.7)	60.8	(1.8)	25.5	(1.9)	13.7	(1.5)	59.1	(1.6)	28.0	(1.6)	12.9	(1.2)
	Tabasco	55.9	(2.4)	34.7	(2.4)	9.4	(1.6)	59.9	(1.5)	32.0	(1.7)	8.0	(1.1)	54.9	(1.4)	36.0	(1.7)	9.1	(1.3)	56.6	(2.1)	32.6	(2.0)	10.8	(1.3)
	Tamaulipas	61.7	(1.7)	25.2	(1.7)	13.1	(1.0)	65.6	(2.0)	22.4	(2.3)	12.0	(1.3)	64.6	(2.4)	23.4	(2.5)	12.0	(1.3)	60.4	(1.7)	26.0	(1.2)	13.7	(1.5)
	Tlaxcala	54.3	(2.4)	31.7	(2.2)	14.0	(1.3)	58.4	(1.5)	30.2	(1.5)	11.4	(1.2)	54.4	(1.9)	33.3	(2.0)	12.3	(1.2)	56.0	(2.4)	32.1	(2.1)	11.9	(1.1)
	Veracruz	49.4	(2.4)	35.8	(2.3)	14.8	(1.4)	57.1	(2.7)	31.0	(2.2)	11.9	(1.1)	52.5	(2.5)	34.2	(2.3)	13.3	(1.4)	58.0	(2.6)	32.1	(2.4)	9.9	(1.5)
	Yucatán	50.5	(3.0)	34.4	(2.7)	15.1	(1.4)	57.5	(2.7)	31.3	(2.5)	11.1	(1.2)	53.4	(2.5)	32.6	(2.2)	13.9	(1.2)	56.8	(2.1)	31.4	(2.2)	11.8	(1.3)
	Zacatecas	59.7	(2.6)	29.9	(2.4)	10.4	(1.4)	66.2	(2.3)	24.1	(1.9)	9.7	(1.4)	64.6	(2.7)	26.1	(2.3)	9.3	(1.3)	62.2	(2.0)	28.9	(2.1)	8.9	(1.0)

• PISA adjudicated region.
Note: See Table IV.3.25 for national data.
StatLink http://dx.doi.org/10.1787/888932957536

[Part 2/2]

Table B2.IV.11 Percentage of students attending after-school lessons (hours per week), by region

Results based on students' self-reports

		Mathematics						Language of instruction						Science						Other subjects					
		No attendance		Less than 4 hours a week		4 hours a week or more		No attendance		Less than 4 hours a week		4 hours a week or more		No attendance		Less than 4 hours a week		4 hours a week or more		No attendance		Less than 4 hours a week		4 hours a week or more	
		%	S.E.	%	S.E.	%	S.E.	%	S.E.	%	S.E.	%	S.E.	%	S.E.	%	S.E.	%	S.E.	%	S.E.	%	S.E.	%	S.E.
OECD	**Portugal**																								
	Alentejo	50.7	(4.3)	36.6	(3.3)	12.7	(2.5)	61.0	(3.9)	29.6	(3.1)	9.5	(2.3)	71.9	(2.9)	24.0	(3.0)	4.1	(1.5)	58.8	(2.0)	35.2	(1.9)	6.0	(1.7)
	Spain																								
	Andalusia•	61.4	(1.9)	26.9	(1.5)	11.6	(1.5)	79.5	(1.5)	15.8	(1.4)	4.7	(0.7)	76.4	(1.6)	16.9	(1.4)	6.7	(0.7)	66.9	(1.8)	24.4	(1.6)	8.7	(1.0)
	Aragon•	61.1	(2.0)	32.8	(2.2)	6.0	(0.8)	83.5	(1.3)	13.0	(1.3)	3.6	(0.7)	74.6	(1.6)	21.3	(1.6)	4.1	(0.5)	60.4	(1.7)	33.7	(1.8)	5.8	(0.9)
	Asturias•	44.6	(2.1)	35.5	(1.5)	19.9	(1.7)	76.9	(1.9)	17.9	(1.6)	5.2	(0.8)	64.4	(2.1)	24.7	(1.7)	10.9	(0.9)	55.1	(1.5)	35.4	(1.7)	9.5	(1.0)
	Balearic Islands•	55.2	(1.9)	39.4	(1.9)	5.4	(0.9)	78.3	(1.8)	17.7	(1.6)	4.0	(0.6)	73.6	(1.4)	21.8	(1.5)	4.5	(0.7)	60.2	(2.3)	33.5	(2.1)	6.3	(0.8)
	Basque Country•	58.2	(1.4)	36.0	(1.3)	5.8	(0.5)	77.5	(1.0)	19.6	(0.9)	2.8	(0.3)	69.8	(1.2)	26.2	(1.2)	4.0	(0.4)	40.1	(1.1)	52.4	(1.1)	7.5	(0.5)
	Cantabria•	47.3	(1.8)	38.2	(1.4)	14.5	(1.0)	73.2	(1.8)	20.0	(1.4)	6.8	(1.0)	67.2	(1.6)	24.7	(1.3)	8.1	(1.0)	52.0	(1.9)	37.6	(1.7)	10.4	(0.9)
	Castile and Leon•	54.4	(2.0)	38.3	(1.7)	7.3	(1.2)	80.8	(1.4)	15.2	(1.3)	4.0	(0.7)	77.4	(1.5)	18.7	(1.3)	3.8	(0.7)	62.2	(1.6)	31.3	(1.6)	6.5	(0.9)
	Catalonia•	70.1	(2.1)	25.9	(2.1)	3.9	(0.7)	82.2	(1.5)	15.8	(1.3)	2.0	(0.6)	85.1	(1.5)	13.0	(1.3)	1.9	(0.5)	55.8	(2.4)	38.5	(2.2)	5.7	(0.6)
	Extremadura•	57.9	(2.2)	28.9	(1.8)	13.2	(1.2)	78.0	(1.8)	16.2	(1.5)	5.8	(0.8)	71.4	(1.7)	21.2	(1.3)	7.4	(0.9)	65.4	(2.0)	27.1	(2.1)	7.5	(0.8)
	Galicia•	50.1	(1.8)	38.0	(1.7)	11.9	(1.1)	80.4	(1.7)	15.4	(1.5)	4.2	(0.8)	67.6	(1.8)	25.1	(1.8)	7.3	(0.9)	62.0	(2.0)	31.0	(2.0)	7.0	(0.9)
	La Rioja•	52.9	(1.7)	39.8	(1.5)	7.3	(0.9)	83.4	(1.2)	13.3	(1.1)	3.3	(0.5)	73.5	(1.5)	22.8	(1.5)	3.8	(0.6)	56.9	(1.8)	37.4	(1.6)	5.7	(0.9)
	Madrid•	65.7	(1.7)	29.7	(1.4)	4.6	(0.7)	84.5	(1.6)	11.8	(1.3)	3.7	(0.6)	79.4	(1.5)	16.5	(1.2)	4.0	(0.6)	62.9	(2.1)	30.3	(2.1)	6.8	(1.0)
	Murcia•	58.2	(1.8)	31.7	(1.7)	10.1	(1.4)	78.0	(2.1)	16.7	(1.9)	5.2	(1.0)	75.2	(1.7)	20.2	(1.4)	4.6	(0.8)	67.9	(1.9)	25.6	(2.2)	6.5	(1.0)
	Navarre•	59.5	(1.5)	35.8	(1.7)	4.7	(0.8)	81.8	(1.4)	15.8	(1.4)	2.3	(0.6)	77.5	(1.3)	19.6	(1.4)	3.0	(0.5)	55.7	(1.9)	38.9	(1.8)	5.4	(0.8)
	United Kingdom																								
	England	58.8	(1.4)	32.4	(1.5)	8.8	(0.8)	66.7	(1.2)	24.9	(1.3)	8.4	(0.8)	65.2	(1.2)	24.0	(1.3)	10.7	(0.9)	49.2	(1.2)	37.0	(1.2)	13.8	(0.7)
	Northern Ireland	55.2	(1.7)	34.8	(1.4)	10.0	(0.9)	65.0	(1.7)	24.8	(1.5)	10.2	(0.9)	66.4	(1.3)	22.6	(0.9)	11.0	(1.0)	53.8	(1.5)	29.6	(1.2)	16.6	(1.2)
	Scotland•	55.7	(1.3)	35.2	(1.3)	9.1	(0.6)	64.8	(1.3)	26.1	(1.3)	9.1	(0.6)	61.3	(1.3)	31.8	(1.2)	6.9	(0.6)	49.1	(1.3)	39.5	(1.2)	11.4	(0.7)
	Wales	55.3	(1.3)	35.2	(1.1)	9.5	(0.7)	67.3	(1.1)	23.3	(1.0)	9.4	(0.7)	68.6	(1.0)	20.5	(0.9)	10.9	(0.7)	53.9	(1.0)	32.5	(0.9)	13.5	(0.7)
	United States																								
	Connecticut•	75.1	(1.3)	20.4	(1.1)	4.5	(0.6)	79.1	(1.1)	15.5	(0.9)	5.4	(0.6)	78.6	(1.1)	16.1	(1.1)	5.4	(0.7)	72.4	(1.2)	20.1	(1.1)	7.5	(0.9)
	Florida•	68.2	(1.8)	26.8	(1.6)	5.0	(0.8)	73.6	(1.5)	20.8	(1.2)	5.7	(0.8)	74.5	(1.6)	21.1	(1.2)	4.4	(0.8)	66.2	(1.9)	22.8	(1.4)	10.9	(1.2)
	Massachusetts•	74.3	(1.2)	20.6	(1.3)	5.2	(0.8)	78.5	(1.2)	16.4	(1.0)	5.0	(0.6)	77.4	(1.3)	18.2	(1.2)	4.4	(0.6)	70.3	(1.4)	21.7	(1.2)	8.0	(0.8)
Partners	**Argentina**																								
	Ciudad Autónoma de Buenos Aires•	59.2	(2.7)	37.5	(2.5)	3.4	(0.6)	79.8	(1.8)	18.1	(1.7)	2.0	(0.7)	79.8	(1.5)	18.0	(1.4)	2.2	(0.6)	64.9	(2.4)	28.2	(2.2)	6.9	(1.0)
	Brazil																								
	Acre	41.1	(2.2)	50.5	(2.5)	8.5	(1.3)	41.0	(1.6)	51.8	(1.9)	7.2	(1.4)	49.1	(2.4)	46.3	(3.0)	4.6	(1.0)	38.4	(2.3)	49.8	(3.2)	11.9	(1.9)
	Alagoas	23.9	(3.0)	55.1	(3.1)	21.0	(3.9)	32.2	(3.3)	49.8	(3.6)	18.0	(3.4)	33.4	(2.0)	61.1	(2.2)	5.6	(1.5)	30.5	(3.5)	51.5	(3.4)	18.0	(1.7)
	Amapá	30.7	(2.9)	52.7	(3.6)	16.6	(2.7)	36.7	(2.7)	47.9	(2.8)	15.3	(2.4)	40.9	(3.5)	52.1	(3.9)	7.0	(1.8)	35.5	(3.4)	48.2	(4.3)	16.3	(2.4)
	Amazonas	35.7	(1.6)	46.0	(1.1)	18.3	(1.4)	41.1	(2.9)	42.6	(2.7)	16.4	(1.7)	46.1	(2.0)	45.2	(2.1)	8.7	(1.2)	35.4	(1.3)	45.6	(2.7)	19.0	(2.7)
	Bahia	38.2	(3.3)	50.4	(3.4)	11.4	(2.4)	43.0	(4.2)	46.4	(3.1)	10.6	(2.7)	45.9	(2.5)	46.9	(2.1)	7.2	(1.4)	41.2	(2.8)	46.2	(3.0)	12.7	(1.6)
	Ceará	24.5	(2.3)	54.5	(2.4)	21.0	(2.3)	29.4	(2.7)	53.8	(2.6)	16.7	(2.5)	34.2	(1.6)	56.4	(1.8)	9.3	(2.1)	25.5	(1.5)	56.9	(2.0)	17.6	(2.2)
	Espírito Santo	45.0	(2.2)	39.7	(2.5)	15.2	(2.5)	51.1	(2.3)	36.3	(2.6)	12.6	(1.5)	53.3	(1.9)	40.2	(2.5)	6.5	(1.2)	43.8	(2.3)	45.6	(3.2)	10.6	(1.5)
	Federal District	43.6	(4.6)	43.1	(4.4)	13.3	(2.2)	50.5	(2.6)	38.8	(2.9)	10.6	(1.3)	47.2	(2.6)	45.4	(2.9)	7.5	(1.1)	36.3	(4.3)	52.7	(5.3)	10.9	(1.6)
	Goiás	43.4	(2.7)	37.5	(2.6)	19.1	(1.9)	48.3	(2.6)	36.9	(2.0)	14.8	(2.2)	52.0	(3.1)	41.8	(3.0)	6.2	(0.9)	43.4	(2.2)	45.2	(2.5)	11.4	(1.0)
	Maranhão	24.9	(2.2)	52.0	(3.0)	23.1	(4.3)	31.0	(2.6)	52.1	(3.9)	16.9	(2.5)	34.8	(2.6)	55.4	(3.2)	9.8	(1.8)	26.5	(2.4)	54.1	(1.8)	19.5	(1.8)
	Mato Grosso	35.2	(2.6)	50.8	(3.3)	14.0	(2.4)	38.5	(2.9)	51.1	(3.3)	10.4	(2.2)	40.5	(3.3)	53.4	(3.9)	6.1	(1.5)	36.7	(2.8)	47.7	(2.0)	15.6	(2.4)
	Mato Grosso do Sul	37.0	(2.7)	50.2	(2.0)	12.8	(1.8)	41.6	(2.5)	47.9	(2.3)	10.5	(2.3)	45.3	(3.0)	45.8	(2.2)	8.9	(1.6)	35.9	(2.8)	53.1	(2.9)	11.0	(1.8)
	Minas Gerais	45.8	(2.9)	40.3	(2.4)	13.9	(2.0)	50.5	(3.1)	39.0	(3.0)	10.6	(1.6)	50.0	(3.1)	41.3	(2.9)	8.8	(0.8)	43.8	(2.9)	45.6	(2.4)	10.7	(1.3)
	Pará	30.2	(2.1)	48.4	(2.1)	21.5	(2.0)	35.5	(2.3)	47.8	(2.2)	16.7	(2.2)	39.1	(2.5)	53.0	(2.4)	7.9	(1.3)	32.0	(2.3)	47.8	(1.8)	20.2	(2.7)
	Paraíba	39.7	(2.3)	42.9	(3.0)	17.4	(2.2)	44.2	(1.8)	42.8	(1.4)	13.0	(2.0)	45.9	(2.4)	41.0	(2.6)	13.1	(2.1)	40.0	(2.1)	42.4	(3.0)	17.6	(2.0)
	Paraná	54.0	(2.3)	37.3	(2.4)	8.8	(1.1)	56.5	(2.9)	36.5	(2.9)	6.9	(1.2)	65.0	(2.9)	30.3	(2.9)	4.7	(0.8)	47.0	(2.7)	41.4	(2.8)	11.7	(1.3)
	Pernambuco	33.1	(2.8)	43.1	(3.8)	23.8	(2.4)	35.1	(3.3)	42.3	(3.4)	22.6	(2.7)	44.9	(4.3)	49.4	(4.2)	5.6	(1.1)	35.5	(2.5)	51.7	(2.8)	12.8	(1.5)
	Piauí	35.5	(1.9)	44.5	(1.9)	20.0	(2.3)	42.5	(2.9)	45.8	(2.9)	11.7	(1.2)	43.3	(3.2)	44.8	(2.9)	11.9	(1.6)	40.6	(3.3)	40.2	(3.4)	19.2	(1.2)
	Rio de Janeiro	30.3	(3.1)	50.9	(1.8)	18.8	(2.2)	36.8	(2.4)	46.4	(1.1)	16.8	(2.2)	44.5	(3.1)	48.4	(3.1)	7.1	(1.0)	31.8	(3.6)	54.9	(2.9)	13.3	(1.4)
	Rio Grande do Norte	34.8	(1.9)	52.9	(2.1)	12.3	(2.5)	38.0	(2.6)	49.7	(2.6)	12.3	(1.9)	43.3	(3.3)	44.5	(2.9)	12.2	(2.5)	35.7	(2.8)	48.8	(3.4)	15.5	(2.4)
	Rio Grande do Sul	52.5	(3.1)	37.7	(3.5)	9.7	(1.9)	55.5	(2.2)	36.7	(2.8)	7.8	(1.6)	58.3	(2.3)	36.0	(2.8)	5.7	(1.3)	49.6	(2.0)	39.4	(2.8)	11.0	(1.8)
	Rondônia	40.0	(3.1)	50.8	(2.6)	9.2	(1.9)	41.0	(2.2)	48.7	(2.6)	10.3	(1.8)	49.4	(3.3)	47.3	(3.0)	3.3	(0.9)	43.2	(2.3)	47.6	(2.3)	9.2	(1.4)
	Roraima	33.9	(3.0)	51.7	(3.0)	14.4	(3.2)	41.0	(3.4)	49.6	(3.6)	9.4	(2.1)	40.7	(4.0)	50.8	(3.3)	8.5	(2.5)	35.4	(3.3)	50.5	(3.4)	14.1	(2.1)
	Santa Catarina	49.4	(2.1)	40.0	(2.2)	10.6	(2.0)	54.9	(2.1)	38.3	(2.1)	6.9	(1.6)	59.8	(1.7)	33.0	(1.7)	7.2	(1.1)	49.7	(2.8)	40.5	(3.3)	9.8	(1.9)
	São Paulo	48.1	(1.9)	34.4	(1.7)	17.5	(1.0)	51.2	(1.7)	33.2	(1.6)	15.6	(1.1)	57.4	(1.7)	37.2	(1.5)	5.5	(0.8)	45.0	(1.6)	45.0	(1.4)	10.0	(1.2)
	Sergipe	30.5	(3.3)	51.9	(2.8)	17.7	(2.0)	31.6	(2.6)	53.2	(4.3)	15.2	(2.4)	33.9	(2.8)	57.5	(2.4)	8.5	(2.1)	33.3	(2.5)	53.8	(3.1)	12.8	(2.4)
	Tocantins	36.9	(2.0)	42.3	(3.1)	20.8	(2.3)	40.5	(2.7)	43.0	(2.5)	16.5	(3.0)	48.3	(2.6)	45.7	(2.2)	6.0	(1.1)	37.6	(1.9)	50.0	(2.0)	12.4	(1.2)
	Colombia																								
	Bogota	42.1	(2.3)	41.9	(2.4)	16.0	(1.5)	51.8	(2.7)	35.8	(1.8)	12.3	(1.8)	44.7	(2.8)	40.7	(2.3)	14.6	(1.6)	45.4	(2.5)	29.9	(2.9)	24.7	(2.6)
	Cali	40.5	(2.3)	40.3	(2.4)	19.2	(2.6)	51.7	(2.1)	35.5	(1.9)	12.8	(1.5)	41.9	(2.4)	41.0	(2.7)	17.0	(2.4)	50.6	(3.1)	32.9	(3.4)	16.5	(2.7)
	Manizales	45.2	(3.6)	35.6	(2.4)	19.2	(2.3)	52.8	(2.6)	31.8	(2.4)	15.4	(0.8)	43.0	(3.9)	41.3	(3.0)	15.7	(1.7)	38.9	(3.0)	26.1	(3.1)	35.1	(2.9)
	Medellin	52.8	(2.3)	32.9	(2.3)	14.2	(1.8)	52.5	(3.3)	35.2	(2.7)	12.3	(1.9)	48.7	(2.4)	36.5	(1.6)	14.8	(1.6)	54.3	(2.8)	23.7	(2.4)	22.0	(2.3)
	Russian Federation																								
	Perm Territory region•	27.7	(2.0)	59.6	(1.8)	12.7	(1.3)	34.8	(2.1)	56.1	(2.0)	9.2	(1.2)	51.7	(1.7)	40.4	(1.7)	7.9	(1.1)	45.0	(1.9)	46.3	(1.9)	8.8	(1.1)
	United Arab Emirates																								
	Abu Dhabi•	53.6	(1.2)	30.0	(0.9)	16.4	(0.8)	68.7	(1.4)	20.8	(1.1)	10.5	(0.8)	59.8	(1.2)	25.5	(0.9)	14.7	(0.8)	59.1	(1.4)	27.6	(1.2)	13.3	(0.7)
	Ajman	49.9	(3.5)	36.0	(2.3)	14.1	(2.2)	69.5	(3.4)	20.4	(2.0)	10.1	(2.3)	59.1	(3.5)	28.8	(2.7)	12.0	(1.5)	59.1	(3.7)	30.1	(2.5)	10.8	(2.0)
	Dubai•	49.2	(1.0)	31.7	(1.1)	19.1	(0.8)	66.6	(0.9)	23.9	(0.8)	9.5	(0.6)	57.8	(0.9)	24.3	(0.9)	17.9	(0.8)	56.2	(0.8)	30.1	(0.9)	13.6	(0.7)
	Fujairah	47.9	(2.6)	39.6	(2.3)	12.5	(1.3)	69.3	(2.8)	23.9	(2.4)	6.8	(0.9)	57.1	(3.8)	31.7	(3.1)	11.2	(1.5)	57.9	(2.8)	29.9	(2.0)	12.2	(2.2)
	Ras Al Khaimah	45.4	(3.1)	38.6	(2.8)	16.0	(2.2)	63.5	(2.8)	25.7	(2.5)	10.8	(2.2)	54.3	(3.1)	31.1	(2.8)	14.5	(1.7)	56.0	(3.0)	29.6	(2.4)	14.4	(2.6)
	Sharjah	46.9	(2.8)	34.5	(2.1)	18.6	(2.2)	67.5	(3.3)	26.0	(2.7)	6.5	(1.1)	57.0	(3.8)	25.7	(2.5)	17.4	(2.3)	58.7	(3.4)	30.1	(2.9)	11.2	(1.4)
	Umm Al Quwain	55.1	(3.4)	35.6	(3.5)	9.3	(1.9)	67.3	(3.1)	24.0	(2.8)	8.7	(2.3)	58.5	(3.3)	33.1	(3.3)	8.4	(1.8)	59.9	(3.4)	31.0	(3.3)	9.2	(2.2)

• PISA adjudicated region.

Note: See Table IV.3.25 for national data.

StatLink http://dx.doi.org/10.1787/888932957536

[Part 1/4]
Index of creative extracurricular activities at school and mathematics performance, by region

Table B2.IV.12   *Results based on school principals' reports*

	Index of creative extracurricular activities at school										Variability in this index	
	All students		Bottom quarter		Second quarter		Third quarter		Top quarter			
	Mean index	S.E.	Mean index	S.E.	Mean index	S.E.	Mean index	S.E.	Mean index	S.E.	Standard deviation	S.E.
Australia												
Australian Capital Territory	2.35	(0.01)	1.42	(0.03)	2.00	(0.01)	2.98	(0.03)	3.00	(0.00)	0.73	(0.01)
New South Wales	1.97	(0.07)	0.77	(0.08)	1.85	(0.14)	2.25	(0.13)	3.00	(0.00)	0.88	(0.04)
Northern Territory	1.53	(0.14)	0.40	(0.08)	1.30	(0.38)	2.00	(0.01)	2.45	(0.26)	0.88	(0.06)
Queensland	2.37	(0.06)	1.51	(0.14)	2.00	(0.09)	2.99	(0.13)	3.00	(0.00)	0.72	(0.05)
South Australia	2.08	(0.07)	1.10	(0.19)	2.00	(0.00)	2.21	(0.18)	3.00	(0.00)	0.77	(0.06)
Tasmania	2.20	(0.03)	1.00	(0.11)	2.00	(0.00)	2.81	(0.06)	3.00	(0.00)	0.86	(0.04)
Victoria	2.29	(0.07)	1.40	(0.16)	2.00	(0.00)	2.75	(0.20)	3.00	(0.00)	0.76	(0.06)
Western Australia	2.27	(0.08)	1.08	(0.18)	2.02	(0.15)	3.00	(0.12)	3.00	(0.00)	0.84	(0.05)
Belgium												
Flemish community●	1.21	(0.07)	0.00	(0.02)	0.93	(0.12)	1.52	(0.15)	2.40	(0.09)	0.95	(0.04)
French community	1.97	(0.07)	0.77	(0.08)	1.85	(0.14)	2.25	(0.13)	3.00	(0.00)	0.88	(0.04)
German-speaking community	2.29	(0.07)	1.40	(0.16)	2.00	(0.00)	2.75	(0.20)	3.00	(0.00)	0.76	(0.06)
Canada												
Alberta	2.65	(0.07)	1.63	(0.21)	2.99	(0.14)	3.00	(0.00)	3.00	(0.00)	0.64	(0.07)
British Columbia	2.59	(0.09)	1.57	(0.17)	2.77	(0.22)	3.00	(0.00)	3.00	(0.00)	0.69	(0.09)
Manitoba	2.74	(0.05)	1.98	(0.20)	3.00	(0.00)	3.00	(0.00)	3.00	(0.00)	0.64	(0.08)
New Brunswick	2.55	(0.07)	1.44	(0.15)	2.77	(0.12)	3.00	(0.00)	3.00	(0.00)	0.75	(0.06)
Newfoundland and Labrador	2.45	(0.11)	1.21	(0.34)	2.58	(0.12)	3.00	(0.00)	3.00	(0.00)	0.89	(0.15)
Nova Scotia	2.74	(0.07)	1.97	(0.26)	3.00	(0.00)	3.00	(0.00)	3.00	(0.00)	0.57	(0.08)
Ontario	2.80	(0.04)	2.19	(0.18)	3.00	(0.00)	3.00	(0.00)	3.00	(0.00)	0.43	(0.05)
Prince Edward Island	2.65	(0.00)	1.98	(0.00)	2.60	(0.02)	3.00	(0.00)	3.00	(0.00)	0.49	(0.00)
Quebec	2.55	(0.05)	1.52	(0.11)	2.68	(0.13)	3.00	(0.00)	3.00	(0.00)	0.72	(0.05)
Saskatchewan	2.50	(0.07)	1.35	(0.20)	2.65	(0.13)	3.00	(0.00)	3.00	(0.00)	0.80	(0.09)
Italy												
Abruzzo	1.41	(0.11)	0.33	(0.22)	1.00	(0.16)	1.98	(0.18)	2.35	(0.15)	0.87	(0.07)
Basilicata	0.97	(0.09)	0.00	(0.00)	0.65	(0.22)	1.04	(0.14)	2.20	(0.11)	0.86	(0.05)
Bolzano	1.39	(0.01)	0.51	(0.02)	1.00	(0.00)	1.29	(0.03)	2.75	(0.02)	0.92	(0.01)
Calabria	1.33	(0.15)	0.23	(0.27)	1.00	(0.00)	1.51	(0.31)	2.59	(0.21)	0.95	(0.09)
Campania	1.15	(0.13)	0.00	(0.13)	0.95	(0.18)	1.35	(0.28)	2.28	(0.15)	0.89	(0.07)
Emilia Romagna	1.57	(0.13)	0.32	(0.20)	1.09	(0.23)	2.00	(0.13)	2.86	(0.20)	1.01	(0.07)
Friuli Venezia Giulia	1.60	(0.10)	0.14	(0.22)	1.14	(0.22)	2.11	(0.12)	3.00	(0.00)	1.11	(0.07)
Lazio	1.53	(0.11)	0.42	(0.21)	1.04	(0.17)	2.00	(0.13)	2.67	(0.24)	0.93	(0.09)
Liguria	1.14	(0.08)	0.23	(0.17)	1.00	(0.00)	1.19	(0.23)	2.13	(0.09)	0.76	(0.06)
Lombardia	1.45	(0.09)	0.52	(0.19)	1.07	(0.17)	2.00	(0.11)	2.23	(0.13)	0.78	(0.08)
Marche	1.53	(0.17)	0.35	(0.23)	1.00	(0.24)	1.99	(0.28)	2.77	(0.23)	0.98	(0.07)
Molise	1.12	(0.02)	0.00	(0.00)	0.70	(0.03)	1.37	(0.03)	2.40	(0.03)	0.98	(0.01)
Piemonte	1.10	(0.11)	0.00	(0.15)	0.97	(0.17)	1.02	(0.14)	2.40	(0.19)	0.90	(0.07)
Puglia	1.28	(0.10)	0.11	(0.19)	1.00	(0.06)	1.71	(0.24)	2.30	(0.10)	0.89	(0.06)
Sardegna	1.25	(0.12)	0.07	(0.19)	1.00	(0.09)	1.72	(0.29)	2.22	(0.13)	0.87	(0.07)
Sicilia	1.57	(0.15)	0.28	(0.23)	1.13	(0.25)	2.00	(0.09)	2.88	(0.21)	1.02	(0.07)
Toscana	1.39	(0.14)	0.30	(0.24)	1.00	(0.11)	1.87	(0.22)	2.41	(0.19)	0.89	(0.07)
Trento	1.41	(0.08)	0.21	(0.13)	1.00	(0.00)	1.76	(0.20)	2.68	(0.10)	0.99	(0.04)
Umbria	1.36	(0.08)	0.26	(0.24)	1.00	(0.00)	1.56	(0.16)	2.63	(0.05)	0.96	(0.05)
Valle d'Aosta	0.83	(0.02)	0.00	(0.00)	0.00	(0.00)	1.22	(0.08)	2.09	(0.01)	0.94	(0.01)
Veneto	1.37	(0.11)	0.10	(0.16)	1.00	(0.16)	1.98	(0.19)	2.42	(0.17)	0.95	(0.07)
Mexico												
Aguascalientes	1.88	(0.16)	0.21	(0.28)	1.88	(0.27)	2.45	(0.25)	3.00	(0.00)	1.11	(0.10)
Baja California	1.79	(0.22)	0.62	(0.18)	1.38	(0.51)	2.18	(0.31)	3.00	(0.11)	0.97	(0.07)
Baja California Sur	1.64	(0.19)	0.00	(0.16)	1.64	(0.41)	2.00	(0.17)	2.93	(0.27)	1.10	(0.07)
Campeche	1.65	(0.17)	0.62	(0.19)	1.03	(0.26)	2.00	(0.26)	2.94	(0.23)	0.94	(0.09)
Chiapas	1.83	(0.15)	0.72	(0.17)	1.36	(0.28)	2.24	(0.33)	3.00	(0.05)	0.95	(0.08)
Chihuahua	2.21	(0.16)	0.89	(0.35)	2.00	(0.23)	2.97	(0.26)	3.00	(0.00)	0.92	(0.10)
Coahuila	1.89	(0.15)	0.54	(0.22)	1.71	(0.33)	2.34	(0.29)	3.00	(0.00)	1.00	(0.10)
Colima	1.51	(0.10)	0.45	(0.23)	1.00	(0.14)	1.96	(0.18)	2.64	(0.11)	0.92	(0.08)
Distrito Federal	2.05	(0.12)	0.86	(0.29)	2.00	(0.13)	2.36	(0.27)	3.00	(0.00)	0.85	(0.09)
Durango	2.00	(0.18)	0.61	(0.14)	1.77	(0.30)	2.62	(0.38)	3.00	(0.00)	1.00	(0.05)
Guanajuato	1.72	(0.18)	0.34	(0.23)	1.29	(0.31)	2.25	(0.34)	3.00	(0.05)	1.08	(0.08)
Guerrero	1.61	(0.24)	0.12	(0.25)	1.00	(0.19)	2.33	(0.67)	3.00	(0.00)	1.19	(0.06)
Hidalgo	1.88	(0.14)	0.66	(0.17)	1.63	(0.26)	2.24	(0.29)	3.00	(0.04)	0.94	(0.08)
Jalisco	1.32	(0.16)	0.00	(0.17)	0.92	(0.29)	1.80	(0.27)	2.58	(0.17)	1.02	(0.08)
Mexico	1.63	(0.18)	0.25	(0.24)	1.06	(0.21)	2.22	(0.41)	3.00	(0.06)	1.10	(0.07)
Morelos	1.99	(0.10)	0.87	(0.32)	2.00	(0.05)	2.08	(0.19)	3.00	(0.07)	0.83	(0.11)
Nayarit	1.55	(0.13)	0.10	(0.21)	1.16	(0.24)	2.00	(0.13)	2.96	(0.16)	1.09	(0.06)
Nuevo León	2.18	(0.14)	0.85	(0.32)	2.00	(0.12)	2.88	(0.23)	3.00	(0.00)	0.93	(0.09)
Puebla	1.89	(0.11)	0.68	(0.15)	1.73	(0.26)	2.16	(0.23)	3.00	(0.05)	0.91	(0.08)
Querétaro	1.81	(0.14)	0.71	(0.20)	1.14	(0.32)	2.41	(0.40)	3.00	(0.00)	1.00	(0.08)
Quintana Roo	1.75	(0.17)	0.49	(0.27)	1.34	(0.37)	2.19	(0.19)	3.00	(0.00)	1.02	(0.09)
San Luis Potosí	1.97	(0.23)	0.51	(0.27)	1.54	(0.41)	2.84	(0.35)	3.00	(0.00)	1.09	(0.09)
Sinaloa	2.06	(0.16)	0.45	(0.38)	2.00	(0.14)	2.81	(0.32)	3.00	(0.00)	1.06	(0.11)
Tabasco	1.71	(0.22)	0.00	(0.12)	1.50	(0.64)	2.35	(0.33)	3.00	(0.00)	1.20	(0.10)
Tamaulipas	1.97	(0.19)	0.71	(0.08)	1.57	(0.39)	2.60	(0.40)	3.00	(0.00)	0.99	(0.04)
Tlaxcala	2.00	(0.12)	0.84	(0.14)	1.87	(0.19)	2.29	(0.26)	3.00	(0.00)	0.85	(0.06)
Veracruz	1.81	(0.17)	0.47	(0.21)	1.71	(0.32)	2.07	(0.25)	3.00	(0.17)	0.98	(0.09)
Yucatán	1.85	(0.20)	0.29	(0.20)	1.56	(0.33)	2.55	(0.38)	3.00	(0.00)	1.12	(0.07)
Zacatecas	1.77	(0.17)	0.33	(0.23)	1.59	(0.29)	2.16	(0.23)	3.00	(0.04)	1.05	(0.07)

● PISA adjudicated region.
Notes: Values that are statistically significant are indicated in bold (see Annex A3).
See Table IV.3.31 for national data.
StatLink ᴬˢᴸᵖ http://dx.doi.org/10.1787/888932957536

[Part 2/4]
Index of creative extracurricular activities at school and mathematics performance, by region
Table B2.IV.12 *Results based on school principals' reports*

| | | Index of creative extracurricular activities at school | | | | | | | | | | Variability in this index | |
| | | All students | | Bottom quarter | | Second quarter | | Third quarter | | Top quarter | | | |
		Mean index	S.E.	Mean index	S.E.	Mean index	S.E.	Mean index	S.E.	Mean index	S.E.	Standard deviation	S.E.
OECD	**Portugal**												
	Alentejo	1.25	(0.21)	0.00	(0.25)	0.91	(0.35)	1.55	(0.37)	2.55	(0.16)	1.00	(0.09)
	Spain												
	Andalusia•	0.90	(0.13)	0.00	(0.00)	0.30	(0.31)	1.21	(0.24)	2.08	(0.09)	0.88	(0.05)
	Aragon•	1.15	(0.14)	0.00	(0.20)	1.00	(0.20)	1.44	(0.32)	2.15	(0.11)	0.84	(0.07)
	Asturias•	0.81	(0.11)	0.00	(0.00)	0.31	(0.26)	1.00	(0.06)	1.94	(0.22)	0.81	(0.06)
	Balearic Islands•	1.00	(0.12)	0.00	(0.00)	0.60	(0.26)	1.24	(0.25)	2.14	(0.10)	0.88	(0.06)
	Basque Country•	0.85	(0.07)	0.00	(0.00)	0.20	(0.15)	1.00	(0.05)	2.22	(0.16)	0.93	(0.04)
	Cantabria•	0.94	(0.10)	0.00	(0.00)	0.63	(0.25)	1.11	(0.21)	2.00	(0.07)	0.78	(0.05)
	Castile and Leon•	1.26	(0.10)	0.22	(0.20)	1.00	(0.00)	1.55	(0.25)	2.27	(0.14)	0.85	(0.07)
	Catalonia•	0.97	(0.12)	0.00	(0.00)	0.56	(0.26)	1.13	(0.23)	2.20	(0.15)	0.89	(0.08)
	Extremadura•	0.73	(0.11)	0.00	(0.00)	0.02	(0.19)	1.00	(0.16)	1.88	(0.26)	0.82	(0.07)
	Galicia•	0.79	(0.10)	0.00	(0.00)	0.54	(0.22)	1.00	(0.00)	1.62	(0.26)	0.75	(0.09)
	La Rioja•	1.10	(0.01)	0.00	(0.00)	0.80	(0.02)	1.00	(0.01)	2.60	(0.03)	1.00	(0.01)
	Madrid•	0.88	(0.12)	0.00	(0.00)	0.48	(0.31)	1.00	(0.05)	2.04	(0.24)	0.84	(0.07)
	Murcia•	1.37	(0.16)	0.00	(0.18)	0.99	(0.19)	1.75	(0.28)	2.74	(0.25)	1.05	(0.08)
	Navarre•	1.22	(0.14)	0.00	(0.01)	0.68	(0.24)	1.68	(0.22)	2.51	(0.16)	1.04	(0.05)
	United Kingdom												
	England	2.78	(0.04)	2.11	(0.17)	3.00	(0.00)	3.00	(0.00)	3.00	(0.00)	0.53	(0.07)
	Northern Ireland	2.45	(0.09)	1.47	(0.17)	2.34	(0.25)	3.00	(0.00)	3.00	(0.00)	0.73	(0.07)
	Scotland•	2.63	(0.06)	1.79	(0.10)	2.73	(0.19)	3.00	(0.00)	3.00	(0.00)	0.60	(0.06)
	Wales	2.72	(0.04)	1.89	(0.10)	2.97	(0.09)	3.00	(0.00)	3.00	(0.00)	0.51	(0.04)
	United States												
	Connecticut•	2.82	(0.05)	2.28	(0.19)	3.00	(0.00)	3.00	(0.00)	3.00	(0.00)	0.39	(0.04)
	Florida•	2.91	(0.04)	2.64	(0.17)	3.00	(0.00)	3.00	(0.00)	3.00	(0.00)	0.29	(0.06)
	Massachusetts•	2.69	(0.11)	1.76	(0.44)	3.00	(0.00)	3.00	(0.00)	3.00	(0.00)	0.71	(0.14)
Partners	**Argentina**												
	Ciudad Autónoma de Buenos Aires•	1.78	(0.17)	0.29	(0.23)	1.34	(0.29)	2.49	(0.30)	3.00	(0.00)	1.13	(0.07)
	Brazil												
	Acre	2.01	(0.21)	0.75	(0.45)	2.00	(0.15)	2.28	(0.46)	3.00	(0.06)	0.90	(0.15)
	Alagoas	1.61	(0.24)	0.52	(0.33)	1.39	(0.52)	2.00	(0.10)	2.53	(0.46)	0.86	(0.15)
	Amapá	1.56	(0.18)	0.32	(0.33)	1.29	(0.34)	2.00	(0.05)	2.64	(0.30)	0.95	(0.12)
	Amazonas	2.01	(0.23)	0.84	(0.49)	2.00	(0.22)	2.22	(0.38)	3.00	(0.11)	0.86	(0.12)
	Bahia	1.46	(0.41)	0.28	(0.47)	1.04	(0.53)	2.00	(0.53)	2.55	(0.54)	0.94	(0.10)
	Ceará	1.58	(0.20)	0.31	(0.25)	1.00	(0.07)	2.01	(0.61)	3.00	(0.17)	1.08	(0.12)
	Espírito Santo	1.00	(0.24)	0.00	(0.00)	0.25	(0.47)	1.71	(0.56)	2.03	(0.02)	0.94	(0.05)
	Federal District	1.61	(0.23)	0.64	(0.26)	1.12	(0.42)	2.00	(0.23)	2.69	(0.49)	0.87	(0.16)
	Goiás	0.95	(0.22)	0.00	(0.03)	0.56	(0.47)	1.00	(0.15)	2.26	(0.48)	0.92	(0.14)
	Maranhão	1.01	(0.27)	0.00	(0.18)	0.83	(0.41)	1.07	(0.39)	c	c	0.83	(0.10)
	Mato Grosso	1.15	(0.17)	0.00	(0.04)	0.79	(0.25)	1.42	(0.40)	2.39	(0.26)	0.96	(0.11)
	Mato Grosso do Sul	0.99	(0.09)	0.10	(0.17)	1.00	(0.08)	1.00	(0.06)	1.85	(0.21)	0.66	(0.06)
	Minas Gerais	1.34	(0.18)	0.29	(0.29)	1.00	(0.07)	1.79	(0.35)	2.30	(0.28)	0.86	(0.12)
	Pará	1.51	(0.35)	0.00	(0.24)	0.98	(0.38)	2.09	(0.99)	c	c	1.18	(0.13)
	Paraíba	1.13	(0.14)	0.00	(0.18)	0.95	(0.26)	1.24	(0.41)	2.35	(0.25)	0.90	(0.12)
	Paraná	0.95	(0.22)	0.00	(0.00)	0.50	(0.42)	1.30	(0.49)	2.00	(0.12)	0.84	(0.07)
	Pernambuco	1.61	(0.34)	0.28	(0.44)	1.58	(0.55)	2.00	(0.08)	2.57	(0.53)	0.94	(0.13)
	Piauí	1.20	(0.24)	0.00	(0.25)	1.00	(0.23)	1.14	(0.41)	2.69	(0.52)	1.00	(0.16)
	Rio de Janeiro	1.44	(0.23)	c	c	1.39	(0.75)	2.00	(0.00)	2.37	(0.26)	1.00	(0.11)
	Rio Grande do Norte	1.43	(0.18)	0.39	(0.36)	1.00	(0.14)	1.87	(0.34)	2.48	(0.32)	0.89	(0.13)
	Rio Grande do Sul	1.05	(0.17)	0.00	(0.00)	0.51	(0.35)	1.50	(0.39)	2.20	(0.20)	0.95	(0.10)
	Rondônia	0.85	(0.18)	0.00	(0.00)	0.28	(0.43)	1.00	(0.18)	2.13	(0.33)	0.88	(0.11)
	Roraima	1.12	(0.22)	0.00	(0.11)	0.67	(0.40)	1.16	(0.33)	2.66	(0.33)	1.05	(0.12)
	Santa Catarina	1.54	(0.14)	0.64	(0.07)	1.30	(0.40)	2.00	(0.08)	2.20	(0.20)	0.73	(0.07)
	São Paulo	1.12	(0.11)	0.02	(0.17)	1.00	(0.15)	1.27	(0.25)	2.18	(0.08)	0.83	(0.06)
	Sergipe	1.41	(0.26)	0.20	(0.29)	1.00	(0.08)	1.58	(0.62)	2.89	(0.45)	1.04	(0.18)
	Tocantins	0.99	(0.15)	0.00	(0.00)	0.62	(0.31)	1.08	(0.20)	2.26	(0.35)	0.90	(0.13)
	Colombia												
	Bogota	1.80	(0.16)	0.31	(0.26)	1.73	(0.28)	2.16	(0.24)	3.00	(0.04)	1.04	(0.09)
	Cali	1.95	(0.11)	0.78	(0.13)	1.59	(0.26)	2.45	(0.24)	3.00	(0.00)	0.94	(0.06)
	Manizales	1.58	(0.19)	0.01	(0.21)	1.14	(0.33)	2.18	(0.29)	3.00	(0.10)	1.15	(0.07)
	Medellin	1.60	(0.17)	0.28	(0.26)	1.16	(0.25)	2.00	(0.23)	2.97	(0.16)	1.04	(0.08)
	Russian Federation												
	Perm Territory region•	1.44	(0.13)	0.01	(0.14)	1.00	(0.21)	2.00	(0.18)	2.76	(0.21)	1.06	(0.07)
	United Arab Emirates												
	Abu Dhabi•	1.31	(0.08)	0.00	(0.06)	0.99	(0.10)	1.91	(0.14)	2.36	(0.10)	0.95	(0.03)
	Ajman	1.33	(0.15)	0.30	(0.27)	1.00	(0.00)	1.48	(0.36)	2.55	(0.07)	0.92	(0.06)
	Dubai•	2.05	(0.00)	0.88	(0.00)	1.72	(0.01)	2.60	(0.01)	3.00	(0.00)	0.90	(0.00)
	Fujairah	1.18	(0.08)	0.31	(0.03)	1.00	(0.00)	1.28	(0.29)	2.15	(0.01)	0.75	(0.03)
	Ras Al Khaimah	1.20	(0.16)	0.31	(0.35)	1.00	(0.00)	1.20	(0.30)	2.30	(0.16)	0.81	(0.10)
	Sharjah	1.34	(0.14)	0.08	(0.17)	1.17	(0.35)	2.00	(0.11)	2.14	(0.13)	0.87	(0.07)
	Umm Al Quwain	1.07	(0.01)	c	c	0.96	(0.03)	1.04	(0.02)	c	c	0.87	(0.01)

• PISA adjudicated region.
Notes: Values that are statistically significant are indicated in bold (see Annex A3).
See Table IV.3.31 for national data.
StatLink http://dx.doi.org/10.1787/888932957536

[Part 3/4]

Index of creative extracurricular activities at school and mathematics performance, by region

Table B2.IV.12 · *Results based on school principals' reports*

	Bottom quarter Mean score	S.E.	Second quarter Mean score	S.E.	Third quarter Mean score	S.E.	Top quarter Mean score	S.E.	Change in the mathematics score per unit of this index Score dif.	S.E.	Increased likelihood of students in the bottom quarter of this index scoring in the bottom quarter of the national mathematics performance distribution Ratio	S.E.	Explained variance in student performance (r-squared x 100) %	S.E.
Australia														
Australian Capital Territory	**496**	(7.3)	520	(7.8)	523	(10.2)	**523**	(10.3)	**16.7**	(4.4)	1.4	(0.21)	1.6	(0.87)
New South Wales	**492**	(7.6)	513	(9.3)	518	(8.3)	**516**	(7.0)	**10.4**	(4.7)	1.2	(0.15)	0.8	(0.68)
Northern Territory	448	(20.2)	459	(27.6)	449	(20.0)	453	(31.9)	1.6	(17.5)	1.1	(0.34)	0.0	(1.49)
Queensland	**478**	(7.1)	494	(6.0)	520	(7.9)	**522**	(6.8)	**27.3**	(6.1)	**1.5**	(0.17)	4.4	(1.89)
South Australia	479	(10.6)	493	(9.8)	492	(7.1)	493	(8.2)	9.9	(5.3)	1.3	(0.21)	0.7	(0.77)
Tasmania	**451**	(8.3)	472	(7.5)	493	(9.1)	**498**	(10.6)	**22.6**	(4.1)	**1.6**	(0.19)	4.3	(1.56)
Victoria	**483**	(5.0)	490	(5.7)	513	(8.7)	**520**	(8.1)	**19.1**	(4.7)	1.3	(0.16)	2.6	(1.08)
Western Australia	**489**	(8.4)	510	(8.8)	535	(8.6)	**537**	(9.1)	**24.5**	(5.3)	**1.6**	(0.25)	4.7	(1.98)
Belgium														
Flemish community*	**483**	(9.0)	537	(8.4)	553	(7.7)	**559**	(8.7)	**27.9**	(5.7)	**2.3**	(0.35)	6.6	(2.77)
French community	**492**	(7.7)	515	(9.3)	517	(7.9)	**515**	(6.6)	**10.4**	(4.7)	1.2	(0.15)	0.8	(0.68)
German-speaking community	**487**	(5.5)	487	(6.8)	512	(10.5)	**518**	(8.6)	**19.1**	(4.7)	1.3	(0.14)	2.6	(1.08)
Canada														
Alberta	**495**	(9.8)	525	(8.5)	524	(9.3)	**525**	(6.4)	**23.0**	(6.5)	1.4	(0.25)	2.6	(1.72)
British Columbia	**505**	(8.0)	527	(8.5)	529	(6.8)	**528**	(7.2)	**16.5**	(4.9)	1.4	(0.22)	1.8	(1.21)
Manitoba	494	(6.9)	491	(6.6)	492	(6.5)	492	(6.9)	0.7	(5.5)	0.9	(0.15)	0.0	(0.13)
New Brunswick	500	(5.5)	502	(8.3)	503	(8.3)	504	(9.6)	2.6	(2.9)	1.0	(0.12)	0.1	(0.14)
Newfoundland and Labrador	**459**	(11.3)	496	(7.4)	503	(5.6)	**504**	(7.9)	**26.0**	(4.0)	**2.0**	(0.31)	7.1	(3.47)
Nova Scotia	487	(6.4)	499	(10.3)	500	(8.0)	502	(7.5)	11.4	(4.8)	1.2	(0.19)	0.6	(0.59)
Ontario	513	(6.9)	516	(6.9)	515	(5.8)	514	(6.0)	2.1	(8.1)	1.0	(0.14)	0.0	(0.15)
Prince Edward Island	482	(5.7)	480	(5.6)	481	(7.0)	482	(7.0)	1.2	(4.7)	0.9	(0.11)	0.0	(0.09)
Quebec	**522**	(7.2)	537	(6.7)	543	(5.8)	**542**	(5.5)	**15.9**	(5.1)	1.3	(0.16)	1.6	(1.01)
Saskatchewan	515	(7.0)	504	(7.4)	501	(6.4)	504	(5.9)	-8.3	(4.0)	0.9	(0.10)	0.6	(0.55)
Italy														
Abruzzo	463	(20.3)	501	(16.7)	455	(13.5)	484	(13.7)	8.7	(10.4)	1.3	(0.39)	0.7	(1.89)
Basilicata	471	(11.5)	457	(9.3)	451	(11.9)	478	(10.9)	2.6	(7.3)	1.0	(0.29)	0.1	(0.53)
Bolzano	**485**	(4.3)	504	(6.2)	517	(5.9)	**526**	(4.2)	**16.6**	(2.3)	**1.6**	(0.17)	3.0	(0.80)
Calabria	440	(21.6)	423	(15.4)	428	(11.8)	427	(16.4)	-6.1	(12.4)	0.9	(0.41)	0.4	(2.33)
Campania	467	(11.5)	441	(12.9)	448	(16.2)	468	(16.1)	2.4	(9.0)	**0.6**	(0.19)	0.1	(0.79)
Emilia Romagna	**478**	(14.1)	485	(16.3)	512	(16.9)	**541**	(16.5)	**24.6**	(7.7)	1.5	(0.42)	6.6	(3.93)
Friuli Venezia Giulia	**470**	(20.4)	515	(14.2)	542	(9.2)	**552**	(9.1)	**29.3**	(5.1)	**2.6**	(0.74)	13.4	(4.23)
Lazio	459	(13.7)	475	(15.3)	491	(18.1)	497	(17.4)	16.8	(8.9)	1.4	(0.35)	3.1	(3.26)
Liguria	**462**	(8.8)	492	(12.6)	492	(10.8)	**502**	(15.8)	**19.3**	(8.5)	**1.5**	(0.23)	2.6	(2.22)
Lombardia	502	(13.0)	515	(13.5)	528	(13.3)	529	(12.3)	15.3	(10.2)	1.4	(0.33)	1.9	(2.46)
Marche	498	(15.1)	507	(14.9)	489	(22.0)	503	(10.3)	0.4	(7.9)	1.0	(0.27)	0.0	(0.72)
Molise	461	(8.3)	462	(7.8)	455	(7.1)	455	(6.8)	-3.7	(3.4)	1.3	(0.22)	0.2	(0.39)
Piemonte	**484**	(12.5)	495	(11.7)	491	(12.9)	**524**	(15.4)	12.8	(8.7)	1.2	(0.31)	1.7	(2.21)
Puglia	474	(14.6)	485	(15.1)	484	(10.0)	477	(15.3)	0.7	(9.7)	1.3	(0.35)	0.0	(0.86)
Sardegna	438	(16.1)	470	(14.1)	463	(11.1)	465	(11.3)	12.0	(8.2)	1.7	(0.47)	1.5	(2.27)
Sicilia	429	(14.9)	443	(11.0)	461	(16.1)	456	(12.8)	12.3	(7.7)	1.4	(0.45)	2.3	(3.04)
Toscana	494	(15.4)	486	(13.0)	501	(15.2)	507	(16.3)	6.7	(12.3)	1.0	(0.31)	0.4	(1.72)
Trento	515	(10.9)	516	(14.4)	542	(11.2)	534	(14.4)	8.9	(6.6)	1.3	(0.30)	1.1	(1.60)
Umbria	480	(13.9)	494	(10.6)	498	(15.4)	493	(14.8)	4.7	(7.5)	1.1	(0.34)	0.3	(1.01)
Valle d'Aosta	**514**	(9.4)	515	(10.1)	489	(6.2)	**467**	(6.2)	**-23.7**	(2.7)	**0.6**	(0.14)	6.9	(1.54)
Veneto	494	(12.7)	558	(18.1)	521	(13.6)	518	(17.7)	7.0	(8.6)	1.7	(0.42)	0.5	(1.68)
Mexico														
Aguascalientes	**409**	(13.1)	430	(9.9)	445	(11.0)	**464**	(9.7)	**19.0**	(4.4)	**1.8**	(0.38)	8.3	(3.78)
Baja California	404	(12.3)	407	(15.2)	420	(16.7)	429	(13.9)	9.6	(8.6)	1.1	(0.34)	1.7	(3.08)
Baja California Sur	402	(12.3)	416	(10.2)	415	(10.7)	424	(8.4)	6.7	(4.9)	1.4	(0.34)	1.0	(1.55)
Campeche	**386**	(6.6)	379	(10.2)	400	(12.8)	**418**	(8.0)	**13.9**	(4.2)	1.2	(0.22)	3.4	(1.83)
Chiapas	363	(7.6)	365	(10.9)	373	(19.4)	391	(16.1)	11.9	(7.5)	1.0	(0.28)	2.3	(2.90)
Chihuahua	**389**	(13.0)	417	(13.4)	453	(16.0)	**454**	(12.6)	**31.8**	(7.0)	**2.2**	(0.58)	14.0	(5.78)
Coahuila	414	(16.7)	404	(9.9)	420	(12.6)	435	(18.1)	6.4	(9.0)	1.1	(0.33)	0.8	(2.28)
Colima	**404**	(11.4)	413	(11.6)	439	(11.1)	**461**	(12.7)	**26.6**	(5.9)	**1.6**	(0.45)	10.1	(4.97)
Distrito Federal	**415**	(7.7)	419	(12.2)	432	(8.5)	**446**	(10.5)	**13.5**	(5.0)	1.2	(0.29)	2.5	(2.16)
Durango	**391**	(10.5)	426	(12.3)	441	(10.2)	441	(9.4)	**21.4**	(4.6)	**2.2**	(0.48)	8.8	(3.75)
Guanajuato	396	(13.3)	410	(14.0)	424	(10.3)	416	(14.4)	9.6	(7.1)	1.6	(0.45)	1.9	(2.81)
Guerrero	360	(8.4)	366	(12.0)	368	(8.8)	379	(9.8)	6.1	(4.6)	1.2	(0.29)	1.2	(1.72)
Hidalgo	406	(10.9)	398	(11.8)	404	(13.8)	418	(12.5)	3.9	(7.1)	1.1	(0.29)	0.2	(1.16)
Jalisco	419	(15.4)	426	(9.9)	437	(11.0)	456	(11.0)	14.5	(6.1)	1.5	(0.47)	4.3	(3.62)
Mexico	412	(10.9)	412	(10.2)	423	(8.5)	422	(15.5)	4.4	(6.8)	1.1	(0.29)	0.5	(1.78)
Morelos	441	(22.5)	406	(13.8)	402	(15.8)	437	(13.8)	-0.8	(10.2)	0.8	(0.19)	0.0	(0.82)
Nayarit	**384**	(14.2)	415	(11.1)	415	(9.4)	**447**	(9.5)	**19.5**	(5.1)	1.8	(0.46)	7.6	(3.70)
Nuevo León	409	(14.2)	448	(12.1)	445	(13.0)	443	(17.5)	14.7	(7.5)	1.7	(0.43)	3.4	(3.60)
Puebla	403	(16.6)	410	(9.5)	417	(9.8)	431	(8.2)	10.7	(8.8)	1.4	(0.42)	1.8	(2.89)
Querétaro	**417**	(12.1)	418	(8.4)	440	(15.5)	**463**	(15.7)	**20.6**	(6.8)	1.3	(0.38)	7.5	(4.94)
Quintana Roo	412	(8.7)	399	(9.7)	398	(12.2)	433	(18.8)	6.1	(7.7)	0.8	(0.25)	0.8	(2.17)
San Luis Potosí	396	(12.8)	421	(19.8)	418	(15.4)	413	(10.5)	7.6	(6.5)	1.4	(0.34)	1.2	(2.36)
Sinaloa	**398**	(10.2)	398	(12.2)	421	(10.4)	**430**	(8.5)	**11.2**	(4.5)	1.3	(0.33)	3.0	(2.31)
Tabasco	**362**	(13.0)	367	(10.5)	378	(15.0)	**408**	(8.5)	**13.1**	(5.6)	1.5	(0.53)	4.9	(4.28)
Tamaulipas	397	(15.5)	413	(9.9)	416	(10.1)	418	(15.8)	7.3	(8.4)	1.5	(0.39)	1.0	(2.41)
Tlaxcala	402	(12.1)	406	(12.8)	413	(10.1)	424	(8.2)	12.0	(6.9)	1.3	(0.32)	2.0	(2.36)
Veracruz	**383**	(11.2)	394	(17.6)	408	(12.8)	**424**	(11.0)	**14.9**	(6.4)	1.4	(0.30)	3.8	(2.84)
Yucatán	**393**	(10.3)	408	(8.5)	413	(12.0)	**426**	(10.1)	**11.3**	(4.9)	1.3	(0.31)	2.9	(2.54)
Zacatecas	**389**	(11.7)	407	(7.9)	411	(7.6)	**427**	(7.2)	**13.7**	(4.5)	1.5	(0.31)	4.0	(2.88)

* PISA adjudicated region.

Notes: Values that are statistically significant are indicated in bold (see Annex A3).
See Table IV.3.31 for national data.
StatLink http://dx.doi.org/10.1787/888932957536

[Part 4/4]

Index of creative extracurricular activities at school and mathematics performance, by region

Table B2.IV.12 *Results based on school principals' reports*

| | Performance on the mathematics scale, by national quarters of this index | | | | | | | | Change in the mathematics score per unit of this index | | Increased likelihood of students in the bottom quarter of this index scoring in the bottom quarter of the national mathematics performance distribution | | Explained variance in student performance (r-squared x 100) | |
| | Bottom quarter | | Second quarter | | Third quarter | | Top quarter | | | | | | | |
	Mean score	S.E.	Mean score	S.E.	Mean score	S.E.	Mean score	S.E.	Score dif.	S.E.	Ratio	S.E.	%	S.E.
Portugal														
Alentejo	506	(18.8)	489	(17.4)	482	(18.6)	488	(17.3)	-7.0	(9.6)	0.6	(0.35)	0.6	(2.24)
Spain														
Andalusia•	469	(8.1)	472	(7.5)	474	(9.0)	474	(10.7)	3.1	(5.0)	1.0	(0.18)	0.1	(0.48)
Aragon•	474	(12.4)	500	(10.6)	505	(10.2)	508	(13.3)	14.9	(9.2)	1.5	(0.32)	1.8	(2.16)
Asturias•	492	(10.8)	496	(10.5)	496	(8.0)	516	(12.3)	10.7	(8.6)	1.1	(0.17)	0.9	(1.42)
Balearic Islands•	464	(8.9)	476	(9.3)	486	(9.8)	474	(10.5)	5.5	(5.7)	1.3	(0.23)	0.3	(0.61)
Basque Country•	502	(4.2)	504	(4.6)	504	(5.9)	513	(6.5)	3.7	(3.9)	1.0	(0.09)	0.2	(0.35)
Cantabria•	475	(10.3)	483	(10.2)	497	(9.5)	**510**	(5.4)	**18.1**	(4.4)	**1.5**	(0.19)	2.5	(1.26)
Castile and Leon•	506	(7.0)	506	(9.7)	509	(8.4)	515	(7.3)	5.1	(4.3)	1.1	(0.18)	0.3	(0.47)
Catalonia•	495	(6.9)	495	(8.2)	495	(10.7)	488	(14.5)	-4.2	(6.2)	1.0	(0.15)	0.2	(0.69)
Extremadura•	456	(8.2)	457	(7.8)	467	(15.1)	469	(12.1)	5.8	(6.4)	1.0	(0.20)	0.3	(0.65)
Galicia•	488	(6.8)	486	(8.3)	487	(9.1)	494	(9.1)	2.5	(5.7)	1.0	(0.19)	0.1	(0.28)
La Rioja•	505	(5.2)	506	(5.9)	504	(6.2)	503	(4.4)	-1.1	(2.5)	1.1	(0.11)	0.0	(0.07)
Madrid•	496	(9.4)	501	(8.6)	500	(10.8)	518	(7.7)	**10.2**	(4.9)	1.2	(0.20)	1.0	(0.98)
Murcia•	467	(13.7)	456	(12.0)	461	(11.1)	464	(9.5)	0.2	(6.3)	0.9	(0.23)	0.0	(0.45)
Navarre•	512	(7.4)	511	(7.1)	519	(7.0)	524	(6.9)	4.6	(3.6)	1.0	(0.21)	0.3	(0.49)
United Kingdom														
England	484	(7.0)	500	(8.2)	504	(7.2)	500	(7.5)	**20.6**	(8.1)	1.3	(0.19)	1.3	(1.05)
Northern Ireland	467	(12.0)	489	(10.1)	490	(10.2)	489	(9.1)	17.8	(9.8)	1.4	(0.27)	2.0	(2.29)
Scotland•	489	(6.2)	497	(5.8)	503	(5.3)	503	(5.2)	8.6	(6.0)	1.2	(0.14)	0.4	(0.52)
Wales	466	(3.9)	469	(5.6)	470	(6.3)	469	(4.7)	1.7	(5.0)	1.0	(0.10)	0.0	(0.09)
United States														
Connecticut•	**478**	(13.9)	512	(9.3)	517	(9.4)	**516**	(9.9)	**50.6**	(15.0)	1.6	(0.33)	4.1	(2.52)
Florida•	464	(8.7)	472	(7.7)	468	(8.1)	473	(8.3)	18.1	(14.2)	1.1	(0.18)	0.4	(0.61)
Massachusetts•	488	(14.8)	521	(10.9)	523	(11.0)	521	(9.5)	**24.4**	(10.5)	1.4	(0.28)	3.1	(2.40)
Argentina														
Ciudad Autónoma de Buenos Aires•	395	(14.7)	388	(22.7)	433	(16.9)	**454**	(15.3)	22.5	(7.3)	1.4	(0.28)	7.0	(3.58)
Brazil														
Acre	354	(8.9)	367	(14.0)	367	(13.3)	359	(7.6)	3.9	(3.6)	1.2	(0.25)	0.3	(0.54)
Alagoas	362	(16.4)	375	(21.9)	364	(15.9)	345	(20.2)	-7.7	(10.6)	1.0	(0.31)	1.0	(2.58)
Amapá	367	(24.4)	365	(10.3)	350	(11.9)	362	(17.2)	-3.2	(13.1)	0.9	(0.43)	0.3	(3.05)
Amazonas	359	(11.1)	375	(17.1)	359	(13.7)	360	(14.4)	1.3	(6.9)	1.1	(0.37)	0.1	(0.75)
Bahia	355	(22.8)	369	(32.7)	386	(28.9)	400	(19.7)	20.9	(12.7)	2.0	(0.85)	5.9	(7.22)
Ceará	**369**	(7.9)	372	(9.2)	392	(30.8)	**431**	(25.9)	22.8	(9.3)	1.1	(0.33)	10.7	(7.59)
Espírito Santo	411	(15.8)	409	(12.8)	438	(29.7)	443	(32.7)	16.5	(21.0)	1.0	(0.41)	3.3	(8.26)
Federal District	**392**	(9.8)	405	(25.0)	457	(32.4)	450	(21.1)	28.7	(12.1)	1.7	(0.48)	10.0	(6.73)
Goiás	378	(16.8)	385	(14.3)	392	(16.7)	383	(17.6)	5.8	(11.8)	1.1	(0.36)	0.6	(2.61)
Maranhão	355	(7.2)	337	(22.0)	334	(31.2)	c	c	16.7	(13.3)	0.7	(0.31)	3.6	(4.93)
Mato Grosso	389	(24.1)	355	(11.8)	367	(23.7)	377	(24.0)	-4.0	(11.4)	0.8	(0.35)	0.3	(2.32)
Mato Grosso do Sul	389	(17.0)	429	(13.6)	422	(14.9)	412	(12.0)	15.3	(10.2)	1.7	(0.53)	1.9	(2.66)
Minas Gerais	**386**	(7.3)	393	(7.0)	417	(10.8)	**437**	(17.9)	**26.0**	(5.4)	1.6	(0.36)	10.2	(5.21)
Pará	338	(14.1)	385	(17.9)	398	(10.8)	c	c	15.1	(7.9)	**2.7**	(0.62)	7.8	(8.85)
Paraíba	**347**	(20.4)	403	(23.6)	419	(14.4)	**440**	(20.9)	34.2	(11.8)	**2.9**	(0.81)	15.7	(10.52)
Paraná	390	(8.6)	401	(13.7)	415	(19.5)	426	(40.0)	19.6	(20.4)	1.3	(0.35)	4.2	(8.25)
Pernambuco	372	(10.1)	369	(18.2)	355	(15.2)	374	(17.0)	0.0	(4.6)	0.8	(0.21)	0.0	(0.38)
Piauí	359	(18.6)	423	(24.7)	416	(22.7)	386	(15.6)	4.5	(8.4)	**1.8**	(0.38)	0.3	(1.41)
Rio de Janeiro	c	c	392	(14.5)	383	(17.0)	387	(10.8)	-9.9	(5.7)	**0.4**	(0.19)	2.0	(2.09)
Rio Grande do Norte	**356**	(11.2)	366	(17.0)	412	(25.3)	**425**	(25.5)	31.8	(9.8)	1.7	(0.43)	10.6	(5.49)
Rio Grande do Sul	418	(11.3)	421	(11.8)	409	(13.5)	403	(15.6)	-7.7	(8.4)	0.8	(0.26)	1.2	(2.69)
Rondônia	395	(11.0)	391	(14.2)	378	(9.2)	396	(15.0)	1.8	(8.5)	0.8	(0.31)	0.1	(1.24)
Roraima	376	(28.5)	356	(12.2)	360	(19.5)	391	(17.8)	9.4	(13.6)	1.4	(0.56)	1.9	(5.71)
Santa Catarina	424	(15.1)	427	(14.0)	433	(12.3)	433	(11.6)	3.4	(11.7)	1.1	(0.33)	0.1	(1.33)
São Paulo	387	(9.3)	419	(11.0)	414	(11.5)	399	(9.0)	5.1	(5.9)	1.3	(0.24)	0.3	(0.78)
Sergipe	371	(10.5)	403	(18.9)	391	(15.7)	414	(21.8)	13.1	(8.2)	1.7	(0.38)	3.8	(4.47)
Tocantins	363	(15.1)	366	(13.1)	357	(15.2)	390	(18.0)	10.6	(8.2)	1.1	(0.34)	1.6	(2.47)
Colombia														
Bogota	387	(10.3)	394	(8.4)	393	(7.5)	402	(5.7)	5.3	(3.7)	**1.4**	(0.20)	0.7	(1.03)
Cali	393	(9.9)	388	(13.3)	372	(9.0)	368	(9.2)	**-12.0**	(5.6)	**0.6**	(0.16)	2.6	(2.45)
Manizales	**371**	(5.3)	383	(12.1)	423	(9.8)	**439**	(19.5)	24.1	(6.2)	**2.0**	(0.30)	14.8	(5.90)
Medellin	**362**	(7.3)	379	(11.6)	396	(15.7)	**437**	(21.4)	26.5	(7.1)	**1.7**	(0.33)	11.1	(4.99)
Russian Federation														
Perm Territory region•	467	(6.9)	468	(11.3)	497	(11.9)	502	(16.4)	**14.3**	(6.2)	1.2	(0.24)	2.9	(2.49)
United Arab Emirates														
Abu Dhabi•	**407**	(7.7)	411	(8.9)	431	(7.2)	**465**	(10.2)	**26.0**	(4.7)	1.4	(0.21)	8.2	(2.91)
Ajman	**419**	(9.6)	415	(13.9)	416	(16.7)	**391**	(9.9)	**-12.5**	(4.9)	0.9	(0.29)	2.6	(1.83)
Dubai•	**434**	(3.0)	446	(3.8)	482	(4.7)	**510**	(4.6)	**35.0**	(1.6)	**1.7**	(0.13)	11.6	(0.98)
Fujairah	385	(8.2)	430	(11.2)	430	(10.6)	419	(21.3)	15.3	(8.1)	1.9	(0.47)	2.1	(2.22)
Ras Al Khaimah	**402**	(11.5)	421	(11.6)	424	(11.7)	453	(9.4)	24.8	(3.8)	1.4	(0.30)	8.0	(2.31)
Sharjah	439	(16.5)	417	(13.1)	456	(21.9)	461	(15.6)	13.6	(11.3)	0.8	(0.31)	2.1	(2.52)
Umm Al Quwain	c	c	404	(10.8)	409	(9.6)	c	c	5.4	(5.2)	1.0	(0.35)	0.4	(0.86)

• PISA adjudicated region.

Notes: Values that are statistically significant are indicated in bold (see Annex A3).

See Table IV.3.31 for national data.

StatLink ᴹˢᴾ http://dx.doi.org/10.1787/888932957536

[Part 1/1]
Pre-school attendance, by region
Table B2.IV.14 *Results based on students' self-reports*

Percentage of students reporting that they had attended pre-primary education (ISCED 0)

	No attendance %	S.E.	For one year or less %	S.E.	For more than one year %	S.E.		No attendance %	S.E.	For one year or less %	S.E.	For more than one year %	S.E.
Australia							**Portugal**						
Australian Capital Territory	2.1	(0.6)	46.0	(1.5)	51.8	(1.6)	Alentejo	11.3	(1.6)	17.4	(1.3)	71.3	(2.0)
New South Wales	2.9	(0.4)	40.4	(1.1)	56.7	(1.2)	**Spain**						
Northern Territory	4.9	(1.2)	61.4	(3.3)	33.7	(3.4)	Andalusia•	7.4	(1.2)	10.5	(0.9)	82.1	(1.6)
Queensland	5.2	(0.5)	54.5	(1.2)	40.3	(1.1)	Aragon•	6.1	(0.9)	7.0	(0.8)	87.0	(1.4)
South Australia	5.3	(0.6)	51.4	(1.7)	43.3	(1.7)	Asturias•	2.5	(0.4)	6.0	(0.7)	91.5	(0.8)
Tasmania	4.7	(0.7)	59.9	(1.7)	35.4	(1.8)	Balearic Islands•	7.0	(0.9)	8.3	(1.0)	84.6	(1.5)
Victoria	5.7	(0.5)	36.5	(1.3)	57.8	(1.4)	Basque Country•	10.3	(0.8)	11.4	(0.6)	78.2	(1.1)
Western Australia	5.9	(0.7)	39.4	(1.3)	54.6	(1.4)	Cantabria•	3.9	(0.6)	7.3	(0.8)	88.8	(1.0)
Belgium							Castile and Leon•	4.5	(0.6)	4.8	(0.7)	90.7	(1.0)
Flemish community•	2.1	(0.3)	3.1	(0.3)	94.7	(0.5)	Catalonia•	6.0	(0.9)	5.2	(0.6)	88.8	(1.2)
French community	2.7	(0.4)	6.1	(0.5)	91.2	(0.6)	Extremadura•	3.6	(0.6)	7.4	(0.8)	89.0	(1.2)
German-speaking community	2.3	(0.6)	32.5	(1.9)	65.2	(2.0)	Galicia•	3.5	(0.5)	6.7	(0.7)	89.8	(0.8)
Canada							La Rioja•	7.0	(0.7)	5.5	(0.6)	87.5	(0.9)
Alberta	4.6	(0.5)	57.3	(1.5)	38.1	(1.6)	Madrid•	4.5	(0.7)	9.2	(1.0)	86.3	(1.3)
British Columbia	4.6	(0.6)	50.1	(1.6)	45.3	(1.7)	Murcia•	6.9	(1.2)	8.2	(0.7)	84.9	(1.5)
Manitoba	6.1	(0.7)	53.1	(1.6)	40.8	(1.5)	Navarre•	9.4	(0.9)	9.8	(1.0)	80.8	(1.5)
New Brunswick	7.9	(0.7)	58.8	(1.4)	33.3	(1.5)	**United Kingdom**						
Newfoundland and Labrador	2.9	(0.8)	56.3	(1.9)	40.7	(1.6)	England	5.1	(0.5)	24.7	(0.6)	70.2	(0.8)
Nova Scotia	18.0	(1.1)	43.0	(1.4)	39.0	(1.2)	Northern Ireland	7.7	(0.6)	49.8	(1.3)	42.5	(1.3)
Ontario	5.9	(0.4)	25.7	(1.3)	68.5	(1.2)	Scotland•	3.0	(0.3)	29.7	(1.0)	67.3	(1.0)
Prince Edward Island	3.2	(0.5)	58.8	(1.4)	38.0	(1.4)	Wales	5.8	(0.4)	27.5	(0.8)	66.7	(0.9)
Quebec	19.9	(0.9)	45.0	(1.0)	35.0	(1.3)	**United States**						
Saskatchewan	5.3	(0.7)	54.7	(2.1)	40.0	(1.8)	Connecticut•	1.0	(0.4)	12.8	(0.9)	86.2	(1.1)
Italy							Florida•	1.7	(0.3)	20.9	(1.5)	77.4	(1.5)
Abruzzo	3.7	(0.5)	5.5	(0.5)	90.8	(1.1)	Massachusetts•	1.2	(0.3)	13.7	(1.0)	85.1	(1.1)
Basilicata	1.6	(0.3)	3.5	(0.5)	94.9	(0.6)							
Bolzano	3.1	(0.4)	7.5	(0.6)	89.4	(0.7)	**Argentina**						
Calabria	4.2	(0.5)	6.7	(0.6)	89.1	(0.8)	Ciudad Autónoma de Buenos Aires•	3.8	(0.7)	9.3	(0.9)	86.9	(1.3)
Campania	3.1	(0.5)	9.1	(1.0)	87.9	(1.2)	**Brazil**						
Emilia Romagna	5.8	(0.6)	8.8	(0.8)	85.5	(1.1)	Acre	27.3	(3.5)	35.1	(2.6)	37.6	(3.6)
Friuli Venezia Giulia	4.4	(0.7)	3.8	(0.5)	91.8	(0.8)	Alagoas	29.5	(2.0)	33.9	(2.3)	36.6	(1.9)
Lazio	4.5	(0.7)	8.4	(0.8)	87.0	(0.9)	Amapá	19.2	(2.9)	31.2	(2.1)	49.7	(3.1)
Liguria	6.6	(0.8)	10.5	(1.1)	83.0	(1.2)	Amazonas	32.7	(2.7)	28.4	(1.9)	38.9	(2.8)
Lombardia	3.9	(0.5)	6.8	(0.8)	89.3	(1.0)	Bahia	27.9	(4.8)	29.3	(3.9)	42.9	(5.0)
Marche	6.1	(1.0)	7.0	(0.9)	87.0	(1.1)	Ceará	26.0	(2.0)	25.5	(2.0)	48.6	(2.1)
Molise	3.1	(0.6)	3.7	(0.6)	93.2	(0.8)	Espírito Santo	14.8	(1.1)	21.8	(1.9)	63.3	(2.5)
Piemonte	3.8	(0.7)	8.8	(0.7)	87.4	(1.1)	Federal District	11.4	(0.7)	28.0	(2.0)	60.5	(2.0)
Puglia	2.8	(0.5)	6.9	(0.6)	90.3	(0.7)	Goiás	22.9	(1.4)	36.9	(2.3)	40.3	(2.1)
Sardegna	4.4	(0.8)	6.5	(0.8)	89.1	(1.1)	Maranhão	20.9	(2.3)	26.3	(2.3)	52.8	(2.6)
Sicilia	5.0	(1.0)	13.4	(0.9)	81.6	(1.4)	Mato Grosso	31.3	(2.5)	35.0	(2.6)	33.7	(3.1)
Toscana	4.6	(0.7)	8.4	(0.8)	87.0	(0.9)	Mato Grosso do Sul	22.7	(2.7)	34.1	(2.7)	43.2	(3.6)
Trento	5.1	(0.8)	4.8	(0.6)	90.1	(1.1)	Minas Gerais	12.4	(1.8)	34.3	(2.3)	53.3	(2.6)
Umbria	3.9	(0.4)	8.3	(0.7)	87.8	(0.8)	Pará	24.0	(2.2)	27.1	(2.2)	48.9	(2.1)
Valle d'Aosta	4.3	(0.7)	5.6	(0.8)	90.1	(1.0)	Paraíba	23.5	(2.7)	31.0	(2.7)	45.6	(4.4)
Veneto	5.6	(1.0)	5.7	(0.7)	88.7	(1.2)	Paraná	23.3	(2.4)	38.3	(3.3)	38.4	(3.8)
Mexico							Pernambuco	27.7	(3.0)	31.9	(2.0)	40.4	(3.6)
Aguascalientes	4.9	(0.8)	20.8	(1.3)	74.4	(1.5)	Piauí	14.7	(2.2)	28.9	(1.7)	56.3	(2.1)
Baja California	7.8	(1.5)	26.1	(2.0)	66.1	(2.6)	Rio de Janeiro	21.5	(1.9)	28.2	(2.5)	50.3	(3.4)
Baja California Sur	6.4	(1.1)	17.7	(1.8)	75.9	(2.5)	Rio Grande do Norte	19.5	(1.7)	30.6	(2.2)	49.9	(2.8)
Campeche	16.2	(1.3)	11.7	(1.2)	72.0	(1.6)	Rio Grande do Sul	22.0	(2.1)	45.0	(1.9)	33.0	(2.2)
Chiapas	21.9	(2.1)	12.3	(1.2)	65.8	(2.5)	Rondônia	35.7	(3.5)	28.0	(1.9)	36.4	(3.1)
Chihuahua	13.9	(2.3)	28.4	(3.1)	57.7	(4.8)	Roraima	24.3	(1.9)	27.4	(1.5)	48.3	(2.1)
Coahuila	6.7	(1.0)	18.3	(1.7)	74.9	(2.1)	Santa Catarina	18.3	(2.7)	38.8	(3.0)	42.9	(4.6)
Colima	8.3	(1.1)	14.1	(1.5)	77.7	(1.5)	São Paulo	11.2	(1.0)	35.5	(1.8)	53.3	(1.9)
Distrito Federal	5.6	(0.9)	17.1	(1.1)	77.4	(1.6)	Sergipe	13.1	(1.9)	36.8	(1.9)	50.1	(2.5)
Durango	7.1	(1.2)	18.5	(1.7)	74.4	(2.3)	Tocantins	28.6	(2.4)	38.0	(2.2)	33.4	(2.5)
Guanajuato	8.1	(1.7)	14.2	(1.5)	77.7	(1.8)	**Colombia**						
Guerrero	15.8	(1.7)	14.8	(1.4)	69.3	(2.5)	Bogota	11.0	(1.0)	59.9	(1.6)	29.1	(1.7)
Hidalgo	9.1	(1.3)	26.4	(2.1)	64.4	(2.5)	Cali	16.2	(1.3)	47.3	(1.8)	36.4	(1.7)
Jalisco	7.3	(1.2)	12.7	(1.3)	80.0	(1.4)	Manizales	8.5	(1.4)	52.9	(1.3)	38.5	(1.7)
Mexico	8.5	(1.8)	23.7	(1.7)	67.8	(3.0)	Medellin	8.5	(1.4)	59.5	(1.8)	32.0	(1.9)
Morelos	8.0	(1.0)	21.1	(1.5)	71.0	(2.0)	**Russian Federation**						
Nayarit	6.3	(1.0)	16.5	(1.3)	77.2	(1.8)	Perm Territory region•	10.0	(1.1)	7.0	(0.7)	83.0	(1.4)
Nuevo León	4.2	(0.9)	20.3	(1.5)	75.5	(1.5)	**United Arab Emirates**						
Puebla	11.9	(1.7)	14.0	(1.6)	74.1	(2.7)	Abu Dhabi•	27.1	(1.1)	25.6	(0.9)	47.3	(1.3)
Querétaro	5.1	(1.5)	19.4	(2.0)	75.5	(3.0)	Ajman	41.0	(3.0)	25.7	(1.7)	33.2	(3.5)
Quintana Roo	9.2	(1.4)	21.2	(1.5)	69.7	(1.6)	Dubai•	17.3	(0.6)	28.9	(0.8)	53.8	(0.8)
San Luis Potosí	9.0	(2.2)	12.1	(1.3)	78.9	(3.3)	Fujairah	26.8	(2.8)	20.6	(1.8)	52.5	(2.5)
Sinaloa	8.1	(1.2)	20.1	(1.8)	71.8	(1.7)	Ras Al Khaimah	27.6	(3.6)	22.0	(2.2)	50.3	(3.4)
Tabasco	13.9	(1.6)	11.3	(1.3)	74.8	(1.7)	Sharjah	18.9	(2.4)	29.2	(2.0)	52.0	(3.4)
Tamaulipas	7.8	(2.6)	31.1	(2.7)	61.1	(3.0)	Umm Al Quwain	32.1	(2.3)	20.6	(2.4)	47.3	(2.8)
Tlaxcala	5.7	(0.7)	23.6	(1.2)	70.6	(2.4)							
Veracruz	10.0	(1.6)	20.4	(1.5)	69.6	(1.7)							
Yucatán	10.8	(1.5)	11.7	(1.2)	77.5	(1.8)							
Zacatecas	9.0	(1.3)	13.9	(1.4)	77.1	(2.1)							

• PISA adjudicated region.
Note: See Table IV.3.33 for national data.
StatLink http://dx.doi.org/10.1787/888932957536

[Part 1/4]
Index of school responsibility for curriculum and assessment and mathematics performance, by region

Table B2.IV.16   *Results based on school principals' reports*

	Index of school responsibility for curriculum and assessment										Variability in this index	
	All students		Bottom quarter		Second quarter		Third quarter		Top quarter			
	Mean index	S.E.	Mean index	S.E.	Mean index	S.E.	Mean index	S.E.	Mean index	S.E.	Standard deviation	S.E.
Australia												
Australian Capital Territory	-0.25	(0.01)	-0.82	(0.00)	-0.68	(0.01)	-0.34	(0.01)	0.85	(0.05)	0.75	(0.01)
New South Wales	-0.01	(0.06)	-0.79	(0.02)	-0.48	(0.05)	-0.14	(0.06)	1.35	(0.16)	0.84	(0.04)
Northern Territory	-0.24	(0.14)	-0.79	(0.01)	-0.56	(0.03)	-0.26	(0.10)	0.67	(0.49)	0.66	(0.18)
Queensland	0.10	(0.09)	-0.80	(0.02)	-0.48	(0.07)	0.24	(0.28)	1.44	(0.00)	0.91	(0.03)
South Australia	-0.01	(0.10)	-0.82	(0.01)	-0.58	(0.05)	-0.06	(0.30)	1.44	(0.11)	0.91	(0.05)
Tasmania	0.11	(0.03)	-0.80	(0.01)	-0.56	(0.01)	0.38	(0.11)	1.44	(0.00)	0.96	(0.01)
Victoria	0.43	(0.08)	-0.62	(0.04)	-0.18	(0.08)	1.09	(0.24)	1.44	(0.00)	0.91	(0.02)
Western Australia	0.08	(0.08)	-0.75	(0.03)	-0.43	(0.05)	0.06	(0.25)	1.44	(0.06)	0.87	(0.04)
Belgium												
Flemish community •	0.12	(0.07)	-0.64	(0.04)	-0.42	(0.03)	0.08	(0.22)	1.44	(0.03)	0.83	(0.03)
French community	-0.01	(0.06)	-0.79	(0.02)	-0.48	(0.05)	-0.14	(0.06)	1.35	(0.16)	0.84	(0.04)
German-speaking community	0.43	(0.08)	-0.62	(0.04)	-0.18	(0.08)	1.09	(0.24)	1.44	(0.00)	0.91	(0.02)
Canada												
Alberta	-0.65	(0.04)	-1.00	(0.03)	-0.81	(0.01)	-0.69	(0.04)	-0.11	(0.11)	0.43	(0.06)
British Columbia	-0.39	(0.06)	-0.86	(0.02)	-0.72	(0.03)	-0.39	(0.07)	0.41	(0.20)	0.61	(0.08)
Manitoba	-0.40	(0.04)	-0.88	(0.02)	-0.77	(0.02)	-0.54	(0.04)	0.58	(0.13)	0.69	(0.05)
New Brunswick	-0.88	(0.02)	-1.08	(0.01)	-1.00	(0.01)	-0.88	(0.01)	-0.58	(0.08)	0.29	(0.09)
Newfoundland and Labrador	-0.98	(0.03)	-1.17	(0.01)	-1.04	(0.01)	-0.99	(0.01)	-0.73	(0.10)	0.33	(0.10)
Nova Scotia	-0.84	(0.07)	-1.15	(0.03)	-0.99	(0.04)	-0.84	(0.08)	-0.36	(0.16)	0.37	(0.09)
Ontario	-0.58	(0.06)	-0.99	(0.02)	-0.82	(0.02)	-0.70	(0.05)	0.20	(0.20)	0.62	(0.08)
Prince Edward Island	-0.86	(0.00)	-1.09	(0.00)	-0.85	(0.00)	-0.81	(0.00)	-0.68	(0.01)	0.23	(0.01)
Quebec	-0.18	(0.07)	-0.87	(0.02)	-0.58	(0.04)	-0.26	(0.07)	0.98	(0.19)	0.78	(0.05)
Saskatchewan	-0.63	(0.03)	-1.00	(0.01)	-0.84	(0.02)	-0.74	(0.02)	0.05	(0.12)	0.54	(0.05)
Italy												
Abruzzo	0.46	(0.11)	-0.72	(0.09)	-0.15	(0.19)	1.29	(0.25)	1.44	(0.00)	0.95	(0.04)
Basilicata	0.57	(0.12)	-0.69	(0.07)	0.09	(0.38)	1.44	(0.07)	1.44	(0.00)	0.97	(0.03)
Bolzano	-0.35	(0.01)	-0.82	(0.00)	-0.67	(0.01)	-0.44	(0.01)	0.54	(0.02)	0.64	(0.01)
Calabria	0.51	(0.11)	-0.68	(0.08)	0.07	(0.29)	1.20	(0.13)	1.44	(0.00)	0.91	(0.04)
Campania	0.76	(0.11)	-0.56	(0.18)	0.73	(0.28)	1.44	(0.10)	1.44	(0.00)	0.85	(0.07)
Emilia Romagna	0.42	(0.14)	-0.81	(0.04)	-0.25	(0.33)	1.28	(0.24)	1.44	(0.00)	0.99	(0.03)
Friuli Venezia Giulia	0.06	(0.10)	-0.79	(0.03)	-0.42	(0.08)	0.05	(0.22)	1.40	(0.09)	0.85	(0.04)
Lazio	0.34	(0.13)	-0.78	(0.05)	-0.31	(0.20)	1.02	(0.35)	1.44	(0.00)	0.95	(0.04)
Liguria	0.11	(0.12)	-0.71	(0.06)	-0.39	(0.06)	0.25	(0.29)	1.29	(0.13)	0.81	(0.05)
Lombardia	-0.01	(0.12)	-0.78	(0.04)	-0.48	(0.08)	0.00	(0.27)	1.24	(0.16)	0.80	(0.06)
Marche	0.17	(0.13)	-0.77	(0.05)	-0.26	(0.18)	0.29	(0.35)	1.44	(0.08)	0.86	(0.05)
Molise	0.60	(0.02)	-0.78	(0.01)	0.30	(0.07)	1.44	(0.00)	1.44	(0.00)	0.99	(0.01)
Piemonte	0.26	(0.13)	-0.85	(0.12)	-0.37	(0.12)	0.82	(0.37)	1.44	(0.00)	0.97	(0.05)
Puglia	0.34	(0.14)	-0.76	(0.05)	-0.34	(0.20)	1.04	(0.37)	1.44	(0.00)	0.95	(0.04)
Sardegna	0.18	(0.11)	-0.81	(0.04)	-0.39	(0.14)	0.47	(0.31)	1.44	(0.02)	0.91	(0.05)
Sicilia	0.50	(0.14)	-0.62	(0.08)	-0.09	(0.26)	1.25	(0.28)	1.44	(0.00)	0.90	(0.04)
Toscana	0.44	(0.14)	-0.66	(0.07)	-0.09	(0.28)	1.08	(0.29)	1.44	(0.00)	0.88	(0.04)
Trento	0.22	(0.09)	-0.83	(0.03)	-0.28	(0.17)	0.65	(0.11)	1.37	(0.10)	0.87	(0.02)
Umbria	0.44	(0.11)	-0.73	(0.03)	-0.16	(0.22)	1.23	(0.27)	1.44	(0.00)	0.94	(0.02)
Valle d'Aosta	-0.19	(0.01)	-0.81	(0.00)	-0.61	(0.01)	-0.26	(0.02)	0.91	(0.04)	0.75	(0.01)
Veneto	0.50	(0.12)	-0.54	(0.07)	-0.02	(0.20)	1.12	(0.26)	1.44	(0.00)	0.83	(0.04)
Mexico												
Aguascalientes	-0.78	(0.07)	-1.21	(0.02)	-1.09	(0.03)	-0.84	(0.06)	0.00	(0.20)	0.59	(0.08)
Baja California	-0.85	(0.09)	-1.25	(0.03)	-1.07	(0.11)	-0.83	(0.08)	-0.23	(0.30)	0.59	(0.15)
Baja California Sur	-0.79	(0.09)	-1.17	(0.03)	-1.09	(0.03)	-0.85	(0.10)	-0.05	(0.28)	0.56	(0.11)
Campeche	-0.70	(0.08)	-1.13	(0.02)	-1.02	(0.02)	-0.82	(0.12)	0.17	(0.22)	0.59	(0.09)
Chiapas	-0.89	(0.07)	-1.24	(0.02)	-1.11	(0.02)	-0.92	(0.12)	-0.28	(0.18)	0.45	(0.08)
Chihuahua	-0.87	(0.10)	-1.25	(0.01)	-1.17	(0.06)	-0.96	(0.12)	-0.08	(0.29)	0.59	(0.13)
Coahuila	-0.81	(0.06)	-1.15	(0.03)	-1.07	(0.04)	-0.88	(0.06)	-0.15	(0.21)	0.55	(0.09)
Colima	-0.75	(0.05)	-1.15	(0.02)	-1.02	(0.07)	-0.79	(0.07)	-0.06	(0.11)	0.48	(0.03)
Distrito Federal	-0.95	(0.05)	-1.23	(0.04)	-1.09	(0.03)	-0.90	(0.09)	-0.58	(0.13)	0.30	(0.06)
Durango	-0.73	(0.13)	-1.21	(0.03)	-0.95	(0.08)	-0.80	(0.11)	0.07	(0.37)	0.53	(0.10)
Guanajuato	-0.80	(0.08)	-1.23	(0.03)	-1.09	(0.03)	-0.97	(0.05)	0.09	(0.29)	0.73	(0.12)
Guerrero	-0.92	(0.07)	-1.26	(0.02)	-1.11	(0.05)	-1.02	(0.07)	-0.28	(0.23)	0.52	(0.10)
Hidalgo	-0.89	(0.07)	-1.25	(0.02)	-1.09	(0.04)	-0.90	(0.06)	-0.31	(0.25)	0.51	(0.12)
Jalisco	-0.90	(0.07)	-1.22	(0.05)	-1.04	(0.05)	-0.88	(0.07)	-0.45	(0.19)	0.41	(0.11)
Mexico	-0.93	(0.06)	-1.25	(0.02)	-1.12	(0.04)	-0.91	(0.09)	-0.43	(0.22)	0.46	(0.16)
Morelos	-0.69	(0.09)	-1.13	(0.04)	-0.87	(0.06)	-0.81	(0.03)	0.07	(0.33)	0.59	(0.14)
Nayarit	-0.71	(0.11)	-1.24	(0.03)	-1.05	(0.04)	-0.86	(0.05)	0.31	(0.36)	0.73	(0.11)
Nuevo León	-0.59	(0.15)	-1.20	(0.04)	-0.98	(0.11)	-0.48	(0.17)	0.31	(0.38)	0.70	(0.15)
Puebla	-0.80	(0.11)	-1.23	(0.03)	-1.09	(0.02)	-0.91	(0.06)	0.02	(0.37)	0.66	(0.17)
Querétaro	-0.80	(0.09)	-1.16	(0.02)	-1.09	(0.08)	-0.81	(0.14)	-0.13	(0.23)	0.53	(0.12)
Quintana Roo	-0.89	(0.07)	-1.20	(0.03)	-1.07	(0.04)	-0.87	(0.07)	-0.41	(0.25)	0.52	(0.15)
San Luis Potosí	-0.97	(0.05)	-1.24	(0.02)	-1.11	(0.03)	-0.96	(0.07)	-0.57	(0.13)	0.32	(0.08)
Sinaloa	-0.98	(0.05)	-1.25	(0.01)	-1.13	(0.05)	-0.90	(0.09)	-0.63	(0.09)	0.27	(0.07)
Tabasco	-1.00	(0.05)	-1.26	(0.00)	-1.15	(0.03)	-1.04	(0.08)	-0.54	(0.15)	0.34	(0.08)
Tamaulipas	-0.88	(0.04)	-1.12	(0.01)	-1.06	(0.05)	-0.84	(0.05)	-0.52	(0.10)	0.34	(0.03)
Tlaxcala	-0.88	(0.08)	-1.24	(0.03)	-1.09	(0.01)	-0.97	(0.07)	-0.23	(0.26)	0.56	(0.13)
Veracruz	-1.05	(0.04)	-1.24	(0.02)	-1.10	(0.03)	-1.07	(0.04)	-0.76	(0.09)	0.22	(0.05)
Yucatán	-0.79	(0.11)	-1.25	(0.01)	-1.11	(0.02)	-0.97	(0.12)	0.17	(0.37)	0.67	(0.15)
Zacatecas	-0.79	(0.07)	-1.15	(0.02)	-1.07	(0.02)	-0.90	(0.06)	-0.05	(0.22)	0.57	(0.07)

• PISA adjudicated region.
Notes: Values that are statistically significant are indicated in bold (see Annex A3).
See Table IV.4.3 for national data.
StatLink ⌘⬛ http://dx.doi.org/10.1787/888932957536

[Part 2/4]
Index of school responsibility for curriculum and assessment and mathematics performance, by region

Table B2.IV.16   *Results based on school principals' reports*

| | Index of school responsibility for curriculum and assessment | | | | | | | | | | Variability in this index | |
| | All students | | Bottom quarter | | Second quarter | | Third quarter | | Top quarter | | | |
	Mean index	S.E.	Mean index	S.E.	Mean index	S.E.	Mean index	S.E.	Mean index	S.E.	Standard deviation	S.E.
Portugal												
Alentejo	-0.57	(0.14)	-1.05	(0.03)	-0.90	(0.06)	-0.68	(0.16)	0.36	(0.41)	0.65	(0.14)
Spain												
Andalusia●	-0.64	(0.07)	-1.14	(0.05)	-0.85	(0.07)	-0.60	(0.09)	0.04	(0.16)	0.52	(0.09)
Aragon●	-0.55	(0.09)	-1.08	(0.02)	-0.85	(0.04)	-0.73	(0.08)	0.45	(0.28)	0.73	(0.09)
Asturias●	-0.66	(0.08)	-1.10	(0.02)	-0.86	(0.06)	-0.73	(0.05)	0.05	(0.24)	0.55	(0.11)
Balearic Islands●	-0.43	(0.07)	-0.98	(0.04)	-0.79	(0.03)	-0.52	(0.07)	0.58	(0.23)	0.72	(0.08)
Basque Country●	0.09	(0.07)	-0.80	(0.02)	-0.48	(0.05)	0.20	(0.22)	1.44	(0.01)	0.91	(0.03)
Cantabria●	-0.51	(0.06)	-1.02	(0.06)	-0.76	(0.04)	-0.53	(0.08)	0.27	(0.18)	0.58	(0.08)
Castile and Leon●	-0.44	(0.10)	-1.01	(0.06)	-0.81	(0.01)	-0.55	(0.12)	0.62	(0.31)	0.75	(0.11)
Catalonia●	-0.19	(0.13)	-0.90	(0.03)	-0.70	(0.07)	-0.30	(0.15)	1.15	(0.36)	0.85	(0.10)
Extremadura●	-0.62	(0.08)	-1.12	(0.02)	-0.93	(0.07)	-0.65	(0.12)	0.21	(0.21)	0.58	(0.09)
Galicia●	-0.55	(0.06)	-0.97	(0.04)	-0.79	(0.04)	-0.54	(0.06)	0.09	(0.20)	0.50	(0.10)
La Rioja●	-0.55	(0.01)	-1.03	(0.00)	-0.85	(0.00)	-0.65	(0.00)	0.33	(0.02)	0.67	(0.01)
Madrid●	-0.65	(0.07)	-1.10	(0.04)	-0.83	(0.03)	-0.66	(0.08)	-0.01	(0.22)	0.51	(0.12)
Murcia●	-0.48	(0.09)	-1.04	(0.05)	-0.82	(0.03)	-0.64	(0.06)	0.58	(0.29)	0.74	(0.09)
Navarre●	-0.37	(0.06)	-0.98	(0.04)	-0.74	(0.03)	-0.44	(0.08)	0.66	(0.17)	0.70	(0.05)
United Kingdom												
England	0.99	(0.06)	-0.35	(0.20)	1.44	(0.08)	1.44	(0.00)	1.44	(0.00)	0.81	(0.04)
Northern Ireland	0.89	(0.08)	-0.36	(0.10)	1.05	(0.24)	1.44	(0.00)	1.44	(0.00)	0.82	(0.04)
Scotland●	0.28	(0.08)	-0.68	(0.04)	-0.34	(0.07)	0.71	(0.24)	1.44	(0.00)	0.92	(0.03)
Wales	0.88	(0.06)	-0.27	(0.06)	0.90	(0.21)	1.44	(0.00)	1.44	(0.00)	0.79	(0.03)
United States												
Connecticut●	-0.01	(0.15)	-0.90	(0.05)	-0.66	(0.13)	0.08	(0.43)	1.44	(0.09)	0.94	(0.06)
Florida●	-0.82	(0.05)	-1.15	(0.02)	-0.99	(0.05)	-0.80	(0.04)	-0.35	(0.14)	0.34	(0.04)
Massachusetts●	0.29	(0.09)	-0.74	(0.04)	-0.23	(0.12)	0.71	(0.26)	1.44	(0.00)	0.89	(0.03)
Argentina												
Ciudad Autónoma de Buenos Aires●	-0.11	(0.12)	-0.95	(0.05)	-0.63	(0.11)	-0.12	(0.26)	1.26	(0.19)	0.87	(0.07)
Brazil												
Acre	-0.55	(0.08)	-1.01	(0.04)	-0.88	(0.05)	-0.68	(0.13)	0.38	(0.21)	0.68	(0.08)
Alagoas	-0.25	(0.23)	-1.10	(0.08)	-0.81	(0.08)	-0.16	(0.48)	1.08	(0.44)	0.89	(0.15)
Amapá	-0.29	(0.09)	-0.98	(0.07)	-0.72	(0.11)	-0.32	(0.08)	0.86	(0.29)	0.75	(0.08)
Amazonas	-0.55	(0.19)	-1.16	(0.02)	-1.00	(0.09)	-0.79	(0.12)	0.76	(0.65)	0.87	(0.18)
Bahia	-0.30	(0.17)	-0.99	(0.08)	-0.68	(0.18)	-0.18	(0.22)	c	c	0.69	(0.15)
Ceará	-0.20	(0.11)	-1.00	(0.10)	-0.57	(0.13)	-0.13	(0.18)	0.92	(0.18)	0.78	(0.06)
Espírito Santo	-0.64	(0.20)	-1.11	(0.02)	-1.06	(0.04)	-0.84	(0.08)	0.46	(0.75)	0.80	(0.23)
Federal District	-0.32	(0.16)	-1.10	(0.12)	-0.81	(0.04)	-0.24	(0.32)	0.89	(0.44)	0.83	(0.17)
Goiás	-0.56	(0.17)	-1.12	(0.04)	-0.95	(0.08)	-0.73	(0.09)	0.55	(0.56)	0.80	(0.18)
Maranhão	-0.46	(0.17)	c	c	-0.89	(0.12)	-0.40	(0.26)	0.56	(0.45)	0.74	(0.16)
Mato Grosso	-0.02	(0.21)	-0.91	(0.07)	-0.60	(0.17)	0.13	(0.45)	1.32	(0.27)	0.89	(0.11)
Mato Grosso do Sul	-0.59	(0.11)	-1.07	(0.03)	-0.90	(0.06)	-0.79	(0.05)	0.40	(0.41)	0.72	(0.14)
Minas Gerais	-0.51	(0.15)	-1.04	(0.04)	-0.84	(0.05)	-0.59	(0.18)	0.43	(0.46)	0.68	(0.18)
Pará	-0.16	(0.10)	-0.99	(0.08)	-0.80	(0.07)	-0.29	(0.34)	c	c	1.00	(0.06)
Paraíba	0.12	(0.30)	-0.86	(0.04)	-0.52	(0.34)	0.44	(0.82)	1.44	(0.13)	0.96	(0.09)
Paraná	-0.35	(0.13)	-0.99	(0.10)	-0.69	(0.13)	-0.42	(0.12)	0.70	(0.36)	0.72	(0.11)
Pernambuco	-0.64	(0.11)	-1.11	(0.06)	-0.87	(0.07)	-0.76	(0.08)	0.20	(0.40)	0.64	(0.17)
Piauí	-0.33	(0.16)	-1.07	(0.04)	-0.95	(0.06)	-0.57	(0.41)	1.30	(0.27)	0.99	(0.09)
Rio de Janeiro	-0.55	(0.08)	-1.17	(0.04)	-0.98	(0.07)	-0.57	(0.15)	0.54	(0.11)	0.73	(0.04)
Rio Grande do Norte	0.01	(0.16)	-0.90	(0.07)	-0.55	(0.23)	0.18	(0.36)	1.32	(0.18)	0.89	(0.08)
Rio Grande do Sul	0.02	(0.13)	-0.81	(0.09)	-0.41	(0.09)	0.09	(0.27)	1.21	(0.20)	0.79	(0.06)
Rondônia	-0.38	(0.16)	-1.05	(0.09)	-0.75	(0.11)	-0.47	(0.20)	0.73	(0.39)	0.72	(0.12)
Roraima	-0.46	(0.08)	-1.09	(0.06)	-0.87	(0.08)	-0.49	(0.12)	0.62	(0.21)	0.76	(0.06)
Santa Catarina	-0.64	(0.17)	-1.19	(0.04)	-1.05	(0.08)	-0.73	(0.17)	0.39	(0.53)	0.77	(0.19)
São Paulo	-0.54	(0.08)	-1.09	(0.02)	-0.93	(0.05)	-0.66	(0.09)	0.53	(0.22)	0.75	(0.08)
Sergipe	-0.30	(0.20)	-1.04	(0.11)	-0.78	(0.11)	-0.43	(0.25)	1.06	(0.50)	0.87	(0.14)
Tocantins	-0.53	(0.12)	-1.06	(0.03)	-0.87	(0.07)	-0.67	(0.10)	0.48	(0.36)	0.70	(0.12)
Colombia												
Bogota	-0.11	(0.10)	-1.02	(0.07)	-0.52	(0.13)	0.07	(0.17)	1.05	(0.15)	0.82	(0.05)
Cali	-0.04	(0.13)	-0.94	(0.07)	-0.53	(0.15)	0.13	(0.27)	1.20	(0.15)	0.84	(0.06)
Manizales	-0.14	(0.12)	-1.07	(0.07)	-0.73	(0.08)	0.03	(0.30)	1.21	(0.15)	0.91	(0.05)
Medellin	-0.20	(0.13)	-1.04	(0.07)	-0.71	(0.09)	-0.22	(0.19)	1.16	(0.28)	0.87	(0.09)
Russian Federation												
Perm Territory region●	0.13	(0.10)	-0.75	(0.04)	-0.46	(0.05)	0.29	(0.37)	1.44	(0.02)	0.90	(0.05)
United Arab Emirates												
Abu Dhabi●	-0.62	(0.06)	-1.26	(0.00)	-1.24	(0.02)	-0.89	(0.05)	0.90	(0.20)	0.96	(0.06)
Ajman	-0.91	(0.12)	-1.26	(0.00)	-1.23	(0.05)	-1.04	(0.04)	-0.11	(0.42)	0.60	(0.19)
Dubai●	0.25	(0.00)	-1.18	(0.00)	-0.43	(0.01)	1.15	(0.01)	1.44	(0.00)	1.13	(0.00)
Fujairah	-0.77	(0.18)	-1.26	(0.00)	-1.15	(0.02)	-1.03	(0.04)	0.37	(0.70)	0.85	(0.23)
Ras Al Khaimah	-0.89	(0.02)	-1.26	(0.00)	-1.24	(0.03)	-1.13	(0.02)	0.07	(0.08)	0.80	(0.02)
Sharjah	-0.65	(0.15)	-1.19	(0.03)	-0.90	(0.07)	-0.79	(0.07)	0.29	(0.52)	0.72	(0.18)
Umm Al Quwain	-0.82	(0.01)	-1.26	(0.00)	-1.26	(0.00)	-1.13	(0.00)	0.37	(0.04)	0.91	(0.01)

● PISA adjudicated region.
Notes: Values that are statistically significant are indicated in bold (see Annex A3).
See Table IV.4.3 for national data.
StatLink ⟐⟐ http://dx.doi.org/10.1787/888932957536

[Part 3/4]
Index of school responsibility for curriculum and assessment and mathematics performance, by region
Table B2.IV.16 · *Results based on school principals' reports*

	Performance on the mathematics scale, by national quarters of this index								Change in the mathematics score per unit of this index		Increased likelihood of students in the bottom quarter of this index scoring in the bottom quarter of the national mathematics performance distribution		Explained variance in student performance (r-squared x 100)	
	Bottom quarter		Second quarter		Third quarter		Top quarter							
	Mean score	S.E.	Mean score	S.E.	Mean score	S.E.	Mean score	S.E.	Score dif.	S.E.	Ratio	S.E.	%	S.E.
Australia														
Australian Capital Territory	523	(8.4)	525	(8.1)	515	(8.2)	508	(7.4)	2.3	(4.5)	0.9	(0.15)	0.0	(0.15)
New South Wales	501	(6.8)	516	(10.7)	511	(7.2)	511	(10.3)	1.4	(6.1)	1.0	(0.13)	0.0	(0.26)
Northern Territory	430	(17.1)	434	(16.3)	465	(17.2)	481	(22.6)	26.2	(13.4)	1.5	(0.37)	2.5	(3.38)
Queensland	498	(7.0)	497	(7.5)	505	(7.7)	513	(8.7)	7.3	(4.8)	1.1	(0.15)	0.5	(0.70)
South Australia	490	(6.3)	483	(7.9)	500	(10.3)	484	(12.6)	-1.2	(6.3)	0.9	(0.15)	0.0	(0.35)
Tasmania	484	(6.0)	484	(5.9)	460	(7.6)	484	(8.2)	1.2	(3.2)	0.9	(0.15)	0.0	(0.13)
Victoria	**486**	(6.5)	499	(7.0)	511	(6.9)	**509**	(8.6)	**10.4**	(4.4)	1.3	(0.14)	1.1	(0.93)
Western Australia	500	(9.4)	520	(8.6)	519	(7.7)	526	(10.7)	8.5	(6.4)	1.3	(0.20)	0.6	(0.85)
Belgium														
Flemish community*	534	(10.9)	548	(12.2)	521	(13.8)	522	(9.9)	-7.1	(7.1)	0.9	(0.17)	0.3	(0.88)
French community	501	(6.8)	516	(11.0)	510	(8.1)	511	(10.3)	1.4	(6.1)	1.0	(0.14)	0.0	(0.26)
German-speaking community	**488**	(6.2)	498	(6.7)	509	(7.8)	**510**	(8.2)	**10.4**	(4.4)	1.2	(0.14)	1.1	(0.93)
Canada														
Alberta	520	(9.1)	514	(7.0)	504	(11.5)	531	(12.6)	16.0	(8.7)	0.9	(0.17)	0.6	(0.64)
British Columbia	519	(7.2)	523	(10.5)	524	(8.7)	523	(6.7)	0.5	(6.4)	1.2	(0.16)	0.0	(0.14)
Manitoba	481	(8.3)	494	(8.8)	487	(6.5)	507	(8.3)	11.3	(5.6)	1.1	(0.20)	0.8	(0.76)
New Brunswick	**493**	(6.8)	497	(8.1)	508	(6.3)	**512**	(6.6)	11.9	(9.8)	1.2	(0.18)	0.2	(0.27)
Newfoundland and Labrador	489	(8.5)	486	(13.4)	498	(11.0)	489	(6.2)	27.9	(4.1)	1.1	(0.35)	1.1	(0.77)
Nova Scotia	492	(8.2)	507	(10.1)	501	(11.6)	488	(20.1)	-8.3	(11.9)	1.1	(0.19)	0.2	(0.40)
Ontario	509	(5.9)	524	(8.9)	515	(7.9)	510	(8.8)	-1.2	(5.1)	1.1	(0.13)	0.0	(0.13)
Prince Edward Island	479	(4.8)	481	(5.5)	477	(5.9)	488	(6.0)	14.2	(9.2)	1.1	(0.12)	0.2	(0.21)
Quebec	525	(7.1)	527	(8.3)	545	(10.5)	546	(9.9)	**15.0**	(5.3)	1.1	(0.16)	1.6	(1.27)
Saskatchewan	510	(7.3)	507	(6.4)	511	(7.5)	496	(6.4)	-1.9	(4.6)	0.9	(0.14)	0.0	(0.10)
Italy														
Abruzzo	457	(20.0)	475	(14.8)	488	(14.1)	484	(9.2)	12.4	(9.3)	1.5	(0.47)	1.7	(2.64)
Basilicata	467	(14.2)	488	(12.4)	456	(11.3)	451	(7.5)	-8.0	(7.5)	1.0	(0.27)	0.8	(1.66)
Bolzano	**472**	(4.3)	522	(4.0)	519	(6.8)	**512**	(4.1)	2.2	(2.5)	**1.9**	(0.22)	0.0	(0.07)
Calabria	417	(14.4)	445	(16.9)	432	(13.1)	426	(12.4)	2.0	(9.5)	1.2	(0.35)	0.1	(0.76)
Campania	448	(19.7)	445	(22.9)	460	(13.6)	457	(13.2)	7.1	(9.1)	1.1	(0.33)	0.5	(1.19)
Emilia Romagna	476	(15.2)	502	(20.6)	514	(15.4)	509	(14.5)	12.3	(10.0)	1.5	(0.41)	1.6	(2.57)
Friuli Venezia Giulia	527	(18.7)	508	(8.4)	514	(14.0)	543	(16.6)	13.1	(12.0)	1.0	(0.42)	1.6	(2.88)
Lazio	488	(25.1)	457	(27.0)	470	(20.1)	484	(14.3)	1.9	(10.4)	0.9	(0.33)	0.0	(0.98)
Liguria	**456**	(15.1)	498	(19.6)	482	(10.4)	**516**	(17.6)	22.5	(8.2)	1.7	(0.41)	4.0	(3.06)
Lombardia	496	(22.8)	535	(13.0)	530	(11.4)	506	(14.8)	-2.3	(10.0)	1.6	(0.37)	0.1	(0.96)
Marche	505	(13.6)	486	(12.3)	493	(18.0)	501	(10.6)	3.0	(7.4)	1.0	(0.31)	0.1	(0.46)
Molise	**491**	(4.9)	441	(5.4)	468	(6.8)	**466**	(6.5)	-4.2	(2.6)	**0.4**	(0.08)	0.3	(0.34)
Piemonte	495	(17.9)	491	(9.2)	513	(13.1)	495	(13.1)	6.4	(8.8)	1.2	(0.38)	0.5	(1.53)
Puglia	464	(16.2)	475	(21.5)	486	(11.1)	487	(12.5)	10.3	(7.4)	1.5	(0.47)	1.3	(1.87)
Sardegna	459	(11.7)	463	(13.3)	446	(11.6)	464	(15.8)	1.1	(8.5)	1.0	(0.25)	0.0	(0.61)
Sicilia	460	(15.5)	430	(17.7)	457	(13.7)	440	(12.9)	-1.7	(9.7)	0.7	(0.27)	0.0	(0.93)
Toscana	493	(14.2)	521	(20.4)	465	(19.8)	503	(17.4)	-5.5	(11.0)	1.1	(0.30)	0.3	(1.28)
Trento	482	(12.4)	540	(9.9)	560	(7.7)	515	(20.6)	14.8	(10.2)	**2.5**	(0.71)	2.4	(3.50)
Umbria	**520**	(9.8)	499	(17.0)	482	(21.0)	**468**	(14.6)	**-21.1**	(8.4)	**0.5**	(0.16)	5.0	(3.67)
Valle d'Aosta	481	(5.3)	514	(6.6)	502	(7.5)	471	(5.6)	-7.4	(3.8)	1.0	(0.17)	0.5	(0.46)
Veneto	531	(19.2)	538	(20.4)	517	(18.1)	507	(12.4)	-14.9	(11.1)	0.8	(0.32)	1.9	(2.93)
Mexico														
Aguascalientes	434	(10.4)	406	(15.0)	449	(15.0)	459	(9.8)	**22.3**	(10.8)	1.0	(0.20)	3.2	(2.31)
Baja California	420	(17.6)	405	(16.0)	419	(22.1)	417	(12.7)	12.4	(6.4)	0.8	(0.40)	1.0	(1.16)
Baja California Sur	415	(8.8)	402	(15.9)	440	(11.5)	401	(18.5)	-15.8	(11.2)	1.0	(0.27)	1.5	(2.29)
Campeche	394	(9.0)	397	(9.8)	384	(6.7)	407	(9.8)	**16.9**	(8.3)	1.0	(0.27)	2.0	(1.62)
Chiapas	364	(16.7)	382	(13.5)	362	(18.2)	384	(18.7)	6.7	(14.2)	1.4	(0.50)	0.2	(0.90)
Chihuahua	423	(18.1)	433	(19.0)	431	(17.3)	426	(17.3)	-2.3	(11.8)	0.9	(0.32)	0.0	(0.63)
Coahuila	**402**	(12.2)	410	(13.7)	425	(20.7)	**436**	(12.1)	5.2	(9.1)	1.5	(0.44)	0.2	(0.70)
Colima	423	(14.3)	414	(15.2)	449	(18.6)	431	(10.4)	5.4	(9.7)	1.4	(0.35)	0.1	(0.52)
Distrito Federal	**411**	(11.5)	392	(23.8)	453	(16.8)	**456**	(13.7)	86.1	(11.2)	1.2	(0.48)	12.1	(5.36)
Durango	435	(9.3)	410	(10.6)	408	(15.0)	444	(15.3)	12.2	(12.3)	0.7	(0.19)	0.8	(1.62)
Guanajuato	**388**	(15.1)	402	(15.1)	416	(16.6)	**441**	(10.6)	9.9	(8.1)	1.6	(0.52)	0.9	(1.35)
Guerrero	371	(11.3)	354	(8.4)	374	(13.4)	368	(13.2)	-7.2	(15.4)	0.9	(0.31)	0.3	(1.54)
Hidalgo	**390**	(11.6)	382	(17.9)	434	(13.5)	**420**	(11.8)	19.5	(15.0)	1.3	(0.30)	1.8	(2.75)
Jalisco	436	(18.3)	434	(16.7)	433	(15.3)	436	(12.2)	2.3	(12.0)	1.0	(0.36)	0.0	(0.41)
Mexico	409	(11.4)	410	(7.5)	423	(13.5)	428	(14.6)	34.2	(12.5)	1.3	(0.33)	5.4	(6.02)
Morelos	419	(15.4)	423	(24.6)	403	(17.7)	440	(23.0)	0.1	(8.6)	1.0	(0.26)	0.0	(0.29)
Nayarit	422	(11.6)	396	(13.5)	409	(13.0)	428	(9.5)	10.5	(6.1)	0.7	(0.21)	1.0	(1.25)
Nuevo León	435	(12.4)	416	(17.3)	448	(16.0)	445	(18.2)	2.5	(13.2)	1.0	(0.34)	0.1	(1.21)
Puebla	407	(14.2)	417	(11.8)	416	(11.4)	421	(11.5)	1.9	(8.4)	1.3	(0.42)	0.0	(0.46)
Querétaro	426	(10.2)	437	(18.3)	450	(18.4)	426	(17.7)	6.4	(10.7)	1.1	(0.27)	0.2	(0.80)
Quintana Roo	406	(6.4)	408	(9.6)	405	(11.6)	423	(14.4)	20.5	(6.9)	1.1	(0.24)	2.2	(1.83)
San Luis Potosí	416	(17.1)	389	(20.4)	419	(10.7)	423	(19.2)	18.9	(35.7)	1.0	(0.30)	0.7	(2.82)
Sinaloa	425	(10.8)	417	(15.7)	399	(9.9)	402	(13.1)	-32.5	(25.3)	**0.6**	(0.18)	1.6	(2.55)
Tabasco	384	(7.5)	372	(10.7)	392	(15.0)	365	(21.4)	-16.4	(23.5)	0.8	(0.15)	0.6	(1.98)
Tamaulipas	396	(10.9)	404	(12.4)	419	(15.2)	425	(15.3)	30.4	(16.9)	1.2	(0.29)	2.0	(2.04)
Tlaxcala	422	(9.1)	406	(13.8)	408	(12.2)	409	(12.5)	-2.4	(8.7)	0.7	(0.20)	0.1	(0.43)
Veracruz	415	(15.4)	402	(12.2)	396	(11.2)	396	(16.8)	-28.8	(28.0)	**0.6**	(0.20)	0.7	(1.33)
Yucatán	420	(8.9)	389	(9.0)	400	(16.9)	430	(14.1)	21.4	(6.6)	0.6	(0.20)	3.7	(2.69)
Zacatecas	399	(8.9)	410	(9.7)	413	(11.1)	412	(9.7)	7.2	(8.0)	1.2	(0.24)	0.3	(0.59)

* PISA adjudicated region.
Notes: Values that are statistically significant are indicated in bold (see Annex A3).
See Table IV.4.3 for national data.
StatLink ⬛═ http://dx.doi.org/10.1787/888932957536

[Part 4/4]
Index of school responsibility for curriculum and assessment and mathematics performance, by region
Table B2.IV.16 *Results based on school principals' reports*

| | Performance on the mathematics scale, by national quarters of this index | | | | | | | | Change in the mathematics score per unit of this index | | Increased likelihood of students in the bottom quarter of this index scoring in the bottom quarter of the national mathematics performance distribution | | Explained variance in student performance (r-squared x 100) | |
| | Bottom quarter | | Second quarter | | Third quarter | | Top quarter | | | | | | | |
	Mean score	S.E.	Mean score	S.E.	Mean score	S.E.	Mean score	S.E.	Score dif.	S.E.	Ratio	S.E.	%	S.E.
Portugal														
Alentejo	477	(28.5)	497	(28.6)	500	(17.7)	481	(15.2)	-11.8	(18.0)	1.1	(0.53)	0.7	(2.85)
Spain														
Andalusia•	**456**	(9.7)	483	(11.1)	467	(10.2)	**483**	(8.1)	13.3	(9.3)	1.3	(0.23)	0.7	(0.98)
Aragon•	507	(10.9)	492	(12.5)	481	(10.8)	505	(13.6)	4.1	(7.2)	0.8	(0.15)	0.1	(0.45)
Asturias•	496	(14.6)	496	(8.0)	510	(14.4)	497	(11.3)	4.7	(11.1)	1.0	(0.27)	0.1	(0.50)
Balearic Islands•	**463**	(7.8)	461	(10.0)	470	(13.8)	**507**	(6.6)	24.0	(5.6)	1.3	(0.21)	3.9	(1.46)
Basque Country•	504	(6.1)	510	(4.8)	509	(5.3)	499	(6.0)	-1.4	(3.5)	1.1	(0.12)	0.0	(0.18)
Cantabria•	488	(6.8)	490	(10.9)	485	(9.0)	503	(9.8)	-1.7	(7.3)	1.0	(0.13)	0.0	(0.18)
Castile and Leon•	502	(11.4)	518	(8.9)	498	(11.5)	517	(7.4)	5.7	(5.0)	1.2	(0.25)	0.3	(0.48)
Catalonia•	483	(10.9)	499	(15.0)	486	(9.7)	504	(12.6)	8.9	(6.5)	1.2	(0.21)	0.8	(1.26)
Extremadura•	462	(10.5)	456	(7.5)	469	(8.2)	461	(11.0)	0.8	(13.1)	1.0	(0.21)	0.0	(0.51)
Galicia•	480	(7.4)	472	(11.8)	502	(8.6)	501	(8.8)	15.6	(7.6)	1.3	(0.23)	0.8	(0.66)
La Rioja•	**489**	(5.6)	495	(5.8)	502	(5.4)	**526**	(4.4)	17.6	(3.4)	1.2	(0.14)	1.4	(0.53)
Madrid•	483	(8.8)	505	(8.9)	514	(11.1)	513	(14.0)	23.0	(11.6)	**1.5**	(0.24)	1.8	(2.00)
Murcia•	**452**	(11.8)	453	(8.8)	447	(11.9)	**494**	(17.6)	25.7	(8.0)	1.1	(0.24)	4.4	(2.83)
Navarre•	517	(7.0)	515	(7.6)	521	(7.6)	514	(6.1)	0.5	(5.0)	1.0	(0.12)	0.0	(0.14)
United Kingdom														
England	**471**	(6.1)	501	(9.0)	503	(6.2)	**505**	(6.5)	16.0	(4.1)	1.4	(0.18)	1.9	(0.97)
Northern Ireland	497	(13.2)	478	(9.5)	487	(7.0)	485	(6.8)	-6.7	(8.0)	1.1	(0.21)	0.3	(0.97)
Scotland•	495	(5.7)	498	(6.9)	500	(5.6)	501	(6.5)	2.3	(3.8)	1.0	(0.13)	0.1	(0.28)
Wales	472	(4.9)	470	(4.5)	466	(4.6)	466	(4.7)	-3.0	(3.8)	0.9	(0.11)	0.1	(0.19)
United States														
Connecticut•	506	(17.9)	502	(12.3)	511	(12.4)	504	(12.9)	-0.4	(9.1)	1.1	(0.31)	0.0	(0.60)
Florida•	478	(7.8)	446	(12.4)	470	(15.5)	474	(13.4)	11.3	(13.5)	0.8	(0.15)	0.2	(0.53)
Massachusetts•	500	(12.7)	520	(12.0)	520	(10.6)	513	(18.0)	3.4	(9.4)	1.2	(0.24)	0.1	(0.75)
Argentina														
Ciudad Autónoma de Buenos Aires•	**369**	(23.4)	415	(25.1)	428	(13.5)	**460**	(14.1)	35.2	(8.3)	2.4	(0.62)	10.5	(4.30)
Brazil														
Acre	353	(7.9)	347	(9.5)	363	(12.9)	376	(17.9)	30.9	(10.1)	1.0	(0.25)	9.8	(7.32)
Alagoas	322	(17.2)	361	(20.4)	338	(26.6)	347	(27.4)	1.0	(11.6)	1.5	(0.47)	0.0	(2.01)
Amapá	368	(9.4)	352	(21.7)	363	(14.1)	358	(11.7)	-1.6	(7.6)	0.7	(0.21)	0.1	(0.87)
Amazonas	350	(10.2)	355	(12.5)	361	(18.0)	363	(10.2)	2.9	(6.0)	1.0	(0.24)	0.2	(0.89)
Bahia	378	(24.0)	367	(19.3)	397	(39.5)	c	c	-28.1	(12.9)	0.7	(0.49)	6.2	(5.82)
Ceará	380	(33.9)	372	(41.5)	392	(19.5)	374	(11.0)	-3.1	(11.4)	1.8	(0.63)	0.1	(1.22)
Espírito Santo	383	(9.9)	392	(13.9)	453	(33.4)	444	(46.9)	48.5	(5.1)	1.6	(0.41)	20.4	(12.33)
Federal District	**387**	(17.2)	377	(15.3)	424	(36.6)	**458**	(30.3)	41.6	(14.2)	1.3	(0.41)	17.6	(12.16)
Goiás	380	(15.4)	354	(20.7)	384	(23.0)	401	(19.7)	20.8	(11.3)	0.7	(0.26)	5.3	(5.82)
Maranhão	c	c	357	(36.2)	360	(27.4)	340	(13.6)	-1.5	(11.4)	1.3	(0.39)	0.0	(0.93)
Mato Grosso	360	(7.1)	366	(20.2)	360	(34.0)	395	(28.0)	12.7	(10.3)	1.0	(0.30)	2.4	(4.01)
Mato Grosso do Sul	396	(8.1)	398	(20.6)	421	(16.5)	418	(15.9)	24.6	(8.0)	1.0	(0.34)	5.8	(3.93)
Minas Gerais	392	(8.7)	389	(7.1)	402	(23.8)	430	(20.9)	22.5	(8.7)	1.1	(0.24)	4.7	(3.78)
Pará	**343**	(9.1)	340	(11.0)	342	(15.1)	c	c	34.4	(3.6)	1.3	(0.35)	25.8	(3.59)
Paraíba	397	(30.8)	386	(25.9)	382	(27.2)	416	(21.2)	10.6	(19.4)	1.2	(0.68)	1.7	(6.86)
Paraná	405	(35.9)	423	(57.2)	387	(20.8)	399	(11.8)	-3.7	(14.6)	1.3	(0.40)	0.1	(1.34)
Pernambuco	350	(15.7)	380	(12.6)	371	(14.6)	353	(14.6)	-4.7	(12.5)	1.3	(0.37)	0.2	(1.51)
Piauí	367	(13.6)	369	(15.6)	379	(29.3)	432	(54.5)	27.1	(18.4)	1.2	(0.42)	11.0	(14.35)
Rio de Janeiro	**362**	(10.0)	365	(8.1)	374	(18.7)	**449**	(13.4)	49.7	(8.6)	1.5	(0.43)	26.3	(6.92)
Rio Grande do Norte	**366**	(14.3)	361	(13.5)	372	(32.0)	**428**	(24.7)	28.6	(10.0)	1.1	(0.35)	9.2	(6.01)
Rio Grande do Sul	**396**	(8.3)	392	(15.6)	411	(13.1)	**438**	(10.7)	23.7	(7.1)	1.2	(0.35)	7.7	(4.27)
Rondônia	381	(15.2)	366	(10.4)	388	(12.8)	392	(14.6)	8.4	(10.6)	1.0	(0.47)	0.9	(1.97)
Roraima	**344**	(8.8)	349	(13.3)	360	(11.9)	**395**	(15.8)	38.4	(6.3)	1.2	(0.24)	16.5	(5.30)
Santa Catarina	426	(11.0)	408	(19.4)	394	(28.1)	419	(27.7)	9.6	(15.1)	**0.5**	(0.20)	1.0	(3.42)
São Paulo	**395**	(8.5)	381	(7.6)	393	(19.8)	443	(19.7)	30.4	(8.3)	1.0	(0.21)	8.5	(4.06)
Sergipe	390	(11.3)	404	(28.2)	368	(15.1)	377	(23.7)	-4.3	(13.5)	0.7	(0.27)	0.3	(2.72)
Tocantins	**350**	(11.8)	354	(11.8)	348	(10.8)	**410**	(20.2)	44.1	(11.0)	1.2	(0.29)	16.2	(6.92)
Colombia														
Bogota	389	(6.1)	390	(7.5)	384	(5.8)	407	(10.7)	8.9	(4.9)	1.0	(0.19)	1.2	(1.32)
Cali	**356**	(9.8)	387	(13.1)	376	(14.9)	**397**	(14.2)	13.7	(7.1)	1.5	(0.34)	2.7	(2.86)
Manizales	**392**	(6.2)	382	(9.4)	409	(13.3)	**434**	(10.8)	21.0	(6.8)	1.1	(0.26)	7.0	(4.04)
Medellin	366	(13.0)	406	(19.6)	412	(25.8)	389	(20.4)	4.6	(11.7)	1.6	(0.33)	0.2	(1.51)
Russian Federation														
Perm Territory region•	477	(14.1)	496	(14.3)	475	(10.1)	487	(18.3)	-0.4	(9.6)	1.0	(0.22)	0.0	(0.70)
United Arab Emirates														
Abu Dhabi•	**393**	(4.9)	400	(8.2)	438	(8.6)	**455**	(13.0)	20.2	(6.1)	**1.5**	(0.22)	4.9	(2.83)
Ajman	397	(16.0)	396	(17.3)	407	(14.2)	414	(16.2)	4.1	(21.3)	1.2	(0.41)	0.1	(1.89)
Dubai•	**417**	(2.6)	461	(3.4)	487	(3.5)	**490**	(3.1)	26.4	(1.1)	**2.3**	(0.13)	10.1	(0.84)
Fujairah	410	(8.6)	408	(9.4)	398	(16.2)	427	(21.4)	2.0	(15.9)	1.0	(0.26)	0.1	(1.73)
Ras Al Khaimah	**404**	(12.0)	403	(13.2)	413	(15.0)	**442**	(9.6)	19.3	(7.2)	1.2	(0.30)	4.2	(3.04)
Sharjah	**414**	(14.2)	435	(15.5)	441	(21.6)	**468**	(15.9)	18.6	(12.3)	1.7	(0.41)	2.6	(3.34)
Umm Al Quwain	398	(12.7)	392	(11.8)	420	(10.7)	382	(5.4)	-12.6	(3.3)	1.2	(0.32)	2.3	(1.20)

• PISA adjudicated region.
Notes: Values that are statistically significant are indicated in bold (see Annex A3).
See Table IV.4.3 for national data.
StatLink ⟨ᴍˢˡ⟩ http://dx.doi.org/10.1787/888932957536

[Part 1/1]
School choice, by region
Table B2.IV.17   *Results based on school principals' reports*

Percentage of students in schools whose principal reported on the number of schools competing for students in the same area

	Two or more other schools		One other school		No other schools				Two or more other schools		One other school		No other schools	
	%	S.E.	%	S.E.	%	S.E.			%	S.E.	%	S.E.	%	S.E.
Australia								**Portugal**						
Australian Capital Territory	85.9	(0.8)	10.5	(0.7)	3.6	(0.4)		Alentejo	36.9	(11.0)	36.0	(13.7)	27.1	(10.1)
New South Wales	86.9	(2.5)	6.2	(1.5)	7.0	(2.0)		**Spain**						
Northern Territory	55.4	(3.5)	37.0	(3.1)	7.6	(1.7)		Andalusia•	55.8	(6.0)	14.0	(5.2)	30.3	(5.6)
Queensland	91.6	(1.9)	3.9	(1.7)	4.5	(1.7)		Aragon•	62.8	(6.7)	19.5	(6.5)	17.7	(5.1)
South Australia	87.3	(2.5)	7.8	(2.1)	4.9	(2.1)		Asturias•	61.5	(6.0)	28.3	(6.1)	10.2	(3.6)
Tasmania	79.5	(1.0)	12.0	(0.7)	8.6	(1.0)		Balearic Islands•	56.6	(7.1)	22.0	(5.7)	21.4	(5.8)
Victoria	90.3	(2.7)	4.0	(1.7)	5.7	(2.1)		Basque Country•	75.0	(3.1)	18.4	(2.8)	6.6	(1.9)
Western Australia	89.7	(2.9)	7.5	(2.7)	2.8	(1.2)		Cantabria•	70.6	(4.5)	13.4	(3.5)	16.0	(3.8)
Belgium								Castile and Leon•	71.7	(6.2)	16.5	(5.5)	11.8	(4.9)
Flemish community•	85.1	(2.9)	10.4	(2.4)	4.5	(1.8)		Catalonia•	72.2	(5.0)	11.8	(5.0)	16.0	(4.3)
French community	73.8	(4.1)	19.5	(3.8)	6.8	(2.6)		Extremadura•	53.3	(6.2)	13.1	(4.9)	33.6	(4.7)
German-speaking community	60.6	(0.2)	24.7	(0.1)	14.6	(0.3)		Galicia•	59.3	(4.8)	17.5	(5.2)	23.2	(5.1)
Canada								La Rioja•	69.2	(0.5)	19.2	(0.4)	11.7	(0.6)
Alberta	71.0	(4.7)	16.8	(4.1)	12.2	(3.9)		Madrid•	86.9	(4.8)	6.8	(3.2)	6.4	(3.6)
British Columbia	65.0	(5.7)	4.0	(2.0)	31.0	(5.3)		Murcia•	73.0	(6.0)	18.1	(5.1)	9.0	(3.4)
Manitoba	51.9	(2.4)	24.0	(2.0)	24.1	(1.6)		Navarre•	72.0	(2.7)	14.2	(1.7)	13.8	(3.0)
New Brunswick	29.8	(1.7)	5.8	(0.9)	64.4	(1.8)		**United Kingdom**						
Newfoundland and Labrador	2.9	(1.1)	4.3	(0.8)	92.8	(0.6)		England	85.3	(2.8)	9.3	(2.3)	5.4	(1.8)
Nova Scotia	23.1	(4.0)	20.0	(4.3)	56.9	(7.3)		Northern Ireland	95.0	(2.5)	2.4	(1.8)	2.6	(1.8)
Ontario	75.9	(4.3)	19.4	(4.1)	4.7	(2.2)		Scotland•	47.5	(4.7)	13.6	(3.4)	38.9	(4.8)
Prince Edward Island	2.7	(0.2)	19.9	(0.2)	77.3	(0.3)		Wales	76.9	(3.5)	13.1	(2.4)	10.0	(2.6)
Quebec	71.4	(3.8)	10.4	(2.7)	18.2	(2.9)		**United States**						
Saskatchewan	49.8	(2.8)	12.5	(2.5)	37.7	(3.3)		Connecticut•	76.5	(6.3)	6.4	(3.8)	17.1	(5.1)
Italy								Florida•	54.8	(6.1)	17.9	(4.7)	27.3	(6.2)
Abruzzo	31.3	(5.8)	20.7	(5.0)	48.0	(5.6)		Massachusetts•	80.4	(6.5)	2.2	(2.2)	17.4	(6.2)
Basilicata	34.0	(5.6)	20.6	(5.3)	45.4	(6.0)								
Bolzano	24.7	(0.6)	30.9	(0.9)	44.3	(0.8)		**Argentina**						
Calabria	22.0	(5.0)	23.9	(6.5)	54.1	(8.1)		Ciudad Autónoma de Buenos Aires•	93.6	(3.7)	4.9	(3.4)	1.6	(1.5)
Campania	42.5	(6.0)	9.0	(3.8)	48.5	(7.0)		**Brazil**						
Emilia Romagna	31.4	(6.1)	21.7	(7.1)	46.9	(8.0)		Acre	46.2	(10.5)	12.9	(6.7)	40.9	(9.9)
Friuli Venezia Giulia	49.1	(6.5)	19.0	(4.3)	31.9	(6.4)		Alagoas	57.3	(11.4)	28.2	(8.1)	14.5	(8.6)
Lazio	24.6	(5.8)	26.4	(4.9)	49.1	(6.9)		Amapá	74.3	(7.1)	15.2	(7.9)	10.6	(6.5)
Liguria	38.5	(6.1)	24.1	(5.4)	37.3	(6.4)		Amazonas	62.0	(6.2)	20.7	(6.9)	17.4	(6.3)
Lombardia	47.9	(6.9)	31.8	(7.2)	20.3	(6.9)		Bahia	51.7	(15.7)	7.0	(6.4)	41.3	(13.2)
Marche	23.1	(5.4)	19.0	(6.2)	57.9	(6.9)		Ceará	44.8	(9.8)	34.5	(8.8)	20.7	(9.0)
Molise	17.1	(0.7)	22.0	(0.7)	61.0	(0.9)		Espírito Santo	46.2	(8.6)	19.2	(5.6)	34.7	(9.2)
Piemonte	34.5	(7.2)	19.9	(6.1)	45.6	(7.1)		Federal District	76.2	(7.9)	13.8	(7.6)	10.0	(5.6)
Puglia	34.4	(8.1)	22.1	(7.7)	43.5	(6.1)		Goiás	47.2	(8.7)	23.2	(7.8)	29.6	(7.8)
Sardegna	30.1	(5.2)	13.0	(2.1)	56.9	(6.7)		Maranhão	54.1	(10.8)	19.3	(8.2)	26.6	(9.1)
Sicilia	22.0	(4.2)	19.2	(4.6)	58.8	(5.5)		Mato Grosso	46.1	(9.9)	29.3	(7.8)	24.6	(8.1)
Toscana	37.1	(6.6)	16.3	(3.8)	46.6	(6.1)		Mato Grosso do Sul	79.8	(7.3)	20.2	(7.3)	0.0	c
Trento	44.9	(5.9)	10.3	(0.8)	44.8	(5.9)		Minas Gerais	44.9	(6.9)	19.2	(7.6)	35.9	(7.7)
Umbria	24.0	(4.9)	23.3	(4.2)	52.7	(6.0)		Pará	28.1	(7.6)	24.2	(10.5)	47.6	(13.3)
Valle d'Aosta	3.2	(0.3)	30.1	(1.0)	66.7	(1.0)		Paraíba	35.5	(10.1)	48.7	(11.7)	15.8	(7.5)
Veneto	43.9	(6.0)	28.2	(5.8)	27.9	(5.1)		Paraná	52.8	(10.5)	15.8	(7.4)	31.3	(10.5)
Mexico								Pernambuco	47.1	(9.9)	43.0	(12.9)	9.9	(7.2)
Aguascalientes	78.0	(4.2)	13.4	(2.3)	8.6	(4.3)		Piauí	59.3	(8.3)	31.8	(7.9)	8.9	(7.0)
Baja California	80.3	(9.1)	11.3	(8.6)	8.4	(2.1)		Rio de Janeiro	62.3	(10.7)	12.2	(7.0)	25.6	(9.2)
Baja California Sur	55.0	(7.9)	14.7	(6.6)	30.2	(8.4)		Rio Grande do Norte	73.5	(10.4)	9.4	(5.6)	17.1	(8.6)
Campeche	58.1	(8.8)	23.3	(7.3)	18.6	(6.3)		Rio Grande do Sul	73.7	(7.5)	8.0	(4.7)	18.3	(7.5)
Chiapas	68.7	(5.5)	14.6	(4.8)	16.8	(2.5)		Rondônia	55.0	(10.3)	19.9	(9.1)	25.1	(9.0)
Chihuahua	62.1	(9.2)	21.1	(8.1)	16.9	(4.9)		Roraima	46.8	(9.8)	14.2	(6.9)	39.0	(9.7)
Coahuila	67.8	(9.8)	26.3	(9.6)	5.9	(3.2)		Santa Catarina	25.8	(7.4)	35.0	(10.5)	39.2	(10.8)
Colima	58.6	(5.4)	25.1	(6.9)	16.2	(6.3)		São Paulo	50.6	(5.7)	25.4	(5.2)	24.0	(4.7)
Distrito Federal	87.6	(5.3)	9.7	(6.0)	2.8	(2.7)		Sergipe	49.0	(14.3)	15.7	(8.8)	35.3	(13.1)
Durango	67.2	(7.0)	14.3	(6.1)	18.4	(4.7)		Tocantins	28.4	(7.7)	42.8	(10.5)	28.8	(11.4)
Guanajuato	53.8	(8.6)	28.1	(7.7)	18.1	(6.3)		**Colombia**						
Guerrero	56.7	(8.9)	28.1	(8.2)	15.2	(5.9)		Bogota	90.0	(4.4)	1.7	(1.2)	8.3	(4.2)
Hidalgo	71.5	(6.7)	21.3	(6.0)	7.2	(3.2)		Cali	81.2	(7.2)	11.1	(4.3)	7.8	(6.1)
Jalisco	62.2	(8.0)	24.2	(7.9)	13.6	(4.7)		Manizales	63.1	(8.6)	20.8	(7.9)	16.1	(5.2)
Mexico	78.5	(8.4)	16.2	(7.7)	5.4	(3.5)		Medellin	85.7	(5.2)	7.2	(4.2)	7.1	(4.2)
Morelos	59.4	(8.1)	23.1	(5.9)	17.5	(7.1)		**Russian Federation**						
Nayarit	61.6	(6.9)	15.4	(6.3)	23.0	(4.5)		Perm Territory region•	55.2	(5.9)	22.4	(5.1)	22.4	(5.4)
Nuevo León	80.2	(6.8)	7.3	(3.8)	12.5	(5.7)		**United Arab Emirates**						
Puebla	71.9	(6.0)	17.4	(5.1)	10.7	(4.7)		Abu Dhabi•	74.5	(3.2)	16.1	(3.0)	9.4	(2.4)
Querétaro	65.8	(9.2)	15.3	(4.7)	18.9	(7.8)		Ajman	83.0	(7.8)	17.0	(7.8)	0.0	c
Quintana Roo	59.6	(7.7)	25.2	(7.7)	15.2	(5.4)		Dubai•	80.6	(0.3)	13.2	(0.3)	6.2	(0.1)
San Luis Potosí	78.2	(4.3)	9.3	(3.9)	12.6	(2.6)		Fujairah	47.6	(7.2)	25.6	(7.3)	26.8	(2.7)
Sinaloa	64.0	(6.8)	15.9	(6.7)	20.1	(5.9)		Ras Al Khaimah	59.3	(9.5)	18.4	(7.1)	22.3	(9.4)
Tabasco	71.3	(6.7)	10.6	(5.3)	18.1	(4.2)		Sharjah	84.7	(6.3)	7.4	(5.1)	7.9	(6.0)
Tamaulipas	78.1	(7.8)	12.6	(5.2)	9.3	(5.7)		Umm Al Quwain	47.1	(0.4)	23.5	(0.3)	29.3	(0.2)
Tlaxcala	87.3	(5.7)	12.7	(5.7)	0.0	c								
Veracruz	80.7	(4.6)	8.6	(3.5)	10.7	(3.5)								
Yucatán	75.3	(6.5)	13.1	(5.3)	11.6	(4.8)								
Zacatecas	59.6	(5.6)	12.9	(3.0)	27.5	(5.8)								

• PISA adjudicated region.
Note: See Table IV.4.4 for national data.
StatLink ⟶ http://dx.doi.org/10.1787/888932957536

[Part 1/4]

Table B2.IV.18 School type and performance in mathematics, reading and science, by region

Results based on school principals' reports

	Government or public schools[1]								Government-dependent private schools[2]								Government-independent private schools[3]							
	Percentage of students		Performance on the mathematics scale		Performance on the reading scale		Performance on the science scale		Percentage of students		Performance on the mathematics scale		Performance on the reading scale		Performance on the science scale		Percentage of students		Performance on the mathematics scale		Performance on the reading scale		Performance on the science scale	
	%	S.E.	Mean score	S.E.	Mean score	S.E.	Mean score	S.E.	%	S.E.	Mean score	S.E.	Mean score	S.E.	Mean score	S.E.	%	S.E.	Mean score	S.E.	Mean score	S.E.	Mean score	S.E.
OECD																								
Australia																								
Australian Capital Territory	w	w	w	w	w	w	w	w	w	w	w	w	w	w	w	w	w	w	w	w	w	w	w	w
New South Wales	w	w	w	w	w	w	w	w	w	w	w	w	w	w	w	w	w	w	w	w	w	w	w	w
Northern Territory	w	w	w	w	w	w	w	w	w	w	w	w	w	w	w	w	w	w	w	w	w	w	w	w
Queensland	w	w	w	w	w	w	w	w	w	w	w	w	w	w	w	w	w	w	w	w	w	w	w	w
South Australia	w	w	w	w	w	w	w	w	w	w	w	w	w	w	w	w	w	w	w	w	w	w	w	w
Tasmania	w	w	w	w	w	w	w	w	w	w	w	w	w	w	w	w	w	w	w	w	w	w	w	w
Victoria	w	w	w	w	w	w	w	w	w	w	w	w	w	w	w	w	w	w	w	w	w	w	w	w
Western Australia	w	w	w	w	w	w	w	w	w	w	w	w	w	w	w	w	w	w	w	w	w	w	w	w
Belgium																								
Flemish community•	w	w	w	w	w	w	w	w	w	w	w	w	w	w	w	w	w	w	w	w	w	w	w	w
French community	47.9	(5.3)	469	(7.3)	476	(9.7)	465	(7.3)	52.1	(5.3)	498	(8.8)	505	(9.9)	495	(8.9)	0.0	c	c	c	c	c	c	c
German-speaking community	41.2	(0.3)	482	(3.7)	488	(4.0)	485	(4.1)	58.8	(0.3)	531	(2.9)	508	(3.3)	523	(3.4)	0.0	c	c	c	c	c	c	c
Canada																								
Alberta	98.9	(1.1)	517	(4.6)	525	(4.1)	539	(4.6)	1.1	(1.1)	c	c	c	c	c	c	0.0	c	c	c	c	c	c	c
British Columbia	89.2	(2.5)	519	(4.4)	531	(4.4)	541	(4.0)	6.3	(3.0)	c	c	c	c	c	c	4.5	(2.6)	c	c	c	c	c	c
Manitoba	94.5	(1.6)	488	(2.9)	489	(3.3)	499	(3.2)	2.1	(0.2)	c	c	c	c	c	c	3.4	(1.6)	c	c	c	c	c	c
New Brunswick	99.3	(0.9)	502	(2.5)	496	(2.6)	507	(2.5)	0.0	c	c	c	c	c	c	c	0.7	(0.9)	c	c	c	c	c	c
Newfoundland and Labrador	98.4	(1.1)	489	(3.7)	501	(3.6)	513	(3.6)	0.0	c	c	c	c	c	c	c	1.6	(1.1)	c	c	c	c	c	c
Nova Scotia	100.0	c	497	(4.1)	508	(3.1)	516	(3.0)	0.0	c	c	c	c	c	c	c	0.0	c	c	c	c	c	c	c
Ontario	96.8	(1.5)	514	(4.2)	528	(4.6)	526	(4.5)	0.0	c	c	c	c	c	c	c	3.2	(1.5)	c	c	c	c	c	c
Prince Edward Island	99.4	(0.1)	479	(2.5)	489	(2.7)	490	(2.7)	0.0	c	c	c	c	c	c	c	0.6	(0.1)	c	c	c	c	c	c
Quebec	79.0	(1.1)	522	(3.8)	505	(3.9)	505	(3.7)	14.6	(2.2)	584	(8.1)	574	(11.8)	549	(8.6)	6.4	(2.2)	585	(17.7)	571	(10.0)	563	(17.0)
Saskatchewan	95.5	(1.2)	505	(3.2)	505	(3.0)	516	(3.1)	2.3	(1.7)	c	c	c	c	c	c	2.2	(1.1)	c	c	c	c	c	c
Italy																								
Abruzzo	98.0	(2.0)	473	(6.6)	479	(6.0)	481	(5.9)	0.0	c	c	c	c	c	c	c	2.0	(2.0)	c	c	c	c	c	c
Basilicata	99.4	(0.6)	464	(4.5)	473	(5.5)	463	(4.2)	0.0	c	c	c	c	c	c	c	0.6	(0.6)	c	c	c	c	c	c
Bolzano	96.8	(0.2)	507	(2.2)	497	(2.6)	519	(2.3)	2.5	(0.1)	536	(7.5)	537	(8.7)	559	(8.3)	0.7	(0.1)	c	c	c	c	c	c
Calabria	99.1	(0.9)	431	(5.9)	437	(7.2)	431	(5.4)	0.0	c	c	c	c	c	c	c	0.9	(0.9)	c	c	c	c	c	c
Campania	95.6	(2.9)	455	(7.7)	466	(10.0)	460	(7.2)	0.0	c	c	c	c	c	c	c	4.4	(2.9)	c	c	c	c	c	c
Emilia Romagna	97.0	(2.5)	505	(7.1)	502	(7.5)	515	(6.7)	1.7	(1.8)	c	c	c	c	c	c	1.2	(1.7)	c	c	c	c	c	c
Friuli Venezia Giulia	90.8	(2.4)	525	(5.1)	526	(5.0)	535	(5.0)	6.7	(1.9)	c	c	c	c	c	c	2.5	(1.5)	c	c	c	c	c	c
Lazio	96.5	(2.7)	481	(8.5)	486	(8.4)	487	(8.0)	0.0	c	c	c	c	c	c	c	3.5	(2.7)	c	c	c	c	c	c
Liguria	91.8	(1.6)	487	(6.6)	486	(6.5)	500	(6.6)	4.8	(2.2)	c	c	c	c	c	c	3.4	(0.9)	c	c	c	c	c	c
Lombardia	92.7	(1.7)	517	(8.7)	521	(6.3)	529	(7.6)	0.0	c	c	c	c	c	c	c	7.3	(1.7)	559	(16.4)	568	(16.7)	565	(9.6)
Marche	99.9	(0.0)	499	(5.7)	498	(6.7)	509	(5.4)	0.1	(0.0)	c	c	c	c	c	c	0.0	c	c	c	c	c	c	c
Molise	100.0	c	458	(2.5)	468	(2.8)	463	(2.5)	0.0	c	c	c	c	c	c	c	0.0	c	c	c	c	c	c	c
Piemonte	90.2	(3.9)	502	(4.9)	510	(4.1)	510	(3.8)	6.6	(4.1)	c	c	c	c	c	c	3.1	(0.5)	c	c	c	c	c	c
Puglia	99.8	(0.2)	480	(6.2)	497	(6.0)	486	(4.9)	0.2	(0.2)	c	c	c	c	c	c	0.0	c	c	c	c	c	c	c
Sardegna	98.8	(1.2)	456	(5.6)	461	(6.8)	471	(5.6)	0.0	c	c	c	c	c	c	c	1.2	(1.2)	c	c	c	c	c	c
Sicilia	100.0	c	448	(5.3)	455	(6.0)	454	(6.4)	0.0	c	c	c	c	c	c	c	0.0	c	c	c	c	c	c	c
Toscana	96.3	(2.9)	494	(5.8)	486	(6.5)	501	(4.7)	0.0	c	c	c	c	c	c	c	3.7	(2.9)	c	c	c	c	c	c
Trento	79.4	(4.4)	540	(6.9)	537	(8.1)	548	(6.9)	16.8	(4.2)	484	(12.8)	466	(11.5)	493	(13.3)	3.8	(1.4)	c	c	c	c	c	c
Umbria	99.3	(0.5)	492	(7.1)	489	(7.3)	500	(6.6)	0.0	c	c	c	c	c	c	c	0.7	(0.5)	c	c	c	c	c	c
Valle d'Aosta	84.8	(0.7)	499	(2.8)	503	(3.2)	509	(3.4)	15.2	(0.7)	c	c	c	c	c	c	0.0	c	c	c	c	c	c	c
Veneto	89.1	(3.2)	534	(8.8)	532	(7.0)	541	(7.1)	9.4	(3.0)	426	(4.8)	424	(13.0)	442	(10.6)	1.5	(1.1)	c	c	c	c	c	c
Mexico																								
Aguascalientes	86.8	(4.6)	434	(4.8)	445	(5.5)	432	(4.3)	0.0	c	c	c	c	c	c	c	13.2	(4.6)	450	(20.2)	452	(16.6)	444	(16.7)
Baja California	92.6	(3.0)	416	(6.5)	429	(7.9)	418	(6.4)	0.0	c	c	c	c	c	c	c	7.4	(3.0)	411	(14.4)	424	(4.8)	413	(14.4)
Baja California Sur	92.9	(2.6)	415	(4.9)	425	(5.3)	419	(4.7)	0.0	c	c	c	c	c	c	c	7.1	(2.6)	c	c	c	c	c	c
Campeche	97.2	(2.1)	397	(4.0)	414	(5.4)	406	(4.8)	0.0	c	c	c	c	c	c	c	2.8	(2.1)	c	c	c	c	c	c
Chiapas	95.1	(3.7)	370	(7.5)	369	(9.0)	375	(7.9)	0.0	c	c	c	c	c	c	c	4.9	(3.7)	c	c	c	c	c	c
Chihuahua	91.6	(3.9)	429	(8.4)	444	(10.2)	428	(10.1)	0.0	c	c	c	c	c	c	c	8.4	(3.9)	431	(24.2)	444	(28.1)	443	(27.2)
Coahuila	80.9	(5.3)	410	(6.9)	423	(7.4)	416	(6.7)	0.0	c	c	c	c	c	c	c	19.1	(5.3)	449	(21.2)	464	(17.4)	441	(14.9)
Colima	95.2	(2.8)	422	(4.3)	435	(4.8)	423	(3.9)	0.0	c	c	c	c	c	c	c	4.8	(2.8)	c	c	c	c	c	c
Distrito Federal	81.4	(5.6)	418	(4.9)	440	(6.3)	419	(5.9)	0.0	c	c	c	c	c	c	c	18.6	(5.6)	469	(10.3)	476	(11.2)	458	(8.9)
Durango	96.6	(2.3)	424	(5.7)	435	(7.3)	421	(6.1)	0.0	c	c	c	c	c	c	c	3.4	(2.3)	c	c	c	c	c	c
Guanajuato	86.4	(5.2)	405	(6.3)	406	(7.3)	397	(6.9)	0.0	c	c	c	c	c	c	c	13.6	(5.2)	447	(13.5)	454	(14.8)	438	(11.5)
Guerrero	99.5	(0.5)	365	(3.7)	366	(5.3)	371	(5.5)	0.0	c	c	c	c	c	c	c	0.5	(0.5)	c	c	c	c	c	c
Hidalgo	91.9	(5.4)	402	(6.2)	408	(6.7)	406	(5.8)	4.8	(4.6)	c	c	c	c	c	c	3.3	(3.2)	c	c	c	c	c	c
Jalisco	91.7	(4.7)	433	(6.6)	431	(6.1)	433	(6.4)	0.0	c	c	c	c	c	c	c	8.3	(4.7)	c	c	c	c	c	c
Mexico	90.0	(2.6)	415	(5.2)	435	(5.8)	418	(5.4)	0.0	c	c	c	c	c	c	c	10.0	(2.6)	439	(34.5)	460	(41.1)	448	(27.5)
Morelos	84.7	(5.7)	410	(8.5)	412	(9.9)	413	(9.5)	0.0	c	c	c	c	c	c	c	15.3	(5.7)	466	(31.1)	473	(28.5)	463	(26.6)
Nayarit	95.3	(3.1)	411	(5.9)	414	(7.2)	404	(5.4)	0.0	c	c	c	c	c	c	c	4.7	(3.1)	c	c	c	c	c	c
Nuevo León	86.8	(4.8)	427	(5.6)	437	(7.7)	430	(7.2)	0.0	c	c	c	c	c	c	c	13.2	(4.8)	477	(20.3)	481	(18.2)	471	(17.0)
Puebla	94.3	(2.5)	411	(5.0)	419	(7.0)	418	(6.5)	0.0	c	c	c	c	c	c	c	5.7	(2.5)	c	c	c	c	c	c
Querétaro	89.0	(3.8)	428	(6.2)	444	(9.8)	425	(7.2)	0.0	c	c	c	c	c	c	c	11.0	(3.8)	470	(16.6)	494	(17.8)	472	(13.6)
Quintana Roo	93.8	(2.7)	404	(4.9)	424	(5.5)	410	(6.7)	0.0	c	c	c	c	c	c	c	6.2	(2.7)	c	c	c	c	c	c
San Luis Potosí	87.8	(6.0)	403	(5.6)	414	(5.9)	408	(4.6)	0.0	c	c	c	c	c	c	c	12.2	(6.0)	460	(25.4)	485	(18.7)	460	(22.4)
Sinaloa	97.7	(2.3)	409	(4.3)	415	(5.2)	406	(4.0)	0.0	c	c	c	c	c	c	c	2.3	(2.3)	c	c	c	c	c	c
Tabasco	95.1	(3.7)	373	(3.9)	391	(4.3)	387	(4.2)	0.0	c	c	c	c	c	c	c	4.9	(3.7)	c	c	c	c	c	c
Tamaulipas	89.7	(2.9)	408	(7.7)	417	(6.2)	412	(7.1)	0.0	c	c	c	c	c	c	c	10.3	(2.9)	436	(26.4)	450	(22.6)	432	(24.4)
Tlaxcala	94.3	(3.1)	408	(5.8)	414	(7.2)	408	(5.3)	0.0	c	c	c	c	c	c	c	5.7	(3.1)	430	(13.0)	457	(24.3)	439	(12.8)
Veracruz	92.3	(2.5)	397	(6.1)	403	(5.3)	397	(5.4)	0.0	c	c	c	c	c	c	c	7.7	(2.5)	425	(17.3)	442	(14.1)	425	(8.6)
Yucatán	89.4	(5.1)	404	(4.6)	419	(6.8)	409	(6.1)	0.0	c	c	c	c	c	c	c	10.6	(5.1)	448	(8.2)	474	(11.8)	454	(7.8)
Zacatecas	98.5	(1.0)	407	(4.3)	410	(5.9)	400	(4.8)	0.0	c	c	c	c	c	c	c	1.5	(1.0)	c	c	c	c	c	c

• PISA adjudicated region.

Notes: Values that are statistically significant are indicated in bold (see Annex A3).

See Table IV.4.7 for national data.

1. Schools which are directly controlled or managed by: *i)* a public education authority or agency or *ii)* a government agency directly or a governing body, most of whose members are either appointed by a public authority or elected by public franchise.

2. Schools which receive 50% or more of their core funding (i.e. funding that supports the basic educational services of the institution) from government agencies.

3. Schools which receive less than 50% of their core funding (i.e. funding that supports the basic educational services of the institution) from government agencies.

StatLink http://dx.doi.org/10.1787/888932957536

[Part 2/4]
School type and performance in mathematics, reading and science, by region
Table B2.IV.18   *Results based on school principals' reports*

	Government or public schools[1]				Government-dependent private schools[2]				Government-independent private schools[3]			
	Percentage of students	Performance on the mathematics scale	Performance on the reading scale	Performance on the science scale	Percentage of students	Performance on the mathematics scale	Performance on the reading scale	Performance on the science scale	Percentage of students	Performance on the mathematics scale	Performance on the reading scale	Performance on the science scale
	% S.E.	Mean score S.E.	Mean score S.E.	Mean score S.E.	% S.E.	Mean score S.E.	Mean score S.E.	Mean score S.E.	% S.E.	Mean score S.E.	Mean score S.E.	Mean score S.E.
Portugal												
Alentejo	91.7 (4.4)	487 (10.9)	491 (9.6)	493 (9.0)	8.3 (4.4)	c c	c c	c c	0.0 c	c c	c c	c c
Spain												
Andalusia•	73.1 (0.9)	463 (4.3)	467 (5.7)	476 (5.0)	20.8 (3.6)	486 (9.6)	495 (8.4)	504 (11.4)	6.0 (3.5)	c c	c c	c c
Aragon•	70.9 (2.5)	485 (6.4)	483 (6.7)	494 (6.2)	21.9 (4.6)	512 (10.4)	501 (14.2)	513 (8.9)	7.3 (3.7)	c c	c c	c c
Asturias•	65.0 (2.2)	489 (5.3)	490 (5.8)	510 (5.3)	29.7 (5.0)	517 (7.3)	526 (8.5)	527 (7.3)	5.3 (3.6)	c c	c c	c c
Balearic Islands•	65.3 (2.2)	461 (6.7)	457 (5.4)	469 (6.1)	27.0 (3.7)	499 (7.9)	505 (10.7)	506 (8.2)	7.7 (2.9)	c c	c c	c c
Basque Country•	46.6 (0.8)	488 (3.1)	479 (4.0)	490 (3.4)	53.0 (0.9)	519 (3.9)	514 (4.0)	518 (3.6)	0.3 (0.4)	c c	c c	c c
Cantabria•	64.7 (1.8)	489 (3.4)	479 (4.3)	499 (4.3)	35.3 (1.8)	497 (7.3)	499 (5.4)	505 (7.0)	0.0 c	c c	c c	c c
Castile and Leon•	64.8 (1.6)	505 (5.9)	497 (7.7)	512 (5.4)	24.3 (4.7)	521 (6.9)	523 (7.6)	535 (6.3)	10.9 (4.5)	506 (8.7)	512 (13.6)	528 (11.6)
Catalonia•	62.6 (2.9)	477 (7.2)	487 (6.8)	479 (6.1)	27.6 (3.8)	518 (9.1)	523 (6.5)	513 (6.2)	9.8 (3.5)	523 (9.3)	528 (14.7)	512 (12.9)
Extremadura•	79.7 (1.7)	451 (5.3)	446 (5.5)	472 (5.5)	18.3 (0.8)	491 (8.4)	486 (12.4)	513 (6.0)	2.0 (2.0)	c c	c c	c c
Galicia•	74.6 (1.9)	481 (5.3)	490 (6.0)	505 (5.6)	22.2 (3.1)	506 (9.5)	522 (9.0)	526 (10.9)	3.2 (2.3)	c c	c c	c c
La Rioja•	66.7 (0.3)	494 (2.8)	479 (3.3)	504 (2.7)	30.1 (0.3)	518 (4.0)	505 (3.8)	517 (3.8)	3.2 (0.0)	c c	c c	c c
Madrid•	58.5 (2.8)	484 (5.0)	497 (6.3)	503 (5.2)	16.7 (4.1)	524 (8.9)	523 (11.6)	531 (9.7)	24.8 (4.4)	535 (8.5)	538 (9.4)	542 (6.6)
Murcia•	75.1 (1.8)	453 (4.8)	452 (6.0)	471 (5.5)	24.9 (1.8)	491 (13.1)	493 (10.2)	504 (10.2)	0.0 c	c c	c c	c c
Navarre•	62.7 (3.4)	506 (4.4)	497 (4.5)	499 (4.6)	37.3 (3.4)	532 (5.0)	527 (5.5)	537 (4.7)	0.0 c	c c	c c	c c
United Kingdom												
England	48.2 (3.6)	485 (5.1)	492 (5.8)	508 (5.8)	43.1 (3.7)	494 (7.7)	498 (8.9)	515 (8.1)	8.7 (0.9)	570 (13.5)	578 (12.6)	593 (11.8)
Northern Ireland	93.5 (3.0)	480 (4.5)	492 (5.0)	501 (5.0)	6.5 (3.0)	532 (16.8)	532 (18.8)	555 (23.0)	0.0 c	c c	c c	c c
Scotland•	94.3 (0.2)	495 (2.7)	503 (3.0)	510 (3.1)	0.0 c	c c	c c	c c	5.7 (0.2)	553 (14.2)	563 (15.7)	573 (15.5)
Wales	98.8 (0.7)	467 (2.1)	479 (2.7)	490 (3.0)	0.0 c	c c	c c	c c	1.2 (0.7)	c c	c c	c c
United States												
Connecticut•	100.0 c	506 (6.2)	521 (6.5)	521 (5.7)	0.0 c	c c	c c	c c	0.0 c	c c	c c	c c
Florida•	100.0 c	469 (5.8)	495 (6.0)	488 (6.4)	0.0 c	c c	c c	c c	0.0 c	c c	c c	c c
Massachusetts•	100.0 c	514 (6.2)	527 (6.1)	527 (6.0)	0.0 c	c c	c c	c c	0.0 c	c c	c c	c c
Argentina												
Ciudad Autónoma de Buenos Aires•	56.4 (5.5)	378 (14.5)	381 (20.5)	379 (17.9)	27.0 (5.3)	459 (8.3)	479 (7.9)	470 (10.3)	16.6 (6.5)	473 (14.2)	492 (19.4)	490 (18.2)
Brazil												
Acre	98.3 (1.7)	354 (4.5)	379 (6.7)	376 (6.1)	0.0 c	c c	c c	c c	1.7 (1.7)	c c	c c	c c
Alagoas	89.1 (4.7)	325 (5.7)	339 (8.5)	332 (9.3)	0.0 c	c c	c c	c c	10.9 (4.7)	c c	c c	c c
Amapá	94.4 (5.5)	359 (9.7)	395 (12.0)	381 (11.3)	0.0 c	c c	c c	c c	5.6 (5.5)	c c	c c	c c
Amazonas	97.4 (2.6)	350 (4.8)	376 (6.2)	370 (4.8)	0.0 c	c c	c c	c c	2.6 (2.6)	c c	c c	c c
Bahia	92.3 (6.2)	354 (10.7)	366 (11.3)	371 (9.8)	0.0 c	c c	c c	c c	7.7 (6.2)	c c	c c	c c
Ceará	86.8 (7.9)	375 (10.0)	389 (12.0)	380 (10.8)	0.0 c	c c	c c	c c	13.2 (7.9)	c c	c c	c c
Espírito Santo	87.7 (7.6)	395 (9.2)	410 (9.4)	409 (6.3)	0.0 c	c c	c c	c c	12.3 (7.6)	c c	c c	c c
Federal District	88.6 (9.1)	384 (8.5)	401 (11.0)	397 (8.0)	0.0 c	c c	c c	c c	11.4 (9.1)	c c	c c	c c
Goiás	82.9 (2.0)	362 (6.7)	379 (7.8)	378 (7.8)	0.0 c	c c	c c	c c	17.1 (2.0)	c c	c c	c c
Maranhão	90.9 (8.4)	332 (8.4)	358 (9.9)	349 (10.1)	0.0 c	c c	c c	c c	9.1 (8.4)	c c	c c	c c
Mato Grosso	93.1 (4.8)	358 (6.7)	369 (7.5)	368 (5.9)	0.0 c	c c	c c	c c	6.9 (4.8)	c c	c c	c c
Mato Grosso do Sul	79.8 (5.4)	387 (5.8)	409 (6.0)	397 (6.1)	0.5 (0.7)	c c	c c	c c	19.8 (5.2)	c c	c c	c c
Minas Gerais	91.6 (4.9)	394 (8.0)	419 (8.7)	410 (8.8)	2.9 (3.0)	c c	c c	c c	5.6 (3.9)	c c	c c	c c
Pará	84.1 (9.7)	339 (4.8)	365 (7.7)	357 (5.0)	0.0 c	c c	c c	c c	15.9 (9.7)	c c	c c	c c
Paraíba	68.7 (8.6)	362 (9.9)	375 (12.0)	380 (11.9)	0.0 c	c c	c c	c c	31.3 (8.6)	457 (17.1)	477 (19.3)	467 (16.7)
Paraná	91.7 (7.6)	387 (6.1)	406 (7.4)	399 (6.6)	0.0 c	c c	c c	c c	8.3 (7.6)	c c	c c	c c
Pernambuco	91.7 (5.8)	357 (8.3)	371 (7.3)	367 (8.2)	0.0 c	c c	c c	c c	8.3 (5.8)	c c	c c	c c
Piauí	93.3 (6.5)	359 (6.2)	380 (7.6)	381 (6.0)	0.0 c	c c	c c	c c	6.7 (6.5)	c c	c c	c c
Rio de Janeiro	72.2 (5.3)	362 (5.5)	381 (9.6)	373 (6.0)	0.0 c	c c	c c	c c	27.8 (5.3)	430 (4.2)	455 (6.1)	447 (7.5)
Rio Grande do Norte	77.7 (4.6)	351 (3.6)	368 (5.3)	362 (4.5)	0.0 c	c c	c c	c c	22.3 (4.6)	484 (26.1)	482 (21.6)	475 (18.9)
Rio Grande do Sul	85.0 (1.5)	399 (6.1)	423 (6.8)	413 (5.9)	4.8 (3.5)	c c	c c	c c	10.2 (4.1)	c c	c c	c c
Rondônia	94.3 (5.5)	380 (5.4)	398 (6.7)	387 (6.4)	0.0 c	c c	c c	c c	5.7 (5.5)	c c	c c	c c
Roraima	96.2 (3.7)	350 (5.6)	364 (7.9)	361 (6.5)	0.0 c	c c	c c	c c	3.8 (3.7)	c c	c c	c c
Santa Catarina	89.6 (6.8)	405 (7.8)	411 (10.9)	410 (8.6)	0.0 c	c c	c c	c c	10.4 (6.8)	c c	c c	c c
São Paulo	85.1 (2.4)	388 (3.5)	407 (4.1)	403 (4.5)	0.0 c	c c	c c	c c	14.9 (2.4)	476 (12.5)	490 (12.3)	485 (10.3)
Sergipe	83.6 (3.9)	370 (6.3)	384 (6.4)	380 (6.1)	3.9 (3.8)	c c	c c	c c	12.5 (2.1)	c c	c c	c c
Tocantins	94.5 (0.9)	360 (7.4)	375 (7.6)	374 (6.6)	0.0 c	c c	c c	c c	5.5 (0.9)	c c	c c	c c
Colombia												
Bogota	83.5 (1.5)	389 (3.2)	421 (3.8)	409 (4.2)	8.3 (3.8)	c c	c c	c c	8.3 (2.7)	c c	c c	c c
Cali	52.9 (4.8)	375 (7.3)	401 (7.3)	397 (8.0)	27.2 (4.6)	359 (9.1)	394 (13.1)	379 (13.1)	19.8 (5.2)	417 (16.1)	454 (16.8)	440 (17.6)
Manizales	82.0 (4.9)	383 (3.5)	415 (4.8)	413 (3.6)	0.0 c	c c	c c	c c	18.0 (4.9)	456 (26.0)	476 (18.1)	468 (29.5)
Medellin	75.4 (4.1)	374 (5.4)	406 (4.4)	402 (4.4)	12.9 (3.4)	364 (8.9)	385 (12.5)	385 (6.7)	11.7 (2.4)	498 (29.7)	529 (14.4)	507 (26.1)
Russian Federation												
Perm Territory region•	100.0 c	484 (5.5)	482 (6.0)	480 (5.3)	0.0 c	c c	c c	c c	0.0 c	c c	c c	c c
United Arab Emirates												
Abu Dhabi•	66.9 (2.7)	395 (3.5)	413 (4.0)	420 (4.2)	0.9 (0.9)	c c	c c	c c	32.2 (2.7)	447 (8.9)	447 (10.7)	454 (10.9)
Ajman	67.5 (5.5)	402 (15.2)	421 (16.8)	428 (15.9)	0.0 c	c c	c c	c c	32.5 (5.5)	395 (7.2)	389 (11.3)	394 (10.8)
Dubai•	25.4 (0.1)	395 (2.9)	403 (3.3)	410 (3.1)	1.1 (0.0)	c c	c c	c c	73.5 (0.1)	482 (1.7)	483 (1.7)	492 (1.7)
Fujairah	85.8 (6.4)	400 (4.2)	413 (4.2)	416 (4.3)	0.0 c	c c	c c	c c	14.2 (6.4)	410 (45.6)	383 (54.4)	430 (44.0)
Ras Al Khaimah	88.8 (3.8)	409 (8.0)	410 (7.9)	425 (8.1)	0.0 c	c c	c c	c c	11.2 (3.8)	454 (7.3)	446 (10.1)	458 (8.9)
Sharjah	37.7 (5.8)	403 (11.2)	422 (10.9)	417 (10.6)	0.0 c	c c	c c	c c	62.3 (5.8)	456 (11.7)	469 (11.8)	465 (15.2)
Umm Al Quwain	81.5 (0.3)	397 (4.8)	396 (4.7)	413 (4.5)	0.0 c	c c	c c	c c	18.5 (0.3)	c c	c c	c c

• PISA adjudicated region.
Notes: Values that are statistically significant are indicated in bold (see Annex A3).
See Table IV.4.7 for national data.
1. Schools which are directly controlled or managed by: *i)* a public education authority or agency or *ii)* a government agency directly or a governing body, most of whose members are either appointed by a public authority or elected by public franchise.
2. Schools which receive 50% or more of their core funding (i.e. funding that supports the basic educational services of the institution) from government agencies.
3. Schools which receive less than 50% of their core funding (i.e. funding that supports the basic educational services of the institution) from government agencies.
StatLink ⟦ᓫᔅᒪ⟧ http://dx.doi.org/10.1787/888932957536

[Part 3/4]
School type and performance in mathematics, reading and science, by region

Table B2.IV.18 *Results based on school principals' reports*

| | Difference in performance on the mathematics scale between public and private schools (government-dependent and government-independent schools combined) | | PISA index of economic, social and cultural status | | | | | | Difference in performance on the mathematics scale between public and private schools after accounting for the PISA index of economic, social and cultural status of: | | | |
| | | | Public schools | | Private schools (government-dependent and government-independent) | | Difference | | Students | | Students and schools | |
	Dif. (Pub. - Priv.)	S.E.	Mean index	S.E.	Mean index	S.E.	Dif. (Pub. - Priv.)	S.E.	Dif. (Pub. - Priv.)	S.E.	Dif. (Pub. - Priv.)	S.E.
Australia												
Australian Capital Territory	w	w	w	w	w	w	w	w	w	w	w	w
New South Wales	w	w	w	w	w	w	w	w	w	w	w	w
Northern Territory	w	w	w	w	w	w	w	w	w	w	w	w
Queensland	w	w	w	w	w	w	w	w	w	w	w	w
South Australia	w	w	w	w	w	w	w	w	w	w	w	w
Tasmania	w	w	w	w	w	w	w	w	w	w	w	w
Victoria	w	w	w	w	w	w	w	w	w	w	w	w
Western Australia	w	w	w	w	w	w	w	w	w	w	w	w
Belgium												
Flemish community*	w	w	w	w	w	w	w	w	w	w	w	w
French community	-29	(14.4)	0.02	(0.1)	0.11	(0.1)	-0.09	(0.1)	-24	(10.0)	-19	(7.3)
German-speaking community	-49	(5.1)	0.22	(0.0)	0.33	(0.0)	-0.12	(0.1)	-46	(5.3)	-33	(5.0)
Canada												
Alberta	c	c	0.52	(0.0)	c	c	c	c	c	c	c	c
British Columbia	-33	(13.3)	0.43	(0.0)	0.71	(0.2)	-0.27	(0.2)	-24	(10.5)	-17	(9.4)
Manitoba	-69	(17.2)	0.20	(0.0)	1.01	(0.2)	-0.81	(0.2)	-38	(12.4)	-16	(9.6)
New Brunswick	c	c	0.36	(0.0)	c	c	c	c	c	c	c	c
Newfoundland and Labrador	c	c	0.26	(0.0)	c	c	c	c	c	c	c	c
Nova Scotia	0	(0.0)	0.31	(0.0)	c	c	c	c	0	(0.0)	0	(0.0)
Ontario	c	c	0.42	(0.0)	c	c	c	c	c	c	c	c
Prince Edward Island	c	c	0.33	(0.0)	c	c	c	c	c	c	c	c
Quebec	-62	(8.8)	0.19	(0.0)	0.84	(0.0)	-0.65	(0.1)	-40	(8.2)	-9	(9.8)
Saskatchewan	-16	(10.4)	0.39	(0.0)	0.73	(0.1)	-0.34	(0.2)	-4	(10.3)	-3	(11.0)
Italy												
Abruzzo	c	c	0.03	(0.0)	c	c	c	c	c	c	c	c
Basilicata	c	c	-0.23	(0.0)	c	c	c	c	c	c	c	c
Bolzano	-11	(7.8)	-0.08	(0.0)	0.54	(0.1)	-0.62	(0.1)	7	(8.4)	60	(7.9)
Calabria	c	c	-0.21	(0.0)	c	c	c	c	c	c	c	c
Campania	c	c	-0.20	(0.1)	c	c	c	c	c	c	c	c
Emilia Romagna	c	c	-0.01	(0.0)	c	c	c	c	c	c	c	c
Friuli Venezia Giulia	c	c	0.09	(0.0)	c	c	c	c	c	c	c	c
Lazio	c	c	0.16	(0.1)	c	c	c	c	c	c	c	c
Liguria	-5	(23.5)	0.01	(0.0)	0.35	(0.1)	-0.35	(0.1)	4	(21.3)	31	(21.5)
Lombardia	-43	(18.5)	-0.02	(0.1)	1.01	(0.2)	-1.03	(0.2)	-10	(16.0)	53	(16.6)
Marche	c	c	-0.06	(0.0)	c	c	c	c	c	c	c	c
Molise	0	(0.0)	-0.20	(0.0)	c	c	c	c	0	(0.0)	0	(0.0)
Piemonte	c	c	-0.08	(0.0)	c	c	c	c	c	c	c	c
Puglia	c	c	-0.27	(0.0)	c	c	c	c	c	c	c	c
Sardegna	c	c	-0.16	(0.1)	c	c	c	c	c	c	c	c
Sicilia	0	(0.0)	-0.10	(0.0)	c	c	c	c	0	(0.0)	0	(0.0)
Toscana	c	c	-0.04	(0.0)	c	c	c	c	c	c	c	c
Trento	52	(13.9)	0.13	(0.0)	-0.35	(0.1)	0.48	(0.1)	43	(13.1)	9	(15.5)
Umbria	c	c	0.08	(0.0)	c	c	c	c	c	c	c	c
Valle d'Aosta	c	c	-0.18	(0.0)	c	c	c	c	c	c	c	c
Veneto	94	(12.8)	-0.04	(0.0)	-0.57	(0.2)	0.53	(0.2)	80	(10.1)	35	(14.8)
Mexico												
Aguascalientes	-16	(22.0)	-0.91	(0.1)	-0.17	(0.3)	-0.73	(0.3)	-1	(17.1)	20	(14.3)
Baja California	4	(16.7)	-0.79	(0.1)	0.04	(0.2)	-0.84	(0.2)	16	(15.4)	43	(16.0)
Baja California Sur	c	c	-0.81	(0.1)	c	c	c	c	c	c	c	c
Campeche	c	c	-1.39	(0.1)	c	c	c	c	c	c	c	c
Chiapas	c	c	-1.82	(0.1)	c	c	c	c	c	c	c	c
Chihuahua	-3	(25.6)	-0.83	(0.1)	-0.72	(0.3)	-0.11	(0.4)	0	(18.5)	4	(10.6)
Coahuila	-39	(22.2)	-1.05	(0.1)	0.05	(0.2)	-1.10	(0.2)	-17	(18.2)	17	(17.3)
Colima	c	c	-0.90	(0.0)	c	c	c	c	c	c	c	c
Distrito Federal	-51	(12.0)	-0.91	(0.1)	0.75	(0.2)	-1.67	(0.2)	-27	(14.6)	58	(29.6)
Durango	c	c	-1.05	(0.1)	c	c	c	c	c	c	c	c
Guanajuato	-42	(16.1)	-1.58	(0.1)	0.21	(0.3)	-1.79	(0.3)	-3	(15.5)	44	(19.7)
Guerrero	c	c	-1.70	(0.1)	c	c	c	c	c	c	c	c
Hidalgo	c	c	-1.63	(0.1)	c	c	c	c	c	c	c	c
Jalisco	c	c	-1.24	(0.1)	c	c	c	c	c	c	c	c
Mexico	-24	(34.8)	-1.20	(0.1)	0.15	(0.3)	-1.35	(0.3)	-9	(28.2)	35	(20.8)
Morelos	-56	(33.4)	-1.23	(0.1)	0.34	(0.3)	-1.57	(0.3)	-20	(26.8)	31	(22.8)
Nayarit	c	c	-1.10	(0.1)	c	c	c	c	c	c	c	c
Nuevo León	-50	(20.9)	-0.67	(0.1)	0.62	(0.3)	-1.29	(0.3)	-29	(18.0)	14	(12.1)
Puebla	c	c	-1.72	(0.1)	c	c	c	c	c	c	c	c
Querétaro	-42	(18.3)	-1.18	(0.2)	0.55	(0.2)	-1.72	(0.3)	-14	(19.9)	14	(21.8)
Quintana Roo	c	c	-1.13	(0.1)	c	c	c	c	c	c	c	c
San Luis Potosí	-58	(24.9)	-1.57	(0.1)	0.08	(0.5)	-1.64	(0.6)	-21	(15.4)	13	(12.0)
Sinaloa	c	c	-1.00	(0.1)	c	c	c	c	c	c	c	c
Tabasco	c	c	-1.31	(0.1)	c	c	c	c	c	c	c	c
Tamaulipas	-28	(27.7)	-1.00	(0.1)	0.06	(0.4)	-1.06	(0.4)	-10	(22.2)	24	(16.2)
Tlaxcala	-21	(12.5)	-1.33	(0.1)	0.07	(0.4)	-1.41	(0.4)	1	(9.6)	48	(14.2)
Veracruz	-27	(18.5)	-1.73	(0.1)	0.11	(0.3)	-1.84	(0.3)	0	(15.4)	17	(16.8)
Yucatán	-44	(9.6)	-1.39	(0.1)	0.36	(0.2)	-1.74	(0.3)	-13	(8.1)	13	(14.1)
Zacatecas	c	c	-1.24	(0.1)	c	c	c	c	c	c	c	c

* PISA adjudicated region.

Notes: Values that are statistically significant are indicated in bold (see Annex A3).

See Table IV.4.7 for national data.

1. Schools which are directly controlled or managed by: *i)* a public education authority or agency or *ii)* a government agency directly or a governing body, most of whose members are either appointed by a public authority or elected by public franchise.

2. Schools which receive 50% or more of their core funding (i.e. funding that supports the basic educational services of the institution) from government agencies.

3. Schools which receive less than 50% of their core funding (i.e. funding that supports the basic educational services of the institution) from government agencies.

StatLink ⌸ http://dx.doi.org/10.1787/888932957536

[Part 4/4]
School type and performance in mathematics, reading and science, by region
Table B2.IV.18   *Results based on school principals' reports*

| | | Difference in performance on the mathematics scale between public and private schools (government-dependent and government-independent schools combined) | | PISA index of economic, social and cultural status | | | | | | Difference in performance on the mathematics scale between public and private schools after accounting for the PISA index of economic, social and cultural status of: | | | |
| | | | | Public schools | | Private schools (government-dependent and government-independent) | | Difference | | Students | | Students and schools | |
		Dif. (Pub. - Priv.)	S.E.	Mean index	S.E.	Mean index	S.E.	Dif. (Pub. - Priv.)	S.E.	Dif. (Pub. - Priv.)	S.E.	Dif. (Pub. - Priv.)	S.E.
OECD	**Portugal**												
	Alentejo	c	c	-0.34	(0.1)	c	c	c	c	c	c	c	c
	Spain												
	Andalusia•	-28	(9.9)	-0.52	(0.1)	0.00	(0.2)	-0.52	(0.2)	-12	(8.2)	-8	(10.0)
	Aragon•	-30	(12.0)	-0.28	(0.1)	0.34	(0.2)	-0.63	(0.2)	-9	(8.3)	8	(8.5)
	Asturias•	-32	(9.0)	-0.24	(0.1)	0.38	(0.1)	-0.62	(0.1)	-11	(6.8)	7	(7.0)
	Balearic Islands•	-38	(9.4)	-0.35	(0.1)	0.21	(0.1)	-0.57	(0.1)	-21	(8.3)	-13	(9.4)
	Basque Country•	-31	(4.9)	-0.17	(0.0)	0.21	(0.0)	-0.38	(0.1)	-19	(4.3)	-9	(4.5)
	Cantabria•	-8	(8.0)	-0.23	(0.0)	0.22	(0.1)	-0.45	(0.1)	7	(7.4)	17	(9.0)
	Castile and Leon•	-12	(8.2)	-0.28	(0.1)	0.20	(0.1)	-0.47	(0.1)	2	(7.5)	14	(8.8)
	Catalonia•	-42	(9.8)	-0.33	(0.1)	0.18	(0.1)	-0.51	(0.2)	-27	(7.6)	-16	(8.9)
	Extremadura•	-44	(9.9)	-0.64	(0.0)	0.10	(0.2)	-0.74	(0.2)	-20	(7.2)	-8	(9.3)
	Galicia•	-27	(9.9)	-0.34	(0.1)	0.18	(0.1)	-0.52	(0.1)	-14	(8.4)	-4	(8.1)
	La Rioja•	-25	(5.4)	-0.34	(0.0)	0.12	(0.0)	-0.46	(0.0)	-7	(5.6)	12	(5.7)
	Madrid•	-46	(7.6)	-0.17	(0.1)	0.52	(0.1)	-0.69	(0.1)	-24	(6.9)	-19	(8.2)
	Murcia•	-38	(14.0)	-0.60	(0.1)	-0.19	(0.1)	-0.41	(0.1)	-24	(12.7)	-18	(11.5)
	Navarre•	-26	(6.8)	-0.35	(0.0)	0.26	(0.1)	-0.61	(0.1)	-7	(6.1)	2	(6.7)
	United Kingdom												
	England	-21	(8.9)	0.20	(0.0)	0.39	(0.0)	-0.19	(0.0)	-12	(6.6)	-1	(5.8)
	Northern Ireland	-52	(18.4)	0.25	(0.0)	0.73	(0.1)	-0.49	(0.1)	-30	(15.3)	15	(16.5)
	Scotland•	-59	(14.5)	0.08	(0.0)	0.94	(0.0)	-0.86	(0.0)	-27	(13.3)	15	(13.2)
	Wales	c	c	0.18	(0.0)	c	c	c	c	c	c	c	c
	United States												
	Connecticut•	0	(0.0)	0.49	(0.1)	c	c	c	c	0	(0.0)	0	(0.0)
	Florida•	0	(0.0)	0.22	(0.1)	c	c	c	c	0	(0.0)	0	(0.0)
	Massachusetts•	0	(0.0)	0.44	(0.1)	c	c	c	c	0	(0.0)	0	(0.0)
Partners	**Argentina**												
	Ciudad Autónoma de Buenos Aires•	-86	(15.8)	-0.77	(0.2)	0.39	(0.1)	-1.17	(0.2)	-45	(13.5)	-3	(18.3)
	Brazil												
	Acre	c	c	-1.46	(0.1)	c	c	c	c	c	c	c	c
	Alagoas	c	c	-2.02	(0.1)	c	c	c	c	c	c	c	c
	Amapá	c	c	-0.93	(0.1)	c	c	c	c	c	c	c	c
	Amazonas	c	c	-1.14	(0.1)	c	c	c	c	c	c	c	c
	Bahia	c	c	-1.88	(0.1)	c	c	c	c	c	c	c	c
	Ceará	c	c	-1.77	(0.1)	c	c	c	c	c	c	c	c
	Espírito Santo	c	c	-1.51	(0.1)	c	c	c	c	c	c	c	c
	Federal District	c	c	-1.11	(0.1)	c	c	c	c	c	c	c	c
	Goiás	c	c	-1.51	(0.1)	c	c	c	c	c	c	c	c
	Maranhão	c	c	-1.58	(0.1)	c	c	c	c	c	c	c	c
	Mato Grosso	c	c	-1.51	(0.0)	c	c	c	c	c	c	c	c
	Mato Grosso do Sul	-96	(11.0)	-1.32	(0.1)	0.27	(0.1)	-1.59	(0.1)	-70	(11.6)	-25	(22.8)
	Minas Gerais	c	c	-1.51	(0.1)	c	c	c	c	c	c	c	c
	Pará	c	c	-1.49	(0.1)	c	c	c	c	c	c	c	c
	Paraíba	-95	(19.6)	-1.79	(0.1)	-0.04	(0.2)	-1.75	(0.3)	-62	(12.6)	-1	(23.3)
	Paraná	c	c	-1.31	(0.1)	c	c	c	c	c	c	c	c
	Pernambuco	c	c	-1.75	(0.1)	c	c	c	c	c	c	c	c
	Piauí	c	c	-1.70	(0.1)	c	c	c	c	c	c	c	c
	Rio de Janeiro	-67	(7.0)	-1.20	(0.0)	-0.65	(0.2)	-0.54	(0.2)	-62	(6.9)	-42	(8.4)
	Rio Grande do Norte	-133	(26.3)	-1.72	(0.1)	0.10	(0.2)	-1.82	(0.2)	-110	(25.3)	-43	(36.7)
	Rio Grande do Sul	c	c	-1.39	(0.1)	c	c	c	c	c	c	c	c
	Rondônia	c	c	-1.48	(0.1)	c	c	c	c	c	c	c	c
	Roraima	c	c	-1.21	(0.1)	c	c	c	c	c	c	c	c
	Santa Catarina	c	c	-1.40	(0.1)	c	c	c	c	c	c	c	c
	São Paulo	-88	(13.1)	-1.19	(0.0)	0.25	(0.1)	-1.44	(0.1)	-68	(14.1)	-18	(19.0)
	Sergipe	c	c	-1.55	(0.1)	c	c	c	c	c	c	c	c
	Tocantins	c	c	-1.39	(0.1)	c	c	c	c	c	c	c	c
	Colombia												
	Bogota	-9	(6.8)	-1.12	(0.0)	-1.10	(0.1)	-0.02	(0.1)	-7	(5.4)	-7	(4.5)
	Cali	-9	(13.4)	-0.98	(0.1)	-0.66	(0.1)	-0.32	(0.2)	1	(10.6)	9	(9.4)
	Manizales	-73	(26.2)	-1.09	(0.1)	0.16	(0.1)	-1.25	(0.1)	-49	(24.1)	-26	(22.8)
	Medellin	-54	(19.3)	-1.17	(0.1)	-0.62	(0.2)	-0.54	(0.2)	-38	(13.1)	-21	(10.1)
	Russian Federation												
	Perm Territory region•	0	(0.0)	-0.12	(0.0)	c	c	c	c	0	(0.0)	0	(0.0)
	United Arab Emirates												
	Abu Dhabi•	-53	(9.3)	0.10	(0.0)	0.53	(0.1)	-0.43	(0.1)	-44	(8.7)	-23	(8.6)
	Ajman	7	(17.4)	-0.08	(0.1)	-0.26	(0.1)	0.18	(0.1)	3	(16.5)	-4	(16.7)
	Dubai•	-87	(3.5)	0.06	(0.0)	0.64	(0.0)	-0.58	(0.0)	-69	(3.6)	-34	(4.7)
	Fujairah	-10	(45.6)	-0.11	(0.0)	0.29	(0.1)	-0.41	(0.1)	-6	(44.5)	9	(42.5)
	Ras Al Khaimah	-45	(11.0)	0.00	(0.1)	0.29	(0.2)	-0.29	(0.2)	-39	(11.7)	-30	(14.9)
	Sharjah	-53	(16.3)	0.06	(0.1)	0.60	(0.1)	-0.54	(0.1)	-44	(16.0)	-46	(21.6)
	Umm Al Quwain	c	c	-0.12	(0.1)	c	c	c	c	c	c	c	c

• PISA adjudicated region.
Notes: Values that are statistically significant are indicated in bold (see Annex A3).
See Table IV.4.7 for national data.
1. Schools which are directly controlled or managed by: *i)* a public education authority or agency or *ii)* a government agency directly or a governing body, most of whose members are either appointed by a public authority or elected by public franchise.
2. Schools which receive 50% or more of their core funding (i.e. funding that supports the basic educational services of the institution) from government agencies.
3. Schools which receive less than 50% of their core funding (i.e. funding that supports the basic educational services of the institution) from government agencies.
StatLink ᐱᓴ http://dx.doi.org/10.1787/888932957536

[Part 1/1]
Use of achievement data for accountability purposes, by region

Table B2.IV.21   *Results based on school principals' reports*

	Percentage of students in schools that use achievement data in the following ways:									
	Posted publicly		Tracked over time by an administrative authority				Posted publicly		Tracked over time by an administrative authority	
	%	S.E.	%	S.E.			%	S.E.	%	S.E.
Australia						**Portugal**				
Australian Capital Territory	74.1	(0.9)	87.4	(0.7)		Alentejo	39.1	(10.4)	82.2	(7.6)
New South Wales	65.6	(4.0)	90.1	(2.2)		**Spain**				
Northern Territory	68.0	(2.9)	83.3	(2.2)		Andalusia•	20.3	(5.4)	80.5	(6.2)
Queensland	73.5	(3.8)	95.1	(1.3)		Aragon•	6.5	(3.8)	80.7	(4.1)
South Australia	49.9	(5.0)	77.9	(4.2)		Asturias•	7.5	(2.7)	77.0	(6.5)
Tasmania	50.4	(1.6)	87.0	(1.5)		Balearic Islands•	6.3	(3.6)	73.0	(6.1)
Victoria	74.7	(3.6)	94.0	(2.2)		Basque Country•	13.9	(2.9)	87.4	(2.4)
Western Australia	72.9	(5.2)	95.8	(2.2)		Cantabria•	20.2	(4.4)	87.7	(4.3)
Belgium						Castile and Leon•	12.3	(4.2)	83.6	(4.9)
Flemish community•	1.7	(0.9)	63.7	(3.5)		Catalonia•	10.9	(4.5)	94.5	(3.2)
French community	5.1	(2.4)	34.7	(4.9)		Extremadura•	17.0	(4.9)	66.8	(8.1)
German-speaking community	0.0	c	8.8	(0.3)		Galicia•	7.4	(3.8)	59.7	(6.6)
Canada						La Rioja•	16.2	(0.4)	63.2	(0.5)
Alberta	70.8	(5.0)	97.6	(1.1)		Madrid•	18.2	(5.3)	94.4	(3.4)
British Columbia	59.5	(6.4)	95.0	(3.1)		Murcia•	13.3	(5.3)	65.2	(6.0)
Manitoba	10.4	(1.6)	74.1	(3.1)		Navarre•	24.9	(3.5)	79.0	(4.6)
New Brunswick	61.7	(1.6)	96.1	(0.3)		**United Kingdom**				
Newfoundland and Labrador	52.5	(4.7)	96.5	(0.3)		England	88.3	(2.6)	89.5	(2.4)
Nova Scotia	50.2	(8.4)	90.2	(3.1)		Northern Ireland	79.7	(4.7)	93.9	(2.7)
Ontario	73.8	(4.9)	95.3	(1.2)		Scotland•	82.9	(4.1)	87.8	(3.1)
Prince Edward Island	10.4	(0.3)	39.3	(0.5)		Wales	77.3	(3.7)	98.3	(0.5)
Quebec	52.3	(4.2)	88.8	(2.5)		**United States**				
Saskatchewan	21.6	(2.9)	91.8	(1.6)		Connecticut•	98.2	(1.8)	98.2	(1.8)
Italy						Florida•	94.7	(3.1)	100.0	c
Abruzzo	30.6	(5.1)	25.6	(7.1)		Massachusetts•	94.7	(3.1)	98.1	(1.9)
Basilicata	23.8	(4.7)	24.0	(4.5)						
Bolzano	14.1	(0.5)	49.5	(0.9)		**Argentina**				
Calabria	28.6	(5.6)	14.7	(4.4)		Ciudad Autónoma de Buenos Aires•	15.8	(6.2)	66.2	(7.1)
Campania	28.8	(5.7)	36.5	(8.0)		**Brazil**				
Emilia Romagna	40.8	(8.1)	29.5	(7.7)		Acre	35.7	(8.6)	86.4	(7.5)
Friuli Venezia Giulia	47.1	(4.2)	27.5	(5.9)		Alagoas	27.5	(10.8)	91.0	(8.1)
Lazio	36.5	(7.3)	37.5	(7.4)		Amapá	32.1	(9.1)	84.1	(3.5)
Liguria	38.7	(6.2)	16.9	(6.4)		Amazonas	48.4	(11.4)	98.2	(1.8)
Lombardia	53.2	(5.7)	34.2	(7.6)		Bahia	46.7	(18.5)	72.7	(14.2)
Marche	31.2	(7.5)	23.0	(7.2)		Ceará	47.1	(12.4)	98.3	(1.3)
Molise	2.6	(0.2)	22.1	(0.8)		Espírito Santo	41.6	(9.1)	100.0	c
Piemonte	61.8	(5.8)	26.5	(5.1)		Federal District	37.7	(11.9)	91.4	(6.0)
Puglia	36.8	(7.6)	21.9	(6.5)		Goiás	36.1	(10.8)	89.1	(7.2)
Sardegna	45.9	(7.7)	27.0	(7.5)		Maranhão	29.7	(12.3)	91.1	(5.6)
Sicilia	32.9	(6.5)	32.6	(7.0)		Mato Grosso	23.9	(7.2)	92.4	(5.8)
Toscana	38.5	(8.0)	30.2	(7.1)		Mato Grosso do Sul	29.1	(9.0)	93.7	(6.2)
Trento	45.5	(4.3)	29.2	(3.6)		Minas Gerais	39.2	(10.6)	100.0	c
Umbria	34.5	(5.0)	32.1	(6.4)		Pará	21.6	(13.2)	74.3	(11.9)
Valle d'Aosta	35.6	(1.0)	43.7	(1.0)		Paraíba	37.0	(13.8)	93.9	(2.0)
Veneto	47.0	(7.3)	26.1	(7.2)		Paraná	19.3	(7.4)	87.5	(5.1)
Mexico						Pernambuco	28.4	(8.8)	94.4	(5.5)
Aguascalientes	38.5	(7.7)	93.0	(2.4)		Piauí	40.5	(9.8)	91.5	(6.1)
Baja California	57.1	(8.9)	99.8	(0.2)		Rio de Janeiro	58.4	(11.0)	96.6	(3.8)
Baja California Sur	41.2	(6.4)	95.1	(1.7)		Rio Grande do Norte	17.5	(7.9)	82.8	(8.8)
Campeche	44.6	(9.7)	95.5	(2.2)		Rio Grande do Sul	13.3	(7.2)	84.9	(7.0)
Chiapas	39.6	(8.8)	94.0	(3.0)		Rondônia	33.5	(6.9)	81.9	(9.0)
Chihuahua	41.4	(9.5)	96.0	(2.3)		Roraima	16.7	(8.1)	97.5	(2.4)
Coahuila	29.7	(7.9)	98.9	(1.2)		Santa Catarina	17.8	(8.1)	70.4	(10.1)
Colima	29.3	(6.0)	85.9	(3.0)		São Paulo	58.2	(6.4)	97.9	(1.4)
Distrito Federal	59.1	(9.2)	94.3	(4.7)		Sergipe	46.0	(11.1)	93.3	(5.1)
Durango	35.9	(7.0)	85.2	(10.2)		Tocantins	33.8	(9.9)	96.0	(4.0)
Guanajuato	33.3	(7.4)	96.9	(1.9)		**Colombia**				
Guerrero	49.5	(8.6)	86.8	(6.9)		Bogota	53.8	(7.5)	83.0	(4.2)
Hidalgo	46.2	(8.7)	95.3	(3.2)		Cali	44.9	(8.9)	89.1	(4.4)
Jalisco	30.3	(9.2)	91.1	(3.7)		Manizales	49.2	(9.5)	82.8	(6.8)
Mexico	51.6	(7.9)	99.8	(0.2)		Medellin	52.4	(7.8)	87.2	(4.3)
Morelos	47.6	(6.8)	96.0	(3.1)		**Russian Federation**				
Nayarit	29.7	(5.9)	87.1	(4.0)		Perm Territory region•	86.9	(4.7)	100.0	c
Nuevo León	39.4	(9.8)	88.6	(4.7)		**United Arab Emirates**				
Puebla	37.2	(8.2)	90.0	(4.6)		Abu Dhabi•	45.3	(4.4)	91.2	(2.8)
Querétaro	28.9	(8.0)	93.8	(5.6)		Ajman	54.6	(6.6)	94.0	(6.0)
Quintana Roo	43.4	(9.9)	96.0	(1.7)		Dubai•	45.9	(0.3)	94.4	(0.1)
San Luis Potosí	37.8	(6.7)	91.1	(3.3)		Fujairah	39.4	(7.9)	94.3	(5.3)
Sinaloa	37.0	(7.7)	97.0	(1.9)		Ras Al Khaimah	47.2	(9.5)	96.7	(3.4)
Tabasco	31.2	(7.1)	91.9	(3.6)		Sharjah	50.1	(10.6)	84.6	(7.7)
Tamaulipas	38.7	(9.7)	89.0	(9.1)		Umm Al Quwain	48.4	(0.4)	99.3	(0.2)
Tlaxcala	40.6	(7.7)	98.0	(1.8)						
Veracruz	44.0	(8.5)	79.3	(5.8)						
Yucatán	47.6	(7.2)	89.9	(4.4)						
Zacatecas	37.9	(7.1)	96.2	(1.9)						

• PISA adjudicated region.
Note: See Table IV.4.31 for national data.
StatLink ⑤ http://dx.doi.org/10.1787/888932957536

[Part 1/2]
Table B2.IV.22 Quality assurance and school improvement, by region
Results based on school principals' reports

Percentage of students in schools whose principal reported that their schools have the following measures aimed at quality assurance and improvement:

		Written specification of the school's curriculum and educational goals		Written specification of student-performance standards		Systematic recording of data, including teacher and student attendance and graduation rates, test results and professional development of teachers		Internal evaluation/ self-evaluation		External evaluation		Seeking written feed-back from students (e.g. regarding lessons, teachers or resources)		Teacher mentoring		Regular consultation with one or more experts over a period of at least six months with the aim of improving the school		Implementation of a standardised policy for mathematics (i.e. school curriculum with shared instructional materials accompanied by staff development and training)	
		%	S.E.	%	S.E.	%	S.E.	%	S.E.	%	S.E.	%	S.E.	%	S.E.	%	S.E.	%	S.E.
OECD	**Australia**																		
	Australian Capital Territory	99.8	(0.1)	95.9	(0.3)	100.0	c	94.7	(0.5)	94.7	(0.4)	73.9	(1.0)	97.9	(0.3)	59.8	(1.1)	89.9	(0.7)
	New South Wales	98.2	(0.9)	90.7	(2.2)	99.0	(0.7)	95.8	(1.6)	68.4	(3.7)	68.8	(3.4)	93.3	(1.8)	69.0	(3.6)	71.1	(3.8)
	Northern Territory	98.5	(1.3)	98.6	(0.5)	96.7	(0.7)	79.4	(6.0)	70.5	(5.5)	40.1	(9.8)	94.0	(0.7)	75.2	(9.6)	61.6	(3.4)
	Queensland	96.5	(1.6)	93.8	(2.2)	98.0	(1.1)	91.9	(2.3)	67.1	(3.8)	61.0	(4.3)	91.4	(2.5)	73.9	(4.1)	86.7	(3.1)
	South Australia	93.9	(2.7)	89.1	(3.2)	91.3	(3.2)	97.8	(1.4)	65.8	(4.9)	72.2	(5.0)	83.5	(4.3)	70.0	(5.3)	75.2	(4.6)
	Tasmania	97.4	(0.7)	86.9	(2.0)	96.5	(0.2)	92.9	(0.6)	46.9	(1.7)	53.3	(2.3)	96.4	(0.7)	64.5	(1.4)	90.9	(1.7)
	Victoria	96.9	(1.6)	88.8	(2.5)	98.5	(1.0)	94.9	(2.0)	73.3	(3.8)	83.4	(3.4)	95.1	(1.6)	79.1	(3.6)	74.6	(3.6)
	Western Australia	91.0	(3.4)	83.2	(4.4)	99.5	(0.6)	93.9	(2.7)	75.2	(4.7)	55.6	(4.4)	89.7	(2.8)	66.8	(5.6)	75.9	(4.8)
	Belgium																		
	Flemish community•	84.2	(2.9)	53.6	(4.2)	93.6	(1.8)	90.3	(2.1)	63.7	(3.8)	52.3	(4.3)	95.1	(1.7)	52.1	(4.0)	40.6	(3.7)
	French community	79.9	(3.9)	41.8	(5.2)	54.1	(4.9)	64.3	(5.4)	76.7	(4.3)	13.0	(3.5)	37.7	(5.7)	23.0	(5.0)	43.4	(5.2)
	German-speaking community	83.1	(0.2)	22.2	(0.3)	66.9	(0.3)	72.9	(0.4)	85.1	(0.3)	23.5	(0.2)	100.0	c	66.0	(0.4)	77.0	(0.3)
	Canada																		
	Alberta	94.9	(2.3)	91.9	(2.8)	91.9	(2.8)	90.9	(2.8)	77.7	(4.7)	65.0	(4.7)	89.9	(2.9)	78.3	(4.7)	90.7	(3.1)
	British Columbia	94.0	(1.2)	89.9	(4.0)	87.0	(4.4)	71.5	(5.6)	48.9	(5.5)	49.2	(4.9)	81.3	(5.0)	48.6	(6.0)	69.2	(6.1)
	Manitoba	87.7	(2.7)	65.0	(3.3)	84.4	(2.8)	92.4	(2.0)	62.4	(2.9)	66.7	(3.3)	90.1	(1.7)	48.9	(3.2)	80.2	(2.7)
	New Brunswick	93.8	(0.3)	89.6	(0.5)	82.4	(1.4)	79.0	(1.4)	89.7	(1.1)	51.3	(2.2)	79.5	(1.2)	66.9	(1.9)	94.5	(0.3)
	Newfoundland and Labrador	94.6	(1.6)	84.7	(3.3)	94.6	(5.5)	98.4	(0.4)	94.4	(1.4)	50.6	(3.0)	87.8	(3.2)	66.7	(3.8)	90.8	(3.2)
	Nova Scotia	92.2	(3.6)	77.0	(4.9)	90.2	(3.2)	97.8	(0.4)	81.8	(4.4)	44.8	(7.2)	90.2	(1.5)	90.0	(3.2)	85.7	(3.8)
	Ontario	97.1	(1.9)	90.5	(3.2)	94.8	(2.3)	89.2	(3.3)	74.9	(4.2)	38.8	(5.2)	93.8	(2.3)	90.3	(2.8)	85.9	(3.6)
	Prince Edward Island	67.9	(0.5)	73.6	(0.4)	60.4	(0.4)	85.4	(0.3)	68.9	(0.4)	52.5	(0.4)	96.3	(0.2)	80.7	(0.3)	71.0	(0.4)
	Quebec	92.5	(2.3)	78.3	(3.9)	84.0	(3.2)	61.5	(4.3)	33.7	(3.5)	23.9	(3.6)	72.4	(4.0)	38.4	(3.6)	68.0	(3.8)
	Saskatchewan	98.4	(0.2)	61.6	(3.7)	85.6	(2.8)	80.7	(3.1)	50.0	(3.6)	51.8	(3.6)	81.9	(4.0)	70.5	(2.8)	81.2	(3.4)
	Italy																		
	Abruzzo	97.4	(2.6)	84.1	(2.8)	38.4	(7.1)	74.7	(5.4)	25.0	(6.0)	47.1	(4.7)	76.8	(3.3)	18.1	(5.3)	46.9	(6.3)
	Basilicata	94.0	(3.2)	93.5	(2.2)	43.8	(4.0)	64.4	(5.1)	15.9	(2.5)	29.4	(3.2)	75.0	(5.2)	16.7	(5.6)	36.9	(5.3)
	Bolzano	86.0	(0.5)	50.5	(0.8)	73.1	(1.0)	95.6	(0.2)	54.5	(0.8)	70.2	(0.6)	97.1	(0.2)	40.5	(0.7)	61.2	(0.8)
	Calabria	97.7	(2.3)	87.4	(5.2)	77.1	(5.9)	87.5	(5.0)	27.2	(6.5)	43.1	(7.7)	84.1	(5.9)	26.6	(6.9)	54.1	(7.4)
	Campania	100.0	c	97.2	(2.2)	42.0	(7.0)	71.7	(8.8)	29.8	(7.1)	34.3	(6.8)	84.2	(5.0)	12.0	(4.2)	59.4	(7.3)
	Emilia Romagna	100.0	c	75.6	(7.6)	48.8	(7.9)	64.7	(8.4)	18.8	(5.8)	37.1	(7.8)	89.2	(4.6)	21.5	(5.7)	54.7	(8.1)
	Friuli Venezia Giulia	98.0	(1.9)	77.7	(5.4)	29.2	(5.4)	59.0	(5.6)	23.2	(4.0)	45.9	(5.7)	83.7	(2.2)	22.7	(6.5)	42.3	(5.4)
	Lazio	96.0	(2.9)	92.6	(3.7)	58.1	(8.4)	74.1	(7.0)	33.8	(7.5)	37.5	(7.2)	69.6	(5.0)	22.6	(6.7)	57.5	(8.7)
	Liguria	96.8	(2.7)	79.9	(5.9)	30.4	(7.9)	66.5	(6.8)	24.8	(7.3)	33.6	(6.8)	75.4	(6.5)	24.8	(6.6)	42.5	(6.3)
	Lombardia	100.0	c	79.5	(7.6)	50.0	(7.9)	83.6	(5.1)	61.0	(7.4)	49.9	(7.6)	81.2	(6.0)	26.5	(6.9)	76.6	(6.7)
	Marche	99.7	(0.3)	78.9	(6.8)	53.5	(7.6)	81.0	(6.4)	36.5	(7.6)	48.7	(6.8)	72.1	(6.9)	33.3	(6.8)	68.3	(5.9)
	Molise	98.0	(0.2)	81.1	(0.7)	74.5	(0.8)	61.2	(0.9)	10.0	(0.6)	29.8	(1.1)	87.3	(0.6)	21.1	(0.6)	39.7	(0.9)
	Piemonte	96.2	(2.7)	92.0	(3.9)	49.9	(6.8)	80.8	(5.5)	25.5	(7.1)	51.9	(8.3)	72.4	(6.9)	23.2	(5.8)	47.0	(6.9)
	Puglia	98.0	(2.0)	86.2	(4.4)	63.2	(6.9)	81.0	(5.7)	35.1	(7.3)	47.9	(6.6)	74.7	(7.7)	10.4	(4.6)	47.2	(8.2)
	Sardegna	99.6	(0.4)	83.5	(6.0)	57.4	(8.0)	60.0	(8.7)	25.6	(6.3)	27.5	(7.3)	66.9	(7.5)	9.6	(3.7)	40.3	(7.2)
	Sicilia	100.0	c	89.0	(4.7)	62.3	(6.6)	84.5	(5.1)	25.4	(6.8)	33.7	(6.3)	74.0	(7.5)	34.5	(7.0)	54.6	(7.8)
	Toscana	96.3	(2.8)	75.2	(6.9)	46.8	(7.4)	62.3	(7.4)	31.8	(7.9)	33.7	(6.9)	69.0	(7.4)	23.3	(5.7)	47.2	(8.8)
	Trento	95.9	(1.4)	55.0	(4.6)	48.2	(4.3)	86.2	(3.7)	29.6	(5.4)	44.1	(3.8)	81.3	(2.6)	28.3	(3.8)	70.8	(4.7)
	Umbria	91.7	(4.3)	81.9	(4.4)	51.0	(6.3)	66.7	(6.4)	26.5	(5.6)	28.0	(4.9)	70.1	(5.3)	20.9	(3.9)	50.5	(5.1)
	Valle d'Aosta	97.7	(0.3)	82.3	(0.8)	41.0	(1.0)	80.2	(0.9)	30.2	(1.0)	33.3	(1.0)	65.9	(0.9)	29.0	(0.8)	34.6	(1.0)
	Veneto	99.5	(0.5)	76.7	(6.6)	52.9	(6.8)	75.8	(6.1)	32.9	(6.8)	30.2	(7.3)	76.1	(6.9)	30.9	(5.7)	54.2	(7.4)
	Mexico																		
	Aguascalientes	94.4	(3.8)	83.1	(5.8)	99.0	(0.9)	95.0	(0.3)	78.4	(5.2)	80.2	(6.2)	44.3	(6.8)	47.9	(6.9)	61.4	(7.3)
	Baja California	96.5	(3.3)	78.2	(7.0)	84.7	(7.9)	92.8	(4.8)	92.0	(4.4)	66.8	(6.5)	58.4	(11.9)	56.1	(6.4)	86.4	(7.4)
	Baja California Sur	96.3	(2.7)	80.5	(4.7)	99.3	(0.7)	90.0	(5.6)	74.6	(4.9)	82.3	(7.7)	50.0	(6.4)	56.7	(7.2)	78.4	(6.3)
	Campeche	86.0	(6.0)	80.4	(5.2)	100.0	c	96.6	(2.4)	71.1	(5.5)	85.2	(5.9)	43.6	(8.0)	46.8	(9.3)	60.7	(6.6)
	Chiapas	88.0	(3.7)	82.4	(6.1)	93.6	(3.3)	94.6	(1.4)	74.0	(8.6)	68.4	(8.4)	49.4	(7.6)	66.5	(5.2)	68.6	(6.7)
	Chihuahua	94.4	(3.6)	85.0	(6.4)	97.7	(1.9)	100.0	c	75.1	(9.9)	75.2	(8.3)	76.9	(7.2)	62.1	(9.2)	84.4	(5.2)
	Coahuila	89.9	(5.4)	84.0	(6.6)	99.1	(0.6)	96.3	(3.7)	67.2	(7.6)	82.5	(7.2)	55.4	(9.0)	52.5	(8.4)	66.1	(9.4)
	Colima	85.1	(4.1)	75.8	(6.5)	84.6	(4.1)	74.3	(2.5)	62.8	(5.6)	69.6	(4.4)	55.5	(7.2)	45.9	(5.9)	70.3	(6.8)
	Distrito Federal	93.1	(3.5)	89.3	(5.9)	97.6	(2.0)	95.0	(3.3)	84.9	(6.3)	82.2	(7.5)	57.7	(9.9)	59.4	(9.7)	66.2	(9.0)
	Durango	97.8	(1.9)	67.4	(9.6)	96.6	(2.6)	93.8	(4.9)	93.8	(3.3)	82.5	(6.0)	53.1	(9.1)	51.6	(7.9)	62.6	(9.8)
	Guanajuato	91.2	(5.8)	87.6	(4.8)	89.6	(3.7)	98.0	(2.0)	76.9	(6.6)	75.1	(7.9)	48.8	(8.9)	32.0	(7.1)	62.9	(6.7)
	Guerrero	83.2	(7.6)	77.5	(8.2)	92.1	(5.6)	90.3	(7.0)	68.3	(10.3)	62.3	(9.8)	57.9	(10.2)	42.7	(8.8)	77.5	(6.9)
	Hidalgo	94.9	(2.6)	90.1	(4.7)	94.1	(3.1)	87.4	(3.9)	79.3	(6.7)	77.9	(7.2)	37.6	(7.5)	40.8	(7.4)	62.4	(7.8)
	Jalisco	98.1	(1.9)	81.8	(7.2)	97.3	(1.9)	94.8	(2.9)	82.5	(4.7)	71.9	(9.5)	50.1	(9.5)	42.9	(7.4)	73.0	(7.8)
	Mexico	98.8	(0.7)	75.4	(8.3)	93.2	(3.9)	100.0	c	55.2	(7.8)	64.5	(7.0)	41.8	(7.3)	54.0	(6.0)	64.4	(6.0)
	Morelos	83.5	(5.8)	87.5	(5.5)	91.9	(4.7)	86.0	(4.8)	66.4	(7.5)	74.6	(8.0)	60.8	(7.1)	64.1	(8.2)	71.8	(7.0)
	Nayarit	78.0	(5.2)	75.1	(4.7)	86.1	(4.8)	81.4	(5.0)	85.2	(4.1)	72.9	(6.4)	55.9	(5.9)	43.9	(7.4)	58.3	(5.7)
	Nuevo León	100.0	c	97.1	(2.3)	93.3	(5.5)	91.2	(5.8)	92.6	(3.7)	83.6	(7.4)	72.0	(8.6)	63.4	(7.7)	85.1	(6.6)
	Puebla	92.5	(4.0)	82.9	(4.7)	95.1	(2.4)	94.5	(3.5)	74.9	(6.3)	69.6	(6.5)	57.2	(7.7)	46.3	(7.4)	69.6	(6.3)
	Querétaro	97.8	(2.3)	86.3	(5.9)	91.4	(5.4)	90.8	(5.5)	69.4	(8.0)	68.6	(12.8)	55.6	(6.9)	41.6	(10.8)	53.4	(12.2)
	Quintana Roo	91.4	(4.9)	78.2	(7.8)	98.7	(0.9)	86.3	(7.5)	77.9	(7.4)	75.4	(7.0)	44.0	(8.3)	53.2	(7.4)	62.4	(8.5)
	San Luis Potosí	96.2	(2.3)	88.7	(4.2)	92.7	(3.0)	95.4	(3.3)	83.1	(5.4)	75.4	(7.1)	72.0	(5.1)	56.5	(7.7)	65.8	(8.9)
	Sinaloa	90.1	(5.1)	82.4	(5.3)	100.0	c	98.1	(1.3)	78.8	(6.8)	85.5	(5.8)	61.8	(7.8)	65.1	(7.9)	68.7	(7.3)
	Tabasco	88.3	(6.0)	85.7	(6.7)	92.9	(3.6)	92.7	(5.1)	71.9	(8.1)	68.4	(8.0)	53.0	(9.9)	59.6	(8.9)	66.4	(6.5)
	Tamaulipas	90.6	(5.3)	76.6	(10.1)	89.5	(8.8)	96.3	(2.7)	56.1	(11.3)	71.0	(10.9)	71.1	(9.2)	74.5	(8.1)	80.1	(4.1)
	Tlaxcala	91.7	(3.8)	75.3	(7.6)	96.4	(1.9)	95.9	(2.6)	87.5	(5.3)	89.7	(3.6)	56.2	(8.3)	55.0	(7.5)	76.1	(6.1)
	Veracruz	85.5	(6.6)	82.5	(7.0)	99.4	(0.6)	93.4	(3.1)	77.3	(6.2)	66.9	(7.5)	49.9	(8.1)	48.0	(8.4)	55.4	(8.0)
	Yucatán	96.1	(3.3)	88.7	(5.1)	93.6	(3.2)	88.3	(5.3)	70.7	(9.2)	58.5	(9.0)	64.1	(8.3)	44.2	(8.6)	72.4	(7.1)
	Zacatecas	87.2	(6.8)	76.9	(7.9)	92.0	(2.5)	89.8	(2.6)	58.9	(7.9)	58.2	(6.9)	36.2	(7.2)	42.1	(6.4)	62.2	(6.5)

• PISA adjudicated region.
Note: See Table IV.4.32 for national data.
StatLink http://dx.doi.org/10.1787/888932957536

[Part 2/2]
Quality assurance and school improvement, by region
Table B2.IV.22 *Results based on school principals' reports*

Percentage of students in schools whose principal reported that their schools have the following measures aimed at quality assurance and improvement:

	Written specification of the school's curriculum and educational goals		Written specification of student-performance standards		Systematic recording of data, including teacher and student attendance and graduation rates, test results and professional development of teachers		Internal evaluation/ self-evaluation		External evaluation		Seeking written feed-back from students (e.g. regarding lessons, teachers or resources)		Teacher mentoring		Regular consultation with one or more experts over a period of at least six months with the aim of improving the school		Implementation of a standardised policy for mathematics (i.e. school curriculum with shared instructional materials accompanied by staff development and training)	
	%	S.E.	%	S.E.	%	S.E.	%	S.E.	%	S.E.	%	S.E.	%	S.E.	%	S.E.	%	S.E.
Portugal																		
Alentejo	94.4	(5.0)	73.4	(11.7)	96.1	(4.2)	100.0	c	97.0	(4.4)	66.0	(12.9)	70.6	(10.4)	19.6	(10.0)	77.1	(9.5)
Spain																		
Andalusia•	95.7	(3.1)	81.8	(5.3)	93.8	(3.5)	98.2	(1.8)	84.0	(5.6)	72.4	(6.2)	17.3	(4.4)	29.7	(7.1)	50.8	(6.1)
Aragon•	97.6	(2.4)	70.9	(7.9)	90.0	(4.5)	70.3	(6.6)	58.4	(7.5)	71.9	(6.4)	16.2	(5.5)	18.2	(4.7)	41.4	(7.3)
Asturias•	100.0	c	85.0	(4.7)	96.1	(2.7)	91.6	(3.8)	77.8	(5.4)	67.4	(5.8)	22.5	(4.6)	26.8	(4.8)	45.0	(6.9)
Balearic Islands•	94.2	(3.4)	59.8	(7.3)	75.3	(5.9)	81.6	(6.0)	62.8	(7.2)	74.5	(6.4)	34.4	(6.6)	28.9	(5.7)	35.7	(7.2)
Basque Country•	96.2	(1.2)	78.0	(3.1)	95.0	(1.7)	77.8	(2.9)	84.0	(2.6)	74.6	(3.1)	58.3	(3.7)	54.9	(3.8)	66.8	(3.8)
Cantabria•	98.0	(1.9)	82.1	(4.9)	94.8	(3.0)	76.8	(5.3)	82.7	(5.1)	61.1	(5.7)	26.2	(5.1)	16.9	(5.0)	35.0	(6.3)
Castile and Leon•	100.0	c	78.3	(6.1)	96.6	(2.3)	78.6	(5.7)	56.2	(6.6)	76.3	(4.4)	25.1	(5.2)	18.9	(4.4)	38.9	(6.7)
Catalonia•	91.7	(4.1)	73.9	(5.9)	90.2	(4.6)	83.8	(4.5)	94.0	(3.5)	49.4	(8.2)	28.4	(6.5)	36.6	(6.9)	32.8	(7.8)
Extremadura•	98.0	(1.9)	74.2	(6.7)	96.6	(2.4)	70.6	(6.4)	75.3	(5.5)	53.4	(7.3)	16.7	(5.6)	12.9	(5.0)	39.3	(6.2)
Galicia•	92.9	(3.6)	76.6	(6.0)	78.1	(6.0)	65.4	(6.8)	65.7	(6.8)	42.5	(7.2)	59.7	(7.3)	15.9	(5.2)	16.5	(5.0)
La Rioja•	94.3	(0.3)	76.6	(0.4)	93.2	(0.3)	74.1	(0.5)	84.5	(0.4)	69.5	(0.5)	21.2	(0.5)	32.8	(0.4)	34.8	(0.5)
Madrid•	96.2	(2.7)	98.1	(1.9)	92.8	(3.6)	81.5	(5.6)	84.6	(4.8)	66.4	(6.3)	29.5	(6.3)	20.7	(5.2)	34.5	(5.9)
Murcia•	93.8	(3.6)	80.8	(5.4)	88.0	(4.1)	82.9	(5.5)	51.2	(5.6)	70.6	(6.9)	10.8	(4.9)	22.1	(6.8)	35.4	(6.7)
Navarre•	97.2	(2.0)	64.1	(4.9)	90.6	(3.5)	84.8	(2.4)	91.3	(2.5)	70.7	(4.4)	35.6	(5.7)	35.7	(4.1)	44.2	(5.4)
United Kingdom																		
England	97.8	(1.1)	94.1	(1.9)	100.0	c	100.0	c	91.7	(2.4)	71.2	(3.9)	98.4	(0.9)	81.4	(2.8)	74.7	(3.7)
Northern Ireland	96.9	(2.8)	94.3	(3.3)	97.3	(2.0)	100.0	c	82.8	(4.0)	65.1	(5.4)	79.5	(3.9)	72.1	(4.9)	77.9	(4.7)
Scotland•	94.5	(2.1)	81.4	(4.0)	96.9	(1.8)	100.0	c	92.2	(2.7)	91.2	(2.8)	85.0	(3.3)	67.9	(4.5)	67.7	(4.2)
Wales	96.6	(1.2)	94.8	(2.0)	99.3	(0.7)	100.0	c	92.2	(1.5)	81.8	(2.9)	91.4	(2.0)	85.8	(2.8)	76.9	(3.4)
United States																		
Connecticut•	100.0	c	91.6	(3.2)	97.8	(2.5)	98.2	(1.8)	86.5	(4.7)	44.0	(7.2)	100.0	c	75.9	(6.6)	87.0	(3.4)
Florida•	98.1	(1.9)	98.1	(1.9)	97.9	(2.1)	98.2	(1.8)	92.7	(3.6)	78.8	(6.1)	100.0	c	81.6	(6.8)	94.8	(3.1)
Massachusetts•	98.0	(2.0)	93.9	(3.5)	98.5	(1.5)	94.5	(3.2)	81.7	(5.4)	49.9	(7.2)	96.7	(2.6)	64.8	(6.8)	88.6	(4.6)
Argentina																		
Ciudad Autónoma de Buenos Aires•	92.5	(5.0)	60.3	(8.2)	85.2	(6.2)	82.8	(5.9)	34.7	(6.9)	38.7	(7.6)	82.1	(7.0)	68.7	(6.8)	69.7	(7.9)
Brazil																		
Acre	87.1	(7.4)	78.9	(9.6)	91.9	(5.4)	94.8	(0.7)	95.9	(4.0)	69.3	(9.0)	73.9	(7.7)	55.3	(9.2)	77.5	(8.6)
Alagoas	92.5	(5.5)	70.8	(9.6)	75.6	(11.3)	80.2	(6.4)	65.3	(13.3)	72.5	(9.9)	84.8	(3.0)	26.7	(11.0)	58.4	(13.1)
Amapá	96.3	(4.0)	73.8	(10.8)	74.3	(8.8)	96.2	(3.4)	70.2	(8.1)	81.2	(9.3)	98.0	(2.1)	64.8	(9.7)	76.4	(4.5)
Amazonas	94.9	(3.9)	65.1	(11.6)	65.0	(10.8)	94.6	(5.6)	68.4	(11.8)	68.9	(11.2)	93.8	(4.7)	47.7	(10.6)	76.9	(8.8)
Bahia	89.4	(7.3)	86.9	(11.4)	80.4	(11.2)	100.0	c	82.9	(10.9)	58.7	(12.7)	100.0	c	33.8	(17.6)	68.5	(15.6)
Ceará	94.5	(3.7)	72.4	(6.6)	88.4	(3.3)	87.3	(5.8)	88.8	(6.0)	61.1	(9.1)	93.9	(5.3)	16.6	(4.7)	65.3	(9.0)
Espírito Santo	91.2	(5.1)	83.3	(8.7)	83.9	(6.6)	80.5	(5.8)	59.9	(11.4)	74.7	(7.0)	91.8	(5.0)	47.8	(11.4)	83.1	(7.5)
Federal District	93.7	(5.8)	65.8	(12.8)	76.4	(7.2)	99.5	(0.5)	76.2	(9.9)	64.8	(8.3)	93.2	(4.0)	51.7	(8.2)	67.8	(7.2)
Goiás	95.8	(4.2)	92.2	(5.2)	96.2	(3.7)	100.0	c	93.7	(4.3)	66.5	(10.8)	85.2	(7.5)	55.2	(12.0)	87.3	(6.7)
Maranhão	100.0	c	63.9	(11.8)	85.8	(7.2)	100.0	c	59.2	(12.2)	78.1	(9.0)	70.0	(8.8)	54.6	(14.2)	81.7	(9.2)
Mato Grosso	100.0	c	82.3	(8.4)	77.1	(10.9)	86.9	(7.6)	53.2	(8.5)	63.4	(10.7)	93.3	(4.8)	42.6	(13.0)	61.9	(11.3)
Mato Grosso do Sul	91.6	(5.8)	72.4	(11.2)	75.1	(10.7)	98.3	(1.7)	86.3	(7.7)	78.9	(7.7)	98.2	(2.0)	49.7	(9.4)	60.6	(9.2)
Minas Gerais	97.7	(2.5)	81.6	(7.8)	84.9	(4.5)	100.0	c	97.7	(2.2)	79.5	(8.1)	91.4	(5.4)	69.0	(10.1)	74.4	(8.5)
Pará	99.2	(0.9)	74.0	(8.3)	80.2	(6.3)	93.9	(4.1)	61.8	(7.2)	73.2	(6.6)	89.3	(4.5)	55.3	(13.7)	55.9	(8.9)
Paraíba	86.9	(10.7)	78.8	(11.3)	69.8	(11.1)	94.3	(4.1)	44.7	(14.2)	81.6	(7.7)	94.5	(4.1)	45.8	(10.6)	76.1	(11.5)
Paraná	100.0	c	68.6	(10.1)	76.2	(8.4)	96.1	(3.6)	72.9	(9.1)	67.7	(8.4)	99.9	(0.1)	55.6	(9.5)	82.5	(7.0)
Pernambuco	100.0	c	77.1	(10.5)	82.8	(8.9)	100.0	c	79.7	(7.5)	67.1	(10.6)	97.4	(2.6)	45.6	(10.0)	79.1	(9.7)
Piauí	94.8	(4.3)	70.6	(9.7)	74.1	(9.2)	91.5	(5.0)	57.3	(10.7)	53.9	(12.9)	92.9	(5.7)	48.3	(14.6)	63.7	(9.3)
Rio de Janeiro	100.0	c	79.9	(8.6)	91.7	(6.3)	96.4	(2.2)	93.9	(5.4)	76.7	(10.7)	75.7	(7.4)	57.4	(9.4)	77.1	(9.1)
Rio Grande do Norte	80.2	(10.5)	74.1	(11.8)	54.0	(9.7)	76.9	(9.0)	65.8	(10.3)	58.5	(10.6)	84.1	(8.2)	60.4	(11.8)	48.0	(9.7)
Rio Grande do Sul	87.8	(6.9)	57.0	(9.5)	62.4	(11.5)	85.8	(4.8)	66.5	(10.0)	75.1	(8.7)	97.1	(2.4)	23.6	(9.3)	66.8	(9.6)
Rondônia	100.0	c	74.8	(9.9)	76.9	(7.9)	85.6	(5.9)	80.1	(9.6)	72.0	(7.7)	87.0	(7.6)	42.3	(9.7)	56.8	(7.2)
Roraima	96.2	(3.7)	78.4	(10.7)	83.6	(4.2)	90.2	(4.4)	68.6	(6.4)	70.4	(11.0)	91.0	(5.2)	64.8	(10.7)	63.8	(8.7)
Santa Catarina	90.9	(6.6)	51.2	(10.4)	71.3	(9.7)	88.1	(5.9)	38.3	(8.5)	66.1	(10.7)	93.1	(4.3)	38.1	(7.7)	45.7	(8.3)
São Paulo	88.9	(3.7)	73.5	(5.9)	89.1	(4.4)	100.0	c	95.1	(2.6)	64.1	(6.4)	97.2	(2.0)	55.2	(5.9)	74.8	(5.6)
Sergipe	87.3	(7.5)	69.2	(12.9)	81.7	(9.2)	86.3	(8.1)	62.3	(9.3)	71.8	(10.0)	96.2	(3.8)	45.7	(11.4)	63.4	(8.1)
Tocantins	87.0	(6.7)	58.1	(6.4)	77.6	(5.4)	85.5	(8.0)	90.7	(6.3)	80.4	(9.1)	93.4	(4.6)	37.0	(11.9)	85.5	(7.1)
Colombia																		
Bogota	89.4	(4.7)	90.9	(4.3)	91.0	(4.1)	100.0	c	90.1	(5.3)	67.1	(6.8)	58.8	(6.7)	59.0	(5.0)	63.5	(7.4)
Cali	99.3	(0.8)	99.3	(0.8)	96.7	(2.1)	99.3	(0.8)	78.3	(7.0)	81.1	(3.6)	74.6	(7.2)	67.5	(6.3)	75.2	(6.5)
Manizales	100.0	c	95.9	(3.1)	87.4	(5.3)	95.1	(3.5)	77.0	(7.3)	69.8	(7.3)	75.9	(3.9)	62.9	(8.4)	56.3	(7.2)
Medellin	92.8	(3.6)	96.4	(2.8)	85.2	(6.5)	98.1	(2.0)	80.7	(6.7)	80.0	(5.6)	67.9	(5.9)	55.6	(6.7)	59.4	(8.1)
Russian Federation																		
Perm Territory region•	91.6	(3.8)	90.9	(4.0)	99.6	(0.4)	96.6	(2.4)	93.2	(3.4)	79.8	(5.0)	98.9	(1.1)	50.7	(5.7)	89.2	(3.4)
United Arab Emirates																		
Abu Dhabi•	97.1	(1.5)	96.4	(1.8)	98.5	(0.9)	95.6	(1.7)	95.0	(2.1)	80.4	(3.3)	92.8	(2.0)	82.4	(3.5)	84.5	(3.1)
Ajman	91.5	(3.9)	91.0	(5.1)	97.5	(1.8)	90.1	(5.5)	90.5	(5.1)	80.1	(8.7)	89.6	(3.8)	29.7	(9.6)	66.6	(5.7)
Dubai•	96.0	(0.0)	93.4	(0.1)	98.9	(0.0)	99.3	(0.0)	94.2	(0.1)	78.7	(0.3)	92.9	(0.1)	81.0	(0.1)	87.9	(0.1)
Fujairah	100.0	c	100.0	c	100.0	c	99.6	(0.1)	88.4	(6.4)	85.1	(3.7)	86.0	(5.3)	45.7	(7.3)	78.3	(4.0)
Ras Al Khaimah	90.4	(6.7)	99.8	(0.0)	100.0	c	100.0	c	91.8	(5.6)	68.8	(9.4)	90.2	(5.3)	49.3	(8.7)	71.1	(7.9)
Sharjah	92.8	(5.3)	96.4	(3.5)	100.0	c	100.0	c	94.2	(3.0)	69.0	(8.7)	92.7	(1.4)	70.2	(6.7)	78.4	(9.4)
Umm Al Quwain	91.0	(0.1)	99.3	(0.2)	99.3	(0.2)	95.5	(0.3)	96.1	(0.2)	83.5	(0.3)	76.2	(0.3)	15.7	(0.3)	46.0	(0.4)

• PISA adjudicated region.
Note: See Table IV.4.32 for national data.
StatLink ㎳ http://dx.doi.org/10.1787/888932957536

[Part 1/4]
Index of disciplinary climate and mathematics performance, by region
Table B2.IV.24   *Results based on students' self-reports*

	All students		Bottom quarter		Second quarter		Third quarter		Top quarter		Variability in this index	
	Mean index	S.E.	Mean index	S.E.	Mean index	S.E.	Mean index	S.E.	Mean index	S.E.	Standard deviation	S.E.
Australia												
Australian Capital Territory	-0.26	(0.05)	-1.55	(0.07)	-0.57	(0.05)	0.04	(0.06)	1.07	(0.07)	1.04	(0.03)
New South Wales	-0.16	(0.03)	-1.52	(0.04)	-0.51	(0.04)	0.19	(0.04)	1.21	(0.04)	1.07	(0.02)
Northern Territory	-0.11	(0.11)	-1.29	(0.15)	-0.37	(0.11)	0.22	(0.12)	1.03	(0.11)	0.92	(0.05)
Queensland	-0.13	(0.03)	-1.48	(0.05)	-0.42	(0.03)	0.19	(0.03)	1.21	(0.05)	1.05	(0.02)
South Australia	-0.14	(0.04)	-1.38	(0.06)	-0.45	(0.05)	0.14	(0.04)	1.13	(0.05)	0.99	(0.02)
Tasmania	-0.19	(0.04)	-1.44	(0.05)	-0.51	(0.05)	0.12	(0.04)	1.06	(0.05)	0.99	(0.02)
Victoria	-0.14	(0.04)	-1.37	(0.04)	-0.46	(0.04)	0.17	(0.03)	1.12	(0.05)	0.98	(0.02)
Western Australia	-0.06	(0.03)	-1.35	(0.05)	-0.32	(0.04)	0.25	(0.04)	1.20	(0.05)	1.01	(0.02)
Belgium												
Flemish community*	0.08	(0.03)	-1.17	(0.04)	-0.26	(0.02)	0.39	(0.04)	1.37	(0.03)	1.00	(0.02)
French community	-0.16	(0.03)	-1.52	(0.04)	-0.51	(0.04)	0.19	(0.04)	1.21	(0.04)	1.07	(0.02)
German-speaking community	-0.14	(0.04)	-1.37	(0.04)	-0.46	(0.04)	0.17	(0.03)	1.12	(0.05)	0.98	(0.02)
Canada												
Alberta	0.04	(0.04)	-1.19	(0.06)	-0.22	(0.03)	0.33	(0.06)	1.27	(0.04)	0.97	(0.02)
British Columbia	0.02	(0.03)	-1.19	(0.05)	-0.24	(0.03)	0.33	(0.04)	1.18	(0.04)	0.94	(0.02)
Manitoba	0.03	(0.04)	-1.17	(0.05)	-0.26	(0.03)	0.29	(0.06)	1.28	(0.04)	0.96	(0.02)
New Brunswick	-0.04	(0.04)	-1.28	(0.07)	-0.27	(0.03)	0.26	(0.04)	1.13	(0.06)	0.96	(0.03)
Newfoundland and Labrador	-0.08	(0.04)	-1.44	(0.06)	-0.40	(0.04)	0.26	(0.05)	1.28	(0.04)	1.06	(0.03)
Nova Scotia	-0.09	(0.06)	-1.48	(0.07)	-0.37	(0.07)	0.27	(0.05)	1.23	(0.08)	1.06	(0.03)
Ontario	-0.02	(0.03)	-1.21	(0.04)	-0.31	(0.02)	0.22	(0.03)	1.22	(0.04)	0.95	(0.02)
Prince Edward Island	-0.12	(0.03)	-1.36	(0.06)	-0.37	(0.04)	0.14	(0.03)	1.11	(0.05)	0.98	(0.02)
Quebec	0.05	(0.03)	-1.20	(0.03)	-0.30	(0.03)	0.38	(0.05)	1.33	(0.04)	0.99	(0.01)
Saskatchewan	0.05	(0.04)	-1.08	(0.06)	-0.24	(0.04)	0.29	(0.05)	1.21	(0.05)	0.91	(0.02)
Italy												
Abruzzo	-0.09	(0.05)	-1.34	(0.05)	-0.42	(0.06)	0.24	(0.07)	1.16	(0.04)	0.98	(0.02)
Basilicata	0.05	(0.05)	-1.22	(0.06)	-0.29	(0.07)	0.45	(0.05)	1.29	(0.05)	1.00	(0.03)
Bolzano	0.05	(0.03)	-1.20	(0.04)	-0.33	(0.04)	0.41	(0.04)	1.34	(0.03)	1.00	(0.02)
Calabria	0.04	(0.05)	-1.22	(0.07)	-0.30	(0.05)	0.39	(0.08)	1.28	(0.05)	0.99	(0.03)
Campania	0.10	(0.05)	-1.15	(0.05)	-0.26	(0.07)	0.51	(0.07)	1.31	(0.06)	0.98	(0.03)
Emilia Romagna	-0.11	(0.04)	-1.31	(0.05)	-0.51	(0.06)	0.20	(0.05)	1.20	(0.06)	0.99	(0.03)
Friuli Venezia Giulia	-0.09	(0.04)	-1.40	(0.05)	-0.47	(0.06)	0.28	(0.06)	1.24	(0.05)	1.04	(0.03)
Lazio	-0.07	(0.04)	-1.32	(0.04)	-0.40	(0.05)	0.26	(0.07)	1.18	(0.05)	0.98	(0.02)
Liguria	-0.20	(0.06)	-1.44	(0.08)	-0.55	(0.07)	0.14	(0.06)	1.08	(0.07)	1.00	(0.03)
Lombardia	-0.01	(0.05)	-1.34	(0.06)	-0.36	(0.06)	0.38	(0.07)	1.27	(0.03)	1.03	(0.02)
Marche	-0.21	(0.05)	-1.44	(0.06)	-0.59	(0.06)	0.14	(0.08)	1.04	(0.04)	0.98	(0.02)
Molise	0.09	(0.04)	-1.18	(0.06)	-0.19	(0.06)	0.45	(0.05)	1.29	(0.05)	0.97	(0.03)
Piemonte	-0.10	(0.08)	-1.38	(0.07)	-0.44	(0.09)	0.23	(0.08)	1.19	(0.09)	1.01	(0.02)
Puglia	0.02	(0.04)	-1.16	(0.05)	-0.31	(0.04)	0.35	(0.06)	1.21	(0.04)	0.94	(0.02)
Sardegna	-0.28	(0.05)	-1.52	(0.06)	-0.65	(0.06)	0.04	(0.06)	1.03	(0.05)	1.01	(0.03)
Sicilia	0.08	(0.05)	-1.16	(0.05)	-0.26	(0.06)	0.44	(0.06)	1.30	(0.05)	0.97	(0.02)
Toscana	-0.22	(0.05)	-1.39	(0.06)	-0.55	(0.05)	0.09	(0.07)	0.99	(0.06)	0.94	(0.02)
Trento	0.02	(0.05)	-1.28	(0.06)	-0.31	(0.06)	0.39	(0.07)	1.26	(0.05)	1.00	(0.03)
Umbria	-0.12	(0.05)	-1.36	(0.06)	-0.45	(0.06)	0.24	(0.05)	1.10	(0.05)	0.97	(0.02)
Valle d'Aosta	-0.29	(0.04)	-1.54	(0.07)	-0.60	(0.05)	-0.02	(0.05)	1.00	(0.06)	0.99	(0.03)
Veneto	-0.12	(0.08)	-1.39	(0.10)	-0.45	(0.09)	0.21	(0.07)	1.14	(0.08)	1.00	(0.03)
Mexico												
Aguascalientes	0.00	(0.06)	-1.11	(0.07)	-0.26	(0.04)	0.27	(0.07)	1.13	(0.08)	0.89	(0.03)
Baja California	-0.03	(0.05)	-1.17	(0.05)	-0.35	(0.06)	0.19	(0.05)	1.22	(0.08)	0.93	(0.03)
Baja California Sur	-0.13	(0.05)	-1.29	(0.07)	-0.45	(0.06)	0.17	(0.04)	1.05	(0.05)	0.92	(0.03)
Campeche	0.02	(0.04)	-1.13	(0.05)	-0.31	(0.05)	0.24	(0.05)	1.27	(0.08)	0.94	(0.03)
Chiapas	0.04	(0.04)	-1.11	(0.07)	-0.18	(0.06)	0.33	(0.04)	1.12	(0.06)	0.88	(0.03)
Chihuahua	0.09	(0.05)	-1.14	(0.07)	-0.19	(0.07)	0.42	(0.06)	1.27	(0.06)	0.96	(0.03)
Coahuila	0.02	(0.05)	-1.10	(0.08)	-0.26	(0.05)	0.28	(0.06)	1.15	(0.08)	0.89	(0.03)
Colima	0.12	(0.08)	-1.09	(0.12)	-0.22	(0.09)	0.48	(0.08)	1.32	(0.06)	0.95	(0.04)
Distrito Federal	0.00	(0.04)	-1.16	(0.05)	-0.33	(0.05)	0.26	(0.06)	1.22	(0.06)	0.94	(0.03)
Durango	0.12	(0.06)	-1.06	(0.08)	-0.18	(0.07)	0.42	(0.07)	1.31	(0.07)	0.94	(0.04)
Guanajuato	0.04	(0.06)	-1.13	(0.08)	-0.27	(0.05)	0.30	(0.08)	1.26	(0.10)	0.93	(0.04)
Guerrero	-0.06	(0.05)	-1.15	(0.06)	-0.31	(0.05)	0.20	(0.05)	1.04	(0.07)	0.88	(0.03)
Hidalgo	0.16	(0.06)	-0.97	(0.07)	-0.11	(0.06)	0.45	(0.07)	1.29	(0.08)	0.90	(0.03)
Jalisco	0.02	(0.04)	-1.15	(0.07)	-0.26	(0.04)	0.31	(0.07)	1.19	(0.07)	0.92	(0.03)
Mexico	0.03	(0.05)	-1.01	(0.06)	-0.24	(0.05)	0.27	(0.06)	1.12	(0.07)	0.85	(0.03)
Morelos	-0.04	(0.06)	-1.17	(0.08)	-0.31	(0.07)	0.24	(0.07)	1.11	(0.07)	0.91	(0.03)
Nayarit	0.04	(0.08)	-1.15	(0.08)	-0.34	(0.07)	0.37	(0.10)	1.31	(0.08)	0.98	(0.03)
Nuevo León	0.16	(0.06)	-1.09	(0.04)	-0.15	(0.07)	0.46	(0.08)	1.43	(0.09)	0.99	(0.03)
Puebla	0.14	(0.05)	-0.91	(0.07)	-0.11	(0.05)	0.40	(0.05)	1.17	(0.05)	0.83	(0.03)
Querétaro	0.20	(0.08)	-1.03	(0.08)	-0.07	(0.09)	0.50	(0.07)	1.40	(0.09)	0.96	(0.03)
Quintana Roo	0.04	(0.06)	-1.07	(0.07)	-0.30	(0.05)	0.28	(0.08)	1.25	(0.08)	0.91	(0.03)
San Luis Potosí	0.10	(0.05)	-1.09	(0.06)	-0.19	(0.06)	0.42	(0.05)	1.28	(0.06)	0.93	(0.03)
Sinaloa	-0.12	(0.07)	-1.27	(0.07)	-0.44	(0.08)	0.16	(0.07)	1.10	(0.10)	0.94	(0.03)
Tabasco	-0.12	(0.05)	-1.26	(0.08)	-0.45	(0.07)	0.16	(0.06)	1.07	(0.07)	0.92	(0.04)
Tamaulipas	0.08	(0.06)	-1.08	(0.06)	-0.24	(0.08)	0.39	(0.09)	1.24	(0.06)	0.92	(0.02)
Tlaxcala	0.14	(0.05)	-1.04	(0.07)	-0.16	(0.07)	0.47	(0.07)	1.28	(0.05)	0.92	(0.03)
Veracruz	0.22	(0.05)	-0.85	(0.05)	-0.07	(0.06)	0.49	(0.06)	1.32	(0.08)	0.86	(0.03)
Yucatán	0.01	(0.06)	-1.16	(0.10)	-0.26	(0.04)	0.27	(0.07)	1.21	(0.07)	0.94	(0.03)
Zacatecas	-0.01	(0.05)	-1.16	(0.07)	-0.30	(0.04)	0.27	(0.06)	1.16	(0.08)	0.91	(0.03)

* PISA adjudicated region.
Notes: Values that are statistically significant are indicated in bold (see Annex A3).
See Table IV.5.6 for national data.
StatLink ᵐˢᴸ http://dx.doi.org/10.1787/888932957536

[Part 2/4]
Index of disciplinary climate and mathematics performance, by region
Table B2.IV.24 *Results based on students' self-reports*

| | Index of disciplinary climate | | | | | | | | | | Variability in this index | |
| | All students | | Bottom quarter | | Second quarter | | Third quarter | | Top quarter | | | |
	Mean index	S.E.	Mean index	S.E.	Mean index	S.E.	Mean index	S.E.	Mean index	S.E.	Standard deviation	S.E.
Portugal												
Alentejo	0.06	(0.08)	-1.09	(0.09)	-0.26	(0.05)	0.33	(0.11)	1.26	(0.09)	0.93	(0.04)
Spain												
Andalusia•	0.03	(0.07)	-1.41	(0.08)	-0.31	(0.07)	0.47	(0.08)	1.39	(0.08)	1.10	(0.03)
Aragon•	-0.03	(0.06)	-1.23	(0.07)	-0.36	(0.07)	0.24	(0.08)	1.25	(0.07)	0.97	(0.03)
Asturias•	0.01	(0.05)	-1.23	(0.05)	-0.37	(0.05)	0.35	(0.08)	1.28	(0.06)	0.99	(0.03)
Balearic Islands•	-0.06	(0.05)	-1.47	(0.08)	-0.42	(0.05)	0.32	(0.07)	1.32	(0.05)	1.09	(0.03)
Basque Country•	-0.15	(0.03)	-1.24	(0.03)	-0.45	(0.03)	0.08	(0.03)	1.01	(0.04)	0.90	(0.01)
Cantabria•	0.09	(0.05)	-1.25	(0.06)	-0.24	(0.08)	0.48	(0.05)	1.38	(0.05)	1.03	(0.03)
Castile and Leon•	0.00	(0.05)	-1.28	(0.07)	-0.35	(0.05)	0.36	(0.07)	1.27	(0.05)	1.01	(0.03)
Catalonia•	-0.16	(0.08)	-1.43	(0.09)	-0.50	(0.09)	0.18	(0.08)	1.11	(0.08)	1.00	(0.03)
Extremadura•	0.02	(0.05)	-1.27	(0.06)	-0.32	(0.05)	0.34	(0.08)	1.31	(0.05)	1.01	(0.03)
Galicia•	-0.05	(0.06)	-1.41	(0.07)	-0.36	(0.06)	0.28	(0.08)	1.29	(0.05)	1.05	(0.03)
La Rioja•	0.04	(0.03)	-1.26	(0.05)	-0.29	(0.04)	0.39	(0.05)	1.30	(0.04)	1.01	(0.02)
Madrid•	0.03	(0.06)	-1.18	(0.06)	-0.29	(0.05)	0.31	(0.09)	1.28	(0.07)	0.97	(0.02)
Murcia•	-0.07	(0.05)	-1.35	(0.06)	-0.39	(0.05)	0.28	(0.05)	1.18	(0.05)	0.99	(0.02)
Navarre•	0.03	(0.05)	-1.24	(0.05)	-0.34	(0.05)	0.37	(0.08)	1.34	(0.05)	1.02	(0.02)
United Kingdom												
England	0.15	(0.03)	-1.24	(0.04)	-0.16	(0.04)	0.55	(0.03)	1.46	(0.03)	1.06	(0.02)
Northern Ireland	0.21	(0.05)	-1.20	(0.06)	-0.09	(0.06)	0.62	(0.05)	1.51	(0.05)	1.06	(0.02)
Scotland•	0.10	(0.04)	-1.33	(0.05)	-0.20	(0.05)	0.51	(0.04)	1.40	(0.04)	1.07	(0.02)
Wales	0.11	(0.03)	-1.27	(0.05)	-0.23	(0.04)	0.48	(0.03)	1.44	(0.04)	1.06	(0.02)
United States												
Connecticut•	0.30	(0.05)	-0.98	(0.08)	-0.02	(0.04)	0.67	(0.08)	1.55	(0.03)	0.99	(0.03)
Florida•	-0.01	(0.05)	-1.31	(0.06)	-0.33	(0.05)	0.26	(0.07)	1.32	(0.05)	1.03	(0.02)
Massachusetts•	0.32	(0.05)	-1.04	(0.09)	0.01	(0.06)	0.73	(0.06)	1.58	(0.03)	1.04	(0.03)
Argentina												
Ciudad Autónoma de Buenos Aires•	-0.45	(0.04)	-1.56	(0.06)	-0.76	(0.04)	-0.17	(0.05)	0.69	(0.07)	0.90	(0.03)
Brazil												
Acre	-0.32	(0.07)	-1.39	(0.09)	-0.68	(0.06)	-0.13	(0.07)	0.93	(0.10)	0.93	(0.03)
Alagoas	-0.45	(0.06)	-1.54	(0.08)	-0.82	(0.06)	-0.24	(0.08)	0.79	(0.08)	0.92	(0.04)
Amapá	-0.31	(0.05)	-1.30	(0.06)	-0.59	(0.07)	-0.06	(0.05)	0.74	(0.08)	0.81	(0.04)
Amazonas	-0.49	(0.06)	-1.59	(0.08)	-0.81	(0.05)	-0.24	(0.06)	0.68	(0.11)	0.91	(0.04)
Bahia	-0.37	(0.13)	-1.38	(0.16)	-0.59	(0.10)	-0.16	(0.13)	0.65	(0.17)	0.82	(0.04)
Ceará	-0.25	(0.06)	-1.50	(0.09)	-0.62	(0.07)	0.01	(0.08)	1.12	(0.06)	1.02	(0.03)
Espírito Santo	-0.44	(0.07)	-1.62	(0.10)	-0.74	(0.08)	-0.15	(0.08)	0.77	(0.06)	0.95	(0.03)
Federal District	-0.19	(0.10)	-1.29	(0.10)	-0.53	(0.09)	0.08	(0.10)	1.00	(0.14)	0.91	(0.05)
Goiás	-0.45	(0.07)	-1.54	(0.08)	-0.69	(0.05)	-0.22	(0.07)	0.66	(0.11)	0.87	(0.04)
Maranhão	-0.31	(0.06)	-1.28	(0.08)	-0.63	(0.07)	-0.11	(0.06)	0.77	(0.08)	0.83	(0.04)
Mato Grosso	-0.47	(0.06)	-1.61	(0.09)	-0.77	(0.06)	-0.23	(0.05)	0.73	(0.10)	0.94	(0.05)
Mato Grosso do Sul	-0.20	(0.06)	-1.40	(0.07)	-0.56	(0.07)	0.11	(0.07)	1.06	(0.07)	0.97	(0.03)
Minas Gerais	-0.27	(0.06)	-1.41	(0.09)	-0.55	(0.06)	0.00	(0.07)	0.91	(0.09)	0.92	(0.03)
Pará	-0.34	(0.15)	-1.40	(0.10)	-0.70	(0.09)	-0.13	(0.14)	0.90	(0.29)	0.92	(0.08)
Paraíba	-0.25	(0.06)	-1.33	(0.07)	-0.56	(0.07)	0.05	(0.08)	0.88	(0.07)	0.88	(0.03)
Paraná	-0.49	(0.05)	-1.56	(0.06)	-0.82	(0.06)	-0.28	(0.05)	0.71	(0.10)	0.92	(0.04)
Pernambuco	-0.30	(0.09)	-1.46	(0.08)	-0.66	(0.10)	-0.09	(0.12)	1.04	(0.11)	0.99	(0.03)
Piauí	-0.23	(0.05)	-1.24	(0.08)	-0.56	(0.04)	-0.02	(0.05)	0.92	(0.13)	0.87	(0.06)
Rio de Janeiro	-0.37	(0.08)	-1.58	(0.09)	-0.67	(0.08)	-0.07	(0.10)	0.85	(0.10)	0.96	(0.04)
Rio Grande do Norte	-0.22	(0.11)	-1.39	(0.08)	-0.62	(0.08)	-0.05	(0.14)	1.18	(0.20)	1.02	(0.06)
Rio Grande do Sul	-0.35	(0.05)	-1.41	(0.08)	-0.62	(0.06)	-0.11	(0.05)	0.74	(0.05)	0.86	(0.03)
Rondônia	-0.32	(0.06)	-1.43	(0.08)	-0.65	(0.05)	-0.09	(0.07)	0.89	(0.11)	0.92	(0.03)
Roraima	-0.44	(0.08)	-1.50	(0.12)	-0.73	(0.07)	-0.23	(0.08)	0.72	(0.12)	0.89	(0.06)
Santa Catarina	-0.22	(0.08)	-1.28	(0.07)	-0.48	(0.09)	0.03	(0.07)	0.87	(0.15)	0.86	(0.05)
São Paulo	-0.36	(0.04)	-1.55	(0.04)	-0.69	(0.05)	-0.10	(0.04)	0.91	(0.09)	0.98	(0.03)
Sergipe	-0.40	(0.08)	-1.43	(0.11)	-0.69	(0.09)	-0.11	(0.09)	0.66	(0.09)	0.85	(0.05)
Tocantins	-0.47	(0.07)	-1.53	(0.08)	-0.76	(0.08)	-0.25	(0.08)	0.66	(0.08)	0.87	(0.03)
Colombia												
Bogota	-0.05	(0.04)	-1.10	(0.05)	-0.28	(0.04)	0.21	(0.05)	0.97	(0.06)	0.83	(0.02)
Cali	0.06	(0.06)	-0.96	(0.06)	-0.23	(0.05)	0.33	(0.07)	1.10	(0.09)	0.82	(0.02)
Manizales	0.01	(0.05)	-0.98	(0.07)	-0.26	(0.04)	0.21	(0.05)	1.06	(0.08)	0.81	(0.02)
Medellin	-0.10	(0.07)	-1.15	(0.07)	-0.38	(0.07)	0.13	(0.06)	1.02	(0.08)	0.86	(0.02)
Russian Federation												
Perm Territory region•	0.23	(0.05)	-1.11	(0.06)	-0.09	(0.05)	0.59	(0.06)	1.53	(0.06)	1.03	(0.02)
United Arab Emirates												
Abu Dhabi•	-0.07	(0.04)	-1.43	(0.04)	-0.47	(0.05)	0.29	(0.06)	1.33	(0.04)	1.09	(0.01)
Ajman•	-0.07	(0.06)	-1.20	(0.09)	-0.46	(0.08)	0.19	(0.05)	1.21	(0.09)	0.95	(0.04)
Dubai•	0.09	(0.02)	-1.18	(0.04)	-0.27	(0.02)	0.44	(0.03)	1.36	(0.03)	1.00	(0.01)
Fujairah	0.02	(0.09)	-1.30	(0.12)	-0.40	(0.08)	0.32	(0.12)	1.47	(0.11)	1.08	(0.05)
Ras Al Khaimah	-0.09	(0.07)	-1.37	(0.08)	-0.53	(0.08)	0.23	(0.09)	1.32	(0.08)	1.05	(0.03)
Sharjah	0.19	(0.08)	-1.09	(0.09)	-0.16	(0.11)	0.52	(0.13)	1.49	(0.08)	0.99	(0.04)
Umm Al Quwain	-0.14	(0.07)	-1.28	(0.07)	-0.55	(0.09)	0.15	(0.10)	1.18	(0.11)	0.98	(0.04)

• PISA adjudicated region.
Notes: Values that are statistically significant are indicated in bold (see Annex A3).
See Table IV.5.6 for national data.
StatLink ⟨⟩ http://dx.doi.org/10.1787/888932957536

[Part 3/4]
Index of disciplinary climate and mathematics performance, by region
Table B2.IV.24 *Results based on students' self-reports*

| | School variability in the distribution of this index | Performance on the mathematics scale, by national quarters of this index | | | | | | | | Change in the mathematics score per unit of this index | | Increased likelihood of students in the bottom quarter of this index scoring in the bottom quarter of the national mathematics performance distribution | | Explained variance in student performance (r-squared x 100) | |
| | | Bottom quarter | | Second quarter | | Third quarter | | Top quarter | | | | | | | |
	Percentage of the index variance between schools	Mean score	S.E.	Mean score	S.E.	Mean score	S.E.	Mean score	S.E.	Score dif.	S.E.	Ratio	S.E.	%	S.E.
Australia															
Australian Capital Territory	6.84	**474**	(10.4)	512	(10.6)	522	(9.0)	**556**	(10.2)	**30.1**	(4.4)	**2.3**	(0.38)	11.0	(3.03)
New South Wales	10.25	**464**	(5.2)	491	(5.5)	522	(6.5)	**554**	(6.2)	**31.9**	(2.3)	**2.0**	(0.18)	11.8	(1.59)
Northern Territory	3.68	**429**	(20.5)	449	(18.1)	459	(22.5)	**496**	(17.8)	25.9	(8.9)	1.4	(0.30)	5.6	(3.49)
Queensland	2.47	**459**	(5.5)	493	(5.4)	516	(7.1)	**548**	(5.4)	**30.7**	(2.3)	**2.2**	(0.21)	12.0	(1.51)
South Australia	0.46	**459**	(6.2)	475	(7.5)	497	(7.6)	**529**	(6.8)	27.8	(3.1)	1.7	(0.22)	9.2	(2.07)
Tasmania	6.62	**457**	(8.0)	458	(9.0)	490	(10.7)	**523**	(9.0)	25.7	(3.7)	1.4	(0.21)	7.0	(1.93)
Victoria	7.82	**469**	(5.2)	490	(6.2)	509	(5.8)	**538**	(7.0)	27.1	(2.8)	1.7	(0.20)	8.7	(1.67)
Western Australia	8.69	**479**	(6.2)	505	(6.3)	532	(7.7)	**553**	(7.9)	27.9	(3.6)	1.8	(0.24)	8.9	(2.20)
Belgium															
Flemish community•	6.10	**517**	(5.4)	532	(4.7)	543	(4.9)	**556**	(5.3)	14.5	(2.7)	1.4	(0.11)	2.1	(0.71)
French community	7.03	**464**	(5.0)	491	(5.6)	521	(6.5)	**554**	(6.2)	31.9	(2.3)	2.0	(0.16)	11.8	(1.59)
German-speaking community	5.86	**469**	(5.2)	490	(5.7)	510	(6.0)	**538**	(7.0)	27.1	(2.8)	1.7	(0.20)	8.7	(1.67)
Canada															
Alberta	3.57	**497**	(7.3)	510	(7.1)	536	(7.8)	**541**	(7.9)	16.9	(4.2)	1.6	(0.23)	3.5	(1.70)
British Columbia	8.87	**502**	(7.6)	528	(6.7)	530	(6.0)	**540**	(7.4)	14.1	(2.7)	1.6	(0.18)	2.5	(1.01)
Manitoba	5.42	**468**	(6.0)	485	(5.8)	504	(5.9)	**525**	(8.2)	22.6	(3.7)	1.5	(0.22)	5.9	(1.85)
New Brunswick	3.18	**482**	(6.9)	498	(7.5)	517	(8.4)	**523**	(7.6)	17.2	(3.7)	1.7	(0.32)	4.0	(1.62)
Newfoundland and Labrador	4.88	**483**	(11.0)	495	(8.6)	506	(7.4)	**491**	(7.0)	2.2	(3.9)	1.3	(0.23)	0.1	(0.35)
Nova Scotia	7.08	**461**	(13.2)	500	(6.0)	510	(8.3)	**533**	(6.2)	22.4	(4.4)	2.3	(0.63)	8.8	(3.15)
Ontario	3.79	**493**	(5.7)	508	(5.7)	520	(7.2)	**541**	(5.9)	18.6	(2.3)	1.6	(0.14)	4.2	(0.99)
Prince Edward Island	9.34	**457**	(6.2)	481	(8.0)	494	(6.2)	**500**	(5.6)	17.5	(2.9)	1.7	(0.23)	4.4	(1.41)
Quebec	6.56	**513**	(5.0)	530	(5.5)	551	(6.2)	**563**	(6.0)	18.8	(2.6)	1.6	(0.19)	4.3	(1.15)
Saskatchewan	5.39	**493**	(5.1)	509	(6.9)	520	(7.3)	**518**	(7.2)	11.1	(3.0)	1.3	(0.17)	1.6	(0.88)
Italy															
Abruzzo	2.54	**444**	(9.3)	472	(7.9)	485	(10.7)	**514**	(10.6)	25.2	(4.1)	1.7	(0.25)	7.4	(2.15)
Basilicata	8.57	**452**	(8.2)	451	(7.8)	472	(7.0)	**490**	(7.0)	15.4	(3.0)	1.3	(0.21)	3.4	(1.26)
Bolzano	3.55	**484**	(5.1)	496	(5.4)	516	(6.2)	**537**	(5.2)	20.9	(2.5)	1.6	(0.21)	5.8	(1.28)
Calabria	6.10	**402**	(9.0)	423	(7.9)	446	(10.7)	**458**	(7.4)	20.5	(4.0)	2.0	(0.31)	5.4	(1.96)
Campania	2.54	**430**	(8.4)	453	(11.2)	462	(9.5)	**471**	(13.6)	15.1	(3.8)	1.5	(0.26)	2.8	(1.40)
Emilia Romagna	4.75	**483**	(8.5)	486	(11.4)	509	(10.6)	**532**	(8.2)	18.6	(3.6)	1.2	(0.18)	3.7	(1.21)
Friuli Venezia Giulia	6.95	**496**	(6.7)	512	(9.2)	528	(7.8)	**555**	(8.0)	20.4	(2.9)	1.6	(0.22)	5.5	(1.48)
Lazio	8.22	**450**	(9.7)	453	(9.0)	490	(10.4)	**513**	(7.1)	24.9	(3.3)	1.8	(0.25)	7.2	(1.79)
Liguria	6.94	**472**	(9.3)	476	(9.2)	503	(8.3)	**506**	(9.7)	11.8	(4.9)	1.4	(0.22)	1.7	(1.35)
Lombardia	3.18	**483**	(10.6)	507	(10.5)	527	(11.4)	**553**	(10.4)	26.6	(3.8)	2.1	(0.42)	10.2	(2.66)
Marche	4.43	**472**	(7.4)	481	(8.9)	508	(10.0)	**522**	(7.3)	19.2	(3.2)	1.5	(0.21)	4.8	(1.40)
Molise	5.39	**445**	(7.0)	462	(7.2)	480	(8.8)	**480**	(7.8)	14.3	(3.7)	1.8	(0.29)	2.7	(1.37)
Piemonte	3.68	**467**	(9.0)	495	(9.3)	509	(12.6)	**526**	(8.2)	20.8	(2.9)	1.8	(0.20)	5.8	(1.68)
Puglia	4.81	**457**	(9.8)	470	(8.1)	491	(8.5)	**501**	(8.2)	16.4	(4.0)	1.5	(0.20)	3.1	(1.40)
Sardegna	6.80	**447**	(10.1)	443	(12.3)	460	(9.2)	**485**	(7.0)	14.6	(4.5)	1.3	(0.22)	2.8	(1.77)
Sicilia	7.82	**434**	(7.9)	439	(7.5)	458	(7.6)	**468**	(9.5)	12.3	(3.8)	1.4	(0.20)	2.1	(1.24)
Toscana	10.27	**479**	(8.3)	491	(8.4)	505	(7.8)	**531**	(8.5)	19.2	(4.8)	1.4	(0.25)	4.1	(2.01)
Trento	3.55	**501**	(6.2)	506	(7.5)	545	(8.5)	**545**	(7.1)	17.9	(3.0)	1.4	(0.18)	4.8	(1.52)
Umbria	5.68	**474**	(7.0)	495	(8.7)	496	(11.1)	**513**	(11.2)	13.4	(5.1)	1.4	(0.25)	2.2	(1.74)
Valle d'Aosta	6.97	**476**	(8.0)	487	(7.1)	488	(8.7)	**529**	(7.8)	19.1	(3.7)	1.4	(0.35)	5.5	(2.15)
Veneto	8.35	**500**	(9.4)	516	(12.8)	539	(12.8)	**547**	(8.5)	19.3	(4.9)	1.5	(0.23)	4.4	(2.05)
Mexico															
Aguascalientes	5.58	**428**	(7.2)	433	(7.4)	446	(9.9)	**453**	(10.6)	12.1	(4.0)	1.1	(0.20)	2.1	(1.37)
Baja California	3.80	411	(9.4)	412	(8.5)	414	(8.4)	424	(7.5)	5.2	(4.0)	1.1	(0.21)	0.5	(0.74)
Baja California Sur	4.88	397	(10.9)	414	(9.4)	413	(8.6)	431	(7.2)	14.6	(3.3)	1.5	(0.32)	3.7	(1.66)
Campeche	9.02	379	(7.1)	387	(7.9)	398	(7.9)	418	(6.9)	15.1	(3.2)	1.5	(0.27)	4.1	(1.72)
Chiapas	6.05	**346**	(10.9)	375	(10.1)	388	(8.6)	**388**	(8.9)	18.5	(3.6)	1.9	(0.33)	4.8	(1.92)
Chihuahua	9.11	**417**	(15.0)	426	(12.0)	432	(8.1)	**448**	(9.0)	11.7	(6.2)	1.2	(0.27)	2.1	(2.22)
Coahuila	8.33	**408**	(9.8)	421	(12.0)	411	(10.4)	**434**	(12.7)	9.2	(3.8)	1.3	(0.30)	1.3	(1.03)
Colima	6.06	416	(15.1)	422	(10.1)	439	(6.6)	447	(6.8)	11.6	(7.1)	1.7	(0.39)	2.0	(2.43)
Distrito Federal	6.49	422	(8.1)	429	(8.2)	431	(8.1)	433	(7.1)	3.2	(3.9)	1.2	(0.25)	0.2	(0.60)
Durango	3.87	**402**	(10.8)	423	(6.8)	430	(13.1)	**456**	(7.7)	19.3	(3.9)	2.0	(0.34)	6.2	(2.29)
Guanajuato	8.69	**397**	(11.1)	408	(8.9)	426	(8.8)	**422**	(8.1)	12.2	(4.7)	1.6	(0.31)	2.3	(1.68)
Guerrero	6.05	**351**	(6.9)	372	(6.9)	374	(8.3)	**380**	(6.1)	11.8	(3.9)	1.7	(0.33)	2.4	(1.48)
Hidalgo	6.22	**391**	(10.3)	402	(7.7)	407	(9.9)	**425**	(10.3)	16.8	(5.3)	1.6	(0.29)	4.2	(2.53)
Jalisco	6.73	**424**	(10.2)	438	(14.8)	435	(7.2)	**454**	(8.3)	12.1	(4.3)	1.5	(0.32)	2.3	(1.56)
Mexico	4.11	**401**	(7.9)	417	(7.6)	418	(7.1)	**429**	(7.3)	14.3	(3.4)	1.4	(0.24)	3.5	(1.65)
Morelos	8.35	415	(18.3)	425	(10.1)	427	(10.2)	420	(5.7)	4.7	(6.8)	1.5	(0.30)	0.3	(1.02)
Nayarit	4.31	**395**	(10.1)	408	(10.2)	426	(10.1)	**438**	(7.3)	14.7	(3.8)	1.6	(0.28)	3.6	(1.68)
Nuevo León	7.22	**413**	(13.8)	428	(9.9)	449	(9.7)	**460**	(7.9)	17.3	(4.6)	1.8	(0.34)	5.3	(3.01)
Puebla	5.68	411	(9.2)	412	(8.7)	417	(8.2)	431	(7.9)	8.5	(5.7)	1.2	(0.26)	1.0	(1.25)
Querétaro	6.84	**422**	(10.3)	434	(10.1)	439	(10.9)	**446**	(8.6)	7.0	(3.9)	1.6	(0.40)	0.8	(0.95)
Quintana Roo	4.75	**397**	(6.3)	414	(8.8)	420	(8.5)	**421**	(6.9)	10.1	(4.0)	1.4	(0.27)	1.7	(1.25)
San Luis Potosí	3.42	408	(11.5)	412	(11.8)	416	(10.6)	421	(8.5)	6.3	(4.5)	1.3	(0.20)	0.6	(0.93)
Sinaloa	5.05	**393**	(6.9)	409	(7.5)	420	(7.3)	**421**	(6.4)	11.9	(2.7)	1.5	(0.22)	2.7	(1.26)
Tabasco	3.87	**364**	(8.5)	365	(8.9)	384	(7.6)	**404**	(6.9)	18.6	(3.1)	1.6	(0.28)	5.9	(1.75)
Tamaulipas	5.42	**399**	(10.9)	403	(8.2)	423	(11.9)	**420**	(8.7)	11.1	(3.5)	1.3	(0.36)	1.9	(1.18)
Tlaxcala	4.81	**397**	(7.0)	396	(8.8)	428	(9.3)	**426**	(7.6)	15.8	(3.4)	1.6	(0.23)	4.1	(1.79)
Veracruz	10.29	400	(8.0)	392	(10.7)	401	(7.9)	419	(12.8)	10.2	(6.0)	1.2	(0.24)	1.4	(1.70)
Yucatán	2.47	**399**	(8.6)	413	(9.0)	414	(7.6)	**420**	(6.2)	8.0	(3.7)	1.3	(0.24)	1.0	(1.04)
Zacatecas	6.22	**400**	(7.3)	412	(8.8)	423	(7.5)	**421**	(8.2)	10.1	(3.7)	1.3	(0.25)	1.7	(1.22)

• PISA adjudicated region.
Notes: Values that are statistically significant are indicated in bold (see Annex A3).
See Table IV.5.6 for national data.
StatLink ⌐ऻ⅁⌐ http://dx.doi.org/10.1787/888932957536

[Part 4/4]
Index of disciplinary climate and mathematics performance, by region
Table B2.IV.24 *Results based on students' self-reports*

| | School variability in the distribution of this index | Performance on the mathematics scale, by national quarters of this index | | | | | | | Change in the mathematics score per unit of this index | | Increased likelihood of students in the bottom quarter of this index scoring in the bottom quarter of the national mathematics performance distribution | | Explained variance in student performance (r-squared x 100) | |
| | | Bottom quarter | | Second quarter | | Third quarter | | Top quarter | | | | | | | |
	Percentage of the index variance between schools	Mean score	S.E.	Mean score	S.E.	Mean score	S.E.	Mean score	S.E.	Score dif.	S.E.	Ratio	S.E.	%	S.E.
Portugal															
Alentejo	6.53	469	(20.0)	488	(13.0)	491	(12.3)	508	(18.6)	**18.6**	(9.3)	**1.8**	(0.38)	3.8	(3.87)
Spain															
Andalusia•	0.18	**455**	(9.8)	463	(6.4)	481	(6.4)	**501**	(8.5)	**14.5**	(4.8)	**1.5**	(0.27)	3.7	(2.40)
Aragon•	7.41	483	(9.2)	500	(8.7)	495	(9.7)	504	(8.0)	5.5	(5.0)	1.3	(0.26)	0.3	(0.64)
Asturias•	4.20	485	(8.1)	498	(9.4)	511	(10.5)	512	(9.7)	**11.0**	(5.2)	1.4	(0.20)	1.4	(1.31)
Balearic Islands•	1.67	**459**	(7.9)	465	(7.6)	480	(7.4)	**504**	(7.1)	**15.2**	(3.4)	**1.5**	(0.23)	3.9	(1.71)
Basque Country•	10.29	**491**	(4.1)	506	(4.2)	508	(4.8)	**522**	(4.8)	**11.4**	(2.5)	**1.4**	(0.14)	1.5	(0.68)
Cantabria•	7.38	**474**	(6.5)	479	(8.2)	501	(7.0)	**506**	(7.3)	**11.9**	(3.2)	**1.4**	(0.19)	2.0	(1.05)
Castile and Leon•	11.44	**491**	(8.6)	502	(8.1)	521	(6.8)	**523**	(6.7)	**11.9**	(3.7)	**1.5**	(0.21)	2.1	(1.24)
Catalonia•	8.13	**479**	(8.9)	490	(10.2)	498	(8.3)	**512**	(6.8)	**11.6**	(2.9)	**1.5**	(0.26)	2.0	(0.94)
Extremadura•	5.58	**432**	(10.0)	462	(7.4)	480	(6.1)	**487**	(6.9)	**20.8**	(4.2)	**1.8**	(0.27)	5.2	(2.10)
Galicia•	4.80	**481**	(7.7)	493	(7.7)	488	(7.9)	**508**	(6.6)	7.5	(3.0)	1.3	(0.18)	0.9	(0.72)
La Rioja•	4.11	**473**	(7.3)	496	(8.3)	504	(6.5)	**538**	(7.0)	**22.6**	(3.4)	**1.7**	(0.22)	5.4	(1.58)
Madrid•	3.57	**478**	(7.2)	495	(9.1)	510	(8.1)	**530**	(9.5)	**19.1**	(3.2)	**1.7**	(0.28)	4.6	(1.53)
Murcia•	7.38	**451**	(7.5)	453	(8.4)	458	(9.4)	**485**	(6.4)	**11.8**	(3.6)	**1.2**	(0.18)	1.8	(1.10)
Navarre•	5.86	**493**	(5.4)	508	(6.0)	523	(6.8)	**540**	(7.0)	**19.1**	(3.3)	**1.4**	(0.17)	5.4	(1.85)
United Kingdom															
England	6.62	**467**	(5.1)	487	(5.0)	515	(5.6)	**527**	(6.2)	**22.8**	(2.3)	**1.8**	(0.16)	6.6	(1.27)
Northern Ireland	4.20	**451**	(7.1)	471	(5.9)	509	(6.3)	**524**	(5.1)	**28.5**	(2.9)	**2.0**	(0.22)	10.6	(2.01)
Scotland•	4.43	**463**	(5.1)	491	(5.9)	515	(4.6)	**533**	(4.6)	**25.0**	(2.1)	**2.0**	(0.21)	10.0	(1.59)
Wales	1.61	**440**	(4.1)	463	(4.7)	479	(4.2)	**500**	(3.8)	**20.4**	(2.0)	**1.9**	(0.15)	6.7	(1.26)
United States															
Connecticut•	6.84	**466**	(8.8)	482	(8.3)	524	(9.9)	**542**	(7.7)	**31.4**	(3.5)	**1.9**	(0.22)	10.5	(1.82)
Florida•	7.37	**431**	(6.3)	460	(8.3)	476	(9.6)	**492**	(8.3)	**20.7**	(3.3)	**1.9**	(0.24)	6.6	(1.93)
Massachusetts•	6.80	**465**	(7.4)	509	(10.3)	540	(9.5)	**545**	(7.3)	**29.6**	(2.9)	**2.4**	(0.29)	10.1	(1.86)
Argentina															
Ciudad Autónoma de Buenos Aires•	6.49	**406**	(12.3)	415	(8.6)	420	(10.3)	**440**	(10.3)	12.6	(6.6)	1.2	(0.24)	1.6	(1.59)
Brazil															
Acre	3.79	360	(8.9)	360	(9.7)	352	(9.2)	379	(9.4)	7.1	(4.7)	1.2	(0.20)	1.1	(1.40)
Alagoas	4.31	**331**	(9.6)	330	(10.7)	347	(9.7)	**365**	(12.9)	**14.6**	(6.1)	1.4	(0.35)	3.7	(3.02)
Amapá	6.94	**341**	(13.6)	363	(11.1)	380	(11.6)	**376**	(13.4)	**15.7**	(5.7)	**1.9**	(0.44)	4.0	(2.71)
Amazonas	3.42	347	(10.7)	352	(7.7)	368	(6.7)	367	(13.3)	8.6	(5.3)	1.5	(0.31)	1.5	(1.57)
Bahia	7.37	366	(20.7)	399	(21.9)	373	(17.0)	392	(20.4)	11.4	(9.8)	1.3	(0.44)	1.4	(2.23)
Ceará	7.08	345	(11.8)	374	(11.1)	394	(16.4)	**401**	(13.2)	**19.0**	(5.6)	**2.0**	(0.49)	6.0	(2.88)
Espírito Santo	6.84	387	(19.5)	398	(12.8)	437	(20.5)	433	(16.4)	19.8	(10.9)	1.7	(0.56)	4.9	(5.14)
Federal District	2.54	404	(20.2)	404	(13.6)	432	(16.8)	428	(11.7)	12.6	(8.3)	1.7	(0.50)	1.9	(3.19)
Goiás	4.70	367	(11.0)	374	(9.6)	390	(11.1)	395	(11.5)	**13.4**	(3.7)	1.3	(0.39)	2.7	(1.64)
Maranhão	7.77	**335**	(15.5)	336	(17.5)	341	(16.6)	**368**	(13.3)	**12.2**	(4.8)	1.2	(0.28)	1.7	(1.35)
Mato Grosso	10.25	**353**	(12.7)	381	(17.0)	375	(9.1)	**391**	(16.3)	**13.5**	(5.4)	**1.9**	(0.37)	3.2	(2.16)
Mato Grosso do Sul	8.33	**386**	(9.5)	392	(11.4)	425	(11.6)	**434**	(12.1)	**18.9**	(4.6)	1.5	(0.27)	6.0	(2.41)
Minas Gerais	4.80	395	(11.2)	402	(8.5)	409	(9.0)	410	(8.8)	5.8	(5.0)	1.2	(0.20)	0.6	(0.97)
Pará	1.61	352	(13.4)	365	(9.3)	360	(10.0)	378	(20.8)	9.5	(11.9)	1.4	(0.29)	1.9	(4.96)
Paraíba	7.41	385	(21.0)	412	(13.1)	408	(12.2)	396	(8.4)	6.4	(6.4)	1.7	(0.40)	0.5	(0.98)
Paraná	8.13	392	(11.7)	406	(16.8)	398	(12.8)	410	(14.4)	4.1	(4.2)	1.2	(0.23)	0.2	(0.42)
Pernambuco	1.98	**354**	(14.2)	361	(10.5)	366	(12.0)	**384**	(13.1)	**13.0**	(3.4)	1.4	(0.43)	3.5	(1.86)
Piauí	8.22	**369**	(11.6)	375	(10.0)	396	(17.2)	**399**	(11.4)	**15.4**	(6.3)	1.5	(0.36)	2.8	(2.04)
Rio de Janeiro	6.73	386	(12.4)	394	(10.4)	396	(9.8)	380	(7.8)	-1.3	(4.1)	1.2	(0.30)	0.1	(0.35)
Rio Grande do Norte	7.03	367	(9.1)	369	(9.5)	379	(12.7)	413	(30.0)	17.2	(10.0)	1.3	(0.40)	4.6	(4.79)
Rio Grande do Sul	11.44	396	(13.4)	409	(8.6)	409	(11.7)	414	(7.5)	7.6	(6.8)	1.4	(0.37)	1.0	(1.65)
Rondônia	6.06	369	(8.4)	379	(9.4)	393	(11.8)	402	(8.3)	**12.9**	(3.7)	1.6	(0.33)	3.5	(1.88)
Roraima	0.18	**343**	(8.0)	350	(7.4)	368	(12.4)	**395**	(11.8)	**19.9**	(5.0)	1.4	(0.30)	6.4	(3.08)
Santa Catarina	5.05	**389**	(12.6)	428	(17.6)	420	(14.4)	**440**	(12.1)	**19.1**	(4.0)	**2.2**	(0.56)	4.6	(2.10)
São Paulo	6.56	**380**	(5.8)	402	(8.1)	410	(8.0)	**422**	(7.4)	**15.7**	(3.3)	**1.7**	(0.23)	3.8	(1.63)
Sergipe	4.70	**374**	(11.2)	364	(11.4)	387	(13.9)	**407**	(14.2)	**19.6**	(6.1)	1.5	(0.38)	5.7	(2.71)
Tocantins	2.54	350	(8.6)	355	(10.5)	373	(11.5)	394	(14.3)	**17.3**	(3.9)	1.6	(0.39)	3.8	(1.60)
Colombia															
Bogota	6.53	**382**	(6.8)	396	(6.0)	395	(5.2)	**404**	(5.5)	8.8	(3.5)	1.5	(0.27)	1.3	(1.10)
Cali	7.22	**372**	(8.2)	380	(7.6)	386	(9.4)	**400**	(7.4)	**14.6**	(3.9)	1.5	(0.25)	3.1	(1.71)
Manizales	9.11	399	(6.7)	401	(9.1)	407	(9.6)	420	(8.9)	10.1	(4.9)	1.2	(0.29)	1.4	(1.24)
Medellin	6.95	**374**	(7.7)	386	(8.0)	400	(11.0)	**428**	(14.6)	**22.2**	(6.4)	1.6	(0.28)	5.3	(2.64)
Russian Federation															
Perm Territory region•	1.98	**456**	(8.6)	480	(8.9)	496	(7.3)	**507**	(7.1)	**20.0**	(2.5)	**1.7**	(0.22)	5.2	(1.32)
United Arab Emirates															
Abu Dhabi•	10.27	**392**	(4.9)	413	(6.5)	441	(5.4)	**448**	(7.3)	**20.2**	(2.7)	**1.7**	(0.17)	6.5	(1.54)
Ajman	7.77	390	(13.1)	403	(11.3)	417	(10.0)	406	(8.9)	6.0	(3.6)	1.3	(0.31)	0.6	(0.75)
Dubai•	3.80	**434**	(4.1)	461	(4.5)	479	(4.7)	**489**	(3.9)	**19.9**	(2.1)	**1.8**	(0.16)	4.6	(0.94)
Fujairah	8.87	**386**	(17.9)	410	(10.7)	423	(12.0)	**428**	(11.6)	**16.5**	(4.5)	2.1	(0.59)	4.9	(2.80)
Ras Al Khaimah	6.97	**386**	(10.1)	397	(13.5)	428	(10.6)	**449**	(12.8)	**22.9**	(5.1)	1.7	(0.44)	10.1	(4.06)
Sharjah	1.67	414	(13.2)	445	(10.5)	450	(15.9)	450	(15.5)	13.9	(7.3)	1.6	(0.39)	2.9	(3.20)
Umm Al Quwain	9.34	**369**	(10.5)	391	(12.3)	410	(13.7)	**430**	(12.8)	**22.4**	(5.4)	1.7	(0.56)	8.5	(3.57)

• PISA adjudicated region.

Notes: Values that are statistically significant are indicated in bold (see Annex A3).
See Table IV.5.6 for national data.
StatLink ⟦⟧ http://dx.doi.org/10.1787/888932957536

ANNEX B3
LIST OF TABLES AVAILABLE ON LINE

The following tables are available in electronic form only.

Chapter 1 How resources, policies and practices are related to education outcomes

http://dx.doi.org/10.1787/888932957384

WEB	Table IV.1.7a	Variation in mathematics performance and variation explained by selecting and grouping students
WEB	Table IV.1.7b	Relationship between selecting and grouping students and mathematics performance
WEB	Table IV.1.7c	Relationship among selecting and grouping students, mathematics performance, and student and school characteristics
WEB	Table IV.1.8a	Variation in mathematics performance and variation explained by resources invested in education
WEB	Table IV.1.8b	Relationship between resources invested in education and mathematics performance
WEB	Table IV.1.8c	Relationship among resources invested in education, mathematics performance, and student and school characteristics
WEB	Table IV.1.9a	Variation in mathematics performance and variation explained by school governance
WEB	Table IV.1.9b	Relationship between school governance and mathematics performance
WEB	Table IV.1.9c	Relationship among school governance, mathematics performance, and student and school characteristics
WEB	Table IV.1.10a	Variation in mathematics performance and variation explained by assessment and accountability policies
WEB	Table IV.1.10b	Relationship between assessment and accountability policies and mathematics performance
WEB	Table IV.1.10c	Relationship among assessment and accountability policies, mathematics performance, and student and school characteristics
WEB	Table IV.1.11a	Variation in mathematics performance and variation explained by the learning environment
WEB	Table IV.1.11b	Relationship between the learning environment and mathematics performance
WEB	Table IV.1.11c	Relationship among the learning environment, mathematics performance, and student and school characteristics
WEB	Table IV.1.19	Correlations among selected system-level characteristics, OECD countries
WEB	Table IV.1.20	Correlations among selected system-level characteristics, all countries and economies that participated in PISA 2012
WEB	Table IV.1.30	Change between 2003 and 2012 in mathematics performance and monitoring mathematics teachers' practice
WEB	Table IV.1.31	Mathematics performance and school admittance policies

Chapter 2 Selecting and grouping students

http://dx.doi.org/10.1787/888932957441

WEB	Table IV.2.12	Correlation between stratification indicators
WEB	Table IV.2.13	Correlation between stratification and variation in socio-economic status and mathematics performance
WEB	Table IV.2.15	Correlation between stratification and students' motivation, after accounting for mathematics performance

Chapter 3 Resources invested in education [Part 1/2]

http://dx.doi.org/10.1787/888932957460

WEB	Table IV.3.7	Socio-economically advantaged, average and disadvantaged schools
WEB	Table IV.3.23	Class size of language-of-instruction lessons
WEB	Table IV.3.24	Class size of language-of-instruction lessons, by school features
WEB	Table IV.3.26	Percentage of students not attending after-school lessons, by school features
WEB	Table IV.3.28	Hours of after-school study time per week, by school features

Chapter 3 Resources invested in education [Part 2/2]

http://dx.doi.org/10.1787/888932957479

WEB	Table IV.3.36	Change between 2003 and 2012 in student-teacher ratio, by school features
WEB	Table IV.3.38 (1)	Change between 2003 and 2012 in teacher shortage, by school features (1/2)
WEB	Table IV.3.38 (2)	Change between 2003 and 2012 in teacher shortage, by school features (2/2)
WEB	Table IV.3.39	Change between 2003 and 2012 in index of teacher shortage, by school features
WEB	Table IV.3.41 (1)	Change between 2003 and 2012 in the quality of physical infrastructure, by school features (1/2)
WEB	Table IV.3.41 (2)	Change between 2003 and 2012 in the quality of physical infrastructure, by school features (2/2)
WEB	Table IV.3.42	Change between 2003 and 2012 in index of quality of physical infrastructure, by school features
WEB	Table IV.3.44 (1)	Change between 2003 and 2012 in the quality of schools' educational resources, by school features (1/3)
WEB	Table IV.3.44 (2)	Change between 2003 and 2012 in the quality of schools' educational resources, by school features (2/3)
WEB	Table IV.3.44 (3)	Change between 2003 and 2012 in the quality of schools' educational resources, by school features (3/3)
WEB	Table IV.3.45	Change between 2003 and 2012 in index of quality of schools' educational resources, by school features
WEB	Table IV.3.47 (1)	Change between 2003 and 2012 in students' learning time in school, by school features (1/2)
WEB	Table IV.3.47 (2)	Change between 2003 and 2012 in students' learning time in school, by school features (2/2)
WEB	Table IV.3.49	Change between 2003 and 2012 in hours of after-school study time per week, by school features

...

These tables, as well as additional material, may be found at: *www.pisa.oecd.org.*

Annex C

THE DEVELOPMENT AND IMPLEMENTATION OF PISA – A COLLABORATIVE EFFORT

PISA is a collaborative effort, bringing together experts from the participating countries, steered jointly by their governments on the basis of shared, policy-driven interests.

A PISA Governing Board, on which each country is represented, determines the policy priorities for PISA, in the context of OECD objectives, and oversees adherence to these priorities during the implementation of the programme. This includes setting priorities for the development of indicators, for establishing the assessment instruments, and for reporting the results.

Experts from participating countries also serve on working groups that are charged with linking policy objectives with the best internationally available technical expertise. By participating in these expert groups, countries ensure that the instruments are internationally valid and take into account the cultural and educational contexts in OECD member and partner countries and economies, that the assessment materials have strong measurement properties, and that the instruments place emphasise authenticity and educational validity.

Through National Project Managers, participating countries and economies implement PISA at the national level subject to the agreed administration procedures. National Project Managers play a vital role in ensuring that the implementation of the survey is of high quality, and verify and evaluate the survey results, analyses, reports and publications.

The design and implementation of the surveys, within the framework established by the PISA Governing Board, is the responsibility of external contractors. For PISA 2012, the development and implementation of the cognitive assessment and questionnaires, and of the international options, was carried out by a consortium led by the Australian Council for Educational Research (ACER). Other partners in this Consortium include cApStAn Linguistic Quality Control in Belgium, the Centre de Recherche Public Henri Tudor (CRP-HT) in Luxembourg, the Department of Teacher Education and School Research (ILS) at the University of Oslo in Norway, the Deutsches Institut für Internationale Pädagogische Forschung (DIPF) in Germany, the Educational Testing Service (ETS) in the United States, the Leibniz Institute for Science and Mathematics Education (IPN) in Germany, the National Institute for Educational Policy Research in Japan (NIER), the Unité d'analyse des systèmes et des pratiques d'enseignement (aSPe) at the University of Liège in Belgium, and WESTAT in the United States, as well as individual consultants from several countries. ACER also collaborated with Achieve, Inc. in the United States to develop the mathematics framework for PISA 2012.

The OECD Secretariat has overall managerial responsibility for the programme, monitors its implementation daily, acts as the secretariat for the PISA Governing Board, builds consensus among countries and serves as the interlocutor between the PISA Governing Board and the international Consortium charged with implementing the activities. The OECD Secretariat also produces the indicators and analyses and prepares the international reports and publications in co-operation with the PISA Consortium and in close consultation with member and partner countries and economies both at the policy level (PISA Governing Board) and at the level of implementation (National Project Managers).

PISA Governing Board

Chair of the PISA Governing Board: Lorna Bertrand

OECD countries

Australia: Tony Zanderigo

Austria: Mark Német

Belgium: Christiane Blondin and Isabelle Erauw

Canada: Pierre Brochu, Patrick Bussiere and Tomasz Gluszynski

Chile: Leonor Cariola Huerta

Czech Republic: Jana Paleckova

Denmark: Tine Bak and Elsebeth Aller

Estonia: Maie Kitsing

Finland: Tommi Karjalainen

France: Bruno Trosseille

Germany: Elfriede Ohrnberger and Susanne von Below

Greece: Vassilia Hatzinikita and Chryssa Sofianopoulou

Hungary: Benõ Csapó

Iceland: Júlíus Björnsson

Ireland: Jude Cosgrove and Gerry Shiel

Israel: Michal Beller and Hagit Glickman

Italy: Paolo Sestito

Japan: Ryo Watanabe

Korea: Sungsook Kim and Keunwoo Lee

Luxembourg: Amina Kafai

Mexico: Francisco Ciscomani and Eduardo Backhoff Escudero

Netherlands: Paul van Oijen

New Zealand: Lynne Whitney

Norway : Anne-Berit Kavli and Alette Schreiner

Poland: Stanislaw Drzazdzewski and Hania Bouacid

Portugal: Luisa Canto and Castro Loura

Slovak Republic: Romana Kanovska and Paulina Korsnakova

Slovenia: Andreja Barle Lakota

Spain: Ismael Sanz Labrador

Sweden: Anita Wester

Switzerland: Vera Husfeldt and Claudia Zahner Rossier

Turkey: Nurcan Devici and Mustafa Nadir Çalis

United Kingdom: Lorna Bertrand and Jonathan Wright

United States: Jack Buckley, Dana Kelly and Daniel McGrath

Observers

Albania: Ermal Elezi

Argentina: Liliana Pascual

Brazil: Luiz Claudio Costa

Bulgaria: Neda Kristanova

Chinese Taipei: Gwo-Dong Chen and Chih-Wei Hue

Colombia: Adriana Molina

Costa Rica: Leonardo Garnier Rimolo

Croatia: Michelle Bras Roth

Hong Kong-China: Esther Sui-chu Ho

Indonesia: Khairil Anwar Notodiputro

Jordan: Khattab Mohammad Abulibdeh

Kazakhstan: Almagul Kultumanova

Latvia: Andris Kangro, Ennata Kivrina and Dita Traidas

Lithuania: Rita Dukynaite

Macao-China: Leong Lai

Montenegro: Zeljko Jacimovic

Panama: Arturo Rivera

Peru: Liliana Miranda Molina

Qatar: Hamda Al Sulaiti

Romania: Roxana Mihail

Russian Federation: Isak Froumin and Galina Kovaleva

Serbia: Dragica Pavlovic-Babic

Shanghai-China: Minxuan Zhang

Singapore: Khah Gek Low

Thailand: Precharn Dechsri

United Arab Emirates: Moza al Ghufly and Ayesha G. Khalfan Almerri

Uruguay: Andrés Peri and Maria Helvecia Sanchez Nunez

Viet Nam: Le Thi My Ha

PISA 2012 National Project Managers

Albania: Alfonso Harizaj

Argentina: Liliana Pascual

Australia: Sue Thomson

Austria: Ursula Schwantner

Belgium: Inge De Meyer and Ariane Baye

Brazil: João Galvão Bacchetto

Bulgaria: Svetla Petrova

Canada: Pierre Brochu and Tamara Knighton

Chile: Ema Lagos Campos

Colombia: Francisco Reyes

Costa Rica: Lilliam Mora

Croatia: Michelle Bras Roth

Czech Republic: Jana Paleckova

Denmark: Niels Egelund

Estonia: Gunda Tire

Finland: Jouni Välijärvi

France: Ginette Bourny

Germany: Christine Sälzer and Manfred Prenzel

Greece: Vassilia Hatzinikita

Hong Kong-China: Esther Sui-chu Ho

Hungary: Ildikó Balazsi

Iceland: Almar Midvik Halldorsson

Indonesia: Yulia Wardhani Nugaan and Hari Setiadi

Ireland: Gerry Shiel and Rachel Perkins

Israel: Joel Rapp and Inbal Ron-Kaplan

Italy: Carlo Di Chiacchio

Japan: Ryo Watanabe

Jordan: Khattab Mohammad Abulibdeh

Kazakhstan: Gulmira Berdibayeva and Zhannur Azmagambetova

Korea: Ji-Min Cho and Mi-Young Song

Latvia: Andris Kangro

Liechtenstein: Christian Nidegger

Lithuania: Mindaugas Stundza

Luxembourg: Bettina Boehm

Macao-China: Kwok Cheung Cheung

Malaysia: Ihsan Ismail and Muhamad Zaini Md Zain

Mexico: María Antonieta Díaz Gutierrez

Montenegro: Divna Paljevic Sturm

Netherlands: Jesse Koops

New Zealand: Kate Lang and Steven May

Norway: Marit Kjaernsli

Peru: Liliana Miranda Molina

Poland: Michal Federowicz

Portugal: Ana Sousa Ferreira

Qatar: Aysha Al-Hashemi and Assad Tounakti

Romania: Silviu Cristian Mirescu

Russian Federation: Galina Kovaleva

Scotland: Rebecca Wheater

Serbia: Dragica Pavlovic-Babic

Shanghai-China: Jing Lu and Minxuan Zhang

Singapore: Chew Leng Poon and Sean Tan

Slovak Republic: Julia Miklovicova and Jana Ferencova

Slovenia: Mojca Straus

Spain: Lis Cercadillo Pérez

Sweden: Magnus Oskarsson

Switzerland: Christian Nidegger

Chinese Taipei: Pi-Hsia Hung

Thailand: Sunee Klainin

Tunisia: Mohamed Kamel Essid

Turkey: Serdar Aztekin

United Arab Emirates: Moza al Ghufly

United Kingdom: Rebecca Wheater

United States: Dana Kelly and Holly Xie

Uruguay: Maria Helvecia Sánchez Nunez

Viet Nam: Thi My Ha Le

OECD Secretariat

Andreas Schleicher (Strategic development)

Marilyn Achiron (Editorial support)

Francesco Avvisati (Analytic services)

Brigitte Beyeler (Administrative support)

Simone Bloem (Analytic services)

Marika Boiron (Translation support)

Francesca Borgonovi (Analytic services)

Jenny Bradshaw (Project management)

Célia Braga-Schich (Production support)

Claire Chetcuti (Administrative support)

Michael Davidson (Project management and analytic services)

Cassandra Davis (Dissemination co-ordination)

Elizabeth Del Bourgo (Production support)

Juliet Evans (Administration and partner country/economy relations)

Tue Halgreen (Project management)

Miyako Ikeda (Analytic services)

Tadakazu Miki (Analytic services)

Guillermo Montt (Analytic services)

Giannina Rech (Analytic services)

Diana Tramontano (Administration)

Sophie Vayssettes (Analytic services)

Elisabeth Villoutreix (Production co-ordination)

Pablo Zoido (Analytic services)

PISA 2012 mathematics expert group

Kaye Stacey (Chair) (University of Melbourne, Australia)

Caroline Bardini (University of Melbourne, Australia)

Werner Blum (University of Kassel, Germany)

Joan Ferrini-Mundy (Michigan State University, United States)

Solomon Garfunkel (COMAP, United States)

Toshikazu Ikeda (Yokohama National University, Japan)

Zbigniew Marciniak (Warsaw University, Poland)

Mogens Niss (Roskilde University, Denmark)

Martin Ripley (World Class Arena Limited, United Kingdom)

William Schmidt (Michigan State University, United States)

PISA 2012 problem solving expert group

Joachim Funke (Chair) (University of Heidelberg, Germany)

Benő Csapó (University of Szeged, Hungary)

John Dossey (Illinois State University, United States)

Arthur Graesser (The University of Memphis United States)

Detlev Leutner (Duisburg-Essen University, Germany)

Romain Martin (Université de Luxembourg FLSHASE, Luxembourg)

Richard Mayer (University of California, United States)

Ming Ming Tan (Ministry of Education, Singapore)

PISA 2012 financial literacy expert group

Annamaria Lusardi (Chair) (The George Washington University School of Business, United States)

Jean-Pierre Boisivon (Université de Paris II Panthéon-Assas, France)

Diana Crossan (Commission for Financial Literacy and Retirement Income, New Zealand)

Peter Cuzner (Australian Securities and Investments Commission, Australia)

Jeanne Hogarth (Federal Reserve System, United States)

Dušan Hradil (Ministry of Finance, Czech Republic)

Stan Jones (Consultant, Canada)

Sue Lewis (Consultant, United Kingdom)

PISA 2012 questionnaire expert group

Eckhard Klieme (Chair) (Deutsches Institut für Internationale Pädagogische Forschung (DIPF), Germany)

Eduardo Backhoff (University of Baja California at the Institute of Educational Research and Development, Mexico)

Ying-yi Hong (Nanyang Business School of Nanyang Technological University, Singapore)

David Kaplan (University of Wisconsin – Madison, United States)

Henry Levin (Columbia University, United States)

Jaap Scheerens (University of Twente, Netherlands)

William Schmidt (Michigan State University, United States)

Fons van de Vijver (Tilburg University, Netherlands)

Technical advisory group

Keith Rust (Chair) (Westat, United States)

Ray Adams (ACER, Australia)

Cees Glas (University of Twente, Netherlands)

John de Jong (Language Testing Services, Netherlands)

David Kaplan (University of Wisconsin – Madison, United States)

Christian Monseur (University of Liège, Belgium)

Sophia Rabe-Hesketh (University of California – Berkeley, United States)

Thierry Rocher (Ministry of Education, France)

Norman Verhelst (CITO, Netherlands)

Kentaro Yamamoto (ETS, United States)

Rebecca Zwick (University of California, United States)

PISA 2012 Consortium

Australian Council for Educational Research

Ray Adams (International Project Director)

Susan Bates (Project administration)

Alla Berezner (Data management and analysis)

Yan Bibby (Data processing and analysis)

Phillipe Bickham (IT services)

Esther Brakey (Administrative support)

Robin Buckley (IT services)

Mark Butler (Financial literacy instruments and test development)

Wei Buttress (Project administration and quality monitoring)

Renee Chow (Data processing and analysis)

John Cresswell (Reporting and dissemination)

Alex Daraganov (Data processing and analysis)

Jorge Fallas (Data processing and analysis)

Kate Fitzgerald (Data processing and sampling)

Kim Fitzgerald (IT Services)

Paul Golden (IT and helpdesk support)

Jennifer Hong (Data processing and sampling)

Nora Kovarcikova (Survey operations)

Winson Lam (IT services)

Petra Lietz (Questionnaire development)

Tom Lumley (Reading instruments and test development)

Greg Macaskill (Data management and processing and sampling)

Ron Martin (Science instruments and test development)

Barry McCrae (Problem solving and science instruments and test development)

Louise McDonald (Graphic design)

Juliette Mendelovits (Reading and financial literacy instruments and test development)

Martin Murphy (Field operations and sampling)

Thoa Nguyen (Data processing and analysis)

Stephen Oakes (IT management and support)

Elizabeth O'Grady (Questionnaire development and project support)

Penny Pearson (Administrative support)

Ray Peck (Mathematics and financial literacy instruments and test development)

Fei Peng (Quality monitoring and project support)

Ray Philpot (Problem Solving instruments and test development)

Anna Plotka (Graphic design)

Dara Ramalingam (Reading instruments and test development)

Sima Rodrigues (Data processing and analysis)

Alla Routitsky (Data management and processing)

James Spithill (Mathematics instruments and test development)

Rachel Stanyon (Project support)

Naoko Tabata (Survey operations)

Stephanie Templeton (Project administration and support)

Mollie Tobin (Questionnaire development and project support)

David Tout (Mathematics instruments and test development)

Ross Turner (Management, mathematics instruments and test development)

Maryanne Van Grunsven (Project support)

Charlotte Waters (Project administration, data processing and analysis)

Maurice Walker (Management, computer-based assessment)

Louise Wenn (Data processing and analysis)

Yan Wiwecka (IT services)

cApStAn Linguistic Quality Control (BELGIUM)

Raphael Choppinet (Computer-based verification management)

Steve Dept (Translation and verification operations)

Andrea Ferrari (Linguistic quality assurance and quality control designs)

Musab Hayatli (Right-to-left scripts, cultural adaptations)

Elica Krajceva (Questionnaire verification co-ordinator)

Shinoh Lee (Cognitive test verification co-ordinator)

Irene Liberati (Manuals verification co-ordinator)

Laura Wayrynen (Verifier training and verification procedures)

Educational Testing Service (ETS)

Jonas Bertling (Questionnaire instruments and test development)

Irwin Kirsch (Reading Components)

Patricia Klag (Problem-solving instruments and test development)

Patrick Kyllonen (Questionnaire instruments and test development)

Marylou Lennon (Questionnaire instruments and test development)

Richard Roberts (Questionnaire instruments and test development)

Matthias von Davier (Questionnaire instruments and test development)

Kentaro Yamamoto (Member TAG, problem-solving instruments and test development)

Deutches Institut für Internationale Pädagogische Forschung (DIPF, GERMANY)

Frank Goldhammer (Test developer, problem solving)

Eckhard Klieme (Chair of Questionnaire Expert Group)

Silke Hertel (Questionnaire development)

Jean-Paul Reeff (International Consultant)

Heiko Rolke (Software Design & Software Development

Management [Delivery System, Translation System])

Brigitte Steinert (Questionnaire development)

Svenja Vieluf (Questionnaire development)

Institutt for Lærerutdanning Og Skoleutvikling (ILS, NORWAY)

Bjornar Alseth (Mathematics instruments and test development)

Ole Kristian Bergem (Mathematics instruments and test development)

Knut Skrindo (Mathematics instruments and test development)

Rolf V. Olsen (Mathematics instruments and test development)

Arne Hole (Mathematics instruments and test development)

Therese Hopfenbeck (Problem-solving instruments and test development)

Leibniz Institute for Science and Mathematics Education (IPN, GERMANY)

Christoph Duchhardt (Mathematics instruments and test development)

Aiso Heinze (Mathematics instruments and test development)

Eva Knopp (Mathematics instruments and test development)

Martin Senkbeil (Mathematics instruments and test development)

National Institute for Educational Policy Research (NIER, JAPAN)

Keiichi Nishimura (Mathematics instruments and test development)

Yuji Surata (Mathematics instruments and test development)

The TAO Initiative: Henry Tudor Public Research Centre, University of Luxembourg (LUXEMBOURG)

Joel Billard (Software Engineer, School Questionnaire)

Marilyn Binkley (Project Consultant, Assessment Expert)

Jerome Bogaerts (Software Engineer, TAO Platform)

Gilbert Busana (Electronic Instruments, Usability)

Christophe Henry (System Engineer, School Questionnaire and Hosting)

Raynald Jadoul (Technical Lead, School Questionnaire and Electronic Instruments)

Isabelle Jars (Project Manager)

Vincent Koenig (Electronic Instruments, Usability)

Thibaud Latour (Project Leader, TAO Platform)

Lionel Lecaque (Software Engineer, Quality)

Primael Lorbat (Software Engineer, Electronic Instruments)

Romain Martin (Problem Solving Expert Group Member)

Matteo Melis (Software Engineer, School Questionnaire)

Patrick Plichart (Software Architect, TAO Platform)

Vincent Porro (Software Engineer, Electronic Instruments)

Igor Ribassin (Software Engineer, Electronic Instruments)

Somsack Sipasseuth (Software Engineer, Electronic Instruments)

Unité d'analyse des Systèmes et des Pratiques d'enseignement (ASPE, BELGIUM)

Isabelle Demonty (Mathematics instruments and test development)

Annick Fagnant (Mathematics instruments and test development)

Anne Matoul (French source development)

Christian Monseur (Member of Technical Advisory Group)

WESTAT

Susan Fuss (Sampling and weighting)

Amita Gopinath (Weighting)

Jing Kang (Sampling and weighting)

Sheila Krawchuk (Sampling, weighting and quality monitoring)

Thanh Le (Sampling, weighting and quality monitoring)

John Lopdell (Sampling and weighting)

Keith Rust (Director of the PISA Consortium for sampling and weighting)

Erin Willey (Sampling and weighting)

Shawn Lu (Weighting)

Teresa Strickler (Weighting)

Yumiko Sugawara (Weighting)

Joel Wakesberg (Sampling and weighting)

Sergey Yagodin (Weighting)

Achieve Inc.

Michael Cohen (Mathematics framework development)

Kaye Forgione (Mathematics framework development)

Morgan Saxby (Mathematics framework development)

Laura Slover (Mathematics framework development)

Bonnie Verrico (Project support)

HallStat SPRL

Beatrice Halleux (Consultant, translation/verification referee, French source development)

University of Heidelberg

Joachim Funke (Chair, Problem Solving Expert Group)

Samuel Greiff (Problem-solving instruments and test development)

University of Melbourne

Caroline Bardini (Member Mathematics Expert Group)

John Dowsey (Mathematics instruments and test development)

Derek Holton (Mathematics instruments and test development)

Kaye Stacey (Chair Mathematics Expert Group)

Other experts

Michael Besser (Mathematics instruments and test development, University of Kassel, Germany)

Khurrem Jehangir (Data analysis for TAG, University of Twente, Netherlands)

Kees Lagerwaard (Mathematics instruments and test development, Institute for Educational Measurement of Netherlands, Netherlands)

Dominik Leiss (Mathematics instruments and test development, University of Kassel, Germany)

Anne-Laure Monnier (Consultant French source development, France)

Hanako Senuma (Mathematics instruments and test development, Tamagawa University, Japan)

Publication layout

Fung Kwan Tam

ORGANISATION FOR ECONOMIC CO-OPERATION AND DEVELOPMENT

The OECD is a unique forum where governments work together to address the economic, social and environmental challenges of globalisation. The OECD is also at the forefront of efforts to understand and to help governments respond to new developments and concerns, such as corporate governance, the information economy and the challenges of an ageing population. The Organisation provides a setting where governments can compare policy experiences, seek answers to common problems, identify good practice and work to co-ordinate domestic and international policies.

The OECD member countries are: Australia, Austria, Belgium, Canada, Chile, the Czech Republic, Denmark, Estonia, Finland, France, Germany, Greece, Hungary, Iceland, Ireland, Israel, Italy, Japan, Korea, Luxembourg, Mexico, the Netherlands, New Zealand, Norway, Poland, Portugal, the Slovak Republic, Slovenia, Spain, Sweden, Switzerland, Turkey, the United Kingdom and the United States. The European Union takes part in the work of the OECD.

OECD Publishing disseminates widely the results of the Organisation's statistics gathering and research on economic, social and environmental issues, as well as the conventions, guidelines and standards agreed by its members.

OECD PUBLISHING, 2, rue André-Pascal, 75775 PARIS CEDEX 16
(98 2013 06 1P) ISBN 978-92-64 20114-9 – No. 60971   2013– 04